shuf·fle 1. *v/t Karten* mischen; *Papiere etc* umordnen, hierhin oder dorthin legen; **shuffle one's feet** schlurfen; *v/i* schlurfen; *Karten* mischen; **2.** Schlurfen *n*, schlurfender Gang; Mischen *n*

Indicating words in *italics*

evening class·es Abendkurs *m*, Abendunterricht *m*
evening dress Gesellschaftsanzug *m*; Frack *m*, Smoking *m*; Abendkleid *n*

Compounds

kultivieren [kʊltiˈviːrən] *v/t (no -ge-, h)* cultivate
Künstler [ˈkʏnstlɐ] *m (-s; -)*, **Künstlerin** [ˈkʏnstlərɪn] *f (-; -nen)* artist, MUS, THEA *a.* performer

Grammatical information

shy 1. scheu; schüchtern; **2.** scheuen (*at* vor *dat*); **shy away from** *fig* zurückschrecken vor (*dat*)

Entries divided into grammatical categories

Kumpel [ˈkʊmpəl] *m (-s; -)* miner; F mate, buddy, pal

Register labels

Abschlusszeugnis *n Am* diploma, *Br* school-leaving certificate

American and British variants

German
Concise Dictionary

German – English
Englisch – Deutsch

Berlitz Publishing
New York · Munich · Singapore

Edited by the Langenscheidt editorial staff

Activity section by Jessie McGuire

Book in cover photo: © Punchstock/Medioimages

Neither the presence nor the absence of a designation
indicating that any entered word constitutes a trademark
should be regarded as affecting the legal status thereof.

Berlitz Publishing
193 Morris Avenue
Springfield, NJ 07081
USA

Printed in Germany
ISBN-13: 978-981-268-016-7
ISBN-10: 981-268-016-0

07

08

09 10

11

5.

4.

3.

2.

1.

Preface

This new dictionary of English and German is a tool with more than 55,000 references for learners of the German language at beginner's or intermediate level.

Thousands of colloquial and idiomatic expressions have been included and the new German spelling has been used. The user-friendly layout with all headwords in blue allows the user to have quick access to all the words, expressions and their translations.

Clarity of presentation has been a major objective. Is the *mouse* you need for your computer, for example, the same in German as the *mouse* you don't want in the house? This dictionary is rich in sense distinctions like this – and in translation options tied to specific, identified senses.

Vocabulary needs grammar to back it up. In this dictionary you will find extra grammar information on German declension and conjugation as well as on German irregular verb forms.

Another feature is the special quick-reference section listing the States of Germany and Austria and the Cantons of Switzerland, German weights and measures etc.

The additional activity section provides the user with an opportunity to develop language skills with a selection of engaging word puzzles. The games are designed specifically to improve vocabulary, spelling, grammar and comprehension in an enjoyable style.

Designed for a wide variety of uses, this dictionary will be of great value to those who wish to learn German and have fun at the same time.

Contents

Guide for the User

This dictionary endeavors to do everything it can to help you find the words and translations you are looking for as quickly and as easily as possible.

To enable you to get the most out of your dictionary, you will be shown exactly where and how to find the information that will help you choose the right translation in every situation – whether at school or at home, when writing letters, or in everyday conversation.

1. German and English headwords

1.1 When you are looking for a particular word it is important to know that the dictionary entries are arranged in strict **alphabetical order:**

> Aal – ab
> beugen – biegen
> hay – haze

In the German-English section the umlauts *ä ö ü* are treated as *a o u*. *ß* is treated as *ss*.

1.2 Besides the headwords and their derivatives and compounds, the past tense and past participle of irregular German verbs are also given as individual entries in alphabetical order in the German-English section, e.g. **ging, gegangen.**

1.3 Many German and English proper names and abbreviations are included in the vocabulary.

1.4 How then do you go about finding a particular word? Take a look at the words in bold print at the top of each page. These are the so-called **running heads** and they serve as a guide to tracing your word as quickly as possible. The running head on the top left gives you the first headword on the left-hand page, while the one on the top right gives you the last word on the right-hand page, e.g.

Gesundheit – Glanz

1.5 What about entries comprising hyphenated expressions or two or more words, such as **D-Zug, left-handed** or **mass media?** Expressions of this kind are treated in the same way as single words and thus appear in strict alphabetical order. Should you be unable to find a compound in the dictionary, just break it down into its components and look these up separately. In this way the meaning of many compound expressions can be derived indirectly.

2. Spelling

2.1 Where American and British spelling of a word differs, the American spelling is given first as in

> **center,** *Br* **centre**
> **center** (*Br* **centre**) **forward**
> **dialog,** *Br* **dialogue**

or in the English-German section as a separate headword, e.g. **theater, defense** etc.

A 'u' or an 'l' in parentheses in a word also indicates variant spellings:

> **colo(u)red** means: *American* **colored,** *British* **coloured**
> **travel(l)er** means: *American* **traveler,** *British* **traveller**

2.2 Word division in a German word is possible after each syllable, e.g.

> **ein-hül-len, Zu-cker, ba-cken, tes-ten**

In the English-German section the centered dots within a headword indicate syllabification breaks.

3. The different typefaces and their functions

3.1 **Bold type** is used for the German and English headwords and for Arabic numerals separating different parts of speech (nouns, transitive and intransitive verbs, adjectives and adverbs etc.) and different grammatical forms of a word:

> **bieten 1.** *v/t* ... **2.** *v/i* ...
> **hängen 1.** *v/i* (*irr, ge-, h*) hang (**an** *dat* on...);
> **2.** *v/t* (*ge-, h*) hang (**an** *acc* on)
> **feed 1.** Futter *n*; ... **2.** *v/t* füttern

3.2 *Italics* are used for

a) grammatical and other abbreviations: *v/t, v/i, adj, adv, appr, fig* etc.
b) gender labels (masculine, feminine and neuter): *m, f, n*
c) grammatical references in brackets in the German-English section
d) any additional information preceding or following a translation (including dative or accusative objects):

> **knacken** *v/t and v/i* ... *twig*: snap; *fire, radio*: crackle
> **Etikett** *n* ... label (*a. fig*)
> **Gedanke** *m* (*-n; -n*) ...
> **geben** (*irr, ge-, h*) ...

befolgen ... follow, take (*advice*); observe
(*rule etc*)
file ... *Briefe etc* ablegen
labored schwerfällig (*style etc*); mühsam
(*breathing etc*)

3.3 *Boldface italics* are used for phraseology etc., notes on German grammar and prepositions taken by the headword:

Lage *f* ... *in der Lage sein zu inf* be able to *inf*
BLZ ... ABBR *of Bankleitzahl*
abheben (*irr*, *heben*, *sep*, *-ge-*, *h*)
abfahren ... (*irr*, *fahren*, *sep*, *-ge-*, *sein*) leave, depart (*both*: *nach* for)
line ... *hold the line* TEL bleiben Sie am Apparat
agree ... sich einigen (*on* über *acc*)

3.4 Normal type is used for translations of the headwords.

4. Pronunciation

When you have found the headword you are looking for in the German-English section, you will notice that very often this word is followed by certain symbols enclosed in square brackets. This is the phonetic transcription of the word, which tells you how it is pronounced. And one phonetic alphabet has come to be used internationally, namely that of the International Phonetic Association. This phonetic system is known by the abbreviation **IPA**. The symbols used in this dictionary are listed in the following tables on page 8 and 9.

4.1 The length of vowels is indicated by [ː] following the vowel symbol.

4.1.1 Stress is indicated by [ˈ] or [ˌ] preceding the stressed syllable. [ˈ] stands for strong stress, [ˌ] for weak stress:

Kabel [ˈkaːbəl] – **Kabine** [kaˈbiːnə]
ˈnachsehen – Beˈsitz – beˈsprechen
Jusˈtizminisˌterium – Miˈnisterpräsiˌdent

4.1.2 The glottal stop [ʔ] is the forced stop between one word or syllable and a following one beginning with a vowel, as in

Analphabet [anʔalfaˈbeːt]
beeindrucken [bəˈʔaindrʊkən]

4.2 No transcription of compounds is given if the parts appear as separate entries. Each individual part should be looked up, as with

'Blumenbeet (= Blume and Beet)

4.2.1 If only part of the pronunciation changes or if a compound word consists of a new component, only the pronunciation of the changed or new part is given:

Demonstrant [demɔn'strant]
Demonstration [-stra'tsjoːn]
'Kinderhort [-hɔrt]

4.3 Guide to pronunciation for the German-English section

A. Vowels

[a] as in French *carte*: **Mann** [man]

[aː] as in *father*: **Wagen** ['vaːgən]

[e] as in *bed*: **Tenor** [te'noːɐ]

[eː] resembles the first sound in English [eɪ]: **Weg** [veːk]

[ə] unstressed e as in *ago*: **Bitte** ['bɪtə]

[ɛ] as in *fair*: **männlich** ['mɛnlɪç], **Geld** [gɛlt]

[ɛː] same sound but long: **zählen** ['tsɛːlən]

[ɪ] as in *it*: **Wind** [vɪnt]

[i] short, otherwise like [iː]: **Kapital** [kapi'taːl]

[iː] long, as in *meet*: **Vieh** [fiː]

[ɔ] as in *long*: **Ort** [ɔrt]

[o] as in *molest*: **Moral** [mo'raːl]

[oː] resembles the English sound in *go* [gəʊ] but without the [ʊ]: **Boot** [boːt]

[øː] as in French *feu*. The sound may be acquired by saying [e] through closely rounded lips: **schön** [ʃøːn]

[ø] same sound but short: **ökumenisch** [øku'meːnɪʃ]

[œ] as in French *neuf*. The sound resembles the English vowel in *her*. Lips, however, must be well rounded as for [ɒ]: **öffnen** ['œfnən]

[ʊ] as in *book*: **Mutter** ['mʊtɐ]

[u] short, otherwise like [uː]: **Musik** [mu'ziːk]

[uː] long, as in *boot*: **Uhr** [uːɐ]

[ʏ] short, opener than [yː]: **Hütte** ['hʏtə]

[y] almost like the French u as in *sur*. It may be acquired by saying [ɪ] through fairly closely rounded lips: **Büro** [by'roː]

[yː] same sound but long: **führen** ['fyːrən]

B. Diphthongs

[aɪ] as in *like*: **Mai** [maɪ]

[aʊ] as in *mouse*: **Maus** [maʊs]

[ɔʏ] as in *boy*: **Beute** ['bɔʏtə], **Läufer** ['lɔʏfɐ]

C. Consonants

[b] as in *better*: **besser** ['bɛsɐ]

[d] as in *dance*: **du** [duː]

[f] as in *find*: **finden** ['findən], **Vater** ['faːtɐ], **Philosoph** [filo'zoːf]

[g] as in *gold*: **Gold** [gɔlt]

[ʒ] as in *measure*: **Genie** [ʒe'niː]

[h] as in *house* but not aspirated: **Haus** [haʊs]

[ç] an approximation to this sound may be acquired by assuming the mouth-configuration for [ɪ] and emitting a strong current of breath: **Licht** [lɪçt], **Mönch** [mœnç], **lustig** ['lʊstɪç]

[x] as in Scottish *loch*. Whereas [ç] is pronounced at the front of the mouth, [x] is pronounced in the throat: **Loch** [lɔx]

[j] as in *year*: **ja** [jaː]

[k] as in *kick*: **keck** [kɛk], **Tag** [taːk], **Chronik** ['kroːnɪk], **Café** [ka'feː]

[l] as in *lump*. Pronounced like English initial „clear l": **lassen** ['lasən]

[m] as in *mouse*: **Maus** [maʊs]

[n] as in *not*: **nein** [naɪn]

[ŋ] as in *sing*, *drink*: **singen** ['zɪŋən], **trinken** ['trɪŋkən]

[p] as in *pass*: **Pass** [pas], **Trieb** [triːp], **obgleich** [ɔp'glaɪç]

[r] as in *rot*. There are two pronunciations: the frontal or lingual r: **rot** [roːt] and the uvular r [ɐ] (unknown in the English language): **Mauer** ['maʊɐ]

[s] as in *miss*. Unvoiced when final, doubled, or next a voiceless consonant: **Glas** [glaːs], **Masse** ['masə], **Mast** [mast], **nass** [nas]

[z] as in *zero*. S voiced when initial in a word or syllable: **Sohn** [zoːn], **Rose** ['roːzə]

[ʃ] as in *ship*: **Schiff** [ʃɪf], **Charme** [ʃarm], **Spiel** [ʃpiːl], **Stein** [ʃtaɪn]

[t] as in *tea*: **Tee** [teː], **Thron** [troːn], **Stadt** [ʃtat], **Bad** [baːt], **Findling** ['fɪntlɪŋ], **Wind** [vɪnt]

[v] as in *vast*: **Vase** ['vaːze], **Winter** ['vɪntɐ]

[ã, ɛ̃, õ] are nasalized vowels. Examples: **Ensemble** [ã'sãːbəl], **Terrain** [tɛ'rɛ̃ː], **Bonbon** [bõ'bõː]

4.3.1 Phonetic changes in plurals

singular		plural		example
-g	[-k]	-ge	[-gə]	Flug – Flüge
-d	[-t]	-de	[-də]	Grund – Gründe, Abend – Abende
-b	[-p]	-be	[-bə]	Stab – Stäbe
-s	[-s]	-se	[-zə]	Los – Lose
-ch	[-x]	-che	[-çə]	Bach – Bäche
-iv	[-iːf]	-ive	[-iːvə]	Stativ – Stative

4.3.2 The German alphabet

a [aː], b [beː], c [tseː], d [deː], e [eː], f [ɛf], g [geː], h [haː], i [iː], j [jɔt], k [kaː], l [ɛl], m [ɛm], n [ɛn], o [oː], p [peː], q [kuː], r [ɛr], s [ɛs], t [teː], u [uː], v [fau], w [veː], x [ɪks], y ['ʏpsilɔn], z [tsɛt]

4.3.3 List of suffixes

The German suffixes are not transcribed unless they are parts of headwords.

-bar	[-baːɐ]	-isch	[-ɪʃ]
-chen	[-çən]	-ist	[-ɪst]
-d	[-t]	-keit	[-kaɪt]
-de	[-də]	-lich	[-lɪç]
-ei	[-aɪ]	-ling	[-lɪŋ]
-en	[-ən]	-losigkeit	[-loːzɪçkaɪt]
-end	[-ənt]	-nis	[-nɪs]
-er	[-ɐ]	-sal	[-zaːl]
-haft	[-haft]	-sam	[-zaːm]
-heit	[-haɪt]	-schaft	[-ʃaft]
-icht	[-ɪçt]	-sieren	[-ziːrən]
-ie	[-iː]	-ste	[-stə]
-ieren	[-iːrən]	-tät	[-tɛːt]
-ig	[-ɪç]	-tum	[-tuːm]
-ik	[-ɪk]	-ung	[-ʊŋ]
-in	[-ɪn]	-ungs-	[-ʊŋs-]
		-wärts	[-vɛrts]

5. Abbreviations of grammatical terms and subject areas are designed to help the user choose the appropriate headword or translation of a word.

In the dictionary words which are predominantly used in British English are marked by the abbreviation *Br*:

> **Bürgersteig** *m* sidewalk, *Br* pavement
> **girl guide** *Br* Pfadfinderin *f*

List of abbreviations

a.	*also*, auch
ABBR	*abbreviation*, Abkürzung
acc	*accusative (case)*, Akkusativ
adj	*adjective*, Adjektiv
adv	*adverb*, Adverb
AGR	*agriculture*, Landwirtschaft
Am	*American English*, amerikanisches Englisch
ANAT	*anatomy*, Anatomie
appr	*approximately*, etwa
ARCH	*architecture*, Architektur
art	*article*, Artikel
ASTR	*astrology*, Astrologie; *astronomy*, Astronomie
attr	*attributively* , attributiv
AVIAT	*aviation*, Luftfahrt
BIOL	*biology*, Biologie
BOT	*botany*, Botanik
Br	*British English*, britisches Englisch
CHEM	*chemistry*, Chemie

cj	*conjunction*, Konjunktion
coll	*collectively*, als Sammelwort
comp	*comparative*, Komparativ
contp	*contemptuously*, verächtlich
cpds	*compounds*, Zusammensetzungen
dat	*dative (case)*, Dativ
ECON	*economy*, Wirtschaft
EDP	*electronic data processing*, Elektronische Datenverarbeitung
e-e	*a(n)*, eine
e.g.	*for example*, zum Beispiel
ELECTR	*electrical engineering*, Elektrotechnik
e-m	*einem*, to a(n)
e-n	*einen*, a(n)
e-r	*einer*, of a(n), to a(n)
e-s	*eines*, of a(n)
esp.	*especially*, besonders
et., *et.*	etwas, *something*
etc	*et cetera, and so on*, usw., und so weiter

11

F	*colloquial*, umgangssprachlich	PHYS	*physics*, Physik
f	*feminine*, weiblich	pl	*plural*, Plural
fig	*figuratively*, übertragen	POET	*poetry*, Dichtung
		POL	*politics*, Politik
GASTR	*gastronomy*, Kochkunst	poss	*possessive*, besitzanzeigend
gen	*genitive (case)*, Genitiv	POST	*post and telecommunications*,
GEOGR	*geography*, Geografie		Postwesen
GEOL	*geology*, Geologie	*pp*	*past participle*, Partizip Perfekt
ger	*gerund*, Gerundium	*pred*	*predicative*, prädikativ
GR	*grammar*, Grammatik	*pres*	*present*, Präsens
h	*haben*, have	*pres p*	*present participle*, Partizip Präsens
HIST	*history*, Geschichte	*pret*	*preterit(e)*, Präteritum
HUMOR	*humorous*, humorvoll	PRINT	*printing*, Druckwesen
		pron	*pronoun*, Pronomen
impers	*impersonal*, unpersönlich	*prp*	*preposition*, Präposition
indef	*indefinite*, unbestimmt	PSYCH	*psychology*, Psychologie
inf	*infinitive (mood)*, Infinitiv		
int	*interjection*, Interjektion	RAIL	*railroad, railway*, Eisenbahn
interr	*interrogative*, fragend	*refl*	*reflexive*, reflexiv
irr	*irregular*, unregelmäßig	REL	*religion*, Religion
		RHET	*rhetoric*, Rhetorik
j-m	*jemandem*, to someone		
j-n	*jemanden*, someone	*s-e*	*seine*, his, one's
j-s	*jemandes*, someone's	*sep*	*separable*, abtrennbar
JUR	*jurisprudence*, Recht	*sg*	*singular*, Singular
		sl	*slang*, Slang
LING	*linguistics*, Sprachwissenschaft	*s-m*	*seinem*, to his, to one's
LIT	*literary*, nur in der Schrift-	*s-n*	*seinen*, his, one's
	sprache vorkommend	s.o., *s.o.*	*someone*, jemand(en)
		SPORT	*sports*, Sport
m	*masculine*, männlich	*s-r*	*seiner*, of his, of one's, to his,
MAR	*maritime term*, Schifffahrt		to one's
MATH	*mathematics*, Mathematik	*s-s*	*seines*, of his, of one's
m-e	*my*, meine	s.th., *s.th.*	*something*, etwas
MED	*medicine*, Medizin	*su*	*substantive*, Substantiv
METEOR	*meteorology*, Meteorologie	*subj*	*subjunctive (mood)*, Konjunktiv
MIL	*military term*, militärisch	*sup*	*superlative*, Superlativ
MOT	*motoring*, Kraftfahrwesen	TECH	*technology*, Technik
m-r	*meiner*, of my, to my	TEL	*telegraphy*, Telegrafie;
mst	*mostly*, *usually*, meistens		*telephony*, Fernsprechwesen
MUS	*music*, Musik	THEA	*theater*, Theater
n	*neuter*, sächlich	TV	*television*, Fernsehen
neg!	*negative*, *usually considered*	u., *u.*	*und*, and
	offensive, kann als beleidigend	UNIV	*university*, Hochschulwesen,
	empfunden werden		Studentensprache
nom	*nominative (case)*, Nominativ		
num	*numeral*, Zahlwort	V	*vulgar*, vulgär, unanständig
		v/aux	*auxiliary verb*, Hilfsverb
OPT	*optics*, Optik	*vb*	*verb*, Verb
o.s., *o.s.*	*oneself*, sich	VET	*veterinary medicine*, Veterinär-
			medizin, Tiermedizin
PAINT	*painting*, Malerei	*v/i*	*intransitive verb*, intransitives Verb
PARL	*parliamentary term*, parlamen-	*v/refl*	*reflexive verb*, reflexives Verb
	tarischer Ausdruck	*v/t*	*transitive verb*, transitives Verb
pass	*passive voice*, Passiv		
PED	*pedagogy*, Schulwesen	ZO	*zoology*, Zoologie
pers	*personal*, persönlich	→	*see, refer to*, siehe
PHARM	*pharmacy*, Pharmazie		
PHIL	*philosophy*, Philosophie	®	*registered trademark*, eingetra-
PHOT	*photography*, Fotografie		gene Marke

6. Translations and phraseology

After the boldface headword in the German-English section, the phonetic transcription of this word, its part of speech label, and its grammar, we finally come to the most important part of the entry: **the translation(s).**

6.1 It is quite rare for a headword to be given just one translation. Usually a word will have several related translations, which are separated by a **comma.**

6.2 Different senses of a word are indicated by

a) **semicolons:**

> **Fest** ... celebration; party; REL festival
> **balance** ... Waage *f*; Gleichgewicht *n*

b) italics for **definitions:**

> **Läufer** ... runner (*a . carpet*); *chess*: bishop
> **call** ... Berufung *f* (*to* in *ein Amt*; auf *einen Lehrstuhl*)
> **cake** ... Tafel *f Schokolade*, Stück *n Seife*

c) **abbreviations** of subject areas:

> **Bug** *m* ... MAR bow; AVIAT nose
> **Gespräch** *n* talk (*a.* POL); ... TEL call
> **daisy** BOT Gänseblümchen *n*
> **duck** ... ZO Ente *f*

6.2.1 Where a word has fundamentally different meanings, it very often appears as two or more separate entries distinguished by **exponents** or raised figures:

> **betreten**[1] *v/t* ... step on; enter
> **betreten**[2] *adj* embarrassed
> **Bauer**[1] *m* ... farmer
> **Bauer**[2] *n, m* ... (bird)cage
> **chap**[1] ... Riss *m*
> **chap**[2] ... *Br* F Bursche *m*

This does not apply to senses which have directly evolved from the primary meaning of the word.

6.3 When a headword can be several different parts of speech, these are distinguished by boldface **Arabic numerals** (see also the section on p.6, paragraph 3.1 concerning the different typefaces):

> **geräuschlos**   **1.** *adj* noiseless (*adjective*)
>   **2.** without a sound (*adverb*)
>
> **work**   **1.** Arbeit *f* (*noun*)
>   **2.** *v/i* arbeiten (*verb*)
>
> **green**   **1.** grün (*adjective*)
>   **2.** Grün *n* (*noun*)

6.3.1 In the German-English section boldface Arabic numerals are also used to distinguish between transitive, intransitive and reflexive verbs (if this affects their translation) and to show that where there is a change of meaning a verb may be differently conjugated:

> **fahren** (*irr, ge-*) **1.** *v/i* (*sein*) go; *bus etc*: run;
> ... **2.** *v/t* (*h*) drive (*car etc*) ...

If grammatical indications come before the subdivision they refer to all translations that follow:

> **bauen** (*ge-*, *h*) **1.** *v/t* build ...; **2.** *fig v/i*:
> **bauen auf** ...

6.3.2 Boldface Arabic numerals are also used to indicate the different meanings of nouns which can occur in more than one gender and to show that where there is a change of meaning a noun may be differently inflected:

> **Halfter 1.** *m, n* (-*s*; -) halter; **2.** *n* (-*s*; -), *f* (-;
> -*n*) holster

6.4 Illustrative phrases in boldface italics are generally given within the respective categories of the dictionary article:

> **baden 1.** *v/i* ... **baden gehen** go swimming;
> **2.** *v/t* ...
> **good 1.** ... **real good** F echt gut (= *adjective*); **2.** ... **for good** für immer (= *noun*)

7. Grammatical references

Knowing what to do with the grammatical information available in the dictionary will enable the user to get the most out of this dictionary.

7.1 Verbs (see the list of irregular German verbs on page 662).

Verbs have been treated in the following ways:

a) **bändigen** *v/t* (*ge-*, *h*)

The past participle of this word is formed by means of the prefix *ge-* and the auxiliary verb *haben*: **er hat gebändigt.**

b) **abfassen** *v/t* (*sep*, *-ge-*, *h*)

In conjugation the prefix *ab* must be separated from the primary verb *fassen*: **sie fasst ab; sie hat abgefasst.**

c) **finden** *v/t* (*irr, ge-*, *h*)

irr following a verb means that it is an irregular verb. The principal parts of this particular word can be found as an individual headword in the main part of the German-English section and in the list of irregular German verbs on page 662: **sie fand; sie hat gefunden.**

d) **abfallen** *v/i* (*irr*, **fallen**, *sep*, *-ge-*, *sein*)

A reference such as *irr*, **fallen** indicates that the compound word **abfallen** is conjugated in exactly the same way as the primary verb **fallen** as given in the list of irregular German verbs on page 662: **er fiel ab; er ist abgefallen.**

e) **senden** *v/t* ([*irr*,] *ge*-, *h*)

The square brackets indicate that **senden** can be treated as a regular or an irregular verb: *sie sandte* or *sie sendete; sie hat gesandt* or *sie hat gesendet.*

7.2 Nouns

The inflectional forms (*genitive singular; nominative plural*) follow immediately after the indication of gender. No forms are given for compounds if the parts appear as separate headwords.

The horizontal stroke replaces the part of the word which remains unchanged in the inflection:

Affäre *f* (-; -*n*)
Keks *m, n* (-*es*; -*e*)
Bau *m* (-[*e*]*s*; *Bauten*)
Blatt *n* (-[*e*]*s*; *Blätter* ['blɛtɐ])

The inflectional forms of German nouns ending in **-in** are given in the following ways:

Ärztin *f* (-; -*nen*)
Chemiker(in) (-*s*; -/-; -*nen*) = **Chemiker** *m*
(-*s*; -) and **Chemikerin** *f* (-; -*nen*)

7.3 Prepositions

If, for instance, a headword (verb, adjective or noun) is governed by certain prepositions, these are given in boldface italics and in brackets together with their English or German translations and placed next to the appropriate translation. If the German or English preposition is the same for all or several translations, it is given only once before or after the first translation and then also applies to the translations which follow it:

abrücken ... **1.** *v/t* (*h*) move away (**von** from)
befestigen *v/t* (*no* -*ge*-, *h*) fasten (**an** *dat* to), fix (to), attach (to)
dissent ... **2.** anderer Meinung sein (**from** als)
dissimilar (**to**) unähnlich (*dat*); verschieden (von)

With German prepositions which can take the dative or the accusative, the case is given in brackets:

fürchten ... **sich fürchten** ... be afraid (**vor** *dat* of)
bauen ... **bauen auf** (*acc*) rely *or* count on

We hope that this somewhat lengthy introduction has shown you that this dictionary contains a great deal more than simple one-to-one translations, and that you are now well-equipped to make the most of all it has to offer.

A

à [a] *prp* **5 Karten à Euro 20** 5 tickets at 20 euros each *or* a piece

Aal [aːl] *m* (-[e]s; -e) ZO eel

aalen ['aːlən] *v/refl* (*ge-, h*) **sich in der Sonne aalen** bask in the sun

'**aal'glatt** *fig adj* (as) slippery as an eel

Aas [aːs] *n* (-[e]s) a) *no pl* carrion, b) F *contp pl* **Äser** beast, *sl* bastard

'**Aasgeier** *m* ZO vulture (*a. fig*)

ab [ap] *prp and adv*: **München ab 13.55** departure from Munich (at) 1.55; **ab 7 Uhr** from 7 o'clock (on); **ab morgen** (**1. März**) starting tomorrow (March 1st); **von jetzt ab** from now on; **ab und zu** now and then; **ein Film ab 18** an X(-rated) film; **ein Knopf ist ab** a button has come off

'**abarbeiten** *v/t* (*sep, -ge-, h*) work out *or* off (*debts*); **sich abarbeiten** wear o.s. out

Abart ['ap?art] *f* (-; en) variety

abartig ['ap?artıç] *adj* abnormal

Abb. ABBR *of* **Abbildung** fig., illustration

'**Abbau** *m* (-[e]s; *no pl*) mining; TECH dismantling; *fig* overcoming (*of prejudices etc*); reduction (*of expenditure, staff etc*)

'**abbauen** *v/t* (*sep, -ge-, h*) mine; TECH dismantle; *fig* overcome (*prejudices etc*); reduce (*expenditure, staff etc*); **sich abbauen** BIOL break down

'**abbeißen** *v/t* (*irr, beißen, sep, -ge-, h*) bite off

'**abbeizen** *v/t* (*sep, -ge-, h*) remove *old paint etc* with corrosives

'**abbekommen** *v/t* (*irr, kommen, sep, no -ge-, h*) get off; **s-n Teil** *or* **et. abbekommen** get one's share; **et. abbekommen** *fig* get hurt, get damaged

'**abberufen** *v/t* (*irr, rufen, sep, no -ge-, h*), '**Abberufung** *f* recall

'**abbestellen** *v/t* (*sep, no -ge-, h*) cancel one's subscription (*or* order) for

'**Abbestellung** *f* cancellation

'**abbiegen** *v/i* (*irr, biegen, sep, -ge-, sein*) turn (off); **nach rechts** (**links**) **abbiegen** turn right (left)

'**abbilden** *v/t* (*sep, -ge-, h*) show, depict

'**Abbildung** *f* (-; -en) picture, illustration

'**Abbitte** *f* apology; **j-m Abbitte leisten wegen** apologize to s.o. for

'**abblasen** F *v/t* (*irr, blasen, sep, -ge-, h*) call off, cancel

'**abblättern** *v/i* (*sep, -ge-, sein*) *paint etc*: flake off

'**abblenden 1.** *v/t* (*sep, -ge-, h*) dim; **2.** *v/i* MOT dim (*Br* dip) the headlights

'**Abblendlicht** *n* MOT dimmed (*Br* dipped) headlights *pl*, low beam

'**abbrechen** *v/t* (*irr, brechen, sep, -ge-*) **1.** *v/t* (*h*) break off (*a. fig*); pull down, demolish (*building etc*); strike (*camp, tent*); **2.** *v/i* a) (*sein*) break off, b) (*h*) *fig* stop

'**abbremsen** *v/t* (*sep, -ge-, h*) slow down

'**abbrennen** *v/t* (*irr, brennen, sep, -ge-*) **1.** *v/i* (*sein*) burn down; **2.** *v/t* (*h*) burn down (*building etc*); let *or* set off (*fireworks*)

'**abbringen** *v/t* (*irr, bringen, sep, -ge-, h*) **j-n von e-r Sache abbringen** talk s.o. out of (doing) s.th.; **j-n vom Thema abbringen** get s.o. off a subject

'**Abbruch** *m* (-[e]s; *no pl*) breaking off; demolition

'**abbruchreif** *adj* derelict, due for demolition

'**abbuchen** *v/t* (*sep, -ge-, h*) debit (**von** to)

'**Abbuchung** *f* debit

'**abbürsten** *v/t* (*sep, -ge-, h*) brush off (*dust etc*); brush (*coat etc*)

Abc [aːbeː'tseː] *n* (-; *no pl*) ABC, alphabet

ABC-Waffen *pl* MIL nuclear, biological and chemical weapons

'**abdanken** *v/i* (*sep, -ge-, h*) resign; *king etc*: abdicate

'**Abdankung** *f* (-; -en) resignation; abdication

'**abdecken** *v/t* (*sep, -ge-, h*) uncover; untile (*roof*); unroof (*house*); clear (*the table*); ECON cover (up)

'**abdichten** *v/t* (*sep, -ge-, h*) TECH seal

'**abdrängen** *v/t* (*sep, -ge-, h*) push aside

'**abdrehen 1.** *v/t* (*sep, -ge-, h*) turn *or* switch off (*light, water etc*); **2.** *v/i* (*a. sein*) *ship, plane*: change one's course

'**Abdruck** *m* print, mark

'**abdrucken** *v/t* (*sep, -ge-, h*) print

'**abdrücken** (*sep, -ge-, h*) **1.** *v/t* fire (*gun*); **2.** *v/i* pull the trigger

Abend ['aːbənt] *m* (-[e]s; -e) evening; **am Abend** in the evening, at night; **heute Abend** tonight; **morgen** (**gestern**) **Abend** tomorrow (last) night; → **bunt**, **essen**

Abendbrot *n* (-[e]s; *no pl*), **Abendessen** *n* supper, dinner, *Br a.* high tea

Abendkasse *f* THEA *etc* box office

Abendkleid *n* evening dress *or* gown

Abendkurs *m* evening classes *pl*

'**Abendland** *n* (-[e]s; *no pl*) West, Occi-

°dent

'**abendländisch** [-lɛndɪʃ] *adj* Western, Occidental

'**Abendmahl** *n* (-[e]s; *no pl*) *the* (Holy) Communion, *the* Lord's Supper; *das Abendmahl empfangen* receive Communion

abends ['aːbənts] *adv* in the evening, at night; *dienstags abends* (on) Tuesday evenings

'**Abendschule** *f* evening classes *pl*, night school

Abenteuer ['aːbəntɔʏɐ] *n* (-s; -) adventure (*a. in cpds …ferien, …spielplatz*)

'**abenteuerlich** *adj* adventurous; *fig* risky; fantastic

Abenteurer ['aːbəntɔʏrɐ] *m* (-s; -) adventurer

'**Abenteurerin** [-rərm] *f* (-; -nen) adventuress

aber ['aːbɐ] *cj and adv* but; *oder aber* or else; *aber, aber!* now then!; *aber nein!* not at all!

'**Aberglaube** *m* superstition

abergläubisch ['aːbɐglɔʏbɪʃ] *adj* superstitious

'**aberkennen** *v/t* (*irr,* **kennen,** *sep, no -ge-, h*) *j-m et. aberkennen* deprive s.o. of s.th. (*a.* JUR)

'**Aberkennung** *f* (-; -en) deprivation (*a.* JUR)

abermalig ['aːbɐmaːlɪç] *adj* repeated

abermals ['aːbɐmaːls] *adv* once more *or* again

'**aber'tausend** *adj:* *tausende und abertausende* thousands upon thousands

'**abfahren** (*irr,* **fahren,** *sep, -ge-*) **1.** *v/i* (*sein*) leave, depart (*both:* **nach** for); F (*voll*) *abfahren auf* (*acc*) really go for; **2.** *v/t* (*h*) carry *or* cart away

'**Abfahrt** *f* departure (**nach** for), start (for); *skiing:* descent

'**Abfahrtslauf** *m* downhill skiing (*or* race)

'**Abfahrtszeit** *f* (time of) departure

'**Abfall** *m* waste, refuse, garbage, trash, *Br a.* rubbish

'**Abfallbeseitigung** *f* waste disposal

'**Abfalleimer** *m* → *Mülleimer*

'**abfallen** *v/i* (*irr,* **fallen,** *sep, -ge-, sein*) fall (off); *terrain:* slope (down); *fig* fall away (**von** from); *esp* POL secede (from); *vom Glauben abfallen* renounce one's faith; *abfallen gegen* compare badly with

'**abfällig 1.** *adj* derogatory; **2.** *adv:* *abfällig von j-m sprechen* run s.o. down

'**Abfallpro,dukt** *n* waste product

'**abfälschen** *v/t* (*sep, -ge-, h*) SPORT deflect

'**abfangen** *v/t* (*irr,* **fangen,** *sep, -ge-, h*) catch, intercept; MOT, AVIAT right

'**abfärben** *v/i* (*sep, -ge-, h*) *color etc:* run, *material:* a. bleed; *fig* *abfärben auf* (*acc*) rub off on

'**abfassen** *v/t* (*sep, -ge-, h*) compose, word, write

'**abfertigen** *v/t* (*sep, -ge-, h*) dispatch; *customs:* clear; serve (*customers*); check in (*passengers etc*); *j-n kurz abfertigen* be short with s.o.

'**Abfertigung** *f* dispatch; clearance; check-in

'**abfeuern** *v/t* (*sep, -ge-, h*) fire (off); launch (*rocket*)

'**abfinden** *v/t* (*irr,* **finden,** *sep, -ge-, h*) ECON pay off (*creditor*); buy out (*partner*); compensate; *sich mit e-r Sache abfinden* put up with s.th.

'**Abfindung** *f* (-; -en) ECON satisfaction; compensation

'**abflachen** *v/t and v/refl* (*sep, -ge-, h*) flatten

'**abflauen** *v/i* (*sep, -ge-, sein*) *wind etc:* drop (*a. fig*)

'**abfliegen** *v/i* (*irr,* **fliegen,** *sep, -ge-, sein*) AVIAT leave, depart

'**abfließen** *v/i* (*irr,* **fließen,** *sep, -ge-, sein*) flow off, drain (off *or* away)

'**Abflug** *m* AVIAT departure

'**Abfluss** *m* (-es; *Abflüsse*) a) *no pl* flowing off, b) TECH drain

'**Abflussrohr** *n* wastepipe, drain(pipe)

'**abfragen** *v/t* (*sep, -ge-, h*) quiz *or* question s.o. (*über acc* about), test *s.o.* orally

Abfuhr ['apfuːɐ] *f* (-; -en) removal; *j-m e-e Abfuhr erteilen* rebuff (F SPORT lick) s.o.

'**abführen** *v/t* (*sep, -ge-, h*) **1.** *v/t* lead *or* take away; ECON pay (over) (**an** *acc* to); **2.** *v/i* MED move one's bowels; act as a laxative

'**abführend** *adj,* '**Abführmittel** *n* MED laxative

'**abfüllen** *v/t* (*sep, -ge-, h*) bottle; can

'**Abgabe** *f* (-; -n) a) *no pl* handing in, b) SPORT pass, c) ECON rate; duty

'**abgabenfrei** *adj* tax-free

'**abgabenpflichtig** *adj* dutiable

'**Abgang** *m* (-[e]s; *Abgänge*) a) *no pl* departure; *Am* graduation, *Br* school-leaving; THEA exit (*a. fig*), b) SPORT dismount

Abgänger ['apgɛŋɐ] *m* (-s; -) *Am* graduate, *Br* school-leaver

'**Abgas** *n* waste gas; *pl* emission(s *pl*); MOT exhaust fumes *pl*

'**abgasfrei** *adj* emission-free

'**Abgasuntersuchung** *f* MOT *Am* emissions test, *Br* exhaust emission test

'**abgearbeitet** *adj* worn out

'**abgeben** *v/t* (*irr,* **geben,** *sep, -ge-, h*) leave (*bei* with); hand in; deposit (*one's baggage etc*), hand over (*ticket etc*) (*an* *acc* to); cast (*vote*); pass (*ball*); *give* off, emit (*heat etc*); make (*offer, statement etc*); *j-m et.* **abgeben von** share s.th. with s.o.; *sich* **abgeben mit** concern o.s. with *s.th.*, associate with *s.o.*

'**abgebrannt** *adj* burnt down; F *fig* broke
abgebrüht *fig adj* hard-boiled
abgedroschen *adj* hackneyed
abgefahren *adj tires*: worn out
abgegriffen *adj* worn
abgehackt *fig adj* disjointed
abgehangen *adj*: **gut abgehangenes Fleisch** well-hung meat
abgehärtet *adj* hardened (**gegen** to)
'**abgehen** *v/i* (*irr,* **gehen,** *sep, -ge-, sein*) *train etc*: leave; *mail, goods*: get off; THEA go off (stage); *button etc*: come off; *path etc*: branch off; **von der Schule abgehen** leave school; **abgehen von** drop (*plan etc*); **von s-r Meinung abgehen** change one's mind *or* opinion; **ihm geht ... ab** he lacks ...; **gut abgehen** end well, pass off well
'**abgehetzt, abgekämpft** *adj* exhausted, worn out
abgekartet ['apgəkartət] F *adj*: **abgekartete Sache** put-up job
abgelegen *adj* remote, distant
abgemacht *adj* fixed; **abgemacht!** it's a deal!
abgemagert *adj* emaciated
abgeneigt *adj*: **e-r Sache abgeneigt sein** be averse to s.th.; **ich wäre nicht abgeneigt, et. zu tun** I wouldn't mind doing s.th.
abgenutzt *adj* worn out
Abgeordnete ['apgə^ʔɔrdnətə] *m, f* (*-n; -n*) *Am* representative, congress|man (-woman), *Br* Member of Parliament (ABBR MP)
'**Abgeordnetenhaus** *n Am* House of Representatives, *Br* House of Commons
'**abgepackt** *adj* prepack(ag)ed
'**abgeschieden** *adj* secluded
'**Abgeschiedenheit** *f* (*-; no pl*) seclusion
'**abgeschlossen** *adj* completed; **abgeschlossene Wohnung** self-contained apartment (*Br* flat)
abgesehen *adj*: **abgesehen von** aside (*Br a.* apart) from; **ganz abgesehen von** not to mention, let alone
abgespannt *adj* exhausted, weary
abgestanden *adj* stale
abgestorben *adj* dead (*tree etc*); numb (*leg etc*)
abgestumpft *adj* insensitive, indifferent (**gegen** to)
abgetragen, abgewetzt *adj* worn out; threadbare, shabby

abgewöhnen *v/t* (*sep, -ge-, h*) *j-m et.* **abgewöhnen** make s.o. give up s.th.; *sich* (*dat*) **das Rauchen abgewöhnen** stop *or* give up smoking
'**Abgott** *m* idol (*a. fig*)
abgöttisch ['apgœtɪʃ] *adv*: *j-n* **abgöttisch lieben** idolize s.o.
'**abgrasen** *v/t* (*sep, -ge-, h*) graze; *fig* scour
'**abgrenzen** *v/t* (*sep, -ge-, h*) mark off; delimit (**gegen** from)
'**Abgrund** *m* abyss, chasm, gulf (*all a. fig*); **am Rande des Abgrunds** *fig* on the brink of disaster
'**abgrund'tief** *adj* abysmal
'**abgucken** F *v/t* (*sep, -ge-, h*) *j-m et.* **abgucken** learn s.th. from (watching) s.o.; → **abschreiben**
'**Abguss** *m* cast
'**abhaben** F *v/t* (*irr,* **haben,** *sep, -ge-, h*) **willst du et. abhaben?** do you want some (of it)? '**abhacken** *v/t* (*sep, -ge-, h*) chop *or* cut off
'**abhaken** *v/t* (*sep, -ge-, h*) check (*Br* tick) off; F forget
'**abhalten** *v/t* (*irr,* **halten,** *sep, -ge-, h*) hold (*meeting etc*); *j-n* **von der Arbeit abhalten** keep s.o. from his work; *j-n* **davon abhalten, et. zu tun** keep s.o. from doing s.th.
'**abhandeln** *v/t* (*sep, -ge-, h*) treat (*subject etc*); *j-m et.* **abhandeln** make a deal with s.o. for s.th.
'**Abhandlung** *f* treatise (**über** *acc* on)
'**Abhang** *m* slope
'**abhängen**[1] *v/t* (*sep, -ge-, h*) take down (*picture etc*); RAIL *etc* uncouple; F shake *s.o.* off
'**abhängen**[2] *v/i* (*irr,* **hängen,** *sep, -ge-, h*) **abhängen von** depend on; **das hängt davon ab** that depends
abhängig ['aphɛŋɪç] *adj*: **abhängig von** dependent on; *a.* addicted to *drugs etc*
'**Abhängigkeit** *f* (*-; -en*) dependence (**von** on); addiction (to)
'**abhärten** *v/t* (*sep, -ge-, h*) *sich* **abhärten** harden o.s. (**gegen** to)
'**abhauen** (*irr,* **hauen,** *sep, -ge-*) **1.** *v/t* (*h*) cut *or* chop off; **2.** F *v/i* (*sein*) make off (**mit** with), run away (with); **hau ab!** beat it!, scram!
'**abheben** (*irr,* **heben,** *sep, -ge-, h*) **1.** *v/t* lift *or* take off; pick up (*receiver*); (with)-draw (*money*); cut (*cards*); *sich* **abheben** stand out (**von** among, from), *fig a.* contrast with; **2.** *v/i* cut the cards; answer the phone; *plane*: take (*esp rocket*: lift) off
'**abheften** *v/t* (*sep, -ge-, h*) file
'**abheilen** *v/i* (*sep, -ge-, sein*) heal (up)
'**abhetzen** *v/refl* (*sep, -ge-, h*) wear o.s. out

'**Abhilfe** f remedy; **Abhilfe schaffen** take remedial measures
'**Abholdienst** m pickup service
'**abholen** v/t (sep, -ge-, h) pick up, collect; **j-n von der Bahn abholen** meet s.o. at the station
'**abholzen** v/t (sep, -ge-, h) fell, cut down (trees); deforest (area)
'**abhorchen** v/t (sep, -ge-, h) MED auscultate, sound
'**abhören** v/t (sep, -ge-, h) listen in on, tap (telephone conversation), F bug; → **abfragen**
'**Abhörgerät** n bugging device, F bug
Abitur [abi'tuːɐ] n (-s; -e) school-leaving examination (qualifying for university entrance)
'**abjagen** v/t (sep, -ge-, h) **j-m et. abjagen** recover s.th. from s.o.
'**abkanzeln** F v/t (sep, -ge-, h) tell s.o. off
'**abkaufen** v/t (sep, -ge-, h) **j-m et. abkaufen** buy s.th. from s.o.
Abkehr ['apkeːɐ] f (-; no pl) break (**von** with)
'**abkehren** v/refl (sep, -ge-, h) **sich abkehren von** turn away from
'**abklingen** v/i (irr, **klingen**, sep, -ge-, sein) fade away; pain etc: ease off
'**abklopfen** v/t (sep, -ge-, h) MED sound
'**abknallen** F v/t (sep, -ge-, h) pick off
'**abknicken** v/t (sep, -ge-, h) snap or break off; bend
'**abkochen** v/t (sep, -ge-, h) boil
'**abkommandieren** v/t (sep, no -ge-, h) MIL detach (**zu** for)
'**abkommen** v/i (irr, **kommen**, sep, -ge-, sein) **abkommen von** get off; drop (plan etc); **vom Thema abkommen** stray from the point; → **Weg**
'**Abkommen** n (-s; -) agreement, treaty; **ein Abkommen schließen** make an agreement
Abkömmling ['apkœmlɪŋ] m (-s; -e) descendant
'**abkoppeln** v/t (sep, -ge-, h) uncouple (**von** from); undock (spacecraft)
'**abkratzen** (sep, -ge-) **1.** v/t (h) scrape off; **2.** F v/i (sein) kick the bucket
'**abkühlen** v/t and v/refl (sep, -ge-, h) cool down (a. fig)
'**Abkühlung** f cooling
'**abkürzen** v/t (sep, -ge-, h) shorten; abbreviate; **den Weg abkürzen** take a short cut
'**Abkürzung** f abbreviation; short cut
'**abladen** v/t (irr, **laden**, sep, -ge-, h) unload; dump (waste etc)
'**Ablage** f (-; -n) a) no pl filing, b) filing tray, c) Swiss → **Zweigstelle**

'**ablagern** (sep, -ge-, h) **1.** v/t season (wood); let wine age; GEOL etc deposit; **sich ablagern** settle, be deposited; **2.** v/i (a. sein) season; age
'**Ablagerung** f (-; -en) CHEM, GEOL deposit, sediment
'**ablassen** (irr, **lassen**, sep, -ge-, h) **1.** v/t drain off (liquid); let off (steam); drain (pond etc); **2.** v/i: **von et.** (**j-m**) **ablassen** stop doing s.th. (leave s.o. alone)
'**Ablauf** m (-[e]s; Abläufe) a) course; process; order of events, b) no pl expiration, Br expiry, c) → **Abfluss**
'**ablaufen** (irr, **laufen**, sep, -ge-) **1.** v/i (sein) water etc: run off; performance etc: go, proceed; come to an end; period, passport etc: expire; time, record, tape: run out; clock: run down; **gut ablaufen** turn out well; **2.** v/t (h) wear down
'**ablecken** v/t (sep, -ge-, h) lick (off)
'**ablegen** (sep, -ge-, h) **1.** v/t take off (clothes); file (letters etc); give up (habit etc); take (examination, oath); **abgelegte Kleider** cast-offs pl; **2.** v/i take off one's (hat and) coat; MAR put out, sail
'**Ableger** m (-s; -) BOT layer; offshoot (a. fig)
'**ablehnen** v/t (sep, -ge-, h) refuse; turn down (application etc); PARL reject; object to; condemn
ablehnend adj negative
'**Ablehnung** f (-; -en) refusal; rejection; objection (gen to)
'**ableiten** v/t (sep, -ge-, h) divert; LING, MATH derive (**aus** dat, **von** from) (a. fig)
'**Ableitung** f diversion; LING, MATH derivation (a. fig)
'**ablenken** v/t (sep, -ge-, h) divert (**von** from); soccer: turn away (ball); deflect (rays etc); **j-n von der Arbeit ablenken** distract s.o. from his work; **er lässt sich leicht ablenken** he is easily diverted
'**Ablenkung** f diversion
'**ablesen** v/t (irr, **lesen**, sep, -ge-, h) read
'**abliefern** v/t (sep, -ge-, h) deliver (**bei** to, at); hand over (to)
'**ablösbar** adj detachable
'**ablösen** v/t (sep, -ge-, h) detach; take off; take s.o.'s place, take over from s.o.; esp MIL relieve; replace; **sich ablösen** take turns (driving etc)
'**Ablösesumme** f SPORT transfer fee
'**Ablösung** f relief
'**abmachen** v/t (sep, -ge-, h) remove, take off; settle, arrange
'**Abmachung** f (-; -en) arrangement, agreement, deal
'**abmagern** v/i (sep, -ge-, sein) get thin
'**Abmagerung** f (-; -en) emaciation

'**Abmagerungskur** *f* slimming diet

'**abmähen** *v/t* (*sep*, *-ge-*, *h*) mow

'**abmalen** *v/t* (*sep*, *-ge-*, *h*) copy

'**Abmarsch** *m* (-[*e*]*s*; *no pl*) start; MIL marching off

'**abmar,schieren** *v/i* (*sep*, *no -ge-*, *sein*) start; MIL march off

'**abmelden** *v/t* (*sep*, *-ge-*, *h*) cancel the registration of (*car etc*); cancel s.o.'s membership (*in a club etc*); give notice of s.o.'s withdrawal (from school); *sich abmelden* give notice of change of address; report off duty

'**Abmeldung** *f* notice of withdrawal; notice of change of address

'**abmessen** *v/t* (*irr*, *messen*, *sep*, *-ge-*, *h*) measure

'**Abmessung** *f* measurement; *pl* dimensions

'**abmon,tieren** *v/t* (*sep*, *no -ge-*, *h*) take off; take down; TECH dismantle

'**abmühen** *v/refl* (*sep*, *-ge-*, *h*) work very hard; try hard (*to do s.th.*); struggle (*mit* with)

'**abnagen** *v/t* (*sep*, *-ge-*, *h*) gnaw (at)

Abnahme ['apna:mə] *f* (-; *-n*) reduction, decrease; loss (*a. of weight*); ECON purchase; TECH acceptance

'**abnehmbar** *adj* removable

'**abnehmen** (*irr*, *nehmen*, *sep*, *-ge-*, *h*) **1.** *v/t* take off (*a.* MED), remove; pick up (*receiver*); TECH accept; ECON buy; *j-m et. abnehmen* take s.th. (away) from s.o.; **2.** *v/i* decrease, diminish; lose weight; answer the phone; *moon*: wane

'**Abnehmer** *m* (-*s*; -) buyer; customer

'**Abneigung** *f* (*gegen*) dislike (of, for); aversion (to)

abnorm [ap'nɔrm] *adj* abnormal; exceptional, unusual

Abnormität [apnɔrmi'tɛːt] *f* (-; *-en*) abnormality

'**abnutzen**, '**abnützen** *v/t and v/refl* (*sep*, *-ge-*, *h*) wear out

'**Abnutzung**, '**Abnützung** *f* (-; *no pl*) wear (and tear) (*a. fig*)

Abonnement [abɔnə'mãː] *n* (-*s*; -*s*) subscription (*auf acc* to)

Abonnent [abɔ'nɛnt] *m* (-*en*; -*en*) subscriber; THEA season-ticket holder

abonnieren [abɔ'niːrən] *v/t* (*no -ge-*, *h*) subscribe to

Abordnung *f* (-; *-en*) delegation

Abort [a'bɔrt] *m* (-[*e*]*s*; -*e*) lavatory, toilet

'**abpassen** *v/t* (*sep*, *-ge-*, *h*) watch *or* wait for (*s.o.*, *s.th.*); waylay s.o. (*a. fig*)

'**abpfeifen** *v/t and v/i* (*irr*, *pfeifen*, *sep*, *-ge-*, *h*) SPORT blow the final whistle; stop the game

'**abplagen** *v/refl* (*sep*, *-ge-*, *h*) struggle (*mit* with)

'**abprallen** *v/i* (*sep*, *-ge-*, *sein*) rebound, bounce (off); *bullet*: ricochet

'**abputzen** *v/t* (*sep*, *-ge-*, *h*) wipe off; clean

'**abraten** *v/i* (*irr*, *raten*, *sep*, *-ge-*, *h*) *j-m abraten von* advise *or* warn s.o. against

'**abräumen** *v/t* (*sep*, *-ge-*, *h*) clear away; clear (*the table*)

'**abrea,gieren** *v/t* (*sep*, *no -ge-*, *h*) work off (*one's anger etc*) (*an dat* on); *sich abreagieren* F let off steam

'**abrechnen** (*sep*, *-ge-*, *h*) **1.** *v/t* deduct, subtract; claim (*expenses*); **2.** *v/i*: *mit j-m abrechnen* settle accounts (*fig a.* get even) with s.o.

'**Abrechnung** *f* settlement; F *fig* showdown

'**abreiben** *v/t* (*irr*, *reiben*, *sep*, *-ge-*, *h*) rub off; rub down (*body*); polish

'**Abreise** *f* departure (*nach* for)

'**abreisen** *v/i* (*sep*, *-ge-*, *sein*) depart, leave, start, set out (*all*: *nach* for)

'**abreißen** (*irr*, *reißen*, *sep*, *-ge-*) **1.** *v/t* (*h*) tear *or* pull off; pull down (*building*); **2.** *v/i* (*sein*) break; *button etc*: come off

'**Abreißka,lender** *m* tear-off calendar

'**abrichten** *v/t* (*sep*, *-ge-*, *h*) train (*animal*), *a.* break *a horse* in

'**abriegeln** *v/t* (*sep*, *-ge-*, *h*) block off, cordon off

'**Abriss** *m* (-*es*; -*e*) a) (*no pl*) demolition, b) outline, summary

'**abrollen** *v/i* (*sep*, *-ge-*, *sein*) *and v/t* (*h*) unroll (*a. fig*)

'**abrücken** (*sep*, *-ge-*) **1.** *v/t* (*h*) move away (*von* from); **2.** *v/i* (*sein*) draw away (*von* from); MIL march off

'**Abruf** *m*: *auf Abruf* ECON on call

'**abrufen** *v/t* (*irr*, *rufen*, *sep*, *-ge-*, *h*) call away; EDP recall, fetch, retrieve

'**abrunden** *v/t* (*sep*, *-ge-*, *h*) round (off)

'**abrupfen** *v/t* (*sep*, *-ge-*, *h*) pluck (off)

abrupt [ap'rʊpt] *adj* abrupt

'**abrüsten** *v/t* (*sep*, *-ge-*, *h*) MIL disarm

'**Abrüstung** *f* (-; *no pl*) MIL disarmament

'**abrutschen** *v/i* (*sep*, *-ge-*, *sein*) slide down; slip (off) (*von* from)

ABS [aːbeː'ɛs] → *Antiblockiersystem*

Absage ['apzaːgə] *f* (-; *-n*) refusal; cancellation

'**absagen** (*sep*, *-ge-*, *h*) **1.** *v/t* call off, cancel (*event etc*); **2.** *v/i* call off; *j-m absagen a.* cancel one's appointment with s.o.; decline (the invitation)

'**absägen** *v/t* (*sep*, *-ge-*, *h*) saw off; F *fig* oust, sack s.o.

'**absahnen** F *v/i* (*sep*, *-ge-*, *h*) cash in

'**Absatz** *m* paragraph; ECON sales *pl*; shoe:

heel; *stairs*: landing

'**abschaben** *v/t* (*sep*, -*ge*-, *h*) scrape off

'**abschaffen** *v/t* (*sep*, -*ge*-, *h*) do away with, abolish; repeal (*law*); put an end to (*abuses etc*)

'**Abschaffung** *f* (-; *no pl*) abolition; repeal

'**abschalten** (*sep*, -*ge*-, *h*) **1.** *v/t* switch *or* turn off; **2.** F *v/i* relax, switch off

'**abschätzen** *v/t* (*sep*, -*ge*-, *h*) estimate; assess; size up

abschätzig ['apʃɛtsɪç] *adj* contemptuous; derogatory

Abschaum *m* (-*s*; *no pl*) scum (*a. fig*)

'**Abscheu** *m* (-*s*; *no pl*) disgust (*vor, gegen* at, for); *e-n Abscheu haben vor* abhor, detest; *Abscheu erregend* → *abscheuerregend*

'**abscheuerregend** *adj* revolting, repulsive

ab'scheulich *adj* abominable, despicable (*a. person*), *a.* atrocious (*crime*)

'**abschicken** *v/t* (*sep*, -*ge*-, *h*) → *absenden*

'**abschieben** *fig v/t* (*irr*, *schieben*, *sep*, -*ge*-, *h*) push away; get rid of; deport; *et. auf j-n abschieben* shove s.th. off on (to) s.o.

Abschied ['apʃiːt] *m* (-[*e*]*s*; -*e*) parting, farewell; *Abschied nehmen* (*von*) say goodbye (to), take leave (of); *s-n Abschied nehmen* resign, retire

'**Abschiedsfeier** *f* farewell party

'**Abschiedskuss** *m* goodbye kiss

'**abschießen** *v/t* (*irr*, *schießen*, *sep*, -*ge*-, *h*) shoot off (AVIAT down); launch (*rocket*); shoot, kill (*deer*); F pick s.o. off; *fig* oust; get rid of s.o.

'**abschirmen** *v/t* (*sep*, -*ge*-, *h*) shield (*gegen* from); *fig* protect (*gegen* against, from)

'**Abschirmung** *f* (-; -*en*) shield, screen; *fig* protection

'**abschlachten** *v/t* (*sep*, -*ge*-, *h*) slaughter (*a. fig*)

'**Abschlag** *m* SPORT kickout; ECON down payment

'**abschlagen** *v/t* (*irr*, *schlagen*, *sep*, -*ge*-, *h*) knock off; cut off (*head*); cut down (*tree*); refuse (*request etc*), turn s.th. down

'**abschleifen** *v/t* (*irr*, *schleifen*, *sep*, -*ge*-, *h*) grind off; sand(paper), smooth

'**Abschleppdienst** *m* MOT emergency road (*Br* breakdown) service

'**abschleppen** *v/t* (*sep*, -*ge*-, *h*) MOT (give s.o. a) tow; *police*: tow away

'**Abschleppseil** *n* towrope

Abschleppwagen *m Am* tow truck, *Br* breakdown lorry

'**abschließen** (*irr*, *schließen*, *sep*, -*ge*-, *h*) **1.** *v/t* lock (up); close, finish; complete;

take out (*insurance*); conclude (*research etc*); *e-n Handel abschließen* strike a bargain; *sich abschließen* shut o.s. off; → *Wette*; **2.** *v/i* close, finish

abschließend 1. *adj* concluding; final; **2.** *adv*: *abschließend sagte er* he concluded by saying

'**Abschluss** *m* conclusion, close

Abschlussprüfung *f* final examination, finals *pl*, *esp Am a.* graduation; *s-e Abschlussprüfung machen* graduate (*an dat* from)

Abschlusszeugnis *n Am* diploma, *Br* school-leaving certificate

'**abschmecken** *v/t* (*sep*, -*ge*-, *h*) season

'**abschmieren** *v/t* (*sep*, -*ge*-, *h*) TECH lubricate, grease

'**abschminken** *v/t* (*sep*, -*ge*-, *h*) *sich abschminken* remove one's make-up

'**abschnallen** *v/t* (*sep*, -*ge*-, *h*) undo; take off (*skis*); *sich abschnallen* MOT, AVIAT unfasten one's seat belt

'**abschneiden** (*irr*, *schneiden*, *sep*, -*ge*-, *h*) **1.** *v/t* cut (off) (*a. fig*); *j-m das Wort abschneiden* cut s.o. short; **2.** *v/i*: *gut abschneiden* come off well

'**Abschnitt** *m* passage, section (*of book etc*); paragraph; MATH, BIOL segment; period (*of time*), stage (*of journey*), phase (*of development*); coupon, slip, stub (*of check etc*)

'**abschnittweise** *adv* section by section

'**abschrauben** *v/t* (*sep*, -*ge*-, *h*) unscrew

'**abschrecken** *v/t* (*sep*, -*ge*-, *h*) deter (*von* from); GASTR douse *eggs etc* with cold water

abschreckend *adj* deterrent; *abschreckendes Beispiel* warning example

'**Abschreckung** *f* (-; -*en*) deterrence

'**abschreiben** *v/t* (*irr*, *schreiben*, *sep*, -*ge*-, *h*) copy; PED crib; ECON write off (*a.* F *fig*)

'**Abschrift** *f* copy, duplicate

'**abschürfen** *v/t* (*sep*, -*ge*-, *h*) graze

'**Abschürfung** *f* (-; -*en*) abrasion

Abschuss *m* launch(ing) (*of rocket*); AVIAT shooting down, downing; kill

Abschussbasis *f* MIL launching base

abschüssig ['apʃʏsɪç] *adj* sloping; steep

'**Abschussliste** F *f*: *auf der Abschussliste stehen* be on the hit list

'**Abschussrampe** *f* MIL launching pad

'**abschütteln** *v/t* (*sep*, -*ge*-, *h*) shake off

'**abschwächen** *v/t* (*sep*, -*ge*-, *h*) lessen, diminish

'**abschweifen** *fig v/i* (*sep*, -*ge*-, *sein*) digress (*von* from)

'**Abschweifung** *f* (-; -*en*) digression

absehbar ['apzeːbaːɐ] *adj* foreseeable; *in absehbarer* (*auf absehbare*) *Zeit* in the (for the) foreseeable future

'**absehen** *v/t* (*irr*, **sehen**, *sep*, -*ge*-, *h*) foresee; *es ist kein Ende abzusehen* there is no end in sight; *es abgesehen haben auf* (*acc*) be after; *absehen von* refrain from

'**abseilen** *v/refl* (*sep*, -*ge*-, *h*) descend by a rope, *Br a.* abseil; F make a getaway

abseits ['apzaɪts] *adv and prp* away *or* remote from

'**Abseitsfalle** *f soccer*: offside trap

abseitsstehen *v/i* (*irr*, **stehen**, *sep*, -*ge*-, *h*) *soccer*: be offside; *fig* be left out

'**absenden** *v/t* ([*irr*, **senden**,] *sep*, -*ge*-, *h*) send (off), dispatch; mail, *esp Br* post (*letter etc*)

'**Absender** *m* (-*s*; -) sender

absetzbar ['apzɛtsbaːɐ] *adj*: *steuerlich absetzbar* deductible from tax

'**absetzen** (*sep*, -*ge*-, *h*) **1.** *v/t* take off (*hat, glasses etc*); set *or* put down (*bag etc*); drop (*passenger*); dismiss (*employee*); THEA, *film*: take off; deduct (*from tax*); depose (*king etc*); ECON sell; *sich absetzen* CHEM, GEOL settle, be deposited; **2.** *v/i*: *ohne abzusetzen* without stopping

'**Absetzung** *f* (-; -*en*) dismissal; deposition; THEA, *film*: withdrawal

'**Absicht** *f* (-; -*en*) intention; *mit Absicht* on purpose

'**absichtlich 1.** *adj* intentional; **2.** *adv* on purpose

'**absitzen** (*irr*, **sitzen**, *sep*, -*ge*-) **1.** *v/i* (*sein*) dismount (*von* from); **2.** *v/t* (*h*) serve (*sentence*); F sit out (*play etc*)

absolut [apzoˈluːt] *adj* absolute

Absolvent [apzɔlˈvɛnt] *m* (-*en*; -*en*), **Absolˈventin** *f* (-; -*nen*) graduate

absolvieren [apzɔlˈviːrən] *v/t* (*no* -*ge*-, *h*) attend (*school*); complete (*studies*); graduate from (*college etc*)

'**absondern** *v/t* (*sep*, -*ge*-, *h*) separate; MED, BIOL secrete; *sich absondern* cut o.s. off (*von* from)

'**Absonderung** *f* (-; -*en*) separation; MED, BIOL secretion

absorbieren [apzɔrˈbiːrən] *v/t* (*no* -*ge*-, *h*) absorb (*a. fig*)

'**abspeichern** *v/t* (*sep*, -*ge*-, *h*) EDP store, save

abspenstig ['apʃpɛnstɪç] *adj*: *j-m die Freundin abspenstig machen* steal s.o.'s girlfriend

absperren *v/t* (*sep*, -*ge*-, *h*) lock; turn off (*water, gas etc*); block off (*road*); cordon off

'**Absperrung** *f* (-; -*en*) barrier; cordon

'**abspielen** *v/t* (*sep*, -*ge*-, *h*) play (*record etc*); SPORT pass (*the ball*); *sich abspielen*

happen, take place

'**Absprache** *f* agreement

'**absprechen** *v/t* (*irr*, **sprechen**, *sep*, -*ge*-, *h*) agree upon; arrange; *j-m die Fähigkeit etc absprechen* dispute s.o.'s ability etc

'**abspringen** *v/i* (*irr*, **springen**, *sep*, -*ge*-, *sein*) jump off; AVIAT jump, bail out; *fig* back out (*von* of)

'**Absprung** *m* jump; SPORT take-off; *fig* *den Absprung schaffen* make it

'**abspülen** *v/t* (*sep*, -*ge*-, *h*) rinse; wash up

abstammen *v/i* (*sep*, *no past participle*) be descended (*von* from); CHEM, LING derive

'**Abstammung** *f* (-; *no pl*) descent; derivation

'**Abstammungslehre** *f* theory of the origin of species

'**Abstand** *m* distance (*a. fig*); interval; *Abstand halten* keep one's distance; *fig* *mit Abstand* by far

abstatten ['apʃtatən] *v/t* (*sep*, -*ge*-, *h*) *j-m e-n Besuch abstatten* pay a visit to s.o.

'**abstauben** *v/t* (*sep*, -*ge*-, *h*) dust; F *fig* sponge; swipe

'**Abstauber** F *m* (-*s*; -), '**Abstaubertor** *n* SPORT opportunist goal

'**abstechen** (*irr*, **stechen**, *sep*, -*ge*-, *h*) **1.** *v/t* stick (*pig etc*); **2.** *v/i* contrast (*von* with)

'**Abstecher** *m* (-*s*; -) side-trip, excursion (*a. fig*)

'**abstecken** *v/t* (*sep*, -*ge*-, *h*) mark out

'**abstehen** *v/i* (*irr*, **stehen**, *sep*, -*ge*-, *h*) stick out, protrude; → *abgestanden*

'**absteigen** *v/i* (*irr*, **steigen**, *sep*, -*ge*-, *sein*) get off (*a horse etc*); climb down; stay (*in* dat at); SPORT *Am* be moved down to a lower division, *Br* be relegated

'**Absteiger** *m* (-*s*; -) SPORT *Br* relegated club

'**abstellen** *v/t* (*sep*, -*ge*-, *h*) put down; leave (*s.th. with s.o.*); turn off (*gas etc*); park (*car*); *fig* put an end to *s.th.*

'**Abstellgleis** *n* RAIL siding; *j-n aufs Abstellgleis schieben* F push s.o. aside

'**Abstellraum** *m* storeroom

'**abstempeln** *v/t* (*sep*, -*ge*-, *h*) stamp

'**absterben** *v/i* (*irr*, **sterben**, *sep*, -*ge*-, *sein*) die off; *limb*: go numb

Abstieg ['apʃtiːk] *m* (-[*e*]*s*; -*e*) descent; *fig* decline; SPORT *Br* relegation

'**abstimmen** *v/i* (*sep*, -*ge*-, *h*) vote (*über* acc on)

'**Abstimmung** *f* vote; *radio*: tuning

Abstinenzler [apstiˈnɛntslɐ] *m* (-*s*; -) teetotal(l)er

'**Abstoß** *m* SPORT goal-kick

'**abstoßen** *v/t* (*irr*, **stoßen**, *sep*, -*ge*-, *h*) re-

pel; MED reject; push off (*boat*); F get rid
of *s.th.*
abstoßend *fig adj* repulsive
abstrakt [ap'strakt] *adj* abstract
'**abstreiten** *v/t* (*irr,* **streiten,** *sep, -ge-, h*)
deny
'**Abstrich** *m* MED smear; *pl* ECON cuts; *fig*
reservations
'**abstufen** *v/t* (*sep, -ge-, h*) graduate; gra-
date (*colors*)
'**abstumpfen** (*sep, -ge-*) **1.** *v/t* (*h*) blunt,
dull (*a. fig*); **2.** *fig v/i* (*sein*) become unfeeling
'**Absturz** *m,* '**abstürzen** *v/i* (*sep, -ge-, sein*)
fall; AVIAT, EDP crash
'**absuchen** *v/t* (*sep, -ge-, h*) search (**nach**
for)
absurd [ap'zʊrt] *adj* absurd, preposterous
Abszess [aps'tsɛs] *m* (*-es; -e*) MED abscess
Abt [apt] *m* (*-[e]s; Äbte* ['ɛptə]) REL abbot
'**abtasten** *v/t* (*sep, -ge-, h*) feel (for); MED
palpate; frisk; TECH, EDP scan
'**abtauen** *v/t* (*sep, -ge-, h*) defrost
Abtei [ap'tai] *f* (*-; -en*) REL abbey
Abteil [ap'tail] *n* (*-[e]s; -e*) RAIL compartment
'**abteilen** *v/t* (*sep, -ge-, h*) divide; ARCH partition off
Ab'teilung *f* (*-; -en*) department (*a.* ECON);
ward (*of hospital*); MIL detachment
Ab'teilungsleiter *m* head of (a) department; *Am* floorwalker, *Br* shopwalker
Äbtissin [ɛp'tɪsɪn] *f* (*-; -nen*) REL abbess
'**abtöten** *v/t* (*sep, -ge-, h*) kill (*bacteria etc*);
fig deaden (*feelings etc*)
'**abtragen** *v/t* (*irr,* **tragen,** *sep, -ge-, h*)
wear out (*clothes*); clear away (*dishes
etc*); pay off (*debt*)
'**Abtrans,port** *m* transportation
'**abtreiben** (*irr,* **treiben,** *sep, -ge-*) **1.** *v/i*
MED (*h*) have an abortion; MAR, AVIAT
(*sein*) be blown off course; **2.** *v/t* (*h*)
MED abort
'**Abtreibung** *f* (*-; -en*) abortion; **e-e Abtreibung vornehmen** perform an abortion
'**abtrennen** *v/t* (*sep, -ge-, h*) detach; separate; MED sever
'**abtreten** (*irr,* **treten,** *sep, -ge-*) **1.** *v/t* (*h*)
wear down (*heels*); wipe (*one's feet*); *fig*
give up (**an** *acc* to); **2.** *v/i* (*sein*) resign;
THEA; exit
'**Abtreter** *m* (*-s; -*) doormat
'**abtrocknen** (*sep, -ge-, h*) **1.** *v/t* dry; **sich
abtrocknen** dry o.s. off; **2.** *v/i* dry the
dishes, *Br a.* dry up
abtrünnig ['aptrʏnɪç] *adj* unfaithful, disloyal
'**Abtrünnige** [-nɪgə] *m, f* (*-n; -n*) renegade,

turncoat
abtun *v/t* (*irr,* **tun,** *sep, -ge-, h*) dismiss (**als**
as), brush *s.o., s.th.* aside
abwägen ['apvɛːgən] *v/t* (*irr,* **wägen,** *sep,
-ge-, h*) weigh (**gegen** against)
'**abwählen** *v/t* (*sep, -ge-, h*) vote out
'**abwälzen** *v/t* (*sep, -ge-, h*) **et. auf j-n abwälzen** shove *s.th.* off on (to) *s.o.*
'**abwandeln** *v/t* (*sep, -ge-, h*) vary, modify
'**abwandern** *v/i* (*sep, -ge-, sein*) migrate
(**von** from; **nach** to)
'**Abwanderung** *f* migration
'**Abwandlung** *f* modification, variation
'**Abwärme** *f* TECH waste heat
Abwart ['apvart] *m* (*-s; -e*) *Swiss* → **Hausmeister**
'**abwarten** (*sep, -ge-, h*) **1.** *v/t* wait for,
await; **2.** *v/i* wait; **warten wir ab!** let's
wait and see!; **wart nur ab!** just wait!
abwärts ['apvɛrts] *adv* down, down-
-ward(s)
Abwasch ['apvaʃ] *m* (*-[e]s; no pl*) **den
Abwasch machen** do the washing-up
'**abwaschbar** *adj* washable
'**abwaschen** (*irr,* **waschen,** *sep, -ge-, h*) **1.**
v/t wash off; **2.** *v/i* do the dishes, *Br a.*
wash up
'**Abwaschwasser** *n* dishwater
'**Abwasser** *n* TECH waste water, sewage
Abwasseraufbereitung *f* TECH sewage
treatment
'**abwechseln** *v/i* (*sep, -ge-, h*) alternate;
sich mit j-m abwechseln take turns
(**bei et.** at [doing] *s.th.*)
abwechselnd *adv* by turns
'**Abwechslung** *f* (*-; -en*) change; **zur Abwechslung** for a change
'**abwechslungsreich** *adj* varied;
colo(u)rful
'**Abweg** *m:* **auf Abwege geraten** go astray
abwegig ['apveːgɪç] *adj* absurd, unrealistic
'**Abwehr** *f* (*-; no pl*) defen|se, *Br* -ce (*a.*
SPORT); warding off (*of blow etc*); save
(*of ball*)
'**abwehren** *v/t* (*sep, -ge-, h*) ward off (*blow
etc*); beat off; SPORT block
'**Abwehrfehler** *m* SPORT defensive error
Abwehrkräfte *pl* MED resistance
Abwehrspieler *m* SPORT defender
Abwehrstoffe *pl* MED antibodies
'**abweichen** *v/i* (*irr,* **weichen,** *sep, -ge-,
sein*) deviate (**von** from); digress
'**Abweichung** *f* (*-; -en*) deviation
'**abweisen** *v/t* (*irr,* **weisen,** *sep, -ge-, h*)
turn away; rebuff; decline, turn down
(*request, offer etc*)
abweisend *adj* unfriendly
'**abwenden** *v/t* ([*irr,* **wenden,**] *sep, -ge-, h*)

turn away (a. **sich abwenden**) (**von** from); avert (*tragedy etc*)

'**abwerfen** v/t (*irr*, **werfen**, *sep*, -*ge*-, *h*) throw off; AVIAT drop; BOT shed (*leaves*); ECON yield (*profit*)

'**abwerten** v/t (*sep*, -*ge*-, *h*) ECON devalue

abwertend *fig adj* disparaging

'**Abwertung** *f* ECON devaluation

'**abwesend** *adj* absent

'**Abwesenheit** *f* (-; *no pl*) absence

abwickeln v/t (*sep*, -*ge*-, *h*) unwind; ECON handle; transact (*business*)

'**abwiegen** v/t (*irr*, **wiegen**, *sep*, -*ge*-, *h*) weigh (out)

'**abwischen** v/t (*sep*, -*ge*-, *h*) wipe (off)

'**Abwurf** *m* dropping; *soccer*: throw-out

'**abwürgen** F v/t (*sep*, -*ge*-, *h*) MOT stall; *fig* stifle

'**abzahlen** v/t (*sep*, -*ge*-, *h*) make *monthly etc* payments for; pay off

'**abzählen** v/t (*sep*, -*ge*-, *h*) count

'**Abzahlung** *f*: *et. auf Abzahlung kaufen Am* buy s.th. on the instalment plan (*Br* on hire purchase)

'**abzapfen** v/t (*sep*, -*ge*-, *h*) tap, draw off

'**Abzeichen** *n* badge; medal

'**abzeichnen** v/t (*sep*, -*ge*-, *h*) copy, draw; sign, initial; **sich abzeichnen** (begin to) show; stand out (**gegen** against)

'**Abziehbild** *n Am* decal, *Br* transfer

'**abziehen** (*irr*, **ziehen**, *sep*, -*ge*-) **1.** v/t (*h*) take off, remove; MATH subtract; strip (*bed*); take out (*key*); **das Fell abziehen** skin; **2.** v/i (*sein*) go away; MIL withdraw; *smoke*: escape; *storm*, *clouds*: move off

'**Abzug** *m* ECON deduction; discount; MIL withdrawal; PRINT copy; PHOT print; *gun*: trigger; TECH vent, outlet; cooker hood

abzüglich ['aptsy:klɪç] *prp* less, minus

'**abzweigen** (*sep*, -*ge*-) **1.** v/t (*h*) divert (*resources etc*) (**für** to); **2.** v/i (*sein*) *path etc*: branch off

'**Abzweigung** *f* (-; -*en*) junction

ach [ax] *int* oh!; **ach je!** oh dear!; **ach so!** I see; **ach was!** *surprised*: really?, annoyed: of course not!, nonsense!

Achse ['aksə] *f* (-; -*n*) TECH axle; MATH *etc* axis; F **auf Achse sein** be on the move

Achsel ['aksəl] *f* (-; -*n*) ANAT shoulder; **die Achseln zucken** shrug one's shoulders

'**Achselhöhle** *f* ANAT armpit

acht [axt] *adj* eight; **heute in acht Tagen** a week from today, *esp Br* today week; (**heute**) **vor acht Tagen** a week ago (today)

Acht *f*: **Acht geben** → **achtgeben**; **außer Acht lassen** disregard; **sich in Acht nehmen** be careful, look *or* watch out (**vor** *dat* for)

achtgeben v/i (*irr*, **geben**, *sep*, -*ge*-, *h*) be careful; pay attention (**auf** *acc* to); take care (**auf** *acc* of); **gib acht!** look *or* watch out!, be careful!

achte ['axtə] *adj* eighth

'**achteckig** *adj* octagonal

Achtel ['axtəl] *n* (-*s*; -) eighth (part)

achten (*ge*-, *h*) **1.** v/t respect; **2.** v/i: **achten auf** (*acc*) pay attention to; keep an eye on; watch; be careful with; **darauf achten, dass** see to it that

ächten ['ɛçtən] v/t (*ge*-, *h*) ban; *esp* HIST outlaw

Achter ['axtɐ] *m* (-*s*; -) *rowing*: eight

'**Achterbahn** *f* roller coaster

'**achtfach** *adj and adv* eightfold

'**achtlos** *adj* careless, heedless

'**Achtung** *f* (-; *no pl*) respect (**vor** *dat* for); **Achtung!** look out!; MIL attention!; **Achtung! Achtung!** attention please!; **Achtung! Fertig! Los!** On your marks! Get set! Go!; **Achtung Stufe!** *Am* caution: step!, *Br* mind the step!

'**achtzehn** *adj* eighteen

'**achtzehnte** *adj* eighteenth

achtzig ['axtsɪç] *adj* eighty; **die achtziger Jahre** the eighties

achtzigste *adj* eightieth

ächzen ['ɛçtsən] v/i (*ge*-, *h*) groan (**vor** *dat* with)

Acker ['akɐ] *m* (-*s*; Äcker ['ɛkɐ]) field

Ackerbau *m* (-[*e*]*s*; *no pl*) agriculture; farming; **Ackerbau und Viehzucht** crop and stock farming

Ackerland *n* (-[*e*]*s*; *no pl*) farmland

'**ackern** F v/i (*ge*-, *h*) slog (away)

Adapter [a'daptɐ] *m* (-*s*; -) TECH adapter

addieren [a'di:rən] v/t (*no* -*ge*-, *h*) add (up)

Addition [adi'tsio:n] *f* (-; -*en*) addition, adding up

Adel ['a:dəl] *m* (-*s*; *no pl*) aristocracy

'**adeln** v/t (*ge*-, *h*) ennoble (a. *fig*); *Br* knight

Ader ['a:dɐ] *f* (-; -*n*) ANAT blood vessel, vein

Adjektiv ['atjɛkti:f] *n* (-*s*; -*e*) LING adjective

Adler ['a:dlɐ] *m* (-*s*; -) ZO eagle

adlig ['a:dlɪç] *adj* noble

Adlige ['a:dlɪgə] *m*, *f* (-*n*; -*n*) noble|man (-woman)

Admiral [atmi'ra:l] *m* (-*s*; -*e*) MAR admiral

adoptieren [adɔp'ti:rən] v/t (*no* -*ge*-, *h*) adopt

Adoptivkind [adɔp'ti:f-] *n* adopted child

Adressbuch [a'drɛs-] *n* directory

Adresse [a'drɛsə] *f* (-; -*n*) address

adressieren [adrɛ'si:rən] v/t (*no* -*ge*-, *h*)

address (*an acc* to)

Advent [at'vɛnt] *m* (-[e]*s*; *no pl*) REL Advent; **Advent Sunday**

Ad'ventszeit *f* Christmas season

Adverb [at'vɛrp] *n* (-*s*; *Adverbien* [at'vɛrbĭən]) LING adverb

Aerobic [ɛ'roːbɪk] *n* (-*s*; *no pl*) aerobics

Affäre [a'fɛːrə] *f* (-; -*n*) affair

Affe ['afə] *m* (-*n*; -*n*) ZO monkey; ape

Affekt [a'fɛkt] *m* (-[e]*s*; -*e*) *im Affekt* in the heat of passion (*a.* JUR)

affektiert [afɛk'tiːɐt] *adj* affected

Afrika ['aːfrika] Africa

Afrikaner [afri'kaːnɐ] *m* (-*s*; -), **Afri'kanerin** [-nərɪn] *f* (-; -*nen*), **afri'kanisch** *adj* African

After ['aftɐ] *m* (-*s*; -) ANAT anus

AG ABBR *of* **Aktiengesellschaft** *Am* (stock) corporation, *Br* PLC, public limited company

Agent [a'gɛnt] *m* (-*en*; -*en*), **A'gentin** *f* (-; -*nen*) agent; POL (secret) agent

Agentur [agɛn'tuːɐ] *f* (-; -*en*) agency

Aggression [agrɛ'sĭoːn] *f* (-; -*en*) aggression

aggressiv [agrɛ'siːf] *adj* aggressive

Aggressivität [agrɛsivi'tɛːt] *f* (-; *no pl*) aggressiveness

Agitator [agi'taːtoːɐ] *m* (-*s*; -*en* [-ta'toːrən]) agitator

ah [aː] *int* ah!

äh [ɛː] *int* er; *disgusted:* ugh!

aha [a'ha] *int* I see!, oh!

A'ha-Erlebnis *n* aha-experience

Ahn [aːn] *m* (-[e]*s*; -*en*; -*en*) ancestor, *pl a.* forefathers

ähneln ['ɛːnəln] *v/i* (*ge-*, *h*) resemble, look like

ahnen ['aːnən] *v/t* (*ge-*, *h*) suspect; foresee, know

ähnlich ['ɛːnlɪç] *adj* similar (*dat* to); *j-m ähnlich sehen* look like s.o.

'Ähnlichkeit *f* (-; -*en*) likeness, resemblance, similarity (*mit* to)

'Ahnung *f* (-; -*en*) presentiment, *a.* foreboding; notion, idea; *ich habe keine Ahnung* I have no idea

'ahnungslos *adj* unsuspecting, innocent

Ahorn ['aːhɔrn] *m* (-*s*, -*e*) BOT maple

Ähre ['ɛːrə] *f* (-; -*n*) BOT ear; spike

Aids [eɪdz] *n* (-; *no pl*) MED AIDS

'Aids-Kranke *m*, *f* MED AIDS victim *or* sufferer

Aidstest *m* MED AIDS test

Airbag ['ɛəbæg] *m* (-*s*; -*s*) MOT airbag

Akademie [akade'miː] *f* (-; -*n*) academy, college

Akademiker(in) [aka'deːmikɐ (-kərɪn)] (-*s*; -/-; -*nen*) university graduate

akademisch [-'deːmɪʃ] *adj* academic

akklimatisieren [aklimati'ziːrən] *v/refl* (*no -ge-*, *h*) acclimatize (*an acc* to)

Akkord [a'kɔrt] *m* (-[e]*s*; -*e*) MUS chord; *im Akkord* ECON by the piece *or* job

Akkordarbeit *f* ECON piecework

Akkordarbeiter(in) ECON pieceworker

Akkordeon [a'kɔrdeɔn] *n* (-*s*; -*s*) MUS accordion

Ak'kordlohn *m* ECON piece wages

Akku ['aku] F *m* (-*s*; -*s*), **Akkumulator** [akumu'laːtoːɐ] *m* (-*s*; -*en* [-la'toːrən]) TECH (storage) battery, *Br a.* accumulator

Akkusativ ['akuzatiːf] *m* (-*s*; -*e*) LING accusative (case)

Akne ['aknə] *f* (-; -*n*) MED acne

Akrobat [akro'baːt] *m* (-*en*; -*en*), **Akro'batin** *f* (-; -*nen*) acrobat

akro'batisch *adj* acrobatic

Akt [akt] *m* (-[e]*s*; -*e*) act(ion); THEA act; PAINT, PHOT nude

Akte ['aktə] *f* (-; -*n*) file; *pl.* files, records; *zu den Akten legen* file

'Aktendeckel *m* folder

Aktenkoffer *m* attaché case

Aktenordner *m* file

Aktentasche *f* briefcase

Aktenzeichen *n* reference (number)

Aktie ['aktsĭə] *f* (-; -*n*) ECON share, *esp Am* stock

'Aktiengesellschaft *f* *Am* corporation, *Br* joint-stock company

Aktion [ak'tsĭoːn] *f* (-; -*en*) campaign, drive; MIL *ect* operation; *in Aktion* in action

Aktionär [aktsĭo'nɛːɐ] *m* (-*s*; -*e*), **Aktio'närin** *f* (-; -*nen*) ECON shareholder, *esp Am* stockholder

aktiv [ak'tiːf] *adj* active

Aktiv ['aktiːf] *n* (-*s*; *no pl*) LING active voice

Aktivist [akti'vist] *m* (-*en*; -*en*) *esp* POL activist

Ak'tivurlaub *m* activity vacation

aktualisieren [aktŭali'ziːrən] *v/t* (*no -ge-*, *h*) update

aktuell [aktŭ'ɛl] *adj* topical; current; up-to-date; TV, *radio:* *e-e aktuelle Sendung* a current affairs *or* news feature

Akupunktur [akupʊŋk'tuːɐ] *f* (-; -*en*) MED acupuncture

Akustik [a'kʊstɪk] *f* (-; *no pl*) acoustics

a'kustisch *adj* acoustic

akut [a'kuːt] *adj* urgent (*problem etc*); *a.* MED acute

Akzent [ak'tsɛnt] *m* (-[e]*s*; -*e*) accent; stress (*a. fig*)

akzeptabel [aktsɛp'taːbəl] *adj* acceptable; reasonable (*price etc*)

akzeptieren [aktsɛp'tiːrən] *v/t* (*no -ge-, h*) accept

Alarm [a'larm] *m* (-[*e*]*s*; -*e*) alarm; *Alarm schlagen* sound the alarm

Alarmanlage *f* alarm system

Alarmbereitschaft *f*: *in Alarmbereitschaft* on standby, on the alert

alarmieren [alar'miːrən] *v/t* (*no -ge-, h*) call; alert

alarmierend *adj* alarming

albern ['albɐn] *adj* silly, foolish

Album ['albʊm] *n* (-*s*; *Alben* ['albən]) album (*a. record*)

Algen ['algən] *pl* BOT algae

Algenpest *f* plague of algae, algal bloom

Algebra ['algəbra] *f* (-; *no pl*) MATH algebra

Alibi ['aːlibi] *n* (-*s*; -*s*) JUR alibi

Alimente [ali'mɛntə] *pl* JUR alimony

Alkohol ['alkohoːl] *m* (-*s*; *no pl*) alcohol

'alkoholfrei *adj* nonalcoholic, soft

Alkoholiker(in) [alko'hoːlikɐ (-kərɪn)] (-*s*; -/-; -*nen*) alcoholic

alko'holisch *adj* alcoholic

Alkoholismus [alkoho'lɪsmʊs] *m* (-; *no pl*) alcoholism

alkoholsüchtig *adj* addicted to alcohol

Alkoholtest *m* MOT breath test

all [al] *indef pron and adj* all; *alles* everything; *alles* (*Beliebige*) anything; *alle* (*Leute*) everybody; anybody; *alle beide* both of them; *wir alle* all of us; *alles in allem* all in all; *auf alle Fälle* in any case; *alle drei Tage* every three days; → *Art, Gute, vor*

All *n* (-*s*; *no pl*) universe; (outer) space

alle ['alə] F *adj*: *alle sein* be all gone; *mein Geld ist alle* I'm out of money

Allee [a'leː] *f* (-; -*n*) avenue

allein [a'lain] *adj and adv* alone; lonely; by o.s.; *ganz allein* all alone; *er hat es ganz allein gemacht* he did it all by himself; *allein stehend* → *alleinstehend*

Al'leinerziehende *m*, *f* (-*n*; -*n*) single parent

Alleingang *m*: *im Alleingang* single-handedly, solo

alleinig [a'lainɪç] *adj* sole

Al'leinsein *n* (-*s*; *no pl*) loneliness

alleinstehend *adj* single

Allerbeste ['alɐ'bɛstə]: *der* (*die, das*) *Allerbeste* the best of all, the very best

allerdings ['alɐ'dɪŋs] *adv* however, though; *allerdings!* certainly!, *esp Am* F sure!

'aller'erste *adj* very first

Allergie [alɐr'giː] *f* (-; -*n*) MED allergy (*gegen* to)

allergisch [a'lɛrgɪʃ] *adj* allergic (*gegen* to)

'aller'hand F *adj* a good deal (of); *das ist ja allerhand!* that's a bit much!

'Aller'heiligen *n* REL All Saints' Day

allerlei ['alɐ'lai] *adj* all kinds *or* sorts of

'aller'letzte *adj* last of all, very last

aller'liebst 1. *adj* (most) lovely; **2.** *adv*: *am allerliebsten mögen* like best of all

aller'meiste *adj* (by far the) most

aller'nächste *adj* very next; *in allernächster Zeit* in the very near future

aller'neu(e)ste *adj* very latest

'Aller'seelen *n* REL All Souls' Day

allerseits ['alɐ'zaits] *adv* F: *Tag allerseits!* hi, everybody!

'aller'wenigst *adv*: *am allerwenigsten* least of all

allesamt ['alə'zamt] *adv* all together

'allge'mein 1. *adj* general; common; universal; **2.** *adv*: *im Allgemeinen* in general, generally; *allgemein verständlich* intelligible (to all), popular

'Allge'meinbildung *f* general education

'Allge'meinheit *f* (-; *no pl*) (general) public

allgemeinver'ständlich *adj* → *allgemein*

All'heilmittel *n* cure-all (*a. fig*)

Allianz [a'ljants] *f* (-; -*en*) alliance

Alligator [ali'gaːtoːɐ] *m* (-*s*; -*en*) alligator

Alliierte [ali'iːɐtə]: *die Alliierten pl* POL the Allies

'all'jährlich *adv* every year; *alljährlich stattfindend* annual

all'mächtig *adj* omnipotent; Almighty (*God*)

allmählich [al'mɛːlɪç] **1.** *adj* gradual; **2.** *adv* gradually

'Allradantrieb *m* MOT four-wheel drive

allseitig ['alzaitɪç] *adv*: *allseitig interessiert sein* have all-round interests

'Alltag *m* everyday life

'all'täglich *adj* everyday; *fig a.* ordinary

all'wissend *adj* omniscient

'allzu *adv* (all) too; *allzu viel* too much

Alm [alm] *f* (-; -*en*) alpine pasture, alp

Almosen ['almoːzən] *n* (-*s*; -) alms

'Alpdruck *m* (-[*e*]*s*; *no pl*) nightmare (*a. fig*)

Alphabet [alfa'beːt] *n* (-[*e*]*s*; -*e*) alphabet

alpha'betisch *adj* alphabetical

alpin [al'piːn] *adj* alpine

'Alptraum *m* nightmare (*a. fig*)

als [als] *cj time*: when; while; *after comp*: than; *als ich ankam* when I arrived; *als Kind* (*Geschenk*) as a child (present); *älter als* older than; *als ob* as if, as though; *nichts als* nothing but

also ['alzo] *cj* so, therefore; F well, you

know; **also gut!** very well (then)!, all right (then)!; **also doch** so ... after all; **du willst also gehen** etc? so you want to go etc?

alt [alt] adj old; HIST ancient; classical (language); **ein 12 Jahre alter Junge** a twelve-year-old boy

Alt m (-s; no pl) MUS alto

Altar [al'taːɐ̯] m (-s; Altäre [al'tɛːrə]) REL altar

'**Alte** m, f (-n; -n) **der Alte** the old man (a. fig); the boss; **die Alte** the old woman (a. fig); **die Alten** pl the old

'**Altenheim** n → **Altersheim**

'**Altenpfleger(in)** geriatric nurse

Alter ['altɐ] n (-s; no pl) age; old age; **im Alter von** ... at the age of ...; **er ist in deinem Alter** he's your age

älter ['ɛltɐ] adj older; **mein älterer Bruder** my elder brother; **ein älterer Herr** an elderly gentleman

'**altern** v/i (ge-, sein) grow old, age

alternativ [altɛrna'tiːf] adj alternative; POL ecological, green; a. counter-culture (movement etc)

Alternative[1] [altɛrna'tiːvə] f (-; -n) alternative; option, choice

Alterna'tive[2] m, f (-n; -n) ecologist, member of the counterculture movement

'**Altersgrenze** f age limit; retirement age

Altersheim n old people's home

Altersrente f old-age pension

Altersschwäche f (-; no pl) infirmity; **an Altersschwäche sterben** die of old age

Altersversorgung f old age pension (scheme)

'**Altertum** n (-s; no pl) antiquity

'**Altglascon,tainer** m Am glass recycling bin, Br bottle bank

'**altklug** adj precocious

'**Altlasten** pl residual pollution

'**Altme,tall** n scrap (metal)

'**altmodisch** adj old-fashioned

'**Altöl** n waste oil

'**Altpa,pier** n waste paper

'**altsprachlich** adj: **altsprachliches Gymnasium** appr classical secondary school

'**Altstadt** f old town

Altstadtsa,nierung f town-cent|er (Br -re) rehabilitation

'**Altwarenhändler** m second-hand dealer

Alt'weibersommer m Indian summer; gossamer

Aluminium [alu'miːnjʊm] n (-s; no pl) alumin(i)um

am [am] prp at the (window etc); time: in the (morning etc); at the (weekend etc); on (Sunday etc); **am 1. Mai** on May 1st; **am Tage** during the day; **am Himmel** in the sky; **am meisten** most; **am Leben** alive

Amateur [ama'tøːɐ̯] m (-s; -e) amateur

Amateurfunker m radio amateur, F radio ham

Amboss ['ambɔs] m (-es; -e) anvil

ambulant [ambu'lant] adv: **ambulant behandelt werden** MED get outpatient treatment

Ambulanz [ambu'lants] f (-; -en) MED outpatients' department; MOT ambulance

Ameise ['aːmaizə] f (-; -n) ZO ant

'**Ameisenhaufen** m ZO anthill

Amerika [a'meːrika] America

Amerikaner [ameri'kaːnɐ] m (-s; -), Ameri'kanerin [-nərm] f (-; -nen), ameri'kanisch adj American

Amnestie [amnɛs'tiː] f (-; -n), amnes'tieren v/t (no -ge-, h) JUR amnesty

Amok ['aːmɔk] m: **Amok laufen** run amok

Ampel ['ampəl] f (-; -n) traffic light(s)

Amphibie [am'fiːbjə] f (-; -n) ZO amphibian

Ampulle [am'pʊlə] f (-; -n) ampoule

Amputation [amputa'tsjoːn] f (-; -en) MED amputation

amputieren [ampu'tiːrən] v/t (no -ge-, h) MED amputate

Amsel ['amzəl] f (-; -n) ZO blackbird

Amt [amt] n (-[e]s; Ämter ['ɛmtɐ]) office, department, esp Am bureau; position; duty, function; TEL exchange

'**amtlich** adj official

'**Amtsarzt** m medical examiner (Br officer)

Amtseinführung f inauguration

Amtsgeheimnis n official secret

Amtsgeschäfte pl official duties

Amtszeichen n TEL dial (Br dialling) tone

Amtszeit f term (of office)

Amulett [amu'lɛt] n (-[e]s; -e) amulet, (lucky) charm

amüsant [amy'zant] adj amusing, entertaining

amüsieren [amy'ziːrən] v/t (no -ge-, h) amuse; **sich amüsieren** enjoy o.s., have a good time; **sich amüsieren über** (acc) laugh at

an [an] **1.** prp: **an der Themse (Küste, Wand)** on the Thames (coast, wall); **an s-m Schreibtisch** at his desk; **an der Hand** by the hand; **an der Arbeit** at work; **an den Hausaufgaben sitzen** sit over one's homework; **et. schicken an** (acc) send s.th. to; **sich lehnen an** (acc) lean against; **an die Tür** etc **klopfen** knock at the door etc; **an e-m Sonntagmorgen** on a Sunday morning; **an dem**

Tag, ... on the day ...; *an Weihnachten etc* at Christmas *etc*; → *Mangel, Stelle, sterben*; **2.** *adv* on (*a. light etc*); *von jetzt* (*da, heute*) *an* from now (that time, today) on; *München an 16.45* arrival Munich 4.45 p.m.

Anabolikum [ana'boːlikʊm] *n* (-*s*; -*ka*) PHARM anabolic steroid

analog [ana'loːk] *adj* analogous

Ana'log... *in cpds* analog(ue) (*computer etc*)

Analphabet [anʔalfa'beːt] *m* (-*en*; -*en*), **Analpha'betin** *f* (-; -*nen*) illiterate (person)

Analyse [ana'lyːzə] *f* (-; -*n*) analysis

analysieren [analy'ziːrən] *v/t* (*no* -ge-, *h*) analy|ze, *Br* -se

Ananas ['ananas] *f* (-; -, -*se*) BOT pineapple

Anarchie [anar'çiː] *f* (-; -*n*) anarchy

Anatomie [anato'miː] *f* (-; -*n*) anatomy

anatomisch [ana'toːmɪʃ] *adj* anatomical

'anbahnen *v/t* (*sep*, -ge-, *h*) pave the way for; *sich anbahnen* be developing; be impending

'Anbau *m* (-[*e*]*s*; -*ten*) a) AGR (*no pl*) cultivation, b) ARCH annex, extension

'anbauen *v/t* (*sep*, -ge-, *h*) AGR cultivate, grow; ARCH add (*an acc* to), build on

'anbehalten *v/t* (*irr*, *halten*, *sep*, *no* -ge-, *h*) keep on

an'bei *adv* ECON enclosed

'anbeißen (*irr*, *beißen*, *sep*, -ge-, *h*) **1.** *v/t* take a bite of; **2.** *v/i fish*: bite; *fig* take the bait

'anbellen *v/t* (*sep*, -ge-, *h*) bark at

'anbeten *v/t* (*sep*, -ge-, *h*) adore, worship (*a. fig*)

'Anbetracht *m*: *in Anbetracht* (*dessen, dass*) considering (that)

'anbetteln *v/t* (*sep*, -ge-, *h*) *j-n um et. anbetteln* beg s.o. for s.th.

'anbiedern [-biːdɐn] *v/refl* (*sep*, -ge-, *h*) curry favo(u)r (*bei* with)

'anbieten *v/t* (*irr*, *bieten*, *sep*, -ge-, *h*) offer

'anbinden *v/t* (*irr*, *binden*, *sep*, -ge-, *h*) tie up; *anbinden an* (*acc or dat*) tie to

'Anblick *m* sight

'anblicken *v/t* (*sep*, -ge-, *h*) look at; glance at

'anbohren *v/t* (*sep*, -ge-, *h*) tap

'anbrechen (*irr*, *brechen*, *sep*, -ge-) **1.** *v/t* (*h*) break into (*supplies*); open; **2.** *v/i* (*sein*) begin; *day*: break; *night*: fall

'anbrennen *v/i* (*irr*, *brennen*, *sep*, -ge-, *sein*) burn (*a. anbrennen lassen*)

'anbringen *v/t* (*irr*, *bringen*, *sep*, -ge-, *h*) fix (*an dat* to)

'Anbruch *m* (-[*e*]*s*; *no pl*) beginning; *bei Anbruch der Nacht* at nightfall

'anbrüllen *v/t* (*sep*, -ge-, *h*) roar at

Andacht ['andaxt] *f* (-; -*en*) REL a) (*no pl*) devotion, b) service; prayers

andächtig ['andɛçtɪç] *adj* REL devout

'andauern *v/i* (*sep*, -ge-, *h*) continue, go on, last

andauernd *adj and adv* → *dauernd*

'Andenken *n* (-*s*; -) keepsake; souvenir (*both: an acc* of); *zum Andenken an* (*acc*) in memory of

andere ['andərə] *adj and indef pron* other; different; *mit anderen Worten* in other words; *am anderen Morgen* the next morning; *et.* (*nichts*) *anderes* s.th. (nothing) else; *nichts anderes als* nothing but; *die anderen* the others; *alle anderen* everybody else

andererseits ['andərɐ'zaɪts] *adv* on the other hand

ändern ['ɛndɐn] *v/t* (-ge-, *h*) change; alter (*clothes*); *ich kann es nicht ändern* I can't help it; *sich ändern* change

'andern'falls *adv* otherwise

anders ['andɐs] *adv* different(ly); *jemand anders* somebody else; *anders werden* change; *anders sein* (*als*) be different (from); *es geht nicht anders* there is no other way

andersherum 1. *adv* the other way round; **2.** F *adj* queer

anderswo(hin) *adv* elsewhere

anderthalb ['andɐt'halp] *adj* one and a half

'Änderung *f* (-; -*en*) change; alteration

'andeuten *v/t* (*sep*, -ge-, *h*) hint (at), suggest; indicate; *j-m andeuten, dass* give s.o. a hint that

'Andeutung *f* (-; -*en*) hint, suggestion

'Andrang *m* (-[*e*]*s*; *no pl*) crush; ECON rush (*nach* for), run (*zu, nach* on)

'andrehen *v/t* (*sep*, -ge-, *h*) turn on; F *j-m et. andrehen* fob s.th. off on s.o.

'androhen *v/t* (*sep*, -ge-, *h*) *j-m et. androhen* threaten s.o. with s.th.

'aneignen *v/refl* (*sep*, -ge-, *h*) acquire; *esp* JUR appropriate

anei'nander *adv* tie *etc* together; *aneinander denken* think of each other; *aneinandergeraten* *v/i* (*irr*, *geraten*, *sep*, *sein*) clash (*mit* with)

Anekdote [anɛk'doːtə] *f* (-; -*n*) anecdote

'anekeln *v/t* (*sep*, -ge-, *h*) disgust, sicken; *es ekelt mich an* it makes me sick

'anerkannt *adj* acknowledged, recognized

'anerkennen *v/t* (*irr*, *kennen*, *sep*, *no* -ge-, *h*) acknowledge, recognize; appreciate

anerkennend *adj* appreciative

'Anerkennung *f* (-; -*en*) acknowledg(e)-ment, recognition; appreciation

'anfahren (*irr*, **fahren**, *sep*, -ge-) **1.** *v/i* (*sein*) start; **2.** *v/t* (*h*) deliver; MOT *etc* hit, *car etc*: a. run into; *fig* **j-n anfahren** jump on s.o.

'Anfahrt *f* journey, ride

'Anfall *m* MED fit, attack

'anfallen *v/t* (*irr*, **fallen**, *sep*, -ge-, *h*) attack, assault; *dog*: go for

'anfällig *adj* delicate; **anfällig für** susceptible to

'Anfang *m* beginning, start; **am Anfang** at the beginning; **Anfang Mai** early in May; **Anfang nächsten Jahres** early next year; **Anfang der neunziger Jahre** in the early nineties; **er ist Anfang 20** he is in his early twenties; **von Anfang an** from the beginning *or* start

'anfangen *v/t and v/i* (*irr*, **fangen**, *sep*, -ge-, *h*) begin, start; do

'Anfänger *m* (-s; -), 'Anfängerin *f* (-; -nen) beginner

'anfangs *adv* at first

'Anfangsbuchstabe *m* initial (letter); **großer Anfangsbuchstabe** capital (letter)

Anfangsstadium *n*: **im Anfangsstadium** at an early stage

'anfassen *v/t* (*sep*, -ge-, *h*) touch; take (hold of); **sich anfassen** take each other by the hands; F **zum Anfassen** everyman's

'anfechtbar *adj* contestable

'anfechten *v/t* (*irr*, **fechten**, *sep*, -ge-, *h*) contest

'Anfechtung *f* (-; -en) contesting

'anfertigen *v/t* (*sep*, -ge-, *h*) make, manufacture

'anfeuchten *v/t* (*sep*, -ge-, *h*) moisten

'anfeuern *fig v/t* (*sep*, -ge-, *h*) cheer

'anflehen *v/t* (*sep*, -ge-, *h*) implore

'anfliegen *v/t* (*irr*, **fliegen**, *sep*, -ge-, *h*) AVIAT approach; fly (regularly) to

'Anflug *m* AVIAT approach; *fig* touch

'anfordern *v/t* (*sep*, -ge-, *h*) demand; request

'Anforderung *f* (-; -en) demand; request; *pl* requirements, qualifications

'Anfrage *f* (-; -n) inquiry

'anfragen *v/i* (*sep*, -ge-, *h*) inquire (**bei j-m nach et.** of s.o. about s.th.)

'anfreunden *v/refl* (*sep*, -ge-, *h*) make friends (**mit** with)

'anfühlen *v/refl* (*sep*, -ge-, *h*) feel; **es fühlt sich weich an** it feels soft

'anführen *v/t* (*sep*, -ge-, *h*) lead; state; F fool

'Anführer(in) leader

'Anführungszeichen *pl* quotation marks, inverted commas

'Angabe *f* (-; -n) statement; indication; F big talk; *tennis*: service; *pl* information, data; TECH specifications

'angeben (*irr*, **geben**, *sep*, -ge-, *h*) **1.** *v/t* give, state; *customs*: declare; indicate; quote (*price*); **2.** *v/i* F *fig* brag, show off; *tennis*: serve

'Angeber F *m* (-s; -) braggart, show-off

Angeberei [ange:bəˈrai] F *f* (-; *no pl*) bragging, showing off

angeblich [ˈange:plɪç] *adj* alleged

angeblich ist er ... he is said to be ...

'angeboren *adj* innate, inborn; MED congenital

'Angebot *n* (-[e]s, -e) offer (*a*. ECON); **Angebot und Nachfrage** supply and demand

'angebracht *adj* appropriate

angebunden *adj*: **kurz angebunden** curt

angegossen F *adj*: **wie angegossen sitzen** fit like a glove

angeheitert *adj* tipsy, Br *a*. (slightly) merry

'angehen (*irr*, **gehen**, *sep*, -ge-, *sein*) **1.** F *v/i* light *etc*: go on; **2.** *v/t* concern; **das geht dich nichts an** that is none of your business

angehend *adj* future; **angehender Arzt** doctor-to-be

'angehören *v/i* (*sep*, *no* -ge-, *h*) belong to

'Angehörige *m*, *f* (-n; -n) relative; member; **die nächsten Angehörigen** next of kin

'Angeklagte *m*, *f* (-n; -n) JUR defendant

Angel [ˈaŋəl] *f* (-; -n) fishing tackle; TECH hinge

'Angelegenheit *f* (-; -en) matter, affair

angelehnt *adj door etc*: ajar

'angelernt *adj* semi-skilled (*worker*)

'Angelhaken *m* fishhook

'angeln (-ge-, *h*) **1.** *v/i* (**nach** for) fish, angle (*both a. fig*); **2.** *v/t* catch, hook

'Angelrute *f* fishing rod

'Angelsachse [-zaksə] *m* (-n; -n), 'angelsächsisch [-zɛksɪʃ] *adj* Anglo-Saxon

'Angelschein *m* fishing permit

'Angelschnur *f* fishing line

angemessen *adj* proper, suitable; just (*punishment*); reasonable (*price*)

'angenehm *adj* pleasant, agreeable; **angenehm!** pleased to meet you

'angenommen *cj* (let's) suppose, supposing

angeregt *adj* animated; lively

angeschrieben *adj*: **bei j-m gut (schlecht) angeschrieben sein** be in s.o.'s good (bad) books

angesehen *adj* respected

'angesichts *prp* (*gen*) in view of

'**Angestellte** *m*, *f* (*-n*; *-n*) employee (*bei* with), *pl* the staff

'**angetan** *adj*: *ganz angetan sein von* be taken with

angetrunken *adj* (slightly) drunk; *in angetrunkenem Zustand* under the influence of alcohol

angewandt *adj* applied

angewiesen *adj*: *angewiesen auf* (*acc*) dependent (up)on

'**angewöhnen** *v/t* (*sep*, *no* -ge-, *h*) *sich* (*j-m*) *angewöhnen*, *et. zu tun* get (s.o.) used to doing s.th.; *sich das Rauchen angewöhnen* take to smoking

'**Angewohnheit** *f* habit

Angina [aŋ'giːna] *f* (-; -nen) MED tonsillitis

'**angleichen** *v/t* (*irr*, *gleichen*, *sep*, -ge-, *h*) adjust (*an acc* to)

Angler ['aŋlɐ] *m* (-*s*; -) angler

Anglist [aŋ'glɪst] *m* (-*en*; -*en*), **An'glistin** *f* (-; -nen) student of (*or* graduate in) English

'**angreifen** *v/t* (*irr*, *greifen*, *sep*, -ge-, *h*) attack (*a.* SPORT *and fig*); affect (*health etc*); touch (*supplies*)

'**Angreifer** *m* (-*s*; -) attacker, SPORT *a.* offensive player; *esp* POL aggressor

'**angrenzend** *adj* adjacent (*an acc* to)

'**Angriff** *m* attack (*a.* SPORT *and fig*); MIL assault, charge; *in Angriff nehmen* set about

'**angriffslustig** *adj* aggressive

Angst [aŋst] *f* (-; *Ängste* ['ɛŋstə]) fear (*vor dat* of); *Angst haben* (*vor dat*) be afraid *or* scared (of); *j-m Angst einjagen* frighten *or* scare s.o.; (*hab*) *keine Angst!* don't be afraid!

Angsthase F *m* chicken

ängstigen ['ɛŋstɪɡən] *v/t* (*ge-*, *h*) frighten, scare; *sich ängstigen* be afraid (*vor dat* of); be worried (*um* about)

ängstlich ['ɛŋstlɪç] *adj* timid, fearful; anxious

'**anhaben** F *v/t* (*irr*, *haben*, *sep*, -ge-, *h*) have on (*a. light etc*), *a.* wear, be wearing (*dress etc*)

'**anhalten** (*irr*, *halten*, *sep*, -ge-, *h*) **1.** *v/t* stop; *den Atem anhalten* hold one's breath; **2.** *v/i* stop; continue

anhaltend *adj* continual

'**Anhalter** *m* (-*s*; -) hitchhiker; F *per Anhalter fahren* hitchhike

'**Anhaltspunkt** *m* clue

an'hand *prp* (*gen*) by means of

'**Anhang** *m* a) appendix, b) (*no pl*) relations

'**anhängen** *v/t* (*sep*, -ge-, *h*) add; hang up; RAIL, MOT couple (*an acc* to)

'**Anhänger** *m* (-*s*; -) follower, supporter (*a.*

SPORT); pendant; label, tag; MOT trailer

'**anhänglich** *adj* affectionate; *contp* clinging

'**anhäufen** *v/t and v/refl* (*sep*, -ge-, *h*) heap up, accumulate

'**Anhäufung** *f* (-; -en) accumulation

'**anheben** *v/t* (*irr*, *heben*, *sep*, -ge-, *h*) lift, raise (*a. price*); MOT jack up

'**anheften** *v/t* (*sep*, -ge-, *h*) attach, tack (*both: an acc* to)

Anhieb *m*: *auf Anhieb* on the first try

'**anhimmeln** F *v/t* (*sep*, -ge-, *h*) idolize, worship

'**Anhöhe** *f* rise, hill, elevation

anhören *v/t* (*sep*, -ge-, *h*) listen to; *mit anhören* overhear; *es hört sich ... an* it sounds ...

'**Anhörung** *f* (-; -en) hearing

animieren [ani'miːrən] *v/t* (*no* -ge-, *h*) encourage; stimulate

'**ankämpfen** *v/i* (*sep*, -ge-, *h*) *ankämpfen gegen* fight s.th.

'**Ankauf** *m* purchase

Anker ['aŋkɐ] *m* (-*s*; -) MAR anchor; *vor Anker gehen* drop anchor

'**ankern** *v/i* (*ge-*, *h*) MAR anchor

'**anketten** *v/t* (*sep*, -ge-, *h*) chain up

'**Anklage** *f* (-; *no pl*) JUR accusation, charge (*a. fig*)

'**anklagen** *v/t* (*sep*, -ge-, *h*) JUR accuse (*wegen* of), charge (with) (*both a. fig.*)

'**anklammern** *v/t* (*sep*, -ge-, *h*) clip s.th. on; *sich anklammern* (*an acc*) cling (to)

Anklang *m*: *Anklang finden* meet with approval

'**ankleben** *v/t* (*sep*, -ge-, *h*) stick on (*an dat or acc* to)

'**anklicken** *v/t* (*sep*, -ge-, *h*) EDP click

'**anklopfen** *v/i* (*sep*, -ge-, *h*) knock (*an dat or acc* at)

'**anknipsen** *v/t* (*sep*, -ge-, *h*) switch on

'**anknüpfen** *v/t* (*sep*, -ge-, *h*) tie (*an acc* to); *fig* begin; *Beziehungen anknüpfen* (*zu*) establish contacts (with)

'**ankommen** *v/i* (*irr*, *kommen*, *sep*, -ge-, *sein*) arrive; *nicht gegen j-n ankommen* be no match for s.o.; *es kommt (ganz) darauf an* it (all) depends; *es kommt darauf an, dass* what matters is; *darauf kommt es nicht an* that doesn't matter; *es darauf ankommen lassen* take a chance; *gut ankommen* (*bei*) *fig* go down well (with)

'**ankündigen** *v/t* (*sep*, -ge-, *h*) announce; advertise

'**Ankündigung** *f* announcement; advertisement

Ankunft ['ankʊnft] *f* (-; *no pl*) arrival

'**anlächeln**, '**anlachen** *v/t* (*sep*, -ge-, *h*)

smile at

'**Anlage** *f* arrangement; facility; plant; TECH system; (stereo *etc*) set; ECON investment; enclosure; *fig* gift; *pl* park, gardens; **sanitäre Anlagen** sanitary facilities

Anlass ['anlas] *m* (*-es*; *Anlässe* ['anlɛsə]) occasion; cause

'**anlassen** *v/t* (*irr*, *lassen*, *sep*, *-ge-*, *h*) MOT start; F keep on, leave on (*a. light etc*)

'**Anlasser** *m* (*-s*; *-*) MOT starter

anlässlich ['anlɛslɪç] *prp* (*gen*) on the occasion of

'**Anlauf** *m* SPORT run-up; *fig* start

'**anlaufen** (*irr*, *laufen*, *sep*, *-ge-*) **1.** *v/i* (*sein*) run up; *fig* start; *metal*: tarnish; *glasses etc*: steam up; **2.** *v/t* (*h*) MAR call *or* touch at

'**anlegen** (*sep*, *-ge-*, *h*) **1.** *v/t* put on (*dress etc*); lay out (garden *etc*); build (*road etc*); invest (*money*); found (*town etc*); MED apply (*dressing etc*); lay in (*supplies*); **sich mit j-m anlegen** pick a quarrel with s.o.; **2.** *v/i* MAR land; moor; **es anlegen auf** (*acc*) aim at

'**Anleger** *m* (*-s*; *-*) ECON investor; MAR landing stage

'**anlehnen** *v/t* (*sep*, *-ge-*, *h*) lean (**an** *acc* against); leave *door etc* ajar; **sich anlehnen an** (*acc*) lean against, *fig* lean on *s.o.*

Anleihe ['anlaiə] *f* (*-*; *-n*) ECON loan

'**Anleitung** *f* (*-*; *-en*) guidance, instruction; *written* instructions

'**Anliegen** *n* (*-s*; *-*) request; message (*of a film etc*)

Anlieger ['anli:gɐ] *m* (*-s*; *-*) resident

'**anlocken** *v/t* (*sep*, *-ge-*, *h*) attract, lure

'**anmachen** *v/t* (*sep*, *-ge-*, *h*) light (*fire etc*); turn on (*light etc*); dress (*salad*); F chat *s.o.* up; turn *s.o.* on

'**anmalen** *v/t* (*sep*, *-ge-*, *h*) paint

'**Anmarsch** *m*: **im Anmarsch** on the way

anmaßen *v/t* (*sep*, *-ge-*, *h*) **sich anmaßen** assume; claim (*right*); **sich anmaßen, et. zu tun** presume to do s.th.

anmaßend *adj* arrogant

'**anmelden** *v/t* (*sep*, *-ge-*, *h*) announce (*visitor*); register (*birth etc*); *customs*: declare; **sich anmelden** enrol(l) (*for classes etc*); register (*at a hotel*); **sich anmelden bei** make an appointment with (*doctor etc*)

'**Anmeldung** *f* announcement; registration, enrol(l)ment

'**anmerken** *v/t* (*sep*, *-ge-*, *h*) **j-m et. anmerken** notice s.th. in s.o.; **sich et. (nichts) anmerken lassen** (not) let it show

'**Anmerkung** *f* (*-*; *-en*) note; annotation, footnote

Anmut ['anmu:t] *f* (*-*; *no pl*) grace

'**anmutig** *adj* graceful

'**annähen** *v/t* (*sep*, *-ge-*, *h*) sew on (**an** *acc* to)

'**annähernd** *adv* approximately

'**Annäherung** *f* (*-*; *-en*) approach (**an** *acc* to)

'**Annäherungsversuche** *pl* advances, F pass

Annahme ['anna:mə] *f* (*-*; *-n*) a) (*no pl*) acceptance (*a. fig*), b) assumption

'**annehmbar** *adj* acceptable; reasonable (*price etc*)

'**annehmen** *v/t* (*irr*, *nehmen*, *sep*, *-ge-*, *h*) accept; suppose; adopt (*child*, *name*); take (*ball*); take on (*color*, *look etc*); **sich e-r Sache** *or* **j-s annehmen** take care of s.th. *or* s.o.

'**Annehmlichkeiten** *pl* comforts, amenities

Annonce [a'nõ:sə] *f* (*-*; *-n*) advertisement

annullieren [anʊ'li:rən] *v/t* (*no -ge-*, *h*) annul; ECON cancel

anöden ['an̩ʔø:dən] F *v/t* (*sep*, *-ge-*, *h*) bore *s.o.* to death

anonym [ano'ny:m] *adj* anonymous

Anonymität [anonymi'tɛ:t] *f* (*-*; *no pl*) anonymity

Anorak ['anorak] *m* (*-s*; *-s*) anorak

'**anordnen** *v/t* (*sep*, *-ge-*, *h*) arrange; give order(s), order

'**Anordnung** *f* (*-*; *-en*) arrangement; direction, order

'**anorganisch** *adj* CHEM inorganic

'**anpacken** F *fig* (*sep*, *-ge-*, *h*) **1.** *v/t* tackle; **2.** *v/i*: **mit anpacken** lend a hand

'**anpassen** *v/t* (*sep*, *-ge-*, *h*) adapt, adjust (*both a. sich anpassen*) (*dat*, **an** *acc* to)

'**Anpassung** *f* (*-*; *-en*) adaptation, adjustment

'**anpassungsfähig** *adj* adaptable

'**Anpassungsfähigkeit** *f* adaptability

'**Anpfiff** *m* SPORT starting whistle; F *fig* dressing-down

'**anpflanzen** *v/t* (*sep*, *-ge-*, *h*) cultivate, plant

'**Anpflanzung** *f* cultivation

'**anpöbeln** *v/t* (*sep*, *-ge-*, *h*) accost; shout abuse at

anprangern ['anpraŋɐn] *v/t* (*sep*, *-ge-*, *h*) denounce

'**anpreisen** *v/t* (*irr*, *preisen*, *sep*, *-ge-*, *h*) push; plug

'**anpro,bieren** *v/t* (*no -ge-*, *h*) try on

'**anpumpen** F *v/t* (*sep*, *-ge-*, *h*) touch *s.o.* (**um** for)

'**anraten** *v/t* (*irr*, *raten*, *sep*, *-ge-*, *h*) advise

'**anrechnen** *v/t* (*sep*, *-ge-*, *h*) charge; allow

'**Anrecht** *n*: **ein Anrecht haben auf** (*acc*)

be entitled to

'**Anrede** *f* address

'**anreden** *v/t* (*sep*, -ge-, *h*) address (*mit Namen* by name)

'**anregen** *v/t* (*sep*, -ge-, *h*) stimulate; suggest

anregend *adj* stimulating

'**Anregung** *f* stimulation; suggestion

'**Anregungsmittel** *n* PHARM stimulant

'**Anreiz** *m* incentive

'**anrichten** *v/t* (*sep*, -ge-, *h*) GASTR prepare, dress; cause, do (*damage etc*)

anrüchig ['anrʏçɪç] *adj* disreputable

'**Anruf** *m* call (*a*. TEL)

Anrufbeantworter *m* TEL answering machine

'**anrufen** *v/t* (*irr*, **rufen**, *sep*, -ge-, *h*) TEL call *or* ring up, phone

'**anrühren** *v/t* (*sep*, -ge-, *h*) touch; mix

'**Ansage** *f* announcement

'**ansagen** *v/t* (*sep*, -ge-, *h*) announce

Ansager ['anzaːgɐ] *m* (-*s*; -), '**Ansagerin** [-gərɪn] *f* (-; -*nen*) announcer

'**ansammeln** *v/t and v/refl* (*sep*, -ge-, *h*) accumulate

'**Ansammlung** *f* collection, accumulation; crowd

'**Ansatz** *m* start (**zu** of); attempt (**zu** at); approach; TECH attachment; MATH set--up; *pl* first signs

'**anschaffen** *v/t* (*sep*, -ge-, *h*) get; **sich et. anschaffen** buy *or* get (o.s.) s.th.

'**Anschaffung** *f* (-; -*en*) purchase, buy

'**anschauen** *v/t* (*sep*, -ge-, *h*) → **ansehen**

'**anschaulich** *adj* graphic (*account etc*)

'**Anschauung** *f* (-; -*en*) (**von**) view (of), opinion (about, of)

'**Anschauungsmateri,al** *n* PED visual aids

'**Anschein** *m* (-[*e*]*s*; *no pl*) appearance; **allem Anschein nach** to all appearances; **den Anschein erwecken, als** (**ob**) give the impression of …

'**anscheinend** *adv* apparently

'**anschieben** *v/t* (*irr*, **shieben**, *sep*, -ge-, *h*) give a push (*a*. MOT)

'**Anschlag** *m* attack; poster; bill; notice; *typewriter*: stroke; MUS, *swimming*: touch; **e-n Anschlag auf j-n verüben** make an attempt on s.o.'s life

Anschlagbrett *n* bulletin (*esp Br* notice) board

'**anschlagen** (*irr*, **schlagen**, *sep*, -ge-, *h*) **1.** *v/t* post; MUS strike; chip (*cup etc*); **2.** *v/i* *dog*: bark; take (effect) (*a*. MED); *swimming*: touch the wall

'**anschließen** *v/t* (*irr*, **schließen**, *sep*, -ge-, *h*) ELECTR, TECH connect; **sich anschließen** follow; agree with; **sich j-m** *or* **e-r Sache anschließen** join s.o. or s.th.

'**anschließend** **1.** *adj* following; **2.** *adv* then, afterwards

'**Anschluss** *m* connection; **im Anschluss an** (*acc*) following; **Anschluss finden** (**bei**) make contact *or* friends (with); **Anschluss bekommen** TEL get through

'**anschmiegen** *v/refl* (*sep*, -ge-, *h*) snuggle up (**an** *acc* to)

'**anschmiegsam** *adj* affectionate

'**anschnallen** *v/t* (*sep*, -ge-, *h*) strap on, put on (*a. ski*); **sich anschnallen** AVIAT, MOT fasten one's seat belt

'**anschnauzen** F *v/t* (*sep*, -ge-, *h*) tell s.o. off, *Am a*. bawl s.o. out

'**anschneiden** *v/t* (*irr*, **schneiden**, *sep*, -ge-, *h*) cut; *fig* bring up

'**anschrauben** *v/t* (*sep*, -ge-, *h*) screw on (**an** *acc* to)

'**anschreiben** *v/t* (*irr*, **schreiben**, *sep*, -ge-, *h*) write on the (black)board; **j-n anschreiben** write to s.o.; (*et.*) **anschreiben lassen** buy (s.th.) on credit; → **angeschrieben**

'**anschreien** *v/t* (*irr*, **schreien**, *sep*, -ge-, *h*) shout at

'**Anschrift** *f* address

'**Anschuldigung** *f* (-; -*en*) accusation

'**anschwellen** *v/i* (*irr*, **schwellen**, *sep*, -ge-, *sein*) swell (*a. fig*)

'**anschwemmen** *v/t* (*sep*, -ge-, *h*) wash ashore

'**ansehen** *v/t* (*irr*, **sehen**, *sep*, -ge-, *h*) look at, have *or* take a look at; watch; see (*all a*. **sich** [*dat*] **ansehen**); **ansehen als** look upon as; **et. mit ansehen** watch *or* witness s.th.; **man sieht ihm an, dass** … one can see that …

'**Ansehen** *n* (-*s*; *no pl*) reputation

ansehnlich ['anzeːnlɪç] *adj* considerable

'**anseilen** *v/t and v/refl* (*sep*, -ge-, *h*) rope

'**ansetzen** (*sep*, -ge-, *h*) **1.** *v/t* put (**an** *acc* to); put on, add; fix, set (*date etc*); **Fett** *etc* **ansetzen** put on weight *etc*; **2.** *v/i*: **ansetzen zu** prepare for (*landing etc*)

'**Ansicht** *f* (-; -*en*) view, *a*. opinion, *a*. sight; **der Ansicht sein, dass** … be of the opinion that …; **meiner Ansicht nach** in my opinion; **zur Ansicht** ECON on approval

'**Ansichtskarte** *f* picture postcard

Ansichtssache *f* matter of opinion

'**anspannen** *v/t* (*sep*, -ge-, *h*) strain

'**Anspannung** *f* (-; -*en*) strain, exertion

'**anspielen** *v/i* (*sep*, -ge-, *h*) *soccer*: kick off; **anspielen auf** (*acc*) allude to, hint at

'**Anspielung** *f* (-; -*en*) allusion, hint

'**anspitzen** *v/t* (*sep*, -ge-, *h*) sharpen

'**Ansporn** *m* (-[*e*]*s*; *no pl*) incentive

'**anspornen** *v/t* (*sep*, -ge-, *h*) encourage,

spur *s.o.* on

'Ansprache *f* address, speech; *e-e An-sprache halten* deliver an address

'ansprechen *v/t* (*irr*, *sprechen*, *sep*, *-ge-*, *h*) address, speak to; *fig* appeal to

ansprechend *adj* attractive

'Ansprechpartner *m* s.o. to talk to, contact

'anspringen (*irr*, *springen*, *sep*, *-ge-*) **1.** *v/i* (*sein*) *engine*: start; **2.** *v/t* (*h*) jump (up)on

'anspritzen *v/t* (*sep*, *-ge-*, *h*) spatter

'Anspruch *m* claim (*auf acc* to) (*a.* JUR); *Anspruch haben auf* (*acc*) be entitled to; *Anspruch erheben auf* (*acc*) claim; *Zeit in Anspruch nehmen* take up time

'anspruchslos *adj* modest; light, undemanding (*reading etc*); *contp* trivial

'anspruchsvoll *adj* demanding; sophisticated, refined (*tastes etc*)

Anstalt ['anʃtalt] *f* (*-*; *-en*) establishment, institution; mental hospital; *Anstalten machen zu* get ready for

'Anstand *m* (*-[e]s*; *no pl*) decency; manners

'anständig *adj* decent (*a. fig*)

'anstandslos *adv* unhesitatingly; without difficulty

'anstarren *v/t* (*sep*, *-ge-*, *h*) stare at

an'statt *prp* (*gen*) *and cj* instead of

'anstechen *v/t* (*irr*, *stechen*, *sep*, *-ge-*, *h*) tap (*barrel*)

'anstecken *v/t* (*sep*, *-ge-*, *h*) stick on; put on (*ring*); light; set fire to; MED infect; *sich bei j-m anstecken* MED catch s.th. from s.o.

ansteckend *adj* MED infectious, contagious, catching (*all a. fig*)

'Anstecknadel *f* pin, button

'Ansteckung *f* (*-*; *no pl*) MED infection, contagion

'anstehen *v/i* (*irr*, *stehen*, *sep*, *-ge-*, *h*) (*nach* for) stand in line, *Br* queue up

'ansteigen *v/i* (*irr*, *steigen*, *sep*, *-ge-*, *sein*) rise

'anstellen *v/t* (*sep*, *-ge-*, *h*) engage, employ; TV *etc*: turn on; MOT start; F be up to (*s.th. illegal etc*); make (*inquiries etc*); *sich anstellen* line up (*nach* for), *Br* queue up (for); F (make a) fuss

'Anstellung *f* job, position; *e-e Anstellung finden* find employment

Anstieg ['anʃtiːk] *m* (*-[e]s*; *no pl*) rise, increase

'anstiften *v/t* (*sep*, *-ge-*, *h*) incite

'Anstifter *m* instigator

'Anstiftung *f* incitement

'anstimmen *v/t* (*sep*, *-ge-*, *h*) MUS strike up

'Anstoß *m* soccer: kickoff; *fig* initiative,

impulse; offen|se, *Br* -ce; *Anstoß erre-gen* give offense (*bei* to); *Anstoß neh-men an* take offense at; *den Anstoß zu et. geben* start s.th., initiate s.th.

'anstoßen (*irr*, *stoßen*, *sep*, *-ge-*) **1.** *v/t* (*h*) nudge *s.o.*; **2.** *v/i* a) (*sein*) knock, bump, b) (*h*) clink glasses; *anstoßen auf* (*acc*) drink to *s.o. or s.th.*

anstößig ['anʃtøːsɪç] *adj* offensive

'anstrahlen *v/t* (*sep*, *-ge-*, *h*) illuminate; beam at *s.o.*

'anstreichen *v/t* (*irr*, *streichen*, *sep*, *-ge-*, *h*) paint; PED mark (*mistakes etc*)

'Anstreicher *m* (house)painter

'anstrengen *v/refl* (*sep*, *-ge-*, *h*) try (hard), make an effort

anstrengend *adj* strenuous, hard

'Anstrengung *f* (*-*; *-en*) exertion, strain; effort

Ansturm *fig m* (*-[e]s*; *no pl*) rush (*auf acc* for)

'Anteil *m* share (*a.* ECON); portion; *Anteil nehmen an* (*dat*) take an interest in; sympathize with

Anteilnahme [*-naːmə*] *f* (*-*; *no pl*) sympathy; interest

Antenne [an'tɛnə] *f* (*-*; *-n*) antenna, *Br* aerial

Anti..., anti... *in cpds* anti...

Antialko'holiker *m* teetotal(l)er

Anti'babypille F *f* birth control pill, F the pill

Anti'biotikum *n* MED antibiotic

Antiblo'ckiersys,tem *n* MOT anti-lock braking system

antik [an'tiːk] *adj* antique, HIST *a.* ancient

An'tike *f* (*-*; *no pl*) ancient world

'Antikörper *m* MED antibody

Antilope [anti'loːpə] *f* (*-*; *-n*) zo antelope

Antipathie [antipa'tiː] *f* (*-*; *-n*) antipathy

Antiquariat [antikva'rjaːt] *n* (*-[e]s*; *-e*) second-hand bookshop

antiquarisch [anti'kvaːrɪʃ] *adj and adv* second-hand

Antiquitäten [antikvi'tɛːtən] *pl* antiques

Antiquitätenladen *m* antique shop

Antisemit [*-ze'miːt*] *m* (*-en*; *-en*) anti--Semite

antise'mitisch *adj* anti-Semitic

Antisemitismus [*-zemi'tɪsmʊs*] *m* (*-*; *no pl*) anti-Semitism

Antrag ['antraːk] *m* (*-[e]s*; *Anträge* ['an-trɛːgə]) application; PARL motion; proposal; *Antrag stellen auf* (*acc*) make an application for; PARL move for

Antragsteller(in) [*-ʃtɛlɐ* (*-lərɪn*)] *m* (*-s*; *-/-*; *-nen*) applicant; PARL mover

'antreiben (*irr*, *treiben*, *sep*, *-ge-*) **1.** *v/t* (*h*) TECH drive; urge *s.o.* (on); **2.** *v/i* (*sein*) float ashore

'**antreten** (*irr*, ***treten***, *sep*, *-ge-*) **1.** *v/t* (*h*) enter upon (*office etc*); take up (*position*); set out on (*journey*); **2.** *v/i* (*sein*) take one's place; MIL line up

'**Antrieb** *m* TECH drive (*a. fig*), propulsion; *fig* motive, impulse; ***aus eigenem Antrieb*** of one's own accord

'**antun** *v/t* (*irr*, ***tun***, *sep*, *-ge-*, *h*) ***j-m et. antun*** do s.th. to s.o.; ***sich et. antun*** lay hands on o.s.

Antwort ['antvɔrt] *f* (-; *-en*) answer (***auf*** *acc* to), reply (to)

'**antworten** *v/i* (*ge-*, *h*) answer (***j-m*** s.o., ***auf et.*** s.th.), reply (to s.o. *or* s.th.)

'**anvertrauen** *v/t* (*sep*, *no -ge-*, *h*) ***j-m et. anvertrauen*** (en)trust s.o. with s.th.; confide s.th. to s.o.

'**anwachsen** *v/i* (*irr*, ***wachsen***, *sep*, *-ge-*, *sein*) BOT take root; *fig* increase

Anwalt ['anvalt] *m* (-*[e]s*; *Anwälte* ['anvɛltə]) → ***Rechtsanwalt***

'**Anwärter** *m* candidate (***auf*** *acc* for)

'**anweisen** *v/t* (*irr*, ***weisen***, *sep*, *-ge-*, *h*) instruct; direct, order

'**Anweisung** *f* instruction; order

'**anwenden** *v/t* ([*irr*, ***wenden***,] *sep*, *-ge-*, *h*) use; apply (***auf*** *acc* to)

'**Anwendung** *f* use; application

'**anwerben** *v/t* (*irr*, ***werben***, *sep*, *-ge-*, *h*) recruit (*a. fig*)

'**Anwesen** *n* (-*s*; -) estate; property

'**anwesend** *adj* present

'**Anwesenheit** *f* (-; *no pl*) presence; PED attendance; ***die Anwesenheit feststellen*** call the roll

'**Anwesenheitsliste** *f* attendance record (*Br* list)

anwidern ['anviːdɐn] *v/t* (*sep*, *-ge-*, *h*) make *s.o.* sick

'**Anzahl** *f* (-; *no pl*) number, quantity

'**anzahlen** *v/t* (*sep*, *-ge-*, *h*) pay on account

'**Anzahlung** *f* down payment

'**anzapfen** *v/t* (*sep*, *-ge-*, *h*) tap

'**Anzeichen** *n* symptom (*a.* MED), sign

Anzeige ['antsaigə] *f* (-; *-n*) advertisement; announcement; JUR information; EDP display; TECH reading

'**anzeigen** *v/t* (*sep*, *-ge-*, *h*) announce; report to the police; TECH indicate, show

'**anziehen** *v/t* (*irr*, ***ziehen***, *sep*, *-ge-*, *h*) put on (*dress etc*); dress *s.o.*; *fig* attract, draw; tighten (*screw*); pull (*lever etc*); ***sich anziehen*** get dressed; dress

anziehend *adj* attractive

'**Anziehung** *f* (-; *no pl*), '**Anziehungskraft** *f* (-; *no pl*) PHYS attraction, *fig a.* appeal

'**Anzug** *m* suit

anzüglich ['antsyːklɪç] *adj* suggestive (*joke*); personal, offensive (*remark etc*)

'**anzünden** *v/t* (*sep*, *-ge-*, *h*) light; set on fire

apart [a'part] *adj* striking

Apartment [a'partmənt] *n* (-*s*; -*s*) studio (apartment *or Br* flat)

apathisch [a'paːtɪʃ] *adj* apathetic

Apfel ['apfəl] *m* (-*s*; *Äpfel* ['ɛpfəl]) BOT apple

Apfelmus *n* GASTR apple sauce

Apfelsine [apfəl'ziːnə] *f* (-; *-n*) BOT orange

'**Apfelwein** *m* cider

Apostel [a'pɔstəl] *m* (-*s*; -) REL apostle

Apostroph [apo'stroːf] *m* (-*s*; -*e*) apostrophe

Apotheke [apo'teːkə] *f* (-; *-n*) pharmacy, drugstore, *Br* chemist's

Apotheker [apo'teːkɐ] *m* (-*s*; -), **Apo'thekerin** *f* (-; *-nen*) pharmacist, druggist, *Br* chemist

App. ABBR *of* **Apparat** TEL ext., extension

Apparat [apa'raːt] *m* (-*[e]s*; -*e*) apparatus; device; (tele)phone; radio; TV set; camera; POL *etc* machine(ry); ***am Apparat!*** TEL speaking!; ***am Apparat bleiben*** TEL hold the line

Appell [a'pɛl] *m* (-*s*; -*e*) appeal (***an*** *acc* to); MIL roll call

appellieren [apɛ'liːrən] *v/i* (*no -ge-*, *h*) (make an) appeal (***an*** *acc* to)

Appetit [ape'tiːt] *m* (-*[e]s*; *no pl*) appetite (***auf*** *acc* for); ***Appetit auf et. haben*** feel like s.th.; ***guten Appetit!*** enjoy your meal!

appe'titanregend *adj* appetizing

Appe'tithappen *m* GASTR appetizer

appe'titlich *adj* appetizing, savo(u)ry, *fig a.* inviting

applaudieren [aplau'diːrən] *v/i* (*no -ge-*, *h*) applaud

Applaus [a'plaus] *m* (-*es*; *no pl*) applause

Aprikose [apri'koːzə] *f* (-; *-n*) BOT apricot

April [a'prɪl] *m* (-*[s]*; *no pl*) April; ***April! April!*** April fool!

Aquaplaning [akva'plaːnɪŋ] *n* (-*[s]*; *no pl*) MOT hydroplaning, *Br* aquaplaning

Aquarell [akva'rɛl] *n* (-*s*; -*e*) watercolo(u)r

Aquarium [a'kvaːrjʊm] *n* (-*s*; -*ien*) aquarium

Äquator [ɛ'kvaːtoːɐ] *m* (-*s*; *no pl*) equator

Ära ['ɛːra] *f* (-; *no pl*) era

Araber ['arabɐ] *m* (-*s*; -), '**Araberin** [-bə-rɪn] *f* (-; *-nen*) Arab

arabisch [a'raːbɪʃ] *adj* Arabian; Arabic

Arbeit ['arbait] *f* (-; *-en*) work, ECON, POL *a.* labo(u)r; employment, job; PED test; *scientific etc* paper; workmanship; ***bei der Arbeit*** at work; ***zur Arbeit gehen***

or **fahren** go to work; *gute Arbeit leis-ten* make a good job of it; *sich an die Arbeit machen* set to work

'**arbeiten** *v/i* (*ge-, h*) work (*an dat* at, on)

'**Arbeiter** *m* (*-s*; *-*), '**Arbeiterin** *f* (*-*; *-nen*) worker

'**Arbeitgeber** *m* (*-s*; *-*) employer

'**Arbeitnehmer** *m* (*-s*; *-*) employee

'**Arbeitsamt** *n Am* labor office, *Br* job centre

Arbeitsblatt *n* PED worksheet

Arbeitserlaubnis *f* green card, *Br* work permit

'**arbeitsfähig** *adj* fit for work

'**Arbeitsgang** *m* TECH operation

Arbeitsgemeinschaft *f* work *or* study group

Arbeitsgericht *n* JUR labor court, *Br* industrial tribunal

Arbeitshose *f* overalls

Arbeitskleidung *f* working clothes

Arbeitskräfte *pl* workers, labo(u)r

'**arbeitslos** *adj* unemployed, out of work

'**Arbeitslose** *m, f* (*-n*; *-n*) *die Arbeitslosen pl* the unemployed

'**Arbeitslosengeld** *n* unemployment compensation (*Br* benefit); *Arbeitslosengeld beziehen* F be on the dole

'**Arbeitslosigkeit** *f* (*-*; *no pl*) unemployment

'**Arbeitsmarkt** *m* labo(u)r market

Arbeitsmi,nister *m Am* Secretary of Labor; *Br* Minister of Labour

Arbeitsniederlegung *f* strike, walkout

Arbeitspause *f* break, intermission

Arbeitsplatz *m* workplace; job

'**arbeitsscheu** *adj* work-shy

'**Arbeitsspeicher** *m* EDP main memory

Arbeitssuche *f*: *er ist auf Arbeitssuche* he is looking for a job

Arbeitssüchtige *m, f* workaholic

Arbeitstag *m* workday

'**arbeitsunfähig** *adj* unfit for work; *permanently* disabled

'**Arbeitsweise** *f* method (of working)

Arbeitszeit *f* (*gleitende* flexible) working hours

Arbeitszeitverkürzung *f* fewer working hours

Arbeitszimmer *n* study

Archäologe [arçεo'loːgə] *m* (*-n*; *-n*) arch(a)eologist

Archäologie [arçεolo'giː] *f* (*-*; *no pl*) arch(a)eology

Archäo'login *f* (*-*; *-nen*) arch(a)eologist

Arche ['arçə] *f* (*-*; *-n*) ark; *die Arche Noah* Noah's ark

Architekt [arçi'tεkt] *m* (*-en*; *-en*), **Architektin** *f* (*-*; *-nen*) architect

architektonisch [-tεk'toːnɪʃ] *adj* architectural

Architektur [-tεk'tuːɐ] *f* (*-*; *-en*) architecture

Archiv [ar'çiːf] *n* (*-s*; *-e*) archives; record office

Arena [a'reːna] *f* (*-*; *-nen*) ring

Ärger ['εrgɐ] *m* (*-s*; *no pl*) anger (*über acc* at); trouble; F *j-m Ärger machen* cause s.o. trouble

'**ärgerlich** *adj* angry (*über, auf acc* at *s.th.*; with *s.o.*); annoying

'**ärgern** *v/t* (*ge-, h*) annoy; *sich ärgern* be annoyed (*über acc* at, about *s.th.*, with *s.o.*)

'**Ärgernis** *n* (*-ses*; *-se*) nuisance

arglos ['arkloːs] *adj* innocent

Argwohn ['arkvoːn] *m* (*-[e]s*; *no pl*) suspicion (*gegen* of)

'**argwöhnisch** [-vøːnɪʃ] *adj* suspicious

Arie ['aːrjə] *f* (*-*; *-n*) MUS aria

Aristokratie [arɪstokra'tiː] *f* (*-*; *-n*) aristocracy

arm [arm] *adj* poor; *die Armen* the poor

Arm *m* (*-[e]s*; *-e*) ANAT arm; GEOGR branch; F *j-n auf den Arm nehmen* pull s.o.'s leg

Armaturen [arma'tuːrən] *pl* TECH instruments; (plumbing) fixtures

Armaturenbrett *n* MOT dashboard

'**Armband** *n* bracelet

'**Armbanduhr** *f* wrist-watch

Armee [ar'meː] *f* (*-*; *-n*) MIL armed forces; army

Ärmel ['εrməl] *m* (*-s*; *-*) sleeve

ärmlich ['εrmlɪç] *adj* poor (*a. fig*); shabby

'**Armreif(en)** *m* bangle

'**armselig** *adj* wretched, miserable

Armut ['armuːt] *f* (*-*; *no pl*) poverty; *Armut an* (*dat*) lack of

Aroma [a'roːma] *n* (*-s*; *-men*) flavo(u)r; aroma

Arrest [a'rεst] *m* (*-[e]s*; *-e*) PED detention; *Arrest bekommen* be kept in

arrogant [aro'gant] *adj* arrogant, conceited

Arsch [arʃ] V *m* (*-es*; *Ärsche* ['εrʃə]) ass, *Br* arse

Arschloch V *n* asshole, *Br* arsehole

Art [art] *f* (*-*; *-en*) way, manner; kind, sort; BIOL species; *auf diese Art* (in) this way; *e-e Art ...* a sort of ...; *Geräte aller Art* all kinds *or* sorts of tools

'**Artenschutz** *m* protection of endangered species

Arterie [ar'teːrjə] *f* (*-*; *-n*) ANAT artery

Ar'terienverkalkung *f* MED arteriosclerosis

Arthritis [ar'triːtɪs] *f* (*-*; *-tiden*) MED arthritis

artig ['artɪç] *adj* good, well-behaved; *sei artig!* be good!, be a good boy (*or* girl)!

Artikel [ar'tiːkəl] *m* (*-s*; -) article

Artillerie ['artɪləriː] *f* (-; *no pl*) MIL artillery

Artist [ar'tɪst] *m* (*-en*; *-en*), **Ar'tistin** *f* (-; *-nen*) acrobat, (circus) performer

Arznei [aːɐts'nai] *f* (-; *-en*), **Arzneimittel** *n* medicine, drug

Arzt [aːɐtst] *m* (*-es*; *Ärzte* ['ɛːɐtstə]) doctor, physician

Ärztin ['ɛːɐtstɪn] *f* (-; *-nen*) (lady) doctor *or* physician

'ärztlich *adj* medical; *sich ärztlich behandeln lassen* undergo treatment

As [as] *n* (-; -) MUS A flat

Asbest [as'bɛst] *m* (*-[e]s*; *-e*) asbestos

Asche ['aʃə] *f* (-; *-n*) ash(es)

'Aschenbahn *f* SPORT cinder-track, MOT dirt track

Aschenbecher *m* ashtray

Ascher'mittwoch *m* Ash Wednesday

äsen ['ɛːzən] *v/i* (*ge-*, *h*) HUNT feed, browse

Asiat [a'zjaːt] *m* (*-en*; *-en*), **Asi'atin** *f* (-; *-nen*) Asian

asi'atisch *adj* Asian, Asiatic

Asien ['aːzjən] *n* (*-s*; *no pl*) Asia

Asket [as'keːt] *m* (*-en*; *-en*), **as'ketisch** *adj* ascetic

'asozial *adj* antisocial

Asphalt [as'falt] *m* (*-s*; *-e*) asphalt

asphaltieren [asfal'tiːrən] *v/t* (*no -ge-*, *h*) (cover with) asphalt

Ass [as] *n* (*-es*; *-e*) ace (*a. tennis and fig*)

aß [aːs] *pret of* **essen**

Assistent [asɪs'tɛnt] *m* (*-en*; *-en*), **Assis'tentin** *f* (-; *-nen*) assistant

Assis'tenzarzt *m Am* intern, *Br* houseman

Ast [ast] *m* (*-es*; *Äste* ['ɛstə]) BOT branch

Astronaut [astro'naut] *m* (*-en*; *-en*), **Astro'nautin** *f* (-; *-nen*) astronaut

Astronom [astro'noːm] *m* (*-en*; *-en*) astronomer

Astronomie [-no'miː] *f* (-; *no pl*) astronomy

ASU ['aːzu] ABBR *of* **Abgas-Sonder-Untersuchung** MOT *Am* emissions test, *Br* exhaust emission test

Asyl [a'zyːl] *n* (*-s*; *-e*) asylum

Asylant [azy'lant] *m* (*-en*; *-en*), **Asy'lantin** *f* (-; *-nen*) asylum seeker, (political) refugee

A'sylbewerber(in) asylum seeker

Asylrecht *n* right of (political) asylum

Atelier [ate'lje:] *n* (*-s*; *-s*) studio

Atem ['aːtəm] *m* (*-s*; *no pl*) breath; *außer Atem* out of breath; *(tief) Atem holen* take a (deep) breath

'atemberaubend *adj* breathtaking

'Atemgerät *n* MED respirator

'atemlos *adj* breathless

'Atempause *f* F breather

'Atemzug *m* breath

Äther ['ɛːtɐ] *m* (*-s*; *no pl*) CHEM ether; *radio etc*: air

Athlet [at'leːt] *m* (*-en*; *-en*), **Ath'letin** *f* (-; *-nen*) SPORT athlete

ath'letisch *adj* athletic

Atlas ['atlas] *m* (*-ses*; *-se*, *Atlanten*) atlas

atmen ['aːtmən] *v/i and v/t* (*ge-*, *h*) breathe

Atmosphäre [atmo'sfɛːrə] *f* (-; *-n*) atmosphere

'Atmung *f* (-; *no pl*) breathing, respiration

Atoll [a'tɔl] *n* (*-s*; *-e*) atoll

Atom [a'toːm] *n* (*-s*; *-e*) atom

A'tom... *in cpds* *-energie*, *-forschung*, *-kraft*, *-krieg*, *-müll*, *-rakete*, *-reaktor*, *-waffen etc* nuclear ...

atomar [ato'maːɐ] *adj* atomic, nuclear

A'tombombe *f* MIL atom(ic) bomb

A'tomkern *m* PHYS (atomic) nucleus

a'tomwaffenfrei *adj* nuclear-free

Attentat ['atəntaːt] *n* (*-[e]s*; *-e*) assassination attempt, attempt on *s.o.'s* life; *Opfer e-s Attentats werden* be assassinated

'Attentäter *m* (*-s*; -) assassin

Attest [a'tɛst] *n* (*-[e]s*; *-e*) (doctor's) certificate

Attraktion [atrak'tsjoːn] *f* (-; *-en*) attraction

attraktiv [-'tiːf] *adj* attractive

Attrappe [a'trapə] *f* (-; *-n*) dummy

Attribut [atri'buːt] *n* (*-[e]s*; *-e*) LING attribute (*a. fig*)

ätzend ['ɛtsənt] *adj* corrosive, caustic (*a. fig*); F gross; *das ist echt ätzend* it's the pits

au [au] *int* ouch!; *au fein!* oh, good!

Aubergine [obɛr'ʒiːnə] *f* (-; *-n*) BOT eggplant, *Br* aubergine

auch [aux] *cj* also, too, as well; *ich auch* so am (*or* do) I, F me too; *auch nicht* not ... either; *wenn auch* even if; *wo auch (immer)* wherever; *ist es auch wahr?* is it really true?

Audienz [au'djɛnts] *f* (-; *-en*) audience (*bei* with)

auf [auf] *prp* (*dat and acc*) *and adv* on; in; at; open; up; *auf Seite 20* on page 20; *auf der Straße* on (*Br* in) the street; on the road; *auf der Welt* in the world; *auf See* at sea; *auf dem Lande* in the country; *auf dem Bahnhof etc* at the station *etc*; *auf Urlaub* on vacation; *die Uhr stellen auf* (*acc*) set the watch to; *auf*

deutsch in German; **auf deinen Wunsch** at your request; **auf die Sekunde genau** to the second; **auf und ab** up and down

'**aufarbeiten** v/t (sep, -ge-, h) catch up on (backlog); refurbish

aufatmen v/i (sep, -ge-, h) heave a sigh of relief

'**Aufbau** m (-[e]s; no pl) building (up); structure

'**aufbauen** v/t (sep, -ge-, h) build (up) (a. fig); set up; construct

'**aufbauschen** v/t (sep, -ge-, h) exaggerate

aufbekommen v/t (irr, **kommen**, sep, no -ge-, h) get door etc open; be given (a task etc)

aufbereiten v/t (sep, no -ge-, h) process, clean, treat

aufbessern v/t (sep, -ge-, h) raise (salary etc)

aufbewahren v/t (sep, no -ge-, h) keep

aufbieten v/t (irr, **bieten**, sep, -ge-, h) muster

aufblasen v/t (irr, **blasen**, sep, -ge-, h) blow up

aufbleiben v/i (irr, **bleiben**, sep, -ge-, sein) stay up; door etc: remain open

aufblenden v/i (sep, -ge-, h) MOT turn the headlights up

aufblicken v/i (sep, -ge-, h) look up (**zu** at) (a. fig)

aufblitzen v/i (sep, -ge-, h, sein) flash (a. fig)

'**aufbrausen** v/i (sep, -ge-, sein) fly into a temper

aufbrausend adj irascible

'**aufbrechen** (irr, **brechen**, sep, -ge-) **1.** v/t (h) break or force open; **2.** v/i (sein) burst open; fig leave (**nach** for)

'**aufbringen** v/t (irr, **bringen**, sep, -ge-, h) raise (money); muster (courage etc); start (fashion etc); → **aufgebracht**

'**Aufbruch** m (-[e]s; no pl) departure, start

'**aufbrühen** v/t (sep, -ge-, h) make

aufbürden v/t (sep, -ge-, h) **j-m et. aufbürden** burden s.o. with s.th.

aufdecken v/t (sep, -ge-, h) uncover

aufdrängen v/t (sep, -ge-, h) **j-m et. aufdrängen** force s.th. on s.o.; **sich j-m aufdrängen** impose on s.o.; **sich aufdrängen** fig suggest itself

aufdrehen F (sep, -ge-, h) **1.** v/t turn on; **2.** v/i MOT step on the gas

'**aufdringlich** adj obtrusive

'**Aufdruck** m imprint; on stamps: overprint, surcharge

aufei'nander adv on top of each other; one after another; **aufeinanderfolgend** adj successive

Aufenthalt ['aufɛnthalt] m (-[e]s; -e) stay; RAIL stop

'**Aufenthaltsgenehmigung** f residence permit

Aufenthaltsraum m lounge, recreation room

'**auferstehen** v/i (irr, **stehen**, sep, no -ge-, sein) rise (from the dead)

'**Auferstehung** f (-; -en) REL resurrection

'**aufessen** v/t (irr, **essen**, sep, -ge-, h) eat up

'**auffahren** v/i (irr, **fahren**, sep, -ge-, sein) crash (**auf** acc into); fig start up

'**Auffahrt** f approach; driveway, Br drive

'**Auffahrunfall** m MOT rear-end collision; pileup

'**auffallen** v/i (irr, **fallen**, sep, -ge-, sein) attract attention; **j-m auffallen** strike s.o.

'**auffallend**, '**auffällig** adj striking; conspicuous; flashy (clothes)

'**auffangen** v/t (irr, **fangen**, sep, -ge-, h) catch (a. fig)

'**auffassen** v/t (sep, -ge-, h) understand (**als** as)

'**Auffassung** f view; interpretation

'**auffinden** v/t (irr, **finden**, sep, -ge-, h) find, discover

'**auffordern** v/t (sep, -ge-, h) **j-n auffordern, et. zu tun** ask (or tell) s.o. to do s.th.

'**Aufforderung** f request; demand

'**auffrischen** v/t (sep, -ge-, h) freshen up; brush up

'**aufführen** v/t (sep, -ge-, h) THEA etc perform, present; state; **sich aufführen** behave

'**Aufführung** f THEA etc performance; film: showing

'**Aufgabe** f task, job; duty; PED task, assignment; MATH problem; fig surrender; **es sich zur Aufgabe machen** make it one's business

'**Aufgang** m staircase; AST rising

'**aufgeben** (irr, **geben**, sep, -ge-, h) **1.** v/t give up; mail, send, Br post; check (baggage); PED set, give, assign (homework etc); ECON place (order etc); **2.** v/i give up or in

'**aufgebracht** adj furious

aufgedreht F adj excited

aufgedunsen ['aufgədʊnzən] adj puffed(-up)

'**aufgehen** v/i (irr, **gehen**, sep, -ge-, sein) open; sun, dough etc: rise; MATH come out even; **in Flammen aufgehen** go up in flames

'**aufgehoben** fig adj: **gut aufgehoben sein bei** be in good hands with

aufgelegt adj: **zu et. aufgelegt sein** feel

like (doing) s.th.; **gut (schlecht) aufgelegt** in a good (bad) mood
aufgeregt *adj* excited; nervous
aufgeschlossen *fig adj* open-minded; **aufgeschlossen für** open to
aufgeweckt *fig adj* bright
'**aufgreifen** *v/t* (*irr*, **greifen**, *sep*, -*ge*-, *h*) pick up
auf'grund (*gen*) because of
'**aufhaben** F *v/t* (*irr*, **haben**, *sep*, -*ge*-, *h*) have on, wear; PED have *homework etc* to do
aufhalten *v/t* (*irr*, **halten**, *sep*, -*ge*-, *h*) stop, hold up (*a. traffic, thief etc*); keep open; **sich aufhalten** (**bei j-m**) stay (with s.o.)
aufhängen *v/t* (*sep*, -*ge*-, *h*) hang (up); **j-n aufhängen** hang s.o.
aufheben *v/t* (*irr*, **heben**, *sep*, -*ge*-, *h*) pick up; keep; abolish (*law etc*); break up (*meeting etc*); **sich gegenseitig aufheben** neutralize each other; → **aufgehoben**
'**Aufheben** *n* (-*s*; *no pl*) **viel Aufhebens machen** make a fuss (**von** about)
'**aufheitern** *v/t* (*sep*, -*ge*-, *h*) cheer up; **sich aufheitern** *weather*: clear up
aufhelfen *v/i* (*irr*, **helfen**, *sep*, -*ge*-, *h*) help s.o. up
aufhellen *v/t and v/refl* (*sep*, -*ge*-, *h*) brighten
aufhetzen *v/t* (*sep*, -*ge*-, *h*) **j-n aufhetzen gegen** set s.o. against
aufholen (*sep*, -*ge*-, *h*) **1.** *v/t* make up for; **2.** *v/i* catch up (**gegen** with)
aufhorchen *v/i* (*sep*, -*ge*-, *h*) prick (up) one's ears; **aufhorchen lassen** make s.o. sit up
aufhören *v/i* (*sep*, -*ge*-, *h*) stop, end, finish, quit; **mit et. aufhören** stop (doing) s.th.; **hör(t) auf!** stop it!
aufkaufen *v/t* (*sep*, -*ge*-, *h*) buy up
'**aufklären** *v/t* (*sep*, -*ge*-, *h*) clear up, *a*. solve (*crime*); **j-n aufklären über** (*acc*) inform s.o. about; **j-n (sexuell) aufklären** F tell s.o. the facts of life
'**Aufklärung** *f* (-; *no pl*) clearing up, solution; information; sex education; PHILOS Enlightenment; MIL reconnaissance
'**aufkleben** *v/t* (*sep*, -*ge*-, *h*) paste *or* stick on
'**Aufkleber** *m* (-*s*; -) sticker
'**aufknöpfen** *v/t* (*sep*, -*ge*-, *h*) unbutton
'**aufkommen** *v/i* (*irr*, **kommen**, *sep*, -*ge*-, *sein*) come up; come into fashion *or* use; *rumo(u)r etc*: arise; **aufkommen für** pay (for)
'**aufladen** *v/t* (*irr*, **laden**, *sep*, -*ge*-, *h*) load; ELECTR charge
'**Auflage** *f* edition; circulation

'**auflassen** F *v/t* (*irr*, **lassen**, *sep*, -*ge*-, *h*) leave *door etc* open; keep *one's hat etc* on
auflauern *v/i* (*sep*, -*ge*-, *h*) **j-m auflauern** waylay s.o.
'**Auflauf** *m* crowd; GASTR soufflé, pudding
'**auflaufen** *v/i* (*irr*, **laufen**, *sep*, -*ge*-, *sein*) MAR run aground
aufleben *v/i* (*sep*, -*ge*-, *sein*) *a*. (**wieder**) **aufleben lassen** revive
auflegen (*sep*, -*ge*-, *h*) **1.** *v/t* put on, lay on; **2.** *v/i* TEL hang up
'**auflehnen** *v/t and v/refl* (*sep*, -*ge*-, *h*) lean (**auf** *acc* on); **sich auflehnen** rebel, revolt (**gegen** against)
'**Auflehnung** *f* (-; -*en*) rebellion, revolt
'**auflesen** *v/t* (*irr*, **lesen**, *sep*, -*ge*-, *h*) pick up (*a. fig*)
aufleuchten *v/i* (*sep*, -*ge*-, *h*) flash (up)
auflisten *v/t* (*sep*, -*ge*-, *h*) list (a. EDP)
auflockern *v/t* (*sep*, -*ge*-, *h*) loosen up; *fig* liven up
'**auflösen** *v/t* (*sep*, -*ge*-, *h*) dissolve; solve (*a.* MATH); disintegrate
'**Auflösung** *f* (dis)solution; disintegration
'**aufmachen** F *v/t* (*sep*, -*ge*-, *h*) open; **sich aufmachen** set out
'**Aufmachung** *f* (-; -*en*) get-up
'**aufmerksam** *adj* attentive (**auf** *acc* to); thoughtful; **j-n aufmerksam machen auf** (*acc*) call s.o.'s attention to
'**Aufmerksamkeit** *f* (-; -*en*) *a*) (*no pl*) attention, *b*) small present
'**aufmuntern** *v/t* (*sep*, -*ge*-, *h*) encourage; cheer up
Aufnahme ['aufnaːmə] *f* (-; -*n*) taking up; reception (*a.* MED *etc*); admission; photo (-graph); recording; *film*: shooting
'**aufnahmefähig** *adj* receptive (**für** of)
'**Aufnahmegebühr** *f* admission fee
Aufnahmeprüfung *f* entrance exam(ination)
'**aufnehmen** *v/t* (*irr*, **nehmen**, *sep*, -*ge*-, *h*) take up (*a. post etc*); pick up; put *s.o.* up; hold; take *s.th.* in; receive; PED *etc* admit; PHOT take a picture of; record; take (*the ball*); **es aufnehmen mit** be a match for
'**aufpassen** *v/i* (*sep*, -*ge*-, *h*) pay attention; take care; **aufpassen auf** (*acc*) take care of, look after; keep an eye on; **pass auf!** look out!
'**Aufprall** *m* (-[*e*]*s*; *no pl*) impact
'**aufprallen** *v/i* (*sep*, -*ge*-, *sein*) **aufprallen auf** (*dat or acc*) hit
'**aufpumpen** *v/t* (*sep*, -*ge*-, *h*) pump up
'**aufputschen** *v/t* (*sep*, -*ge*-, *h*) pep up
'**Aufputschmittel** *n* PHARM stimulant, pep pill
'**aufraffen** *v/refl* (*sep*, -*ge*-, *h*) **sich aufraffen zu** bring o.s. to *do* s.th.

aufräumen *v/t* (*sep*, *-ge-*, *h*) tidy up; clear
'aufrecht *adj and adv* upright (*a. fig*)
aufrechterhalten *v/t* (*irr*, **halten**, *sep*, *no
-ge-*, *h*) maintain, keep up
'aufregen *v/t* (*sep*, *-ge-*, *h*) excite, upset;
sich aufregen get excited *or* upset (**über**
acc about)
aufregend *adj* exciting
'Aufregung *f* excitement; fuss
'aufreiben *fig v/t* (*irr*, **reiben**, *sep*, *-ge-*, *h*)
wear down
aufreibend *adj* stressful
'aufreißen *v/t* (*irr*, **reißen**, *sep*, *-ge-*, *h*) tear
open; fling *door etc* open; open *one's
eyes* wide; F pick *s.o.* up
'aufreizend *adj* provocative
'aufrichten *v/t* (*sep*, *-ge-*, *h*) put up, raise;
sich aufrichten straighten up; sit up
'aufrichtig *adj* sincere; frank
'Aufrichtigkeit *f* (*-*; *no pl*) sincerity; frankness
'Aufriss *m* (*-es*; *-e*) ARCH elevation
'aufrollen *v/t and v/refl* (*sep*, *-ge-*, *h*) roll
up
'Aufruf *m* call; appeal (**zu** for)
'aufrufen *v/t* (*irr*, **rufen**, *sep*, *-ge-*, *h*) call
on
Aufruhr ['aufruːɐ] *m* (*-s*; *no pl*) revolt; riot; turmoil
'Aufrührer *m* (*-s*; *-*) rebel; rioter
aufrührerisch ['aufryːrərɪʃ] *adj* rebellious
'aufrunden *v/t* (*sep*, *-ge-*, *h*) round off
'aufrüsten *v/t and v/i* (*sep*, *-ge-*, *h*) (re)arm
'Aufrüstung *f* (re)armament
'aufrütteln *fig v/t* (*sep*, *-ge-*, *h*) shake up,
rouse
aufsagen *v/t* (*sep*, *-ge-*, *h*) say; *a.* recite
(*poem*)
aufsässig ['aufzɛsɪç] *adj* rebellious
'Aufsatz *m* PED essay, *Am a.* theme; (*newspaper etc*) article; TECH top
'aufsaugen *v/t* (*sep*, *-ge-*, *h*) absorb (*a. fig*)
aufscheuern *v/t* (*sep*, *-ge-*, *h*) chafe
aufschichten *v/t* (*sep*, *-ge-*, *h*) pile up
aufschieben *fig v/t* (*irr*, **schieben**, *sep*,
-ge-, *h*) put off, postpone; delay
'Aufschlag *m* impact; ECON extra charge;
lapel; cuff, *Br* turnup; *tennis*: service
'aufschlagen (*irr*, **schlagen**, *sep*, *-ge-*, *h*)
1. *v/t* open (*book, eyes etc*); pitch (*tent*);
cut (*one's knee etc*); **Seite 3 aufschlagen**
open at page 3; **2.** *v/i tennis*: serve; **auf
dem Boden aufschlagen** hit the ground
'aufschließen *v/t* (*irr*, **schließen**, *sep*,
-ge-, *h*) unlock, open
aufschlitzen *v/t* (*sep*, *-ge-*, *h*) slit *or* rip
open
'Aufschluss *m* information (**über** *acc* on)

'aufschnappen F *fig v/t* (*sep*, *-ge-*, *h*) pick
up
aufschneiden (*irr*, **schneiden**, *sep*, *-ge-*,
h) **1.** *v/t* cut open; GASTR cut up; **2.** F *fig*
v/i brag, boast, talk big
'Aufschnitt *m* (*-[e]s*; *no pl*) GASTR cold
cuts, *Br* (slices of) cold meat
'aufschnüren *v/t* (*sep*, *-ge-*, *h*) untie; un-
lace
aufschrauben *v/t* (*sep*, *-ge-*, *h*) unscrew
aufschrecken (*sep*, *-ge-*) **1.** *v/t* (*h*) startle;
2. *v/i* (*sein*) start (up)
'Aufschrei *m* yell; scream, outcry (*a. fig*)
'aufschreiben *v/t* (*irr*, **schreiben**, *sep*,
-ge-, *h*) write down
aufschreien *v/i* (*irr*, **schreien**, *sep*, *-ge-*, *h*)
cry out, scream
'Aufschrift *f* inscription
'Aufschub *m* postponement; delay; adjournment; respite
'Aufschwung *m* SPORT swing-up; *esp* ECON
recovery, upswing; boom
'Aufsehen *n* (*-s*; *no pl*) **Aufsehen erregen** attract attention; cause a sensation;
Aufsehen erregend → **aufsehenerregend**
'aufsehenerregend *adj* sensational
'Aufseher *m* (*-s*; *-*), '**Aufseherin** *f* (*-*; *-nen*)
guard
'aufsetzen (*sep*, *-ge-*, *h*) **1.** *v/t* put on; draw
up (*letter etc*); **sich aufsetzen** sit up; **2.**
v/i AVIAT touch down
'Aufsetzer *m* (*-s*; *-*) SPORT awkward bounc-
ing ball
'Aufsicht *f* (*-*; *no pl*) supervision, control;
Aufsicht führen PED *etc* be on (break)
duty; proctor, *Br* invigilate
'Aufsichtsbehörde *f* supervisory board
Aufsichtsrat *m* ECON board of directors;
supervisory board
'aufsitzen *v/i* (*irr*, **sitzen**, *sep*, *-ge-*, *sein*)
mount
aufspannen *v/t* (*sep*, *-ge-*, *h*) stretch; put
up (*umbrella*); spread
aufsparen *v/t* (*sep*, *-ge-*, *h*) save
aufsperren *v/t* (*sep*, *-ge-*, *h*) unlock; F open
wide
aufspielen *v/refl* (*sep*, *-ge-*, *h*) show off;
sich aufspielen als play
aufspießen *v/t* (*sep*, *-ge-*, *h*) spear, skewer;
animal: gore
aufspringen *v/i* (*irr*, **springen**, *sep*, *-ge-*,
sein) jump up; *door etc*: fly open; *lips
etc*: chap
aufspüren *v/t* (*sep*, *-ge-*, *h*) track down
aufstacheln *v/t* (*sep*, *-ge-*, *h*) goad (*s.o. into doing s.th.*)
aufstampfen *v/i* (*sep*, *-ge-*, *h*) stamp (one's
foot)

'**Aufstand** *m* revolt, rebellion
'**Aufständische** *m, f* (*-n; -n*) rebel
'**aufstapeln** *v/t* (*sep, -ge-, h*) pile up
aufstechen *v/t* (*irr,* **stechen,** *sep, -ge-, h*) puncture, prick open; MED lance
aufstecken *v/t* (*sep, -ge-, h*) put up (*hair*); F *fig* give up
aufstehen *v/i* (*irr,* **stehen,** *sep, -ge-, sein*) get up, rise
aufsteigen *v/i* (*irr,* **steigen,** *sep, -ge-, sein*) rise (*a. fig*); get on (*horse, bicycle*); be promoted; SPORT *Am a.* be moved up to a higher division
'**aufstellen** *v/t* (*sep, -ge-, h*) set up, put up; post (*guard*); set (*trap, record etc*); nominate *s.o.*; draw up (*table, list etc*)
'**Aufstellung** *f* putting up; nomination; list; SPORT line-up
Aufstieg ['aufʃtiːk] *m* (*-[e]s; -e*) ascent, *fig a.* rise
'**aufstöbern** *fig v/t* (*sep, -ge-, h*) ferret out
aufstoßen (*irr,* **stoßen,** *sep, -ge-, h*) **1.** *v/t* push open; **2.** *v/i* belch
aufstützen *v/refl* (*sep, -ge-, h*) lean (**auf** *acc or dat* on)
aufsuchen *v/t* (*sep, -ge-, h*) visit; see
'**Auftakt** *m* MUS upbeat; *fig* prelude
'**auftanken** *v/t* (*sep, -ge-, h*) fill up; MOT, AVIAT refuel
auftauchen *v/i* (*sep, -ge-, sein*) appear; MAR surface
auftauen *v/t* (*sep, -ge-, h*) thaw; GASTR defrost
aufteilen *v/t* (*sep, -ge-, h*) divide (up)
Auftrag ['auftraːk] *m* (*-[e]s; Aufträge* ['auftrɛːɡə]*)* instructions, order (*a.* ECON); MIL mission; *im* **Auftrag von** on behalf of
auftragen *v/t* (*irr,* **tragen,** *sep, -ge-, h*) serve (up) (*food*); apply (*paint*); *j-m et.* **auftragen** ask (*or* tell) s.o. to do s.th; F *dick* **auftragen** exaggerate
'**Auftraggeber** *m* (*-s; -*) principal; customer
'**auftreffen** *v/i* (*irr,* **treffen,** *sep, -ge-, sein*) strike, hit
auftreiben F *v/t* (*irr,* **treiben,** *sep, -ge-, h*) get hold of; raise (*money*)
auftrennen *v/t* (*sep, -ge-, h*) undo (*seam*), cut open
auftreten *v/i* (*irr,* **treten,** *sep, -ge-, sein*) THEA *etc* appear (**als** as); behave, act; occur
'**Auftreten** *n* (*-s; no pl*) appearance; behavio(u)r; occurrence
'**Auftrieb** *m* (*-[e]s; no pl*) PHYS buoyancy (*a. fig*); AVIAT lift; *fig* impetus
'**Auftritt** *m* THEA entrance
'**auftun** *v/refl* (*irr,* **tun,** *sep, -ge-, h*) open (*a.*

fig); *abyss:* yawn
auftürmen *v/t* (*sep, -ge-, h*) pile *or* heap up; *sich* **auftürmen** pile up
aufwachen *v/i* (*sep, -ge-, sein*) wake up
aufwachsen *v/i* (*irr,* **wachsen,** *sep, -ge-, sein*) grow up
Aufwand ['aufvant] *m* (*-[e]s; no pl*) expenditure (**an** *dat* of), *a.* expense; pomp
aufwändig ['aufvɛndɪç] *adj* costly; extravagant (*lifestyle*)
'**aufwärmen** *v/t* (*sep, -ge-, h*) warm up; F *fig contp* bring up
aufwärts ['aufvɛrts] *adv* upward(s); **aufwärtsgehen** *v/i* (*irr,* **gehen,** *sep, -ge-, sein*) *fig* improve
'**aufwecken** *v/t* (*sep, -ge-, h*) wake (up)
aufweichen *v/t* (*sep, -ge-, h*) soften; soak
aufweisen *v/t* (*irr,* **weisen,** *sep, -ge-, h*) show, have
aufwenden *v/t* ([*irr,* **wenden,**] *sep, -ge-, h*) spend (**für** on); *Mühe* **aufwenden** take pains
aufwendig → **aufwändig**
'**aufwerfen** *v/t* (*irr,* **werfen,** *sep, -ge-, h*) raise (*question etc*)
'**aufwerten** *v/t* (*sep, -ge-, h*) ECON revalue; *fig* increase the value of
'**Aufwertung** *f* revaluation
'**aufwickeln** *v/t and v/refl* (*sep, -ge-, h*) wind up, roll up; put *hair* in curlers
aufwiegeln ['aufviːɡəln] *v/t* (*sep, -ge-, h*) stir up, incite, instigate
'**aufwiegen** *v/t* (*irr,* **wiegen,** *sep, -ge-, h*) make up for
Aufwiegler ['aufviːɡlɐ] *m* (*-s; -*) agitator; instigator
'**Aufwind** *m* upwind; *im* **Aufwind** *fig* on the upswing
'**aufwirbeln** *v/t* (*sep, -ge-, h*) whirl up; *fig* (*viel*) *Staub* **aufwirbeln** make (quite) a stir
aufwischen *v/t* (*sep, -ge-, h*) wipe up
aufwühlen *fig v/t* (*sep, -ge-, h*) stir, move
'**aufzählen** *v/t* (*sep, -ge-, h*) name (one by one), list
'**Aufzählung** *f* enumeration, list
'**aufzeichnen** *v/t* (*sep, -ge-, h*) TV, *radio etc*: record, tape; draw
'**Aufzeichnung** *f* recording; *pl* notes
'**aufzeigen** *v/t* (*sep, -ge-, h*) show; demonstrate; point out (*mistake etc*)
'**aufziehen** (*irr,* **ziehen,** *sep, -ge-*) **1.** *v/t* (*h*) draw *or* pull up; (pull) open; bring up (*child*); wind (up) (*clock*); mount (*photo etc*); *j-n* **aufziehen** tease s.o.; **2.** *v/i* (*sein*) come up
'**Aufzug** *m* elevator, *Br* lift; THEA act; F *contp* get-up
'**aufzwingen** *v/t* (*irr,* **zwingen,** *sep, -ge-, h*)

j-m et. aufzwingen force s.th. upon s.o.

Augapfel ['auk-] *m* ANAT eyeball

Auge ['augə] *n* (*-s*; *-n*) ANAT eye; *ein blaues Auge* a black eye; *mit bloßem Auge* with the naked eye; *mit verbundenen Augen* blindfold; *in meinen Augen* in my view; *mit anderen Augen* in a different light; *aus den Augen verlieren* lose sight of; *ein Auge zudrücken* turn a blind eye; *unter vier Augen* in private; F *ins Auge gehen* go wrong

'**Augenarzt** *m* eye specialist

'**Augenblick** *m* moment, instant

'**augenblicklich 1.** *adj* present; immediate; momentary; **2.** *adv* at present, at the moment; immediately

'**Augenbraue** *f* eyebrow

Augenlicht *n* (*-[e]s*; *no pl*) eyesight

Augenlid *n* eyelid

Augenmaß *n*: *ein gutes Augenmaß* a sure eye; *nach dem Augenmaß* by the eye

Augenmerk *n*: *sein Augenmerk richten auf* (*acc*) turn one's attention to, *fig a.* have in view

Augenschein *m* (*-s*; *no pl*) appearance; *in Augenschein nehmen* examine, inspect

Augenzeuge *m* eyewitness

August [au'gʊst] *m* (*-*; *no pl*) August

Auktion [auk'tsjoːn] *f* (*-*; *-en*) auction

Auktionator [auktsjo'naːtoːɐ] *m* (*-s*; *-en* [-na'toːrən]) auctioneer

Aula ['aula] *f* (*-*; *-s, Aulen*) auditorium, *Br* (assembly) hall

aus [aus] *prp* (*dat*) *and adv mst* out of, from; of (*silk etc*); out of (*spite etc*); *light etc*: out, off; *play etc*: over, finished; SPORT out; *aus dem Fenster etc* out of the window *etc*; *aus München* from Munich; *aus Holz* (made) of wood; *aus Mitleid* out of pity; *aus Spaß* for fun; *aus Versehen* by mistake; *aus diesem Grunde* for this reason; *von hier aus* from here; F *von mir aus!* I don't care!; *aus der Mode* out of fashion; F *aus sein* be over; be out; *aus sein auf* (*acc*) be out for; be after (*s.o.'s money etc*); *die Schule* (*das Spiel*) *ist aus* school (the game) is over; *einlaus* TECH on / off

Aus *n*: *im Aus ball*: out of play

'**ausarbeiten** *v/t* (*sep, -ge-, h*) work out; prepare

ausarten *v/i* (*sep, -ge-, sein*) get out of hand

ausatmen *v/t and v/i* (*sep, -ge-, h*) breathe out

ausbaden F *v/t* (*sep, -ge-, h*) *et. ausbaden müssen* take the rap for s.th.

'**Ausbau** *m* (*-[e]s*; *no pl*) extension; completion; removal

'**ausbauen** *v/t* (*sep, -ge-, h*) extend; complete; remove; improve

'**ausbaufähig** *adj*: *et. ist ausbaufähig* there is potential for growth *or* development

'**ausbessern** *v/t* (*sep, -ge-, h*) mend, repair, F *a.* fix

'**Ausbesserung** *f* (*-*; *-en*) repair(ing)

'**Ausbeute** *f* (*-*; *no pl*) gain, profit; yield

'**ausbeuten** *v/t* (*sep, -ge-, h*) exploit (*a. contp*)

'**Ausbeutung** *f* (*-*; *no pl*) exploitation

'**ausbilden** *v/t* (*sep, -ge-, h*) train, instruct; *j-n ausbilden zu* train s.o. to be

'**Ausbilder** *m* (*-s*; *-*) instructor

'**Ausbildung** *f* (*-*; *-en*) training, instruction

'**ausbleiben** *v/i* (*irr, bleiben, sep, -ge-, sein*) stay out; fail to come; *es konnte nicht ausbleiben* it was inevitable

'**Ausblick** *m* view (*auf acc* of); *fig* outlook (*for*)

'**ausbrechen** *v/i* (*irr, brechen, sep, -ge-, sein*) break out (*a. fig*); *in Tränen ausbrechen* burst into tears

'**Ausbrecher** *m* (*-s*; *-*) escaped prisoner

'**ausbreiten** *v/t* (*sep, -ge-, h*) spread (out); *sich ausbreiten* spread

'**Ausbreitung** *f* (*-*; *no pl*) spreading

'**ausbrennen** *v/t* (*irr, brennen, sep, -ge-, sein*) burn out

'**Ausbruch** *m* escape, breakout; outbreak (*of fire etc*); eruption (*of volcano*); (out)-burst (*of resentment etc*)

'**ausbrüten** *v/t* (*sep, -ge-, h*) hatch (*a. fig*)

'**Ausdauer** *f* perseverance, stamina, *esp* SPORT *a.* staying power

'**ausdauernd** *adj* persevering; SPORT tireless

'**ausdehnen** *v/t and v/refl* (*sep, -ge-, h*) stretch; *fig* expand, extend

'**Ausdehnung** *f* expansion; extension

'**ausdenken** *v/t* (*irr, denken, sep, -ge-, h*) think s.th. up; invent (*a. fig*)

'**Ausdruck** *m* expression, term; EDP print--out

'**ausdrucken** *v/t* (*sep, -ge-, h*) EDP print out

'**ausdrücken** *v/t* (*sep, -ge-, h*) stub out (*cigarette etc*); *fig* express

ausdrücklich ['ausdrʏklɪç] *adj* express, explicit

'**ausdruckslos** *adj* expressionless, blank

ausdrucksvoll *adj* expressive

'**Ausdrucksweise** *f* language, style

'**Ausdünstung** *f* (*-*; *-en*) exhalation; perspiration; odo(u)r

auseinander [aus?ai'nandɐ] *adv* apart; separate(d); *auseinanderbringen* *v/t* (*irr, bringen, sep, -ge-, h*) separate, *aus-*

einandergehen *v/i* (*irr*, **gehen**, *sep*, *-ge-*, *sein*) part; *meeting etc*: break up; *opinions etc*: differ; *married couple*: separate; **auseinanderhalten** *v/t* (*irr*, **halten**, *sep*, *-ge-*, *h*) tell apart; **auseinandernehmen** *v/t* (*irr*, **nehmen**, *sep*, *-ge-*, *h*) take apart (*a. fig*); **auseinandersetzen** *v/t* (*irr*, **setzen**, *sep*, *-ge-*, *h*) explain; *sich auseinander setzen mit* *v/refl* deal with; argue with *s.o.*

Ausei'nandersetzung *f* (-; *-en*) argument
'**auserlesen** *adj* choice, exquisite
'**ausfahren** (*irr*, **fahren**, *sep*, *-ge-*) **1.** *v/i* (*sein*) go for a drive *or* ride; **2.** *v/t* (*h*) take *s.o.* out; AVIAT extend (*landing gear*)
'**Ausfahrt** *f* drive, ride; MOT exit
'**Ausfall** *m* TECH, MOT, SPORT failure; loss
'**ausfallen** *v/i* (*irr*, **fallen**, *sep*, *-ge-*, *sein*) fall out; not take place, be cancelled; TECH, MOT break down, fail; *gut etc ausfallen* turn out well *etc*; *ausfallen lassen* cancel; *die Schule fällt aus* there is no school
'**ausfallend**, '**ausfällig** *adj* insulting
'**ausfertigen** *v/t* (*sep*, *-ge-*, *h*) draw up (*contract etc*); make out (*check etc*)
'**Ausfertigung** *f* drawing up; copy; *in doppelter Ausfertigung* in duplicate
'**ausfindig** *adj*: *ausfindig machen* find
ausflippen ['ausflɪpən] F *v/i* (*sep*, *-ge-*, *sein*) freak out
Ausflüchte ['ausflʏçtə] *pl* excuses
'**Ausflug** *m* trip, excursion, outing
Ausflügler ['ausflyːklɐ] *m* (*-s*; -) daytripper
'**Ausfluss** *m* TECH outlet; MED discharge
'**ausfragen** *v/t* (*sep*, *-ge-*, *h*) question (*über acc* about); sound out
ausfransen *v/i* (*sep*, *-ge-*, *sein*) fray
ausfressen F *v/t* (*irr*, **fressen**, *sep*, *-ge-*, *h*) *et. ausfressen* be up to no good
Ausfuhr ['ausfuːɐ] *f* (-; *-en*) ECON export(ation)
'**ausführbar** *adj* practicable
'**ausführen** *v/t* (*sep*, *-ge-*, *h*) take *s.o.* out; carry out (*task etc*); ECON export; explain
ausführlich ['ausfyːɐlɪç] **1.** *adj* detailed; comprehensive; **2.** *adv* in detail
'**Ausführlichkeit** *f*: *in aller Ausführlichkeit* in great detail
'**Ausführung** *f* execution, performance; type, model, design
'**ausfüllen** *v/t* (*sep*, *-ge-*, *h*) fill out (*Br* in) (*form*)
'**Ausgabe** *f* distribution; edition; expense; issue; EDP output
'**Ausgang** *m* exit, way out; end; result, outcome; TECH, ELECTR output, outlet
'**Ausgangspunkt** *m* starting point

Ausgangssperre *f* POL curfew
'**ausgeben** *v/t* (*irr*, **geben**, *sep*, *-ge-*, *h*) give out; spend; F *j-m e-n ausgeben* buy *s.o.* a drink; *sich ausgeben als* pass *o.s.* off as
'**ausgebeult** *adj* baggy
ausgebildet *adj* trained, skilled
ausgebucht *adj* booked up
ausgedehnt *adj* extensive
ausgedient *adj*: *ausgedient haben* *fig* have had its day
ausgefallen *adj* odd, unusual
ausgeglichen *adj* (well-)balanced
'**ausgehen** *v/i* (*irr*, **gehen**, *sep*, *-ge-*, *sein*) go out; end; *hair*: fall out; *money*, *supplies*: run out; *leer ausgehen* get nothing; *ausgehen von* start from *or* at; come from; *davon ausgehen, dass* assume that; *ihm ging das Geld aus* he ran out of money
'**ausgekocht** *fig adj* cunning; out-and-out (*villain etc*)
ausgelassen *fig adj* cheerful; hilarious; *ausgelassen sein* be in high spirits
ausgemacht *adj* agreed(-on); downright (*nonsense*)
ausgeprägt *adj* marked, pronounced
ausgerechnet *adv*: *ausgerechnet er* he of all people; *ausgerechnet heute* today of all days
ausgeschlossen *adj* out of the question
ausgestorben *adj* extinct
ausgesucht *adj* select, choice
ausgewachsen *adj* fullgrown
ausgewogen *adj* (well-)balanced
ausgezeichnet *adj* excellent
ausgiebig ['ausgiːbɪç] *adj* extensive, thorough; substantial (*meal*)
'**ausgießen** *v/t* (*irr*, **gießen**, *sep*, *-ge-*, *h*) pour out
'**Ausgleich** *m* (-[*e*]*s*; *no pl*) compensation; SPORT even score, *Br* equalization; *tennis*: deuce
'**ausgleichen** *v/t and v/i* (*irr*, **gleichen**, *sep*, *-ge-*, *h*) compensate; equalize (*Br a.* SPORT); ECON balance; SPORT make the score even
'**Ausgleichssport** *m* remedial exercises
Ausgleichstor *n*, **Ausgleichstreffer** *m* SPORT tying point, *Br* equalizer
'**ausgraben** *v/t* (*irr*, **graben**, *sep*, *-ge-*, *h*) dig out *or* up (*a. fig*)
'**Ausgrabungen** *pl* excavations
'**ausgrenzen** *v/t* (*sep*, *-ge-*, *h*) isolate
'**Ausguss** *m* (kitchen) sink
'**aushalten** (*irr*, **halten**, *sep*, *-ge-*, *h*) **1.** *v/t* bear, stand; keep (*mistress etc*); *nicht auszuhalten sein* be unbearable; **2.** *v/i* hold out

aushändigen ['aushɛndɪgən] v/t (sep, -ge-, h) hand over

'**Aushang** m notice; bulletin

'**aushängen** v/t (sep, -ge-, h) hang out, put up; unhinge (door)

'**ausheben** v/t (irr, **heben**, sep, -ge-, h) dig (trench); raid (place etc)

aushelfen v/i (irr, **helfen**, sep, -ge-, h) help out

'**Aushilfe** f (temporary) help

'**Aushilfs**... in cpds -kellner etc: temporary

'**ausholen** v/i (sep, -ge-, h) **zum Schlag ausholen** swing (to strike); fig **weit ausholen** go far back

aushorchen v/t (sep, -ge-, h) sound (**über** acc on)

aushungern v/t (sep, -ge-, h) starve out

auskennen v/refl (irr, **kennen**, sep, -ge-, h) **sich auskennen** (**in** dat) know one's way (about); fig know a lot (about)

ausklingen v/i (irr, **klingen**, sep, -ge-, sein) draw to a close

ausklopfen v/t (sep, -ge-, h) knock out

auskommen v/i (irr, **kommen**, sep, -ge-, sein) get by; **auskommen mit** manage with s.th.; get along with s.o.

Auskunft ['auskʊnft] f (-; Auskünfte ['auskʏnftə]) a) information, b) (no pl) information desk; TEL inquiries

'**auslachen** v/t (sep, -ge-, h) laugh at (**wegen** for)

ausladen v/t (irr, **laden**, sep, -ge-, h) unload

'**Auslage** f window display; pl expenses

'**Ausland** n (-[e]s; no pl) **das Ausland** foreign countries; **ins Ausland, im Ausland** abroad

Ausländer ['auslɛndɐ] m (-s; -) foreigner

Ausländerfeindlichkeit f hostility to foreigners, xenophobia

Ausländerin ['auslɛndərɪn] f (-; -nen) foreigner

'**ausländisch** [-lɛndɪʃ] adj foreign

'**Auslandsgespräch** n international call

Auslandskorrespondent(in) foreign correspondent

'**auslassen** v/t (irr, **lassen**, sep, -ge-, h) leave out; melt (butter etc); let out (seam); **s-n Zorn an j-m auslassen** take it out on s.o.; **sich auslassen über** (acc) express o.s. on

'**Auslassung** f (-; -en) omission

'**Auslassungszeichen** n LING apostrophe

'**Auslauf** m room to move about; dog: exercise

'**auslaufen** v/i (irr, **laufen**, sep, -ge-, sein) MAR leave port; pot etc: leak; liquid etc: run out

'**Ausläufer** m METEOR ridge, trough; pl GEOGR foothills

'**Auslaufmo,dell** n ECON close-out (Br phase-out) model

'**auslegen** v/t (sep, -ge-, h) lay out; carpet; line (with paper etc); display (goods); interpret (text etc); advance (money)

'**Auslegung** f (-; -en) interpretation

'**ausleihen** v/t (irr, **leihen**, sep, -ge-, h) lend (out), loan; **sich** (dat) **et. ausleihen** borrow s.th.

auslernen v/i (sep, -ge-, h) complete one's training; **man lernt nie aus** we live and learn

'**Auslese** f choice, selection; fig pick

'**auslesen** v/t (irr, **lesen**, sep, -ge-, h) pick out, select; finish (book etc)

'**ausliefern** v/t (sep, -ge-, h) hand or turn over, deliver (up); POL extradite

'**Auslieferung** f delivery; extradition

'**ausliegen** v/i (irr, **liegen**, sep, -ge-, h) be laid out

auslöschen v/t (sep, -ge-, h) put out; fig wipe out

auslosen v/t (sep, -ge-, h) draw (lots) for

'**auslösen** v/t (sep, -ge-, h) TECH release; ransom, redeem; cause, start, trigger s.th. off

'**Auslöser** m (PHOT shutter) release; trigger

'**ausmachen** v/t (sep, -ge-, h) put out (fire); turn off (light etc); arrange (date etc); agree on (price etc); make up; amount to; settle (dispute); sight, spot; **macht es Ihnen et. aus** (, **wenn...**)? do you mind (if ...)?; **es macht mir nichts aus** I don't mind; **das macht (gar) nichts aus** that doesn't matter (at all)

'**ausmalen** v/t (sep, -ge-, h) paint; **sich et. ausmalen** imagine s.th.

'**Ausmaß** n extent; pl proportions

ausmerzen ['ausmɛrtsən] v/t (sep, -ge-, h) eliminate

ausmessen v/t (irr, **messen**, sep, -ge-, h) measure

Ausnahme ['ausnaːmə] f (-; -n) exception

Ausnahmezustand m POL state of emergency

'**ausnahmslos** adv without exception

'**ausnahmsweise** adv by way of exception; just this once

'**ausnehmen** v/t (irr, **nehmen**, sep, -ge-, h) clean (chicken etc); except; F contp fleece s.o.

ausnehmend adv exceptionally

'**ausnutzen** v/t (sep, -ge-, h) use; take advantage of (a. contp); exploit

auspacken (sep, -ge-, h) **1.** v/t unpack; **2.** F

v/i talk

auspfeifen *v/t* (*irr*, **pfeifen**, *sep*, -*ge*-, *h*) boo, hiss

ausplaudern *v/t* (*sep*, -*ge*-, *h*) blab out

ausplündern *v/t* (*sep*, -*ge*-, *h*) plunder, rob

auspro,bieren *v/t* (*sep*, *no* -*ge*-, *h*) try (out), test

'Auspuff *m* MOT exhaust

Auspuffgase *pl* MOT exhaust fumes

Auspuffrohr *n* MOT exhaust pipe

Auspufftopf *m* MOT muffler, *Br* silencer

'ausquar,tieren *v/t* (*sep*, *no* -*ge*-, *h*) move out

ausra,dieren *v/t* (*sep*, *no* -*ge*-, *h*) erase; *fig* wipe out

ausran,gieren *v/t* (*sep*, *no* -*ge*-, *h*) discard

ausrauben *v/t* (*sep*, -*ge*-, *h*) rob

ausräumen *v/t* (*sep*, -*ge*-, *h*) empty; clear out (*room etc*); *fig* clear up (*doubt etc*)

ausrechnen *v/t* (*sep*, -*ge*-, *h*) work out

'Ausrede *f* excuse

'ausreden (*sep*, -*ge*-, *h*) **1.** *v/i* finish speaking; *j-n ausreden lassen* hear s.o. out; **2.** *v/t*: *j-m et. ausreden* talk s.o. out of s.th.

'ausreichen *v/t* (*sep*, -*ge*-, *h*) be enough

ausreichend *adj* sufficient, enough; *grade*: (barely) passing, only average, weak, D

'Ausreise *f* departure

'ausreisen *v/i* (*sep*, -*ge*-, *sein*) leave (a *or* one's country)

'Ausreisevisum *n* exit visa

'ausreißen (*irr*, **reißen**, *sep*, -*ge*-) **1.** *v/t* (*h*) pull *or* tear out; **2.** F *v/i* (*sein*) run away

'Ausreißer *m* (-*s*; -) runaway

'ausrenken *v/t* (*sep*, -*ge*-, *h*) MED dislocate

ausrichten *v/t* (*sep*, -*ge*-, *h*) tell *s.o. s.th.*; deliver (*message*); accomplish; arrange (*party etc*); *richte ihr e-n Gruß von mir aus!* give her my regards!; *kann ich et. ausrichten?* can I take a message

'ausrotten *v/t* (*sep*, -*ge*-, *h*) exterminate

'Ausrottung *f* (-; -*en*) extermination

'ausrücken *v/i* (*sep*, -*ge*-, *sein*) F run away; MIL march out

'Ausruf *m* cry, shout

'ausrufen *v/t* (*irr*, **rufen**, *sep*, -*ge*-, *h*) cry, shout, exclaim; call out (*name*); POL proclaim

'Ausrufung *f* (-; -*en*) POL proclamation

'Ausrufungszeichen *n* LING exclamation mark

'ausruhen *v/i*, *v/t and v/refl* (*sep*, -*ge*-, *h*) rest

'ausrüsten *v/t* (*sep*, -*ge*-, *h*) equip

'Ausrüstung *f* equipment

'ausrutschen *v/i* (*sep*, -*ge*-, *sein*) slip

'Aussage *f* statement; JUR evidence

'aussagen *v/t* (*sep*, -*ge*-, *h*) state, declare; JUR testify

ausschalten *v/t* (*sep*, -*ge*-, *h*) switch off; *fig* eliminate

'Ausschau *f*: *Ausschau halten nach* →

'ausschauen *v/i* (*sep*, -*ge*-, *h*) *Ausschau nach* look out for, watch out for

'ausscheiden (*irr*, **scheiden**, *sep*, -*ge*-) **1.** *v/i* (*sein*) be ruled out; SPORT *etc* drop out (*aus dat* of); retire (*aus dat* from *office etc*); *ausscheiden aus* (*dat*) leave (*a firm etc*); **2.** *v/t* (*h*) eliminate; MED *etc* secrete, exude

'Ausscheidung *f* elimination (*a.* SPORT); MED secretion

'Ausscheidungs... *in cpds* ...*spiel etc*: SPORT qualifying ...

'ausschlachten *fig v/t* (*sep*, -*ge*-, *h*) salvage, *Br a.* cannibalize; *contp* exploit

ausschlafen (*irr*, **schlafen**, *sep*, -*ge*-, *h*) **1.** *v/i* sleep in; **2.** *v/t* sleep off

'Ausschlag *m* MED rash; TECH deflection; *den Ausschlag geben* decide it

'ausschlagen (*irr*, **schlagen**, *sep*, -*ge*-, *h*) **1.** *v/t* knock out (*tooth etc*); *fig* refuse, decline (*offer etc*); **2.** *v/i* horse: kick; BOT bud; TECH deflect

'ausschlaggebend *adj* decisive

'ausschließen *v/t* (*irr*, **schließen**, *sep*, -*ge*-, *h*) lock out; *fig* exclude; expel; SPORT disqualify

'ausschließlich *adj* exclusive

'Ausschluss *m* exclusion; expulsion; SPORT disqualification; *unter Ausschluss der Öffentlichkeit* in closed session

'ausschmücken *v/t* (*sep*, -*ge*-, *h*) decorate; *fig* embellish

ausschneiden *v/t* (*irr*, **schneiden**, *sep*, -*ge*-, *h*) cut out

'Ausschnitt *m clothing*: neck; (*press*) clipping (*Br* cutting); *fig* part; extract; *mit tiefem Ausschnitt* low-necked

'ausschreiben *v/t* (*irr*, **schreiben**, *sep*, -*ge*-, *h*) write out (*a.* check *etc*); advertise (*post etc*)

'Ausschreibung *f* advertisement

'Ausschreitungen *pl* violence, riots

'Ausschuss *m* committee, board; TECH (*no pl*) refuse, waste, rejects

'ausschütteln *v/t* (*sep*, -*ge*-, *h*) shake out

ausschütten *v/t* (*sep*, -*ge*-, *h*) pour out (*a. fig*); spill; ECON pay; *sich vor Lachen ausschütten* split one's sides

'ausschweifend *adj* dissolute

'Ausschweifung *f* (-; -*en*) debauchery, excess

'aussehen *v/i* (*irr*, **sehen**, *sep*, -*ge*-, *h*) look; *krank* (*traurig*) *aussehen* look ill (sad); *aussehen wie ...* look like ...;

wie sieht er aus? what does he look like? **'Aussehen** *n* (*-s*; *no pl*) look(s), appearance

außen ['ausən] *adv* outside; *nach außen* (*hin*) outward(s); *fig* outwardly

'Außenbordmotor *m* outboard motor

aussenden *v/t* ([*irr,* **senden**,] *sep, -ge-, h*) send out

'Außendienst *m* field service

Außenhandel *m* foreign trade

Außenmi,nister *m Am* Secretary of State, *Br* Foreign Secretary

Außenminis,terium *n Am* State Department, *Br* Foreign Office

Außenpoli,tik *f* foreign affairs; foreign policy

'außenpo,litisch *adj* foreign-policy

'Außenseite *f* outside

'Außenseiter [-zaitɐ] *m* (*-s*; *-*) outsider

'Außenspiegel *m* MOT outside rearview mirror

Außenstände *pl* ECON receivables

Außenstelle *f* branch

Außenstürmer *m* SPORT winger

Außenwelt *f* outside world

außer ['ausɐ] **1.** *prp* (*dat*) out of; aside from, *Br* beside(s); except; *außer sich sein* be beside o.s. (*vor Freude* with joy); *alle außer e-m* all but one; → *Betrieb, Gefahr*; **2.** *cj*: *außer dass* except that; *außer wenn* unless

'außerdem *cj* besides, moreover

äußere ['ɔysərə] *adj* exterior, outer, outward

'Äußere *n* (*-n*; *no pl*) exterior, outside; (outward) appearance

'außergewöhnlich *adj* unusual

'außerhalb *prp* (*gen*) *and adv* outside; out of; beyond

'außerirdisch *adj* extraterrestrial

'äußerlich *adj* external, outward

'Äußerlichkeit *f* (*-*; *-en*) formality; minor detail

äußern ['ɔysɐn] *v/t* (*ge-, h*) utter, express; *sich äußern* say s.th.; *sich äußern zu or über* (*acc*) express o.s. on

'außer'ordentlich *adj* extraordinary

'außerplanmäßig *adj* unscheduled

äußerst ['ɔysɐst] **1.** *adj* outermost; *fig* extreme; *im äußersten Fall* at (the) worst; at (the) most **2.** *adv* extremely

außer'stande *adj*: *außerstande sein* be unable

'Äußerung *f* (*-*; *-en*) utterance, remark

'aussetzen (*sep, -ge-, h*) **1.** *v/t* abandon; expose (*dat* to); *et. auszusetzen haben an* (*dat*) find fault with; **2.** *v/i* stop, break off; MOT, TECH fail

'Aussicht *f* view (*auf acc* of); *fig* prospect

(of), chance (*auf Erfolg* of success)

'aussichtslos *adj* hopeless, desperate

'Aussichtspunkt *m* vantage point

'aussichtsreich *adj* promising

'Aussichtsturm *m* lookout tower

'Aussiedler *m* resettler, evacuee

'aussitzen *v/t* (*irr,* **sitzen**, *sep, -ge-, h*) sit *s.th.* out

aussöhnen ['auszø:nən] *v/refl* (*sep, -ge-, h*) *sich aussöhnen* (*mit*) become reconciled (with), F make it up (with)

'Aussöhnung *f* (*-*; *-en*) reconciliation

'aussor,tieren *v/t* (*sep, no -ge-, h*) sort out

ausspannen (*sep, -ge-, h*) **1.** *v/t* unharness; **2.** *fig v/i* (take a) rest, relax

'aussperren *v/t* (*sep, -ge-, h*) lock out (*a.* ECON)

'Aussperrung *f* (*-*; *-en*) ECON lock-out

'ausspielen (*sep, -ge-, h*) **1.** *v/t* play; *j-n gegen j-n ausspielen* play s.o. off against s.o.; **2.** *v/i* card game: lead; *er hat ausgespielt* *fig* he is done for

ausspio,nieren *v/t* (*sep, no -ge-, h*) spy out

'Aussprache *f* pronunciation; discussion; *private* heart-to-heart (talk)

'aussprechen *v/t* (*irr,* **sprechen**, *sep, -ge-, h*) pronounce; express; *sich aussprechen für* (*gegen*) speak for (against); *sich mit j-m gründlich aussprechen* have a heart-to-heart talk with s.o.

'Ausspruch *m* saying; remark

'ausspucken *v/i and v/t* (*sep, -ge-, h*) spit out

ausspülen *v/t* (*sep, -ge-, h*) rinse

'Ausstand *m* strike, F walkout

'ausstatten *v/t* (*sep, -ge-, h*) fit out, equip, furnish

'Ausstatung *f* (*-*; *-en*) equipment, furnishings; design

'ausstechen *v/t* (*irr,* **stechen**, *sep, -ge-, h*) GASTR cut out (*a. fig*); put out (*eyes*)

ausstehen (*irr,* **stehen**, *sep, -ge-, h*) **1.** *v/t* stand, endure; F *ich kann ihn* (*es*) *nicht ausstehen* I can't stand him (it); **2.** *v/i*: (*noch*) *ausstehen* be outstanding *or* overdue

'aussteigen *v/i* (*irr,* **steigen**, *sep, -ge-, sien*) get out (*aus dat* of); (*a. aussteigen aus dat*) get off *a bus, train*; F *fig* drop out

'Aussteiger F *m* (*-s*; *-*) drop-out

'ausstellen *v/t* (*sep, -ge-, h*) exhibit, display, show; make out (*check etc*); issue (*passport*)

'Aussteller *m* (*-s*; *-*) exhibitor; issuer; drawer (*of check*)

'Ausstellung *f* exhibition, show

'aussterben *v/i* (*irr,* **sterben**, *sep, -ge-, sein*) die out, become extinct (*both a. fig*)

'Aussteuer *f* trousseau; dowry

'**aussteuern** v/t (sep, -ge-, h) ELECTR modulate

'**Aussteuerung** f ELECTR modulation; level control

Ausstieg ['ausʃtiːk] m (-[e]s; -e) exit; fig withdrawal (**aus** dat from)

'**ausstopfen** v/t (sep, -ge-, h) stuff; pad

'**Ausstoß** m TECH, PHYS discharge, ejection; ECON output

'**ausstoßen** v/t (irr, **stoßen**, sep, -ge-, h) TECH, PHYS give off, eject, emit; ECON turn out; give (cry, sigh); expel

'**ausstrahlen** v/t (sep, -ge-, h) radiate (happiness etc); TV, radio: broadcast, transmit

'**Ausstrahlung** f radiation; broadcast; fig magnetism, charisma

'**ausstrecken** v/t (sep, -ge-, h) stretch (out)

ausstreichen v/t (irr, **streichen**, sep, -ge-, h) strike out

ausströmen v/i (sep, -ge-, sein) escape (**aus** dat from)

aussuchen v/t (sep, -ge-, h) choose, pick

'**Austausch** m (-[e]s; no pl) exchange

'**austauschbar** adj exchangeable

'**austauschen** v/t (sep, -ge-, h) exchange (**gegen** for)

'**Austauschschüler(in)** exchange student

'**austeilen** v/t (sep, -ge-, h) distribute, hand out; deal (out) (cards, blows)

Auster ['austɐ] f (-; -n) ZO oyster

'**austragen** v/t (irr, **tragen**, sep, -ge-, h) deliver (mail); settle (dispute etc); hold (contest etc); **das Kind austragen** have the baby

'**Austragungsort** m SPORT venue

Australien [aus'traːljən] Australia

Australier [aus'traːljɐ] m (-s; -), **Aust'ralierin** [-ljərɪn] f (-; -nen), **aust'ralisch** adj Australian

'**austreiben** v/t (irr, **treiben**, sep, -ge-, h) exorcise; F **j-m et. austreiben** cure s.o. of s.th.

austreten (irr, **treten**, sep, -ge-) **1.** v/t (h) tread or stamp out (fire); wear out (shoes); **2.** v/i (sein) escape (**aus** dat from); F go to the bathroom (Br toilet); **austreten aus** (dat) leave (a club etc); resign from

austrinken v/t (irr, **trinken**, sep, -ge-, h) drink up; empty

'**Austritt** m leaving; resignation; escape

'**austrocknen** v/t (sep, -ge-, h) and v/i (sein) dry up

'**ausüben** v/t (sep, -ge-, h) practi|ce, Br -se; hold (office); exercise (power etc); exert (pressure etc)

'**Ausübung** f (-; no pl) practice; exercise

'**Ausverkauf** m ECON (clearance) sale

'**ausverkauft** adj ECON, THEA sold out; **vor ausverkauftem Haus spielen** play to a full house

'**Auswahl** f choice, selection (both a. ECON); SPORT representative team

'**auswählen** v/t (sep, -ge-, h) choose, select

'**Auswanderer** m emigrant

'**auswandern** v/i (sep, -ge-, sein) emigrate

'**Auswanderung** f emigration

auswärtig ['ausvɛrtɪç] adj out-of-town; POL foreign

'**auswärts** adv out of town

'**Auswärtssieg** m SPORT away victory

Auswärtsspiel n SPORT away game

'**auswechseln** v/t (sep, -ge-, h) exchange (**gegen** for); change (tire); replace; **A gegen B auswechseln** SPORT substitute B for A; **wie ausgewechselt** (like) a different person

'**Auswechselspieler** m SPORT substitute

'**Ausweg** m way out

'**ausweglos** adj hopeless

'**Ausweglosigkeit** f (-; no pl) hopelessness

'**ausweichen** v/i (irr, **weichen**, sep, -ge-, sein) make way (dat for); fig avoid s.o.; evade (question)

ausweichend adj evasive

'**ausweinen** v/refl (sep, -ge-, h) have a good cry

Ausweis ['ausvais] m (-es; -e) identification (card); card

'**ausweisen** v/t (irr, **weisen**, sep, -ge-, h) expel; **sich ausweisen** identify o.s.

'**Ausweispa,piere** pl documents

'**Ausweisung** f (-; -en) expulsion

'**ausweiten** fig v/t (sep, -ge-, h) expand

'**auswendig** adv by heart; **et. auswendig können** know s.th. by heart; **auswendig lernen** memorize; learn by heart

'**auswerfen** v/t (irr, **werfen**, sep, -ge-, h) throw out; cast (anchor); TECH eject

'**auswerten** v/t (sep, -ge-, h) evaluate, analyze, interpret; utilize, exploit

'**Auswertung** f evaluation; utilization

'**auswickeln** v/t (sep, -ge-, h) unwrap

'**auswirken** v/refl (sep, -ge-, h) **sich auswirken auf** (acc) affect; **sich positiv auswirken** have a favo(u)rable effect

'**Auswirkung** f effect

'**auswischen** v/t (sep, -ge-, h) wipe out

'**auswringen** v/t (irr, **wringen**, sep, -ge-, h) wring out

'**Auswuchs** m (-es; Auswüchse ['ausvyːksə]) excrescence; fig pl excesses

'**auswuchten** v/t (sep, -ge-, h) TECH balance: **auszahlen** v/t (sep, -ge-, h) pay (out); pay s.o. off; **sich auswuchten** pay

auszählen v/t (sep, -ge-, h) count; boxing:

count out
'**Auszahlung** f payment; paying off
'**auszeichnen** v/t (sep, -ge-, h) price, mark
(out) (goods); **sich auszeichnen** distinguish o.s.; **j-n mit et. auszeichnen** award
s.th. to s.o.
'**Auszeichnung** f marking; fig distinction,
hono(u)r; award; decoration
'**ausziehen** (irr, **ziehen**, sep, -ge-) **1.** v/t (h)
take off (coat etc); pull out (table etc);
sich ausziehen undress; **2.** v/i (sein)
move out
'**Auszubildende** m, f (-n; -n) apprentice,
trainee
'**Auszug** m move, removal; extract, excerpt; statement (of account)
authentisch [au'tɛntɪʃ] adj authentic,
genuine
Autismus [au'tɪsmʊs] m PSYCH autism
autistisch [au'tɪstɪʃ] adj PSYCH autistic
Auto ['auto] n (-s; -s) car, auto(mobile);
(**mit dem**) **Auto fahren** drive, go by car
'**Autobahn** f Am expressway, Br motorway
Autobahndreieck n interchange
Autobahngebühr f toll
Autobahnkreuz n interchange
Autobiogra'phie f autobiography
'**Autobombe** f car bomb
Autobus m → **Bus**
Autofähre f car ferry
Autofahrer(in) motorist, driver
Autofahrt f drive

Autofriedhof F m car dump, auto junkyard
Autogramm [auto'gram] n autograph
Autogrammjäger m autograph hunter
'**Autokarte** f road map
Autokino n drive-in theater (Br cinema)
Automat [auto'maːt] m (-en; -en) vending
(Br a. slot) machine; TECH robot; →
Spielautomat
Automatik [auto'maːtɪk] f (-; no pl) automatic (system or control); MOT automatic
transmission; automatic
Automation [automa'tsjoːn] f (-; no pl)
automation
auto'**matisch** adj automatic
'**Autome,chaniker** m car mechanic
autonom [auto'noːm] adj autonomous
'**Autonummer** f license (Br licence) number
Autor ['autoːɐ] m (-s; -en [au'toːrən]) author
'**Autorepara,turwerkstatt** f garage, car
repair shop
Autorin [au'toːrɪn] f (-; -nen) author(ess)
autorisieren [autori'ziːrən] v/t (no -ge-, h)
authorize
autoritär [autori'tɛːɐ] adj authoritarian
Autorität [autori'tɛːt] f (-; -en) authority
'**Autotele,fon** n car phone
Autovermietung f car rental (Br hire) service
Autowaschanlage f car wash
Axt [akst] f (-; Äxte ['ɛkstə]) ax(e)

B

Bach [bax] m (-[e]s; Bäche ['bɛçə]) brook,
stream, Am a. creek
'**Backblech** n baking sheet
'**Backbord** n (-s; no pl) MAR port
Backe ['bakə] f (-; -n) ANAT cheek
backen v/t and v/i ([irr, **backen**,] -ge-, h)
bake
'**Backenzahn** m ANAT molar (tooth)
Bäcker ['bɛkɐ] m (-s; -) baker; **beim Bäcker** at the baker's
Bäckerei [bɛkə'rai] f (-; -en) bakery,
baker's (shop)
'**Backform** f baking tin
Backhendl ['bakhɛndl] Austrian n (-s; -n)
fried chicken
Backobst n dried fruit

Backofen m oven
Backpflaume f prune
Backpulver n baking powder
Backstein m brick
backte ['baktə] pret of **backen**
'**Backwaren** pl breads and pastries
Bad [baːt] n (-[e]; Bäder ['bɛːdɐ]) bath;
swim; bathroom; → **Badeort**; **ein Bad
nehmen** → **baden 1**
'**Badeanstalt** f swimming pool, public
baths
Badeanzug m swimsuit
Badehose f bathing trunks
Badekappe f bathing cap
Bademantel m bathrobe
Bademeister m pool or bath attendant

baden ['baːdən] (*ge-*, *h*) **1.** *v/i* bathe, take *or* have a bath; swim; **baden gehen** go swimming; **2.** *v/t* bathe (*a.* MED); *Br a.* bath

'Badeort *m* seaside (*or* health) resort

Badetuch *n* bath towel

Badewanne *f* bathtub

Badezimmer *n* bathroom

baff [baf] *adj*: F **baff sein** be flabbergasted

Bagatelle [baga'tɛlə] *f* (-; *-n*) trifle

Baga'tellschaden *m* superficial damage

Bagger ['bagɐ] *m* (-*s*; -) TECH excavator; dredge(r)

'baggern *v/i* (*ge-*, *h*) TECH excavate; dredge

Bahn [baːn] *f* (-; *-en*) railroad, *Br* railway; train; way, path, course; SPORT track; **mit der Bahn** by rail; **Bahn frei!** make way!; *cpds* → *a.* **Eisenbahn**

'bahnbrechend *adj* epoch-making

'Bahndamm *m* railroad (*Br* railway) embankment

'bahnen *v/t* (*ge-*, *h*) **den Weg bahnen** clear the way (*dat* for *s.o.* or *s.th.*); **sich e-n Weg bahnen** force *or* work one's way

'Bahnhof *m* (railroad, *Br* railway) station

Bahnlinie *f* railroad (*Br* railway) line

Bahnsteig [-ʃtaik] *m* (-[*e*]*s*; *-e*) platform

Bahnübergang *m* grade (*Br* level) crossing

Bahre ['baːrə] *f* (-; *-n*) stretcher; bier

Baisse ['bɛːsə] *f* (-; *-n*) ECON fall, slump

Bakterien [bak'teːrjən] *pl* MED bacteria, germs

balancieren [balã'siːrən] *v/t and v/i* (*no -ge-*, *h*) balance

bald [balt] *adv* soon; F almost, nearly; **so bald wie möglich** as soon as possible

baldig ['baldɪç] *adj* speedy; **baldige Antwort** ECON early reply; **auf (ein) baldiges Wiedersehen!** see you again soon!

balgen ['balgən] *v/refl* (*ge-*, *h*) scuffle (**um** for)

Balken ['balkən] *m* (-*s*; -) beam

Balkon [bal'kɔŋ] *m* (-*s*; *-s*, *-e* [-'koːnə]) balcony

Balkontür *f* French window

Ball [bal] *m* (-[*e*]*s*; **Bälle** ['bɛlə]) ball; dance; **am Ball sein** SPORT have the ball; **am Ball bleiben** *fig* stick to it

Ballade [ba'laːdə] *f* (-; *-n*) ballad

Ballast ['balast] *m* (-[*e*]*s*; *no pl*) ballast, *fig a.* burden

Ballaststoffe *pl* MED roughage, bulk

ballen ['balən] *v/t* (*ge-*, *h*) clench (*fist*)

'Ballen *m* (-*s*; -) bale; ANAT ball

Ballett [ba'lɛt] *n* (-[*e*]*s*; *-e*) ballet

Ballon [ba'lɔŋ] *m* (-*s*; *-s*) balloon

'Ballungsraum *m*, **Ballungszentrum** *n* congested area, conurbation

Balsam ['balzaːm] *m* (-*s*; *no pl*) balm

Bambus ['bambʊs] *m* (-*ses*, -; *-se*) BOT bamboo

Bambusrohr *n* BOT bamboo (cane)

banal [ba'naːl] *adj* banal, trite

Banane [ba'naːnə] *f* (-; *-n*) BOT banana

Banause [ba'nauzə] *m* (-*n*; *-n*) philistine

band [bant] *pret of* **binden**

Band[1] *n* (-[*e*]*s*; **Bänder** ['bɛndɐ]) ribbon; tape; (*hat*) band; ANAT ligament; *fig* tie, link; **auf Band aufnehmen** tape; **am laufenden Band** *fig* continuously

Band[2] *m* (-[*e*]*s*; **Bände** ['bɛndə]) volume

Bandage [ban'daːʒə] *f* (-; *-n*) bandage

bandagieren [banda'ʒiːrən] *v/t* (*no -ge-*, *h*) bandage (up)

'Bandbreite *f* ELECTR bandwidth; *fig* range

Bande ['bandə] *f* (-; *-n*) gang; *billiards*: cushions; *ice hockey*: boards; *bowling*: gutter

'Bänderriss *m* MED torn ligament

bändigen ['bɛndigən] *v/t* (*ge-*, *h*) tame (*a. fig*); restrain, control (*children etc*)

Bandit [ban'diːt] *m* (-*en*; *-en*) bandit, outlaw

'Bandmaß *n* tape measure

Bandscheibe *f* ANAT (intervertebral) disk (*Br* disc)

Bandscheibenschaden *m*, **Bandscheibenvorfall** *m* MED slipped disk

Bandwurm *m* ZO tapeworm

bange ['baŋə] *adj* afraid; anxious

'Bange *f*: **j-m Bange machen** frighten *or* scare s.o.; **keine Bange!** (have) no fear!

'bangen *v/i* (*ge-*, *h*) be anxious *or* worried (**um** about)

Bank[1] [baŋk] *f* (-; **Bänke** ['bɛŋkə]) bench; F **durch die Bank** without exception; **auf die lange Bank schieben** put off

Bank[2] *f* (-; *-en*) bank; **auf der Bank** in the bank

'Bankangestellte *m*, *f* bank clerk *or* employee

'Bankauto,mat *m* → **Geldautomat**

Bankett [baŋ'ket] *n* (-[*e*]*s*; *-e*) banquet

'Bankgeschäfte *pl* banking transactions

Bankier [baŋ'kjeː] *m* (-*s*; *-s*) banker

'Bankkonto *n* bank(ing) account

Bankleitzahl *f* A.B.A. number, *Br* bank (sorting) code

Banknote *f* bill, *Br* (bank) note

Bankraub *m* bank robbery

bankrott [baŋ'krɔt] *adj* ECON bankrupt

Bank'rott *m* (-[*e*]*s*; *-e*) ECON bankruptcy; **Bankrott machen** go bankrupt

'**Bankverbindung** f account(s), account details

Bann [ban] m (-[e]s; no pl) ban; spell

'**bannen** v/t (ge-, h) ward off; (**wie**) **gebannt** spellbound

Banner ['banɐ] n (-s; -) banner (a. fig)

bar [baːɐ] adj (in) cash; **gegen bar** for cash

Bar f (-; -s) bar; nightclub

Bär [bɛːɐ] m (-en; -en) zo bear

Baracke [ba'rakə] f (-; -n) hut; contp shack

Barbar [bar'baːɐ] m (-en; -en) barbarian

barbarisch [bar'baːrɪʃ] adj barbarous, a. atrocious (crime etc)

'**Bardame** f barmaid

'**barfuß** adj and adv barefoot

barg [bark] pret of **bergen**

'**Bargeld** n cash

'**bargeldlos** adj noncash

'**Barhocker** m bar stool

Bariton ['baːritɔn] m (-s; -e [-toːnə]) MUS baritone

Barkasse [bar'kasə] f (-; -n) MAR launch

barm'herzig adj merciful; charitable

Barm'herzigkeit f (-; no pl) mercy; charity

'**Barmixer** m barman

Barometer [baro'meːtɐ] n (-s; -) barometer

Baron [ba'roːn] m (-s; -e) baron

Ba'ronin f (-; -nen) baroness

Barren ['barən] m (-s; -) bar, ingot, a. gold, silver bullion; SPORT parallel bars

Barriere [ba'rjeːrə] f (-; -n) barrier

Barrikade [bari'kaːdə] f (-; -n) barricade

barsch [barʃ] adj rough, gruff, brusque

Barsch m (-[e]s; -e) zo perch

'**Barscheck** m (negotiable) check, Br open cheque

barst [barst] pret of **bersten**

Bart [baːɐt] m (-[e]s; Bärte ['bɛːɐtə]) beard; TECH bit; **sich e-n Bart wachsen lassen** grow a beard

bärtig ['bɛːɐtɪç] adj bearded

'**Barzahlung** f cash payment

Basar [ba'zaːɐ] m (-s; -e) bazaar

Base ['baːzə] f (-; -n) cousin; CHEM base

basieren [ba'ziːrən] v/i (no -ge-, h) **basieren auf** (dat) be based on

Basis ['baːzɪs] f (-; Basen) basis; MIL, ARCH base

Baskenmütze ['baskən-] f beret

Bass [bas] m (-es; Bässe ['bɛsə]) MUS bass

Bassin [ba'sɛ̃ː] n (-s; -s) basin; (swimming) pool

Bassist [ba'sɪst] m (-en; -en) MUS bass singer or player

Bast [bast] m (-[e]s; -e) bast; HUNT velvet

Bastard ['bastart] m (-s; -e) BIOL hybrid; mongrel; V bastard

basteln ['bastəln] (ge-, h) **1.** v/i make or repair things o.s.; **2.** v/t build, make

Bastler ['bastlɐ] m (-s; -) home handyman, do-it-yourselfer

bat [baːt] pret of **bitten**

Batik ['baːtɪk] m (-s; -en), f (-; -en) batik

Batist [ba'tɪst] m (-[e]s; -e) cambric

Batterie [batə'riː] f (-; -n) ELECTR, MIL battery

Bau [bau] m (-[e]s; Bauten) a) (no pl) building, construction; build, frame, b) building, c) zo (pl Baue) hole, den; **im Bau** under construction

Bauarbeiten pl construction work; road works

Bauarbeiter m construction worker

Bauart f style (of construction); type, model

Bauch [baux] m (-[e]s; Bäuche ['bɔʏçə]) belly (a. fig); ANAT abdomen; F tummy

'**bauchig** adj bulgy

'**Bauchlandung** f AVIAT belly landing

Bauchredner m ventriloquist

Bauchschmerzen pl stomachache

Bauchtanz m belly dancing

bauen ['bauən] (ge-, h) **1.** v/t build, construct, a. make (furniture etc); **2.** fig v/i: **bauen auf** (acc) rely or count on

Bauer[1] ['bauɐ] m (-n; -n) farmer; chess: pawn

'**Bauer**[2] n, m (-s; -) (bird)cage

Bäuerin ['bɔʏərɪn] f (-; -nen) farmer's wife; farmer

bäuerlich ['bɔʏɐlɪç] adj rural; rustic

'**Bauernfänger** contp m trickster, conman

Bauernhaus n farmhouse

Bauernhof m farm

Bauernmöbel pl rustic furniture

'**baufällig** adj dilapidated

'**Baufirma** f builders and contractors

Baugenehmigung f building permit

Baugerüst n scaffold(ing)

Bauherr m owner

Bauholz n lumber, Br a. timber

Bauinge,nieur m civil engineer

Baujahr n year of construction; **Baujahr 1995** 1995 model

Baukasten m box of building blocks (Br bricks); TECH construction set; kit

Bauleiter m building supervisor

'**baulich** adj structural

Baum [baum] m (-[e]s; Bäume ['bɔʏmə]) BOT tree

'**Baumarkt** m do-it-yourself superstore

baumeln ['bauməln] v/i (ge-, h) dangle, swing; **mit den Beinen baumeln** dangle one's legs

'Baumschule *f* nursery
Baumstamm *m* trunk; log
Baumwolle *f* cotton
'Bauplan *m* architectural drawing; blueprints
Bauplatz *m* building site
Bausch [bauʃ] *m* (-[e]s; -e) wad, ball; *in Bausch und Bogen* lock, stock and barrel
'Bausparkasse *f* building and loan association, *Br* building society
'Baustein *m* brick; (building) block; *fig* element
Baustelle *f* building site; MOT construction zone, *Br* roadworks
Baustil *m* (architectural) style
Baustoff *m* building material
Bautechniker *m* engineer
Bauteil *n* component (part), unit, module
Bauunternehmer *m* building contractor
Bauvorschriften *pl* building regulations
Bauwerk *n* building
Bauzaun *m* hoarding
Bauzeichner *m* draftsman, *Br* draughtsman
Bayern ['baiɐn] Bavaria
Bayer ['baiɐ] *m* (-n; -n), Bayerin ['baiərin] *f* (-; -nen), bay(e)risch ['bai(ə)riʃ] *adj* Bavarian
Bazillus [ba'tsilus] *m* (-; -len) MED bacillus, germ
beabsichtigen [bə'ʔapzıçtıgən] *v/t* (*no -ge-, h*) intend, plan; *es war beabsichtigt* it was intentional
be'achten *v/t* (*no -ge-, h*) pay attention to; observe, follow (*rule etc*); *beachten Sie, dass ...* note that ...; *nicht beachten* take no notice of; disregard
be'achtlich *adj* remarkable; considerable
Be'achtung *f* (-; *no pl*) attention; consideration; observance
Beamte [bə'ʔamtə] *m* (-n; -n), Be'amtin *f* (-; -nen) official; (*police etc*) officer; civil servant
be'ängstigend *adj* alarming
beanspruchen [bə'ʔanʃpruxən] *v/t* (*no -ge-, h*) claim; take up (*time etc*); TECH stress
Be'anspruchung *f* (-; -en) claim; TECH stress, strain (*a. fig*)
beanstanden [bə'ʔanʃtandən] *v/t* (*no -ge-, h*) complain about; object to
beantragen [bə'ʔantra:gən] *v/t* (*no -ge-, h*) apply for; JUR, PARL move (for); propose
be'antworten *v/t* (*no -ge-, h*) answer, reply to
be'arbeiten *v/t* (*no -ge-, h*) work; AGR till; hew (*stone*); process; be in charge of (*a*

case etc); treat (*subject*); revise; THEA adapt (*nach* from); *esp* MUS arrange; F *j-n bearbeiten* work on s.o.
Be'arbeitung *f* (-; -en) working; revision; THEA adaptation; *esp* MUS arrangement; TECH processing, treatment
be'atmen *v/t* (*no -ge-, h*) MED give artificial respiration to s.o.
beaufsichtigen [bə'ʔaufzıçtıgən] *v/t* (*no -ge-, h*) supervise; look after
Be'aufsichtigung *f* (-; -en) supervision; looking after
be'auftragen *v/t* (*no -ge-, h*) commission; instruct; *beauftragen mit* put s.o. in charge of.
Be'auftragte [-tra:ktə] *m, f* (-n; -n) agent; representative; commissioner
be'bauen *v/t* (*no -ge-, h*) build on; AGR cultivate
beben ['be:bən] *v/i* (*ge-, h*) shake, tremble; shiver (*all: vor* with); *earth*: quake
bebildern [bə'bıldɐn] *v/t* (*no -ge-, h*) illustrate
Becher ['bɛçɐ] *m* (-s; -) cup, mug
Becken ['bɛkən] *n* (-s; -) basin, bowl; pool; ANAT pelvis; MUS cymbal(s)
bedacht [bə'daxt] *adj*: *darauf bedacht sein zu inf* be anxious to *inf*
bedächtig [bə'dɛçtıç] *adj* deliberate; measured
bedang [bə'daŋ] *pret of bedingen*
be'danken *v/refl* (*no -ge-, h*) *sich bei j-m für et. bedanken* thank s.o. for s.th.
Bedarf [bə'darf] *m* (-[e]s; *no pl*) need (*an dat* of), want (of); ECON demand (for); *bei Bedarf* if necessary
Be'darfshaltestelle *f* request stop
bedauerlich [bə'dauɐlıç] *adj* regrettable
be'dauerlicher'weise *adv* unfortunately
be'dauern *v/t* (*no -ge-, h*) feel *or* be sorry for *s.o.*, pity *s.o.*; regret *s.th.*
Be'dauern *n* (-s; *no pl*) regret (*über acc* at)
be'dauernswert *adj* pitiable, deplorable
be'decken *v/t* (*no -ge-, h*) cover
be'deckt *adj* METEOR overcast
be'denken *v/t* (*irr, denken, no -ge-, h*) consider, think *s.th.* over
Be'denken *pl* doubts; scruples; objections
be'denkenlos *adv* unhesitatingly; without scruples
be'denklich *adj* doubtful; serious, critical; alarming
Be'denkzeit *f*: *e-e Stunde Bedenkzeit* one hour to think it over
be'deuten *v/t* (*no -ge-, h*) mean
bedeutend *adj* important; considerable; distinguished
Be'deutung *f* (-; -en) meaning; impor-

tance

be'deutungslos *adj* insignificant; meaningless

be'deutungsvoll *adj* significant; meaningful

be'dienen (*no -ge-, h*) **1.** *v/t* serve, wait on *s.o.*; TECH operate, work; *sich bedienen* help o.s.; *bedienen Sie sich!* help yourself! **2.** *v/i* serve; wait (at table); *card games*: follow suit

Be'dienung *f* (-; *-en*) a) (*no pl*) service, b) waiter, waitress; shop assistant, clerk, c) TECH operation, control

Be'dienungsanleitung *f* operating instructions

bedingen [bə'dɪŋən] *v/t* ([*irr,*] *no -ge-, h*) require; cause; imply, involve

be'dingt *adj*: *bedingt durch* caused by, due to

Be'dingung *f* (-; *-en*) condition; *pl* ECON terms; requirements; conditions; *unter einer Bedingung* on one condition

be'dingungslos *adj* unconditional

be'drängen *v/t* (*no -ge-, h*) press (hard)

be'drohen *v/t* (*no -ge-, h*) threaten, menace

be'drohlich *adj* threatening

Be'drohung *f* threat, menace (*gen* to)

be'drücken *v/t* (*no -ge-, h*) depress, sadden

bedungen [bə'dʊŋən] *pp of* **bedingen**

Bedürfnis [bə'dʏrfnɪs] *n* (-*ses; -se*) need, necessity (*für, nach* for)

Bedürfnisanstalt *f* comfort station, *Br* public convenience (*or* toilets)

be'dürftig *adj* needy, poor

be'eilen *v/refl* (*no -ge-, h*) hurry (up)

beeindrucken [bə'ʔaindrʊkən] *v/t* (*no -ge-, h*) impress

beeinflussen [bə'ʔainflʊsən] *v/t* (*no -ge-, h*) influence; affect

beeinträchtigen [bə'ʔaintrɛçtɪgən] *v/t* (*no -ge-, h*) affect, impair

be'end(ig)en *v/t* (*no -ge-, h*) (bring to an) end, finish, conclude, close

beengen [bə'ɛŋən] *v/t* (*no -ge-, h*) make *s.o.* (feel) uncomfortable

be'engt *adj*: *beengt wohnen* live in cramped quarters

be'erben *v/t* (*no -ge-, h*) *j-n beerben* be s.o.'s heir

beerdigen [bə'ʔeːrdɪgən] *v/t* (*no -ge-, h*) bury

Be'erdigung *f* (-; *-en*) burial, funeral

Beere ['beːrə] *f* (-; *-n*) BOT berry; grape

Beet [beːt] *n* (-[*e*]*s; -e*) bed, patch

befähigen [bə'fɛːɪgən] *v/t* (*no -ge-, h*) enable; qualify (*für, zu* for)

be'fähigt *adj* (cap)able; *zu et. befähigt* fit

or qualified for s.th.

Be'fähigung *f* (-; *no pl*) qualification(s), (cap)ability

befahl [bə'faːl] *pret of* **befehlen**

be'fahrbar *adj* passable, practicable; MAR navigable

be'fahren *v/t* (*irr, fahren, no -ge-, h*) drive *or* travel on; MAR navigate

be'fallen *v/t* (*irr, fallen, no -ge-, h*) attack, seize (*a. fig*)

be'fangen *adj* self-conscious; prejudiced, JUR *a.* bias(s)ed

Be'fangenheit *f* (-; *no pl*) self-consciousness; JUR bias, prejudice

be'fassen *v/refl* (*no -ge-, h*) *sich befassen mit* engage *or* occupy o.s. with; work on *s.th.*; deal with *s.o., s.th.*

Befehl [bə'feːl] *m* (-[*e*]*s; -e*) order; command (*über acc* of)

be'fehlen *v/t* (*irr, no -ge-, h*) order; command

Be'fehlshaber *m* (-*s; -*) MIL commander

be'festigen *v/t* (*no -ge-, h*) fasten (*an dat* to), fix (to), attach (to); MIL fortify

Be'festigung *f* (-; *-en*) fixing, fastening; MIL fortification

be'feuchten *v/t* (*no -ge-, h*) moisten, damp

be'finden *v/refl* (*irr, finden, no -ge-, h*) be (situated)

Be'finden *n* (-*s; no pl*) (state of) health

be'flecken *v/t* (*no -ge-, h*) stain; *fig a.* sully

befohlen [bə'foːlən] *pp of* **befehlen**

be'folgen *v/t* (*no -ge-, h*) follow, take (*advice*); observe (*rule etc*); REL keep

Be'folgung *f* (-; *no pl*) following; observance

be'fördern *v/t* (*no -ge-, h*) carry, transport; haul, ship; promote (*zu* to)

Be'förderung *f* (-; *-en*) a) (*no pl*) transport(ation); shipment, b) promotion

be'fragen *v/t* (*no -ge-, h*) question, interview

be'freien *v/t* (*no -ge-, h*) free, liberate; rescue; exempt (*von* from)

Be'freiung *f* (-; *no pl*) liberation; exemption

Befremden [bə'frɛmdən] *n* (-*s; no pl*) irritation, displeasure

be'fremdet *adj* irritated, displeased

befreunden [bə'frɔyndən] *v/refl* (*no -ge-, h*) *sich befreunden mit* make friends with; *fig* warm to

be'freundet *adj* friendly; *befreundet sein* be friends

befriedigen [bə'friːdɪgən] *v/t* (*no -ge-, h*) satisfy; *sich selbst befriedigen* masturbate

befriedigend *adj* satisfactory; *grade*: fair

befriedigt [bə'fri:dıçt] *adj* satisfied, pleased

Be'friedigung *f* (-; *no pl*) satisfaction

be'fristet *adj* limited (**auf** *acc* to), temporary

be'fruchten *v/t* (*no -ge-, h*) BIOL fertilize, inseminate

Be'fruchtung *f* (-; *-en*) BIOL fertilization, insemination

Befugnis [bə'fu:knıs] *f* (-; *-se*) authority; *esp* JUR competence

befugt [bə'fu:kt] *adj* authorized; competent

be'fühlen *v/t* (*no -ge-, h*) feel, touch

Be'fund *m* finding(s) (*a*. MED, JUR)

be'fürchten *v/t* (*no -ge-, h*) fear, be afraid of; suspect

Be'fürchtung *f* (-; *-en*) fear, suspicion

befürworten [bə'fy:ɐvɔrtən] *v/t* (*no -ge-, h*) advocate, speak *or* plead for

Be'fürworter *m* (*-s*; -) advocate

begabt [bə'ga:pt] *adj* gifted, talented

Be'gabung *f* (-; *-en*) gift, talent(s)

begann [bə'gan] *pret of* **beginnen**

be'geben *v/refl* (*irr*, **geben**, *no -ge-, h*) **sich in Gefahr begeben** expose o.s. to danger

Be'gebenheit *f* (-; *-en*) incident, event

begegnen [bə'ge:gnən] *v/i* (*no -ge-, sein*) meet (*a. fig* **mit** with); **sich begegnen** meet

Be'gegnung *f* (-; *-en*) meeting, encounter (*a.* SPORT)

be'gehen *v/t* (*irr*, **gehen**, *no -ge-, h*) walk (on); celebrate (*birthday etc*); commit (*crime*); make (*mistake*); **ein Unrecht begehen** do wrong

begehren [bə'ge:rən] *v/t* (*no -ge-, h*) desire

be'gehrenswert *adj* desirable

be'gehrlich *adj* desirous, covetous

begehrt [bə'ge:ɐt] *adj* (very) popular, (much) in demand

begeistern [bə'gaistɐn] *v/t* (*no -ge-, h*) fill with enthusiasm; carry away (*audience*); **sich begeistern für** be enthusiastic about

be'geistert *adj* enthusiastic

Be'geisterung *f* (-; *no pl*) enthusiasm

Begierde [bə'gi:ɐdə] *f* (-; *-n*) desire (**nach** for), appetite (for)

be'gierig *adj* greedy; eager (**nach, auf** *acc* for; **zu** *inf* to *inf*)

be'gießen *v/t* (*irr*, **gießen**, *no -ge-, h*) water; GASTR baste; F *fig* celebrate *s.th.* (with a drink)

Beginn [bə'gın] *m* (*-[e]s*; *no pl*) beginning, start; **zu Beginn** at the beginning

be'ginnen *v/t and v/i* (*irr, no -ge-, h*) begin, start

beglaubigen [bə'glaubıgən] *v/t* (*no -ge-, h*) attest, certify

Be'glaubigung *f* (-; *-en*) attestation, certification

be'gleichen *v/t* (*irr*, **gleichen**, *no -ge-, h*) pay, settle

be'gleiten *v/t* (*no -ge-, h*) accompany (*a.* MUS **auf** *dat* on); **j-n nach Hause begleiten** see s.o. home

Be'gleiter(in) (*-s*; -/-; *-nen*) companion; MUS accompanist

Be'gleiterscheinung *f* concomitant; MED side effect

Begleitschreiben *n* covering letter

Be'gleitung *f* (-; *-en*) company; *esp* MIL escort; MUS accompaniment

be'glückwünschen *v/t* (*no -ge-, h*) congratulate (**zu** on)

begnadigen [bə'gna:dıgən] *v/t* (*no -ge-, h*), **Be'gnadigung** *f* (-; *-en*) JUR pardon; amnesty

begnügen [bə'gny:gən] *v/refl* (*no -ge-, h*) **sich begnügen mit** be satisfied with; make do with

begonnen [bə'gɔnən] *pp of* **beginnen**

be'graben *v/t* (*irr*, **graben**, *no -ge-, h*) bury (*a. fig*)

Begräbnis [bə'grɛ:pnıs] *n* (*-ses*; *-se*) burial; funeral

begradigen [bə'gra:dıgən] *v/t* (*no -ge-, h*) straighten

be'greifen *v/t* (*irr*, **greifen**, *no -ge-, h*) comprehend, understand

be'greiflich *adj* understandable

be'grenzen *v/t* (*no -ge-, h*) limit, restrict (**auf** *acc* to)

be'grenzt *adj* limited

Be'griff *m* (*-[e]s*; *-e*) idea, notion; term (*a.* MATH); **im Begriff sein zu** *inf* be about to *inf*

be'griffsstutzig *contp adj* F slow on the uptake

be'gründen *v/t* (*no -ge-, h*) give reasons for

be'gründet *adj* well-founded, justified

Be'gründung *f* (-; *-en*) reasons, arguments

be'grünen *v/t* (*no -ge-, h*) landscape

be'grüßen *v/t* (*no -ge-, h*) greet, welcome (*a. fig*)

Be'grüßung *f* (-; *-en*) greeting, welcome

begünstigen [bə'gynstıgən] *v/t* (*no -ge-, h*) favo(u)r

be'gutachten *v/t* (*no -ge-, h*) give an (expert's) opinion on; examine; **begutachten lassen** obtain expert opinion on

begütert [bə'gy:tɐt] *adj* wealthy

be'haart *adj* hairy

behäbig [bə'hɛːbɪç] *adj* slow; portly

be'haftet *adj*: **mit Fehlern behaftet** flawed

behagen [bə'haːgən] *v/i* (*no -ge-, h*) **j-m behagen** please *or* suit s.o.

Be'hagen *n* (*-s; no pl*) pleasure, enjoyment

behaglich [bə'haːklɪç] *adj* comfortable; cozy, snug

be'halten *v/t* (*irr*, **halten**, *no -ge-, h*) keep (*fig* **für sich** to o.s.); remember

Behälter [bə'hɛltɐ] *m* (*-s; -*) container, receptacle

be'handeln *v/t* (*no -ge-, h*) handle; treat (*a.* MED); **sich (ärztlich) behandeln lassen** undergo (medical) treatment

Be'handlung *f* (*-; -en*) handling; *a.* MED treatment

beharren [bə'harən] *v/i* (*no -ge-, h*) insist (**auf** *dat* on)

be'harrlich *adj* persistent

behaupten [bə'hauptən] *v/t* (*no -ge-, h*) claim; pretend

Be'hauptung *f* (*-; -en*) statement, claim

be'heben *v/t* (*irr*, **heben**, *no -ge-, h*) repair (*damage etc*)

be'heizen *v/t* (*no -ge-, h*) heat

be'helfen *v/refl* (*irr*, **helfen**, *no -ge-, h*) **sich behelfen mit** make do with; **sich behelfen ohne** do without

Be'helfs... *in cpds mst* temporary

beherbergen [bə'hɛrbɛrgən] *v/t* (*no -ge-, h*) accommodate

be'herrschen *v/t* (*no -ge-, h*) rule (over), govern; ECON dominate, control; have (a good) command of (*language*); **sich beherrschen** control o.s.

Be'herrschung *f* (*-; no pl*) command, control

beherzigen [bə'hɛrtsɪgən] *v/t* (*no -ge-, h*) take to heart, mind

be'hilflich *adj*: **j-m behilflich sein** help s.o. (**bei** with, in)

be'hindern *v/t* (*no -ge-, h*) hinder; obstruct (*a.* SPORT)

be'hindert *adj* MED handicapped; disabled

Be'hinderung *f* (*-; -en*) obstruction; MED handicap

Behörde [bə'høːɐdə] *f* (*-; -n*) authority, *mst the* authorities; board

be'hüten *v/t* (*no -ge-, h*) guard (**vor** *dat* from)

behutsam [bə'huːtzaːm] *adj* careful; gentle

bei [bai] *prp* (*dat*) near; at; with; by; *time*: during; at; **bei München** near Munich; **wohnen bei** stay (*or* live) with; **bei mir (ihr)** at my (her) place; **bei uns (zu Hause)** at home; **arbeiten bei** work for; **e-e Stelle bei** a job with; **bei der Marine** in the navy; **bei Familie Müller** at the Müllers'; **bei Müller** c/o Müller; **ich habe kein Geld bei mir** I have no money with *or* on me; **bei e-r Tasse Tee** over a cup of tea; **wir haben Englisch bei Herrn X** we have Mr X for English; **bei Licht** by light; **bei Tag** during the day; **bei Nacht (Sonnenaufgang)** at night (sunrise); **bei s-r Geburt** at his birth; **bei Regen (Gefahr)** in case of rain (danger); **bei 100 Grad** at a hundred degrees; → **Arbeit, beim, weit**

'beibehalten *v/t* (*irr*, **halten**, *sep, no -ge-, h*) keep up, retain

'beibringen *v/t* (*irr*, **bringen**, *sep, no -ge-, h*) teach; tell; inflict (*dat* on)

Beichte ['baiçtə] *f* (*-; -n*) REL confession

'beichten *v/t and v/i* (*ge-, h*) REL confess (*a. fig*)

'Beichtstuhl *m* REL confessional

beide ['baidə] *adj and pron* both; **m-e beiden Brüder** my two brothers; **wir beide** the two of us; both of us; **keiner von beiden** neither of them; **30 beide** *tennis*: 30 all

beiei'nander *adv* together

'Beifahrer *m* front(-seat) passenger

'Beifall *m* (*-[e]s; no pl*) applause; *fig* approval

'Beifallssturm *m* (standing) ovation

'beifügen *v/t* (*sep, -ge-, h*) enclose (*dat* with)

beige [beːʃ] *adj* beige

'beigeben (*irr*, **geben**, *sep, -ge-, h*) **1.** *v/t* add; **2.** F *v/i*: **klein beigeben** knuckle under

'Beigeschmack *m* smack (**von** of) (*a. fig*)

Beihilfe *f* aid, allowance; JUR aiding and abetting

Beil [bail] *n* (*-[e]s; -e*) hatchet; ax(e)

'Beilage *f* supplement; GASTR side dish; vegetables

'beiläufig *adj* casual

'beilegen *v/t* (*sep, -ge-, h*) add (*dat* to); enclose (with); settle (*dispute*)

'Beilegung *f* (*-; -en*) settlement

'Beileid *n* (*-[e]s; no pl*) condolence; **herzliches Beileid** my deepest sympathy

'beiliegen *v/i* (*irr*, **liegen**, *sep, -ge-, h*) be enclosed (*dat* with)

beim [baim] *prp*: **beim Bäcker** at the baker's; **beim Sprechen** *etc* while speaking *etc*; **beim Spielen** at play; → *a.* **bei**

'beimessen *v/t* (*irr*, **messen**, *sep, -ge-, h*) attach *importance etc* (*dat* to)

Bein [bain] *n* (*-[e]s; -e*) ANAT leg; bone

beinah(e) ['baina:(ə)] *adv* almost, nearly

'Beinbruch *m* MED fracture of the leg

'beipflichten *v/i* (*sep*, *-ge-*, *h*) agree (*dat* with)

be'irren *v/t* (*no -ge-*, *h*) confuse

beisammen [bai'zamən] *adv* together

Bei'sammensein *n*: **geselliges Beisammensein** get-together

'Beischlaf *m* JUR sexual intercourse

bei'seite *adv* aside; **beiseiteschaffen** *v/t* (*sep*, *-ge-*, *h*) remove; liquidate *s.o.*

'beisetzen *v/t* (*sep*, *-ge-*, *h*) bury

'Beisetzung *f* (*-; -en*) funeral

'Beispiel *n* (*-[e]s; -e*) example; **zum Beispiel** for example, for instance; **sich an j-m ein Beispiel nehmen** follow s.o.'s example

'beispielhaft *adj* exemplary

beispiellos *adj* unprecedented, unparalleled

'beispielsweise *adv* such as

beißen ['baisən] *v/t and v/i* (*irr*, *-ge-*, *h*) bite (*a. fig*); **sich beißen** colors: clash

beißend *adj* biting, pungent (*both a. fig*)

'Beistand *m* (*-[e]s; no pl*) assistance

'beistehen *v/i* (*irr*, **stehen**, *sep*, *-ge-*, *h*) **j-m beistehen** assist *or* help s.o.

beisteuern *v/t* (*sep*, *-ge-*, *h*) contribute (**zu** to)

Beitrag ['baitraːk] *m* (*-[e]s; Beiträge* ['baitrɛːgə]) contribution; dues, *Br* subscription

'beitragen *v/t* (*irr*, **tragen**, *sep*, *-ge-*, *h*) contribute (**zu** to)

'beitreten *v/i* (*irr*, **treten**, *sep*, *-ge-*, *sein*) join

'Beitritt *m* (*-[e]s; -e*) joining

'Beiwagen *m* MOT sidecar

bei'zeiten *adv* early, in good time

beizen ['baitsən] *v/t* (*ge-*, *h*) stain (*wood*); pickle (*meat*)

bejahen [bə'jaːən] *v/t* (*no -ge-*, *h*) answer in the affirmative, affirm

bejahend *adj* affirmative

be'kämpfen *v/t* (*no -ge-*, *h*) fight (against)

bekannt [bə'kant] *adj* (well-)known; familiar; **et. bekannt geben** announce s.th.; **j-n mit j-m bekannt machen** introduce s.o. to s.o.

Be'kannte *m*, *f* (*-n; -n*) acquaintance, *mst* friend

be'kanntgeben *v/t* (*irr*, **geben**, *sep*, *-ge-*, *h*) →**bekannt**

be'kanntlich *adv* as you know

be'kanntmachen *v/t* (*sep*, *-ge-*, *h*) → **bekannt**; Be'kanntmachung *f* (*-; -en*) announcement

Be'kanntschaft *f* (*-; -en*) acquaintance

be'kehren *v/t* (*no -ge-*, *h*) convert

be'kennen *v/t* (*irr*, **kennen**, *no -ge-*, *h*) confess (*a.* REL); admit; **sich schuldig bekennen** JUR plead guilty; **sich bekennen zu** profess *s.th.*; claim responsibility for

Be'kennerbrief *m* letter claiming responsibility

Be'kenntnis *n* (*-ses; -se*) confession, REL *a.* denomination

be'klagen *v/t* (*no -ge-*, *h*) deplore; **sich beklagen** complain (**über** *acc* about)

be'klagenswert *adj* deplorable

be'kleben *v/t* (*no -ge-*, *h*) stick (*or* paste) on *s.th.*; **mit Etiketten bekleben** label *s.th.*

be'kleckern F *v/t* (*no -ge-*, *h*) stain; **sich bekleckern mit** spill *s.th.* over o.s.

Be'kleidung *f* (*-; -en*) clothing, clothes

be'kommen (*irr*, **kommen**, *no -ge-*) **1.** *v/t* (*h*) get, receive; MED catch; be having (*baby*); **2.** *v/i* (*sein*) **j-m** (**gut**) **bekommen** agree with s.o.

bekömmlich [bə'kœmlıç] *adj* wholesome

be'kräftigen *v/t* (*no -ge-*, *h*) confirm

be'kreuzigen *v/refl* (*no -ge-*, *h*) cross o.s.

bekümmert [bə'kʏmɐt] *adj* worried

be'laden *v/t* (*irr*, **laden**, *no -ge-*, *h*) load, *fig a.* burden

Belag [bə'laːk] *m* (*-[e]s; Beläge* [bə'lɛːgə]) covering; TECH coat(ing); MOT lining; (*road*) surface; MED fur; plaque; GASTR topping; spread; (*sandwich*) filling

be'lagern *v/t* (*no -ge-*, *h*) MIL besiege (*a. fig*)

Be'lagerung *f* (*-; -en*) MIL siege

be'lassen *v/t* (*irr*, **lassen**, *no -ge-*, *h*) leave; **es dabei belassen** leave it at that

be'langlos *adj* irrelevant

be'lastbar *adj* resistant to strain *or* stress; TECH loadable

be'lasten *v/t* (*no -ge-*, *h*) load; *fig* burden; JUR incriminate; pollute; damage; **j-s Konto belasten mit** charge *s.th.* to s.o.'s account

belästigen [bə'lɛstıgən] *v/t* (*no -ge-*, *h*) molest; annoy; disturb, bother

Be'lästigung *f* (*-; -en*) molestation; annoyance; disturbance

Be'lastung *f* (*-; -en*) load (*a.* TECH); *fig* burden; strain; stress; JUR incrimination; pollution, contamination

Be'lastungszeuge *m* JUR witness for the prosecution

be'laufen *v/refl* (*irr*, **laufen**, *no -ge-*, *h*) **sich belaufen auf** (*acc*) amount to

be'lauschen *v/t* (*no -ge-*, *h*) eavesdrop on

be'leben *fig v/t* (*no -ge-*, *h*) stimulate

belebend *adj* stimulating

belebt [bə'leːpt] *adj* busy, crowded

Beleg [bə'leːk] *m* (*-[e]s; -e*) proof; receipt;

B

document
be'legen v/t (no -ge-, h) cover; reserve
(seat); prove; enrol(l) for, take (classes);
GASTR put s.th. on; **den ersten** etc **Platz belegen** SPORT take first etc place
Be'legschaft f (-; -en) staff
be'legt adj taken,.occupied; hotel etc: full;
TEL busy, Br engaged; MED coated; **belegtes Brot** sandwich
be'lehren v/t (no -ge-, h) teach, instruct,
inform; **sich belehren lassen** take advice
beleidigen [bə'laidɪgən] v/t (no -ge-, h) offend (a. fig), insult
beleidigend adj offensive, insulting
Be'leidigung f (-; -en) offense, Br offence,
insult
be'lesen adj well-read
be'leuchten v/t (no -ge-, h) light (up), illuminate (a. fig); fig throw light on
Be'leuchtung f (-; -en) light(ing); illumination
Belgien ['bɛlgjən] Belgium
Belgier ['bɛlgjɐ] m (-s; -), **'Belgierin**
[-gjərɪn] f (-; -nen), **'belgisch** adj Belgian
be'lichten v/t (no -ge-, h) PHOT expose
Be'lichtungsmesser m PHOT exposure
meter
Be'lieben n: **nach Belieben** at will
beliebig [bə'liːbɪç] adj any; optional; **jeder beliebige** anyone
beliebt [bə'liːpt] adj popular (**bei** with)
Be'liebtheit f (-; no pl) popularity
be'liefern v/t (no -ge-, h) supply, furnish
(**mit** with)
Be'lieferung f supply
bellen ['bɛlən] v/i (ge-, h) bark (a. fig)
be'lohnen v/t (no -ge-, h) reward
Be'lohnung f (-; -en) reward; **zur Belohnung** as a reward
be'lügen v/t (irr, **lügen**, no -ge-, h) **j-n belügen** lie to s.o.
belustigen [bə'lʊstɪgən] v/t (no -ge-, h)
amuse
be'lustigt [-tɪçt] adj amused
Be'lustigung f (-; -en) amusement
bemächtigen [bə'mɛçtɪgən] v/refl (no
-ge-, h) get hold of, seize
be'malen v/t (no -ge-, h) paint
bemängeln [bə'mɛŋəln] v/t (no -ge-, h)
find fault with
bemannt [bə'mant] adj manned
be'merkbar adj noticeable; **sich bemerkbar machen** draw attention to o.s.; begin
to show
be'merken v/t (no -ge-, h) notice; remark
be'merkenswert adj remarkable
Be'merkung f (-; -en) remark (**über** acc
about)

be'mitleiden v/t (no -ge-, h) pity, feel sorry for
be'mitleidenswert adj pitiable
be'mühen v/refl (no -ge-, h) try (hard);
sich bemühen um try to get s.th.; try
to help s.o.; **bitte bemühen Sie sich nicht!** please don't bother
Be'mühung f (-; -en) effort; **danke für Ihre Bemühungen!** thank you for your
trouble
be'muttern v/t (no -ge-, h) mother s.o.
be'nachbart adj neighbo(u)ring
benachrichtigen [bə'naːxrɪçtɪgən] v/t
(no -ge-, h) inform, notify
Be'nachrichtigung f (-; -en) information,
notification
benachteiligen [bə'naːxtailɪgən] v/t (no
-ge-, h) place s.o. at a disadvantage; discriminate against s.o.
benachteiligt [bə'naːxtailɪçt] adj disadvantaged; **die Benachteiligten** the underprivileged
Be'nachteiligung f (-; -en) disadvantage;
discrimination
be'nehmen v/refl (irr, **nehmen**, no -ge-, h)
behave (o.s.)
Be'nehmen n (-s; no pl) behavio(u)r;
manners
be'neiden v/t (no -ge-, h) **j-n um et. beneiden** envy s.o. s.th.
be'neidenswert adj enviable
BENELUX ['beːnelʊks] ABBR of **Belgien, Niederlande, Luxemburg** Belgium,
the Netherlands and Luxembourg
be'nennen v/t (irr, **nennen**, no -ge-, h)
name
Bengel ['bɛŋəl] m (-s; -) (little) rascal, urchin
benommen [bə'nɔmən] adj dazed, F
dopey
be'noten v/t (no -ge-, h) grade, Br mark
be'nötigen v/t (no -ge-, h) need, want, require
be'nutzen v/t (no -ge-, h) use
Be'nutzer m (-s; -) user
be'nutzerfreundlich adj user-friendly
Be'nutzeroberfläche f EDP user interface
Be'nutzung f use
Benzin [bɛn'tsiːn] n (-s; -e) gasoline, F gas,
Br petrol
beobachten [bə'ʔoːbaxtən] v/t (no -ge-,
h) watch; observe
Be'obachter m (-s; -) observer
Be'obachtung f (-; -en) observation
be'pflanzen v/t (no -ge-, h) plant (**mit**
with)
bequem [bə'kveːm] adj comfortable;
easy; lazy
be'quemen v/refl (no -ge-, h) **sich beque-**

men zu inf bring o.s. to inf
Be'quemlichkeit f (-; -en) a) comfort; *alle Bequemlichkeiten* all conveniences, b) (*no pl*) laziness
be'raten v/t (*irr*, *raten*, *no -ge-*, *h*) advise s.o.; debate, discuss *s.th.*; *sich beraten* confer (*mit j-m* with s.o.; *über et.* on s.th.)
Be'rater m (-s; -) adviser, consultant
Be'ratung f (-; -en) advice (*a.* MED); debate; consultation, conference
Be'ratungsstelle f counsel(l)ing center (*Br* centre)
be'rauben v/t (*no -ge-*, *h*) rob
be'rauschend *adj* intoxicating; F *fig* **nicht gerade berauschend!** not so hot!
be'rauscht *fig adj*: **berauscht von** drunk with
be'rechnen v/t (*no -ge-*, *h*) calculate; ECON charge (*zu* at)
berechnend *adj* calculating
Be'rechnung f calculation (*a. fig*)
berechtigen [bə'rɛçtɪgən] v/t: *j-n berechtigen zu* entitle (*or* authorize) s.o. to
be'rechtigt [-tɪçt] *adj* entitled (*zu* to); authorized (to); legitimate
Be'rechtigung f (-; *no pl*) right (*zu* to); authority
Beredsamkeit [bə'reːtzaːmkait] f (-; *no pl*) eloquence
beredt [bə'reːt] *adj* eloquent (*a. fig*)
Be'reich m (-[e]s; -e) area; range; field
bereichern [bə'raiçɐn] v/t (*no -ge-*, *h*) enrich; *sich bereichern* get rich (*an dat* on)
Be'reicherung [bə'raiçərʊŋ] f (-; *no pl*) enrichment
Be'reifung f (-; -en) (set of) tires (*Br* tyres)
be'reinigen v/t (*no -ge-*, *h*) settle
be'reisen v/t (*no -ge-*, *h*) tour; cover
bereit [bə'rait] *adj* ready, prepared; willing
be'reiten v/t (*no -ge-*, *h*) prepare; cause
be'reithalten v/t (*irr*, *halten*, *sep*, *-ge-*, *h*) have *s.th.* ready; *sich bereithalten* stand by
be'reits *adv* already
Be'reitschaft f (-; *no pl*) readiness; *in Bereitschaft* on standby
Be'reitschaftsdienst m: *Bereitschaftsdienst haben* doctor etc: be on call
be'reitstellen v/t (*sep*, *-ge-*, *h*) provide
be'reitwillig *adj* ready, willing
be'reuen v/t (*no -ge-*, *h*) repent (of); regret
Berg [bɛrk] m (-[e]s; -e) mountain; *Berge von* F loads of; *die Haare standen ihm zu Berge* his hair stood on end
berg'ab *adv* downhill (*a. fig*)
'Bergarbeiter m miner
berg'auf *adv* uphill

'Bergbahn f mountain railroad (*Br* railway)
Bergbau m (-[e]s; *no pl*) mining
bergen ['bɛrgən] v/t (*irr*, *ge-* *h*) rescue, save *s.o.*; salvage *s.th.*; recover (*body*)
'Bergführer m mountain guide
bergig ['bɛrgɪç] *adj* mountainous
'Bergkette f mountain range
Bergmann m (-[e]s; *-leute*) miner
Bergrutsch m landslide
Bergschuhe *pl* mountain(eering) boots
Bergspitze f (mountain) peak
Bergsteigen n mountaineering, (mountain) climbing
Bergsteiger m (-s; -) mountaineer, (mountain) climber
'Bergung f (-; -en) recovery; rescue
'Bergungsarbeiten *pl* rescue work; salvage operations
'Bergwacht f alpine rescue service
'Bergwerk n mine
Bericht [bə'rɪçt] m (-[e]s; -e) report (*über acc* on), account (of)
be'richten v/t and v/i (*no -ge-*, *h*) report (*über acc* on); *j-m et. berichten* inform s.o. of s.th.; tell s.o. about s.th.
Be'richterstatter m (-s; -) reporter; correspondent
Berichterstattung f (-; -en) report(ing)
berichtigen [bə'rɪçtɪgən] v/t (*no -ge-*, *h*) correct
Be'richtigung f (-; -en) correction
be'rieseln v/t (*no -ge-*, *h*) sprinkle
Bernstein ['bɛrnʃtain] m (-s; *no pl*) amber
bersten ['bɛrstən] v/i (*irr*, *-ge-*, *sein*) burst (*fig vor dat* with)
berüchtigt [bə'ryçtɪçt] *adj* notorious (*wegen* for)
berücksichtigen [bə'rykzɪçtɪgən] v/t (*no -ge-*, *h*) take into consideration; *nicht berücksichtigen* disregard
Be'rücksichtigung f: *unter Berücksichtigung* (*gen*) in consideration of
Be'ruf m (-[e]s; -e) job, occupation; trade; profession
be'rufen v/t (*irr*, *rufen*, *no -ge-*, *h*) appoint (*zu* [as] *s.o.*; to *s.th.*); *sich berufen auf* (*acc*) refer to
be'ruflich *adj* professional; *beruflich unterwegs* away on business
Be'rufs... in cpds ...*sportler* etc: professional ...
Berufsausbildung f vocational (*or* professional) training
Berufsberater m careers advisor
Berufsberatung f careers guidance
Berufsbezeichnung f job designation *or* title
Berufskleidung f work clothes

Berufskrankheit *f* occupational disease

Berufsschule *f* vocational school

be'rufstätig *adj*: **berufstätig sein** (go to) work, have a job

Be'rufstätige *m*, *f* (*-n*; *-n*) working person, *pl* working people

Be'rufsverkehr *m* rush-hour traffic

Be'rufung *f* (*-*; *-en*) appointment (**zu** to); JUR appeal (**bei** to); **unter Berufung auf** (*acc*) with reference to; on the grounds of

be'ruhen *v/i* (*no -ge-*, *h*) **beruhen auf** (*dat*) be based on; **et. auf sich beruhen lassen** let s.th. rest

beruhigen [bə'ruːɪɡən] *v/t* (*no -ge-*, *h*) quiet(en), calm, soothe; reassure *s.o.*; **sich beruhigen** calm down

beruhigend *adj* reassuring; MED sedative

Be'ruhigung *f* (*-*; *-en*) calming (down); soothing; relief

Be'ruhigungsmittel *n* MED sedative; tranquil(l)izer

berühmt [bə'ryːmt] *adj* famous (**wegen** for)

Be'rühmtheit *f* (*-*; *-en*) a) (*no pl*) fame, b) celebrity, star

be'rühren *v/t* (*no -ge-*, *h*) touch (*a. fig*); concern

Be'rührung *f* (*-*; *-en*) touch; **in Berührung kommen** come into contact

Be'rührungsangst *f* fear of contact

Berührungspunkt *m* point of contact

besänftigen [bə'zɛnftɪɡən] *v/t* (*no -ge-*, *h*) appease, calm, soothe

Be'satzung *f* (*-*; *-en*) AVIAT, MAR crew; MIL occupying forces

Be'satzungsmacht *f* MIL occupying power

Besatzungstruppen *pl* MIL occupying forces

be'saufen F *v/refl* (*irr*, **saufen**, *no -ge-*, *h*) get drunk, get bombed

be'schädigen *v/t* (*no -ge-*, *h*) damage

Be'schädigung *f* (*-*; *-en*) damage

be'schaffen *v/t* (*no -ge-*, *h*) provide, get; raise (*money*)

Be'schaffenheit *f* (*-*; *no pl*) state, condition

beschäftigen [bə'ʃɛftɪɡən] *v/t* (*no -ge-*, *h*) employ; keep *s.o.* busy; **sich beschäftigen** occupy o.s.

be'schäftigt [-tɪçt] *adj* busy, occupied

Be'schäftigte *m*, *f* (*-n*; *-n*) employed person, *pl* employed people

Be'schäftigung *f* (*-*; *-en*) employment; occupation

be'schämen *v/t* (*no -ge-*, *h*) shame *s.o.*, make *s.o.* feel ashamed

beschämend *adj* shameful; humiliating

be'schämt *adj* ashamed (**über** *acc* of)

be'schatten *fig v/t* (*no -ge-*, *h*) shadow, F tail

Bescheid [bə'ʃait] *m* (*-[e]s*; *-e*) answer; JUR decision; information (**über** *acc* on, about); **sagen Sie mir Bescheid** let me know; (**gut**) **Bescheid wissen über** (*acc*) know all about

be'scheiden *adj* modest (*a. fig*); humble

Be'scheidenheit *f* (*-*; *no pl*) modesty

bescheinigen [bə'ʃainɪɡən] *v/t* (*no -ge-*, *h*) certify

Be'scheinigung *f* (*-*; *-en*) a) (*no pl*) certification, b) certificate

be'scheißen V *v/t* (*irr*, **scheißen**, *no -ge-*, *h*) cheat; **j-n bescheißen um** do s.o. out of

be'schenken *v/t* (*no -ge-*, *h*) **j-n** (**reich**) **beschenken** give s.o. (shower s.o. with) presents

Be'scherung *f* (*-*; *-en*) distribution of (Christmas) presents; F *fig* mess

be'schichten *v/t* (*no -ge-*, *h*) TECH coat

Be'schichtung *f* (*-*; *-en*) TECH coat

be'schießen *v/t* (*irr*, **schießen**, *no -ge-*, *h*) MIL fire *or* shoot at; bombard (*a*. PHYS), shell

be'schimpfen *v/t* (*no -ge-*, *h*) abuse, insult; swear at

Be'schimpfung *f* (*-*; *-en*) abuse, insult

be'schissen V *adj* lousy, rotten

Be'schlag *m* TECH metal fitting(s); **in Beschlag nehmen** *fig* monopolize *s.o.*; bag; occupy

be'schlagen (*irr*, **schlagen**, *no -ge-*) **1.** *v/t* (*h*) cover; TECH fit, mount; shoe (*horse*); **2.** *v/i* (*sein*) window etc: steam up; **3.** *adj* steamed-up; *fig* well-versed (**auf**, **in** *dat* in)

Be'schlagnahme [bə'ʃlaːknaːmə] *f* (*-*; *-n*) confiscation

be'schlagnahmen *v/t* (*no -ge-*, *h*) confiscate

beschleunigen [bə'ʃlɔynɪɡən] *v/t and v/i* (*no -ge-*, *h*) accelerate, speed up

Be'schleunigung *f* (*-*; *-en*) acceleration

be'schließen *v/t* (*irr*, **schließen**, *no -ge-*, *h*) decide (on); pass (*law*); conclude

Be'schluss *m* decision

be'schmieren *v/t* (*no -ge-*, *h*) smear, soil; scrawl all over; cover *wall etc* with graffiti; spread (*toast etc*)

be'schmutzen *v/t* (*no -ge-*, *h*) soil (*a. fig*), dirty

be'schneiden *v/t* (*irr*, **schneiden**, *no -ge-*, *h*) clip, cut (*a. fig*); prune; MED circumcise

be'schönigen [bə'ʃøːnɪɡən] *v/t* (*no -ge-*, *h*) gloss over

beschränken [bə'ʃrɛŋkən] *v/t* (*no -ge-*, *h*) confine, limit, restrict; **sich beschrän-**

ken auf (*acc*) confine o.s. to
be'schränkt *adj* limited; *contp* dense; narrow-minded
Be'schränkung *f* (-; *-en*) limitation, restriction
be'schreiben *v/t* (*irr,* **schreiben,** *no -ge-, h*) describe; write on
Be'schreibung *f* (-; *-en*) description
be'schriften *v/t* (*no -ge-, h*) inscribe; mark (*goods*)
Be'schriftung *f* (-; *-en*) inscription
beschuldigen [bə'ʃʊldɪgən] *v/t* (*no -ge-, h*) blame; *j-n e-r Sache beschuldigen* accuse s.o. of s.th. (*a.* JUR)
Be'schuldigung *f* (-; *-en*) accusation
be'schummeln F *v/t* (*no -ge-, h*) cheat
Be'schuss *m*: *unter Beschuss* MIL under fire
be'schützen *v/t* (*no -ge-, h*) protect, shelter, guard (*vor dat* from)
Be'schützer *m* (*-s;* -) protector
Beschwerde [bə'ʃveːɐdə] *f* (-; *-n*) complaint (*über acc* about; *bei* to); *pl* MED complaints, trouble
beschweren [bə'ʃveːrən] *v/t* (*no -ge-, h*) weight *s.th.; sich beschweren* complain (*über acc* about; *bei* to)
be'schwerlich *adj* hard, arduous
beschwichtigen [bə'ʃvɪçtɪgən] *v/t* (*no -ge-, h*) appease (*a.* POL), calm
be'schwindeln *v/t* (*no -ge-, h*) tell a fib *or* lie; cheat
beschwingt [bə'ʃvɪŋt] *adj* buoyant; MUS lively, swinging
beschwipst [bə'ʃvɪpst] F *adj* tipsy
be'schwören *v/t* (*irr,* **schwören,** *no -ge-, h*) swear to; implore; conjure up
beseitigen [bə'zaɪtɪgən] *v/t* (*no -ge-, h*) remove (*a. s.o.*), *a.* dispose of (*waste etc*); eliminate; POL liquidate
Be'seitigung *f* (-; *no pl*) removal; disposal; elimination
Besen ['beːzən] *m* (*-s;* -) broom
'Besenstiel *m* broomstick
besessen [bə'zesən] *adj* obsessed (*von* by, with); *wie besessen* like mad
be'setzen *v/t* (*no -ge-, h*) occupy (*a.* MIL); fill (*post etc*); THEA cast; trim; squat in
be'setzt *adj* occupied; *seat:* taken; *bus etc:* full up; TEL busy, *Br* engaged
Be'setztzeichen *n* TEL busy signal, *Br* engaged tone
Be'setzung *f* (-; *-en*) THEA cast; MIL occupation
besichtigen [bə'zɪçtɪgən] *v/t* (*no -ge-, h*) visit, see the sights of; inspect
Be'sichtigung *f* (-; *-en*) sightseeing; visit (*gen* to); inspection (of)
be'siedeln *v/t* (*no -ge-, h*) settle; colonize;

populate
be'siedelt *adj:* **dicht** (**dünn**) **besiedelt** densely (sparsely) populated
Be'siedlung *f* (-; *-en*) settlement; colonization; population
be'siegeln *v/t* (*no -ge-, h*) seal
be'siegen *v/t* (*no -ge-, h*) defeat, beat; conquer (*a. fig*)
besinnen *v/refl* (*irr,* **sinnen,** *no -ge-, h*) remember; think (*auf acc* about); *sich anders besinnen* change one's mind
be'sinnlich *adj* contemplative
Be'sinnung *f* (-; *no pl*) MED consciousness; (**wieder**) *zur Besinnung kommen* MED come round; *fig* come to one's senses
be'sinnungslos *adj* MED unconscious
Be'sitz *m* (*-es; no pl*) possession; property; *Besitz ergreifen von* take possession of
be'sitzanzeigend *adj* LING possessive
be'sitzen *v/t* (*irr,* **sitzen,** *no -ge-, h*) possess, own
Be'sitzer *m* (*-s;* -) possessor, owner; *den Besitzer wechseln* change hands
besoffen [bə'zɔfən] F *adj* drunk, plastered, stoned
besohlen [bə'zoːlən] *v/t* (*no -ge-, h*) **besohlen lassen** have (re)soled
Be'soldung *f* (-; *-en*) pay; salary
besondere [bə'zɔndərə] *adj* special, particular; peculiar
Be'sonderheit *f* (-; *-en*) peculiarity
be'sonders *adv* especially, particularly; chiefly, mainly
be'sonnen *adj* prudent, level-headed
be'sorgen *v/t* (*no -ge-, h*) get, buy; → **erledigen**
Be'sorgnis [bə'zɔrknɪs] *f* (-; *-se*) concern, alarm, anxiety (*über acc* about, at); *Besorgnis erregend* → **besorgniserregend**
be'sorgniserregend *adj* alarming
besorgt [bə'zɔrkt] *adj* worried, concerned
Be'sorgung *f* (-; *-en*) *Besorgungen machen* go shopping
be'spielen *v/t* (*no -ge-, h*) make a recording on
be'spitzeln *v/t* (*no -ge-, h*) spy on *s.o.*
be'sprechen *v/t* (*irr,* **sprechen,** *no -ge-, h*) discuss, talk *s.th.* over; review (*book etc*)
Be'sprechung *f* (-; *-en*) discussion, talk(s); meeting, conference; review
be'spritzen *v/t* (*no -ge-, h*) spatter
besser ['bɛsɐ] *adj and adv* better; *es ist besser, wir fragen ihn* we had better ask him; *immer besser* better and better; *es geht ihm besser* he is better; *oder bes-*

ser gesagt or rather; *es besser wissen* know better; *es besser machen als* do better than; *besser ist besser* just to be on the safe side

'bessern *v/refl* (*ge-, h*) improve, get better

'Besserung *f* (*-; no pl*) improvement; *auf dem Wege der Besserung* on the way to recovery; *gute Besserung!* get better soon

'Besserwisser [-vɪsɐ] *m* (*-s; -*) F smart aleck

Be'stand *m* a) (*no pl*) (continued) existence, b) stock; *Bestand haben* last, be lasting

be'ständig *adj* constant, steady (*a. character*); settled; *...beständig in cpds* *...-resistant, ...proof*

Be'standsaufnahme *f* ECON stocktaking (*a. fig*); *Bestandsaufnahme machen* take stock (*a. fig*)

Be'standteil *m* part, component

be'stärken *v/t* (*no -ge-, h*) confirm, strengthen, encourage (*in dat* in)

bestätigen [bə'ʃtɛːtɪgən] *v/t* (*no -ge-, h*) confirm; certify; acknowledge (*receipt*); *sich bestätigen* prove (to be) true; come true; *sich bestätigt fühlen* feel affirmed

Be'stätigung *f* (*-; -en*) confirmation; certificate; acknowledg(e-)ment; letter of confirmation

bestatten [bə'ʃtatən] *v/t* (*no -ge-, h*) bury

Be'stattungsinsti,tut *n* funeral home, *Br* undertakers

be'stäuben *v/t* (*no -ge-, h*) dust; BOT pollinate

beste ['bɛstə] *adj and adv* best; *am besten* best; *welches gefällt dir am besten?* which one do you like best?; *am besten nehmen Sie den Bus* it would be best to take a bus

Beste *m, f* (*-n; -n*), *n* (*-n; no pl*) the best; *das Beste geben* do one's best; *das Beste machen aus* make the best of; *(nur) zu deinem Besten* for your own good

be'stechen *v/t* (*irr, stechen, no -ge-, h*) bribe; fascinate (*durch* by)

be'stechlich *adj* corrupt

Be'stechung *f* (*-; -en*) bribery, corruption

Be'stechungsgeld *n* bribe

Besteck [bə'ʃtɛk] *n* (*-[e]s; -e*) (set of) knife, fork and spoon; cutlery

be'stehen (*irr, stehen, no -ge-, h*) **1.** *v/t* pass (*examination etc*); **2.** *v/i* be, exist; *bestehen auf* (*dat*) insist on; *bestehen aus* (*in*) (*dat*) consist of (in); *bestehen bleiben* last, survive

Be'stehen *n* (*-s; no pl*) existence

be'stehlen *v/t* (*irr, stehlen, no -ge-, h*) *j-n*

bestehlen steal s.o.'s money *etc*

be'steigen *v/t* (*irr, steigen, no -ge-, h*) climb; get on *a bus etc*; ascend (*the throne*)

be'stellen *v/t* (*no -ge-, h*) order; book (*room etc*); reserve (*seat etc*); call (*taxi*); give, send (*message etc*); AGR cultivate; *kann ich et. bestellen?* can I take a message?; *bestellen Sie ihm bitte, ...* please tell him ...

Be'stellschein *m* ECON order form

Be'stellung *f* (*-; -en*) booking; reservation; ECON order; *auf Bestellung* to order

'bestenfalls *adv* at best

'bestens *adv* very well

bestialisch [bɛs'tjaːlɪʃ] *adj fig* bestial

Bestie ['bɛstjə] *f* (*-; -n*) beast, *fig a.* brute

be'stimmen *v/t* (*no -ge-, h*) determine, decide; define; choose, pick; *zu bestimmen haben* be in charge, F be the boss; *bestimmt für* meant for

be'stimmt **1.** *adj* determined, firm; LING definite (*article*); *bestimmte Dinge* certain things; **2.** *adv* certainly; *ganz bestimmt* definitely; *er ist bestimmt ...* he must be ...

Be'stimmung *f* (*-; -en*) regulation; destiny

Be'stimmungsort *m* destination

'Bestleistung *f* SPORT (personal) record

be'strafen *v/t* (*no -ge-, h*) punish

Be'strafung *f* (*-; -en*) punishment

be'strahlen *v/t* (*no -ge-, h*) irradiate (*a. MED*)

Be'strahlung *f* (*-; -en*) irradiation; MED ray treatment, radiotherapy

be'streichen *v/t* (*irr, streichen, no -ge-, h*) spread

be'streiten *v/t* (*irr, streiten, no -ge-, h*) challenge; deny; pay for, finance

be'streuen *v/t* (*no -ge-, h*) sprinkle (*mit* with)

be'stürmen *v/t* (*no -ge-, h*) urge; bombard

be'stürzt *adj* dismayed (*über acc* at)

Be'stürzung *f* (*-; no pl*) consternation, dismay

Besuch [bə'zuːx] *m* (*-[e]s; -e*) visit (*gen, bei, in dat* to); call (*bei* on; *in dat* at); attendance (*gen* at); *Besuch haben* have company *or* guests

be'suchen *v/t* (*no -ge-, h*) visit; call on, (go to) see; look s.o. up; attend (*meeting etc*); go to (*pub etc*)

Be'sucher(in) (*-s; -/-; -nen*) visitor, guest

Be'suchszeit *f* visiting hours

be'sucht *adj*: *gut* (*schlecht*) *besucht* well (poorly) attended; much (little) frequented

betagt [bə'taːkt] *adj* aged

be'tasten v/t (no -ge-, h) touch, feel
be'tätigen v/t (no -ge-, h) TECH operate; apply (brake); **sich betätigen** be active
Be'tätigung f (-; -en) activity
betäuben [bə'tɔʏbən] v/t (no -ge-, h) stun (a. fig), daze; MED an(a)esthetize
Be'täubung f (-; -en) MED an(a)esthetization; an(a)esthesia; fig daze, stupor
Be'täubungsmittel n MED an(a)esthetic; narcotic
Bete ['beːtə] f (-; -n) **rote Bete** BOT beet, Br beetroot
beteiligen [bə'tailɪgən] v/t (no -ge-, h) **j-n beteiligen** give s.o. a share (**an** dat in); **sich beteiligen** take part (**an** dat, **bei** in), participate (in) (a. JUR)
beteiligt [bə'tailɪçt] adj concerned; **beteiligt sein an** (dat) be involved in; ECON have a share in
Be'teiligung f (-; -en) participation (a. JUR, ECON); involvement; share (a. ECON)
beten ['beːtən] v/i (ge-, h) pray (**um** for), say one's prayers; say grace
beteuern [bə'tɔʏɐn] v/t (no -ge-, h) protest (one's innocence etc)
Beton [be'tɔŋ] m (-s; -s, -e [be'toːnə]) concrete
betonen [be'toːnən] v/t (no -ge-, h) stress, fig a. emphasize
betonieren [beto'niːrən] v/t (no -ge-, h) (cover with) concrete
Be'tonung f (-; -en) stress; fig emphasis
betören [bə'tøːrən] v/t (no -ge-, h) infatuate, bewitch
Betr. ABBR of **betrifft** re
Betracht [bə'traxt] m: **in Betracht ziehen** take into consideration; **nicht in Betracht kommen** be out of the question
be'trachten v/t (no -ge-, h) look at, fig a. view; **betrachten als** look upon or regard as, consider
Be'trachter m (-s; -) viewer
beträchtlich [bə'trɛçtlɪç] adj considerable
Be'trachtung f (-; -en) view; **bei näherer Betrachtung** on closer inspection
Betrag [bə'traːk] m (-[e]s; Beträge [bə-'trɛːgə]) amount, sum
be'tragen (irr, tragen, no -ge-, h) 1. v/t amount to; 2. v/refl behave (o.s.)
Be'tragen n (-s; no pl) behavio(u)r, conduct
be'trauen v/t (no -ge-, h) entrust (**mit** with)
be'treffen v/t (irr, treffen, no -ge-, h) concern; refer to; **was ... betrifft** as for ..., as to ...; **betrifft** (ABBR **Betr.**) re
betreffend adj concerning; **die betreffenden Personen** etc the people etc concerned

be'treiben v/t (irr, **treiben**, no -ge-, h) operate, run; go in for (sport etc)
be'treten¹ v/t (irr, **treten**, no -ge-, h) step on; enter; **Betreten (des Rasens) verboten!** keep off (the grass!)
be'treten² adj embarrassed
betreuen [bə'trɔʏən] v/t (no -ge-, h) look after, take care of
Be'treuung f (-; no pl) care (gen of, for)
Betrieb [bə'triːp] m (-[e]s; -e) a) business, firm, company, b) (no pl) operation, running, c) (no pl) rush; **in Betrieb sein** (**setzen**) be in (put into) operation; **außer Betrieb** out of order; **im Geschäft war viel Betrieb** the shop was very busy
Be'triebsanleitung f operating instructions
Betriebsberater m business consultant
Betriebsferien pl company (Br a. works) holiday
Betriebsfest n annual company fête
Betriebskapi,tal n working capital
Betriebsklima n working atmosphere
Betriebskosten pl operating costs
Betriebsleitung f management
Betriebsrat m works council
be'triebssicher adj safe to operate
Be'triebsstörung f TECH breakdown
Betriebssys,tem n EDP operating system
Betriebsunfall m industrial accident
Betriebswirtschaft f business administration
be'trinken v/refl (irr, **trinken**, no -ge-, h) get drunk
betroffen [bə'trɔfən] adj affected, concerned; dismayed, shocked
Be'troffenheit f (-; no pl) dismay, shock
betrübt [bə'tryːpt] adj sad, grieved (**über** acc at)
Betrug [bə'truːk] m (-[e]s; no pl) cheat; JUR fraud; deceit
be'trügen v/t (irr, **trügen**, no -ge-, h) deceive; cheat (**beim Kartenspiel** at cards); swindle, trick (**um et.** out of s.th.); be unfaithful to
Be'trüger(in) (-s; -/-; -nen) swindler, trickster
betrunken [bə'truŋkən] adj drunken; **betrunken sein** be drunk
Be'trunkene m, f (-n; -n) drunk
Bett [bɛt] n (-[e]s; -en) bed; **am Bett** at the bedside; **ins Bett gehen** (**bringen**) go (put) to bed
Bettbezug m comforter case, Br duvet cover
Bettdecke f blanket; quilt
betteln ['bɛtəln] v/i (ge-, h) beg (**um** for)
'Bettgestell n bedstead

'bettlägerig [-lɛːɡərɪç] *adj* bedridden
'Bettlaken *n* sheet
Bettler ['bɛtlɐ] *m* (-*s*; -) beggar
'Bettnässer [-nɛsɐ] *m* (-*s*; -) MED bed wetter
Bettruhe *f* bed rest; *j-m Bettruhe verordnen* tell s.o. to stay in bed
Bettvorleger *m* bedside rug
Bettwäsche *f* bed linen
Bettzeug *n* bedding, bedclothes
beugen ['bɔyɡən] *v/t* (ge-, h) bend; LING inflect; *sich beugen* (*vor dat* to) bend, bow
Beule ['bɔylə] *f* (-; -*n*) MED bump; MOT dent
beunruhigen [bə'ʔʊnruːɪɡən] *v/t* (no -ge-, h) alarm, worry
beurlauben [bə'ʔuːɐlaubən] *v/t* give s.o. leave *or* time off; suspend; *sich beurlauben lassen* ask for leave
be'urlaubt [-laupt] *adj* on leave
be'urteilen *v/t* (no -ge-, h) judge (*nach* by); rate
Be'urteilung *f* (-; -*en*) judg(e)ment; evaluation
Beute ['bɔytə] *f* (-; no *pl*) booty, loot; ZO prey (*a. fig*); HUNT bag; *fig a.* victim
Beutel ['bɔytəl] *m* (-*s*; -) bag; pouch
bevölkern [bə'fœlkɐn] *v/t* (no -ge-, h) populate
be'völkert *adj* → *besiedelt*
Be'völkerung *f* (-; -*en*) population
bevollmächtigen [bə'fɔlmɛçtɪɡən] *v/t* (no -ge-, h) authorize
be'vor *cj* before
bevormunden [bə'foːɐmʊndən] *v/t* (no -ge-, h) patronize
bevorstehen *v/i* (irr, *stehen*, sep, -ge-, h) be approaching; lie ahead; be imminent; *j-m bevorstehen* be in store for s.o., await s.o.
be'vorzugen [-tsuːɡən] *v/t* (no -ge-, h) prefer; favo(u)r
Be'vorzugung *f* (-; -*en*) preferential treatment
be'wachen *v/t* (no -ge-, h) guard, watch over
Be'wacher *m* (-*s*; -) guard; SPORT marker
Be'wachung *f* (-; -*en*) a) (no *pl*) guarding; SPORT marking, b) guard
bewaffnen [bə'vafnən] *v/t* (no -ge-, h) arm (*a. fig*)
Be'waffnung *f* (-; -*en*) armament; arms
be'wahren *v/t* (no -ge-, h) keep; *bewahren vor* (*dat*) keep *or* save from
be'währen *v/refl* (no -ge-, h) prove successful; *sich bewähren als* prove to be
bewährt [bə'vɛːɐt] *adj* (well-)tried, reliable; experienced
Be'währung *f* (-; -*en*) JUR probation

Be'währungsfrist *f* JUR (period of) probation
Bewährungshelfer *m* JUR probation officer
Bewährungsprobe *f* (acid) test
bewaldet [bə'valdət] *adj* wooded, woody
bewältigen [bə'vɛltɪɡən] *v/t* (no -ge-, h) manage, cope with; cover (*distance*)
be'wandert *adj* (well-)versed (*in dat* in)
be'wässern *v/t* (no -ge-, h) irrigate
Be'wässerung *f* (-; -*en*) irrigation
bewegen [bə'veːɡən] *v/t and v/refl* (no -ge-, h) move (*a. fig*); *nicht bewegen!* don't move!; (irr) *j-n zu et. bewegen* get s.o. to do s.th.
Be'weggrund *m* motive
beweglich [bə'veːklɪç] *adj* movable; agile; flexible; TECH moving (*parts*)
Be'weglichkeit *f* (-; no *pl*) mobility; agility
be'wegt *adj* rough (*sea*); choked (*voice*); eventful (*life*); *fig* moved, touched
Be'wegung *f* (-; -*en*) movement (*a. POL*); motion (*a. PHYS*); exercise; *fig* emotion; *in Bewegung setzen* set in motion
Be'wegungsfreiheit *f* (-; no *pl*) freedom of movement (*fig a.* of action)
be'wegungslos *adj* motionless
Beweis [bə'vais] *m* (-*es*; -*e*) proof (*für* of); *Beweis(e)* evidence (*esp* JUR)
be'weisen *v/t* (irr, *weisen*, no -ge-, h) prove; show
Be'weismittel *n* JUR (piece of) evidence
Be'weisstück *n* (piece of) evidence, JUR exhibit
be'wenden *v/i*: *es dabei bewenden lassen* leave it at that
be'werben *v/refl* (irr, *werben*, no -ge-, h) *sich bewerben um* apply for
Be'wer-ber(in) (-*s*; -/-*nen*) applicant
Be'werbung *f* (-; -*en*) application
Be'werbungsschreiben *n* (letter of) application
be'werten *v/t* (no -ge-, h) assess; judge
Be'wertung *f* (-; -*en*) assessment
bewilligen [bə'vɪlɪɡən] *v/t* (no -ge-, h) grant, allow
be'wirken *v/t* (no -ge-, h) cause
bewirten [bə'vɪrtən] *v/t* (no -ge-, h) entertain
be'wirtschaften *v/t* (no -ge-, h) run; AGR farm
be'wirtschaftet *adj* open (to the public)
Be'wirtung *f* (-; -*en*) catering; service; hospitality
bewog [bə'voːk] *pret of* **bewegen**
bewogen [bə'voːɡən] *pp of* **bewegen**
be'wohnen *v/t* (no -ge-, h) live in; inhabit
Be'wohner(in) (-*s*; -/-; -*nen*) inhabitant;

occupant

be'wohnt *adj* inhabited; occupied

bewölken [bə'vœlkən] *v/refl (no -ge-, h)* METEOR cloud over (*a. fig*)

be'wölkt *adj* METEOR cloudy, overcast

Be'wölkung *f (-; no pl)* METEOR clouds

Bewunderer [bə'vʊndərɐ] *m (-s; -)* admirer

be'wundern *v/t (no -ge-, h)* admire (**wegen** for)

be'wundernswert *adj* admirable

Be'wunderung *f (-; no pl)* admiration

bewusst [bə'vʊst] *adj* conscious; intentional; *sich e-r Sache bewusst sein* be conscious *or* aware of s.th., realize s.th.; *j-m et. bewusst machen* make s.o. realize s.th.

be'wusstlos *adj* MED unconscious

be'wusstmachen *v/t →* **bewusst**

Be'wusstsein *n (-s; no pl)* MED consciousness; *bei Bewusstsein* conscious

be'zahlen *v/t (no -ge-, h)* pay; pay for (*a. fig*)

be'zahlt *adj: bezahlter Urlaub* paid leave; *es macht sich bezahlt* it pays

Be'zahlung *f (-; no pl)* payment; pay

be'zaubern *v/t (no -ge-, h)* charm

bezaubernd *adj* charming, F sweet, darling

be'zeichnen *v/t (no -ge-, h) bezeichnen als* call, describe as

bezeichnend *adj* characteristic, typical (*für* of)

Be'zeichnung *f (-; -en)* name, term

be'zeugen *v/t (no -ge-, h)* JUR testify to

be'ziehen *v/t (irr, ziehen, no -ge-, h)* cover; put clean sheets on (*bed*); move into; receive; subscribe to (*paper etc*); *beziehen auf (acc)* relate to; *sich beziehen* cloud over; *sich beziehen auf (acc)* refer to

Be'ziehung *f (-; -en)* relation (*zu* to *s.th.*; with *s.o.*); connection (*zu* with); relationship; respect; *Beziehungen haben* have connections

be'ziehungsweise *cj* respectively; or; or rather

Bezirk [bə'tsɪrk] *m (-[e]s; -e)* precinct, Br *a.* district

Bezug [bə'tsuːk] *m (-[e]s; Bezüge* [bə-'tsyːɡə]) a) cover(ing); case, slip, b) (*no pl*) ECON purchase; subscription (*gen* to), c) *pl* earnings; *Bezug nehmen auf (acc)* refer to; *in Bezug auf (acc) →* **bezüglich**

bezüglich [bə'tsyːklɪç] *prp (gen)* regarding, concerning

Be'zugsper,son *f* PSYCH person to relate to; role model

Bezugspunkt *m* reference point

Bezugsquelle *f* source (of supply)

be'zwecken *v/t (no -ge-, h)* aim at, intend

be'zweifeln *v/t (no -ge-, h)* doubt, question

be'zwingen *v/t (irr, zwingen, no -ge-, h)* conquer, defeat

Bibel ['biːbəl] *f (-; -n)* Bible

Biber ['biːbɐ] *m (-s; -)* ZO beaver

Bibliothek [biblio'teːk] *f (-; -en)* library

Bibliothekar [bibliote'kaːɐ] *m (-s; -e),* **Bibliothe'karin** *f (-; -nen)* librarian

biblisch ['biːblɪʃ] *adj* biblical

bieder ['biːdɐ] *adj* honest; square

biegen ['biːɡən] *v/t (irr, ge-, h) and v/i (sein)* bend (*a. sich biegen*), road: *a.* turn; *um die Ecke biegen* turn (round) the corner

biegsam ['biːkzaːm] *adj* flexible

'Biegung *f (-; -en)* curve

Biene ['biːnə] *f (-; -n)* ZO bee

'Bienenkönigin *f* ZO queen (bee)

Bienenkorb *m,* **Bienenstock** *m* (bee)hive

Bienenwachs *n* beeswax

Bier [biːɐ] *n (-[e]s; -e)* beer; *Bier vom Faß* draft (Br draught) beer

Bierdeckel *m* coaster, beer mat

Bierkrug *m* beer mug, stein

Biest [biːst] F *fig n (-[e]s; -er)* beast; (*kleines*) *Biest* brat, little devil, stinker

bieten ['biːtən] (*irr, ge-, h*) 1. *v/t* offer; *sich bieten* present itself; 2. *v/i* auction: (make a) bid

Bigamie [biga'miː] *f (-; -n)* bigamy

Bikini [bi'kiːni] *m (-s; -s)* bikini

Bilanz [bi'lants] *f (-; -en)* ECON balance; *fig* result; *Bilanz ziehen aus (dat) fig* take stock of

Bild [bɪlt] *n (-[e]s; -er* ['bɪldɐ]) picture; image; *sich ein Bild machen von* get an idea of

Bildausfall *m* TV blackout

Bildbericht *m* photo(graphic) essay (Br report)

bilden ['bɪldən] *v/t (ge-, h)* form (*a. sich bilden*); shape; *fig* educate (*sich o.s.*); be, constitute

'Bilderbuch *n* picture book

'Bildfläche *f:* F *auf der Bildfläche erscheinen (von der Bildfläche verschwinden)* appear on (disappear from) the scene

'Bildhauer *m (-s; -),* **'Bildhauerin** *f (-; -nen)* sculptor

'bildlich *adj* graphic; figurative

'Bildnis *n (-ses; -se)* portrait

'Bildplatte *f* videodisk (Br -disc)

'Bildröhre *f* picture tube

'Bildschirm *m* TV screen, EDP *a.* display,

monitor
Bildschirmarbeitsplatz m workstation
Bildschirmgerät n visual display unit, VDU
Bildschirmschoner m (-s; -) screen saver
Bildschirmtext m videotext, Br viewdata
'bild'schön adj most beautiful
'Bildung f (-; -en) a) (no pl) education, b) formation
'Bildungs... in cpds ...chancen, ...reform, ...urlaub etc: educational ...
Bildungslücke f gap in one's knowledge
'Bildunterschrift f caption
Billard ['bɪljart] n (-s; -e) billiards, pool
Billardkugel f billiard ball
Billardstock m cue
Billett [bɪl'jɛt] n (-[e]s; -e) Swiss ticket
billig ['bɪlɪç] adj cheap (a. contp), inexpensive
billigen ['bɪlɪgən] v/t (ge-, h) approve of
'Billigung f (-; no pl) approval
Billion [bɪl'joːn] f (-; -en) trillion
bimmeln ['bɪməln] F v/i (ge-, h) jingle; TEL ring
binär [bi'nɛːɐ] adj MATH, PHYS etc binary
Binde ['bɪndə] f (-; -n) bandage; sling; → **Damenbinde**
Bindegewebe n ANAT connective tissue
Bindeglied n (connecting) link
'Bindehaut f ANAT conjunctiva
Bindehautentzündung f MED conjunctivitis
binden (irr, ge-, h) **1.** v/t bind (a. book), tie (**an** acc to); make (wreath etc); knot (tie); **sich binden** bind or commit o.s.; **2.** v/i bind
'Bindestrich m LING hyphen
'Bindewort n LING conjunction
Bindfaden ['bɪnt-] m string
'Bindung f (-; -en) tie, link, bond; skiing: binding
Binnenhafen ['bɪnən-] m inland port
Binnenhandel m domestic trade
Binnenmarkt m: **Europäischer Binnenmarkt** European single market
Binnenschifffahrt f inland navigation
Binnenverkehr m inland traffic or transport
Binse ['bɪnzə] f (-; -n) BOT rush
'Binsenweisheit f (-; -en) truism
Bio..., **bio...** [bio-] in cpds ...chemie, ...dynamisch, ...sphäre etc: bio...
Biografie, **Biographie** [biogra'fiː] f (-; -n) biography
bio'grafisch, **bio'graphisch** adj biographic(al)
Bioladen ['biːo-] m health food shop or store
Biologe [bio'loːgə] m (-n; -n) biologist

Biologie [biolo'giː] f (-; no pl) biology
Bio'login f (-; -nen) biologist
biologisch [bio'loːgɪʃ] adj biological; AGR organic; **biologisch abbaubar** biodegradable
'Biorhythmus m biorhythms
'Biotechnik f (-; no pl) biotechnology
Biotop [bio'toːp] n (-s; -e) biotope
Birke ['bɪrkə] f (-; -n) BOT birch (tree)
Birne ['bɪrnə] f (-; -n) BOT pear; ELECTR (light) bulb
bis [bɪs] prp (acc) and adv and cj time: till, until, (up) to; space: (up) to, as far as; **von ... bis ...** from ... to ...; **bis auf** (acc) except; **bis zu** up to; **bis später!** see you later!; **bis jetzt** up to now, so far; **bis Montag** by Monday; **zwei bis drei** two or three; **wie weit ist es bis ...?** how far is it to ...?
Bischof ['bɪʃɔf] m (-s; Bischöfe ['bɪʃœfə]) REL bishop
bisexuell [bizɛ'ksuɛl] adj bisexual
bis'her adv up to now, so far; **wie bisher** as before
bisherig [bɪs'heːrɪç] adj previous
Biskuit [bɪs'kviːt] n (-[e]s; -e) sponge cake (mix)
biss [bɪs] pret of **beißen**
Biss m (-es; -e) bite (a. fig)
bisschen ['bɪsçən] adj and adv: **ein bisschen** a little, a (little) bit (of); **nicht ein bisschen** not in the least
Bissen ['bɪsən] m (-s; -) bite; **keinen Bissen** not a thing
bissig ['bɪsɪç] adj fig cutting; **ein bissiger Hund** a dog that bites; **Vorsicht, bissiger Hund!** beware of the dog!
Bistum ['bɪstuːm] n (-s; Bistümer ['bɪstyː-mɐ]) REL bishopric, diocese
bis'weilen adv at times, now and then
Bit [bɪt] n (-[s]; -[s]) EDP bit
bitte ['bɪtə] adv please; **bitte nicht!** please don't!; **bitte (schön)!** that's all right, not at all, you're welcome; here you are; **(wie) bitte?** pardon?; **bitte sehr?** can I help you?
'Bitte f (-; -n) request (**um** for); **ich habe e-e Bitte (an dich)** I have a favo(u)r to ask of you
'bitten v/t (irr, ge-, h) **j-n um et. bitten** ask s.o. for s.th.; **darf ich bitten?** may I have (the pleasure of) this dance?; → **Erlaubnis**
bitter ['bɪtɐ] adj bitter (a. fig), a. biting (cold)
bitter'kalt adj bitterly cold
blähen ['blɛːən] v/refl (ge-, h) swell
'Blähungen pl MED flatulence, Br a. wind
blamabel [bla'maːbəl] adj embarrassing

Blamage [bla'maːʒə] *f* (-; -*n*) disgrace, shame

blamieren [bla'miːrən] *v/t* (*no* -ge-, *h*) *j-n blamieren* make s.o. look like a fool; *sich blamieren* make a fool of o.s.

blank [blaŋk] *adj* shining, shiny, bright; polished; F broke

Blanko... ['blaŋko] *in cpds* ECON blank

Bläschen ['blɛːsçən] *n* (-*s*; -) MED vesicle, small blister

Blase ['blaːzə] *f* (-; -*n*) bubble; ANAT bladder; MED blister

'Blasebalg *m* (pair of) bellows

'blasen *v/t* (*irr, ge-, h*) blow (*a.* MUS)

'Blasinstru,ment *n* MUS wind instrument

Blaska,pelle *f* brass band

Blasrohr *n* blowpipe

blass [blas] *adj* pale (*vor* with); *blass werden* turn pale

Blässe ['blɛsə] *f* (-; *no pl*) paleness, pallor

Blatt [blat] *n* (-[*e*]*s*; *Blätter* ['blɛtɐ]) BOT leaf; piece, sheet (*a.* MUS); (news)paper; *card games*: hand

blättern ['blɛtɐn] *v/i* (*ge-, h*) *blättern in* (*dat*) leaf through

'Blätterteig *m* puff pastry

blau [blau] *adj* blue; F loaded, stoned; *blaues Auge* black eye; *blauer Fleck* bruise; *Fahrt ins Blaue* mystery tour

'blauäugig [-ɔygɪç] *adj* blue-eyed; *fig* starry-eyed

'Blaubeere *f* BOT blueberry, *Br* bilberry

'blaugrau *adj* bluish-gray (*Br* -grey)

bläulich ['blɔylɪç] *adj* bluish

'Blaulicht *n* (-[*e*]*s*; -*er*) flashing light(s)

'Blauhelme *pl* MIL UN soldiers

'blaumachen F *v/i* (*sep, -ge-, h*) stay away from work *or* school

'Blausäure *f* CHEM prussic acid

Blech [blɛç] *n* (-[*e*]*s*; -*e*) sheet metal; *in cpds* ...*dach*, ...*löffel etc*: tin ...; ...*instrument*: MUS brass ...

'blechen F *v/t and v/i* (*ge-, h*) shell out

'Blechbüchse,Blechdose *f* can, *Br a.* tin

Blechschaden *m* MOT bodywork damage

Blei [blai] *n* (-[*e*]*s*; -*e*) lead; *aus Blei* leaden

Bleibe ['blaibə] *f* (-; -*n*) place to stay

'bleiben *v/i* (*irr, ge-, sein*) stay, remain; *bleiben bei* stick to; F *et. bleiben lassen* not do s.th.; *lass das bleiben!* stop that!; *das wirst du schön bleiben lassen!* you'll do nothing of the sort!; → *Apparat, ruhig*

bleibend *adj* lasting, permanent

'bleibenlassen *v/i* → *bleiben*

bleich [blaiç] *adj* pale (*vor dat* with)

'bleichen *v/t* ([*irr,*] *ge-, h*) bleach

bleiern ['blaiɐn] *adj* lead(en *fig*)

'bleifrei *adj* MOT unleaded

'Bleistift *m* pencil

Bleistiftspitzer *m* pencil sharpener

Blende ['blɛndə] *f* (-; -*n*) blind; PHOT aperture; (*bei*) *Blende 8* (at) f-8

'blenden *v/t* (*ge-, h*) blind, dazzle (*both a. fig*)

blendend *adj* dazzling (*a. fig*); brilliant; *blendend aussehen* look great

'blendfrei *adj* OPT antiglare

blich [blɪç] *pret of* **bleichen**

Blick [blɪk] *m* (-[*e*]*s*; -*e*) look (*auf acc* at); view (of); *flüchtiger Blick* glance; *auf den ersten Blick* at first sight

'blicken *v/i* (*ge-, h*) look, glance (*both: auf acc, nach* at)

'Blickfang *m* eye-catcher

'Blickfeld *n* field of vision

blieb [bliːp] *pret of* **bleiben**

blies [bliːs] *pret of* **blasen**

blind [blɪnt] *adj* blind (*a. fig gegen, für* to); *vor dat* with); dull (*mirror etc*); *blinder Alarm* false alarm; *blinder Passagier* stowaway; *auf e-m Auge blind* blind in one eye; *ein Blinder* a blind man; *e-e Blinde* a blind woman; *die Blinden* the blind

'Blinddarm *m* ANAT appendix

Blinddarmentzündung *f* MED appendicitis

Blinddarmoperati,on *f* MED appendectomy

Blindenhund ['blɪndən-] *m* seeing eye (*Br* guide) dog

Blindenschrift *f* braille

'Blindgänger [-gɛŋɐ] *m* (-*s*; -) MIL dud

'Blindheit *f* (-; *no pl*) blindness

blindlings ['blɪntlɪŋs] *adv* blindly

'Blindschleiche *f* ZO blindworm

blinken ['blɪŋkən] *v/i* (*ge-, h*) sparkle, shine; twinkle; flash (a signal); MOT indicate

Blinker ['blɪŋkɐ] *m* (-*s*; -) MOT turn signal, *Br* indicator

blinzeln ['blɪntsəln] *v/i* (*ge-, h*) blink (one's eyes)

Blitz [blɪts] *m* (-*es*; -*e*) (flash of) lightning; PHOT flash

Blitzableiter *m* (-*s*; -) lightning conductor

'blitzen *v/i* (*ge-, h*) flash; *es blitzt* it's lightening

'Blitzgerät *n* PHOT (electronic) flash

Blitzlampe *f* PHOT flashbulb; flash cube

Blitzlicht *n* (-[*e*]*s*; -*er*) PHOT flash(light)

Blitzschlag *m* lightning stroke

'blitz'schnell *adj and adv* like a flash; *attr* split-second

Block [blɔk] *m* (-[*e*]*s*; *Blöcke* ['blœkə]) block; POL, ECON bloc; (*writing*) pad

B

Blockade [blɔ'kaːdə] *f* (-; -*n*) MAR, MIL blockade

'**Blockflöte** *f* recorder

'**Blockhaus** *n* log cabin

blockieren [blɔ'kiːrən] *v/t and v/i* (*no -ge-,* *h*) block; MOT lock

'**Blockschrift** *f* block letters

blöde ['bløːdə] F *adj* silly, stupid

'**blödeln** *v/i* (*ge-, h*) fool *or* clown around

Blödheit ['bløːthait] *f* (-; *no pl*) stupidity

'**Blödsinn** F *m* (-[*e*]*s*; *no pl*) rubbish, nonsense

'**blödsinnig** F *adj* stupid, idiotic

blöken ['bløːkən] *v/i* (*ge-, h*) ZO bleat

blond [blɔnt] *adj* blond, fair

Blondine [blɔn'diːnə] *f* (-; -*n*) blonde

bloß [bloːs] **1.** *adj* bare; naked (*eye*); mere; *bloß legen v/t* (*sep, -ge-, h*) lay bare, expose; **2.** *adv* only, just, merely

Blöße ['bløːsə] *f* (-; -*n*) nakedness; *sich e-e Blöße geben* lay o.s. open to attack *or* criticism

'**bloßlegen** *v/t* → *bloß*

bloßstellen *v/t* (*sep, -ge-, h*) expose, compromise, unmask; *sich bloßstellen* compromise o.s.

blühen ['blyːən] *v/i* (*ge-, h*) (be in) bloom; (be in) blossom; *fig* flourish

Blume ['bluːmə] *f* (-; -*n*) flower; GASTR bouquet; head, froth

'**Blumenbeet** *n* flowerbed

Blumenhändler *m* florist

Blumenkohl *m* BOT cauliflower

Blumenladen *m* flower shop, florist's

Blumenstrauß *m* bunch of flowers; bouquet

Blumentopf *m* flowerpot

Blumenvase *f* vase

Bluse ['bluːzə] *f* (-; -*n*) blouse

Blut [bluːt] *n* (-[*e*]*s*; *no pl*) blood

'**blutarm** *adj* MED an(a)emic (*a. fig*)

'**Blutarmut** *f* MED an(a)emia

Blutbad *n* massacre

Blutbahn *f* ANAT bloodstream

Blutbank *f* (-; -*en*) MED blood bank

'**blutbefleckt** *adj* bloodstained

'**Blutbild** *n* MED blood count

Blutblase *f* MED blood blister

Blutdruck *m* MED blood pressure

Blüte ['blyːtə] *f* (-; -*n*) flower; bloom (*a. fig*); blossom; *fig* height, heyday; *in* (*voller*) *Blüte* in (full) bloom

'**Blutegel** *m* ZO leech

'**bluten** *v/i* (*ge-, h*) bleed (*aus dat* from)

'**Blütenblatt** *n* petal

Blütenstaub *m* pollen

Bluter ['bluːtɐ] *m* (-*s*; -) MED h(a)emophiliac

'**Bluterguss** *m* bruise; MED h(a)ematoma

Blutgefäß *n* ANAT blood vessel

Blutgerinnsel *n* MED blood clot

Blutgruppe *f* MED blood group

Bluthund *m* ZO bloodhound

'**blutig** *adj* bloody; *blutiger Anfänger* rank beginner, F greenhorn

'**Blutkörperchen** *n* MED blood corpuscle

Blutkreislauf *m* MED (blood) circulation

Blutlache *f* pool of blood

'**blutleer** *adj* bloodless

'**Blutprobe** *f* MED blood test

'**blutrünstig** [-rynstɪç] *adj* bloodthirsty, gory

'**Blutschande** *f* JUR incest

'**Blutspender** *m* blood donor

'**Blutsverwandte** *m, f* blood relation

'**Blutübertragung** *f* MED blood transfusion

'**Blutung** *f* (-; -*en*) MED bleeding, h(a)emorrhage

'**blutunterlaufen** *adj* bloodshot

'**Blutvergießen** *n* (-*s*; *no pl*) bloodshed

Blutvergiftung *f* MED blood poisoning

Blutwurst *f* black sausage (*Br* pudding)

BLZ [beːɛl'tsɛt] ABBR *of* **Bankleitzahl** A.B.A. number, *Br* bank (sorting) code

Bö [bøː] *f* (-; -*en*) gust, squall

Bob [bɔp] *m* (-*s*; -*s*) bob(sled)

Bobbahn *f* bob run

Bobfahrer *m* bobber

Bock [bɔk] *m* (-[*e*]*s*; *Böcke* ['bœkə]) ZO buck; he-goat, billy-goat; ram; SPORT buck; F *e-n Bock schießen* (make a) blunder; F *keinen* (*or null*) *Bock auf et. haben* have zero interest in s.th.

'**bocken** *v/i* (*ge-, h*) buck; sulk

'**bockig** *adj* obstinate; sulky

'**Bockspringen** *n* leapfrog

Boden ['boːdən] *m* (-*s*; *Böden* ['bøːdən]) ground; AGR soil; bottom; floor; attic

'**Bodenperso,nal** *n* AVIAT ground crew

Bodenre,form *f* land reform

Bodenschätze *pl* mineral resources

Bodenstati,on *f* AVIAT ground control

Bodenturnen *n* floor exercises

Body ['bɔdi] *m* (-*s*; -*s*) bodysuit

bog [boːk] *pret of* **biegen**

Bogen ['boːgən] *m* (-*s*; *Bögen* ['bøːgən]) bend, curve; MATH arc; ARCH arch; *skiing:* turn; bow; sheet

Bogenschießen *n* archery

Bogenschütze *m* archer

Bohle ['boːlə] *f* (-; -*n*) plank

Bohne ['boːnə] *f* (-; -*n*) BOT bean; *grüne Bohnen* green (*Br a.* French) beans

'**Bohnenstange** *f* beanpole (*a. F*)

bohnern ['boːnɐn] *v/t* (*ge-, h*) polish, wax

'**Bohnerwachs** *n* floor polish

bohren ['boːrən] *v/t* (*ge-, h*) bore, drill (*a.*

dentist)

bohrend *fig adj* piercing (*look*); insistent (*questions etc*)

Bohrer ['boːrɐ] *m* (-*s*; -) TECH drill

'Bohrinsel *f* oil rig

Bohrloch *n* borehole, well(head)

Bohrma schine *f* (electric) drill

Bohrturm *m* derrick

'Bohrung *f* (-; -*en*) drilling; bore

Boje ['boːjə] *f* (-; -*n*) MAR buoy

Bolzen ['bɔltsən] *m* (-*s*; -) TECH bolt

bombardieren [bɔmbar'diːrən] *v/t* (*no* -*ge*-, *h*) bomb; *fig* bombard

Bombe ['bɔmbə] *f* (-; -*n*) bomb; *fig* bombshell

'Bombenangriff *m* air raid

Bombenanschlag *m* bomb attack

Bombenerfolg F *m* roaring success; THEA *etc* smash hit

Bombengeschäft F *n* super deal

'Bombenleger *m* (-*s*; -) bomber

'bombensicher *adj* bombproof

Bomber ['bɔmbɐ] F *m* (-*s*; -) MIL bomber (*a.* SPORT)

Bon [bɔŋ] *m* (-*s*; -*s*) coupon, voucher

Bonbon [bɔŋ'bɔŋ] *m*, *n* (-*s*; -*s*) candy, *Br* sweet

Boot [boːt] *n* (-[*e*]*s*; -*e*) boat

'Bootsmann *m* (-[*e*]*s*; -*leute*) boatswain

Bord[1] [bɔrt] *n* (-[*e*]*s*; -*e*) shelf

Bord[2] *m*: **an Bord** AVIAT, MAR on board; **über Bord** MAR overboard; **von Bord gehen** MAR disembark

Bordell [bɔr'dɛl] *n* (-*s*; -*e*) brothel, F whorehouse

'Bordkarte *f* AVIAT boarding pass

'Bordstein *m* curb, *Br* kerb

borgen ['bɔrgən] *v/t* (*ge*-, *h*) borrow; **sich et. von j-m borgen** borrow s.th. from s.o.; **j-m et. borgen** lend s.th. to s.o.

Borke ['bɔrkə] *f* (-; -*n*) BOT bark

borniert [bɔr'niːɐt] *adj* narrow-minded

Börse ['bœrzə] *f* (-; -*n*) ECON stock exchange

'Börsenbericht *m* market report

Börsenkurs *m* quotation

Börsenmakler *m* stockbroker

Börsenspeku lant *m* stock-jobber

Borste ['bɔrstə] *f* (-; -*n*) bristle

'borstig *adj* bristly

Borte ['bɔrtə] *f* (-; -*n*) border; braid, lace

bösartig ['bøː-] *adj* vicious; MED malignant

Böschung ['bœʃʊŋ] *f* (-; -*en*) slope, bank; RAIL embankment

böse ['bøːzə] *adj* bad, evil, wicked; angry (**über** *acc* about; **auf j-n** with s.o.), mad (**auf** *acc* at); **er meint es nicht böse** he means no harm

'Böse *n* (-*n*; *no pl*) (the) evil

'Bösewicht *m* (-[*e*]*s*; -*er*) villain

boshaft ['boːshaft] *adj* malicious

Bosheit ['boːshait] *f* (-; *no pl*) malice

'böswillig *adj* malicious, JUR *a.* wil(l)ful

bot [boːt] *pret of* **bieten**

Botanik [bo'taːnɪk] *f* (-; *no pl*) botany

Bo taniker *m* (-*s*; -) botanist

bo tanisch *adj* botanical

Bote ['boːtə] *m* (-*n*; -*n*) messenger

'Botengang *m* errand; **Botengänge machen** run errands

Botschaft ['boːtʃaft] *f* (-; -*en*) message; POL embassy

'Botschafter *m* (-*s*; -) POL ambassador (*in dat* to)

'Botschafterin *f* (-; -*nen*) POL ambassadress (*in dat* to)

Bottich ['bɔtɪç] *m* (-*s*; -*e*) tub, vat

Bouillon [bʊl'jɔŋ] *f* (-; -*s*) consommé, bouillon, broth

Boulevardblatt [bulə'vaːɐ-] *n*, **Boulevardzeitung** *f* tabloid

Bowle ['boːlə] *f* (-; -*n*) (cold) punch; bowl

boxen ['bɔksən] (*ge*-, *h*) **1.** *v/i* box; **2.** *v/t* punch

'Boxen *n* (-*s*; *no pl*) boxing

Boxer ['bɔksɐ] *m* (-*s*; -) boxer

'Boxhandschuh *m* boxing glove

Boxkampf *m* boxing match, fight

Boxsport *m* boxing

Boykott [bɔy'kɔt] *m* (-[*e*]*s*; -*e*), **boykottieren** [bɔykɔ'tiːrən] *v/t* (*no* -*ge*-, *h*) boycott

brach [braːx] *pret of* **brechen**

brachliegend *adj* AGR fallow

brachte ['braxtə] *pret of* **bringen**

Branche ['brãːʃə] *f* (-; -*n*) ECON line (of business)

'Branchenverzeichnis *n* TEL yellow pages

Brand [brant] *m* (-[*e*]*s*; *Brände* ['brɛndə]) fire; **in Brand geraten** catch fire; **in Brand stecken** set fire to

Brandblase *f* MED blister

branden ['brandən] *v/i* (*ge*-, *sein*) surge (**gegen** against)

'Brandfleck *m* burn

Brandmal *n* brand

'brandmarken *fig v/t* (*ge*-, *h*) brand, stigmatize

'Brandmauer *f* fire wall

Brandstätte *f*, **Brandstelle** *f* scene of fire

Brandstifter *m* arsonist

Brandstiftung *f* arson

'Brandung *f* (-; *no pl*) surf, surge, breakers

'Brandwunde *f* MED burn; scald

brannte ['brantə] *pret of* **brennen**

'Branntwein *m* brandy, spirits

braten ['braːtən] v/t (irr, ge-, h) roast; grill, broil; fry; **am Spieß braten** roast on a spit, barbecue

'**Braten** m (-s; -) roast (meat); joint

Bratenfett n dripping

Bratensoße f gravy

'**Bratfisch** m fried fish

Brathuhn n roast chicken

Bratkar,toffeln pl fried potatoes

Bratofen m oven

Bratpfanne f frying pan

Bratsche ['braːtʃə] f (-; -n) MUS viola

'**Bratwurst** f grilled sausage

Brauch [braux] m (-[e]s; Bräuche ['brɔʏçə]) custom; habit, practice

'**brauchbar** adj useful

'**brauchen** v/t (ge-, h) need; require; take (time); use; **wie lange wird er brauchen?** how long will it take him?; **du brauchst es nur zu sagen** just say the word; **ihr braucht es nicht zu tun** you don't have to do it; **er hätte nicht zu kommen brauchen** he need not have come

brauen ['brauən] v/t (ge-, h) brew

Brauerei [brauə'raı] f (-; -en) brewery

braun [braun] adj brown; (sun)tanned; **braun werden** (get a) tan

Bräune ['brɔʏnə] f (-; no pl) (sun)tan

'**bräunen** (ge-, h) **1.** v/t brown, tan; **2.** v/i (get a) tan

'**Braunkohle** f brown coal, lignite

'**bräunlich** adj brownish

Brause ['brauzə] f (-; -n) shower; → **Limonade**

'**brausen** v/i a) (ge-, h) roar, b) (sein) rush, c) (h) → **duschen**

Braut [braut] f (-; Bräute ['brɔʏtə]) bride; fiancée

Bräutigam ['brɔʏtɪgam] m (-s; -e) (bride)-groom; fiancé

'**Brautjungfer** f bridesmaid

Brautkleid n wedding-dress

Brautpaar n bride and (bride)groom; engaged couple

brav [braːf] adj good; honest; **sei(d) brav!** be good!

BRD [beː'ʔɛr'deː] ABBR of **Bundesrepublik Deutschland** FRG, Federal Republic of Germany

brechen ['brɛçən] (irr, ge-) **1.** v/t (h) break (a. fig); MED vomit; **sich den Arm brechen** break one's arm; **2.** v/i a) (h) MED vomit, F throw up, Br a. be sick; **mit j-m brechen** break with s.o; **brechend voll** crammed, packed, b) (sein) break, get broken, fracture

'**Brechreiz** m MED nausea

'**Brechstange** f crowbar

'**Brechung** f (-; -en) OPT refraction

Brei [braı] m (-[e]s; -e) pulp, mash; pap; porridge; pudding

'**breiig** adj pulpy, mushy

breit [braıt] adj wide; broad (a. fig)

'**breitbeinig** adj with legs (wide) apart

Breite ['braıtə] f (-; -n) width, breadth; ASTR, GEOGR latitude

'**breiten** v/t (ge-, h) spread

'**Breitengrad** m degree of latitude

Breitenkreis m parallel (of latitude)

breitmachen v/refl (sep, -ge-, h): **sich breitmachenmachen** F spread o.s., take up room

'**Breitwand** f film: wide screen

Bremsbelag ['brɛms-] m brake lining

Bremse ['brɛmzə] f (-; -n) TECH brake; ZO gadfly

'**bremsen** (ge-, h) **1.** v/i MOT brake, put on the brake(s); slow down; **2.** v/t MOT brake; fig curb

'**Bremslicht** n (-[e]s; -er) MOT stop light

Bremspe,dal n MOT brake pedal

Bremsspur f MOT skid marks

Bremsweg m MOT stopping distance

'**brennbar** adj combustible; (in)flammable

brennen ['brɛnən] (irr, ge-, h) **1.** v/t burn; distil(l) (whisky etc); bake (bricks); **2.** v/i burn; be on fire; wound, eyes: smart, burn; F **darauf brennen zu** inf be dying to inf; **es brennt!** fire!

Brenner ['brɛnɐ] m (-s; -) burner

'**Brennholz** n firewood

Brennmateri,al n fuel

Brennnessel f BOT (stinging) nettle

Brennpunkt m focus, focal point

Brennspiritus m methylated spirit

Brennstab m TECH fuel rod

Brennstoff m fuel

brenzlig ['brɛntslɪç] adj burnt; fig hot

Bresche ['brɛʃə] f (-; -n) breach (a. fig), gap

Brett [brɛt] n (-[e]s; -er) board

'**Bretterzaun** m wooden fence

'**Brettspiel** n board game

Brezel ['breːtsəl] f (-; -n) pretzel

Brief [briːf] m (-[e]s; -e) letter

Briefbeschwerer m (-s; -) paperweight

Briefbogen m sheet of (note)paper

Brieffreund(in) pen pal (Br friend)

Briefkasten m mailbox, Br letterbox

'**brieflich** adj and adv by letter

'**Briefmarke** f (postage) stamp

Briefmarkensammlung f stamp collection

Brieföffner m letter opener, Br paper knife

Briefpa,pier *n* stationery
Brieftasche *f* wallet
Brieftaube *f* zo carrier pigeon
Briefträger(in) (*-s*; *-/-*; *-nen*) mailman (mailwoman), *Br* postman (postwoman)
Briefumschlag *m* envelope
Briefwahl *f* postal vote
Briefwechsel *m* correspondence
briet [briːt] *pret of* **braten**
Brikett [briˈkɛt] *n* (*-s*; *-s*) briquet(te)
brillant [brɪlˈjant] *adj* brilliant
Bril'lant *m* (*-en*; *-en*) (cut) diamond
Bril'lantring *m* diamond ring
Brille ['brɪlə] *f* (*-*; *-n*) (pair of) glasses, spectacles; goggles; toilet seat
'Brillenetui *n* eyeglass (*Br* spectacle) case
Brillenträger(in) (*-s*; *-/-*; *-nen*) **Brillenträger sein** wear glasses
bringen ['brɪŋən] *v/t* (*irr, ge-, h*) bring; take; cause; make (*sacrifice*); yield (*profit*); **j-n nach Hause bringen** see (*or* take) s.o. home; **in Ordnung bringen** put in order; **das bringt mich auf e-e Idee** that gives me an idea; **j-n dazu bringen, et. zu tun** get s.o. to do s.th.; **et. mit sich bringen** involve s.th.; **j-n um et. bringen** deprive s.o. of s.th.; **j-n zum Lachen bringen** make s.o. laugh; **j-n wieder zu sich bringen** bring s.o. round; **es zu et. (nichts) bringen** go far (get nowhere); F **es bringen** make it; **das bringt nichts** it's no use
Brise ['briːzə] *f* (*-*; *-n*) breeze
Brite ['brɪtə] *m* (*-n*; *-n*), **'Britin** *f* (*-*; *-nen*) Briton; **die Briten** *pl* the British
'britisch *adj* British
bröckeln ['brœkəln] *v/i* (*ge-, h, sein*) crumble
Brocken ['brɔkən] *m* (*-s*; *-*) piece; lump; rock; GASTR chunk; morsel; **ein paar Brocken Englisch** a few scraps of English; F **ein harter Brocken** a hard nut to crack
Brombeere ['brɔm-] *f* BOT blackberry
Bronchitis [brɔnˈçiːtɪs] *f* (*-*; *-tiden* [brɔn-çiˈtiːdən]) MED bronchitis
Bronze ['brõːsə] *f* (*-*; *-n*) bronze
Bronzezeit *f* (*-*; *no pl*) HIST Bronze Age
Brosche ['brɔʃə] *f* (*-*; *-n*) brooch, pin
broschiert [brɔˈʃiːrt] *adj* paperback
Broschüre [brɔˈʃyːrə] *f* (*-*; *-n*) pamphlet; brochure
Brot [broːt] *n* (*-[e]s*; *-e*) bread; sandwich; **ein (Laib) Brot** a loaf (of bread); **e-e Scheibe Brot** a slice of bread; **sein Brot verdienen** earn one's living
Brötchen ['brøːtçən] *n* (*-s*; *-*) roll
'Brotrinde *f* crust
Brot(schneide)ma,schine *f* bread cutter
Bruch [brʊx] *m* (*-[e]s*; *Brüche* ['brʏçə])

break; MED fracture; hernia; MATH fraction; GEOL fault; *fig* breach (*of promise etc*); JUR violation; **zu Bruch gehen** be wrecked
Bruchbude F *f* dump, hovel
brüchig ['brʏçɪç] *adj* brittle
'Bruchlandung *f* AVIAT crash landing
Bruchrechnung *f* MATH fractional arithmetic, F fractions
'bruchsicher *adj* breakproof
'Bruchstrich *m* MATH fraction bar
Bruchstück *n* fragment
Bruchteil *m* fraction; **im Bruchteil e-r Sekunde** in a split second
Bruchzahl *f* MATH fraction(al) number
Brücke ['brʏkə] *f* (*-*; *-n*) bridge (*a.* SPORT); rug
'Brückenpfeiler *m* pier
Bruder ['bruːdɐ] *m* (*-s*; *Brüder* ['bryːdɐ]) brother (*a.* REL)
Bruderkrieg *m* civil war
brüderlich ['bryːdɐlɪç] **1.** *adj* brotherly; **2.** *adv*: **brüderlich teilen** share and share alike
'Brüderlichkeit *f* (*-*; *no pl*) brotherhood
'Brüderschaft *f*: **Brüderschaft trinken** *agree to use the familiar 'du' form of address*
Brühe ['bryːə] *f* (*-*; *-n*) broth; stock; F dishwater; slops; F filthy water, bilge
'Brühwürfel *m* beef cube
brüllen ['brʏlən] *v/i* (*ge-, h*) roar (**vor Lachen** with laughter); zo bellow; F bawl; **brüllendes Gelächter** roars of laughter
brummen ['brʊmən] *v/i* (*ge-, h*) growl; zo hum, buzz (*a. engine etc*); *head*: be buzzing
'brummig *adj* grumpy
brünett [brʏˈnɛt] *adj* brunette, dark-haired
Brunnen ['brʊnən] *m* (*-s*; *-*) well, spring, fountain
Brunstzeit ['brʊnst-] *f* zo rutting season
Brust [brʊst] *f* (*-*; *Brüste* ['brʏstə]) ANAT a) (*no pl*) chest, b) breast(s), bosom
Brustbein *n* ANAT breastbone
Brustbeutel *m* neck pouch, *Br* money bag
brüsten ['brʏstən] *v/refl* (*ge-, h*) boast, brag (**mit** of)
'Brustkasten *m*, **Brustkorb** *m* ANAT chest, thorax
Brustschwimmen *n* breaststroke
'Brüstung *f* (*-*; *-en*) parapet
'Brustwarze *f* ANAT nipple
Brut [bruːt] *f* (*-*; *-en*) zo brooding; brood (*a.* F), hatch; fry
brutal [bruˈtaːl] *adj* brutal
Brutalität [brutaliˈtɛːt] *f* (*-*; *-en*) brutality
'Brutappa,rat *m* zo incubator

brüten ['bryːtən] v/i (ge-, h) zo brood, sit (on eggs); **brüten über** (dat) fig brood over

'Brutkasten m MED incubator

brutto ['brʊto] adv ECON gross

'Bruttoeinkommen n ECON gross earnings

Bruttosozi‚alpro‚dukt n ECON gross national product

Bube ['buːbə] m (-n; -n) boy, lad; card game: knave, jack

Buch [buːx] n (-[e]s; Bücher ['byːçɐ]) book

Buchbinder m (-s; -) (book)binder

Buchdrucker m printer

Buchdruckerei f print shop, Br printing office

Buche ['buːxə] f (-; -n) BOT beech

'buchen v/t (ge-, h) book; ECON enter

Bücherbord ['byːçɐ-] n bookshelf

Bücherei [byːçə'rai] f (-; -en) library

'Bücherre‚gal n bookshelf

'Bücherschrank m bookcase

'Buchfink m zo chaffinch

Buchhalter(in) bookkeeper

Buchhaltung f (-; no pl) bookkeeping

Buchhändler(in) bookseller

Buchhandlung f bookstore, Br bookshop

Buchmacher m bookmaker

Büchse ['byksə] f (-; -n) can, Br tin; box; rifle

'Büchsenfleisch n canned (Br tinned) meat

Büchsenöffner m can (Br tin) opener

Buchstabe ['buːxʃtaːbə] m (-n; -n) letter; **großer** (**kleiner**) **Buchstabe** capital (small) letter

buchstabieren [buːxʃta'biːrən] v/t (no -ge-, h) spell

buchstäblich ['buːxʃtɛːplɪç] adv literally

'Buchstütze f bookend

Bucht ['bʊxt] f (-; -en) bay; creek; inlet

'Buchung f (-; -en) booking; ECON entry

Buckel ['bʊkəl] m (-s; -) hump, hunch; **e-n Buckel machen** hump or hunch one's back

bücken ['byːkən] v/refl (ge-, h) bend (down), stoop

bucklig ['bʊklɪç] adj hunchbacked

Bucklige ['bʊklɪgə] m, f (-n; -n) hunchback

Bückling ['byːklɪŋ] m (-s; -e) smoked herring, Br kipper

Buddhismus [bʊ'dɪsmʊs] m (-; no pl) Buddhism

Buddhist [bʊ'dɪst] m (-en; -en), bud-'dhistisch adj Buddhist

Bude ['buːdə] f (-n; -n) stall, booth; hut; F pad, Br digs; contp shack, dump, hole

Budget [by'dʒeː] n (-s; -s) budget

Büfett [by'fɛt] n (-[e]s; -s, -e) counter, bar, buffet; sideboard, cupboard; **kaltes Büfett** GASTR cold buffet (meal)

Büffel ['byfəl] m (-s; -) zo buffalo

'büffeln F v/i (ge-, h) grind, cram, swot

Bug [buːk] m (-[e]s; -e) MAR bow; AVIAT nose; zo, GASTR shoulder

Bügel ['byːgəl] m (-s; -) hanger; bow

Bügelbrett n ironing board

Bügeleisen n iron

Bügelfalte f crease

'bügelfrei adj no(n)-iron

'bügeln v/t (ge-, h) iron, press

buh [buː] int boo!

buhen ['buːən] v/i (ge-, h) boo

Bühne ['byːnə] f (-; -n) stage, fig a. scene

'Bühnenbild n (stage) set(ting)

Bühnenbildner(in) (-s; -/-; -nen) stage designer

'Buhrufe pl boos

Bullauge ['bʊl-] n MAR porthole

'Bulldogge f zo bulldog

Bulle ['bʊlə] m (-n; -n) zo bull (a. fig); F contp cop, pl the fuzz

Bummel ['bʊməl] F m (-s; -) stroll

Bummelei [bʊmə'lai] f (-; no pl) F contp dawdling; slackness

'bummeln F v/i a) (ge-, sein) stroll, saunter, b) (ge-, h) contp dawdle; ECON go slow

'Bummelstreik m ECON slowdown, Br go--slow (strike)

Bummler ['bʊmlɐ] F m (-s; -) stroller; contp dawdler, slowpoke, Br slowcoach

bumsen ['bʊmzən] v/i and v/t (ge-, h) F → **krachen**; V screw

Bund[1] [bʊnt] m (-[e]s; Bünde ['byndə]) union, federation, alliance; association; (waist)band; **der Bund** POL the Federal Government; F → **Bundeswehr**

Bund[2] n (-[e]s; -e) bundle; bunch

Bündel ['byndəl] n (-s; -) bundle

'bündeln v/t (ge-, h) bundle (up)

Bundes... ['bʊndəs-] in cpds Federal ...; German ...

Bundesbahn f Federal Railroad(s)

Bundesgenosse m ally

Bundeskanzler(in) Federal Chancellor

Bundesland n appr (federal) state, Land

Bundesliga f SPORT First Division

Bundespost f Federal Postal Administration

Bundespräsi‚dent m Federal President

Bundesrat m Bundesrat, Upper House of German Parliament

Bundesrepu‚blik f Federal Republic

Bundesstaat m federal state; confederation

Bundesstraße f Federal Highway

Bundestag *m* (-[e]*s*; *no pl*) Bundestag, Lower House of German Parliament
Bundestrainer *m* coach of the (German) national team
Bundesverfassungsgericht *n* Federal Constitutional Court, *Am appr* Supreme Court
Bundeswehr *f* (-; *no pl*) MIL (German Federal) Armed Forces
bündig ['bʏndɪç] *adj* TECH flush; *kurz und bündig* terse(ly); point-blank
Bündnis ['bʏntnɪs] *n* (-*ses*; -*se*) alliance
Bunker ['bʊŋkɐ] *m* (-*s*; -) air-raid shelter, bunker
bunt [bʊnt] *adj* colo(u)red; multicolo(u)red; colo(u)rful (*a. fig*); varied; *bunter Abend* evening of entertainment; F *mir wird's zu bunt* that's all I can take
'Buntstift *m* colo(u)red pencil, crayon
Bürde ['bʏrdə] *f* (-; -*n*) burden (*für j-n* to s.o.)
Burg [bʊrk] *f* (-; -*en*) castle
Bürge ['bʏrgə] *m* (-*n*; -*n*) JUR guarantor (*a. fig*)
'bürgen *v/i* (*ge*-, *h*) *für j-n bürgen* JUR stand surety for s.o.; *für et. bürgen* guarantee s.th.
Bürger ['bʏrgɐ] *m* (-*s*; -), **'Bürgerin** *f* (-; -*nen*) citizen
Bürgerinitia,tive *f* (citizen's *or* local) action group
Bürgerkrieg *m* civil war
'bürgerlich *adj* civil; middle-class; *esp contp* bourgeois; *bürgerliche Küche* home cooking
'Bürgerliche *m*, *f* (-*n*; -*n*) commoner
'Bürgermeister *m* mayor
Bürgerrechte *pl* civil rights
Bürgersteig [-ʃtaik] *m* (-[e]*s*; -*e*) sidewalk, *Br* pavement
'Bürgschaft *f* (-; -*en*) JUR surety; bail
Büro [by'roː] *n* (-*s*; -*s*) office
Büroangestellte *m*, *f* (-*n*; -*n*) clerk, office worker
Büroklammer *f* (paper) clip
Bürokrat [byro'kraːt] *m* (-*en*; -*en*) bureaucrat
Bürokratie [byrokra'tiː] *f* (-; -*n*) bureaucracy; *contp* red tape
Bü'rostunden *pl* office hours
Bursche ['bʊrʃə] *m* (-*n*; -*n*) fellow, guy
burschikos [bʊrʃi'koːs] *adj* (tom)boyish, pert
Bürste ['bʏrstə] *f* (-; -*n*) brush
'bürsten *v/t* (*ge*-, *h*) brush
'Bürstenschnitt *m* crew cut
Bus [bʊs] *m* (-*ses*; -*se*) bus; coach
Busch [bʊʃ] *m* (-[e]*s*; *Büsche* ['bʏʃə]) BOT bush, shrub
Büschel ['bʏʃəl] *n* (-*s*; -) bunch; tuft
'buschig *adj* bushy
Busen ['buːzən] *m* (-*s*; -) ANAT bosom, breast(s)
'Busfahrer *m* bus driver
'Bushaltestelle *f* bus stop
Bussard ['busart] *m* (-*s*; -*e*) ZO buzzard
Buße ['buːsə] *f* (-; -*n*) REL penance; repentance; *Buße tun* do penanc
büßen ['byːsən] *v/t* (*ge*-, *h*) pay *or* suffer for *s.th.*; REL repent
'Bußgeld *n* fine, penalty
'Bußtag *m* REL day of repentance
Büste ['byːstə] *f* (-; -*n*) bust
'Büstenhalter *m* bra
Butter ['bʊtɐ] *f* (-; *no pl*) butter
Butterblume *f* BOT buttercup
Butterbrot *n* (slice *or* piece of) bread and butter; F *für ein Butterbrot* for a song
Butterbrotpa,pier *n* greaseproof paper
Butterdose *f* butter dish
Buttermilch *f* buttermilk
b.w. ABBR *of* **bitte wenden** PTO, please turn over
bzw. ABBR *of* **beziehungsweise** resp., respectively

C

C ABBR *of* **Celsius** C, Celsius, centigrade
ca. ABBR *of* **circa** approx., approximately
Café [ka'feː] *n* (-*s*; -*s*) café, coffee house
campen ['kɛmpən] *v/i* (*ge*-, *h*) camp
Camper ['kɛmpɐ] *m* (-*s*; -) camper
Camping... ['kɛmpɪŋ-] *in cpds* ...*bett*, ...*tisch etc* camp ...
Campingbus *m* camper (van *Br*)
Campingplatz *m* campground, *Br* campsite
Catcher ['kɛtʃɐ] *m* (-*s*; -) wrestler
Casino [ka'ziːno] *n* → *Kasino*

CD [tseː'deː] f (-; -s) CD, compact disk (Br disc)

C'D-ROM f CD-ROM

C'D-Spieler m CD player

Cellist [tʃɛ'lɪst] m (-en; -en), Cel'listin f (-; -nen) MUS cellist

Cello ['tʃɛlo] n (-s; -s, Celli) MUS Cello

Celsius ['tsɛlzjʊs] 5 Grad Celsius (ABBR 5° C) five degrees centigrade or Celsius

Cembalo ['tʃɛmbalo] n (-s; -s, -li) MUS harpsichord

Champagner [ʃam'panjɐ] m (-s; -) champagne

Champignon ['ʃampɪnjɔŋ] m (-s; -s) BOT mushroom

Chance ['ʃãːsə] f f (-; -n) chance; die Chancen stehen gleich (3 zu 1) the odds are even (three to one)

'Chancengleichheit f equal opportunities

Chaos ['kaːɔs] n (-; no pl) chaos

Chaot [ka'oːt] m (-en; -en) chaotic person; POL anarchist, pl a. lunatic fringe

cha'otisch adj chaotic

Charakter [ka'raktɐ] m (-s; -e [-'teːrə]) character, nature

charakterisieren [-teri'ziːrən] v/t (no -ge-, h) characterize, describe (als as)

charakteristisch [-te'rɪstɪʃ] adj characteristic, typical (für of)

Cha'rakterzug m trait

charmant [ʃar'mant] adj charming

Charme [ʃarm] m (-s; no pl) charm

Chassis [ʃa'siː] n (-; -) TECH chassis

Chauffeur [ʃɔ'føːɐ] m (-s; -e) chauffeur, driver

Chauvi ['ʃoːvi] m (-s; -s) F male chauvinist (pig)

Chauvinismus [ʃovi'nɪsmʊs] m (-; no pl) chauvinism, POL a. jingoism

Chef [ʃɛf] m (-s; -s) head, chief, F boss

Chefarzt m medical director, Br senior consultant

Chefsekre,tärin f executive secretary

Chemie [çe'miː] f (-; no pl) chemistry

Chemiefaser f synthetic fiber (Br fibre)

Chemikalien [çcmi'kaːljən] pl chemicals

Chemiker(in) ['çeːmikɐ (-kərɪn)] (-s; -/-; -nen) (analytical) chemist

chemisch ['çeːmɪʃ] adj chemical; chemische Reinigung dry cleaning

Chemothera'pie [çemo-] f MED chemotherapy

Chiffre ['ʃɪfrə] f (-; -n) code, cipher; box (number)

chiffrieren [ʃɪ'friːrən] v/t (no -ge-, h) (en)code

China ['çiːna] China

Chinese [çi'neːzə] m (-n; -n), Chi'nesin f (-; -nen), chi'nesisch adj Chinese

Chinin [çi'niːn] n (-s; no pl) PHARM quinine

Chip [tʃɪp] m (-s; -s) a. EDP chip; GASTR pl chips, Br crisps

Chirurg [çi'rʊrk] m (-en; -en) surgeon

Chirurgie [çirʊr'giː] f (-; -n) surgery

Chirurgin [çi'rʊrgɪn] f (-; -nen) surgeon

chirurgisch [çi'rʊrgɪʃ] adj surgical

Chlor [kloːɐ] n (-s; no pl) CHEM chlorine

chloren ['kloːrən] v/t (ge-, h) chlorinate

Cholera ['koːlera] f (-; no pl) MED cholera

cholerisch [ko'leːrɪʃ] adj choleric

Cholesterin [çolɛste'riːn] n (-s; no pl) MED cholesterol

Chor [koːɐ] m (-[e]s; Chöre ['køːrə]) MUS choir (a. ARCH); im Chor in chorus

Choral [ko'raːl] m (-s; Choräle [ko'rɛːlə]) MUS, REL chorale, hymn

Christ [krɪst] m (-en; -en) REL Christian

Christbaum m Christmas tree

'Christenheit: die Christenheit REL Christendom

'Christentum n (-s; no pl) REL Christianity

Christin ['krɪstɪn] f (-; -nen) REL Christian

'Christkind n Infant Jesus; Father Christmas, Santa Claus

'christlich adj REL Christian

Christus ['krɪstʊs] REL Christ; vor Christus B.C.; nach Christus A.D.

Chrom [kroːm] n (-s; no pl) chrome, CHEM a. chromium

Chromosom [kromo'zoːm] n (-s; -en) BIOL chromosome

Chronik ['kroːnɪk] f (-; -en) chronicle

chronisch ['kroːnɪʃ] adj MED chronic

chronologisch [krono'loːgɪʃ] adj chronological

circa → zirka

City ['sɪti] f (-; -s) downtown, (city) center, Br centre

Clique ['klɪkə] f (-; -n) F group, set; contp clique

Clou [kluː] F m (-s; -s) highlight, climax; der Clou daran the whole point of it

Compact Disc, Compact Disk ['kɔmpæktdɪsk] f (-; -s) compact disk (Br disc)

Computer [kɔm'pjuːtɐ] m (-s; -) computer

Computerausdruck m computer printout

com'putergesteuert adj computer-controlled

computergestützt adj computer-aided

Com'putergrafik f computer graphics

computerisieren [kɔmpjutəri'ziːrən] v/t (no -ge-, h) computerize

Com'puterspiel n computer game

Computervirus m EDP computer virus

Conférencier [kõferã'sjeː] *m* (*-s*; *-s*) master of ceremonies, F emcee, MC, *Br* compère
Cord *etc* → **Kord** *etc*
Couch [kautʃ] *f* (-; *-s*) couch
Coupé [ku'peː] *n* (*-s*; *-s*) MOT coupé

Coupon → **Kupon**
Cousin [ku'zɛ̃ː] *m* (*-s*; *-s*), **Cousine** [ku'ziːnə] *f* (-; *-n*) cousin
Creme [kreːm] *f* (-; *-s*) cream (*a. fig*)
Curry ['kari] *m* (*-s*; *-s*) curry powder
Cursor ['kɜːsə] *m* (*-s*; *-s*) EDP cursor

D

da [daː] **1.** *adv space*: there; here; *time*: then, at that time; *da drüben* (*draußen, hinten*) over (out, back) there; *von da aus* from there; *das … da* that … (over there); *da kommt er* here he comes; *da bin ich* here I am; *da sein* be there; exist; *ist noch … da?* is any … left?; *noch nie da gewesen* unprecedented; *er ist gleich wieder da* he'll be right back; *von da an* or *ab* from then on; **2.** *cj* as, since, because
'dabehalten *v/t* (*irr*, *halten*, *sep*, *no -ge-*, *h*) keep; *j-n dabehalten* keep s.o. in
dabei [da'bai] *adv* there, present; near *or* close by; at the same time; included with it; *dabei sein* be there; take part; be in on it; *ich bin dabei!* count me in!; *er ist gerade dabei zu gehen* he's just leaving; *es ist nichts dabei* there's nothing to it; there's no harm in it; *was ist schon dabei?* (so) what of it?; *lassen wir es dabei!* let's leave it at that!
dabeibleiben *v/i* (*irr*, *bleiben*, *sep*, *-ge-*, *sein*) stick to it
dabeihaben F *v/t* (*irr*, *haben*, *sep*, *-ge-*, *h*) have with (*or* on) one
'dableiben *v/i* (*irr*, *bleiben*, *sep*, *-ge-*, *sein*) stay
Dach [dax] *n* (*-[e]s*; *Dächer* ['dɛçɐ]) roof
'Dachboden *m* attic
Dachdecker [-dekɐ] *m* (*-s*; -) roofer
Dachfenster *n* dormer window
Dachgepäckträger *m* MOT roof-rack
'Dachgeschoss *n*, **'Dachgeschoß** *Austrian n* attic
Dachgeschosswohnung *f* loft apartment, *Br* attic flat
'Dachkammer *f* garret
Dachluke *f* skylight
Dachpappe *f* roofing felt
Dachrinne *f* gutter
Dachs [daks] *m* (*-es*; *-e*) ZO badger
'Dachstuhl *m* roof framework

dachte ['daxtə] *pret of* **denken**
'Dachter,rasse *f* roof terrace
'Dachverband *m* ECON *etc* umbrella organization
Dackel ['dakəl] *m* (*-s*; -) ZO dachshund
'dadurch *adv and cj* this *or* that way; for this reason, so; *dadurch, dass* due to the fact that
dafür [da'fyːɐ] *adv* for it, for that; instead; in return, in exchange; *dafür sein* be in favo(u)r of it; *er kann nichts dafür* it is not his fault; *dafür sorgen, dass* see to it that
da'gegen *adv and cj* against it; however, on the other hand; *dagegen sein* be against (*or* opposed to) it; *haben Sie et. dagegen, dass ich …?* do you mind if I …?; *wenn Sie nichts dagegen haben* if you don't mind; *… ist nichts dagegen* … can't compare
da'heim *adv* at home
'daher *adv and cj* from there; that's why
da'hin *adv* there, to that place; gone, past; *bis dahin* till then; up to there
da'hinten *adv* back there
da'hinter *adv* behind it; *es steckt nichts dahinter* there is nothing to it; F *dahinter kommen* find out (about it)
'dalassen F *v/t* (*irr*, *lassen*, *sep*, *-ge-*, *h*) leave behind
damalig ['daːmaːlɪç] *adj* then
damals ['daːmaːls] *adv* then, at that time
Dame ['daːmə] *f* (-; *-n*) lady; partner; *cards*, *chess*: queen; checkers, *Br* draughts
'Damen… *in cpds* ladies' …; SPORT women's …
Damenbinde *f* sanitary napkin (*Br* towel)
'damenhaft *adj* ladylike
'Damentoi,lette *f* ladies' room (*Br* toilet), *the* ladies
Damenwahl *f* ladies' choice
damit 1. ['daːmɪt] *adv* with it *or* that; by it,

with it; **was will er damit sagen?** what's he trying to say?; **wie steht es damit?** how about it?; **damit einverstanden sein** have no objections; **2.** [da'mɪt] *cj* so that; in order to *inf*; **damit nicht** so as not to *inf*

Damm [dam] *m* (-[e]s; *Dämme* ['dɛmə]) dam; embankment

dämmerig ['dɛmərɪç] *adj* dim

'**Dämmerlicht** *n* (-[e]s; *no pl*) twilight

dämmern ['dɛmɐn] *v/i* (*ge-, h*) dawn (*a.* F *j-m* on s.o.); get dark *or* dusky

'**Dämmerung** *f* (-; *-en*) dusk; dawn

Dämon ['dɛ:mɔn] *m* (-s; *-en* [dɛ'mo:nən]) demon

dämonisch [dɛ'mo:nɪʃ] *adj* demoniac(al)

Dampf [dampf] *m* (-[e]s; *Dämpfe* ['dɛmpfə]) steam; PHYS vapo(u)r

'**dampfen** *v/i* (*ge-, h and sein*) steam

dämpfen ['dɛmpfən] *v/t* (*ge-, h*) deaden; muffle (*voice*); soften (*light, sound, blow*); GASTR steam, stew; steam-iron; *fig* put a damper on; curb (*a.* ECON)

Dampfer ['dampfɐ] *m* (-s; -) steamer, steamship

'**Dampfkochtopf** *m* pressure cooker

Dampfma,schine *f* steam engine

Dampfschiff *n* steamer, steamship

da'**nach** *adv* after it *or* that; afterwards; for it; according to it; **ich fragte ihn danach** I asked him about it; F **mir ist nicht danach** I don't feel like it

Däne ['dɛ:nə] *m* (-n; -n) Dane

da'**neben** *adv* next to it, beside it; besides, as well, at the same time; beside the mark

danebenbenehmen F *v/refl* (*irr, nehmen, sep, no -ge-, h*) step out of line

danebengehen F *v/i* (*irr, gehen, sep, -ge-, sien*) miss (the target); F misfire

'**Dänemark** Denmark

Dänin ['dɛ:nɪn] *f* (-; *-nen*) Danish woman *or* girl

'**dänisch** *adj* Danish

dank [daŋk] *prp* (*gen*) thanks to

Dank *m* (-[e]s; *no pl*) thanks; **Gott sei Dank!** thank God!; **vielen Dank!** many thanks!

'**dankbar** *adj* grateful (*j-m* to s.o.); rewarding (*task etc*)

'**Dankbarkeit** *f* (-; *no pl*) gratitude

'**danken** *v/i* (*ge-, h*) thank (*j-m für et.* s.o. for s.th.); **danke** (**schön**) thank you (very much); (**nein,**) **danke** no, thank you; **nichts zu danken** not at all

dann [dan] *adv* then; **dann und wann** (every) now and then

daran [da'ran] *adv* on it; *die, think etc* of it; *believe etc* in it; *suffer etc* from it; →

liegen

darauf [da'rauf] *adv* on (top of) it; after (that); *listen, drink etc* to it; *proud etc* of it; *wait etc* for it; **am Tage darauf** the day after; **zwei Jahre darauf** two years later; **darauf kommt es an** that's what matters

darauf'hin *adv* after that; as a result

daraus [da'raus] *adv* from (*or* out of) it; **was ist daraus geworden?** what has become of it?; **daraus wird nichts!** F nothing doing!

Darbietung ['da:ɐbi:tʊŋ] *f* (-; *-en*) presentation; performance

darin [da'rɪn] *adv* in it; ['da:rɪn] in that

darlegen ['da:ɐ-] *v/t* (*sep, -ge-, h*) explain, set out

Darlehen ['da:ɐle:ən] *n* (-s; -) loan; **ein Darlehen geben** grant a loan

Darm [darm] *m* (-[e]s; *Därme* ['dɛrmə]) ANAT bowel(s), intestine(s); GASTR skin

Darmgrippe *f* MED intestinal flu

darstellen ['da:ɐ-] *v/t* (*sep, -ge-, h*) represent, show, depict; describe; THEA play, do; trace, graph

'**Darsteller(in)** (-s; -/-; *-nen*) THEA performer, actor (actress)

'**Darstellung** *f* (-; *-en*) representation; description; account; portrayal

darüber [da'ry:bɐ] *adv* over *or* above it; across it; in the meantime; *write, talk etc* about it; **... und darüber** ... and more; **darüber werden Jahre vergehen** that will take years

darum [da'rʊm] *adv and cj* (a)round it; because of it, that's why; **darum bitten** ask for it; → **gehen**

darunter [da'rʊntɐ] *adv* under *or* below it, underneath; among them; including; **... und darunter** ... and less; **was verstehst du darunter?** what do you understand by it?

das [das] → **der**

'**Dasein** *n* (-s; *no pl*) life, existence

dass [das] *cj* that; so (that); **es sei denn, dass** unless; **nicht dass ich wüsste** not that I know of

'**dastehen** *v/i* (*irr, stehen, sep, -ge-, h*) stand (there)

Datei [da'tai] *f* (-; *-en*) EDP file

Dateiverwaltung *f* EDP file management

Daten ['da:tən] *pl* data (*a.* EDP), facts; particulars

Datenbank *f* (-; *-en*) EDP database, data bank

Datenschutz *m* JUR data protection

Datenspeicher *m* data memory *or* storage

Datenträger *m* data medium *or* carrier

Datenübertragung *f* data transfer
Datenverarbeitung *f* data processing
datieren [da'tiːrən] *v/t and v/i* (*no -ge-, h*) date
Dativ ['daːtiːf] *m* (*-s; -e*) dative (case)
Dattel ['datəl] *f* (*-; -n*) BOT date
Datum ['daːtʊm] *n* (*-s; Daten* ['daːtən]) date; *welches Datum haben wir heute?* what's the date today?
Dauer ['daʊɐ] *f* (*-; no pl*) duration; continuance; *auf die Dauer* in the long run; *für die Dauer von* for a period *or* term of; *von Dauer sein* last
Dauerarbeitslosigkeit *f* long-term unemployment
Dauerauftrag *m* ECON standing order
Dauergeschwindigkeit *f* MOT *etc* cruising speed
'**dauerhaft** *adj* lasting; durable
'**Dauerkarte** *f* season ticket
Dauerlauf *m* SPORT jogging; *im Dauerlauf* at a jog
Dauerlutscher *m* lollipop
dauern *v/i* (*ge-, h*) last, take; → *lange*
'**Dauerwelle** *f* permanent, *Br* perm
Daumen ['daʊmən] *m* (*-s; -*) ANAT thumb; F *j-m den Daumen halten* keep one's fingers crossed (for s.o.); *am Daumen lutschen* suck one's thumb
Daunen ['daʊnən] *pl* down
'**Daunendecke** *f* eiderdown
da'von *adv* (away) from it; by it; about it; away; of it *or* them; *et. davon haben* get s.th. out of it; *das kommt davon!* there you are!, that will teach you!
davonkommen *v/i* (*irr, kommen, sep, -ge-, sein*) escape, get away
davonlaufen *v/i* (*irr, laufen, sep, -ge-, sein*) run away
da'vor *adv* before it; in front of it; *be afraid, warn s.o. etc* of it
da'zu *adv* for it, for that purpose; in addition; *noch dazu* into the bargain; *dazu ist es da* that's what it's there for; *Salat dazu?* a salad with it?; → *kommen, Lust*
dazugehören *v/i* (*sep, no -ge-, h*) belong to it, be part of it
dazugehörig *adj* belonging to it
dazukommen *v/i* (*irr, kommen, sep, -ge-, sein*) join *s.o.*; be added
da'zwischen *adv* between (them); in between; among them
dazwischenkommen *v/i* (*irr, kommen, sep, -ge-, sein*) intervene, happen; *wenn nichts dazwischenkommt* if all goes well
DB [deː'beː] ABBR *of Deutsche Bahn* German Rail
dealen ['diːlən] *v/i* (*ge-, h*) F push drugs

Dealer ['diːlɐ] *m* (*-s; -*) drug dealer, F pusher
Debatte [de'batə] *f* (*-; -n*) debate
debattieren [deba'tiːrən] *v/i* (*no -ge-, h*) debate (*über acc* on)
Debüt [de'byː] *n* (*-s; -s*) debut; *sein Debüt geben* make your debut
dechiffrieren [deʃɪ'friːrən] *v/t* (*no -ge-, h*) decipher, decode
Deck [dɛk] *n* (*-[e]s; -s*) MAR deck
Decke ['dɛkə] *f* (*-; -n*) blanket; quilt; ARCH ceiling
Deckel ['dɛkəl] *m* (*-s; -*) lid, cover, top
'**decken** *v/t and v/i* (*ge-, h*) cover (*a.* ZO), SPORT *a.* mark; *sich decken (mit)* coincide (with); → *Tisch*
'**Deckung** *f* (*-; no pl*) cover; *boxing*: guard; *in Deckung gehen* take cover
defekt [de'fɛkt] *adj* defective, faulty; TECH out of order
De'fekt *m* (*-[e]s; -e*) defect, fault
defensiv [defɛn'siːf] *adj*, **Defensive** [-'ziːvə] *f* (*-; no pl*) defensive
definieren [defi'niːrən] *v/t* (*no -ge-, h*) define
Definition [defini'tsjoːn] *f* (*-; -en*) definition
Defizit ['deːfitsɪt] *n* (*-s; -e*) deficit; deficiency
Degen ['deːgən] *m* (*-s; -*) sword; *fencing*: épée
degradieren [degra'diːrən] *v/t* (*no -ge-, h*) degrade (*a. fig*)
dehnbar ['deːnbaːɐ] *adj* flexible, elastic (*a. fig*)
dehnen ['deːnən] *v/t* (*ge-, h*) stretch (*a. fig*)
Deich [daɪç] *m* (*-[e]s; -e*) dike
Deichsel ['daɪksəl] *f* (*-; -n*) pole, shaft
dein [daɪn] *poss pron* your; *deiner, deine, dein(e)s* yours
deinerseits ['daɪnɐzaɪts] *adv* on your part
deines'gleichen ['daɪnəs-] *pron contp* the likes of you
deinetwegen ['daɪnət'veːgən] *adv* for your sake; because of you
Dekan [de'kaːn] *m* (*-s; -e*), **De'kanin** *f* (*-; -nen*) REL, UNIV dean
Deklination [deklina'tsjoːn] *f* (*-; -en*) LING declension
deklinieren [dekli'niːrən] *v/t* (*no -ge-, h*) decline
Dekolleté [dekɔl'teː] *n* (*-s; -s*) low neckline
Dekorateur [dekora'tøːɐ] *m* (*-s; -e*), **Dekora'teurin** *f* (*-; -nen*) decorator; window dresser
Dekoration [-'tsjoːn] *f* (*-; -en*) decoration;

(window) display; THEA scenery
dekorativ [-'tiːf] *adj* decorative
dekorieren [deko'riːrən] *v/t (no -ge-, h)* decorate; dress
Delfin → **Delphin**
delikat [deli'kaːt] *adj* delicious, exquisite; *fig* delicate, ticklish
Delikatesse [delika'tɛsə] *f (-; -n)* delicacy
Delika'tessenladen *m* delicatessen, F deli
Delphin [dɛl'fiːn] *m (-s; -e)* zo dolphin
Dementi [de'mɛnti] *n (-s; -s)* (official) denial
dementieren [demɛn'tiːrən] *v/t (no -ge-, h)* deny (officially)
dementsprechend, **demgemäß** ['deːm-] *adv* accordingly
'**demnach** *adv* according to that
'**demnächst** *adv* shortly, before long
Demo ['deːmo] F *f (-; -s)* demo
Demokrat [demo'kraːt] *m (-en; -en)* democrat
Demokratie [demokra'tiː] *f (-; -n)* democracy
Demo'kratin *f (-; -nen)* democrat
demo'kratisch *adj* democratic
demolieren [demo'liːrən] *v/t (no -ge-, h)* demolish, wreck
Demonstrant [demɔn'strant] *m (-en; -en)*, **Demon'strantin** *f (-; -nen)* demonstrator
Demonstration [-stra'tsjoːn] *f (-; -en)* demonstration
demonstrieren [-'striːrən] *v/t and v/i (no -ge-, h)* demonstrate
demontieren [demɔn'tiːrən] *v/t (no -ge-, h)* dismantle
demoralisieren [demorali'ziːrən] *v/t (no -ge-, h)* demoralize
Demoskopie [demosko'piː] *f (-; -n)* public opinion research
Demut ['deːmuːt] *f (-; no pl)* humility, humbleness
demütig ['deːmyːtɪç] *adj* humble
demütigen ['deːmyːtɪɡən] *v/t (ge-, h)* humiliate
'**Demütigung** *f (-; -en)* humiliation
denkbar ['dɛŋkbaːɐ] **1.** *adj* conceivable; **2.** *adv*: **denkbar einfach** most simple
denken ['dɛŋkən] *v/t and v/i (irr, ge-, h)* think (**an** *acc*, **über** *acc* of, about); **daran denken** (**zu** *inf*) remember (to *inf*)
'**Denkfa,brik** *f* think tank
'**Denkmal** *n* monument; memorial
'**denkwürdig** *adj* memorable
denn [dɛn] *cj and adv* for, because; **es sei denn, dass** unless; **mehr denn je** more than ever
dennoch ['dɛnnɔx] *cj* yet, still, nevertheless
Denunziant [denʊn'tsjant] *m (-en; -en)* informer
denunzieren [-'tsiːrən] *v/t (no -ge-, h)* inform on *or* against
Deodorant [deʔodo'rant] *n (-s; -e, -s)* deodorant
Deponie [depo'niː] *f (-; -n)* dump, waste disposal site
deponieren [depo'niːrən] *v/t (no -ge-, h)* deposit, leave
Depot [de'poː] *n (-s; -s)* depot (*a.* MIL); *Swiss:* deposit
Depression [deprɛ'sjoːn] *f (-; -en)* depression (*a.* ECON)
depressiv [deprɛ'siːf] *adj* depressive
deprimieren [depri'miːrən] *v/t (no -ge-, h)* depress
deprimierend *adj* depressing
deprimiert [depri'miːɐt] *adj* depressed
der [deːɐ], **die** [diː], **das** [das] **1.** *art* the; **2.** *dem pron* that, this; he, she, it; **die** *pl* these, those, they; **3.** *rel pron* who, which, that
'**derartig 1.** *adv* so (much); like that; **2.** *adj* such (as this)
derb [dɛrp] *adj* coarse; tough, sturdy
'**der'gleichen** *dem pron*: **nichts dergleichen** nothing of the kind
'**der-**, '**die-**, '**dasjenige** [-jeːnɪɡə] *dem pron* the one; **diejenigen** *pl* the ones, those
dermaßen ['deːɐ'maːsən] *adv* so (much), like that
Dermatologe [dɛrmato'loːɡə] *m (-n; -n)*, **Dermato'login** *f (-; -nen)* dermatologist
der-, **die-**, **dasselbe** [-'zɛlbə] *dem pron* the same
Deserteur [dezɛr'tøːɐ] *m (-s; -e)* MIL deserter
desertieren [dezɛr'tiːrən] *v/i (no -ge-, sein)* MIL desert
deshalb ['dɛs'halp] *cj and adv* therefore, for that reason, that is why, so
Desinfektionsmittel [dɛsʔinfɛk'tsjoːns-] *n* MED disinfectant
desinfizieren [dɛsʔinfi'tsiːrən] *v/t (no -ge-, h)* MED disinfect
'**Desinteresse** *n (-s; no pl)* indifference
'**desinteres,siert** *adj* uninterested, indifferent
destillieren [dɛstɪ'liːrən] *v/t (no -ge-, h)* distil(l)
desto ['dɛsto] *cj and adv* → **je**
'**des'wegen** *cj and adv* → **deshalb**
Detail [de'tai] *n (-s; -s)* detail
detailliert [deta'jiːɐt] *adj* detailed
Detektiv [detɛk'tiːf] *m (-s; -e)* detective
deuten ['dɔytən] *(ge-, h)* **1.** *v/t* interpret; **2.** *v/i*: **deuten auf** *(acc)* point at
'**deutlich** *adj* clear, distinct, plain

deutsch [dɔytʃ] *adj* German; *auf* **Deutsch** in German

'**Deutsche** *m, f* (-*n*; -*n*) German

'**Deutschland** Germany

Devise [de'vi:zə] *f* (-; -*n*) motto

De'visen *pl* ECON foreign currency

Dezember [de'tsɛmbɐ] *m* (-[*s*]; -) December

dezent [de'tsɛnt] *adj* discreet, unobtrusive; conservative (*clothes etc*); soft (*music etc*)

Dezimal... [detsi'ma:l-] MATH *in cpds* ...*bruch,* ...*system etc*: decimal ...

Dezimalstelle *f* MATH decimal (place)

DGB [de:ge:'be:] *abbr of* **Deutscher Gewerkschaftsbund** Federation of German Trade Unions

d. h. ABBR *of das heißt* i. e., that is

Dia ['di:a] *n* (-*s*; -*s*) PHOT slide

Diagnose [dia'gno:zə] *f* (-; -*n*) diagnosis

diagonal [diago'na:l] *adj,* **Diago'nale** *f* (-; -*n*) diagonal

Dialekt [dia'lɛkt] *m* (-[*e*]*s*; -*e*) dialect

Dialog [dia'lo:k] *m* (-[*e*]*s*; -*e*) dialog, *Br* dialogue

Diamant [dia'mant] *m* (-*en*; -*en*) diamond

'**Diapro,jektor** *m* slide projector

Diät [di'ɛ:t] *f* (-; -*en*) diet; *e-e Diät machen* (*Diät leben*) be on (keep to) a diet

Di'äten *pl* PARL allowance

dich [dɪç] *pers pron* you; *dich (selbst)* yourself

dicht [dɪçt] **1.** *adj* dense, *a.* thick (*fog*); heavy (*traffic*); F closed, shut; **2.** *adv*: *dicht an* (*dat*) *or* *bei* close to

'**dichten** *v/t and v/i* (*ge-, h*) write (poetry)

Dichter(in) ['dɪçtɐ (-tərɪn)] (-*s*; -/-; -*nen*) poet; writer

dichterisch ['dɪçtərɪʃ] *adj* poetic; *dichterische Freiheit* poetic licen|se, *Br* -ce

'**dichthalten** F *v/i* (*irr, halten, sep, -ge-, h*) keep mum

'**Dichtung¹** *f* (-; -*en*) TECH seal(ing)

'**Dichtung²** *f* (-; -*en*) poetry

dick [dɪk] *adj* thick; fat; *es macht dick* it's fattening

'**Dicke** *f* (-; -*n*) thickness; fatness;

'**dickfellig** F *adj* thick-skinned

'**dickflüssig** *adj* thick; TECH viscous

Dickicht ['dɪkɪçt] *n* (-[*e*]*s*; -*e*) thicket

'**Dickkopf** *m* stubborn *or* pig-headed person

Dickmilch *f* soured milk

Dieb [di:p] *m* (-[*e*]*s*; -*e* ['di:bə]), **Diebin** ['di:bɪn] *f* (-; -*nen*) thief

diebisch ['di:bɪʃ] *adj* thievish; *fig* malicious (*glee etc*)

Diebstahl ['di:pʃta:l] *m* (-[*e*]*s*; -*stähle* [-ʃtɛ:lə]) theft; JUR *mst* larceny

Diele ['di:lə] *f* (-; -*n*) board, plank; hallway, *Br a.* hall

dienen ['di:nən] *v/i* (*ge-, h*) serve (*j-m* s.o.; *als* as)

Diener ['di:nɐ] *m* (-*s*; -) servant; *fig* bow (*vor dat* to)

Dienst [di:nst] *m* (-[*e*]*s*; -*e*) service; work; *Dienst haben* be on duty; *im (außer) Dienst* on (off) duty; *Dienst tuend* on duty

Dienst... *in cpds* ...*wagen,* ...*wohnung etc*: official ..., company ..., business ...

'**Dienstag** *m* (-[*e*]*s*; -*e*) Tuesday

'**Dienstalter** *n* seniority, length of service

'**dienstbereit** *adj* on duty

diensteifrig *adj* (*contp* over-)eager

'**Dienstgrad** *m* grade, rank (*a.* MIL)

'**Dienstleistung** *f* service

'**dienstlich** *adj* official

'**Dienstreise** *f* business trip

'**Dienststunden** *pl* office hours

'**Dienstweg** *m* official channels

dies [di:s], **dieser** ['di:zɐ], **diese** ['di:zə], **dieses** ['di:zəs] *dem pron* this; this one; *diese pl* these

diesig ['di:zɪç] *adj* hazy, misty

'**diesjährig** [-jɛ:rɪç] *adj* this year's

'**diesmal** *adv* this time

'**diesseits** [-zaits] *prp* (*gen*) on this side of

'**Diesseits** *n* (-; *no pl*) this life *or* world

Dietrich ['di:trɪç] *m* (-*s*; -*e*) TECH picklock, skeleton key

Differenz [difə'rɛnts] *f* (-; -*en*) difference; disagreement

differenzieren [dɪfərɛn'tsi:rən] *v/i* (*no -ge-, h*) distinguish

Digital... [digi'ta:l] *in cpds* ...*anzeige,* ...*uhr etc*: digital ...

Diktat [dɪk'ta:t] *n* (-[*e*]*s*; -*e*) dictation

Diktator [dɪk'ta:to:ɐ] *m* (-*s*; -*en*) [dɪkta-'to:rən] dictator

diktatorisch [dɪkta'to:rɪʃ] *adj* dictatorial

Diktatur [dɪkta'tu:ɐ] *f* (-; -*en*) dictatorship

diktieren [dɪk'ti:rən] *v/t and v/i* (*no -ge-, h*) dictate

Dik'tiergerät *n* Dictaphone®

Dilettant [dilɛ'tant] *m* (-*en*; -*en*) amateur

dilet'tantisch *adj* amateurish

DIN [di:n] ABBR *of Deutsches Institut für Normung* German Institute for Standardization

Ding [dɪŋ] *n* (-[*e*]*s*; -*e*) thing; *vor allen Dingen* above all; F *ein Ding drehen* pull a job

'**Dings(bums)** *m, f, n,* **Dingsda** *m, f, n* F thingamajig, whatchamacallit

Dinosaurier [dino'zaurjɐ] *m* (-*s*; -) ZO dinosaur

Dioxid ['di:'ɔksy:t] *n* (-*s*; -*e*) CHEM dioxide

Dioxin [diɔ'ksiːn] *n* (-*s*; -*e*) CHEM dioxin

Diphtherie [dɪfte'riː] *f* (-; -*n*) MED diphtheria

Diplom [di'ploːm] *n* (-*s*; -*e*) diploma, degree

Diplom... *in cpds* ...*ingenieur etc*: qualified ..., graduate ...

Diplomat [diplo'maːt] *m* (-*en*; -*en*) diplomat

Diplomatie [diploma'tiː] *f* (-; *no pl*) diplomacy

Diplo'matin *f* (-; -*nen*) diplomat

diplo'matisch *adj* diplomatic (*a. fig*)

dir [diːɐ] *pers pron* (to) you; **dir** (**selbst**) yourself

direkt [di'rɛkt] **1.** *adj* direct; TV live; **2.** *adv* direct; *fig* directly, right; TV live; **direkt gegenüber** (**von**) right across

Direktion [dirɛk'tsjoːn] *f* (-; -*en*) management

Direktor [di'rɛktoːɐ] *m* (-*s*; -*en* [dirɛk'toːrən]) director, manager; PED principal, *Br* headmaster

Direktorin [dirɛk'toːrɪn] (-; -*nen*) director, manager; PED principal, *Br* headmistress

Di'rektübertragung *f* TV live transmission *or* broadcast

Dirigent [diri'gɛnt] *m* (-*en*; -*en*) conductor

dirigieren [diri'giːrən] *v/t and v/i* (*no -ge-*, *h*) MUS conduct; *fig* direct

Dirne ['dɪrnə] *f* (-; -*n*) prostitute, whore

Disharmo'nie [dɪs-] *f* MUS dissonance (*a. fig*)

dishar'monisch *adj* MUS discordant

Diskette [dɪs'kɛtə] *f* (-; -*n*) EDP diskette, floppy (disk)

Dis'kettenlaufwerk *n* EDP disk drive

Disko ['dɪsko] *f* (-; -*s*) disco

Diskont [dɪs'kɔnt] *m* (-*s*; -*e*) ECON discount

Diskothek [dɪsko'teːk] (-; -*en*) disco, discotheque

diskret [dɪs'kreːt] *adj* discreet

Diskretion [dɪskre'tsjoːn] *f* (-; *no pl*) discretion

diskriminieren [dɪskrimi'niːrən] *v/t* (*no -ge-*, *h*) discriminate against

Diskrimi'nierung *f* (-; -*en*) discrimination (**von** against)

Diskussion [dɪsku'sjoːn] *f* (-; -*en*) discussion, debate

Diskussi'onsleiter *m* (panel) chairman

Diskussionsrunde *f*, **Diskussionsteilnehmer** *pl* panel

Diskuswerfen ['dɪskus-] *n* (-*s*; *no pl*) SPORT discus throwing

diskutieren [dɪsku'tiːrən] *v/t and v/i* (*no -ge-*, *h*) discuss

Disqualifikati'on *f* SPORT disqualification (**wegen** for)

disqualifi'zieren *v/t* (*no -ge-*, *h*) SPORT disqualify

Dissident [dɪsi'dɛnt] *m* (-*en*; -*en*), **Dissi'dentin** *f* (-; -*nen*) POL dissident

Distanz [dɪs'tants] *f* (-; -*en*) distance

distanzieren [dɪstan'tsiːrən] *v/refl* (*no -ge-*, *h*) distance o.s. (**von** from)

Distel ['dɪstəl] *f* (-; -*n*) BOT thistle

Distrikt [dɪs'trɪkt] *m* (-[*e*]*s*; -*e*) district

Disziplin [dɪstsi'pliːn] *f* (-; -*en*) a) (*no pl*) discipline, b) SPORT event

diszipliniert [dɪstsipli'niːɐt] *adj* disciplined

divers [di'vɛrs] *adj* various; several

Dividende [divi'dɛndə] *f* (-; -*n*) ECON dividend

dividieren [divi'diːrən] *v/t* (*no -ge-*, *h*) MATH divide (**durch** by)

Division [divi'zjoːn] *f* (-; -*en*) MATH, MIL division

DJH [deːjɔt'haː] ABBR *of* **Deutsches Jugendherbergswerk** German Youth Hostel Association

DM [deː'ɛm] ABBR *of* **Deutsche Mark** German mark(s)

doch [dɔx] *cj and adv* but, however, yet; **kommst du nicht** (**mit**)**? - doch!** aren't you coming? - (oh) yes, I am!; **ich war es nicht- doch!** I didn't do it - yes, you did!; **er kam also doch?** so he did come after all?; **du kommst doch?** you're coming, aren't you?; **kommen Sie doch herein!** do come in!; **wenn doch ...!** if only ...!

Docht [dɔxt] *m* (-[*e*]*s*; -*e*) wick

Dock [dɔk] *n* (-*s*; -*s*) MAR dock

Dogge ['dɔgə] *f* (-; -*n*) ZO mastiff; Great Dane

Dogma ['dɔgma] *n* (-*s*; *Dogmen* ['dɔgmən]) dogma

dogmatisch [dɔg'maːtɪʃ] *adj* dogmatic

Dohle ['doːlə] *f* (-; -*n*) ZO (jack)daw

Doktor ['dɔktoːɐ] *m* (-*s*; -*en* [dɔk'toːrən]) doctor; UNIV doctor's degree

Doktorarbeit *f* UNIV (doctoral *or* PhD) thesis

Dokument [doku'mɛnt] *n* (-[*e*]*s*; -*e*) document

Dokumentar... [dokumɛn'taːɐ-] *in cpds* ...*spiel etc*: documentary ...

Dokumentarfilm *m* documentary (film)

Dolch [dɔlç] *m* (-[*e*]*s*; -*e*) dagger

Dollar ['dɔlar] *m* (-[*s*]; -*s*) dollar

dolmetschen ['dɔlmɛtʃən] *v/i* (*ge-*, *h*) interpret

'Dolmetscher(in) (-*s*; -/-; -*nen*) interpreter

Dom [doːm] *m* (-[*e*]*s*; -*e*) cathedral

dominierend [domi'niːrənt] *adj* (pre-)

dominant
Dompteur [dɔmp'tøːɐ] *m* (*-s*; *-e*), **Dompteuse** [dɔmp'tøːzə] *f* (*-*; *-n*) animal tamer *or* trainer
Donner ['dɔnɐ] *m* (*-s*; *no pl*) thunder
'**donnern** *v/i* (*ge-*, *h*) thunder (*a. fig*)
'**Donnerstag** *m* (*-[e]s*; *-e*) Thursday
'**Donnerwetter** F *n* (*-s*; *-*) dressing-down; *Donnerwetter!* wow!
doof [doːf] F *adj* stupid, dumb
Doppel ['dɔpəl] *n* (*-s*; *-*) duplicate; *tennis etc*: doubles
Doppel... *in cpds* ...*bett*, ...*zimmer etc*: double ...
'**Doppeldecker** [-dɛkɐ] *m* (*-s*; *-*) AVIAT biplane; MOT double-decker (bus)
'**Doppelgänger** [-gɛŋɐ] *m* (*-s*; *-*) double, look-alike
'**Doppelhaus** *n* duplex, *Br* pair of semis
Doppelhaushälfte *f* semidetached (house)
'**Doppelpass** *m soccer*: wall pass
Doppelpunkt *m* LING colon
Doppelstecker *m* ELECTR two-way adapter
doppelt *adj* double; *doppelt so viel (wie)* twice as much (as)
'**Doppelverdiener** *pl* two-income family
Dorf [dɔrf] *n* (*-[e]s*; *Dörfer* ['dœrfɐ]) village
Dorfbewohner *m* villager
Dorn [dɔrn] *m* (*-[e]s*; *-en*) BOT thorn (*a. fig*); TECH tongue; spike
'**dornig** *adj* thorny (*a. fig*)
Dorsch [dɔrʃ] m (*-[e]s*; *-e*) ZO cod(fish)
dort [dɔrt] *adv* there
'**dorther** *adv* from there
'**dorthin** *adv* there
Dose ['doːzə] *f* (*-*; *-n*) can, *Br a.* tin
'**Dosen...** *in cpds* canned, *Br a.* tinned
dösen ['døːzən] F *v/i* (*ge-*, *h*) doze
'**Dosenöffner** *m* can (*Br* tin) opener
Dosis ['doːzɪs] *f* (*-*; *Dosen*) MED dose
Dotter ['dɔtɐ] *m*, *n* (*-s*; *-*) yolk
Double ['duːbəl] *n* (*-s*; *-s*) *film*: stunt man (*or* woman)
Dozent [do'tsɛnt] *m* (*-en*; *-en*), **Do'zentin** *f* (*-*; *-nen*) (university) lecturer, assistant professor
Dr. ABBR *of* **Doktor** Dr., Doctor
Drache ['draxə] *m* (*-n*; *-n*) dragon
'**Drachen** *m* (*-s*; *-*) kite; SPORT hang glider; *e-n Drachen steigen lassen* fly a kite
Drachenfliegen *n* SPORT hang gliding
Draht [draːt] *m* (*-[e]s*; *Drähte* ['drɛːtə]) wire; F *auf Draht sein* be on the ball
drahtig ['draːtɪç] *fig adj* wiry
'**drahtlos** *adj* wireless
'**Drahtseil** *n* TECH cable; *circus*: tightrope

Drahtseilbahn *f* cable railway
'**Drahtzieher** *fig m* (*-s*; *-*) wirepuller
drall [dral] *adj* buxom, strapping
Drall *m* (*-[e]s*; *no pl*) twist, spin
Drama ['draːma] *n* (*-s*; *Dramen*) drama
Dramatiker [dra'maːtikɐ] *m* (*-s*; *-*) dramatist, playwright
dra'matisch *adj* dramatic
dran [dran] F *adv* → *daran*; *du bist dran* it's your turn; *fig* you're in for it
drang [draŋ] *pret of* **dringen**
Drang *m* (*-[e]s*; *no pl*) urge, drive (*nach* for)
drängeln ['drɛŋəln] F *v/t and v/i* (*ge-*, *h*) push, shove
drängen ['drɛŋən] *v/t and v/i* (*ge-*, *h*) push, shove; *j-n zu et. drängen* press *or* urge s.o. to do s.th.; *sich drängen* press; force one's way
drängend *adj* pressing
'**drankommen** F *v/i* (*irr*, *kommen*, *sep*, *-ge-*, *sein*) have one's turn; *als erster drankommen* be first
drastisch ['drastɪʃ] *adj* drastic
drauf [drauf] F *adv* → *darauf*; *drauf und dran sein, et. zu tun* be just about to do s.th.
'**Draufgänger** [-gɛŋɐ] *m* (*-s*; *-*) daredevil
draus [draus] F *adv* → *daraus*
draußen ['drausən] *adv* outside; outdoors; *da draußen* out there; *bleib(t) draußen!* keep out!
drechseln ['drɛksəln] *v/t* (*ge-*, *h*) turn (on a lathe)
Drechsler ['drɛkslɐ] *m* (*-s*; *-*) turner
Dreck [drɛk] F *m* (*-[e]s*; *no pl*) dirt; filth (*a. fig*); mud; *fig* trash
dreckig ['drɛkɪç] F *adj* dirty; filthy (*both a. fig*)
Dreharbeiten ['dreː-] *pl film*: shooting
Drehbank *f* (*-*; *-bänke*) TECH lathe
'**drehbar** *adj* revolving, rotating
'**Drehbuch** *n film*: script
drehen ['dreːən] *v/t* (*ge-*, *h*) turn; *film*: shoot; roll; *sich drehen* turn, rotate; spin; *sich drehen um fig* be about; → *Ding*
Dreher ['dreːɐ] *m* (*-s*; *-*) TECH turner
'**Drehkreuz** *n* turnstile
Drehorgel *f* barrel-organ
Drehort *m film*: location
Drehstrom *m* ELECTR three-phase current
Drehstuhl *m* swivel chair
Drehtür *f* revolving door
Drehung *f* (*-*; *-en*) turn; rotation
'**Drehzahl** *f* TECH (number of) revolutions
Drehzahlmesser *m* MOT rev(olution) counter
drei [drai] *adj* three

Drei *f* (-; *-en*) three; *grade*: fair, C

'**dreibeinig** *adj* three-legged

dreidimensio,nal *adj* three-dimensional

'**Dreieck** *n* (-[*e*]*s*; *-e*) triangle

'**dreieckig** *adj* triangular

dreierlei ['draiɐ'lai] *adj* three kinds of

'**dreifach** *adj* threefold, triple

'**Dreigang...** TECH *in cpds* three-speed ...

Dreikampf *m* SPORT triathlon

Dreirad *n* tricycle

Dreisatz *m* (-*es*; *no pl*) MATH rule of three

Dreisprung *m* (-[*e*]*s*; *no pl*) SPORT triple jump

dreißig ['draisɪç] *adj* thirty

'**dreißigste** *adj* thirtieth

dreist [draist] *adj* brazen, impertinent

'**dreistufig** [-ʃtuːfɪç] *adj* three-stage

'**dreizehn(te)** *adj* thirteen(th)

Dresche ['drɛʃə] F *f* (-; *no pl*) thrashing

'**dreschen** *v/t and v/i* (*irr, ge-, h*) AGR thresh; thrash

'**Dreschma,schine** *f* AGR threshing machine

dressieren [drɛ'siːrən] *v/t* (*no -ge-, h*) train

Dressman ['drɛsmən] *m* (-*s*; *-men*) male model

Dressur [drɛ'suːɐ] *f* (-; *-en*) training; act

Dressurreiten *n* dressage

dribbeln ['drɪbəln] *v/i* (*ge-, h*), **Dribbling** *n* (-*s*; *-s*) SPORT dribble

drillen ['drɪlən] *v/t* (*ge-, h*) MIL drill (*a. fig*)

Drillinge ['drɪlɪŋə] *pl* triplets

drin [drɪn] F *adv* → *darin*; *das ist nicht drin!* no way!

dringen ['drɪŋən] *v/i* (*irr, ge-, h*) *dringen auf* (*acc*) insist on; *dringen aus* come from; *dringen durch* force one's way through, penetrate, pierce; *dringen in* (*acc*) penetrate into; *darauf dringen, dass* urge that

dringend *adj* urgent, pressing; strong (*suspicion etc*)

drinnen ['drɪnən] F *adv* inside; indoors

dritte ['drɪtə] *adj* third; *wir sind zu dritt* there are three of us; *die Dritte Welt* the Third World

'**Drittel** *n* (-*s*; -) third

'**drittens** *adv* thirdly

'**Dritte-Welt-Laden** *m* third world shop

Droge ['droːɡə] *f* (-; *-n*) drug

'**drogenabhängig** *adj* addicted to drugs; *drogenabhängig sein* be a drug addict

'**Drogenabhängige** *m, f* (-*n*; *-n*) drug addict

Drogenmissbrauch *m* drug abuse

'**drogensüchtig** → *drogenabhängig*

'**Drogentote** *m, f* drug victim

Drogerie [droɡə'riː] *f* (-; *-n*) drugstore, Br chemist's (shop)

Drogist [dro'ɡɪst] *m* (-*en*; *-en*), **Dro'gistin** *f* (-; *-nen*) chemist

drohen ['droːən] *v/i* (*ge-, h*) threaten, menace

dröhnen ['drøːnən] *v/i* (*ge-, h*) roar

'**Drohung** *f* (-; *-en*) threat (*gegen* to)

drollig ['drɔlɪç] *adj* funny, droll

Dromedar [dromə'daːɐ] *n* (-*s*; *-e*) ZO dromedary

drosch [drɔʃ] *pret of* **dreschen**

Drossel ['drɔsəl] *f* (-; *-n*) ZO thrush

'**drosseln** *v/t* (*ge-, h*) TECH throttle

drüben ['dryːbən] *adv* over there (*a. fig*)

drüber ['dryːbɐ] F *adv* → *darüber, drunter*

Druck [drʊk] *m* (-[*e*]*s*; *-e*) pressure; printing; print

'**Druckbuchstabe** *m* block letter

Drückeberger ['drʏkəbɛrɡɐ] F *m* (-*s*; -) shirker

'**drucken** *v/t* (*ge-, h*) print; *et. drucken lassen* have s.th. printed *or* published

drücken ['drʏkən] (*ge-, h*) **1.** *v/t* press; push; *fig* force down; *j-m die Hand drücken* shake hands with s.o.; **2.** *v/i* pinch; **3.** F *v/refl*: *sich vor et. drücken* shirk (doing) s.th.

drückend *adj* heavy, oppressive

Drucker ['drʊkɐ] *m* (-*s*; -) printer (*a.* EDP)

Drücker ['drʏkɐ] *m* (-*s*; -) latch; trigger; F hawker

Druckerei [drʊkə'rai] *f* (-; *-en*) printers

'**Druckfehler** *m* misprint

Druckkammer *f* pressurized cabin

Druckknopf *m* snap fastener, Br press stud; TECH (push) button

Druckluft *f* TECH compressed air

Drucksache *f* printed (*or* second-class) matter

Druckschrift *f* block letters

Drucktaste *f* TECH push button

drunter ['drʊntɐ] F *adv* → *darunter*; *es ging drunter und drüber* it was absolutely chaotic

Drüse ['dryːzə] *f* (-; *-n*) ANAT gland

Dschungel ['dʒʊŋəl] *m* (-*s*; -) jungle (*a. fig*)

Dschunke ['dʒʊŋkə] *f* (-; *-n*) MAR junk

du [duː] *pers pron* you

Dübel ['dyːbəl] *m* (-*s*; -), '**dübeln** *v/t* (*ge-, h*) TECH dowel

ducken ['dʊkən] *v/refl* (*ge-, h*) duck; *fig* cringe (*vor dat* before); crouch

Duckmäuser ['dʊkmɔyzɐ] *m* (-*s*; -) coward; yes-man

Dudelsack ['duːdəlzak] *m* MUS bagpipes

Duell [du'ɛl] *n* (-*s*; *-e*) duel

duellieren [duɛ'liːrən] *v/refl* (*no -ge-, h*) fight a duel

Duett [du'ɛt] *n* (-[*e*]*s*; -*e*) MUS duet
Duft [dʊft] *m* (-[*e*]*s*; *Düfte* ['dʏftə]) scent, fragrance, smell (*nach* of)
'duften *v/i* (*ge-*, *h*) smell (*nach* of)
'duftend *adj* fragrant
'duftig *adj* dainty
dulden ['dʊldən] *v/t* (*ge-*, *h*) tolerate, put up with; suffer
duldsam ['dʊltzaːm] *adj* tolerant
dumm [dʊm] *adj* stupid, F dumb
'Dummheit *f* (-; -*en*) a) (*no pl*) stupidity, ignorance, b) stupid *or* foolish thing
'Dummkopf *m contp* fool, blockhead
dumpf [dʊmpf] *adj* dull; *fig* vague
Düne ['dyːnə] *f* (-; -*n*) (sand) dune
Dung [dʊŋ] *m* (-[*e*]*s*; *no pl*) dung, manure
düngen ['dʏŋən] *v/t* (*ge-*, *h*) fertilize; manure
Dünger ['dʏŋɐ] *m* (-*s*; -) fertilizer; manure
dunkel ['dʊŋkəl] *adj* dark (*a. fig*)
'Dunkelheit *f* (-; *no pl*) dark(ness)
'Dunkelkammer *f* PHOT darkroom
Dunkelziffer *f* number of unreported cases
dünn [dʏn] *adj* thin; weak (*coffee etc*)
Dunst [dʊnst] *m* (-[*e*]*s*; *Dünste* ['dʏnstə]) haze, mist; CHEM vapo(u)r
dünsten ['dʏnstən] *v/t* (*ge-*, *h*) GASTR stew, braise
'dunstig *adj* hazy, misty
Duplikat [dupli'kaːt] *n* (-[*e*]*s*; -*e*) duplicate; copy
Dur [duːɐ] *n* (-; *no pl*) MUS major (key)
durch [dʊrç] *prp* (*acc*) *and adv* through; across; MATH divided by; GASTR (well) done; *durch j-n* (*et.*) by s.o. (s.th.); *durch und durch* through and through
'durcharbeiten (*sep*, -*ge-*, *h*) **1.** *v/t* study thoroughly; *sich durcharbeiten durch* work (one's way) through a *text etc*; **2.** *v/i* work without a break
durch'aus *adv* absolutely, quite; *durchaus nicht* by no means
'durchblättern *v/t* (*sep*, -*ge-*, *h*) leaf *or* thumb through
'Durchblick *fig m* grasp *of s.th.*
'durchblicken *v/i* (*sep*, -*ge-*, *h*) look through; *durchblicken lassen* give to understand; *ich blicke (da) nicht durch* I don't get it
durch'bohren *v/t* (*no -ge-*, *h*) pierce; perforate
'durchbraten *v/t* (*irr*, *braten*, *sep*, -*ge-*, *h*) roast thoroughly
'durchbrechen[1] (*irr*, *brechen*, *sep*, -*ge-*) **1.** *v/t* (*h*) break (in two); **2.** *v/i* (*sein*) break through *or* apart
durch'brechen[2] *v/t* (*irr*, *brechen*, *no -ge-*, *h*) break through

'durchbrennen *v/i* (*irr*, *brennen*, *sep*, -*ge-*, *sein*) ELECTR blow; *reactor*: melt down; F run away
'durchbringen *v/t* (*irr*, *bringen*, *sep*, -*ge-*, *h*) get (MED pull) *s.o.* through; go through one's money); support (*family*)
'Durchbruch *m* breakthrough (*a. fig*)
durch'dacht *adj* (well) thought-out
'durchdrehen (*sep*, -*ge-*, *h*) **1.** *v/i wheels*: spin; F *fig* crack up, flip; **2.** *v/t* GASTR grind, *Br* mince
'durchdringend *adj* piercing
durchei'nander *adv* confused; (in) a mess
Durchei'nander *n* (-*s*; *no pl*) confusion, mess; *Durcheinanderbringen v/t* (*irr*, *bringen*, *sep*, -*ge-*, *h* confuse, mix up; mess up
durch'fahren[1] *v/t* (*irr*, *fahren*, *no -ge-*, *h*) go (*or* pass, drive) through
'durchfahren[2] *v/i* (*irr*, *fahren*, *sep*, -*ge-*, *sein*) go (*or* pass, drive) through
'Durchfahrt *f* passage; *Durchfahrt verboten* no thoroughfare
'Durchfall *m* MED diarrh(o)ea
'durchfallen *v/i* (*irr*, *fallen*, *sep*, -*ge-*, *sein*) fall through; fail, F flunk (*test etc*); F be a flop; *j-n durchfallen lassen* fail (F flunk) s.o.
durchfragen *v/refl* (*sep*, -*ge-*, *h*) ask one's way (*nach*, *zu* to)
'durchführbar *adj* practicable, feasible
'durchführen *v/t* (*sep*, -*ge-*, *h*) carry out, do
'Durchgang *m* passage
'Durchgangs... *in cpds* ...*verkehr etc*: through ...; ...*lager etc*: transit ...
'durchgebraten *adj* well done
'durchgehen (*irr*, *gehen*, *sep*, -*ge-*, *sein*) **1.** *v/i* go through (*a.* RAIL *and* PARL); *fig* run away (*mit* with); *horse*: bolt; **2.** *v/t* go *or* look through; *durchgehen lassen* tolerate
durchgehend *adj* continuous; *durchgehender Zug* through train; *durchgehend geöffnet* open all day
'durchgreifen *fig v/i* (*irr*, *greifen*, *sep*, -*ge-*, *h*) take drastic measures
durchgreifend *adj* drastic; radical
'durchhalten (*irr*, *halten*, *sep*, -*ge-*, *h*) **1.** *v/t* keep up; **2.** *v/i* hold out
'durchhängen *v/i* (*irr*, *hängen*, *sep*, -*ge-*, *h*) sag; F have a low
'durchkämpfen *v/t* (*sep*, -*ge-*, *h*) fight out; *sich durchkämpfen* fight one's way through
'durchkommen *v/i* (*irr*, *kommen*, *sep*, -*ge-*, *sein*) come through (*a.* MED); get through; get along; get away (*mit e-r Lüge etc* with a lie *etc*)

durch'kreuzen v/t (no -ge-, h) cross, thwart

'**durchlassen** v/t (irr, **lassen**, sep, -ge-, h) let pass, let through

'**durchlässig** adj permeable (**für** to)

'**durchlaufen**[1] (irr, **laufen**, sep, -ge-) 1. v/i (sein) run through; 2. v/t (h) wear through

durch'**laufen**[2] v/t (irr, **laufen**, no -ge-, h) pass through

'**Durchlauferhitzer** m (-s; -) (instant) water heater, Br a. geyser

'**durchlesen** v/t (irr, **lesen**, sep, -ge-, h) read through

durch'**leuchten** v/t (no -ge-, h) MED X-ray; fig screen

durch**löchern** [-'lœçɐn] v/t (no -ge-, h) perforate, make holes in

'**durchmachen** F v/t (sep, -ge-, h) go through; **viel durchmachen** suffer a lot; **die Nacht durchmachen** make a night of it

'**Durchmesser** m (-s; -) diameter

durch'**nässen** v/t (no -ge-, h) soak

'**durchnehmen** v/t (irr, **nehmen**, sep, -ge-, h) PED do, deal with

'**durchpausen** v/t (sep, -ge-, h) trace

durch'**queren** v/t (no, -ge-, h) cross

'**Durchreiche** f (-; -n) hatch

'**Durchreise** f: **ich bin nur auf der Durchreise** I'm only passing through

'**durchreisen** v/i (sep, -ge-, sein) travel through

'**Durchreisevisum** n transit visa

'**durchreißen** (irr, **reißen**, sep, -ge-) 1. v/t (h) tear (in two); 2. v/i (sein) tear, break

durch**ringen** v/refl (irr, **ringen**, sep, -ge-, h) **sich durchringen**, et. **zu tun** bring o.s. to do s.th.

'**Durchsage** f announcement

durch'**schauen** v/t (no -ge-, h) see through s.o. or s.th.

'**durchscheinen** v/i (irr, **scheinen**, sep, -ge-, h) shine through

durch**scheinend** adj transparent

'**durchscheuern** v/t (sep, -ge-, h) chafe; wear through

'**durchschlafen** v/i (irr, **schlafen**, sep, -ge-, h) sleep through

'**Durchschlag** m (carbon) copy

durch'**schlagen**[1] v/t (irr, **schlagen**, no -ge-, h) cut in two; bullet etc: go through, pierce

'**durchschlagen**[2] (irr, **schlagen**, sep, -ge-) 1. v/refl (h): **sich durchschlagen nach** make one's way to; 2. v/i (sein) come through (a. fig)

durch**schlagend** adj sweeping; effective

'**Durchschlagpa,pier** n carbon paper

Durchschlagskraft fig f force, impact

'**durchschneiden** v/t (irr, **schneiden**, sep, -ge-, h) cut (through)

'**Durchschnitt** m average; **im (über, unter dem) Durchschnitt** on an (above, below) average; **im Durchschnitt betragen (verdienen** etc) average

'**durchschnittlich** 1. adj average; ordinary; 2. adv on an average

'**Durchschnitts...** in cpds average ...

'**Durchschrift** f (carbon) copy

'**durchsehen** v/t (irr, **sehen**, sep, -ge-, h) look or go through; check

durch**setzen** v/t (sep, -ge-, h) put (or push) s.th. through; **s-n Kopf durchsetzen** have one's way; **sich durchsetzen** get one's way; be successful; **sich durchsetzen können** have authority (**bei** over)

durch'**setzt** adj: **durchsetzt mit** interspersed with

'**durchsichtig** adj transparent (a. fig); clear; see-through

'**durchsickern** v/i (sep, -ge-, sein) seep through; fig leak out

'**durchstarten** v/i (sep, -ge-, sein) AVIAT climb and reaccelerate

durch'**stechen** v/t (irr, **stechen**, no -ge-, h) pierce

'**durchstecken** v/t (sep, -ge-, h) stick through

durch**stehen** v/t (irr, **stehen**, sep, -ge-, h) go through

durch'**stoßen** v/t (irr, **stoßen**, no -ge-, h) break through

'**durchstreichen** v/t (irr, **streichen**, sep, -ge-, h) cross out

durch'**suchen** v/t (no -ge-, h) search, F frisk

Durch'suchung f (-; -en) search

Durch'suchungsbefehl m search warrant

durch**trieben** [-'triːbən] adj cunning, sly

durch'**wachsen** adj GASTR streaky

'**Durchwahl** f (-; no pl) TEL direct dial-(l)ing

'**durchwählen** v/i (sep, -ge-, h) TEL dial direct

'**durchweg** [-vɛk] adv without exception

durch'**weicht** adj soaked, drenched

durch'**wühlen** v/t (no -ge-, h) rummage through

'**durchzählen** v/t (sep, -ge-, h) count off (Br up)

durch**ziehen** (irr, **ziehen**, sep, -ge-) 1. v/i (sein) pass through; 2. v/t (h) pull s.th. through; fig carry s.th. through (to the end)

durch'**zucken** v/t (no -ge-, h) flash through

'Durchzug *m* (-[e]s; *no pl*) draft, *Br* draught
dürfen ['dʏrfən] **1.** *v/aux* (*irr, no* -ge-, *h*) be allowed *or* permitted to *inf*; **darf ich gehen?** may I go?; **ja(**, **du darfst)** yes, you may; **du darfst nicht** you must not, you aren't allowed to; **dürfte ich ...?** could I ...?; **das dürfte genügen** that should be enough; **2.** *v/i* (*irr*, ge-, *h*) **er darf** (**nicht**) he is (not) allowed to *inf*
durfte ['dʊrftə] *pret of* **dürfen**
dürftig ['dʏrftɪç] *adj* poor; scanty
dürr [dʏr] *adj* dry; barren, arid; skinny
Dürre ['dʏrə] *f* (-; -*n*) a) drought, b) (*no pl*) barrenness
Durst [dʊrst] *m* (-[e]s; *no pl*) thirst (**auf** *acc* for); **Durst haben** be thirsty
'durstig *adj* thirsty
Dusche ['dʊʃə] *f* (-; -*n*) shower
'duschen *v/refl and v/i* (ge-, *h*) have *or* take a shower
Düse ['dyːzə] *f* (-; -*n*) TECH nozzle; jet

'düsen F *v/i* (ge-, *sein*) jet
'Düsenantrieb *m* jet propulsion; **mit Düsenantrieb** jet-propelled
Düsenflugzeug *n* jet (plane)
Düsenjäger *m* MIL jet fighter
Düsentriebwerk *n* jet engine
düster ['dyːstɐ] *adj* dark, gloomy (*both a. fig*); dim (*light*); *fig* dismal
Dutzend ['dʊtsənt] *n* (-*s*; -*e*) dozen
'dutzendweise *adv* by the dozen
duzen ['duːtsən] *v/t* (ge-, *h*) use the familiar 'du' with s.o.; **sich duzen** be on 'du' terms
Dynamik [dy'naːmɪk] *f* (-; *no pl*) PHYS dynamics; *fig* dynamism
dy'namisch *adj* dynamic
Dynamit [dyna'miːt] *n* (-*s*; *no pl*) dynamite
Dynamo [dy'anːmo] *m* (-*s*; -*s*) ELECTR dynamo, generator
D-Zug ['deː-] *m* express train

E

Ebbe ['ɛbə] *f* (-; -*n*) ebb, low tide
eben ['eːbən] **1.** *adj* even; flat; MATH plane; **zu ebener Erde** on the first (*Br* ground) floor; **2.** *adv* just; **an eben dem Tag** on that very day; **so ist es eben** that's the way it is; **gerade eben so** *or* **noch** just barely
'Ebenbild *n* image
'ebenbürtig [-bʏrtɪç] *adj*: **j-m ebenbürtig sein** be a match for s.o., be s.o.'s equal
Ebene ['eːbənə] *f* (-; -*n*) GEOGR plain; MATH plane; *fig* level
'ebenerdig *adj and adv* at street level; on the first (*Br* ground) floor
'ebenfalls *adv* as well, too
'Ebenholz *n* ebony
'Ebenmaß *n* (-*es*; *no pl*) symmetry; harmony; regularity
'ebenmäßig *adj* symmetrical; harmonious; regular
'ebenso *adv and cj* just as; as well; **ebenso wie** in the same way as; **ebenso gern, ebenso gut** just as well; **ebenso sehr, ebenso viel** just as much; **ebenso wenig** just as little *or* few
Eber ['eːbɐ] *m* (-*s*; -) ZO boar
ebnen ['eːbnən] *v/t* (ge-, *h*) even, level; *fig*

smooth
Echo ['ɛço] *n* (-*s*; -*s*) echo; *fig* response
echt [ɛçt] *adj* genuine (*a. fig*), real; true; pure; fast (*color*); authentic; F **echt gut** real good
'Echtheit *f* (-; *no pl*) genuineness; authenticity
Eckball ['ɛk-] *m* SPORT corner (kick)
Ecke ['ɛkə] *f* (-; -*n*) corner; edge; SPORT **lange** (**kurze**) **Ecke** far (near) corner; → **Eckball**
eckig ['ɛkɪç] *adj* square, angular; *fig* awkward
'Eckzahn *m* canine tooth
edel ['eːdəl] *adj* noble; MIN precious
'Edelme,tall *n* precious metal
'Edelstahl *m* stainless steel
'Edelstein *m* precious stone; gem
EDV [eːdeː'fau] ABBR *of* **Elektronische Datenverarbeitung** EDP, electronic data processing
Efeu ['eːfɔy] *m* (-*s*; *no pl*) BOT ivy
Effekt [ɛ'fɛkt] *m* (-[e]s; -*e*) effect
effektiv [ɛfɛk'tiːf] **1.** *adj* effective; **2.** *adv* actually
Effektivität [ɛfɛktivi'tɛːt] *f* (-; *no pl*) effectiveness

ef'fektvoll *adj* effective, striking

Effet [ɛ'feː] *m* (-s; -s) SPORT spin

EG [eː'geː] HIST ABBR *of* **Europäische Gemeinschaft** EC, European Community

egal [e'gaːl] F *adj*: **egal ob** (**warum, wer** *etc*) no matter if (why, who, *etc*); **das ist egal** it doesn't matter; **das ist mir egal** I don't care, it's all the same to me

Egge ['ɛgə] *f* (-; -n), **'eggen** *v/t* (*ge-*, *h*) AGR harrow

Egoismus [ego'ısmʊs] *m* (-; *no pl*) ego-(t)ism

Egoist(in) [ego'ıst(ın)] (-en; -en/-; -nen) ego(t)ist

ego'istisch *adj* selfish, ego(t)istic(al)

ehe ['eːə] *cj* before; **nicht ehe** not until

Ehe ['eːə] *f* (-; -n) marriage (**mit** to)

Eheberatung *f* marriage counseling (*Br* guidance)

Ehebrecher *m* (-s; -) adulterer

Ehebrecherin *f* (-; -nen) adulteress

'ehebrecherisch *adj* adulterous

'Ehebruch *m* adultery

Ehefrau *f* wife

Eheleute *pl* married couple

'ehelich *adj* conjugal; JUR legitimate

ehemalig ['eːəmaːlıç] *adj* former, ex-...

ehemals ['eːəmaːls] *adv* formerly

'Ehemann *m* husband

'Ehepaar *n* (married) couple

eher ['eːɐ] *adv* earlier, sooner; **je eher, desto lieber** the sooner the better; **nicht eher als** not until *or* before

'Ehering *m* wedding ring

ehrbar ['eːɐbaːɐ] *adj* respectable

Ehre ['eːrə] *f* (-; -n) hono(u)r; **zu Ehren** (**von**) in hono(u)r of

'ehren *v/t* (*ge-*, *h*) hono(u)r; respect

'ehrenamtlich *adj* honorary

'Ehrenbürger *m* honorary citizen

Ehrendoktor *m* UNIV honorary doctor

Ehrengast *m* guest of hono(u)r

Ehrenkodex *m* code of hono(u)r

Ehrenmann *m* man of hono(u)r

Ehrenmitglied *n* honorary member

Ehrenplatz *m* place of hono(u)r

Ehrenrechte *pl* civil rights

Ehrenrettung *f* rehabilitation

'ehrenrührig *adj* defamatory

'Ehrenrunde *f esp* SPORT lap of hono(u)r

Ehrensache *f* point of hono(u)r

Ehrentor *n*, Ehrentreffer *m* SPORT consolation goal

'ehrenwert *adj* hono(u)rable

'Ehrenwort *n* (-[e]s; -e) word of hono(u)r; F **Ehrenwort!** cross my heart!

ehrerbietig ['eːɐʔeːbiːtıç] *adj* respectful

Ehrfurcht ['eːɐ-] *f* (-; *no pl*) respect (**vor** *dat* for); awe (of); **Ehrfurcht gebietend** awe-inspiring, awesome

'ehrfürchtig [-fʏrçtıç] *adj* respectful

'Ehrgefühl *n* (-[e]s; *no pl*) sense of hono(u)r

'Ehrgeiz *m* ambition

'ehrgeizig *adj* ambitious

'ehrlich *adj* honest; frank; fair

'Ehrlichkeit *f* (-; *no pl*) honesty; fairness

'Ehrung *f* (-; -en) hono(u)r(ing)

'ehrwürdig *adj* venerable

Ei [ai] *n* (-[e]s; *Eier* ['aiɐ]) egg; V *pl* balls

Eiche ['aiçə] *f* (-; -n) oak(-tree)

Eichel ['aiçəl] *f* (-; -n) BOT acorn; *card games*: club(s); ANAT glans (penis)

eichen ['aiçən] *v/t* (*ge-*, *h*) ga(u)ge

Eichhörnchen ['aiçhœrnçən] *n* (-s; -) ZO squirrel

Eid [ait] *m* (-[e]s; -e) oath; **e-n Eid ablegen** take an oath

Eidechse ['aidɛksə] *f* (-; -n) ZO lizard

eidesstattlich ['aidəs-] *adj*: **eidesstattliche Erklärung** JUR statutory declaration

'Eidotter *m*, *n* (egg) yolk

'Eierbecher *m* eggcup

Eierkuchen *m* pancake

Eierli,kör *m* eggnog

Eierschale *f* eggshell

Eierstock *m* ANAT ovary

Eieruhr *f* egg timer

Eifer ['aifɐ] *m* (-s; *no pl*) zeal, eagerness; **glühender Eifer** ardo(u)r

'Eifersucht *f* (-; *no pl*) jealousy

'eifersüchtig *adj* jealous (**auf** *acc* of)

eifrig *adj* eager, zealous; ardent

'Eigelb *n* (-[e]s; -e) (egg) yolk

eigen ['aigən] *adj* own, of one's own; peculiar; particular, F fussy

...eigen *in cpds staatseigen etc*: ...-owned

'Eigenart *f* peculiarity

'eigenartig *adj* peculiar; strange

'Eigenbedarf *m* personal needs

'Eigengewicht *n* dead weight

'eigenhändig [-hɛndıç] **1.** *adj* personal; **2.** *adv* personally, with one's own hands

'Eigenheim *n* home (of one's own)

Eigenliebe *f* self-love

Eigenlob *n* self-praise

'eigenmächtig *adj* arbitrary

'Eigenname *m* proper noun

'Eigennutz *m* (-es; *no pl*) self-interest

'eigennützig [-nytsıç] *adj* selfish

'eigens *adv* (e)specially, expressly

'Eigenschaft *f* (-; -en) quality; TECH, PHYS, CHEM property; **in s-r Eigenschaft als** in his capacity as

'Eigenschaftswort *n* (-[e]s; -wörter) LING adjective

'Eigensinn *m* (-[e]s; *no pl*) stubbornness

'eigensinnig *adj* stubborn, obstinate

eigentlich ['aigəntlıç] **1.** *adj* actual, true, real; exact; **2.** *adv* actually, really; originally

'**Eigentor** *n* SPORT own goal (*a. fig*)

'**Eigentum** *n* (-[e]*s*; *no pl*) property

Eigentümer ['aigənty:mɐ] *m* (-*s*; -), '**Eigentümerin** *f* (-; -*nen*) owner, proprietor (proprietress)

'**eigentümlich** [-ty:mlıç] *adj* peculiar; strange, odd

'**Eigentümlichkeit** *f* (-; -*en*) peculiarity

'**Eigentumswohnung** *f* condominium, F condo, *Br* owner-occupied flat

'**eigenwillig** *adj* wil(l)ful; individual, original (*style etc*)

eignen ['aignən] *v/refl* (*ge-*, *h*) **sich eignen für** be suited *or* fit for

'**Eignung** *f* (-; *no pl*) suitability; aptitude, qualification

'**Eignungsprüfung** *f*, **Eignungstest** *m* aptitude test

Eilbote ['ail-] *m*: **durch Eilboten** by special delivery

Eilbrief *m* special delivery (*Br* express) letter

Eile ['ailə] *f* (-; *no pl*) haste, hurry

'**eilen** *v/i* a) (*ge-*, *sein*) hurry, hasten, rush, b) (*ge-*, *h*) be urgent

'**eilig** *adj* hurried, hasty; urgent; **es eilig haben** be in a hurry

Eimer ['aimɐ] *m* (-*s*; -) bucket, pail

ein [ain] **1.** *adj* one; **2.** *indef art* a, an; **3.** *adv*: "**einlaus**" "on / off"; **ein und aus gehen** come and go; **nicht mehr ein noch aus wissen** be at one's wits' end

einander [ai'nandɐ] *pron* each other, one another

'**einarbeiten** *v/t* (*sep*, *-ge-*, *h*) train, acquaint *s.o.* with his work, F break *s.o.* in; **sich einarbeiten** work o.s. in

'**einarmig** [-armıç] *adj* one-armed

einäschern ['ainʔɛʃɐn] *v/t* (*sep*, *-ge-*, *h*) cremate

Einäscherung ['ainʔɛʃərʊŋ] *f* (-; -*en*) cremation

'**einatmen** *v/t* (*sep*, *-ge-*, *h*) inhale, breathe

'**einäugig** [-ɔygıç] *adj* one-eyed

'**Einbahnstraße** *f* one-way street

einbalsamieren ['ainbalzami:rən] *v/t* (*no -ge-*, *h*) embalm

'**Einband** *m* (-[e]*s*; *-bände*) binding, cover

'**Einbau** *m* (-[e]*s*; *-bauten*) installation, fitting; **Einbau...** *in cpds* ...*möbel etc*: built-in ...

'**einbauen** *v/t* (*sep*, *-ge-*, *h*) build in, instal(l), fit

'**einberufen** *v/t* (*irr*, **rufen**, *sep*, *no -ge-*, *h*) MIL draft, *Br* call up; call (*meeting etc*)

'**Einberufung** *f* (-; -*en*) MIL draft, *Br* call--up

'**einbeziehen** *v/t* (*irr*, **ziehen**, *sep*, *no -ge-*, *h*) include

einbiegen *v/i* (*irr*, **biegen**, *sep*, *-ge-*, *sein*) turn (*in acc* into)

'**einbilden** *v/refl* (*sep*, *-ge-*, *h*) imagine; **sich et. einbilden auf** (*acc*) be conceited about

'**Einbildung** *f* (-; *no pl*) imagination, fancy; conceit

'**einblenden** *v/t* (*sep*, *-ge-*, *h*) TV fade in

'**Einblick** *m* insight (*in acc* into)

'**einbrechen** *v/i* (*irr*, **brechen**, *sep*, *-ge-*, *sein*) collapse; *winter*: set in; **einbrechen in** (*acc*) break into, burgle; fall through (the ice)

'**Einbrecher** *m* (-*s*; -) burglar

'**einbringen** *v/t* (*irr*, **bringen**, *sep*, *-ge-*, *h*) bring in; yield (*profit etc*)

'**Einbruch** *m* burglary; **bei Einbruch der Nacht** at nightfall

'**einbürgern** [-byrgɐn] *v/t* (*sep*, *-ge-*, *h*) naturalize; **sich einbürgern** *fig* come into use

'**Einbürgerung** *f* (-; -*en*) naturalization

'**Einbuße** *f* (-; -*n*) loss

'**einbüßen** *v/t* (*sep*, *-ge-*, *h*) lose

'**eindämmen** [-dɛmən] *v/t* (*sep*, *-ge-*, *h*) dam (up), *fig a.* get under control

'**eindecken** *fig v/t* (*sep*, *-ge-*, *h*) provide (*mit* with)

'**eindeutig** [-dɔytıç] *adj* clear

'**eindrehen** *v/t* (*sep*, *-ge-*, *h*) put *hair* in curlers

'**eindringen** *v/i* (*irr*, **dringen**, *sep*, *-ge-*, *sein*) **eindringen in** (*acc*) enter (*a. fig*); force one's way into; MIL invade

'**eindringlich** *adj* urgent

'**Eindringling** *m* (-*s*; -*e*) intruder; MIL invader

'**Eindruck** *m* impression

'**eindrücken** *v/t* (*sep*, *-ge-*, *h*) break *or* push in

'**eindrucksvoll** *adj* impressive

eineiig ['ainʔaiıç] *adj* identical (*twins*)

'**einein'halb** *adj* one and a half

einengen ['ainʔɛŋən] *v/t* (*sep*, *-ge-*, *h*) confine, restrict

einer ['ainɐ], **eine** ['ainə], **ein(e)s** ['ain(-ə)s] *indef pron* one

'**Einer** *m* (-*s*; -) MATH unit; *rowing*: single sculls

einerlei ['ainɐ'lai] *adj*: **ganz einerlei** all the same; **einerlei ob** no matter if

'**Einer'lei** *n*: **das tägliche Einerlei** the daily grind *or* rut

'**einer'seits** *adv* on the one hand

'**einfach** *adj* simple; easy; plain; one-way (*Br* single) (*ticket*)

'**Einfachheit** *f* (-; *no pl*) simplicity
'**einfädeln** [-fɛːdəln] *v/t* (*sep*, -ge-, *h*) thread; F start, set afoot; MOT merge
'**einfahren** (*irr*, **fahren**, *sep*, -ge-) **1.** *v/t* (*h*) MOT run in; bring in (*harvest*); **2.** *v/i* (*sein*) come in, RAIL *a*. pull in
'**Einfahrt** *f* entrance, way in
'**Einfall** *m* idea; MIL invasion
'**einfallen** *v/i* (*irr*, **fallen**, *sep*, -ge-, *sein*) fall in; collapse; MUS join in; **einfallen in** (*acc*) MIL invade; **ihm fiel ein, dass** it came to his mind that; **mir fällt nichts ein** I have no ideas; **es fällt mir nicht ein** I can't think of it; **dabei fällt mir ein** that reminds me; **was fällt dir ein?** what's the idea?
einfältig ['ainfɛltɪç] *adj* simple-minded; stupid
Einfa'milienhaus *n* detached house
'**einfarbig** *adj* solid-colored, *Br* self-coloured
'**einfassen** *v/t* (*sep*, -ge-, *h*) border
einfetten *v/t* (*sep*, -ge-, *h*) grease
einfinden *v/refl* (*irr*, **finden**, *sep*, -ge-, *h*) appear, arrive
einflechten *fig v/t* (*irr*, **flechten**, *sep*, -ge-, *h*) work in
einfliegen *v/t* (*irr*, **fliegen**, *sep*, -ge-, *h*) fly in
einfließen *v/i* (*irr*, **fließen**, *sep*, -ge-, *sein*) *fig et.* **einfließen lassen** slip s.th. in
einflößen *v/t* (*sep*, -ge-, *h*) pour (**j-m** into s.o.'s mouth); *fig* fill with (*awe etc*)
'**Einfluss** *fig m* influence
'**einflussreich** *adj* influential
'**einförmig** [-fœrmɪç] *adj* uniform
'**einfrieren** (*irr*, **frieren**, *sep*, -ge-) **1.** *v/i* (*sein*) freeze (in); **2.** *v/t* (*h*) freeze (*a. fig*)
'**einfügen** *v/t* (*sep*, -ge-, *h*) put in; *fig* insert; **sich einfügen** fit in; adjust (o.s.) (**in** *acc* to)
'**Einfügetaste** *f* EDP insert key
einfühlsam ['ainfyːlzaːm] *adj* sympathetic
'**Einfühlungsvermögen** *n* (-s; *no pl*) empathy
Einfuhr ['ainfuːɐ] *f* (-; -en) ECON a) (*no pl*) importation, b) import
'**einführen** *v/t* (*sep*, -ge-, *h*) introduce; instal(l) *s.o.*: insert; ECON import
'**Einfuhrstopp** *m* ECON import ban
'**Einführung** *f* (-; -en) introduction
'**Einführungs...** *in cpds* **...kurs**, **...preis** *etc*: introductory ...
'**Eingabe** *f* petition; EDP input
Eingabetaste *f* EDP enter *or* return key
'**Eingang** *m* entrance; ECON arrival; receipt
'**eingängig** *adj* catchy (*tune etc*)

'**eingangs** *adv* at the beginning
'**eingeben** *v/t* (*irr*, **geben**, *sep*, -ge-, *h*) MED administer (*dat* to); EDP feed, enter
'**eingebildet** *adj* imaginary; conceited (**auf** *acc* of)
'**Eingeborene** *m*, *f* (-n; -n) native
'**Eingebung** *f* (-; -en) inspiration; impulse
'**eingefallen** *adj* sunken, hollow
'**eingefleischt** *adj* confirmed
'**eingehen** (*irr*, **gehen**, *sep*, -ge-, *sein*) **1.** *v/i* ECON come in, arrive; BOT, ZO die; *fabric*: shrink; **eingehen auf** (*acc*) agree to; go into (*detail*); listen to *s.o.*; **2.** *v/t* enter into (*a contract etc*); make (*a bet*); take (*a risk etc*)
eingehend *adj* thorough; detailed
'**eingemacht** *adj* preserved
eingemeinden ['aingəmaindən] *v/t* (*sep*, *no* -ge-, *h*) incorporate (**in** *acc* into)
'**eingenommen** *adj* partial (**für** to); prejudiced (**gegen** against); **von sich eingenommen** full of o.s.
eingeschlossen *adj* locked in; trapped; ECON included
eingeschnappt F *adj* in a huff
eingeschrieben *adj* registered
eingespielt *adj*: (**gut**) **aufeinander eingespielt sein** work well together, be a good team
eingestellt *adj*: **eingestellt auf** (*acc*) prepared for; **eingestellt gegen** opposed to
Eingeweide ['aingəvaidə] *pl* ANAT intestines, guts
'**Eingeweihte** *m*, *f* (-n; -n) insider
'**eingewöhnen** *v/refl* (*sep*, *no* -ge-, *h*) **sich eingewöhnen in** (*acc*) get used to, settle in
'**eingießen** *v/t* (*irr*, **gießen**, *sep*, -ge-, *h*) pour
'**eingleisig** [-glaizɪç] *adj* single-track
'**eingliedern** *v/t* (*sep*, -ge-, *h*) integrate
'**Eingliederung** *f* integration
'**eingraben** *v/t* (*irr*, **graben**, *sep*, -ge-, *h*) bury
eingra,vieren *v/t* (*sep*, *no* -ge-, *h*) engrave
'**eingreifen** *v/i* (*irr*, **greifen**, *sep*, -ge-, *h*) step in, interfere
'**Eingriff** *m* intervention, interference; MED operation
'**einhaken** *v/t* (*sep*, -ge-, *h*) hook in; **sich einhaken** link arms, take s.o.'s arm
'**Einhalt** *m*: **Einhalt gebieten** put a stop (*dat* to)
'**einhalten** *v/t* (*irr*, **halten**, *sep*, -ge-, *h*) keep
'**einhängen** (*sep*, -ge-, *h*) **1.** *v/t* hang in; TEL hang up (*receiver*); **sich einhängen → einhaken**; **2.** *v/i* TEL hang up
'**einheimisch** *adj* native, local; ECON

home, domestic
'Einheimische *m*, *f* (-*n*; -*n*) local, native
'Einheit *f* (-; -*en*) unit; POL unity
'einheitlich *adj* uniform; homogeneous
'Einheits... *in cpds* ...*preis etc*: standard
einhellig ['ainhɛlıç] *adj* unanimous
'einholen *v/t* (*sep*, -*ge*-, *h*) catch up with (*a.*
fig); make up for *lost time*; make (*inqui-ries*) (*über acc* about); seek (*advice*) (*bei*
from); ask for *permission etc*; strike (*sail*);
einholen gehen go shopping
'Einhorn *n* MYTH unicorn
'einhüllen *v/t* (*sep*, -*ge*-, *h*) wrap (up); *fig*
shroud
einig ['ainıç] *adj*: *sich einig sein* agree;
sich nicht einig sein disagree, differ
einige ['ainıɡə] *indef pron* some, a few,
several
einigen ['ainıɡən] *v/t* (*ge*-, *h*) *sich eini-gen über* (*acc*) agree on
einigermaßen ['ainıɡɐ'ma:sən] *adv* quite,
fairly; not too bad
'einiges *indef pron* some, something;
quite a lot
'Einigkeit *f* (-; *no pl*) unity; agreement
'Einigung *f* (-; -*en*) agreement, settle-ment; POL unification
'einjagen *v/t* (*sep*, -*ge*-, *h*) *j-m e-n Schre-cken einjagen* give s.o. a fright, frighten
or scare s.o.
'einjährig [-jɛːrıç] *adj* one-year-old; *ein-jährige Pflanze* annual
'einkalku̱lieren *v/t* (*no -ge*-, *h*) take into
account, allow for
'Einkauf *m* purchase; *Einkäufe machen*
→ *einkaufen 2*
'einkaufen (*sep*, -*ge*-, *h*) **1.** *v/t* buy, ECON *a.*
purchase; **2.** *v/i* go shopping
'Einkaufs... *in cpds* shopping ...
Einkaufsbummel *m* shopping spree
Einkaufspreis *m* ECON purchase price
Einkaufswagen *m* grocery *or* shopping
cart, *Br* (supermarket) trolley
Einkaufszentrum *n* (shopping) mall, *Br*
shopping centre
'einkehren *v/i* (*sep*, -*ge*-, *sein*) stop (*in dat*
at)
einklammern *v/t* (*sep*, -*ge*-, *h*) put in
brackets
'Einklang *m* (-[*e*]*s*; *no pl*) MUS unison; *fig*
harmony
'einkleiden *v/t* (*sep*, -*ge*-, *h*) clothe (*a. fig*)
einklemmen *v/t* (*sep*, -*ge*-, *h*) squeeze,
jam; *eingeklemmt sein* be stuck, be
jammed
einkochen (*sep*, -*ge*-) **1.** *v/t* (*h*) preserve; **2.**
v/i (*sein*) boil down
'Einkommen *n* (-*s*; -) income
Einkommensteuererklärung *f* income-

-tax return
'einkreisen *v/t* (*sep*, -*ge*-, *h*) encircle, sur-round
Einkünfte ['ainkynftə] *pl* income
'einladen *v/t* (*irr*, *laden*, *sep*, -*ge*-, *h*) in-vite; load
einladend *adj* inviting
'Einladung *f* (-; -*en*) invitation
'Einlage *f* (-; -*n*) ECON investment; MED
arch support; THEA, MUS interlude
Einlass ['ainlas] *m* (-*es*; *no pl*) admission,
admittance
'einlassen *v/t* (*irr*, *lassen*, *sep*, -*ge*-, *h*) let
in; run (*a bath*); *sich einlassen auf* (*acc*)
get involved in; let o.s. in for; agree to;
sich mit j-m einlassen get involved with
s.o.
'Einlauf *m* SPORT finish; MED enema
'einlaufen (*irr*, *laufen*, *sep*, -*ge*-) **1.** *v/i*
(*sein*) come in (*a.* SPORT); *water*: run in;
MAR enter port; *fabric*: shrink; **2.** *v/t* (*h*)
break *new shoes* in; *sich einlaufen* warm
up
'einleben *v/refl* (*sep*, -*ge*-, *h*) settle in
'einlegen *v/t* (*sep*, -*ge*-, *h*) put in; set
(*hair*); GASTR pickle; MOT change into
'Einlegesohle *f* insole
'einleiten *v/t* (*sep*, -*ge*-, *h*) start; introduce;
MED induce; TECH dump, discharge (*se-wage*)
einleitend *adj* introductory
'Einleitung *f* introduction
'einlenken *v/i* (*sep*, -*ge*-, *h*) come round
einleuchten *v/i* (*sep*, -*ge*-, *h*) be evident,
be obvious; *das leuchtet mir* (*nicht*)
ein that (doesn't make) sense to
me
einliefern *v/t* (*sep*, -*ge*-, *h*) take (*ins Ge-fängnis* to prison; *in die Klinik* to
[the] hospital)
einlösen *v/t* (*sep*, -*ge*-, *h*) redeem; cash
(*check*)
einmachen *v/t* (*sep*, -*ge*-, *h*) preserve
'einmal *adv* once; some *or* one day, some-time; *auf einmal* suddenly; at the same
time, at once; *noch einmal* once more *or*
again; *noch einmal so ... (wie)* twice as
... (as); *es war einmal* once (upon a
time) there was; *haben Sie schon ein-mal ...?* have you ever ...?; *schon ein-mal dort gewesen sein* have been there
before; *nicht einmal* not even
'Einmal... *in cpds* disposable ...
Einmal'eins *n* (-; *no pl*) multiplication ta-ble
einmalig ['ainma:lıç] *adj* single; *fig*
unique; F fabulous
'Einmann... *in cpds* one-man ...
'Einmarsch *m* entry; MIL invasion

E

'einmar‚schieren *v/i* (*no -ge-*, *sein*) march in; **einmarschieren in** (*acc*) MIL invade
'einmischen *v/refl* (*sep*, *-ge-*, *h*) meddle (**in** *acc* in, with), interfere (with)
'Einmündung *f* junction
'einmütig [-myːtıç] *adj* unanimous
'Einmütigkeit *f* (-; *no pl*) unanimity
Einnahmen ['ainnaːmən] *pl* takings, receipts
'einnehmen *v/t* (*irr*, **nehmen**, *sep*, *-ge-*, *h*) take (*a.* MIL); earn, make
'einnehmend *adj* engaging
'einnicken *v/i* (*sep*, *-ge-*, *sein*) doze off
'einnisten *v/refl* (*sep*, *-ge-*, *h*) **sich bei j-m einnisten** park o.s. on s.o.
'Einöde *f* (-; *-n*) desert, wilderness
'einordnen *v/t* (*sep*, *-ge-*, *h*) put in its proper place; file; **sich einordnen** MOT get in lane
einpacken *v/t* (*sep*, *-ge-*, *h*) pack (up); wrap up
einparken *v/t and v/i* (*sep*, *-ge-*, *h*) park (between two cars)
einpferchen *v/t* (*sep*, *-ge-*, *h*) pen in; coop up
einpflanzen *v/t* (*sep*, *-ge-*, *h*) plant; *fig* implant (*a.* MED)
einplanen *v/t* (*sep*, *-ge-*, *h*) allow for
einprägen *v/t* (*sep*, *-ge-*, *h*) impress; **sich et. einprägen** keep s.th. in mind; memorize s.th.
einquartieren F *v/t* (*no -ge-*, *h*) put *s.o.* up (**bei j-m** at s.o.'s place); **sich einquartieren bei** (*dat*) move in with
einrahmen *v/t* (*sep*, *-ge-*, *h*) frame
einräumen *v/t* (*sep*, *-ge-*, *h*) put away; furnish; *fig* grant, concede
einreden (*sep*, *-ge-*, *h*) **1.** *v/t*: **j-m et. einreden** talk s.o. into (believing) s.th.; **2.** *v/i*: **auf j-n einreden** keep on at s.o.
einreiben *v/t* (*irr*, **reiben**, *sep*, *-ge-*, *h*) rub
einreichen *v/t* (*sep*, *-ge-*, *h*) hand *or* send in
einreihen *v/t* (*sep*, *-ge-*, *h*) place (among); **sich einreihen** take one's place
'einreihig [-raiıç] *adj* single-breasted
'Einreise *f* entry (*a. in cpds*)
'einreisen *v/i* (*sep*, *-ge-*, *sein*) enter (**in ein Land** a country)
'einreißen (*irr*, **reißen**, *sep*, *-ge-*) **1.** *v/t* (*h*) tear; pull down; **2.** *v/i* (*sein*) tear; *fig* spread
einrenken *v/t* (*sep*, *-ge-*, *h*) MED set; *fig* straighten out
'einrichten *v/t* (*sep*, *-ge-*, *h*) furnish; establish; arrange; **sich einrichten** furnish one's home; **sich einrichten auf** (*acc*) prepare for
'Einrichtung *f* (-; *-en*) furnishings; fittings;

TECH installation(s), facilities; institution, facility
'einrücken (*sep*, *-ge-*) **1.** *v/i* (*sein*) MIL join the forces; march in; **2.** *v/t* (*h*) PRINT indent
eins [ains] *pron and adj* one; one thing; **es ist alles eins** it's all the same (thing)
Eins *f* (-; *-en*) one; *grade*: excellent, A
einsam ['ainzaːm] *adj* lonely, lonesome; solitary
'Einsamkeit *f* (-; *no pl*) loneliness; solitude
'einsammeln *v/t* (*sep*, *-ge-*, *h*) collect
'Einsatz *m* TECH inset, insert; stake(s) (*a. fig*); MUS entry; *fig* effort(s), zeal; use, employment; MIL action, mission; deployment; **im Einsatz** in action; **unter Einsatz des Lebens** at the risk of one's life
'einsatzbereit *adj* ready for action
einsatzfreudig *adj* dynamic, zealous
'einschalten *v/t* (*sep*, *-ge-*, *h*) ELECTR switch *or* turn on; call *s.o.* in; **sich einschalten** step in
'Einschaltquote *f* TV rating
'einschärfen *v/t* (*sep*, *-ge-*, *h*) urge (**j-m et.** s.o. to do s.th.)
einschätzen *v/t* (*sep*, *-ge-*, *h*) estimate; judge, rate; **falsch einschätzen** misjudge
einschenken *v/t* (*sep*, *-ge-*, *h*) pour (out)
einschicken *v/t* (*sep*, *-ge-*, *h*) send in
einschieben *v/t* (*irr*, **schieben**, *sep*, *-ge-*, *h*) slip in; insert
einschlafen *v/i* (*irr*, **schlafen**, *sep*, *-ge-*, *sein*) fall asleep, go to sleep
einschläfern [-ʃlɛːfɐn] *v/t* (*sep*, *-ge-*, *h*) put to sleep
einschl. ABBR *of* **einschließlich** incl., including
'Einschlag *m* strike, impact; *fig* touch
'einschlagen (*irr*, **schlagen**, *sep*, *-ge-*, *h*) **1.** *v/t* knock in (*or* out); break (in), smash; wrap up; take (*road etc*); turn (*wheels*); → **Laufbahn**; **2.** *v/i* lightning etc: strike; *fig* be a success
'einschlägig [-ʃlɛːgıç] *adj* relevant
'einschleusen *fig v/t* (*sep*, *-ge-*, *h*) infiltrate (**in** *acc* into)
einschließen *v/t* (*irr*, **schließen**, *sep*, *-ge-*, *h*) lock in *or* up; enclose; MIL surround, encircle; *fig* include
einschließlich *prp* (*gen*) including, ... included
einschmeicheln *v/refl* (*sep*, *-ge-*, *h*) **sich einschmeicheln bei** ingratiate o.s. with
einschnappen *v/i* (*sep*, *-ge-*, *sein*) snap shut; *fig* go into a huff; → **eingeschnappt**

'**einschneidend** *fig adj* drastic; farreaching

'**Einschnitt** *m* cut; notch; *fig* break

'**einschränken** *v/t* (*sep*, *-ge-*, *h*) restrict, reduce (*both*: **auf** *acc* to); cut down on; **sich einschränken** economize

'**Einschränkung** *f* (-; *-en*) restriction, reduction, cut; **ohne Einschränkung** without reservation

'**Einschreibebrief** *m* registered letter

'**einschreiben** *v/t* (*irr*, *schreiben*, *sep*, *-ge-*, *h*) enter; book; enrol(l) (*a.* MIL); (*sich*) **einschreiben lassen** (*für*) enrol(l) (o.s.) (for)

'**einschreiten** *fig v/i* (*irr*, *schreiten*, *sep*, *-ge-*, *sein*) step in, intervene; **einschreiten** (**gegen**) take (legal) measures (against)

'**einschüchtern** *v/t* (*sep*, *-ge-*, *h*) intimidate; bully

'**Einschüchterung** *f* (-; *-en*) intimidation

'**einschulen** *v/t* (*sep*, *-ge-*, *h*) **eingeschult werden** start school

'**Einschuss** *m* bullet hole

'**einschweißen** *v/t* (*sep*, *-ge-*, *h*) shrink-wrap

'**einsegnen** *v/t* (*sep*, *-ge-*, *h*) REL consecrate; confirm

'**Einsegnung** *f* (-; *-en*) REL consecration; confirmation

'**einsehen** *v/t* (*irr*, *sehen*, *sep*, *-ge-*, *h*) see, realize; **das sehe ich nicht ein!** I don't see why!

'**Einsehen** *n*: **ein Einsehen haben** show some understanding

'**einseifen** *v/t* (*sep*, *-ge-*, *h*) soap; lather; F *fig* **j-n einseifen** take s.o. for a ride

'**einseitig** [-zaɪtɪç] *adj* one-sided; MED, POL, JUR unilateral

'**einsenden** *v/t* ([*irr*, *senden*,] *sep*, *-ge-*, *h*) send in

'**Einsendeschluss** *m* closing date (for entries)

'**einsetzen** (*sep*, *-ge-*, *h*) **1.** *v/t* put in, insert; appoint; use, employ; TECH put into service; ECON invest, stake; bet; risk; **sich einsetzen** try hard, make an effort; **sich einsetzen für** stand up for; **2.** *v/i* set in, start

'**Einsicht** *f* (-; *-en*) a) insight, b) (*no pl*) understanding; **zur Einsicht kommen** listen to reason; **Einsicht nehmen in** (*acc*) take a look at

'**einsichtig** *adj* understanding; reasonable

'**Einsiedler** *m* (*-s*; -) hermit

'**einsilbig** [-zɪlbɪç] *adj* monosyllabic; *fig* taciturn

'**einspannen** *v/t* (*sep*, *-ge-*, *h*) harness; TECH clamp, fix; F rope *s.o.* in

einsparen *v/t* (*sep*, *-ge-*, *h*) save, economize on

einsperren *v/t* (*sep*, *-ge-*, *h*) lock *or* shut up

einspielen *v/t* (*sep*, *-ge-*, *h*) bring in; **sich einspielen** warm up; *fig* get going; → **eingespielt**

'**Einspielergebnisse** *pl film*: box-office returns

'**einspringen** *v/i* (*irr*, *springen*, *sep*, *-ge-*, *sein*) **für j-n einspringen** take s.o.'s place

'**Einspritz...** *in cpds* MOT fuel-injection

'**Einspruch** *m* objection (*a.* JUR), protest; POL veto; appeal

'**einspurig** [-ʃpuːrɪç] *adj* RAIL single-track; MOT single-lane

einst [aɪnst] *adv* once, at one time

'**Einstand** *m* start; *tennis*: deuce

'**einstecken** *v/t* (*sep*, *-ge-*, *h*) pocket (*a. fig*); ELECTR plug in; mail, post; *fig* take

einstehen *v/i* (*irr*, *stehen*, *sep*, *-ge-*, *h*) **einstehen für** stand up for

einsteigen *v/i* (*irr*, *steigen*, *sep*, *-ge-*, *sein*) get in; get on (*bus etc*); **alles einsteigen!** RAIL all aboard!

einstellen *v/t* (*sep*, *-ge-*, *h*) engage, employ, hire; give up; stop; SPORT equal; TECH adjust (**auf** *acc* to); *radio*: tune in (to); OPT, PHOT focus (on); **die Arbeit einstellen** (go on) strike, walk out; **das Feuer einstellen** MIL cease fire; **sich einstellen auf** (*acc*) adjust to; be prepared for

'**Einstellung** *f* attitude (**zu** towards); employment; cessation; TECH adjustment; OPT, PHOT focus(s)ing; *film*: take

'**Einstellungsgespräch** *n* interview

Einstieg ['aɪnʃtiːk] *m* (-[*e*]*s*; *-e*) entrance, entry (*a.* POL, ECON)

'**Einstiegsdroge** *f* gateway drug

einstig ['aɪnstɪç] *adj* former, one-time

'**einstimmen** *v/i* (*sep*, *-ge-*, *h*) MUS join in

'**einstimmig** [-ʃtɪmɪç] *adj* unanimous

'**einstöckig** [-ʃtœkɪç] *adj* one-storied, *Br* one-storey(ed)

'**einstu,dieren** *v/t* (*no -ge-*, *h*) THEA rehearse

einstufen *v/t* (*sep*, *-ge-*, *h*) grade, rate

'**Einstufungsprüfung** *f* placement test

'**einstufig** [-ʃtuːfɪç] *adj* single-stage

'**Einsturz** *m*, '**einstürzen** *v/i* (*sep*, *-ge-*, *sein*) collapse

'**einst'weilen** *adv* for the present

'**einstweilig** [-vaɪlɪç] *adj* temporary

'**eintauschen** *v/t* (*sep*, *-ge-*, *h*) exchange (**gegen** for)

einteilen *v/t* (*sep*, *-ge-*, *h*) divide (**in** *acc* into); organize

'**einteilig** [-taɪlɪç] *adj* one-piece

'**Einteilung** *f* (-; *-en*) division; organization; arrangement

'eintönig [-tøːnɪç] *adj* monotonous
'Eintönigkeit *f* (-; *no pl*) monotony
'Eintopf *m* GASTR stew
'Eintracht *f* (-; *no pl*) harmony, unity
'einträchtig *adj* harmonious, peaceful
Eintrag ['aintraːk] *m* (-[e]s; *Einträge* ['aintrɛːgə]) entry (*a*. ECON), registration
'eintragen *v/t* (*irr*, *tragen*, *sep*, -*ge*-, *h*) enter (*in acc* in); register (*bei* with); enrol(l) (with); *fig* earn; *sich eintragen* register, *hotel*: *a*. check in
einträglich ['aintrɛːklɪç] *adj* profitable
'eintreffen *v/i* (*irr*, *treffen*, *sep*, -*ge*-, *sein*) arrive; happen; come true
eintreiben *fig v/t* (*irr*, *treiben*, *sep*, -*ge*-, *h*) collect
eintreten (*irr*, *treten*, *sep*, -*ge*-) **1.** *v/i* (*sein*) enter; happen, take place; *eintreten für* stand up for, support; *eintreten in* (*acc*) join (*club etc*); **2.** *v/t* (*h*) kick in (*door etc*); *sich et. eintreten* run s.th. into one's foot
'Eintritt *m* entry; admission; *Eintritt frei!* admission free!; *Eintritt verboten!* keep out!
'Eintrittsgeld *n* entrance *or* admission (fee)
Eintrittskarte *f* (admission) ticket
'einüben *v/t* (*sep*, -*ge*-, *h*) practise; rehearse
'einverstanden *adj*: *einverstanden sein* agree (*mit* to); *einverstanden!* agreed!
'Einverständnis *n* (-*ses*; *no pl*) agreement
Einwand ['ainvant] *m* (-[e]s; *Einwände* ['ainvɛndə]) objection (*gegen* to)
'Einwanderer *m*, 'Einwanderin *f* immigrant
'einwandern *v/i* (*sep*, -*ge*-, *sein*) immigrate
'Einwanderung *f* immigration
'einwandfrei *adj* perfect, faultless
einwärts ['ainvɛrts] *adv* inward(s)
'Einweg... ...*rasierer*, ...*spritze etc*: disposable
Einwegflasche *f* non-returnable bottle
Einwegpackung *f* throwaway pack
'einweichen *v/t* (*sep*, -*ge*-, *h*) soak
'einweihen *v/t* (*sep*, -*ge*-, *h*) dedicate, *Br* inaugurate; *j-n einweihen in* (*acc*) F let s.o. in on
'Einweihung *f* (-; -*en*) dedication, *Br* inauguration
'einweisen *v/t* (*irr*, *weisen*, *sep*, -*ge*-, *h*) *j-n einweisen in* (*acc*) send (*esp* JUR commit) s.o. to; instruct s.o. in, brief s.o. on
'einwenden *v/t* ([*irr*, *wenden*,] *sep*, -*ge*-, *h*) object (*gegen* to)
'Einwendung *f* (-; -*en*) objection
'einwerfen *v/t* (*irr*, *werfen*, *sep*, -*ge*-, *h*)

throw in (*a*. *fig*, SPORT *a*. *v/i*); break (*window*); mail, *Br* post; insert (*coin*)
'einwickeln *v/t* (*sep*, -*ge*-, *h*) wrap (up); F take *s.o.* in
'Einwickelpa,pier *n* wrapping-paper
einwilligen ['ainvɪlɪgən] *v/i* (*sep*, -*ge*-, *h*) consent (*in acc* to), agree (to)
'Einwilligung *f* (-; -*en*) consent (*in acc* to), agreement
'einwirken *v/i* (*sep*, -*ge*-, *h*) *einwirken auf* (*acc*) act (up)on; *fig* work on *s.o.*
'Einwirkung *f* effect, influence
Einwohner ['ainvoːnɐ] *m* (-*s*; -), 'Einwohnerin *f* (-; -*nen*) inhabitant
'Einwohnermeldeamt *n* registration office
'Einwurf *m* slot; SPORT throw-in
'Einzahl *f* (-; *no pl*) LING singular
'einzahlen *v/t* (*sep*, -*ge*-, *h*) pay in
'Einzahlung *f* payment, deposit
einzäunen ['aintsɔynən] *v/t* (*sep*, -*ge*-, *h*) fence in
Einzel ['aintsəl] *n* (-*s*; -) *tennis*: singles
'Einzel... *in cpds* ...*bett*, ...*zimmer etc*: single ...
Einzelfall *m* special case
Einzelgänger [-gɛŋɐ] *m* (-*s*; -) F loner
Einzelhaft *f* solitary confinement
Einzelhandel *m* retail trade
Einzelhändler *m* retailer
Einzelhaus *n* detached house
'Einzelheit *f* (-; -*en*) detail
'einzeln *adj* single; odd (*shoe etc*); *Einzelne pl* several, some; *der Einzelne* the individual; *einzeln eintreten* enter one at a time; *einzeln angeben* specify; *im Einzelnen* in detail; *jeder Einzelne* each and every one
'einziehen (*irr*, *ziehen*, *sep*, -*ge*-) **1.** *v/t* (*h*) draw in; *esp* TECH retract; duck; strike (*sail etc*); MIL draft, *Br* call up; confiscate; withdraw (*license etc*); make (*inquiries*); **2.** *v/i* (*sein*) move in; march in; soak in
einzig ['aintsɪç] *adj* only; single; *kein Einziger* ... not a single ...; *das Einzige* the only thing; *der* (*die*) *Einzige* the only one
einzigartig *adj* unique, singular
'Einzug *m* moving in; entry
Eis [ais] *n* (-*es*; *no pl*) ice; GASTR ice cream; *Eis am Stiel* ice lolly
Eisbahn *f* skating rink
Eisbär *m* ZO polar bear
Eisbecher *m* sundae
Eisbein *n* GASTR (pickled) pork knuckles
Eisberg *m* iceberg
Eisbrecher *m* (-*s*; -) MAR icebreaker
Eisdiele *f* ice-cream parlo(u)r
Eisen ['aizən] *n* (-*s*; -) iron

'Eisenbahn *f* railroad, *Br* railway; train set

'Eisenbahner [-ba:nɐ] *m* (-s; -) railroadman, *Br* railwayman

'Eisenbahnwagen *m* (railroad) car, *Br* coach, railway carriage

'Eisenerz *n* iron ore

Eisengießerei *f* iron foundry

Eisenhütte *f* TECH ironworks

'Eisenwaren *pl* hardware, ironware

Eisenwarenhandlung *f* hardware store, *Br* ironmonger's

eisern ['aizɐn] *adj* iron (*a. fig*), of iron

'eisgekühlt *adj* iced

'Eishockey *n* hockey, *Br* ice hockey

eisig ['aizɪç] *adj* icy (*a. fig*)

'eis'kalt *adj* ice-cold

'Eiskunstlauf *m* (-[e]s; *no pl*) figure skating

Eiskunstläufer(in) figure skater

'Eismeer *n* polar sea

Eisre‚vue *f* ice show

Eisschnelllauf *m* speed skating

Eisscholle *f* ice floe

Eisverkäufer *m* iceman

Eiswürfel *m* ice cube

Eiszapfen *m* icicle

Eiszeit *f* (-; *no pl*) GEOL ice age

eitel ['aitəl] *adj* vain

'Eitelkeit *f* (-; *no pl*) vanity

Eiter ['aitɐ] *m* (-s; *no pl*) MED pus

'Eiterbeule *f* MED abscess, boil

'eitern *v/i* (ge-, h) MED fester

eitrig ['aitrɪç] *adj* MED purulent, festering

'Eiweiß *n* (-es; *no pl*) white of egg; BIOL protein

'eiweißarm *adj* low in protein, low-protein

eiweißreich *adj* rich in protein, high-protein

'Eizelle *f* BIOL egg cell, ovum

Ekel ['e:kəl] **1.** *m* (-s; *no pl*) disgust (**vor** *dat* at), loathing (for); **Ekel erregend** → **ekelhaft**; **2.** F *n* (-s; -) beast

ekelerregend *adj* → **ekelhaft**

'ekelhaft, 'ek(e)lig *adj* sickening, disgusting, repulsive

'ekeln *v/refl and v/impers* (ge-, h) **ich ekle mich davor** it makes me sick

Ekstase [ɛk'sta:zə] *f* (-; -*n*) ecstasy

Elan [e'la:n] *m* (-s; *no pl*) vigo(u)r

elastisch [e'lastɪʃ] *adj* elastic, flexible

Elch [ɛlç] *m* (-[e]s; -*e*) ZO elk; moose

Elefant [ele'fant] *m* (-en; -en) ZO elephant

Ele'fantenhochzeit F *f* ECON jumbo merger

elegant [ele'gant] *adj* elegant

Eleganz [ele'gants] *f* (-; *no pl*) elegance

Elektriker [e'lɛktrɪkɐ] *m* (-s; -) electrician

elektrisch [e'lɛktrɪʃ] *adj* electrical; electric

elektrisieren [elɛktri'zi:rən] *v/t* (*no -ge-, h*) electrify

Elektrizität [elɛktritsi'tɛ:t] *f* (-; *no pl*) electricity

Elektrizi'tätswerk *n* (electric) power station

Elektrogerät [e'lɛktro-] *n* electric appliance

Elektronik [elɛk'tro:nɪk] *f* electronics; electronic system

elektronisch [elɛk'tro:nɪʃ] *adj* electronic

E'lektrora‚sierer *m* (-s; -) electric razor

Elektro'technik *f* electrical engineering

Elektro'techniker *m* electrical engineer

Element [ele'mɛnt] *n* (-[e]s; -*e*) element

elementar [elemɛn'ta:ɐ] *adj* elementary

elend ['e:lɛnt] *adj* miserable

'Elend *n* (-s; *no pl*) misery

'Elendsviertel *n* slums

elf [ɛlf] *adj* eleven

Elf *f* (-; -*en*) eleven; soccer: team

Elfe ['ɛlfə] *f* (-; -*n*) elf, fairy

'Elfenbein *n* ivory

Elf'meter *m* (-s; -) soccer: penalty

Elfmeterpunkt *m* penalty spot

Elfmeterschießen *n* penalty shoot-out

'elfte *adj* eleventh

Elite [e'li:tə] *f* (-; -*n*) elite

Ellbogen [e'l-] *m* ANAT elbow

Elster ['ɛlstɐ] *f* (-; -*n*) ZO magpie

elterlich ['ɛltɐlɪç] *adj* parental

Eltern ['ɛltɐn] *pl* parents

'Elternhaus *n* (one's parents') home

'elternlos *adj* orphan(ed)

'Elternteil *m* parent

Elternvertretung *f* appr Parent-Teacher Association

Email [e'mai] *n* (-s; -s), Emaille [e'maljə] *f* (-; -*n*) enamel

Emanze [e'mantsə] F *f* (-; -*n*) women's libber

Emanzipation [emantsipa'tsjo:n] *f* (-; -*en*) emancipation; women's lib(eration)

emanzipieren [emantsi'pi:rən] *v/refl* (*no -ge-, h*) become emancipated

Embargo [ɛm'bargo] *n* (-s; -s) ECON embargo

Embolie [ɛmbo'li:] *f* (-; -*n*) MED embolism

Embryo ['ɛmbryo] *m* (-s; -en [ɛmbry'o:-nən]) BIOL embryo

Emigrant [emi'grant] *m* (-en; -en), Emi-'grantin *f* (-; -*nen*) emigrant, *esp* POL refugee

Emigration [emigra'tsjo:n] *f* (-; -*en*) emigration; **in der Emigration** in exile

emigrieren [emi'gri:rən] *v/i* (*no -ge-, sein*) emigrate

Emission [ɛmɪ'sjoːn] f (-; -en) PHYS emission; ECON issue

empfahl [ɛm'pfaːl] pret of **empfehlen**

Empfang [ɛm'pfaŋ] m (-[e]s; Empfänge [ɛm'pfɛŋə]) reception (a. radio, hotel), welcome; receipt (**nach, bei** on)

emp'fangen v/t (irr, **fangen**, no -ge-, h) receive; welcome

Emp'fänger(in) (-s; -/-; -nen) receiver (m a. radio); addressee

emp'fänglich adj susceptible (**für** to)

Empfängnis [ɛm'pfɛŋnɪs] f (-; no pl) MED conception

Empfängnisverhütung f MED contraception, birth control

Emp'fangsbescheinigung f receipt

Empfangsdame f receptionist

empfehlen [ɛm'pfeːlən] v/t (irr, no -ge-, h) recommend

emp'fehlenswert adj advisable

Emp'fehlung f (-; -en) recommendation

empfinden [ɛm'pfɪndən] v/t (irr, **finden**, no -ge-, h) feel (**als** ... to be ...)

empfindlich [ɛm'pfɪntlɪç] adj sensitive (**für, gegen** to) (a. PHOT, CHEM); tender, delicate; touchy; irritable (a. MED); severe (punishment etc); **empfindliche Stelle** sore spot

Emp'findlichkeit f (-; -en) sensitivity; PHOT speed; delicacy; touchiness

empfindsam [ɛm'pfɪntzaːm] adj sensitive

Emp'findung f (-; -en) sensation; perception; feeling, emotion

empfohlen [ɛm'pfoːlən] pp of **empfehlen**

empor [ɛm'poːɐ] adv up, upward(s)

empören [ɛm'pøːrən] v/t (no -ge-, h) outrage; shock; **sich empören (über** acc) be outraged or shocked (at)

empörend adj shocking, outrageous

Em'pörkömmling [-kœmlɪŋ] contp m (-s; -e) upstart

empört [ɛm'pøːɐt] adj indignant (**über** acc at), shocked (at)

Em'pörung f (-; no pl) indignation

emsig ['ɛmzɪç] adj busy

'Emsigkeit f (-; no pl) activity

Ende ['ɛndə] n (-s; no pl) end; film: ending; **am Ende** at the end; in the end, finally; **zu Ende** over; time: up; **zu Ende gehen** come to an end; **zu Ende lesen** finish reading; **er ist Ende zwanzig** he is in his late twenties; **Ende Mai** at the end of May; **Ende der achtziger Jahre** in the late eighties; radio: **Ende!** over!

'enden v/i (ge-, h) (come to an) end; stop, finish; F **enden als** end up as

'Endergebnis n final result

'endgültig adj final, definitive

Endlagerung ['ɛnt-] f final disposal (of

radioactive waste)

'endlich adv finally, at last

'endlos adj endless

'Endrunde f, **Endspiel** n SPORT final(s)

Endspurt m SPORT final spurt (a. fig)

Endstati‚on f RAIL terminus, terminal

Endsumme f (sum) total

'Endung f (-; -en) LING ending

Energie [enɛr'giː] f (-; -n) energy; TECH, ELECTR power; **Energiesparen** n energy saving, conservation of energy

ener'giebewusst adj energy-conscious

Ener'giekrise f energy crisis

ener'gielos adj lacking in energy

Ener'giequelle f source of energy

Energieversorgung f power supply

energisch [e'nɛrgɪʃ] adj energetic, vigorous

eng [ɛŋ] adj narrow; tight; cramped; fig close; **eng beieinander** close(ly) together

Engagement [ãgaʒə'mãː] n (-s; -s) THEA etc engagement; POL commitment

engagieren [ãga'ʒiːrən] v/t (no -ge-, h) engage; **sich engagieren für** be very involved in

engagiert [ãga'ʒiːɐt] adj involved, committed

Enge ['ɛŋə] f (-; no pl) narrowness; cramped conditions; **in die Enge treiben** drive into a corner

Engel ['ɛŋəl] m (-s; -) angel

'England England

Engländer ['ɛŋlɛndɐ] m (-s; -) Englishman; **die Engländer** pl the English

Engländerin ['ɛŋlɛndərɪn] f (-; -nen) Englishwoman

'englisch adj English; **auf Englisch** in English

'Englischunterricht m English lesson(s) or class(es); teaching of English

'Engpass m bottleneck (a. fig)

'engstirnig [-ʃtɪrnɪç] adj narrow-minded

Enkel ['ɛŋkəl] m (-s; -) grandchild; grandson

'Enkelin f (-; -nen) granddaughter

enorm [e'nɔrm] adj enormous; F terrific

Ensemble [ã'sãːbl] n (-s; -s) THEA company; cast

entarten [ɛntʔ'aːɐtən] v/i (no -ge-, sein), **ent'artet** adj degenerate

Ent'artung f (-; -en) degeneration

entbehren [ɛnt'beːrən] v/t (no -ge-, h) do without; spare; miss

entbehrlich [ɛnt'beːɐlɪç] adj dispensable; superfluous

Ent'behrung f (-; -en) want, privation

ent'binden (irr, **binden**, no -ge-, h) **1.** v/i MED have the baby; **2.** v/t: **j-n entbinden**

von fig relieve s.o. of; *entbunden werden von* MED give birth to

Ent'bindung *f* (-; -en) MED delivery

Ent'bindungsstati,on *f* MED maternity ward

entblößen [ɛnt'blø:sən] *v/t* (*no -ge-, h*) bare, uncover

ent'decken *v/t* (*no -ge-, h*) discover

Ent'decker *m* (-s; -), **Ent'deckerin** *f* (-; -nen) discoverer

Ent'deckung *f* (-; -en) discovery

Ente ['ɛntə] *f* (-; -n) ZO duck; F *fig* hoax

ent'ehren *v/t* (*no -ge-, h*) dishono(u)r

enteignen [ɛnt'ʔaignən] *v/t* (*no -ge-, h*) expropriate; dispossess *s.o.*

Ent'eignung *f* (-; -en) expropriation; dispossession

ent'erben *v/t* (*no -ge-, h*) disinherit

entern ['ɛntɐn] *v/t* (*ge-, h*) MAR board

entfachen [ɛnt'faxən] *v/t* (*no -ge-, h*) kindle, *fig a.* rouse

entfallen *v/i* (*irr, fallen, no -ge-, sein*) be cancelled; *entfallen auf* (*acc*) fall to s.o. ('s share); *es ist mir entfallen* it has slipped my memory

entfalten *v/t* (*no -ge-, h*) unfold; *fig* develop; *sich entfalten* unfold; *fig* develop (*zu* into)

entfernen [ɛnt'fɛrnən] *v/t* (*no -ge-, h*) remove (*a. fig*); *sich entfernen* leave

ent'fernt *adj* distant (*a. fig*); *weit* (*zehn Meilen*) *entfernt* far (10 miles) away

Ent'fernung *f* (-; -en) distance; removal

Ent'fernungsmesser *m* (-s; -) PHOT range finder

ent'flammbar *adj* (in)flammable

entfremden [ɛnt'frɛmdən] *v/t* (*no -ge-, h*) estrange (*dat* from)

Ent'fremdung *f* (-; -en) estrangement, alienation

ent'führen *v/t* (*no -ge-, h*) kidnap; AVIAT hijack

Ent'führer *m* (-s; -) kidnapper; AVIAT hijacker

Ent'führung *f* (-; -en) kidnapping; AVIAT hijacking

ent'gegen *prp* (*dat*) *and adv* contrary to; toward(s)

entgegengehen *v/i* (*irr, gehen, sep, -ge-, sein*) go to meet

ent'gegengesetzt *adj* opposite

ent'gegenkommen *v/i* (*irr, kommen, sep, -ge-, sein*) come to meet; *fig j-m entgegenkommen* meet s.o. halfway

entgegenkommend *fig adj* obliging

ent'gegennehmen *v/t* (*irr, nehmen, sep, -ge-, h*) accept, receive

entgegensehen *v/i* (*irr, sehen, sep, -ge-, h*) await; look forward to *s.th.*

entgegensetzen *v/t* (*sep, -ge-, h*) *j-m Widerstand entgegensetzen* put up resistance to s.o.

entgegentreten *v/i* (*irr, treten, sep, -ge-, sein*) walk towards; oppose; face

entgegnen [ɛnt'ge:gnən] *v/i* (*no -ge-, h*) reply, answer; retort

Ent'gegnung *f* (-; -en) reply; retort

ent'gehen *v/i* (*irr, gehen, no -ge-, sein*) escape; miss

entgeistert [ɛnt'gaistɐt] *adj* aghast

Entgelt [ɛnt'gɛlt] *n* (-[e]s; -e) remuneration; fee

entgiften [ɛnt'gɪftən] *v/t* (*no -ge-, h*) decontaminate

entgleisen [ɛnt'glaizən] *v/i* (*no -ge-, sein*) RAIL be derailed; *fig* blunder

ent'gleiten *fig v/i* (*irr, gleiten, no -ge-, sein*) get out of control

entgräten [ɛnt'grɛ:tən] *v/t* (*no -ge-, h*) bone, fil(l)et

ent'halten *v/t* (*irr, halten, no -ge-, h*) contain, hold; include; *sich enthalten* (*gen*) abstain *or* refrain from

ent'haltsam *adj* abstinent; moderate

Ent'haltsamkeit *f* (-; *no pl*) abstinence; moderation

Ent'haltung *f* (-; -en) abstention

ent'härten *v/t* (*no -ge-, h*) soften

enthaupten [ɛnt'hauptən] *v/t* (*no -ge-, h*) behead, decapitate

ent'hüllen *v/t* (*no -ge-, h*) uncover; unveil; *fig* reveal, disclose

Ent'hüllung *f* (-; -en) unveiling; *fig* revelation, disclosure

Enthusiasmus [ɛntu'zjasmʊs] *m* (-; *no pl*) enthusiasm

Enthusiast(in) [-'zjast(-ɪn)] (-en, -en/-; -nen) enthusiast; *film,* SPORT F fan

enthusi'astisch *adj* enthusiastic

ent'kleiden *v/t and v/refl* (*no -ge-, h*) undress, strip

ent'kommen *v/i* (*irr, kommen, no -ge-, sein*) escape (*dat* from)

ent'korken *v/t* (*no -ge-, h*) uncork

entkräften [ɛnt'krɛftən] *v/t* (*no -ge-, h*) weaken (*a. fig*)

Ent'kräftung *f* (-; -en) weakening, exhaustion

ent'laden *v/t* (*irr, laden, no -ge-, h*) unload; *esp* ELECTR discharge; *sich entladen esp* ELECTR discharge; *fig* explode

Ent'ladung *f* (-; -en) unloading; *esp* ELECTR discharge; *fig* explosion

ent'lang *prp* (*dat*) *and adv* along; *hier entlang, bitte!* this way, please!; *die Straße etc entlang* along the street *etc*

entlarven [ɛnt'larfən] *v/t* (*no -ge-, h*) unmask, expose

E

ent'lassen v/t (*irr*, **lassen**, *no -ge-, h*) dismiss, F fire, give *s.o.* the sack; MED discharge; JUR release

Ent'lassung f (-; -en) dismissal; MED discharge; JUR release

ent'lasten v/t (*no -ge-, h*) relieve *s.o.* of some of his work; JUR exonerate, clear *s.o.* of a charge; **den Verkehr entlasten** relieve the traffic congestion

Ent'lastung f (-; -en) relief; JUR exoneration

Ent'lastungszeuge m JUR witness for the defense (*Br* defence)

ent'laufen v/i (*irr*, **laufen**, *no -ge-, sein*) run away (*dat* from)

ent'legen adj remote, distant

ent'locken v/t (*no -ge-, h*) draw, elicit (*dat* from)

ent'lohnen v/t (*no -ge-, h*) pay (off)

ent'lüften v/t (*no -ge-, h*) ventilate

entmachten [ɛnt'maxtən] v/t (*no -ge-, h*) deprive *s.o.* of *his* power

entmilitarisieren [ɛntmilitari'ziːrən] v/t (*no -ge-, h*) demilitarize

entmündigen [ɛnt'mʏndɪgən] v/t (*no -ge-, h*) JUR place under disability

entmutigen [ɛnt'muːtɪgən] v/t (*no -ge-, h*) discourage

ent'nehmen v/t (*irr*, **nehmen**, *no -ge-, h*) take (*dat* from); **entnehmen aus** (with-)- draw from; *fig* gather *or* learn from

ent'puppen v/refl (*no -ge-, h*) **sich entpuppen als** turn out to be

ent'rahmen v/t (*no -ge-, h*) skim

ent'reißen v/t (*irr*, **reißen**, *no -ge-, h*) snatch (away) (*dat* from)

ent'rinnen v/i (*irr*, **rinnen**, *no -ge-, sein*) escape (*dat* from)

ent'rollen v/t (*no -ge-, h*) unroll

ent'rüsten v/t (*no -ge-, h*) fill with indignation; **sich entrüsten** become indignant (**über** acc at *s.th.*, with *s.o.*)

ent'rüstet adj indignant (**über** acc at *s.th.*, with *s.o.*;) **Ent'rüstung** f (-; -en) indignation

Entsafter [ɛnt'zaftɐ] m (-s; -) juice extractor

ent'salzen v/t (*no -ge-, h*) desalinize

ent'schädigen v/t (*no -ge-, h*) compensate

Ent'schädigung f (-; -en) compensation

ent'schärfen v/t (*no -ge-, h*) defuse (*a. fig*)

ent'scheiden v/t and v/i and v/refl (*irr*, **scheiden**, *no -ge-, h*) decide (**für** on, in favo[u]r of; **gegen** against); settle; **er kann sich nicht entscheiden** he can't make up his mind

entscheidend adj decisive; crucial

Ent'scheidung f (-; -en) decision

entschieden [ɛnt'ʃiːdən] adj decided, determined, resolute; **entschieden dafür** strongly in favo(u)r of it

Ent'schiedenheit f (-; *no pl*) determination

ent'schließen v/refl (*irr*, **schließen**, *no -ge-, h*) decide, determine, make up one's mind

Ent'schließung f (-; -en) POL resolution

entschlossen [ɛnt'ʃlɔsən] adj determined, resolute

Ent'schlossenheit f (-; *no pl*) determination, resoluteness

Ent'schluss m decision, resolution

entschlüsseln [ɛnt'ʃlʏsəln] v/t (*no -ge-, h*) decipher, decode

entschuldigen [ɛnt'ʃʊldɪgən] v/t (*no -ge-, h*) excuse; **sich entschuldigen** apologize (**bei** to; **für** for); excuse o.s.; **entschuldigen Sie!** (I'm) sorry!; excuse me!

Ent'schuldigung f (-; -en) excuse; apology; **um Entschuldigung bitten** apologize; **Entschuldigung!** (I'm) sorry!; excuse me!

ent'setzen v/t (*no -ge-, h*) shock; horrify

Ent'setzen n (-s; *no pl*) horror, terror

ent'setzlich adj horrible, dreadful, terrible; atrocious

ent'setzt adj shocked; horrified

ent'sichern v/t (*no -ge-, h*) release the safety catch of

ent'sinnen v/refl (*irr*, **sinnen**, *no -ge-, h*) remember, recall

ent'sorgen v/t (*no -ge-, h*) dispose of

Ent'sorgung f (-; -en) (waste) disposal

ent'spannen v/t and v/refl (*no -ge-, h*) relax; **sich entspannen** a. take it easy; *fig* ease (up)

ent'spannt adj relaxed

Ent'spannung f (-; -en) relaxation; POL détente

ent'spiegelt adj OPT non-glare

ent'sprechen v/i (*irr*, **sprechen**, *no -ge-, h*) correspond to; answer to *a description*; meet (*requirements etc*)

entsprechend adj corresponding (*dat* to); appropriate

Ent'sprechung f (-; -en) equivalent

ent'springen v/i (*irr*, **springen**, *no -ge-, sein*) *river*: rise

entstehen v/i (*irr*, **stehen**, *no -ge-, sein*) come into being; arise; emerge, develop; **entstehen aus** originate from

Ent'stehung f (-; -en) origin

ent'stellen v/t (*no -ge-, h*) disfigure, deform; *fig* distort

Ent'stellung f (-; -en) disfigurement, deformation, distortion (*a. fig*)

entstört [ɛnt'ʃtøːɐt] adj ELECTR interference-free

ent'täuschen *v/t* (*no -ge-, h*) disappoint

Ent'täuschung *f* (-; *-en*) disappointment

entwaffnen [ɛnt'vafnən] *v/t* (*no -ge-, h*) disarm

Ent'warnung *f* all clear (signal)

ent'wässern *v/t* (*no -ge-, h*) drain

Ent'wässerung *f* (-; *-en*) drainage; CHEM dehydration

'entweder *cj*: **entweder ... oder** either ... or

ent'weichen *v/i* (*irr*, **weichen**, *no -ge-, sein*) escape (**aus** from)

ent'weihen *v/t* (*no -ge-, h*) desecrate

ent'wenden *v/t* (*no -ge-, h*) pilfer, steal

ent'werfen *v/t* (*irr*, **werfen**, *no -ge-, h*) design; draw up

ent'werten *v/t* (*no -ge-, h*) lower the value of (*a. fig*); cancel

Ent'wertung *f* (-; *-en*) devaluation; cancellation

ent'wickeln *v/t and v/refl* (*no -ge-, h*) develop (*a.* PHOT) (**zu** into)

Ent'wicklung *f* (-; *-en*) development, BIOL *a.* evolution; adolescence, age of puberty

Ent'wicklungshelfer *m*, **Entwicklungshelferin** *f* POL, ECON development aid volunteer; Peace Corps volunteer, *Br* VSO worker

Entwicklungshilfe *f* development aid

Entwicklungsland *n* POL developing country

entwirren [ɛnt'vɪrən] *v/t* (*no -ge-, h*) disentangle (*a. fig*)

ent'wischen *v/i* (*no -ge-, sein*) get away

ent'würdigend *adj* degrading

Ent'wurf *m* outline, (rough) draft, plan; design; sketch

ent'wurzeln *v/t* (*no -ge-, h*) uproot

ent'ziehen *v/t* (*irr*, **ziehen**, *no -ge-, h*) take away (*dat* from); revoke (*license etc*); deprive of *rights etc*; CHEM extract; **sich j-m (e-r Sache) entziehen** evade s.o. (s.th.)

Ent'ziehungsanstalt *f* substance (*Br* drug) abuse clinic

Entziehungskur *f* detoxi(fi)cation (treatment), *a.* F drying out

entziffern [ɛnt'tsɪfɐn] *v/t* (*no -ge-, h*) decipher, make out

ent'zücken *v/t* (*no -ge-, h*) charm, delight

Ent'zücken *n* (*-s; no pl*) delight

ent'zückend *adj* delightful, charming, F sweet

ent'zückt *adj* delighted (**über** *acc*, **von** at, with)

Ent'zug *m* withdrawal; revocation

Ent'zugserscheinung *f* MED withdrawal symptom

entzündbar [ɛnt'tsʏntbaːɐ] *adj* (in-)

flammable

ent'zünden *v/refl* (*no -ge-, h*) catch fire; MED become inflamed

Ent'zündung *f* (-; *-en*) MED inflammation

ent'zwei *adv* in two, to pieces

Enzyklopädie [ɛntsyklopɛ'diː] *f* (-; *-n*) encyclop(a)edia

Epidemie [epide'miː] *f* (-; *-n*) MED epidemic (disease)

Epilog [epi'loːk] *m* (-[*e*]*s*; *-e* [epi'loːgə]) epilog, *Br* epilogue

episch ['eːpɪʃ] *adj* epic

Episode [epi'zoːdə] *f* (-; *-n*) episode

Epoche [e'pɔxə] *f* (-; *-n*) epoch, period, era

Epos ['eːpɔs] *n* (-; *Epen* ['eːpən]) epic (poem)

er [eːɐ] *pers pron* he; it

Er'achten *n*: **meines Erachtens** in my opinion

Erbanlage ['ɛrp-] *f* BIOL genes, genetic code

erbarmen [ɛɐ'barmən] *v/refl* (*no -ge-, h*) **sich j-s erbarmen** take pity on s.o.

erbärmlich [ɛɐ'bɛrmlɪç] *adj* pitiful, pitiable; miserable; mean

er'barmungslos *adj* pitiless, merciless

er'bauen *v/t* (*no -ge-, h*) build, construct

Er'bauer *m* (-*s*; -) builder, constructor

er'baulich *adj* edifying

Er'bauung *fig f* (-; *-en*) edification, uplift

Erbe ['ɛrbə] **1.** *m* (-*n*; *-n*) heir; **2.** *n* (-*s*; *no pl*) inheritance, heritage

erben ['ɛrbən] *v/t* (*ge-, h*) inherit

erbeuten [ɛɐ'bɔytən] *v/t* (*no -ge-, h*) MIL capture; *thief*: get away with

'Erbfaktor *m* BIOL gene

Erbin ['ɛrbɪn] *f* (-; *-nen*) heir, heiress

er'bitten *v/t* (*irr*, **bitten**, *no -ge-, h*) ask for, request

erbittert [ɛɐ'bɪtɐt] *adj* fierce, furious

'Erbkrankheit *f* MED hereditary disease

erblich ['ɛrplɪç] *adj* hereditary

er'blicken *v/t* (*no -ge-, h*) see, catch sight of

erblinden [ɛɐ'blɪndən] *v/i* (*no -ge-, sein*) go blind

er'brechen *v/t and v/refl* (*irr*, **brechen**, *no -ge-, h*) MED vomit

Erbschaft ['ɛrpʃaft] *f* (-; *-en*) inheritance, heritage

Erbse ['ɛrpsə] *f* (-; *-n*) BOT pea; (**grüne**) **Erbsen** green peas

'Erbstück *n* heirloom

Erdapfel ['eːɐt-] *Austrian m* potato

Erdball *m* (-[*e*]*s*; *no pl*) globe

Erdbeben *n* (-*s*; -) earthquake

Erdbeere *f* BOT strawberry

Erdboden *m* earth, ground

Erde ['eːɐdə] *f* (-; *-n*) a) (*no pl*) earth, b) ground, soil; → **eben**

'erden *v/t* (*ge-, h*) ELECTR earth, ground

erdenklich [ɛɐ'dɛŋklɪç] *adj* imaginable

Erdgas ['eːɐt-] *n* natural gas

Erdgeschoss *n*, **Erdgeschoß** *Austrian n* first (*Br* ground) floor

er'dichten *v/t* (*no -ge-, h*) invent, make up

er'dichtet *adj* invented, made-up

erdig ['eːɐdɪç] *adj* earthy

'Erdklumpen *m* clod, lump of earth

Erdkruste *f* earth's crust

Erdkugel *f* globe

Erdkunde *f* (-; *no pl*) geography

Erdleitung *f* ELECTR ground (*Br* earth) connection; underground pipe(line)

Erdnuss *f* BOT peanut

Erdöl *n* (mineral) oil, petroleum

Erdreich *n* ground, earth

erdreisten [ɛɐ'draistən] *v/refl* (*no -ge-, h*) F have the nerve

er'drosseln *v/t* (*no -ge-, h*) throttle

er'drücken *v/t* (*no -ge-, h*) crush (to death)

erdrückend *fig adj* overwhelming

'Erdrutsch *m* (-[*e*]*s*; *-e*) landslide (*a.* POL)

Erdteil *m* GEOGR continent

er'dulden *v/t* (*no -ge-, h*) suffer, endure

'Erdumlaufbahn *f* earth orbit

'Erdung *f* (-; *-en*) ELECTR grounding, *Br* earthing

'Erdwärme *f* GEOL geothermal energy

er'eifern *v/refl* (*no -ge-, h*) get excited

ereignen [ɛɐ'ʔaignən] *v/refl* (*no -ge-, h*) happen, occur

Ereignis [ɛɐ'ʔaignɪs] *n* (-*ses*; *-se*) event, occurrence

er'eignisreich *adj* eventful

Erektion [erɛk'tsjoːn] *f* (-; *-en*) erection

Eremit [ere'miːt] *m* (-*en*; *-en*) hermit, anchorite

er'fahren[1] *v/t* (*irr*, **fahren**, *no -ge-, h*) hear; learn; experience

er'fahren[2] *adj* experienced

Er'fahrung *f* (-; *-en*) (work) experience

Er'fahrungsaustausch *m* exchange of experience

er'fahrungsgemäß *adv* as experience shows

er'fassen *v/t* (*no -ge-, h*) grasp; record, register; cover, include; EDP collect

er'finden *v/t* (*irr*, **finden**, *no -ge-, h*) invent

Er'finder(in) (-*s*; -/-; *-nen*) inventor

erfinderisch [ɛɐ'fɪndərɪʃ] *adj* inventive

Er'findung *f* (-; *-en*) invention

Er'findungskraft *f* (-; *no pl*) inventiveness

Erfolg [ɛɐ'fɔlk] *m* (-[*e*]*s*; *-e*) success; result; **viel Erfolg!** good luck!; **Erfolg versprechend** promising

er'folgen *v/i* (*no -ge-, sein*) happen, take place

er'folglos *adj* unsuccessful; futile

Er'folglosigkeit *f* (-; *no pl*) lack of success

er'folgreich *adj* successful

Er'folgserlebnis *n* sense of achievement

erforderlich [ɛɐ'fɔrdɐlɪç] *adj* necessary, required

er'fordern *v/t* (*no -ge-, h*) require, demand

Erfordernis [ɛɐ'fɔrdɐnɪs] *n* (-*ses*; *-se*) requirement, demand

er'forschen *v/t* (*no -ge-, h*) explore; investigate, study

Er'forscher *m* explorer

Er'forschung *f* exploration

er'freuen *v/t* (*no -ge-, h*) please

erfreulich [ɛɐ'frɔylɪç] *adj* pleasing, pleasant; gratifying

er'freut *adj* pleased (**über** *acc* at, about); **sehr erfreut!** pleased to meet you

er'frieren *v/i* (*irr*, **frieren**, *no -ge-, sein*) freeze to death

Er'frierung *f* (-; *-en*) MED frostbite

er'frischen *v/t and v/refl* (*no -ge-, h*) refresh (o.s.)

erfrischend *adj* refreshing

Er'frischung *f* (-; *-en*) refreshment

erfroren [ɛɐ'froːrən] *adj* frostbitten; BOT killed by frost

er'füllen *fig v/t* (*no -ge-, h*) fulfil(l); keep (*promise etc*); serve (*purpose etc*); meet (*requirements etc*); **erfüllen mit** fill with; **sich erfüllen** be fulfilled, come true

Er'füllung *f* (-; *-en*) fulfil(l)ment; **in Erfüllung gehen** come true

ergänzen [ɛɐ'gɛntsən] *v/t* (*no -ge-, h*) complement (**einander** each other); supplement, add

ergänzend *adj* complementary, supplementary

Er'gänzung *f* (-; *-en*) completion; supplement, addition

ergattern [ɛɐ'gatɐn] F *v/t* (*no -ge-, h*) (manage to) get hold of

er'geben (*irr*, **geben**, *no -ge-, h*) **1.** *v/t* amount *or* come to; **2.** *v/refl* surrender; *fig* arise; **sich ergeben aus** result from; **sich ergeben in** (*acc*) resign o.s. to

Er'gebenheit *f* (-; *no pl*) devotion

Ergebnis [ɛɐ'geːpnɪs] *n* (-*ses*; *-se*) result, SPORT *a.* score; outcome

er'gebnislos *adj* without result

er'gehen *v/i* (*irr*, **gehen**, *no -ge-, sein*) *order etc*: be issued (**an** *acc* to); **wie ist es dir ergangen?** how did things go with you?; **et. über sich ergehen lassen** (patiently) endure s.th.

ergiebig [ɛɐ'giːbɪç] *adj* productive, rich

Er'giebigkeit *f* (-; *no pl*) (high) yield; productiveness er'gießen *v/refl* (*irr*, **gießen**, *no -ge-*, *h*) **sich ergießen über** (*acc*) pour down on

er'grauen *v/i* (*no -ge-*, *sein*) turn gray (*Br* grey)

er'greifen *v/t* (*irr*, **greifen**, *no -ge-*, *h*) seize, grasp, take hold of; take (*measures etc*); take up; *fig* move, touch

ergriffen [ɛɐˈgrɪfən] *fig adj* moved

Er'griffenheit *f* (*-*; *no pl*) emotion

er'gründen *v/t* (*no -ge-*, *h*) find out, fathom

er'haben *adj* raised, elevated; *fig* sublime; **erhaben sein über** (*acc*) be above

er'halten[1] *v/t* (*irr*, **halten**, *no -ge-*, *h*) get, receive; keep, preserve; protect; support, maintain (*family etc*)

er'halten[2] *adj*: **gut erhalten** in good condition

erhältlich [ɛɐˈhɛltlɪç] *adj* obtainable, available

Er'haltung *f* (*-*; *no pl*) preservation; upkeep

er'hängen *v/t* (*no -ge-*, *h*) hang (**sich** o.s.)

er'heben *v/t* (*irr*, **heben**, *no -ge-*, *h*) raise (*a. voice*), lift; **sich erheben** rise up (**gegen** against)

erheblich [ɛɐˈheːplɪç] *adj* considerable

Er'hebung *f* (*-*; *-en*) survey; revolt

erheitern [ɛɐˈhaitɐn] *v/t* (*no -ge-*, *h*) cheer up, amuse

erhellen [ɛɐˈhɛlən] *v/t* (*no -ge-*, *h*) light up; *fig* throw light upon

erhitzen [ɛɐˈhɪtsən] *v/t* (*no -ge-*, *h*) heat; **sich erhitzen** get hot

er'hoffen *v/t* (*no -ge-*, *h*) hope for

erhöhen [ɛɐˈhøːən] *v/t* (*no -ge-*, *h*) raise; increase

Er'höhung *f* (*-*; *-en*) increase

er'holen *v/refl* (*no -ge-*, *h*) recover; relax, rest

erholsam [ɛɐˈhoːlzaːm] *adj* restful, relaxing

Er'holung *f* (*-*; *no pl*) recovery; relaxation

Er'holungsheim *n* rest home

erinnern [ɛɐˈʔɪnɐn] *v/t* (*no -ge-*, *h*) **j-n erinnern an** (*acc*) remind s.o. of; **sich erinnern an** (*acc*) remember, recall

Erinnerung [ɛɐˈɪnərʊŋ] *f* (*-*; *-en*) memory (**an** *acc* of); remembrance, souvenir; keepsake; **zur Erinnerung an** (*acc*) in memory of

erkalten [ɛɐˈkaltən] *v/i* (*no -ge-*, *sein*) cool down (*a. fig*)

erkälten [ɛɐˈkɛltən] *v/refl* (*no -ge-*, *h*) **sich erkälten** catch (a) cold; (**stark**) **erkältet sein** have a (bad) cold

Er'kältung *f* (*-*; *-en*) cold

erkennbar [ɛɐˈkɛnbaːɐ] *adj* recognizable

er'kennen *v/t* (*irr*, **kennen**, *no -ge-*, *h*) recognize (**an** *dat* by), know (by); see, realize

er'kenntlich *adj*: **sich** (**j-m**) **erkenntlich zeigen** show (s.o.) one's gratitude

Er'kenntnis *f* (*-*; *-se*) realization; discovery; *pl* findings

Er'kennungsdienst *m* (police) records department

Erkennungsmelo,die *f* signature tune

Erkennungszeichen *n* badge; AVIAT markings

Erker ['ɛrkɐ] *m* (*-s*; *-*) ARCH bay

Erkerfenster *n* ARCH bay window

er'klären *v/t* (*no -ge-*, *h*) explain (**j-m** to s.o.); declare; **j-n** (*offiziell*) **für ... erklären** pronounce s.o. ...

erklärend *adj* explanatory

erklärlich [ɛɐˈklɛːɐlɪç] *adj* explainable

er'klärt *adj* declared

Er'klärung *f* (*-*; *-en*) explanation; declaration; definition; **e-e Erklärung abgeben** make a statement

er'klingen *v/i* (*irr*, **klingen**, *no -ge-*, *sein*) (re)sound, ring (out)

erkranken [ɛɐˈkraŋkən] *v/i* (*no -ge-*, *sein*) fall ill, get sick; **erkranken an** (*dat*) get

Er'krankung *f* (*-*; *-en*) illness, sickness

erkunden [ɛɐˈkʊndən] *v/t* (*no -ge-*, *h*) explore

erkundigen [ɛɐˈkʊndɪgən] *v/refl* (*no -ge-*, *h*) inquire (**nach** about s.th.; after s.o.); make inquiries (about); **sich** (**bei j-m**) **nach dem Weg erkundigen** ask (s.o.) the way

Er'kundigung *f* (*-*; *-en*) inquiry

Er'kundung *f* (*-*; *-en*) exploration; MIL reconnaissance

Erlagschein [ɛɐˈlaːk-] *Austrian m* money-order form

er'lahmen *v/i* (*no -ge-*, *sein*) flag

Erlass [ɛɐˈlas] *m* (*-es*; *-e*) decree; JUR remission

er'lassen *v/t* (*irr*, **lassen**, *no -ge-*, *h*) issue; enact (*bill etc*); **j-m et. erlassen** release s.o. from s.th.

erlauben [ɛɐˈlaubən] *v/t* (*no -ge-*, *h*) allow, permit; **sich et. erlauben** permit o.s. (*or* dare) to do s.th.; treat o.s. to s.th.

Erlaubnis [ɛɐˈlaupnɪs] *f* (*-*; *no pl*) permission; authority; **um Erlaubnis bitten** ask s.o.'s permission

Erlaubnisschein *m* permit

erläutern [ɛɐˈlɔytɐn] *v/t* (*no -ge-*, *h*) explain, illustrate

Er'läuterung *f* (*-*; *-en*) explanation; annotation

Erle ['ɛrlə] *f* (*-*; *-n*) BOT alder

er'leben *v/t* (*no -ge-*, *h*) experience; go through; see; have; **das werden wir**

E

nicht mehr erleben we won't live to see that

Erlebnis [ɛɐ'leːpnɪs] *n* (*-ses*; *-se*) experience; adventure

er'lebnisreich *adj* eventful

erledigen [ɛɐ'leːdɪɡən] *v/t* (*no -ge-*, *h*) take care of, do, handle; settle; F finish *s.o.* (*a.* SPORT); do *s.o.* in

erledigt [ɛɐ'leːdɪçt] *adj* finished, settled; F worn out; F *der ist erledigt!* he is done for

Er'ledigung *f* (*-*; *-en*) a) (*no pl*) settlement, b) *pl* things to do, shopping

er'legen *v/t* (*no -ge-*, *h*) HUNT shoot

erleichtern [ɛɐ'laɪçtɐn] *v/t* (*no -ge-*, *h*) ease, relieve

er'leichtert *adj* relieved

Er'leichterung [-təroŋ] *f* (*-*; *no pl*) relief (*über acc* at)

er'leiden *v/t* (*irr*, *leiden*, *no -ge-*, *h*) suffer

er'lesen *adj* choice, select

er'leuchten *v/t* (*no -ge-*, *h*) illuminate

er'liegen *v/i* (*irr*, *liegen*, *no -ge-*, *sein*) succumb to

Er'liegen *n*: *zum Erliegen kommen* (*bringen*) come (bring) to a standstill

erlogen [ɛɐ'loːɡən] *adj* false; *erlogen sein* be a lie

Erlös [ɛɐ'løːs] *m* (*-es*; *-e*) proceeds; profit(s)

erlosch [ɛɐ'lɔʃ] *pret of* **erlöschen**

erloschen [ɛɐ'lɔʃən] **1.** *pp of* **erlöschen**; **2.** *adj* extinct (*volcano*)

er'löschen *v/i* (*irr*, *no -ge-*, *sein*) go out; *fig* die; JUR lapse, expire

er'lösen *v/t* (*no -ge-*, *h*) deliver, free (*both*: *von* from)

Erlöser [ɛɐ'løːzɐ] *m* (*-s*; *no pl*) REL Savio(u)r

Er'lösung *f* (*-*; *no pl*) REL salvation; relief

ermächtigen [ɛɐ'mɛçtɪɡən] *v/t* (*no -ge-*, *h*) authorize

Er'mächtigung *f* (*-*; *-en*) authorization; authority

er'mahnen *v/t* (*no -ge-*, *h*) admonish; reprove, warn (*a.* SPORT)

Er'mahnung *f* (*-*; *-en*) admonition; warning; *esp* SPORT (first) caution

Er'mangelung *f*: *in Ermangelung* (*gen*) for want of

ermäßigt [ɛɐ'mɛːsɪçt] *adj* reduced, cut

Er'mäßigung *f* (*-*; *-en*) reduction, cut

er'messen *v/t* (*irr*, *messen*, *no -ge-*, *h*) assess; judge

Er'messen *n* (*-s*; *no pl*) discretion; *nach eigenem Ermessen* at one's own discretion

er'mitteln (*no -ge-*, *h*) **1.** *v/t* find out; determine; **2.** *v/i esp* JUR investigate

Er'mittlung *f* (*-*; *-en*) finding; JUR investigation

er'möglichen *v/t* (*no -ge-*, *h*) make possible

er'morden *v/t* (*no -ge-*, *h*) murder; *esp* POL assassinate

Er'mordung *f* (*-*; *-en*) murder; *esp* POL assassination

ermüden [ɛɐ'myːdən] (*no -ge-*) **1.** *v/t* (*h*) tire, fatigue; **2.** *v/i* (*sein*) tire, get tired, fatigue (*a.* TECH)

Er'müdung *f* (*-*; *no pl*) fatigue, tiredness

er'muntern [ɛɐ'mʊntɐn] *v/t* (*no -ge-*, *h*) encourage; stimulate

Er'munterung *f* (*-*; *-en*) encouragement; incentive

ermutigen [ɛɐ'muːtɪɡən] *v/t* (*no -ge-*, *h*) encourage

ermutigend *adj* encouraging

Er'mutigung *f* (*-*; *-en*) encouragement

er'nähren *v/t* (*no -ge-*, *h*) feed; support (*family etc*); *sich ernähren von* live on

Er'nährer *m* (*-s*; *-*) breadwinner, supporter

Er'nährung *f* (*-*; *no pl*) nutrition, food, diet

er'nennen *v/t* (*irr*, *nennen*, *no -ge-*, *h*) *j-n ernennen zu* appoint s.o. (to be)

Er'nennung *f* (*-*; *-en*) appointment

erneuern [ɛɐ'nɔʏɐn] *v/t* (*no -ge-*, *h*) renew

Er'neuerung *f* (*-*; *-en*) renewal

er'neut 1. *adj* renewed **2.** *adv* once more

erniedrigen [ɛɐ'niːdrɪɡən] *v/t* (*no -ge-*, *h*) humiliate; *sich erniedrigen* degrade o.s.

Er'niedrigung *f* (*-*; *-en*) humiliation

ernst [ɛrnst] *adj* serious, earnest; *ernst nehmen* take *s.o. or s.th.* seriously

Ernst *m* (*-es*; *no pl*) seriousness, earnest; *im Ernst*(?) seriously(?); *ist das dein Ernst?* are you serious?

'ernsthaft, **'ernstlich** *adj* serious

Ernte ['ɛrntə] *f* (*-*; *-n*) harvest; crop(s)

'Erntedankfest *n* Thanksgiving (Day), *Br* harvest festival

'ernten *v/t* (*ge-*, *h*) harvest, reap (*a. fig*)

er'nüchtern *v/t* (*no -ge-*, *h*) sober, *fig a.* disillusion

Er'nüchterung *f* (*-*; *-en*) sobering up; *fig* disillusionment

Eroberer [ɛɐ'ʔoːbərɐ] *m* (*-s*; *-*) conqueror

erobern [ɛɐ'ʔoːbɐn] *v/t* (*no -ge-*, *h*) conquer

Er'oberung *f* (*-*; *-en*) conquest (*a. fig*)

er'öffnen *v/t* (*no -ge-*, *h*) open; inaugurate; disclose *s.th.* (*j-m* to s.o.)

Er'öffnung *f* (*-*; *-en*) opening; inauguration; disclosure

erörtern [ɛɐ'ʔœrtɐn] *v/t* (*no -ge-*, *h*) discuss

Er'örterung *f* (-; -*en*) discussion

Erotik [e'roːtɪk] *f* (-; *no pl*) eroticism

erotisch [e'roːtɪʃ] *adj* erotic

er'pressen *v/t* (*no -ge-, h*) blackmail; extort

Er'presser(in) (-*s*; -/-; -*nen*) blackmailer

Er'pressung *f* (-; -*en*) blackmail(ing); extortion

er'proben *v/t* (*no -ge-, h*) try, test

er'raten *v/t* (*irr,* **raten**, *no -ge-, h*) guess

er'rechnen *v/t* (*no -ge-, h*) calculate, work *s.th.* out

erregbar [ɛɐ'reːkbaːɐ] *adj* excitable; irritable

er'regen *v/t* (*no -ge-, h*) excite, *sexually:* a. arouse; *fig* rouse; cause; **sich erregen** get excited

erregend *adj* exciting, thrilling

Er'reger *m* (-*s*; -) MED germ, virus

Er'regung *f* (-; -*en*) excitement

erreichbar [ɛɐ'raiçbaːɐ] *adj* within reach (*a. fig*); available; **leicht erreichbar** within easy reach; **nicht erreichbar** out of reach; not available

er'reichen *v/t* (*no -ge-, h*) reach; catch (*train etc*); **es erreichen, dass ...** succeed in *doing s.th.*; *et.* **erreichen** get somewhere; **telefonisch zu erreichen sein** have a (*Br* be on the) phone

er'richten *v/t* (*no -ge-, h*) put up, erect; *fig* found, *esp* ECON set up

Er'richtung *f* (-; -*en*) erection; *fig* establishment

er'ringen *v/t* (*irr,* **ringen**, *no -ge-, h*) win, gain; achieve

er'röten *v/i* (*no -ge-, sein*) blush

Errungenschaft [ɛɐ'rʊŋənʃaft] *f* (-; -*en*) achievement; **m-e neueste Errungenschaft** my latest acquisition

Ersatz [ɛɐ'zats] *m* (-*es*; *no pl*) replacement; substitute; surrogate; compensation; damages; **als Ersatz für** in exchange for

Ersatzdienst *m* → **Zivildienst**

Ersatzmann *m* (-[*e*]*s*; -*leute*) substitute (*a.* SPORT)

Ersatzmine *f* refill

Ersatzreifen *m* MOT spare tire (*Br* tyre)

Ersatzspieler *m* SPORT substitute

Ersatzteil *n* TECH spare part

er'schaffen *v/t* (*irr,* **schaffen**, *no -ge-, h*) create

er'schallen *v/i* ([*irr,* **schallen**,] *no -ge-, sein*) (re)sound, ring (out)

er'scheinen *v/i* (*irr,* **scheinen**, *no -ge-, sein*) appear, F turn up; be published

Er'scheinen *n* (-*s*; *no pl*) appearance; publication

Er'scheinung *f* (-; -*en*) appearance; apparition; phenomenon

er'schießen *v/t* (*irr,* **schießen**, *no -ge-, h*) shoot (dead)

erschlaffen [ɛɐ'ʃlafən] *v/i* (*no -ge-, sein*) go limp; *fig* weaken

er'schlagen *v/t* (*irr,* **schlagen**, *no -ge-, h*) kill

er'schließen *v/t* (*irr,* **schließen**, *no -ge-, h*) open up; develop

erschollen [ɛɐ'ʃɔlən] *pp of* **erschallen**

er'schöpfen *v/t* (*no -ge-, h*) exhaust

er'schöpft *adj* exhausted

Er'schöpfung *f* (-; *no pl*) exhaustion

erschrak [ɛɐ'ʃraːk] *pret of* **erschrecken** 2

er'schrecken 1. *v/t* (*no -ge-, h*) frighten, scare; **2.** *v/i* (*irr, no -ge-, sein*) be frightened (**über** *acc* at)

erschreckend *adj* alarming; terrible

erschrocken [ɛɐ'ʃrɔkən] *pp of* **erschrecken** 2

erschüttern [ɛɐ'ʃʏtɐn] *v/t* (*no -ge-, h*) shake; *fig* a. shock; *fig* move

Er'schütterung *f* (-; -*en*) shock (*a. fig*); TECH vibration

erschweren [ɛɐ'ʃveːrən] *v/t* (*no -ge-, h*) make more difficult; aggravate

er'schwindeln *v/t* (*no -ge-, h*) obtain *s.th.* by fraud; (**sich**) *et.* **von j-m erschwindeln** swindle s.o. out of s.th.

er'schwingen *v/t* (*irr,* **schwingen**, *no -ge-, h*) afford

er'schwinglich *adj* within one's means, affordable; reasonable (*price*)

er'sehen *v/t* (*irr,* **sehen**, *no -ge-, h*) see, learn, gather (*all:* **aus** from)

ersetzbar [ɛɐ'zɛtsbaːɐ] *adj* replaceable; reparable

er'setzen *v/t* (*no -ge-, h*) replace (**durch** by); compensate for; **j-m et. ersetzen** reimburse s.o. for s.th.

er'sichtlich *adj* evident, obvious

er'sparen *v/t* (*no -ge-, h*) save; **j-m et. ersparen** spare s.o. s.th.

Ersparnisse [ɛɐ'ʃpaːɐnɪsə] *pl* savings

erst [eːɐst] *adv* first; at first; **erst jetzt** (**gestern**) only now (yesterday); **erst nächste Woche** not before *or* until next week; **es ist erst neun Uhr** it's only nine o'clock; **eben erst** just (now); **erst recht** all the more; **erst recht nicht** even less; → **einmal**

er'starren *v/i* (*no -ge-, sein*) stiffen; *fig* freeze

er'starrt *adj* stiff; numb

erstatten [ɛɐ'ʃtatən] *v/t* (*no -ge-, h*) refund, reimburse (**j-m et.** s.o. for s.th.); **Bericht erstatten** (give a) report (**über** *acc* on); **Anzeige erstatten** report to the police

E

'**Erstaufführung** *f* THEA first night *or* performance, premiere, *film*: *a.* first run

er'**staunen** *v/t* (*no -ge-*, *h*) surprise, astonish

Er'**staunen** *n* (*-s*; *no pl*) surprise, astonishment; *in* **Erstaunen** (*ver*)**setzen** astonish

er'**staunlich** *adj* surprising, astonishing

er'**staunt** *adj* astonished

'**Erstausgabe** *f* first edition

'**erst'beste** *adj* first; any old

'**erste** *adj* first; *auf den ersten Blick* at first sight; *fürs Erste* for the time being; *als Erste*(*r*) first; *zum ersten Mal*(*e*) for the first time; *am Ersten* on the first

er'**stechen** *v/t* (*irr*, *stechen*, *no -ge-*, *h*) stab

'**erstens** *adv* first(ly), in the first place

'**Erstere**: *der* (*die*, *das*) **Erstere** the former

er'**sticken** *v/t* (*no -ge-*, *h*) *and* *v/i* (*sein*) choke, suffocate

Er'**stickung** *f* (*-*; *no pl*) suffocation

'**erstklassig** [-klasıç] *adj* first-class, F *a.* super

erst**malig** [-maːlıç] *adj* first

erst**mals** [-maːls] *adv* for the first time

er'**streben** *v/t* (*no -ge-*, *h*) strive after

er'**strebenswert** *adj* desirable

er'**strecken** *v/refl* (*no -ge-*, *h*) extend, stretch (*bis*, *auf* *acc* to; *über* *acc* over); *sich erstrecken über* (*acc*) *a.* cover

'**Erstschlag** *m* MIL first strike

er'**suchen** *v/t* (*no -ge-*, *h*) request

er'**tappen** *v/t* (*no -ge-*, *h*) catch; → *Tat*

er'**tönen** *v/i* (*no -ge-*, *sein*) (re)sound

Er**trag** [ɛɐ'traːk] *m* (*-[e]s*; *Erträge* [ɛɐ'trɛːgə]) AGR yield, produce, TECH *a.* output; ECON proceeds, returns

er'**tragen** *v/t* (*irr*, *tragen*, *no -ge-*, *h*) bear, endure; stand

er**träglich** [ɛɐ'trɛːklıç] *adj* bearable, tolerable

er'**tränken** *v/t* (*no -ge-*, *h*) drown

er'**trinken** *v/i* (*irr*, *trinken*, *no -ge-*, *sein*) drown

er**übrigen** [ɛɐ'ʔyːbrıgən] *v/t* (*no -ge-*, *h*) spare; *sich erübrigen* be unnecessary

er'**wachen** *v/i* (*no -ge-*, *sein*) wake (up); *esp fig* awake, awaken

Erw. ABBR *of* **Erwachsene**(*r*) adult(s)

er'**wachsen**[1] *v/i* (*irr*, *wachsen*, *no -ge-*, *sein*) arise (*aus* from)

er'**wachsen**[2] *adj* grown-up, adult

Er'**wachsene** *m*, *f* (*-n*; *-n*) adult; *nur für Erwachsene!* adults only!

Er'**wachsenenbildung** *f* adult education

er**wägen** [ɛɐ'vɛːgən] *v/t* (*irr*, *wägen*, *no -ge-*, *h*) consider, think *s.th.* over

Er'**wägung** *f* (*-*; *-en*) consideration; *in Erwägung ziehen* take into consideration

er**wähnen** [ɛɐ'vɛːnən] *v/t* (*no -ge-*, *h*) mention

Er'**wähnung** *f* (*-*; *-en*) mention(ing)

er'**wärmen** *v/t and v/refl* (*no -ge-*, *h*) warm (up); *fig* **sich erwärmen für** warm to

Er'**wärmung** *f* (*-*; *-en*) warming up; *Erwärmung der Erdatmosphäre* global warming

er'**warten** *v/t* (*no -ge-*, *h*) expect; wait for, await

Er'**wartung** *f* (*-*; *-en*) expectation, anticipation

er'**wartungsvoll** *adj and adv* full of expectation, expectant(ly)

er'**wecken** *fig* *v/t* (*no -ge-*, *h*) awaken; arouse; → *Anschein*

er'**weisen** *v/t* (*irr*, *weisen*, *no -ge-*, *h*) do (*service etc*); show (*respect etc*); *sich erweisen als* prove to be

er**weitern** [ɛɐ'vaitɐn] *v/t and v/refl* (*no -ge-*, *h*) extend, enlarge; *esp* ECON expand

Er'**weiterung** *f* (*-*; *-en*) extension, enlargement, expansion

Er**werb** [ɛɐ'vɛrp] *m* (*-[e]s*; *-e*) acquisition; purchase; income

er'**werben** *v/t* (*irr*, *werben*, *no -ge-*, *h*) acquire (*a. fig*); purchase

er'**werbslos** *adj* unemployed

erwerbs**tätig** *adj* (gainfully) employed, working

erwerbs**unfähig** *adj* unable to work

Er'**werbung** *f* (*-*; *-en*) acquisition; purchase

er**widern** [ɛɐ'viːdɐn] *v/t* (*no -ge-*, *h*) reply, answer; return (*visit etc*)

Er'**widerung** *f* (*-*; *-en*) reply, answer; return

er'**wischen** *v/t* (*no -ge-*, *h*) catch, get; *ihn hat's erwischt* he's had it

er'**wünscht** *adj* desired; desirable; welcome

er'**würgen** *v/t* (*no -ge-*, *h*) strangle

Erz [eːɐts] *n* (*-es*; *-e*) ore

er'**zählen** *v/t* (*no -ge-*, *h*) tell; narrate; *man hat mir erzählt* I was told

Er'**zähler** *m* (*-s*; *-*), Er'**zählerin** *f* (*-*; *-nen*) narrator

Er'**zählung** *f* (*-*; *-en*) (short) story, tale

'**Erzbischof** *m* REL archbishop

'**Erzbistum** *n* REL archbishopric

'**Erzengel** *m* REL archangel

er'**zeugen** *v/t* (*no -ge-*, *h*) ECON produce (*a. fig*); TECH make, manufacture; ELECTR generate; *fig* cause, create

Er'**zeuger** *m* (*-s*; *-*) ECON producer

Er'**zeugnis** *n* (*-ses*; *-se*) ECON product (*a. fig*)

Er'zeugung *f* (-; *-en*) ECON production

er'ziehen *v/t* (*irr*, *ziehen*, *no -ge-*, *h*) bring up, raise; educate; *j-n zu et.* *erziehen* teach s.o. to be *or* to do s.th.

Erzieher [ɛʁ'tsiːʁɐ] *m* (-*s*; -), **Erzieherin** [ɛʁ'tsiːərɪn] *f* (-; *-nen*) educator; teacher; (qualified) kindergarten teacher

er'zieherisch *adj* educational, pedagogic(al)

Er'ziehung *f* (-; *no pl*) upbringing; education

Er'ziehungsanstalt *f* reform (*Br* approved) school

Erziehungsberechtigte *m, f* (*-n*; *-n*) parent or guardian

Erziehungswesen *n* (-*s*; *no pl*) educational system

er'zielen *v/t* (*no -ge-*, *h*) achieve; SPORT score

erzogen [ɛʁ'tsoːɡən] *adj*: *gut erzogen sein* be well-bred; *schlecht erzogen sein* be ill-bred

er'zwingen *v/t* (*irr*, *zwingen*, *no -ge-*, *h*) (en)force

es [ɛs] *pers pron* it; he; she; *es gibt* there is, there are; *ich bin es* it's me; *ich hoffe es* I hope so; *ich kann es* I can (do it)

Esche ['ɛʃə] *f* (-; *-n*) BOT ash (tree)

Esel ['eːzəl] *m* (-*s*; -) ZO donkey, ass (*a.* F)

'Eselsbrücke *f* mnemonic

'Eselsohr *fig n* dog-car

Eskorte [ɛs'kɔrtə] *f* (-; *-n*) MIL escort, MAR *a.* convoy

essbar ['ɛsbaːʁ] *adj* eatable; edible

essen ['ɛsən] *v/t and v/i* (*irr*, *ge-*, *h*) eat; *zu Mittag essen* (have) lunch; *zu Abend essen* have supper (*or* dinner); *essen gehen* eat *or* dine out

'Essen *n* (-*s*; -) food; meal; dish; dinner

'Essensmarke *f* meal ticket

Essenszeit *f* lunchtime; dinner *or* supper time

Essig ['ɛsɪç] *m* (-*s*; *-e*) vinegar

'Essiggurke *f* pickled gherkin, pickle

Esslöffel *m* tablespoon

Essstäbchen *pl* chopsticks

Esstisch *m* dining table

Esszimmer *n* dining room

Estrich ['ɛstrɪç] *m* (-*s*; *-e*) ARCH flooring, subfloor; *Swiss*: loft, attic, garret

etablieren [eta'bliːrən] *v/refl* (*no -ge-*, *h*) establish o.s.

Etage [e'taːʒə] *f* (-; *-n*) floor, stor(e)y; *auf der ersten Etage* on the second (*Br* first) floor

E'tagenbett *n* bunk bed

Etappe [e'tapə] *f* (-; *-n*) stage, SPORT *a.* leg

Etat [e'taː] *m* (-*s*; *-s*) budget

Ethik ['eːtɪk] *f* (-; *no pl*) ethics

ethisch ['eːtɪʃ] *adj* ethical

ethnisch ['ɛtnɪʃ] *adj* ethnic

Etikett [eti'kɛt] *n* (-[*e*]*s*; *-e*[*n*]) label (*a. fig*); (price) tag

Eti'kette *f* (-; *-n*) etiquette

etikettieren [etikɛ'tiːrən] *v/t* (*no -ge-*, *h*) label

etliche ['ɛtlɪçə] *indef pron* several, quite a few

Etui [ɛt'viː] *n* (-*s*; *-s*) case

etwa ['ɛtva] *adv* about, around; perhaps, by any chance; *nicht etwa, dass* not that

etwaig ['ɛtvaɪç] *adj* any

etwas ['ɛtvas] **1.** *indef pron* something; anything; **2.** *adj* some; any; **3.** *adv* a little, somewhat

EU [eː'uː] ABBR *of* **Europäische Union** EU, European Union

euch [ɔyç] *pers pron* you; *euch* (*selbst*) yourselves

euer ['ɔyʁ] *poss pron* your; *der* (*die*, *das*) *Eu(e)re* yours

Eule ['ɔylə] *f* (-; *-n*) ZO owl; *Eulen nach Athen tragen* carry coals to Newcastle

euresgleichen ['ɔyrəs'glaɪçən] *pron* people like you, F *contp* the likes of you

Euro... ['ɔyro] *in cpds* ...*cheque etc*: Euro...

Europa [ɔy'roːpa] Europe; *Europa...* *in cpds* European

Europäer [ɔyro'pɛːʁ] *m* (-*s*; -), **Europäerin** [-'pɛːərɪn] *f* (-; *-nen*), **euro'päisch** *adj* European; *Europäische Gemeinschaft* European Community

Euter ['ɔytɐ] *n* (-*s*; -) udder

ev. ABBR *of* **evangelisch** Prot., Protestant

evakuieren [evaku'iːrən] *v/t* (*no -ge-*, *h*) evacuate

evangelisch [evaŋ'geːlɪʃ] *adj* REL Protestant; *evangelisch-lutherisch* Lutheran

Evangelium [evaŋ'geːljʊm] *n* (-*s*; *-lien*) Gospel

eventuell [evɛntu'ɛl] **1.** *adj* possible; **2.** *adv* possibly, perhaps

evtl. ABBR *of* **eventuell** poss., possibly

ewig ['eːvɪç] *adj* eternal; F constant, endless; *auf ewig* for ever

'Ewigkeit *f* (-; *no pl*) eternity; F *eine Ewigkeit* (for) ages

exakt [ɛ'ksakt] *adj* exact, precise

Ex'aktheit *f* (-; *no pl*) exactness, precision

Examen [ɛ'ksaːmən] *n* (-*s*; *Examina* [ɛ'ksaːmina]) exam, examination

Exekutive [ɛkseku'tiːvə] *f* (-; *-n*) POL executive (power)

Exemplar [ɛksɛm'plaːʁ] *n* (-*s*; *-e*) specimen; copy

exerzieren [ɛksɛr'tsiːrən] *v/i* (*no -ge-*, *h*) MIL drill

Exil [ε'ksi:l] *n* (-*s*; -*e*) exile
Existenz [εksɪs'tɛnts] *f* (-; -*en*) existence; living, livelihood
Existenzkampf *m* struggle for survival
Existenzminimum *n* subsistence level
existieren [εksɪs'ti:rən] *v/i* (*no -ge-, h*) exist; live (**von** on)
exklusiv [εksklu'zi:f] *adj* exclusive, select
exotisch [ε'kso:tɪʃ] *adj* exotic
Expansion [εkspan'zjo:n] *f* (-; -*en*) expansion
Expedition [εkspedi'tsjo:n] *f* (-; -*en*) expedition
Experiment [εksperi'mɛnt] *n* (-[*e*]*s*; -*e*), **experimentieren** [εksperimɛn'ti:rən] *v/i* (*no -ge-, h*) experiment
Experte [εks'pɛrtə] *m* (-*n*; -*n*), **Ex'pertin** *f* (-; -*nen*) expert (**für** on)
explodieren [εksplo'di:rən] *v/i* (*no -ge-, sein*) explode (*a. fig*), burst
Explosion [εksplo'zjo:n] *f* (-; -*en*) explosion (*a. fig*)
explosiv [-'zi:f] *adj* explosive

Export [εks'pɔrt] *m* (-[*e*]*s*; -*e*) a) (*no pl*) export(ation), b) exports
exportieren [εkspɔr'ti:rən] *v/t* (*no -ge-, h*) export
Express [εks'prɛs] *m* (-*es*; *no pl*) RAIL express; **per Express** by special delivery, *Br* express
extra ['εkstra] *adv* extra; separately; F on purpose; **extra für dich** especially for you
Extra *n* (-*s*; -*s*), **Extrablatt** *n* extra
Extrakt [εks'trakt] *m* (-[*e*]*s*; -*e*) extract
extravagant [εkstrava'gant] *adj* flamboyant
extrem [εks'tre:m] *adj*, **Ex'trem** *n* (-*s*; -*e*) extreme
Extremist(in) [εkstre-'mɪst(ɪn)] (-*en*; -*en*/-; -*nen*), **extre'mistisch** *adj* extremist, ultra
Exzellenz [εkstsε'lɛnts] *f* (-; -*en*) Excellency
exzentrisch [εks'tsɛntrɪʃ] *adj* eccentric
Exzess [εks'tsɛs] *m* (-*ses*; -*se*) excess

F

Fa. ABBR *of* **Firma** firm; Messrs.
Fabel ['fa:bəl] *f* (-; -*n*) fable (*a. fig*) '**fabelhaft** *adj* fantastic, wonderful
Fabrik [fa'bri:k] *f* (-; -*en*) factory, works, shop
Fabrikant [fabri'kant] *m* (-*en*; -*en*) factory owner; manufacturer
Fa'brikarbeiter *m* factory worker
Fabrikat [fabri'ka:t] *n* (-[*e*]*s*; -*e*) make, brand; product
Fabrikation [fabrika'tsjo:n] *f* (-; -*en*) manufacturing, production
Fabrikati'onsfehler *m* flaw
Fa'brikbesitzer *m* factory owner
Fabrikware *f* manufactured product(s)
Fach [fax] *n* (-[*e*]*s*; *Fächer* ['fɛçɐ]) compartment; pigeonhole; shelf; PED, UNIV subject; → **Fachgebiet**
Facharbeiter *m* skilled worker
Facharzt *m*, **Fachärztin** *f* specialist (**für** in)
Fachausbildung *f* professional training
Fachausdruck *m* technical term
Fachbuch *n* specialist book
Fächer ['fɛçɐ] *m* (-*s*; -) fan
'**Fachfrau** *f* expert

Fachgebiet *n* line, field; trade, business
Fachgeschäft *n* dealer (specializing in ...)
Fachhochschule *f* appr (technial) college, *esp Br* polytechnic
Fachkenntnisse *pl* specialized knowledge
'**fachkundig** *adj* competent, expert
'**fachlich** *adj* professional, specialized
'**Fachlitera,tur** *f* specialized literature
Fachmann *m* (-[*e*]*s*; -*leute*) expert
'**fachmännisch** [-mɛnɪʃ] *adj* expert
'**Fachschule** *f* technical school *or* college
fachsimpeln ['faxzɪmpəln] *v/i* (*ge-, h*) talk shop
'**Fachwerk** *n* framework
Fachwerkhaus *n* half-timbered house
Fachzeitschrift *f* (professional *or* specialist) journal
Fackel ['fakəl] *f* (-; -*n*) torch
Fackelzug *m* torchlight procession
fade ['fa:də] *adj* GASTR tasteless, flat; stale; *fig* dull, boring
Faden ['fa:dən] *m* (-*s*; *Fäden* ['fɛ:dən]) thread (*a. fig*)
'**fadenscheinig** *adj* threadbare; *fig* flimsy

(*excuse etc*)
fähig ['fɛːɪç] *adj* capable (**zu** of [*doing*] *s.th.*), able (to *do s.th.*)
'**Fähigkeit** *f* (-; -en) (cap)ability; talent, gift
fahl [faːl] *adj* pale; ashen (*face*)
fahnden ['faːndən] *v/i* (*ge-*, *h*) search (**nach** for)
'**Fahndung** *f* (-; -en) search
'**Fahndungsliste** *f* wanted list
Fahne ['faːnə] *f* (-; -n) flag; *mst fig* banner; **F e-e Fahne haben** reek of alcohol
'**Fahnenflucht** *f* (-; *no pl*) MIL desertion
Fahnenstange *f* flagpole, flagstaff
Fahrbahn ['faːɐ-] *f* road(way), pavement; MOT lane
'**fahrbar** *adj* mobile
Fähre ['fɛːrə] *f* (-; -n) ferry(boat)
fahren ['faːrən] (*irr*, *ge-*) **1.** *v/i* (*sein*) go; *bus etc*: run; leave; MOT drive; ride; **mit dem Auto** (**Zug, Bus** *etc*) **fahren** go by car (train, bus *etc*); **über e-e Brücke** *etc* **fahren** cross a bridge *etc*; **mit der Hand über et. fahren** run one's hand over s.th.; **was ist denn in dich gefahren?** what's got into you?; **2.** *v/t* (*h*) drive (*car etc*); ride (*bicycle etc*); carry
Fahrer ['faːrɐ] *m* (-s; -) driver
Fahrerflucht *f* hit-and-run offense (*Br* offence)
'**Fahrerin** *f* (-; -nen) driver
Fahrgast ['faːɐ-] *m* passenger
Fahrgeld *n* fare
Fahrgelegenheit *f* means of transport(ation)
Fahrgemeinschaft *f* car pool
Fahrgestell *n* MOT chassis; AVIAT → **Fahrwerk**
Fahrkarte *f* ticket
'**Fahrkartenauto,mat** *m* ticket machine
Fahrkartenentwerter *m* (-s; -) ticket-cancel(l)ing machine
Fahrkartenschalter *m* ticket window
'**fahrlässig** *adj* careless, reckless (*a.* JUR); **grob fahrlässig** grossly negligent
'**Fahrlehrer** *m* driving instructor
'**Fahrplan** *m* timetable, schedule
'**fahrplanmäßig 1.** *adj* scheduled; **2.** *adv* according to schedule; on time
'**Fahrpreis** *m* fare
Fahrprüfung *f* driving test
Fahrrad *n* bicycle, F bike
Fahrschein *m* ticket
Fahrschule *f* driving school
Fahrschüler *m* MOT student driver, *Br* learner (driver); PED non-local student
Fahrstuhl *m* elevator, *Br* lift
Fahrstunde *f* driving lesson
Fahrt [faːɐt] *f* (-; -en) ride, MOT *a.* drive;

trip, journey, MAR voyage, cruise; speed (*a.* MOT); **in voller Fahrt** at full speed
Fährte ['fɛːɐtə] *f* (-; -n) track (*a. fig*)
'**Fahrtenschreiber** *m* MOT tachograph
'**Fahrwasser** *n* MAR fairway
'**Fahrwerk** *n* AVIAT landing gear
'**Fahrzeug** *n* (-[e]s; -e) vehicle
Fairness ['fɛːrnɪs] *f* (-; *no pl*) fair play
Faktor ['faktoːɐ] *m* (-s; -en [fak'toːrən]) factor
Fakultät [fakʊl'tɛːt] *f* (-; -en) UNIV faculty, department
Falke ['falkə] *m* (-n; -n) ZO hawk, falcon
Fall [fal] *m* (-[e]s; *Fälle* ['fɛlə]) fall; LING, JUR, MED case; **auf jeden Fall** in any case; **auf keinen Fall** on no account; **für den Fall, dass ...** in case ...; **gesetzt den Fall, dass** suppose (that); **zu Fall bringen** *fig* defeat
Falle ['falə] *f* (-; -n) trap (*a. fig*)
fallen ['falən] *v/i* (*irr*, *ge-*, *sein*) fall (*a. rain etc*), drop; **fallen lassen** drop (*a. fig*); MIL be killed (in action); **ein Tor fiel** SPORT a goal was scored
fällen ['fɛlən] *v/t* (*ge-*, *h*) fell, cut down (*tree*); JUR pass (*sentence*); make (*a decision etc*)
fällig ['fɛlɪç] *adj* due; payable
'**fallenlassen** ['faləlasən] *v/i* (*irr*, **fallen**, *no ge-*, *h*) *fig* drop
'**Fallobst** *n* windfall
Fallrückzieher *m* soccer: overhead kick
falls [fals] *cj* if, in case; **falls nicht** unless
'**Fallschirm** *m* parachute
Fallschirmjäger *m* MIL paratrooper
Fallschirmspringen *n* MIL parachuting; SPORT skydiving
Fallschirmspringer *m* MIL parachutist; SPORT skydiver
'**Falltür** *f* trapdoor
falsch [falʃ] *adj and adv* wrong; false (*a. fig*); forged; **falsch gehen** *watch*: be wrong; **et. falsch aussprechen** (**schreiben, verstehen** *etc*) mispronounce (misspell, misunderstand *etc*) s.th.; **falsch verbunden!** TEL sorry, wrong number
fälschen ['fɛlʃən] *v/t* (*ge-*, *h*) forge, fake; counterfeit
'**Fälscher** *m* (-s; -) forger
'**Falschgeld** *n* counterfeit *or* false money
Falschmünzer [-mʏntsɐ] *m* (-s; -) counterfeiter
Falschspieler *m* cheat
'**Fälschung** *f* (-; -en) forgery; counterfeit
'**fälschungssicher** *adj* forgery-proof
Falt... ['falt-] *in cpds* ...**bett**, ...**boot** *etc*: folding ...
Falte ['faltə] *f* (-; -n) fold; wrinkle; pleat; crease

'falten v/t (ge-, h) fold
'Faltenrock m pleated skirt
Falter ['faltɐ] m (-s; -) zo butterfly
faltig ['faltɪç] adj wrinkled
familiär [famiˈljɛːɐ] adj personal; informal; **familiäre Probleme** family problems
Familie [faˈmiːljə] f (-; -n) family (a. zo, bot)
Fa'milienangelegenheit f family affair
Familienanschluss m: **Familienanschluss haben** live as one of the family
Familienname m family (or last) name, surname
Familienpackung f family size (package)
Familienplanung f family planning
Familienstand m marital status
Familienvater m family man
Fanatiker [faˈnaːtikɐ] m (-s; -), **Fa'natikerin** f (-; -nen), **fa'natisch** adj fanatic
Fanatismus [fanaˈtɪsmʊs] m (-; no pl) fanaticism
fand [fant] pret of **finden**
Fang [faŋ] m (-[e]s; Fänge ['fɛŋə]) catch (a. fig)
'fangen v/t (irr, ge-, h) catch (a. fig); **sich wieder fangen** get a grip on o.s. again; **Fangen spielen** play tag (Br catch)
'Fangzahn m zo fang
Fantasie [fantaˈziː] f (-; -n) imagination; fantasy
fanta'sielos adj unimaginative
fanta'sieren v/i (no -ge-, h) daydream; MED be delirious; F talk nonsense
fanta'sievoll adj imaginative
Fantast [fanˈtast] m (-en; -en) dreamer
fan'tastisch adj fantastic, F a. great, terrific
Farbband ['farp-] n (typewriter) ribbon
Farbe ['farbə] f (-; -n) colo(u)r; paint; complexion; tan; card games: suit
'farbecht adj colo(u)r-fast
färben ['fɛrbən] v/t (ge-, h) dye; esp fig colo(u)r; **sich rot färben** turn red; → **abfärben**
'farbenblind adj colo(u)r-blind
farbenfroh, farbenprächtig adj colo(u)rful
'Farbfernsehen n colo(u)r television
Farbfernseher m colo(u)r TV set
Farbfilm m colo(u)r film
Farbfoto n colo(u)r photo
farbig ['farbɪç] adj colo(u)red; stained (glass); fig colo(u)rful
Farbige ['farbɪgə] m, f (-n; -n) → **Schwarze**
'Farbkasten m paintbox
'farblos adj colo(u)rless (a. fig)
'Farbstift m colo(u)red pencil, crayon

'Farbstoff m dye; GASTR colo(u)ring
'Farbton m shade, tint
'Färbung f (-; -en) colo(u)ring; hue
Farnkraut ['farn-] n bot fern
Fasan [faˈzaːn] m (-[e]s; -e[n]) zo pheasant
Faschismus [faˈʃɪsmʊs] m (-; no pl) POL fascism
Faschist [faˈʃɪst] m (-en; -en), **fa'schistisch** adj fascist
faseln ['faːzəln] F v/i (ge-, h) drivel
Faser ['faːzɐ] f (-; -n) fiber, Br fibre; grain
faserig ['faːzərɪç] adj fibrous
'fasern v/i (ge-, h) fray
Fass [fas] n (-es; Fässer ['fɛsɐ]) cask, barrel; **vom Fass** on tap
Fassade [faˈsaːdə] f (-; -n) ARCH facade, front (a. fig)
'Fassbier n draft (Br draught) beer
fassen ['fasən] (ge-, h) **1.** v/t take hold of, grasp; seize; catch (criminal); hold, take; set (jewels); fig grasp, understand; pluck up (courage); make (a decision); **sich fassen** compose o.s.; **sich kurz fassen** be brief; **es ist nicht zu fassen** that's incredible **2.** v/i: **fassen nach** reach for
'Fassung f (-; -en) a) setting; frame (of glasses); ELECTR socket; draft(ing); wording, version, b) (no pl) composure; **die Fassung verlieren** lose one's composure; **j-n aus der Fassung bringen** put s.o. out
'fassungslos adj stunned; speechless
'Fassungsvermögen n capacity
fast [fast] adv almost, nearly; **fast nie (nichts)** hardly ever (anything)
fasten ['fastən] v/i (ge-, h) fast
'Fastenzeit f REL Lent
'Fastnacht f → **Karneval**
fatal [faˈtaːl] adj unfortunate; awkward; disastrous
fauchen ['fauxən] v/i (ge-, h) zo hiss
faul [faul] adj rotten, bad, GASTR a. spoiled; fig lazy; F fishy; **faule Ausrede** lame excuse
'faulen v/i (ge-, h, sein) rot, go bad; decay
faulenzen ['faulɛntsən] v/i (ge-, h) laze, loaf (about)
'Faulenzer(in) [-tsɐ (-tsə-rɪn)] (-s; -/-; -nen) lazybones; contp loafer
'Faulheit f (-; no pl) laziness
faulig ['faulɪç] adj rotten
Fäulnis ['fɔylnɪs] f (-; no pl) rottenness, decay (a. fig)
'Faulpelz F m → **Faulenzer**
'Faultier n zo sloth
Faust [faust] f (-; Fäuste ['fɔystə]) fist; **auf eigene Faust** on one's own initiative
Fausthandschuh m mitten

Faustregel f (*als Faustregel* as a) rule of thumb
Faustschlag m punch
Favorit [favo'riːt] m (*-en*; *-en*), **Favo'ritin** f (*-*; *-nen*) favo(u)rite
Fax [faks] n (*-*; *-[e]*) fax; fax machine
faxen ['faksən] v/i *and* v/t (*ge-*, *h*) fax, send a fax (to)
'Faxgerät n fax machine
FCKW [ɛftseːkaːˈveː] ABBR *of* **Fluorchlorkohlenwasserstoff** chlorofluorocarbon, CFC
Feber ['feːbɐ] *Austrian* m (*-s*; *-*), **Februar** ['feːbruaːɐ] m (*-s*; *-e*) February
fechten ['fɛçtən] v/i (*irr*, *ge-*, *h*) SPORT fence; *fig* fight
'Fechten n (*-s*; *no pl*) SPORT fencing
Fechter(in) ['fɛçtɐ (-tərɪn)] (*-s*; *-/-*; *-nen*) SPORT fencer
Feder ['feːdɐ] f (*-*; *-n*) feather; plume; nib; TECH spring
Federball m SPORT badminton; shuttlecock
Federbett n comforter, *Br* duvet
Federgewicht n SPORT featherweight
Federhalter m penholder
'feder'leicht adj (as) light as a feather
'Federmäppchen [-mɛpçən] n (*-s*; *-*) pencil case
'federn (*ge-*, *h*) **1.** v/i be springy; **2.** v/t TECH spring
federnd adj springy, elastic
'Federstrich m stroke of the pen
Federung ['feːdəruŋ] f (*-*; *-en*) springs; MOT suspension; *e-e gute Federung haben* be well sprung
'Federzeichnung f pen-and-ink drawing
Fee [feː] f (*-*; *-n*) fairy
fegen ['feːgən] v/t (*ge-*, *h*) *and fig* v/i (*sein*) sweep
fehl [feːl] adj: *fehl am Platze* out of place
'Fehlbetrag m deficit
'fehlen v/i (*ge-*, *h*) be missing; be absent; *ihm fehlt (es an)* ... he is lacking ...; *du fehlst uns* we miss you; *was dir fehlt, ist ...* what you need is ...; *was fehlt Ihnen?* what's wrong with you?
Fehler ['feːlɐ] m (*-s*; *-*) mistake; fault, TECH *a.* defect, flaw; EDP error
'fehlerfrei adj faultless, flawless
'fehlerhaft adj faulty; full of mistakes; TECH defective
'Fehlermeldung f EDP error message
'Fehlernährung f malnutrition
Fehlgeburt f MED miscarriage
Fehlgriff m mistake; wrong choice
'Fehlschlag m failure
'fehlschlagen v/i (*irr*, *schlagen*, *sep*, *-ge-*, *sein*) fail

'Fehlstart m false start
Fehltritt m slip; *fig* lapse
Fehlzündung f MOT backfire (*a. Fehlzündung haben*)
Feier ['faiɐ] f (*-*; *-n*) celebration; party
'Feierabend m end of a day's work; closing time; evening (at home); *Feierabend machen* finish (work), F knock off; *nach Feierabend* after work
'feierlich adj solemn; festive
'Feierlichkeit f (*-*; *-en*) a) (*no pl*) solemnity, b) ceremony
'feiern v/t *and* v/i (*ge-*, *h*) celebrate; have a party
'Feiertag m holiday; *gesetzlicher Feiertag* public (*or* legal, *Br a.* bank) holiday
feig [faik], **feige** ['faigə] adj cowardly; *feig sein* be a coward
Feige ['faigə] f (*-*; *-n*) BOT fig
'Feigheit f (*-*; *no pl*) cowardice
'Feigling m (*-s*; *-e*) coward
Feile ['failə] f (*-*; *-n*), **'feilen** v/t *and* v/i (*ge-*, *h*) file
feilschen ['failʃən] v/i (*ge-*, *h*) haggle (*um* about, over)
fein [fain] adj fine; choice, excellent; keen (*ear*); delicate; distinguished, F posh; *fein!* good!, okay!
Feind [faint] m (*-[e]s*; *-e* ['faində]) enemy (*a. fig*)
Feindbild n enemy image
Feindin ['faindɪn] f (*-*; *-nen*) enemy
'feindlich adj hostile; MIL enemy
'Feindschaft f (*-*; *no pl*) hostility
'feindselig adj hostile (*gegen* to)
'Feindseligkeit f (*-*; *no pl*) hostility
feinfühlig ['fainfyːlɪç] adj sensitive
'Feingefühl n (*-[e]s*; *no pl*) sensitiveness
'Feinheit f (*-*; *-en*) a) (*no pl*) fineness; keenness; delicacy, b) *pl* niceties
'Feinkostgeschäft n delicatessen
Feinme,chaniker m precision mechanic
'Feinschmecker m (*-s*; *-*) gourmet
feist [faist] adj fat, stout
Feld [fɛlt] n (*-[e]s*; *-er* ['fɛldɐ]) field (*a. fig*); *chess:* square
Feldarbeit f AGR work in the fields; fieldwork
Feldbett n cot, *Br* camp bed
Feldflasche f water bottle, canteen
Feldlerche f ZO skylark
Feldmarschall m MIL field marshal
'Feldstecher [-ʃtɛçɐ] m (*-s*; *-*) field glasses
'Feldwebel [-veːbəl] m (*-s*; *-*) MIL sergeant
'Feldzug m MIL campaign (*a. fig*)
Felge ['fɛlgə] f (*-*; *-n*) rim; SPORT circle
Fell [fɛl] n (*-[e]s*; *-e*) ZO coat; skin, fur
Fels [fɛls] m (*-en*; *-en*) rock
'Felsbrocken m boulder

Felsen ['fɛlzən] *m* (*-s*; *-*) rock

felsig ['fɛlzɪç] *adj* rocky

'**Felsspalte** *f* crevice

'**Felsvorsprung** *m* ledge

feminin [femi'niːn] *adj* feminine (*a.* LING); *contp* effeminate

Feminismus [femi'nɪsmʊs] *m* (*-*; *no pl*) feminism

Feministin [femi'nɪstɪn] *f* (*-*; *-nen*), **femi-'nistisch** *adj* feminist

Fenchel ['fɛnçəl] *m* (*-s*; *no pl*) BOT fennel

Fenster ['fɛnstɐ] *n* (*-s*; *-*) window

Fensterbank *f* (*-*; *-bänke*), **Fensterbrett** *n* windowsill

'**Fensterflügel** *m* casement

'**Fensterladen** *m* shutter

'**Fensterrahmen** *m* window frame

'**Fensterscheibe** *f* (window)pane

Ferien ['feːrjən] *pl* vacation, *esp Br* holiday(s *pl*); **Ferien haben** be on vacation

Ferienhaus *n* vacation home, cottage

Ferienlager *n* summer camp

Ferienwohnung *f* vacation rental, *Br* holiday apartment

Ferkel ['fɛrkəl] *n* (*-s*; *-*) ZO piglet; F pig

fern [fɛrn] *adj and adv* far(away), far-off, distant; **von fern** from a distance

'**Fernamt** *n* telephone exchange

'**Fernbedienung** *f* remote control

'**fernbleiben** *v/i* (*irr*, **bleiben**, *sep*, *-ge-*, *sein*) stay away (*dat* from)

Ferne ['fɛrnə] *f* (*-*; *no pl*) distance; **aus der Ferne** from a distance

ferner ['fɛrnɐ] *adv* further(more); in addition, also

'**Fernfahrer** *m* long-haul truck driver, F trucker, *Br* long-distance lorry driver

Ferngespräch *n* TEL long-distance call

'**ferngesteuert** *adj* remote-controlled; MIL guided (*missile etc*)

'**Fernglas** *n* binoculars

'**fernhalten** *v/t* (*irr*, **halten**, *sep*, *-ge-*, *h*) keep away (**von** from)

Fernheizung *f* district heating

Fernko,pierer *m* fax machine

Fernkurs *m* correspondence course

Fernlaster F *m* (*-s*; *-*) MOT longhaul truck, *Br* long-distance lorry

Fernlenkung *f* remote control

Fernlicht *n* MOT full (*or* high) beam

'**fernliegen** *v/i* (*irr*, **liegen**, *sep*, *-ge-*, *h*): **es liegt mir fernliegen zu** far be it from me to

'**Fernmeldesatel,lit** *m* communications satellite

Fernmeldetechnik *f*, **Fernmeldewesen** *n* (*-s*; *no pl*) telecommunications

'**Fernrohr** *n* telescope

Fernschreiben *n*, **Fernschreiber** *m* telex

'**fernsehen** *v/i* (*irr*, **sehen**, *sep*, *-ge-*, *h*) watch television

'**Fernsehen** *n* (*-s*; *no pl*) television (**im** on)

'**Fernseher** F *m* (*-s*; *-*) TV (set); TV viewer

'**Fernsehschirm** *m* (TV) screen

Fernsehsendung *f* TV program(me)

Fernsprechamt *n* telephone exchange

'**Fernsteuerung** *f* remote control

'**Fernverkehr** *m* long-distance traffic

Ferse ['fɛrzə] *f* (*-*; *-n*) ANAT heel (*a. fig*)

fertig ['fɛrtɪç] *adj* ready; finished; **fertig bringen** manage; *iro* be capable of; **fertig machen** finish (*a.* F *s.o.*); get *s.th.* ready; F give *s.o.* hell, do *s.o.* in; **sich fertig machen** get ready; (**mit et.**) **fertig sein** have finished (s.th.); **mit et. fertig werden** cope with *a problem etc*; F **völlig fertig** dead beat

'**fertigbringen** *v/t* (*irr*, **bringen**, *sep*, *-ge-*, *h*) → **fertig**

'**Fertiggericht** *n* ready(-to-serve) meal

Fertighaus *n* prefabricated house, F prefab

'**Fertigkeit** *f* (*-*; *-en*) skill

'**fertigmachen** *v/t* (*irr*, **bringen**, *sep*, *-ge-*, *h*) → **fertig**

'**Fertigstellung** *f* (*-*; *no pl*) completion

'**fertigwerden** *v/i* (*irr*, **bringen**, *sep*, *-ge-*, *sein*) → **fertig**

fesch [feʃ] *Austrian adj* smart, chic

Fessel ['fɛsəl] *f* (*-*; *-n*) shackle (*a. fig*); ANAT ankle

'**fesseln** *v/t* (*ge-*, *h*) bind, tie (up); *fig* fascinate

fest [fɛst] *adj* firm (*a. fig*); solid; fast; *fig* fixed (*date etc*); sound (*sleep*); steady (*girlfriend etc*); **fest schlafen** be fast asleep

Fest *n* (*-[e]s*; *-e*) celebration; party; REL festival, feast; → **froh**

'**festbinden** *v/t* (*irr*, **binden**, *sep*, *-ge-*, *h*) fasten, tie (**an** *dat* to)

'**Festessen** *n* banquet, feast

'**festfahren** *v/refl* (*irr*, **fahren**, *sep*, *-ge-*, *h*) get stuck

'**Festhalle** *f* (festival) hall

'**festhalten** (*irr*, **halten**, *sep*, *-ge-*, *h*) **1.** *v/i*: **festhalten an** (*dat*) stick to; **2.** *v/t* hold on to; hold *s.o. or s.th.* tight; **sich festhalten an** (*dat*) hold on to

festigen ['fɛstɪgən] *v/t* (*ge-*, *h*) strengthen; **sich festigen** grow firm *or* strong

Festigkeit ['fɛstɪçkait] *f* (*-*; *no pl*) firmness; strength

'**Festland** *n* mainland; *the* Continent

'**festlegen** *v/t* (*sep*, *-ge-*, *h*) fix, set; **sich festlegen auf** (*acc*) commit o.s. to *s.th.*

'**festlich** *adj* festive

'**festmachen** *v/t* (*sep*, *-ge-*, *h*) fasten, fix

(*an* *dat* to); MAR moor; ECON fix
'**Festnahme** [-na:mə] *f* (-; -*n*), '**festneh-men** *v/t* (*irr*, *nehmen*, *sep*, *-ge-*, *h*) arrest
'**Festplatte** *f* EDP hard disk
'**festschrauben** *v/t* (*sep*, *-ge-*, *h*) screw (on) tight
festsetzen *v/t* (*sep*, *-ge-*, *h*) fix
festsitzen *v/i* (*irr*, *sitzen*, *sep*, *-ge-*, *h*) be stuck; be (left) stranded
'**Festspiele** *pl* festival
'**feststehen** *v/i* (*irr*, *stehen*, *sep*, *-ge-*, *h*) be certain; *date etc*: be fixed
feststehend *adj* established (*fact etc*); set (*phrase etc*)
'**feststellen** *v/t* (*sep*, *-ge-*, *h*) find (out); establish; see, notice; state; TECH lock, arrest
'**Feststellung** *f* (-; -*en*) finding(s); realization; statement
'**Festtag** *m* holiday; REL religious holiday; F red-letter day
'**Festung** *f* (-; -*en*) fortress
'**Festwertspeicher** *m* EDP read-only memory, ROM
'**Festzug** *m* procession
fett [fɛt] *adj* fat (*a. fig*); PRINT bold; *fett gedruckt* boldface, in bold type (*or* print)
Fett *n* (-[*e*]*s*; -*e*) fat; dripping; shortening; TECH grease
'**fettarm** *adj* low-fat, *pred* low in fat
'**Fettfleck** *m* grease spot
fettig ['fɛtɪç] *adj* greasy
'**Fettnäpfchen** *n*: *ins Fettnäpfchen treten* put one's foot in it
Fetzen ['fɛtsən] *m* (-*s*; -) shred; rag; scrap (*of paper etc*)
feucht [fɔʏçt] *adj* moist, damp; humid
Feuchtigkeit ['fɔʏçtɪçkait] *f* (-; *no pl*) moisture; dampness; humidity
feudal [fɔʏ'da:l] *adj* POL feudal; F posh, *Br* swish
Feuer ['fɔʏɐ] *n* (-*s*; -) fire (*a. fig*); *j-m Feuer geben* give s.o. a light; *Feuer fangen* catch fire; *fig* fall for *s.o.*
Feuera,larm *m* fire alarm
Feuerbestattung *f* cremation
Feuereifer *m* ardo(u)r
'**feuerfest** *adj* fireproof, fire-resistant
'**Feuergefahr** *f* danger of fire
'**feuergefährlich** *adj* inflammable
'**Feuerleiter** *f* fire escape
Feuerlöscher [-lœʃɐ] *m* (-*s*; -) fire extinguisher
Feuermelder [-mɛldɐ] *m* (-*s*; -) fire alarm
feuern ['fɔʏɐn] *v/i and v/t* (*ge-*, *h*) fire (*a.* F *s.o.*)
'**feuer'rot** *adj* blazing red; crimson
'**Feuerschiff** *n* lightship
Feuerstein *m* flint

Feuerwache *f* fire station
Feuerwaffe *f* firearm, gun
Feuerwehr *f* (-; -*en*) fire brigade (*or* department); fire truck (*Br* engine)
Feuerwehrmann *m* (-[*e*]*s*, -*männer*, -*leute*) fireman, fire fighter
Feuerwerk *n* fireworks
Feuerwerkskörper *m* firework, firecracker
Feuerzeug *n* (cigarette) lighter
feurig ['fɔʏrɪç] *adj* fiery, ardent
Fiasko ['fjasko] *n* (-*s*; -*s*) fiasco, (complete) failure
Fibel ['fi:bəl] *f* (-; -*n*) primer, first reader
Fiber ['fi:bɐ] *f* fiber, *Br* fibre
Fiberglas *n* fiberglass, *Br* fibreglass
Fichte ['fɪçtə] *f* (-; -*n*) BOT spruce, F *mst* pine *or* fir (tree)
ficken ['fɪkən] V *v/i and v/t* (*ge-*, *h*) fuck
Fieber ['fi:bɐ] *n* (-*s*; *no pl*) MED temperature, fever (*a. fig*); *Fieber haben* (*messen*) have a (take *s.o.'s*) temperature; *Fieber senkend* MED antipyretic
'**fieberhaft** *adj* MED feverish (*a. fig*)
'**fiebern** *v/i* (*ge-*, *h*) MED have *or* run a temperature; *fiebern nach fig* crave for
'**Fieberthermo,meter** *n* fever (*Br* clinical) thermometer
fiel [fi:l] *pret of* **fallen**
fies [fi:s] F *adj* mean, nasty
Figur [fi'guːɐ] *f* (-; -*en*) figure
Filet [fi'le:] *n* (-*s*; -*s*) GASTR fil(l)et
Filiale [fi'lja:lə] *f* (-; -*n*) branch
Film [fɪlm] *m* (-[*e*]*s*; -*e*) film; movie, *esp Br* (motion) picture; *the* movies, *Br the* cinema; *e-n Film einlegen* PHOT load a camera
Filmaufnahme *f* filming, shooting; take, shot
filmen ['fɪlmən] (*ge-*, *h*) **1.** *v/t* film, shoot; **2.** *v/i* make a film
'**Filmgesellschaft** *f* motion-picture (*Br* film) company
Filmkamera *f* motion-picture (*Br* film) camera
Filmkas,sette *f* film magazine, cartridge
Filmpro,jektor *m* film (*or* movie) projector
Filmregis,seur *m* film director
Filmschauspieler(in) film (*or* screen, movie) actor (actress)
Filmstudio *n* film studio(s)
Filmthe,ater *n* → *Kino*
Filmverleih *m* film distributors
Filmvorführer *m* (-*s*; -) projectionist
Filter ['fɪltɐ] *m*, *esp* TECH *n* (-*s*; -) filter
'**Filterkaffee** *m* filter coffee
'**filtern** *v/t* (*ge-*, *h*) filter
'**Filterziga,rette** *f* filter(-tipped) cigarette,

filter tip

Filz [fɪlts] *m* (*-es*; *-e*) felt; F POL corruption, sleaze

'**filzen** F *v/t* (*ge-*, *h*) frisk

'**Filzschreiber** [-ʃraibɐ] *m* (*-s*; -), **Filzstift** *m* felt(-tipped) pen

Finale [fi'naːlə] *n* (*-s*; -) finale; SPORT final(s)

Finanzamt [fi'nants-] *n* tax office; Internal (*Br* Inland) Revenue

Finanzbeamte *m* tax officer

Finanzen [fi'nantsən] *pl* finances

finanziell [finan'tsjɛl] *adj* financial

finanzieren [finan'tsiːrən] *v/t* (*no -ge-*, *h*) finance

Fi'nanzmi,nister *m* minister of finance; Secretary of the Treasury, *Br* Chancellor of the Exchequer

Finanzminis,terium *n* ministry of finance; Treasury Department, *Br* Treasury

Finanzwesen *n* (*-s*; *no pl*) finance

Findelkind ['fɪndəl-] *n* JUR foundling

finden *v/t* (*irr*, *ge-*, *h*) find; think, believe; *ich finde ihn nett* I think he's nice; *wie finden Sie ...?* how do you like ...?; *finden Sie (nicht)?* do (don't) you think so?; *das wird sich finden* we'll see

Finder ['fɪndɐ] *m* (*-s*; -) finder

'**Finderlohn** *m* finder's reward

findig ['fɪndɪç] *adj* clever

fing [fɪŋ] *pret of* **fangen**

Finger ['fɪŋɐ] *m* (*-s*; -) ANAT finger

Fingerabdruck *m* fingerprint

Fingerfertigkeit *f* (-; *no pl*) manual skill

Fingerhut *m* thimble; BOT foxglove

Fingernagel *m* ANAT fingernail

Fingerspitze *f* fingertip

Fingerspitzengefühl *n* (*-[e]s*; *no pl*) sure instinct; tact

fingiert [fɪŋ'giːɐt] *adj* faked; fictitious

Fink [fɪŋk] *m* (*-en*; *-en*) ZO finch

Finne ['fɪnə] *m* (*-n*; *-n*), **Finnin** ['fɪnɪn] *f* (-; *-nen*) Finn

'**finnisch** *adj* Finnish

Finnland ['fɪn-] Finland

finster ['fɪnstɐ] *adj* dark, gloomy; *fig* grim; shady

'**Finsternis** *f* (-; *-se*) darkness, gloom

Finte ['fɪntə] *f* (-; *-n*) trick; SPORT feint

Firma ['fɪrma] (-; *-men*) firm, company

firmen ['fɪrmən] *v/t* (*ge-*, *h*) REL confirm

'**Firmung** *f* (-; *-en*) REL confirmation

First [fɪrst] *m* (*-[e]s*; *-e*) ARCH ridge

Fisch [fɪʃ] *m* (*-[e]s*; *-e*) ZO fish; *pl* ASTR Pisces; *er ist (ein) Fisch* he's (a) Pisces

'**Fischdampfer** *m* trawler

fischen ['fɪʃən] *v/t and v/i* (*ge-*, *h*) fish

Fischer ['fɪʃɐ] *m* (*-s*; -) fisherman; *Fi-*

scher... in cpds ...boot, ...dorf etc: fishing ...

Fischerei [fɪʃə'rai] *f* (-; *no pl*) fishing

'**Fischfang** *m* (*-[e]s*; *no pl*) fishing

Fischgräte *f* fishbone

Fischgrätenmuster *n* herring-bone (pattern)

Fischgründe *pl* fishing grounds

Fischhändler *m* fish dealer, *esp Br* fishmonger

Fischkutter *m* smack

Fischlaich *m* spawn

Fischstäbchen *n* GASTR fish stick (*Br* finger)

Fischzucht *f* fish farming

Fischzug *m* catch, haul (*both a. fig*)

Fisole [fi'zoːlə] *Austrian f* (-; *-n*) BOT string bean

Fistel ['fɪstəl] *f* (-; *-n*) MED fistula

'**Fistelstimme** *f* falsetto

fit [fɪt] *adj* fit; *sich fit halten* keep fit

'**Fitness** *f* (-; *no pl*) fitness

Fitnesscenter *n* health club, fitness center, gym

fix [fɪks] *adj* ECON fixed; F quick; F smart, bright; F *fix und fertig sein* be dead beat; be a nervous wreck; *fixe Idee* PSYCH obsession

fixen ['fɪksən] F *v/i* (*ge-*, *h*) shoot, fix; be a junkie

Fixer ['fɪksɐ] F *m* (*-s*; -) junkie, mainliner

fixieren [fɪ'ksiːrən] *v/t* (*no -ge-*, *h*) fix (*a.* PHOT); stare at *s.o.*

'**Fixstern** *m* ASTR fixed star

FKK [ɛfka:'ka:] *ABBR of* **Freikörperkultur** nudism

FK'K-Strand *m* nudist beach

flach [flax] *adj* flat; level, even, plane; *fig* shallow

Fläche ['flɛçə] *f* (-; *-n*) surface (*a.* MATH); area (*a.* MATH); expanse, space

'**flächendeckend** *adj* exhaustive

'**Flächeninhalt** *m* MATH (surface) area

Flächenmaß *n* square *or* surface measure

'**Flachland** *n* (*-[e]s*; *no pl*) lowland, plain

Flachs [flaks] *m* (*-es*; *no pl*) BOT flax

flackern ['flakɐn] *v/i* (*ge-*, *h*) flicker

Fladenbrot ['flaːdən-] *n* round flat bread (*or* loaf)

Flagge ['flagə] *f* (-; *-n*) flag

'**flaggen** *v/i* (*ge-*, *h*) fly a flag *or* flags

Flak [flak] *f* (-; -) MIL anti-aircraft gun

Flamme ['flamə] *f* (-; *-n*) flame (*a. fig*)

Flanell [fla'nɛl] *m* (*-s*; *-e*) flannel

Flanke ['flaŋkə] *f* (-; *-n*) flank, side; *soccer*: cross; SPORT flank vault

flankieren [flaŋ'kiːrən] *v/t* (*no -ge-*, *h*) flank

Flasche ['flaʃə] *f* (-; *-n*) bottle; baby's bot-

tle; F contp dead loss
'Flaschenbier n bottled beer
Flaschenhals m neck of a bottle
Flaschenöffner m bottle opener
Flaschenpfand n (bottle) deposit
Flaschenzug m TECH block and tackle, pulley
flatterhaft ['flatɐhaft] adj fickle, flighty
flattern ['flatɐn] v/i (ge-, sein) flutter; TECH (h) wobble
flau [flau] adj queasy; fig flat; ECON slack
Flaum [flaum] m (-[e]s; no pl) down, fluff, fuzz
Flausch [flauʃ] m (-es; -e) fleece
flauschig ['flauʃɪç] adj fleecy, fluffy
Flausen ['flauzən] F pl (funny) ideas
Flaute ['flautə] f (-; -n) MAR calm; ECON slack period
Flechte ['flɛçtə] f (-; -n) plait, braid; BOT, MED lichen
'flechten v/t (irr, ge-, h) plait, braid (hair); weave (basket)
Fleck [flɛk] m (-[e]s; -e) stain, mark; speck; dot; blot(ch); fig place, spot; patch; blauer Fleck bruise; vom Fleck weg on the spot; nicht vom Fleck kommen not get anywhere
'Flecken m → Fleck
'Fleckenentferner m stain remover
'fleckenlos adj spotless (a. fig)
fleckig ['flɛkɪç] adj spotted; stained
Fledermaus ['fleːdɐ-] f zo bat
Flegel ['fleːgəl] m (-s; -) lout, boor
'flegelhaft adj loutish
'Flegeljahre pl awkward age
'flegeln F contp v/refl (ge-, h) lounge
flehen ['fleːən] v/i (ge-, h) beg; pray (um for)
flehentlich ['fleːəntlɪç] adj imploring, entreating
Fleisch [flaiʃ] n (-[e]s; no pl) flesh (a. fig); GASTR meat; Fleisch fressend → fleischfressend
Fleischbrühe f (meat) broth, consommé
Fleischer ['flaiʃɐ] m (-s; -) butcher
Fleischerei [flaiʃə'rai] f (-; -en) butcher's (shop)
'fleischfressend adj BOT, ZO carnivorous
'Fleischhauer [-hauɐ] Austrian m (-s; -) butcher
fleischig ['flaiʃɪç] adj fleshy
'Fleischklößchen n (-s; -) meatball
Fleischkon‚serven pl canned (Br tinned) meat
'fleischlos adj meatless
'Fleischwolf m meat grinder, Br mincer
Fleiß [flais] m (-es; no pl) diligence, hard work
fleißig ['flaisɪç] adj diligent, hard-work-

ing; fleißig sein work hard
fletschen ['flɛtʃən] v/t (ge-, h) bare
flexibel [flɛ'ksiːbəl] adj flexible
Flexibilität [flɛksibili'tɛːt] f (-; no pl) flexibility
flicken ['flɪkən] v/t (ge-, h) mend, repair, a. fig patch (up)
'Flicken m (-s; -) patch
'Flickwerk n patchwork (a. fig)
'Flickzeug n TECH repair kit
Flieder ['fliːdɐ] m (-s; -) BOT lilac
Fliege ['fliːgə] f (-; -n) zo fly; bow tie
'fliegen v/i (irr, ge-, sein) and v/t (h) fly (a. fliegen lassen); F fall; F be fired, F get the sack; be kicked out of school; F fliegen auf (acc) really go for; F in die Luft fliegen blow up
'Fliegen n (-s; no pl) flying; aviation
'Fliegenfänger m flypaper
'Fliegenfenster n flyscreen
'Fliegengewicht n SPORT flyweight
'Fliegengitter n wire mesh (screen)
'Fliegenklatsche f flyswatter
'Fliegenpilz m BOT fly agaric
Flieger ['fliːgɐ] m (-s; -) MIL airman; F plane; cycling: sprinter
Fliegerₗlarm m air-raid warning
fliehen ['fliːən] v/i (irr, ge-, sein) flee, run away (both: vor dat from)
'Fliehkraft f PHYS centrifugal force
Fliese ['fliːzə] f (-; -n), 'fliesen v/t (ge-, h) tile
'Fliesenleger m (-s; -) tiler
Fließband ['fliːs-] n (-[e]s; -bänder) TECH assembly line; conveyor belt
fließen ['fliːsən] v/i (irr, ge-, sein) flow (a. fig); run
fließend 1. adj flowing; running; LING fluent; 2. adv: er spricht fließend Englisch he speaks English fluently or fluent English
'Fließheck n MOT fastback
flimmern ['flɪmɐn] v/i (ge-, h) shimmer; film: flicker
flink [flɪŋk] adj quick, nimble
Flinte ['flɪntə] f (-; -n) shotgun; F gun
Flipper ['flɪpɐ] F m (-s; -) pinball machine
'flippern v/i (ge-, h) play pinball
Flirt [flœrt] m (-s; -s) flirtation
flirten ['flœrtən] v/i (ge-, h) flirt
Flittchen ['flɪtçən] F n (-s; -) floozie
Flitter ['flɪtɐ] m (-s; -) tinsel (a. fig), spangles
Flitterwochen pl honeymoon
flitzen ['flɪtsən] F v/i (ge-, sein) flit, whizz, shoot
flocht [flɔxt] pret of flechten
Flocke ['flɔkə] f (-; -n) flake
flockig ['flɔkɪç] adj fluffy, flaky

flog [floːk] *pret of* **fliegen**

floh [floː] *pret of* **fliehen**

Floh *m* (-[e]s; *Flöhe* ['fløːə]) zo flea

'**Flohmarkt** *m* flea market

Florett [flo'rɛt] *n* (-[e]s; -e) foil

florieren [flo'riːrən] *v/i* (*no* -ge-, *h*) flourish, prosper

Floskel ['flɔskəl] *f* (-; -n) empty *or* cliché(d) phrase

floss [flɔs] *pret of* **fließen**

Floß [floːs] *n* (-es; *Flöße* ['fløːsə]) raft, float

Flosse ['flɔsə] *f* (-; -n) zo fin, *a.* SPORT flipper

Flöte ['fløːtə] *f* (-; -n) MUS flute; recorder

flott [flɔt] *adj* brisk (*pace*); F smart, chic; MAR afloat

Flotte ['flɔtə] *f* (-; -n) MAR fleet; navy

'**Flottenstützpunkt** *m* MIL naval base

Fluch [fluːx] *m* (-[e]s; *Flüche* ['flyːçə]) curse; swear word

fluchen ['fluːxən] *v/i* (*ge-*, *h*) swear, curse

Flucht [fluxt] *f* (-; -en) flight (**vor** *dat* from); escape, getaway (**aus** *dat* from)

'**fluchtartig** *adv* hastily

'**Fluchtauto** *n* getaway car

flüchten ['flʏçtən] *v/i* (*ge-*, *sein*) flee (**nach**, **zu** to), run away; escape, get away

flüchtig ['flʏçtɪç] *adj* quick; superficial; careless; fugitive, *criminal etc*: on the run, at large; **flüchtiger Blick** glance; **flüchtiger Eindruck** glimpse

'**Flüchtigkeitsfehler** *m* slip

Flüchtling ['flʏçtlɪŋ] *m* fugitive; POL refugee

'**Flüchtlingslager** *n* refugee camp

Flug [fluːk] *m* (-[e]s; *Flüge* ['flyːgə]) flight; **im Flug(e)** rapidly, quickly

Flugabwehrra,kete *f* MIL anti-aircraft missile

Flugbahn *f* trajectory

Flugball *m* tennis: volley

Flugbegleiter(in) flight attendant

Flugblatt *n* handbill, leaflet

Flugdienst *m* air service

Flügel ['flyːgəl] *m* (-s; -) zo wing (*a.* SPORT); TECH blade; *windmill*: sail; MUS grand piano

Flügelmutter *f* TECH wing nut

Flügelschraube *f* TECH thumb screw

Flügelstürmer *m* SPORT wing forward

'**Flügeltür** *f* folding door

'**Fluggast** *m* (air) passenger

flügge ['flʏgə] *adj* full-fledged

'**Fluggesellschaft** *f* airline

Flughafen *m* airport

Fluglinie *f* air route; → *Fluggesellschaft*

Fluglotse *m* air traffic controller

Flugplan *m* air schedule

Flugplatz *m* airfield, airport

Flugschein *m* (flight) ticket

Flugschreiber *m* (-s; -) flight recorder, black box

Flugsicherung *f* air traffic control

Flugverkehr *m* air traffic

'**Flugzeug** *n* (-[e]s; -e) (air)plane, aircraft, *Br a.* aeroplane; **mit dem Flugzeug** by air *or* plane

Flugzeugabsturz *m* air *or* plane crash

Flugzeugentführung *f* hijacking, skyjacking

Flugzeughalle *f* hangar

Flugzeugträger *m* MAR MIL aircraft carrier

Flunder ['flʊndɐ] *f* (-; -n) zo flounder

flunkern ['flʊŋkɐn] *v/i* (*ge-*, *h*) fib; brag

Fluor ['fluːoːɐ] *n* (-s; *no pl*) CHEM fluorine; fluoride

'**Fluorchlorkohlenwasserstoff** *m* CHEM chlorofluorocarbon, CFC

Flur [fluːɐ] *m* (-[e]s; -e) hall; corridor

Fluss [flʊs] *m* (-es; *Flüsse* ['flʏsə]) river; stream; *im Fluss* fig in (a state of) flux

fluss'abwärts *adv* downstream

fluss'aufwärts *adv* upstream

'**Flussbett** *n* river bed

flüssig ['flʏsɪç] *adj* liquid; melted; *fig* fluent; ECON available

'**Flüssigkeit** *f* (-; -en) a) liquid, b) (*no pl*) liquidity; *fig* fluency

'**Flüssigkris,tallanzeige** *f* liquid crystal display, LCD

'**Flusslauf** *m* course of a river

Flusspferd *n* zo hippopotamus, F hippo

Flussufer *n* riverbank, riverside

flüstern ['flʏstɐn] *v/i and v/t* (*ge-*, *h*) whisper

Flut [fluːt] *f* (-; -en) flood (*a. fig*); high tide; **es ist Flut** the tide is in

Flutlicht *n* floodlights

Flutwelle *f* tidal wave

focht [fɔxt] *pret of* **fechten**

Fohlen ['foːlən] *n* (-s; -) zo foal; colt; filly

Föhn[1] [føːn] *m* (-[e]s; -e) hairdrier

Föhn[2] *m* (-[e]s; -e) METEOR foehn, föhn

föhnen ['føːnən] *v/t* (*ge-*, *h*) blow-dry

Folge ['fɔlgə] *f* (-; -n) result, consequence; effect; succession; order; series; TV *etc*: sequel, episode; aftermath; MED aftereffect

folgen ['fɔlgən] *v/i* (*ge-*, *sein*) follow; obey; **hieraus folgt, dass** from this it follows that; **wie folgt** as follows

folgend *adj* following, subsequent

folgendermaßen ['fɔlgəndɐ'maːsən] *adv* as follows

'**folgenschwer** *adj* momentous

'**folgerichtig** *adj* logical; consistent

folgern ['fɔlgɐn] *v/t* (*ge-*, *h*) conclude (**aus**

dat from)

Folgerung ['fɔlgərʊŋ] *f* (-; *-en*) conclusion

folglich ['fɔlklɪç] *cj* consequently, thus, therefore

folgsam ['fɔlkzaːm] *adj* obedient

Folie ['foːljə] *f* (-; *-n*) foil; transparency

Folter ['fɔltɐ] *f* (-; *-n*) torture; **auf die Folter spannen** tantalize

'**foltern** *v/t* (*ge-*, *h*) torture, *fig a.* torment

Fön® *m* → **Föhn**[1]

Fonds [fõː] *m* (-; -) ECON fund

fönen *v/t* → **föhnen**

Fontäne [fɔn'tɛːnə] *f* (-; *-n*) jet, spout; gush

Förderband ['fœrdɐ-] *n* TECH conveyor belt

Förderkorb *m* *mining*: cage

fordern ['fɔrdɐn] *v/t* (*ge-*, *h*) demand, *esp* JUR *a.* claim; ECON ask, charge

fördern ['fœrdɐn] *v/t* (*ge-*, *h*) promote; support (*a.* UNIV), sponsor; PED tutor, provide remedial classes for; TECH mine

Forderung ['fɔrdərʊŋ] *f* (-; *-en*) demand; claim (*a.* JUR); ECON charge

Förderung ['fœrdərʊŋ] *f* (-; *-en*) promotion, advancement; support, sponsorship; UNIV *etc*: grant; PED tutoring, remedial classes; TECH mining

Forelle [fo'rɛlə] *f* (-; *-n*) ZO trout

Form [fɔrm] *f* (-; *-en*) form, shape, SPORT *a.* condition; TECH mo(u)ld; **gut in Form** in great form

formal [fɔr'maːl] *adj* formal

Formalität [fɔrmali'tɛːt] *f* (-; *-en*) formality

Format [fɔr'maːt] *n* (-[*e*]*s*; -*e*) size; format; *fig* caliber, *Br* calibre

formatieren [fɔrma'tiːrən] *v/t* (*no -ge-*, *h*) EDP format

Forma'tierung *f* (-; *-en*) EDP formatting

Formel ['fɔrməl] *f* (-; *-n*) formula

formell [fɔr'mɛl] *adj* formal

formen ['fɔrmən] *v/t* (*ge-*, *h*) shape, form; *fig* mo(u)ld

'**Formfehler** *m* irregularity

formieren [fɔr'miːrən] *v/t and v/refl* (*no -ge-*, *h*) form (up)

förmlich ['fœrmlɪç] **1.** *adj* formal; *fig* regular; **2.** *adv* formally; *fig* literally

'**formlos** *adj* shapeless; *fig* informal

'**formschön** *adj* well-designed

Formular [fɔrmu'laːɐ] *n* (-*s*; -*e*) form, blank

formulieren [fɔrmu'liːrən] *v/t* (*no -ge-*, *h*) word, phrase; formulate; express

Formu'lierung *f* (-; *-en*) wording, phrasing; formulation; expression, phrase

forsch [fɔrʃ] *adj* dashing

forschen ['fɔrʃən] *v/i* (*ge-*, *h*) research, do

research; **forschen nach** search for

Forscher ['fɔrʃɐ] *m* (-*s*; -), '**Forscherin** *f* (-; *-nen*) explorer; (research) scientist

Forschung ['fɔrʃʊŋ] *f* (-; *-en*) research (work)

Forst [fɔrst] *m* (-[*e*]*s*; -*e*[*n*]) forest

Förster ['fœrstɐ] *m* (-*s*; -) forester; forest ranger

'**Forstwirtschaft** *f* (-; *no pl*) forestry

fort [fɔrt] *adv* off, away; gone; missing

Fort [foːɐ] *n* (-*s*; -*s*) MIL fort

'**fortbestehen** *v/i* (*irr*, **stehen**, *sep*, *no -ge-*, *h*) continue

'**fortbewegen** *v/refl* (*sep*, *no -ge-*, *h*) move

'**Fortbewegung** *f* moving; (loco)motion

'**Fortbildung** *f* (-, *no pl*) further education *or* training

'**fortfahren** *v/i* (*irr*, **fahren**, *sep*, *-ge-*) a) (*sein*) leave, go away, MOT *a.* drive off, b) (*h*) continue, go *or* keep on (**et. zu tun** doing s.th.)

fortführen *v/t* (*sep*, *-ge-*, *h*) continue, carry on

fortgehen *v/i* (*irr*, **gehen**, *sep*, *-ge-*, *sein*) go away, leave

'**fortgeschritten** *adj* advanced

'**fortlaufend** *adj* consecutive, successive

'**fortpflanzen** *v/refl* (*sep*, *-ge-*, *h*) BIOL reproduce; *fig* spread

'**Fortpflanzung** *f* BIOL reproduction

'**fortschreiten** *v/i* (*irr*, **schreiten**, *sep*, *-ge-*, *sein*) advance, proceed, progress

fortschreitend *adj* progressive

'**Fortschritt** *m* progress

'**fortschrittlich** *adj* progressive

'**fortsetzen** *v/t* (*sep*, *-ge-*, *h*) continue, go on with

'**Fortsetzung** *f* (-; *-en*) continuation; *film etc*: sequel; **Fortsetzung folgt** to be continued

'**Fortsetzungsro**,**man** *m* serialized novel

'**fortwährend** *adj* continual, constant

fossil [fɔ'siːl] *adj*, **Fos'sil** *n* (-*s*; *-ien*) GEOL fossil (*a. fig* F)

Foto ['foːto] *n* (-*s*; -*s*) photo(graph); **ein Foto machen (von)** take a photo (of)

'**Fotoalbum** *n* photo album

'**Fotoappa,rat** *m* camera

Fotograf [foto'graːf] *m* (-*en*; -*en*) photographer

Fotografie [fotogra'fiː] *f* (-; *-n*) a) (*no pl*) photography, b) photograph, picture

fotografieren [fotogra'fiːrən] *v/t and v/i* (*no -ge-*, *h*) take a photo(graph) *or* picture (of); **sich fotografieren lassen** have one's picture taken

Foto'grafin *f* (-; *-nen*) photographer

'**Fotohandy** *n* camera phone

Fotoko'pie *f* photocopy

fotoko'pieren v/t (no -ge-, h) (photo)copy
'Fotomo,dell n model
'Fotozelle f photoelectric cell
Fotze ['fɔtsə] V f (-; -n) cunt
Foul [faul] n (-s; -s) SPORT foul
foulen ['faulən] v/t and v/i (ge-, h) SPORT foul
Foyer [foa'je:] n (-s; -s) foyer, lobby, lounge
Fr. ABBR of **Frau** Mrs, Ms
Fracht [fraxt] f (-; -en) freight, load, MAR, AVIAT a. cargo; ECON freight, Br carriage
Frachtbrief m RAIL bill of lading (a. MAR), Br consignment note
Frachter ['fraxtɐ] m (-s; -) MAR freighter
Frack [frak] m (-[e]s; Fräcke ['frɛkə]) tails, tailcoat
Frage ['fra:gə] f (-; -n) question; **e-e Frage stellen** ask a question; → **infrage**
'Fragebogen m question(n)aire
'fragen v/t and v/i (ge-, h) ask (**nach** for; **wegen** about); **nach dem Weg (der Zeit) fragen** ask the way (time); **sich fragen** wonder
'Fragewort n LING interrogative
Fragezeichen n LING question mark
fraglich ['fra:klıç] adj doubtful, uncertain; ... im Frageböger
fraglos ['fra:klo:s] adv undoubtedly, unquestionably
Fragment [fra'gmɛnt] n (-[e]s; -e) fragment
fragwürdig ['fra:k-] adj dubious, F shady
Fraktion [frak'tsjo:n] f (-; -en) (parliamentary) group or party
Frakti'onsführer m PARL floor leader, Br chief whip
Franc [frã:] m (-; -s), **Franken** ['fraŋkən] m (-; -) franc
frankieren [fraŋ'ki:rən] v/t (no -ge-, h) stamp; frank
Frankreich ['fraŋkraiç] France
Franse ['franzə] f (-; -n) fringe
fransig ['franzıç] adj frayed
Franzose [fran'tso:zə] m (-n; -n) Frenchman; **die Franzosen** pl the French
Französin [fran'tsø:zın] f (-; -nen) Frenchwoman
französisch [fran'tsø:zıʃ] adj French
fraß [fra:s] pret of **fressen**
Fraß F contp m (-es; no pl) muck
Fratze ['fratsə] f (-; -n) grimace
Frau [frau] f (-; -en) woman; wife; **Frau X** Mrs (or Ms) X
Frauchen ['frauçən] n mistress (of dog)
'Frauenarzt m, **Frauenärztin** f gyn(a)e-cologist
Frauenbewegung f: **die Frauenbewegung** POL women's lib(eration)

'frauenfeindlich adj sexist
'Frauenhaus n women's shelter (Br refuge)
Frauenklinik f gyn(a)ecological hospital
Frauenrechtlerin [-rɛçtlərın] f (-; -nen) feminist
Fräulein ['frɔʏlain] n (-s; -) Miss
'fraulich adj womanly, feminine
frech [frɛç] adj sassy, Br cheeky
'Frechheit f (-; no pl) F Br cheek
frei [frai] adj free (**von** from, of); independent; freelance; vacant; candid, frank; SPORT unmarked; **ein freier Tag** a day off; **morgen haben wir frei** there is no school tomorrow; **im Freien** outdoors; → **Fuß**; **sich frei machen** undress; **sich frei machen von** free o.s. from; → a, **freibekommen, freigeben, freihaben**; **frei halten** keep clear (exit), → **freihalten**
'Freibad n open-air swimming-pool
'freibekommen v/t (irr, kommen, sep, no -ge-, h) get a day etc off
'freiberuflich adj freelance, self-employed
'Freiexem,plar n free copy
'Freigabe f (-; no pl) release
'freigeben (irr, geben, sep, -ge-, h) **1.** v/t release; **e-n Tag etc freigeben** give a day etc off; **2.** v/i: **j-m freigeben** give s.o. time off
'freigebig [-ge:bıç] adj generous
'Freigepäck n AVIAT baggage allowance
'freihaben F v/i (irr, haben, sep, -ge-, h) have a day off (Br a. a holiday)
'Freihafen m free port
'freihalten v/t (irr, halten, sep, -ge-, h) keep, save (seat etc); treat (s.o.)
'Freihandel m free trade
Freihandelszone f free trade area
'freihändig [-hɛndıç] adv with no hands
'Freiheit f (-; -en) freedom, liberty; **sich Freiheiten herausnehmen gegen** take liberties with
'Freiheitsstrafe f JUR prison sentence
'Freikarte f free ticket
'freikaufen v/t (sep, -ge-, h) ransom
'Freikörperkul,tur f (-; no pl) nudism
'freilassen v/t (irr, lassen, sep, -ge-, h) release, set free
'Freilassung f (-; -en) release
'Freilauf m freewheel (a. **im Freilauf fahren**)
'freilich adv indeed, of course
'Freilicht... in cpds open-air ...
'freimachen v/t (sep, -ge-, h) post: stamp; **sich freimachen** undress; **sich freimachen von** free o.s. from; → **frei**; → **Oberkörper**
'Freimaurer m freemason

'freimütig [-my:tıç] *adj* candid, frank
'freischaffend *adj* freelance
'freischwimmen *v/refl* (*irr*, **schwimmen**, *sep*, -ge-, *h*) pass a 15-minute swimming test
'freisprechen *v/t* (*irr*, **sprechen**, *sep*, -ge-, *h*) *esp* REL absolve (**von** from); JUR acquit (of)
'Freispruch *m* JUR acquittal
'Freistaat *m* POL free state
'freistehen *v/i* (*irr*, **stehen**, *sep*, -ge-, *h*) be unoccupied; SPORT be unmarked; **es steht dir frei zu** *inf* you are free to *inf*
freistellen *v/t* (*sep*, -ge-, *h*) **j-n freistellen** exempt s.o. (**von** from) (*a.* MIL); **j-m et. freistellen** leave s.th. (up) to s.o.
'Freistil *m* freestyle
Freistoß *m* *soccer*: free kick
Freistunde *f* PED free period
Freitag *m* Friday
Freitod *m* suicide
Freitreppe *f* outdoor stairs
Freiübungen *pl* exercises
Freiwild *fig n* fair game
'freiwillig *adj* voluntary; **sich freiwillig melden** volunteer (**zu** for)
Freiwillige ['fraivılıgə] *m*, *f* (-*n*; -*n*) volunteer
'Freizeit *f* free *or* leisure time
Freizeitgestaltung *f* leisure-time activities
Freizeitkleidung *f* leisurewear
Freizeitpark *m* amusement park
Freizeitzentrum *n* leisure center (*Br* centre)
'freizügig *adj* permissive; *film etc*: explicit
fremd [frɛmt] *adj* strange; foreign; unknown; **ich bin auch fremd hier** I'm a stranger here myself
'fremdartig *adj* strange, exotic
Fremde ['frɛmdə] *m*, *f* (-*n*; -*n*) stranger; foreigner
'Fremdenführer *m*, Fremdenführerin *f* (-; -*nen*) (tourist) guide
Fremdenhass *m* xenophobia
Fremdenlegi,on *f* Foreign Legion
Fremdenverkehr *m* tourism
Fremdenverkehrsbü,ro *n* tourist office
Fremdenzimmer *n* guest room; **Fremdenzimmer** (**zu vermieten**) rooms to let
'fremdgehen F *v/i* (*irr*, **gehen**, *sep*, -ge-, *sein*) be unfaithful (to one's wife *or* husband), play around
'Fremdkörper *m* MED foreign body; *fig* alien element
Fremdsprache *f* foreign language
Fremdsprachensekre,tärin *f* bilingual secretary
'fremdsprachig, fremdsprachlich *adj* foreign-language

'Fremdwort *n* (-[*e*]*s*; -*wörter*) foreign word
Frequenz [fre'kvɛnts] *f* (-; -*en*) PHYS frequency
Fresse ['frɛsə] V *f* (-; -*n*) big (fat) mouth
'fressen *v/t* (*irr*, *ge*-, *h*) ZO eat, feed on; F gobble (up); *fig* devour
Freude ['frɔydə] *f* (-; -*n*) joy, delight; pleasure; **Freude haben an** (*dat*) take pleasure in
'Freudengeschrei *n* shouts of joy, cheers
Freudenhaus F *n* brothel
Freudentag *m* red-letter day
Freudentränen *pl* tears of joy
'freudestrahlend *adj* radiant (with joy)
freudig ['frɔydıç] *adj* joyful, cheerful; happy (*event etc*)
freudlos ['frɔyt-] *adj* joyless, cheerless
freuen ['frɔyən] *v/t* (*ge*-, *h*) **es freut mich, dass** I'm glad *or* pleased (that); **sich freuen über** (*acc*) be pleased *or* glad about; **sich freuen auf** (*acc*) look forward to
Freund [frɔynt] *m* (-[*e*]*s*; -*e* ['frɔyndə]) friend; boyfriend
Freundin ['frɔyndın] *f* (-; -*nen*) friend; girlfriend
'freundlich *adj* friendly, kind, nice; *fig* cheerful (*room etc*)
'Freundlichkeit *f* (-; *no pl*) friendliness, kindness
'Freundschaft *f* (-; -*en*) friendship; **Freundschaft schließen** make friends
'freundschaftlich *adj* friendly
'Freundschaftsspiel *n* SPORT friendly (game)
Frevel ['fre:fəl] *m* (-*s*; -) outrage (**an** *dat*, **gegen** on)
Frieden ['fri:dən] *m* (-*s*; *no pl*) peace; **im Frieden** in peacetime; **lass mich in Frieden!** leave me alone!
'Friedensbewegung *f* peace movement
Friedensforschung *f* peace studies
Friedensverhandlungen *pl* peace negotiations *or* talks
Friedensvertrag *m* peace treaty
friedfertig ['fri:t-] *adj* peaceable
'Friedhof *m* cemetery, graveyard
'friedlich *adj* peaceful
'friedliebend *adj* peace-loving
frieren ['fri:rən] *v/i* (*irr*, *ge*-, *h*) freeze; **ich friere** I am *or* feel cold; I'm freezing
Fries [fri:s] *m* (-*es*; -*e*) ARCH frieze
Frikadelle [frika'dɛlə] *f* (-; -*n*) meatball
frisch [frıʃ] *adj* fresh; clean (*shirt etc*); **frisch gestrichen!** wet (*or* fresh) paint!
Frische ['frıʃə] *f* (-; *no pl*) freshness
'Frischhaltebeutel *m* polythene bag
Frischhaltefolie *f* plastic wrap, *Br* cling

film

Friseur [fri'zøːɐ] *m* (-*s*; -*e*) hairdresser; barber

Friseursa,lon *m* hairdresser's (shop), barber's shop

Friseuse [fri'zøːzə] *f* (-; -*n*) hairdresser

frisieren [fri'ziːrən] *v/t* (*no* -*ge*-, *h*) do *s.o.'s* hair; F MOT soup up

Frisör *etc* → **Friseur** *etc*

Frist [frɪst] *f* (-; -*en*) (fixed) period of time; deadline; extension (*a.* ECON)

fristen ['frɪstən] *v/t* (*ge*-, *h*) **sein Dasein fristen** scrape a living

'**fristlos** *adj* without notice

Frisur [fri'zuːɐ] *f* (-; -*en*) hairstyle, hairdo

Fritten ['frɪtən] F *pl* fries, *Br* chips

frittieren [fri'tiːrən] *v/t* (*no* -*ge*-, *h*) deep-fry

frivol [fri'voːl] *adj* frivolous; suggestive

froh [froː] *adj* glad (*über acc* about); cheerful; happy; **frohes Fest!** happy holiday!; Merry Christmas!

fröhlich ['frøːlɪç] *adj* cheerful, happy; merry

'**Fröhlichkeit** *f* (-; *no pl*) cheerfulness, merriment

fromm [frɔm] *adj* pious, devout; meek; steady (*horse*); **frommer Wunsch** pious hope

Frömmigkeit ['frœmɪçkait] *f* (-; *no pl*) religiousness, piety

Fronleichnam ['froːn-] *m* (-[*e*]*s*; *no pl*) REL Corpus Christi

Front [frɔnt] *f* (-; -*en*) front (*a. fig*), ARCH *a.* face, MIL *a.* line; **in Front liegen** SPORT be ahead

frontal [frɔn'taːl] *adj* MOT head-on

Fron'talzusammenstoß *m* MOT head-on collision

'**Frontantrieb** *m* MOT front-wheel drive

fror [froːɐ] *pret of* **frieren**

Frosch [frɔʃ] *m* (-[*e*]*s*; *Frösche* ['frœʃə]) ZO frog

Froschmann *m* frogman

Froschperspek,tive *f* worm's-eye view

Froschschenkel *pl* GASTR frog's legs

Frost [frɔst] *m* (-[*e*]*s*; *Fröste* ['frœstə]) frost

Frostbeule *f* chilblain

frösteln ['frœstəln] *v/i* (*ge*-, *h*) feel chilly, shiver (*a. fig*)

'**frostig** *adj* frosty, *fig a.* chilly

'**Frostschutzmittel** *n* MOT antifreeze

Frottee [frɔ'teː] *n, m* (-[*s*]; -*s*) terry(-cloth)

frottieren [frɔ'tiːrən] *v/t* (*no* -*ge*-, *h*) rub down

Frucht [fruxt] *f* (-; *Früchte* ['frʏçtə]) BOT fruit (*a. fig*)

'**fruchtbar** *adj* BIOL fertile, *esp fig a.* fruit-

ful

'**Fruchtbarkeit** *f* (-; *no pl*) fertility; *fig* fruitfulness

'**fruchtlos** *adj* fruitless, futile

'**Fruchtsaft** *m* fruit juice

früh [fryː] *adj and adv* early; **zu früh kommen** be early; **früh genug** soon enough; **heute** (**morgen**) **früh** this (tomorrow) morning

'**Frühaufsteher** *m* (-*s*; -) early riser (F bird)

Frühe ['fryːə] *f: in aller Frühe* (very) early in the morning

früher ['fryːɐ] **1.** *adj* former; previous; **2.** *adv* in former times, at one time; **früher oder später** sooner or later; **ich habe früher** (**einmal**) … I used to …

'**frühestens** *adv* at the earliest

'**Frühgeburt** *f* MED premature birth; premature baby

Frühjahr *n* spring

Frühjahrsputz *m* spring cleaning

früh'morgens *adv* early in the morning

'**frühreif** *adj* precocious

'**Frühstück** *n* breakfast (**zum** for)

'**frühstücken** *v/i* (*ge*-, *h*) (have) breakfast

Frust [frust] F *m* (-[*e*]*s*; *no pl*) frustration

Frustration [frustra'tsjoːn] *f* (-; -*en*) frustration

frustrieren [frus'triːrən] *v/t* (*no* -*ge*-, *h*) frustrate

frz. ABBR *of* **französisch** Fr., French

Fuchs [fuks] *m* (-*es*; *Füchse* ['fʏksə]) ZO fox (*a. fig*); sorrel

Fuchsjagd *f* foxhunt(ing)

Fuchsschwanz *m* TECH handsaw

'**fuchs'teufels'wild** F *adj* hopping mad

fuchteln ['fuxtəln] *v/i* (*ge*-, *h*) **fuchteln mit** wave *s.th.* around

Fuge ['fuːgə] *f* (-; -*n*) TECH joint; MUS fugue

fügen ['fyːgən] *v/refl* (*ge*-, *h*) submit (**in** *acc, dat* to *s.th.*)

fühlbar ['fyːl-] *adj* noticeable; considerable

fühlen ['fyːlən] *v/t and v/i and v/refl* (*ge*-, *h*) feel, *fig a.* sense; **sich wohl fühlen** → **wohlfühlen**

Fühler ['fyːlɐ] *m* (-*s*; -) ZO feeler (*a. fig*)

fuhr [fuːɐ] *pret of* **fahren**

führen ['fyːrən] (*ge*-, *h*) **1.** *v/t* lead; guide; take; run, manage; ECON sell, deal in; keep (*account, books etc*); have (*a talk etc*); bear (*name etc*); MIL command; **j-n führen durch** show s.o. round; **sich führen** conduct o.s.; **2.** *v/i* lead (**zu** to, *a. fig*), SPORT *a.* be leading, be ahead

führend *adj* leading

Führer ['fyːrɐ] *m* (-*s*; -) leader (*a.* POL);

guide; head, chief; guide(book)
'**Führerschein** *m* MOT driver's license, *Br* driving licence
'**Führung** *f* (-; *-en*) a) (*no pl*) leadership, control; ECON management, b) (guided) tour; *gute Führung* good conduct; *in Führung gehen (sein)* SPORT take (be in) the lead
'**Führungszeugnis** *n* certificate of (good) conduct
Fuhrunternehmen ['fuːɐ-] *n* trucking company, *Br* haulage contractors
'**Fuhrwerk** *n* horse-drawn vehicle
Fülle ['fʏlə] *f* (-; *no pl*) crush; *fig* wealth, abundance; GASTR body
'**füllen** *v/t and v/refl* (*ge-, h*) fill (*a.* MED), stuff (*a.* GASTR)
Füller ['fʏlɐ] *m* (*-s;* -), '**Füllfederhalter** *m* fountain pen
füllig ['fʏlɪç] *adj* stout, portly
'**Füllung** *f* (-; *-en*) filling (*a.* MED), stuffing (*a.* GASTR)
fummeln ['fʊməln] F *v/i* (*ge-, h*) fiddle, tinker (*both: an dat* with); F grope
Fund [fʊnt] *m* (*-[e]s;* *-e* ['fʊndə]) discovery; find
Fundament [fʊndaˈmɛnt] *n* (*-[e]s;* *-e*) ARCH foundation(s), *fig a.* basis
Fundamentalist [fʊndamɛntaˈlɪst] *m* (*-en;* *-en*) fundamentalist
'**Fundbü,ro** *n* lost and found (office), *Br* lost-property office
'**Fundgrube** *fig f* treasure trove
Fundi ['fʊndi] F *m* (*-s;* *-s*) POL radical Green
fundiert [fʊnˈdiːɐt] *adj* well-founded (*argument etc*); sound (*knowledge*)
fünf [fʏnf] *adj* five; *grade:* F, N, *Br* fail, poor, E
'**Fünfeck** *n* (*-[e]s;* *-e*) pentagon
'**fünffach** *adj* fivefold
'**Fünfkampf** *m* SPORT pentathlon
'**Fünflinge** *pl* quintuplets
'**fünfte** *adj* fifth
'**Fünftel** *n* (*-s;* -) fifth
'**fünftens** *adv* fifth(ly), in the fifth place
'**fünfzehn(te)** *adj* fifteen(th)
fünfzig ['fʏnftsɪç] *adj* fifty
'**fünfzigste** *adj* fiftieth
fungieren [fʊŋˈgiːrən] *v/i* (*no -ge-, h*) *fungieren als* act as, function as
Funk [fʊŋk] *m* (*-s; no pl*) radio; *über or durch Funk* by radio
'**Funkama,teur** *m* radio ham
Funke ['fʊŋkə] *m* (*-n;* *-n*) spark; *fig a.* glimmer
funkeln ['fʊŋkəln] *v/i* (*ge-, h*) sparkle, glitter; twinkle
'**funken** *v/t* (*ge-, h*) radio, transmit

Funker ['fʊŋkɐ] *m* (*-s;* -) radio operator
'**Funkgerät** *n* radio set
Funkhaus *n* broadcasting center (*Br* centre)
Funksig,nal *n* radio signal
Funkspruch *m* radio message
Funkstati,on *f* radio station
Funkstreife *f* (radio) patrol car
Funktele,fon *n* cellular phone
Funktion [fʊŋkˈtsjoːn] *f* (-; *-en*) function
Funktionär [fʊŋktsjoˈnɛːɐ] *m* (*-s;* *-e*) functionary, official (*a.* SPORT)
funktionieren [fʊŋktsjoˈniːrən] *v/i* (*no -ge-, h*) work
'**Funkturm** *m* radio tower
'**Funkverkehr** *m* radio communication
für [fyːɐ] *prp* (*acc*) for; in favo(u)r of; on behalf of; *für immer* forever; *Tag für Tag* day by day; *Wort für Wort* word by word; *jeder für sich* everyone by himself; *was für …?* what (kind *or* sort of) …?; *das Für und Wider* the pros and cons
Furche ['fʊrçə] *f* (-; *-n*) furrow; rut
Furcht [fʊrçt] *f* (*-; no pl*) fear, dread (*both: vor dat* of); *aus Furcht*(, *dass*) for fear (that); *Furcht erregend* → *furchterregend*
'**furchtbar** *adj* terrible, awful
fürchten ['fʏrçtən] *v/t and v/i* (*ge-, h*) fear, be afraid of; dread; *fürchten um* fear for; *sich fürchten* be scared; be afraid (*vor dat* of); *ich fürchte, …* I'm afraid …
fürchterlich ['fʏrçtɐlɪç] → *furchtbar*
'**furchterregend** *adj* frightening
furchtlos *adj* fearless
furchtsam *adj* timid
füreiˈnander *adv* for each other
Furnier [fʊrˈniːɐ] *n* (*-[e]s;* *-e*), **furnieren** [fʊrˈniːrən] *v/t* (*no -ge-, h*) veneer
'**Fürsorge** *f* (-; *no pl*) care; *öffentliche Fürsorge* (public) welfare (work)
Fürsorgeempfänger *m* social security beneficiary
'**fürsorglich** [-zɔrklɪç] *adj* considerate
'**Fürsprache** *f* intercession (*für* for; *bei* with)
Fürsprech *m* (*-[e]s;* *-e*) *Swiss:* lawyer
Fürsprecher(in) advocate (*a. fig*)
Fürst [fʏrst] *m* (*-en;* *-en*) prince
'**Fürstentum** *n* (*-s;* *-tümer* [-tyːmɐ]) principality
'**Fürstin** *f* (-; *-nen*) princess
'**fürstlich** *adj* princely (*a. fig*)
Furt [fʊrt] *f* (-; *-en*) ford
Furunkel [fuˈrʊŋkəl] *m* (*-s;* -) MED boil, furuncle
'**Fürwort** *n* (*-[e]s;* *-wörter*) LING pronoun
Furz [fʊrts] *m* (*-es;* *-e*), '**furzen** *v/i* (*ge-, h*) fart

F

Fusion [fu'zjo:n] *f* (-; -*en*) ECON merger, amalgamation

fusionieren [fuzjo'ni:rən] *v/i* (*no -ge-, h*) ECON merge, amalgamate

Fuß [fu:s] *m* (-*es; Füße* ['fy:sə] ANAT foot; stand; stem; *zu Fuß* on foot; *zu Fuß gehen* walk; *gut zu Fuß sein* be a good walker; *Fuß fassen* become established; *auf freiem Fuß* at large

'**Fußball** *m* a) (*no pl*) soccer, *Br* football, b) soccer ball, *Br* football

'**Fußballer** [-balɐ] *m* (-*s*; -) footballer

'**Fußballfeld** *n* football field

Fußballrowdy *m* (football) hooligan

Fußballspiel *n* soccer *or* football match

Fußballspieler(in) football player, footballer

Fußballtoto *n* football pools

'**Fußboden** *m* floor; flooring

Fußbodenheizung *f* underfloor heating

'**Fußbremse** *f* MOT footbrake

Fussel ['fʊsəl] *f* (-; -*n*), *m* (-*s*; -[*n*]) piece of lint (*Br* fluff); *pl* lint, *Br* fluff

'**fusselig** ['fʊsəliç] *adj* linty, *Br* covered in fluff

'**fusseln** *v/i* (*ge-, h*) shed a lot of lint (*Br* fluff), F mo(u)lt

'**Fußgänger** [-gɛŋɐ] *m* (-*s*; -), '**Fußgängerin** *f* (-; -*nen*) pedestrian

'**Fußgängerzone** *f* (pedestrian *or* shopping) mall, *Br* pedestrian precinct

'**Fußgeher** *Austrian m* → **Fußgänger**

'**Fußgelenk** *n* ANAT ankle

Fußmatte *f* doormat

Fußnote *f* footnote

Fußpflege *f* pedicure; MED podiatry, *Br.* chiropody

Fußpfleger(in) podiatrist, *Br* chiropodist

Fußpilz *m* MED athlete's foot

Fußsohle *f* ANAT sole (of the foot)

Fußspur *f* footprint; track

Fußstapfen *pl*: *in j-s Fußstapfen treten* follow in s.o.'s footsteps

Fußtritt *m* kick

Fußweg *m* foothpath; *e-e Stunde Fußweg* an hour's walk

Futter[1] ['fʊtɐ] *n* (-*s; no pl*) AGR feed, fodder, food

'**Futter**[2] *n* (-*s*; -) lining

Futteral [fʊtə'ra:l] *n* (-*s*; -*e*) case; cover

füttern[1] ['fʏtɐn] *v/t* (*ge-, h*) AGR feed

'**füttern**[2] *v/t* (*ge-, h*) line

'**Futternapf** *m* (feeding) bowl

Fütterung ['fʏtərʊŋ] *f* (-; -*en*) feeding (time)

Futur [fu'tu:ɐ] *n* (-*s*; -*e*) future (*a*. LING)

G

gab [ga:p] *pret of* **geben**

Gabe ['ga:bə] *f* (-; -*n*) gift, present; MED dose; *fig* talent, gift; *milde Gabe* alms

Gabel ['ga:bəl] *f* (-; -*n*) fork; TEL cradle

'**gabeln** *v/refl* (*ge-, h*) fork, branch

'**Gabelstapler** [-ʃta:plɐ] *m* (-*s*; -) TECH fork-lift (truck)

Gabelung ['ga:bəlʊŋ] *f* (-; -*en*) fork(ing)

gackern ['gakɐn] *v/i* (*ge-, h*) cluck, cackle (*a. fig*)

gaffen ['gafən] *v/i* (*ge-, h*) gawk, gawp, F rubberneck

Gaffer ['gafɐ] *m* (-*s*; -) F rubberneck(er), *Br* nosy parker

Gage ['ga:ʒə] *f* (-; -*n*) fee

gähnen ['gɛ:nən] *v/i* (*ge-, h*) yawn

Gala ['ga:la] *f* (-; -*s*) gala

galant [ga'lant] *adj* gallant, courteous

Galeere [ga'le:rə] *f* (-; -*n*) MAR galley

Galerie [galə'ri:] *f* (-; -*n*) gallery

Galgen ['galgən] *m* (-*s*; -) gallows

Galgenfrist *f* reprieve

Galgenhu,mor *m* gallows humo(u)r

Galgenvogel F *m* crook

Galle ['galə] *f* (-; -*n*) ANAT gall; bile

'**Gallenblase** *f* ANAT gall bladder

Gallenstein *m* MED gallstone

Gallert ['galɐt] *n* (-[*es*]; -*e*), **Gallerte** [ga-'lɛrtə] *f* (-; -*n*) jelly

Galopp [ga'lɔp] *m* (-*s*; -*s*, -*e*) gallop

galoppieren [galɔ'pi:rən] *v/i* (*no -ge-, sein*) gallop

galt [galt] *pret of* **gelten**

gammeln ['gaməln] F *v/i* (*ge-, h*) loaf (about), bum around

Gammler(in) ['gamlɐ (-lərɪn)] F (-*s*; -/-; -*nen*) loafer, bum

Gämse ['gɛmzə] *f* (-; -*n*) ZO chamois

gang [gaŋ] *adj*: *gang und gäbe* nothing unusual, (quite) usual

Gang [gaŋ] *m* (-[*e*]*s; Gänge* ['gɛŋə]) walk, gait, way *s.o.* walks; ARCH passage, *a.* AVIAT

gastieren

etc aisle; corridor; MOT gear; GASTR course; *et. in Gang bringen* get s.th. going, start s.th.; *in Gang kommen* get started; *im Gang(e) sein* be (going) on, be in progress; *in vollem Gang(e)* in full swing

gängeln ['gɛŋəln] *v/t (ge-, h)* lead *s.o.* by the nose

gängig ['gɛŋɪç] *adj* current; ECON sal(e)able

'Gangschaltung *f* MOT gears

Ganove [ga'noːvə] F *m (-n; -n)* crook

Gans [gans] *f (-; Gänse* ['gɛnzə]) ZO goose

Gänseblümchen ['gɛnzə-] *n* BOT daisy

Gänsebraten *m* roast goose

Gänsehaut *f (-; no pl)* gooseflesh; *dabei kriege ich e-e Gänsehaut* F it gives me the creeps

Gänsemarsch *m (-[e]s; no pl)* single *or* Indian file

Gänserich ['gɛnzərɪç] *m (-s; -e)* ZO gander

ganz [gants] **1.** *adj* whole, entire, total; F undamaged; full (*hour etc*); *den ganzen Tag* all day; *die ganze Zeit* all the time; *auf der ganzen Welt* all over the world; *sein ganzes Geld* all his money; **2.** *adv* completely, totally; very; quite, rather, fairly; *ganz allein* all by oneself; *ganz aus Holz etc* all wood *etc*; *ganz und gar* completely, totally; *ganz und gar nicht* not at all, by no means; *ganz wie du willst* just as you like; *nicht ganz* not quite; → *voll*

Ganze ['gantsə] *n (-n; no pl)* whole; *das Ganze* the whole thing; *im Ganzen* in all, altogether; *im großen Ganzen* on the whole; *aufs Ganze gehen* go all out

gänzlich ['gɛntslɪç] *adv* completely, entirely

'Ganztagsbeschäftigung *f* full-time job

Ganztagsschule *f* all-day school(ing)

gar [gaːɐ] **1.** *adj* GASTR done; **2.** *adv*: *gar nicht* not at all; *gar nichts* nothing at all; *gar zu ...* (a bit) too ...

Garage [ga'raːʒə] *f (-; -n)* garage

Garantie [garan'tiː] *f (-; -n)* guarantee, *esp* ECON warranty

garantieren [garan'tiːrən] *v/t and v/i (no -ge-, h)* guarantee (*für et.* s.th.)

Garbe ['garbə] *f (-; -n)* AGR sheaf

Garde ['gardə] *f (-; -n)* guard; MIL (the) Guards

Garderobe [gardə'roːbə] *f (-; -n)* a) (*no pl*) wardrobe, clothes, b) checkroom, *Br* cloakroom; THEA dressing room

Garde'robenfrau *f* checkroom (*Br* cloakroom) attendant

Garderobenmarke *f* coatcheck (*Br* cloakroom) ticket

Garderobenständer *m* coat stand *or* rack

Gardine [gar'diːnə] *f (-; -n)* curtain

Gar'dinenstange *f* curtain rod

gären ['gɛːrən] *v/i ([irr,] ge-, h, sein)* ferment, work

Garn [garn] *n (-[e]s; -e)* yarn; thread; cotton

Garnele [gar'neːlə] *f (-; -n)* ZO shrimp; prawn

garnieren [gar'niːrən] *v/t (no -ge-, h)* garnish (*a. fig*)

Garnison [garni'zoːn] *f (-; -en)* MIL garrison, post

Garnitur [garni'tuːɐ] *f (-, -en)* set; suite

Garten ['gartən] *m (-s; Gärten* ['gɛrtən]) garden

Gartenarbeit *f* gardening

Gartenbau *m (-[e]s; no pl)* horticulture

Gartenerde *f (garden)* mo(u)ld

Gartenfest *n* garden party

Gartengeräte *pl* gardening tools

Gartenhaus *n* summerhouse

Gartenlo,kal *n* beer garden; outdoor restaurant

Gartenschere *f* pruning shears

Gartenstadt *f* garden city

Gartenzwerg *m* (garden) gnome

Gärtner ['gɛrtnɐ] *m (-s; -)* gardener

Gärtnerei [gɛrtnə'rai] *f (-; -en)* truck farm, *Br* market garden

'Gärtnerin *f (-; -nen)* gardener

Gärung ['gɛːrʊŋ] *f (-; -en)* fermentation

Gas [gaːs] *n (-es; -e* ['gaːzə]) gas; *Gas geben* MOT accelerate, F step on the gas

'gasförmig [-fœrmɪç] *adj* gaseous

'Gashahn *m* gas valve (*or* cock, *Br* tap)

Gasheizung *f* gas heating

Gasherd *m* gas cooker *or* stove

Gaskammer *f* gas chamber

Gasla,terne *f* gas (street) lamp

Gasleitung *f* gas main

Gasmaske *f* gas mask

Gasofen *m* gas stove

Gaspe,dal *n* MOT gas pedal, *Br* accelerator (pedal)

Gasse ['gasə] *f (-; -n)* lane, alley

Gast [gast] *m (-[e]s; Gäste* ['gɛstə]) guest; visitor; customer

'Gastarbeiter *m,* **'Gastarbeiterin** *f* foreign worker

Gästebuch ['gɛstə-] *n* visitors' book

'Gästezimmer *n* guest (*or* spare) room

'gastfreundlich *adj* hospitable

'Gastfreundschaft *f* hospitality

'Gastgeber [-geːbɐ] *m (-s; -)* host

'Gastgeberin [-geːbərɪn] *f (-; -nen)* hostess

'Gasthaus *n,* **Gasthof** *m* restaurant, inn

gastieren [gas'tiːrən] *v/i (no -ge-, h)* give

performances; THEA guest, give a guest performance

'**gastlich** *adj* hospitable

'**Gastmannschaft** *f* SPORT visiting team

Gastspiel *n* THEA guest performance

Gaststätte *f* restaurant

Gaststube *f* taproom; restaurant

Gastwirt *m* landlord

Gastwirtschaft *f* restaurant, inn

'**Gaswerk** *n* TECH gasworks

'**Gaszähler** *m* TECH gas meter

Gatte ['gatə] *m* (*-n*; *-n*) husband

Gatter ['gatɐ] *n* (*-s*; *-*) fence; gate

Gattin ['gatɪn] *f* (*-*; *-nen*) wife

Gattung ['gatʊŋ] *f* (*-*; *-en*) type, class, sort; BIOL genus; species

GAU [gau] (ABBR *of* **größter anzunehmender Unfall**) *m* (*-[s]; no pl*) worst case scenario, *Br* maximum credible accident, MCA

Gaul [gaul] *m* (*-[e]s*; **Gäule** ['gɔylə]) nag

Gaumen ['gaumən] *m* (*-s*; *-*) ANAT palate

Gauner ['gaunɐ] *m* (*-s*, *-*), '**Gaunerin** *f* (*-*; *-nen*) F crook

Gaze ['gaːzə] *f* (*-*; *-n*) gauze

Gazelle [ga'tsɛlə] *f* (*-*; *-n*) ZO gazelle

geb. ABBR *of* **geboren** b., born

Gebäck [gə'bɛk] *n* (*-[e]s*; *-e*) pastry; cookies, *Br* biscuits

ge'backen *pp of* **backen**

Gebälk [gə'bɛlk] *n* (*-[e]s*; *-e*) timberwork, beams

gebar [gə'baːɐ] *pret of* **gebären**

Gebärde [gə'bɛːɐdə] *f* (*-*; *-n*) gesture

ge'bärden *v/refl* (*no -ge-*, *h*) behave, act (**wie** like)

gebären [gə'bɛːrən] *v/t* (*irr*, *no -ge-*, *h*) give birth to

Gebärmutter [gə'bɛːɐ-] *f* ANAT uterus, womb

Gebäude [gə'bɔydə] *n* (*-s*; *-*) building, structure

Ge'beine *pl* bones, mortal remains

geben ['geːbən] *v/t* (*irr*, *ge-*, *h*) give (*j-m et.* s.o. s.th.); hand, pass; deal (*cards*); make; **sich geben** pass; get better; **von sich geben** utter, let out; **j-m die Schuld geben** blame s.o.; **es gibt** there is, there are; **was gibt es?** what's up?; what's for *lunch etc?*; TV *etc* what's on?; **das gibt's nicht** that can't be true; that's out

Gebet [gə'beːt] *n* (*-[e]s*; *-e*) prayer

ge'beten *pp of* **bitten**

Gebiet [gə'biːt] *n* (*-[e]s*; *-e*) region, area; *esp* POL territory; *fig* field

ge'bieterisch *adj* imperious

ge'bietsweise *adv* regionally; **gebietsweise Regen** local showers

Gebilde [gə'bɪldə] *n* (*-s*; *-*) thing, object

gebildet [gə'bɪldət] *adj* educated

Gebirge [gə'bɪrgə] *n* (*-s*; *-*) mountains

gebirgig [gə'bɪrgɪç] *adj* mountainous

Ge'birgsbewohner *m* mountain-dweller

Gebirgszug *m* mountain range

Ge'biss *n* (*-es*; *-e*) (set of) teeth; (set of) false teeth, denture(s)

ge'bissen *pp of* **beißen**

Gebläse [gə'blɛːzə] *n* (*-s*; *-*) TECH blower, (MOT air) fan

ge'blasen *pp of* **blasen**

geblichen [gə'blɪçən] *pp of* **bleichen**

geblieben [gə'bliːbən] *pp of* **bleiben**

geblümt [gə'blyːmt] *adj* floral

gebogen [gə'boːgən] **1.** *pp of* **biegen**; **2.** *adj* bent, curved

geboren [gə'boːrən] **1.** *pp of* **gebären**; **2.** *adj* born; **ein geborener Deutscher** German by birth; **geborene Smith** née Smith; **ich bin am ... geboren** I was born on the ...

geborgen [gə'bɔrgən] **1.** *pp of* **bergen**; **2.** *adj* safe, secure

Ge'borgenheit *f* (*-*; *no pl*) safety, security

geborsten [gə'bɔrstən] *pp of* **bersten**

Gebot [gə'boːt] *n* (*-[e]s*; *-e*) REL commandment; *fig* rule; necessity; *auction etc*: bid

geboten [gə'boːtən] *pp of* **bieten**

gebracht [gə'braxt] *pp of* **bringen**

gebrannt [gə'brant] *pp of* **brennen**

ge'braten *pp of* **braten**

Ge'brauch *m* (*-[e]s*; *no pl*) use; application

ge'brauchen *v/t* (*no -ge-*, *h*) use; employ; **gut (nicht) zu gebrauchen sein** be useful (useless); **ich könnte ... gebrauchen** I could do with ...

gebräuchlich [gə'brɔyçlɪç] *adj* in use; common, usual; current

Ge'brauchsanweisung *f* directions *or* instructions for use

ge'brauchsfertig *adj* ready for use; instant (*coffee etc*)

Ge'brauchsgrafiker *m* commercial artist

ge'braucht *adj* used, ECON *a.* second-hand

Ge'brauchtwagen *m* MOT used *or* second--hand car

Gebrauchtwagenhändler *m* used car dealer

Ge'brechen *n* (*-s*; *-*) defect, handicap

gebrechlich [gə'brɛçlɪç] *adj* frail; infirm

Ge'brechlichkeit *f* (*-*; *no pl*) frailty; infirmity

gebrochen [gə'brɔxən] *pp of* **brechen**

Ge'brüder *pl* brothers

Gebrüll [gə'brʏl] *n* (*-[e]s*; *no pl*) roar(-ing)

Gebühr [gə'byːɐ] *f* (*-*; *-en*) charge (*a.* TEL), fee; postage; due

gebührend [gə'byːrənt] *adj* due; proper
ge'bührenfrei *adj* free of charge; TEL toll--free, *Br* nonchargeable
gebührenpflichtig *adj* chargeable; *gebührenpflichtige Straße* toll road; *gebührenpflichtige Verwarnung* fine
gebunden [gə'bʊndən] **1.** *pp of binden*; **2.** *adj* bound, *fig a.* tied
Geburt [gə'buːɐt] *f* (-; -en) birth; *Deutscher von Geburt* German by birth
Ge'burtenkon,trolle *f*, **Geburtenregelung** *f* birth control
ge'burtenschwach *adj* low-birthrate
geburtenstark *adj*: *geburtenstarke Jahrgänge* baby boom
Ge'burtenziffer *f* birthrate
gebürtig [gə'byrtɪç] *adj* by birth
Ge'burtsanzeige *f* birth announcement
Geburtsdatum *n* date of birth
Geburtsfehler *m* congenital defect
Geburtshelfer(in) obstetrician
Geburtsjahr *n* year of birth
Geburtsland *n* native country
Geburtsort *m* birthplace
Geburtstag *m* birthday
Geburtstagsfeier *f* birthday party
Geburtstagskind *n* birthday boy (*or* girl)
Geburtsurkunde *f* birth certificate
Gebüsch [gə'byʃ] *n* (-[e]s; -e) bushes, shrubbery
gedacht [gə'daxt] *pp of denken*
Gedächtnis [gə'dɛçtnɪs] *n* (-ses; -se) memory; *aus dem Gedächtnis* from memory; *zum Gedächtnis an* (*acc*) in memory (*or* commemoration) of; *im Gedächtnis behalten* keep in mind, remember
Gedächtnislücke *f* memory lapse
Gedächtnisschwund *m* MED amnesia; blackout
Gedächtnisstütze *f* memory aid
Gedanke [gə'daŋkə] *m* (-n; -n) thought; idea; *was für ein Gedanke!* what an idea!; *in Gedanken* absorbed in thought; absent-minded; *sich Gedanken machen über* (*acc*) think about; be worried *or* concerned about; *j-s Gedanken lesen* read s.o.'s mind
Ge'dankenaustausch *m* exchange of ideas
Gedankengang *m* train of thought
ge'dankenlos *adj* thoughtless
Ge'dankenstrich *m* dash
Gedankenübertragung *f* telepathy
Gedeck [gə'dɛk] *n* (-[e]s; -e) cover; *ein Gedeck auflegen* set a place
gedeihen [gə'daiən] *v/i* (*irr, no -ge-, sein*) thrive, prosper; grow; flourish
ge'denken *v/i* (*irr, denken, no -ge-, h*)

(*gen*) think of; commemorate; mention
Gedenkfeier [gə'dɛŋk-] *f* commemoration
Gedenkmi,nute *f*: *e-e Gedenkminute* a moment's (*Br* minute's) silence
Gedenkstätte *f*, **Gedenkstein** *m* memorial
Gedenktafel *f* plaque
Gedicht [gə'dɪçt] *n* (-[e]s; -e) poem
gediegen [gə'diːgən] *adj* solid; tasteful
gedieh [gə'diː] *pret of gedeihen*
gediehen [gə'diːən] *pp of gedeihen*
Gedränge [gə'drɛŋə] *n* (-s; -) crowd, crush
ge'drängt *fig adj* concise
gedroschen [gə'drɔʃən] *pp of dreschen*
ge'drückt *fig adj* depressed
gedrungen [gə'drʊŋən] **1.** *pp of dringen*; **2.** *adj* squat, stocky; thickset
Geduld [gə'dʊlt] *f* (-; *no pl*) patience
ge'dulden *v/refl* (*no -ge-, h*) wait (patiently)
geduldig [gə'dʊldɪç] *adj* patient
Ge'duldspiel *n* puzzle (*a. fig*)
gedurft [gə'dʊrft] *pp of dürfen*
geehrt [gə'ʔeːɐt] *adj* hono(u)red; *Sehr geehrter Herr N.* Dear Mr N.
geeignet [gə'ʔaignət] *adj* suitable; suited, qualified; right
Gefahr [gə'faːɐ] *f* (-; -en) danger; threat; risk; *auf eigene Gefahr* at one's own risk; *außer Gefahr* out of danger, safe
gefährden [gə'fɛːɐdən] *v/t* (*no -ge-, h*) endanger; risk, jeopardize
ge'fahren *pp of fahren*
gefährlich [gə'fɛːɐlɪç] *adj* dangerous; risky
ge'fahrlos *adj* without risk, safe
Gefährte [gə'fɛːɐtə] *m* (-n; -n), **Ge'fährtin** *f* (-; -nen) companion
Gefälle [gə'fɛlə] *n* (-s; -) fall, slope, descent; gradient (*a.* PHYS)
ge'fallen 1. *pp of fallen*; **2.** *v/i* (*irr, fallen, no -ge-, h*) please; *es gefällt mir (nicht)* I (don't) like it; *wie gefällt dir ...?* how do you like ...?; *sich et. gefallen lassen* put up with s.th.
Ge'fallen¹ *m* (-s; -) favo(u)r; *j-n um e-n Gefallen bitten* ask a favo(u)r of s.o.
Ge'fallen² *n*: *Gefallen finden an* (*dat*) enjoy, like
ge'fällig *adj* pleasant, agreeable; obliging, kind; *j-m gefällig sein* do s.o. a favo(u)r
Ge'fälligkeit *f* (-; -en) a) (*no pl*) kindness, b) favo(u)r
ge'fangen 1. *pp of fangen*; **2.** *adj* captive; imprisoned; *gefangen halten* keep *s.o.* prisoner; *gefangen nehmen* take *s.o.* prisoner; *fig* captivate

Ge'fangene *m, f* (*-n*; *-n*) prisoner; convict

Ge'fangennahme *f* (*-*; *no pl*) capture

Ge'fangenschaft *f* (*-*; *no pl*) captivity, imprisonment; *in Gefangenschaft sein* be a prisoner of war

Gefängnis [gə'fɛŋnɪs] *n* (*-ses*; *-se*) prison, jail, *Br a.* gaol; *ins Gefängnis kommen* go to jail *or* prison

Gefängnisdi,rektor *m* governor, warden

Gefängnisstrafe *f* (sentence *or* term of) imprisonment

Gefängniswärter *m* prison guard

Gefäß [gə'fɛːs] *n* (*-es*; *-e*) vessel (*a.* ANAT), container

gefasst [gə'fast] *adj* composed; *gefasst auf* (*acc*) prepared for

Gefecht [gə'fɛçt] *n* (*-[e]s*; *-e*) MIL combat, action

gefedert [gə'feːdɐt] *adj*: *gut gefedert sein* MOT have good suspension

gefeit [gə'fait] *adj*: *gefeit gegen* immune to

Gefieder [gə'fiːdɐ] *n* (*-s*; *-*) ZO plumage, feathers

geflochten [gə'flɔxtən] *pp of* **flechten**

geflogen [gə'floːgən] *pp of* **fliegen**

geflohen [gə'floːən] *pp of* **fliehen**

geflossen [gə'flɔsən] *pp of* **fließen**

Ge'flügel *n* (*-s*; *no pl*) poultry

ge'flügelt *adj*: *geflügeltes Wort* saying

gefochten [gə'fɔxtən] *pp of* **fechten**

Ge'folge *n* (*-s*; *-*) entourage, retinue, train

Gefolgschaft [gə'fɔlkʃaft] *f* (*-*; *-en*) followers

gefragt [gə'fraːkt] *adj* in demand, popular

gefräßig [gə'frɛːsɪç] *adj* greedy, voracious

Gefreite [gə'fraitə] *m* (*-n*; *-n*) MIL private first class, *Br* lance corporal

ge'fressen *pp of* **fressen**

ge'frieren *v/i* (*irr*, **frieren**, *no -ge-*, *sein*) freeze

Gefrierfach [gə'friːr-] *n* freezer, freezing compartment

Gefrierfleisch *n* frozen meat

ge'friergetrocknet *adj* freeze-dried

Ge'frierpunkt *m* freezing point

Gefriertruhe *f* freezer, deep-freeze

gefroren [gə'froːrən] *pp of* **frieren**

Ge'frorene *Austrian n* (*-n*; *no pl*) ice cream

Gefüge [gə'fyːgə] *n* (*-s*; *-*) structure, texture

gefügig [gə'fyːgɪç] *adj* pliant

Ge'fügigkeit *f* (*-*; *no pl*) pliancy

Gefühl [gə'fyːl] *n* (*-[e]s*; *-e*) feeling; sense; sensation; emotion

ge'fühllos *adj* insensible, numb; unfeeling, heartless

ge'fühlsbetont *adj* (highly) emotional

ge'fühlvoll *adj* (full of) feeling; tender; sentimental

gefunden [gə'fundən] *pp of* **finden**

gegangen [gə'gaŋən] *pp of* **gehen**

gegeben [gə'geːbən] *pp of* **geben**

gegen ['geːgən] *prp* (*acc*) against, JUR, SPORT *a.* versus; about, around; (in return) for; MED *etc* for; compared with

'Gegen... *in cpds* ...aktion, ...angriff, ...argument, ...frage *etc*: counter-...

Gegenbesuch *m* return visit

Gegend ['geːgənt] *f* (*-*; *-en*) region, area; countryside; neighbo(u)rhood

gegenei'nander *adv* against one another *or* each other

'Gegenfahrbahn *f* MOT opposite *or* on-coming lane

Gegengewicht *n* counterweight; *ein Gegengewicht bilden zu et.* counterbalance s.th.

Gegenkandi,dat *m* rival candidate

Gegenleistung *f* quid pro quo; *als Gegenleistung* in return

Gegenlicht *n* (*-[e]s*; *no pl*) PHOT back light; *im or bei Gegenlicht* against the light

Gegenmaßnahme *f* countermeasure

Gegenmittel *n* MED antidote (*a. fig*)

Gegenpar,tei *f* other side; POL opposition; SPORT opposite side

Gegenrichtung *f* opposite direction

'Gegensatz *m* contrast; opposite; *im Gegensatz zu* in contrast to *or* with

'gegensätzlich [-zɛtslɪç] *adj* contrary, opposite

'Gegenseite *f* opposite side

'gegenseitig [-zaitɪç] *adj* mutual

'Gegenseitigkeit *f*: *auf Gegenseitigkeit beruhen* be mutual

'Gegenspieler *m*, **Gegenspielerin** *f* SPORT opponent (*a. fig*)

Gegensprechanlage *f* intercom (system)

'Gegenstand *m* object (*a. fig*); *fig* subject

'gegenständlich [-ʃtɛntlɪç] *adj art*: representational

'gegenstandslos *adj* invalid; irrelevant; *art*: abstract, nonrepresentational

'Gegenstimme *f* PARL vote against, no; *nur drei Gegenstimmen* only three noes

Gegenstück *n* counterpart

'Gegenteil *n* opposite; *im Gegenteil* on the contrary

'gegenteilig *adj* contrary, opposite

gegen'über *adv and prp* (*dat*) opposite; *fig* to, toward(s); compared with

Gegen'über *n* (*-s*; *-*) person opposite; neighbo(u)r across the street

gegen'überstehen v/i (irr, **stehen**, sep, -ge-, h) face, be faced with
Gegen'überstellung f confrontation
'**Gegenverkehr** m oncoming traffic
'**Gegenwart** [-vart] f (-; no pl) present (time); presence; LING present (tense)
'**gegenwärtig** [-vɛrtɪç] **1.** adj present, current; **2.** adv at present
'**Gegenwehr** [-veːɐ] f (-; no pl) resistance
Gegenwert m equivalent (value)
Gegenwind m head wind
'**gegenzeichnen** v/t (sep, -ge-, h) countersign
'**Gegenzug** m countermove; RAIL train coming from the opposite direction
gegessen [gə'gɛsən] pp of **essen**
geglichen [gə'glɪçən] pp of **gleichen**
geglitten [gə'glɪtən] pp of **gleiten**
geglommen [gə'glɔmən] pp of **glimmen**
Gegner ['geːgnɐ] m (-s; -), '**Gegnerin** f (-; -nen) opponent (a. SPORT), adversary; MIL enemy
'**gegnerisch** adj opposing; MIL (of the) enemy, hostile
'**Gegnerschaft** f (-; -en) opposition
gegolten [gə'gɔltən] pp of **gelten**
gegoren [gə'goːrən] pp of **gären**
gegossen [gə'gɔsən] pp of **gießen**
ge'graben pp of **graben**
gegriffen [gə'grɪfən] pp of **greifen**
gehabt [gə'haːpt] pp of **haben**
Gehackte [gə'haktə] n → **Hackfleisch**
Gehalt [gə'halt] **1.** m (-[e]s; -e) content; **2.** n (-[e]s; Gehälter [gə'hɛltɐ]) salary
ge'halten pp of **halten**
Ge'haltsempfänger m salaried employee
Gehaltserhöhung f raise, Br increase or rise in salary
ge'haltvoll adj substantial; nutritious
gehangen [gə'haŋən] pp of **hängen** 1
gehässig [gə'hɛsɪç] adj malicious, spiteful
Ge'hässigkeit f (-; no pl) malice, spite (-fulness)
ge'hauen pp of **hauen**
Gehäuse [gə'hɔyzə] n (-s; -) case, box; TECH casing; ZO shell; BOT core
Gehege [gə'heːgə] n (-s; -) enclosure
geheim [gə'haim] adj secret; et. **geheim halten** keep s.th. (a) secret
Ge'heima,gent m secret agent
Geheimdienst m secret service
Geheimnis [gə'haimnɪs] n (-ses; -se) secret; mystery
ge'heimnisvoll adj mysterious
Ge'heimnummer f TEL unlisted (Br ex-directory) number
Geheimpoli,zei f secret police
Geheimschrift f code, cipher

ge'heißen pp of **heißen**
gehemmt [gə'hɛmt] adj inhibited, self--conscious
gehen ['geːən] v/i (irr, ge-, sein) go; walk; leave; TECH work (a. fig); ECON sell; fig last; **einkaufen (schwimmen) gehen** go shopping (swimming); **gehen wir!** let's go!; **wie geht es dir (Ihnen)?** how are you?; **es geht mir gut (schlecht)** I'm fine (not feeling well); **gehen in** (acc) go into
gehen nach road etc: lead to; window etc: face; fig go or judge by; **das geht nicht** that's impossible; **das geht schon** that's o.k.; **es geht nichts über** (acc) … there is nothing like …; **worum geht es?** what is it about?; **darum geht es (nicht)** that's (not) the point; **sich gehen nach lassen** let o.s. go
'**gehenlassen** v/refl (irr, **lassen**, sep, no -ge-, h) → **gehen**
geheuer [gə'hɔyɐ] adj: **nicht (ganz) geheuer** eerie, creepy, F fishy
Geheul [gə'hɔyl] n (-[e]s; no pl) howling
Ge'hirn n (-[e]s; -e) ANAT brain(s)
Gehirnerschütterung f MED concussion (of the brain)
Gehirnschlag m MED (cerebral) apoplexy
Gehirnwäsche f brainwashing
gehoben [gə'hoːbən] **1.** pp of **heben**; **2.** adj elevated; high(er); **gehobene Stimmung** high spirits
Gehöft [gə'hœft] n (-[e]s; -e) farm(stead)
geholfen [gə'hɔlfən] pp of **helfen**
Gehölz [gə'hœlts] n (-es; -e) wood, coppice, copse
Gehör [gə'høːɐ] n (-[e]s; -e) (sense of) hearing; ear; **nach dem Gehör** by ear; **sich Gehör verschaffen** make o.s. heard
ge'horchen v/i (no -ge-, h) obey; **nicht gehorchen** disobey
ge'hören v/i (no -ge-, h) belong (dat or **zu** to); **gehört dir das?** is this yours?; **es gehört sich (nicht)** it is proper or right (not done); **das gehört nicht hierher** that's not to the point
ge'hörig 1. adj due, proper; necessary; decent; **zu et. gehörig** belonging to s.th.; **2.** adv properly, thoroughly
ge'hörlos adj deaf; **die Gehörlosen** the deaf
gehorsam [gə'hoːɐzaːm] adj obedient
Ge'horsam m (-s; no pl) obedience
'**Gehsteig** m, '**Gehweg** m sidewalk, Br pavement
Geier ['gaiɐ] m (-s; -) ZO vulture, buzzard
Geige ['gaigə] f (-; -n) MUS violin, F fiddle; **(auf der) Geige spielen** play (on) the vi-

G

olin
'Geigenbogen m MUS (violin) bow
Geigenkasten m MUS violin case
'Geiger ['gaigɐ] m (-s; -), **Geigerin** ['gai-
gərɪn] f (-; -nen) MUS violinist
'Geigerzähler m PHYS Geiger counter
geil [gail] adj V hot, horny; contp lecher-
ous, lewd; BOT rank; F awesome, Br brill,
ace
Geisel ['gaizəl] f (-; -n) hostage
Geiselnehmer [-neːmɐ] m (-s; -) kidnap-
(p)er
Geißel ['gaisəl] fig f (-; -n) scourge
Geist [gaist] m (-[e]s; -er) a) (no pl) spirit;
soul; mind; intellect; wit, b) ghost; **der
Heilige Geist** REL the Holy Ghost or
Spirit
Geisterbahn ['gaistɐ-] f tunnel of horror,
Br ghost train
Geisterfahrer F m MOT wrong-way driver
'geisterhaft adj ghostly
'geistesabwesend adj absent-minded
'Geistesarbeiter m brainworker
Geistesblitz m brainstorm, Br brainwave
'Geistesgegenwart f presence of mind
'geistesgegenwärtig adj alert; quick-witted
'geistesgestört adj mentally disturbed,
deranged
'geisteskrank adj mentally ill
'Geisteskrankheit f mental illness
'geistesschwach adj feeble-minded
'Geisteswissenschaften pl the arts, the
humanities
'Geisteszustand m mental state
geistig ['gaistɪç] adj mental; intellectual;
spiritual; **geistig behindert** mentally
handicapped; **geistige Getränke** spirits
'geistlich adj religious; spiritual; ecclesiastical; clerical
'Geistliche m (-n; -n) clergyman; priest;
minister; **die Geistlichen** the clergy
'geistlos adj trivial, inane, silly
'geistreich, 'geistvoll adj witty, clever
Geiz [gaits] m (-es; no pl) stinginess
'Geizhals m miser, niggard
geizig ['gaitsɪç] adj stingy, miserly
Ge'jammer F n (-s; no pl) wailing, com-
plaining
gekannt [gə'kant] pp of **kennen**
Gekläff [gə'klɛf] F n (-[e]s; no pl) yapping
Geklapper [gə'klapɐ] F n (-s; no pl) clat-
ter(ing)
Geklimper F n (-s; no pl) tinkling
geklungen [gə'klʊŋən] pp of **klingen**
gekniffen [gə'knɪfən] pp of **kneifen**
ge'kommen pp of **kommen**
gekonnt [gə'kɔnt] **1.** pp of **können**; **2.** adj
masterly

gekränkt [gə'krɛŋkt] adj hurt, offended
Gekritzel [gə'krɪtsəl] contp n (-s; no pl)
scrawl, scribble
gekrochen [gə'krɔxən] pp of **kriechen**
gekünstelt [gə'kʏnstəlt] adj affected; artificial
Gelächter [gə'lɛçtɐ] n (-s; no pl) laughter
ge'laden pp of **laden**
Ge'lage n (-s; -) feast; carouse
Gelände [gə'lɛndə] n (-s; -) area, country,
ground; site; **auf dem Gelände** on the
premises; **Gelände...** in cpds ...lauf,
...ritt, ...wagen etc: cross-country ...
Geländer [gə'lɛndɐ] n (-s; -) banisters;
handrail, rail(ing); parapet
ge'lang pret of **gelingen**
ge'langen v/i (no -ge-, sein) **gelangen an**
(acc) or **nach** reach, arrive at, get or
come to; **gelangen in** (acc) get or come
into; fig **zu et. gelangen** gain or win or
achieve s.th.
ge'lassen 1. pp of **lassen**; **2.** adj calm,
composed, cool
Gelatine [ʒela'tiːnə] f (-; no pl) gelatin(e)
ge'laufen pp of **laufen**
ge'läufig adj common, current; familiar
gelaunt [gə'launt] adj: **schlecht (gut) gelaunt sein** be in a bad (good) mood
gelb [gɛlp] adj yellow
'gelblich adj yellowish
'Gelbsucht f (-; no pl) MED jaundice
Geld [gɛlt] n (-[e]s; -er ['gɛldɐ]) money;
zu Geld machen turn into cash
'Geldangelegenheiten pl money or financial matters or affairs
Geldanlage f investment
Geldausgabe f expense
Geldauto,mat m automatic teller ma-
chine, ATM, autoteller, Br cash dispens-
er
Geldbeutel m, **Geldbörse** f purse
Geldbuße f fine, penalty
Geldgeber(in) [-geːbɐ (-bərɪn)] (-s; -/-;
-nen) financial backer; investor
'geldgierig adj greedy for money
'Geldknappheit f, **Geldmangel** m lack of
money; ECON (financial) stringency
Geldmittel pl funds, means, resources
Geldschein m bill, Br (bank)note
Geldschrank m safe
Geldsendung f remittance
Geldstrafe f fine
Geldstück n coin
Geldverlegenheit f financial embarrass-
ment
Geldverschwendung f waste of money
Geldwaschanlage f money laundering
scheme
Geldwechsel m exchange of money

Geldwechsler [-vɛkslɐ] *m* (*-s*; -) change machine

Gelee [ʒeˈleː] *n, m* (*-s*; *-s*) jelly; gel

geˈlegen 1. *pp of liegen*; **2.** *adj* situated, located; *fig* convenient, opportune

Geˈlegenheit *f* (-; *-en*) occasion; opportunity, chance; *bei Gelegenheit* on occasion

Geˈlegenheitsarbeit *f* casual *or* odd job

Gelegenheitsarbeiter *m* casual labo(u)rer, odd-job man

Gelegenheitskauf *m* bargain

gelegentlich [ɡəˈleːɡəntlɪç] *adv* occasionally

gelehrig [ɡəˈleːrɪç] *adj* docile

Gelehrsamkeit [ɡəˈleːɐzaːmkait] *f* (-; *no pl*) learning

gelehrt [ɡəˈleːɐt] *adj* learned

Geˈlehrte *m, f* (*-n*; *-n*) scholar, learned man *or* woman

Geleise [ɡəˈlaizə] *n* → *Gleis*

Geleit [ɡəˈlait] *n* (*-[e]s*; *-e*) escort

geˈleiten *v/t* (*no -ge-, h*) accompany, conduct, escort

Geˈleitzug *m* MAR, MIL convoy

Gelenk [ɡəˈlɛŋk] *n* (*-[e]s*; *-e*) ANAT, TECH joint

geˈlenkig *adj* flexible (*a.* TECH); lithe, supple

gelernt [ɡəˈlɛrnt] *adj* skilled, trained

geˈlesen *pp of lesen*

geliebt [ɡəˈliːpt] *adj* (be)loved, dear

Geˈliebte 1. *m* (*-n*; *-n*) lover; **2.** *f* (*-n*; *-n*) mistress

geliehen [ɡəˈliːən] *pp of leihen*

gelingen [ɡəˈlɪŋən] *v/i* (*irr, no -ge-, sein*) succeed, manage; turn out well; *es gelang mir, et. zu tun* I succeeded in doing (I managed to do) s.th.

Geˈlingen *n* (*-s*; *no pl*) success; *gutes Gelingen!* good luck!

gelitten [ɡəˈlɪtən] *pp of leiden*

gelogen [ɡəˈloːɡən] *pp of lügen*

gelten [ˈɡɛltən] *v/i and v/t* (*irr, ge-, h*) be worth; *fig* count for; be valid; SPORT count; ECON be effective; *gelten für* apply to; *gelten als* be regarded *or* looked upon as, be considered *or* supposed to be; *gelten lassen* accept (*als* as)

geltend *adj* accepted; *geltend machen* assert; *s-n Einfluss (bei j-m) geltend machen* bring one's influence to bear (on s.o.)

ˈGeltung *f* (-; *no pl*) prestige; weight; *zur Geltung kommen* show to advantage

ˈGeltungsbedürfnis *n* (*-ses*; *no pl*) need for recognition

Gelübde [ɡəˈlʏpdə] *n* (*-s*; -) vow

gelungen [ɡəˈlʊŋən] **1.** *pp of gelingen*; **2.**

adj successful, a success

gemächlich [ɡəˈmɛːçlɪç] *adj* leisurely

geˈmahlen *pp of mahlen*

Gemälde [ɡəˈmɛːldə] *n* (*-s*; -) painting, picture

Gemäldegaleˌrie *f* art (*or* picture) gallery

gemäß [ɡəˈmɛːs] *prp* (*dat*) according to

gemäßigt [ɡəˈmɛːsɪçt] *adj* moderate; temperate (*climate etc*)

gemein [ɡəˈmain] *adj* mean; dirty, filthy (*joke etc*); BOT, ZO common

Gemeinde [ɡəˈmaində] *f* (*-*; *-n*) POL municipality; local government; REL parish; congregation

Gemeinderat *m* (member of the) city (*Br* local) council

Gemeinderätin [-rɛːtɪn] *f* (-; *-nen*) member of the city (*Br* local) council

Gemeindesteuern *pl* local taxes, *Br* (local) rates

geˈmeingefährlich *adj*: *gemeingefährlicher Mensch* public enemy

Geˈmeinheit *f* (-; *-en*) a) (*no pl*) meanness, b) mean thing (to do *or* say), F dirty trick

geˈmeinnützig [-nʏtsɪç] *adj* non-profit, *Br* non-profitmaking

Geˈmeinplatz *m* commonplace

geˈmeinsam 1. *adj* common, joint; mutual; **2.** *adv* together

Geˈmeinschaft *f* (-; *-en*) community

Geˈmeinschaftsarbeit *f* teamwork

Gemeinschaftskunde *f* (-; *no pl*) PED social studies

Gemeinschaftsprodukti̱on *f* coproduction

Gemeinschaftsraum *m* recreation room, lounge

Geˈmeinsinn *m* (*-[e]s*; *no pl*) public spirit; (sense of) solidarity

geˈmeinverständlich *adj* popular

Geˈmeinwohl *n* public welfare

geˈmessen 1. *pp of messen*; **2.** *adj* measured; formal; grave

Gemetzel [ɡəˈmɛtsəl] *n* (*-s*; -) slaughter, massacre

gemieden [ɡəˈmiːdən] *pp of meiden*

Gemisch [ɡəˈmɪʃ] *n* (*-[e]s*; *-e*) mixture (*a.* CHEM)

gemocht [ɡəˈmɔxt] *pp of mögen*

gemolken [ɡəˈmɔlkən] *pp of melken*

Gemse → *Gämse*

Gemurmel [ɡəˈmʊrməl] *n* (*-s*; *no pl*) murmur, mutter

Gemüse [ɡəˈmyːzə] *n* (*-s*; -) vegetable(s); greens

Gemüsehändler *m* greengrocer('s)

gemusst [ɡəˈmʊst] *pp of müssen*

Gemüt [ɡəˈmyːt] *n* (*-[e]s*; *-er*) mind, soul; heart; nature, mentality

ge'mütlich *adj* comfortable, snug, cozy, *Br* cosy; peaceful, pleasant, relaxed; **mach es dir gemütlich** make yourself at home

Ge'mütlichkeit *f* (-; *no pl*) snugness, coziness, *Br* cosiness; cozy (*Br* cosy) *or* relaxed atmosphere

Ge'mütsbewegung *f* emotion

ge'mütskrank *adj* emotionally disturbed

Ge'mütszustand *m* state of mind

Gen [ge:n] *n* (-*s*; -*e*) BIOL gene

genannt [gə'nant] *pp of* **nennen**

genas [gə'naːs] *pret of* **genesen** 1

genau [gə'nau] **1.** *adj* exact, precise, accurate; careful, close; strict; **Genaueres** further details; **2.** *adv:* **genau um 10 Uhr** at 10 o'clock sharp; **genau der ...** that very ...; **genau zuhören** listen closely; **es genau nehmen** (**mit et.**) be particular (about s.th.)

Ge'nauigkeit *f* (-; *no pl*) accuracy, precision, exactness

ge'nauso *adv* → **ebenso**

genehmigen [gə'neːmɪgən] *v/t* (*no -ge-, h*) permit, allow; approve

Ge'nehmigung *f* (-; -*en*) permission; approval; permit; licen|se, *Br* -ce

geneigt [gə'naikt] *adj* inclined (**zu** to)

General [genə'raːl] *m* (-*s*; *Generäle* [genə'rɛːlə]) MIL general

Generaldi,rektor *m* ECON president, *Br* chairman

Generalkonsul *m* consul general

Generalkonsu,lat *n* consulate general

Generalprobe *f* THEA dress rehearsal

Generalsekre,tär *m* secretary-general

Generalstab *m* MIL general staff

Generalstreik *m* general strike

Generalversammlung *f* general meeting

Generalvertreter *m* ECON sole agent

Generation [genəra'tsjoːn] *f* (-; -*en*) generation

Generati'onenkon,flikt *m* generation gap

Generator [genə'raːtoːɐ] *m* (-*s*; -*en* [-ra-'toːrən]) ELECTR generator

generell [genə'rɛl] *adj* general, universal

genesen [gə'neːzən] **1.** *v/i* (*irr, no -ge-, sein*) recover (**von** from), get well; **2.** *pp of* **genesen** 1

Ge'nesung *f* (-; *no pl*) recovery

Genetik [ge'neːtɪk] *f* (-; *no pl*) BIOL genetics

ge'netisch *adj* BIOL genetic; **genetischer Fingerabdruck** genetic fingerprint

genial [ge'njaːl] *adj* brilliant, of genius

Genialität [genjali'tɛːt] *f* (-; *no pl*) genius

Genick [gə'nɪk] *n* (-[*e*]*s*; -*e*) ANAT (back *or* nape of the) neck

Genie [ʒe'niː] *n* (-*s*; -*s*) genius

genieren [ʒe'niːrən] *v/refl* (*no -ge-, h*) be embarrassed

genießen [gə'niːsən] *v/t* (*irr, no -ge-, h*) enjoy

Genießer [gə'niːsɐ] *m* (-*s*; -) gourmet

Genitiv ['geːnitiːf] *m* (-*s*; -*e*) LING genitive *or* possessive (case)

genommen [gə'nɔmən] *pp of* **nehmen**

genormt [gə'nɔrmt] *adj* standardized

genoss [gə'nɔs] *pret of* **genießen**

Genosse [gə'nɔsə] *m* (-*n*; -*n*) POL comrade; F pal, buddy, *Br* mate

genossen [gə'nɔsən] *pp of* **genießen**

Ge'nossenschaft *f* (-; -*en*) cooperative

Ge'nossin *f* (-; -*nen*) POL comrade

'Gentechnik *f*, **'Gentechnolo,gie** *f* genetic engineering

genug [gə'nuːk] *adj* enough, sufficient

Genüge [gə'nyːgə] *f*: **zur Genüge** (well) enough, sufficiently

ge'nügen *v/i* (*no -ge-, h*) be enough, be sufficient; **das genügt** that will do

genügend *adj* enough, sufficient; plenty of

genügsam [gə'nyːkzaːm] *adj* easily satisfied; frugal; modest

Ge'nügsamkeit *f* (-; *no pl*) modesty; frugality

Ge'nugtuung *f* (-; *no pl*) satisfaction

Genus ['geːnʊs] *n* (-; *Genera* ['geːnera]) LING gender

Genuss [gə'nʊs] *m* (-*es*; *Genüsse* [gə'nʏsə]) a) pleasure, b) (*no pl*) consumption; **ein Genuss** a real treat; *food: a.* delicious

Genussmittel *n* excise item, *Br* (semi-)-luxury

Geografie, Geographie [geogra'fiː] *f* (-; *no pl*) geography

geografisch, geographisch [geo'graː-fɪʃ] *adj* geographic(al)

Geologe [geo'loːgə] *m* (-*n*; -*n*) geologist

Geologie [geolo'giː] *f* (-; *no pl*) geology

Geo'login *f* (-; -*nen*) geologist

geologisch [geo'loːgɪʃ] *adj* geologic(al)

Geometrie [geome'triː] *f* (-; *no pl*) geometry

geometrisch [geo'meːtrɪʃ] *adj* geometric(al)

Gepäck [gə'pɛk] *n* (-[*e*]*s*; *no pl*) baggage, luggage

Gepäckablage *f* baggage (*or* luggage) rack

Gepäckaufbewahrung *f* baggage room, *Br* left-luggage office

Gepäckkon,trolle *f* baggage check, *Br* luggage inspection

Gepäckschalter *m* baggage (*or* luggage) counter

Gepäckschein *m* baggage check, *Br* luggage ticket
Gepäckträger *m* porter; *bicycle*: carrier
gepanzert [gə'pantsɐt] *adj* MOT armo(u)red
Gepard ['geːpart] *m* (-*s*; -*e*) ZO cheetah
gepfiffen [gə'pfɪfən] *pp of* **pfeifen**
gepflegt [gə'pfleːkt] *adj* well-groomed, neat; *fig* cultivated
Gepflogenheit [gə'pfloːgənhait] *f* (-; -*en*) habit, custom
Geplapper [gə'plapɐ] F *n* (-*s*; *no pl*) babbling, chatter(ing)
Geplauder [gə'plaudɐ] *n* (-*s*; *no pl*) chat (-ting)
Gepolter [gə'pɔltɐ] *n* (-*s*; *no pl*) rumble
gepriesen [gə'priːzən] *pp of* **preisen**
Gequassel [gə'kvasəl] F *n* (-*s*; *no pl*), **Gequatsche** [gə'kvatʃə] F *n* (-*s*; *no pl*) blather, blabber
gequollen [gə'kvɔlən] *pp of* **quellen**
gerade [gə'raːdə] **1.** *adj* straight (*a. fig*); even (*number*); direct; upright, erect (*posture*); **2.** *adv* just; *nicht gerade* not exactly; *das ist es ja gerade!* that's just it!; *gerade deshalb* that's just why; *gerade rechtzeitig* just in time; *warum gerade ich?* why me of all people?; *da wir gerade von ... sprechen* speaking of ...
Ge'rade *f* (-*n*; -*n*) MATH (straight) line; SPORT straight; *linke* (*rechte*) *Gerade* boxing: straight left (right)
gerade'aus *adv* straight on *or* ahead
geradehe'raus *adj* straightforward, frank
ge'radestehen *v/i* (*irr*, **stehen**, *sep*, -*ge*-, *h*) stand straight; *geradestehen für* answer for
ge'radewegs *adv* straight, directly
ge'radezu *adv* simply
gerannt [gə'rant] *pp of* **rennen**
Gerät [gə'rɛːt] *n* (-[*e*]*s*; -*e*) device; F gadget; appliance; (kitchen) utensil; *radio*, TV set; *coll, a.* SPORT *etc* equipment; SPORT apparatus; TECH tool; instrument
ge'raten 1. *pp of* **raten**; **2.** *v/i* (*irr*, **raten**, *no -ge-, sein*) turn out (*gut* well); *geraten an* (*acc*) come across; *geraten in* (*acc*) get into; *in Brand geraten* catch fire
Ge'räteturnen *n* apparatus gymnastics
Ge'ratewohl *n*: *aufs Geratewohl* at random
geräumig [gə'rɔymɪç] *adj* spacious, roomy
Geräusch [gə'rɔyʃ] *n* (-[*e*]*s*; -*e*) sound, noise
ge'räuschlos 1. *adj* noiseless (*a.* TECH); **2.** *adv* without a sound
ge'räuschvoll *adj* noisy
gerben ['gɛrbən] *v/t* (*ge*-, *h*) tan

Gerberei [gɛrbə'rai] *f* (-; -*en*) tannery
ge'recht *adj* just, fair; (*j-m, e-r Sache*) *gerecht werden* do justice to; meet (*demands etc*)
Ge'rechtigkeit *f* (-; *no pl*) justice
Ge'rede F *n* (-*s*; *no pl*) talk; gossip
gereizt [gə'raitst] *adj* irritable
Ge'reiztheit *f* (-; *no pl*) irritability
Gericht¹ [gə'rɪçt] *n* (-[*e*]*s*; -*e*) GASTR dish
Ge'richt² *n* (-[*e*]*s*; -*e*) JUR court; *vor Gericht stehen* (*stellen*) stand (bring to) trial; *vor Gericht gehen* go to court
ge'richtlich *adj* JUR judicial, legal
Ge'richtsbarkeit *f* (-; *no pl*) JUR jurisdiction
Ge'richtsgebäude *n* JUR law court(s), courthouse
Gerichtshof *m* JUR law court
Gerichtsmedi,zin *f* JUR forensic medicine
Gerichtssaal *m* JUR courtroom
Gerichtsverfahren *n* JUR lawsuit
Gerichtsverhandlung *f* JUR hearing; trial
Gerichtsvollzieher [-fɔltsiːɐ] *m* (-*s*; -) JUR marshal, *Br* bailiff
gerieben [gə'riːbən] *pp of* **reiben**
gering [gə'rɪŋ] *adj* little, small; slight, minor; low; *gering schätzen* think little of
ge'ringfügig *adj* slight, minor; petty
ge'ringschätzen *v/t* (*sep*, -*ge*-, *h*) → **gering**
geringschätzig [-ʃɛtsɪç] *adj* contemptuous
ge'ringst *adj* least; *nicht im Geringsten* not in the least
ge'rinnen *v/i* (*irr*, **rinnen**, *no -ge-, sein*) coagulate; curdle; clot
Ge'rippe *n* (-*s*; -) skeleton (*a. fig*); TECH framework
gerissen [gə'rɪsən] **1.** *pp of* **reißen**; **2.** F *adj* cunning, smart
geritten [gə'rɪtən] *pp of* **reiten**
germanisch [gɛr'maːnɪʃ] *adj* Germanic
Germanist(in) [gɛrma'nɪst(ɪn)] (-*en*; -*en*/-; -*nen*) student of (*or* graduate in) German
gern [gɛrn] *adv* willingly, gladly; *et.* (*sehr*) *gern tun* like (love) to do s.th. *or* doing s.th.; *ich möchte gern* I'd like (to); *gern geschehen!* not at all, (you're) welcome
gernhaben *v/t* (*irr*, **haben**, *sep*, -*ge*-, *h*) like, be fond of;
gerochen [gə'rɔxən] *pp of* **riechen**
Geröll [gə'rœl] *n* (-[*e*]*s*; -*e*) scree; boulders
geronnen [gə'rɔnən] *pp of* **rinnen**
Gerste ['gɛrstə] *f* (-; -*n*) BOT barley
'Gerstenkorn *n* MED sty(e)
Gerte ['gɛrtə] *f* (-; -*n*) switch, rod, twig
Geruch [gə'rux] *m* (-[*e*]*s*; *Gerüche* [gə-'ryçə]) smell; odo(u)r; scent

G

ge'ruchlos *adj* odo(u)rless

Ge'ruchsinn *m* (sense of) smell

Gerücht [gə'ryçt] *n* (-[e]s; -e) rumo(u)r

ge'rufen *pp of* **rufen**

gerührt [gə'ry:ɐt] *adj* touched, moved

Gerümpel [gə'rʏmpəl] *n* (-s; *no pl*) lumber, junk

Gerundium [ge'rʊndiʊm] *n* (-s; -ien) LING gerund

gerungen [gə'rʊŋən] *pp of* **ringen**

Gerüst [gə'ryst] *n* (-[e]s; -e) frame(-work); scaffold(ing); stage

ge'salzen *pp of* **salzen**

gesamt [gə'zamt] *adj* whole, entire, total, all

Ge'samt... *in cpds* ...**ergebnis** *etc: mst* total ...

Gesamtausgabe *f* complete edition

Gesamtschule *f* comprehensive school

gesandt [gə'zant] *pp of* **senden**

Gesandte [gə'zantə] *m, f* (-n; -n) POL envoy

Ge'sandtschaft *f* (-; -en) legation, mission

Gesang [gə'zaŋ] *m* (-[e]s; Gesänge [gə-'zɛŋə]) singing; song; voice

Gesangbuch *n* REL hymn book

Gesang(s)lehrer(in) singing teacher

Gesangverein *m* choral society, glee club

Gesäß [gə'zɛ:s] *n* (-es; -e) ANAT buttocks, bottom

ge'schaffen *pp of* **schaffen**[1]

Geschäft [gə'ʃɛft] *n* (-[e]s; -e) business; store, *Br* shop; bargain

ge'schäftig *adj* busy, active

Ge'schäftigkeit *f* (-; *no pl*) activity

ge'schäftlich 1. *adj* business ...; commercial; **2.** *adv* on business

Ge'schäftsbrief *m* business letter

Geschäftsfrau *f* businesswoman

Geschäftsfreund *m* business friend

Geschäftsführer *m* manager

Geschäftsführung *f* management

Geschäftsinhaber *m* proprietor

Geschäftsmann *m* businessman

ge'schäftsmäßig *adj* businesslike

Ge'schäftsordnung *f* PARL standing orders; rules (of procedure)

Geschäftspartner *m* (business) partner

Geschäftsräume *pl* (business) premises

Geschäftsreise *f* business trip

Geschäftsschluss *m* closing time; **nach Geschäftsschluss** *a.* after business hours

Geschäftsstelle *f* office

Geschäftsstraße *f* shopping street

Geschäftsträger *m* POL chargé d'affaires

'ge'schäftstüchtig *adj* efficient, smart

Ge'schäftsverbindung *f* business connection

Geschäftsviertel *n* commercial district; downtown

Geschäftszeit *f* office *or* business hours

Geschäftszweig *m* branch *or* line (of business)

geschah [gə'ʃa:] *pret of* **geschehen** 1

geschehen [gə'ʃe:ən] **1.** *v/i* (*irr, no* -ge-, *sein*) happen, occur, take place; be done; **es geschieht ihm recht** it serves him right; **2.** *pp of* **geschehen** 1

gescheit [gə'ʃait] *adj* clever, bright, F brainy

Geschenk [gə'ʃɛŋk] *n* (-[e]s; -e) present, gift

Geschenkpackung *f* gift box

Geschichte [gə'ʃɪçtə] *f* (-; -n) a) story, b) (*no pl*) history, c) F business, thing

ge'schichtlich *adj* historical

Ge'schichtsschreiber *m* (-s; -), **Ge'schichtswissenschaftler** *m* historian

Geschick [gə'ʃɪk] *n* (-[e]s; -e) fate, destiny; → **Ge'schicklichkeit** *f* (-; *no pl*) skill; dexterity

ge'schickt *adj* skil(l)ful, skilled; dext(e)rous; clever

geschieden [gə'ʃi:dən] **1.** *pp of* **scheiden**; **2.** *adj* divorced, *marriage:* dissolved

geschienen [gə'ʃi:nən] *pp of* **scheinen**

Geschirr [gə'ʃɪr] *n* (-[e]s; -e) a) dishes, china, b) (*no pl*) kitchen utensils, pots and pans, crockery, c) harness; **Geschirr spülen** wash *or* do the dishes

Ge'schirrspüler *m* (-s; -) dishwasher

geschissen [gə'ʃɪsən] *pp of* **scheißen**

ge'schlafen *pp of* **schlafen**

ge'schlagen *pp of* **schlagen**

Geschlecht [gə'ʃlɛçt] *n* (-[e]s; -er) a) (*no pl*) sex, b) kind, species, c) family, line (-age); generation, d) LING gender

Ge'schlechtskrankheit *f* MED venereal disease

Geschlechtsreife *f* puberty

Geschlechtsteile *pl* genitals

Geschlechtstrieb *m* sexual instinct *or* urge

Geschlechtsverkehr *m* (sexual) intercourse

Geschlechtswort *n* LING article

geschlichen [gə'ʃlɪçən] *pp of* **schleichen**

geschliffen [gə'ʃlɪfən] **1.** *pp of* **schleifen**[2]; **2.** *adj* cut; *fig* polished

geschlossen [gə'ʃlɔsən] **1.** *pp of* **schließen**; **2.** *adj* closed

geschlungen [gə'ʃlʊŋən] *pp of* **schlingen**

Geschmack [gə'ʃmak] *m* (-[e]s; Geschmäcke [gə'ʃmɛkə]) taste (*a. fig*); flavo(u)r; **Geschmack finden an** (*dat*) de-

velop a taste for
ge'schmacklos adj a. fig tasteless
Ge'schmacklosigkeit f (-; no pl) taste-lessness; **das war e-e Geschmacklosig-keit** that was in bad taste
Ge'schmack(s-)sache f matter of taste
ge'schmackvoll adj tasteful, in good taste
geschmeidig [gə'ʃmaidıç] adj supple, pliant
geschmissen [gə'ʃmısən] pp of **schmeißen**
geschmolzen [gə'ʃmɔltsən] pp of **schmelzen**
geschnitten [gə'ʃnıtən] pp of **schneiden**
geschoben [gə'ʃoːbən] pp of **schieben**
Geschöpf [gə'ʃœpf] n (-[e]s; -e) creature
geschoren [gə'ʃoːrən] pp of **scheren**
Geschoss [gə'ʃɔs] n (-es; -e), **Geschoß** [gə'ʃoːs] Austrian n (-es; -e) projectile, missile; stor(e)y, floor
ge'schossen pp of **schießen**
Ge'schrei F n (-s; no pl) shouting, yelling; screams; crying; fig fuss
geschrieben [gə'ʃriːbən] pp of **schreiben**
geschrie(e)n [gə'ʃriː(ə)n] pp of **schreien**
geschritten [gə'ʃrıtən] pp of **schreiten**
geschunden [gə'ʃundən] pp of **schinden**
Geschütz [gə'ʃʏts] n (-es; -e) MIL gun, cannon
Geschwader [gə'ʃvaːdɐ] n (-s; -) MIL MAR squadron; AVIAT group, Br wing
Geschwätz [gə'ʃvɛts] F n (-es; no pl) chatter, babble; gossip; fig nonsense
ge'schwätzig adj talkative; gossipy
geschweige [gə'ʃvaigə] cj: **geschweige (denn)** let alone
geschwiegen [gə'ʃviːgən] pp of **schweigen**
geschwind [gə'ʃvınt] adj quick, swift
Geschwindigkeit [gə'ʃvındıçkait] f (-; -en) speed; fastness, quickness; PHYS velocity; **mit e-r Geschwindigkeit von ...** at a speed or rate of ...
Ge'schwindigkeitsbegrenzung f speed limit
Geschwindigkeitsüberschreitung f MOT speeding
Geschwister [gə'ʃvıstɐ] pl brother(s) and sister(s); JUR siblings
geschwollen [gə'ʃvɔlən] 1. pp of **schwellen** 1; 2. adj MED swollen; fig bombastic, pretentious, pompous
geschwommen [gə'ʃvɔmən] pp of **schwimmen**
geschworen [gə'ʃvoːrən] pp of **schwören**
Ge'schworene m, f (-n; -n) member of a jury; **die Geschworenen** the jury

Geschwulst [gə'ʃvolst] f (-; Geschwülste [gə'ʃvʏlstə]) MED growth, tumo(u)r
geschwunden [gə'ʃvondən] pp of **schwinden**
geschwungen [gə'ʃvoŋən] pp of **schwingen**
Geschwür [gə'ʃvyːɐ] n (-s; -e) MED abscess, ulcer
ge'sehen pp of **sehen**
Geselchte [gə'zɛlçtə] Austrian n (-n; no pl) GASTR smoked meat
Geselle [gə'zɛlə] m (-n; -n) journeyman
ge'sellen v/refl (no -ge-, h) **sich zu j-m gesellen** join s.o.
ge'sellig adj sociable; ZO etc social; **geselliges Beisammensein** get-together
Ge'sellin f (-; -nen) trained woman hairdresser etc, journeywoman
Gesellschaft [gə'zɛlʃaft] f (-; -en) society; company; party; ECON company, corporation; **j-m Gesellschaft leisten** keep s.o. company
ge'sellschaftlich adj social
Ge'sellschafts... in cpds ...kritik, ...ordnung etc: social ...
Gesellschaftsreise f group tour
Gesellschaftsspiel n parlo(u)r game
Gesellschaftstanz m ballroom dance
gesessen [gə'zɛsən] pp of **sitzen**
Gesetz [gə'zɛts] n (-es; -e) JUR law; act
Gesetzbuch n JUR code (of law)
Gesetzentwurf m PARL bill
ge'setzgebend adj JUR legislative
Ge'setzgeber m (-s; -) JUR legislator
Ge'setzgebung f (-; -en) JUR legislation
ge'setzlich 1. adj legal; lawful; 2. adv: **gesetzlich geschützt** JUR patented, registered
ge'setzlos adj lawless
ge'setzmäßig adj legal, lawful
gesetzt [gə'zɛtst] 1. adj staid, dignified; mature (age); 2. cj: **gesetzt den Fall(, dass)** ... supposing (that)
ge'setzwidrig adj illegal, unlawful
Gesicht [gə'zıçt] n (-[e]s; -er) face; **zu Gesicht bekommen** catch sight of
Ge'sichtausdruck m look, expression
Gesichtfarbe f complexion
Gesichtpunkt m point of view, aspect, angle
Gesichtzug m feature
Gesindel [gə'zındəl] n (-s; no pl) trash, the riff-raff
gesinnt [gə'zınt] adj minded; **j-m feindlich gesinnt sein** be ill-disposed towards s.o.
Ge'sinnung f (-; -en) mind; attitude; POL conviction(s)

ge'sinnungslos *adj* unprincipled
ge'sinnungstreu *adj* loyal
Ge'sinnungswechsel *m* about-face, *Br* about-turn
gesittet [gə'zɪtət] *adj* civilized, well-mannered
gesoffen [gə'zɔfən] *pp of* **saufen**
gesogen [gə'zoːgən] *pp of* **saugen**
gesotten [gə'zɔtən] *pp of* **sieden**
gespalten [gə'ʃpaltən] *pp of* **spalten**
Gespann [gə'ʃpan] *n* (-[e]s; -e) team (*a. fig*)
gespannt [gə'ʃpant] *adj* tense (*a. fig*); **gespannt sein auf** (*acc*) be anxious to see; **ich bin gespannt, ob** (**wie**) I wonder if (how)
Gespenst [gə'ʃpɛnst] *n* (-[e]s; -er) ghost, apparition, *esp fig* specter, *Br* spectre
ge'spenstisch *adj* ghostly, F spooky
gespie(e)n [gə'ʃpiː(ə)n] *pp of* **speien**
Gespinst [gə'ʃpɪnst] *n* (-[e]s; -e) web, tissue (*both a. fig*)
gesponnen [gə'ʃpɔnən] *pp of* **spinnen**
Gespött [gə'ʃpœt] *n* (-[e]s; *no pl*) mockery, ridicule; **j-n zum Gespött machen** make a laughingstock of s.o.
Gespräch [gə'ʃprɛːç] *n* (-[e]s; -e) talk (*a. POL*), conversation; *TEL* call
ge'sprächig *adj* talkative
gesprochen [gə'ʃprɔxən] *pp of* **sprechen**
gesprossen [gə'ʃprɔsən] *pp of* **sprießen**
gesprungen [gə'ʃpruŋən] *pp of* **springen**
Gespür [gə'ʃpyːɐ] *n* (-s; *no pl*) flair, nose
Gestalt [gə'ʃtalt] *f* (-; -en) shape, form; figure
ge'stalten *v/t* (*no* -ge-, *h*) arrange; design
Ge'staltung *f* (-; -en) arrangement; design; decoration
gestanden [gə'ʃtandən] *pp of* **stehen**
ge'ständig *adj*: **geständig sein** confess; have confessed
Geständnis [gə'ʃtɛntnɪs] *n* (-ses; -se) confession (*a. fig*)
Gestank [gə'ʃtaŋk] *m* (-[e]s; *no pl*) stench, stink
gestatten [gə'ʃtatən] *v/t* (*no* -ge-, *h*) allow, permit
Geste ['gɛstə] *f* (-; -n) gesture (*a. fig*)
ge'stehen *v/t and v/i* (*irr*, **stehen**, *no* -ge-, *h*) confess
Ge'stein *n* (-[e]s; -e) rock, stone
Gestell [gə'ʃtɛl] *n* (-[e]s; -e) stand, base, pedestal; shelves; frame
gestern ['gɛstɐn] *adv* yesterday; **gestern Abend** last night
gestiegen [gə'ʃtiːgən] *pp of* **steigen**
gestochen [gə'ʃtɔxən] *pp of* **stechen**
gestohlen [gə'ʃtoːlən] *pp of* **stehlen**

gestorben [gə'ʃtɔrbən] *pp of* **sterben**
ge'stoßen *pp of* **stoßen**
gestreift [gə'ʃtraift] *adj* striped
gestrichen [gə'ʃtrɪçən] *pp of* **streichen**
gestrig ['gɛstrɪç] *adj* yesterday's, of yesterday
gestritten [gə'ʃtrɪtən] *pp of* **streiten**
Gestrüpp [gə'ʃtrʏp] *n* (-[e]s; -e) brushwood, undergrowth; *fig* jungle, maze
gestunken [gə'ʃtuŋkən] *pp of* **stinken**
Gestüt [gə'ʃtyːt] *n* (-[e]s; -e) stud
Gesuch [gə'zuːx] *n* (-[e]s; -e) application, request
gesund [gə'zʊnt] *adj* healthy; healthful, *fig a.* sound; **gesunder Menschenverstand** common sense; (**wieder**) **gesund werden** get well (again), recover
Ge'sundheit *f* (-; *no pl*) health; **auf j-s Gesundheit trinken** drink to s.o.'s health; **Gesundheit!** bless you!
ge'sundheitlich 1. *adj*: **gesundheitlicher Zustand** state of health; **aus gesundheitlichen Gründen** for health reasons; **2.** *adv*: **gesundheitlich geht es ihm gut** he is in good health
Ge'sundheitsamt *n* Public Health Department (*Br* Office)
ge'sundheitsschädlich *adj* bad for one's health
Ge'sundheitszeugnis *n* health certificate
Gesundheitszustand *m* state of health
gesungen [gə'zʊŋən] *pp of* **singen**
gesunken [gə'zʊŋkən] *pp of* **sinken**
getan [gə'taːn] *pp of* **tun**
Getöse [gə'tøːzə] *n* (-s; *no pl*) din, (deafening) noise
ge'tragen *pp of* **tragen**
Getränk [gə'trɛŋk] *n* (-[e]s; -e) drink, beverage
Ge'tränkeauto,mat *m* drinks machine
Getreide [gə'traidə] *n* (-s; -) cereals, grain, *Br a.* corn
Getreideernte *f* grain harvest (*or* crop)
ge'treten *pp of* **treten**
Getriebe [gə'triːbə] *n* (-s; -) *MOT* transmission
ge'trieben [gə'triːbən] *pp of* **treiben**
getroffen [gə'trɔfən] *pp of* **treffen**
getrogen [gə'troːgən] *pp of* **trügen**
getrost [gə'troːst] *adv* safely
getrunken [gə'trʊŋkən] *pp of* **trinken**
Getue [gə'tuːə] F *n* (-s; *no pl*) fuss
Getümmel [gə'tʏməl] *n* (-s; -) turmoil
Gewächs [gə'vɛks] *n* (-es; -e) plant; *MED* growth
ge'wachsen 1. *pp of* **wachsen**[1]; **2.** *fig adj*: **j-m gewachsen sein** be a match for s.o.; **e-r Sache gewachsen sein** be equal to s.th., be able to cope with s.th.

Ge'wächshaus *n* greenhouse, hothouse
gewagt [gə'va:kt] *adj* daring; *fig* risqué
gewählt [gə'vɛ:lt] *adj* refined
Gewähr [gə'vɛːɐ] *f:* ***Gewähr überneh-men (für)*** guarantee
ge'währen *v/t* (*no -ge-*, *h*) grant, allow
ge'währleisten *v/t* (*no -ge-*, *h*) guarantee
Gewahrsam [gə'va:ɐza:m] *m: et. (j-n) in Gewahrsam nehmen* take s.th. in safe-keeping (s.o. into custody)
Gewalt [gə'valt] *f* (-; -en) a) (*no pl*) force, violence, b) power; *mit Gewalt* by force; *höhere Gewalt* act of God; *häusliche Gewalt* domestic violence; *in s-e Gewalt bringen* seize by force; *die Gewalt verlieren über* (*acc*) lose control over
Gewaltherrschaft *f* tyranny
ge'waltig *adj* powerful, mighty; enormous
ge'waltlos *adj* nonviolent
Ge'waltlosigkeit *f* (-; *no pl*) nonviolence
ge'waltsam 1. *adj* violent; **2.** *adv* by force; *gewaltsam öffnen* force open
ge'walttätig *adj* violent
Ge'walttätigkeit *f* (-; -en) a) (*no pl*) violence, b) act of violence
Ge'waltverbrechen *n* crime of violence
Gewand [gə'vant] *n* (-[e]s; *Gewänder* [gə'vɛndɐ]) robe, gown; REL vestment
gewandt [gə'vant] **1.** *pp of wenden* (*v/refl*); **2.** *adj* nimble; skil(l)ful; clever
Ge'wandtheit *f* (-; *no pl*) nimbleness; skill; ease
gewann [gə'van] *pret of gewinnen*
ge'waschen *pp of waschen*
Gewässer [gə'vɛsɐ] *n* (-s; -) body of water; *pl* waters
Gewebe [gə've:bə] *n* (-s; -) fabric; BIOL tissue
Gewehr [gə'veːɐ] *n* (-[e]s; -e) gun; rifle; shotgun
Gewehrkolben *m* (rifle) butt
Gewehrlauf *m* (rifle *or* gun) barrel
Geweih [gə'vai] *n* (-[e]s; -e) ZO antlers, horns
Gewerbe [gə'vɛrbə] *n* (-s; -) trade, business
Gewerbeschein *m* trade licen|se, *Br* -ce
Gewerbeschule *f* vocational *or* trade school
gewerblich [gə'vɛrplɪç] *adj* commercial, industrial
gewerbsmäßig [gə'vɛrps-] *adj* professional
Gewerkschaft [gə'vɛrkʃaft] *f* (-; -en) labor union, *Br* (trade) union
Ge'werkschaft(l)er *m* (-s; -), **Ge'werkschaft(l)erin** *f* (-; -nen) labor (*Br* trade) unionist

ge'werkschaftlich *adj*, **Ge'werkschafts...** *in cpds* labor (*Br* trade) union ...
ge'wesen *pp of sein*[1]
gewichen [gə'vɪçən] *pp of weichen*
Gewicht [gə'vɪçt] *n* (-[e]s; -e) weight; importance; *Gewicht legen auf* (*acc*) stress
gewiesen [gə'vi:zən] *pp of weisen*
gewillt [gə'vɪlt] *adj* willing, ready
Gewimmel [gə'vɪməl] *n* (-s; *no pl*) throng
Gewinde [gə'vɪndə] *n* (-s; -) TECH thread; *ein Gewinde bohren in* (*acc*) tap
Gewinn [gə'vɪn] *m* (-[e]s; -e) ECON profit (*a. fig*); gain(s); prize; winnings; *Gewinn bringend → gewinnbringend*
ge'winnbringend *adj* profitable
ge'winnen *v/t and v/i* (*irr, no -ge-*, *h*) win; gain
gewinnend *fig adj* winning, engaging
Gewinner [gə'vɪnɐ] *m* (-s; -), **Ge'winnerin** *f* (-; -nen) winner
Ge'winnzahl *f* winning number
Gewirr [gə'vɪr] *n* (-[e]s; *no pl*) tangle; maze
gewiss [gə'vɪs] **1.** *adj* certain; **2.** *adv* certainly
Ge'wissen *n* (-s; -) conscience
ge'wissenhaft *adj* conscientious
ge'wissenlos *adj* unscrupulous
Ge'wissensbisse *pl* pricks *or* pangs of conscience
Gewissensfrage *f* question of conscience
Gewissensgründe *pl: aus Gewissensgründen* for reasons of conscience
Ge'wissheit *f* (-; *no pl*) certainty; *mit Gewissheit* know etc for certain *or* sure
Gewitter [gə'vɪtɐ] *n* (-s; -) thunderstorm
Gewitterregen *m* thundershower
Gewitterwolke *f* thundercloud
gewoben [gə'vo:bən] *pp of weben*
gewogen [gə'vo:gən] *pp of wiegen*[1] *and wägen*
gewöhnen [gə'vøːnən] *v/t and v/refl* (*no -ge-*, *h*) *sich* (*j-n*) *gewöhnen an* (*acc*) get (s.o.) used to
Gewohnheit [gə'voːnhait] *f* (-; -en) habit (*et. zu tun* of doing s.th.)
ge'wohnheitsmäßig *adj* habitual
gewöhnlich [gə'vøːnlɪç] *adj* common, ordinary, usual; vulgar, F common
gewohnt [gə'voːnt] *adj* usual; *et.* (*zu tun*) *gewohnt sein* be used *or* accustomed to (doing) s.th.
Gewölbe [gə'vœlbə] *n* (-s; -) vault
gewölbt [gə'vœlpt] *adj* arched
gewonnen [gə'vɔnən] *pp of gewinnen*
geworben [gə'vɔrbən] *pp of werben*
geworden [gə'vɔrdən] *pp of werden*
geworfen [gə'vɔrfən] *pp of werfen*

G

gewrungen [gə'vruŋən] *pp of* **wringen**
Gewühl [gə'vy:l] *n* (-[e]s; *no pl*) crowd, crush
gewunden [gə'vundən] **1.** *pp of* **winden**; **2.** *adj* winding
Gewürz [gə'vʏrts] *n* (-es; -e) spice
Gewürzgurke *f* pickle(d gherkin)
gewusst [gə'vust] *pp of* **wissen**
gezackt [gə'tsakt] *adj* jagged, serrated
Ge'zeiten *pl* tide(s)
Gezeter [gə'tse:tɐ] *contp n* (-s; *no pl*) (shrill) clamo(u)r; nagging
geziert [gə'tsi:ɐt] *adj* affected
gezogen [gə'tso:gən] *pp of* **ziehen**
Gezwitscher [gə'tsvɪtʃɐ] *n* (-s; *no pl*) chirp(ing), twitter(ing)
gezwungen [gə'tsvuŋən] **1.** *pp of* **zwingen**; **2.** *adj* forced, unnatural
Gicht [gɪçt] *f* (-; *no pl*) MED gout
Giebel ['gi:bəl] *m* (-s; -) gable
Gier [gi:ɐ] *f* (-; *no pl*) greed(iness) (*nach* for)
gierig ['gi:rɪç] *adj* greedy (*nach, auf* acc for, after)
gießen ['gi:sən] *v/t and v/i* (*irr, ge-, h*) pour; TECH cast; water
Gieße'rei *f* (-; -en) TECH foundry
'Gießkanne *f* watering pot (*Br* can)
Gift [gɪft] *n* (-[e]s; -e) poison, ZO *a.* venom (*a. fig*)
'giftig *adj* poisonous; venomous (*a. fig*); poisoned; MED toxic
'Giftmüll *m* toxic waste
Giftmülldepo,nie *f* toxic waste dump
Giftschlange *f* ZO poisonous *or* venomous snake
Giftstoff *m* poisonous *or* toxic substance; pollutant
Giftzahn *m* ZO poison fang
Gigant [gi'gant] *m* (-en; -en) giant
gi'gantisch *adj* gigantic
ging [gɪŋ] *pret of* **gehen**
Gipfel ['gɪpfəl] *m* (-s; -) top, peak, summit, *fig a.* height
Gipfelkonfe,renz *f* POL summit (meeting *or* conference)
'gipfeln *v/i* (*ge-, h*) culminate (*in* dat in)
Gips [gɪps] *m* (-es; -e) plaster (of Paris); *in Gips* MED in (a) plaster (cast)
Gipsabdruck *m*, **Gipsabguss** *m* plaster cast
'gipsen *v/t* (*ge-, h*) plaster (*a.* F MED)
'Gipsverband *m* MED plaster cast
Giraffe [gi'rafə] *f* (-; -n) ZO giraffe
Girlande [gɪr'landə] *f* (-; -n) garland, festoon
Girokonto ['ʒi:ro-] *n* checking (*or* current) account; postal check (*Br* giro) account
Gischt [gɪʃt] *m* (-[e]s; -e), *f* (-; -en) (sea) spray, spindrift

Gitarre [gi'tarə] *f* (-; -n) MUS guitar
Gitarrist [gita'rɪst] *m* (-en; -en) guitarist
Gitter ['gɪtɐ] *n* (-s; -) lattice; grating; F *hinter Gittern* (*sitzen*) (be) behind bars
'Gitterbett *n* crib, *Br* cot
'Gitterfenster *n* lattice (window)
Glanz [glants] *m* (-es; *no pl*) shine, gloss (*a.* TECH), luster, *Br* lustre, brilliance (*a. fig*); *fig* splendo(u)r, glamo(u)r
glänzen ['glɛntsən] *v/i* (*ge-, h*) shine, gleam; glitter; glisten
glänzend *adj* shining, shiny, bright; PHOT glossy; *fig* brilliant, excellent
'Glanzleistung *f* brilliant achievement
Glanzzeit *f* heyday
Glas [gla:s] *n* (-es; *Gläser* ['glɛ:zɐ]) glass
Glaser ['gla:zɐ] *m* (-s; -) glazier
gläsern ['glɛ:zɐn] *adj* (of) glass
'Glasfaser *f*, **Glasfiber** *f* glass fiber (*Br* fibre)
Glashütte *f* TECH glassworks
glasieren [gla'zi:rən] *v/t* (*no -ge-, h*) glaze; GASTR ice, frost
glasig ['gla:zɪç] *adj* glassy
'glasklar *adj* crystal-clear (*a. fig*)
'Glasscheibe *f* (glass) pane
Glasur [gla'zu:ɐ] *f* (-; -en) glaze; GASTR icing
glatt [glat] *adj* smooth (*a. fig*); slippery; *fig* clear
Glätte ['glɛtə] *f* (-; *no pl*) smoothness (*a. fig*); slipperiness
'Glatteis *n* (glare, *Br* black) ice; *es herrscht Glatteis* the roads are icy; *j-n aufs Glatteis führen* mislead s.o.
glätten ['glɛtən] *v/t* (*ge-, h*) smooth; *Swiss:* → **bügeln**
'glattgehen *v/i* (*irr, sep, -ge-, sein*) F work (out well), go (off) well
Glatze ['glatsə] *f* (-; -n) bald head; *e-e Glatze haben* be bald
Glaube ['glaubə] *m* (-ns; *no pl*) belief, *esp* REL faith (*both: an* acc in)
'glauben *v/t and v/i* (*ge-, h*) believe; think, guess; *glauben an* (acc) believe in (*a.* REL)
'Glaubensbekenntnis *n* REL creed, profession *or* confession of faith
Glaubenslehre *f*, **Glaubenssatz** *m* dogma, doctrine
glaubhaft ['glauphaft] *adj* credible, plausible
gläubig ['glɔʏbɪç] *adj* religious; devout; *die Gläubigen* the faithful
Gläubiger ['glɔʏbɪgɐ] *m* (-s; -), **'Gläubigerin** *f* (-; -nen) ECON creditor
'glaubwürdig *adj* credible; reliable
gleich [glaiç] **1.** *adj* same; equal (*right etc*);

auf die gleiche Art (in) the same way;
zur gleichen Zeit at the same time;
das ist mir gleich it's all the same to
me; *ganz gleich, wann* etc no matter
when etc; *das Gleiche* the same; (*ist*)
gleich ... MATH equals ..., is ...; *gleich
bleibend* → *gleichbleibend*; *gleich gesinnt* like-minded; *gleich lautend* →
gleichlautend; **2.** adv equally, alike; at
once, right away; in a moment or minute;
gleich groß (*alt*) of the same size (age);
gleich nach (*neben*) right after (next
to); *gleich gegenüber* just opposite or
across the street; *es ist gleich 5 Uhr*
it's almost 5 o'clock; *gleich aussehen*
(*gekleidet sein*) look (be dressed) alike;
bis gleich! see you soon or later!
gleichaltrig ['glaiçʔaltrɪç] adj (of) the
same age
'gleichberechtigt adj equal, having equal
rights
'Gleichberechtigung f (-; no pl) equal
rights
'gleichbleibend adj constant, steady
'gleichen v/i (irr, ge-, h) (dat) be or look
like
'gleichfalls adv also, likewise; *danke,
gleichfalls!* (thanks,) the same to you
'gleichförmig [-fœrmɪç] adj uniform
'Gleichgewicht n (-[e]s; no pl) balance (a.
fig)
'gleichgültig adj indifferent (*gegen* to);
careless; *das* (*er*) *ist mir gleichgültig* I
don't care (for him)
'Gleichgültigkeit f (-; no pl) indifference
'Gleichheit f (-; no pl) equality
'gleichkommen v/i (irr, kommen, sep,
-ge-, sein) *e-r Sache gleichkommen*
amount to s.th.; *j-m gleichkommen*
equal s.o. (*an* dat in)
'gleichlautend adj identical
'gleichmäßig adj regular; constant; even
'gleichnamig [-na:mɪç] adj of the same
name
'Gleichnis n (-ses; -se) parable
'gleichsam adv as it were, so to speak
'gleichseitig [-zaitɪç] adj MATH equilateral
'gleichsetzen, gleichstellen v/t (sep, -ge-,
h) equate (*dat* to, with); put *s.o.* on an
equal footing (with)
'Gleichstrom m ELECTR direct current
'Gleichung f (-; -en) MATH equation
'gleichwertig adj equally good; *j-m
gleichwertig sein* be a match for s.o.
(a. SPORT)
'gleichzeitig adj simultaneous; *beide
gleichzeitig* both at the same time
Gleis [glais] n (-es; -e) RAIL rail(s), track(s),
line; platform, gate

gleiten ['glaitən] v/i (irr, ge-, sein) glide,
slide
gleitend adj: *gleitende Arbeitszeit* flexible working hours, flextime, Br a. flexi-
time
'Gleitflug m glide
'Gleitschirmfliegen n paragliding
Gleitschirmflieger m paraglider
Gletscher ['glɛtʃɐ] m (-s; -) glacier
Gletscherspalte f crevasse
glich [glɪç] pret of gleichen
Glied [gli:t] n (-es; Glieder ['gli:dɐ]) ANAT
limb; penis; TECH link
gliedern ['gli:dɐn] v/t (ge-, h) structure;
divide (*in* acc into)
Gliederung ['gli:dərʊŋ] f (-; -en) structure, arrangement; outline
'Gliedmaßen pl ANAT limbs, extremities
glimmen ['glɪmən] v/i ([irr,] ge-, h) glow;
smo(u)lder
'Glimmstängel F m (-s; -) cigarette, Br sl
fag
glimpflich ['glɪmpflɪç] **1.** adj lenient,
mild; **2.** adv: *glimpflich davonkommen*
get off lightly
glitschig ['glɪtʃɪç] adj slippery
glitt [glɪt] pret of gleiten
glitzern ['glɪtsɐn] v/i (ge-, h) glitter, sparkle, glint
global [glo'ba:l] adj global
Globus ['glo:bʊs] m (-[ses]; -se) globe
Glocke ['glɔkə] f (-; -n) bell
'Glockenblume f bluebell
Glockenspiel n chimes
Glockenturm m bell tower, belfry
glomm [glɔm] pret of glimmen
glorreich ['glo:ɐraiç] adj glorious
Glotze ['glɔtsə] F f (-; -n) TV the tube, Br
goggle box
'glotzen F v/i (ge-, h) goggle, gape, stare
Glück [glʏk] n (-[e]s; no pl) (good) luck,
fortune; happiness; *Glück haben* be
lucky; *zum Glück* fortunately; *viel
Glück!* good luck!
Glucke ['glʊkə] f (-; -n) ZO sitting hen; fig
hen
gluckern ['glʊkɐn] v/i (ge-, h) gurgle
'glücklich adj happy; *glücklicher Zufall*
lucky chance
'glücklicher'weise adv fortunately
'Glücksbringer m (-s; -) lucky charm
Glücksfall m lucky chance
Glückspfennig m lucky penny
Glückspilz m lucky fellow
Glücksspiel n game of chance; coll gam-
bling
Glücksspieler m gambler
Glückstag m lucky day
'glückstrahlend adj radiant

G

'Glückwunsch *m* congratulations; *herzlichen Glückwunsch!* congratulations!; happy birthday!

Glühbirne ['gly:-] *f* ELECTR light bulb

glühen ['gly:ən] *v/i* (*ge-*, *h*) glow (*a. fig*)

glühend ['gly:ənt] *adj* glowing; red-hot (*iron*); *fig* burning; *glühend heiß* blazing hot

'Glühwein *m* mulled wine

Glut [glu:t] *f* (-; *-en*) (glowing) fire; embers; live coals; *fig* ardo(u)r

'Gluthitze *f* blazing heat

GmbH [ge:ʔɛmbe:ˈhaː] *ABBR of Gesellschaft mit beschränkter Haftung* private limited liability company

Gnade ['gna:də] *f* (-; *-n*) mercy, *esp* REL *a.* grace; favo(u)r

'Gnadenfrist *f* reprieve

Gnadengesuch *n* JUR petition for mercy

'gnadenlos *adj* merciless

gnädig ['gnɛ:dɪç] *adj* gracious; *esp* REL merciful

Gold [gɔlt] *n* (-[e]s; *no pl*) gold

Goldbarren *m* gold bar *or* ingot; *coll* bullion

golden ['gɔldən] *adj* gold; *fig* golden

'Goldfisch *m* ZO goldfish

'goldgelb *adj* golden (yellow)

'Goldgräber [-grɛ:bɐ] *m* (-s; -) gold digger

Goldgrube *fig f* goldmine, bonanza

goldig ['gɔldɪç] F *adj* sweet, lovely, cute

'Goldmine *f* goldmine

'Goldmünze *f* gold coin

Goldschmied *m* goldsmith

Goldstück *n* gold coin

Golf[1] [gɔlf] *m* (-[e]s; *-e*) GEOGR gulf

Golf[2] *n* (-s; *no pl*) SPORT golf

Golfplatz *m* golf course

Golfschläger *m* golf club

Golfspieler *m* golfer

Gondel ['gɔndəl] *f* (-; *-n*) gondola; cabin

Gong ['gɔŋ-] *m* (-s; -s) gong

gönnen ['gœnən] *v/t* (*ge-*, *h*) *j-m et. gönnen* not (be)grudge s.o. s.th.; *j-m et. nicht gönnen* (be)grudge s.o. s.th.; *sich et. gönnen* allow o.s. s.th., treat o.s. to s.th.

gönnerhaft ['gœnɐhaft] *adj* patronizing

gor [goːɐ] *pret of gären*

Gorilla [goˈrɪla] *m* (-s; -s) ZO gorilla

goss [gɔs] *pret of gießen*

Gosse ['gɔsə] *f* (-; *-n*) gutter (*a. fig*)

Gotik ['goːtɪk] *f* (-; *no pl*) ARCH Gothic style *or* period

'gotisch *adj* Gothic

Gott [gɔt] *m* (-[e]s; *Götter* ['gœtɐ]) REL God, Lord; MYTH god; *Gott sei Dank*(!) thank God(!); *um Gottes Willen!* for heaven's sake!

'gottergeben *adj* resigned (to the will of God)

'Gottesdienst *m* REL (divine) service

'gottesfürchtig [-fʏrçtɪç] *adj* god-fearing

'Gotteslästerer [-lɛstərɐ] *m* (-s; -) blasphemer

'Gotteslästerung *f* (-; *-en*) blasphemy

'Gottheit *f* (-; *-en*) deity, divinity

Göttin ['gœtɪn] *f* (-; *-nen*) goddess

'göttlich ['gœtlɪç] *adj* divine

gott'lob *int* thank God *or* goodness!

'gottlos *adj* godless, wicked

'gottverlassen F *adj* godforsaken

'Gottvertrauen *n* trust in God

Götze ['gœtsə] *m* (-n; -n), 'Götzenbild *n* idol

Gouverneur [guvɛrˈnøːɐ] *m* (-s; -e) governor

Grab [gra:p] *n* (-[e]s; *Gräber* ['grɛ:bɐ]) grave; tomb

graben ['gra:bən] *v/t and v/i* (*irr*, *ge-*, *h*) dig, ZO *a.* burrow

'Graben *m* (-s; *Gräben* ['grɛ:bən]) ditch; MIL trench

'Grabmal *n* monument; tomb

Grabrede *f* funeral address

Grabschrift *f* epitaph

Grabstätte *f* burial place; grave, tomb

Grabstein *m* tombstone, gravestone

Grad [gra:t] *m* (-[e]s; *-e*) degree; MIL *etc* rank, grade; *15 Grad Kälte* 15 degrees below zero

Gradeinteilung *f* graduation

graduell [gra'duɛl] *adj* in degree

Graf [gra:f] *m* (-en; *-en*) count, *Br* earl

Graffiti [gra'fi:ti] *pl* graffiti

Grafik ['gra:fɪk] *f* (-; *-en*) a) (*no pl*) graphic arts, b) print, c) MATH, TECH graph, diagram, d) (*no pl*) art(work), illustrations, e) (*no pl*) EDP graphics

'Grafiker *m* (-s; -), 'Grafikerin *f* (-; *-nen*) graphic artist

Gräfin ['grɛ:fɪn] *f* (-; *-nen*) countess

grafisch ['gra:fɪʃ] *adj* graphic

Grafologie *f → Graphologie*

'Grafschaft *f* (-; *-en*) county

Gramm [gram] *n* (-s; *-e*) gram

Grammatik [gra'matɪk] *f* (-; *-en*) grammar

gram'matisch *adj* grammatical

Granat [gra'na:t] *m* (-[e]s; *-e*) MIN garnet

Gra'nate *f* (-; *-n*) MIL shell

Gra'natsplitter *m* MIL shell splinter

Granatwerfer *m* MIL mortar

grandios [gran'djoːs] *adj* magnificent, grand

Granit [gra'niːt] *m* (-s; *-e*) granite

Graphik *f etc → Grafik etc*

Graphologie [grafolo'gi:] *f* (-; *no pl*) graphology

Gras [graːs] *n* (*-es*; *Gräser* ['grɛːzɐ]) grass
grasen ['graːzən] *v/i* (*ge-*, *h*) graze
'**Grashalm** *m* blade of grass
grassieren [gra'siːrən] *v/i* (*no -ge-*, *h*) rage, be rife
grässlich ['grɛslɪç] *adj* hideous, atrocious
Gräte ['grɛːtə] *f* (*-*; *-n*) (fish)bone
Gratifikation [gratifika'tsjoːn] *f* (*-*; *-en*) gratuity, bonus
gratis ['graːtɪs] *adv* free (of charge)
Grätsche ['grɛːtʃə] *f* (*-*; *-n*), '**grätschen** *v/i* (*ge-*, *h*) straddle; *soccer:* stride tackle
Gratulant [gratu'lant] *m* (*-en*; *-en*), **Gratu'lantin** *f* (*-*; *-nen*) congratulator
Gratulation [-la'tsjoːn] *f* (*-*; *-en*) congratulation
gratulieren [-'liːrən] *v/i* (*no -ge-*, *h*) congratulate (*j-m zu et.* s.o. on s.th.); *j-m zum Geburtstag gratulieren* wish s.o. many happy returns (of the day)
grau [grau] *adj* gray, *Br* grey
'**Graubrot** *n* rye bread
Gräuel ['grɔʏəl] *m* (*-s*; *-*) horror
'**Gräueltat** *f* atrocity
'**grauen** *v/i* (*ge-*, *h*) *mir graut es vor* (*dat*) I dread (the thought of)
'**Grauen** *n* (*-s*; *-*) horror
'**grauenhaft**, '**grauenvoll** *adj* horrible, horrifying
Graupel ['graupəl] *f* (*-*; *-n*) sleet, soft hail
grausam ['grauzaːm] *adj* cruel
'**Grausamkeit** *f* (*-*; *-en*) cruelty
grausig ['grauzɪç] *adj* → *grauenhaft*
'**Grauzone** *f fig* gray (*Br* grey) area
gravieren [gra'viːrən] *v/t* (*no -ge-*, *h*) engrave
gravierend *adj* serious
Gravur [gra'vuːɐ] *f* (*-*; *-en*) engraving
Grazie ['graːtsjə] *f* (*-*; *no pl*) grace
graziös [gra'tsjøːs] *adj* graceful
greifen ['graifən] (*irr*, *ge-*, *h*) **1.** *v/t* seize, grasp, grab, take *or* catch hold of; **2.** *v/i fig* take effect; *greifen nach* reach for; grasp at
Greis [grais] *m* (*-es*; *-e*) (very) old man
greisenhaft ['graizənhaft] *adj* senile (*a.* MED)
Greisin ['graizɪn] *f* (*-*; *-nen*) (very) old woman
grell [grɛl] *adj* glaring; shrill
Grenze ['grɛntsə] *f* (*-*; *-n*) border; boundary; *fig* limit
'**grenzen** *v/i* (*ge-*, *h*) *grenzen an* (*acc*) border on
'**grenzenlos** *adj* boundless
'**Grenzfall** *m* borderline case
Grenzland *n* borderland, frontier
Grenzlinie *f* borderline, POL demarcation line

Grenzstein *m* boundary stone
Grenzübergang *m* frontier crossing (point), checkpoint
Greuel *m* → *Gräuel*
Grieche ['griːçə] *m* (*-n*; *-n*) Greek
'**Griechenland** Greece
'**Griechin** *f* (*-*; *-nen*), '**griechisch** *adj* Greek
Grieß [griːs] *m* (*-es*; *-e*) semolina
griff [grɪf] *pret of greifen*
Griff *m* (*-[e]s*; *-e*) grip, grasp; handle
'**griffbereit** *adj* at hand, handy
Grill [grɪl] *m* (*-s*; *-s*) grill
Grille ['grɪlə] *f* (*-*; *-n*) ZO cricket
'**grillen** *v/t* (*ge-*, *h*) grill, barbecue
Grimasse [gri'masə] *f* (*-*; *-n*) grimace; *Grimassen schneiden* pull faces
grimmig ['grɪmɪç] *adj* grim
grinsen ['grɪnzən] *v/i* (*ge-*, *h*) grin (*über acc* at); *höhnisch or spöttisch grinsen* (*über acc*) sneer (at)
'**Grinsen** *n* (*-s*; *no pl*) grin; *höhnisches or spöttisches Grinsen* sneer
Grippe ['grɪpə] *f* (*-*; *-n*) MED influenza, F flu
Grips [grɪps] F *m* (*-es*; *no pl*) brains
grob [groːp] **1.** *adj* coarse (*a. fig*); *fig* gross; crude; rude; rough; **2.** *adv*: *grob geschätzt* at a rough estimate
'**Grobheit** *f* (*-*; *no pl*) coarseness; roughness; rudeness
grölen ['grøːlən] F *v/t and v/i* (*ge-*, *h*) bawl
Groll [grɔl] *m* (*-[e]s*; *no pl*) grudge, ill will
'**grollen** *v/i* (*ge-*, *h*) *j-m grollen* bear s.o. a grudge
Groschen ['grɔʃən] *m* (*-s*; *-*) *Austrian* groschen; F ten-pfennig piece, ten pfennigs
groß [groːs] *adj* big; large (*a. family*); tall; grown-up; F big (*brother etc*); *fig* great (*a. fun, trouble, pain etc*); capital (*letter*); *großes Geld* bills, *Br* notes; *große Ferien* summer vacation, *Br* summer holiday(s); *Groß und Klein* young and old; *im Großen und Ganzen* on the whole; F *groß in et. sein* be great at (doing) s.th.; *wie groß ist es?* what size is it?; *wie groß bist du?* how tall are you?
'**großartig** *adj* great, F *a.* terrific
'**Großaufnahme** *f film:* close-up
Größe ['grøːsə] *f* (*-*; *-n*) size; height; *esp* MATH quantity; *fig* greatness; celebrity
'**Großeltern** *pl* grandparents
'**großenteils** *adv* to a large *or* great extent, largely
'**Größenwahn** *m* megalomania (*a. fig*)
'**Großfa,milie** *f* extended family
Großhandel *m* ECON wholesale (trade)
Großhändler *m* ECON wholesale dealer, wholesaler

Großhandlung f ECON wholesale business
Großindus,trie f big industry; big business
Großindustri,elle m big industrialist, F tycoon
Großmacht f POL great power
Großmarkt m ECON hypermarket; wholesale market
Großmaul F n braggart
Großmutter f grandmother
Großraum m conurbation, metropolitan area; *der Großraum München* Greater Munich, the Greater Munich area
Großraumflugzeug n wide-bodied jet
'**großschreiben** v/t (*irr, schreiben, sep, -ge-, h*) capitalize
'**Großschreibung** f (use of) capitalization
'**großsprecherisch** [-ʃprɛçərɪʃ] adj boastful
'**großspurig** [-ʃpuːrɪç] adj arrogant
'**Großstadt** f big city
'**großstädtisch** adj of or in a big city, urban
'**größten'teils** adv mostly, mainly
'**großtun** v/i (*irr, tun, sep, -ge-, h*) show off; *sich mit et. großtun* brag about s.th.
'**Großvater** m grandfather
'**Großverdiener** m (-s; -) big earner
'**Großwild** n big game
'**großziehen** v/t (*irr, ziehen, sep, -ge-, h*) raise, rear; bring up
'**großzügig** adj generous, liberal; ... on a large scale; spacious
'**Großzügigkeit** f (-; *no pl*) generosity, liberality; spaciousness
grotesk [gro'tɛsk] adj grotesque
Grotte ['grɔtə] f (-; -n) grotto
grub [gruːp] *pret of graben*
Grübchen ['gryːpçən] n (-s; -) dimple
Grube ['gruːbə] f (-; -n) pit; mine
Grübelei [gryːbə'lai] f (-; -en) pondering, musing
grübeln ['gryːbəln] v/i (ge-, h) ponder, muse (*über acc* on, over)
Gruft [grʊft] f (-; *Grüfte* ['gryftə]) tomb, vault
grün [gryːn] adj green
Grün n (-s; -) green; *im Grünen* in the country
'**Grünanlage** f park
Grund [grʊnt] m (-[e]s; *Gründe* ['gryndə]) reason; cause; ground, AGR *a.* soil; bottom; *Grund und Boden* property, land; *aus diesem Grund(e)* for this reason; *von Grund auf* entirely; *im Grunde (genommen)* actually, basically; → *aufgrund*; → *zugrunde*
'**Grund...** *in cpds* ...bedeutung, ...bedingung, ...regel, ...prinzip, ...wortschatz

etc: mst basic ...
Grundbegriffe *pl* basics, fundamentals
Grundbesitz m property, land
Grundbesitzer m landowner
gründen ['gryndən] v/t (ge-, h) found (*a. family*), set up, establish; *sich gründen auf* (*dat*) be based *or* founded on
Gründer ['gryndɐ] m (-s; -), '**Gründerin** f (-; -nen) founder
'**grund'falsch** adj absolutely wrong
'**Grundfläche** f MATH base; ARCH area
Grundgedanke m basic idea
Grundgeschwindigkeit f AVIAT ground speed
Grundgesetz n POL Basic (Constitutional) Law (for the Federal Republic of Germany)
Grundlage f foundation, *fig a.* basis; *pl* (basic) elements
'**grundlegend** adj fundamental, basic
gründlich ['gryntlɪç] adj thorough
'**Grundlinie** f *tennis etc:* base line
'**grundlos** adj groundless, unfounded
'**Grundmauer** f foundation
Grün'donnerstag m REL Maundy *or* Holy Thursday
'**Grundrechnungsart** f MATH basic arithmetical operation
Grundriss m ARCH ground plan
Grundsatz m principle
grundsätzlich ['grʊntzɛtslɪç] **1.** adj fundamental; **2.** adv: *ich bin grundsätzlich dagegen* I am against it on principle
'**Grundschule** f elementary (*or* grade) school, *Br* primary (*or* junior) school
Grundstein m ARCH foundation stone; *fig* foundations
Grundstück n plot (of land), lot; (building) site; premises
Grundstücksmakler m realtor, *Br* real estate agent
'**Gründung** f (-; -en) foundation, establishment, setting up
'**grundver'schieden** adj totally different
'**Grundwasser** n ground water
Grundzahl f cardinal number
Grundzug m main feature, characteristic
Grüne ['gryːnə] m, f (-n; -n) POL Green
'**Grünfläche** f green space
'**grünlich** adj greenish
'**Grünspan** m (-[e]s; *no pl*) verdigris
grunzen ['grʊntsən] v/i *and* v/t (ge-, h) grunt
Gruppe ['grʊpə] f (-; -n) group
'**Gruppenreise** f group tour
gruppieren [grʊ'piːrən] v/t (*no -ge-, h*) group, arrange in groups; *sich gruppieren* form groups
Grusel... ['gruːzəl-] *in cpds* ...film *etc:*

horror ...

'**gruselig** adj eerie, creepy; spine-chilling

'**gruseln** v/t and v/refl (ge-, h) **es gruselt mich** F it gives me the creeps

Gruß [gruːs] m (-es; **Grüße** ['gryːsə]) greeting(s); MIL salute; **viele Grüße an** (acc) ... give my regards (or love) to ...; **mit freundlichen Grüßen** yours sincerely; **herzliche Grüße** best wishes; love

grüßen ['gryːsən] v/t (ge-, h) greet, F say hello to; MIL salute; **grüßen Sie ihn von mir** give my regards (or love) to him

gucken ['gʊkən] v/i (ge-, h) look

'**Guckloch** n peephole

Güggeli ['gygəli] n (-s; -) Swiss chicken

gültig ['gyltɪç] adj valid; current

'**Gültigkeit** f (-; no pl) validity; **s-e Gültigkeit verlieren** expire

Gummi ['gʊmi] m, n (-s; -[s]) rubber

Gummiband n (-[e]s; -bänder) rubber (esp Br a. elastic) band

Gummibärchen pl gummy bears

Gummibaum m BOT rubber tree; rubber plant

Gummibon,bon m, n gumdrop

gummieren [gʊ'miːrən] v/t (no -ge-, h) gum

'**Gummiknüppel** m truncheon

Gummistiefel m rubber boot, esp Br wellington (boot)

Gummizug m elastic

Gunst [gʊnst] f (-; no pl) favo(u)r, goodwill; → **zugunsten**

günstig ['gynstɪç] adj favo(u)rable (**für** to); convenient; **im günstigsten Fall** at best; **günstige Gelegenheit** chance

Gurgel ['gʊrgəl] f (-; -n) throat; **j-m an die Gurgel springen** fly at s.o.'s throat

'**gurgeln** v/i (ge-, h) MED gargle

Gurke ['gʊrkə] f (-; -n) BOT cucumber

gurren ['gʊrən] v/i (ge-, h) ZO coo

Gurt [gʊrt] m (-[e]s; -e) belt (a. MOT and AVIAT); strap

Gürtel ['gyrtəl] m (-s; -) belt

Gürtelreifen m MOT radial (tire, Br tyre)

GUS [gʊs, geːˀuːˀɛs] ABBR of **Gemeinschaft Unabhängiger Staaten** CIS, Commonwealth of Independent States

Guss [gʊs] m (-es; **Güsse** ['gʏsə]) downpour; TECH casting; GASTR icing; fig **aus e-m Guss** of a piece

'**Gusseisen** n cast iron

'**gusseisern** adj cast-iron

gut [guːt] **1.** adj good; fine; **ganz gut** not bad; **also gut!** all right (then)!; **schon gut!** never mind!; (**wieder**) **gut werden** come right (again), be all right; **gute Reise!** have a nice trip!; **sei bitte so gut und** ... would you be so good as to or good

enough to ...; **in et. gut sein** be good at (doing) s.th.; **2.** adv well; look, taste etc good; **du hast es gut** you are lucky; **es ist gut möglich** it may well be; **es gefällt mir gut** I (do) like it; **gut gebaut** well-built; **gut gelaunt** in a good mood; **gut gemacht!** well done!; **mach's gut!** take care (of yourself!)!; **gut gehen** go (off) well, work out well or all right; **wenn alles gut geht** if nothing goes wrong; **mir geht es gut** I'm (doing) well

Gut n (-[e]s; **Güter** ['gyːtɐ]) estate; pl goods

'**Gutachten** n (-s; -) (expert) opinion; certificate

Gutachter ['guːtˀaxtɐ] m (-s; -) expert

'**gutartig** adj good-natured; MED benign

Gutdünken ['guːtdʏŋkən] n: **nach Gutdünken** at one's discretion

Gute ['guːtə] n (-n; no pl) good; **Gutes tun** do good; **alles Gute!** all the best!, good luck!

Güte ['gyːtə] f (-; no pl) goodness, kindness; ECON quality; F **meine Güte!** good gracious!

Güterbahnhof ['gyːtɐ-] m freight depot, Br goods station

Gütergemeinschaft f JUR community of property

Gütertrennung f JUR separation of property

Güterverkehr m freight (Br goods) traffic

Güterwagen m freight car, Br goods wag(g)on

Güterzug m freight (Br goods) train

'**gutgläubig** adj credulous

'**Guthaben** n (-s; -) ECON credit (balance)

'**gutheißen** v/t (irr, **heißen**, sep, -ge-, h) approve (of)

'**gutherzig** adj kind(-hearted)

gütig ['gyːtɪç] adj good, kind(ly)

gütlich ['gyːtlɪç] adv: **sich gütlich einigen** come to an amicable settlement

'**gutmachen** v/t (sep, -ge-, h) make up for, repay

'**gutmütig** [-myːtɪç] adj good-natured

'**Gutmütigkeit** f (-; no pl) good nature

'**Gutsbesitzer** m, '**Gutsbesitzerin** f (-; -nen) estate owner

'**Gutschein** m coupon, esp Br voucher

'**gutschreiben** v/t (irr, **schreiben**, sep, -ge-, h) **j-m et. gutschreiben** credit s.th. to s.o.'s account

'**Gutschrift** f credit

'**Gutshaus** n manor (house)

'**Gutshof** m estate, manor

'**gutstehen** v/refl (irr, **stehen**, sep, -ge-, h): **sich gutstehen** be well off; F **sich gut mit j-m stehen** → **stehen**

'**Gutsverwalter** *m* steward, manager
'**gutwillig** *adj* willing
Gymnasium [gym'naːzjʊm] *n* (*-s*; *-ien*) high school, *Br appr* grammar school
Gymnastik [gym'nastɪk] *f* (*-*; *no pl*) exercises, gymnastics

gym'nastisch *adj*: *gymnastische Übungen* physical exercises
Gynäkologe [gynɛko'loːgə] *m* (*-n*; *-n*), **Gynäko'login** *f* (*-*; *-nen*) MED gyn(a)ecologist

H

Haar [haːɐ] *n* (*-[e]s*; *-e* ['haːrə]) hair; *sich die Haare kämmen* (*schneiden lassen*) comb one's hair (have one's hair cut); *sich aufs Haar gleichen* look absolutely identical; *um ein Haar* by a hair's breadth
'**Haarausfall** *m* loss of hair
'**Haarbürste** *f* hairbrush
haaren ['haːrən] *v/i and v/refl* (*ge-*, *h*) ZO lose its hair; *fur*: shed hairs
'**Haaresbreite** *f*: *um Haaresbreite* by a hair's breadth
'**haarfein** *adj* (as) fine as a hair
'**Haarfestiger** *m* (*-s*; *-*) setting lotion
'**Haargefäß** *n* ANAT capillary (vessel)
'**haargenau** F *adv* precisely; (*stimmt*) *haargenau!* dead right!
haarig ['haːrɪç] *adj* hairy
'**haarklein** F *adv* to the last detail
'**Haarklemme** *f* bobby pin, *Br* hair clip
Haarnadel *f* hairpin
Haarnadelkurve *f* hairpin bend
Haarnetz *n* hair-net
'**haarscharf** F *adv* by a hair's breadth
'**Haarschnitt** *m* haircut
Haarspalterei *f* (*-*; *no pl*) hair-splitting
Haarspange *f* barrette, *Br* (hair) slide
Haarspray *m*, *n* hairspray
'**haarsträubend** *adj* hair-raising
'**Haarteil** *n* hairpiece
Haartrockner *m* hair dryer
Haarwäsche *f*, **Haarwaschmittel** *n* shampoo
Haarwasser *n* hair tonic
Haarwuchs *m*: *starken Haarwuchs haben* have a lot of hair
Haarwuchsmittel *n* hair restorer
haben ['haːbən] *v/t* (*irr*, *ge-*, *h*) have (got); *Hunger haben* be hungry; *Durst haben* be thirsty; *Ferien* (*Urlaub*) *haben* be on vacation (*Br* holiday); *er hat Geburtstag* it's his birthday; *welche Farbe hat ...?* what colo(u)r is ...?; *zu haben sein* be

available; F *sich haben* make a fuss; F *was hast du?* what's the matter with you?; F *da haben wir's!* there we are!; → *Datum*
'**Haben** *n* (*-s*; *no pl*) ECON credit
Habgier ['haːp-] *f* greed(iness)
'**habgierig** *adj* greedy
Habicht ['haːbɪçt] *m* (*-s*; *-e*) ZO hawk
'**Habseligkeiten** *pl* belongings
Hacke ['hakə] *f* (*-*; *-n*) AGR hoe; (pick-) axe; ANAT heel
'**hacken** *v/t* (*ge-*, *h*) chop; AGR hoe; ZO peck
'**Hackentrick** *m* *soccer*: backheeler
Hacker ['hakɐ] *m* (*-s*; *-*) EDP hacker
'**Hackfleisch** *n* ground (*Br* minced) meat
Hackordnung *f* ZO pecking order
Hafen ['haːfən] *m* (*-s*; *Häfen* ['hɛːfən]) harbo(u)r, port
Hafenarbeiter *m* docker, longshoreman
Hafenstadt *f* (sea)port
Hafer ['haːfɐ] *m* (*-s*; *-*) BOT oats
Haferbrei *m* oatmeal, *Br* porridge
Haferflocken *pl* (rolled) oats
Haferschleim *m* gruel
Haft [haft] *f* (*-*; *no pl*) JUR confinement, imprisonment; *in Haft* under arrest
'**haftbar** *adj* responsible, JUR liable
'**Haftbefehl** *m* JUR warrant of arrest
'**haften** *v/i* (*ge-*, *h*) stick, adhere (*an dat* to); *haften für* JUR answer for, be liable for
Häftling ['hɛftlɪŋ] *m* (*-s*; *-e*) prisoner, convict
'**Haftpflicht** *f* JUR liability
Haftpflichtversicherung *f* liability insurance; MOT third party insurance
'**Haftung** *f* (*-*; *-en*) responsibility, JUR liability; *mit beschränkter Haftung* limited
Hagel ['haːgəl] *m* (*-s*; *no pl*) hail, *fig a.* shower, volley
'**Hagelkorn** *n* hailstone

'hageln v/i (ge-, h) hail (a. fig)
'Hagelschauer m hail shower
hager ['haːgɐ] adj lean, gaunt, haggard
Hahn [haːn] m (-[e]s; Hähne ['hɛːnə]) zo
   cock, rooster; TECH (water) tap, faucet
Hähnchen ['hɛːnçən] n (-s; -) zo chicken
'Hahnenkamm m zo cockscomb
Hai [hai] m (-[e]s; -e), Haifisch m zo shark
häkeln ['hɛːkəln] v/t and v/i (ge-, h) cro-
   chet
Haken ['haːkən] m (-s; -) hook (a. boxing),
   peg; check, Br tick; F snag, catch
'Hakenkreuz n swastika
halb [halp] adj and adv half; e-e halbe
   Stunde half an hour; ein halbes Pfund
   half a pound; zum halben Preis at half-
   -price; auf halbem Wege (entgegenkommen) (meet) halfway; halb so viel
   half as much; F (mit j-m) halbe-halbe
   machen go halves or fifty-fifty (with
   s.o.); halb gar GASTR underdone
'Halbbruder m half-brother
'Halbdunkel n semi-darkness
Halbe ['halbə] f (-n; -n) pint (of beer)
'halbfett adj GASTR medium-fat; PRINT
   semi-bold
'Halbfi₁nale n SPORT semifinal
'Halbgott m demigod
'halbherzig adj half-hearted
halbieren [hal'biːrən] v/t (no -ge-, h)
   halve; MATH bisect
'Halbinsel f peninsula
'Halbjahr n six months
'halbjährig [-jɛːrɪç] adj six-month
'halbjährlich 1. adj half-yearly; 2. adv
   half-yearly, twice a year
'Halbkreis m semicircle
'Halbkugel f hemisphere
'halblaut 1. adj low, subdued; 2. adv in an
   undertone
'Halbleiter m ELECTR semiconductor
'halbmast adv (at) half-mast
'Halbmond m half-moon, crescent
Halbpensi₁on f (-; no pl) esp Br half board
Halbschlaf m doze
Halbschuh m (low) shoe
Halbschwester f half-sister
'halbtags adv: halbtags arbeiten work
   part-time
'Halbtagsarbeit f (-; no pl) part-time job
'Halbtagskraft f part-time worker, F part-
   -timer
'halbwegs [-veːks] adv reasonably
'Halbwüchsige [-vyːksɪgə] m, f (-n; -n)
   adolescent
'Halbzeit f SPORT half (time)
Halbzeitstand m SPORT half-time score
Halde ['haldə] f (-; -n) slope; dump
half [half] pret of helfen

Hälfte ['hɛlftə] f (-; -n) half; die Hälfte
   von half of
Halfter ['halftɐ] 1. m, n (-s; -) halter; 2. n
   (-s; -), f (-; -n) holster
Halle ['halə] f (-; -n) hall; lounge; in der
   Halle SPORT etc indoors
'hallen v/i (ge-, h) resound, reverberate
'Hallenbad n indoor swimming pool
'Hallensport m indoor sports
Halm [halm] m (-[e]s; -e) BOT blade;
   ha(u)lm, stalk; straw
Hals [hals] m (-es; Hälse ['hɛlzə]) ANAT
   neck; throat; Hals über Kopf helter-skel-
   ter; F sich vom Hals schaffen get rid of;
   F es hängt mir zum Hals(e) (he)raus
   I'm fed up with it; fig bis zum Hals
   up to one's neck
Halsband n (-[e]s; -bänder) necklace; collar
Halsentzündung f MED sore throat
Halskette f necklace
Halsschmerzen pl: Halsschmerzen haben have a sore throat
'halsstarrig [-ʃtarɪç] adj stubborn, obstinate
'Halstuch n neckerchief; scarf
Halt [halt] m (-[e]s; -e, -s) a (no pl) hold;
   support (a. fig); fig stability, b) stop
halt [halt] int stop!, MIL halt!
'haltbar adj durable; GASTR not perishable; fig tenable; haltbar bis ... best before ...
'Haltbarkeitsdatum n best-by (or best-before) date
halten ['haltən] (irr, ge-, h) 1. v/t hold;
   keep (animal, promise etc); make
   (speech); give (lecture); take (Br a. in) a
   paper etc; SPORT save; halten für regard
   as; (mis)take for; viel (wenig) halten
   von think highly (little) of; sich halten
   last; GASTR keep; sich gut halten fig do
   well; sich halten an (acc) keep to; 2. v/i
   hold, last; stop, halt; ice: bear; rope etc:
   hold; halten zu stand by, F stick to
Halter(in) ['hal-tɐ(-tərin)] (-s; -/-; -nen)
   owner; TECH holder
'Haltestelle f stop, RAIL a. station
'Halteverbot n MOT no stopping (area)
'haltlos adj unsteady; fig baseless
'haltmachen v/i (sep, -ge-, h) stop; fig vor
   nichts haltmachen stop at nothing
'Haltung f (-; -en) posture; fig attitude (zu
   towards)
hämisch ['hɛːmɪʃ] adj malicious, sneering
Hammel ['haməl] m (-s; -) zo wether
'Hammelfleisch n GASTR mutton
Hammer ['hamɐ] m (-s; Hämmer ['hɛmɐ])
   hammer (a. SPORT)
hämmern ['hɛmɐn] v/t and v/i (ge-, h)

hammer

Hämorrhoiden, Hämorriden [hɛmɔro'iː-dən] *pl* MED h(a)emorrhoids, F *Br* piles

Hampelmann ['hampəl-] *m* jumping jack

Hamster ['hamstɐ] *m* (*-s*; *-*) ZO hamster

'**hamstern** *v/t and v/i* (*ge-*, *h*) hoard

Hand [hant] *f* (*-*; *Hände* ['hɛndə]) hand; *von Hand, mit der Hand* by hand; *an Hand von* (*or gen*) by means of; *zur Hand* at hand; *aus erster* (*zweiter*) *Hand* first-hand (second-hand); *an die Hand nehmen* take by the hand; *sich die Hand geben* shake hands; *aus der Hand legen* lay aside; *Hand breit* → *handbreit*; *Hand voll* → *handvoll*; *Hände hoch* (*weg*)*!* hands up (off)!

Handarbeit *f* a) (*no pl*) manual labo(u)r, b) needlework; *es ist Handarbeit* it is handmade

Handball *m* SPORT (European) handball

Handbetrieb *m* TECH manual operation

Handbreit *f* (*-*; *-*) hand's breadth

Handbremse *f* MOT handbrake

Handbuch *n* manual, handbook

Händedruck ['hɛndə-] *m* (*-[e]s*; *-drücke*) handshake

Handel ['handəl] *m* (*-s*; *no pl*) commerce, business; trade; market; transaction, deal, bargain; *Handel treiben* ECON trade (*mit* with *s.o.*)

'**handeln** *v/i* (*ge-*, *h*) act, take action; bargain (*um* for), haggle (over); *mit j-m handeln* ECON trade with s.o.; *handeln mit* deal in; *handeln von* deal with, be about; *es handelt sich um* it concerns, it is about; it is a matter of

'**Handelsabkommen** *n* trade agreement

Handelsbank *f* (*-*; *-banken*) commercial bank

Handelsbi,lanz *f* balance of trade

'**handelseinig** *adj*: *handelseinig werden* come to terms

'**Handelsgesellschaft** *f* (trading) company

Handelskammer *f* chamber of commerce

Handelsschiff *n* merchant ship

Handelsschule *f* commercial school

Handelsvertreter *m* (traveling) salesman, *Br* sales representative

Handelsware *f* commodity, merchandise

'**Handfeger** [-feːgɐ] *m* (*-s*; *-*) handbrush

Handfertigkeit *f* manual skill

'**handfest** *adj* solid

'**Handfläche** *f* ANAT palm

'**handgearbeitet** *adj* handmade

'**Handgelenk** *n* ANAT wrist

Handgepäck *n* hand baggage (*Br* luggage)

Handgra,nate *f* MIL hand grenade

'**handgreiflich** [-graiflɪç] *adj*: *handgreiflich werden* turn violent, get tough

'**handhaben** *v/t* (*ge-*, *h*) handle, manage; TECH operate

Händler ['hɛndlɐ] *m* (*-s*; *-*), '**Händlerin** *f* (*-*; *-nen*) dealer, trader

'**handlich** *adj* handy, manageable

Handlung ['handlʊŋ] *f* (*-*; *-en*) act, action; *film etc*: story, plot

'**Handlungsreisende** *m* sales representative, travel(l)ing salesman

'**Handrücken** *m* ANAT back of the hand

Handschellen *pl* handcuffs; *j-m Handschellen anlegen* handcuff s.o.

Handschlag *m* handshake

Handschrift *f* hand(writing)

'**handschriftlich** *adj* handwritten

'**Handschuh** *m* glove

Handspiel *n* *soccer*: hand ball

Handstand *m* handstand

Handtasche *f* handbag, purse

Handtuch *n* towel

Handvoll *f* handful

Handwagen *m* handcart

Handwerk *n* craft, trade

'**Handwerker** [-vɛrkɐ] *m* (*-s*; *-*) craftsman; workman

'**Handwerkszeug** *n* (kit of) tools

'**Handwurzel** *f* ANAT wrist

Handy ['hɛndi] *n* (*-s*; *-s*) mobile (phone), cellular phone

Hanf [hanf] *m* (*-es*; *no pl*) BOT hemp; cannabis

Hang [haŋ] *m* (*-[e]s*; *Hänge* ['hɛŋə]) a) slope, b) (*no pl*) *fig* inclination (*zu* for), tendency (towards)

Hängebrücke ['hɛŋə-] *f* suspension bridge

Hängelampe *f* hanging lamp

Hängematte *f* hammock

hängen ['hɛŋən] **1.** *v/i* (*irr*, *ge-*, *h*) hang (*an dat* on *the wall etc*; from *the ceiling etc*); *hängen bleiben* get stuck (*a. fig*); *hängen bleiben an* (*dat*) get caught on; *hängen an* (*dat*) be fond of; be devoted to; *alles, woran ich hänge* everything that is dear to me; **2.** *v/t* (*ge-*, *h*) hang (*an acc* on)

hängenbleiben *v/i* (*irr*, *bleiben*, *sep*, *-ge-*, *sein*) *fig* get stuck; → *hängen*

hänseln ['hɛnzəln] *v/t* (*ge-*, *h*) tease (*wegen* about)

Hanswurst [hans'vʊrst] *m* (*-[e]s*; *-e*) fool, clown

Hantel ['hantəl] *f* (*-*; *-n*) dumbbell

hantieren [han'tiːrən] *v/i* (*no -ge-*, *h*) *hantieren mit* handle; *hantieren an* (*dat*) fiddle about with

Happen ['hapən] *m* (*-s*; *-*) morsel, bite; snack

Hardware ['hɑːdwɛə] *f* (*-*; *-s*) EDP hardware

Harfe ['harfə] *f* (*-*; *-n*) MUS harp

Harfenist [harfə'nɪst] *m* (*-en*; *-en*), **Harfe-'nistin** *f* (*-*; *-nen*) MUS harpist

Harke ['harkə] *f* (*-*; *-n*), '**harken** *v/t* (*ge-*, *h*) rake

harmlos ['harmloːs] *adj* harmless

Harmonie [harmo'niː] *f* (*-*; *-n*) harmony (*a.* MUS)

harmo'nieren *v/i* (*no -ge-*, *h*) harmonize (**mit** with)

harmonisch [har'moːnɪʃ] *adj* harmonious

Harn [harn] *m* (*-[e]s*; *-e*) MED urine

'**Harnblase** *f* ANAT (urinary) bladder

'**Harnröhre** *f* ANAT urethra

Harpune [har'puːnə] *f* (*-*; *-n*) harpoon

harpunieren [harpu'niːrən] *v/t* (*no -ge-*, *h*) harpoon

hart [hart] **1.** *adj* hard, F *a.* tough; SPORT rough; severe; **hart gekocht** hard-boiled; **2.** *adv* hard

Härte ['hɛrtə] *f* (*-*; *-n*) hardness; toughness; roughness; severity; *esp* JUR hardship

Härtefall *m* case of hardship

'**härten** *v/t* (*ge-*, *h*) harden

'**Hartfaserplatte** *f* hardboard

'**Hartgeld** *n* coin(s)

'**hartgesotten** [-gəzɔtən] *adj* hard-boiled

'**hartherzig** *adj* hard-hearted

'**hartnäckig** [-nɛkɪç] *adj* stubborn, obstinate; persistent

Harz [haːrts] *n* (*-es*; *-e*) resin; rosin

'**harzig** *adj* resinous

Hasch [haʃ] F *n* (*-s*; *no pl*) hash

'**haschen** F *v/i* (*ge-*, *h*) smoke hash

Haschisch ['haʃɪʃ] *n* (*-[s]*; *no pl*) hashish

Hase ['haːzə] *m* (*-n*; *-n*) zo hare

Haselmaus ['haːzəl-] *f* zo dormouse

'**Haselnuss** *f* BOT hazelnut

'**Hasenscharte** *f* MED harelip

Hass [has] *m* (*-es*; *no pl*) hatred, hate (**auf** *acc*, **gegen** of, for)

hassen ['hasən] *v/t* (*ge-*, *h*) hate

hässlich ['hɛslɪç] *adj* ugly, *fig a.* nasty

Hast [hast] *f* (*-*; *no pl*) hurry, haste; rush

hasten ['hastən] *v/i* (*ge-*, *sein*) hurry, hasten, rush

'**hastig** *adj* hasty, hurried

hätscheln ['hɛːtʃəln] *v/t* (*ge-*, *h*) fondle; *contp* pamper

hatte ['hatə] *pret of* **haben**

Haube ['haubə] *f* (*-*; *-n*) bonnet (*a. Br* MOT); cap; zo crest; MOT hood

Hauch [haux] *m* (*-[e]s*; *-e*) breath; whiff; *fig* touch, trace

hauchen ['hauxən] *v/t* (*ge-*, *h*) breathe

hauen F *v/t* ([*irr*,] *ge-*, *h*) hit, beat, thrash; TECH hew; **sich hauen** (have a) fight

Haufen ['haufən] *m* (*-s*; *-*) heap, pile (*both a.* F); F crowd

häufen ['hɔyfən] *v/t* (*ge-*, *h*) heap (up), pile (up); **sich häufen** *fig* become more frequent, be on the increase

häufig ['hɔyfiç] **1.** *adj* frequent; **2.** *adv* frequently, often

Haupt [haupt] *n* (*-[e]s*; *Häupter* ['hɔyptɐ]) head, *fig a.* leader

Hauptbahnhof *m* main *or* central station

Hauptbeschäftigung *f* chief occupation

Hauptbestandteil *m* chief ingredient

Hauptdarsteller(in) leading actor (actress), lead

Häuptelsa lat ['hɔyptəl-] *Austrian m* BOT lettuce

'**Hauptfach** *n* UNIV major, *Br* main subject

Hauptfilm *m* feature (film)

Hauptgericht *n* GASTR main course

Hauptgewinn *m* first prize

Hauptgrund *m* main reason

Hauptleitung *f* TECH main

Häuptling ['hɔyptlɪŋ] *m* (*-s*; *-e*) chief

'**Hauptmann** *m* (*-[e]s*; *-leute*) MIL captain

Hauptme,nü *n* EDP main menu

Hauptmerkmal *n* chief characteristic

Hauptper son F *f* center (*Br* centre) of attention

Hauptquar tier *n* headquarters

Hauptrolle *f* THEA *etc* lead(ing part)

'**Hauptsache** *f* main thing *or* point

'**hauptsächlich** *adj* main, chief, principal

'**Hauptsatz** *m* LING main clause

Hauptsendezeit *f* TV prime time, *Br* peak time (*or* viewing hours)

Hauptspeicher *m* EDP main memory

Hauptstadt *f* capital

Hauptstraße *f* main street; main road

Hauptverkehrsstraße *f* arterial road

Hauptverkehrszeit *f* rush *or* peak hour(s)

Hauptversammlung *f* general meeting

Hauptwohnsitz *m* main place of residence

Hauptwort *n* (*-[e]s*; *-wörter*) LING noun

Haus [haus] *n* (*-es*; *Häuser* ['hɔyzɐ]) house; building; **zu Hause** at home, in; **nach Hause kommen** (**bringen**) come *or* get (take) home

Hausangestellte *m*, *f* domestic (servant)

Hausapo,theke *f* medicine cabinet

Hausarbeit *f* housework

Hausarzt *m*, **Hausärztin** *f* family doctor

Hausaufgaben *pl* PED homework, assignment; **s-e Hausaufgabenn machen** *a. fig* do one's homework

Hausbar *f* cocktail cabinet

Hausbesetzer *m* (*-s*; *-*) squatter

Hausbesetzung *f* squatting
Hausbesitzer *m* house owner
Hauseinweihung *f* house-warming (party)
hausen ['hauzən] *v/i* (*ge-*, *h*) live; *fig* play havoc
'**Hausflur** *m* (entrance) hall, hallway
'**Hausfrau** *f* housewife
'**Hausfriedensbruch** *m* JUR trespass
'**hausgemacht** *adj* homemade
'**Haushalt** *m* (-[*e*]*s*; *-e*) household; PARL budget; (*j-m*) *den Haushalt führen* keep house (for s.o.)
'**Haushälterin** [-hɛltərɪn] *f* (-; *-nen*) housekeeper
'**Haushaltsgeld** *n* housekeeping money
Haushaltsplan *m* PARL budget
Haushaltswaren *pl* household articles
'**Hausherr** *m* head of the household; host
Hausherrin *f* lady of the house; hostess
'**haushoch** *adj* huge; crushing (*defeat etc*)
hausieren [hau'ziːrən] *v/i* (*no* -*ge*-, *h*) peddle, hawk (*mit et.* s.th.) (*a. fig*)
Hau'sierer *m* (-*s*; -) pedlar, hawker
häuslich ['hɔyslɪç] *adj* domestic; home-loving
'**Hausmädchen** *n* (house)maid
Hausmann *m* house husband
Hausmannskost *f* plain fare
Hausmeister *m* caretaker, janitor
Hausmittel *n* household remedy
Hausordnung *f* house rules
Hausrat *m* (-[*e*]*s*; *no pl*) household effects
Hausschlüssel *m* front-door key
Hausschuh *m* slipper
Hausse ['hoːs(ə)] *f* (-; *-n*) ECON rise, boom
'**Haussuchung** *f* (-; *-en*) house search
Haustier *n* domestic animal
Haustür *f* front door
Hausverwaltung *f* property management
Hauswirt *m* landlord
Hauswirtin *f* landlady
Hauswirtschaft *f* (-; *no pl*) housekeeping
Hauswirtschaftslehre *f* domestic science, home economics
Hauswirtschaftsschule *f* domestic science (*or* home economics) school
Haut [haut] *f* (-; *Häute* ['hɔytə]) skin; complexion; *bis auf die Haut durchnässt* soaked to the skin
Hautabschürfung *f* MED abrasion
Hautarzt *m*, **Hautärztin** *f* dermatologist
Hautausschlag *m* MED rash
'**hauteng** *adj* skin-tight
'**Hautfarbe** *f* colo(u)r of the skin; complexion
Hautkrankheit *f* skin disease
Hautpflege *f* skin care
Hautschere *f* cuticle scissors

Hbf. ABBR *of* **Hauptbahnhof** cent. sta., central station
H-Bombe ['haːbɔmbə] *f* MIL H-bomb
Hebamme ['heːpʔamə] *f* (-; *-n*) midwife
Hebebühne ['heːbə-] *f* MOT car hoist
Hebel ['heːbəl] *m* (-*s*; -) TECH lever
heben ['heːbən] *v/t* (*irr*, *ge-*, *h*) lift, raise (*a. fig*); heave; hoist; *fig a.* improve; *sich heben* rise, go up
Hecht [hɛçt] *m* (-[*e*]*s*; *-e*) ZO pike
'**hechten** *v/i* (*ge-*, *sein*) dive (*nach* for); SPORT do a long-fly
Heck [hɛk] *n* (-[*e*]*s*; *-e*) MAR stern; AVIAT tail; MOT rear
Hecke ['hɛkə] *f* (-; *-n*) BOT hedge
'**Heckenrose** *f* BOT dogrose
'**Heckenschütze** *m* MIL sniper
'**Heckscheibe** *f* MOT rear window
Heer [heːɐ] *n* (-[*e*]*s*; *-e*) MIL army, *fig a.* host
Hefe ['heːfə] *f* (-; *-n*) yeast
Heft [hɛft] *n* (-[*e*]*s*; *-e*) notebook; exercise book; booklet; issue, number
heften ['hɛftən] *v/t* (*ge-*, *h*) fix, fasten, attach (*an acc* to); pin (to); tack, baste; stitch
Hefter ['hɛftɐ] *m* (-*s*; -) stapler; file
heftig ['hɛftɪç] *adj* violent, fierce; heavy
'**Heftklammer** *f* staple
'**Heftpflaster** *n* bandage, Band Aid®, *Br* (adhesive *or* sticking) plaster
Hehl [heːl] *n*: *kein Hehl aus et. machen* make no secret of s.th.
Hehler ['heːlɐ] *m* (-*s*; -) JUR receiver of stolen goods, *sl* fence
Hehlerei [heːlə'rai] *f* (-; *-en*) JUR receiving stolen goods
Heide[1] ['haidə] *m* (-*n*; *-n*) REL heathen
Heide[2] *f* (-; *-n*) heath(land)
'**Heidekraut** *n* (-[*e*]*s*; *no pl*) BOT heather, heath
'**Heidenangst** F *f*: *e-e Heidenangst haben* be scared stiff
Heidengeld F *n*: *ein Heidengeld* a fortune
Heidenlärm F *m*: *ein Heidenlärm* a hell of a noise
Heidenspaß F *m*: *e-n Heidenspaß haben* have a ball
'**Heidentum** *n* (-*s*; *no pl*) REL heathenism
Heidin ['haidɪn] *f* (-; *-nen*), '**heidnisch** ['haidnɪʃ] *adj* REL heathen
heikel ['haikəl] *adj* delicate, tricky; tender; F fussy
heil [hail] *adj* safe, unhurt; undamaged, whole, intact
Heil *n* (-*s*; *no pl*) REL grace; *sein Heil versuchen* try one's luck
Heiland ['hailant] *m* (-[*e*]*s*; *no pl*) REL Sav-

io(u)r, Redeemer
'**Heilanstalt** f sanatorium, sanitarium; mental home
'**Heilbad** n health resort, spa
'**heilbar** adj curable
heilen ['hailən] **1.** v/t (ge-, h) cure; **2.** v/i (ge-, sein) heal (up)
'**Heilgym,nastik** f physiotherapy
heilig ['hailıç] adj REL holy; sacred (a. fig)
Heilig'abend m Christmas Eve
Heilige ['hailıgə] m, f (-n; -n) REL saint
heiligen ['hailıgən] v/t (ge-, h) REL sanctify (a. fig), hallow
'**heiligsprechen** v/t (irr, **sprechen**, sep, -ge-, h) canonize
'**Heiligtum** n (-s; -tümer [-tyːmɐ]) REL sanctuary, shrine
'**Heilkraft** f healing or curative power
'**heilkräftig** adj curative
'**Heilkraut** n BOT medicinal herb
'**heillos** fig adj utter, hopeless
'**Heilmittel** n remedy, cure (both a. fig)
Heilpraktiker(in) [-praktikɐ (-kərın)] (-s; -/-; -nen) nonmedical practitioner
Heilquelle f (medicinal) mineral spring
'**heilsam** fig adj salutary
'**Heilsar,mee** f Salvation Army
'**Heilung** f (-; -en) cure; healing
heim [haim] adv home
Heim n (-[e]s; -e) a) (no pl) home, b) hostel
Heim... in cpds ...computer, ...mannschaft, ...sieg, ...spiel etc: home
Heimat ['haimaːt] f (-; no pl) home; home country; home town; **in der** (**meiner**) **Heimat** at home
'**heimatlos** adj homeless
'**Heimatstadt** f home town
'**Heimatvertriebene** m, f expellee
heimisch ['haimıʃ] adj home, domestic; BOT, ZO etc native; fig homelike, hom(e)y; **sich heimisch fühlen** feel at home
'**Heimkehr** [-keːɐ] f (-; no pl) return (home)
'**heimkehren** v/i (sep, -ge-, sein) return home, come back
'**heimlich** adj secret
'**Heimlichkeit** f (-; -en) a) (no pl) secrecy, b) pl secrets
'**Heimreise** f journey home
'**heimsuchen** v/t (sep, -ge-, h) strike
'**heimtückisch** adj insidious (a. MED); treacherous
'**heimwärts** [-vɛrts] adv homeward(s)
'**Heimweg** m way home
'**Heimweh** n (-s; no pl) homesickness; **Heimweh haben** be homesick
'**Heimwerker** [-vɛrkɐ] m (-s; -) do-it-yourselfer
Heirat ['hairaːt] f (-; -en) marriage

heiraten ['hairaːtən] v/t and v/i (ge-, h) marry, get married (to)
'**Heiratsantrag** m proposal (of marriage); **j-m e-n Heiratsantrag machen** propose to s.o.
Heiratsschwindler m marriage impostor
Heiratsvermittler(in) (-s; -/-; -nen) marriage broker
Heiratsvermittlung f marriage bureau
heiser ['haizɐ] adj hoarse, husky
'**Heiserkeit** f (-; no pl) hoarseness, huskiness
heiß [hais] adj hot, fig a. passionate, ardent; **mir ist heiß** I am or feel hot
heißen ['haisən] v/i (irr, ge-, h) be called; mean; **wie heißen Sie?** what's your name?; **wie heißt das?** what do you call this?; **was heißt ... auf Englisch?** what is ... in English?; **es heißt im Text** it says in the text; **das heißt** that is (ABBR **d. h.** i. e.)
heiter ['haitɐ] adj cheerful; humorous (film etc); METEOR fair; fig **aus heiterem Himmel** out of the blue
'**Heiterkeit** f (-; no pl) cheerfulness; amusement
heizbar ['haitsbaːɐ] adj heated
heizen ['haitsən] v/t and v/i (ge-, h) heat; **mit Kohlen heizen** burn coal
Heizer ['haitsɐ] m (-s; -) MAR, RAIL stoker
'**Heizkessel** m boiler
'**Heizkissen** n electric cushion
'**Heizkörper** m radiator
'**Heizkraftwerk** n thermal power-station
'**Heizmateri,al** n fuel
'**Heizöl** n fuel oil
'**Heizung** f (-; -en) heating
Held [hɛlt] m (-en; -en ['hɛldən]) hero
heldenhaft ['hɛldənhaft] adj heroic
'**Heldentat** f heroic deed
'**Heldentum** n (-s; no pl) heroism
Heldin ['hɛldın] f (-; -nen) heroine
helfen ['hɛlfən] v/i (irr, ge-, h) help, aid; assist; **j-m bei et. helfen** help s.o. with or in (doing) s.th.; **helfen gegen** MED etc be good for; **er weiß sich zu helfen** he can manage; **es hilft nichts** it's no use
Helfer ['hɛlfɐ] m (-s; -), '**Helferin** f (-; -nen) helper, assistant
'**Helfershelfer** contp m accomplice
hell [hɛl] adj bright (light, flame etc); light (color etc); light-colo(u)red (dress etc); clear (voice etc); pale (beer); fig bright, clever; **es wird schon hell** it's getting light already
'**hellblau** adj light blue
'**hellblond** adj very fair
hellhörig adj quick of hearing; ARCH poorly soundproofed; **hellhörig werden**

prick up one's ears

'Hellseher *m* (*-s*; *-*), **'Hellseherin** *f* (*-*; *-nen*) clairvoyant

Helm [hɛlm] *m* (*-[e]s*; *-e*) helmet

Hemd [hɛmt] *n* (*-[e]s*; *-en* ['hɛmdən]) shirt; vest

Hemdbluse *f* shirt

Hemdblusenkleid *n* shirtwaist, *Br* shirt-waister

Hemisphäre [hemi'sfɛːrə] *f* (*-*; *-n*) hemisphere

hemmen ['hɛmən] *v/t* (*ge-*, *h*) check, stop; hamper

'Hemmung *f* (*-*; *-en*) PSYCH inhibition; scruple

'hemmungslos *adj* unrestrained; unscrupulous

Hengst [hɛŋst] *m* (*-[e]s*; *-e*) zo stallion

Henkel ['hɛŋkəl] *m* (*-s*; *-*) handle

Henker ['hɛŋkɐ] *m* (*-s*; *-*) hangman, executioner

Henne ['hɛnə] *f* (*-*; *-n*) zo hen

her [heːɐ] *adv* here; ***das ist lange her*** that was a long time ago

herab [hɛ'rap] *adv* down

herablassen *fig v/refl* (*irr*, ***lassen***, *sep*, *-ge-*, *h*) condescend

herablassend *adj* condescending

herabsehen *fig v/i* (*irr*, ***sehen***, *sep*, *-ge-*, *h*) ***herabsehen auf*** (*acc*) look down upon

herabsetzen *v/t* (*sep*, *-ge-*, *h*) reduce; *fig* disparage

heran [hɛ'ran] *adv* close, near; ***heran an*** (*acc*) up *or* near to

herangehen *v/i* (*irr*, ***gehen***, *sep*, *-ge-*, *sein*) ***herangehen an*** (*acc*) walk up to; *fig* set about *a task etc*

herankommen *v/i* (*irr*, ***kommen***, *sep*, *-ge-*, *sein*) come near (*a. fig*)

heranwachsen *v/i* (*irr*, ***wachsen***, *sep*, *-ge-*, *sein*) grow (up) (***zu*** into)

He'ranwachsende *m*, *f* (*-n*; *-n*) adolescent

he'ranwinken *v/t* (*sep*, *-ge-*, *h*) hail (*taxi etc*)

herauf [hɛ'rauf] *adv* up (here); upstairs

heraufbeschwören *v/t* (*irr*, ***schwören***, *sep*, *no -ge-*, *h*) call up; bring on, provoke

heraus [hɛ'raus] *adv* out; *fig* ***aus*** (*dat*) ... ***heraus*** out of ...; ***zum Fenster heraus*** out of the window; ***heraus mit der Sprache!*** speak out!, out with it!

herausbekommen *v/t* (*irr*, ***kommen***, *sep*, *no -ge-*, *h*) get out; get back (*change*); *fig* find out

herausbringen *v/t* (*irr*, ***bringen***, *sep*, *-ge-*, *h*) bring out; PRINT publish; THEA stage; *fig* find out

herausfinden (*irr*, ***finden***, *sep*, *-ge-*, *h*) **1.** *v/t* find; *fig* find out, discover; **2.** *v/i* find one's way out

He'rausforderer *m* (*-s*; *-*) challenger

he'rausfordern *v/t* (*sep*, *-ge-*, *h*) challenge; provoke, F ask for it

He'rausforderung *f* challenge; provocation

he'rausgeben *v/t* (*irr*, ***geben***, *sep*, *-ge-*, *h*) give back; give up; PRINT publish; issue; give change (***auf*** *acc* for)

He'rausgeber(in) [-geːbɐ (-bərɪn)] (*-s*; *-/-*; *-nen*) publisher

he'rauskommen *v/i* (*irr*, ***kommen***, *sep*, *-ge-*, *sein*) come out; *book*: be published; *stamps*: be issued; ***herauskommen aus*** get out of; F ***groß herauskommen*** be a great success

herausnehmen *v/t* (*irr*, ***nehmen***, *sep*, *-ge-*, *h*) take out; SPORT take *s.o.* off the team; *fig* ***sich et. herausnehmen*** take liberties, go too far

herausputzen *v/t and v/refl* (*sep*, *-ge-*, *h*) spruce (o.s.) up

herausreden *v/refl* (*sep*, *-ge-*, *h*) make excuses; talk one's way out

herausstellen *v/t* (*sep*, *-ge-*, *h*) put out; *fig* emphasize; ***sich herausstellen als*** turn out *or* prove to be

herausstrecken *v/t* (*sep*, *-ge-*, *h*) stick out

heraussuchen *v/t* (*sep*, *-ge-*, *h*) pick out; ***j-m et. heraussuchen*** find s.o. s.th.

herb [hɛrp] *adj* tart; dry (*wine etc*); *fig* harsh; bitter

her'bei *adv* up, over, here

herbeieilen *v/i* (*sep*, *-ge-*, *sein*) come running up

herbeiführen *fig v/t* (*sep*, *-ge-*, *h*) cause, bring about

Herberge ['hɛrbɛrgə] *f* (*-*; *-n*) inn; lodging; hostel

Herbst [hɛrpst] *m* (*-[e]s*; *-e*) fall, autumn

Herd [heːɐt] *m* (*-[e]s*; *-e*) ['heːɐdə]) cooker, stove; *fig* center, *Br* centre; MED focus, seat

Herde ['heːɐdə] *f* (*-*; *-n*) zo herd (*a. fig contp*); flock (*of sheep, geese etc*)

herein [hɛ'rain] *adv* in (here); ***herein!*** come in!

hereinbrechen *v/i* (*irr*, ***brechen***, *sep*, *-ge-*, *sein*) *night*: fall; ***hereinbrechen über*** (*acc*) befall *s.o.*

hereinfallen F *v/i* (*irr*, ***fallen***, *sep*, *-ge-*, *sein*) be taken in (***auf*** *acc* by)

hereinlegen F *v/t* (*sep*, *-ge-*, *h*) take *s.o.* in

'herfallen *v/i* (*irr*, ***fallen***, *sep*, *-ge-*, *sein*) ***herfallen über*** (*acc*) attack (*a. fig*)

'Hergang *m*: ***j-m den Hergang schildern*** tell s.o. what happened 'hergeben v/t (irr, **geben**, sep, -ge-, h) give up, part with; **sich hergeben zu** lend o.s. to

Hering ['heːrɪŋ] m (-s; -e) zo herring

'herkommen v/i (irr, **kommen**, sep, -ge-, sein) come (here); **herkommen von** come from, fig a. be caused by

'herkömmlich [-kœmlɪç] adj conventional (a. MIL)

'Herkunft [-kʊnft] f (-; no pl) origin; birth, descent

heroisch [heˈroːɪʃ] adj heroic

Herr [hɛr] m (-n; -en) gentleman; master; REL the Lord; **Herr Brown** Mr Brown; **Herr der Lage** master of the situation

'Herrenbekleidung f menswear

Herrendoppel n tennis: men's doubles

Herreneinzel n tennis: men's singles

'herrenlos adj abandoned; stray (dog)

'Herrentoi,lette f men's restroom (Br toilet or lavatory)

'herrichten v/t (sep, -ge-, h) get ready, F fix

herrisch ['hɛrɪʃ] adj imperious

herrlich ['hɛrlɪç] adj marvel(l)ous, wonderful, F fantastic

'Herrlichkeit f (-; -en) glory

'Herrschaft f (-; no pl) rule, power, control (a. fig) (**über** acc over); **die Herrschaft verlieren über** (acc) lose control of

herrschen ['hɛrʃən] v/i (ge-, h) rule; **es herrschte ...** there was ...

Herrscher(in) ['hɛrʃɐ (-ʃərɪn)] (-s; -/-; -nen) ruler; sovereign, monarch

'herrschsüchtig adj domineering, F bossy

'herrühren v/i (sep, -ge-, h) **herrühren von** come from, be due to

'herstellen v/t (sep, -ge-, h) make, produce; fig establish

'Herstellung f (-; no pl) production; fig establishment

'Herstellungskosten pl production cost(s)

herüber [hɛˈryːbɐ] adv over (here), across

herum [hɛˈrʊm] adv (a)round; F **anders herum** the other way round

herumführen v/t (sep, -ge-, h) **j-n (in der Stadt** etc) **herumführen** show s.o. (a)round (the town etc)

herumkommen F v/i (irr, **kommen**, sep, -ge-, sein) (**weit** or **viel**) **herumkommen** get around; **um et. herumkommen** fig get (a)round s.th.

herumkriegen F v/t (sep, -ge-, h) **j-n zu et. herumkriegen** get s.o. round to (doing) s.th.

herumlungern F v/i (sep, -ge-, h) loaf or hang around

herumreichen v/t (sep, -ge-, h) pass or hand round

herumsprechen v/refl (irr, **sprechen**, sep, -ge-, h) get around

herumtreiben F v/refl (irr, **treiben**, sep, -ge-, h) gad or knock about

He'rumtreiber F m (-s; -), **He'rumtreiberin** F f (-; -nen) tramp, loafer

herunter [hɛˈrʊntɐ] adv down; downstairs

heruntergekommen adj run-down; seedy, shabby

herunterhauen F v/t (sep, -ge-, h) **j-m e-e herunterhauen** smack or slap s.o. ('s face)

heruntermachen F v/t (sep, -ge-, h) run s.o. or s.th. down

herunterspielen F v/t (sep, -ge-, h) play s.th. down

hervor [hɛɐˈfoːɐ] adv out of or from, forth

hervorbringen v/t (irr, **bringen**, sep, -ge-, h) bring out, produce (a. fig); yield; utter

hervorgehen v/i (irr, **gehen**, sep, -ge-, sein) **hervorgehen aus** (dat) follow from; **als Sieger hervorgehen** come off victorious

hervorheben v/t (irr, **heben**, sep, -ge-, h) stress, emphasize

hervorragend adj outstanding, excellent, superior; prominent, eminent

hervorrufen v/t (irr, **rufen**, sep, -ge-, h) cause, bring about; create

hervorstechend adj striking

hervortretend adj prominent; protruding, bulging

hervortun v/refl (irr, **tun**, sep, -ge-, h) distinguish o.s. (**als** as)

Herz [hɛrts] n (-ens; -en) ANAT heart (a. fig); cards: heart(s); **j-m das Herz brechen** break s.o.'s heart; **sich ein Herz fassen** take heart; **mit ganzem Herzen** whole-heartedly; **schweren Herzens** with a heavy heart; **sich et. zu Herzen nehmen** take s.th. to heart; **es nicht übers Herz bringen zu** inf not have the heart to inf; **et. auf dem Herzen haben** have s.th. on one's mind; **ins Herz schließen** take to one's heart

Herzanfall m heart attack

'Herzenslust f: **nach Herzenslust** to one's heart's content

Herzenswunsch m heart's desire, dearest wish

'Herzfehler m cardiac defect

'herzhaft adj hearty; savo(u)ry

'herzig adj sweet, lovely, cute

'Herzin,farkt m MED cardiac infarct(-ion), F mst heart attack, coronary

Herzklopfen n (-s; no pl) palpitation; **er hatte Herzklopfen (vor** dat) his heart was throbbing (with)

'**herzkrank** *adj* suffering from (a) heart disease

'**herzlich** **1.** *adj* cordial, hearty; warm, friendly; **2.** *adv:* **herzlich gern** with pleasure

'**herzlos** *adj* heartless

Herzog ['hɛrtsoːk] *m* (*-s; Herzöge* ['hɛrtsøːgə]) duke

Herzogin [hɛrtsoːgɪn] *f* (*-; -nen*) duchess

'**Herzschlag** *m* heartbeat; MED heart failure

Herzschrittmacher *m* MED (cardiac) pacemaker

Herztransplantati,on *f* MED heart transplant

'**herzzerreißend** *adj* heart-rending

Hetze ['hɛtsə] *f* (*-; no pl*) hurry, rush; POL *etc* agitation, campaign(ing) (*gegen* against)

'**hetzen** **1.** *v/t* (*ge-, h*) rush; ZO hunt, chase; **e-n Hund auf j-n hetzen** set a dog on s.o.; **2.** *v/i* a) (*ge-, sein*) hurry, rush, b) (*ge-, h*) POL *etc* agitate (*gegen* against)

'**hetzerisch** *adj* inflammatory

'**Hetzjagd** *f* hunt(ing), chase (*a. fig*); *fig* rush

'**Hetzkam,pagne** *f* POL smear campaign

Heu [hɔy] *n* (*-[e]s; no pl*) hay

'**Heuboden** *m* hayloft

Heuchelei [hɔyçə'lai] *f* (*-; -en*) hypocrisy; cant

heucheln ['hɔyçəln] *v/i and v/t* (*ge-, h*) feign, simulate

Heuchler(in) ['hɔyçlɐ (-lərɪn)] (*-s; -/-; -nen*) hypocrite

heuchlerisch ['hɔyçlərɪʃ] *adj* hypocritical

heuer ['hɔyɐ] *Austrian adv* this year

Heuer ['hɔyɐ] *f* (*-; -n*) MAR pay

'**heuern** *v/t* (*ge-, h*) hire, MAR a. sign on

heulen ['hɔylən] *v/i* (*ge-, h*) howl; F *contp* bawl; MOT roar; *siren:* whine

'**Heuschnupfen** *m* MED hay fever

'**Heuschrecke** *f* (*-; -n*) ZO grasshopper; locust

heute ['hɔytə] *adv* today; **heute Abend** this evening, tonight; **heute früh, heute Morgen** this morning; **heute in acht Tagen** a week from now; **heute vor acht Tagen** a week ago today

heutig ['hɔytɪç] *adj* today's; of today, present(-day)

'**heutzutage** *adv* nowadays, these days

Hexe ['hɛksə] *f* (*-; -n*) witch (*a. fig*); **alte Hexe** (old) hag

'**hexen** *v/i* (*ge-, h*) practice witchcraft; F work miracles

'**Hexenkessel** *m* inferno

Hexenschuss *m* (*-es; no pl*) MED lumbago

hieb [hiːp] *pret of* **hauen**

Hieb [hiːp] *m* (*-[e]s; -e* ['hiːbə]) blow, stroke; punch; lash, cut; *pl* beating; thrashing

hielt [hiːlt] *pret of* **halten**

hier [hiːɐ] *adv* here, in this place; present; **hier entlang!** this way!

hieran ['hiː'ran] *adv* from *or* in this

hierauf ['hiː'rauf] *adv* on it *or* this; after this, then

hieraus ['hiː'raus] *adv* from *or* out of this

'**hier'bei** *adv* here, in this case; on this occasion

'**hier'durch** *adv* by this, hereby, this way

'**hier'für** *adv* for this

'**hier'her** *adv* (over) here, this way; **bis hierher** so far

hierin ['hiː'rɪn] *adv* in this

'**hier'mit** *adv* with this

'**hier'nach** *adv* after this; according to this

hierüber ['hiː'ryːbɐ] *adv* about this (subject)

hierunter ['hiː'rʊntɐ] *adv* under this; among these; *understand etc* by this *or* that

'**hier'von** *adv* of *or* from this

'**hier'zu** *adv* for this; to this

hiesig ['hiːzɪç] *adj* local; **ein Hiesiger** one of the locals

hieß [hiːs] *pret of* **heißen**

Hilfe ['hɪlfə] *f* (*-; -n*) help; aid (*a. ECON*), assistance (*a. MED*), relief (*für* to); **Erste Hilfe** first aid; **um Hilfe rufen** cry for help; **Hilfe!** help!; → **mithilfe**

Hilfeme,nü *n* EDP help menu

Hilferuf *m* call (*or* cry) for help

Hilfestellung *f* support (*a. fig*)

'**hilflos** *adj* helpless

hilfreich *adj* helpful

'**Hilfsakti,on** *f* relief action

'**Hilfsarbeiter** *m*, '**Hilfsarbeiterin** *f* unskilled worker

'**hilfsbedürftig** *adj* needy

'**hilfsbereit** *adj* helpful, ready to help

'**Hilfsbereitschaft** *f* (*-; no pl*) readiness to help, helpfulness

'**Hilfsmittel** *n* aid, TECH *a.* device

Hilfsorganisati,on *f* relief organization

Hilfsverb *n* LING auxiliary (verb)

Himbeere ['hɪmbeːrə] *f* BOT raspberry

Himmel ['hɪməl] *m* (*-s; -*) sky; REL heaven (*a. fig*); **um Himmels willen** for Heaven's sake; → **heiter**

Himmelfahrt REL Ascension (Day)

'**Himmelskörper** *m* AST celestial body

Himmelsrichtung *f* direction; cardinal point

himmlisch ['hɪmlɪʃ] *adj* heavenly, *fig a.* marvel(l)ous

hin [hɪn] **1.** *adv* there; **bis hin zu** as far as;

noch lange hin still a long way off; *auf s-e Bitte (s-n Rat) hin* at his request (advice); *hin und her* to and fro, back and forth; *hin und wieder* now and then; *hin und zurück* there and back; RAIL round trip, round-trip ticket, *esp Br* return (ticket); **2.** F *pred adj* ruined; done for; gone

hi'nab *adv* → *hinunter*

'**hinarbeiten** *v/i* (*sep, -ge-, h*) **hinarbeiten auf** (*acc*) work towards

hi'nauf *adv* up (there); upstairs; *die Straße etc hinauf* up the street *etc*

hinaufgehen *v/i* (*irr, gehen, sep, -ge-, sein*) go up, *fig a.* rise

hi'naus *adv* out; *aus ... hinaus* out of ...; *in* (*acc*) *... hinaus* out into ...; *hinaus* (*mit dir*)! (get) out!, out you go!

hinausgehen *v/i* (*irr, gehen, sep, -ge-, sein*) go out(side); *hinausgehen über* (*acc*) go beyond; *hinausgehen auf* (*acc*) *window etc:* look out onto

hinauslaufen *v/i* (*irr, laufen, sep, -ge-, sein*) run out(side); *hinauslaufen auf* (*acc*) come *or* amount to

hinausschieben *v/t* (*irr, schieben, sep, -ge-, h*) put off, postpone

hinausstellen *v/t* (*sep, -ge-, h*) SPORT send s.o. off (the field)

hinauswerfen *v/t* (*irr, werfen, sep, -ge-, h*) throw out (*aus* of), *fig a.* kick out; (give s.o. the) sack, fire

hinauswollen *v/i* (*sep, -ge-, h*) *hinauswollen auf* (*acc*) aim (*or* drive *or* get) at; *hoch hinauswollen* aim high

'**Hinblick** *m*: *im Hinblick auf* (*acc*) in view of, with regard to

'**hinbringen** *v/t* (*irr, bringen, sep, -ge-, h*) take there

hinderlich ['hɪndɐlɪç] *adj* hindering, impeding; *j-m hinderlich sein* be in s.o.'s way

hindern ['hɪndɐn] *v/t* (*ge-, h*) hinder, hamper; *hindern an* (*dat*) prevent from

Hindernis ['hɪndɐnɪs] *n* (*-ses; -se*) obstacle (*a. fig*)

Hindernisrennen *n* steeplechase

Hindu ['hɪndu] *m* (*-[s]; -[s]*) Hindu

Hinduismus [hɪndu'ɪsmʊs] *m* (*-; no pl*) hinduism

hin'durch *adv* through; *das ganze Jahr etc hindurch* throughout the year *etc*

hi'nein *adv* in; *hinein mit dir!* in you go!

hineingehen *v/i* (*irr, gehen, sep, -ge-, sein*) go in; *hineingehen in* (*acc*) go into

'**hinfallen** *v/i* (*irr, fallen, sep, -ge-, sein*) fall (down)

'**hinfällig** *adj* frail, infirm; invalid

hing [hɪŋ] *pret of* **hängen** 1

'**Hingabe** *f* (*-; no pl*) devotion (*an acc* to)

'**hingeben** *v/t* (*irr, geben, sep, -ge-, h*) give (up); *sich hingeben* (*dat*) give o.s. to; devote o.s. to

'**hinhalten** *v/t* (*irr, halten, sep, -ge-, h*) hold out; *j-n hinhalten* put s.o. off

hinken ['hɪŋkən] *v/i* a) (*ge-, h*) (walk with a) limp, b) (*ge-, sein*) limp

'**hinkommen** *v/i* (*irr, kommen, sep, -ge-, sein*) get there

hinkriegen F *v/t* (*sep, -ge-, h*) manage

'**hinlänglich** *adj* sufficient

'**hinlegen** *v/t* (*sep, -ge-, h*) lay *or* put down; *sich hinlegen* lie down

hinnehmen *v/t* (*irr, nehmen, sep, -ge-, h*) put up with

'**hinreißen** *v/t* (*irr, reißen, sep, -ge-, h*) carry away

hinreißend *adj* entrancing; breathtaking

'**hinrichten** *v/t* (*sep, -ge-, h*) execute

'**Hinrichtung** *f* (*-; -en*) execution

'**hinsetzen** *v/t* (*sep, -ge-, h*) set *or* put down; *sich hinsetzen* sit down

'**Hinsicht** *f* (*-; no pl*) respect; *in gewisser Hinsicht* in a way

'**hinsichtlich** *prp* (*gen*) with respect *or* regard to

'**Hinspiel** *n* SPORT first leg

'**hinstellen** *v/t* (*sep, -ge-, h*) put (down); *hinstellen als* make s.o. *or* s.th. appear to be

hinten ['hɪntən] *adv* at the back; MOT in the back; *von hinten* from behind

hinter ['hɪntɐ] *prp* (*dat*) behind

'**Hinter...** *in cpds* ...*achse*, ...*eingang*, ...*rad etc*: rear ...

Hinterbein *n* hind leg

Hinterbliebenen [-'bliːbənən] *pl the* bereaved; *esp* JUR surviving dependents

hinterei'nander *adv* one after the other; *dreimal hintereinander* three times in a row

'**Hintergedanke** *m* ulterior motive

hinter'gehen *v/t* (*irr, gehen, no -ge-, h*) deceive

'**Hintergrund** *m* background (*a. fig*)

'**Hinterhalt** *m* ambush

'**hinterhältig** [-hɛltɪç] *adj* insidious, underhand(ed)

'**Hinterhaus** *n* rear building

hinter'her *adv* behind, after; afterwards

'**Hinterhof** *m* backyard

'**Hinterkopf** *m* back of the head

hinter'lassen *v/t* (*irr, lassen, no -ge-, h*) leave (behind)

Hinter'lassenschaft *f* (*-; -en*) property (left), estate

hinter'legen *v/t* (*no -ge-, h*) deposit (*bei* with)

H

'**Hinterlist** *f* deceit(fulness); (underhanded) trick

'**hinterlistig** *adj* deceitful; underhand(ed)

'**Hintermann** *m* person (car *etc*) behind (one); *fig mst pl* person behind the scenes, brain(s), mastermind

'**Hintern** F *m* (*-s; -*) bottom, backside, behind, *Br* bum

'**hinterrücks** [-rʏks] *adv* from behind

'**Hinterseite** *f* back

Hinterteil F *n* → **Hintern**

Hintertreppe *f* back stairs

Hintertür *f* back door

hinter'ziehen *v/t* (*irr*, **ziehen**, *no -ge-, h*) evade (*taxes*)

'**Hinterzimmer** *n* back room

hi'nüber *adv* over, across; **hinüber sein** F be ruined; GASTR be spoilt

hi'nunter *adv* down; downstairs; **die Straße hinunter** down the road

Hinweg ['hɪnveːk] *m* way there

hinweg [hɪn'vɛk] *adv*: **über** (*acc*) ... **hinweg** over ...

hinwegkommen *v/i* (*irr*, **kommen** *sep*, *-ge-*, *sein*) **hinwegkommen über** (*acc*) get over

hinwegsehen *v/i* (*irr*, **sehen**, *sep*, *-ge-*, *h*) **hinwegsehen über** (*acc*) ignore

hinwegsetzen *v/refl* (*sep*, *-ge-*, *h*) **sich hinwegsetzen über** (*acc*) ignore, disregard

Hinweis ['hɪnvais] *m* (*-es; -e*) reference (**auf** *acc* to); hint, tip (as to, regarding); indication (of), clue (as to)

'**hinweisen** (*irr*, **weisen**, *sep*, *-ge-*, *h*) **1.** *v/t*: **j-n hinweisen auf** (*acc*) draw *or* call s.o.'s attention to; **2.** *v/i*: **hinweisen auf** (*acc*) point at *or* to, indicate; *fig* point out, indicate; hint at

'**Hinweisschild** *n*, **Hinweistafel** *f* sign, notice

'**hinwerfen** *v/t* (*irr*, **werfen**, *sep*, *-ge-*, *h*) throw down

hinziehen *v/refl* (*irr*, **ziehen**, *sep*, *-ge-*, *h*) extend (**bis zu** to), stretch (to); drag on

hin'zufügen *v/t* (*sep*, *-ge-*, *h*) add (**zu** to) (*a. fig*)

hinzukommen *v/i* (*irr*, **kommen**, *sep*, *-ge-*, *sein*) be added; **hinzu kommt, dass** add to this ..., and what is more, ...

hinzuziehen *v/t* (*irr*, **ziehen**, *sep*, *-ge-*, *h*) call in, consult

Hirn [hɪrn] *n* (*-[e]s; -e*) ANAT brain; *fig* brain(s), mind

Hirngespinst *n* fantasy

Hirsch [hɪrʃ] *m* (*-[e]s; -e*) ZO stag

Hirschgeweih *n* ZO antlers

Hirschkuh *f* ZO hind

Hirse ['hɪrzə] *f* (*-; -n*) BOT millet

Hirte ['hɪrtə] *m* (*-n; -n*) herdsman; shepherd (*a. fig*)

hissen ['hɪsən] *v/t* (*ge-*, *h*) hoist

Historiker [hɪs'toːrike] *m* (*-s; -*), **His'torikerin** *f* (*-; -nen*) historian

his'torisch *adj* historical; historic (*event etc*)

Hitliste ['hɪtlɪstə] *f* top 40 *etc*, charts

Hitze ['hɪtsə] *f* (*-; no pl*) heat

'**Hitzewelle** *f* heat wave

'**hitzig** *adj* hot-tempered, peppery; heated (*debate etc*)

'**Hitzkopf** *m* hothead

'**Hitzschlag** *m* MED heatstroke

HIV-negativ [haːʔiːˈfau-] *adj* MED HIV negative

HIV-positiv *adj* MED HIV positive

HIV-Positive *m*, *f* (*-n; -n*) MED HIV carrier

H-Milch ['haː-] *f* Br long-life milk

hob [hoːp] *pret of* **heben**

Hobby ['hɔbi] *n* (*-s; -s*) hobby

'**Hobby...** *in cpds* amateur ...

Hobel ['hoːbəl] *m* (*-s; -*) TECH plane

'**Hobelbank** *f* (*-; -bänke*) TECH carpenter's bench

'**hobeln** *v/t* (*ge-*, *h*) TECH plane

hoch [hoːx] *adj and adv* high; tall; *fig* heavy (*fine etc*); distinguished (*guest*); great, old (*age*); deep (*snow*); **10 hoch 4** MATH 10 to the power of 4; **3000 Meter hoch** *fly etc* at an altitude of 3,000 meters; **in hohem Maße** highly, greatly; **hoch verschuldet** heavily in debt; F **das ist mir zu hoch** that's above me

Hoch *n* (*-s; -s*) METEOR high (*a. fig*)

'**Hochachtung** *f* (deep) respect (**vor** *dat* for)

'**hochachtungsvoll** *adv* Yours sincerely

'**Hochbau** *m* (*-[e]s; no pl*) **Hoch- und Tiefbau** structural and civil engineering

Hochbetrieb F *m* (*-[e]s; no pl*) rush

'**hochdeutsch** *adj* High *or* standard German

'**Hochdruck** *m* high pressure (*a. fig*)

Hochebene *f* plateau, tableland

Hochform *f*: **in Hochform** in top form *or* shape

Hochfre,quenz *f* ELECTR high frequency

Hochgebirge *n* high mountains

Hochgenuss *m* real treat

'**hochgezüchtet** *adj* ZO, TECH highbred, TECH *a.* sophisticated; MOT tuned up, F souped up

'**hochhackig** [-hakɪç] *adj* high-heeled

'**Hochhaus** *n* high rise, tower block

Hochkonjunk,tur *f* ECON boom

Hochland *n* highlands

Hochleistungs... *in cpds* ...*sport etc*: high-performance ...

'**Hochmut** *m* arrogance
'**hochmütig** [-my:tɪç] *adj* arrogant
'**Hochofen** *m* TECH blast furnace
'**hochpro,zentig** *adj* high-proof
'**Hochrechnung** *f* projection; POL computer prediction
Hochsai,son *f* peak (*or* height of the) season
Hochschulabschluss *m* degree
Hochschulausbildung *f* higher education
Hochschule *f* university; college; academy
Hochseefischerei *f* deep-sea fishing
Hochsommer *m* midsummer
Hochspannung *f* ELECTR high tension (*a. fig*) *or* voltage
Hochsprung *m* SPORT high jump
höchst [hø:çst] **1.** *adj* highest, *fig a.* supreme; extreme; **2.** *adv* highly, most, extremely
'**Höchst...** *in cpds mst* maximum ..., top ...
'**Hochstapler** [-ʃta:plɐ] *m* (*-s*; -), '**Hochstaplerin** *f* (-; *-nen*) impostor, swindler
'**höchstens** *adv* at (the) most, at best
'**Höchstform** *f* SPORT top form *or* shape
Höchstgeschwindigkeit *f* top speed (*mit* at); speed limit
Höchstleistung *f* SPORT record (performance); TECH maximum output
Höchstmaß *n* maximum (*an dat* of)
'**höchstwahr'scheinlich** *adv* most likely *or* probably
'**Hochtechnolo,gie** *f* high technology, hi tech
'**hochtrabend** *adj* pompous
'**Hochverrat** *m* high treason
'**Hochwasser** *n* high tide; flood
'**hochwertig** [-ve:ɐtɪç] *adj* high-grade, high-quality
Hochzeit ['hɔxtsait] *f* (-; *-en*) wedding
'**Hochzeits...** *in cpds* ...*geschenk*, ...*kleid*, ...*tag etc*: wedding ...
Hochzeitsreise *f* honeymoon
Hocke ['hɔkə] *f* (-; *-n*) crouch, squat
'**hocken** *v/i* (*ge-*, h) squat, crouch; F sit
Hocker ['hɔkɐ] *m* (*-s*; -) stool
Höcker ['hœkɐ] *m* (*-s*; -) ZO hump
Hockey ['hɔki] *n* (*-s*; *no pl*) SPORT field hockey, *Br* hockey
Hoden ['ho:dən] *m* (*-s*; -) ANAT testicle
Hof [ho:f] *m* (*-[e]s*; *Höfe* ['hø:fə]) yard; AGR farm; court(yard); court
Hofdame *f* lady-in-waiting
hoffen ['hɔfən] *v/i and v/t* (*ge-*, h) hope (*auf acc* for); trust (in); *das Beste hoffen* hope for the best; *ich hoffe es* I hope so; *ich hoffe nicht, ich will es nicht hoffen*

I hope not
'**hoffentlich** *adv* I hope, let's hope, hopefully
'**Hoffnung** *f* (-; *-en*) hope (*auf acc* of); *sich Hoffnungen machen* have hopes; *die Hoffnung aufgeben* lose hope
'**hoffnungslos** *adj* hopeless
'**hoffnungsvoll** *adj* hopeful; promising
höflich ['hø:flɪç] *adj* polite, courteous (*zu* to)
'**Höflichkeit** *f* (-; *no pl*) politeness, courtesy
Höhe ['hø:ə] *f* (-; *-n*) height; AVIAT, MATH, ASTR, GEOGR altitude; peak (*a. fig*); *fig* amount; level; extent (*of damage etc*); MUS pitch; *auf gleicher Höhe mit* on a level with; *in die Höhe* up; F *ich bin nicht ganz auf der Höhe* I'm not feeling up to the mark
Hoheit ['ho:hait] *f* (-; *no pl*) POL sovereignty; Highness
'**Hoheitsgebiet** *n* territory
Hoheitsgewässer *pl* territorial waters
Hoheitszeichen *n* national emblem
'**Höhenluft** *f* mountain air
Höhenmesser *m* altimeter
Höhenruder *n* AVIAT elevator
Höhensonne *f* MED ultraviolet lamp, sunlamp
Höhenzug *m* mountain chain
'**Höhepunkt** *m* climax, culmination, height, peak; highlight
hohl [ho:l] *adj* hollow (*a. fig*)
Höhle ['hø:lə] *f* (-; *-n*) cave, cavern; ZO hole, burrow; den, lair
'**Hohlmaß** *n* measure of capacity
Hohlraum *m* hollow, cavity
Hohlspiegel *m* concave mirror
Hohn [ho:n] *m* (*-[e]s*; *no pl*) derision, scorn
'**Hohngelächter** *n* jeers, jeering laughter
höhnisch ['hø:nɪʃ] *adj* derisive, scornful; *höhnisches Lächeln* sneer
holen ['ho:lən] *v/t* (*ge-*, h) (go and) get, fetch, go for; draw (*breath*); call (*s.o., the police etc*); *holen lassen* send for; *sich holen* catch, get (*a cold etc*); seek (*advice*)
Holland ['hɔlant] Holland, *the* Netherlands
Holländer ['hɔlɛndɐ] *m* (*-s*; -) Dutchman
'**Hol'länderin** [-dərɪn] *f* (-; *-nen*) Dutchwoman
'**holländisch** *adj* Dutch
Hölle ['hœlə] *f* (-; *no pl*) hell
'**Höllenlärm** F *m* a hell of a noise
Holler ['hɔlɐ] *Austrian m* (*-s*; -) BOT elder
höllisch ['hœlɪʃ] *adj* infernal, F hellish
holperig ['hɔlpərɪç] *adj* bumpy (*a. fig*),

H

rough, uneven; *fig* clumsy (*style etc*)

holpern ['hɔlpɐn] *v/i* (*ge-*, *sein*) jolt, bump; *fig* be bumpy

Holunder [ho'lʊndɐ] *m* (*-s*; -) BOT elder

Holz [hɔlts] *n* (*-es*; *Hölzer* ['hœltsɐ]) wood; lumber, *Br a.* timber; *aus Holz* (made) of wood, wooden; *Holz hacken* chop wood

Holzblasinstru,ment *n* MUS woodwind (instrument)

hölzern ['hœltsɐn] *adj* wooden, *fig a.* clumsy

'Holzfäller [-fɛlɐ] *m* (*-s*; -) woodcutter, lumberjack

Holzhammer *m* mallet; *fig* sledgehammer

holzig ['hɔltsɪç] *adj* woody; stringy

'Holzkohle *f* charcoal

Holzschnitt *m* woodcut

Holzschnitzer *m* wood carver

Holzschuh *m* clog

Holzweg *fig m*: *auf dem Holzweg sein* be barking up the wrong tree

Holzwolle *f* wood shavings, excelsior

Holzwurm *m* ZO woodworm

homöopathisch [homøo'paːtɪʃ] *adj* hom(o)eopathic

homosexuell [homozɛ'ksuɛl] *adj*, **Homosexu'elle** *m*, *f* (*-n*; *-n*) homosexual

Honig ['hoːnɪç] *m* (*-s*; *-e*) honey

'Honigwabe *f* honeycomb

Honorar [hono'raːɐ] *n* (*-s*; *-e*) fee

honorieren [hono'riːrən] *v/t* (*no -ge-*, *h*) pay (a fee to); *fig* appreciate, reward

Hopfen ['hɔpfən] *m* (*-s*; -) BOT hop; *brewing*: hops

hoppla ['hɔpla] *int* (wh)oops!

hopsen ['hɔpsən] F *v/i* (*ge-*, *sein*) hop, jump

Hörappa,rat ['høːɐ-] *m* hearing aid

hörbar ['høːɐbaːɐ] *adj* audible

horchen ['hɔrçən] *v/i* (*ge-*, *h*) listen (*auf acc* to); eavesdrop

Horcher ['hɔrçɐ] *m* (*-s*; -) eavesdropper

Horde ['hɔrdə] *f* (*-*; *-n*) horde (*a.* ZO), *contp a.* mob, gang

hören ['høːrən] *v/i and v/t* (*ge-*, *h*) hear; listen to; obey, listen; *hören auf* (*acc*) listen to; *von j-m hören* hear from (*or* of, about) s.o.; *er hört schwer* his hearing is bad; *hör(t) mal!* listen!; look (here)!; *nun or also hör(t) mal!* wait a minute!, now look *or* listen here!

Hörer ['høːrɐ] *m* (*-s*; -) listener; TEL receiver

'Hörerin [-rərɪn] *f* (*-*; *-nen*) listener

Hörfehler ['høːɐ-] *m* MED hearing defect

Hörgerät *n* hearing aid

hörig ['høːrɪç] *adj*: *j-m hörig sein* be s.o.'s slave

Horizont [hori'tsɔnt] *m* (*-[e]s*; *-e*) horizon (*a. fig*); *s-n Horizont erweitern* broaden one's mind; *das geht über meinen Horizont* that's beyond me

horizontal [horitsɔn'taːl] *adj* horizontal

Hormon [hɔr'moːn] *n* (*-s*; *-e*) hormone

Horn [hɔrn] *n* (*-[e]s*; *Hörner* ['hœrnɐ]) horn

Hornhaut *f* horny skin, callus(es); ANAT cornea

Hornisse [hɔr'nisə] *f* (*-*; *-n*) ZO hornet

Horoskop [horo'skoːp] *n* (*-s*; *-e*) horoscope

Hörrohr ['høːɐ-] *n* MED stethoscope

Hörsaal *m* lecture hall, auditorium

Hörspiel *n* radio play

Hörweite *f*: *in* (*außer*) *Hörweite* within (out of) earshot

Höschen ['høːsçən] *n* (*-s*; -) panties

Hose ['hoːzə] *f* (*-*; *-n*) (*e-e Hose* a pair of) pants, *Br* trousers; slacks; shorts

'Hosenanzug *m* pants (*Br* trouser) suit

Hosenrock *m* (*ein Hosenrock* a pair of) culottes

Hosenschlitz *m* fly

Hosentasche *f* trouser pocket

Hosenträger *pl* (a pair of) suspenders *or Br* braces

Hospital [hɔspi'taːl] *n* (*-s*; *-täler* [-'tɛːlɐ]) hospital

Hostie ['hɔstjə] *f* (*-*; *-n*) REL host

Hotel [ho'tɛl] *n* (*-s*; *-s*) hotel

Hoteldi,rektor *m* hotel manager

Hotelfach *n* (*-[e]s*; *no pl*) hotel business

Hotelzimmer *n* hotel room

HP ABBR *of* *Halbpension* half-board

Hr(n). ABBR *of* *Herrn* Mr

Hubraum ['huːp-] *m* MOT cubic capacity

hübsch [hʏpʃ] *adj* pretty, nice(-looking), cute; *fig* nice, lovely

Hubschrauber ['huːpʃraubɐ] *m* (*-s*; -) helicopter

Hubschrauberlandeplatz *m* heliport

Huf [huːf] *m* (*-[e]s*; *-e*) ZO hoof

'Hufeisen *n* horseshoe

Hüfte ['hʏftə] *f* (*-*; *-n*) ANAT hip

'Hüftgelenk *n* ANAT hip joint

'Hüftgürtel *m* girdle

Hügel ['hyːgəl] *m* (*-s*; -) hill

'hügelig *adj* hilly

'Hügelland *n* downs

Huhn [huːn] *n* (*-[e]s*; *Hühner* ['hyːnɐ]) ZO chicken; hen

Hühnchen ['hyːnçən] *n* (*-s*; -) chicken; F *mit j-m ein Hühnchen zu rupfen haben* have a bone to pick with s.o.

'Hühnerauge *n* MED corn

Hühnerbrühe *f* chicken broth

Hühnerei *n* hen's egg
Hühnerfarm *f* poultry *or* chicken farm
Hühnerhof *m* poultry *or* chicken yard
Hühnerleiter *f* chicken ladder
Hühnerstall *m* henhouse
huldigen ['hʊldɪɡən] *v/i* (*ge-, h*) pay homage to; *fig* indulge in
Hülle ['hʏlə] *f* (-; -*n*) cover(ing), wrap (-ping); jacket, *Br* sleeve; sheath; *in Hülle und Fülle* in abundance
'**hüllen** *v/t* (*ge-, h*) *hüllen in* (*acc*) wrap (-up) in, cover in
Hülse ['hʏlzə] *f* (-; -*n*) BOT pod; husk; TECH case
'**Hülsenfrüchte** *pl* pulse
human [hu'maːn] *adj* humane
humanitär [humani'tɛːɐ] *adj* humanitarian
Humanität [humani'tɛːt] *f* (-; *no pl*) humanity
Hummel ['hʊməl] *f* (-; -*n*) ZO bumblebee
Hummer ['hʊmɐ] *m* (-*s*; -) ZO lobster
Humor [hu'moːɐ] *m* (-*s*; *no pl*) humo(u)r; (*keinen*) *Humor haben* have a (no) sense of humo(u)r
Humorist [humo'rɪst] *m* (-*en*; -*en*) humorist
humo'ristisch, hu'morvoll *adj* humorous
humpeln ['hʊmpəln] *v/i* a) (*ge-, h*) hobble, b) (*ge-, sein*) limp
Hund [hʊnt] *m* (-[*e*]*s*; -*e*) ZO dog
Hundehütte ['hʊndə-] *f* doghouse, *Br* kennel
Hundekuchen *m* dog biscuit
Hundeleine *f* lead, leash
'**hunde'müde** *adj* dog-tired
hundert ['hʊndɐt] *adj* a *or* one hundred; *zu hunderten* by the hundreds
'**hundertfach** *adj* hundredfold
Hundert'jahrfeier *f* centenary, centennial
'**hundertjährig** [-jɛːrɪç] *adj* a hundred years old; a hundred years of
'**hundertste** *adj* hundredth
Hündin ['hʏndɪn] *f* (-; -*nen*) ZO bitch
hündisch ['hʏndɪʃ] *adj* doglike, slavish
Hüne ['hyːnə] *m* (-*n*; -*n*) giant
'**Hünengrab** *n* dolmen
Hunger ['hʊŋɐ] *m* (-*s*; *no pl*) hunger; *Hunger bekommen* get hungry; *Hunger haben* be hungry; *vor Hunger sterben* die of starvation, starve to death
'**Hungerlohn** *m* starvation wages
'**hungern** *v/i* (*ge-, h*) go hungry, starve
'**Hungersnot** *f* famine
'**Hungerstreik** *m* hunger strike
'**Hungertod** *m* (death from) starvation
hungrig ['hʊŋrɪç] *adj* hungry (*nach, auf acc* for)
Hupe ['huːpə] *f* (-; -*n*) MOT horn

'**hupen** *v/i* (*ge-, h*) MOT sound one's horn, hoot, honk
hüpfen ['hʏpfən] *v/i* (*ge, sein*) hop, skip; *ball etc*: bounce
Hürde ['hʏrdə] *f* (-; -*n*) hurdle, *fig a.* obstacle; ZO fold, pen
'**Hürdenlauf** *m* SPORT hurdles
'**Hürdenläufer** *m*, '**Hürdenläuferin** *f* SPORT hurdler
Hure ['huːrə] *f* (-; -*n*) whore, prostitute
huschen ['hʊʃən] *v/i* (*ge-, sein*) flit, dart
hüsteln ['hyːstəln] *v/i* (*ge-, h*) cough slightly; *iro* hem
husten ['huːstən] *v/i* (*ge-, h*), '**Husten** *m* (-*s*; *no pl*) cough
'**Hustenbon,bon** *m, n* cough drop
Hustensaft *m* PHARM cough syrup
Hut[1] [huːt] *m* (-[*e*]*s*; *Hüte* ['hyːtə]) hat; *den Hut aufsetzen* (*abnehmen*) put on (take off) one's hat
Hut[2] *f*: *auf der Hut sein* be on one's guard (*vor dat* against)
hüten ['hyːtən] *v/t* (*ge-, h*) guard, protect, watch over; ZO herd, mind; look after; *das Bett hüten* be confined to (one's) bed; *sich hüten vor* (*dat*) beware of; *sich hüten, et. zu tun* be careful not to do s.th.
'**Hutkrempe** *f* (hat) brim
hutschen ['hʊtʃən] *Austrian v/t and v/i* → **schaukeln**
Hütte ['hʏtə] *f* (-; -*n*) hut; *contp* shack; cottage, cabin; mountain hut; TECH ironworks
Hyäne ['hyɛːnə] *f* (-; -*n*) ZO hy(a)ena
Hyazinthe [hya'tsɪntə] *f* (-; -*n*) BOT hyacinth
Hydrant [hy'drant] *m* (-*en*; -*en*) hydrant
hydraulisch [hy'draulɪʃ] *adj* hydraulic
Hydrokultur ['hyːdro-] *f* hydroponics
Hygiene [hy'gjeːnə] *f* (-; *no pl*) hygiene
hygienisch [hy'gjeːnɪʃ] *adj* hygienic
Hypnose [hʏp'noːzə] *f* (-; -*n*) hypnosis
Hypnotiseur [hʏpnoti'zøːɐ] *m* (-*s*; -*e*) hypnotist
hypnotisieren [hʏpnoti-'ziːrən] *v/t* (*no -ge-, h*) hypnotize
Hypotenuse [hypote'nuːzə] *f* (-; -*n*) MATH hypotenuse
Hypothek [hypo'teːk] *f* (-; -*en*) ECON mortgage; *e-e Hypothek aufnehmen* take out a mortgage
Hypothese [hypo'teːzə] *f* (-; -*n*) hypothesis, supposition
hypothetisch [hypo'teːtɪʃ] *adj* hypothetical
Hysterie [hʏste'riː] *f* (-; -*n*) hysteria
hysterisch [hʏs'teːrɪʃ] *adj* hysterical

H

I

i. A. ABBR *of* **im Auftrag** p. p., per procuration

ICE [iːtseːˈʔeː] ABBR *of* **Intercityexpresszug** intercity express (train)

ich [ɪç] *pers pron* I; **ich selbst** (I) myself; **ich bin's** it's me

ideal [ideˈaːl] *adj*, **Ide'al** *n* (-s; -e) ideal

Idealismus [ideaˈlɪsmʊs] *m* (-; *no pl*) idealism

Idea'list(in) (-en; -en/-; -nen) idealist

Idee [iˈdeː] *f* (-; -n) idea

identifizieren [idɛntifiˈtsiːrən] *v/t* (*no -ge-, h*) identify; **sich identifizieren mit** identify with

identisch [iˈdɛntɪʃ] *adj* identical

Identitätskarte [idɛntiˈtɛːts-] *Austrian f* identity card

Ideologe [ideoˈloːgə] *m* (-n; -n) ideologist

Ideologie [ideoloˈgiː] *f* (-; -n) ideology

ideo'logisch *adj* ideological

idiomatisch [idioˈmaːtɪʃ] *adj* LING idiomatic; **idiomatischer Ausdruck** idiom

Idiot [iˈdjoːt] *m* (-en; -en) idiot

Idi'otenhügel F *m skiing:* nursery slope

idi'otisch *adj* idiotic

Idol [iˈdoːl] *n* (-s; -e) idol

Idyll [iˈdʏl] *n* (-s; -e), **I'dylle** *f* (-; -n) idyl(l)

i'dyllisch *adj* idyllic

Igel [ˈiːgəl] *m* (-s; -) ZO hedgehog

Iglu [ˈiːglu] *m* (-s; -s) igloo

ignorieren [ɪgnoˈriːrən] *v/t* (*no -ge-, h*) ignore, disregard

i. H. ABBR *of* **im Hause** on the premises

ihr [iːɐ] *poss pron* her; *pl* their; **Ihr** your

ihrerseits [ˈiːrɐzaits] *adv* on her (*pl* their) part

ihresgleichen [ˈiːrəs-] *indef pron* her (*pl* their) equals, people like herself (*pl* themselves)

ihretwegen [ˈiːrət-] *adv* for her (*pl* their) sake

Ikone [iˈkoːnə] *f* (-; -n) icon (*a.* EDP)

illegal [ˈɪlegaːl] *adj* JUR illegal

illegitim [ɪlegiˈtiːm] *adj* JUR illegitimate

Illusion [ɪluˈzjoːn] *f* (-; -en) illusion

illusorisch [ɪluˈzoːrɪʃ] *adj* illusory

Illustration [ɪlustraˈtsjoːn] *f* (-; -en) illustration

illustrieren [ɪlʊsˈtriːrən] *v/t* (*no -ge-, h*) illustrate

Illustrierte [ɪlʊsˈtriːɐtə] *f* (-n; -n) magazine

im [ɪm] *prep* in the; **im Bett** in bed; **im Kino** *etc* at the cinema *etc*; **im Erdge-**

schoss on the first (*Br* ground) floor; **im Mai** in May; **im Jahre 1997** in (the year) 1997; **im Stehen** (while) standing up; → *in*

imaginär [imagiˈnɛːɐ] *adj* imaginary

Imbiss [ˈɪmbɪs] *m* (-es; -e) snack

'Imbissstube *f* snack bar

imitieren [imiˈtiːrən] *v/t* (*no -ge-, h*) imitate

Imker [ˈɪmkɐ] *m* (-s; -) beekeeper

immatrikulieren [ɪmatrikuˈliːrən] *v/t and v/refl* (*no -ge-, h*) UNIV enrol(l), register

immer [ˈɪmɐ] *adv* always, all the time; **immer mehr** more and more; **immer wieder** again and again; **für immer** for ever, for good

'Immergrün *n* BOT evergreen

'immer'hin *adv* after all

'immer'zu *adv* all the time, constantly

Immigrant [imiˈgrant] *m* (-en; -en), **Immi'grantin** *f* (-; -nen) immigrant

Immissionen [ɪmiˈsjoːnən] *pl* (harmful effects of) noise, pollutants *etc*

Immobilien [imoˈbiːliən] *pl* real estate

Immobilienmakler *m* realtor, real estate agent

immun [ɪˈmuːn] *adj* immune (**gegen** to, against, from); **immun machen** → **immunisieren** [ɪmuniˈziːrən] *v/t* (*no -ge-, h*) immunize

Immunität [ɪmuniˈtɛːt] *f* (-; *no pl*) immunity

Im'munschwäche *f* (-; -n) **Erworbene Immunschwäche** MED AIDS

Imperativ [ˈɪmperatiːf] *m* (-s; -e) LING imperative (mood)

Imperfekt [ˈɪmpɛrfɛkt] *n* (-s; -e) LING past (tense)

Imperialismus [ɪmperjaˈlɪsmʊs] *m* (-; *no pl*) imperialism

Imperialist [ɪmperjaˈlɪst] *m* (-en; -en), **imperia'listisch** *adj* imperialist

impfen [ˈɪmpfən] *v/t* (*ge-, h*) MED vaccinate

'Impfpass *m* MED vaccination card

Impfschein *m* MED vaccination certificate

Impfstoff *m* MED vaccine, serum

'Impfung *f* (-; -en) MED vaccination

imponieren [ɪmpoˈniːrən] *v/i* (*no -ge-, h*) **j-m imponieren** impress s.o.

Import [ɪmˈport] *m* (-[e]s; -e) ECON import

Importeur [ɪmporˈtøːɐ] *m* (-s; -e) ECON importer

importieren [-'ti:rən] *v/t* (*no -ge-, h*) ECON import

imposant [ɪmpo'zant] *adj* impressive, imposing

imprägnieren [ɪmprɛ'gni:rən] *v/t* (*no -ge-, h*), **imprägniert** [ɪmprɛ'gni:ɐt] *adj* waterproof

improvisieren [ɪmprovi'zi:rən] *v/t and v/i* (*no -ge-, h*) improvise

Impuls [ɪm'pʊls] *m* (*-es; -e*) impulse; stimulus

impulsiv [ɪmpʊl'zi:f] *adj* impulsive

imstande [ɪm'ʃtandə] *adj*: *imstande sein zu inf* be capable of *ger*

in [ɪn] *prp* (*dat and acc*) **1.** in, at; within, inside; into, in; *überall in* all over; *in der Stadt* in town; *in der Schule* at school; *in die Schule* to school; *ins Kino* to the cinema; *in Bett* to bed; *warst du schon mal in ...?* have you ever been to ...?; → *im*; **2.** in, at, during; *in dieser* (*der nächsten*) *Woche* this (next) week; *in diesem Alter* (*Augenblick*) at this age (moment); *in der Nacht* at night; *heute in acht Tagen* a week from now; *heute in e-m Jahr* this time next year; → *im*; **3.** in, at; *gut sein in* (*dat*) be good at; *in Eile* in a hurry; *in Behandlung* (*Reparatur*) under treatment (repair); *ins Deutsche* into German; → *im*; **4.** F *in sein* be in

'Inbegriff *m* epitome

'inbegriffen *adj* ECON included

in'dem *cj* while, as; by *doing s.th.*

Inder ['ɪndɐ] *m* (*-s; -*), **Inderin** ['ɪndərɪn] *f* (*-; -nen*) Indian

Indian ['ɪndja:n] *Austrian m* (*-s; -e*) ZO turkey (cock)

Indianer [ɪn'dja:nɐ] *m* (*-s; -*), **Indianerin** [ɪn'dja:nərɪn] *f* (*-; -nen*) Native American, (American) Indian

Indien ['ɪndjən] India

Indikativ ['ɪndikati:f] *m* (*-s; -e*) LING indicative (mood)

indirekt ['ɪndirɛkt] *adj* indirect, LING *a.* reported

indisch ['ɪndɪʃ] *adj* Indian

indiskret ['ɪndɪskre:t] *adj* indiscreet

Indiskretion [ɪndɪskre'tsjo:n] *f* (*-; -en*) indiscretion

indiskutabel [ɪndɪsku'ta:bəl] *adj* out of the question

individuell [ɪndivi'duɛl] *adj*, **Individuum** [ɪndi'vi:duʊm] *n* (*-s; -en*) individual

indiz [ɪn'di:ts] *n* (*-es; -ien*) indication, sign; *pl* JUR circumstantial evidence

industrialisieren [ɪndʊstriali'zi:rən] *v/t* (*no -ge-, h*) industrialize

Industriali'sierung *f* (*-; no pl*) industrialization

Industrie [ɪndʊs'tri:] *f* (*-; -n*) industry

Indus'triegebiet *n* industrial area

industriell [ɪndʊstri'ɛl] *adj* industrial

Industri'elle *m* (*-n; -n*) industrialist

inei'nander *adv* into one another; *ineinander verliebt* in love with each other; *ineinandergreifen* *v/t* (*irr*, *greifen*, *sep*, *-ge-, h*) TECH interlock (*a. fig*)

Infanterie ['ɪnfantəri:] *f* (*-; -n*) MIL infantry

Infanterist ['ɪnfantərɪst] *m* (*-en; -en*) MIL infantryman

Infektion [ɪnfɛk'tsjo:n] *f* (*-; -en*) MED infection

Infekti'onskrankheit *f* infectious disease

Infinitiv ['ɪnfiniti:f] *m* (*-s; -e*) LING infinitive (mood)

infizieren [ɪnfi'tsi:rən] *v/t* (*no -ge-, h*) MED infect

Inflation [ɪnfla'tsjo:n] *f* (*-; -en*) inflation

in'folge *prp* (*gen*) owing to, due to

infolge'dessen *adv* consequently

Informatik [ɪnfɔr'ma:tɪk] *f* (*-; no pl*) computer science

Infor'matiker(in) [ɪnfɔr'ma:tikɐ (-kərɪn)] (*-s; -/-; -nen*) computer scientist

Information [ɪnfɔrma'tsjo:n] *f* (*-; -en*) information; *die neuesten Informationen* the latest information

informieren [ɪnfɔr'mi:rən] *v/t* (*no -ge-, h*) inform; *falsch informieren* misinform

in'frage: *infrage stellen* question; put in jeopardy; *infrage kommen* be possible (*person*: eligible); *nicht infrage kommen* be out of the question

infrarot ['ɪnfra-] *adj* PHYS infrared

'Infrastruk,tur *f* infrastructure

Ing. ABBR *of* **Ingenieur** eng., engineer

Ingenieur [ɪnʒe'njø:ɐ] *m* (*-s; -e*), **Inge'nieurin** *f* (*-; -nen*) engineer

Ingwer ['ɪŋvɐ] *m* (*-s; no pl*) ginger

Inhaber ['ɪnha:bɐ] *m* (*-s; -*), **'Inhaberin** *f* (*-; -nen*) owner, proprietor (proprietress); holder

Inhalt ['ɪnhalt] *m* (*-[e]s; -e*) contents; volume, capacity; *fig* meaning

'Inhaltsangabe *f* summary

Inhaltsverzeichnis *n* table of contents

Initiative [initsja'ti:və] *f* (*-; -n*) initiative; *die Initiative ergreifen* take the initiative

inklusive [ɪnklu'zi:və] *prp* ECON including

inkonsequent ['ɪnkɔnzekvɛnt] *adj* inconsistent

In-'Kraft-Treten *n* (*-s; no pl*) coming into force, taking effect

'Inland *n* (*-[e]s; no pl*) home (country)

Inlandflug *m* domestic (*or* internal) flight

inländisch ['ɪnlɛndɪʃ] *adj* domestic, home, inland

Inlett ['ɪnlɛt] n (-[e]s; -e) ticking

in'mitten prp (gen) in the middle of

innen ['ɪnən] adv inside; **nach innen** inwards

'**Innenarchi,tekt** m, **Innenarchi,tektin** f interior designer

Innenarchitek,tur f interior design

Innenmi,nister(in) minister of the interior; Secretary of the Interior, Br Home Secretary

Innenminis,terium n ministry of the interior; Department of the Interior, Br Home Office

Innenpoli,tik f domestic politics

'**innenpo,litisch** adj domestic, internal

'**Innenseite** f: **auf der Innenseite** (on the) inside

'**Innenstadt** f downtown, (city or town) center or Br centre

inner ['ɪnɐ] adj inside; fig inner; MED, POL internal

Innere ['ɪnərə] n (-n; no pl) interior, inside

Innereien [ɪnə'raɪən] pl GASTR offal

'**innerhalb** prp (gen) within

'**innerlich** adj internal (a. MED)

innert ['ɪnɐt] Swiss prp (gen or dat) with in

innig ['ɪnɪç] adj tender, affectionate

Innung ['ɪnʊŋ] f (-; -en) guild

'**inoffiziell** adj unofficial

ins [ɪns] → **in**

Insasse ['ɪnzasə] m (-n; -n) inmate; MOT passenger

'**Insassenversicherung** f MOT passenger insurance

'**Insassin** f (-; -nen) inmate; MOT passenger

insbe'sondere adv (e)specially

'**Inschrift** f inscription, legend

Insekt [ɪn'zɛkt] n (-s; -en) ZO insect, bug

In'sektenstich m insect bite

Insel ['ɪnzəl] f (-; -n) island

'**Inselbewohner** m islander

Inserat [ɪnze'raːt] n (-[e]s; -e) advertisement, F ad

inserieren [ɪnze'riːrən] v/t and v/i (no -ge-, h) advertise

insge'heim adv secretly

insge'samt adv altogether, in all

inso'fern 1. adv as far as that goes; **2.** cj: **insofern als** in so far as

Inspektion [ɪnspɛk'tsjoːn] f (-; -en) inspection; MOT service

Inspektor [ɪn'spɛktoːɐ] m (-s; -en [ɪnspɛk'toːrən]), **Inspek'torin** f (-; -nen) inspector

inspizieren [ɪnspi'tsiːrən] v/t (no -ge-, h) inspect

Installateur [ɪnstala'tøːɐ] m (-s; -e) plumber; (gas or electrical) fitter

installieren [ɪnsta'liːrən] v/t (no -ge-, h) put in, fit, instal(l)

instand [ɪn'ʃtant] adv: **instand halten** keep in good condition or repair; TECH maintain; **instand setzen** repair

In'standhaltung f (-; no pl) maintenance

'**inständig** adv: **j-n inständig bitten** implore s.o.

In'standsetzung f (-; -en) repair

Instanz [ɪn'stants] f (-; -en) authority; JUR instance

Instinkt [ɪn'stɪŋkt] m (-[e]s; -e) instinct

instinktiv [ɪnstɪŋk'tiːf] adv instinctively

Institut [ɪnsti'tuːt] n (-[e]s; -e) institute

Institution [ɪnstitu'tsjoːn] f (-; -en) institution

Instrument [ɪnstru'mɛnt] n (-[e]s; -e) instrument

inszenieren [ɪnstse'niːrən] v/t (no -ge-, h) (put on) stage; film: direct; fig stage

Insze'nierung f (-; -en) production

intellektuell [ɪntɛlɛk'tuɛl] adj, **Intellektu'elle** m, f (-n; -n) intellectual, F highbrow

intelligent [ɪntɛli'gɛnt] adj intelligent

Intelligenz [ɪntɛli'gɛnts] f (-; -en) intelligence

Intelligenzquoti,ent m I.Q.

Intendant [ɪntɛn'dant] m (-en; -en), **Inten'dantin** f (-; -nen) THEA etc director

intensiv [ɪntɛn'ziːf] adj intensive; intense

Inten'sivkurs m crash course

interessant [ɪntərɛ'sant] adj interesting

Interesse [ɪntə'rɛsə] n (-s; -n) interest (**an** dat, **für** in)

Inte'ressengebiet n field of interest

Interessent [ɪntərɛ'sɛnt] m (-en; -en), **Interes'sentin** f (-; -nen) interested person; ECON prospect, Br prospective buyer

interessieren [ɪntərɛ'siːrən] v/t (no -ge-, h) interest (**für** in); **sich interessieren für** take an interest in; be interested in

intern [ɪn'tɛrn] adj internal

Internat [ɪntɐ'naːt] n (-[e]s; -e) boarding school

internatio'nal [ɪntɐ-] adj international

Internet ['ɪntɐnɛt] n (-[s]; no pl) Internet

Internist [ɪntɐ'nɪst] m (-en; -en), **Inter'nistin** f (-; -nen) MED internist

Interpretation [ɪntɐpreta'tsjoːn] f (-; -en) interpretation; analysis

interpretieren [ɪntɐpre'tiːrən] v/t (no -ge-, h) interpret, ana,lyze, Br -lyse

Interpunktion [ɪntɐpʊŋk'tsjoːn] f (-; no pl) punctuation

Intervall [ɪntɐ'val] n (-[e]s; -e) interval

intervenieren [ɪntɐve'niːrən] v/i (no -ge-, h) intervene

Interview ['ɪntɐvjuː] n (-s; -s), **interview-**

en [ɪntɐ'vjuːən] v/t (no -ge-, h) interview

intim [ɪn'tiːm] adj intimate (*mit* with) (*a. sexually*)

Intimität [ɪntimi'tɛːt] f (-; no pl) intimacy

In'timsphäre f privacy

intolerant ['ɪntolerant] adj intolerant (*gegen* of)

Intoleranz ['ɪntolerants] f (-; no pl) intolerance

intransitiv ['ɪntranzitiːf] adj LING intransitive

Intrige [ɪn'triːgə] f (-; -n) intrigue, scheme, plot

intrigieren [ɪntri'giːrən] v/i (no -ge-, h) (plot and) scheme

Invalide [ɪnva'liːdə] m (-n; -n) invalid

Inva'lidenrente f disability pension

Invalidität [ɪnvalidi'tɛːt] f (-; no pl) disablement, disability

Inventar [ɪnvɛn'taːɐ] n (-s; -e) inventory, stock

Inventur [ɪnvɛn'tuːɐ] f (-; -en) ECON stocktaking; *Inventur machen* take stock

investieren [ɪnvɛs'tiːrən] v/t (no -ge-, h) ECON invest (*a. fig*)

Investition [ɪnvɛsti'tsjoːn] f (-; -en) ECON investment

inwiefern [ɪnvi'fɛrn] cj and adv in what respect or way

inwie'weit cj and adv to what extent

'Inzucht f inbreeding

in'zwischen adv meanwhile, in the meantime; by now

irdisch ['ɪrdɪʃ] adj earthly, worldly

Ire ['iːrə] m (-n; -n) Irishman; pl the Irish

irgend ['ɪrgənt] adv in cpds: some...; any...; *wenn irgend möglich* if at all possible; *wenn du irgend kannst* if you possibly can; F *irgend so ein ...* some ...

irgend'ein(e) indef pron some(one); any (-one)

irgend'ein(e)s indef pron some; any

irgendetwas something; anything

irgendjemand someone, somebody; anyone, anybody

irgend'wann adv sometime (or other); (at) any time

irgend'wie adv somehow (or other)

irgend'wo adv somewhere; anywhere

Irin ['iːrɪn] f (-; -nen) Irishwoman

irisch ['iːrɪʃ] adj Irish

Irland ['ɪrlant] Ireland

Ironie [iro'niː] f (-; no pl) irony

ironisch [i'roːnɪʃ] adj ironic(al)

irre ['ɪrə] adj mad, crazy, insane; confused; F super, terrific

'Irre m, f (-n; -n) madman (madwoman), lunatic; *wie ein Irrer* like mad or a madman

'irreführen v/t (sep, -ge-, h) mislead, lead astray

irreführend adj misleading

'irregehen v/i (irr, sep, -ge-, sein) go astray, fig a. be wrong

irremachen v/t (sep, -ge-, h) confuse

irren ['ɪrən] **1.** v/i/refl (ge-, h) be wrong, be mistaken; *sich irren* be wrong; *sich in et. irren* get s.th. wrong; **2.** v/i (ge-, sein) wander, stray, err

irritieren [ɪri'tiːrən] v/t (no -ge-, h) irritate; F confuse

'Irrlicht n (-[e]s; -er) will-o'-the-wisp

'Irrsinn m (-[e]s; no pl) madness

'irrsinnig adj insane, mad; F terrific

Irrtum ['ɪrtuːm] m (-s; Irrtümer ['ɪrtyːmɐ]) error, mistake; *im Irrtum sein* be mistaken

'irrtümlich adv by mistake

Ischias ['ɪʃjas] m, n, f (-; no pl) MED sciatica

Islam [ɪs'laːm] m (-[s]; no pl) Islam

Island ['iːslant] Iceland

Isländer ['iːslɛndɐ] m (-s; -), **'Isländerin** [-dərɪn] f (-; -nen) Icelander

'isländisch adj Icelandic

Isolierband [izo'liːɐ-] n (-[e]s; -bänder) insulating tape

isolieren [izo'liːrən] v/t (no -ge-, h) isolate; ELECTR, TECH insulate

Iso'lierstati,on f MED isolation ward

Iso'lierung f (-; -en) isolation; ELECTR, TECH insulation

Israel ['ɪsraeːl] Israel

Israeli [ɪsra'eːli] m (-[s]; -[s]), f (-; -[s]), **israelisch** [ɪsra'eːlɪʃ] adj Israeli

Italien [i'taːljən] Italy

Italiener [ita'ljeːnɐ] m (-s; -), **Itali'enerin** [-nərɪn] f (-; -nen), **itali'enisch** adj Italian

J

ja [jaː] *adv* yes, F *a.* yeah; PARL yea, aye;
wenn ja if so; *da ist er ja!* well, there
he is!; *ich sagte es Ihnen ja* I told you
so; *ich bin ja (schließlich)* ... after all,
I am ...; *tut es 'ja nicht!* don't you dare
do it!; *sei 'ja vorsichtig!* do be careful!;
vergessen Sie es 'ja nicht! be sure not
to forget it!; *ja, weißt du nicht?* why,
don't you know?; *du kommst doch,
ja?* you're coming, aren't you?

Jacht [jaxt] *f* (-; -en) MAR yacht

Jacke ['jakə] *f* (-; -n) jacket; coat

Jackett [ʒa'kɛt] *n* (-s; -s) jacket, coat

Jagd [jaːkt] *f* (-; -en) hunt(ing) (*a. fig*);
shoot(ing); *fig* chase; → *Jagdrevier*;
auf (die) Jagd gehen go hunting *or*
shooting; *Jagd machen auf* (*acc*) hunt
(for); *a.* chase *s.o.*

Jagdaufseher *m* gamekeeper

Jagdflugzeug *n* MIL fighter (plane)

Jagdhund *m* zo hound

Jagdhütte *f* (hunting) lodge

Jagdre,vier *n* hunting ground

Jagdschein *m* hunting *or* shooting li-
cen|se, *Br* -ce

jagen ['jaːgən] *v/t and v/i* (ge-, *h*) hunt;
shoot; *fig* race, dash; hunt, chase; *j-n
aus dem Haus etc jagen* drive *or* chase
s.o. out of the house *etc*

Jäger ['jɛːgɐ] *m* (-s; -) hunter, huntsman

Jaguar ['jaːguaːɐ] *m* (-s; -e) zo jaguar

jäh [jɛː] *adj* sudden; steep

Jahr [jaːɐ] *n* (-[e]s; -e ['jaːrə]) year; *ein
drei viertel Jahr* nine months; *einmal
im Jahr* once a year; *im Jahre 1995* in
(the year) 1995; *ein 10 Jahre altes Auto*
a ten-year-old car; *mit 18 Jahren, im Alter von 18 Jahren* at (the age of) eighteen; *heute vor e-m Jahr* a year ago today; *die 80er-Jahre* the eighties

jahr'aus *adv*: *jahraus, jahrein* year in,
year out; year after year

'Jahrbuch *n* yearbook, annual

jahrelang ['jaːrəlaŋ] **1.** *adj* longstanding,
(many) years of; **2.** *adv* for (many) years

Jahres... ['jaːrəs-] *in cpds* ...bericht, ...bi-
lanz, ...einkommen *etc*: annual ...

Jahresanfang *m* beginning of the year

Jahresende *n* end of the year

Jahrestag *m* anniversary

Jahreswechsel *m* turn of the year

Jahreszahl *f* date, year

Jahreszeit *f* season, time of (the) year

'Jahrgang *m* age group; PED year, class

(*1995* of '95); GASTR vintage

Jahr'hundert *n* (-s; -e) century

Jahrhundertwende *f* turn of the century

jährlich ['jɛːrlɪç] **1.** *adj* annual, yearly; **2.**
adv every year, yearly, once a year

'Jahrmarkt *m* fair

Jahr'tausend *n* (-s; -e) millennium

Jahr'zehnt *n* (-[e]s; -e) decade

'Jähzorn *m* violent (fit of) temper

'jähzornig *adj* hot-tempered

Jalousie [ʒalu'ziː] *f* (-; -n) (venetian) blind

Jammer ['jamɐ] *m* (-s; *no pl*) misery; *es
ist ein Jammer* it is a pity

jämmerlich ['jɛmɐlɪç] *adj* miserable,
wretched; pitiful, sorry; *jämmerlich versagen* fail miserably

'jammern *v/i* (ge-, *h*) moan, lament (*über*
acc over, about); complain (of, about)

jammer'schade *adj*: *es ist jammerscha-
de, dass* it's a crying shame that

Janker ['jaŋkɐ] *Austrian m* (-s; -) jacket

Jänner ['jɛnɐ] *Austrian m* (-s; -), **Januar**
['januaːɐ] *m* (-[s]; -e) January

Japan ['jaːpan] Japan

Japaner [ja'paːnɐ] *m* (-s; -), **Ja'panerin**
[-nərɪn] *f* (-; -nen), **ja'panisch** *adj* Japanese

Jargon [ʒar'gõː] *m* (-s; -s) jargon; slang

'Jastimme *f* PARL aye, yea

jäten ['jɛːtən] *v/t* (ge-, *h*) weed

Jauche ['jauxə] *f* (-; -n) liquid manure

jauchzen ['jauxtsən] *v/i* (ge-, *h*) shout for
or with joy; exult, rejoice

Jause ['jauzə] *Austrian f* (-; -n) snack

ja'wohl *adv* (that's) right, (yes,) indeed

je [jeː] *adv and cj* ever; each; per; *der
beste Film, den ich je gesehen habe*
the best film I have ever seen; *je zwei
(Pfund)* two (pounds) each; *drei Mark
je Kilo* three marks per kilo; *je nach
Größe (Geschmack)* according to size
(taste); *je nachdem(, wie)* it depends
(on how); *je ..., desto ...* the ... the ...

Jeans [dʒiːnz] *pl, a. f* (-; -) (*e-e Jeans* a
pair of) jeans

Jeansjacke *f* denim jacket

jede ['jeːdə], **jeder** ['jeːdɐ], **jedes** ['jeː-
dəs] *indef pron* every; any; each; either;
jeder weiß (das) everybody knows; *du
kannst jeden fragen* (you can) ask anyone; *jeder von uns (euch)* each of us
(you); *jeder, der* whoever; *jeden zweiten Tag* every other day; *jeden Augenblick* any moment now; *jedes Mal* every

time; **jedes Mal wenn** whenever
'jeden'falls *adv* in any case, anyhow
'jedermann *indef pron* everyone, every-body
'jeder'zeit *adv* any time, always
je'doch *cj* however
je'her *adv*: **von jeher** always
jemals ['je:ma:ls] *adv* ever
jemand ['je:mant] *indef pron* someone, somebody; anyone, anybody
jene ['je:nə], jener ['je:nɐ], jenes ['je:-nəs] *dem pron* that (one); *pl* those; **dies und jenes** this and that
jenseitig ['je:nzaitıç] *adj* opposite
jenseits ['je:nzaits] *adv and prp (gen)* on the other side (of), beyond (*a. fig*)
'Jenseits *n* (-; *no pl*) next world, hereafter
jetzig ['jɛtsıç] *adj* present; existing
jetzt [jɛtst] *adv* now, at present; **bis jetzt** up to now, so far; **erst jetzt** only now; **jetzt gleich** right now *or* away; **für jetzt** for the present; **von jetzt an** from now on
jeweilig ['je:'vailıç] *adj* respective
jeweils ['je:'vails] *adv* each; at a time
Jh. ABBR *of* **Jahrhundert** cent., century
Jochbein ['jɔx-] *n* ANAT cheekbone
Jockei ['dʒɔke] *m* (-s; -s) jockey
Jod [jo:t] *n* (-[e]s; *no pl*) CHEM iodine
jodeln ['jo:dəln] *v/i* (ge-, *h*) yodel
Joga → **Yoga**
joggen ['dʒɔgən] *v/i* (ge-, *h*) jog
Jogger ['dʒɔgɐ] *m* (-s; -) jogger
Jogging ['dʒɔgıŋ] *n* (-s; *no pl*) jogging
Jogginganzug *m* tracksuit
Jogginghose *f* tracksuit trousers
Joghurt, Jogurt ['jo:gʊrt] *m, n* (-[s]; -[s]) yog(h)urt, yoghourt
Johannisbeere [jo'hanıs-] *f*: **rote Johannisbeere** redcurrant; **schwarze Johannisbeere** blackcurrant
johlen ['jo:lən] *v/i* (ge-, *h*) howl, yell
Jolle ['jɔlə] *f* (-; -n) MAR dinghy
Jongleur [ʒõ'glø:ɐ] *m* (-s; -e) juggler
jonglieren [ʒõ'gli:rən] *v/t and v/i* (*no* -ge-, *h*) juggle
Joule [dʒu:l] *n* (-[s]; -) PHYS joule
Journalismus [ʒʊrna'lısmʊs] *m* (-; *no pl*) journalism
Journalist(in) [ʒʊrna-'lıst(ın)] (-en; -en/-; -nen) journalist
jr. → **jun.**
Jubel ['ju:bəl] *m* (-s; *no pl*) cheering, cheers; rejoicing
'jubeln *v/i* (ge-, *h*) cheer, shout for joy; rejoice
Jubiläum [jubi'lɛːʊm] *n* (-s; -*läen*) anniversary; **50-jähriges Jubiläum** fiftieth anniversary, (golden) jubilee
jucken ['jʊkən] *v/t and v/i* (ge-, *h*) itch; **es**

juckt mich am ... my ... itches
Jude ['ju:də] *m* (-n; -n) Jewish person; **er ist Jude** he is Jewish
Jüdin ['jy:dın] *f* (-; -nen) Jewish woman *or* girl; **sie ist Jüdin** she is Jewish
jüdisch ['jy:dıʃ] *adj* Jewish
Judo ['ju:do] *n* (-[s]; *no pl*) SPORT judo
Jugend ['ju:gənt] *f* (-; *no pl*) youth; **die Jugend** young people
Jugendamt *n* youth welfare office
Jugendarbeitslosigkeit *f* youth unemployment
'jugendfrei *adj*: **jugendfreier Film** G(-rated) (*Br* U[-rated]) film; **nicht jugendfrei** X-rated
'Jugendfürsorge *f* youth welfare
Jugendgericht *n* JUR juvenile court
Jugendherberge *f* youth hostel
Jugendklub *m* youth club
Jugendkriminali,tät *f* juvenile delinquency
'jugendlich *adj* youthful, young
'Jugendliche *m, f* (-n; -n) young person, *m a.* youth, JUR *a.* juvenile
'Jugendstil *m* (-s; *no pl*) Art Nouveau
Jugendstrafanstalt *f* detention center (*Br* centre), reformatory
Jugendverbot *n* for adults only; → **jugendfrei**
Jugendzentrum *n* youth center (*Br* centre)
Juli ['ju:li] *m* (-[s]; -s) July
Jumbojet ['jʊmbo-] *m* jumbo (jet)
jun. ABBR *of* **junior** Jun., jun., Jnr., Jr., junior
jung [jʊŋ] *adj* young
Junge¹ ['jʊŋə] *m* (-n; -n) boy; lad; *cards*: jack, knave
'Junge² *n* (-n; -n) ZO young; puppy; kitten; cub; **Junge bekommen** *or* **werfen** have young
'jungenhaft *adj* boyish
'Jungenstreich *m* boyish prank
jünger ['jʏŋɐ] *adj* younger
'Jünger *m* (-s; -) REL disciple (*a. fig*)
Jungfer ['jʊŋfɐ] *f* (-; -n) **alte Jungfer** old maid
'Jungfernfahrt *f* MAR maiden voyage
Jungfernflug *m* AVIAT maiden flight
'Jungfrau *f* virgin; ASTR Virgo; **er ist Jungfrau** he's (a) Virgo
Junggeselle *m* bachelor, single (man)
Junggesellin *f* bachelor girl, single (woman); *esp* JUR spinster
jüngste ['jʏŋstə] *adj* youngest; *fig* latest; **in jüngster Zeit** lately, recently; **das Jüngste Gericht** the Last Judg(e)ment; **der Jüngste Tag** Doomsday
Juni ['ju:ni] *m* (-[s]; -s) June

junior ['juːnjoːɐ] *adj*, **'Junior** *m* (*-s*; *-en* [ju'njoːrən]), **Juni'orin** *f* (-; *-nen*) junior (*a.* SPORT)
Jupe [ʒyːp] *Swiss m* (*-s*; *-s*) skirt
Jura ['juːra]: *Jura studieren* study (the) law
juridisch [ju'riːdɪʃ] *Austrian* → *juristisch*
Jurist(in) [ju'rɪst(ɪn)] (*-en*; *-en/-*; *-nen*) lawyer; law student
ju'ristisch *adj* legal
Jurorenkomitee [ju'roːrən-] *Austrian n* → *Jury*
Jury [ʒy'riː] *f* (-; *-s*) jury
justieren [jʊs'tiːrən] *v/t* (*no -ge-*, *h*) TECH

adjust, set
Justiz [jʊs'tiːts] *f* (-; *no pl*) (administration of) justice, (the) law
Justizbeamte *m* judicial officer
Justizirrtum *m* error of justice
Justizmi,nister *m* minister of justice; Attorney General, *Br* Lord Chancellor
Justizminis,terium *n* ministry of justice; Department of Justice
Jute ['juːtə] *f* (-; *no pl*) jute
Juwel [ju'veːl] *m*, *n* (*-s*; *-en*) jewel, gem (*both a. fig*); *pl* jewel(le)ry
Juwelier [juve'liːɐ] *m* (*-s*; *-e*) jewel(l)er

K

Kabarett [kaba'rɛt] *n* (*-s*; *-s*) (political) revue
Kabel ['kaːbəl] *n* (*-s*; -) cable
'Kabelfernsehen *n* cable TV
Kabeljau ['kaːbəljau] *m* (*-s*; *-e*, *-s*) ZO cod(fish)
Kabine [ka'biːnə] *f* (-; *-n*) cabin; cubicle; SPORT dressing room; TECH car; TEL *etc* booth
Ka'binenbahn *f* cable railway
Kabinett [kabi'nɛt] *n* (*-s*; *-e*) POL cabinet
Kabis ['kaːbɪs] *Swiss m* (-; *no pl*) green cabbage
Kabriolett [kabrio'lɛt] *n* (*-s*; *-s*) MOT convertible
Kachel ['kaxəl] *f* (-; *-n*), **'kacheln** *v/t* (*ge-*, *h*) tile
'Kachelofen *m* tiled stove
Kadaver [ka'daːvɐ] *m* (*-s*; -) carcass
Kadett [ka'dɛt] *m* (*-en*; *-en*) MIL cadet
Käfer ['kɛːfɐ] *m* (*-s*; -) ZO beetle, bug
Kaffee ['kafe] *m* (*-s*; *-s*) coffee; *Kaffee kochen* make coffee; *Kaffee mit Milch* white coffee
Kaffeeauto,mat *m* coffee machine
Kaffeebohne *f* coffee bean
Kaffeehaus [ka'fe:-] *Austrian n* café, coffee house
Kaffeekanne *f* coffee pot
Kaffeema,schine *f* cofffeemaker
Kaffeemühle *f* coffee grinder
Käfig ['kɛːfɪç] *m* (*-s*; *-e*) cage (*a. fig*)
kahl [kaːl] *adj* bald; *fig* bare (*rock*, *wall etc*); barren, bleak (*landscape*)
Kahn [kaːn] *m* (*-[e]s*; *Kähne* ['kɛːnə])

boat; barge
Kai [kai] *m* (*-s*; *-s*) quay, wharf
Kaiser ['kaizɐ] *m* (*-s*; -) emperor
Kaiserin ['kaizərɪn] *f* (-; *-nen*) empress
'Kaiserreich *n* empire
Kajüte [ka'jyːtə] *f* (-; *-n*) MAR cabin
Kakao [ka'kau] *m* (*-s*; *-s*) cocoa; (hot) chocolate; chocolate milk
Kaktee [kak'teː] *f* (-; *-n*), **Kaktus** ['kaktʊs] *m* (-; *Kakteen*) BOT cactus
Kalb [kalp] *n* (*-[e]s*; *Kälber* ['kɛlbɐ]) ZO calf
kalben ['kalbən] *v/i* (*ge-*, *h*) calve
'Kalbfleisch *n* veal
'Kalbsbraten *m* roast veal
Kalbsschnitzel *n* veal cutlet; escalope (of veal)
Kaldaunen [kal'daunən] *pl* GASTR tripe
Kalender [ka'lɛndɐ] *m* (*-s*; -) calendar
Kalenderjahr *n* calendar year
Kali ['kaːli] *n* (*-s*; *no pl*) CHEM potash
Kaliber [ka'liːbɐ] *n* (*-s*; -) caliber, *Br* calibre (*a. fig*)
Kalk [kalk] *m* (*-[e]s*; *-e*) lime; GEOL limestone, chalk; MED calcium
'kalken *v/t* (*ge-*, *h*) whitewash; AGR lime
'kalkig *adj* limy
'Kalkstein *m* limestone
Kalorie [kalo'riː] *f* (-; *-n*) calorie
kalo'rienarm *adj*, **kalorienredu,ziert** *adj* low-calorie, low in calories
kalorienreich *adj* high-calorie, high *or* rich in calories
kalt [kalt] *adj* cold; *mir ist kalt* I'm cold; *es (mir) wird kalt* it's (I'm) getting cold;

kalt bleiben *fig* keep (one's) cool; **das lässt mich kalt** that leaves me cold
'kaltblütig [-blyːtɪç] **1.** *adj* cold-blooded (*a. fig*); **2.** *adv* in cold blood
Kälte ['kɛltə] *f* (-; *no pl*) cold; *fig* coldness; **vor Kälte zittern** shiver with cold; **fünf Grad Kälte** five degrees below zero
Kälteeinbruch *m* cold snap
Kältegrad *m* degree below zero
Kälteperi,ode *f* cold spell
'kaltmachen F *v/t* (*sep*, *-ge-*, *h*) bump off
kam [kaːm] *pret of* **kommen**
Kamee [ka'meːə] *f* (-; -*n*) cameo
Kamel [ka'meːl] *n* (-*s*; -*e*) zo camel
Ka'melhaar *n* (-[*e*]*s*; *no pl*) camelhair
Kamera ['kaməra] *f* (-; -*s*) camera
Kamerad [kamə'raːt] *m* (-*en*; -*en* [-'raːdən]) companion, F mate, pal, buddy
Kameradin [-'raːdɪn] *f* (-; -*nen*) companion
Kame'radschaft *f* (-; *no pl*) comradeship
'Kameramann *m* cameraman
'Kamerare,korder *m* (-*s*; -) camcorder
Kamille [ka'mɪlə] *f* (-; -*n*) BOT camomile
Kamin [ka'miːn] *m* (-*s*; -*e*) fireplace; chimney (*a.* MOUNT); **am Kamin** by the fire (-side)
Kaminkehrer [-keːrɐ] *m* (-*s*; -) chimney sweep
Kaminsims *m, n* mantelpiece
Kamm [kam] *m* (-[*e*]*s*; *Kämme* ['kɛmə]) comb, zo *a.* crest (*a. fig*)
kämmen ['kɛmən] *v/t* (*ge-*, *h*) comb; **sich (die Haare) kämmen** comb one's hair
Kammer ['kamɐ] *f* (-; -*n*) (small) room; storeroom, closet; garret; POL, ECON chamber; JUR division
'Kammermu,sik *f* chamber music
'Kammgarn *n* worsted (yarn)
Kampagne [kam'panjə] *f* (-; -*n*) campaign
Kampf [kampf] *m* (-[*e*]*s*; *Kämpfe* ['kɛmpfə]) fight (*a. fig*), struggle (*a. fig*), *esp* MIL combat, battle (*a. fig*); SPORT contest, match; *boxing*: fight, bout; *fig* conflict
'kampfbereit *adj* ready for battle (MIL combat)
kämpfen ['kɛmpfən] *v/i* (*ge-*, *h*) fight (**gegen** against; **mit** with; **um** for) (*a. fig*); struggle (*a. fig*); *fig* contend, wrestle
Kampfer ['kampfɐ] *m* (-*s*; *no pl*) CHEM camphor
Kämpfer ['kɛmpfɐ] *m* (-*s*; -), **'Kämpferin** *f* (-; -*nen*) fighter (*a. fig*)
kämpferisch ['kɛmpfərɪʃ] *adj* fighting, aggressive
'Kampfflugzeug *n* MIL combat aircraft
Kampfkraft *f* (-; *no pl*) fighting strength
Kampfrichter *m* SPORT judge
Kampfsportarten *pl* martial arts

Kanada ['kanada] Canada
Kanadier [ka'naːdjɐ] *m* (-*s*; -), **Ka'nadierin** [-djərɪn] *f* (-; -*nen*), **ka'nadisch** *adj* Canadian
Kanal [ka'naːl] *m* (-*s*; *Kanäle* [ka'nɛːlə]) canal; channel (*a.* TV, TECH, *fig*); sewer, drain; **der Kanal** the (English) Channel
Kanalisation [kanaliza'tsjoːn] *f* (-; -*en*) sewerage (system); canalization
kanalisieren [kanali'ziːrən] *v/t* (*no -ge-*, *h*) sewer; canalize; *fig* channel
Ka'naltunnel *m* Channel Tunnel, F Chunnel
Kanarienvogel [ka'naːrjən-] *m* canary
Kandidat [kandi'daːt] *m* (-*en*; -*en*), **Kandi'datin** *f* (-; -*nen*) candidate
Kandidatur [kandida'tuːɐ] *f* (-; -*en*) candidacy, *Br a.* candidature
kandidieren [kandi'diːrən] *v/i* (*no -ge-*, *h*) stand *or* run for election; **kandidieren für ...** run for the office of ...
Känguru, Känguruh ['kɛŋguru] *n* (-*s*; -*s*) zo kangaroo
Kaninchen [ka'niːnçən] *n* (-*s*; -) zo rabbit
Kanister [ka'nɪstɐ] *m* (-*s*; -) (fuel) can
Kanne ['kanə] *f* (-; -*n*) pot; can
Kannibale [kani'baːlə] *m* (-*n*; -*n*) cannibal
kannte ['kantə] *pret of* **kennen**
Kanon ['kaːnɔn] *m* (-*s*; -*s*) MUS canon
Kanone [ka'noːnə] *f* (-; -*n*) MIL gun; cannon; F *esp* SPORT *a.* crack
Kante ['kantə] *f* (-; -*n*) edge
'kanten *v/t* (*ge-*, *h*) set on edge; tilt; edge (*skis*)
'Kanten *m* (-*s*; -) crust
kantig ['kantɪç] *adj* angular, square(d)
Kantine [kan'tiːnə] *f* (-; -*n*) canteen
Kanton [kan'toːn] *m* (-*s*; -*e*) POL canton
Kanu ['kaːnu] *n* (-*s*; -*s*) canoe
Kanüle [ka'nyːlə] *f* (-; -*n*) MED cannula, (drain) tube
Kanzel ['kantsəl] *f* (-; -*n*) REL pulpit; AVIAT cockpit
Kanzlei [kants'lai] *f* (-; -*en*) office
Kanzler ['kantslɐ] *m* (-*s*; -) chancellor
Kanzlerin ['kantslərɪn] *f* (-; -*nen*) chancellor
Kap [kap] *n* (-*s*; -*s*) cape, headland
Kapazität [kapatsi'tɛːt] *f* (-; -*en*) capacity; *fig* authority
Kapelle [ka'pɛlə] *f* (-; -*n*) REL chapel; MUS band
Ka'pellmeister *m* MUS conductor
kapern ['kaːpɐn] *v/t* (*ge-*, *h*) MAR capture, seize
kapieren [ka'piːrən] F *v/t* (*no -ge-*, *h*) get; **kapiert?** got it?
Kapital [kapi'taːl] *n* (-*s*; -*e*, -*ien*) ECON capital, funds

K

Kapitalanlage *f* investment

Kapitalismus [kapita'lɪsmʊs] *m* (-; *no pl*) capitalism

Kapita'list *m* (-*en*; -*en*), **kapita'listisch** *adj* capitalist

Kapi'talverbrechen *n* capital crime, JUR felony

Kapitän [kapi'tɛːn] *m* (-*s*; -*e*) captain (*a.* SPORT)

Kapitel [ka'pɪtəl] *n* (-*s*; -) chapter (*a. fig*); *fig* story

Kapitulation [kapitula'tsjoːn] *f* (-; -*en*) capitulation, surrender (*a. fig*)

kapitulieren [kapitu'liːrən] *v/i* (*no -ge-, h*) capitulate, surrender (*a. fig*)

Kaplan [ka'plaːn] *m* (-*s*; *Kapläne* [ka-'plɛːnə]) REL curate

Kappe ['kapə] *f* (-; -*n*) cap, TECH *a.* top, hood

'**kappen** *v/t* (*ge-, h*) cut (*rope*); lop, top (*tree*)

Kapsel ['kapsəl] *f* (-; -*n*) capsule

kaputt [ka'pʊt] F *adj* broken (*a. fig*); TECH out of order; *fig* dead beat; ruined; *kaputt machen* F *v/t* (*sep, -ge-, h*) break, wreck (*a. fig*), ruin; *fig* → *kaputtmachen*; **kaputtgehen** F *v/i* (*irr, gehen, sep, -ge-, sein*) break; MOT *etc* break down; *fig* break up

kaputtmachen *v/t* (*sep, -ge-, h*) F *fig* wreck, ruin

Kapuze [ka'puːtsə] *f* (-; -*n*) hood; cowl

Karabiner [kara'biːnɐ] *m* (-*s*; -) carbine

Karabinerhaken *m* karabiner, snaplink

Karaffe [ka'rafə] *f* (-; -*n*) decanter

Karambolage [karambo'laːʒə] *f* (-; -*n*) collision, crash

Karat [ka'raːt] *n* (-[*e*]*s*; -*e*) carat

Karate [ka'raːtə] *n* (-[*s*]; *no pl*) SPORT karate

Karawane [kara'vaːnə] *f* (-; -*n*) caravan

Kardinal [kardi'naːl] *m* (-*s*; *Kardinäle* [kardi'nɛːlə]) REL cardinal

Karfiol [kar'fjoːl] *Austrian m* (-*s*; *no pl*) BOT cauliflower

Kar'freitag [kaːɐ̯-] *m* REL Good Friday

karg [kark], **kärglich** ['kɛrklɪç] *adj* meag|er, *Br* -re, scanty; frugal; poor

kariert [ka'riːɐ̯t] *adj* checked, checkered, *Br* chequered; squared

Karies ['kaːrjɛs] *f* (-; *no pl*) MED (dental) caries

Karikatur [karika'tuːɐ̯] *f* (-; -*en*) *mst* cartoon, *esp fig* caricature

Karikaturist [karikatu'rɪst] *m* (-*en*; -*en*) cartoonist

karikieren [kari'kiːrən] *v/t* (*no -ge-, h*) caricature

Karneval ['karnəval] *m* (-*s*; -*e*, -*s*) carnival

Karo ['kaːro] *n* (-*s*; -*s*) square, check; *cards*: diamonds

Karosserie [karɔsə'riː] *f* (-; -*n*) MOT body

Karotte [ka'rɔtə] *f* (-; -*n*) BOT carrot

Karpfen ['karpfən] *m* (-*s*; -) ZO carp

Karre ['karə] *f* (-; -*n*), '**Karren** *m* (-*s*; -) cart; wheelbarrow; F MOT jalopy

Karriere [ka'rjeːrə] *f* (-; -*n*) career; *Karriere machen* work one's way up, get to the top

Karte ['kartə] *f* (-; -*n*) card; ticket; GEOGR map; chart; GASTR menu; *gute* (*schlechte*) *Karten* a good (bad) hand

Kartei [kar'tai] *f* (-; -*en*) card index

Karteikarte *f* index *or* file card

'**Kartenhaus** *n* house of cards (*a. fig*); MAR chartroom

Kartenspiel *n* card game; deck (*Br* pack) of cards

Kartentele,fon *n* cardphone

Kartenvorverkauf *m* advance booking; box office

Kartoffel [kar'tɔfəl] *f* (-; -*n*) BOT potato

Kartoffelbrei *m* mashed potatoes

Kartoffelchips *pl* (potato) chips, *Br* crisps

Kartoffelkloß *m*, **Kartoffelknödel** *m* potato dumpling

Kartoffelpuffer *m* potato fritter

Kartoffelschalen *pl* potato peelings

Kartoffelschäler *m* potato peeler

Karton [kar'tɔŋ] *m* (-*s*; -*s*) cardboard; pasteboard; cardboard box

Karussell [karʊ'sɛl] *n* (-*s*; -*s*) roundabout, car(r)ousel, merry-go-round

Karwoche ['kaːɐ̯-] *f* REL Holy Week

Kaschmir ['kaʃmiːɐ̯] *m* (-*s*; -*e*) cashmere

Käse ['kɛːzə] *m* (-*s*; -) cheese

Kaserne [ka'zɛrnə] *f* (-; -*n*) barracks

Ka'sernenhof *m* barrack square

käsig ['kɛːzɪç] *adj* cheesy; pasty

Kasino [ka'ziːno] *n* (-*s*; -*s*) casino; MIL (officers') mess

Kasperle ['kaspɐlə] *n*, *m* (-*s*; -) Punch

Kasperlethe,ater *n* Punch and Judy show

Kassa ['kasa] *Austrian f* (-; *Kassen*), **Kasse** ['kasə] *f* (-; -*n*) till; cash register; checkout (counter); cash desk; cashier's counter; THEA *etc* box office; F *gut* (*knapp*) *bei Kasse sein* be flush (be a bit hard up)

'**Kassenbeleg** *m*, **Kassenbon** *m* sales slip, *Br* receipt

Kassenerfolg *m* THEA *etc* box-office success

Kassenpati,ent *m* MED health plan (*Am* medicaid, *Br* NHS) patient

Kassenschlager *m* blockbuster

Kassenwart [-vart] *m* (-[*e*]*s*; -*e*) treasurer

Kassette [ka'sɛtə] *f* (-; -*n*) box, case; MUS,

TV, PHOT *etc* cassette; casket
Kas'setten... *in cpds* *...rekorder etc*: cassette ...
kassieren [ka'siːrən] *v/t and v/i* (*no* -ge-, *h*) collect, take (the money)
Kassierer [ka'siːrɐ] *m* (-*s*; -), **Kas'siererin** *f* (-; -*nen*) cashier; teller; collector
Kastanie [kas'taːnjə] *f* (-; -*n*) BOT chestnut
Kasten ['kastən] *m* (-*s*; *Kästen* ['kɛstən]) box (*a.* F TV, SPORT *etc*); case; chest
kastrieren [kas'triːrən] *v/t* (*no* -ge-, *h*) MED, VET castrate
Kasus ['kaːzʊs] *m* (-; -) LING case
Katalog [kata'loːk] *m* (-[*e*]*s*; -*e*) catalog(ue *Br*)
Katalysator [kataly'zaːtoːɐ] *m* (-*s*; -*en* [-za'toːrən]) CHEM catalyst; MOT catalytic converter
Katapult [kata'pʊlt] *m*, *n* (-[*e*]*s*; -*e*), **katapultieren** [katapʊl'tiːrən] *v/t* (*no* -ge-, *h*) catapult
katastrophal [katastro'faːl] *adj* disastrous (*a. fig*)
Katastrophe [katas'troːfə] *f* (-; -*n*) catastrophe, disaster (*a. fig*)
Kata'strophengebiet *n* disaster area
Katastrophenschutz *m* disaster control
Katechismus [katɛ'çɪsmʊs] *m* (-; -*men*) REL catechism
Kategorie [katego'riː] *f* (-; -*n*) category
Kater ['kaːtɐ] *m* (-*s*; -) ZO male cat, tomcat; F hangover
kath. ABBR *of* **katholisch** Cath., Catholic
Kathedrale [kate'draːlə] *f* (-; -*n*) cathedral
Katholik [kato'liːk] *m* (-*en*; -*en*), **Katho'likin** *f* (-; -*nen*), **katholisch** [ka'toːlɪʃ] *adj* (Roman) Catholic
Kätzchen ['kɛtsçən] *n* (-*s*; -) ZO kitten, pussy (*a.* BOT)
Katze ['katsə] *f* (-; -*n*) ZO cat; kitten
Kauderwelsch ['kaudɐvɛlʃ] *n* (-[*s*]; *no pl*) gibberish
kauen ['kauən] *v/t and v/i* (ge-, *h*) chew
kauern ['kauɐn] *v/i and v/refl* (ge-, *h*) crouch, squat
Kauf [kauf] *m* (-[*e*]*s*; *Käufe* ['kɔʏfə]) purchase (*a.* ECON), F buy; purchasing, buying; *ein guter Kauf* a bargain, F a good buy; *zum Kauf anbieten* offer for sale
'kaufen *v/t* (ge-, *h*) buy (*a. fig*), purchase
Käufer ['kɔʏfɐ] *m* (-*s*; -), **'Käuferin** *f* (-; -*nen*) buyer; customer
'Kauffrau *f* (-; -*en*) businesswoman
'Kaufhaus *n* department store
Kaufkraft *f* (-; *no pl*) ECON purchasing power
käuflich ['kɔʏflɪç] *adj* for sale; *fig* venal
'Kaufmann *m* (-[*e*]*s*; -*leute*) businessman; dealer, trader, merchant; storekeeper, *Br*

mst shopkeeper; grocer
'kaufmännisch [-mɛnɪʃ] *adj* commercial, business; *kaufmännischer Angestellter* clerk
'Kaufvertrag *m* contract of sale
'Kaugummi *m* (-*s*; -*s*) chewing gum
kaum [kaum] *adv* hardly; *kaum zu glauben* hard to believe
Kaution [kau'tsjoːn] *f* (-; -*en*) security; JUR bail
Kautschuk ['kautʃʊk] *m* (-*s*; -*e*) (india) rubber
Kavalier [kava'liːɐ] *m* (-*s*; -*e*) gentleman
Kaviar ['kaːvjar] *m* (-*s*; -*e*) caviar(e)
keck [kɛk] *adj* cheeky, saucy, pert
Kegel ['keːgəl] *m* (-*s*; -) skittle, pin; MATH, TECH cone
Kegelbahn *f* bowling (*esp Br* skittle) alley
'kegelförmig [-fœrmɪç] *adj* conical
'Kegelkugel *f* bowling (*esp Br* skittle) ball
'kegeln *v/i* (ge-, *h*) bowl, go bowling, *esp Br* play (at) skittles *or* ninepins
Kehle ['keːlə] *f* (-; -*n*) ANAT throat
'Kehlkopf *m* ANAT larynx
Kehre ['keːrə] *f* (-; -*n*) (sharp) bend
'kehren *v/t* (ge-, *h*) sweep; *j-m den Rücken kehren* turn one's back on s.o.
Kehricht ['keːrɪçt] *m* (-*s*; *no pl*) sweepings
Kehrichtschaufel *f* dustpan
kehrtmachen ['keːɐt-] *v/i* (*sep*, -ge-, *h*) turn back
keifen ['kaifən] *v/i* (ge-, *h*) nag, bitch
Keil [kail] *m* (-[*e*]*s*; -*e*) wedge; gusset
Keiler ['kailɐ] *m* (-*s*; -) ZO wild boar
'Keilriemen *m* MOT fan belt
Keim [kaim] *m* (-[*e*]*s*; -*e*) BIOL, MED germ; BOT bud, sprout; *fig* seed(s)
'keimen *v/i* (ge-, *h*) BOT germinate, sprout; *fig* form, grow; stir
'keimfrei *adj* MED sterile
'keimtötend *adj* MED germicidal
'Keimzelle *f* BIOL germ cell
kein [kain] *indef pron* **1.** *adj*: *kein(e)* no, not any; *kein anderer* no one else; *kein(e) ... mehr* not any more ...; *kein Geld (keine Zeit) mehr* no money (time) left; *kein Kind mehr* no longer a child; **2.** *su*: *keiner, keine, kein(e)s* none, no one, nobody; *keiner von beiden* neither (of the two); *keiner von uns* none of us
'keines'falls *adv* by no means, under no circumstances
'keineswegs [-'veːks] *adv* by no means, not in the least
'keinmal *adv* not once, not a single time
Keks [keːks] *m*, *n* (-*es*, -*e*) cookie, *Br* biscuit
Kelch [kɛlç] *m* (-[*e*]*s*; -*e*) cup (*a.* BOT); REL chalice

K

Kelle ['kɛlə] *f* (-; -*n*) GASTR ladle, scoop; TECH trowel; signaling disk

Keller ['kɛlɐ] *m* (-*s*; -) cellar; → **Kellergeschoss** *n*, **Kellergeschoß** *Austrian n* basement

Kellerwohnung *f* basement (apartment, *esp Br* flat)

Kellner ['kɛlnɐ] *m* (-*s*; -) waiter

Kellnerin ['kɛlnərɪn] *f* (-; -*nen*) waitress

keltern ['kɛltɐn] *v/t* (*ge-*, *h*) press

kennen ['kɛnən] *v/t* (*irr*, *ge-*, *h*) know, be acquainted with; **kennen lernen** → **kennenlernen**

'**kennenlernen** *v/t* (*sep*, -*ge-*, *h*) get to know, become acquainted with; meet *s.o.*; **als ich ihn kennenlernen lernte** when I first met him

Kenner ['kɛnɐ] *m* (-*s*; -), '**Kennerin** *f* (-; -*nen*) expert

kenntlich ['kɛntlɪç] *adj* recognizable (**an** *dat* by)

Kenntnis *f* (-; -*se*) knowledge; **gute Kenntnisse in** (*dat*) a good knowledge of

'**Kennwort** *n* password

'**Kennzeichen** *n* mark, sign; (distinguishing) feature, characteristic; MOT license (*Br* registration) number

'**kennzeichnen** *v/t* (*ge-*, *h*) mark; *fig* characterize

kentern ['kɛntɐn] *v/i* (*ge-*, *sein*) MAR capsize

Keramik [ke'raːmɪk] *f* (-; -*en*) ceramics

Kerbe ['kɛrbə] *f* (-; -*n*) notch

Kerker ['kɛrkɐ] *m* (-*s*; -) dungeon

Kerl [kɛrl] *F m* (-*s*; -*e*) fellow, guy; **armer Kerl** poor devil; **ein anständiger Kerl** a decent sort

Kern [kɛrn] *m* (-[*e*]*s*; -*e*) BOT pip, seed, stone, kernel; TECH core (*a. fig*); PHYS nucleus

Kern... *in cpds* ...*energie*, ...*forschung*, ...*physik*, ...*reaktor*, ...*technik etc*: nuclear ...

Kernfach *n* PED basic subject

Kernfa,milie *f* nuclear family

Kerngehäuse *n* BOT core

'**kernge'sund** *adj* F (as) sound as a bell

kernig ['kɛrnɪç] *adj* full of seeds (*Br* pips); *fig* robust; pithy

'**Kernkraft** *f* PHYS nuclear power

Kernkraftgegner *m* anti-nuclear activist

Kernkraftwerk *n* nuclear power station *or* plant

'**kernlos** *adj* BOT seedless

'**Kernspaltung** *f* PHYS nuclear fission

'**Kernwaffen** *pl* MIL nuclear weapons

'**kernwaffenfrei** *adj*: **kernwaffenfreie Zone** MIL nuclear-free zone

'**Kernwaffenversuch** *m* MIL nuclear test

'**Kernzeit** *f* ECON core time

Kerze ['kɛrtsə] *f* (-; -*n*) candle; SPORT shoulder stand

kess [kɛs] F *adj* cheeky, saucy, pert

Kessel ['kɛsəl] *m* (-*s*; -) kettle; TECH boiler; tank

Kette ['kɛtə] *f* (-; -*n*) chain (*a. fig*); necklace; **e-e Kette bilden** form a line

'**Ketten...** *in cpds* ...*antrieb*, ...*laden*, ...*rauchen*, ...*raucher*, ...*reaktion etc*: chain ...

'**ketten** *v/t* (*ge-*, *h*) chain (**an** *acc* to)

'**Kettenfahrzeug** *n* tracked vehicle

Ketzer ['kɛtsɐ] *m* (-*s*; -) heretic

Ketzerei [kɛtsə'raɪ] *f* (-; -*en*) heresy

keuchen ['kɔʏçən] *v/i* (*ge-*, *h*) pant, gasp

'**Keuchhusten** *m* MED whooping cough

Keule ['kɔʏlə] *f* (-; -*n*) club; GASTR leg

keusch [kɔʏʃ] *adj* chaste

'**Keuschheit** *f* (-; *no pl*) chastity

Kfz [kaː'ʔɛf'tsɛt] ABBR *of* **Kraftfahrzeug** motor vehicle

Kf'z-Brief *m*, **Kf'z-Schein** *m* vehicle registration document

Kf'z-Steuer *f* road *or* automobile tax

Kf'z-Werkstatt *f* garage

KG [kaː'geː] ABBR *of* **Kommanditgesellschaft** ECON limited partnership

kichern ['kɪçɐn] *v/i* (*ge-*, *h*) giggle

Kiebitz ['kiːbɪts] *m* (-*es*; -*e*) ZO peewit, lapwing; F kibitzer

Kiefer[1] ['kiːfɐ] *m* (-*s*; -) ANAT jaw(bone)

'**Kiefer**[2] *f* (-; -*n*) BOT pine(tree)

Kiel [kiːl] *m* (-[*e*]*s*; -*e*) MAR keel

Kielflosse *f* AVIAT tail fin

'**Kielraum** *m* MAR bilge

'**Kielwasser** *n* (-*s*; -) MAR wake (*a. fig*)

Kieme ['kiːmə] *f* (-; -*n*) ZO gill

Kies [kiːs] *m* (-*es*; -*e*) gravel (*a.* **mit Kies bestreuen**); F dough

Kiesel ['kiːzəl] *m* (-*s*; -) pebble

Kilo ['kiːlo] *n* (-*s*; -) → **Kilogramm**

Kilo'gramm [kilo-] *n* kilogram(me)

Kilohertz [-'hɛrts] *n* (-; -*n*) kilohertz

Kilo'meter *m* kilometer, *Br* kilometre

Kilo'watt *n* ELECTR kilowatt

Kind [kɪnt] *n* (-[*e*]*s*; -*er* ['kɪndɐ]) child; **ein Kind erwarten** be expecting a baby

'**Kinderarzt** *m*, **Kinderärztin** *f* p(a)ediatrician

Kindergarten *m* kindergarten, nursery school

Kindergärtnerin [-gɛrtnərɪn] *f* (-; -*nen*) nursery-school *or* kindergarten teacher

Kindergeld *n* child benefit

Kinderhort [-hɔrt] *m* (-[*e*]*s*; -*e*), **Kinderkrippe** *f* day nursery

Kinderlähmung *f* MED polio(-myelitis)

'**kinderlieb** *adj* fond of children
'**kinderlos** *adj* childless
'**Kindermädchen** *n* nurse(maid), nanny
Kinderspiel *fig n*: **ein Kinderspiel sein** be child's play
Kinderstube *fig f* manners, upbringing
Kinderwagen *m* baby carriage, buggy, *Br* pram
Kinderzimmer *n* children's room
Kindesalter ['kɪndəs-] *n* childhood; infancy
Kindesentführung *f* kidnap(p)ing
Kindesmisshandlung *f* child abuse
'**Kindheit** *f* (-; *no pl*) (**von Kindheit an** from) childhood
kindisch ['kɪndɪʃ] *adj* childish
'**kindlich** *adj* childlike
Kinn [kɪn] *n* (-[e]s; -e) ANAT chin
Kinnbacke *f*, **Kinnbacken** *m* (-s; -) ANAT jaw(-bone)
Kinnhaken *m boxing*: hook (to the chin), uppercut
Kino ['kiːno] *n* (-s; -s) a) (*no pl*) motion pictures, *esp Br* cinema, F *the* movies, b) movie theater, *esp Br* cinema
'**Kinobesucher** *m*, '**Kinogänger** [-gɛŋɐ] *m* (-s; -) moviegoer, *Br* cinemagoer
Kippe ['kɪpə] *f* (-; -n) F butt, *esp Br* stub; SPORT upstart
'**kippen 1.** *v/i* (*ge-, sein*) tip *or* topple (over); **2.** *v/t* (*ge-, h*) tilt, tip over *or* up
Kirche ['kɪrçə] *f* (-; -n) church; **in die Kirche gehen** go to church
'**Kirchenbuch** *n* parish register
Kirchendiener *m* sexton
Kirchengemeinde *f* parish
Kirchenjahr *n* Church *or* ecclesiastical year
Kirchenlied *n* hymn
Kirchenmu,sik *f* sacred *or* church music
Kirchenschiff *n* ARCH nave
Kirchensteuer *f* church tax
Kirchenstuhl *m* pew
Kirchentag *m* church congress
'**Kirchgang** *m* churchgoing
'**Kirchgänger** [-gɛŋɐ] *m* (-s; -) churchgoer
'**kirchlich** *adj* church, ecclesiastical
'**Kirchturm** *m* steeple; spire; church tower
Kirsche ['kɪrʃə] *f* (-; -n) BOT cherry
Kissen ['kɪsən] *n* (-s; -) pillow; cushion
Kissenbezug *m*, **Kissenhülle** *f* pillowcase, pillowslip
Kiste ['kɪstə] *f* (-; -n) box, chest; crate
Kitsch [kɪtʃ] *m* (-[e]s; *no pl*) kitsch; trash; F slush
'**kitschig** *adj* kitschy; trashy; slushy
Kitt [kɪt] *m* (-[e]s; -e) cement; putty
Kittel ['kɪtəl] *m* (-s; -) smock; overall; MED (white) coat

'**kitten** *v/t* (*ge-, h*) cement; putty
Kitzel ['kɪtsəl] *m* (-s; -) tickle, *fig a*. thrill, kick
'**kitzeln** *v/i and v/t* (*ge-, h*) tickle
Kitzler ['kɪtslɐ] *m* (-s; -) ANAT clitoris
kitzlig ['kɪtslɪç] *adj* ticklish (*a. fig*)
kläffen ['klɛfən] *v/i* (*ge-, h*) yap, yelp
klaffend ['klafənt] *adj* gaping; yawning
Klage ['klaːgə] *f* (-; -n) complaint; lament; JUR action, (law)suit
'**klagen** *v/i* (*ge-, h*) complain (**über** *acc* of, about; **bei** to); lament; JUR go to court; **gegen j-n klagen** JUR sue s.o.
Kläger ['klɛːgɐ] *m* (-s; -), '**Klägerin** *f* (-; -nen) JUR plaintiff
kläglich ['klɛːklɪç] → **jämmerlich**
Klamauk [kla'mauk] *m* (-s; *no pl*) racket; THEA *etc* slapstick
klamm [klam] *adj* numb; clammy
Klammer ['klamɐ] *f* (-; -n) TECH cramp, clamp; clip; clothespin, *Br* (clothes) peg; MED brace; MATH, PRINT bracket(s)
'**klammern** *v/t* (*ge-, h*) fasten *or* clip together; **sich klammern an** (*acc*) cling to
klang [klaŋ] *pret of* **klingen**
Klang *m* (-[e]s; **Klänge** ['klɛŋə]) sound; tone; clink; ringing
'**klangvoll** *adj* sonorous; *fig* illustrious
Klappe ['klapə] *f* (-; -n) flap; hinged lid; MOT tailgate, *Br* tailboard; TECH, BOT, ANAT valve; F trap
'**klappen** (*ge-, h*) **1.** *v/t*: **nach oben klappen** lift up, raise; put *or* fold up; **nach unten klappen** lower, put down; **es lässt sich (nach hinten) klappen** it folds (backward); **2.** *v/i* clap, clack; F work, work out (well)
Klapper ['klapɐ] *f* (-; -n) rattle
'**klappern** *v/i* (*ge-, h*) clatter, rattle (**mit et.** s.th.)
'**Klapperschlange** *f* ZO rattlesnake
Klappfahrrad ['klap-] *n* folding bicycle
Klappfenster *n* top-hung window
Klappmesser *n* jack knife, clasp knife
klapprig ['klaprɪç] *adj* MOT rattly, ramshackle; F shaky
'**Klappsitz** *m* folding *or* tip-up seat
'**Klappstuhl** *m* folding chair
'**Klapptisch** *m* folding table
Klaps [klaps] *m* (-es; -e) slap, pat; smack
klar [klaːɐ] *adj* clear (*a. fig*); **ist dir klar, dass …?** do you realize that …?; **das ist mir (nicht ganz) klar** I (don't quite) understand; (**na**) **klar!** of course!; **alles klar?** everything okay?
Kläranlage ['klɛːɐ-] *f* sewage works
klären ['klɛːrən] *v/t* (*ge-, h*) TECH purify, treat; *fig* clear up; settle; SPORT clear
'**Klarheit** *f* (-; *no pl*) clearness, *fig a*. clarity

Klarinette [klari'nɛtə] f (-; -n) MUS clarinet

'Klarsicht... in cpds transparent

Klasse ['klasə] f (-; -n) class (a. POL), PED a.
grade, Br form; classroom; F **klasse sein**
be super, be fantastic

'Klassenarbeit f (classroom) test

Klassenbuch n classbook, Br (class) register

Klassenkame,rad m classmate

Klassenlehrer(in) m homeroom teacher, Br
form teacher, a. form master (mistress)

Klassensprecher m class representative

Klassenzimmer n classroom

klassifizieren [klasifi'tsi:rən] v/t (no -ge-,
h) classify

'Klassifi'zierung f (-; -en) classification

Klassiker ['klasikɐ] m (-s; -) classic

klassisch ['klasɪʃ] adj classic(al)

Klatsch [klatʃ] F m (-es; no pl) gossip

'Klatschbase f gossip

'klatschen v/i and v/t (ge-, h) clap, applaud; F slap, bang; splash; F gossip; **in
die Hände klatschen** clap one's hands

'klatschhaft adj gossipy

'Klatschmaul F n (old) gossip

'klatsch'nass F adj soaking wet

klauben ['klaubən] Austrian v/t (ge-, h)
pick; gather

Klaue ['klauə] f (-; -n) ZO claw; pl fig
clutches

klauen ['klauən] F v/t (ge-, h) pinch

Klausel ['klauzəl] f (-; -n) JUR clause; condition

Klausur [klau'zu:ɐ] f (-; -en) test (paper),
exam(ination)

Klavier [kla'vi:ɐ] n (-s; -e) MUS piano; **Klavier spielen** play the piano

Klavierkon,zert n MUS piano concerto; piano recital

Klebeband ['kle:bə-] n (-[e]s; -bänder)
adhesive tape

kleben ['kle:bən] (ge-, h) **1.** v/t glue, paste;
stick; **2.** v/i stick, cling (**an** dat to) (a. fig)

klebrig ['kle:brɪç] adj sticky

Klebstoff ['kle:p-] m adhesive; glue

Klebstreifen m adhesive tape

kleckern ['klɛkɐn] F (ge-, h) **1.** v/i make a
mess; **2.** v/t spill

Klecks [klɛks] F m (-es; -e) (ink)blot; blob

klecksen ['klɛksən] F v/i (ge-, h) blot,
make blots

Klee [kle:] m (-s; no pl) BOT clover

'Kleeblatt n cloverleaf

Kleid [klait] n (-[e]s; -er ['klaidɐ]) dress; pl
clothes

kleiden ['klaidən] v/t (ge-, h) dress, clothe;
j-n gut kleiden suit s.o.; **sich gut** etc **kleiden** dress well etc

Kleiderbügel ['klaidɐ-] m (coat) hanger

Kleiderbürste f clothes brush

Kleiderhaken m coat hook

Kleiderschrank m wardrobe

Kleiderständer m coat stand

Kleiderstoff m dress material

'kleidsam adj becoming

'Kleidung f (-; no pl) clothes, clothing

'Kleidungsstück n article of clothing

Kleie ['klaiə] f (-; -n) AGR bran

klein [klain] adj small, esp F little (a. finger, brother); short; **von klein auf** from
an early age; **ein klein wenig** a little
bit; **Groß und Klein** young and old;
die Kleinen the little ones; **klein schneiden** cut up (into small pieces)

'Kleinanzeige f want ad, Br small ad

Kleinbildkamera f 35 mm camera

Kleinfa,milie f nuclear family

Kleingeld n (small) change

Kleinholz n matchwood

Kleinigkeit ['klainıçkait] f (-; -en) little
thing, trifle; little something; **e-e Kleinigkeit sein** be nothing, be child's play

'Kleinkind n baby, infant

'Kleinkram F m odds and ends

'kleinlaut adj subdued

'kleinlich adj small-minded, petty; mean;
pedantic, fussy

'kleinschneiden v/t (irr, **schneiden**, sep,
-ge-, h) → **klein**

'Kleinstadt f small town

'kleinstädtisch adj small-town, provincial

'Kleintrans,porter m MOT pick-up

'Kleinwagen m MOT small or compact car,
F runabout

Kleister ['klaistɐ] m (-s; -) paste

Klemme ['klɛmə] f (-; -n) TECH clamp;
(hair) clip; F **in der Klemme sitzen** be
in a fix or tight spot

'klemmen v/i and v/t (ge-, h) jam; stick; be
stuck, be jammed; **sich klemmen** jam
one's finger or hand

Klempner ['klɛmpnɐ] m (-s; -) plumber

Klepper ['klɛpɐ] m (-s; -) ZO nag

Klerus ['kle:rʊs] m (-; no pl) REL clergy

Klette ['klɛtə] f (-; -n) BOT bur(r); fig leech

klettern ['klɛtɐn] v/i (ge-, sein) climb; **auf
e-n Baum klettern** climb (up) a tree

'Kletterpflanze f BOT climber

Klient [kli'ɛnt] m (-en; -en), **Kli'entin** f (-;
-nen) client

Klima ['kli:ma] n (-s; -s) climate, fig a. atmosphere

'Klimaanlage f air-conditioning

klimatisch [kli'ma:tɪʃ] adj climatic

klimpern ['klɪmpɐn] v/i (ge-, h) jingle,
chink (**mit et.** s.th.); F MUS strum (away)
(**auf** dat on)

Klinge ['klɪŋə] f (-; -n) blade

Klingel ['klɪŋəl] f (-; -n) bell
'**Klingelknopf** m bell (push)
'**klingeln** v/i (ge-, h) ring (the bell); **es klingelt** the (door)bell is ringing
'**klingen** v/i (irr, ge-, h) sound; bell, metal etc: ring; glasses etc: clink
Klinik ['kliːnɪk] f (-; -en) hospital; clinic
klinisch ['kliːnɪʃ] adj clinical
Klinke ['klɪŋkə] f (-; -n) (door) handle
Klippe ['klɪpə] f (-; -n) cliff, rock(s); fig obstacle
klirren ['klɪrən] v/i (ge-, h) window: rattle; glasses etc: clink; broken glass: tinkle; swords: clash; keys, coins: jingle
Klischee [kli'ʃeː] n (-s; -s) cliché
klobig ['kloːbɪç] adj bulky, clumsy
klopfen ['klɔpfən] (ge-, h) **1.** v/i heart etc: beat, throb; knock (an acc at, on); tap; pat; **es klopft** there's a knock at the door; **2.** v/t beat; knock; drive (nail etc)
Klosett [klo'zɛt] n (-s; -s) lavatory, toilet
Klosettbrille f toilet seat
Klosettpaͺpier n toilet paper
Kloß [kloːs] m (-es; Klöße ['kløːsə]) clod, lump (a. fig); GASTR dumpling
Kloster ['kloːstɐ] n (-s; Klöster ['kløːstɐ]) REL monastery; convent
Klotz [klɔts] m (-es; Klötze ['klœtsə]) block; log
Klub [klʊb] m (-s; -s) club
'**Klubsessel** m lounge chair
Kluft [klʊft] f (-; Klüfte ['klʏftə]) gap (a. fig); abyss
klug [kluːk] adj intelligent, clever, F bright, smart; wise; **daraus (aus ihm) werde ich nicht klug** I don't know what to make of it (him)
'**Klugheit** f (-; no pl) intelligence, cleverness, F brains; good sense; knowledge
Klumpen ['klʊmpən] m (-s; -) lump; clod; nugget
'**Klumpfuß** m MED club foot
'**klumpig** adj lumpy; cloddish
knabbern ['knabɐn] v/t and v/i (ge-, h) nibble, gnaw
Knabe ['knaːbə] m (-n; -n) boy
'**knabenhaft** adj boyish
Knäckebrot ['knɛkə-] n crispbread
knacken ['knakən] v/t and v/i (ge-, h) crack; twig: snap; fire, radio: crackle
Knacks F m (-es; -e) crack; fig defect
Knall [knal] m (-[e]s; -e) bang; crack, report; pop; F **e-n Knall haben** be nuts
'**Knallbonͺbon** m, n cracker
'**knallen** v/i and v/t (ge-, h) bang; slam; crack; pop; F crash (**gegen** into); F **j-m e-e knallen** slap s.o.('s face)
'**knallig** F adj flashy, loud
'**Knallkörper** m firecracker

knapp [knap] adj scarce; scanty, meager, Br meagre (food, pay etc); bare (a. majority etc); limited (time etc); narrow (escape etc); tight (dress etc); brief; **knapp an Geld** (**Zeit** etc) short of money (time etc); **mit knapper Not** only just, barely
Knappe ['knapə] m (-n; -n) miner
'**knapphalten** v/t (irr, halten, sep, -ge-, h): **j-n knapphalten** halten keep s.o. short
'**Knappheit** f (-; no pl) shortage
Knarre ['knarə] f (-; -n) rattle; F gun
'**knarren** v/i (ge-, h) creak
Knast [knast] F m (-[e]s; Knäste ['knɛstə]) sl clink
'**Knastbruder** F m jailbird
knattern ['knatɐn] v/i (ge-, h) crackle; MOT roar
Knäuel ['knɔyəl] m, n (-s; -) ball; tangle
Knauf [knauf] m (-[e]s; Knäufe ['knɔyfə]) knob; pommel
knaus(e)rig ['knauz(ə)rɪç] F adj stingy
knautschen ['knautʃən] v/t and v/i (ge-, h) crumple
'**Knautschzone** f MOT crumple zone
Knebel ['kneːbəl] m (-s; -), '**knebeln** v/t (ge-, h) gag (a. fig)
Knecht [knɛçt] m (-[e]s; -e) farmhand; fig slave
Knechtschaft fig f (-; no pl) slavery
kneifen ['knaifən] v/t and v/i (irr, ge-, h) pinch (**j-m in den Arm** s.o.'s arm); F chicken out
'**Kneifzange** f pincers
Kneipe ['knaipə] F f (-; -n) saloon, bar, esp Br pub
kneten ['kneːtən] v/t (ge-, h) knead; mo(u)ld
'**Knetmasse** f Plasticine®, Play-Doh®
Knick [knɪk] m (-[e]s; -e, -s) fold, crease; bend
'**knicken** v/t (ge-, h) fold, crease; bend; break; **nicht knicken!** do not bend!
Knicks [knɪks] m (-es; -e) curts(e)y; **e-n Knicks machen** → '**knicksen** v/i (ge-, h) curts(e)y (**vor** dat to)
Knie [kniː] n (-s; - ['kniːə, kniː]) ANAT knee
Kniebeuge f SPORT knee bend
Kniekehle f ANAT hollow of the knee
knien [kniːn] v/i (ge-, h) kneel, be on one's knees (**vor** dat before)
'**Kniescheibe** f ANAT kneecap
'**Kniestrumpf** m knee(-length) sock
kniff [knɪf] pret of **kneifen**
Kniff m (-[e]s; -e) crease, fold; pinch; trick, knack
kniff(e)lig ['knɪf(ə)lɪç] adj tricky
knipsen ['knɪpsən] v/t and v/i (ge-, h) F PHOT take a picture (of); punch, clip
Knirps [knɪrps] m (-es; -e) little guy

knirschen ['knɪrʃən] v/i (ge-, h) crunch; **mit den Zähnen knirschen** grind or gnash one's teeth

knistern ['knɪstɐn] v/i (ge-, h) crackle; rustle

knittern ['knɪtɐn] v/t and v/i (ge-, h) crumple, crease, wrinkle

Knoblauch ['kno:plaux] m (-[e]s; no pl) BOT garlic

Knöchel ['knœçəl] m (-s; -) ANAT ankle; knuckle

Knochen ['knɔxən] m (-s; -) ANAT bone

'Knochenbruch m MED fracture

knochig ['knɔxɪç] adj bony

Knödel ['knøːdəl] m (-s; -) dumpling

Knolle ['knɔlə] f (-; -n) BOT tuber; bulb

Knopf [knɔpf] m (-es; Knöpfe ['knœpfə]), **knöpfen** ['knœpfən] v/t (ge-, h) button

'Knopfloch n buttonhole

Knorpel ['knɔrpəl] m (-s; -) GASTR gristle; ANAT cartilage

knorrig ['knɔrɪç] adj gnarled, knotted

Knospe ['knɔspə] f (-; -n), **'knospen** v/i (ge-, h) BOT bud

knoten [kno:tən] v/t (ge-, h) knot, make a knot in

'Knoten m (-s; -) knot (a. fig)

'Knotenpunkt m center, Br centre; RAIL junction

knüllen ['knʏlən] v/t and v/i (ge-, h) crumple

Knüller ['knʏlɐ] F m (-s; -) smash (hit); scoop

knüpfen ['knʏpfən] v/t (ge-, h) tie; weave

Knüppel ['knʏpəl] m (-s; -) stick, cudgel; truncheon

Knüppelschaltung f floor shift

knurren ['knʊrən] v/i (ge-, h) growl, snarl; fig grumble (**über** acc at); stomach: rumble

knusp(e)rig ['knʊsp(ə)rɪç] adj crisp, crunchy

knutschen ['knu:tʃən] F v/i (ge-, h) pet, neck, smooch

k.o. [ka:'ʔo:] adj knocked out; fig beat

Koalition [koali'tsjo:n] f (-; -en) esp POL coalition

große Koalition grand coalition

Kobold ['ko:bɔlt] m (-[e]s; -e) (hob)goblin, imp (a. fig)

Koch [kɔx] m (-[e]s; Köche ['kœçə]) cook; chef

Kochbuch n cookbook, Br cookery book

'kochen (ge-, h) **1.** v/t cook; boil (eggs etc); make (coffee etc); **2.** v/i cook, do the cooking; boil (a. fig); **gut kochen** be a good cook; F **vor Wut kochen** boil with rage; **kochend heiß** boiling hot

Kocher ['kɔxɐ] m (-s; -) ELECTR cooker

Köchin ['kœçɪn] f (-; -nen) cook; chef

'Kochlöffel m (wooden) spoon

Kochnische f kitchenette

Kochplatte f hotplate

Kochsalz n common salt

Kochtopf m saucepan, pot

Köder ['køːdɐ] m (-s; -) bait, decoy (both a. fig), lure

'ködern v/t (ge-, h) bait, decoy (both a. fig)

Kodex ['ko:dɛks] m (-es; -, -e) code

kodieren [ko'di:rən] v/t (no -ge-, h) (en-)code

Ko'dierung f (-; -en) (en-) coding

Koffein [kɔfe'i:n] n (-s; no pl) caffeine

Koffer ['kɔfɐ] m (-s; -) (suit)case; trunk

Kofferradio n portable (radio)

Kofferraum m MOT trunk, Br booth

Kognak ['kɔnjak] m (-s; -s) (French) brandy, cognac

Kohl [ko:l] m (-[e]s; -e) BOT cabbage

Kohle ['ko:lə] f (-; -n) coal; ELECTR carbon; F dough

'Kohlehy,drat n carbohydrate

'Kohlen... in cpds ...dioxid etc: CHEM carbon ...

Kohlenbergwerk n coalmine, colliery

Kohlenofen m coal-burning stove

'Kohlensäure f CHEM carbonic acid; GASTR F fizz

'kohlensäurehaltig adj carbonated, F fizzy

'Kohlenstoff m CHEM carbon

Kohlenwasserstoff m CHEM hydrocarbon

'Kohlepa,pier n carbon paper

Kohlezeichnung f charcoal drawing

Kohlrabi [-'ra:bi] m (-s; -s) BOT kohlrabi

Koje ['ko:jə] f (-; -n) MAR berth, bunk

Kokain [koka'i:n] n (-s; no pl) cocaine

kokettieren [kokɛ'ti:rən] v/i (no -ge-, h) flirt; fig **kokettieren mit** toy with

Kokosnuss ['ko:kɔs-] f BOT coconut

Koks [ko:ks] m (-es; no pl) coke; F dough; sl coke, snow

Kolben ['kɔlbən] m (-s; -) butt; TECH piston

Kolbenstange f TECH piston rod

Kolibri ['ko:libri] m (-s; -s) ZO humming bird

Kolleg [kɔ'le:k] n (-s; -s) UNIV course (of lectures)

Kollege [kɔ'le:gə] m (-n; -n), **Kol'legin** f (-; -nen) colleague

Kollegium [kɔ'le:gjʊm] n (-s; -ien) UNIV faculty, Br teaching staff

Kollekte [kɔ'lɛktə] f (-; -n) REL collection

Kollektion [kɔlɛk'tsjo:n] f (-; -en) ECON collection; range

kollektiv [kɔlɛk'ti:f] adj, **Kollek'tiv** n (-s; -e) collective (a. in cpds)

Koller ['kɔlɐ] F *m* (-*s*; -) fit; rage

kollidieren [kɔli'diːrən] *v/i* (*no -ge-, sein*) collide

Kollision [kɔli'zjoːn] *f* (-; -*en*) collision, *fig a.* clash, conflict

Kölnischwasser ['kœlnɪʃ-] *n* (-*s*; -) (eau de) cologne

Kolonie [kolo'niː] *f* (-; -*n*) colony

kolonisieren [koloni'ziːrən] *v/t* (*no -ge-, h*) colonize

Koloni'sierung *f* (-; -*en*) colonization

Kolonne [ko'lɔnə] *f* (-; -*n*) column; MIL convoy; gang, crew

Koloss [ko'lɔs] *m* (-*es*; -*e*) colossus, *fig a.* giant (of a man)

kolossal [kolɔ'saːl] *adj* gigantic

Kombi ['kɔmbi] *m* (-[*s*]; -*s*) MOT station wagon, *Br* estate (car)

Kombination [kɔmbina'tsjoːn] *f* (-; -*en*) combination; set; coveralls, *Br* overalls; flying suit; *soccer:* combined move

kombinieren [kɔmbi'niːrən] (*no -ge-, h*) **1.** *v/t* combine; **2.** *v/i* reason

Kombüse [kɔm'byːzə] *f* (-; -*n*) MAR galley

Komet [ko'meːt] *m* (-*en*; -*en*) ASTR comet

Komfort [kɔm'foːɐ] *m* (-*s*; *no pl*) (modern) conveniences; luxury

komfortabel [kɔmfɔr'taːbəl] *adj* comfortable; well-appointed; luxurious

Komik ['koːmɪk] *f* (-; *no pl*) humo(u)r; comic effect

Komiker ['koːmikɐ] *m* (-*s*; -) comedian

komisch ['koːmɪʃ] *adj* comic(al), funny; strange, odd

Komitee [komi'teː] *n* (-*s*; -*s*) committee

Komma ['kɔma] *n* (-*s*; -*s*, -*ta*) comma; *sechs Komma vier* six point four

Kommandant [kɔman'dant] *m* (-*en*; -*en*), **Kommandeur** [kɔman'døːɐ] *m* (-*s*; -*e*) MIL commander, commanding officer

kommandieren [kɔman'diːrən] *v/i and v/t* (*no -ge-, h*) command, be in command of

Kommando [kɔ'mando] *n* (-*s*; -*s*) command; order; MIL commando

Komm'mandobrücke *f* MAR (navigating) bridge

kommen ['kɔmən] *v/i* (*irr, ge-, sein*) come; arrive; get; reach; *zu spät kommen* be late; *weit kommen* get far; *zur Schule kommen* start school; *ins Gefängnis kommen* go to jail; *kommen lassen* send for *s.o.*, call *s.o.*; order *s.th.*; *kommen auf* (*acc*) think of, hit upon; remember; *hinter et. kommen* find s.th. out; *um et. kommen* lose s.th.; miss s.th.; *zu et. kommen* come by s.th.; *wieder zu sich kommen* come round *or* to; *wohin kommt ...?* where does ... go?; *daher kommt es, dass* that's why; *woher*

kommt es, dass ...? why is it that ...?, F how come ...?

'**kommenlassen** *v/t* (*irr, lassen, sep, no -ge-, h*) → **kommen**

Kommentar [kɔmɛn'taːɐ] *m* (-*s*; -*e*) commentary; *kein Kommentar!* no comment

Kommentator [kɔmɛn'taːtoːɐ] *m* (-*s*; -*en* [-ta'toːrən]), **Kommentatorin** [-ta'toːrɪn] *f* (-; -*nen*) commentator

kommentieren [kɔmɛn'tiːrən] *v/t* (*no -ge-, h*) comment (on)

kommerzialisieren [kɔmɛrtsjali'ziːrən] *v/t* (*no -ge-, h*) commercialize

Kommissar [kɔmɪ'saːɐ] *m* (-*s*; -*e*) commissioner; superintendent

Kommission [kɔmɪ'sjoːn] *f* (-; -*en*) commission; committee

Kommode [kɔ'moːdə] *f* (-; -*n*) bureau, *Br* chest (of drawers)

Kommunal... [kɔmu'naːl-] *in cpds ...politik etc:* local ...

Kommune [kɔ'muːnə] *f* (-; -*n*) commune

Kommunikation [kɔmunika'tsjoːn] *f* (-; *no pl*) communication

Kommunion [kɔmu'njoːn] *f* (-; -*en*) REL (Holy) Communion

Kommunismus [kɔmu'nɪsmʊs] *m* (-; *no pl*) POL communism

Kommunist [kɔmu'nɪst] *m* (-*en*; -*en*), **Kommu'nistin** *f* (-; -*nen*), **kommu'nistisch** *adj* POL communist

Komödie [ko'møːdjə] *f* (-; -*n*) comedy; *Komödie spielen* put on an act, play-act

kompakt [kɔm'pakt] *adj* compact

Kom'paktanlage *f* stereo system, music center (*Br* centre)

Kompanie [kɔmpa'niː] *f* (-; -*n*) MIL company

Kompass ['kɔmpas] *m* (-*es*; -*e*) compass

kompatibel [kɔmpa'tiːbəl] *adj* compatible (*a.* EDP)

komplett [kɔm'plɛt] *adj* complete

Komplex [kɔm'plɛks] *m* (-*es*; -*e*) complex (*a.* PSYCH)

Kompliment [kɔmpli'mɛnt] *n* (-[*e*]*s*; -*e*) compliment; *j-m ein Kompliment machen* pay s.o. a compliment

Komplize [kɔm'pliːtsə] *m* (-*n*; -*n*) accomplice

komplizieren [kɔmpli'tsiːrən] *v/t* (*no -ge-, h*) complicate

kompliziert [kɔmpli'tsiːɐt] *adj* complicated, complex

Kom'plizin *f* (-; -*nen*) accomplice

Komplott [kɔm'plɔt] *n* (-[*e*]*s*; -*e*) plot, conspiracy

komponieren [kɔmpo'niːrən] *v/t and v/i* (*no -ge-, h*) MUS compose; write

Komponist [kɔmpo'nɪst] *m* (-en; -en) MUS composer

Komposition [kɔmpozi'tsjoːn] *f* (-; -en) MUS composition

Kompott [kɔm'pɔt] *n* (-[e]s; -e) GASTR compot(e), stewed fruit

Kompresse [kɔm'prɛsə] *f* (-; -n) MED compress

komprimieren [kɔmpri'miːrən] *v/t* (*no -ge-, h*) compress

Kompromiss [kɔmpro'mɪs] *m* (-es; -e) compromise

kompro'misslos *adj* uncompromising

kompromittieren [kɔmprɔmɪ'tiːrən] *v/t* (*no -ge-, h*) compromise (**sich** o.s.)

kompromittierend *adj* compromising

Kondensator [kɔndɛn'zaːtoːɐ] *m* (-s; -en [-zaːtoːrən]) ELECTR capacitor; TECH condenser

kondensieren [kɔndɛn'ziːrən] *v/t* (*no -ge-, h*) condense

Kondensmilch [kɔn'dɛns-] *f* condensed milk

Kondition [kɔndi'tsjoːn] *f* (-; -en) a) condition, b) (*no pl*) SPORT condition, shape, form; **gute Kondition** (great) stamina

konditional [kɔnditsjo'naːl] *adj* LING conditional

Konditi'onstraining *n* fitness training

Konditor [kɔn'diːtoːɐ] *m* (-s; -en [-di'toːrən]) confectioner, pastrycook

Konditorei [kɔndito'rai] *f* (-; -en) cake shop; café, tearoom

Konditoreiwaren *pl* confectionery

Kondom [kɔn'doːm] *n*, *m* (-s; -e) condom

Kondukteur [kɔndʊk'tøːɐ] *Swiss m* (-s; -e) → **Schaffner**

Konfekt [kɔn'fɛkt] *n* (-[e]s; -e) sweets, chocolates

Konfektion [kɔnfɛk'tsjoːn] *f* (-; *no pl*) ready-made clothing

Konfekti'ons... *in cpds* ready-made ..., off-the-peg ...

Konferenz [kɔnfe'rɛnts] *f* (-; -en) conference

Konfession [kɔnfɛ'sjoːn] *f* (-; -en) religion, denomination

konfessionell [kɔnfɛsjo'nɛl] *adj* confessional, denominational

Konfessi'onsschule *f* denominational school

Konfirmand [kɔnfɪr'mant] *m* (-en; -en), **Konfir'mandin** *f* (-; -nen) REL confirmand

Konfirmation [kɔnfɪrma'tsjoːn] *f* (-; -en) REL confirmation

konfirmieren [kɔnfɪr'miːrən] *v/t* (*no -ge-, h*) confirm

konfiszieren [kɔnfɪs'tsiːrən] *v/t* (*no -ge-, h*) JUR confiscate

Konfitüre [kɔnfi'tyːrə] *f* (-; -n) jam

Konflikt [kɔn'flɪkt] *m* (-[e]s; -e) conflict

konfrontieren [kɔnfrɔn'tiːrən] *v/t* (*no -ge-, h*) confront

konfus [kɔn'fuːs] *adj* confused, mixed-up

Kongress [kɔn'grɛs] *m* (-es; -e) convention, *Br* congress

König ['køːnɪç] *m* (-s; -e) king

Königin ['køːnɪgɪn] *f* (-; -nen) queen

königlich ['køːnɪklɪç] *adj* royal

Königreich ['køːnɪk-] *n* kingdom

Konjugation [kɔnjuga'tsjoːn] *f* (-; -en) LING conjugation

konjugieren [kɔnju'giːrən] *v/t* (*no -ge-, h*) LING conjugate

Konjunktiv ['kɔnjʊŋktiːf] *m* (-s; -e) LING subjunctive (mood)

Konjunktur [kɔnjʊŋk'tuːɐ] *f* (-; -en) economic situation

konkret [kɔn'kreːt] *adj* concrete

Konkurrent [kɔnkʊ'rɛnt] *m* (-en; -en), **Konkur'rentin** *f* (-; -nen) competitor, rival

Konkurrenz [kɔnkʊ'rɛnts] *f* (-; *no pl*) competition; **die Konkurrenz** one's competitors; **außer Konkurrenz** not competing; → **konkurrenzlos**

konkur'renzfähig *adj* competitive

Konkur'renzkampf *m* competition

konkur'renzlos *adj* without competition, unrival(l)ed

konkurrieren [kɔnkʊ'riːrən] *v/i* (*no -ge-, h*) compete

Konkurs [kɔn'kurs] *m* (-es; -e) ECON, JUR bankruptcy; **in Konkurs gehen** go bankrupt

Konkursmasse *f* JUR bankrupt's estate

können ['kœnən] *v/t and v/i* (*irr, ge-, h*), *v/aux* (*irr, no -ge-, h*) can, be able to; may, be allowed to; **kann ich gehen** *etc?* can *or* may I go *etc?*; **du kannst nicht** you cannot *or* can't; **ich kann nicht mehr** I can't go on; I can't manage *or* eat any more; **es kann sein** it may be; **ich kann nichts dafür** it's not my fault; **e-e Sprache können** know *or* speak a language

'Können *n* (-s; *no pl*) ability, skill

Könner ['kœnɐ] *m* (-s; -), **'Könnerin** *f* (-; -nen) master, expert; *esp* SPORT ace, crack

konnte ['kɔntə] *pret of* **können**

konsequent [kɔnze'kvɛnt] *adj* consistent

Konsequenz [kɔnze'kvɛnts] *f* (-; -en) a) (*no pl*) consistency, b) consequence

konservativ [kɔnzɛrva'tiːf] *adj* conservative

Konserven [kɔn'zɛrvən] *pl* canned (*Br a.* tinned) foods

Kord

Konservenbüchse *f*, **Konservendose** *f* can, *Br a.* tin

Konservenfa,brik *f* cannery

konservieren [kɔnzɛr'viːrən] *v/t* (*no -ge-*, *h*) preserve

Konser'vierungsmittel *n* preservative

Konsonant [kɔnzo'nant] *m* (-*en*; -*en*) LING consonant

konstruieren [kɔnstru'iːrən] *v/t* (*no -ge-*, *h*) construct; design

Konstrukteur [kɔnstrʊk'tøːɐ] *m* (-*s*; -*e*) TECH designer

Konstruktion [kɔnstrʊk'tsjoːn] *f* (-; -*en*) construction

Konsul ['kɔnzʊl] *m* (-*s*; -*n*) consul

Konsulat [kɔnzu'laːt] *n* (-[*e*]*s*; -*e*) consulate

konsultieren [kɔnzʊl'tiːrən] *v/t* (*no -ge-*, *h*) consult

Konsum[1] [kɔn'zuːm] *m* (-*s*; *no pl*) consumption

Konsum[2] ['kɔnzuːm] *m* (-*s*; -*s*) cooperative (society *or* store), F co-op

Konsument [kɔnzu'mɛnt] *m* (-*en*; -*en*), **Konsu'mentin** *f* (-; -*nen*) consumer

Kon'sumgesellschaft *f* consumer society

konsumieren [kɔnzu'miːrən] *v/t* (*no -ge-*, *h*) consume

Kontakt [kɔn'takt] *m* (-[*e*]*s*; -*e*) contact (*a.* ELECTR); **Kontakt aufnehmen** get in touch; **Kontakt haben** *or* **in Kontakt stehen mit** be in contact *or* touch with; **den Kontakt verlieren** lose touch

kon'taktfreudig *adj* sociable

Kon'taktlinsen *pl* OPT contact lenses

Konter ['kɔntɐ] *m* (-*s*; -), **'kontern** *v/i* (*ge-*, *h*) counter (*a. fig*)

Kontinent [kɔnti'nɛnt] *m* (-[*e*]*s*; -*e*) continent

Konto ['kɔnto] *n* (-*s*; *Konten*) account

'Kontoauszug *m* (bank) statement

Kontrast [kɔn'trast] *m* (-[*e*]*s*; -*e*) contrast (*a.* PHOT, TV *etc*)

Kontrolle [kɔn'trɔlə] *f* (-; -*n*) control; supervision; check(up)

Kontrolleur [kɔntrɔ'løːɐ] *m* (-*s*; -*e*), **Kontrol'leurin** *f* (-; -*nen*) inspector, RAIL *a.* conductor

kontrollieren [kɔntrɔ'liːrən] *v/t* (*no -ge-*, *h*) check; check up on *s.o.*; control

Kon'trollpunkt *m* checkpoint

Kontroverse [kɔntro'vɛrzə] *f* (-; -*n*) controversy

konventionell [kɔnvɛntsjo'nɛl] *adj* conventional

Konversation [kɔnvɛrza'tsjoːn] *f* (-; -*en*) conversation

Konversati'onslexikon *n* encyclop(a)edia

Konzentration [kɔntsɛntra'tsjoːn] *f* (-; -*en*) concentration

Konzentrati'onslager *n* concentration camp

konzentrieren [kɔntsɛn'triːrən] *v/t and v/refl* (*no -ge-*, *h*) concentrate; **sich auf et. konzentrieren** concentrate on *s.th.*

Konzept [kɔn'tsɛpt] *n* (-[*e*]*s*; -*e*) (rough) draft; conception; **j-n aus dem Konzept bringen** put *s.o.* out

Konzern [kɔn'tsɛrn] *m* (-[*e*]*s*; -*e*) ECON combine, group

Konzert [kɔn'tsɛrt] *n* (-[*e*]*s*; -*e*) MUS concert; concerto

Konzerthalle *f*, **Konzertsaal** *m* concert hall, auditorium

Konzession [kɔntsɛ'sjoːn] *f* (-; -*en*) concession; license, *Br* licence

Kopf [kɔpf] *m* (-[*e*]*s*; *Köpfe* ['kœpfə]) head (*a. fig*); top; *fig a.* brains, mind; **Kopf hoch!** chin up!; **j-m über den Kopf wachsen** outgrow *s.o.*; *fig* be too much for *s.o.*; **sich den Kopf zerbrechen** (**über** *acc*) rack one's brains (over); **sich et. aus dem Kopf schlagen** put *s.th.* out of one's mind; **Kopf an Kopf** neck and neck

Kopfball *m* SPORT header; headed goal

Kopfbedeckung *f* headgear; **ohne Kopfbedeckung** bareheaded

köpfen ['kœpfən] *v/t* (*ge-*, *h*) behead, decapitate; SPORT head (**ins Tor** home)

'Kopfende *n* head

Kopfhörer *pl* headphones

Kopfjäger *m* headhunter

Kopfkissen *n* pillow

'kopflos *adj* headless; *fig* panicky

'Kopfrechnen *n* mental arithmetic

Kopfsa,lat *m* BOT lettuce

Kopfschmerzen *pl* headache

Kopfsprung *m* SPORT header

Kopfstand *m* SPORT headstand

Kopftuch *n* scarf, (head)kerchief

kopf'über *adv* headfirst (*a. fig*)

'Kopfweh *n →* **Kopfschmerzen**

'Kopfzerbrechen *n*: **j-m Kopfzerbrechen machen** give *s.o.* a headache

Kopie [ko'piː] *f* (-; -*n*), **ko'pieren** *v/t* (*no -ge-*, *h*) copy

Kopiergerät [ko'piːɐ-] *n* copier

Ko'pierstift *m* indelible pencil

Koppel[1] ['kɔpəl] *f* (-; -*n*) paddock

'Koppel[2] *n* (-*s*; -) MIL belt

'koppeln *v/t* (*ge-*, *h*) couple; dock

Koralle [ko'ralə] *f* (-; -*n*) ZO coral

Korb [kɔrp] *m* (-[*e*]*s*; *Körbe* ['kœrbə]) basket

Korbmöbel *pl* wicker furniture

Kord [kɔrt] *m* (-[*e*]*s*; -*e*) corduroy

Kordel ['kɔrdəl] *f* (-; *-n*) cord
'**Kordhose** *f* corduroys
Korinthe [ko'rıntə] *f* (-; *-n*) currant
Kork [kɔrk] *m* (-[e]*s*; *-e*) BOT cork
'**Korkeiche** *f* BOT cork oak
Korken ['kɔrkən] *m* (-*s*; -) cork
Korkenzieher [-tsi:ɐ] *m* (-*s*; -) corkscrew
Korn[1] [kɔrn] *n* (-[e]*s*; *Körner* ['kœrnɐ])
BOT a) grain; seed, b) (*no pl*) grain, *Br*
a. corn, c) (*pl -e*) TECH front sight
Korn[2] *f m* (-[e]*s*; *-e*) (grain) schnapps
körnig ['kœrnıç] *adj* grainy
Körper ['kœrpɐ] *m* (-*s*; -) body (*a*. PHYS,
CHEM), MATH *a*. solid, **Körperbau** *m*
(-[e]*s*; *no pl*) build, physique
'**körperbehindert** *adj* (physically) disabled *or* handicapped
'**Körpergeruch** *m* body odo(u)r, BO
Körpergröße *f* height
Körperkraft *f* physical strength
'**körperlich** *adj* physical
'**Körperpflege** *f* personal hygiene
'**Körperschaft** *f* (-; *-en*) corporation, (corporate) body
'**Körperteil** *m* part of the body
Körperverletzung *f* JUR bodily injury
korrekt [kɔ'rɛkt] *adj* correct
Korrektur [kɔrɛk'tu:ɐ] *f* (-; *-en*) correction; PED *etc* grading, *Br* marking
Korrespondent [kɔrɛspɔn'dɛnt] *m* (-*en*;
-*en*), **Korrespon'dentin** *f* (-; *-nen*) correspondent
Korrespondenz [-'dɛnts] *f* (-; *-en*) correspondence
korrespondieren [-'di:rən] *v/i* (*no -ge-*, *h*)
correspond (*mit* with)
Korridor ['kɔrido:ɐ] *m* (-*s*; *-e*) corridor;
hall
korrigieren [kɔri'gi:rən] *v/t* (*no -ge-*, *h*)
correct; PED *etc* grade, *Br* mark
korrupt [kɔ'rʊpt] *adj* corrupt(ed)
Korruption [kɔrʊp'tsjo:n] *f* (-; *-en*) corruption
Korsett [kɔr'zɛt] *n* (-*s*; *-s*) corset (*a. fig*)
Kosename ['ko:zə-] *m* pet name
Kosmetik [kɔs'me:tık] *f* (-; *no pl*) beauty
culture; cosmetics, toiletries
Kosmetikerin [kɔs'me:tikərın] *f* (-; *-nen*)
beautician, cosmetician
Kost [kɔst] *f* (-; *no pl*) food, diet; board
'**kostbar** *adj* precious, valuable; costly
'**Kostbarkeit** *f* (-; *-en*) precious object,
treasure (*a. fig*)
kosten[1] ['kɔstən] *v/t* (*ge-*, *h*) cost, be; *fig*
take (*time etc*); **was** *or* **wie viel kostet
…?** how much it …?
'**kosten**[2] *v/t* (*ge-*, *h*) taste, try
'**Kosten** *pl* cost(s); price; expenses; charges; **auf j-s Kosten** at s.o.'s expense

'**kostenlos 1.** *adj* free; **2.** *adv* free of charge
köstlich ['kœstlıç] *adj* delicious; *fig* priceless; **sich köstlich amüsieren** have great
fun, F have a ball
'**Kostprobe** *f* taste, sample (*a. fig*)
'**kostspielig** *adj* expensive, costly
Kostüm [kɔs'ty:m] *n* (-*s*; *-e*) costume,
dress; suit
Kostümfest *n* fancy-dress ball
Kot [ko:t] *m* (-[e]*s*; *no pl*) excrement, ZO *a*.
droppings
Kotelett [kotə'lɛt] *n* (-*s*; *-s*) chop, cutlet
Koteletten [kotə'lɛtən] *pl* sideburns
'**Kotflügel** *m* MOT fender, *Br* wing
kotzen ['kɔtsən] V *v/i* (*ge-*, *h*) puke
Krabbe ['krabə] *f* (-; *-n*) ZO shrimp; prawn
krabbeln ['krabəln] *v/i* (*ge-*, *sein*) crawl
Krach [krax] *m* (-[e]*s*; *Kräche* ['krɛçə]) a)
crash, bang, b) (*no pl*) noise, c) F quarrel,
fight
'**krachen** *v/i* (*ge-*, *h*) crack, bang, crash
Kracher ['kraxɐ] *m* (-*s*; -) (fire)cracker
krächzen ['krɛçtsən] *v/t and v/i* (*ge-*, *h*)
croak
Kraft [kraft] *f* (-; *Kräfte* ['krɛftə])
strength, force (*a*. POL), power (*a*. ELECTR,
TECH, POL); **in Kraft sein** (**setzen**, **treten**)
JUR *etc* be in (put into, come into) force
Kraftbrühe *f* GASTR consommé, clear soup
Kraftfahrer(in) driver, motorist
Kraftfahrzeug *n* motor vehicle
kräftig ['krɛftıç] *adj* strong (*a. fig*), powerful; substantial (*food*); good
'**kraftlos** *adj* weak, feeble
'**Kraftprobe** *f* test of strength
Kraftstoff *m* MOT fuel
Kraftverschwendung *f* waste of energy
Kraftwerk *n* power station
Kragen ['kra:gən] *m* (-*s*; -) collar
Krähe ['krɛ:ə] *f* (-; *-n*) ZO crow
krähen ['krɛ:ən] *v/i* (*ge-*, *h*) crow
Krake ['kra:kə] *m* (-*n*; *-n*) ZO octopus
Kralle ['kralə] *f* (-; *-n*) ZO claw (*a. fig*)
'**krallen** *v/refl* (*ge-*, *h*) cling (**an** *acc* on),
clutch (at)
Kram [kra:m] F *m* (-[e]*s*; *no pl*) stuff,
(one's) things
Krampf [krampf] *m* (-[e]*s*; *Krämpfe*
['krɛmpfə]) MED cramp; spasm, convulsion
Krampfader *f* MED varicose vein
'**krampfhaft** *fig adj* forced (*smile etc*); desperate (*attempt etc*)
Kran [kra:n] *m* (-[e]*s*; *Kräne* ['krɛ:nə])
TECH crane
Kranich ['kra:nıç] *m* (-*s*; *-e*) ZO crane
krank [kraŋk] *adj* ill, sick; **krank werden**
get sick, *Br* fall ill

'**Kranke** *m, f (-n; -n)* sick person, patient; **die Kranken** the sick

kränken ['krɛŋkən] *v/t (ge-, h)* hurt (*s.o.'s* feelings), offend

'**Krankenbett** *n* sickbed

Krankengeld *n* sickness benefit

Krankengym,nastik *f* physiotherapy

Krankenhaus *n* hospital

Krankenkasse *f* health insurance scheme; **in e-r Krankenkasse sein** be a member of a health insurance scheme *or* plan

Krankenpflege *f* nursing

Krankenpfleger *m* male nurse

Krankenschein *m* health insurance certificate

Krankenschwester *f* nurse

Krankenversicherung *f* health insurance

Krankenwagen *m* ambulance

Krankenzimmer *n* sickroom

'**krankhaft** *adj* morbid (*a. fig*)

'**Krankheit** *f (-; -en)* illness, sickness, disease

'**Krankheitsserreger** *m* germ

kränklich ['krɛŋklɪç] *adj* sickly, ailing

Kränkung ['krɛŋkʊŋ] *f (-; -en)* insult, offense, *Br* offence

Kranz [krants] *m (-es; Kränze* ['krɛntsə]) wreath; *fig* ring, circle

krass [kras] *adj* crass, gross; blunt

Krater ['kraːtɐ] *m (-s; -)* crater

kratzen ['kratsən] *v/t and v/refl (ge-, h)* scratch (o.s.); scrape (**von** off)

Kratzer ['kratsɐ] *m (-s; -)* scratch (*a. MED*)

kraulen ['kraulən] **1.** *v/t (ge-, h)* stroke; run one's fingers through; **2.** *v/i (ge-, sein)* SPORT do the crawl

kraus [kraus] *adj* curly (*hair*); wrinkled

Krause ['krauzə] *f (-; -n)* ruff; friz(z)

kräuseln ['krɔyzəln] *v/t and v/refl (ge-, h)* curl, friz(z); *water:* ripple

Kraut [kraut] *n (-[e]s; Kräuter* ['krɔytɐ]) BOT herb; tops, leaves; cabbage

Krawall [kra'val] *m (-s; -e)* riot; F row, racket

Krawatte [kra'vatə] *f (-; -n)* tie

kreativ [krea'tiːf] *adj* creative

Kreativität [kreativi'tɛːt] *f (-; no pl)* creativity

Kreatur [krea'tuːɐ] *f (-; -en)* creature

Krebs [kreːps] *m* ZO crayfish; MED cancer; AST Cancer; **sie ist (ein) Krebs** she's (a) Cancer; **Krebs erregend** → **krebserregend**

Krebs... MED cancerous

krebserregend *adj* MED carcinogenic

Krebsgeschwulst *f* MED carcinoma

Krebskranke *m, f* cancer patient

Kredit [kre'diːt] *m (-[e]s; -e)* ECON credit;

loan

Kredithai *m* loan shark

Kreditkarte *f* credit card, *pl coll* F plastic money

Kreide ['kraidə] *f (-; -n)* chalk; crayon

Kreis [krais] *m (-es; -e)* circle (*a. fig*); POL district, county

Kreisbahn *f* AST orbit

kreischen ['kraiʃən] *v/i (ge-, h)* screech; squeal

Kreisel ['kraizəl] *m (-s; -)* (spinning) top; PHYS gyro(scope)

'**kreiseln** *v/i (ge-, h, sein)* spin around

kreisen ['kraizən] *v/i (ge-, h, sein)* (move in a) circle, revolve, rotate; circulate

'**kreisförmig** [-fœrmɪç] *adj* circular

'**Kreislauf** *m* MED, ECON circulation; BIOL cycle (*a. fig*), TECH, ELECTR *a.* circuit

Kreislaufstörungen *pl* MED circulatory trouble

'**Kreissäge** *f* circular saw

Kreisverkehr *m* traffic circle, *Br* roundabout

Krempe ['krɛmpə] *f (-; -n)* brim

Kren [kreːn] *Austrian m (-[e]s; no pl)* GASTR horseradish

Krepp [krɛp] *m (-s; -s)* crepe

Kreuz [krɔyts] *n (-es; -e)* cross (*a. fig*); ANAT (small of the) back; *cards:* club(s); MUS sharp; **über Kreuz** crosswise; F **j-n aufs Kreuz legen** take s.o. in

kreuzen ['krɔytsən] **1.** *v/t and v/refl (ge-, h)* cross; clash; **2.** *v/i (ge-, sein)* MAR cruise

Kreuzer ['krɔytsɐ] *m (-s; -)* MAR cruiser

'**Kreuzfahrer** *m* HIST crusader

'**Kreuzfahrt** *f* MAR cruise

kreuzigen ['krɔytsɪgən] *v/t (ge-, h)* crucify

'**Kreuzigung** *f (-; -en)* crucifixion

'**Kreuzotter** *f* ZO adder

'**Kreuzschmerzen** *pl* backache

'**Kreuzung** *f (-; -en)* RAIL, MOT crossing; junction; intersection, crossroads; BIOL cross(breed)ing; cross(breed); *fig* cross

'**Kreuzverhör** *n* JUR cross-examination; **ins Kreuzverhör nehmen** cross-examine

'**kreuzweise** *adv* crosswise, crossways

'**Kreuzworträtsel** *n* crossword (puzzle)

Kreuzzug *m* HIST crusade

kriechen ['kriːçən] *v/i (irr, ge-, sein)* creep, crawl; *fig* **vor j-m kriechen** toady to s.o.

Kriecher ['kriːçɐ] *contp m (-s; -)* toady

'**Kriechspur** *f* MOT slow lane

Krieg [kriːk] *m (-[e]s; -e* ['kriːgə]) war; **Krieg führen gegen** be at war with

kriegen ['kriːgən] F *v/t (ge-, h)* get; catch

Krieger ['kriːgɐ] *m (-s; -)* warrior

'**Kriegerdenkmal** *n* war memorial

kriegerisch ['kriːgərɪʃ] *adj* warlike, mar-

K

tial

'Kriegführung f (-; no pl) warfare

'Kriegsbeil fig n: **das Kriegsbeil begra-ben** bury the hatchet

Kriegsdienstverweigerer m (-s; -) conscientious objector

Kriegserklärung f declaration of war

Kriegsgefangene m prisoner of war, P.O.W.

Kriegsgefangenschaft f captivity

Kriegsrecht n JUR martial law

Kriegsschauplatz m theater (Br theatre) of war

Kriegsschiff n warship

Kriegsteilnehmer m (war) veteran, Br ex-serviceman

Kriegstreiber [-traibɐ] m (-s; -) POL warmonger

Kriegsverbrechen n war crime

Kriegsverbrecher m war criminal

Krimi ['kri:mi] F m (-s; -s) (crime) thriller, detective novel

Kriminalbeamte [krimi'na:l-] m detective, plain-clothesman

Kriminalpolizei f criminal investigation department

Kriminalroman m → **Krimi**

kriminell [krimi'nɛl] adj, **Krimi'nelle** m, f (-n; -n) criminal

Krippe ['krɪpə] f (-; -n) crib, manger (a. REL); REL crèche, Br crib

Krise ['kri:zə] f (-; -n) crisis

'Krisenherd m esp POL trouble spot

Kristall[1] [krɪs'tal] m (-s; -e) crystal

Kris'tall[2] n (s; no pl), **Kristallglas** n crystal

kristallisieren [krɪstali'zi:rən] v/i and v/refl (no -ge-, h) crystallize

Kriterium [kri'te:rjʊm] n (-s; -ien) criterion (**für** of)

Kritik [kri'ti:k] f (-; -en) criticism; THEA, MUS etc review, critique; **gute Kritiken** a good press; **Kritik üben an** (dat) criticize

Kritiker(in) ['kri:tikɐ (-kərɪn)] (-s; -/-; -nen) critic

kri'tiklos adj uncritical

kritisch ['kri:tɪʃ] adj critical (a. fig) (**gegenüber** of)

kritisieren [kriti'zi:rən] v/t (no -ge-, h) criticize

kritzeln ['krɪtsəln] v/t and v/i (ge-, h) scrawl, scribble

kroch [krɔx] pret of **kriechen**

Krokodil [kroko'di:l] n (-s; -e) ZO crocodile

Krone ['kro:nə] f (-; -n) crown; coronet

krönen ['krø:nən] v/t (ge-, h) crown; **j-n zum König krönen** crown s.o. king

'Kronleuchter m chandelier

'Kronprinz m crown prince

'Kronprin,zessin f crown princess

'Krönung f (-; -en) coronation; fig crowning event, climax, high point

Kropf [krɔpf] m (-[e]s; Kröpfe ['krœpfə]) MED goiter, Br goitre; ZO crop

Kröte ['krø:tə] f (-; -n) ZO toad

Krücke ['krʏkə] f (-; -n) crutch

Krug [kru:k] m (-[e]s; Krüge ['kry:gə]) jug, pitcher; mug, stein; tankard

Krümel ['kry:məl] m (-s; -) crumb

krümelig ['kry:məlıç] adj crumbly

'krümeln v/t and v/i (ge-, h) crumble

krumm [krʊm] adj crooked (a. fig), bent

'krummbeinig [-bainıç] adj bow-legged

krümmen ['krʏmən] v/t (ge-, h) bend (a. TECH), crook; **sich krümmen** bend; writhe (with pain)

'Krümmung f (-; -en) bend, curve; GEOGR, MATH, MED curvature

Krüppel ['krʏpəl] m (-s; -) cripple

Kruste ['krʊstə] f (-; -n) crust

Kto. ABBR of **Konto** a/c, account

Kübel ['ky:bəl] m (-s; -) bucket, pail; tub

Kubikmeter [ku'bi:k-] n, m cubic meter (Br metre)

Kubikwurzel f MATH cube root

Küche ['kʏçə] f (-; -n) kitchen; GASTR cooking, cuisine; **kalte (warme) Küche** cold (hot) meals

Kuchen ['ku:xən] m (-s; -) cake; tart, pie

'Küchengeräte pl kitchen utensils (or appliances)

Küchengeschirr n kitchen crockery, kitchenware

Küchenherd m cooker

Küchenschrank m (kitchen) cupboard

Kuckuck ['kʊkʊk] m (-s; -s) ZO cuckoo

Kufe ['ku:fə] f (-; -n) runner; AVIAT skid

Kugel ['ku:gəl] f (-; -n) ball; bullet; MATH, GEOGR sphere; SPORT shot

'kugelförmig [-fœrmıç] adj ballshaped, esp ASTR, MATH spheric(al)

'Kugelgelenk n TECH, ANAT ball (and socket) joint

'Kugellager n TECH ball bearing

'kugeln v/i (ge-, sein) and v/t (h) roll

'Kugelschreiber [-ʃraibɐ] m (-s; -) ballpoint (pen)

'kugelsicher adj bulletproof

'Kugelstoßen n (-s; no pl) SPORT shot put(ting)

'Kugelstoßer [-ʃto:sɐ] m (-s; -), **Kugelstoßerin** [-ʃto:sərɪn] f (-; -nen) SPORT shot-putter

Kuh [ku:] f (-; Kühe ['ky:ə]) ZO cow

kühl [ky:l] adj cool (a. fig)

'Kühle f (-; no pl) cool(ness)

'**kühlen** v/t (ge-, h) cool; chill; refrigerate; refresh
Kühler ['ky:lɐ] m (-s; -) MOT radiator
'**Kühlerhaube** f MOT hood, Br bonnet
'**Kühlmittel** n coolant
'**Kühlraum** m cold-storage room
'**Kühlschrank** m fridge, refrigerator
'**Kühltruhe** f deep-freeze, freezer
'**Kühlwasser** n MOT cooling water
kühn [ky:n] adj bold
'**Kühnheit** f (-; no pl) boldness
'**Kuhstall** m cowshed
Küken ['ky:kən] n (-s; -) ZO chick (a. fig)
Kukuruz ['kukuruts] Austrian m → **Mais**
Kuli ['ku:li] F m (-s; -s) ballpoint
Kulissen [ku'lɪsən] pl THEA wings; scenery; **hinter den Kulissen** backstage, esp fig behind the scenes
Kult [kult] m (-[e]s; -e) cult; rite, ritual (act)
kultivieren [kulti'vi:rən] v/t (no -ge-, h) cultivate
Kultur [kul'tu:ɐ] f (-; -en) culture (a. BIOL), civilization; AGR cultivation
Kul'turbeutel m toilet bag
kulturell [kultu'rɛl] adj cultural
Kul'turgeschichte f history of civilization
Kulturvolk n civilized people
Kulturzentrum n cultural center (Br centre)
Kultusmi,nister ['kultus-] m minister of education and cultural affairs
Kummer ['kumɐ] m (-s; no pl) grief, sorrow; trouble, worry; **Kummer haben mit** have trouble or problems with
kümmerlich ['kymɐlɪç] adj miserable; poor, scanty
kümmern ['kymɐn] v/refl and v/t (ge-, h) **sich kümmern um** look after, take care of, mind; care or worry about, be interested in
Kumpel ['kumpəl] m (-s; -) miner; F mate, buddy, pal
Kunde ['kundə] m (-n; -n) customer, client
'**Kundendienst** m after-sales service; (customer) service; service department; TECH servicing
Kundgebung ['kuntge:buŋ] f (-; -en) meeting, rally, demonstration
kündigen ['kyndɪgən] v/i and v/t (ge-, h) cancel; **j-m kündigen** give s.o. his / her / one's notice; dismiss s.o., F sack or fire s.o.
'**Kündigung** f (-; -en) cancellation; (period of) notice
Kundin ['kundɪn] f (-; -nen) customer, client
Kundschaft ['kuntʃaft] f (-; -en) customers, clients

Kunst [kunst] f (-; Künste ['kynstə]) art; skill
Kunst... in cpds ...herz, ...leder, ...licht etc: artificial ...
Kunstakade,mie f academy of arts
Kunstausstellung f art exhibition
Kunstdünger m AGR artificial fertilizer
Kunsterziehung f PED art (education)
Kunstfaser f man-made or synthetic fiber (Br fibre)
Kunstfehler m professional blunder
Kunstfliegen n stunt flying, aerobatics
Kunstgeschichte f history of art
Kunstgewerbe n, **Kunsthandwerk** n arts and crafts
Künstler ['kynstlɐ] m (-s; -), **Künstlerin** ['kynstlərɪn] f (-; -nen) artist, MUS, THEA a. performer
künstlerisch ['kynstlərɪʃ] adj artistic
künstlich ['kynstlɪç] adj artificial; false; synthetic; man-made
'**Kunstschwimmen** n water ballet
Kunstseide f rayon
Kunstspringen n springboard diving
Kunststoff m plastic
Kunststück n trick, stunt, esp fig feat
Kunstturnen n gymnastics
Kunstturner m gymnast
'**kunstvoll** adj artistic; elaborate
'**Kunstwerk** n work of art
Kupfer ['kupfɐ] n (-s; no pl) copper (**aus** of)
Kupferstich m copperplate (engraving)
Kupon [ku'põ:] m (-s; -s) coupon
Kuppe ['kupə] f (-; -n) (rounded) hilltop; ANAT head
Kuppel ['kupəl] f (-; -n) ARCH dome; cupola
Kuppelei [kupə'lai] f (-; -en) JUR procuring
'**kuppeln** v/i (ge-, h) MOT put the clutch in or out
Kupplung ['kupluŋ] f (-; -en) MOT clutch
Kur [ku:ɐ] f (-; -en) course of treatment; cure
Kür [ky:ɐ] f (-; -en) SPORT free skating; free exercises
Kurbel ['kurbəl] f (-; -n) crank, handle
'**kurbeln** v/t (ge-, h) crank; wind (up etc)
'**Kurbelwelle** f TECH crankshaft
Kürbis ['kyrbɪs] m (-ses; -se) BOT pumpkin, gourd, squash
'**Kurgast** m visitor
kurieren [ku'ri:rən] v/t (no -ge-, h) cure (**von** of)
kurios [ku'rjo:s] adj curious, odd, strange
'**Kürlauf** m SPORT free skating
'**Kurort** m health resort, spa
Kurpfuscher ['ku:ɐpfuʃɐ] m (-s; -) quack (doctor)

K

Kurs [kʊrs] *m* (*-es*; *-e*) AVIAT, MAR course (*a. fig*); PED *etc* class(es); ECON (exchange) rate; (stock) price

Kursbuch *n* railroad (*Br* railway) guide

Kürschner ['kʏrʃnɐ] *m* (*-s*; -) furrier

kursieren [kʊr'ziːrən] *v/i* (*no -ge-*, *h*) circulate (*a. fig*)

Kurve ['kʊrvə] *f* (-; *-n*) curve (*a.* MATH *and fig*); bend, turn

'**kurvenreich** *adj* winding, full of bends; F curvaceous

kurz [kʊrts] *adj* short; brief; **kurze Hose** shorts; (*bis*) **vor kurzem** (until) recently; (*erst*) **seit kurzem** (only) for a short time; **kurz vorher** (*darauf*) shortly before (after[wards]); **kurz vor uns** just ahead of us; **kurz nacheinander** in quick succession; **kurz fortgehen** *etc* go away for a short time *or* a moment; **kurz gesagt** in short; **zu kurz kommen** go short; **kurz angebunden** curt

'**Kurzarbeit** *f* ECON short time

'**kurzarbeiten** *v/i* (*sep*, *ge-*, *h*) ECON work short time

'**kurzatmig** [-ʔaːtmɪç] *adj* short of breath

Kürze ['kʏrtsə] *f* (-; *no pl*) shortness; brevity; *in Kürze* soon, shortly, before long

'**kürzen** *v/t* (*ge-*, *h*) shorten (*um* by); abridge; cut, reduce (*a.* MATH)

kurzerhand ['kʊrtsɐ'hant] *adv* without hesitation, on the spot

'**kurzfassen** *v/refl* (*sep*, *-ge-*, *h*): **sich kurzfassen** be brief, put it briefly

'**kurzfristig** 1. *adj* short-term; 2. *adv* at short notice

'**Kurzgeschichte** *f* short story

'**kurzlebig** [-leːbɪç] *adj* short-lived

kürzlich ['kʏrtslɪç] *adv* recently, not long ago

'**Kurznachrichten** *pl* news summary

Kurzschluss *m* ELECTR short circuit, F short

Kurzschrift *f* shorthand

'**kurzsichtig** *adj* nearsighted, *Br* short-sighted

'**Kurzstrecke** *f* short distance

'**Kürzung** *f* (-; *-en*) cut, reduction (*a.* MATH)

'**Kurzwaren** *pl* notions, *Br* haberdashery

'**kurzweilig** [-vailɪç] *adj* entertaining

'**Kurzwelle** *f* PHYS, *radio*: short wave

kuschelig ['kʊʃəlɪç] F *adj* cozy, *Br* cosy, snug

kuscheln ['kʊʃəln] *v/refl* (*ge-*, *h*) snuggle, cuddle (*an acc* up to; *in acc* in)

Kusine *f* → *Cousine*

Kuss [kʊs] *m* (*-es*; *Küsse* ['kʏsə]) kiss

'**kussecht** *adj* kiss-proof

küssen ['kʏsən] *v/t* (*ge-*, *h*) kiss

Küste ['kʏstə] *f* (-; *-n*) coast, shore; *an der Küste* on the coast; *an die Küste* ashore

'**Küstengewässer** *pl* coastal waters

Küstenschifffahrt *f* coastal shipping

Küstenschutz *m*, **Küstenwache** *f* coast guard

Küster ['kʏstɐ] *m* (*-s*; -) REL verger, sexton

Kutsche ['kʊtʃə] *f* (-; *-n*) carriage, coach

Kutscher ['kʊtʃɐ] *m* (*-s*; -) coachman

Kutte ['kʊtə] *f* (-; *-n*) (monk's) habit

Kutteln ['kʊtəln] *pl* GASTR tripe

Kutter ['kʊtɐ] *m* (*-s*; -) MAR cutter

Kuvert [ku'veːɐ] *n* (*-s*; *-s*) envelope

Kybernetik [kybɐr'neːtɪk] *f* (-; *no pl*) cybernetics

L

labil [la'biːl] *adj* unstable

Labor [la'boːɐ] *n* (*-s*; *-e*) laboratory, F lab

Laborant(in) [labo'rant(ɪn)] (*-en*; *-en*/-; *-nen*) laboratory assistant

Labyrinth [laby'rɪnt] *n* (-[*e*]*s*; *-e*) labyrinth, maze (*both a. fig*)

Lache ['laxə] *f* (-; *-n*) pool, puddle

lächeln ['lɛçəln] *v/i* (*ge-*, *h*), '**Lächeln** *n* (*-s*; *no pl*) smile

lachen ['laxən] *v/i* (*ge-*, *h*) laugh (*über acc* at)

'**Lachen** *n* (*-s*; *no pl*) laugh(-ter); *j-n zum Lachen bringen* make s.o. laugh

lächerlich ['lɛçɐlɪç] *adj* ridiculous; *lächerlich machen* ridicule, make fun of; *sich lächerlich machen* make a fool of o.s.

Lachs [laks] *m* (*-es*; *-e*) ZO salmon

Lack [lak] *m* (-[*e*]*s*; *-e*) varnish; lacquer; MOT paint(work)

lackieren [la'kiːrən] *v/t* (*no -ge-*, *h*) varnish; lacquer; paint (*a.* MOT)

'**Lackschuhe** *pl* patent-leather shoes

Ladefläche ['laːdə-] *f* loading space

'**Ladegerät** *n* ELECTR battery charger
'**Ladehemmung** *f* MIL jam
laden ['la:dən] *v/t* (*irr, ge-, h*) load; ELECTR charge; EDP boot (up); *fig et. auf sich laden* burden o.s. with s.th.
'**Laden** *m* (*-s*; *Läden* ['lɛːdən]) store, *Br* shop; shutter
Ladendieb *m* shoplifter
Ladendiebstahl *m* shoplifting
Ladeninhaber *m* storekeeper, *Br* shopkeeper
Ladenkasse *f* till
Ladenschluss *m* closing time; *nach Ladenschluss* after hours
Ladentisch *m* counter
'**Laderampe** *f* loading platform *or* ramp
'**Laderaum** *m* loading space; MAR hold
'**Ladung** *f* (*-*; *-en*) load, freight; AVIAT, MAR cargo; ELECTR, MIL charge; *e-e Ladung ...* a load of ...
lag [la:k] *pret of* **liegen**
Lage ['la:gə] *f* (*-*; *-n*) situation, position (*both a. fig*); location; layer; round (*of beer etc*); *in schöner* (*ruhiger*) *Lage* beautifully (peacefully) situated; *in der Lage sein zu inf* be able to *inf*, be in a position to *inf*
Lager ['la:gɐ] *n* (*-s*; *-*) bed; camp (*a. fig*); ECON stock, store; GEOL deposit; TECH bearing; *et. auf Lager haben* have s.th. in store (*a. fig for s.o.*)
Lagerfeuer *n* campfire
Lagerhaus *n* warehouse
'**lagern** (*ge-, h*) **1.** *v/i* camp; ECON be stored; **2.** *v/t* store, keep; MED lay, rest; *kühl lagern* keep in a cool place
'**Lagerraum** *m* storeroom
Lagerung ['la:gəruŋ] *f* (*-*; *no pl*) storage
Lagune [la'gu:nə] *f* (*-*; *-n*) lagoon
lahm [la:m] *adj* lame
lahmen ['la:mən] *v/i* (*ge-, h*) be lame (*auf dat* in)
'**lahmlegen** *v/t* (*sep, -ge-, h*) → **lähmen**;
lähmen ['lɛːmən] *v/t* (*ge-, h*) paralyze, *Br* paralyse; bring *traffic etc* to a standstill
'**Lähmung** *f* (*-*; *-en*) MED paralysis
Laib [laip] *m* (*-[e]s*; *-e* ['laibə]) loaf
Laich [laiç] *m* (*-[e]s*; *-e*), **laichen** ['laiçən] *v/i* (*ge-, h*) spawn
Laie ['laiə] *m* (*-n*; *-n*) layman; amateur
'**laienhaft** *adj* amateurish
'**Laienspiel** *n* amateur play
Laken ['la:kən] *n* (*-s*; *-*) sheet; bath towel
Lakritze [la'krɪtsə] *f* (*-*; *-n*) liquorice
lallen ['lalən] *v/i and v/t* (*ge-, h*) speak drunkenly; *baby*: babble
Lamm [lam] *n* (*-[e]s*; *Lämmer* ['lɛmɐ]) ZO lamb
Lammfell *n* lambskin

Lampe ['lampə] *f* (*-*; *-n*) lamp, light; bulb
'**Lampenfieber** *n* stage fright
'**Lampenschirm** *m* lampshade
Lampion [lam'pjõ:] *m* (*-s*; *-s*) Chinese lantern
Land [lant] *n* (*-[e]s*; *Länder* ['lɛndɐ]) land; country; AGR ground, soil; ECON land, property; *an Land gehen* MAR go ashore; *auf dem Lande* in the country; *aufs Land fahren* go into the country; *außer Landes gehen* go abroad
Landarbeiter *m* farmhand
Landbevölkerung *f* country *or* rural population
Landebahn ['landə-] *f* AVIAT runway
land'einwärts *adv* up-country, inland
landen ['landən] *v/i* (*ge-, sein*) land; *fig landen in* (*dat*) end up in
'**Landenge** *f* neck of land, isthmus
'**Landeplatz** *m* AVIAT landing field
Länderspiel ['lɛndɐ-] *n* SPORT international match
'**Landesgrenze** *f* national border
Landesinnere *n* interior
Landesre,gierung *f* Land (*Austrian Provincial*) government
Landessprache *f* national language
'**landesüblich** *adj* customary
'**Landesverrat** *m* treason
Landesverräter *m* traitor (to one's country)
Landesverteidigung *f* national defen|se, *Br* -ce
'**Landflucht** *f* rural exodus
'**Landfriedensbruch** *m* JUR breach of the public peace
Landgericht *n* JUR *appr* regional superior court
Landgewinnung *f* reclamation of land
Landhaus *n* country house, cottage
Landkarte *f* map
Landkreis *m* district
'**landläufig** *adj* customary, current, common
ländlich ['lɛntlɪç] *adj* rural; rustic
'**Landrat** *m*, **Landrätin** [-rɛːtɪn] *f* (*-*; *-nen*) *appr* District Administrator
Landratte F *f* MAR landlubber
'**Landschaft** *f* (*-*; *-en*) countryside; scenery; *esp* PAINT landscape
'**landschaftlich** *adj* scenic
'**Landsmann** *m* (*-[e]s*; *-leute*) (fellow) countryman
'**Landsmännin** [-mɛnɪn] *f* (*-*; *-nen*) fellow countrywoman
'**Landstraße** *f* country (*or* ordinary) road
'**Landstreicher(in)** tramp
Landstreitkräfte *pl* MIL land forces
Landtag *m* Land parliament

L

'**Landung** f (-; -en) landing, AVIAT a. touch-down

'**Landungssteg** m MAR gangway

'**Landvermesser** [-fɛɐmɛsɐ] m (-s; -) land surveyor

Landvermessung f (-; -en) land surveying

Landweg m: *auf dem Landwege* by land

Landwirt(in) farmer

'**Landwirtschaft** f (-; no pl) agriculture, farming

'**landwirtschaftlich** adj agricultural

'**Landzunge** f GEOGR promontory, spit

lang [laŋ] adj and adv long; F tall; *drei Jahre (einige Zeit) lang* for three years (some time); *den ganzen Tag lang* all day long; *seit langem* for a long time; *vor langer Zeit* (a) long (time) ago; *über kurz oder lang* sooner or later; *lang ersehnt* long-hoped-for; *lang erwartet* long-awaited; *gleich lang* the same length

'**langatmig** [-ʔaːtmɪç] adj long-winded

lange ['laŋə] adv (for a) long (time); *es ist schon lange her(, seit)* it has been a long time (since); *(noch) nicht lange her* not long ago; *noch lange hin* still a long way off; *es dauert nicht lange* it won't take long; *ich bleibe nicht lange fort* I won't be long; *wie lange noch?* how much longer?

Länge ['lɛŋə] f (-; -n) length; GEOGR longitude; *der Länge nach* (at) full length; *(sich) in die Länge ziehen* stretch (a. fig)

langen ['laŋən] F v/i (ge-, h) reach (*nach* for); be enough; *mir langt es* I've had enough, fig a. I'm sick of it

'**Längengrad** m GEOGR degree of longitude

Längenmaß n linear measure

'**Langeweile** f (-; no pl) boredom; *Langeweile haben* be bored; *aus Langeweile* to pass the time

'**langfristig** adj long-term

'**langjährig** [-jɛːrɪç] adj longstanding; *langjährige Erfahrung* many years of experience

'**Langlauf** m (-[e]s; no pl) SPORT cross-country (skiing)

'**langlebig** [-leːbɪç] adj long-lived

länglich ['lɛŋlɪç] adj longish, oblong

längs [lɛŋs] 1. prp (gen) along(side); 2. adv lengthwise

'**langsam** adj slow; *langsamer werden or fahren* slow down

'**Langschläfer** [-ʃlɛːfɐ] m (-s; -), **Langschläferin** [-fərɪn] f (-; -nen) late riser

Langspielplatte f long-playing record, mst LP

längst [lɛŋst] adv long ago or before; *längst vorbei* long past; *ich weiß es längst* I have known it for a long time

längstens ['lɛŋstəns] adv at (the) most

'**Langstrecken...** in cpds long-distance ...; AVIAT, MIL long-range ...

'**langweilen** v/t (ge-, h) bore; *sich langweilen* be bored

'**langweilig** [-vailɪç] adj boring, dull; *langweilige Person* bore

'**Langwelle** f PHYS, radio: long wave

'**langwierig** [-viːrɪç] adj lengthy, protracted (a. MED)

Lanze ['lantsə] f (-; -n) lance, spear

Lappalie [la'paːljə] f (-; -n) trifle

Lappen ['lapən] m (-s; -) (piece of) cloth; rag (a. fig)

läppisch ['lɛpɪʃ] adj silly; ridiculous

Lärche ['lɛrçə] f (-; -n) BOT larch

Lärm [lɛrm] m (-s; no pl) noise

lärmen ['lɛrmən] v/i (ge-, h) be noisy

lärmend adj noisy

Larve ['larfə] f (-; -n) mask; zo larva

las [laːs] pret of *lesen*

lasch [laʃ] F adj slack, lax

Lasche ['laʃə] f (-; -n) flap; tongue

Laser ['leːzɐ] m (-s; -) PHYS laser

Laserdrucker m EDP laser printer

Laserstrahl m PHYS laser beam

Lasertechnik f laser technology

lassen ['lasən] v/t (irr, ge-, h) and v/aux (irr, no -ge-, h) let, leave; *j-n et. lassen* let s.o. do s.th.; allow s.o. to do s.th.; make s.o. do s.th.; *j-n (et.) zu Hause lassen* leave s.o. (s.th.) at home; *j-n allein (in Ruhe) lassen* leave s.o. alone; *sich die Haare schneiden lassen* have or get one's hair cut; *sein Leben lassen (für)* lose (give) one's life (for); *rufen lassen* send for, call in; *es lässt sich machen* it can be done; *lass alles so, wie (wo) es ist* leave everything as (where) it is; *er kann das Rauchen etc nicht lassen* he can't stop smoking etc; *lass das!* stop it! → *grüßen, kommen*

lässig ['lɛsɪç] adj casual; careless

Last [last] f (-; -en) load, burden, weight (all a. fig); *j-m zur Last fallen* be a burden to s.o.; *j-m et. zur Last legen* charge s.o. with s.th.

lasten ['lastən] v/i (ge-, h) *lasten auf* (dat) a. fig weigh or rest (up)on

'**Lastenaufzug** m freight elevator, Br goods lift

Laster[1] ['lastɐ] m (-s; -) → *Lastwagen*

'**Laster**[2] n (-s; -) vice

lästern ['lɛstɐn] v/i (ge-, h) *lästern über (acc)* run down

lästig ['lɛstɪç] adj troublesome, annoying;

(*j-m*) *lästig sein* be a nuisance (to s.o.)

'**Lastkahn** *m* barge

Lasttier *n* pack animal

Lastwagen *m* MOT truck, *Br a.* lorry

Lastwagenfahrer *m* MOT truck (*Br a.* lorry) driver, trucker

Latein [la'tain] *n* (-*s*; *no pl*) Latin

La'teina,merika Latin America

La'teinameri,kaner(in), **la'teinameri,kanisch** *adj* Latin American

la'teinisch *adj* Latin

Laterne [la'tɛrnə] *f* (-; -*n*) lantern; streetlight

La'ternenpfahl *m* lamppost

Latte ['latə] *f* (-; -*n*) lath; pale; SPORT bar

'**Lattenzaun** *m* paling, picket fence

Lätzchen ['lɛtsçən] *n* (-*s*; -) bib

Laub [laup] *n* (-[*e*]*s*; *no pl*) foliage, leaves

'**Laubbaum** *m* deciduous tree

Laube ['laubə] *f* (-; -*n*) arbo(u)r

'**Laubfrosch** *m* ZO tree frog

'**Laubsäge** *f* fretsaw

Lauch [laux] *m* (-[*e*]*s*; -*e*) BOT leek

Lauer ['lauɐ] *f*: *auf der Lauer liegen or sein* lie in wait

'**lauern** *v/i* (*ge-*, *h*) lurk; *lauern auf* (*acc*) lie in wait for

Lauf [lauf] *m* (-[*e*]*s*; *Läufe* ['lɔyfə]) run; course; *gun*: barrel; *im Lauf(e) der Zeit* in the course of time

Laufbahn *f* career

Laufdiszi,plin *f* SPORT track event

laufen ['laufən] *v/i and v/t* (*irr*, *ge-*, *sein*) run (*a.* TECH, MOT, ECON); walk; *fig* work, run; *j-n laufen lassen* let s.o. go; let s.o. off

laufend 1. *fig adj* present, current (*a.* ECON); continual; *auf dem Laufenden sein* be up to date; **2.** *adv* continuously; regularly; always

'**laufenlassen** *v/t* (*irr*, *lassen*, *sep*, *no -ge-*, *h* → *laufen*

Läufer ['lɔyfɐ] *m* (-*s*; -) runner (*a. carpet*); *chess*: bishop

'**Läuferin** *f* (-; -*nen*) runner

'**Laufgitter** *n* playpen

Laufmasche *f* run, *Br* ladder

Laufschritt *m*: *im Laufschritt* on the double

Laufschuhe *pl* walking shoes; SPORT trainers

Laufsteg *m* footbridge; TECH, *fashion*: catwalk; MAR gangway

Lauge ['laugə] *f* (-; -*n*) suds; CHEM lye

Laune ['launə] *f* (-; -*n*) mood, temper; *gute (schlechte) Laune haben* be in a good (bad) mood *or* temper

launenhaft, '**launisch** *adj* moody; bad--tempered

Laus [laus] *f* (-; *Läuse* ['lɔyzə]) ZO louse

Lauschangriff ['lauʃ-] *m* bugging operation

lauschen ['lauʃən] *v/i* (*ge-*, *h*) listen (*dat* to); eavesdrop

lauschig ['lauʃɪç] *adj* snug, cozy, *Br* cosy

laut[1] [laut] **1.** *adj* loud; noisy; **2.** *adv* loud(ly); *laut vorlesen* read (out) aloud; (*sprich*) *lauter, bitte!* speak up, please!

laut[2] *prp* (*gen or dat*) according to

Laut *m* (-[*e*]*s*; -*e*) sound, noise

lauten ['lautən] *v/i* (*ge-*, *h*) read; be

läuten ['lɔytən] *v/i and v/t* (*ge-*, *h*) ring; *es läutet* (*an der Tür*) the (door)bell is ringing

lauter ['lautɐ] *adv* sheer (*nonsense etc*); nothing but; (so) many

'**lautlos** *adj* silent, soundless; hushed

'**Lautschrift** *f* phonetic transcription

'**Lautsprecher** *m* TECH (loud)speaker

'**Lautstärke** *f* loudness, ELECTR *a.* (sound) volume; *mit voller Lautstärke* (at) full blast

Lautstärkeregler *m* volume control

lauwarm ['lau-] *adj* lukewarm (*a. fig*)

Lava ['la:va] *f* (-; *Laven*) GEOL lava

Lavabo [la'va:bo] *Swiss n* → *Waschbecken*

Lavendel [la'vɛndəl] *m* (-*s*; -) BOT lavender

Lawine [la'vi:nə] *f* (-; -*n*) avalanche

Lazarett [latsa'rɛt] *n* (-[*e*]*s*; -*e*) (military) hospital

leben ['le:bən] (*ge-*, *h*) **1.** *v/i* live; be alive; *von et. leben* live on s.th.; **2.** *v/t* live

'**Leben** *n* (-*s*; -) life; *am Leben bleiben* stay alive; survive; *am Leben sein* be alive; *ums Leben bringen* kill; *sich das Leben nehmen* take one's (own) life, commit suicide; *ums Leben kommen* lose one's life, be killed; *um sein Leben laufen* (*kämpfen*) run (fight) for one's life; *das tägliche Leben* everyday life; *mein Leben lang* all my life

'**lebend** *adj* living

lebendig [le'bɛndɪç] *adj* living, alive; *fig* lively

'**Lebensabend** *m* old age, the last years of one's life

Lebensbedingungen *pl* living conditions

Lebensdauer *f* life-span; TECH (service) life

Lebenserfahrung *f* experience of life

Lebenserwartung *f* life expectancy

'**lebensfähig** *adj* MED viable (*a. fig*)

'**Lebensgefahr** *f* mortal danger; *in (unter) Lebensgefahr* in danger (at the risk) of one's life

'**lebensgefährlich** *adj* dangerous (to life),

L

perilous

'**lebensgroß** *adj* life-size(d)

'**Lebensgröße** *f*: **e-e Statue in Lebensgröße** a life-size(d) statue

'**Lebenshaltungskosten** *pl* cost of living

'**lebenslänglich 1.** *adj* lifelong; **lebenslängliche Freiheitsstrafe** JUR life sentence; **2.** *adv* for life

'**Lebenslauf** *m* personal record, curriculum vitae

'**lebenslustig** *adj* fond of life

'**Lebensmittel** *pl* food(stuffs); groceries

Lebensmittelgeschäft *n* grocery, supermarket

'**lebensmüde** *adj* tired of life

'**Lebensnotwendigkeit** *f* vital necessity

Lebensretter(in) lifesaver, rescuer

Lebensstandard *m* standard of living

Lebensunterhalt *m* livelihood; **s-n Lebensunterhalt verdienen** earn one's living (**als** as; **mit** out of, by)

Lebensversicherung *f* life insurance

Lebensweise *f* way of life

'**lebenswichtig** *adj* vital, essential

'**Lebenszeichen** *n* sign of life

'**Lebenszeit** *f* lifetime; **auf Lebenszeit** for life

Leber ['leːbɐ] *f* (-; -*n*) ANAT liver

Leberfleck *m* mole

Lebertran *m* cod-liver oil

'**Lebewesen** *n* living being, creature

lebhaft ['leːphaft] *adj* lively; heavy (*traffic etc*)

'**Lebkuchen** *m* gingerbread

'**leblos** *adj* lifeless (*a. fig*)

'**Lebzeiten** *pl*: **zu s-n Lebzeiten** in his lifetime

lechzen ['lɛçtsən] *v/i* (*ge-*, *h*) **lechzen nach** thirst for

leck [lɛk] *adj* leaking, leaky

Leck *n* (-[*e*]*s*; -*s*) leak

lecken[1] ['lɛkən] *v/t and v/i* (*ge-*, *h*) *a.* **lecken an** (*dat*) lick

'**lecken**[2] *v/i* (*ge-*, *h*) leak

lecker ['lɛkɐ] *adj* delicious, tasty, F yummy

'**Leckerbissen** *m* delicacy, treat (*a. fig*)

Leder ['leːdɐ] *n* (-*s*; -) leather

'**ledern** *adj* leather(n)

'**Lederwaren** *pl* leather goods

ledig ['leːdɪç] *adj* single, unmarried

lediglich ['leːdɪklɪç] *adv* only, merely

Lee [leː] *f* (-; *no pl*) MAR lee; **nach Lee** leeward

leer [leːɐ] **1.** *adj* empty (*a. fig*); vacant (*house etc*); blank (*page etc*); ELECTR dead, *Br* flat; **leer stehend** unoccupied, vacant; **2.** *adv*: **leer laufen** TECH idle

Leere ['leːrə] *f* (-; *no pl*) emptiness (*a. fig*)

'**leeren** *v/t and v/refl* (*ge-*, *h*) empty

'**Leergut** *n* empties

'**Leerlauf** *m* TECH idling; neutral (gear); *fig* running on the spot

'**Leertaste** *f* space bar

'**Leerung** *f* (-; -*en*) *post* collection

legal [le'gaːl] *adj* legal, lawful

legalisieren [legali'ziːrən] *v/t* (*no -ge-*, *h*) legalize

Legali'sierung *f* (-; -*en*) legalization

Legasthenie [legaste'niː] *f* (-; -*n*) PSYCH dyslexia, F word blindness

Legastheniker [legas'teːnikɐ] *m* (-*s*; -), **Legas'thenikerin** *f* (-; -*nen*) PSYCH dyslexic

legen ['leːgən] *v/t and v/i* (*ge-*, *h*) lay (*a. eggs*); place, put; set (*hair*); **sich legen** lie down; *fig* calm down; *pain*: wear off

Legende [le'gɛndə] *f* (-; -*n*) legend

leger [le'ʒeːɐ] *adj* casual, informal

Legislative [legɪsla'tiːvə] *f* (-; -*n*) legislative power

legitim [legi'tiːm] *adj* legitimate

Lehm [leːm] *m* (-[*e*]*s*; -*e*) loam; clay

'**lehmig** ['leːmɪç] *adj* loamy, F muddy

Lehne ['leːnə] *f* (-; -*n*) back(rest); arm(-rest)

'**lehnen** *v/t and v/i* lean (*a.* **sich lehnen**) rest (**an** *acc*, **gegen** against; **auf** *acc* on); **sich aus dem Fenster lehnen** lean out of the window

'**Lehnsessel** *m*, '**Lehnstuhl** *m* armchair, easy chair

Lehrbuch ['leːɐ-] *n* textbook

Lehre ['leːrə] *f* (-; -*n*) science; theory; REL, POL teachings, doctrine; moral; ECON apprenticeship; **in der Lehre sein** be apprenticed (**bei** to); **das wird ihm e-e Lehre sein** that will teach him a lesson

'**lehren** *v/t* (*ge-*, *h*) teach, instruct; show

Lehrer ['leːrɐ] *m* (-*s*; -) teacher, instructor, *Br a.* master

Lehrerausbildung *f* teacher training

Lehrerin ['leːrərɪn] *f* (-; -*nen*) (lady) teacher, *Br a.* mistress

'**Lehrerkol,legium** *n* (teaching) staff

Lehrerzimmer *n* staff *or* teachers' room

'**Lehrgang** *m* course (of instruction *or* study); training course

Lehrherr *m* master

Lehrjahr *n* year (of apprenticeship)

Lehrling ['leːɐlɪŋ] *m* (-*s*; -*e*) apprentice, trainee

'**Lehrmeister** *m*, **Lehrmeisterin** *f* master; *fig* teacher

Lehrmittel *pl* teaching aids

Lehrplan *m* curriculum, syllabus

Lehrprobe *f* demonstration lesson

'**lehrreich** *adj* informative, instructive

'**Lehrstelle** *f* apprenticeship; vacancy for an apprentice
Lehrstuhl *m* professorship
Lehrtochter *Swiss f* apprentice
Lehrvertrag *m* indenture(s)
Lehrzeit *f* apprenticeship
Leib [laip] *m* (-[e]*s*; *Leiber* ['laibɐ]) body; belly, ANAT abdomen; stomach; *bei lebendigem Leibe* alive; *mit Leib und Seele* (with) heart and soul
Leibeserziehung ['laibəs-] *f* PED physical education, ABBR PE
Leibeskräfte *pl*: *aus Leibeskräften* with all one's might
'**Leibgericht** *n* GASTR favo(u)rite dish
leibhaftig [laip'haftɪç] *adj*: *der leibhaftige Teufel* the devil incarnate; *leibhaftiges Ebenbild* living image; *ich sehe ihn noch leibhaftig vor mir* I can see him (before me) now
'**leiblich** *adj* physical
'**Leibrente** *f* life annuity
Leibwache *f*, **Leibwächter** *m* bodyguard
Leibwäsche *f* underwear
Leiche ['laiçə] *f* (-; -*n*) (dead) body, corpse
'**leichen'blass** *adj* deadly pale
'**Leichenhalle** *f* mortuary
Leichenschauhaus *n* morgue
Leichenverbrennung *f* cremation
Leichenwagen *m* hearse
leicht [laiçt] *adj* light (*a. fig*); easy, simple; slight, minor; TECH light(weight); *möglich* quite possible; *leicht gekränkt* easily offended; *es fällt mir* (*nicht*) *leicht* (*zu inf*) I find it easy (difficult) (to *inf*); *das ist leicht gesagt* it's not as easy as that; *es geht leicht kaputt* it breaks easily; *leicht verständlich* easy to understand
'**Leichtath,let** *m* SPORT (track-and-field) athlete
Leichtath,letik *f* SPORT track and field (events), athletics
Leichtath,letin *f* SPORT (track-and-field) athlete
Leichtgewicht *n* SPORT lightweight
'**leichtgläubig** *adj* credulous
Leichtigkeit ['laiçtɪçkait] *f*: *mit Leichtigkeit* easily, with ease
'**leichtlebig** [-le:bɪç] *adj* happy-go-lucky
'**Leichtme,tall** *n* light metal
'**leichtnehmen** *v/t* (*irr*, **nehmen**, *sep*, *-ge-*, *h*): *et. leichtnehmen* not worry about s.th.; make light of s.th.; *nimm's leichtnehmen!* never mind!, don't worry about it!
'**Leichtsinn** *m* (-[e]*s*; *no pl*) carelessness; recklessness
'**leichtsinnig** *adj* careless; reckless

'**leichtverständlich** *adj* → **leicht**
Leid [lait] *n* (-[e]*s*; *no pl*) sorrow, grief; pain; *es tut mir Leid* I'm sorry (*um* for; *wegen* about; *dass ich zu spät komme* for being late)
leiden ['laidən] *v/t and v/i* (*irr*, *ge-*, *h*) suffer (*an dat*, *unter dat* from); *j-n gut leiden können* like s.o.; *ich kann … nicht leiden* I don't like …; I can't stand …
'**Leiden** *n* (-*s*; -) suffering(s); MED disease
'**Leidenschaft** *f* (-; -*en*) passion
'**leidenschaftlich** *adj* passionate; vehement
'**Leidensgenosse** *m*, '**Leidensgenossin** *f* fellow sufferer
leider ['laidɐ] *adv* unfortunately; *leider ja* (*nein*) I'm afraid so (not)
'**leidlich** *adj* passable, F so-so
'**Leidtragende** *m*, *f* (-*n*; -*n*) mourner; *er ist der Leidtragende dabei* he is the one who suffers for it
'**Leidwesen** *n*: *zu m-m Leidwesen* to my regret
Leierkasten ['laiɐ-] *m* barrel organ
Leierkastenmann *m* organ grinder
leiern ['laiɐn] *v/i and v/t* (*ge-*, *h*) crank (up); *fig* drone
Leihbücherei ['lai-] *f* public library
leihen ['laiən] *v/t* (*irr*, *ge-*, *h*) lend; rent (*Br* hire) out; borrow (*von* from); rent, hire
'**Leihgebühr** *f* rental, lending fee
Leihhaus *n* pawnshop, pawnbroker's (shop)
Leihmutter F *f* surrogate mother
Leihwagen *m* MOT rented (*Br* hire) car
'**leihweise** *adv* on loan
Leim [laim] *m* (-[e]*s*; -*e*), **leimen** ['laimən] *v/t* (*ge-*, *h*) glue
Leine ['lainə] *f* (-; -*n*) line; lead, leash
Leinen ['lainən] *n* (-*s*; -) linen; canvas; *in Leinen gebunden* clothbound
'**Leinenschuh** *m* canvas shoe
'**Leinsamen** *m* BOT linseed
Leintuch *n* (linen) sheet
Leinwand *f* linen; PAINT canvas; screen
leise ['laizə] *adj* quiet, *a.* low, soft (*voice*, *a. music etc*); *fig* slight, faint; *leiser stellen* turn (the volume) down
Leiste ['laistə] *f* (-; -*n*) ledge; ANAT groin
'**leisten** *v/t* (*ge-*, *h*) do, work; achieve, accomplish; render (*service etc*); take (*oath*); *gute Arbeit leisten* do a good job; *sich et. leisten* treat o.s. to s.th.; *ich kann es mir* (*nicht*) *leisten* I can('t) afford it
'**Leistung** *f* (-; -*en*) performance; achievement, PED *a.* (piece of) work, result, TECH *a.* output; service; benefit
'**Leistungsdruck** *m* (-[e]*s*; *no pl*) pressure,

stress
'**leistungsfähig** *adj* efficient; (physically) fit
'**Leistungsfähigkeit** *f* (-; *no pl*) efficiency (*a.* TECH, ECON); fitness
'**Leistungskon,trolle** *f* (achievement *or* proficiency) test
Leistungskurs *m* PED *appr* special subject
Leistungssport *m* competitive sport(s)
Leitar,tikel ['lait-] *m* editorial, *esp Br* leader, leading article
leiten ['laitən] *v/t* (*ge-, h*) lead, guide (*a. fig*), conduct (*a.* PHYS, MUS); run (*a.* PED), be in charge of, manage; TV *etc* direct; host
leitend *adj* leading; PHYS conductive; *leitende Stellung* key position; *leitender Angestellter* executive
Leiter[1] ['laitɐ] *f* (-; *-n*) ladder
'**Leiter**[2] *m* (*-s; -*) leader; conductor (*a.* PHYS, MUS); ECON *etc* head, manager; chairman; → *Schulleiter*
Leiterin ['laitərɪn] *f* (-; *-nen*) leader; head; chairwoman
'**Leitfaden** *m* manual, guide
Leitplanke *f* MOT guardrail, *Br* crash barrier
Leitspruch *m* motto
'**Leitung** *f* (-; *-en*) ECON management; head office; administration; chairmanship; organization; THEA *etc* direction; TECH main, pipe(s); ELECTR, TEL line; *die Leitung haben* be in charge; *unter der Leitung von* MUS conducted by
'**Leitungsrohr** *n* pipe
'**Leitungswasser** *n* tap water
Lektion [lɛk'tsjoːn] *f* (-; *-en*) lesson
Lektüre [lɛk'tyːrə] *f* (-; *-n*) reading (matter); PED reader
Lende ['lɛndə] *f* (-; *-n*) ANAT loin; GASTR sirloin
lenken ['lɛŋkən] *v/t* (*ge-, h*) steer, drive; *fig* guide *s.o.*; direct (*traffic etc*)
Lenker ['lɛŋkɐ] *m* (*-s; -*) handlebar
'**Lenkrad** *n* MOT steering wheel
'**Lenkung** *f* (-; *-en*) MOT steering (system)
Leopard [leo'part] *m* (*-en; -en*) ZO leopard
Lerche ['lɛrçə] *f* (-; *-n*) ZO lark
lernen ['lɛrnən] *v/t and v/i* (*ge-, h*) learn; study; *er lernt leicht* he is a quick learner; *lesen lernen* learn (how) to read
'**Lernmittelfreiheit** *f* free books *etc*
lesbar ['leːsbaːɐ] *adj* readable
Lesbierin ['lɛsbjərɪn] *f* (-; *-nen*), **lesbisch** ['lɛsbɪʃ] *adj* lesbian
Lesebuch ['leːzə-] *n* reader
'**Leselampe** *f* reading lamp
lesen ['leːzən] *v/i and v/t* (*irr, ge-, h*) read; AGR harvest

'**lesenswert** *adj* worth reading
Leser ['leːzɐ] *m* (*-s; -*) reader
'**Leseratte** F *f* bookworm
'**Leserbrief** *m* letter to the editor
'**Leserin** *f* (-; *-nen*) reader
'**leserlich** *adj* legible
'**Lesestoff** *m* reading matter
'**Lesezeichen** *n* bookmark
'**Lesung** *f* (-; *-en*) reading (*a.* PARL)
Letzt [lɛtst] *f*: *zu guter Letzt* in the end
letzte ['lɛtstə] *adj* last; latest; *zum letzten Mal(e)* for the last time; *in letzter Zeit* recently; *als Letzter ankommen etc* arrive *etc* last; *Letzter sein* be last (*a.* SPORT); *das ist das Letzte!* that's the limit!
'**letztens** *adv* finally; *erst letztens* just recently
letztere ['lɛtstərə] *adj* latter; *der (die, das) Letztere* the latter
Leuchtanzeige ['lɔyçt-] *f* luminous *or* LED display light
leuchten ['lɔyçtən] *v/i* (*ge-, h*) shine; glow
'**Leuchten** *n* (*-s; no pl*) shining; glow
'**leuchtend** *adj* shining (*a. fig*); bright
Leuchter ['lɔyçtɐ] *m* (*-s; -*) candlestick
'**Leuchtfarbe** *f* luminous paint
Leuchtre,klame *f* neon sign(s)
Leucht(stoff)röhre *f* ELECTR fluorescent lamp
Leuchtturm *m* lighthouse
Leuchtziffer *f* luminous figure
leugnen ['lɔygnən] *v/t and v/i* (*ge-, h*) deny (*et. getan zu haben* having done s.th.)
Leute ['lɔytə] *pl* people, F folks
Leutnant ['lɔytnant] *m* (*-s; -s*) MIL second lieutenant
Lexikon ['lɛksikɔn] *n* (*-s; -ka, -ken*) encyclop(a)edia; dictionary
Libelle [li'bɛlə] *f* (-; *-n*) ZO dragonfly
liberal [libe'raːl] *adj* liberal
Libero ['liːbero] *m* (*-s; -s*) soccer: sweeper
licht ['lɪçt] *adj* bright; *fig* lucid
Licht *n* (*-[e]s; -er* ['lɪçtɐ]) a) light, b) (*no pl*) brightness; *Licht machen* switch *or* turn on the light(s)
'**Lichtbild** *n* photo(graph); slide
Lichtbildervortrag *m* slide lecture
Lichtblick *m* ray of hope; bright moment
'**lichtempfindlich** *adj* sensitive to light; PHOT sensitive
'**Lichtempfindlichkeit** *f* (light) sensitivity; PHOT speed
lichten ['lɪçtən] *v/t* (*ge-, h*) clear; *den Anker lichten* MAR weigh anchor; *sich lichten* get thin(ner); *fig* be thinning (out)
'**Lichtgeschwindigkeit** *f* speed of light
Lichtgriffel *m* light pen
Lichthupe *f* MOT (headlight) flash(er); *die Lichthupe betätigen* flash one's lights

Lichtjahr *n* light year
Lichtma,schine *f* MOT generator
Lichtorgel *f* colo(u)r organ
Lichtpause *f* blueprint
Lichtschacht *m* well
Lichtschalter *m* (light) switch
'**lichtscheu** *fig adj* shady
'**Lichtschutzfaktor** *m* sun protection factor, SPF
Lichtstrahl *m* ray *or* beam of light (*a. fig*)
'**Lichtung** *f* (-; -*en*) clearing
Lid [li:t] *n* (-[e]*s*; *Lider* ['li:dɐ]) ANAT (eye)-lid
Lidschatten *m* eye shadow
lieb [li:p] *adj* dear; sweet; nice, kind; good; **lieb gewinnen** get fond of; **lieb haben** love, be fond of
Liebe ['li:bə] *f* (-; *no pl*) love (**zu** of, for); **aus Liebe zu** out of love for; **Liebe auf den ersten Blick** love at first sight
'**lieben** *v/t* (*ge-*, *h*) love, *a.* be in love with *s.o.*; make love to
'**liebenswert** *adj* lovable, charming, sweet
'**liebenswürdig** *adj* kind
'**Liebenswürdigkeit** *f* (-; *no pl*) kindness
lieber ['li:bɐ] *adv* rather, sooner; **lieber haben** prefer, like better; **ich möchte lieber (nicht)** ... I'd rather (not) ...; **du solltest lieber (nicht)** ... you had better (not) ...
'**Liebesbrief** *m* love letter
Liebeserklärung *f*: **j-m e-e Liebeserklärung machen** declare one's love to s.o.
Liebeskummer *m*: **Liebeskummer haben** be lovesick
Liebespaar *n* lovers
'**liebevoll** *adj* loving, affectionate
'**liebgewinnen** *v/t* (*irr*, **gewinnen**, *sep*, *h*) → **lieb**
'**liebhaben** *v/t* (*irr*, **haben**, *sep*, -*ge-*, *h*) → **lieb**
Liebhaber ['li:pha:bɐ] *m* (-*s*; -) lover (*a. fig*); **Liebhaber...** *in cpds* ...*preis*, ...*stück etc*: collector's ...
Liebhaberei [li:pha:bə'rai] *f* (-; -*en*) hobby
Liebkosung [li:p'ko:zʊŋ] *f* (-; -*en*) caress
'**lieblich** *adj* lovely, charming, sweet (*a. wine*)
'**Liebling** *m* (-*s*; -*e*) darling; favo(u)rite
'**Lieblings...** *in cpds mst* favo(u)rite
'**lieblos** *adj* unloving, cold; unkind (*words etc*); *fig* careless
Lied [li:t] *n* (-[e]*s*; -*er* ['li:dɐ]) song; tune
liederlich ['li:dɐlɪç] *adj* slovenly, sloppy
Liedermacher ['li:dɐ-] *m* (-*s*; -) singer-songwriter
lief [li:f] *pret of* **laufen**
Lieferant [lifə'rant] *m* (-*en*; -*en*) ECON sup-

plier
lieferbar ['li:fɐba:ɐ] *adj* ECON available
'**Lieferfrist** *f* ECON term of delivery
liefern ['li:fɐn] *v/t* (*ge-*, *h*) ECON deliver; **j-m et. liefern** supply s.o. with s.th.
Lieferung ['li:fərʊŋ] *f* (-; -*en*) ECON delivery; supply
'**Lieferwagen** *m* MOT (delivery) van
Liege ['li:gə] *f* (-; -*n*) couch
liegen ['li:gən] *v/i* (*irr*, *ge-*, *h*) lie, *a.* be (situated); (*krank*) **im Bett liegen** be (ill) in bed; **nach Osten** (**der Straße**) **liegen** face east (the street); **daran liegt es(, dass)** that's (the reason) why; **es (er) liegt mir nicht** F it (he) is not my cup of tea; **mir liegt viel** (**wenig**) **daran** it means a lot (doesn't mean much) to me; **liegen bleiben** stay in bed; be left behind; **liegen lassen** leave (behind); F **j-n links liegen lassen** ignore s.o., give s.o. the cold shoulder
'**liegenbleiben** *v/i* (*irr*, **bleiben**, *sep*, -*ge-*, *sein*) → **liegen**
liegenbleibenlassen *v/i* (*irr*, **lassen**, *sep*, *no* -*ge-*, *h*) → **liegen**
'**Liegesitz** *m* reclining seat
Liegestuhl *m* deckchair
Liegestütz *m* (-*es*; -*e*) SPORT push-up, *Br* press-up
Liegewagen *m* RAIL couchette
lieh [li:] *pret of* **leihen**
ließ [li:s] *pret of* **lassen**
Lift [lɪft] *m* (-[e]*s*; -*e*, -*s*) elevator, *Br* lift; ski lift
Liga ['li:ga] *f* (-; *Ligen*) league, SPORT *a.* division
Likör [li'kø:ɐ] *m* (-*s*; -*e*) liqueur
lila ['li:la] *adj* purple, violet
Lilie ['li:ljə] *f* (-; -*n*) BOT lily
Liliputaner [lilipu'ta:nɐ] *m* (-*s*; -) dwarf, midget
Limonade [limo'na:də] *f* (-; -*n*) pop; lemon soda, *Br* lemonade
Limousine [limu'zi:nə] *f* (-; -*n*) MOT sedan, *Br* saloon car; limousine
Linde ['lɪndə] *f* (-; -*n*) BOT lime (tree), linden
lindern ['lɪndɐn] *v/t* (*ge-*, *h*) relieve, ease, alleviate
Linderung ['lɪndərʊŋ] *f* (-; *no pl*) relief, alleviation
Lineal [line'a:l] *n* (-*s*; -*e*) ruler
Linie ['li:njə] *f* (-; -*n*) line; **auf s-e Linie achten** watch one's weight
'**Linienflug** *m* AVIAT scheduled flight
Linienrichter *m* SPORT linesman
'**linientreu** *adj* POL: **linientreu sein** follow the party line
linieren [li'ni:rən], **liniieren** [lini'i:rən] *v/t*

(*no -ge-, h*) rule, line

linke ['lɪŋkə] *adj* left (*a.* POL); *auf der lin-ken Seite* on the left(-hand side)

'**Linke** *m, f* (*-n; -n*) POL leftist, left-winger

linkisch ['lɪŋkɪʃ] *adj* awkward, clumsy

links [lɪŋks] *adv* on the left (*a.* POL); on the wrong side; *nach links* (to the) left; *links von* to the left of

Links... *in cpds* ...*verkehr etc*: left-hand

Links'außen *m* (*-; -*) SPORT outside left, left wing

'**Linkshänder** [-hɛndɐ] *m* (*-s; -*), '**Links-händerin** *f* (*-; -nen*) left-hander

'**Linksradi,kale** *m, f* (*-n; -n*) POL left-wing extremist

Linse ['lɪnzə] *f* (*-; -n*) BOT lentil; OPT lens

Lippe ['lɪpə] *f* (*-; -n*) ANAT lip

'**Lippenstift** *m* lipstick

liquidieren [likvi'diːrən] *v/t* (*no -ge-, h*) ECON liquidate (*a.* POL)

lispeln ['lɪspəln] *v/i* (*ge-, h*) (have a) lisp

List [lɪst] *f* (*-; -en*) a) trick, b) (*no pl*) cunning

Liste ['lɪstə] *f* (*-; -n*) list; roll

listig ['lɪstɪç] *adj* cunning, tricky, sly

Liter ['liːtɐ] *n, m* (*-s; -*) liter, *Br* litre

literarisch [lɪtə'raːrɪʃ] *adj* literary

Literatur [lɪtəra'tuːɐ] *f* (*-; -en*) literature

Literatur... *in cpds* ...*kritik etc*: *mst* literary

Litfaßsäule ['lɪtfas-] *f* advertising pillar

litt [lɪt] *pret of* **leiden**

Lizenz [li'tsɛnts] *f* (*-; -en*) license, *Br* licence

Lkw, LKW ['ɛlkave] *m* (*-[s]; -*) ABBR *of* **Lastkraftwagen** truck, *Br a.* lorry

Lob [loːp] *n* (*-[e]s; no pl*), **loben** ['loːbən] *v/t* (*ge-, h*) praise

'**lobenswert** *adj* praiseworthy, laudable

Loch [lɔx] *n* (*-[e]s; Löcher* ['lœçɐ]) hole (*a. fig*); puncture

lochen ['lɔxən] *v/t* (*ge-, h*) punch (*a.* TECH)

Locher ['lɔxɐ] *m* (*-s; -*) punch

Locke ['lɔkə] *f* (*-; -n*) curl; lock

locken¹ ['lɔkən] *v/t and v/refl* (*ge-, h*) curl

locken² *v/t* (*ge-, h*) lure, entice, *fig a.* attract, tempt

'**Lockenkopf** *m* curly head

Lockenwickler [-vɪklɐ] *m* (*-s; -*) curler, roller

locker ['lɔkɐ] *adj* loose; slack; *fig* relaxed

'**lockern** *v/t* (*ge-, h*) loosen, slacken; relax (*a. fig*); *sich lockern* loosen, (be)come loose; SPORT limber up; *fig* relax

lockig ['lɔkɪç] *adj* curly, curled

'**Lockvogel** *m* decoy (*a. fig*)

lodern ['loːdɐn] *v/i* (*ge-, h*) blaze, flare

Löffel ['lœfəl] *m* (*-s; -*) spoon; ladle

'**löffeln** *v/t* (*ge-, h*) spoon up

log [loːk] *pret of* **lügen**

Logbuch ['lɔk-] *n* MAR log

Loge ['loːʒə] *f* (*-; -n*) THEA box; lodge

Logik ['loːgɪk] *f* (*-; no pl*) logic

logisch ['loːgɪʃ] *adj* logical

'**logischer'weise** *adv* obviously

Lohn [loːn] *m* (*-[e]s; Löhne* ['løːnə]) ECON wages, pay(ment); *fig* reward

Lohnempfänger *m* wageworker, *Br* wage earner

lohnen ['loːnən] *v/refl* (*ge-, h*) be worth (-while), pay; *es (die Mühe) lohnt sich* it's worth it (the trouble); *das Buch (der Film) lohnt sich* the book (film) is worth reading (seeing)

lohnend *adj* paying; *fig* rewarding

'**Lohnerhöhung** *f* raise, *Br* increase in wages, rise

Lohnsteuer *f* income tax

Lohnstopp *m* wage freeze

Lohntüte *f* pay packet

Loipe ['lɔypə] *f* (*-; -n*) (cross-country) course

Lokal [lo'kaːl] *n* (*-s; -e*) restaurant; bar, saloon, *esp Br* pub

Lo'kal... *in cpds mst* local

Lok [lɔk] *f* (*-; -s*) → **Lokomotive**

Lokführer *m* RAIL engineer, *Br* train driver

Lokomotive [lokomo'tiːvə] *f* (*-; -n*) RAIL engine

Lorbeer ['lɔrbeːɐ] *m* (*-s; -en*) BOT laurel; GASTR bay leaf

Lore ['loːrə] *f* (*-; -n*) TECH tipcart

los [loːs] *adj and adv* off; *dog etc*: loose; *los sein* be rid of; *was ist los?* what's the matter?, F what's up?; what's going on (here)?; *hier ist nicht viel los* there's nothing much going on here; F *da ist was los!* that's where the action is!; F *al-so los!* okay, let's go!

Los [loːs] *n* (*-es; -e* ['loːzə]) lot, *fig a.* fate; (lottery) ticket, number

'**losbinden** *v/t* (*irr, binden, sep, -ge-, h*) untie

Löschblatt ['lœʃ-] *n* blotting paper

löschen ['lœʃən] *v/t* (*ge-, h*) extinguish, put out; quench (*thirst*); blot (*ink*); wipe off *the blackboard*; erase, EDP *a.* delete; slake (*lime*); MAR unload

'**Löschpa,pier** *n* blotting paper

lose ['loːzə] *adj* loose

Lösegeld ['løːzə-] *n* ransom

losen ['loːzən] *v/i* (*ge-, h*) draw lots (*um* for)

lösen ['løːzən] *v/t* (*ge-, h*) undo (*knot etc*); loosen, relax; TECH release; take off; solve (*problem etc*); settle (*conflict etc*); buy, get (*ticket etc*); dissolve (*a.* CHEM);

sich lösen come loose *or* undone; *fig* free o.s. (**von** from)

'**losfahren** *v/i* (*irr*, **fahren**, *sep*, *-ge-*, *sein*) leave; drive off

losgehen *v/i* (*irr*, **gehen**, *sep*, *-ge-*, *sein*) leave; start, begin; *shot etc*: go off; **auf j-n losgehen** go for s.o.; **ich gehe jetzt los** I'm off now

losketten *v/t* (*sep*, *-ge-*, *h*) unchain

loskommen *v/i* (*irr*, **kommen**, *sep*, *-ge-*, *sein*) get away (**von** from)

loslassen *v/t* (*irr*, **lassen**, *sep*, *-ge-*, *h*) let go; **den Hund loslassen auf** (*acc*) set the dog on

loslegen F *v/i* (*sep*, *-ge-*, *h*) get cracking

löslich ['løːslɪç] *adj* CHEM soluble

'**losmachen** *v/t* (*sep*, *-ge-*, *h*) → **lösen**

losreißen *v/t* (*irr*, **reißen**, *sep*, *-ge-*, *h*) tear off; **sich losreißen** break away; *esp fig* tear o.s. away (*both*: **von** from)

lossagen *v/refl* (*sep*, *-ge-*, *h*) **sich lossagen von** break with

losschlagen *v/i* (*irr*, **schlagen**, *sep*, *-ge-*, *h*) strike (**auf j-n** out at s.o.)

losschnallen *v/t* (*sep*, *-ge-*, *h*) unbuckle; **sich losschnallen** MOT, AVIAT unfasten one's seatbelt

losstürzen *v/i* (*sep*, *-ge-*, *sein*) **losstürzen auf** (*acc*) rush at

Losung ['loːzʊŋ] *f* (*-; -en*) MIL password; *fig* slogan

Lösung ['løːzʊŋ] *f* (*-; -en*) solution (*a. fig*); settlement

'**Lösungsmittel** *n* solvent

'**loswerden** *v/t* (*irr*, **werden**, *sep*, *-ge-*, *sein*) get rid of; spend (*money*); lose

'**losziehen** *v/i* (*irr*, **ziehen**, *sep*, *-ge-*, *sein*) set out, take off, march away

Lot [loːt] *n* (*-[e]s; -e*) plumbline

löten ['løːtən] *v/t* (*ge-*, *h*) TECH solder

Lotion [loˈtsjoːn] *f* (*-; -en*) lotion

Lotse ['loːtsə] *m* (*-n; -n*), '**lotsen** *v/t* (*ge-*, *h*) MAR pilot

Lotterie [lɔtəˈriː] *f* (*-; -n*) lottery

Lotteriegewinn *m* prize

Lotterielos *n* lottery ticket

Lotto ['lɔto] *n* (*-s; -s*) lotto, bingo; *Br* national lottery; *in Germany*: Lotto; (**im**) **Lotto spielen** do Lotto

Lottoschein *m* Lotto coupon

Lottoziehung *f* Lotto draw

Löwe ['løːvə] *m* (*-n; -n*) ZO lion; AST Leo; **er ist (ein) Löwe** he's (a) Leo

'**Löwenzahn** *m* BOT dandelion

Löwin ['løːvɪn] *f* (*-; -nen*) ZO lioness

loyal [loaˈjaːl] *adj* loyal, faithful

Luchs [lʊks] *m* (*-es; -e*) ZO lynx

Lücke ['lʏkə] *f* (*-; -n*) gap (*a. fig*)

'**Lückenbüßer** *m* stopgap

'**lückenhaft** *adj* full of gaps; *fig* incomplete

'**lückenlos** *adj* without a gap; *fig* complete

'**Lückentest** *m* PSYCH completion *or* fill-in test

lud [luːt] *pret of* **laden**

Luft [lʊft] *f* (*-; no pl*) air; **an der frischen Luft** (out) in the fresh air; (**frische**) **Luft schöpfen** get a breath of fresh air; **die Luft anhalten** catch (*esp fig a.* hold) one's breath; **tief Luft holen** take a deep breath; **in die Luft sprengen** (F **fliegen**) blow up

'**Luftangriff** *m* air raid

Luftballon *m* balloon

Luftbild *n* aerial photograph *or* view

Luftblase *f* air bubble

Luftbrücke *f* airlift

'**luftdicht** *adj* airtight

'**Luftdruck** *m* (*-[e]s; no pl*) PHYS, TECH air pressure

lüften ['lʏftən] *v/t and v/i* (*ge-*, *h*) air, ventilate; *fig* reveal

'**Luftfahrt** *f* (*-; no pl*) aviation, aeronautics

Luftfeuchtigkeit *f* (atmospheric) humidity

Luftgewehr *n* airgun

'**luftig** *adj* airy; breezy; light (*dress etc*)

'**Luftkissen** *n* air cushion

Luftkissenfahrzeug *n* hovercraft

Luftkrankheit *f* air-sickness

Luftkrieg *m* air warfare

Luftkurort *m* (climatic) health resort

'**luftleer** *adj*: **luftleerer Raum** vacuum

'**Luftlinie** *f*: **50 km Luftlinie** 50 km as the crow flies

Luftpost *f* air mail

Luftpumpe *f* air pump; bicycle pump

Luftröhre *f* ANAT windpipe, trachea

Luftschlange *f* streamer

Luftschloss *n* castle in the air

Luftsprünge *pl*: **Luftsprünge machen vor Freude** jump for joy

'**Lüftung** *f* (*-; -en*) airing; TECH ventilation

'**Luftveränderung** *f* change of air

Luftverkehr *m* air traffic

Luftverschmutzung *f* air pollution

Luftwaffe *f* MIL air force

Luftweg *m*: **auf dem Luftweg** by air

Luftzug *m* draft, *Br* draught

Lüge ['lyːgə] *f* (*-; -n*) lie

'**lügen** *v/i* (*irr*, *ge-*, *h*) lie, tell a lie *or* lies; **das ist gelogen** that's a lie

Lügner(in) ['lyːgnɐ (-nərɪn)] (*-s; -/-; -nen*) liar

'**lügnerisch** [-nərɪʃ] *adj* false

Luke ['luːkə] *f* (*-; -n*) hatch; skylight

Lümmel ['lʏməl] F *m* (*-s; -*) rascal

lumpen ['lʊmpən] F *v/t*: **sich nicht lum-**

L

pen lassen be generous

'**Lumpen** *m* (*-s*; *-*) rag; *in Lumpen* in rags

Lumpenpack F *n sl* bastards

lumpig ['lʊmpɪç] F *adj*: *für lumpige zwei Mark* for a paltry two marks

Lunge ['lʊŋə] *f* (*-*; *-n*) ANAT lungs; (*auf*) *Lunge rauchen* inhale

'**Lungenentzündung** *f* MED pneumonia

Lungenflügel *m* ANAT lung

Lungenzug *m*: *e-n Lungenzug machen* inhale

Lupe ['lu:pə] *f* (*-*; *-n*) magnifying glass; *unter die Lupe nehmen* scrutinize (closely)

Lust [lʊst] *f* (*-*; *Lüste* ['lʏstə]) a) (*no pl*) desire, interest; pleasure, delight, b) lust; *Lust haben auf et.* (*et. zu tun*) feel like (doing) s.th.; *hättest du Lust auszugehen?* would you like to go out?, how about going out?; *ich habe keine Lust* I don't feel like it, I'm not in the mood for it; *die Lust an et. verlieren* (*j-m die Lust an et. nehmen*) (make s.o.) lose

all interest in s.th.

lüstern ['lʏstɐn] *adj* greedy (*nach* for)

lustig ['lʊstɪç] *adj* funny; cheerful; *er ist sehr lustig* he is full of fun; *es war sehr lustig* it was great fun; *sich lustig machen über* (*acc*) make fun of

'**lustlos** *adj* listless, indifferent

'**Lustmord** *m* sex murder

'**Lustspiel** *n* THEA comedy

lutschen ['lʊtʃən] *v/i* and *v/t* (*ge-*, *h*) suck

Luv [lu:f] *f* (*-*; *no pl*) MAR windward, weather side

luxuriös [lʊksu'rjø:s] *adj* luxurious

Luxus ['lʊksʊs] *m* (*-*; *no pl*) luxury

Luxusar,tikel *m* luxury (article)

Luxusausführung *f* deluxe version

Luxusho,tel *n* five-star (*or* luxury) hotel

Lymphdrüse ['lʏmf-] *f* ANAT lymph gland

lynchen ['lʏnçən] *v/t* (*ge-*, *h*) lynch

Lyrik ['ly:rɪk] *f* (*-*; *no pl*) poetry

Lyriker ['ly:rikɐ] *m* (*-s*; *-*), '**Lyrikerin** *f* (*-*; *-nen*) (lyric) poet

lyrisch ['ly:rɪʃ] *adj* lyrical (*a. fig*)

M

machbar ['maxba:ɐ] *adj* feasible

machen ['maxən] *v/t* (*ge-*, *h*) do; make; GASTR make, prepare; fix (*a. fig*); be, come to, amount to; take, pass (*test etc*); make, go on (*a trip etc*); *Hausaufgaben machen* do one's homework; *da* (*-gegen*) *kann man nichts machen* it can't be helped; *mach, was du willst!* do as you please!; (*nun*) *mach mal or schon!* hurry up!, come on *or* along now!; *mach's gut!* take care (of yourself)!, good luck!; (*das*) *macht nichts* it doesn't matter; *mach dir nichts d(a)raus!* never mind!, don't worry!; *das macht mir nichts aus* I don't mind *or* care; *was or wie viel macht das?* how much is it?; *sich et.* (*nichts*) *machen aus* (not) care about; (not) care for

'**Machenschaften** *pl* machinations; *unsaubere Machenschaften* sleaze (*esp* POL)

Macher ['maxɐ] *m* (*-s*; *-*) man of action, doer

Macho ['matʃo] *m* (*-s*; *-s*) macho

Macht [maxt] *f* (*-*; *Mächte* ['mɛçtə]) power (*über acc* of); *an der Macht* in power;

mit aller Macht with all one's might

'**Machthaber** [-ha:bɐ] *m* (*-s*; *-*) POL ruler

mächtig ['mɛçtɪç] *adj* powerful, mighty (*a. F*); enormous, huge

'**Machtkampf** *m* struggle for power

'**machtlos** *adj* powerless

'**Machtmissbrauch** *m* abuse of power

Machtpoli,tik *f* power politics

Machtübernahme *f* takeover

Machtwechsel *m* transition of power

Mädchen ['mɛ:tçən] *n* (*-s*; *-*) girl; maid

'**mädchenhaft** *adj* girlish

'**Mädchenname** *m* girl's name; maiden name

Mädchenschule *f* girls' school

Made ['ma:də] *f* (*-*; *-n*) ZO maggot; worm

Mädel ['mɛ:dəl] *n* (*-s*; *-s*) girl

'**madig** *adj* maggoty, worm-eaten; F'**madigmachen** *v/t* (*sep*, *-ge-*, *h*): F *j-m et. madig* spoil s.th. for s.o.

Magazin [maga'tsi:n] *n* (*-s*; *-e*) magazine (*a*. MIL, PHOT, TV); store(room), warehouse

Magd [ma:kt] *f* (*-*; *Mägde* ['mɛ:ktə]) (female) farmhand

Magen ['ma:gən] *m* (*-s*; *Mägen* ['mɛ:gən])

ANAT stomach

Magenbeschwerden *pl* MED stomach trouble

Magengeschwür *n* MED (stomach) ulcer

Magenschmerzen *pl* stomachache

mager ['maːgɐ] *adj* lean, thin, skinny; GASTR low-fat (*cheese*), lean (*meat*), skim (*milk*); *fig* meager, *Br* meagre

Magie [maˈgiː] *f* (-; *no pl*) magic

magisch ['maːgɪʃ] *adj* magic(al)

Magister [maˈgɪstɐ] *m* (-s; -) UNIV Master of Arts *or* Science; *Austrian* → ***Apotheker***

Magistrat [magɪsˈtraːt] *m* (-[e]s; -e) municipal council

Magnet [maˈgneːt] *m* (-[e]s, -en; -e[n]) magnet (*a. fig*)

Magnet... *in cpds* ...band, ...feld, ...nadel *etc*: magnetic ...

mag'netisch *adj* magnetic (*a. fig*)

magnetisieren [magnetiˈziːrən] *v/t* (*no* -ge-, *h*) magnetize

Mahagoni [mahaˈgoːni] *n* (-s; *no pl*) mahogany

mähen ['mɛːən] *v/t* (ge-, *h*) mow; cut; AGR reap

'Mähdrescher [-drɛʃɐ] *m* (-s; -) AGR combine (harvester)

mahlen ['maːlən] *v/t* (*irr*, ge-, *h*) grind; mill

'Mahlzeit *f* (-; -en) meal; feed(ing)

Mähne ['mɛːnə] *f* (-; -n) ZO mane (*a.* F)

mahnen ['maːnən] *v/t* (ge-, *h*) remind; ECON send *s.o.* a reminder

'Mahngebühr *f* reminder fee

'Mahnmal *n* memorial

'Mahnung *f* (-; -en) reminder

Mai [mai] *m* (-[e]s; -e) May; *der Erste Mai* May Day

Maibaum *m* maypole

Maiglöckchen *n* BOT lily of the valley

Maikäfer *m* ZO cockchafer

Mais [mais] *m* (-es; -e) BOT corn, *Br* maize

Majestät [majɛsˈtɛːt] *f*: *Seine (Ihre, Eure) Majestät* His (Her, Your) Majesty

majes'tätisch *adj* majestic

Majonäse *f* → ***Mayonnaise***

Major [maˈjoːɐ] *m* (-s; -e) MIL major

makaber [maˈkaːbɐ] *adj* macabre

Makel ['maːkəl] *m* (-s; -) blemish (*a. fig*)

mäkelig ['mɛːkəlɪç] F *adj* picky, *esp Br* choos(e)y

'makellos *adj* immaculate (*a. fig*)

mäkeln ['mɛːkəln] F *v/i* (ge-, *h*) carp, pick, nag (*an dat* at)

Makler ['maːklɐ] *m* (-s; -) ECON real estate agent; broker

Maklergebühr *f* fee, commission

'Maklerin *f* (-; -nen) ECON → ***Makler***

mal [maːl] *adv* MATH times, multiplied by;

by; F → *einmal; 12 mal 5 ist (gleich) 60* 12 times *or* multiplied by 5 is *or* equals 60; *ein 7 mal 4 Meter großes Zimmer* a room 7 meters by 4

Mal[1] *n* (-[e]s; -e) time; *zum ersten (letzten) Mal(e)* for the first (last) time; *mit e-m Mal(e)* all of a sudden; *ein für alle Mal(e)* once and for all

Mal[2] *n* mark

malen ['maːlən] *v/t* (ge-, *h*) paint

Maler ['maːlɐ] *m* (-s; -) painter

Malerei [maːləˈrai] *f* (-; -en) painting

Malerin ['maːlərɪn] *f* (-; -nen) (woman) painter

'malerisch *fig adj* picturesque

'Malkasten *m* paintbox

'malnehmen → ***multiplizieren***

Malz [malts] *n* (-es; *no pl*) malt

'Malzbier *n* malt beer

Mama ['mama] F *f* (-; -s) mom(my), *Br* mum(my)

Mammut ['mamʊt] *n* (-s; -e, -s) ZO mammoth

man [man] *indef pron* you, one; they, people; *wie schreibt man das?* how do you spell it?; *man sagt, dass* they *or* people say (that); *man hat mir gesagt* I was told

Manager ['mɛnɪdʒɐ] *m* (-s; -), **'Managerin** *f* (-; -nen) ECON executive; SPORT manager

manch [manç], **mancher** ['mançɐ], **manche** ['mançə], **manches** ['mançəs] *indef pron* (*mst pl*) some; quite a few, many

'manchmal *adv* sometimes, occasionally

Mandant [manˈdant] *m* (-en; -en), **Man'dantin** *f* (-; -nen) JUR client

Mandarine [mandaˈriːnə] *f* (-; -n) BOT tangerine

Mandat [manˈdaːt] *n* (-[e]s; -e) POL mandate; seat

Mandatar [mandaˈtaːɐ] *Austrian m* → ***Abgeordnete***

Mandel ['mandəl] *f* (-; -n) BOT almond; ANAT tonsil

Mandelentzündung *f* MED tonsillitis

Manege [maˈneːʒə] *f* (-; -n) (circus) ring

Mangel[1] ['maŋəl] *m* (-s; *Mängel* ['mɛŋəl]) a) (*no pl*) lack (*an dat* of), shortage, b) TECH defect, fault; shortcoming; *aus Mangel an* (*dat*) for lack of

'Mangel[2] *f* (-; -n) mangle

'mangelhaft *adj* poor (*quality etc*); defective (*goods etc*); PED poor, unsatisfactory, failing

'mangeln *v/t* (ge-, *h*) mangle

'mangels *prp* (*gen*) for lack *or* want of

'Mangelware *f*: *Mangelware sein* be scarce

Manie [maˈniː] *f* (-; -n) mania (*a. fig*)

Manieren [maˈniːrən] *pl* manners

M

manierlich [ma'ni:ɐlıç] *adv*: **sich manierlich betragen** behave (decently)

Manifest [mani'fɛst] *n* (-[e]s; -e) manifesto

manipulieren [manipu'li:rən] *v/t* (*no -ge-, h*) manipulate

Mann [man] *m* (-[e]s; *Männer* ['mɛnɐ]) man; husband

Männchen ['mɛnçən] *n* (-s; -) zo male

'**Manndeckung** *f* sport man-to-man marking

Mannequin ['manəkɛ:] *n* (-s; -s) model

mannigfach ['manıçfax], '**mannigfaltig** *adj* many and various

männlich ['mɛnlıç] *adj* biol male; masculine (*a.* ling)

'**Mannschaft** *f* (-; -en) sport team; mar, aviat crew

Manöver [ma'nø:vɐ] *n* (-s; -), **manövrieren** [manø'vri:rən] *v/i* (*no -ge-, h*) maneuver, *Br* manoeuvre

Mansarde [man'zardə] *f* (-; -n) room *or* apartment in the attic

Manschette [man'ʃɛtə] *f* (-; -n) cuff; tech gasket

Man'schettenknopf *m* cuff-link

Mantel ['mantəl] *m* (-s; *Mäntel* ['mɛntəl]) coat; *tire*: casing, *bicycle*: tire (*Br* tyre) cover; tech jacket, shell

Manuskript [manu'skrıpt] *n* (-[e]s; -e) manuscript; copy

Mappe ['mapə] *f* (-; -n) briefcase; school bag, satchel; folder

Märchen ['mɛ:ɐçən] *n* (-s; -) fairytale (*a. fig*)

Märchenland *n* (-[e]s; *no pl*) fairyland

Marder ['mardɐ] *m* (-s; -) zo marten

Margarine [marga'ri:nə] *f* (-; *no pl*) margarine

Margerite [margə'ri:tə] *f* (-; -n) bot marguerite

Marienkäfer [ma'ri:ən-] *m* zo lady bug, *Br* ladybird

Marihuana [mari'hua:na] *n* (-s; *no pl*) marijuana, *sl* grass

Marihuanaziga,rette *f sl* joint

Marille [ma'rılə] *Austrian f* (-; -n) bot apricot

Marine [ma'ri:nə] *f* (-; -n) mil navy

ma'rineblau *adj* navy blue

Marionette [marjo'nɛtə] *f* (-; -n) puppet (*a. fig*)

Mario'nettenthe,ater *n* puppet show

Mark[1] [mark] *f* (-; -) mark

Mark[2] *n* (-[e]s; *no pl*) marrow; bot pulp

Marke ['markə] *f* (-; -n) econ brand; tech make; trademark; stamp; badge, tag; mark

markieren [mar'ki:rən] *v/t* (*no -ge-, h*)

mark (*a.* sport); F *fig* act

Mar'kierung *f* (-; -en) mark

Markise [mar'ki:zə] *f* (-; -n) awning, sun blind

Markt [markt] *m* (-[e]s; *Märkte* ['mɛrktə]) econ market; **auf den Markt bringen** put on the market

Marktplatz *m* market place

Marktwirtschaft *f* market economy

Marmelade [marmə'la:də] *f* (-; -n) jam

Marmor ['marmo:ɐ] *m* (-s; -e) marble

Marsch[1] [marʃ] *m* (-[e]s; *Märsche* ['mɛrʃə]) march (*a.* mus)

Marsch[2] *f* (-; -en) geogr marsh, fen

Marschall ['marʃal] *m* (-s; *Marschälle* ['marʃɛlə]) mil marshal

'**Marschbefehl** *m* mil marching orders

marschieren [mar'ʃi:rən] *v/i* (*no -ge-, sein*) march

Marsmensch ['mars-] *m* Martian

Marter ['martɐ] *f* (-; -n) torture

'**martern** *v/t* (*ge-, h*) torture

'**Marterpfahl** *m* stake

Martinshorn ['marti:ns-] *n* (police *etc*) siren

Märtyrer ['mɛrtyrɐ] *m* (-s; -), '**Märtyrerin** *f* (-; -nen) martyr (*a. fig*)

Marxismus [mar'ksısmʊs] *m* (-; *no pl*) pol Marxism

Marxist [mar'ksıst] *m* (-en; -en), **mar'xistisch** *adj* pol Marxist

März [mɛrts] *m* (-[es]; -e) March

Marzipan [martsi'pa:n] *n* (-s; -e) marzipan

Masche ['maʃə] *f* (-; -n) stitch; mesh; F trick

'**Maschendraht** *m* wire netting

Maschine [ma'ʃi:nə] *f* (-; -n) machine; mot engine; aviat plane; motorcycle; **Maschine schreiben** type

Ma'schinenbau *m* (-[e]s; *no pl*) mechanical engineering

Maschinengewehr *n* mil machinegun

ma'schinenlesbar *adj* edp machine-readable

Ma'schinenöl *n* engine oil

Maschinenpis,tole *f* mil submachine gun, machine pistol

Maschinenschaden *m* engine trouble *or* failure

Maschinenschlosser *m* (engine) fitter

Masern ['ma:zɐn] *pl* med measles

Maserung ['ma:zərʊŋ] *f* (-; -en) grain

Maske ['maskə] *f* (-; -n) mask (*a.* edp)

'**Maskenball** *m* fancy-dress ball

'**Maskenbildner** [-bıldnɐ] *m* (-s; -), '**Maskenbildnerin** *f* (-; -nen) thea *etc* make-up artist

maskieren [mas'ki:rən] *v/t* (*no -ge-, h*) mask; **sich maskieren** put on a mask

Maus

maskulin [masku'liːn] *adj* masculine (*a.* LING)

maß [maːs] *pret of* **messen**

Maß[1] *n* (*-es; -e*) measure (**für** of); dimensions, measurements, size; *fig* extent, degree; *Maße und Gewichte* weights and measures; *nach Maß* (*gemacht*) made to measure; *in gewissem* (*hohem*) *Maße* to a certain (high) degree; *in zunehmendem Maße* increasingly; *Maß halten* → *maßhalten*

Maß[2] *f* (*-; -[e]*) liter (*Br* litre) of beer

Massage [ma'saːʒə] *f* (*-; -n*) massage

Massaker [ma'saːkɐ] *n* (*-s; -*) massacre

Masse ['masə] *f* (*-; -n*) mass; substance; bulk; F *e-e Masse Geld etc* loads *or* heaps of; *die* (*breite*) *Masse*, POL *die Massen pl* the masses

'Maßeinheit *f* unit of measure(ment)

'Massen... *in cpds* ...*medien*, ...*mörder etc*: mass ...

Massenandrang *m* crush

'massenhaft F *adv* masses *or* loads of

'Massenkarambo,lage *f* MOT pileup

Massenprodukti,on *f* ECON mass production

Masseur [ma'søːɐ] *m* (*-s; -e*) masseur

Masseurin [ma'søːrɪn] *f* (*-; -nen*), **Masseuse** [ma'søːzə] *f* (*-; -n*) masseuse

'maßgebend, **'maßgeblich** [-geːplɪç] *adj* authoritative

'maßhalten *v/i* (*irr*, *halten, sep, -ge-, h*) be moderate (*in dat* in)

massieren [ma'siːrən] *v/t* (*no -ge-, h*) massage

massig ['masɪç] *adj* massive, bulky

mäßig ['mɛːsɪç] *adj* moderate; poor

mäßigen ['mɛːsɪgən] *v/t and v/refl* (*ge-, h*) moderate

'Mäßigung *f* (*-; no pl*) moderation; restraint

massiv [ma'siːf] *adj* solid

Mas'siv *n* (*-s; -e*) GEOL massif

'Maßkrug *m* beer mug, stein

'maßlos *adj* immoderate; gross (*exaggeration*)

'Maßnahme [-naːmə] *f* (*-; -n*) measure, step

'Maßregel *f* rule

'maßregeln *v/t* (*ge-, h*) reprimand; discipline

'Maßstab *m* scale; *fig* standard; *im Maßstab 1:10* on the scale of 1:10

maßstabgetreu *adj* true to scale

'maßvoll *adj* moderate

Mast[1] [mast] *m* (*-[e]s; -en*) MAR, TECH mast

Mast[2] *f* (*-; -en*) AGR fattening

'Mastdarm *m* ANAT rectum

mästen ['mɛstən] *v/t* (*ge-, h*) AGR fatten; F

stuff *s.o.*

masturbieren [mastʊr'biːrən] *v/i* (*no -ge-, h*) masturbate

Match [mɛtʃ] *n* (*-[e]s; -s, -e*) game, *Br* match

Matchball *m tennis*: match point

Material [mate'rjaːl] *n* (*-s; -ien*) material (*a. fig*); TECH materials

Materialismus [materja'lɪsmʊs] *m* (*-; no pl*) PHILOS materialism

Materialist [-'lɪst] *m* (*-en; -en*) materialist

materia'listisch *adj* materialistic

Materie [ma'teːrjə] *f* (*-; -n*) matter (*a. fig*); *fig* subject (matter)

materiell [mate'rjɛl] *adj* material

Mathematik [matema'tiːk] *f* (*-; no pl*) mathematics

Mathematiker [mate'maːtikɐ] *m* (*-s; -*) mathematician

mathe'matisch *adj* mathematical

Matinee [mati'neː] *f* (*-; -n*) THEA *etc* morning performance

Matratze [ma'tratsə] *f* (*-; -n*) mattress

Matrize [ma'triːtsə] *f* (*-; -n*) stencil

Matrose [ma'troːzə] *m* (*-n; -n*) MAR sailor, seaman

Matsch [matʃ] F *m* (*-[e]s; no pl*) mud, slush

'matschig *adj* muddy, slushy

matt [mat] *adj* weak; exhausted, worn out; dull, pale (*color*); PHOT mat(t); frosted (*glass*); *chess*: checkmate

Matte ['matə] *f* (*-; -n*) mat

Mattigkeit ['matɪçkait] *f* (*-; no pl*) exhaustion, weakness

'Mattscheibe *f* screen; PHOT focus(s)ing screen; F (boob) tube, *Br* telly, box

Matura [ma'tuːra] *Austrian, Swiss f* → *Abitur*

Mauer ['mauɐ] *f* (*-; -n*) wall

Mauerblümchen *fig n* wallflower

Mauerwerk *n* (*-[e]s; no pl*) masonry, brickwork

'mauern *v/i* (*ge-, h*) lay bricks

Maul [maul] *n* (*-[e]s; Mäuler* ['mɔylɐ]) ZO mouth; *sl halt's Maul!* shut up!

maulen ['maulən] F *v/i* (*ge-, h*) grumble, sulk, pout

'Maulkorb *m* muzzle (*a. fig*)

Maultier *n* mule

Maulwurf *m* ZO mole

Maulwurfshaufen *m*, **Maulwurfshügel** *m* molehill

Maurer ['maurɐ] *m* (*-s; -*) bricklayer

Maurerkelle *f* trowel

Maurermeister *m* master bricklayer

Maurerpo,lier *m* foreman bricklayer

Maus [maus] *f* (*-; Mäuse* ['mɔyzə]) ZO mouse (*a.* EDP)

M

'**Mausefalle** ['mauzə-] *f* mousetrap

Mauser ['mauzɐ] *f* (-; *no pl*) zo mo(u)lt (-ing); *in der Mauser sein* be mo(u)lting

Maut [maut] *Austrian f* (-; -*en*) toll

Mautstraße *f* turnpike, toll road

maximal [maksi'maːl] **1.** *adj* maximum; **2.** *adv* at (the) most

Maximum ['maksimʊm] *n* (-*s*; -*ma*) maximum

Mayonnaise [majɔ'nɛːzə] *f* (-; -*n*) GASTR mayonnaise

Mäzen [mɛ'tseːn] *m* (-*s*; -*e*) patron; SPORT sponsor

Mechanik [me'çaːnɪk] *f* (-; -*en*) a) (*no pl*) PHYS mechanics, b) TECH mechanism

Mechaniker [me'çaːnikɐ] *m* (-*s*; -) mechanic

mechanisch [me'çaːnɪʃ] *adj* TECH mechanical

mechanisieren [meçani'ziːrən] *v/t* (*no -ge-*, *h*) mechanize

Mechani'sierung *f* (-; -*en*) mechanization

Mechanismus [meça'nɪsmʊs] *m* (-; -*men*) TECH mechanism; works

meckern ['mɛkɐn] *v/i* (*ge-*, *h*) zo bleat; F grumble, bitch (*über acc* at, about)

Medaille [me'daljə] *f* (-; -*n*) medal

Me'daillengewinner *m* medal(l)ist

Medaillon [medal'jõː] *n* (-*s*; -*s*) locket

Medien ['meːdjən] *pl* mass media; teaching aids; audio-visual aids

Medikament [medika'mɛnt] *n* (-[*e*]*s*; -*e*) drug; medicine

meditieren [medi'tiːrən] *v/i* (*no -ge-*, *h*) meditate (*über acc* on)

Medizin [medi'tsiːn] *f* (-; -*en*) a) (*no pl*) (science of) medicine, b) medicine, remedy (*gegen* for)

Mediziner [medi'tsiːnɐ] *m* (-*s*; -), **Medi'zinerin** *f* (-; -*nen*) (medical) doctor; UNIV medical student

medizinisch [medi'tsiːnɪʃ] *adj* medical

Meer [meːɐ] *n* (-[*e*]*s*; -*e* ['meːrə]) sea (*a. fig*), ocean

Meerenge *f* GEOGR straits

Meeresboden ['meːrəs-] *m* seabed

Meeresfrüchte *pl* GASTR seafood

Meeresspiegel *m* sea level

'**Meerjungfrau** *f* MYTH mermaid

'**Meerrettich** *m* (-*s*; -*e*) horseradish

'**Meerschweinchen** [-ʃvainçən] *n* (-*s*; -) zo guinea pig

Megabyte [mega'bait] *n* EDP megabyte

Mehl [meːl] *n* (-[*e*]*s*; -*e*) flour; meal

mehlig ['meːlɪç] *adj* mealy

'**Mehlspeise** *Austrian f* sweet (dish)

mehr [meːɐ] *indef pron and adv* more; *immer mehr* more and more; *nicht mehr* no longer, not any longer (*or more*);

noch mehr even more; *es ist kein ... mehr da* there isn't any ... left

'**mehrdeutig** [-dɔytɪç] *adj* ambiguous

mehrere ['meːrərə] *adj and indef pron* several

'**Mehrheit** *f* (-; -*en*) majority

'**Mehrkosten** *pl* extra costs

'**mehrmals** *adv* several times

'**Mehrwegflasche** *f* returnable (*or* deposit) bottle

Mehrwertsteuer *f* ECON value-added tax (ABBR VAT)

Mehrzahl *f* (-; *no pl*) majority; LING plural (form)

'**Mehrzweck...** *in cpds* ...*fahrzeug etc*: multi-purpose ...

meiden ['maidən] *v/t* (*irr*, *ge-*, *h*) avoid

Meile ['mailə] *f* (-; -*n*) mile

'**meilenweit** *adv* (for) miles

mein [main] *poss pron and adj* my; *das ist meiner* (*meine, mein*[*e*]*s*) that's mine

'**Meineid** *m* JUR perjury

meinen ['mainən] *v/t* (*ge-*, *h*) think, believe; mean; say; *meinen Sie wirklich?* do you (really) think so?; *wie meinen Sie das?* what do you mean by that?; *sie meinen es gut* they mean well; *ich habe es nicht so gemeint* I didn't mean it; *wie meinen Sie?* (I beg your) pardon?

meinet'wegen ['mainət-] *adv* for my sake; because of me; F I don't mind *or* care!

'**Meinung** *f* (-; -*en*) opinion (*über acc*, *von* about, of); *meiner Meinung nach* in my opinion; *der Meinung sein, dass* be of the opinion that, feel *or* believe that; *s-e Meinung äußern* express one's opinion; *s-e Meinung ändern* change one's mind; *ich bin Ihrer* (*anderer*) *Meinung* I (don't) agree with you; *j-m die Meinung sagen* give s.o. a piece of one's mind

'**Meinungsaustausch** *m* exchange of views (*über acc* on)

Meinungsforscher *m* pollster

Meinungsfreiheit *f* (-; *no pl*) freedom of speech *or* opinion

Meinungsumfrage *f* opinion poll

Meinungsverschiedenheit *f* disagreement (*über acc* about)

Meise ['maizə] *f* (-; -*n*) zo titmouse

Meißel ['maisəl] *m* (-*s*; -) chisel

'**meißeln** *v/t and v/i* (*ge-*, *h*) chisel, carve

meist [maist] **1.** *adj* most; *das meiste* (*davon*) most of it; *die meisten* (*von ihnen*) most of them; *die meisten Leute* most people; *die meiste Zeit* most of the time; **2.** *adv* → *meistens*; *am meisten* (the) most; most (of all)

meistens ['maistəns] *adv* usually; most of the time

Meister ['maistɐ] *m* (-s; -) master (*a. fig*); SPORT champion, F champ

'meisterhaft 1. *adj* masterly; **2.** *adv* in a masterly manner *or* way

'Meisterin *f* (-; -nen) master (*a. fig*); SPORT champion

meistern ['maistɐn] *v/t* (*ge-, h*) master

'Meisterschaft *f* (-; -en) a) (*no pl*) mastery, b) SPORT championship, cup; title

'Meisterstück *n*, **Meisterwerk** *n* masterpiece

Melancholie [melaŋko'li:] *f* (-; -n) melancholy

melancholisch [melaŋ'ko:lɪʃ] *adj* melancholy; ***melancholisch sein*** feel depressed, F have the blues

Melange [me'lɑ̃:ʒə] *Austrian f* (-; -n) coffee with milk

melden ['mɛldən] (*ge-, h*) **1.** *v/t* report *s.th. or s.o.* (**bei** to); *radio etc*: announce, report; ***j-m et. melden*** notify s.o. of s.th.; **2.** *v/refl*: ***sich melden*** report (**bei** to, **für, zu** for); register (**bei** with); PED *etc*: put up one's hand; TEL answer the phone; SPORT enter (**für, zu** for); volunteer (**für, zu** for)

'Meldung *f* (-; -en) report, news, announcement; information, notice; notification; registration (**bei** with); SPORT entry (**für, zu** for)

melken ['mɛlkən] *v/t* ([*irr,*] *ge-, h*) milk

Melodie [melo'di:] *f* (-; -n) MUS melody, tune

melodisch [me'lo:dɪʃ] *adj* MUS melodious, melodic

Melone [me'lo:nə] *f* (-; -n) BOT melon; F derby, *Br* bowler (hat)

Memoiren [me'moa:rən] *pl* memoirs

Menge ['mɛŋə] *f* (-; -n) amount, quantity; MATH set; F ***e-e Menge Geld*** plenty (*or* lots) of money; → **Menschenmenge**

'Mengenlehre *f* (-; *no pl*) MATH set theory; PED new math(ematics)

Mensa ['mɛnza] *f* (-; -s, *Mensen*) cafeteria, *Br* refectory, canteen

Mensch [mɛnʃ] *m* (-en; -en) human being; man; person, individual; *pl* people; mankind; ***kein Mensch*** nobody; ***Mensch!*** wow!

Menschenaffe *m* ZO ape

Menschenfresser *m* cannibal

Menschenfreund *m* philanthropist

Menschenhandel *m* slave trade

Menschenkenntnis *f*: ***Menschenkenntnis haben*** know human nature

Menschenleben *n* human life

'menschenleer *adj* deserted

'Menschenmenge *f* crowd

Menschenrechte *pl* human rights

Menschenseele *f*: ***keine Menschenseele*** not a (living) soul

'menschenunwürdig *adj* degrading; *housing etc*: unfit for human beings

'Menschenverstand *m*: ***gesunder Menschenverstand*** common sense

Menschenwürde *f* human dignity

Menschheit: ***die Menschheit*** mankind, the human race

'menschlich *adj* human; humane

'Menschlichkeit *f* (-; *no pl*) humanity

Menstruation [mɛnstrua'tsjo:n] *f* (-; -en) MED menstruation

Mentalität [mɛntali'tɛ:t] *f* (-; -en) mentality

Menü [me'ny:] *n* (-s; -s) set meal (*or* lunch); EDP menu

Meridian [meri'dja:n] *m* (-s; -e) GEOGR, ASTR meridian

merkbar ['mɛrkba:ɐ] *adj* marked, distinct; noticeable

'Merkblatt *n* leaflet

merken ['mɛrkən] *v/t* (*ge-, h*) notice; feel; find (out), discover; ***sich et. merken*** remember s.th., keep *or* bear s.th. in mind

'merklich *adj* → **merkbar**

'Merkmal *n* sign; feature, trait

'merkwürdig *adj* strange, odd, curious

'merkwürdiger'weise *adv* strangely enough

messbar ['mɛsba:ɐ] *adj* measurable

'Messbecher *m* measuring cup

Messe ['mɛsə] *f* (-; -n) ECON fair; REL mass; MIL, MAR mess

messen ['mɛsən] *v/t* (*irr, ge-, h*) measure; take (*temperature etc*); ***sich nicht mit j-m messen können*** be no match for s.o.; ***gemessen an*** (*dat*) compared with

Messer ['mɛsɐ] *n* (-s; -) knife; ***bis aufs Messer*** to the knife; ***auf des Messers Schneide stehen*** be on a razor edge, be touch and go (**ob** whether)

Messerstecherei [-ʃtɛçə'rai] *f* (-; -en) knife fight

'Messerstich *m* stab (with a knife)

Messing ['mɛsɪŋ] *n* (-s; -e) brass

'Messinstru,ment *n* measuring instrument

'Messung *f* (-; -en) measuring; reading

Metall [me'tal] *n* (-s; -e) metal

metallen [me'talən], **me'tallisch** *adj* metallic

Me'tallwaren *pl* hardware

Metamorphose [metamɔr'fo:zə] *f* (-; -n) metamorphosis

Metastase [meta'sta:zə] *f* (-; -n) MED me-

M

tastasis

Meteor [mete'oːɐ] m (-s; -e) ASTR meteor

Meteorit [meteo'riːt] m (-en; -e[n]) ASTR meteorite

Meteorologe [meteoro'loːgə] m (-n; -n) meteorologist

Meteorologie [meteorolo'giː] f (-; no pl) meteorology

Meteoro'login f (-; -nen) meteorologist

Meter ['meːtɐ] n, m (-s; -) meter, Br metre

Metermaß n tape measure

Methode [me'toːdə] f (-; -n) method, TECH a. technique

methodisch [me'toːdɪʃ] adj methodical

metrisch ['meːtrɪʃ] adj metric; **metrisches Maßsystem** metric system

Metropole [metro'poːlə] f (-; -n) metropolis

Metzger ['mɛtsgɐ] m (-s; -) butcher

Metzgerei [mɛtsgə'rai] f (-; -en) butcher's (shop)

Meute ['mɔytə] f (-; -n) pack (of hounds); fig mob, pack

Meuterei [mɔytə'rai] f (-; -en) mutiny

Meuterer ['mɔytərɐ] m (-s; -) mutineer

meutern ['mɔytɐn] v/i (ge-, h) mutiny (**gegen** against)

MEZ ABBR of **Mitteleuropäische Zeit** CET, Central European Time

miau [mi'au] int ZO meow, Br miaow

miauen [mi'auən] v/i (no -ge-, h) ZO meow, Br miaow

mich [mɪç] pers pron me; **mich (selbst)** myself

mied [miːt] pret of **meiden**

Mieder ['miːdɐ] n (-s; -) corset(s); bodice

Miederhöschen n pantie girdle

Miederwaren pl foundation garments

Miene ['miːnə] f (-; -n) expression, look, air; **gute Miene zum bösen Spiel machen** grin and bear it

mies [miːs] F adj rotten, lousy

Miete ['miːtə] f (-; -n) rent; hire charge; **zur Miete wohnen** be a tenant; lodge (**bei** with)

'mieten v/t (ge-, h) rent; (take on) lease; AVIAT, MAR charter; **ein Auto etc mieten** rent (Br hire) a car etc

Mieter(in) ['miːtɐ (-tərɪn)] (-s; -/-; -nen) tenant, lodger

'Mietshaus n apartment building or house, Br block of flats, tenement

'Mietvertrag m lease (contract)

'Mietwohnung f apartment, Br (rented) flat

Migräne [mi'grɛːnə] f (-; -n) MED migraine

Mikro ['miːkro] F n (-s; -s) mike

Mikro... ['miːkro-] in cpds ...chip, ...computer, ...elektronik, ...film, ...prozessor

etc: micro...

Mikrofon [mikro'foːn] n (-s; -e) microphone

Mikroskop [mikro'skoːp] n (-s; -e) microscope

mikro'skopisch adj microscopic(al)

Mikrowelle ['miːkro-] F f, **'Mikrowellenherd** m microwave oven

Milbe ['mɪlbə] f (-; -n) ZO mite

Milch [mɪlç] f (-; no pl) milk

Milchgeschäft n dairy, creamery

Milchglas n frosted glass

milchig ['mɪlçɪç] adj milky

'Milchkaffee m white coffee

Milchkännchen n (milk) jug

Milchkanne f milk can

Milchmann F m milkman

Milchmixgetränk n milk shake

Milchpro,dukte pl dairy products

Milchpulver n powdered milk

Milchreis m rice pudding

Milchstraße f ASTR Milky Way, Galaxy

Milchtüte f milk carton

Milchwirtschaft f dairy farming

Milchzahn m milk tooth

mild [mɪlt] adj mild, soft; gentle

milde ['mɪldə] adv mildly; **milde ausgedrückt** to put it mildly

'Milde f (-; no pl) mildness, gentleness; leniency, mercy

mildern ['mɪldɐn] v/t (ge-, h) lessen, soften

mildernd adj: **mildernde Umstände** JUR mitigating circumstances

'mildtätig adj charitable

Milieu [mi'ljøː] n (-s; -s) environment; social background

Militär [mili'tɛːɐ] n (-s; no pl) the military, armed forces; army

Militärdienst m (-[e]s; no pl) military service

Militärdikta,tur f military dictatorship

Militärgericht n court martial

militärisch [mili'tɛːrɪʃ] adj military

Militarismus [milita'rɪsmʊs] m (-; no pl) militarism

Militarist [milita'rɪst] m (-en; -en) militarist

milita'ristisch adj militaristic

'Mili'tärre'gierung f military government

Milliarde [mɪ'ljardə] f (-; -n) billion, Br old use a. a thousand million(s)

Millimeter [mɪli'meːtɐ] n, m (-s; -) millimet|er, Br -re

Millimeterpa,pier n graph paper

Million [mɪ'lioːn] f (-; -en) million

Millionär [mɪljo'nɛːɐ] m (-s; -e), **Millionä-rin** f (-; -nen) millionaire

Milz [mɪlts] f (-; no pl) ANAT spleen

Mimik ['mi:mɪk] *f* (-; *no pl*) facial expression

minder ['mɪndɐ] **1.** *adj* → **geringer, weniger**; **2.** *adv* less; **nicht minder** no less

'Minderheit *f* (-; -en) minority

'minderjährig [-jɛːrɪç] *adj*: **minderjährig sein** be under age, be a minor

'Minderjährige [-jɛːrɪgə] *m, f* (-*n*; -*n*) minor

'Minderjährigkeit *f* (-; *no pl*) minority

'minderwertig *adj* inferior, of inferior quality

'Minderwertigkeit *f* (-; *no pl*) inferiority; ECON inferior quality

'Minderwertigkeitskom,plex *m* PSYCH inferiority complex

mindest ['mɪndəst] *adj* least; **das Mindeste** the (very) least; **nicht im Mindesten** not in the least, not at all

'Mindest... *in cpds ...alter, ...einkommen, ...lohn etc*: minimum ...

mindestens ['mɪndəstəns] *adv* at least

'Mindesthaltbarkeitsdatum *n* pull date, *Br* best-before (*or* best-by, sell-by) date

Mindestmaß *n* minimum; **auf ein Mindestmaß herabsetzen** reduce to a minimum

Mine ['mi:nə] *f* (-; -*n*) mine (*a.* MAR, MIL); lead; cartridge; refill

Mineral [minə'raːl] *n* (-*s*; -*e*, -*ien*) mineral

Mineralogie [mineralo'giː] *f* (-; *no pl*) mineralogy

Mine'ralöl *n* mineral oil

Mine'ralwasser *n* mineral water

Miniatur [minja'tuːɐ] *f* (-; -*en*) miniature

Minigolf ['mɪni-] *n* miniature (*Br* crazy) golf

minimal [mini'maːl] *adj, adv* minimal; minimum; at least

Minimum ['miːnimʊm] *n* (-*s*; -*ma*) minimum

Minirock ['mɪni-] *m* miniskirt

Minister [mi'nɪstɐ] *m* (-*s*; -), **Mi'nisterin** *f* (-; -*nen*) minister, secretary, *Br a.* secretary of state

Ministerium [minɪs'teːriʊm] *n* (-*s*; -*ien*) ministry, department, *Br a.* office

Mi'nisterpräsi,dent *m*, **Mi'nisterpräsi,dentin** *f* prime minister

minus ['miːnʊs] *adv* MATH minus; **bei 10 Grad minus** at 10 degrees below zero

Minute [mi'nuːtə] *f* (-; -*n*) minute

Mi'nutenzeiger *m* minute hand

Mio ABBR *of* **Million(en)** m, million

mir [miːɐ] *pers pron* (to) me

Mischbatte,rie ['mɪʃ-] *f* mixing faucet, *Br* mixer tap

'Mischbrot *n* wheat and rye bread

mischen ['mɪʃən] *v/t* (ge-, h) mix; blend (*tea etc*); shuffle (*cards*); **sich mischen** mingle *or* mix (**unter** with)

'Mischling *m* (-*s*; -*e*) *esp contp* half-caste; BOT, ZO hybrid; mongrel

'Mischmasch F *m* (-[*e*]*s*; -*e*) hotchpotch, jumble

'Mischma,schine *f* TECH mixer

Mischpult *n* radio, TV: mixer, mixing console

'Mischung *f* (-; -*en*) mixture; blend; assortment

'Mischwald *m* mixed forest

miserabel [mizə'raːbəl] F *adj* lousy, rotten

miss'achten [mɪs-] *v/t* (*no* -ge-, h) disregard, ignore; despise

Miss'achtung *f* disregard; contempt; neglect (*all: gen* of)

'Missbildung *f* (-; -*en*) deformity, malformation

miss'billigen *v/t* (*no* -ge-, h) disapprove of

'Missbrauch *m* abuse (*a.* JUR); misuse

miss'brauchen *v/t* (*no* -ge-, h) abuse; misuse

miss'deuten *v/t* (*no* -ge-, h) misinterpret

'Misserfolg *m* failure; F flop

'Missernte *f* bad harvest, crop failure

miss'fallen *v/i* (*irr,* **fallen,** *no* -ge-, h) **j-m missfallen** displease s.o.

'Missfallen *n* (-*s*; *no pl*) displeasure, dislike

'missgebildet *adj* deformed, malformed

'Missgeburt *f* deformed child *or* animal; freak

'Missgeschick *n* (-[*e*]*s*; -*e*) mishap

miss'glücken *v/i* (*no* -ge-, *sein*) fail

miss'gönnen *v/t* (*no* -ge-, h) **j-m et. missgönnen** envy s.o. s.th.

'Missgriff *m* mistake

miss'handeln *v/t* (*no* -ge-, h) ill-treat, maltreat (*a. fig*); batter

Miss'handlung *f* ill-treatment, maltreatment, *esp* JUR assault and battery

Mission [mɪ'sjoːn] *f* (-; -*en*) mission (*a.* POL *and fig*)

Missionar(in) [mɪsjo'naːɐ (-'naːrɪn)] (-*s*; -*e*/-; -*nen*) missionary

'Missklang *m* dissonance, discord (*both a. fig*)

'Misskre,dit *m* discredit

misslang [mɪs'laŋ] *pret of* **misslingen**

misslingen [mɪs'lɪŋən] *v/i* (*irr, no* -ge-, *sein*) fail

misslungen [mɪs'lʊŋən] *pp of* **misslingen**; **das ist mir misslungen** I've bungled it

'missmutig *adj* bad-tempered, grumpy, glum

miss'raten 1. *v/i* (*irr,* **raten,** *no* -ge-, *sein*)

M

fail; turn out badly; **2.** *adj* wayward

miss'trauen *v/i* (*no -ge-, h*) distrust

'Misstrauen *n* (*-s; no pl*) distrust, suspicion (*both*: **gegenüber** of)

'Misstrauensantrag *m* PARL motion of no confidence

Misstrauensvotum *n* PARL vote of no confidence

misstrauisch ['mɪstrauɪʃ] *adj* distrustful, suspicious

'Missverhältnis *n* disproportion

'Missverständnis *n* (*-ses; -se*) misunderstanding

'missverstehen *v/t* (*irr, stehen, no -ge-, h*) misunderstand

'Misswahl *f* beauty contest *or* competition

Mist [mɪst] *m* (*-[e]s; no p*) AGR dung, manure; F trash, rubbish

'Mistbeet *n* AGR hotbed

Mistel ['mɪstəl] *f* (*-; -n*) BOT mistletoe

'Mistgabel *f* AGR dung fork

'Misthaufen *m* AGR manure heap

mit [mɪt] *prp* (*dat*) *and adv* with; **mit Gewalt** by force; **mit Absicht** on purpose; **mit dem Auto** (**der Bahn** *etc*) by car (train *etc*); **mit 20 Jahren** at (the age of) 20; **mit 100 Stundenkilometern** at 100 kilometers per hour; **mit einem Mal(e)** all of a sudden; (all) at the same time; **mit lauter Stimme** in a loud voice; **mit anderen Worten** in other words; **ein Mann mit dem Namen ...** a man by the name of ...; **j-n mit Namen kennen** know s.o. by name; **mit der Grund dafür, dass** one of the reasons why; **mit der Beste** one of the best

'Mitarbeit *f* cooperation; assistance; PED activity, class participation

'Mitarbeiter *m*, 'Mitarbeiterin *f* colleague; employee; assistant; **freie(r) Mitarbeiter(in)** freelance

'mitbekommen F *v/t* (*irr, kommen, sep, no -ge-, h*) get; catch

mitbenutzen *v/t* (*sep, no -ge-, h*) share

'Mitbestimmungsrecht *n* (right of) codetermination, worker participation

Mitbewerber(in) (rival) competitor; fellow applicant

Mitbewohner(in) roommate, *Br* flatmate

'mitbringen *v/t* (*irr, bringen, sep, -ge-, h*) bring s.th. or s.o. with one; **j-m et. mitbringen** bring s.o. s.th.

Mitbringsel ['mɪtbrɪŋzəl] F *n* (*-s; -*) little present; souvenir

'Mitbürger *m*, 'Mitbürgerin *f* fellow citizen

mitei'nander *adv* with each other, with one another; together, jointly

'miterleben *v/t* (*sep, no -ge-, h*) live to see

'Mitesser *m* MED blackhead

'mitfahren *v/i* (*irr, fahren, sep, -ge-, sein*) **mit j-m mitfahren** drive *or* go with s.o.; **j-n mitfahren lassen** give s.o. a lift

'Mitfahrgelegenheit *f* lift

Mitfahrzen,trale *f* car pool(ing) service

'mitfühlend *adj* sympathetic

'mitgeben *v/t* (*irr, geben, sep, -ge-, h*) **j-m et. mitgeben** give s.o. s.th. (to take along)

'Mitgefühl *n* (*-[e]s; no pl*) sympathy

'mitgehen *v/i* (*irr, gehen, sep, -ge-, sein*) **mit j-m mitgehen** go *or* come along with s.o.; F **et. mitgehen lassen** walk off with s.th.

'Mitgift *f* (*-; -en*) dowry

'Mitglied *n* member (**bei** of)

'Mitgliedsbeitrag *m* subscription

'Mitgliedschaft *f* (*-; -en*) membership

'mithaben *v/t* (*irr, haben, sep, -ge-, h*) **ich habe kein Geld mit** I haven't got any money with me *or* on me

'Mithilfe *f* (*-; no pl*) assistance, help, cooperation (**bei** in; **von** of)

mit'hilfe *prp*: **mithilfe von** (*or gen*) with the help of, *fig a.* by means of

'mithören *v/t* (*sep, -ge-, h*) listen in to; overhear

'Mitinhaber *m*, 'Mitinhaberin *f* joint owner

'mitkommen *v/i* (*irr, kommen, sep, -ge-, sein*) come along (**mit** with); *fig* keep pace (**mit** with), follow; PED get on, keep up (with the class)

'Mitlaut *m* LING consonant

'Mitleid *n* (*-[e]s; no pl*) pity (**mit** for); **aus Mitleid** out of pity; **Mitleid haben mit** feel sorry for

mitleidig ['mɪtlaidɪç] *adj* compassionate, sympathetic

'mitleidslos *adj* pitiless

'mitmachen (*sep, -ge-, h*) **1.** *v/i* join in; **2.** *v/t* take part in; follow (*a fashion etc*); F go through

'Mitmenschen: **die Mitmenschen** one's fellow human beings; people

'mitnehmen *v/t* (*irr, nehmen, sep, -ge-, h*) take s.th. or s.o. with one; **j-n (im Auto) mitnehmen** give s.o. a lift

'mitreden *v/t* (*sep, -ge-, h*) **et. mitzureden haben** (**bei**) have a say (in)

'mitreißen *v/t* (*irr, reißen, sep, -ge-, h*) drag along; *fig* carry away (*mst passive*)

mitreißend *fig adj* electrifying (*speech etc*)

'mitschneiden *v/t* (*irr, schneiden, sep, -ge-, h*) radio, TV record, tape(-record)

'mitschreiben *v/t* (*irr, schreiben, sep, -ge-, h*) **1.** *v/t* take down; take, do (*a test*); **2.**

v/i take notes

'**Mitschuld** *f* (-; *no pl*) partial responsibility

'**mitschuldig** *adj*: *mitschuldig sein* be partly to blame (*an dat* for)

'**Mitschüler** *m*, '**Mitschülerin** *f* classmate; schoolmate, fellow student

'**mitspielen** *v/i* (*sep*, *-ge-*, *h*) SPORT, MUS play; join in *a game etc*; *in e-m Film etc mitspielen* be *or* appear in a film *etc*

'**Mitspieler** *m*, '**Mitspielerin** *f* partner, SPORT *a.* team-mate

Mittag ['mɪtaːk] *m* (-s; -e) noon, midday; *heute Mittag* at noon today; *zu Mittag essen* (have) lunch

Mittagessen *n* lunch; *was gibt es zum Mittagessen?* what's for lunch?

'**mittags** *adv* at noon; *12 Uhr mittags* 12 o'clock noon

'**Mittagspause** *f* lunch break

'**Mittagsruhe** *f* midday rest

Mittagsschlaf *m* after-dinner nap

Mittagszeit *f* lunchtime

Mitte ['mɪtə] *f* (-; *no pl*) middle; center, *Br* centre (*a.* POL); *Mitte Juli* in the middle of July; *Mitte dreißig* in one's mid thirties

'**mitteilen** *v/t* (*sep*, *-ge-*, *h*) *j-m et. mitteilen* inform s.o. of s.th.

'**mitteilsam** *adj* communicative

'**Mitteilung** *f* (-; *-en*) report, information, message

Mittel ['mɪtəl] *n* (-s; -) means, way; measure; PHARM remedy (*gegen* for) (*a. fig*); average; MATH mean; PHYS medium; *pl* means, money

'**Mittelalter** *n* (-s; *no pl*) Middle Ages

'**mittelalterlich** *adj* medi(a)eval

'**Mittelding** *n* cross (*zwischen* between)

Mittelfeld *n* SPORT midfield

Mittelfeldspieler(in) midfield player, midfielder

Mittelfinger *m* ANAT middle finger

'**mittelfristig** *adj* medium-term

'**Mittelgewicht** *n* (-[e]s; *no pl*) SPORT middleweight (class)

'**mittelgroß** *adj* of medium height; medium-sized

'**Mittelklasse** *f* middle class (*a.* MOT)

Mittellinie *f* SPORT halfway line

'**mittellos** *adj* without means

'**mittelmäßig** *adj* average

'**Mittelpunkt** *m* center, *Br* centre (*a. fig*)

'**mittels** *prp* (*gen*) by (means of), through

'**Mittelschule** *f* → *Realschule*

'**Mittelstrecke** *f* SPORT middle distance

Mittelstreckenra‚kete *f* MIL medium-range missile

Mittelstreifen *m* MOT median strip, *Br* central reservation

Mittelstufe *f* PED junior highschool, *Br* middle school

Mittelstürmer(in) SPORT center (*Br* centre) forward

Mittelweg *m* middle course

Mittelwelle *f* *radio*: medium wave (ABBR AM)

Mittelwort *n* (-[e]s; *-wörter*) LING participle

mitten ['mɪtən] *adv*: *mitten in* (*auf, unter dat*) in the midst *or* middle of

mitten'drin F *adv* right in the middle

mitten'durch F *adv* right through (the middle); right in two

Mitternacht ['mɪtɐ-] *f* midnight

mittlere ['mɪtlərə] *adj* middle, central; average, medium

mittlerweile ['mɪtlɐ'vailə] *adv* meanwhile, (in the) meantime

Mittwoch ['mɪtvɔx] *m* (-[s]; -e) Wednesday

mit'unter *adv* now and then

'**Mitverantwortung** *f* share of the responsibility

'**mitwirken** *v/i* (*sep*, *-ge-*, *h*) take part (*bei* in)

'**Mitwirkende** *m*, *f* (-*n*; -*n*) THEA, MUS performer; *pl* THEA the cast

'**Mitwirkung** *f* (-; *no pl*) participation

mixen ['mɪksən] *v/t* (*ge-*, *h*) mix

'**Mixbecher** *m* shaker

Mixer ['mɪksɐ] *m* (-s; -) mixer

'**Mixgetränk** *n* mixed drink, cocktail, shake

Möbel ['møːbəl] *pl* furniture

Möbelspediti‚on *f* removal firm

Möbelstück *n* piece of furniture

Möbelwagen *m* moving (*Br* furniture) van

mobil [mo'biːl] *adj* mobile; *mobil machen* MIL mobilize

Mobiliar [mobi'ljaːɐ] *n* (-s; *no pl*) furniture

Mo'biltele‚fon *n* mobile phone

möblieren [mø'bliːrən] *v/t* (*no -ge-*, *h*) furnish

mochte ['mɔxtə] *pret of* **mögen**

Mode ['moːdə] *f* (-; -*n*) fashion; *in Mode* in fashion; *Mode sein* be in fashion, F be in; *die neueste Mode* the latest fashion; *mit der Mode gehen* follow the fashion; *in (aus der) Mode kommen* come into (go out of) fashion

Modell [mo'dɛl] *n* (-s; -e) model; *j-m Modell stehen* or *sitzen* pose *or* sit for s.o.

Modellbau *m* model construction

Modellbaukasten *m* model construction kit

Modelleisenbahn *f* model railway

M

modellieren [modɛ'liːrən] v/t (no -ge-, h) model

Modem ['moːdɛm] m, n (-s; -s) EDP modem

'Modenschau f fashion show

Moderator [mode'raːtoːɐ] m (-s; -en [modera'toːrən]), **Modera'torin** f (-; -nen) TV etc presenter, host, anchorman (anchorwoman)

moderieren [mode'riːrən] v/t (no -ge-, h) TV etc present, host

moderig ['moːdərɪç] adj musty, mo(u)ldy

modern[1] ['moːdɐn] v/i (ge-, h, sein) mo(u)ld, rot, decay

modern[2] [mo'dɛrn] adj modern; fashionable

modernisieren [modɛrni'ziːrən] v/t (no -ge-, h) modernize, bring up to date

'Modeschmuck m costume jewel(le)ry

Modeschöpfer(in) fashion designer

Modewaren pl fashionwear

Modewort n (-[e]s; -wörter) vogue word, F in word

Modezeichner(in) fashion designer

Modezeitschrift f fashion magazine

modisch ['moːdɪʃ] adj fashionable, stylish

Modul[1] [mo'duːl] n (-s; -e) EDP module

Modul[2] ['moːdʊl] m (-s;-n) MATH, TECH module

Mofa ['moːfa] n (-s; -s) (small) moped, motorized bicycle

mogeln ['moːgəln] F v/i (ge-, h) cheat; crib

mögen ['møːgən] v/t (irr, ge-, h) and v/aux (irr, no -ge-, h) like; **er mag sie (nicht)** he likes (doesn't like) her; **lieber mögen** like better, prefer; **nicht mögen** dislike; **was möchten Sie?** what would you like?; **ich möchte, dass du es weißt** I'd like you to know (it); **ich möchte lieber bleiben** I'd rather stay; **es mag sein (, dass)** it may be (that)

möglich ['møːklɪç] **1.** adj possible; **alle möglichen** all sorts of; **sein Möglichstes tun** do what one can; do one's utmost; **nicht möglich!** you don't say (so)!; **so bald (schnell, oft) wie möglich** as soon (quickly, often) as possible; **2.** adv: **möglichst bald** etc as soon etc as possible

'möglicher'weise adv possibly

'Möglichkeit f (-; -en) possibility; opportunity; chance; **nach Möglichkeit** if possible

Mohammedaner [mohame'daːnɐ] m (-s; -), **mohamme'danisch** adj Muslim

Mohn [moːn] m (-[e]s; -e) BOT poppy

Möhre ['møːrə] f (-; -n), **Mohrrübe** ['moːɐ-] f BOT carrot

Molch [mɔlç] m (-[e]s; -e) ZO salamander

Mole ['moːlə] f (-; -n) MAR mole, jetty

Molekül [mole'kyːl] n (-s; -e) CHEM molecule

molk [mɔlk] pret of **melken**

Molkerei [mɔlkə'rai] f (-; -en) dairy

Moll [mɔl] n (-; no pl) MUS minor (key); **a-Moll** A minor

mollig ['mɔlɪç] F adj snug, cozy, Br cosy; plump, chubby

Moment [mo'mɛnt] m (-[e]s; -e) moment; **(e-n) Moment bitte!** just a moment please!; **im Moment** at the moment

Monarch [mo'narç] m (-en; -en) monarch

Monarchie [monar'çiː] f (-; -n) monarchy

Monarchin [mo'narçɪn] f (-; -nen) monarch

Monarchist [monar'çɪst] m (-en; -en) monarchist

Monat ['moːnat] m (-[e]s; -e) month; **zweimal im** or **pro Monat** twice a month

'monatelang adv for months

'monatlich adj and adv monthly

'Monatsbinde f sanitary napkin (Br towel)

Monatskarte f commuter ticket, Br (monthly) season ticket

Mönch [mœnç] m (-[e]s; -e) monk; friar

Mond [moːnt] m (-[e]s; -e ['moːndə]) moon

Mondfinsternis f lunar eclipse

'mondhell adj moonlit

'Mondlandefähre f lunar module

Mondlandung f moon landing

Mondoberfläche f moon surface, lunar soil

Mondschein m (-[e]s; no pl) moonlight

Mondsichel f crescent

Mondumkreisung f, **Mondumlaufbahn** f lunar orbit

Monitor ['moːnitoːɐ] m (-s; -en [moni'toːrən]) TV etc monitor

Monolog [mono'loːk] m (-[e]s; -e) monolog(ue Br)

Monopol [mono'poːl] n (-s; -e) ECON monopoly

monoton [mono'toːn] adj monotonous

Monotonie [monoto'niː] f (-; -n) monotony

Monoxid ['moːnɔksiːt] n CHEM monoxide

Monster ['mɔnstɐ] n (-s; -) monster

Montag ['moːntaːk] m (-[e]s; -e) Monday

Montage [mɔn'taːʒə] f (-; -n) TECH assembly; installation; **auf Montage sein** be away on a field job

Montageband n (-[e]s; -bänder) TECH assembly line

Montagehalle f TECH assembly shop

Monteur [mɔn'tøːɐ] *m* (*-s*; *-e*) TECH fitter; *esp* MOT, AVIAT mechanic

montieren [mɔn'tiːrən] *v/t* (*no -ge-*, *h*) TECH assemble; fit, attach; install(1)

Moor [moːɐ] *n* (*-[e]s*; *-e*) bog, moor(-land)

moorig ['moːrɪç] *adj* boggy

Moos [moːs] *n* (*-es*; *-e*) BOT moss

moosig ['moːzɪç] *adj* mossy

Moped ['moːpɛt] *n* (*-s*; *-s*) moped

Mops [mɔps] *m* (*-es*; *Möpse* ['mœpsə]) ZO pug(dog)

Moral [mo'raːl] *f* (*-*; *no pl*) morals, moral standards; MIL *etc* morale

mo'ralisch *adj* moral

moralisieren [morali'ziːrən] *v/i* (*no -ge-*, *h*) moralize

Morast [mo'rast] *m* (*-[e]s*; *-e*) morass; mire, mud

Mord [mɔrt] *m* (*-[e]s*; *-e* ['mɔrdə]) murder (**an** *dat* of); **e-n Mord begehen** commit murder

Mordanschlag *m esp* POL assassination attempt

Mörder ['mœrdɐ] *m* (*-s*; *-*), **'Mörderin** *f* (*-*; *-nen*) murderer; (hired) killer; *esp* POL assassin

'Mordkommissi,on *f* homicide division, *Br* murder squad

Mordpro,zess *m* JUR murder trial

'Mordsangst F *f*: **e-e Mordsangst haben** be scared stiff

Mordsglück F *n* stupendous luck

Mordskerl F *m* devil of a fellow

Mordswut F *f*: **e-e Mordswut haben** be in a hell of a rage

'Mordverdacht *m* suspicion of murder

Mordversuch *m* attempted murder

morgen ['mɔrgən] *adv* tomorrow; **morgen Abend** (**früh**) tomorrow night (morning); **morgen Mittag** at noon tomorrow; **morgen in e-r Woche** a week from tomorrow; **morgen um diese Zeit** this time tomorrow; **... von morgen** tomorrow's **...**, **...** of tomorrow

'Morgen *m* (*-s*; *-*) morning; AGR acre; **heute Morgen** this morning; **am** (**frühen**) **Morgen** (early) in the morning; **am nächsten Morgen** the next morning

Morgenessen *Swiss n* breakfast

Morgengrauen *n* dawn; **im** *or* **bei Morgengrauen** at dawn

Morgenland *n* (*-[e]s*; *no pl*) Orient

Morgenmantel *m*, **Morgenrock** *m* dressing gown

'morgens *adv* in the morning; **von morgens bis abends** from morning till night

morgig ['mɔrgɪç] *adj* tomorrow's **...**

Morphium ['mɔrfjʊm] *n* (*-s*; *no pl*) PHARM morphine

morsch [mɔrʃ] *adj* rotten; **morsch werden** rot

Morsealpha,bet ['mɔrzə-] *n* Morse code

Mörser ['mœrzə] *m* (*-s*; *-*) mortar (*a.* MIL)

'Morsezeichen *n* Morse signal

Mörtel ['mœrtəl] *m* (*-s*; *-*) mortar

Mosaik [moza'iːk] *n* (*-s*; *-en*) mosaic

Mosa'ikstein *m* piece

Moschee [mɔ'ʃeː] *f* (*-*; *-n*) mosque

Moskito [mɔs'kiːto] *m* (*-s*; *-s*) ZO mosquito

Moslem ['mɔslɛm] *m* (*-s*; *-s*), **moslemisch** [mɔs'leːmɪʃ] *adj*, **Moslime** [-'liːmə] *f* (*-*; *-n*) Muslim

Most [mɔst] *m* (*-[e]s*; *-e*) grape juice; cider

Motiv [mo'tiːf] *n* (*-s*; *-e*) motive; PAINT, MUS motif

Motivation [motiva'tsjoːn] *f* (*-*; *-en*) motivation

motivieren [moti'viːrən] *v/t* (*no -ge-*, *h*) motivate

Motor ['moːtoːɐ, mo'toːɐ] *m* (*-s*; *-en* [mo'toːrən]) motor, engine

Motorboot *n* motor boat

Motorhaube *f* hood, *Br* bonnet

motorisieren [motori'ziːrən] *v/t* (*no -ge-*, *h*) motorize

'Motorleistung *f* (engine) performance

Motorrad *n* motorcycle, F motorbike; **Motorrad fahren** ride a motorcycle

Motorradfahrer(in) motorcyclist, biker

Motorroller *m* (motor) scooter

Motorsäge *f* power saw

Motorschaden *m* engine trouble (*or* failure)

Motte ['mɔtə] *f* (*-*; *-n*) ZO moth

'Mottenkugel *f* mothball

'mottenzerfressen *adj* moth-eaten

Motto ['mɔto] *n* (*-s*; *-s*) motto

Möwe ['møːvə] *f* (*-*; *-n*) ZO (sea)gull

Mücke ['mʏkə] *f* (*-*; *-n*) ZO gnat, midge, mosquito; **aus e-r Mücke e-n Elefanten machen** make a mountain out of a molehill

'Mückenstich *m* gnat bite

müde ['myːdə] *adj* tired; weary; sleepy; **müde sein** (**werden**) be (get) tired (*fig* **e-r Sache** of s.th.)

'Müdigkeit *f* (*-*; *no pl*) tiredness

Muff [mʊf] *m* (*-[e]s*; *-e*) muff

Muffe ['mʊfə] *f* (*-*; *-n*) TECH sleeve, socket

Muffel ['mʊfəl] F *m* (*-s*; *-*) sourpuss

muff(e)lig ['mʊf(ə)lɪç], **muffig** ['mʊfɪç] F *adj* musty; *contp* sulky, sullen

Mühe ['myːə] *f* (*-*; *-n*) trouble; effort; difficulty (**mit** with *s.th.*); (**nicht**) **der Mühe wert** (not) worth the trouble; **j-m Mühe machen** give s.o. trouble; **sich Mühe geben** try hard; **sich die Mühe sparen** save o.s. the trouble; **mit Mühe und Not**

(just) barely

'**mühelos** *adv* without difficulty

mühen ['myːən] *v/refl* (*ge-*, *h*) struggle, work hard

'**mühevoll** *adj* laborious

Mühle ['myːlə] *f* (-; *-n*) mill; morris

Mühsal ['myːzaːl] *f* (-; *-e*) toil

mühsam ['myːzaːm], '**mühselig 1.** *adj* laborious; **2.** *adv* with difficulty

Mulatte [mu'latə] *m* (*-n*; *-n*), **Mu'lattin** *f* (-; *-nen*) mulatto

Mulde ['muldə] *f* (-; *-n*) hollow

Mull [mul] *m* (*-[e]s*; *-e*) muslin; *esp* MED gauze

Müll [myl] *m* (*-s*; *no pl*) garbage, trash, *Br* refuse, rubbish

Müllabfuhr *f* garbage (*Br* refuse) collection

Müllbeseitigung *f* waste disposal

Müllbeutel *m* garbage bag, *Br* dustbin liner

'**Mullbinde** *f* MED gauze bandage

'**Müllcon,tainer** *m* garbage (*Br* rubbish) skip

Mülldepo,nie *f* dump

Mülleimer *m* garbage can, *Br* dustbin

Müllfahrer *m* garbage man, *Br* dustman

Müllhalde *f* dump

Müllhaufen *m* garbage (*Br* rubbish) heap

Müllkippe *f* dump

Müllschlucker *m* garbage (*Br* refuse) chute

Mülltonne *f* garbage can, *Br* dustbin

Müllverbrennungsanlage *f* (waste) incineration plant

Müllwagen *m* garbage truck, *Br* dustcart

Multiplikation [multiplika'tsjoːn] *f* (-; *-en*) MATH multiplication

multiplizieren [multipli'tsiːrən] *v/t* (*no -ge-*, *h*) MATH multiply (*mit* by)

Mumie ['muːmjə] *f* (-; *-n*) mummy

Mumps [mumps] *m*, *f* (-; *no pl*) MED mumps

Mund [munt] *m* (*-[e]s*; *Münder* ['myndɐ]) mouth; F **den Mund vollnehmen** talk big; **halt den Mund!** shut up!

Mundart *f* dialect

münden ['myndən] *v/i* (*ge-*, *h*, *sein*) **münden in** (*acc*) *river etc*: flow into; *road etc*: lead into

'**Mundgeruch** *m* bad breath

'**Mundhar,monika** *f* MUS mouth organ, harmonica

mündig ['myndɪç] *adj* emancipated; **mündig (werden)** JUR (come) of age

mündlich ['myntlɪç] *adj* oral; verbal

'**Mundstück** *n* mouthpiece; tip

'**Mündung** *f* (-; *-en*) *river*: mouth; *gun*: muzzle

'**Mundwasser** *n* mouthwash

Mundwerk F *n*: **ein gutes Mundwerk haben** have the gift of the gab; **ein loses Mundwerk** a loose tongue

Mundwinkel *m* corner of the mouth

'**Mund-zu-'Mund-Beatmung** *f* (-; *-en*) MED mouth-to-mouth resuscitation, F kiss of life

Munition [muni'tsjoːn] *f* (-; *-en*) ammunition

munkeln ['muŋkəln] F *v/t* (*ge-*, *h*) **man munkelt, dass** rumo(u)r has it that

Münster ['mynstɐ] *n* (*-s*; -) cathedral, minster

munter ['muntɐ] *adj* awake; lively; merry

Münze ['myntsə] *f* (-; *-n*) coin; medal

'**Münzeinwurf** *m* (coin) slot

Münzfernsprecher *m* pay phone

Münztank (**auto,mat**) *m* coin-operated (gas, *Br* petrol) pump

Münzwechsler *m* (*-s*; -) change machine

mürbe ['myrbə] *adj* tender; brittle; GASTR crisp

'**Mürbeteig** *m* short pastry; shortcake

Murmel ['murməl] *f* (-; *-n*) marble

'**murmeln** *v/t and v/i* (*ge-*, *h*) murmur

'**Murmeltier** *n* ZO marmot

murren ['murən] *v/i* (*ge-*, *h*) complain (*über acc* about)

mürrisch ['myrɪʃ] *adj* sullen; grumpy

Mus [muːs] *n* (*-es*; *-e*) mush; stewed fruit

Muschel ['muʃəl] *f* (-; *-n*) ZO mussel; shell

Museum [mu'zeːʊm] *n* (*-s*; *Museen*) museum

Musik [mu'ziːk] *f* (-; *no pl*) music

musikalisch [muzi'kaːlɪʃ] *adj* musical

Mu'sikanlage *f* hi-fi *or* stereo set

Musikauto,mat *m*, **Musikbox** *f* juke box

Musiker ['muːzikɐ] *m* (*-s*; -), '**Musikerin** *f* (-; *-nen*) musician

Mu'sikinstru,ment *n* musical instrument

Musikka,pelle *f* band

Musikkas,sette *f* music cassette

Musiklehrer(in) *m* music teacher

Musikstunde *f* music lesson

musisch ['muːzɪʃ] *adv*: **musisch interessiert (begabt)** fond of (gifted for) fine arts and music

musizieren [muzi'tsiːrən] *v/i* (*no -ge-*, *h*) make music

Muskat [mus'kaːt] *m* (*-[e]s*; *-e*), **Muskatnuss** *f* BOT nutmeg

Muskel ['muskəl] *m* (*-s*; *-n*) ANAT muscle

Muskelkater F *m* aching muscles

Muskelzerrung *f* MED pulled muscle

muskulös [musku'løːs] *adj* muscular, brawny

Müsli ['myːsli] *n* (*-s*; -) GASTR granola, *Br* muesli

Muss *n* (-; *no pl*) necessity; *es ist ein Muss* it is a must

Muße ['muːsə] *f* (-; *no pl*) leisure; spare time

müssen ['mʏsən] *v/i* (*irr*, *ge-*, *h*) *and v/aux* (*irr*, *no -ge-*, *h*) must, have (got) to; *du musst den Film sehen!* you must see the film!; *ich muss jetzt* (*m-e*) *Hausaufgaben machen* I have (got) to do my homework now; *sie muss krank sein* she must be ill; *du musst es nicht tun* you need not do it; *das müsstest du* (*doch*) *wissen* you ought to know (that); *sie müsste zu Hause sein* she should (ought to) be (at) home; *das müsste schön sein!* that would be nice!; *du hättest ihm helfen müssen* you ought to have helped him

müßig ['myːsɪç] *adj* idle; useless

musste ['mʊstə] *pret of* **müssen**

Muster ['mʊstɐ] *n* (-s; -) pattern; sample; model

'**mustergültig, musterhaft** *adj* exemplary; *sich mustergültig benehmen* behave perfectly

'**Musterhaus** *n* showhouse

'**mustern** *v/t* (*ge-*, *h*) eye *s.o.*; size *s.o.* up; MIL *gemustert werden* F have one's medical

Musterung ['mʊstərʊŋ] *f* (-; *-en*) MIL medical (examination for military service)

Mut [muːt] *m* (-[*e*]*s*; *no pl*) courage; *j-m Mut machen* encourage *s.o.*; *den Mut verlieren* lose courage; → *zumute*

mutig ['muːtɪç] *adj* courageous, brave

'**mutlos** *adj* discouraged

'**mutmaßen** *v/t* (*ge-*, *h*) speculate

'**mutmaßlich** *adj* probable; presumed

'**Mutprobe** *f* test of courage

Mutter ['mʊtɐ] *f* (-; *Mütter* ['mʏtɐ]) mother; TECH nut

Mutterboden *m*, **Muttererde** *f* AGR topsoil

mütterlich ['mʏtɐlɪç] *adj* motherly

'**mütterlicherseits** *adv*: *Onkel etc mütterlicherseits* maternal uncle *etc*

'**Mutterliebe** *f* motherly love

'**mutterlos** *adj* motherless

'**Muttermal** *n* birthmark, mole

Muttermilch *f* mother's milk

Mutterschaftsurlaub *m* maternity leave

Mutterschutz *m* JUR legal protection of expectant and nursing mothers

Muttersöhnchen *contp n* sissy

Muttersprache *f* mother tongue

Muttersprachler [-ʃpraːxlɐ] *m* (-s; -) native speaker

Muttertag *m* Mother's Day

Mutti ['mʊti] F *f* (-; *-s*) mom(my), *esp Br* mum(my)

'**mutwillig** *adj* wanton

Mütze ['mʏtsə] *f* (-; *-n*) cap

MwSt ABBR *of* **Mehrwertsteuer** VAT, value-added tax

mysteriös [mʏsteˈrjøːs] adj mysterious

mystisch ['mʏstɪʃ] *adj* mystic(al)

mythisch ['myːtɪʃ] *adj* mythical

Mythologie [mytoloˈɡiː] *f* (-; *-n*) mythology

Mythos ['myːtɔs] *m* (-; *Mythen*) myth

N

N ABBR *of* **Nord(en)** N, north

na [na] *int* well; *na und?* so what?; *na gut!* all right then; *na ja* (oh) well; *na(, na)!* come on!, come now!; *na so* (*et*)*was!* what do you know!, *Br* I say!; *na, dann nicht!* oh, forget it!; *na also!* there you are!; *na, warte!* just you wait!

Nabe ['naːbə] *f* (-; *-n*) TECH hub

Nabel ['naːbəl] *m* (-s; -) ANAT navel

'**Nabelschnur** *f* ANAT umbilical chord

nach [naːx] *prp* (*dat*) *and adv* to, toward(s), for; after; *time*: after, past; according to, by; *nach Hause* home; *abfahren nach* leave for; *nach rechts* (*Sü-* den) to the right (south); *nach oben* up (-stairs); *nach unten* down(stairs); *nach vorn* (*hinten*) to the front (back); *der Reihe nach* one after the other; *s-e Uhr nach dem Radio stellen* set one's watch by the radio; *nach m-r Uhr* by my watch; *suchen* (*fragen*) *nach* look (ask) for; *nach Gewicht* (*Zeit*) by weight (the hour); *riechen* (*schmecken*) *nach* smell (taste) of; *nach und nach* gradually; *nach wie vor* as before, still

'**nachahmen** [-aːmən] *v/t* (*sep*, *-ge-*, *h*) imitate, copy; take off

'**Nachahmung** *f* (-; *-en*) imitation

Nachbar

Nachbar ['naxbaːɐ] *m* (*-n*; *-n*), **Nachbarin** *f* (*-*; *-nen*) neighbo(u)r
Nachbarschaft *f* (*-*; *no pl*) neighbo(u)rhood, vicinity
Nachbau *m* (*-[e]s*; *-ten*) TECH reproduction
nachbauen *v/t* (*sep*, *-ge-*, *h*) copy, reproduce
Nachbildung *f* (*-*; *-en*) copy, imitation; replica; dummy
nachblicken *v/i* (*sep*, *-ge-*, *h*) look after
nachdem *cj* after, when; *je nachdem wie* depending on how
nachdenken *v/i* (*irr*, **denken**, *sep*, *-ge-*, *h*) think; **nachdenken über** (*acc*) think about, think *s.th.* over
nachdenklich *adj* thoughtful; *es macht e-n nachdenklich* it makes you think
Nachdruck[1] *m* (*-[e]s*; *no pl*) emphasis, stress
Nachdruck[2] (*-[e]s*; *-e*) reprint
nachdrucken *v/t* (*sep*, *-ge-*, *h*) reprint
nachdrücklich [*-drʏklɪç*] *adj* emphatic; forceful; **nachdrücklich raten** (**empfehlen**) advise (recommend) strongly
nacheifern *v/i* (*sep*, *-ge-*, *h*) *j-m nacheifern* emulate *s.o.*
nacheinander *adv* one after the other, in (*or* by) turns
nacherzählen *v/t* (*sep*, *no -ge-*, *h*) retell
Nacherzählung *f* (*-*; *-en*) PED reproduction
Nachfolge *f* (*-*; *no pl*) succession; *j-s Nachfolge antreten* succeed s.o.
nachfolgen *v/i* (*sep*, *-ge-*, *sein*) (*dat*) succeed *s.o.*
Nachfolger(in) [*-fɔlgɐ* (*-gərɪn*)] (*-s*; *-/-*; *-nen*) successor
nachforschen *v/i* (*sep*, *-ge-*, *h*) investigate
Nachforschung *f* (*-*; *-en*) investigation, inquiry
Nachfrage *f* (*-*; *-n*) inquiry; ECON demand
nachfragen *v/i* (*sep*, *-ge-*, *h*) inquire, ask
nachfühlen *v/t* (*sep*, *-ge-*, *h*) *j-m et. nachfühlen* understand how s.o. feels
nachfüllen *v/t* (*sep*, *-ge-*, *h*) refill
nachgeben *v/i* (*irr*, **geben**, *sep*, *-ge-*, *h*) give (way); *fig* give in
Nachgebühr *f* (*-*; *-en*) *post* surcharge
nachgehen *v/i* (*irr*, **gehen**, *sep*, *-ge-*, *sein*) follow (*a. fig*); *watch*: be slow; *e-r Sache nachgehen* investigate s.th.; *s-r Arbeit nachgehen* go about one's work
Nachgeschmack *m* (*-[e]s*; *no pl*) aftertaste (*a. fig*)
nachgiebig [*-giːbɪç*] *adj* yielding, soft (*both a. fig*)
Nachgiebigkeit *f* (*-*; *no pl*) yieldingness, softness (*both a. fig*)

nachhaltig [*-haltɪç*] *adj* lasting, enduring
nach hause → *Haus*
nachher *adv* afterwards; *bis nachher!* see you later!, so long!
Nachhilfe *f* help, assistance; PED → **Nachhilfestunden** *pl*, **Nachhilfeunterricht** *m* PED private lesson(s), coaching
nachholen *v/t* (*sep*, *-ge-*, *h*) make up for, catch up on
Nachkomme *m* (*-n*; *-n*) descendant, *pl esp* JUR issue
nachkommen *v/i* (*irr*, **kommen**, *sep*, *-ge-*, *sein*) follow, come later; (*dat*) comply with
Nachkriegs... *in cpds* postwar ...
Nachlass ['naːxlas] *m* (*-es*; *-lässe* [*-lɛsə*]) ECON reduction, discount; JUR estate
nachlassen *v/i* (*irr*, **lassen**, *sep*, *-ge-*, *h*) decrease, diminish, go down; *effect etc*: wear off; *student etc*: slacken one's effort; *interest etc*: flag; *health etc*: fail, deteriorate
nachlässig *adj* careless, negligent
nachlaufen *v/i* (*irr*, **laufen**, *sep*, *-ge-*, *sein*) run after
nachlesen *v/t* (*irr*, **lesen**, *sep*, *-ge-*, *h*) look up
nachmachen *v/t* (*sep*, *-ge-*, *h*) imitate, copy; counterfeit, forge
Nachmittag *m* afternoon; *heute Nachmittag* this afternoon
nachmittags *adv* in the afternoon
Nachnahme ['naːxnaːmə] *f* (*-*; *-n*) ECON cash on delivery; *per Nachnahme schicken* send C.O.D.
Nachname *m* surname, last (*or* family) name
Nachporto *n* surcharge
nachprüfen *v/t* (*sep*, *-ge-*, *h*) check (up), make sure (of)
nachrechnen *v/t* (*sep*, *-ge-*, *h*) check
Nachrede *f*: *üble Nachrede* malicious gossip; JUR defamation (of character), slander
Nachricht ['naːxrɪçt] *f* (*-*; *-en*) news; message; report; information, notice; *pl* news (report), newscast; *e-e gute* (*schlechte*) *Nachricht* good (bad) news; *Sie hören Nachrichten* here is the news
Nachrichtendienst *m* news service; MIL intelligence service
Nachrichtensatellit *m* communications satellite
Nachrichtensprecher(in) newscaster, *esp Br* newsreader
Nachrichtentechnik *f* telecommunications
Nachruf *m* obituary
nachrüsten *v/i* (*sep*, *-ge-*, *h*) POL, MIL close

the armament gap

nachsagen v/t (sep, -ge-, h) **j-m Schlechtes nachsagen** speak badly of s.o.; **man sagt ihm nach, dass er ...** he is said to inf

'**Nachsai,son** f off-peak season; **in der Nachsaison** out of season

'**nachschlagen** (irr, **schlagen**, sep, -ge-, h) **1.** v/t look up; **2.** v/i: **nachschlagen in** (dat) consult

'**Nachschlagewerk** n reference book

'**Nachschlüssel** m duplicate (or skeleton) key

Nachschrift f postscript; dictation

Nachschub m esp MIL supplies

'**nachsehen** (irr, **sehen**, sep, - ge-, h) **1.** v/i follow with one's eyes; (have a) look; **nachsehen ob** (go and) see whether; **2.** v/t look or go over or through; correct, mark; check (a. TECH)

nachsenden v/t ([irr, **senden**,] sep, -ge-, h) send on, forward; **bitte nachsenden!** post please forward!

'**Nachsilbe** f LING suffix

'**nachsitzen** v/i (irr, **sitzen**, sep, -ge-, h) stay in (after school), be kept in; **nachsitzen lassen** keep in, detain

'**Nachspann** m (-[e]s; -e) film: credits pl

'**Nachspiel** n sequel, consequences

'**nachspielen** v/i (sep, -ge-, h) SPORT **5 Minuten nachspielen lassen** allow 5 minutes for injury time

'**Nachspielzeit** f esp soccer: injury time

'**nachspio,nieren** v/i (no -ge-, h) spy (up)-on

nachsprechen v/t (irr, **sprechen**, sep, -ge-, h) **j-m et. nachsprechen** say or repeat s.th. after s.o.

nächst'beste ['nɛːçst-] adj first, F any old; next-best, second-best

nächste ['nɛːçstə] adj next; nearest (a. relative); **in den nächsten Tagen (Jahren)** in the next few days (years); **in nächster Zeit** in the near future; **was kommt als Nächstes?** what comes next?; **der Nächste, bitte!** next please!

'**nachstehen** v/i (irr, **stehen**, sep, -ge-, h) **j-m in nichts nachstehen** be in no way inferior to s.o.

'**nachstellen** (sep, -ge-, h) **1.** v/t put back (watch); TECH (re)adjust; **2.** v/i: **j-m nachstellen** be after s.o.

'**Nachstellung** f (-; -en) persecution

'**Nächstenliebe** f charity

Nacht [naxt] f (-; **Nächte** ['nɛçtə]) night; **Tag und Nacht** night and day; **die ganze Nacht** all night (long); **heute Nacht** tonight; last night

'**Nachtdienst** m night duty; **Nachtdienst**

haben PHARM be open all night

'**Nachteil** m disadvantage, drawback; **im Nachteil sein** be at a disadvantage (**gegenüber** compared with)

'**nachteilig** [-tailɪç] adj disadvantageous

'**Nachtessen** Swiss n → **Abendbrot**

Nachtfalter m ZO moth

Nachthemd n nightgown, nightdress, F nightie; nightshirt

Nachtigall ['naxtigal] f (-; -en) ZO nightingale

'**Nachtisch** m (-[e]s; no pl) dessert; sweet

nächtlich ['nɛçtlɪç] adj nightly; at or by night

'**Nachtlo,kal** n nightclub

Nachtrag ['naːxtraːk] m (-[e]s; -träge [-trɛːgə]) supplement

'**nachtragen** fig v/t (irr, **tragen**, sep, -ge-, h) **j-m et. nachtragen** bear s.o. a grudge

'**nachtragend** adj unforgiving

'**nachträglich** [-trɛːklɪç] adj additional; later; belated

nachts adv at night, in the night(time)

'**Nachtschicht** f night shift; **Nachtschicht haben** be on night shift

'**nachtschlafend** adj: **zu nachtschlafender Zeit** in the middle of the night

'**Nachttisch** m bedside table

'**Nachttopf** m chamber pot

'**Nachtwächter** m night watchman

'**nachwachsen** v/i (irr, **wachsen**, sep, -ge-, sein) grow again

'**Nachwahl** f PARL special election, Br by--election

Nachweis ['naːxvais] m (-es; -e) proof, evidence

'**nachweisbar** adj demonstrable; esp CHEM etc detectable

'**nachweisen** v/t (irr, **weisen**, sep, -ge-, h) prove; esp CHEM etc detect

'**nachweislich** adv as can be proved

'**Nachwelt** f (-; no pl) posterity

Nachwirkung f aftereffect(s), pl a. aftermath

Nachwort n (-[e]s; -worte) epilog(ue)

'**Nachwuchs** m (-es; no pl) young talent, F new blood

Nachwuchs... in cpds ...autor, ...schauspieler etc: talented or promising young ..., up-and-coming ...

'**nachzahlen** v/t (sep, -ge-, h) pay extra

nachzählen v/t (sep, -ge-, h) count over (again), check

'**Nachzahlung** f additional or extra payment

Nachzügler ['naːxtsyːklɐ] m (-s; -) straggler, latecomer

Nacken ['nakən] m (-s; -) ANAT (back or nape of the) neck

Nackenstütze f headrest
nackt [nakt] adj naked; esp PAINT, PHOT nude; bare (a. fig); fig plain; **völlig nackt** stark naked; **sich nackt ausziehen** strip; **nackt baden** swim in the nude; **j-n nackt malen** paint s.o. in the nude
Nadel ['naːdəl] f (-; -n) needle; pin; brooch
Nadelbaum m BOT conifer(ous tree)
Nadelöhr n eye of a needle
Nadelstich m pinprick (a. fig)
Nagel ['naːgəl] m (-s; Nägel ['nɛːgəl]) nail; **an den Nägeln kauen** bite one's nails
Nagellack m nail varnish or polish
'**nageln** v/t (ge-, h) nail (**an** acc, **auf** acc to)
'**nagel'neu** F adj brand-new
'**Nagelpflege** f manicure
nagen ['naːgən] (ge-, h) **1.** v/i gnaw (**an** dat at); **an e-m Knochen nagen** pick a bone; **2.** v/t gnaw
'**Nagetier** n ZO rodent
'**Nahaufnahme** f PHOT etc close-up
nahe [naːə] adj near, close (**bei** to); nearby; **nahe kommen** (dat) come close to; fig →**nahekommen**; →**nahelegen**; →**naheliegen**; →**naheliegend**
Nähe ['nɛːə] f (-; no pl) nearness; neighbo(u)rhood, vicinity; **in der Nähe des Bahnhofs** near the station; **ganz in der Nähe** quite near, close by; **in deiner Nähe** near you
nahegehen v/i (irr, gehen, sep, -ge-, sein): **j-m nahegehen** affect s.o. deeply
'**nahekommen** v/i (irr, kommen, sep, -ge-, sein) fig come close to
'**nahelegen** v/t (sep, -ge-, h) suggest
'**naheliegen** v/i (irr, liegen, sep, -ge-, h) seem likely
'**naheliegend** adj likely, obvious
nahen ['naːən] v/i (ge-, sein) approach
nähen ['nɛːən] v/t and v/i (ge-, h) sew; make
Nähere ['nɛːərə] n (-n; no pl) details, particulars
nähern ['nɛːɐn] v/refl (ge-, h) approach, get near(er) or close(r) (dat to)
'**nahezu** adv nearly, almost
'**Nähgarn** n (sewing) cotton
'**Nahkampf** m MIL close combat
nahm [naːm] pret of **nehmen**
'**Näh·ma,schine** f sewing machine
'**Nähnadel** f (sewing) needle
nähren ['nɛːrən] v/t (ge-, h) feed; fig nurture
nahrhaft ['naːɐhaft] adj nutritious, nourishing
Nährstoff ['nɛːɐ-] m nutrient
Nahrung ['naːrʊŋ] f (-; no pl) food, nourishment; AGR feed; diet

'**Nahrungsmittel** pl food(stuffs)
Nährwert ['nɛːɐ-] m nutritional value
Naht [naːt] f (-; Nähte ['nɛːtə]) seam; MED suture
'**Nahverkehr** m local traffic
'**Nahverkehrszug** m local or commuter train
'**Nähzeug** n sewing kit
naiv [na'iːf] adj naive
Naivität [naivi'tɛːt] f (-; no pl) naivety
Name ['naːmə] m (-ns; -n) name; **im Namen von** on behalf of; **nur dem Namen nach** in name only
'**namenlos** adj nameless, fig a. unspeakable
'**namens** adv by (the) name of, named, called
'**Namenstag** m name day
Namensvetter m namesake
Namenszug m signature
namentlich ['naːməntlɪç] adj and adv by name
nämlich ['nɛːmlɪç] adv that is (to say), namely; you see or know
nannte ['nantə] pret of **nennen**
Napf [napf] m (-[e]s; Näpfe ['nɛpfə]) bowl, basin
Narbe ['narbə] f (-; -n) scar
narbig ['narbɪç] adj scarred
Narkose [nar'koːzə] f (-; -n) MED an(a)esthesia; **in Narkose** under an an(a)esthetic
Narr [nar] m (-en; -en) fool; **j-n zum Narren halten** fool s.o.
'**narrensicher** adj foolproof
närrisch ['nɛrɪʃ] adj foolish; **närrisch vor** (dat) mad with
Narzisse [nar'tsɪsə] f (-; -n) BOT daffodil
nasal [na'zaːl] adj nasal
naschen ['naʃən] v/i and v/t (ge-, h) nibble (**an** dat at); **gern naschen** have a sweet tooth
Naschereien [naʃə'raiən] pl dainties, goodies, sweets
'**naschhaft** adj sweet-toothed
Nase ['naːzə] f (-; -n) ANAT nose (a. fig); **sich die Nase putzen** blow one's nose; **in der Nase bohren** pick one's nose; F **die Nase voll haben** (**von**) be fed up (with)
'**Nasenbluten** n MED nosebleed
Nasenloch n nostril
Nasenspitze f tip of the nose
Nashorn n ZO rhinoceros, F rhino
nass [nas] adj wet; **triefend nass** soaking (wet)
Nässe ['nɛsə] f (-; no pl) wet(-ness)
'**nässen** (ge-, h) **1.** v/t wet; **2.** v/i MED weep
'**nasskalt** adj damp and cold, raw

Nation [na'tsjoːn] *f* (-; *-en*) nation
national [natsjo'naːl] *adj* national
Natio'nalhymne *f* national anthem
Nationalismus [natsjona'lɪsmʊs] *m* (-; *no pl*) nationalism
Nationalität [natsjonali'tɛːt] *f* (-; *-en*) nationality
Natio'nalmannschaft *f* SPORT national team
Nationalpark *m* national park
Natio'nalsozia,lismus *m* HIST National Socialism, *contp* Nazism
Natio'nalsozia,list *m*, **natio'nalsozia,listisch** *adj* HIST National Socialist, *contp* Nazi
Natter ['natɐ] *f* (-; *-n*) zo adder, viper (*a. fig*)
Natur [na'tuːɐ] *f* (-; *-en*) nature; *von Natur* (*aus*) by nature
Naturalismus [natura'lɪsmʊs] *m* (-; *no pl*) naturalism
Na'turereignis *n*, **Naturerscheinung** *f* natural phenomenon
Naturforscher *m* naturalist
Naturgeschichte *f* natural history
Naturgesetz *n* law of nature
na'turgetreu *adj* true to life; lifelike
Na'turkata,strophe *f* (natural) catastrophe *or* disaster, act of God
natürlich [na'tyːɐlɪç] **1.** *adj* natural; **2.** *adv* naturally, of course
Na'turschätze *pl* natural resources
Naturschutz *m* nature conservation; *unter Naturschutz* protected
Naturschützer [-ʃYtsɐ] *m* (-s; -) conservationist
Naturschutzgebiet *n* nature reserve; national park
Naturvolk *n* primitive race
Naturwissenschaft *f* (natural) science
n. Chr. ABBR *of nach Christus* AD, Anno Domini
Nebel ['neːbəl] *m* (-s; -) fog; mist; haze; smoke
Nebelhorn *n* foghorn
Nebelleuchte *f* MOT fog light
neben ['neːbən] *prp* (*dat and acc*) beside, next to; besides, apart from; compared with; *neben anderem* among other things; *setz dich neben mich* sit by me *or* by my side
neben'an *adv* next door
neben'bei *adv* in addition, at the same time; *nebenbei* (*gesagt*) by the way
'Nebenberuf *m* second job, sideline
'nebenberuflich *adv* as a sideline
'Nebenbuhler [-buːlɐ] *m* (-s; -), **'Nebenbuhlerin** *f* (-; *-nen*) rival
'nebenei'nander *adv* side by side; next

(door) to each other; *nebeneinander bestehen* coexist
'Nebeneinkünfte *pl*, **Nebeneinnahmen** *pl* extra money
Nebenfach *n* PED *etc* minor (subject), *Br* subsidiary subject
Nebenfluss *m* tributary
Nebengebäude *n* next-door *or* adjoining building; annex(e)
Nebenhaus *n* house next door
Nebenkosten *pl* extras
Nebenmann *m*: *dein Nebenmann* the person next to you
Nebenpro,dukt *n* by-product
Nebenrolle *f* THEA supporting role, minor part (*a. fig*); cameo (role)
Nebensache *f* minor matter; *das ist Nebensache* that's of little *or* no importance
'nebensächlich *adj* unimportant
'Nebensatz *m* LING subordinate clause
Nebenstelle *f* TEL extension
Nebenstraße *f* side street; minor road
Nebenstrecke *f* RAIL branch line
Nebentisch *m* next table
Nebenverdienst *m* extra earnings
Nebenwirkung *f* side effect
Nebenzimmer *n* adjoining room
neblig ['neːblɪç] *adj* foggy; misty; hazy
necken ['nɛkən] *v/t* (*ge-, h*) tease
Neckerei [nɛkə'rai] *f* (-; *-en*) teasing
'neckisch *adj* playful, teasing
Neffe ['nɛfə] *m* (-*n*; *-n*) nephew
negativ ['neːgatiːf] *adj* negative
'Negativ *n* (-s; *-e*) PHOT negative
Neger ['neːgɐ] *m* (-s; -), **Negerin** ['neːgə-rɪn] *f* (-; *-nen*) → *Schwarze*
nehmen ['neːmən] *v/t* (*irr, ge-, h*) take (*a. sich nehmen*); *j-m et. nehmen* take s.th. (away) from s.o. (*a. fig*); *sich e-n Tag frei nehmen* take a day off; *j-n an die Hand nehmen* take s.o. by the hand
Neid [nait] *m* (-*es*; *no pl*) envy; *reiner Neid* sheer envy; **neidisch** ['naidɪʃ] *adj* envious (*auf acc* of)
Neige ['naigə] *f*: *zur Neige gehen* draw to its close; run out
'neigen (*ge-, h*) **1.** *v/t and refl* bend, incline; **2.** *v/i*: *zu et. neigen* tend to (do) s.th.
'Neigung *f* (-; *-en*) inclination (*a. fig*), slope, incline; *fig* tendency
nein [nain] *adv* no
Nektar ['nɛktaːɐ] *m* (-s; *-e*) BOT nectar
Nelke ['nɛlkə] *f* (-; *-n*) BOT carnation; GASTR clove
nennen ['nɛnən] *v/t* (*irr, ge-, h*) name, call; mention; *sich nennen* call o.s., be called; *man nennt ihn ...* he is called ...;

N

das nenne ich ...! that's what I call ...!

'**nennenswert** *adj* worth mentioning

Nenner ['nɛnɐ] *m* (-*s*; -) MATH denominator

'**Nennwert** *m* ECON nominal *or* face value; *zum Nennwert* at par

Neo..., **neo...** [neo-] *in cpds ...faschist etc*: neo-...

Neon ['ne:ɔn] *n* (-*s*; *no pl*) CHEM neon

'**Neonröhre** *f* neon tube

Nepp [nɛp] F *m* (-*s*; *no pl*) rip-off

neppen ['nɛpən] F *v/t* (*ge-*, *h*) fleece, rip *s.o.* off

Nerv [nɛrf] *m* (-*s*; -*en*) ANAT nerve; *j-m auf die Nerven fallen or gehen* get on s.o.'s nerves; *die Nerven behalten* (*verlieren*) keep (lose) one's head

nerven ['nɛrfən] F *v/t and v/i* (*ge-*, *h*) be a pain in the neck (*j-n* to s.o.)

'**Nervenarzt** *m*, '**Nervenärztin** *f* neurologist

'**nervenaufreibend** *adj* nerve-racking

'**Nervenbelastung** *f* nervous strain

Nervenkitzel *m* thrill, F kick(s)

'**nervenkrank** *adj* mentally ill

'**Nervensäge** F *f* pain in the neck

Nervensys¦tem *n* nervous system

Nervenzusammenbruch *m* nervous breakdown

nervös [nɛr'vø:s] *adj* nervous

Nervosität [nɛrvozi'tɛːt] *f* (-; *no pl*) nervousness

Nerz [nɛrts] *m* (-*es*; -*e*) ZO mink

Nessel ['nɛsəl] *f* (-; -*n*) BOT nettle

Nest [nɛst] *n* (-[*e*]*s*; -*er* ['nɛstɐ]) ZO nest; F *contp* one-horse town

nett [nɛt] *adj* nice; kind; *so nett sein und et.* (*or et. zu*) *tun* be so kind as to do s.th.

netto ['nɛto] *adv* ECON net

Netz [nɛts] *n* (-*es*; -*e*) net; RAIL, TEL, EDP network; ELECTR mains; *am Netz sein* EDP be in the network

Netzhaut *f* ANAT retina

Netzkarte *f* RAIL area season ticket

neu [nɔy] *adj* new; fresh; *fig* modern; *neuere Sprachen* modern languages; *neueste Nachrichten* (*Mode*) latest news (fashion); *von neuem* anew, afresh; *seit neu*(*st*)*em* since (very) recently; *viel Neues* a lot of new things; *was gibt es Neues?* what's the news?, what's new?

'**neuartig** *adj* novel

'**Neubau** *m* (-[*e*]*s*; -*ten*) new building

Neubaugebiet *n* new housing estate

neuerdings ['nɔyɐ'dɪŋs] *adv* lately, recently

Neuerer ['nɔyərɐ] *m* (-*s*; -) innovator

'**Neuerung** *f* (-; -*en*) innovation

'**Neugestaltung** *f* reorganization, reformation

'**Neugier** *f*, **Neugierde** ['nɔygiːɐdə] *f* (-; *no pl*) curiosity

'**neugierig** *adj* curious (*auf acc* about); F *contp* nos(e)y; *ich bin neugierig, ob* I wonder if

'**Neugierige** [-giːrɪgə] *contp pl* rubbernecks

'**Neuheit** *f* (-; -*en*) novelty

Neuigkeit ['nɔyɪçkait] *f* (-; -*en*) (piece of) news

'**Neujahr** *n* New Year('s Day); *Prost Neujahr!* Happy New Year!

'**neulich** *adv* the other day

Neuling ['nɔylɪŋ] *m* (-*s*; -*e*) newcomer, F greenhorn

'**neumodisch** *contp adj* newfangled

'**Neumond** *m* new moon

neun [nɔyn] *adj* nine

'**neunte** *adj* ninth

'**Neuntel** *n* (-*s*; -) ninth (part)

'**neuntens** *adv* ninthly

'**neunzehn** *adj* nineteen

'**neunzehnte** *adj* nineteenth

'**neunzig** *adj* ninety

'**neunzigste** *adj* ninetieth

Neurose [nɔy'roːzə] *f* (-; -*n*) MED neurosis

neurotisch [nɔy'roːtɪʃ] *adj* MED neurotic

'**neusprachlich** *adj* modern-language

neutral [nɔy'traːl] *adj* neutral

Neutralität [nɔytrali'tɛːt] *f* (-; *no pl*) neutrality

Neutronen... [nɔy'troːnən-] PHYS *in cpds ...bombe etc*: neutron ...

Neutrum ['nɔytrum] *n* (-*s*; -*tra*) LING neuter

'**Neuverfilmung** *f* remake

'**neuwertig** *adj* as good as new

'**Neuzeit** *f* (-; *no pl*) modern times

nicht [nɪçt] *adv* not; *überhaupt nicht* not at all; *nicht* (*ein*)*mal, gar nicht erst* not even; *nicht mehr* not any more *or* longer; *sie ist nett* (*wohnt hier*), *nicht* (*wahr*)*?* she's nice (lives here), isn't (doesn't) she?; *nicht so ... wie* not as ... as; *noch nicht* not yet; *nicht besser* (*als*) no (*or* not any) better (than); *ich* (*auch*) *nicht* I don't *or* I'm not (either); (*bitte*) *nicht!* (please) don't!

'**Nicht...** *in cpds ...mitglied*, *...schwimmer etc*: mst non-...

Nichtbeachtung *f* disregard; non-observance

Nichte ['nɪçtə] *f* (-; -*n*) niece

nichtig ['nɪçtɪç] *adj* trivial; JUR void, invalid

'**Nichtraucher** *m*, '**Nichtraucherin** *f* nonsmoker

nichts *indef pron* nothing, not anything; *nichts (anderes) als* nothing but; *gar nichts* nothing at all; F *das ist nichts* that's no good; *nichts sagend* meaningless

Nichts *n* (-s; *no pl*) nothing(ness); *aus dem Nichts* appear *etc* from nowhere; *build etc* from nothing

nichtsdesto'weniger *adv* nevertheless

'**nichtsnutzig** [-nʊtsɪç] *adj* good-for--nothing, worthless

'**nichtssagend** *adj* meaningless

'**Nichtstuer** [-tuːɐ] *m* (-s; -) do-nothing, F bum

nicken ['nɪkən] *v/i* (ge-, h) nod (one's head)

nie [niː] *adv* never, at no time; *fast nie* hardly ever; *nie und nimmer* never ever

nieder ['niːdɐ] **1.** *adj* low; **2.** *adv* down

'**Niedergang** *m* (-[e]s; *no pl*) decline

'**niedergeschlagen** *adj* depressed, (feeling) down

'**Niederlage** *f* defeat, F beating

'**niederlassen** *v/refl* (*irr*, *lassen*, *sep*, *-ge-*, *h*) settle (down); ECON set up (*als* as)

'**Niederlassung** *f* (-; *-en*) ECON establishment; branch

'**niederlegen** *v/t* (*sep*, *-ge-*, *h*) lay down (*a. office etc*); *die Arbeit niederlegen* (go on) strike, down tools, F walk out; *sich niederlegen* lie down; go to bed

niedermetzeln *v/t* (*sep*, *-ge-*, *h*) massacre

'**Niederschlag** *m* METEOR rain(fall); PHYS fallout; CHEM precipitate; *boxing*: knock-down

'**niederschlagen** *v/t* (*irr*, *schlagen*, *sep*, *-ge-*, *h*) knock down; cast down (*eyes*); *fig* put down (*revolt etc*); JUR quash; *sich niederschlagen* CHEM precipitate

'**niederschmettern** *fig v/t* (*sep*, *-ge-*, *h*) shatter, crush

'**niederträchtig** *adj* base, mean

Niederung ['niːdərʊŋ] *f* (-; *-en*) lowland(s)

niedlich ['niːtlɪç] *adj* pretty, sweet, cute

niedrig ['niːdrɪç] *adj* low (*a. fig*); *fig* light (*sentence etc*); *niedrig fliegen* fly low

niemals ['niːmaːls] → *nie*

niemand ['niːmant] *indef pron* nobody, no one, not anybody; *niemand von ihnen* none of them

'**Niemandsland** *n* (-[e]s; *no pl*) no-man's-land

Niere ['niːrə] *f* (-; *-n*) ANAT kidney

nieseln ['niːzəln] *v/i* (ge-, h) drizzle

'**Nieselregen** *m* drizzle

niesen ['niːzən] *v/i* (ge-, h) sneeze

Niete[1] ['niːtə] *f* (-; *-n*) TECH rivet

'**Niete**[2] *f* (-; *-n*) blank; F failure

Nikolaustag ['nɪkolaus-] *m* St. Nicholas' Day

Nikotin [niko'tiːn] *n* (-s; *no pl*) CHEM nicotine

Nilpferd ['niːl-] *n* ZO hippopotamus, F hippo

Nippel ['nɪpəl] *m* (-s; -) TECH nipple

nippen ['nɪpən] *v/i* (ge-, h) sip (*an dat* at)

nirgends ['nɪrgənts] *adv* nowhere

Nische ['niːʃə] *f* (-; *-n*) niche, recess

nisten ['nɪstən] *v/i* (ge-, h) ZO nest

'**Nistplatz** *m* ZO nesting place

Niveau [ni'voː] *n* (-s; -s) level, *fig a.* standard

Nixe ['nɪksə] *f* (-; *-n*) water nymph, mermaid

noch [nɔx] *adv* still; *noch nicht* not yet; *noch nie* never before; *er hat nur noch 5 Mark (Minuten)* he has only 5 marks (minutes) left; (*sonst*) *noch et.?* anything else?; *ich möchte noch et.* (*Tee*) I'd like some more (tea); *noch ein(e, -n)..., bitte* another ..., please; *noch einmal* once more *or* again; *noch zwei Stunden* another two hours, two hours to go; *noch besser* (*schlimmer*) even better (worse); *noch gestern* only yesterday; *und wenn es noch so ... ist* however (*or* no matter how) ... it may be

'**nochmalig** [-maːlɪç] *adj* new, renewed

'**nochmals** *adv* once more *or* again

Nockerl ['nɔkɐl] *Austrian n* (-s; *-n*) GASTR small dumpling

Nomade [no'maːdə] *m* (-n; *-n*), **No'madin** *f* (-; *-nen*) nomad

Nominativ ['noːminatiːf] *m* (-s; *-e*) LING nominative (case)

nominieren [nomi'niːrən] *v/t* (*no -ge-*, *h*) nominate

Nonne ['nɔnə] *f* (-; *-n*) REL nun

'**Nonnenkloster** *n* REL convent

Norden ['nɔrdən] *m* (-s; *no pl*) north; *nach Norden* north(wards)

nordisch ['nɔrdɪʃ] *adj* northern; SPORT *nordische Kombination* Nordic Combined

nördlich ['nœrtlɪç] **1.** *adj* north(ern); northerly; **2.** *adv:* **nördlich von** north of

Nordlicht ['nɔrt-] *n* (-[e]s; *-er*) ASTR northern lights

Nord'osten *m* northeast

nord'östlich *adj* northeast(ern); northeasterly

'**Nordpol** *m* North Pole

Nord'westen *m* northwest

nord'westlich *adj* northwest(ern); northwesterly

'**Nordwind** *m* north wind

nörgeln ['nœrgəln] *v/i* (ge-, h) nag (*an dat*

at)

Nörgler ['nœrglɐ] *m* (-*s*; -), '**Nörglerin** *f* (-; -*nen*) nagger

Norm [nɔrm] *f* (-; -*en*) standard, norm

normal [nɔr'maːl] *adj* normal; F **nicht ganz normal** not quite right in the head

Nor'mal... *esp* TECH *in cpds* ...**maß**, ...**zeit** *etc*: standard ...

Normalben,zin *n* regular (gas, *Br* petrol)

normalerweise [nɔr'maːlɐ'vaizə] *adv* normally, usually

normalisieren [nɔrmali'ziːrən] *v/refl* (*no -ge-*, *h*) return to normal

normen ['nɔrmən] *v/t* (*ge-*, *h*) standardize

Norwegen ['nɔrveːgən] Norway

Norweger ['nɔrveːgɐ] *m* (-*s*; -), '**Norwegerin** [-gərɪn] *f* (-; -*nen*), '**norwegisch** *adj* Norwegian

Not [noːt] *f* (-; *Nöte* ['nøːtə]) need; want; poverty; hardship, misery; difficulty; emergency; distress; **Not leidend** needy; **in Not sein** be in trouble; **zur Not** if need be, if necessary

Notar [no'taːɐ] *m* (-*s*; -*e*), **No'tarin** *f* (-; -*nen*) JUR notary (public)

'**Notaufnahme** *f* MED emergency room, *Br* casualty

Notausgang *m* emergency exit

Notbehelf *m* (-[*e*]*s*; -*e*) makeshift, expedient

Notbremse *f* emergency brake

Notdienst *m* emergency duty

'**notdürftig** *adj* scanty; temporary

Note ['noːtə] *f* (-; -*n*) note (*a.* MUS *and* POL); ECON bill, *esp Br* (bank)note; PED grade, *Br* mark; *pl* MUS (sheet) music; **Noten lesen** read music

Notebook ['noʊtbʊk] *n* (-*s*; -*s*) EDP notebook

'**Notendurchschnitt** *m* PED *etc* average

'**Notenständer** *m* music stand

'**Notfall** *m* emergency

'**notfalls** *adv* if necessary

'**notgedrungen** *adv*: **et. notgedrungen tun** be forced to do s.th.

notieren [no'tiːrən] *v/t* (*no -ge-*, *h*) make a note of, note (down); ECON quote

nötig ['nøːtɪç] *adj* necessary; **nötig haben** need; **nötig brauchen** need badly; **das Nötigste** the (bare) necessities *or* essentials

nötigen ['nøːtɪgən] *v/t* (*ge-*, *h*) force, compel; press, urge

'**Nötigung** *f* (-; -*en*) coercion; JUR intimidation

Notiz [no'tiːts] *f* (-; -*en*) note; **keine Notiz nehmen von** take no notice of, ignore; **sich Notizen machen** take notes

Notizblock *m* memo pad, *Br* notepad

Notizbuch *n* notebook

'**Notlage** *f* awkward (*or* difficult) situation; difficulties; emergency

'**notlanden** *v/i* (-*ge-*, *sein*) AVIAT make an emergency landing

'**Notlandung** *f* AVIAT emergency landing

'**Notlösung** *f* expedient

'**Notlüge** *f* white lie

notorisch [no'toːrɪʃ] *adj* notorious

'**Notruf** *m* TEL emergency call

Notrufsäule *f* TEL emergency phone

Notsig,nal *n* emergency *or* distress signal

Notstand *m* state of (national) emergency

Notstandsgebiet *n* disaster area; ECON depressed area

Notstandsgesetze *pl* POL emergency laws

Notverband *m* MED emergency dressing

'**Notwehr** *f* (-; *no pl*) JUR self-defense, *Br* self-defence

'**notwendig** *adj* necessary

'**Notwendigkeit** *f* (-; -*en*) necessity

'**Notzucht** *f* (-; *no pl*) JUR rape

Novelle [no'vɛlə] *f* (-; -*n*) novella; PARL amendment

November [no'vɛmbɐ] *m* (-[*s*]; -) November

Nr. ABBR *of* **Nummer** No., no., number

Nu [nuː] *m*: **im Nu** in no time

Nuance ['nyãːsə] *f* shade

nüchtern ['nʏçtɐn] *adj* sober (*a. fig*); matter-of-fact; **auf nüchternen Magen** on an empty stomach; **nüchtern werden** (**machen**) sober up

'**Nüchternheit** *f* (-; *no pl*) sobriety

Nudel ['nuːdəl] *f* (-; -*n*) noodle

nuklear [nukle'aːɐ] *adj* nuclear

null [nʊl] *adj* zero, *Br* nought; TEL 0; SPORT nil, nothing; *tennis*: love; **null Grad** zero degrees; **null Fehler** no mistakes; **gleich Null sein** be nil

'**Nulldi,ät** *f* low-calorie (*or* F starvation) diet

Nullpunkt *m* zero (point *or fig* level)

Nullta,rif *m* free fare(s); **zum Nulltarif** free (of charge)

Numerus clausus ['nuːmerʊs 'klauzʊs] *m* (-; *no pl*) UNIV restricted admission(s)

Nummer ['nʊmɐ] *f* (-; -*n*) number; issue; size

nummerieren [nʊmə'riːrən] *v/t* (*no -ge-*, *h*) number

'**Nummernschild** *n* MOT license plate, *Br* numberplate

nun [nuːn] *adv* now; well

nur [nuːɐ] *adv* only, just; merely; nothing but; **er tut nur so** he's just pretending; **nur so** (**zum Spaß**) just for fun; **warte nur!** just you wait!; **mach nur!, nur zu!** go ahead!; → **Erwachsene**

Nuss [nʊs] *f* (-; *Nüsse* ['nʏsə]) BOT nut
Nussbaum *m* walnut (tree)
Nussknacker *m* nutcracker
Nussschale *f* nutshell
Nüstern ['nʏstɐn] *pl* ZO nostrils
Nutte ['nʊtə] F *f* (-; -*n*) hooker, *sl* tart
Nutzanwendung ['nʊts-] *f* practical application
'**nutzbar** *adj* usable; **nutzbar machen** utilize; exploit; harness
'**nutzbringend** *adj* profitable, useful
nütze ['nʏtsə] *adj* useful; **zu nichts nütze sein** be (of) no use; be good for nothing
Nutzen ['nʊtsən] *m* (-*s*; -) use; profit, gain; advantage; **Nutzen ziehen aus** (*dat*)

benefit *or* profit from *or* by; **zum Nutzen von** (*or gen*) for the benefit of
'**nutzen**, '**nützen** (*ge*-, *h*) **1.** *v/i*: **j-m nutzen** be of use to s.o.; **es nützt nichts** (**es zu tun**) it's no use (doing it); **2.** *v/t* use, make use of; take advantage of
nützlich ['nʏtslɪç] *adj* useful, helpful; advantageous; **sich nützlich machen** make o.s. useful
'**nutzlos** *adj* useless, (of) no use
'**Nutzung** *f* (-; -*en*) use, utilization
Nylon® ['nailɔn] *n* (-*s*; *no pl*) nylon
Nylonstrümpfe *pl* nylon stockings
Nymphe ['nʏmfə] *f* (-; -*n*) nymph

O

O ABBR *of* **Osten** E, east
o *int* oh!; **o weh!** oh dear!
o. Ä. ABBR *of* **oder Ähnliche(s)** or the like
Oase [o'a:zə] *f* (-; -*n*) oasis (*a. fig*)
ob [ɔp] *cj* whether, if; **als ob** as if, as though; **und ob!** and how!, you bet!
Obacht ['o:baxt] *f*: **Obacht geben auf** (*acc*) pay attention to; (**gib**) **Obacht!** watch out!
Obdach ['ɔpdax] *n* (-[*e*]*s*; *no pl*) shelter
'**obdachlos** *adj* homeless, without shelter
'**Obdachlose** *m*, *f* (-*n*; -*n*) homeless person
'**Obdachlosen͵syl** *n* shelter for the homeless
Obduktion [ɔpdʊk'tsjoːn] *f* (-; -*en*) MED autopsy
obduzieren [ɔpdu'tsiːrən] *v/t* (*no* -*ge*-, *h*) MED perform an autopsy on
oben ['o:bən] *adv* above; up; on (the) top; at the top (*a. fig*); on the surface; upstairs; **da oben** up there; **von oben bis unten** from top to bottom (*or* toe); **links oben** (at the) top left; **siehe oben** see above; F **oben ohne** topless; **von oben herab** *fig* patronizing(ly), condescending(ly); **oben erwähnt** *or* **genannt** above-mentioned
oben'an *adv* at the top
oben'auf *adv* on the top; on the surface; F feeling great
oben'drein *adv* besides, into the bargain, at that
oben'hin *adv* superficially

Ober ['o:bɐ] *m* (-*s*; -) waiter
'**Oberarm** *m* ANAT upper arm
Oberarzt *m*, **Oberärztin** *f* assistant medical director
Oberbefehl *m* MIL supreme command
Oberbegriff *n* generic term
Oberbürgermeister *m* mayor, *Br* Lord Mayor
obere ['o:bərə] *adj* upper, top, *fig a.* superior
'**Oberfläche** *f* surface (*a. fig*) (**an** *dat* on)
'**oberflächlich** *adj* superficial
'**oberhalb** *prp* (*gen*) above
'**Oberhand** *f*: **die Oberhand gewinnen** (**über** *acc*) get the upper hand (of)
Oberhaupt *n* head, chief
Oberhaus *n* (-*es*; *no pl*) *Br* PARL House of Lords
Oberhemd *n* shirt
Oberherrschaft *f* (-; *no pl*) supremacy
Oberin ['o:bərɪn] *f* (-; -*nen*) REL Mother Superior
'**oberirdisch** *adj* above ground; ELECTR overhead
'**Oberkellner** *m* head waiter
Oberkiefer *m* ANAT upper jaw
Oberkörper *m* upper part of the body; **den Oberkörper frei machen** strip to the waist
Oberleder *n* uppers
Oberleitung *f* chief management; ELECTR overhead contact line
Oberlippe *f* ANAT upper lip
Obers ['o:bɐs] *Austrian n* (-; *no pl*) GASTR

cream
'**Oberschenkel** *m* ANAT thigh
'**Oberschule** *f appr* highschool, *Br* grammar school
Oberst ['oːbɐst] *m* (*-en*; *-en*) MIL colonel
oberste ['oːbɐstə] *adj* up(per)most, top (-most); highest; *fig* chief, first
'**Oberstufe** *f appr* senior highschool, *Br appr* senior classes
Oberteil *n* top
ob'gleich *cj* (al)though
Obhut ['ɔphuːt] *f* (-; *no pl*) care, charge; **in s-e Obhut nehmen** take care *or* charge of
obig ['oːbɪç] *adj* above(-mentioned)
Objekt [ɔp'jɛkt] *n* (*-[e]s*; *-e*) object (*a.* LING); ECON property
objektiv [ɔpjɛk'tiːf] *adj* objective; impartial, unbias(s)ed
Objek'tiv *n* (*-s*; *-e*) PHOT (object) lens
Objektivität [ɔpjɛktivi'tɛːt] *f* (-; *no pl*) objectivity; impartiality
Oblate [o'blaːtə] *f* (-; *-n*) wafer; REL host
obligatorisch [obliga'toːrɪʃ] *adj* compulsory
Oboe [o'boːə] *f* (-; *-n*) MUS oboe
Oboist [obo'ɪst] *m* (*-en*; *-en*) MUS oboist
Observatorium [ɔpzɛrva'toːrjʊm] *n* (*-s*; *-ien*) ASTR observatory
Obst [oːpst] *n* (*-[e]s*; *no pl*) fruit
Obstgarten *m* orchard
Obstkon,serven *pl* canned fruit
Obstladen *m* fruit store, *esp Br* fruiterer's (shop)
Obsttorte *f* fruit pie (*Br* flan)
obszön [ɔps'tsøːn] *adj* obscene, filthy
ob'wohl *cj* (al)though
Occasion [ɔka'zjoːn] *Swiss f* (-; *-en*) bargain, good buy
Ochse ['ɔksə] *m* (*-n*; *-n*) ZO ox, bullock; F blockhead
od. ABBR *of* **oder** or
öde ['øːdə] *adj* deserted, desolate; *fig* dull, dreary, tedious
oder ['oːdɐ] *cj* or; **oder aber** or else, otherwise; **oder vielmehr** or rather; **oder so** or so; **er kommt doch, oder?** he's coming, isn't he?; **du kennst ihn ja nicht, oder doch?** you don't know him, or do you?
Ofen ['oːfən] *m* (*-s*; *Öfen* ['øːfən]) stove; oven; TECH furnace
Ofenheizung *f* stove heating
Ofenrohr *n* stovepipe
offen ['ɔfən] **1.** *adj* open (*a. fig*); vacant (*post*); *fig* frank; **2.** *adv*: **offen gesagt** frankly (speaking); **offen s-e Meinung sagen** speak one's mind (freely); **offen stehen** be open; ECON be outstanding

'**offenbar** *adj* obvious, evident; apparent
offenbaren [-'baːrən] *v/t* (*ge-, h*) reveal, disclose, show
Offen'barung *f* (-; *-en*) revelation
'**Offenheit** *f* (-; *no pl*) openness, frankness
'**offenherzig** *adj* open-hearted, frank, candid; *fig* revealing (*dress*)
'**offensichtlich** *adj* → **offenbar**
offensiv [ɔfɛn'ziːf] *adj*, **Offensive** [ɔfɛn'ziːvə] *f* (-; *-n*) offensive
'**offenstehen** *v/i* (*irr*, **stehen**, *sep*, *-ge-, h*): **j-m offenstehen** *fig* be open to s.o.
öffentlich ['œfəntlɪç] *adj* public; **öffentliche Verkehrsmittel** *pl* public transport; **öffentliche Schulen** *pl* public schools; **öffentlich auftreten** appear in public
'**Öffentlichkeit** *f* (-; *no pl*) the public; **in aller Öffentlichkeit** in public, openly; **an die Öffentlichkeit bringen** make public
offiziell [ɔfi'tsjɛl] *adj* official
Offizier [ɔfi'tsiːɐ] *m* (*-s*; *-e*) MIL (commissioned) officer
öffnen ['œfnən] *v/t and v/refl* (*ge-, h*) open
Öffner ['œfnɐ] *m* (*-s*; -) opener
'**Öffnung** *f* (-; *-en*) opening
'**Öffnungszeiten** *pl* business *or* office hours
oft [ɔft] *adv* often, frequently
oh [oː] *int* o(h)!
ohne ['oːnə] *prp* (*acc*) *and cj* without; **ohne mich!** count me out!; **ohne ein Wort (zu sagen)** without (saying) a word
ohne'gleichen *adv* unequal(l)ed, unparalleled
ohne'hin *adv* anyhow, anyway
Ohnmacht ['oːnmaxt] *f* (-; *-en*) MED unconsciousness; *fig* helplessness; **in Ohnmacht fallen** faint, pass out
'**ohnmächtig** *adj* MED unconscious; *fig* helpless; **ohnmächtig werden** faint, pass out
Ohr [oːɐ] *n* (*-[e]s*; *-en* ['oːrən]) ANAT ear; F **j-n übers Ohr hauen** cheat s.o.; **bis über die Ohren verliebt (verschuldet)** head over heels in love (over your head in debt)
Öhr [øːɐ] *n* (*-[e]s*; *-e* ['øːrə]) eye
Ohrenarzt ['oːrən-] *m* ear specialist
'**ohrenbetäubend** *adj* deafening
'**Ohrenschmerzen** *pl* earache
'**Ohrenschützer** *pl* earmuffs
Ohrenzeuge *m* earwitness
'**Ohrfeige** *f* slap in the face (*a. fig*)
'**ohrfeigen** [-faigən] *v/t* (*ge-, h*) **j-n ohrfeigen** slap s.o.'s face
'**Ohrläppchen** [-lɛpçən] *n* (*-s*; -) ANAT earlobe

Ohrring *m* earring

oje [oˈjeː] *int* oh dear!, dear me!

Ökologe [økoˈloːgə] *m* (-*n*; -*n*) ecologist

Ökologie [økoloˈgiː] *f* (-; *no pl*) ecology

ökologisch [økoˈloːgɪʃ] *adj* ecological

Ökonomie [økonoˈmiː] *f* (-; *no pl*) economy; ECON economics

ökonomisch [økoˈnoːmɪʃ] *adj* economical; ECON economic

Ökosys,tem [ˈøːko-] *n* ecosystem

Oktave [ɔkˈtaːvə] *f* (-; -*n*) MUS octave

Oktober [ɔkˈtoːbɐ] *m* (-[*s*]; -) October

ökumenisch [økuˈmeːnɪʃ] *adj* REL ecumenical

Öl [øːl] *n* (-[*e*]*s*; *Öle*) oil; petroleum; *nach Öl bohren* drill for oil; *auf Öl stoßen* strike oil

'Ölbaum *m* BOT olive (tree)

Oldtimer [ˈoʊldtaɪmɐ] *m* (-*s*; -) MOT veteran car

ölen [ˈøːlən] *v/t* (*ge*-, *h*) oil, TECH *a.* lubricate

'Ölfarbe *f* oil (paint)

Ölfeld *n* oilfield

Ölförderland *n* oil-producing country

Ölförderung *f* oil production

Ölgemälde *n* oil painting

Ölheizung *f* oil heating

ölig [ˈøːlɪç] *adj* oily, greasy (*both a. fig*)

oliv [oˈliːf] *adj* olive

Olive [oˈliːvə] *f* (-; -*n*) BOT olive

'Ölleitung *f* (oil) pipeline

Ölmesstab *m* MOT dipstick

Ölpest *f* oil pollution

Ölquelle *f* oil well

'Ölsar,dine *f* canned (*Br a.* tinned) sardine

Öltanker *m* MAR oil tanker

Ölteppich *m* oil slick

Ölstand *m* oil level

'Ölung *f* (-; *no pl*) oiling, TECH *a.* lubrication; *Letzte Ölung* REL extreme unction

'Ölwanne *f* MOT oil pan, *Br* sump

Ölwechsel *m* MOT oil change

Ölzeug *n* oilskins

Olympia... [oˈlʏmpja-] *in cpds* ...*mannschaft*, ...*medaille etc*: Olympic ...

Olympiade [olʏmˈpjaːdə] *f* (-; -*n*) SPORT Olympic Games, Olympics

Oma [ˈoːma] F *f* (-; -*s*) grandma

Omi [ˈoːmi] F *f* (-; -*s*) granny

Omnibus [ˈɔmnibʊs] *m* → *Bus*

onanieren [onaˈniːrən] *v/i* (*no -ge*-, *h*) masturbate

Onkel [ˈɔŋkəl] *m* (-*s*; -) uncle

Online... [ˈɔnlain-] EDP online ...

Opa [ˈoːpa] F *m* (-*s*; -*s*) grandpa

Oper [ˈoːpɐ] *f* (-; -*n*) MUS opera; opera (house)

Operation [opəraˈtsjoːn] *f* (-; -*en*) MED operation; *e-e Operation vornehmen* perform an operation

Operati'onssaal *m* MED operating room (*Br* theatre)

Operette [opəˈrɛtə] *f* (-; -*n*) MUS operetta

operieren [opəˈriːrən] (*no -ge*-, *h*) **1.** *v/t* MED *j-n operieren* operate on s.o. (*wegen* for); *operiert werden* be operated on, have an operation; *sich operieren lassen* undergo an operation; **2.** *v/i* MED, MIL operate; proceed

'Opernsänger(in) opera singer

Opfer [ˈɔpfɐ] *n* (-*s*; -) sacrifice; offering; victim; *ein Opfer bringen* make a sacrifice; (*dat*) *zum Opfer fallen* fall victim to

'opfern *v/t and v/i* (*ge*-, *h*) sacrifice

Opium [ˈoːpjʊm] *n* (-*s*; *no pl*) opium

Opposition [ɔpoziˈtsjoːn] *f* (-; -*en*) opposition (*a.* PARL)

Optik [ˈɔptik] *f* (-; *no pl*) optics; PHOT optical system

Optiker [ˈɔptikɐ] *m* (-*s*; -), **'Optikerin** *f* (-; -*nen*) optician

optimal [ɔptiˈmaːl] *adj* optimum, best

Optimismus [ɔptiˈmɪsmʊs] *m* (-; *no pl*) optimism

Optimist(in) [ɔptiˈmɪst(ɪn)] (-*en*; -*en*/-; -*nen*) optimist

opti'mistisch *adj* optimistic

Option [ɔpˈtsjoːn] *f* (-; -*en*) option

optisch [ˈɔptiʃ] *adj* optical

Orange [oˈrãːʒə] *f* (-; -*n*) BOT orange

Orchester [ɔrˈkɛstɐ] *n* (-*s*; -) MUS orchestra

Orchidee [ɔrçiˈdeː] *f* (-; -*n*) bot orchid

Orden [ˈɔrdən] *m* (-*s*; -) medal, decoration; *esp* REL order

'Ordensschwester *f* REL sister, nun

ordentlich [ˈɔrdəntlɪç] **1.** *adj* tidy, neat, orderly; proper; thorough; decent (*a.* F); respectable; full (*member etc*); JUR ordinary; reasonable (*performance etc*); F good, sound; **2.** *adv*: *s-e Sache ordentlich machen* do a good job; *sich ordentlich benehmen* (*anziehen*) behave (dress) properly *or* decently

ordinär [ɔrdiˈnɛːɐ] *adj* vulgar; common

ordnen [ˈɔrdnən] *v/t* (*ge*-, *h*) put in order; arrange, sort (out); file; settle

Ordner [ˈɔrdnɐ] *m* (-*s*; -) file; folder; attendant, guard

'Ordnung *f* (-; *no pl*) order; orderliness, tidiness; arrangement; system, set-up; class; *in Ordnung* all right; TECH *etc* in (good) order; *in Ordnung bringen* put right (*a. fig*); tidy up; repair, fix (*a. fig*); *(in) Ordnung halten* keep (in) order; *et. ist nicht in Ordnung (mit)* there is s.th. wrong (with)

O

'**ordnungsgemäß 1.** *adj* correct, regular;
2. *adv* duly, properly
'**Ordnungsstrafe** *f* JUR fine, penalty
Ordnungszahl *f* MATH ordinal number
Organ [ɔr'gaːn] *n* (-*s*; -*e*) organ
Organempfänger *m* MED organ recipient
Organhandel *m* sale of (transplant) organs
Organisation [ɔrganiza'tsjoːn] *f* (-; -*en*) organization
Organisator [ɔrgani'zaːtoːɐ] *m* (-*s*; -*en* [-za'toːrən]) organizer
Organisa'torin *f* (-; -*nen*) organizer
organisatorisch [-za'toːrɪʃ] *adj* organizational
organisch [ɔr'gaːnɪʃ] *adj* organic
organisieren [ɔrgani'ziːrən] *v/t* organize; F get (hold of); ***sich organisieren*** organize; ECON unionize
organisiert [ɔrgani'ziːɐt] *adj* organized; ECON unionized
Organismus [ɔrga'nɪsmʊs] *m* (-; -*men*) BIOL organism
Organist [ɔrga'nɪst] *m* (-*en*; -*en*), **Orga-'nistin** *f* (-; -*nen*) MUS organist
Or'ganspender *m* MED (organ) donor
Orgasmus [ɔr'gasmʊs] *m* (-; -*men*) orgasm
Orgel ['ɔrgəl] *f* (-; -*n*) MUS organ
'**Orgelpfeife** *f* MUS organ pipe
Orgie ['ɔrgjə] *f* (-; -*n*) orgy
Orientale [orjɛn'taːlə] *m* (-*n*; -*n*), **Orien-'talin** *f* (-; -*nen*), **orien'talisch** *adj* oriental
orientieren [orjɛn'tiːrən] *v/t* (*no -ge-, h*) inform (***über*** *acc* about), brief (on); ***sich orientieren*** orient(ate) o.s. (*a. fig*) (***nach*** by); inform o.s.
Orien'tierung *f* (-; *no pl*) orientation, *fig a.* information; ***die Orientierung verlieren*** lose one's bearings
Orien'tierungssinn *m* (-[*e*]*s*; *no pl*) sense of direction
original [origi'naːl] *adj* original; real, genuine; TV live
Origi'nal *n* (-*s*; -*e*) original; *fig* real (*or* quite a) character
Origi'nal... *in cpds* ...*aufnahme*, ...*ausgabe etc*: original ...
Originalübertragung *f* live broadcast *or* program(me)
originell [origi'nɛl] *adj* original; ingenious; witty
Orkan [ɔr'kaːn] *m* (-[*e*]*s*; -*e*) hurricane
or'kanartig *adj* violent; *fig* thunderous

Ort [ɔrt] *m* (-[*e*]*s*; -*e*) place; village, (small) town; spot, point; scene; ***vor Ort*** *mining*: at the (pit) face; *fig* in the field, on the spot
orten ['ɔrtən] *v/t* (*ge-, h*) locate, spot
orthodox [ɔrto'dɔks] *adj* orthodox
Orthographie [ɔrtogra'fiː] *f* (-; -*n*) orthography
Orthopäde [ɔrto'pɛːdə] *m* (-*n*; -*n*), **Or-tho'pädin** *f* (-; -*nen*) MED orthop(a)edic specialist
örtlich ['œrtlɪç] *adj* local
'**Ortsbestimmung** *f* AVIAT, MAR location; LING adverb of place
'**Ortschaft** *f* → **Ort**
'**Ortsgespräch** *n* TEL local call
'**Ortskenntnis** *f*: ***Ortskenntnis besitzen*** know a place
'**Ortsnetz** *n* TEL local exchange
'**Ortszeit** *f* local time
Öse ['øːzə] *f* (-; -*n*) eye; eyelet
Ostblock ['ɔst-] *m* (-[*e*]*s*; *no pl*) HIST POL East(ern) Bloc
Osten ['ɔstən] *m* (-*s*; *no pl*) east; POL *the* East; ***nach Osten*** east(wards)
Osterei ['oːstɐ-] *n* Easter egg
Osterhase *m* Easter bunny *or* rabbit
Ostern ['oːstɐn] *n* (-; -) Easter (***zu, an*** at); ***frohe Ostern!*** Happy Easter!
Österreicher ['øːstəraiçɐ] *m* (-*s*; -), '**Österreicherin** [-raiçərɪn] *f* (-; -*nen*), '**österreichisch** *adj* Austrian
östlich ['œstlɪç] **1.** *adj* east(ern); easterly; **2.** *adv*: ***östlich von*** (to the) east of
ostwärts ['ɔstvɛrts] *adv* east(wards)
'**Ostwind** *m* east wind
Otter ['ɔtɐ] ZO **1.** *m* (-*s*; -) otter; **2.** *f* (-; -*n*) adder, viper
outen ['autən] *v/t* (*ge-, h*) out
Ouvertüre [uvɛr'tyːrə] *f* (-; -*n*) MUS overture
oval [o'vaːl] *adj*, **O'val** *n* (-*s*; -*e*) oval
Oxid [ɔ'ksiːt] *n* (-[*e*]*s*; -*e* [ɔ'ksiːdə]) CHEM oxide
oxidieren [ɔksi'diːrən] *v/t* (*no -ge-, h*) *and v/i* (*h, sein*) CHEM oxidize
Oxyd *n* → **Oxid**
Ozean ['oːtseaːn] *m* (-*s*; -*e*) ocean, sea
Ozon [o'tsoːn] *n* (-*s*; *no pl*) CHEM ozone
o'zonfreundlich *adj* ozone-friendly
O'zonloch *n* ozone hole
Ozonschicht *f* ozone layer
Ozonschild *m* ozone shield
Ozonwerte *pl* ozone levels

P

paar [paːɐ] *indef pron*: **ein paar** a few, some, F a couple of; **ein paar Mal** a few times

Paar *n* (-[e]s; -e) pair; couple; **ein Paar (neue) Schuhe** a (new) pair of shoes

paaren ['paːrən] *v/t and v/refl* (ge-, h) zo mate; *fig* combine

'Paarlauf *m* SPORT pair skating

'Paarung *f* (-; -en) zo mating, copulation; SPORT matching

'paarweise *adv* in pairs, in twos

Pacht [paxt] *f* (-; -en) lease; rent

'pachten *v/t* (ge-, h) (take on) lease

Pächter ['pɛçtɐ] *m* (-s; -), **'Pächterin** *f* (-; -nen) leaseholder; AGR tenant

'Pachtvertrag *m* lease

Pachtzins *m* rent

Pack¹ [pak] *m* → **Packen**

Pack² *contp n* (-[e]s; *no pl*) rabble

Päckchen ['pɛkçən] *n* (-s; -) pack, *Br* packet; small parcel

packen ['pakən] *v/t and v/i* (ge-, h) pack; make up (*parcel etc*); grab, seize (**an** *dat* by); *fig* grip

'Packen *m* (-s; -) pack, pile (*a. fig*)

Packer ['pakɐ] *m* (-s; -) packer; removal man

'Packpa,pier *n* packing *or* brown paper

'Packung *f* (-; -en) package, box; pack, *Br* packet

Pädagoge [pɛda'goːgə] *m* (-n; -n), **Päda-'gogin** *f* (-; -nen) teacher; education(al)ist

päda'gogisch *adj* pedagogic, educational; **pädagogische Hochschule** college of education

Paddel ['padəl] *n* (-s; -) paddle

'Paddelboot *n* canoe

'paddeln *v/i* (ge-, h, sein) paddle, canoe

Page ['paːʒə] *m* (-n; -n) page(boy)

Paket [pa'keːt] *n* (-[e]s; -e) package; parcel

Paketkarte *f* parcel post slip, *Br* parcel mailing form

Paketpost *f* parcel post

Paketschalter *m* parcel counter

Paketzustellung *f* parcel delivery

Pakt [pakt] *m* (-[e]s; -e) POL pact

Palast [pa'last] *m* (-[e]s; *Paläste* [pa'lɛstə]) palace

Palme ['palmə] *f* (-; -n) BOT palm (tree)

Palm'sonntag *m* REL Palm Sunday

Pampelmuse ['pampəlmuːzə] *f* (-; -n) BOT grapefruit

paniert [pa'niːɐt] *adj* GASTR breaded

Panik ['paːnɪk] *f* (-; -en) panic; **in Panik geraten** (**versetzen**) panic; **in Panik** panic-stricken, F panicky

panisch ['paːnɪʃ] *adj*: **panische Angst** mortal terror

Panne ['panə] *f* (-; -n) breakdown, MOT *a.* engine trouble; *fig* mishap

'Pannenhilfe *f* MOT breakdown service

Panter, Panther ['pantɐ] *m* (-s; -) zo panther

Pantoffel [pan'tɔfəl] *m* (-s; -n) slipper

Pantoffelheld F *m* henpecked husband

Pantomime [panto'miːmə] THEA **1.** *f* (-; -n) mime, dumb show; **2.** *m* (-n; -n) mime (artist)

panto'mimisch *adv*: **pantomimisch darstellen** mime

Panzer ['pantsɐ] *m* (-s; -) armo(u)r (*a. fig*); MIL tank; zo shell

Panzerglas *n* bulletproof glass

'panzern *v/t* (ge-, h) armo(u)r; → **gepanzert**

'Panzerschrank *m* safe

Panzerung ['pantsərʊŋ] *f* (-; -en) armo(u)r plating

Papa [pa'paː] F *m* (-s; -s) dad(dy), pa

Papagei [papa'gai] *m* (-en; -en) zo parrot

Papeterie [papɛtə'riː] *Swiss f* (-; -n) stationer('s shop)

Papier [pa'piːɐ] *n* (-s; -e) paper; *pl* papers, documents; identification (paper)

Pa'pier... *in cpds* ...**geld**, ...**handtuch**, ...**serviette**, ...**tüte** *etc*: *mst* paper ...

Papiergeschäft *n* stationer('s store, *Br* shop)

Papierkorb *m* wastepaper basket

Papierkrieg F *m* red tape

Papierschnitzel *pl* scraps of paper

Papierwaren *pl* stationery

Pappe ['papə] *f* (-; -n) cardboard, pasteboard

Pappel ['papəl] *f* (-; -n) BOT poplar

'Pappkar,ton *m* cardboard box, carton

Pappteller *m* paper plate

Paprika ['paprika] *m* (-s; -[s]) a) BOT sweet pepper, b) (*no pl*) GASTR paprika

Papst [paːpst] *m* (-[e]s; *Päpste* ['pɛːpstə]) pope

'päpstlich *adj* papal

Parade [pa'raːdə] *f* (-; -n) parade; *soccer etc*: save; *boxing, fencing*: parry

Paradeiser [para'daizɐ] *Austrian m* (-s; -) BOT tomato

Paradies [para'diːs] *n* (-es; -e) paradise

paradiesisch [para'di:zɪʃ] *fig adj* heavenly, delightful

paradox [para'dɔks] *adj* paradoxical

Paragraph [para'graːf] *m* (-en; -en) JUR article, section; paragraph

parallel [para'leːl] *adj*, **Paral'lele** *f* (-; -n) parallel

Parasit [para'ziːt] *m* (-en; -en) parasite

Parfüm [par'fyːm] *n* (-s; -s) perfume, *Br a.* scent

Parfümerie [parfymə'riː] *f* (-; -n) perfumery

parfümieren [parfy'miːrən] *v/t* (*no -ge-, h*) perfume, scent; **sich parfümieren** put on perfume

parieren [pa'riːrən] *v/t and v/i* (*no -ge-, h*) SPORT parry, *fig a.* counter (**mit** with); pull up (*horse*); obey

Park [park] *m* (-s; -s) park

parken ['parkən] *v/i and v/t* (*ge-, h*) MOT park; **Parken verboten!** no parking!

Parkett [par'kɛt] *n* (-[e]s; -e, -s) parquet (floor); THEA orchestra, *Br* stalls; dance floor

'Parkgebühr *f* parking fee

Park(hoch-)haus *n* parking garage, *Br* multi-storey car park

parkieren [par'kiːrən] *Swiss v/t and v/i* → **parken**

'Parkkralle *f* wheel clamp

Parklücke *f* parking space

Parkplatz *m* parking lot, *Br* car park; → **Parklücke**; **e-n Parkplatz suchen (finden)** look for (find) somewhere to park the car

Parkscheibe *f* parking disk (*Br* disc)

Parksünder *m* parking offender

Parkuhr *f* MOT parking meter

Parkwächter *m* park keeper; MOT parking lot (*Br* car park) attendant

Parlament [parla'mɛnt] *n* (-[e]s; -e) parliament

parlamentarisch [parlamɛn'taːrɪʃ] *adj* parliamentary

Parodie [paro'diː] *f* (-; -n), **paro'dieren** *v/t* (*no -ge-, h*) parody

Parole [pa'roːlə] *f* (-n; -n) MIL password; *fig* watchword, POL *a.* slogan

Partei [par'tai] *f* (-; -en) party (*a.* POL); **j-s Partei ergreifen** take sides with s.o., side with s.o.

par'teiisch *adj* partial (**für** to); prejudiced (**gegen** against)

par'teilos *adj* POL independent

Par'teimitglied *n* POL party member

Parteipro,gramm *n* POL platform

Parteitag *m* POL convention

Parteizugehörigkeit *f* POL party membership

Parterre [par'tɛrə] *n* (-s; -s) first (*Br* ground) floor

Partie [par'tiː] *f* (-; -n) game, SPORT *a.* match; part, passage (*a.* MUS); **e-e gute etc Partie sein** be a good *etc* match

Partisan [parti'zaːn] *m* (-s; -en, -en), **Parti'sanin** *f* (-; -nen) MIL partisan, guerilla

Partitur [parti'tuːɐ] *f* (-; -en) MUS score

Partizip [parti'tsiːp] *n* (-s; -ien) LING participle

Partner ['partnɐ] *m* (-s; -), **'Partnerin** *f* (-; -nen) partner

'Partnerschaft *f* (-; -en) partnership

'Partnerstadt *f* twin town

paschen ['paʃən] *Austrian v/t and v/i* (*ge-, h*) smuggle

Pascher ['paʃɐ] *Austrian m* (-s; -) smuggler

Pass [pas] *m* (-es; *Pässe* ['pɛsə]) passport; SPORT, GEOGR pass; **langer Pass** SPORT long ball

Passage [pa'saːʒə] *f* (-; -n) passage

Passagier [pasa'ʒiːɐ] *m* (-s; -e) passenger

Passagierflugzeug *n* passenger plane; airliner

Passa'gierin *f* (-; -nen) passenger

Passah ['pasa] *n* (-s; *no pl*), **'Passahfest** *n* REL Passover

Passant [pa'sant] *m* (-en; -en), **Pas'santin** *f* (-; -nen) passerby

'Passbild *n* passport photo(graph)

passen ['pasən] **1.** *v/i* (*ge-, h*) fit (**j-m** s.o.); **auf** *or* **für** *or* **zu et.** s.th.); suit (**j-m** s.o.), be convenient; *cards*, SPORT pass; **passen zu** go with, match; **sie passen gut zueinander** they are well suited to each other; **passt es Ihnen morgen?** would tomorrow suit you *or* be all right (with you)?; **das (es) passt mir gar nicht** I don't like that (him) at all; **das passt (nicht) zu ihm** that's just like him (not like him, not his style)

passend *adj* fitting; matching; suitable, right

passierbar [pa'siːɐbaːɐ] *adj* passable

passieren [pa'siːrən] (*no -ge-*) **1.** *v/i* (*sein*) happen; **2.** *v/t* (*h*) pass (through)

Pas'sierschein *m* pass, permit

Passion [pa'sjoːn] *f* (-; -en) passion; REL Passion

passiv ['pasiːf] *adj* passive

'Passiv *n* (-s; *no pl*) LING passive (voice)

Paste ['pastə] *f* (-; -n) paste

Pastell [pas'tɛl] *n* (-[e]s; -e) PAINT pastel

Pastete [pas'teːtə] *f* (-; -n) GASTR pie

Pate ['paːtə] *m* (-n; -n) godfather

'Patenkind *n* godchild

'Patenschaft *f* (-; -en) sponsorship

Patent [pa'tɛnt] *n* (-[e]s; -e) patent; MIL

commission
Patentamt *n* patent office
Patentanwalt *m* JUR patent agent
patentieren [patɛn'tiːrən] *v/t (no -ge-, h)* patent; **(sich) et. patentieren lassen** take out a patent for s.th.
Pa'tentinhaber *m* patentee
pathetisch [pa'teːtɪʃ] *adj* pompous
Patient [pa'tsjɛnt] *m (-en; -en)*, **Pa'tientin** *f (-; -nen)* MED patient
Patin ['paːtɪn] *f (-; -nen)* godmother
Patriot [patri'oːt] *m (-en; -en)* patriot
patri'otisch *adj* patriotic
Patrone [pa'troːnə] *f (-; -n)* cartridge
Patrouille [pa'trʊljə] *f (-; -n)* MIL patrol
patroullieren [patrʊl'jiːrən] *v/i (no -ge-, h)* MIL patrol
Patsche ['patʃə] F *f*: **in der Patsche sitzen** be in a fix *or* jam
'**patschen** F *v/i (ge-, h)* (s)plash
'**patsch'nass** *adj* soaking wet
patzen ['patsən] F *v/i (ge-, h)*, **Patzer** ['patsɐ] F *m (-s; -)* blunder
Pauke ['paukə] *f (-; -n)* MUS bass drum; kettledrum
'**pauken** F *v/i and v/t (ge-, h)* cram
Pauschale [pau'ʃaːlə] *f (-; -n)* lump sum
Pau'schalgebühr *f* flat rate
Pauschalreise *f* package tour
Pauschalurteil *n* sweeping judg(e)ment
Pause[1] ['pauzə] *f (-; -n)* recess, *Br* break, *esp* THEA, SPORT intermission, *Br* interval; pause; rest *(a.* MUS*)*
'**Pause**[2] *f (-; -n)* TECH tracing
'**pausen** *v/t (ge-, h)* TECH trace
'**pausenlos** *adj* uninterrupted, nonstop
'**Pausenzeichen** *n radio:* interval signal; PED bell
pausieren [pau'ziːrən] *v/i (no -ge-, h)* pause, rest
Pavian ['paːvjaːn] *m (-s; -e)* ZO baboon
Pavillon ['pavɪljɔŋ] *m (-s; -s)* pavilion
Pazifist [patsi'fɪst] *m (-en; -en)*, **Pazi'fistin** *f (-; -nen)*, **pazi'fistisch** *adj* pacifist
PC [peː'tseː] *m (-[s]; -[s])* ABBR *of **personal computer** PC*
Pech [pɛç] *n (-s; no pl)* pitch; F bad luck
Pechsträhne F *f* run of bad luck
Pechvogel F *m* unlucky fellow
pedantisch [pe'dantɪʃ] *adj* pedantic, fussy
Pegel ['peːgəl] *m (-s; -)* level *(a. fig)*
peilen ['pailən] *v/t (ge-, h)* sound
peinigen ['painɪgən] *v/t (ge-, h)* torment
Peiniger ['painɪgɐ] *m (-s; -)* tormentor
peinlich ['painlɪç] *adj* embarrassing; **peinlich genau** meticulous *(bei, in dat* in); **es war mir peinlich** I was *or* felt embarrassed

Peitsche ['paitʃə] *f (-; -n)*, '**peitschen** *v/t (ge-, h)* whip
'**Peitschenhieb** *m* lash
Pelle ['pɛlə] *f (-; -n)* skin; peel
'**pellen** *v/t (ge-, h)* peel
'**Pellkar,toffeln** *pl* potatoes (boiled) in their jackets
Pelz [pɛlts] *m (-es; -e)* fur; skin
'**pelzgefüttert** *adj* fur-lined
'**Pelzgeschäft** *n* fur(rier's) store *(Br* shop)
pelzig ['pɛltsɪç] *adj* furry; MED furred
'**Pelzmantel** *m* fur coat
'**Pelztiere** *pl* furred animals, furs
Pendel ['pɛndəl] *n (-s; -)* pendulum
'**pendeln** *v/i (ge-, h)* swing; RAIL *etc* shuttle; commute
'**Pendeltür** *f* swing door
'**Pendelverkehr** *m* RAIL *etc* shuttle service; commuter traffic
Pendler(in) ['pɛndlɐ (-lərɪn)] *(-s; -/-; -nen)* RAIL *etc* commuter
Penis ['peːnɪs] *m (-s; -se)* ANAT penis
Penner ['pɛnɐ] F *m (-s; -)* tramp, bum
Pension [pɑ̃'sjoːn] *f (-; -en)* (old age) pension; boarding-house, private hotel; **in Pension sein** be retired
Pensionär(in) [pɑ̃sjo'nɛːɐ (-'nɛːrɪn)] *(-s; -e/-; -nen)* (old age) pensioner; boarder
Pensionat [pɑ̃sjo'naːt] *n (-[e]s; -e)* boarding school
pensionieren [pɑ̃sjo'niːrən] *v/t (no -ge-, h)* pension (off); **sich pensionieren lassen** retire
Pensio'nierung *f (-; -en)* retirement
Pensionist [pɑ̃sjo'nɪst] *Austrian, Swiss m (-en; -en)* (old age) pensioner
Pensi'onsgast *m* boarder
Pensum ['pɛnzʊm] *n (-s; Pensen, Pensa)* (work) quota, stint
per [pɛr] *prp (acc)* per; by
perfekt [pɛr'fɛkt] *adj* perfect; **perfekt machen** settle
'**Perfekt** *n (-s; -e)* LING present perfect
Pergament [pɛrga'mɛnt] *n (-[e]s; -e)* parchment
Periode [pe'rjoːdə] *f (-; -n)* period, MED *a.* menstruation
periodisch [pe'rjoːdɪʃ] *adj* periodic(al)
Peripherie [perife'riː] *f (-; -n)* periphery, outskirts
Peripheriegeräte *pl* EDP peripheral equipment
Perle ['pɛrlə] *f (-; -n)* pearl; bead
'**perlen** *v/i (ge-, h)* sparkle, bubble
'**Perlenkette** *f* pearl necklace
'**Perlmuschel** *f* ZO pearl oyster
Perlmutt ['pɛrlmʊt] *n (-s; no pl)* mother-of-pearl
Perron [pɛ'rõː] *m (-s; -s)* *Swiss* platform

Perser ['pɛrzɐ] *m* (*-s; -*) Persian; Persian carpet

Perserin ['pɛrzərɪn] *f* (*-; -nen*) Persian (woman)

Persien ['pɛrzjən] Persia

persisch ['pɛrzɪʃ] *adj* Persian

Person [pɛr'zoːn] *f* (*-; -en*) person, THEA *etc a.* character; *ein Tisch für drei Personen* a table for three

Personal [pɛrzoˈnaːl] *n* (*-s; no pl*) staff, personnel; *zu wenig Personal haben* be understaffed

Personalabbau *m* staff reduction

Personalabteilung *f* personnel department

Personalausweis *m* identity card

Personalchef *m* staff manager

Personalien [pɛrzoˈnaːljən] *pl* particulars, personal data

Perso'nalpro,nomen *n* LING personal pronoun

Per'sonen(kraft)wagen (ABBR **PKW**) *m* (*Br a.* motor)car, auto(mobile)

Personenzug *m* passenger train; local *or* commuter train

personifizieren [pɛrzonifiˈtsiːrən] *v/t* (*no -ge-, h*) personify

persönlich [pɛrˈzøːnlɪç] *adj* personal

Per'sönlichkeit *f* (*-; -en*) personality

Perücke [peˈrʏkə] *f* (*-; -n*) wig

pervers [pɛrˈvɛrs] *adj* perverted; *perverser Mensch* pervert

Pessimismus [pɛsiˈmɪsmʊs] *m* (*-; no pl*) pessimism

Pessimist(in) [pɛsiˈmɪst(ɪn)] (*-en; -en/-; -nen*) pessimist

pessi'mistisch *adj* pessimistic

Pest [pɛst] *f* (*-; no pl*) MED plague

Pestizid [pɛstiˈtsiːt] *n* (*-s; -e*) pesticide

Petersilie [peːtɐˈziːljə] *f* (*-; -n*) BOT parsley

Petroleum [peˈtroːleʊm] *n* (*-s; no pl*) kerosene, *Br* paraffin

Petroleumlampe *f* kerosene (*Br* paraffin) lamp

petzen ['pɛtsən] F *v/i* (*ge-, h*) tell tales, *Br a.* sneak

Pfad [pfaːt] *m* (*-[e]s; -e* ['pfaːdə]) path, track

Pfadfinder *m* boy scout

Pfadfinderin [-fɪndərɪn] *f* (*-; -nen*) girl scout, *Br* girl guide

Pfahl [pfaːl] *m* (*-[e]s; Pfähle* ['pfɛːlə]) stake; post; pole

Pfand [pfant] *n* (*-[e]s; Pfänder* ['pfɛndɐ]) security; pawn, pledge; deposit; forfeit

'Pfandbrief *m* ECON mortgage bond

pfänden ['pfɛndən] *v/t* (*ge-, h*) seize

'Pfandhaus *n* → *Leihhaus*

'Pfandleiher [-laiɐ] *m* (*-s; -*) pawnbroker

'Pfandschein *m* pawn ticket

'Pfändung *f* (*-; -en*) JUR seizure

Pfanne ['pfanə] *f* (*-; -n*) pan, skillet

'Pfannkuchen *m* pancake

Pfarrbezirk ['pfar-] *m* parish

Pfarrer ['pfarɐ] *m* (*-s; -*) vicar; pastor; (parish) priest

'Pfarrgemeinde *f* parish

Pfarrhaus *n* parsonage; rectory, vicarage

Pfarrkirche *f* parish church

Pfau [pfau] *m* (*-[e]s; -en*) ZO peacock

Pfeffer ['pfɛfɐ] *m* (*-s; -*) pepper

Pfefferkuchen *m* gingerbread

Pfefferminze [-mɪntsə] *f* (*-; no pl*) BOT peppermint

'pfeffern *v/t* (*ge-, h*) pepper

'Pfefferstreuer *m* (*-s; -*) pepper caster

pfeffrig ['pfɛfrɪç] *adj* peppery

Pfeife ['pfaifə] *f* (*-; -n*) whistle; pipe (*a.* MUS)

'pfeifen *v/i and v/t* (*irr, ge-, h*) whistle (*j-m* to s.o.); F *pfeifen auf* (*acc*) not give a damn about

Pfeil [pfail] *m* (*-[e]s; -e*) arrow

Pfeiler ['pfailɐ] *m* (*-s; -*) pillar; pier

Pfennig ['pfɛnɪç] *m* (*-s; -e*) pfennig; *fig* penny

Pferch [pfɛrç] *m* (*-[e]s; -e*) fold, pen

'pferchen *v/t* (*ge-, h*) cram (*in acc* into)

Pferd [pfeːɐt] *n* (*-[e]s; -e*) ZO horse (*a.* SPORT); *zu Pferde* on horseback

Pferdegeschirr ['pfeːɐdə-] *n* harness

Pferdekoppel *f* paddock

Pferderennen *n* horserace

Pferdestall *m* stable

Pferdestärke *f* TECH horsepower

Pferdewagen *m* (horse-drawn) carriage

pfiff [pfɪf] *pret of* *pfeifen*

Pfiff *m* (*-[e]s; -e*) whistle

pfiffig ['pfɪçɪç] *adj* smart

Pfingsten ['pfɪŋstən] *n* (*-; -*) REL Pentecost, *Br* Whitsun (*zu, an* at)

Pfingst'montag *m* REL Whit Monday

'Pfingstrose *f* BOT peony

Pfingst'sonntag *m* REL Pentecost, *Br* Whit Sunday

Pfirsich ['pfɪrzɪç] *m* (*-s; -e*) BOT peach

Pflanze ['pflantsə] *f* (*-; -n*) plant; *Pflanzen fressend* ZO herbivorous

'pflanzen *v/t* (*ge-, h*) plant

'Pflanzenfett *n* vegetable fat

'pflanzlich *adj* vegetable

'Pflanzung *f* (*-; -en*) plantation

Pflaster ['pflastɐ] *n* (*-s; -*) pavement; MED Band-Aid®, *Br* plaster

'pflastern *v/t* (*ge-, h*) pave

'Pflasterstein *m* paving stone

Pflaume ['pflaumə] *f* (*-; -n*) BOT plum

Pflege ['pfleːgə] *f* (*-; no pl*) care; MED

nursing; *fig* cultivation; TECH maintenance; *j-n in Pflege nehmen* take s.o. into one's care; *Pflege... in cpds ...eltern, ...kind, ...sohn etc:* foster *...; ...heim, ...kosten, ...personal etc:* nursing ...

'pflegebedürftig *adj* needing care

'Pflegefall *m* constant-care patient

'pflegeleicht *adj* wash-and-wear, easy-care

'pflegen *v/t (ge-, h)* care for, look after, *esp* MED *a.* nurse; TECH maintain; *fig* cultivate; keep up *(custom etc); sie pflegte zu sagen* she used to *or* would say

Pfleger ['pfleːgɐ] *m (-s; -)* male nurse

Pflegerin ['pfleːgərɪn] *f (-; -nen)* nurse

'Pflegestelle *f* nursing place

Pflicht [pflɪçt] *f (-; -en)* duty *(gegen* to); SPORT compulsory events

'pflichtbewusst *adj* conscientious

'Pflichtbewusstsein *n* sense of duty

Pflichterfüllung *f* performance of one's duty

Pflichtfach *n* PED compulsory subject

'pflichtgemäß, pflichtgetreu *adj* dutiful

pflichtvergessen *adv: pflichtvergessen handeln* neglect one's duty

'Pflichtversicherung *f* compulsory insurance

Pflock ['pflɔk] *m (-[e]s; Pflöcke* ['pflœkə]) peg, pin; plug

pflücken ['pflʏkən] *v/t (ge-, h)* pick, gather

Pflug [pfluːk] *m (-[e]s; Pflüge* ['pflyːgə]), pflügen ['pflyːgən] *v/t and v/i (ge-, h)* plow, *Br* plough

Pforte ['pfɔrtə] *f (-; -n)* gate, door, entrance

Pförtner ['pfœrtnɐ] *m (-s; -)* doorman, doorkeeper, porter

Pfosten ['pfɔstən] *m (-s; -)* post

Pfote ['pfoːtə] *f (-; -n)* ZO paw *(a.* F)

pfropfen ['pfrɔpfən] *v/t (ge-, h)* stopper; cork; plug; AGR graft; F cram, stuff

'Pfropfen *m (-s; -)* stopper; cork; plug; MED clot

pfui [pfui] *int* ugh!; *audience:* boo!

Pfund [pfʊnt] *n (-[e]s; -e* ['pfʊndə]) pound *(453,59 g);* pound (sterling); *10 Pfund* ten pounds

'pfundweise *adv* by the pound

pfuschen ['pfuʃən] F *v/i (ge-, h),* Pfuscherei [pfʊʃə'rai] F *f (-; -en)* bungle, botch

Pfütze ['pfʏtsə] *f (-; -n)* puddle, pool

Phänomen [fɛno'meːn] *n (-s; -e)* phenomenon

phänomenal [fɛnome'naːl] *adj* phenomenal

Phantasie *etc* → *Fantasie etc*

pharmazeutisch [farma'tsɔytɪʃ] *adj* pharmaceutic(al)

Phase ['faːzə] *f (-; -n)* phase *(a.* ELECTR), stage

Philosoph [filo'zoːf] *m (-en; -en)* philosopher

Philosophie [filozo'fiː] *f (-; -n)* philosophy

philosophieren [filozo'fiːrən] *v/i (no -ge-, h)* philosophize *(über acc* on)

Philo'sophin *f (-; -nen)* (woman) philosopher

philosophisch [filo'zoːfɪʃ] *adj* philosophical

phlegmatisch [flɛ'gmatɪʃ] *adj* phlegmatic

Phonetik [fo'neːtɪk] *f (-; no pl)* phonetics

pho'netisch *adj* phonetic

Phosphor ['fɔsfoːɐ] *m (-s; -e)* CHEM phosphorus

Photo... → *Foto...*

Phrase ['fraːzə] *contp f (-; -n)* cliché (phrase)

Physik [fy'ziːk] *f (-; no pl)* physics

physikalisch [fyzi'kaːlɪʃ] *adj* physical

Physiker ['fyːzikɐ] *m (-s; -),* 'Physikerin *f (-; -nen)* physicist

physisch ['fyːzɪʃ] *adj* physical

Pianist [pja'nɪst] *m (-en; -en),* Pia'nistin *f (-; -nen)* MUS pianist

Piano ['pjaːno] *n (-s; -s)* MUS piano

Picke ['pɪkə] *f (-; -n)* TECH pick(axe)

Pickel[1] ['pɪkəl] *m (-s; -)* TECH pick(axe)

'Pickel[2] *m (-s; -)* MED pimple

pickelig ['pɪkəlɪç] *adj* MED pimpled, pimply

picken ['pɪkən] *v/i and v/t (ge-, h)* ZO peck, pick

Picknick ['pɪknɪk] *n (-s; -e, -s)* picnic

'picknicken *v/i (ge-, h)* (have a) picnic

piekfein ['piːk-] F *adj* posh

piep(s)en ['piːp(s)ən] *v/i (ge-, h)* chirp, cheep; ELECTR bleep

Pietät [pje'tɛːt] *f (-; no pl)* reverence; piety

pie'tätlos *adj* irreverent

pie'tätvoll *adj* reverent

Pik [piːk] *n (-[s]; -[s]) cards:* spade(s)

pikant [pi'kant] *adj* piquant, spicy *(both a. fig)*

Pilger ['pɪlgɐ] *m (-s; -)* pilgrim

'Pilgerfahrt *f* pilgrimage

'Pilgerin *f (-; -nen)* pilgrim

'pilgern *v/i (ge-, sein)* (go on a) pilgrimage

Pille ['pɪlə] *f (-; -n)* pill; F *die Pille nehmen* be on the pill

Pilot [pi'loːt] *m (-en; -en),* Pi'lotin *f (-; -nen)* pilot

Pilz [pɪlts] *m (-es; -e)* BOT mushroom *(a.*

fig); toadstool; MED fungus; *Pilze suchen* (*gehen*) go mushrooming

Pinguin ['pɪŋguiːn] *m* (*-s; -e*) zo penguin

pinkeln ['pɪŋkəln] F *v/i* (*ge-, h*) (have a) pee, piddle

Pinsel ['pɪnzəl] *m* (*-s; -*) (paint)brush

'**Pinselstrich** *m* brushstroke

Pinzette [pɪn'tsɛtə] *f* (*-; -n*) tweezers

Pionier [pjo'niːɐ] *m* (*-s; -e*) pioneer, MIL *a.* engineer

Pirat [pi'raːt] *m* (*-en; -en*) pirate

Pisse ['pɪsə] V *f* (*-; no pl*), '**pissen** V *v/i* (*ge-, h*) piss

Piste ['pɪstə] *f* (*-; -n*) course; AVIAT runway

Pistole [pɪs'toːlə] *f* (*-; -n*) pistol, gun

Pkw, PKW ['peːkaːveː] *ABBR of Personenkraftwagen* (*Br a.* motor)car, automobile

Plache ['plaxə] *Austrian f* (*-; -n*) awning, tarpaulin

placieren *etc* → *platzieren etc*

plädieren [plɛ'diːrən] *v/i* (*no -ge-, h*) JUR plead (*für* for)

Plädoyer [plɛdoa'jeː] *n* (*-s; -s*) JUR final speech, pleading

Plage ['plaːgə] *f* (*-; -n*) trouble, misery; plague; nuisance, F pest

'**plagen** *v/t* (*ge-, h*) trouble; bother; pester; *sich plagen* toil, drudge

Plakat [pla'kaːt] *n* (*-[e]s; -e*) poster, placard, bill

Plakette [pla'kɛtə] *f* (*-; -n*) plaque, badge

Plan [plaːn] *m* (*-[e]s; Pläne* ['plɛːnə]) plan; intention

Plane ['plaːnə] *f* (*-; -n*) awning, tarpaulin

'**planen** *v/t* (*ge-, h*) plan, make plans for

Planet [pla'neːt] *m* (*-en; -en*) ASTR planet

planieren [pla'niːrən] *v/t* (*no -ge-, h*) TECH level, plane, grade

Planke ['plaŋkə] *f* (*-; -n*) plank, (thick) board

plänkeln ['plɛŋkəln] *v/i* (*ge-, h*) skirmish

'**planlos** *adj* without plan; aimless

'**planmäßig 1.** *adj* scheduled (*arrival etc*); **2.** *adv* according to plan

Plan(t)schbecken ['planʃ-] *n* paddling pool

plan(t)schen ['planʃən] *v/i* (*ge-, h*) splash

Plantage [plan'taːʒə] *f* (*-; -n*) plantation

Plappermaul ['plapɐ-] F *n* chatterbox

plappern ['plapɐn] F *v/i* (*ge-, h*) chatter, prattle, babble, jabber

plärren ['plɛrən] F *v/i and v/t* (*ge-, h*) blubber; bawl; *radio:* blare

Plastik[1] ['plastɪk] *f* (*-; -en*) sculpture

'**Plastik**[2] *n* (*-s; no pl*) plastic; *Plastik... in cpds ...besteck etc:* plastic ...

plastisch ['plastɪʃ] *adj* plastic; three-dimensional; *fig* graphic

Platin ['plaːtiːn] *n* (*-s; no pl*) platinum

plätschern ['plɛtʃɐn] *v/i* (*ge-, h*) ripple (*a. fig*), splash

platt [plat] *adj* flat, level, even; *fig* trite; F flabbergasted

Platte ['platə] *f* (*-; -n*) sheet, plate; slab; board; panel; MUS record, disk, *Br* disc; EDP disk; GASTR dish; F bald pate; *kalte Platte* GASTR plate of cold cuts (*Br* meats)

plätten ['plɛtən] *v/t* (*ge-, h*) iron, press

'**Plattenspieler** *m* record player

Plattenteller *m* turntable

'**Plattform** *f* platform

'**Plattfuß** *m* MED flat foot

'**Plattheit** *fig f* (*-; -en*) triviality; platitude

Plättli ['plɛtli] *Swiss n* (*-s; -s*) tile

Platz [plats] *m* (*-es; Plätze* ['plɛtsə]) place, spot; site; room, space; square; circus; seat; *es ist* (*nicht*) *genug Platz* there's (there isn't) enough room; *Platz machen für* make room for; make way for; *Platz nehmen* take a seat, sit down; *ist dieser Platz noch frei?* is this seat taken?; *j-n vom Platz stellen* SPORT send s.o. off; *auf eigenem Platz* SPORT at home; *auf die Plätze, fertig, los!* SPORT on your marks, get set, go!

'**Platzanweiser** *m* (*-s; -*) usher

Platzanweiserin *f* (*-; -nen*) usherette

Plätzchen ['plɛtsçən] *n* (*-s; -*) (little) place, spot; GASTR cookie, *Br* biscuit

platzen ['platsən] *v/i* (*ge-, sein*) burst (*a. fig*); crack, split; explode (*a. fig vor dat* with), blow up; F come to grief *or* nothing, fall through, blow up, *sl* go phut; break up

platzieren [pla'tsiːrən] *v/t* (*no -ge-, h*) place; *sich platzieren* SPORT be placed

Plat'zierung *f* (*-; -en*) place, placing

'**Platzkarte** *f* reservation (ticket)

Plätzli ['plɛtsli] *Swiss n* (*-s; -*) cutlet

'**Platzpa,trone** *f* blank (cartridge)

Platzregen *m* cloudburst, downpour

Platzreser,vierung *f* seat reservation

Platzverweis *m: e-n Platzverweis erhalten* SPORT be sent off

Platzwart *m* (*-s; -e*) SPORT groundkeeper, *Br* groundsman

Platzwunde *f* MED cut, laceration

Plauderei [plaudə'rai] *f* (*-; -en*) chat

plaudern ['plaudɐn] *v/i* (*ge-, h*) (have a) chat

plauschen ['plauʃən] *Austrian v/i* (have a) chat

pleite ['plaitə] F *adj* broke

'**Pleite** F *f* (*-; -n*) bankruptcy; *fig* flop

pleitegehen go broke

Plombe ['plɔmbə] *f* (*-; -n*) TECH seal; MED

filling
plombieren [plɔm'biːrən] v/t (no -ge-, h) TECH seal; MED fill
plötzlich ['plœtslıç] **1.** adj sudden; **2.** adv suddenly, all of a sudden
plump [plʊmp] adj clumsy
plumps int thud, plop
plumpsen ['plʊmpsən] v/i (ge-, sein) thud, plop, flop
Plunder ['plʊndɐ] F m (-s; no pl) trash, junk
Plünderer ['plʏndərɐ] m (-s; -) looter, plunderer
plündern ['plʏndɐn] v/i and v/t (ge-, h) plunder, loot
Plural ['pluːraːl] m (-s; -e) LING plural
plus [plʊs] adv plus
Plusquamperfekt ['plʊskvampɐfɛkt] n (-s; -e) LING past perfect
Pneu [pnɔʏ] Swiss m (-s; -s) tire, Br tyre
Po [poː] F m (-s; -s) bottom, behind
Pöbel ['pøːbəl] m (-s; no pl) mob, rabble
pochen ['pɔxən] v/i (ge-, h) knock, rap (both: **an** acc at)
Pocke ['pɔkə] f (-; -n) MED pock
'Pocken pl MED smallpox
Pockenimpfung f MED smallpox vaccination
Podest [po'dɛst] n, m (-[e]s; -e) platform; fig pedestal
Podium ['poːdjʊm] n (-s; -ien) podium, platform
'Podiumsdiskussi͵on f panel discussion
Poesie [poe'ziː] f (-; -n) poetry
Poet [po'eːt] m (-en; -en), **Po'etin** f (-; -nen) poet
poetisch [po'eːtıʃ] adj poetic(al)
Pointe ['poɛ̃ːtə] f (-; -n) point, punch line
Pokal [po'kaːl] m (-s; -e) goblet; SPORT cup
Pokalendspiel n SPORT cup final
Pokalsieger m SPORT cup winner
Pokalspiel n SPORT cup tie
pökeln ['pøːkəln] v/t (ge-, h) salt
Pol [poːl] m (-s; -e) GEOGR pole
polar [po'laːɐ] adj polar
Pole ['poːlə] m (-n; -n) Pole
'Polen Poland
Polemik [po'leːmık] f (-; -en) polemic(s)
po'lemisch adj polemic(al)
polemisieren [polemi'ziːrən] v/i (no -ge-, h) polemize
Police [po'liːsə] f (-; -n) policy
Polier [po'liːɐ] m (-s; -e) TECH foreman
polieren [po'liːrən] v/t (no -ge-, h) polish
Polin ['poːlın] f (-; -nen) Pole, Polish woman
Politik [poli'tiːk] f (-; no pl) politics; policy (a. fig)
Politiker(in) [po'liːtikɐ (-kərın)] (-s; -/-;

-nen) politician
politisch [po'liːtıʃ] adj political
politisieren [politi'ziːrən] v/i (no -ge-, h) talk politics
Polizei [poli'tsai] f (-; no pl) police
Polizeiauto n police car
Polizeibeamte m, **-in** f police officer
poli'zeilich adj (of or by the) police
Poli'zeiprä͵sidium n police headquarters
Polizeire͵vier n police station; precinct, Br district
Polizeischutz m: **unter Polizeischutz** under police guard
Polizeistreife f police patrol
Polizeistunde f closing time
Polizeiwache f police station
Polizist [poli'tsıst] m (-en; -en) policeman
Poli'zistin f (-; -nen) policewoman
polnisch ['pɔlnıʃ] adj Polish
Polster ['pɔlstɐ] n (-s; -) upholstery; cushion; pad(ding); fig bolster
Polstergarni͵tur f three-piece suite
Polstermöbel pl upholstered furniture
'polstern v/t (ge-, h) upholster; pad
'Polstersessel m easy chair, armchair
Polsterstuhl m upholstered chair
Polsterung ['pɔlstərʊŋ] f (-; -en) upholstery; padding
poltern ['pɔltɐn] v/i (ge-, h) rumble; fig bluster
Pommes frites [pɔm'frıt] pl French fries, French fried potatoes, Br chips
Pomp [pɔmp] m (-[e]s; no pl) pomp
pompös [pɔm'pøːs] adj showy
Pony¹ ['pɔni] n (-s; -s) ZO pony
'Pony² m (-s; -s) fringe, bangs
Popgruppe ['pɔp-] f MUS pop group
'Popmu͵sik f pop music
populär [popu'lɛːɐ] adj popular
Popularität [populari'tɛːt] f (-; no pl) popularity
Pore ['poːrə] f (-; -n) pore
Porno ['pɔrno] F m (-s; -s), **Pornofilm** m porn (film), blue movie
Pornoheft n porn magazine
porös [po'røːs] adj porous
Portemonnaie [pɔrtmɔ'neː] n (-s; -s) purse
Portier [pɔr'tjeː] m (-s; -s) doorman, porter
Portion [pɔr'tsjoːn] f (-; -en) portion, share; helping, serving
Portmonee n → **Portemonnaie**
Porto ['pɔrto] n (-s; -s, -ti) postage
Porträt [pɔr'trɛː] n (-s; -s) portrait
porträtieren [pɔrtrɛ'tiːrən] v/t (no -ge-, h) portray
Portugal ['pɔrtugal] Portugal
Portugiese [pɔrtu'giːzə] m (-n; -n), **Por-**

P

tu'giesin *f* (-; *-nen*), **portu'giesisch** *adj* Portuguese

Porzellan [pɔrtsɛ'laːn] *n* (*-s*; *-e*) china, porcelain

Posaune [po'zaunə] *f* (-; *-n*) MUS trombone; *fig* trumpet

Pose ['poːzə] *f* (-; *-n*) pose, attitude

Position [pozi'tsjoːn] *f* (-; *-en*) position (*a. fig*)

positiv ['poːzitiːf] *adj* positive

possessiv [pɔsɛ'siːf] *adj* LING possessive

Posses'sivpro,nomen *n* LING possessive pronoun

Post [pɔst] *f* (-; *no pl*) mail, *esp Br* post; letters; *mit der Post* by post *or* mail

Postamt *n* post office

Postanweisung *f* money order

Postbeamte *m*, **-in** *f* post office clerk

Postbote *m* mailman, *Br* postman

Posten ['pɔstən] *m* (*-s*; -) post; job, position; MIL sentry; ECON item; lot, parcel

'**Postfach** *n* (PO) box

postieren [pɔs'tiːrən] *v/t* (*no -ge-, h*) post, station, place; *sich postieren* station o.s.

'**Postkarte** *f* postcard

'**Postkutsche** *f* stagecoach

'**postlagernd** *adj* (in care of) general delivery, *Br* poste restante

'**Postleitzahl** *f* zip code, *Br* post(al) code

Postmi,nister *m* Postmaster General

Postscheck *m* postal check (*Br* cheque)

Postsparbuch *n* post-office savings book

Poststempel *m* postmark

'**postwendend** *adv* by return mail, *Br* by return (of post)

'**Postwertzeichen** *n* (postage) stamp

Postzustellung *f* postal *or* mail delivery

Potenz [po'tɛnts] *f* (-; *-en*) a) (*no pl*) MED potency, b) MATH power

Pracht [praxt] *f* (-; *no pl*) splendo(u)r, magnificence

prächtig ['prɛçtɪç] *adj* splendid, magnificent, *fig a.* great, super

Prädikat [prɛdi'kaːt] *n* (*-[e]s*; *-e*) LING predicate

prägen ['prɛːgən] *v/t* (*ge-, h*) stamp, coin (*a. fig*)

prahlen ['praːlən] *v/i* (*ge-, h*) brag, boast (*both: mit* of), talk big, show off

Prahler ['praːlɐ] *m* (*-s*; -) boaster, braggart

Prahlerei [praːlə'rai] *f* (-; *-en*) boasting, bragging

'**prahlerisch** *adj* boastful; showy

Praktikant [prakti'kant] *m* (*-en*; *-en*), **Prakti'kantin** *f* (-; *-nen*) trainee

Praktiken ['praktikən] *pl* practices

'**Praktikum** *n* (*-s*; *-ka*) practical training

'**praktisch 1.** *adj* practical; useful, handy; *praktischer Arzt* general practitioner; **2.** *adv* practically; virtually

praktizieren [prakti'tsiːrən] *v/t* (*no -ge-, h*) practice (*Br* practise) medicine *or* law

Prälat [prɛ'laːt] *m* (*-en*; *-en*) REL prelate

Praline [pra'liːnə] *f* (-; *-n*) chocolate

prall [pral] *adj* tight; well-rounded; bulging; blazing (*sun*)

prallen ['pralən] *v/i* (*ge-, sein*) *prallen gegen* (*or auf* acc) crash *or* bump into

Prämie ['prɛːmjə] *f* (-; *-n*) premium; prize; bonus

prämieren [prɛ'miːrən], **prämiieren** [prɛmi'iːrən] *v/t* (*no -ge-, h*) award a prize to

Pranke ['praŋkə] *f* (-; *-n*) ZO paw (*a.* F)

Präparat [prɛpa'raːt] *n* (*-[e]s*; *-e*) preparation

präparieren [prɛpa'riːrən] *v/t* (*no -ge-, h*) prepare; MED, BOT, ZO dissect

Präposition [prɛpozi'tsjoːn] *f* (-; *-en*) LING preposition

Prärie [prɛ'riː] *f* (-; *-n*) prairie

Präsens ['prɛːzɛns] *n* (-; *-sentia* [prɛ'zɛntsja]) LING present (tense)

präsentieren [prɛzɛn'tiːrən] *v/t* (*no -ge-, h*) present; offer

Präservativ [prɛzɛrva'tiːf] *n* (*-s*; *-e*) condom

Präsident [prɛzi'dɛnt] *m* (*-en*; *-en*), **Präsi'dentin** *f* (-; *-nen*) president; chairman (chairwoman)

präsidieren [prɛzi'diːrən] *v/i* preside (*in dat* over)

Präsidium [prɛ'ziːdjʊm] *n* (*-s*; *-ien*) presidency

prasseln ['prasəln] *v/i* (*ge-, h*) rain etc: patter; *fire*: crackle

Präteritum [prɛ'teːritʊm] *n* (*-s*; *-ta*) LING past (tense)

Praxis ['praksɪs] *f* (-; *Praxen*) a) (*no pl*) practice (*a.* MED, JUR), b) MED doctor's office, *Br* surgery

Präzedenzfall [prɛtse'dɛnts-] *m* precedent

präzis [prɛ'tsiːs], **präzise** [prɛ'tsiːzə] *adj* precise

Präzision [prɛtsi'zjoːn] *f* (-; *no pl*) precision

predigen ['preːdɪgən] *v/i and v/t* (*ge-, h*) preach

Prediger ['preːdɪgɐ] *m* (*-s*, -), '**Predigerin** *f* (-; *-nen*) preacher

Predigt ['preːdɪçt] *f* (-; *-en*) sermon

Preis [prais] *m* (*-es*; *-e*) price (*a. fig*); prize; *film etc*: award; reward; *um jeden Preis* at all costs

'**Preisausschreiben** *n* competition

Preiselbeere ['praizəl-] *f* BOT cranberry

preisen ['praizən] *v/t* (*irr, ge-, h*) praise

'**Preiserhöhung** *f* rise *or* increase in

Profit

price(s)

'**preisgeben** v/t (*irr*, **geben**, *sep*, -*ge*-, *h*) abandon; reveal, give away

'**preisgekrönt** *adj* prize-winning; *film etc*: award-winning

'**Preisgericht** *n* jury

Preislage *f* price range

Preisliste *f* price list

Preisnachlass *m* discount

Preisrätsel *n* competition

Preisrichter(in) judge

Preisschild *n* price tag

Preisstopp *m* price freeze

Preisträger(in) prizewinner

'**preiswert** *adj* cheap

prellen ['prɛlən] v/t (*ge*-, *h*) *fig* cheat (**um** out of); **sich et. prellen** MED bruise s.th.

'**Prellung** *f* (-; -*en*) MED contusion, bruise

Premiere [prə'mjeːrə] *f* (-; -*n*) THEA *etc* first night, première

Premiermi,nister [prə'mjeː-] *m*, **Pre'miermi,nisterin** *f* prime minister

Presse ['prɛsə] *f* (-; -*n*) a) (*no pl*) press, b) squeezer

Presse... *in cpds* ...*agentur*, ...*konferenz*, ...*fotograf etc*: press ...

Pressefreiheit *f* freedom of the press

Pressemeldung *f* news item

'**pressen** v/t (*ge*-, *h*) press; squeeze

'**Pressetri,büne** *f* press box

Pressevertreter *m* reporter

'**Pressluft** *f* compressed air

Pressluft... *in cpds* ...*bohrer*, ...*hammer etc*: pneumatic ...

Prestige [prɛs'tiːʒə] *n* (-*s*; *no pl*) prestige

Prestigeverlust *m* loss of prestige *or* face

Preuße ['prɔysə] *m* (-*n*; -*n*), '**Preußin** *f* (-; -*nen*), '**preußisch** *adj* Prussian

prickeln ['prɪkəln] v/i (*ge*-, *h*) prickle; tingle

pries [priːs] *pret of* **preisen**

Priester ['priːstɐ] *m* (-*s*; -) priest

Priesterin ['priːstərɪn] *f* (-; -*nen*) priestess

'**priesterlich** *adj* priestly

prima ['priːma] F *adj* great, super

primär [pri'mɛːɐ] *adj* primary

Primararzt [pri'maːɐ-] *Austrian m* → **Oberarzt**

Primarschule *Swiss f* → **Grundschule**

Primel ['priːməl] *f* (-; -*n*) BOT primrose

primitiv [primi'tiːf] *adj* primitive

Prinz [prɪnts] *m* (-*en*; -*en*) prince

Prinzessin [prɪn'tsɛsɪn] *f* (-; -*nen*) princess

'**Prinzgemahl** *m* prince consort

Prinzip [prɪn'tsiːp] *n* (-*s*; -*ien*) principle (**aus** on; **im** in)

prinzipiell [prɪntsi'pjɛl] *adv* as a matter of principle

Prise ['priːzə] *f* (-; -*n*) **e-e Prise Salz** *etc* a pinch of salt *etc*

Prisma ['prɪsma] *n* (-*s*; -*men*) prism

Pritsche ['prɪtʃə] *f* (-; -*n*) plank bed; MOT platform

privat [pri'vaːt] *adj* private; personal

Pri'vat... *in cpds* ...*leben*, ...*schule*, ...*detektiv etc*: private ...

Privatangelegenheit *f* personal *or* private matter *or* affair; **das ist m-e Privatangelegenheit** that's my own business

Privileg [privi'leːk] *n* (-[*e*]*s*; -*gien* [privi'leːgjən]) privilege

pro [proː] *prp* (*acc*) per; **2 Mark pro Stück** two marks each

Pro *n*: **das Pro und Kontra** the pros and cons

Probe ['proːbə] *f* (-; -*n*) trial, test; sample; THEA rehearsal; MATH proof; **auf Probe** on probation; **auf die Probe stellen** put to the test

Probea,larm *m* test alarm, fire drill

Probeaufnahmen *pl film*: screen test

Probefahrt *f* test drive

Probeflug *m* test flight

'**proben** v/i *and* v/t (*ge*-, *h*) THEA *etc* rehearse

'**probeweise** *adv* on trial; on probation

'**Probezeit** *f* (time of) probation

probieren [pro'biːrən] v/t (*no* -*ge*-, *h*) try; taste

Problem [pro'bleːm] *n* (-*s*; -*e*) problem

problematisch [proble'maːtɪʃ] *adj* problematic(al)

Produkt [pro'dʊkt] *n* (-[*e*]*s*; -*e*) product (*a.* MATH); result

Produktion [prodʊk'tsjoːn] *f* (-; -*en*) production; output

produktiv [prodʊk'tiːf] *adj* productive

Produktivität [prodʊktivi'tɛːt] *f* (-; *no pl*) productivity

Produzent [produ'tsɛnt] *m* (-*en*; -*en*), **Produ'zentin** *f* (-; -*nen*) producer

produzieren [produ'tsiːrən] v/t (*no* -*ge*-, *h*) produce

professionell [profɛsjo'nɛl] *adj* professional

Professor [pro'fɛsoːɐ] *m* (-*s*; -*en* [profɛ'soːrən]), **Profes'sorin** *f* (-; -*nen*) professor

Professur [profɛ'suːɐ] *f* (-; -*en*) professorship, chair (**für** of)

Profi ['proːfi] *m* (-*s*; -*s*) pro

Profi... *in cpds* ...*boxer*, ...*fußballer etc*: professional

Profil [pro'fiːl] *n* (-*s*; -*e*) profile; MOT tread

profilieren [profi'liːrən] v/refl (*no* -*ge*-, *h*) distinguish o.s.

Profit [pro'fiːt] *m* (-[*e*]*s*; -*e*) profit

P

profitieren 214

profitieren [profi'tiːrən] *v/i* (*no -ge-, h*) profit (*von* or *bei et.* from or by s.th.)

Prognose [pro'gnoːzə] *f* (-; *-n*) prediction; METEOR forecast; MED prognosis

Programm [pro'gram] *n* (*-s; -e*) program(me *Br*), TV *a.* channel; EDP program

Programmfehler *m* EDP program error, bug

programmieren [progra'miːrən] *v/t* (*no -ge-, h*) program (*a.* EDP)

Programmierer [progra'miːrɐ] *m* (*-s; -*), **Program'miererin** *f* (-; *-nen*) EDP programmer

Projekt [pro'jɛkt] *n* (*-[e]s; -e*) project

Projektion [projɛk'tsjoːn] *f* (-; *-en*) projection

Projektor [pro'jɛktoːɐ] *m* (*-s; -en* [projɛk'toːrən]) projector

proklamieren [prokla'miːrən] *v/t* (*no -ge-, h*) proclaim

Prokurist [proku'rɪst] *m* (*-en; -en*), **Proku'ristin** *f* (-; *-nen*) authorized signatory

Proletarier [prole'taːrjɐ] *m* (*-s; -*), **prole-tarisch** [-'taːrɪʃ] *adj* proletarian

Prolog [pro'loːk] *m* (*-[e]s; -e*) prologue

Promillegrenze [pro'mɪlə-] *f* (blood) alcohol limit

prominent [promi'nɛnt] *adj* prominent

Prominenz [promi'nɛnts] *f* (-; *no pl*) notables; high society

Promotion [promo'tsjoːn] *f* (-; *-en*) UNIV doctorate

promovieren [promo'viːrən] *v/i* (*no -ge-, h*) do one's doctorate

prompt [prɔmpt] *adj* prompt; quick

Pronomen [pro'noːmən] *n* (*-s; -mina*) LING pronoun

Propeller [pro'pɛlɐ] *m* (*-s; -*) propeller

Prophet [pro'feːt] *m* (*-en; -en*) prophet

pro'phetisch *adj* prophetic

prophezeien [profe'tsaiən] *v/t* (*no -ge-, h*) prophesy, predict

Prophe'zeiung *f* (-; *-en*) prophecy, prediction

Proportion [propɔr'tsjoːn] *f* (-; *-en*) proportion

Proporz [pro'pɔrts] *m* (*-es; -e*) POL proportional representation

Prosa ['proːza] *f* (-; *no pl*) prose

Prospekt [pro'spɛkt] *m* (*-[e]s; -e*) prospectus; brochure, pamphlet

prost [proːst] *int* cheers!

Prostituierte [prostitu'iːɐtə] *f* (*-n; -n*) prostitute

Protest [pro'tɛst] *m* (*-[e]s; -e*) protest; *aus Protest* in (or as a) protest

Protestant [protɛs'tant] *m* (*-en; -en*), **Protes'tantin** *f* (-; *-nen*), **protes'tantisch** *adj* REL Protestant

protestieren [protɛs'tiːrən] *v/i* (*no -ge-, h*) protest

Prothese [pro'teːzə] *f* (-; *-n*) MED artificial limb; denture

Protokoll [proto'kɔl] *n* (*-s; -e*) record, minutes; protocol; (*das*) *Protokoll führen* take or keep the minutes; *zu Protokoll nehmen* JUR record

Protokollführer *m* keeper of the minutes

protokollieren [protokɔ'liːrən] *v/t* and *v/i* (*no -ge-, h*) take the minutes (of); JUR record

protzen ['prɔtsən] F *v/i* (*ge-, h*) show off (*mit et.* s.th.)

protzig ['prɔtsɪç] *adj* showy, flashy

Proviant [pro'vjant] *m* (*-s; no pl*) provisions, food

Provinz [pro'vɪnts] *f* (-; *-en*) province; *fig* country

provinziell [provɪn'tsjɛl] *adj* provincial (*a. contp*)

Provision [provi'zjoːn] *f* (-; *-en*) ECON commission

provisorisch [provi'zoːrɪʃ] *adj* provisional, temporary

provozieren [provo'tsiːrən] *v/t* (*no -ge-, h*) provoke

Prozent [pro'tsɛnt] *n* (*-[e]s; -e*) per cent; F *pl* discount

Prozentsatz *m* percentage

prozentual [protsɛn'tuaːl] *adj* proportional; *prozentualer Anteil* percentage

Prozess [pro'tsɛs] *m* (*-es; -e*) process (*a.* TECH, CHEM *etc*); JUR action; lawsuit, case; trial; *j-m den Prozess machen* take s.o. to court; *e-n Prozess gewinnen* (*verlieren*) win (lose) a case

prozessieren [protsɛ'siːrən] *v/i* (*no -ge-, h*) JUR go to court; *gegen j-n prozessieren* bring an action against s.o., take s.o. to court

Prozession [protsɛ'sjoːn] *f* (-; *-en*) procession

Prozessor [pro'tsɛsoːɐ] *m* (*-s; -en* [protsɛ'soːrən]) EDP processor

prüde ['pryːdə] *adj* prudish; *prüde sein* be a prude

prüfen ['pryːfən] *v/t* (*ge-, h*) PED *etc* examine, test (*a.* TECH); check; inspect (*a.* TECH); *fig* consider

prüfend *adj* searching

Prüfer ['pryːfɐ] *m* (*-s; -*), **'Prüferin** *f* (-; *-nen*) PED *etc* examiner; *esp* TECH tester

Prüfling ['pryːflɪŋ] *m* (*-s; -e*) candidate

'Prüfstein *m* touchstone (*für* of)

'Prüfung *f* (-; *-en*) examination, F exam; test; check(ing), inspection; *e-e Prüfung machen* (*bestehen, nicht bestehen*) take (pass, fail) an exam(ination)

'**Prüfungsarbeit** *f* examination *or* test paper

Prügel ['pry:gəl] F *pl* (*e-e Tracht*) *Prügel bekommen* get a (good) beating *or* hiding *or* thrashing

Prüge'lei F *f* (-; *-en*) fight

'**prügeln** F *v/t* (*ge-, h*) beat, flog; *sich prügeln* (have a) fight

'**Prügelstrafe** *f* corporal punishment

Prunk [pruŋk] *m* (-[e]s; *no pl*) splendo(u)r, pomp

'**prunkvoll** *adj* splendid, magnificent

PS [pe:'ʔɛs] ABBR *of Pferdestärke* horsepower, HP

Psalm [psalm] *m* (-s; *-en*) REL psalm

Pseudonym [psɔydo'ny:m] *n* (-s; *-e*) pseudonym

pst [pst] *int* sh!, ssh!; psst!

Psyche ['psy:çə] *f* (-; *-n*) mind, psyche

Psychiater [psy'çja:tɐ] *m* (-s; -), **Psy-'chiaterin** *f* (-; *-nen*) psychiatrist

psychiatrisch [psy'çja:trıʃ] *adj* psychiatric

psychisch ['psy:çıʃ] *adj* mental, MED *a.* psychic

Psychoana'lyse [psyço-] *f* psychoanalysis

Psychologe [psyço'lo:gə] *m* (*-n*; *-n*) psychologist (*a. fig*)

Psychologie [psyçolo'gi:] *f* (-; *no pl*) psychology

Psycho'login *f* (-; *-nen*) psychologist

psycho'logisch *adj* psychological

Psychose [psy'ço:zə] *f* (-; *-n*) MED psychosis

psychosomatisch [psyçozo'ma:tıʃ] *adj* MED psychosomatic

Pubertät [pubɛr'tɛ:t] *f* (-; *no pl*) puberty

Publikum ['pu:blikum] *n* (-s; *no pl*) audience, TV *a.* viewers, *radio: a.* listeners; SPORT crowd, spectators; ECON customers; public

publizieren [publi'tsi:rən] *v/t* (*no -ge-, h*) publish

Pudding ['pudıŋ] *m* (-s; *-e, -s*) pudding, *esp Br* blancmange

Pudel ['pu:dəl] *m* (-s; -) ZO poodle

Puder ['pu:dɐ] *m* (-s; -) powder

'**Puderdose** *f* powder compact

'**pudern** *v/t* (*ge-, h*) powder; *sich pudern* powder one's face

'**Puderzucker** *m* confectioner's (*Br* icing) sugar

Puff[1] [puf] F *m* (-s; *-s*) brothel

Puff[2] *m* (-[e]s; *Püffe* ['pyfə]) hump; poke

Puffer ['pufɐ] *m* (-s; -) RAIL buffer (*a. fig*)

'**Puffmais** *m* popcorn

Pulli ['puli] F *m* (-s; *-s*) (light) sweater

Pullover [pu'lo:vɐ] *m* (-s; -) sweater, pullover

Puls [puls] *m* (-es; *-e*) MED pulse; pulse rate

Pulsader *f* ANAT artery

pulsieren [pul'zi:rən] *v/i* (*no -ge-, h*) MED pulsate (*a. fig*)

Pult [pult] *n* (-[e]s; *-e*) desk

Pulver ['pulvɐ] *n* (-s; -) powder; F cash, *sl* dough

pulv(e)rig ['pulv(ə)rıç] *adj* powdery

pulverisieren [pulveri'zi:rən] *v/t* (*no -ge-, h*) pulverize

'**Pulverkaffee** *m* instant coffee

'**Pulverschnee** *m* powder snow

pumm(e)lig ['pum(ə)lıç] F *adj* chubby, plump, tubby

Pumpe ['pumpə] *f* (-; *-n*) TECH pump

'**pumpen** *v/i and v/t* TECH pump; F lend; borrow

Punker ['paŋkɐ] F *m* (-s; -), '**Punkerin** *f* (-; *-nen*) punk

Punkt [puŋkt] *m* (-[e]s; *-e*) point (*a. fig*); dot; full stop, period; *fig* spot, place; *um Punkt zehn (Uhr)* at ten (o'clock) sharp; *nach Punkten gewinnen etc* SPORT win *etc* on points

punktieren [puŋk'ti:rən] *v/t* (*no -ge-, h*) dot; MED puncture

pünktlich ['pyŋktlıç] *adj* punctual; *pünktlich sein* be on time

'**Pünktlichkeit** *f* (-; *no pl*) punctuality

'**Punktsieger** *m* SPORT winner on points

Punktspiel *n* SPORT league game

Pupille [pu'pılə] *f* (-; *-n*) ANAT pupil

Puppe ['pupə] *f* (-; *-n*) doll, F *a.* chick; THEA puppet (*a. fig*); MOT dummy; ZO chrysalis, pupa

'**Puppenspiel** *n* puppet show

Puppenstube *f* doll's house

Puppenwagen *m* doll carriage, *Br* doll's pram

pur [pu:ɐ] *adj* pure (*a. fig*); *whisky etc*: straight, *Br* neat

Purpur ['purpur] *m* (-s; *no pl*) crimson

'**purpurrot** *adj* crimson

Purzelbaum ['purtsəl-] *m* somersault; *e-n Purzelbaum schlagen* turn a somersault

purzeln ['purtsəln] *v/i* (*ge-, sein*) tumble

Pute ['pu:tə] *f* (-; *-n*) ZO turkey (hen)

Puter ['pu:tɐ] *m* (-s; -) ZO turkey (cock)

Putsch [putʃ] *m* (-[e]s; *-e*) putsch, coup (d'état)

'**putschen** *v/i* (*ge-, h*) revolt, make a putsch

Putz [puts] *m* (-es; *no pl*) ARCH plaster (-ing); *unter Putz* ELECTR concealed

putzen ['putsən] (*ge-, h*) **1.** *v/t* clean; polish; wipe; *sich die Nase putzen* blow

P

one's nose; **sich die Zähne putzen** brush one's teeth; **2.** *v/i* do the cleaning; **putzen** (**gehen**) work as a cleaner
'**Putzfrau** *f* cleaner, cleaning woman *or* lady
putzig ['pʊtsɪç] *adj* funny, cute

'**Putzlappen** *m* cleaning rag
'**Putzmittel** *n* clean(s)er; polish
Puzzle ['pazəl] *n* (-*s*; -*s*) jigsaw (puzzle)
Pyjama [py'dʒaːma] *m* (-*s*; -*s*) pajamas, *Br* pyjamas
Pyramide [pyra'miːdə] *f* (-; -*n*) pyramid

Q

Quacksalber ['kvakzalbɐ] *m* (-*s*; -) quack (doctor)
Quadrat [kva'draːt] *n* (-[*e*]*s*; -*e*) square; **ins Quadrat erheben** MATH square; **Quadrat...** *in cpds* ...*meile*, ...*meter*, ...*wurzel*, ...*zahl etc*: square ...
qua'dratisch *adj* square; MATH quadratic
quaken ['kvaːkən] *v/i* (*ge*-, *h*) duck: quack; *frog*: croak
quäken ['kvɛːkən] *v/i* (*ge*-, *h*) squeak
Qual [kvaːl] *f* (-; -*en*) pain, torment, agony; anguish
quälen ['kvɛːlən] *v/t* (*ge*-, *h*) torment (*a. fig*); torture; *fig* pester, plague
Qualifikation [kvalifika'tsjoːn] *f* (-; -*en*) qualification
Qualifikati'ons... *in cpds* ...*spiel etc*: qualifying ...
qualifizieren [kvalifi'tsiːrən] *v/t and v/refl* (*no -ge-*, *h*) qualify
Qualität [kvali'tɛːt] *f* (-; -*en*) quality
qualitativ [kvalita'tiːf] *adj and adv* in quality
Quali'täts... *in cpds* ...*arbeit*, ...*waren etc*: high-quality ...
Qualm [kvalm] *m* (-[*e*]*s*; *no pl*) (thick) smoke
qualmen ['kvalmən] *v/i* (*ge*-, *h*) smoke; F be a heavy smoker
'**qualvoll** *adj* very painful; agonizing
Quantität [kvanti'tɛːt] *f* (-; -*en*) quantity
quantitativ [kvantita'tiːf] *adj and adv* in quantity
Quantum ['kvantʊm] *n* (-*s*; *Quanten*) amount, *fig a.* share
Quarantäne [karan'tɛːnə] *f* (-; -*n*) (**unter Quarantäne stellen** put in) quarantine
Quark [kvark] *m* (-*s*; *no pl*) curd, cottage cheese
Quartal [kvar'taːl] *n* (-*s*; -*e*) quarter (of a year)
Quartett [kvar'tɛt] *n* (-[*e*]*s*; -*e*) quartet(te)

Quartier [kvar'tiːɐ] *n* (-*s*; -*e*) accommodation; *Swiss*: quarter
Quarz [kvaːɐts] *m* (-*es*; -*e*) MIN quartz
Quatsch [kvatʃ] F *m* (-[*e*]*s*; *no pl*) nonsense, rubbish, *sl* rot, crap, bullshit; **Quatsch machen** fool around; joke, F kid
quatschen ['kvatʃən] F *v/i* (*ge*-, *h*) talk rubbish; chat
Quecksilber ['kvɛkzɪlbɐ] *n* (-*s*; *no pl*) mercury, quicksilver
Quelle ['kvɛlə] *f* (-; -*n*) spring, source (*a. fig*), well, *fig a.* origin
'**quellen** *v/i* (*irr*, *ge*-, *sein*) pour (**aus** from)
'**Quellenangabe** *f* reference
quengeln ['kvɛŋəln] F *v/i* (*ge*-, *h*) whine
quer [kveːɐ] *adv* across; crosswise; **kreuz und quer** all over the place; **kreuz und quer durch Deutschland fahren** travel all over Germany
Quere ['kveːrə] *f*: F **j-m in die Quere kommen** get in s.o.'s way
Querfeld'einlauf *m* SPORT cross-country race
'**Querlatte** *f* SPORT crossbar
'**Querschläger** *m* MIL ricochet
'**Querschnitt** *m* cross-section (*a. fig*)
'**querschnitt(s)gelähmt** *adj* MED paraplegic
'**Querstraße** *f* intersecting road; **zweite Querstraße rechts** second turning on the right
Querulant [kveru'lant] *m* (-*en*; -*en*), **Queru'lantin** *f* (-; -*nen*) querulous person
quetschen ['kvɛtʃən] *v/t and v/refl* (*ge*-, *h*) squeeze; MED bruise (o.s.)
'**Quetschung** *f* (-; -*en*) MED bruise
quiek(s)en ['kviːk(s)ən] *v/i* (*ge*-, *h*) squeak, squeal
quietschen ['kviːtʃən] *v/i* (*ge*-, *h*) squeal; screech; squeak, creak
quitt [kvɪt] *adj*: **mit j-m quitt sein** be quits

or even with s.o. (*a. fig*)

quittieren [kvɪ'tiːrən] *v/t* (*no -ge-, h*) ECON give a receipt for

'**Quittung** *f* (*-; -en*) receipt; *fig* answer

quoll [kvɔl] *pret of* **quellen**

Quote ['kvoːtə] *f* (*-; -n*) quota; share; rate

'**Quotenregelung** *f* quota system

Quotient [kvo'tsjɛnt] *m* (*-en; -en*) MATH quotient

R

Rabatt [ra'bat] *m* (*-[e]s; -e*) ECON discount, rebate

Rabe ['raːbə] *m* (*-n; -n*) ZO raven

rabiat [ra'bjaːt] *adj* rough, tough

Rache ['raxə] *f* (*-; no pl*) revenge; *aus Rache für* in revenge for

Rachen ['raxən] *m* (*-s; -*) ANAT throat

rächen ['rɛçən] *v/t* (*ge-, h*) avenge *s.th.*; revenge *s.o.*; *sich an j-m für et. rächen* revenge o.s. *or* take revenge on s.o. for s.th.

Rächer ['rɛçɐ] *m* (*-s; -*) avenger

rachsüchtig ['rax-] *adj* revengeful, vindictive

Rad [raːt] *n* (*-[e]s; Räder* ['rɛːdɐ]) wheel; bicycle, F bike; *Rad fahren* cycle, ride a bicycle, F bike; *ein Rad schlagen peacock*: spread its tail; SPORT turn a (cart)-wheel

Radar [ra'daːɐ] *m, n* (*-s; -e*) radar

Radarfalle *f* MOT speed trap

Radarkon,trolle *f* MOT radar speed check

Radarschirm *m* radar screen

Radarstati,on *f* radar station

radeln ['raːdəln] F *v/i* (*ge-, sein*) bike

Rädelsführer ['rɛːdəls-] *m* ringleader

Räderwerk ['rɛːdɐ-] *n* TECH gearing

'**Radfahrer** *m* (*-s; -*), '**Radfahrerin** *f* (*-; -nen*) cyclist

radieren [ra'diːrən] *v/t* (*no -ge-, h*) erase, rub out; *art*: etch

Radiergummi [ra'diːɐ-] *m* eraser, *Br a.* rubber

Ra'dierung *f* (*-; -en*) *art*: etching

Radieschen [ra'diːsçən] *n* (*-s; -*) BOT (red) radish

radikal [radi'kaːl] *adj*, **Radi'kale** *m, f* (*-n; -n*) radical

Radikalismus [radika'lɪsmʊs] *m* (*-; no pl*) radicalism

Radio ['raːdjo] *n* (*-s; -s*) radio; *im Radio* on the radio; *Radio hören* listen to the radio

radioak'tiv [radjo-] *adj* PHYS radioactive; *radioaktiver Niederschlag* fall-out

Radioaktivi'tät *f* (*-; no pl*) radioactivity

'**Radiowecker** *m* clock radio

Radius ['raːdjʊs] *m* (*-s; Radien*) radius

'**Radkappe** *f* hubcap

Radrennbahn *f* cycling track

Radrennen *n* cycle race

Radsport *m* cycling

Radsportler *m* cyclist

Radweg *m* cycle track *or* path, bikeway

raffen ['rafən] *v/t* (*ge-, h*) gather up; *an sich raffen* grab

Raffinerie [rafinə'riː] *f* (*-; -n*) CHEM refinery

Raffinesse [rafi'nɛsə] *f* (*-; -n*) a) (*no pl*) shrewdness, b) refinement

raffiniert [rafi'niːɐt] *adj* refined (*a. fig*); *fig* shrewd, clever

ragen ['raːgən] *v/i* (*ge-, h*) tower (up), rise (high)

Rahe ['raːə] *f* (*-; -n*) MAR yard

Rahm [raːm] *m* (*-[e]s; no pl*) cream

rahmen ['raːmən] *v/t* (*ge-, h*) frame; PHOT mount

'**Rahmen** *m* (*-s; -*) frame; *fig* framework; setting; scope; *aus dem Rahmen fallen* be out of the ordinary

Rakete [ra'keːtə] *f* (*-; -n*) rocket, MIL *a.* missile; *ferngelenkte Rakete* guided missile; *e-e Rakete abfeuern (starten)* launch a rocket *or* missile

Ra'ketenantrieb *m* rocket propulsion; *mit Raketenantrieb* rocket-propelled

Raketenbasis *f* MIL rocket *or* missile base *or* site

rammen ['ramən] *v/t* (*ge-, h*) ram; MOT *etc* hit, collide with

Rampe ['rampə] *f* (*-; -n*) (loading) ramp

'**Rampenlicht** *n* (*-[e]s; no pl*) THEA footlights; *fig* limelight

Ramsch [ramʃ] F *m* (*-es; no pl*) junk

Rand [rant] *m* (*-[e]s; Ränder* ['rɛndɐ]) edge, border; brink (*a. fig*); rim; brim; margin; *am Rand(e) des Ruins etc* on the brink of ruin *etc*

randalieren [randa'liːrən] *v/i* (*no -ge-, h*) kick up a racket

Randalierer [randa'liːrɐ] *m* (*-s; -*) rowdy, hooligan

'**Randbemerkung** *f* marginal note; *fig* comment

Randgruppe *f* fringe group

'**randlos** *adj* rimless

'**Randstreifen** *m* MOT shoulder

rang [raŋ] *pret of* **ringen**

Rang *m* (*-[e]s; Ränge* ['rɛŋə]) position, rank (*a.* MIL); THEA balcony, *Br* circle; *pl* SPORT terraces

rangieren [raŋ'ʒiːrən] (*no -ge-, h*) **1.** *v/t* RAIL switch, *Br* shunt; **2.** *fig v/i* rank (*vor j-m* before s.o.)

'**Rangordnung** *f* hierarchy

Ranke ['raŋkə] *f* (*-; -n*) BOT tendril

'**ranken** *v/refl* (*ge-, h*) BOT creep, climb

rann [ran] *pret of* **rinnen**

rannte ['rantə] *pret of* **rennen**

Ranzen ['rantsən] *m* (*-s; -*) knapsack; satchel

ranzig ['rantsɪç] *adj* rancid, rank

Rappe ['rapə] *m* (*-n; -n*) ZO black horse

rar [raːɐ] *adj* rare, scarce

Rarität [rari'tɛːt] *f* (*-; -en*) a) curiosity, b) (*no pl*) rarity

rasch [raʃ] *adj* quick, swift; prompt

rascheln ['raʃəln] *v/i* (*ge-, h*) rustle

rasen ['raːzən] *v/i* a) (*ge-, sein*) F MOT race, tear, speed, b) (*ge-, h*) rage; *rasen vor Begeisterung* roar with enthusiasm

'**Rasen** *m* (*-s; -*) lawn, grass

'**rasend** *adj* breakneck; raging; agonizing; splitting; thunderous

'**Rasenmäher** *m* lawn mower

Rasenplatz *m* lawn; *tennis*: grass court

Raserei [raːzə'rai] *f* (*-; -en*) a) (*no pl*) frenzied rage; frenzy, madness, b) F MOT reckless driving

Rasierappa,rat [ra'ziːɐ-] *m* (safety) razor; *esp elektrischer Rasierapparat* shaver

Rasiercreme *f* shaving cream

rasieren [ra'ziːrən] *v/t and v/refl* (*no -ge-, h*) shave

Ra'sierklinge *f* razor blade

Rasiermesser *n* (straight) razor

Rasierpinsel *m* shaving brush

Rasierseife *f* shaving soap

Rasierwasser *n* aftershave (lotion)

Rasse ['rasə] *f* (*-; -n*) race; ZO breed

'**Rassehund** *m* ZO pedigree dog

Rassel ['rasəl] *f* (*-; -n*), '**rasseln** *v/i* (*ge-, h*) rattle

'**Rassen...** *in cpds* ...*diskriminierung*, ...*konflikt*, ...*probleme etc*: *mst* racial ...

Rassentrennung *f* POL (racial) segregation; HIST apartheid

Rassenunruhen *pl* race riots

rassig ['rasɪç] *adj* classy

rassisch ['rasɪʃ] *adj* racial

Rassismus [ra'sɪsmʊs] *m* (*-; no pl*) POL racism

Ras'sist(in) (*-en; -en/-; -nen*), **ras'sistisch** *adj* POL racist

Rast [rast] *f* (*-; -en*) rest, stop; break

rasten ['rastən] *v/i* (*ge-, h*) rest, stop, take a break

'**rastlos** *adj* restless

'**Rastplatz** *m* resting place; MOT rest area, *Br* lay-by

'**Raststätte** *f* MOT service area

Rasur [ra'zuːɐ] *f* (*-; -en*) shave

Rat [raːt] *m* (*-[e]s; Räte* ['rɛːtə]) a) (*no pl*) (piece of) advice, b) council; *j-n um Rat fragen* ask s.o.'s advice; *j-s Rat befolgen* take s.o.'s advice

Rate ['raːtə] *f* (*-; -n*) rate; ECON instal(l)-ment; *auf Raten* by instal(l)ments

raten ['raːtən] *v/t and v/i* (*irr, ge-, h*) advise; guess; solve; *j-m zu et. raten* advise s.o. to do s.th.; *rate mal!* (have a) guess!

'**Ratenzahlung** *f* → *Abzahlung*

'**Rateteam** *n* TV *etc* panel

'**Ratgeber** ['raːt-] *m* (*-s; -*), '**Ratgeberin** *f* (*-; -nen*) adviser, counsel(l)or; *m* guide (*über acc* to)

'**Rathaus** *n* city (*Br* town) hall

ratifizieren [ratifi'tsiːrən] *v/t* (*no -ge-, h*) ratify

Ration [ra'tsjoːn] *f* (*-; -en*) ration

rational [ratsjo'naːl] *adj* rational

rationell [ratsjo'nɛl] *adj* efficient; economical

rationieren [ratsjo'niːrən] *v/t* (*no -ge-, h*) ration

'**ratlos** *adj* at a loss

'**ratsam** *adj* advisable, wise

'**Ratschlag** *m* piece of advice; *ein paar gute Ratschläge* some good advice

Rätsel ['rɛːtsəl] *n* (*-s; -*) puzzle; riddle (*both a. fig*); mystery

'**rätselhaft** *adj* puzzling; mysterious

Ratte ['ratə] *f* (*-; -n*) ZO rat (*a. contp*)

rattern ['ratɐn] *v/i* (*ge-, h, sein*) rattle, clatter

rau [rau] *adj* rough, rugged (*both a. fig*); harsh; chapped; sore

Raub [raup] *m* (*-[e]s; no pl*) robbery; loot, booty; prey

Raubbau *m* (*-[e]s; no pl*) overexploitation (*an dat* of); *Raubbau mit s-r Gesundheit treiben* ruin one's health

rauben ['raubən] *v/t* (*ge-, h*) rob, steal; kidnap; *j-m et. rauben* rob s.o. of s.th. (*a. fig*)

Räuber ['rɔybɐ] *m* (*-s; -*) robber

'**Raubfisch** *m* predatory fish
Raubmord *m* murder with robbery
Raubmörder *m* murderer and robber
Raubtier *n* beast of prey
Raubüberfall *m* holdup, (armed) robbery; mugging
Raubvogel *m* bird of prey
Raubzug *m* raid
Rauch [raux] *m* (-[e]s; *no pl*) smoke; CHEM *etc* fume
rauchen ['rauxən] *v/i and v/t* (*ge-*, *h*) smoke; CHEM *etc* fume; *Rauchen verboten!* no smoking; *Pfeife rauchen* smoke a pipe
Raucher(in) ['rauxɐ (-ɐrɪn)] (-s; -/-; -nen) smoker (*m a.* RAIL)
Räucher... ['rɔʏçɐ-] *in cpds* ...*aal*, ...*speck etc*: smoked ...
'**räuchern** *v/t* (*ge-*, *h*) smoke
'**Räucherstäbchen** *n* joss stick
'**Rauchfahne** *f* trail of smoke
rauchig ['rauxɪç] *adj* smoky
'**Rauchwaren** *pl* tobacco products; furs
Rauchzeichen *n* smoke signal
Räude ['rɔʏdə] *f* (-; -n) VET mange
'**räudig** *adj* VET mangy
raufen ['raufən] (*ge-*, *h*) **1.** *v/t*: *sich die Haare raufen* tear one's hair; **2.** *v/i* fight, scuffle
Rauferei [raufə'rai] *f* (-; -en) fight, scuffle
Raum [raum] *m* (-[e]s; *Räume* ['rɔʏmə]) room; space; area; (outer) space
Raumanzug *m* spacesuit
Raumdeckung *f* SPORT zone marking
räumen ['rɔʏmən] *v/t* (*ge-*, *h*) leave, move out of; check out of; clear (*von* of); evacuate (*a.* MIL); *s-e Sachen in ... (acc) räumen* put one's things (away) in ...
'**Raumfahrer** F *m* spaceman
Raumfahrt *f* (-; *no pl*) space travel *or* flight; astronautics
Raumfahrt... *in cpds* ...*technik*, ...*zentrum etc*: space ...
Raumfähre *f* space shuttle
Raumflug *m* space flight
Rauminhalt *m* volume
Raumkapsel *f* space capsule
Raumla,bor *n* space lab
räumlich ['rɔʏmlɪç] *adj* three-dimensional
'**Raumschiff** *n* spacecraft; spaceship
Raumsonde *f* space probe
Raumstati,on *f* space station
'**Räumung** *f* (-; -en) clearance; evacuation (*a.* MIL); JUR eviction
'**Räumungsverkauf** *m* ECON clearance sale
raunen ['raunən] *v/i* (*ge-*, *h*) whisper, murmur

Raupe ['raupə] *f* (-; -n) ZO caterpillar, TECH *a.* track
'**Raupenschlepper** *m* MOT caterpillar tractor
'**Raureif** *m* hoarfrost
raus [raus] F *int* get out (of here)!
Rausch [rauʃ] *m* (-es; *Räusche* ['rɔʏʃə]) drunkenness, intoxication; F high; *fig* ecstasy; *e-n Rausch haben* be drunk; *s-n Rausch ausschlafen* sleep it off
rauschen ['rauʃən] *v/i* a) (*ge-*, *h*) water *etc*: rush; *brook*: murmur; *storm*: roar, b) (*ge-*, *sein*) sweep
rauschend *adj* thunderous (*applause*); *rauschendes Fest* lavish celebration
'**Rauschgift** *n* drug(s), narcotic(s)
Rauschgiftdezer,nat *n* narcotics *or* drugs squad
Rauschgifthandel *m* drug traffic(king)
Rauschgifthändler *m* drug trafficker, F pusher
räuspern ['rɔʏspɐn] *v/refl* (*ge-*, *h*) clear one's throat
Razzia ['ratsja] *f* (-; -ien) raid, roundup
Reagenzglas [rea'gɛnts-] *n* CHEM test tube
reagieren [rea'giːrən] *v/i* (*no -ge-*, *h*) CHEM, MED react (*auf acc* to), *fig a.* respond (to)
Reaktion [reak'tsjoːn] *f* (-; -en) CHEM, MED, PHYS, POL reaction (*auf acc* to), *fig a.* response (to)
Reaktor [re'aktoːɐ] *m* (-s; -en [reak'toːrən]) PHYS (nuclear *or* atomic) reactor
real [re'aːl] *adj* real; concrete
realisieren [reali'ziːrən] *v/t* (*no -ge-*, *h*) realize
Realismus [rea'lɪsmʊs] *m* (-; *no pl*) realism
rea'listisch *adj* realistic
Realität [reali'tɛːt] *f* (-; *no pl*) reality
Re'alschule *f appr* (junior) highschool, *Br* secondary (modern) school
Rebe ['reːbə] *f* (-; -n) BOT vine
Rebell [re'bɛl] *m* (-en; -en) rebel
rebellieren [rebɛ'liːrən] *v/i* (*no -ge-*, *h*) rebel, revolt, rise (*all: gegen* against)
Re'bellin *f* (-; -nen) rebel
re'bellisch *adj* rebellious
Rebhuhn ['reːp-] *n* ZO partridge
'**Rebstock** *m* BOT vine
Rechen ['rɛçən] *m* (-s; -), '**rechen** *v/t* (*ge-*, *h*) rake
'**Rechenaufgabe** *f* MATH (arithmetical) problem
Rechenfehler *m* MATH arithmetical error, miscalculation
Rechenma,schine *f* calculator; computer
'**Rechenschaft** *f*: *Rechenschaft ablegen*

R

über (*acc*) account for; *zur Rechenschaft ziehen* call to account (*wegen* for)

'**Rechenschieber** *m* MATH slide rule

Rechenwerk *n* EDP arithmetic unit

Rechenzentrum *n* computer center (*Br* centre)

rechnen ['rɛçnən] *v/i and v/t* (*ge-, h*) calculate, reckon; work out, do sums; count; *rechnen mit fig* expect; count on; *mit mir kannst du nicht rechnen!* count me out!

'**Rechnen** *n* (*-s; no pl*) arithmetic

Rechner ['rɛçnɐ] *m* (*-s; -*) calculator; computer

'**rechnerabhängig** *adj* EDP online

rechnerisch ['rɛçnərɪʃ] *adj* arithmetical

'**rechnerunabhängig** *adj* EDP offline

'**Rechnung** *f* (*-; -en*) MATH calculation; problem, sum; ECON invoice, bill, check; *die Rechnung, bitte!* can I have the check, please?; *das geht auf m-e Rechnung* that's on me

recht [rɛçt] **1.** *adj* right; correct; POL right-wing; *auf der rechten Seite* on the right(-hand side); *mir ist es recht* I don't mind; **2.** *adv* right(ly), correctly; rather, quite; *ich weiß nicht recht* I don't really know; *es geschieht ihm recht* it serves him right; *erst recht* all the more; *erst recht nicht* even less; *du kommst gerade recht* (*zu*) you're just in time (for); *j-m recht geben* agree with s.o.; *recht haben* be right

Recht *n* (*-[e]s; -e*) a) right, claim (*both: auf acc* to), b) (*no pl*) JUR law; justice; *gleiches Recht* equal rights; *Recht haben* → *recht*; *j-m Recht geben* → *recht*; *im Recht sein* be in the right; *er hat es mit* (*vollem*) *Recht getan* he was (perfectly) right to do so; *ein Recht auf et. haben* be entitled to s.th.

'**Rechteck** *n* (*-[e]s; -e*) rectangle

'**rechteckig** *adj* rectangular

'**rechtfertigen** *v/t* (*ge-, h*) justify

'**Rechtfertigung** *f* (*-; -en*) justification

'**rechtlich** *adj* JUR legal

'**rechtlos** *adj* without rights; outcast

'**rechtmäßig** *adj* JUR lawful; legitimate; legal

'**Rechtmäßigkeit** *f* (*-; no pl*) JUR lawfulness, legitimacy

rechts [rɛçts] *adv* on the right(-hand side); *nach rechts* to the right

Rechts... *in cpds* POL right-wing ...

Rechtsanspruch *m* legal claim (*auf acc* to)

Rechtsanwalt *m*, **Rechtsanwältin** [-anvɛltɪn] *f* (*-; -nen*) lawyer

Rechts'außen *m* (*-; -*) *soccer:* outside right

'**rechtschaffen** *adj* honest

'**Rechtschreibfehler** *m* spelling mistake

Rechtschreibung *f* (*-; no pl*) spelling, orthography

'**rechtsextre,mistisch** *adj* POL extreme right

'**Rechtsfall** *m* JUR (law) case

'**Rechtshänder** [-hɛndɐ] *m* (*-s; -*), '**Rechtshänderin** *f* (*-; -nen*) right-handed person; *sie ist Rechtshänderin* she is right-handed

'**Rechtsprechung** *f* (*-; no pl*) jurisdiction

'**rechtsradi,kal** *adj* POL extreme right-wing

'**Rechtsschutz** *m* legal protection; legal costs insurance

'**rechtswidrig** *adj* JUR illegal, unlawful

'**rechtwink(e)lig** *adj* rectangular

'**rechtzeitig 1.** *adj* punctual; **2.** *adv* in time (*zu* for)

Reck [rɛk] *n* (*-[e]s; -e*) horizontal bar

recken ['rɛkən] *v/t* (*ge-, h*) stretch; *sich recken* stretch o.s.

recyceln [ri'saikəln] *v/t* (*no -ge-, h*) recycle

Recyclingpa,pier [ri'saiklɪŋ-] *n* recycled paper

Redakteur [redak'tø:ɐ] *m* (*-s; -e*), **Redak'teurin** *f* (*-; -nen*) editor

Redaktion [redak'tsjo:n] *f* (*-; -en*) a) (*no pl*) editing, b) editorial staff, editors, c) editorial office *or* department

redaktionell [redaktsjo'nɛl] *adj* editorial

Rede ['re:də] *f* (*-; -n*) speech, address; talk (*von* of); *e-e Rede halten* make a speech; *direkte* (*indirekte*) *Rede* LING direct (reported *or* indirect) speech; *j-n zur Rede stellen* take s.o. to task; *nicht der Rede wert* not worth mentioning

'**redegewandt** *adj* eloquent

reden ['re:dən] *v/i and v/t* (*ge-, h*) talk, speak (*both: mit* to; *über acc* about, of); *ich möchte mit dir reden* I'd like to talk to you; *die Leute reden* people talk; *j-n zum Reden bringen* make s.o. talk

'**Redensart** *f* saying, phrase

redlich ['re:tlɪç] *adj* upright, honest; *sich redlich(e) Mühe geben* do one's best

Redner ['re:dnɐ] *m* (*-s; -*), '**Rednerin** *f* (*-; -nen*) speaker

'**Rednerpult** *n* speaker's desk

redselig ['re:tze:lɪç] *adj* talkative

reduzieren [redu'tsi:rən] *v/t* (*no -ge-, h*) reduce (*auf acc* to)

Reeder ['re:dɐ] *m* (*-s; -*) shipowner

Reederei [re:də'rai] *f* (*-; -en*) shipping

company
reell [re'ɛl] *adj* reasonable, fair (*price*); real (*chance*); solid (*firm*)
Referat [refe'raːt] *n* (-[e]s; -e) paper; report; lecture; *ein Referat halten* read a paper
Referendar [referɛn'daːɐ] *m* (-s; -e), **Referen'darin** *f* (-; -nen) *appr* trainee teacher
Referent [refe'rɛnt] *m* (-en; -en), **Refe-'rentin** *f* (-; -nen) speaker
Referenz [refe'rɛnts] *f* (-; -en) reference
referieren [refe'riːrən] *v/i* (*no* -ge-, *h*) (give a) report *or* lecture (*über acc* on)
reflektieren [reflɛk'tiːrən] *v/t and v/i* (*no* -ge-, *h*) reflect (*fig über acc* [up]on)
Reflex [re'flɛks] *m* (-es; -e) reflex
reflexiv [reflɛ'ksiːf] *adj* LING reflexive
Reform [re'fɔrm] *f* (-; -en) reform
Reformator [refɔr'maːtoːɐ] *m* (-s; -en [-ma'toːrən]), **Reformer(in)** [re'fɔrmɐ (-mərɪn)] (-s; -/-; -nen) reformer
Re'formhaus *n* health food store (*Br* shop)
reformieren [refɔr'miːrən] *v/t* (*no* -ge-, *h*) reform
Refrain [rə'frɛ̃ː] *m* (-s; -s) refrain, chorus
Regal [re'gaːl] *n* (-s; -e) shelf (unit), shelves
rege ['reːgə] *adj* lively; busy; active
Regel ['reːgəl] *f* (-; -n) rule; MED period, menstruation; *in der Regel* as a rule
'regelmäßig *adj* regular
regeln ['reːgəln] *v/t* (*ge-, h*) regulate, TECH *a.* adjust; ECON settle
'regelrecht *adj* regular (*a.* F)
'Regeltechnik *f* control engineering
'Regelung *f* (-; -en) regulation; adjustment; ECON settlement; TECH control
'regelwidrig *adj* against the rule(s); SPORT unfair; *regelwidriges Spiel* foul play
regen ['reːgən] *v/t and v/refl* (*ge-, h*) move, stir
'Regen *m* (-s; -) rain; *starker Regen* heavy rain(fall)
Regenbogen *m* rainbow
Regenbogenhaut *f* ANAT iris
Regenguss *m* (heavy) shower, downpour
Regenmantel *m* raincoat
Regenschauer *m* shower
Regenschirm *m* umbrella
Regentag *m* rainy day
Regentropfen *m* raindrop
Regenwald *m* rain forest
Regenwasser *n* rainwater
Regenwetter *n* rainy weather
Regenwurm *m* ZO earthworm
Regenzeit *f* rainy season, the rains
Regie [re'ʒiː] *f* (-; *no pl*) THEA, *film etc*: di-

rection; *unter der Regie von* directed by
Re'gieanweisung *f* stage direction
regieren [re'giːrən] (*no* -ge-, *h*) **1.** *v/i* reign; **2.** *v/t* govern (*a.* LING), rule
Re'gierung *f* (-; -en) government, administration; reign
Re'gierungsbezirk *m* administrative district
Regierungschef *m* head of government
Regierungswechsel *m* change of government
Regime [re'ʒiːm] *n* (-s; -) POL regime
Re'gimekritiker *m* POL dissident
Regiment [regi'mɛnt] *n* (-[e]s; -er) a) (*no pl*) rule (*a. fig*), b) MIL regiment
Regisseur [reʒɪ'søːɐ] *m* (-s; -e), **Regis-'seurin** *f* (-; -nen) THEA, *film etc*: director, THEA *Br a.* producer
Register [re'gɪstɐ] *n* (-s; -) register (*a.* MUS), record; index
registrieren [regɪs'triːrən] *v/t* (*no* -ge-, *h*) register, record; *fig* note
Registrierkasse [regɪs'triːɐ-] *f* cash register
Reglement [reglə'mãː] *n* (-s; -s) regulation, order, rule
Regler ['reːglɐ] *m* (-s; -) TECH control
regnen ['reːgnən] *v/i* (*ge-, h*) rain (*a. fig*); *es regnet in Strömen* it's pouring with rain
'regnerisch *adj* rainy
regulär [regu'lɛːɐ] *adj* regular; normal
regulierbar [regu'liːɐbaːɐ] *adj* adjustable; controllable
regulieren [regu'liːrən] *v/t* (*no* -ge-, *h*) regulate, adjust; control
'Regung *f* (-; -en) movement, motion; emotion; impulse
'regungslos *adj* motionless
Reh [reː] *n* (-[e]s; -e) ZO deer, roe; doe; GASTR venison
rehabilitieren [rehabili'tiːrən] *v/t* (*no* -ge-, *h*) rehabilitate
'Rehbock *m* ZO (roe)buck
Rehkeule *f* GASTR leg of venison
Rehkitz *n* ZO fawn
Reibe ['raibə] *f* (-; -n), **Reibeisen** ['raip-] *n* (-s; -) grater, rasp
reiben ['raibən] *v/i and v/t* (*irr, ge-, h*) rub; grate, grind; *sich die Augen (Hände) reiben* rub one's eyes (hands)
'Reibung *f* (-; -en) TECH *etc* friction
'reibungslos *adj* TECH *etc* frictionless; *fig* smooth
reich [raiç] *adj* rich (*an dat* in), wealthy; abundant
Reich *n* (-[e]s; -e) empire, kingdom (*a.* REL, BOT, ZO); *fig* world
reichen ['raiçən] (*ge-, h*) **1.** *v/t* reach;

R

hand, pass; give, hold out (*one's hand*); **2.**
v/i last, do; **reichen bis** reach *or* come up
to; **das reicht** that will do; F **mir reicht's!**
I've had enough

'**reichhaltig** *adj* rich

'**reichlich 1.** *adj* rich, plentiful; plenty of;
2. *adv* rather; generously

'**Reichtum** *m* (-*s*; *no pl*) wealth (**an** *dat* of)
(*a. fig*)

'**Reichweite** *f* reach; AVIAT, MIL *etc* range;
in (**außer**) (**j-s**) **Reichweite** within (out
of) (s.o.'s) reach

reif [raif] *adj* ripe, *esp fig* mature

Reif *m* (-[*e*]*s*; *no pl*) white frost, hoarfrost

Reife ['raifə] *f* (-; *no pl*) ripeness, *esp fig*
maturity

'**reifen** *v/i* (*ge-*, *sein*) ripen, mature (*both a.
fig*)

Reifen ['raifən] *m* (-*s*; -) hoop; MOT *etc* tire,
Br tyre

Reifenpanne *f* MOT flat tire (*Br* tyre),
puncture, F flat

'**Reifeprüfung** *f* → **Abitur**

'**reiflich** *adj* careful

Reihe ['raiə] *f* (-; -*n*) line, row; number;
series; **der Reihe nach** in turn; **ich bin
an der Reihe** it's my turn

'**Reihenfolge** *f* order

'**Reihenhaus** *n* row (*Br* terraced) house

'**reihenweise** *adv* in rows; F *fig* by the doz-
en

Reiher ['raiɐ] *m* (-*s*; -) ZO heron

Reim [raim] *m* (-[*e*]*s*; -*e*) rhyme

reimen ['raimən] *v/t and v/refl* (*ge-*, *h*)
rhyme (**auf** *acc* with)

rein [rain] *adj* pure (*a. fig*); clean; *fig* clear
(*conscience*); plain (*truth*); mere, sheer,
nothing but

'**Reinfall** F *m* flop; let-down

'**Reingewinn** *m* ECON net profit

'**reinhauen** F *v/i* (*sep*, -*ge-*, *h*) tuck in

'**Reinheit** *f* (-; *no pl*) purity (*a. fig*); clean-
ness

reinigen ['rainɪgən] *v/t* (*ge-*, *h*) clean;
cleanse (*a.* MED); dry-clean; *fig* purify

'**Reinigung** *f* (-; -*en*) clean(s)ing; *fig* puri-
fication; (dry) cleaners; **chemische Reinigung** dry cleaning; dry cleaner's

'**Reinigungsmittel** *n* cleaning agent,
cleaner, detergent

'**reinlich** *adj* clean; cleanly

'**reinrassig** *adj* ZO purebred, pedigree;
thoroughbred

'**Reinschrift** *f* fair copy

Reis [rais] *m* (-*es*; -*e*) BOT rice

Reise ['raizə] *f* (-; -*n*) trip; journey; tour;
MAR voyage; **auf Reisen sein** be travel-
(l)ing; **e-e Reise machen** take a trip;
gute Reise! have a nice trip!

Reiseandenken *n* souvenir

Reisebü,ro *n* travel agency *or* bureau

Reiseführer *m* guide(book)

Reisegesellschaft *f* tourist party; tour
operator

Reisekosten *pl* travel(l)ing expenses

Reisekrankheit *f* travel sickness

Reiseleiter(in) tour guide *or* manager, *Br*
courier

'**reisen** *v/i* (*ge-*, *sein*) travel; **durch Frankreich reisen** tour France; **ins Ausland
reisen** go abroad

'**Reisende** *m*, *f* (-*n*; -*n*) travel(l)er; tourist;
passenger

'**Reisepass** *m* passport

Reisescheck *m* travel(l)er's check (*Br*
cheque)

Reisetasche *f* travel(l)ing bag, holdall

Reisig ['raizıç] *n* (-*s*; *no pl*) brushwood

Reißbrett ['rais-] *n* drawing board

reißen ['raisən] (*irr*, *ge-*) **1.** *v/t* (*h*) tear (**in
Stücke** to pieces), rip; pull, drag; ZO kill;
F crack (*jokes*); SPORT knock down; **an
sich reißen** seize, snatch, grab; **2.** *v/i*
(*sein*) break, burst; **sich um et. reißen**
scramble for (*or* to get) s.th.

reißend *adj* torrential

Reißer ['raisɐ] F *m* (-*s*; -) thriller; hit

reißerisch ['raisərıʃ] *adj* sensational, loud

'**Reißverschluss** *m* zipper; **den Reißverschluss an et. öffnen** (**schließen**) unzip
(zip up) s.th.

Reißzwecke *f* thumbtack, *Br* drawing pin

reiten ['raitən] (*irr*, *ge-*) **1.** *v/i* (*sein*) ride,
go on horseback; **2.** *v/t* (*h*) ride

'**Reiten** *n* (-*s*; *no pl*) horseback riding

Reiter ['raitɐ] *m* (-*s*; -) rider, horseman

Reiterin ['raitərın] *f* (-; -*nen*) rider, horse-
woman

'**Reitpferd** *n* saddle *or* riding horse

Reiz [raits] *m* (-*es*; -*e*) charm, attraction,
appeal; thrill; MED, PSYCH stimulus; (**für
j-n**) **den Reiz verlieren** lose one's appeal
(for s.o.)

'**reizbar** *adj* irritable, excitable

reizen ['raitsən] (*ge-*, *h*) **1.** *v/t* irritate (*a.*
MED), annoy; ZO bait; provoke; appeal
to, attract; tempt; challenge; **2.** *v/i cards*:
bid

'**reizend** *adj* charming, delightful; lovely,
sweet, cute

'**reizlos** *adj* unattractive

'**Reizung** *f* (-; -*en*) irritation (*a.* MED)

'**reizvoll** *adj* attractive; challenging

'**Reizwort** *n* (-[*e*]*s*; -*wörter*) emotive word

rekeln ['re:kəln] F *v/refl* (*ge-*, *h*) loll

Reklamation [reklama'tsjo:n] *f* (-; -*en*)
complaint

Reklame [re'kla:mə] *f* (-; -*n*) advertising,

publicity; advertisement, F ad; *Reklame machen für* advertise, promote

reklamieren [rekla'miːrən] *v/i* (*no -ge-, h*) complain (*wegen* about), protest (against)

Rekord [re'kɔrt] *m* (-[e]s; -e) record; *e-n Rekord aufstellen* set *or* establish a record

Rekrut [re'kruːt] *m* (-en; -en) MIL recruit

rekrutieren [rekru'tiːrən] *v/t* (*no -ge-, h*) recruit

Rektor ['rɛktoːɐ] *m* (-s; -en [rɛk'toːrən]) principal, *Br* headmaster; UNIV president, *Br* rector

Rektorin [rɛk'toːrɪn] *f* (-; -nen) principal, *Br* headmistress; UNIV president, *Br* rector

relativ [rela'tiːf] *adj* relative

Relief [re'ljɛf] *n* (-s; -s) relief

Religion [reli'gjoːn] *f* (-; -en) religion

religiös [reli'gjøːs] *adj* religious

Reling ['reːlɪŋ] *f* (-; -s) MAR rail

Reliquie [re'liːkvjə] *f* (-; -n) relic

Rempelei [rɛmpə'lai] F *f* (-; -en), **rempeln** ['rɛmpəln] F *v/t* (*ge-, h*) jostle

Rennbahn ['rɛn-] *f* racecourse, racetrack; cycling track

'Rennboot *n* racing boat; speedboat

rennen ['rɛnən] *v/i and v/t* (*irr, ge-, sein*) run

'Rennen *n* (-s; -) race (*a. fig*); heat

'Rennfahrer *m*, **Rennfahrerin** *f* racing driver; racing cyclist

Rennläufer *m* ski racer

Rennpferd *n* racehorse, racer

Rennrad *n* racing bicycle, racer

Rennsport *m* racing

Rennstall *m* racing stable

Rennwagen *m* race (*Br* racing) car, racer

renommiert [reno'miːɐt] *adj* renowned

renovieren [reno'viːrən] *v/t* (*no -ge-, h*) renovate, F do up; redecorate

rentabel [rɛn'taːbəl] *adj* ECON profitable, paying

Rente ['rɛntə] *f* (-; -n) (old age) pension; *in Rente gehen* retire

'Rentenalter *n* retirement age

Rentenversicherung *f* pension scheme

Rentier ['rɛntiːɐ] *n* (-s; -e) ZO reindeer

rentieren [rɛn'tiːrən] *v/refl* (*no -ge-, h*) ECON pay; *fig* be worth it

Rentner ['rɛntnɐ] *m* (-s; -), **'Rentnerin** [-nərɪn] *f* (-; -nen) (old age) pensioner

Reparatur [repara'tuːɐ] *f* (-; -en) repair

Reparaturwerkstatt *f* repair shop; MOT garage

reparieren [repa'riːrən] *v/t* (*no -ge-, h*) repair, mend, F fix

Reportage [repɔr'taːʒə] *f* (-; -n) report

Reporter [re'pɔrtɐ] *m* (-s; -), **Re'porterin** *f* (-; -nen) reporter

Repräsentant [reprɛzɛn'tant] *m* (-en; -en) representative

Repräsentantenhaus *n* PARL House of Representatives

Repräsen'tantin *f* (-; -nen) representative

repräsentieren [reprɛzɛn'tiːrən] *v/t* (*no -ge-, h*) represent

Repressalie [reprɛ'saːljə] *f* (-; -n) reprisal

Reproduktion [reprodʊk'tsjoːn] *f* (-; -en) reproduction, print

reproduzieren [reprodu'tsiːrən] *v/t* (*no -ge-, h*) reproduce

Reptil [rɛp'tiːl] *n* (-s; -ien) ZO reptile

Republik [repu'bliːk] *f* (-; -en) republic

Republikaner [republi'kaːnɐ] *m* (-s; -), **Republi'kanerin** *f* (-; -nen), **republi'kanisch** *adj* POL republican

Reservat [rezɛr'vaːt] *n* (-[e]s; -e) (p)reserve; reservation

Reserve [re'zɛrvə] *f* (-; -n) reserve (*a.* MIL)

Reserve... *in cpds* ...*kanister*, ...*rad etc*: spare ...

reservieren [rezɛr'viːrən] *v/t* (*no -ge-, h*) reserve (*a. reservieren lassen*); *j-m e-n Platz reservieren* keep *or* save a seat for s.o.

reserviert [rezɛr'viːɐt] *adj* reserved (*a. fig*); aloof

Reser'viertheit *f* (-; *no pl*) aloofness

Residenz [rezi'dɛnts] *f* (-; -en) residence

Resignation [rezɪgna'tsjoːn] *f* (-; *no pl*) resignation

resignieren [rezɪ'gniːrən] *v/i* (*no -ge-, h*) give up

resigniert [rezɪ'gniːɐt] *adj* resigned

Resoziali'sierung *f* (-; -en) rehabilitation

Respekt [re'spɛkt] *m* (-[e]s; *no pl*) respect (*vor* for)

respektieren [respɛk'tiːrən] *v/t* (*no -ge-, h*) respect

re'spektlos *adj* irreverent, disrespectful

re'spektvoll *adj* respectful

Ressort [rɛ'soːɐ] *n* (-s; -s) department, province

Rest [rɛst] *m* (-[e]s; -e) rest; *pl* remains, remnants; GASTR leftovers; F *das gab ihm den Rest* that finished him (off)

Restaurant [rɛsto'rãː] *n* (-s; -s) restaurant

restaurieren [rɛsto'riːrən] *v/t* (*no -ge-, h*) restore

'Restbetrag *m* remainder

'restlich *adj* remaining

'restlos *adv* completely

Resultat [rezʊl'taːt] *n* (-[e]s; -e) result (*a. sport*), outcome

Retorte [re'tɔrtə] *f* (-; -n) CHEM retort

Re'tortenbaby F *n* test-tube baby

R

retten ['rɛtən] v/t (ge-, h) save, rescue (*both*: **aus** dat, **vor** dat from)

Retter ['rɛtɐ] m (-s; -), **'Retterin** f (-; -nen) rescuer

Rettich ['rɛtɪç] m (-s; -e) BOT radish

'Rettung f (-; -en) rescue (**aus** dat, **vor** dat from); **das war s-e Rettung** that saved him

'Rettungsboot n lifeboat

Rettungsmannschaft f rescue party

Rettungsring m life belt, life buoy

Rettungsschwimmer m lifeguard

Reue ['rɔʏə] f (-; no pl) remorse, repentance (*both*: **über** acc for)

reumütig ['rɔʏmyːtɪç] adj repentant

Revanche [re'vãːʃ(ə)] f (-; -n) revenge

revanchieren [revã'ʃiːrən] v/refl (no -ge-, h) have one's revenge (**bei, an** dat on); make it up (**bei j-m** to s.o.)

Revers [re'veːɐ] n, m (-; -) lapel

revidieren [revi'diːrən] v/t (no -ge-, h) revise; ECON audit

Revier [re'viːɐ] n (-s; -e) district; ZO territory (a. fig); → **Polizeirevier**

Revision [revi'zjoːn] f (-; -en) revision; ECON audit; JUR appeal

Revolte [re'vɔltə] f (-; -n), **revoltieren** [revɔl'tiːrən] v/i (no -ge-, h) revolt

Revolution [revolu'tsjoːn] f (-; -en) revolution

revolutionär [revolutsjo'nɛːɐ] adj, **Revolutio'när(in)** (-s; -e/-; -nen) revolutionary

Revolver [re'vɔlvɐ] m (-s; -) revolver, F gun

Revue [re'vyː] f (-; -n) THEA (musical) show

Rezept [re'tsɛpt] n (-[e]s; -e) MED prescription; GASTR recipe (a. fig)

Rezession [retsɛ'sjoːn] f (-; -en) ECON recession

Rhabarber [ra'barbɐ] m (-s; no pl) BOT rhubarb

rhetorisch [re'toːrɪʃ] adj rhetorical

Rheuma ['rɔʏma] n (-s; no pl) MED rheumatism

rhythmisch ['rʏtmɪʃ] adj rhythmic(al)

Rhythmus ['rʏtmʊs] m (-; -men) rhythm

Ribisel ['riːbiːzəl] Austrian f (-; -[n]) → **Johannisbeere**

richten ['rɪçtən] v/t (ge-, h) fix; get s.th. ready, prepare; do (room, one's hair); (**sich**) **richten an** (acc) address (o.s. to); put a question to; **richten auf** (acc) direct or turn to; point or aim camera, gun etc at; **richten gegen** direct against; **sich richten nach** go by, act according to; follow (fashion etc); depend on; **ich richte mich ganz nach dir** I leave it to you

Richter ['rɪçtɐ] m (-s; -), **'Richterin** f (-; -nen) judge

'richterlich adj judicial

'Richtgeschwindigkeit f MOT recommended speed

richtig ['rɪçtɪç] **1.** adj right; correct, proper; true; real; **2.** adv: **richtig nett** (**böse**) really nice (angry); **et. richtig machen** do s.th. right; **m-e Uhr geht richtig** my watch is right

'Richtigkeit f (-; no pl) correctness

richtigstellen v/t (sep, -ge-, h) fig put or set right

'Richtlinien pl guidelines

Richtpreis m ECON recommended price

'Richtung f (-; -en) direction; POL leaning; PAINT etc style

'richtungslos adj aimless, disorient(at)ed

'richtungweisend adj pioneering

rieb [riːp] pret of **reiben**

riechen ['riːçən] v/i and v/t (irr, ge-, h) smell (**nach** of; **an** dat at)

rief [riːf] pret of **rufen**

Riegel ['riːgəl] m (-s; -) bolt, bar

Riemen ['riːmən] m (-s; -) strap; TECH belt; MAR oar

Riese ['riːzə] m (-n; -n) giant (a. fig)

rieseln ['riːzəln] v/i (ge-, sein) trickle; rain: drizzle; snow: fall gently

'Riesen... in cpds mst giant ..., gigantic ..., enormous ...

Riesenerfolg m huge success, film etc: a. smash hit

'riesengroß, 'riesenhaft → **riesig**

'Riesenrad n Ferris wheel

riesig ['riːzɪç] adj enormous, gigantic, giant

'Riesin f (-; -nen) giantess (a. fig)

riet [riːt] pret of **raten**

Riff [rɪf] n (-[e]s; -e) GEOGR reef

Rille ['rɪlə] f (-; -n) groove

Rind [rɪnt] n (-[e]s; -er ['rɪndɐ]) ZO cow, pl cattle; GASTR beef

Rinde ['rɪndə] f (-; -n) BOT bark; GASTR rind; crust

Rinderbraten ['rɪndɐ-] m roast beef

Rinderherde f herd of cattle

'Rindfleisch n GASTR beef

Rind(s)leder n cowhide

Rindvieh n ZO cattle

Ring [rɪŋ] m (-[e]s; -e) ring (a. fig); MOT ring road; subway etc: circle (line)

'Ringbuch n loose-leaf or ring binder

ringeln ['rɪŋəln] v/refl (ge-, h) curl, coil (a. ZO)

'Ringelnatter f ZO grass snake

'Ringelspiel Austrian n → **Karussell**

ringen ['rɪŋən] (irr, ge-, h) **1.** v/i SPORT wrestle (**mit** with), fig a. struggle (against, with; **um** for); **nach Atem rin-**

gen gasp (for breath); **2.** v/t wring

'**Ringen** n (-s; no pl) SPORT wrestling

Ringer ['rɪŋɐ] m (-s; -) SPORT wrestler

'**ringförmig** [-fœrmɪç] adj circular

'**Ringkampf** m SPORT wrestling match

'**Ringrichter** m SPORT referee

rings adv: **rings um** around

'**ringshe'rum**, '**rings'um**, '**ringsum'her** adv all around; everywhere

Rinne ['rɪnə] f (-; -n) groove, channel; gutter

'**rinnen** v/i (irr, ge-, sein) run; flow, stream

Rinnsal ['rɪnzaːl] n (-s; -e) trickle

'**Rinnstein** m gutter

Rippe ['rɪpə] f (-; -n) ANAT rib

'**Rippenfell** n ANAT pleura

Rippenfellentzündung f MED pleurisy

'**Rippenstoß** m nudge in the ribs

Risiko ['riːziko] n (-s; -s, -ken) risk; **ein** (**kein**) **Risiko eingehen** take a risk (no risks); **auf eigenes Risiko** at one's own risk

riskant [rɪs'kant] adj risky

riskieren [rɪs'kiːrən] v/t (no -ge-, h) risk

riss [rɪs] pret of **reißen**

Riss m (-es; -e) tear, rip, split (a. fig); crack; MED chap, laceration

rissig ['rɪsɪç] adj chapped; cracky, cracked

Rist [rɪst] m (-es; -e) ANAT instep

ritt [rɪt] pret of **reiten**

Ritt m (-[e]s; -e) ride (on horseback)

Ritter ['rɪtɐ] m (-s; -) knight; **j-n zum Ritter schlagen** knight s.o.

'**ritterlich** fig adj chivalrous

Ritz [rɪts] m (-es; -e), **Ritze** ['rɪtsə] f (-; -n) crack, chink; gap

Rivale [ri'vaːlə] m (-n; -n), **Ri'valin** f (-; -nen) rival

rivalisieren [rivali'ziːrən] v/i (no -ge-, h) compete

Rivalität [rivali'tɛːt] f (-; -en) rivalry

rk., r.-k. ABBR of **römisch-katholisch** RC, Roman Catholic

Robbe ['rɔbə] f (-; -n) ZO seal

Robe ['roːbə] f (-; -n) robe, gown

Roboter ['rɔbɔtɐ] m (-s; -) robot

robust [ro'bʊst] adj robust, strong, tough

roch [rɔx] pret of **riechen**

röcheln ['rœçəln] (ge-, h) **1.** v/i moan; **2.** v/t gasp

Rock [rɔk] m (-[e]s; Röcke ['rœkə]) skirt

Rodelbahn ['roːdəl-] f toboggan run

rodeln ['roːdəln] v/i (ge-, sein) sled(ge), coast; SPORT toboggan

'**Rodelschlitten** m sled(ge); toboggan

roden ['roːdən] v/t (ge-, h) clear; stub

Rogen ['roːgən] m (-s; -) (hard) roe

Roggen ['rɔgən] m (-s; -) BOT rye

roh [roː] adj raw; rough; fig brutal; **mit roher Gewalt** with brute force

'**Rohbau** m (-[e]s; -ten) carcass

'**Rohkost** f raw vegetables and fruit

'**Rohling** m (-s; -e) TECH blank; fig brute

'**Rohmateri,al** n raw material

'**Rohöl** n crude (oil)

Rohr [roːɐ] n (-[e]s; -e ['roːrə]) TECH pipe, tube; duct; BOT reed; cane

Röhre ['røːrə] f (-; -n) pipe, tube (a. TV), TV etc valve

'**Rohrleitung** f duct, pipe(s); plumbing; pipeline

Rohrstock m cane

Rohrzucker m cane sugar

'**Rohstoff** m raw material

Rollbahn ['rɔl-] f AVIAT runway

Rolle ['rɔlə] f (-; -n) roll (a. SPORT), TECH a. roller; coil; caster, castor; THEA part, role (both a. fig); **e-e Rolle Garn** a spool of thread, Br a reel of cotton; **das spielt keine Rolle** that doesn't matter, that makes no difference; **Geld spielt k-e Rolle** money is no object

'**rollen** v/i (ge-, sein) and v/t (ge-, h) roll

Roller ['rɔlɐ] m (-s; -) (motor) scooter

'**Rollfilm** m PHOT roll film

Rollkragen m turtleneck, esp Br polo neck

Rollladen m rolling shutter

Rollo ['rɔlo] n (-s; -s) shades, Br (roller) blind

'**Rollschuh** m roller skate; **Rollschuh laufen** roller-skate

Rollschuhbahn f roller-skating rink

Rollschuhläufer m roller skater

'**Rollstuhl** m wheelchair

'**Rolltreppe** f escalator

Roman [ro'maːn] m (-s; -e) novel

Romanik [ro'maːnɪk] f (-; no pl) ARCH Romanesque (style or period)

romanisch [ro'maːnɪʃ] adj LING Romance; ARCH Romanesque

Romanist [roma'nɪst] m (-en; -en), **Roma'nistin** f (-; -nen) student of Romance languages

Ro'manschriftsteller m, **Ro'manschriftstellerin** f novelist

Romantik [ro'mantɪk] f (-; no pl) romance; HIST Romanticism

romantisch [ro'mantɪʃ] adj romantic

Römer ['røːmɐ] m (-s; -), '**Römerin** f (-; -nen), **römisch** ['røːmɪʃ] adj Roman

Rommee ['rɔmeː] n (-s; -s) rummy

röntgen ['rɛntgən] v/t (ge-, h) MED X-ray

'**Röntgenappa,rat** m MED X-ray apparatus

Röntgenaufnahme f, **Röntgenbild** n MED X-ray

Röntgenstrahlen *pl* PHYS X-rays
Röntgenuntersuchung *f* MED X-ray
rosa ['roːza] *adj* pink; *fig* rose-colo(u)red
Rose ['roːzə] *f* (-; -*n*) BOT rose
'**Rosenkohl** *m* BOT Brussels sprouts
'**Rosenkranz** *m* REL rosary
rosig ['roːzɪç] *adj* rosy (*a. fig*)
Rosine [ro'ziːnə] *f* (-; -*n*) raisin
'**Rosshaar** *n* (-[*e*]*s*; *no pl*) horsehair
Rost [rɔst] *m* (-[*e*]*s*; -*e*) a) (*no pl*) CHEM
  rust, b) TECH grate; GASTR grid(iron), grill
rosten ['rɔstən] *v/i* (*ge-*, *sein*) rust
rösten ['rœstən] *v/t* (*ge-*, *h*) roast (*a. F*);
  toast; fry
'**Rostfleck** *m* rust stain
'**rostfrei** *adj* rustproof, stainless
'**rostig** *adj* rusty
rot [roːt] *adj* red (*a.* POL); *rot glühend* red-
  -hot; *rot werden* blush; *in den roten Zah-*
  len ECON in the red
Rot *n* (-*s*; -) red; *die Ampel steht auf Rot*
  the lights are red; *bei Rot* at red
'**rotblond** *adj* sandy(-haired)
Röte ['røːtə] *f* (-; *no pl*) redness, red (col-
  o[u]r); *fig* blush
Röteln ['røːtəln] *pl* MED German measles
röten ['røːtən] *v/refl* (*ge-*, *h*) redden; flush
'**rothaarig** *adj* red-haired
'**Rothaarige** *m, f* (-*n*; -*n*) redhead
rotieren [ro'tiːrən] *v/i* (*no -ge-*, *h*) rotate
'**Rotkehlchen** *n* (-*s*; -) zo robin
'**Rotkohl** *m* BOT red cabbage
rötlich ['røːtlɪç] *adj* reddish
'**Rotstift** *m* red crayon *or* pencil
Rotwein *m* red wine
Rotwild *n* zo (red) deer
Rotznase [rɔts-] F *f* snotty nose
Route ['ruːtə] *f* (-; -*n*) route
Routine [ru'tiːnə] *f* (-; *no pl*) routine; ex-
  perience
Routinesache *f* routine (matter)
routiniert [ruti'niːɐt] *adj* experienced
Rübe ['ryːbə] *f* (-; -*n*) BOT turnip; (sugar)
  beet
Rubin [ru'biːn] *m* (-*s*; -*e*) MIN ruby
Rübli ['ryːpli] *Swiss n* (-*s*; -) BOT carrot
Rubrik [ru'briːk] *f* (-; -*en*) heading; col-
  umn
Ruck [rʊk] *m* (-[*e*]*s*; -*e*) jerk, jolt, start; *fig*
  POL swing
Rückantwortschein ['ryk-] *m* reply cou-
  pon
'**ruckartig** *adj* jerky, abrupt
'**rückbezüglich** *adj* LING reflexive
'**Rückblende** *f* flashback (*auf acc* to)
'**Rückblick** *m* review (*auf acc* of); *im*
  Rückblick in retrospect
rücken ['rykən] **1.** *v/t* (*ge-*, *h*) move, shift,
  push; **2.** *v/i* (*ge-*, *sein*) move; move over;

näher rücken approach
'**Rücken** *m* (-*s*; -) ANAT back (*a. fig*)
Rückendeckung *fig f* backing, support
Rückenlehne *f* back(rest)
Rückenmark *n* ANAT spinal cord
Rückenschmerzen *pl* backache
Rückenschwimmen *n* backstroke
Rückenwind *m* following wind, tailwind
Rückenwirbel *m* ANAT dorsal vertebra
'**Rückerstattung** *f* (-; -*en*) refund
Rückfahrkarte *f* round-trip ticket, *Br a.*
  return (ticket)
Rückfahrt *f* return trip; *auf der Rück-*
  fahrt on the way back
Rückfall *m* relapse
'**rückfällig** *adj*: *rückfällig werden* relapse
'**Rückflug** *m* return flight
'**Rückgabe** *f* (-; *no pl*) return
'**Rückgang** *m* drop, fall; ECON recession
'**rückgängig** *adj*: *rückgängig machen*
  cancel
'**Rückgewinnung** *f* (-; *no pl*) recovery
Rückgrat *n* ANAT spine, backbone (*both a.*
  fig)
Rückhalt *m* (-[*e*]*s*; *no pl*) support
Rückhand *f*, **Rückhandschlag** *m* tennis:
  backhand
Rückkauf *m* ECON repurchase
Rückkehr ['rykkeːɐ] *f* (-; *no pl*) return;
  nach s-r Rückkehr aus ... on his return
  from ...
'**Rückkopplung** *f* ELECTR feedback (*a. fig*)
Rücklage *f* (-; -*n*) reserve(s); savings
Rücklauf *m* TECH rewind
'**rückläufig** *adj* falling, downward
'**Rücklicht** *n* (-[*e*]*s*; -*er*) MOT rear light, tail-
  light
rücklings ['ryklɪŋs] *adv* backward(s);
  from behind
'**Rückporto** *n* return postage
'**Rückreise** *f* → *Rückfahrt*
Rucksack ['rʊkzak] *m* rucksack, back-
  pack
Rucksacktou‚rismus *m* backpacking
Rucksacktou‚rist *m* backpacker
'**Rückschlag** *m* SPORT return; *fig* setback
Rückschluss *m* conclusion
Rückschritt *m fig* step back(ward)
Rückseite *f* back; reverse; flip side
Rücksendung *f* return
'**Rücksicht** *f* (-; -*en*) consideration, regard; *aus* (*ohne*) *Rücksicht auf* (*acc*)
  out of (without any) consideration *or* re-
  gard for; *Rücksicht nehmen auf* (*acc*)
  show consideration for
'**rücksichtslos** *adj* inconsiderate (*gegen*
  of), thoughtless (of); ruthless; reckless
'**rücksichtsvoll** *adj* considerate (*gegen*
  of), thoughtful

'**Rücksitz** *m* MOT back seat
Rückspiegel *m* MOT rear-view mirror
Rückspiel *n* SPORT return match
Rückstand *m* CHEM residue; *mit der Arbeit (e-m Tor) im Rückstand sein* be behind with one's work (down by one goal)
'**rückständig** *adj* backward; underdeveloped; *rückständige Miete* arrears of rent
'**Rückstau** *m* MOT tailback
Rückstelltaste *f* backspace key
Rücktriff *m* resignation; withdrawal; TECH → **Rücktrittbremse** *f* coaster (*Br* back--pedal) brake
rückwärts ['rʏkvɛrts] *adv* backward(s); *rückwärts aus* (*dat*) *... fahren* back out of ...; *rückwärts in* (*acc*) *... fahren* back into ...
'**Rückwärtsgang** *m* MOT reverse (gear)
'**Rückweg** *m* way back
'**ruckweise** *adv* jerkily, in jerks
'**rückwirkend** *adj* retroactive
'**Rückwirkung** *f* reaction (*auf acc* upon)
Rückzahlung *f* repayment
Rückzieher *m* (*-s*; *-*) *soccer*: overhead kick; F *e-n Rückzieher machen* back (*or* chicken) out (*von* of)
Rückzug *m* retreat
Rüde ['ryːdə] *m* (*-n*; *-n*) ZO male (dog *ect*)
Rudel ['ruːdəl] *n* (*-s*; *-*) ZO pack; herd
Ruder ['ruːdɐ] *n* (*-s*; *-*) AVIAT, MAR rudder; SPORT oar; *am Ruder* at the helm (*a. fig*)
Ruderboot *n* rowing boat, rowboat
Ruderer ['ruːdərɐ] *m* (*-s*; *-*) rower, oarsman
'**Ruderin** *f* (*-*; *-nen*) rower, oarswoman
'**rudern** *v/i and v/t* (*ge-, h*) row
'**Ruderre,gatta** *f* (rowing) regatta, boat race
Rudersport *m* rowing
Ruf [ruːf] *m* (*-[e]s*; *-e*) call (*a. fig*); cry, shout; *fig* reputation
'**rufen** *v/i and v/t* (*irr, ge-, h*) call (*a. doctor etc*); cry, shout; *rufen nach* call for (*a. fig*); *rufen lassen* send for; *um Hilfe rufen* call *or* cry for help
'**Rufnummer** *f* telephone number
'**Rufweite** *f*: *in* (*außer*) *Rufweite* within (out of) call(ing distance)
Rüge ['ryːgə] *f* (*-*; *-n*) reproof, reproach (*both*: *wegen* for)
'**rügen** *v/t* (*ge-, h*) reprove, reproach
Ruhe ['ruːə] *f* (*-*; *no pl*) quiet, calm; silence; rest; peace; calm(ness); *zur Ruhe kommen* come to rest; *j-n in Ruhe lassen* leave s.o. in peace; *lass mich in Ruhe!* leave me alone!; *et. in Ruhe tun* take one's time (doing s.th.); *die Ruhe behalten* F keep (one's) cool, play it cool; *sich*

zur Ruhe setzen retire; *Ruhe, bitte!* (be) quiet, please!
'**ruhelos** *adj* restless
'**ruhen** *v/i* (*ge-, h*) rest (*auf dat* on)
'**Ruhepause** *f* break
Ruhestand *m* (*-[e]s*; *no pl*) retirement
Ruhestörer *m* (*-s*; *-*) *esp* JUR disturber of the peace
Ruhetag *m* a day's rest; *Montag Ruhetag* closed on Mondays
ruhig ['ruːɪç] *adj* quiet; silent; calm; cool; TECH smooth; *ruhig bleiben* F keep (one's) cool, play it cool
Ruhm [ruːm] *m* (*-[e]s*; *no pl*) fame, *esp* POL, MIL *etc* glory
rühmen ['ryːmən] *v/t* (*ge-, h*) praise (*wegen* for); *sich e-r Sache rühmen* boast of s.th.
rühmlich ['ryːmlɪç] *adj* laudable, praiseworthy
'**ruhmlos** *adj* inglorious
'**ruhmreich** *adj* glorious
Ruhr [ruːɐ] *f* (*-*; *no pl*) MED dysentery
Rühreier ['ryːɐ̯ʔaiɐ] *pl* scrambled eggs
rühren ['ryːrən] *v/t* (*ge-, h*) stir; move (*a. fig*); *fig* touch, affect; *das rührt mich gar nicht* that leaves me cold; *rührt euch!* MIL (stand) at ease!
rührend *fig adj* touching, moving; very kind
rührig ['ryːrɪç] *adj* active, busy
rührselig ['ryːɐ-] *adj* sentimental
'**Rührung** *f* (*-*; *no pl*) emotion
Ruin [ruˈiːn] *m* (*-s*; *no pl*) ruin
Ruine [ruˈiːnə] *f* (*-*; *-n*) ruin
ruinieren [ruiˈniːrən] *v/t* (*no -ge-, h*) ruin
rülpsen ['rʏlpsən] *v/i* (*ge-, h*), **Rülpser** ['rʏlpsɐ] *m* (*-s*; *-*) belch
Rumäne [ruˈmɛːnə] *m* (*-n*; *-n*) Romanian
Rumänien Romania
Ru'mänin *f* (*-*; *-nen*), **ru'mänisch** *adj* Romanian
Rummel ['rʊməl] F *m* (*-s*; *no pl*) (hustle and) bustle; F ballyhoo
Rummelplatz F *m* amusement park, fairground
rumoren [ruˈmoːrən] *v/i* (*no -ge-, h*) rumble
Rumpelkammer ['rʊmpəl-] F *f* lumber room
rumpeln ['rʊmpəln] F *v/i* (*ge-, h, sein*) rumble
Rumpf [rʊmpf] *m* (*-es*; *Rümpfe* ['rʏmpfə]) ANAT trunk; MAR hull; AVIAT fuselage
rümpfen ['rʏmpfən] *v/t* (*ge-, h*) *die Nase rümpfen* turn up one's nose (*über acc* at), sneer (at)
rund [rʊnt] **1.** *adj* round (*a. fig*); **2.** *adv* about; *rund um* (a)round

'**Rundblick** *m* panorama
Runde ['rʊndə] *f* (-; -*n*) round (*a. fig and* SPORT); *racing*: lap; *s-e Runde machen in* (*dat*) patrol; *die Runde machen* go the round(s)
'**Rundfahrt** *f* tour (*durch* round)
'**Rundfunk** *m* (-*s*; *no pl*) radio; broadcasting corporation; *im Rundfunk* on the radio; *im Rundfunk übertragen or senden* broadcast
Rundfunkhörer(in) listener, *pl a.* (radio) audience
Rundfunksender *m* broadcasting *or* radio station
'**Rundgang** *m* tour (*durch* of)
'**rundhe'raus** *adv* frankly, plainly
'**rundhe'rum** *adv* all around
'**rundlich** *adj* plump, chubby
'**Rundreise** *f* tour (*durch* of)
'**Rundschau** *f* review
Rundschreiben *n* circular (letter)
Rundspruch *Swiss m* → *Rundfunk*
'**Rundung** *f* (-; -*en*) curve
'**rundweg** [-'vɛk] *adv* flatly, plainly
runter ['rʊntɐ] F *adv* → *herunter*
Runzel ['rʊntsəl] *f* (-; -*n*) wrinkle
runz(e)lig ['rʊnts(ə)lɪç] *adj* wrinkled
'**runzeln** *v/t* (*ge-*, *h*) *die Stirn runzeln* frown (*über acc* at)
Rüpel ['ryːpəl] *m* (-*s*; -) lout

rupfen ['rʊpfən] *v/t* (*ge-*, *h*) pluck
Rüsche ['ryːʃə] *f* (-; -*n*) frill, ruffle
Ruß ['ruːs] *m* (-*es*; *no pl*) soot
Russe ['rʊsə] *m* (-*n*; -*n*) Russian
Rüssel ['rʏsəl] *m* (-*s*; -) ZO trunk; snout
rußen ['ruːsən] *v/i* (*ge-*, *h*) smoke
rußig ['ruːsɪç] *adj* sooty
Russin ['rʊsɪn] *f* (-; -*nen*), **russisch** ['rʊsɪʃ] *adj* Russian
'**Russland** Russia
rüsten ['rʏstən] (*ge-*, *h*) **1.** *v/i* MIL arm; **2.** *v/refl* get ready, prepare (*zu, für* for); arm o.s. (*gegen* for)
rüstig ['rʏstɪç] *adj* vigorous, sprightly
rustikal [rʊstiˈkaːl] *adj* rustic
'**Rüstung** *f* (-; -*en*) MIL armament; armo(u)r
'**Rüstungsindus,trie** *f* armament industry
Rüstungswettlauf *m* arms race
'**Rüstzeug** *n* equipment
Rute ['ruːtə] *f* (-; -*n*) rod (*a. fig*), switch
Rutschbahn ['rʊtʃ-] *f*, **Rutsche** ['rʊtʃə] *f* (-; -*n*) slide, chute
'**rutschen** *v/i* (*ge-*, *sein*) slide, slip; glide; MOT *etc* skid
rutschig ['rʊtʃɪç] *adj* slippery
'**rutschsicher** *adj* MOT *etc* non-skid
rütteln ['rʏtəln] (*ge-*, *h*) **1.** *v/t* shake; **2.** *v/i* jolt; *an der Tür rütteln* rattle at the door

S

S ABBR *of* **Süd(en)** S, south
S. ABBR *of* **Seite** p., page
s. ABBR *of* **siehe** see
Saal [zaːl] *m* (-[*e*]*s*; *Säle* ['zɛːlə]) hall
Saat [zaːt] *f* (-; -*en*) a) (*no pl*) sowing, b) seed(s) (*a. fig*); crop(s)
Sabbat ['zabat] *m* (-*s*; -*e*) sabbath (day)
sabbern ['zabɐn] F *v/i* (*ge-*, *h*) slobber, slaver
Säbel ['zɛːbəl] *m* (-*s*; -) saber, *Br* sabre (*a.* SPORT), sword
'**säbeln** F *v/t* (*ge-*, *h*) cut, hack
Sabotage [zaboˈtaːʒə] *f* (-; -*n*) sabotage
Saboteur [zaboˈtøːɐ] *m* (-*s*; -*e*) saboteur
sabotieren [zaboˈtiːrən] *v/t* (*no -ge-*, *h*) sabotage
Sachbearbeiter ['zax-] *m*, **Sachbearbeiterin** *f* official in charge
Sachbeschädigung *f* damage to proper-

ty
Sachbuch *n* specialized book, *pl coll* nonfiction
'**sachdienlich** *adj*: *sachdienliche Hinweise* relevant information
Sache ['zaxə] *f* (-; -*n*) thing; matter, business; issue, problem, question; cause; JUR matter, case; *pl* things, clothes; *zur Sache kommen* (*bei der Sache bleiben*) come (keep) to the point; *nicht zur Sache gehören* be irrelevant
'**sachgerecht** *adj* proper
'**Sachkenntnis** *f* expert knowledge
'**sachkundig** *adj* expert
'**sachlich** *adj* matter-of-fact, businesslike; unbias(s)ed, objective; practical, technical; *sachlich richtig* factually correct
sächlich ['zɛçlɪç] *adj* LING neuter
'**Sachre,gister** *n* (subject) index

'Sachschaden *m* damage to property
sacht [zaxt] *adj* soft, gentle; slow
'Sachverhalt *m* (-[e]s; -e) facts (of the case)
Sachverstand *m* know-how
Sachverständige *m*, *f* (-*n*; -*n*) expert; JUR expert witness
Sachwert *m* (-[e]s; *no pl*) real value
Sachzwänge *pl* inherent necessities
Sack [zak] *m* (-[e]s; Säcke ['zɛkə]) sack, bag; V balls
sacken ['zakən] F *v/i* (*ge-, sein*) sink
'Sackgasse *f* blind alley (*a. fig*), dead end (*a. fig*), *fig* impasse
Sadismus [za'dɪsmʊs] *m* (-; *no pl*) sadism
Sadist [za'dɪst] *m* (-*en*; -*en*) sadist
sa'distisch *adj* sadistic
säen ['zɛːən] *v/t and v/i* (*ge-, h*) sow (*a. fig*)
Safari [za'faːri] *f* (-; -s) safari
Safaripark *m* wildlife reserve, safari park
Saft [zaft] *m* (-[e]s; Säfte ['zɛftə]) juice; BOT sap (*both a. fig*)
saftig ['zaftɪç] *adj* juicy (*a. fig*); lush; F fancy (*prices etc*)
Sage ['zaːgə] *f* (-; -*n*) legend, myth
Säge ['zɛːgə] *f* (-; -*n*) saw
'Sägemehl *n* sawdust
sagen ['zaːgən] *v/i and v/t* (*ge-, h*) say; *j-m et. sagen* tell s.o. s.th.; *die Wahrheit sagen* tell the truth; *er lässt dir sagen* he asked me to tell you; *sagen wir ...* (let's) say ...; *man sagt, er sei reich* he is said to be rich; *er lässt sich nichts sagen* he will not listen to reason; *das hat nichts zu sagen* it doesn't matter; *et. (nichts) zu sagen haben (bei)* have a say (no say) (in); *sagen wollen mit* mean by; *das sagt mir nichts* it doesn't mean anything to me; *unter uns gesagt* between you and me
sägen ['zɛːgən] *v/t and v/i* (*ge-, h*) saw
'sagenhaft *adj* legendary; F fabulous, incredible, fantastic
'Sägespäne *pl* sawdust
'Sägewerk *n* sawmill
sah [zaː] *pret of* **sehen**
Sahne ['zaːnə] *f* (-; *no pl*) cream
Saison [zɛ'zõː] *f* (-; -s) season; *in der Saison* in season
sai'sonbedingt *adj* seasonal
Saite ['zaitə] *f* (-; -*n*) MUS string, chord (*a. fig*)
'Saiteninstru‚ment *n* MUS string(ed) instrument
Sakko ['zako] *m, n* (-s; -s) (sports) jacket, sport(s) coat
Sakristei [zakrɪs'tai] *f* (-; -*en*) REL vestry, sacristy
Salat [za'laːt] *m* (-[e]s; -e) BOT lettuce;

GASTR salad
Salatsauce *f* salad dressing
Salbe ['zalbə] *f* (-; -*n*) ointment
'Salbung *f* (-; -*en*) unction
'salbungsvoll *adj* unctuous
Saldo ['zaldo] *m* (-s; -s, -di) ECON balance
Salon [za'lõː] *m* (-s; -s) salon; MAR saloon; drawing room
salopp [za'lɔp] *adj* casual; *contp* sloppy
Salpeter [zal'peːtɐ] *m* (-s; *no pl*) CHEM salt|peter (*Br* -petre), niter, *Br* nitre
Salto ['zalto] *m* (-s; -s, -ti) somersault
Salut [za'luːt] *m* (-[e]s; -e) MIL salute; *Salut schießen* fire a salute
salutieren [zalu'tiːrən] *v/i* (*no -ge-, h*) MIL (give a) salute
Salve ['zalvə] *f* (-; -*n*) MIL volley (*a. fig*); salute
Salz [zalts] *n* (-*es*; -*e*) salt
'Salzbergwerk *n* salt mine
salzen ['zaltsən] *v/t* ([*irr*,] *ge-, h*) salt
salzfrei ['zaltsfrai] *adj* salt-free, no-salt diet
salzig ['zaltsɪç] *adj* salty
'Salzkar‚toffeln *pl* boiled potatoes
Salzsäure *f* (-; *no pl*) CHEM hydrochloric acid
Salzstange *f* pretzel (*Br* salt) stick
Salzstreuer *m* (-s; -) salt shaker, *Br* salt cellar
Salzwasser *n* salt water
Same ['zaːmə] *m* (-*n*; -*n*), 'Samen *m* (-s -) BOT seed (*a. fig*); BIOL sperm, semen
'Samenbank *f* (-; -*en*) MED, VET sperm bank
Samenerguss *m* ejaculation
Samenkorn *n* BOT seedcorn
Sammel... ['zaməl-] *in cpds* ...*begriff*, ...*bestellung*, ...*konto etc*: collective ...
Sammelbüchse *f* collecting box
'sammeln *v/t* (*ge-, h*) collect; gather; pick; accumulate; *sich sammeln* assemble; *fig* compose o.s.
Sammler ['zamlɐ] *m* (-s; -), 'Sammlerin *f* (-; -*nen*) collector
'Sammlung *f* (-; -*en*) collection
Samstag ['zamstaːk] *m* (-[e]s; -e) Saturday
samt [zamt] *prp* (*dat*) together *or* along with
Samt *m* (-[e]s; -e) velvet
sämtlich ['zɛmtlɪç] *adj*: *sämtliche pl* all the; the complete works *etc*
Sanatorium [zana'toːrjʊm] *n* (-s; -*ien*) sanatorium, sanitarium
Sand [zant] *m* (-[e]s; -e) sand
Sandale [zan'daːlə] *f* (-; -*n*) sandal
Sandalette [zanda'lɛtə] *f* (-; -*n*) high-heeled sandal

S

'**Sandbahn** f SPORT dirt track
Sandbank f (-; -bänke) sandbank
Sandboden m sandy soil
Sandburg f sandcastle
sandig ['zandıç] adj sandy
'**Sandmann** m, **Sandmännchen** n sandman
Sandpa,pier n sandpaper
Sandsack m sand bag
Sandstein m sandstone
Sandstrand m sandy beach
sandte ['zantə] pret of **senden**
'**Sanduhr** f hourglass
sanft [zanft] adj gentle, soft; mild; easy (death)
'**sanftmütig** [-my:tıç] adj gentle, mild
sang [zaŋ] pret of **singen**
Sänger ['zɛŋɐ] m (-s; -), **Sängerin** ['zɛŋə-rın] f (-; -nen) singer
sanieren [za'ni:rən] v/t (no -ge-, h) redevelop (a. ECON), rehabilitate (a. ARCH)
Sa'nierung f (-; -en) redevelopment, rehabilitation
Sa'nierungsgebiet n redevelopment area
sanität [zani'tɛːɐ] adj sanitary
Sanitäter [zani'tɛːtɐ] m (-s; -) paramedic; MIL medic, Br medical orderly
sank [zaŋk] pret of **sinken**
Sankt [zaŋkt] Saint, ABBR St
Sardelle [zar'dɛlə] f (-; -n) ZO anchovy
Sardine [zar'di:nə] f (-; -n) ZO sardine
Sarg [zark] m (-[e]s; Särge ['zɛrgə]) casket, esp Br coffin
Sarkasmus [zar'kasmʊs] m (-; no pl) sarcasm
sar'kastisch adj sarcastic
saß [zaːs] pret of **sitzen**
Satan ['zaːtan] m (-s; -e) Satan; fig devil
Satellit [zatɛ'liːt] m (-en; -en) satellite (a. fig); **über Satellit** by or via satellite
Satel'liten... in cpds ...**bild**, ...**staat**, ...**stadt**, ...-**TV**: satellite ...
Satin [za'tɛ̃ː] m (-s; -s) satin; sateen
Satire [za'tiːrə] f (-; -n) satire (**auf** acc upon)
Satiriker [za'tiːrikɐ] m (-s; -) satirist
sa'tirisch adj satiric(al)
satt [zat] adj F full (up); **ich bin satt** I've had enough, F I'm full (up); **sich satt essen** eat one's fill (**an** dat of)
Sattel ['zatəl] m (-s; Sättel ['zɛtəl]) saddle
'**satteln** v/t (ge-, h) saddle
'**Sattelschlepper** m MOT semi-trailer truck, Br articulated lorry
'**satthaben** v/t (irr, **haben**, sep, -ge-, h) F be tired or F sick of, be fed up with
sättigen ['zɛtıgən] (ge-, h) **1.** v/t satisfy; feed; CHEM, PHYS saturate; **2.** v/i be substantial, be filling

'**Sättigung** f (-; -en) satiety; CHEM, ECON saturation (a. fig)
Sattler ['zatlɐ] m (-s; -) saddler
Sattlerei [zatlə'rai] f (-; -en) saddlery
Satz [zats] m (-es; Sätze ['zɛtsə]) leap; LING sentence; tennis etc: set; ECON rate; MUS movement
Satzaussage f LING predicate
Satzbau m (-[e]s; no pl) LING syntax; construction
Satzgegenstand m LING subject
Satzung ['zatsʊŋ] f (-; -en) statute
'**Satzzeichen** n LING punctuation mark
Sau [zau] f (-; Säue ['zɔyə]) ZO sow; HUNT wild sow; F swine, pig
sauber ['zaubɐ] adj clean (a. F fig); pure; neat (a. fig), tidy; decent; iro fine, nice; **sauber halten** keep clean (**sich** o.s.); **sauber machen** clean (up)
'**Sauberkeit** f (-; no pl) clean(li)ness; tidiness, neatness; purity; decency
'**saubermachen** v/t and v/i (sep, -ge-, h) → **sauber**
säubern ['zɔybɐn] v/t (ge-, h) clean (up); cleanse (a. MED); **säubern von** clear (POL a. purge) of
'**Säuberung(sakti,on)** f POL purge
sauer ['zauɐ] adj sour (a. fig), acid (a. CHEM); GASTR pickled; F mad (**auf** acc at), cross (with); **sauer werden** turn sour; F get mad; **saurer Regen** acid rain
säuerlich ['zɔyɐlıç] adj sharp; F wry
'**Sauerstoff** m (-[e]s; no pl) CHEM oxygen
Sauerstoffgerät n MED oxygen apparatus
Sauerstoffzelt n MED oxygen tent
'**Sauerteig** m leaven
saufen ['zaufən] v/t and v/i (irr, ge-, h) ZO drink; F booze
Säufer(in) ['zɔyfɐ (-fərın)] F (-s; -/-; -nen) drunkard, F boozer
saugen ['zaugən] v/i and v/t ([irr,] ge-, h) suck (**an et.** [at] s.th.)
säugen ['zɔygən] v/t (ge-, h) suckle (a. ZO), nurse, breastfeed
'**Säugetier** n mammal
saugfähig ['zauk-] adj absorbent
Säugling ['zɔyklıŋ] m (-s; -e) baby, infant
'**Säuglingsheim** n (baby) nursery
Säuglingspflege f infant care
Säuglingsschwester f baby nurse
Säuglingsstati,on f neonatal care unit
Säuglingssterblichkeit f infant mortality
Säule ['zɔylə] f (-; -n) column; pillar (a. fig)
'**Säulengang** m colonnade
Saum [zaum] m (-[e]s; Säume ['zɔymə]) hem(line); seam
säumen ['zɔymən] v/t (ge-, h) hem; border, edge; line

S

Sauna ['zauna] *f* (-; -s, *Saunen*) sauna

Säure ['zɔyrə] *f* (-; -n) CHEM acid

'**säurehaltig** [-haltɪç] *adj* acid

sausen ['zauzən] *v/i* a) (*ge-, sein*) F rush, dash, b) (*ge-, h*) ears: buzz; *wind:* howl

'**Saustall** *m* pigsty (*a.* F *contp*)

Saxophon [zakso'fo:n] *n* (-s; -e) MUS saxophone, F sax

S-Bahn ['ɛsbaːn] *f* rapid transit, *Br* suburban train

Schabe ['ʃaːbə] *f* (-; -n) ZO cockroach

'**schaben** *v/t* (*ge-, h*) scrape (*von* from)

schäbig ['ʃɛːbɪç] *adj* shabby, *fig a.* mean

Schablone [ʃa'bloːnə] *f* (-; -n) stencil; *fig* stereotype

Schach [ʃax] *n* (-s; *no pl*) chess; *Schach!* check!; *Schach und matt!* checkmate!; *j-n in Schach halten* keep s.o. in check

Schachbrett *n* chessboard

Schachfeld *n* square

Schachfi,gur *f* chessman, piece

schach'matt *adj: j-n schachmatt setzen* checkmate s.o.

'**Schachspiel** *n* (game of) chess; chessboard and men

Schacht [ʃaxt] *m* (-[e]s; *Schächte* ['ʃɛçtə]) shaft, *mining: a.* pit

Schachtel ['ʃaxtəl] *f* (-; -n) box; carton; *e-e Schachtel Zigaretten* a pack (*esp Br* packet) of cigarettes

'**Schachzug** *m* move (*a. fig*)

schade ['ʃaːdə] *pred adj: es ist schade* it's a pity; *wie schade!* what a pity *or* shame!; *zu schade sein für* be too good for

Schädel ['ʃɛːdəl] *m* (-s; -) ANAT skull

Schädelbruch *m* MED fracture of the skull

schaden ['ʃaːdən] *v/i* (*ge-, h*) damage, do damage to, harm, hurt; *der Gesundheit schaden* be bad for one's health; *das schadet nichts* it doesn't matter; *es könnte ihm nicht schaden* it wouldn't hurt him

'**Schaden** *m* (-s; *Schäden* ['ʃɛːdən]) damage (*an dat* to); *esp* TECH trouble, defect (*a.* MED); *fig* disadvantage; ECON loss; *j-m Schaden zufügen* do s.o. harm

Schadenersatz *m* damages; *Schadenersatz leisten* pay damages

Schadenfreude *f: Schadenfreude empfinden über* (*acc*) gloat over

'**schadenfroh** *adv* gloatingly

schadhaft ['ʃaːthaft] *adj* damaged; defective, faulty; leaking (*pipes*)

schädigen ['ʃɛːdɪɡən] *v/t* (*ge-, h*) damage, harm

schädlich ['ʃɛːtlɪç] *adj* harmful, injurious; bad (for your health)

Schädling ['ʃɛːtlɪŋ] *m* (-s; -e) BIOL pest

'**Schädlingsbekämpfung** *f* pest control

Schädlingsbekämpfungsmittel *n* pesticide

Schadstoff ['ʃaːt-] *m* harmful substance; pollutant

'**schadstoffarm** *adj* MOT low-emission

Schaf [ʃaːf] *n* (-[e]s; -e) ZO sheep

'**Schafbock** *m* ZO ram

Schäfer ['ʃɛːfɐ] *m* (-s; -) shepherd

Schäferhund *m* sheepdog; *Deutscher Schäferhund* German shepherd, *esp Br* Alsatian

'**Schaffell** *n* sheepskin; ZO fleece

schaffen¹ ['ʃafən] *v/t* (*irr, ge-, h*) create

'**schaffen²** (*ge-, h*) **1.** *v/t* cause, bring about; manage, get *s.th.* done; take; *es schaffen* make it, *a.* succeed; **2.** *v/i* work; *j-m zu schaffen machen* cause s.o. trouble; *sich zu schaffen machen an* (*dat*) tamper with

Schaffner ['ʃafnɐ] *m* (-s; -), '**Schaffnerin** *f* (-; -nen) conductor; *Br* RAIL guard

Schafott [ʃa'fɔt] *n* (-[e]s; -e) scaffold

Schaft [ʃaft] *m* (-[e]s; *Schäfte* ['ʃɛftə]) shaft; stock; shank; leg

'**Schafwolle** *f* sheep's wool

'**Schafzucht** *f* sheep breeding

schäkern ['ʃɛːkɐn] *v/i* (*ge-, h*) joke; flirt

schal [ʃaːl] *adj* stale, flat, *fig a.* empty

Schal *m* (-s; -s) scarf

Schale ['ʃaːlə] *f* (-; -n) bowl, dish; GASTR shell; peel, skin

schälen ['ʃɛːlən] *v/t* (*ge-, h*) peel, pare; *sich schälen skin:* peel (off)

Schall [ʃal] *m* (-[e]s; -e) sound

Schalldämpfer *m* silencer (*a. Br* MOT), MOT muffler

'**schalldicht** *adj* soundproof

schallen ['ʃalən] *v/i* ([*irr,*] *ge-, h*) sound; ring (out); *schallendes Gelächter* roars of laughter

'**Schallgeschwindigkeit** *f* speed of sound

Schallmauer *f* sound barrier

Schallplatte *f* record, disk, *Br* disc

Schallwelle *f* PHYS sound wave

schalten ['ʃaltən] *v/i and v/t* (*ge-, h*) switch, turn; MOT shift (*esp Br* change) gear; F get it; react

Schalter ['ʃaltɐ] *m* (-s; -) counter; RAIL ticket window; AVIAT desk; ELECTR switch

'**Schalthebel** *m* MOT gear lever; TECH, AVIAT control lever; ELECTR switch lever

Schaltjahr *n* leap year

Schalttafel *f* ELECTR switchboard, control panel

Schaltuhr *f* time switch

'**Schaltung** *f* (-; -en) MOT gearshift; ELECTR circuit

Scham [ʃaːm] *f* (-; *no pl*) shame; *vor*

S

Scham with shame

schämen ['ʃɛːmən] v/refl (ge-, h) be or feel ashamed (gen, **wegen** of); **du solltest dich (was) schämen!** you ought to be ashamed of yourself!

'**Schamgefühl** n (-[e]s; no pl) sense of shame

Schamhaare pl pubic hair

'**schamhaft** adj bashful

'**schamlos** adj shameless; indecent

Schande ['ʃandə] f (-; no pl) shame, disgrace

schänden ['ʃɛndən] v/t (ge-, h) disgrace; desecrate; rape

Schandfleck ['ʃant-] m eyesore

schändlich ['ʃɛntlɪç] adj disgraceful

'**Schandtat** f atrocity

Schanze ['ʃantsə] f (-; -n) SPORT ski jump

Schar [ʃaːɐ] f (-; -en ['ʃaːrən]) troop, band; F horde; crowd; ZO flock

'**scharen** v/refl (ge-, h) **sich scharen um** gather round

scharf [ʃarf] adj sharp (a. fig), PHOT a. in focus; clear; savage, fierce (dog); live (ammunition), armed (bomb etc); GASTR hot; F hot, sexy; F **scharf sein auf** (acc) be keen on; **scharf (ein)stellen** PHOT focus; F **scharfe Sachen** hard liquor

Schärfe ['ʃɛrfə] f (-; -n) sharpness (a. PHOT); fig severity, fierceness

'**schärfen** v/t (ge-, h) sharpen

'**Scharfrichter** m executioner

Scharfschütze m sharpshooter; sniper

'**scharfsichtig** adj sharp-sighted; fig clear-sighted

'**Scharfsinn** m (-[e]s; no pl) acumen

'**scharfsinnig** adj sharp-witted, shrewd

'**scharfstellen** v/t (sep, -ge-, h) → **scharf**

Scharlach ['ʃarlax] m (-s; no pl) scarlet; MED scarlet fever

'**scharlachrot** adj scarlet

Scharlatan ['ʃarlatan] m (-s; -e) charlatan, fraud

Scharnier [ʃar'niːɐ] n (-s; -e) TECH hinge

Schärpe ['ʃɛrpə] f (-; -n) sash

scharren ['ʃarən] v/i (ge-, h) scrape, scratch

schartig ['ʃartɪç] adj jagged, notchy

Schaschlik ['ʃaʃlɪk] m, n (-s; -s) GASTR shish kebab

Schatten ['ʃatən] m (-s; -) shadow (a. fig); shade; **im Schatten** in the shade

'**schattenhaft** adj shadowy

Schattierung [ʃa'tiːrʊŋ] f (-; -en) shade; fig colo(u)r

schattig ['ʃatɪç] adj shady

Schatz [ʃats] m (-es; Schätze ['ʃɛtsə]) treasure; fig darling

Schatzamt n POL Treasury Department, Br Treasury

schätzen ['ʃɛtsən] v/t (ge-, h) estimate, value (both: **auf** acc at); appreciate; think highly of; F reckon, guess

'**Schatzkammer** f treasury (a. fig)

Schatzkanzler m Chancellor of the Exchequer

Schatzmeister(in) treasurer

'**Schätzung** f (-; -en) estimate; valuation

Schau [ʃau] f (-; -en) show, exhibition; **zur Schau stellen** exhibit, display

Schauder ['ʃaudɐ] m (-s; -) shudder

'**schauderhaft** adj horrible, dreadful

'**schaudern** v/i (ge-, h) shudder, shiver (both: **vor** dat with)

schauen ['ʃauən] v/i (ge-, h) look (**auf** acc at)

Schauer ['ʃauɐ] m (-s; -) METEOR shower; shudder, shiver

Schauergeschichte f horror story (a. fig)

'**schauerlich** adj dreadful, horrible

Schaufel ['ʃaufəl] f (-; -n) shovel; dustpan

'**schaufeln** v/t (ge-, h) shovel; dig

'**Schaufenster** n shop window

Schaufensterauslage f window display

Schaufensterbummel m: **e-n Schaufensterbummel machen** go window-shopping

Schaufensterdekoration f window dressing

Schaukel ['ʃaukəl] f (-; -n) swing

'**schaukeln** (ge-, h) **1.** v/i swing; boat etc: rock; **2.** v/t rock

'**Schaukelpferd** n rocking horse

Schaukelstuhl m rocking chair, rocker

'**Schaulustige** [-lʊstɪgə] pl (curious) onlookers, F rubbernecks

Schaum [ʃaum] m (-[e]s; Schäume ['ʃɔymə]) foam; GASTR froth, head; lather; spray

schäumen ['ʃɔymən] v/i (ge-, h) foam (a. fig), froth; lather; spray

'**Schaumgummi** m foam rubber

schaumig ['ʃaumɪç] adj foamy, frothy

'**Schaumlöscher** m foam extinguisher

'**Schauplatz** m scene

'**Schauprozess** m JUR show trial

schaurig ['ʃaurɪç] adj creepy; horrible

'**Schauspiel** n THEA play; fig spectacle

'**Schauspieler(in)** actor (actress)

'**Schauspielschule** f drama school

'**Schausteller** [-ʃtɛlɐ] m (-s; -) showman

Scheck [ʃɛk] m (-s; -s) ECON check, Br cheque

Scheckheft n checkbook, Br chequebook

scheckig ['ʃɛkɪç] adj spotty

'**Scheckkarte** f check cashing (Br cheque) card

scheffeln ['ʃɛfəln] F *v/t* (*ge-, h*) rake in
Scheibe ['ʃaibə] *f* (-; -*n*) disk, *Br* disc; slice; pane; target
'**Scheibenbremse** *f* MOT disk (*Br* disc) brake
Scheibenwischer *m* MOT windshield (*Br* windscreen) wiper
Scheide ['ʃaidə] *f* (-; -*n*) sheath; scabbard; ANAT vagina
'**scheiden** (*irr, ge-*) **1.** *v/t* (*h*) separate, part (*both*: **von** from); divorce; *sich schei-den lassen* get a divorce, *von j-m*: divorce s.o.; **2.** *v/i* (*sein*) part; *scheiden aus* (*dat*) retire from
'**Scheideweg** *m* crossroads
'**Scheidung** *f* (-; -*en*) divorce
'**Scheidungsklage** *f* JUR divorce suit
Schein[1] [ʃain] *m* (-[*e*]*s; -e*) certificate; blank, *Br* form; bill, *Br* note
Schein[2] *m* (-[*e*]*s; no pl*) light; *fig* appearance; *et.* (*nur*) *zum Schein tun* (only) pretend to do s.th.
'**scheinbar** *adj* seeming, apparent
scheinen ['ʃainən] *v/i* (*irr, ge-, h*) shine; *fig* seem, appear, look
'**scheinheilig** *adj* hypocritical
'**Scheinwerfer** *m* searchlight; MOT headlight; THEA spotlight
Scheiß... ['ʃais-] V *in cpds* damn ..., fucking ..., *esp Br* bloody ...
Scheiße ['ʃaisə] V *f* (-; *no pl*), '**scheißen** V *v/i* (*irr, ge-, h*) shit, crap
Scheit [ʃait] *n* (-[*e*]*s; -e*) piece of wood
Scheitel ['ʃaitəl] *m* (-*s; -*) parting
'**scheiteln** *v/t* (*ge-, h*) part
Scheiterhaufen ['ʃaitɐ-] *m* pyre; HIST stake
scheitern ['ʃaitɐn] *v/i* (*ge-, sein*) fail, go wrong
Schelle ['ʃɛlə] *f* (-; -*n*) (little) bell; TECH clamp, clip
Schellfisch ['ʃɛl-] *m* ZO haddock
Schelm [ʃɛlm] *m* (-[*e*]*s; -e*) rascal
schelmisch ['ʃɛlmiʃ] *adj* impish
Schema ['ʃeːma] *n* (-*s; -s, -ta*) pattern, system
schematisch [ʃeˈmaːtiʃ] *adj* schematic; mechanical
Schemel ['ʃeːməl] *m* (-*s; -*) stool
schemenhaft ['ʃeːmən-] *adj* shadowy
Schenkel ['ʃɛŋkəl] *m* (-*s; -*) ANAT thigh; shank; MATH leg
schenken ['ʃɛŋkən] *v/t* (*ge-, h*) give (as a present) (*zu* for)
'**Schenkung** *f* (-; -*en*) JUR donation
Scherbe ['ʃɛrbə] *f* (-; -*n*), '**Scherben** *m* (-*s; -*) (broken) piece, fragment
Schere ['ʃeːrə] *f* (-; -*n*) scissors; ZO claw
scheren[1] ['ʃeːrən] *v/t* (*irr, ge-, h*) ZO shear;

BOT clip; cut
'**scheren**[2] *v/refl* (*ge-, h*) *sich scheren um* bother about
Scherereien [ʃeːrəˈraiən] *pl* trouble, bother
Schermaus ['ʃeːɐ-] *Austrian f* ZO mole
Scherz [ʃɛrts] *m* (-*es; -e*) joke; *im* (*zum*) *Scherz* for fun
scherzen ['ʃɛrtsən] *v/i* (*ge-, h*) joke (*über acc* at)
'**scherzhaft** *adj* joking; *scherzhaft gemeint* meant as a joke
scheu [ʃɔy] *adj* shy (*a*. ZO); bashful; *scheu machen* frighten
Scheu *f* (-; *no pl*) shyness; awe
scheuen ['ʃɔyən] (*ge-, h*) **1.** *v/i* shy (*vor dat* at), take fright (at); **2.** *v/t* shun, avoid; fear; *sich scheuen, et. zu tun* be afraid of doing s.th.
scheuern ['ʃɔyɐn] *v/t and v/i* (*ge-, h*) scrub, scour; chafe
'**Scheuertuch** *n* floor cloth
'**Scheuklappen** *pl* blinders, *Br* blinkers (*both a. fig*)
'**scheumachen** *v/t* (*sep, -ge-, h*) → *scheu*
Scheune ['ʃɔynə] *f* (-; -*n*) barn
Scheusal ['ʃɔyzaːl] *n* (-*s; -e*) monster (*a. fig*); *fig* beast
scheußlich ['ʃɔyslıç] *adj* horrible (*a.* F), atrocious
Schicht [ʃıçt] *f* (-; -*en*) layer; coat; film; ECON shift; class
schichten ['ʃıçtən] *v/t* (*ge-, h*) arrange in layers, pile up
'**schichtweise** *adv* in layers
schick [ʃık] *adj* smart, chic, stylish
schicken ['ʃıkən] *v/t* (*ge-, h*) send (*nach, zu* to); *das schickt sich nicht* that isn't done
Schickeria [ʃıkəˈriːa] F *f* (-; *no pl*) smart set, beautiful people, trendies
Schickimicki [ʃıkiˈmıki] F *contp m* (-*s; -s*) trendy
Schicksal ['ʃıkzaːl] *n* (-*s; -e*) fate, destiny; lot
Schiebedach ['ʃiːbə-] *n* MOT sliding roof, sunroof
Schiebefenster *n* sliding window; sash window
schieben ['ʃiːbən] *v/t* (*irr, ge-, h*) push
Schieber ['ʃiːbɐ] *m* (-*s; -*) TECH slide; bolt; F profiteer
'**Schiebetür** *f* sliding door
'**Schiebung** F *f* (-; -*en*) swindle, fix (*a. SPORT*)
schied [ʃiːt] *pret of scheiden*
Schiedsrichter ['ʃiːts-] *m*, '**Schiedsrichterin** *f* *soccer*: referee; *tennis*: umpire; judge, *esp pl a.* jury

schief [ʃiːf] *adj* crooked, not straight; sloping, oblique (*a.* MATH); leaning; *fig* false

Schiefer [ˈʃiːfɐ] *m* (*-s; -*) GEOL slate

'Schiefertafel *f* slate

'schiefgehen *v/i* (*irr*, **gehen**, *sep*, *-ge-*, *sein*) F go wrong

schielen [ˈʃiːlən] *v/i* (*ge-*, *h*) squint, be cross-eyed

schien [ʃiːn] *pret of* **scheinen**

Schienbein [ˈʃiːn-] *n* ANAT shin(bone)

Schiene [ˈʃiːnə] *f* (*-; -n*) TECH *etc* rail; MED splint

'schienen *v/t* (*ge-*, *h*) MED splint

Schießbude [ˈʃiːs-] *f* shooting gallery

schießen [ˈʃiːsən] *v/i and v/t* (*irr*, *ge-*, *h*) shoot, fire (*both*: **auf** *acc* at); SPORT score

Schießerei [ʃiːsəˈrai] *f* (*-; -en*) shooting; gunfight

'Schießpulver *n* gunpowder

Schießscharte *f* MIL loophole, embrasure

Schießscheibe *f* target

Schießstand *m* shooting range

Schiff [ʃif] *n* (*-[e]s; -e*) MAR ship, boat; ARCH nave; **mit dem Schiff** by boat

Schiffahrt *f* → **Schifffahrt**

'schiffbar *adj* navigable

'Schiffbau *m* (*-[e]s; no pl*) shipbuilding

'Schiffbruch *m* shipwreck (*a. fig*); **Schiffbruch erleiden** be shipwrecked

Schiffer [ˈʃifɐ] *m* (*-s; -*) sailor; skipper

'Schifffahrt *f* (*-; no pl*) shipping, navigation

'Schiffsjunge *m* ship's boy

Schiffsladung *f* shipload; cargo

Schiffsschraube *f* (ship's) propeller

Schiffswerft *f* shipyard

Schikane [ʃiˈkaːnə] *f* (*-; -n*) *a. pl* harassment; **aus reiner Schikane** out of sheer spite; F **mit allen Schikanen** with all the trimmings

schikanieren [ʃikaˈniːrən] *v/t* (*no -ge-*, *h*) harass; bully

Schild¹ [ʃilt] *n* (*-[e]s; -er* [ˈʃildɐ]) sign, plate

Schild² *m* (*-[e]s; -e*) shield

'Schilddrüse *f* ANAT thyroid (gland)

schildern [ˈʃildɐn] *v/t* (*ge-*, *h*) describe; depict, portray

Schilderung [ˈʃildəruŋ] *f* (*-; -en*) description, portrayal; account

'Schildkröte *f* ZO tortoise; turtle

Schilf [ʃilf] *n* (*-[e]s; no pl*) BOT reed(s)

schillern [ˈʃilɐn] *v/i* (*ge-*, *h*) be iridescent

schillernd *adj* iridescent; *fig* dubious

Schimmel [ˈʃiməl] *m* ZO white horse; BOT mo(u)ld

schimm(e)lig [ˈʃim(ə)liç] *adj* mo(u)ldy, musty

'schimmeln *v/i* (*ge-*, *h*, *sein*) go mo(u)ldy

Schimmer [ˈʃimɐ] *m* (*-s; -*) glimmer (*a. fig*), gleam, *fig a.* trace, touch

'schimmern *v/i* (*ge-*, *h*) shimmer, glimmer, gleam

Schimpanse [ʃimˈpanzə] *m* (*-n; -n*) ZO chimpanzee

schimpfen [ˈʃimpfən] *v/i and v/t* (*ge-*, *h*) scold (*mit j-m* s.o.); F tell *s.o.* off, bawl *s.o.* out; **schimpfen über** (*acc*) complain about

'Schimpfwort *n* swearword

Schindel [ˈʃindəl] *f* (*-; -n*) shingle

schinden [ˈʃindən] *v/t* (*irr*, *ge-*, *h*) maltreat; slave-drive; **sich schinden** drudge, slave away

Schinder [ˈʃindɐ] *m* (*-s; -*) slave driver

Schinderei [ʃindəˈrai] *f* (*-; -en*) slavery, drudgery

Schinken [ˈʃiŋkən] *m* (*-s; -*) ham

Schippe [ˈʃipə] *f* (*-; -n*), **'schippen** *v/t* (*ge-*, *h*) shovel

Schirm [ʃirm] *m* (*-[e]s; -e*) umbrella; sunshade; TV, EDP *etc*: screen; shade; peak, visor

Schirmherr(in) patron, sponsor

Schirmherrschaft *f* patronage, sponsorship; **unter der Schirmherrschaft von** under the auspices of

Schirmmütze *f* peaked cap

Schirmständer *m* umbrella stand

schiss [ʃis] *pret of* **scheißen**

Schlacht [ʃlaxt] *f* (*-; -en*) battle (**bei** of)

'schlachten *v/t* (*ge-*, *h*) slaughter, kill, butcher

Schlachter [ˈʃlaxtɐ] *m* (*-s; -*) butcher

'Schlachtfeld *n* MIL battlefield, battleground

Schlachthaus *n*, **Schlachthof** *m* slaughterhouse

Schlachtplan *m* MIL plan of action (*a. fig*)

Schlachtschiff *n* MIL battleship

Schlacke [ˈʃlakə] *f* (*-; -n*) cinders; GEOL, METALL slag

Schlaf [ʃlaːf] *m* (*-[e]s; no pl*) sleep; **e-n leichten (festen) Schlaf haben** be a light (sound) sleeper; F *fig* **im Schlaf** blindfold

'Schlafanzug *m* pajamas, *Br* pyjamas

Schläfe [ˈʃlɛːfə] *f* (*-; -n*) ANAT temple

schlafen [ˈʃlaːfən] *v/i* (*irr*, *ge-*, *h*) sleep (*a. fig*); **schlafen gehen, sich schlafen legen** go to bed; **fest schlafen** be fast asleep; **j-n schlafen legen** put s.o. to bed *or* to sleep

schlaff [ʃlaf] *adj* slack (*a. fig*); flabby; limp

'Schlafgelegenheit *f* sleeping accommodation

Schlafkrankheit *f* MED sleeping sickness
Schlaflied *n* lullaby
'**schlaflos** *adj* sleepless
'**Schlaflosigkeit** *f* (-; *no pl*) sleeplessness, MED insomnia
'**Schlafmittel** *n* MED sleeping pill(s)
'**Schlafmütze** *fig f* sleepyhead; slowpoke, *Br* slowcoach
schläfrig ['ʃlɛ:frɪç] *adj* sleepy, drowsy
'**Schlafsaal** *m* dormitory
Schlafsack *m* sleeping bag
Schlafta,blette *f* sleeping pill
'**schlaftrunken** *adj* (very) drowsy
'**Schlafwagen** *m* RAIL sleeping car, sleeper
Schlafwandler(in) [-vandlɐ (-lərɪn)] (-*s*; -/-; -*nen*) sleepwalker, somnambulist
Schlafzimmer *n* bedroom
Schlag [ʃla:k] *m* (-[e]*s*; *Schläge* ['ʃlɛ:gə]) blow (*a. fig*); slap; punch; pat, tap; *a. tennis*: stroke; ELECTR shock (*a. fig*); MED beat; *pl* beating; → *Schlaganfall*
Schlagader *f* ANAT artery
Schlaganfall *m* MED (apoplectic) stroke
'**schlagartig 1.** *adj* sudden, abrupt; **2.** *adv* all of a sudden, abruptly
'**Schlagbaum** *m* barrier
'**Schlagbohrer** *m* TECH percussion drill
schlagen ['ʃla:gən] (*irr, ge-, h*) **1.** *v/t* hit, beat (*a.* GASTR *and fig*), strike, knock; fell, cut (down); **sich schlagen** fight (*um* over); **sich geschlagen geben** admit defeat; **2.** *v/i* hit, beat (*a. heart etc*), strike (*a. clock*), knock; **an** *or* **gegen et. schlagen** hit s.th., bump *or* crash into s.th.
Schlager ['ʃla:gɐ] *m* (-*s*; -) MUS hit (*a. fig*), (pop) song
Schläger ['ʃlɛ:gɐ] *m* (-*s*; -) *tennis etc*: racket; *table tennis, cricket, baseball*: bat; *golf*: club; *hockey*: stick; *contp* thug
Schlägerei [ʃlɛ:gə'raɪ] *f* (-; -*en*) fight, brawl
'**schlagfertig** *adj* quick-witted; **schlagfertige Antwort** (witty) repartee
'**Schlaginstru,ment** *n* MUS percussion instrument
Schlagkraft *f* (-; *no pl*) striking power (*a.* MIL)
Schlagloch *n* pot-hole
Schlagobers *Austrian n*, **Schlagsahne** *f* whipped cream
Schlagseite *f* MAR list; **Schlagseite haben** be listing
Schlagstock *m* baton, truncheon
Schlagwort *n* catchword, slogan
Schlagzeile *f* headline
'**Schlagzeug** *n* MUS drums
'**Schlagzeuger** [-tsɔygɐ] *m* (-*s*; -) MUS drummer

schlaksig ['ʃla:ksɪç] *adj* lanky, gangling
Schlamm [ʃlam] *m* (-[e]*s*; -*e*) mud
schlammig ['ʃlamɪç] *adj* muddy
Schlampe ['ʃlampə] F *f* (-; -*n*) slut
schlampig ['ʃlampɪç] F *adj* sloppy
schlang [ʃlaŋ] *pret of* **schlingen**
Schlange ['ʃlaŋə] *f* (-; -*n*) ZO snake, serpent (*a. fig*); *fig* line, *esp Br* queue; **Schlange stehen** line up, stand in line, *esp Br* queue (up) (**nach** for)
schlängeln ['ʃlɛŋəln] *v/refl* (*ge-, h*) wind *or* weave (one's way), *person*: worm one's way
'**Schlangenlinie** *f* serpentine line; **in Schlangenlinien fahren** weave
schlank [ʃlaŋk] *adj* slim, slender; **j-n schlank machen** make s.o. look slim; **schlanke Unternehmensstruktur** ECON lean management
'**Schlankheitskur** *f*: **e-e Schlankheitskur machen** be slimming
'**schlankmachen** *v/t* (*sep, -ge-, h*): **j-n schlankmachen** → **schlank**
schlapp [ʃlap] F *adj* worn out; weak
Schlappe ['ʃlapə] F *f* (-; -*n*) setback, beating
'**schlappmachen** F *v/i* (*sep, -ge-, h*) flake out
'**Schlappschwanz** F *m* weakling, wimp
schlau [ʃlau] *adj* clever, smart, bright; sly, cunning, crafty
Schlauch [ʃlaux] *m* (-[e]*s*; *Schläuche* ['ʃlɔyçə]) tube; hose
Schlauchboot *n* (inflatable *or* rubber) dinghy
Schlaufe ['ʃlaufə] *f* (-; -*n*) loop
schlecht [ʃlɛçt] *adj* bad; poor; **mir ist (wird) schlecht** I feel (I'm getting) sick to my stomach; **schlecht aussehen** look ill; **sich schlecht fühlen** feel bad; **schlecht werden** GASTR go bad; **es geht ihm sehr schlecht** he is in a bad way; **schlecht gelaunt** in a bad temper *or* mood, bad-tempered; F **j-n schlecht machen** run s.o. down, backbite s.o.
'**schlechtmachen** *v/t* (*sep, -ge-, h*): F **j-n schlechtmachen machen** run s.o. down, backbite s.o.
schleichen ['ʃlaiçən] *v/i* (*irr, ge-, sein*) creep (*a. fig*), sneak
'**Schleichweg** *m* secret path
'**Schleichwerbung** *f* plugging; **für et. Schleichwerbung machen** plug s.th.
Schleier ['ʃlaiɐ] *m* (-*s*; -) veil (*a. fig*); haze
'**schleierhaft** *adj*: F **es ist mir schleierhaft** it's a mystery to me
Schleife ['ʃlaifə] *f* (-; -*n*) bow; ribbon; AVIAT, EDP, ELECTR, GEOGR loop
schleifen[1] ['ʃlaifən] *v/t and v/i* (*ge-, h*)

S

drag (along); rub

'**schleifen**² *v/t* (*irr, ge-, h*) grind (*a.* TECH), sharpen; sand(paper); cut; F drill *s.o.* hard

Schleifer ['ʃlaifɐ] *m* (*-s; -*), '**Schleifma-,schine** *f* TECH grinder

'**Schleifpa,pier** *n* sandpaper

'**Schleifstein** *m* grindstone; whetstone

Schleim [ʃlaim] *m* (*-[e]s; -e*) slime; MED mucus

'**Schleimhaut** *f* ANAT mucous membrane

schleimig ['ʃlaimɪç] *adj* slimy (*a. fig*); MED mucous

schlemmen ['ʃlɛmən] *v/i* (*ge-, h*) feast

schlendern ['ʃlɛndɐn] *v/i* (*ge-, sein*) stroll, saunter, amble

schlenkern ['ʃlɛŋkɐn] *v/i and v/t* (*ge-, h*) dangle, swing (*mit den Armen* one's arms)

schleppen ['ʃlɛpən] *v/t* (*ge-, h*) drag (*a. fig*); MOT, MAR tow; *sich schleppen* drag (on)

schleppend *adj* dragging; *fig* drawling

Schlepper ['ʃlɛpɐ] *m* (*-s; -*) MAR tug; MOT tractor

'**Schlepplift** *m* T-bar (lift), drag lift, ski tow

Schlepptau *n* tow-rope; *im* (*ins*) *Schlepptau* in tow (*a. fig*)

Schleuder ['ʃlɔydɐ] *f* (*-; -n*) catapult, slingshot; TECH spin drier

'**schleudern** (*ge-, h*) **1.** *v/t* fling, hurl (*both a. fig*); spin-dry; **2.** *v/i* MOT skid

'**Schleudersitz** *m* AVIAT ejection (*esp Br* ejector) seat

schleunigst ['ʃlɔyniçst] *adv* immediately

Schleuse ['ʃlɔyzə] *f* (*-; -n*) sluice; lock

schlich [ʃlɪç] *pret of* **schleichen**

schlicht [ʃlɪçt] *adj* plain, simple

schlichten ['ʃlɪçtən] *v/t* (*ge-, h*) settle

'**Schlichtung** *f* (*-; -en*) settlement

schlief [ʃliːf] *pret of* **schlafen**

schließen ['ʃliːsən] *v/t and v/i* (*irr, ge-, h*) shut, close (down); *fig* close, finish; *schließen aus* (*dat*) conclude from; *nach ... zu schließen* judging by ...

Schließfach ['ʃliːs-] *n* safe-deposit box; RAIL *etc*: (left luggage) locker

schließlich ['ʃliːslɪç] *adv* finally; eventually, in the end; after all

schliff [ʃlɪf] *pret of* **schleifen**²

Schliff *m* (*-[e]s; -e*) cut; polish (*a. fig*)

schlimm [ʃlɪm] *adj* bad; awful; *das ist nicht* or *halb so schlimm* it's not as bad as that; *das Schlimme daran* the bad thing about it

'**schlimmsten'falls** *adv* at (the) worst

Schlinge ['ʃlɪŋə] *f* (*-; -n*) loop; noose; HUNT snare (*a. fig*); MED sling

Schlingel ['ʃlɪŋəl] *m* (*-s; -*) rascal

schlingen ['ʃlɪŋən] *v/t* (*irr, ge-, h*) wind, twist; tie; wrap (*um* [a]round); gobble; *sich um et. schlingen* wind (a)round s.th.

schlingern ['ʃlɪŋɐn] *v/i* (*ge-, h*) MAR roll

'**Schlingpflanze** *f* BOT creeper, climber

Schlips [ʃlɪps] *m* (*-es; -e*) necktie, *esp Br* tie

schlitteln ['ʃlɪtəln] *Swiss v/i* (*ge-, sein*) go sledging, go tobogganing

Schlitten ['ʃlɪtən] *m* (*-s; -*) sled, *Br* sledge; sleigh; SPORT toboggan; *Schlitten fahren* go sledging, go tobogganing

Schlittschuh ['ʃlɪt-] *m* ice-skate (*a. Schlittschuh laufen*)

Schlittschuhläufer(in) ice-skater

Schlitz [ʃlɪts] *m* (*-es; -e*) slit; slot

schlitzen ['ʃlɪtsən] *v/t ge-, h*) slit, slash

schloss [ʃlɔs] *pret of* **schließen**

Schloss *n* (*-es; Schlösser* ['ʃlœsɐ]) TECH lock; ARCH castle, palace; *ins Schloss fallen* door: slam shut; *hinter Schloss und Riegel* locked up, under lock and key

Schlosser ['ʃlɔsɐ] *m* (*-s; -*) metalworker; locksmith

Schlosserei [ʃlɔsə'rai] *f* (*-; -en*) metalwork shop

schlottern ['ʃlɔtɐn] *v/i* (*ge-, h*) shake, tremble (*both: vor* with); bag

Schlucht [ʃlʊxt] *f* (*-; -en*) canyon, gorge, ravine

schluchzen ['ʃlʊxtsən] *v/i* (*ge-, h*), **Schluchzer** ['ʃlʊxtsɐ] *m* (*-s; -*) sob

Schluck [ʃlʊk] *m* (*-[e]s; -e*) draught, swallow; sip; gulp

'**Schluckauf** *m* (*-s; no pl*) hiccups; (*e-n*) *Schluckauf haben* have (the) hiccups

schlucken ['ʃlʊkən] *v/t and v/i* (*ge-, h*) swallow (*a. fig*)

'**Schluckimpfung** *f* MED oral vaccination

schlug [ʃluːk] *pret of* **schlagen**

Schlummer ['ʃlʊmɐ] *m* (*-s; no pl*) slumber

'**schlummern** *v/i* (*ge-, h*) lie asleep; *fig* slumber

schlüpfen ['ʃlʏpfən] *v/i* (*ge-, sein*) slip, slide; zo hatch (out)

Schlüpfer ['ʃlʏpfɐ] *m* (*-s;-*) briefs, panties

schlüpfrig ['ʃlʏpfrɪç] *adj* slippery; *contp* risqué, off-colo(u)r

'**Schlupfwinkel** ['ʃlʊpf-] *m* hiding place

schlurfen ['ʃlʊrfən] *v/i* (*ge-, sein*) shuffle (along)

schlürfen ['ʃlʏrfən] *v/t and v/i* (*ge-, h*) slurp

Schluss [ʃlʊs] *m* (*-es; no pl*) end; conclusion; ending; *Schluss machen* finish; break up; *Schluss machen mit* stop

Schmuggel

s.th., put an end to *s.th.*; **zum Schluss** finally; **(ganz) bis zum Schluss** to the (very) end; **Schluss für heute!** that's all for today!

Schlüssel ['ʃlʏsəl] *m* (-*s*; -) key (**für, zu** to)

Schlüsselbein *n* ANAT collarbone

Schlüsselblume *f* BOT cowslip, primrose

Schlüsselbund *m, n* bunch of keys

Schlüsselkind F *n* latchkey child

Schlüsselloch *n* keyhole

Schlüsselwort *n* keyword, EDP *a.* password

'Schlussfolgerung *f* conclusion

schlüssig ['ʃlʏsɪç] *adj* conclusive; **sich schlüssig werden** make up one's mind (**über** *acc* about)

'Schlusslicht *n* MOT *etc*: tail-light

Schlusspfiff *m* SPORT final whistle

Schlussphase *f* final stage(s)

Schlussverkauf *m* ECON (end-of-season) sale

schmächtig ['ʃmɛçtɪç] *adj* slight, thin, frail

schmackhaft ['ʃmakhaft] *adj* tasty

schmal [ʃmaːl] *adj* narrow; thin, slender (*a. fig*)

schmälern ['ʃmɛːlɐn] *v/t* (*ge-, h*) detract from

'Schmalfilm *m* cinefilm

'Schmalspur *f* RAIL narrow ga(u)ge

'Schmalspur... *fig in cpds* small-time ...

Schmalz [ʃmalts] *n* (-*es*; -*e*) grease; lard

schmalzig ['ʃmaltsɪç] F *adj* schmaltzy, mushy, *Br* soapy

schmarotzen [ʃma'rɔtsən] F *v/i* (*no -ge-, h*) sponge (**bei** on)

Schmarotzer [ʃma'rɔtsɐ] *m* (-*s*; -) BOT, ZO parasite, *fig a.* sponger

schmatzen ['ʃmatsən] *v/i* smack (one's lips), eat noisily

schmecken ['ʃmɛkən] *v/i and v/t* (*ge-, h*) taste (**nach** of); **gut (schlecht) schmecken** taste good (bad); (**wie) schmeckt dir ...?** (how) do you like ...? (*a. fig*), **es schmeckt süß (nach nichts)** it has a sweet (no) taste

Schmeichelei [ʃmaiçə'lai] *f* (-; -*en*) flattery

'schmeichelhaft *adj* flattering

'schmeicheln *v/i* (*ge-, h*) flatter (**j-m** s.o.)

Schmeichler(in) ['ʃmaiçlɐ (-lərɪn)] (-*s*; -/-; -*nen*) flatterer

schmeichlerisch ['ʃmaiçlərɪʃ] *adj* flattering

schmeißen ['ʃmaisən] F *v/t and v/i* (*irr, ge-, h*) throw, chuck; slam; **mit Geld um sich schmeißen** throw one's money about

'Schmeißfliege *f* ZO blowfly, bluebottle

schmelzen ['ʃmɛltsən] *v/i* (*irr, ge-, sein*) *and v/t* (*h*) melt; thaw; TECH smelt

'Schmelzofen *m* (s)melting furnace

Schmelztiegel *m* melting pot (*a. fig*)

Schmerz [ʃmɛrts] *m* (-*es*; -*en*) pain (*a. fig*), ache; *fig* grief, sorrow

schmerzen ['ʃmɛrtsən] *v/i and v/t* (*ge-, h*) hurt (*a. fig*), ache; *esp fig* pain

'schmerzfrei *adj* without pain

'schmerzhaft *adj* painful

'schmerzlich *adj* painful, sad

'schmerzlos *adj* painless

'Schmerzmittel *n* PHARM painkiller

'schmerzstillend *adj* painkilling

Schmetterling ['ʃmɛtɐlɪŋ] *m* (-*s*; -*e*) ZO butterfly

schmettern ['ʃmɛtɐn] (*ge-, h*) **1.** *v/t* smash (*a. tennis*); F MUS belt out; **2.** *v/i* a) (*sein*) crash, slam, b) MUS blare

Schmied [ʃmiːt] *m* (-[*e*]*s*; -*e*) (black-)-smith

Schmiede ['ʃmiːdə] *f* (-; -*n*) forge, smithy

'Schmiedeeisen *n* wrought iron

'schmieden *v/t* (*ge-, h*) forge; *fig* make (*plans etc*)

schmiegen ['ʃmiːgən] *v/refl* (*ge-, h*) **sich schmiegen an** (*acc*) snuggle up to; *dress etc*: cling to

Schmiere ['ʃmiːrə] *f* (-; -*n*) grease

'schmieren *v/t* (*ge-, h*) TECH grease, oil, lubricate; spread (*butter etc*); *contp* scribble, scrawl

Schmiererei [ʃmiːrə'rai] *f* (-; -*en*) scrawl; graffiti

schmierig ['ʃmiːrɪç] *adj* greasy; dirty; filthy; *contp* slimy

Schmiermittel ['ʃmiːɐ-] *n* TECH lubricant

Schminke ['ʃmɪŋkə] *f* (-; -*n*) make-up (*a. THEA*)

'schminken *v/t* (*ge-, h*) make *s.o.* up; **sich schminken** make o.s. *or* one's face up

Schmirgelpa‚pier ['ʃmɪrgəl-] *n* emery paper

schmiss [ʃmɪs] *pret of* **schmeißen**

schmollen ['ʃmɔlən] *v/i* (*ge-, h*) sulk, be sulky, pout

schmolz [ʃmɔlts] *pret of* **schmelzen**

schmoren ['ʃmoːrən] *v/t and v/i* (*ge-, h*) GASTR braise, stew (*a. fig*)

Schmuck [ʃmʊk] *m* (-[*e*]*s*; *no pl*) jewel-(le)ry, jewels; decoration(s), ornament(s)

schmücken ['ʃmʏkən] *v/t* (*ge-, h*) decorate

'schmucklos *adj* unadorned; plain

'Schmuckstück *n* piece of jewel(le)ry; *fig* gem

Schmuggel ['ʃmʊgəl] *m* (-; *no pl*), Schmuggelei [ʃmʊgə'lai] *f* (-; -*en*) smuggling

'**schmuggeln** v/t and v/i (ge-, h) smuggle

'**Schmuggelware** f smuggled goods

Schmuggler ['ʃmʊglɐ] m (-s; -) smuggler

schmunzeln ['ʃmʊntsəln] v/i (ge-, h) smile to o.s.

schmusen ['ʃmuːzən] F v/i (ge-, h) (kiss and) cuddle, smooch

Schmutz [ʃmʊts] m (-es; no pl) dirt, filth, fig a. smut

Schmutzfleck m smudge

schmutzig ['ʃmʊtsɪç] adj dirty, filthy (both a. fig); **schmutzig werden, sich schmutzig machen** get dirty

Schnabel ['ʃnaːbəl] m (-s; Schnäbel ['ʃnɛːbəl]) zo bill, beak

Schnalle ['ʃnalə] f (-; -n) buckle

'**schnallen** v/t (ge-, h) buckle; **et. schnallen an** (acc) strap s.th. to

schnalzen ['ʃnaltsən] v/i (ge-, h) snap one's fingers; click one's tongue

schnappen ['ʃnapən] (ge-, h) **1.** v/i snap, snatch (both: **nach** at); F **nach Luft schnappen** gasp for breath; **2.** F v/t catch

'**Schnappschuss** m PHOT snapshot

Schnaps [ʃnaps] m (-es; Schnäpse ['ʃnɛpsə]) spirits, schnapps, F booze

schnarchen ['ʃnarçən] v/i (ge-, h) snore

schnarren ['ʃnarən] v/i (ge-, h) rattle; voice: rasp

schnattern ['ʃnatɐn] v/i (ge-, h) zo cackle; chatter (a. F)

schnauben ['ʃnaubən] v/i and v/t (ge-, h) snort; **sich die Nase schnauben** blow one's nose

schnaufen ['ʃnaufən] v/i (ge-, h) breathe hard, pant, puff

Schnauze ['ʃnautsə] f (-; -n) zo snout, mouth, muzzle; F AVIAT, MOT nose; TECH spout; V trap, kisser; V **die Schnauze halten** keep one's trap shut

Schnecke ['ʃnɛkə] f (-; -n) zo snail; slug

'**Schneckenhaus** n zo snail shell

Schneckentempo n: **im Schneckentempo** at a snail's pace

Schnee [ʃneː] m (-s; no pl) snow (a. sl); **Schnee räumen** remove snow

Schneeball m snowball

Schneeballschlacht f snowball fight

'**schneebedeckt** adj snow-capped

'**Schneefall** m snowfall

Schneeflocke f snowflake

Schneegestöber [-gəʃtøːbɐ] n (-s; -) snow flurry

Schneeglöckchen n BOT snowdrop

Schneegrenze f snow line

Schneemann m snowman

Schneematsch m slush

Schneemo,bil n snowmobile

Schneepflug m snowplow, Br snowplough

Schneeregen m sleet

Schneesturm m snowstorm, blizzard

Schneeverwehung f snowdrift

'**schnee'weiß** adj snow-white

Schneewittchen [ʃneːˈvɪtçən] n (-s; no pl) Snow White

Schneid [ʃnait] F m (-[e]s; no pl) grit, guts

Schneidbrenner m TECH cutting torch

Schneide ['ʃnaidə] f (-; -n) edge

'**schneiden** v/t and v/i (irr, ge-, h) cut (a. fig), film etc: a. edit; GASTR carve

Schneider ['ʃnaidɐ] m (-s; -) tailor

Schneiderei [ʃnaidəˈrai] f (-; -en) a) (no pl) tailoring, dressmaking, b) tailor's or dressmaker's shop

'**Schneiderin** f (-; -nen) dressmaker; seamstress

'**schneidern** v/i and v/t (ge-, h) do dressmaking; make, sew

'**Schneidezahn** m incisor

schneidig ['ʃnaidɪç] adj dashing; smart

schneien ['ʃnaiən] v/i (ge-, h) snow

schnell [ʃnɛl] adj fast, quick; prompt; rapid; **es geht schnell** it won't take long; (**mach[t]**) **schnell!** hurry up!

'**Schnell...** in cpds ...dienst, ...paket, ...zug etc: mst express ...

schnellen ['ʃnɛlən] v/t (ge-, h) and v/i (ge-, sein) shoot, spring

'**Schnellhefter** m folder

Schnelligkeit ['ʃnɛlɪçkait] f (-; no pl) speed; quickness, rapidity

'**Schnellimbiss** m snack bar

Schnellstraße f expressway, thruway, Br motorway

schnetzeln ['ʃnɛtsəln] esp Swiss v/t (ge-, h) GASTR chop up

Schnippchen ['ʃnɪpçən] n: F **j-m ein Schnippchen schlagen** outwit s.o.

schnippisch ['ʃnɪpɪʃ] adj sassy, pert

schnipsen ['ʃnɪpsən] v/i (ge-, h) snap one's fingers

schnitt [ʃnɪt] pret of **schneiden**

Schnitt m (-[e]s; -e) cut (a. fig); average

'**Schnittblumen** pl cut flowers

Schnitte ['ʃnɪtə] f (-; -n) slice; open sandwich

schnittig ['ʃnɪtɪç] adj stylish; MOT sleek

Schnittlauch m BOT chives

Schnittmuster n pattern

Schnittpunkt m (point of) intersection

Schnittstelle f film etc: cut; EDP interface

Schnittwunde f MED cut

Schnitzel¹ ['ʃnɪtsəl] n (-s; -) GASTR cutlet; **Wiener Schnitzel** schnitzel

'**Schnitzel²** n, m (-s; -) chip; scrap

schnitzen ['ʃnɪtsən] v/t (ge-, h) carve, cut

(in wood)
Schnitzer ['ʃnɪtsɐ] *m* (-*s*; -) (wood) carver
Schnitzerei [ʃnɪtsə'rai] *f* (-; -*en*) (wood) carving
Schnorchel ['ʃnɔrçəl] *m* (-*s*; -); '**schnorcheln** *v/i* (*ge-*, *h*) snorkel
Schnörkel ['ʃnœrkəl] *m* (-*s*; -) flourish; ARCH scroll
schnorren ['ʃnɔrən] F *v/t* (*ge-*, *h*) mooch, *Br* cadge
schnüffeln ['ʃnʏfəln] *v/i* (*ge-*, *h*) sniff (*an dat* at); F snoop (about *or* around)
Schnuller ['ʃnʊlɐ] *m* (-*s*; -) pacifier, *Br* dummy
Schnulze ['ʃnʊltsə] F *f* (-; -*n*) tearjerker; schmal(t)zy song
'**Schnulzensänger** F *m*, '**Schnulzensängerin** *f* crooner
schnulzig ['ʃnʊltsɪç] F *adj* schmal(t)zy
Schnupfen ['ʃnʊpfən] *m* (-*s*; -) MED cold; *e-n Schnupfen haben* (*bekommen*) have a (catch [a]) cold
'**Schnupftabak** *m* snuff
schnuppern ['ʃnʊpɐn] *v/i* (*ge-*, *h*) sniff (*an et.* [at] s.th.)
Schnur [ʃnuːɐ] *f* (-; *Schnüre* ['ʃnyːrə]) string, cord; ELECTR flex
Schnürchen ['ʃnyːɐçən] *n*: *wie am Schnürchen* like clockwork
schnüren ['ʃnyːrən] *v/t* (*ge-*, *h*) lace (up); tie up
'**schnurgerade** *adv* dead straight
'**schnurlos** *adj*: *schnurloses Telefon* cordless phone
Schnürlsamt ['ʃnyːɐl-] *Austrian m* corduroy
schnurrbart ['ʃnʊr-] *m* m(o)ustache
schnurren ['ʃnʊrən] *v/i* (*ge-*, *h*) purr
Schnürschuh ['ʃnyːɐ-] *m* laced shoe
Schnürsenkel [-zeŋkəl] *m* (-*s*; -) shoestring, *Br* shoelace
schnurstracks ['ʃnuːɐ'ʃtraks] *adv* direct(ly), straight; straight away
schob [ʃoːp] *pret of* **schieben**
Schober ['ʃoːbɐ] *m* (-*s*; -) haystack, hayrick; barn
Schock [ʃɔk] *m* (-[*e*]*s*; -*s*) MED shock; *unter Schock stehen* be in (a state of) shock
schocken ['ʃɔkən] F *v/t* (*ge-*, *h*) shock
schockieren [ʃɔ'kiːrən] *v/t* (*no -ge-*, *h*) shock
Schokolade [ʃoko'laːdə] *f* (-; -*n*) chocolate; *e-e Tafel Schokolade* a bar of chocolate
scholl [ʃɔl] *pret of* **schallen**
Scholle ['ʃɔlə] *f* (-; -*n*) clod; (ice)floe; ZO flounder, *Br* plaice
schon [ʃoːn] *adv* already; ever; even;

schon damals even then; **schon 1968** as early as 1968; **schon der Gedanke** the very idea; *ist sie schon da* (*zurück*)? has she come (is she back) yet?; *habt ihr schon gegessen?* have you eaten yet?; *bist du schon einmal dort gewesen?* have you ever been there?; *ich wohne hier schon seit zwei Jahren* I've been living here for two years now; *ich kenne ihn schon, aber* I do know him, but; *er macht das schon* he'll do it all right; *schon gut!* never mind!, all right!
schön [ʃøːn] **1.** *adj* beautiful, lovely; METEOR *a.* fine, fair; nice (*a.* F *iro*); (*na*,) **schön** all right; **2.** *adv*: **schön warm** (*kühl*) nice and warm (cool); **ganz schön teuer** (*schnell*) pretty expensive (fast); *j-n ganz schön erschrecken* (*überraschen*) give s.o. quite a start (surprise)
schonen ['ʃoːnən] *v/t* (*ge-*, *h*) take care of, go easy on (*a.* TECH); spare; *sich schonen* take it easy; save o.s. *or* one's strength
schonend 1. *adj* gentle; mild; **2.** *adv*: *schonend umgehen mit* take (good) care of; handle with care; go easy on
'**Schönheit** *f* (-; -*en*) beauty
'**Schönheitspflege** *f* beauty care
'**Schonung** *f* (-; -*en*) a) (*no pl*) (good) care; rest; preservation, b) tree nursery
'**schonungslos** *adj* relentless, brutal
schöpfen ['ʃœpfən] *v/t* (*ge-*, *h*) scoop, ladle; draw (*water*); → *Luft*, *Verdacht*
Schöpfer ['ʃœpfɐ] *m* (-*s*; -), '**Schöpferin** *f* (-; -*nen*) creator
schöpferisch ['ʃœpfərɪʃ] *adj* creative
'**Schöpfung** *f* (-; -*en*) creation
schor [ʃoːɐ] *pret of* **scheren**
Schorf [ʃɔrf] *m* (-[*e*]*s*; -*e*) MED scab
Schornstein ['ʃɔrnʃtain] *m* chimney; MAR, RAIL funnel
Schornsteinfeger *m* chimneysweep
schoss [ʃɔs] *pret of* **schießen**
Schoß [ʃoːs] *m* (-*es*; *Schöße* ['ʃøːsə]) lap; womb
Schote ['ʃoːtə] *f* (-; -*n*) BOT pod, husk
Schotte ['ʃɔtə] *m* (-*n*; -*n*) Scot(sman); *pl* the Scots, the Scottish (people)
Schotter ['ʃɔtɐ] *m* (-*s*; -) gravel, road metal
Schottin ['ʃɔtɪn] *f* (-; -*nen*) Scotswoman
'**schottisch** *adj* Scots, Scottish; Scotch
'**Schottland** Scotland
schräg [ʃrɛːk] **1.** *adj* slanting, sloping, oblique; diagonal; **2.** *adv*: **schräg gegenüber** diagonally opposite
Schramme ['ʃramə] *f* (-; -*n*), '**schrammen**

S

v/t and v/i (*ge-*, *h*) scratch (*a.* MED)

Schrank [ʃraŋk] *m* (*-[e]s*; *Schränke* ['ʃrɛŋkə]) cupboard; closet; wardrobe

Schranke ['ʃraŋkə] *f* (*-*; *-n*) barrier (*a. fig*), RAIL *a.* gate; JUR bar; *pl* limits, bounds

'**schrankenlos** *fig adj* boundless

'**Schrankenwärter** *m* RAIL gatekeeper

'**Schrankwand** *f* wall units

Schraube ['ʃraubə] *f* (*-*; *-n*), '**schrauben** *v/t* (*ge-*, *h*) TECH screw

'**Schraubenschlüssel** *m* TECH spanner, wrench

Schraubenzieher *m* TECH screwdriver

Schraubstock ['ʃraup-] *m* vise, *Br* vice

Schreck [ʃrɛk] *m* (*-[e]s*; *-e*) fright, shock; *j-m e-n Schreck einjagen* give s.o. a fright, scare s.o.

Schrecken ['ʃrɛkən] *m* (*-s*; *-*) terror, fright; horror(s)

'**Schreckensnachricht** *f* dreadful news

'**schreckhaft** *adj* jumpy; skittish

'**schrecklich** *adj* awful, terrible; horrible, dreadful, atrocious

Schrei [ʃrai] *m* (*-[e]s*; *-e*) cry, shout, yell, scream (*all*: *um, nach* for)

schreiben ['ʃraibən] *v/t and v/i* (*irr, ge-, h*) write (*j-m* to s.o.; *über acc* about); type; spell; *falsch schreiben* misspell; *wie schreibt man …?* how do you spell …?

'**Schreiben** *n* (*-s*; *-*) letter

'**Schreibfehler** *m* spelling mistake

Schreibheft *n* exercise book

Schreibkraft *f* typist

Schreibma,schine *f* typewriter

Schreibmateri,al *n* writing materials, stationery

Schreibschutz *m* EDP write *or* file protection

Schreibtisch *m* desk

'**Schreibung** *f* (*-*; *-en*) spelling

'**Schreibwaren** *pl* stationery

Schreibwarengeschäft *n* stationer's, stationery shop

'**Schreibzen,trale** *f* typing pool

schreien ['ʃraiən] *v/i and v/t* (*irr, ge-, h*) cry, shout, yell, scream (*all*: *um, nach* [out] for); *schreien vor Schmerz* (*Angst*) cry out with pain (in terror); *es war zum Schreien* it was a scream

schreiend *fig adj* loud (*colors*); flagrant (*abuse etc*), glaring (*injustices etc*)

Schreiner ['ʃrainɐ] *m* (*-s*; *-*) → *Tischler*

schreiten ['ʃraitən] *v/i* (*irr, ge-, sein*) stride

schrie [ʃriː] *pret of* **schreien**

schrieb [ʃriːp] *pret of* **schreiben**

Schrift [ʃrift] *f* (*-*; *-en*) (hand)writing, hand; PRINT type; character, letter; *pl* works, writings; *die Heilige Schrift* REL the Scriptures

Schriftart *f* script; PRINT typeface

Schriftdeutsch *n* standard German

'**schriftlich** *adj* written; *schriftlich übersetzen* translate in writing

'**Schriftsteller** [-ʃtɛlɐ] *m* (*-s*; *-*), '**Schriftstellerin** *f* (*-*; *-nen*) author, writer

'**Schriftverkehr** *m*, **Schriftwechsel** *m* correspondence

Schriftzeichen *n* character, letter

schrill [ʃril] *adj* shrill (*a. fig*), piercing

schritt [ʃrit] *pret of* **schreiten**

Schritt *m* (*-[e]s*; *-e*) step (*a. fig*); pace; *fig Schritte unternehmen* take steps; *Schritt fahren!* MOT dead slow

Schrittmacher *m* SPORT pacemaker (*a.* MED), pacesetter

'**schrittweise** *adv* step by step, gradually

schroff [ʃrɔf] *adj* steep; jagged; *fig* gruff

Schrot [ʃroːt] *m, n* (*-[e]s*; *-e*) a) (*no pl*) coarse meal, b) HUNT (small) shot; pellet

Schrotflinte *f* shotgun

Schrott [ʃrɔt] *m* (*-[e]s*; *-e*) scrap (metal)

'**Schrotthaufen** *m* scrap heap

'**Schrottplatz** *m* scrapyard

schrubben ['ʃrubən] *v/t* (*ge-*, *h*) scrub, scour

schrumpfen ['ʃrumpfən] *v/i* (*ge-*, *sein*) shrink

Schub [ʃuːp] *m* (*-[e]s*; *Schübe* ['ʃyːbə]) → *Schubkraft*

Schubfach *n* drawer

Schubkarren *m* wheelbarrow

Schubkasten *m* drawer

Schubkraft *f* PHYS, TECH thrust

Schublade *f* drawer

Schubs [ʃups] F *m* (*-es*; *-e*), **schubsen** ['ʃupsən] F *v/t* (*ge-*, *h*) push

schüchtern ['ʃʏçtɐn] *adj* shy, bashful

'**Schüchternheit** *f* (*-*; *no pl*) shyness, bashfulness

schuf [ʃuːf] *pret of* **schaffen**[1]

Schuft [ʃuft] *m* (*-[e]s*; *-e*) *contp* bastard

schuften ['ʃuftən] F *v/i* (*ge-*, *h*) slave away, drudge

Schuh [ʃuː] *m* (*-[e]s*; *-e*) shoe; *j-m et. in die Schuhe schieben* put the blame for s.th. on s.o.

Schuhanzieher *m* shoehorn

Schuhcreme *f* shoe polish

Schuhgeschäft *n* shoe store (*Br* shop)

Schuhlöffel *m* shoehorn

Schuhmacher *m* shoemaker

Schuhputzer [-putsɐ] *m* (*-s*; *-*) shoeshine boy

'**Schulabbrecher** *m* (*-s*; *-*) dropout

Schulabgänger [-apgɛŋɐ] *m* (*-s*; *-*) school leaver

Schulamt *n* school board, *Br* education authority

S

Schularbeit *f* schoolwork; *pl* homework
Schulbesuch *m* (school) attendance
Schulbildung *f* education
Schulbuch *n* textbook
Schuld [ʃʊlt] *f* (-; -en [ˈʃʊldən]) a) (*no pl*)
JUR guilt, *esp* REL sin, b) *mst pl* debt; *j-m
die Schuld (an et.) geben* blame s.o.
(for s.th.); *es ist (nicht) deine Schuld*
it is(n't) your fault; *Schulden haben
(machen)* be in (run into) debt; → *zuschulden*
'schuldbewusst *adj*: *schuldbewusste
Miene* guilty look
schulden [ˈʃʊldən] *v/t* (*ge-, h*) *j-m et.
schulden* owe s.o. s.th.
schuldig [ˈʃʊldɪç] *adj esp* JUR guilty (*an
dat* of); responsible *or* to blame (for);
j-m et. schuldig sein owe s.o. s.th.
Schuldige [ˈʃʊldɪɡə] *m, f* (-*n*; -*n*) culprit;
JUR guilty person, offender
'schuldlos *adj* innocent
Schuldner [ˈʃʊldnɐ] *m* (-*s*; -)
'Schuldnerin *f* (-; -*nen*) debtor
'Schuldschein *m* ECON promissory note,
IOU (= I owe you)
Schule [ˈʃuːlə] *f* (-; -*n*) school (*a. fig*); *höhere Schule appr* (senior) high school,
Br secondary school; *auf or in der Schu-
le* at school; *in die or zur Schule gehen
(kommen)* go to (start) school
'schulen *v/t* (*ge-, h*) train, school
Schüler [ˈʃyːlɐ] *m* (-*s*; -) student, school-
boy, *esp Br a.* pupil
Schüleraustausch *m* student exchange
(program[me])
Schülerin [ˈʃyːlərɪn] *f* (-; -*nen*) student,
schoolgirl, *esp Br a.* pupil
'Schülervertretung *f appr* student gov-
ernment (*Br* council)
'Schulferien *pl* vacation, *Br* holidays
Schulfernsehen *n* educational TV
Schulfunk *m* schools programmes
Schulgebäude *n* school (building)
Schulgeld *n* school fee(s), tuition
Schulheft *n* exercise book
Schulhof *m* school yard, playground
Schulkame,rad *m* schoolfellow
Schulleiter *m* principal, *Br* headmaster,
head teacher
Schulleiterin *f* principal, *Br* headmistress
Schulmappe *f* schoolbag; satchel
Schulordnung *f* school regulations
'schulpflichtig *adj*: *schulpflichtiges
Kind* school--age child
'Schulschiff *n* training ship
Schulschluss *m* end of school (*or* term);
nach Schulschluss after school
Schulschwänzer [-ʃvɛntsɐ] *m* (-*s*; -) tru-
ant

Schulstunde *f* lesson, class, period
Schultasche *f* schoolbag
Schulter [ˈʃʊltɐ] *f* (-; -*n*) ANAT shoulder
'Schulterblatt *n* ANAT shoulder-blade
'schulterfrei *adj* strapless
'schultern *v/t* (*ge-, h*) shoulder
'Schultertasche *f* shoulder bag
'Schulwesen *n* (-*s; no pl*) education(al system)
schummeln [ˈʃʊməln] F *v/i* (*ge-, h*) cheat
Schund [ʃʊnt] *m* (-[*e*]*s; no pl*) trash, rubbish, junk
schund [ʃʊnt] *pret of* **schinden**
Schuppe [ˈʃʊpə] *f* (-; -*n*) ZO scale; *pl* MED
dandruff
'Schuppen *m* (-*s*; -) shed, *esp* F *contp*
shack
schuppig [ˈʃʊpɪç] *adj* ZO scaly
schüren [ˈʃyːrən] *v/t* (*ge-, h*) stir up (*a. fig*)
schürfen [ˈʃʏrfən] *v/i* (*ge-, h*) prospect
(*nach* for)
'Schürfwunde *f* MED graze, abrasion
Schurke [ˈʃʊrkə] *m* (-*n*; -*n*) *esp* THEA *etc*
villain
Schurwolle [ˈʃuːrˌ] *f* virgin wool
Schürze [ˈʃʏrtsə] *f* (-; -*n*) apron
Schuss [ʃʊs] *m* (-*es*; *Schüsse* [ˈʃʏsə])
shot; GASTR dash; SPORT shot, *soccer: a.*
strike; *skiing:* schuss (*a. Schuss fahren*);
sl shot, fix; F *gut in Schuss sein* be in
good shape
Schüssel [ˈʃʏsəl] *f* (-; -*n*) bowl, dish; basin
'Schusswaffe *f* firearm
Schusswunde *f* MED gunshot *or* bullet
wound
Schuster [ˈʃuːstɐ] *m* (-*s*; -) shoemaker
Schutt [ʃʊt] *m* (-[*e*]*s; no pl*) rubble, debris
'Schüttelfrost *m* MED shivering fit, *the*
shivers
schütteln [ˈʃʏtəln] *v/t* (*ge-, h*) shake
schütten [ˈʃʏtən] *v/t* (*ge-, h*) pour; throw
Schutz [ʃʊts] *m* (-*es; no pl*) protection
(*gegen, vor dat* against), defense, *Br* defence (against, from); shelter (from);
safeguard (against); cover
Schutzblech *n* fender, *Br* mudguard
Schutzbrille *f* goggles
Schütze [ˈʃʏtsə] *m* (-*n*; -*n*) MIL rifleman;
hunter; SPORT scorer; ASTR Sagittarius;
er ist (ein) Schütze he's (a) Sagittarius;
ein guter Schütze a good shot
schützen [ˈʃʏtsən] *v/t* (*ge-, h*) protect (*gegen, vor dat* against, from), defend
(against, from), guard (against, from);
shelter (from); safeguard
'Schutzengel *m* guardian angel
'Schützengraben *m* MIL trench
'Schutzgeld *n* protection money
Schutzgelderpressung *f* protection

S

racket
'**Schutzhaft** f JUR protective custody
Schutzheilige m, f patron (saint)
Schutzimpfung f MED protective inoculation; vaccination
Schutzkleidung f protective clothing
Schützling ['ʃʏtslɪŋ] m (-s; -e) protégé(e)
'**schutzlos** adj unprotected; defenseless, Br defenceless
'**Schutzmaßnahme** f safety measure
Schutzpa͵tron m REL patron (saint)
Schutzumschlag m dust cover
Schutzzoll m ECON protective duty (or tariff)
schwach [ʃvax] adj weak (a. fig); poor; faint; delicate, frail; **schwächer werden** grow weak; decline; fail; fade
Schwäche ['ʃvɛçə] f weakness (a. fig); MED infirmity; fig drawback, shortcoming; **e-e Schwäche haben für** be partial to
'**schwächen** v/t (ge-, h) weaken (a. fig); lessen
'**schwächlich** adj weakly, feeble; delicate, frail
'**Schwächling** m (-s; -e) weakling (a. fig), softy, sissy
'**schwachsinnig** adj feeble-minded; F stupid, idiotic
'**Schwachstrom** m ELECTR low-voltage current
Schwager ['ʃvaːgɐ] m (-s; Schwäger ['ʃvɛːgɐ]) brother-in-law
Schwägerin ['ʃvɛːgərɪn] f (-; -nen) sister-in-law
Schwalbe ['ʃvalbə] f (-; -n) ZO swallow; soccer: dive
Schwall [ʃval] m (-[e]s; -e) gush, esp fig a. torrent
schwamm [ʃvam] pret of **schwimmen**
Schwamm m (-[e]s; Schwämme ['ʃvɛmə]) sponge; BOT fungus; F dry rot
Schwammerl ['ʃvamɐl] Austrian m (-s; -[n]) → **Pilz**
schwammig ['ʃvamɪç] adj spongy; puffy; fig woolly
Schwan [ʃvaːn] m (-[e]s; Schwäne ['ʃvɛːnə]) ZO swan
schwand [ʃvant] pret of **schwinden**
schwang [ʃvaŋ] pret of **schwingen**
schwanger ['ʃvaŋɐ] adj pregnant
'**Schwangerschaft** f (-; -en) pregnancy
'**Schwangerschaftsabbruch** m abortion
schwanken ['ʃvaŋkən] v/i (ge-, h) sway, roll (a. MAR); stagger; fig **schwanken zwischen ... und ...** waver between ... and ...; prices: range from ... to ...
'**Schwankung** f (-; -en) change, variation (a. ECON)

Schwanz [ʃvants] m (-es; Schwänze ['ʃvɛntsə]) ZO tail (a. AVIAT, ASTR); V cock
schwänzen ['ʃvɛntsən] v/i and v/t (ge-, h) (**die Schule**) **schwänzen** play truant (F hooky)
Schwarm [ʃvarm] m (-[e]s; Schwärme ['ʃvɛrmə]) swarm; crowd, F bunch; ZO shoal, school; F dream; idol
schwärmen ['ʃvɛrmən] v/i a) (ge-, sein) ZO swarm, b) (ge-, h) **schwärmen für** be mad about; dream of; have a crush on s.o.; **schwärmen von** rave about
Schwarte ['ʃvartə] f (-; -n) rind; F contp (old) tome
schwarz [ʃvarts] adj black (a. fig); **Schwarzes Brett** bulletin board, Br notice board; **schwarz auf weiß** in black and white
'**Schwarzarbeit** f (-; no pl) illicit work
'**Schwarzbrot** n rye bread
Schwarze ['ʃvartsə] m, f (-n; -n) black (man or woman); pl the Blacks
schwärzen ['ʃvɛrtsən] v/t (ge-, h) blacken
'**Schwarzfahrer** m fare dodger
Schwarzhändler m black marketeer
Schwarzmarkt m black market
Schwarzseher m pessimist; (TV) license (Br licence) dodger
Schwarz'weiß... in cpds ...film, ...fernseher etc: black-and-white ...
schwatzen ['ʃvatsən], **schwätzen** ['ʃvɛtsən] v/i (ge-, h) chat(ter); PED talk
Schwätzer ['ʃvɛtsɐ] contp m (-s; -), '**Schwätzerin** f (-; -nen) loudmouth
schwatzhaft ['ʃvatshaft] adj chatty
Schwebebahn ['ʃveːbə-] f cableway, ropeway
Schwebebalken m SPORT beam
schweben ['ʃveːbən] v/i (ge-, h) be suspended; ZO, AVIAT hover (a. fig); glide; esp JUR be pending; **in Gefahr schweben** be in danger
Schwede ['ʃveːdə] m (-n; -n) Swede
Schweden ['ʃveːdən] Sweden
Schwedin ['ʃveːdɪn] f (-; -nen) Swede
'**schwedisch** adj Swedish
Schwefel ['ʃveːfəl] m (-s; no pl) CHEM sulfur, Br sulphur
Schwefelsäure f CHEM sulfuric (Br sulphuric) acid
Schweif [ʃvaif] m (-[e]s; -e) ZO tail (a. ASTR)
schweifen ['ʃvaifən] v/i (ge-, sein) wander (a. fig), roam
schweigen ['ʃvaigən] v/i (irr, ge-, h) be silent
'**Schweigen** n (-s; no pl) silence
'**schweigend** adj silent
schweigsam ['ʃvaikzaːm] adj quiet, taci-

turn, reticent
Schwein [ʃvain] n (-[e]s; -e) zo pig, hog; F
contp (filthy) pig; swine, bastard; F
Schwein haben be lucky
'**Schweinebraten** m roast pork
'**Schweinefleisch** n pork
Schweinerei [ʃvainə'rai] F f (-; -en) mess;
fig dirty trick; dirty *or* crying shame;
filth(y story *or* joke)
'**Schweinestall** m pigsty (*a. fig*)
'**schweinisch** F *adj* filthy, obscene
'**Schweinsleder** n pigskin
Schweiß [ʃvais] m (-es; *no pl*) sweat, per-
spiration
schweißen v/t (ge-, h) TECH weld
Schweißer m (-s; -) TECH welder
'**schweißgebadet** *adj* soaked in sweat
'**Schweißgeruch** m body odo(u)r, BO
Schweiz [ʃvaits] Switzerland
Schweizer ['ʃvaitsɐ] m (-s; -), *adj* Swiss
Schweizerin ['ʃvaitsərɪn] f (-; -nen) Swiss
woman *or* girl
schweizerisch ['ʃvaitsərɪʃ] *adj* Swiss
schwelen ['ʃveːlən] v/i (ge-, h) smo(u)l-
der (*a. fig*)
schwelgen ['ʃvɛlgən] v/i (ge-, h) **schwel-**
gen in (*dat*) revel in
Schwelle ['ʃvɛlə] f (-; -n) threshold (*a.*
fig); RAIL tie, *Br* sleeper
'**schwellen 1.** v/i (*irr, ge-, sein*) swell; **2.** v/t
(ge-, h) swell
'**Schwellung** f (-; -en) MED swelling
Schwemme ['ʃvɛmə] f (-; -n) ECON glut,
oversupply
'**schwemmen** v/t (ge-, h) **an Land**
schwemmen wash ashore
Schwengel ['ʃvɛŋəl] m (-s; -) clapper;
handle
schwenken ['ʃvɛŋkən] v/t (ge-, h) *and* v/i
(ge-, sein) swing, wave
schwer [ʃveːɐ] **1.** *adj* heavy; *fig* difficult,
hard; GASTR strong, rich; MED *etc* serious,
severe; heavy, violent (*storm etc*);
schwere Zeiten hard times; ***es schwer***
haben have a bad time; ***100 Pfund***
schwer sein weigh a hundred pounds;
2. *adv*: ***schwer arbeiten*** work hard; →
schwerfallen; → ***hören***; ***schwer be-***
schädigt → ***schwerbeschädigt***;
schwer verdaulich indigestible, heavy
(*both a. fig*); ***schwer verständlich*** difficult *or* hard to understand; ***schwer ver-***
wundet seriously wounded
'**schwerbeschädigt** *adj* seriously disabled
Schwere ['ʃveːrə] f (-; *no pl*) weight (*a.*
fig); *fig* seriousness
'**schwerfallen** v/i (*irr, fallen, sep, -ge-,*
sein): ***j-m schwerfallen*** be difficult for

s.o.; ***es fällt ihm schwer zu ...*** he finds
it difficult to ...
'**schwerfällig** *adj* awkward, clumsy
'**Schwergewicht** n (-[e]s; *no pl*) heavy-
weight; *fig* (main) emphasis
'**schwerhörig** *adj* hard of hearing
'**Schwerindus,trie** f heavy industry
Schwerkraft f (-; *no pl*) PHYS gravity
Schwerme,tall n heavy metal
'**schwermütig** [-myːtɪç] *adj* melancholy;
schwermütig sein have the blues
'**Schwerpunkt** m center (*Br* centre) of
gravity; *fig* (main) emphasis
Schwert [ʃveːɐt] n (-[e]s; -er) sword
'**Schwerverbrecher** m dangerous criminal, JUR felon
'**schwerverdaulich** *adj* → **schwer**
schwerverständlich *adj* → **schwer**
schwerver,wundet *adj* → **schwer**
'**schwerwiegend** *fig adj* weighty, serious
Schwester ['ʃvɛstɐ] f (-; -n) sister, REL *a.*
nun; MED nurse
schwieg [ʃviːk] *pret of* **schweigen**
Schwieger... ['ʃviːgɐ-] *in cpds* ...**eltern,**
...**mutter,** ...**sohn** etc: ...**-in-law**
Schwiele ['ʃviːlə] f (-; -n) MED callus
schwielig ['ʃviːlɪç] *adj* horny
schwierig ['ʃviːrɪç] *adj* difficult, hard
'**Schwierigkeit** f (-; -en) difficulty, trouble; ***in Schwierigkeiten geraten*** get *or*
run into trouble; ***Schwierigkeiten ha-***
ben, et. zu tun have difficulty in doing
s.th.
Schwimmbad ['ʃvɪm-] n (indoor) swimming pool
schwimmen ['ʃvɪmən] v/i (*irr, ge-, sein*)
swim; float; ***schwimmen gehen*** go
swimming
'**Schwimmflosse** f swimfin, *Br* flipper
Schwimmgürtel m swimming belt
Schwimmhaut f zo web
Schwimmlehrer m swimming instructor
Schwimmweste f life jacket
Schwindel ['ʃvɪndəl] m (-s; *no pl*) MED
giddiness, dizziness; F swindle, fraud;
Schwindel erregend dizzy
'**schwindeler,regend** *adj* dizzy
'**schwindeln** F v/i (ge-, h) fib, tell fibs
schwinden ['ʃvɪndən] v/i (*irr, ge-, sein*)
dwindle, decline
Schwindler ['ʃvɪndlɐ] F m (-s; -),
'**Schwindlerin** f (-; -nen) swindler, crook;
liar
schwindlig ['ʃvɪndlɪç] *adj* MED dizzy, giddy; ***mir ist schwindlig*** I feel dizzy
Schwinge ['ʃvɪŋə] f (-; -n) zo wing
'**schwingen** v/i *and* v/t (*irr, ge-, h*) swing;
wave; PHYS oscillate; vibrate
'**Schwingung** f (-; -en) PHYS oscillation;

vibration

Schwips [ʃvɪps] F *m*: *e-n Schwips haben* be tipsy

schwirren ['ʃvɪrən] *v/i* a) (*ge-*, *sein*) whirr, whizz, *esp* zo buzz (*a. fig*), b) (*ge-*, *h*) *mir schwirrt der Kopf* my head is buzzing

schwitzen ['ʃvɪtsən] *v/i* (*ge-*, *h*) sweat, perspire

schwoll [ʃvɔl] *pret of* **schwellen** 1

schwor [ʃvoːɐ] *pret of* **schwören**

schwören ['ʃvøːrən] *v/t and v/i* (*irr*, *ge-*, *h*) swear; JUR take an *or* the oath; *fig* **schwören auf** (*acc*) swear by

schwul [ʃvuːl] F *adj* gay; *contp* queer

schwül [ʃvyːl] *adj* sultry (*a. fig*), close

schwülstig ['ʃvʏlstɪç] *adj* bombastic, pompous

Schwung [ʃvʊŋ] *m* (-[e]s; *Schwünge* ['ʃvʏŋə]) swing; *fig* verve, pep; drive; *in Schwung kommen* get going; *et. in Schwung bringen* get s.th. going

'**schwungvoll** *adj* full of energy *or* verve; MUS swinging

Schwur [ʃvuːɐ] *m* (-[e]s; *Schwüre* ['ʃvyː-rə]) oath

Schwurgericht *n* JUR jury court

sechs [zɛks] *adj* six; *grade*: F, *Br a.* poor

'**Sechseck** *n* (-[e]s; *-e*) hexagon

'**sechseckig** *adj* hexagonal

'**sechsfach** *adj* sixfold

'**sechsmal** *adv* six times

Sechs'tagerennen *n* SPORT six-day race

'**sechstägig** [-tɛːgɪç] *adj* lasting *or* of six days

'**sechste** *adj* sixth

Sechstel ['zɛkstəl] *n* (-s; -) sixth (part)

'**sechstens** *adv* sixthly, in the sixth place

sechzehn(te) ['zɛçtseːn(tə)] *adj* sixteen(th)

sechzig ['zɛçtsɪç] *adj* sixty

'**sechzigste** *adj* sixtieth

See[1] [zeː] *m* (-s; -n) lake

See[2] *f* (-; *no pl*) sea, ocean; *auf See* at sea; *auf hoher See* on the high seas; *an der See* at the seaside; *zur See gehen (fahren)* go to sea (be a sailor); *in See stechen* put to sea

Seebad *n* seaside resort

Seefahrt *f* navigation

Seegang *m* (-[e]s; *no pl*): *hoher Seegang* heavy sea

Seehafen *m* seaport

Seehund *m* zo seal

Seekarte *f* nautical chart

'**seekrank** *adj* seasick

'**Seekrankheit** *f* seasickness

Seele ['zeːlə] *f* (-; *-n*) soul (*a. fig*)

'**seelenlos** *adj* soulless

'**Seelenruhe** *f* peace of mind; *in aller*

Seelenruhe as cool as you please

seelisch ['zeːlɪʃ] *adj* mental

'**Seelsorge** *f* (-; *no pl*) pastoral care

'**Seelsorger** [-zɔrgɐ] *m* (-s; -), '**Seelsorgerin** *f* (-; -*nen*) pastor

'**Seemacht** *f* sea power

Seemann *m* (-[e]s; *-leute*) seaman, sailor

Seemeile *f* nautical mile

Seenot *f* (-; *no pl*) distress (at sea)

Seenotkreuzer *m* MAR rescue cruiser

Seeräuber *m* pirate

Seereise *f* voyage, cruise

Seerose *f* BOT water lily

Seesack *m* kit bag

Seeschlacht *f* MIL naval battle

Seestreitkräfte *pl* MIL naval forces, navy

'**seetüchtig** *adj* seaworthy

'**Seewarte** *f* naval observatory

Seeweg *m* sea route; *auf dem Seeweg* by sea

Seezeichen *n* seamark

Seezunge *f* zo sole

Segel ['zeːgəl] *n* (-s; -) sail

Segelboot *n* sailboat, *Br* sailing boat

Segelfliegen *n* gliding

Segelflugzeug *n* glider

'**segeln** *v/i* (*ge-*, *sein*) sail, SPORT *a.* yacht

'**Segelschiff** *n* sailing ship; sailing vessel

Segelsport *m* sailing, yachting

Segeltuch *n* canvas, sailcloth

Segen ['zeːgən] *m* (-s; -) blessing (*a. fig*)

Segler ['zeːglɐ] *m* (-s; -) yachtsman

Seglerin ['zeːglərɪn] *f* (-; -*nen*) yachtswoman

segnen ['zeːgnən] *v/t* (*ge-*, *h*) bless

'**Segnung** *f* (-; -*nen*) blessing

Sehbeteiligung ['zeː-] *f* (TV) ratings

sehen ['zeːən] *v/i and v/t* (*irr*, *ge-*, *h*) see; watch; notice; *sehen nach* look after; look for; *sich sehen lassen* show up; *das sieht man (kaum)* it (hardly) shows; *siehst du* (you) see; I told you; *siehe oben (unten, Seite ...)* see above (below, page ...)

'**sehenlassen** *v/refl* (*irr*, *lassen*, *sep*, *no -ge-*, *h*) → **sehen**

'**sehenswert** *adj* worth seeing

'**Sehenswürdigkeit** *f* (-; -*en*) place *etc* worth seeing, sight, *pl* sights

'**Sehkraft** *f* (-; *no pl*) eyesight, vision

Sehne ['zeːnə] *f* (-; *-n*) ANAT sinew; string

sehnen ['zeːnən] *v/refl* (*ge-*, *h*) long (*nach* for), yearn (for); *sich danach sehnen zu inf* be longing to *inf*

'**Sehnerv** *m* ANAT optic nerve

sehnig ['zeːnɪç] *adj* sinewy, GASTR *a.* stringy

sehnlichst ['zeːnlɪçst] *adj* dearest

'**Sehnsucht** *f*, '**sehnsüchtig** *adj* longing,

yearning

sehr [zeːɐ] *adv before adj and adv*: very; *with verbs*: very much, greatly

'Sehtest *m* sight test

seicht [zaiçt] *adj* shallow (*a. fig*)

Seide ['zaidə] *f* (-; -*n*), **'seiden** *adj* silk

'Seidenpa,pier *n* tissue paper

'Seidenraupe *f* zo silkworm

seidig ['zaidıç] *adj* silky

Seife ['zaifə] *f* (-; -*n*) soap

'Seifenblase *f* soap bubble

Seifenlauge *f* (soap)suds

Seifenoper *f* TV soap opera

Seifenschale *f* soap dish

Seifenschaum *m* lather

seifig ['zaifıç] *adj* soapy

Seil [zail] *n* (-[*e*]*s*; -*e*) rope

'Seilbahn *f* cable railway

'seilspringen *v/i* (*only inf*) skip

sein¹ [zain] *v/i* (*irr, ge-, sein*) be; exist; *et. sein lassen* stop *or* quit (doing) s.th.

sein² *poss pron* his, her, its; *seiner, seine, sein(e)s* his, hers

Sein *n* (-*s*; *no pl*) being; existence

seinerseits ['zainɐzaits] *adv* for his part

seiner'zeit *adv* then, in those days

seines'gleichen ['zainəs-] *pron* his equals

seinet'wegen ['zainət-] → *meinetwegen*

'seinlassen *v/t* (*irr, sep, -ge-, h*): *et. seinlassen* → *sein*

seit [zait] *prp and cj* since; *seit 1982* since 1982; *seit drei Jahren* for three years (now); *seit langem (kurzem)* for a long (short) time

seit'dem 1. *adv* since then, since that time, ever since; **2.** *cj* since

Seite ['zaitə] *f* (-; -*n*) side (*a. fig*); page; *auf der linken Seite* on the left(-hand side); *fig auf der e-n (anderen) Seite* on the one (other) hand

'Seitenansicht *f* side view, profile

Seitenblick *m* sidelong glance

Seitenhieb *m* sideswipe

Seitenlinie *f esp soccer*: touchline

seitens ['zaitəns] *prp* (*gen*) on the part of, by

'Seitensprung F *m*: *e-n Seitensprung machen* cheat (on one's wife *or* husband)

'Seitenstechen *n* (-*s*; *no pl*) MED a stitch (in the side)

'seitlich *adj* side …, at the side(s)

'seitwärts [-vɛrts] *adv* sideways, to the side

Sekretär [zekre'tɛːɐ] *m* (-*s*; -*e*) secretary; bureau

Sekretariat [-ta'rjaːt] *n* (-[*e*]*s*; -*e*) (secretary's) office

Sekretärin [-'tɛːrın] *f* (-; -*nen*) secretary

Sekt [zɛkt] *m* (-[*e*]*s*; -*e*) sparkling wine, champagne

Sekte ['zɛktə] *f* (-; -*n*) sect

Sektion [zɛk'tsjoːn] *f* (-; -*en*) section; MED autopsy

Sektor ['zɛktoːɐ] *m* (-*s*; -*en* [zɛk'toːrən]) sector; *fig* field

Sekunde [ze'kʊndə] *f* (-; -*n*) second; *auf die Sekunde* to the second

Se'kundenzeiger *m* second(s) hand

selbe ['zɛlbə] *adj* same

selber ['zɛlbɐ] *pron* → *selbst 1*

selbst [zɛlbst] **1.** *pron*: *ich (du etc) selbst* I (you *etc*) myself (yourself *etc*); *mach es selbst* do it yourself; *et. selbst tun* do s.th. by oneself; *von selbst* by itself; *selbst gemacht* homemade; **2.** *adv* even

'Selbstachtung *f* self-respect

'selbständig *etc* → *selbstständig etc*

'Selbstbedienung(sladen *m*) *f* self-service (store, *Br* shop)

Selbstbefriedigung *f* masturbation

Selbstbeherrschung *f* self-control

Selbstbestimmung *f* self-determination

'selbstbewusst *adj* self-confident, self--assured

'Selbstbewusstsein *n* self-confidence

'Selbstbildnis *n* self-portrait

Selbsterhaltungstrieb *m* survival instinct

Selbsterkenntnis *f* (-; *no pl*) self-knowledge

'selbstgerecht *adj* self-righteous

'Selbsthilfe *f* self-help

Selbsthilfegruppe *f* self-help group

Selbstkostenpreis *m*: *zum Selbstkostenpreis* ECON at cost (price)

'selbstkritisch *adj* self-critical

'Selbstlaut *m* LING vowel

'selbstlos *adj* unselfish

'Selbstmord *m*, **Selbstmörder(in)** suicide

'selbstmörderisch *adj* suicidal

'selbstsicher *adj* self-confident, self-assured

'selbstständig *adj* independent, self-reliant; self-employed

'Selbstständigkeit *f* (-; *no pl*) independence

'Selbststudium *n* (-*s*; *no pl*) self-study

'selbstsüchtig *adj* selfish, ego(t)istic(al)

selbsttätig *adj* automatic

'Selbsttäuschung *f* self-deception

'selbstverständlich 1. *adj* natural; *das ist selbstverständlich* that's a matter of course; **2.** *adv* of course, naturally; *selbstverständlich!* a. by all means!

'Selbstverständlichkeit *f* (-; -*en*) matter

'**Selbstverteidigung** *f* self-defense, *Br* self-defence

Selbstvertrauen *n* self-confidence, self--reliance

Selbstverwaltung *f* self-government, autonomy

Selbstwähldienst *m* TEL automatic long--distance dial(l)ing service

'**selbstzufrieden** *adj* self-satisfied

selchen ['zɛlçən] *Austrian* → **räuchern**

selig ['zeːlɪç] *adj* REL blessed; late; *fig* overjoyed

'**Sellerie** ['zɛləri] *m* (-s; -[s]), *f* (-; -) BOT celeriac; celery

selten ['zɛltən] **1.** *adj* rare; **selten sein** be rare, be scarce; **2.** *adv* rarely, seldom

'**Seltenheit** *f* (-; *no pl*) rarity

seltsam ['zɛltzaːm] *adj* strange, odd

Semester [ze'mɛstɐ] *n* (-s; -) UNIV semester, *esp Br* term

Semikolon [zemi'koːlɔn] *n* (-s; -s) LING semicolon

Seminar [zemi'naːɐ] *n* (-s; -e) UNIV department; seminar; REL seminary; teacher training college

sen. ABBR *of* **senior** sen., Sen., Sr, Snr, senior

Senat [ze'naːt] *m* (-[e]s; -e) senate

Senator [ze'naːtoːɐ] *m* (-s; -en [zena'toːrən]), **Sena'torin** *f* (-; -nen) senator

Sendemast *m* ELECTR mast

senden ['zɛndən] *v/t* ([*irr*,] *ge-*, *h*) send (**mit der Post** by mail, *Br* by post); ELECTR broadcast, transmit, *a.* televise

Sender ['zɛndɐ] *m* (-s; -) radio *or* television station; ELECTR transmitter

'**Sendereihe** *f* TV *or* radio series

Sendeschluss *m* close-down, F sign-off

Sendezeichen *n* call letters (*Br* sign)

Sendezeit *f* air time

'**Sendung** *f* (-; -en) broadcast, program(-me), *a.* telecast; ECON consignment, shipment; **auf Sendung sein** be on the air

Senf [zɛnf] *m* (-[e]s; -e) mustard (*a.* BOT)

senil [ze'niːl] *adj* senile

Senilität [zenili'tɛːt] *f* (-; *no pl*) senility

Senior ['zeːnjoːɐ] **1.** *m* (-s; -en [ze'njoːrən]) senior (*a.* SPORT); senior citizen; **2.** *adj* senior

Seni'orenheim *n* old people's home

Seni'orin *f* (-; -nen) senior citizen

Senke ['zɛŋkə] *f* (-; -n) GEOGR depression, hollow

'**senken** *v/t* (*ge-*, *h*) lower (*a.* one's voice), *a.* bow (one's head); ECON *a.* reduce, cut; **sich senken** drop, go *or* come down

'**senkrecht** *adj* vertical

Sensation [zɛnza'tsjoːn] *f* (-; -en) sensation

sensationell [zɛnzatsjo'nɛl] *adj*, **Sensati'ons...** *in cpds* ...*blatt etc*: sensational (...)

Sense ['zɛnzə] *f* (-; -n) AGR scythe

sensibel [zɛn'ziːbəl] *adj* sensitive

sensibilisieren [zɛnzibili'ziːrən] *v/t* (*no -ge-*, *h*) sensitize (**für** to)

sentimental [zɛntimɛn'taːl] *adj* sentimental

Sentimentalität [zɛntimɛntali'tɛːt] *f* (-; -en) sentimentality

September [zɛp'tɛmbɐ] *m* (-[s]; -) September

Serenade [zere'naːdə] *f* (-; -n) MUS serenade

Serie ['zeːrjə] *f* (-; -n) series, TV *etc a.* serial; set; **in Serie** produce *etc* in series

'**serienmäßig** *adj* series(-produced); standard

'**Seriennummer** *f* serial number

Serienwagen *m* MOT standard-type car

seriös [ze'rjøːs] *adj* respectable; honest; serious

Serum ['zeːrʊm] *n* (-s; -ren, -ra) serum

Service[1] ['zœr'viːs] *n* (-[s]; -) set; service

Service[2] ['zøːɐvis] *m*, *n* (-; -s) service

servieren [zɛr'viːrən] *v/t* (*no -ge-*, *h*) serve

Serviererin [zɛr'viːrərɪn] *f* (-; -nen) waitress

Serviertochter [zɛr'viːɐ-] *Swiss f* waitress

Serviette [zɛr'vjɛtə] *f* (-; -n) napkin, *esp Br* serviette

Servobremse ['zɛrvo-] *f* MOT servo *or* power brake

Servolenkung *f* MOT servo(-assisted) *or* power steering

Sessel ['zɛsəl] *m* (-s; -) armchair, easy chair

Sessellift *m* chair lift

sesshaft ['zɛshaft] *adj*: **sesshaft werden** settle (down)

Set [zɛt] *n*, *m* (-s; -s) place mat

setzen ['zɛtsən] *v/t and v/i* (*ge-*, *h*) put, set (*a.* PRINT, AGR, MAR), AGR *a.* plant; place; seat *s.o.*; **setzen über** (*acc*) jump over; cross (*river*); **setzen auf** (*acc*) bet on, back; **sich setzen** sit down; CHEM *etc* settle; **sich setzen auf** (*acc*) get on, mount; **sich setzen in** (*acc*) get into; **sich zu j-m setzen** sit beside *or* with s.o.; **setzen Sie sich bitte!** take *or* have a seat!

Setzer ['zɛtsɐ] *m* (-s; -) PRINT compositor, typesetter

Setzerei [zɛtsə'rai] *f* (-; -en) PRINT composing room

Seuche ['zɔyçə] *f* (-; -n) epidemic (disease)

seufzen ['zɔyftsən] *v/i* (*ge-*, *h*), **Seufzer** ['zɔyftsɐ] *m* (*-s*; *-*) sigh

Sexismus [zɛ'ksɪsmʊs] *m* (*-*; *no pl*) sexism

Sexist [zɛ'ksɪst] *m* (*-en*; *-en*), **se'xistisch** *adj* sexist

Sexual... [zɛ'ksua:l-] *in cpds* ...*erziehung*, ...*leben*, ...*trieb etc*: sex(ual) ...

Sexualverbrechen *n* sex crime

sexuell [zɛ'ksuɛl] *adj* sexual; **sexuelle Belästigung** (sexual) harassment

sexy ['zɛksi] *adj* sexy

sezieren [ze'tsi:rən] *v/t* (*no -ge-*, *h*) MED dissect (*a. fig*); perform an autopsy on

Showgeschäft ['ʃou-] *n* (*-[e]s*; *no pl*) show business

sich [zɪç] *refl pron* oneself; himself, herself, itself; *pl* themselves; yourself, *pl* yourselves; **sich ansehen** look at oneself; look at each other

Sichel ['zɪçəl] *f* (*-*; *-n*) AGR sickle; ASTR crescent

sicher ['zɪçɐ] **1.** *adj* safe (*vor dat* from), secure (from); *esp* TECH proof (*gegen* against); *fig* certain, sure; reliable; (*sich*) **sicher sein** be sure (*e-r Sache* of s.th.; **dass** that); **2.** *adv* safely; **sicher!** of course, sure(ly); certainly; probably; **du hast** (**bist**) **sicher ...** you must have (be) ...

'Sicherheit *f* (*-*; *-en*) a) (*no pl*) security (*a.* MIL, POL, ECON); safety (*a.* TECH); *fig* certainty; skill; (*sich*) **in Sicherheit bringen** get to safety, b) ECON cover

'Sicherheits... *esp* TECH *in cpds* ...*glas*, ...*nadel*, ...*schloss etc*: safety ...

Sicherheitsgurt *m* seat belt, safety belt

Sicherheitsmaßnahme *f* safety (POL security) measure

'sicherlich *adv* → **sicher** 2

'sichern *v/t* (*ge-*, *h*) protect, safeguard; secure (*a.* MIL, TECH); EDP save; **sich sichern** secure o.s. (*gegen*, *vor dat* against, from)

'sicherstellen *v/t* (*sep*, *-ge-*, *h*) secure; guarantee

Sicherung ['zɪçərʊŋ] *f* (*-*; *-en*) securing; safeguard(-ing); TECH safety device; ELECTR fuse

'Sicherungskasten *m* ELECTR fuse box

Sicherungsko,pie *f* EDP backup; **e-e Sicherungskopie machen** (**von**) back up

Sicht [zɪçt] *f* (*-*; *no pl*) visibility; view; **in Sicht kommen** come into sight *or* view; **auf lange Sicht** in the long run

'sichtbar *adj* visible

'sichten ['zɪçtən] *v/t* (*ge-*, *h*) sight; *fig* sort (through *or* out)

'Sichtkarte *f* season ticket

'sichtlich *adv* visibly

'Sichtweite *f* visibility; **in** (**außer**) **Sichtweite** within (out of) sight

sickern ['zɪkɐn] *v/i* (*ge-*, *sein*) trickle, ooze, seep

sie [zi:] *pers pron* she; it; *pl* they; **Sie** you

Sieb [zi:p] *n* (*-[e]s*; *-e*) sieve; strainer

sieben[1] ['zi:bən] *v/t* (*ge-*, *h*) sieve, sift

'sieben[2] *adj* seven

Sieben'meter *m* SPORT penalty shot *or* throw

siebte ['zi:ptə] *adj*, **'Siebtel** *n* (*-s*; *-*) seventh

siebzehn(te) ['zi:p-] *adj* seventeen(th)

siebzig ['zi:ptsɪç] *adj* seventy

'siebzigste *adj* seventieth

siedeln ['zi:dəln] *v/i* (*ge-*, *h*) settle

sieden ['zi:dən] *v/t and v/i* ([*irr*,] *ge-*, *h*) boil, simmer

'Siedepunkt *m* boiling point (*a. fig*)

Siedler ['zi:dlɐ] *m* (*-s*; *-*) settler

Siedlung ['zi:dlʊŋ] *f* (*-*; *-en*) settlement; housing development

Sieg [zi:k] *m* (*-[e]s*; *-e*) victory, SPORT *a.* win

Siegel ['zi:gəl] *n* (*-s*; *-*) seal, signet

'Siegellack *m* sealing wax

'siegeln *v/t* (*ge-*, *h*) seal

siegen ['zi:gən] *v/i* (*ge-*, *h*) win

Sieger ['zi:gɐ] *m* (*-s*; *-*), **Siegerin** ['zi:gə-rɪn] *f* (*-*; *-nen*) winner

'siegreich *adj* winning; victorious

Signal [zɪ'gna:l] *n* (*-s*; *-e*), **signalisieren** [zɪgnali'zi:rən] *v/t* (*no -ge-*, *h*) signal

signieren [zɪ'gni:rən] *v/t* (*no -ge-*, *h*) sign

Silbe ['zɪlbə] *f* (*-*; *-n*) syllable

'Silbentrennung *f* LING syllabification

Silber ['zɪlbɐ] *n* (*-s*; *no pl*) silver; silverware

'silbergrau *adj* silver-gray (*Br* -grey)

'Silberhochzeit *f* silver wedding

'silbern *adj* silver

Silhouette [zi'luɛtə] *f* (*-*; *-n*) silhouette; skyline

Silikon [zili'ko:n] *n* (*-s*; *-e*) CHEM silicone

Silizium [zi'li:tsjʊm] *n* (*-s*; *no pl*) CHEM silicon

Silvester [zɪl'vɛstɐ] *n* (*-s*; *-*) New Year's Eve

Sims [zɪms] *m*, *n* (*-es*; *-e*) ledge; windowsill

simulieren [zimu'li:rən] *v/t and v/i* TECH *etc* simulate; sham

simultan [zimʊl'ta:n] *adj* simultaneous

Sinfonie [zɪnfo'ni:] *f* (*-*; *-n*) MUS symphony

singen ['zɪŋən] *v/t and v/i* (*irr*, *ge-*, *h*) sing (**richtig** [**falsch**] in [out of] tune)

Singular ['zɪŋgulaɐ] *m* (*-s*; *-e*) LING singular

Singvogel ['zɪŋ-] *m* zo songbird

sinken ['zɪŋkən] *v/i* (*irr*, ge-, sein) sink (*a. fig*), go down (*a.* ECON), ASTR *a.* set; *prices etc*: fall, drop

Sinn [zɪn] *m* (-[e]s; -e) sense (*für* of); mind; meaning; point, idea; *im Sinn haben* have in mind; *es hat keinen Sinn* (*zu warten etc*) it's no use *or* good (waiting *etc*)

'**Sinnbild** *n* symbol

'**sinnentstellend** *adj* distorting

Sinnesorgan ['zɪnəs-] *n* sense organ

Sinnestäuschung *f* hallucination

Sinneswandel *m* change of mind

'**sinnlich** *adj* sensuous; sensory; sensual

'**Sinnlichkeit** *f* (-; *no pl*) sensuality

'**sinnlos** *adj* senseless; useless

'**sinnverwandt** *adj* synonymous

'**sinnvoll** *adj* meaningful; useful; wise, sensible

Sintflut ['zɪnt-] *f the* Flood

Sippe ['zɪpə] *f* (-; -n) (extended) family, clan

Sirene [zi're:nə] *f* (-; -n) siren

Sirup ['zi:rʊp] *m* (-s; -e) sirup, *Br* syrup; treacle, molasses

Sitte ['zɪtə] *f* (-; -n) custom, tradition; *pl* morals; manners

'**Sittenlosigkeit** *f* (-; *no pl*) immorality

'**Sittenpoli,zei** *f* vice squad

'**sittenwidrig** *adj* immoral

'**Sittlichkeitsverbrechen** *n* sex crime

Situation [zitua'tsjo:n] *f* (-; -en) situation; position

Sitz [zɪts] *m* (-es; -e) seat; fit

Sitzblo,ckade *f* sit-down demonstration

sitzen ['zɪtsən] *v/i* (*irr*, ge-, h) sit (*an dat* at; *auf dat* on); be; fit; F do time; *sitzen bleiben* keep one's seat; PED have to repeat a year; F *sitzen bleiben auf* (*dat*) be left with; F *j-n sitzen lassen* leave s.o. in the lurch, let s.o. down

'**sitzenbleiben** *v/i* (*irr*, **bleiben**, sep, -ge-, sein*) → **sitzen**

sitzenlassen *v/i* (*irr*, **lassen**, sep, *no -ge-*, sein*) *a. fig → **sitzen**

'**Sitzplatz** *m* seat

'**Sitzstreik** *m* sit-down strike

'**Sitzung** *f* (-; -en) session (*a.* PARL), meeting, conference

Skala ['ska:la] *f* (-; -en) scale, *fig a.* range

Skalp [skalp] *m* (-s; -e), **skalpieren** [skal-'pi:rən] *v/t* (*no -ge-*, h) scalp

Skandal [skan'da:l] *m* (-s; -e) scandal; *ein Skandal sein* be scandalous

skandalös [skanda'lø:s] *adj* scandalous, shocking

Skelett [ske'lɛt] *n* (-[e]s; -e) skeleton

Skepsis ['skɛpsɪs] *f* (-; *no pl*) skepticism, *Br* scepticism

Skeptiker ['skɛptikɐ] *m* (-s; -) skeptic, *Br* sceptic

skeptisch ['skɛptɪʃ] *adj* skeptical, *Br* sceptical

Ski [ʃi:] *m* (-s; -er ['ʃi:ɐ]) ski; *Ski laufen or fahren* ski

Skifahrer(in) skier

Skifliegen *n* ski flying

Skilift *m* ski lift

Skipiste *f* ski run

Skischuh *m* ski boot

Skisport *m* skiing

Skispringen *n* ski jumping

Skizze ['skɪtsə] *f* (-; -n), **skizzieren** [skɪ-'tsi:rən] *v/t* (*no -ge-*, h) sketch

Sklave ['skla:və] *m* (-n; -n) slave (*a. fig*)

Sklaverei [skla:və'rai] *f* (-; *no pl*) slavery

'**Sklavin** *f* (-; -nen) slave (*a. fig*)

'**sklavisch** *adj* slavish (*a. fig*)

Skonto ['skɔnto] *m, n* (-s; -s) ECON (cash) discount

Skorpion [skɔr'pjo:n] *m* (-s; -e) zo scorpion; ASTR Scorpio; *er ist (ein) Skorpion* he's (a) Scorpio

Skrupel ['skru:pəl] *m* (-s; -) scruple, qualm

'**skrupellos** *adj* unscrupulous

Skulptur [skʊlp'tu:ɐ] *f* (-; -en) sculpture

Slalom ['sla:lɔm] *m* (-s; -s) slalom

Slawe ['sla:və] *m* (-n; -n), '**Slawin** *f* (-; -nen) Slav

'**slawisch** *adj* Slav(ic)

Slip [slɪp] *m* (-s; -s) briefs, panties

'**Slipeinlage** *f* panty liner

Slipper ['slɪpɐ] *m* (-s; -) loafer, *esp Br* slip--on (shoe)

Slowake [slo'va:kə] *m* (-n; -n) Slovak

Slowakei [slova'kai] *f* Slovakia

Slo'wakin *f* (-; -nen), **slo'wakisch** *adj* Slovak

Smaragd [sma'rakt] *m* (-[e]s; -e) MIN, **sma'ragdgrün** *adj* emerald

Smoking ['smo:kɪŋ] *m* (-s; -s) tuxedo, *Br* dinner jacket

Snob [snɔp] *m* (-s; -s) snob

Snobismus [sno'bɪsmʊs] *m* (-; *no pl*) snobbery

sno'bistisch *adj* snobbish

so [zo:] **1.** *adv* so; like this *or* that, this *or* that way; thus; such; (*nicht*) *so groß wie* (not) as big as; *so ein(e)* such a; *so sehr* so (F that) much; *und so weiter* and so on; *oder so et.* or s.th. like that; *oder so* or so; *so, fangen wir an!* well *or* all right, let's begin!; F *so weit sein* be ready; *es ist so weit* it's time; *so genannt* so-called; *doppelt so viel* twice as much; *so viel wie möglich* as much

as possible; **2.** *cj* so, therefore; **so dass**
so that; **3.** *int:* **so!** all right!, o.k.!; that's
it!; **ach so!** I see

s.o. ABBR *of* **siehe oben** see above
so'bald [zo-] *cj* as soon as
Socke ['zɔkə] *f* (-; *-n*) sock
Sockel ['zɔkəl] *m* (*-s*; -) base; pedestal
Sodbrennen ['zo:t-] *n* (*-s*; *no pl*) MED
  heartburn
soeben [zo'e:bən] *adv* just (now)
Sofa ['zo:fa] *n* (*-s*; *-s*) sofa, settee, daven-
  port
sofern [zo'fɛrn] *cj* if, provided that; **so-**
fern nicht unless
soff [zɔf] *pret of* **saufen**
sofort [zo'fɔrt] *adv* at once, immediately,
  right away
So'fortbildkamera *f* PHOT instant camera
Software ['zɔftwɛːɐ] *f* EDP software
Softwarepa,ket *n* software package
sog [zo:k] *pret of* **saugen**
Sog *m* (*-[e]s*; *-e*) suction, MAR *a.* wake
sogar [zo'ga:ɐ] *adv* even
Sohle ['zo:lə] *f* (-; *-n*) sole; *mining:* floor
Sohn [zo:n] *m* (*-[e]s*; *Söhne* ['zøːnə]) son
Sojabohne ['zo:ja-] *f* BOT soybean
so'lange [zo-] *cj* as long as
Solar... [zo'la:ɐ-] *in cpds* ...*energie etc:* solar ...
solch [zɔlç] *dem pron* such, like this *or*
  that
Sold [zɔlt] *m* (*-[e]s*; *-e*) MIL pay
Soldat [zɔl'da:t] *m* (*-en*; *-en*), **Sol'datin** *f*
  (-; *-nen*) soldier
Söldner ['zœldnɐ] *m* (*-s*; -) MIL mercenary
Sole ['zo:lə] *f* (-; *-n*) brine, salt water
solidarisch [zoli'da:rɪʃ] *adj:* **sich solida-**
risch erklären mit declare one's solidarity with
solíde [zo'li:də] *adj* solid, *fig a.* sound;
  reasonable (*prices*); steady (*person*)
Solist [zo'lɪst] *m* (*-en*; *-en*), **So'listin** *f* (-;
  -nen) soloist
Soll [zɔl] *n* (*-[s]*; *-[s]*) ECON debit; target,
  quota; **Soll und Haben** debit and credit
sollen ['zɔlən] *v/i* (*ge-*, *h*) *and v/aux* (*irr*,
  no -ge-, *h*) be to; be supposed to; **(was)**
soll ich ...? (what) shall I ...?; **du soll-**
test (**nicht**) ... you should(n't) ...; you
  ought(n't) to; **was soll das?** what's the
  idea?
Solo ['zo:lo] *n* (*-s*, *-s*, *Soli*) *esp* MUS solo;
  SPORT solo attempt *etc*
so'mit [zo-] *cj* thus, so, consequently
Sommer ['zɔmɐ] *m* (*-s*; -) summer (time);
  im Sommer in (the) summer
Sommerferien *pl* summer vacation (*Br*
  holidays)
Sommerfrische *f* summer resort

'**sommerlich** *adj* summery
'**Sommersprosse** *f* freckle
'**sommersprossig** *adj* freckled
'**Sommerzeit** *f* summertime; daylight saving (*Br* summer) time
Sonate [zo'na:tə] *f* (-; *-n*) MUS sonata
Sonde ['zɔndə] *f* (-; *-n*) probe (*a.* MED)
Sonder... ['zɔndɐ-] *in cpds* ...*angebot*,
  ...*ausgabe*, ...*flug*, ...*preis*, ...*wunsch*,
  ...*zug etc:* special ...
'**sonderbar** *adj* strange, F funny
'**Sonderling** *m* (*-s*; *-e*) eccentric
'**Sondermüll** *m* hazardous (*or* special tox-
  ic) waste
Sondermülldepo,nie *f* special waste
  dump
sondern ['zɔndɐn] *cj* but; **nicht nur ...,**
sondern auch ... not only ... but also ...
'**Sonderschule** *f* special school (for the
  handicapped *etc*)
Sonnabend ['zɔn-] *m* Saturday
Sonne ['zɔnə] *f* (-; *-n*) sun
sonnen ['zɔnən] *v/refl* (*ge-*, *h*) sunbathe
'**Sonnenaufgang** *m* (**bei Sonnenauf-**
gang at) sunrise
'**Sonnenbad** *n:* **ein Sonnenbad nehmen**
  sunbathe
Sonnenbank *f* (-; *-bänke*) sunbed
Sonnenblume *f* BOT sunflower
Sonnenbrand *m* sunburn
Sonnenbräune *f* suntan
Sonnenbrille *f* sunglasses
Sonnencreme *f* suntan lotion, *Br* sun
  cream
Sonnenener,gie *f* solar energy
Sonnenfinsternis *f* solar eclipse
'**sonnen'klar** F *adj* (as) clear as daylight
'**Sonnenkol,lektor** *m* solar panel
Sonnenlicht *n* (*-[e]s*, *no pl*) sunlight
Sonnenöl *n* suntan oil
Sonnenschein *m* sunshine
Sonnenschirm *m* sunshade
Sonnenschutz *m* suntan lotion
Sonnenseite *f* sunny side (*a. fig*)
Sonnenstich *m* sunstroke
Sonnenstrahl *m* sunbeam
Sonnensys,tem *n* solar system
Sonnenuhr *f* sundial
Sonnenuntergang *m* sunset
sonnig ['zɔnɪç] *adj* sunny (*a. fig*)
Sonntag ['zɔn-] *m* Sunday; (**am**) **Sonntag**
  on Sunday
'**sonntags** *adv* on Sundays
'**Sonntagsfahrer** *contp m* MOT Sunday
  driver
sonst [zɔnst] *adv* else; otherwise, or
  (else); normally, usually; **sonst noch**
et. (jemand)? anything (anyone) else?;
sonst noch Fragen? any other ques-

S

tions?; **sonst nichts** nothing else; **alles wie sonst** everything as usual; **nichts ist wie sonst** nothing is as it used to be

'sonstig *adj* other

Sopran [zo'pra:n] *m* (*-s; -e*) MUS, **Sopranistin** [zopra'nıstın] *f* (*-; -nen*) MUS soprano

Sorge ['zɔrgə] *f* (*-; -n*) worry; sorrow; trouble; care; **sich Sorgen machen (um)** worry *or* be worried (about); **keine Sorge!** don't worry!

sorgen ['zɔrgən] (*ge-, h*) **1.** *v/i*: **sorgen für** care for, take care of; **dafür sorgen, dass** see (to it) that; **2.** *v/refl*: **sich sorgen um** worry *or* be worried about

'Sorgenkind *n* problem child

Sorgfalt ['zɔrkfalt] *f* (*-; no pl*) care

sorgfältig ['zɔrkfɛltıç] *adj* careful

sorglos ['zɔrk-] *adj* carefree; careless

Sorte ['zɔrtə] *f* (*-; -n*) sort, kind, type

sortieren [zɔr'ti:rən] *v/t* (*no -ge-, h*) sort; arrange

Sortiment [zɔrti'mɛnt] *n* (*-[e]s; -e*) ECON assortment

Soße ['zo:sə] *f* (*-; -n*) sauce; gravy

sott [zɔt] *pret of* **sieden**

Souffleur [zu'flø:ɐ] *m* (*-s; -e*), **Souffleuse** [zu'flø:zə] *f* (*-; -n*) THEA prompter

soufflieren [zu'fli:rən] *v/i* (*no -ge-, h*) THEA prompt (*j-m* s.o.)

souverän [zuvə'rɛ:n] *adj* POL sovereign

Souveränität [zuvərɛni'tɛ:t] *f* (*-; no pl*) POL sovereignty

so'viel [zo-] *cj* as far as; → **so**

so'weit *cj* as far as; → **so**

so'wie *cj* as well as, and ... as well; as soon as

sowie'so *adv* anyway, anyhow, in any case

Sowjet [zɔ'vjɛt] *m* (*-s; -s*), **sow'jetisch** *adj* HIST Soviet

so'wohl [zo-] *cj*: **sowohl Lehrer als (auch) Schüler** both teachers and students

sozial [zo'tsja:l] *adj* social

Sozi'al... *in cpds* ...**arbeiter**, ...**demokrat**, ...**versicherung** *etc*: social ...

Sozialhilfe *f* welfare, *Br* social security; **Sozialhilfe beziehen** be on welfare (*Br* social security)

Sozialismus [zotsja'lısmʊs] *m* (*-; no pl*) socialism

Sozialist(in) (*-en/-; -en/ -nen*), **sozia'listisch** *adj* socialist

Sozi'alkunde *f* PED social studies

Sozi'alstaat *m* welfare state

Soziologe [zotsjo'lo:gə] *m* (*-n; -n*) sociologist

Soziologie [zotsjolo'gi:] *f* (*-; no pl*) sociology

Sozio'login *f* (*-; -nen*) sociologist

soziologisch [zotsjo'lo:gıʃ] *adj* sociological

sozu'sagen *adv* so to speak

Spagat [ʃpa'ga:t] *m*: **Spagat machen** do the splits

Spalier [ʃpa'li:ɐ] *n* (*-s; -e*) BOT espalier; MIL *etc* lane

Spalt [ʃpalt] *m* (*-[e]s; -e*) crack, gap

Spalte ['ʃpaltə] *f* (*-; -n*) → **Spalt**; PRINT column

'**spalten** *v/t* ([*irr,*] *ge-, h*) split (*a. fig*); POL divide; **sich spalten** split (up)

'**Spaltung** *f* (*-; -en*) split(ting); PHYS fission; *fig* split; POL division

Span [ʃpa:n] *m* (*-[e]s; Späne* ['ʃpɛ:nə]) chip; *pl* TECH shavings

Spange ['ʃpaŋə] *f* (*-; -n*) clasp

Spaniel ['ʃpa:njəl] *m* (*-s; -s*) ZO spaniel

Spanien ['ʃpa:njən] Spain

Spanier ['ʃpa:njɐ] *m* (*-s; -*), **Spanierin** ['ʃpa:njərın] *f* (*-; -nen*) Spaniard

spanisch ['ʃpa:nıʃ] *adj* Spanish

spann [ʃpan] *pret of* **spinnen**

Spann *m* (*-[e]s; -e*) ANAT instep

Spanne ['ʃpanə] *f* (*-; -n*) span

'**spannen** (*ge-, h*) **1.** *v/t* stretch, tighten; put up (*line*); cock (*gun*); draw, bend (*bow*); **2.** *v/i* be (too) tight

spannend *adj* exciting, thrilling, gripping

'**Spannung** *f* (*-; -en*) tension (*a.* TECH, POL, PSYCH); ELECTR voltage; *fig* suspense, excitement

'**Spannweite** *f* span, *fig a.* range

Sparbuch ['ʃpa:ɐ-] *n* savings book

Sparbüchse *f esp Br* money box

sparen ['ʃpa:rən] *v/i and v/t* (*ge-, h*) save; economize; **sparen für** *or* **auf** (*acc*) save up for

Sparer(in) ['ʃpa:rɐ (-rərın)] (*-s; -/-; -nen*) saver

'**Sparschwein(chen)** *n* piggy bank

Spargel ['ʃpargəl] *m* (*-s; -*) BOT asparagus

'**Sparkasse** *f* savings bank

'**Sparkonto** *n* savings account

spärlich ['ʃpɛ:rlıç] *adj* sparse, scant; scanty; poor (*attendance*)

sparsam ['ʃpa:rza:m] *adj* economical (**mit** of); **sparsam leben** lead a frugal life; **sparsam umgehen mit** use sparingly; go easy on

'**Sparsamkeit** *f* (*-; no pl*) economy

Spaß [ʃpa:s] *m* (*-es; Späße* ['ʃpɛ:sə]), *Austrian a.* **Spass** fun; joke; **aus** (**nur zum**) **Spaß** (just) for fun; **es macht viel** (**keinen**) **Spaß** it's great (no) fun; **j-m den Spaß verderben** spoil s.o.'s fun; **er macht nur Spaß** he is only joking (F kidding); **keinen Spaß verstehen** have no sense of humo(u)r**spaßen** ['ʃpaːsən] *v/i* (*ge-*, *h*) joke

spaßig ['ʃpaːsɪç] *adj* funny

'**Spaßvogel** *m* joker

spät [ʃpɛːt] *adj and adv* late; *am späten Nachmittag* late in the afternoon; *wie spät ist es?* what time is it?; *von früh bis spät* from morning till night; (*fünf Minuten*) *zu spät kommen* be (five minutes) late; *bis später!* see you (later)!; → *früher*

Spaten ['ʃpaːtən] *m* (*-s*; -) spade

'**spätestens** *adv* at the latest

Spatz [ʃpats] *m* (*-en*; *-en*) ZO sparrow

spazieren [ʃpa'tsiːrən]: *spazieren fahren* go (take *s.o.*) for a drive; take *s.o.* out; *spazieren gehen* go for a walk

Spazierfahrt [ʃpa'tsiːɐ-] *f* drive, ride

Spa'ziergang *m* walk; *e-n Spaziergang machen* go for a walk

Spa'ziergänger(in) [-gɛŋɐ (-ŋərɪn)] (*-s*; -/-; *-nen*) walker

Specht [ʃpɛçt] *m* (*-[e]s*; *-e*) ZO woodpecker

Speck [ʃpɛk] *m* (*-[e]s*; *-e*) bacon

speckig ['ʃpɛkɪç] *fig adj* greasy

Spediteur [ʃpedi'tøːɐ] *m* (*-s*; *-e*) shipping agent; remover

Spedition [ʃpedi'tsjoːn] *f* (*-*; *-en*) shipping agency; moving (*Br* removal) firm

Speer [ʃpeːɐ] *m* (*-[e]s*; *-e*) spear; SPORT javelin

Speiche ['ʃpaiçə] *f* (*-*; *-n*) spoke

Speichel ['ʃpaiçəl] *m* (*-s*; *no pl*) saliva, spit

Speicher ['ʃpaiçɐ] *m* (*-s*; -) storehouse; tank, reservoir; ARCH attic; EDP memory, store

Speicherdichte *f* EDP bit density

Speicherkapazi,**tät** *f* EDP memory capacity

'**speichern** *v/t* (*ge-*, *h*) store (up)

Speicherung ['ʃpaiçərʊŋ] *f* (*-*; *-en*) storage

speien ['ʃpaiən] *v/t* (*irr*, *ge-*, *h*) spit; spout; *volcano etc*: belch

Speise ['ʃpaizə] *f* (*-*; *-n*) food; dish

Speiseeis *n* ice cream

Speisekammer *f* larder, pantry

Speisekarte *f* menu

'**speisen** (*ge-*, *h*) **1.** *v/i* dine; **2.** *v/t* feed (*a.* ELECTR *etc*)

'**Speiseröhre** *f* ANAT gullet

Speisesaal *m* dining hall

Speisewagen *m* RAIL diner, *esp Br* dining car

Spekulant [ʃpeku'lant] *m* (*-en*; *-en*) ECON speculator

Spekulation [ʃpekula'tsjoːn] *f* (*-*; *-en*) speculation, ECON *a.* venture

spekulieren [ʃpeku'liːrən] *v/i* (*no -ge-*, *h*) ECON speculate (*auf acc* on; *mit* in)

Spende ['ʃpɛndə] *f* (*-*; *-n*) gift; contribution; donation

'**spenden** *v/t* (*ge-*, *h*) give (*a. fig*); donate (*a.* MED)

Spender ['ʃpɛndɐ] *m* (*-s*; -) giver; donor (*a.* MED), **Spenderin** *f* (*-*; *-nen*) donor (*a.* MED)

spendieren [ʃpɛn'diːrən] *v/t* (*no -ge-*, *h*) *j-m et. spendieren* treat s.o. to s.th.

Spengler ['ʃpɛŋlɐ] *Austrian m* → **Klempner**

Sperling ['ʃpɛrlɪŋ] *m* (*-s*; *-e*) ZO sparrow

Sperre ['ʃpɛrə] *f* (*-*; *-n*) barrier, RAIL *a.* gate; *fig* stop; TECH lock(ing device); barricade; SPORT suspension; PSYCH mental block; ECON embargo

'**sperren** *v/t* (*ge-*, *h*) close; ECON embargo; cut off; stop (*check*); SPORT suspend; obstruct; *sperren in* (*acc*) lock (up) in

'**Sperrholz** *n* plywood

Sperrmüllabfuhr *f* removal of bulky refuse

'**Sperrung** *f* (*-*; *-en*) closing

Spesen ['ʃpeːzən] *pl* expenses

Spezi ['ʃpeːtsi] F *m* (*-s*; *-[s]*) buddy, pal

Spezialausbildung [ʃpe'tsjaːl-] *f* special training

Spezialgebiet *n* special field, special(i)ty

Spezialgeschäft *n* specialized shop *or* store

spezialisieren [ʃpetsjali'ziːrən] *v/refl* (*no -ge-*, *h*) specialize (*auf acc* in)

Spezialist(in) [ʃpetsja'lɪst(ɪn)] (*-en*; *-en*/-; *-nen*) specialist

Spezialität [ʃpetsjali'tɛːt] *f* (*-*; *-en*) special(i)ty

speziell [ʃpe'tsjɛl] *adj* specific, particular

spezifisch [ʃpe'tsiːfɪʃ] *adj* specific; *spezifisches Gewicht* specific gravity

Sphäre ['sfɛːrə] *f* (*-*; *-n*) sphere (*a. fig*)

spicken ['ʃpɪkən] (*ge-*, *h*) **1.** *v/t* GASTR lard (*a. fig*); **2.** F *v/i* PED crib

spie [ʃpiː] *pret of* **speien**

Spiegel ['ʃpiːgəl] *m* (*-s*; -) mirror (*a. fig*)

'**Spiegelbild** *n* reflection (*a. fig*)

'**Spiegelei** *n* GASTR fried egg

'**spiegel'glatt** *adj* glassy; icy

'**spiegeln** *v/i and v/t* (*ge-*, *h*) reflect (*a. fig*); shine; *sich spiegeln* be reflected (*a. fig*)

'**Spiegelung** *f* (*-*; *-en*) reflection

Spiel [ʃpiːl] *n* (*-[e]s*; *-e*) game (*a. fig*); match; play (*a.* THEA *etc*); gambling; *fig* gamble; *auf dem Spiel stehen* be at stake; *aufs Spiel setzen* risk

spielen ['ʃpiːlən] *v/i and v/t* (*ge-*, *h*) play (*a. fig*) (*um* for); THEA act; perform; gam-

S

ble; do (*the pools etc*); **Klavier** *etc* **spie-len** play the piano *etc*

'**spielend** *fig adv* easily

Spieler ['ʃpiːlɐ] *m* (*-s*; -), **Spielerin** ['ʃpiː-lərɪn] *f* (-; *-nen*) player; gambler

'**Spielfeld** *n* (playing) field, pitch

Spielca,sino *n* casino

Spielfilm *m* feature film

Spielhalle *f* amusement arcade, game room

Spielkame,rad(in) playmate

Spielkarte *f* playing card

Spielka,sino *n* casino

Spielmarke *f* counter, chip

Spielplan *m* THEA *etc* program(me)

Spielplatz *m* playground

Spielraum *fig m* play, scope

Spielregel *f* rule (of the game)

Spielsachen *pl* toys

Spielstand *m* score

Spieluhr *f* music (*Br* musical) box

Spielverderber(in) (*-s*; -/-; *-nen*) spoil-sport

Spielwaren *pl* toys

Spielzeit *f* THEA, SPORT season; playing (*film*: running) time

'**Spielzeug** *n* toy(s); **Spielzeug...** *in cpds* ...pistole *etc*: toy ...

Spieß [ʃpiːs] *m* (*-es*; *-e*) MIL spear; GASTR spit; skewer

spießen ['ʃpiːsən] *v/t* (*ge-*, *h*) skewer

Spießer ['ʃpiːsɐ] F *contp m* (*-s*; -), '**spie-ßig** F *contp adj* philistine

Spinat [ʃpi'naːt] *m* (*-[e]s*; *-e*) BOT spinach

Spind [ʃpɪnt] *n*, *m* (*-[e]s*; *-e*) locker

Spindel ['ʃpɪndəl] *f* (-; *-n*) spindle

Spinne ['ʃpɪnə] *f* (-; *-n*) ZO spider

'**spinnen** (*irr, ge-, h*) **1.** *v/t* spin (*a. fig*); **2.** F *contp v/i* be nuts; talk nonsense

Spinner ['ʃpɪnɐ] *m* (*-s*; -), '**Spinnerin** *f* (-; *-nen*) spinner; F *contp* nut, crackpot

'**Spinnrad** *n* spinning wheel

'**Spinnwebe** *f* (-; *-n*) cobweb

Spion [ʃpjoːn] *m* (*-s*; *-e*) spy

Spionage [ʃpjo'naːʒə] *f* (-; *no pl*) espionage

spionieren [ʃpjo'niːrən] *v/i* (*no -ge-*, *h*) spy; F snoop

Spi'onin *f* (-; *-nen*) spy

Spirale [ʃpi'raːlə] *f* (-; *-n*), **spi'ralförmig** [-fœrmɪç] *adj* spiral

Spirituosen [ʃpiri'tuoːzən] *pl* spirits

Spiritus ['ʃpiːrɪtʊs] *m* spirit

Spital [ʃpi'taːl] *Austrian, Swiss n* (*-s*; *Spi-täler* [ʃpi'tɛːlɐ]) hospital

spitz [ʃpɪts] *adj* pointed (*a. fig*); MATH acute; **spitze Zunge** sharp tongue

'**Spitzbogen** *m* ARCH pointed arch

Spitze ['ʃpɪtsə] *f* (-; *-n*) point; tip; ARCH

spire; BOT, GEOGR top; head (*a. fig*); lace; F MOT top speed; **spitze sein** F be super, be (the) tops; **an der Spitze** at the top (*a. fig*)

Spitzel ['ʃpɪtsəl] *m* (*-s*; -) informer, F stoolpigeon

spitzen ['ʃpɪtsən] *v/t* (*ge-*, *h*) point, sharpen; purse; ZO prick up (*its ears*)

'**Spitzen...** *in cpds* top ...; hi-tech ...

Spitzentechnolo,gie *f* high technology, hi tech

'**spitzfindig** *adj* quibbling

'**Spitzfindigkeit** *f* (-; *-en*) subtlety

'**Spitzhacke** *f* pickax(e), pick

'**Spitzname** *m* nickname

Splitter ['ʃplɪtɐ] *m* (*-s*; -), '**splittern** *v/i* (*ge-*, *h*, *sein*) splinter

'**splitter'nackt** F *adj* stark naked

sponsern ['ʃpɔnzɐn] *v/t* (*ge-*, *h*) sponsor

Sponsor ['ʃpɔnzɐ] *m* (*-s*; *-en* [ʃpɔn'zoː-rən]) sponsor

spontan [ʃpɔn'taːn] *adj* spontaneous

Sporen ['ʃpoːrən] *pl* spurs (*a.* ZO); BIOL spores

Sport [ʃpɔrt] *m* (*-[e]s*; *no pl*) sport(s); PED physical education; **Sport treiben** do sports

'**Sport...** *in cpds* ...ereignis, ...geschäft, ...hemd, ...verein, ...zentrum *etc*: *mst* sports ...

Sportkleidung *f* sportswear

'**Sportler** ['ʃpɔrtlɐ] *m* (*-s*; -), **Sportlerin** ['ʃpɔrtlərɪn] *f* (-; *-nen*) athlete

'**sportlich** *adj* athletic; casual, sporty

'**Sportnachrichten** *pl* sports news

Sportplatz *m* sports grounds

Sporttauchen *n* scuba diving

Sportwagen *m* stroller, *Br* pushchair; MOT sports car

Spott [ʃpɔt] *m* (*-[e]s*; *no pl*) mockery; derision

'**spott'billig** F *adj* dirt cheap

spotten ['ʃpɔtən] *v/i* (*ge-*, *h*) mock (**über** *acc* at), scoff (at); make fun (of)

Spötter ['ʃpœtɐ] *m* (*-s*; -) mocker, scoffer

'**spöttisch** *adj* mocking, derisive

'**Spottpreis** *m*: **für e-n Spottpreis** dirt cheap

sprach [ʃpraːx] *pret of* **sprechen**

Sprache ['ʃpraːxə] *f* (-; *-n*) language (*a. fig*); speech; **zur Sprache kommen** (**bringen**) come up (bring *s.th.* up)

'**Sprachfehler** *m* speech defect

Sprachgebrauch *m* usage

Sprachla,bor *n* language laboratory

Sprachlehre *f* grammar

Sprachlehrer(in) language teacher

'**sprachlich 1.** *adj* language ...; **2.** *adv*: **sprachlich richtig** grammatically cor-

rect
'**sprachlos** *adj* speechless
'**Sprachrohr** *fig n* mouthpiece
Sprachunterricht *m* language teaching
Sprachwissenschaft *f* linguistics
sprang [ʃpraŋ] *pret of* **springen**
Spraydose [ˈʃpreː-] *f* spray can, aerosol (can)
Sprechanlage [ˈʃprɛç-] *f* intercom
sprechen [ˈʃprɛçən] *v/t and v/i* (*irr, ge-, h*) speak (*j-n, mit j-m* to s.o.); talk (to) (*both: über acc, von* about, of); *nicht zu sprechen sein* be busy
Sprecher(in) [ˈʃprɛçɐ (-çərɪn)] (*-s; -/-; -nen*) speaker; announcer; spokesman (spokeswoman)
'**Sprechstunde** *f* office hours; MED office (*Br* consulting) hours, *Br* surgery
'**Sprechzimmer** *n* office, *Br a.* consulting room
spreizen [ˈʃpraitsən] *v/t* (*ge-, h*) spread
sprengen [ˈʃprɛŋən] *v/t* (*ge-, h*) blow up; blast; sprinkle; water; *fig* break up
'**Sprengkopf** *m* MIL warhead
'**Sprengstoff** *m* MIL explosive
'**Sprengung** *f* (*-; -en*) blasting; blowing up
sprenkeln [ˈʃprɛŋkəln] *v/t* (*ge-, h*) speck (-le), spot, dot
Spreu [ʃprɔʏ] *f* (*-; no pl*) chaff (*a. fig*)
Sprichwort [ˈʃprɪç-] *n* proverb, saying
'**sprichwörtlich** *adj* proverbial (*a. fig*)
sprießen [ˈʃpriːsən] *v/i* (*irr, ge-, sein*) BOT sprout
'**Springbrunnen** *m* fountain
springen [ˈʃprɪŋən] *v/i* (*irr, ge-, sein*) jump, leap; *ball etc:* bounce; SPORT dive; *glass etc:* crack; break; burst; *in die Höhe (zur Seite) springen* jump up (aside)
Springer [ˈʃprɪŋɐ] *m* (*-s; -*) jumper; diver; *chess:* knight
'**Springflut** *f* spring tide
'**Springreiten** *n* show jumping
Spritze [ˈʃprɪtsə] *f* (*-; -n*) MED injection, F shot; syringe
'**spritzen 1.** *v/i and v/t* (*ge-, h*) splash; spray (*a.* TECH, AGR); MED inject; give s.o. an injection of; **2.** *v/i* (*ge-, sein*) spatter; gush (*aus* from)
Spritzer [ˈʃprɪtsɐ] *m* (*-s; -*) splash; dash
'**Spritzpis,tole** *f* TECH spray gun
'**Spritztour** F *f* MOT spin
spröde [ˈʃprøːdə] *adj* brittle (*a. fig*); rough
spross [ʃprɔs] *pret of* **sprießen**
Sprosse [ˈʃprɔsə] *f* (*-; -n*) rung
Spruch [ʃprʊx] *m* (*-[e]s; Sprüche* [ˈʃprʏçə]) saying; decision
Spruchband *n* banner
Sprudel [ˈʃpruːdəl] *m* (*-s; -*) mineral water
'**sprudeln** *v/i* (*ge-, sein*) bubble

Sprühdose [ˈʃpryː-] *f* spray can, aerosol (can)
sprühen [ˈʃpryːən] *v/t and v/i* (*ge-, h*) spray; throw out (*sparks*)
'**Sprühregen** *m* drizzle
Sprung [ʃprʊŋ] *m* (*-[e]s; Sprünge* [ˈʃprʏŋə]) jump, leap; SPORT dive; crack, fissure
Sprungbrett *n* SPORT diving board; springboard; *fig* stepping stone
Sprungschanze *f* ski jump
Spucke [ˈʃpʊkə] F *f* (*-; no pl*) spit
'**spucken** *v/i and v/t* (*ge-, h*) spit; F throw up
Spuk [ʃpuːk] *m* (*-[e]s; -e*) apparition, ghost
spuken [ˈʃpuːkən] *v/i* (*ge-, h*) *spuken in (dat)* haunt; *hier spukt es* this place is haunted
Spule [ˈʃpuːlə] *f* (*-; -n*) spool, reel; bobbin; ELECTR coil
'**spulen** *v/t* (*ge-, h*) spool, wind, reel
spülen [ˈʃpyːlən] *v/t and v/i* (*ge-, h*) wash up, do the dishes; rinse; flush the toilet
'**Spülma,schine** *f* dishwasher
Spur [ʃpuːɐ] *f* (*-; -en*) track(s); trail; print; lane; trace (*a. fig*); *j-m auf der Spur sein* be on s.o.'s trail
spüren [ˈʃpyːrən] *v/t* (*ge-, h*) feel, sense; notice
'**spurlos** *adv* without leaving a trace
'**Spurweite** *f* RAIL ga(u)ge; MOT track
St. ABBR *of* **Sankt** St, Saint
Staat [ʃtaːt] *m* (*-[e]s; -en*) state; POL government
'**Staatenbund** *m* confederacy, confederation
'**staatenlos** *adj* stateless
'**staatlich 1.** *adj* state ...; public, national; **2.** *adv:* *staatlich geprüft* qualified, registered
'**Staatsangehörige** *m, f* national, citizen; subject
Staatsangehörigkeit *f* (*-; no pl*) nationality
Staatsanwalt *m* JUR district attorney, *Br* (public) prosecutor
Staatsbesuch *m* official *or* state visit
Staatsbürger(in) citizen
Staatschef *m* head of state
Staatsdienst *m* civil (*or* public) service
'**staatseigen** *adj* state-owned
'**Staatsfeind** *m* public enemy
'**staatsfeindlich** *adj* subversive
'**Staatshaushalt** *m* budget
Staatskasse *f* treasury
Staatsmann *m* statesman
Staatsoberhaupt *n* head of (the) state
Staatssekre,tär(in) undersecretary of

S

state
Staatsstreich *m* coup d'état
Staatsvertrag *m* treaty
Staatswissenschaft *f* political science
Stab [ʃtaːp] *m* (-[e]s; *Stäbe* ['ʃtɛːbə]) staff
(*a. fig*); bar; SPORT, MUS baton; SPORT pole
Stäbchen ['ʃtɛːpçən] *pl* chopstick
'**Stabhochsprung** *m* SPORT pole vault
stabil [ʃtaˈbiːl] *adj* stable (*a.* ECON, POL);
solid, strong; sound
stabilisieren [ʃtabiliˈziːrən] *v/t* (*no* -ge-,
h) stabilize
Stabilität [-ˈtɛːt] *f* (-; *no pl*) stability
stach [ʃtaːx] *pret of* **stechen**
Stachel ['ʃtaxəl] *m* (-*s*; -*n*) BOT, ZO spine,
prick; ZO sting
Stachelbeere *f* BOT gooseberry
Stacheldraht *m* barbed wire
stachelig ['ʃtaxəliç] *adj* prickly
'**Stachelschwein** *n* ZO porcupine
Stadel ['ʃtaːdəl] *Austrian m* (-*s*; -[*n*]) barn
Stadion ['ʃtaːdjɔn] *n* (-*s*; -*ien*) stadium
Stadium ['ʃtaːdjʊm] *n* (-*s*; -*ien*) stage,
phase
Stadt [ʃtat] *f* (-; *Städte* ['ʃtɛːtə]) town;
city; *die Stadt Berlin* the city of Berlin;
in die Stadt fahren go downtown, *esp Br*
go (in)to town
Stadtbahn *f* urban railway
Städter ['ʃtɛːtɐ] *m* (-*s*; -), '**Städterin** *f* (-;
-*nen*) city dweller, F townie, *often contp*
city slicker
'**Stadtgebiet** *n* urban area
Stadtgespräch *fig n* talk of the town
städtisch ['ʃtɛːtɪʃ] *adj* urban; POL munic-
ipal
'**Stadtplan** *m* city map
Stadtrand *m* outskirts
Stadtrat *m* town council; city councilman,
Br town council(l)or
Stadtrundfahrt *f* sightseeing tour
Stadtstreicher(in) city vagrant
Stadtteil *m*, **Stadtviertel** *n* quarter
Staffel ['ʃtafəl] *f* (-; -*n*) SPORT relay race *or*
team; MIL, AVIAT squadron
Staffelei [ʃtafəˈlai] *f* (-; -*en*) PAINT easel
'**staffeln** *v/t* (*ge-*, *h*) grade, scale
stahl [ʃtaːl] *pret of* **stehlen**
Stahl *m* (-[*e*]*s*; *Stähle* ['ʃtɛːlə]) steel
'**Stahlwerk** *n* steelworks
stak [ʃtaːk] *pret of* **stecken** 2
Stall [ʃtal] *m* (-[*e*]*s*; *Ställe* ['ʃtɛlə]) stable
'**Stallknecht** *m* stableman
Stamm [ʃtam] *m* (-[*e*]*s*; *Stämme* ['ʃtɛmə])
BOT stem (*a.* LING), trunk; tribe, stock; *fig*
regulars; *Stamm...* *in cpds* *...gast*,
...kunde, *...spieler etc*: regular ...
Stammbaum *m* family tree; ZO pedigree
stammeln ['ʃtaməln] *v/t* (*ge-*, *h*) stammer

stammen ['ʃta,ən] *v/i* (*ge-*, *h*) **stammen
aus** (**von**) come from; be from; **stammen von** *work of art etc*: be by
'**Stammformen** *pl* LING principal parts,
mst tenses
stämmig ['ʃtɛmɪç] *adj* sturdy; stout
'**Stammkneipe** F *f* Br local
stampfen ['ʃtampfən] (*ge-*, *h*) **1.** *v/t* mash;
2. *v/i* stamp (*mit dem Fuß* one's foot)
stand [ʃtant] *pret of* **stehen**
Stand *m* (-[*e*]*s*; *Stände* ['ʃtɛndə]) a) (*no
pl*) stand(ing), standing *or* upright position; footing, foothold; ASTR position;
TECH *etc*: height, level (*a. fig*); reading;
SPORT score; *racing*: standings; *fig* state;
social standing, status, b) stand, stall, *c*)
class; profession; *auf den neuesten
Stand bringen* bring up to date; *e-n
schweren Stand haben* have a hard
time (of it); → *außerstande*; → *imstan-
de*; → *instand*; → *zustande*
Standard ['ʃtandart] *m* (-*s*; -*s*) standard
'**Standbild** *n* statue
Ständchen ['ʃtɛntçən] *n* (-*s*; -) MUS serenade
Ständer ['ʃtɛndɐ] *m* (-*s*; -) stand; rack
Standesamt ['ʃtandəs-] *n* marriage license bureau, *Br* registry office
'**standesamtlich** *adj*: *standesamtliche
Trauung* civil marriage
'**Standesbeamte** *m*, -**in** *f* civil magistrate,
Br registrar
'**Standfoto** *n* still
'**standhaft** *adj* steadfast, firm; *standhaft
bleiben* resist temptation
'**standhalten** *v/i* (*irr*, *halten*, *sep*, -ge-, *h*)
withstand, resist
ständig ['ʃtɛndɪç] *adj* constant; perma-
nent (*address*)
'**Standlicht** *n* (-[*e*]*s*; *no pl*) MOT parking
light
Standort *m* position; location; MIL post,
garrison
Standpauke F *f*: *j-m e-e Standpauke hal-
ten* give s.o. a talking-to
Standplatz *m* stand
Standpunkt *m* (point of) view, standpoint
Standrecht *n* (-[*e*]*s*; *no pl*) MIL martial law
Standspur *f* MOT (*Br* hard) shoulder
Standuhr *f* grandfather clock
Stange ['ʃtaŋə] *f* (-; -*n*) pole; staff; rod,
bar; carton (*of cigarettes*)
Stängel ['ʃtɛŋəl] *m* (-*s*; -) BOT stalk, stem
stank [ʃtaŋk] *pret of* **stinken**
Stanniol [ʃtaˈnjoːl] *n* (-*s*; -*e*) tin foil
Stanze ['ʃtantsə] *f* (-; -*n*), '**stanzen** *v/t*
(*ge-*, *h*) TECH punch
Stapel ['ʃtaːpəl] *m* (-*s*; -) pile, stack; heap;
vom Stapel lassen MAR launch (*a. fig*);

vom Stapel laufen MAR be launched

'**Stapellauf** *m* MAR launch

'**stapeln** *v/t* (*ge-*, *h*) pile (up), stack

stapfen ['ʃtapfən] *v/i* (*ge-*, *sein*) trudge

Star[1] [ʃtaːɐ] *m* (-[*e*]*s*; *-e*) ZO starling; MED cataract

Star[2] *m* (-*s*; -*s*) THEA *etc*: star

starb [ʃtarp] *pret of* **sterben**

stark [ʃtark] **1.** *adj* strong (*a.* GASTR); powerful; *fig* heavy; F super, great; **2.** *adv*: **stark beeindruckt** greatly impressed; **stark beschädigt** badly damaged

Stärke ['ʃtɛrkə] *f* (-; -*n*) a) (*no pl*) strength, power; intensity, b) degree, c) CHEM starch

'**stärken** *v/t* (*ge-*, *h*) strengthen (*a. fig*); starch; **sich stärken** take some refreshment

'**Starkstrom** *m* ELECTR high-voltage (*or* heavy) current

Stärkung *f* (-; -*en*) strengthening; refreshment

'**Stärkungsmittel** *n* MED tonic

starr [ʃtar] *adj* stiff; rigid (*a.* TECH); frozen (*face*); **starrer Blick** (fixed) stare; **starr vor Kälte** (**Entsetzen**) frozen (scared) stiff

'**starren** *v/i* (*ge-*, *h*) stare (**auf** *acc* at)

'**starrköpfig** [-kœpfɪç] *adj* stubborn, obstinate

'**Starrsinn** *m* (-[*e*]*s*; *no pl*) stubbornness, obstinacy

Start [ʃtart] *m* (-[*e*]*s*; -*s*) start (*a. fig*); AVIAT take-off; *rocket*: lift-off

'**Startbahn** *f* AVIAT runway

'**startbereit** *adj* ready to start; AVIAT ready for take-off

starten ['ʃtartən] *v/i* (*ge-*, *sein*) *and v/t* (*ge-*, *h*) start (*a.* F); AVIAT take off; lift off; launch (*a. fig*)

Station [ʃtaˈtsjoːn] *f* (-; -*en*) station; MED ward

stationär [ʃtatsjoˈnɛːɐ] *adj*: **stationärer Patient** MED in-patient

stationieren [ʃtatsjoˈniːrən] *v/t* (*no -ge-*, *h*) MIL station; deploy

Stationsvorsteher *m* RAIL stationmaster

Statist [ʃtaˈtɪst] *m* (-*en*; -*en*) THEA extra

Statistik [ʃtaˈtɪstɪk] *f* (-; -*en*) statistics

Sta'tistiker [-tikɐ] *m* (-*s*; -) statistician

sta'tistisch *adj* statistical

Stativ [ʃtaˈtiːf] *n* (-*s*; -*e*) PHOT tripod

statt [ʃtat] *prp* instead of; **statt et. zu tun** instead of doing s.th.

statt'dessen instead

Stätte ['ʃtɛtə] *f* (-; -*n*) place; scene

'**stattfinden** *v/i* (*irr*, **finden**, *sep*, *-ge-*, *h*) take place; happen

'**stattlich** *adj* imposing; handsome

Statue ['ʃtaːtuə] *f* (-; -*n*) statue

Statur [ʃtaˈtuːɐ] *f* (-; -*en*) build

Status ['ʃtaːtʊs] *m* (-; -) state; status

Statussym.bol *n* status symbol

Statuszeile *f* EDP status line

Stau [ʃtau] *m* (-[*e*]*s*; -*s*, -*e*) MOT traffic jam *or* congestion

Staub [ʃtaup] *m* (-[*e*]*s*; TECH -*e*, *Stäube* ['ʃtɔʏbə]) dust (*a.* **Staub wischen**)

'**Staubecken** *n* reservoir

stauben ['ʃtaubən] *v/i* (*ge-*, *h*) give off *or* make dust

staubig ['ʃtaubɪç] *adj* dusty

'**staubsaugen** *v/i and v/t* (*ge-*, *h*) vacuum, F *Br* hoover

'**Staubsauger** *m* vacuum cleaner, F *Br* hoover

'**Staubtuch** *n* duster

'**Staudamm** *m* dam

Staude ['ʃtaudə] *f* (-; -*n*) BOT herbacious plant

stauen ['ʃtauən] *v/t* (*ge-*, *h*) dam up; **sich stauen** MOT *etc* be stacked up

staunen ['ʃtaunən] *v/i* (*ge-*, *h*) be astonished *or* surprised (**über** *acc* at)

'**Staunen** *n* (-*s*; *no pl*) astonishment, amazement

Staupe ['ʃtaupə] *f* (-; -*n*) VET distemper

'**Stausee** *m* reservoir

stechen ['ʃtɛçən] *v/i and v/t* (*irr*, *ge-*, *h*) prick; ZO sting, bite; stab; pierce; **mit et. stechen in** (*acc*) stick s.th. in(to); **sich stechen** prick o.s.

stechend *fig adj* piercing (*look*); stabbing (*pain*)

'**Stechuhr** *f* time clock

Steckbrief ['ʃtɛk-] *m* JUR „wanted" poster

'**steckbrieflich** *adv*: **er wird steckbrieflich gesucht** JUR a warrant is out against him

'**Steckdose** *f* ELECTR (wall) socket

stecken ['ʃtɛkən] (*ge-*, *h*) **1.** *v/t* stick; put; *esp* TECH insert (**in** *acc* into); pin (**an** *acc* to, on); AGR set, plant; **2.** *v/i* ([*irr*]) be; stick, be stuck; **stecken bleiben** get stuck

'**steckenbleiben** *v/i* (*irr*, **bleiben**, *sep*, *-ge-*, *sein*) *fig* get stuck

'**Steckenpferd** *n* hobby horse; *fig* hobby

'**Stecker** ['ʃtɛkɐ] *m* (-*s*; -) ELECTR plug

'**Steckkon.takt** *m* ELECTR plug (connection)

Stecknadel *f* pin

Steckplatz *m* EDP slot

Steg [ʃteːk] *m* (-[*e*]*s*; -*e*) footbridge

Stegreif ['ʃteːkraif] *m*: **aus dem Stegreif** extempore, ad-lib; **aus dem Stegreif sprechen** *or* **spielen** *etc* extemporize, ad-lib

S

stehen ['ʃteːən] *v/i* (*irr, ge-, h*) stand; be; stand up; *es steht ihr* it suits (*or* looks well on) her; *wie steht es* (*or das Spiel*)? what's the score?; *hier steht, dass* it says here that; *wo steht das?* where does it say so *or* that?; *sich schlecht stehen* be badly off; F *sich gut mit j-m stehen* get along well with s.o.; *wie steht es mit ...?* what about ...?; F *darauf stehe ich* it turns me on; *stehen bleiben* stop; *esp* TECH come to a standstill (*a. fig*); *stehen lassen* leave (untouched); leave behind; *alles stehen und liegen lassen* drop everything; *lass e-n Bart stehen lassen* grow a beard

'**stehenbleiben** *v/i* (*irr, bleiben, sep, -ge-, sein*) → *stehen*

stehenlassen *v/t* (*irr, lassen, sep, no -ge-, h*) → *stehen*

'**Stehkragen** *m* stand-up collar

Stehlampe *f* floor (*Br* standard) lamp

Stehleiter *f* step ladder

stehlen ['ʃteːlən] *v/t and v/i* (*irr, ge-, h*) steal (*a. fig* **sich stehlen**)

'**Stehplatz** *m* standing ticket; *pl* standing room

steif [ʃtaif] *adj* stiff (*vor dat* with)

Steigbügel ['ʃtaik-] *m* stirrup

steigen ['ʃtaigən] *v/i* (*irr, ge-, sein*) go, step; climb (*a.* AVIAT); *fig* rise, go up; *steigen in* (*auf*) (*acc*) get on (*bus, bike etc*); *steigen aus* (*von*) get off (*bus, horse etc*); *aus dem Bett steigen* get out of bed

steigern ['ʃtaigən] *v/t* (*ge-, h*) raise, increase; heighten; improve; LING compare; *sich steigern* improve, get better

Steigerung ['ʃtaigərʊŋ] *f* (*-; -en*) rise, increase; heightening; improvement; LING comparison

'**Steigung** *f* (*-; -en*) gradient; slope

steil [ʃtail] *adj* steep (*a. fig*)

Stein [ʃtain] *m* (*-[e]s; -e*) stone (*a.* BOT, MED), rock

Steinbock *m* ZO rock goat; ASTR Capricorn; *er ist (ein) Steinbock* he's (a) Capricorn

Steinbruch *m* quarry

steinern ['ʃtainən] *adj* (of) stone; *fig* stony

'**Steingut** *n* (*-[e]s; -e*) earthenware

steinig ['ʃtainɪç] *adj* stony

steinigen ['ʃtainɪgən] *v/t* (*ge-, h*) stone

'**Steinkohle** *f* (hard) coal

'**Steinmetz** [-mɛts] *m* (*-en; -en*) stonemason

'**Steinzeit** *f* (*-; no pl*) Stone Age

Stellage [ʃtɛˈlaːʒə] *Austrian f* (*-; -n*) stand, rack, shelf

Stelle ['ʃtɛlə] *f* (*-; -n*) place; spot; point; job; authority; MATH figure; *freie Stelle* vacancy, opening; *auf der* (*zur*) *Stelle* on the spot; *an erster Stelle stehen* (*kommen*) be (come) first; *an j-s Stelle* in s.o.'s place; *ich an deiner Stelle* if I were you

'**stellen** *v/t* (*ge-, h*) put; set (*trap, clock, task etc*); turn (*up, down etc*); ask (*question*); provide; corner, hunt down (*criminal etc*); *sich stellen* give o.s. up, turn o.s. in; *sich gegen* (*hinter*) *j-n stellen* *fig* oppose (back) s.o.; *sich schlafend etc stellen* pretend to be asleep *etc*; *stell dich dorthin!* (go and) stand over there!

'**Stellenangebot** *n* vacancy; *ich habe ein Stellenangebot* I was offered a job

Stellenanzeige *f* job ad(vertisement), employment ad

Stellengesuch *n* application for a job

'**stellenweise** *adv* partly, in places

'**Stellung** *f* (*-; -en*) position; post, job; *Stellung nehmen zu* comment on, give one's opinion of

Stellungnahme [-naːmə] *f* (*-; -n*) comment, opinion (*both:* **zu** on)

'**stellungslos** *adj* unemployed, jobless

'**stellvertretend** *adj* acting, deputy, vice-...

'**Stellvertreter(in)** (*-s; -/-; -nen*) representative; deputy

Stelze ['ʃtɛltsə] *f* (*-; -n*) stilt

'**stelzen** *v/i* (*ge-, sein*) stalk

stemmen ['ʃtɛmən] *v/t* (*ge-, h*) lift (*weight*); *sich stemmen gegen* press o.s. against; *fig* resist *or* oppose s.th.

Stempel ['ʃtɛmpəl] *m* (*-s; -*) stamp; postmark; hallmark; BOT pistil

'**Stempelkissen** *n* ink pad

'**stempeln** (*ge-, h*) **1.** *v/t* stamp; cancel; hallmark; **2.** F *v/i*: *stempeln gehen* be on the dole

Stengel → *Stängel*

Stenografie [ʃtenograˈfiː] *f* (*-; -n*) shorthand

stenograˈfieren *v/t* (*no -ge-, h*) take down in shorthand

Stenogramm [ʃtenoˈgram] *n* (*-[e]s; -e*) shorthand notes

Stenotypistin [-tyˈpɪstɪn] *f* (*-; -nen*) shorthand typist

Steppdecke ['ʃtɛp-] *f* quilt

steppen ['ʃtɛpən] (*ge-, h*) **1.** *v/t* quilt; stitch; **2.** *v/i* tap dance

'**Stepptanz** *m* tap dancing

Sterbebett ['ʃtɛrbə-] *n* deathbed

'**Sterbeklinik** *f* MED hospice

sterben ['ʃtɛrbən] *v/i* (*irr, ge-, sein*) die (*an dat* of) (*a. fig*); *im Sterben liegen* be dying

sterblich [ˈʃtɛrplɪç] *adj* mortal
'Sterblichkeit *f* (-; *no pl*) mortality
Stereo [ˈʃteːreo] *n* (-*s*; -*s*) stereo
steril [ʃteˈriːl] *adj* sterile
Sterilisation [ʃteriliza'tsjoːn] *f* (-; -*en*) sterilization
sterilisieren [ʃteriliˈziːrən] *v/t* (*no -ge-*, *h*) sterilize
Stern [ʃtɛrn] *m* (-[*e*]*s*; -*e*) star (*a. fig*)
'Sternbild *n* ASTR constellation; sign of the zodiac
'Sternchen *n* (-*s*; -) PRINT asterisk
'Sternenbanner *n* Star-Spangled Banner, Stars and Stripes
'Sternenhimmel *m* starry sky
'sternklar *adj* starry
'Sternkunde *f* (-; *no pl*) astronomy
Sternschnuppe *f* (-; -*n*) shooting *or* falling star
Sternwarte *f* (-; -*n*) observatory
stetig [ˈʃteːtɪç] *adj* continual, constant; steady
stets [ʃteːts] *adv* always
Steuer¹ [ˈʃtɔʏɐ] *n* (-*s*; -) MOT (steering) wheel; MAR helm, rudder
'Steuer² *f* (-; -*n*) tax (*auf acc* on)
'Steuerbeamte *m* revenue officer
Steuerberater *m* tax adviser
'Steuerbord *n* MAR starboard
'Steuererklärung *f* tax return
Steuerermäßigung *f* tax allowance
'steuerfrei *adj* tax-free
'Steuerhinterziehung *f* tax evasion
'Steuerknüppel *m* AVIAT control column *or* stick
Steuermann *m* MAR helmsman; *rowing*: cox, coxswain
'steuern *v/t and v/i* (*ge-*, *h*) steer, AVIAT, MAR *a.* navigate, pilot, MOT *a.* drive; TECH control (*a. fig*); *fig* direct
'steuerpflichtig *adj* taxable
'Steuerrad *n* MOT steering wheel
'Steuerruder *n* MAR helm, rudder
'Steuersenkung *f* tax reduction
Steuerung [ˈʃtɔʏərʊŋ] *f* (-; -*en*) steering (system); ELECTR, TECH control (*a. fig*)
'Steuerzahler *m*, **'Steuerzahlerin** *f* taxpayer
Stich [ʃtɪç] *m* (-[*e*]*s*; -*e*) prick; ZO sting, bite; stab; stitch; *cards*: trick; engraving; *im Stich lassen* desert *or* abandon *s.o.*, *s.th.*, leave *s.o.* in the lurch, let *s.o.* down
Stichelei [ʃtɪçə'lai] F *f* (-; -*en*) dig, gibe
sticheln [ˈʃɪçəln] F *v/i* (*ge-*, *h*) make digs, gibe (*gegen* at)
'Stichflamme *f* jet of flame
'stichhaltig *adj* valid, sound; watertight; *nicht stichhaltig sein* F not hold water
'Stichprobe *f* spot check

Stichtag *m* cutoff date; deadline
Stichwahl *f* POL run-off
Stichwort *n* a) (-[*e*]*s*; -*e*) THEA cue, b) (-[*e*]*s*; -*wörter*) headword; *Stichworte pl* notes; *das Wichtigste in Stichworten* an outline of the main points
Stichwortverzeichnis *n* index
Stichwunde *f* MED stab
sticken [ˈʃtɪkən] *v/t and v/i* (*ge-*, *h*) embroider
Stickerei [ʃtɪkə'rai] *f* (-; -*en*) embroidery
stickig [ˈʃtɪkɪç] *adj* stuffy
'Stickstoff *m* (-[*e*]*s*; *no pl*) CHEM nitrogen
Stief... [ʃtiːf-] *in cpds ...mutter etc*: step...
Stiefel [ˈʃtiːfəl] *m* (-*s*; -) boot
'Stiefmütterchen [-mʏtɐçən] *n* (-*s*; -) BOT pansy
stieg [ʃtiːk] *pret of* **steigen**
Stiege [ˈʃtiːgə] *Austrian f* (-; -*n*) → *Treppe*
Stiel [ʃtiːl] *m* (-[*e*]*s*; -*e*) handle; stick; stem; BOT stalk
Stier [ʃtiːɐ] *m* (-[*e*]*s*; -*e*) ZO bull; ASTR Taurus; *er ist (ein) Stier* he's (a) Taurus
'Stierkampf *m* bullfight
stieß [ʃtiːs] *pret of* **stoßen**
Stift [ʃtɪft] *m* (-[*e*]*s*; -*e*) pen; pencil; crayon; TECH pin; peg
stiften [ˈʃtɪftən] *v/t* (*ge-*, *h*) donate; *fig* cause
'Stiftung *f* (-; -*en*) donation
Stil [ʃtiːl] *m* (-[*e*]*s*; -*e*) style (*a. fig*); *in großem Stil* in (grand) style; *fig* on a large scale
stilistisch [ʃtiˈlɪstɪʃ] *adj* stylistic
still [ʃtɪl] *adj* quiet, silent; still; *sei(d) still!* be quiet!; *halt still!* keep still!; *sich still verhalten* keep quiet (*or* still)
Stille [ˈʃtɪlə] *f* (-; *no pl*) silence, quiet (-ness); *in aller Stille* quietly; secretly
Stilleben *n* → *Stillleben*
stillen [ˈʃtɪlən] *v/t* (*ge-*, *h*) nurse, breastfeed; *fig* relieve (*pain*); satisfy (*curiosity etc*); quench (*one's thirst*)
'stillhalten *v/i* (*irr*, **halten**, *sep*, *-ge-*, *h*) keep still
'Stillleben *n* PAINT still life
'stilllegen *v/t* (*sep*, *-ge-*, *h*) close down
'stillos *adj* lacking style, tasteless
'stillschweigend *adj* tacit
'Stillstand *m* (-[*e*]*s*; *no pl*) standstill, stop, *fig a.* stagnation (*a.* ECON); deadlock
'stillstehen *v/i* (*irr*, **stehen**, *sep*, *-ge-*, *h*) (have) stop(ped), (have) come to a standstill
'Stilmöbel *pl* period furniture
'stilvoll *adj* stylish; *stilvoll sein* have style
'Stimmband *n* ANAT vocal cord
'stimmberechtigt *adj* entitled to vote
Stimme [ˈʃtɪmə] *f* (-; -*n*) voice; POL vote;

S

sich der Stimme enthalten abstain
'stimmen (*ge-, h*) **1.** *v/i* be right, be true, be correct; POL vote (*für* for; *gegen* against); *es stimmt et. nicht* (*damit or mit ihm*) there's s.th. wrong (with it *or* him); **2.** *v/t* MUS tune; *j-n traurig etc stimmen* make s.o. sad *etc*
'Stimmenthaltung *f* abstention
'Stimmrecht *n* right to vote
'Stimmung *f* (-; *-en*) mood; atmosphere; feeling
'stimmungsvoll *adj* atmospheric
'Stimmzettel *m* ballot (paper)
stinken ['ʃtɪŋkən] *v/i* (*irr, ge-, h*) stink (*a. fig*) (*nach* of)
Stipendium [ʃti'pɛndjʊm] *n* (-*s*; *-ien*) UNIV scholarship, grant
stippen ['ʃtɪpən] *v/t* (*ge-, h*) dip
'Stippvi,site F *f* flying visit
Stirn [ʃtɪrn] *f* (-; *-en*) ANAT forehead; *die Stirn runzeln* frown
stöbern ['ʃtøːbɐn] F *v/i* (*ge-, h*) rummage (about)
stochern ['ʃtɔxɐn] *v/i* (*ge-, h*) *im Feuer stochern* poke the fire; *im Essen stochern* pick at one's food; *in den Zähnen stochern* pick one's teeth
Stock [ʃtɔk] *m* (-[*e*]*s*; *Stöcke* ['ʃtœkə]) stick; cane; ARCH stor(e)y, floor; *im ersten Stock* on the second (*Br* first) floor
'stock'dunkel F *adj* pitch-dark
stocken ['ʃtɔkən] *v/i* (*ge-, h*) stop (short); falter; *traffic*: be jammed
stockend **1.** *adj* halting; **2.** *adv: stockend lesen* stumble through a text; *stockend sprechen* speak haltingly
'Stockfleck *m* mo(u)ld stain
'Stockung *f* (-; *-en*) holdup, delay
'Stockwerk *n* stor(e)y, floor
Stoff [ʃtɔf] *m* (-[*e*]*s*; *-e*) material, stuff (*a. F*); fabric, textile; cloth; CHEM, PHYS *etc* substance; *fig* subject (matter)
'stofflich *adj* material
'Stofftier *n* soft toy animal
'Stoffwechsel *m* BIOL metabolism
stöhnen ['ʃtøːnən] *v/i* (*ge-, h*) groan, moan (*a. fig*)
Stollen ['ʃtɔlən] *m* (-*s*; -) tunnel, gallery
stolpern ['ʃtɔlpɐn] *v/i* (*ge-, sein*) stumble (*über* acc over), trip (over) (*both a. fig*)
stolz [ʃtɔlts] *adj* proud (*auf* acc of)
Stolz *m* (-*es*; *no pl*) pride (*auf* acc in)
stolzieren [ʃtɔl'tsiːrən] *v/i* (*no -ge-, sein*) strut, stalk
stopfen ['ʃtɔpfən] *v/t* (*ge-, h*) darn, mend; stuff, fill (*a. pipe*)
Stoppel ['ʃtɔpəl] *f* (-; -*n*) stubble
'Stoppelbart F *m* stubbly beard
'stoppelig *adj* stubbly, bristly

'Stoppelzieher *Austrian m* corkscrew
stoppen ['ʃtɔpən] *v/i and v/t* (*ge-, h*) stop (*a. fig*); *esp* SPORT time
'Stopplicht *n* (-[*e*]*s*; *-er*) MOT stop light
Stoppschild *n* stop sign
Stoppuhr *f* stopwatch
Stöpsel ['ʃtœpsəl] *m* (-*s*; -) stopper; plug
Storch [ʃtɔrç] *m* (-[*e*]*s*; *Störche* ['ʃtœrçəl]) ZO stork
stören ['ʃtøːrən] *v/t and v/i* (*ge-, h*) disturb; trouble; bother, annoy; be in the way; *lassen Sie sich nicht stören!* don't let me disturb you!; *darf ich Sie kurz stören?* may I trouble you for a minute?; *es (er) stört mich nicht* it (he) doesn't bother me, I don't mind (him); *stört es Sie(, wenn ich rauche)?* do you mind (my smoking *or* if I smoke)?
'Störenfried [-friːt] *m* (-[*e*]*s*; -*e*) troublemaker; intruder
Störfall ['ʃtøːɐ-] *m* TECH accident
störrisch ['ʃtœrɪʃ] *adj* stubborn, obstinate
'Störung *f* (-; -*en*) disturbance; trouble (*a.* TECH); TECH breakdown; TV, *radio*: interference
Stoß [ʃtoːs] *m* (-*es*; *Stöße* ['ʃtøːsə]) push, shove; thrust; kick; butt; blow, knock; shock; MOT jolt; bump, *esp* TECH, PHYS impact; pile, stack
'Stoßdämpfer *m* MOT shock absorber
stoßen ['ʃtoːsən] *v/t* (*irr, ge-, h*) *and v/i* (*sein*) push, shove; thrust; kick; butt; knock, strike; pound; *stoßen gegen or an* (acc) bump *or* run into *or* against; *sich den Kopf stoßen* (*an dat*) knock one's head (against); *stoßen auf* (acc) strike (*oil etc*); *fig* come across; meet with
'stoßgesichert *adj* shockproof, shock-resistant
'Stoßstange *f* MOT bumper
'Stoßzahn *m* ZO tusk
'Stoßzeit *f* rush hour, peak hours
stottern ['ʃtɔtɐn] *v/i and v/t* (*ge-, h*) stutter
Str. ABBR *of* **Straße** St, Street; Rd, Road
'Strafanstalt *f* prison, penitentiary
'strafbar *adj* punishable, penal; *sich strafbar machen* commit an offense (*Br* offence)
Strafe ['ʃtraːfə] *f* (-; -*n*) punishment; JUR, ECON, SPORT penalty (*a. fig*); fine; *20 Mark Strafe zahlen müssen* be fined 20 marks; *zur Strafe* as a punishment
'strafen *v/t* (*ge-, h*) punish
straff [ʃtraf] *adj* tight; *fig* strict
'straffrei *adj: straffrei ausgehen* go unpunished
'Strafgefangene *m, f* prisoner, convict
Strafgesetz *n* criminal law

sträflich ['ʃtrɛːflɪç] **1.** *adj* inexcusable; **2.** *adv:* **sträflich vernachlässigen** neglect badly

'**Strafmi,nute** *f* SPORT penalty minute

Strafpro,zess *m* JUR criminal action, trial

Strafraum *m* SPORT penalty area (F box)

Strafstoß *m* SPORT penalty kick

Straftat *f* JUR criminal offense (*Br* offence); crime

Strafzettel *m* ticket

Strahl [ʃtraːl] *m* (-[e]s, -en) ray (*a. fig*); beam; flash; jet

strahlen ['ʃtraːlən] *v/i* (*ge-, h*) radiate; shine (brightly); *fig* beam (**vor** with)

'**Strahlen...** *in cpds* PHYS \133*schutz etc:* radiation ...

'**Strahlung** *f* (-; -en) PHYS radiation

Strähne ['ʃtrɛːnə] *f* (-; -n) strand; streak

stramm [ʃtram] *adj* tight

strammstehen MIL stand to attention

strampeln ['ʃtrampəln] *v/i* (*ge-, h*) kick

Strand [ʃtrant] *m* (-[e]s; *Strände* ['ʃtrɛndə]) beach; **am Strand** on the beach

stranden ['ʃtrandən] *v/i* (*ge-, sein*) MAR strand; *fig* fail

'**Strandgut** *n* flotsam and jetsam (*a. fig*)

Strandkorb *m* roofed wicker beach chair

Strang [ʃtraŋ] *m* (-[e]s; *Stränge* ['ʃtrɛŋə]) rope; *esp* ANAT cord

Strapaze [ʃtra'paːtsə] *f* (-; -n) strain, exertion, hardship

strapazieren [ʃtrapa'tsiːrən] *v/t* (*no -ge-, h*) wear *s.o. or s.th.* out, be hard on

strapazierfähig *adj* longwearing, *Br* hardwearing

strapaziös [ʃtrapa'tsjøːs] *adj* strenuous

Straße ['ʃtraːsə] *f* (-; -n) road; street; GEOGR strait; **auf der Straße** on the road; on (*Br a.* in) the street

'**Straßenarbeiten** *pl* roadworks

Straßenbahn *f* streetcar, *Br* tram

Straßenca,fé *n* sidewalk (*Br* pavement) café

Straßenkarte *f* road map

Straßenkehrer [-keːrɐ] *m* (-s; -) street sweeper

Straßenkreuzung *f* crossroads; intersection

Straßenlage *f* MOT roadholding

Straßenrand *m* roadside; **am Straßenrand** at *or* by the roadside

Straßensperre *f* road block

strategisch [ʃtra'teːgɪʃ] *adj* strategic

sträuben ['ʃtrɔʏbən] *v/t and v/refl* (*ge-, h*) ruffle (up); bristle (up); **sich sträuben gegen** struggle against

Strauch [ʃtraux] *m* (-[e]s; *Sträucher* ['ʃtrɔʏçɐ]) BOT shrub, bush

straucheln ['ʃtrauxəln] *v/i* (*ge-, sein*) stumble

Strauß[1] [ʃtraus] *m* (-es; -e) ZO ostrich

Strauß[2] *m* (-es; *Sträuße* ['ʃtrɔʏsə]) bunch, bouquet

Strebe ['ʃtreːbə] *f* (-; -n) prop, stay (*a.* AVIAT, MAR)

'**streben** *v/i* (*ge-, h*) strive (**nach** for, after)

Streber ['ʃtreːbɐ] *m* (-s; -) pusher; PED *etc* grind, *Br* swot

strebsam ['ʃtreːp-] *adj* ambitious

Strecke ['ʃtrɛkə] *f* (-; -n) distance (*a.* SPORT, MATH), way; route; RAIL line; SPORT course; stretch; **zur Strecke bringen** kill; *esp fig* hunt down

'**strecken** *v/t* (*ge-, h*) stretch (out), extend

Streich [ʃtraiç] *m* (-[e]s; -e) trick, prank, practical joke; **j-m e-n Streich spielen** play a trick *or* joke on s.o.

streicheln ['ʃtraiçəln] *v/t* (*ge-, h*) stroke, caress

streichen ['ʃtraiçən] *v/t and v/i* (*irr, ge-, h*) paint; spread; cross out; cancel; MAR strike; MUS bow; **mit der Hand streichen über** (*acc*) run one's hand over; **streichen durch** roam (*acc*)

Streicher(in) ['ʃtraiçɐ (-çərɪn)] (-s; -/-; -nen) MUS string player, *pl the* strings

'**Streichholz** *n* match

Streichinstru,ment *n* MUS string instrument

Streichor,chester *n* MUS string orchestra

'**Streichung** *f* (-; -en) cancellation; cut

Streife ['ʃtraifə] *f* (-; -n) patrol; **auf Streife gehen** go on patrol; **auf Streife sein in** (*dat*) patrol

'**streifen** *v/t and v/i* (*ge-, h*) touch, brush (against); MOT scrape against; graze; slip (**von** off); *fig* touch on; **streifen durch** roam (*acc*), wander through

'**Streifen** *m* (-s; -) stripe; strip

'**Streifenwagen** *m* squad (*Br* patrol) car

'**Streifschuss** *m* MED graze

'**Streifzug** *m* tour (**durch** of)

Streik [ʃtraik] *m* (-[e]s; -s) strike, walkout; **wilder Streik** wildcat strike

'**Streikbrecher** *m* strikebreaker, *Br* blackleg, *contp* scab

streiken ['ʃtraikən] *v/i* (*ge-, h*) (go *or* be on) strike; F *fig* refuse (to work etc)

'**Streikende** *m, f* (-n; -n) striker

'**Streikposten** *m* picket

Streit [ʃtrait] *m* (-[e]s; -e) quarrel; argument; fight; POL *etc* dispute; **Streit anfangen** pick a fight *or* quarrel; **Streit suchen** be looking for trouble

streiten ['ʃtraitən] *v/i and v/refl* (*irr, ge-, h*) quarrel, argue, fight (*all:* **wegen**, **über** *acc* about, over); **sich streiten um** fight for

'Streitfrage *f* (point at) issue
streitig ['ʃtraitɪç] *adj*: *j-m et. streitig machen* dispute s.o.'s right to s.th.
'Streitkräfte *pl* MIL (armed) forces
'streitshüctig *adj* quarrelsome
streng [ʃtrɛŋ] *adj* strict; severe; harsh; rigid; *streng genommen* strictly speaking
Strenge ['ʃtrɛŋə] *f* (-; *no pl*) strictness; severity; harshness; rigidity
'strenggläubig *adj* REL orthodox
Stress [ʃtrɛs] *m* (-*es*; *no pl*) stress; *im Stress* under stress
Streu [ʃtrɔy] *f* (-; -*en*) AGR litter
'streuen *v/t and v/i* (*ge-*, *h*) scatter (*a.* PHYS); spread; sprinkle; grit
streunen ['ʃtrɔynən] *v/i* (*ge-*, *sein*), streunend *adj* stray
strich [ʃtrɪç] *pret of* streichen
Strich *m* (-[*e*]*s*; -*e*) line; stroke; F redlight district; F *auf den Strich gehen* walk the streets
Strichkode *m* bar code
Strichjunge F *m* male prostitute
'strichweise *adv* in parts; *strichweise Regen* scattered showers
Strick [ʃtrɪk] *m* (-[*e*]*s*; -*e*) cord; rope
stricken ['ʃtrɪkən] *v/t and v/i* (*ge-*, *h*) knit
'Strickjacke *f* cardigan
'Strickleiter *f* rope ladder
'Stricknadel *f* knitting needle
'Strickwaren *pl* knitwear
'Strickzeug *n* knitting (things)
Striemen ['ʃtriːmən] *m* (-*s*; -) welt, weal
stritt [ʃtrɪt] *pret of* streiten
strittig ['ʃtrɪtɪç] *adj* controversial; *strittiger Punkt* point at issue
Stroh [ʃtroː] *n* (-[*e*]*s*; *no pl*) straw; thatch
Strohdach *n* thatch(ed) roof
Strohhalm *m* straw
Strohhut *m* straw hat
Strohwitwe F *f* grass widow
Strohwitwer F *m* grass widower
Strom [ʃtroːm] *m* (-[*e*]*s*; Ströme ['ʃtrøːmə]) (large) river; current (*a.* fig); *ein Strom von* a stream of (*a.* fig); *es gießt in Strömen* it's pouring (with rain)
strom'ab(wärts) *adv* downstream
strom'auf(wärts) *adv* upstream
'Stromausfall *m* ELECTR power failure, blackout
strömen ['ʃtrøːmən] *v/i* (*ge-*, *sein*) stream (*a.* fig), flow, run; pour (*a.* fig)
'Stromkreis *m* ELECTR circuit
'stromlinienförmig *adj* streamlined
'Stromschnelle *f* (-; -*n*) GEOGR rapid
'Stromstärke *f* ELECTR amperage
'Strömung *f* (-; -*en*) current, fig *a.* trend
Strophe ['ʃtroːfə] *f* (-; -*n*) stanza, verse

strotzen ['ʃtrɔtsən] *v/i* (*ge-*, *h*) *strotzen von* be full of, abound with; *strotzen vor* (*dat*) be bursting with
Strudel ['ʃtruːdəl] *m* (-*s*; -) whirlpool (*a.* fig), eddy
Struktur [ʃtrʊk'tuːɐ] *f* (-; -*en*) structure, pattern
Strumpf [ʃtrʊmpf] *m* (-[*e*]*s*; Strümpfe ['ʃtrʏmpfə]) stocking
'Strumpfhose *f* pantyhose, *Br* tights
struppig ['ʃtrʊpɪç] *adj* shaggy
Stück [ʃtʏk] *n* (-[*e*]*s*; -*e*) piece; part; lump; AGR head (*a.* pl); THEA play; *2 Mark das Stück* 2 marks each; *im or am Stück* in one piece; *in Stücke schlagen* (*reißen*) smash (tear) to pieces
'stückweise *adv* bit by bit (*a.* fig); ECON by the piece
Student [ʃtu'dɛnt] *m* (-*en*; -*en*), Stu'dentin *f* (-; -*nen*) student
Studie ['ʃtuːdjə] *f* (-; -*n*) study (*über acc* of)
'Studienplatz *m* university *or* college place
studieren [ʃtu'diːrən] *v/t and v/i* (*no -ge-*, *h*) study, be a student (of) (*an dat* at)
Studium ['ʃtuːdjʊm] *n* (-*s*; -*ien*) studies; *das Studium der Medizin* etc the study of medicine etc
Stufe ['ʃtuːfə] *f* (-; -*n*) step; level; stage
'Stufenbarren *m* SPORT uneven parallel bars
Stuhl [ʃtuːl] *m* (-[*e*]*s*; Stühle ['ʃtyːlə]) chair; MED stool
Stuhlgang *m* (-[*e*]*s*; *no pl*) MED (bowel) movement
Stuhllehne *f* back of a chair
stülpen ['ʃtʏlpən] *v/t* (*ge-*, *h*) put (*auf acc*, *über acc* over, on)
stumm [ʃtʊm] *adj* dumb, mute; fig silent
Stummel ['ʃtʊməl] *m* (-*s*; -) stub, stump, butt
'Stummfilm *m* silent film
Stümper ['ʃtʏmpɐ] F *m* (-*s*; -) bungler
stumpf [ʃtʊmpf] *adj* blunt, dull (*a.* fig)
Stumpf *m* (-[*e*]*s*; Stümpfe ['ʃtʏmpfə]) stump, stub
'stumpfsinnig *adj* dull; monotonous
Stunde ['ʃtʊndə] *f* (-; -*n*) hour; PED class, lesson; period
'Stundenkilo,meter *m* kilometer (*Br* kilometre) per hour
'stundenlang 1. *adj*: *nach stundenlangem Warten* after hours of waiting; 2. *adv* for hours (and hours)
'Stundenlohn *m* hourly wage
'Stundenplan *m* schedule, *Br* timetable
'stundenweise *adv* by the hour
'Stundenzeiger *m* hour hand

stündlich ['ʃtʏntlɪç] **1.** *adj* hourly; **2.** *adv* hourly, every hour

Stupsnase ['ʃtʊps-] F *f* snub nose

stur [ʃtuːɐ] F *adj* pigheaded

Sturm [ʃtʊrm] *m* (-[e]s; *Stürme* ['ʃtʏrmə]) storm (*a. fig*)

stürmen ['ʃtʏrmən] *v/t* (*ge-*, *h*) *and v/i* (*ge-*, *sein*) storm; SPORT attack; rush

Stürmer(in) ['ʃtʏrmɐ (-mərɪn)] (-*s*; -/-; -*nen*) SPORT forward; *esp soccer*: striker

stürmisch ['ʃtʏrmɪʃ] *adj* stormy; *fig* wild, vehement

Sturz [ʃtʊrts] *m* (-*es*; *Stürze* ['ʃtʏrtsə]) fall (*a. fig*); POL *etc*: overthrow

stürzen ['ʃtʏrtsən] **1.** *v/i* (*ge-*, *sein*) fall; crash; rush, dash; *schwer stürzen* have a bad fall; **2.** *v/t* (*ge-*, *h*) throw; POL *etc*: overthrow; *j-n ins Unglück stürzen* ruin s.o.; *sich stürzen aus* throw o.s. out of; *sich stürzen auf* (*acc*) throw o.s. at

'**Sturzflug** *m* AVIAT nosedive

'**Sturzhelm** *m* crash helmet

Stute ['ʃtuːtə] *f* (-; -*n*) ZO mare

Stütze ['ʃtʏtsə] *f* (-; -*n*) support, prop; *fig a*. aid

stutzen ['ʃtʊtsən] (*ge-*, *h*) **1.** *v/t* trim, clip; **2.** *v/i* stop short; (begin to) wonder

stützen ['ʃtʏtsən] *v/t* (*ge-*, *h*) support (*a. fig*); *sich stützen auf* (*acc*) lean on; *fig* be based on

'**Stützpfeiler** *m* ARCH supporting column

Stützpunkt *m* MIL base (*a. fig*)

Styropor® [ʃtyro'poːɐ] *n* (-*s*; *no pl*) Styrofoam®, *Br* polystyrene

s. u. ABBR *of* **siehe unten** see below

Subjekt [zʊp'jɛkt] *n* (-[e]*s*; -*e*) LING subject; *contp* character

subjektiv [zʊpjɛk'tiːf] *adj* subjective

Substantiv ['zʊpstantiːf] *n* (-*s*; -*e*) LING noun

Substanz [zʊp'stants] *f* (-; -*en*) substance (*a. fig*)

subtrahieren [zʊptra'hiːrən] *v/t* (*no -ge-*, *h*) MATH subtract

Subtraktion [zʊptrak'tsjoːn] *f* (-; -*en*) MATH subtraction

subventionieren [zʊpvɛntsjo'niːrən] *v/t* (*no -ge-*, *h*) subsidize

Suche ['zuːxə] *f* (-; *no pl*) search (*nach* for); *auf der Suche nach* in search of

'**suchen** *v/t and v/i* (*ge-*, *h*) look for; search for; *gesucht:* ... wanted: ...; *was hat er hier zu suchen?* what's he doing here?; *er hat hier nichts zu suchen* he has no business to be here

Sucher ['zuːxɐ] *m* (-*s*; -) PHOT viewfinder

Sucht [zʊxt] *f* (-; *Süchte* ['zʏçtə]) addiction (*nach* to); mania (for)

süchtig ['zʏçtɪç] *adj*: *süchtig sein* be ad-

dicted to *drugs etc*, be a *drug etc* addict

Süchtige ['zʏçtɪgə] *m*, *f* (-*n*; -*n*) addict

Süden ['zyːdən] *m* (-*s*; *no pl*) south; *nach Süden* south(wards)

Südfrüchte ['zyːt-] *pl* tropical *or* southern fruits

'**südlich 1.** *adj* south(ern); southerly; **2.** *adv*: *südlich von* (to the) south of

Süd'osten *m* southeast

süd'östlich *adj* southeast(ern); southeasterly

'**Südpol** *m* South Pole

'**südwärts** [-vɛrts] *adv* southward(s)

Süd'westen *m* southwest

süd'westlich *adj* southwest(ern); southwesterly

'**Südwind** *m* south wind

Sülze ['zʏltsə] *f* (-; -*n*) GASTR jellied meat

Summe ['zʊmə] *f* (-; -*n*) sum (*a. fig*); amount; (sum) total

summen ['zʊmən] *v/i and v/t* (*ge-*, *h*) buzz, hum

summieren [zʊ'miːrən] *v/refl* (*no -ge-*, *h*) add up (*auf acc* to)

Sumpf [zʊmpf] *m* (-*es*; *Sümpfe* ['zʏmpfə]) swamp, bog

'**sumpfig** *adj* swampy, marshy

Sünde ['zʏndə] *f* (-; -*n*) sin (*a. fig*)

'**Sündenbock** F *m* scapegoat

Sünder ['zʏndɐ] *m* (-*s*; -), '**Sünderin** *f* (-; -*nen*) sinner

sündig ['zʏndɪç] *adj* sinful

sündigen ['zʏndɪgən] *v/i* (*ge-*, *h*) (commit a) sin

Super... ['zuːpɐ-] *in cpds* ...*macht etc*: mst super...

'**Super** *n* (-*s*; *no pl*), **Superben,zin** *n* super *or* premium (gasoline), *Br* four-star (petrol)

Superlativ ['zuːpɐlatiːf] *m* (-*s*; -*e*) LING superlative (*a. fig*)

'**Supermarkt** *m* supermarket

Suppe ['zʊpə] *f* (-; -*n*) soup

'**Suppen...** *in cpds* ...*löffel*, ...*teller*, ...*küche etc*: soup ...

Surfbrett ['zøːɐf-] *n* sail board; surfboard

'**surfen** *v/i* (*ge-*, *h*) go surfing

surren ['zʊrən] *v/i* (*ge-*, *h*) whirr; buzz

süß [zyːs] *adj* sweet, sugary (*both a. fig*)

Süße ['zyːsə] *f* (-; *no pl*) sweetness

'**süßen** *v/t* (*ge-*, *h*) sweeten

Süßigkeiten ['zyːsɪçkaitən] *pl* sweets, candy

'**süßlich** *adj* sweetish; *contp* mawkish, sugary

'**süß'sauer** *adj* GASTR sweet-and-sour

'**Süßstoff** *m* sweetener

'**Süßwasser** *n* fresh water

Symbol [zʏm'boːl] *n* (-*s*; -*e*) symbol

S

Symbolik [zʏmˈboːlɪk] *f* (-; *no pl*) symbolism

sym'bolisch *adj* symbolic(al)

Symmetrie [zʏmeˈtriː] *f* (-; -*n*) symmetry

symmetrisch [zʏˈmeːtrɪʃ] *adj* symmetric(al)

Sympathie [zʏmpaˈtiː] *f* (-; -*n*) liking (*für* for); sympathy

Sympathisant(in) [zʏmpatiˈzant(ɪn)] (-*en*; -*en*/-; -*nen*) sympathizer

sympathisch [zʏmˈpaːtɪʃ] *adj* nice, likable; *er ist mir sympathisch* I like him

Symphonie [zʏmfoˈniː] *f* (-; -*n*) *etc* → *Sinfonie*

Symptom [zʏmpˈtoːm] *n* (-*s*; -*e*) symptom

Synagoge [zynaˈɡoːɡə] *f* (-; -*n*) synagogue

synchron [zʏnˈkroːn] *adj* TECH synchronous

synchronisieren [zʏnkroniˈziːrən] *v/t* (*no* -*ge*-, *h*) synchronize; *film etc*: dub

synonym [zynoˈnyːm] *adj* synonymous

Syno'nym *n* (-*s*; -*e*) synonym

Synthese [zʏnˈteːzə] *f* (-; -*n*) synthesis

synthetisch [zʏnˈteːtɪʃ] *adj* synthetic

System [zʏsˈteːm] *n* (-*s*; -*e*) system

systematisch [zʏsteˈmaːtɪʃ] *adj* systematic, methodical

Sys'temfehler *m* EDP system error

Szene [ˈstseːnə] *f* (-; -*n*) scene (*a. fig*)

Szenerie [stsenəˈriː] *f* (-; -*n*) scenery; setting

T

Tabak [ˈtaːbak] *m* (-*s*; -*e*) tobacco

Tabakgeschäft *n* tobacconist's

Tabakwaren *pl* tobacco products

Tabelle [taˈbɛlə] *f* (-; -*n*) table (*a.* MATH, SPORT)

Ta'bellenkalkulati₁on *f* EDP spreadsheet

Tabellenplatz *m* SPORT position

Tablett [taˈblɛt] *n* (-[*e*]*s*; -*s*) tray

Tablette [taˈblɛtə] *f* (-; -*n*) tablet

tabu [taˈbuː] *adj*, **Ta'bu** *n* (-*s*; -*s*) taboo

Tabulator [tabuˈlaːtoːɐ] *m* (-*s*; -*en* [-laˈtoːrən]) tabulator

Tachometer [taxoˈmeːtɐ] *m*, *n* (-*s*; -) MOT speedometer

Tadel [ˈtaːdəl] *m* (-*s*; -) blame; censure, reproof, rebuke

'tadellos *adj* faultless; blameless; excellent; perfect

'tadeln *v/t* (*ge*-, *h*) criticize, blame; censure, reprove, rebuke (*all*: *wegen* for)

Tafel [ˈtaːfəl] *f* PED *etc*: blackboard; (bulletin, *esp Br* notice) board; sign; tablet, plaque; GASTR bar (*of chocolate*)

täfeln [ˈtɛːfəln] *v/t* (*ge*-, *h*) panel

'Täfelung *f* (-; -*en*) panel(l)ing

Taft [taft] *m* (-[*e*]*s*; -*e*) taffeta

Tag [taːk] *m* (-[*e*]*s*; -*e* [ˈtaːɡə]) day; daylight; *welchen Tag haben wir heute?* what day is it today?; *heute* (*morgen*) *in 14 Tagen* two weeks from today (tomorrow); *e-s Tages* one day; *den ganzen Tag* all day; *am Tage* during the day; *Tag und Nacht* night and day; *am*

helllichten Tag in broad daylight; *ein freier Tag* a day off; *guten Tag!* hello!, hi!; how do you do?; (*j-m*) *guten Tag sagen* say hello (to s.o.); F *sie hat ihre Tage* she has her period; *unter Tage* underground; → *zutage*

Tagebau [ˈtaːɡə-] *m* (-[*e*]*s*; -*e*) opencast mining

Tagebuch *n* diary; *Tagebuch führen* keep a diary

'tagelang *adv* for days

'tagen *v/i* (*ge*-, *h*) meet, hold a meeting; JUR be in session

'Tagesanbruch *m*: *bei Tagesanbruch* at daybreak, at dawn

Tagesgespräch *n* talk of the day

Tageskarte *f* day ticket; GASTR menu for the day

Tageslicht *n* (-[*e*]*s*; *no pl*) daylight

Tagesmutter *f* childminder

Tagesordnung *f* agenda

Tagesstätte *f* day care center (*Br* centre)

Tagestour *f* day trip

Tageszeit *f* time of day; *zu jeder Tageszeit* at any hour

Tageszeitung *f* daily (paper)

'tageweise *adv* by the day

täglich [ˈtɛːklɪç] *adj and adv* daily

'Tagschicht *f* ECON day shift

'tagsüber *adv* during the day

'Tagung *f* (-; -*en*) conference

Taille [ˈtaljə] *f* (-; -*n*) waist; waistline

tailliert [taˈjiːɐt] *adj* waisted, tapered

Takelage [takə'laːʒə] *f* (-; *-n*) MAR rigging

Takt [takt] *m* (*-[e]s*; *-e*) a) (*no pl*) MUS time, measure, beat, b) MUS bar, c) MOT stroke, d) (*no pl*) tact; *den Takt halten* MUS keep time

Taktik ['taktɪk] *f* (-; *-en*) MIL tactics (*a. fig*)

'**taktisch** *adj* tactical

'**taktlos** *adj* tactless

'**Taktstock** *m* MUS baton

'**Taktstrich** *m* MUS bar

'**taktvoll** *adj* tactful

Tal [taːl] *n* (*-[e]s*; *Täler* ['tɛːlɐ]) valley

Talar [ta'laːɐ] *m* (*-s*; *-e*) robe, gown

Talent [ta'lɛnt] *n* (*-[e]s*; *-e*) talent (*a. person*), gift

talentiert [talɛn'tiːɐt] *adj* talented, gifted

Talg [talk] *m* (*-[e]s*; *-e*) tallow; GASTR suet

Talisman ['taːlɪsman] *m* (*-s*; *-e*) talisman, charm

Talkmaster ['tɔːk-] *m* (*-s*; -) TV talk (*Br* chat) show host

Talkshow [-ʃoʊ] *f* (-; *-s*) TV talk (*Br* chat) show

'**Talsperre** *f* dam, barrage

Tampon ['tampɔn] *m* (*-s*; *-s*) tampon

Tandler ['tandlɐ] *Austrian m* (*-s*; -) second-hand dealer

Tang [taŋ] *m* (*-[e]s*; *-e*) BOT seaweed

Tank [taŋk] *m* (*-s*; *-s*) tank

tanken ['taŋkən] *v/t* (*ge-*, *h*) get some gasoline (*Br* petrol), fill up

Tanker ['taŋkɐ] *m* (*-s*; -) MAR tanker

'**Tankstelle** *f* filling (*or* gas, *Br* petrol) station

'**Tankwart** *m* (*-[e]s*; *-e*) gas station (*Br* petrol pump) attendant

Tanne ['tanə] *f* (-; *-n*) BOT fir (tree)

'**Tannenbaum** *m* Christmas tree

'**Tannenzapfen** *m* BOT fir cone

Tante ['tantə] *f* (-; *-n*) aunt; *Tante Lindy* Aunt Lindy

Tante-Emma-Laden F *m* mom-and-pop store, *Br* corner shop

Tantiemen [tã'tjeːmən] *pl* royalties

Tanz [tants] *m* (*-es*; *Tänze* ['tɛntsə]), **tanzen** ['tantsən] *v/i* (*ge-*, *h*, *sein*) *and v/t* (*ge-*, *h*) dance

Tänzer ['tɛntsɐ] *m* (*-s*; -), **Tänzerin** ['tɛntsərɪn] *f* (-; *-nen*) dancer

'**Tanzfläche** *f* dance floor

Tanzkurs *m* dancing lessons

Tanzmu,sik *f* dance music

Tanzschule *f* dancing school

Tapete [ta'peːtə] *f* (-; *-n*), **tapezieren** [tape'tsiːrən] *v/t* (*no -ge-*, *h*) wallpaper

tapfer ['tapfɐ] *adj* brave; courageous

'**Tapferkeit** *f* (-; *no pl*) bravery; courage

Tarif [ta'riːf] *m* (*-[e]s*; *-e*) rate(s), tariff; (wage) scale

Tariflohn *m* standard wage(s)

Tarifverhandlungen *pl* wage negotiations, collective bargaining

tarnen ['tarnən] *v/t* (*ge-*, *h*) camouflage; *fig* disguise

'**Tarnung** *f* (-; *-en*) camouflage

Tasche ['taʃə] *f* (-; *-n*) bag; pocket

'**Taschenbuch** *n* paperback

Taschendieb *m* pickpocket

Taschengeld *n* allowance, *Br* pocket money

Taschenlampe *f* flashlight, *Br* torch

Taschenmesser *n* penknife, pocketknife

Taschenrechner *m* pocket calculator

Taschenschirm *m* telescopic umbrella

Taschentuch *n* handkerchief, F hankie

Taschenuhr *f* pocket watch

Tasse ['tasə] *f* (-; *-n*) cup; *e-e Tasse Tee etc* a cup of tea *etc*

Tastatur [tasta'tuːɐ] *f* (-; *-en*) keyboard, keys

Taste ['tastə] *f* (-; *-n*) key

tasten ['tastən] (*ge-*, *h*) **1.** *v/i* grope (*nach* for), feel (for); fumble (for); **2.** *v/t* touch, feel; *sich tasten* feel *or* grope (*a. fig*) one's way

'**Tastentele,fon** *n* push-button phone

'**Tastsinn** *m* (*-[e]s*; *no pl*) sense of touch

tat [taːt] *pret of* **tun**

Tat *f* (-; *-en*) act, deed; action; JUR offense, *Br* offence; *j-n auf frischer Tat ertappen* catch s.o. in the act

'**tatenlos** *adj* inactive, passive

Täter ['tɛːtɐ] *m* (*-s*, -), '**Täterin** *f* (-; *-nen*) culprit; JUR offender

tätig ['tɛːtɪç] *adj* active; busy; *tätig sein bei* be employed with; *tätig werden* act, take action

'**Tätigkeit** *f* (-; *-en*) activity; work; occupation, job; *in Tätigkeit* in action

'**Tatkraft** *f* (-; *no pl*) energy

'**tatkräftig** *adj* energetic, active

tätlich ['tɛːtlɪç] *adj* violent; *tätlich werden gegen* assault

'**Tätlichkeiten** *pl* (acts of) violence; JUR assault (and battery)

'**Tatort** *m* JUR scene of the crime

tätowieren [tɛto'viːrən] *v/t* (*no -ge-*, *h*), **Täto'wierung** *f* (-; *-en*) tattoo

'**Tatsache** *f* fact

'**tatsächlich 1.** *adj* actual, real; **2.** *adv* actually, in fact; really

tätscheln ['tɛːtʃəln] *v/t* (*ge-*, *h*) pat, pet

Tatze ['tatsə] *f* (-; *-n*) ZO paw (*a. fig*)

Tau[1] [tau] *n* (*-[e]s*; *-e*) rope

Tau[2] *m* (*-[e]s*; *no pl*) dew

taub [taup] *adj* deaf (*fig gegen* to); numb, benumbed

Taube ['taubə] *f* (-; *-n*) ZO pigeon; *esp fig*

dove

'Taubenschlag *m* pigeonhouse

'Taubheit *f* (-; *no pl*) deafness; numbness

'taubstumm *adj* deaf-and-dumb

'Taubstumme *m*, *f* (-*n*; -*n*) deaf mute

tauchen ['tauxən] **1.** *v/i* (*ge-*, *h*, *sein*) dive (*nach* for); SPORT skin-dive; *submarine*: *a.* submerge; stay underwater; **2.** *v/t* (*h*) dip (*in acc* into); duck

Taucher ['tauxɐ] *m* (-*s*; -) (SPORT skin) diver

'Tauchsport *m* skin diving

tauen ['tauən] *v/i* (*ge-*, *sein*) *and v/t* (*ge-*, *h*) thaw, melt

Taufe ['taufə] *f* (-; -*n*) baptism, christening

'taufen *v/t* (*ge-*, *h*) baptize, christen

'Taufpate *m* godfather

'Taufpatin *f* godmother

'Taufschein *m* certificate of baptism

taugen ['taugən] *v/i* (*ge-*, *h*) be good *or* fit *or* of use *or* suited (*all*: *zu*, *für* for); *nichts taugen* be no good; F *taugt es was?* is it any good?

tauglich ['tauklɪç] *adj esp* MIL fit (for service)

Taumel ['tauməl] *m* (-*s*; *no pl*) dizziness; rapture, ecstasy

'taumelig *adj* dizzy

'taumeln *v/i* (*ge-*, *sein*) stagger, reel

Tausch [tauʃ] *m* (-[*e*]*s*; -*e*) exchange, F swap

tauschen ['tauʃən] *v/t* (*ge-*, *h*) exchange, F swap (*both*: *gegen* for); switch; change; *ich möchte nicht mit ihm tauschen* I wouldn't like to be in his shoes

täuschen ['tɔyʃən] *v/t* (*ge-*, *h*) deceive, fool; delude; cheat; *a.* SPORT feint; *sich täuschen* deceive o.s.; be mistaken; *sich täuschen lassen von* be taken in by; *täuschende Ähnlichkeit* striking similarity

'Täuschung *f* (-; -*en*) deception; delusion; JUR deceit; *a.* PED cheating

tausend ['tauzənt] *adj* a thousand

'tausendst *adj* thousandth

'Tausendstel *n* (-*s*; -) thousandth (part)

'Tautropfen *m* dewdrop

'Tauwetter *n* thaw

'Tauziehen *n* (-*s*; *no pl*) SPORT tug-of-war (*a. fig*)

Taxi ['taksi] *n* (-*s*; -*s*) taxi(cab), cab

taxieren [ta'ksiːrən] *v/t* (*no -ge-*, *h*) rate, estimate (*auf acc* at)

'Taxistand *m* cabstand, *esp Br* taxi rank

Technik ['tɛçnɪk] *f* (-; -*en*) a) (*no pl*) technology, engineering, b) technique (*a.* SPORT *etc*)

Techniker ['tɛçnikɐ] *m* (-*s*; -), 'Technikerin *f* (-; -*nen*) engineer; technician (*a.* SPORT *etc*)

technisch ['tɛçnɪʃ] *adj* technical; technological; *technische Hochschule* school *etc* of technology

Technologie [tɛçnolo'giː] *f* (-; -*n*) technology

technologisch [tɛçno'loːgɪʃ] *adj* technological

Tee [teː] *m* (-*s*; -*s*) tea; (*e-n*) *Tee trinken* have some tea; (*e-n*) *Tee machen* or *kochen* make some tea

Teebeutel *m* teabag

Teekanne *f* teapot

Teelöffel *m* teaspoon

Teer [teːɐ] *m* (-[*e*]*s*; -*e*), teeren ['teːrən] *v/t* (*ge-*, *h*) tar

'Teesieb *n* tea strainer

'Teetasse *f* teacup

Teich [taiç] *m* (-[*e*]*s*; -*e*) pool, pond

Teig [taik] *m* (-[*e*]*s*; -*e*) dough, paste

teigig ['taigɪç] *adj* doughy, pasty

'Teigwaren *pl* pasta

Teil [tail] *m*, *n* (-[*e*]*s*; -*e*) part; portion; share; component; *zum Teil* partly, in part

Teil... *in cpds* ...erfolg *etc*: partial ...

'teilbar *adj* divisible

'Teilchen *n* (-*s*; -) particle

teilen ['tailən] *v/t* (*ge-*, *h*) divide; share

'teilhaben *v/i* (*irr*, *haben*, *sep*, *-ge-*, *h*) *teilhaben an* (*dat*) (have a) share in

'Teilhaber(in) [-haːbɐ (-bərɪn)] (-*s*; -/-; -*nen*) ECON partner

'Teilnahme [-naːmə] *f* (-; *no pl*) participation (*an dat* in); *fig* interest (in); sympathy (for)

'teilnahmslos *adj* indifferent; *esp* MED apathetic

'Teilnahmslosigkeit *f* (-; *no pl*) indifference; apathy

'teilnehmen *v/i* (*irr*, *nehmen*, *sep*, *-ge-*, *h*) *teilnehmen an* (*dat*) take part *or* participate in; share (in)

'Teilnehmer(in) [-neːmɐ (-mərɪn)] (-*s*; -/-; -*nen*) participant; UNIV student; SPORT competitor

teils *adv* partly

'Teilstrecke *f* stage, leg

'Teilung *f* (-; -*en*) division

'teilweise *adv* partly, in part

'Teilzahlung *f* → *Abzahlung*, *Rate*

Teint [tɛ̃ː] *m* (-*s*; -*s*) complexion

Tel. ABBR *of Telefon* tel., telephone

Telefon [tele'foːn] *n* (-*s*; -*e*) telephone, phone; *am Telefon* on the (tele)phone; *Telefon haben* have a (*Br* be on the) (tele)phone; *ans Telefon gehen* answer the (tele)phone

Telefonanruf *m* (tele)phone call

Telefonanschluss *m* telephone connection

Telefonappa,rat *m* telephone, phone

Telefonat [telefo'naːt] *n* (-[*e*]*s*; *-e*) → **Telefongespräch**

Tele'fonbuch *n* telephone directory, phone book

Telefongebühr *f* telephone charge

Telefongespräch *n* (tele)phone call

telefonieren [telefo'niːrən] *v/i* (*no -ge-*, *h*) (tele)phone; be on the phone; **mit j-m telefonieren** talk to s.o. on the phone

telefonisch [tele'foːnɪʃ] **1.** *adj* telephonic, telephone …; **2.** *adv* by (tele)phone, over the (tele)phone

Telefonist [telefo'nɪst] *m* (-*en*; -*en*), **Telefo'nistin** *f* (-; -*nen*) (telephone) operator

Tele'fonkarte *f* phonecard

Telefonleitung *f* telephone line

Telefonnetz *n* telephone network

Telefonnummer *f* (tele)phone number

Telefonzelle *f* (tele)phone booth, *esp Br* (tele)phone box, *Br* call box

Telefonzen,trale *f* switchboard

telegrafieren [telegra'fiːrən] *v/t and v/i* (*no -ge-*, *h*) telegraph, wire; cable

telegrafisch [tele'graːfɪʃ] *adj and adv* by telegraph, by wire, by cable

Telegramm [tele'gram] *n* (-*s*; *-e*) telegram, wire, cable(gram)

Teleobjektiv ['teːlə-] *n* telephoto lens

Telephon *n* → **Telefon**

Teletext ['teːlə-] *m* teletext

Teller ['tɛlɐ] *m* (-*s*; -) plate

Tellerwäscher [-vɛʃɐ] *m* (-*s*; -) dishwasher

Tempel ['tɛmpəl] *m* (-*s*; -) temple

Temperament [tɛmpəra'mɛnt] *n* (-[*e*]*s*; *-e*) temper(ament); life, F pep

tempera'mentlos *adj* lifeless, dull

temperamentvoll *adj* full of life *or* F pep

Temperatur [tɛmpəra'tuːɐ] *f* (-; *-en*) temperature; **j-s Temperatur messen** take s.o.'s temperature

Tempo ['tɛmpo] *n* (-*s*; -*s*, *-pi*) speed; MUS time; **mit Tempo** … at a speed of … an hour

Tendenz [tɛn'dɛnts] *f* (-; *-en*) tendency, trend; leaning

tendenziös [tɛndɛn'tsjøːs] *adj* tendentious

tendieren [tɛn'diːrən] *v/i* (*no -ge-*, *h*) tend (**zu** towards; **dazu, et. zu tun** to do s.th.)

Tennis ['tɛnɪs] *n* (-; *no pl*) tennis

Tennisplatz *m* tennis court

Tennisschläger *m* tennis racket

Tennisspieler(in) tennis player

Tenor [te'noːɐ] *m* (-*s*; *Tenöre* [te'nøːrə]) MUS tenor

Teppich ['tɛpɪç] *m* (-*s*; *-e*) carpet

'**Teppichboden** *m* fitted carpet, wall-to-wall carpeting

Termin [tɛr'miːn] *m* (-*s*; *-e*) date; deadline; engagement; **e-n Termin vereinbaren (einhalten, absagen)** make (keep, cancel) an appointment

Terminal ['tøːɐmɪnəl] a) *m*, *n* (-*s*; *-s*) AVIAT terminal, b) *n* (-*s*; *-s*) EDP terminal

Terrasse [tɛ'rasə] *f* (-; *-n*) terrace

ter'rassenförmig [-fœrmɪç] *adj* terraced, in terraces

Terrine [tɛ'riːnə] *f* (-; *-n*) tureen

Territorium [tɛri'toːrjʊm] *n* (-*s*; *-ien*) territory

Terror ['tɛroːɐ] *m* (-*s*; *no pl*) terror

terrorisieren [tɛrori'ziːrən] *v/t* (*no -ge-*, *h*) terrorize

Terrorismus [tɛro'rɪsmʊs] *m* (-; *no pl*) terrorism

Terrorist(in) [-'rɪst(ɪn)] (-*en*; -*en*/-; *-nen*), **terro'ristisch** *adj* terrorist

Testament [tɛsta'mɛnt] *n* (-[*e*]*s*; *-e*) (last) will; JUR last will and testament

testamentarisch [tɛstamɛn'taːrɪʃ] *adv* by will

Testa'mentsvollstrecker *m* executor

Testbild ['tɛst-] *n* TV test card

testen ['tɛstən] *v/t* (*no -ge-*, *h*) test

'**Testpi,lot** *m* test pilot

Tetanus ['teːtanʊs] *m* (-; *no pl*) MED tetanus

teuer ['tɔyɐ] *adj* expensive; **wie teuer ist es?** how much is it?

Teufel ['tɔyfəl] *m* (-*s*; -) devil (*a. fig*); **wer (wo, was) zum Teufel …?** who (where, what) the hell …?

'**Teufelskerl** F *m* devil of a fellow

'**Teufelskreis** *m* vicious circle

teuflisch ['tɔyflɪʃ] *adj* devilish, diabolic(al)

Text [tɛkst] *m* (-[*e*]*s*; *-e*) text; MUS words, lyrics

Texter ['tɛkstɐ] *m* (-*s*; -), '**Texterin** *f* (-; -*nen*) MUS songwriter

Textil… [tɛks'tiːl-] *in cpds* textile …

Textilien [tɛks'tiːljən] *pl* textiles

'**Textverarbeitung** *f* EDP word processing

'**Textverarbeitungsgerät** *n* EDP word processor

Theater [te'aːtɐ] *n* (-*s*; -) theater, *Br* theatre; F **Theater machen (um)** make a fuss (about)

Theaterbesucher *m* theatergoer, *Br* theatregoer

Theaterkarte *f* theater (*Br* theatre) ticket

Theaterkasse *f* box office

Theaterstück *n* play

Thema ['teːma] *n* (-*s*; *Themen*) subject, topic; MUS theme; **das Thema wechseln**

change the subject
Theologe [teo'lo:gə] *m* (*-n*; *-n*) theologian
Theologie [teolo'gi:] *f* (*-*; *-n*) theology
Theo'login *f* (*-*; *-nen*) theologian
theo'logisch *adj* theological
Theoretiker [teo're:tikɐ] *m* (*-s*; *-*) theorist
theo'retisch *adj* theoretical
Theorie [teo'ri:] *f* (*-*; *-n*) theory
Therapeut [tera'pɔyt] *m* (*-en*; *-en*), **Therapeutin** *f* (*-*; *-nen*) therapist
Therapie [-'pi:] *f* (*-*; *-n*) therapy
Thermometer [tɛrmo'me:tɐ] *n* (*-s*; *-*) thermometer
Thermosflasche® ['tɛrmɔs-] *f* thermos®
These ['te:zə] *f* (*-*; *-n*) thesis
Thon [to:n] *Swiss m* (*-s*; *-s*) tuna (fish)
Thrombose [trɔm'bo:zə] *f* (*-*; *-n*) MED thrombosis
Thron [tro:n] *m* (*-[e]s*; *-e*) throne
'Thronfolger [-fɔlgɐ] *m* (*-s*; *-*), **'Thronfolgerin** [-fɔlgərɪn] *f* (*-*; *-nen*) successor to the throne
Thunfisch ['tu:n-] *m* tuna (fish)
Tick [tɪk] F *m* (*-[e]s*; *-s*) quirk
ticken ['tɪkən] *v/i* (*ge-*, *h*) tick
Tiebreak, **Tie-Break** ['taɪbreɪk] *m*, *n tennis*: tiebreak(er)
tief [ti:f] *adj* deep (*a. fig*); low
Tief *n* (*-s*; *-s*) METEOR depression (*a.* PSYCH, ECON), low (*a. fig*)
Tiefe ['ti:fə] *f* (*-*; *-n*) depth (*a. fig*)
'Tiefebene *f* lowland(s)
Tiefflieger *m* low-flying air plane
Tiefgang *m* MAR draft, *Br* draught; *fig* depth
Tiefga,rage *f* parking *or* underground garage, *Br* underground car park
'tiefgekühlt *adj* deep-frozen
'Tiefkühlfach *n* freezing compartment
Tiefkühlschrank *m*, **Tiefkühltruhe** *f* freezer, deep-freeze
Tiefkühlkost *f* frozen foods
Tier [ti:ɐ] *n* (*-[e]s*; *-e*) animal; F *hohes Tier* bigwig, big shot
Tierarzt *m*, **-ärztin** *f* veterinarian, *Br* veterinary surgeon, F vet
Tierfreund *m* animal lover
Tiergarten *m* → *Zoo*
Tierheim *n* animal shelter
tierisch ['ti:rɪʃ] *adj* animal; *fig* bestial, brutish
'Tierkreis *m* ASTR zodiac
Tierkreiszeichen *n* sign of the zodiac
'Tiermedi,zin *f* veterinary medicine
Tierquäle'rei *f* cruelty to animals
'Tierreich *n* animal kingdom
Tierschutz *m* protection of animals
Tierschutzverein *m* society for the prevention of cruelty to animals

Tierversuch *m* MED experiment with animals
Tiger ['ti:gɐ] *m* (*-s*; *-*) ZO tiger
Tigerin ['ti:gərɪn] *f* (*-*; *-nen*) ZO tigress
tilgen ['tɪlgən] *v/t* (*ge-*, *h*) ECON pay off
Tinte ['tɪntə] *f* (*-*; *-n*) ink
'Tintenfisch *m* ZO squid
Tipp [tɪp] *m* (*-s*; *-s*) hint, tip; tip-off; *j-m e-n Tipp geben* tip s.o. off
tippen ['tɪpən] *v/i and v/t* (*ge-*, *h*) tap; type; F guess; do *lotto etc*
Tisch [tɪʃ] *m* (*-[e]s*; *-e*) table; *am Tisch sitzen* sit at the table; *bei Tisch* at table; *den Tisch decken* (*abräumen*) lay (clear) the table
Tischdecke *f* tablecloth
Tischgebet *n* REL grace: *das Tischgebet sprechen* say grace
Tischler ['tɪʃlɐ] *m* (*-s*; *-*) joiner; cabinet-marker
'Tischplatte *f* tabletop
Tischrechner *m* desktop computer
Tischtennis *n* table tennis
Tischtuch *n* tablecloth
Titel ['ti:təl] *m* (*-s*; *-*) title
Titelbild *n* cover picture
Titelblatt *n*, **Titelseite** *f* title page; cover, front page
Toast [to:st] *m* (*-[e]s*; *-s*), **toasten** ['to:stən] *v/t* (*ge-*, *h*) toast
toben ['to:bən] *v/i* (*ge-*, *h*) rage (*a. fig*); romp
tobsüchtig ['to:p-] *adj* raving mad
'Tobsuchtsanfall *m* tantrum
Tochter ['tɔxtɐ] *f* (*-*; *Töchter* ['tœçtɐ]) daughter
Tochtergesellschaft *f* ECON subsidiary (company)
Tod [to:t] *m* (*-[e]s*; *no pl*) death (*a. fig*) (*durch* from)
tod... *in cpds ...ernst, ...müde, ...sicher:* dead ...
Todesängste ['to:dəs-] *pl*: *Todesängste ausstehen* be scared to death
Todesanzeige *f* obituary (notice)
Todesfall *m* (case of) death
Todeskampf *m* agony
Todesopfer *n* casualty
Todesstrafe *f* JUR capital punishment; death penalty
Todesursache *f* cause of death
Todesurteil *n* JUR death sentence
'Todfeind *m* deadly enemy
'tod'krank *adj* mortally ill
tödlich ['tø:tlɪç] *adj* fatal; deadly; *esp fig* mortal
'Todsünde *f* mortal *or* deadly sin
Toilette [toa'lɛtə] *f* (*-*; *-n*) bathroom, *Br* toilet, lavatory; *pl* rest rooms, *Br* ladies'

T

or men's rooms

Toi'letten... *in cpds* ...*papier,* ...*seife etc*: toilet ...

Toilettentisch *m* dressing table

tolerant [tole'rant] *adj* tolerant (*gegen* of, towards)

Toleranz [tole'rants] *f* (-; -*en*) tolerance (*a.* TECH)

tolerieren [tole'ri:rən] *v/t* (*no* -*ge*-, *h*) tolerate

toll [tɔl] *adj* wild; F great, fantastic

'tollkühn *adj* daredevil

'Tollwut *f* VET rabies

'tollwütig [-vy:tɪç] *adj* VET rabid

Tomate [to'ma:tə] *f* (-; -*n*) BOT tomato

Ton[1] [to:n] *m* (-[*e*]*s*; -*e*) clay

Ton[2] *m* (-[*e*]*s*; *Töne* ['tø:nə]) tone (*a.* MUS, PAINT), PAINT *a.* shade; sound (*a.* TV, *film*); note; stress; *kein Ton* not a word

Tonabnehmer *m* ELECTR pickup

Tonart *f* MUS key

Tonband *n* (-[*e*]*s*; -*bänder*) (recording) tape

Tonbandgerät *n* tape recorder

tönen ['tø:nən] (*ge*-, *h*) **1.** *v/i* sound, ring; **2.** *v/t* tinge, tint, shade

'Tonfall *m* tone (of voice); accent

Tonfilm *m* sound film

Tonkopf *m* ELECTR (magnetic) head

Tonlage *f* MUS pitch

Tonleiter *f* MUS scale

Tonne ['tɔnə] *f* (-; -*n*) barrel; (metric) ton

'Tontechniker *m* sound engineer

'Tönung *f* (-; -*en*) tint, tinge, shade

Topf [tɔpf] *m* (-[*e*]*s*; *Töpfe* ['tœpfə]) pot; saucepan

Topfen ['tɔpfən] *Austrian m* (-*s*; *no pl*) GASTR curd(s)

Töpfer ['tœpfɐ] *m* (-*s*; -) potter

Töpferei [tœpfə'rai] *f* (-; -*en*) pottery

'Töpferin *f* (-; -*nen*) potter

'Töpferscheibe *f* potter's wheel

'Töpferware *f* pottery, earthenware

Tor [to:ɐ] *n* (-[*e*]*s*; -*e*) gate; *soccer etc*: goal; *ein Tor schießen* score (a goal); *im Tor stehen* keep goal

Torf [tɔrf] *m* (-[*e*]*s*; -*e*) peat

'Torfmull *m* peat dust

'Torhüter [-hy:tɐ] *m* → **Torwart**

torkeln ['tɔrkəln] F *v/i* (*ge*-, *h*, *sein*) reel, stagger

'Torlatte *f* SPORT crossbar

'Torlinie *f* SPORT goal line

torpedieren [tɔrpe'di:rən] *v/t* (*no* -*ge*-, *h*) MIL torpedo (*a. fig*)

'Torpfosten *m* SPORT goalpost

Torraum *m* SPORT goalmouth

Torschuss *m* SPORT shot at goal

Torschütze *m* SPORT scorer

Torte ['tɔrtə] *f* (-; -*n*) pie, *esp Br* flan; cream cake, gateau

'Torwart [-vart] *m* (-[*e*]*s*; -*e*) SPORT goalkeeper, F goalie

tosen ['to:zən] *v/i* (*ge*-, *h*) roar; thunder

tosend *adj* thunderous (*applause*)

tot [to:t] *adj* dead (*a. fig*); late; *tot geboren* MED stillborn; *tot umfallen* drop dead

total [to'ta:l] *adj* total, complete

totalitär [totali'tɛ:ɐ] *adj* POL totalitarian

'Tote *m, f* (-*n*; -*n*) dead man *or* woman; (dead) body, corpse; *mst pl* casualty; *pl the* dead

töten ['tø:tən] *v/t* (*ge*-, *h*) kill

'Totenbett *n* deathbed

'toten'blass *adj* deadly pale

'Totengräber [-grɛ:bɐ] *m* (-*s*; -) gravedigger

Totenkopf *m* skull; skull and crossbones

Totenmaske *f* death mask

Totenmesse *f* REL mass for the dead, requiem (*a.* MUS)

Totenschädel *m* skull

Totenschein *m* death certificate

'toten'still *adj* deathly still

'totlachen F *v/refl* (*sep*, -*ge*-, *h*) kill o.s. laughing

Toto ['to:to] *m*, F *n* (-*s*; -*s*) football pools

'Totschlag *m* (-[*e*]*s*; *no pl*) JUR manslaughter

'totschlagen *v/t* (*irr*, *schlagen*, *sep*, -*ge*-, *h*) kill; *j-n totschlagen* beat s.o. to death; *die Zeit totschlagen* kill time

'totschweigen *v/t* (*irr*, *schweigen*, *sep*, -*ge*-, *h*) hush up

Toupet [tu'pe:] *n* (-*s*; -*s*) toupee

toupieren [tu'pi:rən] *v/t* (*no* -*ge*-, *h*) Br backcomb

Tour [tu:ɐ] *f* (-; -*en*) tour (*durch* of), trip; excursion; TECH. turn, revolution; *auf Touren kommen* MOT pick up speed; F *krumme Touren* underhand methods

Touren... ['tu:rən-] *in cpds* ...*rad etc*: touring ...

Tourismus [tu'rɪsmʊs] *m* (-; *no pl*) tourism

Tourismusgeschäft *n* tourist industry

Tourist [tu'rɪst] *m* (-*en*; -*en*), **Tou'ristin** *f* (-; -*nen*) tourist

tou'ristisch *adj* touristic

Tournee [tʊr'ne:] *f* (-; -*s*, -*n*) tour; *auf Tournee gehen* go on tour

Trab [tra:p] *m* (-[*e*]*s*; *no pl*) trot

Trabant [tra'bant] *m* (-*en*; -*en*) ASTR satellite

Tra'bantenstadt *f* satellite town

traben ['tra:bən] *v/i* (*ge*-, *sein*) trot

Traber ['tra:bɐ] *m* (-*s*; -) ZO trotter

'**Trabrennen** *n* trotting race

Tracht [traxt] *f* (-; *-en*) costume; uniform; dress; F *e-e Tracht Prügel* a thrashing

trächtig ['trɛçtıç] *adj* zo with young, pregnant

Tradition [tradi'tsjoːn] *f* (-; *-en*) tradition

traditionell [traditsjoʼnɛl] *adj* traditional

traf [traːf] *pret of* **treffen**

Trafik [tra'fɪk] *Austrian f* (-; *-en*) → *Tabakgeschäft*

Trafikant [trafi'kant] *Austrian m* (*-en*; *-en*) tobacconist

Tragbahre ['traːk-] *f* stretcher

'**tragbar** *adj* portable; wearable; *fig* bearable; *person*: acceptable

Trage ['traːgə] *f* (-; *-n*) stretcher

träge ['trɛːgə] *adj* lazy, indolent; PHYS inert (*a. fig*)

tragen [traːgən] (*irr, ge-, h*) **1.** *v/t* carry; wear; *fig* bear; *sich gut tragen* wear well; **2.** *v/i* BOT bear fruit; *fig* hold

tragend *adj* ARCH supporting; THEA leading

Träger ['trɛːgɐ] *m* (*-s*; -) carrier; porter; (shoulder) strap; TECH support; ARCH girder; *fig* bearer

'**trägerlos** *adj* strapless

'**Tragetasche** *f* carrier bag; carrycot

'**tragfähig** *adj* load-bearing; *fig* sound

'**Tragfläche** *f* AVIAT wing

Trägheit ['trɛːkhait] *f* (-; *no pl*) laziness, indolence; PHYS inertia (*a. fig*)

Tragik ['traːgık] *f* (-; *no pl*) tragedy

tragisch ['traːgıʃ] *adj* tragic

Tragödie [tra'gøːdjə] *f* (-; *-n*) tragedy

'**Tragriemen** *m* strap; sling

'**Tragweite** *f* range; *fig* significance

Trainer ['trɛːnɐ] *m* (*-s*; -), '**Trainerin** *f* (-; *-nen*) SPORT trainer, coach

trainieren [trɛ'niːrən] *v/i and v/t* (*no -ge-, h*) SPORT train, coach

'**Training** *n* (*-s*; *-s*) training

'**Trainingsanzug** *m* track suit

Traktor ['traktoːɐ] *m* (*-s*; *-en* [trak'toːrən]) MOT tractor

trällern ['trɛlɐn] *v/t and v/i* (*ge-*, *h*) warble, trill

Tram [tram] *Austrian f* (-; *-s*), *Swiss n* (*-s*; *-s*) streetcar, *Br* tram

trampeln ['trampəln] *v/i* (*ge-*, *h*) trample, stamp

'**Trampelpfad** *m* beaten track

trampen ['trɛmpən] *v/i* (*ge-*, *sein*) hitchhike

Tramper(in) ['trɛmpɐ (-pərın)] (*-s*; -/-; *-nen*) hitchhiker

Träne ['trɛːnə] *f* (-; *-n*) tear; *in Tränen ausbrechen* burst into tears

'**tränen** *v/i* (*ge-*, *h*) water

'**Tränengas** *n* tear gas

trank [traŋk] *pret of* **trinken**

Tränke ['trɛŋkə] *f* (-; *-n*) watering place

'**tränken** *v/t* (*ge-*, *h*) zo water; soak, drench

Transfer [trans'feːɐ] *m* (*-s*; *-s*) transfer (*a.* SPORT)

Transformator [transfɔr'maːtoːɐ] *m* (*-s*; *-en* [-ma'toːrən]) ELECTR transformer

Transfusion [transfu'zjoːn] *f* (-; *-en*) MED transfusion

Transistor [tran'zıstoːɐ] *m* (*-s*; *-en* [-zıs'toːrən]) ELECTR transistor

Transit [tran'ziːt] *m* (*-s*; *-e*) transit

transitiv ['tranzitiːf] *adj* LING transitive

transparent [transpa'rɛnt] *adj* transparent

Transpa'rent *n* (*-[e]s*; *-e*) banner

Transplantation [transplanta'tsjoːn] *f* (-; *-en*), **transplantieren** [-'tiːrən] *v/t* (*no -ge-, h*) MED transplant

Transport [trans'pɔrt] *m* (*-[e]s*; *-e*) transport; shipment

transportabel [transpɔr'taːbəl], **trans'portfähig** *adj* transportable

transportieren [transpɔr'tiːrən] *v/t* (*no -ge-, h*) transport, ship, carry, MOT *a.* haul

Trans'portmittel *n* (means of) transport(ation)

Transportunternehmen *n* hauler, *Br* haulier

Trapez [tra'peːts] *n* (*-es*; *-e*) MATH trapezoid, *Br* trapezium; SPORT trapeze

trappeln ['trapəln] *v/i* (*ge-*, *sein*) clatter; patter

trat [traːt] *pret of* **treten**

Traube ['traubə] *f* (-; *-n*) BOT bunch of grapes; grape; *pl* grapes; *fig* cluster

Traubensaft *m* grape juice

'**Traubenzucker** *m* glucose

trauen ['trauən] (*ge-*, *h*) **1.** *v/t* marry; **2.** *v/i* trust (*j-m* s.o.); *sich trauen, et. zu tun* dare (to) do s.th.; *ich traute meinen Augen nicht* I couldn't believe my eyes

Trauer ['trauɐ] *f* (-; *no pl*) grief, sorrow; mourning; *in Trauer* in mourning

Trauerfall *m* death

Trauerfeier *f* funeral service

Trauermarsch *m* MUS funeral march

'**trauern** *v/i* (*ge-*, *h*) mourn (*um* for)

'**Trauerrede** *f* funeral oration

'**Trauerzug** *m* funeral procession

träufeln ['trɔyfəln] *v/t* (*ge-*, *h*) drip, trickle

Traum [traum] *m* (*-[e]s*; *Träume* ['trɔymə]) dream (*a. fig*)

Traum... *in cpds* ...*beruf*, ...*mann etc*: dream ..., ... of one's dreams

träumen ['trɔymən] *v/i and v/t* (*ge-*, *h*) dream (*a. fig*) (*von* about, of); *schlecht*

träumen have bad dreams
Träumer ['trɔymɐ] *m* (-*s*; -) dreamer (*a.*
  fig)
Träumerei [trɔymə'rai] *fig f* (day)-
  dream(s), reverie (*a.* mus)
träumerisch ['trɔymərɪʃ] *adj* dreamy
traurig ['traurɪç] *adj* sad (**über** *acc*, **wegen** about)
'**Traurigkeit** *f* (-; *no pl*) sadness
Trauring ['trau-] *m* wedding ring
'**Trauschein** *m* marriage certificate
'**Trauung** *f* (-; -*en*) marriage, wedding
'**Trauzeuge** *m*, '**Trauzeugin** *f* witness to a
  marriage
Trecker ['trɛkɐ] *m* (-*s*; -) mot tractor
Treff [trɛf] F *m* (-*s*; -*s*) meeting place
treffen ['trɛfən] *v/t and v/i* (*irr, ge-, h*) hit
  (*a. fig*); hurt; meet *s.o.*; take (*measures
  etc*); **nicht treffen** miss; **sich treffen**
  (**mit** *j-m*) meet (s.o.); **gut treffen** phot
  etc: capture well
'**Treffen** *n* (-*s*; -) meeting
'**treffend 1.** *adj* apt (*remark etc*); **2.** *adv*:
  treffend gesagt well put
Treffer ['trɛfɐ] *m* (-*s*; -) hit (*a. fig*); sport
  goal; win
'**Treffpunkt** *m* meeting place
Treibeis ['traip-] *n* drift ice
treiben ['traibən] (*irr, ge-*) **1.** *v/t* (*h*) drive
  (*a.* tech *and fig*); sport *etc*: do; push,
  press *s.o.*; bot put forth; F do, be up to;
  2. *v/i* (*sein*) drift (*a. fig*), float; bot shoot
  (up); **sich treiben lassen** drift along (*a.
  fig*); **treibende Kraft** driving force
'**Treiben** *n* (-*s*; *no pl*) doings, goingson;
  geschäftiges Treiben bustle
'**treibenlassen** *v/refl* (*irr, lassen, sep, no
  -ge-, h*) → **treiben**
'**Treibhaus** *n* hothouse
Treibhausef‚fekt *m* greenhouse effect
Treibholz *n* driftwood
Treibriemen *m* tech driving belt
Treibsand *m* quicksand
Treibstoff *m* fuel
trennen ['trɛnən] *v/t* (*ge-, h*) separate;
  sever; part; divide (*a.* ling, pol); segre-
  gate; tel disconnect; **sich trennen** sep-
  arate (**von** from), part (*a. fig*); **sich tren-
  nen von** part with *s.th.*; leave *s.o.*
'**Trennung** *f* (-; -*en*) separation; division;
  segregation
'**Trennwand** *f* partition
Treppe ['trɛpə] *f* (-; -*n*) staircase, stairs
'**Treppenabsatz** *m* landing
Treppengeländer *n* banisters
Treppenhaus *n* staircase; hall
Tresor [tre'zoːɐ] *m* (-*s*; -*e*) safe; strong-
  room, vault
treten ['treːtən] *v/i and v/t* (*irr, ge-, h*) kick;

step (**aus** out of; **in** *acc* into; **auf** *acc* on[-
  to]); pedal (away)
treu [trɔy] *adj* faithful (*a. fig*); loyal; devot-
  ed
Treue ['trɔyə] *f* (-; *no pl*) fidelity, faithful-
  ness, loyalty
'**Treuhänder** [-hɛndɐ] *m* (-*s*; -) jur trustee
'**treulos** *adj* faithless, disloyal, unfaithful
  (*all*: **gegen** to)
Tribüne [tri'byːnə] *f* (-; -*n*) platform; stand
Trichter ['trɪçtɐ] *m* (-*s*; -) funnel; crater
Trick [trɪk] *m* (-*s*; -*s*) trick
Trickaufnahme *f* trick shot
Trickbetrüger(in) confidence trickster
trieb [triːp] *pret of* **treiben**
Trieb *m* (-[*e*]*s*; -*e* ['triːbə]) bot (young)
  shoot, sprout; *fig* impulse, drive; sex
  drive
Triebfeder *f* mainspring (*a. fig*)
triefen ['triːfən] *v/i* (*ge-, h*) drip, be dripping (**von** with)
triftig ['trɪftɪç] *adj* weighty; good
Trikot [tri'koː] *n* (-*s*; -*s*) sport shirt, jersey;
  leotard
Triller ['trɪlɐ] *m* (-*s*; -) mus trill
'**trillern** *v/i and v/t* (*ge-, h*) trill; zo warble
trimmen ['trɪmən] *v/refl* (*ge-, h*) keep fit
'**Trimmpfad** *m* fitness trail
trinkbar ['trɪŋkbaːɐ] *adj* drinkable
trinken ['trɪŋkən] *v/t and v/i* (*irr, ge-, h*)
  drink (**auf** *acc* to); have; **et. zu trinken**
  a drink
Trinker(in) ['trɪŋkɐ (-kərɪn)] (-*s*; -/-; -*nen*)
  drinker, alcoholic
'**Trinkgeld** *n* tip; **j-m** (**e-e Mark**) **Trinkgeld
  geben** tip s.o. (one mark)
Trinkspruch *m* toast
Trinkwasser *n* drinking water
Trio ['triːo] *n* (-*s*; -*s*) mus trio (*a. fig*)
trippeln ['trɪpəln] *v/i* (*ge-, sein*) mince
Tripper ['trɪpɐ] *m* (-*s*; -) med gonorrh(o)ea
Tritt [trɪt] *m* (-[*e*]*s*; -*e*) kick; step
'**Trittbrett** *n* step; mot running board
'**Trittleiter** *f* stepladder
Triumph [tri'umf] *m* (-[*e*]*s*; -*e*) triumph
triumphal [trium'faːl] *adj* triumphant
triumphieren [trium'fiːrən] *v/i* (*no -ge-, h*)
  triumph (**über** *acc* over)
trocken ['trɔkən] *adj* dry (*a. fig*)
'**Trocken...** *in cpds* dried ...; drying ...
'**Trockenhaube** *f* hairdryer
'**Trockenheit** *f* (-; *no pl*) dryness; agr
  drought
'**trockenlegen** *v/t* (*sep, -ge-, h*) drain;
  change (*a baby*)
trocknen ['trɔknən] *v/t* (*ge-, h*) *and v/i*
  (*sein*) dry
Trockner ['trɔknɐ] *m* (-*s*; -) dryer
Troddel ['trɔdəl] *f* (-; -*n*) tassel

T

Trödel ['trøːdəl] m (-s; no pl) junk

trödeln ['trøːdəln] v/i (ge-, h) dawdle

Trödler ['trøːdlɐ] m (-s; -) junk dealer; dawdler

trog [troːk] pret of **trügen**

Trog m (-[e]s; Tröge ['trøːgə]) trough

Trommel ['trɔməl] f (-; -n) MUS drum (a. TECH)

Trommelfell n ANAT eardrum

'trommeln v/i and v/t (ge-, h) drum

Trommler ['trɔmlɐ] m (-s; -) drummer

Trompete [trɔm'peːtə] f (-; -n) MUS trumpet

trom'peten v/i and v/t (no -ge-, h) trumpet (a. ZO)

Trompeter [trɔm'peːtɐ] m (-s; -) trumpeter

Tropen ['troːpən]: **die Tropen** pl the tropics

'Tropen... in cpds tropical ...

Tropf [trɔpf] m (-[e]s; Tröpfe ['trœpfə]) MED drip

Tröpfchen ['trœpfçən] n (-s; -) droplet

tröpfeln ['trœpfəln] v/i and v/t (ge-, h) drip; **es tröpfelt** it's spitting

tropfen ['trɔpfən] v/i and v/t (ge-, h) drip, drop

'Tropfen m (-s; -) drop (a. fig); **ein Tropfen auf den heißen Stein** a drop in the bucket

'tropfenweise adv in drops, drop by drop

Trophäe [tro'fɛːə] f (-; -n) trophy (a. fig)

tropisch ['troːpɪʃ] adj tropical

Trosse ['trɔsə] f (-; -n) cable

Trost [troːst] m (-[e]s; no pl) comfort, consolation; **ein schwacher Trost** cold comfort

trösten ['trøːstən] v/t (ge-, h) comfort, console; **sich trösten** console o.s. (**mit** with)

tröstlich ['trøːstlɪç] adj comforting

'trostlos adj miserable; desolate

Trott [trɔt] m (-[e]s; -e) trot; F **der alte Trott** the old routine

Trottel ['trɔtəl] F m (-s; -) dope

trottelig ['trɔtəlɪç] F adj dopey

trotten ['trɔtən] v/i (ge-, sein) trot

Trottinett ['trɔtinɛt] Swiss n (-s; -e) scooter

Trottoir [trɔ'toaːɐ] Swiss n (-s; -e, -s) sidewalk, Br pavement

trotz [trɔts] prp (gen) in spite of, despite

Trotz m (-es; no pl) defiance; **j-m zum Trotz** to spite s.o.

'trotzdem adv in spite of it, nevertheless, F anyhow, anyway

trotzen ['trɔtsən] v/i (ge-, h) defy (dat s.o. or s.th.); sulk

trotzig ['trɔtsɪç] adj defiant; sulky

trüb [tryːp], **trübe** ['tryːbə] adj cloudy; muddy; dim; dull, fig a. gloomy

Trubel ['truːbəl] m (-s; no pl) (hustle and) bustle

trüben ['tryːbən] v/t (ge-, h) cloud; fig spoil, mar

Trübsal ['tryːpzaːl] f: **Trübsal blasen** mope

'trübselig adj sad, gloomy; dreary

'Trübsinn m (-[e]s; no pl) melancholy, gloom, low spirits

'trübsinnig adj melancholy, gloomy

trug [truːk] pret of **tragen**

trügen ['tryːgən] (irr, ge-, h) **1.** v/t deceive; **2.** v/i be deceptive

trügerisch ['tryːgərɪʃ] adj deceptive

'Trugschluss m fallacy

Truhe ['truːə] f (-; -n) chest

Trümmer ['trymɐ] pl ruins; debris; pieces, bits

Trumpf [trʊmpf] m (-[e]s; Trümpfe ['trympfə]) trump (card) (a. fig); **Trumpf sein** be trumps; fig **s-n Trumpf ausspielen** play one's trump card

Trunkenheit ['trʊŋkənhait] f (-; no pl) esp JUR; **Trunkenheit am Steuer** drunk (Br drink) driving

'Trunksucht f (-; no pl) alcoholism

Trupp [trʊp] m (-s; -s) band, party; group

Truppe ['trʊpə] f (-; -n) MIL troop, pl troops, forces; THEA company, troupe

'Truppengattung f MIL branch (of service)

Truppenübungsplatz m training area

Truthahn ['truːt-] m ZO turkey

Tscheche ['tʃɛçə] m (-n; -n) Czech

Tschechien ['tʃɛçjən] Czech Republic

'Tschechin f (-; -nen) Czech

'tschechisch adj Czech; **Tschechische Republik** Czech Republic

Tube ['tuːbə] f (-; -n) tube

Tuberkulose [tubɛrku'loːzə] f (-; -n) MED tuberculosis

Tuch [tuːx] n (-[e]s) a) (pl -e) cloth, b) (pl Tücher ['tyːçɐ]) scarf

'Tuchfühlung f: **auf Tuchfühlung** in close contact

tüchtig ['tyçtɪç] adj (cap)able, competent; skil(l)ful; efficient; F fig good

'Tüchtigkeit f (-; no pl) (cap)ability, qualities; skill; efficiency

tückisch ['tykɪʃ] adj malicious; MED insidious; treacherous

tüfteln ['tyftəln] F v/i (ge-, h) puzzle (**an** dat over)

Tugend ['tuːgənt] f (-; -en) virtue (a. fig)

Tulpe ['tʊlpə] f (-; -n) BOT tulip

Tumor ['tuːmoːɐ] m (-s; -en [tu'moːrən]) MED tumo(u)r

Tümpel ['tympəl] m (-s; -) pool

Tumult [tu'mʊlt] m (-[e]s; -e) tumult, uproar

tun [tuːn] v/t and v/i (irr, ge-, h) do; take (a step etc); F put; **zu tun haben** have work to do; be busy; **ich weiß (nicht)**, **was ich tun soll** or **muss** I (don't) know what to do; **so tun, als ob** pretend to inf

Tünche ['tʏnçə] f (-; -n), **'tünchen** v/t (ge-, h) whitewash

Tunfisch m → **Thunfisch**

Tunke ['tʊŋkə] f (-; -n) sauce

Tunnel ['tʊnəl] m (-s; -) tunnel

Tüpfelchen ['tʏpfəlçən] n: **das Tüpfelchen auf dem i** the icing on the cake

tupfen ['tʊpfən] v/t (ge-, h) dab

'Tupfen m (-s; -) dot, spot

Tupfer ['tʊpfɐ] m (-s; -) MED swab

Tür [tyːɐ] f (-; -en ['tyːrən]) door (a. fig); **die Tür(en) knallen** slam the door(s); F **j-n vor die Tür setzen** throw s.o. out; **Tag der offenen Tür** open house (Br day)

Turban ['tʊrbaːn] m (-s; -e) turban

Turbine [tʊr'biːnə] f (-; -n) TECH turbine

Turbolader ['tʊrbolaːdɐ] m (-s; -) MOT turbo(charger)

Türke ['tʏrkə] m (-n; -n) Turk

Türkei [tʏr'kai] f Turkey

Türkin ['tʏrkɪn] f (-; -nen) Turk(ish woman)

'türkisch adj Turkish

'Türklingel f doorbell

Türklinke f door handle

Türknauf m doorknob

Turm [tʊrm] m (-[e]s; **Türme** ['tʏrmə]) tower; steeple; chess: castle, rook

türmen ['tʏrmən] v/t (ge-, h) pile up (a. **sich türmen**)

'Turmspitze f spire

'Turmspringen n SPORT platform diving

turnen ['tʊrnən] v/i (ge-, h) SPORT do gymnastics

'Turnen n (-s; no pl) SPORT gymnastics; PED physical education (ABBR PE)

Turner ['tʊrnɐ] m (-s; -), **Turnerin** ['tʊrnərɪn] f (-; -nen) SPORT gymnast

'Turnhalle f gymnasium, F gym

'Turnhemd n gym shirt

'Turnhose f gym shorts

Turnier [tʊr'niːɐ] n (-s; -e) tournament

Tur'niertanz m ballroom dancing

'Turnlehrer(in) gym(nastics) or PE teacher

Turnschuh m sneaker, Br trainer

Turnverein m gymnastics club

'Türpfosten m doorpost

Türrahmen m doorframe

Türschild n doorplate

Türsprechanlage f entryphone

Tusche ['tʊʃə] f (-; -n) Indian ink; water-colo(u)r

'Tuschkasten m paintbox

Tüte ['tyːtə] f (-; -n) (paper or plastic) bag; **e-e Tüte ...** a bag of ...

TÜV [tʏf] ABBR of **Technischer Überwachungs-Verein** Br appr MOT (test), compulsory car inspection; **(nicht) durch den TÜV kommen** pass (fail) its or one's MOT

Typ [typ] m (-s; -en) type; model; F fellow, guy

Type ['tyːpə] f (-; -n) TECH type; F character

Typhus ['tyːfʊs] m (-; no pl) MED typhoid (fever)

typisch ['tyːpɪʃ] adj typical (**für** of)

Tyrann [ty'ran] m (-en; -en) tyrant

Tyrannei [tyra'nai] f (-; -en) tyranny

tyrannisch [ty'ranɪʃ] adj tyrannical

tyrannisieren [tyrani'ziːrən] v/t (no -ge-, h) tyrannize, bully

U

u. a. ABBR of **unter anderem** among other things; **und andere** and others

U-Bahn ['uːbaːn] f underground, subway, in London: tube

übel ['yːbəl] adj bad; **mir ist übel** I feel sick; **et. übel nehmen** be offended by s.th.; **übel riechend** foul-smelling, foul

'Übel n (-s; -) evil

'Übelkeit f (-; -en) nausea

'übelnehmen v/t (irr, **nehmen**, sep, -ge-, h) → **übel**

'Übeltäter m, **'Übeltäterin** f esp iro culprit

üben ['yːbən] v/t and v/i (ge-, h) practice, Br practise; **Klavier** etc **üben** practice the piano etc

über ['yːbɐ] prp (dat or acc) over; above (a. fig); more than; across; fig about, of, lecture etc a. on; **sprechen (nachdenken** etc) **über** (acc) talk (think etc) about; **über Nacht bleiben** stay overnight; **über**

München nach Rom to Rome via Munich

über'all *adv* everywhere; *überall in ...* (*dat*) a. throughout ..., all over ...

über'anstrengen *v/t and v/refl* (*no -ge-, h*) overstrain (o.s.)

über'arbeiten *v/t* (*no -ge-, h*) revise; *sich überarbeiten* overwork o.s.

'überaus *adv* most, extremely

'überbelichten *v/t* (*no -ge-, h*) PHOT overexpose

über'bieten *v/t* (*irr, bieten, no -ge-, h*) at auction: outbid (*um* by); *fig* beat, a. outdo *s.o.*

'Überblick *m* view; *fig* overview (*über acc* of); general idea, outline

über'blicken *v/t* (*no -ge-, h*) overlook; *fig* be able to calculate

über'bringen *v/t* (*irr, bringen, no -ge-, h*) deliver

Über'bringer(in) (*-s; -/-; -nen*) ECON bearer

über'brücken *v/t* (*no -ge-, h*) bridge (*a. fig*)

überdacht [-'daxt] *adj* roofed, covered

über'dauern *v/t* (*no -ge-, h*) outlast, survive

über'denken *v/t* (*irr, denken, no -ge-, h*) think *s.th.* over

'überdimensio,nal *adj* oversized

'Überdosis *f* MED overdose

'überdrüssig [-drvsıç] *adj*: *überdrüssig sein* be weary *or* sick (*gen* of)

'überdurchschnittlich *adj* above--average

übereifrig *adj* overzealous

über'eilen *v/t* (*no -ge-, h*) rush; *nichts übereilen!* don't rush things!

über'eilt *adj* rash, hasty

überei'nander *adv* on top of each other; *talk etc* about one another

übereinanderschlagen *v/t* (*irr, schlagen, sep, -ge-, h*): *die Beine übereinanderschlagen* cross one's legs

über'einkommen *v/i* (*irr, kommen, sep, -ge-, sein*) agree

Über'einkommen *n* (*-s; -*), Über'einkunft *f* (*-; -künfte*) agreement

über'einstimmen *v/i* (*sep, -ge-, h*) tally, correspond (with); *mit j-m übereinstimmen* agree with s.o. (*in dat* on)

Über'einstimmung *f* (*-; -en*) agreement; correspondence; *in Übereinstimmung mit* in accordance with

über'fahren *v/t* (*irr, fahren, no -ge-, h*) run *s.o.* over, knock *s.o.* down

'Überfahrt *f* MAR crossing

'Überfall *m* assault (*auf acc* on); hold-up (on, of); mugging (of); MIL raid (on); invasion (of)

über'fallen *v/t* (*irr, fallen, no -ge-, h*) attack, assault; hold up; mug; MIL raid; invade

'überfällig *adj* overdue

über'fliegen *v/t* (*irr, fliegen, no -ge-, h*) fly over *or* across; *fig* glance over, skim (through)

'überfließen *v/i* (*irr, fließen, sep, -ge-, sein*) overflow

'Überfluss *m* (*-es; no pl*) abundance (*an dat* of); affluence; *im Überfluss haben* abound in

'überflüssig *adj* superfluous

über'fluten *v/t* (*no -ge-, h*) flood (*a. fig*)

über'fordern *v/t* (*no -ge-, h*) overtax

überfragt [-'fra:kt] *adj*: F *da bin ich überfragt* you've got me there

über'führen *v/t* (*no -ge-, h*) transport; JUR convict (*e-r Tat* of a crime)

Über'führung *f* (*-; -en*) transfer; JUR conviction; MOT overpass, *Br* flyover; footbridge

über'füllt *adj* overcrowded, packed

über'füttern *v/t* (*no -ge-, h*) overfeed

'Übergang *m* crossing; *fig* transition

über'geben *v/t* (*irr, geben, no -ge-, h*) hand over; MIL surrender; *sich übergeben* vomit

über'gehen¹ *v/t* (*irr, gehen, no -ge-, h*) pass over, ignore

'übergehen² *v/i* (*irr, gehen, sep, -ge-, sein*) pass (*zu* on to); *übergehen in* (*acc*) change *or* turn (in)to

'übergeschnappt F *adj* cracked

'Übergewicht *n* (*Übergewicht haben* be) overweight; *fig* predominance

'übergewichtig *adj* overweight

'überglücklich *adj* overjoyed

'übergreifen *v/i* (*irr, greifen, sep, -ge-, h*) *übergreifen auf* (*acc*) spread to

'Übergriff *m* infringement (*auf acc* of); (act of) violence

'Übergröße *f* outsize; *in Übergrößen* outsized, oversize(d)

über'handnehmen *v/i* (*irr, nehmen, sep, -ge-, h*) become rampant

über'häufen *v/t* (*no -ge-, h*) swamp; shower

über'haupt *adv* ... at all; anyway; *überhaupt nicht* (*nichts*) not (nothing) at all

überheblich [-'he:plıç] *adj* arrogant

Über'heblichkeit *f* (*-; no pl*) arrogance

über'hitzen *v/t* (*no -ge-, h*) overheat (*a. fig*)

überhöht [-'hø:t] *adj* excessive

über'holen *v/t* (*no -ge-, h*) pass, overtake (*a.* SPORT); TECH overhaul, service

über'holt *adj* outdated, antiquated

über'hören v/t (no -ge-, h) miss, not catch or get; ignore

'überirdisch adj supernatural

über'kleben v/t (no -ge-, h) paste up, cover

'überkochen v/i (sep, -ge-, sein) boil over

über'kommen v/t (irr, **kommen**, no -ge-, h) ... **überkam ihn** he was seized with or overcome by ...

über'laden v/t (irr, **laden**, no -ge-, h) overload (a. ELECTR); fig clutter

über'lassen v/t (irr, **lassen**, no -ge-, h) **j-m et. überlassen** let s.o. have s.th., leave s.th. to s.o. (a. fig); **j-n sich selbst überlassen** leave s.o. to himself; **j-n s-m Schicksal überlassen** leave s.o. to his fate

über'lasten v/t (no -ge-, h) overload (a. ELECTR); fig overburden

'überlaufen¹ v/i (irr, **laufen**, sep, -ge-, sein) run or flow over; MIL desert

über'laufen² v/t (irr, **laufen**, no -ge-, h) **es überlief mich heiß und kalt** I went hot and cold

über'laufen³ adj overcrowded

'Überläufer m MIL deserter; POL defector

über'leben v/t and v/i (no -ge-, h) survive (a. fig); live through s.th.

Über'lebende m, f (-n; -n) survivor

'überlebensgroß adj larger than life

über'legen¹ v/t and v/i (no -ge-, h) think about s.th., think s.th. over; consider; **lassen Sie mich überlegen** let me think; **ich habe es mir (anders) überlegt** I've made up (changed) my mind

über'legen² adj superior (**j-m** to s.o.)

Über'legenheit f (-; no pl) superiority

über'legt adj deliberate; prudent

Über'legung f (-; -en) consideration, reflection

'überleiten v/i (sep, -ge-, h) **überleiten zu** lead up or over to

über'liefern v/t (no -ge-, h) hand down, pass on

Über'lieferung f (-; -en) tradition

über'listen v/t (no -ge-, h) outwit

'Übermacht f (-; no pl) superiority; esp MIL superior forces; **in der Übermacht sein** be superior in numbers

'übermächtig adj superior; fig overpowering

'Übermaß n (-es; no pl) excess (**an** dat of)

'übermäßig adj excessive

'übermenschlich adj superhuman

über'mitteln v/t (no -ge-, h) convey

'übermorgen adv the day after tomorrow

über'müdet adj overtired

'übermütig [-my:tɪç] adj high-spirited

'übernächst adj the next but one; **über-**

nächste Woche the week after next

übernachten [-'naxtən] v/i (no -ge-, h) stay overnight (**bei j-m** at s.o.'s [house], with s.o.), spend the night (at, with)

Über'nachtung f (-; -en) night; **Übernachtung und Frühstück** bed and breakfast

Übernahme ['y:bəna:mə] f (-; -n) taking (over); adoption

'überna,türlich adj supernatural

über'nehmen v/t (irr, **nehmen**, no -ge-, h) take over; adopt; take (responsibility etc); undertake to do

über'prüfen v/t (no -ge-, h) check, examine; verify; esp POL screen

Über'prüfung f check, examination; verification; screening

über'queren v/t (no -ge-, h) cross

über'ragen v/t (no -ge-, h) tower above (a. fig)

über'ragend adj outstanding

überraschen [y:bɐ'raʃən] v/t (no -ge-, h) surprise; **j-n bei et. überraschen** a. catch s.o. doing s.th.

Über'raschung f (-; -en) surprise

über'reden v/t (no -ge-, h) persuade (**et. zu tun** to do s.th.); **j-n zu et. überreden** talk s.o. into (doing) s.th.

Über'redung f (-; no pl) persuasion

'überregio,nal adj national

über'reichen v/t (no -ge-, h) present, hand s.th. over (**dat** to)

über'reizen v/t (no -ge-, h) overexcite

über'reizt adj overwrought, F on edge

'Überrest m remains; pl relics; GASTR leftovers

über'rumpeln v/t (no -ge-, h) (take s.o. by) surprise

über'runden v/t (no -ge-, h) SPORT lap

übersät [-'zɛːt] adj: **übersät mit** strewn with garbage; studded with stars

übersättigt [-'zɛtɪçt] adj sated, surfeited

'Überschall... in cpds supersonic ...

über'schatten v/t (no -ge-, h) overshadow (a. fig)

über'schätzen v/t (no -ge-, h) overrate, overestimate

'Überschlag m AVIAT loop; SPORT somersault; ECON rough estimate

'überschlagen¹ (irr, **schlagen**, sep, -ge-) **1.** v/t (h) cross (one's legs); **2.** v/i (sein) fig **überschlagen in** (acc) turn into

über'schlagen² (no -ge-, h) **1.** v/t skip; ECON make a rough estimate of; **2.** v/refl turn (right) over; go head over heels; voice: break

'überschnappen F v/i (no -ge-, sein) crack up

über'schneiden v/refl (irr, **schneiden**, no

-ge-, h) overlap (a. fig); intersect

über'schreiben v/t (irr, **schreiben**, no -ge-, h) make s.th. over (dat to)

über'schreiten v/t (irr, **schreiten**, no -ge-, h) cross; fig go beyond; pass; break (the speed limit etc)

'Überschrift f heading, title; headline; caption

'Überschuss m, **'überschüssig** [-ʃʏsɪç] adj surplus

über'schütten v/t (no -ge-, h) **überschütten mit** cover with; shower with; heap s.th. on

'überschwänglich [-ʃvɛŋlɪç] adj effusive

über'schwemmen v/t (no -ge-, h), **Über'schwemmung** f (-; -en) flood

'überschwenglich → **überschwänglich**

'Übersee: in (nach) Übersee oversea

über'sehen v/t (irr, **sehen**, no -ge-, h) overlook; ignore

über'setzen¹ v/t (no -ge-, h) translate (**in** acc into)

'übersetzen² (sep, -ge-) 1. v/i (h, sein) cross (**über e-n Fluss** a river); 2. v/t (h) take over

Übersetzer [-'zɛtsɐ] m (-s; -), **Über'setzerin** f (-; -nen) translator

Über'setzung f (-; -en) translation (**aus** dat from; **in** acc into)

'Übersicht f (-; -en) overview (**über** acc of); outline, summary

'übersichtlich adj clear(ly arranged)

'übersiedeln v/i (sep, -ge-, sein) move (**nach** to)

'Übersied(e)lung f move

über'spannen v/t (no -ge-, h) span

über'spannt fig adj eccentric; extravagant

über'spielen v/t (no -ge-, h) record; tape; fig cover up

über'spitzt adj exaggerated

über'springen v/t (irr, **springen**, no -ge-, h) jump (over), esp SPORT a. clear; fig skip

über'stehen¹ v/t (irr, **stehen**, no -ge-, h) get over; survive (a. fig), live through

'überstehen² v/i (irr, **stehen**, sep, -ge-, h) jut out

über'steigen fig v/t (irr, **steigen**, no -ge-, h) exceed

über'stimmen v/t (no -ge-, h) outvote

'überstreifen v/t (sep, -ge-, h) slip s.th. on

überströmen v/i (sep, -ge-, sein) overflow (**vor** dat with)

'Überstunden pl overtime; **Überstunden machen** work overtime

über'stürzen v/t (no -ge-, h) et. **überstürzen** rush things; **sich überstürzen** events: follow in rapid succession

über'stürzt adj (over)hasty; rash

über'teuert adj overpriced

über'tönen v/t (no -ge-, h) drown (out)

über'tragbar adj transferable; MED contagious

über'tragen¹ adj figurative

über'tragen² v/t (irr, **tragen**, no -ge-, h) broadcast, a. televise; translate; MED, TECH transmit; MED transfuse (blood); JUR, ECON transfer

Über'tragung f (-; -en) radio, TV broadcast; transmission; translation; MED transfusion; JUR, ECON transfer

über'treffen v/t (irr, **treffen**, no -ge-, h) outstrip, outdo, surpass, beat

über'treiben v/i and v/t (irr, **treiben**, no -ge-, h) exaggerate; overdo

Über'treibung f (-; -en) exaggeration

'übertreten¹ v/i (irr, **treten**, sep, -ge-, sein) **übertreten zu** go over to, REL convert to

über'treten² (irr, **treten**, no -ge-, h) 1. v/t break, violate; 2. v/i SPORT foul (a jump or throw)

Über'tretung f (-; -en) violation, JUR a. offen|se, Br -ce

'Übertritt m change (**zu** to); REL, POL conversion (to)

übervölkert [-'fœlkɐt] adj overpopulated

über'wachen v/t (no -ge-, h) supervise, oversee; control; observe

Über'wachung f (-; -en) supervision, control; observance; surveillance

überwältigen [-'vɛltɪgən] v/t (no -ge-, h) overwhelm, overpower, fig a. overcome

überwältigend adj overwhelming, overpowering

über'weisen v/t (irr, **weisen**, no -ge-, h) ECON transfer (**an j-n** to s.o.'s account); remit; MED refer (**an** acc to)

Über'weisung f (-; -en) ECON transfer; remittance; MED referral

'überwerfen¹ v/t (irr, **werfen**, sep, -ge-, h) slip s.th. on

über'werfen² v/refl (irr, **werfen**, no -ge-, h) **sich überwerfen (mit j-m)** fall out with each other (with s.o.)

über'wiegen v/i (irr, **wiegen**, no -ge-, h) predominate

überwiegend adj predominant; vast (majority)

über'winden v/t (irr, **winden**, no -ge-, h) overcome (a. fig); defeat; **sich überwinden zu** inf bring o.s. to inf

überwintern [-'vɪntɐn] v/i (no -ge-, h) spend the winter (**in** dat in)

über'wuchern v/t (no -ge-, h) overgrow

'Überzahl f (-; no pl) majority; **in der Überzahl sein** outnumber s.o.

über'zeugen v/t (no -ge-, h) convince (**von** of), persuade; **sich überzeugen, dass** make sure that; **sich selbst über-**

zeugen (go and) see for o.s.

überzeugt [-'tsɔʏkt] *adj* convinced; **über-zeugt sein** a. be *or* feel (quite) sure

Über'zeugung *f* (-; -en) conviction

'überziehen[1] *v/t* (*irr*, **ziehen**, *sep*, -ge-, *h*) put *s.th.* on

über'ziehen[2] *v/t* (*irr*, **ziehen**, *no*, -ge-, *h*) TECH *etc* cover; ECON overdraw

Über'ziehungskre‚dit *m* ECON overdraft (facility)

'Überzug *m* cover; coat(ing)

üblich ['y:plɪç] *adj* usual, normal; **es ist üblich** it's the custom; **wie üblich** as usu-al

'U-Boot *n* submarine

übrig ['y:brɪç] *adj* remaining; **die Übri-gen** *pl* the others, the rest; **übrig sein** (**haben**) be (have) left; **übrig bleiben** be left, remain; **es bleibt mir nichts an-deres übrig** (**als zu** *inf*) there is nothing else I can do (but *inf*); **übrig lassen** leave

übrigens ['y:brɪgəns] *adv* by the way

'übriglassen *v/i* (*irr*, **lassen**, *sep*, -ge-, *sein*) (*a. fig*) → **übrig**

Übung ['y:bʊŋ] *f* (-; -en) exercise; prac-tice; **in** (**aus der**) **Übung** in (out of) prac-tice

Ufer ['u:fɐ] *n* (-s; -) shore; bank; **ans Ufer** ashore

Uhr [u:ɐ] *f* (-; -en ['u:rən]) clock; watch; **um vier Uhr** at four o'clock

'Uhrarmband *n* watchstrap

Uhrmacher *m* (-s; -) watchmaker

Uhrwerk *n* clockwork

Uhrzeiger *m* hand

Uhrzeigersinn *m*: **im Uhrzeigersinn** clockwise; **entgegen dem Uhrzeiger-sinn** counterclockwise, *Br* anticlockwise

Uhu ['u:hu] *m* (-s; -s) ZO eagle owl

UKW [u:ka:'ve:] *abbr of* **Ultrakurzwelle** VHF, very high frequency

Ulk [ʊlk] *m* (-s; -e) joke; hoax

ulkig ['ʊlkɪç] *adj* funny

Ulme ['ʊlmə] *f* (-; -n) BOT elm

Ultimatum [ʊlti'ma:tʊm] *n* (-s; -ten) ulti-matum; **j-m ein Ultimatum stellen** deliv-er an ultimatum to s.o.

um [ʊm] *prp* (*acc*) *and cj* (a)round; at; about, around; **um Geld** for money; **um e-e Stunde** (**10 cm**) by an hour (10 cm); **um ... willen** for the sake of ...; **um zu** *inf* (in order) to *inf*; **um sein** F be over; **die Zeit ist um** time's up; → **umso**

umarmen [ʊm'ʔarmən] *v/t* (*no* -ge-, *h*) (*a.* **sich umarmen**) embrace, hug

Um'armung *f* (-; -en) embrace, hug

'Umbau *m* (-[e]s; -e, -ten) rebuilding, re-construction

'umbauen *v/t* (*sep*, -ge-, *h*) rebuild, recon-struct

'umbinden *v/t* (*irr*, **binden**, *sep*, -ge-, *h*) put *s.th.* on

umblättern *v/i* (*sep*, -ge-, *h*) turn (over) the page

umbringen *v/t* (*irr*, **bringen**, *sep*, -ge-, *h*) kill; **sich umbringen** kill o.s.

umbuchen *v/t* (*sep*, -ge-, *h*) change; ECON transfer (**auf** *acc* to)

umdenken *v/i* (*irr*, **denken**, *sep*, -ge-, *h*) change one's way of thinking

umdispo‚nieren *v/i* (*sep*, *no* -ge-, *h*) change one's plans

umdrehen *v/t* (*sep*, -ge-, *h*) turn (round); **sich umdrehen** turn round

Um'drehung *f* (-; -en) turn; PHYS, TECH ro-tation, revolution

umei'nander *adv* care *etc* about *or* for each other

'umfahren[1] *v/t* (*irr*, **fahren**, *sep*, -ge-, *h*) run down

um'fahren[2] *v/t* (*irr*, **fahren**, *no* -ge-, *h*) drive (MAR sail) round

'umfallen *v/i* (*irr*, **fallen**, *sep*, -ge-, *sein*) fall down *or* over; collapse; **tot umfallen** drop dead

'Umfang *m* circumference; size; extent; **in großem Umfang** on a large scale

'umfangreich *adj* extensive; voluminous

um'fassen *fig v/t* (*no* -ge-, *h*) cover; in-clude

umfassend *adj* comprehensive; complete

'umformen *v/t* (*sep*, -ge-, *h*) turn, change; ELECTR, LING, MATH *a.* transform, convert (*all*: **in** *acc* [in]to)

'Umformer *m* (-s; -) ELECTR converter

'Umfrage *f* opinion poll

'Umgang *m* (-[e]s; *no pl*) company; **Um-gang haben mit** associate with; **beim Umgang mit** when dealing with

'umgänglich [-gɛŋlɪç] *adj* sociable

'Umgangsformen *pl* manners

Umgangssprache *f* colloquial speech; **die englische Umgangssprache** collo-quial English

um'geben *v/t* (*irr*, **geben**, *no* -ge-, *h*) sur-round (**mit** with)

Um'gebung *f* (-; -en) surroundings; envi-ronment

'umgehen[1] *v/i* (*irr*, **gehen**, *sep*, -ge-, *sein*) **umgehen mit** deal with, handle; **umge-hen können mit** have a way with, be good with

um'gehen[2] *v/t* (*irr*, **gehen**, *no* -ge-, *h*) avoid; bypass

'umgehend *adv* immediately

Um'gehungsstraße *f* bypass; beltway, *Br*

ring road
umgekehrt ['ʊmgəkeːɐt] **1.** *adj* reverse;
opposite; (*genau*) *umgekehrt* (just)
the other way round; **2.** *adv* the other
way round; *und umgekehrt* and vice versa
'**umgraben** *v/t* (*irr*, *graben*, *sep*, *-ge-*, *h*)
dig (up), break up
'**Umhang** *m* cape
'**umhängen** *v/t* (*sep*, *-ge-*, *h*) put around *or*
over s.o.'s shoulders *etc*; rehang
'**umhauen** *v/t* (*irr*, *hauen*, *sep*, *-ge-*, *h*) fell,
cut down; F knock *s.o.* out
um'her *adv* (a)round, about
um'herstreifen *v/i* (*sep*, *-ge-*, *sein*) roam *or*
wander around
'**umkehren** (*sep*, *-ge-*) **1.** *v/i* (*sein*) turn
back; **2.** *v/t* (*h*) reverse
'**Umkehrung** *f* (*-*; *-en*) reversal (*a. fig*)
'**umkippen** (*sep*, *-ge-*) **1.** *v/t* (*h*) tip over,
upset; **2.** *v/i* (*sein*) fall down *or* over, overturn
um'klammern *v/t* (*no -ge-*, *h*), **Um'klammerung** *f* (*-*; *-en*) clasp, clutch, clench
'**Umkleideka,bine** *f* changing cubicle
Umkleideraum *m esp* SPORT changing *or*
locker room; THEA dressing room
'**umkommen** *v/i* (*irr*, *kommen*, *sep*, *-ge-*,
sein) be killed (*bei* in), die (in); F *umkommen vor* (*dat*) be dying with
'**Umkreis** *m*: *im Umkreis von* within a radius of
um'kreisen *v/t* (*no -ge-*, *h*) circle; ASTR revolve around; *satellite etc*: orbit
'**umkrempeln** *v/t* (*sep*, *-ge-*, *h*) roll up
'**Umlauf** *m* circulation; PHYS, TECH rotation; ECON circular; *im* (*in*) *Umlauf sein*
(*bringen*) be in (put into) circulation, circulate
Umlaufbahn *f* ASTR orbit
'**umlaufen** *v/i* (*irr*, *laufen*, *sep*, *-ge-*, *sein*)
circulate
umlegen *v/t* (*sep*, *-ge-*, *h*) put on; move;
share (*expenses etc*); TECH pull; F do *s.o.*
in, bump *s.o.* off
'**umleiten** *v/t* (*sep*, *-ge-*, *h*) divert
'**Umleitung** *f* (*-*; *-en*) detour, *Br* diversion
'**umliegend** *adj* surrounding
'**umpacken** *v/t* (*sep*, *-ge-*, *h*) repack
'**umpflanzen** *v/t* (*sep*, *-ge-*, *h*) repot
umranden [ʊm'randən] *v/t* (*no -ge-*, *h*),
Um'randung *f* (*-*; *-en*) edge, border
'**umräumen** *v/t* (*sep*, *-ge-*, *h*) rearrange
'**umrechnen** *v/t* (*sep*, *-ge-*, *h*) convert (*in*
acc into)
'**Umrechnung** *f* (*-*; *-en*) conversion
'**Umrechnungskurs** *m* exchange rate
'**umreißen** *v/t* (*irr*, *reißen*, *sep*, *-ge-*, *h*)
knock *s.o.* down

um'ringen *v/t* (*no -ge-*, *h*) surround
'**Umriss** *m* outline (*a. fig*), contour
'**umrühren** *v/t* (*sep*, *-ge-*, *h*) stir
umrüsten *v/t* (*sep*, *-ge-*, *h*) TECH convert
(*auf acc* to)
umsatteln F *v/i* (*sep*, *-ge-*, *h*) *umsatteln*
von ... auf (*acc*) ... switch from ... to ...
'**Umsatz** *m* ECON sales
'**umschalten** *v/t and v/i* (*sep*, *-ge-*, *h*)
switch (over) (*auf acc* to) (*a. fig*)
'**Umschlag** *m* envelope; cover, wrapper;
jacket; cuff, *Br* turn-up; MED compress;
ECON handling
'**umschlagen** (*irr*, *schlagen*, *sep*, *-ge-*) **1.**
v/t (*h*) cut down, fell; turn up; turn down;
ECON handle; **2.** *v/i* (*sein*) turn over; *fig*
change (suddenly)
'**Umschlagplatz** *m* trading center (*Br*
centre)
'**umschnallen** *v/t* (*sep*, *-ge-*, *h*) buckle on
'**umschreiben**[1] *v/t* (*irr*, *schreiben*, *sep*,
-ge-, *h*) rewrite
um'schreiben[2] *v/t* (*irr*, *schreiben*, *no*
-ge-, *h*) paraphrase
Um'schreibung *f* (*-*; *-en*) paraphrase
'**Umschrift** *f* transcription
'**umschulen** *v/t* (*sep*, *-ge-*, *h*) retrain; transfer to another school
umschwärmt [ʊm'ʃvɛrmt] *adj* idolized
'**Umschwung** *m* (drastic) change, *esp* POL
a. swing
um'segeln *v/t* (*no -ge-*, *h*) sail round; circumnavigate
'**umsehen** *v/refl* (*irr*, *sehen*, *sep*, *-ge-*, *h*)
look around (*in e-m Laden* a shop; *nach*
for); look back (*nach* at); *sich umsehen*
nach be looking for
umsetzen *v/t* (*sep*, *-ge-*, *h*) move (*a.* PED);
ECON sell; *umsetzen in* (*acc*) convert (in)to; *in die Tat umsetzen* put into action;
sich umsetzen change places
'**umsiedeln** *v/i* (*sep*, *-ge-*, *sein*) *and v/t* (*h*)
resettle; → *umziehen*
'**Umsied(e)lung** *f* (*-*; *-en*) resettlement
'**Umsiedler** *m* (*-s*; *-*) resettler
'**umso 1.** *je später etc*, *umso schlechter*
etc the later *etc* the worse *etc*; **2.** *umso*
besser so much the better
um'sonst *adv* free (of charge), for nothing; F for free; *fig* in vain
um'spannen *v/t* (*no -ge-*, *h*) span (*a. fig*)
'**umspringen** *v/i* (*irr*, *springen*, *sep*, *-ge-*,
sein) shift, change (suddenly) (*a. fig*);
umspringen mit treat (badly)
'**Umstand** *m* circumstance; fact; detail;
unter diesen (*keinen*) *Umständen* under the (no) circumstances; *unter Umständen* possibly; *keine Umstände machen* not cause *s.o.* any trouble; not go to

any trouble; no put o.s. out; *in anderen Umständen sein* be expecting

umständlich ['ʊmʃtɛntlɪç] *adj* awkward; complicated; long-winded; *das ist (mir) viel zu umständlich* that's far too much trouble (for me)

'**Umstandskleid** *n* maternity dress

Umstandswort *n* (-[*e*]*s*; -*wörter*) LING adverb

'**Umstehende**: *die Umstehenden pl* the bystanders

'**umsteigen** *v/i* (*irr*, *steigen*, *sep*, -*ge*-, *sein*) change (*nach* for), RAIL *a.* change trains (for)

'**umstellen** *v/t* (*sep*, -*ge*-, *h*) change (*auf acc* to), make a change *or* changes in, *esp* TECH *a.* switch (over) (to), convert (to); adjust (to); rearrange (*a. furniture*), reorganize; reset (*watch*); *sich umstellen auf* (*acc*) change *or* switch (over) to; adjust (o.s.) to, get used to

'**Umstellung** *f* (-; -*en*) change; switch, conversion; adjustment; rearrangement, reorganization

'**umstimmen** *v/t* (*sep*, -*ge*-, *h*) *j-n umstimmen* change s.o.'s mind

'**umstoßen** *v/t* (*irr*, *stoßen*, *sep*, -*ge*-, *h*) knock over, upset (*a. fig*)

umstritten [ʊm'ʃtrɪtən] *adj* controversial

'**Umsturz** *m* overthrow

'**umstürzen** *v/i* (*sep*, -*ge*-, *sein*) overturn, fall over

'**Umtausch** *m*, '**umtauschen** *v/t* (*sep*, -*ge*-, *h*) exchange (*gegen* for)

'**umwälzend** *adj* revolutionary

'**Umwälzung** *f* (-; -*en*) radical change

'**umwandeln** *v/t* (*sep*, -*ge*-, *h*) turn (*in acc* into), transform (into), *esp* CHEM, ELECTR, PHYS *a.* convert ([in]to)

'**Umwandlung** *f* (-; -*en*) transformation, conversion

'**Umweg** *m* roundabout route *or* way (*a. fig*), *esp* MOT *a.* detour; *ein Umweg von 10 Minuten* ten minutes out of the way; *fig auf Umwegen* in a roundabout way

'**Umwelt** *f* (-; *no pl*) environment

'**Umwelt...** *in cpds mst* environmental ...

Umweltforschung *f* ecology

'**umweltfreundlich** *adj* environment-friendly, non-polluting

umweltschädlich *adj* harmful, noxious, polluting

'**Umweltschutz** *m* conservation, environmental protection, pollution control

Umweltschützer *m* environmentalist, conservationist

Umweltschutzpa₁pier *n* recycled paper

Umweltsünder *m* (environmental) pollut-er

Umweltverschmutzer *m* (-*s*; -) polluter

Umweltverschmutzung *f* (environmental) pollution

Umweltzerstörung *f* ecocide

'**umziehen** (*irr*, *ziehen*, *sep* -*ge*-) **1.** *v/i* (*sein*) move (*nach* to); **2.** *v/refl* (*h*) change (one's clothes)

umzingeln [ʊm'tsɪŋəln] *v/t* (*no* -*ge*-, *h*) surround, encircle

'**Umzug** *m* move (*nach* to), removal (to); parade

unabhängig ['ʊn-] *adj* independent (*von* of); *unabhängig davon, ob* (*was*) regardless of whether (what)

'**Unabhängigkeit** *f* (-; *no pl*) independence (*von* from)

'**unabsichtlich** *adj* unintentional; *et. unabsichtlich tun* do s.th. by mistake

unab'wendbar *adj* inevitable

'**unachtsam** *adj* careless, negligent

'**Unachtsamkeit** *f* (-; *no pl*) carelessness, negligence

unan'fechtbar *adj* incontestable

'**unangebracht** *adj* inappropriate; *unangebracht sein* be out of place

unangemessen *adj* unreasonable; inadequate

unangenehm *adj* unpleasant; embarrassing

unan'nehmbar *adj* unacceptable

Unannehmlichkeiten ['ʊnʔanneːmlɪçkaitən] *pl* trouble, difficulties

'**unansehnlich** *adj* unsightly

'**unanständig** *adj* indecent, obscene

unan'tastbar *adj* inviolable

'**unappetitlich** *adj* unappetizing

Unart ['ʊnʔart] *f* (-; -*en*) bad habit

'**unartig** *adj* naughty, bad

'**unaufdringlich** *adj* unobtrusive

'**unauffällig** *adj* inconspicuous, unobtrusive

unauf'findbar *adj* not to be found, untraceable

'**unaufgefordert** *adv* without being asked, of one's own accord

unaufhörlich [ʊnʔauf'høːɐlɪç] *adj* continuous

'**unaufmerksam** *adj* inattentive

'**Unaufmerksamkeit** *f* (-; *no pl*) inattention, inattentiveness

'**unaufrichtig** *adj* insincere

unauslöschlich [ʊnʔaus'lœʃlɪç] *adj* indelible

unausstehlich [-'ʃteːlɪç] *adj* unbearable

'**unbarmherzig** *adj* merciless

'**unbeabsichtigt** *adj* unintentional

unbeachtet *adj* unnoticed

unbeaufsichtigt *adj* unattended

unbebaut *adj* undeveloped

unbedacht [-bədaxt] *adj* thoughtless

unbedenklich 1. *adj* safe; **2.** *adv* without hesitation

unbedeutend *adj* insignificant; minor

unbedingt 1. *adj* unconditional, absolute; **2.** *adv* by all means, absolutely; *need etc* badly

unbefahrbar *adj* impassable

unbefangen *adj* unprejudiced, unbias(s)ed; unembarrassed

unbefriedigend *adj* unsatisfactory

unbefriedigt *adj* dissatisfied

unbegabt *adj* untalented

unbegreiflich *adj* inconceivable, incomprehensible

unbegrenzt *adj* unlimited, boundless

unbegründet *adj* unfounded

'Unbehagen *n* (*-s; no pl*) uneasiness, discomfort

'unbehaglich *adj* uneasy, uncomfortable

unbehelligt [ʊnbə'hɛlıçt] *adj* unmolested

'unbeherrscht *adj* uncontrolled, lacking self-control

unbeholfen [-bəhɔlfən] *adj* clumsy, awkward

unbeirrt *adj* unwavering

unbekannt *adj* unknown

'Unbekannte *f* (*-; -n*) MATH unknown quantity

'unbekümmert *adj* light-hearted, cheerful

unbelehrbar *adj*: **er ist unbelehrbar** he'll never learn

unbeliebt *adj* unpopular; **er ist überall unbeliebt** nobody likes him

unbemannt *adj* unmanned

unbemerkt *adj* unnoticed

unbenutzt *adj* unused

unbequem *adj* uncomfortable; inconvenient

unberechenbar *adj* unpredictable

unberechtigt *adj* unauthorized; unjustified

unbeschädigt *adj* undamaged

unbescheiden *adj* immodest

unbe'schränkt *adj* unlimited; absolute (*power*)

unbeschreiblich [-bə'ʃraiplıç] *adj* indescribable

unbe'sehen *adv* unseen

unbesiegbar [-bə'ziːkbaːɐ] *adj* invincible

'unbesonnen *adj* thoughtless, imprudent; rash

unbe'spielbar *adj* SPORT unplayable

unbeständig *adj* unstable; METEOR changeable, unsettled

unbestätigt *adj* unconfirmed

unbe'stechlich *adj* incorruptible

'unbestimmt *adj* indefinite (*a.* LING); uncertain; vague

unbe'streitbar *adj* indisputable

unbestritten [-bə'ʃtrıtən] *adj* undisputed

'unbeteiligt *adj* not involved; indifferent

unbetont *adj* unstressed

unbeugsam [ʊn'bɔʏkzaːm] *adj* inflexible

'unbewacht *adj* unwatched, unguarded (*a. fig*)

unbewaffnet *adj* unarmed

unbeweglich *adj* immovable; motionless

unbe'wohnbar *adj* uninhabitable

'unbewohnt *adj* uninhabited; unoccupied, vacant

'unbewusst *adj* unconscious

unbe'zahlbar *fig adj* invaluable, priceless

'unbezahlt *adj* unpaid

'unblutig 1. *adj* bloodless; **2.** *adv* without bloodshed

'unbrauchbar *adj* useless

und [ʊnt] *cj* and; F **na und?** so what?

'undankbar *adj* ungrateful (**gegen** to); thankless

'Undankbarkeit *f* (*-; no pl*) ingratitude, ungratefulness

undefi'nierbar *adj* undefinable

un'denkbar *adj* unthinkable

'undeutlich *adj* indistinct; inarticulate; *fig* vague

'undicht *adj* leaky

'unduldsam *adj* intolerant

'Unduldsamkeit *f* (*-; no pl*) intolerance

undurch'dringlich *adj* impenetrable

undurch'führbar *adj* impracticable

'undurchlässig *adj* impervious, impermeable

undurchsichtig *adj* opaque; *fig* mysterious

'uneben *adj* uneven

'Unebenheit *f* a) (*-; no pl*) unevenness, b) (*-; -en*) bump

'unecht *adj* false; artificial; imitation ...; F *contp* fake, phon(e)y

'unehelich *adj* illegitimate

'unehrenhaft *adj* dishono(u)rable

'unehrlich *adj* dishonest

'uneigennützig *adj* unselfish

'uneinig *adj*: (**sich**) **uneinig sein** disagree (**über** *acc* on)

'Uneinigkeit *f* (*-; no pl*) disagreement; dissension

unein'nehmbar *adj* impregnable

'unempfänglich *adj* insusceptible (**für** to)

unempfindlich *adj* insensitive (**gegen** to)

un'endlich *adj* infinite; endless, never-ending

Un'endlichkeit *f* (*-; no pl*) infinity (*a. fig*)

unentbehrlich [ʊn'ʔɛnt'beːɐlıç] *adj* indispensable

unentgeltlich [-'gɛltlɪç] *adj and adv* free (of charge)

'**unentschieden** *adj* undecided; **unentschieden enden** SPORT end in a draw *or* tie; **es steht unentschieden** the score is even

'**Unentschieden** *n* (-s; -) SPORT draw, tie

'**unentschlossen** *adj* irresolute

unent'schuldbar *adj* inexcusable

unentwegt [ʊnʔɛnt'veːkt] *adv* untiringly; continuously

'**unerfahren** *adj* inexperienced

unerfreulich *adj* unpleasant

unerfüllt *adj* unfulfilled

unergiebig *adj* unproductive

unerheblich *adj* irrelevant (*für* to); insignificant

unerhört ['ʊnʔɛːɐ'høːɐt] *adj* outrageous

'**unerkannt** *adj* unrecognized

unerklärlich *adj* inexplicable

unerlässlich *adj* essential, indispensable

unerlaubt *adj* unallowed; unauthorized

unerledigt *adj* unsettled (*a.* ECON)

uner'messlich *adj* immeasurable

unermüdlich [ʊnʔɛɐ'myːtlɪç] *adj* indefatigable; untiring

uner'reichbar *adj* inaccessible; *esp fig* unattainable

uner'reicht *adj* unequal(l)ed

unersättlich [ʊnʔɛɐ'zɛtlɪç] *adj* insatiable

'**unerschlossen** *adj* undeveloped

unerschöpflich [ʊnʔɛɐ'ʃœpflɪç] *adj* inexhaustible

unerschütterlich [-'ʃʏtɐlɪç] *adj* imperturbable

unerschwinglich [-'ʃvɪŋlɪç] *adj* exorbitant; **für j-n unerschwinglich sein** be beyond s.o.'s means

unersetzlich [-'zɛtslɪç] *adj* irreplaceable

unerträglich [-'trɛːklɪç] *adj* unbearable

'**unerwartet** *adj* unexpected

'**unerwünscht** *adj* unwanted

'**unfähig** *adj* incompetent; incapable (*zu tun* of doing), unable (to *inf*)

'**Unfähigkeit** *f* (-; *no pl*) incompetence; incapacity, inability

'**Unfall** *m* accident; crash

'**Unfallstelle** *f* scene of the accident

un'fehlbar *adj* infallible (*a.* REL); unfailing

unförmig ['ʊnfœrmɪç] *adj* shapeless; misshapen; monstrous

'**unfrankiert** *adj* unstamped

'**unfrei** *adj* not free; *post* unpaid

'**unfreiwillig** *adj* involuntary; unconscious (*humor*)

'**unfreundlich** *adj* unfriendly (*zu* to), unkind (to); *fig* cheerless

'**Unfrieden** *m* (-s; *no pl*) discord; **Unfrieden stiften** make mischief

'**unfruchtbar** *adj* infertile

'**Unfruchtbarkeit** *f* (-; *no pl*) infertility

Unfug ['ʊnfuːk] *m* (-[e]s; *no pl*) nonsense; **Unfug treiben** be up to mischief, fool around

Ungar ['ʊŋgar] *m* (-*n*; -*n*), '**Ungarin** *f* (-; -*nen*), '**ungarisch** *adj* Hungarian

'**Ungarn** Hungary

'**ungastlich** *adj* inhospitable

'**ungeachtet** *prp* (*gen*) regardless of; despite

ungeahnt *adj* unthought-of

ungebeten *adj* uninvited, unasked

ungebildet *adj* uneducated

ungeboren *adj* unborn

ungebräuchlich *adj* uncommon, unusual

ungebührlich [-gəby:ɐlɪç] *adj* unseemly

ungebunden *fig adj* free, independent; **frei und ungebunden** footloose and fancy-free

ungedeckt *adj* ECON uncovered; SPORT unmarked

'**Ungeduld** *f* (-; *no pl*) impatience

'**ungeduldig** *adj* impatient

'**ungeeignet** *adj* unfit; unqualified; inappropriate

ungefähr ['ʊngəfɛːɐ] **1.** *adj* approximate; rough; **2.** *adv* approximately, roughly, about, around, ... or so; **so ungefähr** something like that

'**ungefährlich** *adj* harmless; safe

'**ungeheuer** *adj* enormous (*a. fig*), huge, vast

'**Ungeheuer** *n* (-s; -) monster (*a. fig*)

unge'heuerlich *adj* monstrous

'**ungehindert** *adj and adv* unhindered

'**ungehobelt** *fig adj* uncouth, rough

'**ungehörig** *adj* improper, unseemly

'**ungehorsam** *adj* disobedient

Ungehorsam *m* (-s; *no pl*) disobedience

'**ungekocht** *adj* uncooked

ungekünstelt *adj* unaffected

ungekürzt *adj* unabridged

ungelegen *adj* inconvenient; **j-m ungelegen kommen** be inconvenient for s.o.

ungelenk ['ʊngəlɛŋk] *adj* awkward, clumsy

'**ungelernt** *adj* unskilled

'**ungemütlich** *adj* uncomfortable; F **ungemütlich werden** get nasty

'**ungenau** *adj* inaccurate; *fig* vague

'**Ungenauigkeit** *f* (-; -*en*) inaccuracy

ungeniert ['ʊnʒeniːɐt] *adj* uninhibited

'**ungenießbar** *adj* uneatable; undrinkable; F unbearable

ungenügend *adj* insufficient; PED poor, unsatisfactory; *grade: a.* F

ungepflegt *adj* neglected; untidy, unkempt

ungerade *adj* uneven; odd
ungerecht *adj* unfair, unjust
'**Ungerechtigkeit** *f* (-; *no pl*) injustice, unfairness
'**ungern** *adv* unwillingly; *et. ungern tun* hate *or* not like to do s.th.
'**ungeschehen** *adj*: *ungeschehen machen* undo
ungeschickt *adj* awkward, clumsy
ungeschliffen *adj* uncut (*diamond etc*); unpolished (*a. fig*)
ungeschminkt *adj* without make-up; *fig* unvarnished, plain (*truth*)
ungesetzlich *adj* illegal, unlawful
ungestört *adj* undisturbed
ungestraft *adj*: *ungestraft davonkommen* get off unpunished (F scot-free)
ungesund *adj* unhealthy (*a. fig*)
ungeteilt *adj* undivided (*a. fig*)
Ungetüm ['ʊŋgəty:m] *n* (-s; -e) monster, *fig a.* monstrosity
'**ungewiss** *adj* uncertain; *j-n im Ungewissen lassen* keep s.o. in the dark (*über acc* about)
'**Ungewissheit** *f* (-; *no pl*) uncertainty
'**ungewöhnlich** *adj* unusual
'**ungewohnt** *adj* strange, unfamiliar;
Ungeziefer ['ʊŋgətsi:fɐ] *n* (-s; *no pl*) vermin
'**ungezogen** *adj* naughty, bad; spoilt
'**ungezwungen** *adj* relaxed, informal; easygoing
'**ungläubig** *adj* incredulous, unbelieving (*a.* REL)
unglaublich [ʊn'glauplɪç] *adj* incredible, unbelievable
'**unglaubwürdig** *adj* implausible; unreliable (*witness etc*)
'**ungleich** *adj* unequal, different; unlike
ungleichmäßig *adj* uneven; irregular
'**Unglück** *n* (-[e]s; -e) a) (*no pl*) bad luck, misfortune; misery, b) accident; disaster
'**unglücklich** *adj* unhappy, miserable; unfortunate
'**unglücklicher'weise** *adv* unfortunately
'**ungültig** *adj* invalid; *für ungültig erklären* JUR invalidate
'**Ungunst** *f*: *zu Ungunsten* → *zuungunsten*
'**ungünstig** *adj* unfavo(u)rable; disadvantageous
'**ungut** *adj*: *ungutes Gefühl* misgivings (*bei et.* about s.th.); *nichts für ungut!* no offense (*Br* offence) meant!
'**unhaltbar** *adj* untenable; intolerable; SPORT unstoppable
'**unhandlich** *adj* unwieldy
'**unhar,monisch** *adj* MUS discordant
'**Unheil** *n* (-s; *no pl*) mischief; evil; disaster

'**unheilbar** *adj* MED incurable
'**unheilvoll** *adj* disastrous; sinister
'**unheimlich** *adj* creepy, spooky, eerie; F tremendous; F *unheimlich gut* terrific, fantastic
'**unhöflich** *adj* impolite; rude
'**Unhöflichkeit** *f* (-; *no pl*) impoliteness; rudeness
un'**hörbar** *adj* inaudible
'**unhygienisch** *adj* insanitary
Uniform [uni'fɔrm] *f* (-; -en) uniform
'**uninteressant** *adj* uninteresting
uninteressiert ['ʊnʔɪntərɛsi:ɐt] *adj* uninterested (*an dat* in)
Union [u'njo:n] *f* (-; -en) union
Universität [univɛrzi'tɛ:t] *f* (-; -en) university
Universum [uni'vɛrzʊm] *n* (-s; *no pl*) universe
Unke ['ʊŋkə] *f* (-; -n) ZO toad
'**unkenntlich** *adj* unrecognizable
'**Unkenntnis** *f* (-; *no pl*) ignorance
'**unklar** *adj* unclear; uncertain; confused, muddled; *im Unklaren sein* (*lassen*) be (leave *s.o.*) in the dark
'**unklug** *adj* imprudent, unwise
'**Unkosten** *pl* expenses, costs
'**Unkraut** *n* (-[e]s; *no pl*) weed(s); *Unkraut jäten* weed (the garden)
unkündbar ['ʊnkʏntba:ɐ] *adj* permanent (*post*)
'**unlängst** *adv* lately, recently
'**unleserlich** *adj* illegible
'**unlogisch** *adj* illogical
un'**lösbar** *adj* insoluble
'**unmännlich** *adj* unmanly, effeminate
'**unmäßig** *adj* excessive
'**Unmenge** *f* vast quantity *or* number(s) (*von* of), F loads (of), tons (of)
'**Unmensch** *m* monster, brute
'**unmenschlich** *adj* inhuman, cruel
'**Unmenschlichkeit** *f* (-; -en) a) (*no pl*) inhumanity, b) cruelty
un'**merklich** *adj* imperceptible
'**unmissverständlich** *adj* unmistakable
'**unmittelbar 1.** *adj* immediate, direct; **2.** *adv*: *unmittelbar nach* (*hinter*) right after (behind)
'**unmöbliert** *adj* unfurnished
'**unmodern** *adj* out of fashion *or* style
'**unmöglich 1.** *adj* impossible; **2.** *adv*: *ich kann es unmöglich tun* I can't possibly do it
'**unmoralisch** *adj* immoral
'**unmündig** *adj* JUR under age
'**unmusikalisch** *adj* unmusical
'**unnachahmlich** *adj* inimitable
'**unnachgiebig** *adj* unyielding
'**unnachsichtig** *adj* strict, severe

unnahbar [ʊn'naːbaːɐ] *adj* standoffish, cold

'**unnatürlich** *adj* unnatural (*a. fig*); affected

'**unnötig** *adj* unnecessary, needless

unnütz ['ʊnnʏts] *adj* useless

'**unordentlich** *adj* untidy; ***unordentlich sein*** *room etc*: be (in) a mess

'**Unordnung** *f* (-; *no pl*) disorder, mess

'**unparteiisch** *adj* impartial, unbias(s)ed

'**Unparteiische** *m, f* (-*n*; -*n*) SPORT referee

'**unpassend** *adj* unsuitable; improper; inappropriate

'**unpassierbar** *adj* impassable

unpässlich ['ʊnpɛslɪç] *adj* indisposed

'**unpersönlich** *adj* impersonal (*a.* LING)

'**unpolitisch** *adj* unpolitical

'**unpraktisch** *adj* impractical

'**unpünktlich** *adj* unpunctual

'**unrecht** *adj* wrong; ***unrecht haben*** be wrong; ***j-m unrecht tun*** do s.o. wrong

'**Unrecht** *n* (-[e]*s*; *no pl*) injustice, wrong; ***zu Unrecht*** wrong(ful)ly; ***Unrecht haben → unrecht***; ***unrecht tun → unrecht***

'**unrechtmäßig** *adj* unlawful

'**unregelmäßig** *adj* irregular (*a.* LING)

'**Unregelmäßigkeit** *f* (-; -*en*) irregularity

'**unreif** *adj* unripe; *fig* immature

'**Unreife** *fig f* immaturity

'**unrein** *adj* unclean; impure (*a.* REL)

'**Unreinheit** *f* (-; -*en*) impurity

'**unrichtig** *adj* incorrect, wrong

'**Unruhe** *f* (-; -*n*) a) (*no pl*) restlessness, unrest (*a.* POL); anxiety, alarm, b) *pl* disturbances, riots

'**unruhig** *adj* restless; uneasy; worried, alarmed; MAR rough

uns [ʊns] *pers pron* (to) us; each other; ***uns (selbst)*** (to) ourselves; ***ein Freund von uns*** a friend of ours

'**unsachgemäß** *adj* improper

unsachlich *adj* unobjective

unsanft *adj* rude, rough

unsauber *adj* unclean, *esp fig a.* impure; SPORT unfair; *fig* underhand

unschädlich *adj* harmless

unscharf *adj* PHOT blurred, out of focus

un'schätzbar *adj* inestimable, invaluable

'**unscheinbar** *adj* inconspicuous; plain

unschicklich *adj* indecent

unschlüssig *adj* irresolute; undecided

unschön *adj* unsightly; *fig* unpleasant

'**Unschuld** *f* (-; *no pl*) innocence; *fig* virginity

'**unschuldig** *adj* innocent (***an*** *dat* of)

'**unselbstständig** *adj* dependent on others

'**Unselbstständigkeit** *f* lack of independence, dependence on others

unser ['ʊnzɐ] *poss pron* our; ***unserer, unsere, unseres*** ours

'**unsicher** *adj* unsafe, insecure; self-conscious; uncertain

'**Unsicherheit** *f* (-; -*en*) a) (*no pl*) insecurity, unsafeness; self-consciousness, b) uncertainty

'**unsichtbar** *adj* invisible

'**Unsinn** *m* (-[e]*s*; *no pl*) nonsense

'**unsinnig** *adj* nonsensical, stupid; absurd

'**Unsitte** *f* bad habit; abuse

'**unsittlich** *adj* immoral, indecent

'**unsozial** *adj* unsocial

'**unsportlich** *adj* unathletic; *fig* unfair

'**unsterblich** **1.** *adj* immortal (*a. fig*); **2.** *adv:* ***unsterblich verliebt*** madly in love (***in*** *acc* with)

'**Unsterblichkeit** *f* immortality

'**Unstimmigkeit** *f* (-; -*en*) discrepancy; *pl* disagreements

'**unsympathisch** *adj* disagreeable; ***er (es) ist mir unsympathisch*** I don't like him (it)

'**untätig** *adj* inactive; idle

'**Untätigkeit** *f* (-; *no pl*) inactivity

'**untauglich** *adj* unfit (*a.* MIL); incompetent

un'teilbar *adj* indivisible

unten ['ʊntən] *adv* (down) below, down (*a.* ***nach unten***); downstairs; ***unten auf*** (*dat*) at the bottom of *the page etc*; ***siehe unten*** see below; ***von oben bis unten*** from top to bottom

unter ['ʊntɐ] *prp* under; below (*a. fig*); among; *fig* less than; ***unter anderem*** among other things; ***unter uns (gesagt)*** between you and me; ***unter Wasser*** underwater

'**Unterarm** *m* ANAT forearm

'**unterbelichtet** *adj* PHOT underexposed

unterbesetzt *adj* understaffed

'**Unterbewusstsein** *n* subconscious; ***im Unterbewusstsein*** subconsciously

unter'bieten *v/t* (*irr*, **bieten**, *no* -*ge*-, *h*) underbid; undercut; beat (*record*)

unter'binden *fig v/t* (*irr*, **binden**, *no* -*ge*-, *h*) put a stop to; prevent

unter'brechen *v/t* (*irr*, **brechen**, *no* -*ge*-, *h*) interrupt

Unter'brechung *f* (-; -*en*) interruption

'**unterbringen** *v/i* (*irr*, **bringen**, *sep*, -*ge*-, *h*) accommodate, put *s.o.* up; find a place for, put (***in*** *acc* into)

'**Unterbringung** *f* (-; -*en*) accommodation

unter'dessen *adv* in the meantime, meanwhile

unter'drücken *v/t* (*no* -*ge*-, *h*) oppress; suppress

Unter'drücker *m* (-*s*; -) oppressor

U

Unter'drückung f (-; -en) oppression; suppression

untere ['ʊntərə] adj lower (a. fig)

'unterentwickelt adj underdeveloped

'unterernährt adj undernourished, underfed

'Unterernährung f (-; no pl) undernourishment, malnutrition

Unter'führung f (-; -en) underpass, Br a. subway

'Untergang m ASTR setting; MAR sinking; fig downfall; decline; fall

'untergehen v/i (irr, **gehen**, sep, -ge-, sein) go down (a. fig), ASTR a. set, MAR a. sink

'untergeordnet adj subordinate, inferior; secondary

'Untergewicht n (-[e]s; no pl), **'untergewichtig** adj underweight

unter'graben fig v/t (irr, **graben**, no -ge-, h) undermine

'Untergrund m subsoil; POL underground; **in den Untergrund gehen** go underground

Untergrundbahn f → **U-Bahn**

'unterhalb prp (gen) below, under

'Unterhalt m (-[e]s; no pl) support, maintenance (a. JUR)

unter'halten v/t (irr, **halten**, no -ge-, h) entertain; support; **sich unterhalten (mit)** talk (to, with); **sich (gut) unterhalten** enjoy o.s., have a good time

unter'haltsam adj entertaining

Unter'haltung f (-; -en) talk, conversation; entertainment

Unter'haltungsindus,trie f show business

'Unterhändler m negotiator

Unterhaus n (-es; no pl) Br PARL House of Commons

Unterhemd n undershirt, Br vest

Unterholz n (-es; no pl) undergrowth

Unterhose f shorts, esp Br underpants, panties, Br pants; **e-e lange Unterhose, lange Unterhose** (a pair of) long johns

'unterirdisch adj underground

'Unterkiefer m ANAT lower jaw

'Unterkleid n slip

'unterkommen v/i (irr, **kommen**, sep, -ge-, sein) find accommodation; find work or a job (**bei** with)

Unterkunft ['ʊntɛkʊnft] f (-; -künfte [-kʏnftə]) accommodation, lodging(s); MIL quarters; **Unterkunft und Verpflegung** board and lodging

'Unterlage f TECH base; pl documents; data

unter'lassen v/t (irr, **lassen**, no -ge-, h) omit, fail to do s.th.; stop or quit doing s.th.

Unter'lassung f (-; -en) omission (a. JUR)

'unterlegen[1] v/t (sep, -ge-, h) underlay

unter'legen[2] adj inferior (dat to)

Unter'legenheit f (-; no pl) inferiority

'Unterleib m ANAT abdomen, belly

unter'liegen v/i (irr, **liegen**, no -ge-, sein) be defeated (**j-m** by s.o.), lose (to s.o.); fig be subject to

'Unterlippe f ANAT lower lip

'Untermieter m, **'Untermieterin** f roomer, Br lodger

unter'nehmen v/t (irr, **nehmen**, no -ge-, h) make, take, go on a trip etc; **et. unternehmen** do s.th. (**gegen** about s.th.), take action (against s.o.)

Unter'nehmen n (-s; -) firm, business; venture; undertaking, enterprise; MIL operation

Unter'nehmensberater(in) management consultant

Unter'nehmer m (-s; -) businessman, entrepreneur; employer

Unter'nehmerin f (-; -nen) businesswoman

unter'nehmungslustig adj active, dynamic; adventurous

'Unteroffizier m MIL non-commissioned officer

'unterordnen v/t and v/refl (sep, -ge-, h) subordinate (o.s.) (dat to)

Unter'redung f (-; -en) talk(s)

Unterricht ['ʊntərɪçt] m (-[e]s; no pl) instruction, teaching; PED school, classes, lessons

unter'richten v/i and v/t (no -ge-, h) teach; give lessons; inform (**über** acc of)

'Unterrichtsstunde f lesson, PED a. class, period

'Unterrock m slip

unter'sagen v/t (no -ge-, h) prohibit

unter'schätzen v/t (no -ge-, h) underestimate; underrate

unter'scheiden v/t and v/i (irr, **scheiden**, no -ge-, h) distinguish (**zwischen** between; **von** from); tell apart; **sich unterscheiden** differ (**von** from; **in** dat in; **durch** by)

Unter'scheidung f (-; -en) distinction

Unterschied ['ʊntəʃiːt] m (-[e]s; -e) difference; **im Unterschied zu** unlike, as opposed to

'unterschiedlich adj different; varying

unter'schlagen v/t (irr, **schlagen**, no -ge-, h) embezzle

Unter'schlagung f (-; -en) embezzlement

Unterschlupf ['ʊntəʃlʊpf] m (-[e]s; no pl) hiding place

unter'schreiben v/t and v/i (irr, **schreiben**, no -ge-, h) sign

'Unterschrift f signature; caption

'**Unterseeboot** *n* → *U-Boot*
Untersetzer ['ʊntɐzɛtsɐ] *m* (-s; -) coaster; saucer
unter'setzt *adj* thickset, stocky
'**Unterstand** *m* shelter, MIL *a*. dugout
unter'stehen (*irr*, **stehen**, *no -ge-*, *h*) **1.** *v/i* (*dat*) be under (the control of); **2.** *v/refl* dare; **unterstehen Sie sich** (*et. zu tun*)*!* don't you dare ([to] do s.th.)*!*
'**unterstellen**[1] *v/t* (*sep*, *-ge-*, *h*) put *s.th.* in; store; **sich unterstellen** take shelter
unter'stellen[2] *v/t* (*no -ge-*, *h*) assume; *j-m* **unterstellen, dass er ...** insinuate that s.o. ...
Unter'stellung *f* (-; *-en*) insinuation
unter'streichen *v/t* (*irr*, **streichen**, *no -ge-*, *h*) underline (*a. fig*)
unter'stützen *v/t* (*no -ge-*, *h*) support; back (up)
Unter'stützung *f* (-; *-en*) support; aid; welfare (payments)
unter'suchen *v/t* (*no -ge-*, *h*) examine (*a.* MED), investigate (*a.* JUR); search; CHEM analyze
Unter'suchung *f* (-; *-en*) examination (*a.* MED), investigation (*a.* JUR), *a.* (medical) checkup; CHEM analysis
Unter'suchungsgefangene *m*, *f* JUR prisoner on remand
Untersuchungsgefängnis *n* JUR remand prison
Untersuchungshaft *f*: **in Untersuchungshaft sein** JUR be on remand
Untersuchungsrichter *m* JUR examining magistrate
Untertan ['ʊntɐta:n] *m* (-s; *-en*) subject
'**Untertasse** *f* saucer
'**untertauchen** (*sep*, *-ge-*) **1.** *v/i* (*sein*) dive, submerge; *fig* disappear; *esp* POL go underground; **2.** *v/t* (*h*) duck
'**Unterteil** *n*, *m* lower part, bottom
unter'teilen *v/t* (*no -ge-*, *h*) subdivide
Unter'teilung *f* (-; *-en*) subdivision
'**Untertitel** *m* subtitle, *film*: *a*. caption
'**Unterton** *m* undertone
Unter'treibung *f* (-; *-en*) understatement
'**untervermieten** *v/t* (*no -ge-*, *h*) sublet
unter'wandern *v/t* (*no -ge-*, *h*) infiltrate
'**Unterwäsche** *f* underwear
'**Unterwasser...** *in cpds* underwater ...
unterwegs [ʊntɐ've:ks] *adv* on the *or* one's way (**nach** to)
unter'weisen *v/t* (*irr*, **weisen**, *no -ge-*, *h*) instruct
Unter'weisung *f* (-; *-en*) instruction
'**Unterwelt** *f* (-; *no pl*) underworld
unter'werfen *v/t* (*irr*, **werfen**, *no -ge-*, *h*) subject (*dat* to); subjugate; **sich unterwerfen** submit (to)

Unter'werfung *f* (-; *-en*) subjection; submission (**unter** *acc* to)
unterwürfig [ʊntɐ'vyrfɪç] *adj* servile
unter'zeichnen *v/t* (*no -ge-*, *h*) sign
Unter'zeichnete *m*, *f* (-*n*; *-n*) the undersigned
Unter'zeichnung *f* (-; *-en*) signing
'**unterziehen**[1] *v/t* (*irr*, **ziehen**, *sep*, *-ge-*, *h*) put *s.th.* on underneath
unter'ziehen[2] *v/t* (*irr*, **ziehen**, *no -ge-*, *h*) **sich** *e-r Behandlung, Prüfung etc* **unterziehen** undergo (*treatment etc*), take (*an examination etc*)
'**Untiefe** *f* shallow, shoal
un'tragbar *adj* unbearable, intolerable
un'trennbar *adj* inseparable
'**untreu** *adj* unfaithful (*dat* to)
un'tröstlich *adj* inconsolable
untrüglich [ʊn'try:klɪç] *adj* unmistakable
'**Untugend** *f* vice, bad habit
'**unüberlegt** *adj* thoughtless
unübersichtlich *adj* blind (*bend etc*)
unübertrefflich [ʊn?y:bɐ'trɛflɪç] *adj* unsurpassable, matchless
unübertroffen [-'trɔfən] *adj* unequal(l)ed
unüberwindlich [-'vɪntlɪç] *adj* insuperable, invincible
unumgänglich [ʊn?ʊm'gɛŋlɪç] *adj* inevitable
unumschränkt [-'ʃrɛŋkt] *adj* unlimited; POL absolute
unumstritten [-'ʃtrɪtən] *adj* undisputed
unumwunden [-'vʊndən] *adv* straight out, frankly
ununterbrochen ['ʊn?ʊntɐbrɔxən] *adj* uninterrupted; continuous
unver'änderlich *adj* unchanging
unver'antwortlich *adj* irresponsible
unver'besserlich *adj* incorrigible
unver'bindlich *adj* noncommittal, ECON not binding
unver'daulich *adj* indigestible (*a. fig*)
'**unverdient** *adj* undeserved
'**unverdünnt** *adj* undiluted; straight
unver'einbar *adj* incompatible
'**unverfälscht** *adj* unadulterated
'**unverfänglich** *adj* harmless
'**unverfroren** *adj* brazen, impertinent
unver'gänglich *adj* immortal, eternal
unver'gesslich *adj* unforgettable
unver'gleichlich *adj* incomparable
'**unverhältnismäßig** *adv* disproportionately; **unverhältnismäßig hoch** excessive
'**unverheiratet** *adj* unmarried, single
unverhofft ['ʊnfɛɐhɔft] *adj* unhoped-for; unexpected
unverhohlen ['ʊnfɛɐho:lən] *adj* undisguised, open

U

'unver**käuflich** *adj* not for sale; unsal(e)-able

unver'**kennbar** *adj* unmistakable

'unver**letzt** *adj* unhurt

unver**meidlich** [ʊnfɛɐ̯'maitlɪç] *adj* inevitable

'unver**mindert** *adj* undiminished

'unver**mittelt** *adj* abrupt, sudden

'Unver**mögen** *n* (-s; *no pl*) inability, incapacity

'unver**mutet** *adj* unexpected

'unver**nünftig** *adj* unreasonable; foolish

'unver**schämt** *adj* rude, impertinent; outrageous (*price etc*)

'Unver**schämtheit** *f* (-; *-en*) impertinence; *die Unverschämtheit haben zu inf* have the nerve to *inf*

'unver**schuldet** *adj* through no fault of one's own

unver**sehens** ['ʊnfɛɐ̯zeːəns] *adv* unexpectedly, all of a sudden

'unver**sehrt** *adj* unhurt; undamaged

unver**söhnlich** *adj* irreconcilable (*a. fig*), implacable

unver**sorgt** *adj* unprovided for

unver**ständlich** *adj* unintelligible; *es ist mir unverständlich* I can't see how *or* why, F it beats me

unver**sucht** *adj*: *nichts unversucht lassen* leave nothing undone

unver'**wundbar** *adj* invulnerable

unver**wüstlich** [ʊnfɛɐ̯'vyːstlɪç] *adj* indestructible

unver**zeihlich** [-'tsailɪç] *adj* inexcusable

unver**züglich** [-'tsyːklɪç] **1.** *adj* immediate, prompt; **2.** *adv* immediately, without delay

'unvoll**endet** *adj* unfinished

'unvoll**kommen** *adj* imperfect

'unvoll**ständig** *adj* incomplete

'unvor**bereitet** *adj* unprepared

'unvor**eingenommen** *adj* unprejudiced, unbias(s)ed

'unvor**hergesehen** *adj* unforeseen

'unvor**hersehbar** *adj* unforeseeable

'unvor**sichtig** *adj* careless

'Unvor**sichtigkeit** *f* (-; *no pl*) carelessness

unvor'**stellbar** *adj* unthinkable

'unvor**teilhaft** *adj* unbecoming

'un**wahr** *adj* untrue

'Un**wahrheit** *f* untruth

'unwahr**scheinlich** *adj* improbable, unlikely; F fantastic

unweg**sam** ['ʊnveːkzaːm] *adj* difficult, rough (*terrain*)

unweiger**lich** [ʊn'vaigɐlɪç] *adv* inevitably

'un**weit** *prp* (*gen*) not far from

'Un**wetter** *n* (-s; -) disastrous (thunder)-storm

'un**wichtig** *adj* unimportant

unwider**legbar** [ʊnviːdɐ'leːkbaɐ̯] *adj* irrefutable

unwider**ruflich** [-'ruːflɪç] *adj* irrevocable

unwider**stehlich** [-'ʃteːlɪç] *adj* irresistible

'Un**wille(n)** *m* indignation (*über acc* at)

'un**willig** *adj* indignant (*über acc* at); unwilling, reluctant

'unwill**kürlich** *adj* involuntary

'un**wirklich** *adj* unreal

'un**wirksam** *adj* ineffective

un**wirsch** ['ʊnvɪrʃ] *adj* surly, gruff

un**wirtlich** ['ʊnvɪrtlɪç] *adj* inhospitable

'unwirt**schaftlich** *adj* uneconomic(al)

'un**wissend** *adj* ignorant

'Un**wissenheit** *f* (-; *no pl*) ignorance

'un**wohl** *adj* unwell; uneasy

'un**würdig** *adj* unworthy (*gen* of)

un**zählig** [ʊn'tsɛːlɪç] *adj* innumerable, countless

unzer'**brechlich** *adj* unbreakable

unzer'**reißbar** *adj* untearable

unzer'**störbar** *adj* indestructible

unzer'**trennlich** *adj* inseparable

'Un**zucht** *f* (-; *no pl*) sexual offense (*Br* offence)

'un**züchtig** *adj* indecent; obscene

'un**zufrieden** *adj* discontent(ed) (*mit* with), dissatisfied (with)

'Un**zufriedenheit** *f* discontent, dissatisfaction

'un**zugänglich** *adj* inaccessible

'un**zulänglich** *adj* inadequate

'un**zulässig** *adj* inadmissible

unzu'**mutbar** *adj* unacceptable; unreasonable

'unzurechnungs**fähig** *adj* JUR irresponsible

'Unzurechnungs**fähigkeit** *f* (-; *no pl*) JUR irresponsibility

'un**zureichend** *adj* insufficient

'unzu**sammenhängend** *adj* incoherent

'unzu**verlässig** *adj* unreliable, untrustworthy; uncertain

üppig ['ʏpɪç] *adj* luxuriant, lush (*both a. fig*); voluptuous, luscious; opulent; rich

uralt ['uːɐ̯'alt] *adj* ancient (*a. iro*)

Uran [u'raːn] *n* (-s; *no pl*) uranium

'**Uraufführung** *f* première, first performance (*film*: showing)

urbar ['uːɐ̯baːɐ̯] *adj* arable; *urbar machen* cultivate; reclaim

'**Urbevölkerung** *f*, '**Ureinwohner** *pl* aboriginal inhabitants; *in Australia*: Aborigines

'**Urenkel** *m* great-grandson

'**Urenkelin** *f* great-granddaughter

'**Urgroß...** *in cpds* **...eltern**, **...mutter**, **...vater**: great-grand...

Urheberrechte ['uːɐheːbɐ-] *pl* copyright (*an dat* on, for)

Urin [u'riːn] *m* (*-s*; *-e*) urine

urinieren [uri'niːrən] *v/i* (*no -ge-*, *h*) urinate

Urkunde ['uːɐkʊndə] *f* (*-*; *-n*) document; diploma

'**Urkundenfälschung** *f* forgery of documents

Urlaub ['uːɐlaup] *m* (*-[e]s*; *-e*) vacation, *Br* holiday(s); MIL leave; *in or im Urlaub sein (auf Urlaub gehen)* be (go) on vacation (*Br* holiday); *e-n Tag (ein paar Tage) Urlaub nehmen* take a day (a few days) off

Urlauber(in) ['uːɐlaubɐ (-bərɪn)] (*-s*; *-/-*; *-nen*) vacationist, vacationer, *Br* holidaymaker

Urne ['ʊrnə] *f* (*-*; *-n*) urn; ballot box

'**Ursache** *f* (*-*; *-n*) cause; reason; *keine Ursache!* not at all, you're welcome

'**Ursprung** *m* origin

ursprünglich ['uːɐʃprʏŋlɪç] *adj* original; natural, unspoilt

Urteil ['ʊrtail] *n* (*-[e]s*; *-e*) judg(e)ment; JUR sentence; *sich ein Urteil bilden* form a judg(e)ment (*über acc* about)

'**urteilen** *v/i* (*ge-*, *h*) judge (*über j-n, et.* s.o., s.th.; *nach* by)

'**Urwald** *m* primeval forest; jungle

urwüchsig ['uːɐvyːksɪç] *adj* coarse, earthy

'**Urzeit** *f* prehistoric times

usw. ABBR *of und so weiter* etc, and so on

Utensilien [utɛn'ziːljən] *pl* utensils

Utopie [uto'piː] *f* (*-*; *-n*) illusion

utopisch [u'toːpɪʃ] *adj* utopian; fantastic

V

Vagabund [vaga'bʊnt] *m* (*-en*; *-en*) vagabond, tramp, F bum

vage ['vaːgə] *adj* vague

Vakuum ['vaːkuʊm] *n* (*-s*; *-kua*, *-kuen*) vacuum

Vampir ['vampiːɐ] *m* (*-s*; *-e*) ZO vampire (*a. fig*)

Vanille [va'nɪljə] *f* (*-*; *no pl*) vanilla

variabel [va'rjaːbəl] *adj* variable

Variante [va'rjantə] *f* (*-*; *-n*) variant

Variation [varja'tsioːn] *f* (*-*; *-en*) variation

Varietee [varje'teː] *n* (*-s*; *-s*), **Varieté**, *a.* vaudeville, *Br* variety theatre, music hall

variieren [vari'iːrən] *v/i and v/t* (*no -ge-*, *h*) vary

Vase ['vaːzə] *f* (*-*; *-n*) vase

Vater ['faːtɐ] *m* (*-s*; *Väter* ['fɛːtɐ]) father

'**Vaterland** *n* native country

'**Vaterlandsliebe** *f* patriotism

väterlich ['fɛːtɐlɪç] *adj* fatherly, paternal

'**Vaterschaft** *f* (*-*; *-en*) JUR paternity

'**Vater'unser** *n* (*-s*; *-*) REL Lord's Prayer

v. Chr. ABBR *of vor Christus* BC, before Christ

V-Ausschnitt ['fau-] *m* V-neck

Vegetarier [vege'taːrjɐ] *m* (*-s*; *-*), **Vege'tarierin** *f* (*-*; *-nen*), **vegetarisch** [vege'taːrɪʃ] *adj* vegetarian

Vegetation [vegeta'tsioːn] *f* (*-*; *-en*) vegetation

vegetieren [vege'tiːrən] *v/i* (*no -ge-*, *h*) vegetate

Veilchen ['failçən] *n* (*-s*; *-*) BOT violet

Velo ['veːlo] *Swiss n* (*-s*; *-s*) bicycle, F bike

Ventil [vɛn'tiːl] *n* (*-s*; *-e*) TECH valve; *fig* vent, outlet

Ventilation [vɛntila'tsioːn] *f* (*-*; *-en*) ventilation

Ventilator [vɛnti'laːtoːɐ] *m* (*-s*; *-en* [-la-'toːrən]) fan

verabreden [fɛɐ'ʔap-] *v/t* (*no -ge-*, *h*) agree (up)on, arrange; appoint, fix; *sich verabreden* make a date (*or* an appointment) (*mit* with)

Ver'abredung *f* (*-*; *-en*) appointment; date

ver'abreichen *v/t* (*no -ge-*, *h*) give; MED administer

verabscheuen *v/t* (*no -ge-*, *h*) loathe, detest

verabschieden [fɛɐ'ʔapʃiːdən] *v/t* (*no -ge-*, *h*) say goodbye to (*a. sich verabschieden von*); dismiss; JUR pass

Ver'abschiedung *f* (*-*; *-en*) dismissal; JUR passing

ver'achten *v/t* (*no -ge-*, *h*) despise

verächtlich [fɛɐ'ʔɛçtlɪç] *adj* contemptuous

Ver'achtung *f* (*-*; *no pl*) contempt

verallgemeinern [fɛɐ'ʔalgə'mainɐn] *v/t* (*no -ge-*, *h*) generalize

ver'altet *adj* antiquated, out of date

Veranda [ve'randa] *f* (-; -*den*) porch, *Br* veranda(h)

veränderlich [fɛɐ̯'ʔɛndɐlɪç] *adj* changeable (*a*. METEOR), variable (*a*. MATH, LING)

ver'ändern *v/t and v/refl* (*no -ge-, h*), **Ver-'änderung** *f* change

verängstigt [fɛɐ̯'ʔɛŋstɪçt] *adj* frightened, scared

ver'anlagen *v/t* (*no -ge-, h*) ECON assess

veranlagt [fɛɐ̯'ʔanlaːkt] *adj* inclined (**zu**, **für** to); **künstlerisch** (**musikalisch**) **veranlagt sein** have a gift *or* bent for art (music)

Ver'anlagung *f* (-; -*en*) (pre)disposition (*a*. MED); talent, gift; ECON assessment

ver'anlassen *v/t* (*no -ge-, h*) make arrangements (*or* arrange) for *s.th.*; **j-n zu et. veranlassen** make s.o. do s.th.

Ver'anlassung *f* (-; -*en*) cause (**zu** for)

ver'anschaulichen *v/t* (*no -ge-, h*) illustrate

ver'anschlagen *v/t* (*no -ge-, h*) estimate (**auf** *acc* at)

ver'anstalten *v/t* (*no -ge-, h*) arrange, organize; hold, give (*concert, party etc*)

Ver'anstaltung *f* (-; -*en*) event, SPORT *a*. meet, *Br* meeting

ver'antworten *v/t* (*no -ge-, h*) take the responsibility for

ver'antwortlich *adj* responsible; **j-n verantwortlich machen für** hold s.o. responsible for

Ver'antwortung *f* (-; *no pl*) responsibility; **auf eigene Verantwortung** at one's own risk; **j-n zur Verantwortung ziehen** call s.o. to account

Ver'antwortungsgefühl *n* (-[*e*]*s*; *no pl*) sense of responsibility

ver'antwortungslos *adj* irresponsible

ver'arbeiten *v/t* (*no -ge-, h*) process; *fig* digest; **et. verarbeiten zu** manufacture (*or* make) s.th. into

ver'ärgern *v/t* (*no -ge-, h*) make s.o. angry, annoy

ver'armt *adj* impoverished

ver'arschen *v/t* (*no -ge-, h*) **j-n verarschen** take the piss out of s.o.

Verb [vɛrp] *n* (-*s*; -*en* ['vɛrbən]) LING verb

Verband [fɛɐ̯'bant] *m* (-*es*; *Verbände* [fɛɐ̯-'bɛndə]) MED dressing, bandage; ECON association; MIL formation, unit

Verband(s)kasten *m* MED first-aid kit *or* box

Verband(s)zeug *n* MED dressing material

ver'bannen *v/t* (*no -ge-, h*) banish (*a*. *fig*), exile

Ver'bannung *f* (-; -*en*) banishment, exile

verbarrika'dieren *v/t* (*no -ge-, h*) barricade; block

ver'bergen *v/t* (*irr*, **bergen**, *no -ge-, h*) hide (*a*. **sich verbergen**), conceal

ver'bessern *v/t* (*no -ge-, h*) improve; correct

Ver'besserung *f* (-; -*en*) improvement; correction

ver'beugen *v/refl* (*no -ge-, h*), **Ver'beugung** *f* (-; -*en*) bow (**vor** to)

ver'biegen *v/t* (*irr*, **biegen**, *no -ge-, h*) twist

ver'bieten *v/t* (*irr*, **bieten**, *no -ge-, h*) forbid; prohibit; → **verboten**

ver'billigen *v/t* (*no -ge-, h*) reduce in price

verbilligt [-'bɪlɪçt] *adj* reduced, at reduced prices

verbinden *v/t* (*irr*, **binden**, *no -ge-, h*) MED dress, bandage; bandage *s.o.* up; *a*. TECH connect, join, link (up); TEL put *s.o.* through (**mit** to); combine (*a*. CHEM **sich verbinden**); *fig* unite; associate; **j-m die Augen verbinden** blindfold s.o.; **damit sind beträchtliche Kosten verbunden** that involves considerable cost(s *pl*); **falsch verbunden!** wrong number!

verbindlich [fɛɐ̯'bɪntlɪç] *adj* obligatory, compulsory (*a*. PED); obliging

Ver'bindlichkeit *f* (-; -*en*) a) (*no pl*) obligingness, b) *pl* ECON liabilities

Ver'bindung *f* (-; -*en*) connection; combination; CHEM compound; UNIV fraternity, *Br* society; **sich in Verbindung setzen mit** get in touch with; **in Verbindung stehen** (**bleiben**) be (keep) in touch

verbissen [fɛɐ̯'bɪsən] *adj* dogged

ver'bittert *adj* bitter, embittered

verblassen [fɛɐ̯'blasən] *v/i* (*no -ge-, sein*) fade (*a*. *fig*)

Verbleib [fɛɐ̯'blaip] *m* (-[*e*]*s*; *no pl*) whereabouts

ver'bleiben *v/i* (*irr*, **bleiben**, *no -ge-, sein*) remain

verbleit [fɛɐ̯'blait] *adj* leaded

ver'blendet *fig adj* blind

Ver'blendung *fig f* (-; -*en*) blindness

verblichen [fɛɐ̯'blɪçən] *adj* faded

verblüffen [fɛɐ̯'blʏfən] *v/t* (*no -ge-, h*) amaze, F flabbergast

Ver'blüffung *f* (-; -*en*) amazement

ver'blühen *v/i* (*no -ge-, sein*) fade, wither (*both a*. *fig*)

ver'bluten *v/i* (*no -ge-, sein*) MED bleed to death

verborgen [fɛɐ̯'bɔrgən] *adj* hidden, concealed; **im Verborgenen** in secret

Verbot [fɛɐ̯'boːt] *n* (-[*e*]*s*; -*e*) prohibition, ban (**on** *s.th.*)

ver'boten *adj*: **Rauchen verboten** no smoking

verdrossen

Ver'brauch *m* (-[e]s; *no pl*) consumption (*an dat* of)

ver'brauchen *v/t* (*no -ge-, h*) consume, use up

Verbraucher [fɛɐˈbrauxɐ] *m* (-s; -), **Ver-'braucherin** *f* (-; -nen) consumer

Verbraucherschutz *m* consumer protection

Ver'brechen *n* (-s; -) crime; *ein Verbrechen begehen* commit a crime

Ver'brecher(in) (-s; -/-; -nen), **ver'brecherisch** *adj* criminal

ver'breiten *v/t and v/refl* (*no -ge-, h*) spread (*in dat, über acc* over, through); circulate

verbreitern [fɛɐˈbraitɐn] *v/t and v/refl* (*no -ge-, h*) widen, broaden

Ver'breitung *f* (-; *no pl*) spread(ing); circulation

ver'brennen *v/i* (*irr, brennen, no -ge-, sein*) *and v/t* (*h*) burn (up); cremate

Ver'brennung *f* (-; -en) burning; cremation; *TECH* combustion; *MED* burn

ver'bringen *v/t* (*irr, bringen, no -ge-, h*) spend, pass

verbrüdern [fɛɐˈbryːdɐn] *v/refl* (*no -ge-, h*) fraternize

Verbrüderung [fɛɐˈbryːdərʊŋ] *f* (-; -en) fraternization

ver'brühen *v/t* (*no -ge-, h*) scald

ver'buchen *v/t* (*no -ge-, h*) book

verbünden [fɛɐˈbʏndən] *v/refl* (*no -ge-, h*) ally o.s. (*mit* to, with)

Ver'bündete *m, f* (-n; -n) ally (*a. fig*)

ver'bürgen *v/refl* (*no -ge-, h*) *sich verbürgen für* vouch for, guarantee

ver'büßen *v/t* (*no -ge-, h*) *e-e Strafe verbüßen* serve a sentence, serve time

verchromt [fɛɐˈkroːmt] *adj* chromium-plated

Verdacht [fɛɐˈdaxt] *m* (-[e]s; -e) suspicion; *Verdacht schöpfen* become suspicious

verdächtig [fɛɐˈdɛçtɪç] *adj* suspicious, suspect

Verdächtige [fɛɐˈdɛçtɪgə] *m, f* (-n; -n) suspect

ver'dächtigen *v/t* (*no -ge-, h*) suspect (*j-n e-r Tat* s.o. of [doing] s.th.)

Ver'dächtigung *f* (-; -en) suspicion

verdammen [fɛɐˈdamən] *v/t* (*no -ge-, h*) condemn (*zu* to), damn (*a. REL*)

Ver'dammnis *f* (-; *no pl*) *REL* damnation

ver'dammt **1.** *adj* damned, F *a.* damn, darn(ed), *Br sl a.* bloody; F *verdammt* (*noch mal*)*!* damn (it)!; **2.** *adv:* *verdammt gut etc* damn (*Br sl a.* bloody) good *etc*

Ver'dammung *f* (-; -en) condemnation; *REL* damnation

ver'dampfen *v/t* (*no -ge-, h*) *and v/i* (*sein*) evaporate

ver'danken *v/t* (*no -ge-, h*) *j-m* (*e-m Umstand*) *et. verdanken* owe s.th. to s.o. (s.th.)

verdarb [fɛɐˈdarp] *pret of* **verderben**

verdauen [fɛɐˈdauən] *v/t* (*no -ge-, h*) digest (*a. fig*)

ver'daulich *adj* digestible; *leicht* (*schwer*) *verdaulich* easy (hard) to digest

Ver'dauung *f* (-; *no pl*) digestion

Ver'deck *n* (-[e]s; -e) top

ver'decken *v/t* (*no -ge-, h*) cover (up) (*a. fig*)

ver'denken *v/t* (*irr, denken, no -ge-, h*) *ich kann es ihm nicht verdenken*(, *dass er …*) I can't blame him (for *doing*)

verderben [fɛɐˈdɛrbən] (*irr, no -ge-*) **1.** *v/i* (*sein*) spoil (*a. fig*); *GASTR* go bad; **2.** *v/t* (*h*) spoil (*a. fig*), ruin; *sich den Magen verderben* upset one's stomach

Ver'derben *n* (-s; *no pl*) ruin

verderblich [fɛɐˈdɛrplɪç] *adj* perishable; *leicht verderbliche Lebensmittel* perishables

ver'dichten *v/t* (*no -ge-, h*) compress, condense

ver'dienen *v/t* (*no -ge-, h*) earn, make; *fig* deserve

Ver'dienst[1] *m* (-[e]s; -e) earnings; salary; wages; gain, profit

Ver'dienst[2] *n* (-[e]s; -e) merit; *es ist sein Verdienst, dass* it is thanks to him that

ver'dient *adj* (well-)deserved

ver'doppeln *v/t and v/refl* (*no -ge-, h*) double

verdorben [fɛɐˈdɔrbən] **1.** *pp of* **verderben**; **2.** *adj GASTR* spoilt, bad (*both a. fig*); *MED* upset

verdorren [fɛɐˈdɔrən] *v/i* (*no -ge-, sein*) wither, dry up

ver'drängen *v/t* (*no -ge-, h*) supplant, supersede; replace; *PHYS* displace; *PSYCH* repress, suppress

ver'drehen *v/t* (*no -ge-, h*) twist, *fig a.* distort; *die Augen verdrehen* roll one's eyes; *j-m den Kopf verdrehen* turn s.o.'s head

ver'dreht F *fig adj* mixed up

ver'dreifachen *v/t and v/refl* (*no -ge-, h*) treble, triple

verdrießen [fɛɐˈdriːsən] *v/t* (*irr, no -ge-, h*) annoy

verdrießlich [fɛɐˈdriːslɪç] *adj* glum, morose, sullen

verdross [fɛɐˈdrɔs] *pret of* **verdrießen**

verdrossen [fɛɐˈdrɔsən] **1.** *pp of* **verdrießen**; **2.** *adj* grumpy, sullen

V

Verdruss [fɛɐ'drʊs] *m* (*-es*; *-e*) annoyance

ver'dummen (*no -ge-*) **1.** *v/t* (*h*) make stupid, stultify; **2.** *v/i* (*sein*) become stultified

ver'dunkeln *v/t and v/refl* (*no -ge-*, *h*) darken; black out; *fig* obscure

Ver'dunk(e)lung *f* (*-*; *-en*) darkening; blackout; JUR collusion

ver'dünnen *v/t* (*no -ge-*, *h*) dilute

ver'dunsten *v/i* (*no -ge-*, *sein*) evaporate

ver'dursten *v/i* (*no -ge-*, *sein*) die of thirst

verdutzt [fɛɐ'dʊtst] *adj* puzzled

ver'edeln *v/t* (*no -ge-*, *h*) BOT graft; TECH process, refine

Ver'ed(e)lung *f* (*-*; *-en*) BOT grafting; TECH processing, refinement

ver'ehren *v/t* (*no -ge-*, *h*) admire; adore, worship (*both a. fig*), *esp* REL *a.* revere, venerate

Ver'ehrer(in) (*-s*; *-/-*; *-nen*) admirer, *esp film etc*: *a.* fan

Ver'ehrung *f* (*-*; *no pl*) admiration; adoration, worship; *esp* REL reverence, veneration

vereidigen [fɛɐ'ʔaidɪgən] *v/t* (*no -ge-*, *h*) swear *s.o.* in; JUR put *s.o.* under an oath

Verein [fɛɐ'ʔain] *m* (*-[e]s*; *-e*) club (*a.* SPORT); society, association

vereinbar [fɛɐ'ʔainbaːɐ] *adj* compatible (***mit*** with)

vereinbaren [fɛɐ'ʔainbaːrən] *v/t* (*no -ge-*, *h*) agree (up)on, arrange

Ver'einbarung *f* (*-*; *-en*) agreement, arrangement

ver'einen → ***vereinigen***

ver'einfachen *v/t* (*no -ge-*, *h*) simplify

Ver'einfachung *f* (*-*; *-en*) simplification

ver'einheitlichen *v/t* (*no -ge-*, *h*) standardize

ver'einigen *v/t and v/refl* (*no -ge-*, *h*) unite (***zu*** into); combine, join

Ver'einigung *f* (*-*; *-en*) union; combination; alliance

ver'einsamen *v/i* (*no -ge-*, *sein*) become lonely *or* isolated

vereinzelt [fɛɐ'ʔaintsəlt] *adj* occasional, odd; ***vereinzelt Regen*** scattered showers

ver'eiteln *v/t* (*no -ge-*, *h*) prevent; frustrate

ver'enden *v/i* (*no -ge-*, *sein*) *esp* ZO die, perish

ver'engen *v/t and v/refl* (*no -ge-*, *h*) narrow

ver'erben *v/t* (*no -ge-*, *h*) ***j-m et. vererben*** leave (BIOL transmit) s.th. to s.o.; ***sich vererben*** (***auf*** *acc*) be passed on *or* down (to) (*a.* BIOL *and fig*)

Ver'erbung *f* (*-*; *no pl*) BIOL heredity

Ver'erbungslehre *f* BIOL genetics

verewigen [fɛɐ'ʔeːvɪgən] *v/t* (*no -ge-*, *h*) immortalize

ver'fahren (*irr*, ***fahren***, *no -ge-*) **1.** *v/i* (*sein*) proceed; ***verfahren mit*** deal with; **2.** *v/refl* (*h*) MOT get lost

Ver'fahren *n* (*-s*; *-*) procedure, method, *esp* TECH *a.* technique, way; JUR (legal) proceedings (***gegen*** against)

Ver'fall *m* (*-[e]s*; *no pl*) decay (*a. fig*); dilapidation; *fig* decline; ECON *etc* expiry

ver'fallen (*irr*, ***fallen***, *no -ge-*, *sein*) **1.** *v/i* decay (*a. fig*), dilapidate; *esp fig* decline; ECON expire; MED waste away; become addicted to; (***wieder***) ***verfallen in*** (*acc*) fall (back) into; ***verfallen auf*** (*acc*) hit (up)on; **2.** *adj* decayed; dilapidated; ***j-m verfallen sein*** be s.o.'s slave

Ver'fallsdatum *n* expiry date; GASTR pull date, *Br* best-before (*or* best-by) date; PHARM sell-by date

ver'fälschen *v/t* (*no -ge-*, *h*) falsify; distort; GASTR adulterate

verfänglich [fɛɐ'fɛŋlɪç] *adj* delicate, tricky; embarrassing, compromising

ver'färben *v/refl* (*no -ge-*, *h*) discolo(u)r

ver'fassen *v/t* (*no -ge-*, *h*) write

Verfasser [fɛɐ'fasɐ] *m* (*-s*; *-*), **Ver'fasserin** *f* (*-*; *-nen*) author

Ver'fassung *f* (*-*; *-en*) state (of health *or* of mind), condition; POL constitution

ver'fassungsmäßig *adj* POL constitutional

verfassungswidrig *adj* unconstitutional

ver'faulen *v/i* (*no -ge-*, *sein*) rot, decay

ver'fechten *v/t* (*irr*, ***fechten***, *no -ge-*, *h*), **Ver'fechter(in)** (*-s*; *-/-*; *-nen*) advocate

ver'fehlen *v/t* (*no -ge-*, *h*) miss (***sich*** each other)

Ver'fehlung *f* (*-*; *-en*) offense, *Br* offence

verfeinden [fɛɐ'faindən] *v/refl* (*no -ge-*, *h*) become enemies

ver'feindet *adj* hostile; ***verfeindet sein*** be enemies

ver'feinern [fɛɐ'fainɐn] *v/t and v/refl* (*no -ge-*, *h*) refine

ver'filmen *v/t* (*no -ge-*, *h*) film

Ver'filmung *f* (*-*; *-en*) filming; film version

ver'flechten *v/t* (*irr*, ***flechten***, *no -ge-*, *h*) intertwine (*a.* ***sich verflechten***)

ver'fluchen *v/t* (*no -ge-*, *h*) curse

ver'flucht → ***verdammt***

ver'folgen *v/t* (*no -ge-*, *h*) pursue (*a. fig*); chase, hunt (*both a. fig*); POL, REL persecute; follow (*track etc*); *fear etc*: haunt *s.o.*; ***j-n gerichtlich verfolgen*** prosecute s.o.

Verfolger [fɛɐ'fɔlgɐ] *m* (*-s*; *-*) pursuer; persecutor

verhalten

Ver'folgung f (-; -en) pursuit (a. cycling); chase, hunt; persecution; **gerichtliche Verfolgung** prosecution
ver'frachten v/t (no -ge-, h) freight, ship; F bundle s.o., s.th. (**in** acc into)
verfremden [fɛɐ̯'frɛmdən] v/t (no -ge-, h) esp art: alienate
ver'früht adj premature
verfügbar [fɛɐ̯'fy:kba:ɐ̯] adj available
ver'fügen (no -ge-, h) **1.** v/t decree, order; **2.** v/i: **verfügen über** (acc) have at one's disposal
Ver'fügung f (-; -en) a) decree, order, b) (no pl) disposal; **j-m zur Verfügung stehen (stellen)** be (place) at s.o. 's disposal
ver'führen v/t (no -ge-, h) seduce (**et. zu tun** into doing s.th.)
Ver'führer m (-s; -) seducer
Ver'führerin f (-; -nen) seductress
ver'führerisch adj seductive; tempting
Ver'führung f (-; -en) seduction
vergangen [fɛɐ̯'gaŋən] adj gone, past; **im vergangenen Jahr** last year
Ver'gangenheit f (-; no pl) past; LING past tense
vergänglich [fɛɐ̯'gɛŋlɪç] adj transitory, transient
vergasen [fɛɐ̯'ga:zən] v/t (no -ge-, h) gas; CHEM gasify
Vergaser [fɛɐ̯'ga:zɐ] m (-s; -) MOT carburet(t)or
vergaß [fɛɐ̯'ga:s] pret of **vergessen**
ver'geben v/t (irr, **geben**, no -ge-, h) give away (a. fig); award (prize etc); forgive
ver'gebens adv in vain
vergeblich [fɛɐ̯'ge:plɪç] **1.** adj futile; **2.** adv in vain
Ver'gebung f (-; -en) forgiveness, pardon
ver'gehen (irr, **gehen**, no -ge-, sein) **1.** v/i time etc: go by, pass; pain, effect etc: wear off; **vergehen vor** (dat) be dying with; **wie die Zeit vergeht!** how time flies!; **2.** v/refl **sich vergehen an** (dat) violate; rape
Vergehen n (-s; -) JUR offen|se, Br -ce
ver'gelten v/t (irr, **gelten**, no -ge-, h) repay; reward
Ver'geltung f (-; -en) retaliation (a. MIL)
vergessen [fɛɐ̯'gɛsən] **1.** v/t (irr, no -ge-, h) forget; leave; **2.** pp of **vergessen** 1
Ver'gessenheit f: **in Vergessenheit geraten** fall into oblivion
vergesslich [fɛɐ̯'gɛslɪç] adj forgetful
vergeuden [fɛɐ̯'gɔydən] v/t (no -ge-, h), **Ver'geudung** f (-; -en) waste
vergewaltigen [fɛɐ̯gə'valtɪgən] v/t (no -ge-, h) rape, violate (a. fig)
Verge'waltigung f (-; -en) rape, violation (a. fig)

vergewissern [fɛɐ̯gə'vɪsɐn] v/refl (no -ge-, h) make sure (**e-r Sache** of s.th.; **ob** whether; **dass** that)
ver'gießen v/t (irr, **gießen**, no -ge-, h) shed (blood, tears); spill
ver'giften v/t (no -ge-, h) poison (a. fig); contaminate
Ver'giftung f (-; -en) poisoning (a. fig); contamination
ver'gittert adj barred (window etc)
Ver'gleich m (-[e]s; -e) comparison; JUR compromise
ver'gleichbar adj comparable (**mit** to, with)
ver'gleichen v/t (irr, **gleichen**, no -ge-, h) compare (**mit** with or to); **... ist nicht zu vergleichen mit** ... cannot be compared to; ... cannot compare with; **verglichen mit** compared to or with
ver'gleichsweise adv comparatively, relatively
ver'glühen v/i (no -ge-, sein) burn out (or up)
vergnügen [fɛɐ̯'gny:gən] v/refl (no -ge-, h) enjoy o.s. (**mit et.** doing s.th.)
Ver'gnügen n (-s; -) pleasure, enjoyment, fun; **mit Vergnügen** with pleasure; **viel Vergnügen!** have fun!, have a good time!
vergnügt [fɛɐ̯'gny:kt] adj cheerful
Ver'gnügung f (-; -en) pleasure, amusement, entertainment
Ver'gnügungspark m amusement park
ver'gnügungssüchtig adj pleasure-seeking
Ver'gnügungsviertel n nightlife district
ver'golden v/t (no -ge-, h) gild
vergöttern [fɛɐ̯'gœtɐn] v/t (no -ge-, h) idolize, adore
ver'graben v/t (irr, **graben**, no -ge-, h) bury (a. fig)
ver'greifen v/refl (irr, **greifen**, no -ge-, h) **sich vergreifen an** (dat) lay hands on
vergriffen [fɛɐ̯'grɪfən] adj out of print
vergrößern [fɛɐ̯'grø:sɐn] v/t (no -ge-, h) enlarge (a. PHOT); increase; OPT magnify; **sich vergrößern** increase, grow, expand
Ver'größerung f (-; -en) increase; PHOT enlargement; OPT magnification
Ver'größerungsglas n OPT magnifying glass
Vergünstigung [fɛɐ̯'gynstɪguŋ] f (-; -en) privilege
vergüten [fɛɐ̯'gy:tən] v/t (no -ge-, h) reimburse, pay (for)
Ver'gütung f (-; -en) reimbursement
ver'haften v/t (no -ge-, h), **Ver'haftung** f (-; -en) arrest
ver'halten[1] v/refl (irr, **halten**, no -ge-, h) behave, conduct o.s., act; **sich ruhig ver-**

halten keep quiet
ver'halten² *adj* restrained; subdued
Ver'halten *n* (*-s; no pl*) behavio(u)r, conduct
Ver'haltensforschung *f* behavio(u)ral science
ver'haltensgestört *adj* disturbed, maladjusted
Verhältnis [fɛɐ'hɛltnɪs] *n* (*-ses; -se*) relationship, relations; attitude; proportion, relation, *esp* MATH ratio; F affair; *pl* circumstances, conditions; *über j-s Verhältnisse* beyond s.o.'s means
ver'hältnismäßig *adv* comparatively, relatively
Ver'hältniswort *n* (*-[e]s; -wörter*) LING preposition
ver'handeln *no* (*-ge-, h*) **1.** *v/i* negotiate; **2.** *v/t* JUR hear
Ver'handlung *f* (*-; -en*) negotiation, talk; JUR hearing; trial
Ver'handlungsbasis *f* ECON asking price
ver'hängen *v/t* (*no -ge-, h*) cover (*mit* with); impose (*über acc* on)
Verhängnis [fɛɐ'hɛŋnɪs] *n* (*-ses; -se*) fate; disaster
ver'hängnisvoll *adj* fatal, disastrous
verharmlosen [fɛɐ'harmloːzən] *v/t* (*no -ge-, h*) play *s.th.* down
verhärmt [fɛɐ'hɛrmt] *adj* careworn
ver'hasst *adj* hated; hateful
ver'hätscheln *v/t* (*no -ge-, h*) coddle, pamper, spoil
ver'hauen F *v/t* (*no -ge-, h*) spank
verheerend [fɛɐ'heːrənt] *adj* disastrous
ver'heilen *v/i* (*no -ge-, sein*) heal (up)
verheimlichen [fɛɐ'haimlɪçən] *v/t* (*no -ge-, h*) hide, conceal
ver'heiraten *v/t* (*no -ge-, h*) marry (*s.o.* off) (*mit* to); *sich verheiraten* get married
ver'heiratet *adj* married (*mit* to)
ver'heißungsvoll *adj* promising
ver'helfen *v/i* (*irr, helfen, no -ge-, h*) *j-m zu et. verhelfen* help s.o. to get s.th.
ver'herrlichen *v/t* (*no -ge-, h*) glorify, *contp a.* idolize
Ver'herrlichung *f* (*-; -en*) glorification
ver'hexen *v/t* (*no -ge-, h*) bewitch
ver'hindern *v/t* (*no -ge-, h*) prevent (*dass j. et. tut* s.o. from doing s.th.)
ver'hindert *adj* unable to come; F *ein verhinderter ...* a would-be ...
Ver'hinderung *f* (*-; -en*) prevention
ver'höhnen *v/t* (*no -ge-, h*) deride, mock (at), jeer (at)
Verhör [fɛɐ'høːɐ] *n* (*-[e]s; -e*) JUR interrogation
ver'hören (*no -ge-, h*) **1.** *v/t* interrogate,

question; **2.** *v/refl* get it wrong
ver'hüllen *v/t* (*no -ge-, h*) cover, veil
ver'hungern *v/i* (*no -ge-, sein*) die of hunger, starve (to death)
Ver'hungern *n* (*-s; no pl*) starvation
ver'hüten *v/t* (*no -ge-, h*) prevent
Ver'hütung *f* (*-; -en*) prevention
Ver'hütungsmittel *n* MED contraceptive
ver'irren *v/refl* (*no -ge-, h*) get lost, lose one's way, go astray (*a. fig*)
Ver'irrung *f* (*-; -en*) aberration
ver'jagen *v/t* (*no -ge-, h*) chase *or* drive away
verjähren [fɛɐ'jɛːrən] *v/i* (*no -ge-, sein*) JUR come under the statute of limitations
ver'jährt *adj* JUR statute-barred
verjüngen [fɛɐ'jʏŋən] *v/t* (*no -ge-, h*) make *s.o.* (look) younger, rejuvenate; *sich verjüngen* ARCH, TECH taper (off)
ver'kabeln *v/t* (*no -ge-, h*) ELECTR cable
Ver'kauf *m* sale
ver'kaufen *v/t* (*no -ge-, h*) sell; *zu verkaufen* for sale; *sich gut verkaufen* sell well
Ver'käufer *m* (*-s; -*) (sales)clerk, salesman, *Br* shop assistant; ECON seller
Ver'käuferin *f* (*-; -nen*) (sales)clerk, saleslady, *Br* shop assistant
ver'käuflich *adj* for sale; *schwer verkäuflich* hard to sell
Verkehr [fɛɐ'keːɐ] *m* (*-s; no pl*) traffic; transportation, *Br* transport; *fig* contact, dealings; intercourse; circulation; *starker (schwacher) Verkehr* heavy (light) traffic
ver'kehren (*no -ge-, h*) **1.** *v/i* bus etc: run; *verkehren in* (*dat*) frequent; *verkehren mit* associate *or* mix with; have intercourse with; **2.** *v/t* turn (*in acc* into); *ins Gegenteil verkehren* reverse
Ver'kehrsader *f* arterial road
Ver'kehrsampel *f* traffic light(s)
Ver'kehrsbehinderung *f* hold-up, delay; JUR obstruction of traffic
Ver'kehrsde,likt *n* traffic offense (*Br* offence)
Ver'kehrsflugzeug *n* airliner
Ver'kehrsfunk *m* traffic bulletin
Ver'kehrsinsel *f* traffic island
Ver'kehrsmeldung *f* traffic announcement, flash
Ver'kehrsmi,nister *m* minister of transportation
Ver'kehrsminis,terium *n* ministry of transportation
Ver'kehrsmittel *n* means of transportation; *öffentliche Verkehrsmittel* public transportation
Ver'kehrsopfer *n* road casualty
Ver'kehrspoli,zei *f* traffic police

Verkehrsrowdy *m* F road hog
ver'kehrssicher *adj* MOT roadworthy
Ver'kehrssicherheit *f* MOT road safety;
roadworthiness
Verkehrsstau *m* traffic jam
Verkehrssünder(in) F traffic offender
Verkehrsteilnehmer(in) road user
Verkehrsunfall *m* traffic accident; (car)
crash
Verkehrsunterricht *m* traffic instruction
Verkehrszeichen *n* traffic sign
ver'kehrt *adj and adv* wrong; upside
down; inside out
ver'kennen *v/t* (*irr*, **kennen**, *no -ge-, h*)
mistake, misjudge
ver'klagen *v/t* (*no -ge-, h*) JUR sue (*auf acc*,
wegen for)
ver'klappen *v/t* (*no -ge-, h*) dump (into the
sea)
ver'kleben *v/t* (*no -ge-, h*) glue (together)
ver'kleiden *v/t* (*no -ge-, h*) disguise (*als*
as), dress *s.o.* up (as); TECH cover, (en-)-
case; panel; *sich verkleiden* disguise
o.s., dress (o.s.) up
Ver'kleidung *f* (*-; -en*) disguise; TECH cover, encasement; panel(1)ing; MOT fairing
verkleinern [fɛɐ̯'klaɪnɐn] *v/t* (*no -ge-, h*)
make smaller, reduce, diminish
Ver'kleinerung [fɛɐ̯'klaɪnɐrʊŋ] *f* (*-; -en*)
reduction
ver'klingen *v/i* (*irr*, **klingen**, *no -ge-, sein*)
die away
ver'knallt F *adj*: *verknallt sein in* (*acc*) be
madly in love with, have a crush on
ver'knoten *v/t* (*no -ge-, h*) knot
ver'knüpfen *v/t* (*no -ge-, h*) knot together;
fig connect, combine
ver'kohlen *v/i* (*no -ge-, sein*) char
ver'kommen 1. *v/i* (*irr*, **kommen**, *no -ge-,
sein*) become run-down *or* dilapidated;
go to seed; GASTR go bad; **2.** *adj* run-
-down, dilapidated; neglected; depraved,
rotten (to the core)
ver'korken *v/t* (*no -ge-, h*) cork (up)
ver'körpern *v/t* (*no -ge-, h*) personify; em-
body; *esp* THEA impersonate
ver'kriechen *v/refl* (*irr*, **kriechen**, *no -ge-,
h*) hide
ver'krümmt *adj* crooked, curved (*a.* MED)
ver'krüppelt *adj* crippled
ver'kümmern *v/i* (*no -ge-, sein*) BIOL become stunted
ver'kümmert *adj* BIOL stunted
verkünden [fɛɐ̯'kʏndən] *v/t* (*no -ge-, h*)
announce; proclaim; JUR pronounce;
REL preach
Ver'kündung *f* (*-; -en*) announcement;
proclamation; JUR pronouncement; REL
preaching

ver'kürzen *v/t* (*no -ge-, h*) shorten; reduce
ver'laden *v/t* (*irr*, **laden**, *no -ge-, h*) load
(*auf acc* onto; *in acc* into)
Verlag [fɛɐ̯'laːk] *m* (*-[e]s; -e* [-'laːɡə]) publishing house *or* company, publisher(s)
ver'lagern *v/t and v/refl* (*no -ge-, h*) shift
(*auf acc* to)
ver'langen *v/t* (*no -ge-, h*) ask for; demand; claim; charge; take, call for
Ver'langen *n* (*-s; -*) desire (*nach* for);
longing (for), yearning (for); *auf Verlangen* by request; ECON on demand
verlängern [fɛɐ̯'lɛŋɐn] *v/t* (*no -ge-, h*)
lengthen, make longer; prolong, extend
(*a.* ECON)
Ver'längerung [fɛɐ̯'lɛŋɐrʊŋ] *f* (*-; -en*)
lengthening; prolongation, extension;
SPORT overtime, *Br* extra time
ver'langsamen *v/t and v/refl* (*no -ge-, h*)
slacken, slow down (*both a. fig*)
ver'lassen (*irr*, **lassen**, *no -ge-, h*) **1.** *v/t*
leave; abandon, desert; **2.** *v/refl*: *sich
verlassen auf* (*acc*) rely *or* depend on
verlässlich [fɛɐ̯'lɛslɪç] *adj* reliable, dependable
Ver'lauf *m* course
ver'laufen (*irr*, **laufen**, *no -ge-*) **1.** *v/i* (*sein*)
run; go; end (up); **2.** *v/refl* (*h*) get lost,
lose one's way
ver'leben *v/t* (*no -ge-, h*) spend; have
ver'legen¹ *v/t* (*no -ge-, h*) move; mislay;
TECH lay; put off, postpone; publish
ver'legen² *adj* embarrassed
Ver'legenheit *f* (*-; -en*) a) (*no pl*) embar-
rassment, b) embarrassing situation
Verleger [fɛɐ̯'leːɡɐ] *m* (*-s; -*), **Ver'legerin** *f*
(*-; -nen*) publisher
Verleih [fɛɐ̯'laɪ] *m* (*-[e]s; -e*) a) (*no pl*) hire,
rental, b) *film*: distributor(s)
ver'leihen *v/t* (*irr*, **leihen**, *no -ge-, h*) lend,
loan; MOT *etc* rent (*Br* hire) out; award
(*prize etc*); grant (*privilege etc*)
Ver'leihung *f* (*-; -en*) award(ing), presentation; grant(ing)
ver'leiten *v/t* (*no -ge-, h*) *j-n zu et. verleiten* make s.o. do s.th., lead s.o. to do s.th.
ver'lernen *v/t* (*no -ge-, h*) forget
ver'lesen (*irr*, **lesen**, *no -ge-, h*) **1.** *v/t* read
(*or* call) out; **2.** *v/refl* make a slip (in reading); misread *s.th.*
verletzen [fɛɐ̯'lɛtsən] *v/t* (*no -ge-, h*) hurt,
injure, *fig a.* offend; *sich verletzen* hurt
o.s., get hurt
verletzend *adj* offensive
Ver'letzte *m, f* (*-n; -n*) injured person; *pl
the* injured
Ver'letzung *f* (*-; -en*) injury, *esp pl a.* hurt;
JUR violation
ver'leugnen *v/t* (*no -ge-, h*) deny; re-

V

nounce

verleumden [fɛɐ̯'lɔʏmdən] v/t (no -ge-, h) defame; JUR slander, libel

ver'leumderisch adj JUR slanderous, libel(l)ous

Ver'leumdung f (-; -en) JUR slander; libel

ver'lieben v/refl (no -ge-, h) fall in love (*in* acc with)

verliebt [fɛɐ̯'liːpt] adj in love (*in* acc with); amorous (*look etc*)

Ver'liebte m, f (-n; -n) lover

verlieren [fɛɐ̯'liːrən] v/t and v/i (irr, no -ge-, h) lose

Ver'lierer(in) (-s; -/-; -nen) loser

ver'loben v/refl (no -ge-, h) get engaged (*mit* to)

Verlobte [fɛɐ̯'loːptə] 1. m (-n; -n) fiancé; 2. f (-n; -n) fiancée

Ver'lobung f (-; -en) engagement

ver'locken v/t (no -ge-, h) tempt

verlockend adj tempting

Ver'lockung f (-; -en) temptation

verlogen [fɛɐ̯'loːgən] adj untruthful, lying

verlor [fɛɐ̯'loːɐ̯] pret of **verlieren**

verloren [fɛɐ̯'loːrən] 1. pp of **verlieren**; 2. adj lost; wasted; **verloren gehen** be or get lost

ver'lorengehen v/i (irr, **gehen**, sep, -ge-, sein) → **verloren**

ver'losen v/t (no -ge-, h) raffle (off)

Ver'losung f (-; -en) raffle

Verlust [fɛɐ̯'lʊst] m (-[e]s; -e) loss (a. fig); pl esp MIL casualties

ver'machen v/t (no -ge-, h) leave, will

Vermächtnis [fɛɐ̯'mɛçtnɪs] n (-ses; -se) legacy (a. fig)

ver'markten v/t (no -ge-, h) market, merchandize

Ver'marktung f (-; -en) marketing, merchandizing

ver'mehren v/t and v/refl increase (*um* by), multiply (by) (a. BIOL); BIOL reproduce, esp ZO a. breed

Ver'mehrung f (-; -en) increase; BIOL reproduction

vermeidbar [fɛɐ̯'maitbaːɐ̯] adj avoidable

ver'meiden v/t (irr, **meiden**, no -ge-, h) avoid

vermeintlich [fɛɐ̯'maintɪç] adj supposed, alleged

ver'mengen v/t (no -ge-, h) mix, mingle, blend

Vermerk [fɛɐ̯'mɛrk] m (-[e]s; -e) note

ver'merken v/t (no -ge-, h) make a note of

ver'messen¹ v/t (irr, **messen**, no -ge-, h) measure; survey

ver'messen² adj presumptuous

Ver'messung f (-; -en) measuring; sur-

vey(ing)

ver'mieten v/t (no -ge-, h) let, rent, lease (out); rent (*Br* hire) out (*cars etc*); **zu vermieten** for rent, *Br* to let, for hire

Ver'mieter n (-s; -) landlord

Ver'mieterin f (-; -nen) landlady

Ver'mietung f (-; -en) letting, renting

ver'mischen v/t and v/refl (no -ge-, h) mix, mingle, blend (*mit* with)

ver'mischt adj mixed; miscellaneous

vermissen [fɛɐ̯'mɪsən] v/t (no -ge-, h) miss

ver'misst adj missing; **die Vermissten** pl the missing

ver'mitteln (no -ge-, h) 1. v/t arrange; give, convey (*impression etc*); **j-m et. vermitteln** get or find s.o. s.th.; 2. v/i mediate (*zwischen* between)

Ver'mittler m (-s; -) mediator, go-between; ECON agent, broker

Ver'mittlung f (-; -en) mediation; arrangement; agency, office; (telephone) exchange; operator

ver'modern v/i (no -ge-, sein) rot, mo(u)lder

Ver'mögen n (-s; -) fortune, property, possessions; ECON assets

ver'mögend adj well-to-do, well-off

vermummen [fɛɐ̯'mʊmən] v/refl (no -ge-, h) mask o.s., disguise o.s.

vermuten [fɛɐ̯'muːtən] v/t (no -ge-, h) suppose, expect, think, guess

ver'mutlich adv probably

Ver'mutung f (-; -en) supposition; speculation

vernachlässigen [fɛɐ̯'naːxlɛsɪgən] v/t (no -ge-, h), **Ver'nachlässigung** f (-; -en) neglect

ver'narben v/i (no -ge-, sein) scar over; fig heal

ver'narrt adj: **vernarrt in** (acc) mad or crazy about

ver'nehmen v/t (irr, **nehmen**, no -ge-, h) JUR question, interrogate

ver'nehmlich adj clear, distinct

Ver'nehmung f (-; -en) JUR interrogation, examination

ver'neigen v/refl (no -ge-, h), **Ver'neigung** f (-; -en) bow (**vor** dat to) (a. fig)

ver'neinen (no -ge-, h) 1. v/t deny; 2. v/i say no, answer in the negative

verneinend adj negative

Ver'neinung f (-; -en) denial, negative (a. LING)

ver'nichten v/t (no -ge-, h) destroy

vernichtend adj devastating (a. fig); crushing

Ver'nichtung f (-; -en) destruction; extermination

Vernunft [fɛɐ̯'nʊnft] *f* (-; *no pl*) reason; **Vernunft annehmen** listen to reason; *j-n zur Vernunft bringen* bring s.o. to reason

vernünftig [fɛɐ̯'nʏnftɪç] *adj* sensible, reasonable (*a.* ECON); F decent

ver'öden *v/i* (*no -ge-, sein*) become deserted

ver'öffentlichen *v/t* (*no -ge-, h*) publish

Ver'öffentlichung *f* (-; *-en*) publication

ver'ordnen *v/t* (*no -ge-, h*) order, MED *a.* prescribe (*gegen* for)

Ver'ordnung *f* (-; *-en*) order; MED prescription

ver'pachten *v/t* (*no -ge-, h*) lease

Ver'pächter *m* lessor

ver'packen *v/t* (*no -ge-, h*) pack (up); TECH package; wrap up

Ver'packung *f* (-; *-en*) pack(ag)ing; wrapping

Ver'packungsmüll *m* superfluous packaging

ver'passen *v/t* (*no -ge-, h*) miss

ver'patzen F *v/t* (*no -ge-, h*) mess up, spoil

verpesten [fɛɐ̯'pɛstən] *v/t* (*no -ge-, h*) pollute, foul, contaminate; stink up (*Br* out)

ver'petzen F *v/t* (*no -ge-, h*) *j-n verpetzen* tell on s.o. (*bei* to)

ver'pfänden *v/t* (*no -ge-, h*) pawn; *fig* pledge

ver'pflanzen *v/t* (*no -ge-, h*), **Ver'pflanzung** *f* (-; *-en*) transplant (*a.* MED)

ver'pflegen *v/t* (*no -ge-, h*) feed

Ver'pflegung *f* (-; *-en*) food

ver'pflichten *v/t* (*no -ge-, h*) oblige; engage; *sich verpflichten, et. zu tun* undertake (ECON agree) to do s.th.

ver'pflichtet *adj*: *verpflichtet sein* (*sich verpflichtet fühlen*) *et. zu tun* be (feel) obliged to do s.th.

Ver'pflichtung *f* (-; *-en*) obligation; duty; ECON, JUR liability; engagement, commitment

ver'pfuschen F *v/t* (*no -ge-, h*) bungle, botch

ver'plappern *v/refl* (*no -ge-, h*) blab

verpönt [fɛɐ̯'pø:nt] *adj* taboo

ver'prügeln F *v/t* (*no -ge-, h*) beat *s.o.* up

Ver'putz *m* (*-es; no pl*), **ver'putzen** *v/t* (*no -ge-, h*) ARCH plaster

verquollen [fɛɐ̯'kvɔlən] *adj face etc*: puffy, swollen; *wood*: warped

Verrat [fɛɐ̯'ra:t] *m* (*-[e]s; no pl*) betrayal (*an dat* of); treachery (to); JUR treason (to)

ver'raten *v/t* (*irr*, *raten*, *no -ge-, h*) betray, give away (*both a. fig*); *sich verraten* betray o.s., give o.s. away

Verräter [fɛɐ̯'rɛ:tɐ] *m* (*-s; -*), **Ver'räterin** *f* (-; *-nen*) traitor

verräterisch [fɛɐ̯'rɛ:tərɪʃ] *adj* treacherous; *fig* telltale

ver'rechnen (*no -ge-, h*) **1.** *v/t* offset (*mit* against); **2.** *v/refl* miscalculate, make a mistake (*a. fig*); *sich um e-e Mark verrechnen* be one mark out

Ver'rechnungsscheck *m* ECON voucher check, *Br* crossed cheque

ver'regnet *adj* rainy

ver'reisen *v/i* (*no -ge-, sein*) go away (*geschäftlich* on business)

ver'reist *adj* away (*geschäftlich* on business)

verrenken [fɛɐ̯'rɛŋkən] *v/t* (*no -ge-, h*) MED dislocate, luxate; *sich et. verrenken* MED dislocate s.th.; *sich den Hals verrenken* crane one's neck

Ver'renkung *f* (-; *-en*) MED dislocation, luxation

ver'richten *v/t* (*no -ge-, h*) do, perform, carry out

ver'riegeln *v/t* (*no -ge-, h*) bolt, bar

verringern [fɛɐ̯'rɪŋɐn] *v/t* (*no -ge-, h*) decrease, lessen (*both a. sich verringern*), reduce, cut down

Ver'ringerung *f* (-; *-en*) reduction, decrease

ver'rosten *v/t* (*no -ge-, sein*) rust, get rusty (*a. fig*)

verrotten [fɛɐ̯'rɔtən] *v/i* (*no -ge-, sein*) rot

ver'rottet *adj* rotten

ver'rücken *v/t* (*no -ge-, h*) move, shift

ver'rückt *adj* mad, crazy (*both a. fig nach* about); *wie verrückt* like mad; *verrückt werden* go mad, go crazy; *j-n verrückt machen* drive s.o. mad

Ver'rückte *m*, *f* (*-n; -n*) madman (madwoman), lunatic, maniac (*all a.* F)

Ver'rücktheit *f* (-; *-en*) a) (*no pl*) madness, craziness, b) crazy thing

Ver'ruf *m*: *in Verruf bringen* bring discredit (up)on; *in Verruf kommen* get into discredit

ver'rufen *adj* disreputable, notorious

ver'rutschen *v/i* (*no -ge-, sein*) slip, get out of place

Vers [fɛrs] *m* (*-es; -e* ['fɛrzə]) verse; line

ver'sagen (*no -ge-, h*) **1.** *v/i* fail (*a.* MED), MOT *etc a.* break down; *gun etc*: misfire; **2.** *v/t* deny, refuse

Ver'sagen *n* (*-s; no pl*) failure

Ver'sager *m* (*-s; -*) failure

ver'salzen *v/t* (*no -ge-, h*) oversalt

ver'sammeln *v/t* (*no -ge-, h*) gather, assemble; *sich versammeln a.* meet

Ver'sammlung *f* (-; *-en*) assembly, meeting

Versand [fɛɐ̯'zant] *m* (*-[e]s; no pl*) dis-

patch, shipment; **Versand...** *in cpds*
...haus, ...katalog *etc*: mail-order ...
ver'**säumen** *v/t* (*no -ge-*, *h*) miss; **versäu-**
men et. zu tun fail to do s.th.
Versäumnis [fɛɐ̯'zɔymnɪs] *n* (*-ses*; *-se*)
omission
ver'**schaffen** *v/t* (*no -ge-*, *h*) get, find; **sich**
verschaffen *a.* obtain
ver'**schämt** *adj* bashful
ver'**schanzen** *v/refl* (*no -ge-*, *h*) entrench
o.s. (*a. fig **hinter*** behind)
ver'**schärfen** *v/t* (*no -ge-*, *h*) aggravate;
tighten up; increase; **sich verschärfen**
get worse
ver'**schenken** *v/t* (*no -ge-*, *h*) give away (*a.*
fig)
ver'**scherzen** *v/t* (*no -ge-*, *h*) forfeit
ver'**scheuchen** *v/t* (*no -ge-*, *h*) chase away
(*a. fig*)
ver'**schicken** *v/t* (*no -ge-*, *h*) send off, *esp*
ECON *a.* dispatch
ver'**schieben** *v/t* (*irr*, **schieben**, *no -ge-*,
h) move, shift (*a. **sich verschieben***);
postpone, put off
Ver'**schiebung** *f* (*-*; *-en*) shift(ing); postponement
verschieden [fɛɐ̯'ʃiːdən] *adj* different
(**von** from); **verschiedene ...** *pl* various
..., several...
verschiedenartig *adj* different; various
Ver'**schiedenheit** *f* (*-*; *-en*) difference
ver'**schiedentlich** *adv* repeatedly
ver'**schiffen** *v/t* (*no -ge-*, *h*) ship
Ver'**schiffung** *f* (*-*; *-en*) shipment
ver'**schimmeln** *v/i* (*no -ge-*, *sein*) get
mo(u)ldy
ver'**schlafen** (*irr*, **schlafen**, *no -ge-*, *h*) **1.**
v/i oversleep; **2.** *v/t* sleep through; **3.** *adj*
sleepy (*a. fig*)
Ver'**schlag** *m* shed
ver'**schlagen**¹ *v/t* (*irr*, **schlagen**, *no -ge-*,
h) **j-m den Atem verschlagen** take s.o.'s
breath away; **j-m die Sprache verschla-**
gen leave s.o. speechless; **es hat ihn**
nach X verschlagen he ended up in X
ver'**schlagen**² *adj* sly, cunning
verschlechtern [fɛɐ̯'ʃlɛçtɐn] *v/t and*
v/refl (*no -ge-*, *h*) make (*refl* get) worse,
worsen, deteriorate
Ver'**schlechterung** *f* (*-*; *-en*) deteriora-
tion; change for the worse
ver'**schleiern** *v/t* (*no -ge-*, *h*) veil (*a. fig*)
Ver'**schleiß** [fɛɐ̯'ʃlais] *m* (*-es*; *no pl*) wear
(and tear)
ver'**schleißen** *v/t* (*irr*, *no -ge-*, *h*) wear out
ver'**schleppen** *v/t* (*no -ge-*, *h*) carry off;
POL displace; draw out, delay; MED neglect
ver'**schleudern** *v/t* (*no -ge-*, *h*) waste;

ECON sell dirt cheap
ver'**schließen** *v/t* (*irr*, **schließen**, *no -ge-*,
h) close (*a. fig one's eyes*); lock (up)
ver'**schlingen** *v/t* (*irr*, **schlingen**, *no -ge-*,
h) devour (*a. fig*); gulp (down)
verschliss [fɛɐ̯'ʃlɪs] *pret of* **verschleißen**
verschlissen [fɛɐ̯'ʃlɪsən] *pp of* **ver-**
schleißen
verschlossen [fɛɐ̯'ʃlɔsən] *adj* closed; *fig*
aloof, reserved
Ver'**schlossenheit** *f* (*-*; *no pl*) aloofness
ver'**schlucken** (*no -ge-*, *h*) **1.** *v/t* swallow
(*fig* up); **2.** *v/refl* choke; **ich habe mich**
verschluckt it went down the wrong way
Ver'**schluss** *m* fastener; clasp; catch; lock;
cover, lid; cap, top; PHOT shutter; **unter**
Verschluss under lock and key
ver'**schlüsseln** *v/t* (*no -ge-*, *h*) (en)code,
(en)cipher
verschmähen [fɛɐ̯'ʃmɛːən] *v/t* (*no -ge-*, *h*)
disdain, scorn
ver'**schmelzen** *v/i* (*irr*, **schmelzen**, *no*
-ge-, *sein*) and *v/t* (*h*) merge, fuse (*both*
a. ECON, POL *etc*), melt
Ver'**schmelzung** *f* (*-*; *-en*) fusion (*a. fig*)
ver'**schmerzen** *v/t* (*no -ge-*, *h*) get over
s.th.
ver'**schmieren** *v/t* (*no -ge-*, *h*) smear,
smudge
verschmitzt [fɛɐ̯'ʃmɪtst] *adj* mischievous
ver'**schmutzen** (*no -ge-*) **1.** *v/t* (*h*) soil,
dirty; pollute; **2.** *v/i* (*sein*) get dirty; get
polluted
ver'**schnaufen** F *v/i and v/refl* (*no -ge-*, *h*)
stop for breath
ver'**schneit** *adj* snow-covered, snowy
Ver'**schnitt** *m* blend; waste
verschnupft [fɛɐ̯'ʃnʊpft] *adj*: **ver-**
schnupft sein MED have a cold; F be
in a huff
ver'**schnüren** *v/t* (*no -ge-*, *h*) tie up
verschollen [fɛɐ̯'ʃɔlən] *adj* missing; JUR
presumed dead
ver'**schonen** *v/t* (*no -ge-*, *h*) spare; **j-n mit**
et. verschonen spare s.o. s.th.
verschönern [fɛɐ̯'ʃøːnɐn] *v/t* (*no -ge-*, *h*)
embellish
Ver'**schönerung** [fɛɐ̯'ʃøːnərʊŋ] *f* (*-*; *-en*)
embellishment
verschossen [fɛɐ̯'ʃɔsən] *adj* faded; F **ver-**
schossen sein in (*acc*) have a crush on
verschränken [fɛɐ̯'ʃrɛŋkən] *v/t* (*no -ge-*,
h) fold; cross (*one's legs*)
ver'**schreiben** (*irr*, **schreiben**, *no -ge-*, *h*)
1. *v/t* MED prescribe (**gegen** for); **2.** *v/refl*
make a slip of the pen
ver'**schreibungspflichtig** *adj* PHARM
available on prescription only
verschroben [fɛɐ̯'ʃroːbən] *adj* eccentric,

V

odd
ver'schrotten v/t (no -ge-, h) scrap
ver'schüchtert adj intimidated
ver'schulden v/t (no -ge-, h) be responsible for, cause, be the cause of; **sich verschulden** get into debt
ver'schuldet adj in debt
ver'schütten v/t (no -ge-, h) spill; bury s.o. (alive)
verschwägert [fɛɐ'ʃvɛːɡɐt] adj related by marriage
ver'schweigen v/t (irr, **schweigen**, no -ge-, h) keep s.th. a secret, hide
verschwenden [fɛɐ'ʃvɛndən] v/t (no -ge-, h) waste
Verschwender [fɛɐ'ʃvɛndɐ] m (-s; -) spendthrift
verschwenderisch [fɛɐ'ʃvɛndərɪʃ] adj wasteful, extravagant; lavish
Ver'schwendung f (-; -en) waste
verschwiegen [fɛɐ'ʃviːɡən] adj discreet; hidden, secret
Ver'schwiegenheit f (-; no pl) secrecy, discretion
ver'schwimmen v/i (irr, **schwimmen**, no -ge-, sein) become blurred
ver'schwinden v/i (irr, **schwinden**, no -ge-, sein) disappear, vanish; F **verschwinde!** beat it!
Ver'schwinden n (-s; no pl) disappearance
verschwommen [fɛɐ'ʃvɔmən] adj blurred (a. PHOT), fig a. vague, hazy
ver'schwören v/refl (irr, **schwören**, no -ge-, h) conspire, plot
Verschwörer [fɛɐ'ʃvøːrɐ] m (-s; -) conspirator
Ver'schwörung f (-; -en) conspiracy, plot
verschwunden [fɛɐ'ʃvʊndən] adj missing
ver'sehen (irr, **sehen**, no -ge-, h) **1.** v/t hold (an office etc); **versehen mit** provide with; **2.** v/refl make a mistake
Ver'sehen n (-s; -) mistake, error; **aus Versehen** → **versehentlich** [fɛɐ'zeːənt-lɪç] adv by mistake, unintentionally
Versehrte [fɛɐ'zeːɐtə] m, f (-n; -n) disabled person
ver'sengen v/t (no -ge-, h) singe, scorch
ver'senken v/t (no -ge-, h) sink; **sich versenken in** (acc) become absorbed in
versessen [fɛɐ'zɛsən] adj: **versessen auf** (acc) keen on, mad or crazy about
ver'setzen v/t (no -ge-, h) move, shift; transfer; PED promote, Br move s.o. up; give (s.o. a kick etc); pawn; AGR transplant; F **j-n versetzen** stand s.o. up; **j-n in die Lage versetzen zu** inf put s.o. in a position to inf, enable s.o. to inf; **sich in j-s Lage versetzen** put o.s. in

s.o.'s place
Ver'setzung f (-; -en) transfer; PED promotion
ver'seuchen v/t (no -ge-, h) contaminate
Ver'seuchung f (-; -en) contamination
ver'sichern v/t (no -ge-, h) ECON insure (**bei** with); assure (**j-m et.** s.o. of s.th.), assert; **sich versichern** insure o.s.; make sure (**dass** that)
Ver'sicherte m, f (-n; -n) the insured
Ver'sicherung f (-; -en) insurance; assurance, assertion
Ver'sicherungsgesellschaft f insurance company
Versicherungspo,lice f, **Versicherungsschein** m insurance policy
ver'sickern v/i (no -ge-, sein) trickle away
ver'siegeln v/t (no -ge-, h) seal
ver'siegen v/i (no -ge-, sein) dry up, run dry
ver'silbern v/t (no -ge-, h) silver-plate; F turn s.th. into cash
ver'sinken v/i (irr, **sinken**, no -ge-, sein) sink; → **versunken**
Version [vɛr'zjoːn] f (-; -en) version
'Versmaß n meter, Br metre
versöhnen [fɛɐ'zøːnən] v/t (no -ge-, h) reconcile; **sich (wieder) versöhnen** make it up (**mit** with)
ver'söhnlich adj conciliatory
Ver'söhnung f (-; -en) reconciliation; esp POL appeasement
ver'sorgen v/t (no -ge-, h) provide (**mit** with), supply (with); support; take care of, look after
Ver'sorgung f (-; no pl) supply (**mit** with); support; care
ver'späten v/refl (no -ge-, h) be late
ver'spätet adj belated, late, RAIL etc a. delayed
Ver'spätung f (-; -en) being or coming late, RAIL etc delay; **20 Minuten Verspätung haben** be 20 minutes late
ver'speisen v/t (no -ge-, h) eat (up)
ver'sperren v/t (no -ge-, h) bar, block (up), obstruct (a. view); lock
ver'spielen v/t (no -ge-, h) lose
ver'spielt adj playful
ver'spotten v/t (no -ge-, h) make fun of, ridicule
ver'sprechen (irr, **sprechen**, no -ge-, h) **1.** v/t promise (a. fig); **sich zu viel versprechen (von)** expect too much (of); **2.** v/refl make a mistake or slip
Ver'sprechen n (-s; -) promise; **ein Versprechen geben (halten, brechen)** make (keep, break) a promise
Ver'sprecher F m (-s; -) slip (of the tongue)

V

ver'staatlichen v/t (no -ge-, h) ECON nationalize

Ver'staatlichung f (-; -en) ECON nationalization

Verstädterung [fɛɐ'ʃtɛːtərʊŋ] f (-; -en) urbanization

Verstand [fɛɐ'ʃtant] m (-[e]s; no pl) mind, intellect; reason, (common) sense; intelligence, brains; *nicht bei Verstand* out of one's mind, not in one's right mind; *den Verstand verlieren* go out of one's mind

verstandesmäßig [fɛɐ'ʃtandəsmɛːsɪç] adj rational

ver'ständig adj reasonable, sensible

verständigen [fɛɐ'ʃtɛndɪɡən] v/t (no -ge-, h) inform (*von* of), notify (of); call (*doctor, police etc*); *sich verständigen* communicate; come to an agreement (*über acc* on)

Ver'ständigung f (-; no pl) communication (a. TEL); agreement

verständlich [fɛɐ'ʃtɛntlɪç] adj audible; intelligible; comprehensible; understandable; *schwer (leicht) verständlich* difficult (easy) to understand; *j-m et. verständlich machen* make s.th. clear to s.o.; *sich verständlich machen* make o.s. understood

Verständnis [fɛɐ'ʃtɛntnɪs] n (-ses; no pl) comprehension, understanding; sympathy; (*viel) Verständnis haben* be (very) understanding; *Verständnis haben für* understand; appreciate

ver'ständnislos adj uncomprehending; blank (*look etc*)

ver'ständnisvoll adj understanding, sympathetic; knowing (*look etc*)

ver'stärken v/t (no -ge-, h) reinforce (a. TECH, MIL); strengthen (a. TECH); radio, PHYS amplify; intensify

Ver'stärker m (-s; -) amplifier

Ver'stärkung f (-; -en) strengthening; reinforcement(s MIL); amplification; intensification

ver'stauben v/i (no -ge-, sein) get dusty

verstauchen [fɛɐ'ʃtauxən] v/t (no -ge-, h), **Ver'stauchung** f (-; -en) MED sprain

ver'stauen v/t (no -ge-, h) stow away

Versteck [fɛɐ'ʃtɛk] n (-[e]s; -e) hiding place, hideout, hideaway

ver'stecken v/t and v/refl (no -ge-, h) hide (a. fig); *Verstecken spielen* play (at) hide-and-seek

ver'stehen v/t (irr, stehen, no -ge-, h) understand, F get; catch; see; realize; know; *es verstehen zu inf* know how to inf; *zu verstehen geben* give s.o. to understand, suggest; *ich verstehe!* I see!;

falsch verstehen misunderstand; *was verstehen Sie unter ...?* what do you mean or understand by ...?; *sich (gut) verstehen* get along (well) (*mit* with); *es versteht sich von selbst* it goes without saying

ver'steifen (no -ge-, h) **1.** v/t stiffen (a. *sich versteifen*); TECH strut, brace; **2.** v/refl: *sich auf et. versteifen* insist on (doing) s.th.

ver'steigern v/t (no -ge-, h) auction off

Ver'steigerung f (-; -en) auction (sale)

ver'steinern v/i (no -ge-, sein) petrify (a. fig)

ver'stellbar adj adjustable

ver'stellen v/t (no -ge-, h) block; move; set s.th. wrong or the wrong way; TECH adjust, regulate; disguise (*one's voice etc*); *sich verstellen* pretend

Ver'stellung f (-; no pl) disguise, make-believe, (false) show

ver'steuern v/t (no -ge-, h) pay duty or tax on

verstiegen [fɛɐ'ʃtiːɡən] adj high-flown

ver'stimmen v/t (no -ge-, h) MUS put out of tune; fig annoy

ver'stimmt adj annoyed; MUS out of tune; MED upset

Ver'stimmung f (-; -en) annoyance

verstockt [fɛɐ'ʃtɔkt] adj stubborn, obstinate

verstohlen [fɛɐ'ʃtoːlən] adj furtive, stealthy

ver'stopfen v/t (no -ge-, h) plug (up); block, jam; MED constipate

ver'stopft adj MED constipated

Ver'stopfung f (-; -en) block(age); MED constipation

verstorben [fɛɐ'ʃtɔrbən] adj late, deceased

Ver'storbene m, f (-n; -n) the deceased; *die Verstorbenen* the deceased

verstört [fɛɐ'ʃtøːɐt] adj upset; distracted; wild (*look etc*)

Ver'stoß m offense, Br offence (*gegen* against), violation (of)

ver'stoßen (irr, stoßen, no -ge-, h) **1.** v/t expel (*aus* from); disown; **2.** v/i: *verstoßen gegen* offend against, violate

ver'strahlt adj (radioactively) contaminated

ver'streichen (irr, streichen, no -ge-) **1.** v/i (sein) time: pass, go by; date: expire; **2.** v/t (h) spread

ver'streuen v/t (no -ge-, h) scatter

verstümmeln [fɛɐ'ʃtʏməln] v/t (no -ge-, h) mutilate (a. fig)

Ver'stümmelung f (-; -en) mutilation (a. fig)

ver'stummen v/i (no -ge-, sein) grow silent; stop; die down

Versuch [fɛɐˈzuːx] m (-[e]s; -e) attempt, try; trial, test; PHYS experiment; **mit et.** **(j-m) e-n Versuch machen** give s.th. (s.o.) a try

ver'suchen v/t (no -ge-, h) try, attempt; taste; REL tempt; **es versuchen** have a try (at it)

Ver'suchs... in cpds ...bohrung etc: test ..., trial ...

Versuchska,ninchen n guinea pig

Versuchsstadium n experimental stage

Versuchstier n laboratory or test animal

ver'suchsweise adv by way of trial

Ver'suchung f (-; -en) temptation; **j-n in** **Versuchung führen** tempt s.o.

versunken [fɛɐˈzʊŋkən] fig adj: **versunken in** (acc) absorbed or lost in

ver'süßen v/t (no -ge-, h) sweeten

ver'tagen v/t and v/refl (no -ge-, h) adjourn

Ver'tagung f (-; -en) adjournment

ver'tauschen v/t (no -ge-, h) exchange (**mit** for)

verteidigen [fɛɐˈtaidɪɡən] v/t (no -ge-, h) defend (**sich** o.s.)

Verteidiger(in) [fɛɐˈtaidɪɡɐ (-ɡərɪn)] (-s; -/-; -nen) defender, SPORT a. back; fig advocate

Ver'teidigung f (-; -en) defense, Br defence

Ver'teidigungs... in cpds ...politik etc: mst defense ..., Br defence ...

Verteidigungsmi,nister m Secretary of Defense, Br Minister of Defence

Verteidigungsminis,terium n Department of Defense, Br Ministry of Defence

ver'teilen v/t (no -ge-, h) distribute; hand out

Ver'teiler m (-s; -) distributor

Ver'teilung f (-; -en) distribution

ver'tiefen v/t and v/refl (no -ge-, h) deepen (a. fig); **sich vertiefen in** (acc) become absorbed in

Ver'tiefung f (-; -en) hollow, depression, dent; fig deepening

vertikal [vɛrtiˈkaːl] adj, **Verti'kale** f (-; -n) vertical

ver'tilgen v/t (no -ge-, h) exterminate; F consume

Ver'tilgung f (-; no pl) extermination

vertonen [fɛɐˈtoːnən] v/t (no -ge-, h) set to music

Vertrag [fɛɐˈtraːk] m (-[e]s; Verträge [fɛɐˈtrɛːɡə]) contract; POL treaty

ver'tragen v/t (irr, tragen, no -ge-, h) endure, bear, stand; **ich kann ... nicht vertragen** ... doesn't agree with me; I can't

stand ...; **er kann viel vertragen** he can take a lot; he can hold his drink; F **ich** **(es) könnte ... vertragen** I (it) could do with ...; **sich (gut) vertragen** get along (well) (**mit** with); **sich wieder vertragen** make it up

ver'traglich adv by contract

verträglich [fɛɐˈtrɛːklɪç] adj easy to get on with; GASTR (easily) digestible

ver'trauen v/i (no -ge-, h) trust (**auf** acc in)

Ver'trauen n (-s; no pl) confidence, trust, faith; **im Vertrauen (gesagt)** between you and me; **wenig Vertrauen erweckend aussehen** inspire little confidence

Ver'trauensfrage f: **die Vertrauensfrage stellen** PARL ask for a vote of confidence

Vertrauenssache f: **das ist Vertrauenssache** that is a matter of confidence

Vertrauensstellung f position of trust

ver'trauensvoll adj trustful, trusting

Ver'trauensvotum n PARL vote of confidence

ver'trauenswürdig adj trustworthy

ver'traulich adj confidential; familiar

ver'traut adj familiar; close

Ver'traute m, f (-n; -n) confidant(e f)

Ver'trautheit f (-; no pl) familiarity

ver'treiben v/t (irr, treiben, no -ge-, h) drive or chase away (a. fig); pass (the time); ECON sell; **vertreiben aus** drive out of

Ver'treibung f (-; -en) expulsion (**aus** from)

ver'treten v/t (irr, treten, no -ge-, h) substitute for, replace, stand in for; POL, ECON represent, PARL a. sit for; JUR act for s.o.; **j-s Sache vertreten** JUR plead s.o.'s cause; **die Ansicht vertreten, dass** argue that; **sich den Fuß vertreten** sprain one's ankle; F **sich die Beine vertreten** stretch one's legs

Ver'treter m (-s; -), **Ver'treterin** f (-; -nen) substitute, deputy; POL, ECON representative, ECON a. agent; MED locum

Ver'tretung f (-; -en) substitution, replacement; substitute, stand-in, a. supply teacher; ECON, POL representation

Vertrieb [fɛɐˈtriːp] m (-[e]s; no pl) ECON sale, distribution

Vertriebene [fɛɐˈtriːbənə] m, f (-n; -n) POL expellee, refugee

ver'trocknen v/i (no -ge-, sein) dry up

ver'trödeln F v/t (no -ge-, h) dawdle away, waste

ver'trösten v/t (no -ge-, h) put s.o. off

ver'tuschen F v/t (no -ge-, h) cover up

ver'übeln v/t (no -ge-, h) take amiss; **ich** **kann es ihr nicht verübeln** I can't blame her for it

ver'üben v/t (no -ge-, h) commit

verunglücken [fɛɐˈʔʊnglʏkən] v/i (no -ge-, sein) have an accident; fig go wrong; **tödlich verunglücken** die in an accident

ver'ursachen v/t (no -ge-, h) cause

ver'urteilen v/t (no -ge-, h) condemn (**zu** to) (a. fig), sentence (to), convict (**wegen** of)

Ver'urteilung f (-; -en) condemnation (a. fig)

ver'vielfachen v/t (no -ge-, h) multiply

vervielfältigen [fɛɐˈfiːlfɛltɪgən] v/t (no -ge-, h) copy, duplicate

Ver'vielfältigung f (-; -en) duplication; copy

ver'vollkommnen v/t (no -ge-, h) perfect; improve

vervollständigen [fɛɐˈfɔlʃtɛndɪgən] v/t (no -ge-, h) complete

ver'wachsen adj MED deformed, crippled; fig **verwachsen mit** deeply rooted in, bound up with

ver'wackelt F adj PHOT blurred

ver'wahren v/t (no -ge-, h) keep (in a safe place); **sich verwahren gegen** protest against

verwahrlost [fɛɐˈvaːɐloːst] adj uncared--for, neglected

ver'walten v/t (no -ge-, h) manage, esp POL a. administer

Ver'walter m (-s; -) manager; administrator

Ver'waltung f (-; -en) administration, management

Ver'waltungs... in cpds ...gericht, ...kosten etc: administrative ...

ver'wandeln v/t (no -ge-, h) change, turn (both a. **sich verwandeln**), esp PHYS, CHEM a. transform, convert (all: **in** acc into)

Ver'wandlung f (-; -en) change, transformation; conversion

verwandt [fɛɐˈvant] adj related (**mit** to)

Ver'wandte m, f (-n; -n) relative; (**alle**) **m-e Verwandten** (all) my relatives or relations; **der nächste Verwandte** the next of kin

Ver'wandtschaft f (-; -en) a) relationship, b) (no pl) relations

ver'warnen v/t (no -ge-, h) Br caution; SPORT book

Ver'warnung f (-; -en) Br caution; SPORT booking

ver'waschen adj washed-out

ver'wässern v/t (no -ge-, h) water down (a. fig)

ver'wechseln v/t (no -ge-, h) confuse (**mit** with), mix up (with), mistake (for)

Ver'wechs(e)lung f (-; -en) mistake, F mix--up

ver'wegen adj daring, bold

Ver'wegenheit f (-; no pl) boldness, daring

ver'weichlicht adj soft

ver'weigern v/t (no -ge-, h) refuse; disobey

Ver'weigerung f (-; -en) denial, refusal

ver'weilen v/i (no -ge-, h) stay; fig rest

Verweis [fɛɐˈvais] m (-es; -e) reprimand, reproof; reference (**auf** acc to)

ver'weisen v/t (irr, weisen, no -ge-, h) refer (**auf** acc, **an** acc to); expel (gen from)

ver'welken v/i (no -ge-, sein) wither, fig a. fade

ver'wenden v/t (no -ge-, h) use; spend (time etc) (**auf** acc on)

Ver'wendung f (-; -en) use; **keine Verwendung haben für** have no use for

ver'werfen v/t (irr, werfen, no -ge-, h) drop, give up; reject

ver'werten v/t (no -ge-, h) use, make use of

verwesen [fɛɐˈveːzən] v/i (no -ge-, sein), Ver'wesung f (-; no pl) decay

ver'wickeln fig v/t (no -ge-, h) involve; **sich verwickeln in** (acc) get caught in

ver'wickelt fig adj complicated; **verwickelt sein (werden) in** (acc) be (get) involved in

Ver'wicklung fig f (-; -en) involvement; complication

ver'wildern v/i (no -ge-, sein) grow (or run) wild

ver'wildert adj wild (a. fig), overgrown

ver'winden v/t (irr, winden, no -ge-, h) get over s.th.

ver'wirklichen v/t (no -ge-, h) realize; **sich verwirklichen** come true; **sich selbst verwirklichen** fulfil(l) o.s.

Ver'wirklichung f (-; -en) realization

ver'wirren v/t (no -ge-, h) tangle (up); fig confuse

ver'wirrt fig adj confused

Ver'wirrung fig f (-; -en) confusion

ver'wischen v/t (no -ge-, h) blur (a. fig); cover (track etc)

verwittern [fɛɐˈvɪtən] v/i (no -ge-, sein) GEOL weather

ver'witwet adj widowed

verwöhnen [fɛɐˈvøːnən] v/t (no -ge-, h) spoil

ver'wöhnt adj spoilt

verworren [fɛɐˈvɔrən] adj confused, muddled; complicated

verwundbar [fɛɐˈvʊntbaːɐ] adj vulnerable (a. fig)

ver'wunden v/t (no -ge-, h) wound

V

ver'wunderlich *adj* surprising
Verwunderung [fɛɐ'vʊndərʊŋ] *f* (-; *no pl*) (*zu m-r etc* **Verwunderung** to my *etc*) surprise
Ver'wundete m, *f* (-n; -n) wounded (person), casualty
Ver'wundung *f* (-; -en) wound, injury
ver'wünschen *v/t* (*no* -ge-, h), **Ver'wünschung** *f* (-; -en) curse
ver'wüsten *v/t* (*no* -ge-, h) lay waste, devastate, ravage
Ver'wüstung *f* (-; -en) devastation, ravage
ver'zählen *v/refl* (*no* -ge-, h) count wrong
verzärteln [fɛɐ'tsɛrtəln] *v/t* (*no* -ge-, h) coddle, pamper
ver'zaubern *v/t* (*no* -ge-, h) enchant, *fig a.* charm; **verzaubern in** (*acc*) turn into
ver'zehren *v/t* (*no* -ge-, h) consume (*a. fig*)
ver'zeichnen *v/t* (*no* -ge-, h) record, keep a record of, list; *fig* achieve; suffer
Ver'zeichnis *n* (-ses; -se) list, catalog(ue); record, register; index
verzeihen [fɛɐ'tsaiən] *v/t and v/i* (*irr, no* -ge-, h) forgive *s.o.*; pardon, excuse *s.th.*
ver'zeihlich *adj* pardonable
Ver'zeihung *f* (-; *no pl*) pardon; (**j-n**) **um Verzeihung bitten** apologize (to s.o.); **Verzeihung!** (I'm) sorry!; excuse me!
ver'zerren *v/t* (*no* -ge-, h) distort (*a. fig*); **sich verzerren** become distorted
Ver'zerrung *f* (-; -en) distortion
Verzicht [fɛɐ'tsɪçt] *m* (-[e]s; -e) renunciation (**auf** *acc* of); *mst* giving up, doing without *etc*
ver'zichten *v/i* (*no* -ge-, h) **verzichten auf** (*acc*) do without; give up; renounce (*a. JUR*)
verzieh [fɛɐ'tsiː] *pret of* **verzeihen**
ver'ziehen (*irr,* **ziehen**, *no* -ge-) **1.** *v/i* (*sein*) move (**nach** to); **2.** *v/t* (h) spoil; **das Gesicht verziehen** make a face; **sich verziehen** *wood*: warp; *storm etc*: pass (over); *F* disappear; **3.** *pp of* **verzeihen**
ver'zieren *v/t* (*no* -ge-, h) decorate
Ver'zierung *f* (-; -en) decoration, ornament
ver'zinsen *v/t* (*no* -ge-, h) pay interest on; **sich verzinsen** yield interest
Ver'zinsung *f* (-; -en) interest
ver'zögern *v/t* (*no* -ge-, h) delay; **sich verzögern** be delayed
Ver'zögerung *f* (-; -en) delay
ver'zollen *v/t* (*no* -ge-, h) pay duty on; **et.** (**nichts**) **zu verzollen haben** have s.th. (nothing) to declare
verzückt [fɛɐ'tsʏkt] *adj* ecstatic
Ver'zückung *f* (-; -en) ecstasy; **in Verzückung geraten** go into ecstasies *or* rap-

tures (**wegen, über** *acc* over)
Verzug [fɛɐ'tsuːk] *m* (-[e]s; *no pl*) delay; ECON default
ver'zweifeln *v/i* (*no* -ge-, h) despair (**an** *dat* of)
ver'zweifelt *adj* desperate, despairing
Ver'zweiflung *f* (-; *no pl*) despair; **j-n zur Verzweiflung bringen** drive s.o. to despair
verzweigen [fɛɐ'tsvaigən] *v/refl* (*no* -ge-, h) branch
verzwickt [fɛɐ'tsvɪkt] F *adj* tricky
Veteran [vete'raːn] *m* (-en; -en) MIL veteran (*a. fig*)
Veterinär [veteri'nɛːɐ] *m* (-s; -e), **Veteri-'närin** *f* (-; -nen) veterinarian, *Br* veterinary surgeon, F vet
Veto ['veːto] *n* (-s; -s) veto; (**s**)**ein Veto einlegen gegen** veto
Vetter ['fɛtɐ] *m* (-s; -n) cousin
'Vetternwirtschaft *f* (-; *no pl*) nepotism
vgl. ABBR *of* **vergleiche** cf., confer
VHS ABBR *of* **Volkshochschule** adult education program(me); adult evening classes
Vibration [vibra'tsjoːn] *f* (-; -en) vibration
vibrieren [vi'briːrən] *v/i* (*no* -ge-, h) vibrate
Video ['viːdeo] *n* (-s; -s) video (*a. in cpds* …*aufnahme*, …*clip*, …*kamera*, …*kassette*, …*recorder etc*); **auf Video aufnehmen** video(tape), tape
Videoband *n* videotape
Videotext *m* teletext
Videothek [video'teːk] *f* (-; -en) video (-tape) library; video store (*Br* shop)
Vieh [fiː] *n* (-[e]s; *no pl*) cattle; **20 Stück Vieh** 20 head of cattle
Viehbestand *m* livestock
Viehhändler *m* cattle dealer
'viehisch *contp adj* bestial, brutal
'Viehmarkt *m* cattle market
Viehzucht *f* cattle breeding, stockbreeding
Viehzüchter *m* cattle breeder, stockbreeder
viel [fiːl] *adj and adv* a lot (of), plenty (of), F lots of; **viele** many; **nicht viel** not much; **nicht viele** not many; **sehr viel** a great deal (of); **sehr viele** very many, a lot (of); **das viele Geld** all that money; **ziemlich viel** quite a lot (of); **ziemlich viele** quite a few; **viel besser** much better; **viel teurer** much more expensive; **e-r zu viel** one too many; **viel zu viel** far too much; **viel zu wenig** not nearly enough; **viel lieber** much rather; **wie viel** how much (*pl* many); **viel beschäftigt** very busy; **viel sagend** meaningful; **viel**

versprechend promising
'**vieldeutig** [-dɔʏtɪç] *adj* ambiguous
vielerlei ['fiːlɐ'lai] *adj* all kinds *or* sorts of
'**vielfach 1.** *adj* multiple; **2.** *adv* in many cases, (very) often
'**Vielfalt** *f* (-; *no pl*) (great) variety (*gen* of)
'**vielfarbig** *adj* multicolo(u)red
vielleicht [fi'laiçt] *adv* perhaps, maybe; *vielleicht ist er* ... he may *or* might be ...
'**vielmals** *adv*: (*ich*) *danke* (*Ihnen*) *vielmals* thank you very much; *entschuldigen Sie vielmals* I'm very sorry, I do apologize
viel'mehr *cj* rather
'**vielsagend** *adj* meaningful
vielversprechend *adj* promising
'**vielseitig** [-zaitɪç] *adj* versatile
'**Vielseitigkeit** *f* (-; *no pl*) versatility
vier [fiːɐ] *adj* four; *zu viert sein* be four; *auf allen vieren* on all fours; *unter vier Augen* in private, privately
'**Vierbeiner** [-bainɐ] *m* (-s; -) zo quadruped, four-legged animal
'**vierbeinig** *adj* four-legged
'**Viereck** *n* quadrangle, quadrilateral
'**viereckig** *adj* quadrangular, square
Vierer ['fiːrɐ] *m* (-s; -) *rowing*: four
'**vierfach** *adj* fourfold; *vierfache Ausfertigung* four copies
'**vierfüßig** [-fyːsɪç] *adj* four-footed
'**Vierfüßler** [-fyːslɐ] *m* (-s; -) zo quadruped
'**vierhändig** [-hɛndɪç] *adj* mus four-handed
'**vierjährig** [-jɛːrɪç] *adj* four-year-old, of four
Vierlinge ['fiːɐlɪŋə] *pl* quadruplets, quads
'**viermal** *adv* four times
'**Vierradantrieb** *m* mot four-wheel drive
'**vierseitig** [-zaitɪç] *adj* math quadrilateral
'**vierspurig** [-ʃpuːrɪç] *adj* mot four-lane
'**vierstöckig** [-ʃtœkɪç] *adj* four-storied, *Br* four-storey ...
'**Viertaktmotor** *m* four-stroke engine
vierte ['fiːɐtə] *adj* fourth
Viertel ['fɪrtəl] *n* (-s; -) fourth (part); quarter; (*ein*) *Viertel vor* (*nach*) (a) quarter to (past)
Viertelfi,nale *n* sport quarter finals
Viertel'jahr *n* three months
'**vierteljährlich 1.** *adj* quarterly; **2.** *adv* every three months, quarterly
vierteln ['fɪrtəln] *v/t* (*ge-*, *h*) quarter
'**Viertelnote** *f* mus quarter note, *Br* crotchet
Viertelpfund *n* quarter of a pound
Viertel'stunde *f* quarter of an hour
viertens ['fiːɐtəns] *adv* fourthly
vierzehn ['fɪrtseːn] *adj* fourteen; *vier-*

zehn Tage two weeks, *esp Br a.* a fortnight
'**vierzehnte** *adj* fourteenth
vierzig ['fɪrtsɪç] *adj* forty
'**vierzigste** *adj* fortieth
Villa ['vɪla] *f* (-; *Villen*) villa
violett [vio'lɛt] *adj* violet, purple
Violine [vio'liːnə] *f* (-; -*n*) mus violin
Virtuelle Realität [vɪr'tuɛlə] *f* EDP virtual reality, Cyberspace
virtuos [vɪr'tuoːs] *adj* virtuoso ..., masterly
Virtuose [vɪr'tuoːzə] *m* (-*n*; -*n*) virtuoso
Virtuosität [vɪrtuozi'tɛːt] *f* (-; *no pl*) virtuosity
Virus ['viːrʊs] *n*, *m* (-; *Viren*) med virus
Visier [vi'ziːɐ] *n* (-s; -*e*) sights; visor
Vision [vi'zjoːn] *f* (-; -*en*) vision
Visite [vi'ziːtə] *f* (-; -*n*) med round
Vi'sitenkarte *f* (visiting) card
Visum ['viːzʊm] *n* (-s; *Visa*) visa
vital [vi'taːl] *adj* vigorous
Vitalität [vitali'tɛːt] *f* (-; *no pl*) vigo(u)r
Vitamin [vita'miːn] *n* (-s; -*e*) vitamin
Vitrine [vi'triːnə] *f* (-; -*n*) (glass) cabinet; showcase
Vize... ['fiːtsɐ-] *in cpds* vice(-)...
Vogel ['foːgəl] *m* (-s; *Vögel* ['føːgəl]) zo bird; F *den Vogel abschießen* take the cake
'**Vogelbauer** *n* birdcage
'**vogelfrei** *adj* outlawed
'**Vogelfutter** *n* birdseed
Vogelgrippe *f* bird flu, avian flu
Vogelkunde *f* ornithology
Vogelkäfig *m* birdcage
vögeln ['føːgəln] V *v/t and v/i* (*ge-*, *h*) screw
'**Vogelnest** *n* bird's nest
Vogelperspektive *f* bird's-eye view
Vogelscheuche *f* scarecrow (*a. fig*)
Vogelschutzgebiet *n* bird sanctuary
Vogelwarte *f* ornithological station
Vogelzug *m* bird migration
Vokabel [vo'kaːbəl] *f* (-; -*n*) word; *pl* → **Vokabular** [vokabu'laːɐ] *n* (-s; -*e*) vocabulary
Vokal [vo'kaːl] *m* (-s; -*e*) ling vowel
Volant [vo'lãː] Austrian *m* → **Lenkrad**
Volk [fɔlk] *n* (-[*e*]s; *Völker* ['fœlkɐ]) people, nation; *the* people; zo swarm; *ein Mann aus dem Volke* a man of the people
Völkerkunde ['fœlkɐ-] *f* ethnology
Völkermord *m* genocide
Völkerrecht *n* (-[*e*]s; *no pl*) international law
Völkerwanderung *f* migration of peoples; F mass exodus

'Volksabstimmung f POL referendum
Volksfest n funfair
Volkshochschule f adult evening classes
Volkslied n folk song
Volksmund m: *im Volksmund* in the vernacular
Volksmu,sik f folk music
Volksrepu,blik f people's republic
Volksschule HIST f → *Grundschule*
Volkssport m popular sport
Volkssprache f vernacular
Volksstamm m tribe, race
Volkstanz m folk dance
Volkstracht f national costume
'volkstümlich [-tyːmlɪç] adj popular, folk ...; traditional
'Volksversammlung f public meeting
Volkswirt m economist
Volkswirtschaft f (national) economy; → *Volkswirtschaftslehre* f economics
Volkszählung f census
voll [fɔl] **1.** adj full (a. fig); full up (a. F); F plastered; thick, rich (hair); *voller* full of, filled with, a. covered with dirt etc; **2.** adv fully; completely, totally, wholly; *pay etc* in full, the full price; *hit etc* full, straight, right; *voll entwickelt* fully developed; *(nicht) für voll nehmen* (not) take seriously
'vollauf adv perfectly, quite
'vollauto,matisch adj fully automatic
'Vollbart m (full) beard
'Vollbeschäftigung f full employment
'Vollblut... in cpds full-blooded (a. fig)
'Vollblüter [-blyːtɐ] m (-s; -) zo thoroughbred
voll'bringen v/t (irr, *bringen*, no -ge-, h) accomplish, achieve; perform
'Volldampf m full steam; F *mit Volldampf* (at) full blast
voll'enden v/t (no -ge-, h) finish, complete
voll'endet adj completed; fig perfect
vollends ['fɔlɛnts] adv completely
Voll'endung f (-; no pl) finishing, completion; fig perfection
voll'führen v/t (no -ge-, h) perform
'vollfüllen v/t (sep, -ge-, h) (*gießen*) fill (up)
'Vollgas n (-es; no pl) MOT full throttle; *Vollgas geben* F step on it
völlig ['fœlɪç] **1.** adj complete, absolute, total; **2.** adv completely; *völlig unmöglich* absolutely impossible
'volljährig [-jɛːrɪç] adj JUR *volljährig sein (werden)* be (come) of age; *noch nicht volljährig* under age
'Volljährigkeit f (-; no pl) JUR majority
voll'kommen adj perfect; → *völlig*
Voll'kommenheit f (-; no pl) perfection

'Vollkornbrot n wholemeal bread
'vollmachen v/t (sep, -ge-, h) fill (up); F soil, dirty; *um das Unglück voll zu machen* to crown it all
Vollmacht f (-; -en) full power(s), authority; JUR power of attorney; *Vollmacht haben* be authorized
Vollmilch f full-cream milk
Vollmond m full moon
'vollpacken v/t (sep, -ge-, h) load (*mit* with) (a. fig)
'Vollpensi,on f full board
'vollschlank adj plump
'vollständig adj complete; → *völlig*
'vollstopfen v/t (sep, -ge-, h) stuff,fig a. cram, pack (*all: mit* with)
voll'strecken v/t (no -ge-, h) JUR execute
Voll'streckung f (-; -en) JUR execution
'volltanken v/t (sep, -ge-, h): *bitte volltanken!* MOT fill her up, please!
'Volltreffer m direct hit; bull's eye (a. fig)
Vollversammlung f plenary session
'vollwertig adj full
'Vollwertkost f wholefoods
vollzählig ['fɔltsɛːlɪç] adj complete
voll'ziehen v/t (irr, *ziehen*, no -ge-, h) execute; perform; *sich vollziehen* take place
Voll'ziehung f (-; no pl), **Voll'zug** m (-[e]s; no pl) execution
Volontär [volɔnˈtɛːɐ] m (-s; -e), **Volon'tärin** f (-; -nen) unpaid trainee
Volt [vɔlt] n (-; -) ELECTR volt
Volumen [voˈluːmən] n (-s; -, -mina) volume; size
von [fɔn] prp from; *instead of gen:* of; *passive:* by; about *s.o.* or *s.th.*; *südlich von* south of; *weit von* far from; *von Hamburg* from Hamburg; *von nun an* from now on; *ein Freund von mir* a friend of mine; *die Freunde von Alice* Alice's friends; *ein Brief (Geschenk) von Tom* a letter (gift) from Tom; *ein Buch (Bild) von Orwell (Picasso)* a book (painting) by Orwell (Picasso); *der König (Bürgermeister etc) von ...* the King (Mayor etc) of ...; *ein Kind von 10 Jahren* a child of ten; *müde von der Arbeit* tired from work; *es war nett (gemein) von dir* it was nice (mean) of you; *reden (hören) von* talk (hear) about *or* of; *von Beruf (Geburt)* by profession (birth); *von selbst* by itself; *von mir aus!* I don't mind *or* care
von'stattengehen v/i (irr, *gehen*, sep, -ge-, sein) go, come off
vor [foːɐ] prp (*dat and acc*) in front of; outside; before; ... ago; with, for; *vor der Klasse* in front of the class; *vor*

der Schule in front of *or* outside the school; before school; *vor kurzem (e-r Stunde)* a short time (an hour) ago; *5 Minuten vor 12* five (minutes) to twelve; *vor j-m liegen* be *or* lie ahead of s.o. (*a. fig and* SPORT); *vor sich hin smile etc* to o.s.; *sicher vor* safe from; *vor Kälte* with cold; *vor Angst* for fear; *vor allem* above all; *vor sich gehen* go on, happen

'**Vorabend** *m* eve (*a. fig*)

'**Vorahnung** *f* presentiment, foreboding

voran [fo'ran] *adv* at the head (*dat* of), in front (of), before; *Kopf voran* head first

vorangehen *v/i* (*irr*, **gehen**, *sep*, *-ge-*, *sein*) go in front *or* first; *esp fig* lead the way

vorankommen *v/i* (*irr*, **kommen**, *sep*, *-ge-*, *sein*) get on *or* along (*a. fig*), make headway

'**Voranzeige** *f* preannouncement; *film*: trailer

'**vorarbeiten** *v/i* (*sep*, *-ge-*, *h*) work in advance; *fig* pave the way

'**Vorarbeiter** *m* foreman

voraus [fo'raus] *adv* ahead (*dat* of); *im Voraus* in advance, beforehand

vo'rausgehen *v/i* (*irr*, **gehen**, *sep*, *-ge-*, *sein*) precede; → *vorangehen*

vo'rausgesetzt *cj*: *vorausgesetzt, dass* provided that

Vo'raussage *f* (*-*; *-n*) prediction; METEOR forecast

vo'raussagen *v/t* (*sep*, *-ge-*, *h*) predict; forecast

vo'rausschicken *v/t* (*sep*, *-ge-*, *h*) send on ahead

voraussehen *v/t* (*irr*, **sehen**, *sep*, *-ge-*, *h*) foresee, see *s.th.* coming

vo'raussetzen *v/t* (*sep*, *-ge-*, *h*) assume; take *s.th.* for granted

Vo'raussetzung *f* (*-*; *-en*) condition, prerequisite; assumption; *die Voraussetzungen erfüllen* meet the requirements

Vo'raussicht *f* (*-*; *no pl*) foresight; *aller Voraussicht nach* in all probability

vo'raussichtlich *adv* probably; *er kommt voraussichtlich morgen* he is expected to arrive tomorrow

Vo'rauszahlung *f* advance payment

'**Vorbedeutung** *f* omen

'**Vorbedingung** *f* prerequisite

Vorbehalt ['fo:rbəhalt] *m* (*-[e]s*; *-e*) reservation

'**vorbehalten 1.** *v/t* (*irr*, **halten**, *sep*, *no -ge-*, *h*) *sich (das Recht) vorbehalten zu inf* reserve the right to *inf*; **2.** *adj* reserved

'**vorbehaltlos 1.** *adj* unconditional; **2.** *adv* without reservation

vor'bei *adv* time: over, past; finished; gone; *space*: past, by; *jetzt ist alles vorbei* it's all over now; *vorbei! missed!*

vorbeifahren *v/i* (*irr*, **fahren**, *sep*, *-ge-*, *sein*) go (*or* drive) past (*an dat s.o. or s.th.*), pass (*s.o. or s.th.*)

vorbeigehen *v/i* (*irr*, **gehen**, *sep*, *-ge-*, *sein*) walk past; *a. fig* go by, pass; *shot etc*: miss

vorbei kommen *v/i* (*irr*, **kommen**, *sep*, *-ge-*, *sein*) pass (*an dat s.th.*); F drop in (*bei j-m* on s.o.); *fig* avoid

vorbei lassen *v/t* (*irr*, **lassen**, *sep*, *-ge-*, *h*) let *s.o.* pass

'**Vorbemerkung** *f* preliminary remark

'**vorbereiten** *v/t and v/refl* (*sep*, *no -ge-*, *h*) prepare (*auf acc* for)

'**Vorbereitung** *f* (*-*; *-en*) preparation (*auf acc* for)

'**vorbestellen** *v/t* (*sep*, *no -ge-*, *h*) book (*or* order) in advance; reserve (*room, seat etc*)

'**Vorbestellung** *f* (*-*; *-en*) advance booking; reservation

'**vorbestraft** *adj*: *vorbestraft sein* have a police record

'**vorbeugen** (*sep*, *-ge-*, *h*) **1.** *v/i* prevent (*e-r Sache* s.th.); **2.** *v/refl* bend forward

vorbeugend *adj* preventive, MED *a.* prophylactic

'**Vorbeugung** *f* (*-*; *-en*) prevention

'**Vorbild** *n* model, pattern; (*j-m*) *ein Vorbild sein* set an example (to s.o.); *sich j-n zum Vorbild nehmen* follow s.o.'s example

'**vorbildlich** *adj* exemplary

'**Vorbildung** *f* education(al background)

'**vorbringen** *v/t* (*irr*, **bringen**, *sep*, *-ge-*, *h*) bring forward; say, state

vorda,tieren *v/t* (*no -ge-*, *h*) antedate; postdate

Vorder... ['fɔrdɐ-] *in cpds* ...*achse*, ...*rad*, ...*sitz*, ...*tür*, ...*zahn etc*: front ...

vordere ['fɔrdərə] *adj* front

'**Vordergrund** *m* foreground (*a. fig*)

Vordermann *m*: *mein Vordermann* the man *or* boy in front of me

Vorderseite *f* front (side); head

'**vordränge(l)n** *v/refl* (*sep*, *-ge-*, *h*) cut into line, *Br* jump the queue

vordringen *v/i* (*irr*, **dringen**, *sep*, *-ge-*, *sein*) advance; *vordringen (bis) zu* work one's way through to (*a. fig*)

vordringlich 1. *adj* (most) urgent; **2.** *adv*: *et. vordringlich behandeln* give s.th. priority

'**Vordruck** *m* (*-[e]s*; *-e*) form, blank

'**voreilig** *adj* hasty, rash, precipitate; *vor-*

eilige Schlüsse ziehen jump to conclusions

'**voreingenommen** *adj* prejudiced, bias(s)ed

'**Voreingenommenheit** *f* (-; *no pl*) prejudice, bias

'**vorenthalten** *v/t* (*irr*, *halten*, *sep*, *no -ge-*, *h*) keep back, withhold (*both*: *j-m et.* s.th. from s.o.)

'**Vorentscheidung** *f* preliminary decision

'**vorerst** *adv* for the present, for the time being

Vorfahr ['fo:ɐfaːɐ] *m* (*-en*; *-en*) ancestor

'**vorfahren** *v/i* (*irr*, *fahren*, *sep*, *-ge-*, *sein*) drive up (*or* on)

'**Vorfahrt** *f* (-; *no pl*) right of way, priority

'**Vorfall** *m* incident, occurrence, event

'**vorfallen** *v/i* (*irr*, *fallen*, *sep*, *-ge-*, *sein*) happen, occur

vorfinden *v/t* (*irr*, *finden*, *sep*, *-ge-*, *h*) find

'**Vorfreude** *f* anticipation

'**vorführen** *v/t* (*sep*, *-ge-*, *h*) show, present; perform (*trick etc*); demonstrate; JUR bring (*j-m* before s.o.)

'**Vorführer** *m* demonstrator

'**Vorführung** *f* presentation, show(ing); performance; demonstration; JUR production

'**Vorführwagen** *m* MOT demonstrator, *Br* demonstration car

'**Vorgabe** *f* handicap

'**Vorgang** *m* event, occurrence, happening; file, record(s); BIOL, TECH process; **e-n Vorgang schildern** give an account of what happened

Vorgänger(in) ['fo:ɐgɛŋɐ (-ŋərɪn)] (*-s*; -/-; *-nen*) predecessor

'**Vorgarten** *m* front yard (*Br* garden)

'**vorgeben** *v/t* (*irr*, *geben*, *sep*, *-ge-*, *h*) SPORT give; *fig* use s.th. as a pretext

'**Vorgebirge** *n* foothills

'**vorgefasst** *adj* preconceived

'**vorgefertigt** *adj* prefabricated

'**Vorgefühl** *n* presentiment

'**vorgehen** *v/i* (*irr*, *gehen*, *sep*, *-ge-*, *sein*) go on; come first; act; JUR sue (*gegen j-n* s.o.); proceed; *watch*: be fast

'**Vorgehen** *n* (*-s*; *no pl*) procedure

'**vorgeschichtlich** *adj* prehistoric

'**Vorgeschmack** *m* foretaste (*auf acc* of)

Vorgesetzte *m*, *f* (*-n*; *-n*) superior, F boss

'**vorgestern** *adv* the day before yesterday

'**vorgreifen** *v/i* (*irr*, *greifen*, *sep*, *-ge-*, *h*) anticipate *s.o. or s.th.*

'**vorhaben** *v/t* (*irr*, *haben*, *sep*, *-ge-*, *h*) plan, intend; **haben Sie heute Abend et. vor?** have you anything on tonight?; **was hat er jetzt wieder vor?** what is he up to now?

'**Vorhaben** *n* (*-s*; -) plan(s), intention; TECH, ECON a. project

'**Vorhalle** *f* (entrance) hall, lobby

'**vorhalten** (*irr*, *halten*, *sep*, *-ge-*, *h*) **1.** *v/t*: *j-m et.* **vorhalten** hold s.th. in front of s.o.; *fig* blame s.o. for (doing) s.th.; **2.** *v/i* last

'**Vorhaltungen** *pl* reproaches; *j-m* **Vorhaltungen machen (für et.)** reproach s.o. (with s.th., for being …)

'**Vorhand** *f* (-; *no pl*) *tennis*: forehand

vorhanden [fo:ɐ'handən] *adj* available; in existence; **vorhanden sein** exist; **es ist nichts mehr vorhanden** there's nothing left

Vor'handensein *n* (*-s*; *no pl*) existence

'**Vorhang** *m* curtain

'**Vorhängeschloss** *n* padlock

vor'her *adv* before, earlier; in advance, beforehand

vor'herbestimmen *v/t* (*sep*, *no -ge-*, *h*) predetermine

vorherig [fo:ɐ'heːrɪç] *adj* previous

'**Vorherrschaft** *f* (-; *no pl*) predominance

'**vorherrschen** *v/i* (*sep*, *-ge-*, *h*) predominate, prevail

'**vorherrschend** *adj* predominant, prevailing

vor'hersehbar *adj* foreseeable

vor'hersehen *v/t* (*irr*, *sehen*, *sep*, *-ge-*, *h*) foresee

vor'hin *adv* a (little) while ago

'**Vorhut** *f* (-; *-en*) MIL vanguard

vorig ['fo:rɪç] *adj* last; former, previous

vorjährig ['fo:ɐjɛːrɪç] *adj* of last year, last year' …

'**Vorkämpfer** *m*, '**Vorkämpferin** *f* champion, pioneer

Vorkehrungen ['fo:ɐkeːruŋən] *pl*: **Vorkehrungen treffen** take precautions

'**Vorkenntnisse** *pl* previous knowledge *or* experience (*in dat* of)

'**vorkommen** *v/i* (*irr*, *kommen*, *sep*, *-ge-*, *sein*) be found; happen; **es kommt mir … vor** it seems … to me

'**Vorkommen** *n* (*-s*; -) MIN deposit(s)

Vorkommnis ['fo:ɐkɔmnɪs] *n* (*-ses*; *-se*) occurrence, incident, event

'**Vorkriegs…** *in cpds* prewar …

'**vorladen** *v/t* (*irr*, *laden*, *sep*, *-ge-*, *h*) JUR summon

'**Vorladung** *f* (-; *-en*) JUR summons

'**Vorlage** *f* model; pattern; copy; presentation; PARL bill; *soccer etc*: pass

'**vorlassen** *v/t* (*irr*, *lassen*, *sep*, *-ge-*, *h*) let s.o. go first; let s.o. pass; **vorgelassen werden** be admitted (*bei* to)

'**Vorlauf** *m* *recorder*: fast-forward; SPORT (preliminary) heat

V

'**Vorläufer** *m* forerunner, precursor
'**vorläufig 1.** *adj* provisional, temporary;
2. *adv* for the present, for the time being
'**vorlaut** *adj* pert, cheeky
'**Vorleben** *n* (-*s*; *no pl*) former life, past
'**vorlegen** *v/t* (*sep*, -*ge*-, *h*) present; produce; show
'**Vorleger** *m* (-*s*; -) rug; mat
'**vorlesen** *v/t* (*irr*, **lesen**, *sep*, -*ge*-, *h*) read out (aloud); *j-m et. vorlesen* read s.th. to s.o.
'**Vorlesung** *f* (-; -*en*) lecture (*über acc* on; *vor dat* to); *e-e Vorlesung halten* (give a) lecture
'**vorletzte** *adj* last but one; *vorletzte Nacht (Woche)* the night (week) before last
'**vorliebnehmen** *v/i* (*irr*, **nehmen**, *sep*, -*ge*-, *h*) *mit* make do with
'**Vorliebe** *f* (-; -*n*) preference, special liking
'**vorliegen** *v/i* (*irr*, **liegen**, *sep*, -*ge*-, *h*) *es liegen (keine) ... vor* there are (no) ...; *was liegt gegen ihn vor?* what is he charged with?
vorliegend *adj* present, in question
'**vorlügen** *v/t* (*irr*, **lügen**, *sep*, -*ge*-, *h*) *j-m et. vorlügen* tell s.o. lies
vormachen *v/t* (*sep*, -*ge*-, *h*) *j-m et. vormachen* show s.th. to s.o., show s.o. how to do s.th.; *fig* fool s.o.
'**Vormachtstellung** *f* supremacy
'**Vormarsch** *m* MIL advance (*a. fig*)
'**vormerken** *v/t* (*sep*, -*ge*-, *h*) *j-n vormerken* put s.o.'s name down
'**Vormittag** *m* morning; *heute Vormittag* this morning
'**vormittags** *adv* in the morning; *sonntags vormittags* on Sunday mornings
'**Vormund** *m* (-[*e*]*s*; -*e*) JUR guardian
Vormundschaft *f* (-; -*en*) JUR guardianship
vorn [fɔrn] *adv* in front; *nach vorn* forward; *von vorn* from the front; from the beginning; *j-n von vorn(e) sehen* see s.o.'s face; *noch einmal von vorn(e) (anfangen)* (start) all over again
'**Vorname** *m* first *or* Christian name, forename
vornehm ['foːɐneːm] *adj* distinguished; noble; fashionable, exclusive, F smart, posh; *die vornehme Gesellschaft* (high) society; *vornehm tun* put on airs
'**vornehmen** *v/t* (*irr*, **nehmen**, *sep*, -*ge*-, *h*) carry out, do; make (*changes etc*); *sich et. vornehmen* decide *or* resolve to do s.th.; make plans for s.th.; *sich fest vorgenommen haben zu inf* have the firm intention to *inf*, be determined to *inf*
'**vornherein** *adv*: *von vornherein* from the start *or* beginning

'**Vorort** *m* suburb
Vorort(s)zug *m* suburban *or* local *or* commuter train
'**Vorposten** *m* outpost (*a.* MIL)
'**vorprogram,mieren** *v/t* (*sep*, *no* -*ge*-, *sein*) (pre)program(me); *fig das war vorprogrammiert* that was bound to happen
'**Vorrang** *m* (-[*e*]*s*; *no pl*) precedence (*vor dat* over), priority (over)
'**Vorrat** *m* (-[*e*]*s*; -*räte*) store, stock, supply (*all: an dat* of); GASTR provisions; ECON resources, reserves; *e-n Vorrat anlegen an (dat)* stockpile
vorrätig ['foːrɛːtɪç] *adj* available; ECON in stock
'**Vorrecht** *n* privilege
'**Vorredner** *m* previous speaker
'**Vorrichtung** *f* TECH device
'**vorrücken** (*sep*, -*ge*-) **1.** *v/t* (*h*) move forward; **2.** *v/i* (*sein*) advance
'**Vorrunde** *f* SPORT preliminary round
'**vorsagen** *v/i* (*sep*, -*ge*-, *h*) *j-m vorsagen* prompt s.o.
'**Vorsai,son** *f* off-peak season
'**Vorsatz** *m* resolution; intention; JUR intent
vorsätzlich ['foːrzɛtslɪç] *adj* intentional; *esp* JUR wil(l)ful
'**Vorschau** *f* preview (*auf acc* of), *film*, TV *a.* trailer
'**Vorschein** *m*: *zum Vorschein bringen* produce; *fig* bring out; *zum Vorschein kommen* appear; *fig* come to light
'**vorschieben** *v/t* (*irr*, **schieben**, *sep*, -*ge*-, *h*) push forward; slip (*bolt*); *fig* use as a pretext
vorschießen F *v/t* (*irr*, **schießen**, *sep*, -*ge*-, *h*) advance (*money*)
'**Vorschlag** *m* suggestion, proposal (*a.* PARL *etc*); *den Vorschlag machen* →
'**vorschlagen** *v/t* (*irr*, **schlagen**, *sep*, -*ge*-, *h*) suggest, propose
'**Vorschlussrunde** *f* SPORT semifinal
'**vorschnell** *adj* hasty, rash
'**vorschreiben** *fig v/t* (*irr*, **schreiben**, *sep*, -*ge*-, *h*) prescribe; tell; *ich lasse mir nichts vorschreiben* I won't be dictated to
'**Vorschrift** *f* rule, regulation; instruction, direction; *Dienst nach Vorschrift machen* work to rule
'**vorschriftsmäßig** *adj* correct, proper
vorschriftswidrig *adj and adv* contrary to regulations
'**Vorschub** *m*: *Vorschub leisten* (*dat*) encourage; JUR aid and abet
'**Vorschul...** *in cpds* pre-school ...
'**Vorschule** *f* preschool

'**Vorschuss** *m* advance
'**vorschützen** *v/t* (*sep, -ge-, h*) use *s.th.* as a pretext
'**vorsehen** (*irr, sehen, sep, -ge-, h*) **1.** *v/t* plan; JUR provide; **vorsehen für** intend (*or* designate) for; **2.** *v/refl* be careful, take care, watch out (**vor** *dat* for)
'**Vorsehung** *f* (-; *no pl*) providence
'**vorsetzen** *v/t* (*sep, -ge-, h*) **j-m et. vorsetzen** put s.th. before s.o.; offer s.o. s.th.
'**Vorsicht** *f* (-; *no pl*) caution, care; **Vorsicht!** look *or* watch out!, (be) careful!; **Vorsicht, Stufe!** mind the step!
'**vorsichtig** *adj* careful, cautious
'**vorsichtshalber** [-halbɐ] *adv* to be on the safe side
'**Vorsichtsmaßnahme** *f* precaution, precautionary measure; **Vorsichtsmaßnahmen treffen** take precautions
'**Vorsilbe** *f* LING prefix
'**vorsingen** *v/t and v/i* (*irr, singen, sep, -ge-, h*) **j-m et. vorsingen** sing s.th. to s.o.; (have an) audition
'**Vorsitz** *m* chair(manship), presidency; **den Vorsitz haben** (**übernehmen**) be in (take) the chair, preside (**bei** over, at)
'**Vorsitzende** *m, f* (-*n*; -*n*) chairman (chairwoman), president
'**Vorsorge** *f* (-; *no pl*) precaution; **Vorsorge treffen** take precautions
Vorsorgeuntersuchung *f* MED preventive checkup
'**vorsorglich 1.** *adj* precautionary; **2.** *adv* as a precaution
'**Vorspann** *m* (-[*e*]*s*; -*e*) *film etc*: credits
'**Vorspeise** *f* hors d'œuvre, *Br* starter
'**Vorspiel** *n* MUS prelude (*a. fig*); foreplay
'**vorspielen** *v/t* (*sep, -ge-, h*) **j-m et. vorspielen** play s.th. to s.o.
'**vorsprechen** (*irr, sprechen, sep, -ge-, h*) **1.** *v/t* pronounce (**j-m** for s.o.); **2.** *v/i* call (**bei** at); THEA (have an) audition
'**vorspringen** *fig v/i* (*irr, springen, sep, -ge-, sein*) project, protrude (*both a.* ARCH)
'**Vorsprung** *m* ARCH projection; SPORT lead; **e-n Vorsprung haben** be leading (**von** by); *esp fig* **e-n Vorsprung von zwei Jahren haben** be two years ahead
'**Vorstadt** *f* suburb
'**Vorstand** *m* ECON board (of directors); managing committee (*of a club etc*)
'**vorstehen** *v/i* (*irr, stehen, sep, -ge-, h*) project, protrude
'**vorstellen** *v/t* (*sep, -ge-, h*) introduce (**sich** o.s.; **j-n j-m** s.o. to s.o.); put *watch* forward (**um** by); *fig* mean; **sich et.** (**j-n als ...**) **vorstellen** imagine s.th. (s.o. as ...); **so stelle ich mir ... vor** that's my

idea of ...; **sich vorstellen bei** have an interview with *a firm etc*
'**Vorstellung** *f* (-; -*en*) introduction; interview; THEA performance, *film etc*: *a.* show; idea; expectation
'**Vorstellungskraft** *f* (-; *no pl*), **Vorstellungsvermögen** *n* (-*s*; *no pl*) imagination
Vorstopper ['foːɐʃtɔpɐ] *m* (-*s*; -) SPORT center (*Br* centre) back
'**Vorstoß** *m* MIL advance; *fig* attempt
'**Vorstrafe** *f* previous conviction
'**vorstrecken** *v/t* (*sep, -ge-, h*) advance (*money*)
'**Vorstufe** *f* preliminary stage
'**vortäuschen** *v/t* (*sep, -ge-, h*) feign, fake
'**Vorteil** *m* advantage (*a.* SPORT); benefit, profit; **die Vorteile und Nachteile** the pros and cons
'**vorteilhaft** *adj* advantageous, profitable
'**Vorteilsregel** *f* SPORT advantage rule
Vortrag ['foːɐtraːk] *m* (-[*e*]*s*; *Vorträge* ['foːɐtrɛːɡə]) talk, *esp* UNIV lecture; MUS *etc* recital; **e-n Vortrag halten** give a talk *or* lecture (**vor** *dat* to; **über** *acc* on)
'**vortragen** *v/t* (*irr, tragen, sep, -ge-, h*) express, state; MUS *etc* perform, play; recite (*poem etc*)
'**vortreten** *v/i* (*irr, treten, sep, -ge-, sein*) step forward; *fig* protrude, stick out
'**Vortritt** *m* (-[*e*]*s*; *no pl*) precedence; **j-m den Vortritt lassen** let s.o. go first
vorüber [fo'ryːbɐ] *adv*: **vorüber sein** be over
vorübergehen *v/i* (*irr, gehen, sep, -ge-, sein*) pass, go by
vorübergehend *adj* temporary
'**Vorübung** *f* preparatory exercise
'**Voruntersuchung** *f* JUR, MED preliminary examination
'**Vorurteil** *n* prejudice
'**vorurteilslos** *adj* unprejudiced, unbias(s)ed
'**Vorverkauf** *m* THEA advance booking
'**vorverlegen** *v/t* (*sep, no -ge-, h*) advance
'**Vorwahl** *f* TEL area (*Br* STD *or* dialling) code; POL primary, *Br* preliminary election
'**Vorwand** *m* pretext, excuse
vorwärts ['foːɐvɛrts] *adv* forward, on (-ward), ahead; **vorwärts!** come on!, let's go!
'**vorwärtskommen** *v/i* (*irr, kommen, sep, -ge-, sein*) make headway (*a. fig*)
vorweg [foːɐ'vɛk] *adv* beforehand
vor'wegnehmen *v/t* (*irr, nehmen, sep, -ge-, h*) anticipate
'**vorweisen** *v/t* (*irr, weisen, sep, -ge-, h*) produce, show; **et. vorweisen können**

boast s.th.

vorwerfen *fig v/t (irr, werfen, sep, -ge-, h)*
j-m et. vorwerfen reproach s.o. with s.th.

'vorwiegend *adv* predominantly, chiefly,
mainly, mostly

'vorwitzig *adj* cheeky, pert

'Vorwort *n (-[e]s; -e)* foreword; preface

'Vorwurf *m* reproach; **j-m Vorwürfe machen (wegen)** reproach s.o. (for)

'vorwurfsvoll *adj* reproachful

'Vorzeichen *n* omen, sign (*a.* MATH)

'vorzeigen *v/t (sep, -ge-, h)* show; produce

'vorzeitig *adj* premature, early

'vorziehen *v/t (irr, ziehen, sep, -ge-, h)*

draw; *fig* prefer

'Vorzimmer *n* anteroom; outer office;
Austrian → **Hausflur**

'Vorzug *m* advantage; merit

vorzüglich [foːɐ̯'tsyːklɪç] *adj* excellent,
exquisite

'vorzugsweise *adv* preferably

Votum ['voːtʊm] *n (-s; -ta, -ten)* vote

VP ABBR *of* **Vollpension** full board; (full)
board and lodging

vulgär [vʊl'ɡɛːɐ̯] *adj* vulgar

Vulkan [vʊl'kaːn] *m (-s; -e)* volcano

Vulkanausbruch *m* volcanic eruption

vul'kanisch *adj* volcanic

W

W ABBR *of* **West(en)** W, west; **Watt** W,
watt(s)

Waage ['vaːɡə] *f (-; -n)* scale(s *Br*); balance; ASTR Libra; **sich die Waage halten**
balance each other; **er ist (e-e) Waage**
he's (a) Libra

'waagerecht *adj* horizontal

Waagschale ['vaːk-] *f* scale

Wabe ['vaːbə] *f (-; -n)* honeycomb

wach [vax] *adj* awake; **wach rütteln**
rouse; *fig →* **wachrütteln; wach werden**
wake (up), *esp fig →* **wachwerden**

Wache ['vaxə] *f (-; -n)* guard (*a.* MIL); sentry; MAR, MED *etc* watch; police station;
Wache haben be on guard (MAR watch);
Wache halten keep watch

'wachen *v/i (ge-, h)* (keep) watch (**über**
acc over)

'Wachhund *m* watchdog

'Wachmann *m (-[e]s; -männer, -leute)*
watchman; *Austrian →* **Polizist**

Wacholder [va'xɔldɐ] *m (-s; -)* BOT juniper

'wachrufen *v/t (irr, rufen, sep, -ge-, h)* call
up, evoke

wachrütteln *v/t (sep, -ge-, h) fig* rouse (*a.
fig*)

Wachs [vaks] *n (-es; -e)* wax

wachsam ['vaxzaːm] *adj* watchful, on
one's guard, vigilant

'Wachsamkeit *f (-; no pl)* watchfulness,
vigilance

wachsen¹ ['vaksən] *v/i (irr, ge-, sein)* grow
(*a.* **sich wachsen lassen**), *fig a.* increase

'wachsen² *v/t (ge-, h)* wax

'Wachsfi,gurenkabi,nett *n* waxworks

Wachstuch *n* oilcloth

'Wachstum *n (-s; no pl)* growth, *fig a.* increase

Wachtel ['vaxtəl] *f (-; -n)* ZO quail

Wächter ['vɛçtɐ] *m (-s; -)* guard

'Wachtmeister *m (-s; no pl)* patrolman,
Br (police) constable

'Wach(t)turm *m* watchtower

'wachwerden *v/i (irr, werden, sep, -ge-,
sein) fig* awake; *→* **wach**

wackelig ['vakəlɪç] *adj* shaky (*a. fig*);
loose (*tooth*)

'wackeln *v/i (ge-, h)* shake; *table etc*: wobble; *tooth*: be loose; PHOT move; **wackeln
mit** waggle

Wade ['vaːdə] *f (-; -n)* ANAT calf

Waffe ['vafə] *f (-; -n)* weapon (*a. fig*), *pl a.*
arms

Waffel ['vafəl] *f (-; -n)* waffle; wafer

'Waffengewalt *f*: **mit Waffengewalt** by
force of arms

Waffenschein *m* gun license (*Br* licence)

Waffenstillstand *m* armistice (*a. fig*);
truce

wagen ['vaːɡən] *v/t (ge-, h)* dare; risk;
sich wagen venture

'Wagen *m (-s; -)* MOT car; RAIL car, *Br* carriage

wägen ['vɛːɡən] *lit v/t (irr, ge-, h)* weigh
(*one's words etc*)

'Wagenheber *m* TECH jack

Wagenladung *f* cartload

Waggon [va'ɡõː] *m (-s, -s)* (railroad) car,
Br (railway) carriage; freight car, *Br*
goods waggon

Wagnis ['vaːknɪs] *n* (*-ses*; *-se*) venture, risk

Wa'gon *m* → **Waggon**

Wahl [vaːl] *f* (*-*; *-en*) choice; alternative; selection; POL election; voting, poll; vote; *die Wahl haben* (*s-e Wahl treffen*) have the (make one's) choice; *keine* (*andere*) *Wahl haben* have no choice *or* alternative

'**wahlberechtigt** *adj* POL entitled to vote

'**Wahlbeteiligung** *f* POL poll, (voter) turnout; *hohe* (*niedrige*) *Wahlbeteiligung* heavy (light) poll

'**Wahlbezirk** *m* → **Wahlkreis**

wählen ['vɛːlən] *v/t and v/i* (*ge-*, *h*) choose, pick, select; POL vote (for); elect; TEL dial

'**Wähler** *m* (*-s*; *-*) voter

'**Wahlergebnis** *n* election result

wählerisch ['vɛːlərɪʃ] *adj* F picky (*in dat* about), *esp Br* choos(e)y

'**Wählerschaft** *f* (*-*; *-en*) electorate, voters

'**Wahlfach** *n* PED *etc* elective, optional subject

Wahlka,bine *f* voting (*esp Br* polling) booth

Wahlkampf *m* election campaign

Wahlkreis *m* electoral district, *Br* constituency

Wahllo,kal *n* polling place (*Br* station)

'**wahllos** *adj* indiscriminate

'**Wahlpro,gramm** *n* election platform

Wahlrecht *n* (*-[e]s*; *no pl*) (right to) vote, suffrage, franchise

Wahlrede *f* election speech

'**Wählscheibe** *f* TEL dial

'**Wahlsieg** *m* election victory

Wahlsieger *m* election winner

Wahlspruch *m* motto

Wahlurne *f* ballot box

Wahlversammlung *f* election rally

'**Wahnsinn** *m* (*-[e]s*; *no pl*) madness (*a.* F), insanity

'**wahnsinnig 1.** *adj* mad (*a.* F), insane, F *a.* crazy; F awful, terrible; **2.** F *adv* terribly, awfully; madly (*in love*)

'**Wahnsinnige** *m*, *f* (*-n*; *-n*) madman (madwoman), lunatic, maniac (*all a.* F)

'**Wahnvorstellung** *f* delusion, hallucination

wahr [vaːɐ] *adj* true; real; genuine

wahren ['vaːrən] *v/t* (*ge-*, *h*) protect; *den Schein wahren* keep up appearances

während ['vɛːrənt] **1.** *prp* (*gen*) during; **2.** *cj* while; whereas

'**wahrhaft**, **wahr'haftig** *adv* really, truly

'**Wahrheit** *f* (*-*; *-en*) truth

'**wahrheitsgemäß**, **wahrheitsgetreu** *adj* true, truthful

wahrheitsliebend *adj* truthful

wahrnehmbar ['vaːɐneːmbaːɐ] *adj* noticeable, perceptible

'**wahrnehmen** *v/t* (*irr*, *nehmen*, *sep*, *-ge-*, *h*) perceive, notice; seize, take (*chance etc*); look after (*s.o.'s interests etc*)

'**Wahrnehmung** *f* (*-*; *-en*) perception

'**wahrsagen** *v/i* (*sep*, *-ge-*, *h*) *j-m wahrsagen* tell s.o. his fortune; *sich wahrsagen lassen* have one's fortune told

'**Wahrsager** [-zaːgɐ] *m* (*-s*; *-*), '**Wahrsagerin** [-zaːgərɪn] *f* (*-*; *-nen*) fortune-teller

wahr'scheinlich 1. *adj* probable, likely; **2.** *adv* probably, (very *or* most) likely; *wahrscheinlich gewinnt er* (*nicht*) he is (not) likely to win

Wahr'scheinlichkeit *f* (*-*; *-en*) probability, likelihood

Währung ['vɛːrʊŋ] *f* (*-*; *-en*) currency

'**Währungs...** *in cpds* ...*politik*, ...*reform etc*: monetary ...

'**Wahrzeichen** *n* landmark

Waise ['vaizə] *f* (*-*; *-n*) orphan; *Waise werden* be orphaned

'**Waisenhaus** *n* orphanage

Wal [vaːl] *m* (*-[e]s*; *-e*) ZO whale

Wald [valt] *m* (*-[e]s*; *Wälder* ['vɛldɐ]) wood(s), forest

Waldbrand *m* forest fire

'**waldreich** *adj* wooded

'**Waldsterben** *n* dying of forests

'**Walfang** *m* whaling

'**Walfänger** *m* whaler

Walkman® *m* (*-s*; *-men*) personal stereo, Walkman®

Wall [val] *m* (*-[e]s*; *Wälle* ['vɛlə]) mound; MIL rampart

Wallach ['valax] *m* (*-[e]s*; *-e*) ZO gelding

wallen ['valən] *v/i* (*ge-*, *sein*) flow

'**Wallfahrer** *m*, '**Wallfahrerin** *f* pilgrim

'**Wallfahrt** *f* pilgrimage

'**Walnuss** *f* BOT walnut

'**Walross** *n* ZO walrus

Walze ['valtsə] *f* (*-*; *-n*) roller; cylinder; TECH, MUS barrel

'**walzen** *v/t* (*ge-*, *h*) roll (*a.* TECH)

wälzen ['vɛltsən] *v/t* (*ge-*, *h*) roll (*a. sich wälzen*); *fig* turn s.th. over in one's mind

Walzer ['valtsɐ] *m* (*-s*; *-*) MUS waltz (*a. Walzer tanzen*)

wand [vant] *pret of* **winden**

Wand *f* (*-*; *Wände* ['vɛndə]) wall, *fig a.* barrier

Wandale [van'daːlə] *m* (*-n*; *-n*) vandal

Wandalismus [vanda'lɪsmʊs] *m* (*-*; *no pl*) vandalism

Wandel ['vandəl] *m* (*-s*; *no pl*), '**wandeln** *v/t and v/refl* (*ge-*, *h*) change

Wanderer ['vandərɐ] *m* (*-s*; *-*), '**Wanderin**

W

f (-; *-nen*) hiker

wandern ['vandɐn] *v/i* (*ge-*, *sein*) hike; ramble (about); *eyes etc*: roam, wander

'**Wanderpo,kal** *m* challenge cup

Wanderpreis *m* challenge trophy

Wanderschuhe *pl* walking shoes

Wandertag *m* (school) outing *or* excursion

'**Wanderung** *f* (-; *-en*) walking tour, hike; zo *etc* migration

'**Wandgemälde** *n* mural

Wandka,lender *m* wall calendar

Wandkarte *f* wallchart

Wandlung ['vandlʊŋ] *f* (-; *-en*) change

'**Wandschrank** *m* closet, *Br* built-in cupboard

Wandtafel *f* blackboard

wandte ['vantə] *pret of* **wenden**

'**Wandteppich** *m* tapestry

Wange ['vaŋə] *f* (-; *-n*) ANAT cheek

Wankelmotor ['vaŋkəl-] *m* rotary piston *or* Wankel engine

wankelmütig ['vaŋkəlmyːtɪç] *adj* fickle

wanken ['vaŋkən] *v/i* (*ge-*, *sein*) stagger, reel; *fig* rock

wann [van] *interr adv* when, (at) what time; *seit wann?* (for) how long?, since when?

Wanne ['vanə] *f* (-; *-n*) tub (*a*. F); bath(tub)

Wanze ['vantsə] *f* (-; *-n*) zo bug (*a*. F)

Wapitihirsch [va'piːti-] *m* zo elk

Wappen ['vapən] *n* (-*s*; -) (coat of) arms

'**Wappenkunde** *f* heraldry

wappnen ['vapnən] *fig v/refl* (*ge-*, *h*) arm o.s.

war [vaːɐ] *pret of* **sein**[1]

warb [varp] *pret of* **werben**

Ware ['vaːrə] *f* (-; *-n*) *coll mst* goods; article; product

'**Warenhaus** *n* department store

Warenlager *n* stock

Warenprobe *f* sample

Warenzeichen *n* trademark

warf [varf] *pret of* **werfen**

warm [varm] *adj* warm (*a. fig*); GASTR hot; *schön warm* nice and warm; *warm halten* keep warm; *warm machen* warm (up)

Wärme ['vɛrmə] *f* (-; *no pl*) warmth; PHYS heat

Wärmeiso,lierung *f* heat insulation

'**wärmen** *v/t* (*ge-*, *h*) warm

'**Wärmflasche** *f* hot-water bottle

'**warmherzig** *adj* warm-hearted

'**warmmachen** *v/t* (*sep*, *-ge-*, *h*) → **warm**

Warm'wasserbereiter *m* (-*s*; -) water heater

Warmwasserversorgung *f* hot-water supply

'**Warnblinkanlage** *f* MOT warning flasher

Warndreieck *n* MOT warning triangle

warnen ['varnən] *v/t* (*ge-*, *h*) warn (*vor dat* of, against); *j-n davor warnen, et. zu tun* warn s.o. not to do s.th.

'**Warnschild** *n* danger sign

Warnsig,nal *n* warning signal

Warnstreik *m* token strike

'**Warnung** *f* (-; *-en*) warning

warten[1] ['vartən] *v/i* (*ge-*, *h*) wait (*auf acc* for); *j-n warten lassen* keep s.o. waiting

'**warten**[2] *v/t* (*ge-*, *h*) TECH service, maintain

Wärter ['vɛrtɐ] *m* (-*s*; -), '**Wärterin** *f* (-; *-nen*) attendant; zo keeper

'**Warteliste** *f* waiting list

Wartesaal *m*, **Wartezimmer** *n* waiting room

'**Wartung** *f* (-; *-en*) TECH maintenance

warum [va'rʊm] *interr adv* why

Warze ['vartsə] *f* (-; *-n*) MED wart

was [vas] **1.** *interr pron* what; *was gibt's?* what is it?, F what's up?; what's for lunch *etc*?; *was soll's?* so what?; *was machen Sie?* what are you doing?; what do you do?; *was kostet ...?* how much is ...?; *was für ...?* what kind *or* sort of ...?; *was für e-e Farbe* (*Größe*)? what col-o(u)r (size)?; *was für ein Unsinn* what nonsense!; *was für e-e gute Idee!* what a good idea!; **2.** *rel pron* what; *was* (*auch*) *immer* whatever; *alles, was ich habe* (*brauche*) all I have (need); *ich weiß nicht, was ich tun* (*sagen*) *soll* I don't know what to do (say); *..., was mich ärgerte...*, which made me angry; **3.** F *indef pron* → *etwas*

waschbar ['vaʃbaːɐ] *adj* washable

'**Waschbecken** *n* washbowl, *Br* washbasin

Wäsche ['vɛʃə] *f* (-; *-n*) a) washing, b) (*no pl*) laundry; linen; underwear; *in der Wäsche* in the wash; *schmutzige Wäsche waschen* wash one's dirty linen in public

'**waschecht** *adj* washable; fast (*color*); *fig* trueborn, genuine

'**Wäscheklammer** *f* clothespin, *Br* clothes peg

Wäscheleine *f* clothesline

waschen ['vaʃən] *v/t and v/refl* (*irr*, *ge-*, *h*) wash; *sich die Haare* (*Hände*) *waschen* wash one's hair (hands)

Wäscherei [vɛʃə'rai] *f* (-; *-en*) laundry

'**Waschlappen** *m* washcloth, *Br* flannel, facecloth

Waschma,schine *f* washing machine, F washer

'**waschma,schinenfest** *adj* machine-

washable
Waschmittel *n*, **Waschpulver** *n* washing powder
Waschraum *m* lavatory, washroom
Waschsa,lon *m* laundromat, *Br* launderette
Waschstraße *f* MOT car wash
Wasser ['vasɐ] *n* (-*s*; -) water
Wasserball *m* beach ball; SPORT water polo
Wasserbett *n* water bed
Wasserdampf *m* steam
'**wasserdicht** *adj* waterproof; *esp* MAR watertight (*a. fig*)
'**Wasserfall** *m* waterfall; falls
Wasserfarbe *f* water colo(u)r
Wasserflugzeug *n* seaplane
Wassergraben *m* SPORT water jump
Wasserhahn *m* tap, faucet
wässerig ['vɛsərɪç] *adj* watery; *j-m den Mund wässerig machen* make s.o.'s mouth water
'**Wasserkessel** *m* kettle
Wasserklo,sett *n* water closet, W.C.
Wasserkraft *f* (-; *no pl*) water power
Wasserkraftwerk *n* hydroelectric power station *or* plant
Wasserlauf *m* watercourse
Wasserleitung *f* waterpipe(s)
Wassermangel *m* (-*s*; *no pl*) water shortage
Wassermann *m* (-[*e*]*s*; *no pl*) ASTR Aquarius; *er ist (ein) Wassermann* he's (an) Aquarius
'**wassern** *v/i* (*ge-*, *h*) AVIAT touch down on water; *spacecraft*: splash down
wässern ['vɛsɐn] *v/t* (*ge-*, *h*) water; AGR irrigate; GASTR soak; PHOT rinse
'**Wasserpflanze** *f* BOT aquatic plant
'**Wasserrohr** *n* TECH water pipe
'**Wasserscheide** *f* GEOGR watershed
'**wasserscheu** *adj* afraid of water
'**Wasserski 1.** *m* water ski; **2.** *n* (-*s*; *no pl*) water skiing; *Wasserski fahren* water-ski
Wasserspiegel *m* water level
Wassersport *m* water *or* aquatic sports, aquatics
Wasserspülung *f* TECH flushing cistern; *Toilette mit Wasserspülung* (flush) toilet, W.C.
Wasserstand *m* water level
Wasserstoff *m* (-[*e*]*s*; *no pl*) CHEM hydrogen
Wasserstoffbombe *f* MIL hydrogen bomb, H-bomb
Wasserstrahl *m* jet of water
Wasserstraße *f* waterway
Wassertier *n* aquatic animal

Wasserverschmutzung *f* water pollution
Wasserversorgung *f* water supply
Wasserwaage *f* (*Br* spirit) level
Wasserweg *m* waterway; *auf dem Wasserweg* by water
Wasserwelle *f* water wave
Wasserwerk(e *pl*) *n* waterworks
Wasserzeichen *n* watermark
waten ['vaːtən] *v/i* (*ge-*, *sein*) wade
watscheln ['vaːtʃəln] *v/i* (*ge-*, *sein*) waddle
Watt[1] [vat] *n* (-*s*; -) ELECTR watt
Watt[2] *n* (-[*e*]*s*; *-en*) GEOGR mud flats
Watte ['vatə] *f* (-; *-n*) cotton wool
wattiert [va'tiːɐt] *adj* padded; quilted
weben ['veːbən] *v/t and v/i* ([*irr*,] *ge-*, *h*) weave
Weber ['veːbɐ] *m* (-*s*; -) weaver
Weberei [veːbə'rai] *f* (-; *-en*) weaving mill
'**Weberin** *f* (-; *-nen*) weaver
Webstuhl ['veːp-] *m* loom
Wechsel ['vɛksəl] *m* (-*s*; -) change; exchange; ECON bill of exchange; allowance
'**Wechselgeld** *n* (small) change
wechselhaft *adj* changeable
'**Wechseljahre** *pl* MED menopause
'**Wechselkurs** *m* ECON exchange rate
'**wechseln** *v/t and v/i* (*ge-*, *h*) change; exchange; vary
wechselnd *adj* varying
'**wechselseitig** [-zaitɪç] *adj* mutual, reciprocal
'**Wechselstrom** *m* ELECTR alternating current
'**Wechselstube** *f* ECON exchange office
Wechselwirkung *f* interaction
wecken ['vɛkən] *v/t* (*ge-*, *h*) wake (up), F call; *fig* awaken (*memories etc*); rouse (*s.o.'s curiosity etc*)
Wecker ['vɛkɐ] *m* (-*s*; -) alarm (clock)
wedeln ['veːdəln] *v/i* (*ge-*, *h*) wave (*mit et.* s.th.); *skiing*: wedel; *mit dem Schwanz wedeln* wag its tail
weder ['veːdɐ] *cj*: *weder ... noch ...* neither ... nor ...
Weg [veːk] *m* (- [*e*]*s*; *-e* ['veːgə]) way (*a. fig*); road (*a. fig*); path; route; walk; *auf friedlichem (legalem) Wege* by peaceful (legal) means; *j-m aus dem Weg gehen* get (*fig* keep) out of s.o.'s way; *j-n aus dem Weg räumen* put s.o. out of the way; *vom Weg abkommen* lose one's way; → *halb*
weg [vɛk] *adv* away; gone; off; F in raptures (*von* over, about); *Finger weg!* (keep your) hands off!; *nichts wie weg!* let's get out of here!; F *weg sein* be out
wegbleiben F *v/i* (*irr*, *bleiben*, *sep*, *-ge-*,

sein) stay away; be left out

wegbringen F *v/t* (*irr*, **bringen**, *sep*, -*ge*-, *h*) take away; **wegbringen von** get *s.o.* away from

wegen ['ve:gən] *prp* (*gen*) because of; for the sake of; due *or* owing to; JUR for

wegfahren *v/i* (*irr*, **fahren**, *sep*, -*ge*-) **1.** *v/i* (*sein*) leave; **2.** *v/t* (*h*) take away, remove

'**wegfallen** *v/i* (*irr*, **fallen**, *sep*, -*ge*-, *sein*) be dropped; stop, be stopped

Weggang ['vɛk-] *m* (-[*e*]*s*; *no pl*) leaving

'**weggehen** *v/i* (*irr*, **gehen**, *sep*, -*ge*-, *sein*) go away (*a. fig*), leave; *stain etc*: come off; ECON sell

wegjagen ['vɛk-] *v/t* (*sep*, -*ge*-, *h*) drive *or* chase away

wegkommen F *v/i* (*irr*, **kommen**, *sep*, -*ge*-, *sein*) get away; get lost; **gut wegkommen** come off well; **mach, dass du wegkommst!** get out of here!, *sl* get lost!

weglassen *v/t* (*irr*, **lassen**, *sep*, -*ge*-, *h*) let *s.o.* go; leave *s.th.* out

weglaufen *v/i* (*irr*, **laufen**, *sep*, -*ge*-, *sein*) run away ([**vor**] *j-m* from s.o.) (*a. fig*)

weglegen *v/t* (*sep*, -*ge*-, *h*) put away

wegnehmen *v/t* (*irr*, **nehmen**, *sep*, -*ge*-, *h*) take away (**von** from); take up (*room*, *time*); steal (*a. s.o.'s girlfriend etc*); **j-m et. wegnehmen** take s.th. (away) from s.o.

wegräumen *v/t* (*sep*, -*ge*-, *h*) clear away, remove

wegschaffen *v/t* (*sep*, -*ge*-, *h*) remove

wegschicken *v/t* (*sep*, -*ge*-, *h*) send away *or* off

wegsehen *v/i* (*irr*, **sehen**, *sep*, -*ge*-, *h*) look away

wegsetzen *v/t* (*sep*, -*ge*-, *h*) move

Wegweiser ['ve:kvaizɐ] *m* (-*s*; -) signpost; *fig* guide

Wegwerf... ['vɛkvɛrf-] *in cpds* ...*geschirr*, ...*besteck*, ...*rasierer etc*: throwaway ..., disposable ...; ...*flasche etc*: non-returnable ...

'**wegwerfen** *v/t* (*irr*, **werfen**, *sep*, -*ge*-, *h*) throw away

wegwischen ['vɛk-] *v/t* (*sep*, -*ge*-, *h*) wipe off

wegziehen (*irr*, **ziehen**, *sep*, -*ge*-) **1.** *v/i* (*sein*) move away; **2.** *v/t* (*h*) pull away

weh [ve:] *adv*: **weh tun** → **wehtun**

wehen ['ve:ən] *v/i* (*ge*-, *h*) blow; wave

'**Wehen** *pl* MED labo(u)r

wehmütig ['ve:my:tɪç] *adj* melancholy; wistful

Wehr[1] [ve:ɐ] *n* (-[*e*]*s*; -*e* ['ve:rə]) weir

Wehr[2] *f*: **sich zur Wehr setzen** → **wehren**

'**Wehrdienst** *m* (-[*e*]*s*; *no pl*) military ser-

vice

Wehrdienstverweigerer *m* (-*s*; -) conscientious objector

wehren ['ve:rən] *v/refl* (*ge*-, *h*) defend o.s. (**gegen** against), fight (*a. fig* **gegen et.** s.th.)

'**wehrlos** *adj* defenseless, *Br* defenceless; *fig* helpless

'**Wehrpflicht** *f* (-; *no pl*) compulsory military service

'**wehrpflichtig** *adj* liable to military service

'**Wehrpflichtige** *m* (-*n*; -*n*) draftee, *Br* conscript

'**wehtun** hurt (*j-m* s.o.; *fig* s.o.'s feelings); be aching; **sich** (**am Finger**) **wehtun** hurt o.s. (hurt one's finger)

Weib [vaip] *n* (-[*e*]*s*; -*er* ['vaibɐ]) *contp* woman; bitch

'**Weibchen** *n* (-*s*; -) ZO female

weibisch ['vaibɪʃ] *adj* effeminate, F sissy

'**weiblich** *adj* female; feminine (*a.* LING)

weich [vaiç] *adj* soft (*a. fig*), tender; GASTR done; soft-boiled (*egg*); **weich werden** soften; *fig* give in

Weiche ['vaiçə] *f* (-; -*n*) RAIL switch, points

weichen ['vaiçən] *v/i* (*irr*, *ge*-, *sein*) give way (*dat* to), yield (to); go (away)

'**weichlich** *adj* soft, effeminate, F sissy

'**Weichling** *m* (-*s*; -*e*) weakling, F softy, sissy

'**weichmachen** *v/t* (*sep*, -*ge*-, *h*): F *j-n* **weichmachen** soften s.o. up

'**Weichspüler** *m* (-*s*; -) fabric softener

'**Weichtier** *n* ZO mollusk, *Br* mollusc

Weide[1] ['vaidə] *f* (-; -*n*) BOT willow

'**Weide**[2] *f* (-; -*n*) AGR pasture; **auf die** (**der**) **Weide** to (at) pasture

'**Weideland** *n* pasture(land), range

'**weiden** *v/t and v/i* (*ge*-, *h*) graze, pasture; *fig* **sich weiden an** (*dat*) feast on; *contp* gloat over

weigern ['vaigɐn] *v/refl* (*ge*-, *h*) refuse

Weigerung ['vaigərʊŋ] *f* (-; -*en*) refusal

Weihe ['vaiə] *f* (-; -*n*) REL consecration; ordination

'**weihen** *v/t* (*ge*-, *h*) consecrate; **zum Priester weihen** ordain s.o. priest

Weiher ['vaiɐ] *m* (-*s*; -) pond

Weihnachten ['vainaxtən] *n* (-; -) Christmas, F Xmas

'**Weihnachtsabend** *m* Christmas Eve

Weihnachtsbaum *m* Christmas tree

Weihnachtseinkäufe *pl* Christmas shopping

Weihnachtsgeschenk *n* Christmas present

Weihnachtslied *n* (Christmas) carol

Weihnachtsmann *m* Father Christmas,

Santa Claus
Weihnachtsmarkt *m* Christmas fair
Weihnachtstag *m* Christmas Day; *zweiter Weihnachtstag* day after Christmas, *esp Br* Boxing Day
Weihnachtszeit *f* Christmas season
'Weihrauch *m* REL incense
Weihwasser *n* (*-s; no pl*) REL holy water
weil [vail] *cj* because; since, as
'Weilchen *n*: *ein Weilchen* a little while
Weile ['vailə] *f*: *e-e Weile* a while
Wein [vain] *m* (*-[e]s; -e*) wine; BOT vine
Wein(an)bau *m* (*-[e]s; no pl*) wine growing
Weinbeere *f* grape
Weinberg *m* vineyard
Weinbrand *m* brandy
weinen ['vainən] *v/i* (*ge-, h*) cry (*vor dat* with; *nach* for; *wegen* about, over); weep (*um* for, over; *über acc* at; *vor dat* for, with)
weinerlich ['vainɐlɪç] *adj* tearful; whining
'Weinfass *n* wine cask *or* barrel
Weinflasche *f* wine bottle
Weinhändler *m* wine merchant
Weinhauer *Austrian m* → *Winzer*
Weinkarte *f* wine list
Weinkeller *m* wine cellar *or* vault, vaults
Weinkellerei *f* winery
Weinkenner *m* wine connoisseur
Weinlese *f* vintage
Weinpresse *f* wine press
Weinprobe *f* wine tasting
Weinrebe *f* BOT vine
'weinrot *adj* claret
Weinstock *m* BOT vine
'Weintraube *f* → *Traube*
weise ['vaizə] *adj* wise
'Weise *f* (*-; -n*) way; MUS tune; *auf diese (die gleiche) Weise* this (the same) way; *auf m-e (s-e) Weise* my (his) way
weisen ['vaizən] *v/t and v/i* (*irr, ge-, h*) show; *j-n von der Schule weisen* expel s.o. from school; *weisen auf* (*acc*) point to *or* at; *von sich weisen* reject; repudiate
Weisheit ['vaishait] *f* (*-; -en*) wisdom; *mit s-r Weisheit am Ende sein* be at one's wit's end
'Weisheitszahn *m* wisdom tooth
weismachen ['vais-] F *v/t*: *j-m weismachen, dass* make s.o. believe that; *du kannst mir nichts weismachen* you can't fool me
weiß [vais] *adj* white; *weiß werden or machen* whiten
'Weißbrot *n* white bread
'Weiße *m*, *f* (*-n; -n*) white, white man (woman), *pl the* whites

'weißen *v/t* (*ge-, h*) whitewash
'Weißkohl *m*, **'Weißkraut** *n* BOT (green, *Br* white) cabbage
'weißlich *adj* whitish
'weißmachen *v/t* (*sep, -ge-, h*) → *weiß*
'Weißwein *m* white wine
Weisung ['vaizʊŋ] *f* (*-; -en*) instruction, directive
weit [vait] **1.** *adj* wide, *clothes*: *a.* big; long (*way, trip etc*); **2.** *adv* far, a long way (*a. time and fig*); *weit weg* far away (*von* from); *von weitem* from a distance; *weit und breit* far and wide; *bei weitem* by far; *bei weitem nicht so ...* not nearly as ...; *weit über* (*acc*) well over; *weit besser* far *or* much better; *zu weit gehen* go too far; *es weit bringen* go far; *wir haben es weit gebracht* we have come a long way; *weit blickend fig* farsighted; *weit reichend* far-reaching; *weit verbreitet* widespread
'weit'ab *adv* far away (*von* from)
'weit'aus *adv* (by) far, much
Weite ['vaitə] *f* (*-; -n*) width; vastness, expanse; *esp* SPORT distance
'weiten *v/t and v/refl* (*ge-, h*) widen
weiter ['vaitɐ] *adv* on, further; (*mach*) *weiter!* go on!; (*geh*) *weiter!* move on!; *und so weiter* and so on *or* forth, et cetera; *nichts weiter* nothing else
weiterarbeiten *v/i* (*sep, -ge-, h*) go on working
weiterbilden *v/refl* (*sep, -ge-, h*) improve one's knowledge; continue one's education *or* training
'Weiterbildung *f* (*-; no pl*) further education *or* training
weitere ['vaitərə] *adj* further, additional; *alles Weitere* the rest; *bis auf weiteres* until further notice; *ohne weiteres* easily; *Weiteres* more, (further) details
'weitergeben *v/t* (*irr, geben, sep, -ge-, h*) pass (*dat, an acc* to) (*a. fig*)
weitergehen *v/i* (*irr, gehen, sep, -ge-, sein*) move on; *fig* continue, go on
'weiter'hin *adv* further(more); *et. weiterhin tun* go on doing s.th., continue to do s.th.
'weiterkommen *v/i* (*irr, kommen, sep, -ge-, sein*) get on (*fig* in life)
weiterleben *v/i* (*sep, -ge-, h*) live on, *fig a.* survive
weitermachen *v/t and v/i* (*sep, -ge-, h*) go *or* carry on, continue
'Weiterverkauf *m* resale
'weitgehend 1. *adj* considerable; **2.** *adv* largely
weitläufig *adj* spacious; distant (*relative*)
weitsichtig *adj* MED farsighted (*a. fig*), *Br*

W

longsighted

'**Weitsprung** *m* broad (*Br* long) jump

'**Weitwinkelobjek,tiv** *n* PHOT wide-angle lens

Weizen ['vaitsən] *m* (-*s*; -) BOT wheat

welche ['vɛlçə], **welcher** ['vɛlçɐ], **welches** ['vɛlçəs] **1.** *interr pron* what, which; *welcher?* which one?; *welcher von beiden?* which of the two?; **2.** *rel pron* who, that; which, that; **3.** F *welche indef pron* some, any

welk [vɛlk] *adj* faded, withered; flabby

welken ['vɛlkən] *v/i* (*ge-, sein*) fade, wither

Wellblech ['vɛl-] *n* corrugated iron

Welle ['vɛlə] *f* (-; -*n*) wave (*a.* PHYS *and fig*); TECH shaft

'**wellen** *v/t and v/refl* (*ge-, h*) wave

'**Wellenlänge** *f* ELECTR wavelength

'**Wellensittich** [-zɪtɪç] *m* (-*s*; -*e*) ZO budgerigar, F budgie

wellig ['vɛlɪç] *adj* wavy

Welt [vɛlt] *f* (-; -*en*) world; *die ganze Welt* the whole world; *auf der ganzen Welt* all over *or* throughout the world; *das beste etc ... der Welt* the best *etc ...* in the world, the world's best *etc ...*; *zur Welt kommen* be born; *zur Welt bringen* give birth to

'**Weltall** *n* universe

'**weltberühmt** *adj* world-famous

Weltergewicht ['vɛltɐ-] *n* (-[*e*]*s*; *no pl*), '**Weltergewichtler** *m* (-*s*; -) SPORT welterweight

'**weltfremd** *adj* naive, unrealistic

'**Weltfriede(n)** *m* world peace

'**Weltgeschichte** *f* world history

'**weltklug** *adj* worldlywise

'**Weltkrieg** *m* world war; *der Zweite Weltkrieg* World War II

'**Weltkugel** *f* globe

'**weltlich** *adj* worldly

'**Weltlitera,tur** *f* world literature

Weltmacht *f* POL world power

Weltmarkt *m* ECON world market

Weltmeer *n* ocean

Weltmeister(in) world champion

Weltmeisterschaft *f* world championship; *esp soccer*: World Cup

Weltraum *m* (-[*e*]*s*; *no pl*) (outer) space

Weltreich *n* empire

Weltreise *f* world trip

Weltre,kord *m* world record

Weltruf *m* (*von Weltruf* of) worldwide reputation

Weltstadt *f* metropolis

Weltuntergang *m* end of the world

'**weltweit** *adj* worldwide

'**Weltwirtschaft** *f* world economy

'**Weltwirtschaftskrise** *f* worldwide economic crisis

'**Weltwunder** *n* wonder of the world .

Wende ['vɛndə] *f* (-; -*n*) turn (*a.* swimming); change

Wendekreis *m* ASTR, GEOGR tropic; MOT turning circle

Wendeltreppe ['vɛndəl-] *f* spiral staircase

'**wenden** *v/t and v/i* (*ge-, h*) *and v/refl* ([*irr,*] *ge-, h*) turn (*nach* to; *gegen* against); MOT turn (round); GASTR turn over; *sich an j-n um Hilfe wenden* turn to s.o. for help; *bitte wenden* please turn over, pto

'**Wendepunkt** *m* turning point

wendig ['vɛndɪç] *adj* MOT, MAR maneuverable, *Br* manoeuvrable; *fig* nimble

'**Wendung** *f* (-; -*en*) turn, *fig a.* change; expression, phrase

wenig ['veːnɪç] *indef pron and adv* little; *wenig(e) pl* few; *nur wenige* only few; only a few; (*in*) *weniger als* (in) less than; *am wenigsten* least of all; *er spricht wenig* he doesn't talk much; (*nur*) *ein* (*klein*) *wenig* (just) a little (bit)

'**wenigstens** *adv* at least

wenn [vɛn] *cj* when; if; *wenn ... nicht* if ... not, unless; *wenn auch* (al)though, even though; *wie or als wenn* as though, as if; *wenn ich nur ... wäre!* if only I were ...!; *wenn auch noch so ...* no matter how ...; *und wenn nun ...?* what if ...?

wer [veːɐ] **1.** *interr pron* who, which; *wer von euch?* which of you?; **2.** *rel pron* who; *wer auch* (*immer*) who(so)ever; **3.** F *indef pron* somebody, anybody

Werbeabteilung ['vɛrbə-] *f* publicity department

Werbeagen,tur *f* advertising agency

Werbefeldzug *m* advertising campaign

Werbefernsehen *n* commercial television

Werbefilm *m* promotion(al) film

Werbefunk *m* radio commercials

werben ['vɛrbən] (*irr, ge-, h*) **1.** *v/i* advertise (*für et.* s.th.), promote (s.th.), give s.th. *or* s.o. publicity; *esp* POL make propaganda (*für* for), canvass (for); *werben um* court (*a. fig*); **2.** *v/t* recruit; canvass, solicit

'**Werbesendung** *f*, '**Werbespot** [-ʃpɔt] *m* (-*s*; -*s*) (TV) commercial

'**Werbung** *f* (-; *no pl*) advertising, (sales) promotion; *a.* POL *etc* publicity, propaganda; recruitment; *Werbung machen für et.* advertise s.th.

Werdegang ['veːɐdə-] *m* career

werden ['veːɐdən] *v/i* (*irr, ge-, sein*) *and v/aux* become, get; turn, go; grow; turn out; *wir werden* we will (*or* shall), we are going to; *geliebt werden* be loved (*von* by); *was willst du werden?* what do you want to be?; *mir wird schlecht* I'm going to be sick; F *es wird schon wieder* (*werden*) it'll be all right

werfen ['vɛrfən] *v/i and v/t* (*irr, ge-, h*) throw (*a.* zo) ([*mit*] *et. nach* s.th. at); drop (*bombs*); cast (*shadow*)

Werft [vɛrft] *f* (-; *-en*) MAR shipyard, dockyard

Werk [vɛrk] *n* (-[e]s; *-e*) work, deed; TECH mechanism; ECON works, factory; *ans Werk gehen* set *or* go to work

Werkbank *f* (-; *-bänke*) TECH workbench

Werkmeister *m* TECH foreman

'**Werkstatt** *f* (-; *-stätten*) workshop; MOT garage

'**Werktag** *m* workday

'**werktags** *adv* on workdays

'**werktätig** *adj* working

'**Werkzeug** *n* tool (*a. fig*); *coll* tools; instrument

Werkzeugmacher *m* toolmaker

wert [veːrt] *adj* worth; *die Mühe* (*e-n Versuch*) *wert* worth the trouble (a try); *fig nichts wert* no good

Wert *m* (-[e]s; *-e*) value, *esp fig a.* worth; use; *pl* data, figures; *... im Wert(e) von 20 Dollar* 20 dollars' worth of ...; *großen Wert legen auf* (*acc*) set great store by

werten ['veːrtən] *v/t* (*ge-, h*) value; *a.* SPORT rate, judge

'**Wertgegenstand** *m* article of value

'**wertlos** *adj* worthless

'**Wertpa,piere** *pl* securities

'**Wertsachen** *pl* valuables

'**Wertung** *f* (-; *-en*) valuation; *a.* SPORT rating, judging; score, points

'**wertvoll** *adj* valuable

Wesen ['veːzən] *n* (-*s*; -) being, creature; *fig* essence; nature, character; *viel Wesens machen um* make a fuss about

'**wesentlich** *adj* essential; considerable; *im Wesentlichen* on the whole

weshalb [vɛs'halp] *interr adv* → *warum*

Wespe ['vɛspə] *f* (-; *-n*) zo wasp

Weste ['vɛstə] *f* (-; *-n*) vest, *Br* waistcoat

Westen ['vɛstən] *m* (-*s*; *no pl*) west; POL West

Western ['vɛstɐn] *m* (-*s*; -) western

'**westlich 1.** *adj* western; westerly; POL West(ern); **2.** *adv*: *westlich von* (to the) west of

'**Westwind** *m* west(erly) wind

Wettbewerb ['vɛtbəvɛrp] *m* (-[e]s; *-e*) competition (*a.* ECON), contest

'**Wettbü,ro** *n* betting office

Wette ['vɛtə] *f* (-; *-n*) bet; *e-e Wette abschließen* make a bet; *um die Wette laufen etc* race (*mit j-m* s.o.)

'**wetteifern** *v/i* (*ge-, h*) compete (*mit* with; *um* for)

'**wetten** *v/i and v/t* (*ge-, h*) bet; *mit j-m um 10 Dollar wetten* bet s.o. ten dollars; *wetten auf* (*acc*) bet on, back

Wetter ['vɛtɐ] *n* (-*s*; -) weather

'**Wetterbericht** *m* weather report

'**Wetterfahne** *f* weather vane

'**wetterfest** *adj* weatherproof

'**Wetterkarte** *f* weather chart

Wetterlage *f* weather situation

Wetterleuchten *n* sheet lightning

Wettervorhersage *f* weather forecast

Wetterwarte *f* weather station

'**Wettkampf** *m* competition, contest

Wettkämpfer(in) contestant, competitor

Wettlauf *m* race (*a. fig mit* against)

Wettläufer(in) runner

'**wettmachen** *v/t* (*sep, -ge-, h*) make up for

'**Wettrennen** *n* race

'**Wettrüsten** *n* (-*s*; *no pl*) arms race

'**Wettstreit** *m* contest, competition

wetzen ['vɛtsən] *v/t* (*ge-, h*) whet, sharpen

wich [vɪç] *pret of* **weichen**

wichtig ['vɪçtɪç] *adj* important

'**Wichtigkeit** *f* (-; *no pl*) importance

'**wickeln** *v/t* (*ge-, h*) change (*baby*); *wickeln in* (*acc*) wrap in; *wickeln um* wrap (a)round

Widder ['vɪdɐ] *m* (-*s*; -) zo ram; ASTR Aries; *er ist* (*ein*) *Widder* he's (an) Aries

wider ['viːdɐ] *prp* (*acc*) *wider Willen* against one's will; *wider Erwarten* contrary to expectations

'**Widerhaken** *m* barb

'**widerhallen** *v/i* (*sep, -ge-, h*) resound (*von* with)

wider'legen *v/t* (*no -ge-, h*) refute, disprove

'**widerlich** *adj* sickening, disgusting

'**widerrechtlich** *adj* illegal, unlawful

'**Widerruf** *m* JUR revocation; withdrawal

wider'rufen *v/t* (*irr, rufen, no -ge-, h*) revoke; withdraw

Widersacher ['viːdɐzaxɐ] *m* (-*s*; -) adversary, rival

'**Widerschein** *m* reflection

wider'setzen *v/refl* (*no -ge-, h*) (*dat*) oppose, resist

'**widersinnig** *adj* absurd

widerspenstig ['viːdɐʃpɛnstɪç] *adj* unruly, stubborn

'**widerspiegeln** *v/t* (*sep, -ge-, h*) reflect (*a. fig*); *sich widerspiegeln in* (*dat*) be reflected in

wider'sprechen *v/i* (*irr, sprechen, no -ge-, h*) (*dat*) contradict

W

'**Widerspruch** *m* contradiction
widersprüchlich ['vi:dɐʃprYçlıç] *adj* contradictory
'**widerspruchslos** *adv* without contradiction
'**Widerstand** *m* resistance (*a.* ELECTR), opposition; **Widerstand leisten** offer resistance (*dat* to)
'**widerstandsfähig** *adj* resistant (*a.* TECH)
wider'stehen *v/i* (*irr,* **stehen**, *no -ge-, h*) (*dat*) resist
wider'streben *v/i* (*no -ge-, h*) **es widerstrebt mir, dies zu tun** I hate doing *or* to do that
widerstrebend *adv* reluctantly
widerwärtig ['vi:dɐvɛrtıç] *adj* disgusting
'**Widerwille** *m* aversion (**gegen** to), dislike (of, for); disgust (at)
'**widerwillig** *adj* reluctant, unwilling
widmen ['vıtmən] *v/t* (*ge-, h*) dedicate
'**Widmung** *f* (-; *-en*) dedication
wie [vi:] **1.** *interr adv* how; **wie geht es Gordon?** how is Gordon?; **wie ist er?** what's he like?; **wie ist das Wetter?** what's the weather like?; **wie heißen Sie?** what's your name?; **wie nennt man ...?** what do you call ...?; **wie wäre (ist, steht) es mit ...?** what *or* how about ...?; **wie viele ...?** how many ...?; **2.** *cj* like; as; **wie neu (verrückt)** like new (mad); **doppelt so ... wie** twice as ... as; **wie (zum Beispiel)** such as, like; **wie üblich** as usual; **wie er sagte** as he said; **ich zeige (sage) dir, wie (...)** I'll show (tell) you how (...)
wieder ['vi:dɐ] *adv* again; *in cpds often* re...; *immer wieder* again and again; **wieder aufbauen** reconstruct; **wieder aufnehmen** resume; **wieder beleben** MED resuscitate, revive (*a. fig*); **wieder erkennen** recognize (**an** *dat* by); **wieder finden** find (what one has lost); *fig* regain; **wieder gutmachen** make up for; **wieder herstellen** restore; **wieder sehen** see *or* meet again; **wieder verwendbar** reusable; **wieder verwerten** TECH recycle
Wieder'aufbau *m* (-[*e*]*s; no pl*) reconstruction, rebuilding
Wieder'aufbereitung *f* TECH recycling, reprocessing (*a.* NUCL)
Wieder'aufbereitungsanlage *f* TECH reprocessing plant
Wieder'aufleben *n* (-*s; no pl*) revival
Wieder'aufnahme *f* (-; *no pl*) resumption
'**wiederbekommen** *v/t* (*irr,* **kommen**, *sep, no -ge-, h*) get back
'**Wiederbelebung** *f* (-; *-en*) MED resuscitation

Wiederbelebungsversuch *m* MED attempt at resuscitation
'**wiederbringen** *v/t* (*irr,* **bringen**, *sep, -ge-, h*) bring back; return
Wieder'einführung *f* reintroduction
'**Wiederentdeckung** *f* rediscovery
'**Wiedergabe** *f* TECH reproduction, playback
'**wiedergeben** *v/t* (*irr,* **geben**, *sep, -ge-, h*) give back, return; *fig* describe; TECH play back, reproduce
Wieder'gutmachung *f* (-; *-en*) reparation
'**wiederholen**[1] *v/t* (*sep, -ge-, h*) (go and) get *s.o. or s.th.* back
wieder'holen[2] *v/t* (*no -ge-, h*) repeat; PED revise, review; THEA replay; **sich wiederholen** repeat o.s. (*a. fig*)
wieder'holt *adv* repeatedly, several times
Wieder'holung *f* (-; *-en*) repetition; PED review; TV *etc* rerun; SPORT replay
Wiederkehr ['vi:dɐke:ɐ] *f* (-; *no pl*) return; recurrence
'**wiederkehren** *v/i* (*sep, -ge-, sein*) return; recur
'**wiederkommen** *v/i* (*irr,* **kommen**, *sep, -ge-, sein*) come back, return
'**Wiedersehen** *n* (-*s; -*) seeing *s.o.* again; reunion; **auf Wiedersehen!** goodbye!
wiederum ['vi:dərʊm] *adv* again; on the other hand
'**Wiedervereinigung** *f* reunion, *esp* POL *a.* reunification
Wiederverkauf *m* resale
Wiederverwendung *f* reuse
Wiederverwertung *f* (-; *-en*) TECH recycling
Wiederwahl *f* POL re-election
Wiege ['vi:gə] *f* (-; *-n*) cradle
wiegen[1] ['vi:gən] *v/t and v/i* (*irr, ge-, h*) weigh
'**wiegen**[2] *v/t* (*ge-, h*) rock (**in den Schlaf** to sleep)
'**Wiegenlied** *n* lullaby
wiehern ['vi:ɐn] *v/i* (*ge-, h*) ZO neigh
wies [vi:s] *pret of* **weisen**
Wiese ['vi:zə] *f* (-; *-n*) meadow
Wiesel ['vi:zəl] *n* (-*s; -*) ZO weasel
wieso [vi'zo:] *interr adv* → **warum**
wievielt [vi'fi:lt] *adj:* **zum wievielten Male?** how many times?
wild [vılt] *adj* wild (*a. fig*) (F **auf** *acc* about); violent; **wilder Streik** wildcat strike
Wild *n* (-[*e*]*s; no pl*) HUNT game; GASTR *mst* venison
Wildbach *m* torrent
Wilde ['vıldə] *m, f* (-*n; -n*) savage; F **wie ein Wilder** like mad
Wilderer ['vıldərɐ] *m* (-*s; -*) poacher

'**wildern** v/i (ge-, h) poach
'**Wildhüter** m gamekeeper
'**Wildkatze** f ZO wild cat
'**Wildleder** n suede
'**Wildnis** f (-; -se) wilderness
'**Wildpark** m, **Wildreser,vat** n game park or reserve
Wildschwein n ZO wild boar
Wille ['vɪlə] m (-ns; -n) will; intention; **s-n Willen durchsetzen** have or get one's own way; **j-m s-n Willen lassen** let s.o. have his (own) way
'**willenlos** adj weak(-willed)
'**Willenskraft** f (-; no pl) willpower; **durch Willenskraft erzwingen** will
'**willensstark** adj strong-willed
willig ['vɪlɪç] adj willing
will'kommen adj welcome (a. **willkommen heißen**) (**in** dat to)
willkürlich ['vɪlkyːɐ̯lɪç] adj arbitrary; random
wimmeln ['vɪməln] v/i (ge-, h) **wimmeln von** be teeming with
wimmern ['vɪmɐn] v/i (ge-, h) whimper
Wimpel ['vɪmpəl] m (-s; -) pennant
Wimper ['vɪmpɐ] f (-; -n) eyelash; **ohne mit der Wimper zu zucken** without turning a hair
'**Wimperntusche** f mascara
Wind [vɪnt] m (-[e]s; -e ['vɪndə]) wind
Winde ['vɪndə] f (-; -n) winch, windlass, hoist
Windel ['vɪndəl] f (-; -n) diaper, Br nappy
winden ['vɪndən] v/t (irr, ge-, h) wind, TECH a. hoist; **sich winden** wind (one's way); writhe (with pain etc)
'**Windhund** m ZO greyhound
windig ['vɪndɪç] adj windy
'**Windmühle** f windmill
Windpocken pl MED chickenpox
Windrichtung f direction of the wind
Windschutzscheibe f MOT windshield, Br windscreen
Windstärke f wind force
'**windstill** adj, '**Windstille** f calm
'**Windstoß** m gust
'**Windsurfen** n windsurfing
'**Windung** f (-; -en) bend, turn (a. TECH)
Wink [vɪŋk] m (-[e]s; -e) sign; fig hint
Winkel ['vɪŋkəl] m (-s; -) corner; MATH angle
'**winkelig** adj angular; crooked
winken ['vɪŋkən] v/i (ge-, h) wave (one's hand etc), signal; beckon
winseln ['vɪnzəln] v/i (ge-, h) whimper, whine
Winter ['vɪntɐ] m (-s; -) winter
'**winterlich** adj wintry
'**Winterreifen** m MOT snow tire (Br tyre)

Winterschlaf m ZO hibernation
Winterspiele pl: **Olympische Winterspiele** SPORT Winter Olympics
Wintersport m winter sports
Winzer ['vɪntsɐ] m (-s; -) winegrower
winzig ['vɪntsɪç] adj tiny, diminutive
Wipfel ['vɪpfəl] m (-s; -) (tree)top
Wippe ['vɪpə] f (-; -n), '**wippen** v/i (ge-, h) seesaw
wir [viːɐ̯] pers pron we; **wir drei** the three of us; F **wir sind's!** it's us!
Wirbel ['vɪrbəl] m (-s; -) whirl (a. fig); ANAT vertebra
'**wirbeln** v/i (ge-, sein) whirl
'**Wirbelsäule** f ANAT spinal column, spine
Wirbelsturm m cyclone, tornado
Wirbeltier n vertebrate
Wirbelwind m whirlwind
wirken ['vɪrkən] (ge-, h) **1.** v/i work; be effective (**gegen** against); look; **anregend etc wirken** have a stimulating etc effect (**auf** acc [up]on); **wirken als** act as; **2.** v/t weave; fig work (miracles etc)
wirklich ['vɪrklɪç] adj real, actual; true, genuine
'**Wirklichkeit** f (-; -en) reality; **in Wirklichkeit** in reality, actually
wirksam ['vɪrkzaːm] adj effective
'**Wirkung** f (-; -en) effect
'**wirkungslos** adj ineffective
'**wirkungsvoll** adj effective
wirr [vɪr] adj confused, mixed-up; hair: tousled
Wirren ['vɪrən] pl disorder, confusion
Wirrwarr ['vɪrvar] m (-s; no pl) confusion, mess, welter
Wirt [vɪrt] m (-[e]s; -e) landlord
'**Wirtin** f (-; -nen) landlady
'**Wirtschaft** f (-; -en) ECON, POL economy; business; → **Gastwirtschaft**
'**wirtschaften** v/i (ge-, h) keep house; manage one's money or affairs or business; economize; **gut (schlecht) wirtschaften** be a good (bad) manager
'**Wirtschafterin** f (-; -nen) housekeeper
'**wirtschaftlich** adj economic; economical
'**Wirtschafts...** ECON in cpds ...gemeinschaft, ...gipfel, ...krise, ...system, ...wunder etc: economic ...
'**Wirtshaus** n → **Gastwirtschaft**
wischen ['vɪʃən] v/t (ge-, h) wipe; **Staub wischen** dust
wispern ['vɪspɐn] v/t and v/i (ge-, h) whisper
wissbegierig ['vɪs-] adj curious
wissen ['vɪsən] v/t and v/i (irr, ge-, h) know; **ich möchte wissen** I'd like to know, I wonder; **soviel ich weiß** as far as I know; **weißt du** you know; **weißt**

W

du noch? (do you) remember?; **woher weißt du das?** how do you know?; **man kann nie wissen** you never know; **ich will davon (von ihm) nichts wissen** I don't want anything to do with it (him)
'**Wissen** n (-s; no pl) knowledge; know--how; **m-s Wissens** as far as I know
'**Wissenschaft** f (-; -en) science
'**Wissenschaftler** m (-s; -), '**Wissenschaftlerin** f (-; -nen) scientist
'**wissenschaftlich** adj scientific
'**wissenswert** adj worth knowing; **Wissenswertes** useful facts; **alles Wissenswerte (über** acc) all you need to know (about)
wittern ['vɪtɐn] v/t (ge-, h) scent, smell (both a. fig)
Witwe ['vɪtvə] f (-; -n) widow
Witwer ['vɪtvɐ] m (-s; -) widower
Witz [vɪts] m (-es; -e) joke; **Witze reißen** crack jokes
witzig ['vɪtsɪç] adj funny; witty
wo [voː] adv where; **wo ... doch** when, although
wob [voːp] pret of **weben**
wobei [vo'bai] adv: **wobei bist du?** what are you at?; **wobei mir einfällt** which reminds me
Woche ['vɔxə] f (-; -n) week
'**Wochen...** in cpds ...lohn, ...markt, ...zeitung etc: weekly ...
Wochenende n weekend; **am Wochenende** on (Br at) the weekend
'**wochenlang 1.** adj: **wochenlanges Warten** (many) weeks of waiting; **2.** adv for weeks
'**Wochenschau** f film: newsreel
'**Wochentag** m weekday
wöchentlich ['vœçəntlɪç] **1.** adj weekly; **2.** adv weekly, every week; **einmal wöchentlich** once a week
wodurch [vo'dʊrç] adv how; through which
wofür [vo'fyːɐ] adv for which; **wofür?** what (...) for?
wog [voːk] pret of **wiegen**[1] and **wägen**
Woge ['voːgə] f (-; -n) wave, esp fig a. surge; breaker
'**wogen** v/i (ge-, h) surge, heave (both a. fig)
woher [vo'heːɐ] adv where ... from; **woher weißt du (das)?** how do you know?
wohin [vo'hɪn] adv where (... to)
wohl [voːl] adv and cj well; probably, I suppose; **sich wohl fühlen** → **wohlfühlen**; **wohl oder übel** willy-nilly, whether you etc like it or not; **wohl kaum** hardly
Wohl n (-[e]s; no pl) well-being; **auf j-s Wohl trinken** drink to s.o.('s health);

zum Wohl! to your health!; F cheers!
'**wohlbehalten** adv safely
'**Wohlfahrtsstaat** m welfare state
'**wohlgemerkt** adv mind you
wohlgenährt adj well-fed
wohlgesinnt adj: **j-m wohlgesinnt sein** be well-disposed towards s.o.
wohlhabend adj well-off, well-to-do
'**wohlfühlen** v/refl (sep, -ge-, h): **sich wohlfühlen** feel well, be well; feel good; feel at home (**bei** with); **ich fühle mich nicht wohl** I don't feel well
wohlig ['voːlɪç] adj snug, cozy, Br cosy
'**Wohlstand** m (-[e]s; no pl) prosperity, affluence
Wohlstandsgesellschaft f affluent society
'**Wohltat** f (-; no pl) pleasure; relief; blessing
'**Wohltäter(in)** benefactor (benefactress)
'**wohltätig** adj charitable; **für wohltätige Zwecke** for charity
'**Wohltätigkeits...** in cpds ...ball, ...konzert etc: charity ...
'**wohltun** v/i (irr, **tun**, sep, -ge-, h): **j-m wohltun** do s.o. good
'**wohlverdient** adj well-deserved
'**wohlwollend** adj benevolent
wohnen ['voːnən] v/i (ge-, h) live (**in** dat in; **bei j-m** with s.o.); stay (**in** dat at; **bei** with)
'**Wohngebiet** n residential area
'**Wohngemeinschaft** f: (**mit j-m) in e-r Wohngemeinschaft leben** share an apartment (Br a flat) or a house (with s.o.)
wohnlich ['voːnlɪç] adj comfortable, snug, cozy, Br cosy
'**Wohnmo,bil** n (-s; -e) camper, motor home (Br caravan)
'**Wohnsiedlung** f housing development (Br estate)
Wohnsitz m residence; **ohne festen Wohnsitz** of no fixed abode
'**Wohnung** f (-; -en) apartment, Br flat; **m-e etc Wohnung** my etc place
'**Wohnungsamt** n housing office
Wohnungsbau m (-[e]s; no pl) house building
Wohnungsnot f housing shortage
'**Wohnwagen** m trailer, Br caravan; mobile home
'**Wohnzimmer** n sitting or living room
wölben ['vœlbən] v/refl (ge-, h), '**Wölbung** f (-; -en) vault, arch
Wolf [vɔlf] m (-[e]s; **Wölfe** ['vœlfə]) zo wolf
Wolke ['vɔlkə] f (-; -n) cloud
'**Wolkenbruch** m cloudburst

'**Wolkenkratzer** *m* (-*s*; -) skyscraper

'**wolkenlos** *adj* cloudless

wolkig ['vɔlkɪç] *adj* cloudy, clouded

Woll... [vɔl-] *in cpds* ...*schal*, ...*socken etc*: wool(l)en ...

Wolldecke *f* blanket

Wolle ['vɔlə] *f* (-; -*n*) wool

wollen ['vɔlən] *v/t and v/i* (*ge*-, *h*) and *v/aux* (*no* -*ge*-, *h*) want (to); *lieber wollen* prefer; *wollen wir* (*gehen etc*)? shall we (go *etc*)?; *wollen Sie bitte* ... will *or* would you please ...; *wie* (*was, wann*) *du willst* as (whatever, whenever) you like; *sie will, dass ich komme* she wants me to come; *ich wollte, ich wäre* (*hätte*) ... I wish I were (had) ...

womit [vo'mɪt] *adv* with which; *womit?* what ... with?

Wonne ['vɔnə] *f* (-; -*n*) joy, delight

woran [vo'ran] *adv*: *woran denkst du?* what are you thinking of?; *woran liegt es, dass ...?* how is it that ...?; *woran sieht man, welche* (*ob*) *...?* how can you tell which (if) ...?

worauf [vo'rauf] *adv* after which; on which; *worauf?* what ... on?; *worauf wartest du?* what are you waiting for?

woraus [vo'raus] *adv* from which; *woraus ist es?* what's it made of?

worin [vo'rɪn] *adv* in which; *worin?* where?

Wort [vɔrt] *n* (-[*e*]*s*; -*e*, *Wörter* ['vœrtɐ]) word; *mit anderen Worten* in other words; *sein Wort geben* (*halten, brechen*) give (keep, break) one's word; *j-n beim Wort nehmen* take s.o. at his word; *ein gutes Wort einlegen für* put in a good word for; *j-m ins Wort fallen* cut s.o. short

'**Wortart** *f* LING part of speech

Wörterbuch ['vœrtɐ-] *n* dictionary

Wörterverzeichnis *n* vocabulary, list of words

'**Wortführer** *m* spokesman

'**Wortführerin** *f* spokeswoman

'**wortkarg** *adj* taciturn

wörtlich ['vœrtlɪç] *adj* literal; *wörtliche Rede* LING direct speech

'**Wortschatz** *m* vocabulary

Wortspiel *n* pun

Wortstellung *f* LING word order

worüber [vo'ry:bɐ] *adv* about which; *worüber lachen Sie?* what are you laughing at *or* about?

worum [vo'rʊm] *adv* about which; *worum handelt es sich?* what is it about?

worunter [vo'rʊntɐ] *adv* among which; *worunter?* what ... under?

wovon [vo'fɔn] *adv* about which; *wovon*

redest du? what are you talking about?

wovor [vo'fo:ɐ] *adv* of which; *wovor hast du Angst?* what are you afraid of?

wozu [vo'tsu:] *adv*: *wozu er mir rät* what he advised me to do; *wozu?* what (...) for?; why?

Wrack [vrak] *n* (-[*e*]*s*; -*s*) MAR wreck (*a. fig*)

wrang [vraŋ] *pret of* **wringen**

wringen ['vrɪŋən] *v/t* (*irr, ge*-, *h*) wring

Wucher ['vu:xɐ] *m* (-*s*; *no pl*) usury

Wucherer ['vu:xəɐ] *m* (-*s*; -) usurer

'**wuchern** *v/i* (*ge*-, *h*) grow (*fig* be) rampant

Wucherung ['vu:xərʊŋ] *f* (-; -*en*) MED growth

Wuchs [vu:ks] *m* (-*es*; *no pl*) growth; build

wuchs [vu:ks] *pret of* **wachsen**[1]

Wucht [vʊxt] *f* (-; *no pl*) force; impact

wuchtig ['vʊxtɪç] *adj* massive; powerful

wühlen ['vy:lən] *v/i* (*ge*-, *h*) dig; ZO root; rummage (*in dat* in, through)

Wulst [vʊlst] *m* (-*es*; *Wülste* ['vʏlstə)], *f* (-; *Wülste*) bulge; roll (*of fat*)

wulstig ['vʊlstɪç] *adj* bulging; thick

wund [vʊnt] *adj* MED sore; *wunde Stelle* MED sore; *wunder Punkt* fig sore point

Wunde ['vʊndə] *f* (-; -*n*) MED wound

Wunder ['vʊndɐ] *n* (-*s*; -) miracle, fig *a*. wonder; *Wunder wirken* work wonders; (*es ist*) *kein Wunder, dass du müde bist* no wonder you are tired

'**wunderbar** *adj* wonderful, marvel(l)ous

'**Wunderkind** *n* infant prodigy

'**wunderlich** *adj* funny, odd; senile

'**wundern** *v/refl* (*ge*-, *h*) be surprised *or* astonished (*über acc* at)

'**wundervoll** *adj* wonderful

'**Wundstarrkrampf** *m* (-*es*; *no pl*) MED tetanus

Wunsch [vʊnʃ] *m* (-[*e*]*s*; *Wünsche* ['vʏnʃə]) wish; request; *auf j-s Wunsch* at s.o.'s request; *auf eigenen Wunsch* at one's own request; (*je*) *nach Wunsch* as desired

wünschen ['vʏnʃən] *v/t* (*ge*-, *h*) wish; *sich et.* (*zu Weihnachten etc*) *wünschen* want s.th. (for Christmas *etc*); *das habe ich mir* (*schon immer*) *gewünscht* that's what I (always) wanted; *alles, was man sich nur wünschen kann* everything one could wish for; *ich wünschte, ich wäre* (*hätte*) ... I wish I were (had) ...

'**wünschenswert** *adj* desirable

wurde ['vʊrdə] *pret of* **werden**

Würde ['vʏrdə] *f* (-; -*n*) dignity

'**würdelos** *adj* undignified

'**Würdenträger** *m* dignitary

W

'**würdevoll** *adj* dignified
würdig ['vʏrdɪç] *adj* worthy (*gen* of); dignified
würdigen ['vʏrdɪgən] *v/t* (*ge-, h*) appreciate; *j-n keines Blickes würdigen* ignore s.o. completely
'**Würdigung** *f* (-; -*en*) appreciation
Wurf [vʊrf] *m* (-[*e*]*s*; *Würfe* ['vʏrfə]) throw; zo litter
Würfel ['vʏrfəl] *m* (-*s*; -) cube (*a.* MATH); dice
'**würfeln** *v/i* (*ge-, h*) throw dice (*um* for); play dice; GASTR dice; *e-e Sechs würfeln* throw a six
'**Würfelzucker** *m* lump sugar
'**Wurfgeschoss** *n* missile
würgen ['vʏrgən] *v/i and v/t* (*ge-, h*) choke; throttle *s.o.*
Wurm [vʊrm] *m* (-[*e*]*s*; *Würmer* ['vʏrmɐ]) zo worm
wurmen ['vʊrmən] F *v/t* (*ge-, h*) gall *s.o.*
'**wurmstichig** ['vʊrmʃtɪçɪç] *adj* worm-eaten
Wurst [vʊrst] *f* (-; *Würste* ['vʏrstə]) sausage

Würstchen ['vʏrstçən] *n* (-*s*; -) small sausage, frankfurter, wiener; hot dog
Würze [vʏrtsə] *f* (-; -*n*) spice (*a. fig*)
Wurzel ['vʊrtsəl] *f* (-; -*n*) root (*a.* MATH); *Wurzeln schlagen* take root (*a. fig*)
'**wurzeln** *v/i* (*ge-, h*) *wurzeln in* (*dat*) be rooted in (*a. fig*)
'**würzen** *v/t* (*ge-, h*) spice, season, flavo(u)r
würzig ['vʏrtsɪç] *adj* spicy, well-seasoned
wusch [vuːʃ] *pret of* **waschen**
wusste ['vʊstə] *pret of* **wissen**
Wust [vuːst] F *m* (-[*e*]*s*; *no pl*) tangled mass
wüst [vyːst] *adj* waste; confused; wild, dissolute
Wüste ['vyːstə] *f* (-; -*n*) desert
Wut [vuːt] *f* (-; *no pl*) rage, fury; *e-e Wut haben* be furious (*auf acc* with)
'**Wutanfall** *m* fit of rage
wüten ['vyːtən] *v/i* (*ge-, h*) rage (*a. fig*)
wütend *adj* furious (*auf acc* with; *über acc* at), F mad (at)
'**wutschnaubend** *adj* fuming

X, Y

X-Beine ['ɪksbainə] *pl* knock-knees; *sie hat X-Beine* she's knock-kneed
x-beinig ['ɪksbainɪç] *adj* knock-kneed
x-be'liebig *adj*: *jede(r, -s) x-Beliebige ...* any ... you like, F any old ...
'**x-mal** F *adv* umpteen times

x-te ['ɪkstə] *adj*: *zum x-ten Male* for the umpteenth time
Xylophon [ksylo'foːn] *n* (-*s*; -*e*) MUS xylophone
Yacht [jaxt] *f* (-; -*en*) MAR yacht
Yoga ['joːga] *m, n* (-[*s*]; *no pl*) yoga

Z

Zacke ['tsakə] *f* (-; -*n*), '**Zacken** *m* (-*s*; -) (sharp) point; tooth
zackig ['tsakɪç] *adj* serrated; jagged; *fig* smart
zaghaft ['tsaːkhaft] *adj* timid
zäh [tsɛː] *adj* tough (*a. fig*)
zähflüssig *adj* thick, viscous; *fig* slow-moving (*traffic*)

Zähigkeit ['tsɛːɪçkait] *f* (-; *no pl*) toughness, *fig a.* stamina
Zahl [tsaːl] *f* (-; -*en*) number; figure
'**zahlbar** *adj* payable (*an acc* to; *bei* at)
zählbar ['tsɛːlbaːɐ] *adj* countable
zahlen ['tsaːlən] *v/i and v/t* (*ge-, h*) pay; *zahlen, bitte!* the check (*Br* bill), please!
zählen ['tsɛːlən] *v/t and v/i* (*ge-, h*) count

(*bis* up to; *fig* **auf** *acc* on); **zählen zu** rank with *the best etc*
'**zahlenmäßig 1.** *adj* numerical; **2.** *adv*: *j-m* **zahlenmäßig überlegen sein** outnumber s.o.
Zähler ['tsɛːlɐ] *m* (*-s*; *-*) counter (*a.* TECH); MATH numerator; ELECTR *etc* meter
'**Zahlkarte** *f post* deposit (*Br* paying-in) slip
'**zahllos** *adj* countless
'**Zahlmeister** *m* MIL paymaster; MAR purser
'**zahlreich 1.** *adj* numerous; **2.** *adv* in great number
'**Zahltag** *m* payday
'**Zahlung** *f* (*-*; *-en*) payment
'**Zählung** *f* (*-*; *-en*) count; POL census
'**Zahlungsaufforderung** *f* request for payment
Zahlungsbedingungen *pl* terms of payment
Zahlungsbefehl *m* order to pay
'**zahlungsfähig** *adj* solvent
'**Zahlungsfrist** *f* term of payment
Zahlungsmittel *n* currency; **gesetzliches Zahlungsmittel** legal tender
Zahlungsschwierigkeiten *pl* financial difficulties
Zahlungster͵min *m* date of payment
'**zahlungsunfähig** *adj* insolvent
'**Zählwerk** *n* TECH counter
'**Zahlwort** *n* LING numeral
zahm [tsaːm] *adj* tame (*a. fig*)
zähmen ['tsɛːmən] *v/t* (*ge-*, *h*) tame (*a. fig*)
'**Zähmung** *f* (*-*; *no pl*) taming
Zahn [tsaːn] *m* (*-[e]s*; *Zähne* ['tsɛːnə]) tooth, TECH *a.* cog
Zahnarzt *m*, **Zahnärztin** *f* dentist, dental surgeon
Zahnbürste *f* toothbrush
Zahncreme *f* toothpaste
zahnen ['tsaːnən] *v/i* (*ge-*, *h*) cut one's teeth, teethe
'**Zahnfleisch** *n* gums
'**zahnlos** *adj* toothless
'**Zahnlücke** *f* gap between the teeth
Zahnmedi͵zin *f* dentistry
Zahnpasta, **Zahnpaste** *f* toothpaste
Zahnradbahn *f* rack railroad
Zahnschmerzen *pl* toothache
Zahnspange *f* MED brace
Zahnstein *m* tartar
Zahnstocher *m* (*-s*; *-*) toothpick
Zange ['tsaŋə] *f* (*-*; *-n*) TECH pliers; pincers; tongs; MED forceps; ZO pincer
zanken ['tsaŋkən] *v/refl* (*ge-*, *h*) quarrel (*wegen* about; *um* over), fight, argue (about; over)

zänkisch ['tsɛŋkɪʃ] *adj* quarrelsome
Zäpfchen ['tsɛpfçən] *n* (*-s*; *-*) ANAT uvula; PHARM suppository
zapfen ['tsapfən] *v/t* (*ge-*, *h*) tap
'**Zapfen** *m* (*-s*; *-*) faucet, *Br* tap; TECH peg, pin; bung; tenon; pivot; BOT cone
'**Zapfenstreich** *m* MIL tattoo, taps
'**Zapfhahn** *m* faucet, *Br* tap; MOT nozzle
Zapfsäule *f* MOT gasoline (*Br* petrol) pump
zappelig ['tsapəlɪç] *adj* fidgety
zappeln ['tsapəln] *v/i* (*ge-*, *h*) fidget, wriggle
zappen ['zɛpən] F *v/i* (*ge-*, *h*) TV zap
zart [tsaːɐt] *adj* tender; gentle; **zart fühlend** sensitive
'**Zartgefühl** *n* (*-[e]s*; *no pl*) delicacy (of feeling), sensitivity, tact
zärtlich ['tsɛːɐtlɪç] *adj* tender, affectionate (*zu* with)
'**Zärtlichkeit** *f* (*-*; *-en*) a) (*no pl*) tenderness, affection, b) caress
Zauber ['tsaubɐ] *m* (*-s*; *-*) magic, spell, charm (*all a. fig*), *fig* enchantment
Zauberei [tsaubə'rai] *f* (*-*; *-en*) magic, witchcraft
Zauberer ['tsaubərɐ] *m* (*-s*; *-*) magician, sorcerer, wizard (*a. fig*)
'**zauberhaft** *fig adj* enchanting, charming
Zauberin ['tsaubərɪn] *f* (*-*; *-nen*) sorceress
'**Zauberkraft** *f* magic power
Zauberkünstler *m* magician, conjurer
Zauberkunststück *n* conjuring trick
'**zaubern** (*ge-*, *h*) **1.** *v/i* practise magic; do conjuring tricks; **2.** *v/t* conjure (up)
'**Zauberspruch** *m* spell
zaudern ['tsaudɐn] *v/i* (*ge-*, *h*) hesitate
Zaum [tsaum] *m* (*-[e]s*; *Zäume* ['tsɔymə]) bridle; **im Zaum halten** control (*sich* o.s.), keep in check
zäumen ['tsɔymən] *v/t* (*ge-*, *h*) bridle
'**Zaumzeug** *n* (*-[e]s*; *-e*) bridle
Zaun [tsaun] *m* (*-[e]s*; *Zäune* ['tsɔynə]) fence
Zaungast *m* onlooker
Zaunpfahl *m* pale
z. B. ABBR *of* **zum Beispiel** e.g., for example, for instance
Zebra ['tseːbra] *n* (*-s*; *-s*) ZO zebra
'**Zebrastreifen** *m* MOT zebra crossing
Zeche ['tsɛçə] *f* (*-*; *-n*) check, *Br* bill; (coal) mine, pit; **die Zeche bezahlen müssen** F have to foot the bill
Zeh [tseː] *m* (*-s*; *-en*), **Zehe** ['tseːə] *f* (*-*; *-n*) ANAT toe; **große** (**kleine**) **Zeh** big (little) toe
'**Zehennagel** *m* ANAT toenail
'**Zehenspitze** *f* tip of the toe; **auf Zehenspitzen gehen** (walk on) tiptoe

Z

zehn

zehn [tse:n] *adj* ten
'zehnfach *adj* tenfold
'zehnjährig [-jɛ:rɪç] *adj* ten-year-old (*boy etc*); ten-year *anniversary etc*; *absence etc* of ten years
Zehnkampf *m* SPORT decathlon
'zehnmal *adv* ten times
'zehnte *adj* tenth
'Zehntel *n* (-s; -) tenth
'zehntens *adv* tenthly
Zeichen ['tsaiçən] *n* (-s; -) sign; mark; signal; *zum Zeichen gen* as a token of
Zeichenblock *m* sketch pad
Zeichenbrett *n* drawing board
Zeichendreieck *n* MATH set square
Zeichenfolge *f* EDP string
Zeichenlehrer(in) art teacher
Zeichensetzung *f* (-; *no pl*) LING punctuation
Zeichensprache *f* sign language
Zeichentrickfilm *m* (animated) cartoon
zeichnen ['tsaiçnən] *v/i* and *v/t* (*ge-, h*) draw; mark (*a. fig*); sign; *fig* leave its mark on *s.o.*
'Zeichnen *n* (-s; *no pl*) drawing; PED art
'Zeichner ['tsaiçnɐ] *m* (-s; -) *mst* graphic artist; draftsman, *Br* draughtsman
'Zeichnung *f* (-; -en) drawing; diagram; ZO marking
Zeigefinger ['tsaigə-] *m* ANAT forefinger, index finger
zeigen ['tsaigən] (*ge-, h*) **1.** *v/t* show (*a. sich zeigen*); **2.** *v/i*: *zeigen nach* point to; (*mit dem Finger*) *zeigen auf* (*acc*) point (one's finger) at
Zeiger ['tsaigɐ] *m* (-s; -) hand; TECH pointer, needle
'Zeigestock *m* pointer
Zeile ['tsailə] *f* (-; -n) line (*a.* TV); *j-m ein paar Zeilen schreiben* drop s.o. a line
Zeit [tsait] *f* (-; -en) time; age, era; LING tense; *vor einiger Zeit* some time ago, a while ago; *in letzter Zeit* lately, recently; *in der* (*or zur*) *Zeit gen* in the days of; *... aller Zeiten ...* of all time; *die Zeit ist um* time's up; *e-e Zeit lang* for some time, for a while; *sich Zeit lassen* take one's time; *es wird Zeit, dass ...* it's time to *inf*; *das waren noch Zeiten* those were the days; *Zeit raubend → zeitraubend*; → *zurzeit*
'Zeitabschnitt *m* period (of time)
Zeitalter *n* age
Zeitbombe *f* time bomb (*a. fig*)
Zeitdruck *m*: *unter Zeitdruck stehen* be pressed for time
Zeitfahren *n* (-s; *no pl*) cycling: time trials
'zeitgemäß *adj* modern, up-to-date
'Zeitgenosse *m*, **'Zeitgenossin** *f*, **'zeit-**

genössisch [-gənœsɪʃ] *adj* contemporary
'Zeitgeschichte *f* (-; *no pl*) contemporary history
Zeitgewinn *m* (-[e]s; *no pl*) gain of time
Zeitkarte *f* season ticket
'Zeitlang *f → Zeit*
zeit'lebens *adv* all one's life
'zeitlich 1. *adj* time ...; **2.** *adv*: *et. zeitlich planen or abstimmen* time s.th.
'zeitlos *adj* timeless; classic
'Zeitlupe *f*: *in Zeitlupe* in slow motion
Zeitnot *f*: *in Zeitnot sein* be pressed for time
Zeitpunkt *m* moment
Zeitraffer *m*: *im Zeitraffer* in quick motion
'zeitraubend *adj* time-consuming
'Zeitraum *m* period (of time)
'Zeitschrift *f* magazine
Zeitung ['tsaitʊŋ] *f* (-; -en) (news)paper
'Zeitungsabonne,ment *n* subscription to a paper
Zeitungsar,tikel *m* newspaper article
Zeitungsausschnitt *m* (newspaper) clipping (*Br* cutting)
Zeitungsjunge *m* paper boy
Zeitungskiosk *m* newspaper kiosk
Zeitungsno,tiz *f* press item
Zeitungspa,pier *n* newspaper
Zeitungsstand *m* newsstand
Zeitungsverkäufer(in) newsdealer, *Br* news vendor
'Zeitverlust *m* (-[e]s; *no pl*) loss of time
'Zeitverschiebung *f* AVIAT time lag
'Zeitverschwendung *f* waste of time
'Zeitvertreib [-fɛɐtraip] *m* (-[e]s; -e) pastime; *zum Zeitvertreib* to pass the time
zeitweilig ['tsaitvailɪç] *adj* temporary
'zeitweise *adv* at times, occasionally
'Zeitwort *n* (-[e]s; -wörter) LING verb
'Zeitzeichen *n* radio: time signal
'Zeitzünder *m* MIL time fuse
Zelle ['tsɛlə] *f* (-; -n) cell
Zellstoff ['tsɛl-] *m*, **Zellulose** [tsɛlu'lo:zə] *f* (-; -n) TECH cellulose
Zelt [tsɛlt] *n* (-[e]s; -e) tent
zelten ['tsɛltən] *v/i* (*ge-, h*) camp
'Zeltlager *n* camp
'Zeltplatz *m* campsite
Zement [tse'mɛnt] *m* (-[e]s; -e), **zementieren** [tsemɛn'ti:rən] *v/t* (*no -ge-, h*) cement
Zenit [tse'ni:t] *m* (-[e]s; *no pl*) zenith
zensieren [tsɛn'zi:rən] *v/t* (*no -ge-, h*) censor; PED mark, grade
Zensor ['tsɛnzo:ɐ] *m* (-s; -en [tsɛn'zo:rən]) censor
Zensur [tsɛn'zu:ɐ] *f* (-; -en [tsɛn'zu:rən])

a) (*no pl*) censorship, b) PED mark, grade
Zentimeter [tsɛnti'meːtɐ] *n, m* (*-s; -*) centimeter, *Br* centimetre
Zentner ['tsɛntnɐ] *m* (*-s; -*) 50 kilograms, metric hundredweight
zentral [tsɛn'traːl] *adj* central
Zentrale [tsɛn'traːlə] *f* (*-; -n*) head office; headquarters; TEL switchboard; TECH control room
Zen'tralheizung *f* central heating
Zentralverriegelung *f* MOT central locking
Zentrum ['tsɛntrʊm] *n* (*-s; Zentren*) center, *Br* centre
Zepter ['tsɛptɐ] *n* (*-s; -*) scepter, *Br* sceptre
zer'brechen *v/i* (*irr, brechen, no -ge-, sein*) *and v/t* (*h*) break; → **Kopf**
zer'brechlich *adj* fragile
zer'bröckeln *v/t* (*no -ge-, h*) *and v/i* (*sein*) crumble
zer'drücken *v/t* (*no -ge-, h*) crush
Zeremonie [tseremo'niː] *f* (*-; -n*) ceremony
zeremoniell [tseremo'njɛl] *adj*, **Zeremoni'ell** *n* (*-s; -e*) ceremonial
Zer'fall *m* (*-[e]s; no pl*) disintegration, decay
zer'fallen *v/i* (*irr, fallen, no -ge-, sein*) disintegrate, decay; **zerfallen in** (*acc*) break up into
zer'fetzen *v/t* (*no -ge-, h*) tear to pieces
zer'fressen *v/t* (*irr, fressen, no -ge-, h*) eat (holes in); CHEM corrode
zer'gehen *v/i* (*irr, gehen, no -ge-, sein*) melt, dissolve
zer'hacken *v/t* (*no -ge-, h*) chop (*a. ELECTR*)
zerknirscht [tsɛɐ'knɪrʃt] *adj* remorseful
zer'knittern *v/t* (*no -ge-, h*) (c)rumple, crease
zer'knüllen *v/t* (*no -ge-, h*) crumple up
zer'kratzen *v/t* (*no -ge-, h*) scratch
zer'krümeln *v/t* (*no -ge-, h*) crumble
zer'lassen *v/t* (*irr, lassen, no -ge-, h*) melt
zer'legen *v/t* (*no -ge-, h*) take apart *or* to pieces; TECH dismantle; GASTR carve; CHEM, LING, *fig* analyze, *Br* analyse
zer'lumpt *adj* ragged, tattered
zer'mahlen *v/t* (*no -ge-, h*) grind
zer'mürben *v/t* (*no -ge-, h*) wear down
zer'quetschen *v/t* (*no -ge-, h*) crush
Zerrbild ['tsɛɐ-] *n* caricature
zer'reiben *v/t* (*irr, reiben, no -ge-, h*) rub to powder, pulverize
zer'reißen (*irr, reißen, no -ge-*) **1.** *v/t* (*h*) tear up *or* to pieces; **sich die Hose zerreißen** tear one's trousers; **2.** *v/i* (*sein*) tear; break

zerren ['tsɛrən] (*ge-, h*) **1.** *v/t* tug, drag, pull (*a. MED*); **2.** *v/i*: **zerren an** (*dat*) tug (*or* strain) at
'Zerrung *f* (*-; -en*) MED pulled muscle
zerrütten [tsɛɐ'rʏtən] *v/t* (*no -ge-, h*) ruin
zer'rüttet *adj*: **zerrüttete Ehe** (*Verhältnisse*) broken marriage (home)
zer'sägen *v/t* (*no -ge-, h*) saw up
zerschellen [-'ʃɛlən] *v/i* (*no -ge-, sein*) be smashed, AVIAT *a.* crash
zer'schlagen 1. *v/t* (*irr, schlagen, no -ge-, h*) smash (to pieces); *fig* smash; **sich zerschlagen** come to nothing; **2.** *adj*: **sich zerschlagen fühlen** be (all) worn out, F be dead beat
zer'schmettern *v/t* (*no -ge-, h*) smash (to pieces), shatter (*a. fig*)
zer'schneiden *v/t* (*irr, schneiden, no -ge-, h*) cut (up)
zer'setzen *v/t* (*no -ge-, h*) CHEM decompose (*a. sich zersetzen*); *fig* corrupt, undermine
zer'splittern *v/t* (*no -ge-, h*) *and v/i* (*sein*) split (up), splinter; shatter
zer'springen *v/i* (*irr, springen, no -ge-, sein*) crack; shatter
zer'stampfen *v/t* (*no -ge-, h*) pound; GASTR mash
zer'stäuben *v/t* (*no -ge-, h*) spray
Zerstäuber [tsɛɐ'ʃtɔybɐ] *m* (*-s; -*) atomizer, sprayer
zer'stören *v/t* (*no -ge-, h*) destroy, ruin (*both a. fig*)
Zer'störer *m* (*-s; -*) destroyer (*a. MAR*)
zer'störerisch *adj* destructive
Zer'störung *f* (*-; -en*) destruction
zer'streuen *v/t and v/refl* (*no -ge-, h*) scatter, disperse; break up (*crowd etc*); *fig* take s.o.'s (*refl* one's) mind off things
zer'streut *fig adj* absent-minded
Zer'streutheit *f* (*-; no pl*) absent-mindedness
Zer'streuung *fig f* (*-; -en*) diversion, distraction
zer'stückeln *v/t* (*no -ge-, h*) cut up *or* (in)to pieces; dismember (*body*)
Zertifikat [tsɛrtifi'kaːt] *n* (*-[e]s; -e*) certificate
zer'treten *v/t* (*irr, treten, no -ge-, h*) crush (*a. fig*)
zer'trümmern *v/t* (*no -ge-, h*) smash
zerzaust [tsɛɐ'tsaust] *adj* tousled, disheveled(l)ed
Zettel ['tsɛtəl] *m* (*-s; -*) slip (of paper); note; label, sticker
Zeug [tsɔʏk] *n* (*-[e]s; -e*) stuff (*a. F*); things; **er hat das Zeug dazu** he's got what it takes; **dummes Zeug** nonsense
Zeuge ['tsɔʏgə] *m* (*-n; -n*) witness

'zeugen¹ v/i (ge-, h) JUR give evidence (**für** for); fig **zeugen von** testify to

'zeugen² v/t (ge-, h) BIOL procreate; father

'Zeugenaussage f JUR testimony, evidence

Zeugenbank f (-; -bänke) JUR witness stand (Br box)

'Zeugin f (-; -nen) JUR (female) witness

Zeugnis ['tsɔyknɪs] n (-ses; -se) report card, Br (school) report; certificate, diploma; reference; pl credentials

'Zeugung f (-; -en) BIOL procreation

z. H(d). ABBR of **zu Händen** attn, attention

Zickzack ['tsɪktsak] m (-[e]s; -e) (a. **im Zickzack fahren**) zigzag

Ziege ['tsiːgə] f (-; -n) ZO (nanny) goat; F contp (**blöde**) **Ziege** (silly old) cow

Ziegel ['tsiːgəl] m (-s; -) brick; tile

'Ziegeldach n tiled roof

Ziegelei [tsiːgə'lai] f (-; -en) brickyard

'Ziegelstein m brick

'Ziegenbock m ZO billy goat

Ziegenleder n kid (leather)

'Ziegenpeter [-peːtɐ] m (-s; -) MED mumps

ziehen ['tsiːən] (irr, -ge-) 1. v/t (h) pull, draw; take off one's hat (**vor** dat to) (a. fig); AGR grow; pull or take out (**aus** of); **j-n ziehen an** (dat) pull s.o. by; **auf sich ziehen** attract (attention etc); **sich ziehen** run; stretch; → **Länge**, **Erwägung**; 2. v/i a) (h) pull (**an** dat at), b) (sein) move; ZO etc migrate; go; travel; wander, roam; **es zieht** there's a draft (Br draught)

Ziehharmonika ['tsiːharmoːnika] f (-; -s) MUS accordion

'Ziehung f (-; -en) draw

Ziel [tsiːl] n (-[e]s; -e) aim, target, mark (all a. fig), fig a. goal, objective; destination; SPORT finish; **sich ein Ziel setzen** set o.s. a goal; **sein Ziel erreichen** reach one's goal; **sich zum Ziel gesetzt haben**, **et. zu tun** aim to do or at doing s.th.

'Zielband n (-[e]s; -bänder) SPORT tape

zielen ['tsiːlən] v/i (ge-, h) (take) aim (**auf** acc at)

'Ziellinie f SPORT finishing line

'ziellos adj aimless

'Zielscheibe f target, fig a. object

zielstrebig ['tsiːlʃtreːbɪç] adj purposeful, determined

ziemlich ['tsiːmlɪç] 1. adj quite a; 2. adv rather, fairly, quite, F pretty; **ziemlich viele** quite a few

Zierde ['tsiːɐdə] f (-; -n) (**zur** as a) decoration

zieren ['tsiːrən] v/t (ge-, h) decorate; **sich zieren** be coy; make a fuss

zierlich ['tsiːɐlɪç] adj dainty; petite

Zierpflanze ['tsiːɐ-] f ornamental plant

Ziffer ['tsɪfɐ] f (-; -n) figure

'Zifferblatt n dial, face

Zigarette [tsiga'rɛtə] f (-; -n) cigarette

Ziga'rettenauto,mat m cigarette machine

Zigarettenstummel m cigarette end, stub, butt

Zigarre [tsi'garə] f (-; -n) cigar

Zigeuner [tsi'gɔynɐ] m (-s; -), Zi'geunerin [-nərɪn] f (-; -nen) gypsy, Br gipsy

Zimmer ['tsɪmɐ] n (-s; -) room; apartment

Zimmereinrichtung f furniture

Zimmermädchen n (chamber)maid

Zimmermann m carpenter

'zimmern v/t (ge-, h) build, make

'Zimmerpflanze f indoor plant

Zimmerservice m room service

Zimmersuche f: **auf Zimmersuche sein** be looking (or hunting) for a room

Zimmervermittlung f accommodation office

zimperlich ['tsɪmpɐlɪç] adj prudish; soft, F sissy

Zimt [tsɪmt] m (-[e]s; -e) cinnamon

Zink ['tsɪŋk] n (-[e]s; no pl) CHEM zinc

Zinke ['tsɪŋkə] f (-; -n) tooth; prong

Zinn [tsɪn] n (-[e]s; no pl) CHEM tin; pewter

Zins [tsɪns] m (-es; -en) ECON interest (a. pl); **3% Zinsen bringen** bear interest at 3%

'zinslos adj ECON interest-free

'Zinssatz m ECON interest rate

Zipfel ['tsɪpfəl] m (-s; -) corner; point; tail; GASTR end

Zipfelmütze f pointed cap

zirka ['tsɪrka] adv about, approximately

Zirkel ['tsɪrkəl] m (-s; -) circle (a. fig); MATH compasses, dividers

zirkulieren [tsɪrku'liːrən] v/i (no -ge-, h) circulate

Zirkus ['tsɪrkʊs] m (-; -se) circus

zirpen ['tsɪrpən] v/i (ge-, h) chirp

zischen ['tsɪʃən] v/i and v/t (ge-, h) hiss; fat etc: sizzle; fig whiz(z)

ziselieren [tsizə'liːrən] v/t (no -ge-, h) TECH chase

Zitat [tsi'taːt] n (-[e]s; -e) quotation, F quote

zitieren [tsi'tiːrən] v/t (no -ge-, h) quote, cite (a. JUR), JUR summon

Zitrone [tsi'troːnə] f (-; -n) BOT lemon

Zi'tronenlimo,nade f lemon soda or pop, Br (fizzy) lemonade

Zitronensaft m lemon juice

Zitronenschale f lemon peel

zitterig ['tsɪtərɪç] adj shaky

zittern ['tsɪtɐn] v/i (ge-, h) tremble, shake (both: **vor** dat with)

zivil [tsi'viːl] adj civil, civilian

Zi'vil *n* (*-s*; *no pl*) civilian clothes; *Polizist in Zivil* plainclothes policeman

Zi'vildienst *m* MIL alternative service (*in lieu of military service*)

Zivilisation [tsiviliza'tsjoːn] *f* (*-*; *-en*) civilization

zivilisieren [tsivili'ziːrən] *v/t* (*no -ge-, h*) civilize

Zivilist [tsivi'lɪst] *m* (*-en*; *-en*) civilian

Zi'vilrecht *n* (*-[e]s*; *no pl*) JUR civil law

Zi'vilschutz *m* civil defen|se, *Br* -ce

Znüni ['tsnyːni] *Swiss m*, *n* (*-s*; *-*) mid-morning snack, tea (*or* coffee) break

zog [tsoːk] *pret of* **ziehen**

zögern ['tsøːgɐn] *v/i* (*ge-, h*) hesitate

'Zögern *n* (*-s*; *no pl*) hesitation

Zoll¹ [tsɔl] *m* (*-[e]s*; *-*) inch

Zoll² *m* (*-[e]s*; *Zölle* ['tsœlə]) a) (*no pl*) customs, b) duty

'Zollabfertigung *f* customs clearance

'Zollbeamte *m* customs officer

'Zollerklärung *f* customs declaration

'zollfrei *adj* duty-free

'Zollkon,trolle *f* customs examination

'zollpflichtig *adj* liable to duty

'Zollstock *m* (folding) rule

Zone ['tsoːnə] *f* (*-*; *-n*) zone

Zoo [tsoː] *m* (*-s*; *-s*) zoo

'Zoohandlung *f* pet shop

Zoologe [tsoo'loːgə] *m* (*-n*; *-n*) zoologist

Zoologie [tsoolo'giː] *f* (*-*; *no pl*) zoology

Zoo'login *f* (*-*; *-nen*) zoologist

zoo'logisch *adj* zoological

Zopf [tsɔpf] *m* (*-[e]s*; *Zöpfe* ['tsœpfə]) plait; pigtail

Zorn [tsɔrn] *m* (*-[e]s*; *no pl*) anger

zornig ['tsɔrnɪç] *adj* angry

Zote ['tsoːtə] *f* (*-*; *-n*) filthy joke, obscenity

zottelig ['tsɔtəlɪç] *adj* shaggy

z. T. ABBR *of* **zum Teil** partly

zu [tsuː] **1.** *prp* (*dat*) to, toward(s); at; *purpose*: for; *zu Fuß* (*Pferd*) on foot (horseback); *zu Hause* (*Ostern etc*) at home (Easter *etc*); *zu Weihnachten* give etc for Christmas; *Tür* (*Schlüssel*) *zu ...* door (key) to ...; *zu m-r Überraschung* to my surprise; *wir sind zu dritt* there are three of us; *zu zweien* two by two; *zu e-r Mark* at *or* for one mark; SPORT *1 zu 1* one all; *2 zu 1 gewinnen* win two one, win by two goals *etc* to one; → *zum, zur*; **2.** *adv* too; F closed, shut; *ein zu großes Risiko* too much of a risk; *zu viel* too much, too many; *zu wenig* too little, too few; **3.** *cj* to; *es ist zu erwarten* it is to be expected

Zubehör ['tsuːbəhøːɐ] *n* (*-[e]s*; *-e*) accessories

'zubereiten *v/t* (*sep, no -ge-, h*) prepare

'Zubereitung *f* (*-*; *-en*) preparation

'zubinden *v/t* (*irr*, *binden*, *sep*, *-ge-, h*) tie (up)

zubleiben *v/i* (*irr*, *bleiben*, *sep*, *-ge-, sein*) stay shut

zublinzeln *v/i* (*sep*, *-ge-, h*) (*dat*) wink at

'Zubringer *m* (*-s*; *-*), **Zubringerstraße** *f* MOT feeder (road), access road

Zucht [tsʊxt] *f* (*-*; *-en*) breed; ZO breeding; BOT cultivation

züchten ['tsʏçtən] *v/t* (*ge-, h*) ZO breed; BOT grow, cultivate

Züchter(in) ['tsʏçtɐ (*-tərɪn*)] *m* (*-s*; *-/-*; *-nen*) ZO breeder; BOT grower

'Zuchtperle *f* culture(d) pearl

zucken ['tsʊkən] *v/i* (*ge-, h*) jerk; twitch (*mit et.* s.th.); wince; *lightning*: flash

zücken ['tsʏkən] *v/t* (*ge-, h*) draw (*weapon*); F pull out (*one's wallet etc*)

Zucker ['tsʊkɐ] *m* (*-s*; *-*) sugar

Zuckerdose *f* sugar bowl

Zuckerguss *m* icing, frosting

'zuckerkrank *adj*, **'Zuckerkranke** *m*, *f* (*-n*; *-n*) MED diabetic

'Zuckerkrankheit *f* MED diabetes

'Zuckermais *m* sweet corn

'zuckern *v/t* (*ge-, h*) sugar

'Zuckerrohr *n* BOT sugarcane

'Zuckerrübe *f* BOT sugar beet

'Zuckerwatte *f* candy floss

'Zuckerzange *f* sugar tongs

'Zuckung *f* (*-*; *-en*) twitch(ing); tic; convulsion, spasm

'zudecken *v/t* (*sep*, *-ge-, h*) cover (up)

zudem [tsu'deːm] *adv* besides, moreover

'zudrehen *v/t* (*sep*, *-ge-, h*) turn off; *j-m den Rücken zudrehen* turn one's back on s.o.

'zudringlich *adj*: *zudringlich werden* F get fresh (*j-m gegenüber* with s.o.)

'zudrücken *v/t* (*sep*, *-ge-, h*) close, push s.th. shut; → *Auge*

zuerst [tsu'ʔeːɐst] *adv* first; at first; first (of all), to begin with

'Zufahrt *f* approach; drive(way)

'Zufahrtsstraße *f* access road

'Zufall *m* chance; *durch Zufall* by chance, by accident

'zufallen *v/i* (*irr*, *fallen*, *sep*, *-ge-, sein*) *door etc*: slam (shut); *fig* fall to s.o.; *mir fallen die Augen zu* I can't keep my eyes open

'zufällig 1. *adj* accidental, chance ...; **2.** *adv* by accident, by chance; *zufällig tun* happen to do

'Zuflucht *f*: *Zuflucht suchen* (*finden*) look for (find) refuge *or* shelter (*vor dat* from; *bei* with); (*s-e*) *Zuflucht nehmen zu* resort to

zufrieden [tsu'friːdən] *adj* content(ed),

satisfied; **zufrieden stellen** satisfy; **zu-frieden stellend** satisfactory

Zu'friedenheit *f* (-; *no pl*) contentment, satisfaction

zu'friedengeben *v/refl* (*irr*, **geben**, *sep*, -*ge*-, *h*): **sich zufriedengeben mit** content o.s. with

zufriedenlassen *v/t* (*irr*, **lassen**, *sep*, -*ge*-, *h*) leave s.o. alone

zufriedenstellen *v/t* (*sep*,-*ge*-, *h*) satisfy

zufriedenstellend *adj* satisfactory

'**zufrieren** *v/i* (*irr*, **frieren**, *sep*, -*ge*-, *sein*) freeze up *or* over

'**zufügen** *v/t* (*sep*, -*ge*-, *h*) do, cause; **j-m Schaden zufügen** *a.* harm s.o.

Zufuhr ['tsuːfuːɐ] *f* (-; -*en*) supply

Zug [tsuːk] *m* (-[*e*]*s*; *Züge* ['tsyːgə]) RAIL train; procession, line; parade; *fig* feature; trait; tendency; *chess etc*: move (*a. fig*); *swimming*: stroke; pull (*a.* TECH), PHYS *a.* tension; *smoking*: puff; draft, *Br* draught; PED stream; **im Zuge** *gen* in the course of; **in e-m Zug** at one go; **Zug um Zug** step by step; **in groben Zügen** in broad outlines

'**Zugabe** *f* addition; THEA encore

'**Zugang** *m* access (*a. fig*)

'**zugänglich** [-gɛŋlɪç] *adj* accessible (**für** to) (*a. fig*)

'**Zugbrücke** *f* drawbridge

'**zugeben** *v/t* (*irr*, **geben**, *sep*, -*ge*-, *h*) add; *fig* admit

'**zugehen** *v/i* (*irr*, **gehen**, *sep*, -*ge*-, *sein*) F *door etc*: close, shut; **zugehen auf** (*acc*) walk up to, approach (*a. fig*); **es geht auf 8 Uhr zu** it's getting on for 8; **es ging lustig zu** we had a lot of fun

'**Zugehörigkeit** *f* (-; *no pl*) membership

Zügel ['tsyːgəl] *m* (-*s*; -) rein (*a. fig*)

'**zügeln 1.** *v/t* (*ge*-, *h*) curb, control, bridle; **2.** *Swiss v/i* (*ge*-, *sein*) move

'**Zugeständnis** *n* concession

'**zugestehen** *v/t* (*irr*, **stehen**, *sep*, *no* -*ge*-, *h*) concede, grant

'**zugetan** *adj* attached (*dat* to)

'**Zugführer** *m* RAIL conductor, *Br* guard

zugig ['tsuːgɪç] *adj* drafty, *Br* draughty

'**Zugkraft** *f* a) TECH traction, b) (*no pl*) attraction, draw, appeal

'**zugkräftig** *adj*: **zugkräftig sein** be a draw

zu'gleich [tsu-] *adv* at the same time

'**Zugluft** *f* (-; *no pl*) draft, *Br* draught

'**Zugma,schine** *f* MOT tractor

'**zugreifen** *v/i* (*irr*, **greifen**, *sep*, -*ge*-, *h*) grab (at) it; *fig* grab the opportunity; **greifen Sie zu!** help yourself!; **mit zu-greifen** lend a hand

'**Zugriffscode** *m* EDP access code

'**Zugriffszeit** *f* EDP access time

zugrunde [tsu'grʊndə] *adv*: **zugrunde gehen** (**an** *dat*) perish (of); **e-r Sache et. zugrunde legen** base s.th. on s.th.; **zugrunde richten** ruin

zugunsten [tsu'gʊnstən] *prp* (*gen*) in favo(u)r of

zu'gute [tsu-] *adv*: **zugute halten** → **zu-gutehalten**; **zugute kommen** → **zugu-tekommen**; **zugutehalten** *v/t* (*irr*, **hal-ten**, *sep*, -*ge*-, *h*): **j-m et. zugute** give s.o. credit for s.th.; make allwances for s.o.'s …

zugutekommen *v/t* (*irr*, **kommen**, *sep*, -*ge*-, *sein*): **j-m zugutekommen** be for the benefit of s.o. '**Zugvogel** *m* zo bird of passage

'**zuhalten** *v/t* (*irr*, **halten**, *sep*, -*ge*-, *h*) keep shut; **sich die Ohren (Augen) zuhalten** cover one's ears (eyes) with one's hands; **sich die Nase zuhalten** hold one's nose

Zuhälter ['tsuːhɛltɐ] *m* (-*s*; -) pimp

Zuhause [tsu'hauzə] *n* (-*s*; *no pl*) home

zu'hause *adv* → **Haus**

'**zuhören** *v/i* (*sep*, -*ge*-, *h*) listen (*dat* to)

'**Zuhörer** *m*, '**Zuhörerin** *f* listener, *pl a. the* audience

'**zujubeln** *v/i* (*sep*, -*ge*-, *h*) cheer

'**zukleben** *v/t* (*sep*, -*ge*-, *h*) seal

'**zuknöpfen** *v/t* (*sep*, -*ge*-, *h*) button (up)

'**zukommen** *v/i* (*irr*, **kommen**, *sep*, -*ge*-, *sein*) **zukommen auf** (*acc*) come up to; *fig* be ahead of; **die Dinge auf sich zu-kommen lassen** wait and see

Zukunft ['tsuːkʊnft] *f* (-; *no pl*) future (*a.* LING)

'**zukünftig 1.** *adj* future; **2.** *adv* in future

'**zulächeln** *v/i* (*sep*, -*ge*-, *h*) smile at

'**Zulage** *f* bonus

'**zulangen** F *v/i* (*sep*, -*ge*-, *h*) tuck in

'**zulassen** *v/t* (*irr*, **lassen**, *sep*, -*ge*-, *h*) F keep s.th. closed; *fig* allow; MOT *etc* license, register; **j-n zu et. zulassen** admit s.o. to s.th.

'**zulässig** *adj* admissible (*a.* JUR); **zulässig sein** be allowed

'**Zulassung** *f* (-; -*en*) admission; MOT *etc* license, *Br* licence

'**zulegen** *v/t* (*sep*, -*ge*-, *h*) add; F **sich … zulegen** get o.s. s.th.; adopt (*name*)

zu'letzt [tsu-] *adv* in the end; *come etc* last; finally; **wann hast du ihn zuletzt gesehen?** when did you last see him?

zu'liebe [tsu-] *adv*: **j-m zuliebe** for s.o.'s sake

zum [tsʊm] *prp* **zu dem** → **zu**; **zum ersten Mal** for the first time; **et. zum Kaffee** s.th. with one's coffee; **zum Schwimmen** *etc* **gehen** go swimming *etc*

'**zumachen** F (*sep*, -*ge*-, *h*) **1.** *v/t* close,

shut; button (up); **2.** *v/i* close (down)
'**zumauern** *v/t* (*sep*, *-ge-*, *h*) brick *or* wall up
zumutbar ['tsuːmuːtbaːɐ] *adj* reasonable
zu'**mute** [tsu-] *adv*: *mir ist … zumute* I feel …
'**zumuten** *v/t* (*sep*, *-ge-*, *h*) *j-m et. zumuten* expect s.th. of s.o.; *sich zu viel zumuten* overtax o.s.
'**Zumutung** *f*: *das ist e-e Zumutung* that's asking *or* expecting a bit much
zu'**nächst** [tsu-] *adv* → *zuerst*
'**zunageln** *v/t* (*sep*, *-ge-*, *h*) nail up
'**zunähen** *v/t* (*sep*, *-ge-*, *h*) sew up
Zunahme ['tsuːnaːmə] *f* (-; *-n*) increase
'**Zuname** *m* surname
zünden ['tsʏndən] *v/i* (*ge-*, *h*) kindle; ELECTR, MOT ignite, fire
zündend *fig adj* stirring
Zünder ['tsʏndɐ] *m* (*-s*; -) MIL fuse; *pl Austrian* matches
Zündholz ['tsʏnt-] *n* match
Zündkerze *f* MOT spark plug
Zündschlüssel *m* MOT ignition key
Zündschnur *f* fuse
'**Zündung** *f* (-; *-en*) MOT ignition
'**zunehmen** *v/i* (*irr*, *nehmen*, *sep*, *-ge-*, *h*) increase (*an dat* in); put on weight; *moon*: wax; *days*: grow longer
'**Zuneigung** *f* (-; *-en*) affection
Zunft [tsʊnft] HIST *f* (-; *Zünfte* ['tsʏnftə]) guild
Zunge [tsʊŋə] *f* (-; *-n*) ANAT tongue; *es liegt mir auf der Zunge* it's on the tip of my tongue
züngeln ['tsʏŋəln] *v/i* (*ge-*, *h*) *flames*: lick, flicker
'**Zungenspitze** *f* tip of the tongue
'**zunicken** *v/i* (*sep*, *-ge-*, *h*) (*dat*) nod at
zunutze [tsu'nʊtsə] *adv*: *sich et. zunutze machen* make (good) use of s.th.; take advantage of s.th.
zupfen [tsʊpfən] *v/t and v/i* (*ge-*, *h*) pull (*an dat* at), pick, pluck (at) (*a.* MUS)
zur [tsuːɐ] *prp zu der* → *zu*; *zur Schule* (*Kirche*) *gehen* go to school (church); *zur Hälfte* half (of it *or* them); *zur Belohnung etc* as a reward *etc*
'**zurechnungsfähig** *adj* JUR responsible
'**Zurechnungsfähigkeit** *f* (-; *no pl*) JUR responsibility
zu'**rechtfinden** *v/refl* (*irr*, *finden*, *sep*, *-ge-*, *h*) find one's way; *fig* cope, manage
zurechtkommen *v/i* (*irr*, *kommen*, *sep*, *-ge-*, *sein*) get along (*mit* with); cope (with)
zurechtlegen *v/t* (*sep*, *-ge-*, *h*) arrange; *fig sich et. zurechtlegen* think s.th. out
zurechtmachen F *v/t* (*sep*, *-ge-*, *h*) get

ready, prepare, fix; *sich zurechtmachen* do o.s. up
zurechtrücken *v/t* (*sep*, *-ge-*, *h*) put s.th. straight (*a. fig*)
zu'**rechtweisen** *v/t* (*irr*, *weisen*, *sep*, *-ge-*, *h*), **Zu**'**rechtweisung** *f* reprimand
'**zureden** *v/i* (*sep*, *-ge-*, *h*) *j-m zureden* encourage s.o.
zureiten *v/t* (*irr*, *reiten*, *sep*, *-ge-*, *h*) break in
zurichten F *fig v/t* (*sep*, *-ge-*, *h*) *übel zurichten* batter, *a.* beat s.o. up badly, *a.* make a mess of s.th., ruin
zurück [tsu'rʏk] *adv* back; behind (*a. fig*)
zurückbehalten *v/t* (*irr*, *halten*, *sep*, *no -ge-*, *h*) keep back, retain
zurückbekommen *v/t* (*irr*, *kommen*, *sep*, *no -ge-*, *h*) get back
zurückbleiben *v/i* (*irr*, *bleiben*, *sep*, *-ge-*, *sein*) stay behind, be left behind; fall behind (*a.* PED *etc*)
zurückblicken *v/i* (*sep*, *-ge-*, *h*) look back (*auf acc* at, *fig* on)
zurückbringen *v/t* (*irr*, *bringen*, *sep*, *-ge-*, *h*) bring *or* take back, return
zurückda,tieren *v/t* (*sep*, *no -ge-*, *h*) backdate (*auf acc* to)
zurückfallen *fig v/i* (*irr*, *fallen*, *sep*, *-ge-*, *sein*) fall behind, SPORT *a.* drop back
zurückfinden *v/i* (*irr*, *finden*, *sep*, *-ge-*, *h*) find one's way back (*nach*, *zu* to); *fig* return (*to*)
zurückfordern *v/t* (*sep*, *-ge-*, *h*) reclaim
zurückführen *v/t* (*sep*, *-ge-*, *h*) lead back; *zurückführen auf* (*acc*) attribute to
zurückgeben *v/t* (*irr*, *geben*, *sep*, *-ge-*, *h*) give back, return
zurückgeblieben *fig adj* backward; retarded
zurückgehen *v/i* (*irr*, *gehen*, *sep*, *-ge-*, *sein*) go back, return; *fig* decrease; go down, drop
zurückgezogen *fig adj* secluded
zurückgreifen *v/i* (*irr*, *greifen*, *sep*, *-ge-*, *h*) *zurückgreifen auf* (*acc*) fall back (up)on
zu'**rückhalten** (*irr*, *halten*, *sep*, *-ge-*, *h*) **1.** *v/t* hold back; **2.** *v/refl* control o.s.; be careful
zurückhaltend *adj* reserved
Zu'**rückhaltung** *f* (-; *no pl*) reserve
zu'**rückkehren** *v/i* (*sep*, *-ge-*, *sein*) return
zurückkommen *v/i* (*irr*, *kommen*, *sep*, *-ge-*, *sein*) come back, return (*both fig auf acc* to)
zurücklassen *v/t* (*irr*, *lassen*, *sep*, *-ge-*, *h*) leave (behind)
zurücklegen *v/t* (*sep*, *-ge-*, *h*) put back; put aside, save (*money*); cover, do (*miles*)

Z

zurücknehmen *v/t* (*irr*, **nehmen**, *sep*, *-ge-*, *h*) take back (*a. fig*)

zurückrufen (*irr*, **rufen**, *sep*, *-ge-*, *h*) **1.** *v/t* call back (*a.* TEL); ECON recall; *ins Gedächtnis zurückrufen* recall; **2.** *v/i* TEL call back

zurückschlagen (*irr*, **schlagen**, *sep*, *-ge-*, *h*) **1.** *v/t* beat off; *tennis*: return; fold back; **2.** *v/i* hit back; MIL retaliate (*a. fig*)

zurückschrecken *v/i* (*sep*, *-ge-*, *sein*) *zurückschrecken vor* (*dat*) shrink from; *vor nichts zurückschrecken* stop at nothing

zurücksetzen *v/t* (*sep*, *-ge-*, *h*) MOT back (up); *fig* neglect *s.o.*

zurückstehen *v/i* (*irr*, **stehen**, *sep*, *-ge-*, *h*) stand aside

zurückstellen *v/t* (*sep*, *-ge-*, *h*) put back (*a.* watch); put aside; MIL defer

zurückstrahlen *v/t* (*sep*, *-ge-*, *h*) reflect

zurücktreten *v/i* (*irr*, **treten**, *sep*, *-ge-*, *sein*) step *or* stand back; resign (*von e-m Amt* [**Posten**] one's office [post]); ECON, JUR withdraw (*von* from)

zurückweichen *v/i* (*irr*, **weichen**, *sep*, *-ge-*, *sein*) fall back (*a.* MIL)

zurückweisen *v/t* (*irr*, **weisen**, *sep*, *-ge-*, *h*) turn down; JUR dismiss

zurückzahlen *v/t* (*sep*, *-ge-*, *h*) pay back (*a. fig*)

zurückziehen *v/t* (*irr*, **ziehen**, *sep*, *-ge-*, *h*) draw back; *fig* withdraw; *sich zurückziehen* retire, withdraw; MIL *a.* retreat

'Zuruf *m* shout

'zurufen *v/t* (*irr*, **rufen**, *sep*, *-ge-*, *h*) *j-m et. zurufen* shout s.th. to s.o.

zur'zeit *adv* at the moment, at present

'Zusage *f* promise; assent

'zusagen *v/i and v/t* (*sep*, *-ge-*, *h*) accept (an invitation); (*dat*) suit, appeal to; *s-e Hilfe zusagen* promise to help

zusammen [tsu'zamən] *adv* together; *alles zusammen* (all) in all; *das macht zusammen ...* that makes ... altogether

Zu'sammenarbeit *f* (*-*; *no pl*) cooperation; *in Zusammenarbeit mit* in collaboration with

zu'sammenarbeiten *v/i* (*sep*, *-ge-*, *h*) cooperate, collaborate

zu'sammenbeißen *v/t* (*irr*, **beißen**, *sep*, *-ge-*, *h*) *die Zähne zusammenbeißen* clench one's teeth

zu'sammenbrechen *v/i* (*irr*, **brechen**, *sep*, *-ge-*, *sein*) break down, collapse (*both a. fig*)

Zu'sammenbruch *m* breakdown, collapse

zu'sammenfallen *v/i* (*irr*, **fallen**, *sep*, *-ge-*, *sein*) coincide

zusammenfalten *v/t* (*sep*, *-ge-*, *h*) fold up

zu'sammenfassen *v/t* (*sep*, *-ge-*, *h*) summarize, sum up

Zu'sammenfassung *f* (*-*; *-en*) summary

zu'sammenfügen *v/t* (*sep*, *-ge-*, *h*) join (together)

zusammengesetzt *adj* compound

zusammenhalten *v/i and v/t* (*irr*, **halten**, *sep*, *-ge-*, *h*) hold together (*a. fig*); F stick together

Zu'sammenhang *m* (*-[e]s*; *-hänge*) connection; context; *im Zusammenhang stehen* (*mit*) be connected (with)

zu'sammenhängen *v/i* (*irr*, **hängen**, *sep*, *-ge-*, *h*) be connected

zusammenhängend *adj* coherent

zu'sammenhang(s)los *adj* incoherent, disconnected

zu'sammenklappen *v/i* (*sep*, *-ge-*, *sein*) *and v/t* (*h*) TECH fold up; F break down

zusammenkommen *v/i* (*irr*, **kommen**, *sep*, *-ge-*, *sein*) meet

Zu'sammenkunft [-kʊnft] *f* (*-*; *-künfte* [-kʏnftə]) meeting

zu'sammenlegen (*sep*, *-ge-*, *h*) **1.** *v/t* combine; fold up; **2.** *v/i* club together

zusammennehmen *v/t* (*irr*, **nehmen**, *sep*, *-ge-*, *h*) muster (up); *sich zusammennehmen* pull o.s. together

zusammenpacken *v/t* (*sep*, *-ge-*, *h*) pack up

zusammenpassen *v/i* (*sep*, *-ge-*, *h*) harmonize; match

zusammenrechnen *v/t* (*sep*, *-ge-*, *h*) add up

zusammenreißen F *v/refl* (*irr*, **reißen**, *sep*, *-ge-*, *h*) pull o.s. together

zusammenrollen *v/t* (*sep*, *-ge-*, *h*) roll up; *sich zusammenrollen* coil up

zusammenrotten [-rɔtən] *v/refl* (*sep*, *-ge-*, *h*) band together

zusammenrücken (*sep*, *-ge-*) **1.** *v/t* (*h*) move closer together; **2.** *v/i* (*sein*) move up

zusammenschlagen *v/t* (*irr*, **schlagen**, *sep*, *-ge-*, *h*) clap (*hands*); click (*one's heels*); beat *s.o.* up; smash (up)

zu'sammenschließen *v/refl* (*irr*, **schließen**, *sep*, *-ge-*, *h*) join, unite

Zu'sammenschluss *m* union

zu'sammenschreiben *v/t* (*irr*, **schreiben**, *sep*, *-ge-*, *h*) write in one word

zusammenschrumpfen *v/i* (*sep*, *-ge-*, *sein*) shrink

zu'sammensetzen *v/t* (*sep*, *-ge-*, *h*) put together; TECH assemble; *sich zusammensetzen aus* (*dat*) consist of, be composed of

Zu'sammensetzung *f* (*-*; *-en*) composition; CHEM, LING compound; TECH assembly

zu'sammenstellen v/t (sep, -ge-, h) put together; arrange

Zu'sammenstoß m collision (a. fig), crash; impact; fig clash

zu'sammenstoßen v/i (irr, **stoßen**, sep, -ge-, sein) collide (a. fig); fig clash; **zusammenstoßen mit** run or bump into; fig have a clash with

zu'sammentreffen v/i (irr, **treffen**, sep, -ge-, sein) meet, encounter; coincide (**mit** with)

Zu'sammentreffen n (-s; -) meeting; coincidence; encounter

zu'sammentreten v/i (irr, **treten**, sep, -ge-, sein) meet

zusammentun v/refl (irr, **tun**, sep, -ge-, h) join (forces), F team up

zusammenwirken v/i (sep, -ge-, h) combine

zusammenzählen v/t (sep, -ge-, h) add up

zusammenziehen (irr, **ziehen**, sep, -ge-) **1.** v/t and v/refl (h) contract; **2.** v/i (sein) move in (**mit** with)

zusammenzucken v/i (sep, -ge-, sein) wince, flinch

'Zusatz m addition; chemical etc additive; **Zusatz...** in cpds mst additional ..., supplementary ...; auxiliary ...

zusätzlich ['tsuːzɛtslɪç] adj additional, extra

'zuschauen v/i (sep, -ge-, h) look on (**bei et.** at s.th.); **j-m zuschauen** watch s.o. (**bei et.** doing s.th.)

Zuschauer ['tsuːʃauɐ] m (-s; -), **'Zuschauerin** f (-; -nen) spectator; TV viewer, pl a. the audience

'Zuschauerraum m auditorium

'Zuschlag m extra charge; RAIL etc excess fare; bonus; auction: knocking down

'zuschlagen v/i (irr, **schlagen**, sep, -ge-, sein) and v/t (h) door etc: slam or bang shut; boxing etc: hit, strike (a blow); fig act; **j-m et. zuschlagen** auction: knock s.th. down to s.o.

'zuschließen v/t (irr, **schließen**, sep, -ge-, h) lock (up)

zuschnallen v/t (sep, -ge-, h) buckle (up)

zuschnappen v/i (sep, -ge-) a) (h) dog: snap, b) (sein) door etc: snap shut

zuschneiden v/t (irr, **schneiden**, sep, -ge-, h) cut out; cut (to size)

zuschnüren v/t (sep, -ge-, h) tie (or lace) up

zuschrauben v/t (sep, -ge-, h) screw shut

zuschreiben v/t (irr, **schreiben**, sep, -ge-, h) ascribe or attribute (dat to)

'Zuschrift f letter

zuschulden [tsu'ʃʊldən] adv: **sich et. (nichts) zuschulden kommen lassen** do s.th. (nothing) wrong

'Zuschuss m allowance; subsidy

'zuschütten v/t (sep, -ge-, h) fill up

'zusehen → zuschauen

zusehends ['tsuːzeːənts] adv noticeably; rapidly

'zusetzen (sep, -ge-, h) **1.** v/t add; lose (money); **2.** v/i lose money; **j-m zusetzen** press s.o. (hard)

'zuspielen v/t (sep, -ge-, h) SPORT pass

'zuspitzen v/t (sep, -ge-, h) point; **sich zuspitzen** become critical

'Zuspruch m (-[e]s; no pl) encouragement; words of comfort

'Zustand m condition, state, F shape

zustande [tsu'ʃtandə] adv: **zustande bringen** bring about, manage (to do); **zustande kommen** come about; **es kam nicht zustande** it didn't come off

'zuständig adj responsible (**für** for), in charge (of)

'zustehen v/i (irr, **stehen**, sep, -ge-, h) **j-m steht et. (zu tun) zu** s.o. is entitled to (do) s.th.

'zustellen v/t (sep, -ge-, h) post: deliver

'Zustellung f post: delivery

'zustimmen v/i (sep, -ge-, h) agree (dat to s.th.; with s.o.)

'Zustimmung f approval, consent; (j-s) **Zustimmung finden** meet with (s.o.'s) approval

'zustoßen v/i (irr, **stoßen**, sep, -ge-, sein) **j-m zustoßen** happen to s.o.

zutage [tsu'taːgə] adv: **zutage bringen** (**kommen**) bring (come) to light

'Zutaten pl ingredients

'zuteilen v/t (sep, -ge-, h) assign, allot

'Zuteilung f (-; -en) allotment; ration

'zutragen v/refl (irr, **tragen**, sep, -ge-, h) happen

'zutrauen v/t (sep, -ge-, h) **j-m et. zutrauen** credit s.o. with s.th.; **sich zu viel zutrauen** overrate o.s.

zutraulich ['tsuːtraulɪç] adj trusting; zo friendly

'zutreffen v/i (irr, **treffen**, sep, -ge-, h) be true; **zutreffen auf** (acc) apply to, go for

zutreffend adj true, correct

'zutrinken v/i (irr, **trinken**, sep, -ge-, h) **j-m zutrinken** drink to s.o.

'Zutritt m (-[e]s; no pl) admission; access; **Zutritt verboten!** no admittance!

zu'ungunsten adv to s.o.'s disadvantage

zuverlässig ['tsuːfɛɐlɛsɪç] adj reliable, dependable; safe

'Zuverlässigkeit f (-; no pl) reliability, dependability

Z

Zuversicht ['tsuːfɛɐzɪçt] *f* (-; *no pl*) confidence

'**zuversichtlich** *adj* confident, optimistic

zuviel → *zu*

zu'vor [tsu-] *adv* before, previously; first

zu'vorkommen *v/i* (*irr*, **kommen**, *sep*, *-ge-*, *sein*) anticipate; prevent; *j-m zuvorkommen a.* F beat s.o. to it

zuvorkommend *adj* obliging; polite

Zuwachs ['tsuːvaks] *m* (*-es*; *no pl*) increase, growth

'**zuwachsen** *v/i* (*irr*, **wachsen**, *sep*, *-ge-*, *sein*) become overgrown; MED close

zu'weilen [tsu-] *adv* occasionally, now and then

'**zuweisen** *v/t* (*irr*, **weisen**, *sep*, *-ge-*, *h*) assign

'**zuwenden** *v/t and v/refl* ([*irr*, **wenden**,] *sep*, *-ge-*, *h*) turn to (*a. fig*)

'**Zuwendung** *f* (-; *-en*) a) payment, b) (*no pl*) attention; (loving) care, love, affection

zuwenig → *zu*

'**zuwerfen** *v/t* (*irr*, **werfen**, *sep*, *-ge-*, *h*) slam (shut); *j-m et. zuwerfen* throw s.o. s.th.; *j-m e-n Blick zuwerfen* cast a glance at s.o.

zu'wider [tsu-] *adj*: *... ist mir zuwider* I hate *or* detest ...

zuwiderhandeln *v/i* (*sep*, *-ge-*, *h*) (*dat*) act contrary to; violate

'**zuwinken** *v/i* (*sep*, *-ge-*, *h*) wave to; signal to

zuzahlen *v/t* (*sep*, *-ge-*, *h*) pay extra

zuziehen (*irr*, **ziehen**, *sep*, *-ge-*) **1.** *v/t* (*h*) draw (*curtains etc*); pull tight; *fig* consult; *sich zuziehen* MED catch; **2.** *v/i* (*sein*) move in

zuzüglich ['tsuːtsyːklɪç] *prp* (*gen*) plus

Zvieri ['tsfiːri] *Swiss m, n* (*-s*; *-s*) afternoon snack, tea *or* coffee break

zwang [tsvaŋ] *pret of* **zwingen**

Zwang *m* (*-[e]s*; *Zwänge* ['tsvɛŋə]) compulsion, constraint; restraint; coercion; force; *Zwang sein* be compulsory

zwängen ['tsvɛŋən] *v/t* (*ge-*, *h*) press, squeeze, force

'**zwanglos** *adj* informal; casual

'**Zwanglosigkeit** *f* (-; *no pl*) informality

'**Zwangsarbeit** *f* JUR hard labo(u)r

Zwangsherrschaft *f* (-; *no pl*) despotism, tyranny

Zwangslage *f* predicament

'**zwangsläufig** *adv* inevitably

'**Zwangsmaßnahme** *f* sanction

Zwangsvollstreckung *f* JUR compulsory execution

Zwangsvorstellung *f* PSYCH obsession

'**zwangsweise** *adv* by force

zwanzig ['tsvantsɪç] *adj* twenty

'**zwanzigste** *adj* twentieth

zwar [tsvaːɐ] *adv*: *ich kenne ihn zwar, aber ...* I do know him, but ..., I know him all right, but ...; *und zwar* that is (to say), namely

Zweck [tsvɛk] *m* (*-[e]s*; *-e*) purpose, aim; *s-n Zweck erfüllen* serve its purpose; *es hat keinen Zweck* (*zu warten etc*) it's no use (waiting *etc*)

'**zwecklos** *adj* useless

'**zweckmäßig** *adj* practical; wise; TECH, ARCH functional

'**Zweckmäßigkeit** *f* (-; *no pl*) practicality, functionality

zwecks *prp* (*gen*) for the purpose of

zwei [tsvai] *adj* two

'**zweibeinig** [-bainɪç] *adj* two-legged

'**Zweibettzimmer** *n* twin-bedded room

'**zweideutig** [-dɔytɪç] *adj* ambiguous; off-colo(u)r

Zweier ['tsvaiɐ] *m* (*-s*; -) *rowing*: pair

zweierlei ['tsvaiɐ'lai] *adj* two kinds of

'**zweifach** *adj* double, twofold

Zweifa'milienhaus *n* duplex, *Br* two-family house

Zweifel ['tsvaifəl] *m* (*-s*; -) doubt

'**zweifelhaft** *adj* doubtful, dubious

'**zweifellos** *adv* undoubtedly, no *or* without doubt

'**zweifeln** *v/i* (*ge-*, *h*) *zweifeln an* (*dat*) doubt *s.th.*, have one's doubts about

Zweig [tsvaik] *m* (*-[e]s*; *-e*) BOT branch (*a. fig*); twig

Zweiggeschäft *n*, **Zweigniederlassung** *f*, **Zweigstelle** *f* branch

'**zweijährig** [-jɛːrɪç] *adj* two-year-old, of two (years)

'**Zweikampf** *m* duel

'**zweimal** *adv* twice

'**zweimalig** *adj* (twice) repeated

'**zweimotorig** [-motoːrɪç] *adj* twin-engined

zweireihig [-raiɪç] *adj* double-breasted (*suit*)

'**zweischneidig** *adj* double-edged, two-edged (*both a. fig*)

zweiseitig [-zaitɪç] *adj* two-sided; reversible; POL bilateral; EDP double-sided

'**Zweisitzer** [-zitsɐ] *m* (*-s*; -) *esp* MOT two-seater

'**zweisprachig** [-ʃpraːxɪç] *adj* bilingual

zweistimmig [-ʃtɪmɪç] *adj* MUS ... for two voices

zweistöckig [-ʃtœkɪç] *adj* two-storied, *Br* two-storey ...

zweit [tsvait] *adj* second; *ein zweiter ...* another ...; *jede(r, -s) zweite ...* every other ...; *aus zweiter Hand* second-hand; *wir sind zu zweit* there are two of us

'zweitbeste *adj* second-best

'zweiteilig *adj* two-piece (*suit etc*)

zweitens ['tsvaitəns] *adv* secondly

'zweitklassig [-klasıç] adj, 'zweitrangig [-raŋıç] *adj* second-class *or* -rate

Zwerchfell ['tsvɛrç-] *n* ANAT diaphragm

Zwerg [tsvɛrk] *m* (-[e]s; -e ['tsvɛrgə]) dwarf; gnome; *fig* midget; *Zwerg... in cpds* BOT dwarf ...; zo pygmy ...

Zwetsch(g)e ['tsvɛtʃ(g)ə] *f* (-; -n) BOT plum

zwicken ['tsvikən] *v/t and v/i* (ge-, h) pinch, nip

Zwieback ['tsvi:bak] *m* (-[e]s; -e, -bäcke [-bɛkə]) rusk, zwieback

Zwiebel ['tsvi:bəl] *f* (-; -n) GASTR onion; BOT bulb

Zwiegespräch ['tsvi:-] *n* dialog(ue)

'Zwielicht *n* (-[e]s; *no pl*) twilight

'Zwiespalt *m* (-[e]s; -e) conflict

'zwiespältig [-ʃpɛltıç] *adj* conflicting

'Zwietracht *f* (-; *no pl*) discord

Zwilling ['tsvilıŋ] *m* (-s; -e) twin; *pl* ASTR Gemini; *er ist (ein) Zwilling* he's (a) Gemini

'Zwillingsbruder *m* twin brother

Zwillingsschwester *f* twin sister

Zwinge ['tsvıŋə] *f* (-; -n) TECH clamp

zwingen ['tsvıŋən] *v/t* (*irr*, ge-, h) force, compel

zwingend *adj* compelling; cogent

Zwinger ['tsvıŋɐ] *m* (-s; -) kennels

zwinkern ['tsvıŋkɐn] *v/i* (ge-, h) wink, blink

Zwirn [tsvırn] *m* (-[e]s; -e) thread, yarn, twist

zwischen ['tsvıʃən] *prp* (*dat and acc*) between; among

'zwischen'durch F *adv* in between

'Zwischenergebnis *n* intermediate result

Zwischenfall *m* incident

Zwischenhändler *m* ECON middleman

Zwischenlandung *f* AVIAT stopover; *ohne Zwischenlandung* nonstop

'Zwischenraum *m* space, interval

Zwischenruf *m* (loud) interruption; *pl* heckling

Zwischenrufer *m* (-s; -) heckler

Zwischenspiel *n* interlude

Zwischenstati̱on *f* stop(over); *Zwischenstation machen* (*in dat*) stop over (in)

Zwischenwand *f* partition (wall)

Zwischenzeit *f*: *in der Zwischenzeit* in the meantime, meanwhile

Zwist [tsvıst] *m* (-[e]s; -e) discord

zwitschern ['tsvıtʃɐn] *v/i* (ge-, h) twitter, chirp

Zwitter ['tsvıtɐ] *m* (-s; -) BIOL hermaphrodite

zwölf [tsvœlf] *adj* twelve; *um zwölf (Uhr)* at twelve (o'clock); at noon; at midnight

'zwölfte *adj* twelfth

Zyankali [tsya:n'ka:li] *n* (-s; *no pl*) CHEM potassium cyanide

Zyklus ['tsy:klʊs] *m* (-; -klen) cycle; series, course

Zylinder [tsi'lındɐ] *m* (-s; -) top hat; MATH, TECH cylinder

zylindrisch [tsi'lındrıʃ] *adj* cylindrical

Zyniker ['tsy:nikɐ] *m* (-s; -) cynic

zynisch ['tsy:nıʃ] *adj* cynical

Zynismus [tsy'nısmʊs] *m* (-; -men) cynicism

Zypresse [tsy'prɛsə] *f* (-; -n) BOT cypress

Zyste ['tsystə] *f* (-; -n) MED cyst

z.Z(t). ABBR *of zur Zeit* at the moment, at present

Z

Activity & Reference Section

The following section contains three parts, each of which will help you in your learning:

Games and puzzles to help you learn to use this dictionary and practice your German-language skills. You'll learn about the different features of this dictionary and how to look something up effectively.

Basic words and expressions to reinforce your learning and help you master the basics.

A short grammar reference to help you use the language correctly.

Using Your Dictionary

Using a bilingual dictionary is important if you want to speak, read or write in a foreign language. Unfortunately, if you don't understand the symbols in your dictionary or the structure of the entries, you'll make mistakes.

What kind of mistakes? Think of some of the words you know in English that sound or look alike. For example, think about the word *ring*. How many meanings can you think of for the word *ring*? Try to list at least three:

a. _____

b. _____

c. _____

Now look up *ring* in the English side of the dictionary. There are more than ten German words that correspond to the single English word *ring*. Some of these German words are listed below in scrambled form.

Unscramble the jumbled German words, then draw a line connecting each German word with the appropriate English meaning or context.

German jumble	*English meanings*
1. LKGENNLI	**a.** a circle around something
2. NGRI	**b.** the action a bell or telephone does (to ring)
3. EGAEMN	**c.** jewelry worn on the finger
4. FEANRNU	**d.** the boxing venue
5. GRNIBXO	**e.** one of the venues at a circus
6. EIKRS	**f.** the action of calling someone

With so many German words to choose from, each meaning something different, you must be careful to choose the right one to fit the context of your translation. Using the wrong word can make it hard for people to understand you. Imagine the confusing sentences you would make if you never looked beyond the first translation.

For example:

The boxer wearily entered the circle.

She always wore the circle left to her by her grandmother.

I was waiting for the phone to circle when there was a knock at the door.

If you choose the wrong meaning, you simply won't be understood. Mistakes like these are easy to avoid once you know what to look for when using your dictionary. The following pages will review the structure of your dictionary and show you how to pick the right word for your context. Read the tips and guidelines, then complete the puzzles and exercises to practice what you have learned.

Identifying Headwords

If you are looking for a single word in the dictionary, you simply look for that word's location in alphabetical order. However, if you are looking for a phrase, or an object that is described by several words, you will have to decide which word to look up.

Two-word terms are listed by their first word. If you are looking for the German equivalent of *shooting star*, you will find it under *shooting*.

So-called phrasal verbs, verbs used in combination with other words, are found in a block under the main verb. The phrasal verbs *go ahead*, *go at*, *go for*, *go on*, *go out*, and *go up* are all found in a block after *go*.

Idiomatic expressions are found under the key word in the expression. The phrase *give someone a ring*, meaning to call someone, is found in the entry for *ring*.

Headwords referring specifically to males or females with the same profession or nationality are listed together in alphabetical order. In German, a male dancer is called a **Tänzer** and a female dancer is a **Tänzerin**. Both of the words are found in alphabetical order under the masculine form, **Tänzer**.

Find the following words and phrases in your bilingual dictionary. Identify the headword that each is found under. Then, try to find all of the headwords in the word-search puzzle on the next page.

1. get the message
2. be in shock
3. give someone a break
4. make a dash for
5. with no strings attached
6. be mixed up with
7. minor key
8. get away with
9. it's going to rain
10. take advantage of
11. charakterisieren
12. 20 Minuten Verspätung haben
13. Hund
14. sich wahrsagen lassen
15. Apotheke

V	X	R	T	R	G	F	Z	N	A	M	D	N	V	W
K	E	V	V	N	E	P	R	C	D	I	D	Y	I	M
A	O	R	I	V	D	K	H	C	V	N	A	E	M	Y
G	K	R	S	A	C	A	E	G	A	O	I	O	E	U
Z	T	N	S	P	R	W	M	H	N	R	G	B	G	Q
S	F	H	K	A	Ä	X	D	W	T	E	O	Y	A	N
E	D	R	K	X	G	T	M	X	A	O	O	B	S	V
W	U	T	I	M	I	P	U	P	G	B	P	C	S	M
Z	E	D	N	U	H	M	A	N	E	Z	Z	A	E	P
R	H	K	J	B	O	Z	N	Q	G	I	E	N	M	T
N	E	G	A	S	R	H	A	W	S	H	O	C	K	E
C	Z	E	A	M	K	E	Q	Z	W	Q	U	Z	Q	G
M	Z	K	N	P	S	A	A	J	D	G	M	I	J	D
F	G	W	K	N	Z	O	P	K	F	N	O	G	X	W
N	P	E	K	C	O	O	P	V	Z	A	P	V	W	N

Alphabetization

The entries in a bilingual dictionary are in alphabetical order. If words begin with the same letter or letters, they are alphabetized from A to Z using the first unique letter in each word.

Umlauts **ä**, **ö**, and **ü** are treated the same as **a**, **o**, and **u**. If they are in a list together, the non-umlauted form goes before the umlauted one (**schon**, **schön**). The "eszet" (**ß**) is alphabetized as if it were **ss**.

Rewrite the following words in alphabetical order. Next to each word also write the number associated with it. Then follow that order to connect the dots on the next page. Not all of the dots will be used, only those whose numbers appear in the word list.

zu	1	langsam	54
anrufen	4	jährlich	56
zusammen	8	Regenmantel	64
schön	11	Gasthaus	65
Jacke	16	schon	68
Gast	22	Mechanikerin	72
Tante	28	Museum	73
interessant	33	Flughafen	76
hin und zurück	34	Bäckerei	78
Badehose	35	können	47
Öl	37	Computer	84
Weißwein	38	Elefant	87
Regenschirm	40	danke	90
trinken	46	wissen	93
kommen	82	Bad	98
fahren	49	Volkswagen	99
Ohrring	53		

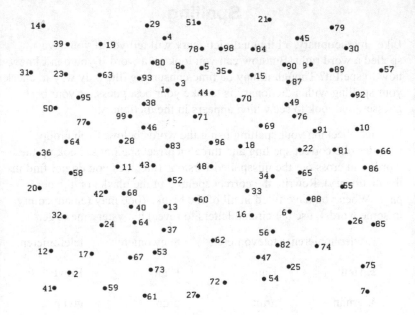

Welches Land sehen Sie?

___ ___ ___ ___ ___ ___ ___ ___ ___ ___

Spelling

Like any dictionary, a bilingual dictionary will tell you if you have spelled a word right. But how can you look up a word if you don't know how to spell it? Though it may be time consuming, the only way to check your spelling with a dictionary is to take your best guess, or your best guesses, and look to see which appears in the dictionary.

Practice checking your spelling using the words below. Each group includes one correct spelling and three incorrect spellings. Look up the words and cross out the misspelled versions (the ones you do not find in the dictionary). Rewrite the correct spelling in the blanks on the next page. When you have filled in all of the blanks (one may remain empty in some words), use the circled letters to reveal a mystery message.

1. telephonieren	televonieren	telewonieren	telefonieren
2. Hout	Haut	Häut	Howt
3. gruhn	gruin	grün	greun
4. Universität	Universitat	Universitaat	Universiteet
5. Addrese	Addresse	Adrässe	Adresse
6. Meßer	Mezser	Mezzer	Messer
7. Räzel	Retsel	Rätsel	Reezel
8. Hilfe	Hülfe	Hilpe	Helfe
9. Esszimmer	Ässzimmer	Eßzimmer	Eszimmer
10. Tish	Tisch	Tich	Tichs
11. Shild	Schildt	Schild	Schilt

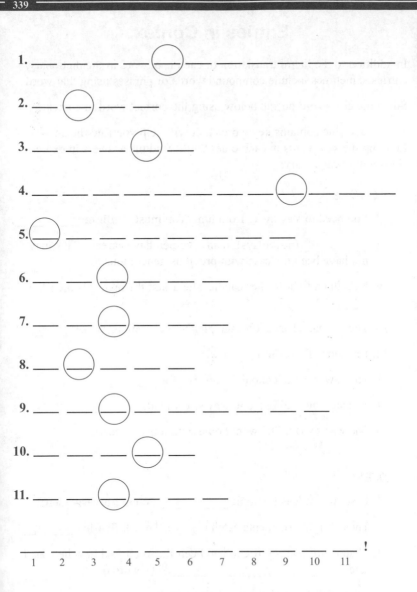

1. ___ ___ ___ ◯ ___ ___ ___ ___ ___ ___

2. ___ ◯ ___ ___ ___ ___

3. ___ ___ ___ ◯ ___ ___

4. ___ ___ ___ ___ ___ ___ ___ ◯ ___ ___ ___

5. ◯ ___ ___ ___ ___ ___ ___ ___

6. ___ ___ ◯ ___ ___ ___

7. ___ ___ ◯ ___ ___ ___

8. ___ ◯ ___ ___ ___

9. ___ ___ ◯ ___ ___ ___ ___ ___

10. ___ ___ ___ ◯ ___

11. ___ ___ ◯ ___ ___ ___

___ ___ ___ ___ ___ ___ ___ ___ ___ ___ ___ !
1 2 3 4 5 6 7 8 9 10 11

Entries in Context

In addition to the literal translation of each headword in the dictionary, entries sometimes include compound words or phrases using that word.

Solve the crossword puzzle below using the correct word in context.

Hint: Each clue contains key words that will help you find the answer. Look up the key words in each clue. You'll find the answers in expressions within each entry.

ACROSS

3. You need to stay away from him. You must **von ihm** _____.

4. _____ (nowadays), many women have careers. This may not have been the case with previous generations.

6. Needing a light for her candle, she asked the man: **"Haben Sie _____?"**

10. The woman chased after the pickpocket, yelling **"Halt! _____!"**

12. I'm sorry. **Es tut mir _____.**

13. To answer the telephone is **ans Telefon _____.**

14. The sign indicating a one-way street reads _____.

15. She was so sad. She went home with a heavy heart, _____**Herzens**.

DOWN

1. Last but not least! **"Nicht _____ , nicht zu vergessen."**

2. Those bright ornaments catch my eye. They **fallen ins _____**.

3. I had heard that my friend had been ill, so I asked how he was. I said: **"_____ _____?"** (4 words)

5. I'd prefer to eat on the open-air patio, **im _____**.

7. When the Germans fall in love, they _____ **sich**.

8. In order to reach my ideal weight, I must **25 Pfund _____**.

9. What a pity! **Wie** _____!

11. I wondered what time it was; I asked a friend, **"Wie** _____ **ist es?"**

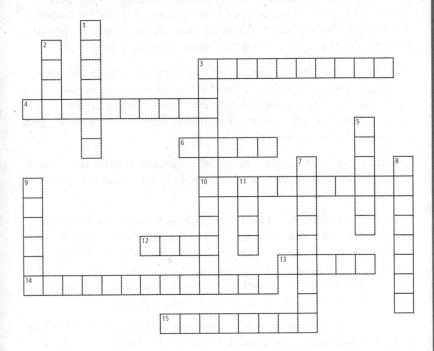

Word Families

Some English words have several related meanings that are represented by different words in German. These related meanings belong to the same word family and are grouped together under a single English head-word. Other words, while they look the same, do not belong to the same word family. These words are written under a separate headword.

Think back to our first example, *ring*. The translations **Ring**, **Boxring**, **Manege** and **Kreis** all refer to related meanings of *ring* in English. They are all circular things, though in different contexts. **Klingeln** and **anrufen**, however, refer to a totally different meaning of *ring* in English: the sound a bell or phone makes.

The word family for circles, with all of its nuanced German translations, is grouped together under *ring¹*. The word family for sounds is grouped together under *ring²*.

Study the lists of words below. Each group includes three German trans-lations belonging to one word family, and one German translation of an identical-looking but unrelated English word. Eliminate the translation that is not in the same word family as the others. Then rewrite the misfit word in the corresponding blanks. When you have filled in all of the blanks, use the circled letters to reveal a bonus message.

Hint: Look up the German words to find out what they mean. Then look up those translations in the English-German side of your dictionary to find the word family that contains the German words.

1. klingeln	Manege	Ring	Kreis
2. leicht	unbedeutend	beleidigen	gering
3. stampfen	Briefmarke	trampeln	stempeln
4. Pause	ausruhen	rasten	Rest
5. Menge	Messe	Masse	Mehrzahl
6. stecken	Stock	Schläger	Zweig

1. 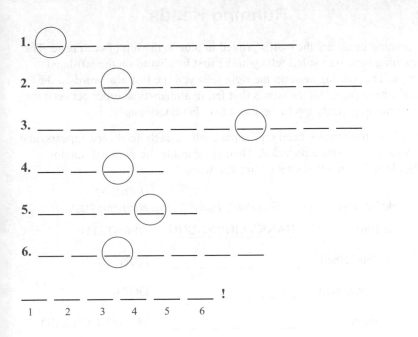 ◯ __ __ __ __ __ __ __

2. __ __ ◯ __ __ __ __ __

3. __ __ __ __ __ ◯ __ __ __

4. __ __ ◯ __

5. __ __ __ ◯ __

6. __ __ ◯ __ __ __ __ __

__ __ __ __ __ __ !
1   2   3   4   5   6

Running Heads

Running heads are the words printed in blue at the top of each page. The running head on the left tells you the first headword on the left-hand page. The running head on the right tells you the last headword on the right-hand page. All the words that fall in alphabetical order between the two running heads appear on those two dictionary pages.

Look up the running head on the page where each headword appears, and write it in the space provided. Then unscramble the jumbled running heads and match them with what you wrote.

Headword	Running head	Jumbled running head
1. Bart	BANKVERBINDUNG	UFRATZPU
2. Dunkelheit		IUJN
3. Gesundheit		DORK
4. Jugend		MENRUDCHKMO
5. Kartoffel		TRAUSSIMNE
6. konventionell		RADIESCHISPA
7. mitbringen		STSON
8. Nachmittag		BEUTANSCHGAL
9. Pass		SINNUNGELOSS
10. quatschen		VERGNUDNIBBNAK
11. Software		BRACHAN
12. Taxistand		PITAKALLANAEG

Pronunciation

Though German has more vowel sounds than English, pronunciation in the two languages is similar. Refer to the pronunciation guide in this dictionary to see equivalent sounds across the two languages. Study the guide to familiarize yourself with the symbols used to give pronunciations in this dictionary.

Practice recognizing pronunciations as they are written in the dictionary. Look at each of the pronunciations below, then connect it to its correct English or German spelling.

1. frend	A. Imbiss
2. ˈevri	B. language
3. æpl	C. Bad
4. naïf	D. every
5. ˈlægwidʒ	E. selig
6. baːt	F. friend
7. ˈɪmbɪs	G. Fang
8. ˈzeˑliç	H. knife
9. faŋ	I. gekränkt
10. gəˈkrɛŋkt	J. apple

Parts of Speech

In German and English, words are categorized into different **parts of speech**. These labels tell us what function a word performs in a sentence. In this dictionary, the part of speech is given before a word's definition.

Nouns are people, places or things. **Verbs** describe actions. **Adjectives** describe nouns in sentences. For example, the adjective *pretty* tells you about the noun *girl* in the phrase *a pretty girl*. **Adverbs** also describe, but they modify verbs, adjectives, and other adverbs. The adverb *quickly* tells you more about how the action is carried out in the phrase *ran quickly*. Adjectives usually take endings when used in a German sentence. Adverbs do not. Most adjectives are also used as adverbs. *The fast (adj) runners ran fast (adv) to the finish line.* The only way to identify whether a particular word is an adjective or adverb is to observe its use in the sentence.

Prepositions specify relationships in time and space. They are words such as *in*, *on*, *before*, or *with*. **Articles** are words that accompany nouns. Words like *the* and *a* or *an* modify the noun, marking it as specific or general, and known or unknown.

Conjunctions are words like *and*, *but*, and *if* that join phrases and sentences together. **Pronouns** take the place of nouns in a sentence.

The following activity uses words from the dictionary in a Sudoku-style puzzle. In Sudoku puzzles, the numbers 1 to 9 are used to fill in grids. All digits 1 to 9 must appear, but cannot be repeated, in each square, row, and column.

In the following puzzles, you are given a set of words for each part of the grid. Look up each word to find out its part of speech. Then arrange the words within the square so that, in the whole puzzle, you do not repeat any part of speech within a column or row.

Hint: If one of the words given in the puzzle is a noun, then you know that no other nouns can be put in that row or column of the grid. Use the process of elimination to figure out where the other parts of speech can go.

Let's try a small puzzle first. Use the categories noun *n*, verb *v*, adjective/adverb *adj/adv*, and preposition *prep* to solve this puzzle. Each section corresponds to one quarter of the puzzle.

Section 1

denken, Hund, schwarz, mit

Section 2

Euro, auf, machen, toll

Section 3

ehrlich, vor, Bilder, spielen

Section 4

Lotterie, staatlich, schaden, nach

denken (v)			**Euro** (n)
		schaden (v)	
ehrlich (adj/adv)			

Now try a larger puzzle. For this puzzle, use the categories noun *n*, verb *v*, adjective/adverb *adj/adv*, preposition *prep*, article *art*, and pronoun *pro*. The sections are numbered from top left to bottom right.

Section 1

Aufzug, attraktiv, **steigen**, **wir**, ein, über

Section 2

andere, ehe, **sortieren**, **Bilder**, das, sie

Section 3

mit, Käse, **planen**, mild, **er**, **eine**

Section 4

schreiben, **exklusiv**, du, die, **Lampen**, ohne

Section 5

nach, diskret, Etappe, wohnen, **ich**, **der**

Section 6

Familie, **ihm**, **zwischen**, gut, kaufen, einen

wir (pron)		**steigen** (v)	**Bilder** (n)		
Aufzug (n)					**sortieren** (v)
	planen (v)			**Lampen** (n)	
eine (art)	**er** (pron)			**exklusiv** (adj/adv)	
nach (prep)		**der** (art)			**ihm** (pron)
		ich (pron)	**zwischen** (prep)		

Pluralization of Nouns

There are sixteen different patterns used to pluralize German nouns. You can familiarize yourself with them in the appendix of this dictionary. The plural form is indicated in parentheses after the gender of the noun in its dictionary entry. First you see an –s, -(e)s or –es. That indicates the genitive form of the noun (the form that says *of the*…). Following that is the abbreviated indicator of the plural form. The symbol –e means that the word adds an –e to become plural. Many feminine nouns add –**en** in the plural. Many masculine and neuter nouns add an umlaut on the stem vowel and then an –e.

Write the plurals of the nouns in the list and then check your spelling by finding them in the following word search.

Singular	*Plural*
1. Kind	_____
2. Mutter	_____
3. Hund	_____
4. Bruder	_____
5. Auto	_____
6. Frau	_____
7. Haus	_____
8. Gericht	_____
9. Arbeiter	_____
10. Lehrerin	_____

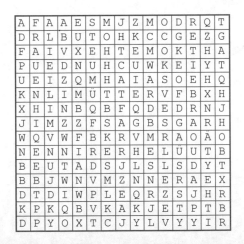

A	F	A	A	E	S	M	J	Z	M	O	D	R	Q	T
D	R	L	B	U	T	O	H	K	C	C	G	E	Z	G
F	A	I	V	X	E	H	T	E	M	O	K	T	H	A
P	U	E	D	N	U	H	C	U	W	K	E	I	Y	T
U	E	I	Z	Q	M	H	A	I	A	S	O	E	H	Q
K	N	L	I	M	Ü	T	T	E	R	V	F	B	X	H
X	H	I	N	B	Q	B	F	Q	D	E	D	R	N	J
J	I	M	Z	Z	F	S	A	G	B	S	G	A	R	H
W	Q	V	W	F	B	K	R	V	M	R	A	O	Ä	O
N	E	N	N	I	R	E	R	H	E	L	Ü	U	T	B
B	E	U	T	A	D	S	J	L	S	L	S	D	Y	T
B	B	J	W	N	V	M	Z	N	N	E	R	A	E	X
D	T	D	I	W	P	L	E	Q	R	Z	S	J	H	R
K	P	K	Q	B	V	K	A	K	J	E	T	P	T	B
D	P	Y	O	X	T	C	J	Y	L	V	Y	Y	I	R

Gender

German nouns are easily recognizable. They are always capitalized, even in the middle of a sentence. They all belong to one of three groups: masculine, feminine, or neuter. A noun's gender is indicated in an entry after the headword or pronunciation with **m** for masculine, **f** for feminine, and **n** for neuter.

Look up the words listed below and mark the gender of each word. Then use the genders to lead you through the puzzle: if a word is masculine, go left; if a word is feminine, go right; if a word is neuter, go up.

	m (go left)	*f* (go right)	*n* (go up)
1. Gericht			
2. Katze			
3. Mond			
4. Sonne			
5. Wagen			
6. Kuchen			
7. Großmutter			
8. Freundschaft			
9. Aufzug			
10. Frühstück			
11. Person			
12. Professor			
13. Bestellung			
14. Reis			

Start

Adjectives

In German, adjectives take different endings in order to agree in gender and number with the noun they modify. In most cases, an –e is added to the adjective for the feminine form, and an –n is added for the plural form. A table of adjective endings can be found in the appendix of this dictionary.

Use the dictionary to determine whether the nouns in the following phrases are masculine or feminine, singular or plural. Then write in the correct form of the adjective to complete the phrase. We have added the correct endings for you. Check your answers against the word search. The correct forms will be found in the puzzle with their endings.

1. a friendly smile = ein _____es Lächeln

2. a blonde woman = eine _____e Frau

3. an important message = eine _____e Nachricht

4. public school = _____e Schule

5. the green car = der _____e Wagen

6. an unforgettable picnic = ein _____es Picknick

7. a pretty girl = ein _____es Mädchen

8. in a good book = in einem _____en Buch

9. an interesting speaker = ein _____er Redner

10. a German piano player = ein _____er Klavierspieler

11. a heavy backback = ein _____er Rucksack

U	E	T	R	Y	G	M	I	E	S	X	O	V	J	X
K	N	H	O	E	A	C	N	F	C	V	H	L	Z	M
S	H	V	M	D	N	N	T	R	H	D	V	V	C	D
F	L	X	E	X	O	U	E	Y	W	G	R	G	Z	E
W	W	Q	F	R	Y	P	R	X	E	F	Q	S	G	H
L	I	M	T	N	G	S	E	G	R	N	M	V	O	C
W	L	C	M	N	C	E	S	R	E	E	G	N	B	I
F	M	N	H	H	K	I	S	S	R	T	R	F	J	L
Q	B	W	Ö	T	B	X	A	S	L	U	J	D	L	T
Z	C	N	Q	H	I	H	N	F	L	G	Y	S	E	N
Q	E	X	Q	J	F	G	T	W	O	I	E	K	T	E
S	E	D	N	O	L	B	E	V	Z	I	C	F	C	F
N	D	U	R	F	U	S	R	M	B	T	O	H	X	F
S	E	H	C	I	L	D	N	U	E	R	F	I	E	Ö
D	E	U	T	S	C	H	E	R	K	L	E	B	C	S

Verbs

Verbs are listed in the dictionary in their infinitive form. To use the verb in a sentence, you must conjugate it and use the form that agrees with the sentence's subject.

Most verbs are regular and conjugate like the chart in the appendix of this dictionary. A few are irregular and require a vowel change in the present tense. A list of all irregular verbs can also be found in the appendix.

For this puzzle, conjugate the given verbs in the present tense. Use the context and the subject pronoun to determine the person and number of the form you need. The correct answer fits in the crossword spaces provided.

ACROSS

2. Am Samstag _____ es auch einen Gemüsemarkt in der Marburger Straße. **geben**

4. Das Kind _____ mit seinen Freunden ins Kino. **gehen**

6. Zur gleichen Zeit _____ ich in die Stadt einkaufen. **fahren**

7. Der Film _____ den Kindern gut. Sie wollen ihn ein zweites Mal sehen. **gefallen**

9. Die Nachbarin _____ dem Ehepaar zum Hochzeitstag. **gratulieren**

12. Was _____ ich meinen Eltern zum Hochzeitstag? Zwei Schiffskarten für eine Kreuzfahrt im Mittelmeer. **schenken**

13. Wir _____ drei Dutzend Eier, da wir backen wollen. **kaufen**

14. Mein Vater _____ seine neue Digitalkamera auf die Reise mit. **nehmen**

17. Die Suppe _____ der Familie sehr gut und ist sehr gesund. **schmecken**

18. Die Feier war so toll, dass alle Gäste nächstes Jahr wieder kommen _____ . **wollen**

DOWN

1. Die Kinder _____ den Film "Superman" am Samstag an. **sehen**

3. Der Supermarkt _____ Eier zum halben Preis an. **bieten**

5. Mein Mann _____ den Kindern immer bei den Hausaufgaben. Er ist Lehrer. **helfen**

6. Die Großeltern _____ am Sonntag ihren fünfzigsten Hochzeitstag. **feiern**

8. Meine Nachbarn _____ den Brokkoli vom Leoni-Markt. **mögen**

10. Bevor sie wegfahren, _____ sie uns immer an und verabschieden sich. **rufen**

11. Katarina _____ früh nach Hause gehen und ihre Hausaufgaben für Montag machen. **müssen**

12. Morgen _____ die ganze Familie nach Ulm zu den Großeltern. **fahren**

16. Meine 10-jährige Tochter _____ jeden Abend in ihr Tagebuch. **schreiben**

17. Seine Bilder _____ sehr gut geworden. **sein**

19. Mein Babysitter muss heute schon früh gehen, also _____ ich nur 15 Minuten auf der Fete. **bleiben**

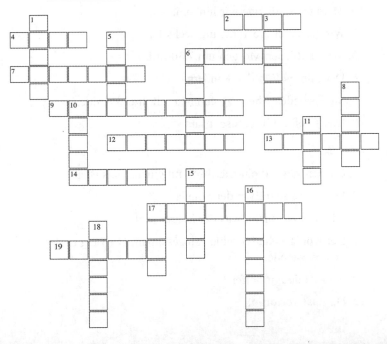

When you are reading German, you face a different challenge. You see a conjugated verb in context and need to determine what its infinitive is in order to understand its meaning.

Often you will see a preposition at the end of the sentence with no object. That's called a separable prefix and is considered part of the verb. **Ich rufe meine Mutter jetzt an.** The verb is **anrufen**. The prefix **an** is separated from the verb in the sentence, but must be added back onto the infinitive in order to insure that you find the correct meaning.

For the next puzzle, you will see conjugated verbs in the sentences. Figure out which verb the conjugated form represents, and write the infinitive (the headword form) in the puzzle.

ACROSS

2. Das Kind **versteckte** seinen Teddybär unter seinem Kopfkissen.

3. Machst du eine Diät? Du **siehst** gut **aus**.

6. Das brave Kind **gehorcht** seinen Eltern immer.

8. Gerd und Gerlinde **kamen** drei Stunden zu spät **an**.

10. Matthias **weiß**, wie wir hinkommen.

11. Wir **rufen** unsere Tante um sechs Uhr **an**.

13. Sie **steht** jeden Morgen um 7.30 **auf**.

16. Der Film **gefällt** den Kindern.

17. Sie **isst** jeden Abend zusammen mit ihrer Familie.

18. Das Telefon **klingelt** sehr laut.

DOWN

1. Carsten **bestellt** ein Käsebrot mit einem Glas Bier.

4. Die Katze **schläft** in der Sonne.

5. Ich **verstehe** nicht, was der Lehrer sagt.

7. Der König **heiratet** seine Prinzessin am Dienstag in der Schlosskapelle.

9. **Kannst** du mir helfen?

12. Du **hast verloren**!

14. Ich **sehe** dich hinter der Couch!

15. Die Schauspielerinnen **sind** sehr hübsch.

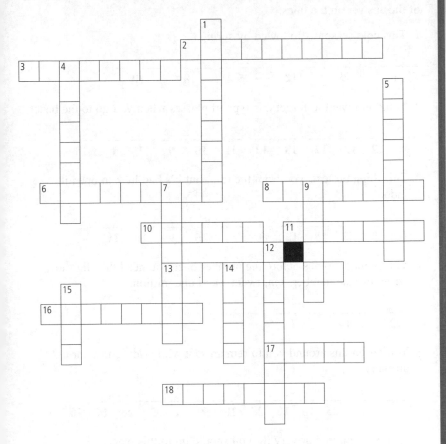

Riddles

Solve the following riddles in English. Then write the German translation of the answer on the lines.

1. This cold season is followed by spring.

6	9	12	5	18	10

2. You don't want to forget this type of glasses when you go to the beach.

3	17	12	12	18	12	11	10	9	1	1	18

3. This thing protects you from the rain, but it's bad luck to open it indoors!

10	18	23	18	12	3	24	25	9	10	21

4. This number comes before the number one. You need this digit to write out the numbers ten, twenty, and one million.

12	14	1	1

5. You fasten this around you to remain safe while riding in a car or airplane.

3	9	24	25	18	10	25	18	9	5	3	23	14	10	5

6. If you are injured or very ill, you should go to this place.

7	10	15	12	7	18	12	25	15	14	3

7. This mode of transportation has only two wheels. It is also good exercise!

13	15	25	10	10	15	2

8. This large mammal lives in the ocean.

___ ___ ___
6   15   1

9. This person is your mother's mother.

___ ___ ___ ___ ___ ___ ___ ___ ___ ___
23 10 17 27 21 14 5 5 18 10

10. There are twelve of these in a year.

___ ___ ___ ___ ___ ___
21 17 12 15 5 18

11. Snow White bit into this red fruit and fell into a long slumber.

___ ___ ___ ___ ___
15 4 13 18 1

12. This professional brings letters and packages to your door.

___ ___ ___ ___ ___ ___ ___ ___ ___ ___ ___
11 10 9 18 13 5 10 8 23 18 10

13. This midday meal falls between breakfast and dinner.

___ ___ ___ ___ ___ ___ ___ ___ ___ ___ ___
21 9 5 5 15 23 18 3 3 18 12

14. A very young cat is referred to as this.

___ ___ ___ ___ ___ ___ ___ ___
7 8 5 16 24 25 28 12

15. An archer uses a bow and this.

___ ___ ___ ___ ___
4 13 18 9 1

16. My mother was married to this relative of mine when she was twenty-three.

___ ___ ___ ___ ___
19 15 5 18 10

Cryptogram

Write the letter that corresponds to each number in the spaces. When you are done, read the German message. It's a quote from a famous German author and expresses our wish that you look forward to your German language experience.

21	15	12		21	14	3	3		9	21	21
18	10		18	5	6	15	3		25	15	11
18	12		6	17	10	15	14	13		21	15
12		3	9	24	25		13	10	18	14	5
	16	9	5	15	5		19	17	12		18
2	14	15	10	2		21	Ö	10	9	7	18

"___ ___ ___ ___ ___ ___ ___ ___ ___ ___ ___ ___

___ ___ ___ ___ ___ ___ ___ ___ ___ ___ ,

___ ___ ___ ___ ___ ___ ___ ___ ___

___ ___ ___ ___ ___ . " ___ ___ ___ ___ ___ ___

___ ___ ___

___ ___ ___ ___ ___ ___ ___ ___ ___ ___

Answer Key

Using Your Dictionary

a–c. Answers will vary

1. klingeln, b
2. Ring, c
3. Manege, e

4. anrufen, f
5. Boxring, d
6. Kreis, a

Identifying Headwords

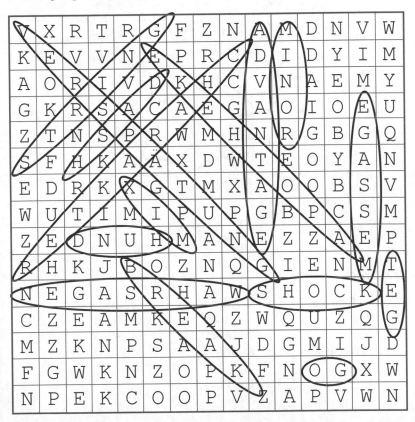

Alphabetization

anrufen, Bäckerei, Bad, Badehose, Computer, danke, Elefant, fahren,
Flughafen, Gast, Gasthaus, hin und zurück, interessant, Jacke,
jährlich, kommen, können, langsam, Mechanikerin, Museum,
Ohrring, Öl, Regenmantel, Regenschirm, schon, schön, Tante, trinken,
Volkswagen, Weißwein, wissen, zu, zusammen

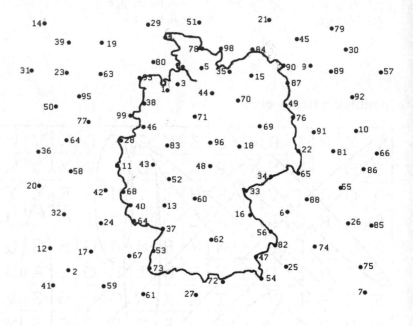

<u>D</u> E <u>U</u> T <u>S</u> C <u>H</u> L A <u>N</u> D

Spelling

1. telefonieren
2. Haut
3. grün
4. Universität
5. Adresse
6. Messer
7. Rätsel
8. Hilfe
9. Esszimmer
10. Tisch
11. Schild

<u>F</u> A <u>N</u> T A <u>S</u> T I <u>S</u> C <u>H</u> !

Entries in Context

Word Families

1. klingeln
2. beleidigen
3. Briefmarke

4. Rest
5. Messe
6. stecken

<u>K</u> <u>L</u> <u>A</u> <u>S</u> <u>S</u> <u>E</u>!

Pronunciation

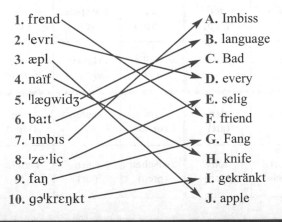

1. frend
2. ˈevri
3. æpl
4. naïf
5. ˈlægwidʒ
6. baːt
7. ˈɪmbɪs
8. ˈzeˑliç
9. faŋ
10. gəˈkrɛŋkt

A. Imbiss
B. language
C. Bad
D. every
E. selig
F. friend
G. Fang
H. knife
I. gekränkt
J. apple

Parts of Speech

Hund (n)	schwarz (adj/adv)	auf (prep)	machen (v)
denken (v)	mit (prep)	toll (adj/adv)	**Euro** (n)
vor (prep)	Bilder (n)	**schaden** (v)	staatlich (adj/adv)
ehrlich (adj/adv)	spielen (v)	Lotterie (n)	nach (prep)

wir (pron)	**ein** (art)	**steigen** (v)	**Bilder** (n)	ehe (prep)	andere (adj/adv)
Aufzug (n)	**über** (prep)	attraktiv (adj/adv)	das (art)	sie (pron)	**sotieren** (v)
mild (adj/adv)	**planen** (v)	mit (prep)	du (pron)	**Lampen** (n)	sie (art)
eine (art)	**er** (pron)	Käse (n)	schreiben (v)	**exklusiv** (adj/adv)	ohne (prep)
nach (prep)	Etappe (n)	**der** (art)	gut (adj/adv)	kaufen (v)	**ihm** (pron)
wohnen (v)	diskret (adj/adv)	**ich** (pron)	**zwischen** (prep)	einen (art)	Familie (n)

Pluralization of Nouns

A	F	A	A	E	S	M	J	Z	M	O	D	R	Q	T
D	R	L	B	U	T	O	H	K	C	C	G	E	Z	G
F	A	I	V	X	E	H	T	E	M	O	K	T	H	A
P	U	E	D	N	U	H	C	U	W	K	E	I	Y	T
U	E	I	Z	Q	M	H	A	I	A	S	O	E	H	Q
K	N	L	I	M	Ü	T	T	E	R	V	F	B	X	H
X	H	I	N	B	Q	B	F	Q	D	E	D	R	N	J
J	I	M	Z	Z	F	S	A	G	B	S	G	A	R	H
W	Q	V	W	F	B	K	R	V	M	R	A	O	A	O
N	E	N	N	I	R	E	R	H	E	L	Ü	U	T	B
B	E	U	T	A	D	S	J	L	S	I	S	D	Y	T
B	B	J	W	N	V	M	Z	N	N	E	R	A	E	X
D	T	D	I	W	P	L	E	Q	R	Z	S	J	H	R
K	P	K	Q	B	V	K	A	K	J	E	T	P	T	B
D	P	Y	O	X	T	C	J	Y	L	V	Y	Y	I	R

Kinder, Mütter, Hunde, Brüder, Autos, Frauen, Häuser,
Gerichte, Arbeiter, Lehrerinnen

Gender

1. Gericht *n* 2. Katze *f* 3. Kind *n* 4. Sonne *f* 5. Auto *n*
6. Kuchen *m* 7. Holz *n* 8. Freundschaft *f* 9. Bett *n*
10. Person *f* 11. Brot *n* 12. Bestellung *f* 13. Pferd *n*

Start

Running Heads

Headword	*Running head*	*Jumbled running head*
1. Bart	BANKVERBINDUNG	UFRATZPU
2. Dunkelheit	DURCHKOMMEN	IUJN
3. Gesundheit	GESINNUNGSLOS	DORK
4. Jugend	JUNI	MENRUDCHKMO
5. Kartoffel	KAPITALANLAGE	TRAUSSIMNE
6. konventionell	KORD	RADIESCHISPA
7. mitbringen	MISSTRAUEN	STSON
8. Nachmittag	NACHBAR	BEUTANSCHGAL
9. Pass	PARADIESISCH	SINNUNGELOSS
10. quatschen	PUTZFRAU	VERGNUDNIBBNAK
11. Software	SONST	BRACHAN
12. Taxistand	TAUBENSCHLAG	PITAKALLANAEG

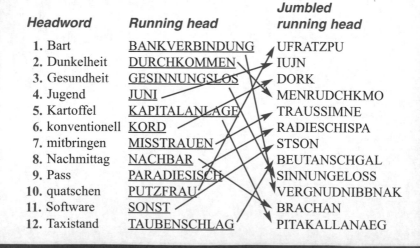

Adjectives

1. ein freundliches Lächeln
2. eine blonde Frau
3. eine wichtige Nachricht
4. öffentliche Schule
5. der grüne Wagen
6. ein unvergessliches Picknick
7. ein schönes Mädchen
8. in einem guten Buch
9. ein interessanter Redner
10. ein deutscher Klavierspieler
11. ein schwerer Rucksack

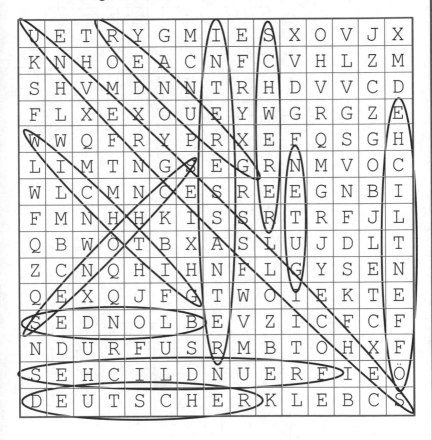

U	E	T	R	Y	G	M	I	E	S	X	O	V	J	X
K	N	H	O	E	A	C	N	F	C	V	H	L	Z	M
S	H	V	M	D	N	N	T	R	H	D	V	V	C	D
F	L	X	E	X	O	U	E	Y	W	G	R	G	Z	E
W	W	Q	F	R	Y	P	R	X	E	F	Q	S	G	H
L	I	M	T	N	G	Q	E	G	R	N	M	V	O	C
W	L	C	M	N	C	E	S	R	E	E	G	N	B	I
F	M	N	H	H	K	I	S	S	R	T	R	F	J	L
Q	B	W	O	T	B	X	A	S	L	U	J	D	L	T
Z	C	N	Q	H	I	H	N	F	L	G	Y	S	E	N
Q	E	X	Q	J	F	G	T	W	O	I	E	K	T	E
S	E	D	N	O	L	B	E	V	Z	I	C	F	C	F
N	D	U	R	F	U	S	R	M	B	T	O	H	X	F
S	E	H	C	I	L	D	N	U	E	R	F	I	E	Ö
D	E	U	T	S	C	H	E	R	K	L	E	B	C	S

Verbs

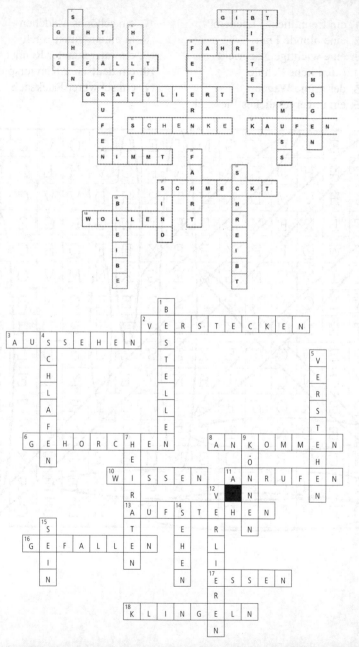

Riddles

1. Winter
2. Sonnenbrille
3. Regenschirm
4. null
5. Sicherheitsgurt
6. Krankenhaus
7. Fahrrad
8. Wal
9. Großmutter
10. Monate
11. Apfel
12. Briefträger
13. Mittagessen
14. Kätzchen
15. Pfeil
16. Vater

Cryptogram

21 M	15 N	12 N		21 M	14 U	3 S	3 S		9 I	21 M	21 M
18 E	10 R		18 E	5 T	6 W	15 A	3 S		25 H	15 A	11 B
18 E	12 N		6 W	17 O	10 R	15 A	14 U	13 F		21 M	15 A
12 N		3 S	9 I	24 C	25 H		13 F	10 R	18 E	14 U	5 T
	16 Z	9 I	5 T	15 A	5 T		19 V	17 O	12 N		18 E
2 D	14 U	15 A	10 R	2 D		21 M		Ö	10 R	9 I	7 K	18 E

„Man muss immer etwas haben, worauf man sich freut." Zitat von Eduard Mörike.

Eduard Mörike was a German lyrical poet who lived from 1805–1875 and wrote that, "One must always have something to look forward to." We hope that you look forward to learning German and to working with this dictionary.

BASIC GERMAN PHRASES & GRAMMAR

Pronunciation

In this section we have used a simplified phonetic system to represent the sounds of German. Simply read the pronunciation as if it were English.

Stress

Generally, as in English, the first syllable is stressed in German, except when short prefixes are added to the beginning of the word. Then the second syllable is stressed (e.g. **bewegen** *to move*, **gesehen** *seen*).

BASIC PHRASES

Essential

Good afternoon!	**Guten Tag!**	goo-ten tahk
Good evening!	**Guten Abend!**	goo-ten ah-bent
Goodbye!	**Auf Wiedersehen!**	owf vee-duh-zay-en
…, please!	**…, bitte!**	bit-tuh
Thank you!	**Danke!**	dahn-kuh
Yes.	**Ja.**	yah
No.	**Nein.**	nine
Sorry!	**Entschuldigung!**	ent-shool-dee-goong
Where are the restrooms?	**Wo ist die Toilette?**	vo ist dee toi-let-tuh
When?	**Wann?**	vahn
What?	**Was?**	vahs
Where?	**Wo?**	vo
Here.	**Hier.**	here
There.	**Dort.**	dawt
On the right.	**Rechts.**	rekhts
On the left.	**Links.**	linx
Do you have …?	**Haben Sie …?**	hah-ben zee
I'd like …	**Ich möchte …**	ikh merkh-tuh
How much is that?	**Was kostet das?**	vahs kaws-tet dahs
Where is …?	**Wo ist …?**	vo ist
Where can I get …?	**Wo gibt es …?**	vo gheept es

Communication Difficulties

Do you speak English?	**Sprechen Sie Englisch?**	shpre-khen zee ayng-lish
Does anyone here speak English?	**Spricht hier jemand Englisch?**	shprikht here yay-mahnt ayng-lish
Did you understand that?	**Haben Sie das verstanden?**	hah-ben zee dahs fair-stahn-den
I understand.	**Ich habe verstanden.**	ikh hah-beh fair-shtahnd-den
I didn't understand that.	**Ich habe das nicht verstanden.**	ikh hah-beh dahs nikht fair-shtahn-den
Could you speak a bit more slowly, please?	**Könnten Sie bitte etwas langsamer sprechen?**	kern-ten zee bit-tuh et-vahs lahng-zah-mer shpre-khen
Could you please repeat that?	**Könnten Sie das bitte wiederholen?**	kern-ten zee dahs bit-tuh veeder-ho-len
What's that in German?	**Wie heißt das auf Deutsch?**	vee highst dahs owf doitch
What does … mean?	**Was bedeutet …?**	vahs buh-doi-tet
Could you write it down for me, blease?	**Könnten Sie es mir bitte aufschreiben?**	kern-ten zee es meer bit-tuh owf-shry-ben

Greetings

Good morning!	**Guten Morgen!**	goo-ten maw-ghen
Good afternoon!	**Guten Tag!**	goo-ten tahk
Good evening!	**Guten Abend!**	goo-ten ah-bent
Goodnight!	**Gute Nacht!**	goo-tuh nakht
Hello!	**Hallo!**	hah-lo
How are you?	**Wie geht es Ihnen / dir?**	vee gate es ee-nen / deer
Fine, thanks. And you?	**Danke, gut. Und Ihnen / dir?**	dahn-kuh goot oont eenen / deer
I'm afraid I have to go.	**Es tut mir Leid, aber ich muss gehen.**	es toot meer lite ah-buh ikh moos gain
Goodbye!	**Auf Wiedersehen!**	owf vee-duh-zay-en
See you soon / tomorrow!	**Bis bald / morgen!**	bis bahlt / maw-ghen
Bye!	**Tschüs!**	chews

It was nice meeting you.	**Schön, Sie / dich kennen gelernt zu haben.**	shern zee / dikh ken-nen guh-lairnt tsoo hah-ben
Have a good trip!	**Gute Reise!**	goo-tuh reye-suh

Meeting People

What's your name?	**Wie heißen Sie / heißt du?**	vee high-sen zee / highst doo
My name is …	**Ich heiße …**	ikh high-suh
May I introduce …	**Darf ich bekannt machen? Das ist …**	dahf ikh buh-kahnt mah-khen dahs ist
– my husband.	**mein Mann.**	mighn mahn
– my wife.	**meine Frau.**	migh-nuh frow
– my boyfriend.	**mein Freund.**	mighn froint
– my girlfriend.	**meine Freundin.**	migh-nuh froin-din
Where are you from?	**Woher sind Sie?**	vo-hair zind zee
I'm from …	**Ich komme aus …**	ikh kom-uh ows
– the US.	**den USA.**	dane oo-es-ah
– Canada.	**Kanada.**	kah-nah-dah
– the UK.	**Großbritannien.**	gross-brit-tahn-ee-en

Expressing Likes and Dislikes

Very good!	**Sehr gut!**	zair goot
I'm very happy.	**Ich bin sehr zufrieden!**	ikh bin zair tsoo-free-den
I like that.	**Das gefällt mir.**	dahs guh-felt meer
What a shame!	**Wie schade!**	vee shah-duh
I'd rather …	**Ich würde lieber …**	ikh vewr-duh lee-buh …
I don't like it.	**Das gefällt mir nicht.**	dahs guh-felt meer nikht
I'd rather not.	**Das möchte ich lieber nicht.**	dahs merkh-tuh ikh lee-buh nisht
Certainly not.	**Auf keinen Fall.**	owf keye-nen fahl

Expressing Requests and Thanks

Thank you very much.	**Vielen Dank.**	fee-len dahnk
Thanks, you too.	**Danke, gleichfalls.**	dahn-kuh gleyekh-fahls
May I?	**Darf ich?**	dahf ikh
Please, …	**Bitte, …**	bit-tuh
No, thank you.	**Nein, danke.**	nine dahn-kuh
Could you help me, please?	**Könnten Sie mir bitte helfen?**	kern-ten zee meer bit-tuh hel-fen
Thank you, that's very nice of you.	**Vielen Dank, das ist sehr nett von Ihnen.**	fee-len dahnk dahs ist zair net fun ee-nen
Thank you very much for all your trouble / help.	**Vielen Dank für Ihre Mühe / Hilfe.**	fee-len dahnk fewr ee-ruh mew-uh / hil-fuh
You're welcome.	**Gern geschehen.**	gehrn guh-shay-en
Sorry!	**Entschuldigung!**	ent-shool-dee-goong
Excuse me!	**Entschuldigen Sie!**	ent-shool-dee-ghen zee
I'm sorry about that.	**Das tut mir Leid.**	dahs toot meer lite
Don't worry about it!	**Macht nichts!**	makht nikhts
How embarrassing!	**Das ist mir sehr unangenehm.**	dahs ist meer zair oon-ahn-guh-name
It was a misunderstanding.	**Das war ein Missverständnis.**	dahs vah eye-n miss-fair-shtent-niss

GRAMMAR

Regular Verbs and Their Tenses

The past is often expressed by using *to have* **haben** + past participle. The future is formed with **werden** + infinitive.

Infinitive:	kaufen *to buy*		arbeiten *to work*
Past Participle:	gekauft *bought*		gearbeitet *worked*

	Present	*Past*	*Future*
ich *I*	kaufe	habe gekauft	werde kaufen
du *you inform.*	kaufst	hast gekauft	wirst kaufen
Sie *you form.*	kaufen	haben gekauft	werden kaufen
er/sie/es *he/she/it*	kauft	hat gekauft	wird kaufen
wir *we*	kaufen	haben gekauft	werden kaufen
ihr *you pl. inform.*	kauft	habt gekauft	werdet kaufen
Sie *you pl. form.*	kaufen	haben gekauft	werden kaufen
sie *they*	kaufen	haben gekauft	werden kaufen

Irregular verbs have to be memorized. Verbs that indicate movement are conjugated with *to be* **sein**, e.g. *to go* **gehen**:

	Present	*Past*	*Future*
ich *I*	gehe	bin gegangen	werde gehen
du *you inform.*	gehst	bist gegangen	wirst gehen
Sie *you form.*	gehen	sind gegangen	werden gehen
er/sie/es *he/she/it*	geht	ist gegangen	wird gehen
wir *we*	gehen	sind gegangen	werden gehen
ihr *you pl. inform.*	geht	seid gegangen	werdet gehen
Sie *you pl. form.*	gehen	sind gegangen	werden gehen
sie *they*	gehen	sind gegangen	werden gehen

To express future, usually the present tense is used together with a time adverb: *I'll work tomorrow.* **Ich arbeite morgen.**

Nouns and Articles

All nouns are written with a capital letter. Their definite articles indicate their gender: **der** (masculine = m), **die** (feminine = f), **das** (neuter = n). The plural article is always **die**, regardless of gender.

Examples:	**Singular**	**Plural**
	der **Mann** *the man*	die **Männer** *the men*
	die **Frau** *the woman*	die **Frauen** *the women*
	das **Kind** *the child*	die **Kinder** *the children*

The indefinite article also indicates the gender of the noun: **ein** (m, n), **eine** (f). There is no indefinite article in the plural.

Examples:	**Singular**	**Plural**
	ein **Zug** *a train*	**Züge** *trains*
	eine **Karte** *a map*	**Karten** *maps*

Possessives also relate to the gender of the noun that follows.

Nominative (m, n/f)	**Accusative** (n/f/m)	**Dative** (m, n/f)
mein/e *my*	**mein/e/en** *my*	**meinem / meiner** *my*
dein/e *your inform.*	**dein/e/en** *your*	**deinem / deiner** *your*
Ihr/e *your form.*	**Ihr/e/en** *your*	**Ihrem / Ihrer** *your*
sein/e *his*	**sein/e/en** *his*	**seinem / seiner** *his*
ihr/e *her*	**ihr/e/en** *her*	**ihrem / ihrer** *her*
sein/e *its*	**sein/e/en** *its*	**seinem / seiner** *its*
unser/e *our*	**unser/e/en** *our*	**unserem / unserer** *our*
euer/e *your pl. inform.*	**euer/e/en** *your*	**eurem / eurer** *your*
Ihr/e *your pl. form.*	**Ihr/e/en** *your*	**Ihrem / Ihrer** *your*
ihr/e *their*	**ihr/e/en** *their*	**ihrem / ihrer** *their*

Examples:	Wo ist meine Fahrkarte?	*Where is my ticket?*
	Ihr Taxi ist hier.	*Your taxi is here.*
	Hier ist euer Pass.	*Here is your passport.*

Word Order

The conjugated verb comes after the subject and before the object. When a sentence doesn't begin with a subject, the word order changes.

Examples:	Er ist in Berlin.	*He is in Berlin.*
	Heute ist er in Berlin.	*Today he is in Berlin.*
	Wir sind in Berlin gewesen.	*We were in Berlin.*

Questions are formed by reversing the order of subject and verb.

Examples:	Haben Sie Bücher?	*Do you have books?*
	Wie ist das Wetter?	*How is the weather?*
	Seid ihr in Köln gewesen?	*Have you been to Cologne?*

Negations

Negative sentences are formed by adding **nicht** (*not*) to that part of the sentence which is to be negated.

Examples:	Wir rauchen nicht.	We don't smoke.
	Der Bus fährt nicht ab.	The bus doesn't leave.
	Warum schreibst du nicht?	Why don't you write?

If a noun is used, the negation is made by adding **kein**. Its ending is defined by the noun's gender.

Examples:	Ich trinke kein Bier.	*I don't drink beer.*
	Wir haben keine Einzelzimmer.	*We don't have any single rooms.*
	Gibt es keinen Zimmerservice?	*Is there no room service?*

Imperatives (Command Form)

du *you sing. inform.*	Geh! *Go!*	Sei still! *Be quiet!*
ihr *you pl. inform.*	Geht! *Go!*	Seid still! *Be quiet!*
Sie *you sing./pl. form.*	Gehen Sie! *Go!*	Seien Sie still! *Be quiet!*
wir *we*	Gehen wir! *Let's go!*	Seien wir still! *Let's be quiet!*

Examples:	Hört mal alle zu!	*Listen everybody!*
	Seid nicht so laut!	*Don't be so noisy!*

Pronouns

Pronouns serve as substitutes for nouns and relate to their gender.

Nominative	**Accusative**	**Dative**
ich *I*	**mich** *me*	**mir** *me*
du *you inform.*	**dich** *you*	**dir** *you*
Sie *you form.*	**Sie** *you*	**Ihnen** *you*

er *he*	**ihn** *him*	**ihm** *him*
sie *she*	**sie** *her*	**ihr** *her*
es *it*	**es** *it*	**ihm** *him*
wir *we*	**uns** *us*	**uns** *us*
ihr *you pl. inform.*	**euch** *you*	**euch** *you*
Sie *you pl. form.*	**Sie** *you*	**Ihnen** *you*
sie *they*	**sie** *them*	**ihnen** *them*

Examples:	**Ich sehe sie.**	*I see them.*
	Hören Sie mich?	*Do you hear me?*

Adjectives

Adjectives describe nouns. Their endings depend on the case.

Examples:	**Wir haben ein altes Auto.**	*We have an old car.*
	Wo ist mein neuer Koffer?	*Where is my new suitcase?*
	Gute Arbeit, Richard!	*Good work, Richard!*

Adverbs and Adverbial Expressions

In German, adverbs are usually identical with adjectives. They describe verbs but, unlike adjectives, their endings don't change.

Examples:	**Linda fährt sehr langsam.**	*Linda drives very slowly.*
	Robert ist sehr nett.	*Robert is very nice.*
	Sie sprechen gut Deutsch.	*You speak German well.*

Some common adverbial time expressions:

zurzeit	*presently*
bald	*soon*
immer noch	*still*
nicht mehr	*not anymore*

Comparisons and Superlatives

Most German adjectives add **–er** for their comparative and **–(e)st** for their superlative. The following list contains only a small selection to illustrate formation and irregularities.

Adjective	Comparative	Superlative
klein *small, little*	kleiner *smaller*	am kleinsten *the smallest*
billig *cheap*	billiger *cheaper*	am billigsten *the cheapest*
neu *new*	neuer *newer*	am neusten *the newest*
schlecht *bad*	schlechter *worse*	am schlechtesten *the worst*
groß *big, large*	größer *bigger*	am größten *the biggest*
alt *old*	älter *older*	am ältesten *the oldest*
lang *long*	länger *longer*	am längsten *the longest*
kurz *short*	kürzer *shorter*	am kürzesten *the shortest*
gut *good*	besser *better*	am besten *the best*
teuer *expensive*	teurer *more expensive*	am teuersten *the most expensive*

Examples:

Diese Postkarten sind billiger. *These postcards are cheaper.*

Wo ist der beste Buchladen? *Where is the best bookstore?*

A

A, a A, a *n*; *from A to Z* von A bis Z

A grade Eins

a *before vowel*: **an** *indef art* ein(e); per, pro, je; *not a(n)* kein(e); *all of a size* alle gleich groß; *100 dollars a year* 100 Dollar im Jahr; *twice a week* zweimal die *or* in der Woche

a·back: *taken aback* überrascht, verblüfft; bestürzt

a·ban·don aufgeben, preisgeben; verlassen; überlassen; *be found abandoned* MOT *etc* verlassen aufgefunden werden

a·base erniedrigen, demütigen

a·base·ment Erniedrigung *f*, Demütigung *f*

a·bashed verlegen

ab·at·toir *Br* Schlachthof *m*

ab·bess REL Äbtissin *f*

ab·bey REL Kloster *n*; Abtei *f*

ab·bot REL Abt *m*

ab·bre·vi·ate (ab)kürzen

ab·bre·vi·a·tion Abkürzung *f*, Kurzform *f*

ABC Abc *n*, Alphabet *n*

ab·di·cate *Amt, Recht etc* aufgeben, verzichten auf (*acc*); *abdicate (from) the throne* abdanken

ab·di·ca·tion Verzicht *m*; Abdankung *f*

ab·do·men ANAT Unterleib *m*

ab·dom·i·nal ANAT Unterleibs...

ab·duct JUR *j-n* entführen

ab·er·ra·tion Verirrung *f*

a·bet → *aid 1*

ab·hor verabscheuen

ab·hor·rence Abscheu *m* (*of* vor *dat*)

ab·hor·rent zuwider (*to dat*); abstoßend

a·bide *v/i*: *abide by the law etc* sich an das Gesetz *etc* halten; *v/t*: *he can't abide him* er kann ihn nicht ausstehen

a·bil·i·ty Fähigkeit *f*

ab·ject verächtlich, erbärmlich; *in abject poverty* in äußerster Armut

ab·jure abschwören; entsagen (*dat*)

a·blaze in Flammen; *fig* glänzend, funkelnd (*with* vor *dat*)

a·ble fähig; geschickt; *be able to inf* in der Lage sein zu *inf*, können

a·ble-bod·ied kräftig

ab·nor·mal abnorm, ungewöhnlich; anomal

a·board an Bord; *all aboard!* MAR alle Mann *or* Reisenden an Bord!; RAIL alles einsteigen!; *aboard a bus* in e-m Bus; *go aboard a train* in e-n Zug einsteigen

a·bode *a. place of abode* Aufenthaltsort *m*, Wohnsitz *m*; *of or with no fixed abode* ohne festen Wohnsitz

a·bol·ish abschaffen, aufheben

ab·o·li·tion Abschaffung *f*, Aufhebung *f*

A-bomb → *atom(ic) bomb*

a·bom·i·na·ble abscheulich, scheußlich

a·bom·i·nate verabscheuen

a·bom·i·na·tion Abscheu *m*

ab·o·rig·i·nal 1. eingeboren, Ur...; **2.** Ureinwohner *m*

ab·o·rig·i·ne Ureinwohner *m*

a·bort *v/t* abbrechen (*a.* MED *Schwangerschaft*); MED *Kind* abtreiben; *v/i* fehlschlagen, scheitern; MED e-e Fehlgeburt haben

a·bor·tion MED Fehlgeburt *f*; Schwangerschaftsabbruch *m*, Abtreibung *f*; *have an abortion* abtreiben (lassen)

a·bor·tive misslungen, erfolglos

a·bound reichlich vorhanden sein; Überfluss haben, reich sein (*in* an *dat*); voll sein (*with* von *dat*)

a·bout 1. *prp* um (... herum); bei (*dat*); (irgendwo) herum in (*dat*); um, gegen, etwa; im Begriff, dabei; über (*acc*); *I had no money about me* ich hatte kein Geld bei mir; **2.** *adv* herum, umher; in der Nähe; etwa, ungefähr

a·bove 1. *prp* über (*dat or acc*), oberhalb (*gen*); *fig* über, erhaben über (*acc*); *above all* vor allem; **2.** *adv* oben; darüber; **3.** *adj* obig, oben erwähnt

a·breast nebeneinander; *keep abreast of, be abreast of fig* Schritt halten mit

a·bridge (ab-, ver)kürzen

a·bridg(e)·ment Kürzung *f*; Kurzfassung *f*

a·broad im *or* ins Ausland; überall(hin); *the news soon spread abroad* die Nachricht verbreitete sich rasch

a·brupt abrupt; jäh; schroff

ab·scess MED Abszess *m*

ab·sence Abwesenheit *f*; Mangel *m*

ab·sent 1. abwesend; fehlend; nicht vorhanden; *be absent* fehlen (*from school* in der Schule; *from work* am Arbeitsplatz); **2.** *absent o.s. from* fernbleiben (*dat*) *or* von

ab·sent-mind·ed zerstreut, geistesabwesend

ab·so·lute absolut; unumschränkt; vollkommen; unbedingt; CHEM rein, unvermischt

ab·so·lu·tion REL Absolution *f*

ab·solve freisprechen, lossprechen
ab·sorb absorbieren, aufsaugen, einsaugen; *fig* ganz in Anspruch nehmen
ab·sorb·ing *fig* fesselnd, packend
ab·stain sich enthalten (*from gen*)
ab·ste·mi·ous enthaltsam; mäßig
ab·sten·tion Enthaltung *f*; POL Stimmenthaltung *f*
ab·sti·nence Abstinenz *f*, Enthaltsamkeit *f*
ab·sti·nent abstinent, enthaltsam
ab·stract 1. abstrakt; 2. *das* Abstrakte; Auszug *m*; 3. abstrahieren; entwenden
ab·stract·ed *fig* zerstreut
ab·strac·tion Abstraktion *f*; abstrakter Begriff
ab·surd absurd; lächerlich
a·bun·dance Überfluss *m*; Fülle *f*; Überschwang *m*
a·bun·dant reich, reichlich
a·buse 1. Missbrauch *m*; Beschimpfung(en *pl*) *f*; *abuse of drugs* Drogenmissbrauch *m*; *abuse of power* Machtmissbrauch *m*; 2. missbrauchen; beschimpfen
a·bu·sive beleidigend, Schimpf...
a·but (an)grenzen (*on* an *acc*)
a·byss Abgrund *m* (*a. fig*)
ac·a·dem·ic 1. Hochschullehrer *m*; 2. akademisch
a·cad·e·mi·cian Akademiemitglied *n*
a·cad·e·my Akademie *f*; *academy of music* Musikhochschule *f*
ac·cede: *accede to* zustimmen (*dat*); Amt antreten; *Thron* besteigen
ac·cel·e·rate *v/t* beschleunigen; *v/i* schneller werden, MOT *a.* beschleunigen, Gas geben
ac·cel·e·ra·tion Beschleunigung *f*
ac·cel·e·ra·tor MOT Gaspedal *n*
ac·cent 1. Akzent *m* (*a.* LING); 2. → **ac·cen·tu·ate** akzentuieren, betonen
ac·cept annehmen; akzeptieren; hinnehmen
ac·cept·a·ble annehmbar; *person:* tragbar
ac·cept·ance Annahme *f*; Aufnahme *f*
ac·cess Zugang *m* (*to* zu); *fig* Zutritt *m* (*to* bei, zu); EDP Zugriff *m* (*to* auf *acc*); *easy of access* zugänglich (*person*)
ac·ces·sa·ry → **accessory**
ac·cess code EDP Zugriffskode *m*
ac·ces·si·ble (leicht) zugänglich
ac·ces·sion (Neu)Anschaffung *f* (*to* für); Zustimmung *f* (*to* zu); Antritt *m* (*e-s Amtes*); *accession to power* Machtübernahme *f*; *accession to the throne* Thronbesteigung *f*
ac·ces·so·ry JUR Komplize *m*, Komplizin *f*, Mitschuldige *m*, *f*; *mst pl* Zubehör *n*,

fashion: a. Accessoires *pl*, TECH a. Zubehörteile *pl*
ac·cess road Zufahrts- *or* Zubringerstraße *f*
access time EDP Zugriffszeit *f*
ac·ci·dent Unfall *m*, Unglück *n*, Unglücksfall *m*; NUCL Störfall *m*; *by accident* zufällig
ac·ci·den·tal zufällig; versehentlich
ac·claim feiern (*as* als)
ac·cla·ma·tion lauter Beifall; Lob *n*
ac·cli·ma·tize (sich) akklimatisieren *or* eingewöhnen
ac·com·mo·date unterbringen; Platz haben für, fassen; anpassen (*to dat or* an *acc*)
ac·com·mo·da·tion Unterkunft *f*, Unterbringung *f*
accommodation of·fice Zimmervermittlung *f*
ac·com·pa·ni·ment MUS Begleitung *f*
ac·com·pa·ny begleiten (*a.* MUS)
ac·com·plice JUR Komplize *m*, Komplizin *f*, Helfershelfer(in)
ac·com·plish erreichen; leisten
ac·com·plished fähig, tüchtig
ac·com·plish·ment Fähigkeit *f*, Talent *n*
ac·cord 1. Übereinstimmung *f*; *of one's own accord* von selbst; *with one accord* einstimmig; 2. übereinstimmen (*with* mit)
ac·cord·ance: *in accordance with* entsprechend (*dat*)
ac·cord·ing: *according to* laut; nach
ac·cord·ing·ly folglich, also; (dem)entsprechend
ac·cost *j-n* ansprechen
ac·count 1. ECON Rechnung *f*, Berechnung *f*; Konto *n*; Rechenschaft *f*; Bericht *m*; *by all accounts* nach allem, was man so hört; *of no account* ohne Bedeutung; *on no account* auf keinen Fall; *on account of* wegen; *take into account, take account of* in Betracht *or* Erwägung ziehen, berücksichtigen; *turn s.th. to (good) account* et. (gut) ausnutzen; *keep accounts* die Bücher führen; *call to account* zur Rechenschaft ziehen; *give (an) account of* Rechenschaft ablegen über (*acc*); *give an account of* Bericht erstatten über (*acc*); 2. *v/i: account for* Rechenschaft über et. ablegen; (sich) erklären
ac·count·a·ble verantwortlich; erklärlich
ac·coun·tant ECON Buchhalter(in)
ac·count·ing ECON Buchführung *f*
acct ABBR *of* **account** Konto *n*
ac·cu·mu·late (sich) (an)häufen *or* ansammeln

ac·cu·mu·la·tion Ansammlung *f*
ac·cu·mu·la·tor ELECTR Akkumulator *m*
ac·cu·ra·cy Genauigkeit *f*
ac·cu·rate genau
ac·cu·sa·tion Anklage *f*; Anschuldigung *f*, Beschuldigung *f*
ac·cu·sa·tive *a. accusative case* LING Akkusativ *m*
ac·cuse JUR anklagen; beschuldigen (*of gen*); *the accused* der *or* die Angeklagte, die Angeklagten *pl*
ac·cus·er JUR Ankläger(in)
ac·cus·ing anklagend, vorwurfsvoll
ac·cus·tom gewöhnen (*to* an *acc*)
ac·cus·tomed gewohnt, üblich; gewöhnt (*to* an *acc*, zu *inf*)
ace Ass *n* (*a. fig*); *have an ace in the hole* (*Br up one's sleeve*) *fig* (noch) e-n Trumpf in der Hand haben; *within an ace* um ein Haar
ache 1. schmerzen, wehtun; **2.** *anhaltender* Schmerz
a·chieve zustande bringen; *Ziel* erreichen
a·chieve·ment Zustandebringen *n*, Leistung *f*, Ausführung *f*
ac·id 1. sauer; *fig* beißend, bissig; **2.** CHEM Säure *f*
a·cid·i·ty Säure *f*
ac·id rain saurer Regen
ac·knowl·edge anerkennen; zugeben; *Empfang* bestätigen
ac·knowl·edg(e)·ment Anerkennung *f*; (Empfangs)Bestätigung *f*; Eingeständnis *n*
a·corn BOT Eichel *f*
a·cous·tics Akustik *f*
ac·quaint bekannt machen; *acquaint s.o. with s.th.* j-m et. mitteilen; *be acquainted with* kennen
ac·quaint·ance Bekanntschaft *f*; Bekannte *m*, *f*
ac·quire erwerben; sich aneignen
ac·qui·si·tion Erwerb *m*; Anschaffung *f*, Errungenschaft *f*
ac·quit JUR freisprechen (*of* von); *acquit o.s. well* s-e Sache gut machen
ac·quit·tal JUR Freispruch *m*
a·cre Acre *m* (*4047 qm*)
ac·rid scharf, beißend
ac·ro·bat Akrobat(in)
ac·ro·bat·ic akrobatisch
a·cross 1. *adv* hinüber, herüber; (quer) durch; drüben, auf der anderen Seite; über Kreuz; **2.** *prp* (quer) über (*acc*); (quer) durch; auf der anderen Seite von (*or gen*), jenseits (*gen*); über (*dat*); *come across, run across fig* stoßen auf (*acc*)
act 1. *v/i* handeln; sich verhalten *or* beneh-

men; (ein)wirken; funktionieren; (Theater) spielen; *v/t* THEA spielen (*a. fig*), *Stück* aufführen; *act as* fungieren als; **2.** Handlung *f*, Tat *f*; JUR Gesetz *n*; THEA Akt *m*
act·ing THEA Spiel(en) *n*
ac·tion Handlung *f* (*a.* THEA), Tat *f*; *film etc*: Action *f*; Funktionieren *n*; (Ein-)Wirkung *f*; JUR Klage *f*, Prozess *m*; MIL Gefecht *n*, Einsatz *m*; *take action* handeln
ac·tive aktiv; tätig, rührig; lebhaft (*a.* ECON), rege; wirksam
ac·tiv·ist *esp* POL Aktivist(in)
ac·tiv·i·ty Tätigkeit *f*; Aktivität *f*; Betriebsamkeit *f*; *esp* ECON Lebhaftigkeit *f*
activity va·ca·tion Aktivurlaub *m*
ac·tor Schauspieler *m*
ac·tress Schauspielerin *f*
ac·tu·al wirklich, tatsächlich, eigentlich
ac·u·men Scharfsinn *m*
ac·u·punc·ture MED Akupunktur *f*
a·cute akut (*shortage, pain etc*); brennend (*problem etc*); scharf (*hearing etc*); scharfsinnig; MATH spitz (*angle*)
ad F → *advertisement*
ad·a·mant unerbittlich
a·dapt anpassen (*to dat or* an *acc*); *Text* bearbeiten (*from* nach); TECH umstellen (*to* auf *acc*); umbauen (*to* für)
a·dapt·a·ble anpassungsfähig
ad·ap·ta·tion Anpassung *f*; Bearbeitung *f*
a·dapt·er, a·dapt·or ELECTR Adapter *m*
add *v/t* hinzufügen; *add up* zusammenzählen, addieren; *v/i*: *add to* vermehren, beitragen zu, hinzukommen zu; *add up* MATH ergeben; F sich summieren; *fig* e-n Sinn ergeben; *add up to fig* hinauslaufen auf (*acc*)
ad·der ZO Natter *f*
ad·dict Süchtige *m*, *f*; *alcohol (drug) addict* Alkoholsüchtige (Drogen- *or* Rauschgiftsüchtige); (*Fußball- etc*) Fanatiker(in), (*Film- etc*)Narr *m*
ad·dict·ed süchtig, abhängig (*to* von); *be addicted to alcohol (drugs)* alkoholsüchtig (drogenabhängig *or* -süchtig) sein
ad·dic·tion Sucht *f*, Süchtigkeit *f*
ad·di·tion Hinzufügen *n*; Zusatz *m*; Zuwachs *m*; ARCH Anbau *m*; MATH Addition *f*; *in addition* außerdem; *in addition to* außer (*dat*)
ad·di·tion·al zusätzlich
ad·dress 1. *Worte* richten (*to* an *acc*), j-n anreden *or* ansprechen; **2.** Adresse *f*, Anschrift *f*; Rede *f*, Ansprache *f*
ad·dress·ee Empfänger(in)
ad·ept erfahren, geschickt (*at, in* in *dat*)

ad·e·qua·cy Angemessenheit *f*
ad·e·quate angemessen
ad·here (*to*) kleben, haften (an *dat*); *fig* festhalten (an *dat*)
ad·her·ence Anhaften *n*; *fig* Festhalten *n*
ad·her·ent Anhänger(in)
ad·he·sive 1. klebend; **2.** Klebstoff *m*
adhesive plas·ter MED Heftpflaster *n*
adhesive tape Klebeband *n*, Klebstreifen *m*; MED Heftpflaster *n*
ad·ja·cent angrenzend, anstoßend (*to* an *acc*); benachbart
ad·jec·tive LING Adjektiv *n*, Eigenschaftswort *n*
ad·join (an)grenzen an (*acc*)
ad·journ *v/t* verschieben, (*v/i* sich) vertagen
ad·journ·ment Vertagung *f*, Verschiebung *f*
ad·just anpassen; TECH einstellen, regulieren
ad·just·a·ble TECH verstellbar, regulierbar
ad·just·ment Anpassung *f*; TECH Einstellung *f*
ad·lib aus dem Stegreif (sprechen *or* spielen)
ad·min·is·ter verwalten; PHARM geben, verabreichen; *administer justice* Recht sprechen
ad·min·is·tra·tion Verwaltung *f*; POL Regierung *f*; Amtsperiode *f*
ad·min·is·tra·tive Verwaltungs...
ad·min·is·tra·tor Verwaltungsbeamte *m*
ad·mi·ra·ble bewundernswert; großartig
ad·mi·ral MAR Admiral *m*
ad·mi·ra·tion Bewunderung *f*
ad·mire bewundern; verehren
ad·mir·er Verehrer *m*
ad·mis·si·ble zulässig
ad·mis·sion Eintritt *m*, Zutritt *m*; Aufnahme *f*; Eintrittsgeld *n*; Eingeständnis *n*; *admission free* Eintritt frei
ad·mit *v/t* zugeben; (her)einlassen (*to, into* in *acc*), eintreten lassen; zulassen (*to* zu)
ad·mit·tance Einlass *m*, Eintritt *m*, Zutritt *m*; *no admittance* Zutritt verboten
ad·mon·ish ermahnen; warnen (*of, against* vor *dat*)
a·do Getue *n*, Lärm *m*; *without more or further ado* ohne weitere Umstände
ad·o·les·cence Jugend *f*, Adoleszenz *f*
ad·o·les·cent 1. jugendlich, heranwachsend; **2.** Jugendliche *m*, *f*
a·dopt adoptieren; übernehmen; *adopted child* Adoptivkind *n*
a·dop·tion Adoption *f*
a·dop·tive par·ents Adoptiveltern *pl*
a·dor·a·ble F bezaubernd, entzückend

ad·o·ra·tion Anbetung *f*, Verehrung *f*
a·dore anbeten, verehren
a·dorn schmücken, zieren
a·dorn·ment Schmuck *m*, Verzierung *f*
a·droit geschickt
ad·ult 1. erwachsen; **2.** Erwachsene *m*, *f*; *adults only* nur für Erwachsene!
adult ed·uca·tion Erwachsenenbildung *f*
a·dul·ter·ate verfälschen, *Wein* panschen
a·dul·ter·er Ehebrecher *m*
a·dul·ter·ess Ehebrecherin *f*
a·dul·ter·ous ehebrecherisch
a·dul·ter·y Ehebruch *m*
ad·vance 1. *v/i* vordringen, vorrücken (*a. time*); Fortschritte machen; *v/t* vorrücken; *Termin etc* vorverlegen; *Argument etc* vorbringen; *Geld* vorstrecken, F vorschießen; (be)fördern; *Preis* erhöhen; *Wachstum etc* beschleunigen; **2.** Vorrücken *n*, Vorstoß *m* (*a. fig*); Fortschritt *m*; ECON Vorschuss *m*; Erhöhung *f*; *in advance* im Voraus
ad·vanced fortgeschritten; *advanced for one's years* weit *or* reif für sein Alter
ad·vance·ment Fortschritt *m*, Verbesserung *f*
ad·van·tage Vorteil *m* (*a.* SPORT); *advantage rule* SPORT Vorteilsregel *f*; *take advantage of* ausnutzen
ad·van·ta·geous vorteilhaft
ad·ven·ture Abenteuer *n*, Wagnis *n*
ad·ven·tur·er Abenteurer *m*
ad·ven·tur·ess Abenteu(r)erin *f*
ad·ven·tur·ous abenteuerlich; verwegen, kühn
ad·verb LING Adverb *n*, Umstandswort *n*
ad·ver·sa·ry Gegner(in)
ad·ver·tise ankündigen, bekannt machen; inserieren; Reklame machen (für)
ad·ver·tise·ment Anzeige *f*, Inserat *n*
ad·ver·tis·ing 1. Reklame *f*, Werbung *f*; **2.** Reklame..., Werbe...
advertising a·gen·cy Werbeagentur *f*
advertising cam·paign Werbefeldzug *m*
ad·vice Rat(schlag) *m*; ECON Benachrichtigung *f*; *take medical advice* e-n Arzt zu Rate ziehen; *take my advice* hör auf mich
ad·vice cen·ter, *Br* **advice cen·tre** Beratungsstelle *f*
ad·vis·a·ble ratsam
ad·vise *v/t j-n* beraten; *j-m* raten; *esp* ECON benachrichtigen, avisieren; *v/i* sich beraten
ad·vis·er *esp Br*, **ad·vis·or** Berater *m*
ad·vi·so·ry beratend
ad·vo·cate 1. befürworten, verfechten; **2.** Befürworter(in), Verfechter(in)
aer·i·al 1. luftig; Luft...; **2.** Antenne *f*

aer·i·al pho·to·graph, aerial view Luftaufnahme *f*, Luftbild *n*

aer·o... Aero..., Luft...

aer·o·bics SPORT Aerobic *n*

aer·o·drome *esp Br* Flugplatz *m*

aer·o·dy·nam·ic aerodynamisch

aer·o·dy·nam·ics Aerodynamik *f*

aer·o·nau·tics Luftfahrt *f*

aer·o·plane *Br* Flugzeug *n*

aer·o·sol Spraydose *f*, Sprühdose *f*

aes·thet·ic *etc* → **esthetic** *etc*

a·far: **from afar** von weit her

af·fair Angelegenheit *f*, Sache *f*; F Ding *n*, Sache *f*; Affäre *f*

af·fect beeinflussen; MED angreifen, befallen; bewegen, rühren; e-e Vorliebe haben für; vortäuschen

af·fec·tion Liebe *f*, Zuneigung *f*

af·fec·tion·ate liebevoll, herzlich

af·fil·i·ate *als Mitglied* aufnehmen; angliedern

af·fin·i·ty Affinität *f*; (geistige) Verwandtschaft; Neigung *f* (**for, to** zu)

af·firm versichern; beteuern; bestätigen

af·fir·ma·tion Versicherung *f*; Beteuerung *f*; Bestätigung *f*

af·fir·ma·tive 1. bejahend; 2. **answer in the affirmative** bejahen

af·fix (**to**) anheften, ankleben (an *acc*), befestigen (an *dat*); beifügen, hinzufügen (*dat*)

af·flict heimsuchen, plagen; **afflicted with** geplagt von, leidend an (*dat*)

af·flic·tion Gebrechen *n*; Elend *n*, Not *f*

af·flu·ence Überfluss *m*; Wohlstand *m*

af·flu·ent reich, reichlich

affluent so·ci·e·ty Wohlstandsgesellschaft *f*

af·ford sich leisten; gewähren, bieten; **I can afford it** ich kann es mir leisten

af·front 1. beleidigen; 2. Beleidigung *f*

a·float MAR flott, schwimmend; **set afloat** MAR flottmachen; *fig Gerücht etc* in Umlauf setzen

a·fraid: **be afraid of** sich fürchten *or* Angst haben vor (*dat*); **I'm afraid she won't come** ich fürchte, sie wird nicht kommen; **I'm afraid I must go now** leider muss ich jetzt gehen

a·fresh von neuem

Af·ri·ca Afrika *n*

Af·ri·can 1. afrikanisch; 2. Afrikaner(in)

af·ter 1. *adv* hinterher, nachher, danach; 2. *prp* nach; hinter (*dat*) (... her); **after all** schließlich (doch); 3. *cj* nachdem; 4. *adj* später; Nach...

after ef·fect MED Nachwirkung *f* (*a. fig*)

af·ter·glow Abendrot *n*

af·ter·math Nachwirkungen *pl*, Folgen *pl*

af·ter·noon Nachmittag *m*; **this afternoon** heute Nachmittag; **good afternoon!** guten Tag!

af·ter·taste Nachgeschmack *m*

af·ter·thought nachträglicher Einfall

af·ter·ward, *Br* **af·ter·wards** nachher, später

a·gain wieder; wiederum; ferner; **again and again, time and again** immer wieder; **as much again** noch einmal so viel

a·gainst gegen; an (*dat or acc*); **as against** verglichen mit; **he was against it** er war dagegen

age 1. (Lebens)Alter *n*; Zeit(alter *n*) *f*; Menschenalter *n*; (**old**) **age** (hohes) Alter; **at the age of** im Alter von; *s.o.* **your age** in deinem *or* Ihrem Alter; (**come**) **of age** mündig *or* volljährig (werden); **be over age** die Altersgrenze überschritten haben; **under age** minderjährig; unmündig; **wait for ages** F e-e Ewigkeit warten; 2. alt werden *or* machen

a·ged[1] alt, betagt

aged[2]: **aged twenty** 20 Jahre alt

age·less zeitlos; ewig jung

a·gen·cy Agentur *f*; Geschäftsstelle *f*, Büro *n*

a·gen·da Tagesordnung *f*

a·gent Agent *m* (*a.* POL), Vertreter *m*; (*Grundstücks- etc*)Makler *m*; CHEM Wirkstoff *m*, Mittel *n*

ag·glom·er·ate (sich) zusammenballen; (sich) (an)häufen

ag·gra·vate erschweren, verschlimmern; F ärgern

ag·gre·gate 1. sich belaufen auf (*acc*); 2. gesamt; 3. Gesamtmenge *f*, Summe *f*; TECH Aggregat *n*

ag·gres·sion Angriff *m*

ag·gres·sive aggressiv, Angriffs...; *fig* energisch

ag·gres·sor Angreifer *m*

ag·grieved verletzt, gekränkt

a·ghast entgeistert, entsetzt

ag·ile flink, behend

a·gil·i·ty Flinkheit *f*, Behendigkeit *f*

ag·i·tate *v/t fig* aufregen, aufwühlen; *Flüssigkeit* schütteln; *v/i* POL agitieren, hetzen (**against** gegen)

ag·i·ta·tion Aufregung *f*; POL Agitation *f*

ag·i·ta·tor POL Agitator *m*

a·glow: **be aglow** strahlen (**with** vor)

a·go: **a year ago** vor e-m Jahr

ag·o·ny Qual *f*; Todeskampf *m*

a·gree *v/i* übereinstimmen; sich vertragen; einig werden, sich einigen (**on** über *acc*); übereinkommen; **agree to** zustimmen (*dat*), einverstanden sein mit

a·gree·a·ble (**to**) angenehm (für); übereinstimmend (mit)

a·gree·ment Übereinstimmung *f*; Vereinbarung *f*; Abkommen *n*

ag·ri·cul·tur·al landwirtschaftlich

ag·ri·cul·ture Landwirtschaft *f*

a·ground MAR gestrandet; *run aground* stranden, auf Grund laufen

a·head vorwärts, voraus; vorn; *go ahead!* nur zu!, mach nur!; *straight ahead* geradeaus

aid 1. unterstützen, *j-m* helfen (*in* bei); fördern; *he was accused of aiding and abetting* JUR er wurde wegen Beihilfe angeklagt; **2.** Hilfe *f*, Unterstützung *f*

AIDS, Aids MED Aids *n*; *person with AIDS* Aids-Kranke *m*, *f*

ail kränklich sein

ail·ment Leiden *n*

aim 1. *v/i* zielen (*at* auf *acc*, nach); *aim at fig* beabsichtigen; *be aiming to do s.th.* vorhaben, et. zu tun; *v/t*: *aim at Waffe etc* richten auf *or* gegen (*acc*); **2.** Ziel *n* (*a. fig*); Absicht *f*; *take aim at* zielen auf (*acc*) *or* nach

aim·less ziellos

air[1] **1.** Luft *f*; Luftzug *m*; Miene *f*, Aussehen *n*; *by air* auf dem Luftwege; *in the open air* im Freien; *on the air* im Rundfunk *or* Fernsehen; *be on the air* senden; in Betrieb sein; *go off the air* die Sendung beenden (*person*); sein Programm beenden (*station*); *give o.s. airs, put on airs* vornehm tun; **2.** (aus)lüften; *fig* an die Öffentlichkeit bringen; erörtern

air[2] MUS Arie *f*, Weise *f*, Melodie *f*

air·bag MOT Airbag *m*

air·base MIL Luftstützpunkt *m*

air·bed Luftmatratze *f*

air·borne AVIAT in der Luft; MIL Luftlande...

air·brake TECH Druckluftbremse *f*

air·bus AVIAT Airbus *m*, Großraumflugzeug *n*

air-con·di·tioned mit Klimaanlage

air-con·di·tion·ing Klimaanlage *f*

air·craft car·ri·er MAR, MIL Flugzeugträger *m*

air·field Flugplatz *m*

air force MIL Luftwaffe *f*

air host·ess AVIAT Stewardess *f*

air jack·et Schwimmweste *f*

air·lift AVIAT Luftbrücke *f*

air·line AVIAT Fluggesellschaft *f*

air·lin·er AVIAT Verkehrsflugzeug *n*

air·mail Luftpost *f*; *by airmail* mit Luftpost

air·man MIL Flieger *m*

air·plane Flugzeug *n*

air·pock·et AVIAT Luftloch *n*

air pol·lu·tion Luftverschmutzung *f*

air·port Flughafen *m*

air raid MIL Luftangriff *m*

air-raid pre·cau·tions MIL Luftschutz *m*

air-raid shel·ter MIL Luftschutzraum *m*

air route AVIAT Flugroute *f*

air·sick luftkrank

air·space Luftraum *m*

air·strip (behelfsmäßige) Start- und Landebahn

air ter·mi·nal Flughafenabfertigungsgebäude *n*

air·tight luftdicht

air time Sendezeit *f*

air traf·fic AVIAT Flugverkehr *m*

air-traf·fic con·trol AVIAT Flugsicherung *f*

air-traffic con·trol·ler AVIAT Fluglotse *m*

air·way AVIAT Fluggesellschaft *f*

air·wor·thy AVIAT flugtüchtig

air·y luftig

aisle ARCH Seitenschiff *n*; Gang *m*

a·jar halb offen, angelehnt

a·kin verwandt (*to* mit)

a·lac·ri·ty Bereitwilligkeit *f*

a·larm 1. Alarm(zeichen *n*) *m*; Wecker *m*; Angst *f*; **2.** alarmieren; beunruhigen

alarm clock Wecker *m*

al·bum Album *n* (*a. record*)

al·bu·mi·nous BIOL eiweißhaltig

al·co·hol Alkohol *m*

al·co·hol·ic 1. alkoholisch; **2.** Alkoholiker(in)

al·co·hol·ism Alkoholismus *m*, Trunksucht *f*

a·lert 1. wachsam; munter; **2.** Alarm *m*; Alarmbereitschaft *f*; *on the alert* auf der Hut; in Alarmbereitschaft; **3.** warnen (*to* vor *dat*), alarmieren

al·ga BOT Alge *f*

al·ge·bra MATH Algebra *f*

al·i·bi JUR Alibi *n*

a·li·en 1. ausländisch; fremd; **2.** Ausländer(in); Außerirdische *m*, *f*

a·li·en·ate veräußern; entfremden; *esp art*: verfremden

a·li·en·a·tion Entfremdung *f*; *esp art*: Verfremdung *f*

a·light 1. in Flammen; **2.** aussteigen; absteigen, absitzen; ZO sich niederlassen; AVIAT landen

a·lign (sich) ausrichten (*with* nach)

a·like 1. *adj* gleich; **2.** *adv* gleich, ebenso

al·i·men·ta·ry nahrhaft

alimentary ca·nal ANAT Verdauungskanal *m*

al·i·mo·ny JUR Unterhalt *m*

a·live lebendig; (noch) am Leben; lebhaft; *alive and kicking* gesund und munter; *be alive with* wimmeln von

all 1. *adj* all; ganz; jede(r, -s); **2.** *pron* alles; alle *pl*; **3.** *adv* ganz, völlig; *all at once* auf einmal; *all the better* desto besser; *all but* beinahe, fast; *all in* F fertig, ganz erledigt; *all right* in Ordnung; *for all that* dessen ungeachtet, trotzdem; *for all I know* soviel ich weiß; *at all* überhaupt; *not at all* überhaupt nicht; *the score was two all* das Spiel stand zwei zu zwei

all-A·mer·i·can typisch amerikanisch; die ganzen USA vertretend

al·lay beruhigen; lindern

al·le·ga·tion *unerwiesene* Behauptung

al·lege behaupten

al·leged angeblich, vermeintlich

al·le·giance Treue *f*

al·ler·gic MED allergisch (*to* gegen)

al·ler·gy MED Allergie *f*

al·le·vi·ate mildern, lindern

al·ley (enge *or* schmale) Gasse; Garten-, Parkweg *m*; *bowling*: Bahn *f*

al·li·ance Bündnis *n*

al·li·ga·tor ZO Alligator *m*

al·lo·cate zuteilen, anweisen

al·lo·ca·tion Zuteilung *f*

al·lot zuteilen, an-, zuweisen

al·lot·ment Zuteilung *f*; Parzelle *f*

al·low erlauben, bewilligen, gewähren; zugeben; ab-, anrechnen, vergüten; *allow for* einplanen, berücksichtigen (*acc*)

al·low·a·ble erlaubt, zulässig

al·low·ance Erlaubnis *f*; Bewilligung *f*; Taschengeld *n*, Zuschuss *m*; Vergütung *f*; *fig* Nachsicht *f*; *make allowance(s) for s.th.* et. berücksichtigen

al·loy TECH **1.** Legierung *f*; **2.** legieren

all·round vielseitig

all·round·er Alleskönner *m*; Allroundsportler *m*, -spieler *m*

al·lude anspielen (*to* auf *acc*)

al·lure locken, an-, verlocken

al·lure·ment Verlockung *f*

al·lu·sion Anspielung *f*

all-wheel drive MOT Allradantrieb *m*

al·ly 1. (sich) vereinigen, verbünden (*to*, *with* mit); **2.** Verbündete *m*, *f*, Bundesgenosse *m*, Bundesgenossin *f*; *the Allies* MIL die Alliierten *pl*

al·might·y allmächtig; *the Almighty* REL der Allmächtige

al·mond BOT Mandel *f*

al·most fast, beinah(e)

alms Almosen *n*

a·loft (hoch) (dr)oben

a·lone allein; *let alone, leave alone* in Ruhe lassen, bleiben lassen; *let alone ...* geschweige denn ...

a·long 1. *adv* weiter, vorwärts; da; dahin; *all along* die ganze Zeit; *along with* (zu-

sammen) mit; *come along* mitkommen, mitgehen; *get along* vorwärtskommen, weiterkommen; auskommen, sich vertragen (*with s.o.* mit j-m); *take along* mitnehmen; **2.** *prp* entlang (*dat*), längs (*gen*)

a·long·side Seite an Seite; neben

a·loof abseits; reserviert, zurückhaltend, verschlossen

a·loof·ness Reserviertheit *f*; Verschlossenheit *f*

a·loud laut

al·pha·bet Alphabet *n*

al·pine (Hoch)Gebirgs..., alpin

al·read·y bereits, schon

al·right → *all right*

Al·sa·tian *esp Br* ZO Deutscher Schäferhund

al·so auch, ferner

al·tar REL Altar *m*

al·ter ändern, sich (ver)ändern; ab-, umändern

al·ter·a·tion Änderung *f* (*to* an *dat*), Veränderung *f*

al·ter·nate 1. abwechseln (lassen); **2.** abwechselnd

al·ter·nat·ing cur·rent ELECTR Wechselstrom *m*

al·ter·na·tion Abwechslung *f*; Wechsel *m*

al·ter·na·tive 1. alternativ, wahlweise; **2.** Alternative *f*, Wahl *f*, Möglichkeit *f*

al·though obwohl, obgleich

al·ti·tude Höhe *f*; *at an altitude of* in e-r Höhe von

al·to·geth·er im Ganzen, insgesamt; ganz (und gar), völlig

a·lu·min·i·um *Br*, **a·lu·mi·num** Aluminium *n*

al·ways immer, stets

am, AM ABBR *of before noon* (*Latin ante meridiem*) morgens, vorm., vormittags

a·mal·gam·ate (sich) zusammenschließen, ECON *a.* fusionieren

a·mass anhäufen, aufhäufen

am·a·teur Amateur(in); Dilettant(in); Hobby...

a·maze in Erstaunen setzen, verblüffen

a·maze·ment Staunen *n*, Verblüffung *f*

a·maz·ing erstaunlich

am·bas·sa·dor POL Botschafter *m* (*to* in *e-m Land*)

am·bas·sa·dress POL Botschafterin *f* (*to* in *e-m Land*)

am·ber Bernstein *m*

am·bi·gu·i·ty Zwei-, Mehrdeutigkeit *f*

am·big·u·ous zwei-, mehr-, vieldeutig

am·bi·tion Ehrgeiz *m*

am·bi·tious ehrgeizig, strebsam

am·ble 1. Passgang *m*; **2.** im Passgang gehen *or* reiten; schlendern

am·bu·lance Krankenwagen *m*

am·bush 1. Hinterhalt *m*; *be or lie in ambush for s.o.* j-m auflauern; **2.** auflauern (*dat*); überfallen

a·men *int* REL amen

a·mend verbessern, berichtigen; PARL abändern, ergänzen

a·mend·ment Bess(e)rung *f*; Verbesserung *f*; PARL Abänderungsantrag *m*, Ergänzungsantrag *m*; Zusatzartikel *m* zur Verfassung

a·mends (Schaden)Ersatz *m*; *make amends* Schadenersatz leisten, es wieder gutmachen; *make amends to s.o. for s.th.* j-n für et. entschädigen

a·men·i·ty *often pl* Annehmlichkeiten *pl*

A·mer·i·ca Amerika *n*

A·mer·i·can 1. amerikanisch; **2.** Amerikaner(in)

A·mer·i·can·is·m LING Amerikanismus *m*

A·mer·i·can·ize (sich) amerikanisieren

A·mer·i·can plan Vollpension *f*

a·mi·a·ble liebenswürdig, freundlich

am·i·ca·ble freundschaftlich, *a.* JUR gütlich

a·mid(st) inmitten (*gen*), (mitten) in *or* unter

a·miss verkehrt, falsch, übel; *take s.th. amiss* et. übel nehmen, et. verübeln

am·mo·ni·a CHEM Ammoniak *n*

am·mu·ni·tion Munition *f*

am·nes·ty JUR **1.** Amnestie *f*; **2.** begnadigen

a·mok: *run amok* Amok laufen

a·mong(st) (mitten) unter, zwischen

am·o·rous verliebt

a·mount 1. (*to*) sich belaufen (auf *acc*); hinauslaufen (auf *acc*); **2.** Betrag *m*, (Gesamt)Summe *f*; Menge *f*

am·per·age ELECTR Stromstärke *f*

am·ple weit, groß, geräumig; reich, reichlich, beträchtlich

am·pli·fi·ca·tion Erweiterung *f*; PHYS Verstärkung *f*

am·pli·fi·er ELECTR Verstärker *m*

am·pli·fy erweitern; ELECTR verstärken

am·pli·tude Umfang *m*, Weite *f*, Fülle *f*; ELECTR, PHYS Amplitude *f*

am·pu·tate MED amputieren

a·muck → *amok*

a·muse (*o.s.*) sich amüsieren, unterhalten, belustigen

a·muse·ment Unterhaltung *f*, Vergnügen *n*, Zeitvertreib *m*

amusement park Vergnügungspark *m*, Freizeitpark *m*

a·mus·ing amüsant, unterhaltend

an → *a*

an·a·bol·ic ster·oid PHARM Anabolikum *n*

a·nae·mi·a *Br* → *anemia*

an·aes·thet·ic *Br* → *anesthetic*

a·nal ANAT anal, Anal...

a·nal·o·gous analog, entsprechend

a·nal·o·gy Analogie *f*, Entsprechung *f*

an·a·lyse *esp Br*, **an·a·lyze** analysieren; zerlegen

a·nal·y·sis Analyse *f*

an·arch·y Anarchie *f*, Gesetzlosigkeit *f*; Chaos *n*

a·nat·o·mize MED zerlegen; zergliedern

a·nat·o·my MED Anatomie *f*; Zergliederung *f*, Analyse *f*

an·ces·tor Vorfahr *m*, Ahn *m*

an·ces·tress Vorfahrin *f*, Ahnfrau *f*

an·chor MAR **1.** Anker *m*; *at anchor* vor Anker; **2.** verankern

an·chor·man TV Moderator *m*

an·chor·wom·an TV Moderatorin *f*

an·cho·vy ZO Anschovis *f*, Sardelle *f*

an·cient 1. alt, antik; uralt; **2.** *the ancients* HIST die Alten, die antiken Klassiker

and und

an·ec·dote Anekdote *f*

a·ne·mi·a MED Blutarmut *f*, Anämie *f*

an·es·thet·ic MED **1.** betäubend, Narkose...; **2.** Betäubungsmittel *n*

an·gel Engel *m*

an·ger 1. Zorn *m*, Ärger *m* (*at* über *acc*); **2.** erzürnen, (ver)ärgern

an·gle¹ Winkel *m* (*a.* MATH)

an·gle² angeln (*for* nach)

an·gler Angler(in)

An·gli·can REL **1.** anglikanisch; **2.** Anglikaner(in)

An·glo-Sax·on 1. angelsächsisch; **2.** Angelsachse *m*

an·gry zornig, verärgert, böse (*at, with* über *acc*, mit *dat*)

an·guish Qual *f*, Schmerz *m*

an·gu·lar winkelig; knochig

an·i·mal 1. Tier *n*; **2.** tierisch

animal lov·er Tierfreund *m*

animal shel·ter Tierheim *n*

an·i·mate beleben; aufmuntern, anregen

an·i·mat·ed lebendig; lebhaft, angeregt

animated car·toon Zeichentrickfilm *m*

an·i·ma·tion Lebhaftigkeit *f*; Animation *f*, Herstellung *f* von (Zeichen-)Trickfilmen; EDP bewegtes Bild

an·i·mos·i·ty Animosität *f*, Feindseligkeit *f*

an·kle ANAT (Fuß)Knöchel *m*

an·nals Jahrbücher *pl*

an·nex 1. anhängen; annektieren; **2.** Anhang *m*; ARCH Anbau *m*

an·ni·ver·sa·ry Jahrestag *m*; Jahresfeier *f*

an·no·tate mit Anmerkungen versehen;

kommentieren

an·nounce ankündigen; bekannt geben; *radio*, TV ansagen; durchsagen

an·nounce·ment Ankündigung *f*; Bekanntgabe *f*; *radio*, TV Ansage *f*; Durchsage *f*

an·nounc·er *radio*, TV Ansager(in), Sprecher(in)

an·noy ärgern; belästigen

an·noy·ance Störung *f*, Belästigung *f*; Ärgernis *n*

an·noy·ing ärgerlich, lästig

an·nu·al 1. jährlich, Jahres…; **2.** einjährige Pflanze; Jahrbuch *n*

an·nu·i·ty (Jahres)Rente *f*

an·nul für ungültig erklären, annullieren

an·nul·ment Annullierung *f*, Aufhebung *f*

an·o·dyne MED **1.** schmerzstillend; **2.** schmerzstillendes Mittel

a·noint REL salben

a·nom·a·lous anomal

a·non·y·mous anonym

an·o·rak Anorak *m*

an·oth·er ein anderer; ein Zweiter; noch eine(r, -s)

an·swer 1. *v/t et.* beantworten; *j-m* antworten; entsprechen (*dat*); *Zweck* erfüllen; TECH *dem Steuer* gehorchen; JUR *e-r Vorladung* Folge leisten; *e-r Beschreibung* entsprechen; ***answer the bell or door*** (die Tür) aufmachen; ***answer the telephone*** ans Telefon gehen; *v/i* antworten (***to*** auf *acc*); entsprechen (***to*** *dat*); ***answer s.o. back*** freche Antworten geben; widersprechen; ***answer for*** einstehen für; **2.** Antwort *f* (***to*** auf *acc*)

an·swer·a·ble verantwortlich

an·swer·ing ma·chine TEL Anrufbeantworter *m*

ant ZO Ameise *f*

an·tag·o·nism Feindschaft *f*

an·tag·o·nist Gegner(in)

an·tag·o·nize bekämpfen; sich *j-n* zum Feind machen

Ant·arc·tic antarktisch

an·te·ced·ent vorhergehend, früher (***to*** als)

an·te·lope ZO Antilope *f*

an·ten·na[1] ZO Fühler *m*

an·ten·na[2] ELECTR Antenne *f*

an·te·ri·or vorhergehend, früher (***to*** als); vorder

an·them MUS Hymne *f*

an·ti… Gegen…, gegen … eingestellt, Anti…, anti…

an·ti·air·craft MIL Fliegerabwehr…, Flugabwehr…

an·ti·bi·ot·ic MED Antibiotikum *n*

an·ti·bod·y BIOL Antikörper *m*, Abwehrstoff *m*

an·tic·i·pate voraussehen, ahnen; erwarten; zuvorkommen; vorwegnehmen

an·tic·i·pa·tion (Vor)Ahnung *f*; Erwartung *f*; Vorwegnahme *f*; Vorfreude *f*; ***in anticipation*** im Voraus

an·ti·clock·wise *Br* entgegen dem Uhrzeigersinn

an·tics Mätzchen *pl*

an·ti·dote Gegengift *n*, Gegenmittel *n*

an·ti·for·eign·er vi·o·lence Gewalt *f* gegen Ausländer

an·ti·freeze Frostschutzmittel *n*

an·ti·lock brak·ing sys·tem MOT Antiblockiersystem *n* (ABBR **ABS**)

an·ti·mis·sile MIL Raketenabwehr…

an·ti·nu·cle·ar ac·tiv·ist Kernkraftgegner(in)

an·tip·a·thy Abneigung *f*

an·ti·quat·ed veraltet

an·tique 1. antik, alt; **2.** Antiquität *f*

an·tique deal·er Antiquitätenhändler(in)

antique shop *esp Br*, **antique store** Antiquitätenladen *m*

an·tiq·ui·ty Altertum *n*, Vorzeit *f*

an·ti·sep·tic MED **1.** antiseptisch; **2.** antiseptisches Mittel

ant·lers ZO Geweih *n*

a·nus ANAT After *m*

an·vil Amboss *m*

anx·i·e·ty Angst *f*, Sorge *f*

anx·ious besorgt, beunruhigt (***about*** wegen); begierig, gespannt (***for*** auf *acc*); bestrebt (***to do*** zu tun)

an·y 1. *adj and pron* (irgend)eine(r, -s), (irgend)welche(r, -s); (irgend)etwas; jede(r, -s) (beliebige); einige *pl*, welche *pl*; ***not any*** keiner; **2.** *adv* irgend(wie), ein wenig, (noch) etwas

an·y·bod·y (irgend)jemand; jeder

an·y·how irgendwie; trotzdem, jedenfalls; wie dem auch sei

an·y·one → ***anybody***

an·y·thing (irgend)etwas; alles; ***anything but*** alles andere als; ***anything else?*** sonst noch etwas?; ***not anything*** nichts

an·y·way → ***anyhow***

an·y·where irgendwo(hin); überall

a·part einzeln, für sich; beiseite; ***apart from*** abgesehen von

a·part·heid POL Apartheid *f*, Politik *f* der Rassentrennung

a·part·ment Wohnung *f*

apartment build·ing, **apartment house** Mietshaus *n*

ap·a·thet·ic apathisch, teilnahmslos, gleichgültig

ap·a·thy Apathie *f*, Teilnahmslosigkeit *f*

ape ZO (Menschen)Affe *m*

ap·er·ture Öffnung *f*

a·pi·a·ry Bienenhaus *n*

a·piece für jedes Stück, pro Stück, je

a·pol·o·gize sich entschuldigen (*for* für; *to* bei)

a·pol·o·gy Entschuldigung *f*; Rechtfertigung *f*; *make an apology (for s.th.)* sich (für et.) entschuldigen

ap·o·plex·y MED Schlaganfall *m*, F Schlag *m*

a·pos·tle REL Apostel *m*

a·pos·tro·phe LING Apostroph *m*

ap·pal(l) erschrecken, entsetzen

ap·pal·ling erschreckend, entsetzlich

ap·pa·ra·tus Apparat *m*, Vorrichtung *f*, Gerät *n*

ap·par·ent offenbar; anscheinend; scheinbar

ap·pa·ri·tion Erscheinung *f*, Gespenst *n*

ap·peal 1. JUR Berufung *or* Revision einlegen, Einspruch erheben, Beschwerde einlegen; appellieren, sich wenden (*to* an *acc*); *appeal to* gefallen (*dat*), zusagen (*dat*), wirken auf (*acc*); *j-n* dringend bitten (*for* um); **2.** JUR Revision *f*, Berufung *f*; Beschwerde *f*; Einspruch *m*; Appell *m* (*to* an *acc*), Aufruf *m*; Wirkung *f*, Reiz *m*; Bitte *f* (*to* an *acc*; *for* um); *appeal for mercy* JUR Gnadengesuch *n*

ap·peal·ing flehend; ansprechend

ap·pear (er)scheinen; sich zeigen; *öffentlich* auftreten; sich ergeben *or* herausstellen

ap·pear·ance Erscheinen *n*; Auftreten *n*; Äußere *n*, Erscheinung *f*, Aussehen *n*; Anschein *m*, äußerer Schein; *keep up appearances* den Schein wahren; *to or by all appearances* allem Anschein nach

ap·pease besänftigen, beschwichtigen; *Durst etc* stillen; *Neugier* befriedigen

ap·pend an-, hinzu-, beifügen

ap·pend·age Anhang *m*; Anhängsel *n*

ap·pen·di·ci·tis MED Blinddarmentzündung *f*

ap·pen·dix Anhang *m*; *a.* **vermiform appendix** ANAT Wurmfortsatz *m*, Blinddarm *m*

ap·pe·tite (*for*) Appetit *m* (auf *acc*); *fig* Verlangen *n* (nach)

ap·pe·tiz·er Appetithappen *m*, appetitanregendes Gericht *or* Getränk

ap·pe·tiz·ing appetitanregend

ap·plaud applaudieren, Beifall spenden; loben

ap·plause Applaus *m*, Beifall *m*

ap·ple BOT Apfel *m*

ap·ple cart: *upset s.o.'s apple cart* F j-s

Pläne über den Haufen werfen

ap·ple pie (*warmer*) gedeckter Apfelkuchen

ap·ple-pie or·der: F *in applepie order* in schönster Ordnung

ap·ple sauce Apfelmus *n*; *sl* Schmus *m*, Quatsch *m*

ap·pli·ance Vorrichtung *f*; Gerät *n*; Mittel *n*

ap·plic·a·ble anwendbar (*to* auf *acc*)

ap·pli·cant Antragsteller(in), Bewerber(in) (*for* um)

ap·pli·ca·tion Anwendung *f* (*to* auf *acc*); Bedeutung *f* (*to* für); Gesuch *n* (*for* um); Bewerbung *f* (*for* um)

ap·ply *v/t* (*to*) (auf)legen, auftragen (auf *acc*); anwenden (auf *acc*); verwenden (für); *apply o.s. to* sich widmen (*dat*); *v/i* (*to*) passen, zutreffen, sich anwenden lassen (auf *acc*); gelten (für); sich wenden (an *acc*); *apply for* sich bewerben um, et. beantragen

ap·point bestimmen, festsetzen; verabreden; ernennen (*s.o. governor* j-n zum ...); berufen (*to* auf *e-n Posten*)

ap·point·ment Bestimmung *f*; Verabredung *f*; Termin *m*; Ernennung *f*, Berufung *f*; Stelle *f*

appointment book Terminkalender *m*

ap·por·tion verteilen, zuteilen

ap·prais·al (Ab)Schätzung *f*

ap·praise (ab)schätzen, taxieren

ap·pre·cia·ble nennenswert, spürbar

ap·pre·ci·ate *v/t* schätzen, würdigen; dankbar sein für; *v/i* im Wert steigen

ap·pre·ci·a·tion Würdigung *f*; Dankbarkeit *f*; (richtige) Beurteilung *f*; ECON Wertsteigerung *f*

ap·pre·hend ergreifen, fassen; begreifen; befürchten

ap·pre·hen·sion Ergreifung *f*, Festnahme *f*; Besorgnis *f*

ap·pre·hen·sive ängstlich, besorgt (*for* um; *that* dass)

ap·pren·tice 1. Auszubildende *m*, *f*, Lehrling *m*, *Swiss* Lehrtochter *f*; **2.** in die Lehre geben

ap·pren·tice·ship Lehrzeit *f*, Lehre *f*, Ausbildung *f*

ap·proach 1. *v/i* näher kommen, sich nähern; *v/t* sich nähern (*dat*); herangehen *or* herantreten an (*acc*); **2.** (Heran)Nahen *n*; Einfahrt *f*, Zufahrt *f*, Auffahrt *f*; Annäherung *f*; Methode *f*

ap·pro·ba·tion Billigung *f*, Beifall *m*

ap·pro·pri·ate 1. sich aneignen; verwenden; PARL bewilligen; **2.** (*for, to*) angemessen (*dat*), passend (für, zu)

ap·prov·al Billigung *f*; Anerkennung *f*,

Beifall *m*
ap·prove billigen, anerkennen
ap·proved bewährt
ap·prox·i·mate annähernd, ungefähr
a·pri·cot BOT Aprikose *f*
A·pril (ABBR **Apr**) April *m*
a·pron Schürze *f*
**apron strings: *be tied to one's mother's
apron strings*** an Mutters Schürzenzipfel hängen
apt geeignet, passend; treffend; begabt;
apt to geneigt zu
ap·ti·tude (***for***) Begabung *f* (für), Befähigung *f* (für), Talent *n* (zu)
ap·ti·tude test Eignungsprüfung *f*
aq·ua·plan·ing *Br* MOT Aquaplaning *n*
a·quar·i·um Aquarium *n*
A·quar·i·us ASTR Wassermann *m*; ***he
(she) is (an) Aquarius*** er (sie) ist (ein)
Wassermann
a·quat·ic Wasser...
a·quat·ic plant Wasserpflanze *f*
a·quat·ics, a·quat·ic sports Wassersport
m
aq·ue·duct Aquädukt *m*
Ar·ab Araber(in)
A·ra·bi·a Arabien *n*
Ar·a·bic 1. arabisch; **2.** LING Arabisch *n*
ar·a·ble AGR anbaufähig; Acker...
ar·bi·tra·ry willkürlich, eigenmächtig
ar·bi·trate entscheiden, schlichten
ar·bi·tra·tion Schlichtung *f*
ar·bi·tra·tor Schiedsrichter *m*; Schlichter
m
ar·bo(u)r Laube *f*
arc Bogen *m*; ELECTR Lichtbogen *m*
ar·cade Arkade *f*; Lauben-, Bogengang
m; Durchgang *m*, Passage *f*
arch¹ 1. Bogen *m*; Gewölbe *n*; **2.** (sich)
wölben; krümmen
arch² erste(r, -s), oberste(r, -s), Haupt...,
Erz...
arch³ schelmisch
ar·cha·ic veraltet
arch·an·gel Erzengel *m*
arch·bish·op REL Erzbischof *m*
ar·cher Bogenschütze *m*
ar·cher·y Bogenschießen *n*
ar·chi·tect Architekt(in)
ar·chi·tec·ture Architektur *f*
ar·chives Archiv *n*
arch·way (Bogen)Gang *m*
arc·tic arktisch, nördlich, Polar...
ar·dent feurig, glühend; *fig* leidenschaftlich, heftig; eifrig
ar·do(u)r Leidenschaft *f*, Glut *f*, Feuer *n*;
Eifer *m*
are *du* bist, *wir or sie or Sie* sind, *ihr* seid
ar·e·a (Boden)Fläche *f*; Gegend *f*, Gebiet

n; Bereich *m*
ar·e·a code TEL Vorwahl(nummer) *f*
Ar·gen·ti·na Argentinien *n*
Ar·gen·tine 1. argentinisch; **2.** Argentinier(in)
a·re·na Arena *f*
ar·gue argumentieren; streiten; diskutieren
ar·gu·ment Argument *n*; Wortwechsel *m*,
Auseinandersetzung *f*
ar·id dürr, trocken (*a. fig*)
Ar·ies ASTR Widder *m*; ***he (she) is (an)
Aries*** er (sie) ist (ein) Widder
a·rise entstehen; auftauchen, auftreten
ar·is·toc·ra·cy Aristokratie *f*, Adel *m*
ar·is·to·crat Aristokrat(in), Adlige *m*, *f*
ar·is·to·crat·ic aristokratisch, adlig
a·rith·me·tic¹ Rechnen *n*
ar·ith·met·ic² arithmetisch, Rechen...
ar·ith·met·ic u·nit EDP Rechenwerk *n*
ark Arche *f*; ***Noah's ark*** die Arche Noah
arm¹ ANAT Arm *m*; Armlehne *f*; ***keep s.o.
at arm's length*** sich j-n vom Leibe halten
arm² MIL (sich) bewaffnen; (auf)rüsten
ar·ma·ment MIL Bewaffnung *f*; Aufrüstung *f*
arm·chair Lehnstuhl *m*, Sessel *m*
ar·mi·stice MIL Waffenstillstand *m*
ar·mo(u)r 1. MIL Rüstung *f*, Panzer *m* (*a.
fig*, ZO); **2.** panzern
ar·mo(u)red car gepanzertes Fahrzeug
arm·pit ANAT Achselhöhle *f*
arms Waffen *pl*; Waffengattung *f*
arms con·trol Rüstungskontrolle *f*
arms race Wettrüsten *n*, Rüstungswettlauf *m*
ar·my MIL Armee *f*, Heer *n*
a·ro·ma Aroma *n*, Duft *m*
ar·o·mat·ic aromatisch, würzig
a·round 1. *adv* (rings)herum, (rund-) herum, ringsumher, überall; umher, herum;
in der Nähe; da; **2.** *prp* um, um... herum,
rund um; in (*dat*) ... herum; ungefähr, etwa
a·rouse (auf)wecken; *fig* aufrütteln, erregen
ar·range (an)ordnen; festlegen, festsetzen; arrangieren (*a.* MUS); vereinbaren;
MUS, THEA bearbeiten
ar·range·ment Anordnung *f*; Vereinbarung *f*; Vorkehrung *f*; MUS Arrangement
n, Bearbeitung *f* (*a.* THEA)
ar·rears Rückstand *m*, Rückstände *pl*
ar·rest JUR **1.** Verhaftung *f*, Festnahme *f*;
2. verhaften, festnehmen
ar·riv·al Ankunft *f*; Erscheinen *n*; Ankömmling *m*; ***arrivals*** AVIAT, RAIL *etc* 'Ankunft' (*timetable*)

ar·rive (an)kommen, eintreffen, erscheinen; *arrive at fig* erreichen (*acc*), kommen zu

ar·ro·gance Arroganz *f*, Überheblichkeit *f*

ar·ro·gant arrogant, überheblich

ar·row Pfeil *m*

ar·row·head Pfeilspitze *f*

ar·se·nic CHEM Arsen *n*

ar·son JUR Brandstiftung *f*

art 1. Kunst *f*; 2. Kunst...; *art exhibition* Kunstausstellung *f*; → *arts*

ar·te·ri·al ANAT Schlagader...

ar·te·ri·al road Hauptverkehrsstraße *f*, Verkehrsader *f*

ar·te·ri·o·scle·ro·sis MED Arteriosklerose *f*, Arterienverkalkung *f*

ar·te·ry ANAT Arterie *f*, Schlagader *f*; (Haupt)Verkehrsader *f*

art·ful schlau, verschmitzt

art gal·le·ry Gemäldegalerie *f*

ar·thri·tis MED Arthritis *f*, Gelenkentzündung *f*

ar·ti·choke BOT Artischocke *f*

ar·ti·cle Artikel *m* (*a.* LING)

ar·tic·u·late 1. deutlich (aus)sprechen; 2. deutlich ausgesprochen; gegliedert

ar·tic·u·lat·ed Gelenk...; *articulated lorry* Br MOT Sattelschlepper *m*

ar·tic·u·la·tion (deutliche) Aussprache; TECH Gelenk *n*

ar·ti·fi·cial künstlich, Kunst...; *artificial person* juristische Person

ar·til·le·ry MIL Artillerie *f*

ar·ti·san Handwerker *m*

art·ist Künstler(in)

ar·tis·tic künstlerisch, Kunst...

art·less schlicht; naiv

arts Geisteswissenschaften *pl*; *Arts Department*, Br *Faculty of Arts* philosophische Fakultät

as 1. *adv* so, ebenso; wie; als; 2. *cj* (gerade) wie; so wie; ebenso wie; als; während; obwohl, obgleich; da, weil; *as ... as* (eben)so ... wie; *as for, as to* was ... (an-)betrifft; *as from* von e-m *Zeitpunkt* an, ab; *as it were* sozusagen; *as Hamlet* THEA als Hamlet

as·bes·tos Asbest *m*

as·cend (auf)steigen; ansteigen; besteigen

as·cen·dan·cy, as·cen·den·cy Überlegenheit *f*; Einfluss *m*

as·cen·sion Aufsteigen *n* (*esp* ASTR); Aufstieg *m*

As·cen·sion (Day) REL Himmelfahrt(stag *m*) *f*

as·cent Aufstieg *m*; Besteigung *f*; Steigung *f*

as·cet·ic asketisch

a·sep·tic MED 1. aseptisch, keimfrei; 2. aseptisches Mittel

ash[1] BOT Esche *f*; Eschenholz *n*

ash[2] *a.* *ashes* Asche *f*

a·shamed beschämt; *be ashamed of* sich schämen für (*or gen*)

ash·en Aschen...; aschfahl, aschgrau

a·shore am *or* ans Ufer *or* Land

ash·tray Asch(en)becher *m*

Ash Wednes·day Aschermittwoch *m*

A·sia Asien *n*

A·sian, A·si·at·ic 1. asiatisch; 2. Asiat(in)

a·side beiseite (*a.* THEA), seitwärts; *aside from* abgesehen von

ask *v/t* fragen (*s.th.* nach et.); verlangen (*of, from s.o.* von j-m); bitten (*s.o.* [*for*] *s.th.* j-n um et.; *that* darum, dass); erbitten; *ask (s.o.) a question* (j-m) e-e Frage stellen; *v/i* bitten um; fragen nach; *he asked for it or for trouble* er wollte es ja so haben; *to be had for the asking* umsonst zu haben sein

a·skance: *look askance at s.o.* j-n schief *or* misstrauisch ansehen

a·skew schief

a·sleep schlafend; *be (fast, sound) asleep* (fest) schlafen; *fall asleep* einschlafen

as·par·a·gus BOT Spargel *m*

as·pect Lage *f*; Aspekt *m*, Seite *f*, Gesichtspunkt *m*

as·phalt 1. Asphalt *m*; 2. asphaltieren

as·pic GASTR Aspik *m*, Gelee *n*

as·pi·rant Bewerber(in)

as·pi·ra·tion Ambition *f*, Bestrebung *f*

as·pire streben (*to, after* nach)

ass ZO Esel *m*

as·sail angreifen; *be assailed with doubts* von Zweifeln befallen werden

as·sail·ant Angreifer(in)

as·sas·sin (*esp* politischer) Mörder, Attentäter *m*

as·sas·sin·ate *esp* POL ermorden; *be assassinated* e-m Attentat *or* Mordanschlag zum Opfer fallen

as·sas·sin·a·tion (*of*) (*esp* politischer) Mord (an *dat*), Ermordung *f* (*gen*), Attentat *n* (auf *acc*)

as·sault 1. Angriff *m*, Überfall *m*; 2. angreifen, überfallen

as·sem·blage Ansammlung *f*; TECH Montage *f*

as·sem·ble (sich) versammeln; TECH montieren

as·sem·bly Versammlung *f*, Gesellschaft *f*; TECH Montage *f*

assembly line TECH Fließband *n*

as·sent 1. Zustimmung *f*; 2. (*to*) zustimmen (*dat*); billigen (*acc*)

as·sert behaupten; geltend machen; **assert o.s.** sich behaupten, sich durchsetzen

as·ser·tion Behauptung *f*; Erklärung *f*; Geltendmachung *f*

as·sess *Kosten etc* festsetzen; *Einkommen etc* (zur Steuer) veranlagen (**at** mit); *fig* abschätzen, beurteilen

as·sess·ment Festsetzung *f*; (Steuer-)Veranlagung *f*; *fig* Einschätzung *f*

as·set ECON Aktivposten *m*; *fig* Plus *n*, Gewinn *m*; *pl* ECON Aktiva *pl*; JUR Vermögen(smasse *f*) *n*; Konkursmasse *f*

as·sid·u·ous emsig, fleißig

as·sign an-, zuweisen; bestimmen; zuschreiben

as·sign·ment An-, Zuweisung *f*; Aufgabe *f*; Auftrag *m*; JUR Abtretung *f*; Übertragung *f*

as·sim·i·late (sich) angleichen *or* anpassen (**to, with** *dat*)

as·sim·i·la·tion Assimilation *f*, Angleichung *f*, Anpassung *f* (*all*: **to** an *acc*)

as·sist *j-m* beistehen, helfen; *j-n* unterstützen

as·sist·ance Beistand *m*, Hilfe *f*

as·sist·ant 1. stellvertretend, Hilfs…; 2. Assistent(in), Mitarbeiter(in); (**shop**) **assistant** *Br* Verkäufer(in)

as·so·ci·ate 1. vereinigen, verbinden, zusammenschließen; assoziieren; **associate with** verkehren mit; 2. Teilhaber(in)

as·so·ci·a·tion Vereinigung *f*, Verbindung *f*; Verein *m*

as·sort sortieren, aussuchen, zusammenstellen

as·sort·ment ECON (**of**) Sortiment *n* (von), Auswahl *f* (an *dat*)

as·sume annehmen, voraussetzen; übernehmen

as·sump·tion Annahme *f*, Voraussetzung *f*; Übernahme *f*; **the Assumption** REL Mariä Himmelfahrt *f*

as·sur·ance Zusicherung *f*, Versicherung *f*; *esp Br* (Lebens)Versicherung *f*; Sicherheit *f*, Gewissheit *f*; Selbstsicherheit *f*

as·sure *j-m* versichern; *esp Br j-s* Leben versichern

as·sured 1. sicher; 2. *esp Br* Versicherte *m*, *f*

as·sur·ed·ly ganz gewiss

as·te·risk PRINT Sternchen *n*

asth·ma MED Asthma *n*

as·ton·ish in Erstaunen setzen; **be astonished** erstaunt sein (**at** über *acc*)

as·ton·ish·ing erstaunlich

as·ton·ish·ment (Er)Staunen *n*, Verwunderung *f*

as·tound verblüffen

a·stray: **go astray** vom Weg abkommen; *fig* auf Abwege geraten; irregehen; **lead astray** *fig* irreführen; verleiten

a·stride rittlings (**of** auf *dat*)

as·trin·gent MED 1. adstringierend; 2. Adstringens *n*

as·trol·o·gy Astrologie *f*

as·tro·naut Astronaut *m*, (Welt)Raumfahrer *m*

as·tron·o·my Astronomie *f*

as·tute scharfsinnig; schlau

a·sun·der auseinander, entzwei

a·sy·lum Asyl *n*; **right of asylum** Asylrecht *n*

a·sy·lum seek·er Asylant(in), Asylbewerber(in)

at *prp place*: in, an, bei, auf; *direction*: auf, nach, gegen, zu; *occupation*: bei, beschäftigt mit; in; *manner, state*: in, bei, zu, unter; *price etc*: für, um; *time, age*: um, bei; **at the baker's** beim Bäcker; **at the door** an der Tür; **at school** in der Schule; **at 10 dollars** für 10 Dollar; **at 18** mit 18 (Jahren); **at the age of** im Alter von; **at 8 o'clock** um 8 Uhr

a·the·ism Atheismus *m*

ath·lete SPORT (Leicht)Athlet(in)

ath·let·ic SPORT athletisch

ath·let·ics SPORT (Leicht)Athletik *f*

At·lan·tic 1. *a.* **Atlantic Ocean** der Atlantik; 2. atlantisch

at·mo·sphere Atmosphäre *f* (*a. fig*)

at·mo·spher·ic atmosphärisch

at·oll Atoll *n*

at·om Atom *n*

atom bomb Atombombe *f*

a·tom·ic atomar, Atom…

atomic age Atomzeitalter *n*

atomic bomb Atombombe *f*

atomic en·er·gy Atomenergie *f*

atomic pile Atomreaktor *m*

atomic pow·er Atomkraft *f*

atomic-pow·ered atomgetrieben

atomic waste Atommüll *m*

atomic weight CHEM Atomgewicht *n*

at·om·ize atomisieren; *Flüssigkeit* zerstäuben

at·om·iz·er Zerstäuber *m*

a·tone: **atone for** büßen für, *et.* sühnen

a·tone·ment Buße *f*, Sühne *f*

a·tro·cious grässlich; grausam

a·troc·i·ty Scheußlichkeit *f*; Greueltat *f*

at sign EDP at-Zeichen *n*

at·tach *v/t* (**to**) anheften, ankleben (an *acc*), befestigen, anbringen (an *dat*); *Wert, Wichtigkeit etc* beimessen (*dat*); **be attached to** *fig* hängen an

at·tach·ment Befestigung *f*; Bindung *f* (**to**

an *acc*); Anhänglichkeit *f* (**to** an *acc*)
at·tack 1. angreifen; **2.** Angriff *m*; MED
Anfall *m*
at·tempt 1. versuchen; **2.** Versuch *m*; *an*
attempt on s.o.'s life ein Mordanschlag
or Attentat auf j-n
at·tend *v/t* (ärztlich) behandeln; *Kranke*
pflegen; teilnehmen an (*dat*), *Schule,*
Vorlesung etc besuchen; *fig* begleiten;
v/i anwesend sein; erscheinen; *attend*
to j-n (*im Laden*) bedienen; *are you be-*
ing attended to? werden Sie schon bedient?; *attend to s.th.* etwas erledigen
at·tend·ance Dienst *m*, Bereitschaft *f*;
Pflege *f*; Anwesenheit *f*, Erscheinen *n*;
Besucher *pl*, Teilnehmer *pl*; Besuch(er-
zahl *f*) *m*, Beteiligung *f*
at·tend·ant Begleiter(in); Aufseher(in);
(*Tank-*)Wart *m*
at·ten·tion Aufmerksamkeit *f* (*a. fig*); *pay*
attention aufpassen
at·ten·tive aufmerksam
at·tic Dachboden *m*; Dachkammer *f*
at·ti·tude (Ein)Stellung *f*; Haltung *f*
at·tor·ney Bevollmächtigte *m*, *f*; JUR
(Rechts)Anwalt *m*, (Rechts)Anwältin *f*;
power of attorney Vollmacht *f*
At·tor·ney Gen·e·ral JUR Justizminister;
Br erster Kronanwalt
at·tract anziehen; *Aufmerksamkeit* erregen; *fig* reizen
at·trac·tion Anziehung *f*, Anziehungskraft *f*, Reiz *m*; Attraktion *f*, THEA *etc*
Zugnummer *f*, Zugstück *n*
at·trac·tive anziehend; attraktiv; reizvoll
at·trib·ute[1] zuschreiben (**to** *dat*); zurückführen (**to** auf *acc*)
at·tri·bute[2] Attribut *n* (*a.* LING), Eigenschaft *f*, Merkmal *n*
at·tune *attune to fig* einstellen auf (*acc*)
au·ber·gine BOT Aubergine *f*
au·burn kastanienbraun
auc·tion 1. Auktion *f*, Versteigerung *f*; **2.**
mst **auction off** versteigern
auc·tion·eer Auktionator *m*
au·da·cious unverfroren, dreist
au·dac·i·ty Unverfrorenheit *f*, Dreistigkeit *f*
au·di·ble hörbar
au·di·ence Publikum *n*, Zuhörer *pl*, Zuschauer *pl*, Besucher *pl*, Leser(kreis *m*)
pl; Audienz *f*
au·di·o·vis·u·al aids audiovisuelle Un-
terrichtsmittel *pl*
au·dit ECON **1.** Buchprüfung *f*; **2.** prüfen
au·di·tion MUS Vorsingen *n*; THEA Vorsprechen *n*; *have an audition* vorsingen,
THEA vorsprechen
au·di·tor ECON Buchprüfer *m*; UNIV Gast-

hörer(in)
au·di·to·ri·um Zuhörer-, Zuschauerraum
m; Vortrags-, Konzertsaal *m*
Aug ABBR *of* **August** Aug., August *m*
au·ger TECH großer Bohrer
Au·gust (ABBR *Aug*) August *m*
aunt Tante *f*
au pair (girl) Au-pair-Mädchen *n*
aus·pic·es: *under the auspices of* unter
der Schirmherrschaft (*gen*)
aus·tere streng; enthaltsam; dürftig; einfach, schmucklos
Aus·tra·li·a Australien
Aus·tra·li·an 1. australisch; **2.** Australi-
er(in)
Aus·tri·a Österreich *n*
Aus·tri·an 1. österreichisch; **2.** Österrei-
cher(in)
au·then·tic authentisch; zuverlässig; echt
au·thor Urheber(in); Autor(in), Verfas-
ser(in), Schriftsteller(in)
au·thor·ess Autorin *f*, Verfasserin *f*,
Schriftstellerin *f*
au·thor·i·ta·tive gebieterisch, herrisch;
maßgebend
au·thor·i·ty Autorität *f*; Nachdruck *m*,
Gewicht *n*; Vollmacht *f*; Einfluss *m* (**over**
auf *acc*); Ansehen *n*; Quelle *f*; Autorität
f, Kapazität *f*; *mst pl* Behörde *f*
au·thor·ize j-n autorisieren, ermächtigen,
bevollmächtigen
au·thor·ship Urheberschaft *f*
au·to Auto *n*
au·to... auto..., selbst..., Auto...,
Selbst...
au·to·bi·og·ra·phy Autobiografie *f*
au·to·graph Autogramm *n*
au·to·mat® Automatenrestaurant *n*
au·to·mate automatisieren
au·to·mat·ic 1. automatisch; **2.** Selbstla-
depistole *f*, -gewehr *n*; Auto *n* mit Automatik
automatic tel·ler ma·chine (ABBR *ATM*)
Geld-, Bankautomat *m*
au·to·ma·tion TECH Automation *f*
au·tom·a·ton Roboter *m*
au·to·mo·bile Auto *n*, Automobil *n*
au·ton·o·my POL Autonomie *f*
au·top·sy MED Autopsie *f*
au·to·tel·ler Geld-, Bankautomat *m*
au·tumn Herbst *m*
au·tum·nal herbstlich, Herbst...
aux·il·i·a·ry helfend, Hilfs...
a·vail: *to no avail* vergeblich
a·vail·a·ble verfügbar, vorhanden; erreichbar; ECON lieferbar, vorrätig, erhältlich
av·a·lanche Lawine *f*
av·a·rice Habsucht *f*

av·a·ri·cious habgierig
a·venge rächen
a·veng·er Rächer(in)
av·e·nue Allee *f*; Boulevard *m*, Prachtstraße *f*
av·e·rage 1. Durchschnitt *m*; **2.** durchschnittlich, Durchschnitts...
a·verse abgeneigt (*to dat*)
a·ver·sion Widerwille *m*, Abneigung *f*
a·vert abwenden (*a. fig*)
avian flu Vogelgrippe *f*
a·vi·a·ry Vogelhaus *n*, Voliere *f*
a·vi·a·tion Luftfahrt *f*
a·vi·a·tor Flieger *m*
av·id gierig (*for* nach); begeistert
av·o·ca·do BOT Avocado *f*
a·void (ver)meiden; ausweichen
a·void·ance Vermeidung *f*
a·vow·al Bekenntnis *n*, (Ein)Geständnis *n*
a·wait erwarten, warten auf (*acc*)
a·wake 1. wach, munter; **2.** *a.* **a·waken** *v/t* (auf)wecken; *v/i* aufwachen, erwachen;
a·wak·en·ing Erwachen *n*

a·ward 1. Belohnung *f*; Preis *m*, Auszeichnung *f*; **2.** zuerkennen, *Preis etc* verleihen
a·ware: *be aware of s.th.* von etwas wissen, sich e-r Sache bewusst sein; *become aware of s.th.* etwas merken
a·way weg, fort; (weit) entfernt; immer weiter, d(a)rauflos; SPORT Auswärts...;
away match SPORT Auswärtsspiel *n*
awe 1. Furcht *f*, Scheu *f*; **2.** *j-m* (Ehr)-Furcht *or* großen Respekt einflößen
aw·ful furchtbar, schrecklich
awk·ward ungeschickt, linkisch; unangenehm; unhandlich, sperrig; ungünstig, ungelegen
awl Ahle *f*, Pfriem *m*
aw·ning Plane *f*; Markise *f*
a·wry schief
ax(e) Axt *f*, Beil *n*
ax·is MATH *etc* Achse *f*
ax·le TECH (Rad)Achse *f*, Welle *f*
ay(e) PARL Jastimme *f*
A-Z *Br appr* Stadtplan *m*
az·ure azurblau, himmelblau

B

B, b B, b *n*
b ABBR *of born* geb., geboren
bab·ble 1. stammeln; plappern, schwatzen; plätschern; **2.** Geplapper *n*, Geschwätz *n*
babe kleines Kind, Baby *n*; F Puppe *f*
ba·boon ZO Pavian *m*
ba·by 1. Baby *n*, Säugling *m*, kleines Kind; F Puppe *f*; **2.** Baby..., Kinder...; klein
baby bug·gy, baby car·riage Kinderwagen *m*
ba·by·hood Säuglingsalter *n*
ba·by·ish *contp* kindisch
ba·by·mind·er *Br* Tagesmutter *f*
ba·by·sit babysitten
ba·by·sit·ter Babysitter(in)
bach·e·lor Junggeselle *m*
back 1. Rücken *m*; Rückseite *f*; (Rück)-Lehne *f*; hinterer *or* rückwärtiger Teil; SPORT Verteidiger *m*; **2.** *adj* Hinter..., Rück..., hintere(r, -s), rückwärtig; ECON rückständig; alt, zurückliegend; **3.** *adv* zurück, rückwärts; **4.** *v/t* mit e-m Rücken versehen; wetten *or* setzen auf (*acc*); *a.*
back up unterstützen; zurückbewegen; MOT zurückstoßen mit; *back up* EDP

e-e Sicherungskopie machen von; *v/i* often *back up* sich rückwärts bewegen, zurückgehen *or* -fahren, MOT *a.* zurückstoßen; *back in(to a parking space)* MOT rückwärts einparken; *back up* EDP e-e Sicherungskopie machen
back·ache Rückenschmerzen *pl*
back·bite verleumden, schlechtmachen
back·bone ANAT Rückgrat *n* (*a. fig*)
back·break·ing erschöpfend, mörderisch
back·chat *Br* freche Antwort(en *pl*)
back·comb *Br* toupieren
back door Hintertür *f*; *fig* Hintertürchen *n*
back·er Unterstützer *m*, Geldgeber *m*
back·fire MOT Früh- *or* Fehlzündung haben; *fig* fehlschlagen
back·ground Hintergrund *m*
back·hand SPORT Rückhand *f*, Rückhandschlag *m*
back·heel·er soccer: Hackentrick *m*
back·ing Unterstützung *f*
back num·ber alte Nummer
back·pack *großer* Rucksack
back·pack·er Rucksacktourist(in)
back·pack·ing Rucksacktourismus *m*

back-ped·al brake Br Rücktritt m, Rücktrittbremse f
back seat MOT Rücksitz m
back·side Gesäß n, F Hintern m, Po m
back·space (key) EDP Rücktaste f
back stairs Hintertreppe f
back street Seitenstraße f
back·stroke Rückenschwimmen n
back talk freche Antwort(en pl)
back·track fig e-n Rückzieher machen
back·up Unterstützung f; TECH Ersatzgerät n; EDP Backup n, Sicherungskopie f; MOT Rückstau m
back·ward 1. adj Rück..., Rückwärts...; zurückgeblieben; rückständig; *a backward glance* ein Blick zurück; **2.** adv a. **backwards** rückwärts, zurück
back·yard Garten m hinter dem Haus; Br Hinterhof m
ba·con Speck m
bac·te·ri·a BIOL Bakterien pl
bad schlecht, böse, schlimm; *go bad* schlecht werden, verderben; *he is in a bad way* es geht ihm schlecht; *he is badly off* es geht ihm finanziell schlecht; *badly wounded* schwer verwundet; *want badly* dringend brauchen
badge Abzeichen n; Dienstmarke f
bad·ger 1. ZO Dachs m; **2.** j-n plagen, j-m zusetzen
bad·min·ton Federball(spiel n) m, SPORT Badminton n
bad-tempered schlecht gelaunt
bag 1. Beutel m, Sack m; Tüte f; Tasche f; *bag and baggage* (mit) Sack und Pack; **2.** in e-n Beutel etc tun; in Beutel verpacken or abfüllen; HUNT zur Strecke bringen; schlottern; a. *bag out* sich bauschen
bag·gage (Reise)Gepäck n
baggage car RAIL Gepäckwagen m
baggage check Gepäckschein m
baggage claim AVIAT Gepäckausgabe f
baggage room RAIL Gepäckaufbewahrung f
bag·gy bauschig; ausgebeult
bag·pipes MUS Dudelsack m
bail 1. Bürge m; JUR Kaution f; *be out on bail* gegen Kaution auf freiem Fuß sein; *go or stand bail for s.o.* für j-n Kaution stellen; **2.** *bail out* JUR j-n gegen Kaution freibekommen; AVIAT (mit dem Fallschirm) abspringen
bai·liff (Guts)Verwalter m; Br JUR Gerichtsvollzieher m
bait 1. Köder m (a. fig); **2.** mit e-m Köder versehen; fig ködern
bake backen, im (Back)Ofen braten; TECH brennen; dörren
bak·er Bäcker m

bak·er·y Bäckerei f
bak·ing pow·der Backpulver n
bal·ance 1. Waage f; Gleichgewicht n (a. fig); ECON Bilanz f; Saldo m, Kontostand m, Guthaben n; Restbetrag m; *keep one's balance* das Gleichgewicht halten; *lose one's balance* das Gleichgewicht verlieren; fig die Fassung verlieren; *balance of payments* ECON Zahlungsbilanz f; *balance of power* POL Kräftegleichgewicht n; *balance of trade* ECON Handelsbilanz f; **2.** v/t abwägen; im Gleichgewicht halten, balancieren; ECON ausgleichen; v/i balancieren; ECON sich ausgleichen; *balance each other* sich die Waage halten
bal·ance sheet ECON Bilanz f
bal·co·ny Balkon m (a. THEA)
bald kahl
bale¹ ECON Ballen m
bale²: *bale out* Br AVIAT (mit dem Fallschirm) abspringen
bale·ful hasserfüllt
balk 1. Balken m; **2.** stutzen; scheuen
ball¹ 1. Ball m; Kugel f; ANAT (Hand-, Fuß)Ballen m; Knäuel m, n; Kloß m; *start the ball rolling* den Stein ins Rollen bringen; *play ball* F mitmachen; *long ball* SPORT langer Pass; **2.** ballen; sich zusammenballen
ball² Ball m, Tanzveranstaltung f
bal·lad Ballade f
bal·last 1. Ballast m; **2.** mit Ballast beladen
ball bear·ing TECH Kugellager n
bal·let Ballett n
bal·lis·tics MIL Ballistik f
bal·loon 1. Ballon m; Sprech-, Denkblase f; **2.** sich (auf)blähen
bal·lot 1. Stimmzettel m; (geheime) Wahl; **2.** (*for*) stimmen (für), (in geheimer Wahl) wählen (acc)
ballot box Wahlurne f
ballot pa·per Stimmzettel m
ball·point (pen) Kugelschreiber m, F Kuli m
ball·room Ballsaal m, Tanzsaal m
balls V Eier pl
balm Balsam m (a. fig)
balm·y lind, mild
ba·lo·ney F Quatsch m
bal·us·trade Balustrade f, Brüstung f, Geländer n
bam·boo BOT Bambus(rohr n) m
bam·boo·zle F betrügen, j-n übers Ohr hauen
ban 1. (amtliches) Verbot, Sperre f; REL Bann m; **2.** verbieten
ba·nal banal, abgedroschen

ba·na·na BOT Banane f

band 1. Band n; Streifen m; Schar f, Gruppe f; contp Bande f; (Musik)Kapelle f, (Tanz-, Unterhaltungs)Orchester n, (Jazz-, Rock)Band f; **2. band together** sich zusammentun or -rotten

ban·dage MED **1.** Bandage f; Binde f; Verband m; (Heft)Pflaster n; **2.** bandagieren; verbinden

'Band-Aid® MED (Heft)Pflaster n

b & b, B & B ABBR of bed and breakfast Übernachtung f mit Frühstück

ban·dit Bandit m

band·lead·er MUS Bandleader m

band·mas·ter MUS Kapellmeister m

ban·dy krumm

ban·dy-legged säbelbeinig, o-beinig

bang 1. heftiger Schlag; Knall m; mst pl Pony m; **2.** dröhnend (zu)schlagen

ban·gle Armreif m, Fußreif m

ban·ish verbannen

ban·ish·ment Verbannung f

ban·is·ter a. pl Treppengeländer n

ban·jo MUS Banjo n

bank[1] ECON **1.** Bank f (a. MED); **2.** v/t bei e-r Bank einzahlen; v/i ein Bankkonto haben (**with** bei)

bank[2] (Erd)Wall m; Böschung f; (Flussetc)Ufer n; (Sand-, Wolken)Bank f

bank ac·count Bankkonto n

bank bill Banknote f, Geldschein m

bank·book Sparbuch n

bank code ECON Bankleitzahl f

bank·er Bankier m, Banker m; **banker's card** Scheckkarte f

bank hol·i·day Br gesetzlicher Feiertag m

bank·ing ECON **1.** Bankgeschäft n, Bankwesen n; **2.** Bank...

bank note Br → **bank bill**

bank rate ECON Diskontsatz m

bank·rupt JUR **1.** Konkursschuldner m; **2.** bankrott; **go bankrupt** in Konkurs gehen, Bankrott machen; **3.** j-n, Unternehmen Bankrott machen

bank·rupt·cy JUR Bankrott m, Konkurs m

bank sort·ing code → **bank code**

ban·ner Transparent n

banns Aufgebot n

ban·quet Bankett n

ban·ter necken

bap·tism REL Taufe f

bap·tize REL taufen

bar 1. Stange f, Stab m; SPORT (Tor-, Quer-, Sprung)Latte f; Riegel m; Schranke f, Sperre f; fig Hindernis n; (Gold- etc)Barren m; MUS Taktstrich m; ein Takt m; dicker Strich; JUR (Gerichts)Schranke f; JUR Anwaltschaft f; Bar f; Lokal n, Imbissstube f; pl Gitter n; **a bar of choco-**

late ein Riegel or e-e Tafel Schokolade; **a bar of soap** ein Stück Seife; **2.** zuriegeln, verriegeln; versperren; einsperren; (ver)hindern); ausschließen

barb Widerhaken m

bar·bar·i·an 1. barbarisch; **2.** Barbar(in)

bar·be·cue 1. Bratrost m, Grill m; Barbecue n; **2.** auf dem Rost or am Spieß braten, grillen

barbed wire Stacheldraht m

bar·ber (Herren)Friseur m, (-)Frisör m

bar code Strichkode m

bare 1. nackt, bloß; kahl; leer; **2.** entblößen

bare·faced unverschämt, schamlos

bare·foot, bare·foot·ed barfuß

bare·head·ed barhäuptig

bare·ly kaum

bar·gain 1. Geschäft n, Handel m; vorteilhaftes Geschäft, Gelegenheitskauf m; **a (dead) bargain** spottbillig; **it's a bargain!** abgemacht!; **into the bargain** obendrein; **2.** (ver)handeln

bargain sale Verkauf m zu herabgesetzten Preisen; Ausverkauf m

barge 1. Lastkahn m; **2. barge in** F hereinplatzen (**on** bei)

bark[1] BOT Borke f, Rinde f

bark[2] **1.** bellen; **bark up the wrong tree** F auf dem Holzweg sein; an der falschen Adresse sein; **2.** Bellen n

bar·ley BOT Gerste f; Graupe f

barn Scheune f; (Vieh)Stall m

ba·rom·e·ter Barometer n

bar·on Baron m; Freiherr m

bar·on·ess Baronin f; Freifrau f

bar·racks MIL Kaserne f; contp Mietskaserne f

bar·rage Staudamm m; MIL Sperrfeuer n; fig (Wort- etc)Schwall m

bar·rel Fass n, Tonne f; (Gewehr)Lauf m; TECH Trommel f, Walze f

bar·rel or·gan MUS Drehorgel f

bar·ren unfruchtbar; trocken

bar·rette Haarspange f

bar·ri·cade 1. Barrikade f; **2.** verbarrikadieren; sperren

bar·ri·er Schranke f (a. fig), Barriere f, Sperre f; Hindernis n

bar·ris·ter Br JUR Barrister m

bar·row Karre f

bar·ter 1. Tausch(handel) m; **2.** tauschen (**for** gegen)

base[1] gemein

base[2] **1.** Basis f; Grundlage f; Fundament n; Fuß m; MIL Standort m; MIL Stützpunkt m; **2.** gründen, stützen (**on** auf acc)

base[3] CHEM Base f

base·ball SPORT Baseball(spiel n) m

B

base·board Scheuerleiste *f*
base·less grundlos
base·line *tennis etc*: Grundlinie *f*
base·ment ARCH Fundament *n*; Kellergeschoss *n*
bash·ful scheu, schüchtern
ba·sic[1] **1.** Grund..., grundlegend; **2.** *pl*
Grundlagen *pl*
ba·sic[2] CHEM basisch
ba·sic·al·ly im Grunde
ba·sin Becken *n*, Schale *f*, Schüssel *f*; Tal-,
Wasser-, Hafenbecken *n*
ba·sis Basis *f*; Grundlage *f*
bask sich sonnen (*a. fig*)
bas·ket Korb *m*
bas·ket·ball SPORT Basketball(spiel *n*) *m*
bass[1] MUS Bass *m*
bass[2] ZO (Fluss-, See)Barsch *m*
bas·tard Bastard *m*
baste[1] GASTR mit Fett begießen
baste[2] (an)heften
bat[1] ZO Fledermaus *f*; **as blind as a bat**
stockblind
bat[2] *baseball, cricket* **1.** Schlagholz *n*,
Schläger *m*; F **right off the bat** sofort;
2. am Schlagen sein
batch Stapel *m*, Stoß *m*
batch pro·cessing EDP Stapelverarbei-
tung *f*
bate: with bated breath mit angehalte-
nem Atem
bath 1. (Wannen)Bad *n*; *pl* Bad *n*, Badeanstalt *f*; Badeort *m*; **have a bath** *Br*, **take a
bath** baden, ein Bad nehmen; **2.** *Br v/t*
j-n baden; *v/i* baden, ein Bad nehmen
bathe *v/t* baden (*a.* MED); *v/i* baden, ein
Bad nehmen; schwimmen
bath·ing 1. Baden *n*; **2.** Bade...
bath·ing suit → *swimsuit*
bath·robe Bademantel *m*; Morgenrock
m, Schlafrock *m*
bath·room Badezimmer *n*; Toilette *f*
bath·tub Badewanne *f*
bat·on Stab *m*; MUS Taktstock *m*; Schlagstock *m*, Gummiknüppel *m*
bat·tal·i·on MIL Bataillon *n*
bat·ten Latte *f*
bat·ter[1] heftig schlagen; misshandeln;
verbeulen; **batter down, batter in** einschlagen
bat·ter[2] GASTR Rührteig *m*
bat·ter[3] *baseball, cricket*: Schläger *m*,
Schlagmann *m*
bat·ter·y ELECTR Batterie *f*; JUR Tätlich-
keit *f*, Körperverletzung *f*; **assault and
battery** JUR tätliche Beleidigung
bat·ter·y charg·er ELECTR Ladegerät *n*
bat·ter·y-op·e·rat·ed ELECTR batteriebe-
trieben

bat·tle 1. MIL Schlacht *f* (**of** bei); *fig* Kampf
m (**for** um); **2.** kämpfen
bat·tle·field, **bat·tle·ground** MIL
Schlachtfeld *n*
bat·tle·ments ARCH Zinnen *pl*
bat·tle·ship MIL Schlachtschiff *n*
baulk → *balk*
Ba·va·ri·a Bayern *n*
Ba·var·i·an 1. bay(e)risch; **2.** Bayer(in)
bawd·y obszön
bawl brüllen, schreien; **bawl s.o. out** mit
j-m schimpfen
bay[1] GEOGR Bai *f*, Bucht *f*; ARCH Erker *m*
bay[2] *a.* **bay tree** BOT Lorbeer(baum) *m*
bay[3] **1.** ZO bellen, Laut geben; **2. hold or
keep at bay** *j-n* in Schach halten; *et.* von
sich fernhalten
bay[4] **1.** rotbraun; **2.** ZO Braune *m*
bay·o·net MIL Bajonett *n*
bay·ou GEOGR sumpfiger Flussarm
bay win·dow ARCH Erkerfenster *n*
ba·zaar Basar *m*
BC ABBR *of* **before Christ** v. Chr., vor
Christus
be sein; *to form the passive*: werden; stattfinden; **he wants to be a doctor** *etc* er
möchte Arzt *etc* werden; **how much
are the shoes?** was kosten die Schuhe?;
that's five dollars das macht *or* kostet
fünf Dollar; **she is reading** sie liest gerade; **there is, there are** es gibt
beach Strand *m*
beach ball Wasserball *m*
beach bug·gy MOT Strandbuggy *m*
beach·wear Strandkleidung *f*
bea·con Leucht-, Signalfeuer *n*
bead (*Glas-, Schweiß- etc*)Perle *f*; *pl* REL
Rosenkranz *m*
bead·y klein, rund und glänzend
beak ZO Schnabel *m*; TECH Tülle *f*
beam 1. Balken *m*; (Licht)Strahl *m*; AVIAT
etc Peil-, Leit-, Richtstrahl *m*; **2.** ausstrahlen; strahlen (*a. fig* **with** vor *dat*)
bean BOT Bohne *f*; **be full of beans** F auf-
gekrazt sein; → *spill 1*
bear[1] ZO Bär *m*
bear[2] tragen; zur Welt bringen, gebären;
ertragen, aushalten; **I can't bear him
(it)** ich kann ihn (es) nicht ausstehen *or*
leiden; **bear out** bestätigen
bear·a·ble erträglich
beard Bart *m*; BOT Grannen *pl*
beard·ed bärtig
bear·er Träger(in); ECON Überbringer(in),
Inhaber(in)
bear·ing Ertragen *n*; Betragen *n*; (Körper)Haltung *f*; *fig* Beziehung *f*; Lage *f*,
Richtung *f*, Orientierung *f*; **take one's
bearings** sich orientieren; **lose one's**

bearings die Orientierung verlieren

beast (*a. wildes*) Tier; Bestie *f*

beast·ly scheußlich

beast of prey ZO Raubtier *n*

beat 1. schlagen; (ver)prügeln; besiegen; übertreffen; F **beat s.o. to it** j-m zuvorkommen; **beat it!** F hau ab!; **that beats all!** das ist doch der Gipfel *or* die Höhe!; **that beats me** F das ist mir zu hoch; **beat about the bush** wie die Katze um den heißen Brei herumschleichen; **beat down** ECON drücken, herunterhandeln; **beat s.o. up** j-n zusammenschlagen; **2.** Schlag *m*; MUS Takt(schlag) *m*; *jazz*: Beat *m*; Pulsschlag *m*; Runde *f*, Revier *n*; **3.** (**dead**) **beat** F wie erschlagen, fix und fertig

beat·en track Trampelpfad *m*; **off the beaten track** ungewohnt, ungewöhnlich

beat·ing (Tracht *f*) Prügel *pl*

beau·ti·cian Kosmetikerin *f*

beau·ti·ful schön

beaut·y Schönheit *f*; **Sleeping Beauty** Dornröschen *n*

beauty care Schönheitspflege *f*

beauty par·lo(u)r, beauty sal·on Schönheitssalon *m*

bea·ver ZO Biber *m*; Biberpelz *m*

be·cause weil; **because of** wegen (*gen*)

beck·on (zu)winken (*dat*)

be·come *v/i* werden (**of** aus); *v/t* sich schicken für; j-m stehen, j-n kleiden

be·com·ing passend; schicklich; kleidsam

bed 1. Bett *n*; ZO Lager *n*; AGR Beet *n*; Unterlage *f*; **bed and breakfast** Zimmer *n* mit Frühstück; **2. bed down** sein Nachtlager aufschlagen

bed·clothes Bettwäsche *f*

bed·ding Bettzeug *n*; AGR Streu *f*

bed·lam Tollhaus *n*

bed·rid·den bettlägerig

bed·room Schlafzimmer *n*

bed·side: at the bedside am (*a. Kranken*)Bett

bed·side lamp Nachttischlampe *f*

bed·sit F, **bed·sit·ter, bed·sit·ting room** *Br* möbliertes Zimmer; Einzimmerappartement *n*

bed·spread Tagesdecke *f*

bed·stead Bettgestell *n*

bed·time Schlafenszeit *f*

bee ZO Biene *f*; **have a bee in one's bonnet** F e-n Fimmel *or* Tick haben

beech BOT Buche *f*

beech·nut BOT Buchecker *f*

beef GASTR Rindfleisch *n*

beef·bur·ger GASTR *Br* Hamburger *m*

beef tea GASTR (Rind)Fleischbrühe *f*

beef·y F bullig

bee·hive Bienenkorb *m*, Bienenstock *m*

bee·keep·er Imker *m*

bee·line: make a beeline for F schnurstracks losgehen auf (*acc*)

beep·er TECH Piepser *m*

beer Bier *n*

beet BOT Runkelrübe *f*, Rote Bete, Rote Rübe

bee·tle ZO Käfer *m*

beet·root BOT *Br* Rote Bete, Rote Rübe

be·fore 1. *adv space*: vorn, voran; *time*: vorher, früher, schon (früher); **2.** *cj* bevor, ehe, bis; **3.** *prp* vor

be·fore·hand zuvor, im Voraus, vorweg

be·friend sich j-s annehmen

beg *v/t et.* erbitten (**of s.o.** von j-m); betteln um; *j-n* bitten; *v/i* betteln; (dringend) bitten

be·get (er)zeugen

beg·gar 1. Bettler(in); F Kerl *m*; **2. it beggars all description** es spottet jeder Beschreibung

be·gin beginnen, anfangen

be·gin·ner Anfänger(in)

be·gin·ning Beginn *m*, Anfang *m*

be·grudge missgönnen

be·guile täuschen; betrügen (**of, out of** um); sich *die Zeit* vertreiben

be·half: in (*Br* **on**) **behalf of** im Namen von (*or* gen)

be·have sich (gut) benehmen

be·hav·io(u)r Benehmen *n*, Betragen *n*, Verhalten *n*

be·hav·io(u)r·al sci·ence PSYCH Verhaltensforschung *f*

be·head enthaupten

be·hind 1. *adv* hinten, dahinter; zurück; **2.** *prp* hinter (*dat or acc*); **3.** F Hinterteil *n*, Hintern *m*

beige beige

be·ing Sein *n*, Dasein *n*, Existenz *f*; (Le-be)Wesen *n*, Geschöpf *n*; j-s Wesen *n*, Natur *f*

be·lat·ed verspätet

belch 1. aufstoßen, rülpsen; *a.* **belch out** speien, ausstoßen; **2.** Rülpser *m*

bel·fry Glockenturm *m*, -stuhl *m*

Bel·gium Belgien *n*

Bel·gian 1. belgisch; **2.** Belgier(in)

be·lief Glaube *m* (**in** an *acc*)

be·liev·a·ble glaubhaft

be·lieve glauben (**in** an *acc*); **I couldn't believe my ears** (**eyes**) ich traute m-n Ohren (Augen) nicht

be·liev·er REL Gläubige *m, f*

be·lit·tle *fig* herabsetzen

bell Glocke *f*; Klingel *f*

bell·boy *Br*, **bell·hop** (Hotel)Page *m*

B

bel·lig·er·ent kriegerisch; streitlustig, aggressiv; Krieg führend
bel·low 1. brüllen; **2.** Gebrüll *n*
bel·lows Blasebalg *m*
bel·ly 1. Bauch *m*; Magen *m*; **2. belly out** (an)schwellen lassen; bauschen
bel·ly·ache F Bauchweh *n*
be·long gehören; **belong to** gehören *dat or* zu
be·long·ings Habseligkeiten *pl*, Habe *f*
be·loved 1. (innig) geliebt; **2.** Geliebte *m, f*
be·low 1. *adv* unten; **2.** *prp* unter (*dat or acc*)
belt 1. Gürtel *m*; Gurt *m*; GEOGR Zone *f*, Gebiet *n*; TECH (Treib)Riemen *m*; **2. belt out** MUS schmettern; *a.* **belt up** den Gürtel (*gen*) zumachen; **belt up** MOT sich anschnallen
belt·ed mit e-m Gürtel
belt·way Umgehungsstraße *f*; Ringstraße *f*
be·moan betrauern, beklagen
bench Sitzbank *f*, Bank *f* (*a.* SPORT); TECH Werkbank *f*; JUR Richterbank *f*; Richter *m or pl*
bend 1. Biegung *f*, Kurve *f*; **drive s.o. round the bend** F j-n noch wahnsinnig machen; **2.** (sich) biegen *or* krümmen; neigen; beugen; *fig* richten (**to, on** auf *acc*)
be·neath → **below**
ben·e·dic·tion REL Segen *m*
ben·e·fac·tor Wohltäter *m*
be·nef·i·cent wohltätig
ben·e·fi·cial wohltuend, zuträglich, nützlich
ben·e·fit 1. Nutzen *m*, Vorteil *m*; Wohltätigkeitsveranstaltung *f*; (*Sozial-, Versicherungs- etc*)Leistung *f*; (*Arbeitslosen- etc*)Unterstützung *f*; (*Kranken- etc*)Geld *n*; **2.** nützen; **benefit by, benefit from** Vorteil haben von *or* durch, Nutzen ziehen aus
be·nev·o·lence Wohlwollen *n*
be·nev·o·lent wohltätig; wohlwollend
be·nign MED gutartig
bent 1. bent on doing entschlossen zu tun; **2.** Hang *m*, Neigung *f*; Veranlagung *f*
ben·zene CHEM Benzol *n*
ben·zine CHEM Leichtbenzin *n*
be·queath JUR vermachen
be·quest JUR Vermächtnis *n*
be·reave berauben
be·ret Baskenmütze *f*
ber·ry BOT Beere *f*
berth 1. MAR Liege-, Ankerplatz *m*; Koje *f*; RAIL (Schlafwagen)Bett *n*; **2.** MAR festma-

chen, anlegen
be·seech (inständig) bitten (um); anflehen
be·set heimsuchen; **beset with difficulties** mit vielen Schwierigkeiten verbunden
be·side *prp* neben (*dat or acc*); **beside o.s.** außer sich (**with** vor); **beside the point, beside the question** nicht zur Sache gehörig
be·sides 1. *adv* außerdem; **2.** *prp* abgesehen von, außer (*dat*)
be·siege belagern
be·smear beschmieren
be·spat·ter bespritzen
best 1. *adj* beste(r, -s) höchste(r, -s), größte(r, -s), meiste; **best before** GASTR haltbar bis; **2.** *adv* am besten; **3.** *der, die, das* Beste; **all the best!** alles Gute!, viel Glück!; **to the best of ...** nach bestem ...; **make the best of** das Beste machen aus (*dat*); **at best** bestenfalls; **be at one's best** in Hoch- *or* Höchstform sein
best-be·fore date, best-by date Mindesthaltbarkeitsdatum *n*
bes·ti·al *fig* tierisch, bestialisch
be·stow geben, verleihen (**on** *dat*)
best-sell·er Bestseller *m*
bet 1. Wette *f*; **make a bet** e-e Wette abschließen; **2.** wetten; **bet s.o. ten dollars** mit j-m um zehn Dollar wetten; **you bet** F und ob!
be·tray verraten (*a. fig*); verleiten
be·tray·al Verrat *m*
be·tray·er Verräter(in)
bet·ter 1. *adj* besser; **he is better** es geht ihm besser; **better and better** immer besser; **2.** *das* Bessere; **get the better of** die Oberhand gewinnen über (*acc*); *et.* überwinden; **3.** *adv* besser; mehr; **do better than** es besser machen als; **know better** es besser wissen; **so much the better** desto besser; **you had better go** Br, F **you better go** es wäre besser, wenn du gingest; **better off** (finanziell) besser gestellt; **he is better off than I am** es geht ihm besser als mir; **4.** *v/t* verbessern; *v/i* sich bessern
be·tween 1. *adv* dazwischen; **in between** zwischendurch; F **few and far between** (ganz) vereinzelt; **2.** *prp* zwischen (*dat or acc*); unter (*dat*); **between you and me** unter uns *or* im Vertrauen (gesagt)
bev·el TECH abkanten, abschrägen
bev·er·age Getränk *n*
bev·y ZO Schwarm *m*, Schar *f*
be·ware (**of**) sich in Acht nehmen (vor *dat*), sich hüten (vor *dat*); **beware of the dog!** Vorsicht, bissiger Hund!

be·wil·der verwirren
be·wil·der·ment Verwirrung f
be·witch bezaubern, verhexen
be·yond 1. adv darüber hinaus; **2.** prp jenseits (gen); über … (acc) hinaus
bi… zwei, zweifach, zweimal
bi·as Neigung f; Vorurteil n
bi·as(s)ed voreingenommen; JUR befangen
bi·ath·lete SPORT Biathlet m
bi·ath·lon SPORT Biathlon n
bib (Sabber)Lätzchen n
Bi·ble Bibel f
bib·li·cal biblisch, Bibel…
bib·li·og·ra·phy Bibliografie f
bi·car·bon·ate a. **bicarbonate of soda** CHEM doppeltkohlensaures Natron
bi·cen·te·na·ry Br, **bi·cen·ten·ni·al** Zweihundertjahrfeier f
bi·ceps ANAT Bizeps m
bick·er sich zanken or streiten
bi·cy·cle Fahrrad n
bid 1. auction: bieten; **2.** ECON Gebot n, Angebot n
bi·en·ni·al zweijährlich; BOT zweijährig
bi·en·ni·al·ly alle zwei Jahre
bier (Toten)Bahre f
big groß; dick, stark; **talk big** F den Mund voll nehmen
big·a·my Bigamie f
big busi·ness Großunternehmertum n
big·head F Angeber m
big shot, big·wig F hohes Tier
bike F **1.** (Fahr)Rad n; **2.** Rad fahren
bik·er Motorradfahrer(in); Radfahrer(in), Radler(in)
bi·lat·er·al bilateral
bile Galle f (a. fig)
bi·lin·gual zweisprachig
bill[1] ZO Schnabel m
bill[2] ECON Rechnung f; POL (Gesetzes-)Vorlage f; JUR (An)Klageschrift f; Plakat n; Banknote f, (Geld)Schein m
bill·board Reklametafel f
bill·fold Brieftasche f
bil·li·ards Billard(spiel) n
bil·li·on Milliarde f
bill of de·liv·er·y ECON Lieferschein m
bill of ex·change ECON Wechsel m
bill of sale JUR Verkaufsurkunde f
bil·low 1. Woge f; (Rauch- etc) Schwaden m; **2.** a. **billow out** sich bauschen or blähen
bil·ly goat ZO Ziegenbock m
bin (großer) Behälter
bi·na·ry MATH, PHYS etc binär, Binär…
bi·na·ry code EDP Binärcode m
bi·na·ry num·ber MATH Binärzahl f
bind v/t (an-, ein-, um-, auf-, fest-, ver-)

binden; a. vertraglich binden, verpflichten; einfassen; v/i binden
bind·er (esp Buch)Binder(in); Einband m; Aktendeckel m
bind·ing 1. bindend, verbindlich; **2.** Einband m; Einfassung f, Borte f
bin·go Bingo n
bi·noc·u·lars, Fern-, Opernglas n
bi·o·chem·is·try Biochemie f
bi·o·de·gra·da·ble biologisch abbaubar, umweltfreundlich
bi·og·ra·pher Biograf m
bi·og·ra·phy Biografie f
bi·o·log·i·cal biologisch
bi·ol·o·gist Biologe m, Biologin f
bi·ol·o·gy Biologie f
bi·o·rhythms Biorhythmus m
bi·o·tope Biotop n
bi·ped ZO Zweifüßer m
birch BOT Birke f
bird ZO Vogel m
bird·cage Vogelkäfig m
bird flu Vogelgrippe f
bird of pas·sage ZO Zugvogel m
bird of prey ZO Raubvogel m
bird sanc·tu·a·ry Vogelschutzgebiet n
bird·seed Vogelfutter n
bird's-eye view Vogelperspektive f
bi·ro® Kugelschreiber m
birth Geburt f; Herkunft f; **give birth to** gebären, zur Welt bringen
birth cer·tif·i·cate Geburtsurkunde f
birth con·trol Geburtenregelung f
birth control pill MED Antibabypille f
birth·day Geburtstag m; **happy birthday!** alles Gute or herzlichen Glückwunsch zum Geburtstag!
birth·mark Muttermal n
birth·place Geburtsort m
birth·rate Geburtenziffer f
bis·cuit Br Keks m, n, Plätzchen n
bi·sex·u·al bisexuell
bish·op REL Bischof m; chess: Läufer m
bish·op·ric REL Bistum n
bi·son ZO Bison m; Wisent m
bit Bisschen n, Stück(chen) n; Gebiss n (am Zaum); (Schlüssel)Bart m; EDP Bit n; **a (little) bit** ein (kleines) bisschen
bitch ZO Hündin f; F contp Miststück n, Schlampe f
bit den·si·ty EDP Speicherdichte f
bite 1. Beißen n; Biss m; Bissen m, Happen m; TECH Fassen n, Greifen n; **2.** (an-) beißen; ZO stechen; GASTR brennen; fig schneiden (cold etc); beißen (smoke etc); TECH fassen, greifen
bit·ter bitter; fig verbittert
bit·ters GASTR Magenbitter m
biz F → **business**

black 1. schwarz; dunkel; finster; *have s.th. in black and white* et. schwarz auf weiß haben *or* besitzen; *be black and blue* blaue Flecken haben; *beat s.o. black and blue* j-n grün und blau schlagen; **2.** schwärzen; *black out* verdunkeln; **3.** Schwarz *n*; Schwärze *f*; Schwarze *m, f*

black·ber·ry BOT Brombeere *f*

black·bird ZO Amsel *f*

black·board (Schul-, Wand)Tafel *f*

black box AVIAT Flugschreiber *m*

black cur·rant BOT schwarze Johannisbeere

black·en *v/t* schwärzen; *fig* anschwärzen; *v/i* schwarz werden

black eye blaues Auge, Veilchen *n*

black·head MED Mitesser *m*

black ice Glatteis *n*

black·ing schwarze Schuhwichse

black·leg *Br* Streikbrecher *m*

black·mail 1. Erpressung *f*; **2.** *j-n* erpressen

black·mail·er Erpresser(in)

black mar·ket Schwarzmarkt *m*

black·ness Schwärze *f*

black·out Verdunkelung *f*; Black-out *n, m*; ELECTR Stromausfall *m*; Ohnmacht *f*

black pud·ding GASTR Blutwurst *f*

black sheep *fig* schwarzes Schaf

black·smith Schmied *m*

blad·der ANAT Blase *f*

blade TECH Blatt *n*, Schaufel *f*; Klinge *f*; Schneide *f*; BOT Halm *m*

blame 1. Tadel *m*; Schuld *f*; **2.** tadeln; *be to blame for* schuld sein an (*dat*)

blame·less untadelig

blanch *v/t* bleichen; GASTR blanchieren; *v/i* erbleichen, bleich werden

blank 1. leer; unausgefüllt, unbeschrieben; ECON Blanko...; verdutzt; **2.** Leere *f*; leerer Raum, Lücke *f*; unbeschriebenes Blatt, Formular *n*; *lottery*: Niete *f*

blank car·tridge Platzpatrone *f*

blank check (*Br* **cheque**) ECON Blankoscheck *m*

blan·ket 1. (Woll)Decke *f*; **2.** zudecken

blare brüllen, plärren (*radio etc*), schmettern (*trumpet*)

blas·pheme lästern

blas·phe·my Gotteslästerung *f*

blast 1. Windstoß *m*; MUS Ton *m*; TECH Explosion *f*; Druckwelle *f*; Sprengung *f*;**2.** sprengen; *fig* zunichtemachen; *blast off (into space)* in den Weltraum schießen; *blast off* abheben, starten (*rocket*); *blast!* verdammt!; *blast you!* der Teufel soll dich holen!; *blasted* verdammt, verflucht

blast fur·nace TECH Hochofen *m*

blast-off Start *m* (*of a rocket*)

bla·tant offenkundig, eklatant

blaze 1. Flamme(n *pl*) *f*, Feuer *n*; heller Schein; *fig* Ausbruch *m*; **2.** brennen, lodern; leuchten

blaz·er Blazer *m*

bla·zon Wappen *n*

bleach bleichen

bleak öde, kahl; rau; *fig* trüb, freudlos, finster

blear·y trübe, verschwommen

bleat ZO **1.** Blöken *n*; **2.** blöken

bleed *v/i* bluten; *v/t* MED zur Ader lassen; F schröpfen

bleed·ing MED Blutung *f*; Aderlass *m*

bleep 1. Piepton *m*; **2.** *j-n* anpiepsen

bleep·er *Br* F Piepser *m*

blem·ish 1. (*a.* Schönheits)Fehler *m*; Makel *m*; **2.** entstellen

blend 1. (sich) (ver)mischen; GASTR verschneiden; **2.** Mischung *f*; GASTR Verschnitt *m*

blend·er Mixer *m*, Mixgerät *n*

bless segnen; preisen; *be blessed with* gesegnet sein mit; (*God*) *bless you!* alles Gute!; Gesundheit!; *bless me!, bless my heart!, bless my soul!* F du meine Güte!

bless·ed selig, gesegnet; F verflixt

bless·ing Segen *m*

blight BOT Mehltau *m*

blind 1. blind (*fig to* gegen[über]); unübersichtlich; **2.** Rouleau *n*, Rollo *n*; *the blind* die Blinden *pl*; **3.** blenden; *fig* blind machen (*to* für, gegen)

blind al·ley Sackgasse *f*

blind·ers Scheuklappen *pl*

blind·fold 1. blindlings; **2.** *j-m* die Augen verbinden; **3.** Augenbinde *f*

blind·ly *fig* blindlings

blind·ness Blindheit *f*; Verblendung *f*

blind·worm ZO Blindschleiche *f*

blink 1. Blinzeln *n*; **2.** blinzeln, zwinkern; blinken

blink·ers *Br* Scheuklappen *pl*

bliss Seligkeit *f*, Wonne *f*

blis·ter MED, TECH **1.** Blase *f*; **2.** Blasen hervorrufen auf (*dat*); Blasen ziehen *or* TECH werfen

blitz MIL **1.** heftiger Luftangriff; **2.** schwer bombardieren

bliz·zard Blizzard *m*, Schneesturm *m*

bloat·ed (an)geschwollen, (auf)gedunsen; *fig* aufgeblasen

bloat·er GASTR Bückling *m*

blob Klecks *m*

block 1. Block *m*, Klotz *m*; Baustein *m*,

(Bau)Klötzchen *n*; (Schreib-, Notiz-) Block *m*; (Häuser)Block *m*; TECH Verstopfung *f*; *fig geistige etc* Sperre; *block (of flats) Br* Wohn-, Mietshaus *n*; **2.** *a.* **block up** (ab-, ver)sperren, blockieren, verstopfen

block·ade 1. Blockade *f*; **2.** blockieren

block·bust·er F Kassenmagnet *m*, Kassenschlager *m*

block·head F Dummkopf *m*

block let·ters Blockschrift *f*

blond 1. Blonde *m*; **2.** blond; hell (*skin*)

blonde 1. blond; **2.** Blondine *f*

blood Blut *n*; *in cold blood* kaltblütig

blood bank MED Blutbank *f*

blood clot MED Blutgerinnsel *n*

blood cor·pus·cle MED Blutkörperchen *n*

blood·cur·dling grauenhaft

blood do·nor MED Blutspender(in)

blood group MED Blutgruppe *f*

blood·hound ZO Bluthund *m*

blood pres·sure MED Blutdruck *m*

blood·shed Blutvergießen *n*

blood·shot blutunterlaufen

blood·thirst·y blutdürstig

blood ves·sel ANAT Blutgefäß *n*

blood test MED Blutprobe *f*

blood·y blutig; *Br* F verdammt, verflucht

bloom 1. Blume *f*, Blüte *f*; *fig* Blüte(zeit) *f*; **2.** blühen; *fig* (er)strahlen

blos·som 1. Blüte *f*; **2.** blühen; *fig blossom into* erblühen zu

blot 1. Klecks *m*; *fig* Makel *m*; **2.** beklecksen

blotch Klecks *m*; Hautfleck *m*

blotch·y fleckig

blot·ter (Tinten)Löscher *m*

blot·ting pa·per Löschpapier *n*

blouse Bluse *f*

blow¹ Schlag *m* (*a. fig*), Stoß *m*

blow² *v/i* blasen, wehen; keuchen, schnaufen; explodieren; platzen (*tire*); ELECTR durchbrennen; *blow up* in die Luft fliegen; explodieren; *v/t: blow one's nose* sich die Nase putzen; *blow one's top* F an die Decke gehen (*vor Wut*); *blow out* ausblasen; *blow up* sprengen; PHOT vergrößern

blow-dry föhnen

blow·fly ZO Schmeißfliege *f*

blow·pipe Blasrohr *n*

blow-up PHOT Vergrößerung *f*

blud·geon Knüppel *m*

blue 1. blau; F melancholisch, traurig, schwermütig; **2.** Blau *n*; *out of the blue fig* aus heiterem Himmel

blue·ber·ry BOT Blau-, Heidelbeere *f*

blue·bot·tle ZO Schmeißfliege *f*

blue-col·lar work·er Arbeiter(in)

blues MUS Blues *m*; F Melancholie *f*; *have the blues* F den Moralischen haben

bluff¹ Steilufer *n*

bluff² 1. Bluff *m*; **2.** bluffen

blu·ish bläulich

blun·der 1. Fehler *m*, F Schnitzer *m*; **2.** e-n (groben) Fehler machen; verpfuschen, F verpatzen

blunt stumpf; *fig* offen

blunt·ly freiheraus

blur [blɜ:] **1.** *v/t* verwischen; verschmieren; PHOT, TV verwackeln, verzerren; *fig* trüben; **2.** *v/i* verschwimmen (*a. fig*)

blurt: *blurt out* herausplatzen mit

blush 1. Erröten *n*, Schamröte *f*; **2.** erröten, rot werden

blus·ter brausen (*wind*); *fig* poltern, toben

BMX ABBR *of bicycle motocross* Querfeldeinrennen *n*

BMX bike BMX-Rad *n*

BO ABBR → *body odo(u)r*

boar ZO Eber *m*; Keiler *m*

board 1. Brett *n*; (Anschlag)Brett *n*; Konferenztisch *m*; Ausschuss *m*, Kommission *f*; Behörde *f*; Verpflegung *f*; Pappe *f*, Karton *m*; sport (Surf)Board *n*; *on board a train* in e-m Zug; **2.** *v/t* dielen, verschalen; beköstigen; an Bord gehen; MAR entern; RAIL *etc* einsteigen in; *v/i* in Kost sein, wohnen

board·er Kostgänger(in); Pensionsgast *m*; Internatsschüler(in)

board game Brettspiel *n*

board·ing card AVIAT Bordkarte *f*

boarding house Pension *f*, Fremdenheim *n*

boarding school Internat *n*

board of di·rec·tors ECON Aufsichtsrat *m*

Board of Trade Handelskammer *f*; *Br* Handelsministerium *n*

board·walk Strandpromenade *f*

boast 1. Prahlerei *f*; **2.** (*of, about*) sich rühmen (*gen*), prahlen (mit)

boat Boot *n*; Schiff *n*

bob 1. Knicks *m*; kurzer Haarschnitt; *Br* HIST F Schilling *m*; **2.** *v/t Haar* kurz schneiden; *v/i* sich auf und ab bewegen; knicksen

bob·bin Spule *f* (*a.* ELECTR)

bob·sleigh SPORT Bob *m*

bod·ice Mieder *n*; Oberteil *n*

bod·i·ly körperlich

bod·y Körper *m*, Leib *m*; Leiche *f*; JUR Körperschaft *f*; Hauptteil *m*; MOT Karosserie *f*; MIL Truppenkörper *m*

bod·y·guard Leibwache *f*; Leibwächter *m*

bod·y o·do(u)r (ABBR *BO*) Körpergeruch

m

body stock·ing Body *m*
bod·y·work MOT Karosserie *f*
Boer 1. Bure *m*; **2.** Buren...
bog Sumpf *m*, Morast *m*
bo·gus falsch; Schwindel...
boil[1] MED Geschwür *n*, Furunkel *m*, *n*
boil[2] **1.** kochen, sieden; **2.** Kochen *n*, Sieden *n*
boil·er (Dampf)Kessel *m*; Boiler *m*
boil·er suit Overall *m*
boil·ing point Siedepunkt *m* (*a. fig*)
bois·ter·ous ungestüm; heftig, laut; lärmend
bold kühn, verwegen; keck, dreist, unverschämt; steil; PRINT fett; *as bold as brass* F frech wie Oskar; *words in bold print* fett gedruckt
bold·ness Kühnheit *f*, Verwegenheit *f*; Dreistigkeit *f*
bol·ster 1. Keilkissen *n*; **2.** *bolster up fig* (unter)stützen, *j-m* Mut machen
bolt 1. Bolzen *m*; Riegel *m*; Blitz(strahl) *m*; plötzlicher Satz, Fluchtversuch *m*; **2.** *adv*: *bolt upright* kerzengerade; **3.** *v/t* verriegeln; F hinunterschlingen; *v/i* davonlaufen, ausreißen; ZO scheuen, durchgehen
bomb 1. Bombe *f*; *the bomb* die Atombombe; **2.** bombardieren
bom·bard bombardieren
bomb·er AVIAT Bomber *m*; Bombenleger *m*
bomb·proof bombensicher
bomb·shell Bombe *f* (*a. fig*)
bo·nan·za *fig* Goldgrube *f*
bond Bund *m*, Verbindung *f*; ECON Schuldverschreibung *f*, Obligation *f*; *in bond* ECON unter Zollverschluss
bond·age Hörigkeit *f*
bonds *fig* Bande *pl*
bone 1. ANAT Knochen *m*, *pl a*. Gebeine *pl*; ZO Gräte *f*; *bone of contention* Zankapfel *m*; *have a bone to pick with s.o.* mit j-m ein Hühnchen zu rupfen haben; *make no bones about* nicht lange fackeln mit; **2.** die Knochen auslösen (aus); entgräten
bon·fire Feuer *n* im Freien; Freudenfeuer *n*
bon·net Haube *f*; *Br* Motorhaube *f*
bo·nus ECON Bonus *m*, Prämie *f*; Gratifikation *f*
bon·y knöchern; knochig
boo *int* buh!; THEA *boo off the stage*, *soccer*: *boo off the park* auspfeifen
boobs *sl* Titten *pl*
boo·by F Trottel *m*
book 1. Buch *n*; Heft *n*; Liste *f*; Block *m*;

2. buchen; eintragen; SPORT verwarnen; *Fahrkarte etc* lösen; *Platz etc* (vor)bestellen, reservieren lassen; *Gepäck* aufgeben; *book in esp Br* sich (*im Hotel*) eintragen; *book in at* absteigen in (*dat*); *booked up* ausgebucht, ausverkauft, belegt
book·case Bücherschrank *m*
book·ing Buchen *n*, (Vor)Bestellung *f*; SPORT Verwarnung *f*
booking clerk Schalterbeamte *m*, -beamtin *f*
booking of·fice Fahrkartenausgabe *f*, -schalter *m*; THEA Kasse *f*
book·keep·er ECON Buchhalter(in)
book·keep·ing ECON Buchhaltung *f*, Buchführung *f*
book·let Büchlein *n*, Broschüre *f*
book·mak·er Buchmacher *m*
book·mark(·er) Lesezeichen *n*
book·sell·er Buchhändler(in)
book·shelf Bücherregal *n*
book·shop *esp Br*, **book·store** Buchhandlung *f*
book·worm *fig* Bücherwurm *m*
boom[1] ECON **1.** Boom *m*, Aufschwung *m*, Hochkonjunktur *f*, Hausse *f*; **2.** e-n Boom erleben
boom[2] MAR Baum *m*, Spiere *f*; TECH (Kran)Ausleger *m*; *film*, TV (Mikrofon)Galgen *m*
boom[3] dröhnen, donnern
boor·ish ungehobelt
boost 1. hochschieben; ECON in die Höhe treiben; ankurbeln; ELECTR verstärken; TECH erhöhen; *fig* stärken, Auftrieb geben (*dat*); **2.** Erhöhung *f*; Auftrieb *m*; ELECTR Verstärkung *f*
boot[1] Stiefel *m*; *Br* MOT Kofferraum *m*
boot[2]: *boot (up)* EDP laden
boot[3]: *to boot* obendrein
boot·ee (*Damen*)Halbstiefel *m*
booth (Markt- *etc*)Bude *f*; (Messe-) Stand *m*; (Wahl- *etc*)Kabine *f*; (Telefon)Zelle *f*
boot·lace Schnürsenkel *m*
boot·y Beute *f*
booze F **1.** saufen; **2.** Zeug *n*; Sauferei *f*
bor·der 1. Rand *m*, Saum *m*, Einfassung *f*; Rabatte *f*; Grenze *f*; **2.** einfassen; (um)säumen; grenzen (*on* an *acc*)
bore[1] **1.** Bohrloch *n*; TECH Kaliber *n*; **2.** bohren
bore[2] **1.** Langweiler *m*; langweilige *or* lästige Sache; **2.** *j-n* langweilen; *be bored* sich langweilen
bore·dom Lang(e)weile *f*
bor·ing langweilig
bo·rough Stadtteil *m*; Stadtgemeinde *f*; Stadtbezirk *m*

bor·row (sich) *et.* borgen *or* (aus)leihen
bos·om Busen *m*; *fig* Schoß *m*
boss F **1.** Boss *m*, Chef *m*; **2.** *a.* **boss about**, **boss around** herumkommandieren
boss·y F herrisch
bo·tan·i·cal botanisch
bot·a·ny Botanik *f*
botch 1. Pfusch *m*; **2.** verpfuschen
both beide(s); **both ... and ...** sowohl ... als (auch) ...
both·er 1. Belästigung *f*, Störung *f*, Plage *f*, Mühe *f*; **2.** belästigen, stören, plagen; **don't bother!** bemühen Sie sich nicht!
bot·tle 1. Flasche *f*; **2.** in Flaschen abfüllen
bottle bank *Br* Altglascontainer *m*
bot·tle·neck *fig* Engpass *m*
bot·tle o·pen·er Flaschenöffner *m*
bot·tom unterster Teil, Boden *m*, Fuß *m*, Unterseite *f*; Grund *m*; F Hintern *m*, Popo *m*; **be at the bottom of s.th.** hinter e-r Sache stecken; **get to the bottom of s.th.** e-r Sache auf den Grund gehen
bough Ast *m*, Zweig *m*
boul·der Geröllblock *m*, Findling *m*
bounce 1. aufprallen *or* aufspringen (lassen); springen, hüpfen, stürmen; ECON F platzen (*check*); **2.** Sprung *m*, Satz *m*; F Schwung *m*
bounc·ing kräftig, stramm
bound¹ unterwegs (**for** nach)
bound² *mst pl* Grenze *f*, *fig a.* Schranke *f*
bound³ 1. Sprung *m*, Satz *m*; **2.** springen, hüpfen; auf-, abprallen
bound·a·ry Grenze *f*
bound·less grenzenlos
boun·te·ous, **boun·ti·ful** freigebig, reichlich
boun·ty Freigebigkeit *f*; großzügige Spende *f*; Prämie *f*
bou·quet Bukett *n* (*a.* GASTR), Strauß *m*; GASTR Blume *f*
bout SPORT (*Box-*, *Ring*)Kampf *m*; MED Anfall *m*
bou·tique Boutique *f*
bow¹ **1.** Verbeugung *f*; **2.** *v/i* sich verbeugen *or* verneigen (**to** vor *dat*); *fig* sich beugen *or* unterwerfen (**to** *dat*); *v/t* biegen; beugen, neigen
bow² MAR Bug *m*
bow³ Bogen *m*; Schleife *f*
bow·els ANAT Darm *m*; Eingeweide *pl*
bowl¹ Schale *f*, Schüssel *f*, Napf *m*; (*Zucker*)Dose *f*; Becken *n*; (*Pfeifen-*) Kopf *m*
bowl² **1.** (*Bowling-*, *Kegel- etc*)Kugel *f*; **2.** kegeln; rollen (*bowling ball*); *cricket*: werfen

bow-leg·ged o-beinig
bowl·er¹ Bowlingspieler(in); Kegler(in)
bowl·er², *a.* **bowler hat** *esp Br* Bowler *m*, F Melone *f*
bowl·ing Bowling *n*; Kegeln *n*; **go bowling** kegeln
bowling al·ley Kegelbahn *f*
bowling ball Kegelkugel *f*
box¹ Kasten *m*, Kiste *f*; Büchse *f*, Dose *f*, Kästchen *n*; Schachtel *f*; Behälter *m*; TECH Gehäuse *n*; Postfach *n*; *Br* (Telefon)Zelle *f*; JUR Zeugenstand *m*; THEA Loge *f*; MOT, ZO Box *f*
box² **1.** SPORT boxen; F **box s.o.'s ears** j-n ohrfeigen; **2.** F **a box on the ear** e-e Ohrfeige
box³ [bɒks] BOT Buchsbaum *m*
box·er Boxer *m*
box·ing Boxen *n*, Boxsport *m*
Box·ing Day *Br* der zweite Weihnachtsfeiertag
box num·ber Chiffre(nummer) *f*
box of·fice Theaterkasse *f*
boy Junge *m*, Knabe *m*, Bursche *m*
boy·cott 1. boykottieren; **2.** Boykott *m*
boy·friend Freund *m*
boy·hood Knabenjahre *pl*, Jugend(-zeit) *f*
boy·ish jungenhaft
boy scout Pfadfinder *m*
bra BH *m* (*Büstenhalter*)
brace 1. TECH Strebe *f*, Stützbalken *m*; (Zahn)Klammer *f*, (-)Spange *f*; **2.** TECH verstreben, versteifen, stützen
brace·let Armband *n*
brac·es *Br* Hosenträger *pl*
brack·et TECH Träger *m*, Halter *m*, Stütze *f*; PRINT Klammer *f*; (*esp Alters-*, *Steuer*)-Klasse *f*; **lower income bracket** niedrige Einkommensgruppe
brack·ish brackig, salzig
brag prahlen (**about** mit)
brag·gart Prahler *m*, F Angeber *m*
braid 1. Zopf *m*; Borte *f*, Tresse *f*; **2.** flechten; mit Borte besetzen
brain ANAT Gehirn *n*, *often pl fig a.* Verstand *m*, Intelligenz *f*, Kopf *m*
brain·storm Geistesblitz *m*
brain·wash *j-n* e-r Gehirnwäsche unterziehen
brain·wash·ing Gehirnwäsche *f*
brain·wave *Br* Geistesblitz *m*
brain·y F gescheit
braise GASTR schmoren
brake TECH **1.** Bremse *f*; **2.** bremsen
brake·light MOT Bremslicht *n*
bram·ble BOT Brombeerstrauch *m*
bran AGR Kleie *f*
branch 1. Ast *m*, Zweig *m*; *fig* Fach *n*; Linie *f* (*des Stammbaumes*); ECON Zweig-

B

stelle *f*, Filiale *f*; **2.** sich verzweigen; abzweigen

brand 1. ECON (Schutz-, Handels)Marke *f*, Warenzeichen *n*; Markenname *m*; Sorte *f*, Klasse *f*; Brandmal *n*; **2.** einbrennen; brandmarken

bran·dish schwingen

brand name ECON Markenname *m*

brand-new nagelneu

bran·dy Kognak *m*, Weinbrand *m*

brass Messing *n*; F Unverschämtheit *f*

brass band MUS Blaskapelle *f*

bras·sière Büstenhalter *m*

brat *contp* Balg *m*, *n*, Gör *n*

brave 1. tapfer, mutig, unerschrocken; **2.** trotzen; mutig begegnen (*dat*)

brav·er·y Tapferkeit *f*

brawl 1. Krawall *m*; Rauferei *f*; **2.** Krawall machen; raufen

brawn·y muskulös

bray 1. ZO Eselsschrei *m*; **2.** ZO schreien; *fig* wiehern

bra·zen unverschämt, unverfroren, frech

Bra·zil Brasilien *n*

Bra·zil·ian 1. brasilianisch; **2.** Brasilianer(in)

breach 1. Bruch *m*; *fig* Verletzung *f*; MIL Bresche *f*; **2.** e-e Bresche schlagen in (*acc*)

bread Brot *n*; ***brown bread*** Schwarzbrot *n*; ***know which side one's bread is buttered*** F s-n Vorteil (er)kennen

breadth Breite *f*

break 1. Bruch *m*; Lücke *f*; Pause *f* (*Br a.* PED), Unterbrechung *f*; (plötzlicher) Wechsel, Umschwung *m*; (*Tages*)Anbruch *m*; ***bad break*** F Pech *n*; ***lucky break*** F Dusel *m*, Schwein *n*; ***give s.o. a break*** F j-m e-e Chance geben; ***take a break*** e-e Pause machen; ***without a break*** ununterbrochen; **2.** *v/t* (ab-, auf-, durch-, zer)brechen; zerschlagen, kaputt machen; ZO *a.* ***break in*** zähmen, abrichten, zureiten; *Gesetz, Vertrag etc* brechen; *Kode etc* knacken; *schlechte Nachricht* (schonend) beibringen; *v/i* brechen (*a. fig*); (zer-)brechen, (zer)reißen, kaputtgehen; anbrechen (*Tag*); METEOR umschlagen; *fig* ausbrechen (***into*** in *Tränen etc*); ***break away*** ab-, losbrechen; sich losmachen *or* losreißen; ***break down*** ein-, niederreißen, *Haus* abbrechen; zusammenbrechen (*a. fig*); versagen; MOT e-e Panne haben; *fig* scheitern; ***break in*** einbrechen, eindringen; ***break into*** einbrechen in (*ein Haus etc*); ***break off*** abbrechen, *fig a.* Schluss machen mit; ***break out*** ausbrechen; ***break through*** durchbrechen; *fig* den Durchbruch

schaffen; ***break up*** abbrechen, beenden, schließen; (sich) auflösen; *fig* zerbrechen, auseinandergehen

break·a·ble zerbrechlich

break·age Bruch *m*

break·a·way 1. Trennung *f*; **2.** Splitter...

break·down Zusammenbruch *m* (*a. fig*); TECH Maschinenschaden *m*; MOT Panne *f*; ***nervous breakdown*** MED Nervenzusammenbruch *m*

breakdown lor·ry *Br* MOT Abschleppwagen *m*

breakdown ser·vice *Br* MOT Pannendienst *m*, Pannenhilfe *f*

breakdown truck *Br* MOT Abschleppwagen *m*

break·fast 1. Frühstück *n*; ***have breakfast*** → **2.** frühstücken

break·through *fig* Durchbruch *m*

break·up Aufhebung *f*; Auflösung *f*

breast ANAT Brust *f*; Busen *m*; *fig* Herz *n*; ***make a clean breast of s.th.*** et. offen (ein)gestehen

breast·stroke Brustschwimmen *n*

breath Atem(zug) *m*; Hauch *m*; ***be out of breath*** außer Atem sein; ***waste one's breath*** in den Wind reden

breath·a·lyse *Br*, **breath·a·lyze** F (ins Röhrchen) blasen *or* pusten lassen

breath·a·lys·er® *Br*, **breath·alyz·er**® Alkoholtestgerät *n*, F Röhrchen *n*

breathe atmen

breath·less atemlos

breath·tak·ing atemberaubend

breech·es Kniebund-, Reithosen *pl*

breed 1. ZO Rasse *f*, Zucht *f*; **2.** *v/t* BOT, ZO züchten; *v/i* BIOL sich fortpflanzen

breed·er Züchter(in); Zuchttier *n*; PHYS Brüter *m*

breed·ing BIOL Fortpflanzung *f*; (Tier-)Zucht *f*; *fig* Erziehung *f*; (gutes) Benehmen

breeze Brise *f*

breth·ren *esp* REL Brüder *pl*

brew brauen; *Tee* zubereiten, aufbrühen

brew·er (Bier)Brauer *m*

brew·er·y Brauerei *f*

bri·ar → **brier**

bribe 1. Bestechungsgeld *n*, -geschenk *n*; Bestechung *f*; **2.** bestechen

brib·er·y Bestechung *f*

brick 1. Ziegel(stein) *m*, Backstein *m*; *Br* Baustein *m*, (Bau)Klötzchen *n*

brick·lay·er Maurer *m*

brick·yard Ziegelei *f*

brid·al Braut...

bride Braut *f*

bride·groom Bräutigam *m*

brides·maid Brautjungfer *f*

buckskin B

bridge 1. Brücke *f*; **2.** e-e Brücke schlagen über (*acc*); *fig* überbrücken
bri·dle 1. Zaum *m*; Zügel *m*; **2.** (auf)zäumen; zügeln
bridle path Reitweg *m*
brief 1. kurz, bündig; **2.** instruieren, genaue Anweisungen geben (*dat*)
brief·case Aktenmappe *f*
briefs Slip *m*
bri·er BOT Dornstrauch *m*; Wilde Rose
bri·gade MIL Brigade *f*
bright hell, glänzend; klar; heiter; lebhaft; gescheit
bright·en *v/t a.* **brighten up** heller machen, aufhellen, erhellen; aufheitern; *v/i a.* **brighten up** sich aufhellen
bright·ness Helligkeit *f*; Glanz *m*; Heiterkeit *f*; Gescheitheit *f*
brill *Br* F super, toll
bril·liance, bril·lian·cy Glanz *m*; *fig* Brillanz *f*
bril·liant 1. glänzend; hervorragend, brillant; **2.** Brillant *m*
brim 1. Rand *m*; Krempe *f*; **2.** bis zum Rande füllen *or* voll sein
brim·ful(l) randvoll
brine Sole *f*; Lake *f*
bring bringen, mitbringen, herbringen; *j-n* dazu bringen (**to do** zu tun); **bring about** zustande bringen; bewirken; **bring forth** hervorbringen; **bring off** *et.* fertigbringen, schaffen; **bring on** verursachen; **bring out** herausbringen; **bring round** Ohnmächtigen wieder zu sich bringen; *Kranken* wieder auf die Beine bringen; **bring up** auf-, großziehen; erziehen; zur Sprache bringen
brink Rand *m* (*a. fig*)
brisk flott; lebhaft; frisch
bris·tle 1. Borste *f*; (Bart)Stoppel *f*; **2.** *a.* **bristle up** sich sträuben; zornig werden; strotzen, wimmeln (**with** von)
bris·tly stoppelig, Stoppel...
Brit F Brite *m*, Britin *f*
Brit·ain Britannien *n*
Brit·ish britisch; **the British** die Briten *pl*
Brit·on Brite *m*, Britin *f*
brit·tle spröde, zerbrechlich
broach *Thema* anschneiden
broad breit; weit; hell; deutlich (*hint etc*); derb (*humor etc*); stark (*accent*); allgemein; weitherzig; liberal
broad·cast 1. im Rundfunk *or* Fernsehen bringen, ausstrahlen, übertragen; senden; **2.** *radio*, TV Sendung *f*
broad·cast·er Rundfunk-, Fernsehsprecher(in)
broad·en verbreitern, erweitern
broad jump SPORT Weitsprung *m*

broad·mind·ed liberal
bro·cade Brokat *m*
bro·chure Broschüre *f*, Prospekt *m*
brogue fester Straßenschuh
broil grillen
broke F pleite, abgebrannt
bro·ken zerbrochen, kaputt; gebrochen (*a. fig*); zerrüttet
brok·en·heart·ed verzweifelt, untröstlich
bro·ker ECON Makler *m*
bron·chi·tis MED Bronchitis *f*
bronze 1. Bronze *f*; **2.** bronzefarben; Bronze...
brooch Brosche *f*
brood ZO **1.** Brut *f*; **2.** Brut...; **3.** brüten (*a. fig*)
brook Bach *m*
broom Besen *m*
broth GASTR Fleischbrühe *f*
broth·el Bordell *n*
broth·er Bruder *m*; **brother(s) and sister(s)** Geschwister *pl*
broth·er·hood REL Bruderschaft *f*
broth·er·in·law Schwager *m*
broth·er·ly brüderlich
brow ANAT (Augen)Braue *f*; Stirn *f*; GEOGR Rand *m*
brow·beat einschüchtern
brown 1. braun; **2.** Braun *n*; **3.** bräunen; braun werden
browse grasen, weiden; *fig* schmökern
bruise 1. MED Quetschung *f*, blauer Fleck; **2.** quetschen; anstoßen; MED e-e Quetschung *or* e-n blauen Fleck bekommen
brunch Brunch *m*
brush 1. Bürste *f*; Pinsel *m*; ZO (*Fuchs*)-Rute *f*; Scharmützel *n*; Unterholz *n*; **2.** bürsten; fegen; streifen; **brush against s.o.** *j-n* streifen; **brush away, brush off** wegbürsten, abwischen; **brush aside, brush away** *et.* abtun; **brush up (on)** *fig* aufpolieren, auffrischen
brush·wood Gestrüpp *n*, Unterholz *n*
brusque brüsk, barsch
Brus·sels sprouts BOT Rosenkohl *m*
bru·tal brutal, roh
bru·tal·i·ty Brutalität *f*
brute 1. brutal; **with brute force** mit roher Gewalt; **2.** Vieh *n*; F Untier *n*, Scheusal *n*; Rohling *m*
brut·ish *fig* tierisch
bub·ble 1. Blase *f*; **2.** sprudeln
buck[1] **1.** ZO Bock *m*; **2.** bocken
buck[2] F Dollar *m*
buck·et Eimer *m*, Kübel *m*
buck·le 1. Schnalle *f*, Spange *f*; **2.** *a.* **buckle up** zu-, festschnallen; **buckle on** anschnallen
buck·skin Wildleder *n*

bud 1. BOT Knospe *f*; *fig* Keim *m*; **2.** knospen, keimen

bud·dy F Kamerad *m*; Kumpel *m*, Spezi *m*

budge *v/i* sich (von der Stelle) rühren; *v/t* (vom Fleck) bewegen

bud·ger·i·gar ZO Wellensittich *m*

bud·get Budget *n*, Etat *m*; PARL Haushaltsplan *m*

bud·gie F → **budgerigar**

buf·fa·lo ZO Büffel *m*

buff·er TECH Puffer *m*

buf·fet[1] schlagen; **buffet about** durchrütteln, durchschütteln

buf·fet[2] Büfett *n*, Anrichte *f*

buf·fet[3] (*Frühstücks- etc*)Büfett *n*; Theke *f*

bug 1. ZO Wanze *f* (*a*. F *fig*); Insekt *n*; EDP Programmfehler *m*; **2.** F Wanzen anbringen in (*dat*); F ärgern

bug·ging de·vice Abhörgerät *n*

bugging op·e·ra·tion Lauschangriff *m*

bug·gy Kinderwagen *m*; MOT Buggy *m*

bu·gle MUS Wald-, Signalhorn *n*

build 1. (er)bauen, errichten; **2.** Körperbau *m*, Figur *f*, Statur *f*

build·er Erbauer *m*; Bauunternehmer *m*

build·ing 1. (Er)Bauen *n*; Bau *m*, Gebäude *n*; **2.** Bau...

building site Baustelle *f*

built-in eingebaut, Einbau...

built-up: *built-up area* bebautes Gelände *or* Gebiet; geschlossene Ortschaft

bulb BOT Zwiebel *f*, Knolle *f*; ELECTR (Glüh)Birne *f*

bulge 1. (Aus)Bauchung *f*, Ausbuchtung *f*; **2.** sich (aus)bauchen; hervorquellen

bulk Umfang *m*, Größe *f*, Masse *f*; Großteil *m*; *in bulk* ECON lose, unverpackt; en gros

bulk·y sperrig

bull ZO Bulle *m*, Stier *m*

bull·dog ZO Bulldogge *f*

bull·doze planieren; F einschüchtern

bull·doz·er TECH Bulldozer *m*, Planierraupe *f*

bul·let Kugel *f*

bul·le·tin Bulletin *n*, Tagesbericht *m*

bul·le·tin board Schwarzes Brett *n*

bul·let·proof kugelsicher

bull·fight Stierkampf *m*

bul·lion Gold-, Silberbarren *m*

bul·lock ZO Ochse *m*

bull's-eye: *hit the bull's-eye* ins Schwarze treffen (*a. fig*)

bul·ly 1. tyrannische Person, Tyrann *m*; **2.** einschüchtern, tyrannisieren

bul·wark Bollwerk *n* (*a. fig*)

bum F **1.** Gammler *m*; Tippelbruder *m*, Vagabund *m*; Nichtstuer *m*; **2.** *v/t* schnorren; *bum around* herumgammeln

bum·ble·bee ZO Hummel *f*

bump 1. heftiger Schlag *or* Stoß; Beule *f*; Unebenheit *f*; **2.** stoßen; rammen, auf *ein Auto* auffahren; zusammenstoßen; holpern; *bump into fig j-n* zufällig treffen; F *bump s.o. off j-n* umlegen

bump·er MOT Stoßstange *f*

bump·y holp(e)rig

bun süßes Brötchen; (Haar)Knoten *m*

bunch Bund *m*, Bündel *n*; F Verein *m*, Haufen *m*; *bunch of flowers* Blumenstrauß *m*; *bunch of grapes* Weintraube *f*; *bunch of keys* Schlüsselbund *m, n*

bun·dle 1. Bündel *n* (*a. fig*), Bund *n*; **2.** *v/t a. bundle up* bündeln

bun·ga·low Bungalow *m*

bun·gee elastisches Seil

bun·gee jump·ing Bungeespringen *n*

bun·gle 1. Pfusch *m*; **2.** (ver)pfuschen

bunk Koje *f*; → **bunk bed** Etagenbett *n*

bun·ny Häschen *n*

buoy 1. MAR Boje *f*; **2.** *buoy up fig* Auftrieb geben (*dat*)

bur·den 1. Last *f*; Bürde *f*; **2.** belasten

bu·reau Br Schreibtisch *m*; (Spiegel-) Kommode *f*; Büro *n*

bu·reauc·ra·cy Bürokratie *f*

burg·er GASTR Hamburger *m*

bur·glar Einbrecher *m*

bur·glar·ize einbrechen in (*acc*)

bur·glar·y Einbruch *m*

bur·gle *Br* → **burglarize**

bur·i·al Begräbnis *n*

bur·ly stämmig, kräftig

burn 1. MED Verbrennung *f*, Brandwunde *f*; verbrannte Stelle; **2.** (ver-, an-)brennen; *burn down* ab-, niederbrennen; *burn out* ausbrennen; *burn up* auflodern; verbrennen; verglühen (*rocket etc*)

burn·ing brennend (*a. fig*)

burp F rülpsen, aufstoßen; ein Bäuerchen machen (lassen)

bur·row 1. ZO Bau *m*; **2.** graben; sich eingraben *or* vergraben

burst 1. Bersten *n*; Riss *m*; *fig* Ausbruch *m*; **2.** *v/i* bersten, (zer)platzen; zerspringen; explodieren; *burst from* sich losreißen von; *burst in on or upon s.o.* bei j-m hereinplatzen; *burst into tears* in Tränen ausbrechen; *burst out fig* herausplatzen; *v/t* (auf)sprengen

bur·y begraben, vergraben; beerdigen

bus Omnibus *m*, Bus *m*

bus driv·er Busfahrer *m*

bush Busch *m*; Gebüsch *n*

bush·el Bushel *m*, Scheffel *m* (*Am 35,24 l, Br 36,37 l*)

bush·y buschig

busi·ness Geschäft *n*; Arbeit *f*, Beschäftigung *f*, Beruf *m*, Tätigkeit *f*; Angelegenheit *f*; Sache *f*, Aufgabe *f*; *business of the day* Tagesordnung *f*; *on business* geschäftlich, beruflich; *you have no business doing* (*or* *to do*) *that* Sie haben kein recht, das zu tun; *that's none of your business* das geht Sie nichts an; → *mind* 2

busi·ness hours Geschäftszeit *f*
busi·ness·like geschäftsmäßig, sachlich
busi·ness·man Geschäftsmann *m*
busi·ness trip Geschäftsreise *f*
busi·ness·wom·an Geschäftsfrau *f*
bus stop Bushaltestelle *f*
bust[1] Büste *f*
bust[2]: *go bust* F pleitegehen
bus·tle 1. geschäftiges Treiben; **2.** *bustle about* geschäftig hin und her eilen
bus·y 1. beschäftigt; geschäftig; fleißig (*at* bei, an *dat*); belebt (*street*); arbeitsreich (*dat*); TEL besetzt; **2.** (*mst busy o.s.* sich) beschäftigen (*with* mit)
bus·y·bod·y aufdringlicher Mensch, Gschaftlhuber *m*
bus·y sig·nal TEL Besetztzeichen *n*
but 1. *cj* aber, jedoch; sondern; außer, als; ohne dass; dennoch; *but then* and(e)rerseits; *he could not but laugh* er musste einfach lachen; **2.** *prp* außer (*dat*); *all but him* alle außer ihm; *the last but one* der Vorletzte; *the next but one* der Übernächste; *nothing but* nichts als; *but for* wenn nicht … gewesen wäre, ohne; **3.** der (die *or* das) nicht; *there is no one but knows* es gibt niemand, der es nicht weiß; **4.** *adv* nur; erst, gerade; *all but* fast, beinahe
butch·er 1. Fleischer *m*, Metzger *m*; **2.** (*fig* ab)schlachten
but·ler Butler *m*
butt[1] **1.** (*Gewehr*)Kolben *m*; (*Zigarren etc*)Stummel *m*, (*Zigaretten*)Kippe *f*; (*Kopf*)Stoß *m*; **2.** (mit dem Kopf) stoßen; *butt in* F sich einmischen (*on* in *acc*)
butt[2] Wein-, Bierfaß *n*; Regentonne *f*
but·ter 1. Butter *f*; **2.** mit Butter bestreichen
but·ter·cup BOT Butterblume *f*
but·ter·fly ZO Schmetterling *m*, Falter *m*
but·tocks ANAT Gesäß *n*, F *or* ZO Hinter-

teil *n*
but·ton 1. Knopf *m*; Button *m*, (Ansteck)-Plakette *f*, Abzeichen *n*; **2.** *mst button up* zuknöpfen
but·ton·hole Knopfloch *n*
but·tress Strebepfeiler *m*
bux·om drall, stramm
buy 1. F Kauf *m*; **2.** (an-, ein)kaufen (*of, from* von; *at* bei); *Fahrkarte* lösen; *buy out j-n* abfinden, auszahlen; *Firma* aufkaufen; *buy up* aufkaufen
buy·er Käufer(in); ECON Einkäufer(in)
buzz 1. Summen *n*, Surren *n*; Stimmengewirr *n*; **2.** *v/i* summen, surren; *buzz off!* F schwirr ab!, hau ab!
buz·zard ZO Bussard *m*
buzz·er ELECTR Summer *m*
by 1. *prp* (nahe *or* dicht) bei *or* an, neben (*side by side* Seite an Seite); vorbei *or* vorüber an; *time*: bis um, bis spätestens (*be back by 9.30* sei um 9 Uhr 30 zurück); während, bei (*by day* bei Tage); per, mit (*by bus* mit dem Bus; *by rail* per Bahn); nach, …weise (*by the dozen* dutzendweise); nach, gemäß (*by my watch* nach *or* auf m-r Uhr); von (*by nature* von Natur aus); von, durch (*a play by* … ein Stück von …; *by o.s.* allein); um (*by an inch* um e-n Zoll); MATH mal (*2 by 4*); geteilt durch (*6 by 3*); **2.** *adv* vorbei, vorüber (*go by* vorbeigehen, -fahren; *time*: vergehen); beiseite (*put by* beiseitelegen, zurücklegen); *by and large* im Großen und Ganzen
by… Neben…; Seiten…
bye, bye-bye *int* F Wiedersehen!, tschüs(s)!
by-e·lec·tion PARL Nachwahl *f*
by·gone 1. vergangen; **2.** *let bygones be bygones* lass(t) das Vergangene ruhen
by·pass 1. Umgehungsstraße *f*; MED Bypass *m*; **2.** umgehen; vermeiden
by-prod·uct Nebenprodukt *n*
by·road Nebenstraße *f*
by·stand·er Zuschauer(in), *pl die* Umstehenden *pl*
byte EDP Byte *n*
by·way Nebenstraße *f*
by·word Inbegriff *m*; *be a byword for* stehen für

C

C, c C, c *n*

C ABBR *of* **Celsius** C, Celsius; *centigrade* hundertgradig

c ABBR *of* **cent(s)** Cent *m or pl*; *century* Jh., Jahrhundert *n*; *circa* ca., zirca, ungefähr; *cubic* Kubik...

cab Droschke *f*, Taxi *n*; RAIL Führerstand *m*; MOT Fahrerhaus *n*, *a.* TECH Führerhaus *n*

cab·a·ret Varieteedarbietung(en *pl*) *f*

cab·bage BOT Kohl *m*

cab·in Hütte *f*; MAR Kabine *f*, Kajüte *f*; AVIAT Kanzel *f*

cab·i·net Schrank *m*, Vitrine *f*; POL Kabinett *n*

cab·i·net-mak·er Kunsttischler *m*

cab·i·net meet·ing POL Kabinettssitzung *f*

ca·ble 1. Kabel *n*; (Draht)Seil *n*; **2.** telegrafieren; *j-m Geld* telegrafisch anweisen; TV verkabeln

ca·ble car Kabine *f*; Wagen *m*

ca·ble·gram (Übersee)Telegramm *n*

ca·ble rail·way Drahtseil-, Kabinenbahn *f*

cable tel·e·vi·sion, cable TV Kabelfernsehen *n*

cab rank, cab·stand Taxi-, Droschkenstand *m*

cack·la ZO **1.** Gegacker *n*, Geschnatter *n*; **2.** gackern, schnattern

cac·tus BOT Kaktus *m*

ca·dence MUS Kadenz *f*; (Sprech-) Rhythmus *m*

ca·det MIL Kadett *m*

cadge *Br* F schnorren

caf·é, caf·e Café *n*

caf·e·te·ri·a Cafeteria *f*, Selbstbedienungsrestaurant *n*, *a.* Kantine *f*, UNIV Mensa *f*

cage Käfig *m*; *mining*: Förderkorb *m*; **2.** einsperren

cake 1. Kuchen *m*, Torte *f*; Tafel *f Schokolade*, Stück *n* Seife; F *take the cake* den Vogel abschießen; **2.** *caked with mud* schmutzverkrustet

ca·lam·i·ty großes Unglück, Katastrophe *f*

cal·cu·late *v/t* kalkulieren; be-, aus-, errechnen; F vermuten; *v/i*: *calculate on* rechnen mit *or* auf (*acc*), zählen auf (*acc*)

cal·cu·la·tion Berechnung *f* (*a. fig*); ECON Kalkulation *f*; *fig* Überlegung *f*

cal·cu·la·tor TECH (Taschen)Rechner *m*

cal·en·dar Kalender *m*

calf[1] ANAT Wade *f*

calf[2] ZO Kalb *n*

calf·skin Kalb(s)fell *n*

cal·i·ber, *esp Br* **cal·i·bre** Kaliber *n*

call 1. Ruf *m*; TEL Anruf *m*, Gespräch *n*; Ruf *m*, Berufung *f* (*to* in *ein* Amt; auf *e-n Lehrstuhl*); Aufruf *m*, Aufforderung *f*; Signal *n*; (kurzer) Besuch; *on call* auf Abruf; *be on call* MED Bereitschaftsdienst haben; *make a call* telefonieren; **2.** *v/t* (herbei)rufen; (ein)berufen; TEL *j-n* anrufen; *j-n* berufen, ernennen (*to* zu); nennen; *Aufmerksamkeit* lenken (*to* auf *acc*); *be called* heißen; *call s.o. names* j-n beschimpfen, j-n beleidigen; *v/i* rufen; TEL anrufen; e-n (kurzen) Besuch machen (*on s.o., at s.o.'s [house]* bei j-m); *call at a port* MAR e-n Hafen anlaufen; *call for* rufen nach; *et.* anfordern; *et.* abholen; *to be called for* postlagernd; *call on* sich an *j-n* wenden (*for* wegen); appellieren an (*acc*) (*to do* zu tun); *call on s.o.* j-n besuchen

call box *Br* Telefonzelle *f*

call·er Besucher(in); TEL Anrufer(in)

call girl Callgirl *n*

call-in → *phone-in*

call·ing Berufung *f*; Beruf *m*

cal·lous schwielig; *fig* gefühllos

cal·lus Schwiele *f*

calm 1. still, ruhig; **2.** (Wind)Stille *f*, Ruhe *f*; **3.** *often calm down* besänftigen, (sich) beruhigen

cal·o·rie Kalorie *f*; *high or rich in calories* kalorienreich; *low in calories* kalorienarm, kalorienreduziert

cal·o·rie-con·scious kalorienbewusst

calve ZO kalben

cam·cor·der Camcorder *m*, Kamerarekorder *m*

cam·el ZO Kamel *n*

cam·e·o Kamee *f*; THEA, *film*: kleine Nebenrolle, kurze Szene

cam·e·ra Kamera *f*, Fotoapparat *m*

cam·o·mile BOT Kamille *f*

cam·ou·flage 1. Tarnung *f*; **2.** tarnen

camp 1. (*Zelt- etc*)Lager *n*; **2.** lagern; *camp out* zelten, campen

cam·paign 1. MIL Feldzug *m* (*a. fig*); *fig* Kampagne *f*, Aktion *f*; POL Wahlkampf *m*; **2.** *fig* kämpfen (*for* für; *against* gegen)

camp bed *Br*, **camp cot** Feldbett *n*

camp·er (van) Campingbus *m*, Wohnmobil *n*

camp·ground, camp·site Lagerplatz *m*; Zeltplatz *m*, Campingplatz *m*

cam·pus Campus *m*, Universitätsgelände *n*

can[1] *v/aux ich* kann, *du* kannst *etc*; dürfen, können

can[2] **1.** Kanne *f*; (Blech-, Konserven-) Dose *f*, (-)Büchse *f*; **2.** einmachen, eindosen

Can·a·da Kanada *n*

Ca·na·di·an 1. kanadisch; **2.** Kanadier(in)

ca·nal Kanal *m* (*a.* ANAT)

ca·nar·y ZO Kanarienvogel *m*

can·cel (durch-, aus)streichen; entwerten; rückgängig machen; absagen; *be cancel(l)ed* ausfallen

Can·cer ASTR Krebs *m*; *he (she) is (a) Cancer* er (sie) ist (ein) Krebs

can·cer MED Krebs *m*

can·cer·ous MED Krebs…, krebsbefallen

can·cer pa·tient MED Krebskranke *m, f*

can·did aufrichtig, offen

can·di·date Kandidat(in) (*for* für), Bewerber(in) (*for* um)

can·died kandiert

can·dle Kerze *f*; Licht *n*; *burn the candle at both ends* mit s-r Gesundheit Raubbau treiben

can·dle·stick Kerzenleuchter *m*, Kerzenständer *m*

can·do(u)r Aufrichtigkeit *f*, Offenheit *f*

can·dy 1. Kandis(zucker) *m*; Süßigkeiten *pl*; **2.** kandieren

candy floss Zuckerwatte *f*

candy store Süßwarengeschäft *n*

cane BOT Rohr *n*; (Rohr)Stock *m*

ca·nine Hunde…

canned Dosen…, Büchsen…; *canned fruit* Obstkonserven *pl*

can·ne·ry Konservenfabrik *f*

can·ni·bal Kannibale *m*

can·non MIL Kanone *f*

can·ny schlau

ca·noe 1. Kanu *n*, Paddelboot *n*; **2.** Kanu fahren, paddeln

can·on Kanon *m*; Regel *f*

can o·pen·er Dosen-, Büchsenöffner *m*

can·o·py Baldachin *m*

cant Jargon *m*; Phrase(n *pl*) *f*

can·tan·ker·ous F zänkisch, mürrisch

can·teen *esp Br* Kantine *f*; MIL Feldflasche *f*; Besteck(kasten *m*) *n*

can·ter 1. Kanter *m*; **2.** kantern

can·vas Segeltuch *n*; Zelt-, Packleinwand *f*; Segel *pl*; PAINT Leinwand *f*; Gemälde *n*

can·vass 1. POL Wahlfeldzug *m*; ECON Werbefeldzug *m*; **2.** *v/t* eingehend untersuchen *or* erörtern *or* prüfen; POL werben um (*Stimmen*); *v/i* POL e-n Wahlfeldzug

veranstalten

can·yon GEOGR Cañon *m*, Schlucht *f*

cap 1. Kappe *f*; Mütze *f*; Haube *f*; Zündkapsel *f*; **2.** (mit e-r Kappe *etc*) bedecken; *fig* krönen; übertreffen

ca·pa·bil·i·ty Fähigkeit *f*

cap·a·ble fähig (*of* zu)

ca·pac·i·ty (Raum)Inhalt *m*; Fassungsvermögen *n*; Kapazität *f*; Aufnahmefähigkeit *f*; (TECH Leistungs)Fähigkeit *f* (*for ger* zu *inf*); *in my capacity as* in meiner Eigenschaft als

cape[1] GEOGR Kap *n*, Vorgebirge *n*

cape[2] Cape *n*, Umhang *m*

ca·per 1. Kapriole *f*, Luftsprung *m*; *cut capers* → **2.** Freuden- *or* Luftsprünge machen

ca·pil·la·ry ANAT Haar-, Kapillargefäß *n*

cap·i·tal 1. ECON Kapital *n*; Hauptstadt *f*; Großbuchstabe *m*; **2.** Kapital…; Tod(es)…; Haupt…; großartig, prima

capital crime JUR Kapitalverbrechen *n*

cap·i·tal·ism ECON Kapitalismus *m*

cap·i·tal·ist ECON Kapitalist *m*

cap·i·tal·ize großschreiben; ECON kapitalisieren

cap·i·tal let·ter Großbuchstabe *m*

capital pun·ish·ment JUR Todesstrafe *f*

ca·pit·u·late kapitulieren (*to* vor *dat*)

ca·pri·cious launisch

Cap·ri·corn ASTR Steinbock *m*; *he (she) is (a) Capricorn* er (sie) ist (ein) Steinbock

cap·size MAR *v/i* kentern; *v/t* zum Kentern bringen

cap·sule Kapsel *f*

cap·tain (An)Führer *m*; MAR, ECON Kapitän *m*; AVIAT Flugkapitän *m*; MIL Hauptmann *m*; SPORT (Mannschafts-) Kapitän *m*, Spielführer *m*

cap·tion Überschrift *f*, Titel *m*; Bildunterschrift *f*; *film*: Untertitel *m*

cap·ti·vate *fig* gefangen nehmen, fesseln

cap·tive 1. gefangen; gefesselt; *hold captive* gefangen halten; **2.** Gefangene *m, f*

cap·tiv·i·ty Gefangenschaft *f*

cap·ture 1. Eroberung *f*; Gefangennahme *f*; **2.** fangen, gefangen nehmen; erobern; erbeuten; MAR kapern

car Auto *n*, Wagen *m*; (Eisenbahn-, Straßenbahn)Wagen *m*; Gondel *f* (*of a balloon etc*); Kabine *f*; *by car* mit dem Auto, im Auto

car·a·mel Karamell *m*; Karamelle *f*

car·a·van Karawane *f*; *Br* Wohnwagen *m*

caravan site Campingplatz *m* für Wohnwagen

car·a·way BOT Kümmel *m*

car·bine MIL Karabiner *m*

car·bo·hy·drate CHEM Kohle(n)hydrat *n*

car bomb Autobombe f
car·bon CHEM Kohlenstoff m; → **carbon copy, carbon paper**
car·bon cop·y Durchschlag m
car·bon pa·per Kohlepapier n
car·bu·ret·(t)or MOT Vergaser m
car·case Br, **car·cass** Kadaver m, Aas n; GASTR Rumpf m
car·cin·o·genic MED karzinogen, krebserregend
car·ci·no·ma MED Krebsgeschwulst f
card Karte f; **play cards** Karten spielen; **have a card up one's sleeve** fig (noch) e-n Trumpf in der Hand haben
card·board Pappe f
cardboard box Pappschachtel f, Pappkarton m
car·di·ac MED Herz...
cardiac pace·mak·er MED Herzschrittmacher m
car·di·gan Strickjacke f
car·di·nal 1. Grund..., Haupt..., Kardinal...; scharlachrot; **2.** REL Kardinal m
car·di·nal num·ber MATH Kardinalzahl f, Grundzahl f
card in·dex Kartei f
card phone Kartentelefon n
card·sharp·er Falschspieler m
car dump Autofriedhof m
care 1. Sorge f; Sorgfalt f; Vorsicht f; Obhut f, Pflege f; **needing care** MED pflegebedürftig; **medical care** ärztliche Behandlung; **take care of** aufpassen auf (acc); versorgen; **with care!** Vorsicht!; **2.** Lust haben (**to** inf zu inf); **care about** sich kümmern um; **care for** sorgen für, sich kümmern um; sich etwas machen aus; **I don't care!** F meinetwegen!; **I couldn't care less** F es ist mir völlig egal
ca·reer 1. Karriere f, Laufbahn f; **2.** Berufs...; Karriere...; **3.** rasen
ca·reers ad·vice Berufsberatung f
careers ad·vi·sor Berufsberater m
careers guidance Berufsberatung f
careers of·fice Berufsberatungsstelle f
careers of·fi·cer Berufsberater m
care·free sorgenfrei, sorglos
care·ful vorsichtig; sorgsam bedacht (**of** auf acc); sorgfältig; **be careful!** pass auf!
care·less nachlässig, unachtsam; leichtsinnig, unvorsichtig; sorglos
care·less·ness Nachlässigkeit f, Unachtsamkeit f; Leichtsinn m; Sorglosigkeit f
ca·ress 1. Liebkosung f; Zärtlichkeit f; **2.** liebkosen, streicheln
care·tak·er Hausmeister m; (Haus- etc)-Verwalter m
care·worn abgehärmt, verhärmt
car fer·ry Autofähre f

car·go Ladung f
car hire Br Autovermietung f
car·i·ca·ture 1. Karikatur f, Zerrbild n; **2.** karikieren
car·i·ca·tur·ist Karikaturist m
car·ies, a. **dental caries** MED Karies f
car me·chan·ic Automechaniker m
car·mine Karmin(rot) n
car·na·tion BOT Nelke f
car·nap·per F Autoentführer m
car·ni·val Karneval m
car·niv·o·rous ZO fleischfressend
car·ol Weihnachtslied n
carp¹ ZO Karpfen m
carp² nörgeln
car park esp Br Parkplatz m; Parkhaus n
car·pen·ter Zimmermann m
car·pet 1. Teppich m; **fitted carpet** Teppichboden m; **sweep s.th. under the carpet** fig et. unter den Teppich kehren; **2.** mit Teppich(boden) auslegen
car phone Autotelefon n
car pool Fahrgemeinschaft f
car pool(·ing) ser·vice Mitfahrzentrale f
car·port MOT überdachter Abstellplatz
car rent·al Autovermietung f
car re·pair shop Autoreparaturwerkstatt f
car·riage Beförderung f, Transport m; Transportkosten pl; Kutsche f; Br RAIL (Personen)Wagen m; (Körper-)Haltung f
car·riage·way Fahrbahn f
car·ri·er Spediteur m; Gepäckträger m (on a bicycle); MIL Flugzeugträger m
car·ri·er bag Br Trag(e)tasche f, -tüte f
car·ri·on 1. Aas n; **2.** Aas...
car·rot BOT Karotte f, Mohrrübe f
car·ry v/t bringen, führen, tragen (a. v/i), fahren, befördern; (bei sich) haben or tragen; Ansicht durchsetzen; Gewinn, Preis davontragen; Ernte, Zinsen tragen; (weiter)führen, Mauer ziehen; Antrag durchbringen; **be carried** PARL etc angenommen werden; **carry the day** den Sieg davontragen; **carry s.th. too far** et. übertreiben, et. zu weit treiben; **get carried away** fig die Kontrolle über sich verlieren; sich hinreißen lassen; **carry forward, carry over** ECON übertragen; **carry on** fortsetzen, weiterführen; ECON betreiben; **carry out, carry through** aus-, durchführen
car·ry·cot Br (Baby)Trag(e)tasche f
cart 1. Karren m; Wagen m; Einkaufswagen m; **put the cart before the horse** fig das Pferd beim Schwanz aufzäumen; **2.** karren
car·ti·lage ANAT Knorpel m
cart·load Wagenladung f

car·ton Karton *m*; *a carton of cigarettes* e-e Stange Zigaretten

car·toon Cartoon *m*, *n*; Karikatur *f*; Zeichentrickfilm *m*

car·toon·ist Karikaturist *m*

car·tridge Patrone *f* (*a.* MIL); (Film-) Patrone *f*, (Film)Kassette *f*; Tonabnehmer *m*

cart·wheel: *turn cartwheels* Rad schlagen

carve GASTR vorschneiden, zerlegen; TECH schnitzen; meißeln

carv·er (Holz)Schnitzer *m*; Bildhauer *m*; GASTR Tranchierer *m*; Tranchiermesser *n*

carv·ing Schnitzerei *f*

car wash Autowäsche *f*; (Auto)Waschanlage *f*, Waschstraße *f*

cas·cade Wasserfall *m*

case¹ 1. Behälter *m*; Kiste *f*, Kasten *m*; Etui *n*; Gehäuse *n*; Schachtel *f*; (*Glas-*) Schrank *m*; (*Kissen*)Bezug *m*; TECH Verkleidung *f*; **2.** in ein Gehäuse *or* Etui stecken; TECH verkleiden

case² Fall *m* (*a.* JUR), LING *a.* Kasus *m*; MED (Krankheits)Fall *m*, Patient(in); Sache *f*, Angelegenheit *f*

case·ment Fensterflügel *m*; → *casement window* Flügelfenster *n*

cash 1. Bargeld *n*; Barzahlung *f*; *cash down* gegen bar; *cash on delivery* Lieferung *f* gegen bar; (per) Nachnahme *f*; **2.** einlösen

cash·book ECON Kassenbuch *n*

cash desk Kasse *f*

cash dis·pens·er *esp Br* Geld-, Bankautomat *m*

cash·ier Kassierer(in)

cash·less bargeldlos

cash ma·chine Geld-, Bankautomat *m*

cash·mere Kaschmir *m*

cash·point *Br* → *cash machine*

cash reg·is·ter Registrierkasse *f*

cas·ing (Schutz)Hülle *f*; Verschalung *f*, Verkleidung *f*, Gehäuse *n*

cask Fass *n*

cas·ket Kästchen *n*; Sarg *m*

cas·sette (*Film-, Band-, Musik*)Kassette *f*

cassette deck Kassettendeck *n*

cassette player Kassettenrekorder *m*

cassette ra·di·o Radiorekorder *m*

cassette re·cord·er Kassettenrekorder *m*

cas·sock REL Soutane *f*

cast 1. Wurf *m*; TECH Guss(form *f*) *m*; Abguss *m*, Abdruck *m*; Schattierung *f*, Anflug *m*; Form *f*, Art *f*; Auswerfen *n* (*of a fishing line etc*); THEA Besetzung *f*; **2.** (ab-, aus-, hin-, um-, weg)werfen; ZO abwerfen (*skin*); verlieren (*teeth*); verwerfen; gestalten; TECH gießen; *a.* *cast up* ausrechnen, zusammenzählen; THEA

Stück besetzen; *Rollen* verteilen (*to* an *acc*); *cast lots* losen (*for* um); *cast away* wegwerfen; *be cast down* niedergeschlagen sein; *cast off Kleidung* ausrangieren; MAR losmachen; *Freund etc* fallen lassen; *knitting*: abketten; *v/i: cast about for, cast around for* suchen (nach), *fig a.* sich umsehen nach

cas·ta·net Kastagnette *f*

cast·a·way Schiffbrüchige *m*, *f*

caste Kaste *f* (*a. fig*)

cast·er Laufrolle *f*; *Br* (*Salz-, Zucker-etc*)Streuer *m*

cast i·ron Gusseisen *n*

cast-i·ron gusseisern

cas·tle Burg *f*, Schloss *n*; *chess*: Turm *m*

cast·or → *caster*

cast·or oil PHARM Rizinusöl *n*

cas·trate kastrieren

cas·u·al zufällig; gelegentlich; flüchtig; lässig

cas·u·al·ty Unfall *m*; Verunglückte *m*, *f*, Opfer *n*; MIL Verwundete *m*; Gefallene *m*; *casualties* Opfer *pl*, MIL *mst* Verluste *pl*

casualty (de·part·ment) MED Notaufnahme *f*

casualty ward MED Unfallstation *f*

cas·u·al wear Freizeitkleidung *f*

cat ZO Katze *f*

cat·a·log, *esp Br* **cat·a·logue 1.** Katalog *m*; Verzeichnis *n*, Liste *f*; **2.** katalogisieren

cat·a·lyt·ic con·vert·er MOT Katalysator *m*

cat·a·pult *Br* Schleuder *f*; Katapult *n*, *m*

cat·a·ract Wasserfall *m*; Stromschnelle *f*; MED grauer Star

ca·tarrh MED Katarr(h) *m*

ca·tas·tro·phe Katastrophe *f*

catch 1. Fangen *n*; Fang *m*, Beute *f*; Halt *m*, Griff *m*; TECH Haken *m* (*a. fig*); (Tür-)Klinke *f*; Verschluss *m*; **2.** *v/t* (auf-, ein)fangen; packen, fassen, ergreifen; überraschen, ertappen; *Blick etc* auffangen; F *Zug etc* (noch) kriegen, erwischen; *et.* erfassen, verstehen; *Atmosphäre etc* einfangen; sich *e-e Krankheit* holen; *catch (a) cold* sich erkälten; *catch the eye* ins Auge fallen; *catch s.o.'s eye* j-s Aufmerksamkeit auf sich lenken; *catch s.o. up* j-n einholen; *be caught up in* verwickelt sein in (*acc*); *v/i* sich verfangen, hängen bleiben; fassen, greifen; TECH ineinandergreifen; klemmen; einschnappen; *catch up with* einholen

catch·er Fänger *m*

catch·ing packend; MED ansteckend (*a. fig*)

catch·word Schlagwort *n*; Stichwort *n*

catch·y MUS eingängig

cat·e·chis·m REL Katechismus *m*

cat·e·go·ry Kategorie *f*

ca·ter: *cater for* Speisen und Getränke liefern für; *fig* sorgen für

cat·er·pil·lar ZO Raupe *f*

Cat·er·pil·lar® MOT Raupenfahrzeug *n*

Caterpillar trac·tor® MOT Raupenschlepper *m*

cat·gut MUS Darmsaite *f*

ca·the·dral Dom *m*, Kathedrale *f*

Cath·o·lic REL **1.** katholisch; **2.** Katholik(in)

cat·kin BOT Kätzchen *n*

cat·tle Vieh *n*

cattle breed·er Viehzüchter *m*

cattle breed·ing Viehzucht *f*

cattle dealer Viehhändler *m*

cattle mar·ket Viehmarkt *m*

ca(u)l·dron großer Kessel

cau·li·flow·er BOT Blumenkohl *m*

cause 1. Ursache *f*; Grund *m*; Sache *f*; **2.** verursachen; veranlassen

cause·less grundlos

cau·tion 1. Vorsicht *f*; Warnung *f*; Verwarnung *f*; **2.** warnen; verwarnen; JUR belehren

cau·tious behutsam, vorsichtig

cav·al·ry HIST MIL Kavallerie *f*

cave 1. Höhle *f*; **2.** *v/i*: *cave in* einstürzen

cav·ern (große) Höhle

cav·i·ty Höhle *f*; MED Loch *n*

caw ZO **1.** krächzen; **2.** Krächzen *n*

CD ABBR *of compact disk* CD *f*

CD play·er CD-Spieler *m*

CD-ROM ABBR *of compact disk read-only memory* CD-ROM

CD vid·e·o CD-Video *n*

cease aufhören; beenden

cease·fire MIL Feuereinstellung *f*; Waffenruhe *f*

cease·less unaufhörlich

cei·ling (Zimmer)Decke *f*; ECON Höchstgrenze *f*, oberste Preisgrenze

cel·e·brate feiern

cel·e·brat·ed gefeiert, berühmt (*for* für, wegen)

cel·e·bra·tion Feier *f*

ce·leb·ri·ty Berühmtheit *f*

cel·e·ry BOT Sellerie *m*, *f*

ce·les·ti·al himmlisch

cel·i·ba·cy Ehelosigkeit *f*

cell BIOL Zelle *f*, ELECTR *a.* Element *n*

cel·lar Keller *m*

cel·list MUS Cellist(in)

cel·lo MUS (Violon)Cello *n*

cel·lo·phane® Cellophan® *n*

cel·lu·lar BIOL Zell(en)...

cel·lu·lar phone Handy *n*

Cel·tic keltisch

ce·ment 1. Zement *m*; Kitt *m*; **2.** zementieren; (ver)kitten

cem·e·tery Friedhof *m*

cen·sor 1. Zensor *m*; **2.** zensieren

cen·sor·ship Zensur *f*

cen·sure 1. Tadel *m*, Verweis *m*; **2.** tadeln

cen·sus Volkszählung *f*

cent Hundert *n*; Cent *m* (*1/100 Dollar*); *per cent* Prozent *n*

cen·te·na·ry Hundertjahrfeier *f*, hundertjähriges Jubiläum

cen·ten·ni·al 1. hundertjährig; **2.** → *centenary*

cen·ter 1. Zentrum *n*, Mittelpunkt *m*; *soccer:* Flanke *f*; **2.** (sich) konzentrieren; zentrieren

center back *soccer:* Vorstopper *m*

center for·ward SPORT Mittelstürmer(in)

center of grav·i·ty PHYS Schwerpunkt *m*

cen·ti·grade: *10 degrees centigrade* 10 Grad Celsius

cen·ti·me·ter, *Br* **cen·ti·me·tre** Zentimeter *m*, *n*

cen·ti·pede ZO Tausendfüß(l)er *m*

cen·tral zentral; Haupt..., Zentral...; Mittel...

central heat·ing Zentralheizung *f*

cen·tral·ize zentralisieren

cen·tral lock·ing MOT Zentralverriegelung *f*

central res·er·va·tion *Br* MOT Mittelstreifen *m*

cen·tre *Br* → *center*

cen·tu·ry Jahrhundert *n*

ce·ram·ics Keramik *f*, keramische Erzeugnisse *pl*

ce·re·al 1. Getreide...; **2.** BOT Getreide *n*; Getreidepflanze *f*; GASTR Getreideflocken *pl*, Frühstückskost *f*

cer·e·bral ANAT Gehirn...

cer·e·mo·ni·al 1. zeremoniell; **2.** Zeremoniell *n*

cer·e·mo·ni·ous zeremoniell; förmlich

cer·e·mo·ny Zeremonie *f*; Feier *f*, Feierlichkeit *f*; Förmlichkeit(en *pl*) *f*

cer·tain sicher, gewiss; zuverlässig; bestimmt; gewisse(r, -s)

cer·tain·ly sicher, gewiss; *int* sicherlich, bestimmt, natürlich

cer·tain·ty Sicherheit *f*, Bestimmtheit *f*, Gewissheit *f*

cer·tif·i·cate Zeugnis *n*; Bescheinigung *f*; *certificate of (good) conduct* Führungszeugnis *n*; *General Certificate of Education advanced level* (*A level*) *Br* PED *appr* Abitur(zeugnis) *n*; *General Certificate of Education ordinary level*

(*O level*) *Br* PED *appr* mittlere Reife; *medical certificate* ärztliches Attest

cer·ti·fy *et.* bescheinigen; beglaubigen

cer·ti·tude Sicherheit *f*, Bestimmtheit *f*, Gewissheit *f*

CET ABBR *of Central European Time* MEZ, mitteleuropäische Zeit

cf (*Latin confer*) ABBR *of compare* vgl., vergleiche

CFC ABBR *of chlorofluorocarbon* FCKW, Fluorchlorkohlenwasserstoff *m*

chafe *v/t* warm reiben; aufreiben, wund reiben; *v/i* (sich durch)reiben, scheuern

chaff AGR Spreu *f*; Häcksel *n*

chaf·finch ZO Buchfink *m*

chag·rin 1. Ärger *m*; **2.** ärgern

chain 1. Kette *f*; *fig* Fessel *f*; **2.** (an)ketten; fesseln

chain re·ac·tion Kettenreaktion *f*

chain-smoke F Kette rauchen

chain-smok·er Kettenraucher(in)

chain-smok·ing Kettenrauchen *n*

chain store Kettenladen *m*

chair Stuhl *m*; UNIV Lehrstuhl *m*; ECON *etc* Vorsitz *m*; *be in the chair* den Vorsitz führen

chair lift Sessellift *m*

chair·man Vorsitzende *m*, Präsident *m*; Diskussionsleiter *m*; ECON *Br* Generaldirektor *m*

chair·man·ship Vorsitz *m*

chair·wom·an Vorsitzende *f*, Präsidentin *f*; Diskussionsleiterin *f*

chal·ice REL Kelch *m*

chalk 1. Kreide *f*; **2.** mit Kreide schreiben *or* zeichnen

chal·lenge 1. Herausforderung *f*; **2.** herausfordern

chal·len·ger Herausforderer *m*

cham·ber TECH, PARL *etc* Kammer *f*

cham·ber·maid Zimmermädchen *n*

cham·ber of com·merce ECON Handelskammer *f*

cham·ois ZO Gämse *f*

cham·ois (**leath·er**) Fensterleder *n*

champ F SPORT → *champion*

cham·pagne Champagner *m*

cham·pi·on 1. Verfechter(in), Fürsprecher(in); SPORT Meister(in); **2.** verfechten, eintreten für

cham·pi·on·ship SPORT Meisterschaft *f*

chance 1. Zufall *m*; Chance *f*, (günstige) Gelegenheit; Aussicht *f* (*of* auf *acc*); Möglichkeit *f*; Risiko *n*; *by chance* zufällig; *take a chance* es darauf ankommen lassen; *take no chances* nichts riskieren (wollen); **2.** zufällig; **3.** F riskieren

chan·cel·lor Kanzler(in)

chan·de·lier Kronleuchter *m*

change 1. Veränderung *f*, Wechsel *m*; Abwechslung *f*; Wechselgeld *n*; Kleingeld *n*; *for a change* zur Abwechslung; *change for the better* (*worse*) Bess(e)rung *f* (Verschlechterung *f*); **2.** *v/t* (ver)ändern, umändern; (aus)wechseln; (aus-, ver-) tauschen (*for* gegen); umbuchen; MOT, TECH schalten; *change over* umschalten; umstellen; *change trains* umsteigen; *v/i* sich (ver)ändern, wechseln; sich umziehen

change·a·ble veränderlich

change ma·chine Münzwechsler *m*

change·o·ver Umstellung *f* (*to* auf *acc*)

chang·ing room *esp* Umkleidekabine *f*, Umkleideraum *m*

chan·nel 1. Kanal *m* (*a.* *fig*); (*Fernseh- etc*)Kanal *m*, (*Fernseh- etc*)Programm *n*; *fig* Weg *m*; **2.** *fig* lenken

Chan·nel Tun·nel Kanaltunnel *m*, Eurotunnel *m*

chant 1. (Kirchen)Gesang *m*; Singsang *m*; **2.** in Sprechchören rufen

cha·os Chaos *n*

chap[1] **1.** Riss *m*; **2.** rissig machen *or* werden; aufspringen

chap[2] *Br* F Bursche *m*, Kerl *m*

chap·el ARCH Kapelle *f*; REL Gottesdienst *m*

chap·lain REL Kaplan *m*

chap·ter Kapitel *n*

char verkohlen

char·ac·ter Charakter *m*; Ruf *m*, Leumund *m*; Schriftzeichen *n*, Buchstabe *m*; *novel etc*: Figur *f*, Gestalt *f*; THEA Rolle *f*

char·ac·ter·is·tic 1. charakteristisch (*of* für); **2.** Kennzeichen *n*

char·ac·ter·ize charakterisieren

char·coal Holzkohle *f*

charge 1. *v/t* ELECTR (auf)laden; *Gewehr etc* laden; *j-n* beauftragen (*with* mit); *j-n* beschuldigen *or* anklagen (*with* e-r *Sache*) (*a.* JUR); ECON berechnen, verlangen, fordern (*for* für); MIL angreifen; stürmen; *charge s.o. with s.th.* ECON *j-m* et. in Rechnung stellen; *v/i: charge at s.o.* auf *j-n* losgehen; **2.** Ladung *f* (*a.* ELECTR *etc*); (Spreng)Ladung *f*; Beschuldigung *f*, *a.* JUR Anklage(-punkt *m*) *f*; ECON Preis *m*; Forderung *f*; Gebühr *f*; *a. pl* Unkosten *pl*, Spesen *pl*; Verantwortung *f*; Schützling *m*, Mündel *n*, *m*; *free of charge* kostenlos; *be in charge of* verantwortlich sein für; *take charge of* die Leitung *etc* übernehmen, die Sache in die Hand nehmen

char·i·ot HIST Streit-, Triumphwagen *m*

cha·ris·ma Charisma *n*, Ausstrahlung *f*,

Ausstrahlungskraft *f*

char·i·ta·ble wohltätig

char·i·ty Nächstenliebe *f*; Wohltätigkeit *f*; Güte *f*, Nachsicht *f*; milde Gabe

char·la·tan Scharlatan *m*; Quacksalber *m*, Kurpfuscher *m*

charm 1. Zauber *m*; Charme *m*, Reiz *m*; Talisman *m*, Amulett *n*; **2.** bezaubern, entzücken

charm·ing charmant, bezaubernd

chart (*See-*, *Himmels-*, *Wetter*)Karte *f*; Diagramm *n*, Schaubild *n*; *pl* MUS Charts *pl*, Hitliste(n *pl*) *f*

char·ter 1. Urkunde *f*; Charta *f*; Chartern *n*; **2.** chartern, mieten

char·ter flight Charterflug *m*

char·wom·an Putzfrau *f*, Raumpflegerin *f*

chase 1. Jagd *f*; Verfolgung *f*; **2.** *v/t* jagen, hetzen; Jagd machen auf (*acc*); TECH ziselieren; *v/i* rasen, rennen

chasm Kluft *f*, Abgrund *m*

chaste keusch; schlicht

chas·tise züchtigen

chas·ti·ty Keuschheit *f*

chat 1. Geplauder *n*, Schwätzchen *n*, Plauderei *f*; **2.** plaudern

chat show *Br* TV Talkshow *f*

chat show host *Br* TV Talkmaster *m*

chat·ter 1. plappern; schnattern; klappern; **2.** Geplapper *n*; Klappern *n*

chat·ter·box F Plappermaul *n*

chat·ty gesprächig

chauf·feur Chauffeur *m*

chau·vi F Chauvi *m*

chau·vin·ist Chauvinist *m*; F *male chauvinist pig* Chauvi *m*; *contp* Chauvischwein *n*

cheap billig; *fig* schäbig, gemein

cheap·en (sich) verbilligen; *fig* herabsetzen

cheat 1. Betrug *m*, Schwindel *m*; Betrüger(in); **2.** betrügen; F schummeln

check 1. Schach(stellung *f*) *n*; Hemmnis *n*, Hindernis *n* (*on* für); Einhalt *m*; Kontrolle *f* (*on* gen); Kontrollabschnitt *m*, -schein *m*; Gepäckschein *m*; Garderobenmarke *f*; ECON Scheck *m* (*for* über); Häkchen *n* (*on a list etc*); ECON Kassenzettel *m*, Rechnung *f*; karierter Stoff; **2.** *v/i* (plötzlich) innehalten; *check in* sich (*in e-m Hotel*) anmelden; einstempeln; AVIAT einchecken; *check out* (*aus e-m Hotel*) abreisen; ausstempeln; *check up* (*on*) F (*e-e Sache*) nachprüfen, (*e-e Sache, j-n*) überprüfen; *v/t* hemmen, hindern, aufhalten; zurückhalten; checken, kontrollieren, überprüfen; *auf e-r Liste* abhaken; *Mantel etc* in der Garderobe abgeben; *Gepäck* aufgeben

check card ECON Scheckkarte *f*

checked kariert

check·ers Damespiel *n*

check-in Anmeldung *f*; Einstempeln *n*; AVIAT Einchecken *n*

check-in coun·ter, check-in desk AVIAT Abfertigungsschalter *m*

check·ing ac·count ECON Girokonto *n*

check·list Check-, Kontrollliste *f*

check·mate 1. (Schach)Matt *n*; **2.** (schach)matt setzen

check-out Abreise *f*; Ausstempeln *n*

check-out coun·ter Kasse *f*

check·point Kontrollpunkt *m*

check·room Garderobe *f*; Gepäckaufbewahrung *f*

check-up Überprüfung *f*; MED Check-up *m*, Vorsorgeuntersuchung *f*

cheek ANAT Backe *f*, Wange *f*; *Br* Unverschämtheit *f*

cheek·y *Br* frech

cheer 1. Stimmung *f*, Fröhlichkeit *f*; Hoch *n*, Hochruf *m*, Beifall *m*, Beifallsruf *m*; *pl* SPORT Anfeuerungsrufe *pl*; *three cheers!* dreimal hoch!; *cheers!* prost!; **2.** *v/t* mit Beifall begrüßen; *a. cheer on* anspornen; *a. cheer up* aufheitern; *v/i* hoch rufen, jubeln; *a. cheer up* Mut fassen; *cheer up!* Kopf hoch!

cheer·ful vergnügt

cheer·i·o *int Br* F tschüs(s)!

cheer·lead·er SPORT Einpeitscher *m*, Cheerleader *m*

cheer·less freudlos; unfreundlich

cheer·y vergnügt

cheese Käse *m*

chee·tah ZO Gepard *m*

chef Küchenchef *m*; Koch *m*

chem·i·cal 1. chemisch; **2.** Chemikalie *f*

chem·ist Chemiker(in); Apotheker(in); Drogist(in)

chem·is·try Chemie *f*

chem·ist's shop Apotheke *f*; Drogerie *f*

chem·o·ther·a·py MED Chemotherapie *f*

cheque *Br* ECON Scheck *m*; *crossed cheque* Verrechnungsscheck *m*

cheque ac·count *Br* Girokonto *n*

cheque card *Br* Scheckkarte *f*

cher·ry BOT Kirsche *f*

chess Schach(spiel) *n*; *a game of chess* e-e Partie Schach

chess·board Schachbrett *n*

chess·man, chess·piece Schachfigur *f*

chest Kiste *f*; Truhe *f*; ANAT Brust *f*, Brustkasten *m*; *get s.th. off one's chest* F sich et. von der Seele reden

chest·nut 1. BOT Kastanie *f*; **2.** kastanienbraun

chest of drawers Kommode *f*

chew (zer)kauen
chew·ing gum Kaugummi *m*
chic schick, *Austrian* fesch
chick zo Küken *n*, junger Vogel; F Biene *f*, Puppe *f* (*girl*)
chick·en zo Huhn *n*; Küken *n*; GASTR (*Brat*)Hähnchen *n*, (*Brat*)Hühnchen *n*
chick·en·heart·ed furchtsam, feige
chick·en pox MED Windpocken *pl*
chic·o·ry BOT Chicorée *m*, *f*
chief 1. oberste(r, -s), Ober…, Haupt…, Chef…; wichtigste(r, -s); **2.** Chef *m*; Häuptling *m*
chief·ly hauptsächlich
chil·blain MED Frostbeule *f*
child Kind *n*; *from a child* von Kindheit an; *with child* schwanger
child a·buse JUR Kindesmisshandlung *f*
child ben·e·fit *Br* Kindergeld *n*
child·birth Geburt *f*, Niederkunft *f*
child·hood Kindheit *f*; *from childhood* von Kindheit an
child·ish kindlich; kindisch
child·like kindlich
child·mind·er Tagesmutter *f*
chill 1. kalt, frostig, kühl (*a. fig*); **2.** Frösteln *n*; Kälte *f*, Kühle *f* (*a. fig*); MED Erkältung *f*; **3.** abkühlen; *j-n* frösteln lassen; kühlen
chill·y kalt, frostig, kühl (*a. fig*)
chime 1. Glockenspiel *n*; Geläut *n*; **2.** läuten; schlagen (*clock*)
chim·ney Schornstein *m*
chim·ney sweep Schornsteinfeger *m*
chimp F, **chim·pan·zee** zo Schimpanse *m*
chin ANAT Kinn *n*; *chin up!* Kopf hoch!, halt die Ohren steif!
chi·na Porzellan *n*
Chi·na China *n*
Chi·nese 1. chinesisch; **2.** Chinese *m*, Chinesin *f*; LING Chinesisch *n*; *the Chinese* die Chinesen *pl*
chink Ritz *m*, Spalt *m*
chip 1. Splitter *m*, Span *m*, Schnitzel *n*, *m*; dünne Scheibe; Spielmarke *f*; EDP Chip *m*; **2.** *v/t* schnitzeln; anschlagen, abschlagen; *v/i* abbröckeln
chips (Kartoffel)Chips *pl*; *Br* Pommes frites *pl*, F Fritten *pl*
chi·rop·o·dist Fußpfleger(in), Pediküre *f*
chirp zo zirpen, zwitschern, piepsen
chis·el 1. Meißel *m*; **2.** meißeln
chit-chat Plauderei *f*
chiv·al·rous ritterlich
chive(s) BOT Schnittlauch *m*
chlo·ri·nate *Wasser etc* chloren
chlo·rine CHEM Chlor *n*
chlo·ro·fluo·ro·car·bon (ABBR *CFC*) CHEM Fluorchlorkohlenwasserstoff *m*

(ABBR *FCKW*)
chlor·o·form MED **1.** Chloroform *n*; **2.** chloroformieren
choc·o·late Schokolade *f*; Praline *f*; *pl* Pralinen *pl*, Konfekt *n*
choice 1. Wahl *f*; Auswahl *f*; **2.** auserlesen, ausgesucht, vorzüglich
choir ARCH, MUS Chor *m*
choke 1. *v/t* (er)würgen, (*a. v/i*) ersticken; *choke back* Ärger etc unterdrücken, *Tränen* zurückhalten; *choke down* hinunterwürgen; *a. choke up* verstopfen; **2.** MOT Choke *m*, Luftklappe *f*
cho·les·te·rol MED Cholesterin *n*
choose (aus)wählen, aussuchen
choos·(e)y *esp Br* wählerisch
chop 1. Hieb *m*, (Handkanten)Schlag *m*; GASTR Kotelett *n*; **2.** *v/t* (zer)hacken, hauen; *chop down* fällen; *v/i* hacken
chop·per Hackmesser *n*, Hackbeil *n*; F Hubschrauber *m*
chop·py unruhig (*sea*)
chop·stick Essstäbchen *n*
cho·ral MUS Chor…
cho·rale MUS Choral *m*
chord MUS Saite *f*; Akkord *m*
chore schwierige *or* unangenehme Aufgabe; *pl* Hausarbeit *f*
cho·rus MUS Chor *m*; Kehrreim *m*, Refrain *m*; Tanzgruppe *f*
Christ REL Christus *m*
chris·ten REL taufen
chris·ten·ing REL **1.** Taufe *f*; **2.** Tauf…
Chris·tian REL **1.** christlich; **2.** Christ(in)
Chris·ti·an·i·ty REL Christentum *n*
Chris·tian name Vorname *m*
Christ·mas Weihnachten *n and pl*; *at Christmas* zu Weihnachten
Christmas Day erster Weihnachtsfeiertag
Christmas Eve Heiliger Abend
chrome Chrom *m*
chro·mi·um CHEM Chrom *n*
chron·ic chronisch; ständig, (an)dauernd
chron·i·cle Chronik *f*
chron·o·log·i·cal chronologisch
chro·nol·o·gy Zeitrechnung *f*; Zeitfolge *f*
chub·by F rundlich, pumm(e)lig; pausbäckig
chuck F werfen, schmeißen; *chuck out j-n* rausschmeißen; *et.* wegschmeißen; *chuck up Job etc* hinschmeißen
chuck·le 1. *chuckle* (*to o.s.*) (stillvergnügt) in sich hineinlachen; **2.** leises Lachen
chum F Kamerad *m*, Kumpel *m*
chum·my F dick befreundet
chump Holzklotz *m*; F Trottel *m*
chunk Klotz *m*, Klumpen *m*
Chun·nel F → *Channel Tunnel*

church 1. Kirche *f*; **2.** Kirch…, Kirchen…
church ser·vice REL Gottesdienst *m*
church·yard Kirchhof *m*
churl·ish grob, flegelhaft
churn 1. Butterfass *n*; **2.** buttern; *Wellen* aufwühlen, peitschen
chute Stromschnelle *f*; Rutsche *f*, Rutschbahn *f*; F Fallschirm *m*
ci·der *a.* **hard cider** Apfelwein *m*; **(sweet) cider** Apfelmost *m*, Apfelsaft *m*
ci·gar Zigarre *f*
cig·a·rette Zigarette *f*
cinch F todsichere Sache
cin·der Schlacke *f*; *pl* Asche *f*
Cin·de·rel·la Aschenbrödel *n*, Aschenputtel *n*
cin·der track SPORT Aschenbahn *f*
cin·e·cam·e·ra (Schmal)Filmkamera *f*
cin·e·film Schmalfilm *m*
cin·e·ma *Br* Kino *n*; Film *m*
cin·na·mon Zimt *m*
ci·pher Geheimschrift *f*, Chiffre *f*; Null *f* (*a. fig*)
cir·cle 1. Kreis *m*; THEA Rang *m*; *fig* Kreislauf *m*; **2.** (um)kreisen
cir·cuit Kreislauf *m*; ELECTR Stromkreis *m*; Rundreise *f*; SPORT Zirkus *m*; **short circuit** ELECTR Kurzschluss *m*
cir·cu·i·tous gewunden; weitschweifig; **circuitous route** Umweg *m*
cir·cu·lar 1. kreisförmig; Kreis…; **2.** Rundschreiben *n*; Umlauf *m*; (Post-)Wurfsendung *f*
cir·cu·late *v/i* zirkulieren, im Umlauf sein; *v/t* in Umlauf setzen
cir·cu·lat·ing li·bra·ry Leihbücherei *f*
cir·cu·la·tion (*a.* Blut)Kreislauf *m*, Zirkulation *f*; ECON Umlauf *m*; *newspaper etc:* Auflage *f*
cir·cum·fer·ence (Kreis)Umfang *m*
cir·cum·nav·i·gate umschiffen, umsegeln
cir·cum·scribe MATH umschreiben; *fig* begrenzen
cir·cum·spect umsichtig, vorsichtig
cir·cum·stance Umstand *m*; *pl* (Sach-)Lage *f*, Umstände *pl*; Verhältnisse *pl*; **in** *or* **under no circumstances** unter keinen Umständen, auf keinen Fall; **in** *or* **under the circumstances** unter diesen Umständen
cir·cum·stan·tial ausführlich; umständlich
circumstantial ev·i·dence JUR Indizien *pl*, Indizienbeweis *m*
cir·cus Zirkus *m*
CIS ABBR *of* **Commonwealth of Independent States** die GUS, die Gemeinschaft unabhängiger Staaten
cis·tern Wasserbehälter *m*; Spülkasten *m*

ci·ta·tion Zitat *n*; JUR Vorladung *f*
cite zitieren; JUR vorladen
cit·i·zen Bürger(in); Städter(in); Staatsangehörige *m*, *f*
cit·i·zen·ship Staatsangehörigkeit *f*
cit·y 1. (Groß)Stadt *f*; **the City** die (Londoner) City; **2.** städtisch, Stadt…
city cen·tre *Br* Innenstadt *f*, City *f*
city coun·cil·(l)or Stadtrat *m*, Stadträtin *f*
city hall Rathaus *n*; Stadtverwaltung *f*
city slick·er *often contp* Städter(in), Stadtmensch *m*
city va·grant Stadtstreicher(in), Nichtsesshafte *m*, *f*
civ·ic städtisch, Stadt…
civ·ics PED Staatsbürgerkunde *f*
civ·il staatlich, Staats…; (staats)bürgerlich, Bürger…; zivil, Zivil…; JUR zivilrechtlich; höflich
ci·vil·i·an Zivilist *m*
ci·vil·i·ty Höflichkeit *f*
civ·i·li·za·tion Zivilisation *f*, Kultur *f*
civ·i·lize zivilisieren
civ·il rights (Staats)Bürgerrechte *pl*
civil rights ac·tiv·ist Bürgerrechtler(in)
civil rights move·ment Bürgerrechtsbewegung *f*
civ·il ser·vant Staatsbeamte *m*, -beamtin *f*
civil ser·vice Staatsdienst *m*
civil war Bürgerkrieg *m*
clad gekleidet
claim 1. Anspruch *m*; Anrecht *n* (**to** auf *acc*); Forderung *f*; Behauptung *f*; Claim *m*; **2.** beanspruchen; fordern; behaupten
clair·voy·ant 1. hellseherisch; **2.** Hellseher(in)
clam·ber (mühsam) klettern
clam·my feuchtkalt, klamm
clam·o(u)r 1. Geschrei *n*, Lärm *m*; **2.** lautstark verlangen (**for** nach)
clamp TECH Zwinge *f*
clan Clan *m*, Sippe *f*
clan·des·tine heimlich
clang klingen, klirren; erklingen lassen
clank 1. Gerassel *n*, Geklirr *n*; **2.** rasseln *or* klirren (mit)
clap 1. Klatschen *n*; Schlag *m*, Klaps *m*; **2.** schlagen *or* klatschen (mit)
clar·et roter Bordeaux(wein); Rotwein *m*
clar·i·fy *v/t* (auf)klären, klarstellen; *v/i* sich (auf)klären, klar werden
clar·i·net MUS Klarinette *f*
clar·i·ty Klarheit *f*
clash 1. Zusammenstoß *m*; Konflikt *m*; **2.** zusammenstoßen; *fig* nicht zusammenpassen *or* harmonieren
clasp 1. Haken *m*, Schnalle *f*; Schloss *n*, (Schnapp)Verschluss *m*; Umklamme-

rung *f*; **2.** einhaken, zuhaken; ergreifen, umklammern

clasp knife Taschenmesser *n*

class 1. Klasse *f*; (Bevölkerungs-) Schicht *f*; (Schul)Klasse *f*; (Unterrichts)Stunde *f*; Kurs *m*; Jahrgang *m*; **2.** (in Klassen) einteilen, einordnen, einstufen

clas·sic 1. Klassiker *m*; **2.** klassisch

clas·si·cal klassisch

clas·sic car Klassiker *m*

clas·si·fi·ca·tion Klassifizierung *f*, Einteilung *f*

clas·si·fied klassifiziert; MIL, POL geheim

classified ad Kleinanzeige *f*

clas·si·fy klassifizieren, einstufen

class·mate Mitschüler(in)

class·room Klassenzimmer *n*

clat·ter 1. Geklapper *n*; **2.** klappern (mit)

clause JUR Klausel *f*, Bestimmung *f*; LING Satz(teil *n*) *m*

claw 1. ZO Klaue *f*, Kralle *f*; (*Krebs-*) Schere *f*; **2.** (zer)kratzen; umkrallen, packen

clay Ton *m*, Lehm *m*

clean 1. *adj* rein; sauber, glatt, eben; *sl* clean; **2.** *adv* völlig, ganz und gar; **3.** reinigen, säubern, putzen; ***clean out*** reinigen; ***clean up*** gründlich reinigen; aufräumen

clean·er Rein(e)machefrau *f*, (*Fenster- etc*)Putzer *m*; Reinigungsmittel *n*, Reiniger *m*; ***take to the cleaners*** *et.* zur Reinigung bringen; F *j-n* ausnehmen

clean·ing: ***do the cleaning*** sauber machen, putzen

cleaning la·dy, cleaning wom·an Putzfrau *f*

clean·li·ness Reinlichkeit *f*

clean·ly 1. *adv* sauber; **2.** *adj* reinlich

cleanse reinigen, säubern

cleans·er Putzmittel *n*, Reinigungsmittel *n*, Reiniger *m*

clear 1. klar; hell; rein; deutlich; frei (***of*** von); ECON Netto…, Rein…; **2.** *v/t* reinigen, säubern; *Wald* lichten, roden; wegräumen (*a.* ***clear away***); *Tisch* abräumen; räumen, leeren; *Hindernis* nehmen; SPORT klären; ECON verzollen; JUR freisprechen; EDP löschen; *v/i* klar *or* hell werden; METEOR aufklaren; sich verziehen (*fog*); ***clear out*** aufräumen; ausräumen, entfernen; F abhauen; ***clear up*** aufräumen; *Verbrechen etc* aufklären; METEOR aufklaren

clear·ance Räumung *f*; TECH lichter Abstand; Freigabe *f*

clearance sale ECON Räumungsverkauf *m*, Ausverkauf *m*

clear·ing Lichtung *f*

cleave spalten

cleav·er Hackmesser *n*

clef MUS Schlüssel *m*

cleft Spalt *m*, Spalte *f*

clem·en·cy Milde *f*, Nachsicht *f*

clem·ent mild (*a.* METEOR)

clench *Lippen etc* (fest) zusammenpressen; *Zähne* zusammenbeißen; *Faust* ballen

cler·gy REL Klerus *m*, *die* Geistlichen *pl*

cler·gy·man REL Geistliche *m*

clerk Verkäufer(in); (Büro- *etc*)Angestellte *m*, *f*, (Bank-, Post)Beamte *m*, (-)Beamtin *f*

clev·er klug, gescheit; geschickt

click 1. Klicken *n*; **2.** *v/i* klicken; zu-, einschnappen; *mit der Zunge* schnalzen; *v/t* klicken *or* einschnappen lassen; *mit der Zunge* schnalzen; ***click on*** EDP anklicken

cli·ent JUR Klient(in), Mandant(in); Kunde *m*, Kundin *f*, Auftraggeber(in)

cliff Klippe *f*, Felsen *m*

cli·mate Klima *n*

cli·max Höhepunkt *m*; Orgasmus *m*

climb klettern; (er-, be)steigen; ***climb (up) a tree*** auf e-n Baum klettern

climb·er Kletterer *m*, Bergsteiger(in); BOT Kletterpflanze *f*

clinch 1. TECH sicher befestigen; (ver-)nieten; *boxing*: umklammern (*v/i* clinchen); *fig* entscheiden; ***that clinched it*** damit war die Sache entschieden; **2.** *boxing*: Clinch *m*

cling (to) festhalten (an *dat*), sich klammern (an *acc*); sich (an)schmiegen (an *acc*)

cling·film® *esp Br* Frischhaltefolie *f*

clin·ic Klinik *f*

clin·i·cal klinisch

clink 1. Klirren *n*, Klingen *n*; *sl* Knast *m*; **2.** klingen *or* klirren (lassen); klimpern mit

clip[1] **1.** ausschneiden; *Schafe etc* scheren; **2.** Schnitt *m*; Schur *f*; (*Film- etc*) Ausschnitt *m*; (*Video*)Clip *m*

clip[2] **1.** (Heft-, Büro- *etc*)Klammer *f*; (*Ohr*)Klipp *m*; **2.** *a.* ***clip on*** anklammern

clip·per: (***a pair of***) ***clippers*** (e-e) (*Nagel- etc*)Schere *f*, Haarschneidemaschine *f*

clip·pings Abfälle *pl*, Schnitzel *pl*; (*Zeitungs- etc*)Ausschnitte *pl*

clit·o·ris ANAT Klitoris *f*

cloak 1. Umhang *m*; **2.** *fig* verhüllen

cloak·room *Br* Garderobe *f*; Toilette *f*

clock 1. (*Wand-, Stand-, Turm*)Uhr *f*; ***9 o'clock*** 9 Uhr; **2.** SPORT Zeit stoppen; ***clock in, clock on*** einstempeln; ***clock out, clock off*** ausstempeln

clock ra·di·o Radiowecker *m*

clock·wise im Uhrzeigersinn

clock·work Uhrwerk *n*; *like clockwork* wie am Schnürchen

clod (Erd)Klumpen *m*

clog 1. (Holz)Klotz *m*; Holzschuh *m*; **2.** *a.* *clog up* verstopfen

clois·ter ARCH Kreuzgang *m*; REL Kloster *n*

close 1. *adj* geschlossen; knapp (*result etc*); genau, gründlich (*inspection etc*); eng (anliegend); stickig, schwül; eng (*friend*), nah (*relative*); *keep a close watch on* scharf im Auge behalten (*acc*); **2.** *adv* eng, nahe, dicht; *close by* ganz in der Nähe, nahe *or* dicht bei; **3.** Ende *n*, (Ab)Schluss *m*; *come or draw to a close* sich dem Ende nähern; Einfriedung *f*; **4.** *v/t* (ab-, ver-, zu)schließen, zumachen; ECON schließen; *Straße* (ab)sperren; *v/i* sich schließen; schließen, zumachen; enden, zu Ende gehen; *close down* Geschäft *etc* schließen, *Betrieb* stilllegen; *radio*, TV das Programm beenden, Sendeschluss haben; *close in* bedrohlich nahe kommen; hereinbrechen (*night*); *close up* (ab-, ver-, zu)schließen; aufschließen, aufrücken

closed geschlossen, F *pred* zu

clos·et (Wand)Schrank *m*

close-up PHOT, *film*: Großaufnahme *f*

clos·ing date Einsendeschluss *m*

clos·ing time Laden-, Geschäftsschluss *m*; Polizeistunde *f* (*of a pub*)

clot 1. Klumpen *m*, Klümpchen *n*; *clot of blood* MED Blutgerinnsel *n*; **2.** gerinnen; Klumpen bilden

cloth Stoff *m*, Tuch *n*; Lappen *m*

cloth·bound in Leinen gebunden

clothe (an-, be)kleiden; einkleiden

clothes Kleider *pl*, Kleidung *f*; Wäsche *f*

clothes bas·ket Wäschekorb *m*

clothes·horse Wäscheständer *m*

clothes·line Wäscheleine *f*

clothes peg *Br*, **clothes·pin** Wäscheklammer *f*

cloth·ing (Be)Kleidung *f*

cloud 1. Wolke *f*; *fig* Schatten *m*; **2.** (sich) bewölken; (sich) trüben

cloud·burst Wolkenbruch *m*

cloud·less wolkenlos

cloud·y bewölkt; trüb; *fig* unklar

clout F Schlag *m*; POL Einfluss *m*

clove¹ GASTR (Gewürz)Nelke *f*; *clove of garlic* Knoblauchzehe *f*

clo·ven hoof ZO Huf *m* der Paarzeher

clo·ver BOT Klee *m*

clown Clown *m*, Hanswurst *m*

club 1. Keule *f*; Knüppel *m*; SPORT Schlagholz *n*; (*Golf*)Schläger *m*; Klub *m*; *pl* *card game*: Kreuz *n*; **2.** einknüppeln

auf (*acc*), niederknüppeln

club·foot MED Klumpfuß *m*

cluck ZO **1.** gackern; glucken; **2.** Gackern *n*; Glucken *n*

clue Anhaltspunkt *m*, Fingerzeig *m*, Spur *f*

clump 1. Klumpen *m*; (*Baum- etc -*)Gruppe *f*; **2.** trampeln

clum·sy unbeholfen, ungeschickt, plump

clus·ter 1. BOT Traube *f*, Büschel *n*; Haufen *m*; **2.** sich drängen

clutch 1. Griff *m*; TECH Kupplung *f*; *fig* Klaue *f*; **2.** (er)greifen; umklammern

clut·ter *fig* überladen

c/o ABBR *of* *care of* c/o, (wohnhaft) bei

Co ABBR *of* *company* ECON Gesellschaft *f*

coach 1. Reisebus *m*; *Br* RAIL (Personen)Wagen *m*; Kutsche *f*; SPORT Trainer(in); PED Nachhilfelehrer(in); **2.** SPORT trainieren; PED *j-m* Nachhilfeunterricht geben

coach·man Kutscher *m*

co·ag·u·late gerinnen (lassen)

coal (Stein)Kohle *f*; *carry coals to Newcastle* F *Br* Eulen nach Athen tragen

co·a·li·tion POL Koalition *f*; Bündnis *n*, Zusammenschluss *m*

coal·mine, **coal·pit** Kohlengrube *f*

coarse grob; rau; derb; ungeschliffen; gemein

coast 1. Küste *f*; **2.** MAR die Küste entlangfahren; im Leerlauf (*car*) *or* im Freilauf (*bicycle*) fahren; rodeln

coast·er brake Rücktritt(bremse *f*) *m*

coast·guard (Angehörige *m* der) Küstenwache *f*

coast·line Küstenlinie *f*, -strich *m*

coat 1. Mantel *m*; ZO Pelz *m*, Fell *n*; (*Farb-etc*)Überzug *m*, Anstrich *m*, Schicht *f*; **2.** (an)streichen, überziehen, beschichten

coat hang·er Kleiderbügel *m*

coat·ing (*Farb- etc*)Überzug *m*, Anstrich *m*; Schicht *f*; Mantelstoff *m*

coat of arms Wappen(schild *m*, *n*) *n*

coax überreden, beschwatzen

cob Maiskolben *m*

cob·bled: *cobbled street* Straße *f* mit Kopfsteinpflaster

cob·bler (Flick)Schuster *m*

cob·web Spinn(en)gewebe *n*

co·caine Kokain *n*

cock 1. ZO Hahn *m*; V Schwanz *m*; **2.** aufrichten; *cock one's ears* die Ohren spitzen

cock·a·too ZO Kakadu *m*

cock·chaf·er ZO Maikäfer *m*

cock·eyed F schielend; (krumm und) schief

Cock·ney Cockney *m*, waschechter Londoner

cock·pit AVIAT Cockpit *n*
cock·roach ZO Schabe *f*
cock·sure F übertrieben selbstsicher
cock·tail Cocktail *m*
cock·y großspurig, anmaßend
co·co BOT Kokospalme *f*
co·coa Kakao *m*
co·co·nut BOT Kokosnuss *f*
co·coon (*Seiden*)Kokon *m*
cod ZO Kabeljau *m*, Dorsch *m*
COD ABBR *of* **collect** (*Br* **cash**) **on delivery** per Nachnahme
cod·dle verhätscheln, verzärteln
code 1. Kode *m*; **2.** verschlüsseln, chiffrieren; kodieren
cod·fish → **cod**
cod·ing Kodierung *f*
cod-liv·er oil Lebertran *m*
co·ed·u·ca·tion PED Gemeinschaftserziehung *f*
co·ex·ist gleichzeitig *or* nebeneinander bestehen *or* leben
co·ex·ist·ence Koexistenz *f*
cof·fee Kaffee *m*; **black** (**white**) **coffee** Kaffee ohne (mit) Milch
coffee bar *Br* Café *n*; Imbissstube *f*
coffee bean Kaffeebohne *f*
coffee grind·er Kaffeemühle *f*
coffee machine Kaffeeautomat *m*
cof·fee·mak·er Kaffeemaschine *f*
cof·fee pot Kaffeekanne *f*
coffee shop Café *n*; Imbissstube *f*
coffee ta·ble Couchtisch *m*
cof·fin Sarg *m*
cog TECH (Rad)Zahn *m*; → **cog·wheel** TECH Zahnrad *n*
co·her·ence, **co·her·en·cy** Zusammenhang *m*
co·her·ent zusammenhängend
co·he·sion Zusammenhalt *m*
co·he·sive (fest) zusammenhaltend
coif·fure Frisur *f*
coil 1. *a.* **coil up** aufrollen, (auf)wickeln; sich zusammenrollen; **2.** Spirale *f* (*a.* TECH, MED); Rolle *f*, Spule *f*
coin 1. Münze *f*; **2.** prägen
co·in·cide zusammentreffen; übereinstimmen
co·in·ci·dence (zufälliges) Zusammentreffen; Zufall *m*
coin-op·e·rat·ed: **coin-operated** (**gas,** *Br* **petrol**) **pump** Münztank(automat) *m*
coke Koks *m* (*a.* F *cocaine*)
Coke® F Coke *n*, Cola *n*, *f*, Coca *n*, *f*
cold 1. kalt; **2.** Kälte *f*; MED Erkältung *f*; **catch** (**a**) **cold** sich erkälten; **have a cold** erkältet sein
cold-blood·ed kaltblütig
cold cuts GASTR Aufschnitt *m*

cold-heart·ed kaltherzig
cold·ness Kälte *f*
cold sweat Angstschweiß *m*; **he broke out in a cold sweat** ihm brach der Angstschweiß aus
cold war POL kalter Krieg
cold wave METEOR Kältewelle *f*
cole·slaw Krautsalat *m*
col·ic MED Kolik *f*
col·lab·o·rate zusammenarbeiten
col·lab·o·ra·tion Zusammenarbeit *f*; **in collaboration with** gemeinsam mit
col·lapse 1. zusammenbrechen (*a. fig*), einstürzen; umfallen; *fig* scheitern; **2.** Einsturz *m*; *fig* Zusammenbruch *m*
col·lap·si·ble Klapp..., zusammenklappbar
col·lar 1. Kragen *m*; (*Hunde- etc*)Halsband *n*; **2.** beim Kragen packen; *j-n* festnehmen, F schnappen
col·lar·bone ANAT Schlüsselbein *n*
col·league Kollege *m*, Kollegin *f*, Mitarbeiter(in)
col·lect *v/t* (ein)sammeln; *Daten* erfassen; *Geld* kassieren; *j-n or et.* abholen; *Gedanken etc* sammeln; *v/i* sich (ver-)sammeln
col·lect·ed *fig* gefasst
col·lect·ing box Sammelbüchse *f*
col·lec·tion Sammlung *f*; ECON Eintreibung *f*; REL Kollekte *f*; Abholung *f*
col·lec·tive gesammelt; Sammel...; **collective bargaining** ECON Tarifverhandlungen
col·lec·tive·ly insgesamt; zusammen
col·lec·tor Sammler(in); Steuereinnehmer *m*; ELECTR Stromabnehmer *m*
col·lege College *n*; Hochschule *f*; höhere Lehranstalt
col·lide zusammenstoßen, kollidieren (*a. fig*)
col·lie·ry Kohlengrube *f*
col·li·sion Zusammenstoß *m*, Kollision *f* (*a. fig*)
col·lo·qui·al umgangssprachlich
co·lon LING Doppelpunkt *m*
colo·nel MIL Oberst *m*
co·lo·ni·al·is·m POL Kolonialismus *m*
col·o·nize kolonisieren, besiedeln
col·o·ny Kolonie *f*
col·o(u)r 1. Farbe *f*; *pl* MIL Fahne *f*; MAR Flagge *f*; **what colo(u)r is ...?** welche Farbe hat ...?; **2.** *v/t* färben; anmalen, bemalen, anstreichen; *fig* beschönigen; *v/i* sich (ver)färben; erröten
col·o(u)r bar Rassenschranke *f*
col·o(u)r-blind farbenblind
col·o(u)red bunt; farbig
col·o(u)r·fast farbecht

col·o(u)r film PHOT Farbfilm *m*

col·o(u)r·ful farbenprächtig; *fig* farbig, bunt

col·o(u)r·ing Färbung *f*; Farbstoff *m*; Gesichtsfarbe *f*

col·o(u)r·less farblos

col·o(u)r line Rassenschranke *f*

col·o(u)r set Farbfernseher *m*

colo(u)r tel·e·vi·sion Farbfernsehen *n*

colt ZO (Hengst)Fohlen *n*

col·umn Säule *f*; PRINT Spalte *f*; MIL Kolonne *f*

col·umn·ist Kolumnist(in)

comb 1. Kamm *m*; **2.** kämmen; striegeln

com·bat 1. Kampf *m*; *single combat* Zweikampf *m*; **2.** kämpfen gegen, bekämpfen

com·ba·tant MIL Kämpfer *m*

com·bi·na·tion Verbindung *f*, Kombination *f*

com·bine 1. (sich) verbinden; **2.** ECON Konzern *m*; AGR *a.* **combine harvester** Mähdrescher *m*

com·bus·ti·ble 1. brennbar; **2.** Brennstoff *m*, Brennmaterial *n*

com·bus·tion Verbrennung *f*

come kommen; *to come* künftig, kommend; *come and go* kommen und gehen; *come to see* besuchen; *come about* geschehen, passieren; *come across* auf *j-n or et.* stoßen; *come along* mitkommen, mitgehen; *come apart* auseinanderfallen; *come away* sich lösen, ab-, losgehen (*button etc*); *come back* zurückkommen; *come by s.th.* zu et. kommen; *come down* herunterkommen (*a. fig*); einstürzen; sinken (*prices*); überliefert werden; *come down with* F erkranken an (*dat*); *come for* abholen kommen, kommen wegen; *come forward* sich melden; *come from* kommen aus; kommen von; *come home* nach Hause (*Austrian, Swiss a.* nachhause) kommen; *come in* hereinkommen; eintreffen (*news*); einlaufen (*train*); *come in!* herein!; *come loose* sich ablösen, abgehen; *come off* ab-, losgehen (*button etc*); *come on!* los!, vorwärts!, komm!; *come out* herauskommen; *come over* vorbeikommen (*visitor*); *come round* vorbeikommen (*visitor*); wieder zu sich kommen; *come through* durchkommen; *Krankheit etc* überstehen, überleben; *come to* sich belaufen auf (*acc*); wieder zu sich kommen; *come up to* entsprechen (*dat*), heranreichen an (*acc*)

come·back Come-back *n*

co·me·di·an Komiker *m*

com·e·dy Komödie *f*, Lustspiel *n*

come·ly attraktiv, gut aussehend

com·fort 1. Komfort *m*, Bequemlichkeit *f*; Trost *m*; *cold comfort* schwacher Trost; **2.** trösten

com·for·ta·ble komfortabel, behaglich, bequem; tröstlich

com·fort·er Tröster *m*; *esp Br* Schnuller *m*; Steppdecke *f*

com·fort·less unbequem; trostlos

com·fort sta·tion Bedürfnisanstalt *f*

com·ic komisch; Komödien..., Lustspiel...

com·i·cal komisch, spaßig

com·ics Comics *pl*, Comic-Hefte *pl*

com·ma LING Komma *n*

com·mand 1. Befehl *m*; Beherrschung *f*; MIL Kommando *n*; **2.** befehlen; MIL kommandieren; verfügen über (*acc*); beherrschen

com·mand·er MIL Kommandeur *m*, Befehlshaber *m*

commander in chief MIL Oberbefehlshaber *m*

com·mand·ment REL Gebot *n*

com·mand mod·ule Kommandokapsel *f*

com·man·do MIL Kommando *n*

com·mem·o·rate gedenken (*gen*)

com·mem·o·ra·tion: *in commemoration of* zum Gedenken *or* Gedächtnis an (*acc*)

com·mem·o·ra·tive Gedenk..., Erinnerungs...

com·ment 1. (*on*) Kommentar *m* (zu); Bemerkung *f* (zu); Anmerkung *f* (zu); *no comment!* kein Kommentar!; **2.** *v/i comment on* e-n Kommentar abgeben zu, sich äußern über (*acc*); *v/t* bemerken (*that* dass)

com·men·ta·ry Kommentar *m* (*on* zu)

com·men·ta·tor Kommentator *m*, *radio*, TV *a.* Reporter *m*

com·merce ECON Handel *m*

com·mer·cial 1. ECON Handels..., Geschäfts...; kommerziell, finanziell; **2.** *radio*, TV Werbespot *m*, Werbesendung *f*

commercial art Gebrauchsgrafik *f*

commercial art·ist Gebrauchsgrafiker(in)

com·mer·cial·ize kommerzialisieren

com·mer·cial tel·e·vi·sion Werbefernsehen *n*; kommerzielles Fernsehen

com·mis·e·rate: *commiserate with* Mitleid empfinden mit

com·mis·e·ra·tion Mitleid *n* (*for* mit)

com·mis·sion 1. Auftrag *m*; Kommission *f*, Ausschuss *m*; ECON Kommission *f*, Provision *f*; Begehung *f* (*of a crime*); **2.** beauftragen; *et.* in Auftrag geben

com·mis·sion·er Beauftragte *m*, *f*; Kommissar(in)

com·mit anvertrauen, übergeben (*to dat*); JUR *j-n* einweisen (*to* in *acc*); *Verbrechen* begehen; *j-n* verpflichten (*to* zu), *j-n* festlegen (*to* auf *acc*)

com·mit·ment Verpflichtung *f*; Engagement *n*

com·mit·tal JUR Einweisung *f*

com·mit·tee Komitee *n*, Ausschuss *m*

com·mod·i·ty ECON Ware *f*, Artikel *m*

com·mon 1. gemeinsam, gemeinschaftlich; allgemein; alltäglich; gewöhnlich, einfach; **2.** Gemeindeland *n*; *in common* gemeinsam (*with* mit)

com·mon·er Bürgerliche *m*, *f*

com·mon law (ungeschriebenes englisches) Gewohnheitsrecht

Com·mon Mar·ket ECON, POL HIST Gemeinsamer Markt

com·mon·place 1. Gemeinplatz *m*; **2.** alltäglich; abgedroschen

Com·mons: *the Commons, the House of Commons Br* PARL das Unterhaus

com·mon sense gesunder Menschenverstand

Com·mon·wealth: *the Commonwealth (of Nations)* das Commonwealth

com·mo·tion Aufregung *f*; Aufruhr *m*, Tumult *m*

com·mu·nal Gemeinde...; Gemeinschafts...

com·mune Kommune *f*

com·mu·ni·cate *v/t* mitteilen; *v/i* sich besprechen; sich in Verbindung setzen (*with s.o.* mit j-m); (durch e-e Tür) verbunden sein

com·mu·ni·ca·tion Mitteilung *f*; Verständigung *f*, Kommunikation *f*; Verbindung *f*; *pl* Kommunikationsmittel *pl*; Verkehrswege *pl*

com·mu·ni·ca·tions sat·el·lite Nachrichtensatellit *m*

com·mu·ni·ca·tive mitteilsam, gesprächig

Com·mu·nion *a. Holy Communion* REL (heilige) Kommunion, Abendmahl *n*

com·mu·nis·m POL Kommunismus *m*

com·mu·nist POL **1.** Kommunist(in); **2.** kommunistisch

com·mu·ni·ty Gemeinschaft *f*; Gemeinde *f*

com·mute JUR Strafe *mildernd* umwandeln; RAIL *etc* pendeln

com·mut·er Pendler(in)

commuter train Pendlerzug *m*, Nahverkehrszug *m*

com·pact 1. Puderdose *f*; MOT Kleinwagen *m*; **2.** *adj* kompakt; eng, klein; knapp (*style*)

compact car MOT Kleinwagen *m*

compact disk (ABBR *CD*) Compact Disc *f*, CD *f*

compact disk play·er CD-Player *m*, CD--Spieler *m*

com·pan·ion Begleiter(in); Gefährte *m*, Gefährtin *f*; Gesellschafter(in); Handbuch *n*, Leitfaden *m*

com·pan·ion·ship Gesellschaft *f*

com·pa·ny Gesellschaft *f*, ECON *a.* Firma *f*; MIL Kompanie *f*; THEA Truppe *f*; *keep s.o. company* j-m Gesellschaft leisten

com·pa·ra·ble vergleichbar

com·par·a·tive 1. vergleichend; verhältnismäßig; **2.** *a. comparative degree* LING Komparativ *m*

com·par·a·tive·ly vergleichsweise; verhältnismäßig

com·pare 1. *v/t* vergleichen; *compared with* im Vergleich zu; *v/i* sich vergleichen lassen; **2.** *beyond compare, without compare* unvergleichlich

com·pa·ri·son Vergleich *m*

com·part·ment Fach *n*; RAIL Abteil *n*

com·pass Kompass *m*; *pair of compasses* Zirkel *m*

com·pas·sion Mitleid *n*

com·pas·sion·ate mitleidig

com·pat·i·ble vereinbar; *be compatible (with)* passen (zu), zusammenpassen; EDP *etc* kompatibel sein (mit)

com·pat·ri·ot Landsmann *m*, Landsmännin *f*

com·pel (er)zwingen

com·pel·ling bezwingend

com·pen·sate *j-n* entschädigen; *et.* ersetzen; ausgleichen

com·pen·sa·tion Ersatz *m*; Ausgleich *m*; Schadenersatz *m*, Entschädigung *f*; Bezahlung *f*, Gehalt *n*

com·pere *Br* Conférencier *m*

com·pete sich (mit)bewerben (*for* um); konkurrieren; SPORT (am Wettkampf) teilnehmen

com·pe·tence Können *n*, Fähigkeit *f*

com·pe·tent fähig, tüchtig; fachkundig, sachkundig

com·pe·ti·tion Wettbewerb *m*; Konkurrenz *f*

com·pet·i·tive konkurrierend

com·pet·i·tor Mitbewerber(in); Konkurrent(in); SPORT (Wettbewerbs-)Teilnehmer(in)

com·pile kompilieren, zusammentragen, zusammenstellen

com·pla·cence, com·pla·cen·cy Selbstzufriedenheit *f*, Selbstgefälligkeit *f*

com·pla·cent selbstzufrieden, selbstgefällig

com·plain sich beklagen *or* beschweren

C

(*about* über *acc*; *to* bei); klagen (*of* über *acc*)

com·plaint Klage *f*, Beschwerde *f*; MED Leiden *n*, *pl* MED *a*. Beschwerden *pl*

com·ple·ment 1. Ergänzung *f*; **2.** ergänzen

com·ple·men·ta·ry (sich) ergänzend

com·plete 1. vollständig; vollzählig; **2.** vervollständigen; beenden, abschließen

com·ple·tion Vervollständigung *f*; Abschluss *m*

completion test PSYCH Lückentext *m*

com·plex 1. zusammengesetzt; komplex, vielschichtig; **2.** Komplex *m* (*a.* PSYCH)

com·plex·ion Gesichtsfarbe *f*, Teint *m*

com·plex·i·ty Komplexität *f*, Vielschichtigkeit *f*

com·pli·ance Einwilligung *f*; Befolgung *f*; *in compliance with* gemäß (*dat*)

com·pli·ant willfährig

com·pli·cate komplizieren

com·pli·cat·ed kompliziert

com·pli·ca·tion Komplikation *f* (*a.* MED)

com·plic·i·ty JUR Mitschuld *f*, Mittäterschaft *f* (*in* an *dat*)

com·pli·ment 1. Kompliment *n*; Empfehlung *f*; Gruß *m*; **2.** *v/t j-m* ein Kompliment *or* Komplimente machen (*on* über *acc*)

com·ply (with) einwilligen (in *acc*); (*e-e Abmachung etc*) befolgen

com·po·nent Bestandteil *m*; TECH, ELECTR Bauelement *n*

com·pose zusammensetzen, -stellen; MUS komponieren; verfassen; *be composed of* bestehen *or* sich zusammensetzen aus; *compose o.s.* sich beruhigen

com·posed ruhig, gelassen

com·pos·er MUS Komponist(in)

com·po·si·tion Zusammensetzung *f*; MUS Komposition *f*; PED Aufsatz *m*

com·po·sure Fassung *f*, (Gemüts)Ruhe *f*

com·pound¹ Lager *n*; Gefängnishof *m*; (Tier)Gehege *n*

com·pound² 1. Zusammensetzung *f*; Verbindung *f*; LING zusammengesetztes Wort; **2.** zusammengesetzt; *compound interest* ECON Zinseszinsen *pl*; **3.** *v/t* zusammensetzen; steigern, *esp* verschlimmern

com·pre·hend begreifen, verstehen

com·pre·hen·si·ble verständlich

com·pre·hen·sion Verständnis *n*; Begriffsvermögen *n*, Verstand *m*; *past comprehension* unfassbar, unfasslich

com·pre·hen·sive 1. umfassend; **2.** *a*. *comprehensive school* Br Gesamtschule *f*

com·press zusammendrücken, -pressen;

compressed air Druckluft *f*

com·pres·sion PHYS Verdichtung *f*; TECH Druck *m*

com·prise einschließen, umfassen; bestehen aus

com·pro·mise 1. Kompromiss *m*; **2.** *v/t* bloßstellen, kompromittieren; *v/i* e-n Kompromiss schließen

com·pro·mis·ing kompromittierend; verfänglich

com·pul·sion Zwang *m*

com·pul·sive zwingend, Zwangs...; PSYCH zwanghaft

com·pul·so·ry obligatorisch; Pflicht..., Zwangs...

com·punc·tion Gewissensbisse *pl*; Reue *f*; Bedenken *pl*

com·pute berechnen; schätzen

com·put·er Computer *m*, Rechner *m*

com·put·er-aid·ed computergestützt

computer-con·trolled computergesteuert

com·put·er game Computerspiel *n*

computer graph·ics Computergrafik *f*

com·put·er·ize (sich) auf Computer umstellen; computerisieren; mit Hilfe e-s Computers errechnen *or* zusammenstellen

com·put·er pre·dic·tion Hochrechnung *f*

computer sci·ence Informatik *f*

computer sci·en·tist Informatiker *m*

computer vi·rus EDP Computervirus *m*

com·rade Kamerad *m*; (Partei)Genosse *m*

con¹ → **contra**

con² F reinlegen, betrügen

con·ceal verbergen; verheimlichen

con·cede zugestehen, einräumen

con·ceit Einbildung *f*, Dünkel *m*

con·ceit·ed eingebildet (*of* auf *acc*)

con·cei·va·ble denkbar, begreiflich

con·ceive *v/i* schwanger werden; *v/t* Kind empfangen; sich *et*. vorstellen *or* denken

con·cen·trate (sich) konzentrieren

con·cept Begriff *m*; Gedanke *m*

con·cep·tion Vorstellung *f*, Begriff *m*; BIOL Empfängnis *f*

con·cern 1. Angelegenheit *f*; Sorge *f*; ECON Geschäft *n*, Unternehmen *n*; **2.** betreffen, angehen; beunruhigen

con·cerned besorgt; beteiligt (*in* an *dat*)

con·cern·ing *prp* betreffend, hinsichtlich (*gen*), was … (*acc*) (an)betrifft

con·cert MUS Konzert *n*

con·cert hall Konzerthalle *f*, -saal *m*

con·ces·sion Zugeständnis *n*; Konzession *f*

con·cil·i·a·to·ry versöhnlich, vermittelnd

con·cise kurz, knapp

con·cise·ness Kürze f
con·clude schließen, beenden; *Vertrag etc* abschließen; *et.* folgern, schließen (**from** aus); *to be concluded* Schluss folgt
con·clu·sion (Ab)Schluss *m*, Ende *n*; Abschluss *m* (*of a contract etc*); (Schluss)Folgerung *f*; → *jump*
con·clu·sive schlüssig
con·coct (zusammen)brauen; *fig* aushecken, ausbrüten
con·coc·tion Gebräu *n*; *fig* Erfindung *f*
con·crete[1] konkret
con·crete[2] 1. Beton *m*; 2. Beton...; 3. betonieren
con·cur übereinstimmen
con·cur·rence Zusammentreffen *n*; Übereinstimmung *f*
con·cus·sion MED Gehirnerschütterung *f*
con·demn verurteilen (*a.* JUR); verdammen; für unbrauchbar *or* unbewohnbar *etc* erklären; *condemn to death* JUR zum Tode verurteilen
con·dem·na·tion Verurteilung *f* (*a.* JUR); Verdammung *f*
con·den·sa·tion Kondensation *f*; Zusammenfassung *f*
con·dense kondensieren; zusammenfassen
con·densed milk Kondensmilch *f*
con·dens·er TECH Kondensator *m*
con·de·scend sich herablassen
con·de·scend·ing herablassend, gönnerhaft
con·di·ment Gewürz *n*, Würze *f*
con·di·tion 1. Zustand *m*; (*körperlicher or* Gesundheits)Zustand *m*; SPORT Kondition *f*, Form *f*; Bedingung *f*; *pl* Verhältnisse *pl*, Umstände *pl*; *on condition that* unter der Bedingung, dass; *out of condition* in schlechter Verfassung, in schlechtem Zustand; **2.** bedingen; in Form bringen
con·di·tion·al 1. (*on*) bedingt (durch), abhängig (von); **2.** *a.* **conditional clause** LING Bedingungs-, Konditionalsatz *m*; *a.* **conditional mood** LING Konditional *m*
con·do → *condominium*
con·dole kondolieren (**with** *dat*)
con·do·lence Beileid *n*
con·dom Kondom *n, m*
con·do·min·i·um Eigentumswohnanlage *f*; Eigentumswohnung *f*
con·done verzeihen, vergeben
con·du·cive dienlich, förderlich (**to** *dat*)
con·duct 1. Führung *f*; Verhalten *n*, Betragen *n*; **2.** führen; PHYS leiten; MUS dirigieren; *conducted tour* Führung *f* (**of** durch)

con·duc·tor Führer *m*, Leiter *m*; (*Bus-, Straßenbahn*)Schaffner *m*; RAIL Zugbegleiter *m*; MUS Dirigent *m*; PHYS Leiter *m*; ELECTR Blitzableiter *m*
cone Kegel *m*; GASTR Eistüte *f*; BOT Zapfen *m*
con·fec·tion Konfekt *n*
con·fec·tion·er Konditor *m*
con·fec·tion·e·ry Süßigkeiten *pl*, Süß-, Konditoreiwaren *pl*; Konfekt *n*; Konditorei *f*; Süßwarengeschäft *n*
con·fed·e·ra·cy (Staaten)Bund *m*; *the* **Confederacy** HIST die Konföderation
con·fed·er·ate 1. verbündet; **2.** Verbündete *m*, Bundesgenosse *m*; **3.** (sich) verbünden
con·fed·er·a·tion Bund *m*, Bündnis *n*; (Staaten)Bund *m*
con·fer *v/t Titel etc* verleihen (**on** *dat*); *v/i* sich beraten
con·fe·rence Konferenz *f*
con·fess gestehen; beichten
con·fes·sion Geständnis *n*; REL Beichte *f*
con·fes·sion·al REL Beichtstuhl *m*
con·fes·sor REL Beichtvater *m*
con·fi·dant(e) Vertraute *m* (*f*)
con·fide: *confide s.th. to s.o.* j-m et. anvertrauen; *confide in s.o.* sich j-m anvertrauen
con·fi·dence Vertrauen *n*; Selbstvertrauen *n*
confidence man → *conman*
confidence trickster Trickbetrüger *m*
con·fi·dent überzeugt, zuversichtlich
con·fi·den·tial vertraulich
con·fine begrenzen, beschränken; einsperren; *be confined of* entbunden werden von
con·fine·ment Haft *f*; Beschränkung *f*; MED Entbindung *f*
con·firm bestätigen; bekräftigen; REL konfirmieren, firmen
con·fir·ma·tion Bestätigung *f*; REL Konfirmation *f*, Firmung *f*
con·fis·cate beschlagnahmen
con·fis·ca·tion Beschlagnahme *f*
con·flict 1. Konflikt *m*, Zwiespalt *m*; **2.** im Widerspruch stehen (**with** zu)
con·flict·ing widersprüchlich, zwiespältig
con·form (sich) anpassen (**to** *dat*, an *acc*)
con·found verwirren, durcheinanderbringen
con·front gegenübertreten, -stehen (*dat*); sich stellen (*dat*); konfrontieren
con·fron·ta·tion Konfrontation *f*
con·fuse verwechseln; verwirren
con·fused verwirrt; verlegen; verworren
con·fu·sion Verwirrung *f*; Verlegenheit *f*; Verwechslung *f*

con·geal erstarren (lassen); gerinnen (lassen)

con·gest·ed überfüllt; verstopft

con·ges·tion MED Blutandrang *m*; *a.* ***traffic congestion*** Verkehrsstockung *f*, Verkehrsstörung *f*, Verkehrsstau *m*

con·grat·u·late beglückwünschen, *j-m* gratulieren

con·grat·u·la·tion Glückwunsch *m*; ***congratulations!*** ich gratuliere!, herzlichen Glückwunsch!

con·gre·gate (sich) versammeln

con·gre·ga·tion REL Gemeinde *f*

con·gress Kongress *m*; ***Congress*** PARL der Kongress

Con·gress·man PARL Kongressabgeordnete *m*

Con·gress·wom·an PARL Kongressabgeordnete *f*

con·ic, con·i·cal *esp* TECH konisch, kegelförmig

co·ni·fer BOT Nadelbaum *m*

con·jec·ture 1. Vermutung *f*; **2.** vermuten

con·ju·gal ehelich

con·ju·gate LING konjugieren, beugen

con·ju·ga·tion LING Konjugation *f*, Beugung *f*

con·junc·tion Verbindung *f*; LING Konjunktion *f*, Bindewort *n*

con·junc·ti·vi·tis MED Bindehautentzündung *f*

con·jure zaubern; *Teufel etc* beschwören; ***conjure up*** heraufbeschwören (*a. fig*)

con·jur·er *esp Br* → **conjuror**

con·jur·ing trick Zauberkunststück *n*

con·jur·or Zauberer *m*, Zauberin *f*, Zauberkünstler(in)

con·man Betrüger *m*; Hochstapler *m*

con·nect verbinden; ELECTR anschließen, zuschalten; RAIL, AVIAT *etc* Anschluss haben (***with*** an *acc*)

con·nect·ed verbunden; (logisch) zusammenhängend (*speech etc*); ***be well connected*** gute Beziehungen haben

con·nec·tion, *Br* **con·nex·ion** Verbindung *f*, Anschluss *m* (*a.* ELECTR, RAIL, AVIAT, TEL); Zusammenhang *m*; *mst pl* Beziehungen *pl*, Verbindungen *pl*; Verwandte *pl*

con·quer erobern; (be)siegen

con·quer·or Eroberer *m*

con·quest Eroberung *f* (*a. fig*); erobertes Gebiet

con·science Gewissen *n*

con·sci·en·tious gewissenhaft; Gewissens…

con·sci·en·tious·ness Gewissenhaftigkeit *f*

con·sci·en·tious ob·jec·tor MIL Wehrdienstverweigerer *m*

con·scious MED bei Bewusstsein; bewusst; ***be conscious of*** sich bewusst sein (*gen*)

con·scious·ness Bewusstsein *n* (*a.* MED)

con·script MIL **1.** einberufen; **2.** Wehrpflichtige *m*

con·scrip·tion MIL Einberufung *f*; Wehrpflicht *f*

con·se·crate REL weihen; widmen

con·se·cra·tion REL Weihe *f*

con·sec·u·tive aufeinanderfolgend; fortlaufend

con·sent 1. Zustimmung *f*; **2.** einwilligen, zustimmen

con·se·quence Folge *f*, Konsequenz *f*; Bedeutung *f*

con·se·quent·ly folglich, daher

con·ser·va·tion Erhaltung *f*; Naturschutz *m*; Umweltschutz *m*; ***conservation area*** (Natur)Schutzgebiet *n*

con·ser·va·tion·ist Naturschützer(in); Umweltschützer(in)

con·ser·va·tive 1. erhaltend; konservativ; vorsichtig; **2.** ***Conservative*** POL Konservative *m*, *f*

con·ser·va·to·ry Treibhaus *n*, Gewächshaus *n*; Wintergarten *m*

con·serve erhalten

con·sid·er *v/t* nachdenken über (*acc*); betrachten als, halten für; sich überlegen, erwägen; in Betracht ziehen, berücksichtigen; *v/i* nachdenken, überlegen

con·sid·e·ra·ble ansehnlich, beträchtlich

con·sid·e·ra·bly bedeutend, ziemlich, (sehr) viel

con·sid·e·rate rücksichtsvoll

con·sid·e·ra·tion Erwägung *f*, Überlegung *f*; Berücksichtigung *f*; Rücksicht (-nahme) *f*; ***take into consideration*** in Erwägung *or* in Betracht ziehen

con·sid·er·ing in Anbetracht (der Tatsache, dass)

con·sign ECON Waren zusenden

con·sign·ment ECON (Waren)Sendung *f*; Zusendung *f*

con·sist: ***consist in*** bestehen in (*dat*); ***consist of*** bestehen aus

con·sis·tence, con·sis·ten·cy Konsistenz *f*, Beschaffenheit *f*; Übereinstimmung *f*; Konsequenz *f*

con·sis·tent übereinstimmend, vereinbar (***with*** mit); konsequent; SPORT *etc*: beständig

con·so·la·tion Trost *m*

con·sole trösten

con·sol·i·date festigen; *fig* zusammenschließen, -legen

con·so·nant LING Konsonant *m*, Mitlaut

m

con·spic·u·ous deutlich sichtbar; auffallend

con·spi·ra·cy Verschwörung *f*

con·spi·ra·tor Verschwörer *m*

con·spire sich verschwören

con·sta·ble *Br* Polizist *m*

con·stant konstant, gleichbleibend; (be)ständig, (an)dauernd

con·stant-care pa·tient MED Pflegefall *m*

con·ster·na·tion Bestürzung *f*

con·sti·pat·ed MED verstopft

con·sti·pa·tion MED Verstopfung *f*

con·sti·tu·en·cy POL *Br* Wählerschaft *f*; Wahlkreis *m*

con·sti·tu·ent (wesentlicher) Bestandteil; POL Wähler(in)

con·sti·tute ernennen, einsetzen; bilden, ausmachen

con·sti·tu·tion POL Verfassung *f*; Konstitution *f*, körperliche Verfassung

con·sti·tu·tion·al konstitutionell; POL verfassungsmäßig

con·strained gezwungen, unnatürlich

con·strict zusammenziehen

con·stric·tion Zusammenziehung *f*

con·struct bauen, errichten, konstruieren

con·struc·tion Konstruktion *f*; Bau *m*, Bauwerk *n*; **under construction** im Bau (befindlich)

construction site Baustelle *f*

con·struc·tive konstruktiv

con·struc·tor Erbauer *m*, Konstrukteur *m*

con·sul Konsul *m*

con·su·late Konsulat *n*

consulate gen·e·ral Generalkonsulat *n*

con·sul gen·e·ral Generalkonsul *m*

con·sult *v/t* konsultieren, um Rat fragen; in *e-m Buch* nachschlagen; *v/i* (sich) beraten

con·sul·tant (fachmännischer) Berater; *Br* Facharzt *m*

con·sul·ta·tion Konsultation *f*, Beratung *f*, Rücksprache *f*

con·sult·ing beratend

consulting hours *Br* MED Sprechstunde *f*

consulting room *Br* MED Sprechzimmer *n*

con·sume *v/t Essen etc* zu sich nehmen, verzehren (*a. fig*); verbrauchen, konsumieren; zerstören, vernichten

con·sum·er ECON Verbraucher(in)

consumer so·ci·e·ty Konsumgesellschaft *f*

con·sum·mate 1. vollendet; **2.** vollenden; *Ehe* vollziehen

con·sump·tion Verbrauch *m*

cont ABBR *of* **continued** Forts., Fortsetzung *f*; fortgesetzt

con·tact 1. Berührung *f*; Kontakt *m*; Ansprechpartner(in), Kontaktperson *f* (*a.* MED); **make contacts** Verbindungen anknüpfen *or* herstellen; **2.** sich in Verbindung setzen mit, Kontakt aufnehmen mit

contact lens Kontaktlinse *f*, -schale *f*, Haftschale *f*

con·ta·gious MED ansteckend (*a. fig*)

con·tain enthalten; *fig* zügeln, zurückhalten

con·tain·er Behälter *m*; ECON Container *m*

con·tain·er·ize ECON auf Containerbetrieb umstellen; in Containern transportieren

con·tam·i·nate verunreinigen; infizieren, vergiften; (*a.* radioaktiv) verseuchen; **radioactively contaminated** verstrahlt; **contaminated soil** Altlasten *pl*

con·tam·i·na·tion Verunreinigung *f*; Vergiftung *f*; (*a.* radioaktive) Verseuchung

contd ABBR *of* **continued** (→ **cont**)

con·tem·plate (nachdenklich) betrachten; nachdenken über (*acc*); erwägen, beabsichtigen

con·tem·pla·tion (nachdenkliche) Betrachtung; Nachdenken *n*

con·tem·pla·tive nachdenklich

con·tem·po·ra·ry 1. zeitgenössisch; **2.** Zeitgenosse *m*, Zeitgenossin *f*

con·tempt Verachtung *f*

con·temp·ti·ble verachtenswert

con·temp·tu·ous geringschätzig, verächtlich

con·tend kämpfen, ringen (**for** um; **with** mit)

con·tend·er *esp* SPORT Wettkämpfer(in)

con·tent¹ Gehalt *m*, Aussage *f*, *pl* Inhalt *m*; (**table of**) **contents** Inhaltsverzeichnis *n*

con·tent² 1. zufrieden; **2.** befriedigen; **content o.s.** sich begnügen

con·tent·ed zufrieden

con·tent·ment Zufriedenheit *f*

con·test 1. (Wett)Kampf *m*; Wettbewerb *m*; **2.** sich bewerben um; bestreiten, *a.* JUR anfechten

con·tes·tant Wettkämpfer(in), (Wettkampf)Teilnehmer(in)

con·text Zusammenhang *m*

con·ti·nent Kontinent *m*, Erdteil *m*; **the Continent** *Br* das (europäische) Festland

con·ti·nen·tal kontinental, Kontinental...

con·tin·gen·cy Möglichkeit *f*, Eventualität *f*; **contingency plan** Notplan *m*

con·tin·gent 1. be contingent on abhängen von; **2.** Kontingent *n* (*a.* MIL)

con·tin·u·al fortwährend, unaufhörlich

con·tin·u·a·tion Fortsetzung *f*; Fortbestand *m*, Fortdauer *f*

con·tin·ue *v/t* fortsetzen, fortfahren mit; beibehalten; *to be continued* Fortsetzung folgt; *v/i* fortdauern; andauern, anhalten; fortfahren, weitermachen

con·ti·nu·i·ty Kontinuität *f*

con·tin·u·ous ununterbrochen

continuous form LING Verlaufsform *f*

con·tort verdrehen; verzerren

con·tor·tion Verdrehung *f*; Verzerrung *f*

con·tour Umriss *m*

con·tra wider, gegen

con·tra·band ECON Schmuggelware *f*

con·tra·cep·tion MED Empfängnisverhütung *f*

con·tra·cep·tive MED **1.** empfängnisverhütend; **2.** Verhütungsmittel *n*

con·tract 1. Vertrag *m*; **2.** (sich) zusammenziehen; sich *e-e Krankheit* zuziehen; e-n Vertrag abschließen; sich vertraglich verpflichten

con·trac·tion Zusammenziehung *f*

con·trac·tor *a.* **building contractor** Bauunternehmer *m*

con·tra·dict widersprechen (*dat*)

con·tra·dic·tion Widerspruch *m*

con·tra·dic·to·ry (sich) widersprechend

con·tra·ry 1. entgegengesetzt (**to** *dat*); gegensätzlich; **contrary to expectations** wider Erwarten; **2.** Gegenteil *n*; **on the contrary** im Gegenteil

con·trast 1. Gegensatz *m*; Kontrast *m*; **2.** *v/t* gegenüberstellen, vergleichen; *v/i* sich abheben (**with** von, gegen); im Gegensatz stehen (**with** zu)

con·trib·ute beitragen, beisteuern; spenden (**to** für)

con·tri·bu·tion Beitrag *m*; Spende *f*

con·trib·u·tor Beitragende *m*, *f*; Mitarbeiter(in)

con·trib·u·to·ry beitragend

con·trite zerknirscht

con·trive zustande bringen; es fertig bringen

con·trol 1. Kontrolle *f*, Herrschaft *f*, Macht *f*, Gewalt *f*, Beherrschung *f*; Aufsicht *f*; TECH Steuerung *f*; *mst pl* TECH Steuervorrichtung *f*; **get** (**have, keep**) **under control** unter Kontrolle bringen (haben, halten); **get out of control** außer Kontrolle geraten; **lose control of** die Herrschaft *or* Gewalt *or* Kontrolle verlieren über; **2.** beherrschen, die Kontrolle haben über (*acc*); e-r *Sache* Herr werden, (erfolgreich) bekämpfen; kontrollieren, überwachen; ECON (staatlich) lenken, *Preise* binden; ELECTR, TECH steuern, regeln, regulieren

control desk ELECTR Schalt-, Steuerpult *n*

control pan·el ELECTR Schalttafel *f*

control tow·er AVIAT Kontrollturm *m*, Tower *m*

con·tro·ver·sial umstritten

con·tro·ver·sy Kontroverse *f*, Streit *m*

con·tuse MED sich *et.* prellen *or* quetschen

con·tu·sion MED Prellung *f*, Quetschung *f*

con·va·lesce gesund werden, genesen

con·va·les·cence Rekonvaleszenz *f*, Genesung *f*

con·va·les·cent 1. genesend; **2.** Rekonvaleszent(in), Genesende *m*, *f*

con·vene (sich) versammeln; zusammenkommen; *Versammlung* einberufen

con·ve·ni·ence Annehmlichkeit *f*, Bequemlichkeit *f*; *Br* Toilette *f*; **all** (**modern**) **conveniences** aller Komfort; **at your earliest convenience** möglichst bald

con·ve·ni·ent bequem; günstig; passend

con·vent REL (Nonnen)Kloster *n*

con·ven·tion Zusammenkunft *f*, Tagung *f*, Versammlung *f*; Abkommen *n*; Konvention *f*, Sitte *f*

con·ven·tion·al herkömmlich, konventionell

con·verge konvergieren; zusammenlaufen, -strömen

con·ver·sa·tion Gespräch *n*, Unterhaltung *f*

con·ver·sa·tion·al Unterhaltungs…; **conversational English** Umgangsenglisch *n*

con·verse sich unterhalten

con·ver·sion Umwandlung *f*, Verwandlung *f*; Umbau *m*; Umstellung *f* (**to** auf *acc*); REL Bekehrung *f*, Übertritt *m*; MATH Umrechnung *f*

conversion ta·ble Umrechnungstabelle *f*

con·vert (sich) umwandeln *or* verwandeln; umbauen (**into** zu); umstellen (**to** auf *acc*); REL *etc* (sich) bekehren; MATH umrechnen

con·vert·er ELECTR Umformer *m*

con·vert·i·ble 1. umwandelbar, verwandelbar; ECON konvertierbar; **2.** MOT Kabrio(lett) *n*

con·vey befördern, transportieren, bringen; überbringen, übermitteln; *Ideen etc* mitteilen, vermitteln

con·vey·ance Beförderung *f*, Transport *m*; Übermittlung *f*; Verkehrsmittel *n*

con·vey·or belt TECH Förderband *n*

con·vict 1. Verurteilte *m*, *f*; Strafgefangene *m*, *f*; **2.** JUR (**of**) überführen (*gen*); verurteilen (wegen)

con·vic·tion Überzeugung *f*; JUR Verurteilung *f*

con·vince überzeugen
con·voy 1. MAR Geleitzug *m*, Konvoi *m*; MOT (Wagen)Kolonne *f*; (Geleit-) Schutz *m*; **2.** Geleitschutz geben (*dat*), eskortieren
con·vul·sion MED Zuckung *f*, Krampf *m*
con·vul·sive MED krampfhaft, krampfartig, konvulsiv
coo ZO gurren (*a. fig*)
cook 1. Koch *m*; Köchin *f*; **2.** kochen; F *Bericht etc* frisieren; **cook up** F sich ausdenken, erfinden
cook·book Kochbuch *n*
cook·er Br Ofen *m*, Herd *m*
cook·e·ry Kochen *n*; Kochkunst *f*
cook·e·ry book Br Kochbuch *n*
cook·ie (süßer) Keks, Plätzchen *n*
cook·ing GASTR Küche *f*
cook·y → **cookie**
cool 1. kühl; *fig* kalt(blütig), gelassen; abweisend; gleichgültig; F klasse, prima, cool; **2.** Kühle *f*; F (Selbst)Beherrschung *f*; **3.** (sich) abkühlen; **cool down, cool off** sich beruhigen
coon F ZO Waschbär *m*
coop 1. Hühnerstall *m*; **2.** **coop up, coop in** einsperren, einpferchen
co-op F Co-op *m*
co·op·e·rate zusammenarbeiten; mitwirken, helfen
co·op·e·ra·tion Zusammenarbeit *f*; Mitwirkung *f*, Hilfe *f*
co·op·e·ra·tive 1. zusammenarbeitend; kooperativ, hilfsbereit; ECON Gemeinschafts..., Genossenschafts...; **2.** *a.* **cooperative society** Genossenschaft *f*; Co-op *m*, Konsumverein *m*; *a.* **cooperative store** Co-op *m*, Konsumladen *m*
co·or·di·nate 1. koordinieren, aufeinander abstimmen; **2.** koordiniert, gleichgeordnet
co·or·di·na·tion Koordinierung *f*, Koordination *f*; harmonisches Zusammenspiel
cop F Bulle *m*
cope: cope with gewachsen sein (*dat*), fertigwerden mit
cop·i·er Kopiergerät *n*, Kopierer *m*
co·pi·ous reich(lich); weitschweifig
cop·per MIN Kupfer *n*; Kupfermünze *f*; **2.** kupfern, Kupfer...
cop·pice, copse Gehölz *n*
cop·y 1. Kopie *f*; Abschrift *f*; Nachbildung *f*; Durchschlag *m*; Exemplar *n*; (*Zeitungs*)Nummer *f*; PRINT Satzvorlage *f*; **fair copy** Reinschrift *f*; **2.** kopieren; abschreiben, e-e Kopie anfertigen von; EDP *Daten* übertragen; nachbilden; nachahmen

cop·y·book Schreibheft *n*
cop·y·ing Kopier...
cop·y·right Urheberrecht *n*, Copyright *n*
cor·al ZO Koralle *f*
cord 1. Schnur *f* (*a.* ELECTR), Strick *m*; Kordsamt *m*; **2.** ver-, zuschnüren
cor·di·al[1] Fruchtsaftkonzentrat *n*; MED Stärkungsmittel *n*
cor·di·al[2] herzlich
cor·di·al·i·ty Herzlichkeit *f*
cord·less schnurlos
cordless phone schnurloses Telefon
cor·don 1. Kordon *m*, Postenkette *f*; **2.** **cordon off** abriegeln, absperren
cor·du·roy Kord *m*; (**a pair of**) **corduroys** (e-e) Kordhose
core 1. Kerngehäuse *n*; Kern *m*, *fig a.* das Innerste; **2.** entkernen
core time ECON Kernzeit *f*
cork 1. Kork(en) *m*; **2.** *a.* **cork up** zu-, verkorken
cork·screw Korkenzieher *m*
corn[1] **1.** Korn *n*, Getreide *n*; *a.* **Indian corn** Mais *m*; **2.** pökeln
corn[2] MED Hühnerauge *n*
cor·ner 1. Ecke *f*; Winkel *m*; *esp* MOT Kurve *f*; *soccer*: Eckball *m*, Ecke *f*; *fig* schwierige Lage, Klemme *f*; **2.** Eck...; **3.** in die Ecke (*fig* Enge) treiben
corner kick *soccer*: Eckball *m*, Eckstoß *m*
corner shop Br Tante-Emma-Laden *m*
cor·net MUS Kornett *n*; Br GASTR Eistüte *f*
corn·flakes Cornflakes *pl*
cor·nice ARCH Gesims *n*, Sims *m*
cor·o·na·ry 1. ANAT Koronar...; **2.** F MED Herzinfarkt *m*
cor·o·na·tion Krönung *f*
cor·o·net Adelskrone *f*
cor·po·ral MIL Unteroffizier *m*
cor·po·ral **pun·ish·ment** körperliche Züchtigung
cor·po·rate gemeinsam; Firmen...
cor·po·ra·tion JUR Körperschaft *f*; Stadtverwaltung *f*; ECON (Aktien)Gesellschaft *f*
corpse Leichnam *m*, Leiche *f*
cor·pu·lent beleibt
cor·ral 1. Korral *m*, Hürde *f*, Pferch *m*; **2.** *Vieh* in e-n Pferch treiben
cor·rect 1. korrekt, richtig, *a.* genau (*time*); **2.** korrigieren, verbessern, berichtigen
cor·rec·tion Korrektur *f*, Verbess(e)rung *f*; Bestrafung *f*
cor·rect·ness Richtigkeit *f*
cor·re·spond (**with, to**) entsprechen (*dat*), übereinstimmen (mit); korrespondieren (**with** mit)
cor·re·spon·dence Übereinstimmung *f*;

C

Korrespondenz f, Briefwechsel m
cor·re·spon·dence course Fernkurs m
cor·re·spon·dent 1. entsprechend; **2.**
Briefpartner(in); Korrespondent(in)
cor·re·spon·ding entsprechend
cor·ri·dor Korridor m, Gang m
cor·rob·o·rate bekräftigen, bestätigen
cor·rode zerfressen; CHEM korrodieren;
rosten
cor·ro·sion CHEM Korrosion f; Rost m
cor·ro·sive CHEM ätzend; *fig* nagend, zer-
setzend
cor·ru·gat·ed i·ron Wellblech n
cor·rupt 1. korrupt, bestechlich, käuflich;
moralisch verdorben; **2.** bestechen; *moralisch* verderben
cor·rupt·i·ble korrupt, bestechlich, käuflich
cor·rup·tion Verdorbenheit f; Unredlichkeit f; Korruption f; Bestechlichkeit f;
Bestechung f
cor·set Korsett n
cos·met·ic 1. kosmetisch, Schönheits...;
2. kosmetisches Mittel, Schönheitsmittel
n
cos·me·ti·cian Kosmetiker(in)
cos·mo·naut Kosmonaut m, (Welt-)
Raumfahrer m
cos·mo·pol·i·tan 1. kosmopolitisch; **2.**
Weltbürger(in)
cost 1. Preis m; Kosten *pl*; Schaden m; **2.**
kosten
cost·ly kostspielig; teuer erkauft
cost of liv·ing Lebenshaltungskosten *pl*
cos·tume Kostüm n, Kleidung f, Tracht f
costume jew·el·(le)ry Modeschmuck m
co·sy *Br* → **cozy**
cot Feldbett n; *Br* Kinderbett n
cot·tage Cottage n, (kleines) Landhaus;
Ferienhaus n, Ferienhäuschen n
cot·ton 1. Baumwolle f; Baumwollstoff m;
(Baumwoll)Garn n, (Baumwoll-) Zwirn
m; (Verband)Watte f; **2.** baumwollen,
Baumwoll...
cot·ton·wood BOT e-e amer. Pappel
cot·ton wool *Br* (Verband)Watte f
couch Couch f, Sofa n; Liege f
cou·chette RAIL Liegewagenplatz m; *a.*
couchette coach Liegewagen m
cou·gar ZO Puma m
cough 1. Husten m; **2.** husten
coun·cil Rat m, Ratsversammlung f
council house *Br* gemeindeeigenes
Wohnhaus
coun·cil·(l)or Ratsmitglied n, Stadtrat m,
Stadträtin f
coun·sel 1. Beratung f; Rat(schlag) m; *Br*
JUR (Rechts)Anwalt m; **counsel for the
defense** (*Br* **defence**) Verteidiger m;

counsel for the prosecution Anklage-
vertreter m; **2.** *j-m* raten; zu *et.* raten;
coun·seling cen·ter (*Br* **counselling
centre**) Beratungsstelle f
coun·sel·(l)or (*Berufs- etc*)Berater(in);
JUR (Rechts)Anwalt m
count¹ Graf m
count² 1. Zählung f; JUR Anklagepunkt
m; **2.** *v/t* (ab-, auf-, aus-, nach-, zusammen)zählen; aus-, berechnen; *fig* halten
für, betrachten als; *v/i* zählen; gelten;
count ten bis zehn zählen; **count down**
Geld hinzählen; den Count-down durchführen für, letzte (Start)Vorbereitungen
treffen für; **count on** zählen auf (*acc*),
sich verlassen auf (*acc*), sicher rechnen
mit
count·down Count-down m, n, letzte
(Start)Vorbereitungen *pl*
coun·te·nance Gesichtsausdruck m; Fassung f, Haltung f
count·er¹ TECH Zähler m; *Br* Spielmarke f
coun·ter² Ladentisch m; Theke f; (Bank-,
Post)Schalter m
coun·ter³ 1. (ent)gegen, Gegen...; **2.** entgegentreten (*dat*), entgegnen (*dat*), bekämpfen; abwehren
coun·ter·act entgegenwirken (*dat*); neutralisieren
coun·ter·bal·ance 1. Gegengewicht n; **2.**
ein Gegengewicht bilden zu, ausgleichen
coun·ter·clock·wise entgegen dem Uhrzeigersinn
coun·ter·es·pi·o·nage Spionageabwehr f
coun·ter·feit 1. falsch, gefälscht; **2.** Fälschung f; **3.** *Geld, Unterschrift etc* fälschen
counterfeit mon·ey Falschgeld n
coun·ter·foil Kontrollabschnitt m
coun·ter·mand *Befehl etc* widerrufen;
Ware abbestellen
coun·ter·pane Tagesdecke f
coun·ter·part Gegenstück n; genaue Entsprechung
coun·ter·sign gegenzeichnen
coun·tess Gräfin f
count·less zahllos
coun·try 1. Land n, Staat m; Gegend f,
Landschaft f; **in the country** auf dem
Lande; **2.** Land..., ländlich
coun·try·man Landbewohner m; Bauer
m; *a.* **fellow countryman** Landsmann m
coun·try road Landstraße f
coun·try·side (ländliche) Gegend; Landschaft f
coun·try·wom·an Landbewohnerin f;
Bäuerin f; *a.* **fellow countrywoman**
Landsmännin f
coun·ty (Land)Kreis m; *Br* Grafschaft f

county seat Kreis(haupt)stadt *f*
county town *Br* Grafschaftshauptstadt *f*
coup Coup *m*; Putsch *m*
cou·ple 1. Paar *n*; *a couple of* F ein paar; **2.** (zusammen)koppeln; TECH kuppeln; ZO (sich) paaren
cou·pon Gutschein *m*; Kupon *m*, Bestellzettel *m*
cour·age Mut *m*
cou·ra·geous mutig, beherzt
cou·ri·er Kurier *m*, Eilbote *m*; Reiseleiter *m*
course AVIAT, MAR Kurs *m* (*a. fig*); SPORT (*Renn*)Bahn *f*, (*Renn*)Strecke *f*, (*Golf*)-Platz *m*; Verlauf *m*; GASTR Gang *m*; Reihe *f*, Zyklus *m*; Kurs *m*, Lehrgang *m*; *of course* natürlich, selbstverständlich; *the course of events* der Gang der Ereignisse, der Lauf der Dinge
court 1. Hof *m*; kleiner Platz; SPORT Platz *m*, (Spiel)Feld *n*; JUR Gericht *n*, Gerichtshof *m*; *go to court* JUR prozessieren; *take s.o. to court* JUR gegen j-n prozessieren; j-m den Prozess machen; **2.** *j-m* den Hof machen; werben um
cour·te·ous höflich
cour·te·sy Höflichkeit *f*; *by courtesy of* mit freundlicher Genehmigung von (*or gen*)
court·house Gerichtsgebäude *n*
court·ier Höfling *m*
court·ly höfisch; höflich
court mar·tial MIL Kriegsgericht *n*
court·mar·tial MIL vor ein Kriegsgericht stellen
court·room Gerichtssaal *m*
court·ship Werben *n*
court·yard Hof *m*
cous·in Cousin *m*, Vetter *m*; Cousine *f*, Kusine *f*
cove kleine Bucht
cov·er 1. Decke *f*; Deckel *m*; (Buch-)Deckel *m*, Einband *m*; Umschlag *m*; Titelseite *f*; Hülle *f*; Überzug *m*, Bezug *m*; Schutzhaube *f*, Schutzplatte *f*; Abdeckhaube *f*; Briefumschlag *m*; GASTR Gedeck *n*; Deckung *f*; Schutz *m*; *fig* Tarnung *f*; *take cover* in Deckung gehen; *under plain cover* in neutralem Umschlag; *under separate cover* mit getrennter Post; **2.** (be-, zu)decken; einschlagen, einwickeln; verbergen; decken, schützen; ECON (ab)decken; versichern; *Thema* erschöpfend behandeln; *radio*, TV berichten über (*acc*); sich über *e-e Fläche etc* erstrecken; *Strecke* zurücklegen; SPORT *Gegenspieler* decken; j-n beschatten; *cover up* ab-, zudecken; *fig* verheimlichen, vertuschen; *cover up for*

s.o. j-n decken
cov·er·age Berichterstattung *f* (*of* über *acc*)
cov·er girl Covergirl *n*, Titelblattmädchen *n*
cov·er·ing Decke *f*; Überzug *m*; Hülle *f*; (*Fußboden*)Belag *m*
cov·er sto·ry Titelgeschichte *f*
cow[1] ZO Kuh *f*
cow[2] einschüchtern
cow·ard 1. feig(e); **2.** Feigling *m*
cow·ard·ice Feigheit *f*
cow·ard·ly feig(e)
cow·boy Cowboy *m*
cow·er kauern; sich ducken
cow·herd Kuhhirt *m*
cow·hide Rind(s)leder *n*
cow·house Kuhstall *m*
cowl Mönchskutte *f*; Kapuze *f*; TECH Schornsteinkappe *f*
cow·shed Kuhstall *m*
cow·slip BOT Schlüsselblume *f*; Sumpfdotterblume *f*
cox, cox·swain Bootsführer *m*; *rowing:* Steuermann *m*
coy schüchtern, scheu
coy·ote ZO Kojote *m*, Präriewolf *m*
co·zy 1. behaglich, gemütlich; **2.** → *egg cosy*, *tea cosy*
CPU ABBR *of central processing unit* EDP Zentraleinheit *f*
crab ZO Krabbe *f*, Taschenkrebs *m*
crack 1. Knall *m*; Sprung *m*, Riss *m*; Spalt(e *f*) *m*, Ritze *f*; (heftiger) Schlag; **2.** erstklassig; **3.** *v/i* krachen, knallen, knacken; (zer)springen; überschnappen (*voice*); *a. crack up* zusammenbrechen; F *crack up* überschnappen; *get cracking* F loslegen; *v/t* knallen mit (*Peitsche*), knacken mit (*Fingern*); zerbrechen; *Nuss*, F *Kode, Safe etc* knacken; *crack a joke* e-n Witz reißen
crack·er GASTR Cracker *m*, Kräcker *m*; Schwär·mer *m*, Knallfrosch *m*, Knallbonbon *m, n*
crack·le knattern, knistern, prasseln
cra·dle 1. Wiege *f*; **2.** wiegen; betten
craft[1] Boot(e *pl*) *n*; Schiff(e *pl*) *n*; Flugzeug(e *pl*) *n*; (Welt)Raumfahrzeug(e *pl*) *n*
craft[2] Handwerk *n*, Gewerbe *n*; Schlauheit *f*, List *f*
crafts·man (Kunst)Handwerker *m*
craft·y gerissen, listig, schlau
crag Klippe *f*, Felsenspitze *f*
cram *v/t* (voll)stopfen; nudeln, mästen; mit *j-m* pauken; *v/i* pauken, büffeln (*for* für)
cramp 1. MED Krampf *m*; TECH Klammer

f; *fig* Fessel *f*; **2.** einengen, hemmen

cran·ber·ry BOT Preiselbeere *f*

crane[1] TECH Kran *m*

crane[2] **1.** ZO Kranich *m*; **2.** den Hals recken; **crane one's neck** sich den Hals verrenken (**for** nach)

crank 1. TECH Kurbel *f*; TECH Schwengel *m*; F Spinner *m*, komischer Kauz; **2.** (an)kurbeln

crank·shaft TECH Kurbelwelle *f*

crank·y wack(e)lig; verschroben; schlecht gelaunt

cran·ny Riss *m*, Ritze *f*

crape Krepp *m*, Flor *m*

crash 1. Krach *m*, Krachen *n*; MOT Unfall *m*, Zusammenstoß *m*; AVIAT Absturz *m*; ECON Zusammenbruch *m*, (Börsen)-Krach *m*; **2.** *v/t* zertrümmern; e-n Unfall haben mit; AVIAT abstürzen mit; *v/i* krachend einstürzen, zusammenkrachen; *esp* ECON zusammenbrechen; krachen (**against, into** gegen); MOT zusammenstoßen, verunglücken; AVIAT abstürzen; **3.** Schnell..., Sofort...

crash bar·ri·er MOT Leitplanke *f*

crash course Schnell-, Intensivkurs *m*

crash di·et radikale Schlankheitskur

crash hel·met Sturzhelm *m*

crash-land AVIAT e-e Bruchlandung machen (mit)

crash land·ing AVIAT Bruchlandung *f*

crate (Latten)Kiste *f*

cra·ter Krater *m*; Trichter *m*

crave sich sehnen (**for, after** nach)

crav·ing heftiges Verlangen

craw·fish → **crayfish**

crawl 1. Kriechen *n*; **2.** kriechen; krabbeln; kribbeln; wimmeln (**with** von); *swimming*: kraulen; **it makes my skin crawl** F mir läuft e-e Gänsehaut über den Rücken

cray·fish ZO Flusskrebs *m*

cray·on Zeichen-, Buntstift *m*

craze Verrücktheit *f*, F Fimmel *m*; **be the craze** Mode sein

cra·zy verrückt (**about** nach)

creak knarren, quietschen

cream 1. GASTR Rahm *m*, Sahne *f*; Creme *f*; *fig* Auslese *f*, Elite *f*; **2.** creme(farben)

cream·y sahnig; weich

crease 1. (Bügel)Falte *f*; **2.** (zer)knittern

cre·ate (er)schaffen; hervorrufen; verursachen

cre·a·tion Schöpfung *f*

cre·a·tive schöpferisch

cre·a·tor Schöpfer *m*

crea·ture Geschöpf *n*; Kreatur *f*

crèche (Kinder)Krippe *f*; (Weihnachts)-Krippe *f*

cre·den·tials Beglaubigungsschreiben *n*; Referenzen *pl*; Zeugnis *n*; Ausweis *m*, Ausweispapiere *pl*

cred·i·ble glaubwürdig

cred·it 1. Glaube(n) *m*; Ruf *m*, Ansehen *n*; Verdienst *n*; ECON Kredit *m*; Guthaben *n*; **credit (side)** Kredit(seite *f*) *n*, Haben *n*; **on credit** auf Kredit; **2.** *j-m* glauben; *j-m* trauen; ECON gutschreiben; **credit s.o. with s.th.** j-m et. zutrauen; j-m et. zuschreiben

cred·i·ta·ble achtbar, ehrenvoll (**to** für)

cred·it card ECON Kreditkarte *f*

cred·i·tor ECON Gläubiger *m*

cred·its *film*: Vorspann *m*, Nachspann *m*

cred·it·wor·thy ECON kreditwürdig

cred·u·lous leichtgläubig

creed REL Glaubensbekenntnis *n*

creek Bach *m*; *Br* kleine Bucht

creep kriechen; schleichen (*a. fig*); **creep in** (sich) hinein- *or* hereinschleichen; sich einschleichen (*mistake etc*); **it makes my flesh creep** mir läuft e-e Gänsehaut über den Rücken

creep·er BOT Kriech-, Kletterpflanze *f*

creep·y unheimlich

cre·mate verbrennen, einäschern

cres·cent Halbmond *m*

cress BOT Kresse *f*

crest ZO Haube *f*, Büschel *n*; (*Hahnen*-)Kamm *m*; Bergrücken *m*, Kamm *m*; (*Wellen*)Kamm *m*; Federbusch *m*; **family crest** Familienwappen *n*

crest·fal·len niedergeschlagen

cre·vasse GEOL (Gletscher)Spalte *f*

crev·ice GEOL Riss *m*, Spalte *f*

crew AVIAT, MAR Besatzung *f*, Crew *f*, MAR Mannschaft *f*

crib 1. (Futter)Krippe *f*; Kinderbettchen *n*; *esp Br* (Weihnachts)Krippe *f*; F PED Spickzettel *m*; **2.** F abschreiben, spicken

crick: **a crick in one's back** (**neck**) ein steifer Rücken (Hals)

crick·et[1] ZO Grille *f*

crick·et[2] SPORT Kricket *n*

crime JUR Verbrechen *n*; *coll* Verbrechen *pl*

crime nov·el Kriminalroman *m*

crim·i·nal 1. kriminell; Kriminal..., Straf...; **2.** Verbrecher(in), Kriminelle *m, f*

crimp kräuseln

crim·son karmesinrot; puterrot

cringe sich ducken

crin·kle 1. Falte *f*, Fältchen *n*; **2.** (sich) kräuseln; knittern

crip·ple 1. Krüppel *m*; **2.** zum Krüppel machen; *fig* lähmen

cri·sis Krise *f*

crisp knusp(e)rig, mürbe; frisch, knackig (*vegetable*); scharf, frisch (*air*); kraus (*hair*)
crisp·bread Knäckebrot *n*
crisps *a.* *potato crisps* *Br* (Kartoffel)-Chips *pl*
criss-cross 1. Netz *n* sich schneidender Linien; **2.** kreuz und quer ziehen durch; kreuz und quer (ver)laufen
cri·te·ri·on Kriterium *n*
crit·ic Kritiker(in)
crit·i·cal kritisch; bedenklich
crit·i·cis·m Kritik *f* (*of* an *dat*)
crit·i·cize kritisieren; kritisch beurteilen; tadeln
cri·tique Kritik *f*, Besprechung *f*, Rezension *f*
croak zo krächzen; quaken (*both a. fig*)
cro·chet 1. Häkelei *f*; Häkelarbeit *f*; **2.** häkeln
crock·e·ry Geschirr *n*
croc·o·dile zo Krokodil *n*
cro·ny F alter Freund
crook 1. Krümmung *f*; Hirtenstab *m*; F Gauner *m*; **2.** (sich) krümmen *or* biegen
crook·ed gekrümmt krumm; F unehrlich, betrügerisch
croon schmachtend singen; summen
croon·er Schnulzensänger(in)
crop 1. AGR (Feld)Frucht *f*; Ernte *f*; zo Kropf *m*; kurzer Haarschnitt; kurz geschnittenes Haar; **2.** zo abfressen, abweiden; *Haar* kurz schneiden; *crop up fig* plötzlich auftauchen
cross 1. Kreuz *n* (*a. fig*); BIOL Kreuzung *f*; *soccer*: Flanke *f*; **2.** böse, ärgerlich; **3.** (sich) kreuzen; *Straße* überqueren; *Plan etc* durchkreuzen; BIOL kreuzen; *cross off, cross out* ausstreichen, durchstreichen; *cross o.s.* sich bekreuzigen; *cross one's arms* die Arme verschränken; *cross one's legs* die Beine übereinanderschlagen; *keep one's fingers crossed* den Daumen drücken
cross·bar SPORT Tor-, Querlatte *f*
cross·breed Mischling *m*, Kreuzung *f*
cross-coun·try Querfeldein..., Gelände...; *cross-country skiing* Skilanglauf *m*
cross-ex·am·i·na·tion JUR Kreuzverhör *n*
cross-ex·am·ine JUR ins Kreuzverhör nehmen
cross-eyed: *be cross-eyed* schielen
cross·ing (*Straßen- etc*)Kreuzung *f*; Straßenübergang *m*; *Br* Fußgängerübergang *m*; MAR Überfahrt *f*
cross·road Querstraße *f*
cross·roads (Straßen)Kreuzung *f*; *fig* Scheideweg *m*

cross-sec·tion Querschnitt *m*
cross·walk Fußgängerüberweg *m*
cross·wise kreuzweise
cross·word (**puz·zle**) Kreuzworträtsel *n*
crotch ANAT Schritt *m*
crotch·et MUS *Br* Viertelnote *f*
crouch 1. sich ducken; **2.** Hockstellung *f*
crow 1. zo Krähe *f*; Krähen *n*; **2.** krähen
crow·bar TECH Brecheisen *n*
crowd 1. (Menschen)Menge *f*; Masse *f*; Haufen *m*; **2.** sich drängen; *Straßen etc* bevölkern; vollstopfen
crowd·ed überfüllt, voll
crown 1. Krone *f*; **2.** krönen; *Zahn* überkronen; *to crown it all* zu allem Überfluss
cru·cial entscheidend, kritisch
cru·ci·fix REL Kruzifix *n*
cru·ci·fix·ion REL Kreuzigung *f*
cru·ci·fy REL kreuzigen
crude roh, unbearbeitet; *fig* roh, grob
crude (oil) Rohöl *n*
cru·el grausam; roh, gefühllos
cru·el·ty Grausamkeit *f*; *cruelty to animals* Tierquälerei *f*; *society for the prevention of cruelty to animals* Tierschutzverein *m*; *cruelty to children* Kindesmisshandlung *f*
cru·et Essig-, Ölfläschchen *n*
cruise 1. Kreuzfahrt *f*, Seereise *f*; **2.** kreuzen, e-e Kreuzfahrt *or* Seereise machen; AVIAT, MOT mit Reisegeschwindigkeit fliegen *or* fahren
cruise mis·sile MIL Marschflugkörper *m*
cruis·er Kreuzfahrtschiff *n*; MIL MAR Kreuzer *m*; (Funk)Streifenwagen *m*
crumb Krume *f*, Krümel *m*
crum·ble zerkrümeln, zerbröckeln
crum·ple *v/t* zerknittern; *v/i* knittern; zusammengedrückt werden
crumple zone MOT Knautschzone *f*
crunch geräuschvoll (zer)kauen; knirschen
cru·sade HIST Kreuzzug *m* (*a. fig*)
crush 1. Gedränge *n*; *have a crush on s.o.* für j-n schwärmen, F in j-n verknallt sein; **2.** *v/t* zerquetschen, zermalmen, zerdrücken; TECH zerkleinern, zermahlen; auspressen; *fig* nieder-, zerschmettern, vernichten; *v/i* sich drängen
crush bar·ri·er Barriere *f*, Absperrung *f*
crust (Brot)Kruste *f*, (Brot)Rinde *f*
crus·ta·cean zo Krebs-, Krusten-, Schalentier *n*
crust·y krustig
crutch Krücke *f*
cry 1. Schrei *m*, Ruf *m*; Geschrei *n*; Weinen *n*; **2.** schreien, rufen (*for* nach); weinen; heulen, jammern

crypt Gruft *f*, Krypta *f*
crys·tal Kristall *m*; Uhrglas *n*
crys·tal·line kristallen
crys·tal·lize kristallisieren
cub ZO Junge *n*
cube Würfel *m* (*a.* MATH); PHOT Blitzwürfel *m*; MATH Kubikzahl *f*
cube root MATH Kubikwurzel *f*
cu·bic, cu·bi·cal würfelförmig; kubisch; Kubik...
cu·bi·cle Kabine *f*
cuck·oo ZO Kuckuck *m*
cu·cum·ber BOT Gurke *f*; (*as*) *cool as a cucumber* F eiskalt, kühl und gelassen
cud AGR wiedergekäutes Futter; *chew the cud* wiederkäuen; *fig* überlegen
cud·dle *v/t* an sich drücken; schmusen mit; *v/i: cuddle up* sich kuscheln *or* schmiegen (*to* an *acc*)
cud·gel 1. Knüppel *m*; **2.** prügeln
cue[1] THEA *etc* Stichwort *n* (*a. fig*); *fig* Wink *m*
cue[2] *billiards*: Queue *n*
cuff[1] Manschette *f*; (Hosen-, *Br* Ärmel-) Aufschlag *m*
cuff[2] **1.** Klaps *m*; **2.** *j-m* e-n Klaps geben
cuff link Manschettenknopf *m*
cui·sine GASTR Küche *f*
cul·mi·nate gipfeln (*in* in *dat*)
cu·lottes (*a pair of* ein) Hosenrock *m*
cul·prit Schuldige *m*, *f*, Täter(in)
cul·ti·vate AGR anbauen, bebauen; kultivieren; *Freundschaft etc* pflegen
cul·ti·vat·ed AGR bebaut; *fig* gebildet, kultiviert
cul·ti·va·tion AGR Kultivierung *f*, Anbau *m*; *fig* Pflege *f*
cul·tu·ral kulturell; Kultur...
cul·ture Kultur *f* (*a.* BIOL); ZO Zucht *f*
cul·tured kultiviert; gezüchtet; Zucht...
cum·ber·some lästig, hinderlich; klobig
cu·mu·la·tive sich (an)häufend, anwachsend; Zusatz...
cun·ning 1. schlau, listig; **2.** List *f*, Schlauheit *f*
cup 1. Tasse *f*; Becher *m*; Schale *f*; Kelch *m*; SPORT Cup *m*, Pokal *m*; **2.** *die Hand* hohl machen; *she cupped her chin in her hand* sie stützte das Kinn in die Hand
cup·board (Geschirr-, Speise-, *Br a.* Wäsche-, Kleider)Schrank *m*
cup·board bed Schrankbett *n*
cup fi·nal SPORT Pokalendspiel *n*
cu·po·la ARCH Kuppel *f*
cup tie SPORT Pokalspiel *n*
cup win·ner SPORT Pokalsieger *m*
cur Köter *m*; Schurke *m*
cu·ra·ble MED heilbar

cu·rate REL Hilfsgeistliche *m*
cu·ra·tive heilkräftig; *curative power* Heilkraft *f*
curb 1. Kandare *f* (*a. fig*); Bordstein *m*; **2.** an die Kandare legen (*a. fig*); *fig* zügeln
curd *a. pl* Dickmilch *f*, Quark *m*
cur·dle *v/t* Milch gerinnen lassen; *v/i* gerinnen, dick werden; *the sight made my blood curdle* bei dem Anblick erstarrte mir das Blut in den Adern
cure 1. MED Kur *f*; (Heil)Mittel *n*; Heilung *f*; **2.** MED heilen; GASTR pökeln; räuchern; trocknen
cur·few MIL Ausgangsverbot *n*, -sperre *f*
cu·ri·o Rarität *f*
cu·ri·os·i·ty Neugier *f*; Rarität *f*
cu·ri·ous neugierig; wissbegierig; seltsam, merkwürdig
curl 1. Locke *f*; **2.** (sich) kräuseln *or* locken
curl·er Lockenwickler *m*
curl·y gekräuselt; gelockt, lockig
cur·rant BOT Johannisbeere *f*; GASTR Korinthe *f*
cur·ren·cy ECON Währung *f*; *foreign currency* Devisen *pl*
cur·rent 1. laufend; gegenwärtig, aktuell; üblich, gebräuchlich; *current events* Tagesereignisse *pl*; **2.** Strömung *f*, Strom *m* (*both a. fig*); ELECTR Strom *m*
current ac·count *Br* ECON Girokonto *n*
cur·ric·u·lum Lehr-, Stundenplan *m*
curriculum vi·tae Lebenslauf *m*
cur·ry[1] GASTR Curry *m, n*
cur·ry[2] *Pferd* striegeln
curse 1. Fluch *m*, Verwünschung *f*; **2.** (ver)fluchen, verwünschen
curs·ed verflucht
cur·sor EDP Cursor *m*
cur·so·ry flüchtig, oberflächlich
curt knapp; barsch, schroff
cur·tail *Ausgaben etc* kürzen; *Rechte* beschneiden
cur·tain 1. Vorhang *m*, Gardine *f*; *draw the curtains* die Vorhänge auf- *or* zuziehen; **2.** *curtain off* mit Vorhängen abteilen
curt·s(e)y 1. Knicks *m*; **2.** knicksen (*to* vor *dat*)
cur·va·ture Krümmung *f*
curve 1. Kurve *f*; Krümmung *f*, Biegung *f*; **2.** (sich) krümmen *or* biegen
cush·ion 1. Kissen *n*, Polster *n*; **2.** polstern; *Stoß etc* dämpfen
cuss 1. Fluch *m*; **2.** (ver)fluchen
cus·tard Eiercreme *f*, Vanillesoße *f*
cus·to·dy JUR Haft *f*; Sorgerecht *n*
cus·tom Brauch *m*, Gewohnheit *f*; ECON Kundschaft *f*
cus·tom·a·ry üblich

cus·tom-built nach Kundenangaben gefertigt

cus·tom·er Kunde *m*, Kundin *f*, Auftraggeber(in)

cus·tom house Zollamt *n*

cus·tom-made maßgefertigt, Maß...

cus·toms Zoll *m*

customs clear·ance Zollabfertigung *f*

customs of·fi·cer, customs of·fi·cial Zollbeamte *m*

cut 1. Schnitt *m*; MED Schnittwunde *f*; GASTR Schnitte *f*, Stück *n*; (Zu)Schnitt *m* (*clothes*); TECH Schnitt *m*, Schliff *m*; Haarschnitt *m*; *fig* Kürzung *f*, Senkung *f*; *cards*: Abheben *n*; **2.** schneiden; ab-, an-, auf-, aus-, be-, durch-, zer-, zuschneiden; *Edelstein etc* schleifen; *Gras* mähen, *Bäume* fällen, *Holz* hacken; MOT *Kurve* schneiden; *Löhne etc* kürzen; *Preise* herabsetzen, senken; *Karten* abheben; **cut one's teeth** Zähne bekommen, zahnen; **cut s.o. (dead)** *fig* F j-n schneiden; **cut s.o. or s.th. short** j-n *or* et. unterbrechen, j-m ins Wort fallen; **cut across** quer durch ... gehen; **cut back** *Pflanze* beschneiden, stutzen; einschränken; **cut down** *Bäume* fällen; verringern, einschränken, reduzieren; **cut in** F sich einmischen, unterbrechen; **cut in on s.o.** MOT j-n schneiden; **cut off** abschneiden; unterbrechen, trennen; *Strom etc* sperren; **cut out** (her)ausschneiden; *Kleid etc* zuschneiden; **be cut out for** wie geschaffen sein für; **cut up** zerschneiden

cut·back Kürzung *f*

cute F schlau; niedlich, süß

cu·ti·cle Nagelhaut *f*

cut·le·ry (Ess)Besteck *n*

cut·let GASTR Kotelett *n*; (*Kalbs-, Schweine*)Schnitzel *n*; Hacksteak *n*

cut·off date Stichtag *m*

cut-price, cut-rate ECON herabgesetzt, ermäßigt; Billig...

cut·ter Zuschneider *m*; (*Glas-, Diamant*)-Schleifer *m*; Schneidemaschine *f*, -werkzeug *n*; *film*: Cutter(in); MAR Kutter *m*

cut·throat 1. Mörder *m*; Killer *m*; **2.** mörderisch

cut·ting 1. schneidend; scharf; TECH Schneid(e)..., Fräs...; **2.** Schneiden *n*; BOT Steckling *m*; *esp Br* Ausschnitt *m*

cut·tings Schnipsel *pl*; Späne *pl*

cut·ting torch TECH Schneidbrenner *m*

Cy·ber·space → *virtual reality*

cy·cle¹ Zyklus *m*; Kreis(lauf) *m*

cy·cle² 1. Fahrrad *n*; **2.** Rad fahren

cy·cle path, cycle track (Fahr)Radweg *m*

cy·cling Radfahren *n*

cy·clist Radfahrer(in); Motorradfahrer(in)

cy·clone Wirbelsturm *m*

cyl·in·der Zylinder *m*, TECH *a.* Walze *f*, Trommel *f*

cyn·ic Zyniker(in)

cyn·i·cal zynisch

cyn·i·cism Zynismus *m*

cy·press BOT Zypresse *f*

cyst MED Zyste *f*

czar → *tsar*

Czech 1. tschechisch; **Czech Republic** Tschechien *n*, Tschechische Republik; **2.** Tscheche *m*, Tschechin *f*; LING Tschechisch *n*

D

D, d D, d *n*

d ABBR *of* **died** gest., gestorben

dab 1. Klecks *m*, Spritzer *m*; **2.** betupfen, abtupfen

dab·ble bespritzen; **dabble at, dabble in** sich oberflächlich *or contp* in dilettantischer Weise beschäftigen mit

dachs·hund ZO Dackel *m*

dad F, **dad·dy** F Papa *m*, Vati *m*

dad·dy long·legs ZO Schnake *f*; Weberknecht *m*

daf·fo·dil BOT gelbe Narzisse

dag·ger Dolch *m*; **be at daggers drawn** *fig* auf Kriegsfuß stehen (**with** mit)

dai·ly 1. täglich; **the daily grind** *or* **rut** das tägliche Einerlei; **2.** Zeitung *f*; Putzfrau *f*

dain·ty 1. zierlich, reizend; wählerisch; **2.** Leckerbissen *m*

dair·y Molkerei *f*; Milchwirtschaft *f*; Milchgeschäft *n*

dai·sy BOT Gänseblümchen *n*

dal·ly: dally about herumtrödeln

dam 1. (Stau)Damm *m*; **2.** *a.* **dam up** stauen, eindämmen

dam·age 1. Schaden *m*, (Be)Schädigung *f*; *pl* JUR Schadenersatz *m*; **2.** (be)schädigen

dam·ask Damast *m*

damn 1. verdammen; verurteilen; ***damn (it)!*** F verflucht!, verdammt!; **2.** *adj and adv* F → ***damned***; **3.** *I don't care a damn* F das ist mir völlig gleich(gültig) *or* egal

dam·na·tion Verdammung *f*; REL Verdammnis *f*

damned F verdammt

damn·ing vernichtend, belastend

damp 1. feucht, klamm; **2.** Feuchtigkeit *f*; **3.** *a.* damp·en an-, befeuchten; dämpfen

damp·ness Feuchtigkeit *f*

dance 1. Tanz *m*; Tanzveranstaltung *f*; **2.** tanzen

danc·er Tänzer(in)

danc·ing 1. Tanzen *n*; **2.** Tanz…

dan·de·li·on BOT Löwenzahn *m*

dan·druff (Kopf)Schuppen *pl*

Dane Däne *m*, Dänin *f*

dan·ger Gefahr *f*; ***be out of danger*** außer Lebensgefahr sein

danger ar·e·a Gefahrenzone *f*, Gefahrenbereich *m*

dan·ger·ous gefährlich

dan·ger zone → ***danger area***

dan·gle baumeln (lassen)

Da·nish 1. dänisch; **2.** LING Dänisch *n*

dank feucht, nass(kalt)

dare *v/i* es wagen, sich (ge)trauen; ***I dare say*** ich glaube wohl; allerdings; ***how dare you!*** was fällt dir ein!; untersteh dich!; *v/t et.* wagen

dare·dev·il Draufgänger *m*

dar·ing 1. kühn, verwegen, waghalsig; **2.** Mut *m*, Kühnheit *f*, Verwegenheit *f*

dark 1. dunkel; finster; *fig* düster, trüb(e); geheim(nisvoll); **2.** Dunkel *n*, Dunkelheit *f*; ***before*** (***at, after***) ***dark*** vor (bei, nach) Einbruch der Dunkelheit; ***keep s.o. in the dark about s.th.*** j-n über et. im Ungewissen lassen

Dark Ag·es *das* frühe Mittelalter

dark·en (sich) verdunkeln *or* verfinstern

dark·ness Dunkelheit *f*, Finsternis *f*

dark·room PHOT Dunkelkammer *f*

dar·ling 1. Liebling *m*; **2.** lieb; F goldig

darn stopfen, ausbessern

dart 1. Wurfpfeil *m*; Sprung *m*, Satz *m*; ***darts*** Darts *n*; **2.** *v/t* werfen, schleudern; *v/i* schießen, stürzen

dart·board Dartsscheibe *f*

dash 1. Schlag *m*; Klatschen *n*; GASTR Prise *f* (*of salt*), Schuss *m* (*of rum etc*), Spritzer *m* (*of lemon etc*); Gedankenstrich *m*; SPORT Sprint *m*; *fig* Anflug *m*; ***a dash of***

blue ein Stich ins Blaue; ***make a dash for*** losstürzen auf (*acc*); **2.** *v/t* schleudern, schmettern; *Hoffnung etc* zerstören, zunichtemachen; *v/i* stürmen; ***dash off*** davonstürzen

dash·board MOT Armaturenbrett *n*

dash·ing schneidig, forsch

da·ta Daten *pl* (*a.* EDP), Angaben *pl*

data bank, data·base EDP Datenbank *f*

data cap·ture Datenerfassung *f*

data in·put Dateneingabe *f*

data me·di·um Datenträger *m*

data mem·o·ry Datenspeicher *m*

data output Datenausgabe *f*

data pro·cess·ing Datenverarbeitung *f*

data pro·tec·tion JUR Datenschutz *m*

data stor·age Datenspeicher *m*

data trans·fer Datenübertragung *f*

date[1] BOT Dattel *f*

date[2] Datum *n*; Zeit *f*, Zeitpunkt *m*; Termin *m*; Verabredung *f*; F (Verabredungs)Partner(in); ***out of date*** veraltet, unmodern; ***up to date*** zeitgemäß, modern, auf dem Laufenden; **1.** datieren; F sich verabreden mit, (aus)gehen mit

dat·ed veraltet, überholt

da·tive *a.* ***dative case*** LING Dativ *m*, dritter Fall

daub (be)schmieren

daugh·ter Tochter *f*

daugh·ter-in-law Schwiegertochter *f*

daunt entmutigen

dav·en·port Sofa *n*

daw ZO Dohle *f*

daw·dle F (herum)trödeln

dawn 1. (Morgen)Dämmerung *f*; ***at dawn*** bei Tagesanbruch; **2.** dämmern; ***dawn on*** *fig* j-m dämmern

day Tag *m*; *often pl* (Lebens)Zeit *f*; ***any day*** jederzeit; ***these days*** heutzutage; ***the other day*** neulich; ***the day after tomorrow*** übermorgen; ***the day before yesterday*** vorgestern; ***open all day*** durchgehend geöffnet; ***let's call it a day!*** machen wir Schluss für heute!, Feierabend!

day·break Tagesanbruch *m*

day care cen·ter (*Br* **cen·tre**) → ***day nursery***

day·dream 1. Tag-, Wachtraum *m*; **2.** (mit offenen Augen) träumen

day·dream·er Träumer(in)

day·light Tageslicht *n*; ***in broad daylight*** am helllichten Tag

day nur·se·ry (Kinder)Tagesstätte *f*

day off freier Tag

day re·turn *Br* Tagesrückfahrkarte *f*

day·time: ***in the daytime*** am Tag, bei Ta-

ge
daze 1. blenden; betäuben; **2.** *in a daze*
benommen, betäubt
dead 1. tot; unempfindlich (*to* für); matt;
blind (*window etc*); erloschen; ECON flau;
tot (*capital etc*); völlig, total; *dead stop*
völliger Stillstand; *drop dead* tot umfal-
" len; **2.** *adv* völlig, total; plötzlich, abrupt;
genau, direkt; *dead slow* MOT Schritt
fahren!; *dead tired* todmüde; **3.** *the
dead* die Toten *pl*; *in the dead of winter*
im tiefsten Winter; *in the dead of night*
mitten in der Nacht
dead·en abstumpfen; (ab)schwächen;
dämpfen
dead end Sackgasse *f* (*a. fig*)
dead heat SPORT totes Rennen
dead·line letzter (Ablieferungs)Termin;
Stichtag *m*
dead·lock *fig* toter Punkt
dead·locked *fig* festgefahren
dead loss Totalverlust *m*; F *he's a dead
loss* er ist e-e Niete
dead·ly tödlich
deaf 1. taub; **2.** *the deaf* die Tauben *pl*
deaf-and-dumb taubstumm
deaf·en taub machen; betäuben
deaf-mute Taubstumme *m*, *f*
deal 1. F Geschäft *n*, Handel *m*; Menge *f*;
it's a deal! abgemacht!; *a good deal*
ziemlich viel; *a great deal* sehr viel; **2.**
v/t (aus-, ver-, zu)teilen; *j-m Karten* geben; *j-m e-n Schlag* versetzen; *v/i* handeln (*in* mit *e-r Ware*); *sl* dealen; *cards*:
geben; *deal with* sich befassen mit, behandeln; ECON Handel treiben mit, Geschäfte machen mit
deal·er ECON Händler(in); *cards*: Ge-
ber(in); *sl* Dealer *m*
deal·ing *mst pl* Umgang *m*, Beziehungen
pl
dean REL, UNIV Dekan *m*
dear 1. teuer; lieb; *Dear Sir* Sehr geehrter
Herr ...; **2.** Liebste *m*, *f*, Schatz *m*; *my
dear* m-e Liebe, mein Lieber; **3.** *int*
(*oh*) *dear!*, *dear dear!*, *dear me!* F du liebe Zeit!, ach herrje!
dear·est sehnlichst
dear·ly innig, von ganzem Herzen; ECON
teuer
death Tod *m*; Todesfall *m*
death·bed Sterbebett *n*
death cer·tif·i·cate Totenschein *m*
death·ly tödlich; *deathly still* totenstill
death war·rant JUR Hinrichtungsbefehl
m; *fig* Todesurteil *n*
de·bar: *debar s.o. from* j-n ausschließen
aus
de·base erniedrigen; mindern

de·ba·ta·ble umstritten
de·bate 1. Debatte *f*, Diskussion *f*; **2.** debattieren, diskutieren
deb·it ECON **1.** Soll *n*; (Konto)Belastung *f*;
debit and credit Soll und Haben *n*; **2.**
j-n, *ein Konto* belasten
deb·ris Trümmer *pl*, Schutt *m*
debt Schuld *f*; *be in debt* Schulden haben,
verschuldet sein; *be out of debt* schul-
denfrei sein; *get into debt* sich verschulden, Schulden machen
debt·or Schuldner(in)
de·bug TECH, EDP Fehler beseitigen
de·but Debüt *n*
Dec ABBR *of December* Dez., Dezember
m
dec·ade Jahrzehnt *n*
dec·a·dent dekadent
de·caf·fein·at·ed koffeinfrei
de·camp F verschwinden
de·cant abgießen; umfüllen
de·cant·er Karaffe *f*
de·cath·lete SPORT Zehnkämpfer *m*
de·cath·lon SPORT Zehnkampf *m*
de·cay 1. zerfallen; verfaulen; kariös *or*
schlecht werden (*tooth*); **2.** Zerfall *m*;
Verfaulen *n*
de·cease *esp* JUR Tod *m*, Ableben *n*
de·ceased *esp* JUR **1.** *the deceased* der *or*
die Verstorbene; die Verstorbenen *pl*; **2.**
verstorben
de·ceit Betrug *m*; Täuschung *f*
de·ceit·ful betrügerisch
de·ceive betrügen; täuschen
de·ceiv·er Betrüger(in)
De·cem·ber (ABBR *Dec*) Dezember *m*
de·cen·cy Anstand *m*
de·cent anständig; F annehmbar, (ganz)
anständig; F nett
de·cep·tion Täuschung *f*
de·cep·tive trügerisch; *be deceptive* täuschen, trügen
de·cide (sich) entscheiden; bestimmen;
beschließen, sich entschließen
de·cid·ed entschieden; bestimmt; entschlossen
dec·i·mal MATH **1.** *a. decimal fraction* De-
zimalbruch *m*; **2.** Dezimal...
de·ci·pher entziffern
de·ci·sion Entscheidung *f*; Entschluss *m*;
Entschlossenheit *f*; *make a decision* e-e
Entscheidung treffen; *reach or come to
a decision* zu e-m Entschluss kommen
de·ci·sive entscheidend; ausschlaggebend; entschieden
deck 1. MAR Deck *n*; Spiel *n*, Pack *m*
(Spiel)Karten; **2.** *deck out* schmücken
deck-chair Liegestuhl *m*
dec·la·ra·tion Erklärung *f*; Zollerklärung

f

de·clare erklären; deklarieren, verzollen

de·clen·sion LING Deklination *f*

de·cline 1. abnehmen, zurückgehen; fallen; verfallen; (höflich) ablehnen; LING deklinieren; **2.** Abnahme *f*, Rückgang *m*, Verfall *m*

de·cliv·i·ty (Ab)Hang *m*

de·clutch MOT auskuppeln

de·code entschlüsseln

de·com·pose zerlegen; (sich) zersetzen; verwesen

de·con·tam·i·nate entgasen, entgiften, entseuchen, entstrahlen

de·con·tam·i·na·tion Entseuchung *f*

dec·o·rate verzieren, schmücken; tapezieren; (an)streichen; dekorieren

dec·o·ra·tion Verzierung *f*, Schmuck *m*, Dekoration *f*; Orden *m*

dec·o·ra·tive dekorativ; Zier...

dec·o·ra·tor Dekorateur *m*; Maler *m* und Tapezierer *m*

dec·o·rous anständig

de·co·rum Anstand *m*

de·coy 1. Lockvogel *m* (*a. fig*); Köder *m* (*a. fig*); **2.** ködern; locken (*into* in *acc*); verleiten (*into* zu)

de·crease 1. Abnahme *f*; **2.** abnehmen; (sich) vermindern

de·cree 1. Dekret *n*, Erlass *m*, Verfügung *f*; *esp* JUR Entscheid *m*, Urteil *n*; **2.** verfügen

ded·i·cate widmen

ded·i·cat·ed engagiert

ded·i·ca·tion Widmung *f*; Hingabe *f*

de·duce ableiten; folgern

de·duct Betrag abziehen (*from* von)

de·duct·i·ble: *tax-deductible* steuerlich absetzbar

de·duc·tion Abzug *m*; (Schluss-)Folgerung *f*, Schluss *m*

deed Tat *f*; Heldentat *f*; JUR (Übertragungs)Urkunde *f*

deep 1. tief (*a. fig*); **2.** Tiefe *f*

deep·en (sich) vertiefen, *fig a.* (sich) verstärken

deep freeze 1. tiefkühlen, einfrieren; **2.** Tiefkühl-, Gefriertruhe *f*

deep-fro·zen tiefgefroren

deep fry frittieren

deep·ness Tiefe *f*

deer ZO Hirsch *m*; Reh *n*

de·face entstellen; unleserlich machen; ausstreichen

def·a·ma·tion Verleumdung *f*

de·fault 1. JUR Nichterscheinen *n* vor Gericht; SPORT Nichtantreten *n*; ECON Verzug *m*; **2.** s-n Verpflichtungen nicht nachkommen, ECON *a.* im Verzug sein; JUR

nicht vor Gericht erscheinen; SPORT nicht antreten

de·feat 1. Niederlage *f*; **2.** besiegen, schlagen; vereiteln, zunichtemachen

de·fect Defekt *m*, Fehler *m*; Mangel *m*

de·fec·tive mangelhaft; schadhaft, defekt

de·fence *Br* → *defense*

de·fence·less *Br* → *defenseless*

de·fend (*from, against*) verteidigen (gegen), schützen (vor *dat*, gegen)

de·fen·dant Angeklagte *m, f*; Beklagte *m, f*

de·fend·er Verteidiger(in); SPORT Abwehrspieler(in)

de·fense Verteidigung *f* (*a.* MIL, JUR, SPORT), Schutz *m*; SPORT Abwehr *f*; *witness for the defense* Entlastungszeuge *m*

de·fense·less schutzlos, wehrlos

de·fen·sive 1. Defensive *f*, Verteidigung *f*, Abwehr *f*; **2.** defensiv; Verteidigungs..., Abwehr...

de·fer aufschieben, verschieben

de·fi·ance Herausforderung *f*; Trotz *m*

de·fi·ant herausfordernd; trotzig

de·fi·cien·cy Unzulänglichkeit *f*; Mangel *m*

de·fi·cient mangelhaft, unzureichend

def·i·cit ECON Defizit *n*, Fehlbetrag *m*

de·file beschmutzen

de·fine definieren; erklären; bestimmen

def·i·nite bestimmt; endgültig, definitiv

def·i·ni·tion Definition *f*, Bestimmung *f*, Erklärung *f*

de·fin·i·tive endgültig, definitiv

de·flect *v/t* ablenken; *Ball* abfälschen; *v/i* abweichen

de·form entstellen, verunstalten

de·formed deformiert, verunstaltet; verwachsen

de·for·mi·ty Missbildung *f*

de·fraud betrügen (*of* um)

de·frost *v/t* Windschutzscheibe *etc* entfrosten; Kühlschrank *etc* abtauen, Tiefkühlkost *etc* auftauen; *v/i* ab-, auftauen

deft geschickt, gewandt

de·fy herausfordern; trotzen (*dat*)

de·gen·e·rate 1. entarten; **2.** entartet

deg·ra·da·tion Erniedrigung *f*

de·grade erniedrigen, demütigen

de·gree Grad *m*; Stufe *f*; (akademischer) Grad; *by degrees* allmählich; *take one's degree* e-n akademischen Grad erwerben, promovieren

de·hy·drate austrocknen; TECH das Wasser entziehen (*dat*)

de·i·fy vergöttern; vergöttlichen

deign sich herablassen

de·i·ty Gottheit *f*

de·jec·ted niedergeschlagen, mutlos, deprimiert

de·jec·tion Niedergeschlagenheit *f*

de·lay 1. Aufschub *m*; Verzögerung *f*; RAIL *etc* Verspätung *f*; **2.** ver-, aufschieben; verzögern; aufhalten; *be delayed* sich verzögern; RAIL *etc* Verspätung haben

del·e·gate 1. abordnen, delegieren; *Vollmachten etc* übertragen; **2.** Delegierte *m*, *f*, bevollmächtigter Vertreter

del·e·ga·tion Übertragung *f*; Abordnung *f*, Delegation *f*

de·lete (aus)streichen; EDP löschen

de·lib·e·rate absichtlich, vorsätzlich; bedächtig, besonnen

de·lib·e·ra·tion Überlegung *f*; Beratung *f*; Bedächtigkeit *f*

del·i·ca·cy Delikatesse *f*, Leckerbissen *m*; Zartheit *f*; Feingefühl *n*, Takt *m*

del·i·cate delikat (*a.* fig), schmackhaft; zart; fein; zierlich; zerbrechlich; heikel; empfindlich

del·i·ca·tes·sen Delikatessen *pl*, Feinkost *f*; Feinkostgeschäft *n*

de·li·cious köstlich

de·light 1. Vergnügen *n*, Entzücken *n*; **2.** entzücken, erfreuen; *delight in* (große) Freude haben an (*dat*)

de·light·ful entzückend

de·lin·quen·cy Kriminalität *f*

de·lin·quent 1. straffällig; **2.** Straffällige *m*, *f*; → *juvenile 1*

de·lir·i·ous MED im Delirium, fantasierend

de·lir·i·um MED Delirium *n*

de·liv·er ausliefern, (ab)liefern; *Briefe* zustellen; *Rede etc* halten; befreien, erlösen; *be delivered of* MED entbunden werden von

de·liv·er·ance Befreiung *f*

de·liv·er·er Befreier(in)

de·liv·er·y (Ab-, Aus)Lieferung *f*; *post* Zustellung *f*; Halten *n* (*e-r Rede*); Vortrag(sweise *f*) *m*; MED Entbindung *f*

de·liv·er·y van *Br* MOT Lieferwagen *m*

dell kleines Tal

de·lude täuschen

del·uge Überschwemmung *f*; *fig* Flut *f*

de·lu·sion Täuschung *f*; Wahn(vorstellung *f*) *m*

de·mand 1. Forderung *f* (*for* nach); Anforderung *f* (*on* an *acc*); Nachfrage *f* (*for* nach), Bedarf *m* (*for* an *dat*); *on demand* auf Verlangen; **2.** verlangen, fordern; (*fordernd*) fragen nach; erfordern

de·mand·ing anspruchsvoll

de·men·ted wahnsinnig

dem·i... Halb..., halb...

de·mil·i·ta·rize entmilitarisieren

dem·o F Demo *f*

de·mo·bi·lize demobilisieren

de·moc·ra·cy Demokratie *f*

dem·o·crat Demokrat(in)

dem·o·crat·ic demokratisch

de·mol·ish demolieren; ab-, ein-, niederreißen; zerstören

dem·o·li·tion Demolierung *f*; Niederreißen *n*, Abbruch *m*

de·mon Dämon *m*; Teufel *m*

dem·on·strate demonstrieren; beweisen; zeigen; vorführen

dem·on·stra·tion Demonstration *f*, *a.* Kundgebung *f*, *a.* Vorführung *f*

demonstration car *Br* Vorführwagen *m*

de·mon·stra·tive: *be demonstrative* s-e Gefühle (offen) zeigen

dem·on·stra·tor Demonstrant(in); Vorführer(in); MOT Vorführwagen *m*

de·mor·al·ize demoralisieren

de·mote degradieren

de·mure ernst, zurückhaltend

den zo Höhle *f* (*a.* fig); F Bude *f*

de·ni·al Ablehnung *f*; Leugnen *n*; Verweigerung *f*; *official denial* Dementi *n*

den·ims Jeans *pl*

Den·mark Dänemark *n*

de·nom·i·na·tion REL Konfession *f*; ECON Nennwert *m*

de·note bezeichnen; bedeuten

de·nounce (öffentlich) anprangern

dense dicht; *fig* beschränkt, begriffsstutzig

den·si·ty Dichte *f*

dent 1. Beule *f*, Delle *f*; **2.** ver-, einbeulen

den·tal Zahn...

dental plaque Zahnbelag *m*

dental plate (Zahn)Prothese *f*

dental surgeon Zahnarzt *m*, Zahnärztin *f*

den·tist Zahnarzt *m*, Zahnärztin *f*

den·tures (Zahn)Prothese *f*, (künstliches) Gebiss

de·nun·ci·a·tion Denunziation *f*

de·nun·ci·a·tor Denunziant(in)

de·ny abstreiten, bestreiten, dementieren, (ab)leugnen; *j-m et.* verweigern, abschlagen

de·o·do·rant De(s)odorant *n*, Deo *n*

de·part abreisen; abfahren, abfliegen; abweichen (*from* von)

de·part·ment Abteilung *f*, UNIV *a.* Fachbereich *m*; POL Ministerium *n*

De·part·ment of De·fense Verteidigungsministerium *n*

Department of the En·viron·ment *Br* Umweltministerium *n*

Department of the In·te·ri·or Innenministerium *n*

Department of State *a.* *State Depart-*

ment Außenministerium *n*

de·part·ment store Kaufhaus *n*, Warenhaus *n*

de·par·ture Abreise *f*; RAIL *etc* Abfahrt *f*; AVIAT Abflug *m*; *fig* Abweichung *f*; ***departures*** 'Abfahrt'

departure gate AVIAT Flugsteig *m*

departure lounge AVIAT Abflughalle *f*

de·pend: ***depend on*** sich verlassen auf (*acc*); abhängen von; angewiesen sein auf (*acc*); ***that depends*** das kommt darauf an

de·pend·a·ble zuverlässig

de·pend·a·bil·i·ty Zuverlässigkeit *f*

de·pen·dant Angehörige *m*, *f*

de·pen·dence Abhängigkeit *f*; Vertrauen *n*

de·pen·dent 1. (*on*) abhängig (von); angewiesen (auf *acc*); **2.** → **dependant**

de·plor·a·ble bedauerlich, beklagenswert

de·plore beklagen, bedauern

de·pop·u·late entvölkern

de·port ausweisen, *Ausländer a.* abschieben; deportieren

de·pose *j-n* absetzen; JUR unter Eid erklären

de·pos·it 1. absetzen, abstellen; CHEM, GEOL (sich) ablagern *or* absetzen; deponieren, hinterlegen; ECON *Betrag* anzahlen; **2.** CHEM Ablagerung *f*, GEOL *a.* (*Erz- etc*)Lager *n*; Deponierung *f*, Hinterlegung *f*; ECON Anzahlung *f*; ***make a deposit*** e-e Anzahlung leisten (**on** für)

dep·ot Depot *n*; Bahnhof *m*

de·prave *moralisch* verderben

de·pre·ci·ate an Wert verlieren

de·press (nieder)drücken; deprimieren, bedrücken

de·pressed deprimiert, niedergeschlagen; ECON flau (*market*); Not leidend (*industry*)

depressed ar·e·a ECON Notstandsgebiet *n*

de·press·ing deprimierend, bedrückend

de·pres·sion Depression *f*, Niedergeschlagenheit *f*; ECON Depression *f*, Flaute *f*; Senke *f*, Vertiefung *f*; METEOR Tief (-druckgebiet) *n*

de·prive: ***deprive s.o. of s.th.*** j-m et. entziehen *or* nehmen

de·prived benachteiligt

dept, Dept ABBR *of* ***department*** Abt., Abteilung *f*

depth 1. Tiefe *f*; **2.** Tiefen...

dep·u·ta·tion Abordnung *f*

dep·u·tize: ***deputize for s.o.*** j-n vertreten

dep·u·ty (Stell)Vertreter(in); PARL Abgeordnete *m*, *f*; *a.* ***deputy sheriff*** Hilfssheriff *m*

de·rail: ***be derailed*** entgleisen

de·ranged geistesgestört

der·by F Melone *f*

der·e·lict heruntergekommen, baufällig

de·ride verhöhnen, verspotten

de·ri·sion Hohn *m*, Spott *m*

de·ri·sive höhnisch, spöttisch

de·rive herleiten (***from*** von); (sich) ableiten (***from*** von); abstammen (***from*** von); ***derive pleasure from*** Freude finden *or* haben an (*dat*)

der·ma·tol·o·gist Dermatologe *m*, Hautarzt *m*

de·rog·a·to·ry abfällig, geringschätzig

der·rick TECH Derrickkran *m*; MAR Ladebaum *m*; TECH Bohrturm *m*

de·scend herab-, hinabsteigen, herunter-, hinuntersteigen, -gehen, -kommen; AVIAT niedergehen; abstammen, herkommen (***from*** von); ***descend on*** herfallen über (*acc*); überfallen (*acc*) (*visitor etc*)

de·scen·dant Nachkomme *m*

de·scent Herab-, Hinuntersteigen *n*, -gehen *n*; AVIAT Niedergehen *n*; Gefälle *n*; Abstammung *f*, Herkunft *f*

de·scribe beschreiben

de·scrip·tion Beschreibung *f*, Schilderung *f*; Art *f*, Sorte *f*

de·scrip·tive beschreibend; anschaulich

des·e·crate entweihen

de·seg·re·gate die Rassentrennung aufheben in (*dat*)

de·seg·re·ga·tion Aufhebung *f* der Rassentrennung

des·ert¹ 1. Wüste *f*; **2.** Wüsten...

de·sert² *v/t* verlassen, im Stich lassen; *v/i* MIL desertieren

de·sert·er MIL Deserteur *m*

de·ser·tion (JUR *a.* böswilliges) Verlassen; MIL Fahnenflucht *f*

de·serve verdienen

de·serv·ed·ly verdientermaßen

de·serv·ing verdienstvoll

de·sign 1. Design *n*, Entwurf *m*, (TECH Konstruktions)Zeichnung *f*; Design *n*, Muster *n*; (*a.* böse)Absicht *f*; **2.** entwerfen, TECH konstruieren; gestalten; ausdenken; bestimmen, vorsehen (***for*** für)

des·ig·nate *et. or j-n* bestimmen

de·sign·er Designer(in); TECH Konstrukteur *m*; (*Mode*)Schöpfer(in)

de·sir·a·ble erwünscht, wünschenswert; begehrenswert

de·sire 1. Wunsch *m*, Verlangen *n*, Begierde *f* (***for*** nach); **2.** wünschen; begehren

de·sist Abstand nehmen (***from*** von)

desk Schreibtisch *m*; Pult *n*; Empfang *m*, Rezeption *f*; Schalter *m*

desk·top com·put·er Desktop-Computer *m*, Tischcomputer *m*, Tischrechner *m*

desktop pub·lish·ing (ABBR **DTP**) EDP Desktop-Publishing *n*

des·o·late einsam, verlassen; trostlos

de·spair 1. Verzweiflung *f*; *drive s.o. to despair* j-n zur Verzweiflung bringen; **2.** verzweifeln (*of* an *dat*)

de·spair·ing verzweifelt

de·spatch → *dispatch*

des·per·ate verzweifelt; F hoffnungslos, schrecklich

des·per·a·tion Verzweiflung *f*

des·pic·a·ble verachtenswert, verabscheuungswürdig

de·spise verachten

de·spite trotz (*gen*)

de·spon·dent mutlos, verzagt

des·pot Despot *m*, Tyrann *m*

des·sert Nachtisch *m*, Dessert *n*

des·ti·na·tion Bestimmung *f*; Bestimmungsort *m*

des·tined bestimmt; MAR *etc* unterwegs (*for* nach)

des·ti·ny Schicksal *n*

des·ti·tute mittellos

de·stroy zerstören, vernichten; *Tier* töten, einschläfern

de·stroy·er Zerstörer(in); MAR MIL Zerstörer *m*

de·struc·tion Zerstörung *f*, Vernichtung *f*

de·struc·tive zerstörend, vernichtend; zerstörerisch

de·tach (ab-, los)trennen, (los)lösen

de·tached einzeln, frei *or* allein stehend; unvoreingenommen; distanziert; *detached house* Einzelhaus *n*

de·tach·ment (Los)Lösung *f*, (Ab-) Trennung *f*; MIL (Sonder)Kommando *n*

de·tail 1. Detail *n*, Einzelheit *f*; MIL (Sonder)Kommando *n*; *in detail* ausführlich; **2.** genau schildern; MIL abkommandieren

de·tailed detailliert, ausführlich

de·tain aufhalten; JUR in (Untersuchungs)Haft behalten

de·tect entdecken, (heraus)finden

de·tec·tion Entdeckung *f*

de·tec·tive Kriminalbeamte *m*, Detektiv *m*

detective nov·el, detective sto·ry Kriminalroman *m*

de·ten·tion JUR Haft *f*; PED Nachsitzen *n*

de·ter abschrecken (*from* von)

de·ter·gent Reinigungs-, Wasch-, Geschirrspülmittel *n*

de·te·ri·o·rate (sich) verschlechtern, nachlassen; verderben

de·ter·mi·na·tion Entschlossenheit *f*, Bestimmtheit *f*; Entschluss *m*; Feststellung *f*, Ermittlung *f*

de·ter·mine *et.* beschließen, bestimmen; feststellen, ermitteln; (sich) entscheiden; sich entschließen

de·ter·mined entschlossen

de·ter·rence Abschreckung *f*

de·ter·rent 1. abschreckend; **2.** Abschreckungsmittel *n*

de·test verabscheuen

de·throne entthronen

de·to·nate *v/t* zünden; *v/i* detonieren, explodieren

de·tour Umweg *m*; Umleitung *f*

de·tract: *detract from* ablenken von; schmälern (*acc*)

de·tri·ment Nachteil *m*, Schaden *m*

deuce *cards etc*: Zwei *f*; *tennis*: Einstand *m*

de·val·u·a·tion Abwertung *f*

de·val·ue abwerten

dev·a·state verwüsten

dev·a·stat·ing verheerend, vernichtend; F umwerfend, toll

de·vel·op (sich) entwickeln; *Naturschätze, Bauland* erschließen, *Altstadt etc* sanieren

de·vel·op·er PHOT Entwickler *m*; (Stadt)-Planer *m*

de·vel·op·ing Entwicklungs…

developing coun·try, developing nation Entwicklungsland *n*

de·vel·op·ment Entwicklung *f*; Erschließung *f*, Sanierung *f*

de·vi·ate abweichen (*from* von)

de·vi·a·tion Abweichung *f*

de·vice Vorrichtung *f*, Gerät *n*; Plan *m*, Trick *m*; *leave s.o. to his own devices* j-n sich selbst überlassen

dev·il Teufel *m* (*a. fig*)

dev·il·ish teuflisch

de·vi·ous abwegig; gewunden; unaufrichtig; *devious route* Umweg *m*

de·vise (sich) ausdenken

de·void: *devoid of* ohne (*acc*)

de·vote widmen (*to* dat)

de·vot·ed ergeben; hingebungsvoll; eifrig, begeistert

dev·o·tee begeisterter Anhänger

de·vo·tion Ergebenheit *f*; Hingabe *f*; Frömmigkeit *f*, Andacht *f*

de·vour verschlingen

de·vout fromm; sehnlichst, innig

dew Tau *m*

dew·y taufeucht, taufrisch

dex·ter·i·ty Gewandtheit *f*

dex·ter·ous, dex·trous gewandt

di·a·bol·i·cal teuflisch

di·ag·nose diagnostizieren

di·ag·no·sis Diagnose *f*

di·ag·o·nal 1. diagonal; **2.** Diagonale *f*

diagram 440

di·a·gram Diagramm *n*, grafische Darstellung

di·al 1. Zifferblatt *n*; TEL Wählscheibe *f*; TECH Skala *f*; **2.** TEL wählen; *dial direct* durchwählen (*to* nach); *direct dial(l)ing* Durchwahl *f*

di·a·lect Dialekt *m*, Mundart *f*

di·al·ling code *Br* TEL Vorwahl(nummer) *f*

di·a·log, *Br* **di·a·logue** Dialog *m*, (Zwie)-Gespräch *n*

di·am·e·ter Durchmesser *m*; *in diameter* im Durchmesser

di·a·mond Diamant *m*; Raute *f*, Rhombus *m*; *cards:* Karo *n*

di·a·per Windel *f*

di·a·phragm ANAT Zwerchfell *n*; OPT Blende *f*; TEL Membran(e) *f*

di·ar·rh(o)e·a MED Durchfall *m*

di·a·ry Tagebuch *n*

dice 1. Würfel *m*; **2.** GASTR in Würfel schneiden; würfeln

dic·tate diktieren; *fig* vorschreiben

dic·ta·tion Diktat *n*

dic·ta·tor Diktator *m*

dic·ta·tor·ship Diktatur *f*

dic·tion Ausdrucksweise *f*, Stil *m*

dic·tion·a·ry Wörterbuch *n*

die[1] sterben; ZO eingehen, verenden; *die of hunger* verhungern; *die of thirst* verdursten; *die away* sich legen (*wind*); verklingen (*sound*); *die down* nachlassen; herunterbrennen; schwächer werden; *die out* aussterben (*a. fig*)

die[2] Würfel *m*

di·et 1. Diät *f*; Nahrung *f*, Kost *f*; *be on a diet* Diät leben; *put s.o. on a diet* j-m e-e Diät verordnen; **2.** Diät leben

di·e·ti·cian Diätassistent(in)

dif·fer sich unterscheiden; anderer Meinung sein (*with, from* als); abweichen

dif·fe·rence Unterschied *m*; Differenz *f*; Meinungsverschiedenheit *f*

dif·fe·rent verschieden; andere(r, -s); anders (*from* als)

dif·fe·ren·ti·ate (sich) unterscheiden

dif·fi·cult schwierig

dif·fi·cul·ty Schwierigkeit *f*, *pl* Unannehmlichkeiten *pl*

dif·fi·dence Schüchternheit *f*

dif·fi·dent schüchtern

dif·fuse 1. *fig* verbreiten; **2.** diffus; *esp* PHYS zerstreut; weitschweifig

dif·fu·sion CHEM, PHYS (Zer)Streuung *f*

dig 1. graben; *dig (up)* umgraben; *dig (up or out)* ausgraben (*a. fig*); *dig s.o. in the ribs* j-m e-n Rippenstoß geben; **2.** F Puff *m*, Stoß *m*; Seitenhieb *m* (*at* auf *acc*)

di·gest 1. verdauen; *digest well* leicht

verdaulich sein; **2.** Abriss *m*; Auslese *f*, Auswahl *f*

di·gest·i·ble verdaulich

di·ges·tion Verdauung *f*

di·ges·tive verdauungsfördernd; Verdauungs...

dig·ger (*esp* Gold)Gräber *m*

di·git Ziffer *f*; *three-digit number* dreistellige Zahl

dig·i·tal clock, digital watch Digitaluhr *f*

dig·ni·fied würdevoll, würdig

dig·ni·ta·ry Würdenträger(in)

dig·ni·ty Würde *f*

di·gress abschweifen

dike[1] **1.** Deich *m*, Damm *m*; Graben *m*; **2.** eindeichen, eindämmen

dike[2] *sl* Lesbe *f*

di·lap·i·dat·ed verfallen, baufällig, klapp(e)rig

di·late (sich) ausdehnen *or* (aus)weiten; *Augen* weit öffnen

dil·a·to·ry verzögernd, hinhaltend; langsam

dil·i·gence Fleiß *m*

dil·i·gent fleißig, emsig

di·lute 1. verdünnen; *fig* verwässern; **2.** verdünnt; *fig* verwässert

dim 1. (halb)dunkel; düster; undeutlich, verschwommen; schwach, trüb(e) (*light*); **2.** (sich) verdunkeln *or* verdüstern; (sich) trüben; undeutlich werden; *dim one's headlights* MOT abblenden

dime Zehncentstück *n*

di·men·sion Dimension *f*, Maß *n*, Abmessung *f*; *pl a.* Ausmaß *n*

di·min·ish (sich) vermindern *or* verringern

di·min·u·tive klein, winzig

dim·ple Grübchen *n*

din Getöse *n*, Lärm *m*

dine essen, speisen; *dine in* zu Hause essen; *dine out* auswärts essen, essen gehen

din·er Speisende *m*, *f*; Gast *m*; Speiselokal *n*; RAIL Speisewagen *m*

din·ghy MAR Jolle *f*; Dingi *n*; Beiboot *n*; Schlauchboot *n*

din·gy schmutzig, schmudd(e)lig

din·ing car RAIL Speisewagen *m*

din·ing room Ess-, Speisezimmer *n*

din·ner (Mittag-, Abend)Essen *n*; Diner *n*, Festessen *n*

dinner jack·et Smoking *m*

dinner par·ty Dinnerparty *f*, Abendgesellschaft *f*

dinner ser·vice, dinner set Speiseservice *n*, Tafelgeschirr *n*

din·ner·time Essens-, Tischzeit *f*

di·no F → *dinosaur*

di·no·saur ZO Dinosaurier *m*

dip 1. *v/t* (ein)tauchen; senken; schöpfen; *dip one's headlights* Br MOT abblenden; *v/i* (unter)tauchen; sinken; sich neigen, sich senken; **2.** (Ein-, Unter-)Tauchen *n*; F kurzes Bad; Senkung *f*, Neigung *f*, Gefälle *n*; GASTR Dip *m*

diph·ther·i·a MED Diphtherie *f*

di·plo·ma Diplom *n*

di·plo·ma·cy Diplomatie *f*

dip·lo·mat Diplomat *m*

dip·lo·mat·ic diplomatisch

dip·per Schöpfkelle *f*

dire schrecklich; höchste(r, -s), äußerste(r, -s)

di·rect 1. *adj* direkt; gerade; unmittelbar; offen, aufrichtig; **2.** *adv* direkt, unmittelbar; **3.** richten; lenken, steuern; leiten; anordnen; *j-n* anweisen; *j-m* den Weg zeigen; *Brief* adressieren; Regie führen bei

direct cur·rent ELECTR Gleichstrom *m*

direct train durchgehender Zug

di·rec·tion Richtung *f*; Leitung *f*, Führung *f*; *film etc*: Regie *f*; *mst pl* Anweisung *f*, Anleitung *f*; *directions for use* Gebrauchsanweisung *f*; *sense of direction* Ortssinn *m*

direction in·di·ca·tor MOT Fahrtrichtungsanzeiger *m*, Blinker *m*

di·rec·tive Anweisung *f*

di·rect·ly 1. *adv* sofort; **2.** *cj* F sobald, sowie

di·rec·tor Direktor *m*; *film etc*: Regisseur(in)

di·rec·to·ry Adressbuch *n*

di·rect speech LING wörtliche Rede

dirt Schmutz *m*; (lockere) Erde

dirt cheap F spottbillig

dirt·y 1. schmutzig (*a. fig*); **2.** *v/t* beschmutzen; *v/i* schmutzig werden, schmutzen

dis·a·bil·i·ty Unfähigkeit *f*

dis·a·bled 1. arbeitsunfähig, erwerbsunfähig, invalid(e); MIL kriegsversehrt; *körperlich or geistig* behindert; **2.** *the disabled* die Behinderten *pl*

dis·ad·van·tage Nachteil *m*; Schaden *m*

dis·ad·van·ta·geous nachteilig, ungünstig

dis·a·gree nicht übereinstimmen; uneinig sein; nicht bekommen (*with s.o.* j-m)

dis·a·gree·a·ble unangenehm

dis·a·gree·ment Verschiedenheit *f*, Unstimmigkeit *f*, Uneinigkeit *f*; Meinungsverschiedenheit *f*

dis·ap·pear verschwinden

dis·ap·pear·ance Verschwinden *n*

dis·ap·point *j-n* enttäuschen; *Hoffnungen etc* zunichtemachen

dis·ap·point·ing enttäuschend

dis·ap·point·ment Enttäuschung *f*

dis·ap·prov·al Missbilligung *f*

dis·ap·prove missbilligen; dagegen sein

dis·arm *v/t* entwaffnen (*a. fig*); *v/i* MIL, POL abrüsten

dis·ar·ma·ment Entwaffnung *f*; MIL, POL Abrüstung *f*

dis·ar·range in Unordnung bringen

dis·ar·ray Unordnung *f*

di·sas·ter Unglück *n*, Unglücksfall *m*, Katastrophe *f*

disaster ar·e·a Katastrophen-, Notstandsgebiet *n*

disaster con·trol Katastrophenschutz *m*

di·sas·trous katastrophal, verheerend

dis·be·lief Unglaube *m*; Zweifel *m* (*in* an *dat*)

dis·be·lieve *et.* bezweifeln, nicht glauben

disc Br → *disk*

dis·card *Karten* ablegen, *Kleidung etc a.* ausrangieren; *Freund etc* fallen lassen

di·scern wahrnehmen, erkennen

di·scern·ing kritisch, scharfsichtig

di·scern·ment Scharfblick *m*

dis·charge 1. *v/t* entladen, ausladen; *j-n* befreien, entbinden; *j-n* entlassen; *Gewehr etc* abfeuern; von sich geben, ausströmen, -senden, -stoßen; MED absondern; *Pflicht etc* erfüllen; *Zorn etc* auslassen (*on* an *dat*); *v/i* ELECTR sich entladen; sich ergießen, münden (*river*); MED eitern; **2.** MAR Entladung *f*; MIL Abfeuern *n*; Ausströmen *n*; MED Absonderung *f*, Ausfluss *m*; Ausstoßen *n*; ELECTR Entladung *f*; Entlassung *f*; Erfüllung *f* (*e-r Pflicht*)

di·sci·ple Schüler *m*; Jünger *m*

dis·ci·pline 1. Disziplin *f*; **2.** disziplinieren; *well disciplined* diszipliniert; *badly disciplined* disziplinlos, undiszipliniert

dis·claim abstreiten, bestreiten; *Verantwortung* ablehnen; JUR verzichten auf (*acc*)

dis·close bekannt geben *or* machen; enthüllen, aufdecken

dis·clo·sure Enthüllung *f*

dis·co Disko *f*

dis·col·o(u)r (sich) verfärben

dis·com·fort 1. Unbehagen *n*; Unannehmlichkeit *f*; **2.** *j-m* Unbehagen verursachen

dis·con·cert aus der Fassung bringen

dis·con·nect trennen (*a.* ELECTR); TECH auskuppeln; ELECTR *Gerät* abschalten; *Gas, Strom, Telefon* abstellen; TEL *Gespräch* unterbrechen

dis·con·nect·ed zusammenhang(s)los

dis·con·so·late untröstlich

dis·con·tent Unzufriedenheit *f*

dis·con·tent·ed unzufrieden

dis·con·tin·ue aufgeben, aufhören mit; unterbrechen

dis·cord Uneinigkeit *f*, Zwietracht *f*, Zwist *m*; MUS Missklang *m*

dis·cord·ant nicht übereinstimmend; MUS unharmonisch, misstönend

dis·co·theque Diskothek *f*

dis·count ECON Diskont *m*; Preisnachlass *m*, Rabatt *m*, Skonto *m, n*

dis·cour·age entmutigen; abschrecken, abhalten, *j-m* abraten (**from** von)

dis·cour·age·ment Entmutigung *f*; Abschreckung *f*

dis·course 1. Unterhaltung *f*, Gespräch *n*; Vortrag *m*; **2.** e-n Vortrag halten (**on** über *acc*)

dis·cour·te·ous unhöflich

dis·cour·te·sy Unhöflichkeit *f*

dis·cov·er entdecken; ausfindig machen, (heraus)finden

dis·cov·e·ry Entdeckung *f*

dis·cred·it 1. Zweifel *m*; Misskredit *m*, schlechter Ruf; **bring discredit (up)on** in Verruf bringen; **2.** nicht glauben; in Misskredit bringen

di·screet besonnen, vorsichtig; diskret, verschwiegen

di·screp·an·cy Diskrepanz *f*, Widerspruch *m*

di·scre·tion Ermessen *n*, Gutdünken *n*; Diskretion *f*, Verschwiegenheit *f*

di·scrim·i·nate unterscheiden; **discriminate against** benachteiligen, diskriminieren

di·scrim·i·nat·ing kritisch, urteilsfähig

di·scrim·i·na·tion unterschiedliche (*esp* nachteilige) Behandlung; Diskriminierung *f*, Benachteiligung *f*; Urteilsfähigkeit *f*

dis·cus SPORT Diskus *m*

di·scuss diskutieren, erörtern, besprechen

di·scus·sion Diskussion *f*, Besprechung *f*

dis·cus throw SPORT Diskuswerfen *n*

discus throw·er SPORT Diskuswerfer(in)

dis·ease Krankheit *f*

dis·eased krank

dis·em·bark von Bord gehen (lassen); MAR Waren ausladen

dis·en·chant·ed: be disenchanted with sich keine Illusionen mehr machen über (*acc*)

dis·en·gage (sich) frei machen; losmachen; TECH auskuppeln, loskuppeln

dis·en·tan·gle entwirren, (sich) befreien

dis·fa·vo(u)r Missfallen *n*; Ungnade *f*

dis·fig·ure entstellen

dis·grace 1. Schande *f*; Ungnade *f*; **2.** Schande bringen über (*acc*), *j-m* Schande bereiten

dis·grace·ful schändlich; skandalös

dis·guise 1. verkleiden (**as** als); *Stimme etc* verstellen; *et.* verbergen, verschleiern; **2.** Verkleidung *f*; Verstellung *f*; Verschleierung *f*; **in disguise** maskiert, verkleidet; *fig* verkappt; **in the disguise of** verkleidet als

dis·gust 1. Ekel *m*, Abscheu *m*; **2.** (an)ekeln; empören, entrüsten

dis·gust·ing ekelhaft

dish 1. flache Schüssel; (Servier)Platte *f*; GASTR Gericht *n*, Speise *f*; **the dishes** das Geschirr; **wash** or **do the dishes** abspülen, abwaschen; **2. dish out** F austeilen; *often* **dish up** Speisen anrichten, auftragen; F *Geschichte etc* auftischen

dish·cloth Geschirrtuch *n*

dis·heart·en entmutigen

di·shev·el(l)ed zerzaust

dis·hon·est unehrlich, unredlich

dis·hon·est·y Unehrlichkeit *f*; Unredlichkeit *f*

dis·hon·o(u)r 1. Schande *f*; **2.** Schande bringen über (*acc*); ECON *Wechsel* nicht honorieren or einlösen

dis·hon·o(u)·ra·ble schändlich, unehrenhaft

dish·wash·er Tellerwäscher *m*, Spüler(in); TECH Geschirrspülmaschine *f*, Geschirrspüler *m*

dish·wa·ter Spülwasser *n*

dis·il·lu·sion 1. Ernüchterung *f*, Desillusion *f*; **2.** ernüchtern, desillusionieren; **be disillusioned with** sich keine Illusionen mehr machen über (*acc*)

dis·in·clined abgeneigt

dis·in·fect MED desinfizieren

dis·in·fec·tant Desinfektionsmittel *n*

dis·in·her·it JUR enterben

dis·in·te·grate (sich) auflösen; verfallen, zerfallen

dis·in·ter·est·ed uneigennützig, selbstlos; objektiv, unvoreingenommen

disk Scheibe *f*; (Schall)Platte *f*; Parkscheibe *f*; EDP Diskette *f*; ANAT Bandscheibe *f*; **slipped disk** MED Bandscheibenvorfall *m*

disk drive EDP Diskettenlaufwerk *n*

disk·ette EDP Floppy *f*, Diskette *f*

disk jock·ey Diskjockey *m*

disk park·ing MOT Parken *n* mit Parkscheibe

dis·like 1. Abneigung *f*, Widerwille *m* (**of**, **for** gegen); **take a dislike to s.o.** gegen j-n e-e Abneigung fassen; **2.** nicht leiden können, nicht mögen

dis·lo·cate MED sich *den Arm etc* verrenken *or* ausrenken

dis·loy·al treulos, untreu

dis·mal trüb(e), trostlos, elend

dis·man·tle TECH demontieren

dis·may 1. Schreck(en) *m*, Bestürzung *f*; *in dismay, with dismay* bestürzt; *to my dismay* zu m-r Bestürzung; **2.** *v/t* erschrecken, bestürzen

dis·miss *v/t* entlassen; wegschicken; ablehnen; *Thema etc* fallen lassen; JUR abweisen

dis·miss·al Entlassung *f*; Aufgabe *f*; JUR Abweisung *f*

dis·mount *v/i* absteigen, absitzen (*from* von); *v/t* demontieren; TECH auseinandernehmen

dis·o·be·di·ence Ungehorsam *m*

dis·o·be·di·ent ungehorsam

dis·o·bey nicht gehorchen, ungehorsam sein (gegen)

dis·or·der Unordnung *f*; Aufruhr *m*; MED Störung *f*

dis·or·der·ly unordentlich; ordnungswidrig; unruhig; aufrührerisch

dis·or·gan·ize durcheinanderbringen; desorganisieren

dis·own nicht anerkennen; *Kind* verstoßen; ablehnen

di·spar·age verächtlich machen, herabsetzen; gering schätzen

di·spar·i·ty Ungleichheit *f*; *disparity of or in age* Altersunterschied *m*

dis·pas·sion·ate leidenschaftslos; objektiv

di·spatch 1. schnelle Erledigung; (Ab)Sendung *f*; Abfertigung *f*; Eile *f*; (Eil)Botschaft *f*; Bericht *m*; **2.** schnell erledigen; absenden, abschicken, *Telegramm* aufgeben, abfertigen

di·spel *Menge etc* zerstreuen (*a. fig*), *Nebel* zerteilen

di·spen·sa·ble entbehrlich

di·spen·sa·ry Werks-, Krankenhaus-, Schul-, MIL Lazarettapotheke *f*

dis·pen·sa·tion Austeilung *f*; Befreiung *f*; Dispens *m*; *göttliche* Fügung

di·spense austeilen; *Recht* sprechen; *Arzneien* zubereiten und abgeben; *dispense with* auskommen ohne; überflüssig machen

di·spens·er Spender *m*, a. Abroller *m* (*for adhesive tape etc*), (*Briefmarkenetc*)Automat *m*

di·sperse verstreuen; (sich) zerstreuen

di·spir·it·ed entmutigt

dis·place verschieben; ablösen, entlassen; *j-n* verschleppen; ersetzen; verdrän-

gen

dis·play 1. Entfaltung *f*; (Her)Zeigen *n*; (protzige) Zurschaustellung; EDP Display *n*, Bildschirm *m*, Datenanzeige *f*; ECON Display *n*, Auslage *f*; *be on display* ausgestellt sein; **2.** entfalten; zur Schau stellen; zeigen

dis·please *j-m* missfallen

dis·pleased ungehalten

dis·plea·sure Missfallen *n*

dis·pos·a·ble Einweg...; Wegwerf...

dis·pos·al Beseitigung *f*, Entsorgung *f*; Endlagerung *f*; Verfügung(srecht *n*) *f*; *be (put) at s.o.'s disposal* j-m zur Verfügung stehen (stellen)

dis·pose *v/t* (an)ordnen, einrichten; geneigt machen, bewegen; *v/i*: *dispose of* verfügen über (*acc*); erledigen; loswerden; wegschaffen, beseitigen; *Abfall, a. Atommüll etc* entsorgen

dis·posed geneigt; ...gesinnt

dis·po·si·tion Veranlagung *f*

dis·pos·sess enteignen, vertreiben; berauben (*of gen*)

dis·pro·por·tion·ate(·ly) unverhältnismäßig

dis·prove widerlegen

di·spute 1. Disput *m*, Kontroverse *f*; Streit *m*; Auseinandersetzung *f*; **2.** streiten (über *acc*); bezweifeln

dis·qual·i·fy unfähig *or* untauglich machen; für untauglich erklären; SPORT disqualifizieren

dis·re·gard 1. Nichtbeachtung *f*; Missachtung *f*; **2.** nicht beachten

dis·rep·u·ta·ble übel; verrufen

dis·re·pute schlechter Ruf

dis·re·spect Respektlosigkeit *f*; Unhöflichkeit *f*

dis·re·spect·ful respektlos; unhöflich

dis·rupt unterbrechen

dis·sat·is·fac·tion Unzufriedenheit *f*

dis·sat·is·fied unzufrieden (*with* mit)

dis·sect MED sezieren, zerlegen, zergliedern (*a. fig*)

dis·sen·sion Meinungsverschiedenheit(en *pl*) *f*, Differenz(en *pl*) *f*; Uneinigkeit *f*

dis·sent 1. abweichende Meinung; **2.** anderer Meinung sein (*from* als)

dis·sent·er Andersdenkende *m, f*

dis·si·dent Andersdenkende *m, f*; POL Dissident(in), Regime-, Systemkritiker(-in)

dis·sim·i·lar (to) unähnlich (*dat*); verschieden (von)

dis·sim·u·la·tion Verstellung *f*

dis·si·pate (sich) zerstreuen; verschwenden

dis·si·pat·ed ausschweifend, zügellos

dis·so·ci·ate trennen; *dissociate o.s.* sich distanzieren (*from* von)

dis·so·lute → *dissipated*

dis·so·lu·tion Auflösung *f*

dis·solve (sich) auflösen

dis·suade *j-m* abraten (*from* von)

dis·tance 1. Abstand *m*; Entfernung *f*; Ferne *f*; Strecke *f*; *fig* Distanz *f*, Zurückhaltung *f*; *at a distance* von weitem; in einiger Entfernung; *keep s.o. at a distance* j-m gegenüber reserviert sein; **2.** hinter sich lassen

distance race SPORT Langstreckenlauf *m*

distance run·ner SPORT Langstreckenläufer(in), Langstreckler(in)

dis·tant entfernt; fern, Fern...; distanziert

dis·taste Widerwille *m*, Abneigung *f*

dis·taste·ful ekelerregend; unangenehm; *be distasteful to s.o.* j-m zuwider sein

dis·tem·per VET Staupe *f*

dis·tend (sich) (aus)dehnen; (auf)blähen; sich weiten

dis·til(l) destillieren

dis·tinct verschieden; deutlich, klar

dis·tinc·tion Unterscheidung *f*; Unterschied *m*; Auszeichnung *f*; Rang *m*

dis·tinc·tive unterscheidend; kennzeichnend, bezeichnend

dis·tin·guish unterscheiden; auszeichnen; *distinguish o.s.* sich auszeichnen

dis·tin·guished berühmt; ausgezeichnet; vornehm

dis·tort verdrehen; verzerren

dis·tract ablenken

dis·tract·ed beunruhigt, besorgt; (*by, with* vor *dat*) außer sich, wahnsinnig

dis·trac·tion Ablenkung *f*; Zerstreuung *f*; Wahnsinn *m*; *drive s.o. to distraction* j-n wahnsinnig machen

dis·traught → *distracted*

dis·tress 1. Leid *n*, Kummer *m*, Sorge *f*; Not(lage) *f*; **2.** beunruhigen, mit Sorge erfüllen

dis·tressed Not leidend

distressed ar·e·a Notstandsgebiet *n*

dis·tress·ing besorgniserregend

dis·trib·ute ver-, aus-, zuteilen; ECON *Waren* vertreiben, absetzen; *Filme* verleihen

dis·tri·bu·tion Ver-, Aus-, Zuteilung *f*; ECON Vertrieb *m*, Absatz *m*; *film:* Verleih *m*

dis·trict Bezirk *m*; Gegend *f*

dis·trust 1. Misstrauen *n*; **2.** misstrauen (*dat*)

dis·trust·ful misstrauisch

dis·turb stören; beunruhigen

dis·turb·ance Störung *f*; Unruhe *f*; *disturbance of the peace* JUR Störung *f* der öffentlichen Sicherheit und Ordnung; *cause a disturbance* für Unruhe sorgen; ruhestörenden Lärm machen

dis·turbed geistig gestört; verhaltensgestört

dis·used nicht mehr benutzt (*machinery etc*), stillgelegt (*colliery etc*)

ditch Graben *m*

di·van Diwan *m*

divan bed Bettcouch *f*

dive 1. (unter)tauchen; *vom Sprungbrett* springen; e-n Hecht- *or* Kopfsprung machen; hechten (*for* nach); e-n Sturzflug machen; **2.** *swimming:* Springen *n*; Kopfsprung *m*, Hechtsprung *m*; *soccer:* Schwalbe *f*; AVIAT Sturzflug *m*; F Spelunke *f*

div·er Taucher(in); SPORT Wasserspringer(in)

di·verge auseinanderlaufen; abweichen

di·ver·gence Abweichung *f*

di·ver·gent abweichend

di·verse verschieden; mannigfaltig

di·ver·si·fy verschieden(artig) *or* abwechslungsreich gestalten

di·ver·sion Ablenkung *f*; Zeitvertreib *m*; *Br* MOT Umleitung *f*

di·ver·si·ty Verschiedenheit *f*; Mannigfaltigkeit *f*

di·vert ablenken; *j-n* zerstreuen, unterhalten; *Br Verkehr* umleiten

di·vide 1. *v/t* teilen; ver-, aus-, aufteilen; trennen; MATH dividieren, teilen (*by* durch); *v/i* sich teilen; sich aufteilen; MATH sich dividieren *or* teilen lassen (*by* durch); **2.** GEOGR Wasserscheide *f*

di·vid·ed geteilt; *divided highway* Schnellstraße *f*

div·i·dend ECON Dividende *f*

di·vid·ers (*a pair of dividers*) ein Stechzirkel *m*

di·vine göttlich

di·vine ser·vice REL Gottesdienst *m*

div·ing 1. Tauchen *n*; SPORT Wasserspringen *n*; **2.** Taucher...

div·ing·board Sprungbrett *n*

div·ing·suit Taucheranzug *m*

di·vin·i·ty Gottheit *f*; Göttlichkeit *f*; Theologie *f*

di·vis·i·ble teilbar

di·vi·sion Teilung *f*; Trennung *f*; Abteilung *f*; MIL, MATH Division *f*

di·vorce 1. (Ehe)Scheidung *f*; *get a divorce* sich scheiden lassen (*from* von); **2.** JUR *j-n*, *Ehe* scheiden; *get divorced* sich scheiden lassen

di·vor·cee Geschiedene *m*, *f*

DIY ABBR → *do-it-yourself*

DIY store Baumarkt *m*

doting

diz·zy schwind(e)lig

do v/t tun, machen; (zu)bereiten; *Zimmer* aufräumen; *Geschirr* abwaschen; *Wegstrecke* zurücklegen, schaffen; **do you know him? no, I don't** kennst du ihn? nein; **what can I do for you?** was kann ich für Sie tun?, womit kann ich (Ihnen) dienen?; **do London** F London besichtigen; **have one's hair done** sich die Haare machen *or* frisieren lassen; **have done reading** fertig sein mit Lesen; v/i tun, handeln; sich befinden; genügen; **that will do** das genügt; **how do you do?** guten Tag!; **do be quick** beeil dich doch; **do you like New York? I do** gefällt Ihnen New York? ja; **she works hard, doesn't she?** sie arbeitet viel, nicht wahr?; **do well** s-e Sache gut machen; gute Geschäfte machen; **do away with** beseitigen, weg-, abschaffen; **do s.o. in** F j-n umlegen; **I'm done in** F ich bin geschafft; **do up** *Kleid etc* zumachen; *Haus etc* instand setzen; *Päckchen* zurechtmachen; **do o.s. up** sich zurechtmachen; **I could do with ...** ich könnte ... brauchen *or* vertragen; **do without** auskommen *or* sich behelfen ohne

doc F → **doctor**

do·cile gelehrig; fügsam

dock[1] stutzen, kupieren

dock[2] **1.** MAR Dock *n*; Kai *m*, Pier *m*; JUR Anklagebank *f*; **2.** v/t MAR (ein)docken; *Raumschiff* koppeln; v/i MAR anlegen; andocken, ankoppeln (*Raumschiff*)

dock·er Dock-, Hafenarbeiter *m*

dock·ing Docking *n*, Ankopp(e)lung *f*

dock·yard MAR Werft *f*

doc·tor Doktor *m* (*a.* UNIV), Arzt *m*, Ärztin *f*

doc·tor·al: doctoral thesis UNIV Doktorarbeit *f*

doc·trine Doktrin *f*, Lehre *f*

doc·u·ment 1. Urkunde *f*; **2.** (urkundlich) belegen

doc·u·men·ta·ry 1. urkundlich; *film etc:* Dokumentar...; **2.** Dokumentarfilm *m*

dodge (rasch) zur Seite springen, ausweichen; F sich drücken (vor *dat*)

dodg·er Drückeberger *m*

doe ZO (Reh)Geiß *f*, Ricke *f*

dog 1. ZO Hund *m*; **2.** j-n beharrlich verfolgen

dog-eared mit Eselsohren (*book*)

dog·ged verbissen, hartnäckig

dog·ma Dogma *n*; Glaubenssatz *m*

dog·mat·ic dogmatisch

do-it-your·self 1. Heimwerken *n*; **2.** Heimwerker...

do-it-your·self·er Heimwerker *m*

dole 1. milde Gabe; *Br* F Stempelgeld *n*; **go** *or* **be on the dole** *Br* F stempeln gehen; **2. dole out** sparsam ver- *or* austeilen

dole·ful traurig, trübselig

doll Puppe *f*

dol·lar Dollar *m*

dol·phin ZO Delphin *m*

dome Kuppel *f*

do·mes·tic 1. häuslich; inländisch, einheimisch; zahm; **2.** Hausangestellte *m*, *f*

domestic an·i·mal Haustier *n*

do·mes·ti·cate *Tier* zähmen

do·mes·tic flight AVIAT Inlandsflug *m*

domestic mar·ket ECON Binnenmarkt *m*

domestic trade ECON Binnenhandel *m*

domestic vi·olence häusliche Gewalt

dom·i·cile Wohnsitz *m*

dom·i·nant dominierend, (vor)herrschend

dom·i·nate beherrschen; dominieren

dom·i·na·tion (Vor)Herrschaft *f*

dom·i·neer·ing herrisch, tyrannisch

do·nate schenken; stiften; spenden (*a.* MED)

do·na·tion Schenkung *f*

done getan; erledigt; fertig; GASTR gar

don·key ZO Esel *m*

do·nor Spender(in) (*a.* MED)

do-noth·ing F Nichtstuer *m*

doom 1. Schicksal *n*, Verhängnis *n*; **2.** verurteilen, verdammen

Dooms·day der Jüngste Tag

door Tür *f*; Tor *n*; **next door** nebenan

door·bell Türklingel *f*

door han·dle Türklinke *f*

door·keep·er Pförtner *m*

door·knob Türknauf *m*

door·mat (Fuß)Abtreter *m*

door·step Türstufe *f*

door·way Türöffnung *f*

dope 1. F Stoff *m* (*Rauschgift*); Betäubungsmittel *n*; SPORT Dopingmittel *n*; *sl* Trottel *m*; **2.** F j-m Stoff geben; SPORT dopen

dope test SPORT Dopingkontrolle *f*

dor·mant schlafend, ruhend; untätig

dor·mi·to·ry Schlafsaal *m*; Studentenwohnheim *n*

dor·mo·bile® Campingbus *m*, Wohnmobil *n*

dor·mouse ZO Haselmaus *f*

dose 1. Dosis *f*; **2.** j-m e-e Medizin geben

dot 1. Punkt *m*; Fleck *m*; **on the dot** F auf die Sekunde pünktlich; **2.** punktieren; tüpfeln; *fig* sprenkeln; **dotted line** punktierte Linie

dote: dote on vernarrt sein in (*acc*)

dot·ing vernarrt

doub·le 1. doppelt; Doppel...; zweifach; **2.** Doppelte *n*; Doppelgänger(in); *film*, TV Double *n*; **3.** (sich) verdoppeln; *film*, TV *j-n* doubeln; *a.* **double up** falten; *Decke* zusammenlegen; **double back** kehrtmachen; **double up with** sich krümmen vor (*dat*)

dou·ble-breast·ed zweireihig

dou·ble-check genau nachprüfen

dou·ble chin Doppelkinn *n*

dou·ble-cross ein doppeltes *or* falsches Spiel treiben mit

dou·ble-deal·ing 1. betrügerisch; **2.** Betrug *m*

dou·ble-deck·er Doppeldecker *m*

dou·ble-edged zweischneidig (*a. fig*); zweideutig

dou·ble fea·ture *film*: Doppelprogramm *n*

dou·ble-park MOT in zweiter Reihe parken

dou·bles *esp tennis*: Doppel *n*; **men's doubles** Herrendoppel *n*; **women's doubles** Damendoppel *n*

dou·ble-sid·ed EDP zweiseitig

doubt 1. *v/i* zweifeln; *v/t* bezweifeln; misstrauen (*dat*); **2.** Zweifel *m*; **be in doubt about** Zweifel haben an (*dat*); **no doubt** ohne Zweifel

doubt·ful zweifelhaft

doubt·less ohne Zweifel

douche 1. Spülung *f* (*a.* MED); Spülapparat *m*; **2.** spülen (*a.* MED)

dough Teig *m*

dough·nut *appr* Krapfen *m*, Berliner Pfannkuchen, Schmalzkringel *m*

dove ZO Taube *f*

dow·dy unelegant; unmodern

dow·el TECH Dübel *m*

down¹ Daunen *pl*; Flaum *m*

down² 1. *adv* nach unten, herunter, hinunter, herab, hinab, abwärts; unten; **2.** *prp* herab, hinab, herunter, hinunter; **down the river** flussabwärts; **3.** *adj* nach unten gerichtet; deprimiert, niedergeschlagen; **down platform** Abfahrtsbahnsteig *m* (*in London*); **down train** Zug *m* (von London fort); **4.** *v/t* niederschlagen; *Flugzeug* abschießen; F *Getränk* runterkippen; **down tools** die Arbeit niederlegen, in den Streik treten

down·cast niedergeschlagen

down·fall Platzregen *m*; *fig* Sturz *m*

down·heart·ed niedergeschlagen

down·hill 1. *adv* bergab; **2.** *adj* abschüssig; *skiing*: Abfahrts...; **3.** Abhang *m*; *skiing*: Abfahrt *f*

down pay·ment ECON Anzahlung *f*

down·pour Regenguss *m*, Platzregen *m*

down·right 1. *adv* völlig, ganz und gar, ausgesprochen; **2.** *adj* glatt (*lie etc*); ausgesprochen

downs Hügelland *n*

down·stairs die Treppe herunter *or* hinunter; (nach) unten

down·stream stromabwärts

down-to-earth realistisch

down·town 1. *adv* im *or* ins Geschäftsviertel; **2.** *adj* im Geschäftsviertel (gelegen *or* tätig); **3.** Geschäftsviertel *n*, Innenstadt *f*, City *f*

down·ward(s) abwärts, nach unten

down·y flaumig

dow·ry Mitgift *f*

doze 1. dösen, ein Nickerchen machen; **2.** Nickerchen *n*

doz·en Dutzend *n*

drab trist; düster; eintönig

draft 1. Entwurf *m*; (Luft)Zug *m*; Zugluft *f*; Zug *m*, Schluck *m*; MAR Tiefgang *m*; ECON Tratte *f*, Wechsel *m*; MIL Einberufung *f*; **beer on draft, draft beer** Bier *n* vom Fass, Fassbier *n*; **2.** entwerfen; *Brief etc* aufsetzen; MIL einberufen

draft·ee MIL Wehr(dienst)pflichtige *m*

drafts·man TECH Zeichner *m*

drafts·wom·an TECH Zeichnerin *f*

draft·y zugig

drag 1. Schleppen *n*, Zerren *n*; *fig* Hemmschuh *m*; F *et.* Langweiliges; **2.** schleppen, zerren, ziehen, schleifen; *a.* **drag behind** zurückbleiben, nachhinken; **drag on** weiterschleppen; *fig* sich dahinschleppen; *fig* sich in die Länge ziehen

drag lift Schlepplift *m*

drag·on MYTH Drache *m*

drag·on·fly ZO Libelle *f*

drain 1. Abfluss(kanal) *m*, Abflussrohr *n*; Entwässerungsgraben *m*; **2.** *v/t* abfließen lassen; entwässern; austrinken, leeren; *v/i*: **drain off, drain away** abfließen, ablaufen

drain·age Abfließen *n*, Ablaufen *n*, Entwässerung *f*; Entwässerungsanlage *f*, -system *n*

drain·pipe Abflussrohr *n*

drake ZO Enterich *m*, Erpel *m*

dram Schluck *m*

dra·ma Drama *n*

dra·mat·ic dramatisch

dram·a·tist Dramatiker *m*

dram·a·tize dramatisieren

drape 1. drapieren; in Falten legen; **2.** *mst* **drapes** Vorhänge *pl*

drap·er·y *Br* Textilien *pl*

dras·tic drastisch, durchgreifend

draught *Br* → **draft**

draughts *Br* Damespiel *n*

draughts·man *etc* → **draftsman** *etc*

draugh·ty *Br* → **drafty**

draw 1. *v/t* ziehen; *Vorhänge* auf-, zuziehen; *Atem* holen; *Tee* ziehen lassen; *fig Menge* anziehen; *Interesse* auf sich ziehen; zeichnen; *Geld* abheben; *Scheck* ausstellen; *v/i* ziehen; SPORT unentschieden spielen; **draw back** zurückweichen; **draw near** sich nähern; **draw out** *Geld* abheben; *fig* in die Länge ziehen; **draw up** *Schriftstück* aufsetzen; MOT (an)halten; vorfahren; **2.** Ziehen *n*; *lottery*: Ziehung *f*; SPORT Unentschieden *n*; Attraktion *f*, Zugnummer *f*

draw·back Nachteil *m*, Hindernis *n*

draw·bridge Zugbrücke *f*

draw·er¹ Schublade *f*, Schubfach *n*

draw·er² Zeichner(in); ECON Aussteller(-in)

draw·ing Zeichnen *n*; Zeichnung *f*

drawing board Reißbrett *n*

drawing pin *Br* Reißzwecke *f*, Reißnagel *m*, Heftzwecke *f*

drawing room → **living room**; Salon *m*

drawl gedehnt sprechen

drawn abgespannt; SPORT unentschieden

dread 1. (große) Angst, Furcht *f*; **2.** (sich) fürchten

dread·ful schrecklich, furchtbar

dream 1. Traum *m*; **2.** träumen

dream·er Träumer(in)

dream·y träumerisch, verträumt

drear·y trübselig; trüb(e); langweilig

dredge 1. (Schwimm)Bagger *m*; **2.** (aus)baggern

dredg·er (Schwimm)Bagger *m*

dregs Bodensatz *m*; *fig* Abschaum *m*

drench durchnässen

dress 1. Kleidung *f*; Kleid *n*; **2.** (sich) ankleiden *or* anziehen; schmücken, dekorieren; zurechtmachen; GASTR zubereiten, *Salat* anmachen; MED *Wunde* verbinden; *Haare* frisieren; **get dressed** sich anziehen; **dress s.o. down** F j-m e-e Standpauke halten; **dress up** (sich) fein machen; sich kostümieren *or* verkleiden

dress cir·cle THEA erster Rang

dress de·sign·er Modezeichner(in)

dress·er Anrichte *f*; Toilettentisch *m*

dress·ing An-, Zurichten *n*; Ankleiden *n*; MED Verband *m*; GASTR Dressing *n*, Füllung *f*

dressing-down F Standpauke *f*

dress·ing gown *esp Br* Morgenrock *m*, -mantel *m*; SPORT Bademantel *m*

dressing room THEA *etc* (Künstler)Garderobe *f*; SPORT (Umkleide)Kabine *f*

dressing ta·ble Toilettentisch *m*

dress·mak·er (Damen)Schneider(in)

dress re·hears·al THEA *etc* Generalprobe *f*

drib·ble tröpfeln (lassen); sabbern, geifern; *soccer*: dribbeln

dried getrocknet, Dörr…

dri·er → **dryer**

drift 1. (Dahin)Treiben *n*; (Schnee)Verwehung *f*; Schnee-, Sandwehe *f*; *fig* Tendenz *f*; **2.** (dahin)treiben; wehen; sich häufen

drill 1. TECH Bohrer *m*; MIL Drill *m* (*a. fig*), Exerzieren *n*; **2.** bohren; MIL drillen (*a. fig*)

drill·ing site TECH Bohrgelände *n*, Bohrstelle *f*

drink 1. Getränk *n*; **2.** trinken; **drink to s.o.** j-m zuprosten *or* zutrinken

drink-driv·ing *Br* Trunkenheit *f* am Steuer

drink·er Trinker(in)

drinks ma·chine Getränkeautomat *m*

drip 1. Tröpfeln *n*; MED Tropf *m*; **2.** tropfen *or* tröpfeln (lassen); triefen

drip-dry bügelfrei

drip·ping Bratenfett *n*

drive 1. Fahrt *f*; Aus-, Spazierfahrt *f*; Zufahrt(sstraße) *f*; (private) Auffahrt *f*; TECH Antrieb *m*; EDP Laufwerk *n*; MOT (*Links-etc*)Steuerung *f*; PSYCH Trieb *m*; *fig* Kampagne *f*; *fig* Schwung *m*, Elan *m*, Dynamik *f*; **2.** *v/t* treiben; *Auto etc* fahren, lenken, steuern; (im *Auto etc*) fahren; TECH (an)treiben; *a.* **drive off** vertreiben; *v/i* treiben; (Auto) fahren; **drive off** wegfahren; **what are you driving at?** F worauf wollen Sie hinaus?

drive-in 1. Auto…; **drive-in cinema** *Br*, **drive-in motion-picture theater** Autokino *n*; **2.** Autokino *n*; Drive-in-Restaurant *n*; Autoschalter *m*, Drive-in-Schalter *m*

driv·el 1. faseln; **2.** Geschwätz *n*, Gefasel *n*

driv·er MOT Fahrer(in); (*Lokomotiv-*) Führer *m*

driv·er's li·cense Führerschein *m*

driv·ing (an)treibend; TECH Antriebs…, Treib…, Trieb…; MOT Fahr…

driv·ing force *fig* Triebkraft *f*

driv·ing li·cence *Br* Führerschein *m*

driv·ing test Fahrprüfung *f*

driz·zle 1. Sprühregen *m*; **2.** sprühen, nieseln

drone 1. ZO Drohne *f* (*a. fig*); **2.** summen; dröhnen

droop (schlaff) herabhängen

drop 1. Tropfen *m*; Fallen *n*, Fall *m*; *fig* Fall *m*, Sturz *m*; Bonbon *m*, *n*; **fruit drops** Drops *pl*; **2.** *v/t* tropfen (lassen); fallen lassen (*a. fig*); *Brief* einwerfen;

Fahrgast absetzen; senken; *drop s.o. a few lines* j-m ein paar Zeilen schreiben; *v/i* tropfen; herab-, herunterfallen; umsinken, fallen; *drop in* (kurz) hereinschauen; *drop off* abfallen; zurückgehen, nachlassen; F einnicken; *drop out* herausfallen; aussteigen (*of* aus); *a. drop out of school* (*university*) die Schule (das Studium) abbrechen

drop·out Drop-out *m*, Aussteiger *m*; (Schul-, Studien)Abbrecher *m*

drought Trockenheit *f*, Dürre *f*

drown *v/t* ertränken; überschwemmen; *fig* übertönen; *v/i* ertrinken

drow·sy schläfrig; einschläfernd

drudge sich (ab)placken, schuften, sich schinden

drudg·e·ry (stumpfsinnige) Plackerei *or* Schinderei *or* Schufterei

drug 1. Arzneimittel *n*, Medikament *n*; Droge *f*, Rauschgift *n*; *be on drugs* drogenabhängig *or* drogensüchtig sein; *be off drugs* clean sein; **2.** j-m Medikamente geben; *j-n* unter Drogen setzen; ein Betäubungsmittel beimischen (*dat*); betäuben (*a. fig*)

drug a·buse Drogenmissbrauch *m*; Medikamentenmissbrauch *m*

drug ad·dict Drogenabhängige *m, f*, Drogensüchtige *m, f*; *be a drug addict* drogenabhängig *or* drogensüchtig sein

drug·gist Apotheker(in); Inhaber(in) e-s Drugstores

drug·store Apotheke *f*; Drugstore *m*

drug vic·tim Drogentote *m, f*

drum 1. MUS Trommel *f*; ANAT Trommelfell *n*; *pl* MUS Schlagzeug *n*; **2.** trommeln

drum·mer MUS Trommler *m*; Schlagzeuger *m*

drunk 1. *adj* betrunken; *get drunk* sich betrinken; **2.** Betrunkene *m, f*; → *drunkard*

drunk·ard Trinker(in), Säufer(in)

drunk driv·ing Trunkenheit *f* am Steuer

drunk·en betrunken

drunken driv·ing *Br* Trunkenheit *f* am Steuer

dry 1. trocken, GASTR *a.* herb; F durstig; **2.** trocknen; dörren; *dry out* trocknen; e-e Entziehungskur machen, F trocken werden; *dry up* austrocknen; versiegen

dry-clean chemisch reinigen

dry clean·er's chemische Reinigung

dry·er TECH Trockner *m*

dry goods Textilien *pl*

du·al doppelt, Doppel...

dual car·riage·way *Br* Schnellstraße *f*

dub *Film* synchronisieren

du·bi·ous zweifelhaft

duch·ess Herzogin *f*

duck 1. ZO Ente *f*; Ducken *n*; F Schatz *m*; **2.** (unter)tauchen; (sich) ducken

duck·ling ZO Entchen *n*

due 1. zustehend; gebührend; angemessen; ECON fällig; *due to* wegen (*gen*); *be due to* zurückzuführen sein *auf* (*acc*); **2.** *adv* direkt, genau (*nach Osten etc*)

du·el Duell *n*

dues Gebühren *pl*; Beitrag *m*

du·et MUS Duett *n*

duke Herzog *m*

dull 1. dumm; träge, schwerfällig; stumpf; matt (*eyes etc*); schwach (*hearing*); langweilig; abgestumpft, teilnahmslos; dumpf; trüb(e); ECON flau; **2.** stumpf machen *or* werden; (sich) trüben; mildern, dämpfen; *Schmerz* betäuben; *fig* abstumpfen

du·ly ordnungsgemäß; gebührend; rechtzeitig

dumb stumm; sprachlos; F doof, dumm, blöd

dum(b)·found·ed verblüfft, sprachlos

dum·my Attrappe *f*; Kleider-, Schaufensterpuppe *f*; MOT Dummy *m*, Puppe *f*; *Br* Schnuller *m*

dump 1. *v/t* (hin)plumpsen *or* (hin)fallen lassen; auskippen; *Schutt etc* abladen; *Schadstoffe* in e-n *Fluss etc* einleiten, im Meer verklappen (*into* in); ECON *Waren* zu Dumpingpreisen verkaufen; **2.** Plumps *m*; Schuttabladeplatz *m*, Müllkippe *f*, Müllhalde *f*, (Müll)Deponie *f*

dump·ing ECON Dumping *n*, Ausfuhr *f* zu Schleuderpreisen

dune Düne *f*

dung AGR **1.** Dung *m*; **2.** düngen

dun·geon (Burg)Verlies *n*

dupe betrügen, täuschen

du·plex 1. doppelt, Doppel...; **2.** *a.* *duplex apartment* Maisonette *f*, Maisonettewohnung *f*; *a.* *duplex house* Doppel-, Zweifamilienhaus *n*

du·pli·cate 1. doppelt; *duplicate key* Zweit-, Nachschlüssel *m*; **2.** Duplikat *n*; Zweit-, Nachschlüssel *m*; **3.** doppelt ausfertigen; kopieren, vervielfältigen

du·plic·i·ty Doppelzüngigkeit *f*

dur·a·ble haltbar; dauerhaft

du·ra·tion Dauer *f*

du·ress Zwang *m*

dur·ing während

dusk (Abend)Dämmerung *f*

dusk·y dämmerig, düster (*a. fig*); schwärzlich

dust 1. Staub *m*; **2.** *v/t* abstauben; (be)streuen; *v/i* Staub wischen, abstauben

dust·bin *Br* Abfall-, Mülleimer *m*; Ab-

fall-, Mülltonne *f*
dustbin lin·er *Br* Müllbeutel *m*
dust·cart *Br* Müllwagen *m*
dust·er Staubtuch *n*
dust cov·er, dust jack·et Schutzumschlag *m*
dust·man *Br* Müllmann *m*
dust·pan Kehrichtschaufel *f*
dust·y staubig
Dutch 1. *adj* holländisch, niederländisch; **2.** *adv*: **go Dutch** getrennte Kasse machen; **3.** LING Holländisch *n*, Niederländisch *n*; **the Dutch** die Holländer *pl*, die Niederländer *pl*
Dutch·man Holländer *m*, Niederländer *m*
Dutch·wom·an Holländerin *f*, Niederländerin *f*
du·ti·a·ble ECON zollpflichtig
du·ty Pflicht *f*; Ehrerbietung *f*; ECON Abgabe *f*; Zoll *m*; Dienst *m*; **on duty** dienst-

habend; **be on duty** Dienst haben; **be off duty** dienstfrei haben
du·ty-free zollfrei
dwarf 1. Zwerg(in); **2.** verkleinern, klein erscheinen lassen
dwell wohnen; *fig* verweilen (**on** bei)
dwell·ing Wohnung *f*
dwin·dle (dahin)schwinden, abnehmen
dye 1. Farbe *f*; **of the deepest dye** *fig* von der übelsten Sorte; **2.** färben
dy·ing 1. sterbend; Sterbe…; **2.** Sterben *n*; **dying of forests** Waldsterben *n*
dyke → **dike**[1, 2]
dy·nam·ic dynamisch, kraftgeladen
dy·nam·ics Dynamik *f*
dy·na·mite 1. Dynamit *n*; **2.** (mit Dynamit) sprengen
dys·en·te·ry MED Ruhr *f*
dys·pep·si·a MED Verdauungsstörung *f*

E

E, e E, e *n*
each jede(r, -s); **each other** einander, sich; je, pro Person, pro Stück
ea·ger begierig; eifrig
ea·ger·ness Begierde *f*; Eifer *m*
ea·gle ZO Adler *m*; HIST Zehndollarstück *n*
ea·gle-eyed scharfsichtig
ear BOT Ähre *f*; ANAT Ohr *n*; Öhr *n*; Henkel *m*; **keep an ear to the ground** die Ohren offen halten
ear·ache Ohrenschmerzen *pl*
ear·drum ANAT Trommelfell *n*
earl *englischer* Graf
ear·lobe ANAT Ohrläppchen *n*
ear·ly früh; Früh…; Anfangs…, erste(r, -s); bald(ig); **as early as May** schon im Mai; **as early as possible** so bald wie möglich; **early on** schon früh, frühzeitig
ear·ly bird Frühaufsteher(in)
ear·ly warn·ing sys·tem MIL Frühwarnsystem *n*
ear·mark 1. Kennzeichen *n*; Merkmal *n*; **2.** kennzeichnen; zurücklegen (**for** für)
earn verdienen; einbringen
ear·nest 1. ernst, ernstlich, ernsthaft; ernst gemeint; **2.** Ernst *m*; **in earnest** im Ernst; ernsthaft
earn·ings Einkommen *n*

ear·phones Ohrhörer *pl*; Kopfhörer *pl*
ear·piece TEL Hörmuschel *f*
ear·ring Ohrring *m*
ear·shot: **within (out of) earshot** in (außer) Hörweite
earth 1. Erde *f*; Land *n*; **2.** *v/t* ELECTR erden
earth·en irden
earth·en·ware Steingut(geschirr) *n*
earth·ly irdisch, weltlich; F denkbar
earth·quake Erdbeben *n*
earth·worm ZO Regenwurm *m*
ease 1. Bequemlichkeit *f*; (Gemüts)Ruhe *f*; Sorglosigkeit *f*; Leichtigkeit *f*; **at (one's) ease** ruhig, entspannt; unbefangen; **be or feel ill at ease** sich (in s-r Haut) nicht wohlfühlen; **2.** *v/t* erleichtern; beruhigen; *Schmerzen* lindern; *v/i mst* **ease up** nachlassen; sich entspannen (*situation etc*)
ea·sel Staffelei *f*
east 1. Ost, Osten *m*; **2.** *adj* östlich, Ost…; **3.** *adv* nach Osten, ostwärts
Eas·ter Ostern *n*; Oster…
Easter bun·ny Osterhase *m*
Easter egg Osterei *n*
eas·ter·ly östlich, Ost…
east·ern östlich, Ost…
east·ward(s) östlich, nach Osten
eas·y leicht; einfach; bequem; gemäch-

lich, gemütlich; ungezwungen; **go easy
on** schonen, sparsam umgehen mit; **go
easy, take it easy** sich Zeit lassen; **take
it easy!** immer mit der Ruhe!

eas·y chair Sessel *m*

eas·y·go·ing gelassen; ungezwungen

eat essen; (zer)fressen; **eat out** essen gehen; **eat up** aufessen

eat·a·ble essbar, genießbar

eat·er Esser(in)

eaves Dachrinne *f*, Traufe *f*

eaves·drop (heimlich) lauschen *or* horchen; **eavesdrop on** belauschen

ebb 1. Ebbe *f*; **2.** zurückgehen; **ebb away** abnehmen

ebb tide Ebbe *f*

eb·o·ny Ebenholz *n*

ec ABBR *of* **Eurocheque** *Br* Eurocheque *m*

ec·cen·tric 1. exzentrisch; **2.** Exzentriker *m*, Sonderling *m*

ec·cle·si·as·tic, ec·cle·si·as·ti·cal geistlich, kirchlich

ech·o 1. Echo *n*; **2.** widerhallen; *fig* echoen, nachsprechen

e·clipse ASTR (*Sonnen-, Mond*)Finsternis *f*; *fig* Niedergang *m*

e·co·cide Umweltzerstörung *f*

e·co·lo·gi·cal ökologisch, Umwelt...

e·col·o·gist Ökologe *m*

e·col·o·gy Ökologie *f*

ec·o·nom·ic Wirtschafts..., wirtschaftlich; **economic growth** Wirtschaftswachstum *n*

e·co·nom·i·cal wirtschaftlich, sparsam

e·co·nom·ics Volkswirtschaft(slehre) *f*

e·con·o·mist Volkswirt *m*

e·con·o·mize sparsam wirtschaften (mit)

e·con·o·my 1. Wirtschaft *f*; Wirtschaftlichkeit *f*, Sparsamkeit *f*; Einsparung *f*; **2.** Spar...

e·co·sys·tem Ökosystem *n*

ec·sta·sy Ekstase *f*, Verzückung *f*

ec·stat·ic verzückt

ed·dy 1. Wirbel *m*; **2.** wirbeln

edge 1. Schneide *f*; Rand *m*; Kante *f*; Schärfe *f*; **be on edge** nervös *or* gereizt sein; **2.** schärfen; (um)säumen; (sich) drängen

edge·ways, edge·wise seitlich, von der Seite

edg·ing Einfassung *f*; Rand *m*

edg·y scharf(kantig); F nervös; F gereizt

ed·i·ble essbar, genießbar

e·dict Edikt *n*

ed·i·fice Gebäude *n*

ed·it *Text* herausgeben, redigieren; EDP editieren; *Zeitung* als Herausgeber leiten

e·di·tion (*Buch*)Ausgabe *f*; Auflage *f*

ed·i·tor Herausgeber(in); Redakteur(in)

ed·i·to·ri·al 1. Leitartikel *m*; **2.** Redaktions...

EDP ABBR *of* **electronic data processing** EDV, elektronische Datenverarbeitung

ed·u·cate erziehen; unterrichten

ed·u·cat·ed gebildet

ed·u·ca·tion Erziehung *f*; (Aus)Bildung *f*; Bildungs-, Schulwesen *n*; **Ministry of Education** *appr Unterrichtsministerium*

ed·u·ca·tion·al erzieherisch, pädagogisch, Erziehungs...; Bildungs...

ed·u·ca·tion·(al·)ist Pädagoge *m*

eel ZO Aal *m*

ef·fect (Aus)Wirkung *f*; Effekt *m*, Eindruck *m*; *pl* ECON Effekten *pl*; **be in effect** in Kraft sein; **in effect** in Wirklichkeit; **take effect** in Kraft treten

ef·fec·tive wirksam; eindrucksvoll; tatsächlich

ef·fem·i·nate verweichlicht; weibisch

ef·fer·vesce brausen, sprudeln

ef·fer·ves·cent sprudelnd, schäumend

ef·fi·cien·cy Leistung *f*; Leistungsfähigkeit *f*; **efficiency measure** ECON Rationalisierungsmaßnahme *f*

ef·fi·cient wirksam; leistungsfähig, tüchtig

ef·flu·ent Abwasser *n*, Abwässer *pl*

ef·fort Anstrengung *f*, Bemühung *f* (**at** um); Mühe *f*; **without effort → ef·fort·less** mühelos, ohne Anstrengung

ef·fron·te·ry Frechheit *f*

ef·fu·sive überschwänglich

egg[1] Ei *n*; **put all one's eggs in one basket** alles auf eine Karte setzen

egg[2]: **egg on** anstacheln

egg co·sy *Br* Eierwärmer *m*

egg·cup Eierbecher *m*

egg·head F Eierkopf *m*

egg·plant BOT Aubergine *f*

egg·shell Eierschale *f*

egg tim·er Eieruhr *f*

e·go·is·m Egoismus *m*, Selbstsucht *f*

e·go·ist Egoist(in)

E·gypt Ägypten *n*

E·gyp·tian 1. ägyptisch; **2.** Ägypter(in)

ei·der·down Eiderdaunen *pl*; Daunendecke *f*

eight 1. acht; **2.** Acht *f*

eigh·teen 1. achtzehn; **2.** Achtzehn *f*

eigh·teenth achtzehnte(r, -s)

eight·fold achtfach

eighth 1. achte(r, -s); **2.** Achtel *n*

eighth·ly achtens

eigh·ti·eth achtzigste(r, -s)

eigh·ty 1. achtzig; **the eighties** die Achtzigerjahre; **2.** Achtzig *f*

ei·ther jede(r, -s) (*von zweien*): eine(r, -s)

(*von zweien*); beides; **either ... or** entweder ... oder; **not either** auch nicht

e·jac·u·late *v/t Samen* ausstoßen; *v/i* ejakulieren, e-n Samenerguss haben

e·jac·u·la·tion Samenerguss *m*

e·ject *j-n* hinauswerfen; TECH ausstoßen, auswerfen

eke: eke out *Vorräte etc* strecken; *Einkommen* aufbessern; **eke out a living** sich (mühsam) durchschlagen

e·lab·o·rate 1. sorgfältig (aus)gearbeitet; kompliziert; **2.** sorgfältig ausarbeiten

e·lapse verfließen, verstreichen

e·las·tic 1. elastisch, dehnbar; **elastic band** *Br* → **2.** Gummiring *m*, Gummiband *n*

e·las·ti·ci·ty Elastizität *f*

e·lat·ed begeistert (**at, by** von)

el·bow 1. Ellbogen *m*; (scharfe) Biegung; TECH Knie *n*; **at one's elbow** bei der Hand; **2.** mit dem Ellbogen (weg)stoßen; **elbow one's way through** sich (mit den Ellbogen) e-n Weg bahnen durch

el·der[1] **1.** ältere(r, -s); **2.** der, die Ältere; (Kirchen)Älteste(r) *m*

el·der[2] BOT Holunder *m*

el·der·ly ältlich, ältere(r, -s)

el·dest älteste(r, -s)

e·lect 1. gewählt; **2.** (aus-, er)wählen

e·lec·tion Wahl *f*

election vic·to·ry POL Wahlsieg *m*

election win·ner POL Wahlsieger *m*

e·lec·tor Wähler(in); POL Wahlmann *m*; HIST Kurfürst *m*

e·lec·to·ral Wähler..., Wahl...; **electoral college** POL Wahlmänner *pl*; **electoral district** POL Wahlkreis *m*

elec·to·rate POL Wähler(schaft *f*) *pl*

e·lec·tric elektrisch, Elektro...

e·lec·tri·cal elektrisch; Elektro...

electrical en·gi·neer Elektroingenieur *m*, Elektrotechniker *m*

electrical en·gi·neer·ing Eletrotechnik *f*

e·lec·tric chair elektrischer Stuhl

e·lec·tri·cian Elektriker *m*

e·lec·tri·ci·ty Elektrizität *f*

e·lec·tric ra·zor Elektrorasierer *m*

e·lec·tri·fy elektrifizieren; elektrisieren (*a. fig*)

e·lec·tro·cute auf dem elektrischen Stuhl hinrichten; durch elektrischen Strom töten

e·lec·tron Elektron *n*

e·lec·tron·ic elektronisch, Elektronen...

electronic da·ta pro·cess·ing elektronische Datenverarbeitung

e·lec·tron·ics Elektronik *f*

el·e·gance Eleganz *f*

el·egant elegant; geschmackvoll; erstklassig

el·e·ment CHEM Element *n*; Urstoff *m*; (Grund)Bestandteil *m*; *pl* Anfangsgründe *pl*, Grundlage(n *pl*) *f*; Elemente *pl*, Naturkräfte *pl*

el·e·men·tal elementar; wesentlich

el·e·men·ta·ry elementar; Anfangs...

elementary school Grundschule *f*

el·e·phant ZO Elefant *m*

el·e·vate erhöhen; *fig* erheben

el·e·vat·ed erhöht; *fig* gehoben, erhaben

el·e·va·tion Erhebung *f*; Erhöhung *f*; Höhe *f*; Erhabenheit *f*

el·e·va·tor TECH Lift *m*, Fahrstuhl *m*, Aufzug *m*

e·lev·en 1. elf; **2.** Elf *f*

e·leventh 1. elfte(r, -s); **2.** Elftel *n*

elf Elf *m*, Elfe *f*; Kobold *m*

e·li·cit *et.* entlocken (**from** *dat*); ans (Tages)Licht bringen

el·i·gi·ble infrage kommend, geeignet, annehmbar, akzeptabel

e·lim·i·nate entfernen, beseitigen; ausscheiden

e·lim·i·na·tion Entfernung *f*, Beseitigung *f*; Ausscheidung *f*

é·lite Elite *f*; Auslese *f*

elk ZO Elch *m*; Wapitihirsch *m*

elm BOT Ulme *f*

e·lon·gate verlängern

e·lope (mit s-m *or* s-r Geliebten) ausreißen *or* durchbrennen

el·o·quent redegewandt, beredt

else sonst, weiter; andere(r, -s)

else·where anderswo(hin)

e·lude geschickt entgehen, ausweichen, sich entziehen (*all: dat*); *fig* nicht einfallen (*dat*)

e·lu·sive schwer fassbar

e·ma·ci·ated abgezehrt, ausgemergelt

em·a·nate ausströmen; ausgehen (**from** von)

em·a·na·tion Ausströmen *n*; *fig* Ausstrahlung *f*

e·man·ci·pate emanzipieren

e·man·ci·pa·tion Emanzipation *f*

em·balm (ein)balsamieren

em·bank·ment (Bahn-, Straßen-) Damm *m*; (Erd)Damm *m*; Uferstraße *f*

em·bar·go ECON Embargo *n*, (Hafen-, Handels)Sperre *f*

em·bark AVIAT, MAR an Bord nehmen *or* gehen, MAR *a.* (sich) einschiffen; *Waren* verladen; **embark on** *et.* anfangen, *et.* beginnen

em·bar·rass in Verlegenheit bringen, verlegen machen, in e-e peinliche Lage bringen

E

em·bar·rass·ing unangenehm, peinlich; verfänglich

em·bar·rass·ment Verlegenheit *f*

em·bas·sy POL Botschaft *f*

em·bed (ein)betten, (ein)lagern

em·bel·lish verschönern; *fig* ausschmücken, beschönigen

em·bers Glut *f*

em·bez·zle unterschlagen

em·bez·zle·ment Unterschlagung *f*

em·bit·ter verbittern

em·blem Sinnbild *n*; Wahrzeichen *n*

em·bod·y verkörpern; enthalten

em·bo·lis·m MED Embolie *f*

em·brace 1. (sich) umarmen; einschließen; **2.** Umarmung *f*

em·broi·der (be)sticken; *fig* ausschmücken

em·broi·der·y Stickerei *f*; *fig* Ausschmückung *f*

em·broil verwickeln (*in* in *acc*)

e·mend *Texte* verbessern, korrigieren

em·e·rald 1. Smaragd *m*; **2.** smaragdgrün

e·merge auftauchen; sich herausstellen *or* ergeben

e·mer·gen·cy 1. Not *f*, Notlage *f*, Notfall *m*, Notstand *m*; **state of emergency** POL Ausnahmezustand *m*; **2.** Not...

emergency brake Notbremse *f*

emergency call Notruf *m*

emergency ex·it Notausgang *m*

emergency land·ing AVIAT Notlandung *f*

emergency num·ber Notruf(nummer *f*) *m*

emergency room MED Notaufnahme *f*

em·i·grant Auswanderer *m*, *esp* POL Emigrant(in)

em·i·grate auswandern, *esp* POL emigrieren

em·i·gra·tion Auswanderung *f*, *esp* POL Emigration *f*

em·i·nence Berühmtheit *f*, Bedeutung *f*; **Eminence** REL Eminenz *f*

em·i·nent hervorragend, berühmt; bedeutend

eminently ganz besonders, äußerst

e·mis·sion Ausstoß *m*, Ausstrahlung *f*, Ausströmen *n*

emission-free abgasfrei

e·mit aussenden, ausstoßen, ausstrahlen, ausströmen; von sich geben

e·mo·tion (Gemüts)Bewegung *f*, Gefühl *n*, Gefühlsregung *f*; Rührung *f*

e·mo·tion·al emotional; gefühlsmäßig; gefühlsbetont

e·mo·tion·al·ly emotional, gefühlsmäßig; **emotionally disturbed** seelisch gestört

e·mo·tion·less gefühllos

e·mo·tive word PSYCH Reizwort *n*

em·pe·ror Kaiser *m*

em·pha·sis Gewicht *n*; Nachdruck *m*

em·pha·size nachdrücklich betonen

em·phat·ic nachdrücklich; deutlich; bestimmt

em·pire Reich *n*, Imperium *n*; Kaiserreich *n*

em·pir·i·cal erfahrungsgemäß

em·ploy 1. beschäftigen, anstellen; an-, verwenden, gebrauchen; **2.** Beschäftigung *f*; **in the employ of** angestellt bei;

em·ploy·ee Angestellte *m*, *f*, Arbeitnehmer(in)

em·ploy·er Arbeitgeber(in)

em·ploy·ment Beschäftigung *f*, Arbeit *f*

employment ad Stellenanzeige *f*

employment of·fice Arbeitsamt *n*

em·pow·er ermächtigen; befähigen

em·press Kaiserin *f*

emp·ti·ness Leere *f* (*a. fig*)

emp·ty 1. leer (*a. fig*); **2.** leeren, ausleeren, entleeren; sich leeren

em·u·late wetteifern mit; nacheifern (*dat*); es gleichtun (*dat*)

e·mul·sion Emulsion *f*

en·a·ble befähigen, es *j-m* ermöglichen; ermächtigen

en·act *Gesetz* erlassen; verfügen

e·nam·el 1. Email *n*, Emaille *f*; ANAT (Zahn)Schmelz *m*; Glasur *f*, Lack *m*; Nagellack *m*; **2.** emaillieren; glasieren; lackieren

en·am·o(u)red: enamo(u)red of verliebt in (*acc*)

en·camp·ment *esp* MIL (Feld)Lager *n*

en·cased: encased in gehüllt in (*acc*)

en·chant bezaubern

en·chant·ing bezaubernd

en·chant·ment Bezauberung *f*; Zauber *m*

en·cir·cle einkreisen, umzingeln; umfassen, umschlingen

en·close einschließen, umgeben; beilegen, beifügen

en·clo·sure Einzäunung *f*; Anlage *f*

en·code verschlüsseln, chiffrieren; kodieren

en·com·pass umgeben

en·coun·ter 1. Begegnung *f*; Gefecht *n*; **2.** begegnen (*dat*); auf *Schwierigkeiten etc* stoßen; mit *j-m feindlich* zusammenstoßen

en·cour·age ermutigen; fördern

en·cour·age·ment Ermutigung *f*; Anfeuerung *f*; Unterstützung *f*

en·cour·ag·ing ermutigend

en·croach (on) eingreifen (in *j-s Recht etc*), eindringen (in *acc*); über Gebühr in Anspruch nehmen (*acc*)

en·croach·ment Ein-, Übergriff *m*

en·cum·ber belasten; (be)hindern
en·cum·brance Belastung *f*
en·cy·clo·p(a)e·di·a Enzyklopädie *f*
end 1. Ende *n*; Ziel *n*, Zweck *m*; **no end of** unendlich viel(e), unzählige; **at the end of May** Ende Mai; **in the end** am Ende, schließlich; **on end** aufrecht; **stand on end** zu Berge stehen (*hair*); **to no end** vergebens; **go off the deep end** F *fig* in die Luft gehen; **make** (**both**) **ends meet** durchkommen, finanziell über die Runden kommen; **2.** enden; beend(-ig)en
en·dan·ger gefährden
en·dear beliebt machen (**to s.o.** bei j-m)
en·dear·ing gewinnend; liebenswert
en·dear·ment: **words of endearment, endearments** zärtliche Worte *pl*
en·deav·o(u)r 1. Bestreben *n*, Bemühung *f*; **2.** sich bemühen
end·ing Ende *n*; Schluss *m*; LING Endung *f*
en·dive BOT Endivie *f*
end·less endlos, unendlich; TECH ohne Ende
en·dorse ECON *Scheck etc* indossieren; *et.* vermerken (**on** auf der Rückseite); billigen
en·dorse·ment Vermerk *m*; ECON Indossament *n*, Giro *n*
en·dow *fig* ausstatten; **endow s.o. with s.th.** j-m et. stiften
en·dow·ment Stiftung *f*; *mst pl* Begabung *f*, Talent *n*
en·dur·ance Ausdauer *f*; **beyond endurance, past endurance** unerträglich
en·dure ertragen
end us·er Endverbraucher *m*
en·e·my 1. Feind *m*; **2.** feindlich
en·er·get·ic energisch; tatkräftig
en·er·gy Energie *f*
en·er·gy cri·sis Energiekrise *f*
en·er·gy-sav·ing energiesparend
en·er·gy sup·ply Energieversorgung *f*
en·fold einhüllen; umfassen
en·force (mit Nachdruck, *a.* gerichtlich) geltend machen; *Gesetz etc* durchführen; durchsetzen, erzwingen
en·force·ment ECON, JUR Geltendmachung *f*; Durchsetzung *f*, Erzwingung *f*
en·fran·chise *j-m* das Wahlrecht verleihen
en·gage *v/t j-s Aufmerksamkeit* auf sich ziehen; TECH einrasten lassen; MOT *e-n Gang* einlegen; *j-n* einstellen, anstellen, *Künstler* engagieren; *v/i* TECH einrasten, greifen; **engage in** sich einlassen auf (*acc*) *or* in (*acc*); sich beschäftigen mit
en·gaged verlobt (**to** mit); beschäftigt (**in, on** mit); besetzt (*a. Br* TEL); **engaged**

tone *or* **signal** *Br* TEL Besetztzeichen *n*
en·gage·ment Verlobung *f*; Verabredung *f*; MIL Gefecht *n*
en·gag·ing einnehmend; gewinnend
en·gine Maschine *f*; Motor *m*; RAIL Lokomotive *f*
engine driv·er *Br* RAIL Lokomotivführer *m*
en·gi·neer 1. Ingenieur *m*, Techniker *m*, Mechaniker *m*; RAIL Lokomotivführer *m*; MIL Pionier *m*; **2.** bauen; *fig* (geschickt) in die Wege leiten
en·gi·neer·ing Technik *f*, Ingenieurwesen *n*, Maschinen- und Gerätebau *m*
En·gland England *n*
En·glish 1. englisch; **2.** LING Englisch *n*; **the English** die Engländer *pl*; **in plain English** *fig* unverblümt
Eng·lish·man Engländer *m*
Eng·lish·wom·an Engländerin *f*
en·grave (ein)gravieren, (ein)meißeln, (ein)schnitzen; *fig* einprägen
en·grav·er Graveur *m*
en·grav·ing (Kupfer-, Stahl)Stich *m*; Holzschnitt *m*
en·grossed: **engrossed in** (voll) in Anspruch genommen von, vertieft *or* versunken in (*acc*)
en·hance erhöhen, verstärken, steigern
e·nig·ma Rätsel *n*
en·ig·mat·ic rätselhaft
en·joy sich erfreuen an (*dat*); genießen; **did you enjoy it?** hat es Ihnen gefallen?; **enjoy o.s.** sich amüsieren, sich gut unterhalten; **enjoy yourself!** viel Spaß!; **I enjoy my dinner** es schmeckt mir
en·joy·a·ble angenehm, erfreulich
en·joy·ment Vergnügen *n*, Freude *f*; Genuss *m*
en·large (sich) vergrößern *or* erweitern, ausdehnen; PHOT vergrößern; sich verbreiten *or* auslassen (**on** über *acc*)
en·large·ment Erweiterung *f*; Vergrößerung *f* (*a.* PHOT)
en·light·en aufklären, belehren
en·light·en·ment Aufklärung *f*
en·list MIL *v/t* anwerben; *v/i* sich freiwillig melden; **enlisted men** Unteroffiziere *pl* und Mannschaften *pl*
en·liv·en beleben
en·mi·ty Feindschaft *f*
en·no·ble adeln; veredeln
e·nor·mi·ty Ungeheuerlichkeit *f*
e·nor·mous ungeheuer
e·nough genug
en·quire, en·qui·ry → **inquire, inquiry**
en·rage wütend machen
en·raged wütend (**at** über *acc*)
en·rap·ture entzücken, hinreißen

en·rap·tured entzückt, hingerissen

en·rich bereichern; anreichern

en·rol(l) (sich) einschreiben *or* eintragen; UNIV (sich) immatrikulieren

en·sign *esp* (National)Flagge *f*; MIL Leutnant *m* zur See

en·sue (darauf-, nach)folgen

en·sure sichern

en·tail mit sich bringen, zur Folge haben

en·tan·gle verwickeln

en·ter *v/t* hinein-, hereingehen, -kommen, -treten in (*acc*), eintreten, einsteigen in (*acc*), betreten; einreisen in (*acc*); MAR, RAIL einlaufen, einfahren in (*acc*); eindringen in (*acc*); *Namen etc* eintragen, einschreiben; SPORT melden, nennen (**for** für); *fig* eintreten in (*acc*), beitreten (*dat*); EDP eingeben; *v/i* eintreten, herein-, hineinkommen, herein-, hineingehen; THEA auftreten; sich eintragen *or* einschreiben *or* anmelden (**for** für); SPORT melden, nennen (**for** für)

en·ter key EDP Eingabetaste *f*

en·ter·prise Unternehmen *n* (*a.* ECON); ECON Unternehmertum *n*; Unternehmungsgeist *m*

en·ter·pris·ing unternehmungslustig; wagemutig; kühn

en·ter·tain unterhalten; bewirten

en·ter·tain·er Entertainer(in), Unterhaltungskünstler(in)

en·ter·tain·ment Unterhaltung *f*; Entertainment *n*; Bewirtung *f*

en·thral(l) fesseln, bezaubern

en·throne inthronisieren

en·thu·si·asm Begeisterung *f*, Enthusiasmus *m*

en·thu·si·ast Enthusiast(in)

en·thu·si·as·tic begeistert, enthusiastisch

en·tice (ver)locken

en·tice·ment Verlockung *f*, Reiz *m*

en·tire ganz, vollständig; ungeteilt

en·tire·ly völlig; ausschließlich

en·ti·tle betiteln; berechtigen (**to** zu)

en·ti·ty Einheit *f*

en·trails ANAT Eingeweide *pl*

en·trance Eintreten *n*, Eintritt *m*; Eingang *m*, Zugang *m*; Zufahrt *f*; Einlass *m*, Eintritt *m*, Zutritt *m*

en·trance ex·am(·i·na·tion) Aufnahmeprüfung *f*

entrance fee Eintritt *m*, Eintrittsgeld *n*; Aufnahmegebühr *f*

en·treat inständig bitten, anflehen

en·trea·ty dringende *or* inständige Bitte

en·trench MIL verschanzen (*a. fig*)

en·tre·pre·neur ECON Unternehmer(in)

en·tre·pre·neu·ri·al ECON unternehmerisch

en·trust anvertrauen (**s.th. to s.o.** j-m et.); j-n betrauen (**with** mit)

en·try Eintreten *n*, Eintritt *m*; Einreise *f*; Beitritt *m* (**into** zu); Einlass *m*, Zutritt *m*; Zugang *m*, Eingang *m*, Einfahrt *f*; Eintrag(ung *f*) *m*; Stichwort *n*; SPORT Nennung *f*, Meldung *f*; **no entry!** Zutritt verboten!, MOT keine Einfahrt!

en·try per·mit Einreiseerlaubnis *f*, -genehmigung *f*

en·try·phone Türsprechanlage *f*

en·try vi·sa Einreisevisum *n*

en·twine ineinander schlingen

e·nu·me·rate aufzählen

en·vel·op (ein)hüllen, einwickeln

en·ve·lope Briefumschlag *m*

en·vi·a·ble beneidenswert

en·vi·ous neidisch

en·vi·ron·ment Umgebung *f*, *a.* Milieu *n*; Umwelt *f*

en·vi·ron·men·tal Milieu...; Umwelt...

en·vi·ron·men·tal·ist Umweltschützer(in)

en·vi·ron·men·tal law Umweltschutzgesetz *n*

environmental pol·lu·tion Umweltverschmutzung *f*

en·vi·ron·ment friend·ly umweltfreundlich

en·vi·rons Umgebung *f*

en·vis·age sich *et.* vorstellen

en·voy Gesandte *m*, Gesandtin *f*

en·vy 1. Neid *m*; **2.** beneiden

ep·ic 1. episch; **2.** Epos *n*

ep·i·dem·ic MED **1.** seuchenartig; **epidemic disease** → **2.** Epidemie *f*, Seuche *f*

ep·i·der·mis ANAT Oberhaut *f*

ep·i·lep·sy MED Epilepsie *f*

ep·i·log, *Br* **ep·i·logue** Epilog *m*, Nachwort *n*

e·pis·co·pal REL bischöflich

ep·i·sode Episode *f*

ep·i·taph Grabschrift *f*

e·poch Epoche *f*, Zeitalter *n*

e·qua·ble ausgeglichen (*a.* METEOR)

e·qual 1. gleich; gleichmäßig; **equal to** *fig* gewachsen (*dat*); **equal opportunities** Chancengleichheit *f*; **equal rights for women** Gleichberechtigung *f* der Frau; **2.** Gleiche *m*, *f*; **3.** gleichen (*dat*)

e·qual·i·ty Gleichheit *f*

e·qual·i·za·tion Gleichstellung *f*; Ausgleich *m*

e·qual·ize gleichmachen, gleichstellen, angleichen; SPORT ausgleichen

e·qual·iz·er SPORT Ausgleich *m*, Ausgleichstor *n*, -treffer *m*

eq·ua·nim·i·ty Gleichmut *m*

e·qua·tion MATH Gleichung *f*

e·qua·tor Äquator *m*

e·qui·lib·ri·um Gleichgewicht *n*

e·quip ausrüsten

e·quip·ment Ausrüstung *f*, Ausstattung *f*; TECH Einrichtung *f*; *fig* Rüstzeug *n*

e·quiv·a·lent 1. gleichwertig, äquivalent; gleichbedeutend (**to** mit); **2.** Äquivalent *n*, Gegenwert *m*

e·ra Zeitrechnung *f*; Zeitalter *n*

e·rad·i·cate ausrotten

e·rase ausradieren, ausstreichen, löschen (*a.* EDP); *fig* auslöschen

e·ras·er Radiergummi *m*

e·rect 1. aufrecht; **2.** aufrichten; *Denkmal etc* errichten; aufstellen

e·rec·tion Errichtung *f*; MED Erektion *f*

er·mine ZO Hermelin *n*

e·rode GEOL erodieren

e·ro·sion GEOL Erosion *f*

e·rot·ic erotisch

err (sich) irren

er·rand Botengang *m*, Besorgung *f*; **go on an errand, run an errand** e-e Besorgung machen

errand boy Laufbursche *m*

er·rat·ic sprunghaft, unstet, unberechenbar

er·ro·ne·ous irrig

er·ror Irrtum *m*, Fehler *m* (*a.* EDP); **in error** irrtümlicherweise; **error of judg(e)ment** Fehleinschätzung *f*; **errors excepted** ECON Irrtümer vorbehalten

error mes·sage EDP Fehlermeldung *f*

e·rupt ausbrechen (*volcano etc*); durchbrechen (*teeth*)

e·rup·tion (*Vulkan-*) Ausbruch *m*; MED Ausschlag *m*

ESA ABBR *of* **European Space Agency** Europäische Weltraumbehörde

es·ca·late eskalieren; ECON steigen, in die Höhe gehen

es·ca·la·tion Eskalation *f*

es·ca·la·tor Rolltreppe *f*

es·ca·lope GASTR (*esp* Wiener) Schnitzel *n*

es·cape 1. entgehen (*dat*); entkommen, entrinnen (*both dat*); entweichen; *j-m* entfallen; **2.** Entrinnen *n*; Entweichen *n*, Flucht *f*; **have a narrow escape** mit knapper Not davonkommen

es·cape chute AVIAT Notrutsche *f*

es·cape key EDP Escape-Taste *f*

es·cort 1. MIL Eskorte *f*; Geleit(schutz *m*) *n*; **2.** MIL eskortieren; AVIAT, MAR Geleit (-schutz) geben; geleiten

es·cutch·eon Wappenschild *m*, *n*

es·pe·cial besondere(r, -s);

es·pe·cial·ly besonders

es·pi·o·nage Spionage *f*

es·pla·nade (*esp* Strand)Promenade *f*

es·say Aufsatz *m*, kurze Abhandlung, Essay *m*, *n*

es·sence Wesen *n*; Essenz *f*; Extrakt *m*

es·sen·tial 1. wesentlich; unentbehrlich; **2.** *mst pl das* Wesentliche

es·sen·tial·ly im Wesentlichen, in der Hauptsache

es·tab·lish einrichten, errichten; **establish o.s.** sich etablieren *or* niederlassen; beweisen, nachweisen

es·tab·lish·ment Einrichtung *f*, Errichtung *f*; ECON Unternehmen *n*, Firma *f*; **the Establishment** das Establishment, die etablierte Macht, die herrschende Schicht

es·tate (großes) Grundstück, Landsitz *m*, Gut *n*; JUR Besitz *m*, (Erb)Masse *f*, Nachlass *m*; **housing estate** (Wohn)Siedlung *f*; **industrial estate** Industriegebiet *n*; **real estate** Liegenschaften *pl*

estate a·gent *Br* Grundstücks-, Immobilienmakler *m*

estate car *Br* MOT Kombiwagen *m*

es·teem 1. Achtung *f*, Ansehen *n* (**with** bei); **2.** achten, (hoch) schätzen

es·thet·ic ästhetisch

es·thet·ics Ästhetik *f*

es·ti·mate 1. (ab-, ein)schätzen; veranschlagen; **2.** Schätzung *f*; (Kosten)Voranschlag *m*

es·ti·ma·tion Meinung *f*; Achtung *f*, Wertschätzung *f*

es·tranged entfremdet

es·trange·ment Entfremdung *f*

es·tu·a·ry weite Flussmündung

etch ätzen; radieren

etch·ing Radierung *f*; Kupferstich *m*

e·ter·nal ewig

e·ter·ni·ty Ewigkeit *f*

e·ther Äther *m*

e·the·re·al ätherisch (*a. fig*)

eth·i·cal sittlich, ethisch

eth·ics Sittenlehre *f*, Ethik *f*

eu·ro Euro *m*

Eu·ro·cheque *Br* Eurocheque *m*

Eu·rope Europa *n*

Eu·ro·pe·an 1. europäisch; **2.** Europäer(in)

European Com·mu·ni·ty (ABBR *EC*) Europäische Gemeinschaft (ABBR *EG*)

e·vac·u·ate entleeren; evakuieren; *Haus etc* räumen

e·vade (geschickt) ausweichen (*dat*); umgehen

e·val·u·ate schätzen; abschätzen, bewerten, beurteilen

e·vap·o·rate verdunsten, verdampfen (lassen)

evaporated milk Kondensmilch *f*

e·vap·o·ra·tion Verdunstung *f*, Verdamp-

E

fung f

e·va·sion Umgehung f, Vermeidung f; (*Steuer*)Hinterziehung f; Ausflucht f

e·va·sive ausweichend; **be evasive** ausweichen

eve Vorabend m; Vortag m; **on the eve of** unmittelbar vor (*dat*), am Vorabend (*gen*)

e·ven 1. adj eben, gleich; gleichmäßig; ausgeglichen; glatt; gerade (*Zahl*); **get even with s.o.** es j-m heimzahlen; **2.** adv selbst, sogar, auch; **not even** nicht einmal; **even though, even if** wenn auch; **3. even out** sich einpendeln; sich ausgleichen

eve·ning Abend m; **in the evening** am Abend, abends

evening class·es Abendkurs m, Abendunterricht m

evening dress Gesellschaftsanzug m; Frack m, Smoking m; Abendkleid n

e·ven·song REL Abendgottesdienst m

e·vent Ereignis n; Fall m; SPORT Disziplin f; SPORT Wettbewerb m; **at all events** auf alle Fälle; **in the event of** im Falle (*gen*)

e·vent·ful ereignisreich

e·ven·tu·al(·ly) schließlich

ev·er immer (wieder); je(mals); **ever after, ever since** seitdem; **ever so** F sehr, noch so; **for ever** für immer, auf ewig; **Yours ever, ..., Ever yours, ...** Viele Grüße, dein(e) or Ihr(e), ...; **have you ever been to Boston?** bist du schon einmal in Boston gewesen?

ev·er·green 1. immergrün; unverwüstlich, *esp* immer wieder gern gehört; **2.** immergrüne Pflanze; MUS Evergreen m, n

ev·er·last·ing ewig

ev·er·more: (**for**) **evermore** für immer

ev·ery jede(r, -s); alle(r, -s); **every now and then** von Zeit zu Zeit, dann und wann; **every one of them** jeder von ihnen; **every other day** jeden zweiten Tag, alle zwei Tage

ev·ery·bod·y jeder(mann)

ev·ery·day Alltags...

ev·ery·one jeder(mann)

ev·ery·thing alles

ev·ery·where überall(hin)

e·vict JUR zur Räumung zwingen; j-n gewaltsam vertreiben

ev·i·dence Beweis(material n) m, Beweise pl; (Zeugen)Aussage f; **give evidence** (als Zeuge) aussagen

ev·i·dent augenscheinlich, offensichtlich

e·vil 1. übel, schlimm, böse; **2.** Übel n; **das Böse**

e·vil-mind·ed bösartig

e·voke (herauf)beschwören; *Erinnerungen* wachrufen

ev·o·lu·tion Entwicklung f; BIOL Evolution f

e·volve (sich) entwickeln

ewe ZO Mutterschaf n

ex prp ECON ab; **ex works** ab Werk

ex... Ex..., ehemalig

ex·act 1. exakt, genau; **2.** fordern, verlangen

ex·act·ing streng, genau; aufreibend, anstrengend

ex·act·ly exakt, genau; **exactly!** ganz recht!, genau!

ex·act·ness Genauigkeit f

ex·ag·ge·rate übertreiben

ex·ag·ge·ra·tion Übertreibung f

ex·am F Examen n

ex·am·i·na·tion Examen n, Prüfung f; Untersuchung f; JUR Vernehmung f, Verhör n

ex·am·ine untersuchen; JUR vernehmen, verhören; PED etc prüfen (**in** in dat; **on** über acc)

ex·am·ple Beispiel n; Vorbild n, Muster n; **for example** zum Beispiel

ex·as·pe·rate wütend machen

ex·as·pe·rat·ing ärgerlich

ex·ca·vate ausgraben, ausheben, ausschachten

ex·ceed überschreiten; übertreffen

ex·ceed·ing übermäßig

ex·ceed·ing·ly außerordentlich, überaus

ex·cel v/t übertreffen; v/i sich auszeichnen

ex·cel·lence ausgezeichnete Qualität

Ex·cel·lency Exzellenz f

ex·cel·lent ausgezeichnet, hervorragend

ex·cept 1. ausnehmen, ausschließen; **2.** prp ausgenommen, außer; **except for** abgesehen von, bis auf (*acc*)

ex·cept·ing prp ausgenommen

ex·cep·tion Ausnahme f; Einwand m (**to** gegen); **make an exception** e-e Ausnahme machen; **take exception to** Anstoß nehmen an (*dat*); **without exception** ohne Ausnahme, ausnahmslos

ex·cep·tion·al außergewöhnlich

ex·cep·tion·al·ly ungewöhnlich, außergewöhnlich

ex·cerpt Auszug m

ex·cess 1. Übermaß n; Überschuss m; Ausschweifung f; **2.** Mehr...

excess baggage AVIAT Übergepäck n

excess fare (Fahrpreis)Zuschlag m

ex·ces·sive übermäßig, übertrieben

ex·cess lug·gage → **excess baggage**

excess post·age Nachgebühr f

ex·change 1. (aus-, ein-, um)tauschen (**for** gegen); wechseln; **2.** (Aus-, Um-) Tausch m; (*esp* Geld)Wechsel m; ECON a. **bill of**

exchange Wechsel *m*; Börse *f*; Wechselstube *f*; TEL Fernsprechamt *n*; ECON **foreign exchange(s)** Devisen *pl*; **rate of exchange** → **exchange rate**
exchange of·fice Wechselstube *f*
exchange rate Wechselkurs *m*
exchange student Austauschschüler(in), Austauschstudent(in)
Ex·cheq·uer: Chancellor of the Exchequer *Br* Finanzminister *m*
ex·cise Verbrauchssteuer *f*
ex·ci·ta·ble reizbar, (leicht) erregbar
ex·cite erregen, anregen; reizen
ex·cit·ed erregt, aufgeregt
ex·cite·ment Aufregung *f*, Erregung *f*
ex·cit·ing erregend, aufregend, spannend
ex·claim (aus)rufen
ex·cla·ma·tion Ausruf *m*, (Auf)Schrei *m*
exclamation mark, **exclamation point** Ausrufe-, Ausrufungszeichen *n*
ex·clude ausschließen
ex·clu·sion Ausschließung *f*, Ausschluss *m*
ex·clu·sive ausschließlich; exklusiv; Exklusiv…; **exclusive of** abgesehen von, ohne
ex·com·mu·ni·cate REL exkommunizieren
ex·com·mu·ni·ca·tion REL Exkommunikation *f*
ex·cre·ment Kot *m*
ex·crete MED ausscheiden
ex·cur·sion Ausflug *m*
ex·cu·sa·ble entschuldbar
ex·cuse 1. entschuldigen; **excuse me** entschuldige(n Sie); 2. Entschuldigung *f*
ex·di·rec·to·ry num·ber *Br* TEL Geheimnummer *f*
ex·e·cute ausführen; vollziehen; MUS vortragen; hinrichten; JUR *Testament* vollstrecken
ex·e·cu·tion Ausführung *f*; Vollziehung *f*; JUR (Zwangs-) Vollstreckung *f*; Hinrichtung *f*; MUS Vortrag *m*; **put or carry a plan into execution** e-n Plan ausführen *or* verwirklichen
ex·e·cu·tion·er JUR Henker *m*, Scharfrichter *m*
ex·ec·u·tive 1. vollziehend, ausübend, POL Exekutiv…; ECON leitend; 2. POL Exekutive *f*, vollziehende Gewalt; ECON *der, die* leitende Angestellte
ex·em·pla·ry vorbildlich
ex·em·pli·fy veranschaulichen
ex·empt 1. befreit, frei; 2. ausnehmen, befreien
ex·er·cise 1. Übung *f*; Ausübung *f*; PED Übung(sarbeit) *f*, Schulaufgabe *f*; MIL Manöver *n*; (körperliche) Bewegung;

do one's exercises Gymnastik machen; **take exercise** sich Bewegung machen; 2. üben; ausüben; (sich) bewegen; sich Bewegung machen; MIL exerzieren
ex·er·cise book Schul-, Schreibheft *n*
ex·ert *Einfluss etc* ausüben; **exert o.s.** sich anstrengen *or* bemühen
ex·er·tion Ausübung *f*; Anstrengung *f*, Strapaze *f*
ex·hale ausatmen; *Gas, Geruch etc* verströmen; *Rauch* ausstoßen
ex·haust 1. erschöpfen; *Vorräte* ver-, aufbrauchen; 2. TECH Auspuff *m*; *a.* **exhaust fumes** TECH Auspuff-, Abgase *pl*
ex·haust·ed erschöpft, aufgebraucht (*supplies*), vergriffen (*book*)
ex·haus·tion Erschöpfung *f*
ex·haus·tive erschöpfend
ex·haust pipe TECH Auspuffrohr *n*
ex·hib·it 1. ausstellen; vorzeigen; *fig* zeigen, zur Schau stellen; 2. Ausstellungsstück *n*; JUR Beweisstück *n*
ex·hi·bi·tion Ausstellung *f*; Zurschaustellung *f*
ex·hil·a·rat·ing erregend, berauschend
ex·hort ermahnen
ex·ile 1. Exil *n*; im Exil Lebende *m*, *f*; 2. ins Exil schicken
ex·ist existieren; vorhanden sein; leben; bestehen
ex·ist·ence Existenz *f*; Vorhandensein *n*, Vorkommen *n*; Leben *n*, Dasein *n*
ex·ist·ent vorhanden
ex·it 1. Abgang *m*; Ausgang *m*; (Autobahn)Ausfahrt *f*; Ausreise *f*; 2. *v/i* verlassen; EDP (*das Programm*) beenden; **exit Macbeth** THEA Macbeth (geht) ab
ex·o·dus Auszug *m*; Abwanderung *f*; **general exodus** allgemeiner Aufbruch
ex·on·e·rate entlasten, entbinden, befreien
ex·or·bi·tant übertrieben, maßlos; unverschämt (*price etc*)
ex·or·cize *böse Geister* beschwören, austreiben (**from** aus); befreien (**of** von)
ex·ot·ic exotisch; fremd(artig)
ex·pand ausbreiten; (sich) ausdehnen *or* erweitern; ECON *a.* expandieren
ex·panse weite Fläche, Weite *f*
ex·pan·sion Ausbreitung *f*; Ausdehnung *f*, Erweiterung *f*
ex·pan·sive mitteilsam
ex·pat·ri·ate *j-n* ausbürgern, *j-m* die Staatsangehörigkeit aberkennen
ex·pect erwarten; F annehmen; **be expecting** in anderen Umständen sein
ex·pec·tant erwartungsvoll; **expectant mother** werdende Mutter
ex·pec·ta·tion Erwartung *f*; Hoffnung *f*,

Aussicht *f*

ex·pe·dient 1. zweckdienlich, zweckmäßig; ratsam; **2.** (Hilfs)Mittel *n*, (Not)Behelf *m*

ex·pe·di·tion Expedition *f*, (Forschungs-)Reise *f*

ex·pe·di·tious schnell

ex·pel (*from*) vertreiben (aus); ausweisen (aus); ausschließen (von, aus)

ex·pen·di·ture Ausgaben *pl*, (Kosten-)Aufwand *m*

ex·pense Ausgaben *pl*; *pl* ECON Unkosten *pl*, Spesen *pl*, Auslagen *pl*; **at the expense of** auf Kosten (*gen*)

ex·pen·sive kostspielig, teuer

ex·pe·ri·ence 1. Erfahrung *f*; (Le-bens)Praxis *f*; Erlebnis *n*; **2.** erfahren, erleben

ex·pe·rienced erfahren

ex·per·i·ment 1. Versuch *m*; **experiment with animals** MED Tierversuch *m*; **2.** experimentieren

ex·per·i·men·tal Versuchs…

ex·pert 1. erfahren, geschickt; fachmännisch; **2.** Fachmann *m*; Sachverständige *m*, *f*

ex·pi·ra·tion Ablauf *m*, Ende *n*; Verfall *m*

ex·pire ablaufen, erlöschen; verfallen

ex·plain erklären

ex·pla·na·tion Erklärung *f*

ex·pli·cit ausdrücklich; ausführlich; offen, deutlich; (**sexually**) **explicit** freizügig (*film etc*)

ex·plode *v/t* zur Explosion bringen; *v/i* explodieren; *fig* ausbrechen (**with** in *acc*), platzen (**with** vor); *fig* sprunghaft ansteigen

ex·ploit 1. (Helden)Tat *f*; **2.** ausbeuten; *fig* ausnutzen

ex·ploi·ta·tion Ausbeutung *f*, Auswertung *f*, Verwertung *f*, Abbau *m*

ex·plo·ra·tion Erforschung *f*

ex·plore erforschen

ex·plor·er Forscher(in); Forschungsreisende *m*, *f*

ex·plo·sion Explosion *f*; *fig* Ausbruch *m*; *fig* sprunghafter Anstieg

ex·plo·sive 1. explosiv; *fig* aufbrausend; *fig* sprunghaft ansteigend; **2.** Sprengstoff *m*

ex·po·nent MATH Exponent *m*, Hochzahl *f*; Vertreter(in), Verfechter(in)

ex·port ECON **1.** exportieren, ausführen; **2.** Export *m*, Ausfuhr *f*; *mst pl* Export-, Ausfuhrartikel *m*

ex·por·ta·tion ECON Ausfuhr *f*

ex·port·er ECON Exporteur *m*

ex·pose aussetzen; PHOT belichten; *Waren* ausstellen; *j-n* entlarven, bloßstellen, *et.* aufdecken

ex·po·si·tion Ausstellung *f*

ex·po·sure Aussetzen *n*, Ausgesetztsein *n* (**to** *dat*); *fig* Bloßstellung *f*, Aufdeckung *f*, Enthüllung *f*, Entlarvung *f*; PHOT Belichtung *f*; PHOT Aufnahme *f*; **die of exposure** an Unterkühlung sterben

exposure me·ter PHOT Belichtungsmesser *m*

ex·press 1. ausdrücklich, deutlich; Express…, Eil…; **2.** Eilbote *m*; Schnellzug *m*; **by express** → **3.** *adv* durch Eilboten; als Eilgut; **4.** äußern, ausdrücken

ex·pres·sion Ausdruck *m*

ex·pres·sion·less ausdruckslos

ex·pres·sive ausdrucksvoll; **be expressive of** *et.* ausdrücken

ex·press let·ter *Br* Eilbrief *m*

ex·press·ly ausdrücklich, eigens

ex·press train Schnellzug *m*

ex·press·way Schnellstraße *f*

ex·pro·pri·ate JUR enteignen

ex·pul·sion (*from*) Vertreibung *f* (aus); Ausweisung *f* (aus)

ex·pur·gate reinigen

ex·qui·site erlesen; fein

ex·tant noch vorhanden

ex·tem·po·re aus dem Stegreif

ex·tem·po·rize aus dem Stegreif sprechen *or* spielen

ex·tend (aus)dehnen, (aus)weiten; *Hand etc* ausstrecken; *Betrieb etc* vergrößern, ausbauen; *Frist*, *Pass etc* verlängern; sich ausdehnen *or* erstrecken

ex·tend·ed fam·i·ly Großfamilie *f*

ex·ten·sion Ausdehnung *f*; Vergrößerung *f*, Erweiterung *f*; (Frist)Verlängerung *f*; ARCH Erweiterung *f*, Anbau *m*; TEL Nebenanschluss *m*, (-)Apparat *m*; *a.* **extension cord** (*Br* **lead**) ELECTR Verlängerungskabel *n*, -schnur *f*

ex·ten·sive ausgedehnt, umfassend

ex·tent Ausdehnung *f*; Umfang *m*, (Aus-)Maß *n*, Grad *m*; **to some extent, to a certain extent** bis zu e-m gewissen Grade; **to such an extent that** so sehr, dass

ex·ten·u·ate abschwächen, mildern; beschönigen; **extenuating circumstances** JUR mildernde Umstände *pl*

ex·te·ri·or 1. äußerlich, äußere(r, -s), Außen…; **2.** *das* Äußere; Außenseite *f*; äußere Erscheinung

ex·ter·mi·nate ausrotten (*a. fig*), vernichten, *Ungeziefer*, *Unkraut a.* vertilgen

ex·ter·nal äußere(r, -s), äußerlich, Außen…

ex·tinct erloschen; ausgestorben

ex·tinc·tion Erlöschen *n*; Aussterben *n*, Untergang *m*; Vernichtung *f*, Zerstörung *f*

ex·tin·guish (aus)löschen; vernichten
ex·tin·guish·er (*Feuer*)Löscher *m*
ex·tort erpressen (*from* von)
ex·tra 1. *adj* zusätzlich, Extra..., Sonder...; *be extra* gesondert berechnet werden; **2.** *adv* extra, besonders; *charge extra for* et. gesondert berechnen; **3.** Sonderleistung *f*; *esp* MOT Extra *n*; Zuschlag *m*; Extrablatt *n*; THEA, *film*: Statist(in)
ex·tract 1. Auszug *m*; **2.** (heraus)ziehen; herauslocken; ableiten, herleiten
ex·trac·tion (Heraus)Ziehen *n*; Herkunft *f*
ex·tra·dite ausliefern; *j-s* Auslieferung erwirken;
ex·tra·di·tion Auslieferung *f*
extra·or·di·na·ry außerordentlich; ungewöhnlich; Sonder...
ex·tra pay Zulage *f*
ex·tra·ter·res·tri·al außerirdisch
ex·tra time SPORT (Spiel)Verlängerung *f*
ex·trav·a·gance Übertriebenheit *f*; Verschwendung *f*; Extravaganz *f*
ex·trav·a·gant übertrieben, überspannt; verschwenderisch; extravagant
ex·treme 1. äußerste(r, -s), größte(r, -s), höchste(r, -s); außergewöhnlich; *extreme right* POL rechtsextrem(istisch); *extreme right wing* POL rechtsradikal; **2.** *das* Äußerste; Extrem *n*; höchster Grad
ex·treme·ly äußerst, höchst
ex·trem·ism POL Extremismus *m*
ex·trem·ist POL Extremist(in)
ex·trem·i·ties Gliedmaßen *pl*, Extremitäten *pl*
ex·trem·i·ty *das* Äußerste; höchste Not; äußerste Maßnahme
ex·tri·cate herauswinden, herausziehen, befreien
ex·tro·vert Extrovertierte *m*, *f*
ex·u·be·rance Fülle *f*; Überschwang *m*
ex·u·be·rant reichlich, üppig; überschwänglich; ausgelassen
ex·ult frohlocken, jubeln
eye 1. ANAT Auge *n*; Blick *m*; Öhr *n*; Öse *f*; *see eye to eye with s.o.* mit j-m völlig übereinstimmen; *be up to the eyes in work* bis über die Ohren in Arbeit stecken; *with an eye to s.th.* im Hinblick auf et.; **2.** ansehen; mustern
eye·ball ANAT Augapfel *m*
eye·brow ANAT Augenbraue *f*
eye·catch·ing ins Auge fallend, auffallend
eye doc·tor F Augenarzt *m*, -ärztin *f*
eye·glass·es *a.* *pair of eyeglasses* Brille *f*
eye·lash ANAT Augenwimper *f*
eye·lid ANAT Augenlid *n*
eye·lin·er Eyeliner *m*
eye·o·pen·er: *that was an eye-opener to me* das hat mir die Augen geöffnet
eye shad·ow Lidschatten *m*
eye·sight Augen(licht *n*) *pl*, Sehkraft *f*
eye·sore F Schandfleck *m*
eye spe·cial·ist Augenarzt *m*, -ärztin *f*
eye·strain Ermüdung *f or* Überanstrengung *f* der Augen
eye·wit·ness Augenzeuge *m*, -zeugin *f*

F

F, f F, f *n*
fa·ble Fabel *f*; Sage *f*
fab·ric Gewebe *n*, Stoff *m*; Struktur *f*
fab·ri·cate fabrizieren (*mst fig*)
fab·u·lous sagenhaft, der Sage angehörend; fabelhaft
fa·cade, fa·çade ARCH Fassade *f*
face 1. Gesicht *n*; Gesichtsausdruck *m*, Miene *f*; (Ober)Fläche *f*; Vorderseite *f*; Zifferblatt *n*; *face to face with* Auge in Auge mit; *save* (*lose*) *one's face* das Gesicht wahren (verlieren); *on the face of it* auf den ersten Blick; *pull a long face* ein langes Gesicht machen; *have the face to do s.th.* die Stirn haben, et. zu tun; **2.** *v/t* ansehen; gegenüberstehen (*dat*); (hinaus)gehen auf (*acc*); die Stirn bieten (*dat*); einfassen; ARCH bekleiden; *v/i*: *face about* sich umdrehen
face·cloth, *Br* **face flan·nel** Waschlappen *m*
face·lift Facelifting *n*, Gesichtsstraffung *f*; *fig* Renovierung *f*, Verschönerung *f*
fa·ce·tious witzig
fa·cial 1. Gesichts...; **2.** Gesichtsbehand-

lung *f*
fa·cile leicht; oberflächlich
fa·cil·i·tate erleichtern
fa·cil·i·ty Leichtigkeit *f*; Oberflächlichkeit *f*; *mst pl* Erleichterung(en *pl*) *f*; Einrichtung(en *pl*) *f*, Anlage(n *pl*) *f*
fac·ing TECH Verkleidung *f*; *pl* Besatz *m*
fact Tatsache *f*, Wirklichkeit *f*, Wahrheit *f*; Tat *f*; *pl* Daten; **in fact** in der Tat, tatsächlich
fac·tion *esp* POL Splittergruppe *f*; Zwietracht *f*
fac·ti·tious künstlich
fac·tor Faktor *m*
fac·to·ry Fabrik *f*
fac·ul·ty Fähigkeit *f*; Kraft *f*; *fig* Gabe *f*; UNIV Fakultät *f*; Lehrkörper *m*
fad Mode *f*, Modeerscheinung *f*, -torheit *f*; (vorübergehende) Laune
fade (ver)welken (lassen); verschießen, verblassen (*color*); schwinden; immer schwächer werden (*person*); *film, radio,* TV **fade in** auf- *or* eingeblendet werden; auf- *or* einblenden; **fade out** aus- *or* abgeblendet werden; aus- *or* abblenden; **faded jeans** ausgewaschene Jeans *pl*
fail *v/i* versagen; misslingen, fehlschlagen; versiegen; nachlassen; durchfallen (*candidate*); *v/t* im Stich lassen; *j-n in e-r Prüfung* durchfallen lassen; **2. without fail** mit Sicherheit, ganz bestimmt
fail·ure Versagen *n*; Fehlschlag *m*, Misserfolg *m*; Versäumnis *n*; Versager *m*, F Niete *f*
faint 1. schwach, matt; **2.** ohnmächtig werden, in Ohnmacht fallen (**with** vor); **3.** Ohnmacht *f*
faint-heart·ed verzagt
fair[1] gerecht, ehrlich, anständig, fair; recht gut, ansehnlich; schön (*weather*); klar (*sky*); blond (*hair*); hell (*skin*); **play fair** fair spielen; *fig* sich an die Spielregeln halten
fair[2] (Jahr)Markt *m*; Volksfest *n*; Ausstellung *f*, Messe *f*
fair game *fig* Freiwild *n*
fair·ground Rummelplatz *m*
fair·ly gerecht; ziemlich
fair·ness Gerechtigkeit *f*, Fairness *f*
fair play SPORT *and fig* Fair Play *n*, Fairness *f*
fai·ry Fee *f*; Zauberin *f*; Elf *m*, Elfe *f*
fai·ry·land Feen-, Märchenland *n*
fai·ry sto·ry, fairy tale Märchen *n* (*a. fig*)
faith Glaube *m*; Vertrauen *n*
faith·ful treu (**to** *dat*); **Yours faithfully** Hochachtungsvoll (*letter*)
faith·less treulos
fake 1. Schwindel *m*; Fälschung *f*;

Schwindler *m*; **2.** fälschen; imitieren, nachmachen; vortäuschen, simulieren; **3.** gefälscht; fingiert
fal·con ZO Falke *m*
fall 1. Fallen *n*, Fall *m*; Sturz *m*; Verfall *m*; Einsturz *m*; Herbst *m*; ECON Sinken *n* (*of prices etc*); Gefälle *n*; *mst pl* Wasserfall *m*; **2.** fallen, stürzen; ab-, einfallen; sinken; sich legen (*wind*); *in e-n Zustand* verfallen; **fall ill, fall sick** krank werden; **fall in love with** sich verlieben in (*acc*); **fall short of** den Erwartungen *etc* nicht entsprechen; **fall back** zurückweichen; **fall back on** *fig* zurückgreifen auf (*acc*); **fall for** hereinfallen auf (*acc*); F sich in *j-n* verknallen; **fall off** zurückgehen (*business, demand etc*), nachlassen; **fall on** herfallen über (*acc*); **fall out** sich streiten (**with** mit); **fall through** durchfallen (*a. fig*); **fall to** reinhauen, tüchtig zugreifen
fal·la·cious trügerisch
fal·la·cy Trugschluss *m*
fall guy F *der* Lackierte, *der* Dumme
fal·li·ble fehlbar
fall·ing star Sternschnuppe *f*
fall·out Fall-out *m*, radioaktiver Niederschlag
fal·low ZO falb; AGR brach(liegend)
false falsch
false·hood, false·ness Falschheit *f*; Unwahrheit *f*
false start Fehlstart *m*
fal·si·fi·ca·tion (Ver)Fälschung *f*
fal·si·fy (ver)fälschen
fal·si·ty Falschheit *f*, Unwahrheit *f*
fal·ter schwanken; stocken (*voice*); stammeln; *fig* zaudern
fame Ruf *m*, Ruhm *m*
famed berühmt (**for** wegen)
fa·mil·i·ar 1. vertraut; gewohnt; familiär; **2.** Vertraute *m*, *f*
fa·mil·i·ar·i·ty Vertrautheit *f*; (plumpe) Vertraulichkeit
fa·mil·i·ar·ize vertraut machen
fam·i·ly 1. Familie *f*; **2.** Familien..., Haus...; **be in the family way** F in anderen Umständen sein
family al·low·ance → **child benefit**
family doc·tor Hausarzt *m*
family name Familien-, Nachname *m*
family plan·ning Familienplanung *f*
family tree Stammbaum *m*
fam·ine Hungersnot *f*; Knappheit *f* (**of** an *dat*)
fam·ished verhungert; **be famished** F am Verhungern sein
fa·mous berühmt
fan[1] **1.** Fächer *m*; Ventilator *m*; **2.** (zu-)fä-

cheln; anfachen; *fig* entfachen

fan[2] (*Sport- etc*)Fan *m*

fa·nat·ic Fanatiker(in)

fa·nat·i·cal fanatisch

fan belt TECH Keilriemen *m*

fan·ci·er BOT, ZO Liebhaber(in), Züchter(in)

fan·ci·ful fantastisch

fan club Fanklub *m*

fan·cy 1. Fantasie *f*; Einbildung *f*; plötzlicher Einfall, Idee *f*; Laune *f*; Vorliebe *f*, Neigung *f*; **2.** ausgefallen; Fantasie…; **3.** sich vorstellen; sich einbilden; *fancy that!* stell dir vor!, denk nur!; sieh mal einer an!

fan·cy ball Kostümfest *n*, Maskenball *m*

fancy dress (Masken)Kostüm *n*

fan·cy-free → *footloose*

fan·cy goods Modeartikel *pl*, -waren *pl*

fan·cy-work Stickerei *f*

fang ZO Reiß-, Fangzahn *m*; Hauer *m*; Giftzahn *m*

fan mail Fanpost *f*, Verehrerpost *f*

fan·tas·tic fantastisch

fan·ta·sy Fantasie *f*

far 1. *adj* fern, entfernt, weit; **2.** *adv* fern; weit; (sehr) viel; *as far as* bis; *in so far as* insofern als

far·a·way weit entfernt

fare 1. Fahrgeld *n*; Fahrgast *m*; Verpflegung *f*, Kost *f*; **2.** *gut* leben; *he fared well* es (er)ging ihm gut

fare dodg·er Schwarzfahrer(in)

fare·well 1. *int* lebe(n Sie) wohl!; **2.** Abschied *m*, Lebewohl *n*

far-fetched *fig* weit hergeholt, gesucht

farm 1. Bauernhof *m*, Gut *n*, Gehöft *n*, Farm *f*; **2.** *Land, Hof* bewirtschaften

farm·er Bauer *m*, Landwirt *m*, Farmer *m*

farm·hand Landarbeiter(in)

farm·house Bauernhaus *n*

farm·ing 1. Acker…, landwirtschaftlich; 2. Landwirtschaft *f*

farm·stead Bauernhof *m*, Gehöft *n*

farm·yard Wirtschaftshof *m*

far-off entfernt, fern

far right POL rechtsgerichtet

far·sight·ed weitsichtig, *fig a.* weitblickend

fas·ci·nate faszinieren

fas·ci·nat·ing faszinierend

fas·ci·na·tion Zauber *m*, Reiz *m*, Faszination *f*

fas·cism POL Faschismus *m*

fas·cist POL **1.** Faschist *m*; **2.** faschistisch

fash·ion Mode *f*; Art *f* und Weise *f*; *be in fashion* in Mode sein; *out of fashion* unmodern; **1.** formen, gestalten

fash·ion·a·ble modisch, elegant; in Mode

fash·ion pa·rade, **fashion show** Mode(n)-schau *f*

fast[1] **1.** Fasten *n*; **2.** fasten

fast[2] schnell; fest; treu; echt, beständig (*color*); flott; *be fast* vorgehen (*watch*)

fast·back MOT (Wagen *m* mit) Fließheck *n*

fast breed·er (**re·ac·tor**) PHYS Schneller Brüter

fas·ten befestigen, festmachen, anheften, anschnallen, anbinden, zuknöpfen, zu-, verschnüren; *Blick etc* richten (*on* auf *acc*); sich festmachen *or* schließen lassen

fas·ten·er Verschluss *m*

fast food Schnellgericht(e *pl*) *n*

fast-food res·tau·rant Schnellimbiss *m*, Schnellgaststätte *f*

fas·tid·i·ous anspruchsvoll, heikel, wählerisch, verwöhnt

fast lane MOT Überholspur *f*

fat 1. fett; dick; fettig, fetthaltig; **2.** Fett *n*; *be low in fat* fettarm sein

fa·tal tödlich; verhängnisvoll, fatal (*to* für)

fa·tal·i·ty Verhängnis *n*; tödlicher Unfall; (Todes)Opfer *n*

fate Schicksal *n*; Verhängnis *n*

fa·ther Vater *m*

Fa·ther Christ·mas *esp Br* der Weihnachtsmann, der Nikolaus

fa·ther·hood Vaterschaft *f*

fa·ther-in-law Schwiegervater *m*

fa·ther·less vaterlos

fa·ther·ly väterlich

fath·om 1. MAR Faden *m*; **2.** MAR loten; *fig* ergründen

fath·om·less unergründlich

fa·tigue 1. Ermüdung *f*; Strapaze *f*; **2.** ermüden

fat·ten dick *or contp* fett machen *or* werden; mästen

fat·ty fett; fettig

fau·cet TECH (Wasser)Hahn *m*

fault Fehler *m*; Defekt *m*; Schuld *f*; *find fault with* et. auszusetzen haben an (*dat*); *be at fault* Schuld haben

fault·less fehlerfrei, fehlerlos

fault·y fehlerhaft, TECH *a.* defekt

fa·vo(u)r 1. Gunst *f*; Gefallen *m*; Begünstigung *f*; *in favo(u)r of* zu Gunsten von (*or gen*); *do s.o. a favo(u)r* j-m e-n Gefallen tun; **2.** begünstigen; bevorzugen, vorziehen; wohlwollend gegenüberstehen; SPORT favorisieren

fa·vo(u)r·a·ble günstig

fa·vo(u)r·ite 1. Liebling *m*; SPORT Favorit *m*; **2.** Lieblings…

fawn 1. ZO (Reh)Kitz *n*; Rehbraun *n*; **2.** rehbraun

fax 1. Fax *n*; **2.** faxen; *fax s.th.* (*through*)

to s.o. j-m et. faxen
fax (ma·chine) Faxgerät *n*
fear 1. Furcht *f* (**of** vor *dat*); Befürchtung *f*; Angst *f*; **2.** (be)fürchten; sich fürchten vor (*dat*)
fear·ful furchtsam; furchtbar
fear·less furchtlos
fea·si·ble durchführbar
feast 1. REL Fest *n*, Feiertag *m*; Festessen *n*; *fig* Fest *n*, (Hoch)Genuss *m*; **2.** *v/t* festlich bewirten; *v/i* sich gütlich tun (**on** an *dat*), schlemmen
feat große Leistung; (Helden)Tat *f*
fea·ther 1. Feder *f*; *a. pl* Gefieder *n*; **birds of a feather** Leute vom gleichen Schlag; **birds of a feather flock together** Gleich und Gleich gesellt sich gern; **that is a feather in his cap** darauf kann er stolz sein; **2.** mit Federn polstern *or* schmücken; *Pfeil* fiedern
feath·er·bed verhätscheln
feath·er·brained F hohlköpfig
feath·ered ZO gefiedert
feath·er·weight SPORT Federgewicht *n*, Federgewichtler *m*; Leichtgewicht *n* (*person*)
feath·er·y gefiedert; federleicht
fea·ture 1. (Gesichts)Zug *m*; (charakteristisches) Merkmal; *radio*, TV *etc* Feature *n*; Haupt-, Spielfilm *m*; **2.** groß herausbringen; *film:* in der Hauptrolle zeigen
feature film Haupt-, Spielfilm *m*
Feb ABBR *of* **February** Febr., Februar *m*
Feb·ru·a·ry (ABBR **Feb**) Februar *m*
fed·e·ral POL Bundes...
Fed·e·ral Re·pub·lic of Ger·man·y *die* Bundesrepublik Deutschland (ABBR **BRD**)
fed·e·ra·tion POL Bundesstaat *m*; Föderation *f*, Staatenbund *m*; ECON, SPORT *etc* (Dach)Verband *m*
fee Gebühr *f*; Honorar *n*; (Mitglieds-)Beitrag *m*; Eintrittsgeld *n*
fee·ble schwach
feed 1. Futter *n*; Nahrung *f*; Fütterung *f*; TECH Zuführung *f*, Speisung *f*; **2.** *v/t* füttern; ernähren; TECH *Maschine* speisen; EDP eingeben; AGR weiden lassen; **be fed up with s.o.** (**s.th.**) j-n (et.) satthaben; **well fed** wohlgenährt; *v/i* (fr)essen; sich ernähren; weiden
feed·back ELECTR Feed-back *n*, Rückkoppelung *f*; *radio*, TV Reaktion *f*
feed·er Esser *m*
feed·er road Zubringer(straße *f*) *m*
feed·ing bot·tle (Saug)Flasche *f*
feel 1. (sich) fühlen; befühlen; empfinden; sich anfühlen; **feel sorry for s.o.** j-n bedauern *or* bemitleiden; **2.** Gefühl *n*;

Empfindung *f*
feel·er ZO Fühler *m*
feel·ing Gefühl *n*
feign *Interesse etc* vortäuschen, *Krankheit a.* simulieren
feint Finte *f*
fell niederschlagen; fällen
fel·low 1. Gefährte *m*, Gefährtin *f*, Kamerad(in); Gegenstück *n*; F Kerl *m*; **old fellow** F alter Knabe; **the fellow of a glove** der andere Handschuh; **2.** Mit...
fellow be·ing Mitmensch *m*
fellow cit·i·zen Mitbürger *m*
fellow coun·try·man Landsmann *m*
fel·low·ship Gemeinschaft *f*; Kameradschaft *f*
fel·low trav·el·(l)er Mitreisende *m*, *f*, Reisegefährte *m*, -gefährtin *f*; POL Mitläufer(in)
fel·on JUR Schwerverbrecher *m*
fel·o·ny JUR (schweres) Verbrechen, Kapitalverbrechen *n*
felt Filz *m*
felt pen, felt tip, felt-tip(ped) pen Filzstift *m*, Filzschreiber *m*
fe·male 1. weiblich; **2.** *contp* Weib *n*, Weibsbild *n*; ZO Weibchen *n*
fem·i·nine weiblich, Frauen...; feminin
fem·i·nism Feminismus *m*
fem·i·nist 1. Feminist(in); **2.** feministisch
fen Fenn *n*, Sumpf-, Marschland *n*
fence 1. Zaun *m*; *sl* Hehler *m*; **2.** *v/t:* **fence in** einzäunen, umzäunen; einsperren; **fence off** abzäunen; *v/i* SPORT fechten
fenc·er SPORT Fechter *m*
fenc·ing 1. Einfriedung *f*; SPORT Fechten *n*; **2.** Fecht...
fend: fend off abwehren; **fend for o.s.** für sich selbst sorgen
fend·er Schutzvorrichtung *f*; Schutzblech *n*; MOT Kotflügel *m*; Kamingitter *n*, Kaminvorsetzer *m*
fen·nel BOT Fenchel *m*
fer·ment 1. Ferment *n*; Gärung *f*; **2.** gären (lassen)
fer·men·ta·tion Gärung *f*
fern BOT Farn(kraut *n*) *m*
fe·ro·cious wild; grausam
fe·ro·ci·ty Wildheit *f*
fer·ret 1. ZO Frettchen *n*; *fig* Spürhund *m*; **2.** herumstöbern; **ferret out** aufspüren, aufstöbern
fer·ry 1. Fähre *f*; **2.** übersetzen
fer·ry·boat Fährboot *n*, Fähre *f*
fer·ry·man Fährmann *m*
fer·tile fruchtbar (**of, in** an *dat*)
fer·til·i·ty Fruchtbarkeit *f* (*a. fig*)
fer·ti·lize fruchtbar machen; befruchten; AGR düngen

fer·ti·liz·er AGR (*esp* Kunst)Dünger *m*, Düngemittel *n*

fer·vent glühend, leidenschaftlich

fer·vo(u)r Glut *f*; Inbrunst *f*

fes·ter MED eitern

fes·ti·val Fest *n*; Festival *n*, Festspiele *pl*

fes·tive festlich

fes·tiv·i·ty Festlichkeit *f*

fes·toon Girlande *f*

fetch holen; *Preis* erzielen; *Seufzer* ausstoßen

fetch·ing F reizend

fete, fête 1. Fest *n*; *village fete* Dorffest *n*; 2. feiern

fet·id stinkend

fet·ter 1. Fessel *f*; 2. fesseln

feud Fehde *f*

feud·al Feudal..., Lehns...

feu·dal·ism Feudalismus *m*, Feudal-, Lehnssystem *n*

fe·ver MED Fieber *n*

fe·ver·ish MED fieb(e)rig, fieberhaft (*a. fig*)

few wenige; *a few* ein paar, einige; *no fewer than* nicht weniger als; *quite a few, a good few* e-e ganze Menge

fi·an·cé Verlobte *m*

fi·an·cée Verlobte *f*

fi·as·co Fiasko *n*

fib F 1. Flunkerei *f*, Schwindelei *f*; 2. schwindeln, flunkern

fi·ber, *Br* **fi·bre** Faser *f*

fi·ber·glass TECH Fiberglas *n*, Glasfaser *f*

fi·brous faserig

fick·le wankelmütig; unbeständig

fic·tion Erfindung *f*; Prosaliteratur *f*, Belletristik *f*; Romane *pl*

fic·tion·al erdichtet; Roman...

fic·ti·tious erfunden, fiktiv

fid·dle 1. Fiedel *f*, Geige *f*; *play first (second) fiddle esp fig* die erste (zweite) Geige spielen; *(as) fit as a fiddle* kerngesund; 2. MUS fiedeln; *a. fiddle about or around (with)* herumfingern (an *dat*), spielen (mit)

fid·dler Geiger(in)

fi·del·i·ty Treue *f*; Genauigkeit *f*

fid·get F nervös machen; (herum)zappeln

fid·get·y zapp(e)lig, nervös

field Feld *n*; SPORT Spielfeld *n*; Arbeitsfeld *n*; Gebiet *n*; Bereich *m*; *field of vision* OPT Gesichtsfeld *n*

field e·vents SPORT Sprung- und Wurfdisziplinen *pl*

field glass·es *a. pair of field glasses* Feldstecher *m*, Fernglas *n*

field mar·shal MIL Feldmarschall *m*

field·work praktische (wissenschaftliche) Arbeit, *a.* Arbeit *f* im Gelände; ECON Feldarbeit *f*

fiend Satan *m*, Teufel *m*; F (*Frischluftetc*)Fanatiker(in)

fiend·ish teuflisch, boshaft

fierce wild; scharf; heftig

fierce·ness Wildheit *f*, Schärfe *f*; Heftigkeit *f*

fi·er·y feurig; hitzig

fif·teen 1. fünfzehn; 2. Fünfzehn *f*

fif·teenth fünfzehnte(r, -s)

fifth 1. fünfte(r, -s); 2. Fünftel *n*

fifth·ly fünftens

fif·ti·eth fünfzigste(r, -s)

fif·ty 1. fünfzig; 2. Fünfzig *f*

fif·ty-fif·ty F halbe-halbe

fig BOT Feige *f*

fight 1. Kampf *m*; MIL Gefecht *n*; Schlägerei *f*; *boxing:* Kampf *m*, Fight *m*; 2. *v/t* bekämpfen; kämpfen gegen *or* mit, SPORT *a.* boxen gegen; *v/i* kämpfen, sich schlagen; SPORT boxen

fight·er Kämpfer *m*; SPORT Boxer *m*, Fighter *m*; *a. fighter plane* MIL Jagdflugzeug *n*

fight·ing Kampf *m*

fig·u·ra·tive bildlich

fig·ure 1. Figur *f*; Gestalt *f*; Zahl *f*, Ziffer *f*; Preis *m*; *be good at figures* ein guter Rechner sein; 2. *v/t* abbilden, darstellen; F meinen, glauben; sich *et.* vorstellen; *figure out Problem* lösen, F rauskriegen; verstehen; *figure up* zusammenzählen; *v/i* erscheinen, vorkommen; *figure on* rechnen mit

figure skat·er Eiskunstläufer(in)

figure skat·ing Eiskunstlauf *m*

fil·a·ment ELECTR Glühfaden *m*

filch F klauen, stibitzen

file [1] 1. Ordner *m*; Karteikasten *m*; Akte *f*, Akten *pl*; Ablage *f*; EDP Datei *f*; Reihe *f*; MIL Rotte *f*; *on file* bei den Akten; 2. *v/t Briefe etc* ablegen, zu den Akten nehmen, einordnen; *Antrag* einreichen, *Berufung* einlegen; *v/i* hintereinander marschieren

file [2] TECH 1. Feile *f*; 2. feilen

file man·age·ment EDP Dateiverwaltung *f*

file pro·tec·tion EDP Schreibschutz *m*

fil·et GASTR Filet *n*

fi·li·al kindlich, Kindes...

fil·ing Ablegen *n*

fil·ing cab·i·net Aktenschrank *m*

fill 1. (sich) füllen; an-, aus-, erfüllen, vollfüllen; *Pfeife* stopfen; *Zahn* füllen, plombieren; *fill in* einsetzen; *fill out* (*Br in*) *Formular* ausfüllen; *fill up* vollfüllen; sich füllen; *fill her up!* F MOT volltanken, bitte!; 2. Füllung *f*; *eat one's fill* sich satt essen

F

fil·let → *filet*

fill·ing Füllung *f*; MED (Zahn)Füllung *f*, Plombe *f*

filling sta·tion Tankstelle *f*

fil·ly ZO Stutenfohlen *n*

film 1. Häutchen *n*; Membran(e) *f*; Film *m* (*a.* PHOT); *take or shoot a film* e-n Film drehen; **2.** (ver)filmen; sich verfilmen lassen

film star *esp Br* Filmstar *m*

fil·ter 1. Filter *m*; **2.** filtern

fil·ter tip Filter *m*; Filterzigarette *f*

fil·ter·tipped: *filtertipped cigarette* Filterzigarette *f*

filth Schmutz *m*

filth·y schmutzig; *fig* unflätig

fin ZO Flosse *f*; SPORT Schwimmflosse *f*

fi·nal 1. letzte(r, -s); End..., Schluss...; endgültig; **2.** SPORT Finale *n*; *mst pl* Schlussexamen *n*, -prüfung *f*

fi·nal dis·pos·al Endlagerung *f*

fi·nal·ist SPORT Finalist(in)

fi·nal·ly endlich, schließlich; endgültig

fi·nal whis·tle SPORT Schlusspfiff *m*, Abpfiff *m*

fi·nance 1. Finanzwesen *n*; *pl* Finanzen *pl*; **2.** finanzieren

fi·nan·cial finanziell

fi·nan·cier Finanzier *m*

finch ZO Fink *m*

find 1. finden; (an)treffen; herausfinden; JUR *j-n* für (*nicht*) *schuldig* erklären; beschaffen, besorgen; *find out* *v/t et.* herausfinden; *v/i* es herausfinden; **2.** Fund *m*, Entdeckung *f*

find·ings Befund *m*; JUR Feststellung *f*, Spruch *m*

fine¹ 1. *adj* fein; schön; ausgezeichnet, großartig; *I'm fine* mir geht es gut; **2.** *adv* F sehr gut, bestens

fine² 1. Geldstrafe *f*, Bußgeld *n*; **2.** zu e-r Geldstrafe verurteilen

fin·ger 1. ANAT Finger *m*; → *cross 3*; **2.** betasten, (herum)fingern an (*dat*)

fin·ger·nail ANAT Fingernagel *m*

fin·ger·print Fingerabdruck *m*

fin·ger·tip Fingerspitze *f*

fin·i·cky pedantisch; wählerisch

fin·ish 1. (be)enden, aufhören (mit); *a.* *finish off* vollenden, zu Ende führen, erledigen, *Buch etc* auslesen; *a.* *finish off*, *finish up* aufessen, austrinken; **2.** Ende *n*, Schluss *m*; SPORT Endspurt *m*, Finish *n*; Ziel *n*; Vollendung *f*, letzter Schliff

fin·ish·ing line SPORT Ziellinie *f*

Fin·land Finnland *n*

Finn Finne *m*, Finnin *f*

Finn·ish 1. finnisch; **2.** LING Finnisch *n*

fir *a.* *fir tree* BOT Tanne *f*

fir cone BOT Tannenzapfen *m*

fire 1. Feuer *n*; *be on fire* in Flammen stehen, brennen; *catch fire* Feuer fangen, in Brand geraten; *set on fire, set fire to* anzünden; **2.** *v/t* anzünden, entzünden; *fig* anfeuern; abfeuern; *Ziegel etc* brennen; F *j-n* rausschmeißen; heizen; *v/i* Feuer fangen (*a. fig*); feuern

fire a·larm Feueralarm *m*; Feuermelder *m*

fire·arms Schusswaffen *pl*

fire bri·gade *Br* Feuerwehr *f*

fire·bug F Feuerteufel *m*

fire·crack·er Knallfrosch *m*; Knallbonbon *m*, *n*

fire de·part·ment Feuerwehr *f*

fire en·gine *Br* Löschfahrzeug *n*

fire es·cape Feuerleiter *f*, -treppe *f*

fire ex·tin·guish·er Feuerlöscher *m*

fire fight·er Feuerwehrmann *m*

fire·guard *Br* Kamingitter *n*

fire hy·drant *Br* Hydrant *m*

fire·man Feuerwehrmann *m*; Heizer *m*

fire·place (offener) Kamin

fire·plug Hydrant *m*

fire·proof feuerfest

fire·rais·ing *Br* Brandstiftung *f*

fire·screen Kamingitter *n*

fire ser·vice *Br* Feuerwehr *f*

fire·side (offener) Kamin

fire sta·tion Feuerwache *f*

fire truck Löschfahrzeug *n*

fire·wood Brennholz *n*

fire·works Feuerwerk *n*

fir·ing squad MIL Exekutionskommando *n*

firm¹ fest; hart; standhaft

firm² Firma *f*

first 1. *adj* erste(r, -s); beste(r, -s); **2.** *adv* erstens; zuerst; *first of all* an erster Stelle; zu allererst; **3.** Erste(r, -s); *at first* zuerst, anfangs; *from the first* von Anfang an

first aid MED Erste Hilfe

first aid box, **first aid kit** Verband(s)kasten *m*

first·born erstgeborene(r, -s), älteste(r, -s)

first class RAIL *etc* 1. Klasse

first-class erstklassig

first floor Erdgeschoss *n*, *Br* erster Stock; → *second floor*

first·hand aus erster Hand

first leg SPORT Hinspiel *n*

first·ly erstens

first name Vorname *m*

first-rate erstklassig

firth Förde *f*, Meeresarm *m*

fish 1. ZO Fisch *m*; **2.** fischen, angeln

fish·bone Gräte *f*

fish·er·man Fischer *m*

fish·e·ry Fischerei *f*
fish fin·ger *Br* GASTR Fischstäbchen *n*
fish·hook Angelhaken *m*
fish·ing Fischen *n*, Angeln *n*
fishing line Angelschnur *f*
fishing rod Angelrute *f*
fishing tack·le Angelgerät *n*
fish·mon·ger *esp Br* Fischhändler *m*
fish stick GASTR Fischstäbchen *n*
fish·y Fisch...; F verdächtig
fis·sion PHYS Spaltung *f*
fis·sure GEOL Spalt *m*, Riss *m*
fist Faust *f*
fit[1] **1.** geeignet, passend; tauglich; SPORT fit, (gut) in Form; *keep fit* sich fit halten; **2.** *v/t* passend machen (*for* für), anpassen; TECH einpassen, einbauen; anbringen; *fit in* j-m e-n Termin geben, *j-n, et.* einschieben; *a. fit on* anprobieren; *a. fit out* ausrüsten, ausstatten, einrichten (*with* mit); *a. fit up* einrichten (*with* mit); montieren, installieren; *v/i* passen, sitzen (*dress etc*); **3.** Sitz *m*
fit[2] MED Anfall *m*; *give s.o. a fit* F j-n auf die Palme bringen; j-m e-n Schock versetzen
fit·ful unruhig (*sleep etc*)
fit·ness Tauglichkeit *f*; *esp* SPORT Fitness *f*, (gute) Form
fitness cen·ter (*Br* **cen·tre**) Fitnesscenter *n*
fit·ted zugeschnitten; *fitted carpet* Spannteppich *m*, Teppichboden *m*; *fitted kitchen* Einbauküche *f*
fit·ter Monteur *m*; Installateur *m*
fit·ting 1. passend; schicklich; **2.** Montage *f*, Installation *f*; *pl* Ausstattung *f*; Armaturen *pl*
five 1. fünf; **2.** Fünf *f*
fix 1. befestigen, anbringen (*to* an *dat*); *Preis* festsetzen; fixieren; *Blick etc* richten (*on* auf *acc*); *Aufmerksamkeit etc* fesseln; reparieren, in Ordnung bringen (*a. fig*); *Essen* zubereiten; **2.** F Klemme *f*; *sl* Fix *m*
fixed fest; starr
fix·ings GASTR Beilagen *pl*
fix·ture Inventarstück *n*; *lighting fixture* Beleuchtungskörper *m*
fizz zischen, sprudeln
flab·ber·gast F verblüffen; *be flabbergasted* F platt sein
flab·by schlaff
flac·cid schlaff, schlapp
flag[1] **1.** Fahne *f*, Flagge *f*; **2.** beflaggen
flag[2] **1.** (Stein)Platte *f*, Fliese *f*; **2.** mit (Stein)Platten *or* Fliesen belegen, fliesen
flag[3] nachlassen, erlahmen
flag·pole, flag·staff Fahnenstange *f*

flag·stone (Stein)Platte *f*, Fliese *f*
flake 1. Flocke *f*; Schuppe *f*; **2.** *mst flake off* abblättern; F *flake out* schlappmachen
flak·y flockig; blätt(e)rig
flak·y pas·try GASTR Blätterteig *m*
flame 1. Flamme *f* (*a. fig*); *be in flames* in Flammen stehen; **2.** flammen, lodern
flam·ma·ble TECH brennbar, leicht entzündlich, feuergefährlich
flan GASTR Obst-, Käsekuchen *m*
flank 1. Flanke *f*; **2.** flankieren
flan·nel Flanell *m*; *Br* Waschlappen *m*; *pl Br* Flanellhose *f*
flap 1. Flattern *n*, (Flügel)Schlag *m*; Klappe *f*; **2.** mit *den Flügeln etc* schlagen; flattern
flare 1. flackern; sich weiten; *flare up* aufflammen; *fig* aufbrausen; **2.** Lichtsignal *n*
flash 1. Aufblitzen *n*, Aufleuchten *n*, Blitz *m*; *radio etc*: Kurzmeldung *f*; PHOT F Blitz *m*; F Taschenlampe *f*; *like a flash* wie der Blitz; *in a flash* im Nu; *a flash of lightning* ein Blitz; **2.** (auf)blitzen *or* aufleuchten (lassen); zucken; rasen, flitzen
flash·back *film*: Rückblende *f*
flash freeze GASTR schnell einfrieren
flash·light PHOT Blitzlicht *n*; Taschenlampe *f*
flash·y protzig; auffallend
flask Taschenflasche *f*
flat[1] **1.** flach, eben, platt; schal; ECON flau; MOT platt (*tire*); **2.** *adv fall flat* danebengehen; *sing flat* zu tief singen; **3.** Fläche *f*, Ebene *f*; flache Seite; Flachland *n*, Niederung *f*; MOT Reifenpanne *f*
flat[2] *Br* Wohnung *f*
flat·foot·ed plattfüßig
flat·mate *Br* Mitbewohner(in)
flat·ten (ein)ebnen; abflachen; *a. flatten out* flach(er) werden
flat·ter schmeicheln (*dat*)
flat·ter·er Schmeichler(in)
flat·ter·y Schmeichelei *f*
fla·vo(u)r 1. Geschmack *m*; Aroma *n*; Blume *f*; *fig* Beigeschmack *m*; Würze *f*; **2.** würzen
fla·vo(u)r·ing Würze *f*, Aroma *n*
flaw Fehler *m*, TECH *a.* Defekt *m*
flaw·less einwandfrei, tadellos
flax BOT Flachs *m*
flea ZO Floh *m*
flea mar·ket Flohmarkt *m*
fleck Fleck(en) *m*; Tupfen *m*
fledged ZO flügge
fledg(e)·ling ZO Jungvogel *m*; *fig* Grünschnabel *m*
flee fliehen; meiden

fleece 1. Vlies *n*, *esp* Schafsfell *n*; **2.** F *j-n* neppen

fleet MAR Flotte *f*

flesh Fleisch *n*

flesh·y fleischig; dick

flex[1] *esp* ANAT biegen

flex[2] *esp Br* ELECTR (Anschluss-, Verlängerungs)Kabel *n*, (-)Schnur *f*

flex·i·ble flexibel, biegsam; *fig* anpassungsfähig; **flexible working hours** Gleitzeit *f*

flex·i·time *Br*, **flex·time** Gleitzeit *f*

flick schnippen; schnellen

flick·er 1. flackern; TV flimmern; **2.** Flackern *n*; TV Flimmern *n*

fli·er AVIAT Flieger *m*; Reklamezettel *m*

flight Flucht *f*; Flug *m* (*a. fig*); ZO Schwarm *m*; *a.* **flight of stairs** Treppe *f*; **put to flight** in die Flucht schlagen; **take (to) flight** die Flucht ergreifen

flight at·tend·ant AVIAT Flugbegleiter(in)

flight·less flugunfähig

flight re·cord·er AVIAT Flugschreiber *m*

flight·y flatterhaft

flim·sy dünn; zart; *fig* fadenscheinig

flinch (zurück)zucken, zusammenfahren; zurückschrecken (**from** vor *dat*)

fling 1. werfen, schleudern; **fling o.s.** sich stürzen; **fling open (to)** *Tür etc* aufreißen (zuschlagen); **2. have a fling** sich austoben; **have a fling at** es versuchen *or* probieren mit

flint Feuerstein *m*

flip schnippen, schnipsen; *Münze* hochwerfen

flip·pant respektlos, F schnodd(e)rig

flip·per ZO Flosse *f*; Schwimmflosse *f*

flirt 1. flirten; **2. be a flirt** gern flirten

flir·ta·tion Flirt *m*

flit flitzen, huschen

float 1. *v/i* (auf dem Wasser) schwimmen, (im Wasser) treiben; schweben; *a.* ECON in Umlauf sein; *v/t* schwimmen *or* treiben lassen; MAR flottmachen; ECON *Wertpapiere etc* in Umlauf bringen; *Währung* floaten, den Wechselkurs (*gen*) freigeben; **2.** Festwagen *m*

float·ing 1. schwimmend, treibend; ECON umlaufend; frei (*exchange rate*); frei konvertierbar (*currency*); **2.** ECON Floating *n*

float·ing vot·er POL Wechselwähler(in)

flock 1. ZO Herde *f* (*a.* REL); Menge *f*, Schar *f*; **2.** *fig* strömen

floe (treibende) Eisscholle

flog prügeln, schlagen

flog·ging Tracht *f* Prügel

flood 1. *a.* **flood tide** Flut *f*; Überschwemmung *f*; **2.** überfluten, überschwemmen

flood·gate Schleusentor *n*

flood·lights ELECTR Flutlicht *n*

floor 1. (Fuß)Boden *m*; Stock *m*, Stockwerk *n*, Etage *f*; Tanzfläche *f*; → **first floor**, **second floor**; **take the floor** das Wort ergreifen; **2.** e-n (Fuß)Boden legen in; zu Boden schlagen; *fig* F *j-n* umhauen

floor·board (Fußboden)Diele *f*

floor cloth Putzlappen *m*

floor·ing (Fuß)Bodenbelag *m*

floor lamp Stehlampe *f*

floor lead·er PARL Fraktionsführer *m*

floor-length bodenlang

floor show Nachtklubvorstellung *f*

floor·walk·er Aufsicht *f*

flop 1. sich (hin)plumpsen lassen; F durchfallen, danebengehen, ein Reinfall sein; **2.** Plumps *m*; F Flop *m*, Reinfall *m*, Pleite *f*; Versager *m*

flop·py (disk) EDP Floppy Disk *f*, Diskette *f*

flor·id rot, gerötet

flor·ist Blumenhändler(in)

floun·der[1] ZO Flunder *f*

floun·der[2] zappeln; strampeln; *fig* sich verhaspeln

flour (feines) Mehl

flour·ish 1. Schnörkel *m*; MUS Tusch *m*; **2.** *v/i* blühen, gedeihen; *v/t* schwenken

flow 1. fließen, strömen; wallen; **2.** Fluß *m*, Strom *m* (*both a. fig*)

flow·er 1. Blume *f*; Blüte *f* (*a. fig*); **2.** blühen

flow·er·bed Blumenbeet *n*

flow·er·pot Blumentopf *m*

fluc·tu·ate schwanken

fluc·tu·a·tion Schwankung *f*

flu F MED Grippe *f*

flue Rauchfang *m*, Esse *f*

flu·en·cy Flüssigkeit *f*; (Rede)Gewandtheit *f*

flu·ent flüssig; gewandt; **speak fluent French** fließend Französisch sprechen

fluff 1. Flaum *m*; Staubflocke *f*; **2.** ZO aufplustern

fluff·y flaumig

flu·id 1. flüssig; **2.** Flüssigkeit *f*

flunk F durchfallen (lassen)

flu·o·res·cent fluoreszierend

flu·o·ride CHEM Fluor *n*

flu·o·rine CHEM Fluor *n*

flur·ry Windstoß *m*; (*Regen-, Schnee-*) Schauer *m*; *fig* Aufregung *f*, Unruhe *f*

flush 1. (Wasser)Spülung *f*; Erröten *n*; Röte *f*; **2.** *v/t a.* **flush out** (aus)spülen; **flush down** hinunterspülen; **flush the toilet** spülen; *v/i* erröten, rot werden; spülen; **3. be flush** F gut bei Kasse sein

flus·ter 1. nervös machen *or* werden; **2.** Nervosität *f*

flute MUS **1.** Flöte *f*; **2.** (auf der) Flöte spielen

flut·ter 1. flattern; **2.** Flattern *n*; *fig* Erregung *f*

flux *fig* Fluss *m*

fly[1] ZO Fliege *f*

fly[2] Hosenschlitz *m*; Zeltklappe *f*

fly[3] fliegen (lassen); stürmen, stürzen; flattern, wehen; (ver)fliegen (*time*); *Drachen* steigen lassen; *fly at s.o.* auf j-n losgehen; *fly into a passion or rage* in Wut geraten

fly·er → *flier*

fly·ing fliegend; Flug...

flying sau·cer fliegende Untertasse

flying squad Überfallkommando *n*

flying vis·it F Stippvisite *f*

fly·o·ver *Br* (Straßen-, Eisenbahn-) Überführung *f*

fly·screen Fliegenfenster *n*

fly·weight *boxing*: Fliegengewicht *n*, Fliegengewichtler *m*

fly·wheel TECH Schwungrad *n*

foal ZO Fohlen *n*

foam 1. Schaum *m*; **2.** schäumen

foam ex·tin·guish·er Schaumlöscher *m*, -löschgerät *n*

foam rub·ber Schaumgummi *m*

foam·y schaumig

fo·cus 1. Brennpunkt *m*, *fig a.* Mittelpunkt *m*; OPT, PHOT Scharfeinstellung *f*; **2.** OPT, PHOT scharf einstellen; *fig* konzentrieren (*on* auf *acc*)

fod·der AGR (Trocken)Futter *n*

foe POET Feind *m*, Gegner *m*

fog (dichter) Nebel

fog·gy neb(e)lig; *fig* nebelhaft

foi·ble (kleine) Schwäche

foil[1] Folie *f*; *fig* Hintergrund *m*

foil[2] vereiteln

foil[3] *fencing*: Florett *n*

fold[1] **1.** Falte *f*; Falz *m*; **2.** ...fach, ...fältig; **3.** (sich) falten; falzen; *Arme* verschränken; einwickeln; *often* ***fold up*** zusammenfalten, -legen, -klappen

fold[2] AGR Schafhürde *f*, Pferch *m*; REL Herde *f*

fold·er Aktendeckel *m*; Schnellhefter *m*; Faltprospekt *m*, -blatt *n*, Broschüre *f*

fold·ing zusammenlegbar; Klapp...

folding bed Klappbett *n*

folding bi·cy·cle Klapprad *n*

folding boat Faltboot *n*

folding chair Klappstuhl *m*

folding door(s) Falttür *f*

fo·li·age BOT Laub *n*, Laubwerk *n*

folk 1. Leute *pl*; *pl* F *m-e etc* Leute *pl*; **2.** Volks...

folk·lore Volkskunde *f*; Volkssagen *pl*; Folklore *f*

folk mu·sic Volksmusik *f*

folk song Volkslied *n*; Folksong *m*

fol·low folgen (*dat*); folgen auf (*acc*); befolgen; verfolgen; *s-m Beruf etc* nachgehen; *follow through Plan etc* bis zum Ende durchführen; *follow up e-r Sache* nachgehen; *e-e Sache* weiterverfolgen; *as follows* wie folgt

fol·low·er Nachfolger(in); Verfolger(in); Anhänger(in)

fol·low·ing 1. Anhängerschaft *f*, Anhänger *pl*; Gefolge *n*; *the following* das Folgende; die Folgenden *pl*; **2.** folgende(r, -s); **3.** im Anschluss an (*acc*)

fol·ly Torheit *f*

fond zärtlich; vernarrt (*of* in *acc*); *be fond of* gernhaben, lieben

fon·dle liebkosen; streicheln; (ver)hätscheln

fond·ness Zärtlichkeit *f*; Vorliebe *f*

font REL Taufstein *m*, Taufbecken *n*

food Nahrung *f*, Essen *n*; Nahrungs-, Lebensmittel *pl*; AGR Futter *n*

fool 1. Narr *m*, Närrin *f*, Dummkopf *m*; *make a fool of s.o.* j-n zum Narren halten; *make a fool of o.s.* sich lächerlich machen; **2.** zum Narren halten; betrügen (*out of* um); *fool about, fool around* herumtrödeln; Unsinn machen, herumalbern

fool·har·dy tollkühn

fool·ish dumm, töricht; unklug

fool·ish·ness Dummheit *f*

fool·proof kinderleicht; todsicher

foot 1. ANAT Fuß *m* (*a. linear measure = 30,48 cm*); Fußende *n*; *on foot* zu Fuß; **2.** F *Rechnung* bezahlen; *have to foot the bill* die Zeche bezahlen müssen; *foot it* zu Fuß gehen

foot·ball Football(spiel *n*) *m*; *Br* Fußball(-spiel *n*) *m*; Football-Ball *m*; *Br* Fußball *m*

foot·bal·ler *Br* Fußballer *m*

foot·ball hoo·li·gan *Br* Fußballrowdy *m*

football play·er *Br* Fußballspieler *m*

foot·bridge Fußgängerbrücke *f*

foot·fall Tritt *m*, Schritt *m*

foot·hold fester Stand, Halt *m*

foot·ing Halt *m*, Stand *m*; *fig* Grundlage *f*, Basis *f*; *be on a friendly footing with s.o.* ein gutes Verhältnis zu j-m haben; *lose one's footing* den Halt verlieren

foot·lights THEA Rampenlicht(er *pl*) *n*

foot·loose frei, unbeschwert; *footloose and fancy-free* frei und ungebunden

foot·note Fußnote *f*

foot·path (Fuß)Pfad *m*, (Fuß)Weg *m*

foot·print Fußabdruck *m*, *pl a.* Fußspur(en *pl*) *f*

F

foot·sore: *be footsore* wunde Füße haben

foot·step Tritt *m*, Schritt *m*; Fußstapfe *f*

foot·wear Schuhwerk *n*, Schuhe *pl*

fop Geck *m*, F Fatzke *m*

for 1. *prp mst* für; *purpose, direction*: zu; nach; *warten, hoffen etc* auf (*acc*); *sich sehnen etc* nach; *cause*: aus, vor (*dat*), wegen; *time*: *for three days* drei Tage (lang); seit drei Tagen; *distance*: *I walked for a mile* ich ging eine Meile (weit); *exchange*: (an)statt; als; *I for one* ich zum Beispiel; *for sure* sicher!, gewiss!; **2.** *cj* denn, weil

for·age *a.* *forage about* (herum)stöbern, (-)wühlen (*in* in *dat*; *for* nach)

for·ay MIL Einfall *m*, Überfall *m*; *fig* Ausflug *m* (*into* in *politics* in *die Politik*)

for·bid verbieten; hindern

for·bid·ding abstoßend

force 1. Stärke *f*, Kraft *f*, Gewalt *f*, Wucht *f*; *the* (*police*) *force* die Polizei; (*armed*) *forces* MIL Streitkräfte *pl*; *by force* mit Gewalt; *come or put into force* in Kraft treten *or* setzen; **2.** *j-n* zwingen; *et.* erzwingen; zwängen; drängen; *Tempo* beschleunigen; *force s.th. on s.o.* *et.* aufzwingen *or* aufdrängen; *force o.s. on s.o.* sich j-m aufdrängen; *force open* aufbrechen

forced erzwungen; gezwungen, gequält

forced land·ing AVIAT Notlandung *f*

force·ful energisch, kraftvoll; eindrucksvoll, überzeugend

for·ceps MED Zange *f*

for·ci·ble gewaltsam; eindringlich

ford 1. Furt *f*; **2.** durchwaten

fore 1. vorder, Vorder...; vorn; **2.** Vorderteil *m*, Vorderseite *f*, Front *f*

fore·arm ANAT Unterarm *m*

fore·bear *mst pl* Vorfahren *pl*, Ahnen *pl*

fore·bod·ing (böses) Vorzeichen; (*böse*) (Vor)Ahnung

fore·cast 1. voraussagen, vorhersehen; *Wetter* vorhersagen; **2.** Voraussage *f*; METEOR Vorhersage *f*

fore·fa·ther Vorfahr *m*

fore·fin·ger ANAT Zeigefinger *m*

fore·foot ZO Vorderfuß *m*

fore·gone con·clu·sion ausgemachte Sache; *be a foregone conclusion a.* von vornherein feststehen

fore·ground Vordergrund *m*

fore·hand SPORT **1.** Vorhand *f*, Vorhandschlag *m*; **2.** Vorhand...

fore·head ANAT Stirn *f*

for·eign fremd, ausländisch, Außen..., Auslands...

foreign af·fairs Außenpolitik *f*

foreign aid Auslandshilfe *f*

for·eign·er Ausländer(in)

for·eign lan·guage Fremdsprache *f*

foreign min·is·ter POL Außenminister *m*

For·eign Of·fice *Br* POL Außenministerium *n*

for·eign pol·i·cy Außenpolitik *f*

For·eign Sec·re·ta·ry *Br* POL Außenminister *m*

for·eign trade ECON Außenhandel *m*

for·eign work·er Gastarbeiter(in)

fore·knowl·edge vorherige Kenntnis

fore·leg ZO Vorderbein *n*

fore·man TECH Vorarbeiter *m*, Polier *m*; Werkmeister *m*; JUR Sprecher *m*

fore·most vorderste(r, -s), erste(r, -s)

fore·name Vorname *m*

fo·ren·sic JUR Gerichts...

forensic me·dicine Gerichtsmedizin *f*

fore·run·ner Vorläufer(in)

fore·see vorhersehen, voraussehen

fore·see·a·ble vorhersehbar

fore·shad·ow ahnen lassen, andeuten

fore·sight Weitblick *m*; (weise) Voraussicht

for·est Wald *m* (*a. fig*); Forst *m*

fore·stall *et.* vereiteln; *j-m* zuvorkommen

for·est·er Förster *m*

for·est·ry Forstwirtschaft *f*

fore·taste Vorgeschmack *m*

fore·tell vorhersagen

for·ev·er, for ev·er für immer

fore·wom·an TECH Vorarbeiterin *f*

fore·word Vorwort *n*

for·feit verwirken; einbüßen

forge 1. Schmiede *f*; **2.** fälschen; schmieden

forg·er Fälscher *m*

for·ge·ry Fälschen *n*; Fälschung *f*

for·ge·ry-proof fälschungssicher

for·get vergessen

for·get·ful vergesslich

for·get-me-not BOT Vergissmeinnicht *n*

for·give vergeben, verzeihen

for·give·ness Verzeihung *f*; Vergebung *f*

for·giv·ing versöhnlich; nachsichtig

fork 1. Gabel *f*; **2.** (sich) gabeln

fork·lift truck MOT Gabelstapler *m*

form 1. Form *f*; Gestalt *f*; Formular *n*, Vordruck *m*; *Br* (Schul)Klasse *f*; Formalität *f*; Kondition *f*, Verfassung *f*; *in great form* gut in Form; **2.** (sich) formen, (sich) bilden, gestalten

for·mal förmlich; formell

for·mal dress Gesellschaftskleidung *f*

for·mal·i·ty Förmlichkeit *f*; Formalität *f*

for·mat 1. Aufmachung *f*; Format *n*; **2.** EDP formatieren

for·ma·tion Bildung *f*

form·a·tive bildend; gestaltend; **forma-tive years** Entwicklungsjahre pl

for·mat·ting EDP Formatierung f

for·mer 1. früher; ehemalig; **2.** *the former* der *or* die *or* das Erstere

for·mer·ly früher

for·mi·da·ble furchterregend; gewaltig, riesig, gefährlich, schwierig

form mas·ter Br Klassenlehrer m, -leiter m

form mis·tress Br Klassenlehrerin f, -leiterin f

form teach·er Br Klassenlehrer(in), Klassenleiter(in)

for·mu·la Formel f; Rezept n

for·mu·late formulieren

for·sake aufgeben; verlassen

for·swear abschwören, entsagen (*dat*)

fort MIL Fort n, Festung f

forth weiter, fort; (her)vor; *and so forth* und so weiter

forth·com·ing bevorstehend, kommend; in Kürze erscheinend (*book*) *or* anlaufend (*film*)

for·ti·eth vierzigste(r, -s)

for·ti·fi·ca·tion Befestigung f

for·ti·fy MIL befestigen; *fig* (ver)stärken

for·ti·tude (innere) Kraft *or* Stärke

fort·night *esp* Br vierzehn Tage

for·tress MIL Festung f

for·tu·i·tous zufällig

for·tu·nate glücklich; *be fortunate* Glück haben

for·tu·nate·ly glücklicherweise

for·tune Vermögen n; (glücklicher) Zufall, Glück n; Schicksal n

for·tune-tell·er Wahrsager(in)

for·ty 1. vierzig; *have forty winks* F ein Nickerchen machen; **2.** Vierzig f

for·ward 1. *adv* nach vorn, vorwärts; **2.** *adj* Vorwärts...; fortschrittlich; vorlaut, dreist; **3.** *soccer*: Stürmer m; **4.** befördern, (ver)senden, schicken; *Brief etc* nachsenden

for·ward·ing a·gent Spediteur m

fos·sil GEOL Fossil n (*a.* F), Versteinerung f

fos·ter-child Pflegekind n

fos·ter-par·ents Pflegeeltern pl

foul 1. stinkend, widerlich; verpestet, schlecht (*air, water*); GASTR verdorben, faul; schmutzig, verschmutzt; METEOR stürmisch, schlecht; SPORT regelwidrig; *esp* Br F mies; **2.** SPORT Foul n, Regelverstoß m; *vicious foul* böses *or* übles Foul; **3.** beschmutzen, verschmutzen; SPORT foulen

found¹ gründen; stiften

found² TECH gießen

foun·da·tion ARCH Grundmauer f, Funda-ment n; *fig* Gründung f, Errichtung f; (gemeinnützige) Stiftung; *fig* Grundlage f, Basis f

found·er¹ Gründer(in); Stifter(in)

foun·der² MAR sinken; *fig* scheitern

found·ling JUR Findelkind n

foun·dry TECH Gießerei f

foun·tain Springbrunnen m; (*Wasser*-)Strahl m

fountain pen Füllfederhalter m

four 1. vier; **2.** Vier f; *rowing*: Vierer m; *on all fours* auf allen vieren

four star Br F Super n

four-star pet·rol Br Superbenzin n

four-stroke en·gine Viertaktmotor m

four·teen 1. vierzehn; **2.** Vierzehn f

four·teenth vierzehnte(r, -s)

fourth 1. vierte(r, -s); **2.** Viertel n

fourth·ly viertens

four-wheel drive MOT Vierradantrieb m

fowl ZO Geflügel n

fox ZO Fuchs m

fox-glove BOT Fingerhut m

fox·y schlau, gerissen

frac·tion Bruchteil m; MATH Bruch m

frac·ture MED **1.** (Knochen)Bruch m; **2.** brechen

fra·gile zerbrechlich

frag·ment Bruchstück n

fra·grance Wohlgeruch m, Duft m

fra·grant wohlriechend, duftend

frail gebrechlich; zerbrechlich; zart, schwach

frail·ty Zartheit f; Gebrechlichkeit f; Schwäche f

frame 1. Rahmen m; (*Brillen- etc*)Gestell n; Körper(bau) m; *frame of mind* (Gemüts)Verfassung f, (-)Zustand m; **2.** (ein)rahmen; bilden, formen, bauen; *a. frame up* F *j-m* et. anhängen

frame-up F abgekartetes Spiel; Intrige f

frame·work TECH Gerüst n; *fig* Struktur f, System n

franc Franc m; Franken m

France Frankreich n

fran·chise POL Wahlrecht n; ECON Konzession f

frank 1. frei(mütig), offen; *frankly (speaking)* offen gesagt; **2.** *Brief* freistempeln

frank·fur·ter GASTR Frankfurter (Würstchen n) f

frank·ness Offenheit f

fran·tic hektisch; *be frantic* außer sich sein

fra·ter·nal brüderlich

frat·er·nize sich verbrüdern

frat·er·ni·za·tion Verbrüderung f

fra·ter·ni·ty Brüderlichkeit f; Vereinigung

f, Zunft *f*; UNIV Verbindung *f*
fraud Betrug *m*; F Schwindel *m*
fraud·u·lent betrügerisch
fray ausfransen, (sich) durchscheuern
freak 1. Missgeburt *f*; Laune *f*; *in cpds* F
…freak *m*, …fanatiker *m*; Freak *m*, irrer
Typ; *freak of nature* Laune *f* der Natur;
2. F *a.* **freak out** durchdrehen, die Nerven verlieren
freck·le Sommersprosse *f*
freck·led sommersprossig
free 1. frei; ungehindert; ungebunden;
kostenlos, zum Nulltarif; freigebig; *free
and easy* zwanglos; sorglos; *set free*
freilassen; **2.** befreien; freilassen
free·dom Freiheit *f*
free fares Nulltarif *m*
free·lance frei, freiberuflich tätig, freischaffend
Free·ma·son Freimaurer *m*
free skat·ing SPORT Kür *f*
free·style SPORT Freistil *m*
free time Freizeit *f*
free trade ECON Freihandel *m*
free trade ar·e·a ECON Freihandelszone *f*
free·way Schnellstraße *f*
free·wheel im Freilauf fahren
freeze 1. *v/i* (ge)frieren; erstarren; *v/t* gefrieren lassen; GASTR einfrieren (*a.* ECON),
tiefkühlen; **2.** Frost *m*, Kälte *f*; ECON, POL
Einfrieren *n*; *wage freeze, freeze on
wages* ECON Lohnstopp *m*
freeze-dried gefriergetrocknet
freeze-dry gefriertrocknen
freez·er Gefriertruhe *f*, Tiefkühl-, Gefriergerät *n*; Gefrierfach *n*
freez·ing eisig; Gefrier…
freezing com·part·ment Gefrierfach *n*
freezing point Gefrierpunkt *m*
freight 1. Fracht *f*; Frachtgebühr *f*; **2.** Güter…; **3.** beladen; verfrachten
freight car RAIL Güterwagen *m*
freight·er MAR Frachter *m*, Frachtschiff *n*;
AVIAT Transportflugzeug *n*
freight train Güterzug *m*
French 1. französisch; **2.** LING Französisch
n; *the French* die Franzosen *pl*
French doors Terrassen-, Balkontür *f*
French fries GASTR Pommes frites *pl*
French·man Franzose *m*
French win·dows → *French doors*
French·wom·an Französin *f*
fren·zied wahnsinnig, rasend (*with* vor
dat); hektisch
fren·zy Wahnsinn *m*; Ekstase *f*; Raserei *f*
fre·quen·cy Häufigkeit *f*; ELECTR Frequenz *f*
fre·quent 1. häufig; **2.** (oft) besuchen
fresh frisch; neu; unerfahren; frech; *get*

fresh (*with s.o.*) (j-m gegenüber) zudringlich werden
fresh·en auffrischen (*wind*); *freshen*
(*o.s.*) *up* sich frisch machen
fresh·man UNIV Student(in) im ersten
Jahr
fresh·ness Frische *f*; Frechheit *f*
fresh wa·ter Süßwasser *n*
fresh·wa·ter Süßwasser…
fret sich Sorgen machen;
fret·ful verärgert, gereizt; quengelig
FRG ABBR *of Federal Republic of Germany* Bundesrepublik *f* Deutschland
Fri ABBR *of Friday* Fr., Freitag *m*
fri·ar REL Mönch *m*
fric·tion TECH *etc* Reibung *f* (*a. fig*)
Fri·day (ABBR *Fri*) Freitag *m*; *on Friday*
(am) Freitag; *on Fridays* freitags
fridge F Kühlschrank *m*
friend Freund(in); Bekannte *m*, *f*; *make
friends with* sich anfreunden mit,
Freundschaft schließen mit
friend·ly 1. freund(schaft)lich; **2.** *esp Br*
SPORT Freundschaftsspiel *n*
friend·ship Freundschaft *f*
fries F GASTR Fritten *pl*
frig·ate MAR Fregatte *f*
fright Schreck(en) *m*; *look a fright* F verboten aussehen
fright·en erschrecken; *be frightened* erschrecken (*at, by, of* vor *dat*); Angst haben (*of* vor *dat*)
fright·ful schrecklich, fürchterlich
fri·gid PSYCH frigid(e); kalt, frostig
frill Krause *f*, Rüsche *f*
fringe 1. Franse *f*; Rand *m*; Pony *m*; **2.** mit
Fransen besetzen
fringe ben·e·fits ECON Gehalts-, Lohnnebenleistungen *pl*
fringe e·vent Randveranstaltung *f*
fringe group *soziale* Randgruppe *f*
frisk herumtollen; F *j-n* filzen, durchsuchen
frisk·y lebhaft, munter
frit·ter: *fritter away* Geld *etc* vertun, *Zeit*
vertrödeln, *Geld*, *Kräfte* vergeuden
fri·vol·i·ty Frivolität *f*, Leichtfertigkeit *f*
friv·o·lous frivol, leichtfertig
friz·zle F GASTR verbrutzeln
frizz·y gekräuselt, kraus
fro: *to and fro* hin und her
frock REL Kutte *f*
frog ZO Frosch *m*
frog·man Froschmann *m*, MIL *a.* Kampfschwimmer *m*
frol·ic herumtoben, herumtollen
from von; aus; von … aus *or* her; von …
(an), seit; aus, vor (*dat*); *from 9 to 5*
(*o'clock*) von 9 bis 5 (Uhr)

front 1. Vorderseite *f*; Front *f* (*a.* MIL); *at the front, in front* vorn; *in front of* vor; *be in front* in Führung sein; **2.** Vorder...; **3.** *a.* *front on, front to(wards)* gegenüberstehen, gegenüberliegen
front·age ARCH (Vorder)Front *f*
front cov·er Titelseite *f*
front door Haustür *f*, Vordertür *f*
front en·trance Vordereingang *m*
fron·tier 1. (Landes)Grenze *f*; HIST Grenzland *n*, Grenze *f*; **2.** Grenz...
front-page F wichtig, aktuell
front-wheel drive MOT Vorderradantrieb *m*
frost 1. Frost *m*; *a.* *hoar frost, white frost* Reif *m*; **2.** mit Reif überziehen; *Glas* mattieren; GASTR glasieren, mit Zuckerguss überziehen; mit (Puder)Zucker bestreuen
frost·bite MED Erfrierung *f*
frost·bit·ten MED erfroren
frost·ed glass Matt-, Milchglas *n*
frost·y eisig, frostig (*a. fig*)
froth 1. Schaum *m*; **2.** schäumen; zu Schaum schlagen
froth·y schäumend; schaumig
frown 1. Stirnrunzeln *n*; *with a frown* stirnrunzelnd; **2.** *v/i* die Stirn runzeln
fro·zen *adj* (eis)kalt; (ein-, zu)gefroren; Gefrier...
fro·zen foods Tiefkühlkost *f*
fru·gal sparsam; bescheiden; einfach
fruit Frucht *f*; Früchte *pl*; Obst *n*
fruit·er·er Obsthändler *m*
fruit·ful fruchtbar
fruit·less unfruchtbar; erfolglos
fruit juice Fruchtsaft *m*
fruit·y fruchtartig; fruchtig (*wine*)
frus·trate vereiteln; frustrieren
frus·tra·tion Vereitelung *f*; Frustration *f*
fry braten; *fried eggs* Spiegeleier *pl*; *fried potatoes* Bratkartoffeln *pl*
fry·ing pan Bratpfanne *f*
fuch·sia BOT Fuchsie *f*
fuck V ficken, vögeln; *fuck off!* verpiss dich!; *get fucked!* der Teufel soll dich holen!
fuck·ing V Scheiß..., verflucht; *fucking hell!* verdammte Scheiße!
fudge GASTR Fondant *m*
fu·el 1. Brennstoff *m*; MOT Treib-, Kraftstoff *m*; **2.** MOT, AVIAT (auf)tanken
fu·el in·jec·tion en·gine MOT Einspritzmotor *m*
fu·gi·tive 1. flüchtig (*a. fig*); **2.** Flüchtling *m*
ful·fil *Br*, **ful·fill** erfüllen; vollziehen
ful·fil·(l)ing befriedigend
ful·fil(l)-ment Erfüllung *f*, Ausführung *f*

full 1. voll; ganz; Voll...; *full of* voll von, voller; *full (up)* (voll) besetzt (*bus etc*); F voll, satt; *house full!* THEA ausverkauft!; *full of o.s.* (ganz) von sich eingenommen; **2.** *adv* völlig, ganz; **3.** *in full* vollständig, ganz; *write out in full* Wort *etc* ausschreiben
full board Vollpension *f*
full dress Gesellschaftskleidung *f*
full-fledged zo flügge; *fig* richtig
full-grown ausgewachsen
full-length in voller Größe; bodenlang; abendfüllend (*film etc*)
full moon Vollmond *m*
full stop LING Punkt *m*
full time SPORT Spielende *n*
full-time ganztägig, Ganztags...
full-time job Ganztagsbeschäftigung *f*
ful·ly voll, völlig, ganz
ful·ly-fledged *Br* → *full-fledged*
ful·ly-'grown *Br* → *full-grown*
fum·ble tasten; fummeln
fume wütend sein
fumes Dämpfe *pl*, Rauch *m*; Abgase *pl*
fum·ing wutschnaubend
fun Scherz *m*, Spaß *m*; *for fun* aus *or* zum Spaß; *make fun of* sich lustig machen über (*acc*), verspotten
func·tion 1. Funktion *f*; Aufgabe *f*; Veranstaltung *f*; **2.** funktionieren
func·tion·a·ry Funktionär *m*
func·tion key EDP Funktionstaste *f*
fund ECON Fonds *m*; Geld(mittel *pl*) *n*
fun·da·men·tal 1. Grund..., grundlegend; **2.** *fundamentals* Grundlage *f*, Grundbegriffe *pl*
fun·da·men·tal·ist Fundamentalist *m*
fu·ne·ral Begräbnis *n*, Beerdigung *f*
funeral march MUS Trauermarsch *m*
funeral o·ration Trauerrede *f*
funeral pro·ces·sion Trauerzug *m*
funeral ser·vice Trauerfeier *f*
fun·fair Rummelplatz *m*
fun·gus BOT Pilz *m*, Schwamm *m*
fu·nic·u·lar *a.* *funicular railway* (Draht)-Seilbahn *f*
funk·y F irre, schräg, schrill
fun·nel Trichter *m*; MAR, RAIL Schornstein *m*
fun·nies F Comics *pl*
fun·ny komisch, lustig, spaßig; sonderbar
fur Pelz *m*, Fell *n*; MED Belag *m*; TECH Kesselstein *m*
fu·ri·ous wütend
furl *Fahne, Segel* aufrollen, einrollen; *Schirm* zusammenrollen
fur·nace TECH Schmelzofen *m*, Hochofen *m*; (Heiz)Kessel *m*
fur·nish einrichten, möblieren; liefern;

versorgen, ausrüsten, ausstatten (*with* mit)

fur·ni·ture Möbel *pl*; *sectional furniture* Anbaumöbel *pl*

furred MED belegt, pelzig

fur·ri·er Kürschner *m*

fur·row 1. Furche *f*; **2.** furchen

fur·ry pelzig; flauschig

fur·ther 1. weiter; **2.** fördern, unterstützen

further ed·u·ca·tion *Br* Fortbildung *f*, Weiterbildung *f*

fur·ther·more *fig* weiter, überdies

fur·ther·most entfernteste(r, -s), äußerste(r, -s)

fur·tive heimlich, verstohlen

fu·ry Wut *f*, Zorn *m*

fuse 1. Zünder *m*; ELECTR Sicherung *f*; Zündschnur *f*; **2.** schmelzen; ELECTR durchbrennen

fuse box ELECTR Sicherungskasten *m*

fu·se·lage (Flugzeug)Rumpf *m*

fu·sion Verschmelzung *f*, Fusion *f*; PHYS *nuclear fusion* Kernfusion *f*

fuss 1. (unnötige) Aufregung; Wirbel *m*, F Theater *n*; **2.** sich (unnötig) aufregen; viel Aufhebens machen (*about* um, von)

fuss·y aufgeregt, hektisch; kleinlich, pedantisch; heikel, wählerisch

fus·ty muffig; *fig* verstaubt

fu·tile nutzlos, zwecklos

fu·ture 1. (zu)künftig; **2.** Zukunft *f*; LING Futur *n*, Zukunft *f*; *in future* in Zukunft, künftig

fuzz feiner Flaum

fuzz·y kraus, wuschelig; unscharf, verschwommen; flaumig, flauschig

G

G, g G, g *n*

gab F Geschwätz *n*; *have the gift of the gab* ein gutes Mundwerk haben

gab·ar·dine Gabardine *m*

gab·ble 1. Geschnatter *n*, Geschwätz *n*; **2.** schnattern, schwatzen

ga·ble ARCH Giebel *m*

gad: F *gad about* (viel) unterwegs sein (in *dat*), sich herumtreiben

gad·fly ZO Bremse *f*

gad·get TECH Apparat *m*, Gerät *n*, Vorrichtung *f*; *often contp* technische Spielerei

gag 1. Knebel *m* (*a. fig*); F Gag *m*; **2.** knebeln; *fig* mundtot machen

gage 1. Eichmaß *n*; TECH Messgerät *n*, Lehre *f*; TECH Stärke *f*, Dicke *f*; RAIL Spur(weite) *f*; **2.** TECH eichen; (ab-, aus)messen

gai·e·ty Fröhlichkeit *f*

gain 1. gewinnen; erreichen, bekommen; zunehmen an (*dat*); vorgehen (um) (*watch*); *gain speed* schneller werden; *gain 5 pounds* 5 Pfund zunehmen; *gain in* zunehmen an (*dat*); **2.** Gewinn *m*; Zunahme *f*; *gain of time* Zeitgewinn *m*

gait Gang *m*, Gangart *f*; Schritt *m*

gai·ter Gamasche *f*

gal F Mädchen *n*

ga·la 1. Festlichkeit *f*; Gala(veranstaltung) *f*; **2.** Gala...

gal·ax·y ASTR Milchstraße *f*, Galaxis *f*

gale Sturm *m*

gall[1] Frechheit *f*

gall[2] **1.** wund geriebene Stelle; **2.** wund reiben *or* scheuern; *fig* (ver)ärgern

gal·lant tapfer; galant, höflich

gal·lan·try Tapferkeit *f*; Galanterie *f*

gall blad·der ANAT Gallenblase *f*

gal·le·ry Galerie *f*; Empore *f*

gal·ley MAR Galeere *f*; Kombüse *f*; *a. galley proof* PRINT Fahne *f*, Fahnenabzug *m*

gal·lon Gallone *f* (*3,79 l*, *Br 4,55 l*)

gal·lop 1. Galopp *m*; **2.** galoppieren (lassen)

gal·lows Galgen *m*

gal·lows hu·mo(u)r Galgenhumor *m*

ga·lore in rauen Mengen

gam·ble 1. (um Geld) spielen; **2.** Glücksspiel *n*

gam·bler (Glücks)Spieler(in)

gam·bol 1. Luftsprung *m*; **2.** (herum-)tanzen, (herum)hüpfen

game (Karten-, Ball- *etc*)Spiel *n*; (einzelnes) Spiel (*a. fig*); HUNT Wild *n*; Wildbret *n*; *pl* Spiele *pl*; PED Sport *m*

game·keep·er Wildhüter *m*

game park, game re·serve Wildpark *m*; Wildreservat *n*

gan·der ZO Gänserich *m*

gang 1. (Arbeiter)Trupp *m*; Gang *f*, Bande *f*; Clique *f*; Horde *f*; **2.** *gang up* sich zusammentun, *contp* sich zusammenrotten

gan·gling schlaksig

gang·ster Gangster *m*

gang war, gang war·fare Bandenkrieg *m*

gang·way Gang *m*; AVIAT, MAR Gangway *f*

gaol, gaol·bird, gaol·er *Br* → **jail** *etc*

gap Lücke *f*; Kluft *f*; Spalte *f*

gape gähnen; klaffen; gaffen

gar·age 1. Garage *f*; (Reparatur)Werkstatt *f* (und Tankstelle *f*); **2.** *Auto* in e-r Garage ab- *or* unterstellen; *Auto* in die Garage fahren

gar·bage Abfall *m*, Müll *m*

garbage bag Müllbeutel *m*

garbage can Abfalleimer *m*, Mülleimer *m*; Abfalltonne *f*, Mülltonne *f*

garbage truck Müllwagen *m*

gar·den Garten *m*

gar·den·er Gärtner(in)

gar·den·ing Gartenarbeit *f*

gar·gle gurgeln

gar·ish grell, auffallend

gar·land Girlande *f*

gar·lic BOT Knoblauch *m*

gar·ment Kleidungsstück *n*; Gewand *n*

gar·nish GASTR garnieren

gar·ret Dachkammer *f*

gar·ri·son MIL Garnison *f*

gar·ter Strumpfband *n*; Sockenhalter *m*; Strumpfhalter *m*, Straps *m*

gas Gas *n*; F Benzin *n*, Sprit *m*

gas·e·ous gasförmig

gash klaffende Wunde

gas·ket TECH Dichtung(sring *m*) *f*

gas me·ter Gasuhr *f*, Gaszähler *m*

gas·o·lene, gas·o·line Benzin *n*

gasolene pump Zapfsäule *f*

gasp 1. keuchen, röcheln; **gasp (for breath)** nach Atem ringen, F nach Luft schnappen; **2.** Keuchen *n*, Röcheln *n*

gas sta·tion Tankstelle *f*

gas stove Gasofen *m*, Gasherd *m*

gas·works TECH Gaswerk *n*

gate Tor *n*; Pforte *f*; Schranke *f*, Sperre *f*; AVIAT Flugsteig *m*

gate·crash F uneingeladen kommen (zu); sich ohne zu bezahlen hineinschmuggeln (in *acc*)

gate·post Tor-, Türpfosten *m*

gate·way Tor(weg *m*) *n*, Einfahrt *f*

gate·way drug Einstiegsdroge *f*

gath·er *v/t* sammeln, *Informationen* einholen, einziehen; *Personen* versammeln; ernten, pflücken; zusammenziehen, kräuseln; *fig* folgern, schließen (*from* aus); **gather speed** schneller werden; *v/i* sich (ver)sammeln; sich (an)sammeln

gath·er·ing Versammlung *f*; Zusammenkunft *f*

gau·dy auffällig, bunt, grell; protzig

gauge *Br* → **gage**

gaunt hager; ausgemergelt

gaunt·let Schutzhandschuh *m*

gauze Gaze *f*; MED Bandage *f*, Binde *f*

gav·el Hammer *m*

gaw·ky linkisch

gay 1. lustig, fröhlich; bunt, (farben-)prächtig; F schwul; **2.** F Schwule *m*

gaze 1. (starrer) Blick; **2.** starren; **gaze at** starren auf (*acc*), anstarren

ga·zette Amtsblatt *n*

ga·zelle ZO Gazelle *f*

gear TECH Getriebe *n*; MOT Gang *m*; *mst in cpds* Vorrichtung *f*, Gerät *n*; F Kleidung *f*, Aufzug *m*; **shift** (*esp Br* **change**) **gear(s)** MOT schalten; **shift** (*esp Br* **change**) **into second gear** MOT in den zweiten Gang schalten

gear·box MOT Getriebe *n*

gear le·ver *Br*, **gear shift, gear stick** *Br* MOT Schalthebel *m*

Gei·ger count·er PHYS Geigerzähler *m*

geld·ing ZO Wallach *m*

gem Edelstein *m*

Gem·i·ni ASTR Zwillinge *pl*; **he (she) is (a) Gemini** er (sie) ist (ein) Zwilling

gen·der LING Genus *n*, Geschlecht *n*

gene BIOL Gen *n*, Erbfaktor *m*

gen·e·ral 1. allgemein; Haupt..., General...; **2.** MIL General *m*; **in general** im Allgemeinen

general de·liv·er·y: (in care of) general delivery postlagernd

general e·lec·tion *Br* POL Parlamentswahlen *pl*

gen·e·ral·ize verallgemeinern

gen·er·al·ly im Allgemeinen, allgemein

gen·er·al prac·ti·tion·er (ABBR **GP**) *appr* Arzt *m or* Ärztin *f* für Allgemeinmedizin

gen·e·rate erzeugen

gen·e·ra·tion Erzeugung *f*; Generation *f*

gen·e·ra·tor ELECTR Generator *m*; MOT Lichtmaschine *f*

gen·e·ros·i·ty Großzügigkeit *f*

gen·e·rous großzügig; reichlich

ge·net·ic genetisch

genetic code BIOL Erbanlage *f*

genetic en·gin·eer·ing Gentechnologie *f*

genetic fin·ger·print genetischer Fingerabdruck

ge·net·ics BIOL Genetik *f*, Vererbungslehre *f*

ge·ni·al freundlich

gen·i·tive *a.* **genitive case** LING Genitiv *m*, zweiter Fall

ge·ni·us Genie *n*

gen·o·cide Völkermord *m*

G

gent F *esp Br* Herr *m*; **gents** *Br* F Herren-
klo *n*
gen·tle sanft, zart, sacht; mild
gen·tle·man Gentleman *m*; Herr *m*
gen·tle·man·ly gentlemanlike, vornehm
gen·tle·ness Sanftheit *f*, Zartheit *f*; Milde *f*
gen·try *Br* niederer Adel; Oberschicht *f*
gen·u·ine echt; aufrichtig
ge·og·ra·phy Geografie *f*
ge·ol·o·gy Geologie *f*
ge·om·e·try Geometrie *f*
germ BIOL, BOT Keim *m*; MED Bazillus *m*,
Bakterie *f*, (Krankheits)Erreger *m*
Ger·man 1. deutsch; **2.** Deutsche *m*, *f*;
LING Deutsch *n*
German shep·herd ZO Deutscher Schäferhund
Ger·man·y Deutschland *n*
ger·mi·nate BIOL, BOT keimen (lassen)
ger·und LING Gerundium *n*
ges·tic·u·late gestikulieren
ges·ture Geste *f*, Gebärde *f*
get *v/t* bekommen, erhalten; sich *et.* verschaffen *or* besorgen; erwerben, sich aneignen; holen; bringen; F erwischen; F
kapieren, verstehen; *j-n* dazu bringen
(**to do** zu tun); *with pp*: lassen; **get one's
hair cut** sich die Haare schneiden lassen;
get going in Gang bringen; **get s.th. by
heart** *et.* auswendig lernen; **get s.th.
ready** *et.* fertig machen; **have got** haben;
have got to müssen; *v/i* kommen, gelangen; *with pp or adj*: werden; **get tired**
müde werden, ermüden; **get going** in
Gang kommen; *fig* in Schwung kommen;
get home nach Hause kommen; **get
ready** sich fertig machen; **get about** herumkommen; sich herumsprechen *or*
verbreiten (*rumor etc*); **get ahead of**
übertreffen (*acc*); **get along** vorwärts-,
vorankommen; auskommen (**with** mit
j-m); zurechtkommen (**with** mit *et.*); **get
at** herankommen an (*acc*); **what is he
getting at?** worauf will er hinaus?; **get
away** loskommen; entkommen; **get
away with** davonkommen mit; **get back**
zurückkommen; *et.* zurückbekommen;
get in hinein-, hereinkommen; einsteigen (in *acc*); **get off** aussteigen (aus); davonkommen (**with** mit); **get on** einsteigen (in *acc*); → **get along**; **get out** herausgehen, hinausgehen; aussteigen (**of**
aus); *et.* herausbekommen; **get over
s.th.** über *et.* hinwegkommen; **get to**
kommen nach; **get together** zusammenkommen; **get up** aufstehen
get·a·way Flucht *f*; **getaway car** Fluchtauto *n*

get·up Aufmachung *f*
gey·ser GEOL Geysir *m*; *Br* TECH Durchlauferhitzer *m*
ghast·ly grässlich; schrecklich; (toten-)
bleich
gher·kin Gewürzgurke *f*
ghet·to Getto *n*
ghost Geist *m*, Gespenst *n*; *fig* Spur *f*
ghost·ly geisterhaft
gi·ant 1. Riese *m*; **2.** riesig
gib·ber·ish Kauderwelsch *n*
gib·bet Galgen *m*
gibe 1. spotten (**at** über *acc*); **2.** höhnische
Bemerkung, Stichelei *f*
gib·lets GASTR Hühner-, Gänseklein *n*
gid·di·ness MED Schwindel(gefühl *n*) *m*
gid·dy schwindelerregend; **I feel giddy**
mir ist schwind(e)lig
gift Geschenk *n*; Talent *n*
gift·ed begabt
gig F MUS Gig *m*, Auftritt *m*, Konzert *n*
gi·gan·tic gigantisch, riesenhaft, riesig,
gewaltig
gig·gle 1. kichern; **2.** Gekicher *n*
gild vergolden
gill ZO Kieme *f*; BOT Lamelle *f*
gim·mick F Trick *m*; Spielerei *f*
gin Gin *m*
gin·ger 1. Ingwer *m*; **2.** rötlich *or* gelblich
braun;
gin·ger·bread Lebkuchen *m*, Pfefferkuchen *m*
gin·ger·ly behutsam, vorsichtig
gip·sy *Br* → **gypsy**
gi·raffe ZO Giraffe *f*
gir·der TECH Tragbalken *m*
gir·dle Hüfthalter *m*, Hüftgürtel *m*
girl Mädchen *n*
girl·friend Freundin *f*
girl guide *Br* Pfadfinderin *f*
girl·hood Mädchenjahre *pl*, Jugend *f*, Ju-
gendzeit *f*
girl·ish mädchenhaft; Mädchen...
girl scout Pfadfinderin *f*
gi·ro *Br* Postgirodienst *m*
gi·ro ac·count *Br* Postgirokonto *n*
gi·ro cheque *Br* Postscheck *m*
girth (Sattel)Gurt *m*; (*a.* Körper)Umfang
m
gist *das* Wesentliche, Kern *m*
give geben; schenken; spenden; *Leben*
hingeben, opfern; *Befehl etc* geben, erteilen; *Hilfe* leisten; *Schutz* bieten;
Grund etc angeben; THEA *etc* geben, aufführen; *Vortrag* halten; *Schmerzen* bereiten, verursachen; *Grüße etc* übermitteln;
give her my love bestelle ihr herzliche
Grüße von mir; **give birth to** zur Welt
bringen; **give s.o. to understand that**

j-m zu verstehen geben, dass; *give way* nachgeben; *Br* MOT die Vorfahrt lassen (*dat*); *give away* hergeben, weggeben, verschenken; *j-n, et.* verraten; *give back* zurückgeben; *give in Gesuch etc* einreichen; *Prüfungsarbeit etc* abgeben; nachgeben; aufgeben; *give off Geruch* verbreiten; ausstoßen; ausströmen, verströmen; *give on(to)* führen auf *or* nach, gehen nach; *give out* aus-, verteilen; *esp Br* bekannt geben; zu Ende gehen (*supplies, strength etc*); F versagen (*engine etc*); *give up* aufgeben; aufhören mit; *j-n* ausliefern; *give o.s. up* sich (freiwillig) stellen (*to the police* der Polizei)

give-and-take beiderseitiges Entgegenkommen, Kompromiss(bereitschaft *f*) *m*

giv·en: *be given to* neigen zu (*dat*)

giv·en name Vorname *m*

gla·cial eisig; Eis...

gla·ci·er Gletscher *m*

glad froh, erfreut; *be glad of* sich freuen über (*acc*)

glad·ly gern(e)

glam·o(u)r Zauber *m*, Glanz *m*

glam·o(u)r·ous bezaubernd, reizvoll

glance 1. (schneller *or* flüchtiger) Blick (*at* auf *acc*); *at a glance* auf e-n Blick; **2.** (schnell *or* flüchtig) blicken (*at* auf *acc*)

gland ANAT Drüse *f*

glare 1. grell scheinen *or* leuchten; wütend starren; *glare at s.o.* j-n wütend anstarren; **2.** greller Schein, grelles Leuchten; wütender Blick

glar·ing *fig* schreiend

glass 1. Glas *n*; (Trink)Glas *n*; Glas(-gefäß) *n*; (Fern-, Opern)Glas *n*; *Br* F Spiegel *m*; *Br* Barometer *n*; (*a pair of*) *glass-es* (e-e) Brille; **2.** gläsern; Glas...; **3.** *glass in, glass up* verglasen

glass case Vitrine *f*; Schaukasten *m*

glass·ful *ein* Glas (voll)

glass·house Gewächs-, Treibhaus *n*

glass·ware Glaswaren *pl*

glass·y gläsern; glasig

glaze 1. *v/t* verglasen; glasieren; *v/i: a. glaze over* glasig werden (*eyes*); **2.** Glasur *f*

gla·zi·er Glaser *m*

gleam 1. schwacher Schein, Schimmer *m*; **2.** leuchten, schimmern

glean *v/t* sammeln; *v/i* Ähren lesen

glee Fröhlichkeit *f*

glee club Gesangverein *m*

glee·ful ausgelassen, fröhlich

glen enges Bergtal *n*

glib gewandt; schlagfertig

glide 1. gleiten; segeln; **2.** Gleiten *n*; AVIAT Gleitflug *m*

glid·er Segelflugzeug *n*

glid·ing Segelfliegen *n*

glim·mer 1. schimmern; **2.** Schimmer *m*

glimpse 1. (nur) flüchtig zu sehen bekommen; **2.** flüchtiger Blick

glint 1. glitzern, glänzen; **2.** Glitzern *n*, Glanz *m*

glis·ten glitzern, glänzen

glit·ter 1. glitzern, funkeln, glänzen; **2.** Glitzern *n*, Funkeln *n*, Glanz *m*

gloat: *gloat over* sich hämisch *or* diebisch freuen über (*acc*)

gloat·ing hämisch, schadenfroh

glo·bal Welt..., global, weltumspannend; umfassend

global warm·ing Erwärmung *f* der Erdatmosphäre

globe (Erd)Kugel *f*; Globus *m*

gloom Düsterkeit *f*; Dunkelheit *f*; düstere *or* gedrückte Stimmung

gloom·y düster; hoffnungslos; niedergeschlagen; trübsinnig, trübselig

glo·ri·fi·ca·tion Verherrlichung *f*

glo·ri·fy verherrlichen

glo·ri·ous ruhmreich, glorreich; herrlich, prächtig

glo·ry Ruhm *m*; Herrlichkeit *f*, Pracht *f*

gloss 1. Glanz *m*; LING Glosse *f*; **2.** *gloss over* beschönigen, vertuschen

glos·sa·ry Glossar *n*

gloss·y glänzend

glove Handschuh *m*

glove com·part·ment MOT Handschuhfach *n*

glow 1. glühen; **2.** Glühen *n*; Glut *f*

glow·er finster blicken

glow-worm ZO Glühwürmchen *n*

glu·cose Traubenzucker *m*

glue 1. Leim *m*; **2.** kleben

glum bedrückt

glut·ton *fig* Vielfraß *m*

glut·ton·ous gefräßig, unersättlich

gnarled knorrig; knotig (*hands etc*)

gnash knirschen (mit)

gnat ZO (Stech)Mücke *f*

gnaw (zer)nagen; (zer)fressen

gnome Gnom *m*; Gartenzwerg *m*

go 1. gehen, fahren, reisen (*to* nach); (fort)gehen; gehen, führen (*to* nach) (*road etc*); sich erstrecken, gehen (*to* bis zu); verkehren, fahren (*bus etc*); TECH gehen, laufen, funktionieren; vergehen (*time*); harmonieren (*with* mit), passen (*with* zu); ausgehen, ablaufen, ausfallen; werden (*go mad; go blind*); *be going to inf* im Begriff sein zu *inf, tun* wollen, *tun* werden (*go shares* teilen; *go swimming* schwimmen gehen; *it is going to rain* es gibt Regen; *I must be going* ich muss ge-

G

hen; *go for a walk* e-n Spaziergang machen, spazieren gehen; *go to bed* ins Bett gehen; *go to school* zur Schule gehen; *go to see* besuchen; *let go* loslassen; *go after* nachlaufen (*dat*); sich bemühen um; *go ahead* vorangehen; vorausgehen, vorausfahren; *go ahead with* beginnen mit; fortfahren mit; *go at* losgehen auf (*acc*); *go away* weggehen; *go between* vermitteln zwischen (*dat*); *go by* vorbeigehen, vorbeifahren; vergehen (*time*); *fig* sich halten an (*acc*), sich richten nach; *go down* untergehen (*sun*); *go for* holen; *go in* hineingehen; *go in for an examination* e-e Prüfung machen; *go off* fortgehen, weggehen; losgehen (*gun etc*); *go on* weitergehen, weiterfahren; *fig* fortfahren (*doing* zu tun); *fig* vor sich gehen, vorgehen; *go out* hinausgehen; ausgehen (*with* mit); ausgehen (*light etc*); *go through* durchgehen, durchnehmen; durchmachen; *go up* steigen; hinaufgehen, -steigen; *go without* sich behelfen ohne, auskommen ohne; 2. F Schwung *m*, Schmiss *m*; *esp Br* F Versuch *m*; *it's my go esp Br* F ich bin dran *or* an der Reihe; *it's a go!* F abgemacht!; *have a go at s.th. Br* F et. probieren; *be all the go Br* F große Mode sein

goad *fig* anstacheln

go-a-head[1]: *get the go-ahead* grünes Licht bekommen; *give s.o. the go-ahead* j-m grünes Licht geben

go-a-head[2] *Br* zielstrebig; unternehmungslustig

goal Ziel *n* (*a. fig*); SPORT Tor *n*; *keep goal* im Tor stehen; *score a goal* ein Tor schießen *or* erzielen; *consolation goal* Ehrentreffer *m*; *own goal* Eigentor *n*, Eigentreffer *m*; *shot at goal* Torschuss *m*

goal·ie F, **goal·keep·er** SPORT Torwart *m*, Torhüter *m*

goal kick *soccer:* Abstoß *m*

goal line SPORT Torlinie *f*

goal·mouth SPORT Torraum *m*

goal·post SPORT Torpfosten *m*

goat ZO Ziege *f*, Geiß *f*

gob·ble schlingen; *mst* **gobble up** verschlingen (*a. fig*)

go-be·tween Vermittler(in), Mittelsmann *m*

gob·lin Kobold *m*

god REL *God* Gott *m*; *fig* Abgott *m*

god·child Patenkind *n*

god·dess Göttin *f*

god·fa·ther Pate *m* (*a. fig*), Taufpate *m*

god·for·sak·en *contp* gottverlassen

god·head Gottheit *f*

god·less gottlos

god·like gottähnlich; göttlich

god·moth·er (Tauf)Patin *f*

god·pa·rent (Tauf)Pate, (Tauf)Patin *f*

god·send Geschenk *n* des Himmels

gog·gle glotzen

gog·gle box *Br* F TV Glotze *f*

gog·gles Schutzbrille *f*

go·ings-on F Treiben *n*, Vorgänge *pl*

gold 1. Gold *n*; 2. golden

gold·en *mst fig* golden, goldgelb

gold·finch ZO Stieglitz *m*

gold·fish ZO Goldfisch *m*

gold·smith Goldschmied *m*

golf 1. Golf(spiel) *n*; 2. Golf spielen

golf club Golfschläger *m*; Golfklub *m*

golf course, **golf links** Golfplatz *m*

gon·do·la Gondel *f*

gone *adj* fort; F futsch; vergangen; tot; F hoffnungslos

good 1. gut; artig; gütig; gründlich; *good at* geschickt *or* gut in (*dat*); *real good* F echt gut; 2. Nutzen *m*, Wert *m*; *das* Gute; *do* (*no*) *good* (nichts) nützen; *for good* für immer; F *what good is ... ?* was nützt ...?

good·by(e) 1. *wish s.o. goodby*, *say goodby to s.o.* j-m Auf Wiedersehen sagen; 2. *int* (auf) Wiedersehen!

Good Fri·day REL Karfreitag *m*

good-hu·mo(u)red gut gelaunt; gutmütig

good·look·ing gut aussehend

good-na·tured gutmütig

good·ness Güte *f*; *thank goodness!* Gott sei Dank!; (*my*) *goodness!*, *goodness gracious!* du meine Güte!, du lieber Himmel!; *for goodness' sake* um Himmels willen!; *goodness knows* weiß der Himmel

goods ECON Waren *pl*, Güter *pl*

good·will gute Absicht, guter Wille; ECON Firmenwert *m*

good·y F Bonbon *m*, *n*

goose ZO Gans *f*

goose·ber·ry BOT Stachelbeere *f*

goose·flesh, **goose pim·ples** *fig* Gänsehaut *f*

go·pher ZO Taschenratte *f*; Ziesel *m*

gore durchbohren, aufspießen

gorge 1. ANAT Kehle *f*, Schlund *m*; GEOGR enge (Fels)Schlucht; 2. verschlingen; schlingen, (sich) vollstopfen

gor·geous prächtig

go·ril·la ZO Gorilla *m*

gor·y F blutrünstig

gosh *int* F Mensch!, Mann!

gos·ling ZO junge Gans

go-slow *Br* ECON Bummelstreik *m*

Gos·pel REL Evangelium *n*

gos·sa·mer Altweibersommer *m*

gos·sip 1. Klatsch *m*, Tratsch *m*; Klatschbase *f*; **2.** klatschen, tratschen

gos·sip·y geschwätzig; voller Klatsch und Tratsch (*letter etc*)

Goth·ic ARCH **1.** gotisch; *Gothic novel* Schauerroman *m*; **2.** Gotik *f*

gourd BOT Kürbis *m*

gout MED Gicht *f*

gov·ern *v/t* regieren; lenken, leiten; *v/i* herrschen

gov·ern·ess Erzieherin *f*

gov·ern·ment Regierung *f*; Staat *m*

gov·er·nor Gouverneur *m*; Direktor *m*, Leiter *m*; F Alte *m*

gown Kleid *n*; Robe *f*, Talar *m*

grab 1. packen, (hastig *or* gierig) ergreifen, fassen; **2.** (hastiger *or* gieriger) Griff; TECH Greifer *m*

grace 1. Anmut *f*, Grazie *f*; Anstand *m*; ECON Frist *f*, Aufschub *m*; Gnade *f*; REL Tischgebet *n*; **2.** zieren, schmücken

grace·ful anmutig

grace·less ungraziös

gra·cious gnädig

gra·da·tion Abstufung *f*

grade 1. Grad *m*, Rang *m*; Stufe *f*; ECON Qualität *f*; RAIL Steigung *f*, Gefälle *n*; PED Klasse *f*; Note *f*, Zensur *f*; **2.** sortieren, einteilen; abstufen

grade cross·ing RAIL schienengleicher Bahnübergang

grade school Grundschule *f*

gra·di·ent *Br* RAIL *etc* Steigung *f*, Gefälle *n*

grad·u·al stufenweise, allmählich

grad·u·al·ly nach und nach; allmählich

grad·u·ate 1. UNIV Hochschulabsolvent(in), Akademiker(in); Graduierte *m*, *f*; PED Schulabgänger(in); **2.** abstufen, staffeln; UNIV graduieren; PED die Abschlussprüfung bestehen

grad·u·a·tion Abstufung *f*, Staffelung *f*; UNIV Graduierung *f*; PED Absolvieren *n* (*from gen*)

graf·fi·ti Graffiti *pl*, Wandschmierereien *pl*

graft 1. MED Transplantat *n*; AGR Pfropfreis *n*; **2.** MED *Gewebe* verpflanzen, transplantieren; AGR pfropfen

grain (Samen-, *esp* Getreide)Korn *n*; Getreide *n*; (*Sand- etc*)Körnchen *n*, (-)Korn *n*; Maserung *f*; *go against the grain for s.o.* *fig* j-m gegen den Strich gehen

gram Gramm *n*

gram·mar Grammatik *f*

gram·mar school Grundschule *f*; *Br appr* (humanistisches) Gymnasium

gram·mat·i·cal grammatisch, Grammatik...

gramme → *gram*

gra·na·ry Kornspeicher *m*

grand 1. *fig* großartig; erhaben; groß; Groß..., Haupt...; **2.** F Riese *m* (*1000 dollars or pounds*)

grand·child Enkel *m*, Enkelin *f*

grand·daugh·ter Enkelin *f*

gran·deur Größe *f*, Erhabenheit *f*; Großartigkeit *f*

grand·fa·ther Großvater *m*

gran·di·ose großartig

grand·moth·er Großmutter *f*

grand·par·ents Großeltern *pl*

grand·son Enkel *m*

grand·stand SPORT Haupttribüne *f*

gran·ny F Oma *f*

grant 1. bewilligen, gewähren; *Erlaubnis etc* geben; *Bitte etc* erfüllen; *et.* zugeben; *take s.th. for granted* et. als selbstverständlich betrachten *or* hinnehmen; **2.** Stipendium *n*; Bewilligung *f*, Unterstützung *f*

gran·u·lat·ed körnig, granuliert; *granulated sugar* Kristallzucker *m*

gran·ule Körnchen *n*

grape BOT Weinbeere *f*, Weintraube *f*

grape·fruit BOT Grapefruit *f*, Pampelmuse *f*

grape·vine BOT Weinstock *m*

graph grafische Darstellung

graph·ic grafisch; anschaulich; *graphic arts* Grafik *f*

graph·ics EDP Grafik *f*

grap·ple: *grapple with* kämpfen mit, *fig a.* sich herumschlagen mit

grasp 1. (er)greifen, packen; *fig* verstehen, begreifen; **2.** Griff *m*; Reichweite *f* (*a. fig*); *fig* Verständnis *n*

grass Gras *n*; Rasen *m*; Weide(land) *n*) *f*; *sl.* Grass *n* (*marijuana*)

grass·hop·per ZO Heuschrecke *f*

grass roots POL Basis *f*

grass wid·ow Strohwitwe *f*

grass wid·ow·er Strohwitwer *m*

gras·sy grasbedeckt, Gras...

grate 1. (Kamin)Gitter *n*; (Feuer)Rost *m*; **2.** reiben, raspeln; knirschen (mit); *grate on s.o.'s nerves* an j-s Nerven zerren

grate·ful dankbar

grat·er Reibe *f*

grat·i·fi·ca·tion Befriedigung *f*; Freude *f*

grat·i·fy erfreuen; befriedigen

grat·ing¹ kratzend, knirschend, quietschend; schrill; unangenehm

grat·ing² Gitter(werk) *n*

grat·i·tude Dankbarkeit *f*

gra·tu·i·tous unentgeltlich; freiwillig

gra·tu·i·ty Abfindung *f*; Gratifikation *f*;

Trinkgeld *n*

grave[1] ernst; (ge)wichtig; gemessen

grave[2] Grab *n*

grave·dig·ger Totengräber *m*

grav·el 1. Kies *m*; **2.** mit Kies bestreuen

grave·stone Grabstein *m*

grave·yard Friedhof *m*

grav·i·ta·tion PHYS Gravitation *f*, Schwerkraft *f*

grav·i·ty PHYS Schwerkraft *f*; Ernst *m*

gra·vy Bratensaft *m*; Bratensoße *f*

gray 1. grau; **2.** Grau *n*; **3.** grau machen *or* werden

gray·hound ZO Windhund *m*

graze[1] *Vieh* weiden (lassen); (ab)weiden; (ab)grasen

graze[2] **1.** streifen; schrammen; *Haut* (ab-, auf)schürfen, (auf)schrammen; **2.** Abschürfung *f*, Schramme *f*; Streifschuss *m*

grease 1. Fett *n*; TECH Schmierfett *n*, Schmiere *f*; **2.** (ein)fetten; TECH schmieren

greas·y fett(ig), ölig; speckig; schmierig

great groß; Ur(groß)…; F großartig, super

Great Brit·ain Großbritannien *n*

great-grand·child Urenkel(in)

great-grand·par·ents Urgroßeltern *pl*

great·ly sehr

great·ness Größe *f*

Greece Griechenland *n*

greed Gier *f*

greed·y gierig (**for** auf *acc*, nach); habgierig; gefräßig

Greek 1. griechisch; **2.** Grieche *m*, Griechin *f*; LING Griechisch *n*

green 1. grün; *fig* grün, unerfahren; **2.** Grün *n*; Grünfläche *f*, Rasen *m*; *pl* grünes Gemüse, Blattgemüse *n*

green·back F Dollar *m*

green belt Grüngürtel *m*

green card Arbeitserlaubnis *f*

green·gro·cer *esp Br* Obst- und Gemüsehändler(in)

green·horn F Greenhorn *n*, Grünschnabel *m*

green·house Gewächs-, Treibhaus *n*

greenhouse ef·fect Treibhauseffekt *m*

green·ish grünlich

greet grüßen

greet·ing Begrüßung *f*, Gruß *m*; *pl* Grüße *pl*

gre·nade MIL Granate *f*

grey *Br* → **gray**

grid Gitter *n*; ELECTR *etc* Versorgungsnetz *n*; Gitter(netz) *n* (*map etc*)

grid·i·ron Bratrost *m*

grief Kummer *m*

griev·ance (Grund *m* zur) Beschwerde *f*; Missstand *m*

grieve *v/t* betrüben, bekümmern; *v/i* bekümmert sein; **grieve for** trauern um

griev·ous schwer, schlimm

grill 1. grillen; **2.** Grill *m*; Bratrost *m*; GASTR *das* Gegrillte *n*

grim grimmig; schrecklich; erbittert; F schlimm

gri·mace 1. Fratze *f*, Grimasse *f*; **2.** Grimassen schneiden

grime Schmutz *m*; Ruß *m*

grim·y schmutzig; rußig

grin 1. Grinsen *n*; **2.** grinsen

grind 1. *v/t* (zer)mahlen, zerreiben, zerkleinern; *Messer etc* schleifen; *Fleisch* durchdrehen; **grind one's teeth** mit den Zähnen knirschen; *v/i* F schuften, pauken, büffeln; **2.** Schinderei *f*, F Schufterei *f*; **the daily grind** das tägliche Einerlei

grind·er (Messer- *etc*)Schleifer *m*; TECH Schleifmaschine *f*; TECH Mühle *f*

grind·stone Schleifstein *m*

grip 1. packen (*a. fig*); **2.** Griff *m*; *fig* Gewalt *f*, Herrschaft *f*; Reisetasche *f*

grip·ping spannend

gris·ly grässlich, schrecklich

gris·tle GASTR Knorpel *m*

grit 1. Kies *m*, (grober) Sand; *fig* Mut *m*; **2.** streuen; **grit one's teeth** die Zähne zusammenbeißen

griz·zly (bear) ZO Grislibär *m*, Graubär *m*

groan 1. stöhnen, ächzen; **2.** Stöhnen *n*, Ächzen *n*

gro·cer Lebensmittelhändler *m*

gro·cer·ies Lebensmittel *pl*

gro·cer·y Lebensmittelgeschäft *n*

grog·gy F groggy, schwach *or* wackelig (auf den Beinen)

groin ANAT Leiste *f*, Leistengegend *f*

groom 1. Pferdepfleger *m*, Stallbursche *m*; Bräutigam *m*; **2.** *Pferde* versorgen, striegeln; pflegen

groove Rinne *f*, Furche *f*; Rille *f*, Nut *f*

grope tasten; F *Mädchen* befummeln

gross 1. dick, feist; grob, derb; ECON Brutto…; **2.** Gros *n*

gro·tesque grotesk

ground[1] gemahlen (*coffee etc*); **ground meat** Hackfleisch *n*

ground[2] **1.** (Erd)Boden *m*, Erde *f*; Boden *m*, Gebiet *n*; SPORT (*Spiel*)Platz *m*; ELECTR Erdung *f*; (Boden)Satz *m*; *fig* Beweggrund *m*; *pl* Grundstück *n*, Park *m*, Gartenanlage *f*; **on the ground(s) of** aufgrund (*gen*); **hold** *or* **stand one's ground** sich behaupten; **2.** MAR auflaufen; ELECTR erden; *fig* gründen, stützen

ground crew AVIAT Bodenpersonal *n*

ground floor *esp Br* Erdgeschoss *n*

ground forc·es MIL Bodentruppen *pl*, Landstreitkräfte *pl*

ground·hog ZO Amer. Waldmurmeltier *n*

ground·ing ELECTR Erdung *f*; Grundlagen *pl*, Grundkenntnisse *pl*

ground·keep·er SPORT Platzwart *m*

ground·less grundlos

ground·nut *Br* BOT Erdnuss *f*

grounds·man *Br* SPORT Platzwart *m*

ground staff *Br* AVIAT Bodenpersonal *n*

ground sta·tion Bodenstation *f*

ground·work *fig* Grundlage *f*, Fundament *n*

group 1. Gruppe *f*; **2.** (sich) gruppieren

group·ie F Groupie *n*

group·ing Gruppierung *f*

grove Wäldchen *n*, Gehölz *n*

grov·el (am Boden) kriechen

grow *v/i* wachsen; (allmählich) werden; **grow up** aufwachsen, heranwachsen; *v/t* BOT anpflanzen, anbauen, züchten; **grow a beard** sich e-n Bart wachsen lassen

grow·er Züchter *m*, Erzeuger *m*

growl knurren, brummen

grown-up 1. erwachsen; **2.** Erwachsene *m*, *f*

growth Wachsen *n*, Wachstum *n*; Wuchs *m*, Größe *f*; *fig* Zunahme *f*, Anwachsen *n*; MED Gewächs *n*, Wucherung *f*

grub 1. ZO Larve *f*, Made *f*; F Futter *n*; **2.** graben

grub·by schmudd(e)lig

grudge 1. missgönnen (*s.o. s.th.* j-m et.); **2.** Groll *m*

grudg·ing·ly widerwillig

gru·el Haferschleim *m*

gruff grob, schroff, barsch, unwirsch

grum·ble murren, F meckern (**über** *acc* about, at); **grumble at** schimpfen über (*acc*)

grump·y F schlecht gelaunt, mürrisch, missmutig, verdrießlich, verdrossen

grun·gy F schmudd(e)lig-schlampig; MUS schlecht und laut

grunt 1. grunzen; brummen; stöhnen; **2.** Grunzen *n*; Stöhnen *n*

guar·an·tee 1. Garantie *f*; Kaution *f*, Sicherheit *f*; **2.** (sich ver)bürgen für; garantieren

guar·an·tor JUR Bürge *m*, Bürgin *f*

guar·an·ty JUR Garantie *f*; Sicherheit *f*

guard 1. Wache *f*, (Wacht)Posten *m*, Wächter *m*; Wärter *m*, Aufseher *m*; Wache *f*, Bewachung *f*; *Br* Zugbegleiter *m*; Schutz(vorrichtung *f*) *m*; Garde *f*; **be on guard** Wache stehen; **be on (off) one's guard** (nicht) auf der Hut sein; **2.** *v/t* bewachen, (be)schützen (**from** vor *dat*); *v/i*

sich hüten *or* in Acht nehmen *or* schützen (**against** vor *dat*)

guard·ed vorsichtig, zurückhaltend

guard·i·an 1. JUR Vormund *m*; **2.** Schutz...

guard·i·an·ship JUR Vormundschaft *f*

gue(r)·ril·la MIL Guerilla *m*

gue(r)·ril·la war·fare Guerillakrieg *m*

guess 1. (er)raten; vermuten; schätzen; glauben, meinen; **2.** Vermutung *f*

guess·work (reine) Vermutung(en *pl*)

guest Gast *m*

guest·house (Hotel)Pension *f*, Fremdenheim *n*

guest·room Gäste-, Fremdenzimmer *n*

guf·faw 1. schallendes Gelächter; **2.** schallend lachen

guid·ance Führung *f*; (An)Leitung *f*

guide 1. (Reise-, Fremden)Führer(in); (Reise- *etc*)Führer *m* (*book*); Handbuch (**to** *gen*); **a guide to London** ein London-Führer; **2.** leiten; führen; lenken

guide·book (Reise- *etc*)Führer *m*

guid·ed tour Führung *f*

guide·lines Richtlinien *pl* (**on** *gen*)

guild HIST Gilde *f*, Zunft *f*

guile·less arglos

guilt Schuld *f*

guilt·less schuldlos, unschuldig (**of** an *dat*)

guilt·y schuldig (**of** *gen*); schuldbewusst

guin·ea pig ZO Meerschweinchen *n*; *fig* Versuchsperson *f*, F Versuchskaninchen *n*

guise *fig* Gestalt *f*, Maske *f*

gui·tar MUS Gitarre *f*

gulch GEOGR tiefe Schlucht, Klamm *f*

gulf GEOGR Golf *m*; *fig* Kluft *f*

gull ZO Möwe *f*

gul·let ANAT Speiseröhre *f*; Gurgel *f*, Kehle *f*

gulp 1. (großer) Schluck; **2.** *often* **gulp down** *Getränk* hinunterstürzen, *Speise* hinunterschlingen

gum[1] ANAT *mst pl* Zahnfleisch *n*

gum[2] **1.** Gummi *m*, *n*; Klebstoff *m*; Kaugummi *m*; (Frucht)Gummi *m*; **2.** kleben

gump·tion F Grips *m*; Schneid *m*

gun 1. Gewehr *n*; Pistole *f*, Revolver *m*; Geschütz *n*, Kanone *f*; **2. gun down** niederschießen

gun·fight Feuergefecht *n*, Schießerei *f*

gun·fire Schüsse *pl*; MIL Geschützfeuer *n*

gun li·cence *Br*, **gun li·cense** Waffenschein *m*

gun·man Bewaffnete *m*

gun·point: **at gunpoint** mit vorgehaltener Waffe, mit Waffengewalt

gun·pow·der Schießpulver *n*

gun·run·ner Waffenschmuggler *m*

gun·run·ning Waffenschmuggel *m*

G

gun·shot Schuss *m*; *within* (*out of*) *gun-shot* in (außer) Schussweite
gur·gle 1. gurgeln, gluckern, glucksen; **2.** Gurgeln *n*, Gluckern *n*, Glucksen *n*
gush 1. strömen, schießen (*from* aus); **2.** Schwall *m*, Strom *m* (*a. fig*)
gust Windstoß *m*, Bö *f*
gust F Eingeweide *pl*; Schneid *m*, Mumm *m*
gut·ter Gosse *f* (*a. fig*), Rinnstein *m*; Dachrinne *f*
guy F Kerl *m*, Typ *m*
guz·zle F saufen; fressen
gym F Fitnesscenter *n*; → *gymnasium*; →

gymnastics
gym·na·si·um Turn-, Sporthalle *f*
gym·nast Turner(in)
gym·nas·tics Turnen *n*, Gymnastik *f*
gym shirt Turnhemd *n*
gym shorts Turnhose *f*
gy·n(a)e·col·o·gist Gynäkologe *m*, Gynäkologin *f*, Frauenarzt *m*, -ärztin *f*
gy·n(a)e·col·o·gy Gynäkologie *f*, Frauenheilkunde *f*
gyp·sy Zigeuner *m*, Zigeunerin *f*
gy·rate kreisen, sich (im Kreis) drehen, (herum)wirbeln

H

H, h H, h *n*
hab·it (An)Gewohnheit *f*; *esp* (Ordens-)Tracht *f*; *get into* (*out of*) *the habit of smoking* sich das Rauchen angewöhnen (abgewöhnen)
ha·bit·u·al gewohnheitsmäßig, Gewohnheits...
hack¹ hacken
hack² *contp* Schreiberling *m*
hack³ *contp* Klepper *m*
hack·er EDP Hacker *m*
hack·neyed abgedroschen
had·dock zo Schellfisch *m*
h(a)e·mor·rhage MED Blutung *f*
hag hässliches altes Weib, Hexe *f*
hag·gard abgespannt; verhärmt, abgehärmt; hager
hag·gle feilschen, handeln
hail 1. Hagel *m*; **2.** hageln
hail·stone Hagelkorn *n*
hail·storm Hagelschauer *m*
hair *einzelnes* Haar; *coll* Haar *n*, Haare *pl*; *let one's hair down* F aus sich herausgehen; *without turning a hair* ohne mit der Wimper zu zucken
hair·breadth → *hair's breadth*
hair·brush Haarbürste *f*
hair·cut Haarschnitt *m*
hair·do F Frisur *f*
hair·dress·er Friseur(in)
hair·dri·er, hair·dry·er Trockenhaube *f*; Haartrockner *m*, Föhn *m*
hair·grip *Br* Haarklammer *f*, Haarklemme *f*
hair·less ohne Haare, kahl

hair·pin Haarnadel *f*
hairpin bend MOT Haarnadelkurve *f*
hair·rais·ing haarsträubend
hair's breadth: *by a hair's breadth* um Haaresbreite
hair slide *Br* Haarspange *f*
hair·split·ting Haarspalterei *f*
hair·spray Haarspray *m, n*
hair·style Frisur *f*
hair styl·ist Hair-Stylist *m*, Damenfriseur *m*
hair·y behaart, haarig
half 1. Hälfte *f*; *go halves* halbe-halbe machen, teilen; **2.** halb; *half an hour* e-e halbe Stunde; *half a pound* ein halbes Pfund; *half past ten* halb elf (Uhr); *half way up* auf halber Höhe
half-breed Halbblut *n*
half-broth·er Halbbruder *m*
half-caste *esp contp* Mischling *m*
half-heart·ed halbherzig
half time SPORT Halbzeit *f*
half time score SPORT Halbzeitstand *m*
half·way halb; auf halbem Weg, in der Mitte
halfway line *soccer*: Mittellinie *f*
half-wit·ted schwachsinnig
hal·i·but zo Heilbutt *m*
hall Halle *f*, Saal *m*; Flur *m*, Diele *f*; *esp Br* Herrenhaus *n*; *Br* UNIV Speisesaal *m*; *Br* *hall of residence* Studentenheim *n*
hall·mark *fig* Kennzeichen *n*
Hal·low·e'en Abend *m* vor Allerheiligen
hal·lu·ci·na·tion Halluzination *f*
hall·way Halle *f*, Diele *f*; Korridor *m*

ha·lo ASTR Hof *m*; Heiligenschein *m*

halt 1. Halt *m*; **2.** (an)halten

hal·ter Halfter *m*, *n*

halt·ing zögernd, stockend

halve halbieren

ham Schinken *m*; *ham and eggs* Schinken mit (Spiegel)Ei

ham·burg·er GASTR Hamburger *m*; Rinderhack *n*

ham·let Weiler *m*

ham·mer 1. Hammer *m*; **2.** hämmern

ham·mock Hängematte *f*

ham·per¹ (Deckel)Korb *m*; Präsentkorb *m*; Wäschekorb *m*

ham·per² (be)hindern

ham·ster ZO Hamster *m*

hand 1. Hand *f* (*a. fig*); Handschrift *f*; (Uhr)Zeiger *m*; *often in cpds* Arbeiter *m*; Fachmann *m*; *card game*: Blatt *n*, Karten *pl*; *hand in glove* ein Herz und eine Seele; *change hands* den Besitzer wechseln; *give or lend a hand* mit zugreifen, *j-m* helfen (*with* by); *shake hands with j-m* die Hand schütteln *or* geben; *at hand* in Reichweite; nahe; bei der *or* zur Hand; *at first hand* aus erster Hand; *by hand* mit der Hand; *on the one hand* einerseits; *on the other hand* andererseits; *on the right hand* rechts; *hands off!* Hände weg!; *hands up!* Hände hoch!; **2.** aushändigen, (über)geben, (über)reichen; *hand around* herumreichen; *hand down* weitergeben, überliefern; *hand in Prüfungsarbeit etc* abgeben; *Bericht, Gesuch etc* einreichen; *hand on* weiterreichen, weitergeben; überliefern; *hand out* austeilen, verteilen; *hand over* übergeben, aushändigen (*to dat*); *hand up* hinauf-, heraufreichen

hand·bag Handtasche *f*

hand bag·gage Handgepäck *n*

hand·ball SPORT Handball *m*; *soccer*: Handspiel *n*

hand·book Handbuch *n*

hand·bill Handzettel *m*, Flugblatt *n*

hand·brake TECH Handbremse *f*

hand·cart Handwagen *m*

hand·cuffs Handschellen *pl*

hand·ful Handvoll *f*; F Plage *f*

hand gre·nade MIL Handgranate *f*

hand·i·cap 1. Handikap *n*, MED *a.* Behinderung *f*, SPORT *a.* Vorgabe *f*; → *mental handicap, physical handicap*; **2.** behindern, benachteiligen

hand·i·capped 1. gehandikapt, behindert, benachteiligt; → *mental, physical*; **2.** *the handicapped* MED die Behinderten *pl*

hand·ker·chief Taschentuch *n*

han·dle 1. Griff *m*; Stiel *m*; Henkel *m*; Klinke *f*; *fly off the handle* F wütend werden; **2.** anfassen, berühren; hantieren *or* umgehen mit; behandeln

han·dle·bar(s) Lenkstange *f*

hand lug·gage Handgepäck *n*

hand·made handgearbeitet

hand·out Almosen *n*; Handzettel *m*; Hand-out *n*, Informationsmaterial *n*

hand·rail Geländer *n*

hand·shake Händedruck *m*

hand·some gut aussehend; *fig* ansehnlich, beträchtlich (*sum etc*)

hands-on praktisch

hand·spring Handstandüberschlag *m*

hand·stand Handstand *m*

hand·writ·ing Handschrift *f*

hand·writ·ten handgeschrieben

hand·y zur Hand; geschickt; handlich, praktisch; nützlich; *come in handy* sich als nützlich erweisen; (sehr) gelegen kommen

hand·y·man Handwerker *m*; *be a handyman a.* handwerklich geschickt sein

hang (auf-, be-, ein)hängen; *Tapete* ankleben; *j-n* (auf)hängen; *hang o.s.* sich erhängen; *hang about, hang around* herumlungern; *hang on* sich klammern (*to* an *acc*) (*a. fig*), festhalten (*to acc*); TEL am Apparat bleiben; *hang up* TEL einhängen, auflegen; *she hung up on me* sie legte einfach auf

han·gar Hangar *m*, Flugzeughalle *f*

hang·er Kleiderbügel *m*

hang glid·er SPORT (Flug)Drachen *m*; Drachenflieger(in)

hang glid·ing SPORT Drachenfliegen *n*

hang·ing 1. Hänge...; **2.** (Er)Hängen *n*

hang·ings Tapete *f*, Wandbehang *m*, Vorhang *m*

hang·man Henker *m*

hang·nail MED Niednagel *m*

hang·o·ver Katzenjammer *m*, Kater *m*

han·ker F sich sehnen (*after, for* nach)

han·kie, han·ky F Taschentuch *n*

hap·haz·ard willkürlich, planlos, wahllos

hap·pen (zufällig) geschehen; sich ereignen, passieren, vorkommen

hap·pen·ing Ereignis *n*, Vorkommnis *n*; Happening *n*

hap·pi·ly glücklich(erweise)

hap·pi·ness Glück *n*

hap·py glücklich; erfreut

hap·py-go-luck·y unbekümmert, sorglos

ha·rangue 1. (Straf)Predigt *f*; **2.** *v/t j-m* e-e Strafpredigt halten

har·ass ständig belästigen; schikanieren; aufreiben, zermürben

H

har·ass·ment ständige Belästigung; Schikane(n *pl*) *f*; → **sexual harassment**

har·bo(u)r 1. Hafen *m*; Zufluchtsort *m*; **2.** *j-m* Zuflucht *or* Unterschlupf gewähren; *Groll etc* hegen

hard hart (*a. fig*); fest; schwer, schwierig; heftig, stark; streng (*a. winter*); *fig* nüchtern (*facts etc*); **give s.o. a hard time** j-m das Leben schwer machen; **hard of hearing** schwerhörig; **be hard on s.th.** et. strapazieren; **hard up** F in (Geld)Schwierigkeiten, knapp bei Kasse; F **the hard stuff** die harten Sachen (*alcohol, drugs*)

hard·back gebundene Ausgabe

hard-boiled GASTR hart (gekocht); F *fig* hart, unsentimental, nüchtern

hard cash Bargeld *n*; klingende Münze

hard core harter Kern

hard-core zum harten Kern gehörend; hart

hard court *tennis*: Hartplatz *m*

hard·cov·er 1. gebunden; **2.** Hard Cover *n*, gebundene Ausgabe

hard cur·ren·cy ECON harte Währung

hard disk EDP Festplatte *f*

hard·en härten; hart machen *or* werden; (sich) abhärten

hard hat Schutzhelm *m*

hard-head·ed nüchtern, praktisch; starrköpfig, dickköpfig

hard-heart·ed hartherzig

hard la·bo(u)r JUR Zwangsarbeit *f*

hard line *esp* POL harter Kurs

hard-line *esp* POL hart, kompromisslos

hard·ly kaum

hard·ness Härte *f*; Schwierigkeit *f*

hard·ship Not *f*; Härte *f*; Strapaze *f*

hard shoul·der *Br* MOT Standspur *f*

hard·top MOT Hardtop *n, m*

hard·ware Eisenwaren *pl*; Haushaltswaren *pl*; EDP Hardware *f*

hard·wear·ing strapazierfähig

har·dy zäh, robust, abgehärtet; BOT winterhart, winterfest

hare ZO Hase *m*

hare·bell BOT Glockenblume *f*

hare·brained verrückt

hare·lip MED Hasenscharte *f*

harm 1. Schaden *m*; **2.** verletzen; schaden (*dat*)

harm·ful schädlich

harm·less harmlos

har·mo·ni·ous harmonisch

har·mo·nize harmonieren; in Einklang sein *or* bringen

har·mo·ny Harmonie *f*

har·ness 1. (*Pferde- etc*)Geschirr *n*; **die in harness** *fig* in den Sielen sterben; **2.** anschirren; anspannen (**to** an *acc*)

harp 1. MUS Harfe *f*; **2.** MUS Harfe spielen; F **harp on** (**about**) herumreiten auf (*dat*)

har·poon 1. Harpune *f*; **2.** harpunieren

har·row AGR **1.** Egge *f*; **2.** eggen

har·row·ing quälend, qualvoll, erschütternd

harsh rau; grell; streng; schroff, barsch

hart ZO Hirsch *m*

har·vest 1. Ernte(zeit) *f*; (Ernte)Ertrag *m*; **2.** ernten

har·vest·er MOT Mähdrescher *m*

hash¹ GASTR Haschee *n*; F **make a hash of s.th.** et. verpfuschen

hash² F Hasch *n*

hash browns GASTR Brat-, Röstkartoffeln *pl*

hash·ish Haschisch *n*

hasp TECH Haspe *f*

haste Eile *f*, Hast *f*

has·ten *j-n* antreiben; (sich be)eilen; et. beschleunigen

hast·y eilig, hastig, überstürzt; voreilig

hat Hut *m*

hatch¹: *a.* **hatch out** ZO ausbrüten; ausschlüpfen

hatch² Durchreiche *f*; AVIAT, MAR Luke *f*

hatch·back MOT (Wagen *m* mit) Hecktür *f*

hatch·et Beil *n*; **bury the hatchet** das Kriegsbeil begraben

hate 1. Hass *m*; **2.** hassen

hate·ful verhasst; abscheulich

ha·tred Hass *m*

haugh·ty hochmütig, überheblich

haul 1. ziehen, zerren; schleppen; befördern, transportieren; **2.** Ziehen *n*; Fischzug *m*, *fig* F *a.* Fang *m*; Beförderung *f*, Transport *m*; Transportweg *m*

haul·age Beförderung *f*, Transport *m*

haul·er, *Br* **haul·i·er** Transportunternehmer *m*

haunch ANAT Hüfte *f*, Hüftpartie *f*, Hinterbacke *f*; GASTR Keule *f*

haunt 1. spuken in (*dat*); häufig besuchen; *fig* verfolgen, quälen; **2.** häufig besuchter Ort; Schlupfwinkel *m*

haunt·ing quälend; unvergesslich, eindringlich

have *v/t* haben; erhalten, bekommen; essen, trinken; **have breakfast** frühstücken; **have a cup of tea** e-n Tee trinken; *with inf*: müssen (**I have to go now** ich muss jetzt gehen); *with object and pp*: lassen (**I had my hair cut** ich ließ mir die Haare schneiden); **have back** zurückbekommen; **have on** *Kleidungsstück* anhaben, *Hut* aufhaben; *v/aux* haben; *v/i* often sein; **I have come** ich bin gekommen

ha·ven Hafen *m* (*mst fig*)

hav·oc Verwüstung *f*, Zerstörung *f*; **play**

483

heart attack

havoc with verwüsten, zerstören; *fig* verheerend wirken auf (*acc*)

hawk[1] zo Habicht *m*, Falke *m*

hawk[2] hausieren mit; auf der Straße verkaufen

hawk·er Hausierer(in); Straßenhändler(in); Drücker(in)

haw·thorn BOT Weißdorn *m*

hay Heu *n*

hay fe·ver MED Heuschnupfen *m*

hay·loft Heuboden *m*

hay·stack Heuhaufen *m*

haz·ard Gefahr *f*, Risiko *n*

haz·ard·ous gewagt, gefährlich, riskant

hazardous waste Sonder-, Giftmüll *m*

haze Dunst(schleier) *m*

ha·zel 1. BOT Hasel(nuss)strauch *m*; **2.** (hasel)nussbraun

ha·zel·nut BOT Haselnuss *f*

haz·y dunstig, diesig; *fig* unklar, verschwommen

H-bomb H-Bombe *f*, Wasserstoffbombe *f*

he 1. er; **2.** Er *m*; zo Männchen *n*; **he-goat** Ziegenbock *m*

head 1. Kopf *m*; (Ober)Haupt *n*; Chef *m*; (An)Führer(in), Leiter(in); Spitze *f*; Kopf(ende *n*) *m*; Kopf *m* (*of a page, nail etc*); Vorderseite *f*; Überschrift *f*; **20 dollars a head** or **per head** zwanzig Dollar pro Kopf *or* Person; **40 head** (**of cattle**) 40 Stück (Vieh); **heads or tails?** Kopf oder Zahl?; **at the head of** an der Spitze (*gen*); **head over heels** kopfüber; bis über beide Ohren (*verliebt sein*); **bury one's head in the sand** den Kopf in den Sand stecken; **get it into one's head that ...** es sich in den Kopf setzen, dass; **lose one's head** den Kopf *or* die Nerven verlieren; **2.** Ober..., Haupt..., Chef..., oberste(r, -s), erste(r, -s); **3.** *v/t* anführen, an der Spitze stehen von (*or gen*); voran-, vorausgehen (*dat*); (an)führen, leiten; *soccer*: köpfen; *v/i* (**for**) gehen, fahren (nach); lossteuern, losgehen (auf *acc*); MAR Kurs halten (auf *acc*)

head·ache Kopfweh *n*

head·band Stirnband *n*

head·dress Kopfschmuck *m*

head·er Kopfsprung *m*; *soccer*: Kopfball *m*

head·first kopfüber, mit dem Kopf voran; *fig* ungestüm, stürmisch

head·gear Kopfbedeckung *f*

head·ing Überschrift *f*, Titel(zeile *f*) *m*

head·land Landspitze *f*, Landzunge *f*

head·light MOT Scheinwerfer *m*

head·line Schlagzeile *f*; **news headlines** *radio*, TV das Wichtigste in Schlagzeilen

head·long kopfüber; *fig* ungestüm

head·mas·ter *Br* PED Direktor *m*, Rektor *m*

head·mis·tress *Br* PED Direktorin *f*, Rektorin *f*

head-on frontal, Frontal...; **head-on collision** MOT Frontalzusammenstoß *m*

head·phones Kopfhörer *pl*

head·quar·ters (ABBR **HQ**) MIL Hauptquartier *n*; Zentrale *f*

head·rest MOT Kopfstütze *f*

head·set Kopfhörer *pl*

head start SPORT Vorgabe *f*, Vorsprung *m* (*a. fig*)

head·strong halsstarrig

head teach·er → **headmaster**, **headmistress**, **principal**

head·wa·ters GEOGR Quellgebiet *n*

head·way Fortschritt(e *pl*) *m*; **make headway** (gut) vorankommen

head·word Stichwort *n*

head·y zu Kopfe steigend, berauschend

heal heilen; **heal over**, **heal up** (zu)heilen

heal·ing Heilung *f*; **healing power** Heilkraft *f*

health Gesundheit *f*

health cer·tif·i·cate Gesundheitszeugnis *n*

health club Fitnessklub *m*, Fitnesscenter *n*

health food Reform-, Biokost *f*

health food shop *Br*, **health food store** Reformhaus *n*, Bioladen *m*

health·ful gesund; heilsam

health in·su·rance Krankenversicherung *f*

health re·sort Kurort *m*

health service Gesundheitsdienst *m*

health·y gesund

heap 1. Haufe(n) *m*; **2.** *a.* **heap up** aufhäufen, *fig a.* anhäufen

hear hören; anhören, *j-m* zuhören; *Zeugen* vernehmen; *Lektion* abhören

hear·er (Zu)Hörer(in)

hear·ing Gehör *n*; Hören *n*; JUR Verhandlung *f*; JUR Vernehmung *f*; *esp* POL Hearing *n*, Anhörung *f*; **within** (**out of**) **hearing** in (außer) Hörweite

hear·ing aid Hörgerät *n*

hear·say Gerede *n*; **by hearsay** vom Hörensagen *n*

hearse Leichenwagen *m*

heart ANAT Herz *n* (*a. fig*); Kern *m*; *card games*: Herz(karte *f*) *n*, *pl* Herz *n*; **lose heart** den Mut verlieren; **take heart** sich ein Herz fassen; **take s.th. to heart** sich et. zu Herzen nehmen; **with a heavy heart** schweren Herzens

heart·ache Kummer *m*

heart at·tack MED Herzanfall *m*; Herzinfarkt *m*

heart·beat Herzschlag *m*

heart·break Leid *n*, großer Kummer

heart·break·ing herzzerreißend

heart·brok·en gebrochen, verzweifelt

heart·burn MED Sodbrennen *n*

heart·en ermutigen

heart fail·ure MED Herzversagen *n*

heart·felt innig, tief empfunden

hearth Kamin *m*

heart·less herzlos

heart·rend·ing herzzerreißend

heart trans·plant MED Herzverpflanzung *f*, Herztransplantation *f*

heart·y herzlich; gesund; herzhaft

heat 1. Hitze *f*; PHYS Wärme *f*; Eifer *m*; ZO Läufigkeit *f*; SPORT (Einzel)Lauf *m*; **preliminary heat** Vorlauf *m*; **2.** *v/t* heizen; *a.* **heat up** erhitzen, aufwärmen; *v/i* sich erhitzen (*a. fig*)

heat·ed geheizt; heizbar; erhitzt, *fig a.* erregt

heat·er Heizgerät *n*, Heizkörper *m*

heath Heide *f*, Heideland *n*

hea·then REL **1.** Heide *m*, Heidin *f*; **2.** heidnisch

heath·er BOT Heidekraut *n*; Erika *f*

heat·ing 1. Heizung *f*; **2.** Heiz...

heat·proof hitzebeständig

heat shield Hitzeschild *m*

heat·stroke MED Hitzschlag *m*

heat wave Hitzewelle *f*

heave *v/t* (hoch)stemmen, (hoch)hieven; *Anker* lichten; *Seufzer* ausstoßen; *v/i* sich heben und senken, wogen

heav·en Himmel *m*

heav·en·ly himmlisch

heav·y schwer; stark (*rain, smoker, drinker, traffic etc*); hoch (*fine, taxes etc*); schwer (verdaulich); drückend, lastend; Schwer...

heav·y cur·rent ELECTR Starkstrom *m*

heav·y-du·ty TECH Hochleistungs...; strapazierfähig

heav·y-hand·ed ungeschickt

heav·y·weight *boxing*: Schwergewicht *n*, Schwergewichtler *m*

He·brew 1. hebräisch; **2.** Hebräer(in); LING Hebräisch *n*

heck·le *Redner* durch Zwischenrufe *or* Zwischenfragen stören

heck·ler Zwischenrufer *m*

heck·ling Zwischenrufe

hec·tic hektisch

hedge 1. Hecke *f*; **2.** *v/t*: *a.* **hedge in** mit e-r Hecke einfassen; *v/i fig* ausweichen

hedge·hog ZO Stachelschwein *n*; *Br* Igel *m*

hedge·row Hecke *f*

heed 1. beachten, Beachtung schenken (*dat*); **2.** **give** *or* **pay heed to, take heed of** → 1

heed·less: **be heedless of** nicht beachten, *Warnung etc* in den Wind schlagen

heel 1. ANAT Ferse *f*; Absatz *m*; **down at heel** *fig* abgerissen; heruntergekommen; **2.** Absätze machen auf (*acc*)

hef·ty kräftig, stämmig; mächtig (*blow etc*), gewaltig; F saftig (*prices, fine etc*)

heif·er ZO Färse *f*, junge Kuh

height Höhe *f*; (Körper)Größe *f*; Anhöhe *f*; *fig* Höhe(punkt *m*) *f*

height·en erhöhen; vergrößern

heir Erbe *m*; **heir to the throne** Thronerbe *m*, Thronfolger *m*

heir·ess Erbin *f*

heir·loom Erbstück *n*

hel·i·cop·ter AVIAT Hubschrauber *m*, Helikopter *m*

hel·i·port AVIAT Hubschrauberlandeplatz *m*

hell 1. Hölle *f*; **a hell of a noise** F ein Höllenlärm; **what the hell ...?** F was zum Teufel ...?; **raise hell** F e-n Mordskrach schlagen; **2.** Höllen...; **3.** *int* F verdammt!, verflucht!

hell·ish F höllisch

hel·lo *int* hallo!

helm MAR Ruder *n*, Steuer *n*

hel·met Helm *m*

helms·man MAR Steuermann *m*

help 1. Hilfe *f*; Hausangestellte *f*; **a call** *or* **cry for help** ein Hilferuf, ein Hilfeschrei; **2.** helfen; **help o.s.** sich bedienen, zulangen; **I cannot help it** ich kann es nicht ändern; **I could not help laughing** ich musste einfach lachen

help·er Helfer(in)

help·ful hilfreich; nützlich

help·ing Portion *f*

help·less hilflos

help·less·ness Hilflosigkeit *f*

help men·u EDP Hilfemenü *n*

hel·ter-skel·ter 1. *adv* holterdiepolter, Hals über Kopf; **2.** *adj* überstürzt

helve Stiel *m*, Griff *m*

Hel·ve·tian Schweizer ...

hem 1. Saum *m*; **2.** säumen; **hem in** einschließen

hem·i·sphere GEOGR Halbkugel *f*, Hemisphäre *f*

hem·line Saum *m*

hem·lock BOT Schierling *m*

hemp BOT Hanf *m*

hem·stitch Hohlsaum *m*

hen ZO Henne *f*, Huhn *n*; Weibchen *n*

hence daher; **a week hence** in e-r Woche

hence·forth von nun an

H

hen house Hühnerstall *m*

hen·pecked hus·band Pantoffelheld *m*

her sie; ihr; ihr(e); sich

her·ald 1. HIST Herold *m*; 2. ankündigen

her·ald·ry Wappenkunde *f*, Heraldik *f*

herb BOT Kraut *n*; Heilkraut *n*

her·ba·ceous BOT krautartig; **herba-
ceous plant** Staudengewächs *n*

herb·al BOT Kräuter..., Pflanzen...

her·bi·vore ZO Pflanzenfresser *m*

herd 1. Herde *f* (*a. fig*), Rudel *n*; 2. *v/t* Vieh
hüten; *v/i: a.* **herd together** in e-r Herde
leben; sich zusammendrängen

herds·man Hirt *m*

here hier; hierher; **here you are** hier (bitte); **here's to you!** auf dein Wohl!

here·a·bout(s) hier herum, in dieser Gegend

here·af·ter 1. künftig; 2. *das* Jenseits

here·by hiermit

he·red·i·ta·ry BIOL erblich, Erb...

he·red·i·ty BIOL Erblichkeit *f*; ererbte Anlagen *pl*, Erbmasse *f*

here·in hierin

here·of hiervon

her·e·sy REL Ketzerei *f*

her·e·tic REL Ketzer(in)

here·up·on hierauf, darauf(hin)

here·with hiermit

her·i·tage Erbe *n*

her·maph·ro·dite BIOL Zwitter *m*

her·met·ic TECH hermetisch

her·mit Einsiedler *m*

he·ro Held *m*

he·ro·ic heroisch, heldenhaft, Helden...

her·o·in Heroin *n*

her·o·ine Heldin *f*

her·o·is·m Heldentum *n*

her·on ZO Reiher *m*

her·ring ZO Hering *m*

hers ihrs, ihre(r, -s)

her·self sie selbst; ihr selbst; sich (selbst);
by herself von selbst, allein, ohne Hilfe

hes·i·tant zögernd, zaudernd, unschlüssig

hes·i·tate zögern, zaudern, unschlüssig
sein, Bedenken haben

hes·i·ta·tion Zögern *n*, Zaudern *n*, Un-
schlüssigkeit *f*; **without hesitation** ohne
zu zögern, bedenkenlos

hew hauen, hacken; **hew down** fällen,
umhauen

hey *int* F he!, heda!

hey·day Höhepunkt *m*, Gipfel *m*; Blüte
(-zeit) *f*

hi *inf* F hallo!

hi·ber·nate ZO Winterschlaf halten

hic·cough, hic·cup 1. Schluckauf *m*; 2.
den Schluckauf haben

hide[1] (sich) verbergen, verstecken; ver-

heimlichen

hide[2] Haut *f*, Fell *n*

hide-and-seek Versteckspiel *n*

hide·a·way F Versteck *n*

hid·e·ous abscheulich, scheußlich

hide·out Versteck *n*

hid·ing[1] F Tracht *f* Prügel

hid·ing[2]: **be in hiding** sich versteckt halten; **go into hiding** untertauchen

hid·ing place Versteck *n*

hi-fi Hi-Fi *n*, Hi-Fi-Gerät *n*, -Anlage *f*

high 1. hoch; groß (*hopes etc*); GASTR an-
gegangen; F blau; F high; **be in high spirits** in Hochstimmung sein; ausgelassen
or übermütig sein; 2. METEOR Hoch *n*;
Höchststand *m*; High School *f*

high·brow F 1. Intellektuelle *m*, *f*; 2. (be-
tont) intellektuell

high-cal·o·rie kalorienreich

high-class erstklassig

high·er ed·u·ca·tion Hochschulausbildung *f*

high fi·del·i·ty High Fidelity *f*

high-grade hochwertig; erstklassig

high-hand·ed anmaßend, eigenmächtig

high-heeled hochhackig

high jump SPORT Hochsprung *m*

high jump·er SPORT Hochspringer(in)

high·land Hochland *n*

high·light 1. Höhe-, Glanzpunkt *m*; 2.
hervorheben

high·ly *fig* hoch; **think highly of** viel halten von

high·ly-strung reizbar, nervös

high·ness *mst fig* Höhe *f*; **Highness** Hoheit *f* (*title*)

high-pitched schrill; steil (*roof*)

high-pow·ered TECH Hochleistungs...; *fig*
dynamisch

high-pres·sure METEOR, TECH Hochdruck...

high-rank·ing hochrangig

high rise Hochhaus *n*

high road *esp Br* Hauptstraße *f*

high school High School *f*

high sea·son Hochsaison *f*

high so·ci·e·ty High Society *f*

high-spir·it·ed übermütig, ausgelassen

high street *Br* Hauptstraße *f*

high tea *Br* frühes Abendessen

high tech·nol·o·gy Hochtechnologie *f*

high ten·sion ELECTR Hochspannung *f*

high tide Flut *f*

high time: **it is high time** es ist höchste
Zeit

high wa·ter Hochwasser *n*

high·way Highway *m*, Haupt(verkehrs)-
straße *f*

High·way Code *Br* Straßenverkehrsordnung f

hi·jack 1. Flugzeug entführen; j-n, Geldtransport etc überfallen; **2.** (Flugzeug-) Entführung f; Überfall m

hi·jack·er Räuber m; (Flugzeug)Entführer(in)

hike 1. wandern; **2.** Wanderung f

hik·er Wanderer m, Wanderin f

hik·ing Wandern n

hi·lar·i·ous ausgelassen

hi·lar·i·ty Ausgelassenheit f

hill Hügel m, Anhöhe f

hill·bil·ly contp Hinterwäldler m

hill·ock kleiner Hügel

hill·side (Ab)Hang m

hill·top Hügelspitze f

hill·y hügelig

hilt Heft n, Griff m

him ihn; ihm; F er; sich

him·self er or ihm or ihn selbst; sich; sich (selbst); **by himself** von selbst, allein, ohne Hilfe

hind¹ zo Hirschkuh f

hind² Hinter...

hin·der hindern (**from** an dat); hemmen

hind·most hinterste(r, -s), letzte(r, -s)

hin·drance Hindernis n

Hin·du Hindu m

Hin·du·ism Hinduismus m

hinge 1. TECH (Tür)Angel f, Scharnier n; **2. hinge on** fig abhängen von

hint 1. Wink m, Andeutung f; Tipp m; Anspielung f; **take a hint** e-n Wink verstehen; **2.** andeuten; anspielen (**at** auf acc)

hip¹ ANAT Hüfte f

hip² BOT Hagebutte f

hip·po F → **hip·po·pot·a·mus** zo Flusspferd n, Nilpferd n

hire 1. Br Auto etc mieten, Flugzeug etc chartern; j-n anstellen; j-n engagieren, anheuern; **hire out** Br vermieten; **2.** Miete f; Lohn m; **for hire** zu vermieten; frei

hire car Br Leih-, Mietwagen m

hire pur·chase: on hire purchase Br ECON auf Abzahlung, auf Raten

his sein(e); seins, seine(r, -s)

hiss 1. zischen; fauchen (cat); auszischen; **2.** Zischen n; Fauchen n

his·to·ri·an Historiker(in)

his·tor·ic historisch, geschichtlich (bedeutsam)

his·tor·i·cal historisch, geschichtlich (belegt or überliefert); Geschichts...; **historical novel** historischer Roman

his·to·ry Geschichte f; **history of civilization** Kulturgeschichte f; **contemporary history** Zeitgeschichte f

hit 1. schlagen; treffen (a. fig); MOT etc j-n, et. anfahren, et. rammen; F **hit it off** (with

s.o.) sich (mit j-m) gut vertragen; **hit on** (zufällig) auf et. stoßen, et. finden; **2.** Schlag m; fig (Seiten)Hieb m; (Glücks-)Treffer m; Hit m

hit-and-run: hit-and-run driver (unfall)flüchtiger Fahrer; **hit-and-run offense** (Br offence) Fahrerflucht f

hitch 1. befestigen, festmachen, festhaken, anbinden, ankoppeln (**to** an acc); **hitch up** hochziehen; **hitch a ride** or **lift** im Auto mitgenommen werden; **2.** Ruck m, Zug m; Schwierigkeit f, Haken m; **without a hitch** glatt, reibungslos;

hitch·hike per Anhalter fahren, trampen

hitch·hik·er Anhalter(in), Tramper(in)

hi-tech → **high tech**

HIV: HIV carrier HIV-Positive m, f; **HIV negative** HIV-negativ; **HIV positive** HIV-positiv

hive Bienenstock m; Bienenschwarm m

hoard 1. Vorrat m, Schatz m; **2.** a. **hoard up** horten, hamstern

hoard·ing Bauzaun m; Br Reklametafel f

hoar·frost (Rau)Reif m

hoarse heiser, rau

hoax 1. Falschmeldung f; (übler) Scherz; **2.** j-n hereinlegen

hob·ble humpeln, hinken

hob·by Hobby n, Steckenpferd n

hob·by·horse Steckenpferd n (a. fig)

hob·gob·lin Kobold m

ho·bo F Landstreicher m

hock¹ weißer Rheinwein

hock² zo Sprunggelenk n

hock·ey SPORT Eishockey n; esp Br Hockey n

hodge·podge Mischmasch m

hoe AGR **1.** Hacke f; **2.** hacken

hog zo (Haus-, Schlacht)Schwein n

hoist 1. hochziehen; hissen; **2.** TECH Winde f, (Lasten)Aufzug m

hold 1. halten; festhalten; Gewicht etc tragen, aushalten; zurück-, abhalten (**from** von); Wahlen, Versammlung etc abhalten; Stellung halten; SPORT Meisterschaft etc austragen; Aktien, Rechte etc besitzen; Amt bekleiden; Platz einnehmen; Rekord halten; fassen, enthalten; Platz bieten für; der Ansicht sein (**that** dass); halten für; fig fesseln, in Spannung halten; (sich) festhalten; anhalten, andauern (a. fig); **hold one's ground, hold one's own** sich behaupten; **hold the line** TEL am Apparat bleiben; **hold responsible** verantwortlich machen; **hold still** still halten; **hold s.th. against s.o.** j-m et. vorhalten or vorwerfen; j-m et. übel nehmen or nachtragen; **hold back** (sich) zurückhalten; fig zurückhalten mit; **hold

on (sich) festhalten (*to* an *dat*); aus-, durchhalten; andauern; TEL am Apparat bleiben; *hold out* aus-, durchhalten; reichen (*supplies etc*); *hold up* hochheben; hochhalten; hinstellen (*as* als); aufhalten, verzögern; *j-n, Bank etc* überfallen; **2.** Griff *m*, Halt *m*; Stütze *f*; Gewalt *f*, Macht *f*, Einfluss *m*; MAR Laderaum *m*, Frachtraum *m*; *catch* (*get, take*) *hold of s.th.* et. ergreifen, et. zu fassen bekommen

hold·er TECH Halter *m*; *esp* ECON Inhaber(in)

hold·ing Besitz *m*

holding com·pa·ny ECON Holding-, Dachgesellschaft *f*

hold·up (Verkehrs)Stockung *f*; (bewaffneter) (Raub)Überfall

hole 1. Loch *n*; Höhle *f*, Bau *m*; *fig* F Klemme *f*; **2.** durchlöchern

hol·i·day Feiertag *m*; freier Tag; *esp Br mst pl* Ferien *pl*, Urlaub *m*; *be on holiday* im Urlaub sein, Urlaub machen

holiday home Ferienhaus *n*, Ferienwohnung *f*

hol·i·day·mak·er Urlauber(in)

hol·i·ness Heiligkeit *f*; *His Holiness* Seine Heiligkeit

hol·ler F schreien

hol·low 1. hohl; **2.** Hohlraum *m*, (Aus)Höhlung *f*; Mulde *f*, Vertiefung *f*; **3.** *hollow out* aushöhlen

hol·ly BOT Stechpalme *f*

hol·o·caust Massenvernichtung *f*, Massensterben *n*, (*esp* Brand)Katastrophe *f*; *the Holocaust* HIST der Holocaust

hol·ster (Pistolen)Halfter *m, n*

ho·ly heilig

ho·ly wa·ter REL Weihwasser *n*

Ho·ly Week REL Karwoche *f*

home 1. Heim *n*; Haus *n*; Wohnung *f*; Zuhause *n*; Heimat *f*; *at home* zu Hause; *make oneself at home* es sich bequem machen; *at home and abroad* im In- und Ausland; **2.** *adj* häuslich, Heim… (*a.* SPORT); inländisch, Inlands…; Heimat…; **3.** *adv* heim, nach Hause; zu Hause; daheim; *fig* ins Ziel, ins Schwarze; *return home* heimkehren; *strike home* sitzen, treffen

home ad·dress Privatanschrift *f*

home com·put·er Heimcomputer *m*

home·less heimatlos; obdachlos; *homeless person* Obdachlose *m, f*; *shelter for the homeless* Obdachlosenasyl *n*

home·ly einfach; unscheinbar, reizlos

home·made selbst gemacht, Hausmacher…

home mar·ket ECON Binnenmarkt *m*

Home Of·fice *Br* POL Innenministerium *n*

Home Sec·re·ta·ry *Br* POL Innenminister *m*

home·sick: be homesick Heimweh haben

home·sick·ness Heimweh *n*

home team SPORT Gastgeber *pl*

home·ward *adj* Heim…, Rück…

home·ward(s) *adv* nach Hause

home·work Hausaufgabe(n *pl*) *f*; *do one's homework* s-e Hausaufgaben machen (*a. fig*)

hom·i·cide JUR Mord *m*; Totschlag *m*; Mörder(in)

hom·i·cide squad Mordkommission *f*

ho·mo·ge·ne·ous homogen, gleichartig

ho·mo·sex·u·al 1. homosexuell; **2.** Homosexuelle *m, f*

hone TECH fein schleifen

hon·est ehrlich, rechtschaffen; aufrichtig

hon·es·ty Ehrlichkeit *f*, Rechtschaffenheit *f*; Aufrichtigkeit *f*

hon·ey Honig *m*; Liebling *m*, Schatz *m*

hon·ey·comb (Honig)Wabe *f*

hon·eyed *fig* honigsüß

hon·ey·moon 1. Flitterwochen *pl*, Hochzeitsreise *f*; **2.** *be honeymooning* auf Hochzeitsreise sein

hon·ey·suck·le BOT Geißblatt *n*

honk MOT hupen

hon·or·ar·y Ehren…; ehrenamtlich

hon·o(u)r 1. Ehre *f*; Ehrung *f*, Ehre(n *pl*) *f*; *pl* besondere Auszeichnung(en *pl*); *Your Hono(u)r* JUR Euer Ehren; **2.** ehren; auszeichnen; ECON *Scheck etc* honorieren, einlösen

hon·o(u)r·a·ble ehrenvoll, ehrenhaft; ehrenwert

hood Kapuze *f*; MOT Verdeck *n*; (Motor)-Haube *f*; TECH (Schutz)Haube *f*

hood·lum F Rowdy *m*; Ganove *m*

hood·wink *j-n* hinters Licht führen

hoof ZO Huf *m*

hook 1. Haken *m*; Angelhaken *m*; *by hook or by crook* F mit allen Mitteln; **2.** an-, ein-, fest-, zuhaken; angeln (*a. fig*)

hooked krumm, Haken…; F süchtig (*on* nach) (*a. fig*); *hooked on heroin* (*television*) heroinsüchtig (fernsehsüchtig)

hook·er F Nutte *f*

hook·y: play hooky F (die Schule) schwänzen

hoo·li·gan Rowdy *m*

hoo·li·gan·ism Rowdytum *n*

hoop Reif(en) *m*

hoot 1. ZO Schrei *m* (*a. fig*); MOT Hupen *n*; **2.** *v/i* heulen; johlen; ZO schreien; MOT hupen; *v/t* auspfeifen, auszischen

Hoo·ver® *Br* **1.** Staubsauger *m*; **2.** *mst*

hoover (staub)saugen

hop¹ **1.** hüpfen, hopsen; hüpfen über (*acc*); *be hopping mad* F e-e Stinkwut haben; **2.** Sprung *m*

hop² BOT Hopfen *m*

hope **1.** Hoffnung *f* (*of* auf *acc*); **2.** hoffen (*for* auf *acc*); *hope for the best* das Beste hoffen; *I hope so, let's hope so* hoffentlich

hope·ful: *be hopeful that* hoffen, dass

hope·ful·ly hoffnungsvoll; hoffentlich

hope·less hoffnungslos; verzweifelt

horde Horde *f* (*often contp*)

ho·ri·zon Horizont *m*

hor·i·zon·tal horizontal, waag(e)recht

hor·mone BIOL Hormon *n*

horn ZO Horn *n*, *pl* Geweih *n*; MOT Hupe *f*

hor·net ZO Hornisse *f*

horn·y schwielig; V geil

hor·o·scope Horoskop *n*

hor·ri·ble schrecklich, furchtbar, scheußlich

hor·rid *esp Br* grässlich, abscheulich; schrecklich

hor·rif·ic schrecklich, entsetzlich

hor·ri·fy entsetzen

hor·ror Entsetzen *n*; Abscheu *m*, Horror *m*; F Gräuel *m*

horse ZO Pferd *n*; Bock *m*, Gestell *n*; *wild horses couldn't drag me there* keine zehn Pferde bringen mich dort hin

horse·back: *on horseback* zu Pferde, beritten

horse chest·nut BOT Rosskastanie *f*

horse·hair Rosshaar *n*

horse·man (geübter) Reiter

horse·pow·er TECH Pferdestärke *f*

horse race Pferderennen *n*

horse rac·ing Pferderennen *n or pl*

horse·rad·ish BOT Meerrettich *m*

horse·shoe Hufeisen *n*

horse·wom·an (geübte) Reiterin

hor·ti·cul·ture Gartenbau *m*

hose¹ Schlauch *m*

hose² Strümpfe *pl*, Strumpfwaren *f*

ho·sier·y Strumpfwaren *pl*

hos·pice Sterbeklinik *f*

hos·pi·ta·ble gastfreundlich

hos·pi·tal Krankenhaus *n*, Klinik *f*; *in the hospital* im Krankenhaus

hos·pi·tal·i·ty Gastfreundschaft *f*

hos·pi·tal·ize ins Krankenhaus einliefern *or* einweisen

host¹ **1.** Gastgeber *m*; BIOL Wirt *m*; *radio*, TV Talkmaster *m*, Showmaster *m*, Moderator(in); *your host was …* durch die Sendung führte Sie …; **2.** *radio*, TV F *Sendung* moderieren

host² Menge *f*, Masse *f*

host³ REL *often* **Host** Hostie *f*

hos·tage Geisel *m*, *f*; *take s.o. hostage* j-n als Geisel nehmen

hos·tel *esp Br* UNIV (Wohn)Heim *n*; *mst* *youth hostel* Jugendherberge *f*

host·ess Gastgeberin *f*; Hostess *f* (*a.* AVIAT); AVIAT Stewardess *f*

hos·tile feindlich; feindselig (*to* gegen); *hostile to foreigners* ausländerfeindlich

hos·til·i·ty Feindseligkeit *f* (*to* gegen); *hostility to foreigners* Ausländerfeindlichkeit *f*

hot heiß (*a.* fig and sl); GASTR scharf; warm (*meal*); fig hitzig, heftig; ganz neu *or* frisch (*news etc*); *I am or feel hot* mir ist heiß

hot·bed Mistbeet *n*; fig Brutstätte *f*

hotch·potch *Br* → *hodgepodge*

hot dog GASTR Hot Dog *n*, *m*

ho·tel Hotel *n*

hot·head Hitzkopf *m*

hot·house Treib-, Gewächshaus *n*

hot line POL heißer Draht; TEL Hotline *f*

hot·plate Kochplatte *f*

hot spot *esp* POL Unruhe-, Krisenherd *m*

hot spring Thermalquelle *f*

hot-tem·pered jähzornig

hot-wa·ter bot·tle Wärmflasche *f*

hound ZO Jagdhund *m*

hour Stunde *f*; *pl* (Arbeits)Zeit *f*, (Geschäfts)Stunden *pl*

hour·ly stündlich

house **1.** Haus *n*; **2.** unterbringen

house·bound ans Haus gefesselt

house·break·ing Einbruch *m*

house·hold **1.** Haushalt *m*; **2.** Haushalts…

house hus·band Hausmann *m*

house·keep·er Haushälterin *f*

house·keep·ing Haushaltung *f*, Haushaltsführung *f*

house·maid Hausangestellte *f*, Hausmädchen *n*

house·man *Br* MED Assistenzarzt *m*, -ärztin *f*

House of Lords *Br* PARL Oberhaus *n*

house plant Zimmerpflanze *f*

house-warm·ing Hauseinweihung *f*, Einzugsparty *f*

house·wife Hausfrau *f*

house·work Hausarbeit *f*

hous·ing Wohnung *f*

housing de·vel·op·ment, *Br* housing es·tate Wohnsiedlung *f*

hov·er schweben; herumlungern; fig schwanken

hov·er·craft Hovercraft *n*, Luftkissenfahrzeug *n*

how wie; *how are you?* wie geht es dir?;

how about ...? wie steht's mit ...?, wie wäre es mit ...?; *how do you do?* guten Tag!; *how much?* wie viel?; *how many* wie viele?

how·ev·er 1. *adv* wie auch (immer); **2.** *cj* jedoch

howl 1. heulen; brüllen, schreien; **2.** Heulen *n*

howl·er F grober Schnitzer

hub TECH (Rad)Nabe *f*; *fig* Mittelpunkt *m*, Angelpunkt *m*

hub·bub Stimmengewirr *n*; Tumult *m*

hub·by F (Ehe)Mann *m*

huck·le·ber·ry BOT amerikanische Heidelbeere

hud·dle: *huddle together* (sich) zusammendrängen; *huddled up* zusammengekauert

hue[1] Farbe *f*; (Farb)Ton *m*

hue[2]: *hue and cry* *fig* großes Geschrei, heftiger Protest

huff: *in a huff* verärgert, verstimmt

hug 1. (sich) umarmen; an sich drücken; **2.** Umarmung *f*

huge riesig, riesengroß

hulk F Koloss *m*; sperriges Ding; *a hulk of a man* ein ungeschlachter Kerl

hull 1. BOT Schale *f*, Hülse *f*; MAR Rumpf *m*; **2.** enthülsen, schälen

hul·la·ba·loo Lärm *m*, Getöse *n*

hul·lo *int* hallo!

hum summen; brummen

hu·man 1. menschlich, Menschen...; **2.** *a.* *human being* Mensch *m*

hu·mane human, menschlich

hu·man·i·tar·i·an humanitär, menschenfreundlich

hu·man·i·ty die Menschheit, die Menschen *pl*; Humanität *f*, Menschlichkeit *f*; *pl* Geisteswissenschaften *pl*; Altphilologie *f*

hu·man·ly: *humanly possible* menschenmöglich

hu·man rights Menschenrechte *pl*

hum·ble 1. demütig; bescheiden; **2.** demütigen

hum·ble·ness Demut *f*

hum·drum eintönig, langweilig

hu·mid feucht, nass

hu·mid·i·ty Feuchtigkeit *f*

hu·mil·i·ate demütigen, erniedrigen

hu·mil·i·a·tion Demütigung *f*, Erniedrigung *f*

hu·mil·i·ty Demut *f*

hum·ming·bird ZO Kolibri *m*

hu·mor·ous humorvoll, komisch

hu·mo(u)r 1. Humor *m*; Komik *f*; **2.** j-m s-n Willen lassen; eingehen auf (*acc*)

hump ZO Höcker *m*; MED Buckel *m*

hump·back(ed) → *hunchback(ed)*

hunch 1. → *hump*; dickes Stück; (Vor)-Ahnung *f*; **2.** *a.* *hunch up* krümmen; *hunch one's shoulders* die Schultern hochziehen

hunch·back Buckel *m*; Bucklige *m*, *f*

hunch·backed buck(e)lig

hun·dred 1. hundert; **2.** Hundert *f*

hun·dredth 1. hundertste(r, -s); **2.** Hundertstel *n*

hun·dred·weight *appr* Zentner *m* (= *50,8 kg*)

Hun·ga·ri·an 1. ungarisch; **2.** Ungar(in); LING Ungarisch *n*

Hun·ga·ry Ungarn *n*

hun·ger 1. Hunger *m* (*a. fig for* nach); **2.** *fig* hungern (*for, after* nach)

hun·ger strike Hungerstreik *m*

hun·gry hungrig

hunk dickes *or* großes Stück

hunt 1. jagen; Jagd machen auf (*acc*); verfolgen; suchen (*for, after* nach); *hunt down* zur Strecke bringen; *hunt for* Jagd machen auf (*acc*); *hunt out, hunt up* aufspüren; **2.** Jagd *f* (*a. fig*), Jagen *n*; Verfolgung *f*; Suche *f* (*for, after* nach)

hunt·er Jäger *m*; Jagdpferd *n*

hunt·ing 1. Jagen *n*; **2.** Jagd...

hunt·ing ground Jagdrevier *n*

hur·dle SPORT Hürde *f* (*a. fig*)

hur·dler SPORT Hürdenläufer(in)

hur·dle race SPORT Hürdenrennen *n*

hurl schleudern; *hurl abuse at s.o.* j-m Beleidigungen ins Gesicht schleudern

hur·rah, **hur·ray** *int* hurra!

hur·ri·cane Hurrikan *m*, Wirbelsturm *m*; Orkan *m*

hur·ried eilig, hastig, übereilt

hur·ry 1. *v/t* schnell *or* eilig befördern *or* bringen; *often hurry up* j-n antreiben, hetzen; *et.* beschleunigen; *v/i* eilen, hasten; *hurry (up)* sich beeilen; *hurry up!* (mach) schnell!; **2.** (große) Eile, Hast *f*; *be in a hurry* es eilig haben

hurt verletzen, verwunden (*a. fig*); schmerzen, wehtun; schaden (*dat*)

hurt·ful verletzend

hus·band (Ehe)Mann *m*

hush 1. *int* still!; **2.** Stille *f*; **3.** zum Schweigen bringen; *hush up* vertuschen, totschweigen

hush mon·ey Schweigegeld *n*

husk BOT **1.** Hülse *f*, Schote *f*; Schale *f*; **2.** enthülsen, schälen

hus·tle 1. (*in aller Eile*) *wohin* bringen *or* schicken; hasten, hetzen; sich beeilen; **2.** *hustle and bustle* Gedränge *n*; Gehetze *n*; Betrieb *m*, Wirbel *m*

hut Hütte *f*

hutch Stall *m*
hy·a·cinth BOT Hyazinthe *f*
hy·(a)e·na ZO Hyäne *f*
hy·brid BIOL Mischling *m*, Kreuzung *f*
hy·drant Hydrant *m*
hy·draul·ic hydraulisch
hy·draul·ics hydraulik *f*
hy·dro... Wasser...
hy·dro·car·bon CHEM Kohlenwasserstoff *m*
hy·dro·chlor·ic ac·id CHEM Salzsäure *f*
hy·dro·foil MAR Tragflächenboot *n*, Tragflügelboot *n*
hy·dro·gen CHEM Wasserstoff *m*
hydrogen bomb Wasserstoffbombe
hy·dro·plane AVIAT Wasserflugzeug *n*; MAR Gleitboot *n*
hy·dro·plan·ing MOT Aquaplaning *n*
hy·e·na ZO Hyäne *f*
hy·giene Hygiene *f*
hy·gien·ic hygienisch

hymn Kirchenlied *n*, Choral *m*
hype F **1.** *a.* **hype up** (übersteigerte) Publicity machen für; **2.** (übersteigerte) Publicity; *media hype* Medienrummel *m*
hy·per... hyper..., übermäßig
hy·per·mar·ket Br Groß-, Verbrauchermarkt *m*
hy·per·sen·si·tive überempfindlich (*to* gegen)
hy·phen Bindestrich *m*
hy·phen·ate mit Bindestrich schreiben
hyp·no·tize hypnotisieren
hy·po·chon·dri·ac Hypochonder *m*
hy·poc·ri·sy Heuchelei *f*
hyp·o·crite Heuchler(in)
hyp·o·criti·cal heuchlerisch, scheinheilig
hy·poth·e·sis Hypothese *f*
hys·te·ri·a MED Hysterie *f*
hys·ter·i·cal hysterisch
hys·ter·ics hysterischer Anfall; *go into hysterics* hysterisch werden

I

I, i I, i *n*
I ich; *it is I* ich bin es
ice 1. Eis *n*; **2.** *Getränke etc* mit *or* in Eis kühlen; GASTR glasieren, mit Zuckerguss überziehen; *iced over* zugefroren (*lake etc*); *iced up* vereist (*road*)
ice age Eiszeit *f*
ice·berg Eisberg *m* (*a. fig*)
ice·bound eingefroren
ice cream (Speise)Eis *n*
ice-cream par·lo(u)r Eisdiele *f*
ice cube Eiswürfel *m*
iced eisgekühlt
ice floe Eisscholle *f*
ice hock·ey SPORT Eishockey *n*
ice lol·ly Br Eis *n* am Stiel
ice rink (Kunst)Eisbahn *f*
ice skate Schlittschuh *m*
ice-skate Schlittschuh laufen
ice show Eisrevue *f*
i·ci·cle Eiszapfen *m*
ic·ing GASTR Glasur *f*, Zuckerguss *m*; *the icing on the cake* das Tüpfelchen auf dem i
i·con REL Ikone *f*; EDP Ikone *f*, (Bild)-Symbol *n*
i·cy eisig; vereist
ID ABBR *of* **identity** Identität *f*; *ID card*

(Personal)Ausweis *m*
i·dea Idee *f*, Vorstellung *f*, Begriff *m*; Gedanke *m*, Idee *f*; *have no idea* keine Ahnung haben
i·deal 1. ideal; **2.** Ideal *n*
i·deal·ism Idealismus *m*
i·deal·ize idealisieren
i·den·ti·cal identisch (*to, with* mit)
identical twins eineiige Zwillinge *pl*
i·den·ti·fi·ca·tion Identifizierung *f*
identification (pa·pers) Ausweis(papiere *pl*) *m*
i·den·ti·fy identifizieren; *identify o.s.* sich ausweisen
i·den·ti·kit® pic·ture Br JUR Phantombild *n*
i·den·ti·ty Identität *f*
identity card (Personal)Ausweis *m*
i·de·o·log·i·cal ideologisch
i·de·ol·o·gy Ideologie *f*
id·i·om Idiom *n*, idiomatischer Ausdruck, Redewendung *f*
id·i·o·mat·ic idiomatisch
id·i·ot MED Idiot(in), *contp a.* Trottel *m*
id·i·ot·ic MED idiotisch, F *a.* blödsinnig, schwachsinnig
i·dle 1. untätig; faul, träge; nutzlos; leer, hohl (*talk*); TECH stillstehend, außer Be-

trieb; MOT leerlaufend, im Leerlauf; **2.** faulenzen; MOT leerlaufen; *mst idle away Zeit* vertrödeln

i·dol Idol *n* (*a. fig*); Götzenbild *n*

i·dol·ize abgöttisch verehren, vergöttern

i·dyl·lic idyllisch

if wenn, falls; ob; *if I were you* wenn ich du wäre

ig·loo Iglu *m, n*

ig·nite anzünden, (sich) entzünden; MOT zünden

ig·ni·tion MOT Zündung *f*

ig·ni·tion key MOT Zündschlüssel *m*

ig·no·rance Unkenntnis *f*, Unwissenheit *f*

ig·no·rant: be ignorant of s.th. et. nicht wissen *or* kennen, nichts wissen von et.

ig·nore ignorieren, nicht beachten

ill krank; schlimm, schlecht; *fall ill, be taken ill* krank werden, erkranken

ill-ad·vised schlecht beraten; unklug

ill-bred schlecht erzogen; ungezogen

il·le·gal verboten, JUR illegal, ungesetzlich; *illegal parking* Falschparken *n*

il·le·gi·ble unleserlich

il·le·git·i·mate unehelich; unrechtmäßig

ill feel·ing Verstimmung *f*; *cause ill feeling* böses Blut machen

ill-hu·mo(u)red schlecht gelaunt

il·li·cit unerlaubt, verboten

il·lit·e·rate ungebildet

ill-man·nered ungehobelt, ungezogen

ill-na·tured boshaft, bösartig

ill·ness Krankheit *f*

ill-tem·pered schlecht gelaunt

ill-timed ungelegen, unpassend

ill-treat misshandeln

il·lu·mi·nate beleuchten

il·lu·mi·nat·ing aufschlussreich

il·lu·mi·na·tion Beleuchtung *f*; *pl* Illumination *f*, Festbeleuchtung *f*

il·lu·sion Illusion *f*, Täuschung *f*

il·lu·sive, il·lu·so·ry illusorisch, trügerisch

il·lus·trate illustrieren; bebildern; erläutern, veranschaulichen

il·lus·tra·tion Erläuterung *f*; Illustration *f*; Bild *n*, Abbildung *f*

il·lus·tra·tive erläuternd

il·lus·tri·ous berühmt

ill will Feindschaft *f*

im·age Bild *n*; Ebenbild *n*; Image *n*; bildlicher Ausdruck, Metapher *f*

im·age·ry Bildersprache *f*, Metaphorik *f*

i·ma·gi·na·ble vorstellbar, denkbar

i·ma·gi·na·ry eingebildet, imaginär

i·ma·gi·na·tion Einbildung(skraft) *f*; Vorstellungskraft *f*, -vermögen *n*

i·ma·gi·na·tive ideenreich, einfallsreich; fantasievoll

i·ma·gine sich *j-n or et.* vorstellen; sich *et.* einbilden

im·bal·ance Unausgewogenheit *f*; POL *etc* Ungleichgewicht *n*

im·be·cile Idiot *m*, Trottel *m*

im·i·tate nachahmen, nachmachen, imitieren

im·i·ta·tion 1. Nachahmung *f*, Imitation *f*; **2.** nachgemacht, unecht, künstlich, Kunst…

im·mac·u·late unbefleckt, makellos; tadellos, fehlerlos

im·ma·te·ri·al unwesentlich, unerheblich (*to* für)

im·ma·ture unreif

im·mea·su·ra·ble unermesslich

im·me·di·ate unmittelbar; sofortig, umgehend; nächste(r, -s) (*family*)

im·me·di·ate·ly unmittelbar; sofort

im·mense riesig, *fig a.* enorm, immens

im·merse (ein)tauchen; *immerse o.s. in* sich vertiefen in (*acc*)

im·mer·sion Eintauchen *n*

im·mer·sion heat·er Tauchsieder *m*

im·mi·grant Einwanderer *m*, Einwanderin *f*, Immigrant(in)

im·mi·grate einwandern, immigrieren (*into* in *dat*)

im·mi·gra·tion Einwanderung *f*, Immigration *f*

im·mi·nent nahe bevorstehend; *imminent danger* drohende Gefahr

im·mo·bile unbeweglich

im·mod·e·rate maßlos

im·mod·est unbescheiden; schamlos, unanständig

im·mor·al unmoralisch

im·mor·tal 1. unsterblich; **2.** Unsterbliche *m, f*

im·mor·tal·i·ty Unsterblichkeit *f*

im·mov·a·ble unbeweglich; *fig* unerschütterlich; hart, unnachgiebig

im·mune MED immun (*to* gegen); geschützt (*from* vor, gegen)

immune sys·tem MED Immunsystem *n*

im·mu·ni·ty MED Immunität *f*

im·mu·nize MED immunisieren, immun machen (*against* gegen)

imp Kobold *m*; F Racker *m*

im·pact Zusammenprall *m*, Anprall *m*; Aufprall *m*; Wucht *f*; *fig* (Ein)Wirkung *f*, (starker) Einfluss (*on* auf *acc*)

im·pair beeinträchtigen

im·part (*to dat*) mitteilen; vermitteln

im·par·tial unparteiisch, unvoreingenommen

im·par·ti·al·i·ty Unparteilichkeit *f*, Objektivität *f*

im·pass·a·ble unpassierbar

im·passe *fig* Sackgasse *f*; **reach an impasse** in e-e Sackgasse geraten
im·pas·sioned leidenschaftlich
im·pas·sive teilnahmslos; ungerührt; gelassen
im·pa·tience Ungeduld *f*
im·pa·tient ungeduldig
im·peach JUR anklagen (**for, of, with** *gen*); JUR anfechten; infrage stellen, in Zweifel ziehen
im·pec·ca·ble untadelig, einwandfrei
im·pede (be)hindern
im·ped·i·ment Hindernis *n* (**to** für); Behinderung *f*
im·pel antreiben; zwingen
im·pend·ing nahe bevorstehend, drohend
im·pen·e·tra·ble undurchdringlich; *fig* unergründlich
im·per·a·tive 1. unumgänglich, unbedingt erforderlich; gebieterisch; LING Imperativ…; **2.** *a.* **imperative mood** LING Imperativ *m*, Befehlsform *f*
im·per·cep·ti·ble nicht wahrnehmbar, unmerklich
im·per·fect 1. unvollkommen; mangelhaft; **2.** *a.* **imperfect tense** LING Imperfekt *n*, 1. Vergangenheit
im·pe·ri·al·ism POL Imperialismus
im·pe·ri·al·ist POL Imperialist *m*
im·pe·ril gefährden
im·pe·ri·ous herrisch, gebieterisch
im·per·me·a·ble undurchlässig
im·per·son·al unpersönlich
im·per·so·nate *j-n* imitieren, nachahmen; verkörpern, THEA *etc* darstellen
im·per·ti·nence Unverschämtheit *f*, Frechheit *f*
im·per·ti·nent unverschämt, frech
im·per·tur·ba·ble unerschütterlich, gelassen
im·per·vi·ous undurchlässig; *fig* unzugänglich (**to** für)
im·pe·tu·ous ungestüm, heftig; impulsiv; vorschnell
im·pe·tus TECH Antrieb *m*, Impuls *m*
im·pi·e·ty Gottlosigkeit *f*; Pietätlosigkeit *f*, Respektlosigkeit *f* (**to** gegenüber)
im·pinge: impinge on sich auswirken auf (*acc*), beeinflussen (*acc*)
im·pi·ous gottlos; pietätlos, respektlos (**to** gegenüber)
im·plac·a·ble unversöhnlich
im·plant MED implantieren, einpflanzen; *fig* einprägen
im·plau·si·ble unglaubwürdig
im·ple·ment 1. Werkzeug *n*, Gerät *n*; **2.** ausführen
im·pli·cate *j-n* verwickeln, hineinziehen (**in** in *acc*)

im·pli·ca·tion Verwicklung *f*; Folge *f*; Andeutung *f*
im·plic·it vorbehaltlos, bedingungslos; impliziert, (stillschweigend *or* mit) inbegriffen
im·plore *j-n* anflehen; *et.* erflehen
im·ply implizieren, einbeziehen, mit enthalten; andeuten; bedeuten
im·po·lite unhöflich
im·pol·i·tic unklug
im·port ECON **1.** importieren, einführen; **2.** Import *m*, Einfuhr *f*
im·por·tance Wichtigkeit *f*, Bedeutung *f*
im·por·tant wichtig, bedeutend
im·por·ta·tion → **import** 2
im·port du·ty ECON Einfuhrzoll *m*
im·port·er ECON Importeur *m*
im·pose auferlegen, aufbürden (**on** *dat*); *Strafe* verhängen (**on** gegen); *et.* aufdrängen, aufzwingen (**on** *dat*); **impose o.s. on s.o.** sich *j-m* aufdrängen
im·pos·ing imponierend, eindrucksvoll, imposant
im·pos·si·bil·i·ty Unmöglichkeit *f*
im·pos·si·ble unmöglich
im·pos·ter, *Br* **im·pos·tor** Betrüger(in), *esp* Hochstapler(in)
im·po·tence Unvermögen *n*, Unfähigkeit *f*; Hilflosigkeit *f*; MED Impotenz *f*
im·po·tent unfähig; hilflos; MED impotent
im·pov·e·rish arm machen; **be impoverished** verarmen; verarmt sein
im·prac·ti·ca·ble undurchführbar; unpassierbar
im·prac·ti·cal unpraktisch; undurchführbar
im·preg·na·ble uneinnehmbar
im·preg·nate imprägnieren, tränken; BIOL schwängern
im·press aufdrücken, einprägen (*a. fig*); *j-n* beeindrucken; **be impressed with** beeindruckt sein von
im·pres·sion Eindruck *m*; Abdruck *m*; **under the impression that** in der Annahme, dass
im·pres·sive eindrucksvoll
im·print 1. (auf)drücken (**on** auf *acc*); **imprint s.th. on s.o.'s memory** *j-m* et. ins Gedächtnis einprägen; **2.** Abdruck *m*, Eindruck *m*; PRINT Impressum *n*
im·pris·on JUR inhaftieren
im·pris·on·ment Freiheitsstrafe *f*, Gefängnis(strafe *f*) *n*, Haft *f*
im·prob·a·ble unwahrscheinlich
im·prop·er ungeeignet, unpassend; unanständig, unschicklich; unrichtig
im·pro·pri·e·ty Unschicklichkeit *f*
im·prove *v/t* verbessern; *Wert etc* erhöhen, steigern; **improve on** übertreffen; *v/i*

sich (ver)bessern, besser werden, sich erholen

im·prove·ment (Ver)Bess(e)rung *f*; Steigerung *f*; Fortschritt *m* (**on** gegenüber *dat*)

im·pro·vise improvisieren

im·pru·dent unklug

im·pu·dence Unverschämtheit *f*

im·pu·dent unverschämt

im·pulse Impuls *m* (*a. fig*); Anstoß *m*, Anreiz *m*

im·pul·sive impulsiv

im·pu·ni·ty: with impunity straflos, ungestraft

im·pure unrein (*a.* REL), schmutzig; *fig* schlecht, unmoralisch

im·pu·ri·ty Unreinheit *f*

im·pute: impute s.th. to s.o. j-n e-r Sache bezichtigen; j-m et. unterstellen

in 1. *prp place*: in (*dat or acc*), an (*dat*), auf (*dat*): **in New York** in New York; **in the street** auf der Straße; **put it in your pocket** steck es in deine Tasche; *time*: in (*dat*), an (*dat*): **in 1999** 1999; **in two hours** in zwei Stunden; **in the morning** am Morgen; *state, manner*: in (*dat*), auf (*acc*), mit; **in English** auf Englisch; *activity*: in (*dat*), bei, auf (*dat*): **in crossing the road** beim Überqueren der Straße; *author*: bei: **in Shakespeare** bei Shakespeare; *direction*: in (*acc, dat*), auf (*acc*), zu: **have confidence in** Vertrauen haben zu; *purpose*: in (*dat*), zu, als: **in defense of** zur Verteidigung *or* zum Schutz von; *material*: in (*dat*), aus, mit: **dressed in blue** in Blau (gekleidet); *amount etc*: in, von, aus, zu: **three in all** insgesamt *or* im Ganzen drei; **one in ten** eine(r, -s) von zehn; nach, gemäß: **in my opinion** m-r Meinung nach; **2.** *adv* innen, drinnen; hinein, herein; da, (an)gekommen; da, zu Hause; **3.** *adj* F in (Mode)

in·a·bil·i·ty Unfähigkeit *f*

in·ac·ces·si·ble unzugänglich, unerreichbar (**to** für *or dat*)

in·ac·cu·rate ungenau

in·ac·tive untätig

in·ac·tiv·i·ty Untätigkeit *f*

in·ad·e·quate unangemessen; unzulänglich, ungenügend

in·ad·mis·si·ble unzulässig, unstatthaft

in·ad·ver·tent unbeabsichtigt, versehentlich; **inadvertently** *a.* aus Versehen

in·an·i·mate leblos; langweilig

in·ap·pro·pri·ate unpassend, ungeeignet (**for, to** für)

in·apt ungeeignet, unpassend

in·ar·tic·u·late unartikuliert, undeutlich (ausgesprochen), unverständlich; unfä-

hig(, deutlich) zu sprechen

in·at·ten·tive unaufmerksam

in·au·di·ble unhörbar

in·au·gu·ral 1. Eröffnungs..., Antritts...; *inaugural speech* → **2.** Antrittsrede *f*

in·au·gu·rate *j-n* (feierlich) (in sein Amt) einführen; einweihen, eröffnen; einleiten

in·au·gu·ra·tion Amtseinführung *f*; Einweihung *f*, Eröffnung *f*; Beginn *m*; *Inauguration Day* Tag *m* der Amtseinführung des neu gewählten Präsidenten der USA

in·born angeboren

in·cal·cu·la·ble unberechenbar; unermesslich

in·can·des·cent (weiß) glühend

in·ca·pa·ble unfähig (**of** zu *inf or gen*), nicht imstande (**of doing** zu tun)

in·ca·pac·i·tate unfähig *or* untauglich machen

in·ca·pac·i·ty Unfähigkeit *f*, Untauglichkeit *f*

in·car·nate leibhaftig; personifiziert

in·cau·tious unvorsichtig

in·cen·di·a·ry Brand...; *fig* aufwiegelnd, aufhetzend

in·cense¹ REL Weihrauch *m*

in·cense² in Wut bringen, erbosen

in·cen·tive Ansporn *m*, Anreiz *m*

in·ces·sant ständig, unaufhörlich

in·cest Inzest *m*, Blutschande *f*

inch 1. Inch *m* (2,54 *cm*), Zoll *m* (*a. fig*); **by inches, inch by inch** allmählich; **every inch** durch und durch; **2.** (sich) zentimeterweise *or* sehr langsam bewegen

in·ci·dence Vorkommen *n*

in·ci·dent Vorfall *m*, Ereignis *n*; POL Zwischenfall *m*

in·ci·den·tal nebensächlich, Neben...; beiläufig

in·ci·den·tal·ly nebenbei bemerkt, übrigens

in·cin·e·rate verbrennen

in·cin·e·ra·tor TECH Verbrennungsofen *m*; Verbrennungsanlage *f*

in·cise einschneiden; aufschneiden; einritzen, einschnitzen

in·ci·sion (Ein)Schnitt *m*

in·ci·sive schneidend, scharf; *fig* treffend

in·ci·sor ANAT Schneidezahn *m*

in·cite anstiften; aufwiegeln, aufhetzen

in·cite·ment Anstiftung *f*; Aufhetzung *f*, Aufwieg(e)lung *f*

in·clem·ent rau

in·cli·na·tion Neigung *f* (*a. fig*)

in·cline 1. *v/i* sich neigen (**to, towards** nach); *fig* neigen (**to, towards** zu); *v/t* neigen; *fig* veranlassen; **2.** Gefälle *n*;

(Ab)Hang *m*

in·close, in·clos·ure → *enclose, enclosure*

in·clude einschließen, enthalten; aufnehmen (**in** in *e-e Liste etc*); *the group included several ...* zu der Gruppe gehörten einige ...; *tax included* inklusive Steuer

in·clud·ing einschließlich

in·clu·sion Einschluss *m*, Einbeziehung *f*

in·clu·sive einschließlich, inklusive (*of gen*); *be inclusive of* einschließen (*acc*)

in·co·her·ent unzusammenhängend, unklar, unverständlich

in·come ECON Einkommen *n*, Einkünfte *pl*

income tax ECON Einkommensteuer *f*

in·com·ing hereinkommend; ankommend; nachfolgend, neu; *incoming mail* Posteingang *m*

in·com·mu·ni·ca·tive verschlossen

in·com·pa·ra·ble unvergleichlich; unvergleichbar

in·com·pat·i·ble unvereinbar; unverträglich; inkompatibel

in·com·pe·tence Unfähigkeit *f*; Inkompetenz *f*

in·com·pe·tent unfähig; nicht fachkundig *or* sachkundig; unzuständig, inkompetent

in·com·plete unvollständig; unvollendet

in·com·pre·hen·si·ble unbegreiflich, unfassbar

in·com·pre·hen·sion Unverständnis *n*

in·con·cei·va·ble unbegreiflich, unfassbar; undenkbar

in·con·clu·sive nicht überzeugend; ergebnislos, erfolglos

in·con·gru·ous nicht übereinstimmend; unvereinbar

in·con·se·quen·tial unbedeutend

in·con·sid·e·ra·ble unbedeutend

in·con·sid·er·ate unüberlegt; rücksichtslos

in·con·sis·tent unvereinbar; widersprüchlich; inkonsequent

in·con·so·la·ble untröstlich

in·con·spic·u·ous unauffällig

in·con·stant unbeständig, wankelmütig

in·con·test·a·ble unanfechtbar

in·con·ti·nent MED inkontinent

in·con·ve·ni·ence 1. Unbequemlichkeit *f*; Unannehmlichkeit *f*, Ungelegenheit *f*; **2.** *j-m* lästig sein; *j-m* Umstände machen

in·con·ve·ni·ent unbequem; ungelegen, lästig

in·cor·po·rate (sich) vereinigen *or* zusammenschließen; (mit) einbeziehen; enthalten; eingliedern; *Ort* eingemeinden; ECON, JUR als Aktiengesellschaft eintragen (lassen)

in·cor·po·rat·ed com·pa·ny ECON Aktiengesellschaft *f*

in·cor·po·ra·tion Vereinigung *f*, Zusammenschluss *m*; Eingliederung *f*; Eingemeindung *f*; ECON, JUR Eintragung *f* als Aktiengesellschaft

in·cor·rect unrichtig, falsch; inkorrekt

in·cor·ri·gi·ble unverbesserlich

in·cor·rup·ti·ble unbestechlich

in·crease 1. zunehmen, (an)wachsen; steigen; vergrößern, vermehren, erhöhen; **2.** Vergrößerung *f*, Erhöhung *f*, Zunahme *f*, Zuwachs *m*, (An)Wachsen *n*, Steigerung *f*

in·creas·ing·ly immer mehr; *increasingly difficult* immer schwieriger

in·cred·i·ble unglaublich

in·cre·du·li·ty Ungläubigkeit *f*

in·cred·u·lous ungläubig, skeptisch

in·crim·i·nate *j-n* belasten

in·cu·bate ausbrüten

in·cu·ba·tor Brutapparat *m*; MED Brutkasten *m*

in·cur sich *et.* zuziehen, auf sich laden; *Schulden* machen; *Verluste* erleiden

in·cu·ra·ble unheilbar

in·cu·ri·ous nicht neugierig, gleichgültig, uninteressiert

in·cur·sion (feindlicher) Einfall; Eindringen *n*

in·debt·ed (zu Dank) verpflichtet; ECON verschuldet

in·de·cent unanständig, anstößig; JUR unsittlich, unzüchtig; *indecent assault* JUR Sittlichkeitsverbrechen *n*

in·de·ci·sion Unentschlossenheit *f*

in·de·ci·sive unentschlossen; unentschieden; unbestimmt, ungewiss

in·deed 1. *adv* in der Tat, tatsächlich, wirklich; allerdings; *thank you very much indeed!* vielen herzlichen Dank!; **2.** *int* ach wirklich?

in·de·fat·i·ga·ble unermüdlich

in·de·fen·si·ble unhaltbar

in·de·fi·na·ble undefinierbar, unbestimmbar

in·def·i·nite unbestimmt; unbegrenzt

in·def·i·nite·ly auf unbestimmte Zeit

in·del·i·ble unauslöschlich (*a. fig*); *indelible pencil* Tintenstift *m*

in·del·i·cate taktlos; unfein, anstößig

in·dem·ni·fy *j-n* entschädigen, *j-m* Schadenersatz leisten (*for* für)

in·dem·ni·ty Entschädigung *f*

in·dent (ein)kerben, auszacken; PRINT *Zeile* einrücken

in·de·pen·dence Unabhängigkeit *f*; Selbstständigkeit *f*; *Independence Day* Unabhängigkeitstag *m*

in·de·pen·dent unabhängig; selbstständig

in·de·scri·ba·ble unbeschreiblich

in·de·struc·ti·ble unzerstörbar; unverwüstlich

in·de·ter·mi·nate unbestimmt; unklar, vage

in·dex Index *m*, (Inhalts-, Namens-, Stichwort)Verzeichnis *n*, (Sach)Register *n*; (An)Zeichen *n*; *cost of living index* Lebenshaltungsindex *m*

in·dex card Karteikarte *f*

in·dex fin·ger ANAT Zeigefinger *m*

In·di·a Indien *n*

In·di·an 1. indisch; *neg!* indianisch, Indianer…; **2.** Inder(in); *American Indian* Indianer(in)

Indian corn BOT Mais *m*

Indian file: *in Indian file* im Gänsemarsch

Indian sum·mer Altweibersommer *m*, Nachsommer *m*

in·di·a rub·ber Gummi *n*, *m*; Radiergummi *m*

in·di·cate deuten *or* zeigen auf (*acc*); TECH anzeigen; MOT blinken; *fig* hinweisen *or* hindeuten auf (*acc*); andeuten

in·di·ca·tion (An)Zeichen *n*, Hinweis *m*, Andeutung *f*, Indiz *n*

in·dic·a·tive *a. indicative mood* LING Indikativ *m*

in·di·ca·tor TECH Anzeiger *m*; MOT Richtungsanzeiger *m*, Blinker *m*

in·dict JUR anklagen (*for* wegen)

in·dict·ment JUR Anklage *f*

in·dif·fer·ence Gleichgültigkeit *f*

in·dif·fer·ent gleichgültig (*to* gegen); mittelmäßig

in·di·gent arm

in·di·ges·ti·ble unverdaulich

in·di·ges·tion MED Verdauungsstörung *f*, Magenverstimmung *f*

in·dig·nant entrüstet, empört, ungehalten (*about, at, over* über *acc*)

in·dig·na·tion Entrüstung *f*, Empörung *f* (*about, at, over* über *acc*)

in·dig·ni·ty Demütigung *f*, unwürdige Behandlung

in·di·rect indirekt; *by indirect means fig* auf Umwegen

in·dis·creet unbesonnen, unbedacht; indiskret

in·dis·cre·tion Unbesonnenheit *f*; Indiskretion *f*

in·dis·crim·i·nate kritiklos; wahllos

in·di·spen·sa·ble unentbehrlich, unerlässlich

in·dis·posed indisponiert, unpässlich; abgeneigt

in·dis·po·si·tion Unpässlichkeit *f*; Abneigung *f* (*to do* zu tun)

in·dis·pu·ta·ble unbestreitbar, unstreitig

in·dis·tinct undeutlich; unklar, verschwommen

in·dis·tin·guish·a·ble nicht zu unterscheiden(d) (*from* von)

in·di·vid·u·al 1. individuell, einzeln, Einzel…; persönlich; **2.** Individuum *n*, Einzelne *m*, *f*

in·di·vid·u·al·ism Individualismus *m*

in·di·vid·u·al·ist Individualist(in)

in·di·vid·u·al·i·ty Individualität *f*, (persönliche) Note

in·di·vid·u·al·ly einzeln, jede(r, -s) für sich; individuell

in·di·vis·i·ble unteilbar

in·dom·i·ta·ble unbezähmbar, nicht unterzukriegen(d)

in·door Haus…, Zimmer…, Innen…, SPORT Hallen…

in·doors im Haus, drinnen; ins Haus (hinein); SPORT in der Halle

in·dorse → *endorse* etc

in·duce *j-n* veranlassen; verursachen, bewirken

in·duce·ment Anreiz *m*

in·duct einführen, -setzen

in·duc·tion Herbeiführung *f*; Einführung *f*, Einsetzung *f*; ELECTR Induktion *f*

in·dulge nachsichtig sein gegen; *e-r Neigung etc* nachgeben; *indulge in s.th.* sich et. gönnen *or* leisten

in·dul·gence Nachsicht *f*; Luxus *m*; REL Ablass *m*

in·dul·gent nachsichtig, nachgiebig

in·dus·tri·al industriell, Industrie…, Gewerbe…, Betriebs…

in·dus·tri·al ar·e·a Industriegebiet *n*

in·dus·tri·al·ist Industrielle *m*, *f*

in·dus·tri·al·ize industrialisieren

in·dus·tri·ous fleißig

in·dus·try Industrie(zweig *m*) *f*; Gewerbe(zweig *m*) *n*; Fleiß *m*

in·ed·i·ble ungenießbar, nicht essbar

in·ef·fec·tive, **in·ef·fec·tu·al** unwirksam, wirkungslos; unfähig, untauglich

in·ef·fi·cient ineffizient; unfähig, untauglich; unrationell, unwirtschaftlich

in·el·e·gant unelegant

in·el·i·gi·ble nicht berechtigt

in·ept unpassend; ungeschickt; albern, töricht

in·e·qual·i·ty Ungleichheit *f*

in·ert PHYS träge (*a. fig*); inaktiv

in·er·tia PHYS Trägheit *f* (*a. fig*)

in·es·cap·a·ble unvermeidlich

in·es·sen·tial unwesentlich, unwichtig (*to* für)

in·es·ti·ma·ble unschätzbar

in·ev·i·ta·ble unvermeidlich

in·ev·i·ta·bly zwangsläufig

in·ex·act ungenau

in·ex·cu·sa·ble unverzeihlich, unentschuldbar

in·ex·haus·ti·ble unerschöpflich; unermüdlich

in·ex·o·ra·ble unerbittlich

in·ex·pe·di·ent unzweckmäßig; nicht ratsam

in·ex·pen·sive billig, preiswert

in·ex·pe·ri·ence Unerfahrenheit *f*

in·ex·pe·ri·enced unerfahren

in·ex·pert unerfahren; ungeschickt

in·ex·plic·a·ble unerklärlich

in·ex·pres·si·ble unaussprechlich, unbeschreiblich

in·ex·pres·sive ausdruckslos

in·ex·tri·ca·ble unentwirrbar

in·fal·li·ble unfehlbar

in·fa·mous berüchtigt; schändlich, niederträchtig

in·fa·my Ehrlosigkeit *f*; Schande *f*; Niedertracht *f*

in·fan·cy frühe Kindheit; *be in its infancy fig* in den Kinderschuhen stecken

in·fant Säugling *m*; kleines Kind, Kleinkind *n*

in·fan·tile kindlich; Kindes..., Kinder...; infantil, kindisch

in·fan·try MIL Infanterie *f*

in·fat·u·at·ed vernarrt (*with* in *acc*)

in·fect MED *j-n*, *et.* infizieren, *j-n* anstecken (*a. fig*); verseuchen, verunreinigen

in·fec·tion MED Infektion *f*, Ansteckung *f* (*a. fig*)

in·fec·tious MED infektiös, ansteckend (*a. fig*)

in·fer folgern, schließen (*from* aus)

in·fer·ence (Schluss)Folgerung *f*, (Rück-)Schluss *m*

in·fe·ri·or 1. untergeordnet (*to dat*), niedriger (*to* als); weniger wert (*to* als); minderwertig; *be inferior to s.o.* j-m untergeordnet sein; j-m unterlegen sein; **2.** Untergebene *m*, *f*

in·fe·ri·or·i·ty Unterlegenheit *f*; Minderwertigkeit *f*

inferiority com·plex PSYCH Minderwertigkeitskomplex *m*

in·fer·nal höllisch, Höllen...

in·fer·no Inferno *n*, Hölle *f*

in·fer·tile unfruchtbar

in·fest verseuchen, befallen; *fig* überschwemmen (*with* mit)

in·fi·del·i·ty (*esp* eheliche) Untreue

in·fil·trate einsickern in (*acc*); einschleusen (*into* in *acc*); POL unterwandern

in·fi·nite unendlich

in·fin·i·tive *a.* **infinitive mood** LING Infinitiv *m*, Nennform *f*

in·fin·i·ty Unendlichkeit *f*

in·firm schwach, gebrechlich

in·fir·ma·ry Krankenhaus *n*; PED *etc* Krankenzimmer *n*

in·fir·mi·ty Schwäche *f*, Gebrechlichkeit *f*

in·flame entflammen (*mst fig*); erregen; *become inflamed* MED sich entzünden

in·flam·ma·ble brennbar, leicht entzündlich; feuergefährlich

in·flam·ma·tion MED Entzündung *f*

in·flam·ma·to·ry MED entzündlich; *fig* aufrührerisch, Hetz...

in·flate aufpumpen, aufblasen, aufblähen (*a. fig*); ECON *Preise etc* in die Höhe treiben

in·fla·tion ECON Inflation *f*

in·flect LING flektieren, beugen

in·flec·tion LING Flexion *f*, Beugung *f*

in·flex·i·ble unbiegsam, starr (*a. fig*); *fig* inflexibel, unbeweglich, unbeugsam

in·flex·ion *Br* → **inflection**

in·flict (*on*) *Leid*, *Schaden etc* zufügen (*dat*); *Wunde etc* beibringen (*dat*); *Strafe* auferlegen (*dat*), verhängen (*über acc*); aufbürden, aufdrängen (*dat*)

in·flic·tion Zufügung *f*; Verhängung *f*; Plage *f*

in·flu·ence 1. Einfluss *m*; **2.** beeinflussen

in·flu·en·tial einflussreich

in·flux Zustrom *m*, Zufluss *m*, (*Waren-*)Zufuhr *f*

in·form benachrichtigen, unterrichten (*of* von), informieren (*of* über *acc*); *inform against or on s.o.* j-n anzeigen; j-n denunzieren

in·for·mal formlos, zwanglos

in·for·mal·i·ty Formlosigkeit *f*; Ungezwungenheit *f*

in·for·ma·tion Auskunft *f*, Information *f*; Nachricht *f*

information (su·per·)highway EDP Datenautobahn *f*

in·for·ma·tive informativ; lehrreich; mitteilsam

in·form·er Denunziant(in); Spitzel *m*

in·fra·struc·ture Infrastruktur *f*

in·fre·quent selten

in·fringe: *infringe on Rechte, Vertrag etc* verletzen, verstoßen gegen

in·fu·ri·ate wütend machen

in·fuse *Tee* aufgießen

in·fu·sion Aufguss *m*; MED Infusion *f*

in·ge·ni·ous genial; einfallsreich; raffiniert

in·ge·nu·i·ty Genialität *f*; Einfallsreichtum *m*

in·gen·u·ous offen, aufrichtig; naiv

in·got (*Gold- etc*)Barren *m*

in·gra·ti·ate: *ingratiate o.s. with s.o.* sich bei j-m beliebt machen

in·grat·i·tude Undankbarkeit *f*

in·gre·di·ent Bestandteil *m*; GASTR Zutat *f*

in·hab·it bewohnen, leben in (*dat*)

in·hab·it·a·ble bewohnbar

in·hab·i·tant Bewohner(in); Einwohner(in)

in·hale einatmen, MED *a.* inhalieren

in·her·ent innewohnend, eigen (*in dat*)

in·her·it erben

in·her·i·tance Erbe *n*

in·hib·it hemmen (*a.* PSYCH), (ver)hindern

in·hib·it·ed PSYCH gehemmt

in·hi·bi·tion PSYCH Hemmung *f*

in·hos·pi·ta·ble ungastlich; unwirtlich (*region etc*)

in·hu·man unmenschlich

in·hu·mane inhuman, menschenunwürdig

in·im·i·cal feindselig (*to* gegen); nachteilig (*to* für)

in·im·i·ta·ble unnachahmlich

i·ni·tial 1. anfänglich, Anfangs...; **2.** Initiale *f*, (großer) Anfangsbuchstabe

i·ni·tial·ly am *or* zu Anfang, anfänglich

i·ni·ti·ate in die Wege leiten, ins Leben rufen; einführen

i·ni·ti·a·tion Einführung *f*

i·ni·tia·tive Initiative *f*, erster Schritt; *take the initiative* die Initiative ergreifen; *on one's own initiative* aus eigenem Antrieb

in·ject MED injizieren, einspritzen

in·jec·tion MED Injektion *f*, Spritze *f*

in·ju·di·cious unklug, unüberlegt

in·junc·tion JUR gerichtliche Verfügung

in·jure verletzen, verwunden; schaden (*dat*); kränken

in·jured 1. verletzt; **2.** *the injured* die Verletzten *pl*

in·ju·ri·ous schädlich; *be injurious to* schaden (*dat*); *injurious to health* gesundheitsschädlich

in·ju·ry MED Verletzung *f*; Kränkung *f*

injury time *Br esp soccer*: Nachspielzeit *f*

in·jus·tice Ungerechtigkeit *f*; Unrecht *n*; *do s.o. an injustice* j-m unrecht tun

ink Tinte *f*

ink·ling Andeutung *f*; dunkle *or* leise Ahnung

ink pad Stempelkissen *n*

ink·y Tinten...; tinten-, pechschwarz

in·laid eingelegt, Einlege...; *inlaid work* Einlegearbeit *f*

in·land 1. *adj* inländisch, einheimisch; ECON Binnen...; **2.** *adv* landeinwärts

In·land Rev·e·nue *Br* Finanzamt *n*

in·lay Einlegearbeit *f*; MED (Zahn)Füllung *f*, Plombe *f*

in·let GEOGR schmale Bucht; TECH Eingang *m*, Einlass *m*

in·line skate Inliner *m*, Inline Skate *m*

in·mate Insasse *m*, Insassin *f*; Mitbewohner(in)

in·most innerste(r, -s) (*a. fig*)

inn Gasthaus *n*, Wirtshaus *n*

in·nate angeboren

in·ner innere(r, -s); Innen...; verborgen

in·ner·most → *inmost*

in·nings *cricket, baseball*: Spielzeit *f*

inn·keep·er Gastwirt(in)

in·no·cence Unschuld *f*; Harmlosigkeit *f*; Naivität *f*

in·no·cent unschuldig; harmlos; arglos; naiv

in·noc·u·ous harmlos

in·no·va·tion Neuerung *f*

in·nu·en·do (versteckte) Andeutung *f*

in·nu·me·ra·ble unzählig, zahllos

i·noc·u·late MED impfen

i·noc·u·la·tion MED Impfung *f*

in·of·fen·sive harmlos

in·op·e·ra·ble MED inoperabel, nicht operierbar; undurchführbar (*plan etc*)

in·op·por·tune inopportun, unangebracht, ungelegen

in·or·di·nate unmäßig

in·pa·tient MED stationärer Patient, stationäre Patientin

in·put Input *m, n*, EDP *a.* (Daten)Eingabe *f*, ELECTR *a.* Eingangsleistung *f*

in·quest JUR gerichtliche Untersuchung

in·quire fragen *or* sich erkundigen (nach); *inquire into et.* untersuchen, prüfen

in·quir·ing forschend; wissbegierig

in·quir·y Erkundigung *f*, Nachfrage *f*; Untersuchung *f*; Ermittlung *f*; *make inquiries* Erkundigungen einziehen

in·qui·si·tion (amtliche) Untersuchung; Verhör *n*; *Inquisition* REL HIST Inquisition *f*

in·quis·i·tive neugierig, wissbegierig

in·roads (*in*[*to*], *on*) Eingriff *m* (in *acc*), Übergriff *m* (auf *acc*)

in·sane geisteskrank, wahnsinnig

in·san·i·ta·ry unhygienisch

in·san·i·ty Geisteskrankheit *f*, Wahnsinn *m*

in·sa·tia·ble unersättlich

in·scrip·tion Inschrift *f*, Aufschrift *f*; Widmung *f*

in·scru·ta·ble unerforschlich, unergründlich

in·sect zo Insekt *n*

in·sec·ti·cide Insektenvertilgungsmittel *n*, Insektizid *n*

in·se·cure unsicher; nicht sicher *or* fest

in·sen·si·ble unempfindlich (**to** gegen); bewusstlos; unempfänglich (**of, to** für), gleichgültig (**of, to** gegen); unmerklich

in·sen·si·tive unempfindlich (**to** gegen); unempfänglich (**of, to** für), gleichgültig (**of, to** gegen)

in·sep·a·ra·ble untrennbar; unzertrennlich

in·sert 1. einfügen, einsetzen, einführen, (hinein)stecken, *Münze* einwerfen; inserieren; **2.** (Zeitungs)Beilage *f*, (Buch)-Einlage *f*

in·ser·tion Einfügen *n*, Einsetzen *n*, Einführen *n*, Hineinstecken *n*; Einfügung *f*; Einwurf *m*; Anzeige *f*, Inserat *n*

in·sert key EDP Einfügetaste *f*

in·shore an *or* nahe der Küste; Küsten...

in·side 1. Innenseite *f*; *das* Innere; *turn inside out* umkrempeln; auf den Kopf stellen; **2.** *adj* innere(r, -s), Innen...; *Insider*...; **3.** *adv* im Inner(e)n, innen, drinnen; *inside of* F innerhalb (*gen*); **4.** *prp* innerhalb, im Inner(e)n

in·sid·er Insider(in), Eingeweihte *m, f*

in·sid·i·ous heimtückisch

in·sight Einsicht *f*, Einblick *m*; Verständnis *n*

in·sig·ni·a Insignien *pl*; Abzeichen *pl*

in·sig·nif·i·cant bedeutungslos; unbedeutend

in·sin·cere unaufrichtig

in·sin·u·ate andeuten, anspielen auf (*acc*); unterstellen; *insinuate that s.o. ...* j-m unterstellen, dass er ...

in·sin·u·a·tion Anspielung *f*, Andeutung *f*, Unterstellung *f*

in·sip·id geschmacklos, fad

in·sist bestehen, beharren (**on** auf *dat*)

in·sis·tence Bestehen *n*, Beharren *n*; Beharrlichkeit *f*

in·sis·tent beharrlich, hartnäckig

in·sole Einlegesohle *f*; Brandsohle *f*

in·so·lent unverschämt

in·sol·u·ble unlöslich (*substance etc*); unlösbar (*problem etc*)

in·sol·vent ECON zahlungsunfähig, insolvent

in·som·ni·a Schlaflosigkeit *f*

in·spect untersuchen, prüfen, nachsehen; besichtigen, inspizieren

in·spec·tion Prüfung *f*, Untersuchung *f*, Kontrolle *f*; Inspektion *f*

in·spec·tor Aufsichtsbeamte *m*, Inspektor *m*; (Polizei)Inspektor *m*, (Polizei)Kommissar *m*

in·spi·ra·tion Inspiration *f*, (plötzlicher) Einfall

in·spire inspirieren, anregen; *Gefühl etc* auslösen

in·stall TECH installieren, einrichten, aufstellen, einbauen, *Leitung* legen; *j-n in ein Amt etc* einsetzen

in·stal·la·tion TECH Installation *f*, Einrichtung *f*, Einbau *m*; TECH *fertige* Anlage *f*; *fig* Einsetzung *f*, Einführung *f*

in·stall·ment, in·stal·ment Br ECON Rate *f*; (Teil)Lieferung *f*; Fortsetzung *f*; *radio*, TV Folge *f*

in·stall·ment plan: *buy on the installment plan* ECON auf Abzahlung *or* Raten kaufen

in·stance Beispiel *n*; (besonderer) Fall; JUR Instanz *f*; *for instance* zum Beispiel

in·stant 1. Moment *m*, Augenblick *m*; **2.** sofortig, augenblicklich

in·stan·ta·ne·ous sofortig, augenblicklich; *death was instantaneous* der Tod trat sofort ein

in·stant cam·e·ra PHOT Sofortbildkamera *f*

instant cof·fee GASTR Pulver-, Instantkaffee *m*

in·stant·ly sofort, augenblicklich

in·stead stattdessen, dafür; *instead of* anstelle von, (an)statt

in·step ANAT Spann *m*, Rist *m*

in·sti·gate anstiften; aufhetzen; veranlassen

in·sti·ga·tor Anstifter(in); (Auf)Hetzer(in)

in·still Br, **in·stil** beibringen, einflößen (*into dat*)

in·stinct Instinkt *m*

in·stinc·tive instinktiv

in·sti·tute Institut *n*

in·sti·tu·tion Institution *f*, Einrichtung *f*; Institut *n*; Anstalt *f*

in·struct unterrichten, -weisen; ausbilden, schulen; informieren; anweisen

in·struc·tion Unterricht *m*; Ausbildung *f*, Schulung *f*, Unterweisung *f*; Anweisung *f*, Instruktion *f*; EDP Befehl *m*; *instructions for use* Gebrauchsanweisung *f*; *operating instructions* Bedienungsanleitung *f*

in·struc·tive instruktiv, lehrreich

in·struc·tor Lehrer *m*; Ausbilder *m*

in·struc·tress Lehrerin *f*; Ausbilderin *f*

in·stru·ment Instrument *n* (*a.* MUS); Werkzeug *n* (*a. fig*)

in·stru·men·tal MUS Instrumental...; behilflich; *be instrumental in* beitragen zu

in·sub·or·di·nate aufsässig

in·sub·or·di·na·tion Auflehnung *f*, Aufsässigkeit *f*

in·suf·fe·ra·ble unerträglich, unausstehlich

in·suf·fi·cient unzulänglich, ungenügend

in·su·lar Insel...; *fig* engstirnig

in·su·late isolieren

in·su·la·tion Isolierung *f*; Isoliermaterial *n*

in·sult 1. Beleidigung *f*; **2.** beleidigen

in·sur·ance Versicherung *f*; Versicherungssumme *f*; Absicherung *f* (*against* gegen)

insurance com·pa·ny Versicherungsgesellschaft *f*

insurance pol·i·cy Versicherungspolice *f*

in·sure versichern (*against* gegen)

in·sured: *the insured* der *or* die Versicherte

in·sur·gent 1. aufständisch; **2.** Aufständische *m*, *f*

in·sur·moun·ta·ble *fig* unüberwindlich

in·sur·rec·tion Aufstand *m*

in·tact intakt, unversehrt, unbeschädigt, ganz

in·take (*Nahrungs- etc*)Aufnahme *f*; (Neu)Aufnahme(n *pl*) *f*, (Neu)Zugänge *pl*; TECH Einlass(öffnung *f*) *m*

in·te·gral ganz, vollständig; wesentlich

in·te·grate (sich) integrieren; zusammenschließen; eingliedern, einbeziehen; *integrated circuit* ELECTR integrierter Schaltkreis

in·te·gra·tion Integration *f*

in·teg·ri·ty Integrität *f*; Vollständigkeit *f*; Einheit *f*

in·tel·lect Intellekt *m*, Verstand *m*

in·tel·lec·tual 1. intellektuell, Verstandes..., geistig; **2.** Intellektuelle *m*, *f*

in·tel·li·gence Intelligenz *f*; nachrichtendienstliche Informationen *pl*

in·tel·li·gent intelligent, klug

in·tel·li·gi·ble verständlich (*to* für)

in·tem·per·ate unmäßig

in·tend beabsichtigen, vorhaben, planen; *intended for* bestimmt für *or* zu

in·tense intensiv, stark, heftig

in·ten·si·fy intensivieren; (sich) verstärken

in·ten·si·ty Intensität *f*

in·ten·sive intensiv, gründlich

intensive care u·nit MED Intensivstation *f*

in·tent 1. gespannt, aufmerksam; *intent on* fest entschlossen zu (*dat*); konzentriert auf (*acc*); **2.** Absicht *f*, Vorhaben *n*

in·ten·tion Absicht *f*; JUR Vorsatz *m*

in·ten·tion·al absichtlich, vorsätzlich

in·ter bestatten

in·ter... zwischen, Zwischen...; gegenseitig, einander

in·ter·act aufeinander (ein)wirken, sich gegenseitig beeinflussen

in·ter·ac·tion Wechselwirkung *f*

in·ter·cede vermitteln, sich einsetzen (*with* bei; *for* für)

in·ter·cept abfangen

in·ter·ces·sion Fürsprache *f*

in·ter·change 1. austauschen; **2.** Austausch *m*; MOT Autobahnkreuz *n*

in·ter·com Sprechanlage *f*

in·ter·course Verkehr *m*; *a. sexual intercourse* (Geschlechts)Verkehr *m*

in·terest 1. Interesse *n* (*in* an *dat*, für); Wichtigkeit *f*, Bedeutung *f*; Vorteil *m*, Nutzen *m*; ECON Anteil *m*, Beteiligung *f*; ECON Zins(en *pl*) *m*; *take an interest in* sich interessieren für; **2.** interessieren (*in* für *et*)

in·terest·ed interessiert (*in* an *dat*); *be interested in* sich interessieren für

in·terest·ing interessant

in·terest rate ECON Zinssatz *m*

in·ter·face EDP Schnittstelle *f*

in·ter·fere sich einmischen (*with* in *acc*); stören

in·ter·fer·ence Einmischung *f*; Störung *f*

in·te·ri·or 1. innere(r, -s), Innen...; Binnen...; Inlands...; **2.** *das* Innere; Interieur *n*; POL innere Angelegenheiten *pl*; → *Department of the Interior*

interior dec·o·ra·tor Innenarchitekt(in)

in·ter·ject *Bemerkung* einwerfen

in·ter·jec·tion Einwurf *m*; Ausruf *m*; LING Interjektion *f*

in·ter·lace (sich) (ineinander) verflechten

in·ter·lop·er Eindringling *m*

in·ter·lude Zwischenspiel *n*; Pause *f*; *interludes of bright weather* zeitweilig schön

in·ter·me·di·a·ry Vermittler(in), Mittelsmann *m*

in·ter·me·di·ate in der Mitte liegend, Mittel..., Zwischen...; PED für fortgeschrittene Anfänger

in·ter·ment Beerdigung *f*, Bestattung *f*

in·ter·mi·na·ble endlos

in·ter·mis·sion Unterbrechung *f*; THEA *etc* Pause *f*

in·ter·mit·tent mit Unterbrechungen, periodisch (auftretend); *intermittent fever* MED Wechselfieber *n*

in·tern[1] internieren

in·tern[2] Assistenzarzt *m*, -ärztin *f*

in·ter·nal innere(r, -s); einheimisch, Inlands...

in·ter·nal-com·bus·tion en·gine Verbrennungsmotor *m*

in·ter·na·tion·al 1. international; Auslands...; **2.** SPORT Internationale *m*, *f*, Nationalspieler(in); internationaler Wettkampf; Länderspiel *n*

international call TEL Auslandsgespräch *n*

international law JUR Völkerrecht *n*

In·ter·net Internet *n*

in·tern·ist MED Internist *m*

in·ter·per·son·al zwischenmenschlich

in·ter·pret interpretieren, auslegen, erklären; dolmetschen

in·ter·pre·ta·tion Interpretation *f*, Auslegung *f*

in·ter·pret·er Dolmetscher(in)

in·ter·ro·gate verhören, vernehmen; (be)fragen

in·ter·ro·ga·tion Verhör *n*, Vernehmung *f*; Frage *f*

in·ter·rog·a·tive LING Interrogativ..., Frage...

in·ter·rupt unterbrechen

in·ter·rup·tion Unterbrechung *f*

in·ter·sect (durch)schneiden; sich schneiden *or* kreuzen

in·ter·sec·tion Schnittpunkt *m*; (Straßen)Kreuzung *f*

in·ter·sperse einstreuen, hier und da einfügen

in·ter·state 1. zwischenstaatlich; 2. *a.* **interstate highway** Autobahn *f*

in·ter·twine (sich ineinander) verschlingen, sich verflechten

in·ter·val Intervall *n* (*a.* MUS), Abstand *m*; *Br* Pause *f* (*a.* THEA *etc*); **at regular intervals** in regelmäßigen Abständen

in·ter·vene eingreifen, einschreiten, intervenieren; dazwischenkommen

in·ter·ven·tion Eingreifen *n*, Einschreiten *n*, Intervention *f*

in·ter·view 1. Interview *n*; Einstellungsgespräch *n*; 2. interviewen; ein Einstellungsgespräch führen mit

in·ter·view·ee Interviewte *m*, *f*

in·ter·view·er Interviewer(in)

in·ter·weave (miteinander) verweben

in·tes·tate: **die intestate** JUR ohne Hinterlassung e-s Testaments sterben

in·tes·tine ANAT Darm *m*; *pl* Eingeweide *pl*; **large intestine** Dickdarm *m*; **small intestine** Dünndarm *m*

in·ti·ma·cy Intimität *f*, Vertrautheit *f*; (*a. plumpe*) Vertraulichkeit; intime (*sexuelle*) Beziehungen *pl*

in·ti·mate 1. intim (*a. sexually*); vertraut, eng (*friends etc*); (*a. plump*)vertraulich; innerste(r, -s); gründlich, genau (*knowledge etc*); 2. Vertraute *m*, *f*

in·tim·i·date einschüchtern

in·tim·i·da·tion Einschüchterung *f*

in·to in (*acc*), in (*acc*) ... hinein; gegen

(*acc*); MATH in (*acc*); **4 into 20 goes five times** 4 geht fünfmal in 20

in·tol·e·ra·ble unerträglich

in·tol·e·rance Intoleranz *f*, Unduldsamkeit (*of* gegen)

in·tol·e·rant intolerant, unduldsam (*of* gegen)

in·to·na·tion MUS Intonation *f*, LING *a.* Tonfall *m*

in·tox·i·cat·ed berauscht, betrunken

in·tox·i·ca·tion Rausch *m* (*a. fig*)

in·trac·ta·ble eigensinnig; schwer zu handhaben(d)

in·tran·si·tive LING intransitiv

in·tra·ve·nous MED intravenös

in tray: **in the in tray** im Posteingang *etc*

in·trep·id unerschrocken

in·tri·cate verwickelt, kompliziert

in·trigue 1. Intrige *f*; 2. faszinieren, interessieren; intrigieren

in·tro·duce vorstellen (**to** *dat*), *j-n* bekannt machen (**to** mit); einführen

in·tro·duc·tion Vorstellung *f*; Einführung *f*; Einleitung *f*, Vorwort *n*; **letter of introduction** Empfehlungsschreiben *n*

in·tro·duc·to·ry Einführungs...; einleitend, Einleitungs...

in·tro·spec·tion Selbstbeobachtung *f*

in·tro·vert PSYCH introvertierter Mensch

in·tro·vert·ed PSYCH introvertiert, in sich gekehrt

in·trude (sich) aufdrängen; stören; **am I intruding?** störe ich?

in·trud·er Eindringling *m*, Störenfried *m*

in·tru·sion Störung *f*

in·tru·sive aufdringlich

in·tu·i·tion Intuition *f*

in·tu·i·tive intuitiv

In·u·it *a.* **Innuit** Inuit *m*, Eskimo *m*

in·un·date überschwemmen, überfluten (*a. fig*)

in·vade eindringen in (*acc*), einfallen in (*acc*), MIL *a.* einmarschieren in (*acc*); *fig* überlaufen, überschwemmen

in·vad·er Eindringling *m*

in·val·id¹ 1. krank; invalid(e); 2. Kranke *m*; *f*; Invalide *m*, *f*

in·val·id² (rechts)ungültig

in·val·i·date JUR für ungültig erkären

in·val·u·a·ble *fig* unschätzbar, unbezahlbar

in·var·i·a·ble unveränderlich

in·var·i·a·bly ausnahmslos

in·va·sion Invasion *f* (*a.* MIL), Einfall *m*, MIL *a.* Einmarsch *m*; *fig* Eingriff *m*, Verletzung *f*

in·vec·tive Schmähung(en *pl*) *f*, Beschimpfung(en *pl*) *f*

in·vent erfinden

in·ven·tion Erfindung *f*

in·ven·tive erfinderisch; einfallsreich

in·ven·tor Erfinder(in)

in·ven·tory Inventar *n*, Bestand *m*; Bestandsliste *f*; Inventur *f*

in·verse 1. umgekehrt; **2.** Umkehrung *f*, Gegenteil *n*

in·ver·sion Umkehrung *f*; LING Inversion *f*

in·vert umkehren

in·ver·te·brate ZO **1.** wirbellos; **2.** wirbelloses Tier

in·vert·ed com·mas LING Anführungszeichen *pl*

in·vest ECON investieren, anlegen

in·ves·ti·gate untersuchen; überprüfen; Untersuchungen *or* Ermittlungen anstellen (*into* über *acc*), nachforschen

in·ves·ti·ga·tion Untersuchung *f*; Ermittlung *f*, Nachforschung *f*

in·ves·ti·ga·tor: *private investigator* Privatdetektiv *m*

in·vest·ment ECON Investition *f*, (Kapital)Anlage *f*

in·ves·tor ECON Anleger *m*

in·vet·e·rate unverbesserlich; hartnäckig

in·vid·i·ous gehässig, boshaft, gemein

in·vig·o·rate stärken, beleben

in·vin·ci·ble unbesiegbar; unüberwindlich

in·vi·o·la·ble unantastbar

in·vis·i·ble unsichtbar

in·vi·ta·tion Einladung *f*; Aufforderung *f*

in·vite einladen; auffordern; *Gefahr etc* herausfordern; *invite s.o. in* j-n hereinbitten

in·vit·ing einladend, verlockend

in·voice ECON **1.** (Waren)Rechnung *f*; **2.** in Rechnung stellen, berechnen

in·voke flehen um; *Gott etc* anrufen; beschwören

in·vol·un·ta·ry unfreiwillig; unabsichtlich; unwillkürlich

in·volve verwickeln, hineinziehen (*in* *acc*); *j-n, et.* angehen, betreffen; zur Folge haben, mit sich bringen

in·volved kompliziert, verworren

in·volve·ment Verwicklung *f*; Beteiligung *f*

in·vul·ne·ra·ble unverwundbar; *fig* unanfechtbar

in·ward 1. *adj* innere(r, -s), innerlich; **2.** *adv mst* **inwards** einwärts, nach innen

i·o·dine CHEM Jod *n*

i·on PHYS Ion *n*

IOU (= *I owe you*) Schuldschein *m*

IQ ABBR *of* **intelligence quotient** IQ, Intelligenzquotient *m*

I·ran Iran *m*

I·ra·ni·an 1. iranisch; **2.** Iraner(in); LING Iranisch *n*

I·raq Irak *m*

I·ra·qi 1. irakisch; **2.** Iraker(in); LING Irakisch *n*

i·ras·ci·ble jähzornig

i·rate zornig, wütend

Ire·land Irland *n*

ir·i·des·cent schillernd

i·ris ANAT Regenbogenhaut *f*, Iris *f*; BOT Schwertlilie *f*, Iris *f*

I·rish 1. irisch; **2.** LING Irisch *n*; *the Irish* die Iren *pl*

I·rish·man Ire *m*

I·rish·wom·an Irin *f*

i·ron 1. Eisen *n*; Bügeleisen *n*; *strike while the iron is hot fig* das Eisen schmieden, solange es heiß ist; **2.** eisern (*a. fig*), Eisen..., aus Eisen; **3.** bügeln; *iron out* ausbügeln

I·ron Cur·tain POL HIST Eiserner Vorhang

i·ron·ic, **i·ron·i·cal** ironisch, spöttisch

i·ron·ing board Bügelbrett *n*

i·ron·mon·ger *Br* Eisenwarenhändler *m*

i·ron·works TECH Eisenhütte *f*

i·ron·y Ironie *f*

ir·ra·tion·al irrational, unvernünftig

ir·rec·on·ci·la·ble unversöhnlich; unvereinbar

ir·re·cov·e·ra·ble unersetzlich; unwiederbringlich

ir·re·fut·a·ble unwiderlegbar

ir·reg·u·lar unregelmäßig; ungleichmäßig; regelwidrig, vorschriftswidrig

ir·rel·e·vant irrelevant, unerheblich, belanglos (*to* für)

ir·rep·a·ra·ble irreparabel, nicht wieder gutzumachen(d)

ir·re·place·a·ble unersetzlich

ir·re·pres·si·ble nicht zu unterdrücken(d); unbezähmbar

ir·re·proach·a·ble einwandfrei, untadelig

ir·re·sist·i·ble unwiderstehlich

ir·res·o·lute unentschlossen

ir·re·spec·tive: *irrespective of* ohne Rücksicht auf (*acc*); unabhängig von

ir·re·spon·si·ble unverantwortlich; verantwortungslos

ir·re·trie·va·ble unwiederbringlich, unersetzlich

ir·rev·e·rent respektlos

ir·rev·o·ca·ble unwiderruflich, endgültig

ir·ri·gate bewässern

ir·ri·ga·tion Bewässerung *f*

ir·ri·ta·ble reizbar

ir·ri·tant Reizmittel *n*

ir·ri·tate reizen; (ver)ärgern

ir·ri·tat·ing ärgerlich

ir·ri·ta·tion Reizung *f*; Verärgerung *f*; Ärger *m* (**at** über *acc*)

is er, sie, es ist

Is·lam der Islam

is·land Insel *f*; *a.* **traffic island** Verkehrsinsel *f*

is·land·er Inselbewohner(in)

isle POET Insel *f*

i·so·late absondern; isolieren

i·so·lat·ed isoliert, abgeschieden; einzeln; **become isolated** vereinsamen

i·so·la·tion Isolierung *f*, Absonderung *f*

isolation ward MED Isolierstation *f*

Is·rael Israel *n*

Is·rae·li 1. israelisch; **2.** Israeli *m*, *f*

is·sue 1. Streitfrage *f*, Streitpunkt *m*; Ausgabe *f*; Erscheinen *n*; JUR Nachkommen(schaft *f*) *pl*; *fig* Ausgang *m*, Ergebnis *n*; **be at issue** zur Debatte stehen; **point at issue** strittiger Punkt; **die without issue** kinderlos sterben; **2.** *v/t* Zeitung etc herausgeben; *Banknoten etc* ausgeben; *Dokument etc* ausstellen; *v/i* herauskommen, hervorkommen; herausfließen, herausströmen

it es; *s.th. previously mentioned*: es, er, ihn,

sie

I·tal·i·an 1. italienisch; **2.** Italiener(in); LING Italienisch *n*

i·tal·ics PRINT Kursivschrift *f*

It·a·ly Italien *n*

itch 1. Jucken *n*, Juckreiz *m*; **2.** jucken, kratzen; **I itch all over** es juckt mich überall; **be itching for s.th.** F et. unbedingt (haben) wollen; **be itching to** *inf* F darauf brennen zu *inf*

itch·y juckend; kratzend

i·tem Punkt *m* (*on the agenda etc*), Posten *m* (*on a list*); Artikel *m*, Gegenstand *m*; (*Presse-, Zeitungs*)Notiz *f*, (*a. radio*, TV) Nachricht *f*, Meldung *f*

i·tem·ize einzeln angeben *or* aufführen

i·tin·e·ra·ry Reiseweg *m*, Reiseroute *f*; Reiseplan *m*

its sein(e), ihr(e)

it·self sich; sich selbst; selbst; **by itself** (für sich) allein; von selbst; **in itself** an sich

i·vo·ry Elfenbein *n*

i·vy BOT Efeu *m*

J

J, j J, j *n*

jab 1. (hinein)stechen, (hinein)stoßen; **2.** Stich *m*, Stoß *m*

jab·ber F (daher)plappern

jack 1. TECH Hebevorrichtung *f*; MOT Wagenheber *m*; *cards*: Bube *m*; **2.** **jack up** *Auto* aufbocken

jack·al ZO Schakal *m*

jack·ass ZO Esel *m* (*a. fig*)

jack·daw ZO Dohle *f*

jack·et Jacke *f*, Jackett *n*; TECH Mantel *m*; (Schutz)Umschlag *m*; (*Platten-*)Hülle *f*; **jacket potatoes, potatoes (boiled) in their jackets** Pellkartoffeln *pl*

jack knife 1. Klappmesser *n*; **2.** zusammenklappen, -knicken

jack-of-all-trades Hansdampf *m* in allen Gassen

jack·pot Jackpot *m*, Haupttreffer *m*; **hit the jackpot** F den Jackpot gewinnen; *fig* das große Los ziehen

jade MIN Jade *m*, *f*; Jadegrün *n*

jag Zacken *m*

jag·ged gezackt, zackig; schartig

jag·u·ar ZO Jaguar *m*

jail 1. Gefängnis *n*; **2.** einsperren

jail·bird F Knastbruder *m*

jail·er Gefängnisaufseher *m*

jail·house Gefängnis *n*

jam[1] Konfitüre *f*, Marmelade *f*

jam[2] **1.** *v/t* (hinein)pressen, (hinein-) quetschen, (hinein)zwängen, *Menschen a.* (hinein)pferchen; (ein)klemmen, (ein)quetschen; *a.* **jam up** blockieren, verstopfen; *Funkempfang* stören; **jam on the brakes** MOT voll auf die Bremse treten; *v/i* sich (hinein)drängen *or* (hinein-) quetschen; *brake*: blockieren; **2.** Gedränge *n*; TECH Blockierung *f*; Stauung *f*, Stockung *f*; **traffic jam** Verkehrsstau *m*; **be in a jam** F in der Klemme stecken

jamb (Tür-, Fenster)Pfosten *m*

jam·bo·ree Jamboree *n*, Pfadfindertreffen *n*; Fest *n*

Jan ABBR *of* **January** Jan., Januar *m*

jan·gle klimpern *or* klirren (mit)

jan·i·tor Hausmeister *m*

Jan·u·a·ry (ABBR *of* **Jan**) Januar *m*
Ja·pan Japan *n*
Jap·a·nese 1. japanisch; **2.** Japaner(in);
LING Japanisch *n*; *the Japanese* die Japaner *pl*
jar[1] **1.** Gefäß *n*, Krug *m*; (Marmelade- *etc*)-
Glas *n*
jar[2]: *jar on* wehtun (*dat*)
jar·gon Jargon *m*, Fachsprache *f*
jaun·dice MED Gelbsucht *f*
jaunt 1. Ausflug *m*, MOT Spritztour *f*; **2.** e-n
Ausflug *or* e-e Spritztour machen
jaun·ty unbeschwert, unbekümmert; flott
jav·e·lin SPORT Speer *m*; *javelin* (*throw*),
throwing the javelin SPORT Speerwerfen
n
jav·e·lin throw·er SPORT Speerwerfer(in)
jaw ANAT Kiefer *m*; *pl* ZO Rachen *m*, Maul
n; TECH Backen *pl*; *lower jaw* ANAT Unterkiefer *m*; *upper jaw* ANAT Oberkiefer
jaw·bone ANAT Kieferknochen *m*
jay ZO Eichelhäher *m*
jay·walk·er unachtsamer Fußgänger
jazz MUS Jazz *m*
jazz·y F poppig
jeal·ous eifersüchtig (*of* auf acc); neidisch
jeal·ous·y Eifersucht *f*; Neid *m*
jeans Jeans *pl*
jeer 1. (*at*) höhnische Bemerkung(en) machen (über *acc*); höhnisch lachen (über
acc); *jeer* (*at*) verhöhnen; **2.** höhnische
Bemerkung; Hohngelächter *n*
jel·lied GASTR in Aspik, in Sülze
jel·ly Gallert(e *f*) *n*; GASTR Gelee *n*; Aspik
m, *n*, Sülze *f*; Götterspeise *f*
jelly ba·by *Br* Gummibärchen *n*
jelly bean Gummi-, Geleebonbon *m*, *n*
jel·ly·fish ZO Qualle *f*
jeop·ar·dize gefährden
jerk 1. ruckartig ziehen an (*dat*); (zusammen)zucken; sich ruckartig bewegen; **2.**
(plötzlicher) Ruck; Sprung *m*, Satz *m*;
MED Zuckung *f*
jerk·y ruckartig; holprig; rüttelnd
jer·sey Pullover *m*
jest 1. Scherz *m*, Spaß *m*; **2.** scherzen, spaßen
jest·er HIST (Hof)Narr *m*
jet 1. (Wasser-, Gas- *etc*)Strahl *m*; TECH
Düse *f*; AVIAT Jet *m*; **2.** (heraus-, hervor)-
schießen (*from* aus); AVIAT F jetten
jet en·gine AVIAT Düsen-, Strahltriebwerk
n
jet plane AVIAT Düsenflugzeug *n*, Jet *m*
jet-pro·pelled AVIAT mit Düsenantrieb,
Düsen...
jet pro·pul·sion AVIAT Düsen-, Strahlantrieb *m*
jet·ty MAR (Hafen)Mole *f*

Jew Jude *m*, Jüdin *f*
jew·el Juwel *n*, *m*, Edelstein *m*
jew·el·er, *Br* **jew·el·ler** Juwelier *m*
jew·el·lery *Br*, **jew·el·ry** Juwelen *pl*;
Schmuck *m*
Jew·ess Jüdin *f*
Jew·ish jüdisch
jif·fy: F *in a jiffy* im Nu, sofort
jig·saw Laubsäge *f*; → **jig·saw puz·zle**
Puzzle(spiel) *n*
jilt *Mädchen* sitzen lassen; *e-m Liebhaber*
den Laufpass geben
jin·gle 1. klimpern (mit), bimmeln (lassen; **2.** Klimpern *n*, Bimmeln *n*; Werbesong *m*, Werbespruch *m*
jit·ters: F *the jitters* Bammel *m*, e-e Heidenangst
jit·ter·y F nervös; ängstlich
job 1. (*einzelne*) Arbeit; Beruf *m*, Beschäftigung *f*, Stellung *f*, Stelle *f*, Arbeit
f, Job *m* (*a*. EDP); Arbeitsplatz *m*; Aufgabe *f*, Sache *f*, Angelegenheit *f*; *a*. *job
work* Akkordarbeit *f*; *by the job* im Akkord; *out of a job* arbeitslos; **2.** *job
around* jobben
job ad, **job ad·ver·tisement** Stellenanzeige *f*
job·ber *Br* ECON Börsenspekulant *m*
job cen·tre *Br* Arbeitsamt *n*
job hop·ping häufiger Arbeitsplatzwechsel
job·hunt·ing Arbeitssuche *f*; *be jobhunting* auf Arbeitssuche sein
job·less arbeitslos
jock·ey Jockei *m*
jog 1. stoßen an (*acc*) *or* gegen, j-n anstoßen; *mst jog along*, *jog on* dahintrotten,
dahinzuckeln; SPORT joggen; **2.** (leichter)
Stoß, Stups *m*; Trott *m*; SPORT Trimmtrab
m
jog·ger SPORT Jogger(in)
jog·ging SPORT Joggen *n*, Jogging *n*
join 1. *v/t* verbinden, vereinigen, zusammenfügen; sich anschließen (*dat or* an
acc), sich gesellen zu; eintreten in (*acc*),
beitreten; teilnehmen *or* sich beteiligen
an (*dat*), mitmachen bei; *join in* einstimmen in; *v/i* sich vereinigen *or* verbinden;
join in teilnehmen *or* sich beteiligen (an
dat), mitmachen (bei); **2.** Verbindungsstelle *f*, Naht *f*
join·er Tischler *m*, Schreiner *m*
joint 1. Verbindungs-, Nahtstelle *f*; ANAT,
TECH Gelenk *n*; BOT Knoten *m*; *Br* GASTR
Braten *m*; F Laden *m*; Bude *f*, Spelunke
f; *sl* Joint *m*; *out of joint* MED ausgerenkt;
fig aus den Fugen; **2.** gemeinsam, gemeinschaftlich; Mit...
joint·ed gegliedert; Glieder...

J

joint-stock com·pa·ny *Br* ECON Kapital-
or Aktiengesellschaft *f*

joint ven·ture ECON Gemeinschaftsunter-
nehmen *n*

joke Witz *m*; Scherz *m*, Spaß *m*; **practical joke** Streich *m*; **play a joke on s.o.**
j-m e-n Streich spielen; **2.** scherzen, Witze machen

jok·er Spaßvogel *m*, Witzbold *m*; *cards*:
Joker *m*

jol·ly 1. *adj* lustig, fröhlich, vergnügt; **2.**
adv Br F ganz schön; **jolly good** prima

jolt 1. e-n Ruck *or* Stoß geben; durchrütteln, durchschütteln; rütteln, holpern
(*vehicle*); *fig* aufrütteln; **2.** Ruck *m*, Stoß
m; *fig* Schock *m*

joss stick Räucherstäbchen *n*

jos·tle (an)rempeln; dränge(l)n

jot 1. *not a jot* keine Spur; **2.** *jot down* sich
schnell *et.* notieren

joule PHYS Joule *n*

jour·nal Journal *n*; (Fach)Zeitschrift *f*;
Tagebuch *n*

jour·nal·ism Journalismus *m*

jour·nal·ist Journalist(in)

jour·ney 1. Reise *f*; **2.** reisen

jour·ney·man Geselle *m*

joy Freude *f*; **for joy** vor Freude

joy·ful freudig; erfreut

joy·less freudlos, traurig

joy·stick AVIAT Steuerknüppel *m*; EDP Joy-
stick *m*

jub·i·lant jubelnd, überglücklich

ju·bi·lee Jubiläum *n*

judge 1. JUR Richter(in); SPORT Kampf-,
Schieds-, Preisrichter(in); *fig* Kenner(in);
2. JUR *Fall* verhandeln; urteilen, ein Urteil fällen; beurteilen, einschätzen

judg·ment JUR Urteil *n*; Urteilsvermögen
n; Meinung *f*, Ansicht *f*; göttliches
(Straf)Gericht; **the Last Judgment** REL
das Jüngste Gericht

Judgment Day, *a.* **Day of Judgment** REL
Tag *m* des Jüngsten Gerichts, Jüngster
Tag

ju·di·cial JUR gerichtlich, Justiz...; richterlich

ju·di·cia·ry JUR Richter *pl*

ju·di·cious klug, weise

ju·do SPORT Judo *n*

jug Krug *m*; Kanne *f*, Kännchen *n*

jug·gle jonglieren (mit); ECON *Bücher etc*
frisieren

jug·gler Jongleur *m*

juice Saft *m*; MOT F Sprit *m*

juic·y saftig; F pikant (*story etc*); F gepfeffert (*price etc*)

juke·box Musikbox *f*, Musikautomat *m*

Jul ABBR *of* **July** Juli *m*

Ju·ly (ABBR *Jul*) Juli *m*

jum·ble 1. *a.* **jumble together, jumble up**
durcheinanderbringen *or* durcheinan-
derwerfen; **2.** Durcheinander *n*

jumble sale *Br* Wohltätigkeitsbasar *m*

jum·bo 1. riesig, Riesen...; **2.** AVIAT F Jumbo *m*

jumbo jet AVIAT Jumbo-Jet *m*

jum·bo-sized riesig

jump 1. *v/i* springen; hüpfen; zusammenzucken, -fahren, hochfahren (**at** bei);
jump at the chance mit beiden Händen
zugreifen; **jump to conclusions** voreili-
ge Schlüsse ziehen; *v/t* (hinweg)springen
über (*acc*); überspringen; **jump the
queue** *Br* sich vordränge(l)n; **jump the
lights** bei Rot über die Kreuzung fahren;
2. Sprung *m*

jump·er¹ SPORT (*Hoch- etc*)Springer(in)

jump·er² Trägerrock *m*, Trägerkleid *n*; *Br*
Pullover *m*

jump·ing jack Hampelmann *m*

jump·y nervös

Jun ABBR *of* **June** Juni *m*

junc·tion (Straßen)Kreuzung *f*; RAIL Knotenpunkt *m*

junc·ture: **at this juncture** zu diesem
Zeitpunkt

June (ABBR *Jun*) Juni *m*

jun·gle Dschungel *m*

ju·ni·or 1. junior; jüngere(r, -s); untergeordnet; SPORT Junioren..., Jugend...; **2.**
Jüngere *m*, *f*

junior school *Br* Grundschule *f* (*for
children aged 7 to 11*)

junk¹ MAR Dschunke *f*

junk² F Trödel *m*; Schrott *m*; Abfall *m*; *sl*
Stoff *m*

junk food F Junk-Food *n*

junk·ie, junk·y *sl* Junkie *m*, Fixer(in)

junk·yard Schuttabladeplatz *m*; Schrottplatz *m*; **auto junkyard** Autofriedhof *m*

jur·is·dic·tion JUR Gerichtsbarkeit *f*; Zu-
ständigkeit(sbereich *m*) *f*

ju·ris·pru·dence Rechtswissenschaft *f*

ju·ror JUR Geschworene *m*, *f*

ju·ry JUR *die* Geschworenen *pl*; SPORT *etc*
Jury *f*, Preisrichter *pl*

ju·ry·man JUR Geschworene *m*

ju·ry·wom·an JUR Geschworene *f*

just 1. *adj* gerecht; berechtigt; angemessen; **2.** *adv* gerade, (so)eben; genau,
eben; gerade (noch), ganz knapp; nur,
bloß; **just about** ungefähr, etwa; **just like
that** einfach so; **just now** gerade (jetzt),
(so)eben

jus·tice Gerechtigkeit *f*; JUR Richter *m*;
Justice of the Peace Friedensrichter
m; **court of justice** Gericht *n*, Gerichts-

J

hof *m*
jus·ti·fi·ca·tion Rechtfertigung *f*
jus·ti·fy rechtfertigen
just·ly mit *or* zu Recht
jut: *jut out* vorspringen, herausragen
ju·ve·nile 1. jugendlich; Jugend...; 2. Ju-

gendliche *m*, *f*
juvenile court JUR Jugendgericht *n*
juvenile de·lin·quen·cy JUR Jugendkri-
minalität *f*
juvenile de·lin·quent JUR straffälliger Jugendlicher, jugendlicher Straftäter

K

K, k K, k *n*
kan·ga·roo ZO Känguru *n*
ka·ra·te SPORT Karate *n*
keel MAR 1. Kiel *m*; 2. *keel over* umschlagen, kentern
keen scharf (*a. fig*); schneidend (*cold*);
heftig, stark; lebhaft (*interest*); groß (*appetite etc*); begeistert, leidenschaftlich;
keen on versessen *or* scharf auf (*acc*)
keep 1. *v/t* (auf-, fest-, zurück)halten;
(bei)behalten, bewahren; *Gesetze etc*
einhalten, befolgen; *Ware* führen; *Geheimnis* für sich behalten; *Versprechen*,
Wort halten; ECON *Buch* führen; aufheben, aufbewahren; abhalten, hindern
(*from* von); *Tiere* halten; *Bett* hüten; ernähren, erhalten, unterhalten; *keep early hours* früh zu Bett gehen; *keep one's
head* die Ruhe bewahren; *keep one's
temper* sich beherrschen; *keep s.o.
company* j-m Gesellschaft leisten; *keep
s.th. from s.o.* j-m et. vorenthalten *or*
verschweigen *or* verheimlichen; *keep
time* richtig gehen (*watch*); MUS Takt halten; *v/i* bleiben; sich halten; *keep going*
weitergehen; *keep smiling* immer nur
lächeln!; *keep (on) talking* weiterspre-
chen

keep (on) trying es weiterversuchen, es
immer wieder versuchen; *keep s.o.
waiting* j-n warten lassen; *keep away*
(sich) fernhalten (*from* von); *keep back*
zurückhalten (*a. fig*); *keep from doing
s.th.* et. nicht tun; *keep in Schüler(in)*
nachsitzen lassen; *keep off* (sich) fern
halten; *keep off!* Betreten verboten!;
keep on Kleidungsstück anbehalten, anlassen, *Hut* aufbehalten; *Licht* brennen
lassen; *keep on doing* fortfahren zu
tun; *keep out* nicht hinein- *or* hereinlas-
sen; *keep out!* Zutritt verboten!; *keep to*
sich halten an (*acc*); *keep up fig* aufrechterhalten; *Mut* nicht sinken lassen;

fortfahren mit, weitermachen; *keep
s.o. up* j-n nicht schlafen lassen; *keep
it up* so weitermachen; *keep up with*
Schritt halten mit; *keep up with the
Joneses* nicht hinter den Nachbarn zurückstehen (wollen); 1. (Lebens)Unter-
halt *m*; *for keeps* F für immer
keep·er Wärter(in), Wächter(in), Aufse-
her(in); *mst in cpds*: Inhaber(in), Besit-
zer(in)
keep·ing Verwahrung *f*; Obhut *f*; *be in
(out of) keeping with ...* (nicht) übereinstimmen mit ...
keep·sake Andenken *n*
keg Fässchen *n*, kleines Fass
ken·nel Hundehütte *f*; *kennels* Hunde-
zwinger *m*; Hundepension *f*
kerb *Br* → *curb*
ker·chief (Hals-, Kopf)Tuch *n*
ker·nel BOT Kern *m* (*a. fig*)
ker·o·sene Petroleum *n*
ket·tle Kessel *m*
ket·tle·drum MUS (Kessel)Pauke *f*
key 1. Schlüssel *m* (*a. fig*); (*Schreibmaschi-
nen-, Klavier- etc*)Taste *f*; MUS Tonart *f*; 2.
Schlüssel...; 3. anpassen (*to* an *acc*); *key
in* EDP *Daten* eingeben; *keyed up* nervös,
aufgeregt, überdreht
key·board Tastatur *f*
key·hole Schlüsselloch *n*
key·note MUS Grundton *m*; *fig* Grundgedanke *m*, Tenor *m*
key ring Schlüsselring *m*
key·stone ARCH Schlussstein *m*; *fig*
Grundpfeiler *m*
key·word Schlüssel-, Stichwort *n*
kick 1. (mit dem Fuß) stoßen, treten, e-n
Tritt geben *or* versetzen (*dat*); soccer:
schießen, treten, kicken; strampeln; ausschlagen (*horse*); *kick off* von sich
schleudern; *soccer*: anstoßen; *kick out*
F rausschmeißen; *kick up* hochschleu-
dern; *kick up a fuss or row* F Krach

schlagen; **2.** (Fuß)Tritt *m*; Stoß *m*; *soccer*: Schuss *m*; *free kick* Freistoß *m*; *for kicks* F zum Spaß; *they get a kick out of it* es macht ihnen e-n Riesenspaß

kick·off *soccer*: Anstoß *m*

kick·out *soccer*: Abschlag *m*

kid¹ zo Zicklein *n*, Kitz *n*; Ziegenleder *n*; F Kind *n*; *kid brother* F kleiner Bruder

kid² *v/t* j-n auf den Arm nehmen; *kid s.o.* j-m et. vormachen; *v/i* Spaß machen; *he is only kidding* er macht ja nur Spaß; *no kidding!* im Ernst!

kid gloves Glacéhandschuhe *pl* (*a. fig*)

kid·nap entführen, kidnappen

kid·nap·(p)er Entführer(in), Kidnapper(in)

kid·nap·(p)ing Entführung *f*, Kidnapping *n*

kid·ney ANAT Niere *f*

kidney bean BOT Kidneybohne *f*, rote Bohne

kidney ma·chine MED künstliche Niere

kill töten (*a. fig*), umbringen, ermorden; vernichten; zo schlachten; HUNT erlegen, schießen; *be killed in an accident* tödlich verunglücken; *kill time* die Zeit totschlagen

kill·er Mörder(in), Killer(in)

kill·ing mörderisch, tödlich

kill·joy Spielverderber *m*

kiln TECH Brennofen *m*

ki·lo F Kilo *n*

kil·o·gram(me) Kilogramm *n*

kil·o·me·ter, *Br* **kil·o·me·tre** Kilometer *m*

kilt Kilt *m*, Schottenrock *m*

kin Verwandtschaft *f*, Verwandte *pl*; *next of kin der, die* nächste Verwandte, *die* nächsten Angehörigen *pl*

kind¹ freundlich, liebenswürdig, nett; herzlich

kind² Art *f*, Sorte *f*; Wesen *n*; *all kinds of* alle möglichen, allerlei; *nothing of the kind* nichts dergleichen; *kind of* F ein bisschen

kin·der·gar·ten Kindergarten *m*

kind-heart·ed gütig

kin·dle anzünden, (sich) entzünden; *Interesse etc* wecken

kind·ly 1. *adj* freundlich, liebenswürdig, nett; **2.** *adv* → 1; freundlicherweise, liebenswürdigerweise, netterweise

kind·ness Freundlichkeit *f*, Liebenswürdigkeit *f*; Gefälligkeit *f*

kin·dred verwandt; *kindred spirits* Gleichgesinnte *pl*

king König *m*

king·dom Königreich *n*; REL Reich *n* Gottes; *fig* Reich *n*; *animal kingdom* Tierreich *n*; *vegetable kingdom* Pflanzen-

reich *n*

king·ly königlich

king-size(d) Riesen...

kink Knick *m*; *fig* Tick *m*, Spleen *m*

kink·y spleenig; pervers

ki·osk Kiosk *m*; *Br* Telefonzelle *f*

kip·per GASTR Räucherhering *m*

kiss 1. Kuss *m*; **2.** (sich) küssen

kit Ausrüstung *f*; Arbeitsgerät *n*, Werkzeug(e *pl*) *n*; Werkzeugtasche *f*, -kasten *m*; Bastelsatz *m*

kit bag Seesack *m*

kitch·en 1. Küche *f*; **2.** Küchen...

kitch·en·ette Kleinküche *f*, Kochnische *f*

kitch·en gar·den Küchen-, Gemüsegarten *m*

kite Drachen *m*; zo Milan *m*; *fly a kite* e-n Drachen steigen lassen

kit·ten zo Kätzchen *n*

knack Kniff *m*, Trick *m*, F Dreh *m*; Geschick *n*, Talent *n*

knave *card games*: Bube *m*, Unter *m*

knead kneten; massieren

knee ANAT Knie *n*; TECH Knie(stück) *n*

knee·cap ANAT Kniescheibe *f*

knee-deep knietief, bis an die Knie (reichend)

knee joint ANAT Kniegelenk *n* (*a.* TECH)

kneel knien (*to* vor *dat*)

knee-length knielang

knell Totenglocke *f*

knick·er·bock·ers Knickerbocker *pl*, Kniehosen *pl*

knick·ers *Br* F (Damen)Schlüpfer *m*

knick-knack Nippsache *f*

knife 1. Messer *n*; **2.** mit e-m Messer stechen *or* verletzen; erstechen

knight 1. Ritter *m*; *chess*: Springer *m*; **2.** zum Ritter schlagen

knight·hood Ritterwürde *f*, -stand *m*

knit *v/t* stricken; *a.* *knit together* zusammenfügen, verbinden; *knit one's brows* die Stirn runzeln; *v/i* stricken; MED zusammenwachsen

knit·ting 1. Stricken *n*; Strickzeug *n*; **2.** Strick...

knitting nee·dle Stricknadel *f*

knit·wear Strickwaren *pl*

knob Knopf *m*, Knauf *m*, *runder* Griff; GASTR Stück(chen) *n*

knock 1. schlagen, stoßen; pochen, klopfen; *knock at the door* an die Tür klopfen; *knock about*, *knock around* herumstoßen; F sich herumtreiben; F herumliegen; *knock down Gebäude etc* abreißen; umstoßen, umwerfen; niederschlagen; anfahren, umfahren; überfahren; mit *dem Preis* heruntergehen; *auction*: et. zuschlagen (*to s.o.* j-m); *be*

ladylike

knocked down überfahren werden; **knock off** herunter-, abschlagen; F *et.* hinhauen; F aufhören (mit); F Feierabend *or* Schluss machen; **knock out** herausschlagen, -klopfen, *Pfeife* ausklopfen; *j-n* bewusstlos schlagen; *boxing*: k.o. schlagen; *fig* betäuben (*drug etc*); *fig* F umhauen, schocken; **knock over** umwerfen, umstoßen; überfahren; **be knocked over** überfahren werden; **2.** Schlag *m*, Stoß *m*; Klopfen *n*; **there is a knock (on** [*Br* **at**] **the door)** es klopft
knock·er Türklopfer *m*
knock-kneed x-beinig
knock·out *boxing*: K.o. *m*
knoll Hügel *m*
knot 1. Knoten *m*; BOT Astknoten *m*; MAR Knoten *m*, Seemeile *f*; **2.** (ver-)knoten, (ver)knüpfen
knot·ty knotig; knorrig; *fig* verwickelt, kompliziert
know wissen; können; kennen; erfahren, erleben; (wieder) erkennen; verstehen; **know French** Französisch können;

know one's way around sich auskennen in (*a place etc*); **know all about it** genau Bescheid wissen; **get to know** kennenlernen; **know one's business, know the ropes, know a thing or two, know what's what** F sich auskennen, Erfahrung haben; **you know** wissen Sie
know-how Know-how *n*, (Sach-, Spezial)-Kenntnis(se *pl*) *f*
know·ing klug, gescheit; schlau; verständnisvoll
know·ing·ly wissend; wissentlich, absichtlich, bewusst
knowl·edge Kenntnis(se *pl*) *f*; Wissen *n*; **to my knowledge** meines Wissens; **have a good knowledge of** viel verstehen von, sich gut auskennen in (*dat*)
knowl·edge·a·ble: be very knowledgeable about viel verstehen von
knuck·le 1. ANAT (Finger)Knöchel *m*; **2. knuckle down to work** sich an die Arbeit machen
Krem·lin: POL **the Kremlin** der Kreml

L

L, l L, l *n*
L ABBR *of* **large (size)** groß
lab F Labor *n*
la·bel 1. Etikett *n*, (Klebe- *etc*)Zettel *m*, (-)Schild(chen) *n*; (Schall)Plattenfirma *f*;**2.** etikettieren, beschriften; *fig* abstempeln als
la·bor 1. (schwere) Arbeit; Mühe *f*; Arbeiter *pl*, Arbeitskräfte *pl*; MED Wehen *pl*; **2.** (schwer) arbeiten; sich bemühen, sich abmühen, sich anstrengen
la·bor·a·to·ry Labor(atorium) *n*
laboratory assis·tant Laborant(in)
la·bored schwerfällig (*style etc*); mühsam (*breathing etc*)
la·bor·er (*esp* Hilfs)Arbeiter *m*
la·bo·ri·ous mühsam; schwerfällig
la·bor u·ni·on Gewerkschaft *f*
la·bour *Br* → **labor**
Labour *Br* POL die Labour Party
la·boured, la·bour·er *Br* → **labored, laborer**
La·bour Par·ty *Br* POL Labour Party *f*
lace 1. Spitze *f*; Borte *f*; Schnürsenkel *m*; **2. lace up** (zu-, zusammen)schnüren;

Schuh zubinden; **laced with brandy** mit e-m Schuss Weinbrand
la·ce·rate zerschneiden, zerkratzen, aufreißen; *j-s Gefühle* verletzen
lack 1. (*of*) Fehlen *n* (von), Mangel *m* (an *dat*); **2.** *v/t* nicht haben; **he lacks money** es fehlt ihm an Geld; *v/i* **be lacking** fehlen; **he is lacking in courage** ihm fehlt der Mut
lack·lus·ter, *Br* **lack·lus·tre** glanzlos, matt
la·con·ic lakonisch, wortkarg
lac·quer 1. Lack *m*; Haarspray *m*, *n*; **2.** lackieren
lad Bursche *m*, Junge *m*
lad·der Leiter *f*; *Br* Laufmasche *f*
lad·der·proof (lauf)maschenfest
la·den (schwer) beladen
la·dle 1. (Schöpf-, Suppen)Kelle *f*, Schöpflöffel *m*; **2. ladle out** *Suppe* austeilen
la·dy Dame *f*; **Lady** Lady *f*; **lady doctor** Ärztin *f*; **Ladies' room**, *Br* **Ladies(')** Damentoilette *f*
la·dy·bird ZO Marienkäfer *m*
la·dy·like damenhaft

lag 1. *mst* **lag behind** zurückbleiben; **2.** →
time lag

la·ger Lagerbier *n*

la·goon Lagune *f*

lair ZO Lager *n*, Höhle *f*, Bau *m*

la·i·ty Laien *pl*

lake See *m*

lamb ZO **1.** Lamm *n*; **2.** lammen

lame 1. lahm (*a. fig*); **2.** lähmen

la·ment 1. jammern, (weh)klagen; trauern; **2.** Jammer *m*, (Weh)Klage *f*

lam·en·ta·ble beklagenswert; kläglich

lam·en·ta·tion (Weh)Klage *f*

lam·i·nat·ed laminiert, geschichtet, be-
schichtet

laminated glass Verbundglas *n*

lamp Lampe *f*; Laterne *f*

lamp·post Laternenpfahl *m*

lamp·shade Lampenschirm *m*

lance Lanze *f*

land 1. Land *n*, AGR *a.* Boden *m*, POL *a.*
Staat *m*; **by land** auf dem Landweg; **2.**
landen, MAR *a.* anlegen; *Güter* ausladen,
MAR *a.* löschen

land a·gent AGR Gutsverwalter *m*

land·ed Land…, Grund…; *landed gen-
try* Landadel *m*; *landed property*
Grundbesitz *m*

land·ing AVIAT Landung *f*, Landen *n*, MAR
a. Anlegen *n*; Treppenabsatz *m*

landing field AVIAT Landeplatz *m*

landing gear AVIAT Fahrgestell *n*

landing stage MAR Landungsbrücke *f*,
-steg *m*

landing strip AVIAT Landeplatz *m*

land·la·dy Vermieterin *f*; Wirtin *f*

land·lord Vermieter *m*; Wirt *m*; Grundbesitzer *m*

land·lub·ber MAR *contp* Landratte *f*

land·mark Wahrzeichen *n*; *fig* Meilenstein *m*

land·own·er Grundbesitzer(in)

land·scape Landschaft *f* (*a. paint*)

land·slide Erdrutsch *m* (*a.* POL); *a landslide victory* POL ein überwältigender
Wahlsieg

land·slip (kleiner) Erdrutsch

lane (Feld)Weg *m*; Gasse *f*, Sträßchen *n*;
MAR Fahrrinne *f*; AVIAT Flugschneise *f*;
SPORT (*einzelne*) Bahn; MOT (Fahr-) Spur
f; *change lanes* MOT die Spur wechseln;
get in lane MOT sich einordnen

lan·guage Sprache *f*

language la·bor·a·to·ry Sprachlabor *n*

lan·guid matt; träg(e)

lank glatt

lank·y schlaksig

lan·tern Laterne *f*

lap¹ Schoß *m*

lap² SPORT **1.** Runde *f*; *lap of hono(u)r* Ehrenrunde *f*; **2.** *Gegner* überrunden; e-e
Runde zurücklegen

lap³ *v/t:* **lap up** auflecken, aufschlecken;
v/i plätschern

la·pel Revers *n*, *m*, Aufschlag *m*

lapse 1. Versehen *n*, (kleiner) Fehler *or*
Irrtum; Vergehen *n*; Zeitspanne *f*; JUR
Verfall *m*; *lapse of memory, memory
lapse* Gedächtnislücke *f*; **2.** verfallen;
JUR verfallen, erlöschen

lar·ce·ny JUR Diebstahl *m*

larch BOT Lärche *f*

lard 1. Schweinefett *n*, Schweineschmalz
n; **2.** *Fleisch* spicken

lar·der Speisekammer *f*, -schrank *m*

large groß; beträchtlich; reichlich; umfassend, weitgehend; *at large* in Freiheit,
auf freiem Fuß; *fig* (sehr) ausführlich;
in der Gesamtheit

large·ly großenteils, größtenteils

large-mind·ed aufgeschlossen, tolerant

large·ness Größe *f*

lar·i·at Lasso *n*, *m*

lark¹ ZO Lerche *f*

lark² F Jux *m*, Spaß *m*

lark·spur BOT Rittersporn *m*

lar·va ZO Larve *f*

lar·yn·gi·tis MED Kehlkopfentzündung *f*

lar·ynx ANAT Kehlkopf *m*

las·civ·i·ous geil, lüstern

la·ser PHYS Laser *m*

laser beam PHYS Laserstrahl *m*

laser print·er EDP Laserdrucker *m*

laser tech·nol·o·gy Lasertechnik *f*

lash 1. Peitschenschnur *f*; (Peitschen-)
Hieb *m*; Wimper *f*; **2.** peitschen (mit);
(fest)binden; schlagen; *lash out* (wild)
um sich schlagen

las·so Lasso *m*, *n*

last¹ 1. *adj* letzte(r, -s); vorige(r, -s); *last
but one* vorletzte(r, -s); *last night* gestern Abend; letzte Nacht; **2.** *adv* zuletzt,
an letzter Stelle; *last but not least*
nicht zu vergessen; **3.** *der, die, das*
Letzte; *at last* endlich; *to the last* bis
zum Schluss

last² (an-, fort)dauern; (sich) halten;
(aus)reichen

last³ (Schuhmacher)Leisten *m*

last·ing dauerhaft; beständig

last·ly zuletzt, zum Schluss

latch 1. Schnappriegel *m*; Schnappschloss
n; **2.** einklinken, zuklinken

latch·key Haus-, Wohnungsschlüssel *m*

late spät; jüngste(r, -s), letzte(r, -s), frühe-
re(r, -s), ehemalig; verstorben; *be late* zu
spät kommen, sich verspäten; RAIL *etc*
Verspätung haben; *as late as* noch, erst;

L

of late kürzlich; *later on* später

late·ly kürzlich

lath Latte *f*, Leiste *f*

lathe TECH Drehbank *f*

la·ther 1. (Seifen)Schaum *m*; 2. *v/t* einseifen; *v/i* schäumen

Lat·in LING 1. lateinisch; südländisch; 2. Latein(isch) *n*

Latin A·mer·i·ca Lateinamerika *n*

Latin A·mer·i·can 1. lateinamerikanisch; 2. Lateinamerikaner(in)

lat·i·tude GEOGR Breite *f*

lat·ter Letztere(r, -s)

lat·tice Gitter(werk) *n*

lau·da·ble lobenswert

laugh 1. lachen (*at* über *acc*); *laugh at s.o. a.* j-n auslachen; 2. Lachen *n*, Gelächter *n*

laugh·a·ble lächerlich, lachhaft

laugh·ter Lachen *n*, Gelächter *n*

launch[1] 1. MAR vom Stapel lassen; MIL abschießen, *Rakete a.* starten; *fig Projekt etc* in Gang setzen, starten; 2. MAR Stapellauf *m*; MIL Abschuss *m*, Start *m*

launch[2] MAR Barkasse *f*

launch pad → *launching pad*

launch·ing → *launch[1]* 2

launching pad Abschussrampe *f*

launching site Abschussbasis *f*

laun·der *Wäsche* waschen (und bügeln); F *esp Geld* waschen

laun·der·ette, laun·drette *esp Br*, laun·dro·mat® Waschsalon *m*

laun·dry Wäscherei *f*; Wäsche *f*

laur·el BOT Lorbeer *m* (*a. fig*)

la·va GEOL Lava *f*

lav·a·to·ry Toilette *f*, Klosett *n*; *public lavatory* Bedürfnisanstalt *f*

lav·en·der BOT Lavendel *m*

lav·ish 1. sehr freigebig, verschwenderisch; 2. *lavish s.th. on s.o.* j-n mit et. überhäufen *or* überschütten

law Gesetz(e *pl*) *n*; Recht *n*, Rechtssystem *n*; Rechtswissenschaft *f*, Jura; F Bullen *pl* (*police*); F Bulle *m* (*policeman*); Gesetz *n*, Vorschrift *f*; *law and order* Recht *or* Ruhe und Ordnung

law-a·bid·ing gesetzestreu

law·court Gericht *n*, Gerichtshof *m*

law·ful gesetzlich; rechtmäßig, legitim; rechtsgültig

law·less gesetzlos; gesetzwidrig; zügellos

lawn Rasen *m*

lawn·mow·er Rasenmäher *m*

law·suit JUR Prozess *m*

law·yer JUR (Rechts)Anwalt *m*, (Rechts)Anwältin *f*

lax locker, schlaff; lax, lasch

lax·a·tive MED 1. abführend; 2. Abführ-

mittel *n*

lay[1] REL weltlich; Laien…

lay[2] *v/t* legen; *Teppich* verlegen; belegen, auslegen (*with* mit); *Tisch* decken; ZO *Eier* legen; vorlegen (*before dat*), bringen (*before* vor *acc*); *Schuld etc* zuschreiben, zur Last legen (*dat*); *v/i* ZO (Eier) legen; *lay aside* beiseitelegen, zurücklegen; *lay off Arbeiter* (*esp* vorübergehend) entlassen; *Arbeit* einstellen; *lay open* darlegen; *lay out* ausbreiten, auslegen; *Garten etc* anlegen; entwerfen, planen; PRINT das Layout (*gen*) machen; *lay up* anhäufen, (an)sammeln; *be laid up* das Bett hüten müssen

lay-by *Br* MOT Parkbucht *f*, Parkstreifen *m*; Parkplatz *m*, Rastplatz *m*

lay·er Lage *f*, Schicht *f*; BOT Ableger *m*

lay·man Laie *m*

lay-off ECON (*esp* vorübergehende) Entlassung

lay·out Grundriss *m*, Lageplan *m*; PRINT Layout *n*, Gestaltung *f*

la·zy faul, träg(e)

LCD ABBR *of* **liquid crystal display** Flüssigkristallanzeige *f*

lead[1] 1. *v/t* führen; (an)führen, leiten; dazu bringen, veranlassen (*to do* zu tun); *v/i* führen; vorangehen; SPORT an der Spitze *or* in Führung liegen; *lead off* anfangen, beginnen; *lead on* j-m et. vormachen *or* weismachen; *lead to fig* führen zu; *lead up to fig* (allmählich) führen zu; 2. Führung *f*; Leitung *f*; Spitzenposition *f*; Vorbild *n*, Beispiel *n*; THEA Hauptrolle *f*; Hauptdarsteller(in); (Hunde-)Leine *f*; Hinweis *m*, Tipp *m*, Anhaltspunkt *m*; SPORT *and fig* Führung *f*, Vorsprung *m*; *be in the lead* in Führung sein; *take the lead* in Führung gehen, die Führung übernehmen

lead[2] CHEM Blei *n*; MAR Lot *n*

lead·ed verbleit, bleihaltig

lead·en bleiern (*a. fig*), Blei…

lead·er (An)Führer(in), Leiter(in); Erste *m*, *f*; *Br* Leitartikel *m*

lead·er·ship Führung *f*, Leitung *f*

lead-free bleifrei

lead·ing leitend; führend; Haupt…

leaf 1. BOT, PRINT Blatt *n*; (*Tür- etc*)Flügel *m*; (*Tisch*)Klappe *f*, Ausziehplatte *f*; 2. *leaf through* durchblättern

leaf·let Hand-, Reklamezettel *m*; Prospekt *m*

league POL Bund *m*; SPORT Liga *f*

leak 1. lecken, leck sein; tropfen; *leak out* auslaufen; *fig* durchsickern; 2. Leck *n*, undichte Stelle (*a. fig*)

leak·age Auslaufen *n*

leak·y leck, undicht

lean¹ (sich) lehnen; (sich) neigen; **lean on** sich verlassen auf (*acc*)

lean² **1.** mager (*a. fig*); **2.** GASTR das Magere

lean man·age·ment ECON schlanke Unternehmensstruktur

leap **1.** springen; **leap at** *fig* sich stürzen auf (*acc*); **2.** Sprung *m*

leap·frog Bockspringen *n*

leap year Schaltjahr *n*

learn (er)lernen; erfahren, hören

learn·ed gelehrt

learn·er Anfänger(in); Lernende *m*, *f*; **learner driver** *Br* MOT Fahrschüler(in)

learn·ing Gelehrsamkeit *f*

lease **1.** Pacht *f*, Miete *f*; Pacht-, Mietvertrag *m*; **2.** pachten, mieten; leasen; **lease out** verpachten, vermieten

leash (Hunde)Leine *f*

least **1.** *adj* geringste(r, -s), mindeste(r, -s), wenigste(r, -s); **2.** *adv* am wenigsten; **least of all** am allerwenigsten; **3.** *das* Mindeste, *das* wenigste; **at least** wenigstens; **to say the least** gelinde gesagt

leath·er **1.** Leder *n*; **2.** ledern; Leder...

leave **1.** *v/t* (hinter-, über-, ver-, zurück-) lassen, übrig lassen; liegen *or* stehen lassen, vergessen; vermachen, vererben; **be left** übrig bleiben, übrig sein; *v/i* (fort-, weg)gehen, abreisen, abfahren, abfliegen; **leave alone** allein lassen; *j-n, et.* in Ruhe lassen; **leave behind** zurücklassen; **leave on** anlassen; **leave out** draußen lassen; auslassen, weglassen; **2.** Erlaubnis *f*; Urlaub *m*; Abschied *m*; **on leave** auf Urlaub

leav·en Sauerteig *m*

leaves BOT Laub *n*

leav·ings Überreste *pl*

lech·er·ous geil, lüstern

lec·ture **1.** UNIV Vorlesung *f* (**über** *acc* on); Vortrag *m*; Strafpredigt *f*; **2.** *v/i* UNIV e-e Vorlesung *or* Vorlesungen halten (**über** *acc* on; **vor** *dat* to); e-n Vortrag *or* Vorträge halten; *v/t* *j-m* e-e Strafpredigt halten

lec·tur·er UNIV Dozent(in); Redner(in)

ledge Leiste *f*, Sims *m*, *n*

leech ZO Blutegel *m*

leek BOT Lauch *m*, Porree *m*

leer **1.** anzüglicher *or* lüsterner Seitenblick; **2.** anzüglich *or* lüstern blicken *or* schielen (**at** nach)

left **1.** *adj* linke(r, -s), Links...; **2.** *adv* links; **turn left** (sich) nach links wenden; MOT links abbiegen; **3.** *die* Linke *f*, POL, *boxing*), linke Seite; **on the left** links, auf der linken Seite; **to the left** (nach) links;

keep to the left sich links halten; links fahren

left-hand linke(r, -s)

left-hand drive MOT Linkssteuerung *f*

left-hand·ed linkshändig; für Linkshänder; **be left-handed** Linkshänder(in) sein

left lug·gage of·fice *Br* RAIL Gepäckaufbewahrung *f*

left-o·vers (Speise)Reste *pl*

left-wing POL dem linken Flügel angehörend, links..., Links...

leg ANAT Bein *n*; GASTR Keule *f*; MATH Schenkel *m*; **pull s.o.'s leg** F *j-n* auf den Arm nehmen; **stretch one's** sich die Beine vertreten

leg·a·cy *fig* Vermächtnis *n*, Erbe *n*

le·gal legal, gesetzmäßig; gesetzlich, rechtlich; juristisch, Rechts...

le·gal·ize legalisieren

le·gal·i·za·tion Legalisierung *f*

le·gal pro·tec·tion Rechtsschutz *m*

le·ga·tion POL Gesandtschaft *f*

le·gend Legende *f*, Sage *f*

le·gen·da·ry legendär

le·gi·ble leserlich

le·gis·la·tion Gesetzgebung *f*

le·gis·la·tive POL **1.** gesetzgebend, legislativ; **2.** Legislative *f*, gesetzgebende Gewalt

le·gis·la·tor POL Gesetzgeber *m*

le·git·i·mate legitim; gesetzmäßig, rechtmäßig; ehelich

lei·sure freie Zeit; Muße *f*; **at leisure** ohne Hast

leisure cen·tre *Br* Freizeitzentrum *n*

lei·sure·ly gemächlich

lei·sure time Freizeit *f*

lei·sure-time ac·tiv·i·ties Freizeitbeschäftigung *f*, -gestaltung *f*

lei·sure·wear Freizeitkleidung *f*

lem·on BOT **1.** Zitrone *f*; **2.** Zitronen...

lem·on·ade Zitronenlimonade *f*

lend *j-m et.* (ver-, aus)leihen

length Länge *f*; Strecke *f*; (Zeit)Dauer *f*; **at length** ausführlich

length·en verlängern, länger machen; länger werden

length·ways, length·wise der Länge nach

length·y sehr lang

le·ni·ent mild(e), nachsichtig

lens ANAT, PHOT, PHYS Linse *f*; PHOT Objektiv *n*

Lent REL Fastenzeit *f*

len·til BOT Linse *f*

Le·o ASTR Löwe *m*; **he (she) is (a) Leo** er (sie) ist (ein) Löwe

leop·ard ZO Leopard *m*

le·o·tard (Tänzer)Trikot *n*

lep·ro·sy MED Lepra *f*

les·bi·an 1. lesbisch; **2.** Lesbierin *f*, F Lesbe *f*

less 1. *adj and adv* kleiner, geringer, weniger; **2.** *prp* weniger, minus, abzüglich

less·en (sich) vermindern *or* verringern; abnehmen; herabsetzen

less·er kleiner, geringer

les·son Lektion *f*; (Unterrichts)Stunde *f*; *fig* Lehre *f*; *pl* Unterricht *m*

let lassen; *esp Br* vermieten, verpachten; *let alone* j-n, et. in Ruhe lassen; geschweige denn; *let down* hinunterlassen, herunterlassen; *Kleider* verlängern; j-n im Stich lassen, F j-n sitzen lassen; enttäuschen; *let go* loslassen; *let o.s. go* sich gehenlassen; *let's go* gehen wir!; *let in* (her)einlassen; *let o.s. in for s.th.* sich et. einbrocken, sich auf et. einlassen

le·thal tödlich; Todes…

leth·ar·gy Lethargie *f*

let·ter Buchstabe *m*; PRINT Type *f*; Brief *m*

let·ter·box *esp Br* Briefkasten *m*

let·ter car·ri·er Briefträger *m*

let·tuce BOT (*esp Br* Kopf)Salat *m*

leu·k(a)e·mia MED Leukämie *f*

lev·el 1. *adj* eben; gleich (*a. fig*); ausgeglichen; *be level with* auf gleicher Höhe sein mit; *my level best* F mein Möglichstes; **2.** Ebene *f* (*a. fig*), ebene Fläche; Höhe *f* (*a.* GEOGR), (*Wasser- etc*)Spiegel *m*, (-)Stand *m*, (-)Pegel *m*; Wasserwaage *f*; *fig* Niveau *n*, Stufe *f*; *sea level* Meeresspiegel *m*; *on the level* F ehrlich, aufrichtig; **3.** (ein)ebnen, planieren; dem Erdboden gleichmachen; *level at Waffe* richten auf (*acc*); *Beschuldigungen* erheben gegen (*acc*); **4.** *adv*: *level with* in Höhe (*gen*)

lev·el cross·ing *Br* schienengleicher Bahnübergang

lev·el-head·ed vernünftig, nüchtern

le·ver Hebel *m*

lev·y 1. Steuer *f*, Abgabe *f*; **2.** *Steuern* erheben

lewd geil, lüstern; unanständig, obszön

li·a·bil·i·ty ECON, JUR Verpflichtung *f*, Verbindlichkeit *f*; ECON, JUR Haftung *f*, Haftpflicht *f*; Neigung *f* (*to* zu), Anfälligkeit *f* (*to* für)

li·a·ble ECON, JUR haftbar, haftpflichtig; *be liable for* haften für; *be liable to* neigen zu, anfällig sein für

li·ar Lügner(in)

li·bel JUR **1.** (*schriftliche*) Verleumdung *or* Beleidigung; **2.** (*schriftlich*) verleumden *or* beleidigen

lib·e·ral 1. liberal (*a.* POL), aufgeschlossen; großzügig; reichlich; **2.** Liberale *m*, *f* (*a.* POL)

lib·e·rate befreien

lib·e·ra·tion Befreiung *f*

lib·e·ra·tor Befreier *m*

lib·er·ty Freiheit *f*; *take liberties with* sich Freiheiten gegen j-n herausnehmen; willkürlich mit et. umgehen; *be at liberty* frei sein

Li·bra ASTR Waage *f*; *he* (*she*) *is* (*a*) *Libra* er (sie) ist (eine) Waage

li·brar·i·an Bibliothekar(in)

li·bra·ry Bibliothek *f*; Bücherei *f*

li·cence 1. *Br* → *license 1*; **2.** e-e Lizenz *or* Konzession erteilen (*dat*); *behördlich* genehmigen

li·cense 1. Lizenz *f*, Konzession *f*; (*Führer-, Jagd-, Waffen- etc*)Schein *m*; **2.** *Br* → *licence 2*

li·cense plate MOT Nummernschild *n*

li·chen BOT Flechte *f*

lick 1. Lecken *n*; Salzlecke *f*; **2.** *v/t* ab-, auflecken; F verdreschen, verprügeln; F schlagen, besiegen; *v/i* lecken; züngeln (*flames*)

lic·o·rice Lakritze *f*

lid Deckel *m*; ANAT (Augen)Lid *n*

lie¹ 1. lügen; *lie to s.o.* j-n belügen, j-n anlügen; **2.** Lüge *f*; *tell lies, tell a lie* lügen; *give the lie to* j-n, et. Lügen strafen

lie² 1. liegen; *let sleeping dogs lie* schlafende Hunde soll man nicht wecken; *lie behind fig* dahinter stecken; *lie down* sich hinlegen; **2.** Lage *f* (*a. fig*)

lie-down *Br* F Nickerchen *n*

lie-in: *have a lie-in esp Br* F sich gründlich ausschlafen

lieu: *in lieu of* anstelle von (*or gen*)

lieu·ten·ant MIL Leutnant *m*

life Leben *n*; JUR lebenslängliche Freiheitsstrafe; *all her life* ihr ganzes Leben lang; *for life* fürs (ganze) Leben; *esp* JUR lebenslänglich

life as·sur·ance *Br* → *life insurance*

life belt Rettungsgürtel *m*

life·boat Rettungsboot *n*

life·guard Bademeister *m*; Rettungsschwimmer *m*

life im·pris·on·ment JUR lebenslängliche Freiheitsstrafe

life in·sur·ance Lebensversicherung *f*

life jack·et Schwimmweste *f*

life·less leblos; matt, schwung-, lustlos

life·like lebensecht

life·long lebenslang

life pre·serv·er Schwimmweste *f*; Rettungsgürtel *m*

life sen·tence JUR lebenslängliche Frei-

heitsstrafe
life·time Lebenszeit f
lift 1. v/t (hoch-, auf)heben; erheben; Verbot etc aufheben; Gesicht etc liften, straffen; F klauen; v/i sich heben, steigen (a. fog); **lift off** starten (rocket), AVIAT abheben; **2.** (Hoch-, Auf)Heben n; PHYS, AVIAT Auftrieb m; Br Lift m, Aufzug m, Fahrstuhl m; **give s.o. a lift** j-n (im Auto) mitnehmen; F j-n aufmuntern, j-m Auftrieb geben
lift-off Start m, Abheben n
lig·a·ment ANAT Band n
light¹ 1. Licht n (a. fig); Beleuchtung f; Schein m; Feuer n; fig Aspekt m; Br mst pl (Verkehrs)Ampel f; **do you have** (Br **have you got**) **a light?** haben Sie Feuer?; **2.** v/t beleuchten, erleuchten; a. **light up** anzünden; v/i sich entzünden; **light up** fig aufleuchten; **3.** hell, licht
light² leicht (a. fig); **make light of s.th.** et. leichtnehmen; et. bagatellisieren
light·en¹ v/t erhellen; aufhellen; v/i hell(er) werden, sich aufhellen
light·en² leichter machen or werden; erleichtern
light·er Anzünder m; Feuerzeug n
light-head·ed (leicht) benommen; leichtfertig, töricht
light-heart·ed fröhlich, unbeschwert
light·house Leuchtturm m
light·ing Beleuchtung f
light·ness Leichtheit f; Leichtigkeit f
light·ning Blitz m; **like lightning** wie der Blitz; **(as) quick as lightning** blitzschnell
light·ning con·duc·tor Br, **lightning rod** ELECTR Blitzableiter m
light·weight SPORT Leichtgewicht n, Leichtgewichtler m
like¹ 1. v/t gernhaben, mögen; **I like it** es gefällt mir; **I like her** ich kann sie gut leiden; **how do you like it?** wie gefällt es dir?, wie findest du es?; **I like that!** iro das hab ich gern!; **I should** or **would like to know** ich möchte gern wissen; v/i wollen; **(just) as you like** (ganz) wie du willst; **if you like** wenn du willst; **2. likes and dislikes** Neigungen und Abneigungen pl
like² 1. gleich; wie; ähnlich; **like that** so; **feel like** Lust haben auf (acc) or zu; **what is he like?** wie ist er?; **that is just like him!** das sieht ihm ähnlich!; **2.** der, die, das Gleiche; **his like** seinesgleichen; **the like** dergleichen; **the likes of you** Leute wie du
like·li·hood Wahrscheinlichkeit f
like·ly 1. adj wahrscheinlich; geeignet; **2.**

adv wahrscheinlich; **not likely!** F bestimmt nicht!
like·ness Ähnlichkeit f; Abbild n
like·wise ebenso
lik·ing Vorliebe f
li·lac 1. lila; **2.** BOT Flieder m
lil·y BOT Lilie f
lil·y of the val·ley BOT Maiglöckchen n
limb ANAT (Körper)Glied n; BOT Ast m
lime¹ Kalk m
lime² BOT Linde f; Limone f
lime·light fig Rampenlicht n
lim·it 1. Limit n, Grenze f; **within limits** in Grenzen; **off limits** Zutritt verboten (**to** für); **that is the limit!** F das ist der Gipfel!, das ist (doch) die Höhe!; **go to the limit** bis zum Äußersten gehen; **2.** beschränken (**to** auf acc)
lim·i·ta·tion Beschränkung f; fig Grenze f; JUR Verjährung f
lim·it·ed beschränkt, begrenzt; **limited** (**liability**) **company** Br ECON Gesellschaft f mit beschränkter Haftung
lim·it·less grenzenlos
limp¹ 1. hinken, humpeln; **2.** Hinken n, Humpeln n
limp² schlaff, schlapp, F lappig
line¹ 1. Linie f, Strich m; Zeile f; Falte f, Runzel f; Reihe f; (Menschen-, a. Auto)Schlange f; (Abstammungs)Linie f; (Verkehrs-, Eisenbahn- etc)Linie f, Strecke f; (Flug- etc)Gesellschaft f; esp TEL Leitung f; MIL Linie f; Fach n, Gebiet n, Branche f; SPORT (Ziel- etc)Linie f; Leine f; Schnur f; Linie f, Richtung f; fig Grenze f; pl THEA Rolle f, Text m; **the line** der Äquator; **draw the line** Halt machen, die Grenze ziehen (**at** bei); **the line is busy** or **engaged** TEL die Leitung ist besetzt; **hold the line** TEL bleiben Sie am Apparat; **stand in line** anstehen, Schlange stehen (**for** um, nach); **2.** lin(i)ieren; Gesicht zeichnen, (zer)furchen; Straße etc säumen; **line up** (sich) in e-r Reihe or Linie aufstellen, SPORT sich aufstellen; sich anstellen (**for** um, nach)
line² Kleid etc füttern; TECH auskleiden, ausschlagen; MOT Bremsen etc belegen
lin·e·ar linear; Längen...
lin·en 1. Leinen n; (Bett-, Tisch- etc -)Wäsche f; **2.** leinen, Leinen...
lin·en clos·et, Br **linen cup·board** Wäscheschrank m
lin·er MAR Linienschiff n; AVIAT Verkehrsflugzeug n
lines·man SPORT Linienrichter m
lines·wom·an SPORT Linienrichterin f
line-up SPORT Aufstellung f; Gegenüberstellung f (zur Identifizierung)

locate

lin·ger verweilen, sich aufhalten; *a. linger on* dahinsiechen; *linger on* noch dableiben; *fig* fortleben

lin·ge·rie Damenunterwäsche *f*

lin·ing Futter(stoff *m*) *n*; TECH Auskleidung *f*; MOT (*Brems- etc*)Belag *m*

link 1. (Ketten)Glied *n*; Manschettenknopf *m*; *fig* (Binde)Glied *n*, Verbindung *f*; **2.** *a. link up* (sich) verbinden

links → *golf links*

link·up Verbindung *f*

lin·seed BOT Leinsamen *m*

lin·seed oil Leinöl *n*

li·on ZO Löwe *m*

li·on·ess ZO Löwin *f*

lip ANAT Lippe *f*; (*Tassen- etc*)Rand *m*; F Unverschämtheit *f*

lip·stick Lippenstift *m*

liq·ue·fy (sich) verflüssigen

liq·uid 1. Flüssigkeit *f*; **2.** flüssig

liq·ui·date liquidieren (*a.* ECON); *Schulden* tilgen

liq·uid·ize zerkleinern, pürieren

liq·uid·iz·er Mixgerät *n*, Mixer *m*

liq·uor *Br* alkoholische Getränke *pl*, Alkohol *m*; Schnaps *m*, Spirituosen *pl*

liq·uo·rice *Br* → *licorice*

lisp 1. lispeln; **2.** Lispeln *n*

list 1. Liste *f*, Verzeichnis *n*; MAR Schlagseite *f*; **2.** (in e-e Liste) eintragen, erfassen; MAR *be listing* Schlagseite haben

lis·ten hören; *listen in* Radio hören; *listen in to et.* im Radio (an)hören; *listen in on Telefongespräch etc* abhören *or* mithören; *listen to* anhören (*acc*), zuhören (*dat*); hören auf (*acc*)

lis·ten·er Zuhörer(in); (Rundfunk-)Hörer(in)

list·less teilnahmslos, lustlos

li·ter Liter *m*, *n*

lit·e·ral (wort)wörtlich; genau; prosaisch

lit·e·ra·ry literarisch, Literatur...

lit·e·ra·ture Literatur *f*

lithe geschmeidig, gelenkig

li·tre *Br* → *liter*

lit·ter 1. (*esp Papier*)Abfall *m*; AGR Streu *f*; ZO Wurf *m*; Trage *f*; Sänfte *f*; **2.** *et.* herumliegen lassen in (*dat*) *or* auf (*dat*); *be littered with* übersät sein mit

lit·ter bas·ket, litter bin Abfallkorb *m*

lit·tle 1. *adj* klein; wenig; *the little ones* die Kleinen *pl*; **2.** *adv* wenig, kaum; **3.** Kleinigkeit *f*; *a little* ein wenig, ein bisschen; *little by little* (ganz) allmählich, nach und nach; *not a little* nicht wenig

live¹ leben; wohnen (*with* bei); *live to see* erleben; *live on* leben von; weiterleben; *live up to s-n Grundsätzen etc* gemäß leben; *Erwartungen etc* entsprechen; *live with* mit *j-m* zusammenleben; mit *et.* leben

live² 1. *adj* lebend, lebendig; richtig, echt; ELECTR Strom führend; *radio*, TV Direkt..., Live-...; **2.** *adv* direkt, original, live

live·li·hood (Lebens)Unterhalt *m*

live·li·ness Lebhaftigkeit *f*

live·ly lebhaft, lebendig; aufregend

liv·er ANAT Leber *f* (*a.* GASTR)

liv·e·ry Livree *f*

live·stock Vieh *n*, Viehbestand *m*

liv·id bläulich; F fuchsteufelswild

liv·ing 1. lebend; *the living image of* das genaue Ebenbild (*gen*); **2.** Leben *n*, Lebensweise *f*; Lebensunterhalt *m*; *the living* die Lebenden *pl*; *standard of living* Lebensstandard *m*; *earn or make a living* (sich) s-n Lebensunterhalt verdienen

liv·ing room Wohnzimmer *n*

liz·ard ZO Eidechse *f*

load 1. Last *f* (*a. fig*); Ladung *f*; Belastung *f*; **2.** *j-n* überhäufen (*with* mit); *Schusswaffe* laden; *load a camera* e-n Film einlegen; *a. load up* (auf-, be-, ein)laden

loaf¹ Laib *m* (Brot); Brot *n*

loaf² *a. loaf about, loaf around* F herumlungern

loaf·er Müßiggänger(in)

loam Lehm *m*

loam·y lehmig

loan 1. (Ver)Leihen *n*; ECON Kredit *m*, Darlehen *n*; Leihgabe *f*; *on loan* leihweise; **2.** *loan s.o. s.th., loan s.th. to s.o.* j-m et. (aus)leihen; et. an j-n verleihen

loan shark ECON Kredithai *m*

loath: *be loath to do s.th.* et. nur (sehr) ungern tun

loathe verabscheuen, hassen

loath·ing Abscheu *m*

lob *esp tennis*: Lob *m*

lob·by 1. Vorhalle *f*; THEA, *film*: Foyer *n*; Wandelhalle *f*; POL Lobby *f*, Interessengruppe *f*; **2.** POL *Abgeordnete etc* beeinflussen

lobe ANAT, BOT Lappen *m*

lob·ster ZO Hummer *m*

lo·cal 1. örtlich, Orts..., lokal, Lokal...; **2.** Ortsansässige *m*, *f*, Einheimische *m*, *f*; *Br* F Stammkneipe *f*

local call TEL Ortsgespräch *n*

local e·lec·tions POL Kommunalwahlen *pl*

local gov·ern·ment Gemeindeverwaltung *f*

local time Ortszeit *f*

local traf·fic Orts-, Nahverkehr *m*

lo·cate ausfindig machen; orten; *be located* gelegen sein, liegen, sich befinden

L

lo·ca·tion Lage *f*; Standort *m*; Platz *m* (**for** für); *film*, TV Gelände *n* für Außenaufnahmen; **on location** auf Außenaufnahme

lock[1] **1.** (*Tür-, Gewehr- etc*)Schloss *n*; Schleuse(nkammer) *f*; Verschluss *m*; Sperrvorrichtung *f*; **2.** *v/t* zu-, verschließen, zu-, versperren (*a.* **lock up**); umschlingen, umfassen; TECH sperren; *v/i* schließen; abschließbar *or* verschließbar sein; MOT *etc* blockieren; **lock away** wegschließen; **lock in** einschließen, einsperren; **lock out** aussperren; **lock up** abschließen; wegschließen; einsperren

lock[2] (Haar)Locke *f*

lock·er Spind *m*, Schrank *m*; Schließfach *n*

locker room *esp* SPORT Umkleidekabine *f*, Umkleideraum *m*

lock·et Medaillon *n*

lock·out ECON Aussperrung *f*

lock·smith Schlosser *m*

lock·up Arrestzelle *f*

lo·cust ZO Heuschrecke *f*

lodge 1. Portier-, Pförtnerloge *f*; (*Jagd-, Ski- etc*)Hütte *f*; Sommer-, Gartenhaus *n*; (*Freimaurer*)Loge *f*; **2.** *v/i* logieren, (*esp* vorübergehend *or* in Untermiete) wohnen; stecken (bleiben) (*bullet etc*); *v/t* aufnehmen, beherbergen, (für die Nacht) unterbringen; *Beschwerde etc* einreichen; *Berufung*, *Protest* einlegen

lodg·er Untermieter(in)

lodg·ing Unterkunft *f*; *pl esp* möbliertes Zimmer

loft (Dach)Boden *m*; Heuboden *m*; Empore *f*; (**converted**) **loft** Loft *m*, Fabriketage *f*

loft·y hoch; erhaben; stolz; hochmütig

log (Holz)Klotz *m*; (*gefällter*) Baumstamm; (Holz)Scheit *n*; → **log·book** MAR Logbuch *n*; AVIAT Bordbuch *n*; MOT Fahrtenbuch *n*

log cab·in Blockhaus *n*, Blockhütte *f*

log·ger·heads: **be at loggerheads** sich streiten, sich in den Haaren liegen (**with** mit)

lo·gic Logik *f*

lo·gic·al logisch

loin GASTR Lende(nstück *n*) *f*; *pl* ANAT Lende *f*

loi·ter trödeln; herumlungern

loll hängen (*head*), heraushängen (*tongue*); **loll around** *or* **about** F sich rekeln *or* lümmeln

lol·li·pop GASTR Lutscher *m*; *esp Br* Eis *n* am Stiel; **lollipop man** *Br* Schülerlotse *m*; **lollipop woman**, **lollipop lady** *Br* Schülerlotsin *f*

lol·ly GASTR F Lutscher *m*; **ice lolly** Eis *n* am Stiel

lone·li·ness Einsamkeit *f*

lone·ly einsam; **become lonely** vereinsamen

lone·some einsam

long[1] **1.** *adj* lang; weit; langfristig; **2.** *adv* lang(e); **as or so long as** solange wie; vorausgesetzt, dass; **long ago** vor langer Zeit; **so long!** F bis dann!, tschüs(s)!; **3.** (e-e) lange Zeit; **for long** lange; **take long** lange brauchen *or* dauern

long[2] sich sehnen (**for** nach)

long-dis·tance Fern..., Langstrecken...

long-distance call TEL Ferngespräch *n*

long-distance run·ner SPORT Langstreckenläufer(in)

long·hand Schreibschrift *f*

long·ing 1. sehnsüchtig; **2.** Sehnsucht *f*, Verlangen *n*

lon·gi·tude GEOGR Länge *f*

long johns lange Unterhose

long jump SPORT Weitsprung *m*

long-life milk *esp Br* H-Milch *f*

long-play·er, **long-play·ing rec·ord** Langspielplatte *f*

long-range MIL, AVIAT Fern..., Langstrecken...; langfristig

long·shore·man Dock-, Hafenarbeiter *m*

long·sight·ed *esp Br* weitsichtig, *fig a.* weitblickend

long-stand·ing seit langer Zeit bestehend; alt

long-term langfristig, auf lange Sicht

long wave ELECTR Langwelle *f*

long-wear·ing strapazierfähig

long-wind·ed langatmig

look 1. sehen, blicken, schauen (**at, on** auf *acc*, nach); nachschauen, nachsehen; *krank etc* aussehen; nach *e-r Richtung* liegen, gehen (*window etc*); **look here!** schau mal (her); hör mal (zu)!; **look like** aussehen wie; **it looks as if** es sieht (so) aus, als ob; **look after** aufpassen auf (*acc*); sich kümmern um, sorgen für, *den Haushalt etc* versehen; **look ahead** nach vorne sehen; *fig* vorausschauen; **look around** sich umsehen; **look at** ansehen; **look back** sich umsehen; *fig* zurückblicken; **look down** herab-, heruntersehen (*a. fig* **on s.o.** auf j-n); **look for** suchen; **look forward to** sich freuen auf (*acc*); **look in** F hereinschauen (**on** bei); **look into** untersuchen, prüfen; **look on** zusehen, zuschauen (*dat*); betrachten, ansehen (**as** als); **look onto** liegen zu, (hinaus)gehen auf (*acc*) (*window etc*); **look out** hinaus-, heraussehen; aufpassen, sich vorsehen; ausschauen *or*

Ausschau halten (**for** nach); *look over* et.
durchsehen; *j-n* mustern; *look round*
sich umsehen; *look through* et. durchsehen; *look up* aufblicken, aufsehen; et.
nachschlagen; *j-n* aufsuchen; **2.** Blick
m; Miene *f*; (Gesichts)Ausdruck *m*;
(*good*) *looks* gutes Aussehen; *have a*
look at s.th. sich et. ansehen; *I don't like*
the look of it es gefällt mir nicht
look·ing glass Spiegel *m*
look·out Ausguck *m*; Ausschau *f*; *fig* F
Aussicht(en *pl*) *f*; *be on the lookout*
for Ausschau halten nach; *that's his*
own lookout F das ist allein seine Sache
loom¹ Webstuhl *m*
loom² *a.* *loom up* undeutlich sichtbar
werden *or* auftauchen
loop 1. Schlinge *f*, Schleife *f*; Schlaufe *f*;
Öse *f*; AVIAT Looping *m*, *n*; EDP Schleife
f; **2.** (sich) schlingen
loop·hole MIL Schießscharte *f*; *fig* Hintertürchen *n*; *a loophole in the law* e-e Ge-
setzeslücke
loose 1. los(e); locker; weit; frei; *let loose*
loslassen; freilassen; **2.** *be on the loose*
frei herumlaufen
loos·en (sich) lösen *or* lockern; *loosen up*
SPORT Lockerungsübungen machen
loot 1. Beute *f*; **2.** plündern
lop *Baum* beschneiden, stutzen; *lop off*
abhauen, abhacken
lop·sid·ed schief; *fig* einseitig
lord Herr *m*, Gebieter *m*; *Br* Lord *m*; *the*
Lord REL Gott *m* (der Herr); *the Lord's*
Prayer REL das Vaterunser; *the Lord's*
Supper REL das (heilige) Abendmahl;
House of Lords Br POL Oberhaus *n*
Lord Mayor *Br* Oberbürgermeister *m*
lor·ry *Br* MOT Last(kraft)wagen *m*, Lastau-
to *n*, Laster *m*
lose verlieren; verpassen; versäumen;
nachgehen (*watch*); *lose o.s.* sich verirren; sich verlieren
los·er Verlierer(in)
loss Verlust *m*; Schaden *m*; *at a loss* ECON
mit Verlust; *be at a loss* in Verlegenheit
sein (*for* um)
lost verloren; *be lost* sich verirrt haben,
sich nicht mehr zurechtfinden (*a. fig*);
be lost in thought in Gedanken versunken sein; *get lost* sich verirren; *get lost!*
sl hau ab!
lost-and-found (of·fice), *Br* **lost prop-**
er·ty of·fice Fundbüro *n*
lot Los *n*; Parzelle *f*; Grundstück *n*; ECON
Partie *f*, Posten *m*; Gruppe *f*, Gesellschaft *f*; Menge *f*, Haufen *m*; Los *n*,
Schicksal *n*; *the lot* alles, das Ganze; *a*
lot of F, *lots of* F viel, e-e Menge; *a*

bad lot F ein übler Kerl; *cast or draw*
lots losen
loth → *loath*
lo·tion Lotion *f*
lot·te·ry Lotterie *f*
loud laut; *fig* schreiend, grell
loud·mouth *contp* Schwätzer *m*
loud·speak·er Lautsprecher *m*
lounge 1. Wohnzimmer *n*; Aufenthaltsraum *m*, Lounge *f* (*a.* AVIAT); Wartehalle
f; **2.** F *contp* sich flegeln; *lounge about*,
lounge around herumlungern
louse ZO Laus *f*
lou·sy verlaust; F miserabel, saumäßig
lout Flegel *m*, Lümmel *m*, Rüpel *m*
lov·a·ble liebenswert; reizend
love 1. Liebe *f* (*of, for, to, towards* zu);
Liebling *m*, Schatz *m*; *tennis*: null; *be*
in love with s.o. in j-n verliebt sein; *fall*
in love with s.o. sich in j-n verlieben;
make love sich lieben, miteinander
schlafen; *give my love to her* grüße
sie herzlich von mir; *send one's love*
to j-n grüßen lassen; *love from ...* herzliche Grüße von ...; **2.** lieben; gern mögen
love af·fair Liebesaffäre *f*
love·ly (wunder)schön; nett, reizend; F
prima
lov·er Liebhaber *m*, Geliebte *m*, *f*; (*Mu-*
sik- etc)Liebhaber(in), (-)Freund(in); *pl*
Liebende *pl*, Liebespaar *n*
lov·ing liebevoll, liebend
low 1. *adj* niedrig (*a. fig*); tief (*a. fig*);
knapp (*supplies etc*); gedämpft, schwach
(*light*); tief (*sound*); leise (*sound, voice*);
fig gering(schätzig); ordinär; niedergeschlagen, deprimiert; **2.** *adv* niedrig; tief
(*a. fig*); leise **3.** METEOR Tief(druckgebiet)
n; *fig* Tief(punkt *m*) *n*
low·brow F **1.** geistig Anspruchslose *m*, *f*,
Unbedarfte *m*, *f*; **2.** geistig anspruchslos,
unbedarft
low-cal·o·rie kalorienarm, -reduziert
low-e·mis·sion schadstoffarm
low·er 1. niedriger; tiefer; untere(r, -s),
Unter...; **2.** niedriger machen; herab-,
herunterlassen; *Augen, Stimme, Preis*
etc senken; *Standard* herabsetzen; *fig* erniedrigen
low-fat fettarm
low-fly·ing plane AVIAT Tiefflieger *m*
low·land Tief-, Flachland *n*
low·ly niedrig
low-necked (tief) ausgeschnitten
low-pitched MUS tief
low-pres·sure METEOR Tiefdruck...; TECH
Niederdruck...
low-rise ARCH niedrig (gebaut)

L

low-spir·it·ed niedergeschlagen
low tide Ebbe *f*
low wa·ter Niedrigwasser *n*
loy·al loyal, treu
loy·al·ty Loyalität *f*, Treue *f*
loz·enge MATH Raute *f*, Rhombus *m*; GASTR Pastille *f*
lu·bri·cant TECH Schmiermittel *n*
lu·bri·cate TECH schmieren, ölen
lu·bri·ca·tion TECH Schmieren *n*, Ölen *n*
lu·cid klar
luck Schicksal *n*; Glück *n*; *bad luck, hard luck, ill luck* Unglück *n*, Pech *n*; *good luck* Glück *n*; *good luck!* viel Glück!; *be in* (*out of*) *luck* (kein) Glück haben
luck·i·ly glücklicherweise, zum Glück
luck·y glücklich, Glücks...; *be lucky* Glück haben; *lucky day* Glückstag *m*; *lucky fellow* Glückspilz *m*
lu·cra·tive einträglich, lukrativ
lu·di·crous lächerlich
lug zerren, schleppen
luge SPORT Rennrodeln *n*; Rennrodel *m*, Rennschlitten *m*
lug·gage *esp Br* (Reise)Gepäck *n*
luggage rack *esp Br* RAIL *etc* Gepäcknetz *n*, Gepäckablage *f*
luggage van *Br* RAIL Gepäckwagen *m*
luke·warm lau(warm); *fig* lau, mäßig, halbherzig
lull 1. beruhigen; sich legen (*storm*); *mst lull to sleep* einlullen; **2.** Pause *f*; MAR Flaute *f* (*a. fig*)
lul·la·by Wiegenlied *n*
lum·ba·go MED Hexenschuss *m*
lum·ber¹ schwerfällig gehen; (dahin-)rumpeln (*vehicle*)
lum·ber² 1. Bau-, Nutzholz *n*; *esp Br* Gerümpel *n*; **2.** *v/t lumber s.o. with s.th.* *Br* F j-m et. aufhalsen
lum·ber·jack Holzfäller *m*, -arbeiter *m*
lum·ber mill Sägewerk *n*
lum·ber room *esp Br* Rumpelkammer *f*
lum·ber·yard Holzplatz *m*, Holzlager *n*
lu·mi·na·ry *fig* Leuchte *f*, Koryphäe *f*
lu·mi·nous leuchtend, Leucht...
lu·mi·nous di·splay Leuchtanzeige *f*
lu·mi·nous paint Leuchtfarbe *f*
lump 1. Klumpen *m*; Schwellung *f*, Beule *f*; MED Geschwulst *f*, Knoten *m*; GASTR Stück *n*; *in the lump* in Bausch und Bo-

gen, pauschal; **2.** *v/t: lump together* *fig* zusammenwerfen; in e-n Topf werfen; *v/i* Klumpen bilden, klumpen
lump sug·ar Würfelzucker *m*
lump sum Pauschalsumme *f*
lump·y klumpig
lu·na·cy Wahnsinn *m*
lu·nar ASTR Mond...
lu·nar mod·ule Mond(lande)fähre *f*
lu·na·tic *fig* **1.** wahnsinnig, verrückt; **2.** Wahnsinnige *m*, *f*, Verrückte *m*, *f*
lunch, *formal* **lun·cheon 1.** Lunch *m*, Mittagessen *n*; **2.** zu Mittag essen
lunch hour, lunch time Mittagszeit *f*, Mittagspause *f*
lung ANAT Lungenflügel *m*; *pl* die Lunge
lunge sich stürzen (*at* auf *acc*)
lurch 1. taumeln, torkeln; **2.** *leave s.o. in the lurch* j-n im Stich lassen, F j-n sitzen lassen
lure 1. Köder *m*; *fig* Lockung *f*; **2.** ködern, (an)locken
lu·rid grell; grässlich, schauerlich
lurk lauern; *lurk about, lurk around* herumschleichen
lus·cious köstlich, lecker; üppig; F knackig
lush saftig, üppig
lust 1. sinnliche Begierde, Lust *f*; Gier *f*; **2.** *lust after, lust for* begehren; gierig sein nach
lus·ter, *Br* **lus·tre** Glanz *m*, Schimmer *m*
lus·trous glänzend, schimmernd
lust·y kräftig, robust, vital
lute MUS Laute *f*
Lu·ther·an REL lutherisch
lux·u·ri·ant üppig
lux·u·ri·ate schwelgen (*in* in *dat*)
lux·u·ri·ous luxuriös, Luxus...
lux·u·ry 1. Luxus *m*; Komfort *m*; Luxusartikel *m*; **2.** Luxus...
lye Lauge *f*
ly·ing lügnerisch, verlogen
lymph MED Lymphe *f*
lynch lynchen
lynch law Lynchjustiz *f*
lynx ZO Luchs *m*
lyr·ic 1. lyrisch; **2.** lyrisches Gedicht; *pl* Lyrik *f*; (Lied)Text *m*
lyr·i·cal lyrisch, gefühlvoll; schwärmerisch

M

M, m M, m *n*

M ABBR *of* **medium** (**size**) mittelgroß

ma F Mama *f*, Mutti *f*

ma'am → **madam**

ma·cad·am Asphalt *m*

mac·a·ro·ni Makkaroni *pl*

ma·chine 1. Maschine *f*; **2.** maschinell herstellen

ma·chine-gun Maschinengewehr *n*

ma·chine-read·a·ble EDP maschinenlesbar

ma·chin·e·ry Maschinen *pl*; Maschinerie *f*

ma·chin·ist TECH Maschinist *m*

mach·o *contp* Macho *m*

mack·e·rel ZO Makrele *f*

mac·ro... Makro..., (sehr) groß

mad wahnsinnig, verrückt; VET tollwütig; F wütend; *fig* **be mad about** wild *or* versessen sein auf (*acc*), verrückt sein nach; **drive s.o. mad** j-n verrückt machen; **go mad** verrückt werden; **like mad** wie verrückt

mad·am gnädige Frau

mad·cap verrückt

mad cow dis·ease VET Rinderwahn(-sinn) *m*

mad·den verrückt *or* rasend machen

mad·den·ing unerträglich; verrückt *or* rasend machend

made: **made of gold** aus Gold

made-to-meas·ure maßgeschneidert

made-up geschminkt; erfunden

mad·house *fig* F Irrenhaus *n*

mad·ly wie verrückt; F wahnsinnig, schrecklich

mad·man Verrückte *m*

mad·ness Wahnsinn

mad·wom·an Verrückte *f*

mag·a·zine Magazin *n* (*a*. PHOT, MIL), Zeitschrift *f*; Lagerhaus *n*

mag·got ZO Made *f*

Ma·gi: the (**three**) **Magi** die (drei) Weisen aus dem Morgenland, die Heiligen Drei Könige

ma·gic 1. Magie *f*, Zauberei *f*; Zauber *m*; *fig* Wunder *n*; **2.** *a*. **magical** magisch, Zauber...

ma·gi·cian Magier *m*, Zauberer *m*; Zauberkünstler *m*

ma·gis·trate (Friedens)Richter(in)

mag·na·nim·i·ty Großmut *f*

mag·nan·i·mous großmütig

mag·net Magnet *m*

mag·net·ic magnetisch, Magnet...

mag·nif·i·cent großartig, prächtig

mag·ni·fy vergrößern

mag·ni·fy·ing glass Vergrößerungsglas *n*, Lupe *f*

mag·ni·tude Größe *f*; Wichtigkeit *f*

mag·pie ZO Elster *f*

ma·hog·a·ny Mahagoni(holz) *n*

maid (Dienst)Mädchen *n*, Hausangestellte *f*; **maid of all work** *esp fig* Mädchen *n* für alles; **maid of hono(u)r** Hofdame *f*; (erste) Brautjungfer

maid·en Jungfern..., Erstlings...

maid·en name Mädchenname *m*

mail 1. Post(sendung) *f*; **by mail** mit der Post; **2.** mit der Post (zu)schicken, aufgeben, *Brief* einwerfen

mail·bag Postsack *m*; Posttasche *f*

mail·box Briefkasten *m*

mail car·ri·er, **mail·man** Briefträger *m*, Postbote *m*

mail or·der Bestellung *f* bei e-m Versandhaus

mail-or·der firm, **mail-order house** Versandhaus *n*

maim verstümmeln

main 1. Haupt..., wichtigste(r, -s); hauptsächlich; **by main force** mit äußerster Kraft; **2.** *mst pl* Hauptleitung *f*, Hauptgas-, Hauptwasser-, Hauptstromleitung *f*; (Strom)Netz *n*; **in the main** in der Hauptsache, im Wesentlichen

main·frame EDP Großrechner *m*

main·land Festland *n*

main·ly hauptsächlich

main mem·o·ry EDP Hauptspeicher *m*; Arbeitsspeicher *m*

main men·u EDP Hauptmenü *n*

main road Haupt(verkehrs)straße *f*

main·spring TECH Hauptfeder *f*; *fig* (Haupt)Triebfeder *f*

main·stay *fig* Hauptstütze *f*

main street Hauptstraße *f*

main·tain (aufrecht)erhalten, beibehalten; instand halten, pflegen, TECH *a*. warten; *Familie etc* unterhalten, versorgen; *et*. behaupten

main·te·nance (Aufrecht)Erhaltung *f*; Instandhaltung *f*, Pflege *f*, TECH *a*. Wartung *f*; Unterhalt *m*

maize *esp Br* BOT Mais *m*

ma·jes·tic majestätisch

ma·jes·ty Majestät *f*; **His** (**Her, Your**) **Majesty** Seine (Ihre, Eure) Majestät

M

ma·jor 1. größere(r, -s), *fig a.* bedeutend, wichtig; JUR volljährig; *C major* MUS C-Dur *n*; **2.** MIL Major *m*; JUR Volljährige *m*, *f*; UNIV Hauptfach *n*; MUS Dur *n*

major gen·e·ral MIL Generalmajor *m*

ma·jor·i·ty Mehrheit *f*, Mehrzahl *f*; JUR Volljährigkeit *f*

ma·jor league *baseball*: oberste Spielklasse

ma·jor road Haupt(verkehrs)straße *f*

make 1. machen; anfertigen, herstellen, erzeugen; (zu)bereiten; (er)schaffen; ergeben, bilden; machen zu; ernennen zu; *Geld* verdienen; sich erweisen als, abgeben (*person*); schätzen auf (*acc*); *Geschwindigkeit* erreichen; *Fehler* machen; *Frieden etc* schließen; *e-e Rede* halten; F *Strecke* zurücklegen; *with inf:* j-n lassen, veranlassen zu, bringen zu, zwingen zu; *make it* es schaffen; *make do with s.th.* mit et. auskommen, sich mit et. behelfen; *do you make one of us?* machen Sie mit?; *what do you make of it?* was halten Sie davon?; *make believe* vorgeben; *make friends with* sich anfreunden mit; *make good* wieder gutmachen; *Versprechen etc* halten; *make haste* sich beeilen; *make way* Platz machen; *make for* zugehen auf (*acc*); sich aufmachen nach; *make into* verarbeiten zu; *make off* sich davonmachen, sich aus dem Staub machen; *make out Rechnung, Scheck etc* ausstellen; ausmachen, erkennen; aus j-m, e-r *Sache* klug werden; *make over Eigentum* übertragen; *make up* et. zusammenstellen; sich *et.* ausdenken, et. erfinden; (sich) zurechtmachen *or* schminken; *make it up* sich versöhnen *or* wieder vertragen (*with* mit); *make up one's mind* sich entschließen; *be made up of* bestehen aus, sich zusammensetzen aus; *make up for* nachholen, aufholen; für *et.* entschädigen; **2.** Machart *f*, Bauart *f*; Fabrikat *n*, Marke *f*

make-be·lieve Schein *m*, Fantasie *f*

mak·er Hersteller *m*; *Maker* REL Schöpfer *m*

make·shift 1. Notbehelf *m*; **2.** behelfsmäßig, Behelfs...

make-up Make-up *n*, Schminke *f*; Aufmachung *f*; Zusammensetzung *f*

mak·ing Erzeugung *f*, Herstellung *f*, Fabrikation *f*; *be in the making* noch in Arbeit sein; *have the makings of* das Zeug haben zu

mal·ad·just·ed nicht angepasst, verhaltensgestört, milieugestört

mal·ad·min·i·stra·tion schlechte Verwaltung; POL Misswirtschaft *f*

mal·con·tent 1. unzufrieden; **2.** Unzufriedene *m*, *f*

male 1. männlich; **2.** Mann *m*; ZO Männchen *n*

male nurse (Kranken)Pfleger *m*

mal·for·ma·tion Missbildung *f*

mal·ice Bosheit *f*; Groll *m*; JUR böse Absicht, Vorsatz *m*

ma·li·cious boshaft; böswillig

ma·lign verleumden

ma·lig·nant bösartig (*a.* MED); boshaft

mall Einkaufszentrum *n*

mal·le·a·ble TECH verformbar; *fig* formbar

mal·let Holzhammer *m*; (Krocket-, Polo)-Schläger *m*

mal·nu·tri·tion Unterernährung *f*; Fehlernährung *f*

mal·o·dor·ous übel riechend

mal·prac·tice Vernachlässigung *f* der beruflichen Sorgfalt; MED falsche Behandlung, (ärztlicher) Kunstfehler

malt Malz *n*

mal·treat schlecht behandeln; misshandeln

mam·mal ZO Säugetier *n*

mam·moth 1. ZO Mammut *n*; **2.** Mammut..., Riesen..., riesig

mam·my F Mami *f*

man 1. Mann *m*; Mensch(en *pl*) *m*; Menschheit *f*; F (Ehe)Mann *m*; F Geliebte *m*; (*Schach*)Figur *f*; (*Dame*)Stein *m*; *the man on* (*Br in*) *the street* der Mann auf der Straße; **2.** (*Raum*)*Schiff etc* bemannen; *Büro etc* besetzen

man·age *v/t Betrieb etc* leiten, führen; *Künstler, Sportler etc* managen; et. zustande bringen; es fertigbringen (*to do* zu tun); umgehen (können) mit; mit j-m, et. fertigwerden; F *Arbeit, Essen etc* bewältigen, schaffen; *v/i* auskommen (*with* mit; *without* ohne); F es schaffen, zurechtkommen; F es einrichten, es ermöglichen

man·age·a·ble handlich; lenksam

man·age·ment Verwaltung *f*; ECON Management *n*, Unternehmensführung *f*; Geschäftsleitung *f*, Direktion *f*

man·ag·er Verwalter *m*; ECON Manager *m* (*a.* THEA *etc*); Geschäftsführer *m*, Leiter *m*, Direktor *m*; SPORT (Chef-) Trainer *m*; *be a good manager* gut *or* sparsam wirtschaften können

man·a·ge·ri·al ECON geschäftsführend, leitend; *managerial position* leitende Stellung; *managerial staff* leitende Angestellte *pl*

man·ag·ing ECON geschäftsführend, leitend

managing di·rec·tor Generaldirektor *m*, leitender Direktor

man·date Mandat *n*; Auftrag *m*; Vollmacht *f*

man·da·to·ry obligatorisch, zwingend

mane ZO Mähne *f* (*a*. F)

ma·neu·ver *a. fig* **1.** Manöver *n*; **2.** manövrieren

mange VET Räude *f*

man·ger AGR Krippe *f*

man·gle 1. (Wäsche)Mangel *f*; **2.** mangeln; *j-n* übel zurichten, zerfleischen; *fig Text* verstümmeln

mang·y VET räudig; *fig* schäbig

man·hood Mannesalter *n*; Männlichkeit *f*

ma·ni·a Wahnsinn *m*; *fig* (**for**) Sucht *f* (nach), Leidenschaft *f* (für), Manie *f*, Fimmel *m*

ma·ni·ac F Wahnsinnige *m*, *f*, Verrückte *m*, *f*; *fig* Fanatiker(in)

man·i·cure Maniküre *f*, Handpflege *f*

man·i·fest 1. offenkundig; **2.** *v/t* offenbaren, manifestieren

man·i·fold mannigfaltig, vielfältig

ma·nip·u·late manipulieren; (geschickt) handhaben

ma·nip·u·la·tion Manipulation *f*

man·kind die Menschheit, die Menschen *pl*

man·ly männlich

man-made vom Menschen geschaffen, künstlich; **man-made fiber** Kunstfaser *f*

man·ner Art *f* (und Weise *f*); Betragen *n*, Auftreten *n*; *pl* Benehmen *n*, Umgangsformen *pl*, Manieren *pl*; Sitten *pl*

ma·noeu·vre *Br* → **maneuver**

man·or *Br* (Land)Gut *n*; → **man·or house** Herrenhaus *n*

man·pow·er menschliche Arbeitskraft; Arbeitskräfte *pl*

man·sion (herrschaftliches) Wohnhaus

man·slaugh·ter JUR Totschlag *m*, fahrlässige Tötung

man·tel·piece, man·tel·shelf Kaminsims *m*

man·u·al 1. Hand...; mit der Hand (gemacht); **2.** Handbuch *n*

man·u·fac·ture 1. erzeugen, herstellen; **2.** Herstellung *f*, Fertigung *f*; Erzeugnis *n*, Fabrikat *n*

man·u·fac·tur·er Hersteller *m*, Erzeuger *m*

man·u·fac·tur·ing Herstellungs...

ma·nure AGR **1.** Dünger *m*, Mist *m*, Dung *m*; **2.** düngen

man·u·script Manuskript *n*

man·y 1. viel(e); **many a** manche(r, -s), manch eine(r, -s); **many times** oft; **as many** ebenso viel(e); **2.** viele; **a good**

many ziemlich viel(e); **a great many** sehr viele

map 1. (Land- *etc*)Karte *f*; (Stadt- *etc*)Plan *m*; **2.** e-e Karte machen von; auf e-r Karte eintragen; **map out** *fig* (bis in die Einzelheiten) (voraus)planen

ma·ple BOT Ahorn *m*

mar beeinträchtigen; verderben

Mar ABBR *of* **March** März *m*

mar·a·thon SPORT **1.** *a.* **marathon race** Marathonlauf *m*; **2.** Marathon... (*a. fig*)

ma·raud plündern

mar·ble 1. Marmor *m*; Murmel *f*; **2.** marmorn

march 1. marschieren; *fig* fortschreiten; **2.** Marsch *m*; *fig* (Fort)Gang *m*; **the march of events** der Lauf der Dinge

March (ABBR **Mar**) März *m*

mare ZO Stute *f*

mar·ga·rine, *Br* F **marge** Margarine *f*

mar·gin Rand *m* (*a. fig*); Grenze *f* (*a. fig*); *fig* Spielraum *m*; (Gewinn-, Verdienst-)Spanne *f*; **by a wide margin** mit großem Vorsprung

mar·gin·al Rand...; **marginal note** Randbemerkung *f*

mar·i·hua·na, mar·i·jua·na Marihuana *n*

ma·ri·na Boots-, Jachthafen *m*

ma·rine Marine *f*; MIL Marineinfanterist *m*

mar·i·ner Seemann *m*

mar·i·tal ehelich, Ehe...

mar·i·tal sta·tus Familienstand *m*

mar·i·time See...; Küsten...; Schiffahrts...

mark¹ (Deutsche) Mark

mark² 1. Marke *f*, Markierung *f*; (Kenn)Zeichen *n*, Merkmal *n*; (Körper)Mal *n*; Ziel *n* (*a. fig*); Spur *f* (*a. fig*); Fleck *m*; (Fabrik-, Waren)Zeichen *n*, (Schutz-, Handels)Marke *f*; ECON Preisangabe *f*; PED Note *f*, Zensur *f*, Punkt *m*; SPORT Startlinie *f*; *fig* Zeichen *n*; *fig* Norm *f*; **be up to the mark** den Anforderungen gewachsen sein (*person*) *or* genügen (*performance etc*); gesundheitlich auf der Höhe sein; **be wide of the mark** weit danebenschießen; *fig* sich gewaltig irren; weit danebenliegen (*estimate etc*); **hit the mark** (das Ziel) treffen; *fig* ins Schwarze treffen; **miss the mark** danebenschießen, das Ziel verfehlen (*a. fig*); **2.** markieren, anzeichnen; anzeigen; kennzeichnen; *Waren* auszeichnen; *Preis* festsetzen; Spuren hinterlassen auf (*dat*); Flecken machen auf (*dat*); PED benoten, zensieren; SPORT *Gegenspieler* decken, markieren; **mark my words** denk an m-e Worte; **to mark the occasion** zur

Feier des Tages; **mark time** auf der Stelle treten (*a. fig*); **mark down** notieren, vermerken; *im Preis* herabsetzen; **mark off** abgrenzen; *auf e-r Liste* abhaken; **mark out** *durch Striche etc* markieren; bestimmen (**for** für); **mark up** *im Preis* heraufsetzen

marked deutlich, ausgeprägt

mark·er Markierstift *m*; Lesezeichen *n*; SPORT Bewacher(in)

mar·ket 1. Markt *m*; Marktplatz *m*; (Lebensmittel)Geschäft *n*, Laden *m*; ECON Absatz *m*; (**for**) Nachfrage *f* (nach), Bedarf *m* (an *dat*); **on the market** auf dem Markt *or* im Handel; **put on the market** auf den Markt *or* in den Handel bringen; (zum Verkauf) anbieten; **2.** *v/t* auf den Markt *or* in den Handel bringen; verkaufen, vertreiben

mar·ket·a·ble ECON marktgängig

mar·ket gar·den *Br* Gemüse- und Obstgärtnerei *f*

mar·ket·ing ECON Marketing *n*

mark·ing Markierung *f*; ZO Zeichnung *f*; SPORT Deckung *f*; **man-to-man marking** Manndeckung *f*

marks·man guter Schütze

mar·ma·lade *esp* Orangenmarmelade *f*

mar·mot ZO Murmeltier *n*

ma·roon 1. kastanienbraun; **2.** *auf e-r einsamen Insel* aussetzen; **3.** Leuchtrakete *f*

mar·quee Festzelt *n*

mar·quis Marquis *m*

mar·riage Heirat *f*, Hochzeit *f* (**to** mit); Ehe *f*; **civil marriage** standesamtliche Trauung

mar·ri·age·a·ble heiratsfähig

mar·riage cer·tif·i·cate Trauschein *m*, Heiratsurkunde *f*

mar·ried verheiratet; ehelich, Ehe...; **married couple** Ehepaar *n*; **married life** Ehe(leben *n*) *f*

mar·row ANAT (Knochen)Mark *n*; *fig* Kern *m*, *das* Wesentliche

mar·ry *v/t* heiraten; *Paar* trauen; **be married** verheiratet sein (**to** mit); **get married** heiraten; sich verheiraten (**to** mit); *v/i* heiraten

marsh Sumpf(land *n*) *m*, Marsch *f*

mar·shal 1. MIL Marschall *m*; Bezirkspolizeichef *m*; **2.** ordnen; führen

marsh·y sumpfig

mar·ten ZO Marder *m*

mar·tial kriegerisch; Kriegs..., Militär...

martial arts asiatische Kampfsportarten *pl*

martial law Kriegsrecht *n*

mar·tyr REL Märtyrer(in) (*a. fig*)

mar·vel 1. Wunder *n*; **2.** sich wundern, staunen

mar·vel·(l)ous wunderbar; fabelhaft, fantastisch

mar·zi·pan Marzipan *n*, *m*

mas·ca·ra Wimperntusche *f*

mas·cot Maskottchen *n*

mas·cu·line männlich; Männer...; maskulin (*a.* LING)

mash zerdrücken, zerquetschen

mashed po·ta·toes Kartoffelbrei *m*

mask 1. Maske *f* (*a.* EDP); **2.** maskieren; *fig* verbergen, verschleiern

masked maskiert; **masked ball** Maskenball *m*

ma·son Steinmetz *m*; *mst* **Mason** Freimaurer *m*

ma·son·ry Mauerwerk *n*

masque THEA HIST Maskenspiel *n*

mas·que·rade 1. Maskerade *f* (*a. fig*); Verkleidung *f*; **2.** sich ausgeben (**as** als, für)

mass 1. Masse *f*; Menge *f*; Mehrzahl *f*; **the masses** die (breite) Masse; **2.** (sich) (an)sammeln *or* (an)häufen; **3.** Massen...

Mass REL Messe *f*

mas·sa·cre 1. Massaker *n*; **2.** niedermetzeln

mas·sage 1. Massage *f*; **2.** massieren

mas·seur Masseur *m*

mas·seuse Masseurin *f*, Masseuse *f*

mas·sif (Gebirgs)Massiv *n*

mas·sive massiv; groß, gewaltig

mass me·di·a Massenmedien *pl*

mass-pro·duce serienmäßig herstellen

mass pro·duc·tion Massen-, Serienproduktion *f*

mast MAR Mast *m*; *Br* ELECTR Sendemast *m*

mas·ter 1. Meister *m* (*a.* PAINT); Herr *m*; *esp Br* Lehrer *m*; Original(kopie *f*) *n*; UNIV Magister *m*; **Master of Arts** (ABBR **MA**) Magister *m* Artium; **master of ceremonies** Conférencier *m*; **2.** Meister...; Haupt...; **master copy** Originalkopie *f*; **master tape** TECH Mastertape *n*, Originaltonband *n*; **3.** Herr sein über (*acc*); *Sprache etc* beherrschen; *Aufgabe etc* meistern

mas·ter key Hauptschlüssel *m*

mas·ter·ly meisterhaft, virtuos

mas·ter·piece Meisterstück *n*, -werk *n*

mas·ter·y Herrschaft *f*; Oberhand *f*; Beherrschung *f*

mas·tur·bate masturbieren, onanieren

mat¹ 1. Matte *f*; Untersetzer *m*; **2.** sich verfilzen

mat² mattiert, matt

match¹ Streichholz *n*, Zündholz *n*

match² 1. *der, die, das* Gleiche; (dazu) passende Sache *or* Person, Gegenstück *n*; (*Fußball- etc*)Spiel *n*, (*Box- etc* -)

Kampf *m*, (*Tennis- etc*)Match *n*, *m*; Heirat *f*; *gute etc* Partie (*person*); **be a (no) match for s.o.** j-m (nicht) gewachsen sein; **find** *or* **meet one's match** s-n Meister finden; **2.** *v/t j-m, e-r Sache* ebenbürtig *or* gewachsen sein, gleichkommen; *j-m, e-r Sache* entsprechen, passen zu; *v/i* zusammenpassen, übereinstimmen, entsprechen; **gloves to match** dazu passende Handschuhe

match·box Streichholz-, Zündholzschachtel *f*

match·less unvergleichlich, einzigartig

match·mak·er Ehestifter(in)

match point *tennis etc*: Matchball *m*

mate¹ → **checkmate**

mate² **1.** (Arbeits)Kamerad *m*, (-)Kollege *m*; zo Männchen *n*, Weibchen *n*; MAR Maat *m*; **2.** zo (sich) paaren

ma·te·ri·al **1.** Material *n*, Stoff *m*; **writing materials** Schreibmaterial(ien *pl*) *n*; **2.** materiell; leiblich; wesentlich

ma·ter·nal mütterlich, Mutter...; mütterlicherseits

ma·ter·ni·ty **1.** Mutterschaft *f*; **2.** Schwangerschafts..., Umstands...

ma·ter·ni·ty leave Mutterschaftsurlaub *m*

maternity ward Entbindungsstation *f*

math F Mathe *f*

math·e·ma·ti·cian Mathematiker *m*

math·e·mat·ics Mathematik *f*

maths *Br* F Mathe *f*

mat·i·née THEA *etc* Nachmittagsvorstellung *f*

ma·tric·u·late (sich) immatrikulieren

mat·ri·mo·ni·al ehelich, Ehe...

mat·ri·mo·ny Ehe *f*, Ehestand *m*

ma·trix TECH Matrize *f*

ma·tron *Br* MED Oberschwester *f*; Hausmutter *f*; Matrone *f*

mat·ter **1.** Materie *f*, Material *n*, Substanz *f*, Stoff *m*; MED Eiter *m*; Sache *f*, Angelegenheit *f*; **printed matter** Drucksache *f*; **what's the matter (with you)?** was ist los (mit dir)?; **no matter who** gleichgültig, wer; **for that matter** was das betrifft; **a matter of course** e-e Selbstverständlichkeit; **a matter of fact** e-e Tatsache; **as a matter of fact** tatsächlich, eigentlich; **a matter of form** e-e Formsache; **a matter of time** e-e Frage der Zeit; **2.** von Bedeutung sein (**to** für); **it doesn't matter** es macht nichts

mat·ter-of-fact sachlich, nüchtern

mat·tress Matratze *f*

ma·ture **1.** reif (*a. fig*); **2.** (heran)reifen, reif werden

ma·tu·ri·ty Reife *f* (*a. fig*)

maud·lin rührselig

maul übel zurichten; *fig* verreißen

Maun·dy Thurs·day Gründonnerstag *m*

mauve malvenfarbig, mauve

mawk·ish rührselig

max·i... Maxi..., riesig, Riesen...

max·im Grundsatz *m*

max·i·mum **1.** Maximum *n*; **2.** maximal, Maximal..., Höchst...

May Mai *m*

may *v/aux ich* kann / mag / darf *etc*, *du* kannst / magst / darfst etc

may·be vielleicht

may·bug zo Maikäfer *m*

May Day der 1. Mai

may·on·naise Mayonnaise *f*

mayor Bürgermeister *m*

may·pole Maibaum *m*

maze Irrgarten *m*, Labyrinth *n* (*a. fig*)

me mich; mir; F ich

mead·ow Wiese *f*, Weide *f*

mea·ger, *Br* **mea·gre** mager (*a. fig*), dürr; dürftig

meal¹ Mahl(zeit *f*) *n*; Essen *n*

meal² Schrotmehl *n*

mean¹ gemein, niederträchtig; geizig, knauserig; schäbig

mean² meinen; sagen wollen; bedeuten; beabsichtigen, vorhaben; **be meant for** bestimmt sein für; **mean well (ill)** es gut (schlecht) meinen

mean³ **1.** Mitte *f*, Mittel *n*, Durchschnitt *m*; **2.** mittlere(r, -s), Mittel..., durchschnittlich, Durchschnitts...

mean·ing **1.** Sinn *m*, Bedeutung *f*; **2.** bedeutungsvoll, bedeutsam

mean·ing·ful bedeutungsvoll; sinnvoll

mean·ing·less sinnlos

means Mittel *n or pl*, Weg *m*; ECON Mittel *pl*, Vermögen *n*; **by all means** auf alle Fälle, unbedingt; **by no means** keineswegs, auf keinen Fall; **by means of** durch, mit

mean·time **1.** inzwischen; **2. in the meantime** inzwischen

mean·while inzwischen

mea·sles MED Masern *pl*

mea·sur·a·ble messbar

mea·sure **1.** Maß *n* (*a. fig*); TECH Messgerät *n*; MUS Takt *m*; *fig* Maßnahme *f*; **beyond measure** über alle Maßen; **in a great measure** großenteils; **take measures** Maßnahmen treffen *or* ergreifen; **2.** (ab-, aus-, ver-)messen; *j-m* Maß nehmen; **measure up to** den Ansprüchen (*gen*) genügen

measured gemessen; wohlüberlegt; maßvoll

mea·sure·ment (Ver)Messung *f*; Maß *n*

measurement of ca·pac·i·ty Hohlmaß *n*

M

mea·sur·ing tape → *tape measure*

meat GASTR Fleisch *n*; *cold meat* kalter Braten

meat·ball GASTR Fleischklößchen *n*

me·chan·ic Mechaniker *m*

me·chan·i·cal mechanisch; Maschinen...

me·chan·ics PHYS Mechanik *f*

mech·a·nism Mechanismus *m*

mech·a·nize mechanisieren

med·al Medaille *f*; Orden *m*

med·al·(l)ist SPORT Medaillengewinner(in)

med·dle sich einmischen (*with, in* in *acc*)

med·dle·some aufdringlich

me·di·a Medien *pl*

med·i·ae·val → *medieval*

me·di·an *a. median strip* MOT Mittelstreifen *m*

me·di·ate vermitteln

me·di·a·tion Vermittlung *f*

me·di·a·tor Vermittler *m*

med·ic MIL Sanitäter *m*

med·i·cal 1. medizinisch, ärztlich; **2.** ärztliche Untersuchung

med·i·cal cer·tif·i·cate ärztliches Attest

med·i·cated medizinisch

me·di·ci·nal medizinisch, heilkräftig, Heil...

medi·cine Medizin *f*, *a.* Arznei *f*, *a.* Heilkunde *f*

med·i·e·val mittelalterlich

me·di·o·cre mittelmäßig

med·i·tate *v/i* (*on*) nachdenken (über *acc*); meditieren (über *acc*); *v/t* erwägen

med·i·ta·tion Nachdenken *n*; Meditation *f*

med·i·ta·tive nachdenklich

Med·i·ter·ra·ne·an Mittelmeer...

me·di·um 1. Mitte *f*; Mittel *n*; Medium *n*; **2.** mittlere(r, -s), Mittel..., *a.* mittelmäßig; GASTR medium, halb gar

med·ley Gemisch *n*; MUS Medley *n*, Potpourri *n*

meek sanft(mütig), bescheiden

meet *v/t* treffen, sich treffen mit; begegnen (*dat*); *j-n* kennenlernen; *j-n* abholen; zusammentreffen mit, stoßen *or* treffen auf (*acc*); *Wünschen* entgegenkommen, entsprechen; *e-r Forderung, Verpflichtung* nachkommen; *v/i* zusammenkommen, -treten; sich begegnen, sich treffen; (*feindlich*) zusammenstoßen; SPORT aufeinandertreffen; sich kennenlernen; *meet with* zusammentreffen mit; sich treffen mit; stoßen auf (*Schwierigkeiten etc*); erleben, erleiden

meet·ing Begegnung *f*, (Zusammen-) Treffen *n*; Versammlung *f*, Konferenz *f*, Tagung *f*

meeting place Tagungs-, Versammlungsort *m*; Treffpunkt *m*

mel·an·chol·y 1. Melancholie *f*, Schwermut *f*, Trübsinn *m*; **2.** melancholisch, traurig, trübsinnig, wehmütig

mel·low 1. reif, weich; sanft, mild (*light*), zart (*colors*); *fig* gereift (*person*); **2.** reifen (lassen) (*a. fig*); weich *or* sanft werden

me·lo·di·ous melodisch

mel·o·dra·mat·ic melodramatisch

mel·o·dy MUS Melodie *f*

mel·on BOT Melone *f*

melt (zer)schmelzen; *melt down* einschmelzen

mem·ber Mitglied *n*, Angehörige *m*, *f*; ANAT Glied *n*, Gliedmaße *f*; (männliches) Glied; *Member of Parliament Br* Mitglied *n* des Unterhauses, Unterhausabgeordnete *m*, *f*

mem·ber·ship Mitgliedschaft *f*; Mitgliederzahl *f*

mem·brane Membran(e) *f*

mem·o Memo *n*

mem·oirs Memoiren *pl*

mem·o·ra·ble denkwürdig

me·mo·ri·al Denkmal *n*, Ehrenmal *n*, Gedenkstätte *f* (*to* für); Gedenkfeier *f* (*to* für)

mem·o·rize auswendig lernen, sich *et.* einprägen

mem·o·ry Gedächtnis *n*; Erinnerung *f*; Andenken *n*; EDP Speicher *m*; *in memory of* zum Andenken an (*acc*)

memory ca·pac·i·ty EDP Speicherkapazität *f*

men·ace 1. (be)drohen; **2.** (Be)Drohung *f*

mend 1. *v/t* (ver)bessern; ausbessern, reparieren, flicken; *mend one's ways* sich bessern; *v/i* sich bessern; **2.** ausgebesserte Stelle; *on the mend* auf dem Wege der Bess(e)rung

men·di·cant REL Bettelmönch *m*

me·ni·al niedrig, untergeordnet

men·in·gi·tis MED Meningitis *f*, Hirnhautentzündung *f*

men·o·pause MED Wechseljahre *pl*

men·stru·ate menstruieren

men·stru·a·tion Menstruation *f*

men·tal geistig, Geistes...; seelisch, psychisch

mental a·rith·me·tic Kopfrechnen *n*

mental hand·i·cap geistige Behinderung

mental hos·pi·tal psychiatrische Klinik

men·tal·i·ty Mentalität *f*

men·tal·ly: *mentally handicapped* geistig behindert; *mentally ill* geisteskrank

men·tion 1. erwähnen; *don't mention it!* keine Ursache!; **2.** Erwähnung *f*

men·u Speise(n)karte *f*; EDP Menü *n*
me·ow ZO miauen
mer·can·tile Handels...
mer·ce·na·ry 1. geldgierig; **2.** MIL Söldner *m*
mer·chan·dise 1. Ware(n *pl*) *f*; **2.** vermarkten
mer·chan·dis·ing Vermarktung *f*
mer·chant 1. (Groß)Händler *m*, (Groß)-Kaufmann *m*; **2.** Handels...
mer·ci·ful barmherzig, gnädig
mer·ci·less unbarmherzig, erbarmungslos
mer·cu·ry CHEM Quecksilber *n*
mer·cy Barmherzigkeit *f*, Erbarmen *n*, Gnade *f*
mere, mere·ly bloß, nur
merge verschmelzen (*into, with* mit); ECON fusionieren
merg·er ECON Fusion *f*
me·rid·i·an GEOGR Meridian *m*; *fig* Gipfel *m*, Höhepunkt *m*
mer·it 1. Verdienst *n*; Wert *m*; Vorzug *m*; **2.** verdienen
mer·maid Meerjungfrau *f*, Nixe *f*
mer·ri·ment Fröhlichkeit *f*; Gelächter *n*, Heiterkeit *f*
mer·ry lustig, fröhlich, ausgelassen; ***Merry Christmas!*** fröhliche *or* frohe Weihnachten
mer·ry-go-round Karussell *n*
mesh 1. Masche *f*; *fig often pl* Netz *n*, Schlingen *pl*; ***be in mesh*** TECH (ineinander)greifen; **2.** TECH (ineinander)greifen; *fig* passen (***with*** zu), zusammenpassen
mess 1. Unordnung *f*, Durcheinander *n*; Schmutz *m*, F Schweinerei *f*; F Patsche *f*, Klemme *f*; MIL Messe *f*, Kasino *n*; ***make a mess of*** F *fig* verpfuschen, ruinieren, *Pläne etc* über den Haufen werfen; **2. *mess about, mess around*** F herumspielen, herumbasteln (***with*** an *dat*); herumgammeln; ***mess up*** in Unordnung bringen, durcheinanderbringen; *fig* F verpfuschen, ruinieren, *Pläne etc* über den Haufen werfen
mes·sage Mitteilung *f*, Nachricht *f*; Anliegen *n*, Aussage *f*; ***can I take a message?*** kann ich etwas ausrichten?; ***get the message*** F kapieren
mes·sen·ger Bote *m*
mess·y unordentlich; unsauber, schmutzig
me·tab·o·lis·m MED Stoffwechsel *m*
met·al Metall *n*
me·tal·lic metallisch; Metall...
met·a·mor·pho·sis Metamorphose *f*, Verwandlung *f*
met·a·phor Metapher *f*

me·tas·ta·sis MED Metastase *f*
me·te·or Meteor *m*
me·te·or·o·log·i·cal meteorologisch, Wetter..., Witterungs...
meteorological of·fice Wetteramt *n*
me·te·or·ol·o·gy Meteorologie *f*, Wetterkunde *f*
me·ter¹ TECH Messgerät *n*, Zähler *m*
me·ter² Meter *m*, *n*; Versmaß *n*
meth·od Methode *f*, Verfahren *n*; System *n*
me·thod·i·cal methodisch, systematisch, planmäßig
me·tic·u·lous peinlich genau, übergenau
me·tre *Br* → **meter²**
met·ric metrisch
metric sys·tem metrisches (Maß- und Gewichts)System
met·ro·pol·i·tan ... der Hauptstadt
me·trop·o·lis Weltstadt *f*
met·tle Eifer *m*, Mut *m*, Feuer *n*
mew ZO miauen
Mex·i·can 1. mexikanisch; **2.** Mexikaner(in)
Mex·i·co Mexiko *n*
mi·aow ZO miauen
mi·cro... Mikro..., (sehr) klein
mi·cro·chip Mikrochip *m*
mi·cro·e·lec·tron·ics Mikroelektronik *f*
mi·cro·film Mikrofilm *m*
mi·cro·or·gan·ism BIOL Mikroorganismus *m*
mi·cro·phone Mikrofon *n*
mi·cro·pro·ces·sor Mikroprozessor *m*
mi·cro·scope Mikroskop *n*
mi·cro·scop·ic mikroskopisch
mi·cro·wave Mikrowelle *f*
microwave ov·en Mikrowellenherd *m*
mid mittlere(r, -s), Mitt(el)...
mid·air: *in midair* in der Luft
mid·day 1. Mittag *m*; **2.** mittägig, Mittag(s)...
mid·dle 1. mittlere(r, -s), Mittel...; **2.** Mitte *f*
mid·dle-aged mittleren Alters
Mid·dle Ag·es HIST Mittelalter *n*
mid·dle class(·es) Mittelstand *m*
mid·dle·man ECON Zwischenhändler *m*; Mittelsmann *m*
mid·dle name zweiter Vorname *m*
mid·dle-sized mittelgroß
mid·dle·weight *boxing*: Mittelgewicht *n*, Mittelgewichtler *m*
mid·dling F mittelmäßig, Mittel...; leidlich
mid·field *esp soccer*: Mittelfeld *n*
mid·field·er, mid·field play·er *esp soccer*: Mittelfeldspieler *m*
midge ZO Mücke *f*

M

midg·et Zwerg *m*, Knirps *m*
mid·night Mitternacht *f*; **at midnight** um Mitternacht
midst: in the midst of mitten in (*dat*)
mid·sum·mer Hochsommer *m*; ASTR Sommersonnenwende *f*
mid·way auf halbem Wege
mid·wife Hebamme *f*
mid·win·ter Mitte *f* des Winters; ASTR Wintersonnenwende *f*; **in midwinter** mitten im Winter
might Macht *f*, Gewalt *f*; Kraft *f*
might·y mächtig, gewaltig
mi·grate (aus)wandern, (fort)ziehen (*a.* ZO)
mi·gra·tion Wanderung *f* (*a.* ZO)
mi·gra·to·ry Wander...; ZO Zug...
mike F Mikrofon *n*
mild mild, sanft, leicht
mil·dew BOT Mehltau *m*
mild·ness Milde *f*
mile Meile *f* (*1,6 km*)
mile·age zurückgelegte Meilenzahl *or* Fahrtstrecke; Meilenstand *m*; *a.* **mileage allowance** Meilengeld *n*, *appr* Kilometergeld *n*
mile·stone Meilenstein *m* (*a. fig*)
mil·i·tant militant; streitbar, kriegerisch
mil·i·ta·ry 1. militärisch, Militär...; 2. **the military** das Militär
military gov·ern·ment Militärregierung *f*
military po·lice (ABBR **MP**) Militärpolizei *f*
mi·li·tia Miliz *f*, Bürgerwehr *f*
milk 1. Milch *f*; **it's no use crying over spilt milk** geschehen ist geschehen; 2. *v/t* melken; *v/i* Milch geben
milk choc·olate Vollmilchschokolade *f*
milk·man Milchmann *m*
milk pow·der Milchpulver *n*, Trockenmilch *f*
milk shake Milchmixgetränk *n*
milk tooth ANAT Milchzahn *m*
milk·y milchig; Milch...
Milky Way ASTR Milchstraße *f*
mill 1. Mühle *f*; Fabrik *f*; 2. *Korn etc* mahlen; *Metall* verarbeiten; *Münze* rändeln
mil·le·pede → **millipede**
mill·er Müller *m*
mil·let BOT Hirse *f*
mil·li·ner Hutmacherin *f*, Putzmacherin *f*, Modistin *f*
mil·lion Million *f*
mil·lion·aire Millionär(in)
mil·lionth 1. millionste(r, -s); 2. Millionstel *n*
mil·li·pede ZO Tausendfüß(l)er *m*
mill·stone Mühlstein *m*; **be a millstone round s.o.'s neck** *fig* j-m ein Klotz am Bein sein

milt ZO Milch *f*
mime 1. Pantomime *f*; Pantomime *m*; 2. (panto)mimisch darstellen
mim·ic 1. mimisch; Schein...; 2. Imitator *m*; 3. nachahmen; nachäffen
mim·ic·ry Nachahmung *f*; ZO Mimikry *f*
mince 1. *v/t* zerhacken, (zer)schneiden; **he does not mince matters** *or* **his words** er nimmt kein Blatt vor den Mund; *v/i* tänzeln, trippeln; 2. *a.* **minced meat** Hackfleisch *n*
minc·er Fleischwolf *m*
mind 1. Sinn *m*, Gemüt *n*, Herz *n*; Verstand *m*, Geist *m*; Ansicht *f*, Meinung *f*; Absicht *f*, Neigung *f*, Lust *f*; Erinnerung *f*, Gedächtnis *n*; **be out of one's mind** nicht (recht) bei Sinnen sein; **bear** *or* **keep in mind** (immer) denken an (*acc*), *et.* nicht vergessen; **change one's mind** es sich anders überlegen, s-e Meinung ändern; **enter s.o.'s mind** j-m in den Sinn kommen; **give s.o. a piece of one's mind** j-m gründlich die Meinung sagen; **have (half) a mind to** *inf* (nicht übel) Lust haben zu *inf*; **lose one's mind** den Verstand verlieren; **make up one's mind** sich entschließen, e-n Entschluss fassen; **to my mind** meiner Ansicht nach; 2. *v/t* achtgeben auf (*acc*); sehen nach, aufpassen auf (*acc*); *et.* haben gegen; **mind the step!** Vorsicht, Stufe!; **mind your own business!** kümmere dich um deine eigenen Angelegenheiten!; **do you mind if I smoke?, do you mind my smoking?** haben Sie *et.* dagegen *or* stört es Sie, wenn ich rauche?; **would you mind opening the window?** würden Sie bitte das Fenster öffnen?; **would you mind coming** würden Sie bitte kommen?; *v/i* aufpassen; *et.* dagegen haben; **mind (you)** wohlgemerkt, allerdings; **never mind!** macht nichts!, ist schon gut!; **I don't mind** meinetwegen, von mir aus
mind·less gedankenlos, blind; unbekümmert (**of** um), ohne Rücksicht (**of** auf *acc*)
mine[1] meins; **that's mine** das gehört mir
mine[2] 1. Bergwerk *n*, Mine *f*, Zeche *f*, Grube *f*; MIL Mine *f*; *fig* Fundgrube *f*; 2. *v/i* schürfen, graben (**for** nach); *v/t* *Erz, Kohle* abbauen; MIL verminen
min·er Bergmann *m*, Kumpel *m*
min·e·ral 1. Mineral *n*; *pl Br* Mineralwasser *n*; 2. Mineral...
mineral oil Mineralöl *n*
mineral wa·ter Mineralwasser *n*
min·gle *v/t* (ver)mischen; *v/i* sich mischen *or* mengen (**with** unter)

Miss

min·i... Mini..., Klein(st)...; → **miniskirt**
min·i·a·ture 1. Miniatur(gemälde *n*) *f*; **2.** Miniatur...; Klein...
miniature cam·e·ra Kleinbildkamera *f*
min·i·mize auf ein Mindestmaß herabsetzen; herunterspielen, bagatellisieren
min·i·mum 1. Minimum *n*, Mindestmaß *n*; **2.** minimal, Mindest...
min·ing 1. Bergbau *m*; **2.** Berg(bau)..., Bergwerks...; Gruben...
min·i·skirt Minirock *m*
min·is·ter POL Minister(in); Gesandte *m*; REL Geistliche *m*
min·is·try POL Ministerium *n*; REL geistliches Amt
mink ZO Nerz *m*
mi·nor 1. kleinere(r, -s), *fig a.* unbedeutend, geringfügig; JUR minderjährig; *A minor* MUS a-Moll *n*; *minor key* MUS Moll(tonart *f*) *n*; **2.** JUR Minderjährige *m*, *f*; UNIV Nebenfach *n*; MUS Moll *n*
mi·nor·i·ty Minderheit *f*; JUR Minderjährigkeit *f*
min·ster *Br* Münster *n*
mint¹ 1. Münze *f*, Münzanstalt *f*; **2.** prägen
mint² BOT Minze *f*
min·u·et MUS Menuett *n*
mi·nus 1. *prp* minus, weniger; F ohne; **2.** *adj* Minus...; **3.** Minus *n*, *fig a.* Nachteil *m*
min·ute¹ Minute *f*; Augenblick *m*; *in a minute* sofort; *just a minute!* Moment mal!
mi·nute² winzig; sehr genau
min·utes Protokoll *n*; *take* (*or keep*) *the minutes* (das) Protokoll führen
mir·a·cle Wunder *n*
mi·rac·u·lous wunderbar
mi·rac·u·lous·ly wie durch ein Wunder
mi·rage Luftspiegelung *f*, Fata Morgana *f*
mire Schlamm *m*; *drag through the mire fig* in den Schmutz ziehen
mir·ror 1. Spiegel *m*; **2.** (wider)spiegeln (*a. fig*)
mis... miss..., falsch, schlecht
mis·ad·ven·ture Missgeschick *n*; Unglück *n*, Unglücksfall *m*
mis·an·thrope, mis·an·thro·pist Menschenfeind(in)
mis·ap·ply falsch an- *or* verwenden
mis·ap·pre·hend missverstehen
mis·ap·pro·pri·ate unterschlagen, veruntreuen
mis·be·have sich schlecht benehmen
mis·cal·cu·late falsch berechnen; sich verrechnen (in *dat*)
miscar·riage MED Fehlgeburt *f*; Misslingen *n*, Fehlschlag(en *n*) *m*; *miscarriage of justice* JUR Fehlurteil *n*

mis·car·ry MED e-e Fehlgeburt haben; misslingen, scheitern
mis·cel·la·ne·ous gemischt, vermischt; verschiedenartig
mis·cel·la·ny Gemisch *n*; Sammelband *m*
mis·chief Schaden *m*; Unfug *m*; Übermut *m*
mischief-mak·er Unruhestifter(in)
mis·chie·vous boshaft, mutwillig; schelmisch
mis·con·ceive falsch auffassen, missverstehen
mis·con·duct schlechtes Benehmen; schlechte Führung; Verfehlung *f*
mis·con·strue falsch auslegen, missdeuten
mis·de·mea·no(u)r JUR Vergehen *n*
mis·di·rect fehlleiten, irreleiten; *Brief etc* falsch adressieren
mise-en-scène THEA Inszenierung *f*
mi·ser Geizhals *m*
mis·e·ra·ble erbärmlich, kläglich, elend; unglücklich
mi·ser·ly geizig, F knick(e)rig
mis·e·ry Elend *n*, Not *f*
mis·fire versagen (*gun*); MOT fehlzünden, aussetzen; *fig* danebengehen
mis·fit Außenseiter(in)
mis·for·tune Unglück *n*, Unglücksfall *m*; Missgeschick *n*
mis·giv·ing Befürchtung *f*, Zweifel *m*
mis·guid·ed irregeleitet, irrig, unangebracht
mis·hap Unglück *n*; Missgeschick *n*; *without mishap* ohne Zwischenfälle
mis·in·form falsch unterrichten
mis·in·ter·pret missdeuten, falsch auffassen *or* auslegen
mis·lay *et.* verlegen
mis·lead irreführen, täuschen; verleiten
mis·man·age schlecht verwalten *or* führen *or* handhaben
mis·place *et.* an e-e falsche Stelle legen *or* setzen; *et.* verlegen; *misplaced fig* unangebracht, deplatziert
mis·print 1. verdrucken; **2.** Druckfehler *m*
mis·read falsch lesen; falsch deuten, missdeuten
mis·rep·re·sent falsch darstellen; entstellen, verdrehen
miss 1. *v/t* verpassen, versäumen, verfehlen; übersehen, nicht bemerken; überhören; nicht verstehen *or* begreifen; vermissen; *a. miss out* auslassen, übergehen, überspringen; *v/i* nicht treffen; missglücken; *miss out on et.* verpassen; **2.** Fehlschuss *m*, Fehlstoß *m*, Fehlwurf *m* *etc*; Verpassen *n*, Verfehlen *n*
Miss Fräulein *n*

M

mis·shap·en missgebildet
mis·sile 1. Geschoss *n*; Rakete *f*; **2.** Raketen...
miss·ing fehlend; *be missing* fehlen, verschwunden *or* weg sein; (MIL *a.* **missing in action**) vermisst; *be missing* MIL vermisst sein *or* werden
mis·sion (*Militär- etc*)Mission *f*; *esp* POL Auftrag *m*, Mission *f* (*a.* REL); MIL, AVIAT Einsatz *m*
mis·sion·a·ry REL Missionar *m*
mis·spell falsch buchstabieren *or* schreiben
mis·spend falsch verwenden; vergeuden
mist 1. (feiner *or* leichter) Nebel; **2.** *mist over* sich trüben; *mist up* (sich) beschlagen
mis·take 1. verwechseln (*for* mit); verkennen, sich irren in (*dat*); falsch verstehen, missverstehen; **2.** Irrtum *m*, Versehen *n*, Fehler *m*; *by mistake* aus Versehen, irrtümlich
mis·tak·en irrig, falsch (verstanden); *be mistaken* sich irren
mis·tle·toe BOT Mistel *f*
mis·tress Herrin *f*; *esp Br* Lehrerin *f*; Geliebte *f*
mis·trust 1. misstrauen (*dat*); **2.** Misstrauen *n* (*of* gegen)
mis·trust·ful misstrauisch
mist·y (leicht) neb(e)lig; *fig* unklar, verschwommen
mis·un·der·stand missverstehen; *j-n* nicht verstehen
mis·un·der·standing Missverständnis *n*
mis·use 1. missbrauchen; falsch gebrauchen; **2.** Missbrauch *m*
mite ZO Milbe *f*; kleines Ding, Würmchen *n*; *a mite* F ein bisschen
mi·ter, *Br* **mi·tre** REL Mitra *f*, Bischofsmütze *f*
mitt *baseball*: Fanghandschuh *m*; → **mitten** Fausthandschuh *m*
mix 1. (ver)mischen, vermengen; *Getränke* mixen; sich (ver)mischen; sich mischen lassen; verkehren (*with* mit); *mix well* kontaktfreudig sein; *mix up* zusammenmischen, durcheinander mischen; (völlig) durcheinanderbringen; verwechseln (*with* mit); *be mixed up* verwickelt sein *or* werden (*in* in *acc*); (*geistig*) ganz durcheinander sein; **2.** Mischung *f*
mixed gemischt (*a. fig*); vermischt, Misch...
mix·er Mixer *m*; TECH Mischmaschine *f*; *radio*, TV *etc*: Mischpult *n*
mix·ture Mischung *f*; Gemisch *n*
mix-up F Verwechs(e)lung *f*
moan 1. Stöhnen *n*; **2.** stöhnen

moat (Burg-, Stadt)Graben *m*
mob 1. Mob *m*, Pöbel *m*; **2.** herfallen über (*acc*); *j-n* bedrängen, belagern
mo·bile 1. beweglich; MIL mobil, motorisiert; *fig* lebhaft; **2.** → **mobile phone** *or* **telephone**
mobile home Wohnwagen *m*
mobile phone, mobile tel·e·phone Mobiltelefon *n*, Handy *n*
mo·bil·ize mobilisieren, MIL *a.* mobil machen
moc·ca·sin Mokassin *m*
mock 1. *v/t* verspotten; nachäffen; *v/i* sich lustig machen, spotten (*at* über *acc*); **2.** nachgemacht, Schein...
mock·e·ry Spott *m*, Hohn *m*; Gespött *n*
mock·ing·bird ZO Spottdrossel *f*
mode (Art *f* und) Weise *f*; EDP Modus *m*, Betriebsart *f*
mod·el 1. Modell *n*; Muster *n*; Vorbild *n*; Mannequin *n*; Model *n*, (Foto)Modell *n*; TECH Modell *n*, Typ *m*; *male model* Dressman *m*; **2.** Modell..., Muster...; **3.** *v/t* modellieren, *a. fig* formen; *Kleider etc* vorführen; *v/i* Modell stehen *or* sitzen; als Mannequin *or* (Foto)Modell *or* Dressman arbeiten
mo·dem EDP Modem *m*, *n*
mod·e·rate 1. (mittel)mäßig; gemäßigt; vernünftig, angemessen; **2.** (sich) mäßigen
mod·e·ra·tion Mäßigung *f*
mod·ern modern, neu
mod·ern·ize modernisieren
mod·est bescheiden
mod·es·ty Bescheidenheit *f*
mod·i·fi·ca·tion (Ab-, Ver)Änderung *f*
mod·i·fy (ab-, ver)ändern
mod·u·late modulieren
mod·ule TECH Modul *n*, ELECTR *a.* Baustein *m*; (*Kommando- etc*)Kapsel *f*
moist feucht
moist·en *v/t* anfeuchten, befeuchten; *v/i* feucht werden
mois·ture Feuchtigkeit *f*
mo·lar ANAT Backenzahn *m*
mo·las·ses Sirup *m*
mold[1] Schimmel *m*; Moder *m*; Humus (-boden) *m*
mold[2] TECH **1.** (Gieß-, Guss-, Press-) Form *f*; **2.** gießen; formen
mol·der *a.* *molder away* vermodern; zerfallen
mold·y verschimmelt, schimm(e)lig; mod(e)rig
mole[1] ZO Maulwurf *m*
mole[2] Muttermal *n*, Leberfleck *m*
mole[3] Mole *f*, Hafendamm *m*
mol·e·cule Molekül *n*

mortal

mole·hill Maulwurfshügel *m*; *make a mountain out of a molehill* aus e-r Mücke e-n Elefanten machen

mo·lest belästigen

mol·li·fy besänftigen, beschwichtigen

mol·lusc *Br*, **mol·lusk** zo Weichtier *n*

mol·ly·cod·dle F verhätscheln, verzärteln

molt (sich) mausern; *Haare* verlieren

mol·ten geschmolzen

mom F Mami *f*, Mutti *f*

mom-and-pop store Tante-Emma-Laden *m*

mo·ment Moment *m*, Augenblick *m*; Bedeutung *f*; PHYS Moment *n*

mo·men·ta·ry momentan, augenblicklich

mo·men·tous bedeutsam, folgenschwer

mo·men·tum PHYS Moment *n*; Schwung *m*

Mon ABBR *of Monday* Mo., Montag *m*

mon·arch Monarch(in), Herrscher(in)

mon·ar·chy Monarchie *f*

mon·as·tery REL (Mönchs)Kloster *n*

Mon·day (ABBR *Mon*) Montag *m*; *on Monday* (am) Montag; *on Mondays* montags

mon·e·ta·ry ECON Währungs...; Geld...

mon·ey Geld *n*

mon·ey·box *Br* Sparbüchse *f*

mon·ey·chang·er (Geld)Wechsler *m*; TECH Wechselautomat *m*

mon·ey or·der Post- *or* Zahlungsanweisung *f*

mon·grel zo Bastard *m*, *esp* Promenadenmischung *f*

mon·i·tor 1. Monitor *m*; Kontrollgerät *n*, -schirm *m*; **2.** abhören; überwachen

monk REL Mönch *m*

mon·key 1. zo Affe *m*; F (kleiner) Schlingel; *make a monkey* (*out*) *of s.o.* F j-n zum Deppen machen; **2.** *monkey about, monkey around* F (herum)albern; *monkey about or around with* F herumspielen *or* an (*dat*) herummurksen an (*dat*)

monkey wrench TECH Engländer *m*, Franzose *m*; *throw a monkey wrench into s.th.* F et. behindern

mon·o 1. Mono *n*; F Monogerät *n*; F Monoschallplatte *f*; **2.** Mono...

mon·o... ein..., mono...

mon·o·log, *esp Br* **mon·o·logue** Monolog *m*

mo·nop·o·lize monopolisieren; *fig* an sich reißen

mo·nop·o·ly Monopol *n* (*of* auf *acc*)

mo·not·o·nous monoton, eintönig

mo·not·o·ny Monotonie *f*

mon·soon Monsun *m*

mon·ster 1. Monster *n*, Ungeheuer *n* (*a. fig*); Monstrum *n*; **2.** Riesen...

mon·stros·i·ty Ungeheuerlichkeit *f*; Monstrum *n*

mon·strous ungeheuer; *mst contp* ungeheuerlich; scheußlich

month Monat *m*

month·ly 1. monatlich, Monats...; **2.** Monatsschrift *f*

mon·u·ment Monument *n*, Denkmal *n*

mon·u·ment·al monumental; F kolossal, Riesen...; Gedenk...

moo zo muhen

mooch F schnorren

mood Stimmung *f*, Laune *f*; *be in a good* (*bad*) *mood* gute (schlechte) Laune haben, gut (schlecht) aufgelegt sein

mood·y launisch; schlecht gelaunt

moon 1. ASTR Mond *m*; **2.** *moon about, moon around* F herumtrödeln; F ziellos herumstreichen

moon·light Mondlicht *n*, -schein *m*

moon·lit mondhell

moor[1] (Hoch)Moor *n*

moor[2] MAR vertäuen, festmachen

moor·ings MAR Vertäuung *f*; Liegeplatz *m*

moose zo *nordamerikanischer* Elch

mop 1. Mopp *m*; F (Haar)Wust *m*; **2.** wischen; *mop up* aufwischen

mope Trübsal blasen

mo·ped *Br* MOT Moped *n*

mor·al 1. moralisch; Moral..., Sitten...; **2.** Moral *f*, Lehre *f*; *pl* Moral *f*, Sitten *pl*

mo·rale Moral *f*, Stimmung *f*

mor·al·ize moralisieren (*about, on* über *acc*)

mor·bid morbid, krankhaft

more 1. *adj* mehr; noch (mehr); *some more tea* noch etwas Tee; **2.** *adv* mehr; noch; *more and more* immer mehr; *more or less* mehr oder weniger; *once more* noch einmal; *the more so because* umso mehr, da; *more important* wichtiger; *more often* öfter; **3.** Mehr *n* (*of an dat*); *a little more* etwas mehr

mo·rel BOT Morchel *f*

more·o·ver außerdem, weiter, ferner

morgue Leichenschauhaus *n*; F (Zeitungs)Archiv *n*

morn·ing Morgen *m*; Vormittag *m*; *good morning!* guten Morgen!; *in the morning* morgens, am Morgen; vormittags, am Vormittag; *tomorrow morning* morgen früh *or* Vormittag

mo·rose mürrisch, verdrießlich

mor·phi·a, **mor·phine** PHARM Morphium *n*

mor·sel Bissen *m*, Happen *m*; *a morsel of* ein bisschen

mor·tal 1. sterblich; tödlich; Tod(es)...; **2.** Sterbliche *m*, *f*

M

mor·tal·i·ty Sterblichkeit *f*

mor·tar[1] Mörtel *m*

mor·tar[2] Mörser *m*

mort·gage 1. Hypothek *f*; **2.** mit e-r Hypothek belasten, e-e Hypothek aufnehmen auf (*acc*)

mor·ti·cian Leichenbestatter *m*

mor·ti·fi·ca·tion Kränkung *f*; Ärger *m*, Verdruss *m*

mor·ti·fy kränken; ärgern, verdrießen

mor·tu·a·ry Leichenhalle *f*

mo·sa·ic Mosaik *n*

Mos·lem → *Muslim*

mosque Moschee *f*

mos·qui·to ZO Moskito *m*; Stechmücke *f*

moss BOT Moos *n*

moss·y BOT moosig, bemoost

most 1. *adj* meiste(r, -s), größte(r, -s); die meisten; *most people* die meisten Leute; **2.** *adv* am meisten; *most of all* am allermeisten; *before adj*: höchst, äußerst; *the most important point* der wichtigste Punkt; **3.** *das* meiste, *das* Höchste; das meiste, der größte Teil; die meisten *pl*; *at (the) most* höchstens; *make the most of et.* nach Kräften ausnutzen, das Beste herausholen aus

most·ly hauptsächlich, meist(ens)

mo·tel Motel *n*

moth ZO Motte *f*

moth·eat·en mottenzerfressen

moth·er 1. Mutter *f*; **2.** bemuttern

moth·er coun·try Vaterland *n*, Heimatland *n*; Mutterland *n*

moth·er·hood Mutterschaft *f*

moth·er-in-law Schwiegermutter *f*

moth·er·ly mütterlich

moth·er-of-pearl Perlmutter *f*, *n*, Perlmutt *n*

moth·er tongue Muttersprache *f*

mo·tif Motiv *n*

mo·tion 1. Bewegung *f*; PARL Antrag *m*; *in quick motion film*: im Zeitraffer; *in slow motion film*: in Zeitlupe; *put or set in motion* in Gang bringen (*a. fig*), in Bewegung setzen; **2.** *v/t* j-n durch e-n Wink auffordern, *j-m* ein Zeichen geben; *v/i* winken

mo·tion·less bewegungslos, unbeweglich

mo·tion pic·ture Film *m*

mo·ti·vate motivieren, anspornen

mo·ti·va·tion Motivation *f*, Ansporn *m*

mo·tive 1. Motiv *n*, Beweggrund *m*; **2.** treibend (*a. fig*)

mot·ley bunt

mo·to·cross SPORT Motocross *n*

mo·tor 1. Motor *m*, *fig a.* treibende Kraft; **2.** Motor...

mo·tor·bike Moped *n*; *Br* F Motorrad *n*

mo·tor·boat Motorboot *n*

mo·tor·cade Auto-, Wagenkolonne *f*

mo·tor·car *Br* Kraftfahrzeug *n*

mo·tor car·a·van *Br* Wohnmobil *n*

mo·tor·cy·cle Motorrad *n*

mo·tor·cy·clist Motorradfahrer(in)

mo·tor home Wohnmobil *n*

mo·tor·ing Autofahren *n*; *school of motoring* Fahrschule *f*

mo·tor·ist Autofahrer(in)

mo·tor·ize motorisieren

mo·tor launch Motorbarkasse *f*

mo·tor·way *Br* Autobahn *f*

mot·tled gefleckt, gesprenkelt

mould[1] *Br* → *mold*[1]

mould[2] *Br* → *mold*[2]

moul·der *Br* → *molder*

mould·y *Br* → *moldy*

moult *Br* → *molt*

mound Erdhügel *m*, Erdwall *m*

mount 1. *v/t Pferd etc* besteigen, steigen auf (*acc*); montieren; anbringen, befestigen; *Bild etc* aufziehen, aufkleben; *Edelstein* fassen; *mounted police* berittene Polizei; *v/i* aufsitzen (*rider*); steigen, *fig a.* (an)wachsen; *mount up to* sich belaufen auf (*acc*); **2.** Gestell *n*; Fassung *f*; Reittier *n*, Reitpferd *n*

moun·tain 1. Berg *m*, *pl a.* Gebirge *n*; **2.** Berg..., Gebirgs...

moun·tain bike Mountainbike *n*

moun·tain·eer Bergsteiger(in)

moun·tain·eer·ing Bergsteigen *n*

moun·tain·ous bergig, gebirgig

mourn *v/i* trauern (*for, over* um); *v/t* betrauern, trauern um

mourn·er Trauernde *m*, *f*

mourn·ful traurig

mourn·ing Trauer *f*; Trauerkleidung *f*

mouse ZO Maus *f* (*a.* EDP)

mous·tache → *mustache*

mouth Mund *m*; ZO Maul *n*, Schnauze *f*; GEOGR Mündung *f*; Öffnung *f*

mouth·ful *ein* Mundvoll; Bissen *m*

mouth or·gan F Mundharmonika *f*

mouth·piece Mundstück *n*; *fig* Sprachrohr *n*

mouth·wash Mundwasser *n*

mo·va·ble beweglich

move 1. *v/t* (weg)rücken; transportieren; bewegen, rühren (*both a. fig*); *chess etc*: e-n Zug machen mit; PARL beantragen; *move house* umziehen; *move heaven and earth* Himmel und Hölle in Bewegung setzen; *v/i* sich (fort)bewegen; sich rühren; umziehen (*to* nach); *chess etc*: e-n Zug machen; *move away* weg-, fortziehen; *move in* einziehen; *move off* sich in Bewegung setzen;

move on weitergehen; ***move out*** ausziehen; **2.** Bewegung *f*; Umzug *m*; *chess etc*: Zug *m*; *fig* Schritt *m*; ***on the move*** in Bewegung; auf den Beinen; ***get a move on!*** F Tempo!, mach(t) schon!, los!

move·a·ble → *movable*

move·ment Bewegung *f* (*a. fig*); MUS Satz *m*; TECH Werk *n*

mov·ie 1. Film *m*; Kino *n*; **2.** Film..., Kino...

movie cam·e·ra Filmkamera *f*

movie star Filmstar *m*

movie thea·ter Kino *n*

mov·ing sich bewegend, beweglich; *fig* rührend

moving stair·case Rolltreppe *f*

moving van Möbelwagen *m*

mow mähen

mow·er Mähmaschine *f*, *esp* Rasenmäher *m*

Mr. ABBR *of* ***Mister*** Herr *m*

Mrs. Frau *f*

Ms. Frau *f*

much 1. *adj* viel; **2.** *adv* sehr; viel; ***much better*** viel besser; ***very much*** sehr; *I* ***thought as much*** das habe ich mir gedacht; **3.** große Sache; ***nothing much*** nichts Besonderes; ***make much of*** viel Wesens machen von; ***think much of*** viel halten von; *I* ***am not much of a dancer*** F ich bin kein großer Tänzer

muck F *Br* AGR Mist *m*, Dung *m*; *fig* Dreck *m*, Schmutz *m*; F *contp* Fraß *m*

mu·cus (Nasen)Schleim *m*

mud Schlamm *m*, Matsch *m*; Schmutz *m* (*a. fig*)

mud·dle 1. Durcheinander *n*; ***be in a muddle*** durcheinander sein; **2.** *a.* ***muddle up*** durcheinanderbringen; ***muddle through*** F sich durchwursteln

mud·dy schlammig, trüb; schmutzig; *fig* wirr

mud·guard Kotflügel *m*; Schutzblech *n*

mues·li Müsli *n*

muff Muff *m*

muf·fle *Ton etc* dämpfen; *often* ***muffle up*** einhüllen, einwickeln

muf·fler (dicker) Schal; MOT Auspufftopf *m*

mug[1] Krug *m*; Becher *m*; große Tasse; F Visage *f*; V Fresse *f*

mug[2] F überfallen und ausrauben

mug·ger F (Straßen)Räuber *m*

mug·ging F Raubüberfall *m*, *esp* Straßenraub *m*

mug·gy schwül

mul·ber·ry BOT Maulbeerbaum *m*; Maulbeere *f*

mule ZO Maultier *n*; Maulesel *m*

mulled: ***mulled wine*** Glühwein *m*

mul·li·on ARCH Mittelpfosten *m*

mul·ti... viel..., mehr..., Mehrfach..., Multi...

mul·ti·cul·tur·al multikulturell

mul·ti·far·i·ous mannigfaltig, vielfältig

mul·ti·lat·e·ral vielseitig; POL multilateral, mehrseitig

mul·ti·me·di·a multimedial

mul·ti·na·tion·al ECON multinationaler Konzern, F Multi *m*

mul·ti·ple 1. vielfach, mehrfach; **2.** MATH Vielfache *n*

mul·ti·pli·ca·tion Vermehrung *f*; MATH Multiplikation *f*

multiplication table Einmaleins *n*

mul·ti·plic·i·ty Vielfalt *f*; Vielzahl *f*

mul·ti·ply (sich) vermehren, (sich) vervielfachen; MATH multiplizieren, malnehmen (***by*** mit)

mul·ti·pur·pose Mehrzweck...

mul·ti·sto·rey *Br* mehrstöckig

multistorey car park *Br* Park(hoch)haus *n*

mul·ti·tude Vielzahl *f*

mul·ti·tu·di·nous zahlreich

mum[1] *Br* F Mami *f*, Mutti *f*

mum[2] **1.** *int*: ***mum's the word*** Mund halten!, kein Wort darüber!; **2.** *adj*: ***keep mum*** nichts verraten, den Mund halten

mum·ble murmeln, F nuscheln; mümmeln

mum·mi·fy mumifizieren

mum·my[1] Mumie *f*

mum·my[2] *Br* F Mami *f*, Mutti *f*

mumps MED Ziegenpeter *m*, Mumps *m*

munch mampfen

mun·dane alltäglich; weltlich

mu·ni·ci·pal städtisch, Stadt..., kommunal, Gemeinde...; ***municipal council*** Stadt-, Gemeinderat *m*

mu·ni·ci·pal·i·ty Kommunalbehörde *f*; Stadtverwaltung *f*

mu·ral Wandgemälde *n*

mur·der 1. Mord *m*, Ermordung *f*; **2.** Mord...; **3.** ermorden; F verschandeln

mur·der·er Mörder *m*

mur·der·ess Mörderin *f*

mur·der·ous mörderisch

murk·y dunkel, finster

mur·mur 1. Murmeln *n*; Gemurmel *n*; Murren *n*; **2.** murmeln; murren

mus·cle Muskel *m*

mus·cu·lar Muskel...; muskulös

muse[1] (nach)sinnen, (nach)grübeln (***on***, ***over*** über *acc*)

muse[2] *a.* ***Muse*** Muse *f*

mu·se·um Museum *n*

mush Brei *m*, Mus *n*; Maisbrei *m*

mush·room 1. BOT Pilz *m*, *esp* Champig-

M

non *m*; **2.** rasch wachsen; **mushroom up** *fig* (wie Pilze) aus dem Boden schießen

mu·sic Musik *f*; Noten *pl*; **put** *or* **set to music** vertonen

mu·sic·al 1. musikalisch; Musik...; **2.** Musical *n*

musical box *esp Br* Spieldose *f*

musical in·stru·ment Musikinstrument *n*

mu·sic box Spieldose *f*

music cen·ter (*Br* **cen·ter**) Kompaktanlage *f*

music hall *Br* Varietee(theater) *n*

mu·si·cian Musiker(in)

mu·sic stand Notenständer *m*

musk Moschus *m*

musk·rat ZO Bisamratte *f*; Bisampelz *m*

Mus·lim 1. Muslim *m*, Moslem *m*; **2.** muslimisch, moslemisch

mus·sel ZO (Mies)Muschel *f*

must¹ 1. *v/aux* ich muss, *du* musst *etc*; **you must not** (F **mustn't**) du darfst nicht; **2.** Muss *n*

must² Most *m*

mus·tache Schnurrbart *m*

mus·tard Senf *m*

mus·ter 1. muster up *s-e Kraft etc* aufbieten; *s-n Mut* zusammennehmen; **2. pass muster** *fig* Zustimmung finden (**with** bei); den Anforderungen genügen

must·y mod(e)rig, muffig

mu·ta·tion Veränderung *f*; BIOL Mutation *f*

mute 1. stumm; **2.** Stumme *m*, *f*; MUS

Dämpfer *m*

mu·ti·late verstümmeln

mu·ti·la·tion Verstümmelung *f*

mu·ti·neer Meuterer *m*

mu·ti·nous meuternd; rebellisch

mu·ti·ny 1. Meuterei *f*; **2.** meutern

mut·ter 1. murmeln; murren; **2.** Murmeln *n*; Murren *n*

mut·ton GASTR Hammel-, Schafffleisch *n*; **leg of mutton** Hammelkeule *f*

mut·ton chop GASTR Hammelkotelett *n*

mu·tu·al gegenseitig; gemeinsam

muz·zle 1. ZO Maul *n*, Schnauze *f*; Mündung *f* (*of a gun*); Maulkorb *m*; **2.** e-n Maulkorb anlegen (*dat*), *fig a.* j-n mundtot machen

my mein(e)

myrrh BOT Myrrhe *f*

myr·tle BOT Myrte *f*

my·self ich, mich *or* mir selbst; mich; mich (selbst); **by myself** allein

mys·te·ri·ous rätselhaft, unerklärlich; geheimnisvoll, mysteriös

mys·te·ry Geheimnis *n*, Rätsel *n*; REL Mysterium *n*; **mystery tour** Fahrt *f* ins Blaue

mys·tic 1. Mystiker(in); **2.** → **mystic·al** mystisch

mys·ti·fy verwirren, vor ein Rätsel stellen; **be mystified** vor e-m Rätsel stehen

myth Mythos *m*, Sage *f*

my·thol·o·gy Mythologie *f*

N

N, n N, n *n*

nab F schnappen, erwischen

na·dir ASTR Nadir *m*; *fig* Tiefpunkt *m*

nag¹ 1. nörgeln; **nag** (**at**) herumnörgeln an (*dat*); **2.** Nörgler(in)

nag² F Gaul *m*, Klepper *m*

nail 1. ANAT, TECH Nagel *m*; **2.** (an-)nageln (**to** an *acc*)

nail pol·ish Nagellack *m*

nail scis·sors Nagelschere *f*

nail var·nish *Br* Nagellack *m*

na·ive, na·ïve naiv (*a. art*)

na·ked nackt, bloß; kahl; *fig* ungeschminkt

nak·ed·ness Nacktheit *f*

name 1. Name *m*; Ruf *m*; **by name** mit

Namen, namentlich; **by the name of ...** namens ...; **what's your name?** wie heißen Sie?; **call s.o. names** j-n beschimpfen; **2.** (be)nennen; erwähnen; ernennen zu

name·less namenlos; unbekannt

name·ly nämlich

name·plate Namens-, Tür-, Firmenschild *n*

name·sake Namensvetter *m*, Namensschwester *f*

name tag Namensschild *n*

nan·ny Kindermädchen *n*

nan·ny goat ZO Geiß *f*, Ziege *f*

nap 1. Schläfchen *n*; **have** *or* **take a nap** → **2.** ein Nickerchen machen

necklace

nape *mst* **nape of the neck** ANAT Genick *n*, Nacken *m*

nap·kin Serviette *f*

nap·py *Br* Windel *f*

nar·co·sis MED Narkose *f*

nar·cot·ic 1. narkotisch, betäubend, einschläfernd; Rauschgift...; *narcotic addiction* Rauschgiftsucht *f*; 2. Narkotikum *n*, Betäubungsmittel *n*; *often pl* Rauschgift *n*; *narcotics squad* Rauschgiftdezernat *n*

nar·rate erzählen; berichten, schildern

nar·ra·tion Erzählung *f*

nar·ra·tive 1. Erzählung *f*; Bericht *m*, Schilderung *f*; 2. erzählend

nar·ra·tor Erzähler(in)

nar·row 1. eng, schmal; beschränkt; knapp; 2. enger *or* schmäler werden *or* machen, (sich) verengen; beschränken, einschränken

nar·row·ly mit knapper Not

nar·row-mind·ed engstirnig, beschränkt

nar·row·ness Enge *f*; Beschränktheit *f*

na·sal nasal; Nasen...

nas·ty ekelhaft, eklig, widerlich (*smell*, *sight etc*); abscheulich (*weather etc*); böse, schlimm (*accident etc*); hässlich (*character, behavior etc*); gemein, fies; schmutzig, zotig (*language*)

na·tal Geburts...

na·tion Nation *f*, Volk *n*

na·tion·al 1. national, National..., Landes..., Volks...; 2. Staatsangehörige *m*, *f*

national an·them Nationalhymne *f*

na·tion·al·i·ty Nationalität *f*, Staatsangehörigkeit *f*

na·tion·al·ize ECON verstaatlichen

na·tion·al park Nationalpark *m*

national so·cial·ism HIST POL Nationalsozialismus *m*

national so·cial·ist HIST POL Nationalsozialist *m*

national team SPORT Nationalmannschaft *f*

na·tion-wide landesweit

na·tive 1. einheimisch, Landes...; heimatlich, Heimat...; eingeboren, Eingeborenen...; angeboren; 2. Eingeborene *m*, *f*; Einheimische *m*, *f*

native lan·guage Muttersprache *f*

native speak·er Muttersprachler(in)

Na·tiv·i·ty REL *die* Geburt Christi

nat·ty F schick, *Austrian* fesch

nat·u·ral natürlich; angeboren; Natur...

natural gas Erdgas *n*

nat·u·ral·ize naturalisieren, einbürgern

nat·u·ral·ly natürlich; von Natur (aus)

nat·u·ral re·sourc·es Boden- u. Naturschätze *pl*

natural sci·ence Naturwissenschaft *f*

na·ture Natur *f*

nature con·ser·va·tion Naturschutz *m*

nature re·serve Naturschutzgebiet *n*

nature trail Naturlehrpfad *m*

naugh·ty unartig; unanständig

nau·se·a Übelkeit *f*, Brechreiz *m*

nau·se·ate: *nauseate s.o.* j-m Übelkeit verursachen; *fig* j-n anwidern

nau·se·at·ing ekelerregend, widerlich

nau·ti·cal nautisch, See...

na·val MIL Flotten..., Marine...; See...

naval base MIL Flottenstützpunkt *m*

naval offi·cer MIL Marineoffizier *m*

naval pow·er MIL Seemacht *f*

nave ARCH Mittel-, Hauptschiff *n*

na·vel ANAT Nabel *m* (*a. fig*)

nav·i·ga·ble schiffbar

nav·i·gate MAR befahren; AVIAT, MAR steuern, lenken

nav·i·ga·tion Schifffahrt *f*; AVIAT, MAR Navigation *f*

nav·i·ga·tor AVIAT, MAR Navigator *m*

na·vy (Kriegs)Marine *f*; Kriegsflotte *f*

navy blue Marineblau *n*

nay PARL Gegen-, Neinstimme *f*

Na·zi HIST POL *contp* Nazi *m*

Na·zism HIST POL *contp* Nazismus *m*

near 1. *adj* nahe; kurz; nahe (verwandt); *in the near future* in naher Zukunft; *be a near miss* knapp scheitern; 2. *adv* nahe, in der Nähe (*a. near at hand*); nahe (bevorstehend) (*a. near at hand*); beinahe, fast; *near the station etc* in der Nähe des Bahnhofs *etc*; *near you* in deiner Nähe; 3. *prp* nahe (*dat*), in der Nähe von (*or gen*); 4. sich nähern, näher kommen (*dat*)

near·by 1. *adj* nahe (gelegen); 2. *adv* in der Nähe

near·ly beinahe, fast; annähernd

near·sight·ed kurzsichtig

neat ordentlich; sauber; gepflegt; pur (*whisky etc*)

neb·u·lous verschwommen

ne·ces·sar·i·ly notwendigerweise; *not necessarily* nicht unbedingt

ne·ces·sa·ry notwendig, nötig; unvermeidlich

ne·ces·si·tate *et.* erfordern, verlangen

ne·ces·si·ty Notwendigkeit *f*; (dringendes) Bedürfnis; Not *f*

neck 1. ANAT Hals *m* (*a. of bottle etc*); Genick *n*, Nacken *m*; *be neck and neck* F Kopf an Kopf liegen (*a. fig*); *be up to one's neck in debt* F bis zum Hals in Schulden stecken; 2. F knutschen, schmusen

neck·er·chief Halstuch *n*

neck·lace Halskette *f*

neck·let Halskettchen *n*

neck·line Ausschnitt *m*

neck·tie Krawatte *f*, Schlips *m*

née: *née Smith* geborene Smith

need 1. (*of, for*) (dringendes) Bedürfnis (nach), Bedarf *m* (an *dat*); Notwendigkeit *f*; Mangel *m* (*of, for* an *dat*); Not *f*; *be in need of s.th.* et. dringend brauchen; *in need* in Not; *in need of help* hilfs-, hilfebedürftig; **2.** *v/t* benötigen, brauchen; *v/aux* brauchen, müssen

nee·dle 1. Nadel *f* (*a.* BOT, MED); Zeiger *m*; **2.** F *j-n* aufziehen, hänseln

need·less unnötig, überflüssig

nee·dle·wom·an Näherin *f*

nee·dle·work Handarbeit *f*

need·y bedürftig, arm

ne·ga·tion Verneinung *f*

neg·a·tive 1. negativ; verneinend; **2.** Verneinung *f*; PHOT Negativ *n*; *answer in the negative* verneinen

ne·glect 1. vernachlässigen; es versäumen (*doing, to do* zu tun); **2.** Vernachlässigung *f*; Nachlässigkeit *f*

neg·li·gence Nachlässigkeit *f*, Unachtsamkeit *f*

neg·li·gent nachlässig, unachtsam; lässig, salopp

neg·li·gi·ble unbedeutend

ne·go·ti·ate verhandeln (über *acc*)

ne·go·ti·a·tion Verhandlung *f*

ne·go·ti·a·tor Unterhändler(in)

neigh ZO **1.** wiehern; **2.** Wiehern *n*

neigh·bo(u)r Nachbar(in)

neigh·bo(u)r·hood Nachbarschaft *f*, Umgebung *f*

neigh·bo(u)r·ing benachbart, Nachbar…, angrenzend

neigh·bo(u)r·ly (gut)nachbarlich

nei·ther 1. *adj and pron* keine(r, -s) (von beiden); **2.** *cj* ***neither … nor*** weder … noch

ne·on CHEM Neon *n*

neon lamp Neonlampe *f*

neon sign Neon-, Leuchtreklame *f*

neph·ew Neffe *m*

nep·o·tism *contp* Vetternwirtschaft *f*

nerd F Trottel *m*; Computerfreak *m*

nerve Nerv *m*; Mut *m*, Stärke *f*, Selbstbeherrschung *f*; F Frechheit *f*; *get on s.o.'s nerves* j-m auf die Nerven gehen *or* fallen; *lose one's nerve* den Mut *or* die Nerven verlieren; *you've got a nerve!* F Sie haben Nerven!

nerve·less kraftlos; mutlos; ohne Nerven, kaltblütig

ner·vous nervös; Nerven…

ner·vous·ness Nervosität *f*

nest 1. Nest *n*; **2.** nisten

nes·tle (sich) schmiegen *or* kuscheln (*against, on* an *acc*); *a.* **nestle down** sich behaglich niederlassen, es sich bequem machen (*in* in *dat*)

net¹ 1. Netz *n*; *net curtain* Store *m*; **2.** mit e-m Netz fangen *or* abdecken

net² 1. netto, Netto…, Rein…; **2.** netto einbringen

Neth·er·lands die Niederlande *pl*

net·tle 1. BOT Nessel *f*; **2.** F *j-n* ärgern

net·work Netz *n* (*a.* EDP), Netzwerk *n*; (Straßen- *etc*)Netz *n*; *radio*, TV Sendernetz *n*; *be in the network* EDP am Netz sein

neu·ro·sis MED Neurose *f*

neu·rot·ic MED **1.** neurotisch; **2.** Neurotiker(in)

neu·ter 1. LING sächlich; geschlechtslos; **2.** LING Neutrum *n*

neu·tral 1. neutral; **2.** Neutrale *m*, *f*; *a. neutral gear* MOT Leerlauf(stellung *f*) *m*

neu·tral·i·ty Neutralität *f*

neu·tral·ize neutralisieren

neu·tron PHYS Neutron *n*

nev·er nie, niemals

nev·er-end·ing endlos, nicht enden wollend, unendlich

nev·er·the·less nichtsdestoweniger, dennoch, trotzdem

new neu; frisch; unerfahren; *nothing new* nichts Neues

new-born neugeboren

new·com·er Neuankömmling *m*; Neuling *m*

new·ly kürzlich; neu

news Neuigkeit(en *pl*) *f*, Nachricht(en *pl*) *f*

news·a·gent Zeitungshändler(in)

news·boy Zeitungsjunge *m*, Zeitungsausträger *m*

news bul·le·tin Kurznachricht(en *pl*) *f*

news·cast *radio*, TV Nachrichtensendung *f*

news·cast·er *radio*, TV Nachrichtensprecher(in)

news deal·er Zeitungshändler(in)

news·flash *radio*, TV Kurzmeldung *f*

news·let·ter Rundschreiben *n*

news·pa·per Zeitung *f*

news·print Zeitungspapier *n*

news·read·er *esp Br* → **newscaster**

news·reel *film*: Wochenschau *f*

news·room Nachrichtenredaktion *f*

news·stand Zeitungskiosk *m*, -stand *m*

news·ven·dor *esp Br* Zeitungsverkäufer(in)

new year Neujahr *n*, *das* neue Jahr; *New Year's Day* Neujahrstag *m*; *New Year's Eve* Silvester(abend *m*) *m*, *n*

next 1. *adj* nächste(r, -s); (*the*) *next day* am nächsten Tag; *next door* nebenan; *next but one* übernächste(r, -s); *next to* gleich neben *or* nach; beinahe, fast *unmöglich etc*; **2.** *adv* als Nächste(r, -s); demnächst, das nächste Mal; **3.** *der, die, das* Nächste; → *kin*

next-door (von) nebenan

nib·ble *v/i* knabbern (*at* an *dat*); *v/t* Loch *etc* nagen, knabbern (*in* in *acc*)

nice nett, freundlich; hübsch, schön; *fig* fein (*detail etc*)

nice·ly gut, fein; genau, sorgfältig

ni·ce·ty Feinheit *f*; Genauigkeit *f*

niche Nische *f*

nick 1. Kerbe *f*; *in the nick of time* gerade noch rechtzeitig, im letzten Moment; **2.** (ein)kerben; *j-n* streifen (*bullet*); *Br* F *et.* klauen; *Br* F *j-n* schnappen

nick·el 1. MIN Nickel *n*; Fünfcentstück *n*; **2.** TECH vernickeln

nick·el-plate TECH vernickeln

nick-nack → *knick-knack*

nick·name 1. Spitzname *m*; **2.** *j-m* den Spitznamen … geben

niece Nichte *f*

nig·gard Geizhals *m*

nig·gard·ly geizig, knaus(e)rig; schäbig, kümmerlich

night Nacht *f*; Abend *m*; *at night, by night, in the night* in der Nacht, nachts

night·cap Schlummertrunk *m*

night·club Nachtklub *m*, Nachtlokal *n*

night·dress (Damen-, Kinder)Nachthemd *n*

night·fall: *at nightfall* bei Einbruch der Dunkelheit

night·gown → *nightdress*

night·ie F → *nightdress*

nigh·tin·gale ZO Nachtigall *f*

night·ly (all)nächtlich; (all)abendlich; jede Nacht; jeden Abend

night·mare Albtraum *m* (*a. fig*)

night school Abendschule *f*

night shift Nachtschicht *f*

night·shirt (Herren)Nachthemd *n*

night·time: *in the nighttime, at nighttime* nachts

night watch·man Nachtwächter *m*

night·y F → *nightdress*

nil Nichts *n*, Null *f*; *our team won two to nil or by two goals to nil* (*2-0*) unsere Mannschaft gewann zwei zu null (2:0)

nim·ble flink, gewandt; geistig beweglich

nine 1. neun; *nine to five* normale Dienststunden (von 9-5); *a nine-to-five job* e-e (An)Stellung mit geregelter Arbeitszeit; **2.** Neun *f*

nine·pins Kegeln *n*

nine·teen 1. neunzehn; **2.** Neunzehn *f*

nine·teenth neunzehnte(r, -s)

nine·ti·eth neunzigste(r, -s)

nine·ty 1. neunzig; **2.** Neunzig *f*

ninth 1. neunte(r, -s); **2.** Neuntel *n*

ninth·ly neuntens

nip¹ 1. kneifen, zwicken; F flitzen, sausen; *nip off* F abknipsen; *nip in the bud fig* im Keim ersticken; **2.** Kneifen *n*, Zwicken *n*; *it was nip and tuck* F es war ganz knapp; *there's a nip in the air today* heute ist es ganz schön kalt

nip² Schlückchen *n* (*of brandy etc*)

nip·per: (*a pair of*) *nippers* (e-e) (Kneif-)Zange *f*

nip·ple ANAT Brustwarze *f*; (Gummi-)Sauger *m*; TECH Nippel *m*

ni·ter, *Br* **ni·tre** CHEM Salpeter *m*

ni·tro·gen CHEM Stickstoff *m*

no 1. *adv* nein; nicht; **2.** *adj* kein(e); *no one* keiner, niemand; *in no time* im Nu, im Handumdrehen; **3.** Nein *n*

no·bil·i·ty (Hoch)Adel *m*; *fig* Adel *m*

no·ble adlig; edel, nobel; prächtig

no·ble·man Adlige *m*

no·ble·wom·an Adlige *f*

no·bod·y 1. niemand, keiner; **2.** *fig* Niemand *m*, Null *f*

no-cal·o·rie di·et Nulldiät *f*

noc·tur·nal nächtlich, Nacht…

nod 1. nicken (mit); *nod off* einnicken; *have a nodding acquaintance with s.o.* *j-n* flüchtig kennen; **2.** Nicken *n*

node BOT, MED Knoten *m*

noise 1. Krach *m*; Lärm *m*; Geräusch *n*; **2.** *noise about* (*abroad, around*) *Gerücht etc* verbreiten

noise·less geräuschlos

nois·y laut, geräuschvoll

no·mad Nomade *m*, Nomadin *f*

nom·i·nal nominell; *nominal value* ECON Nennwert *m*

nom·i·nate ernennen; nominieren, (zur Wahl) vorschlagen

nom·i·na·tion Ernennung *f*; Nominierung *f*

nom·i·na·tive *a. nominative case* LING Nominativ *m*, erster Fall

nom·i·nee Kandidat(in)

non… nicht…, Nicht…, un…

non·al·co·hol·ic alkoholfrei

non·a·ligned POL blockfrei

non·com·mis·sioned of·fi·cer MIL Unteroffizier *m*

non·com·mit·tal unverbindlich

non·con·duc·tor ELECTR Nichtleiter *m*

non·de·script nichtssagend; unauffällig

none 1. *pron* keine(r, -s), niemand; **2.** *adv* in keiner Weise, keineswegs

N

non·en·ti·ty *fig* Null *f*

none·the·less nichtsdestoweniger, dennoch, trotzdem

non·ex·ist·ence Nichtvorhandensein *n*, Fehlen *n*

non·ex·ist·ent nicht existierend

non·fic·tion Sachbücher *pl*

non·flam·ma·ble, **non·in·flam·mable** nicht brennbar

non·in·ter·fer·ence, **non·in·ter·vention** POL Nichteinmischung *f*

non·i·ron bügelfrei

no-non·sense nüchtern, sachlich

non·par·ti·san POL überparteilich; unparteiisch

non·pay·ment ECON Nicht(be)zahlung *f*

non·plus verblüffen

non·pol·lut·ing umweltfreundlich

non·prof·it, *Br* **non·prof·it·mak·ing** gemeinnützig

non·res·i·dent 1. nicht (orts)ansässig; nicht im Hause wohnend; **2.** Nichtansässige *m*, *f*; nicht im Hause Wohnende *m*, *f*

non·re·turn·a·ble Einweg...

nonreturnable bot·tle Einwegflasche *f*

non·sense Unsinn *m*, dummes Zeug

non·skid rutschfest, rutschsicher

non·smok·er Nichtraucher(in)

non·smok·ing Nichtraucher...

non·stick mit Antihaftbeschichtung

non·stop nonstop, ohne Unterbrechung; RAIL durchgehend; AVIAT ohne Zwischenlandung; **nonstop flight** *a.* Nonstop-Flug *m*

non·u·nion nicht (gewerkschaftlich) organisiert

non·vi·o·lence (Politik *f* der) Gewaltlosigkeit *f*

non·vi·o·lent gewaltlos

noo·dle Nudel *f*

nook Ecke *f*, Winkel *m*

noon Mittag(szeit *f*) *m*; **at noon** um 12 Uhr (mittags)

noose Schlinge *f*

nope F ne(e), nein

nor → **neither** 2; auch nicht

norm Norm *f*

nor·mal normal

nor·mal·ize (sich) normalisieren

north 1. Nord, Norden *m*; **2.** *adj* nördlich, Nord...; **3.** *adv* nach Norden, nordwärts

north·east 1. Nordost, Nordosten *m*; **2.** *a.* **northeastern** nordöstlich

nor·ther·ly, **nor·thern** Nord..., nördlich

North Pole Nordpol *m*

north·ward(s) *adv* nördlich, nach Norden

north·west 1. Nordwest, Nordwesten *m*; **2.** *a.* **northwestern** nordwestlich

Nor·way Norwegen *n*

Nor·we·gian 1. norwegisch; **2.** Norweger(in); LING Norwegisch *n*

nose 1. Nase *f*; ZO Schnauze *f*; *fig* Gespür *n*; **2.** *Auto etc* vorsichtig fahren; *a.* **nose about**, **nose around** *fig* F herumschnüffeln (in *dat*) (**for** nach)

nose·bleed Nasenbluten *n*; **have a nosebleed** Nasenbluten haben

nose·dive AVIAT Sturzflug *m*

nos·ey → **nosy**

nos·tal·gia Nostalgie *f*

nos·tril ANAT Nasenloch *n*, *esp* ZO Nüster *f*

nos·y F neugierig

not nicht; **not a** kein(e)

no·ta·ble bemerkenswert; beachtlich

no·ta·ry *mst* **notary public** Notar *m*

notch 1. Kerbe *f*; GEOL Engpass *m*; **2.** (ein)kerben

note (*mst pl*) Notiz *f*, Aufzeichnung *f*; Anmerkung *f*; Vermerk *m*; Briefchen *n*, Zettel *m*; (diplomatische) Note; Banknote *f*, Geldschein *m*; MUS Note *f*; *fig* Ton *m*; **take notes (of)** sich Notizen machen (über *acc*)

note·book Notizbuch *n*; EDP Notebook *n*

not·ed bekannt, berühmt (**for** wegen)

note·pa·per Briefpapier *n*

note·wor·thy bemerkenswert

noth·ing nichts; **nothing but** nichts als, nur; **nothing much** F nicht viel; **for nothing** umsonst; **to say nothing of** ganz zu schweigen von; **there is nothing like** es geht nichts über (*acc*)

no·tice 1. Ankündigung *f*, Bekanntgabe *f*, Mitteilung *f*, Anzeige *f*; Kündigung(sfrist) *f*; Beachtung *f*; **give or hand in one's notice** kündigen (**to** bei); **give s.o. notice** j-m kündigen; **give s.o. notice to quit** j-m kündigen; **at six months' notice** mit halbjährlicher Kündigungsfrist; **take (no) notice of** (keine) Notiz nehmen von, (nicht) beachten; **at short notice** kurzfristig; **until further notice** bis auf weiteres; **without notice** fristlos; **2.** (es) bemerken; (besonders) beachten *or* achten auf (*acc*)

no·tice·a·ble erkennbar, wahrnehmbar; bemerkenswert

no·tice·board *Br* schwarzes Brett

no·ti·fy *et.* anzeigen, melden, mitteilen; j-n benachrichtigen

no·tion Begriff *m*, Vorstellung *f*; Idee *f*

no·tions Kurzwaren *pl*

no·to·ri·ous berüchtigt (**for** für)

not·with·stand·ing trotz (*gen*)

nought *Br*: **0.4 (nought point four)** 0,4

noun LING Substantiv *n*, Hauptwort *n*

nour·ish (er)nähren; *fig* hegen

nour·ish·ing nahrhaft

nour·ish·ment Ernährung *f*; Nahrung *f*
Nov ABBR *of* **November** Nov., November *m*

nov·el 1. Roman *m*; **2.** (ganz) neu(artig)
nov·el·ist Romanschriftsteller(in)
no·vel·la Novelle *f*
nov·el·ty Neuheit *f*
No·vem·ber (ABBR *Nov*) November *m*
nov·ice Anfänger(in), Neuling *m*; REL Novize *m*, Novizin *f*
now 1. *adv* nun, jetzt; *now and again*, (*every*) *now and then* von Zeit zu Zeit, dann und wann; *by now* inzwischen; *from now* (*on*) von jetzt an; *just now* gerade eben; **2.** *cj a.* *now that* nun da
now·a·days heutzutage
no·where nirgends
nox·ious schädlich
noz·zle TECH Schnauze *f*; Stutzen *m*; Düse *f*; Zapfpistole *f*
nu·ance Nuance *f*
nub springender Punkt
nu·cle·ar Kern..., Atom..., atomar, nuklear, Nuklear...
nuclear en·er·gy PHYS Atomenergie *f*, Kernenergie *f*
nuclear fam·i·ly Kern-, Kleinfamilie *f*
nuclear fis·sion PHYS Kernspaltung *f*
nu·cle·ar-free atomwaffenfrei
nu·cle·ar fu·sion PHYS Kernfusion *f*
nuclear phys·ics Kernphysik *f*
nuclear pow·er PHYS Atomkraft *f*, Kernkraft *f*
nu·cle·ar-pow·ered atomgetrieben
nu·cle·ar pow·er plant ELECTR Atomkraftwerk *n*, Kernkraftwerk *n*
nuclear re·ac·tor PHYS Atomreaktor *m*, Kernreaktor *m*
nuclear war Atomkrieg *m*
nuclear war·head MIL Atomsprengkopf *m*
nuclear waste Atommüll *m*
nuclear weap·ons MIL Atomwaffen *pl*, Kernwaffen *pl*
nu·cle·us BIOL, PHYS Kern *m* (*a. fig*)
nude 1. nackt; **2.** *art*: Akt *m*
nudge 1. *j-n* anstoßen, (an)stupsen; **2.** Stups(er) *m*
nug·get (*esp* Gold)Klumpen *m*
nui·sance Plage *f*, Ärgernis *n*; Nervensäge *f*, Quälgeist *m*; *what a nuisance!* wie

ärgerlich!; *be a nuisance to s.o.* j-m lästig fallen, F j-n nerven; *make a nuisance of o.s.* den Leuten auf die Nerven gehen *or* fallen
nukes F Atom-, Kernwaffen *pl*
null: *null and void esp* JUR null und nichtig
numb 1. starr (*with* vor), taub; *fig* wie betäubt (*with* vor); **2.** starr *or* taub machen
num·ber 1. Zahl *f*, Ziffer *f*; Nummer *f*; (An)Zahl *f*; Ausgabe *f*; (*Bus- etc*)Linie *f*; *sorry, wrong number* TEL falsch verbunden!; **2.** nummerieren; zählen; sich belaufen auf (*acc*)
num·ber·less zahllos
num·ber·plate *esp* Br MOT Nummernschild *n*
nu·me·ral Ziffer *f*; LING Zahlwort *n*
nu·me·ra·tor MATH Zähler *m*
nu·me·rous zahlreich
nun REL Nonne *f*
nun·ne·ry REL Nonnenkloster *n*
nurse 1. (Kranken-, Säuglings)Schwester *f*; Kindermädchen *n*; (Kranken-) Pflegerin *f*; → *male nurse*; *a.* *wet nurse* Amme *f*; **2.** stillen; pflegen; hegen; als Krankenschwester *or* -pfleger arbeiten; *nurse s.o. back to health* j-n gesund pflegen
nur·se·ry Tagesheim *n*, Tagesstätte *f*; Baum-, Pflanzschule *f*
nursery rhyme Kinderlied *n*, Kinderreim *m*
nursery school Br Vorschule *f*
nursery slope *skiing*: F Idiotenhügel *m*
nurs·ing Stillen *n*; (Kranken)Pflege *f*
nursing bot·tle (Saug)Flasche *f*
nursing home Pflegeheim *n*
nut BOT Nuss *f*; TECH (Schrauben)Mutter *f*; F verrückter Kerl; F Birne *f* (*head*); *be off one's nut* F spinnen
nut·crack·er(s) Nussknacker *m*
nut·meg BOT Muskatnuss *f*
nu·tri·ent 1. Nährstoff *m*; **2.** nahrhaft
nu·tri·tion Ernährung *f*
nu·tri·tious, **nu·tri·tive** nahrhaft
nut·shell Nussschale *f*; (*to put it*) *in a nutshell* F kurz gesagt, mit e-m Wort
nut·ty voller Nüsse; Nuss...; F verrückt
ny·lon Nylon *n*
nylon stock·ings Nylonstrümpfe *pl*
nymph Nymphe *f*

O

O, o O, o *n*

o Null *f*

oaf Lümmel *m*, Flegel *m*

oak BOT Eiche *f*

oar Ruder *n*

oars·man SPORT Ruderer *m*

oars·wom·an SPORT Ruderin *f*

o·a·sis Oase *f* (*a. fig*)

oath Eid *m*, Schwur *m*; Fluch *m*; *take an oath* e-n Eid leisten *or* schwören; *be on* or *under oath* JUR unter Eid stehen; *take the oath* JUR schwören

oat·meal Hafermehl *n*, Hafergrütze *f*

oats BOT Hafer *m*; *sow one's wild oats* sich die Hörner abstoßen

o·be·di·ence Gehorsam *m*

o·be·di·ent gehorsam

o·bese fett, fettleibig

o·bes·i·ty Fettleibigkeit *f*

o·bey gehorchen (*dat*), folgen (*dat*); Befehl *etc* befolgen

o·bit·u·a·ry Nachruf *m*; *a. obituary notice* Todesanzeige *f*

ob·ject 1. Objekt *n* (*a.* LING); Gegenstand *m*; Ziel *n*, Zweck *m*, Absicht *f*; 2. einwenden; *et.* dagegen haben

ob·jec·tion Einwand *m*, Einspruch *m* (*a.* JUR)

ob·jec·tion·a·ble nicht einwandfrei; unangenehm; anstößig

ob·jec·tive 1. objektiv, sachlich; 2. Ziel *n*

ob·jec·tive·ness Objektivität *f*

ob·li·ga·tion Verpflichtung *f*; *be under an obligation to s.o.* j-m (zu Dank) verpflichtet sein; *be under an obligation to do* verpflichtet sein, *et.* zu tun

ob·lig·a·to·ry verpflichtend, verbindlich

o·blige nötigen, zwingen; (zu Dank) verpflichten; *oblige s.o.* j-m e-n Gefallen tun; *much obliged* besten Dank

o·blig·ing entgegenkommend, gefällig

o·blique schief, schräg; *fig* indirekt

o·blit·er·ate auslöschen; vernichten, völlig zerstören; verdecken

o·bliv·i·on Vergessen(heit *f*) *n*; *fall into oblivion* in Vergessenheit geraten

o·bliv·i·ous: *be oblivious of* or *to s.th.* sich e-r Sache nicht bewusst sein; *et.* nicht bemerken *or* wahrnehmen

ob·long rechteckig; länglich

ob·nox·ious widerlich

ob·scene obszön, unanständig

ob·scure 1. dunkel, *fig a.* unklar; unbekannt; 2. verdunkeln, verdecken

ob·scu·ri·ty Unbekanntheit *f*; Unklarheit *f*

ob·se·quies Trauerfeier(lichkeiten *pl*) *f*

ob·ser·va·ble wahrnehmbar, merklich

ob·ser·vance Beachtung *f*, Befolgung *f*

ob·ser·vant aufmerksam

ob·ser·va·tion Beobachtung *f*, Überwachung *f*; Bemerkung *f* (*on* über *acc*)

ob·ser·va·to·ry Observatorium *n*, Sternwarte *f*

ob·serve beobachten; überwachen; *Vorschrift etc* beachten, befolgen, einhalten; bemerken, äußern

ob·serv·er Beobachter(in)

ob·sess: *be obsessed by* or *with* besessen sein von

ob·ses·sion PSYCH Besessenheit *f*, fixe Idee, Zwangsvorstellung *f*

ob·ses·sive PSYCH zwanghaft

ob·so·lete veraltet

ob·sta·cle Hindernis *n*

ob·sti·na·cy Starrsinn *m*

ob·sti·nate hartnäckig; halsstarrig, eigensinnig, starrköpfig

ob·struct verstopfen, versperren; blockieren; behindern

ob·struc·tion Verstopfung *f*; Blockierung *f*; Behinderung *f*

ob·struc·tive blockierend; hinderlich

ob·tain erhalten, bekommen, sich *et.* beschaffen

ob·tain·a·ble erhältlich

ob·tru·sive aufdringlich

ob·tuse MATH stumpf; *fig* begriffsstutzig; *be obtuse* sich dumm stellen

ob·vi·ous offensichtlich, klar, einleuchtend

oc·ca·sion Gelegenheit *f*; Anlass *m*; Veranlassung *f*; (festliches) Ereignis; *on the occasion of* anlässlich (*gen*)

oc·ca·sion·al gelegentlich; vereinzelt

oc·ca·sion·al·ly gelegentlich, manchmal

Oc·ci·dent *der* Westen, *der* Okzident, *das* Abendland

oc·ci·den·tal abendländisch, westlich

oc·cu·pant Bewohner(in); Insasse *m*, Insassin *f*

oc·cu·pa·tion Beruf *m*; Beschäftigung *f*; MIL, POL Besetzung *f*, Besatzung *f*, Okkupation *f*

oc·cu·py in Besitz nehmen, MIL, POL besetzen; *Raum* einnehmen; in Anspruch nehmen; beschäftigen; *be occupied* bewohnt sein; besetzt sein (*seat*)

oc·cur sich ereignen; vorkommen; *it occurred to me that* es fiel mir ein *or* mir kam der Gedanke, dass

oc·cur·rence Vorkommen *n*; Ereignis *n*; Vorfall *m*

o·cean Ozean *m*, (Welt)Meer *n*

o'clock: (*at*) *five o'clock* (um) fünf Uhr

Oct ABBR *of* **October** Okt., Oktober *m*

Oc·to·ber (ABBR **Oct**) Oktober *m*

oc·u·lar Augen...

oc·u·list Augenarzt *m*, Augenärztin *f*

OD F *v/i*: **OD on heroin** an e-r Überdosis Heroin sterben

odd sonderbar, seltsam, merkwürdig; einzeln, Einzel...; ungerade (*number*); gelegentlich, Gelegenheits...; *odd jobs* Gelegenheitsarbeiten *pl*; F *30 odd* (et.) über 30, einige 30

odds (Gewinn)Chancen *pl*; *the odds are 10 to 1* die Chancen stehen 10 zu 1; *the odds are that* es ist sehr wahrscheinlich, dass; *against all odds* wider Erwarten, entgegen allen Erwartungen; *be at odds* uneins sein (*with* mit); *odds and ends* Krimskrams *m*

odds-on hoch, klar (*favorite*), aussichtsreichst (*candidate etc*); F *it's odds-on that* es sieht ganz so aus, als ob ...

ode Ode *f*

o·do(u)r Geruch *m*

o·do(u)r·less geruchlos

of *prp* von; *origin*: von, aus; *material*: aus; um (*cheat s.o. of s.th.* j-n um et. betrügen); *cause*: an (*dat*) (*die of* sterben an); aus (*of charity* aus Nächstenliebe); vor (*dat*) (*be afraid of* Angst haben vor); auf (*acc*) (*be proud of* stolz sein auf); über (*acc*) (*be glad of* sich freuen über); nach (*smell of* riechen nach); von, über (*acc*) (*speak of s.th.* von *or* über et. sprechen); an (*acc*) (*think of s.th.* an et. denken); *the city of London* die Stadt London; *the works of Dickens* Dickens' Werke; *your letter of ...* Ihr Schreiben vom ...; *five minutes of twelve* fünf Minuten vor zwölf

off 1. *adv* fort(...), weg(...); ab(...), abgegangen (*button etc*); weg, entfernt (*3 miles off*); ELECTR *etc* aus(...), aus-, abgeschaltet; TECH zu; aus(gegangen), alle; aus, vorbei; verdorben (*food*); frei; *I must be off* ich muss gehen *or* weg; *off with you!* fort mit dir!; *be off* ausfallen, nicht stattfinden; *10% off* ECON 10% Nachlass; *off and on* ab und zu, hin und wieder; *take a day off* sich e-n Tag freinehmen; *be well* (*badly*) *off* gut (schlecht) d(a)ran *or* gestellt *or* situiert sein; **2.** *prp* fort von, weg von, von (...,

ab, weg, herunter); abseits von (*or gen*), von ... weg; MAR vor *der Küste etc*; *be off duty* nicht im Dienst sein, dienstfrei haben; *be off smoking* nicht mehr rauchen; **3.** *adj* frei, arbeits-, dienstfrei; *fig* *have an off day* e-n schlechten Tag haben

of·fal GASTR Innereien *pl*

off-col·o(u)r schlüpfrig, zweideutig

of·fence *Br* → **offense**

of·fend beleidigen, kränken; verstoßen (*against* gegen)

of·fend·er (Übel-, Misse)Täter(in); *first offender* JUR nicht Vorbestrafte *m*, *f*, Ersttäter(in)

of·fense Vergehen *n*, Verstoß *m*; JUR Straftat *f*; Beleidigung *f*, Kränkung *f*; *take offense* Anstoß nehmen (*at* an *dat*)

of·fen·sive 1. beleidigend, anstößig; widerlich (*smell etc*); MIL Offensiv..., Angriffs...; **2.** MIL Offensive *f* (*a. fig*)

of·fer 1. *v/t* anbieten (*a.* ECON); *Preis, Möglichkeit etc* bieten; *Preis, Belohnung* aussetzen; sich bereit erklären (*to do* zu tun); *Widerstand* leisten; *v/i* es *or* sich anbieten; **2.** Angebot *n*

off·hand 1. *adj* lässig; Stegreif...; *be offhand with s.o.* F mit j-m kurz angebunden sein; **2.** *adv* auf Anhieb, so ohne weiteres

of·fice Büro *n*, Geschäftsstelle *f*, (*Anwalts*)Kanzlei *f*; (*esp* öffentliches) Amt, Posten *m*; *mst* **Office** *esp Br* Ministerium *n*

office block *Br*, **office build·ing** Bürohaus *n*

office hours Dienstzeit *f*; Geschäfts-, Öffnungszeiten *pl*

of·fi·cer MIL Offizier *m*; (*Polizei- etc*)Beamte *m*, (-)Beamtin *f*

of·fi·cial 1. Beamte *m*, Beamtin *f*; **2.** offiziell, amtlich, dienstlich

of·fi·ci·ate amtieren

of·fi·cious übereifrig

off-licence *Br* Wein- und Spirituosenhandlung *f*

off·line EDP offline, Offline..., rechnerunabhängig

off-peak: *off-peak electricity* Nachtstrom *m*; *off-peak hours* verkehrsschwache Stunden *pl*

off sea·son Nebensaison *f*

off·set ECON ausgleichen; verrechnen (*against* mit)

off·shoot BOT Ableger *m*, Spross *m*

off·shore vor der Küste

off·side SPORT abseits; *offside position* Abseitsposition *f*, Abseitsstellung *f*; *offside trap* Abseitsfalle *f*

off·spring Nachkomme *m*, Nachkommenschaft *f*

off-the-peg *Br*, **off-the-rack** Konfektions…, … von der Stange

off-the-rec·ord inoffiziell

of·ten oft(mals), häufig

oh *int* oh!

oil 1. Öl *n*; Erdöl *n*; **2.** (ein)ölen, schmieren (*a. fig*)

oil change MOT Ölwechsel *m*

oil·cloth Wachstuch *n*

oil·field Ölfeld *n*

oil paint·ing Ölmalerei *f*; Ölgemälde *n*

oil pan MOT Ölwanne *f*

oil plat·form → *oilrig*

oil pol·lu·tion Ölpest *f*

oil pro·duc·tion Ölförderung *f*

oil-pro·duc·ing coun·try Ölförderland *n*

oil re·fin·e·ry Erdölraffinerie *f*

oil·rig (Öl)Bohrinsel *f*

oil·skins Ölzeug *n*

oil slick Ölteppich *m*

oil well Ölquelle *f*

oil·y ölig; *fig* schmierig, schleimig

oint·ment Salbe *f*

OK, o·kay F **1.** *adj and int* okay(!), o.k.(!), in Ordnung(!); **2.** genehmigen, *e-r Sache* zustimmen; **3.** Okay *n*, O.K. *n*, Genehmigung *f*, Zustimmung *f*

old 1. alt; **2.** *the old* die Alten *pl*

old age (hohes) Alter

old age pen·sion Rente *f*, Pension *f*

old age pen·sion·er Rentner(in), Pensionär(in)

old-fash·ioned altmodisch

old·ish ältlich

old peo·ple's home Altersheim *n*, Altenheim *n*

ol·ive BOT Olive *f*; Olivgrün *n*

O·lym·pic Games SPORT Olympische Spiele *pl*

om·i·nous unheilvoll

o·mis·sion Auslassung *f*; Unterlassung *f*; Versäumnis *n*

o·mit auslassen, weglassen; unterlassen

om·nip·o·tent allmächtig

om·nis·ci·ent allwissend

on 1. *prp* auf (*acc or dat*) (**on the table** auf dem *or* den Tisch); an (*dat*) (**on the wall** an der Wand); in (**on TV** im Fernsehen); *direction, target*: auf (*acc*) … (hin), an (*acc*), nach (*dat*) … (hin) (**march on London** nach London marschieren); *fig* auf (*acc*) … (hin) (**on demand** auf Anfrage); *time*: an (*dat*) (**on Sunday** am Sonntag; **on the 1st of April** am 1. April); (gleich) nach, bei (**on his arrival**); *gehörig* zu, *beschäftigt* bei (**be on a committee** e-m Ausschuss angehören; **be on the „Daily**

Mail" bei der "Daily Mail" beschäftigt sein); *state*: in (*dat*), auf (*dat*) (**on duty** im Dienst; **be on fire** in Flammen stehen); *subject*: über (*acc*) (**talk on a subject** über ein Thema sprechen); nach (*dat*) (**on this model** nach diesem Modell); von (*dat*) (**live on s.th.** von et. leben); **on the street** auf der Straße; **on a train** in e-m Zug; **on hearing it** als ich *etc* es hörte; **have you any money on you?** hast du Geld bei dir?; **2.** *adj and adv* (-geschaltet) (*light etc*), eingeschaltet (*radio etc*), auf (*faucet etc*); (dar)auf(*legen, -schrauben etc*); an(*haben, -ziehen*) (**have a coat on** e-n Mantel anhaben); auf (-*behalten*) (**keep one's hat on** den Hut aufbehalten); weiter(*gehen, -sprechen etc*); **and so on** und so weiter; **on and on** immer weiter; **from this day on** von dem Tage an; **be on** THEA gegeben werden; *film*: laufen; *radio, TV* gesendet werden; **what's on?** was ist los?

once 1. einmal; einst; **once again, once more** noch einmal; **once in a while** ab und zu, hin und wieder; **once and for all** ein für alle Mal; **not once** kein einziges Mal, keinmal; **at once** sofort; auf einmal, gleichzeitig; **all at once** plötzlich; **for once** diesmal, ausnahmsweise; **this once** dieses eine Mal; **once upon a time there was …** es war einmal …; **2.** sobald

one ein(e); einzig; man; Eins *f*, eins; **one's** sein(e); **one day** eines Tages; **one Smith** ein gewisser Smith; **one another** sich (gegenseitig), einander; **one by one, one after another, one after the other** e-r nach dem andern; **I for one** ich zum Beispiel; **the little ones** die Kleinen *pl*

one-horse town F *contp* Nest *n*

one·self sich (selbst); sich selbst; (**all**) **by oneself** ganz allein; **to oneself** ganz für sich (allein)

one-sid·ed einseitig

one·time ehemalig, früher

one-track mind: **have a one-track mind** immer nur dasselbe im Kopf haben

one-two *soccer*: Doppelpass *m*

one-way Einbahn…

one-way street Einbahnstraße *f*

one-way tick·et RAIL *etc* einfache Fahrkarte, AVIAT einfaches Ticket

one-way traf·fic MOT Einbahnverkehr *m*

on·ion BOT Zwiebel *f*

on·line EDP online, Online…, rechnerabhängig

on·look·er Zuschauer(in)

on·ly 1. *adj* einzige(r, -s); **2.** *adv* nur, bloß; erst; **only yesterday** erst gestern; **3.** *cj* F nur, bloß

on·rush Ansturm *m*

on·set Beginn *m*; MED Ausbruch *m*

on·slaught (heftiger) Angriff (*a. fig*)

on·to auf (*acc*)

on·ward(s) *adv* vorwärts, weiter; *from now onward* von nun an

ooze *v/i* sickern; *ooze away fig* schwinden; *v/t* absondern; *fig* ausstrahlen, verströmen

o·paque undurchsichtig; *fig* unverständlich

o·pen 1. offen, *a.* geöffnet, *a.* frei (*country etc*); öffentlich; *fig* offen, *a.* unentschieden, *a.* freimütig; *fig* zugänglich, aufgeschlossen (*to* für *or* dat); *open all day* durchgehend geöffnet; *in the open air* im Freien; **2.** *golf, tennis*: offenes Turnier; *in the open im Freien*; *come out into the open fig* an die Öffentlichkeit treten; **3.** *v/t* öffnen, aufmachen, *Buch etc a.* aufschlagen; eröffnen; *v/i* sich öffnen, aufgehen; öffnen, aufmachen (*store*); anfangen, beginnen; *open into* führen nach *or* in (*acc*); *open onto* hinausgehen auf (*acc*)

o·pen-air im Freien

o·pen-end·ed zeitlich unbegrenzt

o·pen·er (*Dosen- etc*)Öffner *m*

o·pen-eyed mit großen Augen, staunend

o·pen-hand·ed freigebig, großzügig

o·pen-heart·ed offenherzig

o·pen·ing 1. Öffnung *f*; ECON freie Stelle; Eröffnung *f*, Erschließung *f*, Einstieg *m*; **2.** Eröffnungs...; Öffnungs...

o·pen-mind·ed aufgeschlossen

o·pen·ness Offenheit *f*

op·e·ra Oper *f*

opera glass·es Opernglas *n*

opera house Opernhaus *n*, Oper *f*

op·e·rate *v/i* wirksam sein *or* werden; TECH arbeiten, in Betrieb sein, laufen (*machine etc*); MED operieren (*on s.o.* j-n); *v/t Maschine* bedienen, *Schalter etc* betätigen; *Unternehmen, Geschäft* betreiben, führen

op·e·rat·ing room MED Operationssaal *m*

operating sys·tem EDP Betriebssystem *n*

operating thea·tre *Br* MED Operationssaal *m*

op·e·ra·tion TECH Betrieb *m*, Lauf *m*; Bedienung *f*; ECON Tätigkeit *f*, Unternehmen *n*; MED, MIL Operation *f*; *in operation* TECH in Betrieb; *have an operation* MED operiert werden

op·e·ra·tive wirksam; MED operativ

op·e·ra·tor TECH Bedienungsperson *f*; EDP Operator *m*; TEL Vermittlung *f*

o·pin·ion Meinung *f*, Ansicht *f*; Gutach-

ten *n* (*on* über *acc*); *in my opinion* meines Erachtens

op·po·nent Gegner(in)

op·por·tune günstig, passend; rechtzeitig

op·por·tu·ni·ty (günstige) Gelegenheit

op·pose sich widersetzen (*dat*)

op·posed entgegengesetzt; *be opposed to* gegen ... sein

op·po·site 1. Gegenteil *n*, Gegensatz *m*; **2.** *adj* gegenüberliegend; entgegengesetzt; **3.** *adv* gegenüber (*to* dat); **4.** *prp* gegenüber (*dat*)

op·po·si·tion Widerstand *m*, Opposition *f* (*a.* PARL); Gegensatz *m*

op·press unterdrücken

op·pres·sion Unterdrückung *f*

op·pres·sive (be)drückend; hart, grausam; schwül (*weather*)

op·tic Augen..., Seh...; → **op·ti·cal** optisch

op·ti·cian Optiker(in)

op·ti·mism Optimismus *m*

op·ti·mist Optimist(in)

op·ti·mis·tic optimistisch

op·tion Wahl *f*; ECON Option *f*, Vorkaufsrecht *n*; MOT Extra *n*

op·tion·al freiwillig; Wahl...; *be an optional extra* MOT gegen Aufpreis erhältlich sein

optional sub·ject PED *etc* Wahlfach *n*

or oder; *or else* sonst

o·ral mündlich; Mund...

or·ange 1. BOT Orange *f*, Apfelsine *f*; **2.** orange(farben)

or·ange·ade Orangenlimonade *f*

o·ra·tion Rede *f*, Ansprache *f*

or·a·tor Redner(in)

or·bit 1. Kreisbahn *f*, Umlaufbahn *f*; *get or put into orbit* in e-e Umlaufbahn gelangen *or* bringen; **2.** *v/i die Erde etc* umkreisen; *v/i* die Erde *etc* umkreisen, sich auf e-r Umlaufbahn bewegen

or·chard Obstgarten *m*

or·ches·tra MUS Orchester *n*; THEA Parkett *n*

or·chid BOT Orchidee *f*

or·dain: *ordain s.o.* (*priest*) j-n zum Priester weihen

or·deal Qual *f*, Tortur *f*

or·der 1. Ordnung *f*; Reihenfolge *f*; Befehl *m*, Anordnung *f*; ECON Bestellung *f*, Auftrag *m*; PARL *etc* (Geschäfts)Ordnung *f*; REL *etc* Orden *m*; *order to pay* ECON Zahlungsanweisung *f*; *in order to inf* um zu *inf*; *out of order* TECH nicht in Ordnung, defekt; außer Betrieb; *make to order* auf Bestellung *or* nach Maß anfertigen; **2.** *v/t* j-m befehlen (*to do* zu tun), *et.* befehlen, anordnen; j-n

O

schicken, beordern; MED *j-m et.* verordnen; ECON bestellen; *fig* ordnen, in Ordnung bringen; *v/i* bestellen (*in restaurant*)
or·der·ly 1. ordentlich; *fig* gesittet, friedlich; **2.** MED Hilfspfleger *m*
or·di·nal *a.* **ordinal number** MATH Ordnungszahl *f*
or·di·nary üblich, gewöhnlich, normal
ore MIN Erz *n*
or·gan ANAT Organ *n* (*a. fig*); MUS Orgel *f*
organ do·nor MED Organspender *m*
organ grind·er Leierkastenmann *m*
organ recip·i·ent MED Organempfänger *m*
or·gan·ic organisch
or·gan·ism Organismus *m*
or·gan·i·za·tion Organisation *f*
or·gan·ize organisieren; sich (gewerkschaftlich) organisieren
or·gan·iz·er Organisator(in)
or·gasm Orgasmus *m*
o·ri·ent 1. Orient *der* Osten, *der* Orient, *das* Morgenland; **2.** orientieren
o·ri·en·tal 1. orientalisch, östlich; **2. Oriental** Orientale *m*, Orientalin *f*
o·ri·en·tate orientieren
or·i·gin Ursprung *m*, Abstammung *f*, Herkunft *f*
o·rig·i·nal 1. ursprünglich; Original...; originell; **2.** Original *n*
o·rig·i·nal·i·ty Originalität *f*
o·rig·i·nal·ly ursprünglich; originell
o·rig·i·nate *v/t* schaffen, ins Leben rufen; *v/i* zurückgehen (**from** auf *acc*), (her)stammen (**from** von, aus)
or·na·ment 1. Ornament(e *pl*) *n*, Verzierung(en *pl*) *f*, Schmuck *m*; *fig* Zier(de) *f* (**to** für *or gen*); **2.** verzieren, schmücken (**with** mit)
or·na·men·tal dekorativ, schmückend, Zier...
or·nate *fig* überladen
or·phan 1. Waise *f*, Waisenkind *n*; **2. be orphaned** Waise werden
or·phan·age Waisenhaus *n*
or·tho·dox orthodox
os·cil·late PHYS schwingen; *fig* schwanken (**between** zwischen *dat*)
os·prey ZO Fischadler *m*
os·ten·si·ble angeblich, vorgeblich
os·ten·ta·tion (protzige) Zurschaustellung; Protzerei *f*, Prahlerei *f*
os·ten·ta·tious protzend, prahlerisch
os·tra·cize ächten
os·trich ZO Strauß *m*
oth·er andere(r, -s); **the other day** neulich; **the other morning** neulich morgens; **every other day** jeden zweiten Tag, alle zwei Tage

oth·er·wise anders; sonst
ot·ter ZO Otter *m*
ought *v/aux ich* sollte, *du* solltest *etc*; **you ought to have done it** Sie hätten es tun sollen
ounce Unze *f* (*28,35 g*)
our unser
ours unsere(r, -s)
our·selves wir *or* uns selbst; uns (selbst)
oust verdrängen, hinauswerfen (**from** aus); *j-n s-s Amtes* entheben
out 1. *adv, adj* aus; hinaus(*gehen, -werfen etc*); heraus(*kommen etc*); aus(*brechen etc*); draußen; im Freien; nicht zu Hause; SPORT aus, draußen; aus, vorbei; aus, erloschen; ausverkauft; F out, aus der Mode; **out of** aus (... heraus); zu ... hinaus; außerhalb von (*or gen*); außer *Reichweite etc*; außer *Atem, Übung etc*; (hergestellt) aus; aus *Furcht etc*; **be out of bread** kein Brot mehr haben; **in nine out of ten cases** in neun von zehn Fällen; **2.** *prp* F aus (... heraus); zu ... hinaus; **3.** outen
out·bal·ance überwiegen
out·bid überbieten
out·board mo·tor Außenbordmotor *m*
out·break MED, MIL Ausbruch *m*
out·build·ing Nebengebäude *n*
out·burst *fig* Ausbruch *m*
out·cast 1. ausgestoßen; **2.** Ausgestoßene *m*, *f*, Verstoßene *m*, *f*
out·come Ergebnis *n*
out·cry Aufschrei *m*, Schrei *m* der Entrüstung
out·dat·ed überholt, veraltet
out·dis·tance hinter sich lassen
out·do übertreffen
out·door *adj* im Freien, draußen
out·doors *adv* draußen, im Freien
out·er äußere(r, -s)
out·er·most äußerste(r, -s)
out·er space Weltraum *m*
out·fit Ausrüstung *f*, Ausstattung *f*; Kleidung *f*; F (Arbeits)Gruppe *f*
out·fit·ter Ausstatter *m*; **men's outfitter** Herrenausstatter *m*
out·go·ing (aus dem Amt) scheidend
out·grow herauswachsen aus (*dat*); *Angewohnheit etc* ablegen; größer werden als
out·house Nebengebäude *n*
out·ing Ausflug *m*; Outing *n*
out·land·ish befremdlich, sonderbar
out·last überdauern, überleben
out·law HIST Geächtete *m*, *f*
out·lay (Geld)Auslagen *pl*, Ausgaben *pl*
out·let Abfluss *m*, Abzug *m*; *fig* Ventil *n*
out·line 1. Umriss *m*; Überblick *m*; **2.** umreißen, skizzieren
out·live überleben

out·look (Aus)Blick *m*, (Aus)Sicht *f*; Einstellung *f*, Auffassung *f*

out·ly·ing abgelegen, entlegen

out·num·ber in der Überzahl sein; *be outnumbered by s.o.* j-m zahlenmäßig unterlegen sein

out-of-date veraltet, überholt

out-of-the-way abgelegen, entlegen; *fig* ungewöhnlich

out·pa·tient MED ambulanter Patient, ambulante Patientin

out·post Vorposten *m*

out·pour·ing (Gefühls)Erguss *m*

out·put ECON Output *m*, Produktion *f*, Ausstoß *m*, Ertrag *m*; EDP (Daten-)Ausgabe *f*

out·rage 1. Gewalttat *f*, Verbrechen *n*; Empörung *f*; 2. grob verletzen; *j-n* empören

out·ra·geous abscheulich; empörend, unerhört

out·right 1. *adj* völlig, gänzlich, glatt (*lie etc*); 2. *adv* auf der Stelle, sofort; ohne Umschweife

out·run schneller laufen als; *fig* übersteigen, übertreffen

out·set Anfang *m*, Beginn *m*

out·shine überstrahlen, *fig a.* in den Schatten stellen

out·side 1. Außenseite *f*; SPORT Außenstürmer(in); *at the* (*very*) *outside* (aller-)höchstens; *outside left* (*right*) SPORT Linksaußen (Rechtsaußen) *m*; 2. *adj* äußere(r, -s), Außen…; 3. *adv* draußen; heraus, hinaus; 4. *prp* außerhalb

out·sid·er Außenseiter(in)

out·size 1. Übergröße *f*; 2. übergroß

out·skirts Stadtrand *m*, Außenbezirke *pl*

out·spo·ken offen, freimütig

out·spread ausgestreckt, ausgebreitet

out·stand·ing hervorragend; ECON ausstehend; ungeklärt (*problem*); unerledigt (*work*)

out·stay länger bleiben als; → *welcome 4*

out·stretched ausgestreckt

out·strip überholen; *fig* übertreffen

out tray: *in the out tray* im Postausgang *etc*

out·vote überstimmen

out·ward 1. äußere(r, -s); äußerlich; 2. *adv mst* **outwards** auswärts, nach außen

out·ward·ly äußerlich

out·weigh *fig* überwiegen

out·wit überlisten, F reinlegen

out·worn veraltet, überholt

o·val 1. oval; 2. Oval *n*

o·va·tion Ovation *f*; *give s.o. a standing ovation* j-m stehende Ovationen bereiten, j-m stehend Beifall klatschen

ov·en Backofen *m*, Bratofen *m*

ov·en-read·y bratfertig

o·ver 1. *prp* über; über (*acc*), über (*acc*) … (hin)weg; über (*dat*), auf der anderen Seite von (*or gen*); über (*acc*), mehr als; 2. *adv* hinüber, herüber (*to* zu); drüben; darüber, mehr; zu Ende, vorüber, vorbei; über…, um…: *et.* über(*geben etc*); über (*-kochen etc*); um(*fallen, -werfen etc*); herum(*drehen etc*); von Anfang bis Ende, durch(*lesen etc*); (gründlich) über(*legen etc*); (*all*) *over again* noch einmal; *all over* ganz vorbei; *over and over* (*again*) immer wieder; *over and above* obendrein, überdies

o·ver·age zu alt

o·ver·all 1. gesamt, Gesamt…; allgemein; insgesamt; 2. *Br* Arbeitsmantel *m*, Kittel *m*; (*Br* **overalls**) Overall *m*, Arbeitsanzug *m*; Arbeitshose *f*

o·ver·awe einschüchtern

o·ver·bal·ance umstoßen, umkippen; das Gleichgewicht verlieren

o·ver·bear·ing anmaßend

o·ver·board MAR über Bord

o·ver·bur·den *fig* überlasten

o·ver·cast bewölkt, bedeckt

o·ver·charge überlasten, ELECTR *a.* überladen; ECON *j-m* zu viel berechnen; *Betrag* zu viel verlangen

o·ver·coat Mantel *m*

o·ver·come überwinden, überwältigen; *be overcome with emotion* von s-n Gefühlen übermannt werden

o·ver·crowd·ed überfüllt; überlaufen

o·ver·do übertreiben; GASTR zu lange kochen *or* braten; *overdone a.* übergar

o·ver·dose Überdosis *f*

o·ver·draft ECON (Konto)Überziehung *f*; *a.* **overdraft facility** Überziehungskredit *m*

o·ver·draw ECON *Konto* überziehen (*by* um)

o·ver·dress (sich) zu fein anziehen; *overdressed* overdressed, zu fein angezogen

o·ver·drive MOT Overdrive *m*, Schongang *m*

o·ver·due überfällig

o·ver·eat zu viel essen

o·ver·es·ti·mate zu hoch schätzen *or* veranschlagen; *fig* überschätzen

o·ver·ex·pose PHOT überbelichten

o·ver·feed überfüttern

o·ver·flow 1. *v/t* überfluten, überschwemmen; *v/i* überlaufen, überfließen; überquellen (*with* von); 2. TECH Überlauf *m*; Überlaufen *n*, -fließen *n*

o·ver·grown BOT überwachsen, überwuchert

o·ver·hang *v/t* über (*dat*) hängen; *v/i* überhängen

o·ver·haul *Maschine* überholen

o·ver·head **1.** *adv* oben, droben; **2.** *adj* Hoch..., Ober...; ECON **overhead expenses** *or* **costs** Gemeinkosten *pl*; SPORT Überkopf...; **overhead kick** *soccer*: Fallrückzieher *m*; **3.** ECON *esp Br a. pl* Gemeinkosten *pl*

o·ver·hear (zufällig) hören

o·ver·heat·ed überhitzt, überheizt; TECH heiß gelaufen

o·ver·joyed überglücklich

o·ver·lap (sich) überlappen; sich überschneiden

o·ver·leaf umseitig, umstehend

o·ver·load überlasten (*a.* ELECTR), überladen

o·ver·look übersehen; **overlooking the sea** mit Blick aufs Meer

o·ver·night **1.** über Nacht; **stay overnight** über Nacht bleiben, übernachten; **2.** Nacht..., Übernachtungs...; **overnight bag** Reisetasche *f*

o·ver·pass (Straßen-, Eisenbahn-) Überführung *f*

o·ver·pay zu viel (be)zahlen

o·ver·pop·u·lat·ed übervölkert

o·ver·pow·er überwältigen; **overpowering** *fig* überwältigend

o·ver·rate überbewerten, überschätzen

o·ver·reach: **overreach o.s.** sich übernehmen

o·ver·re·act überreagieren, überzogen reagieren (**to** auf *acc*)

o·ver·re·ac·tion Überreaktion *f*, überzogene Reaktion

o·ver·ride sich hinwegsetzen über (*acc*)

o·ver·rule *Entscheidung etc* aufheben, *Einspruch etc* abweisen

o·ver·run länger dauern als vorgesehen; *Signal* überfahren; **be overrun with** wimmeln von

o·ver·seas **1.** *adj* überseeisch, Übersee...; **2.** *adv* in *or* nach Übersee

o·ver·see beaufsichtigen, überwachen

o·ver·shad·ow *fig* überschatten, in den Schatten stellen

o·ver·sight Versehen *n*

o·ver·size(d) übergroß, überdimensional, in Übergröße(n)

o·ver·sleep verschlafen

o·ver·staffed (personell) überbesetzt

o·ver·state übertreiben

o·ver·state·ment Übertreibung *f*

o·ver·stay länger bleiben als; → **welcome**

4

o·ver·step *fig* überschreiten

o·ver·take überholen; *j-n* überraschen

o·ver·tax zu hoch besteuern; *fig* überbeanspruchen, überfordern

o·ver·throw **1.** *Regierung etc* stürzen; **2.** (Um)Sturz *m*

o·ver·time ECON Überstunden *pl*; SPORT (Spiel)Verlängerung *f*; **be on overtime, do overtime, work overtime** Überstunden machen

o·ver·tired übermüdet

o·ver·ture MUS Ouvertüre *f*; Vorspiel *n*

o·ver·turn *v/t* umwerfen, umstoßen; *Regierung etc* stürzen; *v/i* umkippen, MAR kentern

o·ver·view *fig* Überblick *m* (**of** über *acc*)

o·ver·weight Übergewicht *n*; **2.** übergewichtig (*person*), zu schwer (**by** um); **be five pounds overweight** fünf Pfund Übergewicht haben

o·ver·whelm überwältigen (*a. fig*)

o·ver·whelm·ing überwältigend

o·ver·work sich überarbeiten; überanstrengen

o·ver·wrought überreizt

o·ver·zeal·ous übereifrig

owe *j-m et.* schulden, schuldig sein; *et.* verdanken

ow·ing: **owing to** infolge, wegen

owl ZO Eule *f*

own **1.** eigen; **my own** mein Eigentum; (**all**) **on one's own** allein; **2.** besitzen; zugeben, (ein)gestehen

own·er Eigentümer(in), Besitzer(in)

own·er·oc·cu·pied *esp Br* eigengenutzt; **owner-occupied flat** Eigentumswohnung *f*

own·er·ship Besitz *m*; Eigentum *n*; Eigentumsrecht *n*

ox ZO Ochse *m*

ox·ide CHEM Oxid *n*, Oxyd *n*

ox·i·dize CHEM oxidieren

ox·y·gen CHEM Sauerstoff *m*

oxygen ap·pa·ra·tus MED Sauerstoffgerät *n*

oxygen tent MED Sauerstoffzelt *n*

oy·ster ZO Auster *f*

o·zone CHEM Ozon *n*

o·zone-friend·ly FCKW-frei, ohne Treibgas

o·zone hole Ozonloch *n*

ozone lay·er Ozonschicht *f*

ozone lev·els Ozonwerte *pl*

ozone shield Ozonschild *m*

P

P, p P, p *n*

pace 1. Tempo *n*, Geschwindigkeit *f*; Schritt *m*; Gangart *f* (*of a horse*); **2.** *v/t* Zimmer *etc* durchschreiten; *a.* **pace out** abschreiten; *v/i* (einher)schreiten; **pace up and down** auf und ab gehen

pace·mak·er SPORT Schrittmacher(in); MED Herzschrittmacher *m*

pace·set·ter SPORT Schrittmacher(in)

Pa·cif·ic *a.* **Pacific Ocean** der Pazifik, der Pazifische *or* Stille Ozean

pac·i·fi·er Schnuller *m*

pac·i·fist Pazifist(in)

pac·i·fy beruhigen, besänftigen

pack 1. Pack(en) *m*, Paket *n*, Bündel *n*; Packung *f*, Schachtel *f*; zo Meute *f*; Rudel *n*; *contp* Pack *n*, Bande *f*; MED *etc* Packung *f*; (Karten)Spiel *n*; **a pack of lies** ein Haufen Lügen; **2.** *v/t* ein-, zusammenpacken, abpacken, verpacken (*a.* **pack up**); zusammenpferchen; vollstopfen; *Koffer etc* packen; **pack off** F fort-, wegschicken; *v/i* packen; (sich) drängen (**into** in *acc*); **pack up** zusammenpacken; **send s.o. packing** j-n fort- *or* wegjagen

pack·age Paket *n*; Packung *f*; **software package** EDP Software-, Programmpaket *n*

pack·age deal F Pauschalangebot *n*, -arrangement *n*

package hol·i·day Pauschalurlaub *m*

package tour Pauschalreise *f*

pack·et Päckchen *n*; Packung *f*, Schachtel *f*

pack·ing Packen *n*; Verpackung *f*

pact Pakt *m*, POL *a.* Vertrag *m*

pad 1. Polster *n*; SPORT (*Knie- etc*)Schützer *m*; (*Schreib- etc*)Block *m*; (*Stempel*)Kissen *n*; zo Ballen *m*; (*Abschuss-*) Rampe *f*; **2.** (aus)polstern, wattieren

pad·ding Polsterung *f*, Wattierung *f*

pad·dle 1. Paddel *n*; MAR (Rad)Schaufel *f*; **2.** paddeln; plan(t)schen

pad·dock (Pferde)Koppel *f*

pad·lock Vorhängeschloss *n*

pa·gan 1. Heide *m*, Heidin *f*; **2.** heidnisch

page¹ 1. Seite *f*; **2.** paginieren

page² 1. (Hotel)Page *m*; **2.** *j-n* ausrufen (lassen)

pag·eant (*a.* historischer) Festzug

pa·gin·ate paginieren

pail Eimer *m*, Kübel *m*

pain 1. Schmerz(en *pl*) *m*; Kummer *m*; *pl* Mühe *f*, Bemühungen *pl*; **be in (great)** pain (große) Schmerzen haben; **be a pain (in the neck)** F e-m auf den Wecker gehen; **take pains** sich Mühe geben; **2.** *esp fig* schmerzen

pain·ful schmerzhaft, schmerzend; *fig* schmerzlich; peinlich

pain·kill·er Schmerzmittel *n*

pain·less schmerzlos

pains·tak·ing sorgfältig, gewissenhaft

paint 1. Farbe *f*; Anstrich *m*; **2.** *v/t* anmalen, bemalen; (an)streichen; *Auto etc* lackieren; *v/i* malen

paint·box Malkasten *m*

paint·brush (Maler)Pinsel *m*

paint·er (*a.* Kunst)Maler(in), Anstreicher(in)

paint·ing Malerei *f*; Gemälde *n*, Bild *n*

pair 1. Paar *n*; **a pair of ...** ein Paar ..., ein(e) ...; **a pair of scissors** e-e Schere; **2.** *v/i* zo sich paaren; *a.* **pair off, pair up** Paare bilden; *v/t a.* **pair off, pair up** paarweise anordnen; **pair off** *zwei Leute* zusammenbringen, verkuppeln

pa·ja·ma(s) (**a pair of**) **pajamas** (ein) Schlafanzug *m*, (ein) Pyjama *m*

pal Kamerad *m*, F Kumpel *m*, Spezi *m*

pal·ace Palast *m*, Schloss *n*

pal·a·ta·ble schmackhaft (*a. fig*)

pal·ate ANAT Gaumen *m*; *fig* Geschmack *m*

pale¹ 1. blass, *a.* bleich, *a.* hell (*color*); **2.** blass *or* bleich werden

pale² Pfahl *m*; *fig* Grenzen *pl*

pale·ness Blässe *f*

Pal·es·tin·i·an 1. palästinensisch; **2.** Palästinenser(in)

pal·ings Lattenzaun *m*

pal·i·sade Palisade *f*; *pl* Steilufer *n*

pal·let TECH Palette *f*

pal·lid blass

pal·lor Blässe *f*

palm¹ *a.* **palm tree** BOT Palme *f*

palm² 1. ANAT Handfläche *f*; **2.** *et.* in der Hand verschwinden lassen; **palm s.th. off on s.o.** F j-m et. andrehen

pal·pa·ble fühlbar, greifbar

pal·pi·tate MED klopfen, pochen

pal·pi·ta·tions MED Herzklopfen *n*

pal·sy MED Lähmung *f*

pal·try armselig

pam·per verwöhnen

pam·phlet Broschüre *f*

pan Pfanne *f*; Topf *m*

pan·a·ce·a Allheilmittel *n*

pan·cake Pfannkuchen *m*
pan·da zo Panda *m*
pan·da car *Br* (Funk)Streifenwagen *m*
pan·de·mo·ni·um Hölle *f*, Höllenlärm *m*, Tumult *m*, Chaos *n*
pan·der Vorschub leisten (**to** *dat*)
pane (*Fenster*)Scheibe *f*
pan·el **1.** (*Tür*)Füllung *f*, (*Wand*)Täfelung *f*; ELECTR, TECH Instrumentenbrett *n*, (*Schalt-, Kontroll- etc*)Tafel *f*; JUR Liste *f* der Geschworenen; Diskussionsteilnehmer *pl*, Diskussionsrunde *f*; Rateteam *n*; **2.** täfeln
pang stechender Schmerz; *pangs of hunger* nagender Hunger; *pangs of conscience* Gewissensbisse *pl*
pan·han·dle **1.** Pfannenstiel *m*; GEOGR schmaler Fortsatz; **2.** F betteln
pan·ic **1.** panisch; **2.** Panik *f*; **3.** in Panik versetzen *or* geraten
pan·ick·y: F *be panicky* in Panik sein
pan·ic-strick·en von Panik erfasst *or* erfüllt
pan·o·ra·ma Panorama *n*, Ausblick *m*
pan·sy BOT Stiefmütterchen *n*
pant keuchen, schnaufen, nach Luft schnappen
pan·ther zo Panther *m*; Puma *m*; Jaguar *m*
pan·ties (*Damen*)Schlüpfer *m*, Slip *m*; Höschen *n*
pan·to·mime THEA Pantomime *f*; *Br* F Weihnachtsspiel *n*
pan·try Speisekammer *f*
pants Hose *f*; *Br* Unterhose *f*; *Br* Schlüpfer *m*
pant·suit Hosenanzug *m*
pan·ty·hose Strumpfhose *f*
pan·ty·lin·er Slipeinlage *f*
pap Brei *m*
pa·pal päpstlich
pa·per **1.** Papier *n*; Zeitung *f*; (Prüfungs)-Arbeit *f*; UNIV Klausur(arbeit) *f*; Aufsatz *m*; Referat *n*; Tapete *f*; *pl* (Ausweis)Papiere *pl*; **2.** tapezieren
pa·per·back Taschenbuch *n*, Paperback *n*
pa·per bag (Papier)Tüte *f*
pa·per·boy Zeitungsjunge *m*
pa·per clip Büro-, Heftklammer *f*
pa·per cup Pappbecher *m*
pa·per·hang·er Tapezierer *m*
pa·per knife *Br* Brieföffner *m*
pa·per mon·ey Papiergeld *n*
pa·per·weight Briefbeschwerer *m*
par: *at par* zum Nennwert; *be on a par with* gleich *or* ebenbürtig sein (*dat*)
par·a·ble Parabel *f*, Gleichnis *n*
par·a·chute Fallschirm *m*
par·a·chut·ist Fallschirmspringer(in)

pa·rade **1.** Umzug *m*, *esp* MIL Parade *f*; *fig* Zurschaustellung *f*; *make a parade of fig* zur Schau stellen; **2.** ziehen (*through* durch); MIL antreten (lassen), vorbeimarschieren (lassen); zur Schau stellen; *parade* (*through*) stolzieren durch
par·a·dise Paradies *n*
par·af·fin *Br* Petroleum *n*
par·a·glid·er SPORT Gleitschirm *m*; Gleitschirmflieger(in)
par·a·glid·ing SPORT Gleitschirmfliegen *n*
par·a·gon Muster *n* (*of* an *dat*)
par·a·graph Absatz *m*, Abschnitt *m*; (Zeitungs)Notiz *f*
par·al·lel **1.** parallel (*to, with* zu); **2.** MATH Parallele *f* (*a. fig*); *without parallel* ohne Parallele, ohnegleichen; **3.** entsprechen (*dat*), gleichkommen (*dat*)
par·a·lyse *Br*, **par·a·lyze** MED lähmen, *fig a.* lahmlegen, zum Erliegen bringen; *paralysed with fig* starr *or* wie gelähmt vor (*dat*)
pa·ral·y·sis MED Lähmung *f*, *fig a.* Lahmlegung *f*
par·a·med·ic MED Sanitäter *m*
par·a·mount größte(r, -s), übergeordnet; *of paramount importance* von (aller)größter Bedeutung *or* Wichtigkeit
par·a·pet Brüstung *f*
par·a·pher·na·li·a (persönliche) Sachen *pl*; Ausrüstung *f*; *esp Br* F Scherereien *pl*
par·a·phrase **1.** umschreiben; **2.** Umschreibung *f*
par·a·site Parasit *m*, Schmarotzer *m*
par·a·troop·er MIL Fallschirmjäger *m*; *pl* Fallschirmjägertruppe *f*
par·boil halb gar kochen, ankochen
par·cel **1.** Paket *n*; Parzelle *f*; **2.** *parcel out* aufteilen; *parcel up* (als Paket) verpacken
parch ausdörren, austrocknen; vertrocknen
parch·ment Pergament *n*
par·don **1.** JUR Begnadigung *f*; *I beg your pardon* Entschuldigung!, Verzeihung!; erlauben Sie mal!, ich muss doch sehr bitten!; *a. pardon?* F (wie) bitte?; **2.** verzeihen; vergeben; JUR begnadigen; *pardon me → I beg your pardon*; F (wie) bitte?
par·don·a·ble verzeihlich
pare sich *die Nägel* schneiden; *Apfel etc* schälen
par·ent Elternteil *m*, Vater *m*, Mutter *f*; *pl* Eltern *pl*
par·ent·age Abstammung *f*, Herkunft *f*
pa·ren·tal elterlich
pa·ren·the·ses (runde) Klammer *f*
par·ents-in-law Schwiegereltern *pl*

par·ent-teach·er meet·ing PED Eltern-abend *m*

par·ings Schalen *pl*

par·ish REL Gemeinde *f*

par·ish church REL Pfarrkirche *f*

pa·rish·ion·er REL Gemeindemitglied *n*

park 1. Park *m*, (Grün)Anlage(n *pl*) *f*; **2.** MOT parken; *look for somewhere to park the car* e-n Parkplatz suchen

par·ka Parka *m*, *f*

park·ing MOT Parken *n*; *no parking* Parkverbot, Parken verboten

parking disk Parkscheibe *f*

parking fee Parkgebühr *f*

parking garage Park(hoch)haus *n*

parking lot Parkplatz *m*

parking lot at·tend·ant Parkwächter *m*

parking me·ter Parkuhr *f*

parking of·fender Parksünder(in)

parking space Parkplatz *m*, Parklücke *f*

parking tick·et Strafzettel *m*

par·ley *esp* MIL Verhandlung *f*

par·lia·ment Parlament *n*

par·lia·men·tar·i·an Parlamentarier(in)

par·lia·men·ta·ry parlamentarisch, Parlaments...

par·lo(u)r *mst in cpds* Salon *m*

pa·ro·chi·al REL Pfarr..., Gemeinde...; *fig* engstirnig, beschränkt

par·o·dy 1. Parodie *f*; **2.** parodieren

pa·role JUR **1.** Hafturlaub *m*; bedingte Haftentlassung; *he is out on parole* er hat Hafturlaub; er wurde bedingt entlassen; **2.** *parole s.o.* j-m Hafturlaub gewähren; j-n bedingt entlassen

par·quet Parkett *n* (*a.* THEA)

par·quet floor Parkett(fuß)boden *m*

par·rot 1. ZO Papagei *m* (*a. fig*); **2.** *et.* (wie ein Papagei) nachplappern

par·ry abwehren, parieren

par·si·mo·ni·ous geizig

pars·ley BOT Petersilie *f*

par·son REL Pfarrer *m*

par·son·age REL Pfarrhaus *n*

part 1. Teil *m*; TECH Teil *n*, Bau-, Ersatzteil *n*; Anteil *m*; Seite *f*, Partei *f*; THEA, *fig* Rolle *f*; MUS Stimme *f*, Partie *f*; GEOGR Gegend *f*, Teil *m*; (Haar)Scheitel *m*; *for my part* was mich betrifft; *for the most part* größtenteils; meistens; *in part* teilweise, zum Teil; *on the part of* vonseiten, seitens (*gen*); *on my part* von m-r Seite; *take part in s.th.* an e-r Sache teilnehmen; *take s.th. in good part* et. nicht übel nehmen; **2.** *v/t* trennen; (ab-, zer-)teilen; einteilen; *Haar* scheiteln; *part company* sich trennen (*with* von); *v/i* sich trennen (*with* von); **3.** *adj* Teil...; **4.** *adv*: **part ...**, **part** teils ..., teils

par·tial Teil..., teilweise; parteiisch, voreingenommen (*to* für)

par·ti·al·i·ty Parteilichkeit *f*, Voreingenommenheit *f*; Schwäche *f*, besondere Vorliebe (*for* für)

par·tial·ly teilweise, zum Teil

par·tic·i·pant Teilnehmer(in)

par·tic·i·pate teilnehmen, sich beteiligen (*both*: *in* an *dat*)

par·tic·i·pa·tion Teilnahme *f*, Beteiligung *f*

par·ti·ci·ple LING Partizip *n*, Mittelwort *n*

par·ti·cle Teilchen *n*

par·tic·u·lar 1. besondere(r, -s), speziell; genau, eigen, wählerisch; **2.** Einzelheit *f*; *pl* nähere Umstände *pl or* Angaben *pl*; Personalien *pl*; *in particular* insbesondere

par·tic·u·lar·ly besonders

part·ing 1. Trennung *f*, Abschied *m*; *esp Br* (Haar)Scheitel *m*; **2.** Abschieds...

par·ti·san 1. Parteigänger(in); MIL Partisan(in); **2.** parteiisch

par·ti·tion 1. Teilung *f*; Trennwand *f*; **2.** *partition off* abteilen, abtrennen

part·ly teilweise, zum Teil

part·ner Partner(in), ECON *a.* Teilhaber(in)

part·ner·ship Partnerschaft *f*, ECON *a.* Teilhaberschaft *f*

part-own·er Miteigentümer(in)

par·tridge ZO Rebhuhn *n*

part-time 1. *adj* Teilzeit..., Halbtags...; *part-time worker* → *part-timer*; **2.** *adv* halbtags

part-tim·er F Teilzeitbeschäftigte *m*, *f*, Halbtagskraft *f*

par·ty Partei *f* (*a.* POL); (Arbeits-, Reise-) Gruppe *f*; (Rettungs- *etc*)Mannschaft *f*; MIL Kommando *n*, Trupp *m*; Party *f*, Gesellschaft *f*; Teilnehmer(in), Beteiligte *m*, *f*

party line POL Parteilinie *f*

party pol·i·tics Parteipolitik *f*

pass 1. *v/i* vorbeigehen, -fahren, -kommen, -ziehen *etc* (*by* an *dat*); übergehen (*to* auf *acc*), fallen (*to* an *acc*); vergehen (*pain etc, time*); durchkommen, (die Prüfung) bestehen; gelten (*as, for* als), gehalten werden (*as, for* für); PARL Rechtskraft erlangen; unbeanstandet bleiben; SPORT (den Ball) abspielen *or* passen (*to* zu); *card game*: passen (*a. fig*); *let s.o. pass* j-n vorbeilassen; *let s.th. pass* et. durchgehen lassen; *v/t* vorbeigehen, -fahren, -fließen, -kommen, -ziehen *etc* an (*dat*); überholen; *Prüfung* bestehen; *Prüfling* durchkommen lassen (*mit der Hand*) streichen (*over* über *acc*); j-m et. reichen, geben, et. weitergeben; SPORT

Ball abspielen, passen (**to** zu); *Zeit* verbringen; PARL *Gesetz* verabschieden; *Urteil* abgeben, fällen, JUR *a*. sprechen (**on** über *acc*); *fig* hinausgehen über (*acc*), übersteigen, übertreffen; **pass away** sterben; **pass off** *j-n, et*. ausgeben (**as** als); *gut etc* verlaufen; **pass out** ohnmächtig werden; **2.** Passierschein *m*; Bestehen *n* (*examination*); SPORT Pass *m*, Zuspiel *n*; (*Gebirgs*)Pass *m*; **free pass** Frei(fahr)-karte *f*; **things have come to such a pass that** F die Dinge haben sich derart zugespitzt, dass; **make a pass at** F Annäherungsversuche machen bei

pass·a·ble passierbar, befahrbar; passabel, leidlich

pas·sage Passage *f*, Korridor *m*, Gang *m*; Durchgang *m*; (See-, Flug)Reise *f*; Durchfahrt *f*, Durchreise *f*; Passage *f* (*a*. MUS), Stelle *f*; **bird of passage** Zugvogel *m*

pass·book ECON Sparbuch *n*

pas·sen·ger Passagier *m*, Fahrgast *m*, Fluggast *m*, Reisende *m, f*, MOT Insasse *m*, Insassin *f*

pass·er·by Passant(in)

pas·sion Leidenschaft *f*; Wut *f*, Zorn *m*; **Passion** REL Passion *f*; **passions ran high** die Erregung schlug hohe Wellen

pas·sion·ate leidenschaftlich

pas·sive passiv; LING passivisch

Pass·o·ver REL Passah(fest) *n*

pass·port (Reise)Pass *m*

pass·word Kennwort *n* (*a*. EDP), MIL *a*. Parole *f*, Losung *f*

past 1. *adj* vergangen; frühere(r, -s); **be past** *a*. vorüber sein; **for some time past** seit einiger Zeit; **past tense** LING Vergangenheit *f*, Präteritum *n*; **2.** *adv* vorüber, vorbei; **go past** vorbeigehen; **3.** *prp time*: nach, über (*acc*); über ... (*acc*) hinaus; an ... (*dat*) vorbei; **half past two** halb drei; **past hope** hoffnungslos; **4.** Vergangenheit *f* (*a*. LING)

pas·ta Teigwaren *pl*

paste 1. Paste *f*; Kleister *m*; Teig *m*; **2.** kleben (**to, on** an *acc*); **paste up** ankleben

paste·board Karton *m*, Pappe *f*

pas·tel Pastell(zeichnung *f*) *n*

pas·teur·ize pasteurisieren

pas·time Zeitvertreib *m*, Freizeitbeschäftigung *f*

pas·tor REL Pastor *m*, Pfarrer *m*, Seelsorger *m*

pas·tor·al REL seelsorgerisch, pastoral; **pastoral care** Seelsorge *f*

pas·try GASTR (*Blätter-, Mürbe*)Teig *m*; Feingebäck *n*

pastry cook Konditor *m*

pas·ture 1. Weide(land *n*) *f*; **2.** *v/t* weiden (lassen); *v/i* grasen, weiden

pas·ty[1] *esp Br* GASTR (Fleisch)Pastete *f*

past·y[2] blass, F käsig

pat 1. Klaps *m*; GASTR Portion *f*; **2.** tätscheln; klopfen

patch 1. Fleck *m*; Flicken *m*; kleines Stück Land; **in patches** stellenweise; **2.** flicken

pa·tent 1. offenkundig; patentiert; Patent...; **2.** Patent *n*; **take out a patent for s.th.** (sich) et. patentieren lassen; **3.** *et*. patentieren lassen

pa·tent·ee Patentinhaber(in)

pa·tent leath·er Lackleder *n*

pa·ter·nal väterlich; väterlicherseits

pa·ter·ni·ty JUR Vaterschaft *f*

path Pfad *m*; Weg *m*

pa·thet·ic mitleiderregend; kläglich, miserabel

pa·tience Geduld *f*; *esp Br* Patience *f*

pa·tient[1] geduldig

pa·tient[2] MED Patient(in)

pat·i·o Terrasse *f*; Innenhof *m*, Patio *m*

pat·ri·ot Patriot(in)

pat·ri·ot·ic patriotisch

pa·trol 1. Patrouille *f* (*a*. MIL), Streife *f*, Runde *f*; **on patrol** auf Patrouille, auf Streife; **2.** abpatrouillieren, auf Streife sein in (*dat*), s-e Runde machen in (*dat*)

pa·trol car (Funk)Streifenwagen *m*

pa·trol·man Streifenpolizist *m*; *Br* motorisierter Pannenhelfer

pa·tron Schirmherr *m*; Gönner *m*, Förderer *m*; (Stamm)Kunde *m*; Stammgast *m*

pat·ron·age Schirmherrschaft *f*; Förderung *f*

pat·ron·ess Schirmherrin *f*; Gönnerin *f*, Förderin *f*

pat·ron·ize fördern; (Stamm)Kunde *or* Stammgast sein bei *or* in (*dat*); gönnerhaft *or* herablassend behandeln

pa·tron saint REL Schutzheilige *m, f*

pat·ter prasseln (*rain*); trappeln (*feet*)

pat·tern 1. Muster *n* (*a. fig*); Schema *n*; **2.** bilden, formen (**after, on** nach)

paunch (dicker) Bauch

pau·per Arme *m, f*

pause 1. Pause *f*; **2.** innehalten, e-e Pause machen

pave pflastern; **pave the way for** *fig* den Weg ebnen für

pave·ment Fahrbahn *f*; Belag *m*, Pflaster *n*; *Br* Bürgersteig *m*, Gehsteig *m*

pave·ment ca·fé *Br* Straßencafé *n*

paw 1. ZO Pfote *f*, Tatze *f*; **2.** *v/t* Boden scharren; scharren an (*dat*); F betatschen; *v/i* scharren (**at** an *dat*)

pawn[1] *chess*: Bauer *m*; *fig* Schachfigur *f*

pawn[2] **1.** verpfänden, versetzen; **2.** **be in**

pawn verpfändet *or* versetzt sein

pawn·bro·ker Pfandleiher *m*

pawn·shop Leihhaus *n*, Pfandhaus *n*

pay 1. *v/t et.* (be)zahlen; *j-n* bezahlen; *Aufmerksamkeit* schenken; *Besuch* abstatten; *Kompliment* machen; **pay attention** achtgeben auf (*acc*); PED aufpassen; **pay cash** bar bezahlen; *v/i* zahlen; *fig* sich lohnen; **pay for** (*fig* für) *et.* bezahlen; *fig* büßen; **pay in** einzahlen; **pay into** einzahlen auf (*acc*); **pay off** *et.* ab(be)zahlen; *j-n* auszahlen; **2.** Bezahlung *f*, Gehalt *n*, Lohn *m*

pay·a·ble zahlbar, fällig

pay·day Zahltag *m*

pay·ee Zahlungsempfänger(in)

pay en·ve·lope Lohntüte *f*

pay·ing lohnend

pay·mas·ter MIL Zahlmeister *m*

pay·ment (Be)Zahlung *f*

pay pack·et *Br* Lohntüte *f*

pay phone *Br* Münzfernsprecher *m*

pay·roll Lohnliste *f*

pay·slip Lohn-, Gehaltsstreifen *m*

PC ABBR *of* **personal computer** PC *m*, Personal Computer *m*; **PC user** PC-Benutzer *m*

pea BOT Erbse *f*

peace Friede(n) *m*; Ruhe *f*; JUR öffentliche Ruhe und Ordnung; **at peace** in Frieden

peace·a·ble friedlich, friedfertig

peace·ful friedlich

peace·lov·ing friedliebend

peace move·ment Friedensbewegung *f*

peace·time Friedenszeiten *pl*

peach BOT Pfirsich(baum) *m*

pea·cock ZO Pfau *m*, Pfauhahn *m*

pea·hen ZO Pfauhenne *f*

peak Spitze *f*, Gipfel *m*; Schirm *m*; *fig* Höhepunkt *m*, Höchststand *m*

peaked cap Schirmmütze *f*

peak hours Hauptverkehrszeit *f*, Stoßzeit *f*; ELECTR Hauptbelastungszeit *f*

peak time, **peak viewing hours** *Br* TV Haupteinschaltzeit *f*, Hauptsendezeit *f*, beste Sendezeit

peal 1. (*Glocken*)Läuten *n*; (*Donner-*) Schlag *m*; **peals of laughter** schallendes Gelächter; **2.** *a.* **peal out** läuten; krachen

pea·nut BOT Erdnuss *f*; *pl* F lächerliche Summe

pear BOT Birne *f*; Birnbaum *m*

pearl 1. Perle *f*; Perlmutter *f*, Perlmutt *n*; **2.** Perlen...

pearl·y perlenartig, Perlen...

peas·ant Kleinbauer *m*

peat Torf *m*

peb·ble Kiesel(stein) *m*

peck picken, hacken; **peck at one's food** im Essen herumstochern

pe·cu·li·ar eigen, eigentümlich, typisch; eigenartig, seltsam

pe·cu·li·ar·i·ty Eigenheit *f*; Eigentümlichkeit *f*

ped·a·go·gic pädagogisch

ped·al 1. Pedal *n*; **2.** das Pedal treten; (mit dem Rad) fahren, strampeln

pe·dan·tic pedantisch

ped·dle hausieren (gehen) mit; **peddle drugs** mit Drogen handeln

ped·dler Hausierer(in)

ped·es·tal Sockel *m*

pe·des·tri·an 1. Fußgänger(in); **2.** Fußgänger...

pedestrian cross·ing Fußgängerübergang *m*

pedestrian mall, *esp Br* **pedestrian precinct** Fußgängerzone *f*

ped·i·cure Pediküre *f*

ped·i·gree Stammbaum *m* (*a.* ZO)

ped·lar *Br* → **peddler**

pee F **1.** pinkeln; **2. have** (*or* **go for**) **a pee** pinkeln (gehen)

peek 1. kurz *or* verstohlen gucken (**at** auf *acc*); **2. have** *or* **take a peek at** e-n kurzen *or* verstohlenen Blick werfen auf (*acc*)

peel 1. *v/t* schälen; *a.* **peel off** abschälen, *Folie*, *Tapete etc* abziehen; *Kleid* abstreifen; *v/i a.* **peel off** sich lösen (*wallpaper etc*), abblättern (*paint etc*), sich schälen (*skin*); **2.** BOT Schale *f*

peep[1] 1. kurz *or* verstohlen gucken (**at** auf *acc*); *mst* **peep out** (her)vorschauen; **2. take a peep at** e-n kurzen *or* verstohlenen Blick werfen auf (*acc*)

peep[2] 1. Piep(s)en *n*; F Piepser *m*; **2.** piep(s)en

peep·hole Guckloch *n*; (Tür)Spion *m*

peer angestrengt schauen, spähen; **peer at s.o.** j-n anstarren

peer·less unvergleichlich, einzigartig

peev·ish verdrießlich, gereizt

peg 1. (Holz)Stift *m*, Zapfen *m*, Pflock *m*; (Kleider)Haken *m*; *Br* (Wäsche-) Klammer *f*; (Zelt)Hering *m*; **take s.o. down a peg** (**or two**) F j-m e-n Dämpfer aufsetzen; **2.** anpflocken; *Wäsche* anklammern, festklammern

pel·i·can ZO Pelikan *m*

pelican cross·ing *Br* Ampelübergang *m*

pel·let Kügelchen *n*; Schrotkorn *n*

pelt[1] *v/t* bewerfen, *v/i*: **it's pelting** (**down**), *esp Br* **it's pelting with rain** es gießt in Strömen

pelt[2] ZO Fell *n*, Pelz *m*

pel·vis ANAT Becken *n*

P

pen

pen[1] (*Schreib*)Feder *f*; Füller *m*; Kugel-schreiber *m*

pen[2] **1.** Pferch *m*, (*Schaf*)Hürde *f*; **2.** *pen in, pen up Tiere* einpferchen, *Personen* zusammenpferchen

pe·nal JUR Straf...; strafbar

pe·nal code JUR Strafgesetzbuch *n*

pe·nal·ize bestrafen

pen·al·ty Strafe *f*, SPORT *a.* Strafpunkt *m*; *soccer:* Elfmeter *m*

penalty ar·e·a, penalty box F *soccer:* Strafraum *m*

penalty goal *soccer:* Elfmetertor *n*

penalty kick *soccer:* Elfmeter *m*, Straf-stoß *m*

penalty shoot-out *soccer:* Elfmeterschie-ßen *n*

penalty spot *soccer:* Elfmeterpunkt *m*

pen·ance REL Buße *f*

pen·cil 1. Bleistift *m*; **2.** (mit Bleistift) markieren *or* schreiben *or* zeichnen; *Au-genbrauen* nachziehen

pen·cil case Federmäppchen *n*

pen·cil sharp·en·er Bleistiftspitzer *m*

pen·dant, pen·dent (Schmuck)Anhänger *m*

pend·ing 1. *prp* bis zu; **2.** *adj esp* JUR schwebend

pen·du·lum Pendel *n*

pen·e·trate *v/t* eindringen in (*acc*); drin-gen durch, durchdringen; *v/i* eindringen (*into* in *acc*)

pen·e·trat·ing durchdringend; *fig* scharf; scharfsinnig

pen·e·tra·tion Durchdringen *n*, Eindrin-gen *n*; *fig* Scharfsinn *m*

pen friend *Br* Brieffreund(in)

pen·guin ZO Pinguin *m*

pe·nin·su·la Halbinsel *f*

pe·nis ANAT Penis *m*

pen·i·tence Buße *f*, Reue *f*

pen·i·tent 1. reuig, bußfertig; **2.** REL Bü-ßer(in)

pen·i·ten·tia·ry (Staats)Gefängnis *n*, Strafanstalt *f*

pen·knife Taschenmesser *n*

pen name Schriftstellername *m*, Pseudo-nym *n*

pen·nant Wimpel *m*

pen·ni·less (völlig) mittellos

pen·ny *a.* **new penny** *Br* Penny *m*

pen pal Brieffreund(in)

pen·sion 1. Rente *f*, Pension *f*; **2.** *pension off* pensionieren, in den Ruhestand ver-setzen

pen·sion·er Rentner(in), Pensionär(in)

pen·sive nachdenklich

pen·tath·lete SPORT Fünfkämpfer(in)

pen·tath·lon SPORT Fünfkampf *m*

Pen·te·cost REL Pfingsten *n*

pent·house Penthouse *n*, Penthaus *n*

pent-up auf-, angestaut (*emotions*)

pe·o·ny BOT Pfingstrose *f*

peo·ple 1. Volk *n*, Nation *f*; die Menschen *pl*, die Leute *pl*; Leute *pl*, Personen *pl*; man; *the people* das (*gemeine*) Volk; **2.** besiedeln, bevölkern (*with* mit)

peo·ple's re·pub·lic Volksrepublik *f*

pep F **1.** Pep *m*, Schwung *m*; **2.** *mst pep up j-n or et.* in Schwung bringen, aufmöbeln

pep·per 1. Pfeffer *m*; BOT Paprikaschote *f*; **2.** pfeffern

pep·per cast·er Pfefferstreuer *m*

pep·per·mint BOT Pfefferminze *f*; Pfeffer-minz *n*

pep·per·y pfeff(e)rig; *fig* hitzig

pep·pill F Aufputschpille *f*

per per, durch; pro, für, je

per·ceive (be)merken, wahrnehmen; er-kennen

per cent, per·cent Prozent *n*

per·cen·tage Prozentsatz *m*; F Prozente *pl*, (An)Teil *m*

per·cep·ti·ble wahrnehmbar, merklich

per·cep·tion Wahrnehmung *f*; Auffas-sung *f*, Auffassungsgabe *f*

perch[1] **1.** (Sitz)Stange *f*; **2.** (*on*) sich setzen (auf *acc*), sich niederlassen (auf *acc, dat*); F hocken (*on* auf *dat*); *perch o.s.* F sich hocken (*on* auf *acc*)

perch[2] ZO Barsch *m*

per·co·la·tor Kaffeemaschine *f*

per·cus·sion Schlag *m*; Erschütterung *f*; MUS Schlagzeug *n*

percussion drill TECH Schlagbohrer *m*

percussion in·stru·ment MUS Schlagins-trument *n*

pe·remp·to·ry herrisch

pe·ren·ni·al ewig, immer während; BOT mehrjährig

per·fect 1. perfekt, vollkommen, vollen-det; gänzlich, völlig; **2.** vervollkommnen; **3.** *a.* **perfect tense** LING Perfekt *n*

per·fec·tion Vollendung *f*; Vollkommen-heit *f*, Perfektion *f*

per·fo·rate durchbohren, -löchern

per·form *v/t* verrichten, durchführen, tun; *Pflicht etc* erfüllen; THEA, MUS aufführen, spielen, vortragen; *v/i* THEA *etc* e-e Vor-stellung geben, auftreten, spielen

per·form·ance Verrichtung *f*, Durchfüh-rung *f*; Leistung *f*; THEA, MUS Aufführ-ung *f*, Vorstellung *f*, Vortrag *f*

per·form·er THEA, MUS Darsteller(in), Künstler(in)

per·fume 1. Duft *m*; Parfüm *n*; **2.** parfü-mieren

per·fum·er·y Parfümerie *f*

per·haps vielleicht
per·il Gefahr f
per·il·ous gefährlich
pe·ri·od Periode f, Zeit f, Zeitdauer f, Zeitraum m, Zeitspanne f; (Unterrichts)Stunde f; MED Periode f; LING Punkt m
period fur·ni·ture Stilmöbel pl
pe·ri·od·ic periodisch
pe·ri·od·i·cal 1. periodisch; **2.** Zeitschrift f
pe·riph·e·ral EDP Peripheriegerät n
peripheral e·quip·ment EDP Peripheriegeräte pl
pe·riph·e·ry Peripherie f, Rand m
per·ish umkommen; GASTR schlecht werden, verderben; TECH verschleißen
per·ish·a·ble leicht verderblich
per·ish·a·bles leicht verderbliche Lebensmittel
per·jure: *perjure o.s.* JUR e-n Meineid leisten
per·ju·ry JUR Meineid m; *commit perjury* e-n Meineid leisten
perk: *perk up* v/i aufleben, munter werden; v/t j-n munter machen, F aufmöbeln
perk·y F munter, lebhaft; keck, selbstbewusst
perm 1. Dauerwelle f; *get a perm* → **2.** *get one's hair permed* sich e-e Dauerwelle machen lassen
per·ma·nent 1. (be)ständig, dauerhaft, Dauer...; **2.** a. *permanent wave* Dauerwelle f
per·me·a·ble durchlässig (*to* für)
per·me·ate durchdringen; dringen (*into* in acc; *through* durch)
per·mis·si·ble zulässig, erlaubt
per·mis·sion Erlaubnis f
per·mis·sive liberal; (sexuell) freizügig
permissive so·ci·e·ty tabufreie Gesellschaft
per·mit 1. erlauben, gestatten; **2.** Genehmigung f
per·pen·dic·u·lar senkrecht; rechtwink(e)lig (*to* zu)
per·pet·u·al fortwährend, ständig, ewig
per·plex verwirren
per·plex·i·ty Verwirrung f
per·se·cute verfolgen
per·se·cu·tion Verfolgung f
per·se·cu·tor Verfolger(in)
per·se·ver·ance Ausdauer f, Beharrlichkeit f
per·se·vere beharrlich weitermachen
per·sist beharren (*in* auf dat); anhalten
per·sis·tence Beharrlichkeit f
per·sis·tent beharrlich; anhaltend
per·son Person f (a. LING)

per·son·al persönlich (a. LING); Personal...; Privat...
personal com·pu·ter (ABBR *PC*) Personal Computer m
personal da·ta Personalien pl
per·son·al·i·ty Persönlichkeit f; pl anzügliche or persönliche Bemerkungen pl
per·son·al or·ga·ni·zer Notizbuch n, Adressbuch n und Taschenkalender m etc (in einem)
personal pro·noun LING Personalpronomen n
personal ster·e·o Walkman® m
per·son·i·fy personifizieren, verkörpern
per·son·nel Personal n, Belegschaft f; die Personalabteilung
personnel de·part·ment Personalabteilung f
personnel man·ag·er Personalchef m
per·spec·tive Perspektive f; Fernsicht f
per·spi·ra·tion Transpirieren n, Schwitzen n; Schweiß m
per·spire transpirieren, schwitzen
per·suade überreden; überzeugen
per·sua·sion Überredung(skunst) f; Überzeugung f
per·sua·sive überzeugend
pert keck, kess; schnippisch
per·tain: *pertain to s.th.* et. betreffen
per·ti·nent sachdienlich, relevant, zur Sache gehörig
per·turb beunruhigen
per·vade durchdringen, erfüllen
per·verse pervers; eigensinnig
per·ver·sion Verdrehung f; Perversion f
per·ver·si·ty Perversität f; Eigensinn m
per·vert 1. pervertieren; verdrehen; **2.** perverser Mensch
pes·sa·ry MED Pessar n
pes·si·mism Pessimismus m
pes·si·mist Pessimist(in)
pes·si·mis·tic pessimistisch
pest ZO Schädling m; F Nervensäge f; F Plage f
pest con·trol Schädlingsbekämpfung f
pes·ter F j-n belästigen, j-m keine Ruhe lassen
pes·ti·cide Pestizid n, Schädlingsbekämpfungsmittel n
pet 1. (zahmes) (Haus)Tier; often contp Liebling m; **2.** Lieblings...; Tier...; **3.** streicheln; F Petting machen
pet·al BOT Blütenblatt n
pet food Tiernahrung f
pe·ti·tion 1. Eingabe f, Gesuch n, (schriftlicher) Antrag; **2.** ersuchen; ein Gesuch einreichen (*for* um), e-n Antrag stellen (*for* auf acc)
pet name Kosename m

P

pet·ri·fy versteinern
pet·rol *Br* Benzin *n*
pe·tro·le·um Erdöl *n*, Mineralöl *n*
pet·rol pump *Br* Zapfsäule *f*
petrol station *Br* Tankstelle *f*
pet shop Tierhandlung *f*, Zoogeschäft *n*
pet·ti·coat Unterrock *m*
pet·ting F Petting *n*
pet·tish launisch, gereizt
pet·ty belanglos, unbedeutend, JUR *a.* geringfügig; engstirnig
petty cash Portokasse *f*
petty lar·ce·ny JUR einfacher Diebstahl
pet·u·lant launisch, gereizt
pew (Kirchen)Bank *f*
pew·ter Zinn *n*; *a.* **pewter ware** Zinn(-geschirr) *n*
phan·tom Phantom *n*; Geist *m*
phar·ma·cist Apotheker(in)
phar·ma·cy Apotheke *f*
phase Phase *f*
pheas·ant ZO Fasan *m*
phe·nom·e·non Phänomen *n*, Erscheinung *f*
phi·lan·thro·pist Philanthrop(in), Menschenfreund(in)
phil·is·tine F *contp* 1. Spießer *m*; 2. spießig
phi·lol·o·gist Philologe *m*, Philologin *f*
phi·lol·o·gy Philologie *f*
phi·los·o·pher Philosoph(in)
phi·los·o·phy Philosophie *f*
phlegm MED Schleim *m*
phone 1. Telefon *n*; *answer the phone* ans Telefon gehen; *by phone* telefonisch; *on the phone* am Telefon; *be on the phone* Telefon haben; am Telefon sein; 2. telefonieren, anrufen
phone book Telefonbuch *n*
phone booth, *Br* **phone box** Telefonzelle *f*
phone call Anruf *m*, Gespräch *n*
phone·card Telefonkarte *f*
phone-in *radio*, TV Sendung *f* mit telefonischer Zuhörer- *or* Zuschauerbeteiligung
phone num·ber Telefonnummer *f*
pho·net·ics Phonetik *f*
pho·n(e)y F 1. Fälschung *f*; Schwindler(in); 2. falsch, gefälscht, unecht; Schein...
phos·pho·rus CHEM Phosphor *m*
pho·to F Foto *n*, Bild *n*; *in the photo* auf dem Foto; *take a photo* ein Foto machen (*of* von)
pho·to·cop·i·er Fotokopiergerät *n*
pho·to·cop·y 1. Fotokopie *f*; 2. fotokopieren
pho·to·graph 1. Fotografie *f*; 2. fotografieren

pho·tog·ra·pher Fotograf(in)
pho·tog·ra·phy Fotografie *f*
phras·al verb LING Verb *n* mit Adverb (und Präposition)
phrase 1. (Rede)Wendung *f*, Redensart *f*, idiomatischer Ausdruck; 2. ausdrücken
phrase·book Sprachführer *m*
phys·i·cal 1. physisch, körperlich; physikalisch; *physically handicapped* körperbehindert; 2. ärztliche Untersuchung
physical ed·u·ca·tion Leibeserziehung *f*, Sport *m*
physical ex·am·i·na·tion ärztliche Untersuchung
physical hand·i·cap Körperbehinderung *f*
physical train·ing Leibeserziehung *f*, Sport *m*
phy·si·cian Arzt *m*, Ärztin *f*
phys·i·cist Physiker(in)
phys·ics Physik *f*
phy·sique Körper(bau) *m*, Statur *f*
pi·a·nist MUS Pianist(in)
pi·an·o MUS Klavier *n*
pick 1. (auf)hacken; (auf)picken; auflesen, aufnehmen; pflücken; *Knochen* abnagen; bohren *or* stochern in (*dat*); F *Schloss* knacken; aussuchen, auswählen; *pick one's nose* in der Nase bohren; *pick one's teeth* in den Zähnen (herum)stochern; *pick s.o.'s pocket* j-n bestehlen; *have a bone to pick with s.o.* mit j-m ein Hühnchen zu rupfen haben; *pick out* (sich) *et.* auswählen; ausmachen, erkennen; *pick up* aufheben, auflesen, aufnehmen; aufpicken; *Spur* aufnehmen; *j-n* abholen; *Anhalter* mitnehmen; F *Mädchen* aufreißen; *Kenntnisse, Informationen etc* aufschnappen; sich *e-e Krankheit etc* holen; *a.* *pick up speed* MOT schneller werden; 2. (Spitz-)Hacke *f*, Pickel *m*; (Aus)Wahl *f*; *take your pick* suchen Sie sich etwas aus
pick-a-back huckepack
pick·ax, *Br* **pick·axe** (Spitz)Hacke *f*, Pickel *m*
pick·et 1. Pfahl *m*; Streikposten *m*; 2. Streikposten aufstellen vor (*dat*), mit Streikposten besetzen; Streikposten stehen
picket fence Lattenzaun *m*
picket line Streikpostenkette *f*
pick·le GASTR 1. Salzlake *f*; Essigsoße *f*; Essig-, Gewürzgurke *f*; *mst pl esp Br* Pickles *pl*; *be in a* (*pretty*) *pickle* F (ganz schön) in der Patsche sitzen *or* sein *or* stecken; 2. einlegen
pick·lock Einbrecher *m*; TECH Dietrich *m*

pick·pock·et Taschendieb(in)
pick-up Tonabnehmer *m*; Kleintransporter *m*; F (Zufalls)Bekanntschaft *f*
pick·y F wählerisch (*in dat* about)
pic·nic 1. Picknick *n*; **2.** ein Picknick machen, picknicken
pic·ture 1. Bild *n*; Gemälde *n*; PHOT Aufnahme *f*; Film *m*; *pl esp Br* Kino *n*; **2.** darstellen, malen; *fig* sich *j-n*, *et.* vorstellen
picture book Bilderbuch *n*
picture post·card Ansichtskarte *f*
pic·tur·esque malerisch
pie (*Fleisch- etc*)Pastete *f*; (*mst* gedeckter) (*Apfel- etc*)Kuchen
piece 1. Stück *n*; Teil *n* (*of a machine etc*); Teil *m* (*of a set etc*); *chess*: Figur *f*; *board game*: Stein *m*; (Zeitungs)Artikel *m*, (-)Notiz *f*; *by the piece* stückweise; *a piece of advice* ein Rat; *a piece of news* e-e Neuigkeit; *give s.o. a piece of one's mind* j-m gründlich die Meinung sagen; *go to pieces* F zusammenbrechen; *take to pieces* auseinandernehmen; **2.** *piece together* zusammensetzen, -stückeln; *fig* zusammenfügen
piece·meal schrittweise
piece·work Akkordarbeit *f*; *do piecework* im Akkord arbeiten
pier MAR Pier *m*, Landungsbrücke *f*; TECH Pfeiler *m*
pierce durchbohren, durchstechen, durchstoßen; durchdringen
pierc·ing durchdringend, (*Kälte etc a.*) schneidend, (*Schrei a.*) gellend, (*Blick*, *Schmerz etc a.*) stechend
pi·e·ty Frömmigkeit *f*
pig ZO Schwein *n* (*a.* F); F Ferkel *n*; *sl contp* Bulle *m*
pi·geon ZO Taube *f*
pi·geon·hole 1. Fach *n*; **2.** ablegen
pig·gy F Schweinchen *n*
pig·gy·back huckepack
pig·gy bank Sparschwein(chen) *n*
pig·head·ed dickköpfig, stur
pig·let ZO Ferkel *n*
pig·sty Schweinestall *m*, F *contp* Saustall *m*
pig·tail Zopf *m*
pike¹ ZO Hecht *m*
pike² → **turnpike**
pile¹ 1. Stapel *m*, Stoß *m*; F Haufen *m*, Menge *f*; (*atomic*) *pile* Atommeiler *m*; **2.** *pile up* (an-, auf)häufen, (auf)stapeln, aufschichten; sich anhäufen; MOT aufeinander auffahren
pile² Flor *m*
pile³ Pfahl *m*
piles *Br* F MED Hämorrhoiden *pl*

pile·up MOT Massenkarambolage *f*
pil·fer stehlen, klauen
pil·grim Pilger(in)
pil·grim·age Pilgerfahrt *f*, Wallfahrt *f*
pill PHARM Pille *f*; *the pill* F die (*Antibaby*)-Pille; *be on the pill* die Pille nehmen
pil·lar Pfeiler *m*; Säule *f*
pil·li·on MOT Soziussitz *m*
pil·lo·ry 1. HIST Pranger *m*; **2.** *fig* anprangern
pil·low (Kopf)Kissen *n*
pil·low·case, **pil·low slip** (Kopf)Kissenbezug *m*
pi·lot 1. AVIAT Pilot *m*; MAR Lotse *m*; **2.** Versuchs…, Pilot…; **3.** lotsen; steuern
pilot film TV Pilotfilm *m*
pilot scheme Versuchs-, Pilotprojekt *n*
pimp Zuhälter *m*
pim·ple MED Pickel *m*, Pustel *f*
pin 1. (Steck)Nadel *f*; (*Haar-*, *Krawatten-etc*)Nadel *f*; Brosche *f*; TECH Bolzen *m*, Stift *m*; *bowling*: Kegel *m*; Pin *m*; (*Wäsche*)Klammer *f*; *Br* (*Reiß-*)Nagel *m*, (-)Zwecke *f*; **2.** (an)heften, anstecken (*to* an *acc*), befestigen (*to* an *dat*); pressen, drücken (*against*, *to* gegen, an *acc*)
PIN *a.* **PIN number** ABBR *of personal identification number* PIN, persönliche Geheimzahl
pin·a·fore Schürze *f*
pin·ball Flippern *n*; *play pinball* flippern
pin·ball ma·chine Flipper(automat) *m*
pin·cers: (*a pair of pincers* e-e) (Kneif)-Zange
pinch 1. *v/t* kneifen, zwicken; F klauen; *v/i* drücken; **2.** Kneifen *n*, Zwicken *n*; Prise *f*; *fig* Not(lage) *f*
pin·cush·ion Nadelkissen *n*
pine¹ BOT Kiefer *f*, Föhre *f*
pine² sich sehnen (*for* nach)
pine·ap·ple BOT Ananas *f*
pine cone BOT Kiefernzapfen *m*
pine·tree BOT Kiefer *f*, Föhre *f*
pin·ion ZO Schwungfeder *f*
pink 1. rosa(farben); **2.** Rosa *n*; BOT Nelke *f*
pint Pint *n* (*0,47 l*, *Br 0,57 l*); *Br* F Halbe *f*
pi·o·neer 1. Pionier *m*; **2.** den Weg bahnen (für)
pi·ous fromm, religiös
pip¹ *Br* (*Apfel-*, *Orangen- etc*)Kern *m*
pip² (Piep)Ton *m*
pip³ *on cards etc*: Auge *n*, Punkt *m*
pipe 1. TECH Rohr *n*, Röhre *f*; (*Tabaks*)-Pfeife *f*; MUS (*Orgel*)Pfeife *f*; *pl Br* F Dudelsack *m*; **2.** (durch Rohre) leiten
pipe·line Rohrleitung *f*; Pipeline *f*
pip·er MUS Dudelsackpfeifer *m*
pip·ing 1. Rohrleitung *f*, Rohrnetz *n*; **2.**

piping hot kochend heiß, siedend heiß
pi·quant pikant (*a. fig*)
pique 1. *in a fit of pique* gekränkt, verletzt, pikiert; **2.** kränken, verletzen; *be piqued a.* pikiert sein
pi·rate 1. Pirat *m*, Seeräuber *m*; **2.** unerlaubt kopieren *or* nachdrucken *or* nachpressen
pi·rate ra·di·o Piratensender *m or pl*
Pis·ces ASTR Fische *pl*; *he (she) is (a) Pisces* er (sie) ist (ein) Fisch
piss V **1.** Pisse *f*; *take the piss out of s.o.* j-n verarschen; **2.** pissen; *piss off!* verpiss dich!
pis·tol Pistole *f*
pis·ton TECH Kolben *m*
pit¹ 1. Grube *f* (*a.* ANAT), MIN *a.* Zeche *f*; *esp Br* THEA Parkett *n*; *a.* ***orchestra pit*** THEA Orchestergraben *m*; MED (*esp* Pocken)Narbe *f*; *car racing*: Box *f*; *pit stop* Boxenstopp *m*; **2.** mit Narben bedecken
pit² 1. BOT Kern *m*, Stein *m*; **2.** entkernen, entsteinen
pitch¹ 1. *v/t* Zelt, *Lager* aufschlagen; werfen, schleudern; MUS (an)stimmen; *v/i* stürzen, fallen; MAR stampfen; sich neigen (*roof etc*); *pitch in* F sich ins Zeug legen; kräftig zulangen; **2.** *esp Br* SPORT (Spiel)Feld *n*; MUS Tonhöhe *f*; *fig* Grad *m*, Stufe *f*; *esp Br* Stand(platz) *m*; MAR Stampfen *n*; Neigung *f* (*of a roof etc*)
pitch² Pech *n*
pitch-black, **pitch-dark** pechschwarz; stockdunkel
pitch·er¹ Krug *m*
pitch·er² *baseball*: Werfer *m*
pitch·fork Heugabel *f*, Mistgabel *f*
pit·e·ous kläglich
pit·fall Fallgrube *f*; *fig* Falle *f*
pith BOT Mark *n*; weiße innere Haut; *fig* Kern *m*
pith·y markig, prägnant
pit·i·a·ble → *pitiful*
pit·i·ful mitleiderregend, bemitleidenswert; erbärmlich, jämmerlich
pit·i·less unbarmherzig, erbarmungslos
pit·ta bread Fladenbrot *n*
pit·y 1. Mitleid *n* (*on* mit); *it is a (great) pity* es ist (sehr) schade; *what a pity!* wie schade!; **2.** bemitleiden, bedauern
piv·ot 1. TECH Drehzapfen *m*; *fig* Dreh- und Angelpunkt *m*; **2.** sich drehen; *pivot on fig* abhängen von
pix·el EDP Pixel *m*
piz·za Pizza *f*
plac·ard 1. Plakat *n*; Transparent *n*; **2.** mit Plakaten bekleben
place 1. Platz *m*, Ort *m*, Stelle *f*; Stätte *f*; Haus *n*, Wohnung *f*; Wohnort *m*; (*Ar-*

beits-, Lehr)Stelle *f*; *in the first place* erstens; *in third place* SPORT *etc* auf dem dritten Platz; *in place of* anstelle von (*or gen*); *out of place* fehl am Platz; *take place* stattfinden; *take s.o.'s place* j-s Stelle einnehmen; **2.** stellen, setzen; *Auftrag* erteilen (*with dat*), Bestellung aufgeben (*with* bei); *be placed* SPORT sich platzieren (*second* an zweiter Stelle)
place mat Platzdeckchen *n*, Set *n*, *m*
place·ment test Einstufungsprüfung *f*
place name Ortsname *m*
plac·id ruhig; gelassen
pla·gia·rize plagiieren
plague 1. Seuche *f*; Pest *f*; Plage *f*; **2.** plagen
plaice ZO Scholle *f*
plaid Plaid *n or m*
plain 1. *adj* einfach schlicht; klar (und deutlich); offen (und ehrlich); unscheinbar, wenig anziehend; rein, völlig (*nonsense etc*); **2.** *adv* F (ganz) einfach; **3.** Ebene *f*, Flachland *n*
plain choc·o·late *Br* (zart)bittere Schokolade
plain-clothes … in Zivil
plain·tiff JUR Kläger(in)
plain·tive traurig, klagend
plait *esp Br* **1.** Zopf *m*; **2.** flechten
plan 1. Plan *m*; **2.** planen; beabsichtigen
plane¹ Flugzeug *n*; *by plane* mit dem Flugzeug; *go by plane* fliegen
plane² 1. flach, eben; **2.** MATH Ebene *f*; *fig* Stufe *f*, Niveau *n*
plane³ 1. Hobel *m*; **2.** hobeln; *plane down* abhobeln
plan·et ASTR Planet *m*
plank Planke *f*, Bohle *f*
plank bed Pritsche *f*
plank·ing Planken *pl*
plant 1. BOT Pflanze *f*; ECON Werk *n*, Betrieb *m*, Fabrik *f*; **2.** (an-, ein)pflanzen; bepflanzen; *Garten etc* anlegen; aufstellen, postieren; *plant s.th. on s.o* j-m et. (*Belastendes*) unterschieben
plan·ta·tion Plantage *f*, Pflanzung *f*; Schonung *f*
plant·er Plantagenbesitzer(in), Pflanzer(in); Pflanzmaschine *f*; Übertopf *m*
plaque Gedenktafel *f*; MED Zahnbelag *m*
plas·ter 1. MED Pflaster *n*; (Ver)Putz *m*; *a.* *plaster of Paris* Gips *m*; *have one's leg in plaster* MED das Bein in Gips haben; **2.** verputzen; bekleben
plaster cast Gipsabguss *m*, Gipsmodell *n*; MED Gipsverband *m*
plas·tic 1. plastisch; Plastik…; **2.** Plastik *n*, Kunststoff *m*; → *plastic mon·ey* F Plas-

tikgeld *n*, Kreditkarten *pl*
plastic wrap Frischhaltefolie *f*
plate 1. Teller *m*; Platte *f*; (*Namens-, Nummern- etc*)Schild *n*; (Bild)Tafel *f*; (Druck)Platte *f*; Gegenstände *pl* aus Edelmetall; Doublé *n*, Dublee *n*; **2.** *plated with gold, gold-plated* vergoldet
plat·form Plattform *f*; RAIL Bahnsteig *m*; (Redner)Tribüne *f*, Podium *n*; POL Plattform *f*; MOT Pritsche *f*; *party platform* POL Parteiprogramm *n*; *election platform* POL Wahlprogramm *n*
plat·i·num CHEM Platin *n*
pla·toon MIL Zug *m*
plat·ter (Servier)Platte *f*
plau·si·ble plausibel, glaubhaft
play 1. Spiel *n*; Schauspiel *n*, (Theater)-Stück *n*; TECH Spiel *n*; *fig* Spielraum *m*; *at play* beim Spiel(en); *in play* im Spiel (*ball*); *out of play* im Aus (*ball*); **2.** *v/i* spielen (*a.* SPORT, THEA *etc*); *v/t* Karten, Rolle, Stück *etc* spielen, SPORT *Spiel* austragen; *play s.o.* SPORT gegen j-n spielen; *play the guitar* Gitarre spielen; *play a trick on s.o.* j-m e-n Streich spielen; *play back* Ball zurückspielen (*to* zu); *Tonband* abspielen; *play s.th. down* verharmlosen, herunterspielen; *play off fig* ausspielen (*against* gegen); *play on fig* j-s Schwächen ausnutzen
play·back Play-back *n*, Wiedergabe *f*, Abspielen *n*
play·boy Playboy *m*
play·er MUS, SPORT Spieler(in); TECH Plattenspieler *m*
play·fel·low *Br* → *playmate*
play·ful verspielt; scherzhaft
play·go·er Theaterbesucher(in)
play·ground Spielplatz *m* (*a. fig*); Schulhof *m*
play·group *Br* Spielgruppe *f*
play·house THEA Schauspielhaus *n*; Spielhaus *n* (*for children*)
play·ing card Spielkarte *f*
play·ing field Sportplatz *m*, Spielfeld *n*
play·mate Spielkamerad(in)
play·pen Laufgitter *n*, Laufstall *m*
play·thing Spielzeug *n*
play·wright Dramatiker(in)
plc, PLC *Br* ECON ABBR *of public limited company* AG, Aktiengesellschaft *f*
plea: *enter a plea of* (*not*) *guilty* JUR sich schuldig bekennen (s-e Unschuld erklären)
plead *v/i* (dringend) bitten (*for* um); *plead* (*not*) *guilty* JUR sich schuldig bekennen (s-e Unschuld erklären); *v/t a.* JUR zu s-r Verteidigung *or* Entschuldigung anführen, geltend machen; *plead*

s.o.'s case sich für j-n einsetzen; JUR j-n vertreten
pleas·ant angenehm, erfreulich; freundlich; sympathisch
please 1. *j-m* gefallen; *j-m* zusagen, *j-n* erfreuen; zufriedenstellen; *only to please you* nur dir zuliebe; *please o.s.* tun, was man will; *please yourself!* mach, was du willst!; **2.** *int* bitte; (*yes,*) *please* (ja,) bitte; (*oh ja,*) gerne; *please come in!* bitte, treten Sie ein!
pleased erfreut, zufrieden; *be pleased about* sich freuen über (*acc*); *be pleased with* zufrieden sein mit; *I am pleased with it* es gefällt mir; *be pleased to do s.th.* et. gern tun; *pleased to meet you!* angenehm!
pleas·ing angenehm
plea·sure Vergnügen *n*; *at* (*one's*) *pleasure* nach Belieben
pleat (Plissee)Falte *f*
pleat·ed skirt Faltenrock *m*
pledge 1. Pfand *n*; *fig* Unterpfand *n*; Versprechen *n*; **2.** versprechen, zusichern
plen·ti·ful reichlich
plen·ty 1. Überfluss *m*; *in plenty* im Überfluss, in Hülle und Fülle; *plenty of* e-e Menge, viel(e), reichlich; **2.** F reichlich
pleu·ri·sy MED Brustfell-, Rippenfellentzündung *f*
pli·a·ble, pli·ant biegsam; *fig* flexibel; *fig* leicht beeinflussbar
pli·ers (*a pair of pliers* e-e) Beißzange *f*
plight Not *f*, Notlage *f*
plim·soll *Br* Turnschuh *m*
plod *a.* *plod along* sich dahinschleppen; *plod away* sich abplagen (*at* mit), schuften
plop F **1.** Plumps *m*, Platsch *m*; **2.** plumpsen, (*ins Wasser*) platschen
plot 1. Stück *n* Land, Parzelle *f*, Grundstück *n*; THEA, *film etc*: Handlung *f*; Komplott *n*, Verschwörung *f*; EDP grafische Darstellung; **2.** *v/i* sich verschwören (*against* gegen); *v/t* planen; einzeichnen
plot·ter EDP Plotter *m*
plough *Br*, **plow** AGR **1.** Pflug *m*; **2.** (um)-pflügen
plough·share *Br*, **plow·share** AGR Pflugschar *f*
pluck 1. *v/t Geflügel* rupfen; *mst pluck out* ausreißen, ausrupfen, auszupfen; MUS *Saiten* zupfen; *pluck up* (*one's*) *courage* Mut *or* sich ein Herz fassen; *v/i* zupfen (*at* an *dat*); **2.** F Mut *m*, Schneid *m*
pluck·y F mutig
plug 1. Stöpsel *m*; ELECTR Stecker *m*, F Steckdose *f*; F MOT (*Zünd*)Kerze *f*; **2.**

P

v/t F für *et.* Schleichwerbung machen; *a.*
plug up zustöpseln; zustopfen, verstopfen; **plug in** ELECTR anschließen, einstecken
plug·ging F Schleichwerbung *f*
plum BOT Pflaume *f*; Zwetsch(g)e *f*
plum·age Gefieder *n*
plumb 1. (Blei)Lot *n*; **2.** ausloten, *fig a.*
ergründen; **plumb in** *esp Br* Waschma-
schine etc anschließen; **3.** *adj* lotrecht,
senkrecht; **4.** *adv* F (haar)genau
plumb·er Klempner *m*, Installateur *m*
plumb·ing Klempner-, Installateurarbeit
f; Rohre *pl*, Rohrleitungen *pl*
plume (Schmuck)Feder *f*; Federbusch *m*;
(*Rauch*)Fahne *f*
plump 1. *adj* drall, mollig, rund(lich), F
pumm(e)lig; **2.** **plump down** fallen *or*
plumpsen (lassen)
plum pud·ding *Br* Plumpudding *m*
plun·der 1. plündern; **2.** Plünderung *f*;
Beute *f*
plunge 1. (ein-, unter)tauchen; (sich) stürzen (**into** in *acc*); MAR stampfen; **2.**
(Kopf)Sprung *m*; **take the plunge** *fig*
den entscheidenden Schritt wagen
plu·per·fect *a.* **pluperfect tense** LING
Plusquamperfekt *n*, Vorvergangenheit *f*
plu·ral LING Plural *m*, Mehrzahl *f*
plus 1. *prp* plus, und, *esp* ECON zuzüglich;
2. *adj* Plus...; **plus sign** MATH Plus *n*,
Pluszeichen *n*; **3.** MATH Plus *n* (*a.* F), Pluszeichen *n*; F Vorteil *m*
plush Plüsch *m*
ply¹ *regelmäßig* verkehren, fahren (**between** zwischen *dat*)
ply² *mst in cpds* TECH Lage *f*, Schicht *f*;
three-ply dreifach (*thread etc*); dreifach
gewebt (*carpet*)
ply·wood Sperrholz *n*
pm, PM ABBR *of* **after noon** (*Latin* **post
meridiem**) nachm., nachmittags, abends
pneu·mat·ic Luft..., pneumatisch; TECH
Druck..., Pressluft...
pneu·mat·ic drill Pressluftbohrer *m*
pneu·mo·ni·a MED Lungenentzündung *f*
poach¹ GASTR pochieren; **poached eggs**
verlorene Eier *pl*
poach² wildern
poach·er Wilddieb *m*, Wilderer *m*
PO Box Postfach *n*; **write to PO Box 225**
schreiben Sie an Postfach 225
pock MED Pocke *f*, Blatter *f*
pock·et 1. (Hosen- *etc*)Tasche *f*; **2.** *adj* Taschen...; **3.** einstecken, in die Tasche
stecken; *fig* in die eigene Tasche stecken
pock·et·book Notizbuch *n*; Brieftasche *f*
pock·et cal·cu·la·tor Taschenrechner *m*
pocket knife Taschenmesser *n*

pocket money Taschengeld *n*
pod BOT Hülse *f*, Schote *f*
po·di·a·trist Fußpfleger(in)
po·em Gedicht *n*
po·et Dichter(in)
po·et·ic dichterisch
po·et·i·cal dichterisch
po·et·ic jus·tice *fig* ausgleichende Gerechtigkeit
po·et·ry Gedichte *pl*; Poesie *f* (*a. fig*),
Dichtkunst *f*, Dichtung *f*
poi·gnant schmerzlich; ergreifend
point 1. Spitze *f*; GEOGR Landspitze *f*;
LING, MATH, PHYS, SPORT *etc* Punkt *m*;
MATH (Dezimal)Punkt *m*; Grad *m*; MAR
(*Kompass*)Strich *m*; *fig* Punkt *m*, Stelle
f, Ort *m*; Zweck *m*; Ziel *n*, Absicht *f*;
Pointe *f*; springender Punkt; Pointe *f*; **two point
five (2.5)** 2,5; **point of view** Stand-, Gesichtspunkt *m*; **be on the point of doing
s.th.** im Begriff sein, et. zu tun; **to the
point** zur Sache gehörig; **off or beside
the point** nicht zur Sache gehörig; **come
to the point** zur Sache kommen; **that's
not the point** darum geht es nicht;
what's the point? wozu?; **win on points**
SPORT nach Punkten gewinnen; **winner
on points** SPORT Punktsieger *m*; **2.** *v/t*
(zu)spitzen; *Waffe etc* richten (**at** auf
acc); **point one's finger at s.o.** (mit
dem Finger) auf j-n zeigen; **point out**
zeigen; *fig* hinweisen *or* aufmerksam machen auf (*acc*); *v/i* (mit dem Finger) zeigen (**at, to** auf *acc*); **point to** nach e-r
Richtung weisen *or* liegen; *fig* hinweisen
auf (*acc*)
point·ed spitz; Spitz...; *fig* scharf (*remark
etc*); ostentativ
point·er Zeiger *m*; Zeigestock *m*; ZO
Pointer *m*, Vorstehhund *m*
point·less sinnlos, zwecklos
points *Br* RAIL Weiche *f*
poise 1. (Körper)Haltung *f*; *fig* Gelassenheit *f*; **2.** balancieren; **be poised** schweben
poi·son 1. Gift *n*; **2.** vergiften
poi·son·ous giftig (*a. fig*)
poke 1. *v/t* stoßen; *Feuer* schüren; stecken;
v/i **poke about, poke around** F (herum-)
stöbern, (-)wühlen (**in** in *dat*); **2.** Stoß *m*
pok·er Schürhaken *m*
pok·y F eng; schäbig
Po·land Polen *n*
po·lar polar
polar bear ZO Eisbär *m*
pole¹ GEOGR Pol *m*
pole² Stange *f*; Mast *m*; Deichsel *f*; SPORT
(Sprung)Stab *m*
Pole Pole *m*, Polin *f*

pole·cat ZO Iltis *m*; F Skunk *m*, Stinktier *n*

po·lem·ic, po·lem·i·cal polemisch

pole star ASTR Polarstern *m*

pole vault SPORT Stabhochsprung *m*, Stabhochspringen *n*

pole-vault SPORT stabhochspringen

pole vault·er SPORT Stabhochspringer(in)

po·lice 1. Polizei *f*; **2.** überwachen

po·lice car Polizeiauto *n*

po·lice·man Polizist *m*

po·lice of·fi·cer Polizeibeamte *m*, -beamtin *f*, Polizist(in)

police sta·tion Polizeiwache *f*, Polizeirevier *n*

po·lice·wom·an Polizistin *f*

pol·i·cy Politik *f*; Taktik *f*; Klugheit *f*; (Versicherungs)Police *f*

po·li·o MED Polio *f*, Kinderlähmung *f*

pol·ish 1. polieren; *Schuhe* putzen; ***polish up*** aufpolieren (*a. fig*); **2.** Politur *f*; (*Schuh*)Creme *f*; *fig* Schliff *m*

Pol·ish 1. polnisch; **2.** LING Polnisch *n*

po·lite höflich

po·lite·ness Höflichkeit *f*

po·lit·i·cal politisch

pol·i·ti·cian Politiker(in)

pol·i·tics Politik *f*

pol·ka MUS Polka *f*

pol·ka-dot gepunktet, getupft

poll 1. (*Meinungs*)Umfrage *f*; Wahlbeteiligung *f*; *a. pl* Stimmabgabe *f*, Wahl *f*; **2.** befragen; *Stimmen* erhalten

pol·len BOT Pollen *m*, Blütenstaub *m*

poll·ing Stimmabgabe *f*; Wahlbeteiligung *f*

polling booth *esp Br* Wahlkabine *f*

polling day Wahltag *m*

polling place, *esp Br* **polling sta·tion** Wahllokal *n*

polls Wahl *f*; Wahllokal *n*

poll·ster Demoskop(in), Meinungsforscher(in)

pol·lut·ant Schadstoff *m*

pol·lute beschmutzen, verschmutzen; verunreinigen

pol·lut·er *a.* ***environmental polluter*** Umweltsünder(in)

pol·lu·tion (*Luft-, Wasser- etc*)Verschmutzung *f*; Verunreinigung *f*

po·lo SPORT Polo *n*

po·lo neck *a.* ***polo neck sweater*** *esp Br* Rollkragenpullover *m*

pol·yp ZO, MED Polyp *m*

pol·y·sty·rene Styropor® *n*

pom·mel (Sattel- *etc*)Knopf *m*

pomp Pomp *m*, Prunk *m*

pom·pous aufgeblasen, wichtigtuerisch; schwülstig (*speech*)

pond Teich *m*, Weiher *m*

pon·der *v/i* nachdenken (**on, over** über *acc*); *v/t* überlegen

pon·der·ous schwerfällig; schwer

pon·toon Ponton *m*

pon·toon bridge Pontonbrücke *f*

po·ny ZO Pony *n*

po·ny·tail Pferdeschwanz *m*

poo·dle ZO Pudel *m*

pool¹ Teich *m*, Tümpel *m*; Pfütze *f*, (*Blutetc*)Lache *f*; (*Schwimm*)Becken *n*, (*Swimming*)Pool *m*

pool² **1.** (*Arbeits-, Fahr*)Gemeinschaft *f*; (*Mitarbeiter- etc*)Stab *m*; (*Fuhr*)Park *m*; (*Schreib*)Pool *m*; ECON Pool *m*, Kartell *n*; *card games*: Gesamteinsatz *m*; Poolbillard *n*; **2.** *Geld, Unternehmen etc* zusammenlegen; *Kräfte etc* vereinen

pool hall, pool·room Billardspielhalle *f*

pools *a.* ***football pools*** *Br* (Fußball)Toto *n, m*

poor 1. arm; dürftig, mangelhaft, schwach; **2.** ***the poor*** die Armen *pl*

poor·ly 1. *adj esp Br* F kränklich, unpässlich; **2.** *adv* ärmlich, dürftig, schlecht, schwach

pop¹ 1. *v/t* zerknallen; F schnell *wohin* tun *or* stecken; *v/i* knallen; (zer)platzen; ***pop in*** F auf e-n Sprung vorbeikommen; ***pop off*** F (plötzlich) den Löffel weglegen; ***pop up*** (plötzlich) auftauchen; **2.** Knall *m*; F Limo *f*

pop² MUS **1.** Pop *m*; **2.** Schlager…; Pop…

pop³ F Paps *m*, Papa *m*

pop⁴ ABBR *of* ***population*** Einw., Einwohner(zahl *f*) *pl*

pop con·cert MUS Popkonzert *n*

pop·corn Popcorn *n*, Puffmais *m*

Pope REL Papst *m*

pop-eyed F glotzäugig

pop group MUS Popgruppe *f*

pop·lar BOT Pappel *f*

pop mu·sic Popmusik *f*

pop·py BOT Mohn *m*

pop·u·lar populär, beliebt; volkstümlich; allgemein

pop·u·lar·i·ty Popularität *f*, Beliebtheit *f*; Volkstümlichkeit *f*

pop·u·late bevölkern, besiedeln; bewohnen

pop·u·la·tion Bevölkerung *f*

pop·u·lous dicht besiedelt, dicht bevölkert

porce·lain Porzellan *n*

porch überdachter Vorbau; Portal *n*; Veranda *f*

por·cu·pine ZO Stachelschwein *n*

pore¹ Pore *f*

pore²: ***pore over*** vertieft sein in (*acc*), et. eifrig studieren

P

pork GASTR Schweinefleisch *n*
porn F → **porno**
por·no F 1. Porno *m*; 2. Porno...
por·nog·ra·phy Pornografie *f*
po·rous porös
por·poise ZO Tümmler *m*
por·ridge Porridge *m*, *n*, Haferbrei *m*
port[1] Hafen *m*; Hafenstadt *f*
port[2] AVIAT, MAR Backbord *n*
port[3] EDP Port *m*, Anschluss *m*
port[4] Portwein *m*
por·ta·ble tragbar
por·ter (Gepäck)Träger *m*; *esp Br* Pförtner *m*, Portier *m*; RAIL Schlafwagenschaffner *m*
port·hole MAR Bullauge *n*
por·tion 1. (An)Teil *m*; GASTR Portion *f*; 2. **portion out** aufteilen, verteilen (**among**, **between** unter *acc*)
port·ly korpulent
por·trait Porträt *n*, Bild *n*, Bildnis *n*
por·tray porträtieren; darstellen; schildern
por·tray·al THEA Verkörperung *f*, Darstellung *f*; Schilderung *f*
Por·tu·gal Portugal *n*
Por·tu·guese 1. portugiesisch; 2. Portugiese *m*, Portugiesin *f*; LING Portugiesisch *n*; **the Portuguese** die Portugiesen *pl*
pose 1. *v/t* aufstellen; *Problem, Frage* aufwerfen, *Bedrohung, Gefahr etc* darstellen; *v/i* Modell sitzen *or* stehen; **pose as** sich ausgeben als *or* für; 2. Pose *f*
posh *esp Br* F schick, piekfein
po·si·tion 1. Position *f*, Lage *f*, Stellung *f* (*a. fig*); Stand *m*; *fig* Standpunkt *m*; 2. (auf)stellen
pos·i·tive 1. positiv; bestimmt, sicher, eindeutig; greifbar, konkret, konstruktiv; 2. PHOT Positiv *n*
pos·sess besitzen; *fig* beherrschen
pos·sessed *fig* besessen
pos·ses·sion Besitz *m*; *fig* Besessenheit *f*
pos·ses·sive besitzergreifend; LING possessiv, besitzanzeigend
pos·si·bil·i·ty Möglichkeit *f*
pos·si·ble möglich
pos·si·bly möglicherweise, vielleicht; **if I possibly can** wenn ich irgend kann; **I can't possibly do this** ich kann das unmöglich tun
post[1] (*Tür-, Tor-, Ziel- etc*)Pfosten *m*; Pfahl *m*; 1. *a.* **post up** *Plakat etc* anschlagen, ankleben; **be posted missing** AVIAT, MAR als vermisst gemeldet werden
post[2] *esp Br* 1. Post *f*; Postsendung *f*; **by post** mit der Post; 2. mit der Post (zu-)schicken, aufgeben, *Brief* einwerfen

post[3] 1. Stelle *f*, Job *m*; Posten *m*; 2. aufstellen, postieren; *esp Br* versetzen, MIL abkommandieren (**to** nach)
post... nach..., Nach...
post·age Porto *n*
postage stamp Postwertzeichen *n*, Briefmarke *f*
post·al postalisch, Post...
postal or·der *Br* ECON Postanweisung *f*
postal vote POL Briefwahl *f*
post·bag *esp Br* Postsack *m*
post·box *esp Br* Briefkasten *m*
post·card Postkarte *f*; *a.* **picture postcard** Ansichtskarte *f*
post·code *Br* Postleitzahl *f*
post·er Plakat *n*; Poster *n*, *m*
poste res·tante *Br* 1. Abteilung *f* für postlagernde Sendungen; 2. postlagernd
pos·te·ri·or HUMOR Hinterteil *n*
pos·ter·i·ty die Nachwelt
post-free *esp Br* portofrei
post·hu·mous post(h)um
post·man *esp Br* Briefträger *m*, Postbote *m*
post·mark 1. Poststempel *m*; 2. (ab-)stempeln
post·mas·ter Postamtsvorsteher *m*
post of·fice Post *f*; Postamt *n*, -filiale *f*
post of·fice box → **PO Box**
post-paid portofrei
post·pone verschieben, aufschieben
post·pone·ment Verschiebung *f*, Aufschub *m*
post·script Postskript(um) *n*, Nachschrift *f*
pos·ture 1. (Körper)Haltung *f*; Stellung *f*; 2. *fig* sich aufspielen
post·war Nachkriegs...
post·wom·an *esp Br* Briefträgerin *f*, Postbotin *f*
po·sy Sträußchen *n*
pot 1. Topf *m*; Kanne *f*; Kännchen *n* (*Tee etc*); SPORT F Pokal *m*; 2. *Pflanze* eintopfen
po·tas·si·um cy·a·nide CHEM Zyankali *n*
po·ta·to Kartoffel *f*; → **chips**, **crisps**
pot·bel·ly Schmerbauch *m*
po·ten·cy Stärke *f*; Wirksamkeit *f*, Wirkung *f*; MED Potenz *f*
po·tent PHARM stark; MED potent
po·ten·tial 1. potenziell, möglich; 2. Potenzial *n*, Leistungsfähigkeit *f*
pot·hole MOT Schlagloch *n*
po·tion Trank *m*
pot·ter[1] *Br*: **potter about** herumwerkeln
pot·ter[2] Töpfer(in)
pot·ter·y Töpferei *f*; Töpferware(n *pl*) *f*
pouch Beutel *m* (*a.* ZO); ZO (*Backen-*)Tasche *f*

poul·tice MED (warmer) Umschlag *m*
poul·try Geflügel *n*
pounce 1. sich stürzen (*on* auf *acc*); **2.** Satz *m*, Sprung *m*
pound[1] Pfund *n* (453,59 g); **pound** (*sterling*) (ABBR £) Pfund *n*
pound[2] Tierheim *n*; Abstellplatz *m* für (polizeilich) abgeschleppte Fahrzeuge
pound[3] *v/t* zerstoßen, zerstampfen; trommeln *or* hämmern auf (*acc*) *or* an (*acc*) *or* gegen; *v/i* hämmern (*with* vor *dat*)
pour *v/t* gießen, schütten; *pour out* ausgießen, ausschütten; *Getränk* eingießen; *v/i* strömen (*a. fig*)
pout *v/t Lippen* schürzen; *v/i* e-n Schmollmund machen; schmollen
pov·er·ty Armut *f*
pow·der 1. Pulver *n*; Puder *m*; **2.** pulverisieren; (sich) pudern
powder puff Puderquaste *f*
powder room (Damen)Toilette *f*
pow·er 1. Kraft *f*; Macht *f*; Fähigkeit *f*, Vermögen *n*; Gewalt *f*; JUR Befugnis *f*, Vollmacht *f*; MATH Potenz *f*; ELECTR Strom *m*; *in power* POL an der Macht; **2.** TECH antreiben
power cut ELECTR Stromsperre *f*
power fail·ure ELECTR Stromausfall *m*, Netzausfall *m*
pow·er·ful stark, kräftig; mächtig
pow·er·less kraftlos; machtlos
pow·er plant Elektrizitäts-, Kraftwerk *n*
power pol·i·tics Machtpolitik *f*
power sta·tion Br Elektrizitäts-, Kraftwerk *n*
prac·ti·ca·ble durchführbar
prac·ti·cal praktisch
practical joke Streich *m*
prac·ti·cal·ly so gut wie
prac·tice 1. Praxis *f*; Übung *f*; Gewohnheit *f*, Brauch *m*; *it is common practice* es ist allgemein üblich; *put into practice* in die Praxis umsetzen; **2.** *v/t* (ein)üben; *als Beruf* ausüben; *practice law* (*medicine*) als Anwalt (Arzt) praktizieren; *v/i* praktizieren; üben
prac·ticed geübt (*in* in *dat*)
prac·tise *Br* → *practice 2*
prac·tised → *practiced*
prac·ti·tion·er: *general practitioner* praktischer Arzt
prai·rie Prärie *f*
prai·rie schoo·ner HIST Planwagen *m*
praise 1. loben, preisen; **2.** Lob *n*
praise·wor·thy lobenswert
pram *Br* Kinderwagen *m*
prance sich aufbäumen, steigen (*horse*); tänzeln (*horse*); stolzieren
prank Streich *m*

prat·tle: *prattle on* plappern (*about* von)
prawn ZO Garnele *f*
pray beten (*to* zu; *for* für, um)
prayer REL Gebet *n*; *often pl* Andacht *f*; *the Lord's Prayer* das Vaterunser
prayer book REL Gebetbuch *n*
preach predigen (*to* zu, vor *dat*)
preach·er Prediger(in)
pre·am·ble Einleitung *f*
pre·ar·range vorher vereinbaren
pre·car·i·ous prekär, unsicher; gefährlich
pre·cau·tion Vorsichtsmaßnahme *f*; *as a precaution* vorsorglich; *take precautions* Vorsichtsmaßnahmen treffen
pre·cau·tion·a·ry vorbeugend; vorsorglich
pre·cede voraus-, vorangehen (*dat*)
pre·ce·dence Vorrang *m*
pre·ce·dent Präzedenzfall *m*
pre·cept Regel *f*, Richtlinie *f*
pre·cinct (*Wahl*)Bezirk *m*; (*Polizei*)Revier *n*; *pl* Gelände *n*; *esp Br* (*Einkaufs*)-Viertel *n*; (*Fußgänger*)Zone *f*
pre·cious 1. *adj* kostbar, wertvoll; Edel... (*stone etc*); **2.** *adv*: *precious little* F herzlich wenig
pre·ci·pice Abgrund *m*
pre·cip·i·tate 1. *v/t* (hinunter-, herunter)-schleudern; CHEM ausfällen; beschleunigen; stürzen (*into* in *acc*); *v/i* CHEM ausfallen; **2.** *adj* überstürzt; **3.** CHEM Niederschlag *m*
pre·cip·i·ta·tion CHEM Ausfällung *f*; METEOR Niederschlag *m*; Überstürzung *f*, Hast *f*
pre·cip·i·tous steil (abfallend); überstürzt
pré·cis Zusammenfassung *f*
pre·cise genau, präzis
pre·ci·sion Genauigkeit *f*; Präzision *f*
pre·clude ausschließen
pre·co·cious frühreif; altklug
pre·con·ceived vorgefasst
pre·con·cep·tion vorgefasste Meinung
pre·cur·sor Vorläufer(in)
pred·a·to·ry ZO Raub...
pre·de·ces·sor Vorgänger(in)
pre·des·ti·na·tion Vorherbestimmung *f*
pre·des·tined prädestiniert, vorherbestimmt (*to* für, zu)
pre·de·ter·mine vorherbestimmen; vorher vereinbaren
pre·dic·a·ment missliche Lage, Zwangslage *f*
pred·i·cate LING Prädikat *n*, Satzaussage *f*
pre·dic·a·tive LING prädikativ
pre·dict vorhersagen, voraussagen
pre·dic·tion Vorhersage *f*, Voraussage *f*; *computer prediction* Hochrechnung *f*
pre·dis·pose geneigt machen, einneh-

P

men (*in favor of* für); *esp* MED anfällig machen (*to* für)

pre·dis·po·si·tion: *predisposition to* Neigung *f* zu, *esp* MED *a.* Anfälligkeit *f* für

pre·dom·i·nant (vor)herrschend, überwiegend

pre·dom·i·nate vorherrschen, überwiegen; die Oberhand haben

pre·em·i·nent hervorragend, überragend

pre·emp·tive ECON Vorkaufs...; MIL Präventiv...

preen ZO *sich or das Gefieder* putzen

pre·fab F Fertighaus *n*

pre·fab·ri·cate vorfabrizieren, vorfertigen; *prefabricated house* Fertighaus *n*

pref·ace 1. Vorwort *n* (*to* zu); **2.** *Buch, Rede etc* einleiten (*with* mit)

pre·fect *Br* PED Aufsichts-, Vertrauensschüler(in)

pre·fer vorziehen (*to* dat), lieber mögen (*to* als), bevorzugen

pref·e·ra·ble: *be preferable* (*to*) vorzuziehen sein (*dat*), besser sein (als)

pref·e·ra·bly vorzugsweise, lieber, am liebsten

pref·e·rence Vorliebe *f* (*for* für); Vorzug *m*

pre·fix LING Präfix *n*, Vorsilbe *f*

preg·nan·cy MED Schwangerschaft *f*; ZO Trächtigkeit *f*

preg·nant MED schwanger; ZO trächtig

pre·heat *Backofen etc* vorheizen

pre·judge *j-n* vorverurteilen; vorschnell beurteilen

prej·u·dice 1. Vorurteil *n*, Voreingenommenheit *f*, Befangenheit *f*; *to the prejudice of* zum Nachteil *or* Schaden (*gen*); **2.** einnehmen (*in favo*[u]*r of* für; *against* gegen); schaden (*dat*), beeinträchtigen

prej·u·diced (vor)eingenommen, befangen

pre·lim·i·na·ry 1. vorläufig, einleitend, Vor...; **2.** *pl* Vorbereitungen *pl*

prel·ude Vorspiel *n* (*a.* MUS)

pre·mar·i·tal vorehelich

pre·ma·ture vorzeitig, verfrüht; *fig* voreilig

pre·med·i·tat·ed JUR vorsätzlich

pre·med·i·ta·tion: *with premeditation* JUR vorsätzlich

prem·i·er POL Premier(minister) *m*

prem·i·ere, prem·i·ère THEA *etc* Premiere *f*, Ur-, Erstaufführung *f*

prem·is·es Gelände *n*, Grundstück *n*, (*Geschäfts*)Räume *pl*; *on the premises* an Ort und Stelle, im Haus, im Lokal

pre·mi·um Prämie *f*, Bonus *m*

pre·mi·um (**gas·o·line**) MOT Super *n*, Su-

perbenzin *n*

pre·mo·ni·tion (böse) Vorahnung

pre·oc·cu·pa·tion Beschäftigung *f* (*with* mit)

pre·oc·cu·pied gedankenverloren, geistesabwesend

pre·oc·cu·py (stark) beschäftigen

prep *Br* F PED Hausaufgabe(n *pl*) *f*

pre·packed, pre·pack·aged abgepackt

pre·paid *post* frankiert, freigemacht

prepaid envelope Freiumschlag *m*

prep·a·ra·tion Vorbereitung *f* (*for* auf *acc*, für); Zubereitung *f*; CHEM, MED Präparat *n*

pre·par·a·to·ry vorbereitend

pre·pare *v/t* vorbereiten; GASTR zubereiten; *v/i*: *prepare for* sich vorbereiten auf (*acc*); Vorbereitungen treffen für; sich gefasst machen auf (*acc*)

pre·pared vorbereitet; bereit

prep·o·si·tion LING Präposition *f*, Verhältniswort *n*

pre·pos·sess·ing einnehmend, anziehend

pre·pos·ter·ous absurd; lächerlich, grotesk

pre·pro·gram(me) vorprogrammieren

pre·req·ui·site Vorbedingung *f*, Voraussetzung *f*

pre·rog·a·tive Vorrecht *n*

pre·school Vorschule *f*

pre·scribe *et.* vorschreiben; MED *j-m et.* verschreiben

pre·scrip·tion Verordnung *f*, Vorschrift *f*; MED Rezept *n*

pres·ence Gegenwart *f*, Anwesenheit *f*

presence of mind Geistesgegenwart *f*

pres·ent[1] Geschenk *n*

pre·sent[2] präsentieren; (über)reichen, (über)bringen, (über)geben; schenken; vorbringen, vorlegen; zeigen, vorführen, THEA *etc* aufführen; schildern, darstellen; *j-n, Produkt etc* vorstellen; *Programm etc* moderieren

pres·ent[3] **1.** anwesend; vorhanden; gegenwärtig, jetzig; laufend; vorliegend (*case etc*); *present tense* LING Präsens *n*, Gegenwart *f*; **2.** Gegenwart *f*, LING *a.* Präsens *n*; *at present* gegenwärtig, zurzeit; *for the present* vorerst, vorläufig

pre·sen·ta·tion Präsentation *f*; Überreichung *f*; Vorlage *f*; Vorführung *f*, THEA *etc* Aufführung *f*; Schilderung *f*, Darstellung *f*; Vorstellung *f*; *radio*, TV Moderation *f*

pres·ent-day heutig, gegenwärtig, modern

pre·sent·er *esp Br* radio, TV Moderator(in)

pre·sen·ti·ment (böse) Vorahnung

pres·ent·ly zurzeit, jetzt; *Br* bald

pres·er·va·tion Bewahrung *f*; Erhaltung *f*; GASTR Konservierung *f*

pre·ser·va·tive GASTR Konservierungsmittel *n*

pre·serve 1. bewahren, (be)schützen; erhalten; GASTR konservieren, *Obst etc* einmachen, einkochen; **2.** (*Jagd-*)Revier *n*; *fig* Ressort *n*, Reich *n*; *mst pl* GASTR das Eingemachte

pre·side den Vorsitz haben (**at, over** bei)

pres·i·den·cy POL Präsidentschaft *f*; Amtszeit *f*

pres·i·dent Präsident *m*; ECON Generaldirektor *m*

press 1. *v/t* drücken, pressen; *Frucht* (aus)pressen; drücken auf (*acc*); bügeln; drängen; *j-n* (be)drängen; bestehen auf (*dat*); *v/i* drücken; drängen (*time etc*); (sich) drängen; **press for** dringen *or* drängen auf (*acc*); **press on** (zügig) weitermachen; **2.** Druck *m* (*a. fig*); (*Wein- etc*)Presse *f*; Bügeln *n*; *die* Presse; *a. printing press* Druckerpresse *f*

press a·gen·cy Presseagentur *f*

press box Pressetribüne *f*

press con·fe·rence Pressekonferenz *f*

press of·fice Pressebüro *n*, Pressestelle *f*

press of·fi·cer Pressereferent(in)

press·ing dringend

press re·lease Pressemitteilung *f*

press stud *Br* Druckknopf *m*

press-up *esp Br* SPORT Liegestütz *m*

pres·sure PHYS, TECH *etc* Druck *m* (*a. fig*)

pressure cook·er Dampfkochtopf *m*, Schnellkochtopf *m*

pres·tige Prestige *n*, Ansehen *n*

pre·su·ma·bly vermutlich

pre·sume *v/t* annehmen, vermuten; sich erdreisten *or* anmaßen (**to do** zu tun); *v/i* annehmen, vermuten; anmaßend sein; **presume on** et. ausnützen, et. missbrauchen

pre·sump·tion Annahme *f*, Vermutung *f*; Anmaßung *f*

pre·sump·tu·ous anmaßend, vermessen

pre·sup·pose voraussetzen

pre·sup·po·si·tion Voraussetzung *f*

pre·tence *Br* → *pretense*

pre·tend vortäuschen, vorgeben; sich verstellen; Anspruch erheben (**to** auf *acc*); *she is only pretending* sie tut nur so

pre·tend·ed vorgetäuscht, gespielt

pre·tense Verstellung *f*, Vortäuschung *f*; Anspruch *m* (**to** auf *acc*)

pre·ten·sion Anspruch *m* (**to** auf *acc*); Anmaßung *f*

pre·ter·it(e) LING Präteritum *n*

pre·text Vorwand *m*

pret·ty 1. *adj* hübsch; **2.** *adv* ziemlich, ganz schön

pret·zel Brezel *f*

pre·vail vorherrschen, weit verbreitet sein; siegen (**over, against** über *acc*)

pre·vail·ing (vor)herrschend

pre·vent verhindern, verhüten, *e-r Sache* vorbeugen; *j-n* hindern (**from** an *dat*)

pre·ven·tion Verhinderung *f*, Verhütung *f*, Vorbeugung *f*

pre·ven·tive vorbeugend

pre·view *film*, TV Voraufführung *f*; Vorbesichtigung *f*; *film*, TV *etc*: Vorschau *f* (**of** auf *acc*)

pre·vi·ous vorhergehend, vorausgehend, vorherig, vorig; *previous to* bevor, vor (*dat*); *previous knowledge* Vorkenntnisse *pl*

pre·vi·ous·ly vorher, früher

pre-war Vorkriegs…

prey 1. ZO Beute *f*, Opfer *n* (*a. fig*); *be easy prey for or to fig* e-e leichte Beute sein für; **2.** *prey on* ZO Jagd machen auf (*acc*); *fig* nagen an (*dat*); *prey on s.o.'s mind* j-m keine Ruhe lassen

price 1. Preis *m*; **2.** den Preis festsetzen für; auszeichnen (**at** mit)

price·less unbezahlbar

price tag Preisschild *n*

prick 1. Stich *m*; V Schwanz *m*; *pricks of conscience* Gewissensbisse *pl*; **2.** *v/t* (auf-, durch)stechen, stechen in (*acc*); *her conscience pricked her* sie hatte Gewissensbisse; *prick up one's ears* die Ohren spitzen; *v/i* stechen

prick·le BOT, ZO Stachel *m*, Dorn *m*

prick·ly stach(e)lig; prickelnd, kribbelnd

pride 1. Stolz *m*; Hochmut *m*; *take (a) pride in* stolz sein auf (*acc*); **2.** *pride o.s. on* stolz sein auf (*acc*)

priest REL Priester *m*

prig Tugendbold *m*

prig·gish tugendhaft

prim steif, prüde

pri·mae·val *esp Br* → *primeval*

pri·ma·ri·ly in erster Linie, vor allem

pri·ma·ry 1. wichtigste(r, -s), Haupt…; grundlegend, elementar, Grund…; Anfangs…, Ur…; **2.** POL Vorwahl *f*

pri·ma·ry school *Br* Grundschule *f*

prime 1. MATH Primzahl *f*; *fig* Blüte(zeit) *f*; *in the prime of life* in der Blüte s-r Jahre; *be past one's prime* s-e besten Jahre hinter sich haben; **2.** *adj* erste(r, -s), wichtigste(r, -s), Haupt…; erstklassig; **3.** *v/t* TECH grundieren; *j-n* instruieren, vorbereiten

prime min·is·ter (ABBR POL F *PM*) Premierminister(in), Ministerpräsident(in)

P

prime num·ber MATH Primzahl *f*

prim·er Fibel *f*, Elementarbuch *n*

prime time TV Haupteinschaltzeit *f*, Hauptsendezeit *f*, beste Sendezeit

pri·me·val urzeitlich, Ur...

prim·i·tive erste(r, -s), ursprünglich, Ur...; primitiv

prim·rose BOT Primel *f*, *esp* Schlüsselblume *f*

prince Fürst *m*; Prinz *m*

prin·cess Fürstin *f*; Prinzessin *f*

prin·ci·pal 1. wichtigste(r, -s), hauptsächlich, Haupt...; **2.** PED Direktor(in), Rektor(in); THEA Hauptdarsteller(in); MUS Solist(in)

prin·ci·pal·i·ty Fürstentum *n*

prin·ci·ple Prinzip *n*, Grundsatz *m*; **on principle** grundsätzlich, aus Prinzip

print 1. PRINT Druck *m* (*a. art*); Gedruckte *n*; (*Finger- etc*)Abdruck *m*; PHOT Abzug *m*; bedruckter Stoff; **in print** gedruckt; **out of print** vergriffen; **2.** *v/i* drucken; in Druckbuchstaben schreiben; *fig* einprägen (**on** *dat*); *a.* **print off** PHOT abziehen; **print out** EDP ausdrucken

print·ed mat·ter *post* Drucksache *f*

print·er Drucker *m* (*a.* TECH); **printer's error** Druckfehler *m*; **printer's ink** Druckerschwärze *f*

print·ers Druckerei *f*

print·ing Drucken *n*; Auflage *f*

printing ink Druckerschwärze *f*

printing press Druckerpresse *f*

print·out EDP Ausdruck *m*

pri·or frühere(r, -s); vorrangig

pri·or·i·ty Priorität *f*, Vorrang *m*; MOT Vorfahrt *f*; **give s.th. priority** et. vordringlich behandeln

prise *esp Br* → **prize²**

prism Prisma *n*

pris·on Gefängnis *n*, Strafanstalt *f*

pris·on·er Gefangene *m*, *f*, Häftling *m*; **hold prisoner, keep prisoner** gefangen halten; **take prisoner** gefangen nehmen

pri·va·cy Intim-, Privatsphäre *f*; Geheimhaltung *f*

pri·vate 1. privat, Privat...; vertraulich; geheim; **private parts** Geschlechtsteile *pl*; **2.** MIL gemeiner Soldat; **in private** privat; unter vier Augen

pri·va·tion Entbehrung *f*

priv·i·lege Privileg *n*; Vorrecht *n*

priv·i·leged privilegiert

priv·y: be privy to eingeweiht sein in (*acc*)

prize¹ 1. (Sieger-, Sieges)Preis *m*, Prämie *f*, Auszeichnung *f*; (*Lotterie*)Gewinn *m*; **2.** preisgekrönt; Preis...; **3.** (hoch) schätzen

prize²: prize open aufbrechen, aufstemmen

prize·win·ner Preisträger(in)

pro¹ F Profi *m*

pro²: the pros and cons das Pro und Kontra, das Für und Wider

prob·a·bil·i·ty Wahrscheinlichkeit *f*; **in all probability** höchstwahrscheinlich

prob·a·ble *adj* wahrscheinlich

prob·a·bly *adv* wahrscheinlich

pro·ba·tion Probe *f*, Probezeit *f*; JUR Bewährung *f*, Bewährungsfrist *f*

pro·ba·tion of·fi·cer JUR Bewährungshelfer(in)

probe 1. MED, TECH Sonde *f*; *fig* Untersuchung *f* (**into** *gen*); **2.** sondieren; (gründlich) untersuchen

prob·lem Problem *n*; MATH *etc* Aufgabe *f*

prob·lem·at·ic, prob·lem·at·i·cal problematisch

pro·ce·dure Verfahren *n*, Verfahrensweise *f*, Vorgehen *n*

pro·ceed (weiter)gehen, (weiter)fahren; sich begeben (**to** nach, zu); *fig* weitergehen; *fig* fortfahren; *fig* vorgehen; **proceed from** kommen *or* herrühren von; **proceed to do s.th.** sich anschicken *or* et. zu tun

pro·ceed·ing Verfahren *n*, Vorgehen *n*

pro·ceed·ings Vorgänge *pl*, Geschehnisse *pl*; **start** *or* **take (legal) proceedings against** JUR (gerichtlich) vorgehen gegen

pro·ceeds ECON Erlös *m*, Ertrag *m*, Einnahmen *pl*

pro·cess 1. Prozess *m*, Verfahren *n*, Vorgang *m*; **in the process** dabei; **be in process** im Gange sein; **in process of construction** im Bau (befindlich); **2.** TECH *etc* bearbeiten, behandeln; EDP *Daten* verarbeiten; PHOT *Film* entwickeln

pro·ces·sion Prozession *f*

pro·ces·sor EDP Prozessor *m*; (*Wort-, Text*)Verarbeitungsgerät *n*

pro·claim proklamieren, ausrufen

proc·la·ma·tion Proklamation *f*, Bekanntmachung *f*

pro·cure (sich) et. beschaffen *or* besorgen; verkuppeln

prod 1. stoßen; *fig* anstacheln, anspornen (**into** zu); **2.** Stoß *m*

prod·i·gal 1. verschwenderisch; **2.** F Verschwender(in)

pro·di·gious erstaunlich, großartig

prod·i·gy Wunder *n*; **child prodigy** Wunderkind *n*

pro·duce¹ ECON produzieren (*a. film*, TV), herstellen, erzeugen (*a. fig*); hervorholen (**from** aus); *Ausweis etc* (vor)zeigen;

Beweise etc vorlegen; *Zeugen etc* beibringen; *Gewinn etc* (er)bringen, abwerfen; THEA inszenieren; *fig* hervorrufen, *Wirkung* erzielen

prod·uce² *esp* (*Agrar*)Produkt(e *pl*) *n*, (*Agrar*)Erzeugnis(se *pl*) *n*

pro·duc·er Produzent(in) (*a. film*, TV), Hersteller(in); THEA Regisseur(in)

prod·uct Produkt *n*, Erzeugnis *n*

pro·duc·tion ECON Produktion *f* (*a. film*, TV), Erzeugung *f*, Herstellung *f*; Produkt *n*, Erzeugnis *n*; Hervorholen *n*; Vorzeigen *n*, Vorlegen *n*, Beibringung *f*; THEA Inszenierung *f*

pro·duc·tive produktiv (*a. fig*), ergiebig, rentabel; *fig* schöpferisch

pro·duc·tiv·i·ty Produktivität *f*

prof F Prof *m*

pro·fa·na·tion Entweihung *f*

pro·fane **1.** (gottes)lästerlich; profan, weltlich; **2.** entweihen

pro·fan·i·ty: *profanities* Flüche *pl*, Lästerungen *pl*

pro·fess vorgeben, vortäuschen; behaupten (*to be* zu sein); erklären

pro·fessed erklärt (*enemy etc*); angeblich

pro·fes·sion (*esp akademischer*) Beruf; Berufsstand *m*

pro·fes·sion·al **1.** Berufs..., beruflich; Fach..., fachlich; fachmännisch; professionell; **2.** Fachmann *m*, Profi *m*; Berufsspieler(in), -sportler(in), Profi *m*

pro·fes·sor Professor(in); Dozent(in)

pro·fi·cien·cy Können *n*, Tüchtigkeit *f*

pro·fi·cient tüchtig (*at, in* in *dat*)

pro·file Profil *n*; *keep a low profile* Zurückhaltung üben

prof·it **1.** Gewinn *m*, Profit *m*; Vorteil *m*, Nutzen *m*; **2.** *profit by, profit from* Nutzen ziehen aus, profitieren von

prof·it·a·ble gewinnbringend, einträglich; nützlich, vorteilhaft

prof·it·eer *contp* Profitmacher *m*, Schieber *m*

prof·it shar·ing ECON Gewinnbeteiligung *f*

prof·li·gate verschwenderisch

pro·found *fig* tief; tiefgründig; profund (*knowledge etc*)

pro·fuse (über)reich; verschwenderisch

pro·fu·sion Überfülle *f*; *in profusion* in Hülle und Fülle

prog·e·ny Nachkommen(schaft *f*) *pl*

prog·no·sis MED Prognose *f*

pro·gram **1.** Programm *n* (*a.* EDP); *radio*, TV *a.* Sendung *f*; **2.** (vor)programmieren; planen; EDP programmieren

pro·gram·er EDP Programmierer(in)

pro·gramme *Br* → **program**

'**pro·gram·mer** *Br* → **programer**

pro·gress **1.** Fortschritt(e *pl*) *m*; *make slow progress* (nur) langsam vorankommen; *be in progress* im Gange sein; **2.** fortschreiten; Fortschritte machen

pro·gres·sive progressiv, fortschreitend; fortschrittlich

pro·hib·it verbieten; verhindern

pro·hi·bi·tion Verbot *n*

pro·hib·i·tive Schutz... (*Zoll etc*); unerschwinglich

proj·ect¹ Projekt *n*, Vorhaben *n*

pro·ject² *v/i* vorspringen, vorragen, vorstehen; *v/t* werfen, schleudern; planen; projizieren

pro·jec·tile Projektil *n*, Geschoss *n*

pro·jec·tion Vorsprung *m*, vorspringender Teil; Werfen *n*, Schleudern *n*; Planung *f*; *film*: Projektion *f*

pro·jec·tion·ist Filmvorführer *m*

pro·jec·tor *film*: Projektor *m*

pro·le·tar·i·an **1.** proletarisch; **2.** Proletarier(in)

pro·lif·ic fruchtbar

pro·log, *esp Br* **pro·logue** Prolog *m*

pro·long verlängern

prom·e·nade **1.** (Strand)Promenade *f*; **2.** promenieren

prom·i·nent vorspringend, vorstehend; *fig* prominent

pro·mis·cu·ous sexuell freizügig

prom·ise **1.** Versprechen *n*; *fig* Aussicht *f*; **2.** versprechen

prom·is·ing vielversprechend

prom·on·to·ry GEOGR Vorgebirge *n*

pro·mote *j-n* befördern; *Schüler* versetzen; ECON werben für; *Boxkampf, Konzert etc* veranstalten; *et.* fördern; *be promoted* SPORT *esp Br* aufsteigen (*to* in *acc*)

pro·mot·er Promoter(in), Veranstalter(in); ECON Verkaufsförderer *m*

pro·mo·tion Beförderung *f*; PED Versetzung *f*; SPORT Aufstieg *m*; ECON Verkaufsförderung *f*, Werbung *f*

pro·mo·tion(·al) *film* Werbefilm *m*

prompt **1.** *j-n* veranlassen (*to do* zu tun); führen zu, *Gefühle etc* wecken; *j-m* vorsagen; THEA *j-m* soufflieren; **2.** prompt, umgehend, unverzüglich; pünktlich

prompt·er THEA Souffleur *m*, Souffleuse *f*

prone auf dem Bauch *or* mit dem Gesicht nach unten liegend; *be prone to a.* MED neigen zu, anfällig sein für

prong Zinke *f*; (*Geweih*)Sprosse *f*

pro·noun LING Pronomen *n*, Fürwort *n*

pro·nounce aussprechen; erklären für; JUR *Urteil* verkünden

pro·nun·ci·a·tion Aussprache *f*

proof **1.** Beweis(e *pl*) *m*, Nachweis *m*; Probe *f*; PRINT Korrekturfahne *f*, *a*. PHOT Probeabzug *m*; **2.** *adj in cpds* ...fest, ...beständig, ...dicht, ...sicher; → *heatproof*, *soundproof*, *waterproof*; *be proof against* geschützt sein vor (*dat*); **3.** imprägnieren

proof·read PRINT Korrektur lesen

proof·read·er PRINT Korrektor(in)

prop 1. Stütze *f* (*a. fig*); **2.** *a*. *prop up* stützen; *sich or et*. lehnen (*against* gegen)

prop·a·gate BIOL sich fortpflanzen *or* vermehren; verbreiten

prop·a·ga·tion Fortpflanzung *f*, Vermehrung *f*; Verbreitung *f*

pro·pel (an)treiben

pro·pel·lant, pro·pel·lent Treibstoff *m*; Treibgas *n*

pro·pel·ler AVIAT Propeller *m*, MAR *a*. Schraube *f*

pro·pel·ling pen·cil Drehbleistift *m*

pro·pen·si·ty *fig* Neigung *f*

prop·er richtig, passend, geeignet; anständig, schicklich; echt, wirklich, richtig; eigentlich; eigen(tümlich); *esp Br* F ordentlich, tüchtig, gehörig

prop·er name, proper noun Eigenname *m*

prop·er·ty Eigentum *n*, Besitz *m*; Landbesitz *m*, Grundbesitz *m*; Grundstück *n*; *fig* Eigenschaft *f*

proph·e·cy Prophezeiung *f*

proph·e·sy prophezeien

proph·et Prophet *m*

pro·por·tion 1. Verhältnis *n*; (An)Teil *m*; *pl* Größenverhältnisse *pl*, Proportionen *pl*; *in proportion to* im Verhältnis zu; **2.** (*to*) in das richtige Verhältnis bringen (mit, zu); anpassen (*dat*)

pro·por·tion·al proportional; → *proportionate*

pro·por·tion·ate (*to*) im richtigen Verhältnis (zu), entsprechend (*dat*)

pro·pos·al Vorschlag *m*; (Heirats)Antrag *m*

pro·pose *v/t* vorschlagen; beabsichtigen, vorhaben; *Toast* ausbringen (*to* auf *acc*); *propose s.o.'s health* auf j-s Gesundheit trinken; *v/i*: *propose to* j-m e-n (Heirats)Antrag machen

prop·o·si·tion Behauptung *f*; Vorschlag *m*, ECON *a*. Angebot *n*

pro·pri·e·ta·ry ECON gesetzlich *or* patentrechtlich geschützt; *fig* besitzergreifend

pro·pri·e·tor Eigentümer *m*, Besitzer *m*, Geschäftsinhaber *m*

pro·pri·e·tress Eigentümerin *f*, Besitzerin *f*, Geschäftsinhaberin *f*

pro·pri·e·ty Anstand *m*; Richtigkeit *f*

pro·pul·sion TECH Antrieb *m*

pro·sa·ic prosaisch, nüchtern, sachlich

prose Prosa *f*

pros·e·cute JUR strafrechtlich verfolgen, (gerichtlich) belangen (*for* wegen)

pros·e·cu·tion JUR strafrechtliche Verfolgung, Strafverfolgung *f*; *the prosecution* die Staatsanwaltschaft, die Anklage(behörde)

pros·e·cu·tor JUR Staatsanwalt *m*, Staatsanwältin *f*; *public prosecutor* JUR Staatsanwalt *m*, Staatsanwältin *f*

pros·pect 1. Aussicht *f* (*a. fig*); Interessent *m*, ECON möglicher Kunde, potenzieller Käufer; **2.** *prospect for* mining: schürfen nach; bohren nach

pro·spec·tive voraussichtlich

pro·spec·tus (Werbe)Prospekt *m*

pros·per gedeihen; ECON blühen, florieren

pros·per·i·ty Wohlstand *m*

pros·per·ous ECON erfolgreich, blühend, florierend; wohlhabend

pros·ti·tute Prostituierte *f*, Dirne *f*; *male prostitute* Strichjunge *m*

pros·trate 1. hingestreckt; *fig* am Boden liegend; erschöpft; *prostrate with grief* gramgebeugt; **2.** niederwerfen; *fig* erschöpfen; *fig* niederschmettern

pros·y langweilig; weitschweifig

pro·tag·o·nist Vorkämpfer(in); THEA Hauptfigur *f*, Held(in)

pro·tect (be)schützen (*from* vor *dat*; *against* gegen)

pro·tec·tion Schutz *m*; F Schutzgeld *n*; *protection of animals* Tierschutz; *protection of endangered species* Artenschutz *m*

protection money F Schutzgeld *n*

protection rack·et F Schutzgelderpressung *f*

pro·tec·tive (be)schützend; Schutz...

protective cloth·ing Schutzkleidung *f*

protective cus·to·dy JUR Schutzhaft *f*

protective du·ty, protective tar·iff ECON Schutzzoll *m*

pro·tec·tor Beschützer *m*; (*Brust- etc* -) Schutz *m*

pro·tec·to·rate POL Protektorat *n*

pro·test 1. Protest *m*; Einspruch *m*; **2.** *v/i* protestieren (*against* gegen); *v/t* protestieren gegen; beteuern

Prot·es·tant REL **1.** protestantisch; **2.** Protestant(in)

prot·es·ta·tion Beteuerung *f*; Protest *m* (*against* gegen)

pro·to·col Protokoll *n*

pro·to·type Prototyp *m*

pro·tract in die Länge ziehen, hinziehen

pro·trude herausragen, vorstehen (*from* aus)

pro·trud·ing vorstehend (*a. teeth*), vor-

puke

springend (*chin*)
proud stolz (**of** auf *acc*) ´
prove *v/t* be-, er-, nachweisen; *v/i*: *prove*
(**to be**) sich herausstellen *or* erweisen als
prov·en bewährt
prov·erb Sprichwort *n*
pro·vide *v/t* versehen, versorgen, beliefern; zur Verfügung stellen, bereitstel-
len; JUR vorsehen, vorschreiben (*that*
dass); *v/i*: *provide against* Vorsorge treffen gegen; JUR verbieten; *provide for*
sorgen für; vorsorgen für; JUR *et.* vorsehen
· **pro·vid·ed**: *provided* (*that*) vorausge-
setzt(, dass)
pro·vid·er Ernährer(in)
prov·ince Provinz *f*; (Aufgaben-, Wissens)Gebiet *n*
pro·vin·cial **1.** Provinz..., provinziell,
contp provinzlerisch; **2.** *contp* Provinz-
ler(in)
pro·vi·sion Bereitstellung *f*, Beschaffung
f; Vorkehrung *f*, Vorsorge *f*; Bestimmung
f, Vorschrift *f*; *pl* Proviant *m*, Verpflegung *f*; *with the provision that* unter
˙der Bedingung, dass
pro·vi·sion·al provisorisch, vorläufig
pro·vi·so Bedingung *f*, Vorbehalt *m*; *with
the proviso that* unter der Bedingung,
dass
prov·o·ca·tion Provokation *f*
pro·voc·a·tive provozierend, (*a. sexually*)
aufreizend
pro·voke provozieren, reizen
prowl 1. *v/i a.* *prowl about, prowl around*
herumschleichen, herumstreifen; *v/t*
durchstreifen; **2.** Herumstreifen *n*
prowl car (Funk)Streifenwagen *m*
prox·im·i·ty Nähe *f*
prox·y (Handlungs)Vollmacht *f*; (Stell)-
Vertreter(in), Bevollmächtigte *m*, *f*; *by
proxy* durch e-n Bevollmächtigten
prude: *be a prude* prüde sein
pru·dence Klugheit *f*, Vernunft *f*; Beson-
nenheit *f*
pru·dent klug, vernünftig; besonnen
prud·ish prüde
prune[1] BOT (be)schneiden
prune[2] Backpflaume *f*
prus·sic ac·id CHEM Blausäure *f*
pry[1] neugierig sein; *pry about* herumschnüffeln; *pry into* s-e Nase stecken
in (*acc*)
pry[2] → **prize**[2]
psalm REL Psalm *m*
pseu·do·nym Pseudonym *n*, Deckname
m
psy·chi·a·trist Psychiater(in)
psy·chi·a·try Psychiatrie *f*

psy·cho·a·nal·y·sis Psychoanalyse *f*
psy·cho·log·i·cal psychologisch
psy·chol·o·gist Psychologe *m*, Psycholo-
gin *f*
psy·chol·o·gy Psychologie *f*
psy·cho·so·mat·ic psychosomatisch
pub *Br* Pub *n*, *m*, Kneipe *f*
pu·ber·ty Pubertät *f*
pu·bic hair Schamhaare *pl*
pub·lic 1. öffentlich; allgemein bekannt;
make public bekannt machen, an die
Öffentlichkeit bringen; **2.** *die* Öffentlichkeit, *das* Publikum; *in public* öffentlich,
in aller Öffentlichkeit
pub·li·ca·tion Bekanntgabe *f*, Bekanntmachung *f*; Publikation *f*, Veröffentlichung *f*
pub·lic con·ve·ni·ence *Br* öffentliche
Bedürfnisanstalt
public en·e·my Staatsfeind *m*
public health öffentliches Gesundheits-
wesen
public hol·i·day gesetzlicher Feiertag
pub·lic·i·ty Publicity *f*, *a.* Bekanntheit *f*,
ECON *a.* Reklame *f*, Werbung *f*
publicity depart·ment Werbeabteilung *f*
pub·lic li·bra·ry Leihbücherei *f*
public re·la·tions (ABBR *PR*) Public Relations *pl*, Öffentlichkeitsarbeit *f*
public school staatliche Schule; *Br* Public School *f*
public trans·port *esp Br*, **public trans-
por·ta·tion** öffentliche Verkehrsmittel *pl*
pub·lish bekannt geben *or* machen; publizieren, veröffentlichen; *Buch etc* verlegen, herausgeben
pub·lish·er Verleger(in), Herausge-
ber(in); Verlag *m*, Verlagshaus *n*
**pub·lish·er's, pub·lish·ers, publish·ing
house** Verlag *m*, Verlagshaus *n*
puck·er *a.* *pucker up* (sich) verziehen,
(sich) runzeln
pud·ding *Br* GASTR Nachspeise *f*, Nachtisch *m*; (*Reis- etc*)Auflauf *m*; (*Art*)
Fleischpastete *f*; Pudding *m*
pud·dle Pfütze *f*
pu·er·ile infantil, kindisch
puff 1. *v/i* schnaufen, keuchen; *a.* *puff
away* paffen (*at* an *dat*); *puff up* (an)-
schwellen; *v/t Rauch* blasen; *puff out
Kerze etc* ausblasen; *Rauch etc* ausstoßen; *Brust* herausdrücken; **2.** Zug *m*;
(*Wind-*) Hauch *m*, (*Wind*)Stoß *m*; (*Puder*)Quaste *f*; F Puste *f*
puffed sleeve Puffärmel *m*
puff pas·try GASTR Blätterteig *m*
puff·y (an)geschwollen; aufgedunsen
pug ZO Mops *m*
puke F (aus)kotzen

P

pull 1. Ziehen *n*; Zug *m*, Ruck *m*; Anstieg *m*, Steigung *f*; Zuggriff *m*, Zugleine *f*; F Beziehungen *pl*; **2.** ziehen; ziehen an (*dat*); zerren; reißen; *Pflanze* ausreißen; *esp Br Bier* zapfen; *fig* anziehen; **pull ahead of** vorbeiziehen an (*dat*), MOT überholen (*acc*); **pull away** anfahren (*bus etc*); **pull down** *Gebäude* abreißen; **pull in** einfahren (*train*); anhalten; **pull off** F *et*. zustande bringen, schaffen; **pull out** herausziehen (*of* aus); *Tisch* ausziehen; RAIL abfahren; MOT ausscheren; *fig* sich zurückziehen, aussteigen (*of* aus); **pull over** (*s-n Wagen*) an die *or* zur Seite fahren; **pull round** MED durchbringen; durchkommen; **pull through** *j-n* durchbringen; **pull o.s. together** sich zusammennehmen, F sich zusammenreißen; **pull up** MOT anhalten; (an)halten; **pull up to, pull up with** SPORT *j-n* einholen
pull date Mindesthaltbarkeitsdatum *n*
pul·ley TECH Flaschenzug *m*
pull-in *Br* F Raststätte *f*, Rasthaus *n*
pull·o·ver Pullover *m*
pull-up SPORT Klimmzug *m*; **do a pull-up** e-n Klimmzug machen
pulp 1. Fruchtfleisch *n*; Brei *m*; **2.** Schund...; **pulp novel** Schundroman *m*
pul·pit Kanzel *f*
pulp·y breiig
pul·sate pulsieren, vibrieren
pulse Puls *m*; Pulsschlag *m*
pul·ver·ize pulverisieren
pu·ma ZO Puma *m*
pum·mel mit den Fäusten bearbeiten
pump 1. Pumpe *f*; (*Zapf*)Säule *f*; **2.** pumpen; F *j-n* aushorchen; **pump up** aufpumpen
pump at·tend·ant Tankwart *m*
pump·kin BOT Kürbis *m*
pun 1. Wortspiel *n*; **2.** Wortspiele *or* ein Wortspiel machen
punch¹ 1. boxen, (mit der Faust) schlagen; **2.** (Faust)Schlag *m*
punch² 1. lochen; *Loch* stanzen (*in* in *acc*); **punch in** einstempeln; **punch out** ausstempeln; **2.** Locher *m*; Lochzange *f*; Locheisen *n*
punch³ Punsch *m*
Punch *appr* Kasper *m*, Kasperle *n*, *m*; **be as pleased** *or* **proud as Punch** sich freuen wie ein Schneekönig
Punch and Ju·dy show Kasperletheater *n*
punc·tu·al pünktlich
punc·tu·al·i·ty Pünktlichkeit *f*
punc·tu·ate interpunktieren
punc·tu·a·tion LING Interpunktion *f*
punctuation mark LING Satzzeichen *n*
punc·ture 1. (Ein)Stich *m*, Loch *n*; MOT

Reifenpanne *f*; **2.** durchstechen, durchbohren; ein Loch bekommen, platzen; MOT e-n Platten haben
pun·gent scharf, stechend, beißend (*smell, taste*); scharf, bissig (*remark etc*)
pun·ish *j-n* (be)strafen
pun·ish·a·ble strafbar
pun·ish·ment Strafe *f*; Bestrafung *f*
punk Punk *m* (*a.* MUS); Punk(er) *m*
pu·ny schwächlich
pup ZO Welpe *m*, junger Hund
pu·pa ZO Puppe *f*
pu·pil¹ Schüler(in)
pu·pil² ANAT Pupille *f*
pup·pet Handpuppe *f*; Marionette *f* (*a. fig*)
puppet show Marionettentheater *n*, Puppenspiel *n*
pup·pe·teer Puppenspieler(in)
pup·py ZO Welpe *m*, junger Hund
pur·chase 1. kaufen; *fig* erkaufen; **2.** Kauf *m*; **make purchases** Einkäufe machen
pur·chas·er Käufer(in)
pure rein; pur
pure·bred ZO reinrassig
pur·ga·tive MED **1.** abführend; **2.** Abführmittel *n*
pur·ga·to·ry REL Fegefeuer *n*
purge 1. *Partei etc* säubern (*of* von); **2.** Säuberung *f*, Säuberungsaktion *f*
pu·ri·fy reinigen
pu·ri·tan (HIST **Puritan**) **1.** Puritaner(in); **2.** puritanisch
pu·ri·ty Reinheit *f*
purl 1. linke Masche; **2.** links stricken
pur·ple purpurn, purpurrot
pur·pose 1. Absicht *f*, Vorsatz *m*; Zweck *m*, Ziel *n*; Entschlossenheit *f*; **on purpose** absichtlich; **to no purpose** vergeblich; **2.** beabsichtigen, vorhaben
pur·pose·ful entschlossen, zielstrebig
pur·pose·less zwecklos; ziellos
pur·pose·ly absichtlich
purr ZO schnurren; MOT summen, surren
purse¹ Geldbeutel *m*, Geldbörse *f*, Portemonnaie *n*; Handtasche *f*; SPORT Siegprämie *f*; *boxing*: Börse *f*
purse²: **purse (up) one's lips** die Lippen schürzen
purs·er MAR Zahlmeister *m*
pur·su·ance: **in (the) pursuance of his duty** in Ausübung s-r Pflicht
pur·sue verfolgen; *s-m Studium etc* nachgehen; *Absicht, Politik etc* verfolgen; *Angelegenheit etc* weiterführen
pur·su·er Verfolger(in)
pur·suit Verfolgung *f*; Weiterführung *f*
pur·vey *Lebensmittel etc* liefern
pur·vey·or Lieferant *m*

pus MED Eiter *m*

push 1. stoßen, F schubsen; schieben; *Taste etc* drücken; drängen; (an)treiben; F *Rauschgift* pushen; *fig j-n* drängen (*to do* zu tun); *fig* Reklame machen für; *push one's way* sich drängen (*through* durch); *push ahead with* *Plan etc* vorantreiben; *push along* F sich auf die Socken machen; *push around* F herumschubsen; *push for* drängen auf (*acc*); *push forward with* → *push ahead with*; *push o.s. forward fig* sich in den Vordergrund drängen *or* schieben; *push in* F sich vordrängeln; *push off!* F hau ab!; *push on with* → *push ahead with*; *push out fig j-n* hinausdrängen; *push through* *et.* durchsetzen; *push up* *Preise etc* hochtreiben; **2.** Stoß *m*, F Schubs *m*; (*Werbe*)- Kampagne *f*; F Durchsetzungsvermögen *n*, Energie *f*, Tatkraft *f*

push but·ton TECH Druckknopf *m*, Drucktaste *f*

push-but·ton TECH (Druck)Knopf..., (Druck)Tasten...; *push-button (tele)- phone* Tastentelefon *n*

push·chair *Br* Sportwagen *m*

push·er F *contp* Rauschgifthändler *m*

push·o·ver F Kinderspiel *n*

push-up SPORT Liegestütz *m*

puss F ZO Mieze *f*

pus·sy *a.* **pussy cat** F Miezekatze *f*

pus·sy·foot: F *pussyfoot about, pussyfoot around* leisetreten, sich nicht festlegen wollen

put legen, setzen, stecken, stellen, tun; *j-n in e-e Lage etc*, *et. auf den Markt, in Ordnung etc* bringen; *et. in Kraft, in Umlauf etc* setzen; SPORT *Kugel* stoßen; unterwerfen, unterziehen (*to dat*); *et.* ausdrücken, *in Worte* fassen; übersetzen (*into German* ins Deutsche); *Schuld* geben (*on dat*); *put right* in Ordnung bringen; *put s.th. before s.o. fig* j-m et. vorlegen; *put to bed* ins Bett bringen; *put to school* zur Schule schicken; *put about Gerüchte* verbreiten, in Umlauf setzen; *put across et.* verständlich machen; *put ahead* SPORT in Führung bringen; *put aside* beiseitelegen; *Ware* zurücklegen; *fig* beiseiteschieben; *put away* weglegen, wegtun; auf-, wegräumen; *put back* zurücklegen, -stellen, -tun; *Uhr* zurückstellen (*by* um); *put by Geld* zurücklegen; *put down* *v/t* hinlegen, niederlegen, hinsetzen, hinstellen; *j-n* absetzen, aussteigen lassen; (auf-, nieder-) schreiben, eintragen; zuschreiben (*to dat*); *Aufstand* niederschlagen; (*a. v/i*) AVIAT landen; *put forward Plan etc* vorlegen;

Uhr vorstellen (*by* um); *fig* vorverlegen (*two days* um zwei Tage; *to* auf *acc*); *put in v/t* hineinlegen, -stecken, -stellen; *Kassette etc* einlegen; installieren; *Gesuch etc* einreichen, *Forderung etc a.* geltend machen; *Antrag* stellen; *Arbeit, Zeit* verbringen (*on* mit); *Bemerkung* einwerfen; *v/i* MAR einlaufen (*at* in *acc*); *put off et.* verschieben (*until* auf *acc*); *j-m* absagen; *j-n* hinhalten (*with* mit), *j-n* vertrösten; *j-n* aus dem Konzept bringen; *put on Kleider etc* anziehen, *Hut, Brille* aufsetzen; *Licht, Radio etc* anmachen, einschalten; *Sonderzug* einsetzen; THEA *Stück etc* herausbringen; *et.* vortäuschen; F *j-n* auf den Arm nehmen; *put on airs* sich aufspielen; *put on weight* zunehmen; *put out v/t* hinauslegen, -setzen, -stellen; *Hand etc* ausstrecken; *Feuer* löschen; *Licht, Radio etc* ausmachen (*a. cigarette*), ab-, ausschalten; veröffentlichen, herausgeben; *radio, TV* bringen, senden; *j-n* aus der Fassung bringen; *j-n* verärgern; *j-m* Ungelegenheiten bereiten; *j-m* Umstände machen; sich *den Arm etc* verrenken *or* ausrenken; *v/i* MAR auslaufen; *put over* → *put across*; *put through* TEL *j-n* verbinden (*to* mit); durch-, ausführen; *put together* zusammenbauen, -setzen, -stellen; *put up v/t* hinauflegen, -stellen; *Hand* (hoch)heben; *Zelt etc* aufstellen; *Gebäude* errichten; *Bild etc* aufhängen; *Plakat, Bekanntmachung etc* anschlagen; *Schirm* aufspannen; *zum Verkauf* anbieten; *Preis* erhöhen; *Widerstand* leisten; *Kampf* liefern; *j-n* unterbringen, (bei sich) aufnehmen; *v/i* *put up at* absteigen in (*dat*); *put up with* sich gefallen lassen; sich abfinden mit

pu·tre·fy (ver)faulen, verwesen

pu·trid faul, verfault, verwest; F scheußlich, saumäßig

put·ty 1. Kitt *m*; **2.** kitten

put-up job F abgekartetes Spiel

puz·zle 1. Rätsel *n*; Geduld(s)spiel *n*; **2.** *v/t j-n* vor ein Rätsel stellen; verwirren; *be puzzled* vor e-m Rätsel stehen; *puzzle out* herausfinden, herausbringen, F austüfteln; *v/i* sich den Kopf zerbrechen (*about, over* über *dat or acc*)

pyg·my 1. Pygmäe *m*, Pygmäin *f*; Zwerg(in); **2.** *esp* ZO Zwerg...

py·ja·mas *Br* → **pajamas**

py·lon TECH Hochspannungsmast *m*

pyr·a·mid Pyramide *f*

pyre Scheiterhaufen *m*

py·thon ZO Python(schlange) *f*

pyx REL Hostienbehälter *m*

Q

Q, q Q, q *n*
quack[1] ZO **1.** quaken; **2.** Quaken *n*
quack[2] *a.* **quack doctor** Quacksalber *m*, Kurpfuscher *m*
quack·er·y Quacksalberei *f*, Kurpfuscherei *f*
quad·ran·gle Viereck *n*
quad·ran·gu·lar viereckig
quad·ra·phon·ic quadrophon(isch)
quad·rat·ic MATH quadratisch
quad·ri·lat·er·al MATH **1.** vierseitig; **2.** Viereck *n*
quad·ro·phon·ic → **quadraphonic**
quad·ru·ped ZO Vierfüß(l)er *m*; Vierbeiner *m*
quad·ru·ple 1. vierfach; **2.** (sich) vervierfachen
quad·ru·plets Vierlinge *pl*
quads Vierlinge *pl*
quag·mire Morast *m*, Sumpf *m*
quail ZO Wachtel *f*
quaint idyllisch, malerisch
quake 1. zittern, beben (**with, for** vor *dat*; **at** bei); **2.** F Erdbeben *n*
Quak·er REL Quäker(in)
qual·i·fi·ca·tion Qualifikation *f*, Befähigung *f*, Eignung *f* (**for** für, zu); Voraussetzung *f*; Einschränkung *f*
qual·i·fied qualifiziert, geeignet, befähigt (**for** für); berechtigt; bedingt, eingeschränkt
qual·i·fy *v/t* qualifizieren, befähigen (**for** für, zu); berechtigen (**to do** zu tun); einschränken, abschwächen, mildern; *v/i* sich qualifizieren or eignen (**for** für; **as** als); SPORT sich qualifizieren (**for** für)
qual·i·ty Qualität *f*; Eigenschaft *f*
qualms Bedenken *pl*, Skrupel *pl*
quan·da·ry: be in a quandary about what to do nicht wissen, was man tun soll
quan·ti·ty Quantität *f*, Menge *f*
quan·tum PHYS **1.** Quant *n*; **2.** Quanten...
quar·an·tine 1. Quarantäne *f*; **2.** unter Quarantäne stellen
quar·rel 1. Streit *m*, Auseinandersetzung *f*; **2.** (sich) streiten
quar·rel·some streitsüchtig, zänkisch
quar·ry[1] Steinbruch *m*
quar·ry[2] HUNT Beute *f*, *a. fig* Opfer *n*
quart Quart *n* (ABBR **qt**) (*0,95 l, Br 1,14 l*)
quar·ter 1. Viertel *n*, vierter Teil; Quartal *n*, Vierteljahr *n*; Viertelpfund *n*; Vierteldollar *m*; SPORT (Spiel)Viertel *n*; (Him-

mels)Richtung *f*; Gegend *f*, Teil *m*; (Stadt)Viertel *n*; GASTR (*esp* Hinter)Viertel *n*; Gnade *f*, Pardon *m*; *pl* Quartier *n*, Unterkunft *f* (*a.* MIL); **a quarter of an hour** e-e Viertelstunde; **a quarter of** (*Br* **to**) **five** (ein) Viertel vor fünf (*4.45*); **a quarter after** (*Br* **past**) **five** (ein) Viertel nach fünf (*5.15*); **at close quarters** in *or* aus nächster Nähe; **from official quarters** von amtlicher Seite; **2.** vierteln; *esp* MIL einquartieren (**on** bei)
quar·ter·deck MAR Achterdeck *n*
quar·ter·fi·nals SPORT Viertelfinale *n*
quar·ter·ly 1. vierteljährlich; **2.** Vierteljahresschrift *f*
quar·tet(te) MUS Quartett *n*
quartz MIN Quarz *m*
quartz clock Quarzuhr *f*
quartz watch Quarz(armband)uhr *f*
qua·ver 1. *v/i* zittern; *v/t et.* mit zitternder Stimme sagen; **2.** Zittern *n*
quay MAR Kai *m*
quea·sy: I feel queasy mir ist übel *or* F mulmig
queen Königin *f*; *card game, chess*: Dame *f*; F Schwule *m*, Homo *m*
queen bee ZO Bienenkönigin *f*
queen·ly wie e-e Königin, königlich
queer komisch, seltsam; F wunderlich; F schwul
quench Durst löschen, stillen
quer·u·lous nörglerisch
que·ry 1. Frage *f*; Zweifel *m*; **2.** infrage stellen, in Zweifel ziehen
quest 1. Suche *f* (**for** nach); **in quest of** auf der Suche nach; **2.** suchen (**after, for** nach)
ques·tion 1. Frage *f*, *a.* Problem *n*, *a.* Sache *f*, *a.* Zweifel *m*; **only a question of time** nur e-e Frage der Zeit; **this is not the point in question** darum geht es nicht; **there is no question that, it is beyond question that** es steht außer Frage, dass; **there is no question about this** daran besteht kein Zweifel; **be out of the question** nicht infrage kommen; **2.** befragen (**about** über *acc*); JUR vernehmen, verhören (**about** zu); bezweifeln, in Zweifel ziehen, infrage stellen
ques·tion·a·ble fraglich, zweifelhaft; fragwürdig
ques·tion·er Fragesteller(in)
ques·tion mark Fragezeichen *n*
question mas·ter *esp Br* Quizmaster *m*

ques·tion·naire Fragebogen *m*
queue *esp Br* **1.** Schlange *f*; → *jump*; **2.** *mst* **queue up** Schlange stehen, anstehen, sich anstellen
quib·ble sich herumstreiten (**with** mit; *about, over* wegen)
quick 1. *adj* schnell, rasch; aufbrausend, hitzig (*temper*); *be quick!* mach schnell!, beeil dich!; **2.** *adv* schnell, rasch; **3.** *cut s.o.* **to the quick** *fig* j-n tief verletzen
quick·en (sich) beschleunigen
quick·sand Treibsand *m*
quick-tem·pered aufbrausend, hitzig
quick-wit·ted schlagfertig; geistesgegenwärtig
qui·et 1. ruhig, still; *quiet, please* Ruhe, bitte; *be quiet!* sei still!; **2.** Ruhe *f*, Stille *f*; *on the quiet* F heimlich; **3.** *v/t a.* **quiet down** j-n beruhigen; *v/i a.* **quiet down** sich beruhigen
qui·et·en *Br* → **quiet** 3
qui·et·ness Ruhe *f*, Stille *f*
quill zo (Schwung-, Schwanz)Feder *f*; Stachel *m*
quilt Steppdecke *f*
quilt·ed Stepp...
quince BOT Quitte *f*
quin·ine PHARM Chinin *n*
quint F Fünfling *m*
quin·tes·sence Quintessenz *f*; Inbegriff *m*
quin·tet(te) MUS Quintett *n*
quin·tu·ple 1. fünffach; **2.** (sich) verfünf-

fachen
quin·tu·plets Fünflinge *pl*
quip 1. geistreiche *or* witzige Bemerkung; **2.** witzeln, spötteln
quirk Eigenart *f*, Schrulle *f*; *by some quirk of fate* durch e-e Laune des Schicksals, durch e-n verrückten Zufall
quit F *v/t* aufhören mit; *quit one's job* kündigen; *v/i* aufhören; kündigen
quite ganz, völlig; ziemlich; *quite a few* ziemlich viele; *quite nice* ganz nett, recht nett; *quite (so)!* *esp Br* genau, ganz recht; *be quite right* völlig recht haben; *she's quite a beauty* sie ist e-e wirkliche Schönheit
quits F quitt (**with** mit); *call it quits* es gut sein lassen
quit·ter: F *be a quitter* schnell aufgeben
quiv·er¹ zittern (**with** vor *dat*; *at* bei)
quiv·er² Köcher *m*
quiz 1. Quiz *n*; Prüfung *f*, Test *m*; **2.** ausfragen (*about* über *acc*)
quiz·mas·ter Quizmaster *m*
quiz·zi·cal spöttisch-fragend
quo·ta Quote *f*, Kontingent *n*
quo·ta·tion Zitat *n*; ECON Notierung *f*; Kostenvoranschlag *m*
quotation marks LING Anführungszeichen *pl*
quote zitieren; *Beispiel etc* anführen; *Preis* nennen; *be quoted at* ECON notieren mit
quo·tient MATH Quotient *m*

R

R, r R, r *n*
rab·bi REL Rabbiner *m*
rab·bit ZO Kaninchen *n*
rab·ble Pöbel *m*, Mob *m*
rab·ble-rous·ing Hetz..., aufwieglerisch
rab·id VET tollwütig; *fig* fanatisch
ra·bies VET Tollwut *f*
rac·coon ZO Waschbär *m*
race¹ Rasse *f*, Rassenzugehörigkeit *f*; (*Menschen*)Geschlecht *n*
race² 1. (Wett)Rennen *n*, (Wett)Lauf *m*; **2.** *v/i* an (e-m) Rennen teilnehmen; um die Wette laufen *or* fahren *etc*; rasen, rennen; MOT durchdrehen; *v/t* um die Wette laufen *or* fahren *etc* mit; rasen mit
race car MOT Rennwagen *m*

race·course Rennbahn *f*
race·horse Rennpferd *n*
rac·er Rennpferd *n*; Rennrad *n*, Rennwagen *m*
race ri·ots Rassenunruhen *pl*
race·track Rennbahn *f*
ra·cial rassisch, Rassen...
rac·ing 1. Rennsport *m*; **2.** Renn...
rac·ing car *Br* MOT Rennwagen *m*
ra·cism Rassismus *m*
ra·cist 1. Rassist(in); **2.** rassistisch
rack 1. Gestell *n*, (Geschirr-, Zeitungs- *etc*)Ständer *m*, RAIL (Gepäck)Netz *n*, MOT (Dach)Gepäckständer *m*; HIST Folter(bank) *f*; **2.** *be racked by or with* geplagt *or* gequält werden von; *rack one's*

brains sich das Hirn zermartern, sich den Kopf zerbrechen

rack·et[1] *tennis etc*: Schläger *m*

rack·et[2] F Krach *m*, Lärm *m*; Schwindel *m*, Gaunerei *f*; (*Drogen- etc*)Geschäft *n*; organisierte Erpressung

rack·et·eer Gauner *m*; Erpresser *m*

ra·coon → **raccoon**

rac·y spritzig, lebendig; gewagt (*joke*)

ra·dar TECH Radar *m*, *n*

radar screen Radarschirm *m*

radar speed check MOT Radarkontrolle *f*

radar sta·tion Radarstation *f*

radar trap MOT Radarkontrolle *f*

ra·di·al 1. radial, Radial..., strahlenförmig; **2.** MOT Gürtelreifen *m*

ra·di·al tire, *Br* **radial tyre** → **radial** 2

ra·di·ant strahlend, leuchtend (*a. fig* **with** vor *dat*)

ra·di·ate ausstrahlen; strahlenförmig ausgehen (**from** von)

ra·di·a·tion Ausstrahlung *f*

ra·di·a·tor Heizkörper *m*; MOT Kühler *m*

rad·i·cal 1. radikal (*a.* POL); MATH Wurzel...; **2.** POL Radikale *m*, *f*

ra·di·o 1. Radio(apparat *m*) *n*; Funk *m*; Funkgerät *n*; **by radio** über Funk; **on the radio** im Radio; **2.** funken

ra·di·o·ac·tive radioaktiv

radioactive waste Atommüll *m*, radioaktiver Abfall

ra·di·o·ac·tiv·i·ty Radioaktivität *f*

ra·di·o ham Funkamateur *m*

radio play Hörspiel *n*

radio set Radioapparat *m*

radio sta·tion Funkstation *f*; Rundfunksender *m*, -station *f*

radio ther·a·py MED Strahlentherapie *f*, Röntgentherapie *f*

radio tow·er Funkturm *m*

rad·ish BOT Rettich *m*; Radieschen *n*

ra·di·us MATH Radius *m*

raf·fle 1. Tombola *f*; **2.** *a.* **raffle off** verlosen

raft Floß *n*

raf·ter (Dach)Sparren *m*

rag Lumpen *m*, Fetzen *m*; Lappen *m*; **in rags** zerlumpt

rage 1. Wut *f*, Zorn *m*; **fly into a rage** wütend werden; **the latest rage** F der letzte Schrei; **be all the rage** F große Mode sein; **2.** wettern (**against, at** gegen); wüten, toben

rag·ged zerlumpt; struppig; *fig* stümperhaft

raid 1. (**on**) Überfall *m* (auf *acc*), MIL *a.* Angriff *m* (gegen); Razzia *f* (in *dat*); **2.** überfallen, MIL *a.* angreifen; e-e Razzia machen in (*dat*)

rail 1. Geländer *n*; Stange *f*; (*Handtuch*)-Halter *m*; (Eisen)Bahn *f*; RAIL Schiene *f*, *pl a.* Gleis *n*; **by rail** mit der Bahn; **2. rail in** einzäunen; **rail off** abzäunen

rail·ing *often pl* (Gitter)Zaun *m*

rail·road Eisenbahn *f*

railroad line Bahnlinie *f*

railroad·man Eisenbahner *m*

railroad sta·tion Bahnhof *m*

rail·way *Br* → **railroad**

rain 1. Regen *m*, *pl* Regenfälle *pl*; **the rains** die Regenzeit; (**come**) **rain or shine** *fig* was immer auch geschieht; **2.** regnen; **it is raining cats and dogs** F es gießt in Strömen; **it never rains but it pours** es kommt immer gleich knüppeldick, ein Unglück kommt selten allein

rain·bow Regenbogen *m*

rain·coat Regenmantel *m*

rain·fall Niederschlag(smenge *f*) *m*

rain for·est GEOGR Regenwald *m*

rain·proof regendicht, wasserdicht

rain·y regnerisch, verregnet, Regen...; **save s.th. for a rainy day** et. für schlechte Zeiten zurücklegen

raise 1. heben; hochziehen; erheben; *Denkmal etc* errichten; *Staub etc* aufwirbeln; *Gehalt, Miete etc* erhöhen; *Geld* zusammenbringen, beschaffen; *Kinder* aufziehen, großziehen; *Tiere* züchten; *Getreide etc* anbauen; *Frage* aufwerfen, *et.* zur Sprache bringen; *Blockade etc*, *a. Verbot* aufheben; **2.** Lohn- *or* Gehaltserhöhung *f*

rai·sin Rosine *f*

rake 1. Rechen *m*, Harke *f*; **2.** *v/t*: **rake** (**up**) (zusammen)rechen, (zusammen)harken; F **rake in** scheffeln; *v/i*: **rake about, rake around** herumstöbern

rak·ish flott, keck, verwegen

ral·ly 1. (sich) (wieder) sammeln; sich erholen (**from** von) (*a.* ECON); **rally round** sich scharen um; **2.** Kundgebung *f*, (Massen)Versammlung *f*; MOT Rallye *f*; *tennis etc*: Ballwechsel *m*

ram 1. ZO Widder *m*, Schafbock *m*; TECH Ramme *f*; **2.** rammen

ram·ble 1. wandern, umherstreifen; abschweifen; **2.** Wanderung *f*

ram·bler Wanderer *m*; BOT Kletterrose *f*

ram·bling weitschweifig; weitläufig

rambling rose BOT Kletterrose *f*

ramp Rampe *f*; MOT (Autobahn)Auffahrt *f*; (Autobahn)Ausfahrt *f*

ram·page 1. rampage through (wild *or* aufgeregt) trampeln (durch (*elephant etc*); → **2. go on the rampage through** randalierend ziehen durch

ram·pant: *be rampant* wuchern (*plant*); grassieren (*in* in *dat*)

ram·shack·le baufällig (*building*); klapp(e)rig (*vehicle*)

ranch Ranch *f*; (*Geflügel-* etc)Farm *f*

ranch·er Rancher *m*; (*Geflügel-* etc) Züchter *m*

ran·cid ranzig

ran·co(u)r Groll *m*, Erbitterung *f*

ran·dom 1. *adj* ziellos, wahllos; zufällig, Zufalls...; *random sample* Stichprobe *f*; **2.** *at random* aufs Geratewohl

range 1. Reich-, Schuss-, Tragweite *f*; Entfernung *f*; *fig* Bereich *m*, *a.* Spielraum *m*, *a.* Gebiet *n*; (*Schieß*)Stand *m*, (-)Platz *m*; (*Berg*)Kette *f*; offenes Weidegebiet; ECON Kollektion *f*, Sortiment *n*; Küchenherd *m*; *at close range* aus nächster Nähe; *within range of vision* in Sichtweite; *a wide range of ...* eine große Auswahl an ... (*dat*); **2.** *v/i*: *range from ... to ..., range between ... and ...* sich zwischen ... und ... bewegen (*prices* etc); *v/t* aufstellen, anordnen

range find·er PHOT Entfernungsmesser *m*

rang·er Förster *m*; Ranger *m*

rank¹ 1. Rang *m* (*a.* MIL), (soziale) Stellung; Reihe *f*; (*Taxi*)Stand *m*; *of the first rank fig* erstklassig; *the rank and file fig* die Basis; *the ranks fig* das Heer, die Masse;**2.** *v/t* rechnen, zählen (*among* zu); stellen (*above* über *acc*); *v/i* zählen, gehören (*among* zu); gelten (*as* als)

rank² BOT (üppig) wuchernd; übel riechend, übel schmeckend; *fig* krass (*outsider*), blutig (*beginner*)

ran·kle *fig* nagen, wehtun, F wurmen

ran·sack durchwühlen, durchsuchen; plündern

ran·som 1. Lösegeld *n*; **2.** freikaufen, auslösen

rant: *rant (on) about, rant and rave about* eifern gegen

rap 1. Klopfen *n*; Klaps *m*; **2.** klopfen (an *acc*, auf *acc*)

ra·pa·cious habgierig

rape¹ 1. vergewaltigen; **2.** Vergewaltigung *f*

rape² BOT Raps *m*

rap·id schnell, rasch

ra·pid·i·ty Schnelligkeit *f*

rap·ids GEOGR Stromschnellen *pl*

rapt: *with rapt attention* mit gespannter Aufmerksamkeit

rap·ture Entzücken *n*, Verzückung *f*; *go into raptures* in Verzückung geraten

rare¹ selten, rar; dünn (*air*); F Mords...

rare² GASTR blutig (*steak*)

rar·e·fied dünn (*air*)

rar·i·ty Seltenheit *f*; Rarität *f*

ras·cal Schlingel *m*

rash¹ voreilig, vorschnell, unbesonnen

rash² MED (Haut)Ausschlag *m*

rash·er dünne Speckscheibe

rasp 1. raspeln; kratzen; **2.** Raspel *f*; Kratzen *n*

rasp·ber·ry BOT Himbeere *f*

rat ZO Ratte *f* (*a. contp*); F *smell a rat* Lunte *or* den Braten riechen

rate 1. Quote *f*, Rate *f*, (*Geburten-, Sterbe*)Ziffer *f*; (*Steuer-, Zins-* etc)Satz *m*; (*Wechsel*)Kurs *m*; Geschwindigkeit *f*, Tempo *n*; *at any rate* auf jeden Fall; **2.** einschätzen, halten (*as* für); *Lob etc* verdienen; *be rated as* gelten als

rate of ex·change ECON (Umrechnungs-, Wechsel)Kurs *m*

rate of in·terest ECON Zinssatz *m*

ra·ther ziemlich; eher, vielmehr, besser gesagt; *rather! esp Br* F und ob!; *I would or had rather go* ich möchte lieber gehen

rat·i·fy POL ratifizieren

rat·ing Einschätzung *f*; *radio*, TV Einschaltquote *f*

ra·ti·o MATH Verhältnis *n*

ra·tion 1. Ration *f*; **2.** et. rationieren; *ration out* zuteilen (*to dat*)

ra·tion·al rational; vernunftbegabt; vernünftig; verstandesmäßig

ra·tion·al·i·ty Vernunft *f*

ra·tion·al·ize rational erklären; ECON rationalisieren

rat race F endloser Konkurrenzkampf

rat·tle 1. klappern; rasseln *or* klimpern (mit); prasseln (*on* auf *acc*) (*rain* etc); rattern, knattern (*vehicle*); rütteln an (*dat*); F *j-n* verunsichern; *rattle at* rütteln an (*dat*); *rattle off Gedicht etc* herunterrasseln; F *rattle on* quasseln (*about* über *acc*); F *rattle through Rede etc* herunterrasseln; **2.** Klappern *n* (etc → 1); Rassel *f*, Klapper *f*

rat·tle·snake ZO Klapperschlange *f*

rau·cous heiser, rau

rav·age verwüsten

rav·ag·es Verwüstungen *pl*, *a. fig* verheerende Auswirkungen *pl*

rave fantasieren, irrereden; toben; wettern (*against, at* gegen); schwärmen (*about* von)

rav·el (sich) verwickeln *or* verwirren

ra·ven ZO Rabe *m*

rav·e·nous ausgehungert, heißhungrig

ra·vine Schlucht *f*, Klamm *f*

rav·ing mad tobsüchtig

rav·ings irres Gerede, Delirien *pl*

rav·ish·ing *fig* hinreißend

raw GASTR roh, ECON, TECH a. Roh...; MED wund; METEOR nasskalt; *fig* unerfahren; **raw vegetables and fruit** Rohkost *f*

raw-boned knochig, hager

raw·hide Rohleder *n*

raw ma·te·ri·al Rohstoff *m*

ray Strahl *m*; *fig* Schimmer *m*

ray·on Kunstseide *f*

ra·zor Rasiermesser *n*; Rasierapparat *m*; **electric razor** Elektrorasierer *m*

ra·zor blade Rasierklinge *f*

ra·zor('s) edge *fig* kritische Lage; **be on a razor('s) edge** auf des Messers Schneide stehen

re... wieder, noch einmal, neu

reach 1. *v/t* erreichen; reichen *or* gehen bis an (*acc*) *or* zu; **reach down** herunter-, hinunterreichen (**from** von); **reach out** Arm etc ausstrecken; *v/i* reichen, gehen, sich erstrecken; *a.* **reach out** greifen, langen (**for** nach); **reach out** die Hand ausstrecken; **2.** Reichweite *f*; **within (out of) reach** in (außer) Reichweite; **within easy reach** leicht erreichbar

re·act reagieren (**to** auf *acc*; CHEM **with** mit)

re·ac·tion Reaktion *f* (*a.* CHEM)

re·ac·tor PHYS Reaktor *m*

read lesen; TECH (an)zeigen; *Zähler etc* ablesen; UNIV studieren; deuten, verstehen (**as** als); sich *gut etc* lesen (lassen); lauten; **read (s.th.) to s.o.** j-m (et.) vorlesen; **read medicine** Medizin studieren

read·a·ble lesbar; leserlich; lesenswert

read·er Leser(in); Lektor(in); Lesebuch *n*

read·i·ly bereitwillig, gern; leicht, ohne weiteres

read·i·ness Bereitschaft *f*

read·ing 1. Lesen *n*; Lesung *f* (*a.* PARL); TECH Anzeige *f*, (*Thermometer- etc -*) Stand *m*; Auslegung *f*; **2.** Lese...; **reading matter** Lesestoff *m*

re·ad·just TECH nachstellen, korrigieren; **readjust (o.s.) to** sich wieder anpassen (*dat*) *or* an (*acc*), sich wieder einstellen auf (*acc*)

read·y bereit, fertig; bereitwillig; im Begriff (**to do** zu tun); schnell, schlagfertig; **ready for use** gebrauchsfertig; **get ready** (sich) fertig machen

read·y cash → **ready money**

read·y-made Konfektions...

read·y meal Fertiggericht *n*

read·y mon·ey Bargeld *n*

real echt; wirklich, tatsächlich, real; F **for real** echt, im Ernst

real es·tate Grundbesitz *m*, Immobilien *pl*

real estate a·gent Grundstücks-, Immo-

bilienmakler *m*

re·a·lism Realismus *m*

re·al·ist Realist(in)

re·al·is·tic realistisch

re·al·i·ty Realität *f*, Wirklichkeit *f*

re·a·li·za·tion Erkenntnis *f*; Realisierung *f* (*a.* ECON), Verwirklichung *f*

re·al·ize sich klarmachen, erkennen, begreifen, einsehen; realisieren (*a.* ECON), verwirklichen

real·ly wirklich, tatsächlich; **well, really!** ich muss schon sagen!; **really?** im Ernst?

realm Königreich *n*; *fig* Reich *n*

real·tor Grundstücks-, Immobilienmakler *m*

reap *Getreide etc* schneiden; *Feld* abernten; *fig* ernten

re·ap·pear wieder erscheinen

rear 1. *v/t Kind, Tier* aufziehen, großziehen; *Kopf* heben; *v/i* sich aufbäumen (*horse*); **2.** Rückseite *f*, Hinterseite *f*, MOT Heck *n*; **in** (*Br* **at**) **the rear of** hinter (*dat*); **bring up the rear** die Nachhut bilden; **3.** hinter, Hinter..., Rück..., MOT *a.* Heck...

rear-end col·li·sion MOT Auffahrunfall *m*

rear·guard MIL Nachhut *f*

rear light MOT Rücklicht *n*

re·arm MIL (wieder) aufrüsten

re·ar·ma·ment MIL (Wieder)Aufrüstung *f*

rear·most hinterste(r, -s)

rear·view mir·ror MOT Rückspiegel *m*

rear·ward 1. *adj* hintere(r, -s), rückwärtig; **2.** *adv a.* **rearwards** rückwärts

rear-wheel drive MOT Hinterradantrieb *m*

rear win·dow MOT Heckscheibe *f*

rea·son 1. Grund *m*; Verstand *m*; Vernunft *f*; **by reason of** wegen; **for this reason** aus diesem Grund; **listen to reason** Vernunft annehmen; **it stands to reason that** es leuchtet ein, dass; **2.** *v/i* vernünftig *or* logisch denken; vernünftig reden (**with** mit); *v/t* folgern, schließen (**that** dass); **reason s.o. into (out of) s.th.** j-m et. einreden (ausreden)

rea·son·a·ble vernünftig; günstig (*price*); ganz gut, nicht schlecht

re·as·sure beruhigen

re·bate ECON Rabatt *m*, (Preis)Nachlass *m*; Rückzahlung *f*

reb·el[1] **1.** Rebell(in); Aufständische *m*, *f*; **2.** aufständisch

re·bel[2] rebellieren, sich auflehnen (**against** gegen)

re·bel·lion Rebellion *f*, Aufstand *m*

re·bel·lious rebellisch, aufständisch

re·birth Wiedergeburt *f*

re·bound 1. abprallen, zurückprallen (**from** von); *fig* zurückfallen (**on** auf *acc*.); **2.** SPORT Abpraller *m*

re·buff 1. schroffe Abweisung, Abfuhr *f*;
2. schroff abweisen

re·build wieder aufbauen (*a. fig*)

re·buke 1. rügen, tadeln; **2.** Rüge *f*, Tadel
m

re·call 1. zurückrufen, abberufen; MOT (in
die Werkstatt) zurückrufen; sich erinnern an (*acc*); erinnern an (*acc*); **2.** Zu-
rückrufung *f*, Abberufung *f*; Rückrufak-
tion *f*; ***have total recall*** das absolute Gedächtnis haben; ***beyond recall***, ***past recall*** unwiederbringlich *or* unwiderruflich
vorbei

re·ca·pit·u·late rekapitulieren, (kurz) zusammenfassen

re·cap·ture wieder einfangen (*a. fig*);
Häftling wieder fassen; MIL zurückerobern

re·cast TECH umgießen; umformen, neu
gestalten; THEA *etc* umbesetzen, neu besetzen

re·cede schwinden; ***receding chin*** flie-
hendes Kinn

re·ceipt *esp* ECON Empfang *m*, Eingang *m*;
Quittung *f*; *pl* Einnahmen *pl*

re·ceive bekommen, erhalten; empfangen; *j-n* aufnehmen (***into*** in *acc*); *radio*,
TV empfangen

re·ceiv·er Empfänger(in); TEL Hörer *m*;
JUR Hehler(in); *a.* ***official receiver*** Br
JUR Konkursverwalter *m*

re·cent neuere(r, -s); jüngste(r, -s)

re·cent·ly kürzlich, vor kurzem

re·cep·tion Empfang *m*; Aufnahme *f* (***into*** in *acc*); *radio*, TV Empfang *m*; *a.* ***reception desk*** *hotel*: Rezeption *f*, Empfang *m*

re·cep·tion·ist Empfangsdame *f*, -chef *m*;
MED Sprechstundenhilfe *f*

re·cep·tive aufnahmefähig; empfänglich
(***to*** für)

re·cess Unterbrechung *f*, (Schul)Pause *f*;
PARL, JUR Ferien *pl*; Nische *f*

re·ces·sion ECON Rezession *f*

re·ci·pe (Koch)Rezept *n*

re·cip·i·ent Empfänger(in)

re·cip·ro·cal wechselseitig, gegenseitig

re·cip·ro·cate *v/i* TECH sich hin- und herbewegen; sich revanchieren; *v/t Einladung etc* erwidern

re·cit·al Vortrag *m*, (*Klavier- etc*)Konzert
n, (*Lieder*)Abend *m*; Schilderung *f*

re·ci·ta·tion Aufsagen *n*, Hersagen *n*;
Vortrag *m*

re·cite aufsagen, hersagen; vortragen;
aufzählen

reck·less rücksichtslos

reck·on *v/t* (aus-, be)rechnen; glauben;
schätzen; ***reckon up*** zusammenrechnen;

v/i: ***reckon on*** rechnen mit; ***reckon with***
rechnen mit; ***reckon without*** nicht rechnen mit

reck·on·ing (Be)Rechnung *f*; ***be out in
one's reckoning*** sich verrechnet haben

re·claim zurückfordern; *Gepäck etc* abholen; *dem Meer etc Land* abgewinnen;
TECH wiedergewinnen

re·cline sich zurücklehnen

re·cluse Einsiedler(in)

rec·og·ni·tion (Wieder)Erkennen *n*; Anerkennung *f*

rec·og·nize (wieder) erkennen; anerkennen; zugeben, eingestehen

re·coil 1. zurückschrecken (***from*** vor *dat*);
2. Rückstoß *m*

rec·ol·lect sich erinnern an (*acc*)

rec·ol·lec·tion Erinnerung *f* (***of*** an *acc*)

rec·om·mend empfehlen (***as*** als; ***for*** für)

rec·om·men·da·tion Empfehlung *f*

rec·om·pense 1. entschädigen (***for*** für);
2. Entschädigung *f*

rec·on·cile versöhnen, aussöhnen; in Einklang bringen (***with*** mit)

rec·on·cil·i·a·tion Versöhnung *f*, Aussöhnung *f* (***between*** zwischen *dat*; ***with*** mit)

re·con·di·tion TECH (general)überholen

re·con·nais·sance MIL Aufklärung *f*, Er-
kundung *f*

re·con·noi·ter, *Br* **re·con·noi·tre** MIL erkunden, auskundschaften

re·con·sid·er noch einmal überdenken

re·con·struct wieder aufbauen (*a. fig*);
Verbrechen etc rekonstruieren

re·con·struc·tion Wiederaufbau *m*; Re-
konstruktion *f*

rec·ord[1] Aufzeichnung *f*; JUR Protokoll *n*;
Akte *f*; (Schall)Platte *f*; SPORT Rekord *m*;
off the record inoffiziell; ***have a criminal record*** vorbestraft sein

re·cord[2] aufzeichnen, aufschreiben,
schriftlich niederlegen; JUR protokollieren, zu Protokoll nehmen; *auf Schallplatte, Tonband etc* aufnehmen, *Sendung a.*
aufzeichnen, mitschneiden

re·cord·er (*Kassetten*)Rekorder *m*; (*Tonband*)Gerät *n*; MUS Blockflöte *f*

re·cord·ing Aufnahme *f*, Aufzeichnung *f*,
Mitschnitt *m*

rec·ord play·er Plattenspieler *m*

re·count erzählen

re·cov·er *v/t* wiedererlangen, wiederbekommen, wieder finden; *Kosten etc* wie-
dereinbringen; *Fahrzeug, Verunglückten
etc* bergen; ***recover consciousness***
MED wieder zu sich kommen, das Bewusstsein wiedererlangen; *v/i* sich erholen (***from*** von)

re·cov·er·y Wiedererlangen *n*; Wiederfin-

R

den *n*; Bergung *f*; Genesung *f*; Erholung *f*

rec·re·a·tion Entspannung *f*; Unterhaltung *f*, Freizeitbeschäftigung *f*

re·cruit **1.** MIL Rekrut *m*; Neue *m*, *f*, neues Mitglied; **2.** MIL rekrutieren; *Personal* einstellen; *Mitglieder* werben

rec·tan·gle MATH Rechteck *n*

rec·tan·gu·lar rechteckig

rec·ti·fy ELECTR gleichrichten

rec·tor REL Pfarrer *m*

rec·to·ry REL Pfarrhaus *n*

re·cu·pe·rate sich erholen (*from* von) (*a. fig*)

re·cur wiederkehren, wieder auftreten

re·cur·rence Wiederkehr *f*

re·cur·rent wiederkehrend

re·cy·cla·ble TECH recyclebar, wiederverwertbar

re·cy·cle TECH *Abfälle* recyceln, wieder verwerten; *recycled paper* Recyclingpapier *n*, Umwelt(schutz)-papier *n*

re·cy·cling TECH Recycling *n*, Wiederverwertung *f*

red **1.** rot; **2.** Rot *n*; *be in the red* ECON in den roten Zahlen sein

red·breast → *robin*

Red Cres·cent Roter Halbmond

Red Cross Rotes Kreuz

red·cur·rant BOT Rote Johannisbeere

red·den röten, rot färben; rot werden

red·dish rötlich

re·dec·o·rate *Zimmer etc* neu streichen *or* tapezieren

re·deem *Pfand*, *Versprechen etc* einlösen; REL erlösen

Re·deem·er REL Erlöser *m*, Heiland *m*

re·demp·tion Einlösung *f*; REL Erlösung *f*

re·de·vel·op *Gebäude*, *Stadtteil* sanieren

red-faced verlegen, mit rotem Kopf

red-hand·ed: *catch s.o. red-handed* j-n auf frischer Tat ertappen

red·head F Rotschopf *m*, Rothaarige *f*

red-head·ed rothaarig

red her·ring *fig* falsche Fährte *or* Spur

red-hot rot glühend; *fig* glühend; F brandaktuell (*news etc*)

Red In·di·an *contp* Indianer(in)

red-let·ter day Freuden-, Glückstag *m*

red·ness Röte *f*

re·dou·ble verdoppeln

red tape Bürokratismus *m*, F Amtsschimmel *m*

re·duce verkleinern; *Geschwindigkeit*, *Risiko etc* verringern, *Steuern etc* senken, *Preis*, *Waren etc* herabsetzen, reduzieren (*from ... to* von ... auf *acc*), *Gehalt etc* kürzen; verwandeln (*to* in *acc*), machen (*to* zu); reduzieren, zurückführen (*to* auf *acc*)

re·duc·tion Verkleinerung *f*; Verringerung *f*, Senkung *f*, Herabsetzung *f*, Reduzierung *f*, Kürzung *f*

re·dun·dant überflüssig

reed BOT Schilf(rohr) *n*

re·ed·u·cate umerziehen

re·ed·u·ca·tion Umerziehung *f*

reef (Felsen)Riff *n*

reek **1.** Gestank *m*; **2.** stinken (*of* nach)

reel[1] **1.** Rolle *f*, Spule *f*; **2.** *reel off* abrollen, abspulen; *fig* herunterrasseln

reel[2] sich drehen; (sch)wanken, taumeln, torkeln; *my head reeled* mir drehte sich alles

re-e·lect wieder wählen

re-en·ter wieder eintreten in (*acc*), wieder betreten

re-en·try Wiedereintreten *n*, Wiedereintritt *m*

ref F SPORT Schiri *m*

re·fer: *refer to* verweisen *or* hinweisen auf (*acc*); *j-n* verweisen an (*acc*); sich beziehen auf (*acc*); anspielen auf (*acc*); erwähnen (*acc*); nachschlagen in (*dat*)

ref·er·ee SPORT Schiedsrichter *m*, Unparteiische *m*; *boxing*: Ringrichter *m*

ref·er·ence Verweis *m*, Hinweis *m* (*to* auf *acc*); Verweisstelle *f*; Referenz *f*, Empfehlung *f*, Zeugnis *n*; Bezugnahme *f* (*to* auf *acc*); Anspielung *f* (*to* auf *acc*); Erwähnung *f* (*to* gen); Nachschlagen *n* (*to* in *dat*); *list of references* Quellenangabe *f*

reference book Nachschlagewerk *n*

reference li·bra·ry Handbibliothek *f*

reference num·ber Aktenzeichen *n*

ref·e·ren·dum POL Referendum *n*, Volksentscheid *m*

re·fill **1.** wieder füllen, nachfüllen, auffüllen; **2.** (*Ersatz*)Mine *f*; (*Ersatz*)Patrone *f*

re·fine TECH raffinieren; *fig* verfeinern, kultivieren; *refine on* verbessern, verfeinern

re·fined TECH raffiniert; *fig* kultiviert, vornehm

re·fine·ment TECH Raffinierung *f*; *fig* Verbess(e)rung *f*, Verfeinerung *f*; Kultiviertheit *f*, Vornehmheit *f*

re·fin·e·ry TECH Raffinerie *f*

re·flect *v/t* reflektieren, zurückwerfen, -strahlen, (wider)spiegeln; *be reflected in* sich (wider)spiegeln in (*dat*) (*a. fig*); *v/i* nachdenken (*on* über *acc*); *reflect (badly) on* sich nachteilig auswirken auf (*acc*); ein schlechtes Licht werfen auf (*acc*)

re·flec·tion Reflexion *f*, Zurückwerfung *f*, -strahlung *f*, (Wider)Spiegelung *f* (*a. fig*);

Spiegelbild *n*; Überlegung *f*; Betrachtung *f*; *on reflection* nach einigem Nachdenken

re·flec·tive reflektierend; nachdenklich

re·flex Reflex *m*

reflex ac·tion Reflexhandlung *f*

reflex cam·e·ra PHOT Spiegelreflexkamera *f*

re·flex·ive LING reflexiv, rückbezüglich

re·form 1. reformieren, verbessern; sich bessern; 2. Reform *f* (*a*. POL), Besserung *f*

ref·or·ma·tion Reformierung *f*; Besserung *f*; *the Reformation* REL die Reformation

re·form·er *esp* POL Reformer *m*; REL Reformator *m*

re·fract *Strahlen etc* brechen

re·frac·tion (*Strahlen- etc*)Brechung *f*

re·frain¹: *refrain from* sich enthalten (*gen*), unterlassen (*acc*)

re·frain² Kehrreim *m*, Refrain *m*

re·fresh (*o.s.* sich) erfrischen, stärken; *Gedächtnis* auffrischen

re·fresh·ing erfrischend (*a. fig*)

re·fresh·ment Erfrischung *f*

re·frig·e·rate TECH kühlen

re·frig·e·ra·tor Kühlschrank *m*

re·fu·el auftanken

ref·uge Zuflucht *f*, Zufluchtsstätte *f*; *Br* Verkehrsinsel *f*

ref·u·gee Flüchtling *m*

ref·u·gee camp Flüchtlingslager *n*

re·fund 1. Rückzahlung *f*, Rückerstattung *f*; 2. *Geld* zurückzahlen, zurückerstatten; *Auslagen* ersetzen

re·fur·bish aufpolieren (*a. fig*); renovieren

re·fus·al Ablehnung *f*; Weigerung *f*; Verweigerung *f*

re·fuse¹ *v/t* ablehnen; verweigern; sich weigern, es ablehnen (*to do* zu tun); *v/i* ablehnen; sich weigern

ref·use² Abfall *m*, Abfälle *pl*, Müll *m*

ref·use dump Müllabladeplatz *m*

re·fute widerlegen

re·gain wieder-, zurückgewinnen

re·gale: *regale s.o. with s.th.* j-n mit et. erfreuen *or* ergötzen

re·gard 1. Achtung *f*; Rücksicht *f*; *pl* Grüße *pl*; *in this regard* in dieser Hinsicht; *with regard to* im Hinblick auf (*acc*); hinsichtlich (*gen*); *with kind regards* mit freundlichen Grüßen; 2. betrachten (*a. fig*), ansehen; *regard as* betrachten als, halten für; *as regards ...* was ... betrifft

re·gard·ing bezüglich, hinsichtlich (*gen*)

re·gard·less: *regardless of* ohne Rück-

sicht auf (*acc*), ungeachtet (*gen*)

regd ABBR *of registered* ECON eingetragen; *post* eingeschrieben

re·gen·e·rate (sich) erneuern *or* regenerieren

re·gent Regent(in)

re·gi·ment 1. MIL Regiment *n*, *fig a*. Schar *f*; 2. reglementieren, bevormunden

re·gion Gegend *f*, Gebiet *n*, Region *f*

re·gion·al regional, örtlich, Orts...

re·gis·ter 1. Register *n*, Verzeichnis *n*, (*Wähler- etc*)Liste *f*; 2. *v/t* registrieren, eintragen (lassen); *Messwerte* anzeigen; *Brief etc* einschreiben lassen; *v/i* sich eintragen (lassen)

re·gis·tered let·ter Einschreib(e)brief *m*, Einschreiben *n*

re·gis·tra·tion Registrierung *f*, Eintragung *f*; MOT Zulassung *f*

registration fee Anmeldegebühr *f*

registration num·ber MOT (polizeiliches) Kennzeichen

re·gis·try Registratur *f*

re·gis·try of·fice *esp Br* Standesamt *n*

re·gret 1. bedauern; bereuen; 2. Bedauern *n*; Reue *f*

re·gret·ful bedauernd

re·gret·ta·ble bedauerlich

reg·u·lar 1. regelmäßig; geregelt, geordnet; richtig; normal; MIL Berufs...; *regular gas* (*Br petrol*) MOT Normalbenzin *n*; 2. F Stammkunde *m*, Stammkundin *f*; Stammgast *m*; SPORT Stammspieler(in); MIL Berufssoldat *m*; MOT Normal(-benzin) *n*

reg·u·lar·i·ty Regelmäßigkeit *f*

reg·u·late regeln, regulieren; TECH einstellen, regulieren

reg·u·la·tion Reg(e)lung *f*, Regulierung *f*; TECH Einstellung *f*; Vorschrift *f*

reg·u·la·tor TECH Regler *m*

re·hears·al MUS, THEA Probe *f*

re·hearse MUS, THEA proben

reign 1. Regierung *f*, *a. fig* Herrschaft *f*; 2. herrschen, regieren

re·im·burse *Auslagen* erstatten, vergüten

rein 1. Zügel *m*; 2. *rein in Pferd etc* zügeln; *fig* bremsen

rein·deer ZO Ren *n*, Rentier *n*

re·in·force verstärken

re·in·force·ment Verstärkung *f*

re·in·state *j-n* wieder einstellen (*as* als; *in dat*)

re·in·sure rückversichern

re·it·e·rate (ständig) wiederholen

re·ject *j-n, et.* ablehnen, *Bitte* abschlagen, *Plan etc* verwerfen; *j-n* ab-, zurückweisen; MED *Organ etc* abstoßen

re·jec·tion Ablehnung *f*; Verwerfung *f*;

R

Zurückweisung *f*; MED Abstoßung *f*
re·joice sich freuen, jubeln (*at, over* über *acc*)
re·joic·ing(s) Jubel *m*
re·join[1] wieder zusammenfügen; wieder zurückkehren zu
re·join[2] erwidern
re·ju·ve·nate verjüngen
re·kin·dle *Feuer* wieder anzünden; *fig* wieder entfachen
re·lapse 1. zurückfallen, wieder verfallen (*into* in *acc*); rückfällig werden; MED e-n Rückfall bekommen; **2.** Rückfall *m*
re·late *v/t* erzählen, berichten; in Verbindung *or* Zusammenhang bringen (*to* mit); *v/i* sich beziehen (*to* auf *acc*); zusammenhängen (*to* mit)
re·lat·ed verwandt (*to* mit)
re·la·tion Verwandte *m*, *f*; Beziehung *f* (*between* zwischen *dat*; *to* zu); *pl* diplomatische, geschäftliche Beziehungen *pl*; *in or with relation to* in Bezug auf (*acc*)
re·la·tion·ship Verwandtschaft *f*; Beziehung *f*, Verhältnis *n*
rel·a·tive[1] Verwandte *m*, *f*
rel·a·tive[2] relativ, verhältnismäßig; bezüglich (*to gen*); LING Relativ…, bezüglich
rel·a·tive pro·noun LING Relativpronomen *n*, bezügliches Fürwort
re·lax *v/t Muskeln etc* entspannen; *Griff etc* lockern; *fig* nachlassen in (*dat*); *v/i* sich entspannen, *fig a.* ausspannen; sich lockern
re·lax·a·tion Entspannung *f*; Erholung *f*; Lockerung *f*
re·laxed entspannt, zwanglos
re·lay[1] **1.** Ablösung *f*; SPORT Staffel *f*; *radio*, TV Übertragung *f*; ELECTR Relais *n*; **2.** *radio*, TV übertragen
re·lay[2] *Kabel*, *Teppich* neu verlegen
re·lay race SPORT Staffel *f*
re·lease 1. entlassen, freilassen; loslassen; freigeben, herausbringen, veröffentlichen; MOT *Handbremse* lösen; *fig* befreien, erlösen; **2.** Entlassung *f*, Freilassung *f*; Befreiung *f*; Freigabe *f*; Veröffentlichung *f*; TECH, PHOT Auslöser *m*; *film: often first release* Uraufführung *f*
rel·e·gate verbannen; *be relegated* SPORT absteigen (*to* in *acc*)
re·lent nachgeben; nachlassen
re·lent·less unbarmherzig; anhaltend
rel·e·vant relevant, erheblich, wichtig; sachdienlich, zutreffend
re·li·a·bil·i·ty Zuverlässigkeit *f*
re·li·a·ble zuverlässig
re·li·ance Vertrauen *n*; Abhängigkeit *f* (*on* von)

rel·ic Relikt *n*, Überrest *m*; REL Reliquie *f*
re·lief Erleichterung *f*; Unterstützung *f*, Hilfe *f*; Sozialhilfe *f*; Ablösung *f*; Relief *n*
relief map GEOGR Reliefkarte *f*
re·lieve *Schmerz*, *Not* lindern, *j-n*, *Gewissen* erleichtern; *j-n* ablösen
re·li·gion Religion *f*
re·li·gious Religions…; religiös; gewissenhaft
rel·ish 1. *fig* Gefallen *m*, Geschmack *m* (*for* an *dat*); GASTR Würze *f*; Soße *f*; *with relish* mit Genuss; **2.** genießen, sich *et.* schmecken lassen; Geschmack *or* Gefallen finden an (*dat*)
re·luc·tance Widerstreben *n*; *with reluctance* widerwillig, ungern
re·luc·tant widerstrebend, widerwillig
re·ly: *rely on* sich verlassen auf (*acc*)
re·main 1. (ver)bleiben; übrig bleiben; **2.** *pl* (Über)Reste *pl*
re·main·der Rest *m*; Restbetrag *m*
re·make 1. wieder *or* neu machen; **2.** Remake *n*, Neuverfilmung *f*
re·mand JUR **1.** *be remanded in custody* in Untersuchungshaft bleiben; **2.** *be on remand* in Untersuchungshaft sein; *prisoner on remand* Untersuchungsgefangene *m*, *f*
re·mark 1. *v/t* bemerken, äußern; *v/i* sich äußern (*on* über *acc*, zu); **2.** Bemerkung *f*
re·mark·a·ble bemerkenswert; außergewöhnlich
rem·e·dy 1. (Heil-, Hilfs-, Gegen)Mittel *n*; (Ab)Hilfe *f*; **2.** *Schaden etc* beheben; *Missstand* abstellen; *Situation* bereinigen
re·mem·ber sich erinnern an (*acc*); denken an (*acc*); *please remember me to her* grüße sie bitte von mir
re·mem·brance Erinnerung *f*; *in remembrance of* zur Erinnerung an (*acc*)
re·mind erinnern (*of* an *acc*)
re·mind·er Mahnung *f*
rem·i·nis·cences Erinnerungen *pl* (*of* an *acc*)
rem·i·nis·cent: *be reminiscent of* erinnern an (*acc*)
re·mit *Schulden*, *Strafe* erlassen; *Sünden* vergeben; *Geld* überweisen (*to dat or* an *acc*)
re·mit·tance ECON Überweisung *f* (*to* an *acc*)
rem·nant (Über)Rest *m*
re·mod·el umformen, umgestalten
re·morse Gewissensbisse *pl*, Reue *f* (*über acc* for)
re·morse·ful zerknirscht, reumütig

re·morse·less unbarmherzig
re·mote fern, entfernt; abgelegen, entlegen
remote con·trol TECH Fernlenkung *f*, Fernsteuerung *f*; Fernbedienung *f*
re·mov·al Entfernung *f*; Umzug *m*
re·mov·al van Möbelwagen *m*
re·move *v/t* entfernen (*from* von); *Hut, Deckel etc* abnehmen; *Kleidung* ablegen; beseitigen, aus dem Weg räumen; *v/i* (um)ziehen (*from* von; *to* nach)
re·mov·er (*Flecken- etc*)Entferner *m*
Re·nais·sance die Renaissance
ren·der berühmt, schwierig, möglich etc machen; *Dienst* erweisen; *Gedicht, Musikstück* vortragen; übersetzen, übertragen (*into* in *acc*); *mst* **render down** Fett auslassen
ren·der·ing *esp Br* → **rendition**
ren·di·tion MUS *etc* Vortrag *m*; Übersetzung *f*, Übertragung *f*
re·new erneuern; *Gespräch etc* wieder aufnehmen; *Kraft etc* wiedererlangen; *Vertrag, Pass* verlängern (lassen)
re·new·al Erneuerung *f*; Verlängerung *f*
re·nounce verzichten auf (*acc*); *s-m Glauben etc* abschwören
ren·o·vate renovieren
re·nown Ruhm *m*
re·nowned berühmt (*as* als; *for* wegen, für)
rent[1] **1.** Miete *f*; Pacht *f*; Leihgebühr *f*; *for rent* zu vermieten, zu verleihen; **2.** mieten, pachten (*from* von); *a.* **rent out** vermieten, verpachten (*to* an *acc*); **rented car** Miet-, Leihwagen *m*
rent[2] Riss *m*
rent·al Miete *f*; Pacht *f*; Leihgebühr *f*; **rental car** Miet-, Leihwagen *m*
re·nun·ci·a·tion Verzicht *m* (*of* auf *acc*); Abschwören *n*
re·pair 1. reparieren, ausbessern; *fig* wieder gutmachen; **2.** Reparatur *f*; Ausbesserung *f*; *pl* Instandsetzungsarbeiten *pl*; *beyond repair* nicht mehr zu reparieren; *in good* (*bad*) *repair* in gutem (schlechtem) Zustand; *be under repair* in Reparatur sein; *the road is under repair* an der Straße wird gerade gearbeitet
rep·a·ra·tion Wiedergutmachung *f*; Entschädigung *f*; *pl* POL Reparationen *pl*
rep·ar·tee Schlagfertigkeit *f*; schlagfertige Antwort(en *pl*) *f*
re·pay *et.* zurückzahlen; *Besuch* erwidern; *et.* vergelten; *j-n* entschädigen
re·pay·ment Rückzahlung *f*
re·peal *Gesetz etc* aufheben
re·peat 1. *v/t* wiederholen; nachsprechen; **repeat o.s.** sich wiederholen; *v/i* F aufstoßen (*on s.o.* j-m) (*food*); **2.** radio, TV Wiederholung *f*
re·peat·ed wiederholt
re·peat·ed·ly verschiedentlich
re·pel *Angriff, Feind* zurückschlagen; *Wasser etc, fig* j-n abstoßen
re·pel·lent abstoßend
re·pent bereuen
re·pent·ance Reue *f* (*for* über *acc*)
re·pen·tant reuig, reumütig
re·per·cus·sion *mst pl* Auswirkungen *pl* (*on* auf *acc*)
rep·er·toire THEA *etc* Repertoire *n*
rep·er·to·ry the·a·ter (*Br* **the·a·tre**) Repertoiretheater *n*
rep·e·ti·tion Wiederholung *f*
re·place an *j-s* Stelle treten, *j-n, et.* ersetzen; TECH austauschen, ersetzen
re·place·ment TECH Austausch *m*; Ersatz *m*
re·plant umpflanzen
re·play 1. SPORT *Spiel* wiederholen; *Tonband-, Videoaufname etc* abspielen; **2.** SPORT Wiederholung *f*
re·plen·ish (wieder) auffüllen
re·plete satt; angefüllt, ausgestattet (*with* mit)
rep·li·ca art: Originalkopie *f*; Kopie *f*, Nachbildung *f*
re·ply 1. antworten, erwidern (*to* auf *acc*); **2.** Antwort *f*, Erwiderung *f* (*to* auf *acc*); *in reply to* (als Antwort) auf (*acc*)
re·ply cou·pon Rückantwortschein *m*
re·ply-paid en·ve·lope Freiumschlag *m*
re·port 1. Bericht *m*; Meldung *f*, Nachricht *f*; Gerücht *n*; Knall *m*; *report card* PED Zeugnis *n*; **2.** berichten (über *acc*); (sich) melden; anzeigen; *it is reported that* es heißt, dass; *reported speech* LING indirekte Rede
re·port·er Reporter(in), Berichterstatter(in)
re·pose Ruhe *f*; Gelassenheit *f*
re·pos·i·to·ry (Waren)Lager *n*; *fig* Fundgrube *f*, Quelle *f*
rep·re·sent *j-n, Wahlbezirk* vertreten; darstellen; hinstellen (*as, to be* als)
rep·re·sen·ta·tion Vertretung *f*; Darstellung *f*
rep·re·sen·ta·tive 1. repräsentativ (*a.* POL), typisch (*of* für); **2.** (Stell)Vertreter(in); ECON (Handels)Vertreter(in); PARL Abgeordnete *m, f*; *House of Representatives* Repräsentantenhaus *n*
re·press unterdrücken; PSYCH verdrängen
re·pres·sion Unterdrückung *f*; PSYCH Verdrängung *f*
re·prieve JUR **1.** *he was reprieved* er wurde begnadigt; s-e Urteilsvollstreckung

R

wurde ausgesetzt; **2.** Begnadigung *f*; Vollstreckungsaufschub *m*

rep·ri·mand 1. rügen, tadeln (*for* wegen); **2.** Rüge *f*, Tadel *m*, Verweis *m*

re·print 1. neu auflegen *or* drucken, nachdrucken; **2.** Neuauflage *f*, Nachdruck *m*

re·pri·sal Repressalie *f*, Vergeltungsmaßnahme *f*

re·proach 1. Vorwurf *m*; **2.** vorwerfen (*s.o. with s.th.* j-m et.); Vorwürfe machen

re·proach·ful vorwurfsvoll

rep·ro·bate verkommenes Subjekt

re·pro·cess NUCL wieder aufbereiten

re·pro·cess·ing TECH Wiederaufbereitung *f*

reprocessing plant TECH Wiederaufbereitungsanlage *f*

re·pro·duce *v/t* Ton etc wiedergeben; *Bild etc* reproduzieren; **reproduce o.s.** → *v/i* BIOL sich fortpflanzen, sich vermehren

re·pro·duc·tion BIOL Fortpflanzung *f*; Reproduktion *f*; Wiedergabe *f*; PED Nacherzählung *f*

re·pro·duc·tive BIOL Fortpflanzungs...

re·proof Rüge *f*, Tadel *m*

re·prove rügen, tadeln (*for* wegen)

rep·tile ZO Reptil *n*

re·pub·lic Republik *f*

re·pub·li·can 1. republikanisch; **2.** Republikaner(in)

re·pug·nant widerlich, abstoßend

re·pulse 1. *j-n, Angebot etc* zurückweisen; MIL *Angriff* zurückschlagen; **2.** MIL Zurückschlagen *n*; Zurückweisung *f*

re·pul·sion Abscheu *m*, Widerwille *m*; PHYS Abstoßung *f*

re·pul·sive abstoßend, widerlich, widerwärtig; PHYS abstoßend

rep·u·ta·ble angesehen

rep·u·ta·tion (guter) Ruf, Ansehen *n*

re·pute (guter) Ruf

re·put·ed angeblich

re·quest 1. (*for*) Bitte *f* (um), Wunsch *m* (nach); *at the request of s.o., at s.o.'s request* auf j-s Bitte hin; *on request* auf Wunsch; **2.** um et. bitten *or* ersuchen; *j-n* bitten, ersuchen (*to do* zu tun)

re·quest stop *Br* Bedarfshaltestelle *f*

re·quire erfordern; benötigen, brauchen; verlangen; *if required* wenn nötig

re·quire·ment Erfordernis *n*, Bedürfnis *n*; Anforderung *f*

req·ui·site 1. erforderlich; **2.** *mst pl* Artikel *pl*; *toilet requisites* Toilettenartikel *pl*

req·ui·si·tion 1. Anforderung *f*; MIL Requisition *f*, Beschlagnahme *f*; *make a requisition for* et. anfordern; **2.** anfordern; MIL requirieren, beschlagnahmen

re·sale Wieder-, Weiterverkauf *m*

re·scind JUR *Gesetz, Urteil etc* aufheben

res·cue 1. retten (*from* aus, vor *dat*); **2.** Rettung *f*; Hilfe *f*; **3.** Rettungs...

re·search 1. Forschung *f*; **2.** forschen; *et.* erforschen

re·search·er Forscher(in)

re·sem·blance Ähnlichkeit *f* (*to* mit; *between* zwischen *dat*)

re·sem·ble ähnlich sein, ähneln (*both*: *dat*)

re·sent übel nehmen, sich ärgern über (*acc*)

re·sent·ful ärgerlich (*of, at* über *acc*)

re·sent·ment Ärger *m* (*against, at* über *acc*)

res·er·va·tion Reservierung *f*, Vorbestellung *f*; Vorbehalt *m*; (*Indianer-*)Reservat(ion *f*) *n*; (*Wild*)Reservat *n*

re·serve 1. (sich) *et.* aufsparen (*for* für); sich vorbehalten; reservieren (lassen), vorbestellen; **2.** Reserve *f* (*a.* MIL); Vorrat *m*; (*Naturschutz-, Wild*)Reservat *n*; SPORT Reservespieler(in); Reserviertheit *f*, Zurückhaltung *f*

re·served zurückhaltend, reserviert

res·er·voir Reservoir *n* (*a. fig of* an *dat*)

re·set *Uhr* umstellen; *Zeiger etc* zurückstellen (*to* auf *acc*)

re·set·tle umsiedeln

re·side wohnen, ansässig sein, s-n Wohnsitz haben

res·i·dence Wohnsitz *m*, Wohnort *m*; Aufenthalt *m*; Residenz *f*; *official residence* Amtssitz *m*

residence per·mit Aufenthaltsgenehmigung *f*, -erlaubnis *f*

res·i·dent 1. wohnhaft, ansässig; **2.** Bewohner(in), *in a town etc a.* Einwohner(in); (*Hotel*)Gast *m*; MOT Anlieger(in)

res·i·den·tial Wohn...

residential ar·e·a Wohngebiet *n*, Wohngegend *f*

re·sid·u·al übrig (geblieben), restlich, Rest...

residual pol·lu·tion Altlasten *pl*

res·i·due Rest *m*, CHEM A. Rückstand *m*

re·sign *v/i* zurücktreten (*from* von); *v/t Amt etc* niederlegen; aufgeben; verzichten auf (*acc*); *resign o.s. to* sich fügen in (*acc*), sich abfinden mit

res·ig·na·tion Rücktritt *m*; Resignation *f*

re·signed ergeben, resigniert

re·sil·i·ence Elastizität *f*; *fig* Zähigkeit *f*

re·sil·i·ent elastisch; *fig* zäh

res·in Harz *n*

re·sist widerstehen (*dat*); Widerstand leisten, sich widersetzen (*both*: *dat*)

re·sist·ance Widerstand *m* (*a*. ELECTR); MED Widerstandskraft *f*; (*Hitze- etc* -) Beständigkeit *f*, (*Stoß- etc*)Festigkeit *f*; *line of least resistance* Weg *m* des geringsten Widerstands

re·sist·ant widerstandsfähig; (*hitze- etc*) beständig, (*stoß- etc*)fest

res·o·lute resolut, entschlossen

res·o·lu·tion Beschluss *m*, PARL *etc a*. Resolution *f*; Vorsatz *m*; Entschlossenheit *f*; Lösung *f*

re·solve 1. beschließen; *Problem etc* lösen; (sich) auflösen; *resolve on* sich entschließen zu; 2. Vorsatz *m*; Entschlossenheit *f*

res·o·nance Resonanz *f*; voller Klang

res·o·nant voll(tönend); widerhallend

re·sort 1. Erholungsort *m*, Urlaubsort *m*; *have resort to* → 2. *resort to* Zuflucht nehmen zu

re·sound widerhallen (*with* von)

re·source Mittel *n*, Zuflucht *f*; Ausweg *m*; Einfallsreichtum *m*; *pl* Mittel *pl*; (*natürliche*) Reichtümer *pl*, (*Boden-, Natur*)Schätze *pl*

re·source·ful einfallsreich, findig

re·spect 1. Achtung *f*, Respekt *m* (*both: for* vor *dat*); Rücksicht *f* (*for* auf *acc*); Beziehung *f*, Hinsicht *f*; *with respect to ...* was ... anbelangt *or* betrifft; *in this respect* in dieser Hinsicht; *give my respects to ...* e-e Empfehlung an ... (*acc*); 2. *v/t* respektieren, *a*. achten, *a*. berücksichtigen, beachten

re·spect·a·ble ehrbar, anständig, geachtet; F ansehnlich, beachtlich

re·spect·ful respektvoll, ehrerbietig

re·spec·tive jeweilig; *we went to our respective places* jeder ging zu seinem Platz

re·spec·tive·ly beziehungsweise

res·pi·ra·tion Atmung *f*

res·pi·ra·tor Atemschutzgerät *n*

re·spite Pause *f*; Aufschub *m*, Frist *f*; *without respite* ohne Unterbrechung

re·splen·dent glänzend, strahlend

re·spond antworten, erwidern (*to* auf *acc*; *that* dass); reagieren, MED *a*. ansprechen (*to* auf *acc*)

re·sponse Antwort *f*, Erwiderung *f* (*to* auf *acc*); *fig* Reaktion *f* (*to* auf *acc*)

re·spon·si·bil·i·ty Verantwortung *f*; *on one's own responsibility* auf eigene Verantwortung; *sense of responsibility* Verantwortungsgefühl *n*; *take (full) responsibility for* die (volle) Verantwortung übernehmen für

re·spon·si·ble verantwortlich; verantwortungsbewusst; verantwortungsvoll

rest¹ 1. Ruhe(pause) *f*; Erholung *f*; TECH Stütze *f*; (*Telefon*)Gabel *f*; *have or take a rest* sich ausruhen; *set s.o.'s mind at rest* j-n beruhigen; 2. *v/i* ruhen; sich ausruhen; lehnen (*against, on* an *dat*); *let s.th. rest* et. auf sich beruhen lassen; *rest on* ruhen auf (*dat*) (*a. fig*); *fig* beruhen auf (*dat*); *v/t* (aus)ruhen (lassen); lehnen (*against* gegen; *on* an *acc*)

rest² Rest *m*; *all the rest of them* alle Übrigen; *for the rest* im Übrigen

rest ar·e·a MOT Rastplatz *m*

res·tau·rant Restaurant *n*, Gaststätte *f*

rest·ful ruhig, erholsam

rest home Altenpflegeheim *n*; Erholungsheim *n*

res·ti·tu·tion ECON Rückgabe *f*, Rückerstattung *f*

res·tive unruhig, nervös

rest·less ruhelos, rastlos; unruhig

res·to·ra·tion Wiederherstellung *f*; Restaurierung *f*; Rückgabe *f*, Rückerstattung *f*

re·store wiederherstellen; restaurieren; zurückgeben, -erstatten; *be restored* (*to health*) wieder gesund sein

re·strain (*from*) zurückhalten (von), hindern an (*dat*); *I had to restrain myself* ich musste mich beherrschen (*from doing s.th.* um nicht et. zu tun)

re·strained beherrscht; dezent (*color*)

re·straint Beherrschung *f*, Zurückhaltung *f*; ECON Be-, Einschränkung *f*

re·strict ECON beschränken (*to* auf *acc*), einschränken

re·stric·tion ECON Be-, Einschränkung *f*; *without restrictions* uneingeschränkt

rest room Toilette *f*

re·struc·ture umstrukturieren

re·sult 1. Ergebnis *n*, Resultat *n*; Folge *f*; *as a result of* als Folge von (*or gen*); *without result* ergebnislos; 2. folgen, sich ergeben (*from* aus); *result in* zur Folge haben (*acc*), führen zu

re·sume wieder aufnehmen; fortsetzen; *Platz* wieder einnehmen

re·sump·tion Wiederaufnahme *f*; Fortsetzung *f*

Res·ur·rec·tion REL Auferstehung *f*

re·sus·ci·tate MED wieder beleben

re·sus·ci·ta·tion MED Wiederbelebung *f*

re·tail ECON 1. Einzelhandel *m*; *by retail* im Einzelhandel; 2. Einzelhandels...; 3. *adv* im Einzelhandel; 4. *v/t* im Einzelhandel verkaufen (*at, for* für); *v/i* im Einzelhandel verkauft werden (*at, for* für)

re·tail·er ECON Einzelhändler(in)

re·tain (be)halten, bewahren; *Wasser, Wärme* speichern

R

re·tal·i·ate Vergeltung üben, sich revanchieren

re·tal·i·a·tion Vergeltung *f*, Vergeltungsmaßnahmen *pl*

re·tard verzögern, aufhalten, hemmen; **(mentally) retarded** (geistig) zurückgeblieben

retch würgen

re·tell nacherzählen

re·think *et.* noch einmal überdenken

re·ti·cent schweigsam, zurückhaltend

ret·i·nue Gefolge *n*

re·tire *v/i* in Rente *or* Pension gehen, sich pensionieren lassen; sich zurückziehen; **retire from business** sich zur Ruhe setzen; *v/t* in den Ruhestand versetzen, pensionieren

re·tired pensioniert, im Ruhestand (lebend); **be retired** *a.* in Rente *or* Pension sein

re·tire·ment Pensionierung *f*, Ruhestand *m*

re·tir·ing zurückhaltend

re·tort 1. (scharf) entgegnen *or* erwidern; **2.** (scharfe) Entgegnung *or* Erwiderung

re·touch PHOT retuschieren

re·trace *Tathergang etc* rekonstruieren; **retrace one's steps** denselben Weg zurückgehen

re·tract *v/t Angebot* zurückziehen; *Behauptung* zurücknehmen; *Geständnis* widerrufen; *TECH, ZO* einziehen; *v/i TECH, ZO* eingezogen werden

re·train umschulen

re·tread MOT **1.** *Reifen* rundernuern; **2.** rundernuerter Reifen

re·treat 1. MIL Rückzug *m*; Zufluchtsort *m*; **beat a (hasty) retreat** das Feld räumen, F abhauen; **2.** sich zurückziehen; zurückweichen (**from** vor *dat*)

ret·ri·bu·tion Vergeltung *f*

re·trieve zurückholen, wiederbekommen; *Fehler, Verlust etc* wieder gutmachen; HUNT apportieren

ret·ro·ac·tive JUR rückwirkend

ret·ro·grade rückschrittlich

ret·ro·spect: in retrospect im Rückblick

ret·ro·spec·tive rückblickend; JUR rückwirkend

re·try JUR *Fall* erneut verhandeln; neu verhandeln gegen *j-n*

re·turn 1. *v/i* zurückkehren, zurückkommen; zurückgehen; **return to** auf *ein Thema etc* zurückkommen; in *e-e Gewohnheit etc* zurückfallen; in *e-n Zustand etc* zurückkehren; *v/t* zurückgeben (**to** *dat*); zurückbringen (**to** *dat*); zurückschicken, -senden (**to** *dat or* an *acc*); zurücklegen, -stellen; erwidern; *Gewinn etc* abwerfen; → **verdict**; **2.** Rückkehr *f*; *fig* Wiederauftreten *n*; Rückgabe *f*; Zurückbringen *n*; Zurückschicken *n*, -senden *n*; Zurücklegen *n*, -stellen *n*; Erwiderung *f*; *(Steuer)*Erklärung *f*; *tennis etc*: Return *m*, Rückschlag *m*; ECON *a. pl* Gewinn *m*; *Br* → **return ticket**; *Br* **many happy returns (of the day)** herzlichen Glückwunsch zum Geburtstag; **by return (of post)** umgehend, postwendend; **in return for** (als Gegenleistung) für; **3.** *adj* Rück...

re·turn·a·ble *in cpds* Mehrweg...; **returnable bottle** Pfandflasche *f*

re·turn key EDP Eingabetaste *f*

return game, return match SPORT Rückspiel *n*

return tick·et *Br* RAIL Rückfahrkarte *f*; AVIAT Rückflugticket *n*

re·u·ni·fi·ca·tion POL Wiedervereinigung *f*

re·u·nion Treffen *n*, Wiedersehensfeier *f*; Wiedervereinigung *f*

re·us·a·ble wieder verwendbar

rev F MOT **1.** Umdrehung *f*; **rev counter** Drehzahlmesser *m*; **2.** *a.* **rev up** aufheulen (lassen)

re·val·ue ECON *Währung* aufwerten

re·veal den Blick freigeben auf *(acc)*, zeigen; *Geheimnis etc* enthüllen, aufdecken

re·veal·ing aufschlussreich (*remark etc*); offenherzig (*dress etc*)

rev·el: revel in schwelgen in (*dat*); sich weiden an (*dat*)

rev·e·la·tion Enthüllung *f*; REL Offenbarung *f*

re·venge 1. Rache *f*; *esp* SPORT Revanche *f*; **in revenge for** aus Rache für; **take revenge on s.o. for s.th.** sich an j-m für et. rächen; **2.** rächen

re·venge·ful rachsüchtig

rev·e·nue Staatseinkünfte *pl*, Staatseinnahmen *pl*

re·ver·be·rate nach-, widerhallen

re·vere (ver)ehren

rev·er·ence Verehrung *f*; Ehrfurcht *f* (**for** vor *dat*)

Rev·e·rend REL Hochwürden *m*

rev·er·ent ehrfürchtig, ehrfurchtsvoll

rev·er·ie (Tag)Träumerei *f*

re·vers·al Umkehrung *f*; Rückschlag *m*

re·verse 1. *adj* umgekehrt; **in reverse order** in umgekehrter Reihenfolge; **2.** *Wagen* im Rückwärtsgang fahren *or* rückwärtsfahren; *Reihenfolge etc* umkehren; *Urteil etc* aufheben; *Entscheidung etc* umstoßen; **3.** Gegenteil *n*; MOT Rückwärtsgang *m*; Rückseite *f*, Kehrseite *f* (*of a coin*); Rückschlag *m*

reverse gear MOT Rückwärtsgang *m*
reverse side linke (*Stoff*)Seite
re·vers·i·ble doppelseitig (tragbar)
re·vert: *revert to* in *e-n Zustand* zurückkehren; in *e-e Gewohnheit etc* zurückfallen; auf *ein Thema* zurückkommen
re·view 1. Überprüfung *f*; Besprechung *f*,
Kritik *f*, Rezension *f*; MIL Parade *f*; PED
(Stoff)Wiederholung *f* (*for* für *e-e Prüfung*); **2.** überprüfen; besprechen, rezensieren; MIL besichtigen, inspizieren; PED
Stoff wiederholen (*for* für *e-e Prüfung*)
re·view·er Kritiker(in), Rezensent(in)
re·vise revidieren, *Ansicht* ändern, *Buch
etc* überarbeiten; *Br* PED *Stoff* wiederholen (*for* für *e-e Prüfung*)
re·vi·sion Revision *f*, Überarbeitung *f*;
überarbeitete Ausgabe; *Br* PED (Stoff-)
Wiederholung *f* (*for* für *e-e Prüfung*)
re·viv·al Wiederbelebung *f*; Wiederaufleben *n*
re·vive wieder beleben; wieder aufleben
(lassen); *Erinnerungen* wachrufen; MED
wieder zu sich kommen; sich erholen
re·voke widerrufen, zurücknehmen, rückgängig machen
re·volt 1. *v/i* sich auflehnen, revoltieren
(*against* gegen); Abscheu empfinden,
empört sein (*against, at, from* über
acc); *v/t* mit Abscheu erfüllen, abstoßen;
2. Revolte *f*, Aufstand *m*
re·volt·ing abscheulich, abstoßend
rev·o·lu·tion Revolution *f*, Umwälzung *f*;
ASTR Umlauf *m* (*round* um); TECH Umdrehung *f*; *number of revolutions*
Drehzahl *f*; *revolution counter* Drehzahlmesser *m*
rev·o·lu·tion·a·ry 1. revolutionär; Revolutions...; **2.** POL Revolutionär(in)
rev·o·lu·tion·ize revolutionieren
re·volve sich drehen (*on, round* um); *revolve around* *fig* sich drehen um
re·volv·er Revolver *m*
re·volv·ing Dreh...; *revolving door(s)*
Drehtür *f*
re·vue THEA Revue *f*; Kabarett *n*
re·vul·sion Abscheu *m*
re·ward 1. Belohnung *f*; **2.** belohnen
re·ward·ing lohnend
re·write neu schreiben, umschreiben
rhap·so·dy MUS Rhapsodie *f*
rhe·to·ric Rhetorik *f*
rheu·ma·tism MED Rheumatismus *m*, F
Rheuma *n*
rhi·no F, **rhi·no·ce·ros** ZO Rhinozeros *n*,
Nashorn *n*
rhu·barb BOT Rhabarber *m*
rhyme 1. Reim *m*; Vers *m*; *without rhyme
or reason* ohne Sinn und Verstand; **2.**

(sich) reimen
rhyth·m Rhythmus *m*
rhyth·mic, rhyth·mi·cal rhythmisch
rib ANAT Rippe *f*
rib·bon (*a*. Farb-, Ordens)Band *n*; Streifen *m*; Fetzen *m*
rib cage ANAT Brustkorb *m*
rice BOT Reis *m*
rice pud·ding GASTR Milchreis *m*
rich 1. reich (*in* an *dat*); prächtig, kostbar;
GASTR schwer; AGR fruchtbar, fett (*soil*);
voll (*sound*); satt (*color*); *rich* (*in calories*) kalorienreich; **2.** *the rich* die Reichen *pl*
rick (Stroh-, Heu)Schober *m*
rick·ets MED Rachitis *f*
rick·et·y F *fig* gebrechlich; wack(e)lig
rid befreien (*of* von); *get rid of* loswerden
rid·dance: F *good riddance!* den (die,
das) sind wir Gott sei Dank los!
rid·den *in cpds* geplagt von
rid·dle[1] Rätsel *n*
rid·dle[2] **1.** grobes Sieb, Schüttelsieb *n*; **2.**
sieben; durchlöchern, durchsieben
ride 1. *v/i* reiten; fahren (*on* auf *e-m Fahrrad etc*; *on or Br in* in *e-m Bus etc*); *v/t*
reiten (auf *dat*); *Fahrrad, Motorrad* fahren, fahren auf (*dat*); **2.** Ritt *m*; Fahrt *f*
rid·er Reiter(in); (Motorrad-, Rad)Fahrer(in)
ridge GEOGR (*Gebirgs*)Kamm *m*, Grat *m*;
ARCH (*Dach*)First *m*
rid·i·cule 1. Spott *m*; **2.** lächerlich machen,
spotten über (*acc*), verspotten
ri·dic·u·lous lächerlich
rid·ing Reit...
riff-raff *contp* Gesindel *n*
ri·fle[1] Gewehr *n*
ri·fle[2] durchwühlen
rift Spalt *m*, Spalte *f*; *fig* Riss *m*
rig 1. *Schiff* auftakeln; *rig out* *j-n* ausstaffieren; *rig up* F (behelfsmäßig) zusammenbauen (*from* aus); **2.** MAR Takelage
f; TECH Bohrinsel *f*; F Aufmachung *f*
rig·ging MAR Takelage *f*
right 1. *adj* recht; richtig; rechte(r, -s),
Rechts...; *all right!* in Ordnung!, gut!;
that's all right! das macht nichts!, schon
gut!, bitte!; *that's right!* richtig!, ganz
recht!, stimmt!; *be right* recht haben;
put right, set right in Ordnung bringen;
berichtigen, korrigieren; **2.** *adv* (nach)
rechts; richtig, recht; genau; gerade
(-wegs), direkt; ganz, völlig; *right away*
sofort; *right now* im Moment; sofort;
right on geradeaus; *turn right* (sich)
nach rechts wenden; MOT rechts abbiegen; **3.** Recht *n*; *die Rechte* (*a*. POL, *boxing*), rechte Seite; *on the right* rechts,

auf der rechten Seite; *to the right* (nach) rechts; *keep to the right* sich rechts halten; MOT rechts fahren; **4.** aufrichten; *et.* wieder gutmachen; in Ordnung bringen

right an·gle MATH rechter Winkel

right-an·gled MATH rechtwink(e)lig

right·eous gerecht (*anger etc*)

right·ful rechtmäßig

right-hand rechte(r, -s)

right-hand drive MOT Rechtssteuerung *f*

right-hand·ed rechtshändig; für Rechtshänder; *be right-handed* Rechtshänder(in) sein

right·ly richtig; mit Recht

right of way MOT Vorfahrt *f*, Vorfahrtsrecht *n*; Durchgangsrecht *n*

right-wing POL dem rechten Flügel angehörend, Rechts...

rig·id starr, steif; *fig* streng, strikt

rig·a·ma·role Geschwätz *n*; *fig* Theater *n*, Zirkus *m*

rig·or·ous streng; genau

rig·o(u)r Strenge *f*, Härte *f*

rile F ärgern, reizen

rim Rand *m*; TECH Felge *f*

rim·less randlos

rind (*Zitronen- etc*)Schale *f*; (*Käse*)Rinde *f*; (*Speck*)Schwarte *f*

ring[1] **1.** Ring *m*; Kreis *m*; Manege *f*; (Box)Ring *m*; (Spionage- *etc*)Ring *m*; **2.** umringen, umstellen; *Vogel* beringen

ring[2] **1.** läuten; klingeln; klingen (*a. fig*); *Br* TEL anrufen; *the bell is ringing* es läutet *or* klingelt; *ring the bell* läuten, klingeln; *ring back Br* TEL zurückrufen; *ring for* nach *j-m, et.* läuten; *Arzt etc* rufen; *ring off Br* TEL (den Hörer) auflegen, Schluss machen; *ring s.o. (up)* j-n *or* bei j-m anrufen; **2.** Läuten *n*, Klingeln *n*; *fig* Klang *m*; *Br* TEL Anruf *m*; F *give s.o. a ring* j-n anrufen

ring bind·er Ringbuch *n*

ring fin·ger Ringfinger *m*

ring·lead·er Rädelsführer(in)

ring·let (Ringel)Löckchen *n*

ring road *Br* Umgehungsstraße *f*; Ringstraße *f*

ring·side: *at the ringside boxing*: am Ring

rink (Kunst)Eisbahn *f*; Rollschuhbahn *f*

rinse *a. rinse out* (aus)spülen

ri·ot 1. Aufruhr *m*; Krawall *m*; *run riot* randalieren; *run riot through* randalierend ziehen durch; **2.** Krawall machen, randalieren

ri·ot·er Aufrührer(in); Randalierer(in)

ri·ot·ous aufrührerisch; randalierend; ausgelassen, wild

rip 1. *a. rip up* zerreißen; *rip open* aufrei-

ßen; F *rip s.o. off* j-n neppen; **2.** Riss *m*

ripe reif

rip·en reifen (lassen)

rip-off F Nepp *m*

rip·ple 1. (sich) kräuseln; plätschern, rieseln; **2.** kleine Welle; Kräuselung *f*; Plätschern *n*, Rieseln *n*

rise 1. aufstehen, sich erheben; REL auferstehen; aufsteigen (*smoke etc*); sich heben (*curtain, spirits*); ansteigen (*road, river etc*), anschwellen (*river etc*); (an)steigen (*temperature etc*), *prices etc*: an ansteigen; stärker werden (*wind etc*); aufgehen (*sun etc, bread etc*); entspringen (*river etc*); *fig* aufsteigen; *fig* entstehen (*from, out of* aus); *a. rise up* sich erheben (*against* gegen); *rise to the occasion* sich der Lage gewachsen zeigen; **2.** (An)Steigen *n*; Steigung *f*; Anhöhe *f*; ASTR Aufgang *m*; *Br* Lohn- *or* Gehaltserhöhung *f*; *fig* Anstieg *m*; Aufstieg *m*; *give rise to* verursachen, führen zu

ris·er: *early riser* Frühaufsteher(in)

ris·ing 1. Aufstand *m*; **2.** aufstrebend

risk 1. Gefahr *f*, Risiko *n*; *at one's own risk* auf eigene Gefahr; *at the risk of doing s.th.* auf die Gefahr hin, et. zu tun; *be at risk* gefährdet sein; *run the risk of doing s.th.* Gefahr laufen, et. zu tun; *run a risk, take a risk* ein Risiko eingehen; **2.** wagen, riskieren

risk·y riskant

rite Ritus *m*; Zeremonie *f*

rit·u·al 1. rituell; Ritual...; **2.** Ritual *n*

ri·val 1. Rivale *m*, Rivalin *f*, Konkurrent(in); **2.** Konkurrenz..., rivalisierend; **3.** rivalisieren *or* konkurrieren mit

ri·val·ry Rivalität *f*; Konkurrenz *f*; Konkurrenzkampf *m*

riv·er Fluss *m*; Strom *m*

riv·er·side Flussufer *n*; *by the riverside* am Fluss

riv·et 1. TECH Niet *m, n*, Niete *f*; **2.** TECH (ver)nieten; *fig Aufmerksamkeit, Blick* richten (*on* auf *acc*)

road (Auto-, Land)Straße *f*; *fig* Weg *m*; *on the road* auf der Straße; unterwegs; THEA auf Tournee

road ac·ci·dent Verkehrsunfall *m*

road·block Straßensperre *f*

road hog F Verkehrsrowdy *m*

road map Straßenkarte *f*

road safe·ty Verkehrssicherheit *f*

road·side Straßenrand *m*; *at the roadside, by the roadside* am Straßenrand

road toll Straßenbenutzungsgebühr *f*

road·way Fahrbahn *f*

road works Straßenarbeiten *pl*

road·wor·thi·ness Verkehrssicherheit *f*

road·wor·thy verkehrssicher

roam v/i (umher)streifen, (-)wandern; v/t streifen or wandern durch

roar 1. Brüllen n, Gebrüll n; Brausen n, Krachen n, Donnern n; *roars of laughter* brüllendes Gelächter; **2.** brüllen; brausen; donnern (*truck, gun etc*)

roast GASTR **1.** v/t braten (a. v/i); Kaffee etc rösten; **2.** Braten m; **3.** adj gebraten

roast beef GASTR Rinderbraten m

rob Bank etc überfallen; j-n berauben

rob·ber Räuber m

rob·ber·y Raubüberfall m, (Bank-) Raub m, (Bank)Überfall m

robe a. pl Robe f, Talar m

rob·in ZO Rotkehlchen n

ro·bot Roboter m

ro·bust robust, kräftig

rock¹ schaukeln, wiegen; erschüttern (a. fig)

rock² Fels(en) m; Felsen pl; GEOL Gestein n; Felsbrocken m; Stein m; Br Zuckerstange f; pl Klippen pl; F *on the rocks* in ernsten Schwierigkeiten (*business etc*); kaputt (*marriage etc*); GASTR mit Eis

rock³ a. *rock music* Rock(musik f) m; → *rock 'n' roll*

rock·er Kufe f; Schaukelstuhl m; Br Rocker m; *off one's rocker* F übergeschnappt

rock·et 1. Rakete f; **2.** rasen, schießen; a. *rocket up* hochschnellen, in die Höhe schießen (*prices*)

rock·ing chair Schaukelstuhl m

rock·ing horse Schaukelpferd n

rock 'n' roll MUS Rock 'n' Roll m

rock·y felsig; steinhart

rod Rute f; TECH Stab m, Stange f

ro·dent ZO Nagetier n

ro·de·o Rodeo m, n

roe ZO a. *hard roe* Rogen m; a. *soft roe* Milch f

roe·buck ZO Rehbock m

roe deer ZO Reh n

rogue Schurke m, Gauner m; Schlingel m, Spitzbube m

ro·guish schelmisch, spitzbübisch

role THEA etc Rolle f (a. fig)

roll 1. v/i rollen; sich wälzen; fahren; MAR schlingern; (g)rollen (*thunder*); v/t et. rollen; auf-, zusammenrollen; *Zigarette* drehen; *roll down* Ärmel herunterkrempeln; MOT *Fenster* herunterkurbeln; *roll out* ausrollen; *roll up* aufrollen; (sich) zusammenrollen; *Ärmel* hochkrempeln; MOT *Fenster* hochkurbeln; **2.** Rolle f; GASTR Brötchen n, Semmel f; Namens-, Anwesenheitsliste f; (G)Rollen n (*of thunder*); (Trommel)Wirbel m; MAR Schlingern n

roll call Namensaufruf m

roll·er (Locken)Wickler m; TECH Rolle f, Walze f

roll·er coast·er Achterbahn f

roll·er skate Rollschuh m

roll·er-skate Rollschuh laufen

roll·er-skat·ing Rollschuhlaufen n

roll·er tow·el Rollhandtuch n

roll·ing pin Nudelholz n

roll-on Deoroller m

Ro·man 1. römisch; **2.** Römer(in)

ro·mance Abenteuer-, Liebesroman m; Romanze f; Romantik f

Ro·mance LING romanisch

Ro·ma·ni·a Rumänien n

Ro·ma·ni·an 1. rumänisch; **2.** Rumäne m, Rumänin f; LING Rumänisch n

ro·man·tic 1. romantisch; **2.** Romantiker(in)

ro·man·ti·cism Romantik f

romp a. *romp about*, *romp around* herumtollen, herumtoben

romp·ers Spielanzug m

roof 1. Dach n; MOT Verdeck n; **2.** mit e-m Dach versehen; *roof in*, *roof over* überdachen

roof·ing felt Dachpappe f

roof-rack MOT Dachgepäckträger m

rook¹ ZO Saatkrähe f

rook² chess: Turm m

rook³ F j-n betrügen (*of* um)

room 1. Raum m, a. Zimmer n, a. Platz m; fig Spielraum m; **2.** wohnen

room·er Untermieter(in)

room·ing-house Fremdenheim n, Pension f

room·mate Zimmergenosse m, -genossin f

room ser·vice Zimmerservice m

room·y geräumig

roost 1. (Hühner)Stange f; ZO Schlafplatz m; **2.** auf der Stange etc sitzen or schlafen

roost·er ZO (Haus)Hahn m

root 1. Wurzel f; *take root* Wurzeln schlagen (a. fig); **2.** v/i Wurzeln schlagen; wühlen (*for* nach); *root about* herumwühlen (*among* in dat); v/t *root out* fig ausrotten; *root up* mit der Wurzel ausreißen

root·ed: *deeply rooted* fig tief verwurzelt; *stand rooted to the spot* wie angewurzelt dastehen

rope 1. Seil n; MAR Tau n; Strick m; (Perlen- etc)Schnur f; *give s.o. plenty of rope* j-m viel Freiheit or Spielraum lassen; *know the ropes* F sich auskennen; *show s.o. the ropes* F j-n einarbeiten; **2.** festbinden (*to* an dat or acc); *rope*

R

off (durch ein Seil) absperren *or* abgrenzen

rope lad·der Strickleiter *f*

ro·sa·ry REL Rosenkranz *m*

rose 1. BOT Rose *f*; Brause *f*; **2.** rosarot, rosenrot

ros·trum Redner-, Dirigentenpult *n*

ros·y rosig (*a. fig*)

rot 1. *v/t* (ver)faulen *or* verrotten lassen; *v/i a.* **rot away** (ver)faulen, verrotten, morsch werden; **2.** Fäulnis *f*

ro·ta·ry rotierend, sich drehend; Rotations..., Dreh...

ro·tate rotieren (lassen), (sich) drehen; turnusmäßig (aus-) wechseln

ro·ta·tion Rotation *f*, Drehung *f*; Wechsel *m*

ro·tor TECH Rotor *m*

rot·ten verfault, faul; verrottet, morsch; *fig* miserabel; gemein; **feel rotten** F sich mies fühlen

ro·tund rund und dick

rough 1. *adj* rau; uneben (*road etc*); stürmisch (*sea, crossing, weather*); grob; barsch; hart; grob, ungefähr (*estimate etc*); roh, Roh...; **2.** *adv* **sleep rough** im Freien übernachten; **play rough** SPORT hart spielen; **3.** *golf*: Rough *n*; **write it out in rough first** zuerst ins Unreine schreiben; **4. rough it** F primitiv *or* anspruchslos leben; **rough out** entwerfen, skizzieren; **rough up** F *j-n* zusammenschlagen

rough·age MED Ballaststoffe *pl*

rough·cast ARCH Rauputz *m*

rough cop·y Rohentwurf *m*, Konzept *n*

rough draft Rohfassung *f*

rough·en rau werden; rau machen; anrauen, aufrauen

rough·ly grob, *fig a.* ungefähr

rough·neck F Schläger *m*

rough·shod: ride roughshod over *j-n* rücksichtslos behandeln; sich rücksichtslos über *et.* hinwegsetzen

round 1. *adj* rund; **a round dozen** ein rundes Dutzend; **in round figures** aufgerundet, abgerundet, rund(e) ...; **2.** *adv* rund(her)um, rings(her)um; überall, auf *or* von *or* nach allen Seiten; **turn round** sich umdrehen; **invite s.o. round** *j-n* zu sich einladen; **round about** F ungefähr; **all (the) year round** das ganze Jahr hindurch *or* über; **the other way round** umgekehrt; **3.** *prp* (rund) um, um (*acc* ... herum); in *or* auf (*dat*) ... herum; **trip round the world** Weltreise *f*; **4.** Runde *f*, *a.* Rundgang *m*, MED Visite *f*, *a.* Lage *f* (*beer etc*); Schuss *m*; *esp Br* Scheibe *f* (*bread etc*); MUS Kanon *m*; **5.** rund

machen, (ab)runden, *Lippen* spitzen; umfahren, fahren um, *Kurve* nehmen; **round down** *Zahl etc* abrunden (**to** auf *acc*); **round off** *Essen etc* abrunden, beschließen (**with** mit); *Zahl etc* auf- *or* abrunden (**to** auf *acc*); **round up** *Vieh* zusammentreiben; *Leute etc* zusammentrommeln; *Zahl etc* aufrunden (**to** auf *acc*)

round·a·bout 1. *Br* MOT Kreisverkehr *m*; *Br* Karussell *n*; **2. take a roundabout route** e-n Umweg machen; **in a roundabout way** *fig* auf Umwegen

round trip Hin- und Rückfahrt *f*; Hin- und Rückflug *m*

round-trip tick·et Rückfahrkarte *f*; Rückflugticket *n*

round·up Razzia *f*

rouse *j-n* wecken; *fig j-n* aufrütteln, wach rütteln; *j-n* erzürnen, reizen

route Route *f*, Strecke *f*, Weg *m*, (*Bus etc*)Linie *f*

rou·tine 1. Routine *f*; **the same old (daily) routine** das (tägliche) ewige Einerlei; **2.** üblich, routinemäßig, Routine...

rove (umher)streifen, (umher)wandern

row¹ Reihe *f*

row² **1.** rudern; **2.** Kahnfahrt *f*

row³ *Br* **1.** Krach *m*; (lauter) Streit; **2.** (sich) streiten

row·boat Ruderboot *n*

row·er Ruderer *m*, Ruderin *f*

row house Reihenhaus *n*

row·ing boat *Br* Ruderboot *n*

roy·al königlich, Königs...

roy·al·ty die königliche Familie; Tantieme *f* (**on** auf *acc*)

rub 1. *v/t* reiben; abreiben; polieren; **rub dry** trocken reiben; **rub it in** *fig* F darauf herumreiten; **rub shoulders with** F verkehren mit; *v/i* reiben, scheuern (**against, on** an *dat*); **rub down** abreiben, trocken reiben; abschmirgeln, abschleifen; **rub off** abreiben; abgehen (*paint etc*); **rub off on(to)** *fig* abfärben auf (*acc*); **rub out** *Br* ausradieren; **2. give s.th. a rub** *et.* abreiben *or* polieren

rub·ber Gummi *n*, *m*; *esp Br* Radiergummi *m*; Wischtuch *n*; F Gummi *m*

rub·ber band Gummiband *n*

rub·ber din·ghy Schlauchboot *n*

rub·ber·neck F **1.** neugierig gaffen; **2.** *a.* **rubbernecker** Gaffer(in), Schaulustige *m*, *f*

rub·ber·y gummiartig; zäh

rub·bish *Br* Abfall *m*, Abfälle *pl*, Müll *m*; F Schund *m*; Quatsch *m*, Blödsinn *m*

rubbish bin *Br* Mülleimer *m*

rubbish chute *Br* Müllschlucker *m*

rub·ble Schutt *m*; Trümmer *pl*
ru·by Rubin *m*; Rubinrot *n*
ruck·sack *esp Br* Rucksack *m*
rud·der AVIAT, MAR Ruder *n*
rud·dy frisch, gesund
rude unhöflich, grob; unanständig (*joke etc*); bös (*shock etc*)
ru·di·men·ta·ry elementar, Anfangs...; primitiv
ru·di·ments Anfangsgründe *pl*
rue·ful reuevoll, reumütig
ruff Halskrause *f* (*a.* ZO)
ruf·fle 1. kräuseln; *Haar* zerzausen; *Federn* sträuben; *ruffle s.o.'s composure* j-n aus der Fassung bringen; **2.** Rüsche *f*
rug Vorleger *m*, Brücke *f*; *esp Br* dicke Wolldecke
rug·by *a.* *rugby football* SPORT Rugby *n*
rug·ged GEOGR zerklüftet, schroff; TECH robust, stabil; zerfurcht (*face*)
ru·in 1. Ruin *m*; *mst pl* Ruine(n *pl*) *f*, Trümmer *pl*; **2.** ruinieren, zerstören
ru·in·ous ruinös
rule 1. Regel *f*; Spielregel *f*; Vorschrift *f*; Herrschaft *f*; Lineal *n*; *against the rules* regelwidrig; verboten; *as a rule* in der Regel; *as a rule of thumb* als Faustregel; *work to rule* Dienst nach Vorschrift tun; **2.** *v/t* herrschen über (*acc*); *esp* JUR entscheiden; *Papier* lin(i)ieren; *Linie* ziehen; *be ruled by* *fig* sich leiten lassen von; beherrscht werden von; *rule out et.* ausschließen; *v/i* herrschen (*over* über *acc*); *esp* JUR entscheiden
rul·er Herrscher(in); Lineal *n*
rum Rum *m*
rum·ble rumpeln (*vehicle*); (g)rollen (*thunder*); knurren (*stomach*)
ru·mi·nant ZO Wiederkäuer *m*
ru·mi·nate ZO wiederkäuen
rum·mage F **1.** *a.* *rummage about* herumstöbern, herumwühlen (*among, in, through* in *dat*); **2.** Ramsch *m*
rummage sale Wohltätigkeitsbasar *m*
ru·mo(u)r 1. Gerücht *n*; *rumo(u)r has it that* es geht das Gerücht, dass; **2.** *it is rumo(u)red that* es geht das Gerücht, dass; *he is rumo(u)red to be ...* man munkelt, er sei ...
rump F Hinterteil *n*
rum·ple zerknittern, zerknüllen, zerwühlen; *Haar* zerzausen
run 1. *v/i* laufen (*a.* SPORT), rennen; fahren, verkehren, gehen (*train, bus etc*); laufen, fließen; zerfließen, zerlaufen (*butter, paint etc*); TECH laufen (*engine*), in Betrieb *or* Gang sein; verlaufen (*road etc*); *esp* JUR gelten, laufen (*for one year* ein Jahr); THEA *etc* laufen (*for three*

months drei Monate lang); lauten (*text*); gehen (*melody*); POL kandidieren (*for* für); *run dry* austrocknen; *run low* knapp werden; *run short* knapp werden; *run short of gas* (*Br petrol*) kein Benzin mehr haben; *v/t Strecke, Rennen* laufen; *Zug, Bus* fahren *or* verkehren lassen; *Wasser, Maschine etc* laufen lassen; *Geschäft, Hotel etc* führen, leiten; *Zeitungsartikel etc* abdrucken, bringen; *run s.o. home* F j-n nach Hause bringen *or* fahren; *be running a temperature* erhöhte Temperatur *or* Fieber haben; → *errand*; *run across* j-n zufällig treffen; stoßen auf (*acc*); *run after* hinterherlaufen, nachlaufen (*dat*); *run along!* F ab mit dir!; *run away* davonlaufen (*from* vor *dat*); *run away with* durchbrennen mit; durchgehen mit (*feelings etc*); *run down* MOT anfahren, umfahren; F schlechtmachen; ausfindig machen; ablaufen (*watch*); leer werden (*battery*); *run in Wagen etc* einfahren; F *Verbrecher* schnappen; *run into* laufen *or* fahren gegen; j-n zufällig treffen; *fig* geraten in (*acc*); *fig* sich belaufen auf (*acc*); *run off with* → *run away with*; *run on* weitergehen, sich hinziehen (*until* bis); F unaufhörlich reden (*about* über *acc*, von); *run out* ablaufen (*time etc*); ausgehen, zu Ende gehen (*supplies etc*); *run out of gas* (*Br petrol*) kein Benzin mehr haben; *run over* MOT überfahren; überlaufen, überfließen; *run through* überfliegen, durchgehen, durchlesen; *run up Flagge* hissen; *hohe Rechnung, Schulden* machen; *run up against* stoßen auf (*acc*); **2.** Lauf *m* (*a.* SPORT); Fahrt *f*; Spazierfahrt *f*; Ansturm *m*, ECON *a.* Run *m* (*on* auf *acc*); THEA *etc* Laufzeit *f*; Laufmasche *f*; Gehege *n*; Auslauf *m*, (*Hühner*)Hof *m*; SPORT (*Bob-, Rodel-*) Bahn *f*; (*Ski*)Hang *m*; *run of good* (*bad*) *luck* Glückssträhne *f* (Pechsträhne *f*); *in the long run* auf die Dauer; *in the short run* zunächst; *on the run* auf der Flucht
run·a·bout F MOT Stadt-, Kleinwagen *m*
run·a·way Ausreißer(in)
rung Sprosse *f*
run·ner SPORT Läufer(in); Rennpferd *n*; *mst in cpds* Schmuggler(in); (*Schlitten-, Schlittschuh-*)Kufe *f*; Tischläufer *m*; TECH (*Gleit*)Schiene *f*; BOT Ausläufer *m*
runner bean *Br* SPORT grüne Bohne
run-up SPORT Zweite *m*, *f*, Vizemeister(in)
run·ning 1. Laufen *n*, Rennen *n*; Führung *f*, Leitung *f*; **2.** fließend; SPORT Lauf...; *two days running* zwei Tage hintereinander

R

running costs ECON Betriebskosten *pl*, laufende Kosten *pl*

run·ny F flüssig; laufend (*nose*), tränend (*eyes*)

run-off POL Stichwahl *f*

run·way AVIAT Start- und Landebahn *f*, Rollbahn *f*, Piste *f*

rup·ture 1. Bruch *m* (*a.* MED *and fig*), Riss *m*; **2.** bersten, platzen; (zer)reißen; **rup·ture o.s.** MED sich e-n Bruch heben *or* zuziehen

ru·ral ländlich

ruse List *f*, Trick *m*

rush[1] **1.** *v/i* hasten, hetzen, stürmen, rasen; **rush at** losstürzen *or* sich stürzen auf (*acc*); **rush in** hineinstürzen, hineinstürmen, hereinstürzen, hereinstürmen; **rush into** *fig* sich stürzen in (*acc*); *et.* überstürzen; *v/t* antreiben, drängen, hetzen; schnell bringen; *Essen* hinunterschlingen; losstürmen auf (*acc*); **don't rush it** lass dir Zeit dabei; **2.** Ansturm *m*; Hast *f*, Hetze *f*; Hochbetrieb *m*; ECON stürmische Nachfrage; **what's all the**

rush? wozu diese Eile *or* Hetze?

rush[2] BOT Binse *f*

rush hour Rushhour *f*, Hauptverkehrszeit *f*, Stoßzeit *f*

rush-hour traf·fic Stoßverkehr *m*

rusk *esp Br* Zwieback *m*

Rus·sia Russland *n*

Rus·sian 1. russisch; **2.** Russe *m*, Russin *f*; LING Russisch *n*

rust 1. Rost *m*; **2.** *v/t* (ein-, ver)rosten lassen; *v/i* (ein-, ver)rosten

rus·tic ländlich, bäuerlich; rustikal

rus·tle 1. rascheln (mit), knistern; *Vieh* stehlen; **2.** Rascheln *n*

rust·proof rostfrei, nicht rostend

rust·y rostig; *fig* eingerostet

rut[1] **1.** (Rad)Spur *f*, Furche *f*; *fig* (alter) Trott; **the daily rut** das tägliche Einerlei; **2.** furchen; **rutted** ausgefahren

rut[2] ZO Brunft *f*, Brunst *f*

ruth·less unbarmherzig; rücksichtslos, skrupellos

rye BOT Roggen *m*

S

S, s S, s *n*

S ABBR *of* **small (size)** klein

sa·ber, *Br* **sa·bre** Säbel *m*

sa·ble ZO Zobel *m*; Zobelpelz *m*

sab·o·tage 1. Sabotage *f*; **2.** sabotieren

sack 1. Sack *m*; **get the sack** *Br* F rausgeschmissen werden; **give s.o. the sack** *Br* F j-n rausschmeißen; **hit the sack** F sich in die Falle *or* Klappe hauen; **2.** in Säcke füllen, einsacken; *Br* F j-n rausschmeißen

sack·cloth, **sack·ing** Sackleinen *n*

sac·ra·ment REL Sakrament *n*

sa·cred geistlich (*music etc*); heilig

sac·ri·fice 1. Opfer *n*; **2.** opfern

sac·ri·lege REL Sakrileg *n*; Frevel *m*

sac·ris·ty REL Sakristei *f*

sad traurig; schmerzlich; schlimm

sad·dle 1. Sattel *m*; **2.** satteln

sa·dism Sadismus *m*

sa·dist Sadist(in)

sa·dis·tic sadistisch

sad·ness Traurigkeit *f*

sa·fa·ri Safari *f*

safari park Safaripark *m*

safe 1. sicher; **2.** Safe *m, n*, Tresor *m*, Geldschrank *m*

safe con·duct freies Geleit

safe de·pos·it Tresor *m*

safe-de·pos·it box Schließfach *n*

safe·guard 1. Schutz *m* (**against** gegen, vor *dat*); **2.** schützen (**against, from** gegen, vor *dat*)

safe·keep·ing sichere Verwahrung

safe·ty 1. Sicherheit *f*; **2.** Sicherheits...

safety belt → **seat belt**

safety is·land Verkehrsinsel *f*

safety lock Sicherheitsschloss *n*

safety mea·sure Sicherheitsmaßnahme *f*

safety pin Sicherheitsnadel *f*

safety ra·zor Rasierapparat *m*

sag sich senken, absacken; durchhängen; (herab)hängen (*shoulders*); *fig* sinken (*morale*); nachlassen (*interest etc*)

sa·ga·cious scharfsinnig

sa·ga·ci·ty Scharfsinn *m*

sage BOT Salbei *m, f*

Sa·git·tar·i·us ASTR Schütze *m*; **he (she) is (a) Sagittarius** er (sie) ist (ein) Schütze

sail 1. Segel *n*; Segelfahrt *f*; (*Windmüh-*

len)Flügel *m*; **set sail** auslaufen (**for** nach); **go for a sail** segeln gehen; **2.** *v/i* MAR segeln, fahren; auslaufen (**for** nach); gleiten, schweben; **go sailing** segeln gehen; *v/t* MAR befahren; *Schiff* steuern, *Boot* segeln

sail·board Surfbrett *n*

sail·boat Segelboot *n*

sail·ing Segeln *n*; Segelsport *m*; **when is the next sailing to …?** wann fährt das nächste Schiff nach …?

sailing boat *Br* Segelboot *n*

sailing ship Segelschiff *n*

sail·or Seemann *m*, Matrose *m*; **be a good (bad) sailor** (nicht) seefest sein

sail·plane Segelflugzeug *n*

saint Heilige *m*, *f*

saint·ly heilig, fromm

sake: **for the sake of …** um … (*gen*) willen; **for my sake** meinetwegen; **for God's sake** F um Gottes willen

sal·a·ble verkäuflich

sal·ad Salat *m*

salad dress·ing Dressing *n*, Salatsoße *f*

sal·a·ried: **salaried employee** Angestellte *m*, *f*, Gehaltsempfänger(in)

sal·a·ry Gehalt *n*

sale Verkauf *m*; Absatz *m*, Umsatz *m*; (Saison)Schlussverkauf *m*; Auktion *f*, Versteigerung *f*; **for sale** zu verkaufen; **not for sale** unverkäuflich; **be on sale** verkauft werden, erhältlich sein

sale·a·ble → **salable**

sales·clerk (Laden)Verkäufer(in)

sales·girl (Laden)Verkäuferin *f*

sales·man Verkäufer *m*; (Handels-) Vertreter *m*

sales rep·re·sen·ta·tive Handlungsreisende *m*, *f*; (Handels)Vertreter(in)

sales slip ECON Quittung *f*

sales tax ECON Umsatzsteuer *f*

sales·wom·an Verkäuferin *f*; (Handels)-Vertreterin *f*

sa·line salzig, Salz…

sa·li·va Speichel *m*

sal·low gelblich

salm·on ZO Lachs *m*

sal·on (*Schönheits- etc*)Salon *m*

sa·loon *Br* MOT Limousine *f*; HIST Saloon *m*; MAR Salon *m*

sa·loon car *Br* MOT Limousine *f*

salt 1. Salz *n*; **2.** salzen; (ein)pökeln, einsalzen (*a.* **salt down**); *Straße etc* (mit Salz) streuen; **3.** Salz…; gepökelt; salzig, gesalzen

salt·cel·lar *Br* Salzstreuer *m*

salt·pe·ter, *esp Br* **salt·pe·tre** CHEM Salpeter *m*

salt shak·er Salzstreuer *m*

salt wa·ter Salzwasser *n*

salt·y salzig

sal·u·ta·tion Gruß *m*, Begrüßung *f*; Anrede *f*

sa·lute 1. MIL salutieren; (be-)grüßen; **2.** Gruß *m*; MIL Ehrenbezeugung *f*; Salut *m*

sal·vage 1. Bergung *f*; Bergungsgut *n*; **2.** bergen (**from** aus); retten (*a. fig*)

sal·va·tion Rettung *f*; REL Erlösung *f*; (Seelen)Heil *n*

Sal·va·tion Ar·my Heilsarmee *f*

salve (Heil)Salbe *f*

same: **the same** derselbe, dieselbe, dasselbe; **all the same** trotzdem; **it is all the same to me** es ist mir ganz egal

sam·ple 1. Muster *n*, Probe *f*; **2.** kosten, probieren

san·a·to·ri·um Sanatorium *n*

sanc·ti·fy heiligen

sanc·tion 1. Billigung *f*, Zustimmung *f*; *mst pl* Sanktionen *pl*; **2.** billigen, sanktionieren

sanc·ti·ty Heiligkeit *f*

sanc·tu·a·ry Zuflucht *f*, Asyl *n*; ZO Schutzgebiet *n*

sand 1. Sand *m*; *pl* Sandfläche *f*; **2.** *Straße etc* mit Sand (be)streuen; TECH schmirgeln

san·dal Sandale *f*

sand·bag Sandsack *m*

sand·bank GEOGR Sandbank *f*

sand·box Sandkasten *m*

sand·cas·tle Sandburg *f*

sand·man Sandmännchen *n*

sand·pa·per Sand-, Schmirgelpapier *n*

sand·pip·er ZO Strandläufer *m*

sand·pit *Br* Sandkasten *m*; Sandgrube *f*

sand·stone GEOL Sandstein *m*

sand·storm Sandsturm *m*

sand·wich 1. Sandwich *n*; **2.** **be sandwiched between** eingekeilt sein zwischen (*dat*); **sandwich s.th. in between** *fig* et. einschieben zwischen (*acc or dat*)

sand·y sandig; rotblond

sane geistig gesund; JUR zurechnungsfähig; vernünftig

san·i·tar·i·um → **sanatorium**

san·i·ta·ry hygienisch; Gesundheits…

sanitary nap·kin, *Br* **sanitary tow·el** (Damen)Binde *f*

san·i·ta·tion sanitäre Einrichtungen *pl*; Kanalisation *f*

san·i·ty geistige Gesundheit; JUR Zurechnungsfähigkeit *f*

San·ta Claus der Weihnachtsmann, der Nikolaus

sap[1] BOT Saft *m*

sap[2] schwächen

sap·phire Saphir *m*

S

sar·casm Sarkasmus *m*
sar·cas·tic sarkastisch
sar·dine ZO Sardine *f*
sash[1] Schärpe *f*
sash[2] Fensterrahmen *m*
sash win·dow Schiebefenster *n*
sas·sy frech
Sat ABBR *of* **Saturday** Sa., Samstag *m*, Sonnabend *m*
Sa·tan der Satan
satch·el (Schul)Ranzen *m*; Schultasche *f*
sat·ed *fig* übersättigt
sat·el·lite 1. Satellit *m*; **by** *or* **via satellite** über Satellit; **2.** Satelliten...; **satellite dish** F Satellitenschüssel *f*
sat·in Satin *m*
sat·ire Satire *f*
sat·ir·ic, sat·ir·i·cal satirisch
sat·i·rist Satiriker(in)
sat·ir·ize verspotten
sat·is·fac·tion Befriedigung *f*; Genugtuung *f*, Zufriedenheit *f*
sat·is·fac·to·ry befriedigend, zufriedenstellend
sat·is·fy befriedigen, zufrieden stellen; überzeugen; **be satisfied that** davon überzeugt sein, dass
sat·u·rate (durch)tränken (**with** mit); CHEM sättigen (*a. fig*)
Sat·ur·day Sonnabend *m*, Samstag *m*; **on Saturday** (am) Sonnabend *or* Samstag; **on Saturdays** sonnabends, samstags
sauce Soße *f*
sauce·pan Kochtopf *m*
sau·cer Untertasse *f*
sauc·y *Br* frech
saun·ter bummeln, schlendern
saus·age Wurst *f*; *a.* **small sausage** Würstchen *n*
sav·age 1. wild; unzivilisiert; **2.** Wilde *m, f*
sav·ag·e·ry Wildheit *f*; Rohheit *f*, Grausamkeit *f*
save 1. retten (**from** vor *dat*); *Geld, Zeit etc* (ein)sparen; *et.* aufheben, aufsparen (**for** für); *j-m et.* ersparen; EDP (ab)speichern, sichern; SPORT *Schuss* halten, parieren, *Tor* verhindern; **2.** SPORT Parade *f*
sav·er Retter(in); ECON Sparer(in)
sav·ings ECON Ersparnisse *pl*
savings ac·count Sparkonto *n*
savings bank Sparkasse *f*
savings de·pos·it Spareinlage *f*
sa·vio(u)r Retter(in); **the Savio(u)r** REL der Erlöser, der Heiland
sa·vo(u)r mit Genuss essen *or* trinken; **sa·vo(u)r of** *fig* e-n Beigeschmack haben von
sa·vo(u)r·y schmackhaft

saw 1. Säge *f*; **2.** sägen
saw·dust Sägemehl *n*, Sägespäne *pl*
saw·mill Sägewerk *n*
Sax·on 1. (Angel)Sachse *m*, (Angel-)Sächsin *f*; **2.** (angel)sächsisch
say 1. sagen; aufsagen; *Gebet* sprechen, *Vaterunser* beten; **say grace** das Tischgebet sprechen; **what does your watch say?** wie spät ist es auf deiner Uhr?; **he is said to be ...** er soll ... sein; **it says** es lautet (*letter etc*); **it says here** hier heißt es; **it goes without saying** es versteht sich von selbst; **no sooner said than done** gesagt, getan; **that is to say** das heißt; **(and) that's saying s.th.** (und) das will was heißen; **you said it** du sagst es; **you can say that again!** das kannst du laut sagen!; **you don't say (so)!** was du nicht sagst!; **I say** sag(en Sie) mal!; ich muss schon sagen!; **I can't say** das kann ich nicht sagen; **2.** Mitspracherecht *n* (**in** bei); **have one's say** s-e Meinung äußern, zu Wort kommen; **he always has to have his say** er muss immer mitreden
say·ing Sprichwort *n*, Redensart *f*; **as the saying goes** wie man so (schön) sagt
scab MED, BOT Schorf *m*; *contp* Streikbrecher(in)
scaf·fold (Bau)Gerüst *n*; Schafott *n*
scaf·fold·ing (Bau)Gerüst *n*
scald 1. sich *die Zunge etc* verbrühen; *Milch* abkochen; **scalding hot** kochend heiß; **2.** MED Verbrühung *f*
scale[1] **1.** Skala *f* (*a. fig*), Grad- *or* Maßeinteilung *f*; MATH, TECH Maßstab *m* (*a. fig*); Waage *f*; MUS Skala *f*, Tonleiter *f*; *fig* Ausmaß *n*, Umfang *m*; **2.** erklettern; **scale down** *fig* verringern; **scale up** *fig* erhöhen
scale[2] Waagschale *f*; (**a pair of**) **scales** (e-e) Waage
scale[3] **1.** ZO Schuppe *f*; TECH Kesselstein *m*; **the scales fell from my eyes** es fiel mir wie Schuppen von den Augen; **2.** *Fisch* (ab)schuppen
scal·lop ZO Kammmuschel *f*
scalp 1. Kopfhaut *f*; Skalp *m*; **2.** skalpieren
scal·y ZO schuppig (*a. fig*)
scamp F Schlingel *m*, (kleiner) Strolch
scam·per trippeln; huschen
scan 1. *et.* absuchen (**for** nach); *Zeitung etc* überfliegen; EDP, *radar*, TV abtasten, scannen; **2.** MED *etc* Scanning *n*
scan·dal Skandal *m*; Klatsch *m*
scan·dal·ize: be scandalized at s.th. über et. empört *or* entrüstet sein
scan·dal·ous skandalös; **be scandalous**

a. ein Skandal sein (*that* dass)
Scan·di·na·vi·a Skandinavien *n*
Scan·di·na·vi·an 1. skandinavisch; **2.** Skandinavier(in)
scan·ner TECH Scanner *m*
scant dürftig, gering
scant·y dürftig, kärglich, knapp
scape·goat Sündenbock *m*
scar MED **1.** Narbe *f* (*a. fig*); **2.** e-e Narbe *or* Narben hinterlassen auf (*dat*) *or fig* bei *j-m*; ***scar over*** vernarben
scarce knapp (*food etc*); selten; ***be scarce*** Mangelware sein (*a. fig*)
scarce·ly kaum
scar·ci·ty Mangel *m*, Knappheit *f* (***of*** an *dat*)
scare 1. erschrecken; ***be scared*** Angst haben (***of*** vor *dat*); ***scare away, scare off*** verjagen, -scheuchen; **2.** Schreck(en) *m*; Panik *f*
scare·crow Vogelscheuche *f* (*a. fig*)
scarf Schal *m*; Hals-, Kopf-, Schultertuch *n*
scar·let scharlachrot
scarlet fe·ver MED Scharlach *m*
scarred narbig
scath·ing bissig (*remark etc*); vernichtend (*criticism etc*)
scat·ter (sich) zerstreuen (*crowd*); ausstreuen, verstreuen; auseinanderstieben (*birds etc*)
scat·ter·brained F schusselig, schusslig
scat·tered verstreut; vereinzelt
scav·enge: *scavenge on* ZO leben von; ***scavenge for*** suchen (nach)
scene Szene *f*; Schauplatz *m*; *pl* THEA Kulissen *pl*
sce·ne·ry Landschaft *f*, Gegend *f*; THEA Bühnenbild *n*, Kulissen *pl*
scent 1. Duft *m*, Geruch *m*; *esp Br* Parfüm *n*; HUNT Witterung *f*; Fährte *f*, Spur *f* (*a. fig*); **2.** wittern; *esp Br* parfümieren
scent·less geruchlos
scep·ter, *Br* **scep·tre** Zepter *n*
scep·tic, scep·ti·cal *Br* → **skeptic** *etc*
sched·ule 1. Aufstellung *f*, Verzeichnis *n*; (*Arbeits-, Stunden-, Zeit- etc*)Plan *m*; Fahr-, Flugplan *m*; ***ahead of schedule*** dem Zeitplan voraus, früher als vorgesehen; ***be behind schedule*** Verspätung haben; im Verzug *or* Rückstand sein; ***on schedule*** (fahr-) planmäßig, pünktlich; **2.** ***the meeting is scheduled for Monday*** die Sitzung ist für Montag angesetzt; ***it is scheduled to take place tomorrow*** es soll morgen stattfinden
sched·uled de·par·ture (fahr)planmäßige Abfahrt
scheduled flight Linienflug *m*

scheme 1. *esp Br* Programm *n*, Projekt *n*; Schema *n*, System *n*; Intrige *f*, Machenschaft *f*; **2.** intrigieren
schmaltz·y F schnulzig
schnit·zel GASTR Wiener Schnitzel *n*
schol·ar Gelehrte *m*, *f*; UNIV Stipendiat(in)
schol·ar·ly gelehrt
schol·ar·ship Gelehrsamkeit *f*; UNIV Stipendium *n*
school[1] **1.** Schule *f* (*a. fig*); UNIV Fakultät *f*; Hochschule *f*; ***at school*** auf *or* in der Schule; ***go to school*** in die *or* zur Schule gehen; **2.** *j-n* schulen, unterrichten; *Tier* dressieren
school[2] ZO Schule *f*, Schwarm *m*
school·bag Schultasche *f*
school·boy Schüler *m*
school·child Schulkind *n*
school·fel·low → **schoolmate**
school·girl Schülerin *f*
school·ing (Schul)Ausbildung *f*
school·mate Mitschüler(in), Schulkamerad(in)
school·teach·er (Schul)Lehrer(in)
school·yard Schulhof *m*
schoo·ner MAR Schoner *m*
sci·ence Wissenschaft *f*; *a.* ***natural science*** Naturwissenschaft(en *pl*) *f*
science fic·tion (ABBR **SF**) Sciencefiction *f*
sci·en·tif·ic (natur)wissenschaftlich; exakt, systematisch
sci·en·tist (Natur)Wissenschaftler(in)
sci-fi F Sciencefiction *f*
scis·sors: (***a pair of scissors*** e-e) Schere *f*
scoff 1. spotten (***at*** über *acc*); **2.** spöttische Bemerkung
scold schimpfen (mit)
scoop 1. Schöpfkelle *f*; (*Mehl- etc -*) Schaufel *f*; (*Eis- etc*)Portionierer *m*; Kugel *f* (*icecream*); *newspaper, radio,* TV Exklusivmeldung *f*, F Knüller *m*; **2.** schöpfen, schaufeln; ***scoop up*** aufheben, hochheben
scoot·er (Kinder)Roller *m*; (*Motor-*) Roller *m*
scope Bereich *m*; Spielraum *m*
scorch *v/t* ansengen, versengen, verbrennen; ausdörren; *v/i Br* MOT F rasen
score 1. SPORT (Spiel)Stand *m*, (-)Ergebnis *n*; MUS Partitur *f*; Musik *f*; 20 (Stück); *a.* ***score mark*** Kerbe *f*, Rille *f*; ***what is the score?*** wie steht es *or* das Spiel?; ***the score stood at*** *or* ***was 3-2*** das Spiel stand 3:2; ***keep (the) score*** anschreiben; ***scores of*** e-e Menge; ***four score and ten*** neunzig; ***on that score*** deshalb, in dieser Hinsicht; ***have a score to settle***

S

with s.o. e-e alte Rechnung mit j-m zu begleichen haben; **2.** v/t SPORT *Punkte, Treffer* erzielen, *Tor a.* schießen; *Erfolg, Sieg* erringen; MUS instrumentieren; die Musik schreiben zu *or* für; einkerben; v/i SPORT e-n Treffer *etc* erzielen, ein Tor schießen; erfolgreich sein

score·board SPORT Anzeigetafel *f*

scor·er SPORT Torschütze *m*, Torschützin *f*; Anschreiber(in)

scorn Verachtung *f*

scorn·ful verächtlich

Scor·pi·o ASTR Skorpion *m*; **he (she) is (a) Scorpio** er (sie) ist (ein) Skorpion

Scot Schotte *m*, Schottin *f*

Scotch 1. schottisch; **2.** Scotch *m*

scot-free: F **get off scot-free** ungeschoren davonkommen

Scot·land Schottland *n*

Scots schottisch

Scotsman Schotte *m*

Scots·wom·an Schottin *f*

Scot·tish schottisch

scoun·drel Schurke *m*

scour¹ scheuern, schrubben

scour² *Gegend* absuchen, durchkämmen **(for** nach)

scourge 1. Geißel *f* (*a. fig*); **2.** geißeln, *fig a.* heimsuchen

scout 1. *esp* MIL Kundschafter *m*; *Br* motorisierter Pannenhelfer; *a.* **boy scout** Pfadfinder *m*; *a.* **girl scout** Pfadfinderin *f*; *a.* **talent scout** Talentsucher(in); **2.** *scout about, scout around* sich umsehen **(for** nach); *a.* **scout out** MIL auskundschaften

scowl 1. finsteres Gesicht; **2.** finster blicken; **scowl at s.o.** j-n böse *or* finster anschauen

scram·ble 1. klettern; sich drängen **(for** zu); **2.** Kletterei *f*; Drängelei *f*

scram·bled eggs Rührei(er *pl*) *n*

scrap¹ 1. Stückchen *n*, Fetzen *m*; Altmaterial *n*; Schrott *m*; Abfall *m*, Speisereste *pl*; **2.** verschrotten; ausrangieren; *Plan etc* aufgeben, fallen lassen

scrap² F **1.** Streiterei *f*; Balgerei *f*; **2.** sich streiten; sich balgen

scrap·book Sammelalbum *n*

scrape 1. (ab)kratzen, (ab)schaben; sich *die Knie etc* aufschürfen; *Wagen etc* ankratzen; scheuern **(against** an *dat*); (entlang)streifen; scharren; **2.** Kratzen *n*; Kratzer *m*, Schramme *f*; *fig* Klemme *f*

scrap heap Schrotthaufen *m*

scrap met·al Altmetall *n*, Schrott *m*

scrap pa·per *esp Br* Schmierpapier *n*

scrap val·ue Schrottwert *m*

scrap·yard Schrottplatz *m*

scratch 1. (zer)kratzen; abkratzen; *s-n Namen etc* einkratzen; (sich) kratzen; scharren; **2.** Kratzer *m*, Schramme *f*; Gekratze *n*; Kratzen *n*; **from scratch** F ganz von vorn; **3.** (bunt) zusammengewürfelt

scratch·pad Notiz-, Schmierblock *m*

scratch pa·per Schmierpapier *n*

scrawl 1. kritzeln; **2.** Gekritzel *n*

scraw·ny dürr

scream 1. schreien **(with** vor *dat*); *a.* **scream out** schreien; **scream with laughter** vor Lachen brüllen; **2.** Schrei *m*; **screams of laughter** brüllendes Gelächter; **be a scream** F zum Schreien (komisch) sein

screech 1. kreischen (*a. fig*), (gellend) schreien; **2.** Kreischen *n*; (gellender) Schrei

screen 1. Wand-, Ofen-, Schutzschirm *m*; *film*: Leinwand *f*; *radar*, TV, EDP Bildschirm *m*; Fliegenfenster *n*, -gitter *n*; *fig* Tarnung *f*; **2.** abschirmen; *film* zeigen, *Fernsehprogramm a.* senden; *fig* j-n decken; *fig* j-n überprüfen; **screen off** abtrennen

screen·play Drehbuch *n*

screen sav·er EDP Bildschirmschoner *m*

screw 1. TECH Schraube *f*; **he has a screw loose** F bei ihm ist e-e Schraube locker; **2.** (an)schrauben **(to** an *acc*); V bumsen, vögeln; **screw up** *Gesicht* verziehen; *Augen* zusammenkneifen; **screw up one's courage** sich ein Herz fassen

screw·ball F Spinner(in)

screw·driv·er Schraubenzieher *m*

screw top Schraubverschluss *m*

scrib·ble 1. (hin)kritzeln; **2.** Gekritzel *n*

scrimp: **scrimp and save** jeden Pfennig zweimal umdrehen

script Manuskript *n*; film, TV Drehbuch *n*, Skript *n*; THEA Text *m*, Textbuch *n*; Schrift(zeichen *pl*) *f*; *Br* UNIV (schriftliche) Prüfungsarbeit

Scrip·ture *a.* **the Scriptures** REL die Heilige Schrift

scroll 1. Schriftrolle *f*; **2.** **scroll down (up)** EDP zurückrollen (vorrollen)

scro·tum ANAT Hodensack *m*

scrub¹ 1. schrubben, scheuern; **2.** Schrubben *n*, Scheuern *n*

scrub² Gebüsch *n*, Gestrüpp *n*

scru·ple 1. Skrupel *m*, Zweifel *m*, Bedenken *pl*; **2.** Bedenken haben

scru·pu·lous gewissenhaft

scru·ti·nize genau prüfen; mustern

scru·ti·ny genaue Prüfung; prüfender Blick

scu·ba div·ing (Sport)Tauchen *n*

scuf·fle 1. Handgemenge *n*, Rauferei *f*; **2.**

S

sich raufen
scull 1. Skull *n*; Skullboot *n*; **2.** rudern, skullen
sculp·tor Bildhauer *m*
sculp·ture 1. Bildhauerei *f*; Skulptur *f*, Plastik *f*; **2.** hauen, meißeln, formen
scum Schaum *m*; *fig* Abschaum *m*; **the scum of the earth** *fig* der Abschaum der Menschheit
scurf (Kopf)Schuppen *pl*
scur·ri·lous beleidigend; verleumderisch
scur·ry huschen; trippeln
scur·vy MED Skorbut *m*
scut·tle: *scuttle away, scuttle off* davonhuschen
scythe Sense *f*
sea Meer *n* (*a. fig*), See *f*; *at sea* auf See; *be all or completely at sea fig* F völlig ratlos sein; *by sea* auf dem Seeweg; *by the sea* am Meer
sea·food GASTR Meeresfrüchte *pl*
sea·gull ZO Seemöwe *f*
seal¹ ZO Robbe *f*, Seehund *m*
seal² 1. Siegel *n*; TECH Plombe *f*; TECH Dichtung *f*; **2.** (ver)siegeln; TECH plombieren; abdichten; *fig* besiegeln; *sealed envelope* verschlossener Briefumschlag; *seal off Gegend etc* abriegeln
sea lev·el: *above (below) sea level* über (unter) dem Meeresspiegel
seal·ing wax Siegellack *m*
seam Naht *f*; Fuge *f*; GEOL Flöz *n*
sea·man Seemann *m*
seam·stress Näherin *f*
sea·plane Wasserflugzeug *n*
sea·port Seehafen *m*; Hafenstadt *f*
sea pow·er Seemacht *f*
search 1. *v/i* suchen (*for* nach); *search through* durchsuchen; *v/t j-n, et.* durchsuchen (*for* nach); *search me!* F keine Ahnung!; **2.** Suche *f* (*for* nach); Fahndung *f* (*for* nach); Durchsuchung *f*; *in search of* auf der Suche nach
search·ing prüfend (*look*); eingehend (*examination*)
search·light (Such)Scheinwerfer *m*
search par·ty Suchmannschaft *f*
search war·rant JUR Haussuchungs-, Durchsuchungsbefehl *m*
sea·shore Meeresküste *f*
sea·sick seekrank
sea·side: *at or by the seaside* am Meer; *go to the seaside* ans Meer fahren
sea·side re·sort Seebad *n*
sea·son¹ Jahreszeit *f*; Saison *f*, THEA *etc a.* Spielzeit *f*, (*Jagd-, Urlaubs- etc*)Zeit *f*; *in (out of) season* in (außerhalb) der (Hoch)Saison; *cherries are now in season* jetzt ist Kirschenzeit; *Season's*

Greetings! Frohe Weihnachten!; *with the compliments of the season* mit den besten Wünschen zum Fest
sea·son² *Speise* würzen (*with* mit); *Holz* ablagern
sea·son·al saisonbedingt, Saison...
sea·son·ing GASTR Gewürz *n*
sea·son tick·et RAIL *etc* Dauer-, Zeitkarte *f*; THEA Abonnement *n*
seat 1. Sitz(gelegenheit *f*) *m*; (Sitz)Platz *m*; Sitz(fläche *f*) *m*; Hosenboden *m*; Hinterteil *n*; (*Geschäfts-, Regierungs- etc*)-Sitz *m*, PARL Sitz *m*; *take a seat* Platz nehmen; *take one's seat* s-n Platz einnehmen; **2.** *j-n* setzen; Sitzplätze bieten für; *be seated* sitzen; *please be seated* bitte nehmen Sie Platz; *remain seated* sitzen bleiben
seat belt AVIAT, MOT Sicherheitsgurt *m*; *fasten one's seat belt* sich anschnallen
sea ur·chin ZO Seeigel *m*
sea·ward(s) seewärts
sea·weed BOT (See)Tang *m*
sea·wor·thy seetüchtig
sec F Augenblick *m*, Sekunde *f*; *just a sec* Augenblick(, bitte)!
se·cede sich abspalten (*from* von)
se·ces·sion Abspaltung *f*, Sezession *f* (*from* von)
se·clud·ed abgelegen, abgeschieden (*place*); zurückgezogen (*life*)
se·clu·sion Abgeschiedenheit *f*; Zurückgezogenheit *f*
sec·ond¹ 1. *adj* zweite(r, -s); *every second day* jeden zweiten Tag, alle zwei Tage; *second to none* unerreicht, unübertroffen; *but on second thought* (*Br thoughts*) aber wenn ich es mir so überlege; **2.** *adv* als Zweite(r, -s); **3.** *der, die, das* Zweite; MOT zweiter Gang; Sekundant *m*; *pl* ECON Waren *pl* zweiter Wahl; **4.** *Antrag etc* unterstützen
sec·ond² Sekunde *f*; *fig* Augenblick *m*, Sekunde *f*; *just a second* Augenblick(, bitte)!
sec·ond·a·ry sekundär, zweitrangig; PED höher
sec·ond-best zweitbeste(r, -s)
sec·ond class RAIL *etc* zweiter Klasse
sec·ond-class zweitklassig
sec·ond floor erster (*Br* zweiter) Stock
sec·ond hand Sekundenzeiger *m*
sec·ond-hand aus zweiter Hand; gebraucht; antiquarisch
sec·ond·ly zweitens
sec·ond-rate zweitklassig
se·cre·cy Verschwiegenheit *f*; Geheimhaltung *f*
se·cret 1. geheim, Geheim...; heimlich;

S

verschwiegen; **2.** Geheimnis *n*; *in secret* heimlich, im Geheimen; *keep s.th. a secret* et. geheim halten (*from* vor *dat*); *can you keep a secret?* kannst du schweigen?

se·cret a·gent Geheimagent(in)

sec·re·ta·ry Sekretär(in); POL Minister(in)

Sec·re·ta·ry of State POL Außenminister(in); *Br* Minister(in)

se·crete MED absondern

se·cre·tion MED Sekret *n*; Absonderung *f*

se·cre·tive verschlossen

se·cret·ly heimlich

se·cret ser·vice Geheimdienst *m*

sec·tion Teil *m*; Abschnitt *m*; JUR Paragraf *m*; Abteilung *f*; MATH, TECH Schnitt *m*

sec·tor Sektor *m*, Bereich *m*

sec·u·lar weltlich

se·cure 1. sicher (*against, from* vor *dat*); **2.** *Tür etc* fest verschließen; *et.* sichern (*against, from* vor *dat*)

se·cu·ri·ty Sicherheit *f*; *pl* ECON Wertpapiere *pl*

security check Sicherheitskontrolle *f*

security mea·sure Sicherheitsmaßnahme *f*

security risk Sicherheitsrisiko *n*

se·dan MOT Limousine *f*

se·date ruhig, gelassen

sed·a·tive *mst* MED **1.** beruhigend; **2.** Beruhigungsmittel *n*

sed·i·ment (Boden)Satz *m*

se·duce verführen

se·duc·er Verführer(in)

se·duc·tion Verführung *f*

se·duc·tive verführerisch

see[1] *v/i* sehen; nachsehen; *I see!* (ich) verstehe!, ach so!; *you see* weißt du; *let me see* warte mal, lass mich überlegen; *we'll see* mal sehen; *v/t* sehen; besuchen; *j-n* aufsuchen, *j-n* konsultieren; *see s.o. home* j-n nach Hause bringen *or* begleiten; *see you!* bis dann!, auf bald!; *see about* sehen nach, sich kümmern um; *see off j-n* verabschieden (*at* am *Bahnhof etc*); *see out j-n* hinausbringen, hinausbegleiten; *see through j-n, et.* durchschauen; *j-m* hinweghelfen über (*acc*); *see to it that* dafür sorgen, dass

see[2] REL Bistum *n*, Diözese *f*; *Holy See* der Heilige Stuhl

seed 1. BOT Same(n) *m*; AGR Saat *f*, Saatgut *n*; (*Apfel- etc*)Kern *m*; SPORT gesetzter Spieler, gesetzte Spielerin; *go or run to seed* BOT schießen; *go to seed* F herunterkommen, verkommen; **2.** *v/t* besäen; entkernen; SPORT *Spieler* setzen; *v/i* BOT in Samen schießen

seedless BOT kernlos

seed·y F heruntergekommen

seek *Schutz, Wahrheit etc* suchen

seem scheinen

seem·ing scheinbar

seep sickern

see·saw Wippe *f*, Wippschaukel *f*

seethe schäumen (*a. fig*); *fig* kochen

see-through durchsichtig

seg·ment Teil *m, n*; Stück *n*; Abschnitt *m*; Segment *n*

seg·re·gate trennen

seg·re·ga·tion Rassentrennung *f*

seize *j-n, et.* packen, ergreifen; *Macht etc* an sich reißen; *et.* beschlagnahmen; *et.* pfänden

sei·zure Beschlagnahme *f*; Pfändung *f*; MED Anfall *m*

sel·dom *adv* selten

se·lect 1. (aus)wählen; **2.** ausgewählt; exklusiv

se·lec·tion (Aus)Wahl *f*; ECON Auswahl *f* (*of* an *dat*)

self Ich *n*, Selbst *n*

self-as·sured selbstbewusst, -sicher

self-cen·tered, *Br* **self-cen·tred** egozentrisch

self-col·o(u)red einfarbig

self-con·fi·dence Selbstbewusstsein *n*, Selbstvertrauen *n*

self-con·fi·dent selbstbewusst

self-con·scious befangen, gehemmt, unsicher

self-con·tained (in sich) abgeschlossen; *fig* verschlossen; *self-contained flat Br* abgeschlossene Wohnung

self-con·trol Selbstbeherrschung *f*

self-crit·i·cal selbstkritisch

self-de·fence *Br*, **self-de·fense** Selbstverteidigung *f*; *in self-defence* in *or* aus Notwehr

self-de·ter·mi·na·tion POL Selbstbestimmung *f*

self-em·ployed selbstständig

self-es·teem Selbstachtung *f*

self-ev·i·dent selbstverständlich; offensichtlich

self-gov·ern·ment POL Selbstverwaltung *f*

self-help Selbsthilfe *f*

self-help group Selbsthilfegruppe *f*

self-im·por·tant überheblich

self-in·dul·gent nachgiebig gegen sich selbst; zügellos

self-in·terest Eigennutz *m*

self·ish selbstsüchtig, egoistisch

self-knowl·edge Selbsterkenntnis *f*

self-pit·y Selbstmitleid *n*

self-por·trait Selbstporträt *n*

self-pos·sessed selbstbeherrscht

self-re·li·ant selbstständig
self-re·spect Selbstachtung *f*
self-right·eous selbstgerecht
self-sat·is·fied selbstzufrieden
self-serv·ice 1. mit Selbstbedienung, Selbstbedienungs…; **2.** Selbstbedienung *f*
self-stud·y Selbststudium *n*
self-suf·fi·cient ECON autark
self-sup·port·ing finanziell unabhängig
self-willed eigensinnig, eigenwillig
sell *v/t* verkaufen; *v/i* verkauft werden (*at, for* für); sich *gut etc* verkaufen (lassen), gehen; **sell by …** mindestens haltbar bis …; **sell off** (*esp* billig) abstoßen; **sell out** ausverkaufen; **be sold out** ausverkauft sein; **sell up** *esp Br* sein *Geschäft etc* verkaufen
sell-by date Mindesthaltbarkeitsdatum *n*
sell·er Verkäufer(in); **good seller** ECON gut gehender Artikel
sem·blance Anschein *m* (*of* von)
se·men MED Samen(flüssigkeit *f*) *m*, Sperma *n*
se·mes·ter UNIV Semester *n*
sem·i… halb…, Halb…
sem·i·cir·cle Halbkreis *m*
sem·i·co·lon LING Semikolon *n*, Strichpunkt *m*
sem·i·con·duc·tor ELECTR Halbleiter *m*
sem·i·de·tached (house) *Br* Doppelhaushälfte *f*
sem·i·fi·nals SPORT Semi-, Halbfinale *n*
sem·i·nar·y Priesterseminar *n*
sem·i·pre·cious: semi-precious stone Halbedelstein *m*
sem·i-skilled angelernt
sem·o·li·na Grieß *m*
sen·ate POL Senat *m*
sen·a·tor POL Senator *m*
send *et., a. Grüße, Hilfe etc* senden, schicken (*to dat or* an *acc*); *Ware etc* versenden, verschicken (*to* an *acc*); *j-n* schicken (*to* ins *Bett etc*); *with adj or pp*: machen: **send s.o. mad** *j-n* wahnsinnig machen; **send word to s.o.** *j-m* Nachricht geben; **send away** fort-, wegschicken; *Brief etc* absenden, abschicken; **send down** *Preise etc* fallen lassen; **send for** nach *j-m* schicken, *j-n* kommen lassen; *et.* kommen lassen, *et.* anfordern; **send in** einsenden, einschicken, einreichen; **send off** fort-, wegschicken; *Brief etc* absenden, abschicken; SPORT *j-n* vom Platz stellen; **send on** *Brief etc* nachsenden, nachschicken (*to* an *acc*); *Gepäck etc* vorausschicken; **send out** hinausschicken; *Einladungen etc* verschicken; **send up** *Preise etc* steigen lassen

send·er Absender(in)
se·nile senil
se·nil·i·ty Senilität *f*
se·ni·or 1. senior; älter (*to* als); dienstälter; rangälter; Ober…; **2.** Ältere *m, f*; UNIV Student(in) im letzten Jahr; **he is my senior by a year** er ist ein Jahr älter als ich
senior cit·i·zens ältere Mitbürger *pl*, Senioren *pl*
se·ni·or·i·ty (höheres) Alter; (höheres) Dienstalter; (höherer) Rang
se·ni·or part·ner ECON Seniorpartner *m*
sen·sa·tion Empfindung *f*; Gefühl *n*; Sensation *f*
sen·sa·tion·al F großartig, fantastisch; sensationell, Sensations…
sense 1. Sinn *m*; Verstand *m*; Vernunft *f*; Gefühl *n*; Bedeutung *f*; **bring s.o. to his senses** j-n zur Besinnung *or* Vernunft bringen; **come to one's senses** zur Besinnung *or* Vernunft kommen; **in a sense** in gewisser Hinsicht; **make sense** e-n Sinn ergeben; vernünftig sein; **sense of duty** Pflichtgefühl *n*; **sense of security** Gefühl *n* der Sicherheit; **2.** fühlen, spüren
sense·less bewusstlos; sinnlos
sen·si·bil·i·ty Empfindlichkeit *f*; *a. pl* Empfindsamkeit *f*, Zartgefühl *n*
sen·si·ble vernünftig; spürbar, merklich; *esp Br* praktisch (*clothes etc*)
sen·si·tive empfindlich; sensibel, empfindsam, feinfühlig
sen·sor TECH Sensor *m*
sen·su·al sinnlich
sen·su·ous sinnlich
sen·tence 1. LING Satz *m*; JUR Strafe *f*, Urteil *n*; **pass or pronounce sentence** das Urteil fällen (*on* über *acc*); **2.** JUR verurteilen (*to* zu)
sen·ti·ment Gefühle *pl*; Sentimentalität *f*; *a. pl* Ansicht *f*, Meinung *f*
sen·ti·men·tal sentimental; gefühlvoll
sen·ti·men·tal·i·ty Sentimentalität *f*
sen·try MIL Wache *f*, (Wach[t])Posten *m*
sep·a·ra·ble trennbar
sep·a·rate 1. (sich) trennen; (auf-, ein-, zer)teilen (*into* in *acc*); **2.** getrennt, separat; einzeln
sep·a·ra·tion Trennung *f*; (Auf-, Ein-, Zer)Teilung *f*
Sept ABBR *of* **September** Sept., September *m*
Sep·tem·ber September *m*
sep·tic MED vereitert, septisch
se·quel Nachfolgeroman *m*, -film *m*, Fortsetzung *f*; *fig* Folge *f*; Nachspiel *n*
se·quence (Aufeinander-, Reihen)Folge

S

f; film, TV Sequenz *f,* Szene *f;* **sequence of tenses** LING Zeitenfolge *f*
ser·e·nade MUS **1.** Serenade *f,* Ständchen *n;* **2.** *j-m* ein Ständchen bringen
se·rene klar; heiter; gelassen
ser·geant MIL Feldwebel *m;* (Polizei-) Wachtmeister *m*
se·ri·al 1. Fortsetzungsroman *m;* (*Rundfunk-, Fernseh*)Serie *f;* **2.** serienmäßig, Serien..., Fortsetzungs...
se·ries Serie *f,* Reihe *f,* Folge *f;* (*Buch*)-Reihe *f;* (*Rundfunk-, Fernseh*)Serie *f,* Sendereihe *f*
se·ri·ous ernst, ernsthaft; ernstlich; schwer (*illness, damage, crime etc*); **be serious** es ernst meinen (**about** mit)
se·ri·ous·ness Ernst *m,* Ernsthaftigkeit *f;* Schwere *f*
ser·mon REL Predigt *f;* F Moral-, Strafpredigt *f*
ser·pen·tine gewunden, kurvenreich
ser·rat·ed zackig, gezackt
se·rum MED Serum *n*
ser·vant Diener(in) (*a. fig*); Dienstmädchen *n;* → **civil servant**
serve 1. *v/t j-m, s-m Land etc* dienen; *Dienstzeit* (*a.* MIL) ableisten, *Amtszeit etc* durchlaufen; *j-n, et.* versorgen (**with** mit); *Essen* servieren; *Alkohol* ausschenken; *j-n* (*im Laden*) bedienen; JUR *Strafe* verbüßen; *e-m Zweck* dienen; *e-n Zweck* erfüllen; JUR *Vorladung etc* zustellen (**on s.o.** j-m); *tennis etc:* aufschlagen; **are you being served?** werden Sie schon bedient?; (*it*) **serves him right** F (das) geschieht ihm ganz recht; *v/i esp* MIL dienen; servieren; dienen (**as, for** als); *tennis etc:* aufschlagen; **XY to serve** *tennis etc:* Aufschlag XY; **serve on a committee** e-m Ausschuss angehören; **2.** *tennis etc:* Aufschlag *m*
serv·er *tennis etc:* Aufschläger(in); GASTR Servierlöffel *m*
ser·vice 1. Dienst *m* (**to** an *dat*); Dienstleistung *f;* (*Post-, Staats-, Telefon- etc*-) Dienst *m;* (*Zug- etc*)Verkehr *m;* ECON Service *m,* Kundendienst *m;* Bedienung *f;* Betrieb *m;* REL Gottesdienst *m;* TECH Wartung *f,* MOT *a.* Inspektion *f;* (*Tee- etc*) Service *n;* JUR Zustellung *f* (*e-r Vorladung*); *tennis etc:* Aufschlag *m;* *pl* MIL Streitkräfte *pl;* **2.** TECH warten
ser·vice·a·ble brauchbar; strapazierfähig
ser·vice ar·e·a MOT (Autobahn)Raststätte *f*
service charge Bedienung *f,* Bedienungszuschlag *m*
service sta·tion Tankstelle *f;* (Reparatur)Werkstatt *f*

ser·vi·ette *esp Br* Serviette *f*
ser·vile sklavisch (*a. fig*); servil, unterwürfig
serv·ing Portion *f*
ser·vi·tude Knechtschaft *f;* Sklaverei *f*
ses·sion Sitzung *f;* Sitzungsperiode *f;* **be in session** JUR, PARL tagen
set 1. *v/t* setzen, stellen, legen; *in e-n Zustand* versetzen; veranlassen (**doing** zu tun); TECH einstellen, *Uhr* stellen (**by** nach), *Wecker* stellen (**for** auf *acc*); *Tisch* decken; *Preis, Termin etc* festsetzen, festlegen; *Rekord* aufstellen; *Edelstein* fassen (**in** in *dat*); *Ring etc* besetzen (**with** mit); *Flüssigkeit* erstarren lassen; *Haar* legen; *Knochen* einrenken, einrichten; MUS vertonen; PRINT absetzen; *Aufgabe, Frage* stellen; **set at ease** beruhigen; **set an example** ein Beispiel geben; **set s.o. free** j-n freilassen; **set going** in Gang setzen; **set s.o. thinking** j-m zu denken geben; **set one's hopes on** s-e Hoffnung setzen auf (*acc*); **set s.o.'s mind at rest** j-n beruhigen; **set great** (**little**) **store by** großen (geringen) Wert legen auf (*acc*); **the novel is set in** der Roman spielt in (*dat*); *v/i* ASTR untergehen; fest werden, erstarren; HUNT vorstehen; **set about doing s.th.** sich daranmachen, et. zu tun; **set about s.o.** F über j-n herfallen; **set aside** beiseitelegen; JUR *Urteil etc* aufheben; **set back** verzögern; *j-n, et.* zurückwerfen (**by two months** um zwei Monate); **set in** einsetzen; **set off** aufbrechen, sich aufmachen; hervorheben, betonen; *et.* auslösen; **set out** arrangieren, herrichten; aufbrechen, sich aufmachen; **set out to do s.th.** sich daranmachen, et. zu tun; **set up** errichten; *Gerät etc* aufbauen; *Firma etc* gründen; *et.* auslösen, verursachen; *j-n* versorgen (**with** mit); sich niederlassen; **set o.s. up as** sich ausgeben für; **2.** *adj* festgesetzt, festgelegt; F bereit, fertig; starr (*smile etc*); **set lunch** *or* **meal** Br Menü *n;* **set phrase** feststehender Ausdruck; **be set on doing s.th.** (fest) entschlossen sein, et. zu tun; **be all set** F startklar sein; **3.** Satz *m;* (*Möbel- etc*)Garnitur *f,* (*Tee- etc*)Service *n;* (*Fernseh-, Rundfunk-*)Apparat *m,* (-)Gerät *n;* THEA Bühnenbild *n; film,* TV Set *n, m; tennis etc:* Satz *m;* (*Personen*)Kreis *m,* Clique *f;* (*Kopf- etc*)Haltung *f;* **have a shampoo and set** sich die Haare waschen und legen lassen
set·back Rückschlag *m* (**to** für)
set·square Br Winkel *m,* Zeichendreieck *n*
set·tee Sofa *n*

set the·o·ry MATH Mengenlehre *f*
set·ting ASTR Untergang *m*; TECH Einstellung *f*; Umgebung *f*; *film etc*: Schauplatz *m*; (*Gold- etc*)Fassung *f*
set·ting lo·tion Haarfestiger *m*
set·tle *v/i* sich niederlassen (*on* auf *acc or dat*), sich setzen (*on* auf *acc*) (*a.* ***settle down***); sich niederlassen (*in* in *dat*); sich legen (*dust*); sich setzen (*coffee etc*); sich senken (*building etc*); sich beruhigen (*person, stomach etc*), sich legen (*a.* ***settle down***); sich einigen; *v/t j-n, Nerven etc* beruhigen; vereinbaren; *Frage etc* klären, entscheiden; *Streit etc* beilegen; *Land* besiedeln; *Leute* ansiedeln; *Rechnung* begleichen, bezahlen; *Konto* ausgleichen; *Schaden* regulieren; *s-e Angelegenheiten* in Ordnung bringen; ***settle o.s.*** sich niederlassen (*on* auf *acc or dat*), sich setzen (*on* auf *acc*); ***that settles it*** damit ist der Fall erledigt; ***that's settled then*** das ist also klar; ***settle back*** sich (gemütlich) zurücklehnen; ***settle down*** → *v/i*; sesshaft werden; ***settle down to*** sich widmen (*dat*); ***settle for*** sich zufriedengeben *or* begnügen mit; ***settle in*** sich einleben *or* eingewöhnen; ***settle on*** sich einigen auf (*acc*); ***settle up*** (be)zahlen; abrechnen (***with*** mit)
set·tled fest (*ideas etc*); geregelt (*life*); beständig (*weather*)
set·tle·ment Vereinbarung *f*; Klärung *f*; Beilegung *f*; Einigung *f*; Siedlung *f*; Besiedlung *f*; Begleichung *f*, Bezahlung *f*; ***reach a settlement*** sich einigen
set·tler Siedler(in)
sev·en 1. sieben; **2.** Sieben *f*
sev·en·teen 1. siebzehn; **2.** Siebzehn *f*
sev·en·teenth siebzehnte(r, -s)
sev·enth 1. siebente(r, -s), siebte(r, -s); **2.** Siebentel *n*, Siebtel *n*
sev·enth·ly siebentens, siebtens
sev·en·ti·eth siebzigste(r, -s)
sev·en·ty 1. siebzig; **2.** Siebzig *f*
sev·er durchtrennen; abtrennen; *Beziehungen* abbrechen; (zer)reißen
sev·er·al mehrere
sev·er·al·ly einzeln, getrennt
se·vere schwer (*injuries, setback etc*); stark (*pain*); hart, streng (*winter*); streng (*person, discipline etc*); scharf (*criticism etc*)
se·ver·i·ty Schwere *f*; Stärke *f*; Härte *f*; Strenge *f*; Schärfe *f*
sew nähen
sew·age Abwasser *n*
sew·age works Kläranlage *f*
sew·er Abwasserkanal *m*
sew·er·age Kanalisation *f*

sew·ing 1. Nähen *n*; Näharbeit *f*; **2.** Näh...
sewing ma·chine Nähmaschine *f*
sex Geschlecht *n*; Sexualität *f*; Sex *m*; Geschlechtsverkehr *m*
sex·ism Sexismus *m*
sex·ist 1. sexistisch; **2.** Sexist(in)
sex·ton Küster *m* (und Totengräber *m*)
sex·u·al sexuell, Sexual..., geschlechtlich, Geschlechts...
sexual har·ass·ment sexuelle Belästigung
sexual in·ter·course Geschlechtsverkehr *m*
sex·u·al·i·ty Sexualität *f*
sex·y F sexy, aufreizend
shab·by schäbig
shack Hütte *f*, Bude *f*; F *contp* Schuppen *m*
shack·les Fesseln *pl*, Ketten *pl* (*both a. fig*)
shade 1. Schatten *m* (*a. fig*); (*Lampen-*) Schirm *m*; Schattierung *f*; Rouleau *n*; *fig* Nuance *f*; ***a shade*** *fig* ein kleines bisschen, e-e Spur; **2.** abschirmen (***from*** gegen); schattieren; ***shade off*** allmählich übergehen (***into*** in *acc*)
shad·ow 1. Schatten *m* (*a. fig*); ***there's not a*** *or* ***the shadow of a doubt about it*** daran besteht nicht der geringste Zweifel; **2.** *j-n* beschatten
shad·ow·y schattig, dunkel; verschwommen, vage, schemenhaft
shad·y schattig; Schatten spendend; F zwielichtig, fragwürdig
shaft (*Pfeil- etc*)Schaft *m*; (*Hammer- etc*) Stiel *m*; TECH Welle *f*; (*Aufzugs-, Bergwerks- etc*)Schacht *m*; (*Sonnen- etc*) Strahl *m*
shag·gy zottig, struppig
shake 1. *v/t* schütteln; rütteln an (*dat*); erschüttern; ***shake hands*** sich die Hand geben *or* schütteln; *v/i* zittern, beben, wackeln (***with*** vor *dat*); ***shake down*** herunterschütteln; durchsuchen, F filzen; *Br* F kampieren; ***shake off*** abschütteln; *Erkältung etc* loswerden; ***shake up*** *Kissen etc* aufschütteln; *Flasche, Flüssigkeit* (durch-) schütteln; *fig* erschüttern; **2.** Schütteln *n*; F Milchshake *m*; ***shake of the head*** Kopfschütteln *n*
shake·down F Erpressung *f*; Durchsuchung *f*, Filzung *f*; *Br* (Not)Lager *n*
shak·en *a.* ***shaken up*** erschüttert
shak·y wack(e)lig; zitt(e)rig
shall *v/aux future*: ich werde, wir werden; *in questions*: soll ich ...?, sollen wir ...?; ***shall we go?*** gehen wir?
shal·low seicht, flach, *fig a.* oberflächlich

S

shal·lows seichte *or* flache Stelle, Untiefe *f*

sham 1. Farce *f*; Heuchelei *f*; **2.** unecht, falsch; vorgetäuscht, geheuchelt; **3.** *v/t Mitgefühl etc* vortäuschen, heucheln; *Krankheit etc* simulieren; *v/i* sich verstellen, heucheln; *he's only shamming* er tut nur so

sham·bles F Schlachtfeld *n*, wüstes Durcheinander, Chaos *n*

shame 1. Scham *f*, Schamgefühl *n*; Schande *f*; *shame!* pfui!; *shame on you!* pfui!; schäm dich!; *put to shame* → **2.** beschämen; Schande machen (*dat*)

shame·faced betreten, verlegen

shame·ful beschämend; schändlich

shame·less schamlos

sham·poo 1. Shampoo *n*, Schampon *n*, Schampun *n*; Haarwäsche *f*; → *set 3*; **2.** *Haare* waschen; *j-m* die Haare waschen; *Teppich etc* schamponieren

shank TECH Schaft *m*; GASTR Hachse *f*

shan·ty[1] Hütte *f*, Bude *f*

shan·ty[2] Shanty *n*, Seemannslied *n*

shan·ty·town Elendsviertel *n*

shape 1. Form *f*; Gestalt *f*; Verfassung *f*, Zustand *m*; *in good* (*bad*) *shape* in gutem (schlechtem) Zustand; *in* (*out of*) *shape* SPORT (nicht) gut in Form; *take shape fig* Gestalt annehmen; **2.** *v/t* formen; gestalten; *v/i a. shape up* sich *gut etc* machen

shape·less formlos; ausgebeult

shape·ly wohlgeformt

share 1. Anteil *m* (*in, of* an *dat*); *esp Br* ECON Aktie *f*; *go shares* teilen; *have a* (*no*) *share in* (nicht) beteiligt sein an (*dat*); **2.** *v/t* (sich) *et.* teilen (*with* mit); *a. share out* verteilen (*among, between* an *acc*, unter *acc*); *v/i* teilen; *share in* sich teilen in (*acc*)

share·hold·er *esp Br* ECON Aktionär(in)

shark ZO Hai(fisch) *m*; → *loan shark*

sharp 1. *adj* scharf (*a. fig*); spitz; abrupt; schneidend (*wind, frost, command, voice, etc*); beißend (*cold, smell etc*); stechend, heftig (*pain*); gescheit; MUS (*um e-n Halbton*) erhöht; *C sharp* MUS Cis *n*; **2.** *adv* scharf, abrupt; MUS zu hoch; pünktlich, genau; *at eight o'clock sharp* Punkt 8 (Uhr); *look sharp* F sich beeilen; *look sharp!* F mach schnell!, Tempo!; F pass auf!, gib Acht!

sharp·en *Messer etc* schärfen, schleifen; *Bleistift etc* spitzen

sharp·en·er (*Messer- etc*)Schärfer *m*; (*Bleistift*)Spitzer *m*

sharp·ness Schärfe *f* (*a. fig*)

sharp·shoot·er Scharfschütze *m*

sharp-sight·ed scharfsichtig

sharp-wit·ted scharfsinnig

shat·ter *v/t* zerschmettern, zerschlagen; *Hoffnungen etc* zerstören; *v/i* zerspringen, zersplittern

shat·ter·ing vernichtend; erschütternd

shat·ter·proof splitterfrei

shave 1. (sich) rasieren; (glatt) hobeln; *j-n, et.* streifen; **2.** Rasur *f*; *have a shave* sich rasieren; *that was a close shave* das war knapp, das ist gerade noch einmal gut gegangen!

shav·en kahl geschoren

shav·er (*esp* elektrischer) Rasierapparat *m*

shav·ing 1. Rasieren *n*; **2.** Rasier...

shaving bag Kulturbeutel *m*

shaving brush Rasierpinsel *m*

shaving cream Rasiercreme *f*

shav·ings Späne *pl*

shawl Umhängetuch *n*; Kopftuch *n*

she 1. *pron* sie; **2.** Sie *f*; ZO Weibchen *n*; **3.** *adj in cpds* ZO \133weibchen *n*; *she-bear* Bärin *f*

sheaf Bündel *n*; AGR Garbe *f*

shear 1. scheren; **2.** (*a pair of*) *shears* (e-e) große Schere

sheath (*Schwert- etc*)Scheide *f*; Hülle *f*; *Br* Kondom *n, m*

sheathe *Schwert etc* in die Scheide stecken; TECH umhüllen, verkleiden, ummanteln

shed[1] Schuppen *m*; Stall *m*

shed[2] *Tränen etc* vergießen; *Blätter etc* verlieren; *fig Hemmungen etc* ablegen; *shed its skin* sich häuten; *shed a few pounds* ein paar Pfund abnehmen

sheen Glanz *m*

sheep ZO Schaf *n*

sheep·dog ZO Schäferhund *m*

sheep·ish verlegen

sheep·skin Schaffell *n*

sheer rein, bloß; steil, (fast) senkrecht; hauchdünn

sheet Betttuch *n*, (Bett)Laken *n*, Leintuch *n*; (*Glas-, Metall- etc*)Platte *f*; Blatt *n*, Bogen *m*; weite (*Eis- etc*)Fläche; *the rain was coming down in sheets* es regnete in Strömen

sheet light·ning Wetterleuchten *n*

shelf (*Bücher-, Wand- etc*)Brett *n*, (-)Bord *n*; GEOGR Riff *n*; *pl* Regal *n*; *off the shelf* gleich zum Mitnehmen

shell 1. (*Austern-, Eier-, Nuss- etc*)Schale *f*; BOT (*Erbsen- etc*)Hülse *f*; ZO Muschel *f*; (*Schnecken*)Haus *n*; ZO Panzer *m*; MIL Granate *f*; (Geschoss-, Patronen)Hülse *f*; Patrone *f*; TECH Rumpf *m*, Gerippe *n*, ARCH *a.* Rohbau *m*; **2.** schälen, enthül-

sen; mit Granaten beschießen
shell·fish zo Schal(en)tier *n*
shel·ter 1. Zuflucht *f*, Schutz *m*; Unterkunft *f*, Obdach *n*; MIL Unterstand *m*;
run for shelter Schutz suchen; ***take
shelter*** sich unterstellen (***under*** unter
dat); ***bus shelter*** Wartehäuschen *n*; **2.**
v/t schützen (***from*** vor *dat*); *v/i* sich unterstellen
shelve *v/t Bücher* in ein Regal stellen;
Plan etc aufschieben, zurückstellen; *v/i*
sanft abfallen (*garden etc*)
shep·herd 1. Schäfer *m*, Hirt *m*; **2.** *j-n* führen
sher·iff Sheriff *m*
shield 1. Schild *m*; **2.** *j-n* (be)schützen
(***from*** vor *dat*); *j-n* decken
shift 1. *v/t et.* bewegen, schieben, *Möbelstück a.* (ver)rücken; *Schuld etc* (ab-)
schieben (***onto*** auf *acc*); ***shift gear(s)***
MOT schalten; *v/i* sich bewegen; umspringen (*wind*); *fig* sich verlagern *or* verschieben *or* wandeln; MOT schalten (***into,
to*** in *acc*); ***shift from one foot to the other*** von e-m Fuß auf den anderen treten;
shift on one's chair auf s-m Stuhl *ungeduldig etc* hin und her rutschen; **2.** *fig*
Verlagerung *f*, Verschiebung *f*, Wandel
m; ECON Schicht *f*
shift key TECH Umschalttaste *f*
shift work·er Schichtarbeiter(in)
shift·y F verschlagen
shim·mer schimmern; flimmern
shin 1. *a.* **shinbone** ANAT Schienbein *n*; **2.**
shin up hinaufklettern; ***shin down*** he-
runterklettern
shine 1. *v/i* scheinen; leuchten; glänzen (*a.
fig*); *v/t Schuhe etc* polieren; **2.** Glanz *m*
shin·gle[1] grober Strandkies
shin·gle[2] (Dach)Schindel *f*
shin·gles MED Gürtelrose *f*
shin·y blank, glänzend
ship 1. Schiff *n*; **2.** verschiffen, ECON verfrachten, versenden
ship·ment ECON Ladung *f*; Verschiffung *f*,
Verfrachtung *f*, Versand *m*
ship·own·er Reeder *m*; Schiffseigner *m*
ship·ping Schifffahrt *f*; Schiffsbestand *m*;
ECON Verschiffung *f*, Verfrachtung *f*, Versand *m*
ship·wreck Schiffbruch *m*
ship·wrecked 1. ***be shipwrecked*** Schiffbruch erleiden; **2.** schiffbrüchig
ship·yard (Schiffs)Werft *f*
shirk sich drücken (vor *dat*)
shirk·er Drückeberger(in)
shirt Hemd *n*
shirt·sleeve 1. Hemdsärmel *m*; ***in (one's)
shirtsleeves*** in Hemdsärmeln, hemds-

ärmelig; **2.** hemdsärmelig
shish ke·bab GASTR Schaschlik *m, n*
shit V **1.** Scheiße *f* (*a. fig*); *fig* Scheiß *m*; **2.**
(voll)scheißen
shiv·er 1. zittern (***with*** vor *dat*); **2.** Schauer
m; *pl* MED F Schüttelfrost *m*; ***the sight
send shivers (up and) down my spine***
bei dem Anblick überlief es mich eiskalt
shoal[1] Untiefe *f*; Sandbank *f*
shoal[2] zo Schwarm *m*
shock[1] **1.** Schock *m* (*a.* MED); Wucht *f*;
ELECTR Schlag *m*, (*a.* MED Elektro-)
Schock *m*; ***be in (a state of) shock*** unter
Schock stehen; **2.** schockieren, empören;
j-m e-n Schock versetzen
shock[2] (***shock of hair*** Haar)Schopf *m*
shock ab·sorb·er TECH Stoßdämpfer *m*
shock·ing schockierend, empörend, anstößig; F scheußlich
shod·dy minderwertig (*goods*); gemein,
schäbig (*trick etc*)
shoe 1. Schuh *m*; Hufeisen *n*; **2.** *Pferd* beschlagen
shoe·horn Schuhanzieher *m*, -löffel *m*
shoe·lace Schnürsenkel *m*
shoe·mak·er Schuhmacher *m*, Schuster
m
shoe·shine boy Schuhputzer *m*
shoe store (*Br* **shop**) Schuhgeschäft *n*
shoe·string Schnürsenkel *m*
shoot 1. *v/t* schießen, HUNT *a.* erlegen; abfeuern, abschießen; erschießen; *Riegel*
vorschieben; *j-n* fotografieren, aufnehmen, *Film* drehen; *Heroin etc* spritzen;
shoot the lights MOT bei Rot fahren;
v/i schießen (***at*** auf *acc*); jagen; *fig* schießen, rasen; *film*, TV drehen, filmen; BOT
sprießen, treiben; **2.** BOT Trieb *m*; Jagd
f; Jagdrevier *n*
shoot·er F Schießeisen *n*
shoot·ing 1. Schießen *n*; Schießerei *f*; Er-
schießung *f*; Anschlag *m*; Jagd *f*; *film*, TV
Dreharbeiten *pl*, Aufnahmen *pl*; **2.** stechend (*pain*)
shooting gal·le·ry Schießbude *f*
shooting range Schießstand *m*
shooting star ASTR Sternschnuppe *f*
shop 1. *Br* Laden *m*, Geschäft *n*; Werkstatt *f*; Betrieb *m*; ***talk shop*** fachsimpeln; **2.** *mst* ***go shopping*** einkaufen gehen
shop as·sis·tant *Br* Verkäufer(in)
shop·keep·er *Br* Ladenbesitzer(in), La-
deninhaber(in)
shop·lift·er Ladendieb(in)
shop·lift·ing Ladendiebstahl *m*
shop·per Käufer(in)
shop·ping 1. Einkauf *m*, Einkaufen *n*;
Einkäufe *pl* (*items bought*); ***do one's***

S

shopping Br einkaufen, (s-e) Einkäufe machen; **2.** Einkaufs...

shopping bag Einkaufsbeutel *m*, -tasche *f*

shopping cart Einkaufswagen *m*

shopping cen·ter (*Br* **cen·tre**) Einkaufszentrum *n*

shopping list Einkaufsliste *f*, -zettel *m*

shopping mall Einkaufszentrum *n*

shopping precinct *Br* Fußgängerzone *f*

shopping street Geschäfts-, Ladenstraße *f*

shop stew·ard ECON gewerkschaftlicher Vertrauensmann

shop·walk·er *Br* Aufsicht(sperson) *f*

shop win·dow Schaufenster *n*

shore[1] Küste *f*; (*See*)Ufer *n*; *on shore* an Land

shore[2]: *shore up* (ab)stützen

short 1. *adj* kurz; klein (*person*); kurz angebunden, barsch, schroff (*with* zu); GASTR mürbe; *be short for* die Kurzform sein von; *be short of* ... nicht genügend ... haben; **2.** *adv* plötzlich, abrupt; *short of* außer; *cut short* plötzlich unterbrechen; *fall short of et.* nicht erreichen; *stop short* plötzlich innehalten, stutzen; *stop short of or at* zurückschrecken vor (*dat*); → *run 1*; **3.** F Kurzfilm *m*; ELECTR Kurze *m*; *called ... for short* kurz ... genannt; *in short* kurz(um)

short·age Knappheit *f*, Mangel *m* (*of* an *dat*)

short·com·ings Unzulänglichkeiten *pl*, Mängel *pl*, Fehler *pl*

short cut Abkürzung *f*; *take a short cut* (den Weg) abkürzen

short·en *v/t* (ab-, ver)kürzen; *v/i* kürzer werden

short·hand Kurzschrift *f*, Stenografie *f*

shorthand typ·ist Stenotypistin *f*

short·ly bald; barsch, schroff; mit wenigen Worten

short·ness Kürze *f*; Schroffheit *f*

shorts *a. pair of shorts* Shorts *pl*; (Herren-)Unterhose *f*

short·sight·ed *esp Br* kurzsichtig (*a. fig*)

short sto·ry Kurzgeschichte *f*

short-tem·pered aufbrausend, hitzig

short-term ECON kurzfristig

short time ECON Kurzarbeit *f*

short wave ELECTR Kurzwelle *f*

short-wind·ed kurzatmig

shot Schuss *m*; Schrot(kugeln *pl*) *m*, *n*; SPORT Kugel *f*; *guter etc* Schütze *m*; *soccer etc*: Schuss *m*; *basketball etc*: Wurf *m*; *tennis, golf*: Schlag *m*; PHOT Schnappschuss *m*, Aufnahme *f*; *film*, TV Aufnahme *f*, Einstellung *f*; MED F Spritze *f*; F

Schuss *m* (*of drugs*); *fig* F Versuch *m*; *a shot of rum* ein Schluck Rum; *I'll have a shot at it* ich probier's mal; *not by a long shot* F noch lange nicht; → *big shot*

shot·gun Schrotflinte *f*

shot·gun wed·ding F Mussheirat *f*

shot put SPORT Kugelstoßen *n*

shot put·ter SPORT Kugelstoßer(in)

shoul·der 1. ANAT Schulter *f*; MOT Standspur *f*; **2.** schultern; *Kosten, Verantwortung etc* übernehmen; (mit der Schulter) stoßen

shoulder bag Schulter-, Umhängetasche *f*

shoulder blade ANAT Schulterblatt *n*

shoulder strap Träger *m*; Tragriemen *m*

shout 1. *v/i* rufen, schreien (*for* nach; *for help* um Hilfe); *shout at s.o.* j-n anschreien; *v/t* rufen, schreien; **2.** Ruf *m*, Schrei *m*

shove 1. stoßen, F schubsen; *et.* schieben, stopfen; **2.** Stoß *m*, F Schubs *m*

shov·el 1. Schaufel *f*; **2.** schaufeln

show 1. *v/t* zeigen, vorzeigen, anzeigen; *j-n* bringen, führen (*to* zu); ausstellen; zeigen, *film etc a.* vorführen, TV a. bringen; *v/i* zu sehen sein; *be showing* gezeigt werden, laufen; *show around* umführen; *show in* herein-, hineinführen, herein-, hineinbringen; *show off* angeben *or* protzen (mit); vorteilhaft zur Geltung bringen; *show out* heraus-, hinausführen, heraus-, hinausbringen; *show round* herumführen; *show up* *v/t* herauf-, hinaufführen, herauf-, hinaufbringen; sichtbar machen; *j-n* entlarven, bloßstellen; *et.* aufdecken; *j-n* in Verlegenheit bringen; *v/i* zu sehen sein; F aufkreuzen, auftauchen; **2.** THEA *etc* Vorstellung *f*; Show *f*; *radio*, TV Sendung *f*; Ausstellung *f*; Zurschaustellung *f*; Demonstration *f*; *fig leerer* Schein; *be on show* ausgestellt *or* zu besichtigen sein; *steal the show from s.o. fig* j-m die Schau stehlen; *make a show of Anteilnahme, Interesse etc* heucheln; *put up a poor show* F e-e schwache Leistung zeigen; *be in charge of the whole show* F den ganzen Laden schmeißen; **3.** Muster...

show·biz F, **show busi·ness** Showbusiness *n*, Showgeschäft *n*, Unterhaltungsindustrie *f*

show·case Schaukasten *m*, Vitrine *f*

show·down Kraft-, Machtprobe *f*

show·er 1. (Regen- *etc*)Schauer *m*; (*Funken*)Regen *m*; (*Wasser-, Wort- etc*) Schwall *m*; Dusche *f*; (Geschenk-) Party *f*; *have or take a shower* duschen; **2.** *v/t* *j-n mit et.* überschütten *or* überhäufen; *v/i* duschen; **shower down** niederprasseln

show jump·er SPORT Springreiter(in)

show jump·ing SPORT Springreiten *n*

show-off F Angeber(in)

show·room Ausstellungsraum *m*

show tri·al JUR Schauprozess *m*

show·y auffallend

shred 1. Fetzen *m*; **2.** zerfetzen; in (schmale) Streifen schneiden, schnitzeln, schnetzeln; in den Papier- *or* Reißwolf geben

shred·der Schnitzelmaschine *f*; Papier-, Reißwolf *m*

shrewd scharfsinnig; schlau

shriek 1. (gellend) aufschreien; **shriek with laughter** vor Lachen kreischen; **2.** (schriller) Schrei

shrill schrill; *fig* heftig, scharf, lautstark

shrimp ZO Garnele *f*; *fig contp* Knirps *m*

shrine Schrein *m*

shrink 1. (ein-, zusammen)schrumpfen (lassen); einlaufen; *fig* abnehmen; **2.** F Klapsdoktor *m*

shrink·age Schrumpfung *f*; Einlaufen *n*; *fig* Abnahme *f*

shrink-wrap einschweißen

shriv·el schrumpfen (lassen); runz(e)lig werden (lassen)

shroud 1. Leichentuch *n*; **2.** *fig* hüllen

Shrove Tues·day Fastnachts-, Faschingsdienstag *m*

shrub Strauch *m*, Busch *m*

shrub·be·ry BOT Strauch-, Buschwerk *n*, Gebüsch *n*

shrug 1. *a.* **shrug one's shoulders** mit den Achseln *or* Schultern zucken; **2.** Achselzucken *n*, Schulterzucken *n*

shuck BOT **1.** Hülse *f*, Schote *f*; Schale *f*; **2.** enthülsen; schälen

shud·der 1. schaudern; **2.** Schauder *m*

shuf·fle 1. *v/t Karten* mischen; *Papiere etc* umordnen, hierhin oder dorthin legen; **shuffle one's feet** schlurfen; *v/i* schlurfen; *Karten* mischen; **2.** Schlurfen *n*, schlurfender Gang; Mischen *n*

shun *j-n, et.* meiden

shunt *Zug etc* rangieren, verschieben; *a.* **shunt off** F *j-n* abschieben (**to** in *acc*, nach)

shut (sich) schließen; zumachen; **shut down** *Fabrik etc* schließen; **shut off** *Wasser, Gas, Maschine etc* abstellen; **shut up** einschließen; einsperren; *Geschäft* schließen; **shut up!** F halt die Klappe!

shut·ter Fensterladen *m*; PHOT Verschluss *m*

shut·tle 1. Pendelverkehr *m*; (*Raum-*) Fähre *f*, (-)Transporter *m*; TECH Schiffchen *n*; **2.** hin- und herbefördern

shut·tle·cock SPORT Federball *m*

shut·tle ser·vice Pendelverkehr *m*

shy 1. scheu; schüchtern; **2.** scheuen (**at** vor *dat*); **shy away from** *fig* zurückschrecken vor (*dat*)

shy·ness Scheu *f*; Schüchternheit *f*

sick 1. krank; **be sick** *esp Br* sich übergeben; **she was** *or* **felt sick** ihr war schlecht; **get sick** krank werden; **be off sick** krank (geschrieben) sein; **report sick** sich krank melden; **be sick of s.th.** F *et.* satthaben; **it makes me sick** F mir wird schlecht davon, *a. fig* es ekelt *or* widert mich an; **2. the sick** die Kranken *pl*

sick·bed Krankenbett *n*

sick·en *v/t j-n* anekeln, anwidern; *v/i esp Br* krank werden

sick·le ['sɪkl] Sichel *f*

sick leave: be on sick leave krank (geschrieben) sein, wegen Krankheit fehlen

sick·ly kränklich; ungesund; matt; widerlich (*smell etc*)

sick·ness Krankheit *f*; Übelkeit *f*

sickness ben·e·fit *Br* Krankengeld *n*

side 1. Seite *f*; *esp Br* SPORT Mannschaft *f*; **side by side** nebeneinander; **take sides** Partei ergreifen (**with** für; **against** gegen); **2.** Seiten…; Neben…; **3.** Partei ergreifen (**with** für; **against** gegen)

side·board Anrichte *f*, Sideboard *n*

side·car MOT Bei-, Seitenwagen *m*

side dish GASTR Beilage *f*

side·long seitlich; Seiten…

sidelong glance Seitenblick *m*

side street Nebenstraße *f*

side·swipe Seitenhieb *m*

side·track *j-n* ablenken; F *et.* abbiegen; RAIL *etc* rangieren, verschieben

side·walk Bürgersteig *m*, Gehsteig *m*

side·walk ca·fé Straßencafé *n*

side·ways seitlich; seitwärts, nach der *or* zur Seite

sid·ing RAIL Nebengleis *n*

si·dle: sidle up to s.o. sich an *j-n* heranschleichen

siege MIL Belagerung *f*; **lay siege to** belagern (*a. fig*)

sieve 1. Sieb *n*; **2.** (durch)sieben

sift (durch)sieben; *a.* **sift through** *fig* sichten, durchsehen, prüfen

sigh 1. seufzen; **2.** Seufzer *m*

sight 1. Sehvermögen *n*, Sehkraft *f*, Augenlicht *n*; Anblick *m*; Sicht(weite) *f*; *pl* Visier *n*; Sehenswürdigkeiten *pl*; **at sight, on sight** sofort; **at the sight of** beim Anblick von (*or gen*); **at first sight**

auf den ersten Blick; *catch sight of* erblicken; *know by sight* vom Sehen kennen; *lose sight of* aus den Augen verlieren; *be (with)in sight* in Sicht sein (*a. fig*); **2.** sichten

sight-read MUS vom Blatt singen *or* spielen

sight·see·ing Sightseeing *n*, Besichtigung *f* von Sehenswürdigkeiten; *go sightseeing* sich die Sehenswürdigkeiten anschauen

sightseeing tour Sightseeingtour *f*, Besichtigungstour *f*, (Stadt)Rundfahrt *f*

sight·se·er Tourist(in)

sight test Sehtest *m*

sign 1. Zeichen *n*; (*Hinweis-, Warn- etc*) Schild *n*; *fig* (An)Zeichen *n*; **2.** unterschreiben, unterzeichnen; *Scheck* ausstellen; *sign in* sich eintragen; *sign out* sich austragen

sig·nal 1. Signal *n* (*a. fig*); Zeichen *n* (*a. fig*); **2.** (ein) Zeichen geben; signalisieren

sig·na·to·ry Unterzeichner(in)

sig·na·ture Unterschrift *f*; Signatur *f*

signature tune *radio*, TV Kennmelodie *f*

sign·board (Aushänge)Schild *n*

sign·er Unterzeichnete *m, f*

sig·net Siegel *n*

sig·nif·i·cance Bedeutung *f*, Wichtigkeit *f*

sig·nif·i·cant bedeutend, bedeutsam, wichtig; bezeichnend

sig·ni·fy bedeuten; andeuten

sign·post Wegweiser *m*

si·lence 1. Stille *f*; Schweigen *n*; *silence!* Ruhe!; *in silence* schweigend; *reduce to silence* → **2.** zum Schweigen bringen

si·lenc·er TECH Schalldämpfer *m*; *Br* MOT Auspufftopf *m*

si·lent still; schweigend; schweigsam; stumm

silent part·ner ECON stiller Teilhaber

sil·i·con CHEM Silizium *n*

sil·i·cone CHEM Silikon *n*

silk 1. Seide *f*; **2.** Seiden...

silk·worm ZO Seidenraupe *f*

silk·y seidig; samtig (*voice*)

sill (*Fenster*)Brett *n*

sil·ly 1. albern, töricht, dumm; **2.** F Dummerchen *n*

sil·ver 1. Silber *n*; **2.** silbern, Silber...; **3.** versilbern

sil·ver·plat·ed versilbert

sil·ver·ware Tafelsilber *n*

sil·ver·y silberglänzend; *fig* silberhell

sim·i·lar ähnlich (*to dat*)

sim·i·lar·i·ty Ähnlichkeit *f*

sim·i·le Gleichnis *n*, Vergleich *m*

sim·mer leicht kochen, köcheln; *simmer with fig* kochen vor (*rage etc*), fiebern vor (*excitement etc*); *simmer down* F sich beruhigen, F sich abregen

sim·per albern *or* affektiert lächeln

sim·ple einfach, schlicht; leicht; dumm, einfältig; naiv; *the simple fact is that ...* es ist einfach e-e Tatsache, dass ...

sim·ple-mind·ed dumm; naiv

sim·pli·ci·ty Einfachheit *f*, Schlichtheit *f*; Dummheit *f*; Naivität *f*

sim·pli·fi·ca·tion Vereinfachung *f*

sim·pli·fy vereinfachen

sim·ply einfach; bloß, nur

sim·u·late vortäuschen; MIL, TECH simulieren

sim·ul·ta·ne·ous simultan, gleichzeitig

sin 1. Sünde *f*; **2.** sündigen

since 1. *adv a. ever since* seitdem, seither; **2.** *prp* seit (*dat*); **3.** *cj* seit(dem); da

sin·cere aufrichtig, ehrlich, offen

sin·cer·i·ty Aufrichtigkeit *f*; Offenheit *f*

sin·ew ANAT Sehne *f*

sin·ew·y sehnig; *fig* kraftvoll

sin·ful sündig, sündhaft

sing singen; *sing s.th. to s.o.* j-m et. vorsingen

singe (sich *et.*) ansengen *or* versengen

sing·er Sänger(in)

sing·ing Singen *n*, Gesang *m*

sin·gle 1. einzig; einzeln, Einzel...; einfach; ledig, unverheiratet; *in single file* im Gänsemarsch; **2.** *Br* RAIL *etc* einfache Fahrkarte, AVIAT einfaches Ticket (*both a. single ticket*); Single *f*; Single *m*, Unverheiratete *m, f*; **3.** *single out* sich herausgreifen

sin·gle-breast·ed einreihig

sin·gle-en·gined AVIAT einmotorig

sin·gle fam·i·ly home Einfamilienhaus *n*

sin·gle fa·ther allein erziehender Vater

sin·gle-hand·ed eigenhändig, allein

sin·gle-lane MOT einspurig

sin·gle-mind·ed zielstrebig, -bewusst

sin·gle moth·er allein erziehende Mutter

sin·gle pa·rent Alleinerziehende *m, f*

sin·gle room Einzelzimmer *n*

sin·gles *esp tennis*: Einzel *n*; *a singles match* ein Einzel; *men's singles* Herreneinzel *n*; *women's singles* Dameneinzel *n*

sin·glet *Br* ärmelloses Unterhemd *or* Trikot

sin·gle-track eingleisig, einspurig

sin·gu·lar 1. einzigartig, einmalig; **2.** LING Singular *m*, Einzahl *f*

sin·is·ter finster, unheimlich

sink 1. *v/i* sinken, untergehen; sich senken; *sink in* eindringen (*a. fig*); *v/t* versenken; *Brunnen etc* bohren; *Zähne etc* vergraben (*into* in *acc*); **2.** Spülbecken *n*, Spüle *f*; Waschbecken *n*

sin·ner Sünder(in)

sip 1. Schlückchen *n*; **2.** *v/t* nippen an (*dat*) *or* von; schlückchenweise trinken; *v/i* nippen (*at* an *dat or* von)

sir mein Herr; *Dear Sir or Madam* Sehr geehrte Damen und Herren (*address in letters*)

sire zo Vater *m*, Vatertier *n*

si·ren Sirene *f*

sis·sy F Weichling *m*

sis·ter Schwester *f*; *Br* MED Oberschwester *f*; REL (Ordens)Schwester *f*

sis·ter·hood Schwesternschaft *f*

sis·ter-in-law Schwägerin *f*

sis·ter·ly schwesterlich

sit *v/i* sitzen; sich setzen; tagen; *v/t j-n* setzen; *esp Br Prüfung* ablegen, machen; *sit down* sich setzen; *sit for Br Prüfung* ablegen, machen; *sit in* ein Sit-in veranstalten; an e-m Sit-in teilnehmen; *sit in for j-n* vertreten; *sit in on* als Zuhörer teilnehmen an (*dat*); *sit on* sitzen auf (*dat*) (*a. fig*); *sit on a committee* e-m Ausschuss angehören; *sit out Tanz* auslassen; das Ende (*gen*) abwarten; *Krise etc* aussitzen; *sit up* sich *or j-n* aufrichten *or* aufsetzen; aufrecht sitzen; aufbleiben

sit·com → *situation comedy*

sit-down *a.* *sit-down strike* Sitzstreik *m*; *a.* *sit-down demonstration or* F *demo* Sitzblockade *f*

site Platz *m*, Ort *m*, Stelle *f*; (*Ausgrabungs*)Stätte *f*; Baustelle *f*

sit-in Sit-in *n*, Sitzstreik *m*

sit·ting Sitzung *f*

sit·ting room *esp Br* Wohnzimmer *n*

sit·u·at·ed: *be situated* liegen, gelegen sein

sit·u·a·tion Lage *f*, Situation *f*

situation com·e·dy TV *etc* Situationskomödie *f*

six 1. sechs; **2.** Sechs *f*

six·teen 1. sechzehn; **2.** Sechzehn *f*

six·teenth sechzehnte(r, -s)

sixth 1. sechste(r, -s); **2.** Sechstel *n*

sixth·ly sechstens

six·ti·eth sechzigste(r, -s)

six·ty 1. sechzig; **2.** Sechzig *f*

size 1. Größe *f*, *fig a.* Ausmaß *n*, Umfang *m*; **2.** *size up* F abschätzen

siz(e)·a·ble beträchtlich

siz·zle brutzeln

skate 1. Schlittschuh *m*; Rollschuh *m*; **2.** Schlittschuh laufen, eislaufen; Rollschuh laufen

skate·board Skateboard *n*

skat·er Eisläufer(in), Schlittschuhläu-

fer(in); Rollschuhläufer(in)

skat·ing Eislaufen *n*, Schlittschuhlaufen *n*; Rollschuhlaufen *n*; *free skating* Kür *f*, Kürlauf *m*

skating rink (Kunst)Eisbahn *f*; Rollschuhbahn *f*

skel·e·ton Skelett *n*, Gerippe *n*

skep·tic Skeptiker(in)

skep·ti·cal skeptisch

sketch 1. Skizze *f*; THEA *etc* Sketch *m*; **2.** skizzieren

skew·er 1. (Brat)Spieß *m*; **2.** (auf)spießen

ski 1. Ski *m*; **2.** Ski…; **3.** Ski fahren *or* laufen

skid 1. MOT rutschen, schleudern; **2.** MOT Rutschen *n*, Schleudern *n*; TECH Kufe *f*

skid mark(s) MOT Bremsspur *f*

ski·er Skifahrer(in), Skiläufer(in)

ski·ing Skifahren *n*, Skilaufen *n*, Skisport *m*

ski jump (Sprung)Schanze *f*

ski jump·er Skispringer *m*

ski jump·ing Skispringen *n*

skil·ful *Br* → *skillful*

ski lift Skilift *m*

skill Geschicklichkeit *f*, Fertigkeit *f*

skilled geschickt (*at, in* in *dat*)

skilled work·er Facharbeiter(in)

skill·ful geschickt

skim *Fett etc* abschöpfen (*a. skim off*); *Milch* entrahmen; (hin)gleiten über (*acc*); *a. skim over, skim through Bericht etc* überfliegen

skim(med) milk Magermilch *f*

skimp *a. skimp on* sparen an (*dat*)

skimp·y dürftig; knapp

skin 1. ANAT Haut *f*; zo Fell *n*; BOT Schale *f*; **2.** *Tier* abhäuten; *Zwiebel etc* schälen; sich *das Knie etc* aufschürfen

skin-deep (nur) oberflächlich

skin div·ing Sporttauchen *n*

skin·flint Geizhals *m*

skin·ny F dürr, mager

skin·ny-dip F nackt baden

skip 1. *v/i* hüpfen, springen; seilhüpfen, seilspringen; *v/t et.* überspringen, auslassen; **2.** Hüpfer *m*

skip·per MAR, SPORT Kapitän *m*

skir·mish Geplänkel *n*

skirt 1. Rock *m*; **2.** *a. skirt (a)round* umgeben; *Problem etc* umgehen

skirt·ing board *Br* Scheuerleiste *f*

ski run Skipiste *f*

ski tow Schlepplift *m*

skit·tle Kegel *m*

skulk sich herumdrücken, herumschleichen

skull ANAT Schädel *m*

skul(l)·dug·ge·ry F fauler Zauber

skunk zo Skunk *m*, Stinktier *n*
sky *a.* **skies** Himmel *m*
sky·jack *Flugzeug* entführen
sky·jack·er Flugzeugentführer(in)
sky·lark zo Feldlerche *f*
sky·light Dachfenster *n*
sky·line Skyline *f*, Silhouette *f*
sky·rock·et F hochschnellen, in die Höhe schießen
sky·scrap·er Wolkenkratzer *m*
slab (*Stein- etc*)Platte *f*; dickes Stück
slack 1. locker; ECON flau; *fig* lax, lasch, nachlässig; **2.** bummeln; *slack off, slack up fig* nachlassen, (*person a.*) abbauen
slack·en *v/t* lockern; verringern; *slacken speed* langsamer werden; *v/i* locker werden; *a. slacken off* nachlassen
slacks F Hose *f*
slag TECH Schlacke *f*
sla·lom SPORT Slalom *m*
slam 1. *a. slam shut* zuschlagen, F zuknallen; *a. slam down* F *et.* knallen (*on* auf *acc*); *slam on the brakes* F MOT auf die Bremse steigen; **2.** Zuschlagen *n*; Knall *m*
slan·der 1. Verleumdung *f*; **2.** verleumden
slan·der·ous verleumderisch
slang 1. Slang *m*; Jargon *m*; **2.** *esp Br* F *j-n* wüst beschimpfen
slant 1. schräg legen *or* liegen; sich neigen; **2.** schräge Fläche; Abhang *m*; *fig* Einstellung *f*; *at or on a slant* schräg
slant·ing schräg
slap 1. Klaps *m*, Schlag *m*; **2.** e-n Klaps geben (*dat*); schlagen; klatschen (*down on* auf *acc*; *against* gegen)
slap·stick THEA Slapstick *m*, Klamauk *m*
slapstick com·e·dy Slapstickkomödie *f*
slash 1. auf-, zerschlitzen; *Preise* drastisch herabsetzen; *Ausgaben etc* drastisch kürzen; *slash at* schlagen nach; **2.** Hieb *m*; Schlitz *m*
slate 1. Schiefer *m*; Schiefertafel *f*; POL Kandidatenliste *f*; **2.** mit Schiefer decken; *j-n* vorschlagen (*for, to be* als); *et.* planen (*for* für)
slaugh·ter 1. Schlachten *n*; *fig* Blutbad *n*, Gemetzel *n*; **2.** schlachten; *fig* niedermetzeln
slaugh·ter·house Schlachthaus *n*, Schlachthof *m*
Slav 1. Slawe *m*, Slawin *f*; **2.** slawisch
slave 1. Sklave *m*, Sklavin *f* (*a. fig*); **2.** *a. slave away* sich abplagen, F schuften
slav·er geifern, sabbern
sla·ve·ry Sklaverei *f*
slav·ish sklavisch
sleaze unsaubere Machenschaften; Kumpanei *f*; F POL Filz *m*

slea·zy schäbig, heruntergekommen; anrüchig
sled 1. (*a.* Rodel)Schlitten *m*; **2.** Schlitten fahren, rodeln
sledge *Br* → *sled*
sledge·ham·mer TECH Vorschlaghammer *m*
sleek 1. glatt, glänzend; geschmeidig; MOT schnittig; **2.** glätten
sleep 1. Schlaf *m*; *I couldn't get to sleep* ich konnte nicht einschlafen; *go to sleep* einschlafen (F *a. leg etc*); *put to sleep Tier* einschläfern; **2.** *v/i* schlafen; *sleep late* lang *or* länger schlafen; *sleep on Problem etc* überschlafen; *sleep with s.o.* mit *j-m* schlafen; *v/t* Schlafgelegenheit bieten für
sleep·er Schlafende *m*, *f*, Schläfer(in); *Br* RAIL Schwelle *f*; RAIL Schlafwagen *m*
sleep·ing bag Schlafsack *m*
Sleep·ing Beau·ty Dornröschen *n*
sleep·ing car RAIL Schlafwagen *m*
sleeping part·ner *Br* ECON stiller Teilhaber
sleeping pill PHARM Schlaftablette *f*, -mittel *n*
sleeping sick·ness MED Schlafkrankheit *f*
sleep·less schlaflos
sleep·walk·er Schlafwandler(in)
sleep·y schläfrig, müde; verschlafen
sleep·y·head F Schlafmütze *f*
sleet 1. Schneeregen *m*; Graupelschauer *m*; **2.** *it's sleeting* es gibt Schneeregen; es graupelt
sleeve Ärmel *m*; TECH Manschette *f*, Muffe *f*; *esp Br* (*Platten*)Hülle *f*
sleeve·less ärmellos
sleigh (*esp* Pferde)Schlitten *m*
sleight of hand Fingerfertigkeit *f*; *fig* (Taschenspieler)Trick *m*
slen·der schlank; *fig* mager, dürftig; schwach (*hope etc*)
slice 1. Scheibe *f*, Stück *n*; *fig* Anteil *m* (*of* an *dat*); **2.** *a. slice up* in Scheiben *or* Stücke schneiden; *slice off Stück* abschneiden (*from* von)
slick 1. gekonnt; geschickt, raffiniert; glatt (*road etc*); **2.** F (*Öl*)Teppich *m*; **3.** *slick down Haar* glätten, F anklatschen
slick·er Regenmantel *m*
slide 1. gleiten (lassen); rutschen; schlüpfen; schieben; *let things slide fig* die Dinge schleifenlassen; **2.** Gleiten *n*, Rutschen *n*; Rutsche *f*, Rutschbahn *f*; TECH Schieber *m*; PHOT Dia *n*; Objektträger *m*; (*Erd- etc*)Rutsch *m*; *Br* (*Haar*)Spange *f*
slide rule Rechenschieber *m*

slide tack·le *soccer*: Grätsche *f*
slid·ing door Schiebetür *f*
slight 1. leicht, gering(fügig), unbedeutend; **2.** beleidigen, kränken; **3.** Beleidigung *f*, Kränkung *f*
slim 1. schlank; *fig* gering; **2.** *a.* **be slimming**, **be on a slimming diet** e-e Schlankheitskur machen, abnehmen
slime Schleim *m*
slim·y schleimig (*a. fig*)
sling 1. aufhängen; F schleudern; **2.** Schlinge *f*; Tragriemen *m*; Tragetuch *n*; Schleuder *f*
slip¹ 1. *v/i* rutschen, schlittern; ausgleiten, ausrutschen; schlüpfen; *v/t* sich losreißen von; **slip s.th. into s.o.'s hand** j-m et. in die Hand schieben; **slip s.o. s.th.** j-m et. zuschieben; **slip s.o.'s attention** j-m *or* j-s Aufmerksamkeit entgehen; **slip s.o.'s mind** j-m entfallen; **she has slipped a disk** MED sie hat e-n Bandscheibenvorfall; **slip by**, **slip past** verstreichen (*time*); **slip off**, **slip out of** schlüpfen aus; **slip on** überstreifen, schlüpfen in (*acc*); **2.** Ausgleiten *n*, (Aus)Rutschen *n*; Versehen *n*; Unterrock *m*; (*Kissen*)Bezug *m*; **slip of the tongue** Versprecher *m*; **give s.o. the slip** F j-m entwischen
slip² a. **slip of paper** Zettel *m*
slip·case Schuber *m*
slip-on 1. *adj* **slip-on shoe** → **2.** Slipper *m*
slipped disk MED Bandscheibenvorfall *m*
slip·per Hausschuh *m*, Pantoffel *m*
slip·per·y glatt, rutschig, glitschig
slip road *Br* MOT → **ramp**
slip·shod schlampig
slit 1. Schlitz *m*; **2.** schlitzen; **slit open** aufschlitzen
slith·er gleiten, rutschen
sliv·er (*Glas- etc*)Splitter *m*
slob·ber sabbern
slo·gan Slogan *m*
sloop MAR Schaluppe *f*
slop 1. *v/t* verschütten; *v/i* überschwappen; schwappen (**over** über *acc*); **2.** *a. pl* schlabb(e)riges Zeug; (*Tee-, Kaffee-*)Rest(e *pl*) *m*; *esp Br* Schmutzwasser *n*
slope 1. (Ab)Hang *m*; Neigung *f*, Gefälle *n*; **2.** sich neigen, abfallen
slop·py schlampig; F gammelig; F rührselig
slot Schlitz *m*, (Münz)Einwurf *m*; EDP Steckplatz *m*
sloth ZO Faultier *n*
slot ma·chine (Waren-, Spiel)Automat *m*
slouch 1. krumme Haltung; F latschiger Gang; **2.** krumm dasitzen *or* dastehen; F latschen
slough¹: **slough off** *Haut* abstreifen, ZO

sich häuten
slough² Sumpf *m*, Sumpfloch *n*
Slo·vak 1. slowakisch; **2.** Slowake *m*, Slowakin *f*; LING Slowakisch *n*
Slo·va·ki·a Slowakei *f*
slov·en·ly schlampig
slow 1. *adj* langsam; begriffsstutzig; ECON schleppend; **be (ten minutes) slow** (zehn Minuten) nachgehen; **2.** *adv* langsam; **3.** *v/t often* **slow down, slow up** *Geschwindigkeit* verringern; *v/i often* **slow down, slow up** langsamer fahren *or* gehen *or* werden
slow-coach *Br* → **slowpoke**
slow-down ECON Bummelstreik *m*
slow lane MOT Kriechspur *f*
low mo·tion PHOT Zeitlupe *f*
slow-mov·ing kriechend (*traffic*)
slow-poke Langweiler(in)
slow-worm ZO Blindschleiche *f*
sludge Schlamm *m*
slug¹ ZO Nacktschnecke *f*
slug² F (*Gewehr- etc*)Kugel *f*; Schluck *m* (*whisky etc*)
slug³ F *j-m* e-n Faustschlag versetzen
slug·gish träge; ECON schleppend
sluice TECH Schleuse *f*
slum *a. pl* Slums *pl*, Elendsviertel *n or pl*
slum·ber POET **1.** schlummern; **2.** *a. pl* Schlummer *m*
slump 1. ECON stürzen (*prices*), stark zurückgehen (*sales etc*); **sit slumped over** zusammengesunken sitzen über (*dat*); **slump into a chair** sich in e-n Sessel fallen lassen; **2.** ECON starker Konjunkturrückgang; **slump in prices** Preissturz *m*
slur¹ MUS *Töne* binden; **slur one's speech** undeutlich sprechen; lallen; **2.** undeutliche Aussprache
slur² **1.** verleumden; **2.** **slur on s.o.'s reputation** Rufschädigung *f*
slurp F schlürfen
slush Schneematsch *m*; F Kitsch *m*
slush·y F kitschig
slut Schlampe *f*; Nutte *f*
sly gerissen, schlau, listig; **on the sly** heimlich
smack¹ 1. *j-m* e-n Klaps geben; **smack one's lips** sich (geräuschvoll) die Lippen lecken; **smack down** F et. hinklatschen; **2.** klatschendes Geräusch, Knall *m*; F Schmatz *m* (*kiss*); F Klaps *m*
smack²: **smack of** *fig* schmecken *or* riechen nach
small 1. *adj and adv* klein; **small wonder** (*that*) kein Wunder, dass; **feel small** *fig* sich klein (und hässlich) vorkommen; **2.** **small of the back** ANAT Kreuz *n*
small ad Kleinanzeige *f*

small arms Handfeuerwaffen *pl*

small change Kleingeld *n*

small hours: *in the small hours* in den frühen Morgenstunden

small-mind·ed engstirnig; kleinlich

small·pox MED Pocken *pl*

small print *das* Kleingedruckte

small talk Small Talk *m*, *n*, oberflächliche Konversation; *make small talk* plaudern

small-time F klein, unbedeutend; *in cpds* Schmalspur...

small town Kleinstadt *f*

smart 1. schick, fesch; smart, schlau, clever; 2. wehtun; brennen; 3. (brennender) Schmerz

smart al·eck F Besserwisser(in), Klugscheißer(in)

smart·ness Schick *m*; Schlauheit *f*, Cleverness *f*

smash 1. *v/t* zerschlagen (*a. smash up*); schmettern (*a. tennis etc*); *Aufstand etc* niederschlagen, *Drogenring etc* zerschlagen; *smash up one's car* s-n Wagen zu Schrott fahren; *v/i* zerspringen; *smash into* prallen an (*acc*) *or* gegen, krachen gegen; 2. Schlag *m; tennis etc:* Schmetterball *m;* → *smash hit, smash-up*

smash hit Hit *m*

smash-up MOT, RAIL schwerer Unfall

smat·ter·ing: *have a smattering of English* ein paar Brocken Englisch können

smear 1. Fleck *m;* MED Abstrich *m;* Verleumdung *f;* 2. (ein-, ver)schmieren; (sich) verwischen; verleumden

smell 1. *v/i* riechen (*at* an *dat*); duften; stinken; *v/t* riechen (an *dat*); 2. Geruch *m;* Gestank *m;* Duft *m*

smell·y übel riechend, stinkend

smelt Erz schmelzen

smile 1. Lächeln *n;* 2. lächeln; *smile at j-n* anlächeln, *j-m* zulächeln; *j-n, et.* belächeln, lächeln über (*acc*); *smile to o.s.* schmunzeln

smirk (selbstgefällig *or* schadenfroh) grinsen

smith Schmied *m*

smith·e·reens: *smash (in)to smithereens* F in tausend Stücke schlagen *or* zerspringen

smith·y Schmiede *f*

smit·ten verliebt, F verknallt (*with* in *acc*); *be smitten by or with fig* gepackt werden von

smock Kittel *m*

smog Smog *m*

smoke 1. Rauch *m; have a smoke* eine rauchen; 2. rauchen; räuchern

smok·er Raucher(in); RAIL Raucher *m*, Raucherabteil *n*

smoke·stack Schornstein *m*

smok·ing Rauchen *n; no smoking* Rauchen verboten

smoking com·part·ment RAIL Raucher *m*, Raucherabteil *n*

smok·y rauchig; verräuchert

smooch F schmusen

smooth 1. glatt (*a. fig*); ruhig (*a. journey etc*); mild (*wine*); *fig* (aal)glatt; 2. *a. smooth out* glätten, glatt streichen; *smooth away Falten etc* glätten; *Schwierigkeiten etc* aus dem Weg räumen; *smooth down* glatt streichen

smoth·er ersticken

smo(u)l·der glimmen, schwelen

smudge 1. Schmutzfleck *m;* 2. (be-, ver)schmieren; (sich) verwischen

smug selbstgefällig

smug·gle schmuggeln (*into* nach; in *acc*)

smug·gler Schmuggler(in)

smut Rußflocke *f;* Schmutz *m* (*a. fig*)

smut·ty *fig* schmutzig

snack Snack *m*, Imbiss *m; have a snack* e-e Kleinigkeit essen

snack bar Snackbar *f*, Imbissstube *f*

snag 1. *fig* Haken *m;* 2. mit *et.* hängen bleiben (*on* an *dat*)

snail ZO Schnecke *f*

snake ZO Schlange *f*

snap 1. *v/i* (zer)brechen, (zer)reißen; *a. snap shut* zuschnappen; *snap at* schnappen nach; *j-n* anschnauzen; *snap out of it!* F Kopf hoch!, komm, komm!; *snap to it!* mach fix!; *v/t* zerbrechen; PHOT F knipsen; *snap one's fingers* mit den Fingern schnalzen; *snap one's fingers at fig* keinen Respekt haben vor (*dat*), sich hinwegsetzen über (*acc*); *snap off* abbrechen; *snap up et.* schnell entschlossen kaufen; *snap it up!* mach fix!; 2. Krachen *n*, Knacken *n*, Knall *m;* PHOT F Schnappschuss *m;* Druckknopf *m;* F Schwung *m; cold snap* Kälteeinbruch *m*

snap fas·ten·er Druckknopf *m*

snap·pish *fig* bissig

snap·py modisch, schick; *make it snappy!* F mach fix!

snap·shot PHOT Schnappschuss *m*

snare 1. Schlinge *f*, Falle *f* (*a. fig*); 2. in der Schlinge fangen; F *et.* ergattern

snarl 1. knurren; *snarl at s.o.* j-n anknurren; 2. Knurren *n*

snatch 1. *v/t et.* packen; *Gelegenheit* ergreifen; *ein paar Stunden Schlaf etc* ergattern; *snatch s.o.'s handbag* j-m die Handtasche entreißen; *v/i snatch at* (schnell) greifen nach; *Gelegenheit* ergreifen; 2. *make a snatch at* (schnell) greifen nach; *snatch of conversation* Gesprächsfetzen *m*

sneak 1. *v/i* (sich) schleichen; *Br* F petzen; *v/t* F stibitzen; **2.** *Br* F Petze *f*

sneak·er Turnschuh *m*

sneer 1. höhnisch *or* spöttisch grinsen (*at* über *acc*); spotten (*at* über *acc*); **2.** höhnisches *or* spöttisches Grinsen; höhnische *or* spöttische Bemerkung

sneeze 1. niesen; **2.** Niesen *n*

snick·er kichern (*at* über *acc*)

sniff 1. *v/i* schniefen; schnüffeln (*at* an *dat*); *sniff at fig* die Nase rümpfen über (*acc*); *v/t Klebstoff etc* schnüffeln, *Kokain etc* schnupfen; **2.** Schniefen *n*

snif·fle 1. schniefen; **2.** Schniefen *n*; *she's got the sniffles* F ihr läuft dauernd die Nase

snig·ger *esp Br* → **snicker**

snip 1. Schnitt *m*; **2.** durchschnippeln; *snip off* abschnippeln

snipe[1] zo Schnepfe *f*

snipe[2] aus dem Hinterhalt schießen (*at* auf *acc*)

snip·er Heckenschütze *m*

sniv·el greinen, jammern

snob Snob *m*

snob·bish versnobt

snoop: *snoop about, snoop around* F herumschnüffeln

snoop·er F Schnüffler(in)

snooze F **1.** ein Nickerchen machen; **2.** Nickerchen *n*

snore 1. schnarchen; **2.** Schnarchen *n*

snor·kel 1. Schnorchel *m*; **2.** schnorcheln

snort 1. schnauben; **2.** Schnauben *n*

snot·ty nose F Rotznase *f*

snout zo Schnauze *f*, Rüssel *m*

snow 1. Schnee *m* (*a. sl cocaine*); **2.** schneien; *be snowed in or up* eingeschneit sein

snow·ball Schneeball *m*

snowball fight Schneeballschlacht *f*

snow·bound eingeschneit

snow-capped schneebedeckt

snow·drift Schneewehe *f*

snow·drop BOT Schneeglöckchen *n*

snow·fall Schneefall *m*

snow·flake Schneeflocke *f*

snow line Schneegrenze *f*

snow·man Schneemann *m*

snow·mo·bile Schneemobil *n*

snow·plough *Br*, **snow·plow** Schneepflug *m*

snow·storm Schneesturm *m*

snow-white schneeweiß

Snow White Schneewittchen *n*

snow·y schneereich; verschneit

snub *j-n* brüskieren, *j-n* vor den Kopf stoßen

snub nose Stupsnase *f*

snuff[1] Schnupftabak *m*

snuff[2] *Kerze* ausdrücken, löschen; *snuff out Leben* auslöschen

snuf·fle schnüffeln, schniefen

snug gemütlich, behaglich; *clothing*: gut sitzend; eng (anliegend)

snug·gle: *snuggle up to s.o.* sich an j-n kuscheln; *snuggle down in bed* sich ins Bett kuscheln

so so; deshalb; → *hope 2, think; is that so?* wirklich?; *an hour or so* etwa e-e Stunde; *she is tired - so am I* sie ist müde - ich auch; *so far* bisher

soak *v/t* einweichen (*in* in *dat*); durchnässen; *soak up* aufsaugen; *v/i* sickern

soak·ing wet *soaking wet* völlig durchnässt, F klatschnass

soap 1. Seife *f*; F → *soap opera*; **2.** (sich) einseifen

soap op·e·ra *radio*, TV Seifenoper *f*

soap·y Seifen...; seifig; *fig* F schmeichlerisch

soar (hoch) aufsteigen; hochragen; zo, AVIAT segeln, gleiten; *fig* in die Höhe schnellen (*prices etc*)

sob 1. schluchzen; **2.** Schluchzen *n*

so·ber 1. nüchtern (*a. fig*); **2.** ernüchtern; *sober up* nüchtern machen *or* werden

so-called sogenannt

soc·cer Fußball *m*

soc·cer hoo·li·gan Fußballrowdy *m*

so·cia·ble gesellig

so·cial sozial, Sozial...; gesellschaftlich, Gesellschafts...; zo gesellig

social dem·o·crat POL Sozialdemokrat(in)

social insur·ance Sozialversicherung *f*

so·cial·ism Sozialismus *m*

so·cial·ist 1. Sozialist(in); **2.** sozialistisch

so·cial·ize *v/i* gesellschaftlich verkehren (*with* mit); *v/t* sozialisieren

so·cial sci·ence Sozialwissenschaft *f*

social se·cu·ri·ty *Br* Sozialhilfe *f*; *be on social security* Sozialhilfe beziehen

social ser·vic·es *esp Br* Sozialeinrichtungen

social work Sozialarbeit *f*

social work·er Sozialarbeiter(in)

so·ci·e·ty Gesellschaft *f*; Verein *m*

so·ci·ol·o·gy Soziologie *f*

sock Socke *f*

sock·et ELECTR Steckdose *f*; Fassung *f*; (Anschluss)Buchse *f*; ANAT (*Augen-*)Höhle *f*

so·da Soda(wasser) *n*; (*Orangen- etc*)Limonade *f*

sod·den aufgeweicht (*ground*); durchweicht (*clothes*)

S

so·fa Sofa *n*

soft weich; sanft; leise; gedämpft (*light etc*); F leicht, angenehm, ruhig (*job etc*); alkoholfrei (*drink*); F verweichlicht

soft drink Soft Drink *m*, alkoholfreies Getränk

soft·en *v/t* weich machen; *Wasser* enthärten; *Ton, Licht, Stimme etc* dämpfen; **soften up** F *j-n* weich machen; *v/i* weich(er) *or* sanft(er) *or* mild(er) werden

soft·heart·ed weichherzig

soft land·ing weiche Landung

soft·ware EDP Software *f*

software pack·age EDP Softwarepaket *n*

soft·y F Softie *m*, Weichling *m*

sog·gy aufgeweicht, matschig

soil[1] Boden *m*, Erde *f*

soil[2] beschmutzen, schmutzig machen

so·lar Sonnen...

solar en·er·gy Solar-, Sonnenenergie *f*

solar pan·el Sonnenkollektor *m*

solar sys·tem Sonnensystem *n*

sol·der TECH (ver)löten

sol·dier Soldat *m*

sole[1] **1.** (Fuß-, Schuh)Sohle *f*; **2.** besohlen

sole[2] ZO Seezunge *f*

sole[3] einzig; alleinig, Allein...

sole·ly (einzig und) allein, ausschließlich

sol·emn feierlich; ernst

so·lic·it bitten um

so·lic·i·tous besorgt (**about, for** um)

sol·id 1. fest; stabil; massiv; MATH körperlich; gewichtig, triftig (*reason etc*), stichhaltig (*argument etc*); solid(e), gründlich (*work etc*); einmütig, geschlossen; **a solid hour** F e-e geschlagene Stunde; **2.** MATH Körper *m*; *pl* feste Nahrung

sol·i·dar·i·ty Solidarität *f*

so·lid·i·fy fest werden (lassen); *fig* (sich) festigen

so·lil·o·quy Selbstgespräch *n*, *esp* THEA Monolog *m*

sol·i·taire Solitär *m*; Patience *f*

sol·i·ta·ry einsam, (*Leben a.*) zurückgezogen, (*Ort etc a.*) abgelegen; einzig

solitary con·fine·ment JUR Einzelhaft *f*

so·lo MUS Solo *n*; AVIAT Alleinflug *m*

so·lo·ist MUS Solist(in)

sol·u·ble CHEM löslich; *fig* lösbar

so·lu·tion CHEM Lösung *f*; *fig* (Auf)Lösung *f*

solve *Fall etc* lösen

sol·vent 1. ECON zahlungsfähig; **2.** CHEM Lösungsmittel *n*

som·ber, *Br* **som·bre** düster, trüb(e); *fig* trübsinnig

some (irgend)ein; *pl* einige, ein paar; manche; etwas, ein wenig, ein bisschen; ungefähr; **some 20 miles** etwa 20 Meilen; **some more cake** noch ein Stück Kuchen; **to some extent** bis zu e-m gewissen Grade

some·bod·y jemand

some·day eines Tages

some·how irgendwie

some·one jemand

some·place irgendwo, irgendwohin

som·er·sault 1. Salto *m*; Purzelbaum *m*; **turn a somersault** → **2.** e-n Salto machen; e-n Purzelbaum schlagen

some·thing etwas; **something like** ungefähr

some·time irgendwann

some·times manchmal

some·what ein bisschen, ein wenig

some·where irgendwo(hin)

son Sohn *m*; **son of a bitch** V Scheißkerl *m*

so·na·ta MUS Sonate *f*

song MUS Lied *n*; Gesang *m*; **for a song** F für ein Butterbrot

song·bird ZO Singvogel *m*

son·ic Schall...

sonic bang *Br*, **sonic boom** Überschallknall *m*

son-in-law Schwiegersohn *m*

son·net Sonett *n*

so·nor·ous sonor, volltönend

soon bald; **as soon as** sobald; **as soon as possible** so bald wie möglich

soon·er eher, früher; **sooner or later** früher oder später; **the sooner the better** je eher, desto besser; **no sooner ... than** kaum ... als; **no sooner said than done** gesagt, getan

soot Ruß *m*

soothe beruhigen, beschwichtigen (*a.* **soothe down**); *Schmerzen* lindern, mildern

sooth·ing beruhigend; lindernd

soot·y rußig

sop[1] Beschwichtigungsmittel *n* (**to** für)

sop[2]: **sop up** aufsaugen

so·phis·ti·cat·ed anspruchsvoll, kultiviert; intellektuell; TECH raffiniert, hoch entwickelt

soph·o·more Student(in) im zweiten Jahr

sop·o·rif·ic einschläfernd

sop·ping *a.* **sopping wet** F klatschnass

sor·cer·er Zauberer *m*, Hexenmeister *m*, Hexer *m*

sor·cer·ess Zauberin *f*, Hexe *f*

sor·cer·y Zauberei *f*, Hexerei *f*

sor·did schmutzig; schäbig

sore 1. weh, wund (*a. fig*); entzündet; F *fig* sauer; **I'm sore all over** mir tut alles weh; **sore throat** Halsentzündung *f*; **have a sore throat** *a.* Halsschmerzen haben;

2. wunde Stelle, Wunde *f*

sor·rel[1] BOT Sauerampfer *m*

sor·rel[2] **1.** ZO Fuchs *m* (*horse*); **2.** rotbraun

sor·row Kummer *m*, Leid *n*, Schmerz *m*, Trauer *f*

sor·row·ful traurig, betrübt

sor·ry 1. *adj* traurig, jämmerlich; *be or feel sorry for s.o.* j-n bedauern *or* bemitleiden; *I'm sorry for her* sie tut mir leid; *I am sorry to say* ich muss leider sagen; *I'm sorry* → **2.** *int* (es) tut mir leid!; Entschuldigung!, Verzeihung!; *sorry? esp Br* wie bitte?

sort 1. Sorte *f*, Art *f*; *sort of* F irgendwie; *of a sort, of sorts* F so etwas Ähnliches wie; *all sorts of things* alles Mögliche; *nothing of the sort* nichts dergleichen; *what sort of (a) man is he?* wie ist er?; *be out of sorts* F nicht auf der Höhe *or* auf dem Damm sein; *be completely out of sorts* SPORT F völlig außer Form sein; **2.** sortieren; *sort out* aussortieren; *Problem etc* lösen, *Frage etc* klären

SOS SOS *n*; *send an SOS* ein SOS funken; *SOS call or message* SOS-Ruf *m*

soul Seele *f* (*a. fig*); MUS Soul *m*

sound[1] **1.** Geräusch *n*; Laut *m*; PHYS Schall *m*; *radio*, TV Ton *m*; MUS Klang *m*, Sound *m*; **2.** *v/i* (er)klingen, (er)tönen; *sich gut etc* anhören; *v/t* LING (aus)sprechen; MAR (aus)loten; MED abhorchen; *sound one's horn* MOT hupen

sound[2] gesund; intakt, in Ordnung; solid(e), stabil, sicher; klug, vernünftig (*person, advice etc*); gründlich (*training etc*); gehörig (*beating*); vernichtend (*defeat*); fest, tief (*sleep*)

sound bar·ri·er Schallgrenze *f*, Schallmauer *f*

sound film Tonfilm *m*

sound·less lautlos

sound·proof schalldicht

sound·track Filmmusik *f*; Tonspur *f*

sound wave Schallwelle *f*

soup 1. Suppe *f*; **2.** *soup up* F *Motor* frisieren

sour 1. sauer; *fig* mürrisch; **2.** sauer werden (lassen); *fig* trüben, verbittern

source Quelle *f*, *fig a.* Ursache *f*, Ursprung *m*

south 1. Süd, Süden *m*; **2.** *adj* südlich, Süd...; **3.** *adv* nach Süden, südwärts

south·east 1. Südost, Südosten *m*; **2.** *a.*

south·east·ern südöstlich

south·er·ly, south·ern südlich, Süd...

south·ern·most südlichste(r, -s)

South Pole Südpol *m*

south·ward(s) südlich, nach Süden

south·west 1. Südwest, Südwesten *m*; **2.**

a. **south·west·ern** südwestlich

sou·ve·nir Souvenir *n*, Andenken *n* (*of* an *acc*)

sove·reign 1. Monarch(in), Landesherr(in); **2.** POL souverän

sove·reign·ty Souveränität *f*

So·vi·et HIST POL sowjetisch, Sowjet...

sow[1] (aus)säen

sow[2] ZO Sau *f*

soy bean BOT Sojabohne *f*

spa (Heil)Bad *n*

space 1. Raum *m*, Platz *m*; (Welt-) Raum *m*; Zwischenraum *m*; Zeitraum *m*; **2.** *a. space out* in Abständen anordnen; PRINT sperren

space age Weltraumzeitalter *n*

space bar TECH Leertaste *f*

space cap·sule Raumkapsel *f*

space cen·ter (*Br* **cen·tre**) Raumfahrtzentrum *n*

space·craft (Welt)Raumfahrzeug *n*

space flight (Welt)Raumflug *m*

space·lab Raumlabor *n*

space·man F Raumfahrer *m*; Außerirdische *m*

space probe (Welt)Raumsonde *f*

space re·search (Welt)Raumforschung *f*

space·ship Raumschiff *n*

space shut·tle Raumfähre *f*, Raumtransporter *m*

space sta·tion (Welt)Raumstation *f*

space·suit Raumanzug *m*

space walk Weltraumspaziergang *m*

space·wom·an F (Welt)Raumfahrerin *f*; Außerirdische *f*

spa·cious geräumig

spade Spaten *m*; *card game*: Pik *n*, Grün *n*; *king of spades* Pikkönig *m*; *call a spade a spade* das Kind beim (rechten) Namen nennen

Spain Spanien *n*

span 1. Spanne *f*; Spannweite *f*; **2.** *Fluss etc* überspannen; *fig* sich erstrecken über (*acc*)

span·gle 1. Flitter *m*, Paillette *f*; **2.** mit Flitter *or* Pailletten besetzen; *fig* übersäen (*with* mit)

Span·iard Spanier(in)

span·iel ZO Spaniel *m*

Span·ish 1. spanisch; **2.** LING Spanisch *n*; *the Spanish* die Spanier *pl*

spank *j-m* den Hintern versohlen

spank·ing Tracht *f* Prügel

span·ner *esp Br* Schraubenschlüssel *m*; *put or throw a spanner in the works* F *j-m* in die Quere kommen

spar *boxing*: sparren (*with* mit); *fig* sich ein Wortgefecht liefern (*with* mit)

spare 1. *j-n, et.* entbehren; *Geld, Zeit etc*

S

übrig haben; *keine Kosten, Mühen etc scheuen*; *spare s.o. s.th.* j-m et. ersparen; **2.** Ersatz..., Reserve...; überschüssig; **3.** MOT Ersatz-, Reservereifen *m*; *esp Br* → *spare part* TECH Ersatzteil *n, m*
spare room Gästezimmer *n*
spare time Freizeit *f*
spar·ing sparsam; *use sparingly* sparsam umgehen mit
spark 1. Funke(n) *m* (*a. fig*); **2.** Funken sprühen
spark·ing plug *Br* → *spark plug*
spar·kle 1. funkeln, blitzen (*with* vor *dat*); perlen (*drink*); **2.** Funkeln *n*, Blitzen *n*
spar·kling funkelnd, blitzend; (geist)sprühend, spritzig; *sparkling wine* Sekt *m*, Schaumwein *m*
spark plug MOT Zündkerze *f*
spar·row ZO Spatz *m*, Sperling *m*
spar·row·hawk ZO Sperber *m*
sparse spärlich, dünn
spasm MED Krampf *m*; Anfall *m*
spas·mod·ic MED krampfartig; *fig* sporadisch, unregelmäßig
spas·tic MED **1.** spastisch; **2.** Spastiker(in)
spa·tial räumlich
spat·ter (be)spritzen
spawn 1. ZO laichen; *fig* hervorbringen; **2.** ZO Laich *m*
speak *v/i* sprechen, reden (*to, with* mit; *about* über *acc*); sprechen (*to* vor *dat*; *about, on* über *acc*); *so to speak* sozusagen; *speaking!* TEL am Apparat!; *speak up* lauter sprechen; *v/t* sprechen, sagen; *Sprache* sprechen
speak·er Sprecher(in), Redner(in)
spear 1. Speer *m*; **2.** aufspießen; durchbohren
spear·head Speerspitze *f*; MIL Angriffsspitze *f*; SPORT (Sturm-, Angriffs)Spitze *f*
spear·mint BOT Grüne Minze
spe·cial 1. besondere(r, -s); speziell; Sonder...; Spezial...; **2.** Sonderbus *m*, Sonderzug *m*; *radio*, TV Sondersendung *f*; ECON F Sonderangebot *n*; *be on special* ECON im Angebot sein
spe·cial·ist Spezialist(in), MED *a.* Facharzt *m*, Fachärztin *f* (*in* für)
spe·ci·al·i·ty *Br* → *specialty*
spe·cial·ize sich spezialisieren (*in* auf *acc*)
spe·cial·ty Spezialgebiet *n*; GASTR Spezialität *f*
spe·cies Art *f*, Spezies *f*
spe·cif·ic konkret, präzis; spezifisch, speziell, besondere(r, -s); eigen (*to* *dat*)
spe·ci·fy genau beschreiben *or* angeben *or* festlegen
spe·ci·men Exemplar *n*; Probe *f*, Muster *n*

speck kleiner Fleck, (*Staub*)Korn *n*; Punkt *m* (*on the horizon* am Horizont)
speck·led gefleckt, gesprenkelt
spec·ta·cle Schauspiel *n*; Anblick *m*; (*a pair of*) *spectacles* (e-e) Brille
spec·tac·u·lar 1. spektakulär; **2.** große (*Fernseh- etc*)Show
spec·ta·tor Zuschauer(in)
spec·ter (*fig a. Schreck*)Gespenst *n*
spec·tral geisterhaft, gespenstisch
spec·tre *Br* → *specter*
spec·u·late spekulieren, Vermutungen anstellen (*about, on* über *acc*); ECON spekulieren (*in* mit)
spec·u·la·tion Spekulation *f* (*a.* ECON), Vermutung *f*
spec·u·la·tive spekulativ, ECON *a.* Spekulations...
spec·u·la·tor ECON Spekulant(in)
speech Sprache *f*; Rede *f*, Ansprache *f*; *make a speech* e-e Rede halten
speech day *Br* PED (Jahres)Schlussfeier *f*
speech·less sprachlos (*with* vor *dat*)
speed 1. Geschwindigkeit *f*, Tempo *n*, Schnelligkeit *f*; TECH Drehzahl *f*; PHOT Lichtempfindlichkeit *f*; *sl* Speed *n*; MOT *etc* Gang *m*; *five-speed gearbox* Fünfganggetriebe *n*; *at a speed of* mit e-r Geschwindigkeit von; *at full or top speed* mit Höchstgeschwindigkeit; **2.** *v/i* rasen; *be speeding* MOT zu schnell fahren; *speed up* beschleunigen, schneller werden; *v/t* rasch bringen *or* befördern; *speed up et.* beschleunigen
speed·boat Rennboot *n*
speed·ing MOT zu schnelles Fahren, Geschwindigkeitsüberschreitung *f*
speed lim·it MOT Geschwindigkeitsbegrenzung *f*, Tempolimit *n*
speed·om·e·ter MOT Tachometer *m, n*
speed trap MOT Radarfalle *f*
speed·y schnell, (*reply etc a.*) prompt
spell¹ *a.* *spell out* buchstabieren; (*orthographisch* richtig) schreiben
spell² Weile *f*; (*Husten- etc*)Anfall *m*; *for a spell* e-e Zeit lang; *a spell of fine weather* e-e Schönwetterperiode; *hot spell* Hitzewelle *f*
spell³ Zauber *m* (*a. fig*)
spell·bound wie gebannt
spell·er EDP Speller *m*, Rechtschreibsystem *n*; *be a good* (*bad*) *speller* in Rechtschreibung gut (schlecht) sein
spell·ing Buchstabieren *n*; Rechtschreibung *f*; Schreibung *f*, Schreibweise *f*
spelling mis·take (Recht)Schreibfehler *m*
spend *Geld* ausgeben (*on* für); *Urlaub, Zeit* verbringen

S

spend·ing Ausgaben *pl*
spend·thrift Verschwender(in)
spent verbraucht
sperm BIOL Sperma *n*, Samen *m*
sphere Kugel *f*; *fig* (*Einfluss- etc*)Sphäre *f*, (*Einfluss- etc*)Bereich *m*, Gebiet *n*
spher·i·cal kugelförmig
spice 1. Gewürz *n*; *fig* Würze *f*; **2.** würzen
spick-and-span blitzsauber
spic·y gut gewürzt, würzig; *fig* pikant
spi·der ZO Spinne *f*
spike 1. Spitze *f*; Dorn *m*; Stachel *m*; SPORT Spike *m*, Dorn *m*; *pl* Spikes *pl*, Rennschuhe *pl*; **2.** aufspießen
spill 1. *v/t* ausschütten, verschütten; *spill the beans* F alles ausplaudern, singen; → *milk 1*; *v/i fig* strömen (*out of* aus); *spill over* überlaufen; *fig* übergreifen (*into* auf *acc*); **2.** F Sturz *m*
spin 1. *v/t* drehen; *Wäsche* schleudern; *Münze* hochwerfen; *Fäden, Wolle etc* spinnen; *spin out Arbeit etc* in die Länge ziehen; *Geld etc* strecken; *v/i* sich drehen; spinnen; *my head was spinning* mir drehte sich alles; *spin along* MOT dahinrasen; *spin round* herumwirbeln; **2.** (schnelle) Drehung; SPORT Effet *m*; TECH Schleudern *n*; AVIAT Trudeln *n*; *be in a (flat) spin esp Br* F am Rotieren sein; *go for a spin* MOT F e-e Spritztour machen
spin·ach BOT Spinat *m*
spin·al ANAT Rückgrat...
spinal col·umn ANAT Wirbelsäule *f*, Rückgrat *n*
spinal cord, spinal mar·row ANAT Rückenmark *n*
spin·dle Spindel *f*
spin-dri·er (Wäsche)Schleuder *f*
spin-dry *Wäsche* schleudern
spin-dry·er → *spin-drier*
spine ANAT Wirbelsäule *f*, Rückgrat *n*; ZO Stachel *m*, BOT *a.* Dorn *m*; (*Buch-*) Rücken *m*
spin·ning mill TECH Spinnerei *f*
spinning top Kreisel *m*
spinning wheel Spinnrad *n*
spin·ster ältere unverheiratete Frau, *contp* alte Jungfer, spätes Mädchen
spin·y ZO stach(e)lig, BOT *a.* dornig
spi·ral 1. spiralförmig, Spiral...; **2.** (*a.* ECON *Preis- etc*)Spirale *f*
spi·ral stair·case Wendeltreppe *f*
spire (*Kirch*)Turmspitze *f*
spir·it Geist *m*; Stimmung *f*, Einstellung *f*; Schwung *m*; Elan *m*; CHEM Spiritus *m*; *mst pl* Spirituosen *pl*
spir·it·ed energisch; erregt (*debate etc*)
spir·it·less temperamentlos; mutlos

spir·its Laune *f*, Stimmung *f*; *be in high spirits* in Hochstimmung sein; ausgelassen *or* übermütig sein; *be in low spirits* niedergeschlagen sein
spir·i·tu·al 1. geistig; geistlich; **2.** MUS Spiritual *n*
spit¹ 1. spucken; knistern (*fire*), brutzeln (*meat etc*); *a.* *spit out* ausspucken; *spit at s.o.* j-n anspucken; *it is spitting (with rain)* es tröpfelt; **2.** Spucke *f*
spit² (*Brat*)Spieß *m*; GEOGR Landzunge *f*
spite 1. Bosheit *f*, Gehässigkeit *f*; *out of or from pure spite* aus reiner Bosheit; *in spite of* trotz (*gen*); **2.** j-n ärgern
spite·ful boshaft, gehässig
spit·ting im·age Ebenbild *n*; *she is the spitting image of her mother* sie ist ihrer Mutter wie aus dem Gesicht geschnitten
spit·tle Speichel *m*, Spucke *f*
splash 1. (be)spritzen; klatschen; plan(t)-schen; platschen; *splash down* wassern; **2.** Klatschen *n*, Platschen *n*; Spritzer *m*, Spritzfleck *m*; *esp Br* GASTR Spritzer *m*, Schuss *m*
splash·down Wasserung *f*
splay *a.* *splay out* Finger, Zehen spreizen
spleen ANAT Milz *f*
splen·did großartig, herrlich, prächtig
splen·do(u)r Pracht *f*
splice miteinander verbinden, *Film etc* (zusammen)kleben
splint MED Schiene *f*; *put in a splint, put in splints* schienen
splin·ter 1. Splitter *m*; **2.** (zer)splittern; *splinter off* absplittern; *fig* sich abspalten (*from* von)
split 1. *v/t* (zer)spalten; zerreißen; *a.* *split up* aufteilen (*between* unter *acc*; *into* in *acc*); sich *et.* teilen; *split hairs* Haarspalterei treiben; *split one's sides* F sich vor Lachen biegen; *v/i* sich spalten; zerreißen; sich teilen (*into* in *acc*); *a.* *split up (with)* Schluss machen (mit), sich trennen (von); **2.** Riss *m*; Spalt *m*; Aufteilung *f*; *fig* Bruch *m*; *fig* Spaltung *f*
split·ting heftig, rasend (*headache etc*)
splut·ter stottern (*a.* MOT); zischen
spoil 1. *v/t* verderben; ruinieren; j-n verwöhnen, *Kind a.* verziehen; *v/i* verderben, schlecht werden; **2.** *mst pl* Beute *f*
spoil·er MOT Spoiler *m*
spoil-sport F Spielverderber(in)
spoke TECH Speiche *f*
spokes·man Sprecher *m*
spokes·wom·an Sprecherin *f*
sponge 1. Schwamm *m*; Schnorrer(in); *Br* → *sponge cake*; **2.** *v/t a.* *sponge down* (mit e-m Schwamm) abwaschen;

S

sponge off weg-, abwischen; **sponge (up)** aufsaugen, aufwischen (**from** von); *et.* schnorren (**from, off, on** von, bei); *v/i* schnorren (**from, off, on** bei)

sponge cake Biskuitkuchen *m*

spong·er Schnorrer(in)

spong·y schwammig; weich

spon·sor 1. Bürge *m*, Bürgin *f*; Sponsor(in), Geldgeber(in); Spender(in); **2.** bürgen für; sponsern

spon·ta·ne·ous spontan

spook F Geist *m*

spook·y F gespenstisch, unheimlich

spool Spule *f*; **spool of thread** Garnrolle *f*

spoon 1. Löffel *m*; **2.** löffeln

spoon-feed *Kind etc* füttern

spoon·ful (*ein*) Löffel (voll)

spo·rad·ic sporadisch, gelegentlich

spore BOT Spore *f*

sport 1. Sport *m*; Sportart *f*; F feiner Kerl; *pl* Sport *m*; **2.** herumlaufen mit; protzen mit

sports Sport...

sports car MOT Sportwagen *m*

sports cen·ter (*Br* **cen·tre**) Sportzentrum *n*

sports·man Sportler *m*

sports·wear Sportkleidung *f*

sports·wom·an Sportlerin *f*

spot 1. Punkt *m*, Tupfen *m*; Fleck *m*; MED Pickel *m*; Ort *m*, Platz *m*, Stelle *f*; *radio*, TV (Werbe)Spot *m*; F Spot *m*; **a spot of** *Br* F ein bisschen; **on the spot** auf der Stelle, sofort; zur Stelle; an Ort und Stelle, vor Ort; auf der Stelle; **be in a spot** F in Schwulitäten sein; **soft spot** *fig* Schwäche *f* (**for** für); **tender spot** empfindliche Stelle; **weak spot** schwacher Punkt; Schwäche *f*; **2.** entdecken, sehen

spot check Stichprobe *f*

spot·less tadellos sauber; *fig* untad(e)lig

spot·light Spotlight *n*, Scheinwerfer *m*; Scheinwerferlicht *n*

spot·ted getüpfelt; fleckig

spot·ter Beobachter *m*

spot·ty pick(e)lig

spouse Gatte *m*, Gattin *f*, Gemahl(in)

spout 1. *v/t* Wasser *etc* (heraus)spritzen; *v/i* spritzen (**from** aus); **2.** Schnauze *f*, Tülle *f*; (*Wasser- etc*)Strahl *m*

sprain MED **1.** sich *et.* verstauchen; **2.** Verstauchung *f*

sprat ZO Sprotte *f*

sprawl ausgestreckt liegen *or* sitzen (*a.* **sprawl out**); sich ausbreiten

spray 1. (be)sprühen; spritzen; sich *die Haare* sprayen; *Parfüm etc* versprühen, zerstäuben; **2.** Sprühnebel *m*; Gischt

m, f; Spray *m, n*; → **sprayer**

spray can → **spray·er** Sprüh-, Spraydose *f*, Zerstäuber *m*

spread 1. *v/t* ausbreiten, *Arme a.* ausstrecken, *Finger etc* spreizen (*all a.* **spread out**); *Furcht, Krankheit, Nachricht etc* verbreiten, *Gerücht a.* ausstreuen; *Butter etc* streichen (**on** auf *acc*); *Brot etc* (be)streichen (**with** mit); *v/i* sich ausbreiten (*a.* **spread out**); sich erstrecken (**over** über *acc*); sich verbreiten, übergreifen (**to** auf *acc*); sich streichen lassen (*butter etc*); **2.** Ausbreitung *f*, Verbreitung *f*; Ausdehnung *f*; Spannweite *f*; GASTR Aufstrich *m*

spread·sheet EDP Tabellenkalkulation *f*, Tabellenkalkulationsprogramm *n*

spree: **go (out) on a spree** F e-e Sauftour machen; **go on a buying** (*or* **shopping, spending**) **spree** wie verrückt einkaufen

sprig BOT kleiner Zweig

spright·ly lebhaft; rüstig

spring 1. *v/i* springen; **spring from** herrühren von; **spring up** aufkommen (*wind*); aus dem Boden schießen (*building etc*); *v/t*: **spring a leak** ein Leck bekommen; **spring a surprise on s.o.** j-n überraschen; **2.** Frühling *m*, Frühjahr *n*; Quelle *f*; TECH Feder *f*; Elastizität *f*; Federung *f*; Sprung *m*, Satz *m*; **in (the) spring** im Frühling

spring·board Sprungbrett *n*

spring-clean gründlich putzen, Frühjahrsputz machen (*in dat*)

spring tide Springflut *f*

spring·time Frühling *m*, Frühlingszeit *f*, Frühjahr *n*

spring·y elastisch, federnd

sprin·kle 1. Wasser *etc* sprengen (**on** auf *acc*); Salz *etc* streuen (**on** auf *acc*); *et.* (be)sprengen *or* bestreuen (**with** mit); **it is sprinkling** es tröpfelt; **2.** Sprühregen *m*

sprin·kler (*Rasen*)Sprenger *m*; Sprinkler *m*, Berieselungsanlage *f*

sprin·kling: a sprinkling of ein bisschen, ein paar

sprint SPORT **1.** sprinten; spurten; **2.** Sprint *m*; Spurt *m*

sprint·er SPORT Sprinter(in)

sprite Kobold *m*

sprout 1. sprießen (*a. fig*), keimen; wachsen lassen; **2.** Spross *m*; (**Brussels**) **sprouts** Rosenkohl *m*

spruce[1] BOT Fichte *f*; Rottanne *f*

spruce[2] adrett

spry rüstig, lebhaft

spur 1. Sporn *m* (*a.* ZO); *fig* Ansporn *m* (**to**

zu); **on the spur of the moment** spontan; **2.** *e-m Pferd* die Sporen geben; *often* **spur on** *fig* anspornen (**to** zu)

spurt[1] **1.** spurten, sprinten; **2.** plötzliche Aktivität, (*Arbeits*)Anfall *m*; Spurt *m*, Sprint *m*

spurt[2] **1.** spritzen (**from** aus); **2.** (*Wasser etc*)Strahl *m*

sput·ter stottern (*a.* MOT); zischen

spy 1. Spion(in); **2.** spionieren, Spionage treiben (**for** für); **spy into** *fig* herumspionieren in (*dat*); **spy on** j-m nachspionieren

spy·hole (Tür)Spion *m*

squab·ble (sich) streiten (**about, over** um, wegen)

squad Mannschaft *f*, Trupp *m*; (*Überfall etc*)Kommando *n*; Dezernat *n*

squad car (Funk)Streifenwagen *m*

squad·ron MIL, AVIAT Staffel *f*; MAR Geschwader *n*

squal·id schmutzig, verwahrlost, verkommen, armselig

squall Bö *f*

squan·der *Geld, Zeit etc* verschwenden, *Chance* vertun

square 1. Quadrat *n*; Viereck *n*; *öffentlicher* Platz; MATH Quadrat(zahl *f*) *n*; *board game*: Feld *n*; TECH Winkel(maß *n*) *m*; **2.** quadratisch, Quadrat...; viereckig; rechtwink(e)lig; eckig (*shoulders etc*); *fig* fair, gerecht; **be** (**all**) **square** quitt sein; **3.** quadratisch *or* rechtwink(e)lig machen (*a.* **square off** *or* **up**); in Quadrate einteilen (*a.* **square off**); MATH *Zahl* ins Quadrat erheben; *Schultern* straffen; *Konto* ausgleichen; *Schulden* begleichen; *fig* in Einklang bringen *or* stehen (**with** mit); **square up** F abrechnen; **square up to** sich j-m, e-m Problem *etc* stellen

square root MATH Quadratwurzel *f*

squash[1] **1.** zerdrücken, zerquetschen; quetschen, zwängen (**into** in *acc*); **squash flat** flach drücken, F platt walzen; **2.** Gedränge *n*; SPORT Squash *n*

squash[2] BOT Kürbis *m*

squat 1. hocken, kauern; *leer stehendes Haus* besetzen; **squat down** sich (hin)kauern *or* (hin)hocken; **2.** gedrungen, untersetzt

squat·ter Hausbesetzer(in)

squaw Squaw *f*

squawk kreischen, schreien; F lautstark protestieren (**about** gegen)

squeak 1. piep(s)en (*mouse etc*); quietschen (*door etc*); **2.** Piep(s)en *n*; Piep(s) *m*; Quietschen *n*

squeak·y piepsig (*voice*); quietschend

(*door etc*)

squeal 1. kreischen (**with** vor *dat*); **squeal on s.o.** *fig* F j-n verpfeifen; **2.** Kreischen *n*; Schrei *m*

squeam·ish empfindlich, zart besaitet

squeeze 1. drücken; auspressen, ausquetschen; (sich) quetschen *or* zwängen (**into** in *acc*); **2.** Druck *m*; GASTR Spritzer *m*; Gedränge *n*

squeez·er (Frucht)Presse *f*

squid ZO Tintenfisch *m*

squint schielen; blinzeln

squirm sich winden

squir·rel ZO Eichhörnchen *n*

squirt 1. (be)spritzen; **2.** Strahl *m*

stab 1. *v/t* niederstechen; **be stabbed in the arm** e-n Stich in den Arm bekommen; *v/i* stechen (**at** nach); **2.** Stich *m*

sta·bil·i·ty Stabilität *f*; *fig* Dauerhaftigkeit *f*; Ausgeglichenheit *f*

sta·bil·ize (sich) stabilisieren

sta·ble[1] stabil; *fig* dauerhaft; ausgeglichen

sta·ble[2] Stall *m*

stack 1. Stapel *m*, Stoß *m*; **stacks of, a stack of** F jede Menge *Arbeit etc*; **2.** stapeln; voll stapeln (**with** mit); **stack up** aufstapeln

sta·di·um SPORT Stadion *n*

staff 1. Stab *m*; Mitarbeiter(stab *m*) *pl*; Personal *n*, Belegschaft *f*; Lehrkörper *m*; MIL Stab *m*; **2.** besetzen (**with** mit)

staff room Lehrerzimmer *n*

stag ZO Hirsch *m*

stage 1. THEA Bühne *f* (*a. fig*); Etappe *f* (*a. fig*), (Reise)Abschnitt *m*; Teilstrecke *f*, Fahrzone *f* (*bus etc*); *fig* Stufe *f*, Stadium *n*, Phase *f*; **2.** THEA inszenieren; veranstalten

stage·coach Postkutsche *f*

stage di·rec·tion THEA Regieanweisung *f*

stage fright Lampenfieber *n*

stage man·ag·er THEA Inspizient *m*

stag·ger 1. *v/i* (sch)wanken, taumeln, torkeln; *v/t* j-n sprachlos machen, F umhauen; *Arbeitszeit etc* staffeln; **2.** Wanken *n*, Schwanken *n*, Taumeln *n*

stag·nant stehend (*water*); *esp* ECON stagnierend

stag·nate *esp* ECON stagnieren

stain 1. *v/t* beflecken; (ein)färben; *Holz* beizen; *Glas* bemalen; *v/i* Flecken bekommen, schmutzen; **2.** Fleck *m*; TECH Färbemittel *n*; (*Holz*)Beize *f*; Makel *m*

stained glass Bunt-, Farbglas *n*

stain·less nicht rostend, rostfrei

stair (Treppen)Stufe *f*; *pl* Treppe *f*

stair·case, stair·way Treppe *f*; Treppenhaus *n*

stake¹ 1. Pfahl *m*, Pfosten *m*; HIST Marterpfahl *m*; **2. stake off, stake out** abstecken

stake² 1. Anteil *m*, Beteiligung *f* (**in** an *dat*) (*a.* ECON); (Wett- *etc*)Einsatz *m*; **be at stake** *fig* auf dem Spiel stehen; **2.** *Geld etc* setzen (**on** auf *acc*); *Ruf etc* riskieren, aufs Spiel setzen

stale alt(backen); abgestanden, *beer etc*: *a.* schal, *air etc*: *a.* verbraucht

stalk¹ BOT Stängel *m*, Stiel *m*, Halm *m*

stalk² *v/t* sich heranpirschen an (*acc*); verfolgen, hinter *j-m, et.* herschleichen; *v/i* stolzieren

stall¹ 1. (*Obst- etc*)Stand *m*, (*Markt-*)Bude *f*; AGR Box *f*; *pl* REL Chorgestühl *n*; *Br* THEA Parkett *n*; **2.** *v/t Motor* abwürgen; *v/i* MOT absterben

stall² *v/i* Ausflüchte machen; Zeit schinden; *v/t j-n* hinhalten; *et.* hinauszögern

stal·li·on ZO (Zucht)Hengst *m*

stal·wart kräftig, robust; *esp* POL treu

stam·i·na Ausdauer *f*; Durchhaltevermögen *n*, Kondition *f*

stam·mer 1. stottern, stammeln; **2.** Stottern *n*, Stammeln *n*

stamp 1. *v/i* sta(m)pfen, trampeln; *v/t Pass etc* (ab)stempeln; *Datum etc* aufstempeln (**on** auf *acc*); *Brief etc* frankieren; *fig j-n* abstempeln (**as** als, zu); **stamp one's foot** aufstampfen; **stamp out** *Feuer* austreten; TECH ausstanzen; **2.** (*Brief-*)Marke *f*; (*Steuer- etc*)Marke *f*; Stempel *m*; **stamped addressed envelope** Freiumschlag *m*

stam·pede 1. ZO wilde Flucht; wilder Ansturm, Massenansturm *m* (**for** auf *acc*); **2.** *v/i* ZO durchgehen; *v/t* in Panik versetzen

stanch treu, zuverlässig

stand 1. *v/i* aufstehen; *fig fest- etc* bleiben; **stand still** still stehen; *v/t* stellen (**on** auf *acc*); aushalten, ertragen; *e-r Prüfung etc* standhalten; *Probe* bestehen; *Chance* haben; *Drink etc* spendieren; **I can't stand him** (*or* **it**) ich kann ihn (*or* das) nicht ausstehen *or* leiden; **stand around** herumstehen; **stand back** zurücktreten; **stand by** danebenstehen; *fig* zu *j-m* halten; zu *et.* stehen; **stand idly by** tatenlos zusehen; **stand down** verzichten; zurücktreten; JUR den Zeugenstand verlassen; **stand for** stehen für, bedeuten; *sich et.* gefallen lassen, *et.* dulden; *esp Br* kandidieren für; **stand in** einspringen (**for** für); **stand in for s.o.** *a.* j-n vertreten; **stand on** (*fig* be)stehen auf (*dat*); **stand out** hervorstechen; sich abheben (**against** gegen, von); **stand over** überwachen, aufpassen auf (*acc*);

stand together zusammenhalten, -stehen; **stand up** aufstehen, sich erheben; **stand up for** eintreten *or* sich einsetzen für; **stand up to** *j-m* mutig gegenübertreten, *j-m* die Stirn bieten; **2.** (*Obst-, Messe- etc*)Stand *m*; (*Schirm-, Noten- etc*) Ständer *m*; SPORT *etc* Tribüne *f*; (*Taxi-*) Stand(platz) *m*; JUR Zeugenstand *m*; **take a stand** *fig* Position beziehen (**on** zu)

stan·dard¹ 1. Norm *f*, Maßstab *m*; Standard *m*, Niveau *n*; **standard of living, living standard** Lebensstandard *m*; **2.** normal, Normal...; durchschnittlich, Durchschnitts...; Standard...

stan·dard² Standarte *f*, MOT Stander *m*; HIST Banner *n*

stan·dard·ize vereinheitlichen, *esp* TECH standardisieren, normen

stan·dard lamp *Br* Stehlampe *f*

stand·by 1. Reserve *f*; AVIAT Stand-by *n*; **be on standby** in Bereitschaft stehen; **2.** Reserve..., Not...; AVIAT Stand-by...

stand-in *film, TV* Double *n*; Ersatzmann *m*; Vertreter(in)

stand·ing 1. stehend; *fig* ständig; → **ovation**; **2.** Rang *m*, Stellung *f*; Ansehen *n*, Ruf *m*; Dauer *f*; **of long standing** alt, seit langem bestehend

standing or·der ECON Dauerauftrag *m*

standing room: standing room only nur noch Stehplätze

stand·off·ish F (sehr) ablehnend, hochnäsig

stand·point *fig* Standpunkt *m*

stand·still Stillstand *m*; **be at a standstill** stehen (*car etc*); ruhen (*production etc*); **bring to a standstill** *Auto etc* zum Stehen bringen; *Produktion etc* zum Erliegen bringen

stand-up Steh...; **stand-up fight** Schlägerei *f*

stan·za Strophe *f*

sta·ple¹ 1. Hauptnahrungsmittel *n*; ECON Haupterzeugnis *n*; **2.** Haupt...; üblich

sta·ple² 1. Heftklammer *f*; Krampe *f*; **2.** heften

sta·pler TECH (Draht)Hefter *m*

star 1. ASTR Stern *m*; PRINT Sternchen *n*; THEA, SPORT *etc* Star *m*; **2.** *v/t* PRINT mit e-m Sternchen kennzeichnen; **starring** ... in der Hauptrolle *or* in den Hauptrollen ...; **a film starring** ... in Film mit ... in der Hauptrolle *or* den Hauptrollen *v/i* die *or* e-e Hauptrolle spielen (**in** in *dat*)

star·board AVIAT, MAR Steuerbord *n*

starch 1. (*Kartoffel- etc*)Stärke *f*; stärkereiches Nahrungsmittel *n*; (*Wäsche-*) Stärke *f*; **2.** *Wäsche* stärken

stare 1. starren; *stare at j-n* anstarren; **2.** (starrer) Blick, Starren *n*

stark 1. *adj fig* nackt; *be in stark contrast to* in krassem Gegensatz stehen zu; **2.** *adv*: F *stark naked* splitternackt; *stark raving mad, stark staring mad* total verrückt

star·light ASTR Sternenlicht *n*

star·ling ZO Star *m*

star·lit stern(en)klar

star·ry Stern..., Sternen...

star·ry-eyed F blauäugig, naiv

start 1. *v/i* anfangen, beginnen (*a. start off*); aufbrechen (*for* nach) (*a. start off, start out*); RAIL *etc* abfahren, MAR ablegen, AVIAT abfliegen, starten; MOT anspringen; TECH anlaufen; SPORT starten; zusammenfahren, -zucken (*at* bei); *to start with* anfangs, zunächst; erstens; *start from scratch* ganz von vorn anfangen; *v/t* anfangen, beginnen (*a. start off*); in Gang setzen *or* bringen, *Motor etc a.* anlassen, starten; **2.** Anfang *m*, Beginn *m*, (*esp* SPORT) Start *m*; Aufbruch *m*; Auffahren *n*, Aufschrecken *n*; *at the start* am Anfang; SPORT am Start; *for a start* erstens; *from start to finish* von Anfang bis Ende

start·er SPORT Starter(in); MOT Anlasser *m*, Starter *m*; *esp Br* GASTR F Vorspeise *f*; *for starters* zunächst einmal

start·le erschrecken; überraschen, bestürzen

starv·a·tion Hungern *n*; *die of starvation* verhungern; *starvation diet* F Fasten-, Hungerkur *f*, Nulldiät *f*

starve hungern (lassen); *starve (to death)* verhungern (lassen); *I'm starving!* Br F, *I'm starved!* F ich komme um vor Hunger!

state 1. Zustand *m*; Stand *m*, Lage *f*; POL (Bundes-, Einzel)Staat *m*; *often* **State** POL Staat *m*; **2.** Staats..., staatlich; **3.** angeben, nennen; erklären, JUR aussagen (*that* dass); festlegen, festsetzen

State De·part·ment POL Außenministerium *n*

state·ly gemessen, würdevoll; prächtig

state·ment Statement *n*, Erklärung *f*; Angabe *f*; JUR Aussage *f*; ECON (*Bank-, Konto*)Auszug *m*; *make a statement* e-e Erklärung abgeben

state-of-the-art TECH neuest, modernst

states·man POL Staatsmann *m*

stat·ic statisch

sta·tion 1. (*a.* Bus-, U-)Bahnhof *m*, Station *f*; (*Forschungs-, Rettungs- etc*)Station *f*; Tankstelle *f*; (*Feuer*)Wache *f*; (*Polizei*)Revier *n*; (*Wahl*)Lokal *n*; *radio*, TV Sender *m*, Station *f*; **2.** aufstellen, postieren; MIL stationieren

sta·tion·ar·y stehend

sta·tion·er Schreibwarenhändler(in)

sta·tion·er's (shop) Schreibwarenhandlung *f*

sta·tion·er·y Schreibwaren *pl*; Briefpapier *n*

sta·tion·mas·ter RAIL Stations-, Bahnhofsvorsteher *m*

sta·tion wag·on MOT Kombiwagen *m*

sta·tis·ti·cal statistisch

sta·tis·ti·cian Statistiker *m*

sta·tis·tics Statistik(en *pl*) *f*

stat·ue Statue *f*, Standbild *n*

sta·tus Status *m*, Rechtsstellung *f*; (*Familien*)Stand *m*; Stellung *f*, Rang *m*, Status *m*

status line EDP Statuszeile *f*

stat·ute Gesetz *n*; Statut *n*, Satzung *f*

stat·ute of lim·i·ta·tions JUR Verjährungsfrist *f*; *come under the statute of limitations* verjähren

staunch¹ Br → **stanch**

staunch² *Blutung* stillen

stay 1. bleiben (*with s.o.* bei j-m); wohnen (*at* in *dat*; *with s.o.* bei j-m); *stay put* F sich nicht (vom Fleck) rühren; *stay away* wegbleiben, sich fernhalten (*from* von); *stay up* aufbleiben; **2.** Aufenthalt *m*; JUR Aussetzung *f*, Aufschub *m*

stead·fast treu, zuverlässig; fest

stead·y 1. *adj* fest; stabil; ruhig (*hand*), gut (*nerves*); gleichmäßig; **2.** (sich) beruhigen; **3.** *int a.* **steady on!** Br F Vorsicht!; **4.** *adv*: *go steady with s.o.* (fest) mit j-m gehen; **5.** feste Freundin, fester Freund

steak GASTR Steak *n*; (*Fisch*)Filet *n*

steal stehlen (*a. fig*); sich stehlen, (sich) schleichen (*out of* aus)

stealth: *by stealth* heimlich, verstohlen

stealth·y heimlich, verstohlen

steam 1. Dampf *m*; Dunst *m*; *let off steam* Dampf ablassen, *fig a.* sich Luft machen; **2.** Dampf...; **3.** *v/i* dampfen; *steam up* beschlagen (*mirror etc*); *v/t* GASTR dünsten, dämpfen

steam·boat Dampfboot *n*, Dampfer *m*

steam·er Dampfer *m*, Dampfschiff *n*; Dampf-, Schnellkochtopf *m*

steam·ship Dampfer *m*, Dampfschiff *n*

steel 1. Stahl *m*; **2.** *steel o.s. for* sich wappnen gegen

steel·work·er Stahlarbeiter *m*

steel·works Stahlwerk *n*

steep¹ steil; *fig* stark (*rise etc*); F happig

steep² eintauchen (*in* in *acc*); *Wäsche* (ein)weichen

stee·ple Kirchturm *m*

S

stee·ple·chase *horse racing:* Hindernisrennen *n;* SPORT Hindernislauf *m*
steer[1] ZO (junger) Ochse
steer[2] steuern, lenken
steer·ing col·umn MOT Lenksäule *f*
steer·ing wheel MOT Lenkrad *n, a.* MAR Steuerrad *n*
stein Maßkrug *m*
stem 1. BOT Stiel *m (a. of a wine glass etc),* Stängel *m;* LING Stamm *m;* **2. stem from** stammen *or* herrühren von
stench Gestank *m*
sten·cil Schablone *f;* PRINT Matrize *f*
ste·nog·ra·pher Stenotypistin *f*
step 1. Schritt *m (a. fig);* Stufe *f;* Sprosse *f;* (**a pair of**) **steps** (e-e) Tritt- *or* Stufenleiter; **mind the step!** Vorsicht, Stufe!; **step by step** Schritt für Schritt; **take steps** Schritte *or* et. unternehmen; **2.** gehen; treten (**in** in *acc;* **on** auf *acc);* **step on it, step on the gas** MOT F Gas geben, auf die Tube drücken; **step aside** zur Seite treten; *fig* Platz machen; **step down** *fig* Platz machen; **step up** Produktion *etc* steigern
step-by-step *fig* schrittweise
step·fa·ther Stiefvater *m*
step·lad·der Tritt-, Stufenleiter *f*
step·moth·er Stiefmutter *f*
steppes GEOGR Steppe *f*
step·ping-stone *fig* Sprungbrett *n* (**to** für)
ster·e·o 1. Stereo *n;* Stereogerät *n,* Stereoanlage *f;* **2.** Stereo...
stereo sys·tem MUS Kompaktanlage *f*
ster·ile steril (*a. fig*), *a.* unfruchtbar, MED *a.* keimfrei
ste·ril·i·ty Sterilität *f (a. fig),* Unfruchtbarkeit *f*
ster·il·ize MED sterilisieren
ster·ling das Pfund Sterling
stern[1] streng
stern[2] MAR Heck *n*
stew 1. *Fleisch, Gemüse* schmoren, *Obst* dünsten; **stewed apples** Apfelkompott *n;* **2.** Eintopf *m;* **be in a stew** in heller Aufregung sein
stew·ard Ordner *m;* AVIAT, MAR Steward *m*
stew·ard·ess AVIAT, MAR Stewardess *f*
stick[1] trockener Zweig; Stock *m;* ([*Eis*]-*Hockey*)Schläger *m;* (*Besen- etc-*) Stiel *m;* AVIAT (*Steuer*)Knüppel *m;* Stück *n,* Stange *f,* (*Lippen- etc*)Stift *m,* Stäbchen *n*
stick[2] *v/t* mit e-r *Nadel etc* stechen (**into** in *acc);* et. kleben (**on** auf, an *acc);* an-, festkleben (**with** mit); stecken; F tun, stellen, setzen, legen; **I can't stick him** (*or* **it**) *esp Br* F ich kann ihn (*or* das) nicht ausstehen *or* leiden; *v/i* kleben; kleben bleiben (**to**

an *dat);* stecken bleiben; **stick at nothing** vor nichts zurückschrecken; **stick by** F bleiben bei; F zu j-m halten; **stick out** vorstehen; abstehen; *et.* ausstrecken *or* vorstrecken; **stick to** bleiben bei
stick·er Aufkleber *m*
stick·ing plas·ter *Br* Heftpflaster *n*
stick·y klebrig (**with** von); F heikel, unangenehm
stiff 1. *adj* steif; F stark (*drink etc*); schwer, hart (*task, penalty etc*); hartnäckig (*resistance*); F happig, gepfeffert, gesalzen (*price*); **keep a stiff upper lip** *fig* Haltung bewahren; **2.** *adv* äußerst; höchst; **be bored stiff** F sich zu Tode langweilen; **be scared stiff** e-e wahnsinnige Angst haben; **be worried stiff** sich furchtbare Sorgen machen
stiff·en *v/t Wäsche* stärken; versteifen; verstärken; *v/i* steif werden; sich verhärten *or* versteifen
sti·fle ersticken; *fig* unterdrücken
stile Zauntritt *m*
sti·let·to Stilett *n*
stiletto heel Bleistift-, Pfennigabsatz *m*
still[1] **1.** *adv* (immer) noch, noch immer; *with comparative:* noch; **2.** *cj* dennoch, trotzdem
still[2] **1.** *adj* still; ruhig; GASTR ohne Kohlensäure; **2.** *film,* TV Standfoto *n*
still·born MED tot geboren
still life PAINT Stilleben *n*
stilt Stelze *f*
stilt·ed *fig* gestelzt
stim·u·lant MED Stimulans *n,* Anregungs-, Aufputschmittel *n; fig* Anreiz *m,* Ansporn *m* (**to** für)
stim·u·late MED stimulieren (*a. fig*), anregen, *fig a.* anspornen
stim·u·lus Reiz *m; fig* Anreiz *m,* Ansporn *m* (**to** für)
sting 1. stechen (*insect*); brennen (auf *or* in *dat);* **2.** Stachel *m;* Stich *m;* Brennen *n,* brennender Schmerz
stin·gy F knaus(e)rig, knick(e)rig (*person*); mick(e)rig (*meal etc*)
stink 1. stinken (**of** nach); **stink up** (*Br* **out**) verpesten; **2.** Gestank *m*
stint: stint o.s. (**of s.th.**) sich einschränken (mit et.); **stint** (**on**) **s.th.** sparen mit et.
stip·u·late zur Bedingung machen; festsetzen, vereinbaren
stip·u·la·tion Bedingung *f;* Vereinbarung *f*
stir 1. (um)rühren; (sich) rühren *or* bewegen; *j-n* aufwühlen; **stir up** Unruhe stiften; *Streit* entfachen; *Erinnerungen* wachrufen; **2. give s.th. a stir** et. umrüh-

ren; *cause* (*or* *create*) *a stir* für Aufsehen sorgen
stir·rup Steigbügel *m*
stitch 1. Stich *m*; Masche *f*; MED Seitenstechen *n*; **2.** zunähen, *Wunde* nähen (*a.* *stitch up*); heften
stock 1. Vorrat *m* (*of* an *dat*); GASTR Brühe *f*; *a.* *livestock* Viehbestand *m*; (*Gewehr*)Schaft *m*; *fig* Abstammung *f*, Herkunft *f*; ECON Aktie(n *pl*) *f*; *pl* Aktien *pl*, Wertpapiere *pl*; *have s.th. in stock* ECON et. vorrätig *or* auf Lager haben; *take stock* ECON Inventur machen; *take stock of* *fig* sich klar werden über (*acc*); **2.** ECON Ware vorrätig haben, führen; *stock up* sich eindecken *or* versorgen (*on, with* mit); **3.** Serien...; Standard...; stereotyp
stock·breed·er AGR Viehzüchter *m*
stock·breed·ing AGR Viehzucht *f*
stock·brok·er ECON Börsenmakler *m*
stock ex·change ECON Börse *f*
stock·hold·er ECON Aktionär(in)
stock·ing Strumpf *m*
stock mar·ket ECON Börse *f*
stock·pile 1. Vorrat *m* (*of* an *dat*); **2.** e-n Vorrat anlegen an (*dat*)
stock·still regungslos
stock·tak·ing ECON Inventur *f*; *fig* Bestandsaufnahme *f*
stock·y stämmig, untersetzt
stol·id gleichmütig
stom·ach 1. ANAT Magen *m*; Bauch *m*; *fig* Appetit *m* (*for* auf *acc*); **2.** vertragen (*a.* *fig*)
stom·ach·ache MED Magenschmerzen *pl*, Bauchschmerzen *pl*, Bauchweh *n*
stom·ach up·set MED Magenverstimmung *f*
stone 1. Stein *m*, BOT *a.* Kern *m*; (*Hagel*)Korn *n*; **2.** mit Steinen bewerfen; steinigen; entkernen, entsteinen
stone·ma·son Steinmetz *m*
stone·ware Steingut *n*
ston·y steinig; steinern (*face etc*), eisig (*silence*)
stool Hocker *m*, Schemel *m*; MED Stuhl *m*, Stuhlgang *m*
stool·pi·geon F (Polizei)Spitzel *m*
stoop 1. *v/i* sich bücken (*a.* *stoop down*); gebeugt gehen; *stoop to* *fig* sich herablassen *or* hergeben zu; **2.** gebeugte Haltung
stop 1. *v/i* (an)halten, stehen bleiben (*a.* *watch etc*), stoppen; aufhören; *esp Br* bleiben; *stop dead* plötzlich *or* abrupt stehen bleiben; *stop at nothing* vor nichts zurückschrecken; *stop short of doing, stop short at s.th.* zurückschre-

cken vor (*dat*); *v/t* anhalten, stoppen; aufhören mit; ein Ende machen *or* setzen (*dat*); *Blutung* stillen; *Arbeiten, Verkehr etc* zum Erliegen bringen; *et.* verhindern; *j-n* abhalten (*from* von), hindern (*from* an *dat*); *Rohr etc* verstopfen (*a.* *stop up*); *Zahn* füllen, plombieren; *Scheck* sperren (lassen); *stop by* vorbeischauen; *stop in* vorbeischauen (*at* bei); *stop off* F kurz Halt machen; *stop over* kurz Halt machen; Zwischenstation machen; **2.** Halt *m*; (*Bus*)Haltestelle *f*; PHOT Blende *f*; *mst* *full stop* LING Punkt *m*
stop·gap Notbehelf *m*
stop·light MOT Bremslicht *n*; rotes Licht
stop·o·ver Zwischenstation *f*; AVIAT Zwischenlandung *f*
stop·page Unterbrechung *f*, Stopp *m*; Verstopfung *f*; Streik *m*; *Br* (Gehalts-, Lohn)Abzug *m*
stop·per Stöpsel *m*
stop sign MOT Stoppschild *n*
stop·watch Stoppuhr *f*
stor·age ECON Lagerung *f*; Lagergeld *n*; EDP Speicher *m*
store 1. (ein)lagern; *Energie* speichern; EDP (ab)speichern, sichern; *a.* *store up* sich e-n Vorrat anlegen an (*dat*); **2.** Vorrat *m*; Lager *n*, Lagerhalle *f*, Lagerhaus *n*; Laden *m*, Geschäft *n*, *esp Br* Kaufhaus *n*, Warenhaus *n*; *set great store by* großen Wert legen auf (*acc*)
store·house Lagerhaus *n*; *fig* Fundgrube *f*
store·keep·er Ladenbesitzer(in)
store·room Lagerraum *m*
sto·rey *Br* → *story²*
...**sto·reyed** *Br*, ...**sto·ried** mit ... Stockwerken, ...stöckig
stork ZO Storch *m*
storm 1. Unwetter *n*; Gewitter *n*; Sturm *m*; **2.** *v/t* MIL *etc* stürmen; *v/i* stürmen, stürzen
storm·y stürmisch
sto·ry¹ Geschichte *f*; Märchen *n* (*a. fig*); Story *f*, *a.* Handlung *f*, *a.* Bericht *m* (*on* über *acc*)
sto·ry² Stock *m*, Stockwerk *n*, Etage *f*
stout korpulent, vollschlank; *fig* unerschrocken; entschieden
stove Ofen *m*, Herd *m*
stow *a.* *stow away* verstauen
stow·a·way AVIAT, MAR blinder Passagier
strad·dle rittlings sitzen auf (*dat*)
strag·gle verstreut liegen *or* stehen; BOT *etc* wuchern; *straggle in* F einzeln eintrudeln
strag·gler Nachzügler(in)
strag·gly verstreut (liegend); BOT *etc* wu-

S

chernd; struppig (*mustache etc*)

straight 1. *adj* gerade; glatt (*hair*); pur (*whisky etc*); aufrichtig, offen, ehrlich; *sl* hetero(*sexuell*); *sl* clean, sauber; **put straight** in Ordnung bringen; **2.** *adv* gerade; genau, direkt; klar; ehrlich, anständig; **straight ahead** geradeaus; **straight off** F sofort; **straight on** geradeaus; **straight out** F offen, rundheraus; **3.** SPORT (*Gegen-, Ziel*)Gerade *f*

straight·en *v/t* gerade machen, (gerade) richten; **straighten out** in Ordnung bringen; *v/i a.* **straighten out** gerade werden; **straighten up** sich aufrichten

straight·for·ward aufrichtig; einfach

strain 1. *v/t* Seil *etc* (an)spannen; *sich, Augen etc* überanstrengen; sich *e-n Muskel etc* zerren; *Gemüse, Tee etc* abgießen; *v/i* sich anstrengen; **strain at** zerren *or* ziehen an (*dat*); **2.** Spannung *f*; Anspannung *f*; Strapaze *f*; *fig* Belastung *f*; MED Zerrung *f*

strained MED gezerrt; gezwungen (*smile etc*); gespannt (*relations*); **look strained** abgespannt aussehen

strain·er Sieb *n*

strait GEOGR Meerenge *f*, Straße *f*; *pl fig* Notlage *f*

strait·ened: **live in straitened circumstances** in beschränkten Verhältnissen leben

strand Strang *m*; Faden *m*; (*Kabel-*)Draht *m*; (*Haar*)Strähne *f*

strand·ed: **be stranded** MAR gestrandet sein; **be (left) stranded** *fig* festsitzen (**in** *dat*)

strange merkwürdig, seltsam, sonderbar; fremd

strang·er Fremde *m, f*

stran·gle erwürgen

strap 1. Riemen *m*, Gurt *m*; (*Uhr*)Armband *n*; Träger *m*; **2.** festschnallen; anschnallen

stra·te·gic strategisch

strat·e·gy Strategie *f*

stra·tum GEOL Schicht *f* (*a. fig*)

straw Stroh *n*; Strohhalm *m*

straw·ber·ry BOT Erdbeere *f*

stray 1. (herum)streunen; sich verirren; *fig* abschweifen (**from** von); **2.** verirrtes *or* streunendes Tier; **3.** verirrt (*bullet, dog etc*); streunend (*dog etc*); vereinzelt

streak 1. Streifen *m*; Strähne *f*; (*Charakter*)Zug *m*; **a streak of lightning** ein Blitz; **lucky streak** Glückssträhne *f*; **2.** flitzen; streifen

streak·y streifig; GASTR durchwachsen

stream 1. Bach *m*; Strömung *f*; *fig* Strom *m*; **2.** strömen; flattern, wehen

stream·er Luft-, Papierschlange *f*; Wimpel *m*; EDP Streamer *m*

street 1. Straße *f*; **on** (*esp Br* **in**) **the street** auf der Straße; **2.** Straßen...

street·car Straßenbahn(wagen *m*) *f*

street sweep·er Straßenkehrer *m*

strength Stärke *f*, Kraft *f*, Kräfte *pl*

strength·en *v/t* (ver)stärken; *v/i* stärker werden

stren·u·ous anstrengend, strapaziös; unermüdlich

stress 1. *fig* Stress *m*; PHYS, TECH Beanspruchung *f*, Belastung *f*, Druck *m*; LING Betonung *f*; *fig* Nachdruck *m*; **2.** betonen

stress·ful stressig, aufreibend

stretch 1. *v/t* strecken; (aus)weiten, dehnen; spannen; *fig* es nicht allzu genau nehmen mit; **stretch out** ausstrecken; **be fully stretched** *fig* richtig gefordert werden; voll ausgelastet sein; *v/i* dehnen, *a.* länger *or* weiter werden; sich dehnen *or* recken *or* strecken; sich erstrecken; **stretch out** sich ausstrecken; **2.** Dehnbarkeit *f*, Elastizität *f*; Strecke *f*; SPORT (*Gegen-, Ziel*)Gerade *f*; Zeit *f*, Zeitraum *m*, Zeitspanne *f*; **have a stretch** sich dehnen *or* recken *or* strecken

stretch·er Trage *f*

strick·en schwer betroffen; **stricken with** befallen *or* ergriffen von

strict streng, strikt; genau; **strictly** (**speaking**) genau genommen

strict·ness Strenge *f*

stride 1. schreiten, mit großen Schritten gehen; **2.** großer Schritt

strife Streit *m*

strike 1. *v/t* schlagen; treffen; einschlagen in (*acc*) (*lightning*); Streichholz anzünden; MAR auflaufen auf (*acc*); streichen (**from, off** aus, von); stoßen auf (*acc*); *j-n* beeindrucken; *j-m* einfallen, in den Sinn kommen; *Münze* prägen; *Saite etc* anschlagen; *Lager, Zelt* abbrechen; *Flagge, Segel* streichen; **strike out** (aus)streichen; **strike up** Lied *etc* anstimmen; *Freundschaft etc* schließen; *v/i* schlagen; einschlagen; ECON streiken; **strike (out) at s.o.** auf *j-n* einschlagen; **2.** ECON Streik *m*; (*Öl- etc*)Fund *m*; MIL Angriff *m*; *soccer*: Schuss *m*; **be on strike** streiken; **go on strike** streiken, in den Streik treten; **a lucky strike** ein Glückstreffer

strik·er ECON Streikende *m, f*; *soccer*: Stürmer(in)

strik·ing apart; auffallend

string 1. Schnur *f*, Bindfaden *m*; (*Schürzen-, Schuh- etc*)Band *n*; (*Puppenspiel*-)

Faden *m*, Draht *m*; (*Perlen- etc*)Schnur *f*; MUS, SPORT Saite *f*; (*Bogen*)Sehne *f*; BOT Faser *f*; EDP Zeichenfolge *f*; *fig* Reihe *f*, Serie *f*; **the strings** MUS die Streichinstrumente *pl*, die Streicher *pl*; **pull a few strings** *fig* ein paar Beziehungen spielen lassen; **with no strings attached** *fig* ohne Bedingungen; **2.** *Perlen etc* aufreihen; *Gitarre etc* besaiten, *Tennisschläger etc* bespannen; *Bohnen* abziehen; **3.** MUS Streich...

string bean BOT grüne Bohne

strin·gent streng

string·y fas(e)rig

strip 1. *v/i*: *a.* **strip off** sich ausziehen (**to** bis auf *acc*); *v/t* ausziehen; *Farbe etc* abkratzen, *Tapete etc* abreißen (**from, off** von); *a.* **strip down** TECH zerlegen, auseinandernehmen; **strip s.o. of s.th.** j-m et. rauben *or* wegnehmen; **2.** (*Land-, Papier- etc*)Streifen *m*; Strip *m*

stripe Streifen *m*

striped gestreift

strive: **strive for** *or* **after** streben nach

stroke 1. streicheln; streichen über (*acc*); **2.** Schlag *m* (*a.* SPORT); MED Schlag(anfall) *m*; (*Pinsel*)Strich *m*; *swimming:* Zug *m*; TECH Hub *m*; → **four-stroke engine**; **stroke of lightning** Blitzschlag *m*; *a* **stroke of luck** *fig* ein glücklicher Zufall, ein Glücksfall

stroll 1. bummeln, spazieren; **2.** Bummel *m*, Spaziergang *m*

stroll·er Bummler(in), Spaziergänger(in); Sportwagen *m*

strong stark (*a.* GASTR, PHARM); kräftig; mächtig; stabil; fest; robust

strong·box (Geld-, Stahl)Kassette *f*

strong·hold Festung *f*; Stützpunkt *m*; *fig* Hochburg *f*

strong-mind·ed willensstark

strong room Tresor(raum) *m*

struc·ture Struktur *f*; (Auf)Bau *m*, Gliederung *f*; Bau *m*, Konstruktion *f*

strug·gle 1. kämpfen, ringen (**with** mit; **for** um); sich abmühen; sich winden, zappeln; **struggle against** sich sträuben gegen; **2.** Kampf *m*

strum klimpern auf (*dat*) (*or* **on** auf *dat*)

strut¹ stolzieren

strut² TECH Strebe *f*; Stütze *f*

stub 1. (*Bleistift-, Zigaretten- etc*)Stummel *m*; Kontrollabschnitt *m*; **2.** sich *die Zehe* anstoßen; **stub out** *Zigarette* ausdrücken

stub·ble Stoppeln *pl*

stub·bly stoppelig

stub·born eigensinnig, stur; hartnäckig

stub·born·ness Starrsinn *m*

stuck-up F hochnäsig

stud¹ 1. (*Kragen-, Manschetten*)Knopf *m*; *soccer:* Stollen *m*; Beschlagnagel *m*; Ziernagel *m*; *pl* MOT Spikes *pl*; **2.** *be* **studded with** besetzt sein mit; übersät sein mit; **studded tires** Spikesreifen *pl*

stud² Gestüt *n*

stu·dent Student(in); Schüler(in)

stud farm Gestüt *n*

stud horse ZO Zuchthengst *m*

stud·ied wohlüberlegt; gesucht

stu·di·o Studio *n*; Atelier *n*; *a.* **studio apartment**, *Br* **studio flat** Studio *n*, Einzimmerappartement *n*

studio couch Schlafcouch *f*

stu·di·ous fleißig

stud·y 1. Studium *n*; Studie *f*, Untersuchung *f*; Arbeitszimmer *n*; *pl* Studium *n*; **be in a brown study** in Gedanken versunken *or* geistesabwesend sein; **2.** studieren; lernen (**for** für)

stuff 1. Zeug *n*; **2.** (aus)stopfen, stopfen, vollstopfen; füllen (*a.* GASTR); **stuff o.s.** F sich vollstopfen

stuff·ing Füllung *f* (*a.* GASTR)

stuff·y stickig; spießig; prüde

stum·ble 1. stolpern (**on, over**, *fig* **at, over** über *acc*); **stumble across**, **stumble on** stoßen auf (*acc*); **2.** Stolpern *n*

stump 1. Stumpf *m*; Stummel *m*; **2.** stampfen, stapfen

stump·y F kurz und dick

stun betäuben; *fig* sprachlos machen

stun·ning fantastisch; unglaublich

stunt¹ (*das Wachstum gen*) hemmen; **stunted** BIOL verkümmert; **become stunted** BIOL verkümmern

stunt² (*Film*)Stunt *m*; (*gefährliches*) Kunststück; (*Reklame*)Gag *m*

stunt man *film*, TV Stuntman *m*, Double *n*

stunt wom·an *film*, TV Stuntwoman *f*, Double *n*

stu·pid dumm; F blöd

stu·pid·i·ty Dummheit *f*

stu·por Betäubung *f*; **in a drunken stupor** im Vollrausch

stur·dy kräftig, stämmig; *fig* entschlossen, hartnäckig

stut·ter 1. stottern (*a.* MOT); stammeln; **2.** Stottern, Stammeln *n*

sty¹ → **pigsty**

sty², **stye** MED Gerstenkorn *n*

style 1. Stil *m*; Ausführung *f*; Mode *f*; **2.** entwerfen; gestalten

styl·ish stilvoll; modisch, elegant

styl·ist Stilist(in)

Sty·ro·foam® Styropor® *n*

suave verbindlich

sub·con·scious Unterbewusstsein *n*; **subconsciously** im Unterbewusstsein

S

sub·di·vi·sion Unterteilung *f*; Unterabteilung *f*

sub·due unterwerfen; *Ärger etc* unterdrücken

sub·dued gedämpft (*light, voice etc*); ruhig, still (*person*)

sub·ject 1. Thema *n*; PED, UNIV Fach *n*; LING Subjekt *n*, Satzgegenstand *m*; Untertan(in); Staatsangehörige *m, f*, -bürger(in); **2** *adj*: *subject to* anfällig für; *be subject to a.* neigen zu; *be subject to* unterliegen (*dat*); abhängen von; *prices subject to change* Preisänderungen vorbehalten; **1.** unterwerfen; *subject to e-m Test etc* unterziehen; *der Kritik etc* aussetzen

sub·jec·tion Unterwerfung *f*; Abhängigkeit *f* (*to* von)

sub·ju·gate unterjochen, unterwerfen

sub·junc·tive LING *a. subjunctive mood* Konjunktiv *m*

sub·lease, sub·let untervermieten, weitervermieten

sub·lime großartig; *fig* total

sub·ma·chine gun Maschinenpistole *f*

sub·ma·rine 1. unterseeisch; **2.** Unterseeboot *n*, U-Boot *n*

sub·merge tauchen; (ein)tauchen (*in* acc)

sub·mis·sion Einreichung *f*; *boxing etc*: Aufgabe *f*; Unterwerfung *f* (*to* unter)

sub·mis·sive unterwürfig

sub·mit *Gesuch etc* einreichen (*to dat or* bei); sich fügen (*to dat or* in acc); *boxing etc*: aufgeben

sub·or·di·nate 1. untergeordnet (*to dat*); **2.** Untergebene *m, f*; **3.** *subordinate to* unterordnen (*dat*), zurückstellen (hinter *acc*)

subordinate clause LING Nebensatz *m*

sub·scribe *v/t Geld* gegen, spenden (*to* für); *v/i*: *subscribe to Zeitung etc* abonnieren

sub·scrib·er Abonnent(in); TEL Teilnehmer(in)

sub·scrip·tion Abonnement *n*; (Mitglieds)Beitrag *m*

sub·se·quent später

sub·side sich senken (*building, road etc*); zurückgehen (*flood, demand etc*), sich legen (*storm, anger etc*)

sub·sid·i·a·ry 1. Neben...; *subsidiary question* Zusatzfrage *f*; **2.** ECON Tochtergesellschaft *f*

sub·si·dize subventionieren

sub·si·dy Subvention *f*

sub·sist leben, existieren (*on* von)

sub·sis·tence Existenz *f*

sub·stance Substanz *f* (*a. fig*), Stoff *m*;

das Wesentliche, Kern *m*

sub·stan·dard minderwertig

sub·stan·tial solid (*furniture etc*); beträchtlich (*salary etc*), (*changes etc a.*) wesentlich; reichlich, kräftig (*meal*)

sub·stan·ti·ate beweisen

sub·stan·tive LING Substantiv *n*, Hauptwort *n*

sub·sti·tute 1. Ersatz *m*; Stellvertreter(in), Vertretung *f*; SPORT Auswechselspieler(in), Ersatzspieler(in); **2.** *substitute s.th. for s.th.* et. durch et. ersetzen, et. gegen et. austauschen *or* auswechseln; *substitute for* einspringen für, *j-n* vertreten

sub·sti·tu·tion Ersatz *m*; SPORT Austausch *m*, Auswechslung *f*

sub·ter·fuge List *f*

sub·ter·ra·ne·an unterirdisch

sub·ti·tle Untertitel *m*

sub·tle fein (*differences etc*); raffiniert (*plan etc*); scharf (*mind*); scharfsinnig

sub·tract MATH abziehen, subtrahieren (*from* von)

sub·trac·tion MATH Abziehen *n*, Subtraktion *f*

sub·trop·i·cal subtropisch

sub·urb Vorort *m*, Vorstadt *f*

sub·ur·ban Vorort..., vorstädtisch, Vorstadt...

sub·ver·sive umstürzlerisch, subversiv

sub·way Unterführung *f*; U-Bahn *f*

suc·ceed *v/i* Erfolg haben, erfolgreich sein, (*plan etc a.*) gelingen; *succeed to* in *e-m* Amt nachfolgen; *succeed to the throne* auf den Thron folgen; *v/t*: *succeed s.o. as* j-s Nachfolger werden als

suc·cess Erfolg *m*

suc·cess·ful erfolgreich

suc·ces·sion Folge *f*; Erb-, Nach-, Thronfolge *f*; *five times in succession* fünfmal hintereinander; *in quick succession* in rascher Folge

suc·ces·sive aufeinanderfolgend

suc·ces·sor Nachfolger(in); Thronfolger(in)

suc·cu·lent GASTR saftig

such solche(r, -s); derartige(r, -s); so; derart; *such a* so ein(e)

suck 1. *v/t* saugen; lutschen (*an dat*); *v/i* saugen (*at an dat*); **2.** *have or take a suck at* saugen *or* lutschen an (*dat*)

suck·er ZO Saugnapf *m*, Saugorgan *n*; TECH Saugfuß *m*; BOT Wurzelschössling *m*, Wurzelspross *m*; F Trottel *m*, Simpel *m*; Lutscher *m*

suck·le säugen, stillen

suc·tion (An)Saugen *n*; Saugwirkung *f*

suction pump TECH Saugpumpe f
sud·den plötzlich, unvermittelt; *all of a sudden* F ganz plötzlich
sud·den·ly plötzlich
suds Seifenschaum m
sue JUR j-n verklagen (*for* auf acc, wegen); klagen (*for* auf acc)
suede, suède Wildleder n, Velours(-leder) n
su·et GASTR Nierenfett n, Talg m
suf·fer v/i leiden (*from* an dat, unter dat); darunter leiden; v/t erleiden; *Folgen* tragen
suf·fer·er Leidende m, f
suf·fer·ing Leiden n; Leid n
suf·fi·cient genügend, genug, ausreichend; *be sufficient* genügen, (aus)reichen
suf·fix LING Suffix n, Nachsilbe f
suf·fo·cate ersticken
suf·frage POL Wahl-, Stimmrecht n
suf·fuse durchfluten (*light etc*); überziehen (*color etc*)
sug·ar 1. Zucker m; 2. zuckern
sug·ar beet BOT Zuckerrübe f
sug·ar bowl Zuckerdose f
sug·ar·cane BOT Zuckerrohr n
sug·ar tongs Zuckerzange f
sug·ar·y süß; fig süßlich
sug·gest vorschlagen, anregen; hindeuten or hinweisen auf (acc), schließen lassen auf (acc); andeuten
sug·ges·tion Vorschlag m, Anregung f; Anflug m, Spur f; Andeutung f; PSYCH Suggestion f
sug·ges·tive zweideutig (*remark etc*), vielsagend (*look etc*)
su·i·cide Selbstmord m; Selbstmörder(in); *commit suicide* Selbstmord begehen
suit 1. Anzug m; Kostüm n; *card game:* Farbe f; JUR Prozess m; *follow suit* fig dem Beispiel folgen, dasselbe tun; 2. v/t j-m passen (*date etc*); j-n kleiden, j-m stehen; et. anpassen (*to* dat); *suit s.th., be suited to s.th.* geeignet sein or sich eignen für; *suit yourself!* mach, was du willst!
sui·ta·ble passend, geeignet (*for, to* für)
suit·case Koffer m
suite (*Möbel-, Sitz*)Garnitur f; Suite f; Zimmerflucht f; MUS Suite f; Gefolge n
sul·fur CHEM Schwefel m
sul·fu·ric ac·id CHEM Schwefelsäure f
sulk schmollen, F eingeschnappt sein
sulk·y schmollend, F eingeschnappt
sul·len mürrisch, verdrossen
sul·phur Br → **sulfur**
sul·phu·ric ac·id Br → **sulfuric acid**

sul·try schwül; aufreizend (*look etc*)
sum 1. Summe f; Betrag m; (einfache) Rechenaufgabe; *do sums* rechnen; 2. *sum up* zusammenfassen; j-n, et. abschätzen
sum·mar·ize zusammenfassen
sum·ma·ry Zusammenfassung f, (kurze) Inhaltsangabe
sum·mer Sommer m; *in (the) summer* im Sommer
summer camp Ferienlager n
summer hol·i·days Br Sommerferien pl
summer resort Sommerfrische f
summer school Ferienkurs m
sum·mer·time Sommer m, Sommerszeit f; *in (the) summertime* im Sommer
sum·mer time esp Br Sommerzeit f
summer va·ca·tion Sommerferien pl
sum·mer·y sommerlich, Sommer…
sum·mit Gipfel m (a. ECON, POL, fig)
summit con·fe·rence POL Gipfelkonferenz f
summit meet·ing POL Gipfeltreffen n
sum·mon auffordern; *Versammlung etc* einberufen; JUR vorladen; *summon up Kraft, Mut etc* zusammennehmen
sum·mons JUR Vorladung f
sump Br MOT Ölwanne f
sump·tu·ous luxuriös, aufwändig
sun 1. Sonne f; 2. Sonnen…; 3. *sun o.s.* sich sonnen
Sun ABBR *of Sunday* So., Sonntag m
sun·bathe sich sonnen, ein Sonnenbad nehmen
sun·beam Sonnenstrahl m
sun·bed Sonnenbank f
sun·burn Sonnenbrand m
sun cream Sonnencreme f
sun·dae GASTR Eisbecher m
Sun·day (ABBR *Sun*) Sonntag m; *on Sunday* (am) Sonntag; *on Sundays* sonntags
sun·dial Sonnenuhr f
sun·dries Diverses, Verschiedenes
sun·dry diverse, verschiedene
sun·glass·es (*a pair of sunglasses* e-e) Sonnenbrille f
sunk·en MAR gesunken, versunken; versenkt; tief liegend; eingefallen (*cheeks*), (a. *eyes*) eingesunken
sun·light Sonnenlicht n
sun·lit sonnenbeschienen
sun·ny sonnig
sun·rise Sonnenaufgang m; *at sunrise* bei Sonnenaufgang
sun·roof Dachterrasse f; MOT Schiebedach n
sun·set Sonnenuntergang m; *at sunset* bei Sonnenuntergang
sun·shade Sonnenschirm m
sun·shine Sonnenschein m

sun·stroke MED Sonnenstich *m*
sun·tan (Sonnen)Bräune *f*
suntan lo·tion Sonnenschutz *m*, Sonnencreme *f*
suntan oil Sonnenöl *n*
su·per F super, spitze, klasse
su·per... Über..., über...
su·per·a·bun·dant überreichlich
su·per·an·nu·at·ed pensioniert, im Ruhestand
su·perb ausgezeichnet
su·per·charg·er MOT Kompressor *m*
su·per·cil·i·ous hochmütig, F hochnäsig
su·per·fi·cial oberflächlich
su·per·flu·ous überflüssig
su·per·hu·man übermenschlich
su·per·im·pose überlagern; *Bild etc* einblenden (*on* in *acc*)
su·per·in·tend die (Ober)Aufsicht haben über (*acc*), überwachen; leiten
su·per·in·tend·ent Aufsicht *f*, Aufsichtsbeamter *m*, -beamtin *f*; *Br* Kriminalrat *m*
su·pe·ri·or 1. ranghöher (*to* als); überlegen (*to dat*), besser (*to* als); ausgezeichnet, hervorragend; überheblich, überlegen; *Father Superior* REL Superior *m*; *Mother Superior* REL Oberin *f*; 2. Vorgesetzte *m*, *f*
su·peri·or·i·ty Überlegenheit *f* (*over* gegenüber)
su·per·la·tive 1. höchste(r, -s), überragend; 2. *a.* **superlative degree** LING Superlativ *m*
su·per·mar·ket Supermarkt *m*
su·per·nat·u·ral übernatürlich
su·per·nu·me·ra·ry zusätzlich
su·per·sede ablösen, ersetzen, verdrängen
su·per·son·ic AVIAT, PHYS Überschall...
su·per·sti·tion Aberglaube *m*
su·per·sti·tious abergläubisch
su·per·store Großmarkt *m*
su·per·vene dazwischenkommen
su·per·vise beaufsichtigen, überwachen
su·per·vi·sion Beaufsichtigung *f*, Überwachung *f*; *under s.o.'s supervision* unter j-s Aufsicht
su·per·vi·sor Aufseher(in), Aufsicht *f*
sup·per Abendessen *n*; *have supper* zu Abend essen; → *lord*
sup·plant verdrängen
sup·ple gelenkig, geschmeidig, biegsam
sup·ple·ment 1. Ergänzung *f*; Nachtrag *m*, Anhang *m*; Ergänzungsband *m*; (*Zeitungs- etc*)Beilage *f*; 2. ergänzen
sup·ple·men·ta·ry ergänzend, zusätzlich
sup·pli·er ECON Lieferant(in), *a. pl* Lieferfirma *f*
sup·ply 1. liefern; stellen, sorgen für; j-n,

et. versorgen, ECON beliefern (*with* mit); 2. Lieferung *f* (*to* an *acc*); Versorgung *f*; ECON Angebot *n*; *mst pl* Vorrat *m* (*of* an *dat*), *a.* Proviant *m*, MIL Nachschub *m*; *supply and demand* ECON Angebot und Nachfrage
sup·port 1. (ab)stützen, *Gewicht etc* tragen; *Währung* stützen; unterstützen; unterhalten, sorgen für; 2. Stütze *f*; TECH Träger *m*; *fig* Unterstützung *f*
sup·port·er Anhänger(in) (*a.* SPORT), Befürworter(in)
sup·pose 1. annehmen, vermuten; *be supposed to ...* sollen; *what is that supposed to mean?* was soll denn das?; *I suppose so* ich nehme es an, vermutlich; 2. *cj* angenommen; wie wäre es, wenn
sup·posed angeblich, vermeintlich
sup·pos·ing → *suppose* 2
sup·po·si·tion Annahme *f*, Vermutung *f*
sup·pos·i·to·ry PHARM Zäpfchen *n*
sup·press unterdrücken
sup·pres·sion Unterdrückung *f*
sup·pu·rate MED eitern
su·prem·a·cy Vormachtstellung *f*
su·preme höchste(r, -s), oberste(r, -s), Ober...; größte(r, -s)
sur·charge 1. Nachporto *n* od *e-n* Zuschlag erheben (*on* auf *acc*); 2. Aufschlag *m*, Zuschlag *m* (*on* auf *acc*); Nach-, Strafporto *n* (*on* auf *acc*)
sure 1. *adj* sicher; *sure of o.s.* selbstsicher; *sure of winning* siegessicher; *sure thing!* F (aber) klar!; *be or feel sure* sicher sein; *be sure to ...* vergiss nicht zu ...; *for sure* ganz sicher *or* bestimmt; *make sure that* sich (davon) überzeugen, dass; *to be sure* sicher(lich); 2. *adv* F sicher, klar; *sure enough* tatsächlich
sure·ly sicher(lich)
sure·ty JUR Bürge *m*, Bürgin *f*; Bürgschaft *f*, Sicherheit *f*; *stand surety for s.o.* für j-n bürgen
surf 1. Brandung *f*; 2. SPORT surfen
sur·face 1. Oberfläche *f*; (*Straßen*)Belag *m*; 2. auftauchen; *Straße* mit e-m Belag versehen; 3. Oberflächen...; *fig* oberflächlich; *surface mail* gewöhnliche Post
surf·board Surfboard *n*, Surfbrett *n*
surf·er Surfer(in), Wellenreiter(in)
surf·ing Surfen *n*, Wellenreiten *n*
surge 1. *fig* Welle *f*, Woge *f*, (*Gefühls*)Aufwallung *f*; 2. (vorwärts-)drängen; *surge (up)* aufwallen
sur·geon MED Chirurg(in)
sur·ge·ry MED Chirurgie *f*; operativer Eingriff, Operation *f*; *Br* Sprechzimmer *n*; *Br* Sprechstunde *f*; *a.* **doctor's sur-**

sweatshirt

gery Arztpraxis *f*
surgery hours MED *Br* Sprechstunde(n *pl*) *f*
sur·gi·cal MED chirurgisch
sur·ly mürrisch, unwirsch
sure·name Familienname *m*, Nachname *m*, Zuname *m*
sur·pass *Erwartungen etc* übertreffen
sur·plus 1. Überschuss *m* (*of* an *dat*); **2.** überschüssig
sur·prise 1. Überraschung *f*, Verwunderung *f*; *take s.o. by surprise* j-n überraschen; **2.** überraschen; *be surprised at or by* überrascht sein über (*acc*)
sur·ren·der 1. *v/i* **surrender to** MIL, *a. fig* sich ergeben (*dat*), kapitulieren vor (*dat*); *surrender to the police* sich der Polizei stellen; *v/t et.* übergeben, ausliefern (*to dat*); aufgeben, verzichten auf (*acc*); *surrender o.s. to the police* sich der Polizei stellen; **2.** MIL Kapitulation *f* (*a. fig*); Aufgabe *f*, Verzicht *m*
sur·ro·gate Ersatz *m*
sur·ro·gate moth·er Leihmutter *f*
sur·round umgeben; umstellen
sur·round·ing umliegend
sur·round·ings Umgebung *f*
sur·vey 1. (sich) *et.* betrachten (*a. fig*); *Haus etc* begutachten; *Land* vermessen; **2.** Umfrage *f*; Überblick *m* (*of* über *acc*); Begutachtung *f*; Vermessung *f*
sur·vey·or Gutachter *m*; Land(ver)-messer *m*
sur·viv·al Überleben *n* (*a. fig*); Überbleibsel *n*
survival in·stinct Selbsterhaltungstrieb *m*
survival kit Überlebensausrüstung *f*
survival train·ing Überlebenstraining *n*
sur·vive überleben; *Feuer etc* überstehen; erhalten bleiben *or* sein
sur·vi·vor Überlebende *m*, *f* (*from, of gen*)
sus·cep·ti·ble empfänglich, anfällig (*both*: *to* für)
sus·pect 1. *j-n* verdächtigen (*of gen*); *et.* vermuten; *et.* anzweifeln, *et.* bezweifeln; **2.** Verdächtige *m*, *f*; **3.** verdächtig, suspekt
sus·pend *Verkauf, Zahlungen etc* (vorübergehend) einstellen; JUR *Verfahren, Urteil* aussetzen; *Strafe* zur Bewährung aussetzen; *j-n* suspendieren; vorübergehend ausschließen (*from* aus); SPORT *j-n* sperren; (auf)hängen; *be suspended* schweben
sus·pend·er *Br* Strumpfhalter *m*, Straps *m*; Sockenhalter *m*; (*a. a pair of*) *sus·penders* Hosenträger *pl*

sus·pense Spannung *f*; *in suspense* gespannt, voller Spannung
sus·pen·sion (vorübergehende) Einstellung; Suspendierung *f*; vorübergehender Ausschluss; SPORT Sperre *f*; MOT *etc* Aufhängung *f*
suspension bridge Hängebrücke *f*
suspension rail·way *esp Br* Schwebebahn *f*
sus·pi·cion Verdacht *m*; Verdächtigung *f*; Argwohn *m*, Misstrauen *n*; *fig* Hauch *m*, Spur *f*
sus·pi·cious verdächtig; argwöhnisch, misstrauisch; *become suspicious* Verdacht schöpfen
sus·tain *j-n* stärken; *Interesse etc* aufrechterhalten; *Schaden, Verlust* erleiden; JUR *e-m Einspruch etc* stattgeben
swab MED **1.** Tupfer *m*; Abstrich *m*; **2.** *Wunde* abtupfen
swad·dle *Baby* wickeln
swag·ger stolzieren
swal·low¹ 1. schlucken (*a.* F); hinunterschlucken; *swallow up fig* schlucken, verschlingen; **2.** Schluck *m*
swal·low² ZO Schwalbe *f*
swamp 1. Sumpf *m*; **2.** überschwemmen; *be swamped with fig* überschwemmt werden mit
swamp·y sumpfig
swan ZO Schwan *m*
swank 1. F *esp Br* angeben; **2.** F *esp Br* Angeber(in); Angabe *f*; **3.** F piekfein
swank·y F piekfein; *esp Br* angeberisch
swap F **1.** (ein)tauschen; **2.** Tausch *m*
swarm 1. ZO Schwarm *m* (*a. fig*); **2.** ZO schwärmen, *fig a.* strömen; *a. fig* wimmeln (*with* von)
swar·thy dunkel (*skin*), dunkelhäutig (*person*)
swas·ti·ka Hakenkreuz *n*
swat *Fliege etc* totschlagen
sway 1. *v/i* sich wiegen, schaukeln; *sway between fig* schwanken zwischen (*dat*); *v/t* hin- und herbewegen, schwenken; *s-n Körper* wiegen; beeinflussen; **2.** Schwanken *n*, Schaukeln *n*
swear fluchen; schwören; *swear at s.o.* j-n wüst beschimpfen; *swear by fig* F schwören auf (*acc*); *swear s.o. in* JUR j-n vereidigen
sweat 1. *v/i* schwitzen (*with* vor *dat*); *v/t*: *sweat out Krankheit* ausschwitzen; *sweat blood* F sich abrackern (*over* mit); **2.** Schweiß *m*; F Schufterei *f*; *get in(to) a sweat fig* F ins Schwitzen geraten *or* kommen
sweat·er Pullover *m*
sweat·shirt Sweatshirt *n*

S

sweat·y schweißig, verschwitzt; nach Schweiß riechend, Schweiß...; schweißtreibend

Swede Schwede *m*, Schwedin *f*

Swe·den Schweden *n*

Swe·dish 1. schwedisch; **2.** LING Schwedisch *n*

sweep 1. *v/t* kehren, fegen; *fig* fegen über (*acc*) (*storm etc*); *Horizont etc* absuchen (*for* nach); *fig Land etc* überschwemmen; *sweep along* mitreißen; *v/i* kehren, fegen; rauschen (*person*); **2.** Kehren *n*, Fegen *n*; Hieb *m*, Schlag *m*; F Schornsteinfeger *m*, Kaminkehrer *m*; *give the floor a good sweep* den Boden gründlich kehren *or* fegen; *make a clean sweep* gründlich aufräumen; SPORT gründlich abräumen

sweep·er (*Straßen*)Kehrer *m*; Kehrmaschine *f*; *soccer*: Libero *m*

sweep·ing durchgreifend (*changes etc*); pauschal, zu allgemein

sweep·ings Kehricht *m*

sweet 1. süß (*a. fig*); lieblich; lieb; *sweet nothings* Zärtlichkeiten *pl*; *have a sweet tooth* gern naschen; **2.** *Br* Süßigkeit *f*, Bonbon *m, n*; *Br* Nachtisch *m*

sweet corn *esp Br* BOT Zuckermais *m*

sweet·en süßen

sweet·heart Schatz *m*, Liebste *m, f*

sweet pea BOT Gartenwicke *f*

sweet shop *esp Br* Süßwarengeschäft *n*

swell 1. *v/i a. swell up* MED (an)schwellen; *a. swell out* sich blähen; *v/t fig Zahl etc* anwachsen lassen; *a. swell out Segel* blähen; **2.** MAR Dünung *f*; **3.** F klasse

swell·ing MED Schwellung *f*

swel·ter vor Hitze fast umkommen

swerve 1. schwenken (*to the left* nach links), e-n Schwenk machen; *fig* abweichen (*from* von); **2.** Schwenk *m*, Schwenkung *f*, MOT *etc a.* Schlenker *m*

swift schnell

swim 1. *v/i* schwimmen; *fig* verschwimmen; *my head was swimming* mir drehte sich alles; *v/t Strecke* schwimmen; *Fluss etc* durchschwimmen; **2.** Schwimmen *n*; *go for a swim* schwimmen gehen

swim·mer Schwimmer(in)

swim·ming Schwimmen *n*

swimming bath(s) *Br* Schwimmbad *n*, *esp* Hallenbad *n*

swimming cap Badekappe *f*, Bademütze *f*

swimming costume Badeanzug *m*

swimming pool Swimmingpool *m*, Schwimmbecken *n*

swimming trunks Badehose *f*

swim·suit Badeanzug *m*

swin·dle 1. *j-n* beschwindeln (*out of* um); **2.** Schwindel *m*

swine ZO Schwein *n* (*a.* F *fig*)

swing 1. *v/i* (hin- und her)schwingen; sich schwingen; einbiegen, -schwenken (*into* in *acc*); MUS schwungvoll spielen (*band etc*); Schwung haben (*music*); *swing round* sich ruckartig umdrehen; *swing shut* zuschlagen (*door etc*); *v/t et., die Arme etc* schwingen; **2.** Schwingen *n*; Schaukel *f*; *fig* Schwung *m*; *fig* Umschwung *m*; *in full swing* in vollem Gang

swing door Pendeltür *f*

swin·ish ekelhaft

swipe 1. Schlag *m*; **2.** schlagen (*at* nach)

swirl 1. wirbeln; **2.** Wirbel *m*

swish[1] 1. *v/i* sausen, zischen; rascheln (*silk etc*); *v/t* mit *dem Schwanz* schlagen; **2.** Sausen *n*, Zischen *n*; Rascheln *n*; Schlagen *n*

swish[2] *Br* feudal, schick

Swiss 1. schweizerisch, eidgenössisch, Schweizer...; **2.** Schweizer(in); *the Swiss* die Schweizer *pl*

switch 1. ELECTR, TECH Schalter *m*; RAIL Weiche *f*; Gerte *f*, Rute *f*; *fig* Umstellung *f*; **2.** ELECTR, TECH (um)schalten (*a. switch over*) (*to* auf *acc*); RAIL rangieren; wechseln (*to* zu); *switch off* abschalten, ausschalten; *switch on* anschalten, einschalten

switch·board ELECTR Schalttafel *f*; (Telefon)Zentrale *f*

Swit·zer·land die Schweiz

swiv·el (sich) drehen

swiv·el chair Drehstuhl *m*

swoon in Ohnmacht fallen

swoop 1. *fig* F zuschlagen (*police etc*); *a. swoop down* ZO herabstoßen (*on* auf *acc*); *swoop on* F herfallen über (*acc*); **2.** Razzia *f*

swop F → *swap*

sword Schwert *n*

syc·a·more BOT Bergahorn *m*; Platane *f*

syl·la·ble Silbe *f*

syl·la·bus PED, UNIV Lehrplan *m*

sym·bol Symbol *n*

sym·bol·ic symbolisch

sym·bol·is·m Symbolik *f*

sym·bol·ize symbolisieren

sym·met·ri·cal symmetrisch

sym·me·try Symmetrie *f*

sym·pa·thet·ic mitfühlend; verständnisvoll; wohlwollend

sym·pa·thize mitfühlen; sympathisieren

sym·pa·thiz·er Sympathisant(in)

sym·pa·thy Mitgefühl *n*; Verständnis *n*

sym·pho·ny MUS Sinfonie *f*

symphony orches·tra MUS Sinfonieor-

chester *n*
symp·tom Symptom *n*
syn·chro·nize *v/t* aufeinander abstimmen; *Uhren, Film* synchronisieren; *v/i*
synchron gehen *or* sein
syn·o·nym Synonym *n*
sy·non·y·mous synonym; gleichbedeutend
syn·tax LING Syntax *f*, Satzlehre *f*
syn·the·sis Synthese *f*

syn·thet·ic CHEM synthetisch
synthetic fi·ber (*Br* **fi·bre**) Kunstfaser *f*
Syr·i·a Syrien *n*
sy·ringe MED Spritze *f*
syr·up Sirup *m*
sys·tem System *n*; (*Straßen-* *etc*)Netz *n*;
Organismus *m*
sys·te·mat·ic systematisch
sys·tem er·ror EDP Systemfehler *m*

T

T, t T, t *n*
tab Aufhänger *m*, Schlaufe *f*; Lasche *f*;
Etikett *n*, Schildchen *n*; Reiter *m*; F
Rechnung *f*
ta·ble 1. Tisch *m*; (Tisch)Runde *f*; Tabelle
f, Verzeichnis *n*; MATH Einmaleins *n*; *at
table* bei Tisch; *at the table* am Tisch;
turn the tables (*on s.o.*) *fig* den Spieß
umdrehen; 2. *fig* auf den Tisch legen;
esp fig zurückstellen
ta·ble·cloth Tischdecke *f*, Tischtuch *n*
ta·ble·land GEOGR Tafelland *n*, Plateau *n*,
Hochebene *f*
ta·ble lin·en Tischwäsche *f*
ta·ble·mat Untersetzer *m*
ta·ble·spoon Esslöffel *m*
tab·let PHARM Tablette *f*; Stück *n*; (*Stein-
etc*)Tafel *f*
ta·ble ten·nis SPORT Tischtennis *n*
ta·ble·top Tischplatte *f*
ta·ble·ware Geschirr *n* und Besteck *n*
tab·loid Boulevardblatt *n*, -zeitung *f*
tab·loid press Boulevardpresse *f*
ta·boo 1. tabu; 2. Tabu *n*
tab·u·lar tabellarisch
tab·u·late tabellarisch (an)ordnen
tab·u·la·tor Tabulator *m*
tach·o·graph MOT Fahrtenschreiber *m*
ta·chom·e·ter MOT Drehzahlmesser *m*
ta·cit stillschweigend
ta·ci·turn schweigsam, wortkarg
tack 1. Stift *m*, (Reiß)Zwecke *f*; Heftstich
m; 2. heften (*to* an *acc*); *tack on* anfügen
(*to dat*)
tack·le 1. *Problem etc* angehen; *soccer etc*:
ballführenden Gegner angreifen; *j-n* zur
Rede stellen (*about* wegen); 2. TECH Flaschenzug *m*; (*Angel*)Gerät(e *pl*) *n*; *soccer
etc*: Angriff *m*

tack·y klebrig; F schäbig
tact Takt *m*, Feingefühl *n*
tact·ful taktvoll
tac·tics Taktik *f*
tact·less taktlos
tad·pole ZO Kaulquappe *f*
taf·fe·ta Taft *m*
taf·fy Sahnebonbon *m, n*, Toffee *n*
tag 1. Etikett *n*; (*Namens-, Preis*)Schild *n*;
(Schnürsenkel)Stift *m*; stehende Redensart *f*; *a.* *question tag* LING Fragean-
hängsel *n*; 2. etikettieren; *Waren* auszeichnen; anhängen; *tag along* F mitgehen, mitkommen; *tag along behind s.o.*
F hinter j-m hertrotten
tail 1. Schwanz *m*; Schweif *m*; hinterer
Teil; F Schatten *m*, Beschatter(in); *pl*
Rück-, Kehrseite *f*; Frack *m*; *put a tail
on j-n* beschatten lassen; *turn tail fig* sich
auf dem Absatz umdrehen; *with one's
tail between one's legs fig* mit eingezo-
genem Schwanz; 2. F *j-n* beschatten; *tail
back esp Br* MOT sich stauen (*to* bis zu);
tail off schwächer werden, abnehmen,
nachlassen
tail·back *esp Br* MOT Rückstau *m*
tail·coat Frack *m*
tail end Ende *n*, Schluss *m*
tail·light MOT Rücklicht *n*
tai·lor 1. Schneider *m*; 2. schneidern
tai·lor-made Maß...; maßgeschneidert (*a.
fig*)
tail pipe TECH Auspuffrohr *n*
tail·wind Rückenwind *m*
taint·ed GASTR verdorben
take 1. *v/t* nehmen; (weg)nehmen; mitnehmen; bringen; MIL, MED einnehmen;
chess etc: Figur, Stein schlagen; *Gefangene, Prüfung etc* machen; UNIV studieren;

T

Preis etc erringen; *Scheck etc* (an)nehmen; *Rat* annehmen; *et.* hinnehmen; fassen, Platz bieten für; *et.* aushalten, ertragen; PHOT *et.* aufnehmen, *Aufnahme* machen; *Temperatur* messen; *Notiz* machen, niederschreiben; *ein Bad, Zug, Bus, Weg etc* nehmen; *Gelegenheit, Maßnahmen* ergreifen; *Mut* fassen; *Zeit, Geduld etc* erfordern, brauchen; *Zeit* dauern; *it took her four hours* sie brauchte vier Stunden; *I take it that* ich nehme an, dass; *take it or leave it* F mach, was du willst; *taken all in all* im Großen (und) Ganzen; *this seat is taken* dieser Platz ist besetzt; *be taken by or with* angetan sein von; *be taken ill or sick* erkranken, krank werden; *take to bits or pieces* et. auseinandernehmen, zerlegen; *take the blame* die Schuld auf sich nehmen; *take care* vorsichtig sein, aufpassen; *take care!* F mach's gut!; → *care 1*; *take hold of* ergreifen; *take part* teilnehmen (*in* an *dat*); → *part 1*; *take pity on* Mitleid haben mit; *take a walk* e-n Spaziergang machen; *take my word for it* verlass dich drauf; → *advice, bath 1, break 1, lead¹ 2, message, oath, offense, place 1, prisoner, risk 1, seat 1, step 1, trouble 1, turn 2, etc*; *v/i* MED wirken, anschlagen; *take after j-m* nachschlagen, ähneln; *take along* mitnehmen; *take apart* auseinandernehmen (*a. fig* F), zerlegen; *take away* wegnehmen (*from s.o.* j-m); *... to take away* Br ... zum Mitnehmen; *take back* zurückbringen; zurücknehmen; bei *j-m* Erinnerungen wachrufen; *j-n* zurückversetzen (*to* in *acc*); *take down* herunternehmen, abnehmen; *Hose* herunterlassen; auseinandernehmen, zerlegen; (sich) *et.* aufschreiben *or* notieren; sich *Notizen* machen; *what do you take me for?* wofür hältst du mich eigentlich?; *take from j-m et.* wegnehmen; MATH abziehen von; *take in j-n* (bei sich) aufnehmen; *fig et.* einschließen; *Kleidungsstück* enger machen; *et.* begreifen; *j-n* hereinlegen, F *j-n* aufs Kreuz legen; *be taken in by* hereinfallen auf (*acc*); *take off Kleidungsstück* ablegen, ausziehen, *Hut etc* abnehmen; *et.* ab-, wegnehmen; abziehen; AVIAT abheben, SPORT abspringen; F sich davonmachen; *take a day off* sich e-n Tag freinehmen; *take on j-n* einstellen; *Arbeit etc* annehmen, übernehmen; *Farbe, Ausdruck etc* annehmen; sich anlegen mit; *take out* herausnehmen, *Zahn* ziehen; *j-n* ausführen, ausgehen mit *j-m*; *Versicherung* abschließen; *s-n Frust etc* auslassen (*on* an

dat); *take over Amt, Macht, Verantwortung etc* übernehmen; die Macht übernehmen; *take to* Gefallen finden an (*dat*); *take to doing s.th.* anfangen, et. zu tun; *take up Vorschlag etc* aufgreifen; *Zeit etc* in Anspruch nehmen, *Platz* einnehmen; *Erzählung etc* aufnehmen; *take up doing s.th.* anfangen, sich mit et. zu beschäftigen; *take up with* sich einlassen mit; **2.** *film,* TV Einstellung *f*; F Einnahmen *pl*

take·a·way Br **1.** Essen *n* zum Mitnehmen; **2.** Restaurant *n* mit Straßenverkauf

take·off AVIAT Abheben *n*, Start *m*; SPORT Absprung *m*

tak·ings Einnahmen *pl*

tale Erzählung *f*; Geschichte *f*; Lüge *f*, Lügengeschichte *f*, Märchen *n*; *tell tales* petzen

tal·ent Talent *n*, Begabung *f*

tal·ent·ed talentiert, begabt

tal·is·man Talisman *m*

talk 1. *v/i* reden, sprechen, sich unterhalten (*to, with* mit; *about* über *acc*; *of* von); *talk about s.th. a.* et. besprechen; *s.o. to talk to* Ansprechpartner(in); *v/t Unsinn etc* reden; reden *or* sprechen *or* sich unterhalten über (*acc*); *talk s.o. into s.th.* j-n zu et. überreden; *talk s.o. out of s.th.* j-m et. ausreden; *talk s.th. over Problem etc* besprechen (*with* mit); *talk round j-n* bekehren (*to* zu), umstimmen; **2.** Gespräch *n*, Unterhaltung *f* (*with* mit; *about* über *acc*); Vortrag *m*; Sprache *f*, Sprechweise *f*; Gerede *n*, Geschwätz *n*; *give a talk* e-n Vortrag halten (*to* vor *dat*; *about, on* über *acc*); *be the talk of the town* Stadtgespräch sein; *baby talk* Babysprache *f*, kindliches Gebabbel; → *small talk*

talk·a·tive gesprächig, redselig

talk·er: *be a good talker* gut reden können

talk·ing-to F Standpauke *f*; *give s.o. a talking-to* j-m e-e Standpauke halten

talk show TV Talkshow *f*

talk-show host TV Talkmaster *m*

tall groß (*person*), hoch (*building etc*)

tal·low Talg *m*

tal·ly¹ SPORT *etc* Stand *m*; *keep a tally of* Buch führen über (*acc*)

tal·ly² übereinstimmen (*with* mit); *a. tally up* zusammenrechnen, -zählen

tal·on zo Kralle *f*, Klaue *f*

tame 1. ZO zahm; *fig* fad(e), lahm; **2.** ZO zähmen (*a. fig*)

tam·per: *tamper with* sich zu schaffen machen an (*dat*)

tam·pon MED Tampon *m*

teach

tan **1.** *Fell* gerben; bräunen; braun werden; **2.** Gelbbraun *n*; (Sonnen)Bräune *f*; **3.** gelbbraun

tang (scharfer) Geruch *or* Geschmack

tan·gent MATH Tangente *f*; **fly** *or* **go off at a tangent** plötzlich (vom Thema) abschweifen

tan·ge·rine BOT Mandarine *f*

tan·gi·ble greifbar, *fig a.* handfest, klar

tan·gle **1.** (sich) verwirren *or* verheddern, durcheinanderbringen; durcheinanderkommen; **2.** Gewirr *n*, *fig a.* Wirrwarr *m*, Durcheinander *n*

tank MOT *etc* Tank *m*; MIL Panzer *m*

tank·ard (Bier)Humpen *m*

tank·er MAR Tanker *m*, Tankschiff *n*; AVIAT Tankflugzeug *n*; MOT Tankwagen *m*

tan·ner Gerber *m*

tan·ne·ry Gerberei *f*

tan·ta·lize *j-n* aufreizen

tan·ta·liz·ing verlockend

tan·ta·mount: **be tantamount to** gleichbedeutend sein mit, hinauslaufen auf (*acc*)

tan·trum Wut-, Tobsuchtsanfall *m*

tap[1] **1.** TECH Hahn *m*; **beer on tap** Bier *n* vom Fass; **2.** *Naturschätze etc* erschließen; *Vorräte etc* angreifen; *Telefon(leitung)* abhören, F anzapfen; *Fass* anzapfen, anstechen

tap[2] **1.** mit *den Fingern, Füßen* klopfen, mit *den Fingern* trommeln (**on** auf *acc*); antippen; **tap s.o. on the shoulder** j-m auf die Schulter klopfen; **tap on** (leicht) klopfen an (*acc*) *or* auf (*acc*) *or* gegen; **2.** (leichtes) Klopfen; Klaps *m*

tap dance Stepptanz *m*

tape **1.** (schmales) Band; Kleb(e)streifen *m*; (Magnet-, Video-, Ton)Band *n*; (*Video- etc*)Kassette *f*; (Band)Aufnahme *f*; TV Aufzeichnung *f*; SPORT Zielband *n*; → **red tape**; **2.** (auf Band) aufnehmen; TV aufzeichnen; *a.* **tape up** (mit Klebeband) zukleben

tape deck Tapedeck *n*

tape meas·ure Bandmaß *n*, Maßband *n*, Messband *n*

ta·per *a.* **taper off** spitz zulaufen, sich verjüngen; *fig* langsam nachlassen

tape re·cord·er Tonbandgerät *n*

tape re·cord·ing Tonbandaufnahme *f*

ta·pes·try Gobelin *m*, Wandteppich *m*

tape·worm ZO Bandwurm *m*

taps MIL Zapfenstreich *m*

tap wa·ter Leitungswasser *n*

tar **1.** Teer *m*; **2.** teeren

tare ECON Tara *f*

tar·get (Schieß-, Ziel)Scheibe *f*; MIL Ziel *n* (*a. fig*), ECON *a.* Soll *n*; *fig* Zielscheibe *f*

target ar·e·a MIL Zielbereich *m*

target group Zielgruppe *f*

tar·iff ECON Zoll(tarif) *m*; *esp Br* Preisverzeichnis *n*

tar·mac Asphalt *m*; AVIAT Rollfeld *n*, Rollbahn *f*

tar·nish *v/i* anlaufen; *v/t Ansehen etc* beflecken

tart[1] *esp Br* Obstkuchen *m*; Obsttörtchen *n*; F Flittchen *n*, *sl* Nutte *f*

tart[2] herb, sauer; scharf (*a. fig*)

tar·tan Tartan *m*; Schottenstoff *m*; Schottenmuster *n*

tar·tar MED Zahnstein *m*; CHEM Weinstein *m*

task Aufgabe *f*; **take s.o. to task** *fig* j-n zurechtweisen (**for** wegen)

task force MIL *etc* Sonder-, Spezialeinheit *f*

tas·sel Troddel *f*, Quaste *f*

taste **1.** Geschmack *m* (*a. fig*), Geschmackssinn *m*; Kostprobe *f*; Vorliebe *f* (**for** für); **2.** *v/t* kosten, probieren; schmecken; *v/i* schmecken (**of** nach)

taste·ful *fig* geschmackvoll

taste·less geschmacklos (*a. fig*)

tast·y schmackhaft

tat·tered zerlumpt

tat·ters Fetzen *pl*; **in tatters** zerfetzt, in Fetzen; *fig* ruiniert

tat·too[1] **1.** Tätowierung *f*; **2.** (ein)tätowieren

tat·too[2] MIL Zapfenstreich *m*

taunt **1.** verhöhnen, verspotten; **2.** höhnische *or* spöttische Bemerkung

Tau·rus ASTR Stier *m*; **he (she) is (a) Taurus** er (sie) ist (ein) Stier

taut straff; *fig* angespannt

taw·dry (billig und) geschmacklos

taw·ny gelbbraun

tax **1.** Steuer *f* (**on** auf *acc*); **2.** besteuern; *j-s Geduld etc* strapazieren

tax·a·ble steuerpflichtig

tax·a·tion Besteuerung *f*

tax e·va·sion Steuerhinterziehung *f*

tax·i **1.** Taxi *n*, Taxe *f*; **2.** AVIAT rollen

tax·i driv·er Taxifahrer(in)

tax·i rank, tax·i stand Taxistand *m*

tax of·fi·cer Finanzbeamte *m*

tax·pay·er Steuerzahler(in)

tax re·duc·tion Steuersenkung *f*

tax re·turn Steuererklärung *f*

T-bar Bügel *m*; *a.* **T-bar lift** Schlepplift *m*

tea Tee *m*; **have a cup of tea** e-n Tee trinken; **make some tea** e-n Tee machen *or* kochen

tea·bag Teebeutel *m*, Aufgussbeutel *m*

teach lehren, unterrichten (in *dat*); *j-m et.* beibringen; unterrichten (**at** an *dat*)

teach·er Lehrer(in)
tea co·sy Teewärmer *m*
tea·cup Teetasse *f*; **a storm in a teacup** *fig* ein Sturm im Wasserglas
team Team *n, a.* Arbeitsgruppe *f*, SPORT *a.* Mannschaft *f, soccer: a.* Elf *f*
team·ster MOT LKW-Fahrer *m*
team·work Zusammenarbeit *f*, Teamwork *n*; Zusammenspiel *n*
tea·pot Teekanne *f*
tear[1] Träne *f*; **in tears** weinend, in Tränen (aufgelöst)
tear[2] **1.** *v/t* zerreißen; sich *et.* zerreißen (**on** an *dat*); weg-, losreißen (**from** von); *v/i* (zer)reißen; F rasen, sausen; **tear down** Plakat *etc* herunterreißen; *Haus etc* abreißen; **tear off** abreißen; sich *Kleidung* vom Leib reißen; **tear out** (her)ausreißen; **tear up** aufreißen; zerreißen; **2.** Riss *m*
tear·drop Träne *f*
tear·ful weinend; tränenreich
tear·jerk·er F Schnulze *f*
tea·room Teestube *f*
tease necken, hänseln; ärgern
tea·spoon Teelöffel *m*
teat ZO Zitze *f*; *Br* (Gummi)Sauger *m*
tech·ni·cal technisch; fachlich, Fach...
tech·ni·cal·i·ty technische Einzelheit; reine Formsache
tech·ni·cian Techniker(in)
tech·nique Technik *f*, Verfahren *n*
tech·nol·o·gy Technologie *f*; Technik *f*
ted·dy bear Teddybär *m*
te·di·ous langweilig, ermüdend
teem: teem with wimmeln von, strotzen von *or* vor (*dat*)
teen·age(d) im Teenageralter; für Teenager
teen·ag·er Teenager *m*
teens: be in one's teens im Teenageralter sein
tee·ny(-wee·ny) F klitzeklein, winzig
tee shirt → **T-shirt**
teethe zahnen
tee·to·tal·(l)er Abstinenzler(in)
tel·e·cast Fernsehsendung *f*
tel·e·com·mu·ni·ca·tions Telekommunikation *f*, Fernmeldewesen *n*
tel·e·gram Telegramm *n*
tel·e·graph 1. by telegraph telegrafisch; **2.** telegrafieren
tel·e·graph·ic telegrafisch
te·leg·ra·phy Telegrafie *f*
tel·e·phone 1. Telefon *n*; **2.** telefonieren; anrufen
telephone booth, telephone box *Br* Telefonzelle *f*, Fernsprechzelle *f*
telephone call Telefonanruf *n*, Telefonge-sprä ch *n*
telephone di·rec·to·ry → **phone book**
telephone exchange Fernsprechamt *n*
telephone number Telefonnummer *f*
te·leph·o·nist *esp Br* Telefonist(in)
tel·e·pho·to lens PHOT Teleobjektiv *n*
tel·e·print·er Fernschreiber *m*
tel·e·scope Teleskop *n*, Fernrohr *n*
tel·e·text Teletext *m*, Videotext *m*
tel·e·type·writ·er Fernschreiber *m*
tel·e·vise im Fernsehen übertragen *or* bringen
tel·e·vi·sion 1. Fernsehen *n*; *a.* **television set** Fernsehapparat *m*, -gerät *n*, F Fernseher *m*; **on television** im Fernsehen; **watch television** fernsehen; **2.** Fernseh...
tel·ex 1. Telex *n*, Fernschreiben *n*; **2.** telexen (**to** an *acc*), ein Telex schicken (*dat*)
tell *v/t* sagen; erzählen; erkennen (**by** an *dat*); *Namen etc* nennen; *et.* anzeigen; *j-m* sagen, befehlen (**to do** zu tun); **I can't tell one from the other, I can't tell them apart** ich kann sie nicht auseinanderhalten; *v/i* sich auswirken (**on** bei, auf *acc*), sich bemerkbar machen; **who can tell?** wer weiß?; **you can never tell, you never can tell** man kann nie wissen; **tell against** sprechen gegen; von Nachteil sein für; **tell s.o. off** F mit j-m schimpfen (**for** wegen); **tell on s.o.** j-n verpetzen *or* verraten
tell·er Kassierer(in)
tell·ing aufschlussreich
tell·tale 1. verräterisch; **2.** F Petze *f*
tel·ly *Br* F Fernseher *m*
te·mer·i·ty Frechheit *f*, Kühnheit *f*
tem·per 1. Temperament *n*, Wesen *n*, Wesensart *f*; Laune *f*, Stimmung *f*; TECH Härte(grad *m*) *f*; **keep one's temper** sich beherrschen, ruhig bleiben; **lose one's temper** die Beherrschung verlieren; **2.** TECH *Stahl* härten
tem·pe·ra·ment Temperament *n*, Naturell *n*, Wesen *n*, Wesensart *f*
tem·pe·ra·men·tal launisch; von Natur aus
tem·pe·rate gemäßigt (*climate, region*)
tem·pe·ra·ture Temperatur *f*; **have** *or* **be running a temperature** MED erhöhte Temperatur *or* Fieber haben
tem·pest POET (heftiger) Sturm
tem·ple[1] Tempel *m*
tem·ple[2] ANAT Schläfe *f*
tem·po·ral weltlich; LING temporal, der Zeit
tem·po·ra·ry vorübergehend, zeiweilig
tempt *j-n* in Versuchung führen; *j-n* verführen (**to** zu)

temp·ta·tion Versuchung *f*, Verführung *f*
tempt·ing verführerisch
ten 1. zehn; **2.** Zehn *f*
ten·a·ble *fig* haltbar
te·na·cious hartnäckig, zäh
ten·ant Pächter(in), Mieter(in)
tend neigen, tendieren (**to** zu); **tend up-wards** e-e steigende Tendenz haben
ten·den·cy Tendenz *f*; Neigung *f*
ten·der[1] empfindlich, *fig a.* heikel; GASTR zart, weich; sanft, zart, zärtlich
ten·der[2] RAIL, MAR Tender *m*
ten·der[3] ECON **1.** Angebot *n*; **legal tender** gesetzliches Zahlungsmittel; **2.** ein Angebot machen (**for** für)
ten·der·foot F Neuling *m*, Anfänger *m*
ten·der·loin GASTR zartes Lendenstück
ten·der·ness Zartheit *f*; Zärtlichkeit *f*
ten·don ANAT Sehne *f*
ten·dril BOT Ranke *f*
ten·e·ment Mietshaus *n*, *contp* Mietskaserne *f*
ten·nis Tennis *n*
tennis court Tennisplatz *m*
tennis play·er Tennisspieler(in)
ten·or MUS, JUR Tenor *m*, JUR *a.* Wortlaut *m*, Sinn *m*; Verlauf *m*
tense[1] LING Zeit(form) *f*, Tempus *n*
tense[2] gespannt, straff (*rope etc*), (an)gespannt (*a. fig*); (über)nervös, verkrampft (*person*)
ten·sion Spannung *f* (*a.* ELECTR)
tent Zelt *n*
ten·ta·cle ZO Tentakel *m*, *n*, Fangarm *m*
ten·ta·tive vorläufig; vorsichtig, zaghaft
ten·ter·hooks: be on tenterhooks wie auf (glühenden) Kohlen sitzen
tenth 1. zehnte(r, -s); **2.** Zehntel *n*
tenth·ly zehntens
ten·u·ous *fig* lose (*link, relationship etc*)
ten·ure Besitz *m*, Besitzdauer *f*; **tenure of office** Amtsdauer *f*, Dienstzeit *f*
tep·id lau(warm)
term 1. Zeit *f*, Zeitraum *m*, Dauer *f*; JUR Laufzeit *f*; PED, UNIV Semester *n*, *esp Br* Trimester *n*; Ausdruck *m*, Bezeichnung *f*; **term of office** Amtsdauer *f*, Amtsperiode *f*, Amtszeit *f*; *pl* Bedingungen *pl*; **be on good (bad) terms** with gut (schlecht) auskommen mit; **they are not on speaking terms** sie sprechen nicht (mehr) miteinander; **come to terms** sich einigen (**with** mit); **2.** nennen, bezeichnen als
ter·mi·nal 1. End...; letzte(r, -s); MED unheilbar; im Endstadium; **terminally ill** unheilbar krank; **2.** RAIL etc Endstation *f*; Terminal *m*, *n*; ELECTR Pol *m*; EDP Terminal *n*, Datenendstation *f*

ter·mi·nate *v/t* beenden; *Vertrag* kündigen, lösen; MED *Schwangerschaft* unterbrechen; *v/i* enden; ablaufen (*contract*)
ter·mi·na·tion Beendigung *f*; Kündigung *f*, Lösung *f*; Ende *n*; Ablauf *m*
ter·mi·nus RAIL etc Endstation *f*
ter·race Terrasse *f*; Häuserreihe *f*; *mst pl esp Br* SPORT Ränge *pl*
ter·raced house *Br* Reihenhaus *n*
ter·res·tri·al irdisch; Erd...; *esp* BOT, ZO Land...
ter·ri·ble schrecklich
ter·rif·ic F toll, fantastisch; irre (*speed, heat etc*)
ter·ri·fy *j-m* schreckliche Angst einjagen
ter·ri·to·ri·al territorial, Gebiets...
ter·ri·to·ry Territorium *n*, (*a.* Hoheits-, Staats)Gebiet *n*
ter·ror Entsetzen *n*; Schrecken *m*; POL Terror *m*; F Landplage *f*; **in terror** in panischer Angst
ter·ror·is·m Terrorismus *m*
ter·ror·ist Terrorist(in)
ter·ror·ize terrorisieren
terse *fig* knapp, kurz (und bündig)
test 1. Test *m*, Prüfung *f*; Probe *f*; **2.** testen, prüfen; probieren; *j-s Geduld etc* auf e-e harte Probe stellen
tes·ta·ment: last will and testament JUR Letzter Wille, Testament *n*
test an·i·mal Versuchstier *n*
test card TV Testbild *n*
test drive MOT Probefahrt *f*
tes·ti·cle ANAT Hoden *m*
tes·ti·fy JUR aussagen
tes·ti·mo·ni·al Referenz *f*
tes·ti·mo·ny JUR Aussage *f*; Beweis *m*
test pi·lot AVIAT Testpilot *m*
test tube CHEM Reagenzglas *n*
tes·ty gereizt
tet·a·nus MED Tetanus *m*, Wundstarrkrampf *m*
teth·er 1. Strick *m*; Kette *f*; **at the end of one's tether** *fig* mit s-n Kräften *or* Nerven am Ende sein; **2.** *Tier* anbinden; anketten
text Text *m*
text·book Lehrbuch *n*
tex·tile 1. Stoff *m*, *pl* Textilien *pl*; **2.** Textil...
tex·ture Textur *f*, Gewebe *n*; Beschaffenheit *f*; Struktur *f*
than als
thank 1. *j-m* danken, sich bei *j-m* bedanken (**for** für); **thank you** danke; **thank you very much** vielen Dank; **no, thank you** nein, danke; (**yes,**) **thank you** ja, bitte; **2. thanks** Dank *m*; **thanks** danke (schön); **no, thanks** nein, danke; **thanks**

T

to dank (*gen*), wegen (*gen*)
thank·ful dankbar
thank·less undankbar
that 1. *pron and adj* das; jene(r, -s), der, die, das, derjenige, diejenige, dasjenige; **2.** *relative pron* der, die, das, welche(r, -s); **3.** *cj* dass; **4.** *adv* F so, dermaßen; *it's that simple* so einfach ist das
thatch 1. mit Stroh *or* Reet decken; **2.** (Dach)Stroh *n*, Reet *n*; Strohdach *n*, Reetdach *n*
thaw 1. (auf)tauen; **2.** Tauwetter *n*; (Auf)Tauen *n*
the 1. der, die, das, *pl* die; **2.** *adv*: *the ... the ...* je ... desto ...; *the sooner the better* je eher, desto besser
the·a·ter Theater *n*; UNIV (*Hör*)Saal *m*; MIL (Kriegs)Schauplatz *m*
the·a·ter·go·er Theaterbesucher(in)
the·a·tre *Br* → **theater**; MED Operationssaal *m*
the·at·ri·cal Theater...; *fig* theatralisch
theft Diebstahl *m*
their ihr(e)
theirs der (die, das) ihrige *or* ihre
them sie (*acc pl*); ihnen (*dat*)
theme Thema *n*
them·selves sie (*acc pl*) selbst; sich (selbst)
then 1. *adv* dann; da; damals; *by then* bis dahin; *from then on* von da an; → *every, now 1, there*; **2.** *adj* damalig
the·o·lo·gian Theologe *m*, Theologin *f*
the·ol·o·gy Theologie *f*
the·o·ret·i·cal theoretisch
the·o·rist Theoretiker *m*
the·o·ry Theorie *f*
ther·a·peu·tic therapeutisch; F wohltuend; gesund
ther·a·pist Therapeut(in)
ther·a·py Therapie *f*
there 1. da, dort; (da-, dort)hin; *there is, there are* es gibt, es ist, *pl* es sind; *there and then* auf der Stelle; *there you are* hier bitte; siehst du!, na also!; **2.** *int* so; siehst du!, na also!; *there, there* ist ja gut!
there·a·bout(s) so ungefähr
there·af·ter danach
there·by dadurch
there·fore deshalb, daher; folglich
there·up·on darauf(hin)
ther·mal 1. thermisch, Thermo..., Wärme...; **2.** Thermik *f*
ther·mom·e·ter Thermometer *n*
ther·mos® Thermosflasche® *f*
the·sis These *f*; UNIV Dissertation *f*, Doktorarbeit *f*
they sie *pl*; man

thick 1. *adj* dick, (*fog etc a.*) dicht; F dumm; F dick befreundet; *be thick with* wimmeln von; *thick with smoke* verräuchert; *that's a bit thick!* *esp Br* F das ist ein starkes Stück!; **2.** *adv* dick, dicht; *lay it on thick* F dick auftragen; **3.** *in the thick of* mitten in (*dat*); *through thick and thin* durch dick und dünn
thick·en dicker werden, (*fog etc a.*) dichter werden; GASTR eindicken, binden
thick·et Dickicht *n*
thick·head·ed F strohdumm
thick·ness Dicke *f*; Lage *f*, Schicht *f*
thick·set gedrungen, untersetzt
thick-skinned *fig* dickfellig
thief Dieb(in)
thigh ANAT (Ober)Schenkel *m*
thim·ble Fingerhut *m*
thin 1. *adj* dünn; dürr; spärlich, dürftig; schütter (*hair*); schwach, (*excuse etc a.*) fadenscheinig; **2.** *adv* dünn; **3.** verdünnen; dünner werden, (*fog, hair a.*) sich lichten
thing Ding *n*; Sache *f*; *pl* Sachen *pl*, Zeug *n*; *fig* Dinge *pl*, Lage *f*, Umstände *pl*; *I couldn't see a thing* ich konnte überhaupt nichts sehen; *another thing* et. anderes; *the right thing* das Richtige
thing·a·ma·jig F Dings(bums) *m*, *f*, *n*
think *v/i* denken (*of* an *acc*); nachdenken (*about* über *acc*); *I think so* ich glaube *or* denke schon; *I'll think about it* ich überlege es mir; *think of* sich erinnern an (*acc*); *think of doing s.th.* beabsichtigen *or* daran denken, et. zu tun; *what do you think of or about ...?* was halten Sie von ...?; *v/t* denken, glauben, meinen; *j-n, et.* halten für; *think over* nachdenken über (*acc*), sich et. überlegen; *think up* sich et. ausdenken
think tank Beraterstab *m*, Sachverständigenstab *m*, Denkfabrik *f*
third 1. dritte(r, -s); **2.** Drittel *n*
third·ly drittens
third-rate drittklassig
Third World Dritte Welt
thirst Durst *m*
thirst·y durstig; *be thirsty* Durst haben, durstig sein
thir·teen 1. dreizehn; **2.** Dreizehn *f*
thir·teenth dreizehnte(r, -s)
thir·ti·eth dreißigste(r, -s)
thir·ty 1. dreißig; **2.** Dreißig *f*
this diese(r, -s); *this morning* heute Morgen; *this is John speaking* TEL hier (spricht) John
this·tle BOT Distel *f*
thong (Leder)Riemen *m*
thorn Dorn *m*

thorn·y dornig; *fig* schwierig, heikel
thor·ough gründlich, genau; fürchterlich (*mess etc*)
thor·ough·bred ZO Vollblüter *m*
thor·ough·fare Hauptverkehrsstraße *f*; *no thoroughfare!* Durchfahrt verboten!
though 1. *cj* obwohl; (je)doch; *as though* als ob; **2.** *adv* dennoch, trotzdem
thought Denken *n*; Gedanke *m* (*of* an *acc*); *on second thought* wenn ich es mir (recht) überlege
thought·ful nachdenklich; rücksichtsvoll, aufmerksam
thought·les gedankenlos; rücksichtslos
thou·sand 1. tausend; **2.** Tausend *n*
thou·sandth 1. tausendste(r, -s); **2.** Tausendstel *n*
thrash verdreschen, verprügeln; SPORT F *j*-n e-e Abfuhr erteilen; *thrash about, thrash around* sich *im Bett etc* hin und her werfen; um sich schlagen; zappeln (*fish*); *thrash out Problem etc* ausdiskutieren
thrash·ing Dresche *f*, Tracht *f* Prügel
thread 1. Faden *m* (*a. fig*); Garn *n*; TECH Gewinde *n*; **2.** *Nadel* einfädeln; *Perlen etc* auffädeln, aufreihen
thread·bare abgewetzt, abgetragen; *fig* abgedroschen
threat Drohung *f*; Bedrohung *f*, Gefahr *f* (*to gen or* für)
threat·en (be)drohen
threat·en·ing drohend
three 1. drei; **2.** Drei *f*
three·fold dreifach
three-ply → *ply*[2]
three·score sechzig
three-stage dreistufig
thresh AGR dreschen
thresh·ing ma·chine AGR Dreschmaschine *f*
thresh·old Schwelle *f*
thrift Sparsamkeit *f*
thrift·y sparsam
thrill 1. prickelndes Gefühl; Nervenkitzel *m*; aufregendes Erlebnis; **2.** *v/t be thrilled* (ganz) hingerissen sein (*at, about* von)
thrill·er Thriller *m*, F Reißer *m*
thrill·ing spannend, fesselnd, packend
thrive gedeihen; *fig* blühen, florieren
throat ANAT Kehle *f*, Gurgel *f*; Rachen *m*; Hals *m*; *clear one's throat* sich räuspern; → *sore 1*
throb 1. hämmern (*machine*), (*heart etc a.*) pochen, schlagen; pulsieren (*pain*); **2.** Hämmern *n*, Pochen *n*, Schlagen *n*
throm·bo·sis MED Thrombose *f*
throne Thron *m*

throng 1. Schar *f*, Menschenmenge *f*; **2.** sich drängen (in *dat*)
throt·tle 1. erdrosseln; *throttle down* MOT, TECH drosseln, Gas wegnehmen; **2.** TECH Drosselklappe *f*
through 1. *prp* durch (*acc*); bis (einschließlich); *Monday through Friday* von Montag bis Freitag; **2.** *adv* durch; *through and through* durch und durch; *put s.o. through to* TEL j-n verbinden mit; *wet through* völlig durchnässt; **3.** *adj* durchgehend (*train etc*); Durchgangs...
through·out 1. *prp*: *throughout the night* die ganze Nacht hindurch; *throughout the country* im ganzen Land, überall im Land; **2.** *adv* ganz, überall; die ganze Zeit (hindurch)
through traf·fic Durchgangsverkehr *m*
through·way *Br* → *thruway*
throw 1. werfen; *Hebel etc* betätigen; *Reiter* abwerfen; *Party* geben, F schmeißen; *throw a four* e-e Vier würfeln; *throw off Jacke etc* abwerfen; *Verfolger* abschütteln; *Krankheit* loswerden; *throw on* sich e-e *Jacke etc* (hastig) überwerfen; *throw out* hinauswerfen; wegwerfen; *throw up v/t* hochwerfen; F *Job etc* hinschmeißen; F (er)brechen; *v/i* F (sich) (er)brechen; **2.** Wurf *m*
throw·a·way Wegwerf..., Einweg...
throwaway pack Einwegpackung *f*
throw-in *soccer*: Einwurf *m*
thru F → *through*
thrum → *strum*
thrush ZO Drossel *f*
thrust 1. *j*-n, *et.* stoßen (*into* in *acc*); *et.* stecken, schieben (*into* in *acc*); *thrust at* stoßen nach; *thrust s.th. upon s.o.* j-m et. aufdrängen; **2.** Stoß *m*; MIL Vorstoß *m*; PHYS Schub *m*, Schubkraft *f*
thru·way Schnellstraße *f*
thud 1. dumpfes Geräusch, Plumps *m*; **2.** plumpsen
thug Verbrecher *m*, Schläger *m*
thumb 1. ANAT Daumen *m*; **2.** *thumb a lift or ride* per Anhalter fahren, trampen (*to* nach); *thumb through a book* ein Buch durchblättern; *well-thumbed* abgegriffen
thumb·tack Reißzwecke *f*, Reißnagel *m*, Heftzwecke *f*
thump 1. *v/t j*-m e-n Schlag versetzen; *thump out Melodie* herunterhämmern (*on the piano* auf dem Klavier); *v/i* (heftig) schlagen *or* hämmern *or* pochen (*a. heart*); plumpsen; trampeln; **2.** dumpfes Geräusch, Plumps *m*; Schlag *m*
thun·der 1. Donner *m*, Donnern *n*; **2.** donnern

T

thun·der·bolt Blitz *m* und Donner *m*
thun·der·clap Donnerschlag *m*
thun·der·cloud Gewitterwolke *f*
thun·der·ous donnernd (*applause*)
thun·der·storm Gewitter *n*, Unwetter *n*
thun·der·struck wie vom Donner gerührt
Thur(s) ABBR *of* **Thursday** Do., Donnerstag *m*
Thurs·day (ABBR **Thur, Thurs**) Donnerstag *m*; **on Thursday** (am) Donnerstag; **on Thursdays** donnerstags
thus so, auf diese Weise; folglich, somit; **thus far** bisher
thwart durchkreuzen, vereiteln
thyme BOT Thymian *m*
thy·roid (gland) ANAT Schilddrüse *f*
tick¹ 1. Ticken *n*; Haken *m*, Häkchen *n*; **2.** *v/i* ticken; *v/t mst* **tick off** ab-, anhaken
tick² ZO Zecke *f*
tick³: **on tick** *Br* F auf Pump
tick·er·tape pa·rade Konfettiparade *f*
tick·et 1. Fahrkarte *f*, Fahrschein *m*; Flugkarte *f*, Flugschein *m*, Ticket *n*; (*Eintritts-, Theater- etc*)Karte *f*; (*Gepäck*)-Schein *m*; Etikett *n*, (*Preis- etc* -) Schild *n*; POL Wahl-, Kandidatenliste *f*; (*a.* **parking ticket**) MOT Strafzettel *m*; **2.** etikettieren; bestimmen, vorsehen (**for** für)
tick·et·can·cel·(l)ing ma·chine (Fahrschein)Entwerter *m*
tick·et col·lec·tor (Bahnsteig)Schaffner(in)
ticket machine Fahrkartenautomat *m*
ticket of·fice RAIL Fahrkartenschalter *m*
tick·ing Inlett *n*; Matratzenbezug *m*
tick·le kitzeln
tick·lish kitz(e)lig, *fig a.* heikel
tid·al wave Flutwelle *f*
tid·bit Leckerbissen *m*
tide 1. Gezeiten *pl*; Flut *f*; *fig* Strömung *f*, Trend *m*; **high tide** Flut *f*; **low tide** Ebbe *f*; **2. tide over** *fig* j-m hinweghelfen über (*acc*); j-n über Wasser halten
ti·dy 1. sauber, ordentlich, aufgeräumt; F hübsch, beträchtlich (*Sum etc*); **2.** *a.* **tidy up** in Ordnung bringen, (*Zimmer a.*) aufräumen; **tidy away** wegräumen, aufräumen
tie 1. Krawatte *f*, Schlips *m*; Band *n*; Schnur *f*; Stimmengleichheit *f*; SPORT Unentschieden *n*; (*Pokal*)Spiel *n*; RAIL Schwelle *f*; *mst pl fig* Bande *pl*; **2.** *v/t* an-, festbinden; (sich) *Krawatte etc* binden; *fig* verbinden; **the game was tied** SPORT das Spiel ging unentschieden aus; *v/i*: **they tied for second place** SPORT *etc* sie belegten gemeinsam den zweiten Platz; **tie down** *fig* (an)binden; j-n festlegen (**to** auf *acc*); **tie in with** über-

einstimmen mit, passen zu; verbinden *or* koppeln mit; **tie up** *Paket etc* verschnüren; *et.* in Verbindung bringen (**with** mit); *Verkehr etc* lahmlegen; **be tied up** ECON fest angelegt sein (**in** in *dat*)
tie·break(·er) *tennis*: Tie-Break *m, n*
tie-in (enge) Verbindung, (enger) Zusammenhang; ECON Kopplungsgeschäft *n*; **a book movie tie-in** *appr* das Buch zum Film
tie-on Anhänge...
tie·pin Krawattennadel *f*
tier (Sitz)Reihe *f*; Lage *f*, Schicht *f*; *fig* Stufe *f*
tie-up (enge) Verbindung, (enger) Zusammenhang; ECON Fusion *f*
ti·ger ZO Tiger *m*
tight 1. *adj* fest (sitzend), fest angezogen; straff (*rope etc*); eng (*a. dress etc*); knapp (*a. fig*); F knick(e)rig; F blau; **be in a tight corner** in der Klemme sein *or* sitzen *or* stecken; **2.** *adv* fest; F gut; **hold tight** festhalten; **sleep tight!** F schlaf gut!
tight·en festziehen, anziehen; *Seil etc* straffen; **tighten one's belt** *fig* den Gürtel enger schnallen; **tighten up (on)** *Gesetz etc* verschärfen
tight·fist·ed F knick(e)rig
tights (*Tänzer-, Artisten*)Trikot *n*; *esp Br* Strumpfhose *f*
ti·gress ZO Tigerin *f*
tile 1. (Dach)Ziegel *m*; Fliese *f*, Kachel *f*; **2.** (mit Ziegeln) decken; fliesen, kacheln
til·er Dachdecker *m*; Fliesenleger *m*
till¹ → **until**
till² (Laden)Kasse *f*
tilt 1. kippen; sich neigen; **2.** Kippen *n*; **at a tilt** schief, schräg; (**at**) **full tilt** F mit Volldampf
tim·ber *Br* Bau-, Nutzholz *n*; Baumbestand *m*, Bäume *pl*; Balken *m*
time 1. Zeit *f*; Uhrzeit *f*; MUS Takt *m*; Mal *n*; **time after time, time and again** immer wieder; **every time I ...** jedes Mal, wenn ich ...; **how many times?** wie oft?; **next time** nächstes Mal; **this time** diesmal; **three times** dreimal; **three times four equals *or* is twelve** drei mal vier ist zwölf; **what's the time?** wie spät ist es?; **what time?** um wie viel Uhr?; **all the time** die ganze Zeit; **at all times, at any time** jederzeit; **at the time** damals; **at the same time** gleichzeitig; **at times** manchmal; **by the time** wenn; als; **for a time** e-e Zeit lang; **for the time being** vorläufig, fürs Erste; **from time to time** von Zeit zu Zeit; **have a good time** sich gut unterhalten *or* amüsieren; **in time** rechtzeitig; **in no time (at all)** im

Nu; *on time* pünktlich; *some time ago* vor einiger Zeit; *to pass the time* zum Zeitvertreib; *take one's time* sich Zeit lassen; **2.** *et.* timen (*a.* SPORT); (ab)stoppen; zeitlich abstimmen, den richtigen Zeitpunkt wählen *or* bestimmen für
time card Stechkarte *f*
time clock Stechuhr *f*
time lag Zeitdifferenz *f*
time-lapse *film*: Zeitraffer...
time·less immer während, ewig; zeitlos
time lim·it Frist *f*
time·ly (recht)zeitig
time sheet Stechkarte *f*
time sig·nal *radio*: Zeitzeichen *n*
time·ta·ble *Br* Fahrplan *m*, Flugplan *m*; Stundenplan *m*; Zeitplan *m*
tim·id ängstlich, furchtsam, zaghaft
tim·ing Timing *n*
tin 1. Zinn *n*; *Br* (Blech-, Konserven)Dose *f*, (-)Büchse *f*; **2.** verzinnen; *Br* einmachen, eindosen
tinc·ture Tinktur *f*
tin·foil Stanniol(papier) *n*; Alufolie *f*
tinge 1. tönen; *be tinged with fig* e-n Anflug haben von; **2.** Tönung *f*; *fig* Anflug *m*, Spur *f* (*of* von)
tin·gle prickeln, kribbeln
tink·er herumfuschen, herumbasteln (*at* an *dat*)
tin·kle bimmeln; klirren
tinned *Br* Dosen..., Büchsen...
tinned fruit *Br* Obstkonserven *pl*
tin o·pen·er *Br* Dosenöffner *m*, Büchsenöffner *m*
tin·sel Lametta *n*; Flitter *m*
tint 1. (Farb)Ton *m*, Tönung *f*; **2.** tönen
ti·ny winzig
tip¹ 1. Spitze *f*; Filter *m*; *it's on the tip of my tongue fig* es liegt mir auf der Zunge; **2.** mit e-r Spitze versehen
tip² 1. *esp Br* (aus)kippen, schütten; kippen; *tip over* umkippen; **2.** *esp Br* (*Schutt- etc*)Abladeplatz *m*, (-)Halde *f*; *Br fig* F Saustall *m*
tip³ 1. Trinkgeld *n*; **2.** *j-m* ein Trinkgeld geben
tip⁴ 1. Tipp *m*, Rat(schlag) *m*; **2.** tippen auf (*acc*) (*as* als); *tip s.o. off j-m* e-n Tipp *or* Wink geben
tip·sy angeheitert
tip·toe 1. *on tiptoe* auf Zehenspitzen; **2.** auf Zehenspitzen gehen
tire¹ MOT Reifen *m*
tire² ermüden, müde machen *or* werden
tired müde; *be tired of j-n, et.* satt haben
tire·less unermüdlich
tire·some ermüdend; lästig
tis·sue BIOL Gewebe *n*; Papier(taschen)-

tuch *n*; → **tissue pa·per** Seidenpapier *n*
tit¹ F *contp* Titte *f*
tit² ZO Meise *f*
tit·bit *esp Br* → **tidbit**
tit·il·late *j-n* (*sexuell*) anregen
ti·tle Titel *m*; JUR (Rechts)Anspruch *m* (*to* auf *acc*)
ti·tle·hold·er SPORT Titelhalter(in)
ti·tle page Titelseite *f*
ti·tle role THEA *etc* Titelrolle *f*
tit·mouse ZO Meise *f*
tit·ter 1. kichern; **2.** Kichern *n*
to 1. *prp* zu; an (*acc*), auf (*acc*), für, in (*acc*), in (*dat*), nach; (im Verhältnis *or* im Vergleich) zu, gegen(über); *extent, limit, degree*: bis, (bis) zu, (bis) an (*acc*); *time*: bis, bis zu, bis gegen, vor (*dat*); *from Monday to Friday* von Montag bis Freitag; *a quarter to one* (ein) Viertel vor eins, drei viertel eins; *go to Italy* nach Italien fahren; *go to school* in die *or* zur Schule gehen; *have you ever been to Rome?* bist du schon einmal in Rom gewesen?; *to me etc* mir *etc*; *here's to you!* auf Ihr Wohl!, prosit!; **2.** *adv* zu; *pull to Tür etc* zuziehen; *come to* (wieder) zu sich kommen; *to and fro* hin und her, auf und ab; **3.** *with infinitive*: zu; *intention, aim*: um zu; *to go* gehen; *easy to learn* leicht zu lernen; *... to earn money ...* um Geld zu verdienen
toad ZO Kröte *f*, Unke *f*
toad·stool BOT ungenießbarer Pilz; Giftpilz *m*
toad·y 1. Kriecher(in); **2.** *toady to s.o. fig* vor j-m kriechen
toast¹ 1. Toast *m*; **2.** toasten; rösten
toast² 1. Toast *m*, Trinkspruch *m*; **2.** auf j-n *or* j-s Wohl trinken
toast·er TECH Toaster *m*
to·bac·co Tabak *m*
to·bac·co·nist Tabak(waren)händler(in)
to·bog·gan 1. (Rodel)Schlitten *m*; **2.** Schlitten fahren, rodeln
to·day 1. *adv* heute; heutzutage; *a week today, today week* heute in e-r Woche, heute in acht Tagen; **2.** *today's paper* die heutige Zeitung, die Zeitung von heute; *of today, today's* von heute, heutig
tod·dle auf wack(e)ligen *or* unsicheren Beinen gehen
to-do F *fig* Theater *n*
toe ANAT Zehe *f*; Spitze *f*
toe·nail ANAT Zehennagel *m*
tof·fee, tof·fy Sahnebonbon *m*, *n*, Toffee *n*
to·geth·er zusammen; gleichzeitig
toi·let Toilette *f*
toilet pa·per Toilettenpapier *n*
toilet roll *esp Br* Rolle *f* Toilettenpapier

to·ken Zeichen *n*; *as a token, in token of* als *or* zum Zeichen (*gen*); zum Andenken an (*acc*)

token strike Warnstreik *m*

tol·e·ra·ble erträglich

tol·e·rance Toleranz *f*; Nachsicht *f*

tol·e·rant tolerant (*of, towards* gegenüber)

tol·e·rate tolerieren, dulden; ertragen

toll¹ Benutzungsgebühr *f*, Maut *f*; *heavy death toll* große Zahl an Todesopfern; *take its toll (on) fig* s-n Tribut fordern (von); s-e Spuren hinterlassen (bei)

toll² läuten

toll-free TEL gebührenfrei

toll road gebührenpflichtige Straße, Mautstraße *f*

tom F → *tomcat*

to·ma·to BOT Tomate *f*

tomb Grab *n*; Grabmal *n*; Gruft *f*

tom·boy Wildfang *m*

tomb·stone Grabstein *m*

tom·cat ZO Kater *m*

tom·fool·e·ry Unsinn *m*

to·mor·row 1. *adv* morgen; *a week tomorrow, tomorrow week* morgen in e-r Woche, morgen in acht Tagen; *tomorrow morning* morgen früh; *tomorrow night* morgen Abend; 2. *the day after tomorrow* übermorgen; *of tomorrow, tomorrow's* von morgen

ton (ABBR *t, tn*) Tonne *f*

tone 1. Ton *m*; Klang *m*; (Farb)Ton *m*; MUS Note *f*; MED Tonus *m*; *fig* Niveau *n*; 2. *tone down* abschwächen; *tone up* Muskeln *etc* kräftigen

tongs (*a pair of tongs* e-e) Zange *f*

tongue ANAT, TECH Zunge *f*; (*Mutter*)Sprache *f*; Klöppel *m* (*e-r Glocke*); *hold one's tongue* den Mund halten

ton·ic Tonikum *n*, Stärkungsmittel *n*; Tonic *n*; MUS Grundton *m*

to·night heute Abend *or* Nacht

ton·sil ANAT Mandel *f*

ton·sil·li·tis MED Mandelentzündung *f*; Angina *f*

too zu; zu, sehr; auch (noch)

tool Werkzeug *n*, Gerät *n*

tool bag Werkzeugtasche *f*

tool box Werkzeugkasten *m*

tool kit Werkzeug *n*

tool·mak·er Werkzeugmacher *m*

tool·shed Geräteschuppen *m*

toot *esp* MOT hupen

tooth Zahn *m*

tooth·ache Zahnschmerzen *pl*, Zahnweh *n*

tooth·brush Zahnbürste *f*

tooth·less zahnlos

tooth·paste Zahncreme *f*, Zahnpasta *f*

tooth·pick Zahnstocher *m*

top¹ 1. oberer Teil; GEOGR Gipfel *m*, Spitze *f*; BOT Krone *f*, Wipfel *m*; Kopfende *n*, oberes Ende; Oberteil *n*; Oberfläche *f*; Deckel *m*; Verschluss *m*; MOT Verdeck *n*; MOT höchster Gang; *at the top of the page* oben auf der Seite; *at the top of one's voice* aus vollem Hals; *on top* oben(auf); darauf, F drauf; *on top of* (oben) auf (*dat or acc*), über (*dat or acc*); 2. oberste(r, -s); Höchst..., Spitzen..., Top...; 3. bedecken (*with* mit); *fig* übersteigen, übertreffen; *top up Tank etc* auffüllen; F *j-m* nachschenken

top² Kreisel *m* (*toy*)

top hat Zylinder *m*

top-heav·y kopflastig (*a. fig*)

top·ic Thema *n*

top·ic·al aktuell

top·ple: *mst* *topple over* umkippen; *topple the government* die Regierung stürzen

top·sy-tur·vy in e-r heillosen Unordnung

torch Br Taschenlampe *f*; Fackel *f*

torch·light Fackelschein *m*; *torchlight procession* Fackelzug *m*

tor·ment 1. Qual *f*; 2. quälen, peinigen, plagen

tor·na·do Tornado *m*, Wirbelsturm *m*

tor·pe·do MIL 1. Torpedo *m*; 2. torpedieren (*a. fig*)

tor·rent reißender Strom; *fig* Schwall *m*

tor·ren·tial: *torrential rain* sintflutartige Regenfälle *pl*

tor·toise ZO Schildkröte *f*

tor·tu·ous gewunden

tor·ture 1. Folter *f*, Folterung *f*; *fig* Qual *f*, Tortur *f*; 2. foltern; *fig* quälen

toss 1. *v/t* werfen; *Münze* hochwerfen; GASTR schwenken; *toss off* F *Bild etc* hinhauen; *v/i a.* *toss about, toss and turn* sich im *Schlaf* hin und her werfen; *a. toss up* e-e Münze hochwerfen; *toss for s.th.* um et. losen; *toss one's head* den Kopf zurückwerfen; 2. Wurf *m*; Zurückwerfen *n*; Hochwerfen *n*

tot F Knirps *m*

to·tal 1. völlig, total; ganz, gesamt, Gesamt...; 2. Gesamtbetrag *m*, -menge *f*; 3. sich belaufen auf (*acc*); *total up* zusammenrechnen, -zählen

tot·ter schwanken, wanken

touch 1. (sich) berühren; anfassen; *Essen etc* anrühren; *fig* herankommen an (*acc*); *fig* rühren; *touch wood!* toi, toi, toi!; *touch down* AVIAT aufsetzen; *touch up* ausbessern; PHOT retuschieren; 2. Tast-

empfindung *f*; Berührung *f*, MUS *etc* Anschlag *m*; (*Pinsel- etc*)Strich *m*; GASTR Spur *f*; Verbindung *f*, Kontakt *m*; *fig* Note *f*; *fig* Anflug *m*; **a touch of flu** e-e leichte Grippe; **get in touch with s.o.** sich mit j-m in Verbindung setzen
touch-and-go F kritisch, riskant, prekär; *it was touch-and-go whether* es stand auf des Messers Schneide, ob
touch-down AVIAT Aufsetzen *n*, Landung *f*
touched gerührt; F leicht verrückt
touch-ing rührend
touch-line *soccer*: Seitenlinie *f*
touch-stone Prüfstein *m* (*of* für)
touch-y empfindlich; heikel (*subject etc*)
tough zäh; widerstandsfähig; *fig* hart; schwierig (*problem, negotiations etc*)
tough-en *a.* **toughen up** hart *or* zäh machen *or* werden
tour **1.** Tour *f* (*of* durch), (Rund)Reise *f*, (Rund)Fahrt *f*; Ausflug *m*; Rundgang *m* (*of* durch); THEA Tournee *f* (*a.* SPORT); *go on tour* auf Tournee gehen; → **conduct** 2; **2.** bereisen, reisen durch
tour-is-m Tourismus *m*, Fremdenverkehr *m*
tour-ist **1.** Tourist(in); **2.** Touristen…
tourist class AVIAT, MAR Touristenklasse *f*
tourist in-dus-try Tourismusgeschäft *n*
tourist infor-ma-tion of-fice, tourist office Verkehrsverein *m*
tourist sea-son Reisesaison *f*, Reisezeit *f*
tour-na-ment Turnier *n*
tou-sled zerzaust
tow **1.** *Boot etc* schleppen, *Auto etc a.* abschleppen; **2.** *give s.o. a tow* j-n abschleppen; *take in tow* *Auto etc* abschleppen
to-ward, *esp Br* **to-wards** auf (*acc*) … zu, (in) Richtung, zu; *time*: gegen; *fig* gegenüber
tow-el **1.** Handtuch *n*, (*Bade- etc*)Tuch *n*; **2.** (mit e-m Handtuch) abtrocknen *or* abreiben
tow-er **1.** Turm *m*; **1.** *tower above, tower over* überragen
tower block *Br* Hochhaus *n*
tow-er-ing turmhoch; *fig* überragend; *in a towering rage* rasend vor Zorn
town Stadt *f*; Kleinstadt *f*; *go into town* in die Stadt gehen
town cen-tre *Br* Innenstadt *f*, City *f*
town coun-cil *Br* Stadtrat *m*
town coun-ci(l)-lor *Br* Stadtrat *m*, Stadträtin *f*
town hall Rathaus *n*
town-ie F Städter(in), Stadtmensch *m*
town plan-ner Stadtplaner(in)
town plan-ning Stadtplanung *f*

towns-peo-ple Städter *pl*, Stadtbevölkerung *f*
tow-rope MOT Abschleppseil *n*
tox-ic toxisch, giftig; Gift…
tox-ic waste Giftmüll *m*
tox-ic waste dump Giftmülldeponie *f*
toy **1.** Spielzeug *n*, *pl a.* Spielsachen *pl*, ECON Spielwaren *pl*; **2.** Spielzeug…; Miniatur…; Zwerg…; **3.** *toy with* spielen mit (*a. fig*)
trace **1.** (durch)pausen; *j-n, et.* ausfindig machen, aufspüren, *et.* finden; *a.* **trace back** *et.* zurückverfolgen (*to* bis zu); *trace s.th. to* *et.* zurückführen auf (*acc*); **2.** Spur *f* (*a. fig*)
track **1.** Spur *f* (*a. fig*), Fährte *f*; Pfad *m*, Weg *m*; RAIL Gleis *n*, Geleise *n*; TECH Raupe *f*, Raupenkette *f*; SPORT (Renn-, Aschen)Bahn *f*, (*Renn*)Strecke *f*; *tape etc*: Spur *f*; Nummer *f* (*on an LP etc*); **2.** verfolgen; *track down* aufspüren; auftreiben
track and field SPORT Leichtathletik *f*
track e-vent SPORT Laufdisziplin *f*
track-ing sta-tion Bodenstation *f*
track-suit Trainingsanzug *m*
tract Fläche *f*, Gebiet *n*; ANAT (*Verdauungs*)Trakt *m*, (*Atem*)Wege *pl*
trac-tion Ziehen *n*, Zug *m*
trac-tion en-gine Zugmaschine *f*
trac-tor Traktor *m*, Trecker *m*
trade **1.** Handel *m*; Branche *f*, Gewerbe *n*; (*esp* Handwerks)Beruf *m*; **2.** Handel treiben, handeln; *trade on* ausnutzen
trade a-gree-ment Handelsabkommen *n*
trade-mark Warenzeichen *n*
trade name Markenname *m*, Handelsbezeichnung *f*
trade price Großhandelspreis *m*
trad-er Händler(in)
trades-man (Einzel)Händler *m*; Ladeninhaber *m*; Lieferant *m*
trade(s *Br*)| **u-nion** Gewerkschaft *f*
trade u-nion-ist Gewerkschaftler(in)
tra-di-tion Tradition *f*; Überlieferung *f*
tra-di-tion-al traditionell
traf-fic **1.** Verkehr *m*; (*esp* illegaler) Handel (*in* mit); **2.** (*esp* illegal) handeln (*in* mit)
traffic cir-cle MOT Kreisverkehr *m*
traffic in-struc-tion Verkehrsunterricht *m*
traffic is-land Verkehrsinsel *f*
traffic jam (Verkehrs)Stau *m*, Verkehrsstockung *f*
traffic light(s) Verkehrsampel *f*
traffic of-fense (*Br* **of-fence**) Verkehrsdelikt *n*
traffic offend-er Verkehrssünder(in)
traffic reg-ula-tions Straßenverkehrsord-

T

nung *f*
traffic sign Verkehrszeichen *n*, -schild *n*
traffic sig·nal → **traffic light(s)**
traffic war·den *Br* Parküberwacher *m*, Politesse *f*
tra·ge·dy Tragödie *f*
tra·gic tragisch
trail 1. *v/t et.* nachschleifen lassen; verfolgen; SPORT zurückliegen hinter (*dat*) (**by** um); *v/i* sich schleppen; BOT kriechen; SPORT zurückliegen (**by 3-0** 0:3); *trail* (*along*) *behind s.o.* hinter j-m herschleifen; **2.** Spur *f* (*a. fig*), Fährte *f*; Pfad *m*, Weg *m*; *trail of blood* Blutspur *f*; *trail of dust* Staubwolke *f*
trail·er MOT Anhänger *m*; Wohnwagen *m*, Caravan *m*; *film*, TV Trailer *m*, Vorschau *f*
trailer park Standplatz *m* für Wohnwagen
train 1. RAIL Zug *m*; Kolonne *f*, Schlange *f*; Schleppe *f*; *fig* Folge*f*, Kette *f*; *by train* mit der Bahn, mit dem Zug; *train of thought* Gedankengang *m*; **2.** *v/t* j-n ausbilden (*as* als, zum), schulen; SPORT trainieren; *Tier* abrichten, dressieren; *Kamera etc* richten (*on* auf *acc*); *v/i* ausgebildet werden (*as* als, zum); SPORT trainieren (*for* für)
train·ee Auszubildende *m*, *f*
train·er Ausbilder(in); ZO Abrichter(in), Dompteur *m*, Dompteuse *f*; SPORT Trainer(in); *Br* Turnschuh *m*
train·ing Ausbildung *f*, Schulung *f*; Abrichten *n*, Dressur *f*; SPORT Training *n*
trait (Charakter)Zug *m*
trai·tor Verräter *m*
tram *Br* Straßenbahn(wagen *m*) *f*
tram·car *Br* Straßenbahnwagen *m*
tramp 1. sta(m)pfen *or* trampeln (durch); **2.** Tramp *m*, Landstreicher *m*, Vagabund *m*; Wanderung *f*; Flittchen *n*
tram·ple (zer)trampeln
trance Trance *f*
tran·quil ruhig, friedlich
tran·quil·(l)i·ty Ruhe *f*, Frieden *m*
tran·quil·(l)ize beruhigen
tran·quil·(l)iz·er PHARM Beruhigungsmittel *n*
trans·act *Geschäft* abwickeln, *Handel* abschließen
trans·ac·tion Abwicklung *f*, Abschluss *m*; Geschäft *n*, Transaktion *f*
trans·at·lan·tic transatlantisch, Transatlantik..., Übersee...
tran·scribe abschreiben, kopieren; *Stenogramm etc* übertragen
tran·script Abschrift *f*, Kopie *f*
tran·scrip·tion Umschreibung *f*, Umschrift *f*; Abschrift *f*, Kopie *f*
trans·fer 1. *v/t* (*to*) *Betrieb etc* verlegen

(nach); *j-n* versetzen (nach); SPORT *Spieler* transferieren (zu), abgeben (an *acc*); *Geld* überweisen (an *acc*, auf *acc*); JUR *Eigentum*, *Recht* übertragen (auf *acc*); *v/i* SPORT wechseln (**to** zu); umsteigen (**from ... to ...** von ... auf ... *acc*); **2.** Verlegung *f*; Versetzung *f*; SPORT Transfer *m*, Wechsel *m*; ECON Überweisung *f*; JUR Übertragung *f*; Umsteige(fahr)karte *f*
trans·fer·a·ble übertragbar
trans·fixed *fig* versteinert, starr
trans·form umwandeln, verwandeln
trans·for·ma·tion Umwandlung *f*, Verwandlung *f*
trans·form·er ELECTR Transformator *m*
trans·fu·sion MED Bluttransfusion *f*, Blutübertragung *f*
trans·gress verletzen, verstoßen gegen
tran·sient flüchtig, vergänglich
tran·sis·tor Transistor *m*
tran·sit Transit-, Durchgangsverkehr *m*; ECON Transport *m*; *in transit* unterwegs, auf dem Transport
tran·si·tion Übergang *m*
tran·si·tive LING transitiv
tran·si·to·ry → **transient**
trans·late übersetzen (*from English into German* aus dem Englischen ins Deutsche)
trans·la·tion Übersetzung *f*
trans·la·tor Übersetzer(in)
trans·lu·cent lichtdurchlässig
trans·mis·sion MED Übertragung *f*; *radio*, TV Sendung *f*; MOT Getriebe *n*
trans·mit *Signale* (aus)senden; *radio*, TV senden; PHYS *Wärme etc* leiten, *Licht etc* durchlassen; MED *Krankheit* übertragen
trans·mit·ter Sender *m*
trans·par·en·cy Durchsichtigkeit *f* (*a. fig*); *fig* Durchschaubarkeit *f*; Dia(-positiv) *n*; Folie *f*
trans·par·ent durchsichtig (*a. fig*); *fig* durchschaubar
tran·spire transpirieren, schwitzen; *fig* durchsickern; F passieren
trans·plant 1. umpflanzen, verpflanzen (*a. MED*); MED transplantieren; **2.** MED Transplantation *f*, Verpflanzung *f*; Transplantat *n*
trans·port 1. Transport *m*, Beförderung *f*; Beförderungs-, Verkehrsmittel *n or pl*; MIL Transportschiff *n*, -flugzeug *n*, (*Truppen*)Transporter *m*; **2.** transportieren, befördern
trans·port·a·ble transportabel, transportfähig
trans·por·ta·tion Transport *m*, Beförderung *f*

trap 1. Falle *f* (*a. fig*); **set a trap for s.o.**
j-m e-e Falle stellen; **shut one's trap,**
keep one's trap shut F die Schnauze halten; **2.** (in *or* mit e-r Falle) fangen; *fig* in
e-e Falle locken; **be trapped** eingeschlossen sein
trap·door Falltür *f*; THEA Versenkung *f*
tra·peze Trapez *n*
trap·per Trapper *m*, Fallensteller *m*, Pelz-
tierjäger *m*
trap·pings Rangabzeichen *pl*; *fig* Drum
und Dran *n*
trash F Schund *m*; Quatsch *m*, Unsinn *m*;
Abfall *m*, Abfälle *pl*, Müll *m*; Gesindel *n*
trash·can Abfall-, Mülleimer *m*; Abfall-,
Mülltonne *f*
trash·y Schund...
trav·el 1. *v/i* reisen; fahren; TECH *etc* sich
bewegen; *fig* sich verbreiten; *fig* schweifen, wandern; *v/t* bereisen; *Strecke* zurücklegen, fahren; **2.** Reisen *n*; *pl* (*esp*
Auslands)Reisen *pl*
travel a·gen·cy Reisebüro *n*
travel a·gent Reisebüroinhaber(in); Angestellte *m*, *f* in e-m Reisebüro
travel a·gent's, travel bu·reau Reisebüro
n
trav·el·(l)er Reisende *m*, *f*
trav·el·(l)er's check (*Br* **cheque**) Reise-,
Travellerscheck *m*
trav·el·(l)ing bag Reisetasche *f*
travel(l)ing expens·es Reisekosten *pl*
trav·el sick·ness Reisekrankheit *f*
trav·es·ty Zerrbild *n*
trawl 1. Schleppnetz *n*; **2.** mit dem
Schleppnetz fischen
trawl·er MAR Trawler *m*
tray Tablett *n*; Ablagekorb *m*
treach·er·ous verräterisch; tückisch
treach·er·y Verrat *m*
trea·cle *esp Br* Sirup *m*
tread 1. treten (**on** auf *acc*; in *acc*); *Pfad etc*
treten; **2.** Gang *m*; Schritt(e *pl*) *m*; (Reifen)Profil *n*
tread·mill Tretmühle *f* (*a. fig*)
trea·son Landesverrat *m*
trea·sure 1. Schatz *m*; **2.** sehr schätzen; in
Ehren halten
trea·sur·er Schatzmeister(in)
trea·sure trove Schatzfund *m*
Trea·su·ry *Br*, **Treasury De·part·ment** Fi-
nanzministerium *n*
treat 1. *j-n, et.* behandeln; umgehen mit;
et. ansehen, betrachten (**as** als); MED
j-n behandeln (**for** gegen); *j-n* einladen
(**to** zu); **treat s.o. to s.th.** *a.* j-m et. spendieren; **treat o.s. to s.th.** sich et. leisten
or gönnen; **be treated for** MED in ärztlicher Behandlung sein wegen; **2.** (beson-

dere) Freude *or* Überraschung; **this is**
my treat das geht auf meine Rechnung,
ich lade dich *etc* ein
trea·tise Abhandlung *f*
treat·ment Behandlung *f*
treat·y Vertrag *m*
tre·ble¹ 1. dreifach; **2.** (sich) verdreifachen
tre·ble² MUS Knabensopran *m*; *radio:*
(Ton)Höhe *f*
tree BOT Baum *m*
tre·foil BOT Klee *m*
trel·lis BOT Spalier *n*
trem·ble zittern (**with** vor *dat*)
tre·men·dous gewaltig, enorm; F klasse,
toll
trem·or Zittern *n*; Beben *n*
trench Graben *m*; MIL Schützengraben *m*
trend Trend *m*, Entwicklung *f*, Tendenz *f*;
Mode *f*
trend·y F **1.** modern, modisch; **be trendy**
als schick gelten, in sein; **2.** *esp Br contp*
Schickimicki *m*
tres·pass 1. trespass on *Grundstück etc*
unbefugt betreten; *j-s Zeit etc* über Gebühr in Anspruch nehmen; **no trespass-**
ing Betreten verboten!; **2.** unbefugtes
Betreten
tres·pass·er: trespassers will be prose-
cuted Betreten bei Strafe verboten!
tres·tle Bock *m*, Gestell *n*
tri·al 1. JUR Prozess *m*, (Gerichts)Verhand-
lung *f*, (-)Verfahren *n*; Erprobung *f*, Probe *f*, Prüfung *f*, Test *m*; Plage *f*; **on trial**
auf *or* zur Probe; **be on trial** erprobt *or*
getestet werden; **be on trial, stand trial**
vor Gericht stehen (**for** wegen); **by way**
of trial versuchsweise; **2.** Versuchs...,
Probe...
tri·an·gle Dreieck *n*; Winkel *m*, Zeichendreieck *n*
tri·an·gu·lar dreieckig
tri·ath·lon SPORT Triathlon *n, m*, Dreikampf *m*
trib·al Stammes...
tribe (Volks)Stamm *m*
tri·bu·nal JUR Gericht(shof *m*) *n*
trib·u·ta·ry GEOGR Nebenfluss *m*
trib·ute: be a tribute to *j-m* Ehre machen;
pay tribute to j-m Anerkennung zollen
trick 1. Trick *m*; (*Karten- etc*)Kunststück
n; Streich *m*; *card game:* Stich *m*; (merk-
würdige) Angewohnheit, Eigenart *f*;
play a trick on s.o. j-m e-n Streich spielen; **2.** Trick...; **trick question** Fangfrage
f; **3.** überlisten, F reinlegen
trick·e·ry Tricks *pl*
trick·le 1. tröpfeln; rieseln; **2.** Tröpfeln *n*;
Rinnsal *n*
trick·ster Betrüger(in), Schwindler(in)

T

trick·y heikel, schwierig; durchtrieben, raffiniert

tri·cy·cle Dreirad *n*

tri·dent Dreizack *m*

tri·fle 1. Kleinigkeit *f*; Lappalie *f*; *a trifle* ein bisschen, etwas; **2.** *trifle with fig* spielen mit; *he is not to be trifled with* er lässt nicht mit sich spaßen

tri·fling geringfügig, unbedeutend

trig·ger Abzug *m*; *pull the trigger* abdrücken

trig·ger-hap·py F schießwütig

trill 1. Triller *m*; **2.** trillern

trim 1. *Hecke etc* stutzen, beschneiden, sich *den Bart etc* stutzen; *Kleidungsstück* besetzen (*with* mit); *trimmed with fur* pelzbesetzt, mit Pelzbesatz; *trim off* abschneiden; **2.** *give s.th. a trim* et. stutzen, et. (be)schneiden; *be in good trim* F gut in Form sein; **3.** gepflegt

trim·mings Besatz *m*; GASTR Beilagen *pl*

Trin·i·ty REL Dreieinigkeit *f*

trin·ket (*esp* billiges) Schmuckstück

trip 1. *v/i* stolpern (*over* über *acc*); (e-n) Fehler machen; *v/t a.* *trip up* j-m ein Bein stellen (*a. fig*); **2.** (kurze) Reise; Ausflug *m*, Trip *m* (*a. sl*); Stolpern *n*, Fallen *n*

tripe GASTR Kaldaunen *pl*, Kutteln *pl*

trip·le 1. dreifach; **2.** verdreifachen

trip·le jump SPORT Dreisprung *m*

trip·lets Drillinge *pl*

trip·li·cate 1. dreifach; **2.** *in triplicate* in dreifacher Ausfertigung

tri·pod PHOT Stativ *n*

trip·per *esp Br* (*esp Tages*)Ausflügler(in)

trite abgedroschen, banal

tri·umph 1. Triumph *m*, *fig* Sieg *m* (*over* über *acc*); **2.** triumphieren (*over* über *acc*)

tri·um·phal Triumph...

tri·um·phant triumphierend

triv·i·al unbedeutend, bedeutungslos; trivial, alltäglich

trol·ley *esp Br* Einkaufswagen *m*; Gepäckwagen *m*, Kofferkuli *m*; (*Tee- etc*) Wagen *m*; (*supermarket*) *trolley* Einkaufswagen *m*; *shopping trolley* Einkaufsroller *m*

trol·ley·bus Oberleitungsbus *m*, Obus *m*

trom·bone MUS Posaune *f*

troop 1. Schar *f*; *pl* MIL Truppen *pl*; **2.** (*herein- etc*)strömen; *troop the colour Br* MIL e-e Fahnenparade abhalten

troop·er MIL Kavallerist *m*; Panzerjäger *m*; Polizist *m*

tro·phy Trophäe *f*

trop·ic ASTR, GEOGR Wendekreis *m*; *the tropic of Cancer* der Wendekreis des Krebses; *the tropic of Capricorn* der Wendekreis des Steinbocks

trop·i·cal tropisch, Tropen...

trop·ics Tropen *pl*

trot 1. Trab *m*; Trott *m*; **2.** traben (lassen); *trot along* F losziehen

trou·ble 1. Schwierigkeit *f*, Problem *n*, Ärger *m*; Mühe *f*; MED Beschwerden *pl*; *a. pl* POL Unruhen *pl*; *pl* Unannehmlichkeiten *pl*; *be in trouble* in Schwierigkeiten sein; *get into trouble* Schwierigkeiten *or* Ärger bekommen; *j-n* in Schwierigkeiten bringen; *get or run into trouble* in Schwierigkeiten geraten; *have trouble with* Schwierigkeiten *or* Ärger haben mit; *put s.o. to trouble* j-m Mühe *or* Umstände machen; *take the trouble to do s.th.* sich die Mühe machen, et. zu tun; **2.** *v/t j-n* beunruhigen; *j-m* Mühe *or* Umstände machen; *j-n* bemühen (*for* um), bitten (*for* um; *to do* zu tun); *be troubled by* geplagt werden von, leiden an (*dat*); *v/i* sich bemühen (*to do* zu tun), sich Umstände machen (*about* wegen)

trou·ble-mak·er Störenfried *m*, Unruhestifter(in)

trou·ble·some lästig

trou·ble spot *esp* POL Krisenherd *m*

trough Trog *m*; Wellental *n*

trounce SPORT haushoch besiegen

troupe THEA Truppe *f*

trou·ser: (*a pair of*) *trousers* (e-e) Hose *f*

trou·ser suit *Br* Hosenanzug *m*

trous·seau Aussteuer *f*

trout ZO Forelle *f*

trow·el (Maurer)Kelle *f*

tru·ant Schulschwänzer(in); *play truant Br* (die Schule) schwänzen

truce MIL Waffenstillstand *m* (*a. fig*)

truck 1. MOT Lastwagen *m*; Fernlaster *m*; *Br* RAIL (offener) Güterwagen; Transportkarren *m*; **2.** auf *or* mit Lastwagen transportieren

truck driv·er, truck·er MOT Lastwagenfahrer *m*; Fernfahrer *m*

truck farm ECON Gemüse- und Obstgärtnerei *f*

trudge (mühsam) stapfen

true wahr; echt, wirklich; treu (*to dat*); *be true* wahr sein, stimmen; *come true* in Erfüllung gehen; wahr werden; *true to life* lebensecht

tru·ly wahrheitsgemäß; wirklich, wahrhaft; aufrichtig

trump 1. Trumpf(karte *f*) *m*; *pl* Trumpf *m*; **2.** mit e-m Trumpf stechen; *trump up* erfinden

trum·pet 1. MUS Trompete *f*; **1.** trompeten; *fig* ausposaunen

trun·cheon (Gummi)Knüppel *m*, Schlagstock *m*

trun·dle *Karren etc* ziehen

trunk (Baum)Stamm *m*; Schrankkoffer *m*; ZO Rüssel *m*; ANAT Rumpf *m*; MOT Kofferraum *m*

trunk road *Br* Fernstraße *f*

trunks (*a.* ***a pair of trunks*** e-e) (*Bade*)Hose *f*; SPORT Shorts *pl*

truss 1. *a.* ***truss up*** *j-n* fesseln; GASTR *Geflügel etc* dressieren; **2.** MED Bruchband *n*

trust 1. Vertrauen *n* (***in*** zu); JUR Treuhand *f*; ECON Trust *m*; Großkonzern *m*; ***hold s.th. in trust*** et. treuhänderisch verwalten (***for*** für); ***place s.th. in s.o.'s trust*** j-m et. anvertrauen; **2.** *v/t* (ver)trauen (*dat*); sich verlassen auf (*acc*); (zuversichtlich) hoffen; ***trust him!*** das sieht ihm ähnlich!; *v/i:* ***trust in*** vertrauen auf (*acc*); ***trust to*** sich verlassen auf (*acc*)

trust·ee JUR Treuhänder(in); Sachverwalter(in)

trust·ful, trust·ing vertrauensvoll

trust·wor·thy vertrauenswürdig, zuverlässig

truth Wahrheit *f*

truth·ful wahr; wahrheitsliebend

try 1. *v/t* versuchen; et. (aus)probieren; JUR (über) *e-e Sache* verhandeln; *j-m* den Prozess machen (***for*** wegen); *j-n*, *j-s Geduld*, *Nerven etc* auf e-e harte Probe stellen; ***try s.th. on*** *Kleid etc* anprobieren; ***try s.th. out*** et. ausprobieren; *v/i* es versuchen; ***try for*** *Br*, ***try out for*** sich bemühen um; **2.** Versuch *m*; ***give s.o., s.th. a try*** es mit *j-m*, et. versuchen; ***have a try*** es versuchen

try·ing anstrengend

tsar HIST Zar *m*

T-shirt T-Shirt *n*

tub Bottich *m*, Zuber *m*, Tonne *f*; Becher *m*; F (Bade)Wanne *f*

tub·by F pumm(e)lig

tube Röhre *f* (*a.* ANAT), Rohr *n*; Schlauch *m*; Tube *f*; *Br* F U-Bahn *f* (*in London*); F Röhre *f*, Glotze *f*

tube·less schlauchlos

tu·ber BOT Knolle *f*

tu·ber·cu·lo·sis MED Tuberkulose *f*

tu·bu·lar röhrenförmig

tuck 1. stecken; ***tuck away*** F wegstecken; ***tuck in*** *esp Br* F reinhauen, zulangen; ***tuck up*** (***in bed***) *Kind* ins Bett packen; **2.** Biese *f*; Saum *m*; Abnäher *m*

Tue(s) ABBR *of* ***Tuesday*** Di., Dienstag *m*

Tues·day (ABBR ***Tue, Tues***) Dienstag *m*; ***on Tuesday*** (am) Dienstag; ***on Tuesdays*** dienstags

tuft (*Gras-, Haar- etc*)Büschel *n*

tug 1. zerren *or* ziehen (an *dat or* **at** an *dat*); **2.** ***give*** *s.th.* **a tug** zerren *or* ziehen an (*dat*)

tug-of-war SPORT Tauziehen *n* (*a. fig*)

tu·i·tion Unterricht *m*; Unterrichtsgebühr(en *pl*) *f*

tu·lip BOT Tulpe *f*

tum·ble 1. fallen, stürzen; purzeln (*a. fig*); **2.** Fall *m*, Sturz *m*

tum·ble·down baufällig

tum·bler (Trink)Glas *n*

tu·mid MED geschwollen

tum·my F Bauch *m*, Bäuchlein *n*

tu·mo(u)r MED Tumor *m*

tu·mult Tumult *m*

tu·mul·tu·ous tumultartig, (*applause etc*) stürmisch

tu·na ZO Thunfisch *m*

tune 1. MUS Melodie *f*; ***be out of tune*** verstimmt sein; **2.** *v/t mst* ***tune in*** *Radio etc* einstellen (***to*** auf *acc*); *a.* ***tune up*** MUS stimmen; *a.* ***tune up*** *Motor* tunen; *v/i:* ***tune in*** (das Radio *etc*) einschalten; ***tune up*** MUS (die Instrumente) stimmen

tune·ful melodisch

tune·less unmelodisch

tun·er *radio*, TV Tuner *m*

tun·nel 1. Tunnel *m*; **2.** *Berg* durchtunneln; *Fluss etc* untertunneln

tun·ny ZO Thunfisch *m*

tur·ban Turban *m*

tur·bid trüb (*water*); dick, dicht (*smoke etc*); *fig* verworren, wirr

tur·bine TECH Turbine *f*

tur·bo F, **tur·bo·charg·er** MOT Turbolader *m*

tur·bot ZO Steinbutt *m*

tur·bu·lent turbulent

tu·reen (Suppen)Terrine *f*

turf 1. Rasen *m*; Sode *f*, Rasenstück *n*; ***the turf*** die (Pferde)Rennbahn; der Pferderennsport; **2.** mit Rasen bedecken

tur·gid MED geschwollen

Turk Türke *m*, Türkin *f*

Tur·key die Türkei

tur·key ZO Truthahn *m*, Truthenne *f*, Pute *f*, Puter *m*; ***talk turkey*** F offen *or* sachlich reden

Turk·ish 1. türkisch; **2.** LING Türkisch *n*

tur·moil Aufruhr *m*

turn 1. *v/t* drehen, herum-, umdrehen; (um)wenden; *Seite* umblättern; *Schlauch etc* richten (***on*** auf *acc*); *Antenne* ausrichten (***toward[s]*** auf *acc*); *Aufmerksamkeit* zuwenden (***to*** *dat*); verwandeln (***into*** in *acc*); *Laub etc* färben; *Milch* sauer werden lassen; TECH formen, drechseln; ***turn the corner*** um die Ecke biegen; ***turn loose*** los-, freilassen; ***turn s.o.'s stom-***

T

ach j-m den Magen umdrehen; → *inside 1*, *upside down*, *somersault 1*; *v/i* sich (um)drehen; abbiegen; einbiegen (*onto* auf *acc*; *into* in *acc*); MOT wenden; *blass*, *sauer etc* werden; sich verwandeln, *fig a.* umschlagen (*into*, *to* in *acc*); → *left 2*, *righ 2*; *turn against* j-n aufbringen *or* aufhetzen gegen; *fig* sich wenden gegen; *turn away* (sich) abwenden (*from* von); j-n abweisen, wegschicken; *turn back* umkehren; j-n zurückschicken; *Uhr* zurückstellen; *turn down* Radio *etc* leiser stellen; *Gas etc* klein(er) stellen; *Heizung etc* runterschalten; j-n, *Angebot etc* ablehnen; *Kragen* umschlagen; *Bettdecke* zurückschlagen; *turn in* v/t zurückgeben; *Gewinn etc* erzielen, machen; *Arbeit* einreichen, abgeben; *turn o.s. in* sich stellen; *v/i* F sich aufs Ohr legen; *turn off* v/t Gas, Wasser *etc* abdrehen; *Licht*, *Radio etc* ausmachen, ausschalten; *Motor* abstellen; F *j-n* anwidern; F *j-m* die Lust nehmen; *v/i* abbiegen; *turn on* Gas, Wasser *etc* aufdrehen; *Gerät* anstellen; *Licht*, *Radio etc* anmachen, an-, einschalten; F *j-n* antörnen, anmachen; *turn out* v/t Licht ausmachen, ausschalten; j-n hinauswerfen; F *Waren* ausstoßen; *Tasche etc* (aus)leeren; *v/i* kommen (*for* zu); sich erweisen *or* herausstellen als; *turn over* (sich) umdrehen; *Seite* umblättern; wenden; *et.* umkippen; sich *et.* überlegen; *j-n*, *et.* übergeben (*to dat*); *Waren* umsetzen; *turn round* sich umdrehen; *turn one's car round* wenden; *turn to* sich an *j-n* wenden; sich zuwenden (*dat*); *turn up Kragen* hochschlagen; *Ärmel*, *Saum etc* umschlagen; *Radio etc* lauter stellen; *Gas etc* aufdrehen; *fig* auftauchen; 2. (Um)Drehung *f*; Biegung *f*, Kurve *f*, Kehre *f*; Abzweigung *f*; *fig* Wende *f*, Wendung *f*; *at every turn* auf Schritt und Tritt; *by turns* abwechselnd; *in turn* der Reihe nach; abwechselnd; *it is my turn* ich bin an der Reihe *or* F dran; *make a left turn* (nach) links abbiegen; *take turns* sich abwechseln (*at* bei); *take a turn for the better* (*worse*) sich bessern (sich verschlimmern); *do s.o. a good* (*bad*) *turn* j-m e-n guten (schlechten) Dienst erweisen

turn·coat Abtrünnige *m*, *f*, Überläufer(in); (*political*) *turncoat* F Wendehals *m*

turn·er Drechsler *m*; Dreher *m*

turn·ing *esp Br* Abzweigung *f*

turn·ing cir·cle MOT Wendekreis *m*

turn·ing point *fig* Wendepunkt *m*

tur·nip BOT Rübe *f*

turn-off Abzweigung *f*

turn-out Besucher(zahl *f*) *pl*, Beteiligung *f*; Wahlbeteiligung *f*; F Aufmachung *f*

turn·o·ver ECON Umsatz *m*; Personalwechsel *m*, Fluktuation *f*

turn·pike (**road**) gebührenpflichtige Schnellstraße

turn·stile Drehkreuz *n*

turn·ta·ble Plattenteller *m*

turn-up *Br* (Hosen)Aufschlag *m*

tur·pen·tine CHEM Terpentin *n*

tur·quoise MIN Türkis *m*

tur·ret ARCH Ecktürmchen *n*; MIL (Panzer)Turm *m*; MAR Gefechtsturm *m*, Geschützturm *m*

tur·tle ZO (See)Schildkröte *f*

tur·tle·dove ZO Turteltaube *f*

tur·tle·neck Rollkragen(pullover) *m*

tusk ZO Stoßzahn *m*; Hauer *m*

tus·sle F Gerangel *n*

tus·sock Grasbüschel *n*

tu·te·lage (An)Leitung *f*; JUR Vormundschaft *f*

tu·tor Privat-, Hauslehrer(in); *Br* UNIV Tutor(in), Studienleiter(in)

tu·to·ri·al *Br* UNIV Tutorenkurs *m*

tux·e·do Smoking *m*

TV 1. TV *n*, Fernsehen *n*; Fernsehgerät *n*, F Fernseher *m*; *on TV* im Fernsehen; *watch TV* fernsehen; 2. Fernseh...

twang 1. Schwirren *n*; *mst* **nasal twang** näselnde Aussprache; 2. schwirren (lassen)

tweak F zwicken, kneifen

tweet ZO piep(s)en

tweez·ers (*a pair of tweezers* e-e) Pinzette *f*

twelfth 1. zwölfte(r, -s); 2. Zwölftel *n*

twelve 1. zwölf; 2. Zwölf *f*

twen·ti·eth zwanzigste(r, -s)

twen·ty 1. zwanzig; 2. Zwanzig *f*

twice zweimal

twid·dle (herum)spielen mit (*or* **with** mit); *twiddle one's thumbs* Däumchen drehen

twig BOT dünner Zweig, Ästchen *n*

twi·light (*esp* Abend)Dämmerung *f*; Zwielicht *n*, Dämmerlicht *n*

twin 1. Zwilling *m*; *pl* Zwillinge *pl*; 2. Zwillings...; doppelt; 3. *be twinned with* die Partnerstadt sein von

twin-bed·ded room Zweibettzimmer *n*

twin beds zwei Einzelbetten

twin broth·er Zwillingsbruder *m*

twine 1. Bindfaden *m*, Schnur *f*; 2. (sich) schlingen *or* winden (*round* um); *a.* *twine together* zusammendrehen

twin-en·gined AVIAT zweimotorig

twinge stechender Schmerz, Stechen *n*; *a twinge of conscience* Gewissensbisse *pl*

twin·kle 1. glitzern (*stars*), (*a. eyes*) funkeln (**with** vor *dat*); **2.** Glitzern *n*, Funkeln *n*; **with a twinkle in one's eye** augenzwinkernd

twin sis·ter Zwillingsschwester *f*

twin town Partnerstadt *f*

twirl 1. (herum)wirbeln; wirbeln (*round* über *acc*); **2.** Wirbel *m*

twist 1. *v/t* drehen; wickeln (*round* um); *fig* verdrehen; **twist off** abdrehen, *Deckel* abschrauben; **twist one's ankle** (mit dem Fuß) umknicken, sich den Fuß vertreten; **her face was twisted with pain** ihr Gesicht war schmerzverzerrt; *v/i* sich winden, (*river etc a.*) sich schlängeln; **2.** Drehung *f*; Biegung *f*; (*überraschende*) Wendung; MUS Twist *m*

twitch 1. *v/t* zucken (mit); *v/i* zucken (**with** vor); zupfen (**at** an *dat*); **2.** Zucken *n*; Zuckung *f*

twit·ter 1. zwitschern; **2.** Zwitschern *n*, Gezwitscher *n*; **be all of a twitter** F ganz aufgeregt sein

two 1. zwei; **the two cars** die beiden Autos; **the two of us** wir beide; **in twos** zu zweit, paarweise; **cut in two** in zwei Teile schneiden; **put two and two together** zwei und zwei zusammenzählen; **2.** Zwei *f*

two-edged zweischneidig

two-faced falsch, heuchlerisch

two·fold zweifach

two·pence *Br* zwei Pence *pl*

two·pen·ny *Br* F für zwei Pence

two-piece zweiteilig; **two-piece dress** Jackenkleid *n*

two-seat·er AVIAT, MOT Zweisitzer *m*

two-sid·ed zweiseitig

two-sto·ried, *Br* **two-sto·rey** zweistöckig

two-way traf·fic MOT Gegenverkehr *m*

ty·coon (*Industrie- etc*)Magnat *m*

type 1. Art *f*, Sorte *f*; Typ *m*; PRINT Type *f*, Buchstabe *m*; **2.** *v/t et.* mit der Maschine schreiben, tippen; *v/i* Maschine schreiben, tippen

type·writ·er Schreibmaschine *f*

type·writ·ten maschine(n)geschrieben

ty·phoid (fe·ver) MED Typhus *m*

ty·phoon Taifun *m*

ty·phus MED Flecktyphus *m*, -fieber *n*

typ·i·cal typisch, bezeichnend (**of** für)

typ·i·fy typisch sein für, kennzeichnen; verkörpern

typ·ing er·ror Tippfehler *m*

typ·ing pool ECON Schreibzentrale *f*

typ·ist Schreibkraft *f*; Maschinenschreiber(in)

ty·ran·ni·cal tyrannisch

tyr·an·nize tyrannisieren

tyr·an·ny Tyrannei *f*

ty·rant Tyrann(in)

tyre *Br* → **tire¹**

tzar → **tsar**

U

U, u U, u *n*

ud·der ZO Euter *n*

ug·ly hässlich (*a. fig*); bös(e), schlimm (*wound etc*)

ul·cer MED Geschwür *n*

ul·te·ri·or: *ulterior motive* Hintergedanke *m*

ul·ti·mate letzte(r, -s), End...; höchste(r, -s)

ul·ti·mate·ly letztlich; schließlich

ul·ti·ma·tum Ultimatum *n*; **deliver an ultimatum to s.o.** j-m ein Ultimatum stellen

ul·tra·high fre·quen·cy ELECTR Ultrakurzwelle *f*

ul·tra·ma·rine ultramarin

ul·tra·son·ic Ultraschall...

ul·tra·sound PHYS Ultraschall *m*

ul·tra·vi·o·let ultraviolett

um·bil·i·cal cord ANAT Nabelschnur *f*

um·brel·la (Regen)Schirm *m*; *fig* Schutz *m*

um·pire SPORT **1.** Schiedsrichter(in); **2.** als Schiedsrichter(in) fungieren (bei)

un·a·bashed unverfroren

un·a·bat·ed unvermindert

un·a·ble unfähig, außerstande, nicht in der Lage

un·ac·cept·a·ble unzumutbar

un·ac·count·a·ble unerklärlich

un·ac·cus·tomed ungewohnt

un·ac·quaint·ed: **be unacquainted with s.th.** et. nicht kennen, mit e-r Sache nicht vertraut sein

un·ad·vised unbesonnen, unüberlegt
un·af·fect·ed natürlich, ungekünstelt; *be unaffected by* nicht betroffen sein von
un·aid·ed ohne Unterstützung, (ganz) allein
un·al·ter·a·ble unabänderlich
u·nan·i·mous einmütig; einstimmig
un·an·nounced unangemeldet
un·an·swer·a·ble unwiderlegbar; nicht zu beantworten(d)
un·ap·pe·tiz·ing unappetitlich
un·ap·proach·a·ble unnahbar
un·armed unbewaffnet
un·asked ungestellt (*question*); unaufgefordert, ungebeten (*guest etc*)
un·as·sist·ed ohne (fremde) Hilfe, (ganz) allein
un·as·sum·ing bescheiden
un·at·tached ungebunden, frei
un·at·tend·ed unbeaufsichtigt
un·at·trac·tive unattraktiv, wenig anziehend, reizlos
un·au·thor·ized unberechtigt, unbefugt
un·a·void·a·ble unvermeidlich
un·a·ware: *be unaware of s.th.* sich e-r Sache nicht bewusst sein, et. nicht bemerken
un·a·wares: *catch or take s.o. unawares* j-n überraschen
un·bal·ance *j-n* aus dem (seelischen) Gleichgewicht bringen
un·bal·anced unausgeglichen, labil
un·bar aufriegeln, entriegeln
un·bear·a·ble unerträglich; *person*: unausstehlich
un·beat·a·ble unschlagbar
un·beat·en ungeschlagen, unbesiegt
un·be·com·ing unvorteilhaft
un·be·known(st): *unbeknown to s.o.* ohne j-s Wissen
un·be·liev·a·ble unglaublich
un·bend gerade biegen; sich aufrichten; *fig* aus sich herausgehen, auftauen
un·bend·ing unbeugsam
un·bi·as(s)ed unvoreingenommen; JUR unbefangen
un·bind losbinden
un·blem·ished makellos
un·born ungeboren
un·break·a·ble unzerbrechlich
un·bri·dled *fig* ungezügelt, zügellos; *unbridled tongue* lose Zunge
un·bro·ken ununterbrochen; heil, unversehrt; nicht zugeritten (*horse*)
un·buck·le aufschnallen, losschnallen
un·bur·den: *unburden o.s. to s.o.* j-m sein Herz ausschütten
un·but·ton aufknöpfen
un·called-for ungerechtfertigt; unnötig; unpassend
un·can·ny unheimlich
un·cared-for vernachlässigt
un·ceas·ing unaufhörlich
un·cer·e·mo·ni·ous brüsk, unhöflich; überstürzt
un·cer·tain unsicher, ungewiss, unbestimmt; vage; METEOR unbeständig
un·cer·tain·ty Unsicherheit *f*, Ungewissheit *f*
un·chain losketten
un·changed unverändert
un·chang·ing unveränderlich
un·char·i·ta·ble unfair
un·checked ungehindert; ungeprüft
un·chris·tian unchristlich
un·civ·il unhöflich
un·civ·i·lized unzivilisiert
un·cle Onkel *m*
un·com·fort·a·ble unbequem; *feel uncomfortable* sich unbehaglich fühlen
un·com·mon ungewöhnlich
un·com·mu·ni·ca·tive wortkarg, verschlossen
un·com·pre·hend·ing verständnislos
un·com·pro·mis·ing kompromisslos
un·con·cerned: *be unconcerned about* sich keine Gedanken *or* Sorgen machen über (*acc*); *be unconcerned with* uninteressiert sein an (*dat*)
un·con·di·tion·al bedingungslos
un·con·firmed unbestätigt
un·con·scious unbewusst; unbeabsichtigt; MED bewusstlos; *be unconscious of* sich *e-r Sache* nicht bewusst sein, nicht bemerken
un·con·scious·ness MED Bewusstlosigkeit *f*
un·con·sti·tu·tion·al verfassungswidrig
un·con·trol·la·ble unkontrollierbar; nicht zu bändigen(d); unbändig (*rage etc*)
un·con·trolled unkontrolliert
un·con·ven·tion·al unkonventionell
un·con·vinced: *be unconvinced* nicht überzeugt sein (*about* von)
un·con·vinc·ing nicht überzeugend
un·cooked ungekocht, roh
un·cork entkorken
un·count·a·ble unzählbar
un·cou·ple abkoppeln
un·couth *fig* ungehobelt
un·cov·er aufdecken, *fig a.* enthüllen
un·crit·i·cal unkritisch; *be uncritical of s.th.* e-r Sache unkritisch gegenüberstehen
unc·tion REL Salbung *f*
unc·tu·ous salbungsvoll
un·cut ungekürzt (*film, novel etc*); ungeschliffen (*diamond etc*)

un·dam·aged unbeschädigt, unversehrt, heil

un·dat·ed undatiert, ohne Datum

un·daunt·ed unerschrocken, furchtlos

un·de·cid·ed unentschieden, offen; unentschlossen

un·de·mon·stra·tive zurückhaltend, reserviert

un·de·ni·a·ble unbestreitbar

un·der **1.** *prp* unter (*dat or acc*); **2.** *adv* unten; darunter

un·der·age minderjährig

un·der·bid unterbieten

un·der·brush → *undergrowth*

un·der·car·riage AVIAT Fahrwerk *n*, Fahrgestell *n*

un·der·charge zu wenig berechnen; zu wenig verlangen

un·der·clothes, un·der·cloth·ing → *underwear*

un·der·coat Grundierung *f*

un·der·cov·er: *undercover agent* verdeckter Ermittler

un·der·cut *j-n* (im Preis) unterbieten

un·der·de·vel·oped unterentwickelt; *underdeveloped country* Entwicklungsland *n*

un·der·dog Benachteiligte *m, f*

un·der·done nicht durchgebraten

un·der·es·ti·mate zu niedrig schätzen *or* veranschlagen; *fig* unterschätzen

un·der·ex·pose PHOT unterbelichten

un·der·fed unterernährt

un·der·go erleben, durchmachen; MED sich *e-r Operation etc* unterziehen

un·der·grad F, **un·der·grad·u·ate** Student(in)

un·der·ground **1.** *adv* unterirdisch, unter der Erde; **2.** *adj* unterirdisch; *fig* Untergrund...; **3.** *esp Br* Untergrundbahn *f*, U-Bahn *f*; *by underground* mit der U-Bahn

un·der·growth Unterholz *n*

un·der·hand, un·der·hand·ed heimlich; hinterhältig

un·der·line unterstreichen (*a. fig*)

un·der·ling *contp* Untergebene *m, f*

un·der·ly·ing zugrunde liegend

un·der·mine unterspülen; *fig* untergraben, unterminieren

un·der·neath **1.** *prp* unter (*dat or acc*); **2.** *adv* darunter

un·der·nour·ished unterernährt

un·der·pants Unterhose *f*

un·der·pass Unterführung *f*

un·der·pay *j-m* zu wenig bezahlen, *j-n* unterbezahlen

un·der·priv·i·leged unterprivilegiert, benachteiligt

un·der·rate unterbewerten, -schätzen

un·der·sec·re·ta·ry POL Staatssekretär *m*

un·der·sell ECON *Ware* verschleudern, unter Wert verkaufen; *undersell o.s. fig* sich schlecht verkaufen

un·der·shirt Unterhemd *n*

un·der·side Unterseite *f*

un·der·signed: *the undersigned* der *or* die Unterzeichnete, die Unterzeichneten *pl*

un·der·size(d) zu klein

un·der·staffed (personell) unterbesetzt

un·der·stand verstehen; erfahren *or* gehört haben (*that* dass); *make o.s. understood* sich verständlich machen; *am I to understand that* soll das heißen, dass; *give s.o. to understand that* j-m zu verstehen geben, dass

un·der·stand·a·ble verständlich

un·der·stand·ing **1.** Verstand *m*; Verständnis *n*; Abmachung *f*; Verständigung *f*; *come to an understanding* e-e Abmachung treffen (*with* mit); *on the understanding that* unter der Voraussetzung, dass; **2.** verständnisvoll

un·der·state untertreiben, untertrieben darstellen

un·der·state·ment Understatement *n*, Untertreibung *f*

un·der·take *et.* übernehmen; sich verpflichten (*to do* zu tun)

un·der·tak·er Leichenbestatter *m*; Beerdigungs-, Bestattungsinstitut *n*

un·der·tak·ing Unternehmen *n*; Zusicherung *f*

un·der·tone *fig* Unterton *m*; *in an undertone* mit gedämpfter Stimme

un·der·val·ue unterbewerten

un·der·wa·ter **1.** *adj* Unterwasser...; **2.** *adv* unter Wasser

un·der·wear Unterwäsche *f*

un·der·weight **1.** Untergewicht *n*; **2.** untergewichtig, zu leicht (*by* um); *she is five pounds underweight* sie hat fünf Pfund Untergewicht

un·der·world Unterwelt *f*

un·de·served unverdient

un·de·sir·a·ble unerwünscht

un·de·vel·oped unerschlossen (*area*); unentwickelt

un·dies F (Damen)Unterwäsche *f*

un·dig·ni·fied würdelos

un·di·min·ished unvermindert

un·dis·ci·plined undiszipliniert

un·dis·cov·ered unentdeckt

un·dis·guised unverhohlen

un·dis·put·ed unbestritten

un·dis·turbed ungestört

un·di·vid·ed ungeteilt

U

un·do aufmachen, öffnen; *fig* zunichtemachen

un·do·ing: *be s.o.'s undoing* j-s Ruin *or* Verderben sein

un·done unerledigt; offen; *come undone* aufgehen

un·doubt·ed unbestritten

un·doubt·ed·ly zweifellos, ohne (jeden) Zweifel

un·dreamed-of, **un·dreamt-of** ungeahnt

un·dress sich ausziehen; *j-n* ausziehen

un·due übermäßig

un·du·lat·ing sanft (*hills*)

un·dy·ing ewig

un·earned *fig* unverdient

un·earth ausgraben, *fig a.* ausfindig machen, aufstöbern

un·earth·ly überirdisch; unheimlich; *at an unearthly hour* F zu e-r unchristlichen Zeit

un·eas·i·ness Unbehagen *n*

un·eas·y unruhig (*sleep*); unsicher (*peace*); *feel uneasy* sich unbehaglich fühlen; *I'm uneasy about* mir ist nicht wohl bei

un·e·co·nom·ic unwirtschaftlich

un·ed·u·cat·ed ungebildet

un·e·mo·tion·al leidenschaftslos, kühl, beherrscht

un·em·ployed 1. arbeitslos; 2. *the unemployed* die Arbeitslosen *pl*

un·em·ploy·ment Arbeitslosigkeit *f* **unemployment ben·e·fit** *Br*, **unemployment com·pen·sa·tion** Arbeitslosengeld *n*

un·end·ing endlos

un·en·dur·a·ble unerträglich

un·en·vi·a·ble wenig beneidenswert

un·e·qual ungleich (*a. fig*), unterschiedlich; *fig* einseitig; *be unequal to* e-r Aufgabe *etc* nicht gewachsen sein

un·e·qual(l)ed unerreicht, unübertroffen

un·er·ring unfehlbar

un·e·ven uneben; ungleich(mäßig); ungerade (*number*)

un·e·vent·ful ereignislos

un·ex·am·pled beispiellos

un·ex·pec·ted unerwartet

un·ex·posed PHOT unbelichtet

un·fail·ing unerschöpflich; nie versagend

un·fair unfair, ungerecht

un·faith·ful untreu (*to dat*)

un·fa·mil·i·ar ungewohnt; unbekannt; nicht vertraut (*with* mit)

un·fas·ten aufmachen, öffnen; losbinden

un·fa·vo(u)r·a·ble ungünstig; unvorteilhaft (*for, to* für); negativ, ablehnend

un·feel·ing gefühllos, herzlos

un·fin·ished unvollendet; unfertig; unerledigt

un·fit nicht fit, nicht in Form; ungeeignet, untauglich; unfähig

un·flag·ging unermüdlich, unentwegt

un·flap·pa·ble F nicht aus der Ruhe zu bringen(d)

un·fold auffalten, auseinanderfalten; darlegen, enthüllen; sich entfalten

un·fore·seen unvorhergesehen, unerwartet

un·for·get·ta·ble unvergesslich

un·for·got·ten unvergessen

un·for·tu·nate unglücklich; unglückselig; bedauerlich

un·for·tu·nate·ly leider

un·found·ed unbegründet

un·friend·ly unfreundlich (**to, towards** zu)

un·furl *Fahne* aufrollen, entrollen, *Segel* losmachen

un·fur·nished unmöbliert

un·gain·ly linkisch, unbeholfen

un·god·ly gottlos; *at an ungodly hour* F zu e-r unchristlichen Zeit

un·gra·cious ungnädig; unfreundlich

un·grate·ful undankbar

un·guard·ed unbewacht; unbedacht, unüberlegt

un·hap·pi·ly unglücklicherweise, leider

un·hap·py unglücklich

un·harmed unversehrt

un·health·y kränklich, nicht gesund; ungesund; *contp* krankhaft, unnatürlich

un·heard: *go unheard* keine Beachtung finden, unbeachtet bleiben

un·heard-of noch nie da gewesen, beispiellos

un·hinge: *unhinge s.o.('s mind) fig* j-n völlig aus dem Gleichgewicht bringen

un·ho·ly F furchtbar, schrecklich

un·hoped-for unverhofft, unerwartet

un·hurt unverletzt

u·ni·corn Einhorn *n*

un·i·den·ti·fied unbekannt, nicht identifiziert

u·ni·fi·ca·tion Vereinigung *f*

u·ni·form 1. Uniform *f*; 2. gleichmäßig; einheitlich

u·ni·form·i·ty Einheitlichkeit *f*

u·ni·fy verein(ig)en; vereinheitlichen

u·ni·lat·e·ral *fig* einseitig

un·i·ma·gin·a·ble unvorstellbar

un·i·ma·gin·a·tive fantasielos, einfallslos

un·im·por·tant unwichtig

un·im·pressed: *remain unimpressed* unbeeindruckt bleiben (*by* von)

un·in·formed nicht unterrichtet *or* eingeweiht

un·in·hab·it·a·ble unbewohnbar

un·in·hab·it·ed unbewohnt

un·in·jured unverletzt
un·in·tel·li·gi·ble unverständlich
un·in·ten·tion·al unabsichtlich, unbeabsichtigt
un·in·terest·ed uninteressiert (**in** an *dat*); **be uninterested in** a. sich nicht interessieren für
un·in·terest·ing uninteressant
un·in·ter·rupt·ed ununterbrochen
u·nion Vereinigung *f*; Union *f*; Gewerkschaft *f*
u·nion·ist Gewerkschaftler(in)
u·nion·ize (sich) gewerkschaftlich organisieren
u·nique einzigartig; einmalig
u·ni·son: in unison gemeinsam
u·nit Einheit *f*; PED Unit *f*, Lehreinheit *f*; MATH Einer *m*; TECH (Anbau)Element *n*, Teil *n*; **unit furniture** Anbaumöbel *pl*
u·nite verbinden, vereinigen; sich vereinigen *or* zusammentun
u·nit·ed vereinigt, vereint
U·nit·ed King·dom das Vereinigte Königreich (*England, Scotland, Wales and Northern Ireland*)
U·nit·ed States of A·mer·i·ca die Vereinigten Staaten von Amerika
u·ni·ty Einheit *f*; MATH Eins *f*
u·ni·ver·sal allgemein; universal, universell; Welt...
u·ni·verse Universum *n*, Weltall *n*
u·ni·ver·si·ty Universität *f*, Hochschule *f*
university grad·u·ate Akademiker(in)
un·just ungerecht
un·kempt ungekämmt (*hair*); ungepflegt (*clothes etc*)
un·kind unfreundlich
un·known 1. unbekannt (**to** *dat*); **2.** *der, die, das* Unbekannte
unknown quan·ti·ty MATH unbekannte Größe (*a. fig*), Unbekannte *f*
un·law·ful ungesetzlich, gesetzwidrig
un·lead·ed bleifrei
un·learn *Ansichten etc* ablegen, aufgeben
un·less wenn ... nicht, außer wenn ..., es sei denn ...
un·like *prp* im Gegensatz zu; **he is very unlike his father** er ist ganz anders als sein Vater; **that is very unlike him** das sieht ihm gar nicht ähnlich
un·like·ly unwahrscheinlich
un·lim·it·ed unbegrenzt
un·list·ed: be unlisted nicht im Telefonbuch stehen
unlisted num·ber TEL Geheimnummer *f*
un·load entladen, abladen, ausladen; MAR *Ladung* löschen
un·lock aufschließen
un·loos·en losmachen; lockern; lösen

un·loved ungeliebt
un·luck·y unglücklich; **be unlucky** Pech haben
un·made ungemacht
un·manned unbemannt
un·marked nicht gekennzeichnet; SPORT ungedeckt, frei
un·mar·ried unverheiratet, ledig
un·mask *fig* entlarven
un·matched unübertroffen, unvergleichlich
un·men·tio·na·ble Tabu...; **be unmentionable** tabu sein
un·mis·tak·a·ble unverkennbar, unverwechselbar, untrüglich
un·mo·lest·ed unbehelligt
un·moved ungerührt; **she remained unmoved by it** es ließ sie kalt
un·mu·si·cal unmusikalisch
un·named ungenannt
un·nat·u·ral unnatürlich; widernatürlich
un·ne·ces·sa·ry unnötig
un·nerve entnerven
un·no·ticed unbemerkt
un·num·bered unnummeriert
un·ob·tru·sive unauffällig, unaufdringlich
un·oc·cu·pied leer (stehend), unbewohnt; unbeschäftigt
un·of·fi·cial inoffiziell
un·pack auspacken
un·paid unbezahlt; *post* unfrei
un·par·al·leled einmalig, beispiellos
un·par·don·a·ble unverzeihlich
un·per·turbed gelassen, ruhig
un·pick *Naht etc* auftrennen
un·placed: be unplaced SPORT sich nicht platzieren können
un·play·a·ble SPORT unbespielbar
un·pleas·ant unangenehm, unerfreulich; unfreundlich
un·plug den Stecker (*gen*) herausziehen
un·pol·ished unpoliert; *fig* ungehobelt
un·pol·lut·ed sauber, unverschmutzt
un·pop·u·lar unpopulär, unbeliebt
un·pop·u·lar·i·ty Unbeliebtheit *f*
un·prac·ti·cal unpraktisch
un·prac·ticed, *Br* **un·prac·tised** ungeübt
un·pre·ce·dent·ed beispiellos, noch nie da gewesen
un·pre·dict·a·ble unvorhersehbar; unberechenbar (*person*)
un·prej·u·diced unvoreingenommen, JUR unbefangen
un·pre·med·i·tat·ed nicht vorsätzlich; unüberlegt
un·pre·pared unvorbereitet
un·pre·ten·tious bescheiden, einfach, schlicht

un·prin·ci·pled skrupellos, gewissenlos
un·prin·ta·ble nicht druckfähig *or* druckreif
un·pro·duc·tive unproduktiv, unergiebig
un·pro·fes·sion·al unprofessionell; unfachmännisch
un·prof·it·a·ble unrentabel
un·pro·nounce·a·ble unaussprechbar
un·pro·tect·ed ungeschützt
un·proved, un·prov·en unbewiesen
un·pro·voked grundlos
un·pun·ished unbestraft, ungestraft; *go unpunished* straflos bleiben
un·qual·i·fied unqualifiziert, ungeeignet (*for* für); uneingeschränkt
un·ques·tion·a·ble unbestritten
un·ques·tion·ing bedingungslos
un·quote: *quote ... unquote* Zitat ... Zitat Ende
un·rav·el (sich) auftrennen (*pullover etc*); entwirren
un·read·a·ble nicht lesenswert, unlesbar, *a.* unleserlich
un·re·al unwirklich
un·rea·lis·tic unrealistisch
un·rea·son·a·ble unvernünftig; übertrieben, unzumutbar
un·rec·og·niz·a·ble nicht wieder zu erkennen(d)
un·re·lat·ed: *be unrelated* in keinem Zusammenhang stehen (*to* mit)
un·re·lent·ing unvermindert
un·re·li·a·ble unzuverlässig
un·re·lieved ununterbrochen, ständig
un·re·mit·ting unablässig, unaufhörlich
un·re·quit·ed: *unrequited love* unerwiderte Liebe
un·re·served uneingeschränkt; nicht reserviert
un·rest POL *etc* Unruhen *pl*
un·re·strained hemmungslos, ungezügelt
un·re·strict·ed uneingeschränkt
un·ripe unreif
un·ri·val(l)ed unerreicht, unübertroffen, einzigartig
un·roll (sich) aufrollen *or* entrollen; sich entfalten
un·ruf·fled gelassen, ruhig
un·ru·ly ungebärdig, wild; widerspenstig (*hair*)
un·sad·dle *Pferd* absatteln; *Reiter* abwerfen
un·safe unsicher, nicht sicher
un·said unausgesprochen
un·sal(e)·a·ble unverkäuflich
un·salt·ed ungesalzen
un·san·i·tar·y unhygienisch
un·sat·is·fac·to·ry unbefriedigend
un·sat·u·rat·ed CHEM ungesättigt

un·sa·vo(u)r·y anrüchig, unerfreulich
un·scathed unversehrt, unverletzt
un·screw abschrauben, losschrauben
un·scru·pu·lous skrupellos, gewissenlos
un·seat *Reiter* abwerfen; *j-n* s-s Amtes entheben
un·seem·ly ungebührlich
un·self·ish selbstlos, uneigennützig
un·set·tle durcheinanderbringen; beunruhigen; aufregen
un·set·tled ungeklärt, offen (*question etc*); unsicher (*situation etc*); METEOR unbeständig
un·shak(e)·a·ble unerschütterlich
un·shav·en unrasiert
un·shrink·a·ble nicht eingehend *or* einlaufend
un·sight·ly unansehnlich; hässlich
un·skilled: *unskilled worker* ungelernter Arbeiter
un·so·cia·ble ungesellig
un·so·cial: *work unsocial hours* außerhalb der normalen Arbeitszeit arbeiten
un·so·lic·it·ed unaufgefordert ein- *or* zugesandt, ECON *a.* unbestellt
un·solved ungelöst (*problem etc*)
un·so·phis·ti·cat·ed einfach, schlicht; TECH unkompliziert
un·sound nicht gesund; nicht in Ordnung; morsch; unsicher, schwach; nicht stichhaltig (*argument etc*); *of unsound mind* JUR unzurechnungsfähig
un·spar·ing großzügig, freigebig, verschwenderisch; schonungslos, unbarmherzig
un·speak·a·ble unbeschreiblich, entsetzlich
un·spoiled, un·spoilt unverdorben; nicht verwöhnt *or* verzogen
un·sta·ble instabil; unsicher, schwankend; labil (*person*)
un·stead·y wack(e)lig, schwankend, unsicher; unbeständig; ungleichmäßig, unregelmäßig
un·stop *Abfluss etc* frei machen; *Flasche* entstöpseln
un·stressed LING unbetont
un·stuck: *come unstuck* abgehen, sich lösen; *fig* scheitern
un·stud·ied ungekünstelt, natürlich
un·suc·cess·ful erfolglos, ohne Erfolg; vergeblich
un·suit·a·ble unpassend, ungeeignet; unangemessen
un·sure unsicher; *unsure of o.s.* unsicher
un·sur·passed unübertroffen
un·sus·pect·ed unverdächtig; unvermutet

uproot

un·sus·pect·ing nichts ahnend, ahnungslos

un·sus·pi·cious arglos; unverdächtig, harmlos

un·sweet·ened ungesüßt

un·swerv·ing unbeirrbar, unerschütterlich

un·tan·gle entwirren (*a. fig*)

un·tapped unerschlossen (*resource etc*)

un·teach·a·ble unbelehrbar (*person*); nicht lehrbar

un·ten·a·ble unhaltbar (*theory etc*)

un·think·a·ble undenkbar, unvorstellbar

un·think·ing gedankenlos

un·ti·dy unordentlich

un·tie aufknoten, *Knoten etc* lösen; losbinden

un·til *prp, cj* bis; *not until* erst; erst wenn, nicht bevor

un·time·ly vorzeitig, verfrüht; unpassend, ungelegen

un·tir·ing unermüdlich

un·told *fig* unermesslich

un·touched unberührt, unangetastet

un·true unwahr, falsch

un·trust·wor·thy unzuverlässig, nicht vertrauenswürdig

un·used[1] unbenutzt, ungebraucht

un·used[2]: *be unused to s.th.* an et. nicht gewöhnt sein; et. nicht gewohnt sein; *be unused to doing s.th.* es nicht gewohnt sein, et. zu tun

un·u·su·al ungewöhnlich

un·var·nished *fig* ungeschminkt

un·var·y·ing unveränderlich, gleichbleibend

un·veil *Denkmal etc* enthüllen

un·versed unbewandert, unerfahren (*in* in *dat*)

un·voiced unausgesprochen

un·want·ed unerwünscht, ungewollt

un·war·rant·ed ungerechtfertigt

un·washed ungewaschen

un·wel·come unwillkommen

un·well: *be or feel unwell* sich unwohl fühlen *or* nicht wohlfühlen

un·whole·some ungesund (*a. fig*)

un·wield·y unhandlich, sperrig

un·will·ing widerwillig; ungern; *be unwilling to do s.th.* et. nicht tun wollen

un·wind (sich) abwickeln; F abschalten, sich entspannen

un·wise unklug

un·wit·ting unwissentlich; unbeabsichtigt

un·wor·thy unwürdig; *he (she) is unworthy of it* er (sie) verdient es nicht, er (sie) ist es nicht wert

un·wrap auswickeln, auspacken

un·writ·ten ungeschrieben

un·yield·ing unnachgiebig

un·zip den Reißverschluss (*gen*) aufmachen

up 1. *adv* herauf, hinauf, aufwärts, nach oben, hoch, in die Höhe; oben; *up there* dort oben; *jump up and down* hüpfen; *walk up and down* auf und ab gehen, hin und her gehen; *up to* bis zu; *be up to s.th.* F et. vorhaben, et. im Schilde führen; *not to be up to s.th.* e-r Sache nicht gewachsen sein; *it's up to you* das liegt bei dir; **2.** *prp* herauf, hinauf; oben auf (*dat*); *up the river* flussaufwärts; **3.** *adj* nach oben (gerichtet), Aufwärts...; ASTR aufgegangen, ECON gestiegen; *time*: abgelaufen, um; aufgestanden, F auf; *the up train* der Zug nach London; *be up and about* F wieder auf den Beinen sein; *what's up?* F was ist los?; **4.** F *v/t Angebot, Preis etc* erhöhen; **5.** *the ups and downs* F die Höhen und Tiefen *pl* (*of life* des Lebens)

up-and-com·ing aufstrebend, vielversprechend

up·bring·ing Erziehung *f*

up·com·ing bevorstehend

up·coun·try landeinwärts; im Landesinneren

up·date 1. auf den neuesten Stand bringen; aktualisieren; **2.** Lagebericht *m*

up·end hochkant stellen

up·grade *j-n* befördern

up·heav·al *fig* Umwälzung *f*

up·hill aufwärts, bergan; bergauf führend; *fig* mühsam

up·hold *Rechte etc* schützen, wahren; JUR *Urteil* bestätigen

up·hol·ster *Möbel* polstern

up·hol·ster·er Polsterer *m*

up·hol·ster·y Polsterung *f*; Bezug *m*; Polsterei *f*

up·keep Instandhaltung(skosten *pl*) *f*; Unterhalt(ungskosten *pl*) *m*

up·land *mst pl* Hochland *n*

up·lift 1. *j-n* aufrichten, *j-m* Auftrieb geben; **2.** Auftrieb *m*

up·on → *on, once 1*

up·per obere(r, -s), Ober...;

up·per·most 1. *adj* oberste(r, -s), größte(r, -s), höchste(r, -s); *be uppermost* oben sein; *fig* an erster Stelle stehen; **2.** *adv* nach oben

up·right aufrecht, *a.* gerade, *fig a.* rechtschaffen

up·ris·ing Aufstand *m*

up·roar Aufruhr *m*

up·roar·i·ous lärmend, laut; schallend (*laughter*)

up·root ausreißen, entwurzeln; *fig j-n* he-

U

rausreißen (*from* aus)

up·set umkippen, umstoßen, umwerfen; *Pläne etc* durcheinanderbringen, stören; *j-n* aus der Fassung bringen; **the fish has upset me** *or* **my stomach** ich habe mir durch den Fisch den Magen verdorben; **be upset** aufgeregt sein; aus der Fassung *or* durcheinander sein; gekränkt *or* verletzt sein

up·shot Ergebnis *n*

up·side down verkehrt herum; *fig* drunter und drüber; **turn upside down** umdrehen, *a. fig* auf den Kopf stellen

up·stairs 1. die Treppe herauf *or* hinauf, nach oben; oben; **2.** im oberen Stockwerk (gelegen), obere(r, -s)

up·start Emporkömmling *m*

up·state im Norden (e-s Bundesstaats)

up·stream fluss-, stromaufwärts

up·take: F **be quick (slow) on the uptake** schnell begreifen (schwer von Begriff sein)

up-to-date modern; aktuell, auf dem neuesten Stand

up·town in den Wohnvierteln; in die Wohnviertel

up·turn Aufschwung *m*

up·ward(s) aufwärts, nach oben

u·ra·ni·um CHEM Uran *n*

ur·ban städtisch, Stadt...

ur·ban·i·za·tion Verstädterung *f*

ur·chin Bengel *m*

urge 1. *j-n* drängen (**to do** zu tun); drängen auf (*acc*); *a.* **urge on** *j-n* drängen, antreiben; **2.** Drang *m*, Verlangen *n*

ur·gen·cy Dringlichkeit *f*

ur·gent dringend; **be urgent** *a.* eilen

u·ri·nate urinieren

u·rine Urin *m*

urn Urne *f*; Großteemaschine *f*, Großkaffeemaschine *f*

us uns; **all of us** wir alle; **both of us** wir beide

us·age Sprachgebrauch *m*; Behandlung *f*; Verwendung *f*, Gebrauch *m*

use 1. *v/t* benutzen, gebrauchen, anwenden, verwenden; (ver)brauchen; **use up** auf-, verbrauchen; *v/i*: **I used to live here** ich habe früher hier gewohnt; **2.** Benutzung *f*, Gebrauch *m*, Verwendung *f*; Nutzen *m*; **be of use** nützlich *or* von Nutzen sein (**to** für); **it's no use** *doing* es ist nutzlos *or* zwecklos *zu inf*; → **milk** *1*

used¹: be used to *s.th.* an et. gewöhnt sein, et. gewohnt sein; **be used to doing** *s.th.* es gewohnt sein, et. zu tun

used² gebraucht

used car Gebrauchtwagen *m*

used car deal·er Gebrauchtwagenhändler(in)

use·ful nützlich

use·less nutzlos, zwecklos

us·er Benutzer(in); Verbraucher(in)

us·er-friend·ly benutzer- *or* verbraucherfreundlich

us·er in·ter·face EDP Benutzeroberfläche *f*

ush·er 1. Platzanweiser *m*; Gerichtsdiener *m*; **2.** *j-n* führen, geleiten (**into** in *acc*; **to** zu)

ush·er·ette Platzanweiserin *f*

u·su·al gewöhnlich, üblich

u·su·al·ly (für) gewöhnlich, normalerweise

u·sur·er Wucherer *m*

u·su·ry Wucher *m*

u·ten·sil Gerät *n*

u·te·rus ANAT Gebärmutter *f*

u·til·i·ty Nutzen *m*; *pl* Leistungen *pl* der öffentlichen Versorgungsbetriebe

u·til·ize nutzen

ut·most äußerste(r, -s), größte(r, -s), höchste(r, -s)

u·to·pi·an utopisch

ut·ter¹ total, völlig

ut·ter² äußern, *Seufzer etc* ausstoßen, *Wort* sagen

U-turn MOT Wende *f*; *fig* Kehrtwendung *f*

u·vu·la ANAT (Gaumen)Zäpfchen *n*

U

V

V, v V, v *n*

va·can·cy freie *or* offene Stelle; **vacancies** Zimmer frei; **no vacancies** belegt

va·cant leer stehend, unbewohnt; frei (*seat etc*); frei, offen (*job*); *fig* leer (*expression, stare etc*)

va·cate *Hotelzimmer* räumen; *Stelle etc* aufgeben

va·ca·tion 1. Ferien *pl*, Urlaub *m*; *esp Br* UNIV Semesterferien *pl*; JUR Gerichtsferien *pl*; **be on vacation** im Urlaub sein, Urlaub machen; **2.** Urlaub machen, die Ferien verbringen

va·ca·tion·er, va·ca·tion·ist Urlauber(in)

vac·cin·ate MED impfen

vac·cin·a·tion MED (Schutz)Impfung *f*

vac·cine MED Impfstoff *m*

vac·il·late *fig* schwanken

vac·u·um 1. PHYS Vakuum *n*; **2.** F *Teppich, Zimmer etc* saugen

vacuum bot·tle Thermosflasche® *f*

vacuum clean·er Staubsauger *m*

vacuum flask *Br* Thermosflasche® *f*

vacuum-packed vakuumverpackt

vag·a·bond Vagabund *m*, Landstreicher(in)

va·ga·ry *mst pl* Laune *f*; wunderlicher Einfall

va·gi·na ANAT Vagina *f*, Scheide *f*

va·gi·nal ANAT vaginal, Scheiden…

va·grant Nichtsesshafte *m, f*, Landstreicher(in)

vague verschwommen; vage; unklar

vain eingebildet, eitel; vergeblich; **in vain** vergebens, vergeblich

val·en·tine Valentinskarte *f*

va·le·ri·an BOT, PHARM Baldrian *m*

val·et (Kammer)Diener *m*

val·id stichhaltig, triftig; gültig (**for two weeks** zwei Wochen); JUR rechtsgültig, rechtskräftig; **be valid** *a.* gelten

va·lid·i·ty (JUR Rechts)Gültigkeit *f*; Stichhaltigkeit *f*, Triftigkeit *f*

val·ley Tal *n*

val·u·a·ble 1. wertvoll; **2.** *pl* Wertgegenstände *pl*, Wertsachen *pl*

val·u·a·tion Schätzung *f*; Schätzwert *m* (**on** *gen*)

val·ue 1. Wert *m*; **be of value** wertvoll sein (**to** für); **get value for money** reell bedient werden; **2.** *Haus etc* schätzen (**at** auf *acc*); *j-n, j-s Rat etc* schätzen

val·ue-ad·ded tax *Br* ECON (ABBR **VAT**) Mehrwertsteuer *f*

val·ue·less wertlos

valve TECH, MUS Ventil *n*; ANAT (*Herz- etc*) Klappe *f*

vam·pire Vampir *m*

van MOT Lieferwagen *m*, Transporter *m*; *Br* RAIL (geschlossener) Güterwagen

van·dal Wandale *m*, Vandale *m*

van·dal·ism Wandalismus *m*, Vandalismus *m*

van·dal·ize mutwillig beschädigen *or* zerstören

vane TECH (*Propeller- etc*)Flügel *m*; (*Wetter*)Fahne *f*

van·guard MIL Vorhut *f*

va·nil·la Vanille *f*

van·ish verschwinden

van·i·ty Eitelkeit *f*

vanity bag Kosmetiktäschchen *n*

vanity case Kosmetikkoffer *m*

van·tage·point Aussichtspunkt *m*; **from my vantagepoint** *fig* aus m-r Sicht

va·por·ize verdampfen; verdunsten (lassen)

va·po(u)r Dampf *m*, Dunst *m*

vapo(u)r trail AVIAT Kondensstreifen *m*

var·i·a·ble 1. variabel, veränderlich; unbeständig, wechselhaft; TECH einstellbar, regulierbar; **2.** MATH, PHYS Variable *f*, veränderliche Größe (*both a. fig*)

var·i·ance: be at variance with im Gegensatz *or* Widerspruch stehen zu

var·i·ant 1. abweichend, verschieden; **2.** Variante *f*

var·i·a·tion Abweichung *f*; Schwankung *f*; MUS Variation *f*

var·i·cose veins MED Krampfadern *pl*

var·ied unterschiedlich; abwechslungsreich

va·ri·e·ty Abwechslung *f*; Vielfalt *f*; ECON Auswahl *f*, Sortiment *n* (**of** an *dat*); BOT, ZO Art *f*; Varietee *n*; **for a variety of reasons** aus den verschiedensten Gründen

variety show Varieteevorstellung *f*

variety thea·ter (*Br* **thea·tre**) Varietee (-theater) *n*

var·i·ous verschieden; mehrere, verschiedene

var·nish 1. Lack *m*; **2.** lackieren

var·si·ty team SPORT Universitäts-, College-, Schulmannschaft *f*

var·y *v/i* sich (ver)ändern; variieren, auseinandergehen (*opinions etc*) (**on** über *acc*); **vary in size** verschieden groß sein; *v/t* (ver)ändern; variieren

V

vase Vase *f*

vast gewaltig, riesig, (*area a.*) ausgedehnt, weit

vast·ly gewaltig, weitaus

vat (großes) Fass, Bottich *m*

VAT ABBR *of* **value-added tax** ECON Mehrwertsteuer *f*

vau·de·ville Varietee(theater) *n*

vault¹ ARCH Gewölbe *n*; *a. pl* Stahlkammer *f*, Tresorraum *m*; (Keller)Gewölbe *n*; Gruft *f*

vault² **1. vault** (**over**) springen über (*acc*); **2.** *esp* SPORT Sprung *m*

vault·ing horse *gymnastics:* Pferd *n*

vaulting pole SPORT Sprungstab *m*

VCR ABBR *of* **video cassette recorder** Videorekorder *m*, Videogerät *n*

veal GASTR Kalbfleisch *n*; **veal chop** Kalbskotelett *n*; **veal cutlet** Kalbsschnitzel *n*; **roast veal** Kalbsbraten *m*

veer (sich) drehen; MOT ausscheren; **veer to the right** das Steuer nach rechts reißen

veg·e·ta·ble 1. *mst pl* Gemüse *n*; **2.** Gemüse...; Pflanzen...

veg·e·tar·i·an 1. Vegetarier(in); **2.** vegetarisch

veg·e·tate (dahin)vegetieren

veg·e·ta·tion Vegetation *f*

ve·he·mence Vehemenz *f*, Heftigkeit *f*

ve·he·ment vehement, heftig

ve·hi·cle Fahrzeug *n*; *fig* Medium *n*

veil 1. Schleier *m*; **2.** verschleiern (*a. fig*)

vein ANAT Vene *f*, Ader *f* (*a.* BOT, GEOL, *fig*); *fig* (*Charakter*)Zug *m*; Stimmung *f*

ve·loc·i·ty TECH Geschwindigkeit *f*

ve·lour(s) Velours *m*

vel·vet Samt *m*

vel·vet·y samtig

vend·er → **vendor**

vend·ing ma·chine (Verkaufs-, Waren)-Automat *m*

vend·or (*Straßen*)Händler(in), (*Zeitungsetc*)Verkäufer(in)

ve·neer 1. Furnier *n*; *fig* Fassade *f*; **2.** furnieren

ven·e·ra·ble ehrwürdig

ven·e·rate verehren

ven·e·ra·tion Verehrung *f*

ve·no·re·al dis·ease MED Geschlechtskrankheit *f*

Ve·ne·tian 1. Venezianer(in); **2.** venezianisch

Venetian blind (Stab)Jalousie *f*

ven·geance Rache *f*; **take vengeance on** sich rächen an (*dat*); **with a vengeance** mächtig, F wie verrückt

ve·ni·al entschuldbar, verzeihlich; REL lässlich

ven·i·son GASTR Wildbret *n*

ven·om ZO Gift *n*, *fig a.* Gehässigkeit *f*

ven·om·ous giftig, *fig a.* gehässig

ve·nous MED venös

vent 1. *v/t* *s-m Zorn etc* Luft machen, *s-e Wut etc* auslassen, abreagieren (**on** an *dat*); **2.** Schlitz *m* (*in a coat etc*); TECH (Abzugs)Öffnung *f*; **give vent to** *s-m Ärger etc* Luft machen

ven·ti·late (be)lüften; *fig* äußern

ven·ti·la·tion (Be)Lüftung *f*, Ventilation *f*

ven·ti·la·tor Ventilator *m*

ven·tri·cle ANAT Herzkammer *f*

ven·tril·o·quist Bauchredner(in)

ven·ture 1. *esp* ECON Wagnis *n*, Risiko *n*; ECON Unternehmen *n*; → **joint venture**; **2.** sich wagen; riskieren

ven·ue SPORT Austragungsort *m*

verb LING Verb *n*, Zeitwort *n*

verb·al mündlich; wörtlich, Wort...

ver·dict JUR (Urteils)Spruch *m*; *fig* Urteil *n*; **bring in** *or* **return a verdict of** (**not**) **guilty** JUR auf (nicht) schuldig erkennen

ver·di·gris Grünspan *m*

verge 1. Rand *m* (*a. fig*); **be on the verge of** kurz vor (*dat*) stehen; **be on the verge of despair** (**tears**) der Verzweiflung (den Tränen) nahe sein; **2. verge on** *fig* grenzen an (*acc*)

ver·i·fy bestätigen; nachweisen; (über-)prüfen

ver·i·ta·ble wahr

ver·mi·cel·li Fadennudeln *pl*

ver·mi·form ap·pen·dix ANAT Wurmfortsatz *m*, Blinddarm *m*

ver·mil·i·on 1. zinnoberrot; **2.** Zinnoberrot *n*

ver·min Ungeziefer *n*; Schädlinge *pl*; *fig* Gesindel *n*, Pack *n*

ver·min·ous voller Ungeziefer

ver·nac·u·lar Dialekt *m*, Mundart *f*; **in the vernacular** im Volksmund

ver·sa·tile vielseitig; vielseitig verwendbar

verse Versdichtung *f*; Vers *m*; Strophe *f*

versed: be (**well**) **versed in** beschlagen *or* bewandert sein in (*dat*)

ver·sion Version *f*; TECH Ausführung *f*; Darstellung *f* (*of an event*); Fassung *f* (*of a film etc*); Übersetzung *f*

ver·sus (ABBR **v.**, **vs.**) SPORT, JUR gegen

ver·te·bra ANAT Wirbel *m*

ver·te·brate ZO Wirbeltier *n*

ver·ti·cal vertikal, senkrecht

ver·ti·go MED Schwindel *m*; **suffer from vertigo** an *or* unter Schwindel leiden

verve Elan *m*, Schwung *m*

ver·y 1. *adv* sehr; aller...; **I very much hope that** ich hoffe sehr, dass; **the very**

best das Allerbeste; *for the very last time* zum allerletzten Mal; **2.** *adj the very* genau der *or* die *or* das; *the very opposite* genau das Gegenteil; *the very thing* genau das Richtige; *the very thought of* schon der *or* der bloße Gedanke an (*acc*)

ves·i·cle MED Bläschen *n*

ves·sel ANAT, BOT Gefäß *n*; Schiff *n*

vest Weste *f*; *Br* Unterhemd *n*; *kugelsichere* Weste

ves·ti·bule (Vor)Halle *f*

ves·tige *fig* Spur *f*

vest·ment Ornat *n*, Gewand *n*, Robe *f*

ves·try REL Sakristei *f*

vet[1] F Tierarzt *m*, Tierärztin *f*

vet[2] *esp Br* F überprüfen

vet[3] MIL F Veteran *m*

vet·e·ran 1. MIL Veteran *m* (*a. fig*); **2.** altgedient; erfahren

veteran car *Br* Oldtimer *m* (*built before 1905*)

vet·e·ri·nar·i·an Tierarzt *m*, -ärztin *f*

vet·e·ri·na·ry tierärztlich

veterinary sur·geon *Br* Tierarzt *m*, Tierärztin *f*

ve·to 1. Veto *n*; **2.** sein Veto einlegen gegen

vexed ques·tion leidige Frage

vi·a über (*acc*), via

vi·a·duct Viadukt *m*, *n*

vi·al (*esp* Arznei)Fläschchen *n*

vibes F Atmosphäre *f*

vi·brant kräftig (*color etc*); pulsierend (*city etc*)

vi·brate *v/i* vibrieren, zittern; flimmern; *fig* pulsieren; *v/t* in Schwingungen versetzen

vi·bra·tion Vibrieren *n*, Zittern *n*; *pl* F Atmosphäre *f*

vic·ar REL Pfarrer *m*

vic·ar·age Pfarrhaus *n*

vice[1] Laster *n*

vice[2] *esp Br* Schraubstock *m*

vice… Vize…, stellvertretend

vice squad Sittendezernat *n*, Sittenpolizei *f*; Rauschgiftdezernat *n*

vi·ce ver·sa: *and vice versa* und umgekehrt

vi·cin·i·ty Nähe *f*; Nachbarschaft *f*

vi·cious brutal; bösartig

vi·cis·si·tudes *das* Auf und Ab, *die* Wechselfälle *pl*

vic·tim Opfer *n*

vic·tim·ize (ungerechterweise) bestrafen, ungerecht behandeln; schikanieren

vic·to·ri·ous siegreich

vic·to·ry Sieg *m*

vid·e·o 1. Video *n*; Videokassette *f*; F Videoband *n*; *esp Br* Videorekorder *m*, Videogerät *n*; *on video* auf Video; **2.** Video…; **3.** *esp Br* auf Video aufnehmen, aufzeichnen

video cam·e·ra Videokamera *f*

video cas·sette Videokassette *f*

video cas·sette re·cord·er → *video recorder*

video clip Videoclip *m*

vid·eo·disk Bildplatte *f*

vid·e·o game Videospiel *n*

video li·brary Videothek *f*

video re·cord·er Videorekorder *m*, Videogerät *n*

video re·cord·ing Videoaufnahme *f*, Videoaufzeichnung *f*

video shop *Br*, **video store** Videothek *f*

vid·e·o·tape 1. Videokassette *f*; Videoband *n*; **2.** auf Video aufnehmen, aufzeichnen

vid·e·o·text Bildschirmtext *m*

vie wetteifern (*with* mit; *for* um)

Vi·en·nese 1. Wiener(in); **2.** wienerisch, Wiener…

view 1. Sicht *f* (*of* auf *acc*); Aussicht *f*, (Aus)Blick *m* (*of* auf *acc*); Ansicht *f* (*a.* PHOT), Meinung *f* (*about, on* über *acc*); *fig* Überblick *m* (*of* über *acc*); *a room with a view* ein Zimmer mit schöner Aussicht; *be on view* ausgestellt *or* zu besichtigen sein; *be hidden from view* nicht zu sehen sein; *come into view* in Sicht kommen; *in full view of* direkt vor *j-s* Augen; *in view of* *fig* angesichts (*gen*); *in my view* m-r Ansicht nach; *keep in view* et. im Auge behalten; *with a view to* *fig* mit Blick auf (*acc*); **2.** *v/t* Haus *etc* besichtigen; *fig* betrachten (*as* als); *v/i* fernsehen

view·da·ta Bildschirmtext *m*

view·er Fernsehzuschauer(in), F Fernseher(in); TECH (Dia)Betrachter *m*

view·find·er PHOT Sucher *m*

view·point Gesichts-, Standpunkt *m*

vig·il (Nacht)Wache *f*

vig·i·lance Wachsamkeit *f*

vig·i·lant wachsam

vig·or·ous energisch; kräftig

vig·o(u)r Energie *f*

Vi·king 1. Wikinger *m*; **2.** Wikinger…

vile gemein, niederträchtig; F scheußlich

vil·lage Dorf *n*

village green Dorfanger *m*

vil·lag·er Dorfbewohner(in)

vil·lain Bösewicht *m*, Schurke *m*; *Br* F Ganove *m*

vin·di·cate *j-n* rehabilitieren; *et.* rechtfertigen; *et.* Bestätigen

vin·dic·tive rachsüchtig, nachtragend

V

vine BOT (Wein)Rebe *f*; Kletterpflanze *f*
vin·e·gar Essig *m*
vine·grow·er Winzer *m*
vine·yard Weinberg *m*
vin·tage 1. Weinernte *f*, Weinlese *f*; GASTR Jahrgang *m*; **2.** GASTR Jahrgangs...; *fig* hervorragend, glänzend; **a 1994 vintage** ein 1994er Jahrgang *or* Wein
vin·tage car *esp Br* Oldtimer *m* (*built between 1919 and 1930*)
vi·o·la MUS Bratsche *f*
vi·o·late *Vertrag etc* verletzen, *a. Versprechen* brechen, *Gesetz etc* übertreten; *Ruhe etc* stören; *Grab etc* schänden
vi·o·la·tion Verletzung *f*, Bruch *m*, Übertretung *f*
vi·o·lence Gewalt *f*; Gewalttätigkeit *f*; Ausschreitungen *pl*; Heftigkeit *f*
vi·o·lent gewalttätig; gewaltsam; heftig
vi·o·let 1. BOT Veilchen *n*; **2.** violett
vi·o·lin MUS Geige *f*, Violine *f*
vi·o·lin·ist Geiger(in), Violinist(in)
VIP ABBR *of* **very important person** VIP *f*
VIP lounge AVIAT *etc* VIP-Lounge *f*; SPORT Ehrentribüne *f*
vi·per ZO Viper *f*, Natter *f*
vir·gin 1. Jungfrau *f*; **2.** jungfräulich, unberührt (*both a. fig*)
Vir·go ASTR Jungfrau *f*; **he (she) is (a) Virgo** er (sie) ist Jungfrau
vir·ile männlich; potent
vi·ril·i·ty Männlichkeit *f*; Potenz *f*
vir·tu·al eigentlich, praktisch
vir·tu·al·ly praktisch, so gut wie
vir·tu·al re·al·i·ty EDP virtuelle Realität
vir·tue Tugend *f*; Vorzug *m*, Vorteil *m*; **by** *or* **in virtue of** aufgrund (*gen*), kraft (*gen*); **make a virtue of necessity** aus der Not e-e Tugend machen
vir·tu·ous tugendhaft
vir·u·lent MED (akut und) bösartig; schnell wirkend (*poison*); *fig* bösartig, gehässig
vi·rus MED Virus *n, m*
vi·sa Visum *n*, Sichtvermerk *m*
vis·cose Viskose *f*
vis·cous dickflüssig, zähflüssig
vise TECH Schraubstock *m*
vis·i·bil·i·ty Sicht *f*, Sichtverhältnisse *pl*, Sichtweite *f*
vis·i·ble sichtbar; (er)sichtlich
vi·sion Sehkraft *f*; Weitblick *m*; Vision *f*
vi·sion·a·ry 1. weitblickend; eingebildet, unwirklich; **2.** Fantast(in), Träumer(in); Seher(in)
vis·it 1. *v/t* j-n besuchen, *Schloss etc a.* besichtigen; *et.* inspizieren; *v/i:* **be visiting** auf Besuch sein (**with** bei); **visit with** plaudern mit; **2.** Besuch *m*, Besichtigung *f* (**to** *gen*); Plauderei *f*; **for** *or* **on a visit**

auf Besuch; **have a visit from** Besuch haben von; **pay a visit to** j-*n* besuchen, *j-m* e-n Besuch abstatten; *Arzt* aufsuchen
vis·it·ing hours MED Besuchszeit *f*
vis·it·or Besucher(in), Gast *m*
vi·sor Visier *n*; Schirm *m*; MOT (Sonnen)-Blende *f*
vis·u·al Seh...; visuell
visual aids PED Anschauungsmaterial *n*, Lehrmittel *pl*
visual dis·play u·nit EDP Bildschirmgerät *n*, Datensichtgerät *n*
visual in·struc·tion PED Anschauungsunterricht *m*
vis·u·al·ize sich *et.* vorstellen
vi·tal vital, Lebens...; lebenswichtig; unbedingt notwendig; **of vital importance** von größter Wichtigkeit
vi·tal·i·ty Vitalität *f*
vit·a·min Vitamin *n*
vitamin de·fi·cien·cy Vitaminmangel *m*
vit·re·ous Glas...
vi·va·cious lebhaft, temperamentvoll
viv·id hell (*light*); kräftig, leuchtend (*color*); anschaulich (*description*); lebhaft (*imagination*)
vix·en ZO Füchsin *f*
V-neck V-Ausschnitt *m*
V-necked mit V-Ausschnitt
vo·cab·u·la·ry Vokabular *n*, Wortschatz *m*; Wörterverzeichnis *n*
vo·cal Stimm...; F lautstark; MUS Vokal..., Gesang...
vocal cords ANAT Stimmbänder *pl*
vo·cal·ist Sänger(in)
vo·ca·tion Begabung *f* (**for** für); Berufung *f*
vo·ca·tion·al Berufs...
vocational ed·u·ca·tion Berufsausbildung *f*
vocational guid·ance Berufsberatung *f*
vocational train·ing Berufsausbildung *f*
vogue Mode *f*; **be in vogue** Mode sein
voice 1. Stimme *f*; **active voice** LING Aktiv *n*; **passive voice** LING Passiv *n*; **2.** zum Ausdruck bringen; LING (stimmhaft) aussprechen
voiced LING stimmhaft
voice·less LING stimmlos
void 1. leer; JUR ungültig; **void of** ohne; **2.** (Gefühl *n* der) Leere *f*
vol ABBR *of* **volume** Bd., Band *m*
vol·a·tile cholerisch (*person*); explosiv (*situation etc*); CHEM flüchtig
vol·ca·no Vulkan *m*
vol·ley 1. Salve *f*; (*Geschoss- etc*)Hagel *m* (*a. fig*); *tennis*: Volley *m*, Flugball *m*; *soccer*: Volleyschuss *m*; **2.** *Ball* volley schie-

　　　　　　　　　　　　　　　　　waiter

ßen
vol·ley·ball SPORT Volleyball *m*
volt ELECTR Volt *n*
volt·age ELECTR Spannung *f*
vol·u·ble redselig; wortreich
vol·ume Band *m*; Volumen *n*, Rauminhalt *m*; Umfang *m*, große Menge; Lautstärke *f*
vo·lu·mi·nous bauschig (*dress etc*); geräumig; umfangreich (*notes etc*)
vol·un·ta·ry freiwillig; unbezahlt
vol·un·teer 1. *v/i* sich freiwillig melden (*for* zu) (*a.* MIL); *v/t Hilfe etc* anbieten; *et.* von sich aus sagen, F herausrücken mit; **2.** Freiwillige *m*, *f*; freiwilliger Helfer
vo·lup·tu·ous sinnlich (*lips etc*); aufreizend (*gesture etc*); üppig (*body etc*); kurvenreich (*woman*)
vom·it 1. *v/t* erbrechen; *v/i* (sich er)brechen, sich übergeben; **2.** Erbrochene *n*
vo·ra·cious unersättlich (*appetite etc*)
vote 1. Abstimmung *f* (*about, on* über

acc); (Wahl)Stimme *f*; Stimmzettel *m*; *a. pl* Wahlrecht *n*; **vote of no confidence** Misstrauensvotum *n*; **take a vote on s.th.** über et. abstimmen; **2.** *v/i* wählen; **vote for (against)** stimmen für (gegen); **vote on** abstimmen über (*acc*); *v/t* wählen; *et.* bewilligen; **vote out of office** abwählen
vot·er Wähler(in)
vot·ing booth Wahlkabine *f*
vouch: vouch for (sich ver)bürgen für
vouch·er Gutschein *m*, Kupon *m*
vow 1. Gelöbnis *n*; Gelübde *n*; **take a vow, make a vow** ein Gelöbnis *or* Gelübde ablegen; **2.** geloben, schwören (*to do* zu tun)
vow·el LING Vokal *m*, Selbstlaut *m*
voy·age (See)Reise *f*
vul·gar vulgär, ordinär; geschmacklos
vul·ne·ra·ble *fig* verletzbar, verwundbar; verletzlich; anfällig (*to* für)
vul·ture ZO Geier *m*

W

W, w W, w *n*
wad (*Watte- etc*)Bausch *m*; Bündel *n*; (*Papier- etc*)Knäuel *m*, *n*
wad·ding Einlage *f*, Füllmaterial *n*
wad·dle watscheln
wade *v/i* waten; **wade through** waten durch; F sich durchkämpfen durch, *et.* durchackern; *v/t* durchwaten
wa·fer (*esp* Eis)Waffel *f*; Oblate *f*; REL Hostie *f*
waf·fle[1] Waffel *f*
waf·fle[2] *Br* F schwafeln
waft *v/i* ziehen (*smell etc*); *v/t* wehen
wag 1. wedeln (mit); **2. with a wag of its tail** schwanzwedelnd
wage[1] *mst pl* (Arbeits)Lohn *m*
wage[2]: **wage (a) war against** *or* **on** MIL Krieg führen gegen; *fig* e-n Feldzug führen gegen
wage earn·er Lohnempfänger(in); Verdiener(in)
wage freeze Lohnstopp *m*
wage ne·go·ti·a·tions Tarifverhandlungen *pl*
wage pack·et Lohntüte *f*
wage rise Lohnerhöhung *f*

wa·ger Wette *f*
wag·gle F wackeln (mit)
wag·gon *Br* → **wag·on** Fuhrwerk *n*, Wagen *m*; *Br* RAIL (offener) Güterwagen; (*Tee- etc*)Wagen *m*
wag·tail ZO Bachstelze *f*
wail 1. jammern; heulen (*siren, wind*); **2.** Jammern *n*; Heulen *n*
wain·scot (Wand)Täfelung *f*
waist Taille *f*
waist·coat *esp Br* Weste *f*
waist·line Taille *f*
wait 1. *v/i* warten (*for, on* auf *acc*); **wait for s.o.** *a.* j-n erwarten; **keep s.o. waiting** j-n warten lassen; **wait and see!** warte es ab!; **wait on** (*Br* **at**) **table** bedienen, servieren; **wait on s.o.** j-n bedienen; **wait up** F aufbleiben (*for* wegen); *v/t*: **wait one's chance** auf e-e günstige Gelegenheit warten (*to do* zu tun); **wait one's turn** warten, bis man an der Reihe ist; **2.** Wartezeit *f*; **have a long wait** lange warten müssen; **lie in wait for s.o.** j-m auflauern
wait·er Kellner *m*, Ober *m*; **waiter, the check** (*Br* **bill**), **please!** (Herr) Ober,

bitte zahlen!

wait·ing Warten *n*; *no waiting* MOT Halt(e)verbot *n*

waiting list Warteliste *f*

waiting room MED *etc* Wartezimmer *n*; RAIL Wartesaal *m*

wait·ress Kellnerin *f*, Bedienung *f*; *waitress, the check* (*Br bill*), *please!* Fräulein, bitte zahlen!

wake[1] *v/i a.* **wake up** aufwachen, wach werden; *v/t a.* **wake up** (auf)wecken; *fig* wachrufen, wecken

wake[2] MAR Kielwasser *n*; *follow in the wake of fig* folgen auf (*acc*)

wake·ful schlaflos

wak·en *v/i a.* **waken up** aufwachen, wach werden; *v/t a.* **waken up** (auf)wecken

walk 1. *v/i* (zu Fuß) gehen, laufen; spazieren gehen; wandern; *v/t Strecke* gehen, laufen; *j-n* bringen (*to* zu; *home* nach Hause); *Hund* ausführen; *Pferd* im Schritt gehen lassen; *walk away → walk off*; *walk in* hineingehen, hereinkommen; *walk off* fort-, weggehen; *walk off with* F abhauen mit; F *Preis etc* locker gewinnen; *walk out* hinausgehen; (unter Protest) den Saal *etc* verlassen; ECON streiken, in (den) Streik treten; *walk out on s.o.* F j-n verlassen, j-n im Stich lassen; *walk up* hinaufgehen, heraufkommen; *walk up to s.o.* auf j-n zugehen; *walk up!* treten Sie näher!; **2.** Spaziergang *m*; Wanderung *f*; Spazier-, Wanderweg *m*; *go for a walk, take a walk* e-n Spaziergang machen, spazieren gehen; *an hour's walk* e-e Stunde Fußweg *or* zu Fuß; *from all walks of life Leute* aus allen Berufen *or* Schichten

walk·a·way F Spaziergang *m*, leichter Sieg

walk·er Spaziergänger(in); Wanderer *m*, Wand(r)erin *f*; SPORT Geher(in); *be a good walker* gut zu Fuß sein

walk·ie-talk·ie Walkie-Talkie *n*, tragbares Funksprechgerät

walk·ing Gehen *n*, Laufen *n*; Spazierengehen *n*; Wandern *n*

walking pa·pers: *get one's walking papers* F den Laufpass bekommen

walking shoes Wanderschuhe *pl*

walking stick Spazierstock *m*

walking tour Wanderung *f*

Walk·man® Walkman® *m*

walk·out Auszug *m* (*by, of e-r Delegation etc*); ECON Ausstand *m*, Streik *m*

walk·over → walkaway

walk-up F (Miets)Haus *n* ohne Fahrstuhl; Wohnung *f or* Büro *n etc* in e-m Haus ohne Fahrstuhl

wall 1. Wand *f*; Mauer *f*; **2.** *a.* *wall in* mit

e-r Mauer umgeben; *wall up* zumauern

wall cal·en·dar Wandkalender *m*

wall·chart Wandkarte *f*

wal·let Brieftasche *f*

wall·flow·er F Mauerblümchen *n*

wal·lop F *j-m* ein Ding verpassen; SPORT *j-n* erledigen, vernichten (*at* in *dat*)

wal·low sich wälzen; *fig* schwelgen, sich baden (*in* in *dat*)

wall·pa·per 1. Tapete *f*; **2.** tapezieren

wall-to-wall: *wall-to-wall carpet(ing)* Spannteppich *m*, Teppichboden *m*

wal·nut BOT Walnuss(baum *m*) *f*

wal·rus ZO Walross *n*

waltz 1. Walzer *m*; **2.** Walzer tanzen

wand (*Zauber*)Stab *m*

wan·der (herum)wandern, herumlaufen, umherstreifen; *fig* abschweifen; fantasieren

wane 1. ASTR abnehmen; *fig* schwinden; **2.** *be on the wane fig* im Schwinden begriffen sein

wan·gle F deichseln, hinkriegen; *wangle s.th. out of s.o.* j-m et. abluchsen; *wangle one's way out of* sich herauswinden aus

want 1. *v/t et.* wollen; *j-n* brauchen; *j-n* sprechen wollen; F *et.* brauchen, nötig haben; *be wanted* (*polizeilich*) gesucht werden (*for* wegen); *v/i* wollen; *I don't want to* ich will nicht; *he does not want for anything* es fehlt ihm an nichts; **2.** Mangel *m* (*of* an *dat*); Bedürfnis *n*, Wunsch *m*; Not *f*

want ad Kleinanzeige *f*

want·ed (*polizeilich*) gesucht

wan·ton mutwillig

war Krieg *m* (*a. fig*); *fig* Kampf *m* (*against* gegen)

war·ble ZO trillern

ward 1. MED Station *f*; *Br* POL Stadtbezirk *m*; JUR Mündel *n*; **2.** *ward off Schlag etc* abwehren, *Gefahr etc* abwenden

war·den Aufseher(in); Heimleiter(in); (Gefängnis)Direktor(in)

ward·er *Br* Aufsichtsbeamte *m*, -beamtin *f*

war·drobe Kleiderschrank *m*; Garderobe *f*

ware·house Lager(haus) *n*

war·fare Krieg *m*; Kriegführung *f*

war·head MIL Spreng-, Gefechtskopf *m*

war·like kriegerisch; Kriegs...

warm 1. *adj* warm, *fig a.* herzlich; *I am warm, I feel warm* mir ist warm; **2.** *v/t a.* *warm up* wärmen, sich *die Hände etc* wärmen; *Motor* warm laufen lassen; *v/i a.* *warm up* warm *or* wärmer werden, sich erwärmen

warmth Wärme *f*
warm-up SPORT Aufwärmen *n*
warn warnen (*against, of* vor *dat*); *j-n* verständigen
warn·ing Warnung *f* (*of* vor *dat*); Verwarnung *f*; *without warning* ohne Vorwarnung
warning sig·nal Warnsignal *n*
warp sich verziehen *or* werfen
war·rant 1. JUR (Durchsuchungs-, Haft- *etc*)Befehl *m*; **2.** *et.* rechtfertigen
warrant of ar·rest JUR Haftbefehl *m*
war·ran·ty ECON Garantie(erklärung) *f*; *it's still under warranty* darauf ist noch Garantie
war·ri·or Krieger *m*
war·ship Kriegsschiff *n*
wart MED Warze *f*
war·y vorsichtig
was ich, er, sie, es war; *passive: ich, er, sie, es* wurde
wash 1. *v/t* waschen, sich *die Hände etc* waschen; *v/i* sich waschen; sich *gut etc* waschen (lassen); *wash up v/i Br* abwaschen, (das) Geschirr spülen; *v/t* anschwemmen, anspülen; *wash one's dirty linen* schmutzige Wäsche waschen; **2.** Wäsche *f*; MOT Waschanlage *f*, Waschstraße *f*; *be in the wash* in der Wäsche sein; *give s.th. a wash et.* waschen; *have a wash* sich waschen
wash·a·ble (ab)waschbar
wash-and-wear bügelfrei; pflegeleicht
wash·ba·sin *Br*, **wash·bowl** Waschbecken *n*
wash·cloth Waschlappen *m*
wash·er Waschmaschine *f*; TECH Unterlegscheibe *f*
wash·ing 1. Wäsche *f*; **2.** Wasch…
wash·ing ma·chine Waschmaschine *f*
washing pow·der Waschpulver *n*, -mittel *n*
washing-up *Br* Abwasch *m*; *do the washing-up* den Abwasch machen
wash·room Toilette *f*
wasp ZO Wespe *f*
waste 1. Verschwendung *f*; Abfall *m*; Müll *m*; *waste of time* Zeitverschwendung *f*; *hazardous waste, special toxic waste* Sondermüll *m*; *special waste dump* Sondermülldeponie *f*; **2.** *v/t* verschwenden, vergeuden; *j-n* auszehren; *v/i waste away* immer schwächer werden (*person*); **3.** überschüssig; Abfall…; brachliegend, öde; *lay waste* verwüsten
waste dis·pos·al Abfall-, Müllbeseitigung *f*; Entsorgung *f*
waste disposal site Deponie *f*
waste·ful verschwenderisch

waste gas Abgas *n*
waste pa·per Abfallpapier *n*; Altpapier *n*
waste·pa·per bas·ket Papierkorb *m*
waste pipe Abflussrohr *n*
watch 1. *v/i* zuschauen; *watch for* warten auf (*acc*); *watch out! pass auf!*, Vorsicht!; *watch out for* Ausschau halten nach; sich in Acht nehmen vor (*dat*); *v/t* beobachten; zuschauen bei, *et.* ansehen; → *television*; **2.** (*Armband-, Taschen-*)Uhr *f*; Wache *f*; *keep watch* Wache halten, wachen (*over* über *acc*); *be on the watch for* Ausschau halten nach; auf der Hut sein vor (*dat*); *keep (a) careful or close watch on* genau beobachten, scharf im Auge behalten
watch·dog Wachhund *m*
watch·ful wachsam
watch·mak·er Uhrmacher(in)
watch·man Wachmann *m*, Wächter *m*
watch·tow·er Wach(t)turm *m*
wa·ter 1. Wasser *n*; **2.** *v/t Blumen* gießen, *Rasen etc* sprengen; *Vieh* tränken; *water down* verdünnen, verwässern; *fig* abschwächen; *v/i* tränen (*eyes*); *make s.o.'s mouth water* j-m den Mund wässerig machen
wa·ter bird ZO Wasservogel *m*
wa·ter·col·o(u)r Wasser-, Aquarellfarbe *f*; Aquarellmalerei *f*; Aquarell *n*
wa·ter·course Wasserlauf *m*
wa·ter·cress BOT Brunnenkresse *f*
wa·ter·fall Wasserfall *m*
wa·ter·front Hafenviertel *n*; *along the waterfront* am Wasser entlang
wa·ter·hole Wasserloch *n*
wa·ter·ing can Gießkanne *f*
wa·ter jump SPORT Wassergraben *m*
wa·ter lev·el Wasserstand *m*
wa·ter lil·y BOT Seerose *f*
wa·ter·mark Wasserzeichen *n*
wa·ter·mel·on BOT Wassermelone *f*
wa·ter pol·lu·tion Wasserverschmutzung *f*
water po·lo SPORT Wasserball(spiel *n*) *m*
wa·ter·proof 1. wasserdicht; **2.** *Br* Regenmantel *m*; **3.** imprägnieren
wa·ters Gewässer *pl*; Wasser *pl*
wa·ter·shed GEOGR Wasserscheide *f*; *fig* Wendepunkt *m*
wa·ter·side Ufer *n*
wa·ter ski·ing SPORT Wasserskilaufen *n*
wa·ter·tight wasserdicht, *fig a.* hieb- und stichfest
wa·ter·way Wasserstraße *f*
wa·ter·works Wasserwerk *n*; *turn on the waterworks* F zu heulen anfangen
wa·ter·y wäss(e)rig
watt ELECTR Watt *n*

W

wave 1. *v/t* schwenken; winken mit; *Haar* wellen, in Wellen legen; **wave one's hand** winken; **wave s.o. aside** j-n beiseitewinken; *v/i* winken; wehen (*flag etc*); sich wellen (*hair*); **wave at s.o.**, **wave to s.o.** j-m zuwinken; **2.** Welle *f* (*a. fig*); Winken *n*

wave·length PHYS Wellenlänge *f* (*a. fig*)

wa·ver flackern; schwanken

wav·y wellig, gewellt

wax¹ 1. Wachs *n*; (*Ohren*)Schmalz *n*; **2.** wachsen; bohnern

wax² ASTR zunehmen

wax·en wächsern

wax·works Wachsfigurenkabinett *n*

wax·y wächsern

way 1. Weg *m*; Richtung *f*, Seite *f*; Entfernung *f*, Strecke *f*; Art *f*, Weise *f*; **ways and means** Mittel und Wege *pl*; **way back** Rückweg *m*, Rückfahrt *f*; **way home** Heimweg *m*; **way in** Eingang *m*; **way out** Ausgang *m*; **be on the way to, be on one's way to** unterwegs sein nach; **by way of** über (*acc*), via; *esp Br* statt; **by the way** übrigens; **give way** nachgeben; *Br* MOT die Vorfahrt lassen; **in a way** in gewisser Hinsicht; **in no way** in keiner Weise; **lead the way** vorangehen; **let s.o. have his (own) way** j-m s-n Willen lassen; **lose one's way** sich verlaufen *or* verirren; **make way** Platz machen (**for** für); **no way!** F kommt überhaupt nicht in Frage!; **out of the way** ungewöhnlich; **this way** hierher; hier entlang; **2.** *adv* weit

way·bill ECON Frachtbrief *m*

way·lay j-m auflauern; j-n abfangen, abpassen

way·ward eigensinnig, launisch

we wir *pl*

weak schwach (**at, in** in *dat*), GASTR *a.* dünn

weak·en *v/t* schwächen (*a. fig*); *v/i* schwächer werden; *fig* nachgeben

weak·ling Schwächling *m*, F Schlappschwanz *n*

weak·ness Schwäche *f*

weal Striemen *m*

wealth Reichtum *m*; *fig* Fülle *f* (**of** von)

wealth·y reich

wean entwöhnen; **wean s.o. from** *or* **off s.th.** j-m et. abgewöhnen

weap·on Waffe *f* (*a. fig*)

wear 1. *v/t* Bart, Brille, Schmuck *etc* tragen, Mantel *etc a.* anhaben, Hut *etc a.* aufhaben; abnutzen, abtragen; **wear the pants** (*Br* **trousers**) F die Hosen anhaben; **wear an angry expression** verärgert dreinschauen; *v/i* sich abnutzen, ver-

schleißen; sich gut *etc* halten; **s.th. to wear** et. zum Anziehen; **wear away** (sich) abtragen *or* abschleifen; **wear down** (sich) abtreten (*stairs*), (sich) ablaufen (*heels*), (sich) abfahren (*tires*); abschleifen; j-n zermürben; **wear off** nachlassen (*pain etc*); **wear on** sich hinziehen (**all day** über den ganzen Tag); **wear out** (sich) abnutzen *or* abtragen; *fig* j-n erschöpfen; **2.** *often in cpds* Kleidung *f*; *a.* **wear and tear** Abnutzung *f*, Verschleiß *m*; **the worse for wear** abgenutzt, verschlissen; F lädiert

wear·i·some ermüdend; langweilig; lästig

wear·y erschöpft, müde; ermüdend, anstrengend; **be weary of s.th.** F et. satthaben

wea·sel ZO Wiesel *n*

weath·er 1. Wetter *n*; Witterung *f*; **2.** *v/t* dem Wetter aussetzen; *fig Krise etc* überstehen; *v/i* verwittern

weath·er-beat·en verwittert

weath·er chart METEOR Wetterkarte *f*

weather fore·cast METEOR Wettervorhersage *f*; Wetterbericht *m*

weath·er·man *radio,* TV Wetteransager *m*

weath·er·proof 1. wetterfest; **2.** wetterfest machen

weath·er re·port METEOR Wetterbericht *m*

weather sta·tion METEOR Wetterwarte *f*

weather vane Wetterfahne *f*

weave weben; *Netz* spinnen; *Korb* flechten; **weave one's way through** sich schlängeln durch

weav·er Weber(in)

web Netz *n* (*a. fig*), Gewebe *n*; ZO Schwimmhaut *f*

wed heiraten

Wed(s) ABBR *of* **Wednesday** Mi., Mittwoch *m*

wed·ding 1. Hochzeit *f*; **2.** Hochzeits..., Braut..., Ehe..., Trau...

wed·ding ring Ehering *m*, Trauring *m*

wedge 1. Keil *m*; **2.** verkeilen, mit e-m Keil festklemmen; **wedge in** einkeilen, einzwängen

wed·lock: born in (out of) wedlock ehelich (unehelich) geboren

Wednes·day (ABBR **Wed, Weds**) Mittwoch *m*; **on Wednesday** (am) Mittwoch; **on Wednesdays** mittwochs

wee¹ F klein, winzig; **a wee bit** ein (kleines) bisschen

wee² F 1. Pipi machen; **2. do** *or* **have a wee** Pipi machen

weed 1. Unkraut *n*; **2.** jäten

weed·kill·er Unkrautvertilgungsmittel *n*

weed·y voll Unkraut; F schmächtig; F rückgratlos

week Woche *f*; **week after week** Woche um Woche; **a week today, today week** heute in e-r Woche *or* in acht Tagen; **every other week** jede zweite Woche; **for weeks** wochenlang; **four times a week** viermal die Woche; **in a week('s time)** in e-r Woche

week·day Wochentag *m*

week·end Wochenende *n*; **on** (*Br* **at**) **the weekend** am Wochenende

week·end·er Wochenendausflügler(in)

week·ly 1. Wochen...; wöchentlich; **2.** Wochenblatt *n*, Wochen(zeit)schrift *f*, Wochenzeitung *f*

weep weinen (**for** um *j-n*; **over** über *acc*); MED nässen

weep·ing wil·low BOT Trauerweide *f*

weep·y F weinerlich; rührselig

wee-wee F → **wee²**

weigh *v/t* (ab)wiegen; *fig* abwägen (**against** gegen); **weigh anchor** MAR den Anker lichten; **be weighed down with** *fig* niedergedrückt werden von; *v/i* ... *Kilo etc* wiegen; **weigh on** *fig* lasten auf (*dat*)

weight 1. Gewicht *n*; Last *f* (*a. fig*); *fig* Bedeutung *f*; **gain weight, put on weight** zunehmen; **lose weight** abnehmen; **2.** beschweren

weight·less schwerelos

weight·less·ness Schwerelosigkeit *f*

weight lift·er SPORT Gewichtheber *m*

weight lift·ing SPORT Gewichtheben *n*

weight·y schwer; *fig* schwerwiegend

weir Wehr *n*

weird unheimlich; F sonderbar, verrückt

wel·come 1. *int* **welcome back!, welcome home!** willkommen zu Hause!; **welcome to England!** willkommen in England!; **2.** *v/t* begrüßen (*a. fig*), willkommen heißen; **3.** *adj* willkommen; **you are welcome to do it** Sie können es gerne tun; **you're welcome!** nichts zu danken!, keine Ursache!, bitte sehr!; **4.** Empfang *m*, Willkommen *n*; **outstay** *or* **overstay one's welcome** j-s Gastfreundschaft überstrapazieren *or* zu lange in Anspruch nehmen

weld TECH schweißen

wel·fare Wohl(ergehen) *n*; Sozialhilfe *f*; **be on welfare** Sozialhilfe beziehen

welfare state Wohlfahrtsstaat *m*

welfare work Sozialarbeit *f*

welfare work·er Sozialarbeiter(in)

well¹ 1. *adv* gut; gründlich; **as well** ebenso, auch; **as well as ...** sowohl ... als auch ...; nicht nur ..., sondern auch ...; **very well** also gut, na gut; **well done!** bravo!; → **off** *1*; **2.** *int* nun, also; **well, well!** na so

was!; **3.** *adj* gesund; **feel well** sich wohlfühlen

well² 1. Brunnen *m*; (*Öl*)Quelle *f*; (*Aufzugs- etc*)Schacht *m*; **2.** *a.* **well out** quellen (**from** aus); **tears welled (up) in their eyes** die Tränen stiegen ihnen in die Augen

well-bal·anced ausgeglichen (*person*); ausgewogen (*diet*)

well-be·haved artig, gut erzogen

well-be·ing Wohl(befinden) *n*

well-dis·posed: be well-disposed towards s.o. j-m wohlgesinnt sein

well-done GASTR durchgebraten

well-earned wohlverdient

well-fed gut genährt

well-found·ed (wohl) begründet

well-in·formed gut unterrichtet; gebildet

well-known (wohl) bekannt

well-mean·ing wohlmeinend, gut gemeint

well-meant gut gemeint

well-off 1. wohlhabend, vermögend, bessergestellt; **be well-off for** gut versorgt sein mit; **2. the well-off** die Wohlhabenden *pl*

well-read belesen

well-timed (zeitlich) günstig, im richtigen Augenblick

well-to-do wohlhabend, reich

well-worn abgetragen; *fig* abgedroschen

Welsh 1. walisisch; **2.** LING Walisisch *n*; **the Welsh** die Waliser *pl*

welt Striemen *m*

wel·ter Wirrwarr *m*, Durcheinander *n*

wel·ter·weight SPORT Weltergewicht *n*; Weltergewichtler *m*

were *du* warst, *Sie* waren, *wir, sie* waren, *ihr* wart

west 1. West, Westen *m*; **the West** POL der Westen; die Weststaaten *pl*; **2.** *adj* westlich, West...; **3.** *adv* nach Westen, westwärts

west·er·ly West..., westlich

west·ern 1. westlich, West...; **2.** Western *m*

west·ward(s) westlich, nach Westen

wet 1. nass, feucht; **2.** Nässe *f*; **3.** nass machen, anfeuchten

weth·er ZO Hammel *m*

wet nurse Amme *f*

whack (knallender) Schlag; F Anteil *m*

whacked F fertig, erledigt

whack·ing 1. *Br* F Mords...; **2.** (Tracht *f*) Prügel *pl*

whale ZO Wal *m*

wharf Kai *m*

what 1. *pron* was; **what about ...?** wie wärs mit ...?; **what for?** wozu?; **so**

what? na und?; **know what's what** F wissen, was Sache ist; **2.** *adj* was für ein(e), welche(r, -s); alle, die; alles, was

what·cha·ma·call·it F → **whatsit**

what·ev·er 1. *pron* was (auch immer); alles, was; egal, was; **2.** *adj* welche(r, -s) ... auch (immer); **no ... whatever** überhaupt kein(e) ...

whats·it F Dings(bums, -da) *m, f, n*

what·so·ev·er → **whatever**

wheat BOT Weizen *m*

whee·dle beschwatzen; **wheedle s.th. out of s.o.** j-m et. abschwatzen

wheel 1. Rad *n*; MOT, MAR Steuer *n*; **2.** schieben, rollen; kreisen; **wheel about, wheel (a)round** herumfahren, herumwirbeln

wheel·bar·row Schubkarre(n *m*) *f*

wheel·chair Rollstuhl *m*

wheel clamp MOT Parkkralle *f*

wheeled mit Rädern; fahrbar; *in cpds* ...räd(e)rig

wheeze keuchen, pfeifend atmen

whelp ZO Welpe *m*, Junge *n*

when wann; als; wenn; obwohl; **since when?** seit wann?

when·ev·er wann auch (immer); jedes Mal, wenn

where wo; wohin; **where ... (from)?** woher?; **where ... (to)?** wohin?

where·a·bouts 1. *adv* wo etwa; **2.** Verbleib *m*; Aufenthalt *m*, Aufenthaltsort *m*

where·as während, wohingegen

where·by wodurch, womit; wonach

where·u·pon worauf, woraufhin

wher·ev·er wo *or* wohin auch (immer); ganz gleich wo *or* wohin

whet *Messer etc* schärfen; *fig Appetit* anregen

wheth·er ob

whey Molke *f*

which welche(r, -s); der, die, das; was; **which of you?** wer von euch?

which·ev·er welche(r, -s) auch (immer); ganz gleich, welche(r, -s)

whiff Luftzug *m*; Hauch *m* (*a. fig of* von); Duft *m*, Duftwolke *f*

while 1. Weile *f*; **for a while** e-e Zeit lang; **2.** *cj* während; obwohl; **3.** *mst* **while away** sich *die Zeit* vertreiben (**by doing s.th.** mit et.)

whim Laune *f*

whim·per 1. wimmern; ZO winseln; **2.** Wimmern *n*; ZO Winseln *n*

whim·si·cal wunderlich; launisch

whine 1. ZO jaulen; jammern (**about** über *acc*); **2.** ZO Jaulen *n*; Gejammer *n*

whin·ny ZO **1.** wiehern; **2.** Wiehern *n*

whip 1. Peitsche *f*; GASTR Creme *f*; **2.** *v/t* (aus)peitschen; GASTR schlagen; *v/i* sausen, flitzen, (*wind*) fegen

whipped cream Schlagsahne *f*, Schlagrahm *m*

whipped eggs Eischnee *m*

whip·ping (Tracht *f*) Prügel *pl*

whip·ping boy Prügelknabe *m*

whip·ping cream Schlagsahne *f*, Schlagrahm *m*

whir → **whirr**

whirl 1. wirbeln; **my head is whirling** mir schwirrt der Kopf; **2.** Wirbeln *n*; Wirbel *m* (*a. fig*); **my head's in a whirl** mir schwirrt der Kopf

whirl·pool Strudel *m*; Whirlpool *m*

whirl·wind Wirbelsturm *m*

whirr schwirren

whisk 1. schnelle Bewegung; Wedel *m*; GASTR Schneebesen *m*; **2.** GASTR schlagen; **whisk its tail** ZO mit dem Schwanz schlagen; **whisk away** *Fliegen etc* verscheuchen *or* wegscheuchen; *et.* schnell verschwinden lassen *or* wegnehmen

whis·ker ZO Schnurr- *or* Barthaar *n*; *pl* Backenbart *m*

whis·k(e)y Whisky *m*

whis·per 1. flüstern; **2.** Flüstern *n*; **say s.th. in a whisper** et. im Flüsterton sagen

whis·tle 1. Pfeife *f*; Pfiff *m*; **2.** pfeifen

white 1. weiß; **2.** Weiß(e) *n*; Weiße *m, f*; Eiweiß *n*

white bread Weißbrot *n*

white coffee *Br* Milchkaffee *m*, Kaffee *m* mit Milch

white-col·lar work·er (Büro)Angestellte *m, f*

white lie Notlüge *f*

whit·en weiß machen *or* werden

white·wash 1. Tünche *f*; **2.** tünchen, anstreichen; weißen; *fig* beschönigen

whit·ish weißlich

Whit·sun Pfingstsonntag *m*; Pfingsten *n or pl*

Whit Sunday Pfingstsonntag *m*

Whit·sun·tide Pfingsten *n or pl*

whit·tle (zurecht)schnitzen; **whittle away** *Gewinn etc* allmählich aufzehren; **whittle down** *et.* reduzieren (**to** auf *acc*)

whiz(z) F **1.** **whiz by, whiz past** vorbeizischen, vorbeidüsen; **2.** Ass *n*, Kanone *f* (**at** in *dat*)

whiz kid F Senkrechtstarter(in)

who wer; wen; wem; welche(r, -s); der, die, das

who·dun·(n)it F Krimi *m*

who·ev·er wer *or* wen *or* wem auch (immer); egal, wer *or* wen *or* wem

whole 1. *adj* ganz; **2.** *das* Ganze; **the**

whole of London ganz London; *on the whole* im Großen (und) Ganzen

whole-heart-ed ungeteilt (*attention*), voll (*support*), ernsthaft (*effort etc*)

whole-heart-ed-ly uneingeschränkt, voll und ganz

whole-meal Vollkorn...; *wholemeal bread* Vollkornbrot *n*

whole-sale ECON **1.** Großhandel *m*; **2.** Großhandels...

wholesale mar-ket ECON Großmarkt *m*

whole-sal-er ECON Großhändler *m*

whole-some gesund

whole wheat → *wholemeal*

whol-ly gänzlich, völlig

whoop 1. schreien, *esp* jauchzen; *whoop it up* F auf den Putz hauen; **2.** (*esp* Freuden)Schrei *m*

whoop-ee: F *make whoopee* auf den Putz hauen

whoop-ing cough MED Keuchhusten *m*

whore Hure *f*

why warum, weshalb; *that's why* deshalb

wick Docht *m*

wick-ed gemein, niederträchtig

wich-er-work Korbwaren *pl*

wick-et *cricket*: Tor *n*

wide 1. *adj* breit; weit offen, aufgerissen (*eyes*); *fig* umfangreich (*knowledge etc*), vielfältig (*interests etc*); **1.** *adv* weit; *go wide* danebengehen; *go wide of the goal* SPORT am Tor vorbeigehen

wide-an-gle lens PHOT Weitwinkelobjektiv *n*

wide-a-wake hellwach; *fig* aufgeweckt, wach

wide-eyed mit großen *or* aufgerissenen Augen; naiv

wid-en verbreitern; breiter werden

wide-o-pen weit offen, aufgerissen (*eyes*)

wide-spread weit verbreitet

wid-ow Witwe *f*

wid-owed verwitwet; *be widowed* verwitwet sein; Witwe(r) werden

wid-ow-er Witwer *m*

width Breite *f*; Bahn *f*

wield *Einfluss etc* ausüben

wife (Ehe)Frau *f*, Gattin *f*

wig Perücke *f*

wild 1. *adj* wild; stürmisch (*wind, applause etc*); außer sich (*with* vor *dat*); verrückt (*idea etc*); *make a wild guess* einfach drauflosraten; *be wild about* (ganz) verrückt sein nach; **2.** *adv*: *go wild* ausflippen; *let one's children run wild* s-e Kinder machen lassen, was sie wollen; **3.** *in the wild* in freier Wildbahn; *the wilds* die Wildnis

wild-cat ZO Wildkatze *f*

wild-cat strike ECON wilder Streik

wil-der-ness Wildnis *f*

wild-fire: *spread like wildfire* sich wie ein Lauffeuer verbreiten

wild-life Tier- und Pflanzenwelt *f*

wil-ful *Br* → *willful*

will¹ *v/aux* ich, *du* will(st) *etc*; *ich* werde ... *etc*

will² Wille *m*; Testament *n*; *of one's own free will* aus freien Stücken

will³ durch Willenskraft erzwingen; JUR vermachen

will-ful eigensinnig; absichtlich, *esp* JUR vorsätzlich

will-ing bereit (*to do* zu tun); (bereit)willig

will-o'-the-wisp Irrlicht *n*

wil-low BOT Weide *f*

wil-low-y *fig* gertenschlank

will-pow-er Willenskraft *f*

wil-ly-nil-ly wohl oder übel

wilt verwelken, welk werden

wi-ly gerissen, raffiniert

wimp F Schlappschwanz *m*

win 1. *v/t* gewinnen; *win s.o. over or round to* j-n gewinnen für; *v/i* gewinnen, siegen; *OK, you win* okay, du hast gewonnen; **2.** *esp* SPORT Sieg *m*

wince zusammenzucken (*at* bei)

winch TECH Winde *f*

wind¹ **1.** Wind *m*; Atem *m*, Luft *f*; MED Blähungen *pl*; *the wind* MUS die Bläser *pl*; **2.** *j-m* den Atem nehmen *or* verschlagen; HUNT wittern

wind² **1.** *v/t* drehen (an *dat*); Uhr *etc* aufziehen; wickeln (*round* um); *v/i* sich winden *or* schlängeln; *wind back* Film *etc* zurückspulen; *wind down* Autofenster *etc* herunterdrehen, -kurbeln; *Produktion etc* reduzieren; sich entspannen; *wind forward* Film *etc* weiterspulen; *wind up* *v/t* Autofenster *etc* hochdrehen, -kurbeln; Uhr *etc* aufziehen; *Versammlung etc* schließen (*with* mit); *Unternehmen* liquidieren, auflösen; *v/i* F enden, landen; (*esp* s-e Rede) schließen (*by saying* mit den Worten); **2.** Umdrehung *f*

wind-bag F Schwätzer(in)

wind-fall BOT Fallobst *n*; unverhofftes Geschenk; unverhoffter Gewinn

wind-ing gewunden

wind-ing stairs Wendeltreppe *f*

wind in-stru-ment MUS Blasinstrument *n*

wind-lass TECH Winde *f*

wind-mill Windmühle *f*

win-dow Fenster *n*; Schaufenster *n*; Schalter *m*

window clean-er Fensterputzer *m*

window dress-er Schaufensterdekora-

W

teur(in)

window dress·ing Schaufensterdekoration *f*; *fig* F Mache *f*

win·dow·pane Fensterscheibe *f*

win·dow seat Fensterplatz *m*

win·dow shade Rouleau *n*

win·dow-shop: *go window-shopping* e-n Schaufensterbummel machen

win·dow·sill Fensterbank *f*, -brett *n*

wind·pipe ANAT Luftröhre *f*

wind·screen *Br* MOT Windschutzscheibe *f*

windscreen wip·er *Br* MOT Scheibenwischer *m*

wind·shield MOT Windschutzscheibe *f*

windshield wip·er MOT Scheibenwischer *m*

wind·surf·ing SPORT Windsurfing *n*, Windsurfen *n*

wind·y windig; MED blähend

wine Wein *m*

wine cel·lar Weinkeller *m*

wine list Weinkarte *f*

wine mer·chant Weinhändler *m*

win·er·y Weinkellerei *f*

wine tast·ing Weinprobe *f*

wing ZO Flügel *m*, Schwinge *f*; *Br* MOT Kotflügel *m*; AVIAT Tragfläche *f*; AVIAT MIL Geschwader *n*; *pl* THEA Seitenkulisse *f*

wing·er SPORT Außenstürmer(in), Flügelstürmer(in)

wink 1. zwinkern; *wink at j-m* zuzwinkern; *et.* geflissentlich übersehen; *wink one's lights Br* MOT blinken; **2.** Zwinkern *n*; *I didn't get a wink of sleep last night, I didn't sleep a wink last night* ich habe letzte Nacht kein Auge zugetan; → *forty 1*

win·ner Gewinner(in), *esp* SPORT Sieger(in)

win·ning 1. einnehmend, gewinnend; **2.** *pl* Gewinn *m*

win·ter 1. Winter *m*; *in (the) winter* im Winter; **2.** überwintern; den Winter verbringen

winter sports Wintersport *m*

win·ter·time Winter *m*; Winterzeit *f*; *in (the) wintertime* im Winter

win·try winterlich; *fig* frostig

wipe (ab-, auf)wischen; *wipe off* ab-, wegwischen; *wipe out* auswischen; auslöschen, ausrotten; *wipe up* aufwischen

wip·er MOT (Scheiben)Wischer *m*

wire 1. Draht *m*; ELECTR Leitung *f*; Telegramm *n*; **2.** Leitungen verlegen in (*dat*) (a. *wire up*); *j-m* ein Telegramm schicken; *j-m et.* telegrafieren

wire·less drahtlos, Funk...

wire net·ting Maschendraht *m*

wire-tap *j-n*, *j-s Telefon* abhören

wir·y *fig* drahtig

wis·dom Weisheit *f*, Klugheit *f*

wis·dom tooth Weisheitszahn *m*

wise weise, klug

wise·crack F **1.** Witzelei *f*; **2.** witzeln

wise guy F Klugscheißer *m*

wish 1. wünschen; wollen; *wish s.o. well* j-m alles Gute wünschen; *if you wish (to)* wenn du willst; *wish for s.th.* sich et. wünschen; **2.** Wunsch *m* (*for* nach)

wish·ful think·ing Wunschdenken *n*

wish·y-wash·y F labb(e)rig, wäss(e)rig; *fig* lasch (*person*); verschwommen

wisp (*Gras-, Haar*)Büschel *n*

wist·ful wehmütig

wit Geist *m*, Witz *m*; geistreicher Mensch; *a. pl* Verstand *m*; *be at one's wits' end* mit s-r Weisheit am Ende sein; *keep one's wits about one* e-n klaren Kopf behalten

witch Hexe *f*

witch·craft Hexerei *f*

with mit; bei; vor (*dat*)

with·draw *v/t Geld* abheben (*from* von); *Angebot etc* zurückziehen, *Anschuldigung etc* zurücknehmen; MIL *Truppen* zurückziehen, abziehen; *v/i* sich zurückziehen; zurücktreten (*from* von)

with·draw·al Rücknahme *f*; *esp* MIL Abzug *m*, Rückzug *m*; Rücktritt *m* (*from* von), Ausstieg *m* (*from* aus); MED Entziehung *f*, Entzug *m*; *make a withdrawal* Geld abheben (*from* von)

withdrawal cure MED Entziehungskur *f*

withdrawal symp·toms MED Entzugserscheinungen *pl*

with·er eingehen *or* verdorren *or* (ver)welken (lassen)

with·hold zurückhalten; *withhold s.th. from s.o.* j-m et. vorenthalten

with·in innerhalb (*gen*)

with·out ohne (*acc*)

with·stand *e-m Angriff etc* standhalten; *Beanspruchung etc* aushalten

wit·ness 1. Zeuge *m*, Zeugin *f*; *witness for the defense* (*Br defence*) JUR Entlastungszeuge *m*, -zeugin *f*; *witness for the prosecution* JUR Belastungszeuge *m*, -zeugin *f*; **2.** Zeuge sein von *et.*; *et.* bezeugen, *Unterschrift* beglaubigen; *witness box Br*, *witness stand* JUR Zeugenstand *m*

wit·ti·cis·m geistreiche *or* witzige Bemerkung

wit·ty geistreich, witzig

wiz·ard Zauberer *m*; *fig* Genie *n* (*at* in *dat*)

wiz·ened verhutzelt

wob·ble *v/i* wackeln, zittern (*a. voice*), schwabbeln; MOT flattern; *fig* schwanken; *v/t* wackeln an (*dat*)

woe·ful traurig; bedauerlich

wolf 1. ZO Wolf *m*; *lone wolf fig* Einzelgänger(in); **2.** *a. wolf down* F *Essen* hinunterschlingen

wom·an Frau *f*

woman doc·tor Ärztin *f*

woman driv·er Frau *f* am Steuer

wom·an·ish weibisch

wom·an·ly fraulich; weiblich

womb ANAT Gebärmutter *f*

women's lib·ber F Emanze *f*

women's move·ment Frauenbewegung *f*

women's ref·uge *Br*, **women's shel·ter** Frauenhaus *n*

won·der 1. neugierig *or* gespannt sein, gern wissen mögen; sich fragen, überlegen; sich wundern, erstaunt sein (*about* über *acc*); *I wonder if you could help me* vielleicht können Sie mir helfen; **2.** Staunen *n*, Verwunderung *f*; Wunder *n*; *do or work wonders* wahre Wunder vollbringen, Wunder wirken (*for* bei)

won·der·ful wunderbar, wundervoll

wont 1. *be wont to do s.th.* et. zu tun pflegen; **2.** *as was his wont* wie es s-e Gewohnheit war

woo umwerben, werben um

wood Holz *n*; Holzfass *n*; *a. pl* Wald *m*, Gehölz *n*; *touch wood!* unberufen!, toi, toi, toi!; *he can't see the wood for the trees* er sieht den Wald vor lauter Bäumen nicht

wood·cut Holzschnitt *m*

wood·cut·ter Holzfäller *m*

wood·ed bewaldet

wood·en hölzern (*a. fig*), aus Holz, Holz...

wood·peck·er ZO Specht *m*

wood·wind: *the woodwind* MUS die Holzblasinstrumente *pl*, die Holzbläser *pl*; *woodwind instrument* Holzblasinstrument *n*

wood·work Holzarbeit *f*

wood·y waldig; BOT holzig

wool Wolle *f*

wool·(l)en 1. wollen, Woll...; **2.** *pl* Wollsachen *pl*, Wollkleidung *f*

wool·(l)y 1. wollig; *fig* schwammig; **2.** *pl* F Wollsachen *pl*

word 1. Wort *n*; Nachricht *f*; Losung *f*, Losungswort *n*; Versprechen *n*; Befehl *m*; *pl* MUS *etc* Text *m*; *have a word or a few words with s.o.* mit j-m sprechen; **2.** *et.* ausdrücken, *Text* abfassen, formulieren

word·ing Wortlaut *m*

word or·der LING Wortstellung *f*

word pro·cess·ing EDP Textverarbeitung *f*

word pro·ces·sor EDP Textverarbeitungsgerät *n*

word·y wortreich, langatmig

work 1. Arbeit *f*; Werk *n*; *pl* TECH Werk *n*, Getriebe *n*; ECON Werk *n*, Fabrik *f*; *at work* bei der Arbeit; *be in work* Arbeit haben; *be out of work* arbeitslos sein; *go or set to work* an die Arbeit gehen; **2.** *v/i* arbeiten (*at, on* an *dat*); TECH funktionieren (*a. fig*); wirken; *work to rule* Dienst nach Vorschrift tun; *v/t j-n* arbeiten lassen; *Maschine etc* bedienen, et. betätigen; et. bearbeiten; bewirken, herbeiführen; *work one's way* sich durcharbeiten *or* durchkämpfen; *work off Schulden* abarbeiten; *Wut etc* abreagieren; *work out v/t* ausrechnen; *Aufgabe* lösen; *Plan etc* ausarbeiten; *fig* sich et. zusammenreimen; *v/i* gut gehen, F klappen; aufgehen; F SPORT trainieren; *work up Zuhörer etc* aufpeitschen, aufwühlen; et. ausarbeiten (*into* zu); *be worked up* aufgeregt *or* nervös sein (*about* wegen)

work·a·ble formbar; *fig* durchführbar

work·a·day Alltags...

work·a·hol·ic F Arbeitssüchtige *m*, *f*

work·bench TECH Werkbank *f*

work·book PED Arbeitsheft *n*

work·day Arbeitstag *m*; Werktag *m*; *on workdays* werktags

work·er Arbeiter(in); Angestellte *m*, *f*

work ex·pe·ri·ence Erfahrung *f*

work·ing werktätig; Arbeits...; *working knowledge* Grundkenntnisse *pl*; *in working order* in betriebsfähigem Zustand

working class Arbeiterklasse *f*

working day → *workday*

working hours Arbeitszeit *f*; *fewer working hours* Arbeitszeitverkürzung *f*; *reduced working hours* Kurzarbeit *f*

work·ings Arbeits-, Funktionsweise *f*

work·man Handwerker *m*

work·man·like fachmännisch

work·man·ship fachmännische Arbeit

work of art Kunstwerk *n*

work·out F SPORT Training *n*

work·place Arbeitsplatz *m*; *at the workplace* am Arbeitsplatz

works coun·cil Betriebsrat *m*

work·sheet PED *etc* Arbeitsblatt *n*

work·shop Werkstatt *f*; Workshop *m*

work·shy arbeitsscheu

work·sta·tion EDP Bildschirmarbeitsplatz *m*

work-to-rule *Br* Dienst *m* nach Vorschrift

W

world 1. Welt *f*; *all over the world* in der ganzen Welt; *bring into the world* auf die Welt bringen; *do s.o. a or the world of good* j-m unwahrscheinlich guttun; *mean all the world to s.o.* j-m alles bedeuten; *they are worlds apart* zwischen ihnen liegen Welten; *think the world of* große Stücke halten von; *what in the world ...?* was um alles in der Welt ...?; **2.** Welt...

world cham·pi·on SPORT Weltmeister *m*

world cham·pi·onship SPORT Weltmeisterschaft *f*

World Cup Fußballweltmeisterschaft *f*; *skiing*: Weltcup *m*

world-fa·mous weltberühmt

world lit·er·a·ture Weltliteratur *f*

world·ly weltlich; irdisch

world·ly·wise weltklug

world mar·ket ECON Weltmarkt *m*

world pow·er POL Weltmacht *f*

world rec·ord SPORT Weltrekord *m*

world trip Weltreise *f*

world war Weltkrieg *m*

world·wide weltweit; auf der ganzen Welt

worm 1. ZO Wurm *m*; **2.** *Hund etc* entwurmen; *worm one's way through* sich schlängeln *or* zwängen durch; *worm o.s. into s.o.'s confidence* sich in j-s Vertrauen einschleichen; *worm s.th. out of s.o.* j-m et. entlocken

worm-eat·en wurmstichig

worm's-eye view Froschperspektive *f*

worn-out abgenutzt, abgetragen; *fig* erschöpft

wor·ried besorgt, beunruhigt

wor·ry 1. beunruhigen; (sich) Sorgen machen; *don't worry!* keine Angst!, keine Sorge!; **2.** Sorge *f*

worse schlechter, schlimmer; *worse still* was noch schlimmer ist; *to make matters worse* zu allem Übel

wors·en schlechter machen *or* werden, (sich) verschlechtern

wor·ship 1. Verehrung *f*; Gottesdienst *m*; **2.** *v/t* anbeten, verehren; *v/i* den Gottesdienst besuchen

wor·ship·(p)er Anbeter(in), Verehrer(in); Kirchgänger(in)

worst 1. *adj* schlechteste(r, -s), schlimmste(r, -s); **2.** *adv* am schlechtesten, am schlimmsten; **3.** *der, die, das* Schlechteste *or* Schlimmste; *at (the) worst* schlimmstenfalls

wor·sted Kammgarn *n*

worth 1. wert; *worth reading* lesenswert; **2.** Wert *m*

worth·less wertlos

worth·while lohnend; *be worthwhile* sich

lohnen

worth·y würdig

would-be Möchtegern...

wound 1. Wunde *f*, Verletzung *f*; **2.** verwunden, verletzen

wow *int* F wow!, Mensch!, toll!

wran·gle 1. (sich) streiten; **2.** Streit *m*

wrap 1. *v/t a. wrap up* (ein)packen, (ein)wickeln (*in* in *dat*); *et.* wickeln ([a]*round* um); *v/i: wrap up* sich warm anziehen; **2.** Umhang *m*

wrap·per (Schutz)Umschlag *m*

wrap·ping Verpackung *f*

wrapping pa·per Einwickel-, Pack-, Geschenkpapier *n*

wrath Zorn *m*

wreath Kranz *m*

wreck 1. MAR Wrack *n* (*a. fig*); **2.** *Pläne etc* zunichtemachen; *be wrecked* MAR zerschellen; Schiffbruch erleiden

wreck·age Trümmer *pl* (*a. fig*), Wrackteile *pl*

wreck·er MOT Abschleppwagen *m*

wreck·ing com·pa·ny Abbruchfirma *f*

wrecking ser·vice MOT Abschleppdienst *m*

wren ZO Zaunkönig *m*

wrench 1. MED sich *das Knie etc* verrenken; *wrench s.th. from or out of s.o.'s hands* j-m et. aus den Händen winden, j-m et. entwinden; *wrench off et.* mit e-m Ruck abreißen *or* wegreißen; *wrench open* aufreißen; **2.** Ruck *m*; MED Verrenkung *f*; *Br* TECH Schraubenschlüssel *m*

wrest: wrest s.th. from or out of s.o.'s hands j-m et. aus den Händen reißen, j-m et. entreißen *or* entwinden

wres·tle *v/i* SPORT ringen (*with* mit), *fig a.* kämpfen (*with* mit); *v/t* SPORT ringen gegen

wres·tler SPORT Ringer *m*

wres·tling SPORT Ringen *n*

wretch *often* HUMOR Schuft *m*, Wicht *m*; *a. poor wretch* armer Teufel

wretch·ed elend; (tod)unglücklich; scheußlich; verdammt, verflixt

wrig·gle *v/i* sich winden; zappeln; *wriggle out of fig* F sich herauswinden aus; *v/t* mit *den Zehen* wackeln

wring j-m die Hand drücken; *die Hände* ringen; *den Hals* umdrehen; *wring out Wäsche etc* auswringen; *wring s.o.'s heart* j-m zu Herzen gehen

wrin·kle 1. Falte *f*, Runzel *f*; **2.** runzeln; *Nase* krausziehen, rümpfen; faltig *or* runz(e)lig werden

wrist ANAT Handgelenk *n*

wrist·band Bündchen *n*, (Hemd)Manschette *f*; Armband *n*
wrist·watch Armbanduhr *f*
writ JUR Befehl *m*, Verfügung *f*
write schreiben; **write down** auf-, niederschreiben; **write off** *j-n*, ECON *et.* abschreiben; **write out** Namen *etc* ausschreiben; *Bericht etc* ausarbeiten; *j-m e-e Quittung etc* ausstellen
write pro·tec·tion EDP Schreibschutz *m*
writ·er Schreiber(in), Verfasser(in), Autor(in); Schriftsteller(in)
writhe sich krümmen *or* winden (*in*, *with* vor *dat*)
writ·ing **1.** Schreiben *n*; (Hand)Schrift *f*; Schriftstück *n*; *pl* Werke *pl*; *in writing* schriftlich; **2.** Schreib…
writing case Schreibmappe *f*
writing desk Schreibtisch *m*
writing pad Schreibblock *m*
writing pa·per Briefpapier *n*, Schreibpapier *n*
writ·ten schriftlich
wrong 1. *adj* falsch; unrecht; *be wrong*

falsch sein, nicht stimmen; unrecht haben; falsch gehen (*watch*); *be on the wrong side of forty* über 40 (Jahre alt) sein; *is anything wrong?* ist et. nicht in Ordnung?; *what's wrong with her?* was ist los mit ihr?, was hat sie?; **2.** *adv* falsch; *get wrong j-n, et.* falsch verstehen; *go wrong* e-n Fehler machen; kaputtgehen; *fig* F schiefgehen; **3.** Unrecht *n*; *be in the wrong* im Unrecht sein; **4.** *j-m* unrecht tun
wrong·ful ungerechtfertigt; gesetzwidrig
wrong-way driv·er MOT F Geisterfahrer(in)
wrought i·ron Schmiedeeisen *n*
wrought-i·ron schmiedeeisern
wry süßsauer (*smile*); ironisch, sarkastisch (*humor etc*)
wt ABBR *of* **weight** Gew., Gewicht *n*
WWF ABBR *of* **World Wide Fund for Nature** WWF *m*
WYSIWYG ABBR *of* **what you see is what you get** EDP was du (*auf dem Bildschirm*) siehst, bekommst du (*auch ausgedruckt*)

X, Y

X, x X, x *n*
xen·o·pho·bi·a Fremdenhass *m*; Ausländerfeindlichkeit *f*
XL ABBR *of* **extra large** (**size**) extragroß
X·mas F → **Christmas**
X-ray MED **1.** röntgen; **2.** Röntgenstrahl *m*; Röntgenaufnahme *f*, -bild *n*; Röntgenuntersuchung *f*
xy·lo·phone MUS Xylophon *n*
Y, y Y, y *n*
yacht MAR **1.** (Segel)Boot *n*; Jacht *f*; **2.** segeln; *go yachting* segeln gehen
yacht club Segelklub *m*, Jachtklub *m*
yacht·ing Segeln *n*, Segelsport *m*
Yan·kee F Yankee *m*, Ami *m*
yap kläffen; F quasseln
yard[1] (ABBR **yd**) Yard *n* (*91, 44 cm*)
yard[2] Hof *m*; (*Bau-, Stapel- etc*)Platz *m*; Garten *m*
yard·stick *fig* Maßstab *m*
yarn Garn *n*; *spin s.o. a yarn about j-m e-e abenteuerliche Geschichte or e-e Lügengeschichte erzählen von
yawn 1. gähnen; **2.** Gähnen *n*
yeah F ja

year Jahr *n*; *all the year round* das ganze Jahr hindurch; *year after year* Jahr für Jahr; *year in year out* jahraus, jahrein; *this year* dieses Jahr; *this year's* diesjährige(r, -s)
year·ly jährlich
yearn sich sehnen (*for* nach; *to do* danach, zu tun)
yearn·ing 1. Sehnsucht *f*; **2.** sehnsüchtig
yeast Hefe *f*
yell 1. schreien, brüllen (*with* vor *dat*); *yell at s.o.* j-n anschreien *or* anbrüllen; *yell (out)* et. schreien, brüllen; **2.** Schrei *m*
yel·low 1. gelb; F feig(e); **2.** Gelb *n*; *at yellow* MOT bei Gelb; **3.** (sich) gelb färben; gelb werden; vergilben
yel·low fe·ver MED Gelbfieber *n*
yel·low·ish gelblich
Yel·low Pag·es® TEL *die* Gelben Seiten *pl*, Branchenverzeichnis *n*
yel·low press Sensationspresse *f*
yelp 1. (auf)jaulen; aufschreien; **2.** (Auf-) Jaulen *n*; Aufschrei *m*
yes 1. ja; doch; **2.** Ja *n*
yes·ter·day gestern; *yesterday morning*

(**afternoon**) gestern Morgen (Nachmittag); **the day before yesterday** vorgestern

yet 1. *adv in questions*: schon; noch; (doch) noch; doch, aber; **as yet** bis jetzt, bisher; **not yet** noch nicht; **2.** *cj* aber, doch

yew BOT Eibe *f*

yield 1. *v/t Früchte* tragen; *Gewinn* abwerfen; *Resultat etc* ergeben, liefern; *v/i* nachgeben; **yield to** MOT *j-m* die Vorfahrt lassen; **2.** Ertrag *m*

yip·pee *int* F hurra!

yo·del 1. jodeln; **2.** Jodler *m*

yo·ga Joga *m, n*, Yoga *m, n*

yog·h(o)urt, yog·urt Jog(h)urt *m, n*

yoke Joch *n* (*a. fig*)

yolk (Ei)Dotter *m, n*, Eigelb *n*

you du, ihr, Sie; (*dat*) dir, euch, Ihnen; (*acc*) dich, euch, Sie; man

young 1. jung; **2.** ZO Junge *pl*; **with young** ZO trächtig; **the young** die jungen Leute *pl*, die Jugend

young·ster Junge *m*

your dein(e); *pl* euer, eure; Ihr(e) (*a. pl*)

yours deine(r, -s); *pl* euer eure(s); Ihre(r, -s) (*a. pl*); **a friend of yours** ein Freund von dir; **Yours, Bill** Dein Bill

your·self selbst; dir, dich, sich; **by yourself** allein

youth Jugend *f*; Jugendliche *m*

youth club Jugendklub *m*

youth·ful jugendlich

youth hos·tel Jugendherberge *f*

yuck·y F *contp* scheußlich

Yu·go·slav 1. jugoslawisch; **2.** Jugoslawe *m*, Jugoslawin *f*

Yu·go·sla·vi·a Jugoslawien *n*

yup·pie, yup·py ABBR *of* **young upwardly-mobile** *or* **urban professional** junger, aufstrebender *or* städtischer Karrieremensch, Yuppie *m*

Z

Z, z Z, z *n*

zap F *esp computer game etc*: abknallen, fertigmachen; MOT beschleunigen (**from ... to ...** von ... auf *acc* ...); jagen, hetzen; TV *Fernbedienung* bedienen; TV zappen, umschalten; **zap off** abzischen; **zap to** düsen *or* jagen *or* hetzen nach

zap·per TV F Fernbedienung *f*

zap·py Br F voller Pep, schmissig, fetzig

zeal Eifer *m*

zeal·ot Fanatiker(in), Eiferer *m*, Eiferin *f*

zeal·ous eifrig; **be zealous to do s.th.** eifrig darum bemüht sein, et. zu tun

ze·bra ZO Zebra *n*

ze·bra cross·ing Br Zebrastreifen *m*

zen·ith Zenit *m* (*a. fig*)

ze·ro 1. Null *f*; Nullpunkt *m*; **20 degrees below zero** 20 Grad unter Null; **2.** Null...

zero growth Nullwachstum *n*

zero in·terest: have zero interest in s.th. F null Bock auf et. haben

zero op·tion POL Nulllösung *f*

zest *fig* Würze *f*; Begeisterung *f*; **zest for life** Lebensfreude *f*

zig·zag 1. Zickzack *m*; **2.** Zickzack...; **3.** im Zickzack fahren, laufen *etc*, zickzack-förmig verlaufen

zinc CHEM Zink *n*

zip¹ 1. Reißverschluss *m*; **2. zip the bag open** (**shut**) den Reißverschluss der Tasche aufmachen (zumachen); **zip s.o. up** j-m den Reißverschluss zumachen

zip² 1. Zischen *n*, Schwirren *n*; F Schwung *m*; **2.** zischen, schwirren; **zip by, zip past** vorbeiflitzen

zip code Postleitzahl *f*

zip fas·ten·er *esp Br* → **zipper**

zip·per Reißverschluss *m*

zo·di·ac ASTR Tierkreis *m*; **signs of the zodiac** Tierkreiszeichen *pl*

zone Zone *f*

zoo Zoo *m*, Tierpark *m*

zo·o·log·i·cal zoologisch

zoological gar·dens Tierpark *m*, zoologischer Garten

zo·ol·o·gist Zoologe *m*, Zoologin *f*

zo·ol·o·gy Zoologie *f*

zoom 1. surren; F sausen; F *fig* in die Höhe schnellen; PHOT zoomen; **zoom by, zoom past** F vorbeisausen; **zoom in on** PHOT *et.* heranholen; **2.** Surren *n*; *a.* **zoom lens** PHOT Zoom *n*, Zoomobjektiv *n*

States of the
Federal Republic of Germany

Baden-Württemberg ['baːdən'vʏrtəm-
bɛrk] Baden-Württemberg
Bayern ['baɪɐn] Bavaria
Berlin [bɛr'liːn] Berlin
Brandenburg ['brandənbʊrk] Branden-
burg
Bremen ['breːmən] Bremen
Hamburg ['hambʊrk] Hamburg
Hessen ['hɛsən] Hesse
Mecklenburg-Vorpommern ['meːklən-
bʊrk'foːɐpɔmɐn] Mecklenburg-Western
Pomerania
Niedersachsen ['niːdɐzaksən] Lower

Saxony
Nordrhein-Westfalen ['nɔrtraɪnvɛst-
'faːlən] North Rhine-Westphalia
Rheinland-Pfalz ['raɪnlant'pfalts] Rhine-
land-Palatinate
Saarland ['zaːɐlant]: *das Saarland* the
Saarland
Sachsen ['zaksən] Saxony
Sachsen-Anhalt ['zaksən'anhalt] Saxony-
Anhalt
Schleswig-Holstein ['ʃleːsvɪç'hɔlʃtaɪn]
Schleswig-Holstein
Thüringen ['tyːrɪŋən] Thuringia

States of the Republic of Austria

Burgenland ['bʊrgənlant]: *das Burgen-
land* the Burgenland
Kärnten ['kɛrntən] Carinthia
Niederösterreich ['niːdɐ'øːstəraɪç] Lo-
wer Austria
Oberösterreich ['oːbɐ'øːstəraɪç] Upper
Austria

Salzburg ['zaltsbʊrk] Salzburg
Steiermark ['ʃtaɪɐmark]: *die Steiermark*
Styria
Tirol [ti'roːl] Tyrol
Vorarlberg ['foːɐ'arlbɛrk] Vorarlberg
Wien [viːn] Vienna

Cantons of the Swiss Confederation

Aargau ['aːɐgaʊ]: *der Aargau* the Aargau
Appenzell [apən'tsɛl] Appenzell
Basel ['baːzəl] Basel, Basle
Bern [bɛrn] Bern(e)
Freiburg ['fraɪbʊrk], *French* **Fribourg**
[fri'buːr] Fribourg
Genf [gɛnf], *French* **Genève** [ʒə'nɛːv]
Geneva
Glarus ['glaːrʊs] Glarus
Graubünden [graʊ'byndən] Graubünden,
Grisons
Jura ['juːra]: *der Jura* the Jura
Luzern [lu'tsɛrn] Lucerne
Neuenburg ['nɔyənbʊrk], *French* **Neu-
châtel** [nøʃa'tɛl] Neuchâtel
St. Gallen [zaŋkt 'galən] St Gallen, St Gall

Schaffhausen [ʃaf'haʊzən] Schaffhausen
Schwyz [ʃviːts] Schwyz
Solothurn ['zoːlotʊrn] Solothurn
Tessin [tɛ'siːn]: *der Tessin* the Ticino,
Italian **Ticino** [ti'tʃiːno]: *das Tessin* the
Ticino
Thurgau ['tuːɐgaʊ]: *der Thurgau* the
Thurgau
Unterwalden ['ʊntɐvaldən] Unterwalden
Uri ['uːri] Uri
Waadt [va(ː)t], *French* **Vaud** [vo] Vaud
Wallis ['valɪs], *French* **Valais** [va'lɛ]: *das
Valais* the Valais, Wallis
Zug [tsuːk] Zug
Zürich ['tsyːrɪç] Zurich

Alphabetical List of the German Irregular Verbs

Infinitive – Past Tense – Past Participle

backen – backt/bäckt – backte – gebacken
bedingen – bedingt – bedang (bedingte) – bedungen (*conditional*: bedingt)
befehlen – befiehlt – befahl – befohlen
beginnen – beginnt – begann – begonnen
beißen – beißt – biss – gebissen
bergen – birgt – barg – geborgen
bersten – birst – barst – geborsten
bewegen – bewegt – bewog – bewogen
biegen – biegt – bog – gebogen
bieten – bietet – bot – geboten
binden – bindet – band – gebunden
bitten – bittet – bat – gebeten
blasen – bläst – blies – geblasen
bleiben – bleibt – blieb – geblieben
bleichen – bleicht – blich – geblichen
braten – brät – briet – gebraten
brauchen – braucht – brauchte – gebraucht (*v/aux* brauchen)
brechen – bricht – brach – gebrochen
brennen – brennt – brannte – gebrannt
bringen – bringt – brachte – gebracht
denken – denkt – dachte – gedacht
dreschen – drischt – drosch – gedroschen
dringen – dringt – drang – gedrungen
dürfen – darf – durfte – gedurft (*v/aux* dürfen)
empfehlen – empfiehlt – empfahl – empfohlen
erlöschen – erlischt – erlosch – erloschen
erschrecken – erschrickt/erschreckt – erschrak – erschrocken
essen – isst – aß – gegessen
fahren – fährt – fuhr – gefahren
fallen – fällt – fiel – gefallen
fangen – fängt – fing – gefangen
fechten – ficht – focht – gefochten
finden – findet – fand – gefunden
flechten – flicht – flocht – geflochten
fliegen – fliegt – flog – geflogen
fliehen – flieht – floh – geflohen
fließen – fließt – floss – geflossen
fressen – frisst – fraß – gefressen
frieren – friert – fror – gefroren
gären – gärt – gor (*esp fig* gärte) – gegoren (*esp fig* gegärt)
gebären – gebärt/gebiert – gebar – geboren
geben – gibt – gab – gegeben
gedeihen – gedeiht – gedieh – gediehen
gehen – geht – ging – gegangen
gelingen – gelingt – gelang – gelungen
gelten – gilt – galt – gegolten
genesen – genest – genas – genesen

genießen – genießt – genoss – genossen
geschehen – geschieht – geschah – geschehen
gewinnen – gewinnt – gewann – gewonnen
gießen – gießt – goss – gegossen
gleichen – gleicht – glich – geglichen
gleiten – gleitet – glitt – geglitten
glimmen – glimmt – glomm – geglommen
graben – gräbt – grub – gegraben
greifen – greift – griff – gegriffen
haben – hat – hatte – gehabt
halten – hält – hielt – gehalten
hängen – hängt – hing – gehangen
hauen – haut – haute (hieb) – gehauen
heben – hebt – hob – gehoben
heißen – heißt – hieß – geheißen
helfen – hilft – half – geholfen
kennen – kennt – kannte – gekannt
klingen – klingt – klang – geklungen
kneifen – kneift – kniff – gekniffen
kommen – kommt – kam – gekommen
können – kann – konnte – gekonnt (*v/aux* können)
kriechen – kriecht – kroch – gekrochen
laden – lädt – lud – geladen
lassen – lässt – ließ – gelassen (*v/aux* lassen)
laufen – läuft – lief – gelaufen
leiden – leidet – litt – gelitten
leihen – leiht – lieh – geliehen
lesen – liest – las – gelesen
liegen – liegt – lag – gelegen
lügen – lügt – log – gelogen
mahlen – mahlt – mahlte – gemahlen
meiden – meidet – mied – gemieden
melken – melkt – melkte (molk) – gemolken (gemelkt)
messen – misst – maß – gemessen
misslingen – misslingt – misslang – misslungen
mögen – mag – mochte – gemocht (*v/aux* mögen)
müssen – muss – musste – gemusst (*v/aux* müssen)
nehmen – nimmt – nahm – genommen
nennen – nennt – nannte – genannt
pfeifen – pfeift – pfiff – gepfiffen
preisen – preist – pries – gepriesen
quellen – quillt – quoll – gequollen
raten – rät – riet – geraten
reiben – reibt – rieb – gerieben
reißen – reißt – riss – gerissen
reiten – reitet – ritt – geritten

rennen – rennt – rannte – gerannt
riechen – riecht – roch – gerochen
ringen – ringt – rang – gerungen
rinnen – rinnt – rann – geronnen
rufen – ruft – rief – gerufen
salzen – salzt – salzte – gesalzen (gesalzt)
saufen – säuft – soff – gesoffen
saugen – saugt – sog – gesogen
schaffen – schafft – schuf – geschaffen
schallen – schallt – schallte (scholl) – ge-
schallt (for **erschallen** a. erschollen)
scheiden – scheidet – schied – geschieden
scheinen – scheint – schien – geschienen
scheißen – scheißt – schiss – geschissen
scheren – schert – schor – geschoren
schieben – schiebt – schob – geschoben
schießen – schießt – schoss – geschossen
schinden – schindet – schund – geschunden
schlafen – schläft – schlief – geschlafen
schlagen – schlägt – schlug – geschlagen
schleichen – schleicht – schlich – geschlichen
schleifen – schleift – schliff – geschliffen
schließen – schließt – schloss – geschlossen
schlingen – schlingt – schlang – geschlungen
schmeißen – schmeißt – schmiss – geschmissen
schmelzen – schmilzt – schmolz – geschmolzen
schneiden – schneidet – schnitt – geschnitten
schrecken – schrickt/schreckt – schrak – *rare*
geschrocken
schreiben – schreibt – schrieb – geschrieben
schreien – schreit – schrie – geschrie(e)n
schreiten – schreitet – schritt – geschritten
schweigen – schweigt – schwieg – geschwiegen
schwellen – schwillt – schwoll – geschwollen
schwimmen – schwimmt – schwamm –
geschwommen
schwinden – schwindet – schwand – geschwunden
schwingen – schwingt – schwang – geschwungen
schwören – schwört – schwor – geschworen
sehen – sieht – sah – gesehen
sein – ist – war – gewesen
senden – sendet – sandte – gesandt
sieden – siedet – sott – gesotten
singen – singt – sang – gesungen
sinken – sinkt – sank – gesunken
sinnen – sinnt – sann – gesonnen
sitzen – sitzt – saß – gesessen

sollen – soll – sollte – gesollt (*v/aux* sollen)
spalten – spaltet – spaltete – gespalten
(gespaltet)
speien – speit – spie – gespie(e)n
spinnen – spinnt – spann – gesponnen
sprechen – spricht – sprach – gesprochen
sprießen – sprießt – spross – gesprossen
springen – springt – sprang – gesprungen
stechen – sticht – stach – gestochen
stecken – steckt – steckte (stak) – gesteckt
stehen – steht – stand – gestanden
stehlen – stiehlt – stahl – gestohlen
steigen – steigt – stieg – gestiegen
sterben – stirbt – starb – gestorben
stinken – stinkt – stank – gestunken
stoßen – stößt – stieß – gestoßen
streichen – streicht – strich – gestrichen
streiten – streitet – stritt – gestritten
tragen – trägt – trug – getragen
treffen – trifft – traf – getroffen
treiben – treibt – trieb – getrieben
treten – tritt – trat – getreten
trinken – trinkt – trank – getrunken
trügen – trügt – trog – getrogen
tun – tut – tat – getan
verderben – verdirbt – verdarb – verdorben
verdrießen – verdrießt – verdross – verdrossen
vergessen – vergisst – vergaß – vergessen
verlieren – verliert – verlor – verloren
verschleißen – verschleißt – verschliss –
verschlissen
verzeihen – verzeiht – verzieh – verziehen
wachsen – wächst – wuchs – gewachsen
wägen – wägt – wog (*rare* wägte) – gewogen
(*rare* gewägt)
waschen – wäscht – wusch – gewaschen
weben – webt – wob – gewoben
weichen – weicht – wich – gewichen
weisen – weist – wies – gewiesen
wenden – wendet – wandte – gewandt
werben – wirbt – warb – geworben
werden – wird – wurde – geworden (worden*)
werfen – wirft – warf – geworfen
wiegen – wiegt – wog – gewogen
winden – windet – wand – gewunden
wissen – weiß – wusste – gewusst
wollen – will – wollte – gewollt (*v/aux*
wollen)
wringen – wringt – wrang – gewrungen
ziehen – zieht – zog – gezogen
zwingen – zwingt – zwang – gezwungen

* only in connection with the past participles of other verbs, *e.g.* **er ist
gesehen worden** he has been seen.

Examples of German Declension and Conjugation

A. Declension

Order of cases: *nom, gen, dat, acc, sg* and *pl*. – Compound nouns and adjectives (e.g. *Eisbär, Ausgang, abfällig* etc.) inflect like their last elements (*Bär, Gang, fällig*). *dem* = demonstrative, *imp* = imperative, *ind* = indicative, *perf* = perfect, *pres* = present, *pres p* = present participle, *rel* = relative, *su* = substantive; the swung dash or tilde(~) represents the preceding word.

I. Nouns

1 Bild ~(e)s¹ ~(e) ~
Bilder² ~ ~n ~

1 **es only**: Geist, Geistes.
2 **a, o, u ⟩ ä, ö, ü**: Rand, Ränder; Haupt, Häupter; Dorf, Dörfer; Wurm, Würmer.

---

2 Reis* ~es ['-zəs] ~(e) ~
Reiser¹ ['-zɐ] ~ ~n ~

1 **a, o ⟩ ä, ö**: Glas, Gläser ['glɛːzɐ]; Haus, Häuser ['hɔʏzɐ]; Fass, Fässer; Schloss, Schlösser.
* Fass, Fasse(s).

---

3 Arm ~(e)s¹,² ~(e)¹ ~
Arme³ ~ ~n ~

1 **without e**: Billard, Billard(s).
2 **es only**: Maß, Maßes.
3 **a, o, u ⟩ ä, ö, ü**: Gang, Gänge; Saal, Säle; Gebrauch, Gebräuche [gə'brɔʏçə]; Sohn, Söhne; Hut, Hüte.

---

4 Greis¹* ~es ['-zəs] ~(e) ~
Greise² ['-zə] ~ ~n ~

1 **s ⟩ ss**: Kürbis, Kürbisse(s).
2 **a, o, u ⟩ ä, ö, ü**: Hals, Hälse; Bass, Bässe; Schoß, Schöße; Fuchs, Füchse; Schuss, Schüsse.
* Ross, Rosse(s).

---

5 Strahl ~(e)s¹,² ~(e)² ~
Strahlen³ ~ ~ ~

1 **es only**: Schmerz, Schmerzes.
2 **without e**: Juwel, Juwel(s).
3 Sporn, Sporen.

---

6 Lappen ~s ~ ~*
Lappen¹ ~ ~ ~

1 **a, o ⟩ ä, ö**: Graben, Gräben; Boden, Böden.

---

* **Infinitives used as nouns have no** *pl* : Geschehen, Befinden etc.

---

7 Maler ~s ~ ~
Maler¹ ~ ~n ~

1 **a, o, u ⟩ ä, ö, ü**: Vater, Väter; Kloster, Klöster; Bruder, Brüder.

---

8 Untertan ~s ~ ~
Untertanen¹,² ~ ~ ~

1 **with change of accent**: Pro'fessor, Profes'soren [-'soːrən]; 'Dämon ['dɛːmɔn], Dä'monen [dɛ'moːnən].
2 *pl* **ien** [-jən]: Kolleg, Kollegien [-'leːgjən]; Mineral, Mineralien.

---

9 Studium ~s ~ ~
Studien¹,² ['-djən] ~ ~ ~

1 **a and o(n) ⟩ en**: Drama, Dramen; Stadion, Stadien.
2 **on and um ⟩ a**: Lexikon, Lexika; Neutrum, Neutra.

---

10 Auge ~s ~ ~
Augen ~ ~ ~

---

11 Genie ~s¹* ~ ~
Genies²* ~ ~ ~

1 **without inflection**: Bouillon etc.
2 *pl* **s or ta**: Komma, Kommas **or** Kommata; **but**: 'Klima, Klimate [kli'maːtə] (3).
* **s is pronounced**: [ʒe'niːs].

---

12 Bär* ~en¹ ~en¹ ~en¹
Bären ~ ~ ~

1 Herr, *sg mst* Herrn; Herz, *gen* Herzens, *acc* Herz.

* ...'log *as well as* ... 'loge (13), e.g. Biolog(e).

13 Knabe   ~n[1] ~n ~n
Knaben   ~ ~ ~
[1] **ns**: Name, Namens.

---

14 Trübsal   ~ ~ ~
Trübsale[1, 2, 3] ~ ~n ~

[1] **a, o, u** 〉 **ä, ö, ü:** Hand, Hände; Braut, Bräute; Not, Nöte; Luft, Lüfte; Nuss, Nüsse; **without e:** Tochter, Töchter; Mutter, Mütter.

[2] **s** 〉 **ss:** Kenntnis, Kenntnisse; Nimbus, Nimbusse.

[3] **is** *or* **us** 〉 **e:** Kultus, Kulte; *with change of accent*: Di'akonus, Dia'kone [-'koːnə].

15 Blume   ~   ~   ~
Blumen ~   ~   ~

...ee: eː, *pl* eːən, *e.g.* I'dee, I'deen.

...ie ⎰ **stressed syllable:** iː, *pl* iːən, *e.g.* Batte'rie(n).
     ⎱ **unstressed syllable:** jə, *pl* jən, *e.g.* Ar'terie(n).

---

16 Frau   ~   ~   ~
Frauen[1, 2, 3] ~   ~   ~

[1] **in** 〉 **innen:** Freundin, Freundinnen.

[2] **a, is, os** *and* **us** 〉 **en:** Firma, Firmen; Krisis, Krisen; Epos, Epen; Genius, Genien; *with change of accent*: 'Heros, He'roen [he'roːən]; Di'akonus, Dia'konen [-'koːnən].

[3] **s** 〉 **ss:** Kirmes, Kirmessen.

<h2 style="text-align:center">II. Proper nouns</h2>

17 *In general proper nouns have no* pl.

The following form the gen sg *with* s:

1. *Proper nouns without a definite article:* Friedrichs, Paulas, (Friedrich von) Schillers, Deutschlands, Berlins;

2. *Proper nouns, masculine and neuter (except the names of countries) with a definite article and an adjective:* des braven Friedrichs Bruder, des jungen Deutschlands (Söhne).

After s, sch, ß, tz, x, *and* z *the* gen sg *ends in* -ens *or* '*(instead of* ' *it is more advisable to use the definite article or* von), e.g. die Werke des [*or* von] Sokrates, Voß *or* Sokrates', Voß' [*not* Sokratessens, **seldom** Vossens] Werke; *but*: die Umgebung von Mainz.

Feminine names ending in a consonant or the vowel e *form the* gen sg *with* (en)s *or* (n)s; *in the* dat *and* acc sg *such names may end in* (e)n (pl = a).

If a proper noun is followed by a title, only the following forms are inflected:

1. *the title when used* with *a definite article*:
der Kaiser Karl (der Große)
des   ~s ~ (des   ~n)
etc.

2. *the* (last) *name when used* with-out *an article*:
Kaiser Karl   (der Große)
    ~s (des   ~n) etc.
(*but*: Herrn Lehmanns Brief).

<h2 style="text-align:center">III. Adjectives and participles
(also used as nouns*), pronouns, etc.</h2>

18

	m	*f*	*n*	*pl*
a) gut	er[1,2]	~e	~es	~e°
	en**	~er	~en**	~er
	em	~er	~em	~en
	en	~e	~es	~e

without article, after prepositions, personal pronouns, and invariables

$$\left.\begin{array}{llll} e^{1,2} & \smallsmile e & \smallsmile e & \smallsmile en \\ en & \smallsmile en & \smallsmile en & \smallsmile en \\ en & \smallsmile en & \smallsmile en & \smallsmile en \\ en & \smallsmile e & \smallsmile e & \smallsmile en \end{array}\right\}$$

b) gut

with definite article (22) **or with pronoun** (21)

$$\left.\begin{array}{llll} er^{1,2} & \smallsmile e & \smallsmile es & \smallsmile en \\ en & \smallsmile en & \smallsmile en & \smallsmile en \\ en & \smallsmile en & \smallsmile en & \smallsmile en \\ en & \smallsmile e & \smallsmile es & \smallsmile en \end{array}\right\}$$

c) gut

with indefinite article or with pronoun
(20)

[1] krass, krasse(r, ~s, ~st etc.).

[2] **a, o, u > ä, ö, ü when forming the** comp and sup: alt, älter(e, ~es etc.), ältest (der ~e, am ~en); grob, gröber(e, ~es etc.), gröbst (der ~e, am ~en); kurz, kürzer(e, ~es etc.), kürzest (der ~e, am ~en).

* e.g. Böse(r) su: der (die, eine) Böse, ein Böser; Böse(s) n: das Böse, **without** article Böses; **in the same way** Abgesandte(r) su, Angestellte(r) su etc.; **in some cases the use varies.**

** **Sometimes the** gen sg **ends in** ~es **instead of** ~en: gutes (**or** guten) Mutes sein.

° **In** böse, böse(r, ~s, ~st etc.) **one e is dropped.**

The Grades of Comparison

The endings of the comparative **and** superlative **are:**

$$\left.\begin{array}{lll} & \text{reich} & \text{schön} \\ comp & \text{reicher} & \text{schöner} \\ sup & \text{reichst} & \text{schönst} \end{array}\right\}$$ **inflected according to** (18²).

After vowels (except e [18°]) **and after** d, s, sch, ß, st, t, tz, x, y, z **the** sup **ends in** ~est, **but in unstressed syllables after** d, sch **and** t **generally in** ~st: blau, 'blauest; rund, 'rundest; rasch, 'raschest etc.; **but:** 'dringend, 'dringendst; 'närrisch, 'närrischst; ge'eignet, ge'eignetst.

Note. – **The adjectives ending in** ~el, ~en (**except** ~nen) **and** ~er (e.g. dunkel, eben, heiter), **and also the possessive adjectives** unser **and** euer **generally drop** e.

Inflection:	~e	~em	~en	~er	~es, and
~el >	~le	~lem*	~len*	~ler	~les
~en >	~(e)ne	~(e)nem	~(e)nen	~(e)ner°	~(e)nes
~er >	~(e)re	~rem*	~ren*	~(e)rer°	~(e)res

* **or** ~elm, ~eln, ~erm, ~ern; e.g. dunk|el: ~le, ~lem (**or** ~elm), ~len (**or** ~eln), ~ler, ~les; eb|en: ~(e)ne, ~(e)nem etc.; heit|er: ~(e)re, ~rem (**or** ~erm) etc.

° **The inflected** comp **ends in** ~ner **and** ~rer **only:** eben, ebnere(r, ~s etc.); heiter, heitrere(r, ~s etc.); **but** sup ebenst, heiterst.

19

	1st pers. m, f, n	2nd pers. m, f, n	3rd pers. m	f	n
sg	ich	du	er	sie	es
	meiner*	deiner*	seiner*	ihrer	seiner*
	mir	dir	ihm	ihr	ihm°
	mich	dich	ihn	sie	es°
pl	wir	ihr	sie	(Sie)	
	unser	euer	ihrer	(Ihrer)	
	uns	euch	ihnen	(Ihnen)°	
	uns	euch	sie	(Sie)°	

* **In poetry sometimes without inflection**: gedenke mein!; **also es instead of** seiner *n* (= *e-r Sache*): ich bin es überdrüssig.
° **Reflexive form**: sich.

20 *m*		*f*	*n*	*pl*
mein		~e	~	~e*
dein	es	~er	~es	~er
sein	em	~er	~em	~en
(k)ein	en	~e	~	~e

* **The indefinite article** ein **has no** *pl* . - **In poetry** mein, dein **and** sein **may stand behind the** *su* **without inflection**: die Mutter (Kinder) mein, **or as predicate**: der Hut [*die Tasche, das Buch*] ist mein; **without** *su*: meiner *m*, meine *f*, mein(e)s *n*, meine *pl* etc.: *wem gehört der Hut* [*die Tasche, das Buch*]? es ist meiner (meine, mein[e]s); **or with definite article**: der (die, das) meine, *pl* die meinen (18b). **Regarding** unser **and** euer **see note** (18).

21 *m*		*f*	*n*	*pl*
dies	er	~e	~es*	~e**
jen	es	~er	~es	~er¹
manch	em	~er	~em	~en¹
welch	en	~e	~es*	~e

¹ derjenige, derselbe - desjenigen, demjenigen, desselben, demselben etc. (18b).

23 **Relative pronoun**

m	*f*	*n*	*pl*
der	die	das	die
dessen*	deren	dessen*	deren¹
dem	der	dem	denen
den	die	das	die

¹ **welche(r, s)** as *rel pron*: *gen sg* dessen, deren, *gen pl* deren, *dat pl* denen (23).

* **Used as** *su*, dies **is preferable to** dieses.

** manch, solch, welch **frequently are uninflected**:

manch	guter	(ein	guter)	Mann	
solch	~en	(	~es	~en)	~es
welch	~em	(	~em	~en)	~e
			etc. (18)		

Similarly all:

all der (dies**er**, mein) Schmerz			
~	des (	~**es**,	~**es**)	~**es**

22 *m*	*f*	*n*	*pl*	
der	die	das	die¹	
des	der	des	der	**definite**
dem	der	dem	den	**article**
den	die	das	die	

¹ **also** derer, **when used as** *dem pron*
* **also** des.

24 wer	was	jemand, niemand	
wessen*	wessen	~(e)s	
wem	–	~(em°)	
wen	was	~(en°)	

* **also** wes.
° **preferably without inflection**.

B. Conjugation

In the conjugation tables (25-30) only the simple verbs may be found; in the alphabetical list of the German irregular verbs compound verbs are only included when no simple verb exists (e.g. **beginnen**; *ginnen* does not exist). In order to find the conjugation of any compound verb (with separable or inseparable prefix, regular or irregular) look up the respective simple verb.

Verbs with separable and stressed prefixes such as '**ab-**, '**an-**, '**auf-**, '**aus-**, '**bei-**, **be'vor-**, '**dar-**, '**ein-**, **em'por-**, **ent-** '**gegen-**, '**fort-**, '**her-**, **he'rab-** etc. and also '**klar-**[*legen*], '**los-**[*schießen*], '**sitzen** [*bleiben*], **über'hand** [*nehmen*] etc. (but not the verbs derived from compound nouns as *be'antragen* or *be'ratschlagen* from *Antrag* and *Ratschlag* etc.) take the preposition **zu** (in the *inf* and the *pres p*) and the syllable **ge** (in the *pp* and in the passive voice) between the stressed prefix and their root.

Verbs with inseparable and unstressed prefixes such as **be-, emp-, ent-, er-, ge-, ver-, zer-** and generally **miss-** (in spite of its being stressed) take the preposition **zu** before the prefix and drop the syllable **ge** in the *pp* and in the passive voice. The prefixes **durch-, hinter-, über-, um-, unter-, voll-, wi(e)der-** are separable when stressed and inseparable when unstressed, e.g.

geben: *zu geben, zu gebend; gegeben; ich gebe, du gibst* etc.;

'abgeben: *'abzugeben, 'abzugebend; 'abgegeben; ich gebe (du gibst* etc.*) ab;*

ver'geben: *zu ver'geben, zu ver'gebend; ver'geben; ich ver'gebe, du ver'gibst* etc.;

'umgehen: *'umzugehen, 'umzugehend; 'umgegangen; ich gehe (du gehst* etc.*) um;*

um'gehen: *zu um'gehen, zu um'gehend; um'gangen; ich um'gehe, du um'gehst* etc.

The same rules apply to verbs with two prefixes, e.g.

zu'rückbehalten [see *halten*]: *zu'rückzubehalten, zu'rückzubehaltend; zu-'rückbehalten; ich behalte (du behältst* etc.*) zurück;*

wieder 'aufheben [see *heben*]: *wieder 'aufzuheben, wieder 'aufzuhebend; wieder 'aufgehoben; ich hebe (du hebst* etc.*) wieder auf.*

The forms in parentheses ( ) follow the same rules.

a) 'Weak' Conjugation

25   loben

| *pres ind* | lobe | lobst | lobt |
| | loben | lobt | loben |

| *pres subj* | lobe | lobest | lobe |
| | loben | lobet | loben |

| *pret ind* | lobte | lobtest | lobte |
| *and subj* | lobten | lobtet | lobten |

imp sg lob(e), *pl* lob(e)t, loben Sie;
inf pres loben; *inf perf* gelobt haben;
pres p lobend; *pp* gelobt (18; 29**).

26   reden

| *pres ind* | rede | redest | redet |
| | reden | redet | reden |

| *pres subj* | rede | redest | rede |
| | reden | redet | reden |

| *pret ind* | redete | redetest | redete |
| *and subj* | redeten | redetet | redeten |

imp sg rede, *pl* redet, reden Sie;
inf pres reden; *inf perf* geredet haben;
pres p redend; *pp* geredet (18; 29**).

27   reisen

| *pres ind* | reise | rei(se)st* | reist |
| | reisen | reist | reisen |

| *pres subj* | reise | reisest | reise |
| | reisen | reiset | reisen |

| *pret ind* | reiste | reistest | reisten |
| *and subj* | reisten | reistet | reisten |

imp sg reise, *pl* reist, reisen Sie;
inf pres reisen; *inf perf* gereist sein *or now rare* haben; *pres p* reisend; *pp* gereist (18; 29**).

  * **sch:** naschen, nasch(e)st; **ß:** spa-ßen, spaßt (spaßest); **tz:** ritzen, ritzt (ritzest); **x:** hexen, hext (hexest); **z:** reizen, reizt (reizest); faulenzen, faulenzt (faulenzest).

28   fassen

| *pres ind* | fasse | fasst | (fassest)fasst |
| | fassen | fasst | fassen |

| *pres subj* | fasse | fassest | fasse |
| | fassen | fasset | fassen |

| *pret ind* | fasste | fasstest | fasste |
| *and subj* | fassten | fasstet | fassten |

imp sg fasse (fass), *pl* fasst, fassen Sie;
inf pres fassen; *inf perf* gefasst haben;
pres p fassend; *pp* gefasst (18; 29**).

29   handeln

pres ind		
handle*	handelst	handelt
handeln	handelt	handeln

pres subj		
handle*	handelst	handle*
handeln	handelt	handeln

	pret ind and *subj*	
handelte	handeltest	handelte
handelten	handeltet	handelten

imp sg handle, *pl* handelt, handeln Sie; *inf pres* handeln; *inf perf* gehandelt haben; *pres p* handelnd; *pp* gehandet (18).

* *Also* handele; wandern, wand(e)re; bessern, bessere (bessre); donnern, donnere.

** Without ge, when the first syllable is unstressed, e.g. be'grüßen, be'grüßt; ent-'stehen, ent'standen; stu'dieren, studiert

(*not* gestudiert); trom'peten, trom'petet (*also* **when preceded by a stressed prefix**: 'austrompeten, 'austrompetet, *not* 'ausgetrompetet). **In some weak verbs the** *pp* **ends in en instead of t**, e.g. mahlen, gemahlen. **With the verbs** brauchen, dürfen, heißen, helfen, hören, können, lassen, lehren, lernen, machen, mögen, müssen, sehen, sollen, wollen *the pp* **is replaced by** *inf* (**without** ge), **when used in connection with another** *inf* , e.g. ich habe ihn singen hören, du hättest es tun können, er hat gehen müssen, ich hätte ihn laufen lassen sollen.

b) 'Strong' Conjugation

30   **fahren**

pres ind	{	fahre	fährst	fährt
		fahren	fahrt	fahren

pres subj	{	fahre	fahrest	fahre
		fahren	fahret	fahren

pret ind	{	fuhr	fuhr(e)st	fuhr
		fuhren	fuhrt	fuhren

pres subj	{	führe	führest	führe
		führen	führet	führen

imp sg fahr(e), *pl* fahr(e)t, fahren Sie; *inf pres* fahren; *inf perf* gefahren haben *or* sein; *pres p* fahrend; *pp* gefahren (18; 29**).

German Weights and Measures

I Linear Measure

1 mm *Millimeter* millimeter, *Br* millimetre
= $^1/_{1000}$ meter (*Br* metre)
= 0.003 feet
= 0.039 inches

1 cm *Zentimeter* centimeter, *Br* centimetre
= $^1/_{100}$ meter (*Br* metre)
= 0.39 inches

1 dm *Dezimeter* decimeter, *Br* decimetre
= $^1/_{10}$ meter (*Br* metre)
= 3.94 inches

1 m *Meter* meter, *Br* metre
= 1.094 yards
= 3.28 feet
= 39.37 inches

1 km *Kilometer* kilometer, *Br* kilometre
= 1,000 meters (*Br* metres)
= 1,093.637 yards
= 0.621 (statute) miles

1 sm *Seemeile* nautical mile
= 1,852 meters (*Br* metres)

II Square Measure

1 mm² *Quadratmillimeter* square millimeter (*Br* millimetre)
= 0.0015 square inches

1 cm² *Quadratzentimeter* square centimeter (*Br* centimetre)
= 0.155 square inches

1 m² *Quadratmeter* square meter (*Br* metre)
= 1.195 square yards
= 10.76 square feet

1 a *Ar* are
= 100 square meters (*Br* metres)
= 119.59 square yards
= 1,076.40 square feet

1 ha *Hektar* hectare
= 100 ares
= 10,000 square meters (*Br* metres)
= 11,959.90 square yards
= 2.47 acres

1 km² *Quadratkilometer* square kilometer (*Br* kilometre)
= 100 hectares
= 1,000,000 square meters (*Br* metres)
= 247.11 acres
= 0.386 square miles

III Cubic Measure

1 cm³ *Kubikzentimeter* cubic centimeter (*Br* centimetre)
= 1,000 cubic millimeters (*Br* millimetres)
= 0.061 cubic inches

1 dm³ *Kubikdezimeter* cubic decimeter (*Br* decimetre)
= 1,000 cubic centimeters (*Br* centimetres)
= 61.025 cubic inches

1 m³ *Kubikmeter*
1 rm *Raummeter* } cubic meter (*Br* metre)
1 fm *Festmeter*
= 1,000 cubic decimeters (*Br* decimetres)
= 1.307 cubic yards
= 35.31 cubic feet

1 RT *Registertonne* register ton
= 2.832 m³
= 100 cubic feet

IV Measure of Capacity

1 l *Liter* liter, *Br* litre
= 10 deciliters (*Br* decilitres)
= 2.11 pints (*Am*)
= 8.45 gills (*Am*)
= 1.06 quarts (*Am*)
= 0.26 gallons (*Am*)
= 1.76 pints (*Br*)
= 7.04 gills (*Br*)
= 0.88 quarts (*Br*)
= 0.22 gallons (*Br*)

1 hl *Hektoliter* hectoliter, *Br* hectolitre
= 100 liters (*Br* litres)
= 26.42 gallons (*Am*)
= 2.84 bushels (*Am*)
= 22.009 gallons (*Br*)
= 2.75 bushels (*Br*)

V Weight

1 mg *Milligramm* milligram(me)
= $^1/_{1000}$ gram(me)
= 0.015 grains

1 g *Gramm* gram(me)
= $^1/_{1000}$ kilogram(me)
= 15.43 grains

1 Pfd *Pfund* pound (German)
= $^1/_2$ kilogram(me)
= 500 gram(me)s
= 1.102 pounds (1b)

1 kg *Kilogramm*, *Kilo* kilogram(me)
= 1,000 gram(me)s
= 2.204 pounds (1b)

1 Ztr. *Zentner* centner
= 100 pounds (German)
= 50 kilogram(me)s
= 110.23 pounds (1b)
= 1.102 US hundredweights
= 0.98 British hundredweights

1 t *Tonne* ton
= 1,000 kilogram(me)s
= 1.102 US tons
= 0.984 British tons

Conversion Tables for Temperatures

°C (Celsius)	°F (Fahrenheit)
100	212
95	203
90	194
85	185
80	176
75	167
70	158
65	149
60	140
55	131
50	122
45	113
40	104
35	95
30	86
25	77
20	68
15	59
10	50
5	41
0	32
− 5	23
−10	14
−15	5
−17.8	0
−20	− 4
−25	−13
−30	−22
−35	−31
−40	−40
−45	−49
−50	−58

Clinical Thermometer

°C (Celsius)	°F (Fahrenheit)
42.0	107.6
41.8	107.2
41.6	106.9
41.4	106.5
41.2	106.2
41.0	105.8
40.8	105.4
40.6	105.1
40.4	104.7
40.2	104.4
40.0	104.0
39.8	103.6
39.6	103.3
39.4	102.9
39.2	102.6
39.0	102.2
38.8	101.8
38.6	101.5
38.4	101.1
38.2	100.8
38.0	100.4
37.8	100.0
37.6	99.7
37.4	99.3
37.2	99.0
37.0	98.6
36.8	98.2
36.6	97.9

Rules for Conversion

$$°F = \frac{9}{5} °C + 32$$
$$°C = (°F - 32)\frac{5}{9}$$

Numerals

Cardinal Numbers

0 null *nought, zero*
1 eins *one*
2 zwei *two*
3 drei *three*
4 vier *four*
5 fünf *five*
6 sechs *six*
7 sieben *seven*
8 acht *eight*
9 neun *nine*
10 zehn *ten*
11 elf *eleven*
12 zwölf *twelve*
13 dreizehn *thirteen*
14 vierzehn *fourteen*
15 fünfzehn *fifteen*
16 sechzehn *sixteen*
17 siebzehn *seventeen*
18 achtzehn *eighteen*
19 neunzehn *nineteen*
20 zwanzig *twenty*
21 einundzwanzig *twenty-one*
22 zweiundzwanzig *twenty-two*
30 dreißig *thirty*
31 einunddreißig *thirty-one*
40 vierzig *forty*

41 einundvierzig *forty-one*
50 fünfzig *fifty*
51 einundfünfzig *fifty-one*
60 sechzig *sixty*
61 einundsechzig *sixty-one*
70 siebzig *seventy*
71 einundsiebzig *seventy-one*
80 achtzig *eighty*
81 einundachtzig *eighty-one*
90 neunzig *ninety*
91 einundneunzig *ninety-one*
100 hundert *a* or *one hundred*
101 hunderteins *a hundred and one*
200 zweihundert *two hundred*
300 dreihundert *three hundred*
572 fünfhundertzweiundsiebzig *five hundred and seventy-two*
1000 tausend *a* or *one thousand*
1999 neunzehnhundertneunundneunzig *nineteen hundred and ninetynine*
2000 zweitausend *two thousand*
5044 TEL fünfzig vierundvierzig *five O (or zero) double four*
1 000 000 eine Million *one million*
2 000 000 zwei Millionen *two million*

Ordinal Numbers

1. erste *first* (*1st*)
2. zweite *second* (*2nd*)
3. dritte *third* (*3rd*)
4. vierte *fourth* (*4th*)
5. fünfte *fifth* (*5th*) etc.
6. sechste *sixth*
7. siebente *seventh*
8. achte *eighth*
9. neunte *ninth*
10. zehnte *tenth*
11. elfte *eleventh*
12. zwölfte *twelfth*
13. dreizehnte *thirteenth*
14. vierzehnte *fourteenth*
15. fünfzehnte *fifteenth*
16. sechzehnte *sixteenth*
17. siebzehnte *seventeenth*
18. achtzehnte *eighteenth*
19. neunzehnte *nineteenth*
20. zwanzigste *twentieth*
21. einundzwanzigste *twenty-first*
22. zweiundzwanzigste *twenty-second*
23. dreiundzwanzigste *twenty-third*
30. dreißigste *thirtieth*
31. einunddreißigste *thirty-first*

40. vierzigste *fortieth*
41. einundvierzigste *forty-first*
50. fünfzigste *fiftieth*
51. einundfünfzigste *fifty-first*
60. sechzigste *sixtieth*
61. einundsechzigste *sixty-first*
70. siebzigste *seventieth*
71. einundsiebzigste *seventy-first*
80. achtzigste *eightieth*
81. einundachtzigste *eighty-first*
90. neunzigste *ninetieth*
100. hundertste *(one) hundredth*
101. hundert(und)erste *(one) hundred and first*
200. zweihundertste *two hundredth*
300. dreihundertste *three hundredth*
572. fünfhundert(und)zweiundsiebzigste *five hundred and seventysecond*
1000. tausendste *(one) thousandth*
1970. neunzehnhundert(und)siebzigste *nineteen hundred and seventieth*
500 000. fünfhunderttausendste *five hundred thousandth*
1 000 000. millionste *(one) millionth*